Baseball America's

1999 Almanac

A Comprehensive Review Of the 1998 Season, Featuring Statistics and Commentary

Distributed by Simon & Schuster

For additional copies, send $12.95 plus $5.00 shipping and handling to:
Baseball America, P.O. Box 2089, Durham, N.C 27702

Baseball America's
1999 Almanac

PUBLISHED BY
Baseball America Inc.

EDITOR
Allan Simpson

ASSOCIATE EDITOR
James Bailey

ASSISTANT EDITORS
Mark Derewicz, John Royster

CONTRIBUTING EDITORS
Will Lingo, Lacy Lusk, John Manuel

CONTRIBUTING WRITERS
Mike Berardino, John Perrotto, David Rawnsley, Alan Schwarz

PRODUCTION
Brandon Donnell, Valerie Holbert, Casey Mansfield Thomas

STATISTICAL PRODUCTION CONSULTANT
Howe Sportsdata International,
Boston, Mass.

Baseball America

PUBLISHER/Lee Folger
EDITOR/Allan Simpson
MANAGING EDITOR/Will Lingo
PRODUCTION DIRECTOR/Valerie Holbert
ADVERTISING DIRECTOR/Kris Howard

COVER PHOTO/Mark McGwire by Ron Vesely

EDITOR'S NOTE

Major league statistics are based on final, unofficial 1998 averages. Minor league statistics are official.

The organization statistics, which begin on Page 51, include all players who participated in at least one game during the 1998 season. Pitchers' batting statistics are not included, nor are the pitching statistics of field players who pitched on rare occasions. For players who played with more than one team in the same league, the player's cumulative statistics appear on the line immediately after the player's last-team statistics.

Innings have been rounded off to the nearest full inning.

Contents

Major Leagues

1998 SEASON

McGwire, Sosa, Yankees highlight exciting campaign

BY MIKE BERARDINO

This was the season you will tell your grandchildren about.

If you never have grandchildren, this was the season you will tell somebody else's grandchildren about. Or the mailman. Or the cab driver. Or the kid one bench over at the mega-mall.

Yes, it's true, the crass dismantling of the Florida Marlins got 1998 off to a lousy start. Thanks to the cynicism of owner H. Wayne Huizenga, the defending World Series champions lost 108 games, 20 more than the previous worst follow-up act (1991 Cincinnati Reds).

But everywhere else you looked, baseball seemingly bent over backward to make up for that affront.

This was the season Mark McGwire and Sammy Sosa swung for the fences and captured our hearts.

This was the season the New York Yankees finished 75 games over .500, swept the World Series in four games from the San Diego Padres and staked their claim to the title of Greatest Team Ever.

This was the season Bud Selig, after nearly six years as an interim commissioner, finally stopped temping and accepted the full-time job. Suddenly, columnists and studio-show wags weren't making baseball jokes anymore. They were mocking the NBA and its lockout instead.

This was the season 38-year-old Cal Ripken finally took a day off. He did this after 16 years and 2,632 consecutive games in the Baltimore Orioles lineup.

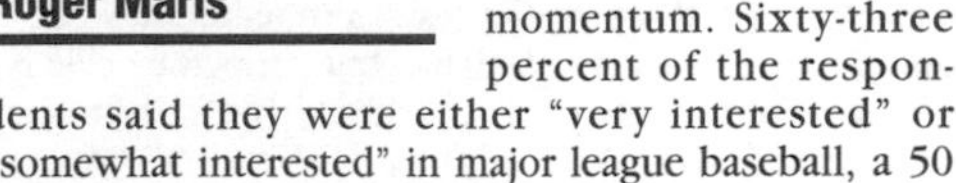

MEL BAILEY

Roger Maris

Over and over and over again . . . this was the season.

America accepted the peace offering. Per-game attendance was more than 29,000, up almost 4 percent from 1997 and the third-highest figure in major league history.

A New York Times/CBS News poll of 960 American adults reinforced the feeling of momentum. Sixty-three percent of the respondents said they were either "very interested" or "somewhat interested" in major league baseball, a 50 percent increase from 1997 figures.

Just 38 percent said they were not interested in the least, down from 58 percent.

Mark And Sammy

How could any true sports fan ignore baseball in 1998? It was virtually impossible.

This was the year one of the most hallowed achievements in sports, Roger Maris' 37-year-old single-season home run record, fell victim to not one but two worthy challengers.

LARRY GOREN

70 Setting a new standard
Mark McGwire was the man

Mark McGwire and Sammy Sosa, two Bunyanesque sluggers who became fast friends, marched in near lockstep to a September crescendo. McGwire, the St. Louis Cardinals first baseman, blew past the Maris Line first on Sept. 8, hitting his 62nd home run against Cubs righthander Steve Trachsel before an adoring crowd at Busch Stadium.

But the pyrotechnics were far from finished.

Slammin' Sammy Sosa came back to tie McGwire at 62 and 65, and even took the lead for 45 minutes on

HOME RUN LEADERS

SINGLE SEASON

	Player, Team, Year	
1.	**Mark McGwire, Cardinals, 1998**	**70**
2.	**Sammy Sosa, Cubs, 1998**	**66**
3.	Roger Maris, Yankees, 1961	61
4.	Babe Ruth, Yankees, 1927	60
5.	Babe Ruth, Yankees, 1921	59
6.	Jimmie Foxx, Athletics, 1932	58
	Hank Greenberg, Tigers, 1938	58
	Mark McGwire, Athletics/Cardinals, 1997	58
9.	Hack Wilson, Cubs, 1930	56
	Ken Griffey, Mariners, 1997	56
	Ken Griffey, Mariners, 1998	**56**

Player of the Year

Even McGwire can't believe it all

More than numbers
Mark McGwire enjoyed an amazing year

It wasn't just that Mark McGwire hit 70 home runs in 1998, shattering a record that had stood for 37 years.

It was more the way he did it.

It was the way no one wanted to be at the concession stand when his name was announced. It was the way fans stopped what they were doing to watch his at-bats on TV. And it was the way the giant of a man grew as the season progressed to fill the ever-expanding spotlight, somehow managing to remain humble at the same time.

"I don't believe I did it. Do you?" McGwire asked after hitting No. 70, one of two he hit on the final day of the season.

From the start of 1998, when he hit four home runs in the first four games, to the end, when he hit five in the final three games, McGwire did a lot of unbelievable things.

And he had fun doing them.

That's what made it so enjoyable for everyone else. Suddenly everyone—everywhere—was tuning in to see what he would do next. And they were all pulling for the St. Louis slugger, who seemed to genuinely love every minute of it.

"It's been amazing," McGwire said, "that a guy who just swings the bat could have had this impact on the country, on people's lives."

When the season ended, McGwire stood front and center as the most inspiring story of one of the most amazing seasons in baseball history. For that he was chosen as Baseball America's first Major League Player of the Year.

The Great Home Run Chase of '98, a two-horse race between McGwire and Cubs outfielder Sammy Sosa, pushed politics, football and all things not baseball to the background.

Spurred on by Sosa, who hit 66, McGwire rewrote the standard by which all power hitters shall be measured. He held the lead nearly wire-to-wire, but for a couple of brief moments when Sosa snuck ahead.

In September the entire world tuned in to see what McGwire would do next. And he never disappointed. He hit three historic home runs—Nos. 60, 61 and 62—before his hometown St. Louis fans over Labor Day weekend, ignoring all the pressure and attention once he stepped into the batters box

Fittingly, Sosa was in right field on Sept. 8 when Big Red launched No. 62, breaking Roger Maris' existing mark and sending Busch Stadium into a frenzy. When McGwire wrapped his friend and rival in a massive bear hug after crossing the plate, it gave real meaning to the accomplishment.

McGwire's season wasn't simply about numbers or records. It was about sportsmanship and a love of the game. Regardless of whether his mark stands for all time, that's what will be remembered, and appreciated, most.

—JAMES BAILEY

the third-to-last day of the regular season. But McGwire, as he did each time before, answered the challenge.

Big Mac pounded out a pair of double-barreled salvos on the final weekend against the Montreal Expos to finish with an unbelievable 70 homers. Expos rookie righthander Carl Pavano surrendered No. 70.

Sosa, who electrified his countrymen back home in the Dominican Republic and delighted Americans, finished with 66.

Incredibly, just about every milestone baseball was returned to the bashers themselves by suddenly greed-free fans.

"Mark is the man," was Sosa's mantra throughout the chase.

By September, the ebullient slugger amended that slightly.

"Mark is the man in the United States," he said. "I am the man in the Dominican Republic."

McGwire amazed all observers, including himself, with his powers of concentration. Forced to give near-daily press briefings to the traveling media circus that followed him from city to city, McGwire held up remarkably well.

His biggest challenge came in late August when a wire-service reporter noticed a bottle of Androstenedione in McGwire's locker. The slugger quickly admitted taking the testosterone-building substance, which is legal in baseball but banned by several other sports' governing bodies, including the International Olympic Committee, NFL and NCAA.

A week-long firestorm of debate ensued, but McGwire refused to stop taking the daily supplement, which he claimed cut his recovery time from a strenuous workout regimen.

Through it all, he kept his focus—and he kept hitting moon shots.

"I think the magnitude of this will probably not sink in or be understood for a while," McGwire said

Kodak moment for Cubs slugger
Sammy Sosa draws a crowd while receiving the ball he hit for No. 63 in San Diego

at season's end. "I mean, it's unheard of for somebody to hit 70 home runs, so I'm like in awe of myself right now."

So immense were the accomplishments of Sosa and McGwire, that Seattle's Ken Griffey hit 56 homers and San Diego's Greg Vaughn hit 50 and were treated as afterthoughts.

You can blame this surge on expansion-diluted pitching, but that would not be an accurate explanation. Even with the Arizona Diamondbacks and Tampa Bay Devil Rays joining the fold, average home runs per game increased only slightly from 1997. They were actually down a tick from 1996.

More Than Home Runs

This 1998 season will be remembered primarily for the longball, but it offered so much more.

This was the season the Atlanta Braves swept to their seventh consecutive division title, the Cleveland Indians rolled to their fourth straight and the Texas Rangers, after a quarter century without winning anything, took the American League West for the second time in three years.

In Houston, the Astros won 100 games for the first time in their 37-year history. They outfoxed a handful of more likely suitors at the trade deadine and landed the Big Unit, Seattle ace Randy Johnson. Baseball's most dominant lefthander only went 10-1 down the stretch before suffering Division Series disappointment against the Padres.

In San Diego, the successful push for a new stadium gathered momentum as the Padres rolled to their second division crown in three years. Energized by the Qualcomm Stadium-throbbing backbeat of AC/DC and the late-innings excellence of closer Trevor Hoffman, the Padres made just the second World Series appearance in their 30-year history.

A zany, three-way race for the National League wild card spilled over into a Giants-Cubs one-game playoff. You could almost sense the hand of fate as the Cubs wore sleeve patches to honor longtime broadcasters Harry Caray and Jack Brickhouse, who died earlier in the year.

Meanwhile the Boston Red Sox wrapped up the AL wild card behind ace righthander Pedro Martinez, who signed baseball's richest contract (six years, $75 million) before the season.

The Yankees' Year

But none of those teams could compare with the mighty Yankees, winners of 125 games and the 24th World Series in their illustrious history, including their second in three years. Along the way they produced a season-long testament to sustained excellence.

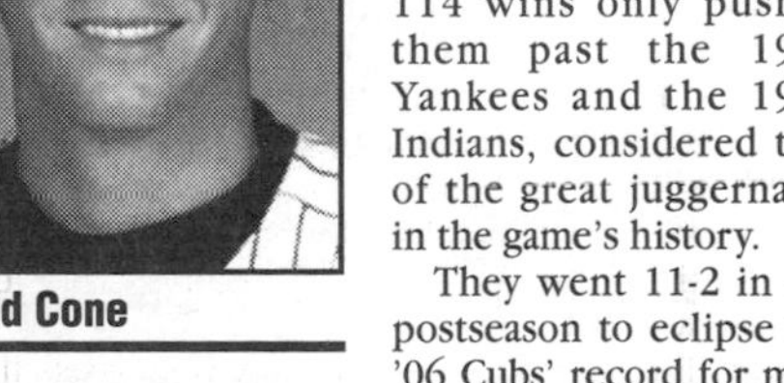
David Cone

Selfless and seemingly fundamentally flawless, they threatened to break the 1906 Chicago Cubs' regular-season record of 116 wins before finally settling for new franchise and AL records. Those 114 wins only pushed them past the 1927 Yankees and the 1954 Indians, considered two of the great juggernauts in the game's history.

They went 11-2 in the postseason to eclipse the '06 Cubs' record for most wins in a single season (118).

"We made our mark. Where it fits, I don't know," said David Cone, the Yankees' unoffical captain and only 20-game winner. "We heard it since the all-star break. People have been comparing us to the greatest teams. That created enormous pressure for us down the stretch. Still we were able to come through."

George Steinbrenner, the Yankees principal owner,

1998 MAJOR LEAGUE ALL-STARS

JOHN WILLIAMSON

Baseball's best catcher
Ivan Rodriguez hit .321 for Texas

LARRY GOREN

Padres Ace
Kevin Brown went 18-7 for San Diego

Selected by Baseball America

FIRST TEAM

Pos.	Player, Team	B-T	Ht.	Wt.	Age	AVG	AB	R	H	2B	3B	HR	RBI	SB
C	Ivan Rodriguez, Rangers	R-R	5-9	205	26	.321	579	88	186	40	4	21	91	9
1B	Mark McGwire, Cardinals	R-R	6-5	225	34	.299	509	130	152	21	0	70	147	1
2B	Craig Biggio, Astros	R-R	5-11	180	32	.325	646	123	210	51	2	20	88	50
3B	Vinny Castilla, Rockies	R-R	6-1	185	30	.319	645	108	206	28	4	46	144	5
SS	Alex Rodriguez, Mariners	R-R	6-2	190	22	.310	686	123	213	35	5	42	124	46
LF	Albert Belle, White Sox	R-R	6-2	210	31	.328	609	113	200	48	2	49	152	6
CF	Ken Griffey, Mariners	L-L	6-3	205	28	.284	633	120	180	33	3	56	146	20
RF	Sammy Sosa, Cubs	R-R	6-0	200	29	.308	643	134	198	20	0	66	158	18
DH	Juan Gonzalez, Rangers	R-R	6-3	210	28	.318	606	110	193	50	2	45	157	2

Pos.	Player, Team	B-T	Ht.	Wt.	Age	W	L	ERA	G	SV	IP	H	BB	SO
SP	Kevin Brown, Padres	R-R	6-4	195	33	18	7	2.38	36	0	257	225	49	257
	Roger Clemens, Blue Jays	R-R	6-4	220	35	20	6	2.65	33	0	235	169	88	271
	Pedro Martinez, Red Sox	R-R	5-11	170	26	19	7	2.89	33	0	234	188	67	251
	David Wells, Yankees	L-L	6-4	225	35	18	4	3.49	30	0	214	195	29	163
RP	Trevor Hoffman, Padres	R-R	6-0	195	30	4	2	1.48	66	53	73	41	21	86

SECOND TEAM

Pos.	Player, Team	B-T	Ht.	Wt.	Age	AVG	AB	R	H	2B	3B	HR	RBI	SB
C	Mike Piazza, Dodgers/Mets	R-R	6-3	200	29	.328	561	88	184	38	1	32	111	1
1B	Mo Vaughn, Red Sox	L-R	6-1	240	30	.337	609	107	205	31	2	40	115	0
2B	Jeff Kent, Giants	R-R	6-1	185	30	.297	526	94	156	37	3	31	128	9
3B	Chipper Jones, Braves	B-R	6-3	195	26	.313	601	123	188	29	5	34	107	16
SS	Nomar Garciaparra, Red Sox	R-R	6-0	200	24	.323	604	111	195	37	8	35	122	12
LF	Barry Bonds, Giants	L-L	6-1	185	33	.303	552	120	167	44	7	37	122	28
CF	Bernie Williams, Yankees	B-R	6-2	196	29	.339	499	101	169	30	5	26	97	15
RF	Vladimir Guerrero, Expos	R-R	6-2	195	22	.324	623	108	202	37	7	38	109	11
DH	Manny Ramirez, Indians	R-R	6-0	190	26	.294	571	108	168	35	2	45	145	5

Pos.	Player, Team	B-T	Ht.	Wt.	Age	W	L	ERA	G	SV	IP	H	BB	SO
SP	Tom Glavine, Braves	L-L	6-1	185	32	20	6	2.47	33	0	229	202	74	157
	Randy Johnson, Mariners/Astros	R-L	6-10	225	34	19	11	3.28	34	0	244	203	86	329
	Al Leiter, Mets	L-L	6-1	190	32	17	6	2.47	28	0	193	151	71	174
	Greg Maddux, Braves	R-R	6-0	175	32	18	9	2.22	34	0	251	201	45	204
RP	John Wetteland, Rangers	R-R	6-2	215	32	3	1	2.03	63	42	62	47	14	72

Ages as of July 1, 1998.

Player of the Year: Mark McGwire, 1b, Cardinals. **Pitcher of the Year:** Roger Clemens, rhp, Blue Jays. **Rookie of the Year:** Kerry Wood, rhp, Cubs. **Manager of the Year:** Larry Dierker, Astros. **Executive of the Year:** Doug Melvin, Rangers.

RON VESELY

Not just acting
Bud Selig finally became full-time commissioner

was less restrained.

"New York is a city full of battlers," Steinbrenner said. "You battle in the morning to get a cab. You battle to get a seat at the lunch counter. Well, this was a team of battlers. This team was designed for New York. They are one of the truly great teams in the history of the game."

Interim No More

After what seemed like a million denials of interest in the full-time job, Selig finally was elected baseball's ninth commissioner on July 9. He had served as acting commissioner since Sept. 9, 1992, two days after Fay Vincent's ouster.

Selig placed his shares of the Milwaukee Brewers into a blind trust. Wendy Selig-Prieb, his daughter, was named to run the franchise in her father's stead.

Selig endorsed the continuation of interleague play, which was only slightly less successful in its second year. Selig also stressed the importance of eventual realignment in order to cut down on travel costs and foster natural geographical rivalries.

The Brewers, the only club to switch leagues in Phase 1 of Selig's plan, finished fifth in the National League Central after becoming the first team to change leagues since 1903.

Increased revenue sharing, or finding some other way to close the ever-widening gap between the game's haves and have-nots, remained another point of emphasis.

At the bottom stood the Montreal Expos, who paid just $9 million to their youthful collection of players and finished fourth in the NL East. The Orioles paid their aging collection of underachievers almost $65 million more and finished fourth in the AL East.

Selig also commissioned MLB president Paul Beeston to further study the feasibility of a baseball world cup. Sandy Alderson, the architect of the Oakland Athletics dynasty of the late 1980s and early '90s, was added to the commissioner's office as well.

Iron Man Ends Streak

The end came Sept. 20 at Camden Yards, almost three years to the day after Cal Ripken eclipsed Lou Gehrig's all-time Iron Man record.

About 30 minutes before the Orioles' final home game of the season, Ripken poked his head into manager Ray Miller's office and asked to be taken out of the lineup.

"I think," Ripken said, "the time is right."

Rookie Ryan Minor replaced Ripken at third base. When they realized what was happening, the Yankees convened on the top step of the visitors dugout and gave Ripken an ovation.

An even louder salute came from another sellout crowd at Camden Yards.

"The streak was born out of a desire to play and a lot of managers wanting to put me in the lineup," said Ripken, who was in perfect health but simply wanted to end his increasingly controversial streak on his terms. "It's your job to come to the ballpark and be available, and if the manager wants to put you in there, you play. I feel very proud, not necessarily with the numbers the streak is, but very proud that my teammates and my manager could count on me."

Gehrig's record stood for 56 years. Ripken, 38, did not sound confident his mark will stand as long, even if most everyone else in the game believes 2,632 will never be broken.

"If I did it someone else can do it. I don't see myself as superhuman," Ripken said after sitting out an Orioles game for the first time since May 29, 1982. "It's a special set of circumstances. You have to be worthy of being in the lineup. You have to have a determination and desire to be in there. You have to have a love of the game. You have to be persistent. You have to be stubborn. Everything has to go your way."

MORRIS FOSTOFF

Ryan Minor

The death of the streak came near the end of a tremendously disappointing season for the big-spending Orioles. Ripken's run production was among the worst for any third baseman in the game, and he had been subjected to another year of criticism from local columnists who considered him selfish.

"I was shocked," Orioles second baseman Roberto Alomar said. "I didn't expect the record to end that way. But there was a lot of criticism of him and I think that's why he ended it. That's sad, because people don't know his work ethic."

A huge weight lifted from his shoulders, Ripken looked to the waning years of his career with his customary enthusiasm.

YANKEES '98: DAY-BY-DAY

APRIL

Date	Opponent	Pitcher	Score	Record
1	at Anaheim	Andy Pettitte	Angels, 4-1	0-1
2	at Anaheim	David Wells	Angels, 10-2	0-2
4	at Oakland	David Cone	Athletics, 7-3	0-3
5	**at Oakland**	**Jeff Nelson**	**Yankees, 9-7**	**1-3**
6	at Seattle	Andy Pettitte	Mariners, 8-0	1-4
7	**at Seattle**	**David Wells**	**Yankees, 13-7**	**2-4**
8	**at Seattle**	**Graeme Lloyd**	**Yankees, 4-3**	**3-4**
10	**Oakland**	**Mike Buddie**	**Yankees, 17-13**	**4-4**
11	**Oakland**	**Andy Pettitte**	**Yankees, 3-1**	**5-4**
12	**Oakland**	**Mike Buddie**	**Yankees, 7-5**	**6-4**
15	**Anaheim**	**David Wells**	**Yankees, 6-3**	**7-4**
17	**at Detroit**	**Andy Pettitte**	**Yankees, 11-2**	**8-4**
18	**at Detroit**	**David Cone**	**Yankees, 8-3**	**9-4**
19	at Detroit	Darren Holmes	Tigers, 2-1	9-5
20	**at Toronto**	**Willie Banks**	**Yankees, 3-2**	**10-5**
21	**at Toronto**	**Mike Stanton**	**Yankees, 5-3**	**11-5**
22	**at Toronto**	**Andy Pettitte**	**Yankees, 9-1**	**12-5**
24	**Detroit**	**David Cone**	**Yankees, 8-4**	**13-5**
25	**Detroit**	**David Wells**	**Yankees, 5-4**	**14-5**
27	**Toronto**	**Andy Pettitte**	**Yankees, 1-0**	**15-5**
28	Toronto	Ramiro Mendoza	Blue Jays, 5-2	15-6
29	**Seattle**	**David Cone**	**Yankees, 8-5**	**16-6**
30	**Seattle**	**Mariano Rivera**	**Yankees, 9-8**	**17-6**

MAY

Date	Opponent	Pitcher	Score	Record
1	**at Kansas City**	**Hideki Irabu**	**Yankees, 2-1**	**18-6**
2	**at Kansas City**	**Andy Pettitte**	**Yankees, 12-6**	**19-6**
3	**at Kansas City**	**Ramiro Mendoza**	**Yankees, 10-1**	**20-6**
5	**at Texas**	**David Cone**	**Yankees, 7-2**	**21-6**
6	**at Texas**	**Mike Stanton**	**Yankees, 15-13**	**22-6**
8	**at Minnesota**	**Hideki Irabu**	**Yankees, 5-1**	**23-6**
9	at Minnesota	Andy Pettitte	Twins, 8-1	23-7
10	**at Minnesota**	**Ramiro Mendoza**	**Yankees, 7-0**	**24-7**
12	**Kansas City**	**David Wells**	**Yankees, 3-2**	**25-7**
13	**Texas**	**David Cone**	**Yankees, 8-6**	**26-7**
14	Texas	Willie Banks	Rangers, 7-5	26-8
15	Minnesota	Andy Pettitte	Twins, 7-6	26-9
16	**Minnesota**	**Ramiro Mendoza**	**Yankees, 5-2**	**27-9**
17	**Minnesota**	**David Wells**	**Yankees, 4-0**	**28-9**
19	**Baltimore**	**Mike Stanton**	**Yankees, 9-5**	**29-9**
20	**Baltimore**	**Hideki Irabu**	**Yankees, 9-6**	**30-9**
21	**Baltimore**	**Andy Pettitte**	**Yankees, 3-1**	**31-9**
22	at Boston	Jeff Nelson	Red Sox, 5-4	31-10
23	**at Boston**	**David Wells**	**Yankees, 12-3**	**32-10**
24	**at Boston**	**David Cone**	**Yankees, 14-4**	**33-10**
25	**at White Sox**	**Hideki Irabu**	**Yankees, 12-0**	**34-10**
26	**at White Sox**	**Jeff Nelson**	**Yankees, 7-5**	**35-10**
27	at White Sox	Jeff Nelson	White Sox, 12-9	35-11
28	**Boston**	**David Wells**	**Yankees, 8-3**	**36-11**
29	**Boston**	**David Cone**	**Yankees, 6-2**	**37-11**
30	Boston	Hideki Irabu	Red Sox, 3-2	37-12
31	Boston	Andy Pettitte	Red Sox, 13-7	37-13

JUNE

Date	Opponent	Pitcher	Score	Record
1	**White Sox**	**Jeff Nelson**	**Yankees, 5-4**	**38-13**
2	**White Sox**	**David Wells**	**Yankees, 6-3**	**39-13**
3	**Tampa Bay**	**Orlando Hernandez**	**Yankees, 7-1**	**40-13**
4	**Tampa Bay**	**Hideki Irabu**	**Yankees, 6-1**	**41-13**
5	**Florida**	**Andy Pettitte**	**Yankees, 5-1**	**42-13**
6	**Florida**	**Ramiro Mendoza**	**Yankees, 4-2**	**43-13**
7	**Florida**	**David Cone**	**Yankees, 4-1**	**44-13**
9	**at Montreal**	**Orlando Hernandez**	**Yankees, 11-1**	**45-13**
10	**at Montreal**	**Hideki Irabu**	**Yankees, 6-2**	**46-13**
11	at Montreal	Jeff Nelson	Expos, 7-5	46-14
14	**Cleveland**	**David Cone**	**Yankees, 4-2**	**47-14**
15	at Baltimore	David Wells	Orioles, 7-4	47-15
16	at Baltimore	Hideki Irabu	Orioles, 2-0	47-16
17	**at Baltimore**	**Andy Pettitte**	**Yankees, 5-3**	**48-16**
18	**at Cleveland**	**Jeff Nelson**	**Yankees, 5-2**	**49-16**
19	at Cleveland	David Cone	Indians, 7-4	49-17
20	**at Cleveland**	**David Wells**	**Yankees, 5-3**	**50-17**
21	at Cleveland	Hideki Irabu	Indians, 11-0	50-18
22	**Atlanta**	**Jeff Nelson**	**Yankees, 6-4**	**51-18**
23	Atlanta	Orlando Hernandez	Braves, 7-2	51-19
24	**at Atlanta**	**David Cone**	**Yankees, 10-6**	**52-19**
25	**at Atlanta**	**David Wells**	**Yankees, 6-0**	**53-19**
26	**at Mets**	**Ramiro Mendoza**	**Yankees, 8-4**	**54-19**
27	**at Mets**	**Andy Pettitte**	**Yankees, 7-2**	**55-19**
28	at Mets	Ramiro Mendoza	Mets, 2-1	55-20
30	**Philadelphia**	**David Cone**	**Yankees, 9-2**	**56-20**

JULY

Date	Opponent	Pitcher	Score	Record
1	**Philadelphia**	**David Wells**	**Yankees, 5-2**	**57-20**
2	**Philadelphia**	**Mike Buddie**	**Yankees, 9-8**	**58-20**
3	**Baltimore**	**Andy Pettitte**	**Yankees, 3-2**	**59-20**
4	**Baltimore**	**Orlando Hernandez**	**Yankees, 4-3**	**60-20**
5	**Baltimore**	**David Cone**	**Yankees, 1-0**	**61-20**
9	**at Tampa Bay**	**Andy Pettitte**	**Yankees, 2-0**	**62-20**
10	**at Tampa Bay**	**Hideki Irabu**	**Yankees, 8-4**	**63-20**
11	**at Tampa Bay**	**David Cone**	**Yankees, 2-0**	**64-20**
12	**at Tampa Bay**	**Mike Stanton**	**Yankees, 9-2**	**65-20**
13	at Cleveland	Orlando Hernandez	Indians, 4-1	65-21
14	**at Cleveland**	**Andy Pettitte**	**Yankees, 7-1**	**66-21**
15	**at Detroit**	**Hideki Irabu**	**Yankees, 11-0**	**67-21**
16	at Detroit	David Cone	Tigers, 3-1	67-22
17	at Toronto	Darren Holmes	Blue Jays, 9-6	67-23
18	**at Toronto**	**Orlando Hernandez**	**Yankees, 10-3**	**68-23**
19	at Toronto	Andy Pettitte	Blue Jays, 9-3	68-24
20	Detroit	Darren Holmes	Tigers, 4-3	68-25
20	**Detroit**	**Hideki Irabu**	**Yankees, 4-3**	**69-25**
21	**Detroit**	**David Cone**	**Yankees, 5-1**	**70-25**
22	**Detroit**	**Orlando Hernandez**	**Yankees, 13-2**	**71-25**
24	**White Sox**	**Andy Pettitte**	**Yankees, 5-4**	**72-25**
25	White Sox	Hideki Irabu	White Sox, 6-2	72-26
26	**White Sox**	**David Wells**	**Yankees, 6-3**	**73-26**
28	**at Anaheim**	**David Cone**	**Yankees, 9-3**	**74-26**
29	at Anaheim	Orlando Hernandez	Angels, 10-5	74-27
30	**at Anaheim**	**Ramiro Mendoza**	**Yankees, 3-0**	**75-27**
31	**at Seattle**	**Hideki Irabu**	**Yankees, 5-3**	**76-27**

AUGUST

Date	Opponent	Pitcher	Score	Record
1	**at Seattle**	**David Wells**	**Yankees, 5-2**	**77-27**
2	at Seattle	David Cone	Mariners, 6-3	77-28
3	**at Oakland**	**Orlando Hernandez**	**Yankees, 14-1**	**78-28**
4	**at Oakland**	**Ramiro Mendoza**	**Yankees, 10-4**	**79-28**
4	**at Oakland**	**Graeme Lloyd**	**Yankees, 10-5**	**80-28**
5	at Oakland	Hideki Irabu	Athletics, 3-1	80-29
7	**Kansas City**	**David Cone**	**Yankees, 8-2**	**81-29**
7	**Kansas City**	**David Wells**	**Yankees, 14-2**	**82-29**
8	**Kansas City**	**Orlando Hernandez**	**Yankees, 14-1**	**83-29**
9	**Kansas City**	**Ramiro Mendoza**	**Yankees, 5-4**	**84-29**
10	**Minnesota**	**Hideki Irabu**	**Yankees, 7-3**	**85-29**
11	**Minnesota**	**David Wells**	**Yankees, 7-0**	**86-29**
12	**Minnesota**	**David Cone**	**Yankees, 11-2**	**87-29**
13	**Texas**	**Orlando Hernandez**	**Yankees, 2-0**	**88-29**
14	**Texas**	**Andy Pettitte**	**Yankees, 6-4**	**89-29**
15	Texas	Hideki Irabu	Rangers, 16-5	89-30
16	**Texas**	**Mariano Rivera**	**Yankees, 6-5**	**90-30**
17	**at Kansas City**	**David Cone**	**Yankees, 7-1**	**91-30**
18	**at Kansas City**	**Joe Borowski**	**Yankees, 3-2**	**92-30**
19	at Minnesota	Andy Pettitte	Twins, 5-3	92-31
20	at Minnesota	Mike Buddie	Twins, 9-4	92-32
21	**at Texas**	**David Wells**	**Yankees, 5-0**	**93-32**
22	**at Texas**	**Ryan Bradley**	**Yankees, 12-9**	**94-32**
23	at Texas	Orlando Hernandez	Rangers, 12-10	94-33
24	Anaheim	Andy Pettitte	Angels, 7-3	94-34
25	Anaheim	Mike Stanton	Angels, 7-6	94-35
26	Anaheim	Ryan Bradley	Angels, 6-4	94-36
26	**Anaheim**	**Mariano Rivera**	**Yankees, 7-6**	**95-36**
27	**Anaheim**	**Jay Tessmer**	**Yankees, 6-5**	**96-36**
28	**Seattle**	**Orlando Hernandez**	**Yankees, 10-3**	**97-36**
29	**Seattle**	**Andy Pettitte**	**Yankees, 11-6**	**98-36**
30	Seattle	Hideki Irabu	Mariners, 13-3	98-37

SEPTEMBER

Date	Opponent	Pitcher	Score	Record
1	**Oakland**	**David Wells**	**Yankees, 7-0**	**99-37**
2	Oakland	David Cone	Athletics, 2-0	99-38
4	**at White Sox**	**Graeme Lloyd**	**Yankees, 11-6**	**100-38**
5	at White Sox	Andy Pettitte	White Sox, 9-5	100-39
6	at White Sox	Hideki Irabu	White Sox, 6-5	100-40
7	at Boston	David Wells	Red Sox, 4-3	100-41
8	**at Boston**	**David Cone**	**Yankees, 3-2**	**101-41**
9	**at Boston**	**Ramiro Mendoza**	**Yankees, 7-5**	**102-41**
10	**Toronto**	**Andy Pettitte**	**Yankees, 8-5**	**103-41**
11	Toronto	Hideki Irabu	Blue Jays, 5-4	103-42
12	Toronto	David Wells	Blue Jays, 5-3	103-43
13	Toronto	David Cone	Blue Jays, 5-3	103-44
14	**Boston**	**Orlando Hernandez**	**Yankees, 3-0**	**104-44**
15	Boston	Mike Jerzembeck	Red Sox, 9-4	104-45
16	at Tampa Bay	Andy Pettitte	Devil Rays, 7-0	104-46
17	**at Tampa Bay**	**Hideki Irabu**	**Yankees, 4-0**	**105-46**
18	**at Baltimore**	**David Wells**	**Yankees, 15-5**	**106-46**
19	at Baltimore	David Cone	Orioles, 5-3	106-47
20	**at Baltimore**	**Orlando Hernandez**	**Yankees, 5-4**	**107-47**
21	Cleveland	Andy Pettitte	Indians, 4-1	107-48
22	**Cleveland**	**Ramiro Mendoza**	**Yankees, 10-4**	**108-48**
22	**Cleveland**	**Hideki Irabu**	**Yankees, 5-1**	**109-48**
23	**Cleveland**	**Ryan Bradley**	**Yankees, 8-4**	**110-48**
24	**Tampa Bay**	**Mike Buddie**	**Yankees, 5-2**	**111-48**
25	**Tampa Bay**	**Orlando Hernandez**	**Yankees, 6-1**	**112-48**
26	**Tampa Bay**	**David Cone**	**Yankees, 3-1**	**113-48**
27	**Tampa Bay**	**Jim Bruske**	**Yankees, 8-3**	**114-48**

Wins in **boldface** type

"It's not going to change who I am. It's not going to change the way I approach the game of baseball," he said. "I still consider myself an everyday player. I plan on coming out every single day and proving that on a daily basis."

A new streak began the very next day.

More Great Performances

Hitters weren't the only ones making big news in 1998.

This was the season Orlando "El Duque" Hernandez, barely five months removed from a dangerous escape by raft from Cuba, made his big league debut in Yankee Stadium. The older half-brother of Marlins postseason hero Livan Hernandez mowed down the Devil Rays in his June 3 debut and later topped that with two postseason wins.

Hernandez, signed in early March to a four-year, $6.6 million contract after a bidding war that included the Angels and Indians, lived up to the hype. A movie about his remarkable life story was in the early stages of production. Oscar-winning actor Cuba Gooding Jr. was said to be preparing to play Hernandez.

"There's sort of this mystery intangible with El Duque," said Yankees teammate David Cone. "Who knows what that raft was like? What that treacherous ride was really like? What pitching on the Cuban national team was like? Nobody really knows what he's been through."

Meanwhile, a disheveled, slightly zany Yankees lefty named David Wells threw a perfect game against the Minnesota Twins on May 17 at Yankee Stadium. An overflow crowd was on hand for Beanie Baby Day.

Wells joined Don Larsen as the only pitchers in club history to achieve perfection. Wells' gem was just the 15th perfecto in big league history and the first since 1994.

"He's a blue-collar guy," Yankees manager Joe Torre said. "The rough edges I think (fans) like more than anything else. But The Boomer can pitch. There's never any doubt about that."

Wells' performance came less than two weeks after a highly publicized flap with Torre and Yankees pitching coach Mel Stottlemyre. Wells was unhappy when he was pulled in the third inning of a game against the Rangers.

After not speaking to either man for 72 hours, the problem was smoothed over during a 45-minute summit meeting in the visiting manager's office in Minneapolis.

Wells' gem stole the spotlight from a Cubs rookie named Kerry Wood, who tied a major league record by striking out 20 Houston Astros in a one-hit shutout on May 6.

Wood, a square-jawed Texan out of the Nolan Ryan mold, continued his "K" parade until September, when a tired right arm finally forced him to rest. He still finished with 233 strikeouts and a 13-6 record.

Longtime Blue Jays scout Gordon Lakey called Wood "the best first-

BASEBALL'S LONGEST STREAK ENDS

DIAMOND IMAGES

On Sept. 20, 1998, during the Orioles' final home game of the season, something unusual happened in Baltimore: third baseman Cal Ripken sat back and watched a game. Since May 30, 1982, Ripken had appeared in every game for the Orioles. His streak was credited with helping revive baseball in 1995 after the players' strike. The countdown to 2,131 began years before he actually broke Lou Gehrig's mark of 2,130 consecutive games on Sept. 6, 1995. But there was no advance warning when The Streak ended after 2,632 games. Ripken's name was originally in manager Ray Miller's lineup, but the Ironman opted out after deciding the situation was perfect to bring the string to a conclusion. Rookie Ryan Minor started at third base in the 5-4 loss to the New York Yankees. Ripken enjoyed the game from the dugout and later the Orioles bullpen.

SINGLE-GAME STRIKEOUTS

The top single-game strikeouts performances of all-time:

Pitcher, Team	Opponent	Date	Strikeouts
Kerry Wood, Cubs	**Astros**	**May 6, 1998**	**20**
Roger Clemens, Red Sox	Tigers	Sept. 18, 1996	20
Roger Clemens, Red Sox	Mariners	April 29, 1986	20
Randy Johnson, Mariners	White Sox	Aug. 8, 1997	19
Randy Johnson, Mariners	Athletics	June 24, 1997	19
David Cone, Mets	Phillies	Oct. 6, 1991	19
Nolan Ryan, Angels	Red Sox	Aug. 12, 1974	19
Tom Seaver, Mets	Padres	April 22, 1970	19
Steve Carlton, Cardinals	Mets	Sept. 15, 1969	19

MARK McGWIRE SCOREBOARD

A home run-by-home run accounting of Mark McGwire's record-shattering 1998 season:

No.	Date	Opponent	H/A	Pitcher	Inn.	Outs	Count	ROB*	Dist.	Score
1.	March 31	Los Angeles	H	Ramon Martinez	5	2	1-0	3	360	Cardinals, 6-0
2.	April 2	Los Angeles	H	Frank Lankford	12	2	0-1	2	370	Cardinals, 8-5 (12)
3.	April 3	San Diego	H	Mark Langston	5	0	3-2	1	370	Padres, 13-5
4.	April 4	San Diego	H	Don Wengert	6	0	2-1	2	430	Cardinals, 8-6
5.	April 14	Arizona	H	Jeff Suppan	3	1	1-2	1	420	Cardinals, 15-5
6.	April 14	Arizona	H	Jeff Suppan	5	2	1-1	0	340	Cardinals, 15-5
7.	April 14	Arizona	H	Barry Manuel	8	0	2-0	1	460	Cardinals, 15-5
8.	April 17	Philadelphia	H	Matt Whiteside	4	2	2-2	1	410	Cardinals, 8-5
9.	April 21	Montreal	A	Trey Moore	3	2	0-0	1	440	Cardinals, 5-3
10.	April 25	Philadelphia	A	Jerry Spradlin	7	2	1-2	1	410	Cardinals, 8-5
11.	April 30	Chicago (N)	A	Marc Pisciotta	8	1	2-1	1	380	Cubs, 8-3
12.	May 1	Chicago (N)	A	Rod Beck	9	2	1-2	1	360	Cubs, 6-5
13.	May 8	New York (N)	A	Rick Reed	3	1	0-2	1	350	Mets, 9-2
14.	May 12	Milwaukee	H	Paul Wagner	5	0	1-2	2	527	Cardinals, 6-5 (10)
15.	May 14	Atlanta	H	Kevin Millwood	4	0	1-1	0	380	Braves, 7-3
16.	May 16	Florida	H	Livan Hernandez	4	0	1-0	0	550	Cardinals, 5-4
17.	May 18	Florida	H	Jesus Sanchez	4	0	2-0	0	478	Marlins, 7-3
18.	May 19	Philadelphia	A	Tyler Green	3	1	2-0	1	420	Phillies, 10-8
19.	May 19	Philadelphia	A	Tyler Green	5	0	0-2	1	390	Phillies, 10-8
20.	May 19	Philadelphia	A	Wayne Gomes	8	0	0-0	1	420	Phillies, 10-8
21.	May 22	San Francisco	H	Mark Gardner	6	1	1-1	1	425	Cardinals, 4-3 (12)
22.	May 23	San Francisco	H	Rich Rodriguez	4	1	1-0	0	370	Cardinals, 11-10
23.	May 23	San Francisco	H	John Johnstone	5	1	2-2	2	480	Cardinals, 11-10
24.	May 24	San Francisco	H	Robb Nen	12	2	2-2	1	390	Giants, 9-6 (17)
25.	May 25	Colorado	H	John Thomson	1	2	2-2	0	430	Rockies, 6-1
26.	May 29	San Diego	A	Dan Miceli	9	1	0-1	1	388	Cardinals, 8-3
27.	May 30	San Diego	A	Andy Ashby	1	2	0-1	0	423	Padres, 3-2
28.	June 5	San Francisco	H	Orel Hershiser	1	1	1-2	1	410	Giants, 3-2
29.	June 8	Chicago (A)	A	Jason Bere	4	0	0-0	1	360	White Sox, 8-6
30.	June 10	Chicago (A)	A	Jim Parque	3	1	1-0	2	410	White Sox, 10-8 (11)
31.	June 12	Arizona	A	Andy Benes	3	1	1-0	3	450	Cardinals, 9-4
32.	June 17	Houston	A	Jose Lima	3	2	1-2	0	350	Astros, 6-5
33.	June 18	Houston	A	Shane Reynolds	5	0	1-1	0	450	Cardinals, 7-6
34.	June 24	Cleveland	A	Jaret Wright	4	1	1-1	0	430	Indians, 14-3
35.	June 25	Cleveland	A	Dave Burba	1	2	2-2	0	461	Indians, 8-2
36.	June 27	Minnesota	A	Mike Trombley	7	2	2-2	1	430	Cardinals, 7-2
37.	June 30	Kansas City	H	Glendon Rusch	7	0	0-1	0	470	Royals, 6-1
38.	July 11	Houston	H	Billy Wagner	11	1	0-2	1	440	Cardinals, 4-3 (11)
39.	July 12	Houston	H	Sean Bergman	1	2	0-0	0	400	Cardinals, 6-4
40.	July 12	Houston	H	Scott Elarton	7	0	2-1	0	390	Cardinals, 6-4
41.	July 17	Los Angeles	H	Brian Bohanon	1	2	0-0	0	510	Cardinals, 4-1
42.	July 17	Los Angeles	H	Antonio Osuna	8	1	1-0	0	430	Cardinals, 4-1
43.	July 20	San Diego	A	Brian Boehringer	5	0	2-1	1	450	Cardinals, 13-1
44.	July 26	Colorado	A	John Thomson	4	2	0-0	0	452	Cardinals, 3-1
45.	July 28	Milwaukee	H	Mike Myers	8	1	2-2	0	420	Brewers, 13-10
46.	Aug. 8	Chicago (N)	H	Mark Clark	4	0	2-1	0	380	Cardinals, 9-8 (13)
47.	Aug. 11	New York (N)	H	Bobby Jones	4	0	1-0	0	470	Mets, 8-3
48.	Aug. 19	Chicago (N)	A	Matt Karchner	8	1	3-1	0	398	Cardinals, 8-6 (10)
49.	Aug. 19	Chicago (N)	A	Terry Mulholland	10	1	2-0	0	409	Cardinals, 8-6 (10)
50.	Aug. 20	New York (N)	A	Rick Reed	1	2	3-2	0	385	Mets, 5-4
51.	Aug. 20	New York (N)	A	Willie Blair	7	0	2-1	0	369	Mets, 5-4
52.	Aug. 22	Pittsburgh	A	Francisco Cordova	1	2	0-2	0	460	Pirates, 14-4
53.	Aug. 23	Pittsburgh	A	Ricardo Rincon	8	2	2-2	0	390	Pirates, 4-3
54.	Aug. 26	Florida	H	Justin Speier	8	0	0-1	1	510	Marlins, 7-6 (10)
55.	Aug. 30	Atlanta	H	Dennis Martinez	7	0	1-0	2	500	Cardinals, 8-7
56.	Sept. 1	Florida	A	Livan Hernandez	7	0	1-1	0	450	Cardinals, 7-1
57.	Sept. 1	Florida	A	Donn Pall	9	1	0-0	0	470	Cardinals, 7-1
58.	Sept. 2	Florida	A	Brian Edmondson	7	2	2-1	1	430	Cardinals, 14-4
59.	Sept. 2	Florida	A	Robby Stanifer	8	2	0-0	1	458	Cardinals, 14-4
60.	Sept. 5	Cincinnati	H	Dennis Reyes	1	1	2-0	1	380	Cardinals, 7-0
61.	Sept. 7	Chicago (N)	H	Mike Morgan	1	2	1-1	0	430	Cardinals, 3-2
62.	Sept. 8	Chicago (N)	H	Steve Trachsel	4	2	0-0	0	341	Cardinals, 6-3
63.	Sept. 15	Pittsburgh	H	Jason Christiansen	9	1	1-0	0	385	Cardinals, 9-3
64.	Sept. 18	Milwaukee	H	Rafael Roque	4	0	3-1	1	410	Cardinals, 7-4
65.	Sept. 20	Milwaukee	H	Scott Karl	1	1	2-1	1	420	Cardinals, 11-6
66.	Sept. 25	Montreal	H	Shayne Bennett	5	2	1-2	1	380	Cardinals, 6-5
67.	Sept. 26	Montreal	H	Dustin Hermanson	4	1	0-0	0	400	Expos, 7-6
68.	Sept. 26	Montreal	H	Kirk Bullinger	7	2	1-1	1	440	Expos, 7-6
69.	Sept. 27	Montreal	H	Mike Thurman	3	2	1-1	0	377	Cardinals, 6-3
70.	Sept. 27	Montreal	H	Carl Pavano	7	2	0-0	2	370	Cardinals, 6-3

***ROB**—Runners on Base

year pitcher" he'd ever seen.

"There's a new term being used in baseball these days: electric," Lakey said. "Like, 'This guy has an electric fastball' or 'This guy has an electric curveball.' Well, this guy ain't electric. He's nuclear."

This was the year classy Braves shortstop Walt Weiss made his first All-Star Game appearance–and a nation cried tears of joy. Brody Weiss, the shortstop's 3-year-old son, was in the Coors Field stands that July night, just two weeks after being exposed to potentially fatal e.coli bacteria at an Atlanta-area water park.

PERFECT GAMES

A complete list of the 15 perfect games in major league history, including the one spun May 17, 1998, by the Yankees' David Wells.

Pitcher, Team	Opponent	Date	Score
John Richmond, Worcester	Cleveland	June 12, 1880	1-0
John Ward, Providence	Buffalo	June 17, 1880	5-0
Cy Young, Boston (AL)	Philadelphia	May 5, 1904	3-0
Addie Joss, Cleveland (AL)	Chicago	Oct. 2, 1908	1-0
Charles Robertson, Chicago (AL)	Detroit	April 30, 1922	2-0
Don Larsen, New York (AL)	Brooklyn	Oct. 8, 1956	2-0
Jim Bunning, Philadelphia	New York (NL)	June 21, 1964	6-0
Sandy Koufax, Los Angeles	Chicago (NL)	Sept. 9, 1965	1-0
Jim "Catfish" Hunter, Oakland	Minnesota	May 8, 1968	4-0
Len Barker, Cleveland	Toronto	May 15, 1981	3-0
Mike Witt, California	Texas	Sept. 30, 1984	1-0
Tom Browning, Cincinnati	Los Angeles	Sept. 16, 1988	1-0
Dennis Martinez, Montreal	Los Angeles	July 28, 1991	2-0
Kenny Rogers, Texas	California	July 28, 1994	4-0
David Wells, New York (AL)	**Minnesota**	**May 17, 1998**	**4-0**

This was the year Phillies ace Curt Schilling became the fifth pitcher in baseball history to record 300 strikeouts in consecutive seasons. It took him until his last start of the season, but he got there.

This was the year Mariners shortstop Alex Rodriguez became the first player at his position to hit 40 home runs and steal 40 bases. He finished with 42 homers and 46 steals.

This was the year Giants outfielder Barry Bonds moved into his very own club: the 400-400 Club. Bonds, still going strong at age 34, set his sights on 500 homers and 500 stolen bases.

"That's a nice combination of speed and power and your ability to run that much and hit that much," Giants manager Dusty Baker said. "The amount of pressure on your legs is incredible. You've got to be in tremendous shape to go for that long a period of time. You have to play a lot and stay off the disabled list."

Said Giants teammate Joe Carter, who retired at the end of the year: "You can say what you want to about Barry Bonds, but he's had a heck of a career and his stats back it up. I mean, he talks a lot. He's very confident. He's not going to be short on words but he's a guy that backs up what he talks about. That's what it comes down to."

It's Still A Business

The Fox Group, the people who gave us Bart Simpson and Melrose Place, proved almost as dastardly in their first year of running the Los Angeles Dodgers.

Baseball owners formally welcomed media mogul Rupert Murdoch to their clique in March, his $311 million purchase of the Dodgers from Peter O'Malley setting an industry record. Peter Chernin and Chase Carey, Murdoch's lieutenants, promised Fox would do its best to continue the blue-blood tradition crafted in a half-century of O'Malley family ownership.

PERFECTO

JOHN KLEIN

Yankees lefthander David Wells made history on May 17 when he became just the 15th major leaguer to record a perfect game. Wells struck out 11 Twins in the performance, including catcher Javier Valentin in all three of his at-bats. Minnesota shortstop Pat Meares flew out to right fielder Paul O'Neill to seal the masterpiece.

MINN.	ab	r	h	bi	bb	so	NEW YORK	ab	r	h	bi	bb	so
Lawton cf	3	0	0	0	0	0	Knoblauch 2b	4	0	0	0	0	0
Gates 2b	3	0	0	0	0	1	Jeter ss	3	0	1	0	1	2
Molitor dh	3	0	0	0	0	1	O'Neill rf	4	0	0	0	0	2
Cordova lf	3	0	0	0	0	1	Martinez 1b	4	0	0	0	0	0
Coomer 1b	3	0	0	0	0	2	Williams cf	3	3	3	1	0	0
Ochoa rf	3	0	0	0	0	0	Strawberry dh	3	1	1	1	0	0
Shave 3b	3	0	0	0	0	2	Curtis lf	3	0	1	1	0	0
Valentin c	3	0	0	0	0	3	Posada c	3	0	0	0	0	1
Meares ss	3	0	0	0	0	1	Brosius 3b	3	0	0	0	0	1
Totals	**27**	**0**	**0**	**0**	**0**	**11**	**Totals**	**30**	**4**	**6**	**3**	**1**	**6**

Minnesota	**000 000 000—0**
New York	**010 100 20x—4**

LOB—New York 3. **2B**—Williams 2. **3B**—Strawberry. **HR**—Williams. **SB**—Jeter, Curtis.

Minnesota	ip	h	r	er	bb	so	New York	ip	h	r	er	bb	so
Hawkins L	7	6	4	4	0	5	Wells W	9	0	0	0	0	11
Naulty	⅓	0	0	0	1	0							
Swindell	⅔	0	0	0	0	1							

PB—Valentin. **WP**—Hawkins.

Umpires: HP—McClelland; **1B**—Hirschbeck; **2B**—Garcia; **3B**—Reilly. **T**—2:40. **A**—49,820.

SAMMY SOSA SCOREBOARD

A home run-by-home run listing of Sammy Sosa's near-record chase for the single-season record:

No.	Date	Opponent	H/A	Pitcher	Inn.	Outs	Count	ROB*	Dist.	Score
1.	April 4	Montreal	H	Marc Valdes	3	2	2-1	0	371	Cubs, 3-1
2.	April 11	Montreal	A	Anthony Telford	7	1	1-2	0	350	Expos, 5-4 (10)
3.	April 15	New York (N)	A	Dennis Cook	8	2	3-2	0	430	Mets, 2-1
4.	April 23	San Diego	H	Dan Miceli	9	0	0-1	0	420	Padres, 4-1
5.	April 24	Los Angeles	A	Ismael Valdes	1	2	3-1	0	430	Dodgers, 12-4
6.	April 27	San Diego	A	Joey Hamilton	1	1	0-1	1	434	Cubs, 3-1
7.	May 3	St. Louis	H	Cliff Politte	1	2	2-1	0	370	Cardinals, 8-5
8.	May 16	Cincinnati	A	Scott Sullivan	3	1	2-1	2	420	Cubs, 5-4
9.	May 22	Atlanta	A	Greg Maddux	1	2	2-2	0	440	Braves, 8-2
10.	May 25	Atlanta	A	Kevin Millwood	4	0	2-2	0	410	Braves, 9-5
11.	May 25	Atlanta	A	Mike Cather	8	2	0-1	2	420	Braves, 9-5
12.	May 27	Philadelphia	H	Darrin Winston	8	0	1-2	0	460	Phillies, 10-5
13.	May 27	Philadelphia	H	Wayne Gomes	9	2	0-0	1	400	Phillies, 10-5
14.	June 1	Florida	H	Ryan Dempster	1	1	1-0	1	430	Cubs, 10-2
15.	June 1	Florida	H	Oscar Henriquez	8	2	1-0	2	410	Cubs, 10-2
16.	June 3	Florida	H	Livan Hernandez	5	0	1-0	1	370	Cubs, 5-1
17.	June 5	Chicago (A)	H	Jim Parque	5	0	1-2	1	370	Cubs, 6-5 (12)
18.	June 6	Chicago (A)	H	Carlos Castillo	7	2	2-2	0	410	Cubs, 7-6
19.	June 7	Chicago (A)	H	James Baldwin	5	1	3-2	2	380	Cubs, 13-7
20.	June 8	Minnesota	A	LaTroy Hawkins	3	1	0-2	0	340	Cubs, 8-1
21.	June 13	Philadelphia	A	Mark Portugal	6	0	0-1	1	350	Cubs, 10-8 (10)
22.	June 15	Milwaukee	H	Cal Eldred	1	2	1-0	0	420	Cubs, 6-5
23.	June 15	Milwaukee	H	Cal Eldred	3	1	2-1	0	410	Cubs, 6-5
24.	June 15	Milwaukee	H	Cal Eldred	7	2	2-1	0	415	Cubs, 6-5
25.	June 17	Milwaukee	H	Bronswell Patrick	4	0	2-2	0	430	Brewers, 6-5
26.	June 19	Philadelphia	H	Carlton Loewer	1	2	2-2	0	380	Phillies, 9-8 (12)
27.	June 19	Philadelphia	H	Carlton Loewer	5	1	1-0	1	380	Phillies, 9-8 (12)
28.	June 20	Philadelphia	H	Matt Beech	3	2	3-2	1	366	Cubs, 9-4
29.	June 20	Philadelphia	H	Toby Borland	6	1	2-0	2	500	Cubs, 9-4
30.	June 21	Philadelphia	H	Tyler Green	4	2	2-2	0	380	Phillies, 7-2
31.	June 24	Detroit	A	Seth Greisinger	1	1	0-2	0	390	Tigers, 7-6 (11)
32.	June 25	Detroit	A	Brian Moehler	7	0	1-0	0	400	Tigers, 6-4
33.	June 30	Arizona	H	Alan Embree	8	1	3-2	0	364	Diamondbacks, 7-4
34.	July 9	Milwaukee	A	Jeff Juden	2	2	0-2	1	430	Brewers, 12-9
35.	July 10	Milwaukee	A	Scott Karl	2	0	1-0	0	450	Brewers, 6-5
36.	July 17	Florida	A	Kirt Ojala	6	2	2-1	1	440	Cubs, 6-1
37.	July 22	Montreal	H	Miguel Batista	8	2	1-0	2	365	Cubs, 9-5
38.	July 26	New York (N)	H	Rick Reed	6	1	2-2	1	420	Cubs, 3-1
39.	July 27	Arizona	A	Willie Blair	6	2	1-1	1	350	Cubs, 6-2
40.	July 27	Arizona	A	Alan Embree	8	0	0-0	3	420	Cubs, 6-2
41.	July 28	Arizona	A	Bob Wolcott	5	1	3-1	3	400	Diamondbacks, 7-5
42.	July 31	Colorado	H	Jamey Wright	1	2	3-2	0	380	Cubs, 9-1
43.	Aug. 5	Arizona	H	Andy Benes	3	2	3-2	1	380	Diamondbacks, 10-7
44.	Aug. 8	St. Louis	A	Rich Croushore	9	0	1-0	1	400	Cardinals, 9-8 (13)
45.	Aug. 10	San Francisco	A	Russ Ortiz	5	2	3-1	0	370	Cubs, 8-5
46.	Aug. 10	San Francisco	A	Chris Brock	7	2	2-1	0	420	Cubs, 8-5
47.	Aug. 16	Houston	A	Sean Bergman	4	1	0-1	0	360	Cubs, 2-1 (11)
48.	Aug. 19	St. Louis	H	Kent Bottenfield	5	2	0-0	1	368	Cardinals, 8-6 (10)
49.	Aug. 21	San Francisco	H	Orel Hershiser	5	1	3-2	1	430	Cubs, 6-5
50.	Aug. 23	Houston	H	Jose Lima	5	2	3-2	0	433	Astros, 13-3
51.	Aug. 23	Houston	H	Jose Lima	8	0	1-0	0	388	Astros, 13-3
52.	Aug. 26	Cincinnati	A	Brett Tomko	3	2	1-1	0	440	Cubs, 9-2
53.	Aug. 28	Colorado	A	John Thomson	1	2	1-2	0	414	Cubs, 10-5
54.	Aug. 30	Colorado	A	Darryl Kile	1	1	1-2	1	482	Cubs, 4-3
55.	Aug. 31	Cincinnati	H	Brett Tomko	3	2	0-1	1	364	Cubs, 5-4
56.	Sept. 2	Cincinnati	H	Jason Bere	6	0	0-1	0	370	Cubs, 4-2
57.	Sept. 4	Pittsburgh	A	Jason Schmidt	1	2	2-0	0	400	Cubs, 8-4
58.	Sept. 5	Pittsburgh	A	Sean Lawrence	6	0	3-1	0	405	Pirates, 4-3
59.	Sept. 11	Milwaukee	H	Bill Pulsipher	5	1	0-1	0	433	Brewers, 13-11
60.	Sept. 12	Milwaukee	H	V. de los Santos	7	1	3-2	2	390	Cubs, 15-12
61.	Sept. 13	Milwaukee	H	Bronswell Patrick	5	0	0-1	1	480	Cubs, 11-10
62.	Sept. 13	Milwaukee	H	Eric Plunk	9	1	2-1	0	480	Cubs, 11-10
63.	Sept. 16	San Diego	A	Brian Boehringer	8	2	1-0	3	434	Cubs, 6-3
64.	Sept. 23	Milwaukee	A	Rafael Roque	5	1	1-0	0	344	Brewers, 8-7
65.	Sept. 23	Milwaukee	A	Rod Henderson	6	2	2-2	0	410	Brewers, 8-7
66.	Sept. 25	Houston	A	Jose Lima	4	0	0-1	0	420	Astros, 6-2

***ROB**—Runners on Base

It did not take Fox long to stand that notion on its head, along with the rest of the game.

On May 15 the Dodgers and Florida Marlins pulled off the so-called Deal of the Century. More than $114 million in combined salary obligation changed hands as the Dodgers shipped prospective free agent Mike Piazza and third baseman Todd Zeile east in exchange for five players, including all-stars Gary Sheffield and Charles Johnson.

The Marlins dealt Piazza to the New York Mets a week later for three prospects. By late October, Piazza provided the starter's pistol for the free-agency frenzy. He re-signed with the Mets for $91 million over seven years. His deal included use of a luxury suite at Shea Stadium and his own hotel suite on the road.

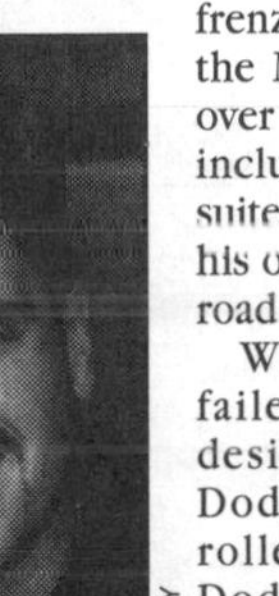
MEL BAILEY

Mike Piazza

When the Piazza deal failed to produce the desired results for the Dodgers, more heads rolled. A month later, Dodgers manager Bill Russell and general manager Fred Claire were toppled in a stunning coup. Russell became the first Dodgers manager fired in midseason since 1948.

Glenn Hoffman was promoted from Triple-A Albuquerque to take over as manager, while Hall of Fame manager Tommy Lasorda came out of semi-retirement to take the GM reins on an interim basis.

Claire, whose 11-year reign was the longest by a GM with his current team, was held accountable for a deal in which he had little, if any, input. Claire got a measure of revenge when Lasorda bungled through a series of midseason trades.

Lasorda plundered the Dodgers farm system in trades for Jeff Shaw, Carlos Perez and Mark Grudzielanek, guaranteed a playoff berth for the club, then watched the Dodgers wilt down the stretch.

Kevin Malone, the former Baltimore assistant GM, was hired as Dodgers GM at season's end. His manager search proved frustrating as Jim Leyland twice refused invitations to interview and Felipe Alou, with whom Malone had worked in Montreal, spurned the Dodgers' offer at the last minute to sign a lucrative extension with the Expos.

Davey Johnson, whose dugout career has been laden with both controversy and success in stops with the Mets, Reds and Orioles, wound up as the compromise choice for Dodgers manager.

Leyland, meanwhile, exercised a $300,000 escape clause in his contract and bolted the Marlins after two seasons for a three-year, $6 million deal with the Colorado Rockies. Leyland, a 13-8 loser as National League manager at the 1998 All-Star Game in Coors Field, nonetheless opted to pursue his second World Series ring with the pitching-challenged organization.

Don Baylor, who had been the only manager in

ON THE REBOUND

Baseball's most exciting season in years led to an all-time total attendance record in 1998. The per-game average was third best all-time, however, and significantly trailed pre-strike levels established in 1993-94.

Year	Total Attendance	Per Game
1993	70,256,459	31,337
1994	50,009,023	31,612
1995	50,282,795	26,202
1996	60,096,451	26,889
1997	63,016,136	28,288
1998	70,589,505	29,376

KID K

LARRY GOREN

In just his fifth major league start, Chicago Cubs righthander Kerry Wood matched his age in strikeouts, whiffing one Astro batter for each of his 20 years. The one hit he allowed was an infield single off the glove of third baseman Kevin Orie that many felt should have been ruled an error. Wood was most pleased by the fact that he didn't walk a batter.

HOUSTON	ab	r	h	bi	bb	so	CHICAGO	ab	r	h	bi	bb	so
Biggio 2b	3	0	0	0	0	1	Brown cf	4	0	2	0	0	1
Bell rf	4	0	0	0	0	2	Morandini 2b	4	1	1	0	0	2
Bagwell 1b	3	0	0	0	0	3	Sosa rf	4	0	1	0	0	2
Howell 3b	3	0	0	0	0	3	Grace 1b	3	1	2	0	1	0
Alou cf	3	0	0	0	0	3	Rodriguez lf	2	0	0	1	0	2
Clark lf	3	0	0	0	0	2	Hernandez lf	1	0	0	1	0	0
Gutierrez ss	3	0	1	0	0	2	Blauser ss	3	0	2	0	0	0
Ausmus c	3	0	0	0	0	2	Martinez c	2	0	0	0	1	0
Reynolds p	1	0	0	0	0	1	Orie 3b	3	0	0	0	0	2
Spiers ph	1	0	0	0	0	1	Wood p	3	0	0	0	0	1
Totals	**27**	**0**	**1**	**0**	**0**	**20**	**Totals**	**29**	**2**	**8**	**2**	**2**	**10**

Houston	**000 000 000—0**
Chicago	**010 000 01x—2**

E—Clark. **DP**—Houston 1. **LOB**—Houston 2, Chicago 6. **2B**—Grace, Blauser. **CS**—Hernandez. **SH**—Reynolds. **SF**—Rodriguez.

Houston	ip	h	r	er	bb	so	Chicago	ip	h	r	er	bb	so
Reynolds L	8	8	2	1	2	10	Wood W	9	1	0	0	0	20

HBP—Biggio (by Wood). **Balk**—Wood.

Umpires: HP—Meals; **1B**—Tata; **2B**—Davis; **3B**—Bell. **T**—2:19. **A**—15,758.

Organization of the Year

Yankees spend money wisely in building system

Talk to enough people in baseball about how the Yankees operate, and the No. 1 topic is money. Teams without the financial means the Yankees have, or teams that refuse to spend, rationalize the Yankees' success by saying they write checks to fill needs.

While it's true that principal owner George Steinbrenner adheres to the philosophy that in order to make money you have to spend it, other teams have no problem doling out dollars.

So to say that the Yankees were Baseball America's 1998 Organization of the Year simply because they spend money isn't correct.

"Everything we do is based on a foundation of principles," Yankees vice president for player development Mark Newman said. "We have a plan and a profile in terms of where we want to go as far as signing players and the development of players. That plan runs throughout the organization."

PREVIOUS WINNERS

1982—Oakland Athletics
1983—New York Mets
1984—New York Mets
1985—Milwaukee Brewers
1986—Milwaukee Brewers
1987—Milwaukee Brewers
1988—Montreal Expos
1989—Texas Rangers
1990—Montreal Expos
1991—Atlanta Braves
1992—Cleveland Indians
1993—Toronto Blue Jays
1994—Kansas City Royals
1995—New York Mets
1996—Atlanta Braves
1997—Detroit Tigers

At the heart of the Yankees' plan is The Bronx. Whether it's a Tampa minicamp, injured minor league players working at the Tampa complex during the winter, or scouts watching a high school game while sitting in a cold April Indiana rain, the goal remains crystal clear.

"Everything is New York-driven," said Newman, who has been running the player-development department since 1996. "We need to know how players will react to the pressure. We are trying to win all the time, but we have to know if we have good enough players to play on a championship club. We are not looking for average guys."

Little about the '98 Yankees was average. En route to an unbelievable 125-50 record between the regular season and postseason, they won their second World Series in three years and 24th in the storied franchise's history. They swept two of their three playoff series, including a four-game dismissal of the Padres in the World Series.

However, look past the major league success for a moment and you find one of the premier player-development setups going. Steinbrenner doesn't shortchange that end of the spectrum, though other clubs do spend more at the minor league level than the Yankees. And just as he demands results from the big club, The Boss follows his minor league system very closely.

Steinbrenner trusts his inner circle of general manager Brian Cashman, superscout Gene Michael, scouting director Lin Garrett, player-personnel director Gordon Blakeley, organizational pitching coordinator Billy Connors and Newman.

Many of the key players on the '98 club were home grown. Several others were picked in exchange for organization products.

As for the next installment of prospects, the Yankees aren't short. Triple-A third baseman Mike Lowell was ready for the big leagues and Class A first baseman Nick Johnson was on the fast track. Righthander Ryan Bradley sailed through three levels to make it to The Bronx in his second pro season. Class A outfielder Jackson Melian, whom the Yankees gave $1.6 million as a 16-year-old in 1996, continued to progress. The lower levels were teeming with talent.

The Yankees' tentacles are everywhere. They are major players on the international market, as Orlando Hernandez, Hideki Irabu and Mariano Rivera prove. Yes, they spend a lot of money at home and abroad. But because they have a detailed plan, the money hasn't been wasted.

—GEORGE KING

Rockies history, was dismissed after six years, including a wild-card berth in 1995. He landed in Atlanta, where he supplanted Clarence Jones as Braves hitting coach.

The Tigers, a year removed from one of the greatest turnarounds in baseball history, dismissed manager Buddy Bell in September. Interim choice Larry Parrish was retained as the full-time replacement.

Dismantling A Champion

Leyland took his leave from Florida after enduring a surreal victory lap. The Marlins became the biggest year-after flop in World Series history, going from the World Series title to a 54-108 nightmare thanks to a series of one-sided deals.

After spending $150 million on free agents and contract extensions en route to winning the 1997 World Series, the Marlins slashed their payroll from almost $54 million to just $13 million by the end of July. Among the players dealt away in a dizzying six-month period: pitchers Kevin Brown, Al Leiter, Robb Nen and Jay Powell; outfielders Sheffield, Moises Alou and Devon White; third baseman Bobby Bonilla; and Johnson, the Gold Glove catcher.

Rookie of the Year

Cubs cautiously excited about Wood's future

Rookie of the Year coronations usually are a time for giddy prognostication, the dreamy look into a player's wide-open future. But 1998 was a little different. When the Cubs talked about freshman sensation Kerry Wood, they did so cautiously.

First baseman Mark Grace: "If his elbow stays healthy, he's gonna be a Hall of Famer. Hands down."

Cubs general manager Ed Lynch: "I just want to see Kerry stay healthy. That's the most important thing. Because if he stays healthy, with the physical skills that he has now, he is going to be a perennial all-star type pitcher."

Cubs manager Jim Riggleman: "I just want him to be healthy. Then everything will fall into place."

Everything fell into place on May 6, when, in his fifth major league start, Wood tied Roger Clemens' major league record with 20 strikeouts in a one-hitter against the Astros. If anyone had any lingering doubts whether he was ready for the big leagues, they disappeared that day.

Wood's masterpiece was arguably the most dominant pitching performance of all time. One hit, an infield single that tipped the glove of third baseman Kevin Orie and could have been ruled an error; no walks; one hit batter; 20 strikeouts; 84 strikes among 122 pitches.

Wood became an overnight celebrity, but he kept his composure and focus, which endeared him to his teammates.

"Rookies, a lot of them nowadays, come up and act like they've been here 10 years," closer Rod Beck said. "Kerry comes up and he's an old-school player. He's levelheaded, very mature for his age. It's very refreshing to see."

Less refreshing, however, was when Wood began experiencing what was termed a "tired arm" in August. Then, after a win over the Reds on Aug. 31, Wood complained of pain in his pitching elbow. The diagnosis: a strained ligament. The prescription: complete shutdown.

Wood didn't pitch in a game the rest of the regular season. The Cubs waited 32 days before throwing their 6-foot-5, 225-pound horse again, when the team trailed the Braves two games to none in the National League Division Series. Wood took the loss while yielding three hits and one run in five innings, striking out five. Chicago lost 6-2, ending its season.

Wood, who threw 93 pitches in that game, was protected by the Cubs like a royal heir. Which he was, in a sense. From the same Texas lineage as strikeout kings Nolan Ryan and Clemens, Wood probably will recover fully from his injury, however scary it might have been in September.

He should begin 1999 not just as the reigning Baseball America Rookie of the Year, but ready to bring all those predictions to life.

—ALAN SCHWARZ

MEL BAILEY

Kerry Wood

PREVIOUS WINNERS

1989—Gregg Olson, rhp, Orioles
1990—Sandy Alomar, c, Indians
1991—Jeff Bagwell, 1b, Astros
1992—Pat Listach, ss, Brewers
1993—Mike Piazza, c, Dodgers
1994—Raul Mondesi, of, Dodgers
1995—Hideo Nomo, rhp, Dodgers
1996—Derek Jeter, ss, Yankees
1997—Nomar Garciaparra, ss, Red Sox

TOP 20 ROOKIES

Selected by Baseball America

1. Kerry Wood, rhp, Cubs
2. Todd Helton, 1b, Rockies
3. Ben Grieve, of, Athletics
4. Orlando Hernandez, rhp, Yankees
5. Rolando Arrojo, rhp, Devil Rays
6. Kerry Ligtenberg, rhp, Braves
7. Mike Caruso, ss, White Sox
8. Mark Kotsay, of, Marlins
9. Brad Fullmer, 1b, Expos
10. Travis Lee, 1b, Diamondbacks
11. Magglio Ordonez, of, White Sox
12. Steve Woodard, rhp, Brewers
13. Derrek Lee, 1b, Marlins
14. Sean Casey, 1b, Reds
15. Bobby Smith, 3b-ss, Devil Rays
16. Desi Relaford, ss, Phillies
17. David Dellucci, of, Diamondbacks
18. Carl Pavano, rhp, Expos
19. Randy Winn, of, Devil Rays
20. Bobby Howry, rhp, White Sox

Huizenga mandated the cost-cutting trades after putting the team up for sale and claiming $34 million in 1997 losses. Marlins president Don Smiley spent nearly 10 months trying to put together a group to buy the club before finally bowing out in early September.

South Florida financial wizard John Henry, a minority owner of the Yankees, concluded a handshake agreement in late September to buy the Marlins for $160 million. Henry vowed to keep the team in South Florida, even if it meant building a new baseball-only stadium with his own funds.

Less problematic was the sale of the Rangers. Tom Hicks, who also owns the NHL's Dallas Stars, bought the club from a group led by Texas Governor George W. Bush. Hicks was approved in June, and a month later Rangers GM Doug Melvin completed a flurry of deadline deals that netted the club Todd Stottlemyre, Royce Clayton, Todd Zeile and Esteban Loaiza.

The Rangers rallied to overtake the Anaheim Angels for their second AL West title in three years, then were swept out of the Division Series by the Yankees.

Meanwhile, new stadiums were either under construction or in the planning stages in San Diego, Seattle, San Francisco, Detroit, Pittsburgh, Houston, Cincinnati and Milwaukee.

1998 MAJOR LEAGUE ALL-STAR GAME

American League wins slugfest at Colorado's Coors Field

Fans who were expecting a lot of offense when the game's best hitters met at Denver's Coors Field for the 1998 All-Star Game didn't go home disappointed. The American League slugged its way to a 13-8 win to take its second consecutive midsummer classic.

For the second straight year, an Alomar won MVP honors. Baltimore second baseman Roberto Alomar went 3-for-4 with two runs and a solo home run off Padres closer Trevor Hoffman in the seventh. Brother Sandy Alomar won the award in 1997 after hitting a game-winning two-run homer in front of his hometown Cleveland fans.

TOP VOTE-GETTERS

AMERICAN LEAGUE

CATCHER: 1. Ivan Rodriguez, Rangers, 3,012,549; 2. Sandy Alomar, Indians, 2,053,805; 3. Joe Girardi, Yankees, 555,499.

FIRST BASE: 1. Jim Thome, Indians, 1,193,823; 2. Tino Martinez, Yankees, 993,944; 3. Frank Thomas, White Sox, 872,908.

SECOND BASE: 1. Roberto Alomar, Orioles, 1,834,970; 2. Chuck Knoblauch, Yankees, 1,650,428; 3. Joey Cora, Mariners, 861,200.

THIRD BASE: 1. Cal Ripken, Orioles, 3,402,657; 2. Travis Fryman, Indians, 843,642; 3. Scott Brosius, Yankees, 455,761.

SHORTSTOP: 1. Alex Rodriguez, Mariners, 2,099,561; 2. Derek Jeter, Yankees, 1,229,865; 3. Omar Vizquel, Indians, 1,204,997.

OUTFIELD: 1. Ken Griffey, Mariners, 4,202,830; 2. Juan Gonzalez, Rangers, 1,900,735; 3. Kenny Lofton, Indians, 1,802,565; 4. David Justice, Indians, 1,467,423; 5. Brady Anderson, Orioles, 923,331; 6. Bernie Williams, Yankees, 878,902; 7. Manny Ramirez, Indians, 804,312; 8. Paul O'Neill, Yankees, 785,884; 9. Darryl Strawberry, Yankees, 718,535.

NATIONAL LEAGUE

CATCHER: 1. Mike Piazza, Mets, 2,731,073; 2. Charles Johnson, Dodgers, 811,813; 3. Javy Lopez, Braves, 758,629.

FIRST BASE: 1. Mark McGwire, Cardinals, 3,377,145; 2. Andres Galarraga, Braves, 880,142; 3. Jeff Bagwell, Astros, 799,069.

SECOND BASE: 1. Craig Biggio, Astros, 2,298,691; 2. Carlos Baerga, Mets, 744,568; 3. Eric Young, Dodgers, 470,869.

THIRD BASE: 1. Chipper Jones, Braves, 1,574,512; 2. Vinny Castilla, Rockies, 1,343,129; 3. Ken Caminiti, Padres, 959,653.

SHORTSTOP: 1. Walt Weiss, Braves, 1,159,960; 2. Barry Larkin, Reds, 997,591; 3. Rey Ordonez, Mets, 798,804.

OUTFIELD: 1. Tony Gwynn, Padres, 2,485,229; 2. Barry Bonds, Giants, 1,897,156; 3. Larry Walker, Rockies, 1,744,949; 4. Dante Bichette, Rockies, 1,213,700; 5. Moises Alou, Astros, 1,205,369; 6. Sammy Sosa, Cubs, 1,112,234; 7. Gary Sheffield, Dodgers, 821,151; 8. Derek Bell, Astros, 675,158; 9. Marquis Grissom, Brewers, 613,044.

ROSTERS

AMERICAN LEAGUE

MANAGER: Mike Hargrove, Indians.

PITCHERS: Rolando Arrojo, Devil Rays; Roger Clemens, Blue Jays; Bartolo Colon, Indians; Tom Gordon, Red Sox; Pedro Martinez, Red Sox; Troy Percival, Angels; Brad Radke, Twins; Aaron Sele, Rangers; **David Wells, Yankees**; John Wetteland, Rangers.

CATCHERS: Sandy Alomar, Indians; **Ivan Rodriguez, Rangers**.

INFIELDERS: **Roberto Alomar (2b), Orioles**; Scott Brosius, Yankees; Ray Durham, White Sox; Damion Easley, Tigers; Derek Jeter, Yankees; Dean Palmer, Royals; y-Rafael Palmeiro, Orioles; **Cal Ripken (3b), Orioles**; **Alex Rodriguez (ss), Mariners**; **Jim Thome (1b), Indians**; x-Mo Vaughn, Red Sox; Omar Vizquel, Indians.

OUTFIELDERS: Darin Erstad, Angels; **Juan Gonzalez (rf), Rangers**; Ben Grieve, Athletics; **Ken Griffey (cf), Mariners**; **Kenny Lofton (lf), Indians**; Paul O'Neill, Yankees; Manny Ramirez, Indians; x-Bernie Williams, Yankees.

NATIONAL LEAGUE

MANAGER: Jim Leyland, Marlins.

PITCHERS: Andy Ashby, Padres; Kevin Brown, Padres; Tom Glavine, Braves; Trevor Hoffman, Padres; **Greg Maddux, Braves**; Robb Nen, Giants; Rick Reed, Mets; Curt Schilling, Phillies; Jeff Shaw, Reds; Ugueth Urbina, Expos.

CATCHERS: Jason Kendall, Pirates; Javy Lopez, Braves; **Mike Piazza, Mets.**

INFIELDERS: **Craig Biggio (2b), Astros**; Bret Boone, Reds; Vinny Castilla, Rockies; Andres Galarraga, Braves; **Chipper Jones (3b), Braves**; **Mark McGwire (1b), Cardinals**; Edgar Renteria, Marlins; Fernando Vina, Brewers; **Walt Weiss (ss), Braves.**

OUTFIELDERS: Moises Alou, Astros; Dante Bichette, Rockies; **Barry Bonds (lf), Giants**; **Tony Gwynn (rf), Padres**; Gary Sheffield, Dodgers; x-Sammy Sosa, Cubs; y-Greg Vaughn, Padres; **Larry Walker (cf), Rockies**; Devon White, Diamondbacks.

Starters in **boldface**. x-injured, did not play; y-injury replacement.

July 7 in Denver
American League 13, National League 8

AMERICAN	ab	r	h	bi	NATIONAL	ab	r	h	bi
Lofton lf	3	0	1	0	Biggio 2b	3	0	0	0
Erstad lf-cf	2	1	0	0	Hoffman p	0	0	0	0
R. Alomar 2b	4	2	3	1	Shaw p	0	0	0	0
Durham 2b	1	1	1	1	G. Vaughn lf	1	0	1	2
Griffey cf	3	1	2	1	Gwynn rf	2	0	1	2
O'Neill lf	2	0	0	0	White cf	3	1	3	0
Gonzalez rf	3	0	0	1	Nen p	0	0	0	0
Ramirez rf	1	0	0	1	McGwire 1b	2	1	0	0
Thome 1b	2	1	0	0	Galarraga 1b	2	0	0	0
Palmiero 1b	2	1	2	1	Bonds lf	2	1	1	3
A. Rodriguez ss	3	2	2	1	Bichette lf-rf	2	0	0	0
Jeter ss	1	0	0	0	Jones 3b	2	1	0	0
Vizquel ss	2	0	1	0	Castilla 3b	2	0	0	0
I. Rodriguez c	4	1	3	1	Piazza c	3	0	1	0
S. Alomar c	1	0	1	1	Lopez c	1	0	0	0
Ripken 3b	4	1	1	2	Kendall ph	1	0	1	0
Arrojo p	0	0	0	0	Walker cf-rf	1	1	0	0
Wetteland p	0	0	0	0	Alou rf-cf	3	1	1	0
Palmer ph	1	0	0	0	Weiss ss	3	1	2	1
Gordon p	0	0	0	0	Renteria ss	1	1	0	0
Percival p	0	0	0	0	Maddux p	0	0	0	0
Wells p	1	0	0	0	Glavine p	0	0	0	0
Clemens p	0	0	0	0	Brown p	0	0	0	0
Easley ph	1	1	1	0	Sheffield ph	1	0	0	0
Radke p	0	0	0	0	Ashby p	0	0	0	0
Grieve ph	0	0	0	0	Urbina p	0	0	0	0
Colon p	0	0	0	0	Vina 2b	1	0	1	0
Brosius 3b	2	1	1	0					
Totals	**43**	**13**	**19**	**11**	**Totals**	**36**	**8**	**12**	**8**

American	**000 413 113—13**
National	**002 130 020— 8**

E—Brosius, Griffey, Vina. **DP**—American 2, National 2. **LOB**—American 11, National 8. **2B**—Ripken. **3B**—White. **HR**—A. Rodriguez, R. Alomar, Bonds. **SB**—Lofton, Griffey, R. Alomar, I. Rodriguez, Brosius. **S**—Glavine. **SF**—Gonzalez, Ramirez.

American	ip	h	r	er	bb	so	National	ip	h	r	er	bb	so
Wells	2	0	0	0	1	1	Maddux	2	3	0	0	1	1
Clemens	1	2	2	2	1	1	Glavine	1⅓	5	4	4	3	0
Radke	1	2	1	1	1	1	Brown	⅔	0	0	0	0	1
Colon W	1	2	3	3	1	1	Ashby	1	1	1	1	1	0
Arrojo	1	2	0	0	0	1	Urbina L	1	3	3	3	1	2
Wetteland	1	0	0	0	0	1	Hoffman	1	1	1	1	0	1
Gordon	1	3	2	1	1	0	Shaw	1	3	1	1	0	0
Percival	1	1	0	0	0	2	Nen	1	3	3	1	0	0

WP—Urbina. **PB**—Lopez. **HBP**—Biggio (by Clemens).

Umpires: HP—Ed Montague; **1B**—Derryl Cousins; **2B**—Brian Gorman; **3B**—Rick Reed; **LF**—Rich Rieker; **RF**—Tim McClelland.

T—3:38. **A**—51,267.

The Rangers' dubious distinction as the last baseball franchise to relocate (1972, from Washington, D.C.) appeared in danger when Montreal politicians repeatedly nixed proposals to replace Olympic Stadium.

The Expos posted the game's worst average attendance (11,293) and seemed headed to Northern Virginia unless some last-minute finagling paid off. Unpopular team president Claude Brochu was ousted and new personalities were vying to make the stadium plan work.

In Minneapolis, owner Carl Pohlad's plans to sell the Twins to a group led by North Carolina businessman Don Beaver fell through after voters in Beaver's home state overwhelmingly rejected a proposal to build a new ballpark with taxpayer funds in the Triad region (Greensboro/Winston-Salem/High Point). Pohlad opted to extend the Twins' Metrodome lease through 2000 as he continued to search for a local buyer.

MEL BAILEY

They finally made it to Cooperstown
The wait for the Hall of Fame was worth it for Larry Doby (left) and Don Sutton

Hall Class Of '98

Cooperstown welcomed five more members, including two whose inclusion seemed well overdue.

Outfielder Larry Doby, who became the first black player in the American League just 11 weeks after Jackie Robinson broke baseball's color barrier, was voted in by the veterans committee. Doby, 74, was a seven-time all-star in a 13-year career with the Indians. He had 253 homers, 969 RBIs and won two AL home-run titles.

Indians owner Bill Veeck bought Doby's contract from the Newark Eagles of the Negro leagues on July 3, 1947. Two days later, Doby was in the majors. He struck out in a pinch-hit appearance, then played first base in the second game of a doubleheader.

"My intention was to play the game as best I could, and be able to live in a society where things are not as easy as they should be," Doby said.

Despite winning 324 games in a 23-year career with five teams, it took Don Sutton five tries to make the Hall of Fame. The baseball writers finally honored him in 1998.

Sutton, 51, never won a Cy Young Award and had only one 20-win season. But he believed his induction sent a message about Cooperstown.

"If you want to show up on time, work your butt off, don't miss starts and grind it out, even if you're not as spectacular as Nolan Ryan or as glamorous as Tom Seaver or as overpowering as Steve Carlton—there's still a spot," Sutton said.

Sutton tied Ryan for 12th place on the all-time victory list and finished with 3,574 strikeouts, fifth all-time.

Former AL president Lee MacPhail, Negro Leagues star "Bullet" Joe Rogan and turn-of-the-century shortstop "Gorgeous" George Davis were the other veterans committee selections.

GROUND BREAKERS

Since 1989, the "top" salary in major league baseball has been claimed by no less than 19 different players. Roger Clemens and Barry Bonds have held the distinction twice.

Mike Piazza became the latest to break new ground when he signed a seven-year, $91 million deal with the New York Mets shortly after the end of the 1998 season.

Salaries listed are average annual values of multiyear deals.

Date	Player	Club	Salary
Oct. 26, 1998	Mike Piazza	Mets	$13,000,000
Dec. 12, 1997	Pedro Martinez	Red Sox	12,500,000
Aug. 10, 1997	Greg Maddux	Braves	11,500,000
Feb. 20, 1997	Barry Bonds	Giants	11,450,000
Nov. 19, 1996	Albert Belle	White Sox	11,000,000
Jan. 31, 1996	Ken Griffey	Mariners	8,500,000
Dec. 8, 1992	Barry Bonds	Giants	7,291,666
March 2, 1992	Ryne Sandberg	Cubs	7,100,000
Dec. 2, 1991	Bobby Bonilla	Mets	5,800,000
Feb. 8, 1991	Roger Clemens	Red Sox	5,380,250
June 27, 1990	Jose Canseco	Athletics	4,700,000
April 9, 1990	Don Mattingly	Yankees	3,860,000
Jan. 22, 1990	Will Clark	Giants	3,750,000
Jan. 17, 1990	Dave Stewart	Athletics	3,550,000
Dec. 11, 1989	Mark Davis	Royals	3,250,000
Dec. 1, 1989	Mark Langston	Angels	3,250,000
Nov. 28, 1989	Rickey Henderson	Athletics	3,000,000
Nov. 22, 1989	Kirby Puckett	Twins	3,000,000
Nov. 17, 1989	Bret Saberhagen	Royals	2,966,667
Feb. 16, 1989	Orel Hershiser	Dodgers	2,633,333
Feb. 15, 1989	Roger Clemens	Red Sox	2,500,000

Welcome Aboard

For the second time in six seasons, baseball welcomed two expansion teams to its ranks. Both teams avoided 100 losses, but still managed to finish last in their respective divisions.

Jerry Colangelo's Arizona Diamondbacks came onto the scene talking tough and ruffling feathers. Having already stolen top amateur talent like Travis Lee and John Patterson through draft loopholes, they signed pitcher Andy Benes away from the Cardinals (thanks to another loophole) and lavished a five-year, $34 million contract on shortstop Jay Bell, who was coming off a career year in 1997.

The Diamondbacks filled glittering Bank One Ballpark on most nights, its retractable dome and right-field area swimming pool coming in handy amid the 110-degree desert heat. Even with respected manager Buck Showalter, they failed to approach .500, as GM

MAJOR LEAGUE DEBUTS, 1998

AMERICAN LEAGUE

Anaheim Angels
Justin Baughman, 2b — May 17
Troy Glaus, 3b — July 31
Ben Molina, c — Sept. 21
Jarrod Washburn, lhp — June 2

Baltimore Orioles
Joel Bennett, rhp — July 15
Radhames Dykhoff, lhp — June 7
P.J. Forbes, 2b — July 21
Chris Fussell, rhp — Sept. 15
Jerry Hairston, 2b — Sept. 11
Ryan Minor, 3b — Sept. 13
Willis Otanez, 3b — Aug. 25
Calvin Pickering, 1b — Sept. 12
Sidney Ponson, rhp — April 19

Boston Red Sox
Brian Barkley, lhp — May 28
Jin Ho Cho, rhp — July 4
Keith Johns, ss — May 23
Lou Merloni, 2b — May 10
Donnie Sadler, 2b — April 1

Chicago White Sox
Chad Bradford, rhp — Aug. 1
Mike Caruso, ss — March 31
Mike Heathcott, rhp — Aug. 28
Bobby Howry, rhp — June 21
Mark Johnson, c — Sept. 14
Jim Parque, lhp — May 26
Todd Rizzo, lhp — April 2
Brian Simmons, of — Sept. 21
John Snyder, rhp — June 30
Bryan Ward, lhp — July 3
Craig Wilson, ss — Sept. 5

Cleveland Indians
Russ Branyan, 3b — Sept. 26
Jolbert Cabrera, ss — April 12
Jason Rakers, rhp — May 6
Alex Ramirez, of — Sept. 19

Detroit Tigers
Gabe Alvarez, 3b — June 22
Matt Anderson, rhp — June 25
Paul Bako, c — April 30
Dean Crow, rhp — May 29
Robert Fick, c — Sept. 19
Seth Greisinger, rhp — June 3
Denny Harriger, rhp — June 16
Gabe Kapler, of — Sept. 20
Brian Powell, rhp — June 27
Sean Runyan, lhp — March 31
Marino Santana, rhp — Sept. 4

Kansas City Royals
Carlos Beltran, of — Sept. 14
Dermal Brown, of — Sept. 14
Tim Byrdak, lhp — Aug. 7
Bart Evans, rhp — June 16
Carlos Febles, 2b — Sept. 14
Jeremy Giambi, of — Sept. 1
Chris Hatcher, of — Sept. 6
Mendy Lopez, ss — June 3
Hector Ortiz, c — Sept. 14

Minnesota Twins
Travis Baptist, lhp — Aug. 1
Corey Koskie, 3b — Sept. 9
Doug Mientkiewicz, 1b — Sept. 18
Eric Milton, lhp — April 5
A.J. Pierzynski, c — Sept. 9
Benj Sampson, lhp — Sept. 9

New York Yankees
Ryan Bradley, rhp — Aug. 22
Mike Buddie, rhp — April 6
Orlando Hernandez, rhp — June 3
Mike Jerzembeck, rhp — Aug. 8
Ricky Ledee, of — June 14
Mike Lowell, 3b — Sept. 13
Shane Spencer, of — April 10
Jay Tessmer, rhp — Aug. 27

Oakland Athletics
Eric Chavez, 3b — Sept. 8
Ryan Christenson, of — April 20
Steve Connelly, rhp — June 28
A.J. Hinch, c — April 1
Mike Neill, of — July 27
Blake Stein, rhp — May 10
Jason Wood, 3b — April 1

Seattle Mariners
Rickey Cradle, of — July 1
Steve Gajkowski, rhp — May 25
Charles Gipson, of — March 31
Carlos Guillen, 2b — Sept. 6
David Holdridge, rhp — Aug. 8
Shane Monahan, of — July 9
Ryan Radmanovich, of — April 13

Tampa Bay Devil Rays
Rolando Arrojo, rhp — April 1
Mike Duvall, lhp — Sept. 22
Scott McClain, 3b — May 14
Kerry Robinson, of — Sept. 22
Bobby Smith, 3b — March 31
Randy Winn, of — May 11

Texas Rangers
Jonathan Johnson, rhp — Sept. 27
Rob Sasser, 3b — July 31

Toronto Blue Jays
Roy Halladay, rhp — Sept. 20
Steve Sinclair, lhp — April 25
Shannon Withem, rhp — Sept. 18
Kevin Witt, 1b — Sept. 15

NATIONAL LEAGUE

Arizona Diamondbacks
Bryan Corey, rhp — May 13
Edwin Diaz, 2b — March 31
Ben Ford, rhp — Aug. 20
Danny Klassen, ss — July 4
Travis Lee, 1b — March 31
Chris Michalak, lhp — Aug. 22
Vladimir Nunez, rhp — Sept. 11
Ricky Pickett, lhp — April 28
Neil Weber, lhp — Sept. 11

Atlanta Braves
Adam Butler, lhp — March 31
Bruce Chen, lhp — Sept. 7
Mark DeRosa, ss — Sept. 2
Brian Edmondson, rhp — April 2
Wes Helms, 3b — Sept. 5
Damon Hollins, of — April 24
George Lombard, of — Sept. 4
Marty Malloy, 2b — Sept. 6
Odaliz Perez, lhp — Sept. 1
John Rocker, lhp — May 5

Chicago Cubs
Jason Maxwell, 2b — Sept. 1
Jose Nieves, ss — Aug. 7
Justin Speier, rhp — May 27
Kennie Streenstra, rhp — May 21
Kerry Wood, rhp — April 12

Cincinnati Reds
Stephen Larkin, 1b — Sept. 27
Eddie Priest, lhp — May 27
Mike Frank, of — June 19
Guillermo Garcia, c — July 19
Keith Glauber, rhp — Sept. 8

Colorado Rockies
Mark Brownson, rhp — July 21
Edgard Clemente, of — Sept. 10
Derrick Gibson, of — Sept. 8
Lariel Gonzalez, rhp — Sept. 22
Fred Rath, rhp — July 29
Mike Saipe, rhp — June 25
Jim Stoops. rhp — Sept. 9
Mark Strittmatter, c — Sept. 3

Florida Marlins
Dave Berg, 3b — April 2
Vic Darensbourg, lhp — April 1
Brian Daubach, of — Sept. 10
Ryan Dempster, rhp — May 23
Joe Fontenot, lhp — May 23
Alex Gonzalez, ss — Aug. 25
Gabe Gonzalez, lhp — April 1
Ryan Jackson, 1b — March 31
Brian Meadows, rhp — April 4
Rafael Medina, rhp — April 2
Kevin Millar, 3b — April 11
Mike Redmond, c — May 31
John Roskos, 1b — April 20
Jesus Sanchez, lhp — March 31

Houston Astros
Scott Elarton, rhp — June 20
Mike Grzanich, rhp — May 14
John Halama, lhp — April 2
Mitch Meluskey, c — Aug. 30
Daryle Ward, of — May 14

Los Angeles Dodgers
Adrian Beltre, 3b — June 24
Will Brunson, lhp — June 21
Alex Cora, ss — June 7
Jeff Kubenka, lhp — Sept. 6
Frank Lankford, rhp — March 31
Paul LoDuca, c — June 21
Mike Metcalfe, 2b — Sept. 18
Angel Pena, c — Sept. 8
Gary Rath, lhp — June 2
Eric Weaver, rhp — May 30

Milwaukee Brewers
Ron Belliard, 2b — Sept. 12
Valerio de los Santos, lhp — July 31
Bobby Hughes, c — April 2
Geoff Jenkins, of — April 24
Bronswell Patrick, rhp — May 18
Greg Martinez, of — March 31
Greg Mullins, lhp — Sept. 18
Rafael Roque, lhp — Aug. 1
Travis Smith, rhp — June 21

Montreal Expos
Michael Barrett, c — Sept. 19
Kirk Bullinger, rhp — Aug. 30
Bob Henley, c — July 19
Trey Moore, lhp — April 5
Carl Pavano, rhp — May 23
Jeremy Powell, rhp — July 23
Fernando Seguignol, 1b — Sept. 5
DaRond Stovall, of — April 1
Javier Vazquez, rhp — April 3
Tim Young, lhp — Sept. 5

New York Mets
Benny Agbayani, of — June 17
Mike Kinkade, 3b — Sept. 8
Jay Payton, of — Sept. 1
Jeff Tam, rhp — June 30
Preston Wilson, of — May 7
Masato Yoshii, rhp — April 5

Philadelphia Phillies
Marlon Anderson, 2b — Sept. 8
Robert Dodd, lhp — May 28
Carlton Loewer, rhp — June 14
Mike Welch, rhp — July 17

Pittsburgh Pirates
Sean Lawrence, lhp — Aug. 25
Javier Martinez, rhp — April 2
Aramis Ramirez, 3b — May 26
Chance Sanford, 3b — April 30

St. Louis Cardinals
Rick Croushore, rhp — May 18
J.D. Drew, of — Sept. 8
Jose Jimenez, rhp — Sept. 9
Mark Little, of — Sept. 12
Braden Looper, rhp — March 31
Joe McEwing, of — Sept. 2
Placido Polanco, ss — July 3
Cliff Politte, rhp — April 2

San Diego Padres
Matt Clement, rhp — Sept. 6
Ben Davis, c — Sept. 25
Stan Spencer, rhp — Aug. 27
Roberto Ramirez, lhp — June 12

San Francisco Giants
Jeff Ball, 1b — June 10
Ramon Martinez, 2b — June 20
Russ Ortiz, rhp — April 2
Armando Rios, of — Sept. 1

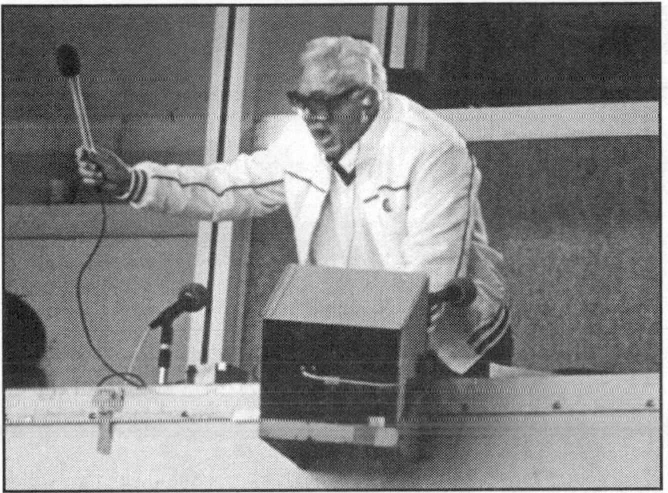
RON VESELY

Seventh-inning stretch wasn't the same
Harry Caray was dearly missed at Wrigley Field in 1998

Angels founder and longtime owner Gene Autry died Oct. 2 at age 91. The Singing Cowboy made his mark in Hollywood as a hero of cinematic westerns but he never realized his dream of a World Series despite unsurpassed generosity.

Autry's baseball career was marked by splashy free-agent signings and heartbreaking defeats, none more so than the 1986 ALCS, when the Angels were one strike away from their first World Series trip until Dave Henderson's ninth-inning homer saved the Boston Red Sox.

We also lost sportswriting giants Jim Murray and Shirley Povich, as well as former Dodgers GM Al Campanis, whose ignorant comments on a 1987 edition of "Nightline" cost him his job but spurred a sustained period of affirmative action within the sport.

Playing greats like Buck Leonard, Mark Belanger and Dan Quisenberry also passed. Leonard starred in the old Negro Leagues. Belanger won eight Gold Gloves as an Orioles shortstop, then worked tirelessly for the Players Association until his death.

Quisenberry, the quirky relief ace of the Kansas City Royals, tried valiantly for more than a year to fight brain cancer. His wit and wisdom included this gem: "I have seen the future and it is a lot like the present–only longer."

Joe Garagiola Jr. had predicted, and seemed to be backing off their win-now philosophy by season's end.

In Tampa Bay, the Devil Rays brought home such local products as Wade Boggs and Fred McGriff but were still disappointed with the turnout at the deceptively named Tropicana Field. Not a field at all but a dome, The Trop was plagued by an antiseptic feel and a meddlesome system of looming catwalks that deflected a number of would-be home runs.

The ground rules were finally adjusted in late May, but not until after the club was forced to endure significant embarrassment and an "arena baseball" taunt from Orioles manager Ray Miller.

In September, the Devil Rays announced the hiring of minor league showman Mike Veeck to oversee their sales and promotions departments. Veeck had been ostracized from the majors since his late father, the legendary Bill Veeck, sold the Chicago White Sox in 1980.

Good-bye Harry

The year marked the passing of too many baseball greats, unforgettable people who made their reputation both on the field and off.

Harry Caray, the lovable Chicago Cubs broadcaster, died on the eve of spring training after suffering a stroke. Caray, an unabashed homer, surely must have caused quite a ruckus in St. Peter's Pub as Sammy Sosa went wild and his beloved Cubbies grabbed the NL wild card in a one-game playoff with the Giants.

The Cubs wore a commemorative patch on their uniform to honor Caray all season, and Wrigley Field fans were treated to a series of cameo performances of Caray's signature "Take Me Out to the Ballgame" during each seventh-inning stretch. Best version? Probably Bill Murray. The worst? Former Chicago Bears coach Mike Ditka, without a doubt.

Retired broadcaster Jack Brickhouse, who called Cubs games even longer than Caray, his fellow Hall of Famer, died Aug. 6 at age 82. His signature "Hey-Hey" call came to mind with each Sosa blast, and the club honored him as well with a uniform patch.

This Was The Season

This was the season Beanie mania came to ballparks across the land. A promotional Beanie Baby given away the night Wells threw his perfect game found its way to the Hall of Fame. And a stuffed bear named Glory caused such a stir at the All-Star Game in Denver, several people were arrested.

This was the season baseball crossed into the realm of Rodmania. Platinum-blond hair became a huge fad. At one point eight Toronto Blue Jays dyed their hair, all at the urging of . . . Roger Clemens.

Around the same time as this silliness, Clemens, 36, launched a 15-game winning streak that carried him to his record fifth Cy Young Award.

Three-fifths of the Anaheim Angels starting rotation went bright white as well. Perhaps the Angels' latest September swoon will halt the unsightly fad. (We can only hope.)

This was the season deposed Atlanta closer Mark Wohlers was placed on the disabled list with the following malady: "inability to pitch." The Marlins, Tigers, Twins and a dozen other clubs immediately kicked themselves for not dreaming that one up first.

This was the season that required no hyperbole. In fact, it might work best to tone things down a bit for future generations. For who could possibly believe 70 home runs . . . 125 wins . . . 2,632 consecutive games?

This was the season.

All grandchildren, present and future, should consider themselves forewarned.

WORLD SERIES

Series sweep stamps Yankees as a club for the ages

BY JOHN PERROTTO

Did anyone really expect the 1998 season to end any other way?

When it was over, there were the New York Yankees joyously piled up in the infield of San Diego's Qualcomm Stadium, having swept the Padres in the World Series. That had seemed like their destiny since the season's early weeks.

After starting off 0-3, the Yankees steamrolled through the American League East. They set an AL record for wins in a 114-48 season and finished an incredible 22 games in front of a Boston Red Sox club that was good enough to get into the playoffs as the wild card.

The Yankees continued their rampage in the postseason.

First, they swept the Rangers in three games in the AL Division Series, limiting Texas to one measly run in 27 innings. They did so despite learning before Game Three that outfielder Darryl Strawberry had been diagnosed with colon cancer. Then, the Yankees rallied from a 2-1 deficit to polish off the Cleveland Indians in six games in the AL Championship Series.

The final tally had the Yankees with 125 wins and 50 losses. No team had ever won more games in a season.

"I picked up the newspaper this morning and saw a win would make us 125-50," manager Joe Torre said after the Yankees' 3-0 win in the decisive Game Four. "I just kept staring at those numbers. I couldn't believe it. It just looked too perfect, 125-50. It's amazing. Those are two nice round numbers. There's a nice look to it."

Yes, 125-50 is very pretty. And 125-50 led to one question once the Series was over: Are the 1998 Yankees the greatest team of all-time?

"We won more games than anyone else ever, so why not?," Yankees lefthander David Wells said in the midst of the raucous postgame celebration.

However, most of the Yankees weren't ready to declare themselves the No. 1 team in baseball.

"I only have about 40 years of history," Torre said. "It's the best club I've ever been around. The 1927 Yankees, they may have been a better club but we had the best record. To me, that was the standard I was looking to pass, because it's more important to have the Yankees' record than anything else. When we broke the '27 team's record of 110 wins, that was big for me.

"There's a certain aura about being the all-time winningest team in Yankees history. Everyone knows the New York Yankees. Even people who don't pay any attention to baseball can tell you who the New York Yankees are.

"When you look at the various great clubs in history, though, you look at the Oakland A's that won three world championships in a row (1972-74) and the Cincinnati Reds that won back-to-back World Series (1975-76) and kept coming at you. That '76 Reds team was always a standard for me. I think we have better pitching than they had but we have to take a back seat to no one in my lifetime.

LARRY GOREN

Heavenly celebration
Joe Girardi and Mariano Rivera embrace after final out

"Let's put it this way: We may not be the greatest team ever but no one has ever had a better single season than us. We've created our spot in history."

The Yankees' players were also happy just to say they won more games in a season than any other team.

"I think you could debate who's the greatest team of all time forever and there really is no clear-cut answer," third baseman and Series MVP Scott Brosius said. "The comparisons will go on and on and there will probably never be a definite answer. But you can look at this year and say we had the best single season of any other team. That's a great accomplishment."

"I'm a little young to know about the teams back in the early 1900s," shortstop Derek Jeter said. "But we were 125-50 and no other team could ever say that.

WORLD SERIES YEAR-BY-YEAR

Year	Winner	Manager	Loser	Manager	Result	MVP
1903	Boston (AL)	Jimmy Collins	Pittsburgh (NL)	Fred Clarke	5-3	None Selected
1904	NO SERIES					
1905	New York (NL)	John McGraw	Philadelphia (AL)	Connie Mack	4-1	None Selected
1906	Chicago (AL)	Fielder Jones	Chicago (NL)	Frank Chance	4-2	None Selected
1907	Chicago (NL)	Frank Chance	Detroit (AL)	Hugh Jennings	4-0	None Selected
1908	Chicago (NL)	Frank Chance	Detroit (AL)	Hugh Jennings	4-1	None Selected
1909	Pittsburgh (NL)	Fred Clarke	Detroit (AL)	Hugh Jennings	4-3	None Selected
1910	Philadelphia (AL)	Connie Mack	Chicago (NL)	Frank Chance	4-1	None Selected
1911	Philadelphia (AL)	Connie Mack	New York (NL)	John McGraw	4-2	None Selected
1912	Boston (AL)	Jake Stahl	New York (NL)	John McGraw	4-3-1	None Selected
1913	Philadelphia (AL)	Connie Mack	New York (NL)	John McGraw	4-1	None Selected
1914	Boston (NL)	George Stallings	Philadelphia (AL)	Connie Mack	4-0	None Selected
1915	Boston (AL)	Bill Carrigan	Philadelphia (NL)	Pat Moran	4-1	None Selected
1916	Boston (AL)	Bill Carrigan	Brooklyn (NL)	Wilbert Robinson	4-1	None Selected
1917	Chicago (AL)	Pants Rowland	New York (NL)	John McGraw	4-2	None Selected
1918	Boston (AL)	Ed Barrow	Chicago (NL)	Fred Mitchell	4-2	None Selected
1919	Cincinnati (NL)	Pat Moran	Chicago (AL)	Kid Gleason	5-3	None Selected
1920	Cleveland (AL)	Tris Speaker	Brooklyn (NL)	Wilbert Robinson	5-2	None Selected
1921	New York (NL)	John McGraw	New York (AL)	Miller Huggins	5-3	None Selected
1922	New York (NL)	John McGraw	New York (AL)	Miller Huggins	4-0	None Selected
1923	New York (AL)	Miller Huggins	New York (NL)	John McGraw	4-2	None Selected
1924	Washington (AL)	Bucky Harris	New York (NL)	John McGraw	4-3	None Selected
1925	Pittsburgh (NL)	Bill McKechnie	Washington (AL)	Bucky Harris	4-3	None Selected
1926	St. Louis (NL)	Rogers Hornsby	New York (AL)	Miller Huggins	4-3	None Selected
1927	New York (AL)	Miller Huggins	Pittsburgh (NL)	Donie Bush	4-0	None Selected
1928	New York (AL)	Miller Huggins	St. Louis (NL)	Bill McKechnie	4-0	None Selected
1929	Philadelphia (AL)	Connie Mack	Chicago (NL)	Joe McCarthy	4-1	None Selected
1930	Philadelphia (AL)	Connie Mack	St. Louis (NL)	Gabby Street	4-2	None Selected
1931	St. Louis (NL)	Gabby Street	Philadelphia (AL)	Connie Mack	4-3	None Selected
1932	New York (AL)	Joe McCarthy	Chicago (NL)	Charlie Grimm	4-0	None Selected
1933	New York (NL)	Bill Terry	Washington (AL)	Joe Cronin	4-1	None Selected
1934	St. Louis (NL)	Frankie Frisch	Detroit (AL)	Mickey Cochrane	4-3	None Selected
1935	Detroit (AL)	Mickey Cochrane	Chicago (NL)	Charlie Grimm	4-2	None Selected
1936	New York (AL)	Joe McCarthy	New York (NL)	Bill Terry	4-2	None Selected
1937	New York (AL)	Joe McCarthy	New York (NL)	Bill Terry	4-1	None Selected
1938	New York (AL)	Joe McCarthy	Chicago (NL)	Gabby Hartnett	4-0	None Selected
1939	New York (AL)	Joe McCarthy	Cincinnati (NL)	Bill McKechnie	4-0	None Selected
1940	Cincinnati (NL)	Bill McKechnie	Detroit (AL)	Del Baker	4-3	None Selected
1941	New York (AL)	Joe McCarthy	Brooklyn (NL)	Leo Durocher	4-1	None Selected
1942	St. Louis (NL)	Billy Southworth	New York (AL)	Joe McCarthy	4-1	None Selected
1943	New York (AL)	Joe McCarthy	St. Louis (NL)	Billy Southworth	4-1	None Selected
1944	St. Louis (NL)	Billy Southworth	St. Louis (AL)	Luke Sewell	4-2	None Selected
1945	Detroit (AL)	Steve O'Neill	Chicago (NL)	Charlie Grimm	4-3	None Selected
1946	St. Louis (NL)	Eddie Dyer	Boston (AL)	Joe Cronin	4-3	None Selected
1947	New York (AL)	Bucky Harris	Brooklyn (NL)	Burt Shotton	4-3	None Selected
1948	Cleveland (AL)	Lou Boudreau	Boston (NL)	Billy Southworth	4-2	None Selected
1949	New York (AL)	Casey Stengel	Brooklyn (NL)	Burt Shotton	4-1	None Selected
1950	New York (AL)	Casey Stengel	Philadelphia (NL)	Eddie Sawyer	4-0	None Selected

Year	Winner	Manager	Loser	Manager	Result	MVP
1951	New York (AL)	Casey Stengel	New York (NL)	Leo Durocher	4-2	None Selected
1952	New York (AL)	Casey Stengel	Brooklyn (NL)	Chuck Dressen	4-3	None Selected
1953	New York (AL)	Casey Stengel	Brooklyn (NL)	Chuck Dressen	4-2	None Selected
1954	New York (NL)	Leo Durocher	Cleveland (AL)	Al Lopez	4-0	None Selected
1955	Brooklyn (NL)	Walter Alston	New York (AL)	Casey Stengel	4-3	Johnny Podres, p, Brooklyn
1956	New York (AL)	Casey Stengel	Brooklyn (NL)	Walter Alston	4-3	Don Larsen, p, New York
1957	Milwaukee (NL)	Fred Haney	New York (AL)	Casey Stengel	4-3	Lew Burdette, p, Milwaukee
1958	New York (AL)	Casey Stengel	Milwaukee (NL)	Fred Haney	4-3	Bob Turley, p, New York
1959	Los Angeles (NL)	Walter Alston	Chicago (AL)	Al Lopez	4-2	Larry Sherry, p, Los Angeles
1960	Pittsburgh (NL)	Danny Murtaugh	New York (AL)	Casey Stengel	4-3	Bobby Richardson, 2b, New York
1961	New York (AL)	Ralph Houk	Cincinnati (NL)	Fred Hutchinson	4-1	Whitey Ford, p, New York
1962	New York (AL)	Ralph Houk	San Francisco (NL)	Alvin Dark	4-3	Ralph Terry, p, New York
1963	Los Angeles (NL)	Walter Alston	New York (AL)	Ralph Houk	4-0	Sandy Koufax, p, Los Angeles
1964	St. Louis (NL)	Johnny Keene	New York (AL)	Yogi Berra	4-3	Bob Gibson, p, St. Louis
1965	Los Angeles (NL)	Walter Alston	Minnesota (AL)	Sam Mele	4-3	Sandy Koufax, p, Los Angeles
1966	Baltimore (AL)	Hank Bauer	Los Angeles (NL)	Walter Alston	4-0	Frank Robinson, of, Baltimore
1967	St. Louis (NL)	Red Schoendienst	Boston (AL)	Dick Williams	4-3	Bob Gibson, p, St. Louis
1968	Detroit (AL)	Mayo Smith	St. Louis (NL)	Red Schoendienst	4-3	Mickey Lolich, p, Detroit
1969	New York (NL)	Gil Hodges	Baltimore (AL)	Earl Weaver	4-1	Donn Clendenon, 1b, New York
1970	Baltimore (AL)	Earl Weaver	Cincinnati (NL)	Sparky Anderson	4-1	Brooks Robinson, 3b, Baltimore
1971	Pittsburgh (NL)	Danny Murtaugh	Baltimore (AL)	Earl Weaver	4-3	Roberto Clemente, of, Pittsburgh
1972	Oakland (AL)	Dick Williams	Cincinnati (NL)	Sparky Anderson	4-3	Gene Tenace, c, Oakland
1973	Oakland (AL)	Dick Williams	New York (NL)	Yogi Berra	4-3	Reggie Jackson, of, Oakland
1974	Oakland (AL)	Alvin Dark	Los Angeles (NL)	Walter Alston	4-1	Rollie Fingers, p, Oakland
1975	Cincinnati (NL)	Sparky Anderson	Boston (AL)	Darrell Johnson	4-3	Pete Rose, 3b, Cincinnati
1976	Cincinnati (NL)	Sparky Anderson	New York (AL)	Billy Martin	4-0	Johnny Bench, c, Cincinnati
1977	New York (AL)	Billy Martin	Los Angeles (NL)	Tom Lasorda	4-2	Reggie Jackson, of, New York
1978	New York (AL)	Bob Lemon	Los Angeles (NL)	Tom Lasorda	4-2	Bucky Dent, ss, New York
1979	Pittsburgh (NL)	Chuck Tanner	Baltimore (AL)	Earl Weaver	4-3	Willie Stargell, 1b, Pittsburgh
1980	Philadelphia (NL)	Dallas Green	Kansas City (AL)	Jim Frey	4-2	Mike Schmidt, 3b, Philadelphia
1981	Los Angeles (NL)	Tom Lasorda	New York (AL)	Bob Lemon	4-2	Cey/Guerrero/Yeager, L.A.
1982	St. Louis (NL)	Whitey Herzog	Milwaukee (AL)	Harvey Kuenn	4-3	Darrell Porter, c, St. Louis
1983	Baltimore (AL)	Joe Altobelli	Philadelphia (NL)	Paul Owens	4-1	Rick Dempsey, c, Baltimore
1984	Detroit (AL)	Sparky Anderson	San Diego (NL)	Dick Williams	4-1	Alan Trammell, ss, Detroit
1985	Kansas City (AL)	Dick Howser	St. Louis (NL)	Whitey Herzog	4-3	Bret Saberhagen, p, Kansas City
1986	New York (NL)	Dave Johnson	Boston (AL)	John McNamara	4-3	Ray Knight, 3b, New York
1987	Minnesota (AL)	Tom Kelly	St. Louis (NL)	Whitey Herzog	4-3	Frank Viola, p, Minnesota
1988	Los Angeles (NL)	Tom Lasorda	Oakland (AL)	Tony La Russa	4-1	Orel Hershiser, p, Los Angeles
1989	Oakland (AL)	Tony La Russa	San Francisco (NL)	Roger Craig	4-0	Dave Stewart, p, Oakland
1990	Cincinnati (NL)	Lou Piniella	Oakland (AL)	Tony La Russa	4-0	Jose Rijo, p, Cincinnati
1991	Minnesota (AL)	Tom Kelly	Atlanta (NL)	Bobby Cox	4-3	Jack Morris, p, Minnesota
1992	Toronto (AL)	Cito Gaston	Atlanta (NL)	Bobby Cox	4-2	Pat Borders, c, Toronto
1993	Toronto (AL)	Cito Gaston	Philadelphia (NL)	Jim Fregosi	4-2	Paul Molitor, dh, Toronto
1994	NO SERIES					
1995	Atlanta (NL)	Bobby Cox	Cleveland (AL)	Mike Hargrove	4-2	Tom Glavine, p, Atlanta
1996	New York (AL)	Joe Torre	Atlanta (NL)	Bobby Cox	4-2	John Wetteland, p, New York
1997	Florida (NL)	Jim Leyland	Cleveland (AL)	Mike Hargrove	4-3	Livan Hernandez, p, Florida
1998	New York (AL)	Joe Torre	San Diego (NL)	Bruce Bochy	4-0	Scott Brosius, 3b, New York

So, I think we can argue our point that we were the greatest ever.

"But I don't think it really matters to the guys on this team. All we were concerned about from the first day of spring training was winning a championship and that's what we accomplished. Nobody cared about individual achievements or anything else. We just wanted to win."

Steady, Not Spectacular

That is exactly how the Yankees played in the Series. They didn't do anything spectacular but they continually got the job done as they hit .309 and had a 2.75 ERA.

"It was just an incredible year for the Yankees," San Diego manager Bruce Bochy said. "They did it all season and they did it in the postseason. They have to go down as one of the greatest teams of all time. We had them on the ropes in two of the four games and they came back on us.

"They had no weakness on that club. They had starting pitching, their relief pitching shut us down and there was no weak spot in their lineup. They did a great job and I tip my hat to them."

"The Yankees were just so impressive," Padres right fielder Tony Gwynn said. "They just did everything right. They never made a mistake. They never gave us an opening. We had the misfortunate of running into one of the greatest teams ever when they were on top of their game."

While the Yankees won their 24th World Series and second in three years with their first Series sweep since dusting the "Whiz Kid" Philadelphia Phillies in 1950, San Diego continued to search for its first title since joining the National League as an expansion franchise in 1969.

LARRY GOREN

Close call at first base
Paul O'Neill's infield single in Game Four touched off an argument

LARRY GOREN

Short-lived hero
Greg Vaughn's homers gave the Padres an early lead

The Padres' only other trip to the Series was a five-game defeat at the hands of the Detroit Tigers in 1984.

"Even though you get beat, I can look back at this as a positive experience," said Gwynn, the last San Diego holdover from '84, who hit .500 (8-for-16) in this Series. "Getting back to the World Series, playing the Yankees tough, making them earn it. The World Series just reconfirmed what I always thought: This is what the game's all about, having the opportunity to play for a ring."

Seven-Run Seventh

Through six innings of Game One, it appeared the Padres might be the team wearing the ring as they built a 5-2 lead at Yankee Stadium on two homers by Greg Vaughn and a two-run shot by Gwynn.

However, the Yankees struck for seven runs in the seventh against San Diego's shaky bullpen to pull out a 9-6 win. Chuck Knoblauch's three-run homer off loser Donne Wall tied it at 5-5 before Tino Martinez's grand slam off Mark Langston won it.

Wells got the win despite giving up five runs in seven innings. Mariano Rivera recorded the final four outs for the save.

The Yankees then coasted to a 9-3 win in Game Two as loser Andy Ashby was tagged for seven runs in 2⅔ innings. Bernie Williams and Jorge Posada homered to lead the rout.

Orlando "El Duque" Hernandez gave up only one run in seven innings for the win, just 10 months after making a daring defection from Cuba on a 20-foot boat.

The series shifted to San Diego for Game Three and the Yankees made another late-inning rally, turning a 3-0 deficit into a 5-4 win and a 3-0 series lead.

Brosius started the comeback with a solo homer in a two-run seventh. He then blasted a three-run homer off relief ace Trevor Hoffman in the eighth that made it 5-3.

Ramiro Mendoza got the win in relief and Rivera pitched 1⅓ scoreless innings for the save.

Brosius Earns MVP Honors

The heroic effort by Brosius was enough to get him the MVP trophy as he went 8-for-17 in the Series with six RBIs.

That capped a dramatic one-year reversal for Brosius, acquired the previous winter from Oakland in a trade that dumped $2.5 million of lefthander Kenny Rogers' $5 million salary on the Athletics. Brosius hit just .203 for Oakland in 1997 but batted .300 with 19 homers and 98 RBIs in 152 regular season games with the Yankees.

"I think it's every player's dream to get to the World Series and feel like you've played a part in the team getting there and the team winning," Brosius said. "So there's certainly some satisfaction in how this has worked out but I also just feel very lucky to be in this position. How things have changed from last year, it's just an unbelievable turnaround."

LARRY GOREN

Series MVP
Scott Brosius

Down 3-0, the Padres hoped for an unbelievable turnaround. It didn't happen, though, as the Yankees completed the first World Series sweep since Cincinnati surprised Oakland in 1990.

Williams broke up a scoreless duel in the sixth inning when his infield chopper off loser Kevin Brown drove in a run. The Yankees added two insurance runs in the eighth as Brosius stroked an RBI single and Ricky Ledee added a sacrifice fly.

Andy Pettitte pitched 7⅓ shutout innings for the win and Rivera got the last four outs for his third save of the Series.

"The most impressive things about us coming in and getting a sweep is the enormous amount of pressure we were under," Yankees righthander David Cone said. "I don't think people realize what was at stake for us. We had everything to lose in the whole postseason. If we didn't win the World Series then everyone would have said we were the biggest flops ever after winning 114 games in the regular season. We had to win it all. There was no other alternative."

Yet, the Yankees fulfilled the great expectations in grand style.

"When I was out there after the game was over, just about every player came up and said 'thank you' to me," Torre said. "They said it before I said it. That knocked me off my stilts a little bit that they thanked me for this.

"I've never been around a more courageous group and more determined group. To have the record going during the course of the year, and to continue playing well and never taking a day off, that to me was a helluva indication that we were special.

"We were that way from the first day until the last day."

WORLD SERIES

BOX SCORES

GAME ONE: October 17
Yankees 9, Padres 6

San Diego	ab	r	h	bi	bb	so	New York	ab	r	h	bi	bb	so
Veras 2b	4	1	1	0	1	0	Knoblauch 2b	4	1	2	3	0	1
Gwynn rf	4	1	3	2	0	0	Jeter ss	4	1	1	0	1	0
Vaughn lf	4	3	2	3	0	0	O'Neill rf	5	0	0	0	0	1
Caminiti 3b	3	0	0	0	1	2	Williams cf	4	1	0	0	1	3
Leyritz dh	4	0	0	0	0	2	Davis dh	3	2	1	0	1	0
Joyner 1b	3	0	0	0	1	1	Martinez 1b	3	2	1	4	1	1
Finley cf	4	0	1	0	0	0	Brosius 3b	4	0	1	0	0	1
Hernandez c	3	0	0	0	0	0	Posada c	3	1	1	0	1	1
G. Myers ph	1	0	0	0	0	1	Ledee lf	3	1	2	2	1	0
Gomez ss	3	1	1	0	0	0							
Vander Wal ph	1	0	0	0	0	1							
Totals	**34**	**6**	**8**	**5**	**3**	**7**	**Totals**	**33**	**9**	**9**	**9**	**6**	**8**

San Diego	**002 030 010—6**
New York	**020 000 70x—9**

E—Vaughn (1), Knoblauch (1). **DP**—New York 2. **LOB**—San Diego 4, New York 7. **2B**—Finley (1), Ledee (1). **HR**—Martinez (1), Knoblauch (1), Gwynn (1), Vaughn 2 (2).

San Diego	ip	h	r	er	bb	so	New York	ip	h	r	er	bb	so
Brown	6⅓	6	4	4	3	5	Wells W	7	7	5	5	2	4
Wall L	0	2	2	2	0	0	Nelson	⅔	1	1	0	1	1
Langston	⅔	1	3	3	2	0	Rivera S	1⅓	0	0	0	0	2
Boehringer	⅓	0	0	0	1	1							
R. Myers	⅔	0	0	0	0	2							

WP—Langston. **HBP**—Knoblauch (by Boehringer).

Umpires: HP—Garcia; **1B**—Hirschbeck; **2B**—Scott; **3B**—DeMuth; **LF**—Tschida; **RF**—Crawford.

T—3:29. **A**—56,712.

GAME TWO: October 10
Yankees 9, Padres 3

San Diego	ab	r	h	bi	bb	so	New York	ab	r	h	bi	bb	so
Veras 2b	5	0	1	1	0	3	Knoblauch 2b	3	2	2	0	2	1
Gwynn rf	4	0	1	0	1	0	Jeter ss	5	1	2	1	0	1
Vaughn lf	4	0	0	0	1	1	O'Neill rf	5	1	1	0	0	0
Caminiti 3b	5	1	1	0	0	2	Williams cf	4	1	1	2	1	0
Joyner 1b	2	0	0	0	1	0	Davis dh	3	1	1	1	2	2
Leyritz ph-1b	1	0	0	0	0	1	Bush pr-dh	0	0	0	0	0	0
Finley cf	4	0	0	0	0	1	Martinez 1b	5	1	3	0	0	0
Vander Wal lf	3	0	2	0	0	1	Brosius 3b	5	1	3	1	0	1
R. Rivera ph-lf	1	1	1	1	0	0	Posada c	4	1	1	2	1	0
G. Myers c	3	0	0	0	0	1	Ledee lf	3	0	2	1	1	0
Hernandez ph-c	1	0	1	0	0	0							
Gomez ss	3	1	2	0	0	0							
Sweeney ph	1	0	1	1	0	0							
Sheets ss	0	0	0	0	0	0							
Totals	**37**	**3**	**10**	**3**	**3**	**10**	**Totals**	**37**	**9**	**16**	**8**	**7**	**5**

San Diego	**000 010 020—3**
New York	**331 020 00x—9**

E—Caminiti (1). **DP**—San Diego 3. **LOB**—San Diego 10, New York 11. **2B**—Veras (1), Caminiti (1), Vander Wal (1), R. Rivera (1), Ledee (2). **3B**—Gomez (1). **HR**—Posada (1), Williams (1). **SB**—Knoblauch (1). **CS**—Ledee (1).

San Diego	ip	h	r	er	bb	so	New York	ip	h	r	er	bb	so
Ashby L	2⅔	10	7	4	1	1	O. Hernandez W	7	6	1	1	3	7
Boehringer	1⅔	4	2	2	1	2	Stanton	⅔	3	2	2	0	1
Wall	2⅔	1	0	0	3	1	Nelson	1⅓	1	0	0	0	2
Miceli	1	1	0	0	2	1							

Umpires: HP—Hirschbeck; **1B**—Scott; **2B**—DeMuth; **3B**—Tschida; **LF**—Crawford; **RF**—Garcia.

T—3:31. **A**—56,692.

GAME THREE: October 20
Yankees 5, Padres 4

New York	ab	r	h	bi	bb	so	San Diego	ab	r	h	bi	bb	so
Knoblauch 2b	4	0	1	0	1	0	Veras 2b	3	2	1	0	1	0
Jeter ss	4	0	1	0	1	1	Gwynn rf	4	1	2	1	0	0
O'Neill rf	4	1	1	0	1	1	R. Rivera pr-rf	0	0	0	0	0	0
Williams cf	4	0	0	0	0	2	Vaughn lf	3	0	0	1	0	0
Martinez 1b	3	1	0	0	1	0	Caminiti 3b	2	0	0	1	1	2
Brosius 3b	4	2	3	4	0	0	Joyner 1b	3	0	0	0	1	0
Spencer lf	3	1	1	0	0	2	Finley cf	4	0	0	0	0	1
Ledee ph-lf	1	0	0	0	0	0	Leyritz c	2	0	0	0	0	1
Girardi c	2	0	0	0	0	1	Hernandez c	2	0	1	0	0	1
Posada ph-c	2	0	1	0	0	1	Vander Wal pr	0	0	0	0	0	0

Major Leagues

Cone p	2	0	1	0	0	0	Gomez ss	3	0	1	0	0	1
Davis ph	1	0	0	1	0	0	Hoffman p	0	0	0	0	0	0
Bush pr	0	0	0	0	0	0	Sweeney ph	1	0	1	0	0	0
Lloyd p	0	0	0	0	0	0	Hitchcock p	2	1	1	0	0	0
Mendoza p	1	0	0	0	0	0	Hamilton p	0	0	0	0	0	0
M. Rivera p	0	0	0	0	0	0	R. Myers p	0	0	0	0	0	0
							Sheets ss	2	0	0	0	0	1
Totals	**35**	**5**	**9**	**5**	**4**	**8**	**Totals**	**31**	**4**	**7**	**3**	**3**	**7**

New York	**000 000 230—5**
San Diego	**000 003 010—4**

E—O'Neill (1), Caminiti (2). **DP**—San Diego 2. **LOB**—New York 7, San Diego 5. **2B**—Spencer (1), Veras (2). **HR**—Brosius 2 (2). **SB**—Finley (1). **SF**—Vaughn, Caminiti.

New York	ip	h	r	er	bb	so	San Diego	ip	h	r	er	bb	so
Cone	6	2	3	2	3	4	Hitchcock	6	7	2	1	1	7
Lloyd	⅓	0	0	0	0	0	Hamilton	1	0	0	0	1	1
Mendoza W	1	2	1	1	0	1	R. Myers	0	0	1	1	1	0
M. Rivera S	2⅔	3	0	0	0	2	Hoffman L	2	2	2	2	1	0

Hitchcock pitched to two batters in the seventh, R. Myers pitched to one batter in the eighth.

PB—Leyritz.

Umpires: HP—Scott; **1B**—DeMuth; **2B**—Tschida; **3B**—Crawford; **LF**—Garcia; **RF**—Hirschbeck.

T—3:14. **A**—64,667.

GAME FOUR: October 21
Yankees 3, Padres 0

New York	ab	r	h	bi	bb	so	San Diego	ab	r	h	bi	bb	so
Knoblauch 2b	5	0	1	0	0	0	Veras 2b	3	0	0	0	1	1
Jeter ss	4	2	2	0	1	1	Gwynn rf	4	0	2	0	0	0
O'Neill rf	5	1	2	0	0	0	Vaughn lf	4	0	0	0	0	1
Williams cf	4	0	0	1	0	0	Caminiti 3b	4	0	1	0	0	1
Martinez 1b	2	0	1	0	2	1	Leyritz 1b	3	0	0	0	1	0
Brosius 3b	4	0	1	1	0	2	R. Rivera cf	4	0	3	0	0	0
Ledee lf	3	0	2	1	0	1	Hernandez c	4	0	0	0	0	2
Girardi c	4	0	0	0	0	1	Gomez ss	2	0	0	0	1	0
Pettitte p	2	0	0	0	0	2	Sweeney ph	1	0	0	0	0	0
Nelson p	0	0	0	0	0	0	Brown p	2	0	1	0	0	0
M. Rivera p	1	0	0	0	0	0	Vander Wal ph	1	0	0	0	0	0
							Miceli p	0	0	0	0	0	0
							R. Myers p	0	0	0	0	0	0
Totals	**34**	**3**	**9**	**3**	**3**	**8**	**Totals**	**32**	**0**	**7**	**0**	**3**	**5**

New York	**000 001 020—3**
San Diego	**000 000 000—0**

DP—New York 2. **LOB**—New York 9, San Diego 8. **2B**—Ledee (3), O'Neill (1), R. Rivera (2). **S**—Pettitte. **SF**—Ledee.

New York	ip	h	r	er	bb	so	San Diego	ip	h	r	er	bb	so
Pettitte W	7⅓	5	0	0	3	4	Brown L	8	8	3	3	3	8
Nelson	⅓	0	0	0	0	1	Miceli	⅔	1	0	0	0	0
M. Rivera S	1⅓	2	0	0	0	0	R. Myers	⅓	0	0	0	0	0

Umpires: HP—DeMuth **1B**—Tschida; **2B**—Crawford; **3B**—Garcia; **LF**—Hirschbeck; **RF**—Scott.

T—2:58. **A**—65,427.

COMPOSITE BOX

NEW YORK

Player, Pos.	AVG	G	AB	R	H	2B	3B	HR	RBI	BB	SO	SB
Ricky Ledee, lf	.600	4	10	1	6	3	0	0	4	2	1	0
David Cone, p	.500	1	2	0	1	0	0	0	0	0	0	0
Scott Brosius, 3b	.471	4	17	3	8	0	0	2	6	0	4	0
Tino Martinez, 1b	.385	4	13	4	5	0	0	1	4	4	2	0
Chuck Knoblauch, 2b	.375	4	16	3	6	0	0	1	3	3	2	1
Derek Jeter, ss	.353	4	17	4	6	0	0	0	1	3	3	0
Jorge Posada, c	.333	3	9	2	3	0	0	1	2	2	2	0
Shane Spencer, lf	.333	1	3	1	1	1	0	0	0	0	2	0
Chili Davis, dh	.286	3	7	3	2	0	0	0	2	3	2	0
Paul O'Neill, rf	.211	4	19	3	4	1	0	0	0	1	2	0
Bernie Williams, cf	.063	4	16	2	1	0	0	1	3	2	5	0
Mariano Rivera, p	.000	3	1	0	0	0	0	0	0	0	0	0
Ramiro Mendoza, p	.000	1	1	0	0	0	0	0	0	0	0	0
Andy Pettitte, p	.000	1	2	0	0	0	0	0	0	0	2	0
Joe Girardi, c	.000	2	6	0	0	0	0	0	0	0	2	0
Homer Bush, pr	.000	2	0	0	0	0	0	0	0	0	0	0
Totals	**.309**	**4**	**139**	**26**	**43**	**5**	**0**	**6**	**25**	**20**	**29**	**1**

Pitching	W	L	ERA	G	GS	SV	IP	H	R	ER	BB	SO
Andy Pettitte	1	0	0.00	1	1	0	7	5	0	0	3	4
Mariano Rivera	0	0	0.00	3	0	3	4	5	0	0	0	4
Jeff Nelson	0	0	0.00	3	0	0	2	2	1	0	1	4
Graeme Lloyd	0	0	0.00	1	0	0	0	0	0	0	0	0
Orlando Hernandez	1	0	1.29	1	1	0	7	6	1	1	3	7
David Cone	0	0	3.00	1	1	0	6	2	3	2	3	4
David Wells	1	0	6.43	1	1	0	7	7	5	5	2	4
Ramiro Mendoza	1	0	9.00	1	0	0	1	2	1	1	0	1
Mike Stanton	0	0	27.00	1	0	0	1	3	2	2	0	1
Totals	**4**	**0**	**2.75**	**4**	**4**	**3**	**36**	**32**	**13**	**11**	**12**	**29**

LARRY GOREN

Hail to the Yankee skipper
Joe Torre takes a bow for four-game sweep

SAN DIEGO

Player, Pos.	AVG	G	AB	R	H	2B	3B	HR	RBI	BB	SO	SB
Ruben Rivera, lf	.800	3	5	1	4	2	0	0	1	0	0	0
Mark Sweeney, ph	.667	3	3	0	2	0	0	0	1	0	0	0
Tony Gwynn, rf	.500	4	16	2	8	0	0	1	3	1	0	0
Kevin Brown, p	.500	2	2	0	1	0	0	0	0	0	0	0
Sterling Hitchcock, p	.500	1	2	1	1	0	0	0	0	0	0	0
John Vander Wal, lf	.400	4	5	0	2	1	0	0	0	0	2	0
Chris Gomez, ss	.364	4	11	2	4	0	1	0	0	1	1	0
Quilvio Veras, 2b	.200	2	15	3	3	2	0	0	1	3	4	0
Carlos Hernandez, c	.200	4	10	0	2	0	0	0	0	0	3	0
Ken Caminiti, 3b	.143	4	14	1	2	1	0	0	1	2	7	0
Greg Vaughn, lf	.133	4	15	3	2	0	0	2	4	1	2	0
Steve Finley, cf	.083	3	12	0	1	1	0	0	0	0	2	1
Andy Sheets, ss	.000	2	2	0	0	0	0	0	0	0	1	0
Greg Myers, c	.000	2	4	0	0	0	0	0	0	0	2	0
Wally Joyner, 1b	.000	3	8	0	0	0	0	0	0	3	1	0
Jim Leyritz, c-1b	.000	4	10	0	0	0	0	0	0	1	4	0
Totals	**.239**	**4**	**134**	**13**	**32**	**7**	**1**	**3**	**11**	**12**	**29**	**1**

Pitching	W	L	ERA	G	GS	SV	IP	H	R	ER	BB	SO
Danny Miceli	0	0	0.00	2	0	0	2	2	0	0	2	1
Joey Hamilton	0	0	0.00	1	0	0	1	0	0	0	1	1
Sterling Hitchcock	0	0	1.50	1	1	0	6	7	2	1	1	7
Kevin Brown	0	1	4.40	2	2	0	14	14	7	7	6	13
Donne Wall	0	1	6.75	2	0	0	3	3	2	2	3	1
Brian Boehringer	0	0	9.00	2	0	0	2	4	2	2	2	3
Trevor Hoffman	0	1	9.00	1	0	0	2	2	2	2	1	0
Randy Myers	0	0	9.00	3	0	0	1	0	1	1	1	2
Andy Ashby	0	1	13.50	1	1	0	3	10	7	4	1	1
Mark Langston	0	0	40.50	1	0	0	1	1	3	3	2	0
Totals	**0**	**4**	**5.82**	**4**	**4**	**0**	**34**	**43**	**26**	**22**	**20**	**29**

SCORE BY INNINGS

New York	**351 021 950—26**
San Diego	**002 043 040—13**

DP—New York 4, San Diego 5. **LOB**—New York 34, San Diego 27. **E**—Caminiti 2, Vaughn, Knoblauch, O'Neill. **CS**—Ledee. **S**—Pettitte. **SF**—Caminiti, Vaughn, Ledee. **PB**—Leyritz.

Umpires—Gerry Crawford, Dana DeMuth, Richie Garcia, Mark Hirschbeck, Dale Scott, Tim Tschida.

AMERICAN LEAGUE

Yankees run table with record 114 wins, playoff sweep

BY JOHN ROYSTER

The Cleveland Indians did more than just win the American League Central in 1998. They actually managed to give the New York Yankees some competition.

The Yankees took the AL East by 22 games, winning 114 times along the way. They swept the Texas Rangers in the Division Series, allowing one run in 27 innings. They swept the San Diego Padres in a World Series that was an anticlimax to an historic season. Only in the AL Championship Series did their pinstripes get a little tight around their necks.

That's because the Indians had them by the collar. Cleveland led two games to one before being done in by poor pitching, good Yankees pitching and a big error from an unlikely source. New York won the last three games and the series 4-2.

"I think because we won 114 games, everybody assumed we were just going to run through everyone," Yankees manager Joe Torre said. "And that's not the case. If we felt that, we'd have been run over by now."

Things looked deceivingly simple for the Yankees in the opening minutes of the series. They scored five runs the first time they came to bat, getting singles from their first four hitters. Lefthander David Wells, who had pitched eight shutout innings in his only Division Series appearance against the Rangers, duplicated the feat before giving up a two-run homer to Indians outfielder Manny Ramirez in the ninth. New York won 7-2.

Chuck Knoblauch

But Game Two put the Indians back in business and provided the most memorable video clip of the series. With the score 1-1 and no outs in the top of the 12th inning, Cleveland third baseman Travis Fryman laid down a bunt to advance pinch runner Enrique Wilson. First baseman Tino Martinez' throw hit Fryman in the back of the shoulder and bounced away. Yankees second baseman Chuck Knoblauch argued for interference as the ball rolled away, and Wilson staggered home with the go-ahead run. Cleveland scored twice more in the inning and won 4-1.

The New York tabloids the next morning predictably labeled Knoblauch a "Blauch Head." And nobody in New York was particularly happy with the no-call by umpire Ted Hendry.

"I don't feel like I didn't play the ball out. I didn't know where it was," Knoblauch said. "I'm pretty shocked. I was kind of dumbfounded. The guy's running right at me, and it seemed to me he was running out of the baseline."

MEL BAILEY

El Duque to the rescue
Orlando Hernandez threw seven shutout innings in the AL Championship Series

If Game Two was given to the Indians, they took Game Three, which was something of a postseason coming-out party for 23-year-old righthander Bartolo Colon. He allowed a manufactured run in the first inning, then nothing the rest of the way. Cleveland hit three home runs after having two out and the bases empty in the fifth, and won 6-1.

The home runs were vintage Indians. But the ease with which they won was–dare we say it?–vintage Yankees.

But that was before El Duque rode to the rescue in Game Four. While his half-brother Livan was beating the Indians twice in last year's World Series, Orlando Hernandez was wasting away in Cuba, suspended from international and Cuban league play by the government.

A couple of months later, he made a daring boat trip out of the country and eventually signed with the Yankees. He capped off his journey with a brilliant postseason, including seven shutout innings to tie the ALCS. Lefty Mike Stanton and ace closer Mariano Rivera finished up New York's 4-0 win.

It was in Game Five that the stress caused Cleveland to crack at its weakest point–starting pitching. Righthander Jaret Wright had taken just two weeks to

AMERICAN LEAGUE CHAMPIONS, 1901-1998

	Pennant	Pct.	GA
1901	Chicago	.610	4
1902	Philadelphia	.610	5
1903	Boston	.659	14½
1904	Boston	.617	1½
1905	Philadelphia	.622	2
1906	Chicago	.616	3
1907	Detroit	.613	1½
1908	Detroit	.588	½
1909	Detroit	.645	3½
1910	Philadelphia	.680	14½
1911	Philadelphia	.669	13½
1912	Boston	.691	14
1913	Philadelphia	.627	6½
1914	Philadelphia	.651	8½
1915	Boston	.669	2½
1916	Boston	.591	2
1917	Chicago	.649	9
1918	Boston	.595	2½
1919	Chicago	.629	3½
1920	Cleveland	.636	2
1921	New York	.641	4½
1922	New York	.610	1
1923	New York	.645	16
1924	Washington	.597	2
1925	Washington	.636	8½
1926	New York	.591	3
1927	New York	.714	19
1928	New York	.656	2½
1929	Philadelphia	.693	18
1930	Philadelphia	.662	8

	Pennant	Pct.	GA	MVP
1931	Philadelphia	.704	13 ½	Lefty Grove, lhp, Philadelphia
1932	New York	.695	13	Jimmie Foxx, 1b, Philadelphia
1933	Washington	.651	7	Jimmie Foxx, 1b, Philadelphia
1934	Detroit	.656	7	Mickey Cochrane, c, Detroit
1935	Detroit	.616	3	Hank Greenberg, 1b, Detroit
1936	New York	.667	19 ½	Lou Gehrig, 1b, New York
1937	New York	.662	13	Charlie Gehringer, 2b, Detroit
1938	New York	.651	9 ½	Jimmie Foxx, 1b, Boston
1939	New York	.702	17	Joe DiMaggio, of, New York
1940	Detroit	.584	1	Hank Greenberg, 1b, Detroit
1941	New York	.656	17	Joe DiMaggio, of, New York
1942	New York	.669	9	Joe Gordon, 2b, New York
1943	New York	.636	13 ½	Spud Chandler, rhp, New York
1944	St. Louis	.578	1	Hal Newhouser, lhp, Detroit
1945	Detroit	.575	1 ½	Hal Newhouher, lhp, Detroit
1946	Boston	.675	12	Ted Williams, of, Boston
1947	New York	.630	12	Joe DiMaggio, of, New York
1948	Cleveland	.626	1	Lou Boudreau, ss, Cleveland
1949	New York	.630	1	Ted Williams, of, Boston
1950	New York	.636	3	Phil Rizzuto, ss, New York
1951	New York	.636	5	Yogi Berra, c, New York
1952	New York	.617	2	Bobby Shantz, lhp, Philadelphia
1953	New York	.656	8 ½	Al Rosen, 3b, Cleveland
1954	Cleveland	.721	8	Yogi Berra, c, New York
1955	New York	.623	3	Yogi Berra, c, New York
1956	New York	.630	9	Mickey Mantle, of, New York
1957	New York	.636	8	Mickey Mantle, of, New York
1958	New York	.597	10	Jackie Jensen, of, Boston
1959	Chicago	.610	5	Nellie Fox, 2b, Chicago
1960	New York	.630	8	Roger Maris, of, New York
1961	New York	.673	8	Roger Maris, of, New York
1962	New York	.593	5	Mickey Mantle, of, New York
1963	New York	.646	10 ½	Elston Howard, c, New York
1964	New York	.611	1	Brooks Robinson, 3b, Baltimore
1965	Minnesota	.630	7	Zoilo Versalles, ss, Minnesota
1966	Baltimore	.606	9	Frank Robinson, of, Baltimore
1967	Boston	.568	1	Carl Yastrzemski, of, Boston
1968	Detroit	.636	12	Denny McLain, rhp, Detroit

	East. Div.	PCT	GA	West. Div.	PCT	GA	Pennant		MVP
1969	Baltimore	.673	19	Minnesota	.599	9	Baltimore	3-0	Harmon Killebrew, 1b-3b, Minnesota
1970	Baltimore	.667	15	Minnesota	.605	9	Baltimore	3-0	Boog Powell, 1b, Baltimore
1971	Baltimore	.639	12	Oakland	.627	16	Baltimore	3-0	Vida Blue, lhp, Oakland
1972	Detroit	.551	½	Oakland	.600	5½	Oakland	3-2	Dick Allen, 1b, Chicago
1973	Baltimore	.599	8	Oakland	.580	6	Oakland	3-2	Reggie Jackson, of, Oakland
1974	Baltimore	.562	2	Oakland	.556	5	Oakland	3-1	Jeff Burroughs, of, Texas
1975	Boston	.594	4½	Oakland	.605	7	Boston	3-0	Fred Lynn, of, Boston
1976	New York	.610	10½	Kansas City	.556	2½	New York	3-2	Thurman Munson, c, New York
1977	New York	.617	2½	Kansas City	.630	8	New York	3-2	Rod Carew, 1b, Minnesota
1978	New York	.613	1	Kansas City	.568	5	New York	3-1	Jim Rice, of, Boston
1979	Baltimore	.642	8	California	.543	3	Baltimore	3-1	Don Baylor, dh, California
1980	New York	.636	3	Kansas City	.599	14	Kansas City	3-0	George Brett, 3b, Kansas City
1981	New York*	.607	2	Oakland**	.587	—	New York	3-0	Rollie Fingers, rhp, Milwaukee
	Milwaukee	.585	1½	Kansas City	.566	1			
1982	Milwaukee	.586	1	California	.574	3	Milwaukee	3-2	Robin Yount, ss, Milwaukee
1983	Baltimore	.605	6	Chicago	.611	20	Baltimore	3-1	Cal Ripken Jr., ss, Baltimore
1984	Detroit	.642	15	Kansas City	.519	3	Detroit	3-0	Willie Hernandez, lhp, Detroit
1985	Toronto	.615	2	Kansas City	.562	1	Kansas City	4-3	Don Mattingly, 1b, New York
1986	Boston	.590	5½	California	.568	5	Boston	4-3	Roger Clemens, rhp, Boston
1987	Detroit	.605	2	Minnesota	.525	2	Minnesota	4-1	George Bell, of, Toronto
1988	Boston	.549	1	Oakland	.642	13	Oakland	4-0	Jose Canseco, of, Oakland
1989	Toronto	.549	2	Oakland	.611	7	Oakland	4-1	Robin Yount, of, Milwaukee
1990	Boston	.543	2	Oakland	.636	9	Oakland	4-0	Rickey Henderson, of, Oakland
1991	Toronto	.562	7	Minnesota	.586	8	Minnesota	4-1	Cal Ripken Jr., ss, Baltimore
1992	Toronto	.593	4	Oakland	.593	6	Toronto	4-2	Dennis Eckersley, rhp, Oakland
1993	Toronto	.586	7	Chicago	.580	8	Toronto	4-2	Frank Thomas, 1b, Chicago

	East Div.	PCT	GA	Central Div.	PCT	GA	West Div.	PCT	GA	MVP
1994	New York	.619	6½	Chicago	.593	1	Texas	.456	1	Frank Thomas, 1b, Chicago
1995	Boston	.597	7	Cleveland#	.694	30	Seattle	.545	1	Mo Vaughn, 1b, Boston
1996	New York@	.568	4	Cleveland	.615	14 ½	Texas	.556	4	Juan Gonzalez, of, Texas
1997	Baltimore	.605	2	Cleveland†	.534	6	Seattle	.556	6	Ken Griffey, of, Seattle
1998	New York&	.704	22	Cleveland	.549	9	Texas	.543	3	Juan Gonzalez, of, Texas

*Won first half; defeated Milwaukee 3-2 in best-of-5 playoff. **Won first half, defeated Kansas City 3-0 in best-of-5 playoff.
Won AL pennant, defeating Seattle 4-2. @ Won AL pennant, defeating Baltimore 4-1. † Won AL pennant, defeating Baltimore 4-2
& Won AL pennant, defeating Cleveland 4-2

STANDINGS

Page	EAST	W	L	PCT	GB	Manager	General Manager	Attend./Dates	Last Penn.
172	New York Yankees	114	48	.704	—	Joe Torre	Brian Cashman	2,949,734 (80)	1998
80	Boston Red Sox*	92	70	.568	22	Jimy Williams	Dan Duquette	2,314,721 (80)	1986
245	Toronto Blue Jays	88	74	.543	26	Tim Johnson	Gord Ash	2,454,303 (81)	1993
73	Baltimore Orioles	79	83	.488	35	Ray Miller	Pat Gillick	3,685,194 (81)	1983
231	Tampa Bay Devil Rays	63	99	.389	51	Larry Rothschild	Chuck LaMar	2,506,023 (81)	None
Page	**CENTRAL**	**W**	**L**	**PCT**	**GB**	**Manager(s)**	**General Manager**	**Attend./Dates**	**Last Penn.**
106	Cleveland Indians	89	73	.549	—	Mike Hargrove	John Hart	3,467,299 (81)	1997
87	Chicago White Sox	80	82	.494	9	Jerry Manuel	Ron Schueler	1,391,146 (79)	1959
139	Kansas City Royals	72	89	.447	16½	Tony Muser	Herk Robinson	1,494,875 (79)	1985
159	Minnesota Twins	70	92	.432	19	Tom Kelly	Terry Ryan	1,165,980 (81)	1991
119	Detroit Tigers	65	97	.401	24	B. Bell/Larry Parrish	Randy Smith	1,409,391 (79)	1984
Page	**WEST**	**W**	**L**	**PCT**	**GB**	**Manager**	**General Manager**	**Attend./Dates**	**Last Penn.**
238	Texas Rangers	88	74	.543	—	Johnny Oates	Doug Melvin	2,927,409 (81)	None
52	Anaheim Angels	85	77	.525	3	Terry Collins	Bill Bavasi	2,519,210 (81)	None
224	Seattle Mariners	76	85	.472	11½	Lou Piniella	Woody Woodward	2,644,166 (81)	None
187	Oakland Athletics	74	88	.457	14	Art Howe	Billy Beane	1,232,339 (79)	1990

*Won wild-card playoff berth

NOTE: Team's individual batting, pitching and fielding statistics can be found on page indicated in lefthand column.

fall from the opening starter in the Division Series to the bullpen. His replacement, righthander Chad Ogea, gave up four runs in 1⅓ innings.

As if to add insult to manager Mike Hargrove's injury, Wright gave up just one run in six innings in relief of Ogea. But it was too little and too late. New York won 5-3. And in truth, Wright was lucky. He got away with seven walks, and five Tribe pitchers gave up an ALCS record-tying 11 walks and hit two batters.

The Yankees took a 6-0 lead in the first three innings of Game Six, and still the Indians had some fight left in them. Cleveland opened the fifth inning with three singles and a walk, and closed it with a Jim Thome grand slam. Just like that, it was 6-5.

But then came the second-most-memorable video clip of the series. Yankees third baseman Scott Brosius led off the bottom of the sixth with a routine grounder to shortstop Omar Vizquel. The equally routine throw from Vizquel, who had never committed an error in the postseason, sailed high and to the left of Thome at first base.

JOHN WILLIAMSON

Almost automatic
Juan Gonzalez led the league with 157 RBIs

A walk and an out later came another, fatal, defensive gaffe. Yankees shortstop Derek Jeter hit a drive to deep right that Ramirez at first appeared to judge a home run. He recovered enough to make a leap at the fence as the ball landed on the warning track.

Jim Thome

Triple, two runs, followed by another run, ballgame, series.

The 9-5 loss was difficult to take for the Indians, who lost the World Series in both 1995 and '97.

"You just keep going," Thome said. "You can't dwell on how we haven't accomplished what we want to. When we do, it will be that much more special."

Rangers Hang In There

The Rangers played credibly against the Yankees, too. Sure, they scored only one run in three Division Series games. But they only gave up nine in losing 2-0, 3-1 and 4-0.

Other than that, the series will be remembered most for the exploits of Yankees left fielder Shane Spencer, who spent nine years in the minor leagues before gaining his 15 minutes of fame.

Spencer accounted for five of New York's last seven runs in the series, hitting a solo home run and scoring another run in Game Two, and hitting a three-run homer in Game Three. By the World Series he had lost his starting job to the equally unlikely Ricky Ledee. And darned if Ledee didn't become a hitting hero on that stage.

The Rangers scored in the fifth inning of Game Two, when catcher Ivan Rodriguez singled home

AMERICAN LEAGUE YEAR-BY-YEAR BATTING LEADERS

Year	Batting Average		Home Runs		RBIs	
1901	Nap Lajoie, Philadelphia	.422	Nap Lajoie, Philadelphia	14	Nap Lajoie, Philadelphia	125
1902	Ed Delahanty, Wash.	.376	Socks Seybold, Philadelphia	16	Buck Freeman, Boston	121
1903	Nap Lajoie, Cleveland	.355	Buck Freeman, Boston	13	Buck Freeman, Boston	104
1904	Nap Lajoie, Cleveland	.381	Harry Davis, Philadelphia	10	Nap Lajoie, Cleveland	102
1905	Elmer Flick, Cleveland	.306	Harry Davis, Philadelphia	8	Harry Davis, Philadelphia	83
1906	George Stone, St. Louis	.358	Harry Davis, Philadelphia	12	Harry Davis, Philadelphia	96
1907	Ty Cobb, Detroit	.350	Harry Davis, Philadelphia	8	Ty Cobb, Detroit	116
1908	Ty Cobb, Detroit	.324	Sam Crawford, Detroit	7	Ty Cobb, Detroit	101
1909	Ty Cobb, Detroit	.377	Ty Cobb, Detroit	9	Ty Cobb, Detroit	115
1910	Ty Cobb, Detroit	.385	Jake Stahl, Boston	10	Sam Crawford, Detroit	115
1911	TyCobb, Detroit	.420	Frank Baker, Philadelphia	11	Ty Cobb, Detroit	144
1912	Ty Cobb, Detroit	.410	2 tied at	10	Frank Baker, Philadelphia	133
1913	Ty Cobb, Detroit	.390	Frank Baker, Philadelphia	12	Frank Baker, Philadelphia	126
1914	Ty Cobb, Detroit	.368	Frank Baker, Philadelphia	9	Sam Crawford, Detroit	112
1915	Ty Cobb, Detroit	.370	Braggo Roth, Cleveland	7	Sam Crawford, Detroit	116
1916	Tris Speaker, Cleveland	.386	Wally Pipp, New York	12	Wally Pipp, New York	99
1917	Ty Cobb, Detroit	.383	Wally Pipp, New York	9	Bob Veah, Detroit	115
1918	Ty Cobb, Detroit	.382	2 tied at	11	2 tied at	74
1919	Ty Cobb, Detroit	.384	Babe Ruth, Boston	29	Babe Ruth, Boston	112
1920	George Sisler, St. Louis	.407	Babe Ruth, New York	54	Babe Ruth, New York	137
1921	Harry Heilmann, Detroit	.394	Babe Ruth, New York	59	Babe Ruth, New York	171
1922	George Sisler, St. Louis	.420	Kenny Williams, St. Louis	39	Kenny Williams, St. Louis	155
1923	Harry Heilmann, Detroit	.403	Babe Ruth, New York	43	Babe Ruth, New York	131
1924	Babe Ruth, New York	.378	Babe Ruth, New York	46	Goose Goslin, Wash.	129
1925	Harry Heilmann, Detroit	.393	Bob Meusel, New York	33	Bob Meusel, New York	138
1926	Heinie Manush, Detroit	.377	Babe Ruth, New York	47	Babe Ruth, New York	145
1927	Harry Heilmann, Detroit	.398	Babe Ruth, New York	60	Lou Gehrig, New York	175
1928	Goose Goslin, Wash.	.379	Babe Ruth, New York	54	2 tied at	142
1929	Lew Fonseca, Cleveland	.369	Babe Ruth, New York	46	Al Simmons, Philadelphia	157
1930	Al Simmons, Philadelphia	.381	Babe Ruth, New York	49	Lou Gehrig, New York	174
1931	Al Simmons, Philadelphia	.390	2 tied at	46	Lou Gehrig, New York	184
1932	Dale Alexander, Det.-Bos.	.367	Jimmie Foxx, Philadelphia	58	Jimmie Foxx, Philadelphia	169
1933	Jimmie Foxx, Philadelphia	.356	Jimmie Foxx, Philadelphia	48	Jimmie Foxx, Philadelphia	163
1934	Lou Gehrig, New York	.363	Lou Gehrig, New York	49	Lou Gehrig, New York	165
1935	Buddy Myer, Washington	.349	2 tied at	36	Hank Greenberg, Detroit	170
1936	Luke Appling, Chicago	.388	Lou Gehrig, New York	49	Hal Trosky, Cleveland	162
1937	Charlie Gehringer, Detroit	.371	Joe DiMaggio, New York	46	Hank Greenberg, Detroit	183
1938	Jimmie Foxx, Boston	.349	Hank Greenberg, Detroit	58	Jimmie Foxx, Boston	175
1939	Joe DiMaggio, New York	.381	Jimmie Foxx, Boston	35	Ted Williams, Boston	145
1940	Joe DiMaggio, New York	.352	Hank Greenberg, Detroit	41	Hank Greenberg, Detroit	150
1941	Ted Williams, Boston	.406	Ted Williams, Boston	37	Joe DiMaggio, New York	125
1942	Ted Williams, Boston	.356	Ted Williams, Boston	36	Ted Williams, Boston	137
1943	Luke Appling, Chicago	.328	Rudy York, Detroit	34	Rudy York, Detroit	118
1944	Lou Boudreau, Cleve.	.327	Nick Etten, New York	22	Vern Stephens, St. Louis	109
1945	Snuffy Stirnweiss, N.Y.	.309	Vern Stephens, St. Louis	24	Nick Etten, New York	111
1946	Mickey Vernon, Wash.	.352	Hank Greenberg, Detroit	44	Hank Greenberg, Detroit	127
1947	Ted Williams, Boston	.343	Ted Williams, Boston	32	Ted Williams, Boston	114
1948	Ted Williams, Boston	.369	Joe DiMaggio, New York	39	Joe DiMaggio, New York	155
1949	George Kell, Detroit	.343	Ted Williams, Boston	43	2 tied at	159
1950	Billy Goodman, Boston	.354	Al Rosen, Cleveland	37	2 tied at	144
1951	Ferris Fain, Philadelphia	.344	Gus Zernial, Chi.-Phil.	33	Gus Zernial, Chi.-Phil.	129
1952	Ferris Fain, Philadelphia	.327	Larry Doby, Cleveland	32	Al Rosen, Cleveland	105
1953	Mickey Vernon, Wash.	.337	Al Rosen, Cleveland	43	Al Rosen, Cleveland	145
1954	Bobby Avila, Cleveland	.341	Larry Doby, Cleveland	32	Larry Doby, Cleveland	126
1955	Al Kaline, Detroit	.340	Mickey Mantle, New York	37	2 tied at	116
1956	Mickey Mantle, New York	.353	Mickey Mantle, New York	52	Mickey Mantle, New York	130
1957	Ted Williams, Boston	.388	Roy Sievers, Washington	42	Roy Sievers, Washington	114
1958	Ted Williams, Boston	.328	Mickey Mantle, New York	42	Jackie Jensen, Boston	122
1959	Harvey Kuenn, Detroit	.353	2 tied at	42	Jackie Jensen, Boston	112
1960	Pete Runnels, Boston	.320	Mickey Mantle, New York	40	Roger Maris, New York	112
1961	Norm Cash, Detroit	.361	Roger Maris, New York	61	Roger Maris, New York	142
1962	Pete Runnels, Boston	.326	Harmon Killebrew, Minn.	48	Harmon Killebrew, Minn.	126
1963	Carl Yastrzemski, Boston	.321	Harmon Killebrew, Minn.	45	Dick Stuart, Boston	118
1964	Tony Oliva, Minnesota	.323	Harmon Killebrew, Minn.	49	Brooks Robinson, Balt.	118
1965	Tony Oliva, Minnesota	.321	Tony Conigliaro, Boston	32	Rocky Colavito, Cleveland	108
1966	Frank Robinson, Balt.	.316	Frank Robinson, Baltimore	49	Frank Robinson, Baltimore	122
1967	Carl Yastrzemski, Boston	.326	2 tied at	44	Carl Yastrzemski, Boston	121
1968	Carl Yastrzemski, Boston	.301	Frank Howard, Washington	44	Ken Harrelson, Boston	109
1969	Rod Carew, Minnesota	.332	Harmon Killebrew, Minn.	49	Harmon Killebrew, Minn.	140
1970	Alex Johnson, California	.329	Frank Howard, Washington	44	Frank Howard, Washington	126
1971	Tony Oliva, Minnesota	.337	Bill Melton, Chicago	33	Harmon Killebrew, Minn.	119
1972	Rod Carew, Minnesota	.318	Dick Allen, Chicago	37	Dick Allen, Chicago	113
1973	Rod Carew, Minnesota	.350	Reggie Jackson, Oakland	32	Reggie Jackson, Oakland	117
1974	Rod Carew, Minnesota	.364	Dick Allen, Chicago	32	Jeff Burroughs, Texas	118
1975	Rod Carew, Minnesota	.359	2 tied at	36	George Scott, Milwaukee	109
1976	George Brett, Kansas City	.333	Graig Nettles, New York	32	Lee May, Baltimore	109
1977	Rod Carew, Minnesota	.388	Jim Rice, Boston	39	Larry Hisle, Minnesota	119
1978	Rod Carew, Minnesota	.333	Jim Rice, Boston	46	Jim Rice, Boston	139
1979	Fred Lynn, Boston	.333	Gorman Thomas, Mil.	45	Don Baylor, California	139
1980	George Brett, Kansas City	.390	2 tied at	41	Cecil Cooper, Milwaukee	122
1981	Carney Lansford, Boston	.336	4 tied at	22	Eddie Murray, Baltimore	78
1982	Willie Wilson, Kansas City	.332	2 tied at	39	Hal McRae, Kansas City	133
1983	Wade Boggs, Boston	.361	Jim Rice, Boston	39	2 tied at	126
1984	Don Mattingly, New York	.343	Tony Armas, Boston	43	Tony Armas, Boston	123
1985	Wade Boggs, Boston	.368	Darrell Evans, Detroit	40	Don Mattingly, New York	145
1986	Wade Boggs, Boston	.357	Jesse Barfield, Toronto	40	Joe Carter, Cleveland	121
1987	Wade Boggs, Boston	.363	Mark McGwire, Oakland	49	George Bell, Toronto	134
1988	Wade Boggs, Boston	.366	Jose Canseco, Oakland	42	Jose Canseco, Oakland	124
1989	Kirby Puckett, Minn.	.339	Fred McGriff, Toronto	36	Ruben Sierra, Texas	119
1990	George Brett, Kansas City	.329	Cecil Fielder, Detroit	51	Cecil Fielder, Detroit	132
1991	Julio Franco, Texas	.341	2 tied at	44	Cecil Fielder, Detroit	133
1992	Edgar Martinez, Seattle	.343	Juan Gonzalez, Texas	43	Cecil Fielder, Detroit	124
1993	John Olerud, Toronto	.363	Juan Gonzalez, Texas	46	Albert Belle, Cleveland	129
1994	Paul O'Neill, New York	.359	Ken Griffey, Seattle	40	Kirby Puckett, Minnesota	112
1995	Edgar Martinez, Seattle	.356	Albert Belle, Cleveland	50	2 tied at	126
1996	Alex Rodriguez, Seattle	.358	Mark McGwire Oakland	52	Albert Belle, Cleveland	148
1997	Frank Thomas, Chicago	.347	Ken Griffey, Seattle	56	Ken Griffey, Seattle	147
1998	Bernie Williams, New York	.339	Ken Griffey, Seattle	56	Juan Gonzalez, Texas	157

AMERICAN LEAGUE YEAR-BY-YEAR PITCHING LEADERS

Year	Wins		ERA		Strikeouts	
1901	Cy Young, Boston	33	Cy Young, Boston	1.63	Cy Young, Boston	158
1902	Cy Young, Boston	32	Ed Siever, Detroit	1.91	Rube Waddell, Philadelphia	210
1903	Cy Young, Boston	28	Earl Moore, Cleveland	1.77	Rube Waddell, Philadelphia	302
1904	Jack Chesbro, New York	41	Addie Joss, Cleveland	1.59	Rube Waddell, Philadelphia	349
1905	Rube Waddell, Phil.	26	Rube Waddell, Philadelphia	1.48	Rue Waddell, Philadelphia	287
1906	Al Orth, New York	27	Doc White, Chicago	1.52	Rube Waddell, Philadelphia	196
1907	2 tied at	27	Ed Walsh, Chicago	1.60	Rube Waddell, Philadelphia	232
1908	Ed Walsh, Chicago	40	Addie Joss, Cleveland	1.16	Ed Walsh, Chicago	269
1909	George Mullin, Detroit	29	Harry Krause, Philadelphia	1.39	Frank Smith, Chicago	177
1910	Jack Coombs, Phil.	31	Ed Walsh, Chicago	1.27	Walter Johnson, Washington	313
1911	Jack Coombs, Phil.	28	Vean Gregg, Cleveland	1.81	Ed Walsh, Chicago	255
1912	Joe Wood, Boston	34	Walter Johnson, Wash.	1.39	Walter Johnson, Washington	303
1913	Walter Johnson, Wash.	36	Walter Johnson, Wash.	1.14	Walter Johnson, Washington	243
1914	Walter Johnson, Wash.	28	Dutch Leonard, Bos.	1.00	Walter Johnson, Washington	225
1915	Walter Johnson, Wash.	27	Joe Wood, Boston	1.49	Walter Johnson, Washington	203
1916	Walter Johnson, Wash.	25	Babe Ruth, Boston	1.75	Walter Johnson, Washington	228
1917	Ed Cicotte, Chicago	28	Ed Cicotte, Chicago	1.53	Walter Johnson, Washington	188
1918	Walter Johnson, Wash.	23	Walter Johnson, Wash.	1.27	Walter Johnson, Washington	162
1919	Ed Cicotte, Chicago	29	Walter Johnson, Wash.	1.49	Walter Johnson, Washington	147
1920	Jim Bagby, Cleveland	31	Bob Shawkey, New York	2.45	Stan Coveleski, Claveland	133
1921	2 tied at	27	Red Faber, Chicago	2.48	Walter Johnson, Washington	143
1922	Eddie Rommel, Phil.	27	Red Faber, Chicago	2.80	Urban Shocker, St. Louis	149
1923	George Uhle, Cleveland	26	Stan Coveleski, Claveland	2.76	Walter Johnson, Washington	130
1924	Walter Johnson, Wash.	23	Walter Johnson, Wash.	2.72	Walter Johnson, Washington	158
1925	2 tied at	21	Stan Coveleski, Wash.	2.84	Lefty Grove, Philadelphia	116
1926	George Uhle, Claveland	27	Lefty Grove, Philadelphia	2.51	Lefty Grove, Philadelphia	194
1927	2 tied at	22	Wilcy Moore, New York	2.28	Lefty Grove, Philadelphia	174
1928	2 tied at	24	Garland Braxton, Wash.	2.52	Lefty Grove, Philadelphia	183
1929	George Earnshaw, Phil.	24	Lefty Grove, Philadelphia	2.82	Lefty Grove, Philadelphia	170
1930	Lefty Grove, Philadelphia	28	Lefty Grove, Philadelphia	2.54	Lefty Grove, Philadelphia	209
1931	Lefty Grove, Philadelphia	31	Lefty Grove, Philadelphia	2.05	Lefty Grove, Philadelphia	175
1932	General Crowder, Wash.	26	Lefty Grove, Philadelphia	2.84	Red Ruffing, New York	190
1933	2 tied at	24	Monte Pearson, Claveland	2.33	Lefty Gomez, New York	163
1934	Lefty Gomez, New York	26	Lefty Gomez, New York	2.33	Lefty Gomez, New York	158
1935	Wes Ferrell, Boston	25	Lefty Grove, Boston.	2.70	Tommy Bridges, Detroit	163
1936	Tommy Bridges, Detroit	23	Lefty Grove, Boston.	2.81	Tommy Bridges, Detroit	175
1937	Lefty Gomez, New York	21	Lefty Gomez, New York	2.33	Lefty Gomez, New York	194
1938	Red Ruffing, New York	21	Lefty Grove, Philadelphia	3.07	Bob Feller, Cleveland	240
1939	Bob Feller, Cleveland	24	Lefty Grove, Philadelphia	2.54	Bob Feller, Cleveland	246
1940	Bob Feller, Cleveland	27	Bob Feller, Cleveland	2.62	Bob Feller, Cleveland	261
1941	Bob Feller, Cleveland	25	Thornton Lee, Chicago	2.37	Bob Feller, Cleveland	260
1942	Tex Hughson, Boston	22	Ted Lyons, Chicago	2.10	2 tied at	113
1943	2 tied at	20	Spud Chandler, New York	1.64	Allie Reynolds, Cleveland	151
1944	Hal Newhouser, Detroit	29	Dizzy Trout, Detroit	2.12	Hal Newhouser, Detroit	187
1945	Hal Newhouser, Detroit	25	Hal Newhouser, Detroit	1.81	Hal Newhouser, Detroit	212
1946	2 tied at	26	Hal Newhouser, Detroit	1.94	Bob Feller, Cleveland	348
1947	Bob Feller, Cleveland	20	Spud Chandler, New York	2.46	Bob Feller, Cleveland	196
1948	Hal Newhouser, Detroit	21	Gene Bearden, Cleveland	2.43	Bob Feller, Cleveland	164
1949	Mel Parnell, Boston	25	Mel Parnell, Boston	2.78	Virgil Trucks, Detroit	153

Year	Wins		ERA		Strikeouts	
1950	Bob Lemon, Cleveland	23	Early Wynn, Cleveland	3.20	Bob Lemon, Cleveland	170
1951	Bob Feller, Cleveland	22	Saul Rogovin, Det.-Chi.	2.78	Vic Raschi, New York	164
1952	Bobby Shantz, Phil.	24	Allie Reynolds, New York	2.07	Allie Reynolds, New York	160
1953	Bob Porterfield, Wash.	22	Eddie Lopat, New York	2.43	Billy Pierce, Chicago	186
1954	2 tied at	23	Mike Garcia, Cleveland	2.64	Bob Turley, Baltimore	185
1955	3 tied at	18	Billy Pierce, Chicago	1.97	Herb Score, Cleveland	245
1956	Frank Lary, Detroit	21	Whitey Ford, New York	2.47	Herb Score, Cleveland	263
1957	2 tied at	20	Bobby Shantz, New York	2.45	Early Wynn, Cleveland	184
1958	Bob Turley, New York	21	Whitey Ford, New York	2.01	Early Wynn, Chicago	179
1959	Early Wynn, Chicago	22	Hoyt Wilhelm, Balt.	2.19	Jim Bunning, Detroit	201
1960	2 tied at	18	Frank Baumann, Chicago	2.68	Jim Bunning, Detroit	201
1961	Whitey Ford, New York	25	Dick Donovan, Washington	2.40	Camilo Pascual, Minnesota	221
1962	Ralph Terry, New York	23	Hank Aguirre, Detroit	2.21	Camilo Pascual, Minnesota	206
1963	Whitey Ford, New York	24	Gary Peters, Chicago	2.33	Camilo Pascual, Minnesota	202
1964	2 tied at	20	Dean Chance, L.A.	1.65	Al Downing, New York	217
1965	Mudcat Grant, Minnesota	21	Sam McDowell, Claveland	2.18	Sam McDowell, Cleveland	325
1966	Jim Kaat, Minnesota	25	Gary Peters, Chicago	1.98	Sam McDowell, Cleveland	225
1967	2 tied at	22	Joel Horlen, Chicago	2.06	Jim Lonborg, Boston	246
1968	Denny McLain, Detroit	31	Luis Tiant, Cleveland	1.60	Sam McDowell, Cleveland	283
1969	Denny McLain, Detroit	24	Dick Bosman, Washington	2.19	Sam McDowell, Cleveland	279
1970	3 tied at	24	Diego Segui, Oakland	2.56	Sam McDowell, Cleveland	304
1971	Mickey Lolich, Detroit	25	Vida Blue, Oakland	1.82	Mickey Lolich, Detroit	308
1972	2 tied at	24	Luis Tiant, Boston	1.91	Nolan Ryan, California	329
1973	Wilbur Wood, Chicago	24	Jim Palmer, Baltimore	2.40	Nolan Ryan, California	383
1974	2 tied at	25	Catfish Hunter, Oakland	2.49	Nolan Ryan, California	367
1975	2 tied at	23	Jim Palmer, Baltimore	2.09	Frank Tanana, California	269
1976	Jim Palmer, Baltimore	22	Mark Fidrych, Detroit	2.34	Nolan Ryan, California	327
1977	3 tied at	20	Frank Tanana, California	2.54	Nolan Ryan, California	341
1978	Ron Guidry, New York	25	Ron Guidry, New York	1.74	Nolan Ryan, California	260
1979	Mike Flanagan, Baltimore	23	Ron Guidry, New York	2.78	Nolan Ryan, California	223
1980	Steve Stone, Baltimore	25	Rudy May, New York	2.47	Len Barker, Cleveland	187
1981	Steve McCatty, Oakland	14	Steve McCatty, Oak.	2.32	Len Barker, Cleveland	127
1982	LaMarr Hoyt, Chicago	19	Rick Sutcliffe, Claveland	2.96	Floyd Bannister, Seattle	209
1983	LaMarr Hoyt, Chicago	21	Rick Honeycutt, Texas	2.42	Jack Morris, Detroit	232
1984	Mike Boddicker, Balt.	20	Mike Boddicker, Balt.	2.79	Mark Langston, Seattle	204
1985	Ron Guidry, New York	22	Dave Stieb, Toronto	2.48	Bert Blyleven, Cleve.-Minn.	206
1986	Roger Clemens, Boston	24	Roger Clemens, Boston	2.48	Mark Langston, Seattle	245
1987	2 tied at	20	Jimmy Key, Toronto	2.76	Mark Langston, Seattle	262
1988	Frank Viola, Minnesota	24	Allan Anderson, Minnesota	2.45	Roger Clemens, Boston	291
1989	Bret Saberhagen, K.C.	23	Bret Saberhagen, K.C.	2.16	Nolan Ryan, Texas	301
1990	Bob Welch, Oakland	27	Roger Clemens, Boston	1.93	Nolan Ryan, Texas	232
1991	2 tied at	20	Roger Clemens, Boston	2.62	Roger Clemens, Boston	241
1992	2 tied at	21	Roger Clemens, Boston	2.41	Randy Johnson, Seattle	241
1993	Jack McDowell, Chicago	22	Kevin Appier, Kansas City	2.56	Randy Johnson, Seattle	308
1994	Jimmy Key, New York	17	Steve Ontiveros, Oakland	2.65	Randy Johnson, Seattle	204
1995	Mike Mussina, Baltimore	19	Randy Johnson, Seattle	2.48	Randy Johnson, Seattle	294
1996	Andy Pettitte, New York	21	Juan Guzman, Toronto	2.93	Roger Clemens, Boston	257
1997	Roger Clemens, Toronto	21	Roger Clemens, Toronto	2.05	Roger Clemens, Toronto	292
1998	3 tied at	20	Roger Clemens, Toronto	2.65	Roger Clemens, Toronto	271

right fielder Juan Gonzalez. Which was fitting, because those two were key players as Texas overcame the Angels to win the AL West.

For much of the season, it looked as though Gonzalez might break Hack Wilson's single-season major league record of 190 RBIs, and that the Angels might win the division. Neither turned out to be so.

JOHN WILLIAMSON

Fan favorite
Alex Rodriguez became the first shortstop to ever hit 40 homers and steal 40 bases

Gonzalez was still on pace to break Wilson's record when he reached 101 by the all-star break. His batting average rose after that, but his RBIs tailed off and he finished at .318 with 45 home runs and 157 RBIs.

The league's hottest hitter in the second half turned out to be Chicago White Sox left fielder Albert Belle, who batted .387 with 31 homers and 86 RBIs after the break.

The Rangers fell behind the Angels during a tough spell of road games in May and June, even as the Angels were enduring a brutal spate of injuries.

But the schedule turned the other way down the stretch, and so did the race. The Angels played 44 of their last 76 games on the road, with three east coast trips in a one-month span.

LARRY GOREN

Beantown's new ace
Pedro Martinez helped the Red Sox to the postseason

They still led Texas by 3½ games with 19 to play, but five of them were against the Rangers. Texas won all five, and Anaheim lost 13 of its last 19 to finish three games behind.

Their September collapse was nothing new. It was the third time in four years that they relinquished a September lead and watched the playoffs from home.

"We're not going to get (the reputation) out of people's heads until we play through it," Anaheim manager Terry Collins said. "Until we do, people are going to talk and talk and talk about it. We don't do well in September. It's right there in black and white. It's history."

Pedro-mania

Another team with a history of heartbreak, the Boston Red Sox, had a pretty good year. They made the biggest splash of the offseason, trading for Montreal Expos righthander Pedro Martinez and giving him a six-year, $75 million contract.

It gave Boston a pitching star to go with first baseman Mo Vaughn and shortstop Nomar Garciaparra. All three delivered good seasons, Vaughn while unsuccessfully negotiating a new contract with the club. The Red Sox easily won the AL wild card, despite finishing 22 games behind the Yankees in the East.

Martinez went 19-7 with a 2.89 ERA and 251 strikeouts in 234 innings, and pitched well in the opening game of the Division Series against the Indians. Boston won that game 11-3, but it would be their last win of the season.

Cleveland seemed to unravel further when Hargrove and starting pitcher Dwight Gooden were ejected in the first inning of Game Two. Hargrove was shown the door just three pitches into the game, backing up Gooden after the righthander argued umpire Joe Brinkman's calls on the second and third pitches.

Gooden was run later in the inning, after Brinkman

called the Red Sox' John Valentin safe on a play at the plate.

"I don't want to say the umps were against us, but we looked across the field and we knew the Red Sox were against us," Indians left fielder David Justice said. "We realized we were going to have to just take the game."

They took the next three, and Justice was largely responsible. He hit an important three-run homer as the Indians overcame the ejections and won the second game 9-5.

Then he almost singlehandedly won the clinching Game Four. He drove in both runs in a 2-1 victory with a double in the eighth inning, and earlier threw out a Boston runner at the plate. He batted .313 with six RBIs in the series, and played brilliantly in left field after DHing for most of the second half of the season.

Like Fine Wine

The Red Sox undoubtedly felt some pressure to acquire Martinez after letting righthander Roger Clemens walk as a free agent two winters before.

It's a good thing Martinez delivered because Clemens, formerly a Boston icon, had his second straight stellar season for the Blue Jays at age 35.

Clemens actually outperformed Martinez in almost exactly the same number of innings. He went 20-6 with a 2.65 ERA and struck out 271 in 235 innings.

He also allowed fewer hits, 169-188, and produced a couple of impressive streaks. Clemens became the fourth pitcher since 1951 to go 20 straight starts without a loss. And he went from July 12-Sept. 16 without allowing a home run. Mark McGwire and Sammy Sosa hit a combined 50 in that span.

JOHN WILLIAMSON

Golden Age shortstop

Derek Jeter led the AL with 127 runs while committing just nine errors

Talk of baseball being in a Golden Age may be a bit premature, but one thing can be said: We're in a Golden Age for AL shortstops, and it might last for a while.

Alex Rodriguez of the Seattle Mariners, Derek Jeter of the Yankees and Nomar Garciaparra of the Red Sox might become known as the best trio of shortstops to play in the same league at the same time, ever. If they aren't already.

That's a pretty strong statement, but at a position heretofore known for defense, here's where they ranked among the offensive leaders in 1998:

Batting: Jeter fifth, Garciaparra sixth.
Runs: Jeter first, Rodriguez third.
Hits: Rodriguez first, Jeter third, Garciaparra fifth.
Triples: Garciaparra and Jeter tied for fourth.
RBIs: Rodriguez fifth.
Stolen Bases: Rodriguez fourth.
Total Bases: Rodriguez third.
Extra-Base Hits: Rodriguez fourth.

AL: BEST TOOLS

A Baseball America survey of American League managers, conducted at midseason 1998, ranked AL players with the best tools:

BEST HITTER
1. Ivan Rodriguez, Rangers
2. Bernie Williams, Yankees
3. Paul O'Neill, Yankees

BEST POWER HITTER
1. Ken Griffey, Mariners
2. Juan Gonzalez, Rangers
3. Jim Thome, Indians

BEST BUNTER
1. Kenny Lofton, Indians
2. Omar Vizquel, Indians
3. Roberto Alomar, Orioles

BEST HIT-AND-RUN ARTIST
1. Omar Vizquel, Indians
2. Joe Girardi, Yankees
3. Gary DiSarcina, Angels

BEST BASERUNNER
1. Rickey Henderson, Athletics
2. Tom Goodwin, Rangers
3. Kenny Lofton, Indians

FASTEST BASERUNNER
1. Tom Goodwin, Rangers
2. Brian Hunter, Tigers
3. Kenny Lofton, Indians

BEST PITCHER
1. Pedro Martinez, Red Sox
2. Rolando Arrojo, Devil Rays
3. David Wells, Yankees

BEST FASTBALL
1. Bartolo Colon, Indians
2. Troy Percival, Angels
3. Randy Johnson, Mariners

BEST CURVEBALL
1. Tom Gordon, Red Sox
2. Aaron Sele, Rangers
3. Mike Mussina, Orioles

BEST SLIDER
1. David Cone, Yankees
2. Rolando Arrojo, Devil Rays
3. Randy Johnson, Mariners

BEST CHANGEUP
1. Pedro Martinez, Red Sox
2. Jamie Moyer, Mariners
3. Mike Mussina, Orioles

BEST CONTROL
1. Bob Tewksbury, Twins
2. Brad Radke, Twins
3. Jamie Moyer, Mariners

BEST PICKOFF MOVE
1. Andy Pettitte, Yankees
2. Kenny Rogers, Athletics
3. Jimmy Key, Orioles

BEST RELIEVER
1. John Wetteland, Rangers
2. Tom Gordon, Red Sox
3. Troy Percival, Angels

BEST DEFENSIVE C
1. Ivan Rodriguez, Rangers
2. Dan Wilson, Mariners
3. Sandy Alomar, Indians

BEST DEFENSIVE 1B
1. David Segui, Mariners
2. Rafael Palmeiro, Orioles
3. Will Clark, Rangers

BEST DEFENSIVE 2B
1. Roberto Alomar, Orioles
2. Chuck Knoblauch, Yankees
3. Damion Easley, Tigers

BEST DEFENSIVE 3B
1. Scott Brosius, Yankees
2. Travis Fryman, Indians
3. Robin Ventura, White Sox

BEST DEFENSIVE SS
1. Omar Vizquel, Indians
2. Alex Rodriguez, Mariners
3. Nomar Garciaparra, Red Sox

BEST INFIELD ARM
1. Alex Rodriguez, Mariners
2. Nomar Garciaparra, Red Sox
3. Mike Blowers, Athletics

BEST DEFENSIVE OF
1. Ken Griffey, Mariners
2. Jim Edmonds, Angels
3. Bernie Williams, Yankees

BEST OUTFIELD ARM
1. Jay Buhner, Mariners
2. Ken Griffey, Mariners
3. Mark Whiten, Indians

MOST EXCITING PLAYER
1. Ken Griffey, Mariners
2. Bernie Williams, Yankees
3. Alex Rodriguez, Mariners

BEST MANAGER
1. Joe Torre, Yankees
2. Tom Kelly, Twins
3. Mike Hargrove, Indians

AMERICAN LEAGUE
DEPARTMENT LEADERS

BATTING

GAMES
- Albert Belle, Chicago 162
- Rafael Palmeiro, Baltimore 162
- B.J. Surhoff, Baltimore 162
- Johnny Damon, Kansas City 161
- Ken Griffey, Seattle 161
- Cal Ripken, Baltimore 161
- Alex Rodriguez, Seattle 161
- Robin Ventura, Chicago 161

AT-BATS
- Alex Rodriguez, Seattle 686
- Johnny Damon, Kansas City 642
- Ray Durham, Chicago 635
- Ken Griffey, Seattle 633
- Shawn Green, Toronto 630

RUNS
- Derek Jeter, New York 127
- Ray Durham, Chicago 125
- Alex Rodriguez, Seattle 123
- Ken Griffey, Seattle 120
- Chuck Knoblauch, New York 117

HITS
- Alex Rodriguez, Seattle 213
- Mo Vaughn, Boston 205
- Derek Jeter, New York 203
- Albert Belle, Chicago 200
- Nomar Garciaparra, Boston 195

TOTAL BASES
- Albert Belle, Chicago 399
- Ken Griffey, Seattle 387
- Alex Rodriguez, Seattle 384
- Juan Gonzalez, Texas 382
- Mo Vaughn, Boston 360

EXTRA-BASE HITS
- Albert Belle, Chicago 99
- Juan Gonzalez, Texas 97
- Ken Griffey, Seattle 92
- Carlos Delgado, Toronto 82
- Manny Ramirez, Cleveland 82
- Alex Rodriguez, Seattle 82

SINGLES
- Derek Jeter, New York 151
- Jose Offerman, Kansas City 143
- Tom Goodwin, Rangers 133
- Mike Caruso, Chicago 132
- Mo Vaughn, Boston 132

DOUBLES
- Juan Gonzalez, Texas 50
- Albert Belle, Chicago 48
- Edgar Martinez, Seattle 46
- John Valentin, Boston 44
- Carlos Delgado, Toronto 43

Ken Griffey
56 home runs

TRIPLES
- Jose Offerman, Kansas City 13
- Johnny Damon, Kansas City 10
- Randy Winn, Tampa Bay 9
- Ray Durham, Chicago 8
- Nomar Garciaparra, Boston 8
- Derek Jeter, New York 8
- Troy O'Leary, Boston 8

HOME RUNS
- Ken Griffey, Seattle 56
- Albert Belle, Chicago 49
- Jose Canseco, Toronto 46
- Juan Gonzalez, Texas 45
- Manny Ramirez, Cleveland 45

HOME RUN RATIO
(At-Bats per Home Runs)
- Ken Griffey, Seattle 11.3
- Albert Belle, Chicago 12.4
- Jose Canseco, Toronto 12.7
- Manny Ramirez, Cleveland 12.7
- Juan Gonzalez, Texas 13.5

RUNS BATTED IN
- Juan Gonzalez, Texas 157
- Albert Belle, Chicago 152
- Ken Griffey, Seattle 146
- Manny Ramirez, Cleveland 145
- Alex Rodriguez, Seattle 124

SACRIFICE BUNTS
- Mike Bordick, Baltimore 15
- Mike Benjamin, Boston 13
- Alex Gonzalez, Toronto 13
- A.J. Hinch, Oakland 13
- Joey Cora, Seattle/Cleveland 12
- Gary DiSarcina, Anaheim 12
- Mark McLemore, Texas 12
- Omar Vizquel, Cleveland 12

SACRIFICE FLIES
- Albert Belle, Chicago 15
- Dean Palmer, Kansas City 13
- Juan Gonzalez, Texas 11
- Paul O'Neill, New York 11
- Frank Thomas, Chicago 11

HIT BY PITCH
- Chuck Knoblauch, New York 18
- Damion Easley, Detroit 16
- Sal Fasano, Kansas City 16
- Brady Anderson, Baltimore 15
- Matt Lawton, Minnesota 15
- Shannon Stewart, Toronto 15

WALKS
- Rickey Henderson, Oakland 118
- Frank Thomas, Chicago 110
- Edgar Martinez, Seattle 106
- Tim Salmon, Anaheim 90
- Jim Thome, Cleveland 90

INTENTIONAL WALKS
- Robin Ventura, Chicago 15
- Carlos Delgado, Toronto 13
- Mo Vaughn, Boston 13
- Ken Griffey, Seattle 11
- Albert Belle, Chicago 10

STRIKEOUTS
- Jose Canseco, Toronto 159
- Mo Vaughn, Boston 144
- Shawn Green, Toronto 142
- Jim Thome, Cleveland 141
- Carlos Delgado, Toronto 139

TOUGHEST TO STRIKE OUT
(Plate Appearances per SO)
- Mike Caruso, Chicago 14.6
- Paul Molitor, Minnesota 13.6

Albert Belle
.655 slugging percentage

- Miguel Cairo, Tampa Bay 12.7
- Joey Cora, Cleveland 11.8
- Gary DiSarcina, Anaheim 11.7

STOLEN BASES
- Rickey Henderson, Oakland 66
- Kenny Lofton, Cleveland 54
- Shannon Stewart, Toronto 51
- Alex Rodriguez, Seattle 46
- Jose Offerman, Kansas City 45

CAUGHT STEALING
- Tom Goodwin, Texas 20
- Shannon Stewart, Toronto 18
- Jose Canseco, Toronto 17
- Rickey Henderson, Oakland 13
- Alex Rodriguez, Seattle 13

GIDP
- Ron Coomer, Minnesota 22
- Paul O'Neill, New York 22
- Nomar Garciaparra, Boston 20
- Juan Gonzalez, Texas 20
- Darrin Fletcher, Toronto 19
- Paul Molitor, Minnesota 19
- Magglio Ordonez, Chicago 19
- Bernie Williams, New York 19

HITTING STREAKS
- Eric Davis, Baltimore 30
- Garret Anderson, Anaheim 28
- Jose Offerman, Kansas City 27
- Nomar Garciaparra, Boston 24
- Joey Cora, Seattle 21

MULTIPLE-HIT GAMES
- Alex Rodriguez, Seattle 64
- Derek Jeter, New York 60
- Mo Vaughn, Boston 60
- Albert Belle, Chicago 59
- Juan Gonzalez, Texas 58
- Paul O'Neill, New York 58

SLUGGING PERCENTAGE
- Albert Belle, Chicago .655
- Juan Gonzalez, Texas .630
- Ken Griffey, Seattle .611
- Manny Ramirez, Cleveland .599
- Carlos Delgado, Toronto .592

ON-BASE PERCENTAGE
- Edgar Martinez, Seattle .429
- Bernie Williams, New York .422
- Jim Thome, Cleveland .413
- Tim Salmon, Anaheim .410
- Jose Offerman, Kansas City .403

PITCHING

WINS
Roger Clemens, Toronto 20
David Cone, New York 20
Rick Helling, Texas 20
Pedro Martinez, Boston 19
Aaron Sele, Texas 19

LOSSES
Tom Candiotti, Oakland 16
Juan Guzman, Toronto/Baltimore 16
Jaime Navarro, Chicago 16
Glendon Rusch, Kansas City 15
Tony Saunders, Tampa Bay 15
Mike Sirotka, Chicago 15
Justin Thompson, Detroit 15

WINNING PERCENTAGE
David Wells, New York .... .818
Roger Clemens, Toronto .... .769
Orlando Hernandez, New York .... .750
David Cone, New York .... .741
Rick Helling, Texas .... .741

GAMES
Sean Runyan, Detroit 88
Paul Quantrill, Toronto 82
Greg Swindell, Boston 81
Eddie Guardado, Minnesota 79
Dan Plesac, Toronto 78

GAMES STARTED
Scott Erickson, Baltimore 36
Tim Belcher, Kansas City 34
Chuck Finley, Anaheim 34
Jamie Moyer, Seattle 34
Kenny Rogers, Oakland 34
Justin Thompson, Detroit 34

COMPLETE GAMES
Scott Erickson, Baltimore 11
David Wells, New York 8
Jeff Fassero, Seattle 7
Kenny Rogers, Oakland 7
Bartolo Colon, Cleveland 6
Randy Johnson, Seattle 6

SHUTOUTS
David Wells, New York 5
Roger Clemens, Toronto 3
Brian Moehler, Detroit 3
Jamie Moyer, Seattle 3

GAMES FINISHED
Tom Gordon, Boston 69
Rick Aguilera, Minnesota 64
Troy Percival, Anaheim 60
John Wetteland, Texas 59
Roberto Hernandez, Tampa Bay 58
Billy Taylor, Oakland 58

SAVES
Tom Gordon, Boston 46
Troy Percival, Anaheim 42
John Wetteland, Texas 42
Mike Jackson, Cleveland 40
Rick Aguilera, Minnesota 38

Tom Gordon
46 saves

Scott Erickson
251 innings, 36 starts

INNINGS PITCHED
Scott Erickson, Baltimore 251
Kenny Rogers, Oakland 239
Roger Clemens, Toronto 235
Jamie Moyer, Seattle 234
Tim Belcher, Kansas City 234

HITS ALLOWED
Scott Erickson, Baltimore 284
Mike Sirotka, Chicago 255
Charles Nagy, Cleveland 250
Tim Belcher, Kansas City 247
Aaron Sele, Texas 239

RUNS ALLOWED
Charles Nagy, Cleveland 139
Mike Sirotka, Chicago 137
Jaime Navarro, Chicago 135
John Burkett, Texas 131
Tim Belcher, Kansas City 127

HOME RUNS ALLOWED
Tim Belcher, Kansas City 37
Woody Williams, Toronto 36
Charles Nagy, Cleveland 34
Jeff Fassero, Seattle 33
Dave Burba, Cleveland 30
Tom Candiotti, Oakland 30
Brian Moehler, Detroit 30
Jaime Navarro, Chicago 30
Mike Sirotka, Chicago 30
Tim Wakefield, Boston 30

WALKS
Tony Saunders, Tampa Bay 111
Chuck Finley, Anaheim 109
Pat Rapp, Kansas City 107
Juan Guzman, Toronto/Baltimore 98
Omar Olivares, Anaheim 91

FEWEST WALKS PER 9 INNINGS
David Wells, New York 1.2
Bret Saberhagen, Boston 1.5
Jamie Moyer, Seattle 1.6
Mike Mussina, Baltimore 1.8
Brad Radke, Minnesota 1.8

HIT BATSMEN
Rolando Arrojo, Tampa Bay 19
David Cone, New York 15
Tim Wakefield, Boston 14
Scott Erickson, Baltimore 13
Aaron Sele, Texas 13

STRIKEOUTS
Roger Clemens, Toronto 271
Pedro Martinez, Boston 251
Randy Johnson, Seattle 213
Chuck Finley, Anaheim 212
David Cone, New York 209

STRIKEOUTS PER 9 INNINGS
Roger Clemens, Toronto 10.4
Pedro Martinez, Boston 9.7
David Cone, New York 9.1
Chuck Finley, Anaheim 8.5
Tony Saunders, Tampa Bay 8.0

PICKOFFS
Justin Thompson, Detroit 12
Kenny Rogers, Oakland 10
Jeff Fassero, Seattle 8
Jim Parque, Chicago 8
Andy Pettitte, New York 8

WILD PITCHES
Jaime Navarro, Chicago 18
Blake Stein, Oakland 15
Tom Candiotti, Oakland 14
Pat Rapp, Kansas City 14
Jeff Fassero, Seattle 12

BALKS
Carlos Castillo, Chicago 3
Mike Jackson, Cleveland 3
Jim Parque, Chicago 3

OPPONENTS BATTING AVERAGE
Roger Clemens, Toronto .... .198
Pedro Martinez, Boston .... .217
Hideki Irabu, New York .... .233
David Cone, New York .... .237
David Wells, New York .... .239

FIELDING

PITCHER
PCT Mike Mussina, Baltimore 1.000
PO Scott Erickson, Baltimore 24
A Kenny Rogers, Oakland 66
E Randy Johnson, Seattle 8
TC Kenny Rogers, Oakland 88
DP Several tied at 5

CATCHER
PCT Chris Hoiles, Baltimore .... .995
PO Ivan Rodriguez, Texas 864
A Ivan Rodriguez, Texas 71
E Two tied at 9
TC Ivan Rodriguez, Texas 941
DP A.J. Hinch, Oakland 8
PB Phil Nevin, Anaheim 20

FIRST BASE
PCT David Segui, Seattle .... .999
PO Rafael Palmeiro, Baltimore 1433
A Rafael Palmeiro, Baltimore 125
E Jason Giambi, Oakland 14
TC Rafael Palmeiro, Baltimore 1567
DP Tony Clark, Detroit 134

SECOND BASE
PCT Damion Easley, Detroit .... .985
PO Damion Easley, Detroit 285
A Roberto Alomar, Baltimore 449
E Joey Cora, Seattle/Cleve. 20
TC Ray Durham, Chicago 738
DP Ray Durham, Chicago 129

THIRD BASE
PCT Cal Ripken, Baltimore .... .979
PO John Valentin, Boston 121
A Robin Ventura, Chicago 328
E Russ Davis, Seattle 32
TC Robin Ventura, Chicago 444
DP Robin Ventura, Chicago 38

SHORTSTOP
PCT Omar Vizquel, Cleveland .... .993
PO Two tied at 271
A Alex Rodriguez, Seattle 447
E Mike Caruso, Chicago 35
TC Alex Rodriguez, Seattle 736
DP Gary DiSarcina, Anaheim 103

OUTFIELD
PCT Darren Bragg, Boston .... .996
PO Ken Griffey, Seattle 408
A Three tied at 18
E Two tied at 8
TC Ken Griffey, Seattle 424
DP Two tied at 5

1998 American League Statistics

CLUB BATTING

	AVG	G	AB	R	H	2B	3B	HR	BB	SO	SB
Texas	.289	162	5672	940	1637	314	32	201	595	1045	82
New York	.288	162	5643	965	1625	290	31	207	653	1025	153
Boston	.280	162	5601	876	1568	338	35	205	541	1049	72
Seattle	.276	161	5628	859	1553	321	28	234	558	1081	115
Baltimore	.273	162	5565	817	1520	303	11	214	593	903	86
Cleveland	.272	162	5616	850	1530	334	30	198	631	1061	143
Anaheim	.272	162	5630	787	1530	314	27	147	510	1028	93
Chicago	.271	163	5585	861	1516	291	38	198	551	916	127
Minnesota	.266	162	5641	734	1499	285	32	115	506	915	112
Toronto	.266	163	5580	816	1482	316	19	221	564	1132	184
Detroit	.264	162	5664	722	1494	306	29	165	455	1070	122
Kansas City	.263	161	5546	714	1459	274	40	134	475	984	135
Tampa Bay	.261	162	5555	620	1450	267	43	111	473	1107	120
Oakland	.257	162	5490	804	1413	295	13	149	633	1122	131

CLUB PITCHING

	ERA	G	CG	SHO	SV	IP	H	R	ER	BB	SO
New York	3.82	162	22	16	48	1457	1357	656	619	466	1080
Boston	4.18	162	5	8	53	1436	1406	729	667	504	1025
Toronto	4.28	163	10	11	47	1465	1443	768	697	587	1154
Tampa Bay	4.35	162	7	7	28	1443	1425	751	698	643	1008
Cleveland	4.44	162	9	4	47	1460	1552	779	721	563	1037
Anaheim	4.49	162	3	5	52	1444	1481	783	720	630	1091
Baltimore	4.74	162	16	10	37	1431	1505	785	754	535	1065
Minnesota	4.75	162	7	8	42	1448	1622	818	764	458	952
Oakland	4.81	162	12	4	39	1434	1555	866	766	529	922
Detroit	4.93	162	9	4	32	1446	1551	863	792	595	947
Seattle	4.93	161	17	7	31	1424	1530	855	781	528	1156
Texas	4.99	162	10	8	46	1431	1624	871	794	519	994
Kansas City	5.15	161	6	5	46	1436	1590	899	822	568	999
Chicago	5.22	163	8	4	42	1439	1569	931	835	580	911

CLUB FIELDING

	PCT	PO	A	E	DP		PCT	PO	A	E	DP
Baltimore	.987	4294	1758	81	144	Detroit	.982	4339	1812	115	164
Tampa Bay	.985	4329	1763	94	178	Texas	.980	4294	1580	121	140
New York	.984	4370	1639	98	146	Kansas City	.980	4309	1689	125	172
Boston	.983	4308	1624	105	128	Toronto	.979	4395	1531	125	131
Anaheim	.983	4332	1646	106	146	Seattle	.979	4273	1571	125	139
Cleveland	.982	4380	1727	110	146	Chicago	.977	4316	1706	140	161
Minnesota	.982	4343	1585	108	135	Oakland	.977	4302	1654	141	155

INDIVIDUAL BATTING LEADERS

(Minimum 502 Plate Appearances)

	AVG	G	AB	R	H	2B	3B	HR	RBI	BB	SO	SB
Williams, Bernie, New York	.339	128	499	101	169	30	5	26	97	74	81	15
Vaughn, Mo, Boston	.337	154	609	107	205	31	2	40	115	61	144	0
Belle, Albert, Chicago	.328	163	609	113	200	48	2	49	152	81	84	6
Davis, Eric, Baltimore	.327	131	452	81	148	29	1	28	89	44	108	7
Jeter, Derek, New York	.324	149	626	127	203	25	8	19	84	57	119	30
Garciaparra, Nomar, Boston	.323	143	604	111	195	37	8	35	122	33	62	12
Martinez, Edgar, Seattle	.322	154	556	86	179	46	1	29	102	106	96	1
Rodriguez, Ivan, Texas	.321	145	579	88	186	40	4	21	91	32	88	9
Fernandez, Tony, Toronto	.321	138	486	71	156	36	2	9	72	45	53	13
Gonzalez, Juan, Texas	.318	154	606	110	193	50	2	45	157	46	126	2

INDIVIDUAL PITCHING LEADERS

(Minimum 162 Innings Pitched)

	W	L	ERA	G	GS	CG	SV	IP	H	R	ER	BB	SO
Clemens, Roger, Toronto	20	6	2.65	33	33	5	0	235	169	78	69	88	271
Martinez, Pedro, Boston	19	7	2.89	33	33	3	0	234	188	82	75	67	251
Rogers, Kenny, Oakland	16	8	3.17	34	34	7	0	239	215	96	84	67	138
Finley, Chuck, Anaheim	11	9	3.39	34	34	1	0	223	210	97	84	109	212
Wells, David, New York	18	4	3.49	30	30	8	0	214	195	86	83	29	163
Mussina, Mike, Baltimore	13	10	3.49	29	29	4	0	206	189	85	80	41	175
Moyer, Jamie, Seattle	15	9	3.53	34	34	4	0	234	234	99	92	42	158
Cone, David, New York	20	7	3.55	31	31	3	0	208	186	89	82	59	209
Arrojo, Rolando, Tampa Bay	14	12	3.56	32	32	2	0	202	195	84	80	65	152
Colon, Bartolo, Cleveland	14	9	3.71	31	31	6	0	204	205	91	84	79	158

AWARD WINNERS

Selected by Baseball Writers Association of America

MVP

Player, Team	1st	2nd	3rd	Total
Juan Gonzalez, Tex.	21	7	0	357
Nomar Garciaparra, Bos.	5	7	7	232
Derek Jeter, N.Y.	2	6	3	180
Mo Vaughn, Bos.	0	3	1	135
Ken Griffey, Sea.	0	0	4	135
Manny Ramirez, Cle.	0	1	3	127
Bernie Williams, N.Y.	0	1	3	103
Albert Belle, Chi.	0	0	4	96
Alex Rodriguez, Sea.	0	2	1	92
Ivan Rodriguez, Tex.	0	0	0	60
Roger Clemens, Tor.	0	1	1	49
Paul O'Neill, N.Y.	0	0	0	36
Tom Gordon, Bos.	0	0	1	27
Darin Erstad, Ana.	0	0	0	7
Tim Salmon, Ana.	0	0	0	7
David Wells, N.Y.	0	0	0	3
John Wetteland, Tex.	0	0	0	3
Eric Davis, Balt.	0	0	0	2
Travis Fryman, Cle.	0	0	0	2
Rafael Palmeiro, Balt.	0	0	0	2
Carlos Delgado, Tor.	0	0	0	1
Rick Helling, Tex.	0	0	0	1
Mike Jackson, Cle.	0	0	0	1
Pedro Martinez, Bos.	0	0	0	1
Jim Thome, Cle.	0	0	0	1

CY YOUNG AWARD

Player, Team	1st	2nd	3rd	Total
Roger Clemens, Tor.	28	0	0	140
Pedro Martinez, Bos.	0	20	5	65
David Wells, N.Y.	0	4	19	31
David Cone, N.Y.	0	4	4	16

ROOKIE OF THE YEAR

Player, Team	1st	2nd	3rd	Total
Ben Grieve, Oak.	23	5	0	130
Rolando Arrojo, T.B.	4	10	11	61
Mike Caruso, Chi.	0	9	7	34
Orlando Hernandez, N.Y.	1	4	8	25
Magglio Ordonez, Chi.	0	0	1	1
Sidney Ponson, Balt.	0	0	1	1

MANAGER OF THE YEAR

Manager, Team	1st	2nd	3rd	Total
Joe Torre, N.Y.	23	4	1	128
Jimy Williams, Bos.	3	12	8	59
Terry Collins, Ana.	2	7	7	38
Johnny Oates, Tex.	0	2	5	11
Mike Hargrove, Cle.	0	1	5	8
Tim Johnson, Tor.	0	1	1	4
Jerry Manuel, Chi.	0	1	1	4

NOTE: MVP balloting based on 14 points for first-place vote, nine for second, eight for third, etc.; Cy Young Award, Rookie of the Year and Manager of the Year balloting based on five points for first-place vote, three for second and one for third.

GOLD GLOVE AWARDS

Selected by AL managers

C—Ivan Rodriguez, Texas. **1B**—Rafael Palmeiro, Baltimore. **2B**—Roberto Alomar, Baltimore. **3B**—Robin Ventura, Chicago. **SS**—Omar Vizquel, Cleveland. **OF**—Jim Edmonds, Anaheim; Ken Griffey, Seattle; Bernie Williams, New York. **P**—Mike Mussina, Baltimore.

Multi-hit games: Rodriguez first, Jeter second.

Garciaparra had the league's fourth-longest hitting streak.

And it's not like the these guys are slouches on defense. Jeter in particular cemented his reputation with a memorable throw from the hole in the World Series, after committing just nine errors during the regular season.

And here's the kicker: Garciaparra is the oldest at 25.

Camden Place

The Baltimore Orioles were the major leagues' feel-bad team of the year. With a meddling owner, a dead clubhouse and a crippled pitching rotation, the team with a $77 million payroll finished 79-83, in a different hemisphere from the Yankees and 13 games out of the wild card.

The offense relied almost totally on the home run, and the pitchers worked about as fast as Congress on Valium. Other than that, they were a joy to watch. The Orioles still attracted a league-best 3.685 million fans.

As has often been the case in the tenure of owner Peter Angelos, significant changes were made after the season. General manager Pat Gillick had already planned to retire. His assistant, Kevin Malone, was compelled to work all year without a contract despite being Gillick's obvious successor. He bolted for the GM job with the Los Angeles Dodgers, and Angelos hired former Marlins assistant Frank Wren as GM.

Scouting director Gary Nickels was fired. Manager Ray Miller was left standing, but hitting coach Rick Down was fired and first-base coach Carlos Bernhardt was reassigned to a scouting job.

All that was before any changes to the playing roster. But those were expected to come over the winter, since the O's finished below .500 with the majors' oldest team.

Odds And Ends

■ One of the few bumps in the Yankees' road occurred on April 13, when a 500-pound steel expansion joint fell through the ceiling of the loge level at Yankee Stadium, obliterating a seat below and gouging out a hole in the floor below that.

It occurred at a fortuitous time, about four hours before a game when the seat might have been occupied.

The damage was repaired remarkably quickly, though not before the Yankees and Mets both played games on the same day across town at Shea Stadium. It also gave players on the Yankees' Double-A Norwich team a chance to play at Yankee Stadium, albeit a mostly empty Yankee Stadium. During their downtime, the Yankees had the Norwich team come up for a scrimmage.

■ In a major upset, only one AL team fired its manager in 1998. The Tigers canned Buddy Bell in early September, replacing him with bench coach Larry Parrish on an interim basis.

The team was 52-85 when Bell was let go. After the season, Parrish was named the permanent manager.

There were just two changes among general managers. In addition to the substitution of Wren for Gillick in Baltimore, Brian Cashman replaced Bob Watson in New York before the season.

LARRY GOREN

Went 3-0 in AL playoffs
Yankees lefthander David Wells

AMERICAN LEAGUE

DIVISION SERIES

NEW YORK vs. TEXAS

COMPOSITE BOX

NEW YORK

Player, Pos.	AVG	G	AB	R	H	2B	3B	HR	RBI	BB	SO	SB
Chad Curtis, lf	.667	3	3	1	2	1	0	0	0	1	1	1
Shane Spencer, lf	.500	2	6	3	3	0	0	2	4	0	1	0
Joe Girardi, c	.429	2	7	0	3	0	0	0	0	0	1	0
Scott Brosius, 3b	.400	3	10	1	4	0	0	1	3	0	3	0
Paul O'Neill, rf	.364	3	11	1	4	2	0	1	1	1	1	0
Tino Martinez, 1b	.273	3	11	1	3	2	0	0	0	0	2	0
Tim Raines, ph-lf	.250	2	4	1	1	1	0	0	0	1	1	0
Chili Davis, dh	.167	2	6	0	1	0	0	0	0	0	2	0
Derek Jeter, ss	.111	3	9	0	1	0	0	0	0	2	2	0
Chuck Knoblauch, 2b	.091	3	11	0	1	0	0	0	0	0	4	0
Jorge Posada, c	.000	1	2	1	0	0	0	0	0	1	2	0
Bernie Williams, cf	.000	3	11	0	0	0	0	0	0	1	4	0
Homer Bush, pr	.000	1	0	0	0	0	0	0	0	0	0	1
Totals	**253**	**3**	**91**	**9**	**23**	**6**	**0**	**4**	**8**	**7**	**24**	**2**

Pitcher	W	L	ERA	G	GS	SV	IP	H	R	ER	BB	SO
David Cone	1	0	0.00	1	1	0	6	2	0	0	1	6
Graeme Lloyd	0	0	0.00	1	0	0	0	0	0	0	0	0
Jeff Nelson	0	0	0.00	2	0	0	3	2	0	0	1	2
Mariano Rivera	0	0	0.00	3	0	2	3	1	0	0	1	2
David Wells	1	0	0.00	1	1	0	8	5	0	0	1	9
Andy Pettitte	1	0	1.29	1	1	0	7	3	1	1	0	8
Totals	**3**	**0**	**0.33**	**3**	**3**	**2**	**27**	**13**	**1**	**1**	**4**	**27**

TEXAS

Player, Pos.	AVG	G	AB	R	H	2B	3B	HR	RBI	BB	SO	SB
Todd Zeile, 3b	.333	3	9	0	3	0	0	0	0	0	2	0
Tom Goodwin, cf	.250	2	4	0	1	0	0	0	0	0	1	0
Royce Clayton, ss	.222	3	9	0	2	0	0	0	0	0	4	0
Mike Simms, dh	.200	2	5	0	1	0	0	0	0	0	2	0
Roberto Kelly, lf	.143	2	7	0	1	1	0	0	0	0	2	0
Mark McLemore, 2b	.100	3	10	0	1	1	0	0	0	2	3	0
Ivan Rodriguez, c	.100	3	10	0	1	0	0	0	1	0	5	0
Will Clark, 1b	.091	3	11	0	1	0	0	0	0	1	2	0

Player, Pos.	AVG	G	AB	R	H	2B	3B	HR	RBI	BB	SO	SB
Rusty Greer, lf	.091	3	11	0	1	0	0	0	0	1	2	0
Juan Gonzalez, rf	.083	3	12	1	1	1	0	0	0	0	3	0
Luis Alicea, ph	.000	1	1	0	0	0	0	0	0	0	0	0
Lee Stevens, 1b	.000	1	3	0	0	0	0	0	0	0	1	0
Totals	**.140**	**3**	**92**	**1**	**13**	**3**	**0**	**0**	**1**	**4**	**27**	**0**

Pitcher	W	L	ERA	G	GS	SV	IP	H	R	ER	BB	SO
Tim Crabtree	0	0	0.00	2	0	0	4	1	0	0	0	2
John Wetteland	0	0	0.00	1	0	0	1	0	0	0	1	1
Todd Stottlemyre	0	1	2.25	1	1	0	8	6	2	2	4	8
Rick Helling	0	1	4.50	1	1	0	6	8	3	3	1	9
Aaron Sele	0	1	6.00	1	1	0	6	8	4	4	1	4
Totals	**0**	**3**	**3.24**	**3**	**3**	**0**	**25**	**23**	**9**	**9**	**7**	**24**

SCORE BY INNINGS	
New York	**030 204 000—9**
Texas	**000 010 000—1**

DP—Texas 4, New York 2. **LOB**—New York 16, Texas 15. **E**—Clayton, Knoblauch. **S**—Jeter, Goodwin. **CS**—Brosius, Curtis, Zeile. **HBP**—Knoblauch (by Stottlemyre). **PB**—Rodriguez.

CLEVELAND vs. BOSTON

COMPOSITE BOX

BOSTON

Player, Pos.	AVG	G	AB	R	H	2B	3B	HR	RBI	BB	SO	SB
John Valentin, 3b	.467	4	15	5	7	1	0	0	0	3	1	0
Mo Vaughn, 1b	.412	4	17	3	7	2	0	2	7	1	5	0
Darren Lewis, cf	.357	4	14	4	5	2	0	0	0	1	3	1
Nomar Garciaparra, ss	.333	4	15	4	5	1	0	3	11	1	0	0
Trot Nixon, rf	.333	2	3	0	1	0	0	0	0	1	0	0
Mike Stanley, dh	.267	4	15	1	4	0	0	0	0	2	5	0
Jason Varitek, c	.250	1	4	0	1	0	0	0	1	0	1	0
Scott Hatteberg, c	.111	3	9	0	1	0	0	0	0	3	1	0
Mike Benjamin, 2b	.091	4	11	1	1	0	0	0	0	1	3	0
Darren Bragg, rf	.083	3	12	0	1	0	0	0	0	0	5	0
Troy O'Leary, lf	.063	4	16	0	1	0	0	0	0	1	4	0
Damon Buford, cf	.000	3	1	2	0	0	0	0	0	0	0	0
Midre Cummings, ph	.000	3	3	0	0	0	0	0	0	0	0	0
Totals	**.252**	**4**	**135**	**20**	**34**	**6**	**0**	**5**	**19**	**14**	**28**	**1**

Pitcher	W	L	ERA	G	GS	SV	IP	H	R	ER	BB	SO
Jim Corsi	0	0	0.00	2	0	0	3	1	0	0	1	2
Pete Schourek	0	0	0.00	1	1	0	5	2	0	0	4	1
Greg Swindell	0	0	0.00	1	0	0	1	0	0	0	1	1
Derek Lowe	0	0	2.08	2	0	0	4	3	1	1	1	2
Pedro Martinez	1	0	3.86	1	1	0	7	6	3	3	0	8
Bret Saberhagen	0	1	3.86	1	1	0	7	4	3	3	1	7
Dennis Eckersley	0	0	9.00	1	0	0	1	1	1	1	0	1
Tom Gordon	0	1	9.00	2	0	0	3	4	3	3	4	1
John Wasdin	0	0	10.80	1	0	0	2	2	2	2	1	2
Tim Wakefield	0	1	33.75	1	1	0	1	3	5	5	2	1
Totals	**1**	**3**	**4.63**	**4**	**4**	**0**	**35**	**26**	**18**	**18**	**15**	**26**

CLEVELAND

Player, Pos.	AVG	G	AB	R	H	2B	3B	HR	RBI	BB	SO	SB
Kenny Lofton, cf	.375	4	16	5	6	1	0	2	4	1	1	2
Manny Ramirez, rf	.357	4	14	2	5	2	0	2	3	1	4	0
David Justice, lf	.313	4	16	2	5	4	0	1	6	0	1	0
Sandy Alomar, c	.231	4	13	2	3	3	0	0	2	1	4	0
Brian Giles, of	.200	3	10	1	2	1	0	0	0	1	4	0
Travis Fryman, 3b	.154	4	13	1	2	1	0	0	0	3	4	1
Jim Thome, 1b-dh	.133	4	15	2	2	0	0	2	2	2	5	0
Omar Vizquel, ss	.067	4	15	1	1	0	0	0	0	1	0	0
Joey Cora, 2b	.000	4	10	2	0	0	0	0	0	3	2	0
Richie Sexson, 1b	.000	3	2	0	0	0	0	0	0	2	1	0
Enrique Wilson, 2b	.000	1	2	0	0	0	0	0	0	0	0	0
Totals	**.206**	**4**	**126**	**18**	**26**	**12**	**0**	**7**	**17**	**15**	**26**	**3**

Pitcher	W	L	ERA	G	GS	SV	IP	H	R	ER	BB	SO
Paul Assenmacher	0	0	0.00	3	0	0	1	2	0	0	0	2
Jim Poole	0	0	0.00	2	0	0	1	1	0	0	1	2
Paul Shuey	0	0	0.00	3	0	0	3	3	0	0	1	4
Charles Nagy	1	0	1.13	1	1	0	8	4	1	1	0	3
Bartolo Colon	0	0	1.59	1	1	0	6	5	1	1	3	3
Mike Jackson	0	0	4.50	3	0	3	4	3	2	2	1	1
Dave Burba	1	0	5.06	1	0	0	5	4	3	3	2	4
Doug Jones	0	0	6.75	1	0	0	3	3	2	2	1	1
Jaret Wright	0	1	12.46	1	1	0	4	7	6	6	2	6
Steve Reed	1	0	40.50	2	0	0	1	1	3	3	1	1
Dwight Gooden	0	0	54.00	1	1	0	0	1	2	2	2	1
Totals	**3**	**1**	**5.00**	**4**	**4**	**3**	**36**	**34**	**19**	**20**	**14**	**28**

SCORE BY INNINGS	
Cleveland	**151 014 231—18**
Boston	**501 234 032—20**

DP—Boston 4, Cleveland 3. **LOB**—Boston 26, Cleveland 22. **E**—Alomar. **CS**—Fryman. **SF**—Garciaparra 2, Justice. **S**—Benjamin. **PB**—Varitek 2. **WP**—Martinez, Gordon. **HBP**—Ramirez (by Wakefield, Wasdin), Giles (by Lowe), Lewis (by Wright), Buford (by Reed).

CHAMPIONSHIP SERIES

NEW YORK vs. CLEVELAND

COMPOSITE BOX

NEW YORK

Player, Pos.	AVG	G	AB	R	H	2B	3B	HR	RBI	BB	SO	SB
Bernie Williams, cf	.381	6	21	4	8	1	0	0	5	7	4	1
Scott Brosius, 3b	.300	6	20	2	6	1	0	1	6	2	4	0
Chili Davis, dh	.286	5	14	2	4	1	0	1	5	2	3	0
Paul O'Neill, rf	.280	6	25	6	7	2	0	1	3	3	4	2
Joe Girardi, c	.250	3	8	2	2	0	0	0	0	1	0	0
Derek Jeter, ss	.200	6	25	3	5	1	1	0	2	2	5	3
Chuck Knoblauch, 2b	.200	6	25	4	5	1	0	0	0	4	2	0
Jorge Posada, c	.182	5	11	1	2	0	0	1	2	4	2	0
Tino Martinez, 1b	.105	6	19	1	2	1	0	0	1	6	8	2
Tim Raines, dh-lf	.100	3	10	0	1	0	0	0	1	2	5	0
Shane Spencer, lf	.100	3	10	1	1	0	0	0	0	1	3	0
Chad Curtis, lf	.000	2	4	0	0	0	0	0	0	1	2	0
Ricky Ledee, lf	.000	3	5	0	0	0	0	0	0	0	0	0
Homer Bush, pr-dh	.000	2	0	1	0	0	0	0	0	0	0	1
Totals	**.218**	**6**	**197**	**27**	**43**	**8**	**1**	**4**	**25**	**35**	**42**	**9**

Pitcher	W	L	ERA	G	GS	SV	IP	H	R	ER	BB	SO
Orlando Hernandez	1	0	0.00	1	1	0	7	3	0	0	2	6
Mariano Rivera	0	0	0.00	4	0	1	6	0	0	0	1	5
Ramiro Mendoza	0	0	0.00	2	0	0	4	4	0	0	0	1
Mike Stanton	0	0	0.00	3	0	0	4	2	0	0	1	4
Graeme Lloyd	0	0	0.00	1	0	0	1	1	0	0	0	0
David Wells	2	0	2.87	2	2	0	16	12	5	5	2	18
David Cone	1	0	4.15	2	2	0	13	12	6	6	6	13
Andy Pettitte	0	1	11.75	1	1	0	5	8	6	6	3	1
Jeff Nelson	0	1	20.26	3	0	0	1	3	3	3	1	3
Totals	**4**	**2**	**3.21**	**6**	**6**	**1**	**56**	**45**	**20**	**20**	**16**	**51**

CLEVELAND

Player, Pos.	AVG	G	AB	R	H	2B	3B	HR	RBI	BB	SO	SB
Omar Vizquel, ss	.440	6	25	2	11	0	1	0	0	1	3	4
Manny Ramirez, rf	.333	6	21	2	7	1	0	2	4	4	9	0
Jim Thome, 1b-dh	.304	6	23	4	7	0	0	4	8	1	8	0
Mark Whiten, lf	.286	2	7	2	2	1	0	1	1	1	3	0
Enrique Wilson, 2b	.214	5	14	2	3	0	0	0	1	1	3	0
Kenny Lofton, cf	.185	6	27	2	5	1	0	1	3	1	7	1
Travis Fryman, 3b	.174	6	23	2	4	0	0	0	0	1	5	1
David Justice, dh-lf	.158	6	19	2	3	0	0	1	2	3	3	0
Joey Cora, 2b	.143	2	7	1	1	0	0	0	0	2	1	0
Brian Giles, lf	.083	4	12	0	1	0	0	0	0	1	3	0
Sandy Alomar, c	.063	5	16	1	1	0	0	0	0	0	2	0
Jeff Branson, ph	.000	1	1	0	0	0	0	0	0	0	0	0
Einar Diaz, c	.000	5	4	0	0	0	0	0	0	0	1	0
Richie Sexson, 1b	.000	3	6	0	0	0	0	0	0	0	3	0
Totals	**.220**	**6**	**205**	**20**	**45**	**3**	**1**	**9**	**19**	**16**	**51**	**6**

Pitcher	W	L	ERA	G	GS	SV	IP	H	R	ER	BB	SO
Paul Shuey	0	0	0.00	5	0	0	6	4	0	0	7	7
Paul Assenmacher	0	0	0.00	3	0	0	2	0	0	0	0	3
Steve Reed	0	0	0.00	3	0	0	2	0	0	0	1	0
Jim Poole	0	0	0.00	4	0	0	1	0	0	0	1	2
Mike Jackson	0	0	0.00	1	0	1	1	0	0	0	0	2
Bartolo Colon	1	0	1.00	1	1	0	9	4	1	1	4	3
Dave Burba	1	0	3.00	3	0	0	6	3	4	2	5	8
Charles Nagy	0	1	3.72	2	2	0	10	13	7	4	1	6
Dwight Gooden	0	1	5.79	1	1	0	5	3	3	3	3	3
Chad Ogea	0	1	8.10	2	1	0	7	9	6	6	5	4
Jaret Wright	0	1	8.10	2	1	0	7	7	6	6	8	4
Totals	**2**	**4**	**3.60**	**6**	**6**	**1**	**55**	**43**	**27**	**22**	**35**	**42**

SCORE BY INNINGS	
New York	**(12)23 304 201 000—27**
Cleveland	**220 191 002 003—20**

DP—Cleveland 7, New York, 5. **LOB**—Cleveland 39, New York 48. **E**—Alomar 2, Fryman, Lofton, Vizquel, Giles, Wilson, Martinez, Brosius. **CS**—Vizquel, Posada, Williams. **S**—Jeter 2, Brosius. **SF**—Ramirez, Martinez, Brosius, Davis. **HBP**—Thome (by Wells), Alomar (by Nelson). **WP**—Shuey, Burba 2, Wright, Wells.

NATIONAL LEAGUE

Padres hold off Braves to win first pennant since '84

BY LACY LUSK

The San Diego Padres had their ace in waiting, but they were in jeopardy of making the kind of baseball history no one wants to make. Lefthander Sterling Hitchcock helped make sure they'd never have to worry about that.

LARRY GOREN

Rocker rolls 'em
San Diego catcher Carlos Hernandez is launched by Atlanta reliever John Rocker's powerful slide in Game Five of the Championship Series.

After San Diego lost its grip on the 1998 National League Championship Series by dropping two straight games to the Atlanta Braves, Hitchcock started a combined two-hitter in Game Six as the Padres won 5-0 to take their second-ever pennant.

Atlanta was trying to become the first team to recover from a 3-0 deficit in major league playoff history. Of the 21 previous teams in that hole, 10 lost Game Four. None of them forced Game Six until the Braves did it.

"There's no pressure on me," Hitchcock said before each of his starts. "I'm not expected to win."

He took the ball in Game Six on three days rest, and bested Atlanta's Tom Glavine.

At Atlanta's Turner Field in the final game, Hitchcock lasted five innings before Brian Boehringer, Mark Langston, Joey Hamilton and Trevor Hoffman pitched four hitless innings of relief.

Hitchcock, the series MVP, had won Game Three in San Diego. It looked like that would be his last outing in the NLCS, especially when righthander Kevin Brown came in from the bullpen in the seventh inning of Game Five.

Kevin Brown

After breezing through the seventh, Brown allowed a game-turning, three-run homer to Michael Tucker with one out in the eighth. That shot gave Atlanta a 5-4 lead, and they went ahead 7-4 before San Diego scored two in the ninth off closer Kerry Ligtenberg. With the score 7-6, four-time Cy Young Award winner Greg Maddux nailed down his first career save.

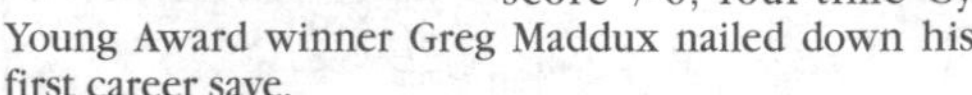

"That was the best game I've been a part of," Padres first baseman Wally Joyner said. "It was like a chess game played with real people."

Brown and Maddux also were the scheduled starters if the series went seven games, but that matchup never materialized. The Padres liked their chances in that game, too, because Brown had jump started their pennant run.

In Game One of the NL Division Series, Brown struck out 16 Astros in eight scoreless innings as San Diego beat Randy Johnson 2-1. The Padres went on to win the best-of-five series, three games to one.

Catcher Jim Leyritz, a hero for the Yankees in the 1996 World Series when he hit a three-run home run to tie Game Four against the Braves, was strong in the postseason again. He hit a game-tying homer off Billy Wagner in Game Two in Houston, but the Astros still won the game. Leyritz followed that up with a seventh-inning home run for the decisive run in Game Three.

As if that weren't enough, the Padres' midseason acquisition homered off Johnson in a 6-1 win in Game Four. San Diego added Leyritz in a June trade with the Red Sox for relievers Carlos Reyes and Dario Veras and catcher Mandy Romero.

The Padres went 98-64 as they won their third NL West title. Knocking off the Astros and Braves, two teams with more than 100 wins apiece, sent them to their only World Series aside from 1984. Right fielder Tony Gwynn was on both those San Diego teams–and every one in between.

"Now I realize how hard it is to get to the World Series," Gwynn said. "It makes you appreciate it even more."

NATIONAL LEAGUE CHAMPIONS, 1901-1998

	Pennant	Pct.	GA
1901	Pittsburgh	.647	½
1902	Pittsburgh	.741	27½
1903	Pittsburgh	.650	6½
1904	New York	.693	13
1905	New York	.686	9
1906	Chicago	.763	20
1907	Chicago	.704	17
1908	Chicago	.643	1
1909	Pittsburgh	.724	6½
1910	Chicago	.675	13
1911	New York	.647	7½
1912	New York	.682	10
1913	New York	.664	12½
1914	Boston	.614	10½
1915	Philadelphia	.592	7
1916	Brooklyn	.610	2½
1917	New York	.636	10
1918	Chicago	.651	10½
1919	Cincinnati	.686	9
1920	Brooklyn	.604	7
1921	New York	.614	4
1922	New York	.604	7
1923	New York	.621	4½
1924	New York	.608	1½
1925	Pittsburgh	.621	8½
1926	St. Louis	.578	2
1927	Pittsburgh	.610	1½
1928	St. Louis	.617	2
1929	Chicago	.645	10½
1930	St. Louis	.597	2

	Pennant	Pct.	GA	MVP
1931	St. Louis	.656	13	Frankie Frisch, 2b, St.Louis
1932	Chicago	.584	4	Chuck Klein, of, Philadelphia
1933	New York	.599	5	Carl Hubbell, lhp, New York
1934	St. Louis	.621	2	Dizzy Dean, rhp, St.Louis
1935	Chicago	.649	4	Gabby Hartnett, c, Chicago
1936	New York	.597	5	Carl Hubbell, lhp, New York
1937	New York	.625	3	Joe Medwick, of, St. Louis
1938	Chicago	.586	2	Ernie Lombardi, c, Cincinnati
1939	Cincinnati	.630	4½	Bucky Walters, rhp, Cincinnati
1940	Cincinnati	.654	12	Frank McCormick, 1b, Cincinnati
1941	Brooklyn	.649	2½	Dolf Camilli, 1b, Brooklyn
1942	St. Louis	.688	2	Mort Cooper, rhp, St. Louis
1943	St. Louis	.682	18	Stan Musial, of, St. Louis
1944	St. Louis	.682	14½	Marty Marion, ss, St. Louis
1945	Chicago	.636	3	Phil Cavarretta, 1b, Chicago
1946	St. Louis	.628	2	Stan Musial, 1b, St. Louis
1947	Brooklyn	.610	5	Bob Elliott, 3b, Boston
1948	Boston	.595	6½	Stan Musial, of, St. Louis
1949	Brooklyn	.630	1	Jackie Robinson, 2b, Brooklyn
1950	Philadelphia	.591	2	Jim Konstanty, rhp, Philadelphia
1951	New York	.624	1	Roy Campanella, c, Brooklyn
1952	Brooklyn	.627	4½	Hank Sauer, of, Chicago
1953	Brooklyn	.682	13	Roy Campanella, c, Brooklyn
1954	New York	.630	5	Willie Mays, of, New York
1955	Brooklyn	.641	13½	Roy Campanella, c, Brooklyn
1956	Brooklyn	.604	1	Don Newcombe, rhp, Brooklyn
1957	Milwaukee	.617	8	Hank Aaron, of, Milwaukee
1958	Milwaukee	.597	8	Ernie Banks, ss, Chicago
1959	Los Angeles	.564	2	Ernie Banks, ss, Chicago
1960	Pittsburgh	.617	7	Dick Groat, ss, Pittsburgh
1961	Cincinnati	.604	4	Frank Robinson, of, Cincinnati
1962	San Francisco	.624	1	Maury Wills, ss, Los Angeles
1963	Los Angeles	.611	6	Sandy Koufax, lhp, Los Angeles
1964	St. Louis	.574	1	Ken Boyer, 3b, St. Louis
1965	Los Angeles	.599	2	Willie Mays, of, San Francisco
1966	Los Angeles	.586	1½	Roberto Clemente, of, Pittsburgh
1967	St. Louis	.627	10½	Orlando Cepeda, 1b, St. Louis
1968	St. Louis	.599	9	Bob Gibson, rhp, St. Louis

	East. Div.	PCT	GA	West. Div.	PCT	GA	Pennant		MVP
1969	New York	.617	8	Atlanta	.574	3	New York	3-0	Willie McCovey, 1b, San Francisco
1970	Pittsburgh	.549	5	Cincinnati	.630	14½	Cincinnati	3-0	Johnny Bench, c, Cincinnati
1971	Pittsburgh	.599	7	San Francisco	.556	1	Pittsburgh	3-1	Joe Torre, 3b, St. Louis
1972	Pittsburgh	.619	11	Cincinnati	.617	10½	Cincinnati	3-2	Johnny Bench, c, Cincinnati
1973	New York	.509	1½	Cincinnati	.611	3½	New York	3-2	Pete Rose, of, Cincinnati
1974	Pittsburgh	.543	1½	Los Angeles	.630	4	Los Angeles	3-1	Steve Garvey, 1b, Los Angeles
1975	Pittsburgh	.571	6½	Cincinnati	.667	20	Cincinnati	3-0	Joe Morgan, 2b, Cincinnati
1976	Philadelphia	.623	9	Cincinnati	.630	10	Cincinnati	3-0	Joe Morgan, 2b, Cincinnati
1977	Philadelphia	.623	5	Los Angeles	.605	10	Los Angeles	3-1	George Foster, of, Cincinnati
1978	Philadelphia	.556	1½	Los Angeles	.586	2½	Los Angeles	3-1	Dave Parker, of, Pittsburgh
1979	Pittsburgh	.605	2	Cincinnati	.559	1½	Pittsburgh	3-0	Hernandez, St. Louis; Stargell, Pittsburgh
1980	Philadelphia	.562	1	Houston	.571	1	Philadelphia	3-2	Mike Schmidt, 3b, Philadelphia
1981	Montreal*	.566	½	Los Angeles**	.632	½	Los Angeles	3-2	Mike Schmidt, 3b, Philadelphia
	Philadelphia	.618	1½	Houston	.623	1			
1982	St. Louis	.568	3	Atlanta	.549	1	St. Louis	3-0	Dale Murphy, of, Atlanta
1983	Philadelphia	.556	6	Los Angeles	.562	3	Philadelphia	3-1	Dale Murphy, of, Atlanta
1984	Chicago	.596	6½	San Diego	.568	12	San Diego	3-2	Ryne Sandberg, 2b, Chicago
1985	St. Louis	.623	3	Los Angeles	.586	5½	St. Louis	4-2	Willie McGee, of, St. Louis
1986	New York	.667	21½	Houston	.593	10	New York	4-2	Mike Schmidt, 3b, Philadelphia
1987	St. Louis	.586	3	San Francisco	.556	6	St. Louis	4-3	Andre Dawson, of, Chicago
1988	New York	.625	15	Los Angeles	.584	7	Los Angeles	4-3	Kirk Gibson, of, Los Angeles
1989	Chicago	.571	6	San Francisco	.568	3	San Francisco	4-1	Kevin Mitchell, of, San Francisco
1990	Pittsburgh	.586	4	Cincinnati	.562	5	Cincinnati	4-2	Barry Bonds, of, Pittsburgh
1991	Pittsburgh	.605	14	Atlanta	.580	1	Atlanta	4-3	Terry Pendleton, 3b, Atlanta
1992	Pittsburgh	.593	9	Atlanta	.605	8	Atlanta	4-3	Barry Bonds, of, Pittsburgh
1993	Philadelphia	.599	3	Atlanta	.642	1	Philadelphia	4-2	Barry Bonds, of, San Francisco

East Div.		PCT	GA	Central Div.	PCT	GA	West Div.	PCT	GA	MVP
1994	Montreal	.649	6	Cincinnati	.593	½	Los Angeles	.509	3½	Jeff Bagwell, 1b, Houston
1995	Atlanta#	.625	21	Cincinnati	.590	9	Los Angeles	.542	1	Barry Larkin, ss, Cincinnati
1996	Atlanta@	.593	8	St. Louis	.543	6	San Diego	.562	1	Ken Caminiti, 3b, San Diego
1997	Atlanta†	.623	9	Houston	.519	5	San Francisco	.556	2	Larry Walker, Colorado
1998	Atlanta	.654	18	Houston	.630	12½	San Diego●	.605	9½	Sammy Sosa, Chicago

*Won second half; defeated Philadelphia 3-2 in best-of-5 playoff. **Won first half; defeated Houston 3-2 in best-of-5 playoff.
#Won NL pennant, defeating Cincinnati 4-2. @ Won NL pennant, defeating St. Louis 4-3.
† Florida (wild card) won NL pennant, defeating Atlanta 4-2. ●Won NL pennant, defeating Atlanta 4-2.

STANDINGS

Page	EAST	W	L	PCT	GB	Manager	General Manager	Attend./Dates	Last Penn.
66	Atlanta Braves	106	56	.654	—	Bobby Cox	John Schuerholz	3,361,350 (81)	1996
179	New York Mets	88	74	.543	18	Bobby Valentine	Steve Phillips	2,287,942(77)	1986
193	Philadelphia Phillies	75	87	.463	31	Terry Francona	Ed Wade	1,715,702 (79)	1993
165	Montreal Expos	65	97	.401	41	Felipe Alou	Jim Beattie	914,717 (81)	None
125	Florida Marlins	54	108	.333	52	Jim Leyland	Dave Dombrowski	1,750,395 (79)	1997
Page	**CENTRAL**	**W**	**L**	**PCT**	**GB**	**Manager**	**General Manager**	**Attend./Dates**	**Last Penn.**
132	Houston Astros	102	60	.630	—	Larry Dierker	Gerry Hunsicker	2,450,451 (80)	None
93	Chicago Cubs*	90	73	.552	12 ½	Jim Riggleman	Ed Lynch	2,623,000 (80)	1945
206	St. Louis Cardinals	83	79	.512	19	Tony La Russa	Walt Jocketty	3,195,021 (80)	1987
100	Cincinnati Reds	77	85	.475	25	Jack McKeon	Jim Bowden	1,793,679 (81)	1990
153	Milwaukee Brewers	74	88	.457	28	Phil Garner	Sal Bando	1,811,548 (79)	None
199	Pittsburgh Pirates	69	93	.426	33	Gene Lamont	Cam Bonifay	1,560,950 (80)	1979
Page	**WEST**	**W**	**L**	**PCT**	**GB**	**Manager**	**General Manager**	**Attend./Dates**	**Last Penn.**
212	San Diego Padres	98	64	.605	—	Bruce Bochy	Kevin Towers	2,555,901 (79)	1998
218	San Francisco Giants	89	74	.546	9 ½	Dusty Baker	Brian Sabean	1,925,634 (80)	1989
146	Los Angeles Dodgers	83	79	.512	15	Russell/Hoffman	Claire/Lasorda	3,089,222 (81)	1988
113	Colorado Rockies	77	85	.475	21	Don Baylor	Bob Gebhard	3,789,347 (81)	None
59	Arizona Diamondbacks	65	97	.401	33	Buck Showalter	Joe Garagiola Jr.	3,602,856 (81)	None

*Won wild-card playoff berth

NOTE: Team's individual batting, pitching and fielding statistics can be found on page indicated in lefthand column.

The Other Race

The 1998 National League season ended with the Padres and Braves fighting for the pennant, but most fans outside San Diego were more interested in another race–the one between Mark McGwire and Sammy Sosa.

MEL BAILEY

Hired gun
Randy Johnson went 10-1 for Houston

Roger Maris' major league record of 61 home runs stood for 37 years, but two NL sluggers eclipsed that total in the same season. They also sailed by Hack Wilson's league standard of 56 homers, which had been in the record books since 1930.

Their chase for immortality captivated both the United States and the Dominican Republic, Sosa's homeland.

Sosa was able to break Wilson's Cubs record by 10 home runs, and he had the major league single-season mark for all of 46 minutes on the last Friday of the season. But his 66-65 lead was obliterated when McGwire homered five times against the Montreal Expos in his last 11 at-bats to finish with 70. Righthander Carl Pavano served up the 70th.

"I just hope he hits 75 next year so people will forget I gave up No. 70," Pavano said.

Sosa trailed McGwire by as many as 15 home runs (24-9 on May 24), but his 20 blasts in June–the most by any player in any month in major league history–closed the gap in a hurry.

Sosa first passed McGwire in Wrigley Field on Aug. 19 when he homered to take a 48-47 lead. But the Chicago Cubs were playing the St. Louis Cardinals that day, and McGwire one-upped Sosa by hitting two homers in the game.

On Sept. 8, McGwire passed Maris with his 62nd home run. His shot off Cubs righthander Steve Trachsel barely cleared the left-field wall in Busch Stadium. Of all of his homers, which had a combined distance slightly more than the height of Mount Everest (29,141 feet), that one was the shortest.

"This is a season I will never, ever forget, and I hope everybody in baseball never forgets," McGwire said.

Across the country, the home run chase was largely hailed as an event that "saved baseball"–or at least helped it grow again, if Cal Ripken gets credit for saving the game in 1995 by breaking Lou Gehrig's consecutive games record. Cubs lefthander Terry Mulholland, who gave up McGwire's 49th, had a more lighthearted take.

"Matt Karchner got him rolling (by giving up No.

NATIONAL LEAGUE YEAR-BY-YEAR BATTING LEADERS

Year	Batting Average	Home Runs	RBIs
1901	Jesse Burkett, St. Louis .382	Sam Crawford, Cincinnati 16	Honus Wagner, Pittsburgh 126
1902	Ginger Beaumont, Pitt. .357	Tom Leach, Pittsburgh 6	Honus Wagner, Pittsburgh 91
1903	Honus Wagner, Pitt. .355	Jim Sheckard, Brooklyn 9	Sam Mertes, New York 104
1904	Honus Wagner, Pitt. .349	Harry Lumley, Brooklyn 9	Bill Dahlen, New York 80
1905	Cy Seymour, Cincinnati .377	Fred Odwell, Cincinnati 9	Cy Seymour, Cincinnati 121
1906	Honus Wagner, Pitt. .339	Tim Jordan, Brooklyn 12	2 tied at 83
1907	Honus Wagner, Pitt. .350	Dave Brain, Boston 10	Sherry Magee, Philadelphia 85
1908	Honus Wagner, Pitt. .354	Tim Jordan, Brooklyn 12	Honus Wagner, Pittsburgh 109
1909	Honus Wagner, Pitt. .339	Red Murray, New York 7	Honus Wagner, Pittsburgh 100
1910	Sherry Magee, Phil. .331	2 tied at 10	Sherry Magee, Philadelphia 123
1911	Honus Wagner, Pitt. .334	Wildfire Schulte, Chicago 21	Wildfire Schulte, Chicago 121
1912	Heinie Zimmerman, Chi. .372	Heinie Zimmerman, Chicago 14	Heinie Zimmerman, Chi. 103
1913	Jake Daubert, Brooklyn .350	Gavvy Cravath, Philadelphia 19	Gavvy Cravath, Phil. 128
1914	Jake Daubert, Brooklyn .329	Gavvy Cravath, Philadelphia 19	Sherry Magee, Phil. 103
1915	Larry Doyle, New York .320	Gavvy Cravath, Philadelphia 24	Gavvy Cravath, Phil. 115
1916	Hal Chase, Cincinnati .339	2 tied at 12	Heinie Zimmerman, Chi.-N.Y. 83
1917	Edd Roush, Cincinnati .341	2 tied at 12	Heinie Zimmerman, N.Y. 102
1918	Zack Wheat, Brooklyn .335	Gavvy Cravath, Philadelphia 8	Sherry Magee, Cincinnati 76
1919	Edd Roush, Cincinnati .321	Gavvy Cravath, Philadelphia 12	Hy Myers, Brooklyn 73
1920	Rogers Hornsby, St.L .370	Cy Williams, Philadelphia 15	2 tied at 94
1921	Rogers Hornsby, St.L .397	George Kelly, New York 23	Rogers Hornsby, St. Louis 126
1922	Rogers Hornsby, St.L .401	Rogers Hornsby, St. Louis 42	Rogers Hornsby, St. Louis 155
1923	Rogers Hornsby, St.L .384	Cy Williams, Philadelphia 41	Emil Meusel, New York 125
1924	Rogers Hornsby, St.L .424	Jack Fournier, Brooklyn 27	George Kelly, New York 136
1925	Rogers Hornsby, St.L .403	Rogers Hornsby, St. Louis 39	Rogers Hornsby, St. Louis 143
1926	Bubbles Hargrave, Cinc. .353	Hack Wilson, Chicago 21	Jim Bottomley, St. Louis 120
1927	Paul Waner, Pittsburgh .380	2 tied at 30	Paul Waner, Pittsburgh 131
1928	Rogers Hornsby, St.L .370	2 tied at 31	Jim Bottomley, St. Louis 136
1929	Lefty ODoul, Philadelphia .398	Chuck Klein, Philadelphia 43	Hack Wilson, Chicago 159
1930	Bill Terry, New York .401	Hack Wilson, Chicago 56	Hack Wilson, Chicago 190
1931	Chick Hafey, St. Louis .349	Chuck Klein, Philadelphia 31	Chuck Klein, Philadelphia 121
1932	Lefty ODoul, Brooklyn .368	2 tied at 38	Frank Hurst, Philadelphia 143
1933	Chuck Klein, Philadelphia .368	Chuck Klein, Philadelphia 28	Chuck Klein, Philadelphia 120
1934	Paul Waner, Pittsburgh .362	2 tied at 35	Mel Ott, New York 135
1935	Arky Vaughan, Pittsburgh .385	Wally Berger, Boston 34	Wally Berger, Boston 130
1936	Paul Waner, Pittsburgh .373	Mel Ott, New York 33	Joe Medwick, St. Louis 138
1937	Joe Medwick, St. Louis .374	2 tied at 31	Joe Medwick, St. Louis 154
1938	Ernie Lombardi, Cinc. .342	Mel Ott, New York 36	Joe Medwick, St. Louis 122
1939	Johnny Mize, St. Louis .349	Johnny Mize, St. Louis 28	Frank McCormick, Cinc. 128
1940	Debs Garms, Pittsburgh .355	Johnny Mize, St. Louis 43	Johnny Mize, St. Louis 137
1941	Pete Reiser, Brooklyn .343	Dolf Camilli, Brooklyn 34	Dolf Camilli, Brooklyn 120
1942	Ernie Lombardi, Boston .330	Mel Ott, New York 30	Johnny Mize, New York 110
1943	Stan Musial, St. Louis .357	Bill Nicholson, Chicago 29	Bill Nicholson, Chicago 128
1944	Dixie Walker, Brooklyn .357	Bill Nicholson, Chicago 33	Bill Nicholson, Chicago 122
1945	Phil Cavarretta, Chicago .355	Tommy Holmes, Boston 28	Dixie Walker, Brooklyn 124
1946	Stan Musial, St. Louis .365	Ralph Kiner, Pittsburgh 23	Enos Slaughter, St. Louis 130
1947	Harry Walker, St.L-Phil. .363	2 tied at 51	Johnny Mize, New York 138
1948	Stan Musial, St. Louis .376	2 tied at 40	Stan Musial, St. Louis 131
1949	Jackie Robinson, Brook. .342	Ralph Kiner, Pittsburgh 54	Ralph Kiner, Pittsburgh 127
1950	Stan Musial, St. Louis .346	Ralph Kiner, Pittsburgh 47	Del Ennis, Philadelphia 126
1951	Stan Musial, St. Louis .355	Ralph Kiner, Pittsburgh 42	Monte Irvin, New York 121
1952	Stan Musial, St. Louis .336	2 tied at 37	Hank Sauer, Chicago 121
1953	Carl Furillo, Brooklyn .344	Eddie Mathews, Milwaukee 47	Roy Campanella, Brooklyn 142
1954	Willie Mays, New York .345	Ted Kluszewski, Cincinnati 49	Ted Kluszewski, Cincinnati 141
1955	Richie Ashburn, Phil. .338	Willie Mays, New York 51	Duke Snider, Brooklyn 136
1956	Hank Aaron, Milwaukee .328	Duke Snider, Brooklyn 43	Stan Musial, St. Louis 109
1957	Stan Musial, St. Louis .351	Hank Aaron, Milwaukee 44	Hank Aaron, Milwaukee 132
1958	Richie Ashburn, Phil. .350	Ernie Banks, Chicago 47	Ernie Banks, Chicago 129
1959	Hank Aaron, Milwaukee .355	Eddie Mathews, Milwaukee 46	Ernie Banks, Chicago 143
1960	Dick Groat, Pittsburgh .325	Ernie Banks, Chicago 41	Hank Aaron, Milwaukee 126
1961	Roberto Clemente, Pitt. .351	Orlando Cepeda, San Fran. 46	Orlando Cepeda, San Fran. 142
1962	Tommy Davis, L.A. .346	Willie Mays, San Francisco 49	Tommy Davis, Los Angeles 153
1963	Tommy Davis, L.A. .326	2 tied at 44	Hank Aaron, Milwaukee 130
1964	Roberto Clemente, Pitt. .339	Willie Mays, San Francisco 47	Ken Boyer, St Louis 119
1965	Roberto Clemente, Pitt. .329	Willie Mays, San Francisco 52	Deron Johnson, Cincinnati 130
1966	Matty Alou, Pittsburgh .342	Hank Aaron, Atlanta 44	Hank Aaron, Atlanta 127
1967	Roberto Clemente, Pitt. .357	Hank Aaron, Atlanta 39	Orlando Cepeda, San Fran. 111
1968	Pete Rose, Cincinnati .335	Willie McCovey, San Fran. 36	Willie McCovey, San Fran. 105
1969	Pete Rose, Cincinnati .348	Willie McCovey, San Fran. 45	Willie McCovey, San Fran. 126
1970	Rico Carty, Atlanta .366	Johnny Bench, Cincinnati 45	Johnny Bench, Cincinnati 148
1971	Joe Torre, St. Louis .363	Willie Stargell, Pittsburgh 48	Joe Torre, St. Louis 137
1972	Billy Williams, Chicago .333	Johnny Bench, Cincinnati 40	Johnny Bench, Cincinnati 125
1973	Pete Rose, Cincinnati .338	Willie Stargell, Pittsburgh 44	Willie Stargell, Pittsburgh 119
1974	Ralph Garr, Atlanta .353	Mike Schmidt, Philadelphia 36	Johnny Bench, Cincinnati 129
1975	Bill Madlock, Chicago .354	Mike Schmidt, Philadelphia 38	Greg Luzinski, Philadelphia 120
1976	Bill Madlock, Chicago .339	Mike Schmidt, Philadelphia 38	George Foster, Cincinnati 121
1977	Dave Parker, Pittsburgh .338	George Foster, Cincinnati 52	George Foster, Cincinnati 149
1978	Dave Parker, Pittsburgh .334	George Foster, Cincinnati 40	George Foster, Cincinnati 120
1979	Keith Hernandez, St.L .344	Dave Kingman, Chicago 48	Dave Winfield, San Diego 118
1980	Bill Buckner, Chicago .324	Mike Schmidt, Philadelphia 48	Mike Schmidt, Philadelphia 121
1981	Bill Madlock, Pittsburgh .341	Mike Schmidt, Philadelphia 31	Mike Schmidt, Philadelphia 91
1982	Al Oliver, Montreal .331	Dave Kingman, New York 37	2 tied at 109
1983	Bill Madlock, Pittsburgh .323	Mike Schmidt, Philadelphia 40	Dale Murphy, Atlanta 121
1984	Tony Gwynn, San Diego .351	2 tied at 36	2 tied at 106
1985	Willie McGee, St. Louis .353	Dale Murphy, Atlanta 37	Dave Parker, Cincinnati 125
1986	Tim Raines, Montreal .334	Mike Schmidt, Philadelphia 37	Mike Schmidt, Philadelphia 119
1987	Tony Gwynn, San Diego .370	Andre Dawson, Chicago 49	Andre Dawson, Chicago 137
1988	Tony Gwynn, San Diego .313	Darryl Strawberry, New York 39	Will Clark, San Francisco 109
1989	Tony Gwynn, San Diego .336	Kevin Mitchell, S.F. 47	Kevin Mitchell, S.F. 125
1990	Willie McGee, St. Louis .335	Ryne Sandberg, Chicago 40	Matt Williams, S.F. 122
1991	Terry Pendleton, Atlanta .319	Howard Johnson, New York 38	Howard Johnson, New York 117
1992	Gary Sheffield, S.D. .330	Fred McGriff, San Diego 35	Darren Daulton, Phil. 109
1993	Andres Galarraga, Colo. .370	Barry Bonds, San Francisco 46	Barry Bonds, S.F. 123
1994	Tony Gwynn, San Diego .394	Matt Williams, S.F. 43	Jeff Bagwell, Houston 116
1995	Tony Gwynn, San Diego .368	Dante Bichette, Colorado 40	Dante Bichette, Colorado 128
1996	Tony Gwynn, San Diego .353	Andres Galarraga, Colorado 47	Andres Galarraga, Colorado 150
1997	Tony Gwynn, San Diego .372	Larry Walker, Colorado 49	Andres Galarraga, Colorado 140
1998	Larry Walker, Colorado .363	Mark McGwire, St. Louis 70	Sammy Sosa, Chicago 158

NATIONAL LEAGUE YEAR-BY-YEAR PITCHING LEADERS

Year	Wins		ERA		Strikeouts	
1901	Bill Donovan, Brooklyn	25	Jesse Tannehill, Pittsburgh	2.18	Noodles Hahn, Cin.	233
1902	Jack Chesbro, Pittsburgh	28	Jack Taylor, Chicago	1.33	Vic Willis, Boston	226
1903	Joe McGinnity, New York	31	Sam Leever, Pittsburgh	2.06	Christy Mathewson, N.Y.	267
1904	Joe McGinnity, New York	35	Joe McGinnity, New York	1.61	Christy Mathewson, N.Y	212
1905	Christy Mathewson, N.Y.	32	Christy Mathewson, N.Y.	1.27	Christy Mathewson, N.Y	206
1906	Joe McGinnity, New York	27	Mordecai Brown, Chicago	1.04	Fred Beebe, Chi.-St.L	171
1907	Christy Mathewson, N.Y.	24	Jack Pfiester, Chicago	1.15	Christy Mathewson, N.Y.	178
1908	Christy Mathewson, N.Y.	37	Christy Mathewson, N.Y.	1.43	Christy Mathewson, N.Y.	259
1909	Mordecai Brown, Chicago	27	Christy Mathewson, N.Y.	1.14	Orval Overall, Chicago	205
1910	Christy Mathewson, N.Y.	27	George McQuillan, Phil.	1.60	Christy Mathewson, N.Y.	190
1911	Grover Alexander, Phil.	28	Christy Mathewson, N.Y.	1.99	Rube Marquard, New York	237
1912	2 tied at	26	Jeff Tesreau, New York	1.96	Grover Alexander, Phil.	195
1913	Tom Seaton, Philadelphia	27	Christy Mathewson, N.Y.	2.06	Tom Seaton, Philadelphia	168
1914	2 tied at	27	Bill Doak, St. Louis.	1.72	Grover Alexander, Phil.	214
1915	Grover Alexander, Phil.	31	Grover Alexander, Phil.	1.22	Grover Alexander, Phil.	241
1916	Grover Alexander, Phil.	33	Grover Alexander, Phil.	1.55	Grover Alexander, Phil.	167
1917	Grover Alexander, Phil.	30	Grover Alexander, Phil.	1.85	Grover Alexander, Phil	200
1918	Hippo Vaughn, Chicago	22	Hippo Vaughn, Chicago	1.74	Hippo Vaughn, Chicago	148
1919	Jesse Barnes, New York	25	Grover Alexander, Chicago	1.72	Hippo Vaughn, Chicago	141
1920	Grover Alexander, Chicago	27	Grover Alexander, Chicago	1.91	Grover Alexander, Chicago	173
1921	2 tied at	22	Bill Doak, St. Louis	2.58	Burleigh Grimes, Brooklyn	136
1922	Eppa Rixey, Cincinnati	25	Rosy Ryan, New York	3.00	Dazzy Vance, Brooklyn	134
1923	Dolf Luque, Cincinnati	27	Dolf Luque, Cincinnati	1.93	Dazzy Vance, Brooklyn	197
1924	Dazzy Vance, Brooklyn	28	Dazzy Vance, Brooklyn	2.16	Dazzy Vance, Brooklyn	262
1925	Dazzy Vance, Brooklyn	22	Dolf Luque, Cincinnati	2.63	Dazzy Vance, Brooklyn	221
1926	4 tied at	20	Ray Kremer, Pittsburgh	2.61	Dazzy Vance, Brooklyn	140
1927	Charlie Root, Chicago	26	Ray Kremer, Pittsburgh	2.47	Dazzy Vance, Brooklyn	184
1928	2 tied at	25	Dazzy Vance, Brooklyn	2.09	Dazzy Vance, Brooklyn	200
1929	Pat Malone, Chicago	22	Bill Walker, New York	3.08	Pat Malone, Chicago	166
1930	2 tied at	20	Dazzy Vance, Brooklyn	2.61	Bill Hallahan, St. Louis	177
1931	3 tied at	19	Bill Walker, New York	2.26	Bill Hallahan, St. Louis	159
1932	Lon Warneke, Chicago	22	Lon Warneke, Chicago	2.37	Dizzy Dean, St. Louis	191
1933	Carl Hubbell, New York	23	Carl Hubbell, New York	1.66	Dizzy Dean, St. Louis	199
1934	Dizzy Dean, St. Louis	30	Carl Hubbell, New York	2.30	Dizzy Dean, St. Louis	195
1935	Dizzy Dean, St. Louis	28	Cy Blanton, Pittsburgh	2.59	Dizzy Dean, St. Louis	182
1936	Carl Hubbell, New York	26	Carl Hubbell, New York	2.31	Van Lingle Mungo, Brooklyn	238
1937	Carl Hubbell, New York	22	Jim Turner, Boston	2.38	Carl Hubbell, New York	159
1938	Bill Lee, Chicago	22	Bill Lee, Chicago	2.66	Clay Bryant, Chicago	135
1939	Bucky Walters, Cincinnati	27	Bucky Walters, Cincinnati	2.29	2 tied at	137
1940	Bucky Walters, Cincinnati	22	Bucky Walters, Cincinnati	2.48	Kirby Higbe, Philadelphia	137
1941	2 tied at	22	Elmer Riddle, Cincinnati	2.24	Johnny Vander Meer, Cin.	202
1942	Mort Cooper, St. Louis	22	Mort Cooper, St. Louis	1.77	Johnny Vander Meer, Cin.	186
1943	3 tied at	21	Howie Pollet, St. Louis	1.75	Johnny Vander Meer, Cin.	174
1944	Bucky Walters, Cincinnati	23	Ed Heusser, Cincinnati	2.38	Bill Voiselle, New York	161
1945	Red Barrett, Bos.-St.L.	23	Hank Borowy, Chicago	2.14	Preacher Roe, Pittsburgh	148
1946	Howie Pollet, St. Louis	21	Howie Pollet, St. Louis	2.10	John Schmitz, Chicago	135
1947	Ewell Blackwell, Cincinnati	22	Warren Spahn, Boston	2.33	Ewell Blackwell, Cincinnati	193
1948	Johnny Sain, Boston	24	Harry Brecheen, St. Louis	2.24	Harry Brecheen, St. Louis	149
1949	Warren Spahn, Boston	21	Dave Koslo, New York	2.50	Warren Spahn, Boston	151

Year	Wins		ERA		Strikeouts	
1950	Warren Spahn, Boston	21	Jim Hearn, St.L.-N.Y.	2.49	Warren Spahn, Boston	191
1951	2 tied at	23	Chet Nichols, Boston	2.88	2 tied at	164
1952	Robin Roberts, Phil.	28	Hoyt Wilhelm, New York	2.43	Warren Spahn, Boston	183
1953	2 tied at	23	Warren Spahn, Milwaukee	2.10	Robin Roberts, Philadelphia	198
1954	Robin Roberts, Phil.	23	John Antonelli, New York	2.29	Robin Roberts, Philadelphia	185
1955	Robin Roberts, Phil.	23	Bob Friend, Pittsburgh	2.84	Sam Jones, Chicago	198
1956	Don Newcombe, Brooklyn	27	Lew Burdette, Milwaukee	2.71	Sam Jones, Chicago	176
1957	Warren Spahn, Milwaukee	21	Johnny Podres, Brooklyn	2.66	Jack Sanford, Philadelphia	188
1958	2 tied	22	Stu Miller, San Francisco	2.47	Sam Jones, St. Louis	225
1959	3 tied at	21	Sam Jones, S.F.	2.82	Don Drysdale, L.A.	242
1960	2 tied at	21	Mike McCormick, S.F.	2.70	Don Drysdale, L.A.	246
1961	2 tied at	21	Warren Spahn, Milwaukee	3.01	Sandy Koufax, L.A.	269
1962	Don Drysdale, Los Angeles	25	Sandy Koufax, L.A.	2.54	Don Drysdale, L.A.	232
1963	2 tied at	25	Sandy Koufax, L.A.	1.88	Sandy Koufax, L.A.	306
1964	Larry Jackson, Chicago	24	Sandy Koufax, L.A.	1.74	Bob Veale, Pittsburgh	250
1965	Sandy Koufax, L.A.	26	Sandy Koufax, L.A.	2.04	Sandy Koufax, Los Angeles	382
1966	Sandy Koufax, L.A.	27	Sandy Koufax, L.A.	1.73	Sandy Koufax, Los Angeles	317
1967	Mike McCormick, S.F.	22	Phil Niekro, Atlanta	1.87	Jim Bunning, Philadelphia	253
1968	Juan Marichal, San Fran.	26	Bob Gibson, St. Louis	1.12	Bob Gibson, St. Louis	268
1969	Tom Seaver, New York	25	Juan Marichal, San Fran.	2.10	Ferguson Jenkins, Chicago	273
1970	2 tied at	23	Tom Seaver, New York	2.81	Tom Seaver, New York	283
1971	Ferguson Jenkins, Chicago	24	Tom Seaver, New York	1.76	Tom Seaver, New York	289
1972	Steve Carlton, Phil.	27	Steve Carlton, Phil.	1.98	Steve Carlton, Phil.	310
1973	Ron Bryant, San Francisco	24	Tom Seaver, New York	2.08	Tom Seaver, New York	251
1974	2 tied at	20	Buzz Capra, Atlanta	2.28	Steve Carlton, Phil.	240
1975	Tom Seaver, New York	23	Randy Jones, San Diego	2.24	Tom Seaver, New York	243
1976	Randy Jones, San Diego	22	John Denny, St. Louis	2.52	Tom Seaver, New York	235
1977	Steve Carlton, Phil.	23	John Candelaria, Pitt.	2.34	Phil Niekro, Atlanta	252
1978	Gaylord Perry, San Diego	21	Craig Swan, New York	2.43	J.R. Richard, Houston	303
1979	2 tied at	21	J.R. Richard, Houston	2.71	J.R. Richard, Houston	313
1980	Steve Carlton, Phil.	24	Don Sutton, Los Angeles	2.21	Steve Carlton, Phil.	286
1981	Tom Seaver, Cincinnati	14	Nolan Ryan, Houston	1.69	Fernando Valenzuela, L.A.	180
1982	Steve Carlton, Phil.	23	Steve Rogers, Montreal	2.40	Steve Carlton, Phil.	286
1983	John Denny, Phil.	19	Atlee Hammaker, S.F.	2.25	Steve Carlton, Phil.	275
1984	Joaquin Andujar, St. Louis	20	Alejandro Pena, L.A.	2.48	Dwight Gooden, New York	276
1985	Dwight Gooden, New York	24	Dwight Gooden, New York	1.53	Dwight Gooden, New York	268
1986	Fernando Valenzuela, L.A.	21	Mike Scott, Houston	2.22	Mike Scott, Houston	306
1987	Rick Sutcliffe, Chicago	18	Nolan Ryan, Houston	2.76	Nolan Ryan, Houston	270
1988	2 tied at	23	Joe Magrane, St. Louis	2.18	Nolan Ryan, Houston	228
1989	Mike Scott, Houston	20	Scott Garrelts, San Fran.	2.28	Jose DeLeon, St. Louis	201
1990	Doug Drabek, Pittsburgh	22	Danny Darwin, Houston	2.21	David Cone, New York	233
1991	2 tied at	20	Dennis Martinez, Mon.	2.39	David Cone, New York	241
1992	2 tied at	20	Bill Swift, San Francisco	2.08	John Smoltz, Atlanta	215
1993	2 tied at	22	Greg Maddux, Atlanta	2.36	Jose Rijo, Cincinnati	227
1994	2 tied at	16	Greg Maddux, Atlanta	1.56	Andy Benes, San Diego	189
1995	Greg Maddux, Atlanta	19	Greg Maddux, Atlanta	1.63	Hideo Nomo, Los Angeles	236
1996	John Smoltz, Atlanta	24	Kevin Brown, Florida	1.89	John Smoltz, Atlanta	276
1997	Denny Neagle, Atlanta	20	Pedro Martinez, Montreal	1.90	Curt Schilling, Philadelphia	319
1998	Tom Glavine, Atlanta	20	Greg Maddux, Atlanta	2.22	Curt Schilling, Philadelphia	300

47). I got him locked in. So when you really analyze it, I saved baseball."

At least pitchers could have a sense of humor about facing the 1990s' Paul Bunyan, or maybe more appropriately, the 1990s' Babe Ruth.

Bold Maneuver

While the 6-foot-5 McGwire was all the rage throughout baseball in 1998, the Astros had their own lofty goals in mind when they acquired the 6-foot-10 Johnson on July 31.

Houston, having never won a playoff series, sent minor league infielder Carlos Guillen and pitchers Freddy Garcia and John Halama to the Mariners in a deadline deal. Before the trade, most of the rumors were of Johnson going to the Cleveland Indians or New York Yankees. The Astros surprised many when they landed the hard-throwing lefty.

In the regular season, Johnson was all any Astros fan could have wanted. He went 10-1 with a 1.28 ERA in 11 starts as he cranked the intensity up a notch in Houston. In 84 innings, he struck out 116 while allowing just 57 hits and 26 walks. Combined with his Mariners numbers, Johnson went 19-11, 3.28 with a career-high 329 strikeouts.

And Johnson wasn't a one-man team in Houston. The Astros were in first place before the trade. They finished 102-60 and led the league with 874 runs. First baseman Jeff Bagwell and outfielders Moises Alou and Derek Bell all drove in more than 100 runs. Second baseman Craig Biggio led the league in doubles (51) and was second in steals (50). The only other major leaguer to ever accomplish Biggio's 50-50 was Tris Speaker in 1912.

"I don't know how anyone ever beats them," Milwaukee Brewers manager Phil Garner said. "They're playing like a team that's going to win it all. If you make a mistake against them, they'll kill you."

In the end, however, Houston had nothing to show for the deal. Johnson lost twice in the Division Series to the Padres, as his postseason losing streak reached five games. The Astros' potent lineup struggled against Kevin Brown in Games One and Three, and the team was unable to recover. Johnson became a free agent at the end of the season.

Down To The Wire

With the Braves, Astros and Padres giving the NL three 98-game winners for the first time since 1962, the best team race was for the wild card.

A team from each division–the Cubs, New York Mets and San Francisco Giants–entered the last scheduled day of the regular season with a chance at the playoffs.

On that final Sunday, all three lost. The Mets, who finished one game out, fell for the third time in a sweep at the hands of the Braves. Later in the day, the Cubs and Giants lost within a minute of each other.

Several Giants were in their clubhouse watching the television feed of the Astros' 4-3, 11-inning win over Chicago. Richard Hidalgo's sacrifice fly led to a celebration in Denver, but as the players got to the dugout they saw Rockies shortstop Neifi Perez hit a game-ending solo homer to beat San Francisco 9-8.

The Giants had squandered a 7-0 lead in Coors Field, the hardest place to keep a lead in baseball. But they had one more chance with a regular season playoff the next night in Wrigley Field. The last NL one-game playoff was an Astros win over the Dodgers in 1980.

JOHN WILLIAMSON

50-50 club
Craig Biggio hit 51 doubles and stole 50 bases

In the extra game, the Cubs held on to win 5-3. Trachsel, who had given up McGwire's 62nd home run, picked up the victory. He did not allow a run in his 6⅓ innings. Five Cubs pitchers later, Rod Beck retired both batters he faced. In the previous day's loss to the Astros, Beck had pitched 2⅔ innings.

Beck's 51 saves made him the fifth closer with 50 or more in a year. The 245-pound Beck had saved 199 games as a Giant from 1991-97.

"I'm never gonna look like Sammy Sosa," Beck said. "When I signed I weighed 185 pounds and they complained about my weight. Now I'm 245 pounds and they still complain. But you know what? Here I am because I've persevered. I've seen guys with a lot more talent than me. But I haven't seen too many guys who wanted it more."

The Cubs, trying to reach their first World Series since 1945, were swept by the Braves in an NL Division Series. Their best chance was in Game Two, when Kevin Tapani held a 1-0 lead until Javier Lopez homered off him in the ninth. Atlanta won that game 2-1 in extra innings, and finished off the sweep in Chicago.

Dismantling A Champion

It didn't take long for the Marlins' 1997 World Series title to become a distant memory.

By Opening Day, Florida already had a totally new look as owner Wayne Huizenga scrapped the roster in an effort to bring down the payroll so he could sell the club. Alou was gone to the Astros, Brown to the Padres, lefthander Al Leiter to the Mets, closer Robb Nen to the Giants and so on and so forth.

"Other teams had to be looking at us like, 'Who are those kids?' " said first baseman Derrek Lee, who came over from San Diego in the Brown trade. "I don't think anybody in this clubhouse has ever been through a season like this. Us all being the same age, that's what made it fun."

By the end of the season, just five of the 20 Marlins who played in Game Seven of the 1997 World Series—catcher Gregg Zaun, second baseman Craig Counsell, shortstop Edgar Renteria, outfielder Cliff Floyd and righthander Antonio Alfonseca—were still with the club. The team's 27 rookies represented an expansion-era record.

The results: Florida went from 92-70 to 54-108. The Marlins became the first World Series champion to lose 100 games the next year. When it was all over, manager Jim Leyland left for the Rockies but general manager Dave Dombrowski stayed. With an overload of prospects picked up in the salary-dumping deals, Dombrowski was optimistic Florida could build a solid system that would last for the long haul—unlike the $96.5 million spent before 1997 to land six free agents and Leyland.

Among the postseason exits was third-base coach Rich Donnelly, who went with Leyland to Colorado. He said the Marlins had nothing to be ashamed of.

"The fans will look at the team picture and think one thing, but we'll think another," Donnelly said. "We're not going to think, 'There's the worst team that ever played.' No, they don't deserve that. They went out and busted their tails to the end. They did the best they could under the circumstances and didn't back off one day."

As for the sale of the team, club president Don Smiley was unable to raise the necessary money. Boca Raton, Fla., commodities trader John Henry came in with a $150 million offer toward the end of the season to nail down the deal.

Not To Be Forgotten

■ While McGwire and Sosa took aim on Maris' record, Padres outfielder Greg Vaughn put on a power display of his own. He hit 50 home runs, with the 50th coming in his last at-bat of the year. One year earlier, the Padres tried to trade him to the Yankees but he failed a physical. San Diego's old home run record was 40 by Ken Caminiti in 1996.

■ McGwire did more than hit home runs. He drew a NL-record 162 walks—eight shy of Ruth's major league mark. McGwire finished the year with a .752 slugging percentage—the highest in the majors since Ruth and Lou Gehrig slugged .772 and .765 for the '27 Yankees.

MEL BAILEY

Greg Vaughn

■ Cubs rookie righthander Kerry Wood pitched what might have been the best single game in the sport's history. He joined Bob Feller as the only pitcher to strike out his age (20) when he one-hit the Astros on May 6. The 20 strikeouts tied Roger Clemens' twice-accomplished record for the most in a nine-inning game. He went on to fan 233 in 167 innings.

■ The only two NL pitchers with more strikeouts than Wood were Curt Schilling (300) and the Padres' Brown (257). The Phillies' Schilling became the first major leaguer with back-to-back 300-strikeout seasons since J.R. Richard in 1978-79.

■ Giants outfielder Barry Bonds started his own club. He became the first major leaguer with more than 400 home runs and more than 400 stolen bases in his career. With 37 homers and 28 steals in 1998, he came within two stolen bases of a sixth straight 30-30 season.

■ Bonds also became just the second major leaguer to receive an intentional walk with the bases loaded. Diamondbacks closer Gregg Olson issued the free pass with an 8-6 lead in the bottom of the ninth on May 28. Arizona held on for an 8-7 win.

■ Mike Piazza, coming off one of the best offensive seasons for a catcher in the history of baseball, played for three NL teams. The Dodgers sent him to the Marlins as they acquired Bobby Bonilla, Jim Eisenreich, Charles Johnson and Gary Sheffield. Then,

NL: BEST TOOLS

A Baseball America survey of National League managers, conducted at midseason 1998, ranked NL players with the best tools:

BEST HITTER
1. Tony Gwynn, Padres
2. Mike Piazza, Mets
3. Larry Walker, Rockies

BEST POWER HITTER
1. Mark McGwire, Cardinals
2. Sammy Sosa, Cubs
3. Andres Galarraga, Braves

BEST BUNTER
1. Tony Womack, Pirates
2. Craig Biggio, Astros
3. Walt Weiss, Braves

BEST HIT-AND-RUN ARTIST
1. Tony Gwynn, Padres
2. Craig Biggio, Astros
3. Walt Weiss, Braves

BEST BASERUNNER
1. Craig Biggio, Astros
2. Larry Walker, Rockies
3. Barry Larkin, Reds

FASTEST BASERUNNER
1. Tony Womack, Pirates
2. Eric Young, Dodgers
3. Delino DeShields, Cardinals

BEST PITCHER
1. Greg Maddux, Braves
2. Curt Schilling, Phillies
3. Andy Ashby, Padres

BEST FASTBALL
1. Robb Nen, Giants
2. Kerry Wood, Cubs
3. Curt Schilling, Phillies

BEST CURVEBALL
1. Darryl Kile, Rockies
2. Kerry Wood, Cubs
3. Bobby Jones, Mets

BEST SLIDER
1. John Smoltz, Braves
2. Kevin Brown, Padres
3. Curt Schilling, Phillies

BEST CHANGEUP
1. Greg Maddux, Braves
2. Tom Glavine, Braves
3. Trevor Hoffman, Padres

BEST CONTROL
1. Greg Maddux, Braves
2. Tom Glavine, Braves
3. Rick Reed, Mets

BEST PICKOFF MOVE
1. Terry Mulholland, Cubs
2. Mark Langston, Padres
3. Jamey Wright, Rockies

BEST RELIEVER
1. Trevor Hoffman, Padres
2. Robb Nen, Giants
3. Jeff Shaw, Dodgers

BEST DEFENSIVE C
1. Charles Johnson, Dodgers
2. Brad Ausmus, Astros
3. Jason Kendall, Pirates

BEST DEFENSIVE 1B
1. Mark Grace, Cubs
2. Andres Galarraga, Braves
3. J.T. Snow, Giants

BEST DEFENSIVE 2B
1. Craig Biggio, Astros
2. Bret Boone, Reds
3. Mickey Morandini, Cubs

BEST DEFENSIVE 3B
1. Scott Rolen, Phillies
2. Ken Caminiti, Padres
3. Matt Williams, D'backs

BEST DEFENSIVE SS
1. Rey Ordonez, Mets
2. Barry Larkin, Reds
3. Edgar Renteria, Marlins

BEST INFIELD ARM
1. Ken Caminiti, Padres
2. Scott Rolen, Phillies
3. Desi Relaford, Phillies

BEST DEFENSIVE OF
1. Larry Walker, Rockies
2. Andruw Jones, Braves
3. Barry Bonds, Giants

BEST OUTFIELD ARM
1. Vladimir Guerrero, Expos
2. Raul Mondesi, Dodgers
3. Larry Walker, Rockies

MOST EXCITING PLAYER
1. Mark McGwire, Cardinals
2. Larry Walker, Rockies
3. Sammy Sosa, Cubs

BEST MANAGER
1. Bobby Cox, Braves
2. Dusty Baker, Giants
3. Bruce Bochy, Padres

NATIONAL LEAGUE
DEPARTMENT LEADERS

BATTING

GAMES
Vinny Castilla, Colorado	162
Neifi Perez, Colorado	162
Dante Bichette, Colorado	161
Jeromy Burnitz, Milwaukee	161
Craig Biggio, Houston	160
Chipper Jones, Atlanta	160
John Olerud, New York	160
Scott Rolen, Philadelphia	160

AT-BATS
Doug Glanville, Philadelphia	678
Dante Bichette, Colorado	662
Tony Womack, Pittsburgh	655
Neifi Perez, Colorado	647
Craig Biggio, Houston	646

RUNS
Sammy Sosa, Chicago	134
Mark McGwire, St. Louis	130
Jeff Bagwell, Houston	124
Craig Biggio, Houston	123
Chipper Jones, Atlanta	123

HITS
Dante Bichette, Colorado	219
Craig Biggio, Houston	210
Vinny Castilla, Colorado	206
Vladimir Guerrero, Montreal	202
Derek Bell, Houston	198
Sammy Sosa, Chicago	198
Fernando Vina, Milwaukee	198

TOTAL BASES
Sammy Sosa, Chicago	416
Mark McGwire, St. Louis	383
Vinny Castilla, Colorado	380
Vladimir Guerrero, Montreal	367
Greg Vaughn, San Diego	342

EXTRA-BASE HITS
Mark McGwire, St. Louis	91
Barry Bonds, San Francisco	88
Sammy Sosa, Chicago	86
Vladimir Guerrero, Montreal	82
Greg Vaughn, San Diego	82

SINGLES
Tony Womack, Pittsburgh	149
Jeff Cirillo, Milwaukee	148
Dante Bichette, Colorado	147
Doug Glanville, Philadelphia	146
Fernando Vina, Milwaukee	145
Mickey Morandini, Chicago	140

MEL BAILEY

John Olerud
23-game hitting streak

Dante Bichette
219 hits

DOUBLES
Craig Biggio, Houston	51
Dante Bichette, Colorado	48
Dmitri Young, Cincinnati	48
Larry Walker, Colorado	46
Cliff Floyd, Florida	45
Scott Rolen, Philadelphia	45

TRIPLES
David Dellucci, Arizona	12
Barry Larkin, Cincinnati	10
Wilton Guerrero, L.A./Montreal	9
Neifi Perez, Colorado	9
Delino DeShields, St. Louis	8
Karim Garcia, Arizona	8
Andruw Jones, Atlanta	8

HOME RUNS
Mark McGwire, St. Louis	70
Sammy Sosa, Chicago	66
Greg Vaughn, San Diego	50
Vinny Castilla, Colorado	46
Andres Galarraga, Atlanta	44

HOME RUN RATIO
(At-Bats per Home Run)

Mark McGwire, St. Louis	7.3
Sammy Sosa, Chicago	9.7
Greg Vaughn, San Diego	11.5
Andres Galarraga, Atlanta	12.6
Vinny Castilla, Colorado	14.0

RUNS BATTED IN
Sammy Sosa, Chicago	158
Mark McGwire, St. Louis	147
Vinny Castilla, Colorado	144
Jeff Kent, San Francisco	128
Jeromy Burnitz, Milwaukee	125

SACRIFICE BUNTS
Neifi Perez, Colorado	22
Terry Jones, Montreal	15
Rey Ordonez, New York	15
Tom Glavine, Atlanta	14
Carlos Perez, Mon./Los Angeles	14

SACRIFICE FLIES
Derek Bell, Houston	10
Rico Brogna, Philadelphia	10
Jeff Kent, San Francisco	10
Ellis Burks, Colo./San Francisco	9
Gary Sheffield, Fla./Los Angeles	9
Kevin Young, Pittsburgh	9

HIT BY PITCH
Jason Kendall, Pittsburgh	31
Andres Galarraga, Atlanta	25
Fernando Vina, Milwaukee	25
Craig Biggio, Houston	23
F.P. Santangelo, Montreal	23

WALKS
Mark McGwire, St. Louis	162
Barry Bonds, San Francisco	130
Jeff Bagwell, Houston	109
Chipper Jones, Atlanta	96
John Olerud, New York	95
Gary Sheffield, Fla./Los Angeles	95

INTENTIONAL WALKS
Barry Bonds, San Francisco	29
Mark McGwire, St. Louis	28
Bob Abreu, Philadelphia	14
Mike Piazza, L.A./Fla./New York	14
Sammy Sosa, Chicago	14

STRIKEOUTS
Sammy Sosa, Chicago	171
Jeromy Burnitz, Milwaukee	158
Mark McGwire, St. Louis	155
Ray Lankford, St. Louis	151
Andres Galarraga, Atlanta	146

TOUGHEST TO STRIKE OUT
(Plate Appearances per SO)

Tony Gwynn, San Diego	28.1
Gregg Jefferies, Philadelphia	19.3
Eric Young, Los Angeles	16.0
Fernando Vina, Milwaukee	15.7
Mark Grace, Chicago	12.5

STOLEN BASES
Tony Womack, Pittsburgh	58
Craig Biggio, Houston	50
Eric Young, Los Angeles	42
Edgar Renteria, Florida	41
Barry Bonds, San Francisco	28

CAUGHT STEALING
Edgar Renteria, Florida	22
Fernando Vina, Milwaukee	16
Cliff Floyd, Florida	14
Eric Young, Los Angeles	13
Barry Bonds, San Francisco	12
Carl Everett, Houston	12

GIDP
Jeff Cirillo, Milwaukee	26
Vinny Castilla, Colorado	24
Bret Boone, Cincinnati	23
Dante Bichette, Colorado	22
Javy Lopez, Atlanta	22

HITTING STREAKS
John Olerud, New York	23
Larry Walker, Colorado	20
Delino DeShields, St. Louis	18
Doug Glanville, Philadelphia	18

MULTIPLE-HIT GAMES
Dante Bichette, Colorado	66
Sammy Sosa, Chicago	66
Vladimir Guerrero, Montreal	64
Derek Bell, Houston	61
Vinny Castilla, Colorado	61

SLUGGING PERCENTAGE
Mark McGwire, St. Louis	.752
Sammy Sosa, Chicago	.647
Larry Walker, Colorado	.630
Barry Bonds, San Francisco	.609
Greg Vaughn, San Diego	.597

ON-BASE PERCENTAGE
Mark McGwire, St. Louis	.470
John Olerud, New York	.446
Larry Walker, Colorado	.445
Barry Bonds, San Francisco	.438
Gary Sheffield, Los Angeles	.428

PITCHING

WINS
Tom Glavine, Atlanta	20

Shane Reynolds, Houston 19
Kevin Tapani, Chicago........................ 19
Kevin Brown, San Diego 18
Greg Maddux, Atlanta 18

LOSSES

Darryl Kile, Colorado 17
Willie Blair, Arizona/New York 16
Mike Remlinger, Cincinnati 15
Javier Vazquez, Montreal 15

WINNING PERCENTAGE

John Smoltz, Atlanta....................... .850
Tom Glavine, Atlanta .... .769
Al Leiter, New York .... .739
Kevin Brown, San Diego................. .720
Shane Reynolds, Houston .... .704

GAMES

Rod Beck, Chicago 81
Steve Kline, Montreal......................... 78
Chuck McElroy, Colorado 78
Robb Nen, San Francisco 78
Anthony Telford, Montreal 77

GAMES STARTED

Kevin Brown, San Diego 35
Darryl Kile, Colorado 35
Shane Reynolds, Houston 35
Curt Schilling, Philadelphia 35

COMPLETE GAMES

Curt Schilling, Philadelphia 15
Livan Hernandez, Florida...................... 9
Greg Maddux, Atlanta 9
Kevin Brown, San Diego 7
Carlos Perez, Mon./Los Angeles 7

SHUTOUTS

Greg Maddux, Atlanta 5
Randy Johnson, Houston 4
Kevin Brown, San Diego 3
Tom Glavine, Atlanta 3

GAMES FINISHED

Rod Beck, Chicago 70
Jeff Shaw, Cincinnati/L.A. 69
Robb Nen, San Francisco 67
Trevor Hoffman, San Diego 61
Ugueth Urbina, Montreal 59

SAVES

Trevor Hoffman, San Diego 53
Rod Beck, Chicago 51
Jeff Shaw, Montreal/L.A. 48
Robb Nen, San Francisco 40
John Franco, New York 38

INNINGS PITCHED

Curt Schilling, Philadelphia 269
Kevin Brown, San Diego 257
Greg Maddux, Atlanta 251
Carlos Perez, Mon./Los Angeles 241

Tom Glavine
20 wins

John Smoltz
.850 winning percentage

Livan Hernandez, Florida.................. 234

HITS ALLOWED

Livan Hernandez, Florida.................. 265
Darryl Kile, Colorado 257
Shane Reynolds, Houston 257
Pedro Astacio, Colorado 245
Carlos Perez, Mon./Los Angeles 244
Kevin Tapani, Chicago...................... 244

RUNS ALLOWED

Pedro Astacio, Colorado 160
Jamey Wright, Colorado 143
Darryl Kile, Colorado 141
Livan Hernandez, Florida.................. 100
Javier Vazquez, Montreal 121

HOME RUNS ALLOWED

Brian Anderson, Arizona 39
Pedro Astacio, Colorado 39
Livan Hernandez, Florida.................... 37
Jose Lima, Houston 34
Willie Blair, Arizona/New York 31
Javier Vazquez, Montreal 31

WALKS

Joey Hamilton, San Diego 106
Livan Hernandez, Florida................. 104
Chan Ho Park, Las Vegas 97
Darryl Kile, Colorado 96
Jamey Wright, Colorado 95

FEWEST WALKS PER 9 INNINGS

Brian Anderson, Arizona.................... 1.0
Jose Lima, Houston 1.2
Rick Reed, New York 1.2
Greg Maddux, Atlanta 1.6
Kevin Brown, San Diego.................... 1.7
Mark Portugal, Philadelphia 1.7

HIT BATSMEN

Pedro Astacio, Colorado 17
Orel Hershiser, San Francisco........... 13
Brian Bohanon, N.Y./Los Angeles 11
Al Leiter, New York 11
Chan Ho Park, Los Angeles................ 11
Javier Vazquez, Montreal 11
Kerry Wood, Chicago.......................... 11
Jamey Wright, Colorado 11

STRIKEOUTS

Curt Schilling, Philadelphia 300
Kevin Brown, San Diego 257
Kerry Wood, Chicago........................ 233
Shane Reynolds, Houston 209
Greg Maddux, Atlanta 204

STRIKEOUTS PER 9 INNINGS

Kerry Wood, Chicago 12.6
Curt Schilling, Philadelphia 10.0
John Smoltz, Atlanta 9.3
Kevin Brown, San Diego...................... 9.0
Darren Dreifort, Los Angeles 8.4
Kevin Millwood, Atlanta...................... 8.4

PICKOFFS

Brian Anderson, Arizona 12
Jesus Sanchez, Florida 12
Carlos Perez, Mon./Los Angeles 9
Jamey Wright, Colorado 8
Dennis Reyes, L.A./Cincinnati 6
Steve Trachsel, Chicago 6

WILD PITCHES

Jason Schmidt, Pittsburgh 15
Hideo Nomo, L.A./New York 13
Orel Hershiser, San Francisco............ 12
Darryl Kile, Colorado 12
Curt Schilling, Philadelphia 12

BALKS

Brian Anderson, Arizona 6
Jesus Sanchez, Florida 5
Kent Mercker, St. Louis 4
Hideo Nomo, L.A./New York 4

OPPONENTS BATTING AVERAGE

Kerry Wood, Chicago .... .196
Al Leiter, New York .... .216
Greg Maddux, Atlanta .... .220
Pete Harnisch, Cincinnati................ ..228
John Smoltz, Atlanta .... .231

FIELDING

PITCHER

PCT Pedro Astacio, Colorado...... 1.000
PO Two tied at 31
A Greg Maddux, Atlanta 63
E Several tied at 4
TC Greg Maddux, Atlanta 98
DP Shane Reynolds, Houston 9

CATCHER

PCT Javy Lopez, Atlanta .... .995
PO Jason Kendall, Pittsburgh 1015
A Two tied at 68
E Chris Widger, Montreal 14
TC Jason Kendall, Pittsburgh 1082
DP Two tied at 12
PB Chris Widger, Montreal 14

FIRST BASE

PCT J.T. Snow, San Francisco...... .999
PO Kevin Young, Pittsburgh 1335
A Todd Helton, Colorado............ 146
E Brad Fullmer, Montreal 17
TC Mark McGwire, St. Louis 1434
DP Todd Helton, Colorado............ 156

SECOND BASE

PCT Mickey Morandini, Chicago.... .993
PO Fernando Vina, Milwaukee 404
A Fernando Vina, Milwaukee 468
E Jeff Kent, San Francisco 20
TC Fernando Vina, Milwaukee 884
DP Fernando Vina, Milwaukee 135

THIRD BASE

PCT Gary Gaetti, St. Louis/Chi. ..... .983
PO Scott Rolen, Philadelphia........ 135
A Jeff Cirillo, Milwaukee 339
E Ken Caminiti, San Diego 21
TC Scott Rolen, Philadelphia........ 467
DP Jeff Cirillo, Milwaukee 45

SHORTSTOP

PCT Chris Gomez, San Diego ...... .980
PO Neifi Perez, Colorado.............. 271
A Neifi Perez, Colorado.............. 517
E Desi Relaford, Philadelphia 24
TC Neifi Perez, Colorado.............. 808
DP Neifi Perez, Colorado.............. 127

OUTFIELD

PCT Darryl Hamilton, S.F./Colo. ..... .997
PO Andruw Jones, Atlanta............ 413
A Two tied at 20
E Vladimir Guerrero, Montreal 17
TC Andruw Jones, Atlanta............ 435
DP Three tied at................................ 6

1998 National League Statistics

CLUB BATTING

	AVG	G	AB	R	H	2B	3B	HR	BB	SO	SB
Colorado	.291	162	5632	826	1640	333	36	183	469	949	67
Houston	.280	162	5641	874	1578	326	28	166	621	1122	155
San Francisco	.274	163	5628	845	1540	292	26	161	678	1040	102
Atlanta	.272	162	5484	826	1489	297	26	215	548	1062	98
Chicago	.264	163	5649	831	1494	250	34	212	601	1223	65
Phiadelphia	.264	162	5617	713	1482	286	36	126	508	1080	97
Cincinnati	.262	162	5496	750	1441	298	28	138	608	1107	95
Milwaukee	.260	162	5541	707	1439	266	17	152	532	1039	81
New York	.259	162	5510	706	1425	289	24	136	571	1049	62
St. Louis	.258	163	5593	810	1444	292	30	223	676	1179	133
Pittsburgh	.254	163	5493	650	1395	271	35	107	393	1060	159
San Diego	.253	162	5490	749	1390	292	30	167	604	1072	79
Los Angeles	.252	162	5459	669	1374	209	27	159	447	1056	137
Montreal	.249	162	5418	644	1348	280	32	147	439	1058	91
Florida	.248	162	5558	667	1381	277	36	114	525	1120	115
Arizona	.246	162	5491	665	1353	235	46	159	489	1239	73

CLUB PITCHING

	ERA	G	CG	SHO	SV	IP	H	R	ER	BB	SO
Atlanta	3.25	162	24	23	45	1439	1291	581	520	466	1232
Houston	3.50	162	12	11	44	1471	1435	620	572	465	1187
San Diego	3.63	162	14	11	59	1455	1384	635	587	501	1217
New York	3.76	162	9	16	46	1458	1381	645	609	532	1129
Los Angeles	3.81	162	16	10	47	1447	1332	678	612	587	1178
Pittsburgh	3.91	163	7	10	41	1449	1433	718	629	530	1112
San Francisco	4.18	163	6	6	44	1477	1457	739	686	562	1089
St. Louis	4.31	163	6	10	44	1470	1513	782	703	558	972
Montreal	4.38	162	4	5	39	1427	1448	783	695	533	1017
Cincinnati	4.44	162	6	8	42	1441	1400	760	711	573	1098
Chicago	4.47	163	7	7	56	1477	1528	792	733	575	1207
Milwaukee	4.63	162	2	2	39	1451	1538	812	746	550	1063
Arizona	4.63	162	7	6	37	1432	1463	812	737	489	908
Philadelphia	4.64	162	21	10	32	1463	1476	808	754	544	1176
Colorado	4.99	162	9	5	36	1433	1583	855	794	562	951
Florida	5.18	162	11	3	24	1450	1617	923	834	715	1016

CLUB FIELDING

	PCT	PO	A	E	DP
Atlanta	.985	4316	1681	91	139
San Francisco	.984	4431	1806	101	157
Arizona	.984	4297	1718	100	125
Chicago	.984	4432	1622	101	107
New York	.984	4374	1672	101	151
Colorado	.984	4298	1795	102	193
San Diego	.983	4364	1727	104	155
Houston	.983	4414	1782	108	144
Philadelphia	.982	4389	1747	110	131
Milwaukee	.982	4353	1761	110	192
Cincinnati	.980	4324	1563	122	142
Florida	.979	4349	1738	129	177
Los Angeles	.978	4342	1731	134	154
St. Louis	.978	4409	1781	142	160
Pittsburgh	.977	4347	1698	140	161
Montreal	.975	4281	1686	155	127

INDIVIDUAL BATTING LEADERS

(Minimum 502 Plate Appearances)

	AVG	G	AB	R	H	2B	3B	HR	RBI	BB	SO	SB
Walker, Larry, Colorado	.363	130	454	113	165	46	3	23	67	64	61	14
Olerud, John, New York	.353	160	558	91	197	36	4	22	93	95	73	2
Bichette, Dante, Colorado	.331	161	662	97	219	48	2	22	122	28	76	14
Piazza, Mike, L.A./Fla./N.Y.	.329	151	560	88	184	38	1	32	111	58	80	1
Kendall, Jason, Pittsburgh	.327	149	535	95	175	36	3	12	75	51	51	26
Biggio, Craig, Houston	.325	160	646	123	210	51	2	20	88	64	113	50
Guerrero, Vladimir, Montreal	.324	159	623	107	202	37	7	38	109	42	95	11
Cirillo, Jeff, Milwaukee	.321	156	604	97	194	31	1	14	68	79	88	10
Gwynn, Tony, San Diego	.321	127	461	65	148	35	0	16	69	35	18	3
Castilla, Vinny, Colorado	.319	162	645	108	206	28	4	46	144	40	89	5

INDIVIDUAL PITCHING LEADERS

(Minimum 162 Innings Pitched)

	W	L	ERA	G	GS	CG	SV	IP	H	R	ER	BB	SO
Maddux, Greg, Atlanta	18	9	2.22	34	34	9	0	251	201	75	62	45	204
Brown, Kevin, San Diego	18	7	2.38	36	35	7	0	257	225	77	68	49	257
Leiter, Al, New York	17	6	2.47	28	28	4	0	193	151	55	53	71	174
Glavine, Tom, Atlanta	20	6	2.47	33	33	4	0	229	202	67	63	74	157
Daal, Omar, Arizona	8	12	2.88	33	23	3	0	163	146	60	52	51	132
Smoltz, John, Atlanta	17	3	2.90	26	26	2	0	168	145	58	54	44	173
Hermanson, Dustin, Montreal	14	11	3.13	32	30	1	0	187	163	80	65	56	154
Harnisch, Pete, Cincinnati	14	7	3.14	32	32	2	0	209	176	79	73	64	157
Schilling, Curt, Philadelphia	15	14	3.25	35	35	15	0	269	236	101	97	61	300
Cordova, Francisco, Pittsburgh	13	14	3.31	33	33	3	0	220	204	91	81	69	157

AWARD WINNERS

Selected by Baseball Writers Association of America

MVP

Player, Team	1st	2nd	3rd	Total
Sammy Sosa, Chi.	30	2	0	438
Mark McGwire, St.L.	2	20	3	272
Moises Alou, Hou.	0	6	8	215
Greg Vaughn, S.D.	0	0	7	185
Craig Biggio, Hou.	0	3	5	163
Andres Galarraga, Atl.	0	0	1	147
Trevor Hoffman, S.D.	0	0	5	117
Barry Bonds, S.F.	0	1	0	66
Chipper Jones, Atl.	0	0	2	56
Jeff Kent, S.F.	0	0	1	56
Vinny Castilla, Col.	0	0	0	49
John Olerud, N.Y.	0	0	0	38
Vladimir Guerrero, Mon.	0	0	0	25
Mike Piazza, N.Y.	0	0	0	15
Tony Gwynn, S.D.	0	0	0	11
Kevin Brown, S.D.	0	0	0	8
Larry Walker, Col.	0	0	0	7
Rod Beck, Chi.	0	0	0	5
Jeromy Burnitz, Mil.	0	0	0	4
Scott Rolen, Phi.	0	0	0	3
Tom Glavine, Atl.	0	0	0	2
Randy Johnson, Hou.	0	0	0	2
Dante Bichette, Col.	0	0	0	2
Javy Lopez, Atl.	0	0	0	1
Mickey Morandini, Chi.	0	0	0	1

CY YOUNG AWARD

Player, Team	1st	2nd	3rd	Total
Tom Glavine, Atl.	11	13	5	99
Trevor Hoffman, S.D.	13	5	8	88
Kevin Brown, S.D.	8	8	12	76
John Smoltz, Atl.	0	3	1	10
Greg Maddux, Atl.	0	2	4	10
Al Leiter, N.Y.	0	1	0	3
Randy Johnson, Hou.	0	0	2	2

ROOKIE OF THE YEAR

Player, Team	1st	2nd	3rd	Total
Kerry Wood, Chi.	16	16	0	128
Todd Helton, Col.	15	14	2	119
Travis Lee, Ariz.	0	2	15	21
Kerry Ligtenberg, Atl.	1	0	13	18
Brad Fullmer, Mon.	0	0	2	2

MANAGER OF THE YEAR

Manager, Team	1st	2nd	3rd	Total
Larry Dierker, Hou.	16	6	4	102
Bruce Bochy, S.D.	5	13	6	70
Jim Riggleman, Chi.	5	7	9	55
Dusty Baker, S.F.	6	2	3	39
Bobby Cox, Atl.	0	3	8	17
Bobby Valentine, N.Y.	0	1	2	5

NOTE: MVP balloting based on 14 points for first place vote, nine of second, eight for third, etc.; Cy Young Award, Rookie of the Year and Manager of the Year balloting based on five points for first-place vote, three for second and one for third.

GOLD GLOVE AWARDS

Selected by NL managers

C—Charles Johnson, Florida/Los Angeles. **1B**—J.T. Snow, San Francisco. **2B**—Bret Boone, Cincinnati. **3B**—Scott Rolen, Philadelphia. **SS**—Rey Ordonez, New York. **OF**—Barry Bonds, San Francisco; Andruw Jones, Atlanta; Larry Walker, Colorado. **P**—Greg Maddux, Atlanta.

Florida saved more cost by shipping Piazza to the Mets for minor leaguers Geoff Goetz, Preston Wilson and Ed Yarnall. Piazza, who hit a combined .329 with 32 homers and 111 RBIs, signed a seven-year, $91 million deal with the Mets after the season ended.

■ The Piazza trade was far from the only change in Los Angeles. Just before the season, the team was sold to FOX and Rupert Murdoch for a record $350 million.

MEL BAILEY

Mike Piazza

During the year, manager Bill Russell and longtime GM Fred Claire were fired. Interim GM Tommy Lasorda traded several prospects, most notably 1997 Minor League Player of the Year Paul Konerko, in an effort to land a wild-card berth. The team failed to contend, though. After the season, Kevin Malone was hired as GM and the Dodgers hired Davey Johnson as manager after making an offer to Expos manager Felipe Alou. Montreal kept Alou with a three-year contract and a significant raise.

■ The Rockies also failed to live up to preseason standards in 1998. Don Baylor, the franchise's only manager in its six seasons, was replaced by Leyland after Colorado went 77-85. One bright spot for the Rockies: Larry Walker, playing all year with excruciating pain in his right elbow after offseason surgery, hit .363 to win the batting title. He denied runner-up John Olerud, who hit .353 for the Mets, in his bid to become the first player to win a batting crown in each league this century.

■ The NL's two new teams, the Brewers and Arizona Diamondbacks, both had cause to celebrate in 1998. The Diamondbacks, playing under the retractable roof at brand-new Bank One Ballpark in Phoenix, avoided 100 losses despite striking out a major league record 1,239 times. Their 65-97 record was 11 games better than the defending World Series champion Marlins. Arizona drew 3.6 million fans, while Milwaukee's 1.8 million fans were more than in any of the club's last five American League seasons.

■ Hoffman, the Padres' closer, tied an NL record with 53 saves in his 4-2, 1.48 season. Randy Myers, who set the mark with the Cubs in 1993, finished the year as one of Hoffman's teammates after an in-season deal with the Blue Jays.

■ Braves righthander Dennis Martinez broke the record for career wins by a Latin American pitcher. After being released in May 1997 by the Mariners, he found a spot in Atlanta's bullpen out of spring training. He went 4-6 to move to 245-193 in his career. Juan Marichal went 243-142 from 1960-75.

■ Expos outfielder Vladimir Guerrero showed he might be the league's newest young star. In his second season, he hit .324 with 38 homers and 109 RBIs. Montreal signed the 22-year-old to a five-year contract.

■ Another second-year big leaguer, Pittsburgh Pirates second baseman Tony Womack, won his second straight NL stolen-base title by swiping 58.

NATIONAL LEAGUE

DIVISION SERIES

ATLANTA vs. CHICAGO

COMPOSITE BOX

ATLANTA

Player, Pos.	AVG	G	AB	R	H	2B	3B	HR	RBI	BB	SO	SB
Danny Bautista, ph	.500	2	2	0	1	1	0	0	0	0	0	0
John Smoltz, p	.500	1	2	0	1	0	0	0	1	1	1	0
Gerald Williams, lf	.500	2	2	1	1	0	0	0	0	0	1	0
Keith Lockhart, 2b	.333	3	12	2	4	0	0	0	0	1	0	0
Javy Lopez, c	.286	2	7	1	2	0	0	1	1	1	1	0
Ryan Klesko, lf	.273	3	11	1	3	0	0	1	4	0	3	0
Andres Galarraga, 1b	.250	3	12	1	3	0	0	0	0	1	3	0
Greg Maddux, p	.250	1	4	1	1	1	0	0	0	0	1	0
Michael Tucker, rf	.250	3	8	1	2	0	0	1	2	2	0	1
Chipper Jones, 3b	.200	3	10	2	2	0	0	0	1	4	3	0
Eddie Perez, c	.200	1	5	1	1	0	0	1	4	0	2	0
Walt Weiss, ss	.154	3	13	2	2	0	0	0	0	1	3	0
Greg Colbrunn, ph	.000	2	2	0	0	0	0	0	0	0	0	0
Tom Glavine, p	.000	1	1	0	0	0	0	0	0	0	0	0
Ozzie Guillen, ph-ss	.000	1	1	0	0	0	0	0	0	0	0	0
Andruw Jones, cf	.000	3	9	2	0	0	0	0	1	3	2	2
Graffanino, Tony, pr	.000	1	0	0	0	0	0	0	0	0	0	0
Totals	**.228**	**3**	**101**	**15**	**23**	**2**	**0**	**4**	**14**	**14**	**20**	**3**

Pitcher	W	L	ERA	G	GS	SV	IP	H	R	ER	BB	SO
Kerry Ligtenberg	0	0	0.00	3	0	0	3	1	0	0	4	3
Odaliz Perez	1	0	0.00	1	0	0	1	0	0	0	0	1
John Rocker	0	0	0.00	2	0	0	1	1	0	0	0	2
Rudy Seanez	0	0	0.00	1	0	0	1	0	0	0	0	0
John Smoltz	1	0	1.17	1	1	0	8	5	1	1	0	6
Tom Glavine	0	0	1.29	1	1	0	7	3	1	1	1	8
Greg Maddux	1	0	2.57	1	1	0	7	7	2	2	0	4
Totals	**3**	**0**	**1.29**	**3**	**3**	**0**	**28**	**17**	**4**	**4**	**5**	**24**

CHICAGO

Player, Pos.	AVG	G	AB	R	H	2B	3B	HR	RBI	BB	SO	SB
Sandy Martinez, ph	1.000	1	1	1	1	0	0	0	0	0	0	0
Scott Servais, c	.667	1	3	0	2	0	0	0	0	0	0	0
Mark Clark, p	.500	1	2	0	1	0	0	0	0	0	0	0
Glenallen Hill, of	.333	1	3	0	1	0	0	0	0	1	2	1
Jose Hernandez, ss	.286	2	7	1	2	0	0	0	0	0	2	0
Mickey Morandini, 2b	.222	3	9	1	2	0	0	0	1	2	2	0
Sammy Sosa, rf	.182	3	11	0	2	1	0	0	0	1	4	0
Tyler Houston, c	.167	3	6	1	1	0	0	1	1	0	3	0
Lance Johnson, cf	.167	3	12	0	2	0	0	0	1	0	1	0
Henry Rodriguez, lf	.143	3	7	0	1	1	0	0	0	1	2	0
Gary Gaetti, 3b	.091	3	11	0	1	0	0	0	0	0	4	0
Mark Grace, 1b	.083	3	12	0	1	0	0	0	1	0	2	0
Manny Alexander, ss	.000	2	5	0	0	0	0	0	0	0	1	0
Jeff Blauser, ph	.000	2	2	0	0	0	0	0	0	0	1	0
Brant Brown, ph	.000	1	1	0	0	0	0	0	0	0	0	0
Kevin Tapani, p	.000	1	1	0	0	0	0	0	0	0	0	0
Kerry Wood, p	.000	1	1	0	0	0	0	0	0	0	0	0
Totals	**.181**	**3**	**94**	**4**	**17**	**2**	**0**	**1**	**4**	**5**	**24**	**1**

Pitcher	W	L	ERA	G	GS	SV	IP	H	R	ER	BB	SO
Mike Morgan	0	0	0.00	2	0	0	1	0	0	0	0	1
Kevin Tapani	0	0	1.00	1	1	0	9	5	1	1	3	6
Kerry Wood	0	1	1.80	1	1	0	5	3	1	1	4	5
Mark Clark	0	1	3.00	1	1	0	6	7	4	2	1	4
Terry Mulholland	0	1	11.57	2	0	0	2	2	3	3	2	2
Matt Karchner	0	0	13.50	1	0	0	1	1	1	1	0	1
Rod Beck	0	0	16.20	1	0	0	2	5	3	3	2	1
Felix Heredia	0	0	54.00	1	0	0	0	0	2	2	2	0
Totals	**0**	**3**	**4.44**	**3**	**3**	**0**	**26**	**23**	**15**	**13**	**14**	**20**

SCORE BY INNINGS	
Chicago	**000 001 030 0— 4**
Atlanta	**021 001 451 1—15**

DP—Atlanta 2, Chicago 1. **LOB**—Atlanta 24, Chicago 15. **E**—Hernandez 2, Gaetti, Mulholland. **CS**—Sosa 2, Morandini. **S**—Tapani 2, Gaetti, Glavine, Graffanino. **SF**—A. Jones, Morandini. **PB**—Houston. **Balk**—Tapani.

SAN DIEGO vs. HOUSTON

COMPOSITE BOX

SAN DIEGO

Player, Pos.	AVG	G	AB	R	H	2B	3B	HR	RBI	BB	SO	SB
Carlos Hernandez, c..	.417	4	12	0	5	0	0	0	0	0	0	0
Jim Leyritz, 1b-c	.400	4	10	0	4	0	0	0	0	0	0	0
John Vander Wal, lf	.333	3	3	1	1	0	1	0	2	0	1	0
Greg Vaughn, lf	.333	4	15	2	5	1	0	1	1	0	4	0
Chris Gomez, ss	.273	4	11	1	3	0	0	0	0	4	1	0
Tony Gwynn, rf	.200	4	15	1	3	2	0	0	2	0	2	0
Wally Joyner, 1b	.167	4	6	1	1	0	0	1	2	1	2	0
Ken Caminiti, 3b	.143	4	14	2	2	0	0	0	0	1	3	0
Quilvio Veras, 2b	.133	4	15	1	2	0	0	0	0	1	6	0
Steve Finley, cf	.100	4	10	2	1	1	0	0	1	1	4	0
George Arias, ph	.000	1	1	0	0	0	0	0	0	0	1	0
Andy Ashby, p	.000	1	1	0	0	0	0	0	0	0	0	0
Kevin Brown, p	.000	2	3	0	0	0	0	0	0	0	2	0
Joey Hamilton, p	.000	1	0	0	0	0	0	0	0	0	0	0
Sterling Hitchcock, p..	.000	1	2	0	0	0	0	0	0	0	1	0
Ruben Rivera, lf	.000	3	6	0	0	0	0	0	0	0	3	0
Mark Sweeney, ph	.000	2	1	0	0	0	0	0	0	1	0	0
Donne Wall, p	.000	1	0	0	0	0	0	0	0	0	0	0
Greg Myers, pr	.000	1	0	0	0	0	0	0	0	0	0	0
Andy Sheets, ss	.000	2	0	0	0	0	0	0	0	0	0	0
Totals	**.216**	**4**	**125**	**14**	**27**	**4**	**1**	**5**	**13**	**9**	**32**	**0**

Pitcher	W	L	ERA	G	GS	SV	IP	H	R	ER	BB	SO
Joey Hamilton	0	0	0.00	2	0	0	3	1	0	0	2	3
Trevor Hoffman	0	0	0.00	4	0	2	3	3	1	0	1	4
Kevin Brown	1	0	0.61	2	2	0	15	5	1	1	7	21
Sterling Hitchcock	1	0	1.50	1	1	0	6	3	1	1	0	11
Danny Miceli	1	1	2.70	3	0	0	3	2	1	1	0	4
Andy Ashby	0	0	6.75	1	1	0	4	6	3	3	1	4
Donne Wall	0	0	9.00	1	0	0	1	2	1	1	0	2
Totals	**3**	**1**	**1.80**	**4**	**4**	**2**	**35**	**22**	**8**	**7**	**11**	**49**

HOUSTON

Player, Pos.	AVG	G	AB	R	H	2B	3B	HR	RBI	BB	SO	SB
Tony Eusebio, c	.333	1	3	0	1	1	0	0	0	0	2	0
Ricky Gutierrez, ss	.300	4	10	1	3	0	0	0	0	3	7	1
Bill Spiers, 3b	.286	4	14	2	4	3	0	0	1	1	3	0
Richard Hidalgo, of	.250	1	4	0	1	0	0	0	0	0	1	0
Brad Ausmus, c	.222	4	9	0	2	0	0	0	0	0	4	0
Moises Alou, lf	.188	4	16	0	3	0	0	0	0	0	2	0
Craig Biggio, 2b	.182	4	11	3	2	1	0	0	1	4	4	0
Carl Everett, cf	.154	4	13	1	2	0	0	0	0	0	4	0
Jeff Bagwell, 1b	.143	4	14	0	2	0	0	0	0	4	1	6	0
Derek Bell, rf	.125	4	16	1	2	0	0	1	1	0	7	0
Sean Berry, 3b	.000	1	2	0	0	0	0	0	0	0	1	0
Mike Hampton, p	.000	1	2	0	0	0	0	0	0	0	2	0
Randy Johnson, p	.000	2	4	0	0	0	0	0	0	0	4	0
Pete Incaviglia, ph	.000	1	1	0	0	0	0	0	0	0	1	0
Doug Henry, p	.000	1	0	0	0	0	0	0	0	0	0	0
Travis Miller, p	.000	1	0	0	0	0	0	0	0	0	0	0
Jay Powell, p	.000	1	0	0	0	0	0	0	0	0	0	0
Shane Reynolds, p	.000	1	2	0	0	0	0	0	0	0	1	0
Dave Clark, ph	.000	2	0	0	0	0	0	0	0	2	0	0
Totals	**.182**	**4**	**121**	**8**	**22**	**5**	**0**	**1**	**7**	**11**	**49**	**1**

Pitcher	W	L	ERA	G	GS	SV	IP	H	R	ER	BB	SO
Mike Hampton	0	0	1.50	1	1	0	6	2	1	1	1	2
Randy Johnson	0	2	1.93	2	2	0	14	12	4	3	2	17
Shane Reynolds	0	0	2.57	1	1	0	7	4	2	2	1	5
Scott Elarton	0	1	4.50	1	0	0	2	1	1	1	1	3
Doug Henry	0	0	5.40	2	0	0	2	2	1	1	0	1
Jay Powell	0	0	11.57	3	0	0	2	2	3	3	3	3
Billy Wagner	1	0	18.00	1	0	0	1	4	2	2	0	1
Travis Miller	0	0	—	1	0	0	0	0	0	0	1	0
Totals	**1**	**3**	**3.44**	**4**	**4**	**0**	**34**	**27**	**14**	**13**	**9**	**32**

SCORE BY INNINGS

San Diego	**010 005 152—14**
Houston	**102 100 112— 8**

DP—San Diego 5, Houston 1. **LOB**—San Diego 23, Houston 25. **E**—Gomez, Berry, Biggio, Joyner, Caminiti. **CS**—Vaughn, Sweeney. **S**—Brown 2. **SF**—Leyritz. **PB**—Hernandez 2. **HBP**—Biggio (by Brown, Hitchcock), Veras (by Powell), Eusebio (by Ashby), Bagwell (by Brown), Gutierrez (by Brown), Hernandez (by Elarton). **WP**—Powell, Hampton.

CHAMPIONSHIP SERIES

ATLANTA vs. SAN DIEGO

COMPOSITE BOX

ATLANTA

Player, Pos.	AVG	G	AB	R	H	2B	3B	HR	RBI	BB	SO	SB
Eddie Perez, c	.750	3	4	0	3	0	0	0	0	0	0	0
Ozzie Guillen, ss	.417	4	12	1	5	0	0	0	1	0	1	0
Michael Tucker, rf	.385	6	13	1	5	1	0	1	5	2	5	0
Greg Colbrunn, ph	.333	6	6	0	2	0	0	0	0	0	2	0
Tony Graffanino, 2b	.333	4	3	2	1	1	0	0	1	2	1	0
Javy Lopez, c	.300	6	20	2	6	0	0	1	1	0	7	0
Andruw Jones, cf	.273	6	22	3	6	0	0	1	2	1	4	1
Tom Glavine, p	.250	3	4	0	1	0	0	0	0	1	2	0
Keith Lockhart, 2b	.235	6	17	2	4	1	1	0	0	0	4	0
Chipper Jones, 3b	.208	6	24	2	5	1	0	0	1	4	5	0
Walt Weiss, ss	.200	4	15	0	3	0	0	0	1	2	5	1
John Smoltz, p	.200	2	5	0	1	0	0	0	0	0	1	0
Gerald Williams, lf-rf	.154	5	13	0	2	0	0	0	0	1	6	1
Andres Galarraga, 1b	.095	6	21	1	2	0	0	1	4	6	6	0
Ryan Klesko, lf	.083	5	12	2	1	0	0	0	1	6	3	0
Greg Maddux, p	.000	2	1	0	0	0	0	0	0	0	0	0
Marty Malloy, 2b	.000	4	1	1	0	0	0	0	0	0	1	0
Denny Neagle, p	.000	2	2	0	0	0	0	0	0	0	0	0
Dannny Bautista, lf	.000	5	5	0	0	0	0	0	0	0	1	0
John Rocker, p	.000	6	0	1	0	0	0	0	0	1	0	0
Totals	**.235**	**6**	**200**	**18**	**47**	**4**	**1**	**4**	**17**	**26**	**54**	**3**

Pitching	W	L	ERA	G	GS	SV	IP	H	R	ER	BB	SO
John Rocker	1	0	0.00	6	0	0	5	3	0	0	1	5
Dennis Martinez	1	0	0.00	4	0	0	3	1	0	0	1	0
Tom Glavine	0	2	2.31	2	2	0	12	13	6	3	9	8
Greg Maddux	0	1	3.00	2	1	1	6	5	2	2	3	4
Denny Neagle	0	0	3.52	2	1	0	8	8	3	3	2	9
John Smoltz	0	0	3.95	2	2	0	14	13	6	6	6	13
Rudy Seanez	0	0	6.00	4	0	0	3	2	2	2	1	4
Kerry Ligtenberg	0	1	7.36	4	0	0	4	3	3	3	2	5
Odaliz Perez	0	0	54.00	2	0	0	0	5	2	2	2	0
Totals	**2**	**4**	**3.50**	**6**	**6**	**1**	**54**	**53**	**24**	**21**	**27**	**48**

SAN DIEGO

Player, Pos.	AVG	G	AB	R	H	2B	3B	HR	RBI	BB	SO	SB
Greg Myers, ph	1.000	2	1	1	1	0	0	1	2	1	0	0
Kevin Brown, p	.500	2	4	1	2	0	0	0	0	0	1	0
John Vander Wal, lf	.429	3	7	1	3	0	0	1	2	0	2	0
Steve Finley, cf	.333	6	21	3	7	1	0	0	2	6	2	1
Carlos Hernandez, c.	.333	6	18	2	6	2	0	0	0	1	5	0
Wally Joyner, 1b	.313	6	16	3	5	0	0	0	2	4	3	0
Ken Caminiti, 3b	.273	6	22	3	6	0	0	2	4	5	4	0
Quilvio Veras, 2b	.250	6	24	2	6	1	0	0	2	5	7	0
Greg Vaughn, lf	.250	3	8	1	2	0	0	0	0	1	1	0
Tony Gwynn, rf	.231	6	26	1	6	1	0	0	2	1	2	0
Ruben Rivera, of	.231	6	13	1	3	2	0	0	0	0	7	1
Sterling Hitchcock, p..	.200	2	5	1	1	0	0	0	0	0	0	0
Jim Leyritz, c-1b	.167	5	12	1	2	0	0	1	4	0	2	0
Chris Gomez, ss	.150	6	20	2	3	0	0	0	0	2	5	0
Joey Hamilton, p	.000	2	2	0	0	0	0	0	0	0	1	0
Mark Sweeney, ph	.000	3	2	1	0	0	0	0	0	1	1	0
Andy Sheets, ss	.000	3	3	0	0	0	0	0	0	0	1	0
Andy Ashby, p	.000	2	4	0	0	0	0	0	0	0	4	0
Totals	**.255**	**6**	**208**	**24**	**53**	**7**	**0**	**5**	**20**	**27**	**48**	**2**

Pitching	W	L	ERA	G	GS	SV	IP	H	R	ER	BB	SO
Brian Boehringer	0	0	0.00	3	0	0	3	3	0	0	1	1
Mark Langston	0	0	0.00	3	0	0	1	1	0	0	0	1
Sterling Hitchcock	2	0	0.90	2	2	0	10	5	1	1	8	14
Andy Ashby	0	0	2.08	2	2	0	13	14	3	3	2	5
Trevor Hoffman	1	0	2.08	3	0	1	4	2	1	1	2	7
Kevin Brown	1	1	2.61	2	2	0	10	5	3	3	4	12
Donne Wall	0	0	3.00	3	0	1	3	3	2	1	4	4
Joey Hamilton	0	1	4.91	2	1	0	7	7	4	4	3	6
Randy Myers	0	0	13.50	4	0	0	2	3	3	3	2	3
Danny Miceli	0	0	13.50	3	0	0	1	4	1	1	0	1
Totals	**4**	**2**	**2.78**	**4**	**4**	**2**	**55**	**47**	**18**	**17**	**26**	**54**

SCORE BY INNINGS

Atlanta	**002 202 651 0—18**
San Diego	**202 039 034 1—24**

DP—San Diego 6, Atlanta 6. **LOB**—San Diego 52, Atlanta 46. **E**—Galarraga 4, Klesko, Smoltz, Lopez, Gomez, Bautista. **CS**—Veras, A. Jones. **SF**—A. Jones. **S**—Maddux, E. Perez, Ashby, Gwynn. **HBP**—Leyritz (by Maddux), **PB**—Lopez. **WP**—Hitchcock 2, Brown, R. Myers. **Balk**—Ligtenberg.

Organization Statistics

ANAHEIM ANGELS

Angels disappointed with another second-place showing

BY BILL SHAIKIN

It was deja vu all over again for the Anaheim Angels in 1998. For the third time in four years, they fell out of first place in the waning days of the season, this time finishing three games behind the Texas Rangers.

Again, it came down to head-to-head competition in September. And again, the Angels failed to win the must-win games. The Rangers won all five games between the two clubs down the stretch, ending any hope of a postseason appearance for Anaheim.

The words that softened the colossal collapse of 1995, words like "young" and "emerging" and "potential," were words that stung this time.

Angels general manager Bill Bavasi took some heat for his failure to acquire stretch-drive help, but he said he refused to deal away his club's future. So while the Rangers picked up third baseman Todd Zeile, shortstop Royce Clayton and righthander Todd Stottlemyre—who beat the Angels twice in September—Bavasi countered with veteran outfielder Gregg Jefferies.

But the season was far from a complete disappointment. Young first baseman-outfielder Darin Erstad broke through on the field and as a clubhouse leader in just his third major league season.

Third baseman Troy Glaus, the third overall pick of the 1997 draft, ascended to Anaheim in July after pausing in the minor leagues for four months—and 35 home runs. Glaus made his professional debut at Double-A Midland in 1998 after signing late the previous summer.

Erstad and Glaus were just the tip of the iceberg. In fact, the Angels were one of the rare clubs capable of fielding an entirely homegrown lineup in 1998: Todd Greene catching, Erstad at first, Justin Baughman at second, Glaus at third, Gary DiSarcina at shortstop and Garret Anderson, Jim Edmonds and Tim Salmon in the outfield. And Bavasi wisely signed several of the young core players to multiyear contracts at bargain prices.

The club's biggest need, pitching, was addressed in the '98 draft, when the Angels selected University of Southern California righthander Seth Etherton with their first-round pick.

Two Midland players who posted strong numbers were second baseman Keith Luuloa and first baseman Danny Buxbaum. Luuloa led the organization in several offensive categories, including average, total bases, runs and RBIs. Buxbaum hit .330 with 17 home runs for Midland.

Triple-A Vancouver experienced a disappointing season, as the club finished last in the 16-team Pacific Coast League. Just two Angels farm clubs finished above .500, with short-season Boise the lone team in the organization to advance to the postseason.

Boise ran through the Northwest League during the regular season at a .618 clip but fell to Salem-Keizer in two straight in the league's title series.

The organization was saddened in October by the passing of beloved owner Gene Autry. The Walt Disney Co., which assumed management control of the franchise in 1996, completed its purchase of the Angels after Autry's death.

Disney committed $200 million to buy the Angels and renovate Anaheim Stadium, and the remodeled and renamed Edison Field attracted 2.5 million fans in 1998, the club's highest total in eight years.

Darin Erstad

MEL BAILEY

Troy Glaus

Players of the Year

Major League: Darin Erstad, of
Erstad hit .296 with 19 homers and led the Angels with 20 steals while emerging as a young team leader.

Minor League: Troy Glaus, 3b, Vancouver/Midland
Anaheim's top prospect hit 35 home runs at Double-A Midland and Triple-A Vancouver before earning a call to the big leagues.

ORGANIZATION LEADERS

BATTING		
*AVG	Keith Luuloa, Vancouver/Midland	.334
R	Keith Luuloa, Vancouver/Midland	89
H	Keith Luuloa, Vancouver/Midland	170
TB	Keith Luuloa, Vancouver/Midland	285
2B	Keith Luuloa, Vancouver/Midland	44
3B	Three tied at	10
HR	Troy Glaus, Vancouver/Midland	35
RBI	Keith Luuloa, Vancouver/Midland	105
BB	Jeff Guiel, Lake Elsinore	83
SO	Jason Herrick, Vancouver/Midland	140
SB	Juan Tolentino, Cedar Rapids	49
PITCHING		
W	Mark Harriger, Lake Elsinore/Cedar Rapids	13
L	Tommy Darrell, Lake Elsinore/Cedar Rapids	15
#ERA	Steve Fish, Cedar Rapids	2.47
G	Scot Shields, Cedar Rapids	58
CG	Two tied at	6
SV	Anthony Chavez, Vancouver	22
IP	Mark Harriger, Lake Elsinore/Cedar Rapids	198
BB	Keith Volkman, Lake Elsinore/Cedar Rapids	76
SO	Mark Harriger, Lake Elsinore/Cedar Rapids	173

*Minimum 250 At-Bats #Minimum 75 Innings

Anaheim ANGELS

Manager: Terry Collins **1998 Record:** 85-77, .525 (2nd, AL West).

BATTING	AVG	G	AB	R	H	2B	3B	HR	RBI	BB	SO	SB	CS	B	T	HT	WT	DOB	1st Yr	Resides
Anderson, Garret	.294	156	622	62	183	41	7	15	79	29	80	8	3	L	L	6-3	190	6-30-72	1990	Granada Hills, Calif.
Baughman, Justin	.255	63	196	24	50	9	1	1	20	6	36	10	4	R	R	5-11	175	8-1-74	1995	Reno, Nev.
Bolick, Frank	.156	21	45	3	7	2	0	1	2	11	8	0	0	B	R	5-10	177	6-28-66	1987	Mount Carmel, Pa.
DiSarcina, Gary	.287	157	551	73	158	39	3	3	56	21	51	11	7	R	R	6-1	178	11-19-67	1988	Malden, Mass.
Edmonds, Jim	.307	154	599	115	184	42	1	25	91	57	114	7	5	L	L	6-1	190	6-27-70	1988	Diamond Bar, Calif.
Erstad, Darin	.296	133	537	84	159	39	3	19	82	43	77	20	6	L	L	6-2	195	6-4-74	1995	Jamestown, N.D.
Fielder, Cecil	.241	103	381	48	92	16	1	17	68	52	98	0	1	R	R	6-3	250	9-21-63	1982	Grosse Pointe Farms, Mich.
Garcia, Carlos	.143	19	35	4	5	1	0	0	0	3	11	2	0	R	R	6-1	193	10-15-67	1987	Lancaster, N.Y.
Glaus, Troy	.218	48	165	19	36	9	0	1	23	15	51	1	0	R	R	6-5	220	8-3-76	1997	Newport Beach, Calif.
Greene, Todd	.201	29	69	3	18	4	0	1	7	2	19	0	0	R	R	5-10	195	5-8-71	1993	Martinez, Ga.
Hollins, Dave	.242	101	363	60	88	16	2	11	39	44	69	11	3	B	R	6-1	207	5-25-66	1987	Orchard Park, N.Y.
Jefferies, Gregg	.347	19	72	7	25	6	0	1	10	0	5	1	0	B	R	5-10	185	8-1-67	1985	Pleasanton, Calif.
Johnson, Mark	.071	10	14	1	1	0	0	0	0	0	6	0	0	L	L	6-4	230	10-17-67	1990	Pittsburgh, Pa.
Kreuter, Chad	.143	3	7	1	1	1	0	0	0	1	4	0	0	B	R	6-2	200	8-26-64	1985	La Quinta, Calif.
2-team (93 Chicago)	.250	96	252	27	63	10	1	2	33	33	49	1	0							
Martin, Norberto	.215	79	195	20	42	2	0	1	13	6	29	3	1	B	R	5-10	164	12-10-66	1984	Hato Rey, P.R.
Mashore, Damon	.235	43	98	13	23	6	0	2	11	9	22	1	0	R	R	5-11	195	10-31-69	1991	Concord, Calif.
Molina, Ben	.000	1	0	0	0	0	0	0	0	0	0	0	0	R	R	5-11	190	7-20-74	1993	Vega Alta, P.R.
Nevin, Phil	.228	75	237	27	54	8	1	8	27	17	67	0	0	R	R	6-2	185	1-19-71	1992	Placentia, Calif.
O'Brien, Charlie	.182	5	11	1	2	0	0	0	0	1	2	0	0	R	R	6-2	205	5-1-61	1982	Tulsa, Okla.
2-team (57 Chicago)	.257	62	175	13	45	9	0	4	18	10	33	0	0							
Palmeiro, Orlando	.321	75	165	28	53	7	2	0	21	20	11	5	4	L	R	5-11	155	1-19-69	1991	Miami, Fla.
Pritchett, Chris	.288	31	80	12	23	2	1	2	8	4	16	2	0	L	R	6-4	185	1-31-70	1991	Modesto, Calif.
Salmon, Tim	.300	136	463	83	139	28	1	26	88	90	100	0	1	R	R	6-3	220	8-24-68	1989	Phoenix, Ariz.
Shipley, Craig	.259	77	147	18	38	7	1	2	17	5	22	0	4	R	R	6-0	168	1-7-63	1984	Jupiter, Fla.
Velarde, Randy	.261	51	188	29	49	13	1	4	26	34	42	7	2	R	R	6-0	185	11-24-62	1985	Midland, Texas
Walbeck, Matt	.257	108	338	41	87	15	2	6	46	30	68	1	1	B	R	5-11	188	10-2-69	1987	Sacramento, Calif.
Williams, Reggie	.342	29	38	7	13	1	0	1	5	7	12	3	3	B	R	6-1	180	5-5-66	1988	Laurens, S.C.

PITCHING	W	L	ERA	G	GS	CG	SV	IP	H	R	ER	BB	SO	B	T	HT	WT	DOB	1st Yr	Resides
Cadaret, Greg	1	2	4.14	39	0	0	1	37	38	17	17	15	37	L	L	6-3	215	2-27-62	1983	Mesa, Ariz.
DeLucia, Rich	2	6	4.27	61	0	0	3	72	56	36	34	46	73	R	R	6-0	185	10-7-64	1986	Shillington, Pa.
Dickson, Jason	10	10	6.05	27	18	0	0	122	147	89	82	41	61	L	R	6-0	190	3-30-73	1994	Chatham, N.B.
Fetters, Mike	1	2	5.56	12	0	0	0	11	14	8	7	4	9	R	R	6-4	226	12-19-64	1986	Gilbert, Ariz.
2-team (48 Oakland)	2	8	4.30	60	0	0	5	59	62	34	28	25	43							
Finley, Chuck	11	9	3.39	34	34	1	0	223	210	97	84	109	212	L	L	6-6	214	11-26-62	1985	Newport Beach, Calif.
Harris, Pep	3	1	4.35	49	0	0	0	60	55	32	29	23	34	R	R	6-2	235	9-23-72	1991	Lancaster, S.C.
Hasegawa, Shigetoshi	8	3	3.14	61	0	0	5	97	86	37	34	32	73	R	R	5-11	160	8-1-68	1997	Kobe, Japan
Hill, Ken	9	6	4.98	19	19	0	0	103	123	60	57	47	57	R	R	6-2	175	12-14-65	1985	Lynn, Mass.
Holtz, Mike	2	2	4.75	53	0	0	1	30	38	16	16	15	29	L	L	5-9	172	10-10-72	1994	Ebensburg, Ark.
James, Mike	0	0	1.93	11	0	0	0	14	10	3	3	7	12	R	R	6-3	180	8-15-67	1988	Mary Esther, Fla.
Juden, Jeff	1	3	6.75	8	6	0	0	40	33	32	30	18	39	B	R	6-8	265	1-19-71	1989	Salem, Mass.
McDowell, Jack	5	3	5.09	14	14	0	0	76	96	45	43	19	45	R	R	6-5	185	1-16-66	1987	Chicago, Ill.
Olivares, Omar	9	9	4.03	37	26	1	0	183	189	92	82	91	112	R	R	6-1	183	7-6-67	1987	San German, P.R.
Percival, Troy	2	7	3.65	67	0	0	42	67	45	31	27	37	87	R	R	6-3	200	8-9-69	1990	Moreno Valley, Calif.
Robertson, Rich	0	0	15.88	5	0	0	0	6	11	11	10	2	3	L	L	6-4	175	9-15-68	1990	Waller, Texas
Sparks, Steve	9	4	4.34	22	20	0	0	129	130	66	62	58	90	R	R	6-0	180	7-2-65	1987	Tulsa, Okla.
Washburn, Jarrod	6	3	4.62	15	11	0	0	74	70	40	38	27	48	L	L	6-1	185	8-13-74	1995	Webster, Wis.
Watson, Allen	6	7	6.04	28	14	1	0	92	122	67	62	34	64	L	L	6-3	195	11-18-70	1991	Middle Village, N.Y.
Wilson, Trevor	0	0	3.52	15	0	0	0	8	8	4	3	5	6	L	L	6-0	204	6-7-66	1985	Scottsdale, Ariz.

FIELDING

Catcher	PCT	G	PO	A	E	DP	PB
Kreuter	.882	3	14	1	2	0	0
Molina	1.000	2	1	0	0	0	0
Nevin	.989	69	399	32	5	3	20
O'Brien	1.000	5	20	2	0	0	0
Walbeck	.990	104	682	46	7	3	8

First Base	PCT	G	PO	A	E	DP
Erstad	.996	72	463	38	2	46
Fielder	.997	72	550	39	2	60
Greene	1.000	3	16	1	0	2
Hollins	.980	7	44	5	1	4
Jefferies	1.000	3	23	2	0	2
Johnson	1.000	5	13	1	0	2
Nevin	1.000	2	3	0	0	2
Pritchett	.995	29	190	20	1	12
Shipley	.968	8	27	3	1	3

Second Base	PCT	G	PO	A	E	DP
Baughman	.977	59	104	153	6	22
Garcia	.978	11	19	25	1	7
Martin	.983	54	88	138	4	31
Shipley	1.000	11	20	31	0	11
Velarde	.982	51	88	132	4	25

Third Base	PCT	G	PO	A	E	DP
Bolick	1.000	7	6	7	0	0
Glaus	.941	48	27	85	7	7
Hollins	.929	91	63	145	16	13
Martin	1.000	5	2	4	0	0
Shipley	.963	48	15	37	2	1

Shortstop	PCT	G	PO	A	E	DP
Baughman	.667	3	2	2	2	0
DiSarcina	.980	157	253	438	14	103
Garcia	1.000	5	5	8	0	2
Martin	1.000	2	1	2	0	0
Shipley	1.000	5	6	5	0	4

Outfield	PCT	G	PO	A	E	DP
Anderson	.983	155	326	11	6	3
Bolick	1.000	1	2	0	0	0
Edmonds	.988	153	389	10	5	1
Erstad	.992	72	116	4	1	2
Greene	1.000	12	12	0	0	0
Jefferies	1.000	15	25	0	0	0
Martin	1.000	5	2	0	0	0
Mashore	1.000	35	54	1	0	0
Palmeiro	1.000	54	92	0	0	0
Salmon	.958	19	45	1	2	0
Shipley	1.000	2	4	0	0	0
Williams	1.000	24	25	0	0	0

Anaheim's Jim Edmonds
Led club with 91 RBIs

LEE SCHMID

Midland's Danny Buxbaum
Batted .330 with 17 home runs

FARM SYSTEM

Director of Player Development: Jeff Parker

Class	Farm Team	League	W	L	Pct.	Finish*	Manager	First Yr
AAA	Vancouver (B.C.) Canadians	Pacific Coast	53	90	.371	16th (16)	Mitch Seoane	1993
AA	Midland (Texas) Angels	Texas	64	76	.457	7th (8)	Don Long	1985
A#	Lake Elsinore (Calif.) Storm	California	66	74	.471	t-7th (10)	Mario Mendoza	1994
A	Cedar Rapids (Iowa) Kernels	Midwest	71	69	.507	t-8th (14)	Garry Templeton	1993
A	Boise (Idaho) Hawks	Northwest	47	29	.618	t-1st (8)	Tom Kotchman	1989
Rookie#	Butte (Mont.) Copper Kings	Pioneer	26	50	.342	7th (8)	Bill Lachemann	1997

*Finish in overall standings (No. of teams in league) #Advanced level

VANCOUVER Class AAA

PACIFIC COAST LEAGUE

BATTING	AVG	G	AB	R	H	2B	3B	HR	RBI	BB	SO	SB	CS	B	T	HT	WT	DOB	1st Yr	Resides
Baughman, Justin	.297	54	222	35	66	10	4	0	15	13	28	26	8	R	R	5-11	175	8-1-74	1995	Reno, Nev.
Betten, Randy	.100	10	10	1	1	1	0	0	2	2	2	1	1	R	R	5-11	170	7-28-71	1995	Highland, Calif.
Bolick, Frank	.264	75	269	40	71	10	2	13	29	28	47	0	1	B	R	5-10	177	6-28-66	1987	Mount Carmel, Pa.
Burke, Jamie	.216	61	162	16	35	6	0	2	14	13	25	0	1	R	R	6-0	195	9-24-71	1993	Roseburg, Ore.
Buxbaum, Danny	.320	27	100	10	32	4	0	2	17	2	17	0	1	R	R	6-4	217	1-17-73	1995	Alachua, Fla.
Carvajal, Jovino	.267	115	389	47	104	20	5	6	34	20	72	20	11	B	R	6-1	160	9-2-68	1987	La Romana, D.R.
Cruz, Fausto	.262	117	420	47	110	26	6	4	43	28	76	7	4	R	R	5-11	165	1-5-72	1990	Villa Vasquez, D.R.
Encarnacion, Angelo	.240	8	25	3	6	2	0	0	2	0	2	0	1	R	R	5-8	180	4-18-73	1990	Santo Domingo, D.R.
Garcia, Carlos	.255	44	161	18	41	6	0	3	15	8	22	2	5	R	R	6-1	193	10-15-67	1987	Lancaster, N.Y.
Glaus, Troy	.306	59	219	33	67	16	0	16	42	21	55	3	2	R	R	6-5	220	8-3-76	1997	Newport Beach, Calif.
Greene, Todd	.278	30	108	16	30	12	0	7	20	12	17	1	0	R	R	5-10	195	5-8-71	1993	Martinez, Ga.
Helfand, Eric	.400	2	5	2	2	0	0	0	1	3	1	0	0	L	R	6-0	210	3-25-69	1990	San Diego, Calif.
Hemphill, Bret	.252	47	155	16	39	10	2	4	12	12	33	0	1	B	R	6-3	210	12-17-71	1994	Santa Clara, Calif.
Herrick, Jason	.217	59	207	17	45	8	3	6	19	4	65	0	4	L	L	6-0	175	7-29-73	1991	Franklin, Wis.
Hutchins, Norm	.207	7	29	4	6	0	0	1	3	2	9	1	2	L	L	6-2	185	11-20-75	1994	Greenburgh, N.Y.
Luuloa, Keith	.333	8	30	4	10	1	0	0	3	4	3	1	1	R	R	6-1	175	12-24-74	1994	Kaunakakai, Hawaii
Mashore, Damon	.273	42	143	19	39	7	0	2	15	18	28	1	1	R	R	5-11	195	10-31-69	1991	Concord, Calif.
Molina, Ben	.293	49	184	13	54	9	1	1	22	5	14	1	1	R	R	5-11	190	7-20-74	1993	Vega Alta, P.R.
Neel, Troy	.244	14	45	9	11	1	0	5	13	9	10	0	0	L	R	6-4	210	9-14-65	1986	El Campo, Texas
Nevers, Tom	.202	30	89	7	18	0	0	1	4	5	18	1	0	R	R	6-1	175	9-13-71	1990	Edina, Minn.
Norton, Chris	.209	43	148	14	31	11	0	5	17	18	46	0	0	R	R	6-2	215	9-21-70	1992	Maitland, Fla.
Palmeiro, Orlando	.300	43	140	21	42	13	3	1	29	16	10	3	1	L	R	5-11	155	1-19-69	1991	Miami, Fla.
Pritchett, Chris	.259	104	374	42	97	21	1	7	41	37	72	2	2	L	R	6-4	185	1-31-70	1991	Modesto, Calif.
Scarsone, Steve	.270	115	407	50	110	24	4	20	55	34	112	4	2	R	R	6-2	170	4-11-66	1986	Anaheim, Calif.

BATTING	AVG	G	AB	R	H	2B	3B	HR	RBI	BB	SO	SB	CS	B	T	HT	WT	DOB	1st Yr	Resides
Thurman, Gary	.220	58	182	24	40	6	2	1	16	20	42	8	1	R	R	5-10	180	11-12-64	1983	Indianapolis, Ind.
Thurston, Jerrey	.160	9	25	0	4	1	0	0	1	3	8	0	0	R	R	6-4	200	4-17-72	1990	Longwood, Fla.
Tinsley, Lee	.180	24	89	5	16	4	1	1	8	10	28	6	1	B	R	5-10	180	3-4-69	1987	Shelbyville, Ky.
Velarde, Randy	.250	4	16	0	4	2	0	0	2	1	4	1	1	R	R	6-0	185	11-24-62	1985	Midland, Texas
Williams, Reggie	.282	100	373	58	105	25	5	5	39	53	98	13	12	B	R	6-1	180	5-5-66	1988	Laurens, S.C.

PITCHING	W	L	ERA	G	GS	CG	SV	IP	H	R	ER	BB	SO	B	T	HT	WT	DOB	1st Yr	Resides
Alvarez, Juan	1	1	5.02	18	0	0	0	14	14	9	8	8	12	L	L	6-1	180	8-9-73	1995	Miami, Fla.
Bonanno, Rob	0	3	7.53	3	3	0	0	14	23	12	12	5	6	L	R	6-0	195	1-5-71	1994	Tampa, Fla.
Bovee, Mike	3	12	5.59	48	8	1	1	95	109	61	59	50	76	R	R	5-10	200	8-21-73	1991	Mira Mesa, Calif.
Brosnan, Jason	0	0	3.46	10	0	0	0	13	13	6	5	5	11	L	L	6-1	190	1-26-68	1989	San Leandro, Calif.
Butcher, Mike	1	4	4.91	37	1	0	0	59	71	37	32	33	50	R	R	6-1	200	5-10-65	1986	Phoenix, Ariz.
Cadaret, Greg	2	1	0.00	9	0	0	1	10	4	2	0	3	12	L	L	6-3	215	2-27-62	1983	Mesa, Ariz.
Chavez, Anthony	1	4	2.63	53	0	0	22	51	44	20	15	17	42	R	R	5-11	180	10-22-70	1992	Merced, Calif.
Dickson, Jason	2	1	1.78	4	4	0	0	25	26	5	5	4	18	L	R	6-0	190	3-30-73	1994	Chatham, N.B.
Edsell, Geoff	4	8	4.17	56	0	0	4	69	63	45	32	33	64	L	R	6-2	195	12-10-71	1993	Muncy, Pa.
Hanson, Erik	5	5	4.50	14	14	2	0	82	82	43	41	36	60	R	R	6-6	215	5-18-65	1986	Kirkland, Wash.
Harris, Pep	1	0	2.84	2	0	0	1	6	4	2	2	3	7	R	R	6-2	235	9-23-72	1991	Lancaster, S.C.
Holtz, Mike	0	0	1.74	10	0	0	2	10	10	4	2	6	18	L	L	5-9	172	10-10-72	1994	Ebensburg, Ark.
Jacobsen, Joe	0	0	2.70	2	0	0	0	3	3	1	1	0	0	R	R	6-3	225	12-26-71	1992	Clovis, Calif.
McDowell, Jack	0	0	6.00	1	1	0	0	3	4	2	2	2	0	R	R	6-5	185	1-16-66	1987	Chicago, Ill.
Mimbs, Mike	1	1	4.70	19	0	0	0	23	25	12	12	14	18	L	L	6-2	188	2-13-69	1990	Macon, Ga.
Robertson, Rich	11	12	3.81	27	27	2	0	175	171	85	74	68	123	L	L	6-4	175	9-15-68	1990	Waller, Texas
Schmidt, Jeff	0	1	6.60	18	0	0	0	30	47	31	22	11	16	R	R	6-5	210	2-21-71	1992	La Crosse, Wis.
Schoeneweis, Scott	11	8	4.50	27	27	2	0	180	188	102	90	59	133	L	L	6-0	180	10-2-73	1996	Mount Laurel, N.J.
Sparks, Steve	0	4	2.89	4	4	2	0	28	23	11	9	6	19	R	R	6-0	180	7-2-65	1987	Tulsa, Okla.
Vanlandingham, William	0	6	11.23	9	8	0	0	34	48	46	42	44	12	R	R	6-2	210	7-16-70	1991	Franklin, Tenn.
Washburn, Jarrod	4	5	4.32	14	14	2	0	92	91	44	44	43	66	L	L	6-1	185	8-13-74	1995	Webster, Wis.
Watson, Allen	0	1	4.50	1	1	0	0	6	6	3	3	2	8	L	L	6-3	195	11-18-70	1991	Middle Village, N.Y.
Williams, Shad	1	4	3.18	14	10	1	0	68	65	30	24	18	29	R	R	6-0	198	3-10-71	1991	Fresno, Calif.
Wilson, Trevor	5	9	3.62	21	21	4	0	142	130	67	57	59	94	L	L	6-0	204	6-7-66	1985	Scottsdale, Ariz.

FIELDING

Catcher	PCT	G	PO	A	E	DP	PB
Burke	.993	51	264	18	2	2	8
Encarnacion	.977	8	39	3	1	0	0
Greene	1.000	4	15	1	0	2	0
Helfand	1.000	2	4	1	0	0	0
Hemphill	.988	40	236	15	3	5	3
Molina	.986	44	316	24	5	2	1
Thurston	1.000	9	52	0	0	0	1

First Base	PCT	G	PO	A	E	DP
Betten	1.000	2	6	0	0	1
Bolick	.927	4	35	3	3	2
Burke	.857	1	6	0	1	1
Buxbaum	1.000	23	180	11	0	27
Greene	.988	9	75	5	1	7
Neel	.992	13	106	12	1	14
Norton	1.000	5	33	2	0	5
Pritchett	.988	88	739	55	10	80
Scarsone	1.000	1	12	0	0	1

Second Base	PCT	G	PO	A	E	DP
Baughman	.985	46	124	140	4	41
Betten	.800	1	3	1	1	1
Cruz	.974	19	31	43	2	10
Garcia	.929	4	7	6	1	1
Luuloa	1.000	6	16	17	0	9
Nevers	.944	9	11	23	2	3
Scarsone	.907	60	110	144	9	38
Velarde	1.000	3	3	7	0	0
Williams	1.000	2	1	4	0	1

Third Base	PCT	G	PO	A	E	DP
Bolick	.970	29	21	76	3	9
Burke	.950	9	8	30	2	7
Glaus	.932	58	46	131	13	12
Luuloa	1.000	1	1	5	0	0
Nevers	.741	8	2	18	7	2
Scarsone	.912	42	22	92	11	9

Shortstop	PCT	G	PO	A	E	DP
Baughman	.950	8	12	26	2	6
Betten	1.000	1	2	2	0	0
Cruz	.964	84	123	252	14	57
Garcia	.949	39	71	97	9	25
Luuloa	1.000	1	1	0	0	0
Nevers	.929	14	19	33	4	11

Outfield	PCT	G	PO	A	E	DP
Betten	1.000	3	5	1	0	0
Bolick	.929	14	26	0	2	0
Carvajal	.982	103	214	7	4	2
Cruz	.972	13	32	3	1	1
Greene	1.000	4	7	1	0	0
Herrick	.991	57	102	4	1	1
Hutchins	1.000	7	12	0	0	0
Mashore	.985	37	62	4	1	2
Palmeiro	1.000	39	70	4	0	1
Scarsone	1.000	1	1	0	0	0
Thurman	.977	50	82	3	2	1
Tinsley	.977	22	39	3	1	0
Williams	.991	95	220	9	2	2

MIDLAND — Class AA

TEXAS LEAGUE

BATTING	AVG	G	AB	R	H	2B	3B	HR	RBI	BB	SO	SB	CS	B	T	HT	WT	DOB	1st Yr	Resides
Abbott, Chuck	.263	132	525	74	138	21	9	2	62	38	135	16	9	B	R	6-1	180	1-26-75	1996	Schaumburg, Ill.
Barnes, Larry	.273	69	245	29	67	16	4	6	35	28	54	4	2	L	L	6-1	195	7-23-74	1995	Bakersfield, Calif.
Betten, Randy	.230	76	209	30	48	16	2	2	19	18	50	3	2	R	R	5-11	170	7-28-71	1995	Highland, Calif.
Burke, Jamie	.244	12	41	7	10	1	0	0	4	7	4	0	0	R	R	6-0	195	9-24-71	1993	Roseburg, Ore.
Buxbaum, Danny	.330	76	297	58	98	19	2	17	53	28	33	1	1	R	R	6-4	217	1-17-73	1995	Alachua, Fla.
Christian, Eddie	.333	105	400	80	133	39	4	5	49	49	61	13	11	B	L	5-11	180	8-26-71	1992	Richmond, Calif.
Curtis, Matt	.262	113	431	53	113	19	5	10	65	33	72	2	2	B	R	6-0	195	8-14-74	1996	Visalia, Calif.
Dalton, Jed	.295	80	258	43	76	11	2	4	34	38	48	7	5	R	R	6-1	190	4-3-73	1995	Omaha, Neb.
Diaz, Freddie	.182	4	11	3	2	0	0	0	2	3	4	0	0	B	R	5-11	190	9-10-72	1992	El Monte, Calif.
Durrington, Trent	.225	112	351	62	79	10	1	1	30	50	74	24	12	B	R	5-10	185	8-27-75	1994	Broadbeach Waters, Australia
Encarnacion, Angelo	.215	28	93	9	20	1	0	2	7	8	11	0	0	R	R	5-8	180	4-18-73	1990	Santo Domingo, D.R.
Glaus, Troy	.309	50	188	51	58	11	2	19	51	39	41	4	2	R	R	6-5	220	8-3-76	1997	Newport Beach, Calif.
Graves, Bryan	.224	29	85	8	19	3	0	1	6	16	18	0	1	R	R	6-0	215	10-8-74	1995	Bogalusa, La.
Herrick, Jason	.332	71	274	61	91	20	7	18	73	20	75	5	5	L	L	6-0	175	7-29-73	1991	Franklin, Wis.
Hutchins, Norm	.312	89	394	74	123	20	10	10	50	14	84	32	10	L	L	6-2	185	11-20-75	1994	Greenburgh, N.Y.
Luuloa, Keith	.334	130	479	85	160	43	10	17	102	75	54	6	5	R	R	6-1	175	12-24-74	1994	Kaunakakai, Hawaii
Molina, Ben	.357	41	154	28	55	8	0	9	39	14	7	0	1	R	R	5-11	190	7-20-74	1993	Vega Alta, P.R.
Morris, Greg	.274	31	106	13	29	6	1	2	12	22	14	1	0	R	R	6-4	210	1-29-72	1994	Concord, Calif.
Norton, Chris	.317	17	60	10	19	1	0	4	12	9	23	0	0	R	R	6-2	215	9-21-70	1992	Maitland, Fla.
O'Brien, Charlie	.118	5	17	1	2	0	0	0	2	2	4	1	0	R	R	6-2	205	5-1-61	1982	Tulsa, Okla.
Sturdivant, Marcus	.250	17	68	7	17	5	0	0	8	2	8	2	1	L	L	5-10	150	10-29-73	1992	Oakboro, N.C.
Thurston, Jerrey	.316	29	95	20	30	4	0	2	22	8	24	0	0	R	R	6-4	200	4-17-72	1990	Longwood, Fla.
Tinsley, Lee	.262	11	42	2	11	4	1	0	5	2	7	3	1	B	R	5-10	180	3-4-69	1987	Shelbyville, Ky.
Vallone, Gar	.167	2	6	0	1	0	0	0	0	0	2	0	0	B	R	6-0	190	5-9-73	1995	Placentia, Calif.
Wooten, Shawn	.321	8	28	3	9	4	0	1	6	3	4	0	0	R	R	5-11	205	7-24-72	1993	La Verne, Calif.

Place
postage
here

Baseball America
P.O. Box 2089
Durham, N.C. 27702

PITCHING	W	L	ERA	G	GS	CG	SV	IP	H	R	ER	BB	SO	B	T	HT	WT	DOB	1st Yr	Resides
Greene, Danny	1	0	2.19	11	0	0	6	12	9	3	3	1	22	R	R	6-3	220	2-24-73	1996	Nashua, N.H.
Harriger, Mark	5	5	4.09	13	12	3	0	81	86	43	37	23	68	R	R	6-2	196	4-29-75	1996	Lakewood, Calif.
Harris, Pep	0	1	0.00	4	1	0	0	9	9	5	0	2	12	R	R	6-2	235	9-23-72	1991	Lancaster, S.C.
Hill, Ken	0	0	6.75	1	1	0	0	4	5	4	3	5	2	R	R	6-2	175	12-14-65	1985	Lynn, Mass.
Johnson, Greg	3	3	4.28	37	1	0	0	76	78	40	36	23	63	L	L	6-0	185	4-28-74	1996	Frostburg, Md.
Leyva, Edgar	8	5	4.76	33	13	0	2	121	125	72	64	48	99	R	R	6-1	215	7-27-77	1995	Guasave, Mexico
McDowell, Jack	0	1	9.00	1	1	0	0	5	7	5	5	0	4	R	R	6-5	185	1-16-66	1987	Chicago, Ill.
Nickle, Doug	3	4	4.48	11	10	1	0	66	68	40	33	25	69	R	R	6-4	210	10-2-74	1997	Sonoma, Calif.
Perozo, Felix	0	1	2.25	10	0	0	2	12	11	4	3	6	12	R	R	6-6	192	3-24-74	1991	Santo Domingo, D.R.
Stephens, Jason	7	6	4.10	35	13	1	0	123	128	72	56	47	89	R	R	6-0	180	9-10-75	1996	Springhill, La.
Stockstill, Jason	8	5	4.41	25	16	1	0	100	111	65	49	45	77	L	L	6-5	215	11-13-76	1995	Anaheim, Calif.
Tokarse, Brian	9	9	5.74	22	22	2	0	125	150	93	80	42	97	R	R	6-3	180	2-28-75	1997	Whittier, Calif.
Volkman, Keith	1	0	6.02	20	2	0	0	43	46	40	29	41	34	L	L	6-2	215	1-13-76	1994	Pasadena, Md.
Watson, Allen	1	0	0.00	1	1	0	0	5	3	0	0	1	6	L	L	6-3	195	11-18-70	1991	Middle Village, N.Y.

CEDAR RAPIDS — Class A

MIDWEST LEAGUE

BATTING	AVG	G	AB	R	H	2B	3B	HR	RBI	BB	SO	SB	CS	B	T	HT	WT	DOB	1st Yr	Resides
Arguelles, Rudy	.198	28	86	12	17	1	1	0	4	12	15	4	1	B	R	5-9	170	1-14-72	1998	Corona, Calif.
Betancourt, Oscar	.206	92	339	33	70	13	0	3	32	26	62	1	2	R	R	6-1	200	7-9-75	1997	San Diego, Calif.
Brewer, Brad	.188	28	69	12	13	0	0	1	8	11	18	0	0	R	R	5-10	170	11-19-75	1997	Fairfield, Calif.
Child, Casey	.201	51	179	14	36	3	1	2	16	9	34	5	5	R	R	6-2	185	2-11-76	1997	Orem, Utah
Colangelo, Mike	.277	22	83	13	23	8	0	4	8	12	16	5	1	R	R	6-1	185	10-22-76	1997	Dumfries, Va.
Delgado, Ariel	.234	133	509	54	119	25	4	5	67	40	105	24	13	L	L	6-2	205	9-11-76	1994	Carolina, P.R.
Diaz, Angel	.333	5	15	2	5	0	0	2	3	3	7	0	0	R	R	6-0	198	7-27-76	1998	Lakeland, Fla.
Dougherty, Jeb	.252	107	425	62	107	12	3	2	42	26	69	40	8	R	R	6-0	180	7-16-75	1997	Yucca Valley, Calif.
Garrick, Matt	.245	61	212	27	52	13	0	4	25	29	55	5	1	R	R	6-0	185	8-19-75	1997	Duncanville, Texas
Johnson, Patrick	.230	47	148	16	34	4	0	2	20	21	26	2	3	R	R	6-3	200	4-18-75	1996	Taylorsville, Utah
Knight, Marcus	.239	97	364	38	87	19	1	8	51	24	59	5	6	B	R	5-11	195	9-10-78	1996	Pembroke Pines, Fla.
Lawrence, Mike	.250	75	248	31	62	12	0	2	25	25	57	1	2	R	R	6-5	200	2-18-76	1995	Chico, Calif.
Leggett, Adam	.273	125	443	83	121	26	3	11	50	80	83	24	14	B	R	6-0	190	4-3-76	1997	Longview, Texas
Martin, Casey	.247	97	336	40	83	18	1	10	46	36	97	3	2	R	R	6-2	220	12-24-75	1997	Lakewood, Calif.
Medosch, Keith	.208	71	178	19	37	9	3	1	14	30	37	1	6	R	R	5-11	175	1-31-75	1997	St. Petersburg, Fla.
Philip-Guide, Sheldon	.140	13	43	5	6	0	0	0	2	2	15	0	0	R	R	6-0	208	2-17-74	1997	Santa Monica, Calif.
Serrano, Danny	.265	9	34	3	9	2	0	1	2	2	8	0	0	B	R	5-10	190	2-16-75	1996	Arecibo, P.R.
Stewart, Paxton	.200	9	30	4	6	2	0	0	2	4	4	4	1	L	R	6-3	185	5-4-74	1995	New York, N.Y.
t'Hoen, E.J.	.218	130	441	57	96	22	1	18	55	50	129	10	5	R	R	6-2	184	11-8-75	1996	Alphen Aan Denryn, Netherlands
Tolentino, Juan	.261	133	495	82	129	27	6	11	57	51	135	49	25	R	R	5-11	175	3-12-76	1995	Bronx, N.Y.

GAMES BY POSITION: C—Diaz 1, Garrick 59, Johnson 44, Martin 40, Serrano 4. **1B**—Delgado 128, Martin 18. **2B**—Brewer 9, Leggett 123, Medosch 14. **3B**—Betancourt 88, Lawrence 55, Medosch 2. **SS**—Brewer 16, Medosch 6, t'Hoen 127. **OF**—Arguelles 28, Child 50, Colangelo 17, Delgado 5, Dougherty 105, Knight 32, Martin 1, Medosch 47, Philip-Guide 11, Stewart 6, Tolentino 132.

PITCHING	W	L	ERA	G	GS	CG	SV	IP	H	R	ER	BB	SO	B	T	HT	WT	DOB	1st Yr	Resides
Dane, Jaymie	1	2	3.75	19	0	0	0	24	21	15	10	12	18	R	L	5-11	170	2-19-75	1997	Scottsdale, Ariz.
Cowsill, Brendon	7	3	2.88	17	12	2	1	91	79	35	29	29	61	R	R	6-3	190	1-7-75	1994	Pasadena, Calif.
Darrell, Tommy	3	4	4.05	9	9	3	0	67	68	35	30	17	44	R	R	6-6	220	7-21-76	1995	Dunbar, Pa.
Dobson, Dwayne	4	7	3.40	23	14	1	0	101	87	43	38	30	67	R	R	6-5	205	2-23-76	1997	Clearwater, Fla.
Duarte, Renney	3	1	0.56	4	4	2	0	32	17	7	2	1	28	R	R	6-0	185	11-7-78	1996	Maracaibo, Ven.
Fish, Steve	10	4	2.47	30	14	3	0	128	111	52	35	28	121	R	R	6-1	190	10-25-74	1997	Bend, Ore.
Green, Steve	2	6	4.54	18	10	1	0	83	86	49	42	25	61	R	R	6-2	180	1-26-78	1997	Longueuil, Quebec
Harriger, Mark	8	4	2.23	16	16	3	0	117	86	37	29	38	105	R	R	6-2	196	4-29-75	1996	Lakewood, Calif.
Hill, Ken	0	0	1.23	2	2	0	0	7	7	1	1	1	6	R	R	6-2	175	12-14-65	1985	Lynn, Mass.
Lubozynski, Matt	2	0	2.53	19	0	0	1	21	17	10	6	5	12	L	L	6-3	180	11-9-76	1998	San Antonio, Texas
McGuire, Brandon	0	2	6.75	5	2	0	0	12	18	13	9	6	8	B	R	6-4	220	8-10-77	1995	Big Spring, Texas
Miller, Ernie	3	2	3.74	8	8	0	0	43	49	24	18	9	25	L	L	6-5	195	7-19-75	1997	Jackson Heights, N.Y.
Nickle, Doug	8	4	3.78	20	7	1	0	69	66	30	29	20	59	R	R	6-4	210	10-2-74	1997	Sonoma, Calif.
Perozo, Felix	0	3	2.52	26	0	0	16	25	16	10	7	12	23	R	R	6-6	192	3-24-74	1991	Santo Domingo, D.R.
Porter, Aaron	0	0	8.80	22	0	0	0	31	40	30	30	16	21	R	R	6-1	185	2-3-75	1997	Sacramento, Calif.
Ricks, Ron	1	2	3.00	12	4	0	0	36	34	13	12	10	29	R	R	6-5	225	3-23-75	1997	Tallahassee, Fla.
Rodriguez, Hector	3	1	2.57	33	0	0	1	56	32	23	16	31	75	R	R	6-2	225	3-21-75	1996	Caguas, P.R.
Shields, Scot	6	5	3.65	58	0	0	7	74	62	33	30	29	81	R	R	6-1	175	7-22-75	1997	Fort Lauderdale, Fla.
Timmerman, Heath	7	13	4.30	27	27	4	0	161	170	100	77	61	132	R	R	6-2	190	8-29-77	1997	Skiatook, Okla.
Volkman, Keith	3	6	4.92	11	11	1	0	64	66	46	35	35	57	L	L	6-2	215	1-13-76	1994	Pasadena, Md.

BOISE — Short-Season Class A

NORTHWEST LEAGUE

BATTING	AVG	G	AB	R	H	2B	3B	HR	RBI	BB	SO	SB	CS	B	T	HT	WT	DOB	1st Yr	Resides
Blakely, Darren	.277	71	267	50	74	9	6	5	33	34	69	9	3	B	R	6-0	190	3-14-77	1998	Honolulu, Hawaii
Child, Casey	.214	74	280	37	60	10	1	8	36	24	61	7	5	R	R	6-2	185	2-11-76	1997	Orem, Utah
Christensen, Mike	.262	70	286	47	75	22	0	9	47	18	63	1	0	R	R	6-2	190	5-24-76	1998	Fort Myers, Fla.
Condon, Mike	.234	33	94	19	22	7	0	1	11	16	15	0	1	R	R	5-10	180	2-13-74	1997	Brielle, N.J.
Croud, Will	.243	65	255	52	62	13	2	2	23	46	48	17	6	B	R	5-11	170	12-29-75	1998	Miramar, Fla.
Diaz, Angel	.200	3	10	3	2	0	0	1	1	3	4	0	1	R	R	6-0	198	7-27-76	1998	Lakeland, Fla.
Diaz, Michael	.221	32	86	20	19	2	1	0	11	16	16	4	2	L	L	5-10	160	8-5-76	1998	Tampa, Fla.
Fox, Brian	.246	24	61	9	15	3	1	3	14	12	11	0	0	L	R	6-2	200	3-5-77	1997	Lubbock, Texas
Hill, Jason	.261	57	203	30	53	17	0	7	39	22	45	1	0	R	R	6-3	210	3-17-77	1998	Danville, Calif.
Hood, Jay	.197	41	132	20	26	6	0	3	19	23	22	1	1	R	R	6-0	185	3-8-77	1998	Germantown, Tenn.
Huisman, Jason	.325	73	292	47	95	20	2	5	59	27	52	5	0	R	R	6-3	196	4-16-76	1998	Palos Heights, Ill.
Kelley, Casey	.224	55	161	31	36	13	0	7	37	32	64	1	0	L	R	6-2	220	11-4-76	1998	Ellensburg, Wash.
Mott, Bill	.304	63	207	54	63	11	0	7	37	48	41	21	1	L	R	6-1	180	1-2-76	1998	San Luis Obispo, Calif.
O'Neil, John	.220	20	41	4	9	2	0	0	3	1	7	0	0	R	R	6-0	205	8-30-75	1998	Middleburg, Fla.

BATTING	AVG	G	AB	R	H	2B	3B	HR	RBI	BB	SO	SB	CS	B	T	HT	WT	DOB	1st Yr	Resides
Oliver, Brian	.259	17	54	6	14	3	1	0	5	8	6	0	1	R	R	5-10	170	11-7-76	1998	Antioch, Calif.
Oliver, William	.289	43	121	23	35	7	0	8	27	14	46	0	1	R	R	6-2	205	5-27-75	1998	San Jose, Calif.
Schwieder, Nicholas	.000	1	0	1	0	0	0	0	0	1	0	0	0	R	R	6-2	190	11-18-75	1998	Wildwood, Mo.
Wade, Bryn	.234	14	47	6	11	4	0	1	3	3	16	1	0	R	R	6-1	195	7-1-75	1998	Newbury Park, Calif.

GAMES BY POSITION: C—A. Diaz 3, Fox 23, Hill 49, O'Neil 18, Schwieder 1. **1B**—Condon 1, M. Diaz 1, Fox 2, Huisman 1, Kelley 54, W. Oliver 36. **2B**—Condon 31, Hood 3, Huisman 37, B. Oliver 3, Wade 14. **3B**—Christensen 67, Huisman 9. **SS**—Condon 1, Hood 37, Huisman 27, B. Oliver 15. **OF**—Blakely 70, Child 74, Croud 64, M. Diaz 29, Mott 1.

PITCHING	W	L	ERA	G	GS	CG	SV	IP	H	R	ER	BB	SO	B	T	HT	WT	DOB	1st Yr	Resides
Bond, Tommy	6	6	4.71	15	15	0	0	80	99	57	42	14	57	R	R	6-4	200	3-2-76	1998	Ocala, Fla.
Bridges, Doug	6	2	2.98	15	15	0	0	82	73	37	27	35	63	L	L	6-2	185	7-20-76	1998	Columbia, S.C.
Brunet, Michael	0	0	10.80	4	0	0	0	3	4	4	4	3	4	R	R	6-2	165	3-5-77	1997	Land O'Lakes, Fla.
Demouy, Chris	5	1	1.54	20	0	0	9	23	11	5	4	11	29	R	L	6-1	205	11-3-75	1998	Baton Rouge, La.
Emanuel, Brandon	4	5	4.59	15	15	0	0	80	96	59	41	21	42	R	R	6-3	215	4-9-76	1998	Panama City, Fla.
Gilich, Denny	1	1	3.24	13	0	0	1	17	11	9	6	9	27	R	R	6-7	210	8-21-75	1998	Gig Harbor, Wash.
Harwas, Oliver	1	3	3.16	20	1	0	0	37	42	19	13	12	29	R	R	6-3	210	8-7-75	1998	Okeechobee, Fla.
Hundley, Jeff	8	3	3.40	16	16	0	0	93	77	42	35	27	89	L	L	6-2	205	2-19-77	1998	Warren, Ohio
Jacobs, Greg	3	2	4.24	25	0	0	0	23	23	16	11	20	16	L	L	5-10	180	10-9-76	1998	Anaheim Hills, Calif.
Jones, Greg	0	2	4.93	22	0	0	1	35	37	22	19	13	28	R	R	6-2	190	11-15-76	1997	Seminole, Fla.
Leach, Mike	4	2	4.50	15	14	1	0	70	79	49	35	26	45	R	R	6-3	205	2-21-76	1998	Seminole, Fla.
Lubozynski, Matt	2	1	1.63	9	0	0	1	28	17	5	5	7	21	L	L	6-3	180	11-9-76	1998	San Antonio, Texas
McGuire, Brandon	0	0	5.27	8	0	0	0	14	13	9	8	9	6	B	R	6-4	220	8-10-77	1995	Big Spring, Texas
Morrison, Cody	5	1	1.78	30	0	0	6	35	25	10	7	16	40	R	R	6-2	200	9-26-74	1998	Kelso, Wash.
Romero, John	0	0	5.93	10	0	0	0	14	24	12	9	6	8	R	R	6-2	175	9-1-75	1995	Sylmar, Calif.
Suarez, Luis	0	0	3.86	11	0	0	1	16	15	7	7	3	18	R	R	6-2	180	3-12-76	1998	Sunrise, Fla.
Williams, Kris	2	0	5.52	10	0	0	0	15	19	9	9	5	12	R	R	6-0	195	9-28-76	1997	Westfield, N.J.

BUTTE — Rookie

PIONEER LEAGUE

BATTING	AVG	G	AB	R	H	2B	3B	HR	RBI	BB	SO	SB	CS	B	T	HT	WT	DOB	1st Yr	Resides
Ahlers, Steve	.205	61	215	35	44	7	0	0	25	33	37	6	1	R	R	6-0	175	11-18-78	1997	Livermore, Calif.
Arballo, Carlos	.000	5	10	1	0	0	0	0	0	1	7	0	0	L	R	5-11	188	10-12-74	1997	Mexicali, Mexico
Bast, Ryan	.222	15	36	9	8	2	2	0	1	4	12	6	0	R	R	5-10	160	11-25-78	1998	Auburn, Calif.
Corley, Kenny	.300	63	213	40	64	17	1	5	47	40	36	3	2	R	R	6-2	185	3-30-76	1998	Phoenix, Ariz.
Diaz, Angel	.306	50	160	38	49	10	3	6	33	28	36	0	1	R	R	6-0	198	7-27-76	1998	Lakeland, Fla.
Downing, Brad	.302	70	235	38	71	15	1	5	42	50	55	1	1	L	R	6-0	200	5-10-76	1998	Celina, Texas
Encarnacion, Bienvenido	.313	69	291	46	91	10	2	5	44	27	40	13	6	B	R	5-11	165	2-24-78	1995	Nizao, D.R.
Guzman, Elpidio	.331	69	299	70	99	16	5	9	61	24	44	40	9	L	L	6-2	166	2-24-79	1996	Santo Domingo, D.R.
Lombardi, Dominick	.219	43	96	19	21	0	0	1	10	37	18	0	0	R	R	5-10	205	3-10-76	1998	Mission Viejo, Calif.
Nizov, Alexander	.207	33	92	15	19	6	1	0	9	6	15	5	0	R	R	6-0	162	7-12-74	1996	Novgorod, Russia
Nolasco, Jose	.167	16	36	7	6	2	0	1	4	4	16	0	0	R	R	6-2	190	8-17-79	1997	Chihuahua, Mexico
Peckham, Chris	.229	65	205	36	47	10	5	5	27	39	39	4	1	R	R	5-10	195	9-17-75	1997	West Bridgewater, Mass.
Pichardo, Gilbert	.154	24	52	9	8	2	0	0	8	7	21	0	0	R	R	6-1	195	1-8-79	1997	Brooklyn, N.Y.
Ross, Justin	.309	65	220	53	68	13	4	1	42	81	31	7	2	L	L	6-2	193	12-24-76	1998	Wexford, Pa.
Santos, Jose	.262	37	130	26	34	9	4	4	21	15	41	0	0	R	R	6-1	200	5-12-77	1995	San Pedro de Macoris, D.R.
Tena, Luis	.194	14	36	7	7	1	0	0	0	8	15	0	0	R	R	5-10	155	10-19-78	1997	Cuauhtemoc, Mexico
Wade, Bryn	.202	26	89	11	18	2	1	1	15	11	30	0	1	R	R	6-1	195	7-1-75	1998	Newbury Park, Calif.
Yount, Jason	.237	40	135	20	32	2	0	2	16	15	35	2	1	R	R	6-2	220	3-22-77	1998	Milpitas, Calif.

GAMES BY POSITION: C—Diaz 39, Lombardi 43, Nolasco 13, Santos 3. **1B**—Corley 42, Nolasco 3, Yount 35. **2B**—Ahlers 37, Bast 6, Encarnacion 3, Nizov 27, Tena 5, Wade 9. **3B**—Ahlers 19, Bast 3, Corley 16, Nizov 1, Peckham 24, Santos 5, Tena 4, Wade 14. **SS**—Ahlers 8, Bast 2, Encarnacion 65, Tena 4. **OF**—Arballo 3, Downing 30, Encarnacion 1, Guzman 69, Nizov 2, Peckham 41, Pichardo 21, Ross 65, Santos 10, Yount 2.

PITCHING	W	L	ERA	G	GS	CG	SV	IP	H	R	ER	BB	SO	B	T	HT	WT	DOB	1st Yr	Resides
Anderson, Jason	1	1	7.76	23	0	0	0	29	30	27	25	27	33	R	R	6-3	215	5-16-75	1997	Clark Lake, Mich.
Aronson, Christopher	2	1	10.80	8	0	0	0	10	18	21	12	4	9	R	R	6-0	185	9-3-75	1998	Milford, Conn.
Berryman, Chad	0	4	12.10	11	8	0	0	39	85	63	52	15	24	R	R	6-3	190	8-2-76	1998	Kannapolis, N.C.
Brooks, Jacob	2	7	7.08	28	3	0	4	55	64	53	43	39	63	R	R	6-1	175	3-23-78	1998	Largo, Fla.
Callier, Jeremy	3	9	3.54	19	11	2	0	102	102	51	40	26	78	R	R	6-0	195	11-18-75	1998	Ballwin, Mo.
Easton, Eric	0	0	9.27	14	0	0	0	22	42	28	23	20	16	R	R	6-7	210	3-6-79	1998	Tarpon Springs, Fla.
Elias, Javier	0	0	18.56	4	0	0	0	5	13	11	11	1	4	R	R	6-0	177	2-21-79	1997	Mexicali, Mexico
Figueroa, Claudio	0	0	9.00	7	0	0	0	11	21	13	11	5	7	R	R	5-11	200	11-2-78	1997	San Luis Rio Colorado, Mexico
Harris, John	1	0	8.16	16	0	0	0	29	35	27	26	9	22	R	R	5-11	165	6-29-76	1998	San Jose, Calif.
Harris, Julian	2	7	7.69	16	13	0	0	62	77	61	53	57	39	L	L	6-3	175	9-26-77	1998	San Jose, Calif.
Hurtado, Ed	2	3	9.73	27	0	0	6	29	41	40	31	24	24	R	R	6-1	200	9-29-76	1998	Corona, Calif.
McClain, Kevin	0	2	24.00	8	5	0	0	12	23	33	32	21	12	R	R	6-4	180	2-22-78	1998	Palm Bay, Fla.
Ozuna, Adrian	3	4	9.30	16	16	0	0	61	94	75	63	41	63	R	R	5-11	160	7-27-80	1997	Mazatlan, Mexico
Padilla, Charly	1	6	7.97	19	6	0	0	50	71	60	44	23	46	R	R	6-4	180	9-11-78	1996	Urachiche, Ven.
Salter, Cody	4	2	3.51	9	5	3	0	49	48	21	19	10	31	R	R	6-4	200	10-8-75	1998	Plainfield, Ill.
Wakefield, Doug	1	1	7.42	15	1	0	0	30	47	33	25	21	23	R	L	6-7	240	8-17-76	1998	Apple Valley, Calif.
Williams, Kris	4	3	5.51	9	8	0	0	47	64	36	29	9	40	R	R	6-0	195	9-28-76	1997	Westfield, N.J.

ARIZONA DIAMONDBACKS

Expansion franchise can build on solid first-year showing

BY JACK MAGRUDER

The Diamondbacks were not the best expansion team in history. They were hardly the worst. They spent their inaugural season proving what baseball folks already knew—a $30 million payroll can buy an 80-home-run infield and a record-setting righthander, but building an infrastructure takes time.

The Diamondbacks, 65-97, were the fourth-winningest team among the 14 expansion franchises since 1961, and pleased themsevles by getting better as the 1998 season went along. They were 57-66 after a disastrous first six weeks.

The turnaround began during a homestand in mid-May when several key pieces were discovered—righthander Gregg Olson became the closer and handyman Andy Fox stepped into the leadoff spot in the batting order. From then on, the Diamondbacks were respectable.

Olson was hardly the only pither to excel. Righthander Andy Benes tied Tampa Bay righthander Rolando Arrojo for the most victories by a pitcher on an expansion team, 14, and ended the season with a streak of 27⅓ scoreless innings.

Lefthander Brian Anderson, Arizona's first pick in the expansion draft, won 12 games, giving the Diamondbacks the winningest tandem in expansion history. Lefthander Omar Daal finished fifth in the NL ERA race at 2.88.

Center fielder Devon White had arguably the best of his 13 major league seasons, hitting .279 with 22 homers, 85 RBIs and 22 stolen bases.

Every starting infielder had at least 18 homers, something no other team in the NL could say. Third baseman Matt Williams had 20 for the ninth straight season, while rookie first baseman Travis Lee did it for the first time. Both Lee and Williams had more than 100 strikeouts as the D'backs set a league record with 1,239.

Jay Bell, who signed a five-year, $34 million contract the day before the expansion draft, switched positions with Tony Batista in September, moving to second base while Batista took over at short. The move appears permanent, if Batista can hold off prospect Danny Klassen in the spring.

Playing in state-of-the-art Bank One Ballpark with its retractable dome, the Diamondbacks drew 3,602,856, second to Colorado (1993) among expansion entries. Only four franchises—the Rockies, Blue Jays, Orioles and Dodgers—have ever drawn more.

The organization made significant strides in the lower levels of the minor leagues, where both Class A High Desert and Rookie-level Lethbridge made the playoffs for the second consecutive season.

Righthander Brad Penny was the co-MVP in the California League after going 14-5 with a 2.96 ERA and striking out 207 in 164 innings. Penny and teammate John Patterson were ranked as the top two prospects in the league.

Outfielder Jason Conti, on loan to Double-A Tulsa because the Diamondbacks didn't field a Double-A team of their own, led the minor leagues with 125 runs and set a Tulsa record with 167 hits.

At Lethbridge, 1997 first-round pick Jack Cust stole the show, hitting .345 with 11 homers and 56 RBIs while drawing 86 walks.

Devon White

Brad Penny

Players of the Year

Major League: Devon White, of

White supplied more than just leadership and defense, hitting .279 and leading the Diamondbacks in runs and RBIs.

Minor League: Brad Penny, rhp, High Desert

Penny struck out 207 batters in 164 innings while going 14-5 with a 2.96 ERA for Class A High Desert.

ORGANIZATION LEADERS

BATTING		
*AVG	Jarrod Patterson, High Desert	.335
R	†Jason Conti, Tulsa	125
H	†Jason Conti, Tulsa	167
TB	Jarrod Patterson, High Desert	271
2B	Jarrod Patterson, High Desert	34
3B	Two tied at	12
HR	Rod Barajas, High Desert	23
RBI	Jarrod Patterson, High Desert	102
BB	†Junior Spivey, Tulsa/High Desert	92
SO	Jhensy Sandoval, High Desert	129
SB	†Junior Spivey, Tulsa/High Desert	42
PITCHING		
W	Brad Penny, High Desert	14
L	Marc Van Wormer, South Bend	15
#ERA	John Patterson, High Desert	2.83
G	Two tied at	48
CG	Bob Wolcott, Tucson	2
SV	Two tied at	13
IP	Brad Penny, High Desert	164
BB	Nick Bierbrodt, High Desert	64
SO	Brad Penny, High Desert	207

*Minimum 250 At-Bats #Minimum 75 Innings
†On loan to Rangers organization

Arizona DIAMONDBACKS

Manager: Buck Showalter

1998 Record: 65-97, .401 (5th, NL West)

BATTING	AVG	G	AB	R	H	2B	3B	HR	RBI	BB	SO	SB	CS	B	T	HT	WT	DOB	1st Yr	Resides
Batista, Tony	.273	106	293	46	80	16	1	18	41	18	52	1	1	R	R	6-0	195	12-9-73	1992	Mao Valverde, D.R.
Bell, Jay	.251	155	549	79	138	29	5	20	67	81	129	3	5	R	R	6-0	182	12-11-65	1984	Valrico, Fla.
Benitez, Yamil	.199	91	206	17	41	7	1	9	30	14	46	2	2	R	R	6-2	195	10-5-72	1990	Rio Piedras, P.R.
Brede, Brent	.226	98	212	23	48	9	3	2	17	24	43	1	0	L	L	6-4	208	9-13-71	1990	Trenton, Ill.
Dellucci, David	.260	124	416	43	108	19	12	5	51	33	103	3	5	L	L	5-10	180	10-31-73	1995	Baton Rouge, La.
Diaz, Edwin	.000	3	7	0	0	0	0	0	0	0	2	0	0	R	R	5-11	170	1-15-75	1993	Vega Alta, P.R.
Fabregas, Jorge	.199	50	151	8	30	4	0	1	15	13	26	0	0	L	R	6-3	215	3-13-70	1991	Miami, Fla.
Fox, Andy	.277	139	502	67	139	21	6	9	44	43	97	14	7	L	R	6-4	185	1-12-71	1989	Sacramento, Calif.
Frias, Hanley	.130	15	23	4	3	0	1	1	2	0	5	0	0	B	R	6-0	165	12-5-73	1991	Villa Ariagracia, D.R.
Garcia, Karim	.222	113	333	39	74	10	8	9	43	18	78	5	4	L	L	6-0	172	10-29-75	1993	Ciudad Obregon, Mexico
Gilkey, Bernard	.248	29	101	8	25	0	0	1	5	11	14	4	2	R	R	6-0	200	9-24-66	1985	St. Louis, Mo.
2-team (83 New York)	.233	111	365	41	85	15	0	5	33	43	80	9	3							
Jones, Chris	.194	20	31	3	6	1	0	0	3	3	9	0	0	R	R	6-2	210	11-16-65	1984	Phoenix, Ariz.
Klassen, Danny	.194	29	108	12	21	2	1	3	8	9	33	1	1	R	R	6-0	175	9-22-75	1993	Stuart, Fla.
Lee, Travis	.269	146	562	71	151	20	2	22	72	67	123	8	1	L	L	6-3	210	5-26-75	1997	Olympia, Wash.
Meulens, Hensley	.067	7	15	1	1	0	0	1	1	0	6	0	0	R	R	6-3	210	6-23-67	1986	Coral Springs, Fla.
Miller, Damian	.286	57	168	17	48	14	2	3	14	11	43	1	0	R	R	6-2	190	10-13-69	1990	La Crosse, Wis.
Robertson, Mike	.154	11	13	0	2	0	0	0	0	0	2	0	0	L	L	6-0	189	10-9-70	1991	Las Vegas, Nev.
Stankiewicz, Andy	.207	77	145	9	30	5	0	0	8	7	33	1	0	R	R	5-9	165	8-10-64	1986	Gilbert, Ariz.
Stinnett, Kelly	.259	92	274	35	71	14	1	11	34	35	74	0	1	R	R	5-11	195	2-4-70	1990	Lawton, Okla.
White, Devon	.279	146	563	84	157	32	1	22	85	42	102	22	8	B	R	6-2	190	12-29-62	1981	Paradise Valley, Ariz.
Williams, Matt	.267	135	510	72	136	26	1	20	71	43	102	5	1	R	R	6-2	210	11-28-65	1986	Scottsdale, Ariz.

PITCHING	W	L	ERA	G	GS	CG	SV	IP	H	R	ER	BB	SO	B	T	HT	WT	DOB	1st Yr	Resides
Adamson, Joel	0	3	8.22	5	5	0	0	23	25	21	21	11	14	L	L	6-4	185	7-2-71	1990	Phoenix, Ariz.
Anderson, Brian	12	13	4.33	32	32	2	0	208	221	109	100	24	95	B	L	6-1	190	4-26-72	1993	North Olmstead, Ohio
Banks, Willie	1	2	3.09	33	0	0	1	44	34	21	15	25	32	R	R	6-1	200	2-27-69	1987	Miami, Fla.
Benes, Andy	14	13	3.97	34	34	1	0	231	221	111	102	74	164	R	R	6-6	245	8-20-67	1989	Phoenix, Ariz.
Blair, Willie	4	15	5.34	23	23	0	0	147	165	91	87	51	71	R	R	6-1	185	12-18-65	1986	Lexington, Ky.
Brow, Scott	1	0	7.17	17	0	0	0	21	22	17	17	14	13	R	R	6-3	200	3-17-69	1990	Hillsboro, Ore.
Chouinard, Bobby	0	2	4.23	26	2	0	0	38	41	23	18	11	26	R	R	6-1	188	5-1-72	1990	Forest Grove, Ore.
2-team (1 Milwaukee)	0	2	4.14	27	2	0	0	41	46	24	19	11	27							
Corey, Bryan	0	0	9.00	3	0	0	0	4	6	4	4	2	1	R	R	6-0	170	10-21-73	1993	Thousand Oaks, Calif.
Daal, Omar	8	12	2.88	33	23	3	0	163	146	60	52	51	132	L	L	6-3	185	3-1-72	1990	Maracaibo, Ven.
Embree, Alan	3	2	4.11	35	0	0	1	35	33	18	16	13	24	L	L	6-2	190	1-23-70	1990	Vancouver, Wash.
2-team (20 Atlanta)	4	2	4.19	55	0	0	1	54	56	32	25	23	43							
Ford, Ben	0	0	9.90	8	0	0	0	10	13	12	11	3	5	R	R	6-7	200	8-15-75	1994	Cedar Rapids, Iowa
Manuel, Barry	1	0	7.47	13	0	0	0	16	17	14	13	14	12	R	R	5-11	185	8-12-65	1987	Mamou, La.
Michalak, Chris	0	0	11.81	5	0	0	0	5	9	7	7	4	5	L	L	6-2	195	1-4-71	1993	Lemont, Ill.
Nunez, Vladimir	0	0	10.13	4	0	0	0	5	7	6	6	2	2	R	R	6-4	235	3-15-75	1996	Santo Domingo, D.R.
Olson, Gregg	3	4	3.01	64	0	0	30	69	56	25	23	25	55	R	R	6-4	210	10-11-66	1988	Reisterstown, Md.
Pickett, Ricky	0	0	81.00	2	0	0	0	1	3	6	6	4	2	L	L	6-1	200	1-19-70	1992	Greenville, Fla.
Rodriguez, Felix	0	2	6.14	43	0	0	5	44	44	31	30	29	36	R	R	6-1	180	12-5-72	1990	Montecristi, D.R.
Small, Aaron	3	1	3.69	23	0	0	0	32	32	14	13	8	14	R	R	6-5	226	11-23-71	1989	Loudon, Tenn.
Sodowsky, Clint	3	6	5.68	45	6	0	0	78	86	56	49	39	42	L	R	6-4	200	7-13-72	1991	Lamont, Okla.
Springer, Russ	4	3	4.13	26	0	0	0	33	29	16	15	14	37	R	R	6-4	205	11-7-68	1989	Pollack, La.
Suppan, Jeff	1	7	6.68	13	13	1	0	66	82	55	49	21	39	R	R	6-2	210	1-2-75	1993	West Hills, Calif.
Telemaco, Amaury	6	9	3.94	27	18	0	0	121	127	63	53	33	60	R	R	6-3	210	1-19-74	1991	La Romana, D.R.
2-team (14 Chicago)	7	10	3.93	41	18	0	0	149	150	75	65	46	78							
Valdez, Efrain	0	0	4.15	6	0	0	0	4	7	2	2	1	2	L	L	5-11	170	6-11-66	1983	San Carlos, D.R.
Weber, Neil	0	0	11.57	4	0	0	0	2	5	3	3	3	4	L	L	6-5	215	12-6-72	1993	Harrisburg, Pa.
Wolcott, Bob	1	3	7.09	6	6	0	0	33	32	27	26	13	21	R	R	6-0	190	9-8-73	1992	Kent, Wash.

FIELDING

Catcher	PCT	G	PO	A	E	DP	PB
Fabregas	.996	41	228	30	1	2	0
Miller	.986	46	255	26	4	2	6
Stinnett	.984	86	458	38	8	3	1

First Base	PCT	G	PO	A	E	DP
Brede	.984	12	58	5	1	4
Fox	1.000	12	104	6	0	7
Lee	.998	146	1270	98	3	104
Miller	1.000	1	0	1	0	0

Second Base	PCT	G	PO	A	E	DP
Batista	.994	41	72	83	1	23
Bell	.985	15	28	38	1	7
Diaz	.933	3	6	8	1	2
Fox	.982	60	103	119	4	23
Frias	1.000	3	5	5	0	2
Klassen	.964	29	60	73	5	16
Stankiewicz	.994	61	61	94	1	17

Third Base	PCT	G	PO	A	E	DP
Batista	.974	15	9	28	1	1
Fox	.973	26	23	48	2	4
Frias	1.000	2	0	1	0	0
Williams	.972	134	99	281	11	18

Shortstop	PCT	G	PO	A	E	DP
Batista	.971	34	43	93	4	13
Bell	.971	138	197	397	18	77
Frias	1.000	2	3	4	0	0

Outfield	PCT	G	PO	A	E	DP
Benitez	.972	62	101	4	3	1
Brede	.964	58	78	2	3	1
Dellucci	.987	117	230	3	3	3
Fox	.975	48	76	3	2	0
Garcia	.975	103	192	6	5	1
Gilkey	.981	27	49	3	1	0
Jones	1.000	8	11	0	0	0
Meulens	1.000	4	6	1	0	0
Miller	.000	2	0	0	0	0
White	.987	144	371	3	5	0

FARM SYSTEM

Director of Player Development: Mel Didier

Class	Farm Team	League	W	L	Pct.	Finish*	Manager	First Yr
AAA	Tucson (Ariz.) Sidewinders	Pacific Coast	57	85	.401	14th (16)	Chris Speier	1998
A#	High Desert (Calif.) Mavericks	California	82	58	.586	2nd (10)	Don Wakamatsu	1997
A	South Bend (Ind.) Silver Hawks	Midwest	40	100	.286	14th (14)	Roly de Armas	1997
Rookie#	Lethbridge (Alta.) Black Diamonds	Pioneer	43	32	.573	3rd (8)	Joe Almaraz	1996
Rookie	Peoria (Ariz.) Diamondbacks	Arizona	24	31	.436	5th (8)	Mike Brumley	1996

*Finish in overall standings (No. of teams in league) #Advanced level

TUCSON Class AAA

PACIFIC COAST LEAGUE

BATTING	AVG	G	AB	R	H	2B	3B	HR	RBI	BB	SO	SB	CS	B	T	HT	WT	DOB	1st Yr	Resides
Allison, Brad	.000	4	6	1	0	0	0	0	0	1	3	0	0	R	R	5-11	220	11-24-73	1996	Cynthiana, Ky.
Bautista, Juan	.150	9	20	1	3	0	0	0	1	2	5	0	0	R	R	6-1	160	7-20-78	1996	San Francisco de Macoris, D.R.
Brede, Brent	.313	29	96	16	30	8	1	2	16	21	20	2	1	L	L	6-4	208	9-13-71	1990	Trenton, Ill.
Cookson, Brent	.360	36	100	24	36	12	0	6	19	18	26	0	0	R	R	5-11	200	9-7-69	1991	Santa Paula, Calif.
Dellucci, David	.306	17	72	17	22	4	3	1	11	5	8	4	0	L	L	5-10	180	10-31-73	1995	Baton Rouge, La.
Diaz, Edwin	.263	131	510	61	134	31	12	2	49	27	105	9	6	R	R	5-11	170	1-15-75	1993	Vega Alta, P.R.
Fabregas, Jorge	.250	6	20	2	5	1	0	0	3	3	1	0	0	L	R	6-3	215	3-13-70	1991	Miami, Fla.
Florez, Tim	.282	77	227	31	64	5	1	3	23	18	49	4	2	R	R	5-10	170	7-23-69	1991	Goleta, Calif.
Frias, Hanley	.289	63	253	32	73	10	4	1	21	24	41	16	7	B	R	6-0	165	12-5-73	1991	Villa Ariagracia, D.R.
Garcia, Karim	.311	27	106	21	33	4	2	10	27	15	24	5	1	L	L	6-0	172	10-29-75	1993	Ciudad Obregon, Mexico
Hartman, Ron	.269	126	438	54	118	21	0	9	55	22	53	1	3	R	R	6-1	200	12-12-74	1996	Baltimore, Md.
Huson, Jeff	.305	27	82	7	25	4	1	1	12	5	14	0	2	L	R	6-1	180	8-15-64	1986	Parker, Colo.
Hyers, Tim	.222	19	27	7	6	1	0	1	5	5	5	1	0	L	L	6-1	195	10-3-71	1990	Covington, Ga.
Hyzdu, Adam	.340	34	100	21	34	7	1	4	14	15	23	0	1	R	R	6-2	210	12-6-71	1990	Mesa, Ariz.
Klassen, Danny	.292	73	281	47	82	25	2	10	47	19	54	6	2	R	R	6-0	175	9-22-75	1993	Stuart, Fla.
Maddox, Garry	.264	81	269	36	71	13	4	4	18	15	57	4	3	L	R	6-3	180	10-24-74	1996	Philadelphia, Pa.
McAffee, Josh	.000	1	1	0	0	0	0	0	0	0	0	0	0	R	R	6-1	215	11-4-77	1996	Rock Springs, Wyo.
Meier, Dan	.207	10	29	5	6	3	0	0	2	1	9	0	0	L	L	6-0	180	8-13-77	1998	Aurora, Colo.
Meulens, Hensley	.250	76	268	45	67	16	2	13	37	30	67	2	1	R	R	6-3	210	6-23-67	1986	Coral Springs, Fla.
Miller, Damian	.349	18	63	14	22	7	1	0	11	9	9	0	0	R	R	6-2	190	10-13-69	1990	La Crosse, Wis.
O'Neal, Troy	.229	55	118	15	27	5	0	1	14	14	33	0	2	R	R	5-11	185	4-24-72	1995	Newark, Del.
Quire, Jeremy	.222	4	9	0	2	1	0	0	0	0	3	0	0	R	R	6-2	205	4-8-75	1997	Anderson, Ind.
Robertson, Mike	.273	111	411	49	112	14	3	13	70	33	56	1	0	L	L	6-0	189	10-9-70	1991	Las Vegas, Nev.
Ryan, Rob	.317	116	394	71	125	18	2	17	66	63	61	9	3	L	L	5-11	190	6-24-73	1996	Spokane, Wash.
Smith, Bubba	.148	9	27	3	4	0	0	1	6	6	7	0	0	R	R	6-2	225	12-18-69	1991	Winston-Salem, N.C.
Stankiewicz, Andy	.300	5	20	1	6	0	0	0	2	0	0	0	0	R	R	5-9	165	8-10-64	1986	Gilbert, Ariz.
Stoner, Mike	.312	106	394	46	123	22	3	5	49	27	52	3	0	R	R	6-0	200	5-23-73	1996	Simpsonville, Ky.
Vicente, Audo	.143	4	7	0	1	0	0	0	0	0	6	0	0	B	R	6-1	155	8-1-79	1996	Santo Domingo, D.R.
Williams, Matt	.200	2	5	0	1	0	0	0	0	0	0	0	0	R	R	6-2	210	11-28-65	1986	Scottsdale, Ariz.
Wilson, Tom	.303	111	370	59	112	17	3	12	54	41	81	3	1	R	R	6-3	210	12-19-70	1991	Fullerton, Calif.

PITCHING	W	L	ERA	G	GS	CG	SV	IP	H	R	ER	BB	SO	B	T	HT	WT	DOB	1st Yr	Resides
Barndollar, Jeff	0	1	9.00	1	1	0	0	4	7	4	4	4	2	R	R	6-4	195	4-29-77	1998	Mission Viejo, Calif.
Boyd, Jason	2	2	6.23	15	0	0	0	22	28	22	15	14	13	R	R	6-3	170	2-23-73	1994	Edwardsville, Ill.
Chouinard, Bobby	0	0	4.26	4	0	0	1	6	6	3	3	0	6	R	R	6-1	188	5-1-72	1990	Forest Grove, Ore.
Clemons, Chris	3	9	6.15	20	19	0	0	86	103	69	59	44	79	R	R	6-4	225	10-31-72	1994	Waco, Texas
Corey, Bryan	4	6	5.44	39	10	0	2	88	116	61	53	24	50	R	R	6-0	170	10-21-73	1993	Thousand Oaks, Calif.
Cornelius, Reid	4	7	5.94	19	16	0	0	94	108	70	62	26	65	R	R	6-0	200	6-2-70	1989	West Palm Beach, Fla.
Cornett, Brad	1	2	7.86	6	6	0	0	26	44	25	23	6	12	R	R	6-3	190	2-4-69	1992	Odessa, Texas
Daal, Omar	0	0	3.00	1	1	0	0	3	3	2	1	1	4	L	L	6-3	185	3-1-72	1990	Maracaibo, Ven.
Figueroa, Nelson	2	2	3.70	7	7	0	0	41	46	22	17	16	29	B	R	6-1	155	5-18-74	1995	Brooklyn, N.Y.
Florez, Tim	0	0	135.00	2	0	0	0	0	4	5	5	1	0	R	R	5-10	170	7-23-69	1991	Goleta, Calif.
Ford, Ben	2	5	4.35	48	0	0	13	68	68	41	33	33	63	R	R	6-7	200	8-15-75	1994	Cedar Rapids, Iowa
Hartman, Ron	0	0	5.79	2	0	0	0	4	7	3	3	2	1	R	R	6-1	200	12-12-74	1996	Baltimore, Md.
Hernandez, Fernando	0	1	15.30	3	2	0	0	10	23	17	17	1	13	R	R	6-2	185	6-16-71	1990	Santiago, D.R.
Johnson, Barry	0	1	6.94	5	1	0	0	12	16	12	9	5	10	R	R	6-4	200	8-21-69	1991	Joliet, Ill.
2-team (31 Oklahoma)	2	9	6.67	36	8	1	1	89	112	78	66	26	64							
Lidle, Cory	0	0	0.00	1	1	0	0	5	2	0	0	2	2	R	R	5-11	180	3-22-72	1991	West Covina, Calif.
Manuel, Barry	3	2	2.61	23	0	0	0	41	28	12	12	16	40	R	R	5-11	185	8-12-65	1987	Mamou, La.
Marrero, Kenny	4	2	5.33	34	1	0	0	54	60	39	32	39	45	R	R	6-3	208	5-13-70	1991	Dorado, P.R.
Martines, Jason	0	0	0.00	1	0	0	0	1	0	0	0	2	2	L	R	6-2	190	1-21-76	1997	Hanover, Mich.
Meier, Dan	1	0	2.70	2	0	0	0	3	3	2	1	0	2	L	L	6-0	180	8-13-77	1998	Aurora, Colo.
Michalak, Chris	3	8	5.03	29	9	0	0	73	91	47	41	29	50	L	L	6-2	195	1-4-71	1993	Lemont, Ill.
Nunez, Vladimir	4	4	4.91	31	13	1	2	95	103	58	52	37	78	R	R	6-4	235	3-15-75	1996	Santo Domingo, D.R.
Oleksik, George	0	0	22.09	2	0	0	0	4	8	9	9	3	1	R	R	6-4	215	4-19-74	1996	McMinnville, Tenn.
Pavlas, Dave	0	2	8.64	9	0	0	1	8	15	11	8	5	8	R	R	6-7	205	8-12-62	1985	Shiner, Texas
Peters, Don	1	1	7.59	13	0	0	0	21	27	18	18	7	4	R	R	6-0	190	10-7-69	1990	Crestwood, Ill.
Pickett, Ricky	0	0	15.43	5	0	0	0	5	7	8	8	9	5	L	L	6-1	200	1-19-70	1992	Greenville, Fla.
Randolph, Steve	1	3	3.18	17	1	0	0	23	16	11	8	19	23	L	L	6-3	185	5-1-74	1995	Austin, Texas
Rodriguez, Felix	0	0	9.00	1	0	0	0	1	1	1	1	2	0	R	R	6-1	180	12-5-72	1990	Montecristi, D.R.
Rooney, Mike	0	2	4.60	3	3	0	0	16	20	10	8	9	6	R	R	6-1	175	10-6-75	1997	Stony Point, N.Y.
Sabel, Erik	1	0	8.71	7	0	0	0	10	17	10	10	5	7	R	R	6-3	193	10-14-74	1996	West Lafayette, Ind.
Sodowsky, Clint	0	1	3.86	2	2	0	0	9	11	4	4	3	7	L	R	6-4	200	7-13-72	1991	Lamont, Okla.
Suppan, Jeff	4	3	3.63	13	12	0	0	67	75	29	27	17	62	R	R	6-2	210	1-2-75	1993	West Hills, Calif.
Tuttle, Dave	1	2	6.84	10	3	0	0	26	32	20	20	16	8	R	R	6-3	190	9-29-69	1992	Los Gatos, Calif.
Valdez, Efrain	1	4	4.37	28	2	0	0	58	59	31	28	18	41	L	L	5-11	170	6-11-66	1983	San Carlos, D.R.
Verplancke, Joe	1	0	0.00	1	0	0	0	3	2	2	0	2	3	R	R	6-2	200	5-11-75	1996	Ontario, Calif.

PITCHING	W	L	ERA	G	GS	CG	SV	IP	H	R	ER	BB	SO	B	T	HT	WT	DOB	1st Yr	Resides
Weber, Neil	5	9	5.11	46	11	1	1	113	116	82	64	55	79	L	L	6-5	215	12-6-72	1993	Harrisburg, Pa.
Wolcott, Bob	8	6	5.18	23	21	2	0	129	156	79	74	26	100	R	R	6-0	190	9-8-73	1992	Kent, Wash.

FIELDING

Catcher	PCT	G	PO	A	E	DP	PB
Allison	1.000	4	14	1	0	0	0
Fabregas	1.000	5	28	3	0	1	2
Miller	.973	18	95	15	3	0	2
O'Neal	.972	45	224	19	7	3	1
Quire	1.000	3	9	1	0	0	0
Wilson	.981	94	565	48	12	5	9

First Base	PCT	G	PO	A	E	DP
Brede	.900	3	9	0	1	0
Florez	.987	12	77	0	1	10
Hartman	.980	12	91	8	2	17
Hyers	1.000	2	4	0	0	1
Meier	.984	8	58	3	1	6
Meulens	.958	3	19	4	1	5
Robertson	.993	107	862	55	6	79
Smith	1.000	3	20	0	0	1
Wilson	.969	13	88	6	3	9

Second Base	PCT	G	PO	A	E	DP
Bautista	.000	1	0	0	0	0
Diaz	.961	108	229	293	21	68
Florez	.979	13	20	26	1	4
Frias	1.000	1	0	1	0	1
Huson	1.000	8	13	21	0	2
Klassen	.991	21	49	67	1	22
Stankiewicz	1.000	3	11	9	0	3

Third Base	PCT	G	PO	A	E	DP
Bautista	1.000	1	0	1	0	0
Diaz	.919	15	6	28	3	3
Florez	.933	14	6	22	2	0
Frias	.950	6	3	16	1	2
Hartman	.906	103	62	170	24	13
Huson	.909	3	2	8	1	0
Meulens	1.000	2	1	7	0	2
Smith	1.000	8	6	12	0	0
Vicente	1.000	1	0	3	0	0
Williams	1.000	2	0	1	0	0
Wilson	.750	1	1	2	1	0

Shortstop	PCT	G	PO	A	E	DP
Bautista	.870	6	9	11	3	2
Diaz	.889	8	12	20	4	9
Florez	.893	15	20	47	8	12
Frias	.957	55	80	155	11	38
Huson	.906	13	23	25	5	6
Klassen	.968	51	79	135	7	29
Vicente	1.000	2	2	2	0	2

Outfield	PCT	G	PO	A	E	DP
Brede	1.000	26	48	6	0	0
Cookson	1.000	29	50	0	0	0
Dellucci	1.000	17	38	0	0	0
Florez	1.000	2	1	0	0	0
Garcia	.958	27	67	1	3	1
Huson	1.000	1	1	0	0	0
Hyers	1.000	10	7	0	0	0
Hyzdu	.974	27	38	0	1	0
Maddox	.973	71	143	2	4	0
Meier	.000	1	0	0	0	0
Meulens	.914	47	71	3	7	0
Robertson	.000	1	0	0	0	0
Ryan	.983	110	224	3	4	0
Stoner	.969	98	152	5	5	0
Wilson	1.000	3	1	0	0	0

TULSA — Class AA

TEXAS LEAGUE

BATTING	AVG	G	AB	R	H	2B	3B	HR	RBI	BB	SO	SB	CS	B	T	HT	WT	DOB	1st Yr	Resides
Conti, Jason	.315	130	530	125	167	31	12	15	67	63	96	19	13	L	R	5-11	180	1-27-75	1996	Cranberry Township, Pa.
Goligoski, Jason	.218	65	202	21	44	4	2	0	10	21	44	0	2	L	R	6-1	175	10-2-71	1993	Hamilton, Mont.
Koeyers, Ramsey	.250	55	164	25	41	2	0	4	18	13	45	1	0	R	R	6-1	187	8-7-74	1991	Willemstad, Curacao

GAMES BY POSITION: C—Koeyers 50. **1B**—Goligoski 1, Koeyers 1. **2B**—Goligoski 8. **3B**—Goligoski 3. **SS**—Goligoski 49. **OF**—Conti 115.

PITCHING	W	L	ERA	G	GS	CG	SV	IP	H	R	ER	BB	SO	B	T	HT	WT	DOB	1st Yr	Resides
Michalak, Chris	1	2	1.83	10	0	0	0	20	10	4	4	2	15	L	L	6-2	195	1-4-71	1993	Lemont, Ill.
Tuttle, Dave	1	2	2.69	36	2	0	4	74	73	30	22	29	47	R	R	6-3	190	9-29-69	1992	Los Gatos, Calif.

Players property of Diamondbacks; on loan to Tulsa. For complete Tulsa statistics, see Page 241.

HIGH DESERT — Class A

CALIFORNIA LEAGUE

BATTING	AVG	G	AB	R	H	2B	3B	HR	RBI	BB	SO	SB	CS	B	T	HT	WT	DOB	1st Yr	Resides
Adams, John	.267	76	303	50	81	19	11	11	43	24	98	8	3	R	R	6-5	225	8-10-76	1997	Olathe, Kan.
Allison, Brad	.265	21	68	10	18	6	2	0	14	10	20	0	0	R	R	5-11	220	11-24-73	1996	Cynthiana, Ky.
Barajas, Rod	.303	113	442	67	134	26	0	23	81	25	81	1	1	R	R	6-2	220	9-5-75	1996	Norwalk, Calif.
Bautista, Juan	.111	6	18	1	2	0	0	1	1	1	5	0	0	R	R	6-1	160	7-20-78	1996	San Francisco de Macoris, D.R.
Calloway, Ron	.282	44	156	30	44	8	2	3	27	12	38	2	4	L	L	6-1	190	9-6-76	1997	San Jose, Calif.
Clark, Kevin	.265	127	498	72	132	24	5	20	98	36	121	1	0	R	R	6-1	200	4-30-73	1993	Henderson, Nev.
Cuntz, Casey	.290	47	176	34	51	10	2	5	25	20	45	6	2	R	R	6-3	185	2-4-75	1997	Metairie, La.
Gann, Jamie	.221	59	217	25	48	8	3	6	25	8	59	9	4	R	R	6-3	190	5-1-75	1996	Norman, Okla.
Garcia, Juan	.167	8	30	5	5	0	0	0	0	7	11	4	1	R	R	5-9	170	9-25-78	1996	San Francisco de Macoris, D.R.
Hudson, Bert	.147	35	116	10	17	5	1	0	3	10	31	4	0	R	R	5-11	185	10-6-77	1996	Jay, Fla.
Lopez, Jose	.273	12	44	3	12	3	0	0	5	0	8	0	0	R	R	5-10	187	12-23-78	1996	San Francisco de Macoris, D.R.
Maddox, Garry	.625	2	8	3	5	2	0	1	4	1	1	1	0	L	R	6-3	180	10-24-74	1996	Philadelphia, Pa.
Martin, Jared	.244	50	168	30	41	7	5	3	21	19	37	3	3	B	R	5-11	180	3-3-75	1997	Tallahassee, Fla.
Martinez, Tony	.133	9	30	2	4	1	0	0	0	6	11	0	1	R	R	6-2	190	11-27-73	1996	Fullerton, Calif.
Matos, Julius	.301	111	439	70	132	27	4	4	60	23	40	19	13	R	R	5-11	175	12-12-74	1994	Racine, Wis.
McAffee, Josh	.222	4	9	3	2	1	0	0	2	2	5	0	0	R	R	6-1	215	11-4-77	1996	Rock Springs, Wyo.
Neubart, Adam	.326	39	141	24	46	7	4	2	21	9	35	4	2	R	R	5-11	165	7-23-77	1998	Livingston, N.J.
Patterson, Jarrod	.335	131	492	89	165	34	9	18	102	66	97	9	2	L	R	6-1	195	9-7-73	1993	Clanton, Ala.
Rexrode, Jackie	.341	53	208	51	71	5	4	1	23	46	42	19	1	L	R	5-11	175	9-16-78	1996	Laurel, Md.
Rodriguez, Miguel	.255	15	55	11	14	2	0	3	6	3	21	2	1	R	R	5-10	170	5-27-78	1996	El Sombrero, Ven.
Sandoval, Jhensy	.276	107	398	49	110	20	2	5	53	15	129	10	10	R	R	6-0	200	9-11-78	1996	Santo Domingo, D.R.
Spivey, Junior	.281	79	285	64	80	14	5	5	35	64	61	34	12	R	R	6-0	185	1-28-75	1996	Oklahoma City, Okla.
Sweeney, Kevin	.267	98	333	59	89	25	3	9	38	60	73	6	3	L	L	5-11	195	3-30-74	1996	Kettering, Ohio
Sykes, Jamie	.168	36	125	13	21	5	2	3	16	19	33	5	2	R	R	5-11	190	1-14-75	1997	Kankakee, Ill.
Wilson, Keith	.067	17	45	4	3	1	0	1	3	5	13	0	0	R	R	6-0	200	12-31-73	1996	Buckeye, Ariz.

GAMES BY POSITION: C—Allison 20, Barajas 95, Clark 14, Lopez 8, McAffee 3, Wilson 9. **1B**—Allison 1, Clark 95, Martinez 1, Patterson 42, Sweeney 4, Wilson 3. **2B**—Bautista 3, Cuntz 3, Martin 17, Patterson 1, Rexrode 42, Spivey 75. **3B**—Clark 1, Cuntz 29, Martin 19, Martinez 3, Patterson 81, Rexrode 11, Spivey 2. **SS**—Bautista 3, Cuntz 15, Martin 13, Matos 110, Spivey 2. **OF**—Adams 31, Calloway 43, Gann 59, Garcia 8, Hudson 35, Maddox 2, Neubart 39, Patterson 7, Rodriguez 15, Sandoval 106, Sweeney 54, Sykes 35.

PITCHING	W	L	ERA	G	GS	CG	SV	IP	H	R	ER	BB	SO	B	T	HT	WT	DOB	1st Yr	Resides
Andrews, Jeff	1	1	4.32	6	3	0	0	25	36	19	12	7	8	R	R	6-2	175	9-1-74	1997	Beverly, Mass.
Bierbrodt, Nick	8	7	3.40	24	23	1	0	130	122	66	49	64	88	L	L	6-5	190	5-16-78	1996	Long Beach, Calif.
Crews, Jason	7	7	4.17	48	0	0	2	86	100	62	40	22	58	R	R	6-2	205	8-28-73	1996	Plantation, Fla.
Grieve, Tim	4	2	4.73	27	0	0	6	46	43	29	24	22	61	R	R	5-11	180	8-17-71	1994	Arlington, Texas
Jacob, Russell	3	2	4.41	31	7	0	1	67	78	42	33	26	64	R	R	6-6	240	1-2-75	1994	Winter Haven, Fla.
Knott, Eric	12	7	4.52	28	22	1	0	143	175	84	72	28	96	L	L	6-1	170	9-23-74	1997	Sebring, Fla.

STEVE MOORE

Arizona's Travis Lee

Rookie first baseman hit .269 with 22 homers

LEE SCHMID

Tulsa's Jason Conti

Led organization with 125 runs, 167 hits

PITCHING	W	L	ERA	G	GS	CG	SV	IP	H	R	ER	BB	SO	B	T	HT	WT	DOB	1st Yr	Resides
Lidle, Cory	0	0	0.00	1	1	0	0	3	2	1	0	2	6	R	R	5-11	180	3-22-72	1991	West Covina, Calif.
Lisio, Joe	1	2	5.87	11	0	0	0	15	19	11	10	11	17	R	R	6-2	205	8-5-73	1994	West Hempstead, N.Y.
Martines, Jason	0	1	7.59	5	0	0	0	11	16	10	9	3	7	L	R	6-2	190	1-21-76	1997	Hanover, Mich.
Norris, Ben	2	2	5.53	9	6	0	1	41	48	27	25	18	17	L	L	6-3	185	12-6-77	1996	Austin, Texas
Oleksik, George	3	3	4.46	41	1	0	0	73	82	51	36	31	57	R	R	6-4	215	4-19-74	1996	McMinnville, Tenn.
Patterson, John	8	7	2.83	25	25	0	0	127	102	54	40	42	148	R	R	6-6	197	1-30-78	1996	Orange, Texas
Penny, Brad	14	5	2.96	28	28	1	0	164	138	65	54	35	207	R	R	6-4	200	5-24-78	1996	Broken Arrow, Okla.
Peters, Don	0	1	2.21	21	0	0	8	20	24	11	5	7	20	R	R	6-0	190	10-7-69	1990	Crestwood, Ill.
Puorto, Jamie	0	0	7.71	1	0	0	0	2	4	2	2	1	2	L	L	6-3	190	6-21-75	1997	Chicago, Ill.
Randolph, Stephen	4	4	3.59	17	17	0	0	85	71	44	34	42	104	L	L	6-3	185	5-1-74	1995	Austin, Texas
Rodriguez, Larry	0	2	5.08	6	5	0	0	28	29	19	16	5	15	R	R	6-2	195	9-9-74	1996	Isla De Margarita, Ven.
Sabel, Erik	0	1	3.18	14	0	0	4	23	25	8	8	4	18	R	R	6-3	193	10-14-74	1996	West Lafayette, Ind.
Sanchez, Martin	3	0	3.05	35	0	0	11	44	36	16	15	21	35	R	R	6-2	180	1-19-77	1994	Santo Domingo, D.R.
Verplancke, Joe	10	4	3.65	42	2	0	1	81	65	41	33	40	87	R	R	6-2	200	5-11-75	1996	Ontario, Calif.
Wilson, Jeff	2	0	5.23	12	0	0	0	21	28	14	12	8	18	R	L	6-2	180	5-30-76	1997	Greensboro, N.C.

SOUTH BEND — Class A

MIDWEST LEAGUE

BATTING	AVG	G	AB	R	H	2B	3B	HR	RBI	BB	SO	SB	CS	B	T	HT	WT	DOB	1st Yr	Resides
Allison, Brad	.163	29	86	6	14	1	0	0	5	8	21	0	0	R	R	5-11	220	11-24-73	1996	Cynthiana, Ky.
Bautista, Juan	.213	71	235	22	50	13	0	1	11	19	60	7	5	R	R	6-1	160	7-20-78	1996	San Francisco de Macoris, D.R.
Bolling, Kirk	.189	44	143	18	27	4	0	4	21	14	49	2	1	R	R	6-3	185	4-14-77	1998	Torrance, Calif.
Brock, J.J.	.260	91	354	45	92	19	3	2	21	26	75	4	8	R	R	5-11	175	12-4-74	1998	South Bend, Ind.
Calloway, Ron	.263	69	251	29	66	12	2	3	33	25	50	6	5	L	L	6-1	190	9-6-76	1997	San Jose, Calif.
Closser, J.D.	.214	4	14	3	3	1	0	0	2	2	7	0	0	B	R	5-11	175	1-15-80	1998	Alexandria, Ind.
Cust, Jack	.242	16	62	5	15	3	0	0	4	5	20	0	1	L	R	6-2	200	1-16-79	1997	Flemington, N.J.
Gordon, Brian	.280	126	468	46	131	23	6	8	61	14	100	6	4	L	R	6-1	180	8-16-78	1997	Round Rock, Texas
Guzman, Julio	.196	17	56	6	11	0	0	1	4	4	25	2	0	R	R	6-3	205	4-28-76	1997	Homestead, Fla.
Hudson, Bert	.210	80	271	35	57	13	3	6	32	21	82	1	0	R	R	5-11	185	10-6-77	1996	Jay, Fla.
Jones, Keith	.222	55	189	19	42	13	0	4	30	24	70	2	2	R	R	6-2	190	1-30-76	1997	Whittier, Calif.
Koerner, Pat	.152	9	33	6	5	2	0	0	4	3	2	0	0	R	R	6-2	245	6-3-75	1997	Blanchard, Okla.
Lopez, Jose	.201	43	144	12	29	5	2	1	20	4	35	0	3	R	R	5-10	187	12-23-78	1996	San Francisco de Macoris, D.R.
Lopez, Omar	.143	11	35	4	5	2	0	0	2	5	8	0	0	R	R	6-0	180	1-3-77	1994	Valencia, Ven.
Martin, Jared	.234	15	47	8	11	0	0	0	4	8	6	1	0	B	R	5-11	180	3-3-75	1997	Tallahassee, Fla.
Martinez, Belvani	.250	18	80	11	20	2	0	0	6	3	22	5	1	R	R	5-11	164	12-14-78	1996	San Cristobal, D.R.
Martinez, Tony	.220	24	82	13	18	1	0	2	15	17	18	0	0	R	R	6-2	190	11-27-73	1996	Fullerton, Calif.
McAffee, Josh	.091	21	66	3	6	1	0	2	4	7	31	0	0	R	R	6-1	215	11-4-77	1996	Rock Springs, Wyo.
Meier, Dan	.179	22	56	7	10	3	0	0	5	11	20	0	0	L	L	6-0	180	8-13-77	1998	Aurora, Colo.
Nunez, Abraham	.255	110	364	44	93	14	2	9	47	67	81	12	14	B	R	6-2	165	2-5-80	1996	Haina, D.R.
Osborne, Mark	.241	78	270	33	65	11	0	3	28	43	65	4	4	L	R	6-3	210	2-1-78	1996	Sanford, N.C.
Quire, Jeremy	.192	57	177	11	34	9	0	1	17	6	44	0	0	R	R	6-2	205	4-8-75	1997	Anderson, Ind.
Rexrode, Jackie	.291	50	175	33	51	7	2	0	7	45	31	22	3	L	R	5-11	175	9-16-78	1996	Laurel, Md.
Rinne, Jim	.273	18	55	10	15	4	0	0	5	12	17	1	2	R	R	6-3	215	7-29-76	1998	Bloomington, Ill.
Rodriguez, Miguel	.232	29	99	12	23	9	0	1	8	7	32	3	2	R	R	5-10	170	5-27-78	1996	El Sombrero, Ven.
Santonocito, Justin	.170	47	153	13	26	2	2	1	9	2	43	0	2	L	R	6-1	195	12-15-76	1998	Santo Domingo, D.R.

BATTING	AVG	G	AB	R	H	2B	3B	HR	RBI	BB	SO	SB	CS	B	T	HT	WT	DOB	1st Yr	Resides
Steelmon, Wyley	.277	90	307	36	85	18	1	9	47	51	77	0	0	L	R	6-3	225	8-29-75	1997	Enid, Okla.
Sykes, Jamie	.204	26	93	12	19	2	3	2	10	16	20	5	0	R	R	5-11	190	1-14-75	1997	Kankakee, Ill.
Taveras, Jose	.191	26	68	7	13	2	1	0	6	8	22	0	0	R	R	6-3	203	4-3-79	1997	San Francisco de Macoris, D.R.
Urquiola, Carlos	.319	39	166	28	53	8	4	0	16	10	15	10	8	L	R	5-8	150	4-22-80	1997	Caracas, Ven.

GAMES BY POSITION: C—Allison 28, Closser 3, Hudson 1, J. Lopez 36, McAffee 21, Osborne 15, Quire 47. **1B**—Allison 1, Bautista 3, Cust 16, K. Jones 10, Koerner 4, T. Martinez 11, Maier [illegible], Osborne [illegible], Quire [illegible], Steelmon [illegible], Taveras 2. **2B**—Bautista 25, Martin 7, Rexrode 49, Santonocito 26, Urquiola 39. **3B**—Bautista 10, Bolling 30, Gordon 1, K. Jones 29, J. Lopez 4, O. Lopez 11, Martin 3, T. Martinez 6, Santonocito 16, Taveras 20. **SS**—Bautista 29, Brock 91, Martin 4, B. Martinez 18, Santonocito 2. **OF**—Bautista 1, Calloway 58, Gordon 115, Guzman 15, Hudson 63, J. Lopez 1, T. Martinez 3, Nunez 109, Rinne 17, Rodriguez 23, Sykes 26.

PITCHING	W	L	ERA	G	GS	CG	SV	IP	H	R	ER	BB	SO	B	T	HT	WT	DOB	1st Yr	Resides
Andrews, Jeff	3	8	2.85	20	17	0	0	123	130	62	39	28	68	R	R	6-2	175	9-1-74	1997	Beverly, Mass.
Bloomer, Chris	2	6	2.79	34	0	0	10	42	36	18	13	13	46	R	R	6-4	215	5-6-75	1997	White Bear Lake, Minn.
Cepeda, Wellington	4	2	3.88	40	0	0	2	60	66	35	26	20	47	R	R	6-2	195	11-25-77	1996	Santo Domingo, D.R.
Cervantes, Chris	2	2	1.34	21	0	0	2	34	29	8	5	6	37	L	L	6-3	165	2-4-79	1998	Tucson, Ariz.
De la Cruz, Ynocencio	3	2	4.09	10	10	0	0	51	48	29	23	12	33	R	R	6-2	165	2-28-77	1994	Puerto Plata, D.R.
Fleming, John	0	1	8.10	3	2	0	0	10	18	10	9	1	5	R	R	6-4	175	1-20-78	1996	Chula Vista, Calif.
Good, Andrew	0	1	3.00	2	0	0	0	6	7	4	2	1	6	R	R	6-3	175	9-19-79	1998	Rochester Hills, Mich.
Jensen, Jason	4	11	4.18	28	26	1	0	153	174	91	71	59	115	L	L	6-2	175	11-4-75	1997	Portland, Maine
Jones, Charlie	4	6	4.23	39	5	0	1	87	79	52	41	36	86	L	R	6-0	188	2-6-76	1997	Vero Beach, Fla.
Lopez, Javier	2	4	6.55	16	9	0	0	44	60	36	32	30	31	L	L	6-5	215	7-11-77	1998	Fairfax, Va.
Martines, Jason	0	2	3.51	21	0	0	0	33	33	16	13	15	31	L	R	6-2	190	1-21-76	1997	Hanover, Mich.
McCall, Travis	0	4	7.33	15	2	0	0	27	37	26	22	5	21	L	L	5-11	185	12-20-77	1996	Chino Hills, Calif.
McCutcheon, Mike	3	3	3.65	13	6	0	0	49	53	30	20	22	32	L	L	6-0	165	7-5-77	1996	Mauna Loa, Hawaii
Mendoza, Hatuey	0	4	5.25	4	4	0	0	24	29	21	14	15	20	R	R	6-0	164	3-16-80	1997	Santo Domingo, D.R.
Norris, Ben	1	5	3.32	15	15	0	0	89	98	44	33	27	53	L	L	6-3	185	12-6-77	1996	Austin, Texas
Pass, Jeff	0	0	4.50	2	0	0	0	2	1	1	1	1	1	L	L	6-1	168	1-3-80	1998	Muncie, Ind.
Puorto, Jamie	3	8	3.68	37	3	0	1	81	99	46	33	13	80	L	L	6-3	190	6-21-75	1997	Chicago, Ill.
Rodriguez, Larry	0	2	7.36	5	2	0	0	15	25	15	12	2	11	R	R	6-2	195	9-9-74	1996	Isla de Margarita, Ven.
Rooney, Mike	4	9	5.20	21	20	1	0	106	122	75	61	35	72	R	R	6-1	175	10-6-75	1997	Stony Point, N.Y.
Sanchez, Martin	1	0	8.74	9	0	0	2	11	14	11	11	3	14	R	R	6-2	180	1-19-77	1994	Santo Domingo, D.R.
Sanchez, Simon	0	0	4.85	3	2	0	0	13	18	7	7	3	8	R	R	6-1	182	3-24-78	1996	San Francisco de Macoris, D.R.
Van Wormer, Marc	3	15	8.09	34	13	0	1	89	130	95	80	51	66	R	R	6-8	240	8-21-77	1996	Prescott, Ariz.
White, Matt	0	0	7.71	3	0	0	0	7	12	6	6	2	6	R	R	6-1	170	9-15-77	1998	Portland, Ore.
Wilson, Jeff	1	5	2.56	12	4	0	0	39	34	17	11	13	30	R	L	6-2	180	5-30-76	1997	Greensboro, N.C.

LETHBRIDGE — Rookie

PIONEER LEAGUE

BATTING	AVG	G	AB	R	H	2B	3B	HR	RBI	BB	SO	SB	CS	B	T	HT	WT	DOB	1st Yr	Resides
Beasley, Justin	.260	17	50	9	13	2	0	1	5	4	11	0	1	R	R	6-1	215	10-13-75	1998	Olmsted, Ohio
Brooks, Jeff	.256	68	242	33	62	10	1	2	38	25	52	0	1	R	R	6-5	220	9-4-79	1997	Nottingham, Pa.
Cintron, Alex	.264	67	258	41	68	11	4	3	34	20	32	8	4	B	R	6-3	165	12-17-78	1997	Yabucoa, P.R.
Conyer, Darryl	.273	11	22	6	6	3	1	0	4	7	6	2	0	L	L	5-10	190	12-10-79	1998	San Diego, Calif.
Cust, Jack	.345	73	223	75	77	20	2	11	56	86	71	15	8	L	R	6-2	200	1-16-79	1997	Flemington, N.J.
Downing, Lance	.234	47	145	20	34	5	3	1	19	26	26	4	4	L	R	6-0	185	3-9-79	1997	Pine Bluff, Ark.
Fox, Brian	.000	1	2	0	0	0	0	0	0	0	1	0	0	L	R	6-2	200	3-5-77	1997	Lubbock, Texas
Guzman, Antonio	.276	35	127	25	35	6	1	6	26	13	24	11	2	R	R	5-11	165	1-11-78	1996	Santo Domingo, D.R.
Guzman, Julio	.258	36	93	16	24	4	0	3	17	15	35	1	2	R	R	6-3	205	4-28-76	1997	Homestead, Fla.
Hammock, Robert	.286	62	227	46	65	14	2	10	56	28	34	5	4	R	R	5-11	180	5-13-77	1998	Marietta, Ga.
Joseph, Adolfo	.186	22	70	10	13	2	1	1	9	5	24	1	1	R	R	6-3	175	10-6-80	1998	Higuey, D.R.
Martinez, Belvani	.305	63	256	56	78	11	3	5	25	12	30	30	10	R	R	5-11	164	12-14-78	1996	San Cristobal, D.R.
McAffee, Josh	.179	17	56	9	10	1	0	2	5	7	23	0	0	R	R	6-1	215	11-4-77	1996	Rock Springs, Wyo.
Mendez, Francisco	.233	20	60	13	14	2	0	3	10	14	8	2	1	L	R	6-3	198	1-6-78	1998	Caborca, Mexico
Neal, Steve	.250	43	148	16	37	8	0	3	20	28	50	5	4	L	L	6-2	260	2-14-77	1998	Pine Bluff, Ark.
Rinne, Jim	.221	23	68	14	15	3	0	0	6	14	24	1	2	R	R	6-3	215	7-29-76	1998	Bloomington, Ill.
Rodriguez, Miguel	.375	5	16	3	6	0	0	1	2	2	4	1	1	R	R	5-10	170	5-27-78	1996	El Sombrero, Ven.
Santonocito, Justin	.231	12	39	6	9	3	0	1	5	2	6	0	0	L	R	6-1	195	12-15-76	1998	Santo Domingo, D.R.
Singletary, Dan	.310	58	213	53	66	9	6	8	44	37	34	15	4	L	L	6-0	180	8-23-75	1998	Paterson, N.J.
Weichard, Paul	.293	54	188	37	55	10	2	0	28	38	45	19	4	B	L	5-11	195	11-7-79	1997	Melbourne, Australia
Wilson, Keith	1.000	2	2	1	2	0	0	0	0	0	0	0	0	R	R	6-0	200	12-31-73	1996	Buckeye, Ariz.

GAMES BY POSITION: C—Beasley 10, Hammock 52, McAffee 17, Santonocito 1, Wilson 1. **1B**—Cust 1, Downing 8, J. Guzman 2, Mendez 20, Neal 43, Santonocito 3, Singletary 4. **2B**—Cintron 1, Downing 37, Martinez 48. **3B**—Brooks 67, Hammock 1, Martinez 8, Santonocito 7. **SS**—Cintron 66, Martinez 11, Santonocito 1. **OF**—Conyer 11, Cust 61, A. Guzman 27, J. Guzman 28, Joseph 13, Rinne 15, Rodriguez 1, Singletary 39, Weichard 53.

PITCHING	W	L	ERA	G	GS	CG	SV	IP	H	R	ER	BB	SO	B	T	HT	WT	DOB	1st Yr	Resides
Abeyta, Scott	2	1	4.54	24	0	0	3	36	43	24	18	15	38	L	L	6-0	190	3-14-77	1997	Vallejo, Calif.
Barndollar, Jeff	0	0	8.18	6	1	0	0	11	15	13	10	10	4	R	R	6-4	195	4-29-77	1998	Mission Viejo, Calif.
Bido, Jose	4	6	4.14	18	7	1	0	63	64	38	29	19	48	R	R	6-3	170	12-20-78	1996	San Francisco de Macoris, D.R.
Davis, Phil	2	2	6.81	20	0	0	1	36	33	31	27	31	36	R	R	6-2	200	9-22-75	1998	Cayucos, Calif.
Fuller, Jody	5	1	3.95	18	7	0	0	55	45	26	24	24	41	R	R	6-3	220	9-12-76	1998	Huntingdon, Tenn.
Giambalvo, Paul	5	1	2.48	22	0	0	2	36	28	14	10	12	41	R	R	6-1	170	3-17-75	1998	Winter Park, Fla.
Kees, Justin	5	3	4.32	17	10	0	0	50	45	33	24	41	46	R	R	6-1	190	8-5-77	1998	Danville, Ill.
Kohl, Doug	2	1	4.66	13	13	1	0	64	72	42	33	27	43	R	R	6-4	210	7-9-79	1997	Henderson, Nev.
Koplove, Mike	1	2	3.54	12	1	0	2	28	23	12	11	3	22	R	R	6-0	160	8-30-76	1998	Philadelphia, Pa.
McCall, Travis	0	1	13.50	1	1	0	0	3	5	7	4	2	3	L	L	5-11	185	12-20-77	1996	Chino Hills, Calif.
McCutcheon, Mike	5	3	5.43	17	10	0	0	65	66	45	39	34	40	L	L	6-0	165	7-5-77	1996	Mauna Loa, Hawaii
Mendoza, Hatuey	0	1	27.00	1	1	0	0	1	2	4	2	3	1	R	R	6-0	164	3-16-80	1997	Santo Domingo, D.R.
Niehaus, Troy	1	1	5.63	19	0	0	1	38	52	36	24	18	23	L	L	6-6	200	5-16-77	1998	Manchester, Mich.
Prinz, Bret	4	2	3.09	11	10	0	0	47	49	26	16	13	30	R	R	6-3	200	6-15-77	1998	Peoria, Ariz.
Sanchez, Simon	5	3	4.11	13	13	0	0	61	72	39	28	25	37	R	R	6-1	182	3-24-78	1996	San Francisco de Macoris, D.R.
Tate, Seth	0	4	7.06	9	1	0	0	22	30	18	17	13	18	R	R	6-0	185	1-7-77	1997	Wenatchee, Wash.
Verigood, Steve	2	0	1.16	15	0	0	3	23	11	5	3	12	17	R	L	6-6	195	4-13-76	1997	Columbia, S.C.

TUCSON — Rookie

ARIZONA LEAGUE

BATTING	AVG	G	AB	R	H	2B	3B	HR	RBI	BB	SO	SB	CS	B	T	HT	WT	DOB	1st Yr	Resides
Beasley, Justin	.231	3	13	1	3	1	0	0	1	1	2	0	0	R	R	6-1	215	10-13-75	1998	Olmsted, Ohio
Closser, J.D.	.313	45	150	26	47	13	2	4	21	37	36	3	2	B	R	5-11	175	1-15-80	1998	Alexandria, Ind.
Conyer, Darryl	.216	26	102	20	22	1	6	0	12	17	46	18	2	L	L	5-10	190	12-10-79	1998	San Diego, Calif.
Corbett, Heath	.289	34	121	13	35	9	0	2	25	11	40	3	1	R	R	6-4	195	4-24-80	1998	Riceville, Tenn.
Egly, John	.172	35	122	14	21	2	1	1	9	9	58	4	2	B	R	6-4	190	12-23-79	1998	Mountain View, Mo.
Gann, Jamie	.429	2	7	1	3	1	0	0	1	0	2	0	0	R	R	6-3	190	5-1-75	1996	Norman, Okla.
Hall, Victor	.188	28	101	10	19	1	1	0	10	10	29	14	2	L	L	5-10	160	9-16-80	1998	Arleta, Calif.
Heintzelman, Brian	.289	15	38	6	11	0	0	1	10	5	11	1	1	R	R	6-0	198	8-15-75	1998	Scottsdale, Ariz.
Joseph, Adolfo	.331	28	124	31	41	8	4	3	28	4	39	10	0	R	R	6-3	175	10-6-80	1998	Higuey, D.R.
Kail, Tom	.265	26	102	13	27	2	4	0	13	5	18	2	2	R	R	6-4	210	7-22-79	1998	Pittsburgh, Pa.
Knorr, Mario	.289	41	149	28	43	3	3	0	15	22	35	11	4	L	R	5-11	175	12-4-79	1998	Lakeside, Calif.
Lopez, Miguel	.355	22	76	8	27	9	1	2	16	5	9	3	2	R	R	5-11	180	10-12-78	1996	Scottsdale, Ariz.
McCarty, Brock	.226	43	146	19	33	4	1	1	15	11	43	16	4	R	R	6-2	205	10-1-79	1998	Monroe, La.
Meier, Dan	.343	12	35	10	12	3	0	1	5	11	8	1	0	L	L	6-0	180	8-13-77	1998	Aurora, Colo.
Moye, Tutu	.224	24	85	10	19	4	0	2	13	5	21	1	0	R	R	6-0	190	9-8-78	1997	Greenville, N.C.
Neal, Steve	.319	12	47	8	15	4	0	0	8	6	13	4	0	L	L	6-2	260	2-14-77	1998	Pine Bluff, Ark.
Neubart, Adam	.158	6	19	6	3	2	0	0	0	3	2	1	0	R	R	5-11	165	7-23-77	1998	Livingston, N.J.
Noboa, Joel	.276	39	152	19	42	9	2	3	20	10	49	4	3	R	R	6-0	172	11-27-79	1997	Santo Domingo, D.R.
Proctor, Jerry	.167	3	6	1	1	0	0	0	1	0	1	0	0	R	R	6-5	200	3-5-78	1996	Pasadena, Calif.
Stankiewicz, Andy	.300	3	10	2	3	0	0	0	3	0	0	0	0	R	R	5-9	165	8-10-64	1986	Gilbert, Ariz.
Urquiola, Carlos	.618	9	34	14	21	3	4	0	10	5	5	13	1	L	R	5-8	150	4-22-80	1997	Caracas, Ven.
Valera, Gregori	.282	45	163	20	46	11	1	0	11	7	34	2	1	R	R	6-0	150	4-11-79	1996	Palenque, D.R.
Vicente, Audo	.271	24	85	20	23	3	1	0	5	9	18	12	3	B	R	6-1	155	8-1-79	1996	Santo Domingo, D.R.

GAMES BY POSITION: C—Beasley 3, Closser 37, Heintzelman 8, Lopez 10. **1B**—Closser 2, Egly 16, Heintzelman 2, Meier 11, Moye 10, Neal 11, Vicente 5. **2B**—Knorr 30, McCarty 1, Moye 6, Stankiewicz 3, Urquiola 9, Vicente 10. **3B**—Egly 19, Moye 3, Noboa 37. **SS**—Neubart 2, Valera 45, Vicente 9. **OF**—Conyer 22, Corbett 28, Gann 2, Hall 23, Heintzelman 3, Joseph 23, Kail 17, Knorr 7, Lopez 1, McCarty 38, Moye 6, Neubart 4, Proctor 3.

PITCHING	W	L	ERA	G	GS	CG	SV	IP	H	R	ER	BB	SO	B	T	HT	WT	DOB	1st Yr	Resides
Barndollar, Jeff	2	1	4.01	9	6	0	0	43	43	22	19	15	46	R	R	6-4	195	4-29-77	1998	Mission Viejo, Calif.
Bevis, P.J.	3	3	5.96	14	9	0	0	45	55	39	30	10	48	R	R	6-2	175	7-28-80	1998	Capalaba, Australia
Crivello, Justin	0	2	3.86	20	0	0	3	30	30	15	13	16	42	L	L	5-8	170	9-8-78	1998	Woodinville, Wash.
Fleming, John	0	0	0.00	1	0	0	1	1	2	0	0	1	2	R	R	6-4	175	1-20-78	1996	Chula Vista, Calif.
Good, Andrew	1	3	4.28	9	8	0	0	34	46	25	16	7	25	R	R	6-3	175	9-19-79	1998	Rochester Hills, Mich.
Griman, Carlos	0	1	5.14	2	2	0	0	7	8	6	4	5	7	R	R	6-2	166	1-26-79	1996	Carabobo, Ven.
Jimenez, Francisco	3	4	6.43	12	3	0	0	28	36	24	20	7	18	R	R	6-1	160	3-13-78	1996	San Juan de la Maguan, D.R.
Jones, Keith	0	0	27.00	2	0	0	0	1	7	4	4	0	2	R	R	6-2	190	1-30-76	1997	Whittier, Calif.
Kelley, Brenton	0	2	2.70	17	0	0	6	23	24	10	7	4	27	R	R	6-1	180	3-28-76	1998	Texarkana, Texas
Koplove, Mike	0	0	9.00	2	0	0	0	4	4	4	4	2	5	R	R	6-0	160	8-30-76	1998	Philadelphia, Pa.
Manuel, Barry	0	0	0.00	1	0	0	0	2	1	0	0	0	2	R	R	5-11	185	8-12-65	1987	Mamou, La.
Mendoza, Hatuey	2	3	3.65	11	10	0	0	44	43	30	18	23	54	R	R	6-0	164	3-16-80	1997	Santo Domingo, D.R.
Morel, Francis	3	2	4.13	15	6	0	0	57	64	32	26	17	41	R	R	6-5	196	12-22-78	1996	Cabrera, D.R.
Pass, Jeff	4	1	8.78	16	0	0	1	27	27	31	26	26	28	L	L	6-1	168	1-3-80	1998	Muncie, Ind.
Prinz, Bret	0	0	3.38	4	0	0	0	5	7	3	2	0	3	R	R	6-3	200	6-15-77	1998	Peoria, Ariz.
Rhodes, Kendall	2	1	3.32	13	0	0	0	22	24	18	8	12	20	R	R	6-1	175	5-29-77	1998	Crockett, Texas
Robinson, Ken	0	0	0.00	1	1	0	0	2	0	0	0	0	6	R	R	5-9	170	11-3-69	1991	Jacksonville, Fla.
Rodriguez, Felix	0	0	4.15	3	2	0	0	4	3	4	2	2	5	R	R	6-1	180	12-5-72	1990	Montecristi, D.R.
Stockman, Phil	0	0	0.00	1	0	0	0	0	0	0	0	2	1	R	R	6-5	180	1-25-80	1997	Mount Warren Park, Australia
Trejo, Francisco	2	5	6.42	13	6	0	0	41	45	37	29	27	48	L	L	5-11	142	3-6-80	1997	Santo Domingo, D.R.
Verigood, Steve	0	1	5.68	4	0	0	0	6	7	5	4	0	9	R	L	6-6	195	4-13-76	1997	Columbia, S.C.
White, Matt	2	1	4.60	15	2	0	0	43	46	28	22	19	40	R	R	6-1	170	9-15-77	1998	Portland, Ore.

ATLANTA BRAVES

Familiar ending haunts Braves despite record 106 wins

BY BILL BALLEW

The 1998 season proved to be the same old song for the Atlanta Braves.

After setting a franchise record by winning 106 games during the regular season and sweeping their third straight Division Series, the Braves lost the National League Championship Series in six games for the second straight year, this time to San Diego. Padres pitchers offset Atlanta's strong starting rotation by shutting out the Braves twice and holding them to 18 runs in six games. The hitting woes were most evident with Andres Galarraga and Chipper Jones, who went a combined 7-for-45 with five RBIs, four of which came on Galarraga's grand slam in Game Four.

Despite the bitter end to the campaign, the Braves continued to be the most consistent team of the 1990s. Atlanta extended its major league record by reaching the playoffs for the seventh straight year. Behind Galarraga, who hit 44 home runs and drove in 121 runs in his first season with the club, the Braves established franchise marks for homers (215, second in the NL), RBIs (794, third) and fielding percentage (.985, first).

Atlanta also led the league in ERA (3.25) for the second straight season and the third time in four years. The Braves became the first team since the 1930 Washington Senators to boast five 15-game winners. Tom Glavine led the way as the NL's only 20-game winner. John Smoltz showed no ill effects from his second elbow surgery in three years and finished with an .850 winning percentage after a late start. An uncharacteristic late-season slump was the only thing that kept Greg Maddux (18-9 with a league-best 2.22 ERA) from a fifth Cy Young Award.

Chipper Jones

JIM McLEAN

Bruce Chen

Players of the Year

Major League: Chipper Jones, 3b

Jones led the Braves with a .404 on-base percentage and 123 runs scored while hitting 34 homers.

Minor League: Bruce Chen, lhp, Rich./Green.

Chen wound up in Atlanta after combining to go 15-8 with a 3.09 ERA and 193 strikeouts at two minor league stops.

The Braves avoided disaster in the bullpen when Kerry Ligtenberg became the first rookie to save 30 games since Todd Worrell in 1986. Ligtenberg, a graduate of the now-defunct independent Prairie League, was pressed into the closer's role when Mark Wohlers succumbed to a side injury in May and could not regain his control after returning from the disabled list. Wohlers' struggles were reminiscent of Steve Blass' bizarre control problems in the early 1970s.

Atlanta's seven minor league teams tied the Dodgers for the worst winning percentage (.439) among the 30 organizations, with only Class A Macon reaching postseason play.

Despite the disappointing record, the organization continued to produce major league talent. In addition to Ligtenberg, John Rocker was promoted to Atlanta in May and established himself as the key lefthander in the bullpen.

The Braves had more help on the way. Lefthander Bruce Chen was named the Double-A Southern League's top pitcher after leading the league in wins and strikeouts at the time of his promotion from Greenville to Triple-A Richmond in early August. He finished the season in Atlanta. Lefthander Odaliz Perez mirrored Chen's season by going from Greenville to Atlanta during the year.

Outfielder George Lombard hit 22 home runs and stole 35 bases for Greenville, but his numbers weren't the best in the organization. Macon second baseman Marcus Giles was named the South Atlantic League's MVP after setting a team record with 37 homers and 108 RBIs.

ORGANIZATION LEADERS

BATTING		
*AVG	Travis Wilson, Macon/Danville (R)	.330
R	Marcus Giles, Macon	111
H	Marcus Giles, Macon	166
TB	Marcus Giles, Macon	321
2B	Marcus Giles, Macon	38
3B	Tyrone Pendergrass, Greenville/Danville (A)	10
HR	Marcus Giles, Macon	37
RBI	Marcus Giles, Macon	108
BB	Marcus Giles, Macon	85
SO	Mike Hessman, Danville (A)	172
SB	Rafael Furcal, Danville (R)	60
PITCHING		
W	Bruce Chen, Richmond/Greenville	15
L	Horacio Ramirez, Macon/Eugene	14
#ERA	Richard Dishman, Danville (A)/Macon	2.55
G	Ray Beasley, Richmond/Danville (A)	56
CG	Three tied at	2
SV	Joe Winkelsas, Greenville/Danville (A)	22
IP	Rob Bell, Danville (A)	178
BB	Dwayne Jacobs, Danville (A)	89
SO	Rob Bell, Danville (A)	197

*Minimum 250 At-Bats #Minimum 75 Innings

Atlanta BRAVES

Manager: Bobby Cox

1998 Record: 106-56, .654 (1st, NL East)

BATTING	AVG	G	AB	R	H	2B	3B	HR	RBI	BB	SO	SB	CS	B	T	HT	WT	DOB	1st Yr	Resides
Bautista, Danny	.250	82	144	17	36	11	0	3	17	7	21	1	0	R	R	5-11	170	5-24-72	1989	Santo Domingo, D.R.
Belliard, Rafael	.250	7	20	1	5	0	0	0	1	0	1	0	0	R	R	5-6	160	10-24-61	1980	Boca Raton, Fla.
Colbrunn, Greg	.295	28	44	6	13	3	0	1	10	2	11	1	0	R	R	6-0	200	7-26-69	1988	Weston, Fla.
2-team (62 Colo.)	.307	90	166	18	51	11	2	3	23	10	34	4	3							
DeRosa, Mark	.333	5	3	2	1	0	0	0	0	0	1	0	0	R	R	6-1	185	2-26-75	1996	Carlstadt, N.J.
Galarraga, Andres	.305	153	555	103	169	27	1	44	121	63	146	7	6	R	R	6-3	235	6-18-61	1979	Caracas, Ven.
Graffanino, Tony	.211	105	289	32	61	14	1	5	22	24	68	1	4	R	R	6-1	200	6-6-72	1990	Marietta, Ga.
Guillen, Ozzie	.277	83	264	35	73	15	1	1	22	24	25	1	4	L	R	5-11	165	1-20-64	1981	Caracas, Ven.
Helms, Wes	.308	7	13	2	4	1	0	1	2	0	4	0	0	R	R	6-4	230	5-12-76	1994	Gastonia, N.C.
Holbert, Ray	.133	8	15	2	2	0	0	0	1	2	4	0	0	R	R	6-0	175	9-25-70	1988	Phoenix, Ariz.
Hollins, Damon	.167	3	6	0	1	0	0	0	0	0	1	0	0	R	L	5-11	180	6-12-74	1992	Vallejo, Calif.
Jones, Andruw	.271	159	582	89	158	33	8	31	90	40	129	27	4	R	R	6-1	185	4-23-77	1994	Willemstad, Neth. Antilles
Jones, Chipper	.313	160	601	123	188	29	5	34	107	96	93	16	6	B	R	6-4	210	4-24-72	1990	Alpharetta, Ga.
Klesko, Ryan	.274	129	427	69	117	29	1	18	70	56	66	5	3	L	L	6-3	220	6-12-71	1989	Boynton Beach, Fla.
Lockhart, Keith	.257	109	366	50	94	21	0	9	37	29	37	2	2	L	R	5-10	170	11-10-64	1986	Overland Park, Kan.
Lombard, George	.333	6	6	2	2	0	0	1	1	0	1	1	0	L	R	6-0	208	9-14-75	1994	Atlanta, Ga.
Lopez, Javy	.284	133	489	73	139	21	1	34	106	30	85	5	3	R	R	6-3	200	11-5-70	1988	Ponce, P.R.
Malloy, Marty	.179	11	28	3	5	1	0	1	1	2	2	0	0	L	R	5-10	160	7-6-72	1992	Trenton, Fla.
Perez, Eddie	.336	61	149	18	50	12	0	6	32	15	28	1	1	R	R	6-1	185	5-4-68	1987	Maracaibo, Ven.
Pride, Curtis	.252	70	107	19	27	6	1	3	9	9	29	4	0	L	R	6-0	210	12-17-68	1986	West Palm Beach, Fla.
Simon, Randall	.188	7	16	2	3	0	0	0	4	0	1	0	0	L	L	6-0	180	5-26-75	1993	Willemstad, Neth. Antilles
Tucker, Michael	.244	130	414	54	101	27	3	13	46	49	112	8	3	L	R	6-2	185	6-25-71	1992	Lehigh Acres, Fla.
Weiss, Walt	.280	96	347	64	97	18	2	0	27	59	53	7	1	B	R	6-0	178	11-28-63	1985	Aurora, Colo.
Williams, Gerald	.305	129	266	46	81	19	2	10	44	17	48	11	5	R	R	6-2	185	8-10-66	1987	La Place, La.

PITCHING	W	L	ERA	G	GS	CG	SV	IP	H	R	ER	BB	SO	B	T	HT	WT	DOB	1st Yr	Resides
Butler, Adam	0	1	10.80	8	0	0	0	5	5	7	6	6	7	L	L	6-2	225	8-17-73	1995	Burke, Va.
Byrd, Paul	0	0	13.50	1	0	0	0	2	4	3	3	1	1	R	R	6-1	185	12-3-70	1991	Louisville, Ky.
Cather, Mike	2	2	3.92	36	0	0	0	41	30	21	18	12	33	R	R	6-2	195	12-17-70	1993	Folsom, Calif.
Charlton, Norm	0	0	1.38	13	0	0	1	13	7	2	2	8	6	B	L	6-3	205	1-6-63	1984	Tilden, Texas
Chen, Bruce	2	0	3.98	4	4	0	0	20	23	9	9	9	17	B	L	6-2	150	6-19-77	1994	Panama City, Panama
Edmondson, Brian	0	1	4.32	10	0	0	0	17	14	10	8	8	8	R	R	6-2	175	1-29-73	1991	Riverside, Calif.
Embree, Alan	1	0	4.34	20	0	0	0	19	23	14	9	10	19	L	L	6-2	190	1-23-70	1990	Vancouver, Wash.
Glavine, Tom	20	6	2.47	33	33	4	0	229	202	67	63	74	157	L	L	6-1	185	3-25-66	1984	Alpharetta, Ga.
Ligtenberg, Kerry	3	2	2.71	75	0	0	30	73	51	24	22	24	79	R	R	6-2	205	5-11-71	1994	Cottage Grove, Minn.
Maddux, Greg	18	9	2.22	34	34	9	0	251	201	75	62	45	204	R	R	6-0	175	4-14-66	1984	Las Vegas, Nev.
Martinez, Dennis	4	6	4.45	53	5	1	2	91	109	53	45	19	62	R	R	6-1	183	5-14-55	1974	Miami, Fla.
Millwood, Kevin	17	8	4.08	31	29	3	0	174	175	86	79	56	163	R	R	6-4	220	12-24-74	1993	Bessemer City, N.C.
Neagle, Denny	16	11	3.55	32	31	5	0	210	196	91	83	60	165	L	L	6-2	225	9-13-68	1989	Alpharetta, Ga.
Perez, Odaliz	0	1	4.22	10	0	0	0	11	10	5	5	4	5	L	L	6-0	150	6-7-78	1994	Las Matas de Farfan, D.R.
Rocker, John	1	3	2.13	47	0	0	2	38	22	10	9	22	42	R	L	6-4	210	10-17-74	1994	Macon, Ga.
Seanez, Rudy	4	1	2.75	34	0	0	2	36	25	13	11	15	50	R	R	5-10	185	10-20-68	1986	El Centro, Calif.
Smoltz, John	17	3	2.90	26	26	2	0	168	145	58	54	44	173	R	R	6-3	205	5-15-67	1986	Duluth, Ga.
Springer, Russ	1	1	4.05	22	0	0	0	20	22	10	9	16	19	R	R	6-4	205	11-7-68	1989	Pollack, La.
2-team (26 Houston)	5	4	4.10	48	0	0	0	53	51	26	24	30	56							
Wohlers, Mark	0	1	10.18	27	0	0	8	20	18	23	23	33	22	R	R	6-4	207	1-23-70	1988	Alpharetta, Ga.

FIELDING

Catcher	PCT	G	PO	A	E	DP	PB
Lopez	.995	128	978	68	5	6	11
Perez	.997	45	275	28	1	2	2

First Base	PCT	G	PO	A	E	DP
Colbrunn	1.000	9	55	4	0	2
Galarraga	.992	149	1219	81	11	114
Guillen	1.000	1	2	0	0	0
Klesko	.981	7	48	4	1	4
Perez	.938	8	15	0	1	1
Simon	1.000	4	36	1	0	3

Second Base	PCT	G	PO	A	E	DP
Graffanino	.971	93	139	227	11	41
Guillen	1.000	2	1	5	0	1
Lockhart	.984	97	130	250	6	56
Malloy	1.000	10	16	22	0	4

Third Base	PCT	G	PO	A	E	DP
Graffanino	.000	1	0	0	0	0
Guillen	1.000	1	1	1	0	0
Helms	.750	4	1	2	1	0
C. Jones	.971	159	105	291	12	28
Lockhart	.000	1	0	0	0	0

Shortstop	PCT	G	PO	A	E	DP
Belliard	.952	7	7	13	1	4
De Rosa	1.000	4	1	1	0	0
Graffanino	1.000	2	0	1	0	0
Guillen	.977	71	93	160	6	25
Holbert	.952	7	6	14	1	3
Weiss	.967	96	96	255	12	63

Outfield	PCT	G	PO	A	E	DP
Bautista	.959	58	47	0	2	0
Colbrunn	1.000	1	2	0	0	0
A. Jones	.995	159	413	20	2	6
Klesko	.994	120	146	9	1	1
Lombard	1.000	2	2	0	0	0
Pride	1.000	22	41	0	0	0
Tucker	.995	118	194	5	1	1
Williams	.970	120	159	2	5	0

DAVID SEELIG

Tom Glavine

Atlanta's Andres Galarraga
First baseman led Braves with 44 homers, 121 RBIs

Greenville's George Lombard
Led Double-A club with 22 homers, 35 steals

FARM SYSTEM

Director, Minor League Operations: Deric Ladnier

Class	Farm Team	League	W	L	Pct.	Finish*	Manager	First Yr
AAA	Richmond (Va.) Braves	International	64	80	.444	13th (14)	Jeff Cox	1966
AA	Greenville (S.C.) Braves	Southern	67	72	.482	6th (10)	Randy Ingle	1984
A#	Danville (Va.) 97s	Carolina	58	82	.414	8th (8)	Paul Runge	1998
A	Macon (Ga.) Braves	South Atlantic	69	72	.489	8th (14)	Brian Snitker	1991
A	Eugene (Ore.) Emeralds	Northwest	24	52	.316	8th (8)	Jim Saul	1995
Rookie#	Danville (Va.) Braves	Appalachian	30	38	.441	8th (10)	Franklin Stubbs	1993
Rookie	Orlando (Fla.) Braves	Gulf Coast	25	35	.417	12th (14)	Rick Albert	1976

*Finish in overall standings (No. of teams in league) #Advanced level

RICHMOND — Class AAA

INTERNATIONAL LEAGUE

BATTING	AVG	G	AB	R	H	2B	3B	HR	RBI	BB	SO	SB	CS	B	T	HT	WT	DOB	1st Yr	Resides
Belliard, Rafael	.140	13	43	6	6	0	0	1	2	0	6	0	0	R	R	5-6	160	10-24-61	1980	Boca Raton, Fla.
Hanel, Marcus	.212	29	85	9	18	3	0	0	7	11	23	0	0	R	R	6-4	205	10-19-71	1989	Racine, Wis.
Helms, Wes	.275	125	451	56	124	27	1	13	75	35	103	6	2	R	R	6-4	230	5-12-76	1994	Gastonia, N.C.
Holbert, Ray	.000	1	1	1	0	0	0	0	0	2	1	0	0	R	R	6-0	175	9-25-70	1988	Phoenix, Ariz.
Holifield, Rick	.231	70	186	27	43	9	5	1	11	34	52	15	2	L	L	6-2	165	3-25-70	1988	Montclair, Calif.
Hollins, Damon	.264	119	436	61	115	26	3	13	48	45	85	10	2	R	L	5-11	180	6-12-74	1992	Vallejo, Calif.
Magdaleno, Ricky	.293	73	249	32	73	11	1	5	29	23	63	1	3	R	R	6-0	185	7-6-74	1993	Baldwin Park, Calif.
Mahoney, Mike	.212	71	208	26	44	10	0	5	28	24	49	1	1	R	R	6-1	200	12-5-72	1995	Des Moines, Iowa
Malloy, Marty	.290	124	483	75	140	25	3	7	54	51	65	20	7	L	R	5-10	160	7-6-72	1992	Trenton, Fla.
Martinez, Pablo	.278	15	36	3	10	1	0	0	3	2	10	1	2	B	R	5-10	155	6-29-69	1989	Sabana Grande, D.R.
2-team (63 Louisville)	.243	78	222	25	54	5	1	2	12	20	41	7	5							
Mateo, Jose	.143	6	7	0	1	0	0	0	0	1	3	0	0	B	R	6-0	160	12-28-76	1994	Santo Domingo, D.R.
Olmeda, Jose	.271	111	373	41	101	17	3	4	34	29	55	7	7	B	R	5-9	155	6-20-68	1989	Gurabo, P.R.
Pride, Curtis	.244	21	78	11	19	2	1	2	6	15	17	8	0	L	R	6-0	210	12-17-68	1986	West Palm Beach, Fla.
Schall, Gene	.300	100	340	60	102	22	0	22	73	37	80	1	3	R	R	6-3	190	6-5-70	1991	Willow Grove, Pa.
Simon, Randall	.256	126	484	52	124	20	1	13	70	24	62	4	4	L	L	6-0	180	5-26-75	1993	Willemstad, Neth. Antilles
Tejero, Fausto	.224	77	223	19	50	14	0	4	26	21	48	1	2	R	R	6-2	205	10-26-68	1990	Miami Lakes, Fla.
Tomberlin, Andy	.260	39	104	12	27	3	0	4	15	15	29	1	1	L	L	5-11	185	11-7-66	1986	Monroe, N.C.
2-team (14 Toledo)	.285	53	151	25	43	5	1	6	19	23	44	2	2							
Warner, Mike	.220	96	322	42	71	16	5	6	27	47	85	7	5	L	L	5-10	170	5-9-71	1992	Palm Beach Gardens, Fla.
Whatley, Gabe	.265	135	475	64	126	36	4	10	54	53	93	11	4	L	R	6-0	180	12-29-71	1993	Stone Mountain, Ga.

PITCHING	W	L	ERA	G	GS	CG	SV	IP	H	R	ER	BB	SO	B	T	HT	WT	DOB	1st Yr	Resides
Arnold, Jamie	1	0	9.58	9	2	0	1	21	30	22	22	17	10	R	R	6-2	188	3-24-74	1992	Kissimmee, Fla.
Beasley, Ray	0	0	4.50	2	0	0	0	6	8	3	3	2	8	R	L	5-11	168	10-26-76	1996	Lake City, Fla.

PITCHING	W	L	ERA	G	GS	CG	SV	IP	H	R	ER	BB	SO	B	T	HT	WT	DOB	1st Yr	Resides
Borbon, Pedro	0	1	5.70	20	0	0	0	24	29	17	15	8	15	L	L	6-1	205	11-15-67	1988	Houston, Texas
Briggs, Anthony	7	10	5.33	28	21	0	0	122	125	82	72	57	91	R	R	6-1	155	9-14-73	1994	Manning, S.C.
Buckley, Travis	1	2	3.79	4	3	0	0	19	21	11	8	4	7	R	R	6-4	208	6-15-70	1989	Overland Park, Kan.
Bullard, Jason	1	2	4.91	36	0	0	0	55	56	36	30	22	48	R	R	6-2	185	10-23-68	1991	Sweeny, Texas
Butler, Adam	3	7	3.60	48	4	0	14	100	96	41	40	28	92	L	L	6-2	225	8-17-73	1995	Burke, Va.
Byrd, Paul	5	5	3.69	17	17	2	0	102	92	44	42	36	84	R	R	6-1	185	12-3-70	1991	Louisville, Ky.
Carlyle, Ken	6	12	5.17	30	30	0	0	157	206	104	90	46	76	R	R	6-1	195	4-16-71	1992	Cordova, Tenn.
Cather, Mike	0	1	5.87	11	0	0	0	15	22	12	10	6	10	R	R	6-2	195	12-17-70	1993	Folsom, Calif.
Charlton, Norm	0	0	0.00	2	0	0	0	2	2	0	0	0	1	B	L	6-3	205	1-6-63	1984	Tilden, Texas
Chen, Bruce	2	1	1.88	4	4	0	0	24	17	5	5	19	29	B	L	6-2	150	6-19-77	1994	Panama City, Panama
Cortes, David	3	3	2.82	29	0	0	4	45	37	15	14	14	46	R	R	5-11	195	10-15-73	1996	El Centro, Calif.
Dedrick, Jim	2	3	5.30	26	0	0	0	37	36	24	22	15	27	B	R	6-0	185	4-4-68	1990	Everett, Wash.
Ebert, Derrin	9	9	4.51	29	29	0	0	164	195	94	82	49	88	R	L	6-3	200	8-21-76	1994	Hesperia, Calif.
Harrison, Tommy	2	0	4.50	2	2	0	0	10	9	5	5	3	11	R	R	6-2	185	9-30-71	1993	Miamisburg, Ohio
Jacobs, Ryan	0	0	18.69	2	0	0	0	4	9	9	9	6	1	R	L	6-2	175	2-3-74	1992	Louisville, Ky.
Mix, Greg	2	4	2.92	28	2	0	2	65	52	24	21	19	59	R	R	6-4	225	8-21-71	1993	Albuquerque, N.M.
Perez, Odaliz	1	2	2.96	13	0	0	3	24	26	10	8	7	22	L	L	6-0	150	6-7-78	1994	Las Matas de Farfan, D.R.
Purdy, Shawn	3	1	1.83	16	1	0	0	34	27	9	7	8	20	R	R	6-0	205	7-30-68	1991	St. Cloud, Fla.
Ratliff, Jon	12	13	4.94	29	29	2	0	151	167	90	83	65	143	R	R	6-4	195	10-23-68	1993	Clay, N.Y.
Rocker, John	1	1	1.42	9	0	0	1	19	13	4	3	10	22	R	L	6-4	210	10-17-74	1994	Macon, Ga.
Seanez, Rudy	2	0	1.29	16	0	0	7	21	13	9	3	7	33	R	R	5-10	185	10-20-68	1986	El Centro, Calif.
Wagner, Paul	1	0	1.98	8	0	0	0	14	11	4	3	3	9	R	R	6-1	202	11-14-67	1989	Germantown, Wis.
2-team (3 Louisville)	2	0	5.19	11	3	0	0	26	28	16	15	8	15							
Wohlers, Mark	0	3	20.43	16	0	0	0	12	21	28	28	36	16	R	R	6-4	207	1-23-70	1988	Alpharetta, Ga.

FIELDING

Catcher	PCT	G	PO	A	E	DP	PB
Hanel	.994	25	146	17	1	0	3
Mahoney	.984	65	379	44	7	2	3
Tejero	.983	63	483	42	9	10	4

First Base	PCT	G	PO	A	E	DP
Hanel	1.000	1	8	0	0	0
Schall	.991	26	188	21	2	23
Simon	.989	118	981	51	11	95
Tejero	1.000	3	20	3	0	3
Whatley	1.000	1	7	0	0	1

Second Base	PCT	G	PO	A	E	DP
Magdaleno	.900	3	3	6	1	1
Malloy	.977	123	206	351	13	75
Martinez	1.000	3	7	7	0	1
Olmeda	1.000	14	22	36	0	11
Whatley	1.000	5	6	14	0	1

Third Base	PCT	G	PO	A	E	DP
Helms	.952	124	75	220	15	24
Magdaleno	.667	1	2	0	1	0
Olmeda	.929	7	4	9	1	3
Whatley	.917	17	8	25	3	4

Shortstop	PCT	G	PO	A	E	DP
Belliard	.980	13	20	28	1	4
Holbert	.833	1	2	3	1	0
Magdaleno	.910	58	77	156	23	34
Martinez	1.000	6	1	8	0	1
Mateo	1.000	2	0	2	0	0
Olmeda	.935	77	128	229	25	43

Outfield	PCT	G	PO	A	E	DP
Holifield	.953	51	100	2	5	1
Hollins	.980	113	233	8	5	2
Magdaleno	1.000	6	12	0	0	0
Olmeda	1.000	8	16	1	0	0
Pride	1.000	14	28	1	0	1
Schall	1.000	43	55	2	0	0
Tejero	.000	1	0	0	0	0
Tomberlin	.981	28	50	1	1	0
Warner	.991	89	210	9	2	3
Whatley	.991	107	207	14	2	2

GREENVILLE — Class AA

SOUTHERN LEAGUE

BATTING	AVG	G	AB	R	H	2B	3B	HR	RBI	BB	SO	SB	CS	B	T	HT	WT	DOB	1st Yr	Resides
Bass, Jayson	.227	86	233	27	53	10	1	5	18	37	60	11	6	B	R	6-0	180	6-2-76	1994	Fayette, Ala.
Battle, Howard	.330	79	291	41	96	27	2	10	50	35	51	3	2	R	R	6-0	197	3-25-72	1990	Ocean Springs, Miss.
2-team (12 Birm.)	.312	91	330	47	103	31	2	11	55	39	58	3	2							
Bautista, Danny	.333	2	6	1	2	0	0	1	2	1	1	0	0	R	R	5-11	170	5-24-72	1989	Santo Domingo, D.R.
Delgado, Jose	.125	21	64	3	8	3	0	1	5	11	7	2	2	B	R	5-11	155	3-20-75	1993	Carolina, P.R.
DeRosa, Mark	.267	125	461	67	123	26	2	8	49	60	57	7	13	R	R	6-1	185	2-26-75	1996	Carlstadt, N.J.
Eaglin, Mike	.256	129	492	84	126	22	2	9	47	51	107	30	19	R	R	5-10	170	4-25-73	1992	Vallejo, Calif.
Goodell, Steve	.278	5	18	7	5	1	0	3	6	3	3	0	0	R	R	6-3	196	4-23-75	1995	Danville, Calif.
Johnson, Adam	.253	121	411	67	104	21	3	19	77	42	71	7	7	L	L	6-0	185	7-18-75	1996	Naples, Fla.
Katz, Jason	.091	18	33	3	3	0	0	0	5	6	12	2	0	B	R	5-10	180	10-7-73	1996	Bayside, N.Y.
Lombard, George	.308	122	422	84	130	25	4	22	65	71	140	35	5	L	R	6-0	208	9-14-75	1994	Atlanta, Ga.
Mahoney, Mike	.216	20	74	3	16	5	0	1	6	1	20	1	1	R	R	6-1	200	12-5-72	1995	Des Moines, Iowa
Matos, Pascual	.249	99	338	40	84	16	1	12	58	14	102	4	1	R	R	6-2	160	12-23-74	1992	Barahona, D.R.
Norris, Dax	.231	64	199	30	46	15	0	6	26	15	43	1	2	R	R	5-10	190	1-14-73	1996	La Grange, Ga.
Pendergrass, Tyrone	.125	5	16	3	2	0	0	0	0	2	4	1	0	B	R	6-1	174	7-31-76	1995	Hartsville, S.C.
Roberts, Lonell	.291	47	182	26	53	9	5	2	17	11	42	4	4	B	R	6-0	172	6-7-71	1989	Bloomington, Calif.
Rumfield, Toby	.290	125	462	61	134	32	0	10	66	43	67	9	4	R	R	6-3	190	9-4-72	1991	Belton, Texas
Rust, Brian	.257	95	265	43	68	19	1	9	39	35	93	10	1	R	R	6-2	205	8-1-74	1995	Portland, Ore.
Salzano, Jerry	.302	101	324	48	98	19	3	7	49	46	67	14	8	R	R	6-0	175	10-27-74	1992	Trenton, N.J.
Trippy, Joe	.217	64	175	19	38	4	0	1	9	27	33	2	8	L	L	5-10	185	7-31-73	1995	Seattle, Wash.
Warner, Mike	.256	23	78	12	20	6	1	2	5	17	19	3	3	L	L	5-10	170	5-9-71	1992	Palm Beach Gardens, Fla.

PITCHING	W	L	ERA	G	GS	CG	SV	IP	H	R	ER	BB	SO	B	T	HT	WT	DOB	1st Yr	Resides
Arnold, Jamie	1	4	4.43	32	6	0	1	83	93	51	41	46	48	R	R	6-2	188	3-24-74	1992	Kissimmee, Fla.
Borbon, Pedro	0	2	4.74	16	0	0	0	19	21	14	10	14	10	L	L	6-1	205	11-15-67	1988	Houston, Texas
Bowie, Micah	11	6	3.48	30	29	1	0	163	132	73	63	64	160	L	L	6-4	185	11-10-74	1993	Humble, Texas
Briggs, Anthony	1	0	5.68	6	0	0	0	13	12	9	8	8	10	R	R	6-1	155	9-14-73	1994	Manning, S.C.
Brooks, Antone	6	3	3.55	26	0	0	1	38	42	16	15	19	37	L	L	6-0	176	12-20-73	1995	Florence, S.C.
Bullard, Jason	1	1	1.06	17	0	0	10	17	9	3	2	8	13	R	R	6-2	185	10-23-68	1991	Sweeny, Texas
Chen, Bruce	13	7	3.29	24	23	1	0	139	106	57	51	48	164	B	L	6-2	150	6-19-77	1994	Panama City, Panama
Cruz, Charlie	3	3	3.33	49	1	0	4	73	80	33	27	31	57	L	L	5-10	175	10-22-73	1995	Miami, Fla.
Flach, Jason	0	0	0.00	1	0	0	0	1	3	0	0	0	4	R	R	6-0	165	11-25-73	1996	Davenport, Iowa
Jacobs, Ryan	6	9	5.35	35	15	0	0	101	104	73	60	72	74	R	L	6-2	175	2-3-74	1992	Louisville, Ky.
Manzano, Adrian	1	5	4.92	39	5	0	8	64	72	43	35	29	57	R	R	5-9	184	11-27-78	1996	Jalisco, Mexico
McGlinchy, Kevin	1	1	5.18	6	6	0	0	33	35	19	19	15	20	R	R	6-5	220	6-28-77	1996	Ocala, Fla.
Mix, Greg	1	1	5.04	22	0	0	2	25	32	19	14	11	18	R	R	6-4	225	8-21-71	1993	Albuquerque, N.M.
Nelson, Erick	1	2	9.82	4	0	0	0	11	14	13	12	6	3	L	L	6-2	185	5-22-72	1997	Bemidji, Minn.
Nelson, Joe	6	9	4.98	45	12	1	2	108	124	76	60	69	74	R	R	6-2	185	10-25-74	1996	Alameda, Calif.
Olszewski, Eric	1	3	7.18	24	0	0	1	31	26	27	25	37	31	L	R	6-3	185	11-4-74	1993	Spring, Texas

PITCHING	W	L	ERA	G	GS	CG	SV	IP	H	R	ER	BB	SO	B	T	HT	WT	DOB	1st Yr	Resides
Perez, Odaliz	6	5	4.02	23	21	0	0	132	127	67	59	53	143	L	L	6-0	150	6-7-78	1994	Las Matas de Farfan, D.R.
Schutz, Carl	1	3	5.59	33	0	0	4	37	41	29	23	32	33	L	L	5-11	200	8-22-71	1993	Paulina, La.
Shumate, Jacob	0	1	15.43	2	0	0	0	2	3	4	4	4	1	R	R	6-2	190	1-22-76	1994	Hartsville, S.C.
Smoltz, John	0	1	2.57	3	3	0	0	14	11	4	4	3	16	R	R	6-3	205	5-15-67	1986	Duluth, Ga.
Villegas, Ismael	7	6	5.28	40	17	1	3	124	134	78	73	71	120	R	R	6-0	188	8-12-76	1995	Caguas, P.R.
Winkelsas, Joe	0	0	4.15	4	0	0	0	1	3	2	2	1	3	R	R	6-3	188	9-14-73	1996	Buffalo, N.Y.
Wohlers, Mark	0	0	0.00	1	1	0	0	1	1	1	0	1	1	R	R	6-4	207	1-23-70	1988	Alpharetta, Ga.

FIELDING

Catcher	PCT	G	PO	A	E	DP	PB
Mahoney	.987	18	140	14	2	1	2
Matos	.981	95	690	99	15	11	12
Norris	.984	32	219	29	4	2	3
Rumfield	1.000	6	32	2	0	1	1

First Base	PCT	G	PO	A	E	DP
Johnson	.955	7	39	3	2	6
Norris	.960	5	23	1	1	2
Rumfield	.985	114	867	64	14	77
Rust	.989	25	160	12	2	18
Salzano	.973	5	36	0	1	5

Second Base	PCT	G	PO	A	E	DP
Battle	1.000	1	1	1	0	0
Delgado	.984	12	28	32	1	10
Eaglin	.961	124	258	329	24	71
Katz	1.000	3	5	4	0	2
Rumfield	1.000	1	0	2	0	0
Rust	1.000	1	0	1	0	0
Salzano	.864	7	9	10	3	2

Third Base	PCT	G	PO	A	E	DP
Battle	.922	68	39	126	14	16
Rust	.944	56	37	98	8	16
Salzano	.863	30	19	50	11	3

Shortstop	PCT	G	PO	A	E	DP
Battle	1.000	7	7	11	0	2
Delgado	.875	3	2	5	1	1
DeRosa	.964	125	195	338	20	76
Goodell	1.000	5	2	16	0	4
Salzano	1.000	3	3	10	0	1

Outfield	PCT	G	PO	A	E	DP
Bass	.968	79	150	3	5	1
Bautista	1.000	2	6	0	0	0
Eaglin	1.000	1	2	0	0	0
Johnson	.979	91	184	2	4	0
Katz	1.000	7	13	0	0	0
Lombard	.947	119	170	8	10	1
Pendergrass	.889	5	8	0	1	0
Roberts	.981	44	98	3	2	1
Salzano	.943	45	65	1	4	0
Trippy	.978	48	83	6	2	2
Warner	1.000	20	42	0	0	0

DANVILLE — Class A

CAROLINA LEAGUE

BATTING	AVG	G	AB	R	H	2B	3B	HR	RBI	BB	SO	SB	CS	B	T	HT	WT	DOB	1st Yr	Resides
Bass, Jayson	.158	10	38	3	6	1	1	0	1	0	12	2	1	B	R	6-0	180	6-2-76	1994	Fayette, Ala.
Borges, Alex	.108	21	37	0	4	0	0	0	1	2	15	1	0	R	R	6-1	185	7-2-74	1996	Miramar, Fla.
Burke, Mark	.108	13	37	2	4	1	0	0	1	0	14	1	0	L	L	6-0	195	6-7-75	1997	Portland, Ore.
Delgado, Jose	.241	82	303	26	73	10	1	3	18	19	45	9	7	B	R	5-11	155	3-20-75	1993	Carolina, P.R.
Goodell, Steve	.298	54	198	21	59	14	2	5	20	17	42	3	4	R	R	6-3	196	4-23-75	1995	Danville, Calif.
Hessman, Mike	.200	118	445	47	89	21	0	20	63	30	172	3	3	R	R	6-5	215	3-5-78	1996	Westminster, Calif.
Katz, Jason	.200	6	15	2	3	0	1	0	2	1	4	0	0	B	R	5-10	180	10-7-73	1996	Bayside, N.Y.
Lunar, Fernando	.220	91	286	19	63	9	0	3	28	6	52	1	1	R	R	6-1	195	5-25-77	1994	Anaco, Ven.
Mateo, Jose	.221	74	217	22	48	8	0	0	10	27	57	13	14	B	R	6-0	160	12-28-76	1994	Santo Domingo, D.R.
Mortimer, Mark	.237	98	338	32	80	11	2	6	33	41	53	0	4	R	R	6-1	215	9-15-75	1997	Forest Park, Ga.
Norris, Dax	.326	28	92	9	30	12	1	3	21	7	15	1	2	R	R	5-10	190	1-14-73	1996	La Grange, Ga.
Pendergrass, Tyrone	.276	132	518	74	143	23	10	4	35	43	91	39	18	B	R	6-1	174	7-31-76	1995	Hartsville, S.C.
Ross, Jason	.212	115	378	36	80	14	3	6	34	15	107	11	5	R	R	6-4	215	6-10-74	1996	Augusta, Ga.
Scharrer, Jim	.193	115	409	28	79	23	0	6	31	17	118	1	5	R	R	6-4	220	11-5-76	1995	Erie, Pa.
Stevenson, Chad	.103	9	29	2	3	0	0	0	0	0	11	0	0	R	R	6-4	215	2-3-76	1994	Henderson, Nev.
Stewart, Colin	.333	4	12	3	4	0	0	0	1	3	2	4	1	R	R	6-1	185	9-2-76	1998	San Jose, Calif.
Terhune, Mike	.220	107	368	44	81	9	0	3	26	17	67	8	5	B	R	6-1	185	10-14-75	1996	Pocono Manor, Pa.
Trippy, Joe	.189	31	106	8	20	2	0	0	5	11	22	10	4	L	L	5-10	185	7-31-73	1995	Seattle, Wash.
Williams, Glenn	.215	134	470	40	101	26	1	9	44	37	132	1	3	R	R	6-2	170	7-18-77	1994	Chipping North, Australia
Wong, Jerrod	.239	81	297	34	71	9	4	5	33	10	62	6	1	L	L	6-3	200	5-29-74	1996	Boise, Idaho

GAMES BY POSITION: C—Borges 11, Lunar 90, Mortimer 39, Norris 13, Stevenson 9. **1B**—Burke 2, Goodell 15, Mortimer 17, Scharrer 96, Wong 16. **2B**—Delgado 5, Mateo 3, Terhune 12, Williams 126. **3B**—Goodell 4, Hessman 112, Terhune 27. **SS**—Delgado 34, Goodell 33, Mateo 64, Terhune 17. **OF**—Bass 10, Borges 2, Burke 2, Delgado 15, Goodell 5, Katz 4, Mateo 6, Mortimer 22, Pendergrass 129, Ross 115, Stewart 4, Terhune 35, Trippy 31, Wong 59.

PITCHING	W	L	ERA	G	GS	CG	SV	IP	H	R	ER	BB	SO	B	T	HT	WT	DOB	1st Yr	Resides
Beasley, Ray	6	8	3.56	54	0	0	8	56	54	26	22	24	55	R	L	5-11	168	10-26-76	1996	Lake City, Fla.
Bell, Rob	7	9	3.28	28	28	2	0	178	169	79	65	46	197	R	R	6-5	225	1-17-77	1995	Marlboro, N.Y.
Corey, Michael	1	0	0.00	2	0	0	0	3	3	0	0	0	2	R	R	6-2	215	9-29-74	1998	Pendleton, Ore.
Culp, Wes	2	4	5.37	37	0	0	0	57	67	42	34	43	33	R	R	6-2	175	12-23-74	1994	Austin, Texas
Dishman, Richard	3	2	1.86	20	11	0	0	77	54	20	16	28	85	R	R	6-5	220	4-26-75	1997	Roosevelt Island, N.Y.
Flach, Jason	5	5	3.14	37	11	0	1	106	110	43	37	31	108	R	R	6-0	165	11-25-73	1996	Davenport, Iowa
Jacobs, Dwayne	5	10	4.99	31	19	0	0	110	92	71	61	89	112	R	R	6-10	210	7-17-76	1994	Jacksonville, Fla.
Marquis, Jason	2	12	4.87	22	22	1	0	115	120	65	62	41	135	L	R	6-1	185	8-21-78	1996	Coral Springs, Fla.
McGlinchy, Kevin	9	8	2.91	22	22	1	0	142	122	55	46	29	129	R	R	6-5	220	6-28-77	1996	Ocala, Fla.
Milburn, Adam	0	2	4.05	45	0	0	2	53	62	32	24	27	33	R	L	6-1	195	4-27-74	1996	Springfield, Ky.
Nelson, Erick	3	1	2.61	10	8	0	0	41	42	17	12	11	38	L	L	6-2	185	5-22-72	1997	Bemidji, Minn.
Onley, Shawn	6	8	3.86	44	2	1	2	93	89	48	40	47	77	R	R	6-5	190	9-10-74	1996	Mount Pleasant, Texas
Porzio, Mike	3	2	2.51	26	11	1	2	97	74	34	27	30	95	L	L	6-3	190	8-20-72	1993	Norwalk, Conn.
Quevedo, Ruben	0	2	3.58	6	6	0	0	33	28	22	13	13	35	R	R	6-1	180	1-5-79	1996	Valencia, Ven.
Tryon, Eric	0	0	11.57	6	0	0	0	5	11	6	6	5	1	R	L	6-0	195	9-3-75	1997	Terre Haute, Ind.
Winkelsas, Joe	6	9	2.22	50	0	0	22	69	66	26	17	24	53	R	R	6-3	188	9-14-73	1996	Buffalo, N.Y.

MACON — Class A

SOUTH ATLANTIC LEAGUE

BATTING	AVG	G	AB	R	H	2B	3B	HR	RBI	BB	SO	SB	CS	B	T	HT	WT	DOB	1st Yr	Resides
Brooks, Anthony	.255	133	502	74	128	26	4	13	55	24	164	17	15	R	R	6-0	195	1-25-77	1996	Pensacola, Fla.
Burke, Mark	.277	65	235	47	65	15	0	8	36	35	36	2	2	L	L	6-0	195	6-7-75	1997	Portland, Ore.
Cameron, Troy	.222	133	472	70	105	20	3	21	65	66	162	4	3	B	R	5-11	180	8-31-78	1997	Plantation, Fla.
Ewan, Bry	.212	19	66	4	14	2	0	1	9	2	27	1	0	R	R	6-2	205	8-2-78	1997	Georgetown, Texas
Giles, Marcus	.329	135	505	111	166	38	3	37	108	85	103	12	5	R	R	5-8	180	5-18-78	1997	El Cajon, Calif.
Hairston, Jason	.240	109	413	61	99	21	2	21	76	32	136	9	7	R	R	6-2	212	5-3-76	1997	Portland, Ore.
Lehr, Ryan	.285	115	400	60	114	26	1	13	69	42	67	1	4	R	R	5-11	205	2-15-79	1997	La Mesa, Calif.

BATTING	AVG	G	AB	R	H	2B	3B	HR	RBI	BB	SO	SB	CS	B	T	HT	WT	DOB	1st Yr	Resides
Mortimer, Mark	.298	28	94	21	28	7	0	5	26	18	11	1	0	R	R	6-1	215	9-15-75	1997	Forest Park, Ga.
Pugh, Josh	.231	40	134	20	31	7	1	0	11	14	38	0	0	R	R	6-0	200	9-10-77	1996	Lexington, Ky.
Sanchez, Manuel	.174	13	46	5	8	1	1	1	4	7	5	1	1	L	R	5-11	160	10-4-76	1994	San Pedro de Macoris, D.R.
Smothers, Stewart	.204	139	506	61	103	17	3	9	60	46	145	17	12	R	R	5-10	180	4-29-76	1997	Los Angeles, Calif.
Spencer, Jeff	.261	115	437	94	114	21	2	28	79	47	143	11	5	R	R	6-2	170	6-25-77	1995	Melbourne, Australia
Stevenson, Chad	.206	32	102	9	21	7	0	0	8	5	26	0	0	R	R	6-4	215	2-3-76	1994	Henderson, Nev.
Thorpe, A.D.	.268	128	519	94	139	21	4	2	34	43	70	21	15	B	R	5-11	160	6-19-77	1996	Rougemont, N.C.
Torrealba, Steve	.273	67	209	28	57	10	0	10	37	20	31	3	0	R	R	6-0	175	2-24-78	1995	Barquisimeto, Ven.
Wilson, Travis	.462	3	13	2	6	0	0	1	4	0	3	0	0	R	R	6-2	185	7-10-77	1996	Christchurch, New Zealand
Zapp, A.J.	.260	20	73	9	19	6	1	3	12	8	18	1	0	L	R	6-3	190	4-24-78	1996	Greenwood, Ind.

GAMES BY POSITION: C—Ewan 13, Mortimer 3, Pugh 39, Stevenson 31, Torrealba 62. **1B**—Burke 39, Lehr 60, Mortimer 18, Spencer 9, Zapp 17. **2B**—Giles 127, Sanchez 3, Thorpe 14. **3B**—Cameron 61, Lehr 41, Mortimer 2, Sanchez 5, Thorpe 36, Torrealba 1, Wilson 2. **SS**—Cameron 70, Thorpe 73. **OF**—Brooks 133, Hairston 63, Mortimer 2, Smothers 139, Spencer 90, Thorpe 2.

PITCHING	W	L	ERA	G	GS	CG	SV	IP	H	R	ER	BB	SO	B	T	HT	WT	DOB	1st Yr	Resides
Bauldree, Joe	1	0	4.05	29	0	0	3	53	49	30	24	19	53	R	R	6-5	175	3-23-77	1995	Wake Forest, N.C.
Borbon, Pedro	0	0	9.00	3	0	0	0	3	4	3	3	1	3	L	L	6-1	205	11-15-67	1988	Houston, Texas
Ciravolo, Jon	1	2	5.02	16	1	0	1	29	37	19	16	17	30	B	R	6-1	190	9-26-75	1997	Kenilworth, N.J.
Dishman, Richard	1	1	3.89	18	0	0	1	39	38	22	17	17	44	R	R	6-5	220	4-26-75	1997	Roosevelt Island, N.Y.
Embry, Byron	2	5	4.39	50	0	0	6	70	51	49	34	50	71	R	R	6-2	240	9-5-76	1997	Richmond, Ky.
Fleck, Will	7	0	2.65	48	0	0	14	71	56	26	21	27	91	R	R	6-0	175	8-29-76	1997	Milford, N.J.
Greene, Ryan	3	3	2.89	22	0	0	2	37	40	19	12	6	46	R	R	6-4	215	8-6-74	1997	Menlo Park, Calif.
Lewis, Derrick	5	6	3.81	23	23	0	0	113	108	64	48	55	100	R	R	6-5	215	5-7-76	1997	Montgomery, Ala.
Nation, Joey	6	12	5.03	29	28	1	0	143	179	102	80	39	141	L	L	6-2	175	9-28-78	1997	Oklahoma City, Okla.
Pacheco, Delvis	7	4	4.97	18	10	0	0	63	67	39	35	14	42	R	R	6-2	180	6-25-78	1995	Maracay, Ven.
Quevedo, Ruben	11	3	3.13	25	15	1	0	112	114	50	39	31	117	R	R	6-1	180	1-5-79	1996	Valencia, Ven.
Ramirez, Horacio	1	7	5.86	12	12	0	0	55	70	50	36	16	38	L	L	6-1	170	11-24-79	1997	Inglewood, Calif.
Rivera, Luis	5	5	3.98	20	20	0	0	93	78	53	41	41	118	R	R	6-3	163	6-21-78	1995	Chihuahua, Mexico
Scarce, Bubba	4	4	4.25	20	1	0	0	36	34	19	17	23	29	R	R	5-11	188	9-30-76	1998	Danville, Va.
Schurman, Ryan	2	4	4.34	17	9	1	0	64	64	43	31	26	53	R	R	6-3	180	8-28-76	1995	Tualatin, Ore.
Shiell, Jason	0	1	4.50	4	3	0	0	8	7	4	4	1	8	R	R	6-0	180	10-19-76	1995	Savannah, Ga.
Shumate, Jacob	5	4	6.75	44	0	0	0	51	44	54	38	75	65	R	R	6-2	190	1-22-76	1994	Hartsville, S.C.
Smoltz, John	0	0	3.60	2	2	0	0	10	7	4	4	1	14	R	R	6-3	205	5-15-67	1986	Duluth, Ga.
Thieme, Richard	0	4	8.29	16	6	0	0	34	41	43	31	28	19	L	L	6-1	216	10-10-75	1997	Lakemont, Ga.
Wyatt, Ben	4	6	7.83	40	9	0	1	87	119	94	76	52	66	L	L	6-4	185	11-14-76	1995	Little Rock, Ark.
Yankosky, L.J.	4	1	2.87	20	2	0	4	47	33	22	15	18	37	R	R	6-2	208	2-1-75	1998	Springfield, Va.

EUGENE — Short-Season Class A

NORTHWEST LEAGUE

BATTING	AVG	G	AB	R	H	2B	3B	HR	RBI	BB	SO	SB	CS	B	T	HT	WT	DOB	1st Yr	Resides
Alvarez, German	.224	23	76	9	17	4	0	0	14	18	11	4	0	L	L	5-11	180	6-6-75	1998	Miami, Fla.
Brignac, Junior	.233	70	270	36	63	13	1	3	29	23	74	15	7	R	R	6-3	175	2-15-78	1996	Sun Valley, Calif.
Castro, Al	.260	74	296	33	77	10	1	3	33	22	49	8	1	B	R	6-1	160	10-23-79	1996	Valencia, Ven.
Cheshier, Casey	.253	55	190	22	48	7	2	6	23	9	51	5	1	R	R	6-3	190	7-13-76	1998	Glendale, Calif.
Cox, Brian	.260	59	208	34	54	11	1	3	23	30	36	7	2	R	R	6-2	180	11-30-75	1998	Shelby, N.C.
Ewan, Bry	.219	56	210	26	46	9	1	6	33	20	72	0	2	R	R	6-2	205	8-2-78	1997	Georgetown, Texas
Gregory, Rich	.221	25	68	11	15	2	1	2	7	8	20	3	0	R	R	6-2	235	7-10-75	1998	Sacramento, Calif.
Hanseen, Tye	.237	38	118	12	28	6	0	0	12	11	21	1	0	R	R	5-10	190	11-22-74	1998	Orem, Utah
Maluchnik, Gregg	.255	58	184	25	47	15	0	2	19	20	55	2	3	R	R	6-3	200	9-14-76	1998	Raleigh, N.C.
Oropeza, Asdrubal	.287	28	108	20	31	6	0	6	24	11	31	0	0	R	R	6-2	170	7-3-80	1996	Barquisimeto, Ven.
Sanchez, Manuel	.259	60	201	28	52	7	4	6	24	12	35	12	5	L	R	5-11	160	10-4-76	1994	San Pedro de Macoris, D.R.
Simmons, Jerry	.275	73	284	48	78	14	3	11	40	25	65	26	11	R	R	5-11	195	6-4-76	1998	Charleston, S.C.
Stewart, Colin	.265	60	204	29	54	7	1	2	23	22	33	12	3	R	R	6-1	185	9-2-76	1998	San Jose, Calif.
Strickland, Greg	.300	56	217	34	65	11	3	2	20	15	57	14	5	L	L	5-10	175	11-8-75	1997	McKenzie, Tenn.

GAMES BY POSITION: C—Ewen 12, Hanseen 36, Maluchnik 32. **1B**—Alvarez 22, Cheshier 26, Gregory 11, Maluchnik 24. **2B**—Castro 37, Cheshier 1, Hanseen 1, Sanchez 48. **3B**—Castro 31, Cheshier 16, Oropeza 28, Sanchez 6. **SS**—Brignac 68, Castro 10. **OF**—Alvarez 1, Cheshier 2, Cox 59, Gregory 9, Maluchnik 1, Simmons 71, Stewart 50, Strickland 44.

PITCHING	W	L	ERA	G	GS	CG	SV	IP	H	R	ER	BB	SO	B	T	HT	WT	DOB	1st Yr	Resides
Abreu, Winston	0	4	6.35	17	10	0	0	45	39	36	32	31	52	R	R	6-2	155	4-5-77	1994	Cotui, D.R.
Birrell, Simon	0	1	9.59	13	0	0	0	25	32	30	27	22	24	R	R	6-6	185	10-7-77	1995	Ephrata, Wash.
Brummitt, Travis	1	7	7.08	17	6	0	1	55	73	60	43	32	34	R	R	6-7	225	4-27-76	1997	Knoxville, Tenn.
Corey, Michael	1	0	1.69	20	0	0	7	32	28	8	6	9	27	R	R	6-2	215	9-29-74	1998	Pendleton, Ore.
Dickinson, Rodney	3	0	3.16	13	0	0	0	26	17	11	9	18	21	R	R	5-10	170	1-9-75	1998	Lawrenceville, Ga.
Frachiseur, Zach	5	4	5.09	23	1	0	1	58	74	45	33	21	74	R	R	6-0	190	9-30-76	1998	Conyers, Ga.
Garmong, Aaron	2	2	4.44	24	2	0	6	47	50	28	23	33	24	L	L	5-11	180	6-3-76	1998	Omaha, Neb.
Holden, Brian	3	4	5.13	17	6	0	1	53	62	41	30	24	37	L	L	6-1	180	6-10-77	1998	West Palm Beach, Fla.
Johnson, Jeremiah	0	1	5.68	7	1	0	0	6	8	6	4	4	3	R	R	6-6	230	7-19-77	1996	Litchfield, Mich.
Lee, Garrett	2	3	6.32	9	9	0	0	47	56	41	33	11	47	R	R	6-5	210	8-17-76	1996	Montrose, Calif.
Mazone, Brian	1	6	5.53	20	9	0	0	68	91	50	42	27	32	L	L	6-4	205	7-26-76	1998	Encinitas, Calif.
Ramirez, Horacio	2	7	6.31	16	8	0	0	56	84	51	39	17	39	L	L	6-1	170	11-24-79	1997	Inglewood, Calif.
Sobkowiak, Scott	3	2	1.55	8	8	0	0	41	25	12	7	13	55	R	R	6-5	230	10-26-77	1998	Loveland, Ohio
Soto, Seferino	1	0	9.09	20	0	0	0	35	44	46	35	53	28	R	R	6-1	185	8-26-75	1995	Escondido, Calif.
Sylvester, Billy	0	11	6.51	16	16	0	0	55	73	61	40	24	42	R	R	6-5	218	10-1-76	1997	Florence, S.C.
Voyles, Brad	0	0	3.09	7	0	0	0	12	9	5	4	10	22	R	R	6-0	195	12-30-76	1998	Green Bay, Wis.

DANVILLE — Rookie

APPALACHIAN LEAGUE

BATTING	AVG	G	AB	R	H	2B	3B	HR	RBI	BB	SO	SB	CS	B	T	HT	WT	DOB	1st Yr	Resides
Aldridge, Cory	.294	60	214	37	63	16	1	3	33	29	48	16	2	L	R	6-0	210	6-13-79	1997	Abilene, Texas
Allen, Troy	.271	63	236	32	64	17	0	3	32	32	63	2	2	L	R	6-5	225	10-8-75	1997	Reston, Va.
Boscan, Jean	.218	51	170	35	37	3	0	4	24	37	44	2	3	R	R	6-2	160	12-26-79	1996	Maracaibo, Ven.

BATTING	AVG	G	AB	R	H	2B	3B	HR	RBI	BB	SO	SB	CS	B	T	HT	WT	DOB	1st Yr	Resides
Furcal, Rafael	.328	66	268	56	88	15	4	0	23	36	29	60	15	B	R	5-10	150	8-24-80	1997	Loma de Cabrera, D.R.
James, Drue	.178	27	73	6	13	2	0	1	9	17	25	1	0	R	R	5-10	215	7-1-76	1998	Blanchard, Okla.
Massimo, Ryan	.206	22	63	6	13	2	0	0	6	4	18	1	0	R	R	6-2	200	2-1-75	1998	Manatee, Fla.
Milton, Prinz	.255	58	220	24	56	5	0	4	33	7	77	10	2	R	R	6-3	225	3-2-79	1997	Gardena, Calif.
Poulsen, Chris	.271	19	70	7	19	3	1	0	9	5	12	0	0	R	R	6-1	190	6-13-76	1998	Fresno, Calif.
Velazquez, Juan	.248	65	230	31	57	8	3	2	21	22	36	16	5	B	R	5-11	150	8-22-78	1997	San Lorenzo, P.R.
Villar, Jose	.172	39	151	22	26	6	3	3	20	12	61	14	7	R	R	6-1	170	5-1-79	1996	Santo Domingo, D.R.
Ward, Greg	.185	52	168	25	31	8	0	3	19	25	58	5	0	R	R	6-5	215	4-8-78	1996	Avon, Conn.
Wilson, Travis	.323	65	269	48	87	25	5	9	48	17	54	16	5	R	R	6-2	185	7-10-77	1996	Christchurch, New Zealand
Zydowsky, John	.212	49	165	27	35	4	0	0	14	23	38	8	4	R	R	5-11	170	4-18-78	1996	Pardeeville, Wis.

GAMES BY POSITION: C—Boscan 49, James 23. **1B**—Allen 50, Massimo 17, Zydowsky 7. **2B**—Furcal 65, Massimo 1, Zydowsky 4. **3B**—Massimo 1, Wilson 65, Zydowsky 2. **SS**—Massimo 1, Velazquez 65, Zydowsky 6. **OF**—Aldridge 58, James 1, Milton 46, Villar 39, Ward 39, Zydowsky 31.

PITCHING	W	L	ERA	G	GS	CG	SV	IP	H	R	ER	BB	SO	B	T	HT	WT	DOB	1st Yr	Resides
Birrell, Simon	3	0	0.96	14	0	0	2	28	14	8	3	15	26	R	R	6-6	185	10-7-77	1995	Ephrata, Wash.
Bowers, Jason	1	0	9.31	13	0	0	0	19	32	23	20	14	9	L	L	6-1	175	1-12-78	1997	Concord, N.C.
Colon, Roman	1	7	5.77	13	13	0	0	73	92	59	47	28	53	R	R	6-3	170	8-13-79	1996	Montecristi, D.R.
Dent, Doug	5	3	3.61	9	9	1	0	47	57	28	19	19	29	R	R	6-8	210	3-23-77	1998	Citrus Heights, Calif.
Gray, Michael	0	3	4.23	20	1	0	4	28	27	15	13	11	41	L	L	6-1	170	12-6-76	1999	Paso Robles, Calif.
Harden, Nathan	0	0	6.60	11	0	0	0	15	12	11	11	14	12	R	R	6-2	185	1-13-78	1996	Dripping Springs, Texas
Herndon, Eric	1	3	5.31	21	0	0	3	42	45	29	25	22	48	L	R	6-1	190	10-4-76	1998	Upper Marlboro, Md.
Holden, Brian	2	0	3.86	4	0	0	0	7	10	3	3	2	10	L	L	6-1	180	6-10-77	1998	West Palm Beach, Fla.
Holzbauer, Joseph	1	0	4.73	17	0	0	0	27	22	17	14	24	24	R	R	6-2	185	4-27-76	1997	Oceanside, Calif.
Phillips, Randy	1	2	9.95	13	0	0	0	19	19	23	21	24	14	L	L	6-2	180	7-21-76	1997	Franklin, Ind.
Scarce, Bubba	0	0	0.00	2	0	0	2	3	1	0	0	2	3	R	R	5-11	188	9-30-76	1998	Danville, Va.
Schmidt, Pat	2	1	5.59	12	0	0	0	19	14	14	12	15	16	L	L	6-3	185	4-3-79	1997	Bellefontaine, Ohio
Simpson, Cory	6	1	5.02	14	6	1	1	52	47	29	29	34	44	R	R	6-5	215	2-1-78	1997	Kentwood, La.
Taylor, Aaron	3	6	6.25	14	14	1	0	72	87	60	50	36	55	R	R	6-5	205	8-20-77	1996	Hahira, Ga.
Truitt, Derrick	0	7	6.91	13	12	0	0	55	72	51	42	27	38	R	R	6-1	170	2-2-78	1998	Columbia, Tenn.
Willoughby, Justin	4	5	4.03	13	13	0	0	74	87	42	33	20	53	L	L	6-3	170	4-9-78	1996	Princeton, N.C.

ORLANDO — Rookie

GULF COAST LEAGUE

BATTING	AVG	G	AB	R	H	2B	3B	HR	RBI	BB	SO	SB	CS	B	T	HT	WT	DOB	1st Yr	Resides
Betemit, Wilson	.220	51	173	23	38	8	4	5	16	20	49	6	5	B	R	6-2	155	7-28-80	1996	Santo Domingo, D.R.
Bronowicz, Scott	.256	27	78	6	20	6	0	0	6	3	18	0	0	L	R	5-11	195	4-14-76	1998	Pittsburgh, Pa.
Burke, Paul	.171	33	76	8	13	8	0	1	5	14	18	0	1	R	R	6-2	200	9-2-77	1998	Louisville, Ky.
Clark, Tommy	.130	33	92	10	12	2	0	1	8	8	40	2	1	R	R	6-2	205	12-21-79	1998	Brunswick, Ga.
Donato, Gregorio	.210	19	62	6	13	4	0	1	6	5	17	1	1	R	R	6-0	185	11-10-80	1998	Clovis, Calif.
Elorduy, Daniel	.237	43	152	18	36	8	0	6	20	6	30	2	1	R	R	6-4	220	11-2-75	1998	Sacramento, Calif.
Frawley, Scott	.287	33	108	11	31	11	1	1	12	9	26	0	2	R	R	6-1	205	9-7-77	1997	Orland Hills, Ill.
Heffernan, Christian	.280	38	82	13	23	5	2	1	10	9	21	5	3	L	R	6-2	193	6-15-78	1997	London, Ontario
Jones, Damien	.271	50	192	25	52	4	1	1	7	10	48	15	7	L	L	6-2	200	7-10-79	1998	Mobile, Ala.
Langerhans, Ryan	.277	43	148	15	41	10	4	2	19	19	38	2	5	L	L	6-3	195	2-20-80	1998	Round Rock, Texas
Lopez, Guuillermo	.179	23	56	2	10	2	0	0	4	5	18	1	1	R	R	6-1	210	4-10-79	1998	Miami, Fla.
McLaughlin, Erik	.100	19	50	1	5	2	0	0	1	4	26	1	1	R	R	6-5	225	8-3-78	1996	Dover, Del.
Mundo, Alberto	.201	44	169	14	34	4	0	2	17	13	35	7	0	B	R	5-11	150	7-3-77	1995	San Carlos, Ven.
Oropeza, Asdrubal	.268	35	127	18	34	10	1	2	13	13	27	4	1	R	R	6-2	170	7-3-80	1996	Barquisimeto, Ven.
Resendez, Carlos	.214	6	14	0	3	0	0	0	2	1	6	0	0	R	R	5-11	190	11-26-76	1997	Victoria, Mexico
Rivas, Justo	.186	37	113	11	21	6	2	0	11	16	31	6	3	R	R	6-1	175	1-9-80	1997	Masaya, Nicaragua
Smith, Toebius	.152	20	46	6	7	1	0	0	0	8	17	0	2	R	R	6-0	188	10-27-79	1998	Clarkton, N.C.
Torres, Luis	.243	48	169	15	41	13	0	1	13	6	26	6	7	B	R	5-10	180	10-20-79	1997	Barranquilla, Colombia

GAMES BY POSITION: C—Bronowicz 16, Burke 29, Frawley 7, Lopez 22, Resendez 5. **1B**—Elorduy 41, Frawley 12, Oropeza 3, Torres 4. **2B**—Mundo 34, Oropeza 1, Torres 28. **3B**—Bronowicz 1, Donato 14, Elorduy 1, Oropeza 31, Torres 14. **SS**—Betemit 50, Mundo 12, Torres 1. **OF**—Bronowicz 1, Clark 26, Heffernan 25, Jones 47, Langerhans 42, McLaughlin 8, Rivas 32, Smith 12.

PITCHING	W	L	ERA	G	GS	CG	SV	IP	H	R	ER	BB	SO	B	T	HT	WT	DOB	1st Yr	Resides
Bong, Jung	1	1	1.49	11	10	0	0	48	31	9	8	14	56	L	L	6-3	175	7-15-80	1997	Norcross, Ga.
Brito, Yorbis	1	0	20.25	3	0	0	0	3	7	6	6	0	2	R	R	6-2	170	6-1-79	1996	San Cristobal, D.R.
Curtis, Daniel	2	1	3.15	14	0	0	2	40	33	17	14	9	32	R	R	6-3	215	11-3-79	1998	Chattanooga, Tenn.
Dansby, Justin	2	2	5.64	15	0	0	1	22	29	15	14	14	23	R	R	6-1	190	2-28-78	1998	Ada, Okla.
Dent, Doug	0	2	4.30	4	4	0	0	15	14	11	7	4	16	R	R	6-8	210	3-23-77	1998	Citrus Heights, Calif.
Dukeman, Greg	3	2	2.32	18	0	0	7	31	26	10	8	8	19	R	R	6-7	175	12-6-78	1998	Costa Mesa, Calif.
Ennis, John	0	3	4.62	8	2	0	0	25	30	16	13	6	18	R	R	6-5	220	10-17-79	1998	North Hills, Calif.
Lelless, Alex	4	0	4.41	14	0	0	2	33	32	16	16	8	21	R	R	6-3	195	11-22-79	1998	Cambridge, Mass.
Martinez, Lionel	0	0	6.00	3	0	0	0	3	3	2	2	1	4	R	R	6-3	165	11-28-79	1996	San Felix, Ven.
Mayi, Leonardo	2	7	3.67	12	12	0	0	56	63	29	23	9	54	L	L	6-0	160	12-20-79	1996	Santo Domingo, D.R.
McGinnis, Johnny	2	6	1.89	13	11	0	0	62	40	23	13	17	53	R	R	6-3	208	9-23-79	1998	Stone Mountain, Ga.
Mendez, David	2	2	5.66	11	8	0	0	41	39	31	26	19	41	L	L	6-2	192	10-1-79	1996	Pubelo Nuevo, Panama
Perez, Elvis	0	1	5.50	11	2	0	0	36	43	23	22	12	26	R	R	6-3	160	7-4-79	1996	Santo Domingo, D.R.
Schmidt, Pat	1	1	8.44	3	0	0	0	5	8	5	5	4	6	L	L	6-3	185	4-3-79	1997	Bellefontaine, Ohio
Targac, Matt	2	2	3.99	13	2	0	0	38	22	20	17	13	48	B	L	6-3	210	6-25-80	1998	Delano, Calif.
Vianna, Marcel	3	4	2.51	12	8	0	1	47	35	17	13	13	49	R	R	6-2	175	3-23-81	1997	Sao Paulo, Brazil

BALTIMORE ORIOLES

Money can't buy playoff appearance for disappointing O's

BY ROCH KUBATKO

The oldest and most expensive team in baseball history became one of its most disappointing, finishing 79-83 after two straight appearances in the American League Championship Series.

The Orioles were a streaky bunch, losing 10, nine and eight games in a row at various points in the 1998 season. They started out 10-2, went 28-48 to close the first half, then began the second half with a 30-8 surge to jump into the wild-card race. Worn thin, they closed at 11-25 to continue frustrating first-year manager Ray Miller with an inconsistancy that didn't match their $70 million payroll and lofty preseason expectations.

The free-agent signings of veterans Joe Carter, Norm Charlton, Doug Drabek and Ozzie Guillen were disasters. Only Drabek made it through the season, and he wound up with a 6-11 record and 7.29 ERA, buried in the bullpen after a stop on the disabled list.

Drabek had lots of company when it came to injuries. The Orioles used the disabled list 17 times, including twice with ace Mike Mussina, who was sidelined by a wart on his pitching hand and again after being hit above the right eye by a line drive from the Indians' Sandy Alomar. Of the original starting rotation, only Scott Erickson made it through the entire season, becoming the first Oriole to lead the AL in innings pitched since Jim Palmer in 1978.

The season might best be remembered for Cal Ripken's decision to end his record consecutive-games streak at 2,632. He walked into Miller's office shortly before the last home game on Sept. 20 against the Yankees, and asked to be removed from the lineup. Rookie Ryan Minor took his place at third base.

On the same night that Ripken sat, Pat Gillick announced he wouldn't be returning as general manager in 1999. The front office already was minus its assistant GM, Kevin Malone, who left to become the Dodgers' GM after working all season without a contract. The upheaval didn't help a club with eight pending free agents including Rafael Palmeiro, who was voted the Orioles' MVP after batting .296 with 43 home runs and 121 RBIs, and outfielder Eric Davis, who put together a 30-game hitting streak and finished at .327 with 28 homers and 89 RBIs.

The club may have found a replacement for Palmeiro in Calvin Pickering, who was named the Double-A Eastern League MVP after hitting .309 with 31 homers and 114 RBIs at Bowie. Pickering and Bowie teammate Jerry Hairston were summoned to Baltimore in September as reward for their fine minor league seasons.

Lefthander Matt Riley, 19, emerged as the Orioles' top pitching prospect after going 5-4 with a 1.19 ERA and 136 strikeouts in 83 innings in his first professional season at Class A Delmarva. He was the Orioles' third-round pick in the 1997 draft and didn't sign until May 1998.

Two other 1997 draft picks joined Riley as Delmarva players named to the South Atlantic League's Top 10 Prospects list. Catcher Jayson Werth was ranked No. 4, while outfielder Darnell McDonald was No. 8. Riley was third on the list.

Delmarva was the organization's only minor league team to make the playoffs, but the club failed to defend its SAL title. Triple-A Rochester went 70-74 and missed the International League playoffs for the first time since 1994.

Rafael Palmeiro

JOHN SPEAR
Calvin Pickering

Players of the Year

Major League: Rafael Palmeiro, 1b

Palmeiro led the Orioles with 43 homers, 121 RBIs and 98 runs while playing in all 162 games.

Minor League: Calvin Pickering, 1b, Bowie

The giant first baseman led Orioles minor leaguers with 31 homers, 114 RBIs and 98 walks at Double-A Bowie.

ORGANIZATION LEADERS

*AVG	Joey Hammond, Fred./Delmarva/Bluefield	.310
R	Jerry Hairston, Bowie/Frederick	98
H	Jerry Hairston, Bowie/Frederick	155
TB	Calvin Pickering, Bowie	276
2B	P.J. Forbes, Rochester	37
3B	Two tied at	9
HR	Calvin Pickering, Bowie	31
RBI	Calvin Pickering, Bowie	114
BB	Calvin Pickering, Bowie	98
SO	Ryan Minor, Bowie	152
SB	Luis Matos, Bowie/Delmarva	43
PITCHING		
W	Three tied at	11
L	Two tied at	10
#ERA	Matt Riley, Delmarva	1.19
G	Jeremy Halpin, Delmarva	57
CG	Matt Snyder, Rochester/Bowie	4
SV	Derek Brown, Delmarva	33
IP	Josh Towers, Bowie/Frederick	163
BB	Chris Fussell, Rochester/Bowie	80
SO	Matt Riley, Delmarva	136

*Minimum 250 At-Bats #Minimum 75 Innings

Baltimore ORIOLES

Manager: Ray Miller

1998 Record: 79-83, .488 (4th, AL East)

BATTING	AVG	G	AB	R	H	2B	3B	HR	RBI	BB	SO	SB	CS	B	T	HT	WT	DOB	1st Yr	Resides
Alomar, Roberto	.282	147	588	86	166	36	1	14	56	59	70	18	5	B	R	6-0	185	2-5-68	1985	Salinas, P.R.
Anderson, Brady	.236	133	479	84	113	28	3	18	51	75	78	21	7	L	L	6-1	202	1-18-64	1985	Lake Tahoe, Nev.
Baines, Harold	.300	104	293	40	88	17	0	9	57	32	40	0	0	L	L	6-2	195	3-15-59	1977	St. Michaels, Md.
Becker, Rich	.204	79	113	22	23	1	0	3	11	22	34	2	0	L	L	5-10	193	2-1-72	1990	Cape Coral, Fla.
Bordick, Mike	.260	151	465	59	121	29	1	13	51	39	65	6	7	R	R	5-11	175	7-21-65	1986	Ruxton, Md.
Carter, Joe	.247	85	283	36	70	15	1	11	34	18	48	3	1	R	R	6-3	215	3-7-60	1981	Leawood, Kan.
Clyburn, Danny	.280	11	25	6	7	0	0	1	3	1	10	0	0	R	R	6-4	220	4-6-74	1992	Lancaster, S.C.
Davis, Eric	.327	131	452	81	148	29	1	28	89	44	108	7	6	R	R	6-3	200	5-29-62	1980	Woodland Hills, Calif.
Forbes, P.J.	.100	9	10	0	1	0	0	0	2	0	0	0	0	R	R	5-10	160	9-22-67	1990	Pittsburg, Kan.
Greene, Charlie	.190	13	21	1	4	1	0	0	0	0	8	0	0	R	R	6-2	190	1-23-71	1991	Miami, Fla.
Greene, Willie	.154	24	39	8	6	1	0	1	5	13	10	1	0	L	R	5-11	192	9-23-71	1989	Haddock, Ga.
Guillen, Ozzie	.063	12	16	2	1	0	0	0	0	1	2	0	1	L	R	5-11	165	1-20-64	1981	Caracas, Ven.
Hairston, Jerry	.000	6	7	2	0	0	0	0	0	0	1	0	0	R	R	5-10	172	5-29-76	1997	Naperville, Ill.
Hammonds, Jeffrey	.269	63	171	36	46	12	1	6	28	26	38	7	2	R	R	6-0	195	3-5-71	1992	Scotch Plains, N.J.
Hoiles, Chris	.262	97	267	36	70	12	0	15	56	38	50	0	1	R	R	6-0	220	3-20-65	1986	Bowling Green, Ohio
Kingsale, Eugene	.000	11	2	1	0	0	0	0	0	0	1	0	0	B	R	6-3	190	8-20-76	1994	Oranjestad, Aruba
Minor, Ryan	.429	9	14	3	6	1	0	0	1	0	3	0	0	R	R	6-7	225	1-5-74	1996	Edmond, Okla.
Mouton, Lyle	.308	18	39	5	12	2	0	2	7	4	8	0	0	R	R	6-4	240	5-13-69	1991	Lafayette, La.
Otanez, Willis	.200	3	5	0	1	0	0	0	0	0	2	0	0	R	R	6-1	200	4-19-73	1990	Las Vega Baja, D.R.
Palmeiro, Rafael	.296	162	619	98	183	36	1	43	121	79	91	11	7	L	L	6-0	190	9-24-64	1985	Colleyville, Texas
Pickering, Calvin	.238	9	21	4	5	0	0	2	3	3	4	1	0	L	L	6-5	283	9-29-76	1995	Temple Terrace, Fla.
Reboulet, Jeff	.244	79	127	20	31	6	0	1	8	19	34	0	1	R	R	6-0	175	4-30-64	1986	Kettering, Ohio
Ripken, Cal	.271	161	601	65	163	27	1	14	61	51	68	0	2	R	R	6-4	220	8-24-60	1978	Reisterstown, Md.
Surhoff, B.J.	.279	162	573	79	160	34	1	22	92	49	81	9	7	L	R	6-1	200	8-4-64	1985	Cockeysville, Md.
Tavarez, Jesus	.182	8	11	2	2	0	0	1	1	2	3	0	1	B	R	6-0	170	3-26-71	1990	Santo Domingo, D.R.
Webster, Lenny	.285	108	309	37	88	16	0	10	46	15	38	0	0	R	R	5-9	195	2-10-65	1986	Charlotte, N.C.

PITCHING	W	L	ERA	G	GS	CG	SV	IP	H	R	ER	BB	SO	B	T	HT	WT	DOB	1st Yr	Resides
Benitez, Armando	5	6	3.82	71	0	0	22	68	48	29	29	39	87	R	R	6-4	225	11-3-72	1990	San Pedro de Macoris, D.R.
Bennett, Joel	0	0	4.50	2	0	0	0	2	2	1	1	3	0	R	R	6-1	161	1-31-70	1991	Sydney, N.Y.
Charlton, Norm	2	1	6.94	36	0	0	0	35	46	27	27	25	41	B	L	6-3	205	1-6-63	1984	Tilden, Texas
Coppinger, Rocky	0	0	5.17	6	1	0	0	16	16	9	9	7	13	R	R	6-5	245	3-19-74	1994	El Paso, Texas
Drabek, Doug	6	11	7.29	23	21	1	0	109	138	90	88	29	55	R	R	6-1	190	7-25-62	1983	The Woodlands, Texas
Dykhoff, Radhames	0	0	18.00	1	0	0	0	1	2	2	2	1	1	L	L	6-0	160	9-27-74	1993	Oranjestad, Aruba
Erickson, Scott	16	13	4.01	36	36	11	0	251	284	125	112	69	186	R	R	6-4	230	2-2-68	1989	Stateline, Nev.
Fussell, Chris	0	1	8.38	3	2	0	0	10	11	9	9	9	8	R	R	6-2	200	5-19-76	1994	Oregon, Ohio
Guzman, Juan	4	4	4.23	11	11	0	0	66	60	34	31	33	55	R	R	5-11	195	10-28-66	1985	Miami, Fla.
2-team (22 Toronto)	10	16	4.35	33	33	2	0	211	193	117	102	98	168							
Johns, Doug	3	3	4.57	31	10	0	1	87	108	46	44	32	34	R	L	6-2	195	12-19-67	1990	Plantation, Fla.
Kamieniecki, Scott	2	6	6.75	12	11	0	0	55	67	41	41	26	25	R	R	6-0	200	4-19-64	1987	Flint, Mich.
Key, Jimmy	6	3	4.20	25	11	0	0	79	77	39	37	23	53	R	L	6-1	190	4-22-61	1982	Tarpon Springs, Fla.
Lewis, Richie	0	0	15.43	2	1	0	0	5	8	8	8	5	4	R	R	5-10	175	1-25-66	1987	Fort Lauderdale, Fla.
Mathews, Terry	0	1	6.20	17	0	0	0	20	26	15	14	8	10	L	R	6-2	225	10-5-64	1987	Alexandria, La.
Mills, Alan	3	4	3.74	72	0	0	2	77	55	32	32	50	57	B	R	6-1	195	10-18-66	1986	Lakeland, Fla.
Munoz, Bobby	0	0	9.75	9	1	0	0	12	18	13	13	6	6	R	R	6-7	210	3-3-68	1989	Hialeah, Fla.
Mussina, Mike	13	10	3.49	29	29	4	0	206	189	85	80	41	175	B	R	6-2	185	12-8-68	1990	Montoursville, Pa.
Orosco, Jesse	4	1	3.18	69	0	0	7	57	46	20	20	28	50	R	L	6-2	205	4-21-57	1978	San Diego, Calif.
Ponson, Sidney	8	9	5.27	31	20	0	1	135	157	82	79	42	85	R	R	6-1	220	11-2-76	1994	Oranjestad, Aruba
Rhodes, Arthur	4	4	3.51	45	0	0	4	77	65	30	30	34	83	L	L	6-2	204	10-24-69	1988	Sarasota, Fla.
Rodriguez, Nerio	1	3	8.05	6	4	0	0	19	25	17	17	9	8	R	R	6-1	195	3-22-73	1991	San Pedro de Macoris, D.R.
Smith, Pete	2	3	6.20	27	4	0	0	45	57	31	31	16	29	R	R	6-2	200	2-27-66	1984	Smyrna, Ga.

FIELDING

Catcher	PCT	G	PO	A	E	DP	PB
Greene	1.000	13	57	5	0	0	1
Hoiles	.995	83	516	39	3	6	2
Webster	.993	102	529	38	4	5	9

First Base	PCT	G	PO	A	E	DP
Carter	1.000	1	3	1	0	0
Hoiles	1.000	6	13	0	0	3
Minor	1.000	3	5	1	0	2
Palmeiro	.994	159	1433	125	9	127
Pickering	.969	5	31	0	1	3
Surhoff	1.000	1	2	0	0	0

Second Base	PCT	G	PO	A	E	DP
Alomar	.985	144	250	449	11	86
Forbes	1.000	7	6	9	0	2
Hairston	.750	4	4	2	2	1
Reboulet	.974	28	27	49	2	13

Third Base	PCT	G	PO	A	E	DP
Forbes	.000	1	0	0	0	0
Guillen	.000	1	0	0	0	0
Minor	.833	6	1	4	1	0
Reboulet	.900	23	1	8	1	2
Ripken	.979	161	101	266	8	23

Shortstop	PCT	G	PO	A	E	DP
Bordick	.990	150	236	445	7	90
Forbes	.000	1	0	0	0	0
Guillen	.933	6	3	11	1	1
Reboulet	.967	28	25	63	3	8

Outfield	PCT	G	PO	A	E	DP
Anderson	.985	130	269	1	4	0
Becker	.984	60	59	1	1	0
Carter	.962	50	96	4	4	1
Clyburn	1.000	8	11	0	0	0
Davis	.992	72	119	4	1	0
Greene	.941	14	15	1	1	0
Hammonds	.980	53	94	2	2	1
Kingsale	1.000	4	2	0	0	0
Mouton	1.000	16	19	1	0	0
Otanez	1.000	2	1	0	0	0
Surhoff	.989	157	253	12	3	2
Tavarez	1.000	8	7	0	0	0

FARM SYSTEM

Director of Player Development: Syd Thrift

Class	Farm Team	League	W	L	Pct.	Finish*	Manager(s)	First Yr
AAA	Rochester (N.Y.) Red Wings	International	70	74	.486	9th (14)	Marv Foley	1961
AA	Bowie (Md.) Baysox	Eastern	71	71	.500	6th (10)	Joe Ferguson	1993
A#	Frederick (Md.) Keys	Carolina	64	76	.457	6th (8)	Tommy Shields	1989
A	Delmarva (Md.) Shorebirds	South Atlantic	81	61	.570	3rd (14)	Dave Machemer	1997
Rookie#	Bluefield (W.Va.) Orioles	Appalachian	33	34	.493	5th (10)	Andy Etchebarren	1958
Rookie	Sarasota (Fla.) Orioles	Gulf Coast	28	32	.467	t-8th (14)	Butch Davis	1991

*Finish in overall standings (No. of teams in league) #Advanced level

ROCHESTER — Class AAA

INTERNATIONAL LEAGUE

BATTING	AVG	G	AB	R	H	2B	3B	HR	RBI	BB	SO	SB	CS	B	T	HT	WT	DOB	1st Yr	Resides
Bogle, Bryan	.267	10	30	5	8	2	0	1	4	1	8	0	0	R	R	6-1	205	5-18-73	1994	Melbourne, Fla.
Clark, Howie	.232	30	95	13	22	4	1	3	8	9	11	1	2	L	R	5-10	179	2-13-74	1992	Huntington Beach, Calif.
Clyburn, Danny	.286	84	322	58	92	21	1	14	54	34	72	11	5	R	R	6-4	220	4-6-74	1992	Lancaster, S.C.
DeCinces, Tim	.095	7	21	1	2	1	0	0	0	2	6	0	0	L	R	6-2	195	4-26-74	1996	Newport Beach, Calif.
Dodson, Bo	.276	116	387	57	107	26	2	8	48	62	65	5	2	L	L	6-2	195	12-7-70	1989	West Sacramento, Calif.
Forbes, P.J.	.293	116	460	74	135	37	3	6	52	36	54	10	2	R	R	5-10	160	9-22-67	1990	Pittsburg, Kan.
Foster, Jim	.235	43	153	22	36	9	0	5	26	18	22	3	1	R	R	6-3	220	8-18-71	1993	Warwick, R.I.
Garcia, Jesse	.294	44	160	20	47	6	4	0	18	7	22	7	5	R	R	5-10	155	9-24-73	1993	Robstown, Texas
Greene, Charlie	.212	77	250	23	53	10	0	4	28	9	54	1	1	R	R	6-2	190	1-23-71	1991	Miami, Fla.
Isom, Johnny	.225	39	142	13	32	4	0	2	13	18	31	2	0	R	R	5-11	210	8-9-73	1995	Fort Worth, Texas
Kingsale, Eugene	.218	18	55	3	12	1	1	0	2	4	8	3	3	B	R	6-3	190	8-20-76	1994	Oranjestad, Aruba
Lamb, David	.298	48	178	24	53	7	1	1	16	17	25	1	5	B	R	6-2	165	6-6-75	1993	Newbury Park, Calif.
Lawrence, Chip	.300	13	30	1	9	1	0	0	2	7	6	0	0	R	R	6-2	192	11-14-74	1996	St. Petersburg, Fla.
Lee, Derek	.283	107	364	63	103	17	3	18	57	49	61	5	6	L	R	6-1	200	7-28-66	1988	Reston, Va.
Luzinski, Ryan	.000	4	12	0	0	0	0	0	1	0	3	0	0	R	R	6-1	215	8-22-73	1992	Medford, N.J.
Lydy, Scott	.136	20	66	3	9	5	0	1	8	4	15	1	0	R	R	6-5	195	10-26-68	1989	Chandler, Ariz.
Miller, Orlando	.294	37	143	21	42	4	1	5	25	9	31	3	1	R	R	6-3	205	1-13-69	1988	Estafeta del Dorado, Panama
Mouton, Lyle	.321	37	137	23	44	9	2	7	32	13	31	1	1	R	R	6-4	240	5-13-69	1991	Lafayette, La.
Murphy, Mike	.379	8	29	3	11	0	0	1	2	3	7	1	1	R	R	6-2	185	1-23-72	1990	Albuquerque, N.M.
Otanez, Willis	.285	124	481	87	137	24	2	27	100	41	104	1	0	R	R	6-1	200	4-19-73	1990	Las Vega Baja, D.R.
Otero, Ricky	.288	87	354	53	102	25	6	4	45	21	30	10	5	B	L	5-7	150	4-15-72	1991	Vega Baja, P.R.
Ramirez, Roberto	.268	13	41	5	11	0	0	0	3	1	10	0	1	R	R	6-2	180	3-18-70	1989	Phoenix, Ariz.
Rosario, Mel	.248	34	113	10	28	4	0	3	10	6	24	5	2	B	R	6-0	200	5-25-73	1992	Miami, Fla.
Short, Rick	.176	13	34	3	6	1	0	1	4	4	4	0	0	R	R	6-0	190	12-6-72	1994	Peoria, Ill.
Simons, Mitch	.216	59	190	21	41	8	2	1	16	20	16	7	2	R	R	5-9	172	12-13-68	1991	Midwest City, Okla.
Smith, Dwight	.174	20	69	5	12	2	0	0	8	7	20	2	0	L	R	5-11	177	11-8-63	1984	Atlanta, Ga.
Tavarez, Jesus	.280	102	364	62	102	17	6	1	30	27	59	22	3	B	R	6-0	170	3-26-71	1990	Santo Domingo, D.R.
Utting, Andy	.278	5	18	4	5	1	0	1	3	2	5	0	0	B	R	6-1	175	9-9-77	1995	Melbourne, Australia
Vinas, Julio	.352	62	199	26	70	15	4	6	40	12	30	2	1	R	R	6-1	205	2-14-73	1991	Hialeah, Fla.

PITCHING	W	L	ERA	G	GS	CG	SV	IP	H	R	ER	BB	SO	B	T	HT	WT	DOB	1st Yr	Resides
Bennett, Joel	10	0	3.64	18	15	1	0	101	99	46	41	37	99	R	R	6-1	161	1-31-70	1991	Sydney, N.Y.
Blood, Darin	3	2	2.48	6	6	1	0	33	24	11	9	13	14	B	R	6-2	200	8-31-74	1995	Scottsdale, Ariz.
Burrows, Terry	9	6	2.92	29	15	1	0	132	104	49	43	42	112	L	L	6-1	190	11-28-68	1990	Lake Charles, La.
Converse, Jim	2	8	4.90	33	6	0	1	83	86	51	45	40	74	L	R	5-9	180	8-17-71	1990	Citrus Heights, Calif.
Coppinger, Rocky	8	3	3.50	14	13	1	0	87	80	38	34	43	64	R	R	6-5	245	3-19-74	1994	El Paso, Texas
Curtis, Chris	2	6	7.67	18	7	0	0	54	68	48	46	21	23	R	R	6-2	195	5-8-71	1991	Duncanville, Texas
Dodson, Bo	0	0	0.00	3	0	0	0	3	1	0	0	1	0	L	L	6-2	195	12-7-70	1989	West Sacramento, Calif.
Fleming, Dave	0	0	3.86	4	0	0	0	7	8	3	3	3	3	L	L	6-3	205	11-7-69	1990	Mahopac, N.Y.
2-team (4 Pawtucket)	1	1	6.58	8	4	0	0	26	29	21	19	16	7							
Fussell, Chris	5	2	3.99	10	10	0	0	59	50	30	26	28	51	R	R	6-2	200	5-19-76	1994	Oregon, Ohio
Gallaher, Kevin	2	6	7.55	13	8	0	0	39	32	40	33	43	28	R	R	6-3	190	8-1-68	1991	Vienna, Va.
Horsman, Vince	0	0	2.92	6	0	0	0	12	13	5	4	1	8	R	L	6-2	180	3-9-67	1985	Palm Harbor, Fla.
Johns, Doug	0	1	1.69	2	2	0	0	11	7	3	2	6	4	R	L	6-2	195	12-19-67	1990	Plantation, Fla.
Kelley, Rich	1	3	5.45	15	3	0	1	38	34	28	23	17	24	L	L	6-3	210	5-27-70	1991	Scituate, Mass.
Lewis, Richie	5	7	5.01	21	21	2	0	124	107	77	69	42	131	R	R	5-10	175	1-25-66	1987	Fort Lauderdale, Fla.
Mathews, Terry	0	1	3.00	1	1	0	0	3	4	1	1	2	4	L	R	6-2	225	10-5-64	1987	Alexandria, La.
Montgomery, Steve	4	6	4.40	51	4	0	8	88	79	50	43	24	66	R	R	6-4	200	12-25-70	1992	Corona del Mar, Calif.
Munoz, Bobby	3	1	1.06	44	0	0	19	59	40	9	7	13	46	R	R	6-7	210	3-3-68	1989	Hialeah, Fla.
Ontiveros, Steve	5	1	3.68	16	14	0	1	81	77	35	33	25	64	R	R	6-0	180	3-5-61	1982	Stafford, Texas
Osteen, Gavin	1	2	3.96	44	0	0	2	73	74	37	32	25	46	R	L	6-0	195	11-27-69	1989	Bethany Beach, Del.
Ponson, Sidney	1	0	0.00	1	1	0	0	5	4	0	0	1	3	R	R	6-1	220	11-2-76	1994	Oranjestad, Aruba
Rhodes, Arthur	0	0	4.50	1	1	0	0	2	3	1	1	1	1	L	L	6-2	204	10-24-69	1988	Sarasota, Fla.
Rodriguez, Nerio	1	4	5.47	5	5	0	0	25	24	16	15	10	19	R	R	6-1	195	3-22-73	1991	San Pedro de Macoris, D.R.
Sackinsky, Brian	0	2	6.46	7	2	0	0	15	22	12	11	4	9	R	R	6-4	220	6-22-71	1992	Bethel Park, Pa.
Snyder, Matt	2	1	3.66	12	0	0	0	20	17	9	8	6	13	R	R	5-11	190	7-7-74	1995	Newton, Pa.
Steph, Rod	3	4	3.32	14	0	0	0	22	25	11	8	2	17	R	R	5-11	185	8-27-69	1991	Lubbock, Texas
Stull, Everett	1	4	8.86	21	7	0	0	43	49	44	42	45	39	R	R	6-3	200	8-24-71	1992	Stone Mountain, Ga.
Taylor, Scott	1	1	11.37	3	0	0	0	6	9	8	8	8	3	R	R	6-3	200	10-3-66	1989	Wichita, Kan.
Turgeon, Dave	1	1	3.18	4	2	0	0	17	15	6	6	4	9	R	R	6-2	180	5-15-65	1987	Fort Lauderdale, Fla.
Young, Ray	0	2	8.03	5	1	0	1	12	18	11	11	6	10	R	R	6-3	180	5-27-64	1984	Tempe, Ariz.

FIELDING

Catcher	PCT	G	PO	A	E	DP	PB
DeCinces	1.000	7	49	2	0	2	0
Foster	.991	31	198	23	2	3	1
Greene	.988	77	517	55	7	6	3
Luzinski	.950	4	18	1	1	0	1
Rosario	.984	26	172	18	3	3	7
Utting	1.000	5	35	2	0	0	2
Vinas	1.000	5	35	2	0	0	3

First Base	PCT	G	PO	A	E	DP
Clark	1.000	10	83	3	0	5
Dodson	.990	112	885	69	10	87
Foster	1.000	6	38	5	0	5
Otanez	.963	4	26	0	1	3
Short	1.000	1	8	0	0	1
Vinas	.993	22	136	5	1	15

Second Base	PCT	G	PO	A	E	DP
Clark	.929	7	14	12	2	6
Forbes	.990	84	170	231	4	48
Garcia	.969	44	102	145	8	44
Lamb	1.000	3	6	7	0	1
Simons	.930	11	21	19	3	1
Tavarez	1.000	1	1	1	0	0

Third Base	PCT	G	PO	A	E	DP
Clark	1.000	1	1	1	0	0
Forbes	.973	16	6	30	1	1
Lamb	.875	4	2	5	1	1
Lawrence	1.000	1	1	2	0	1
Otanez	.968	116	91	240	11	17
Short	1.000	12	8	19	0	0

Shortstop	PCT	G	PO	A	E	DP
Forbes	.974	20	31	44	2	14
Lamb	.965	40	61	104	6	31
Lawrence	.900	12	14	22	4	4
Miller	.939	35	61	77	9	20
Simons	.929	47	58	138	15	19

Outfield	PCT	G	PO	A	E	DP
Bogle	.917	8	10	1	1	0
Clyburn	.970	72	125	4	4	0
Dodson	1.000	1	1	0	0	0
Isom	.983	37	54	3	1	0
Kingsale	1.000	16	[illegible]	[illegible]	0	[illegible]
Lamb	1.000	2	5	0	0	0
Lee	.968	53	90	1	3	0
Lydy	.976	15	40	0	1	0
Mouton	.983	28	56	1	1	0
Murphy	1.000	7	16	1	0	0
Otanez	1.000	2	5	0	0	0
Otero	.995	87	187	5	1	1
Ramirez	.964	12	26	1	1	0
Smith	.923	6	11	1	1	0
Tavarez	.974	99	182	3	5	0

BOWIE — Class AA

EASTERN LEAGUE

BATTING	AVG	G	AB	R	H	2B	3B	HR	RBI	BB	SO	SB	CS	B	T	HT	WT	DOB	1st Yr	Resides
Almonte, Wady	.048	7	21	2	1	0	0	1	2	4	9	0	0	R	R	6-0	195	4-20-75	1993	Higuey, D.R.
Bogle, Bryan	.254	21	67	12	17	3	0	4	16	3	19	0	0	R	R	6-1	205	5-18-73	1994	Melbourne, Fla.
Clark, Howie	.286	88	276	37	79	16	0	9	45	29	42	1	1	L	R	5-10	179	2-13-74	1992	Huntington Beach, Calif.
Clark, Tim	.316	52	174	28	55	10	0	10	39	23	40	1	1	L	L	6-3	210	2-10-69	1990	Philadelphia, Pa.
Conner, Decomba	.250	65	208	31	52	5	2	5	27	16	42	10	3	R	R	5-10	185	7-17-73	1994	Mooresville, N.C.
Davis, Tommy	.280	37	132	12	37	11	0	1	15	13	27	0	0	R	R	6-1	195	5-21-73	1994	Semmes, Ala.
DeCinces, Tim	.333	5	18	5	6	1	0	1	4	1	5	0	0	L	R	6-2	195	4-26-74	1996	Newport Beach, Calif.
Foster, Jim	.240	66	221	24	53	17	0	5	33	31	38	1	1	R	R	6-3	220	8-18-71	1993	Warwick, R.I.
Garcia, Jesse	.283	86	258	46	73	13	1	2	20	34	37	12	3	R	R	5-10	155	9-24-73	1993	Robstown, Texas
Garland, Tim	.262	59	164	18	43	4	3	2	8	25	24	8	7	R	R	6-0	185	7-15-68	1989	Danville, Va.
Hairston, Jerry	.326	55	221	42	72	12	3	5	37	20	25	6	4	R	R	5-10	172	5-29-76	1997	Naperville, Ill.
Hammonds, Jeffrey	.333	3	6	4	2	0	0	0	0	2	2	3	1	R	R	6-0	195	3-5-71	1992	Scotch Plains, N.J.
Isom, Johnny	.240	93	325	47	78	12	1	13	39	29	72	1	3	R	R	5-11	210	8-9-73	1995	Fort Worth, Texas
Kingsale, Eugene	.262	111	427	69	112	11	5	1	34	48	79	29	12	B	R	6-3	190	8-20-76	1994	Oranjestad, Aruba
Lamb, David	.303	66	241	29	73	10	1	2	25	27	33	1	3	B	R	6-2	165	6-6-75	1993	Newbury Park, Calif.
Lawrence, Chip	.250	6	12	0	3	1	0	0	0	0	3	0	0	R	R	6-2	192	11-14-74	1996	St. Petersburg, Fla.
Luzinski, Ryan	.240	72	233	25	56	3	0	7	25	20	72	3	3	R	R	6-1	215	8-22-73	1992	Medford, N.J.
Martinez, Eddy	.286	5	14	1	4	0	0	0	1	1	3	0	0	R	R	6-2	150	10-23-77	1995	San Pedro de Macoris, D.R.
Matos, Luis	.263	5	19	2	5	0	0	1	3	1	1	1	1	R	R	6-0	155	10-30-78	1996	Bayamon, P.R.
Minor, Ryan	.250	138	521	73	130	20	3	17	71	34	152	2	3	R	R	6-7	225	1-5-74	1996	Edmond, Okla.
Ojeda, Augie	.256	73	254	36	65	10	2	1	19	36	30	0	3	B	R	5-9	165	12-20-74	1996	South Gate, Calif.
Perez, Danny	.216	22	74	8	16	3	1	0	6	8	12	1	0	R	R	5-9	175	2-26-71	1992	El Paso, Texas
Pickering, Calvin	.309	139	488	93	151	28	2	31	114	98	119	4	6	L	L	6-5	283	9-29-76	1995	Temple Terrace, Fla.
Ramirez, Roberto	.286	6	21	4	6	0	0	1	1	2	5	0	0	R	R	6-2	180	3-18-70	1989	Phoenix, Ariz.
Rosario, Mel	.269	39	130	22	35	5	4	5	25	9	31	2	1	B	R	6-0	200	5-25-73	1992	Miami, Fla.
Short, Rick	.230	34	87	12	20	4	0	2	18	13	18	0	0	R	R	6-0	190	12-6-72	1994	Peoria, Ill.
Utting, Andy	.250	2	4	1	1	0	0	0	0	1	1	1	0	B	R	6-1	175	9-9-77	1995	Melbourne, Australia
Werth, Jayson	.158	5	19	2	3	2	0	0	1	2	6	1	0	R	R	6-6	191	5-20-79	1997	Chatham, Ill.

PITCHING	W	L	ERA	G	GS	CG	SV	IP	H	R	ER	BB	SO	B	T	HT	WT	DOB	1st Yr	Resides
Converse, Jim	0	0	7.20	1	1	0	0	5	9	4	4	1	2	L	R	5-9	180	8-17-71	1990	Citrus Heights, Calif.
Coppinger, Rocky	2	2	4.35	7	6	0	0	31	26	18	15	11	30	R	R	6-5	245	3-19-74	1994	El Paso, Texas
Curtis, Chris	0	2	6.95	12	1	0	0	22	27	18	17	11	11	R	R	6-2	195	5-8-71	1991	Duncanville, Texas
Delahoya, Javier	4	1	3.82	6	4	1	0	31	32	13	13	7	33	R	R	6-2	160	2-21-70	1989	North Hollywood, Calif.
Drabek, Doug	0	0	0.00	1	1	0	0	5	0	0	0	0	3	R	R	6-1	190	7-25-62	1983	The Woodlands, Texas
Dykhoff, Radhames	3	7	4.71	38	8	0	1	94	83	51	49	52	98	L	L	6-0	160	9-27-74	1993	Oranjestad, Aruba
Eibey, Scott	1	1	4.21	24	0	0	0	36	40	20	17	14	29	L	L	6-4	210	1-19-74	1995	Waterloo, Iowa
Estes, Eric	5	2	4.38	9	9	1	0	49	53	28	24	8	29	R	R	6-4	185	9-4-72	1997	Vancouver, Wash.
Evans, Dave	1	1	1.96	14	0	0	0	18	17	9	4	6	26	R	R	6-3	205	1-1-68	1990	Houston, Texas
Fussell, Chris	3	7	4.26	18	18	0	0	93	87	54	44	52	84	R	R	6-2	200	5-19-76	1994	Oregon, Ohio
Gallaher, Kevin	2	0	5.06	9	0	0	0	16	12	9	9	17	18	R	R	6-3	190	8-1-68	1991	Vienna, Va.
Heredia, Maximo	1	1	6.23	5	4	0	0	13	18	9	9	2	7	R	R	6-0	163	9-27-76	1994	San Pedro de Macoris, D.R.
Hernandez, Francis	3	3	4.76	21	0	0	0	34	34	22	18	20	19	R	R	6-0	160	12-17-76	1994	San Pedro de Macoris, D.R.
Kamieniecki, Scott	1	0	4.76	3	3	0	0	11	13	6	6	2	5	R	R	6-0	200	4-19-64	1987	Flint, Mich.
Kelley, Rich	8	2	3.71	18	13	0	0	85	80	38	35	34	56	L	L	6-3	210	5-27-70	1991	Scituate, Mass.
Kohlmeier, Ryan	4	4	6.12	42	0	0	7	50	52	37	34	16	56	R	R	6-2	195	6-25-77	1996	Cottonwood Falls, Kan.
Lane, Aaron	1	1	6.26	15	0	0	0	23	29	19	16	14	11	L	L	6-1	180	6-2-71	1992	Taylorville, Ill.
Mathews, Terry	0	0	6.00	1	1	0	0	3	3	2	2	1	2	L	R	6-2	225	10-5-64	1987	Alexandria, La.
McCommon, Jason	8	8	4.28	23	19	2	0	124	113	63	59	42	73	R	R	6-0	190	8-9-71	1994	Memphis, Tenn.
2-team (6 Harrisburg)	9	8	4.24	29	19	2	1	134	121	67	63	48	80							
Medina, Carlos	1	0	0.00	1	1	0	0	5	1	0	0	0	6	L	L	6-2	160	5-16-77	1994	La Vega, D.R.
Mitchell, Larry	0	0	9.64	4	1	0	0	5	6	5	5	11	2	R	R	6-1	219	10-16-71	1992	Charlottesville, Va.
Molina, Gabe	3	2	3.36	47	0	0	24	62	48	24	23	27	75	R	R	5-11	190	5-3-75	1996	Denver, Colo.
Paronto, Chad	1	3	5.80	8	7	0	1	36	38	30	23	23	28	R	R	6-5	250	7-28-75	1996	North Haverhill, N.H.
Rodriguez, Nerio	0	1	4.50	2	2	0	0	4	6	2	2	0	7	R	R	6-1	195	3-22-73	1991	San Pedro de Macoris, D.R.
Rogers, Jason	4	3	3.20	38	0	0	3	56	40	22	20	20	46	L	L	6-6	220	4-5-73	1994	Reno, Nev.
Sackinsky, Brian	0	0	0.00	1	1	0	0	1	0	0	0	0	0	R	R	6-4	220	6-22-71	1992	Bethel Park, Pa.
Shepherd, Alvie	0	2	3.32	6	3	0	0	19	13	8	7	14	12	R	R	6-7	220	5-12-74	1996	Bellwood, Ill.
Smith, Hut	0	3	6.90	6	5	0	0	30	32	23	23	6	12	R	R	6-3	195	6-8-73	1992	Kannapolis, N.C.
Snyder, Matt	9	6	4.35	22	20	4	0	120	127	66	58	30	116	R	R	5-11	190	7-7-74	1995	Newton, Pa.

PITCHING	W	L	ERA	G	GS	CG	SV	IP	H	R	ER	BB	SO	B	T	HT	WT	DOB	1st Yr	Resides
Steinmetz, Earl	0	0	0.00	1	0	0	0	0	2	0	0	1	0	R	R	6-3	175	5-17-71	1989	San Antonio, Texas
Stewart, Rachaad	0	4	10.80	5	5	0	0	20	27	25	24	11	7	L	L	6-4	212	10-8-74	1994	Elgin, Ill.
Towers, Josh	2	1	3.50	5	2	0	0	18	20	9	7	4	7	R	R	6-1	150	2-26-77	1996	Port Hueneme, Calif.
Twiggs, Greg	4	4	4.12	31	7	0	0	74	85	43	34	23	59	R	L	5-11	165	10-15-71	1993	Winter Springs, Fla.

FIELDING

Catcher	PCT	G	PO	A	E	DP	PB
Davis	.969	23	150	7	5	0	9
Foster	.990	25	177	18	2	3	1
Luzinski	.993	61	371	45	3	0	6
Rosario	.973	35	216	38	7	3	8
Utting	1.000	1	2	0	0	0	0
Werth	1.000	5	49	4	0	1	1

First Base	PCT	G	PO	A	E	DP
Bogle	1.000	1	11	0	0	2
H. Clark	1.000	8	12	0	0	0
T. Clark	.981	7	49	2	1	4
Davis	1.000	7	56	3	0	6
Pickering	.983	128	1063	60	20	90

Second Base	PCT	G	PO	A	E	DP
H. Clark	1.000	8	10	16	0	2
Garcia	.978	83	128	190	7	42
Hairston	.984	54	109	133	4	34
Lawrence	1.000	3	2	4	0	0
Short	.909	9	5	5	1	1

Third Base	PCT	G	PO	A	E	DP
H. Clark	.700	5	2	5	3	1
DeCinces	.667	1	0	2	1	0
Minor	.928	135	89	245	26	27
Ojeda	.929	5	4	9	1	2
Short	.667	3	1	1	1	0

Shortstop	PCT	G	PO	A	E	DP
Garcia	.818	7	3	6	2	0
Hairston	.667	1	0	2	1	0
Lamb	.946	65	73	171	14	30
Lawrence	1.000	3	1	4	0	0
Martinez	.917	5	5	6	1	2
Ojeda	.966	69	91	190	10	34

Outfield	PCT	G	PO	A	E	DP
Almonte	.929	7	12	1	1	1
Bogle	.977	19	41	1	1	1
H. Clark	.963	55	76	3	3	1
Conner	.984	61	118	2	2	0
DeCinces	.000	1	0	0	0	0
Garcia	1.000	1	2	0	0	0
Garland	1.000	55	108	2	0	0
Hammonds	1.000	3	3	0	0	0
Isom	.994	92	151	12	1	5
Kingsale	.980	111	279	9	6	4
Luzinski	.000	1	0	0	0	0
Matos	.833	5	4	1	1	1
Perez	1.000	19	24	0	0	0
Pickering	.714	6	5	0	2	0
Ramirez	1.000	6	5	0	0	0
Short	1.000	12	23	0	0	0

FREDERICK — Class A

CAROLINA LEAGUE

BATTING	AVG	G	AB	R	H	2B	3B	HR	RBI	BB	SO	SB	CS	B	T	HT	WT	DOB	1st Yr	Resides
Alley, Chip	.262	112	340	42	89	23	1	9	47	60	60	0	2	B	R	6-3	190	12-20-76	1995	West Palm Beach, Fla.
Benham, Jason	.250	4	16	2	4	0	0	0	2	1	3	1	0	L	R	6-1	190	10-13-75	1998	Garland, Texas
Bryant, Chris	.259	135	483	66	125	22	0	13	81	52	127	11	3	R	R	6-2	195	12-15-72	1995	Middlesex, N.C.
Casimiro, Carlos	.236	131	478	44	113	23	9	15	61	25	98	10	7	R	R	5-11	175	11-8-76	1994	San Pedro de Macoris, D.R.
Coffie, Ivanon	.256	130	473	62	121	19	2	16	75	48	109	17	12	L	R	6-1	170	5-16-77	1995	Curacao, Neth. Antilles
Conner, Decomba	.298	32	121	16	36	7	2	2	11	10	21	10	5	R	R	5-10	185	7-17-73	1994	Mooresville, N.C.
Daedelow, Craig	.270	40	122	12	33	4	0	1	15	15	18	2	0	R	R	5-11	165	4-3-76	1994	Huntington Beach, Calif.
Davison, Ashanti	.167	9	18	4	3	1	0	0	3	1	4	0	0	R	R	5-10	170	10-31-78	1996	Stockton, Calif.
Dent, Darrell	.246	131	456	65	112	19	1	0	24	43	95	33	16	L	L	6-2	172	5-26-77	1995	Panorama City, Calif.
DeCinces, Tim	.267	110	374	50	100	25	0	16	64	59	90	3	4	L	R	6-2	195	4-26-74	1996	Newport Beach, Calif.
Diaz, Maikell	.213	13	47	3	10	0	0	0	4	1	10	1	1	R	R	5-10	158	9-29-78	1996	Miranda, Ven.
Figueroa, Franky	.158	4	19	2	3	1	0	1	3	0	4	0	0	R	R	6-6	225	2-9-77	1996	Hialeah, Fla.
Fowler, Maleke	.186	84	210	25	39	5	1	0	8	20	40	25	6	R	R	5-11	180	12-2-78	1996	Baton Rouge, La.
Garavito, Eddy	.211	4	19	4	4	1	1	0	2	1	5	0	1	B	R	5-8	170	12-2-78	1996	Manrreza, D.R.
Garland, Tim	.263	11	38	4	10	1	0	0	5	3	5	6	1	R	R	6-0	185	7-15-68	1989	Danville, Va.
Hage, Tom	.288	45	163	15	47	12	0	2	27	12	27	0	0	L	R	6-0	220	8-2-74	1996	Bronx, N.Y.
Hairston, Jerry	.283	80	293	56	83	22	3	5	33	28	32	13	7	R	R	5-10	172	5-29-76	1997	Naperville, Ill.
Hammond, Joey	.300	3	10	3	3	1	0	0	2	3	2	1	0	R	R	6-0	180	10-27-77	1998	Frederick, Md.
Lawrence, Chip	.221	48	104	9	23	1	0	0	6	4	24	0	2	R	R	6-2	192	11-14-74	1996	St. Petersburg, Fla.
LeCronier, Jason	.208	54	154	12	32	4	1	4	14	8	52	0	1	L	R	6-0	180	3-30-73	1995	Lafayette, La.
McDonald, Darnell	.222	4	18	3	4	2	0	1	2	3	6	2	0	R	R	5-11	190	11-17-78	1997	Glendale, Colo.
Mejia, Miguel	.196	49	138	15	27	4	0	1	8	9	43	7	3	R	R	6-1	155	3-25-75	1992	San Pedro de Macoris, D.R.
Ndungidi, Ntema	.000	1	2	0	0	0	0	0	0	0	1	0	0	L	R	6-2	165	3-15-79	1997	Montreal, Quebec
O'Toole, Bobby	.138	14	29	1	4	0	0	0	0	2	12	0	0	R	R	6-1	200	5-19-74	1995	Newton, Mass.
Paz, Richard	.245	40	143	31	35	10	0	3	8	21	22	6	3	R	R	5-8	130	7-30-77	1994	Los Teques, Ven.
Rivera, Roberto	.333	3	6	1	2	0	0	1	1	1	1	0	0	R	R	6-2	160	11-25-76	1994	La Romana, D.R.
Rumfield, Brock	.000	5	12	0	0	0	0	0	0	0	4	0	0	R	R	6-1	185	11-20-75	1998	Belton, Texas
Short, Rick	.308	59	221	36	68	14	0	6	28	18	29	3	2	R	R	6-0	190	12-6-72	1994	Peoria, Ill.
Utting, Andy	.108	15	37	2	4	0	0	0	1	4	6	0	0	B	R	6-1	175	9-9-77	1995	Melbourne, Australia
Wade, Michael	.133	14	30	1	4	0	0	1	2	0	10	0	0	R	R	6-5	200	10-31-75	1998	Moore, Okla.

GAMES BY POSITION: G—Alley 95, Bryant 1, DeCinces 40, O'Toole 9, Utting 5, Wade 12. **1B**—Bryant 82, Daedelow 1, DeCinces 15, Figueroa 4, Hage 42, Lawrence 2, Short 4, Utting 5. **2B**—Casimiro 114, Daedelow 1, DeCinces 1, Garavito 4, Hairston 14, Lawrence 9, Short 5. **3B**—Benham 3, Bryant 7, Casimiro 14, Coffie 52, Daedelow 7, DeCinces 3, Diaz 9, Hammond 3, Lawrence 12, Paz 30, Rumfield 5, Short 10. **SS**—Benham 1, Casimiro 1, Coffie 50, Daedelow 2, Diaz 3, Hairston 65, Lawrence 18, Paz 11. **OF**—Bryant 50, Conner 27, Daedelow 18, Davison 7, Dent 131, Fowler 73, Garland 11, Lawrence 4, LeCronier 45, McDonald 4, Mejia 48, Ndungidi 1, Rivera 3, Short 43.

PITCHING	W	L	ERA	G	GS	CG	SV	IP	H	R	ER	BB	SO	B	T	HT	WT	DOB	1st Yr	Resides
Bell, Mike	7	4	2.69	38	0	0	7	60	53	22	18	13	38	L	L	6-2	195	10-14-72	1995	Sarasota, Fla.
Eibey, Scott	1	2	3.86	21	0	0	1	35	47	17	15	8	20	L	L	6-4	210	1-19-74	1995	Waterloo, Iowa
Falkenborg, Brian	5	5	4.50	15	14	1	0	78	83	42	39	18	70	R	R	6-6	187	1-18-78	1996	Redmond, Wash.
Forbes, Cameron	2	3	3.22	14	3	0	0	36	38	20	13	21	16	R	R	6-1	170	2-28-77	1996	Lara, Australia
Hacen, Abraham	7	10	4.46	30	26	0	0	145	138	83	72	74	93	R	R	6-2	175	1-22-76	1993	La Romana, D.R.
Heredia, Maximo	1	3	4.92	29	3	0	3	64	71	44	35	19	36	R	R	6-0	163	9-27-76	1994	San Pedro de Macoris, D.R.
Hernandez, Francis	0	1	5.79	5	0	0	1	5	4	3	3	3	3	R	R	6-0	160	12-17-76	1994	San Pedro de Macoris, D.R.
Key, Jimmy	1	0	3.00	1	1	0	0	6	4	2	2	2	6	R	L	6-1	190	4-22-61	1982	Tarpon Springs, Fla.
Kohlmeier, Ryan	1	2	7.45	9	0	0	5	10	10	9	8	3	15	R	R	6-2	195	6-25-77	1996	Cottonwood Falls, Kan.
Lane, Aaron	1	1	2.70	5	1	0	1	13	9	5	4	7	6	L	L	6-1	180	6-2-71	1992	Taylorville, Ill.
Lee, Chris	0	0	4.50	2	0	0	0	4	3	2	2	2	4	R	R	6-1	235	9-8-75	1997	La Grange, Ga.
Mastrolonardo, David	1	6	5.01	48	0	0	15	56	59	34	31	29	69	R	R	6-4	220	8-23-74	1997	Satellite Beach, Fla.
McNatt, Josh	11	8	3.15	27	26	3	0	157	141	78	55	70	118	B	L	6-4	200	7-23-77	1996	Jackson, Tenn.
Olszewski, Tim	3	4	4.70	34	0	0	1	61	83	46	32	14	37	R	R	6-2	200	2-24-74	1995	Germantown, Wis.
Paronto, Chad	7	6	3.13	18	18	0	0	104	116	44	36	39	87	R	R	6-5	250	7-28-75	1996	North Haverhill, N.H.
Parrish, John	4	4	3.27	16	16	1	0	83	77	39	30	27	81	L	L	5-11	165	11-26-77	1996	Lancaster, Pa.
Peguero, Americo	0	1	6.43	5	4	0	0	14	10	11	10	11	15	R	R	6-0	140	5-20-77	1995	La Romana, D.R.
Richardson, Kasey	1	0	5.30	22	0	0	1	37	44	29	22	14	38	L	L	6-3	191	8-27-76	1994	Huntington, Md.

PITCHING	W	L	ERA	G	GS	CG	SV	IP	H	R	ER	BB	SO	B	T	HT	WT	DOB	1st Yr	Resides
Rogers, Jason	0	3	3.98	17	0	0	0	20	19	12	9	7	19	L	L	6-6	220	4-5-73	1994	Reno, Nev.
Romero, Jordan	2	5	3.04	15	8	0	0	50	45	19	17	21	58	R	R	6-1	170	10-8-76	1997	San Jose, Calif.
Sims, Kenny	0	0	1.35	3	0	0	1	7	6	2	1	0	8	R	R	6-4	187	7-24-75	1996	Union, S.C.
Steinmetz, Earl	1	1	3.13	13	0	0	0	23	23	13	8	6	20	R	R	6-3	175	5-17-71	1989	San Antonio, Texas
Tapia, Rafael	0	0	0.00	1	0	0	0	1	1	0	0	0	1	R	R	6-2	160	4-28-78	1995	San Pedro de Macoris, D.R.
Towers, Josh	0	7	[illegible]	[illegible]	[illegible]	0	1	[illegible]	[illegible]	[illegible]	[illegible]	[illegible]	[illegible]	R	R	6-1	[illegible]	[illegible]	[illegible]	Port Hueneme, Calif.

DELMARVA — Class A

SOUTH ATLANTIC LEAGUE

BATTING	AVG	G	AB	R	H	2B	3B	HR	RBI	BB	SO	SB	CS	B	T	HT	WT	DOB	1st Yr	Resides
Charles, Curtis	.179	10	28	4	5	0	1	0	1	1	10	2	2	R	R	6-1	179	3-15-76	1995	Caracas, Ven.
Davison, Ashanti	.154	7	26	1	4	0	1	0	1	1	6	0	1	R	R	5-10	170	10-31-78	1996	Stockton, Calif.
Diaz, Maikell	.243	59	169	26	41	7	4	3	24	20	40	4	2	R	R	5-10	158	9-29-78	1996	Miranda, Ven.
Figueroa, Franky	.276	137	515	61	142	29	4	13	94	14	113	8	0	R	R	6-6	225	2-9-77	1996	Hialeah, Fla.
Garavito, Eddy	.247	135	481	81	119	20	8	9	66	44	93	25	15	B	R	5-8	170	12-2-78	1996	Manrreza, D.R.
Haman, Mack	.000	2	6	0	0	0	0	0	0	0	4	0	0	R	R	6-4	205	12-11-75	1997	Newark, Del.
Hammond, Joey	.237	38	135	19	32	6	1	1	15	16	21	1	2	R	R	6-0	180	10-27-77	1998	Frederick, Md.
Hoch, Corey	.206	16	34	6	7	3	0	1	4	4	6	0	0	R	R	6-0	190	9-10-75	1998	Salisbury, Md.
Hooper, Daren	.207	96	319	36	66	13	1	8	36	26	147	1	2	R	R	6-1	230	5-15-77	1996	Woodside, Calif.
Hughes, Brian	.289	38	121	14	35	6	1	1	20	13	17	7	2	R	R	5-9	180	8-5-75	1998	Metairie, La.
Martinez, Eddy	.263	113	361	46	95	16	1	2	39	33	66	21	7	R	R	6-2	150	10-23-77	1995	San Pedro de Macoris, D.R.
Matos, Luis	.272	133	503	73	137	26	6	7	62	38	90	42	14	R	R	6-0	155	10-30-78	1996	Bayamon, P.R.
McDonald, Darnell	.261	134	528	87	138	24	5	6	44	33	117	35	11	R	R	5-11	190	11-17-78	1997	Glendale, Colo.
McGee, Tom	.268	50	123	16	33	5	0	2	14	9	23	4	2	R	R	5-11	190	1-29-75	1997	Rialto, Calif.
Pacheco, Juan	.000	1	3	1	0	0	0	0	0	1	3	0	0	R	R	6-0	170	11-4-76	1997	Newark, N.J.
Paxton, Chris	.259	63	170	20	44	11	0	1	19	27	39	0	1	L	R	6-2	210	12-11-76	1995	Palmdale, Calif.
Paz, Richard	.320	98	325	55	104	10	4	5	56	75	42	22	7	R	R	5-8	130	7-30-77	1994	Los Teques, Ven.
Perez, Richard	.114	23	35	6	4	0	0	0	4	2	13	1	2	R	R	6-0	155	2-18-78	1995	San Pedro de Macoris, D.R.
Rivera, Roberto	.238	110	390	55	93	21	5	7	50	25	99	17	4	R	R	6-2	160	11-25-76	1994	La Romana, D.R.
Werth, Jayson	.265	120	408	71	108	20	3	8	53	50	92	21	6	R	R	6-6	191	5-20-79	1997	Chatham, Ill.

GAMES BY POSITION: C—McGee 39, Paxton 4, Werth 111. **1B**—Figueroa 137, Paxton 15. **2B**—Diaz 4, Garavito 131, Hammond 3, Paz 10. **3B**—Diaz 23, Garavito 1, Hammond 35, Hoch 7, Paxton 1, Paz 88. **SS**—Diaz 34, Hoch 2, Martinez 113, Paz 1. **OF**—Charles 8, Davison 7, Haman 1, Hooper 24, Hughes 38, Matos 131, McDonald 119, McGee 2, Perez 14, Rivera 104.

PITCHING	W	L	ERA	G	GS	CG	SV	IP	H	R	ER	BB	SO	B	T	HT	WT	DOB	1st Yr	Resides
Achilles, Matt	8	7	3.78	26	25	2	0	150	143	71	63	70	125	R	R	6-3	175	8-18-76	1996	Moline, Ill.
Bauer, Richard	5	8	4.73	22	22	1	0	118	127	69	62	44	81	R	R	6-5	190	1-10-77	1997	Eagle, Idaho
Bello, Jilberto	1	0	4.50	3	0	0	0	4	6	2	2	2	4	R	R	6-3	150	2-26-77	1994	San Pedro de Macoris, D.R.
Brown, Derek	3	4	1.85	55	0	0	33	68	55	19	14	13	63	R	R	6-1	180	7-23-76	1994	Clear Spring, Md.
Fontaine, Tom	0	2	15.88	6	0	0	0	6	9	10	10	8	7	R	R	5-11	175	3-17-75	1997	Greenville, Pa.
Garcia, Sonny	2	0	2.52	4	4	1	0	25	17	9	7	9	21	R	R	6-3	220	9-10-76	1998	Houston, Texas
Halpin, Jeremy	9	5	3.97	57	0	0	7	93	93	45	41	17	104	R	R	6-3	190	11-20-74	1997	Rome, N.Y.
Huntsman, Brandon	7	6	3.94	23	17	0	0	98	114	59	43	53	71	R	R	6-4	195	11-19-75	1994	Pleasant Grove, Utah
Lee, Chris	3	0	3.79	19	0	0	1	36	27	17	15	21	39	R	R	6-1	235	9-8-75	1997	La Grange, Ga.
Medina, Carlos	4	6	3.79	22	11	0	0	81	70	41	34	39	85	L	L	6-2	160	5-16-77	1994	La Vega, D.R.
Murphy, Darren	0	0	4.32	5	0	0	0	8	11	4	4	4	4	L	L	6-3	170	9-13-76	1997	Santee, Calif.
Peguero, Americo	2	1	6.00	15	2	0	2	36	38	26	24	22	37	R	R	6-0	140	5-20-77	1995	La Romana, D.R.
Perez, Norberto	5	2	4.06	24	4	0	0	51	54	29	23	26	52	R	R	6-4	175	10-10-77	1995	El Seibo, D.R.
Richardson, Kasey	2	2	2.68	16	3	0	2	40	23	13	12	11	47	L	L	6-3	191	8-27-76	1994	Huntington, Md.
Riley, Matt	5	4	1.19	16	14	0	0	83	42	19	11	44	136	L	L	6-1	205	8-2-79	1998	Oakley, Calif.
Romero, Jordan	4	5	5.33	15	14	0	0	79	87	50	47	31	70	R	R	6-1	170	10-8-76	1997	San Jose, Calif.
Spurgeon, Jay	11	3	2.64	27	20	0	0	136	112	49	40	48	103	R	R	6-6	225	7-5-76	1997	Coarsegold, Calif.
Stephens, John	1	2	2.60	6	6	1	0	35	25	11	10	13	40	R	R	6-1	175	11-15-79	1996	Berala, Australia
Tapia, Rafael	1	0	5.40	2	0	0	0	2	3	1	1	1	0	R	R	6-2	160	4-28-78	1995	San Pedro de Macoris, D.R.
Theodile, Simeon	2	1	6.48	19	0	0	0	25	30	19	18	11	21	R	R	6-2	190	4-15-77	1997	Jeanerette, La.
Wise, William	6	3	4.67	34	0	0	1	62	74	35	32	18	40	R	R	6-4	203	9-10-75	1994	Plains, Ga.

BLUEFIELD — Rookie

APPALACHIAN LEAGUE

BATTING	AVG	G	AB	R	H	2B	3B	HR	RBI	BB	SO	SB	CS	B	T	HT	WT	DOB	1st Yr	Resides
Benham, Jason	.223	57	202	38	45	6	3	6	28	21	36	3	1	L	R	6-1	190	10-13-75	1998	Garland, Texas
Bonilla, Juan	.269	37	119	16	32	8	0	3	16	7	21	0	1	R	R	6-1	200	5-6-78	1998	Crestview, Fla.
Carter, Shannon	.247	36	150	23	37	2	0	1	10	9	35	14	3	L	L	6-0	170	3-23-79	1997	El Reno, Okla.
Davison, Ashanti	.255	50	196	30	50	8	3	1	17	24	32	16	8	R	R	5-10	170	10-31-78	1996	Stockton, Calif.
Diaz, Maikell	.300	11	40	4	12	1	0	0	6	4	6	2	1	R	R	5-10	158	9-29-78	1996	Miranda, Ven.
Escalante, Jaime	.247	53	166	24	41	9	0	3	12	17	46	3	1	B	R	6-2	210	4-5-77	1997	Federalsburg, Md.
Hage, Tom	.364	28	107	26	39	8	1	10	37	15	9	1	0	L	R	6-0	220	8-2-74	1996	Bronx, N.Y.
Haman, Mack	.225	38	120	19	27	6	0	2	11	9	33	1	1	R	R	6-4	205	12-11-75	1997	Newark, Del.
Hammond, Joey	.388	31	129	23	50	5	0	1	16	12	15	4	2	B	R	6-0	180	10-27-77	1998	Frederick, Md.
Kirkpatrick, Michael	.279	14	43	9	12	1	1	1	6	3	15	1	1	L	L	6-0	180	11-12-77	1996	New Castle, Del.
Koone, Chuck	.143	16	42	4	6	0	0	0	2	8	14	0	1	B	R	6-0	175	9-19-75	1998	Marion, N.C.
Martin, Tommy	.280	18	50	8	14	2	0	0	5	7	12	4	2	R	R	5-10	175	9-12-75	1997	Ypsilanti, Mich.
Ndungidi, Ntema	.295	59	210	26	62	10	5	7	35	35	52	6	5	L	R	6-2	165	3-15-79	1997	Montreal, Quebec
Nolasco, Regino	.233	66	215	27	50	7	3	0	26	15	40	12	5	R	R	6-0	145	7-28-79	1996	San Pedro de Macoris, D.R.
Pacheco, Juan	.227	12	44	7	10	1	0	0	3	3	5	0	0	R	R	6-0	170	11-4-76	1997	Newark, N.J.
Ramirez, Luis	.187	46	150	16	28	5	2	3	20	17	50	1	3	R	R	6-3	180	9-26-78	1996	Arroyo, P.R.
Utting, Andy	.245	40	147	16	36	6	0	3	22	22	29	2	5	B	R	6-1	175	9-9-77	1995	Melbourne, Australia
Wilson, Cliff	.225	23	80	13	18	4	1	4	11	9	20	0	0	L	R	6-2	198	4-10-77	1997	Lyman, S.C.

GAMES BY POSITION: C—Bonilla 13, Escalante 47, Utting 9. **1B**—Bonilla 16, Escalante 5, Hage 28, Ramirez 2, Utting 18. **2B**—Benham 1, Hammond 29, Martin 15, Nolasco 13, Pacheco 11. **3B**—Benham 52, Martin 1, Pacheco 1, Ramirez 1, Wilson 15. **SS**—Benham 3, Diaz 11, Hammond 2, Nolasco 53, Pacheco 2. **OF**—Benham 1, Carter 36, Davison 50, Haman 25, Kirkpatrick 7, Koone 15, Martin 1, Ndungidi 48, Ramirez 31.

PITCHING	W	L	ERA	G	GS	CG	SV	IP	H	R	ER	BB	SO	B	T	HT	WT	DOB	1st Yr	Resides
Bello, Jilberto	1	2	5.01	26	0	0	10	32	22	18	18	14	43	R	R	6-3	150	2-26-77	1994	San Pedro de Macoris, D.R.
Casteel, Ricky	5	3	4.02	13	13	0	0	69	66	38	31	26	50	R	R	6-2	190	10-29-77	1997	Texarkana, Texas
Dixon, Derek	0	0	27.00	2	0	0	0	1	1	4	4	1	2	R	R	6-3	195	9-24-75	1998	Chickasha, Okla.
Douglass, Sean	2	2	3.23	10	10	0	0	53	45	20	19	14	62	R	R	6-6	200	4-28-79	1997	Lancaster, Calif.
Garcia, Sonny	4	2	2.04	12	8	0	0	57	39	15	13	19	77	R	R	6-3	220	9-10-76	1998	Houston, Texas
Guzman, Juan	1	2	1.42	15	0	0	1	25	22	12	4	7	26	R	R	6-2	160	3-4-78	1995	Los Llanos, D.R.
Jones, Sean	4	2	9.76	14	6	0	0	40	62	49	43	20	30	R	R	6-7	180	4-12-78	1997	Hamilton, Ontario
Murphy, Brian	3	4	3.32	14	6	3	0	57	65	29	21	7	41	L	R	6-6	200	1-20-76	1998	North Street, Mich.
Murphy, Darren	2	0	4.12	16	0	0	0	20	25	9	9	5	16	L	L	6-3	170	9-13-76	1997	Santee, Calif.
Myers, Gene	0	2	7.83	17	1	0	0	23	35	27	20	24	25	R	R	6-3	205	6-22-76	1997	Newark, Del.
Perez, Norberto	1	1	4.97	6	0	0	0	13	8	7	7	4	11	R	R	6-4	175	10-10-77	1995	El Seibo, D.R.
Ratliff, Craig	0	0	5.14	3	3	0	0	14	18	12	8	5	11	R	R	6-7	215	1-19-78	1996	West Van Lear, Ky.
Ryba, Jason	3	3	5.24	12	9	0	0	46	46	36	27	25	41	R	R	6-3	190	10-5-78	1997	Brooklyn Heights, Ohio
Sims, Kenny	5	3	3.10	19	1	0	0	49	49	20	17	14	32	R	R	6-4	187	7-24-75	1996	Union, S.C.
Tapia, Rafael	0	2	5.48	4	4	0	0	21	24	18	13	11	20	R	R	6-2	160	4-28-78	1995	San Pedro de Macoris, D.R.
Theodile, Simeon	2	5	2.96	18	6	0	1	55	47	24	18	15	61	R	R	6-2	190	4-15-77	1997	Jeanerette, La.

SARASOTA — Rookie

GULF COAST LEAGUE

BATTING	AVG	G	AB	R	H	2B	3B	HR	RBI	BB	SO	SB	CS	B	T	HT	WT	DOB	1st Yr	Resides
Berrien, Samuel	.236	45	148	22	35	5	2	2	21	28	31	4	4	L	L	6-0	235	4-30-79	1998	Philadelphia, Pa.
Cabrera, Raymond	.272	49	184	21	50	9	1	2	30	2	25	5	0	R	R	6-3	170	11-10-78	1996	Upata, Ven.
Calzado, Napolean	.230	31	113	15	26	6	4	1	18	10	17	1	1	R	R	6-3	165	2-9-80	1996	Santo Domingo, D.R.
Davison, Ashanti	.214	4	14	2	3	0	0	0	1	2	2	4	0	R	R	5-10	170	10-31-78	1996	Stockton, Calif.
Elder, Rick	.340	29	106	19	36	5	4	3	26	12	20	3	2	L	L	6-6	230	2-24-80	1998	Marietta, Ga.
Green, Richard	.173	18	52	1	9	1	0	0	1	5	21	2	2	R	R	6-2	185	12-6-78	1998	Tullahoma, Tenn.
Gutierrez, Derrick	.241	32	112	15	27	2	2	0	14	9	27	3	1	R	R	5-11	175	10-6-78	1998	Jacksonville, Fla.
Gutierrez, Fernando	.185	32	92	10	17	3	0	0	5	9	19	2	1	R	R	6-2	175	9-25-80	1997	Araure, Ven.
Hoch, Corey	.353	19	68	9	24	8	1	0	11	7	10	3	1	R	R	6-0	190	9-10-75	1998	Salisbury, Md.
Hughes, Brian	.341	21	85	22	29	5	1	0	7	10	10	15	3	R	R	5-9	180	8-5-75	1998	Metairie, La.
Koone, Chuck	.208	31	96	14	20	3	2	1	14	16	31	6	2	B	R	6-0	175	9-19-75	1998	Marion, N.C.
Leon, Alfredo	.071	9	28	3	2	0	0	0	1	1	4	0	0	R	R	6-0	170	3-14-80	1996	Puerto Ordaz, Ven.
Lopez, Radhames	.204	14	49	4	10	1	0	0	3	7	13	2	0	B	R	5-10	170	11-21-78	1998	Baltimore, Md.
Mack, Antonio	.181	40	127	18	23	2	0	1	9	9	46	4	4	R	R	5-11	185	3-19-79	1998	Orlando, Fla.
Martin, Tommy	.197	24	76	11	15	3	0	0	11	9	19	9	2	R	R	5-10	175	9-12-75	1997	Ypsilanti, Mich.
Monzon, Francisco	.117	32	77	3	9	1	0	0	5	5	17	0	0	R	R	6-0	175	11-8-79	1998	Carolina, P.R.
Ojeda, Augie	.400	4	15	6	6	2	0	0	2	3	1	3	0	B	R	5-9	165	12-20-74	1996	South Gate, Calif.
Pacheco, Juan	.267	31	116	20	31	6	1	2	11	9	17	5	3	R	R	6-0	170	11-4-76	1997	Newark, N.J.
Raines, Tim	.244	56	197	40	48	7	4	1	13	30	53	37	4	R	R	5-10	175	8-31-79	1998	Sanford, Fla.
Rumfield, Brock	.232	49	185	26	43	10	0	3	25	9	23	3	4	R	R	6-1	185	11-20-75	1998	Belton, Texas
Tucker, Mamon	.143	12	42	5	6	0	0	0	2	1	17	1	0	R	R	6-3	190	10-18-79	1998	Austin, Texas
Wade, Michael	.118	7	17	3	2	0	0	1	1	2	5	0	1	R	R	6-5	200	10-31-75	1998	Moore, Okla.

GAMES BY POSITION: C—Green 13, D. Gutierrez 1, F. Gutierrez 30, Monzon 29, Wade 5. **1B**—Berrien 44, Calzado 1, Elder 3, Hoch 0, Pacheco 1, Rumfield 3, Tucker 3, Wade 2. **2B**—D. Gutierrez 4, Lopez 14, Martin 12, Pacheco 29, Rumfield 3. **3B**—Calzado 21, Hoch 4, Leon 2, Martin 2, Rumfield 36. **SS**—Calzado 11, D. Gutierrez 23, F. Gutierrez 1, Hoch 6, Leon 7, Martin 9, Ojeda 4. **OF**—Cabrera 33, Davison 4, Elder 15, Green 4, Hughes 18, Koone 22, Mack 37, Raines 52, Tucker 2.

PITCHING	W	L	ERA	G	GS	CG	SV	IP	H	R	ER	BB	SO	B	T	HT	WT	DOB	1st Yr	Resides
Bechler, Steve	2	4	2.72	9	9	0	0	50	51	22	15	8	39	R	R	6-2	195	11-18-79	1998	Medford, Ore.
Brewer, Dustin	0	4	5.90	14	9	0	0	50	64	36	33	25	29	R	R	6-5	225	7-14-80	1998	Granite City, Ill.
Escalona, Jesus	1	1	3.86	3	2	0	0	12	9	7	5	7	6	R	R	5-11	165	12-2-80	1997	Barquisimeto, Ven.
Fischer, Sean	4	3	3.21	17	3	0	2	42	32	17	15	26	31	L	L	6-1	205	12-13-77	1998	Philadelphia, Pa.
Houle, Marc	0	1	6.43	9	0	0	3	14	17	11	10	7	11	R	R	6-5	210	2-18-78	1998	Montreal, Quebec
Huntsman, Brandon	0	0	.00	1	1	0	0	2	0	0	0	1	3	R	R	6-4	195	11-19-75	1994	Pleasant Grove, Utah
Lluberes, Alberto	0	1	9.00	2	0	0	0	3	5	4	3	0	2	R	R	6-4	179	1-24-79	1996	San Pedro de Macoris, D.R.
Murphy, Brian	0	0	1.42	3	0	0	1	6	7	3	1	2	2	L	R	6-6	200	1-20-76	1998	North Street, Mich.
Paz, Rolando	0	0	.00	1	0	0	0	1	2	0	0	1	2	R	R	6-2	180	1-31-79	1997	Vacamonte, Panama
Perez, Randy	0	2	4.50	8	0	0	2	24	29	13	12	7	17	L	L	6-1	170	4-13-80	1998	Lakeside, Calif.
Pruitt, Jason	4	3	4.08	17	3	0	1	46	44	21	21	17	47	L	L	6-3	190	8-6-80	1998	Philadelphia, Pa.
Ratliff, Craig	5	4	3.07	10	10	0	0	56	53	31	19	21	33	R	R	6-7	215	1-19-78	1996	West Van Lear, Ky.
Saneaux, Francisco	2	0	3.45	3	3	0	0	16	15	6	6	8	10	R	R	6-3	175	11-24-79	1996	La Romana, D.R.
Schwager, Matt	0	2	6.75	12	1	0	3	24	31	19	18	13	20	R	R	6-5	215	10-10-77	1998	Rio Piedras, P.R.
Shepherd, Alvie	0	0	4.76	3	3	0	0	6	7	3	3	3	4	R	R	6-7	220	5-12-74	1996	Bellwood, Ill.
Tapia, Rafael	2	0	5.23	11	2	0	0	33	42	24	19	9	22	R	R	6-2	160	4-28-78	1995	San Pedro de Macoris, D.R.
Tomaszewski, Eliot	0	1	7.16	16	1	0	1	28	29	28	22	32	19	R	R	6-4	190	1-13-80	1998	Albuquerque, N.M.
Trinidad, Fernando	1	0	4.50	3	0	0	0	6	4	3	3	6	1	R	R	6-2	180	11-1-79	1997	Hato Mayor, D.R.
Whitecotton, Billy	4	2	6.14	10	7	0	0	48	52	35	33	12	29	R	R	6-3	170	8-18-80	1998	Baltimore, Md.
Yarno, Josh	3	4	4.37	16	6	0	0	58	71	40	28	20	46	R	R	6-5	205	11-16-79	1998	Decatur, Ga.

BOSTON RED SOX

Red Sox fit pieces together to secure return to postseason

BY TONY MASSAROTTI

The season ended like so many others, yet there was so much progress in Boston during the summer of 1998.

In one year, the Red Sox climbed from fourth place in the American League East to second, from 78 wins to 92. They transformed themselves from also-rans to playoff contenders, finishing with the second-best record in the AL.

"Nobody was really prepared to go home," said veteran righthander Bret Saberhagen after the Sox were eliminated in four games by the Cleveland Indians in the AL Division Series. "I've been on teams where everybody was picking up and getting ready to go home, and that never really happened this year. We accomplished a lot. A lot of guys have a lot to be proud of."

Indeed, even the most cynical, staid New Englanders could not help but embrace these Red Sox. Managed by Jimy Williams, the Sox established themselves with an improbable 14-1 April surge that began with a game-winning grand slam by Mo Vaughn in the home opener on April 10. During their first homestand, the Sox went 9-1, winning six times in their final at-bat.

Along the way, ace Pedro Martinez (19-7, 2.89) established himself as a Cy Young candidate, shortstop Nomar Garciaparra (.323-35-122) emerged as an MVP threat and reliever Tom Gordon blossomed into one of the finest closers in the game. Gordon collected a club-record 46 saves, including a major league record 43 straight to end the season.

Nonetheless, the Sox were not without their usual lot of uncertainty. While Martinez, Garciaparra, Gordon, Saberhagen, outfielder Troy O'Leary, infielders John Valentin and Jeff Frye, and righthander Tim Wakefield were all signed to long-term contracts before or during the season, cornerstone Vaughn was eligible for free agency.

"We were a close-knit bunch of guys this year and next year it's going to be like a family reunion," Saberhagen said. "I truly hope Mo comes back."

General manager Dan Duquette faced the prospect of going outside the organization for a first baseman if he failed to bring Vaughn back. The only position player in the minors who appeared ready to take over a major league job in 1999 was outfielder Trot Nixon, who hit .259 in 27 September at-bats for Boston. Nixon had his finest pro season in 1998, batting .310 with 23 homers and 74 RBIs for Triple-A Pawtucket.

Several other players excited the Red Sox with productive years down on the farm. Outfielder Dernell Stenson hit .257 with 24 homers for Double-A Trenton, enhancing his prospect status. And catcher Shea Hillenbrand hit .349 with 19 homers and 92 RBIs at Class A Michigan.

But the year saw the Red Sox lose several promising young pitchers in trade as righthanders Tony Armas, Matt Kinney, Peter Munro, Carl Pavano and Jay Yennaco were sent packing in exchange for veteran players. Righthander Brian Rose, the top pitcher left in the system, missed most of 1998 due to injury.

Farm director Bob Schaefer, who lost a power struggle with Duquette in July, was forced out of his position. Schaefer had been with the organization since 1993. He was replaced by Kent Qualls.

Nomar Garciaparra

Trot Nixon

Players of the Year

Major League: Nomar Garciaparra, ss

The key to Boston's strong showing, Garciaparra hit .323 and drove in 122 runs in his second full major league season.

Minor League: Trot Nixon, of, Pawtucket

Nixon finally had the season the Red Sox were waiting for, hitting .310 with 23 homers and 24 steals at Triple-A.

ORGANIZATION LEADERS

BATTING

*AVG	Shea Hillenbrand, Michigan	.349
R	David Eckstein, Sarasota	99
H	Shea Hillenbrand, Michigan	174
TB	Shea Hillenbrand, Michigan	272
2B	Two tied at	33
3B	Roy Marsh, Sarasota	7
HR	Dernell Stenson, Trenton	24
RBI	Shea Hillenbrand, Michigan	92
BB	David Eckstein, Sarasota	87
SO	Steve Lomasney, Sarasota	145
SB	David Eckstein, Sarasota	45

PITCHING

W	Jim Farrell, Pawtucket	14
L	Two tied at	12
#ERA	Jeff Taglienti, Michigan	1.89
G	Sal Urso, Trenton	69
CG	Two tied at	5
SV	Jeff Taglienti, Michigan	30
IP	Jim Farrell, Pawtucket	163
BB	John Curtice, Michigan	79
SO	Rob Ramsay, Trenton	166

*Minimum 250 At-Bats #Minimum 75 Innings

Boston RED SOX

Manager: Jimy Williams

1998 Record: 92-70, .568 (2nd, AL East)

BATTING	AVG	G	AB	R	H	2B	3B	HR	RBI	BB	SO	SB	CS	B	T	HT	WT	DOB	1st Yr	Resides
Ashley, Billy	.292	13	24	3	7	3	0	3	7	2	11	0	0	R	R	6-7	230	7-11-70	1988	Belleville, Mich.
Benjamin, Mike	.272	124	349	46	95	23	0	4	39	15	73	3	0	R	R	6-0	169	11-22-65	1987	Chandler, Ariz.
Bragg, Darren	.279	129	409	51	114	29	3	8	57	42	99	5	3	L	R	5-9	180	9-7-69	1991	Phoenix, Ariz.
Buford, Damon	.282	86	216	37	61	14	4	10	42	22	43	5	5	R	R	5-10	170	6-12-70	1990	Phoenix, Ariz.
Cummings, Midre	.283	67	120	20	34	8	0	5	15	17	19	3	3	L	R	6-0	190	10-14-71	1990	Clearwater, Fla.
Garciaparra, Nomar	.323	143	604	111	195	37	8	35	122	33	62	12	6	R	R	6-0	175	7-23-73	1994	Las Vegas, Nev.
Hatteberg, Scott	.276	112	359	46	99	23	1	12	43	43	58	0	0	L	R	6-1	195	12-14-69	1991	Tacoma, Wash.
Jefferson, Reggie	.306	62	196	24	60	16	1	8	31	21	40	0	0	L	L	6-4	215	9-25-68	1986	Tallahassee, Fla.
Johns, Keith	.000	2	0	0	0	0	0	0	0	1	0	0	0	R	R	6-1	175	7-19-71	1992	St. Louis, Mo.
Lemke, Mark	.187	31	91	10	17	4	0	0	7	6	15	0	1	B	R	5-9	167	8-13-65	1983	Atlanta, Ga.
Lewis, Darren	.268	155	585	95	157	25	3	8	63	70	94	29	12	R	R	6-0	189	8-28-67	1988	San Carlos, Calif.
Leyritz, Jim	.287	52	129	17	37	6	0	8	24	21	34	0	0	R	R	6-0	195	12-27-63	1986	Cooper City, Fla.
Merced, Orlando	.000	9	9	0	0	0	0	0	2	2	3	0	0	L	R	6-1	195	11-2-66	1985	Orlando, Fla.
2-team (63 Minn.)	.277	72	213	22	59	12	0	5	35	19	32	1	4							
Merloni, Lou	.281	39	96	10	27	6	0	1	15	7	20	1	0	R	R	5-10	194	4-6-71	1993	Framingham, Mass.
Mitchell, Keith	.273	23	33	4	9	2	0	0	6	7	5	1	0	R	R	5-10	195	8-6-69	1987	San Diego, Calif.
Nixon, Trot	.259	13	27	3	7	1	0	0	0	1	3	0	0	L	L	6-2	196	4-11-74	1993	Charlotte, N.C.
O'Leary, Troy	.270	156	611	95	165	36	8	23	83	36	108	2	2	L	L	6-0	190	8-4-69	1987	Phoenix, Ariz.
Romero, Mandy	.231	12	13	2	3	1	0	0	1	3	3	0	0	B	R	5-11	196	10-19-67	1988	Miami, Fla.
Sadler, Donnie	.226	58	124	20	28	4	4	3	15	6	28	4	0	R	R	5-6	165	6-17-75	1994	Valley Mills, Texas
Snopek, Chris	.167	8	12	2	2	0	0	0	2	2	5	0	0	R	R	6-1	185	9-20-70	1992	Cynthiana, Ky.
2-team (53 Chicago)	.201	61	137	19	20	2	0	1	6	18	29	3	0							
Stanley, Mike	.288	47	156	25	45	12	0	7	32	26	43	1	0	R	R	6-0	190	6-25-63	1985	Maitland, Fla.
2-team (98 Toronto)	.256	145	497	74	127	25	0	29	79	82	129	3	1							
Valentin, John	.247	153	588	113	145	44	1	23	73	77	82	4	5	R	R	6-0	180	2-18-67	1988	Homdel, N.J.
Varitek, Jason	.253	86	221	31	56	13	0	7	33	17	45	2	2	B	R	6-2	210	4-11-72	1995	Longwood, Fla.
Vaughn, Mo	.337	154	609	107	205	31	2	40	115	61	144	0	0	L	R	6-1	240	12-15-67	1989	Easton, Mass.

PITCHING	W	L	ERA	G	GS	CG	SV	IP	H	R	ER	BB	SO	B	T	HT	WT	DOB	1st Yr	Resides
Avery, Steve	10	7	5.02	34	23	0	0	124	128	74	69	64	57	L	L	6-4	205	4-14-70	1988	Taylor, Mich.
Barkley, Brian	0	0	9.82	6	0	0	0	11	16	13	12	9	2	L	L	6-2	180	12-8-75	1994	Waco, Texas
Checo, Robinson	0	2	9.39	2	2	0	0	8	11	8	8	5	5	R	R	6-1	185	9-9-71	1989	Santiago, D.R.
Cho, Jin Ho	0	3	8.20	4	4	0	0	19	28	17	17	3	15	R	R	6-3	207	8-16-75	1998	Jun Ju City, Korea
Corsi, Jim	3	2	2.59	59	0	0	0	66	58	23	19	23	49	R	R	6-1	220	9-9-61	1982	Natick, Mass.
Eckersley, Dennis	4	1	4.76	50	0	0	1	40	46	21	21	8	22	R	R	6-2	195	10-3-54	1972	Sudbury, Mass.
Garces, Rich	1	1	3.33	30	0	0	1	46	36	19	17	27	34	R	R	6-0	215	5-18-71	1988	Maracay, Ven.
Gordon, Tom	7	4	2.72	73	0	0	46	79	55	24	24	25	78	R	R	5-9	180	11-18-67	1986	Avon Park, Fla.
Henry, Butch	0	0	4.00	2	2	0	0	9	8	4	4	3	6	L	L	6-1	205	10-7-68	1987	El Paso, Texas
Lowe, Derek	3	9	4.02	63	10	0	4	123	126	65	55	42	77	R	R	6-6	170	6-1-73	1991	Dearborn, Mich.
Mahay, Ron	1	1	3.46	29	0	0	1	26	26	16	10	15	14	L	L	6-2	185	6-28-71	1991	Crestwood, Ill.
Martinez, Pedro	19	7	2.89	33	33	3	0	234	188	82	75	67	251	R	R	5-11	170	10-25-71	1988	Santo Domingo, D.R.
Reyes, Carlos	1	1	3.52	24	0	0	0	38	35	15	15	14	23	B	R	6-1	190	4-19-69	1991	Tampa, Fla.
Rose, Brian	1	4	6.93	8	8	0	0	38	43	32	29	14	18	R	R	6-3	215	2-13-76	1995	Dartmouth, Mass.
Saberhagen, Bret	15	8	3.96	31	31	0	0	175	181	82	77	29	100	R	R	6-1	200	4-11-64	1983	Babylon, N.Y.
Schourek, Pete	1	3	4.30	10	8	0	0	44	45	21	21	14	36	L	L	6-5	205	5-10-69	1987	Clifton, Va.
Shouse, Brian	0	1	5.63	7	0	0	0	8	9	5	5	4	5	L	L	5-11	180	9-26-68	1990	Peoria, Ill.
Swindell, Greg	2	3	3.38	29	0	0	0	24	25	13	9	13	18	R	L	6-3	230	1-2-65	1986	Houston, Texas
2-team (52 Minn.)	5	6	3.59	81	0	0	2	90	92	40	36	31	63							
Valdez, Carlos	1	0	0.00	4	0	0	0	3	1	0	0	5	4	R	R	5-11	191	12-26-71	1990	Nizao, D.R.
Veras, Dario	0	1	10.13	7	0	0	0	8	12	9	9	7	2	R	R	6-2	155	3-13-73	1991	Villa Vasquez, D.R.
Wakefield, Tim	17	8	4.58	36	33	2	0	216	211	123	110	79	146	R	R	6-2	204	8-2-66	1988	Melbourne, Fla.
Wasdin, John	6	4	5.25	47	8	0	0	96	111	57	56	27	59	R	R	6-2	195	8-5-72	1993	Jacksonville, Fla.
West, David	0	0	27.00	6	0	0	0	2	7	6	6	7	4	L	L	6-6	247	9-1-64	1983	Palm City, Fla.

FIELDING

Catcher	PCT	G	PO	A	E	DP	PB
Hatteberg	.993	108	665	60	5	7	17
Leyritz	1.000	1	10	0	0	0	0
Romero	1.000	4	11	0	0	0	0
Varitek	.988	75	367	32	5	3	18

First Base	PCT	G	PO	A	E	DP
Ashley	.857	2	6	0	1	2
Benjamin	1.000	10	41	9	0	3
Jefferson	.953	7	37	4	2	2
Leyritz	1.000	1	3	0	0	1
Stanley	1.000	13	108	6	0	14
Vaughn	.991	142	1176	87	12	91

Second Base	PCT	G	PO	A	E	DP
Benjamin	.994	87	159	189	2	40
Buford	.000	1	0	0	0	0
Johns	1.000	1	1	1	0	1
Lemke	1.000	31	38	71	0	15
Merloni	.974	32	47	66	3	10
Sadler	.972	50	77	96	5	17
Snopek	.750	3	1	2	1	0
Valentin	.000	1	0	0	0	0

Third Base	PCT	G	PO	A	E	DP
Benjamin	1.000	11	6	19	0	0
Buford	.000	1	0	0	0	0
Merloni	.857	5	5	7	2	0
Snopek	1.000	3	0	2	0	0
Valentin	.965	153	121	289	15	26

Shortstop	PCT	G	PO	A	E	DP
Benjamin	.988	20	26	59	1	11
Garciaparra	.962	143	228	401	25	67
Merloni	.000	1	0	0	0	0
Sadler	1.000	4	5	6	0	2

Outfield	PCT	G	PO	A	E	DP
Ashley	1.000	2	0	1	0	0
Bragg	.996	124	219	6	1	2
Buford	1.000	67	133	4	0	1
Cummings	.941	17	16	0	1	0
Lewis	.992	152	382	6	3	0
Merced	1.000	1	2	0	0	0
Mitchell	1.000	10	6	0	0	0
Nixon	1.000	7	16	0	0	0
O'Leary	.990	155	302	9	3	1

LARRY GOREN

Boston's Mo Vaughn
Led team with 40 home runs

DIAMOND IMAGES

Trenton's Dernell Stenson
Hit 24 homers in Double-A

FARM SYSTEM

Director of Player Development: Bob Schaefer/Kent Qualls

Class	Farm Team	League	W	L	Pct.	Finish*	Manager	First Yr
AAA	Pawtucket (R.I.) Red Sox	International	77	64	.546	4th (14)	Ken Macha	1973
AA	Trenton (N.J.) Thunder	Eastern	71	70	.504	5th (10)	DeMarlo Hale	1995
A#	Sarasota (Fla.) Red Sox	Florida State	76	61	.555	5th (14)	Bob Geren	1994
A	Michigan Battle Cats	Midwest	79	61	.564	t-2nd (14)	Billy Gardner Jr.	1995
A	Lowell (Mass.) Spinners	New York-Penn	32	44	.421	13th (14)	Dick Berardino	1996
Rookie	Fort Myers (Fla.) Red Sox	Gulf Coast	27	33	.450	10th (14)	Luis Aguayo	1993

*Finish in overall standings (No. of teams in league) #Advanced level

PAWTUCKET — Class AAA

INTERNATIONAL LEAGUE

BATTING	AVG	G	AB	R	H	2B	3B	HR	RBI	BB	SO	SB	CS	B	T	HT	WT	DOB	1st Yr	Resides
Abad, Andy	.307	111	365	71	112	18	1	16	66	68	70	10	6	L	L	6-1	176	8-25-72	1993	Jupiter, Fla.
Ashley, Billy	.271	63	218	40	59	12	0	14	51	35	72	1	0	R	R	6-7	230	7-11-70	1988	Belleville, Mich.
Borrero, Richie	.176	6	17	3	3	0	0	0	0	1	5	0	0	R	R	6-1	195	1-5-73	1990	Hormigueros, P.R.
Bryant, Pat	.224	75	259	43	58	8	1	8	26	33	63	13	5	R	R	5-11	182	10-27-72	1990	Sherman Oaks, Calif.
Carey, Todd	.205	28	83	10	17	4	0	4	10	5	13	2	0	L	R	6-1	180	8-14-71	1992	Cumberland, R.I.
Coleman, Michael	.253	93	340	47	86	13	0	14	37	27	92	12	9	R	R	5-11	207	8-16-75	1994	Nashville, Tenn.
DePastino, Joe	.242	9	33	1	8	1	0	0	4	0	8	1	1	R	R	6-2	210	9-4-73	1992	Sarasota, Fla.
Diaz, Eddy	.295	33	139	30	41	9	1	4	13	11	12	5	1	R	R	5-10	160	9-29-71	1991	Barquisimeto, Ven.
2-team (86 Louisville)	.257	119	416	61	107	24	2	9	53	39	39	13	6							
Hulse, David	.329	21	85	9	28	6	2	1	13	2	18	3	1	L	L	5-11	170	2-25-68	1990	San Angelo, Texas
Hurst, Jimmy	.286	103	360	61	103	11	1	20	67	59	98	22	9	R	R	6-6	225	3-1-72	1991	Tuscaloosa, Ala.
Jackson, Gavin	.238	67	206	21	49	4	1	3	24	27	40	3	2	R	R	5-10	170	7-19-73	1993	Sylvester, Ga.
Johns, Keith	.228	96	329	31	75	12	1	8	38	28	82	2	6	R	R	6-1	175	7-19-71	1992	St. Louis, Mo.
Liniak, Cole	.261	112	429	65	112	31	1	17	59	39	71	4	4	R	R	6-1	181	8-23-76	1995	Encinitas, Calif.
McKeel, Walt	.288	48	170	26	49	10	1	4	26	21	27	1	2	R	R	6-2	200	1-17-72	1990	Stantonsburg, N.C.
Merloni, Lou	.386	27	88	17	34	3	1	8	22	16	13	2	2	R	R	5-10	194	4-6-71	1993	Framingham, Mass.
Mitchell, Keith	.313	63	211	55	66	15	0	12	45	44	37	3	3	R	R	5-10	195	8-6-69	1987	San Diego, Calif.
Nixon, Trot	.310	135	509	97	158	26	4	23	74	76	81	26	13	L	L	6-2	196	4-11-74	1993	Charlotte, N.C.
Pozo, Arquimedez	.305	90	348	53	106	20	5	12	51	22	44	4	2	R	R	5-10	160	8-24-73	1991	Santo Domingo, D.R.
Romero, Mandy	.331	45	139	20	46	5	0	8	27	24	15	0	0	B	R	5-11	196	10-19-67	1988	Miami, Fla.
Sadler, Donnie	.221	36	131	25	29	5	1	2	10	26	23	11	1	R	R	5-6	165	6-17-75	1994	Valley Mills, Texas
Tebbs, Nate	.281	17	57	7	16	2	0	0	4	3	13	5	2	B	R	5-10	170	12-14-72	1993	Riverton, Utah
Waszgis, B.J.	.202	66	208	31	42	9	0	9	41	26	52	2	4	R	R	6-2	210	8-24-70	1991	Omaha, Neb.

PITCHING	W	L	ERA	G	GS	CG	SV	IP	H	R	ER	BB	SO	B	T	HT	WT	DOB	1st Yr	Resides
Avery, Steve	0	2	5.56	3	3	0	0	11	9	9	7	9	6	L	L	6-4	205	4-14-70	1988	Taylor, Mich.
Barkley, Brian	7	9	4.91	23	23	1	0	139	161	81	76	50	88	L	L	6-2	180	12-8-75	1994	Waco, Texas
Blais, Mike	0	1	7.71	2	0	0	0	2	4	2	2	2	0	R	R	6-5	226	10-2-71	1993	East Lyme, Conn.
Checo, Robinson	6	2	4.56	11	10	0	0	53	48	30	27	26	46	R	R	6-1	185	9-9-71	1989	Santiago, D.R.
Corsi, Jim	0	0	.00	1	1	0	0	2	3	0	0	0	1	R	R	6-1	220	9-9-61	1982	Natick, Mass.
Cummings, John	0	5	6.16	10	8	0	0	38	46	28	26	12	17	L	L	6-3	200	5-10-69	1990	Laguna Niguel, Calif.
2-team (21 Buffalo)	0	6	6.03	31	8	0	0	57	71	43	38	16	32							
Eckersley, Dennis	0	0	4.50	2	0	0	0	2	2	1	1	0	2	R	R	6-2	195	10-3-54	1972	Sudbury, Mass.
Farrell, Jim	14	8	5.51	28	25	2	0	163	176	106	100	52	142	R	R	6-1	180	11-1-73	1995	Hartville, Ohio
Fernandez, Jared	1	1	4.74	5	2	0	0	25	26	16	13	7	15	R	R	6-2	230	2-2-72	1994	West Valley, Utah
Fleming, Dave	1	1	7.58	4	4	0	0	19	21	18	16	13	4	L	L	6-3	205	11-7-69	1990	Mahopac, N.Y.
Flury, Pat	0	0	5.64	17	0	0	0	22	23	15	14	16	22	R	R	6-1	220	3-14-73	1993	Sparks, Nev.
Frey, Steve	4	2	3.88	50	0	0	2	63	66	29	27	22	42	L	L	5-9	170	7-29-63	1983	Newtown, Pa.
Garces, Rich	0	1	5.40	7	0	0	3	8	6	5	5	2	10	R	R	6-0	215	5-18-71	1988	Maracay, Ven.
Hudson, Joe	2	2	4.53	46	0	0	10	48	57	32	24	23	32	R	R	6-1	180	9-29-70	1992	Medford, N.J.
Mahay, Ron	3	1	4.17	23	1	0	3	41	37	20	19	19	41	L	L	6-2	185	6-28-71	1991	Crestwood, Ill.
Munro, Peter	5	4	4.05	18	17	0	0	107	111	49	48	35	75	R	R	6-2	193	6-14-75	1994	Little Neck, N.Y.
Pena, Juan	8	10	4.38	24	23	1	0	140	141	73	68	51	146	R	R	6-5	211	6-27-77	1995	Miami, Fla.
Rose, Brian	0	3	7.64	6	6	0	0	18	24	19	15	4	17	R	R	6-3	215	2-13-76	1995	Dartmouth, Mass.
Schrenk, Steve	8	3	2.82	34	0	0	1	61	60	27	19	23	45	R	R	6-3	185	11-20-68	1987	Aurora, Ore.
Shouse, Brian	2	0	2.90	22	1	0	6	31	21	11	10	7	25	L	L	5-11	180	9-26-68	1990	Peoria, Ill.
Thompson, Chris	0	0	3.00	2	0	0	0	3	3	1	1	1	3	R	R	6-2	202	9-29-72	1996	Elyria, Ohio
Valdez, Carlos	4	3	4.10	37	5	0	0	75	74	38	34	22	75	R	R	5-11	191	12-26-71	1990	Nizao, D.R.
Veras, Dario	2	0	3.72	23	0	0	7	29	30	12	12	11	27	R	R	6-2	155	3-13-73	1991	Villa Vasquez, D.R.
Walker, Pete	1	4	5.94	22	0	0	0	33	34	26	22	17	19	R	R	6-2	195	4-8-69	1990	East Lyme, Conn.
Wasdin, John	1	0	3.00	4	2	0	0	12	11	6	4	5	10	R	R	6-2	195	8-5-72	1993	Jacksonville, Fla.
West, David	5	0	1.13	17	0	0	3	24	19	4	3	12	23	L	L	6-6	247	9-1-64	1983	Palm City, Fla.
Yennaco, Jay	3	2	5.82	11	11	1	0	60	77	43	39	16	34	R	R	6-4	238	11-17-75	1996	Windham, N.H.

FIELDING

Catcher	PCT	G	PO	A	E	DP	PB
Borrero	.944	6	29	5	2	2	0
DePastino	1.000	9	47	3	0	0	0
McKeel	.980	36	220	23	5	0	6
Romero	.991	38	311	27	3	4	3
Waszgis	.984	62	386	32	7	5	3

First Base	PCT	G	PO	A	E	DP
Abad	.993	86	683	64	5	65
Ashley	.980	25	187	12	4	18
Carey	.988	22	154	10	2	14
Johns	1.000	9	33	3	0	3
McKeel	.989	13	85	4	1	4
Mitchell	1.000	1	6	0	0	0
Nixon	1.000	1	1	0	0	0
Waszgis	1.000	4	14	2	0	1

Second Base	PCT	G	PO	A	E	DP
Carey	1.000	1	1	3	0	1
Diaz	1.000	10	21	27	0	6
Jackson	.973	32	30	70	0	17
Merloni	.974	10	11	26	1	7
Pozo	.963	53	121	138	10	37
Sadler	.975	32	67	92	4	14
Tebbs	1.000	11	24	19	0	4

Third Base	PCT	G	PO	A	E	DP
Diaz	.930	21	18	35	4	0
Johns	1.000	2	1	4	0	0
Liniak	.939	106	86	192	18	13
McKeel	.000	1	0	0	0	0
Merloni	.000	1	0	0	0	0
Pozo	.879	9	7	22	4	1
Tebbs	.778	4	3	4	2	0

Shortstop	PCT	G	PO	A	E	DP
Carey	1.000	4	6	8	0	4
Diaz	.818	2	3	6	2	0
Jackson	.955	36	48	99	7	21
Johns	.964	88	136	263	15	57
Merloni	.979	15	16	30	1	3
Sadler	1.000	4	6	12	0	2

Outfield	PCT	G	PO	A	E	DP
Abad	1.000	27	43	2	0	0
Ashley	1.000	6	11	0	0	0
Bryant	.986	71	140	4	2	0
Coleman	.978	88	173	9	4	1
Hulse	1.000	7	11	0	0	0
Hurst	.947	78	150	11	9	2
Mitchell	.989	41	79	8	1	1
Nixon	.956	126	230	11	11	3
Tebbs	1.000	2	3	0	0	0

TRENTON — Class AA

EASTERN LEAGUE

BATTING	AVG	G	AB	R	H	2B	3B	HR	RBI	BB	SO	SB	CS	B	T	HT	WT	DOB	1st Yr	Resides
Barnes, John	.274	100	380	53	104	18	0	14	36	40	47	3	8	R	R	6-1	205	4-24-76	1996	El Cajon, Calif.
Borrero, Richie	.247	51	162	21	40	6	0	6	24	6	32	3	3	R	R	6-1	195	1-5-73	1990	Hormigueros, P.R.
Bryant, Pat	.295	26	88	17	26	5	0	3	14	12	20	3	3	R	R	5-11	182	10-27-72	1990	Sherman Oaks, Calif.
Chamblee, Jim	.241	136	489	71	118	33	3	17	65	62	144	9	5	R	R	6-4	175	5-6-75	1995	Denton, Texas
Chevalier, Virgil	.274	30	117	19	32	7	2	2	16	4	17	2	2	R	R	6-2	240	10-31-73	1995	Burnt Hills, N.Y.
DeLeon, Jorge	.291	29	86	11	25	7	0	0	10	5	3	2	1	R	R	6-2	170	9-26-74	1997	Guayama, P.R.
DePastino, Joe	.295	73	275	34	81	16	0	10	43	28	51	3	0	R	R	6-2	210	9-4-73	1992	Sarasota, Fla.
DeRosso, Tony	.107	9	28	3	3	0	0	1	3	2	12	0	0	R	R	6-3	216	11-7-75	1994	Moultrie, Ga.
Epperson, Chad	.253	109	383	53	97	27	2	15	57	38	129	2	8	B	R	6-3	221	3-26-72	1992	Fort Myers, Fla.
Everson, Darin	.273	9	33	4	9	3	0	0	2	5	5	0	0	L	R	6-3	238	4-22-71	1994	Ada, Minn.
Gibralter, David	.260	100	385	48	100	16	0	15	61	25	91	2	3	R	R	6-3	215	6-19-75	1993	Duncanville, Texas
Hamilton, Joe	.174	30	92	10	16	3	0	3	10	11	33	1	3	L	R	6-0	185	7-12-74	1992	Rehoboth, Mass.
Jackson, Gavin	.244	50	168	12	41	7	1	0	17	18	21	3	1	R	R	5-10	170	7-19-73	1993	Sylvester, Ga.
Maness, Dwight	.246	85	313	48	77	12	5	11	32	37	80	15	6	R	R	6-3	188	4-3-74	1992	New Castle, Del.
2-team (27 Binghamton)	.244	112	406	63	99	15	5	14	42	51	108	18	11							
Martinez, Rafael	.204	15	49	5	10	3	0	0	3	6	13	0	0	L	L	6-3	185	8-24-75	1991	Santo Domingo, D.R.
Mitchell, Keith	.195	12	41	4	8	2	0	2	7	8	5	0	0	R	R	5-10	195	8-6-69	1987	San Diego, Calif.
Ortiz, Nick	.229	39	131	17	30	6	0	1	9	14	27	0	0	R	R	6-0	165	7-9-73	1991	Cidra, P.R.
2-team (56 Harrisburg)	.252	95	294	35	74	17	2	7	33	32	64	2	3							
Raifstanger, John	.159	20	44	4	7	2	0	1	7	6	13	0	0	R	R	6-0	190	6-2-73	1994	Great Barrington, Mass.
Sapp, Damian	.242	28	91	9	22	5	0	5	10	9	35	0	0	R	R	6-3	219	5-20-76	1994	Pleasant Grove, Utah
Stenson, Dernell	.257	138	505	90	130	21	1	24	71	84	135	5	3	L	L	6-1	230	6-17-78	1996	La Grange, Ga.
Tebbs, Nate	.256	104	394	44	101	21	2	2	31	36	63	14	13	B	R	5-10	170	12-14-72	1993	Riverton, Utah
Veras, Wilton	.291	126	470	70	137	27	4	16	67	15	66	5	4	R	R	6-2	186	1-19-78	1995	Santo Domingo, D.R.

PITCHING	W	L	ERA	G	GS	CG	SV	IP	H	R	ER	BB	SO	B	T	HT	WT	DOB	1st Yr	Resides
Beale, Chuck	5	3	3.26	43	0	0	1	69	54	31	25	31	39	R	R	6-0	210	3-19-74	1996	Dublin, Ga.
Betancourt, Rafael	0	0	6.75	7	0	0	0	9	9	7	7	3	9	R	R	6-2	176	4-29-75	1994	Cumana, Ven.
Blais, Mike	2	1	3.95	22	0	0	2	27	36	14	12	10	14	R	R	6-5	226	10-2-71	1993	East Lyme, Conn.
Cho, Jin Ho	5	2	2.19	13	13	1	0	74	59	21	18	19	62	R	R	6-3	207	8-16-75	1998	Jun Ju City, Korea
Crawford, Paxton	6	5	4.17	22	20	1	0	108	104	53	50	39	82	R	R	6-3	193	8-4-77	1995	Morrialton, Ark.
Cressend, Jack	10	11	4.34	29	29	1	0	149	168	86	72	55	130	R	R	6-1	185	5-13-75	1996	Covington, La.
De la Cruz, Fernando	0	0	0.00	3	0	0	1	4	3	0	0	1	3	R	R	6-0	175	1-25-71	1993	La Romana, D.R.

PITCHING	W	L	ERA	G	GS	CG	SV	IP	H	R	ER	BB	SO	B	T	HT	WT	DOB	1st Yr	Resides
Fernandez, Jared	3	7	5.25	36	7	0	1	118	132	80	69	51	70	R	R	6-2	230	2-2-72	1994	West Valley, Utah
Flury, Pat	0	0	1.76	26	0	0	16	31	24	6	6	11	37	R	R	6-1	220	3-14-73	1993	Sparks, Nev.
Miadich, Bart	1	6	5.96	22	8	0	1	54	66	39	36	26	33	R	R	6-4	205	2-3-76	1997	Lake Oswego, Ore.
Ramsay, Rob	12	6	3.49	27	27	1	0	163	137	67	63	50	166	L	L	6-5	230	12-3-73	1996	Washougal, Wash.
Rose, Brian	3	5	3.90	24	0	0	2	32	39	16	14	16	23	R	R	6-1	190	10-7-72	1994	Potsdam, N.Y.
Sekany, Jason	10	10	5.21	28	28	1	0	149	151	101	[illegible]	87	110	R	R	[illegible]	200	7-20-75	1996	Fort Myers, Fla.
Smetana, Steve	2	3	4.46	49	0	0	12	77	88	40	38	23	51	L	L	6-0	205	4-14-73	1996	Chardon, Ohio
Tweedlie, Brad	1	2	5.93	35	0	0	2	41	47	33	27	27	29	R	R	6-2	210	12-9-71	1993	Agawam, Mass.
Urso, Sal	8	6	4.10	69	0	0	3	83	86	45	38	32	86	R	L	5-11	195	1-19-72	1990	Tampa, Fla.
Yennaco, Jay	3	3	4.86	9	9	0	0	54	50	30	29	19	23	R	R	6-4	238	11-17-75	1996	Windham, N.H.

FIELDING

Catcher	PCT	G	PO	A	E	DP	PB
Borrero	.981	49	338	32	7	4	11
Chevalier	.909	2	9	1	1	0	0
DePastino	.986	56	368	53	6	6	14
Epperson	.993	19	135	13	1	0	5
Raifstanger	.000	1	0	0	0	0	0
Sapp	.962	22	132	21	6	0	12

First Base	PCT	G	PO	A	E	DP
Chevalier	1.000	12	74	4	0	8
DePastino	1.000	1	1	0	0	0
Epperson	.994	17	152	12	1	10
Everson	1.000	6	56	4	0	5
Gibralter	.990	90	837	44	9	70
Martinez	.976	15	111	10	3	11
Raifstanger	1.000	2	6	2	0	1
Sapp	1.000	2	12	1	0	2

Second Base	PCT	G	PO	A	E	DP
Chamblee	.974	131	247	352	16	92
Raifstanger	.571	1	2	2	3	0
Tebbs	.964	12	22	32	2	5

Third Base	PCT	G	PO	A	E	DP
Gibralter	.778	5	4	10	4	1
Raifstanger	.000	1	0	0	0	0
Tebbs	.897	13	9	26	4	1
Veras	.952	125	100	259	18	25

Shortstop	PCT	G	PO	A	E	DP
Chamblee	1.000	1	0	1	0	1
De Leon	.968	29	43	79	4	16
Jackson	.972	50	86	155	7	31
Ortiz	.923	38	65	102	14	21
Tebbs	.954	31	36	88	6	15

Outfield	PCT	G	PO	A	E	DP
Barnes	.979	94	134	6	3	1
Bryant	.979	24	45	2	1	0
Chamblee	.000	1	0	0	0	0
Chevalier	.857	11	12	0	2	0
DeRosso	1.000	3	1	0	0	0
Epperson	1.000	6	6	0	0	0
Gibralter	.000	1	0	0	0	0
Hamilton	.982	29	55	1	1	0
Maness	.973	83	209	11	6	3
Mitchell	1.000	10	22	1	0	0
Raifstanger	1.000	4	7	0	0	0
Stenson	.975	131	218	15	6	1
Tebbs	.991	49	100	6	1	0

SARASOTA — Class A

FLORIDA STATE LEAGUE

BATTING	AVG	G	AB	R	H	2B	3B	HR	RBI	BB	SO	SB	CS	B	T	HT	WT	DOB	1st Yr	Resides
Bazzani, Matt	.200	2	5	0	1	0	1	0	1	0	3	0	0	R	R	6-0	205	9-17-73	1994	Foster City, Calif.
Chevalier, Virgil	.327	81	327	59	107	22	4	8	59	27	59	13	4	R	R	6-2	240	10-31-73	1995	Burnt Hills, N.Y.
Choi, Kyung	.271	63	181	25	49	10	1	4	23	17	32	7	0	L	L	6-0	182	5-12-72	1997	Seoul, South Korea
DeRosso, Tony	.308	4	13	1	4	3	0	0	5	3	1	0	0	R	R	6-3	216	11-7-75	1994	Moultrie, Ga.
Eckstein, David	.306	135	503	99	154	29	4	3	58	87	51	45	16	R	R	5-8	168	1-20-75	1997	Sanford, Fla.
Espinal, Juan	.278	127	508	76	141	32	1	16	88	37	107	3	1	R	R	5-11	165	4-15-75	1992	La Vega, D.R.
Everson, Darin	.351	17	57	16	20	5	1	5	17	5	9	1	0	L	R	6-3	238	4-22-71	1994	Ada, Minn.
Faggett, Ethan	.279	62	233	42	65	12	1	4	25	25	55	13	5	L	L	6-0	190	8-21-74	1992	Burleson, Texas
Fuentes, Javier	.275	82	251	45	69	14	1	4	29	38	38	5	2	R	R	6-1	185	9-27-74	1996	Austin, Texas
Jefferson, Reggie	.357	4	14	2	5	0	0	0	2	1	3	0	0	L	L	6-4	215	9-25-68	1986	Tallahassee, Fla.
Jenkins, Corey	.175	79	252	24	44	7	2	3	28	25	109	2	1	R	R	6-2	200	8-25-76	1995	Columbia, S.C.
Larned, Andrew	.154	8	13	0	2	0	0	0	2	5	2	0	0	R	R	6-0	195	11-13-75	1998	Mentor, Ohio
Lomasney, Steve	.239	122	443	74	106	22	1	22	63	59	145	13	4	R	R	6-0	185	8-29-77	1995	Peabody, Mass.
Marsh, Roy	.277	109	357	63	99	13	7	1	35	43	56	27	9	R	R	5-8	191	11-6-73	1994	Baltimore, Md.
Martinez, Rafael	.267	98	329	49	88	9	2	5	40	49	59	6	4	L	L	6-3	185	8-24-75	1991	Santo Domingo, D.R.
Olmeda, Jose	.209	113	358	37	75	18	4	5	42	19	112	8	5	B	R	6-1	155	7-7-77	1995	Fajardo, P.R.
Padilla, Roy	.255	109	365	46	93	17	3	3	53	28	66	12	2	L	L	6-5	227	8-4-75	1993	Panama City, Panama
Raifstanger, John	.255	43	145	23	37	12	0	4	24	33	37	4	3	R	R	6-0	190	6-2-73	1994	Great Barrington, Mass.
Rojas, Mo	.118	5	17	1	2	1	0	0	2	1	5	2	0	R	R	5-11	180	11-25-76	1995	Hialeah, Fla.
Sapp, Damian	.244	35	127	18	31	9	0	7	23	15	38	1	0	R	R	6-3	219	5-20-76	1994	Pleasant Grove, Utah
Uccello, Jeff	.229	36	109	11	25	2	0	1	7	6	21	2	0	R	R	6-3	205	6-16-75	1997	Newington, Conn.

GAMES BY POSITION: C—Bazzani 1, Chevalier 17, Larned 4, Lomasney 80, Raifstanger 1, Sapp 18, Uccello 32. **1B**—Chevalier 14, Espinal 1, Everson 16, Lomasney 3, Martinez 97, Raifstanger 4, Sapp 13, Uccello 1. **2B**—Eckstein 115, Fuentes 26, Raifstanger 6. **3B**—Espinal 125, Fuentes 15, Raifstanger 1. **SS**—Eckstein 16, Fuentes 24, Olmedo 113, Raifstanger 1. **OF**—Chevalier 18, Choi 36, DeRosso 3, Faggett 61, Jenkins 73, Marsh 105, Padilla 107, Raifstanger 26, Rojas 5.

PITCHING	W	L	ERA	G	GS	CG	SV	IP	H	R	ER	BB	SO	B	T	HT	WT	DOB	1st Yr	Resides
Betancourt, Rafael	3	1	3.54	20	0	0	2	28	22	12	11	6	33	R	R	6-2	176	4-29-75	1994	Cumana, Ven.
Betti, Rich	1	2	11.45	4	4	0	0	11	19	14	14	3	11	R	L	5-11	170	9-16-73	1993	Milford, Mass.
Cannon, Kevan	5	1	4.08	44	0	0	10	57	57	29	26	26	60	L	L	6-1	222	8-24-74	1995	Columbus, Ohio
Checo, Robinson	0	1	9.00	1	1	0	0	2	3	2	2	1	4	R	R	6-1	185	9-9-71	1989	Santiago, D.R.
Cho, Jin Ho	3	1	3.09	5	5	0	0	32	33	14	11	5	30	R	R	6-3	207	8-16-75	1998	Jun Ju City, Korea
De la Cruz, Fernando	0	0	1.04	12	0	0	4	17	10	2	2	7	10	R	R	6-0	175	1-25-71	1993	La Romana, D.R.
Garrett, Josh	8	12	5.21	26	25	5	0	155	182	108	90	40	68	R	R	6-4	195	1-12-78	1997	Richland, Ind.
Hayden, Terry	1	2	4.70	13	1	0	0	23	25	13	12	7	20	L	L	6-6	215	6-26-75	1997	Taylor, Mich.
Hazlett, Andy	11	7	3.19	30	22	4	1	161	154	76	57	25	135	L	L	6-3	195	8-27-75	1997	The Dalles, Ore.
Henry, Butch	0	1	1.35	1	1	0	0	7	4	2	1	0	5	L	L	6-1	205	10-7-68	1987	El Paso, Texas
Hunter, Germaine	0	1	4.61	7	0	0	0	14	15	12	7	9	14	R	R	5-11	175	1-9-74	1996	Paducah, Ky.
Kim, Sun	12	8	4.82	26	24	5	0	153	159	88	82	40	132	R	R	6-2	180	9-4-77	1997	Seoul, Korea
Kinney, Matt	9	6	4.01	22	20	2	1	121	109	70	54	75	96	R	R	6-4	190	12-16-76	1995	Bangor, Maine
Lyons, Jonathan	1	0	4.50	7	0	0	0	12	15	7	6	2	14	R	R	6-3	215	1-13-75	1997	Olive Branch, Miss.
McMullen, Jerry	3	1	2.73	39	0	0	2	63	53	23	19	36	60	L	L	6-2	190	10-13-73	1995	Redmond, Ore.
Miadich, Bart	3	2	3.14	22	0	0	7	49	40	20	17	15	64	R	R	6-4	205	2-3-76	1997	Lake Oswego, Ore.
Musgrave, Scott	2	3	6.30	28	4	0	0	60	73	46	42	31	34	L	L	5-10	190	4-24-74	1996	Princeton, N.C.
Pineda, Isauro	4	2	5.23	10	9	0	0	41	43	30	24	20	22	R	R	6-0	168	11-10-78	1997	Mazatlan, Mexico
Rahilly, Michael	1	0	1.59	7	0	0	1	17	17	7	3	2	13	R	R	6-6	230	12-3-76	1996	Cape Coral, Fla.
Reitsma, Chris	0	0	2.84	8	8	0	0	13	12	6	4	5	9	R	R	6-5	195	12-31-77	1996	Calgary, Alberta
Rose, Brian	0	2	1.49	22	0	0	4	36	35	16	6	12	37	R	R	6-1	190	10-7-72	1994	Potsdam, N.Y.
Thompson, Chris	5	2	3.18	30	0	0	4	45	48	19	16	17	28	R	R	6-2	202	9-29-72	1996	Elyria, Ohio
Welch, Robb	4	6	6.75	20	13	0	1	76	70	66	57	72	64	R	R	6-4	201	12-30-75	1994	Twin Falls, Idaho

MICHIGAN — Class A

MIDWEST LEAGUE

BATTING	AVG	G	AB	R	H	2B	3B	HR	RBI	BB	SO	SB	CS	B	T	HT	WT	DOB	1st Yr	Resides
Ahumada, Alejandro	.277	111	390	45	108	22	2	0	35	25	91	4	7	R	R	6-1	160	1-20-79	1996	Culiacan, Mexico
Alevras, Chad	.249	85	281	35	70	14	1	7	39	27	70	1	1	R	R	6-1	195	1-8-75	1997	Littleton, Colo.
Capista, Aaron	.261	127	471	58	123	25	5	5	68	23	47	5	3	B	R	6-2	185	5-31-79	1997	Shorewood, Ill.
DeLeon, Jorge	.265	50	185	23	49	8	1	2	19	15	19	4	0	R	R	6-2	170	9-26-74	1997	Guayama, P.R.
Fischer, Mark	.253	102	379	52	96	19	2	8	50	36	93	9	6	R	R	6-1	205	4-15-76	1997	Atlanta, Ga.
Gancasz, Michael	.261	26	46	7	12	1	1	0	3	5	17	0	0	R	R	6-1	210	5-16-74	1997	Royersford, Pa.
Graham, Jess	.261	113	414	73	108	22	5	8	61	50	96	10	4	L	L	6-0	185	10-12-75	1997	Fairmont, W.Va.
Haas, Danny	.234	96	299	39	70	14	1	3	29	22	55	1	2	L	R	5-11	184	1-4-76	1997	Paducah, Ky.
Habig, Keith	.083	6	12	2	1	0	0	0	1	0	2	0	0	R	R	6-0	165	10-23-73	1997	Las Vegas, Nev.
Hamilton, Joe	.271	63	203	36	55	12	0	9	34	28	68	3	1	L	R	6-0	185	7-12-74	1992	Rehoboth, Mass.
Hillenbrand, Shea	.349	129	498	80	174	33	4	19	93	19	49	13	7	R	R	6-1	175	7-27-75	1996	Mesa, Ariz.
Howard, Marcus	.202	30	94	7	19	1	1	1	10	8	24	2	2	R	R	6-0	200	10-3-75	1997	Toledo, Ohio
Johnson, Rontrez	.271	85	306	65	83	15	5	5	32	66	46	24	8	R	R	5-10	165	12-8-76	1995	Marshall, Texas
Keaveney, Jeff	.252	112	373	61	94	24	0	15	54	65	104	0	2	R	R	6-5	240	10-7-75	1996	Framingham, Mass.
Leon, Carlos	.250	107	372	59	93	7	3	3	37	50	81	10	10	B	R	5-10	169	8-31-79	1997	Cabimas, Ven.
LoCurto, Gary	.186	60	188	20	35	8	0	0	15	31	52	1	3	L	R	6-1	200	5-25-78	1996	San Diego, Calif.
Marino, Larry	.180	53	139	15	25	3	0	1	13	22	26	0	0	R	R	5-10	185	10-11-74	1997	Lutherville, Md.
McDaniels, Paul	.172	12	29	4	5	1	0	0	1	4	11	2	0	L	R	6-2	200	3-2-77	1998	Costa Mesa, Calif.
Uccello, Jeff	.220	21	41	4	9	3	0	0	1	3	6	3	2	R	R	6-3	205	6-16-75	1997	Newington, Conn.

GAMES BY POSITION: C—Alevras 49, Gancasz 12, Hillenbrand 87, Uccello 9. **1B**—Alevras 20, Gancasz 14, Hamilton 21, Hillenbrand 12, Keaveney 26, LoCurto 59, Uccello 6. **2B**—Ahumada 26, DeLeon 18, Leon 107, Marino 1. **3B**—Ahumada 81, DeLeon 26, Habig 1, Hillenbrand 2, Marino 52. **SS**—Ahumada 15, Capista 126, DeLeon 5, Leon 1. **OF**—Alevras 1, Fischer 95, Graham 109, Haas 71, Habig 3, Hamilton 41, Howard 29, Johnson 82, McDaniels 12, Uccello 3.

PITCHING	W	L	ERA	G	GS	CG	SV	IP	H	R	ER	BB	SO	B	T	HT	WT	DOB	1st Yr	Resides
Arias, Rafael	7	7	5.09	34	12	0	1	110	130	68	62	31	69	R	R	6-4	180	2-4-77	1996	San Pedro de Macoris, D.R.
Cisar, Mark	1	1	4.91	6	0	0	1	7	8	4	4	8	4	R	R	5-11	185	5-22-75	1998	New Martinsville, W.Va.
Curtice, John	6	6	3.37	25	25	1	0	134	96	61	50	79	146	L	L	6-2	210	11-1-79	1997	Chesapeake, Va.
Duchscherer, Justin	7	12	4.79	30	26	0	0	143	166	87	76	47	106	R	R	6-3	150	11-19-77	1996	Lubbock, Texas
Hayden, Terry	2	2	7.70	20	0	0	1	31	40	29	27	10	30	L	L	6-0	215	6-20-75	1997	Taylor, Mich.
Hunter, Germaine	2	0	1.19	22	0	0	2	30	23	5	4	14	31	R	R	5-11	175	1-9-74	1996	Paducah, Ky.
Lyons, Jonathan	3	4	2.77	41	0	0	3	65	63	29	20	27	57	R	R	6-3	215	1-13-75	1997	Olive Branch, Miss.
McLeary, Marty	5	7	4.16	37	7	0	0	89	99	58	41	35	54	R	R	6-5	220	10-26-74	1997	Mansfield, Ohio
Miller, Tom	0	0	6.35	11	0	0	0	17	28	13	12	7	10	R	L	6-1	195	5-18-75	1997	Eagle, Mich.
Norton, Jason	3	1	1.93	7	7	0	0	42	34	14	9	12	36	R	R	6-3	205	4-9-76	1998	Mobile, Ala.
O'Dette, Rick	0	0	9.00	1	1	0	0	2	0	2	2	6	2	R	L	6-3	178	2-11-76	1997	Tinley Park, Ill.
Partenheimer, Brian	7	5	3.62	60	0	0	6	82	79	35	33	21	61	R	L	6-5	230	4-13-75	1997	Birdseye, Ind.
Rahilly, Michael	2	0	8.84	12	1	0	0	18	25	18	18	0	10	R	R	6-6	230	12-3-76	1996	Cape Coral, Fla.
Rayborn, Kenny	4	2	4.56	17	8	0	0	49	62	27	25	13	34	R	R	6-4	210	11-22-74	1997	Purvis, Miss.
Rupp, Michael	6	1	5.03	11	11	0	0	48	51	28	27	30	48	R	R	6-3	170	2-21-78	1997	Spring Valley, Calif.
Santana, Pedro	5	3	5.11	15	9	0	0	62	77	41	35	19	39	R	R	6-3	190	11-22-77	1995	San Pedro de Macoris, D.R.
Surridge, Lance	3	3	2.81	18	8	0	2	64	59	26	20	27	43	L	R	6-4	200	7-17-76	1998	Burnsville, Minn.
Taglienti, Jeff	4	2	1.89	57	0	0	30	76	54	19	16	17	111	R	R	6-0	208	11-13-75	1997	Walpole, Mass.
Thomas, Joe	12	5	3.25	20	20	1	0	130	126	52	47	36	100	L	L	6-3	225	1-25-75	1997	Kenmore, N.Y.
Tribe, Byron	0	0	5.04	5	5	0	0	25	17	15	14	15	25	R	R	6-3	210	3-21-75	1996	Katy, Texas

LOWELL — Short-Season Class A

NEW YORK-PENN LEAGUE

BATTING	AVG	G	AB	R	H	2B	3B	HR	RBI	BB	SO	SB	CS	B	T	HT	WT	DOB	1st Yr	Resides
Adeeb, Josh	.250	3	8	1	2	0	0	0	0	0	2	0	0	R	R	6-1	190	8-17-75	1998	Jacksonville, Fla.
Benham, David	.275	41	131	17	36	12	0	2	6	7	23	1	0	R	R	6-2	190	10-12-75	1998	Garland, Texas
Everett, Adam	.296	21	71	11	21	6	2	0	9	11	13	2	1	R	R	6-1	167	2-6-77	1998	Kennesaw, Ga.
Falcon, Edwin	.225	64	213	21	48	13	1	3	32	25	70	1	0	R	R	6-1	225	8-28-78	1996	Bayamon, P.R.
Flores, Jose	.147	49	116	17	17	5	0	0	2	7	31	2	1	B	R	6-1	170	4-24-78	1995	Ciudad Guayana, Ven.
Hart, Keith	.273	41	165	14	45	12	0	3	30	3	34	0	1	R	R	6-0	220	2-4-76	1998	Baytown, Texas
James, Tony	.272	68	235	42	64	13	0	8	34	27	45	7	1	R	R	5-10	180	5-16-76	1998	Victorville, Calif.
Johnson, Chad	.200	38	110	16	22	2	0	3	13	13	37	1	0	R	R	6-5	225	5-11-76	1998	Moline, Ill.
Larned, Andrew	.222	21	54	4	12	3	0	0	5	2	12	0	0	R	R	6-0	195	11-13-75	1998	Mentor, Ohio
Ledesma, Philip	.202	54	129	17	26	4	1	2	12	13	35	4	2	R	R	5-11	175	3-14-75	1998	Upland, Calif.
McDaniels, Paul	.241	58	170	33	41	8	2	7	24	27	49	1	1	L	R	6-2	200	3-2-77	1998	Costa Mesa, Calif.
Mendoza, Angel	.297	69	256	29	76	20	4	2	36	9	70	7	3	R	R	6-2	165	11-30-78	1996	San Pedro de Macoris, D.R.
Pena, Rodolfo	.229	15	35	3	8	3	0	1	4	3	8	0	0	R	R	6-0	180	3-7-79	1997	Montecristi, D.R.
Rodriguez, Ronny	.083	5	12	3	1	0	0	0	1	3	5	0	0	R	R	6-0	172	1-7-81	1998	Maracaibo, Ven.
Rojas, Mo	.270	63	241	27	65	21	1	5	27	10	57	0	0	R	R	5-11	180	11-25-76	1995	Hialeah, Fla.
Roush, Ryan	.229	39	118	8	27	6	0	1	8	14	28	2	2	R	R	6-1	190	9-5-76	1998	West Columbia, W.Va.
Santoro, Patrick	.247	55	190	24	47	7	6	2	19	26	54	4	0	R	R	6-0	175	11-9-78	1998	River Forest, Ill.
Santos, Angel	.245	28	102	19	25	4	1	1	12	9	12	2	1	B	R	5-11	185	8-14-79	1997	Cayey, P.R.
Terni, Chaz	.255	46	165	22	42	7	1	3	14	12	38	2	1	R	R	5-10	175	10-1-78	1997	Uncasville, Conn.
Thompson, Sonny	.105	8	19	1	2	0	0	0	0	0	7	0	0	R	R	6-2	180	4-28-76	1997	Grand Rapids, Mich.
Warren, Chris	.000	1	1	0	0	0	0	0	0	0	0	0	0	R	R	6-3	205	9-30-76	1998	Fayetteville, N.C.
Wright, Bryan	.034	11	29	1	1	0	0	0	0	0	11	0	0	R	R	5-11	165	5-17-76	1998	Destin, Fla.

GAMES BY POSITION: C—Benham 30, Falcon 3, Johnson 28, Larned 20, Pena 15. **1B**—Benham 3, Falcon 35, Hart 33, Rojas 8. **2B**—James 48, Roush 1, Santoro 28, Santos 8. **3B**—Hart 4, James 1, Rodriguez 4, Rojas 8, Roush 1, Santoro 9, Santos 5, Terni 46, Wright 6. **SS**—Everett 21, James 5, Rodriguez 1, Roush 36, Santoro 2, Santos 16, Wright 6. **OF**—Adeeb 3, Flores 42, Johnson 1, Ledesma 50, McDaniels 51, Mendoza 68, Rojas 42, Thompson 6.

PITCHING	W	L	ERA	G	GS	CG	SV	IP	H	R	ER	BB	SO	B	T	HT	WT	DOB	1st Yr	Resides
Cisar, Mark	2	1	1.42	22	0	0	9	38	22	11	6	10	42	R	R	5-11	185	5-22-75	1998	New Martinsville, W.Va.
Donahoo, Matt	0	3	6.49	16	1	0	0	35	49	29	25	18	36	L	L	6-1	180	4-17-76	1998	Chattanooga, Tenn.
Flores, Benito	1	5	4.68	20	4	0	3	42	46	26	22	20	47	L	L	6-1	185	1-24-76	1998	Placentia, Calif.

PITCHING	W	L	ERA	G	GS	CG	SV	IP	H	R	ER	BB	SO	B	T	HT	WT	DOB	1st Yr	Resides
Hancock, Josh	0	1	2.25	1	1	0	0	4	5	2	1	4	4	R	R	6-3	210	4-11-78	1998	Tupelo, Miss.
Hill, Terrance	0	4	2.00	19	7	0	0	63	60	28	14	33	61	L	L	5-10	170	10-17-75	1998	Thibodaux, La.
Lampley, Danny	7	2	2.39	13	11	0	0	64	51	25	17	22	95	R	R	6-5	235	11-1-75	1998	Rockingham, N.C.
Linarelli, Tom	2	4	7.06	18	6	0	0	51	78	51	40	28	44	R	R	6-3	210	11-11-76	1998	Kirkland, Wash.
Maroth, Mike	2	3	2.90	6	6	0	0	31	22	13	10	13	34	L	L	6-0	180	8-17-77	1998	Orlando, Fla.
Miller, Tom	2	4	3.81	16	6	0	1	50	51	24	21	20	57	R	L	6-1	195	5-18-75	1997	Eagle, Mich.
Molina, Primitivo	3	2	1.96	15	0	0	2	23	21	6	5	6	16	R	R	6-2	170	12-10-77	1997	La Paz, Mexico
Mowel, Mike	2	6	4.46	15	13	0	0	67	65	39	33	20	46	R	R	6-0	190	7-16-79	1997	East Hartford, Conn.
Norton, Jason	1	1	4.62	6	4	0	0	25	22	17	13	7	33	R	R	6-3	205	4-9-76	1998	Mobile, Ala.
O'Dette, Rick	0	2	11.34	9	1	0	0	17	14	23	21	32	16	R	L	6-3	178	2-11-76	1997	Tinley Park, Ill.
Phillips, Matt	4	4	4.21	15	14	0	0	73	81	44	34	27	57	R	R	6-1	210	5-22-75	1998	Seaford, Del.
Slomkowski, Robert	3	0	9.39	22	0	0	3	31	42	38	32	12	32	R	R	6-4	205	2-5-75	1998	Rutherford, N.J.
Zallie, Chris	3	2	4.01	20	2	0	0	49	56	24	22	24	67	L	L	6-1	195	2-4-75	1998	Harleysville, Pa.

FORT MYERS — Rookie

GULF COAST LEAGUE

BATTING	AVG	G	AB	R	H	2B	3B	HR	RBI	BB	SO	SB	CS	B	T	HT	WT	DOB	1st Yr	Resides
Benham, David	.364	6	22	3	8	3	0	1	3	2	1	0	0	R	R	6-2	190	10-12-75	1998	Garland, Texas
Borjas, Henry	.242	42	124	20	30	3	0	0	8	18	26	5	3	B	R	6-0	193	6-5-79	1997	Barquisimeto, Ven.
Brown, Tonayne	.316	54	225	43	71	12	4	8	38	8	32	15	6	R	L	5-11	190	8-24-77	1998	Tallahassee, Fla.
Caridi, Tony	.136	13	22	1	3	1	0	0	0	1	7	0	0	B	R	6-3	175	10-26-79	1998	Spring, Texas
DePastino, Joe	.294	6	17	2	5	1	1	1	1	5	3	0	0	R	R	6-2	210	9-4-73	1992	Sarasota, Fla.
DeRosso, Tony	.467	4	15	4	7	2	0	0	3	1	3	0	0	R	R	6-3	216	11-7-75	1994	Moultrie, Ga.
Fischer, Mark	.192	7	26	5	5	0	0	2	5	4	8	2	0	R	R	6-1	205	4-15-76	1997	Atlanta, Ga.
Garcia, Manuel	.204	18	49	5	10	3	0	0	2	2	10	2	0	B	R	5-11	175	12-24-80	1997	Santiago, D.R.
Guerrero, Julio	.207	39	145	21	30	4	0	0	13	11	21	12	1	R	R	6-3	170	10-18-80	1998	Don Gregorio, D.R.
Jefferson, Reggie	.000	1	4	0	0	0	0	0	0	0	1	0	0	L	L	6-4	215	9-25-68	1986	Tallahassee, Fla.
Kawabata, Kenichiro	.252	39	107	16	27	4	1	0	10	17	24	10	5	B	L	6-2	170	5-8-79	1997	Osaka, Japan
Larned, Andrew	.125	2	8	1	1	0	0	0	0	1	1	1	0	R	R	6-0	195	11-13-75	1998	Mentor, Ohio
Liniak, Cole	.000	2	8	1	0	0	0	0	0	0	1	0	0	R	R	6-1	181	8-23-76	1995	Encinitas, Calif.
McKeel, Walt	.250	13	36	1	9	2	0	1	4	4	8	0	0	R	R	6-2	200	1-17-72	1990	Stantonsburg, N.C.
Merloni, Lou	.000	1	1	0	0	0	0	0	0	0	0	0	0	R	R	5-10	194	4-6-71	1993	Framingham, Mass.
Pena, Jose	.344	48	160	28	55	12	3	4	21	14	33	6	5	R	R	6-1	175	2-10-80	1997	Don Gregorio, D.R.
Pena, Rodolfo	.349	24	83	15	29	5	2	0	14	3	11	1	1	R	R	6-0	180	3-7-79	1997	Montecristi, D.R.
Penna, Shaun	.212	31	99	13	21	5	0	0	10	9	24	1	1	R	R	6-0	180	11-2-74	1998	Pittsfield, Mass.
Rix, Derek	.283	44	152	28	43	8	4	8	38	19	48	2	0	L	R	6-3	208	1-18-78	1998	Jacksonville, Fla.
Rodriguez, Carlos	.325	54	197	35	64	14	2	8	37	11	37	14	3	R	R	6-2	210	6-12-77	1998	Louisville, Ky.
Rodriguez, Ronny	.287	27	87	12	25	8	1	1	17	8	15	1	1	R	R	6-0	172	1-7-81	1998	Maracaibo, Ven.
Santos, Angel	.351	23	77	14	27	5	1	0	13	13	10	7	3	B	R	5-11	185	8-14-79	1997	Cayey, P.R.
Terni, Chaz	.317	17	63	14	20	4	1	0	13	8	12	1	0	R	R	5-10	175	10-1-78	1997	Uncasville, Conn.
Tyson, Torre	.322	36	118	29	38	9	0	2	18	30	8	8	4	B	R	5-10	185	12-31-75	1998	St. Louis, Mo.
Warren, Chris	.298	32	114	23	34	2	2	3	16	12	20	4	0	R	R	6-3	205	9-30-76	1998	Fayetteville, N.C.
Whitby, Corey	.386	18	44	13	17	0	1	0	6	15	3	7	1	L	R	5-8	180	1-27-76	1998	Richmond, Va.

GAMES BY POSITION: C—Benham 3, Caridi 12, DePastino 4, Garcia 17, Larned 2, McKeel 6, R. Pena 19, Whitby 15. **1B**—Benham 3, Borjas 8, McKeel 1, R. Pena 8, Rix 41, C. Rodriguez 8. **2B**—Borjas 23, Merloni 1, R. Rodriguez 3, Santos 8, Tyson 34. **3B**—Borjas 10, Penna 30, Santos 5, Terni 17. **SS**—Guerrero 35, R. Rodriguez 18, Santos 12. **OF**—Borjas 3, Brown 51, DeRosso 3, Fischer 2, Kawabata 33, J. Pena 44, C. Rodriguez 35, Warren 19.

PITCHING	W	L	ERA	G	GS	CG	SV	IP	H	R	ER	BB	SO	B	T	HT	WT	DOB	1st Yr	Resides
Betancourt, Rafael	0	2	7.20	4	3	0	0	5	6	5	4	1	4	R	R	6-2	176	4-29-75	1994	Cumana, Ven.
Betti, Rich	0	1	10.50	3	1	0	0	6	3	7	7	6	6	R	L	5-11	170	9-16-73	1993	Milford, Mass.
Cadena, Nathan	0	0	3.60	4	0	0	0	5	3	2	2	1	5	R	R	6-3	195	12-3-79	1998	Anaheim, Calif.
Checketts, Andrew	0	0	0.00	2	0	0	0	2	2	0	0	2	5	R	R	5-10	185	10-8-75	1998	West Linn, Ore.
Checo, Robinson	1	0	3.00	3	3	0	0	9	9	5	3	0	13	R	R	6-1	185	9-9-71	1989	Santiago, D.R.
De la Cruz, Fernando	0	0	13.50	1	0	0	0	2	4	3	3	0	2	R	R	6-0	175	1-25-71	1993	La Romana, D.R.
Gamble, Jerome	2	3	4.43	11	6	0	1	43	33	24	21	19	49	R	R	6-3	190	4-5-80	1998	Concord, Mass.
Garces, Rich	0	0	3.27	7	7	0	0	11	11	4	4	0	8	R	R	6-0	215	5-18-71	1988	Maracay, Ven.
Glaser, Eric	2	3	4.18	15	1	0	5	32	28	19	15	12	29	R	R	6-6	208	1-23-78	1997	Fort Thomas, Ky.
Hancock, Josh	1	1	3.38	5	1	0	0	13	9	5	5	3	21	R	R	6-3	210	4-11-78	1998	Tupelo, Miss.
Hunter, Germaine	1	0	0.00	1	0	0	0	2	0	0	0	0	4	R	R	5-11	175	1-9-74	1996	Paducah, Ky.
Kim, Jae	0	1	5.25	5	1	0	0	12	12	14	7	5	3	R	R	6-3	182	6-11-79	1998	Seoul, Korea
Lampley, Danny	1	0	0.00	1	0	0	0	3	1	0	0	0	3	R	R	6-5	235	11-1-75	1998	Rockingham, N.C.
Maroth, Mike	1	1	0.00	4	2	0	0	13	9	3	0	2	14	L	L	6-0	180	8-17-77	1998	Orlando, Fla.
Martinez, Anastacio	2	3	3.18	12	10	0	0	51	45	28	18	12	50	R	R	6-2	180	11-3-80	1998	Santo Domingo, D.R.
Miller, Greg	6	0	2.49	11	7	0	0	43	33	18	12	18	47	L	L	6-5	215	9-30-79	1997	Aurora, Ill.
Norris, Shon	0	2	2.25	15	0	0	2	24	22	10	6	9	14	R	R	6-2	185	6-29-77	1998	Pittsburgh, Pa.
Norton, Jason	1	1	1.50	3	0	0	0	6	2	1	1	1	9	R	R	6-3	205	4-9-76	1998	Mobile, Ala.
Otanez, Ender	0	3	5.59	13	2	0	0	29	27	21	18	11	30	R	R	6-2	165	7-29-80	1997	Cotui, D.R.
Peguero, Kerbin	1	1	2.55	9	0	0	0	18	13	8	5	11	9	L	L	6-2	175	5-9-80	1998	San Pedro de Macoris, D.R.
Pineda, Isauro	0	0	3.38	4	0	0	0	13	11	7	5	5	16	R	R	6-0	168	11-10-78	1997	Mazatlan, Mexico
Roller, Adam	0	2	4.85	15	2	0	1	39	51	31	21	22	27	R	R	6-2	205	6-27-78	1997	Lakeland, Fla.
Seybt, Paul	1	2	3.00	16	0	0	1	27	32	12	9	11	24	R	R	6-0	185	8-18-75	1998	Lexington, S.C.
Silverthorn, Will	4	4	4.84	11	8	0	0	45	52	26	24	13	39	L	L	6-1	190	4-9-79	1998	Richardson, Texas
Solano, Alexander	3	3	3.51	12	6	0	1	51	65	35	20	17	35	R	R	6-1	150	4-22-80	1997	La Romana, D.R.

CHICAGO WHITE SOX

Strong second half provides hope for young White Sox

BY PHIL ROGERS

When Jerry Manuel closed the clubhouse doors and addressed the 1998 White Sox for one last time, he offered a simple message. "Struggle," Manuel told the players, "breeds character."

With Manuel giving direction, Albert Belle leading the thundering run-production and the controversial White Flag trade of 1997 providing a ton of young talent, the Sox turned a lost season into the most positive one for the franchise since the 1994 strike cost Jerry Reinsdorf's team the chance to play in October.

The South Siders wound up with their second consecutive losing campaign, but the 80-82 record in Manuel's rookie season was a marked improvement from the 80-81 year that got Terry Bevington fired.

Rather than jousting at windmills with a corps of aging veterans, general manager Ron Schueler committed the organization to developing kids like shortstop Mike Caruso, right fielder Magglio Ordonez and pitchers Mike Sirokta, Jim Parque and Bobby Howry.

It was an unexpected bonus that a devastating second half by Belle and the emergence of righthander James Baldwin allowed Manuel's team to go 45-31 after the all-star break, which ranked behind only the Yankees in the American League. The Sox wound up with their third consecutive second-place finish in the AL Central, nine games behind the Indians.

"Going into the all-star break, I was really concerned where we'd end up," Manuel said. "Somebody mentioned we were on pace to lose 100 games. That was scary for me. To finish strong after that, it makes me optimistic for next season."

For the second year in a row, Belle got off to a slow start. His lack of production was a major factor in the Sox' 10-15 record in April. But once he got his swing worked out, he was the kind of force Reinsdorf envisioned when he signed him to his $55 million deal after the 1996 season.

In the second half of the season, Belle hit .387 with 31 homers and 86 RBIs over 76 games. He finished the year hitting .328 with 49 homers and 152 RBIs, giving him the team record for home runs, which Frank Thomas had set in 1993, and RBIs, which Zeke Bonura had held since 1936.

Thomas endured the worst season of his career. His batting average plummeted from a league-leading .347 in 1997 to .265.

Caruso, Howry and Keith Foulke, who were acquired with three other minor leaguers in the much-criticized trade that sent Roberto Hernandez, Wilson Alvarez and Danny Darwin to the Giants in July 1997, paid big dividends. Caruso made the jump from Class A with remarkable ease, hitting .306 as the regular shortstop.

At the minor league level, the Sox produced a championship in the Rookie-level Appalachian League and narrowly missed another in the Triple-A Pacific Coast League.

Bristol marched to the Appy League title with the oldest club in the league. Led by Rookie-level veterans Manny Lutz and Jeff Newkirk, Bristol had the league's best record and swept Princeton in the finals.

Calgary, led by third baseman Olmedo Saenz, recovered from a poor start to land a playoff spot. The Cannons took New Orleans to the decisive fifth game of the PCL championship series before bowing out.

Albert Belle

Joe Crede

Players of the Year

Major League: Albert Belle, of

Belle caught fire in the second half and finished 1998 with 49 home runs and 152 RBIs, both second-best in the AL.

Minor League: Joe Crede, 3b, Winston-Salem

Crede was named MVP of the Class A Carolina League after hitting .315 with 20 homers and 88 RBIs.

ORGANIZATION LEADERS

BATTING

*AVG	Jim Terrell, Winston-Salem/Hickory	.341
R	Joe Crede, Winston-Salem	92
H	Jim Terrell, Winston-Salem/Hickory	174
TB	Carlos Lee, Birmingham	266
2B	Two tied at	36
3B	Jeff Newkirk, Hickory/Bristol	10
HR	Olmedo Saenz, Calgary	29
RBI	Carlos Lee, Birmingham	106
BB	Mark Johnson, Birmingham	105
SO	J.R. Mounts, Hickory	154
SB	Lou Frazier, Calgary	42

PITCHING

W	Three tied at	13
L	Three tied at	12
#ERA	Mario Iglesias, Winston-Salem	2.31
G	David Lundquist, Calgary/Birm./Win.-Salem	51
CG	Two tied at	4
SV	Jose Bautista, Calgary	15
IP	Hansel Izquierdo, Winston-Salem/Hickory	177
BB	Two tied at	91
SO	Hansel Izquierdo, Winston-Salem/Hickory	188

*Minimum 250 At-Bats #Minimum 75 Innings

Chicago WHITE SOX

Manager: Jerry Manuel

1998 Record: 80-82, .494 (2nd, AL Central)

BATTING	AVG	G	AB	R	H	2B	3B	HR	RBI	BB	SO	SB	CS	B	T	HT	WT	DOB	1st Yr	Resides
Abbott, Jeff	.279	89	244	33	68	14	1	12	41	9	28	3	3	R	L	6-2	190	8-17-72	1994	Dunwoody, Ga.
Belle, Albert	.328	163	609	113	200	48	2	49	152	81	84	6	4	R	R	6-2	210	8-25-66	1987	Euclid, Ohio
Cameron, Mike	.210	141	396	53	83	16	5	8	43	37	101	27	11	R	R	6-2	190	1-8-73	1991	La Grange, Ga.
Caruso, Mike	.306	133	523	80	160	17	6	5	55	14	38	22	6	L	R	6-1	172	5-27-77	1996	Coral Springs, Fla.
Cordero, Wil	.267	96	341	58	91	18	2	13	49	22	66	2	1	R	R	6-2	185	10-3-71	1988	Mayaguez, P.R.
Durham, Ray	.285	158	635	125	181	35	8	19	67	73	105	36	9	B	R	5-8	170	11-30-71	1990	Charlotte, N.C.
Frazier, Lou	.000	7	7	0	0	0	0	0	0	2	6	4	0	B	R	6-2	175	1-26-65	1986	Chandler, Ariz.
Johnson, Mark	.087	7	23	2	2	0	2	0	1	1	8	0	0	L	R	6-0	185	9-12-75	1994	Warner Robins, Ga.
Kreuter, Chad	.253	93	245	26	62	9	1	2	33	32	45	1	0	B	R	6-2	200	8-26-64	1985	La Quinta, Calif.
Machado, Robert	.207	34	111	14	23	6	0	3	15	7	22	0	0	R	R	6-1	205	6-3-73	1989	Caracas, Ven.
Norton, Greg	.237	105	299	38	71	17	2	9	36	26	77	3	3	B	R	6-1	190	7-6-72	1993	Norman, Okla.
O'Brien, Charlie	.262	57	164	12	43	9	0	4	18	9	31	0	0	R	R	6-2	205	5-1-61	1982	Tulsa, Okla.
Ordonez, Magglio	.282	145	535	70	151	25	2	14	65	28	53	9	7	R	R	5-11	170	1-28-74	1991	Coro, Ven.
Sierra, Ruben	.216	27	74	7	16	4	1	4	11	3	11	2	0	B	R	6-1	200	10-6-65	1983	San Juan, P.R.
Simmons, Brian	.368	5	19	4	7	0	0	2	6	0	2	0	1	B	R	6-2	190	9-4-73	1995	McMurray, Pa.
Snopek, Chris	.208	53	125	17	26	2	0	1	4	14	24	3	0	R	R	6-1	185	9-20-70	1992	Cynthiana, Ky.
Thomas, Frank	.265	160	585	109	155	35	2	29	109	110	93	7	0	R	R	6-5	270	5-27-68	1989	Oak Brook, Ill.
Ventura, Robin	.263	161	590	84	155	31	4	21	91	79	111	1	1	L	R	6-1	198	7-14-67	1989	Santa Maria, Calif.
Wilson, Craig	.468	13	47	14	22	5	0	3	10	3	6	1	0	R	R	6-0	185	9-3-70	1992	Phoenix, Ariz.

PITCHING	W	L	ERA	G	GS	CG	SV	IP	H	R	ER	BB	SO	B	T	HT	WT	DOB	1st Yr	Resides
Abbott, Jim	5	0	4.55	5	5	0	0	32	35	16	16	12	14	L	L	6-3	210	9-19-67	1989	Newport Beach, Calif.
Baldwin, James	13	6	5.32	37	24	1	0	159	176	103	94	60	108	R	R	6-3	210	7-15-71	1990	Southern Pines, N.C.
Bere, Jason	3	7	6.45	18	15	0	0	84	98	71	60	58	53	R	R	6-3	215	5-26-71	1990	Wilmington, Mass.
Bradford, Chad	2	1	3.23	29	0	0	1	31	27	16	11	7	11	R	R	6-5	205	9-14-74	1996	Jackson, Miss.
Casian, Larry	0	0	11.25	4	0	0	0	4	8	5	5	1	6	R	L	6-0	175	10-28-65	1987	Salem, Ore.
Castillo, Carlos	6	4	5.11	54	2	0	0	100	94	61	57	35	64	R	R	6-2	250	4-21-75	1994	Miami, Fla.
Castillo, Tony	1	2	8.00	25	0	0	0	27	38	25	24	11	14	L	L	5-10	190	3-1-63	1983	Lara, Ven.
Eyre, Scott	3	8	5.38	33	17	0	0	107	114	78	64	64	73	L	L	6-1	190	5-30-72	1991	West Valley, Utah
Fordham, Tom	1	2	6.75	29	5	0	0	48	51	36	36	42	23	L	L	6-2	205	2-20-74	1993	El Cajon, Calif.
Foulke, Keith	3	2	4.13	54	0	0	1	65	51	31	30	20	57	R	R	6-0	200	10-19-72	1994	Huffman, Texas
Heathcott, Mike	0	0	3.00	1	0	0	0	3	2	1	1	1	3	R	R	6-3	180	5-16-69	1991	Chicago, Ill.
Howry, Bobby	0	3	3.15	44	0	0	9	54	37	20	19	19	51	L	R	6-5	215	8-4-73	1994	Glendale, Ariz.
Karchner, Matt	2	4	5.15	32	0	0	11	37	33	21	21	19	30	R	R	6-4	210	6-28-67	1989	Manassas, Va.
Navarro, Jaime	8	16	6.36	37	27	1	1	173	223	135	122	77	71	R	R	6-4	230	3-27-68	1986	Milwaukee, Wis.
Parque, Jim	7	5	5.10	21	21	0	0	113	135	72	64	49	77	L	L	5-11	165	2-8-75	1997	La Crescenta, Calif.
Rizzo, Todd	0	0	13.50	9	0	0	0	7	12	12	10	6	3	R	L	6-2	220	5-24-71	1992	Conshohocken, Pa.
Simas, Bill	4	3	3.57	60	0	0	18	71	54	29	28	22	56	L	R	6-3	220	11-28-71	1992	Fresno, Calif.
Sirotka, Mike	14	15	5.06	33	33	5	0	212	255	137	119	47	128	L	L	6-1	200	5-13-71	1993	Houston, Texas
Snyder, John	7	2	4.80	15	14	1	0	86	96	49	46	23	52	R	R	6-3	185	8-16-74	1992	Thousand Oaks, Calif.
Ward, Bryan	1	2	3.33	28	0	0	1	27	30	13	10	7	17	L	L	6-2	210	1-25-72	1993	Mount Holly, N.J.

FIELDING

Catcher	PCT	G	PO	A	E	DP	PB
Johnson	1.000	7	36	2	0	1	0
Kreuter	.985	91	424	35	7	4	5
Machado	.981	34	189	17	4	1	3
O'Brien	.988	57	305	22	4	3	1

First Base	PCT	G	PO	A	E	DP
Cordero	.992	83	698	67	6	78
Norton	.994	79	643	30	4	57
Snopek	1.000	1	9	0	0	1
Thomas	.984	14	116	6	2	12

Second Base	PCT	G	PO	A	E	DP
Durham	.976	158	282	438	18	129
Norton	1.000	1	0	2	0	0
Snopek	.962	12	6	19	1	3
Wilson	1.000	4	7	9	0	4

Third Base	PCT	G	PO	A	E	DP
Norton	.917	11	12	10	2	0
Snopek	.000	3	0	0	0	0
Ventura	.966	161	101	328	15	38
Wilson	1.000	2	0	1	0	0

Shortstop	PCT	G	PO	A	E	DP
Caruso	.944	131	217	377	35	91
Snopek	.972	33	47	93	4	16
Wilson	1.000	8	13	17	0	4

Outfield	PCT	G	PO	A	E	DP
Abbott	.971	76	132	0	4	0
Belle	.976	159	315	11	8	3
Cameron	.988	138	313	5	4	0
Cordero	.938	11	15	0	1	0
Frazier	1.000	3	5	0	0	0
Ordonez	.985	145	323	10	5	2
Sierra	1.000	14	19	1	0	0
Simmons	1.000	5	13	0	0	0
Snopek	.000	1	0	0	0	0

DAVID SEELIG

James Baldwin

FARM SYSTEM

Vice President, Player Development: Ken Williams

Class	Farm Team	League	W	L	Pct.	Finish*	Manager(s)	First Yr
AAA	Calgary (Alberta) Cannons	Pacific Coast	81	62	.566	t-2nd (16)	Tom Spencer	1998
AA	Birmingham (Ala.) Barons	Southern	58	82	.414	10th (10)	Dave Huppert	1986
A#	Winston-Salem (N.C.) Warthogs	Carolina	79	60	.568	2nd (8)	Chris Cron	1997
A	Hickory (N.C.) Crawdads	South Atlantic	56	84	.400	15th (16)	Mark Haley	1993
Rookie#	Bristol (Va.) Sox	Appalachian	42	24	.636	+1st (10)	Nick Capra	1995
Rookie	Tucson (Ariz.) White Sox	Arizona	20	34	.370	8th (8)	Tony Pena	1998

*Finish in overall standings (No. of teams in league) #Advanced level +Won league championship

CALGARY — Class AAA

PACIFIC COAST LEAGUE

BATTING	AVG	G	AB	R	H	2B	3B	HR	RBI	BB	SO	SB	CS	B	T	HT	WT	DOB	1st Yr	Resides
Christopherson, Eric	.352	21	54	12	19	2	1	5	14	7	7	0	0	R	R	6-1	190	4-25-69	1990	Westminster, Calif.
Evans, Jason	.252	127	424	62	107	27	6	3	52	49	96	10	4	B	R	5-11	185	2-11-71	1992	Los Angeles, Calif.
Finn, John	.311	45	148	31	46	9	1	1	11	20	9	3	2	R	R	5-8	168	10-18-67	1989	Oakland, Calif.
Frazier, Lou	.270	101	397	81	107	26	3	14	50	57	84	42	8	B	R	6-2	175	1-26-65	1986	Chandler, Ariz.
Gil, Benji	.248	128	460	80	114	24	5	14	69	41	90	11	4	R	R	6-2	190	10-6-72	1991	San Diego, Calif.
Gonzales, Rene	.205	15	44	4	9	1	0	0	1	11	8	0	0	R	R	6-3	220	9-3-61	1982	Hollywood Hills, Calif.
Hunter, Brian	.097	11	31	1	3	1	0	0	6	2	9	0	0	R	L	6-0	195	3-4-68	1987	Anaheim, Calif.
Liefer, Jeff	.258	8	31	3	8	3	0	1	10	2	12	0	0	L	R	6-3	195	8-17-74	1996	Upland, Calif.
Machado, Robert	.264	66	239	31	63	19	0	4	27	20	33	2	2	R	R	6-1	205	6-3-73	1989	Caracas, Ven.
Meulens, Hensley	.375	2	8	3	3	1	0	2	3	0	2	0	0	R	R	6-3	210	6-23-67	1986	Coral Springs, Fla.
2-team (76 Tucson)	.254	78	276	48	70	17	2	15	40	30	69	2	1							
Moore, Brandon	.209	86	244	37	51	4	1	2	19	20	30	5	3	R	R	5-11	175	8-23-72	1994	Springville, Ala.
Pearson, Eddie	.291	99	354	32	103	21	1	7	53	22	63	1	2	B	R	6-3	225	1-31-74	1992	Mobile, Ala.
Roberson, Kevin	.271	119	431	84	117	36	0	27	97	37	128	5	1	B	R	6-4	200	1-29-68	1988	Tempe, Ariz.
Saenz, Olmedo	.313	124	466	89	140	29	0	29	102	45	49	3	3	R	R	6-0	185	10-8-70	1990	Chitre, Panama
Simmons, Brian	.290	94	355	72	103	21	4	13	51	41	82	10	6	B	R	6-2	190	9-4-73	1995	McMurray, Pa.
Smith, Demond	.059	5	17	0	1	0	0	0	0	1	6	0	0	B	R	5-11	170	11-6-72	1990	Rialto, Calif.
Toth, Dave	.232	72	246	31	57	12	0	6	30	24	44	3	2	R	R	6-2	208	12-8-69	1990	Macon, Ga.
Valdez, Mario	.330	123	448	86	148	32	0	20	81	60	102	1	2	L	R	6-2	190	11-19-74	1994	Hialeah, Fla.
Wilson, Craig	.306	120	432	67	132	21	1	14	69	37	41	4	2	R	R	6-0	185	9-3-70	1992	Phoenix, Ariz.

PITCHING	W	L	ERA	G	GS	CG	SV	IP	H	R	ER	BB	SO	B	T	HT	WT	DOB	1st Yr	Resides
Abbott, Jim	2	2	2.61	5	5	1	0	31	31	9	9	9	20	L	L	6-3	210	9-19-67	1989	Newport Beach, Calif.
Andujar, Luis	3	3	6.26	13	9	0	0	50	62	38	35	15	46	R	R	6-2	215	11-22-72	1991	Bani, D.R.
Bautista, Jose	3	3	3.92	35	0	0	15	41	52	24	18	4	23	R	R	6-2	207	7-25-64	1981	Cooper City, Fla.
Beirne, Kevin	0	0	4.50	2	2	0	0	8	12	5	4	4	6	L	R	6-4	210	1-1-74	1996	The Woodlands, Texas
Bertotti, Mike	3	2	5.94	43	6	0	3	80	90	56	53	50	64	L	L	6-1	185	1-18-70	1991	Highland Mills, N.Y.
Bradford, Chad	4	1	1.94	29	0	0	0	51	50	12	11	11	27	R	R	6-5	205	9-14-74	1996	Jackson, Miss.
Casian, Larry	4	1	3.63	43	0	0	4	52	53	22	21	16	44	R	L	6-0	175	10-28-65	1987	Salem, Ore.
Castillo, Carlos	1	1	9.00	2	2	0	0	8	12	8	8	4	4	R	R	6-2	250	4-21-75	1994	Miami, Fla.
Cruz, Nelson	10	6	5.33	35	18	2	0	127	159	85	75	40	101	R	R	6-1	185	9-13-72	1991	Washington, D.C.
Fordham, Tom	4	2	3.02	9	9	0	0	57	38	21	19	26	39	L	L	6-2	205	2-20-74	1993	El Cajon, Calif.
Hasselhoff, Derek	2	0	6.63	13	0	0	0	19	23	15	14	8	24	R	R	6-2	185	10-10-73	1995	Pasadena, Md.
Heathcott, Mike	9	6	5.04	39	13	1	1	109	113	65	61	51	77	R	R	6-3	180	5-16-69	1991	Chicago, Ill.
Herbert, Russ	9	10	5.06	28	28	2	0	164	182	100	92	74	147	R	R	6-3	195	4-21-72	1994	Mentor, Ohio
Howry, Bobby	1	2	3.41	23	0	0	5	32	25	12	12	10	22	L	R	6-5	215	8-4-73	1994	Glendale, Ariz.
Lundquist, David	3	0	3.60	12	0	0	2	15	12	6	6	7	12	R	R	6-2	200	6-4-73	1993	Carson City, Nev.
Parque, Jim	2	3	3.94	8	8	0	0	48	49	26	21	25	31	L	L	5-11	165	2-8-75	1997	La Crescenta, Calif.
Pratt, Rich	6	12	6.29	29	23	1	0	133	191	112	93	44	76	L	L	6-3	201	5-7-71	1993	East Hartford, Conn.
Rizzo, Todd	7	3	6.75	50	0	0	4	72	102	62	54	39	58	R	L	6-2	220	5-24-71	1992	Conshohocken, Pa.
Simas, Bill	1	0	0.00	5	0	0	1	9	3	1	0	2	11	L	R	6-3	220	11-28-71	1992	Fresno, Calif.
Snyder, John	7	3	4.36	15	15	1	0	97	112	49	47	34	63	R	R	6-3	185	8-16-74	1992	Thousand Oaks, Calif.
Theodile, Robert	0	2	7.68	17	5	0	0	39	36	35	33	31	24	R	R	6-3	190	9-16-72	1992	Jeanerette, La.

FIELDING

Catcher	PCT	G	PO	A	E	DP	PB
Christopherson	.983	18	107	9	2	0	2
Machado	.987	61	409	39	6	4	5
Toth	.992	68	423	52	4	8	12

First Base	PCT	G	PO	A	E	DP
Hunter	1.000	2	8	0	0	0
Liefer	1.000	2	19	3	0	0
Pearson	1.000	12	83	8	0	8
Valdez	.987	117	1002	75	14	107
Wilson	1.000	18	123	5	0	17

Second Base	PCT	G	PO	A	E	DP
Finn	1.000	23	47	58	0	18
Gonzales	1.000	1	0	1	0	0
Moore	.992	79	175	206	3	54
Wilson	.987	57	116	119	3	30

Third Base	PCT	G	PO	A	E	DP
Evans	.500	1	0	1	1	0
Finn	1.000	12	4	18	0	0
Gonzales	1.000	1	0	5	0	0
Saenz	.937	113	75	235	21	24
Wilson	.949	26	6	31	2	4

Shortstop	PCT	G	PO	A	E	DP
Gil	.943	117	160	319	29	69
Moore	1.000	3	7	10	0	1
Wilson	.969	33	32	92	4	22

Outfield	PCT	G	PO	A	E	DP
Christopherson	1.000	1	1	0	0	0
Evans	.986	120	199	6	3	0
Finn	.867	11	13	0	2	0
Frazier	.969	73	153	3	5	0
Gil	.500	2	1	0	1	0
Gonzales	.938	12	15	0	1	0
Hunter	1.000	9	18	2	0	0
Liefer	1.000	4	7	0	0	0
Meulens	1.000	2	1	0	0	0
Roberson	.980	115	236	9	5	3
Simmons	.967	92	197	6	7	0
Smith	1.000	3	4	0	0	0
Valdez	.500	2	1	0	1	0
Wilson	1.000	2	2	1	0	0

BIRMINGHAM — Class AA

SOUTHERN LEAGUE

BATTING	AVG	G	AB	R	H	2B	3B	HR	RBI	BB	SO	SB	CS	B	T	HT	WT	DOB	1st Yr	Resides
Battle, Howard	.179	12	39	6	7	4	0	1	5	4	7	0	0	R	R	6-0	197	3-25-72	1990	Ocean Springs, Miss.

BATTING	AVG	G	AB	R	H	2B	3B	HR	RBI	BB	SO	SB	CS	B	T	HT	WT	DOB	1st Yr	Resides
Bautista, Juan	.255	120	420	46	107	13	1	5	34	18	98	6	12	R	R	6-0	170	6-24-75	1992	San Pedro de Macoris, D.R.
Cardenas, Johnny	.200	17	55	3	11	2	0	0	8	1	8	0	0	R	R	6-3	210	7-23-70	1993	Fort Worth, Texas
Cordero, Wil	.286	11	35	6	10	2	0	2	11	7	3	0	0	R	R	6-2	185	10-3-71	1988	Mayaguez, P.R.
Downs, Brian	.297	10	37	3	11	1	0	0	3	2	7	0	0	R	R	6-2	210	4-10-75	1995	Chino, Calif.
Finn, John	.274	44	146	37	40	6	1	3	15	34	12	4	4	R	R	5-8	168	10-18-67	1989	Oakland, Calif.
Gonzalez, Manny	.302	102	371	51	112	24	2	2	55	20	[illegible]	0	7	[illegible]	[illegible]	[illegible]	[illegible]	5-5-76	1994	Santo Domingo, D.R.
Gonzalez, Ricky	.219	23	73	5	16	2	0	0	11	7	10	0	0	R	R	6-0	185	11-13-74	1995	Miami, Fla.
Heller, Brad	.364	6	11	1	4	0	0	0	0	0	2	0	0	R	R	5-11	190	12-8-71	1995	Tucson, Ariz.
Inglin, Jeff	.245	139	494	75	121	22	6	24	100	78	101	3	2	R	R	5-11	185	10-8-75	1996	Petaluma, Calif.
Jenkins, Corey	.154	7	26	3	4	1	0	0	1	2	17	0	0	R	R	6-2	200	8-25-76	1995	Columbia, S.C.
Johnson, Mark	.283	117	382	68	108	17	3	9	59	105	72	0	1	L	R	6-0	185	9-12-75	1994	Warner Robins, Ga.
Lee, Carlos	.302	138	549	77	166	33	2	21	106	39	55	11	5	R	R	6-2	202	6-20-76	1994	Aguadulce, Panama
Liefer, Jeff	.291	127	471	84	137	33	6	21	89	60	125	1	2	L	R	6-3	195	8-17-74	1996	Upland, Calif.
Manning, Brian	.186	12	43	2	8	1	0	0	2	2	8	0	0	R	R	6-2	200	2-1-75	1996	Hazlet, N.J.
McKinnon, Sandy	.200	57	200	21	40	8	0	1	18	19	41	11	3	R	R	5-8	175	9-20-72	1993	Nicholls, Ga.
Nunez, Sergio	.244	115	435	57	106	8	0	1	32	38	59	26	7	R	R	5-10	170	1-3-75	1991	Santo Domingo, D.R.
Polidor, Wil	.231	31	104	8	24	0	0	0	4	1	15	0	0	B	R	6-1	158	9-23-73	1991	Caracas, Ven.
Seefried, Tate	.238	66	231	21	55	14	0	4	36	32	61	0	1	L	R	6-4	180	4-22-72	1990	Tampa, Fla.
Smith, Demond	.308	84	321	75	99	23	7	5	30	48	67	25	14	B	R	5-11	170	11-6-72	1990	Rialto, Calif.
Whittaker, Jerry	.239	57	205	21	49	12	2	9	26	9	65	3	3	R	R	6-2	190	11-17-73	1994	Long Beach, Calif.

PITCHING	W	L	ERA	G	GS	CG	SV	IP	H	R	ER	BB	SO	B	T	HT	WT	DOB	1st Yr	Resides
Abbott, Jim	2	3	5.40	8	8	0	0	42	53	33	25	21	35	L	L	6-3	210	9-19-67	1989	Newport Beach, Calif.
Ambrose, John	9	12	5.18	31	22	0	0	141	156	90	81	69	103	R	R	6-5	180	11-1-74	1994	St. Petersburg, Fla.
Beirne, Kevin	13	9	3.44	26	26	2	0	167	142	77	64	87	153	L	R	6-4	210	1-1-74	1995	The Woodlands, Texas
Bradford, Chad	1	1	2.60	10	0	0	1	17	13	6	5	8	14	R	R	6-5	205	9-14-74	1996	Jackson, Miss.
Buteaux, Shane	0	1	5.68	13	1	0	0	25	36	28	16	11	12	R	R	6-3	202	12-28-71	1994	New Iberia, La.
Chantres, Carlos	2	4	5.81	20	5	0	1	53	58	35	34	42	49	R	R	6-3	175	4-1-76	1994	Miami, Fla.
Davenport, Joe	3	2	7.22	26	0	0	1	39	54	36	31	30	22	R	R	6-5	225	3-24-76	1994	Santee, Calif.
Farley, Joe	1	2	11.15	6	1	0	0	15	20	19	19	15	7	L	L	6-2	185	9-12-74	1996	Montoursville, Pa.
Lakman, Jason	0	10	7.96	15	15	0	0	72	89	70	64	40	79	R	R	6-4	220	10-17-76	1995	Woodinville, Wash.
Lundquist, David	1	1	3.29	33	0	0	10	41	28	15	15	15	41	R	R	6-2	200	6-4-73	1993	Carson City, Nev.
Mitchell, Larry	0	0	63.00	2	0	0	0	1	4	7	7	5	0	R	R	6-1	219	10-16-71	1992	Charlottesville, Va.
Nichols, Jamie	0	0	7.50	5	1	0	0	12	15	11	10	8	12	R	R	6-5	215	1-22-76	1995	Bear, Del.
Olsen, Jason	8	10	4.69	28	28	4	0	159	188	95	83	53	134	R	R	6-4	210	3-16-75	1995	Fairfield, Calif.
Pena, Jesus	0	2	3.86	22	0	0	2	23	20	12	10	10	28	L	L	6-0	170	3-8-75	1993	Santo Domingo, D.R.
Secoda, Jason	2	3	6.34	39	0	0	1	65	78	50	46	39	45	R	R	6-1	195	9-2-74	1995	Fullerton, Calif.
Theodile, Robert	0	1	7.56	8	0	0	0	17	18	18	14	16	17	R	R	6-3	190	9-16-72	1992	Jeanerette, La.
Tucker, Julien	4	6	6.82	34	5	0	3	66	77	66	50	45	47	L	R	6-7	200	4-19-73	1993	Chateauguay, Quebec
Vining, Ken	10	12	4.07	29	28	1	0	173	187	103	78	91	133	L	L	6-0	180	12-5-74	1996	Hopkins, S.C.
Ward, Bryan	2	3	2.36	29	0	0	12	42	33	19	11	25	40	L	L	6-2	210	1-25-72	1993	Mount Holly, N.J.
Woods, Brian	0	0	11.45	7	0	0	0	11	15	15	14	11	10	L	R	6-6	212	6-7-71	1993	West Caldwell, N.J.
Zolecki, Mike	0	0	7.88	14	0	0	0	24	20	22	21	29	11	R	R	6-2	195	12-6-71	1993	South Milwaukee, Wis.

FIELDING

Catcher	PCT	G	PO	A	E	DP	PB
Cardenas	1.000	17	105	12	0	1	2
R. Gonzalez	.984	23	170	13	3	2	1
Heller	.950	5	17	2	1	0	0
Johnson	.990	103	717	65	8	4	19

First Base	PCT	G	PO	A	E	DP
Battle	.947	2	16	2	1	4
Cordero	.989	10	81	9	1	7
Downs	.974	5	35	3	1	4
Johnson	1.000	1	6	0	0	1
Liefer	.987	100	753	59	11	68
Polidor	1.000	3	7	0	0	0
Seefried	.991	24	207	19	2	20

Second Base	PCT	G	PO	A	E	DP
Finn	1.000	13	30	25	0	6
Nunez	.963	115	236	344	22	80
Polidor	.938	16	25	36	4	8

Third Base	PCT	G	PO	A	E	DP
Battle	1.000	3	2	1	0	0
Finn	.950	7	7	12	1	2
Lee	.902	127	99	223	35	16
Polidor	.917	4	2	9	1	1

Shortstop	PCT	G	PO	A	E	DP
Bautista	.943	120	173	342	31	76
Finn	.961	12	11	38	2	7
Polidor	.972	9	15	20	1	6

Outfield	PCT	G	PO	A	E	DP
Finn	1.000	2	2	0	0	0
M. Gonzalez	.959	95	169	18	8	1
Inglin	.986	115	204	10	3	1
Jenkins	.857	7	6	0	1	0
Liefer	1.000	10	10	1	0	0
Manning	.933	8	14	0	1	0
McKinnon	.966	56	106	6	4	2
Smith	.979	83	185	4	4	2
Whittaker	.978	52	128	5	3	0

WINSTON-SALEM — Class A

CAROLINA LEAGUE

BATTING	AVG	G	AB	R	H	2B	3B	HR	RBI	BB	SO	SB	CS	B	T	HT	WT	DOB	1st Yr	Resides
Albert, Rashad	.273	18	55	10	15	0	4	1	10	1	16	3	1	R	R	6-1	165	9-18-75	1994	Fernandina Beach, Fla.
Christensen, McKay	.285	95	361	69	103	17	6	4	32	53	54	20	10	L	L	5-11	180	8-14-75	1995	Clovis, Calif.
Connacher, Kevin	.241	80	212	45	51	9	3	7	23	34	63	15	5	R	R	5-9	175	4-6-75	1997	West Palm Beach, Fla.
Crede, Joe	.315	137	492	92	155	32	3	20	88	53	98	9	7	R	R	6-3	190	4-26-78	1996	Westphalia, Mo.
Dellaero, Jason	.208	121	428	45	89	23	3	10	49	25	147	12	4	B	R	6-2	195	12-17-76	1997	Brewster, N.Y.
Downs, Brian	.259	9	27	3	7	3	0	2	8	1	9	0	0	R	R	6-2	210	4-10-75	1995	Chino, Calif.
Garcia, Luis	.270	106	389	49	105	29	1	10	58	13	68	8	5	R	R	6-3	200	9-22-75	1995	Hermosillo, Mexico
Gomez, Ramon	.218	43	124	21	27	5	2	0	10	12	36	13	3	R	R	6-2	175	10-6-75	1994	San Pedro de Macoris, D.R.
Gonzalez, Jose	.267	14	30	3	8	2	0	0	5	1	8	0	2	R	R	5-10	170	9-24-77	1996	Barcelona, Ven.
Heintz, Chris	.289	130	508	66	147	21	4	8	79	31	87	10	8	R	R	6-1	200	8-6-74	1996	Clearwater, Fla.
Klee, Chuck	.200	28	65	7	13	4	1	0	1	7	22	0	0	R	R	6-3	175	5-15-77	1995	Lighthouse Point, Fla.
Manning, Brian	.272	80	265	32	72	15	2	6	39	20	48	6	10	R	R	6-2	200	2-1-75	1996	Hazlet, N.J.
McKinnon, Sandy	.262	45	149	18	39	8	1	1	15	12	37	3	2	R	R	5-8	175	9-20-72	1993	Nicholls, Ga.
Olson, Dan	.260	117	404	73	105	33	5	18	68	41	152	5	6	L	L	6-2	210	4-10-75	1996	Cape May, N.J.
Paul, Josh	.255	123	444	66	113	20	7	11	63	38	91	20	8	R	R	6-1	185	5-19-75	1996	Buffalo Grove, Ill.
Rodriguez, Liu	.279	112	420	62	117	27	3	2	43	45	40	15	10	B	R	5-9	170	11-5-76	1995	Caracas, Ven.
Sheppard, Greg	.265	89	260	29	69	13	1	7	27	30	82	2	2	R	R	6-0	190	3-1-75	1996	Palmdale, Calif.
Terrell, Jim	.455	3	11	1	5	3	1	0	2	0	2	0	0	L	R	6-1	175	9-8-77	1996	Miami, Fla.

GAMES BY POSITION: C—Downs 4, Heintz 34, Paul 109, Shepard 3. **1B**—Downs 2, Heintz 101, Klee 10, Olson 7, Rodriguez 1, Shepard 35. **2B**—Connacher 50, Gonzalez 3, Klee 1, Rodriguez 96. **3B**—Connacher 6, Crede 132, Gonzalez 5, Heintz 5, Klee 3, Terrell 1. **SS**—Dellaero 121, Gonzalez 3, Klee 15, Rodriguez 12. **OF**—Albert 15, Christensen 95, Garcia 100, Gomez 39, Klee 1, Manning 58, McKinnon 43, Olson 82, Terrell 2.

PITCHING	W	L	ERA	G	GS	CG	SV	IP	H	R	ER	BB	SO	B	T	HT	WT	DOB	1st Yr	Resides
Abbott, Jim	2	1	5.40	4	4	0	0	22	17	13	13	7	13	L	L	6-3	210	9-19-67	1989	Newport Beach, Calif.
Biddle, Rocky	4	5	4.57	16	16	0	0	83	92	55	42	45	72	R	R	6-3	230	5-21-76	1997	Arcadia, Calif.
Chantres, Carlos	5	5	3.77	13	13	1	0	88	71	43	37	41	86	R	R	6-3	175	4-1-76	1994	Miami, Fla.
Daneker, Pat	5	0	2.04	7	7	2	0	53	51	13	12	5	43	R	R	6-3	195	1-14-76	1997	Williamsport, Pa.
Davenport, Joe	2	0	1.38	20	0	0	2	26	25	9	4	4	26	R	R	6-5	225	3-24-76	1994	Santee, Calif.
Farley, Joe	5	6	4.99	21	19	1	0	119	126	73	66	55	70	L	L	6-2	185	9-12-74	1996	Montoursville, Pa.
Fogg, Josh	0	1	0.00	1	0	0	0	1	2	2	0	0	2	R	R	6-2	195	12-13-76	1998	Margate, Fla.
Hasselhoff, Derek	0	0	0.00	1	0	0	0	2	3	0	0	0	3	R	R	6-2	185	10-10-73	1995	Pasadena, Md.
Hunt, Jon	1	1	9.00	6	0	0	0	8	11	8	8	3	6	L	L	6-1	190	5-5-74	1995	Ironton, Ohio
Iglesias, Mario	13	1	2.31	35	0	0	5	78	51	24	20	19	90	B	R	6-3	195	6-2-74	1996	Castro Valley, Calif.
Izquierdo, Hansel	0	0	0.00	1	0	0	1	2	1	0	0	1	2	R	R	6-2	205	1-2-77	1995	Miami, Fla.
Lakman, Jason	3	2	3.77	13	13	1	0	86	62	37	36	30	98	R	R	6-4	220	10-17-76	1995	Woodinville, Wash.
Lundquist, David	1	0	2.53	6	0	0	0	11	9	4	3	3	9	R	R	6-2	200	6-4-73	1993	Carson City, Nev.
Meyer, Jake	0	1	2.92	11	0	0	2	12	12	6	4	3	13	R	R	6-1	195	1-7-75	1997	San Diego, Calif.
Myette, Aaron	4	2	2.01	6	6	1	0	45	32	14	10	14	54	R	R	6-4	195	9-26-77	1997	Gig Harbor, Wash.
Nichols, Jamie	3	3	5.50	19	4	0	0	54	71	34	33	11	39	R	R	6-5	215	1-22-76	1995	Bear, Del.
Ochsenfeld, Chris	0	0	4.50	17	0	0	2	26	26	15	13	12	16	L	L	6-2	210	8-21-76	1994	Hampton, Va.
Pena, Jesus	3	4	3.13	23	0	0	7	32	20	11	11	12	37	L	L	6-0	170	3-8-75	1993	Santo Domingo, D.R.
Roberts, Mark	9	9	3.92	27	25	2	0	165	165	88	72	50	142	R	R	6-2	205	9-29-75	1996	Zephyrhills, Fla.
Schmack, Brian	5	5	2.20	42	0	0	10	61	48	23	15	17	52	R	R	6-2	195	12-7-73	1996	Barrington, Ill.
Scott, Brian	6	6	4.93	19	19	0	0	100	116	70	55	43	76	R	R	6-3	190	4-29-76	1997	Ramona, Calif.
Secoda, Jason	2	0	1.59	6	0	0	0	11	8	2	2	2	8	R	R	6-1	195	9-2-74	1995	Fullerton, Calif.
Virchis, Adam	5	6	3.39	22	13	1	0	104	104	54	39	20	73	R	R	6-3	185	10-15-73	1995	Chula Vista, Calif.
Whitley, Curtis	0	1	0.63	10	0	0	0	14	11	2	1	6	21	L	L	6-4	240	1-9-74	1997	Goldsboro, N.C.
Zolecki, Mike	1	1	4.30	8	0	0	0	15	17	9	7	8	6	R	R	6-2	195	12-6-71	1993	South Milwaukee, Wis.

HICKORY — Class A

SOUTH ATLANTIC LEAGUE

BATTING	AVG	G	AB	R	H	2B	3B	HR	RBI	BB	SO	SB	CS	B	T	HT	WT	DOB	1st Yr	Resides
Albert, Rashad	.259	106	390	48	101	18	4	6	39	14	96	23	11	R	R	6-1	165	9-18-75	1994	Fernandina Beach, Fla.
Berger, Matt	.299	126	469	72	140	30	0	24	94	50	111	3	2	R	R	6-1	195	10-2-74	1997	Fort Mitchell, Ky.
Borges, Elio	.212	22	52	7	11	3	0	0	7	2	18	2	1	B	R	6-0	180	10-7-77	1997	Hialeah, Fla.
Caradonna, Brett	.266	116	447	43	119	21	1	3	35	45	84	15	11	L	R	6-1	185	12-3-78	1997	San Diego, Calif.
Downs, Brian	.278	91	331	35	92	15	0	9	39	17	68	2	4	R	R	6-2	210	4-10-75	1995	Chino, Calif.
Durham, Chad	.233	117	480	57	112	7	4	2	34	29	74	33	16	R	R	5-8	175	6-23-78	1997	Charlotte, N.C.
Fauske, Josh	.269	104	375	55	101	18	0	15	60	36	65	2	2	R	R	6-4	230	3-16-74	1995	Mercer Island, Wash.
Hollins, Darontaye	.220	45	150	17	33	6	1	3	13	10	40	7	6	R	R	6-0	200	9-6-74	1995	Roseville, Calif.
Klee, Chuck	.190	49	163	11	31	7	2	2	18	6	42	1	1	R	R	6-3	175	5-15-77	1995	Lighthouse Point, Fla.
Kopacz, Derek	.149	13	47	3	7	2	0	0	8	3	19	0	0	R	R	5-11	185	4-2-75	1995	Orland Park, Ill.
Mounts, J.R.	.240	110	430	57	103	20	2	11	43	27	154	20	7	R	R	6-0	190	11-13-78	1997	Key West, Fla.
Newkirk, Jeff	.215	26	93	11	20	8	2	1	7	10	20	2	4	L	L	5-10	185	8-1-75	1997	Kinston, N.C.
Rowand, Aaron	.342	61	222	42	76	13	3	5	32	21	36	7	3	R	R	6-1	215	8-29-77	1998	Fullerton, Calif.
Sandoval, Danny	.230	126	430	43	99	12	2	0	30	29	88	13	15	B	R	5-11	160	4-7-79	1997	Lara, Ven.
Sutton, Joe	.231	76	238	29	55	14	2	4	22	31	75	1	1	L	R	6-3	225	10-17-74	1996	El Paso, Texas
Terrell, Jim	.338	131	500	84	169	21	4	13	64	53	90	25	8	L	R	6-1	175	9-8-77	1996	Miami, Fla.

GAMES BY POSITION: C—Downs 61, Fauske 34, Sutton 56. **1B**—Berger 94, Downs 7, Fauske 34, Klee 1, Kopacz 7, Terrell 2. **2B**—Borges 4, Durham 117, Klee 3, Terrell 20. **3B**—Berger 28, Borges 14, Klee 22, Terrell 84. **SS**—Klee 12, Sandoval 126, Terrell 7. **OF**—Albert 97, Caradonna 98, Hollins 43, Mounts 106, Newkirk 21, Rowand 46, Terrell 18.

PITCHING	W	L	ERA	G	GS	CG	SV	IP	H	R	ER	BB	SO	B	T	HT	WT	DOB	1st Yr	Resides
Abbott, Jim	0	0	2.25	1	1	0	0	4	3	1	1	2	2	L	L	6-3	210	9-19-67	1989	Newport Beach, Calif.
Borne, Matt	2	1	8.86	15	0	0	1	21	36	24	21	11	16	R	R	6-3	190	9-12-76	1998	Lexington, Ky.
Cardona, Steve	3	5	4.59	44	0	0	6	65	57	35	33	28	65	R	R	6-3	190	2-18-74	1996	Stockton, Calif.
Currens, Tim	1	2	5.71	28	0	0	1	58	71	46	37	24	36	L	R	6-4	195	10-2-75	1997	Bowling Green, Ky.
Daneker, Pat	6	6	3.15	17	17	2	0	117	115	50	41	16	95	R	R	6-3	195	1-14-76	1997	Williamsport, Pa.
Felix, Miguel	3	11	6.47	21	19	1	0	97	111	90	70	64	86	R	R	6-1	155	12-30-76	1995	La Romana, D.R.
Fitzpatrick, Luke	2	0	3.14	20	0	0	0	29	37	14	10	16	21	L	L	6-0	190	4-30-76	1997	Long Beach, Calif.
Fogg, Josh	1	3	2.18	8	8	0	0	41	36	17	10	13	29	R	R	6-2	195	12-13-76	1998	Margate, Fla.
Garcia, Ariel	0	6	4.89	9	7	0	0	39	44	31	21	14	14	R	R	6-5	206	10-3-75	1993	Panama City, Panama
Garland, Jon	1	4	5.40	5	5	0	0	27	36	20	16	13	19	R	R	6-6	200	9-27-79	1997	Granada Hills, Calif.
Izquierdo, Hansel	9	11	4.37	28	27	2	0	175	159	104	85	76	186	R	R	6-2	205	1-2-77	1995	Miami, Fla.
Lopez, Jose	4	3	4.50	33	0	0	5	46	43	23	23	16	33	B	R	6-2	185	4-16-76	1996	Ridgewood, N.Y.
Meyer, Jake	0	6	3.21	35	0	0	11	56	58	30	20	22	47	R	R	6-1	195	1-7-75	1997	San Diego, Calif.
Myette, Aaron	9	4	2.47	17	17	0	0	102	84	43	28	30	103	R	R	6-4	195	9-26-77	1997	Gig Harbor, Wash.
Nichols, Jamie	0	1	3.79	11	0	0	1	19	15	8	8	12	19	R	R	6-5	215	1-22-76	1995	Bear, Del.
Perez, Elvis	0	0	10.80	3	0	0	0	3	8	6	4	4	2	L	L	6-2	190	2-9-78	1996	Hialeah, Fla.
Schorzman, Steve	2	2	6.54	23	0	0	0	43	37	32	31	24	35	R	R	6-2	185	7-6-74	1996	Cambridge, Idaho
Scott, Brian	4	2	2.79	6	6	0	0	39	33	16	12	11	38	R	R	6-3	190	4-29-76	1997	Ramona, Calif.
Stockstill, Jason	0	0	5.79	10	0	0	3	14	13	10	9	11	8	L	L	6-5	215	11-13-76	1995	Anaheim, Calif.
Tellez, Eloy	0	0	10.13	4	0	0	0	5	11	6	6	3	3	L	R	6-3	220	1-29-76	1996	El Paso, Texas
Tokarse, Brian	0	1	7.36	2	2	0	0	4	3	3	3	3	3	R	R	6-3	180	2-28-75	1997	Whittier, Calif.
Virchis, Adam	1	3	3.38	9	0	0	1	19	16	8	7	5	19	R	R	6-3	185	10-15-73	1995	Chula Vista, Calif.
Weymouth, Marty	4	5	4.34	31	14	0	3	112	125	74	54	32	99	R	R	6-2	180	8-6-77	1995	Romeo, Mich.
Whitley, Curtis	4	8	4.17	22	17	1	1	112	111	70	52	58	87	L	L	6-4	240	1-9-74	1997	Goldsboro, N.C.

BRISTOL — Rookie

APPALACHIAN LEAGUE

BATTING	AVG	G	AB	R	H	2B	3B	HR	RBI	BB	SO	SB	CS	B	T	HT	WT	DOB	1st Yr	Resides
Aceves, Jonathan	.296	43	135	29	40	12	3	4	30	29	38	1	3	R	R	6-2	187	3-7-78	1997	Sonora, Mexico
Fennell, Jason	.318	47	170	40	54	8	1	7	33	23	25	0	1	B	R	6-3	210	11-15-77	1996	Pittsburgh, Pa.
Gonzalez, Jose	.312	51	205	39	64	14	0	1	24	18	35	16	5	R	R	5-10	170	9-24-77	1996	Barcelona, Ven.
Hankins, Ryan	.255	50	188	40	48	4	1	13	38	36	47	4	1	R	R	5-11	200	6-30-76	1997	Simi Valley, Calif.
Hyde, Brandon	.372	27	94	21	35	9	0	5	26	21	20	0	1	R	R	6-3	210	10-3-73	1997	Santa Rosa, Calif.

BATTING	AVG	G	AB	R	H	2B	3B	HR	RBI	BB	SO	SB	CS	B	T	HT	WT	DOB	1st Yr	Resides
Lutz, Manny	.305	65	279	52	85	21	0	17	58	14	56	2	1	L	R	6-2	230	6-14-76	1995	Spring Valley, Calif.
Medrano, Ricardo	.230	40	148	34	34	0	0	0	11	29	23	28	4	B	R	5-9	165	4-23-78	1996	Maracay, Ven.
Merriman, Terrell	.227	37	128	24	29	9	0	1	14	17	33	10	1	L	L	6-0	180	7-30-77	1998	Cheraw, S.C.
Newkirk, Jeff	.266	59	222	40	59	8	8	4	33	27	32	19	1	L	L	5-10	185	8-1-75	1997	Kinston, N.C.
Roman, Junior	.222	7	27	8	6	0	0	0	1	4	6	0	3	B	R	5-11	160	8-30-80	1997	Mao Valverde, D.R.
Romero, Marty	.239	19	71	9	17	2	0	6	19	6	21	1	0	R	R	6-2	187	10-6-76	1994	Caracas, Ven.
Suarez, Luis	.253	59	198	35	50	5	1	1	25	22	40	7	1	R	R	6-1	175	9-5-78	1998	Hialeah, Fla.
Valenzuela, Mario	.330	61	233	44	77	13	1	10	46	24	49	6	4	R	R	6-2	190	3-10-77	1996	Isla San Marcos, Mexico
Wallace, Derek	.221	52	204	32	45	12	2	7	32	12	52	6	2	R	R	6-3	195	9-24-76	1996	Monroe, La.

GAMES BY POSITION: C—Aceves 43, Hyde 8, Romero 17. **1B**—Fennell 1, Hyde 1, Lutz 65, Romero 1. **2B**—Gonzalez 21, Hankins 3, Medrano 40, Roman 7. **3B**—Gonzalez 30, Hankins 41, Lutz 1. **SS**—Gonzalez 1, Hankins 8, Romero 1, Suarez 59. **OF**—Fennell 4, Merriman 35, Newkirk 59, Valenzuela 59, Wallace 45.

PITCHING	W	L	ERA	G	GS	CG	SV	IP	H	R	ER	BB	SO	B	T	HT	WT	DOB	1st Yr	Resides
Almonte, Edwin	3	0	3.38	8	3	0	0	27	29	14	10	4	26	R	R	6-3	200	12-17-76	1998	New York, N.Y.
Duenas, Alain	1	2	7.48	6	3	0	0	22	37	19	18	3	14	R	R	6-1	180	9-27-75	1997	Coral Gables, Fla.
Felix, Miguel	1	1	4.57	5	4	0	0	22	20	16	11	15	23	R	R	6-1	155	12-30-76	1995	La Romana, D.R.
Figueroa, Juan	5	5	5.06	13	13	2	0	80	87	58	45	22	102	R	R	6-3	150	6-24-79	1996	Santo Domingo, D.R.
Fischer, Eric	0	1	6.35	4	0	0	0	6	10	5	4	1	5	B	L	6-6	215	2-19-80	1998	Cincinnati, Ohio
Freeman, Kai	6	2	3.28	11	9	1	0	58	56	28	21	21	44	R	R	6-1	180	3-11-77	1998	Shorewood, Ill.
Garcia, Ariel	0	1	11.12	3	2	0	0	6	10	9	7	1	4	R	R	6-5	206	10-3-75	1993	Panama City, Panama
Jacobson, Andrew	4	3	3.52	12	8	2	0	64	72	38	25	24	38	R	R	6-8	210	1-25-76	1997	McRain, Mich.
Johnson, Solomon	2	2	3.74	14	7	0	0	43	38	22	18	26	38	L	L	6-0	210	8-27-78	1998	Mexia, Texas
Kane, Kyle	1	0	5.32	13	0	0	0	24	34	21	14	8	17	L	R	6-3	210	2-4-76	1997	Temecula, Calif.
Lopez, Jose	2	0	3.12	5	0	0	1	9	10	6	3	3	4	B	R	6-2	185	4-16-76	1996	Ridgewood, N.Y.
Mendoza, Geronimo	5	2	3.83	13	13	0	0	80	78	40	34	30	70	L	R	6-4	160	1-23-78	1995	Santo Domingo, D.R.
Rodgers, Marcus	3	0	4.18	18	0	0	1	28	11	14	13	10	39	R	R	6-3	225	11-1-76	1996	Saraland, Ala.
Smith, Jamie	1	0	8.38	8	0	0	0	10	16	9	9	3	12	R	R	6-2	193	2-2-76	1997	San Antonio, Texas
Tellez, Eloy	4	2	6.59	14	0	0	0	27	39	23	20	9	18	L	R	6-3	220	1-29-76	1996	El Paso, Texas
Williams, Mike	3	1	3.49	24	0	0	9	39	28	16	15	16	43	R	R	6-3	190	8-9-78	1998	Cypress, Texas
Williams, Tom	1	0	7.71	4	4	0	0	16	23	18	14	7	12	R	R	6-1	220	1-30-76	1997	Lake Charles, La.
Wylie, Mitchell	0	2	3.30	20	0	0	6	30	34	12	11	11	32	R	R	6-3	190	1-14-77	1998	Davenport, Iowa

TUCSON — Rookie

ARIZONA LEAGUE

BATTING	AVG	G	AB	R	H	2B	3B	HR	RBI	BB	SO	SB	CS	B	T	HT	WT	DOB	1st Yr	Resides
Aguirregaviria, Frank	.202	37	104	18	21	4	0	0	9	15	36	2	4	R	R	6-1	180	2-11-78	1997	Miami, Fla.
Battersby, Eric	.375	43	136	34	51	15	3	5	27	29	32	4	2	R	L	6-2	205	2-28-76	1998	San Antonio, Texas
Borges, Elio	.000	1	1	0	0	0	0	0	0	0	0	0	0	B	R	6-0	180	10-7-77	1997	Hialeah, Fla.
Cabrera, Mayron	.333	30	72	10	24	3	0	0	11	2	15	3	2	R	R	5-11	205	8-10-79	1997	Colon, Panama
Cline, Carlos	.263	39	118	9	31	6	0	0	12	16	39	4	3	L	L	6-2	210	12-27-77	1998	Nutley, N.J.
Delgado, Chris	.302	38	129	28	39	12	0	5	25	20	30	6	1	R	R	6-3	215	10-8-77	1997	Pembroke Pines, Fla.
Garcia, Tony	.250	36	120	21	30	5	2	3	21	15	31	5	4	R	R	6-1	213	3-12-78	1998	Miami, Fla.
Garza, Rolando	.354	53	206	41	73	11	2	3	33	18	35	17	7	R	R	6-3	180	12-14-79	1997	Coachella, Calif.
Lowe, Ernesto	.225	29	80	11	18	2	0	1	11	18	21	6	2	R	R	6-1	180	10-1-78	1997	Miami, Fla.
Manuel, Marcellous	.299	44	137	29	41	11	1	5	26	13	19	5	3	L	L	5-10	165	10-9-75	1998	Stone Mountain, Ga.
Mosley, Gus	.230	32	87	14	20	1	1	0	3	6	30	3	3	R	R	6-2	185	9-29-79	1998	Crawfordsville, Fla.
Perez, Rafael	.263	40	118	19	31	4	4	2	18	10	47	5	6	L	R	6-3	175	10-15-79	1998	Santo Domingo, D.R.
Rapp, Travis	.243	18	37	5	9	5	0	0	3	6	15	0	1	R	R	6-2	205	1-28-75	1997	Sebring, Fla.
Rodriguez, Mervin	.283	23	53	8	15	1	0	0	7	4	16	1	1	R	R	6-1	180	1-9-80	1997	Nizao, D.R.
Roman, Junior	.354	36	130	28	46	3	1	1	15	24	23	17	8	B	R	5-11	160	8-30-80	1997	Mao Valverde, D.R.
Santamarina, Juan	.200	41	165	15	33	4	0	2	20	9	36	3	1	L	R	6-1	180	10-3-79	1998	Miami, Fla.
Simmons, Brian	.167	5	12	1	2	0	0	0	0	1	1	0	0	B	R	6-2	190	9-4-73	1995	McMurray, Pa.
Tineo, Esmerlin	.214	32	98	11	21	5	1	0	6	7	15	4	5	L	L	6-0	160	6-22-80	1997	Montecristi, D.R.

GAMES BY POSITION: C—Aguirregaviria 17, Garcia 36, Rapp 14. **1B**—Battersby 2, Cline 30, Delgado 26, Garza 1, Manuel 2, Perez 1, Tineo 1. **2B**—Aguirregaviria 15, Borges 1, Garza 14, Lowe 2, Rapp 1, Rodriguez 16, Roman 12. **3B**—Aguirregaviria 3, Cabrera 1, Delgado 5, Garza 9, Rapp 1, Santamarina 41. **SS**—Garza 31, Rodriguez 5, Roman 24. **OF**—Battersby 28, Cabrera 20, Cline 1, Lowe 24, Manuel 21, Mosley 27, Perez 36, Simmons 4, Tineo 27.

PITCHING	W	L	ERA	G	GS	CG	SV	IP	H	R	ER	BB	SO	B	T	HT	WT	DOB	1st Yr	Resides
Almonte, Edwin	0	0	0.93	5	0	0	0	10	6	5	1	1	8	R	R	6-3	200	12-17-76	1998	New York, N.Y.
Barcelo, Lorenzo	0	1	1.50	3	3	0	0	6	6	1	1	0	9	R	R	6-4	220	8-10-77	1994	San Pedro de Macoris, D.R.
Biddle, Rocky	1	0	3.94	5	2	0	0	16	15	9	7	8	18	R	R	6-3	230	5-21-76	1997	Arcadia, Calif.
Borne, Matt	0	0	4.50	2	0	0	0	4	3	3	2	4	3	R	R	6-3	190	9-12-76	1998	Lexington, Ky.
Brown, Tighe	0	0	4.26	5	0	0	0	6	7	8	3	4	10	R	R	6-4	195	9-10-76	1995	Louisville, Ky.
Caraballo, Angel	3	5	7.49	14	13	0	0	64	90	71	53	36	57	R	L	6-2	195	1-20-80	1997	Guanta, Ven.
Duenas, Alain	0	0	2.25	6	0	0	0	8	8	2	2	2	11	R	R	6-1	180	9-27-75	1997	Coral Gables, Fla.
Ferrand, Dario	2	2	4.60	16	0	0	1	31	49	18	16	4	19	R	R	6-1	160	9-19-81	1998	Santo Domingo, D.R.
Fischer, Eric	0	1	5.20	8	8	0	0	28	30	18	16	14	31	B	L	6-6	215	2-19-80	1998	Cincinnati, Ohio
Fogg, Josh	1	0	0.00	2	0	0	0	4	0	0	0	1	5	R	R	6-2	195	12-13-76	1998	Margate, Fla.
Freeman, Kai	0	0	4.50	1	0	0	0	2	1	1	1	1	2	R	R	6-1	180	3-11-77	1998	Shorewood, Ill.
Frias, Yovany	1	1	8.13	11	4	0	0	28	41	30	25	22	21	R	R	6-4	190	8-20-78	1994	San Pedro de Macoris, D.R.
Gonzalez, Martin	0	1	28.42	7	0	0	0	6	24	25	20	8	9	R	R	6-1	180	7-15-81	1998	Guaymas, Mexico
Hasselhoff, Derek	0	0	0.00	6	1	0	0	10	6	1	0	0	16	R	R	6-2	185	10-10-73	1995	Pasadena, Md.
Kvasnicka, Jay	0	2	9.00	7	0	0	1	8	11	10	8	2	8	R	R	6-4	180	7-21-76	1997	Chicago Heights, Ill.
Perez, Elvis	2	3	6.75	14	8	0	0	48	60	38	36	33	42	L	L	6-2	190	2-9-78	1996	Hialeah, Fla.
Reyes, Hipolito	2	1	6.65	14	1	0	1	22	33	21	16	13	16	R	R	6-2	170	6-17-81	1998	Hato Mayor, D.R.
Rodgers, Marcus	0	0	6.35	2	1	0	0	6	8	5	4	2	6	R	R	6-3	225	11-1-76	1996	Saraland, Ala.
Rohling, Stuart	3	5	8.06	13	6	0	0	45	63	51	40	30	41	R	R	6-4	185	6-29-78	1998	Leoma, Tenn.
Santana, Fausto	0	2	7.20	12	0	0	2	15	19	14	12	10	12	R	R	5-11	175	2-6-78	1996	Puerto Plata, D.R.
Simpson, Andre	3	6	6.20	14	6	0	0	41	47	36	28	20	35	R	R	6-3	170	7-1-80	1998	Lemon Grove, Calif.
Smith, Jamie	0	2	7.27	5	0	0	0	9	14	9	7	4	16	R	R	6-2	193	2-2-76	1997	San Antonio, Texas
Whatley, Brannon	1	2	2.91	16	0	0	2	34	35	14	11	19	32	R	R	6-1	170	10-11-76	1998	Marietta, Ga.
Williams, Tom	0	0	0.00	1	0	0	0	2	2	2	0	1	1	R	R	6-1	220	1-30-76	1997	Lake Charles, La.

CHICAGO CUBS

Sosa and Wood meant excitement at Wrigley in 1998

BY BARRY ROZNER

Sammy Sosa. Kerry Wood. The two took turns in the spotlight for the Cubs in 1998, but neither drew the focus from the team's ultimate goal—its first postseason berth since 1989.

Even though they lasted just three quiet games against the Braves in the Division Series, the Cubs will consider 1998 a successful season.

"Absolutely," Cubs general manager Ed Lynch said. "Based on the fact that we were 68-94 (in 1997) and then to win 90 games and go to the postseason.

"Yeah, it was a successful year, and yes, we're disappointed we got swept by the Braves in the playoffs. We got to the postseason. Does that mean we're going to rest on our laurels? No, it doesn't."

Wood's 20-strikeout performance against the Astros on May 6 set the tone for the season and gave the Cubs the confidence they lacked. That was followed in June by Sosa's record-setting, 20-homer performance that carried the Cubs into the second half. Sosa finished with 66 home runs and led the majors in RBIs with 158, while leading the Cubs to the wild card.

The winning attitude caught on at Triple-A Iowa, where the Cubs finished first in the Pacific Coast League with an 85-59 record. Like their major league counterparts, the I-Cubs fell in the first round of the postseason to eventual PCL champ New Orleans.

Iowa manager Terry Kennedy was honored as BA's Minor League Manager of the Year and is regarded as a bright managerial prospect. Minor league veterans like Kurt Miller and Dave Swartzbaugh, who each won 14 games, helped Kennedy look smart, as did outfielder Micah Franklin and first baseman Rod McCall, who combined for 59 home runs.

Sammy Sosa

Brian McNichol

Players of the Year

Major League: Sammy Sosa, of
Sosa may have finished second in the home run chase with 66, but his season was one of the best of all time.

Minor League: Brian McNichol, lhp, Iowa/West Tenn
McNichol tied for the organization lead in strikeouts with 173 while going 12-9 at two minor league stops.

Other organization highlights included lefthander Brian McNichol going 12-9 with a 3.72 ERA and 168 strikeouts for Double-A West Tenn and second baseman Chad Meyers scoring 102 runs and stealing 60 bases at two levels.

But none of those players seem likely to step in and offer immediate help in 1999. Career years from Kevin Tapani, Rod Beck, Mickey Morandini, Brant Brown and Henry Rodriguez helped the Cubs overlook several glaring holes in the lineup. Questions need to be addressed for the 1999 season, most notably what to do about a bullpen that collapsed down the stretch and nearly cost the club a shot at the playoffs.

The Cubs picked up two relievers at the trade deadline—Matt Karchner and Felix Heredia—by trading former first-round picks Todd Noel and Jon Garland, a price many felt was too high.

The team can't afford to trade more top prospects to fill the holes at catcher, third base, shortstop, left field or in the rotation.

Two-fifths of the rotation was out of action down the stretch, when Jeremi Gonzalez went down with season-ending elbow surgery and Wood missed September because of soreness in his right elbow. But Wood's arm was healthy and he came back to start Game Three against the Braves in the NL Division Series.

The Cubs had two affiliation changes in the offseason, moving their short-season club from Williamsport in the New York-Penn League to Eugene in the Northwest League, and switching their low Class A team from Rockford to Lansing in the Midwest League.

ORGANIZATION LEADERS

BATTING		
*AVG	Derrick White, Iowa	.363
R	Chad Meyers, West Tenn/Daytona	102
H	Julio Zuleta, West Tenn/Daytona	167
TB	Julio Zuleta, West Tenn/Daytona	257
2B	Two tied at	40
3B	Bo Porter, Iowa/West Tenn	11
HR	Rod McCall, Iowa	30
RBI	Julio Zuleta, West Tenn/Daytona	106
BB	Chad Meyers, West Tenn/Daytona	91
SO	Rod McCall, Iowa	151
SB	Chad Meyers, West Tenn/Daytona	60
PITCHING		
W	Two tied at	14
L	Jason Ryan, West Tenn	13
#ERA	Kyle Lohse, Rockford	3.22
G	Richie Barker, Iowa/West Tenn	67
CG	Brian McNichol, Iowa/West Tenn	4
SV	Chad Ricketts, West Tenn/Daytona	25
IP	Phillip Norton, West Tenn/Daytona	186
BB	Courtney Duncan, West Tenn	108
SO	Two tied at	173

*Minimum 250 At-Bats #Minimum 75 Innings

Chicago CUBS

Manager: Jim Riggleman

1998 Record: 89-73, .549 (2nd, NL Central)

BATTING	AVG	G	AB	R	H	2B	3B	HR	RBI	BB	SO	SB	CS	B	T	HT	WT	DOB	1st Yr	Resides
Alexander, Manny	.227	108	264	34	60	10	1	5	25	18	66	4	1	R	R	5-10	175	3-20-71	1988	San Pedro de Macoris, D.R.
Blauser, Jeff	.219	119	361	49	79	11	3	4	26	60	93	2	2	R	R	6-1	180	11-8-65	1984	Alpharetta, Ga.
Brown, Brant	.291	124	347	56	101	17	7	14	48	30	95	4	5	L	L	6-3	205	6-22-71	1992	Porterville, Calif.
Gaetti, Gary	.320	37	128	21	41	11	0	8	27	12	23	0	0	R	R	6-0	200	8-19-58	1979	Raleigh, N.C.
2-team (91 St. Louis)	.281	128	434	60	122	34	1	19	70	43	62	1	1							
Grace, Mark	.309	158	595	92	184	39	3	17	89	93	56	4	7	L	L	6-2	200	6-28-64	1986	Chicago, Ill.
Hardtke, Jason	.238	18	21	2	5	0	0	0	2	2	6	0	0	B	R	5-10	175	9-15-71	1990	Port Washington, N.Y.
Hernandez, Jose	.254	149	488	76	124	23	7	23	75	40	140	4	6	R	R	6-0	185	7-14-69	1987	Dorado, P.R.
Hill, Glenallen	.351	48	131	26	46	5	0	8	23	14	34	0	0	R	R	6-2	225	3-22-65	1983	Santa Cruz, Calif.
Houston, Tyler	.255	95	255	26	65	7	1	9	33	13	53	2	2	L	R	6-2	205	1-17-71	1989	Las Vegas, Nev.
Johnson, Lance	.280	85	304	51	85	8	4	2	21	26	22	10	6	L	L	5-11	165	7-6-63	1984	Mobile, Ala.
Lowery, Terrell	.200	24	15	2	3	1	0	0	1	3	7	0	0	R	R	6-3	195	10-25-70	1991	Vallejo, Calif.
Martinez, Sandy	.264	45	87	7	23	9	1	0	7	13	21	1	0	L	R	6-2	205	10-3-72	1990	Santo Domingo, D.R.
Maxwell, Jason	.333	7	3	2	1	0	0	1	2	0	2	0	0	R	R	6-0	185	3-26-72	1993	Lewisburg, Tenn.
Merced, Orlando	.300	12	10	2	3	0	0	1	5	1	2	0	0	L	R	6-1	195	11-2-66	1985	Orlando, Fla.
Mieske, Matt	.299	77	97	16	29	7	0	1	12	11	17	0	0	R	R	6-0	195	2-13-68	1990	Mesa, Ariz.
Morandini, Mickey	.296	154	582	93	172	20	4	8	53	72	84	13	1	L	R	5-11	175	4-22-66	1989	Valparaiso, Ind.
Nieves, Jose	.000	2	1	0	0	0	0	0	0	0	0	0	0	R	R	6-1	180	6-16-75	1992	Guacara, Ven.
Orie, Kevin	.181	64	204	24	37	14	0	2	21	18	35	1	1	R	R	6-4	215	9-1-72	1993	West Chester, Pa.
Rodriguez, Henry	.251	128	415	56	104	21	1	31	85	54	113	1	3	L	L	6-2	220	11-8-67	1986	Santo Domingo, D.R.
Servais, Scott	.222	113	325	35	72	15	1	7	36	26	51	1	0	R	R	6-2	210	6-4-67	1989	Castle Rock, Colo.
Sosa, Sammy	.308	159	643	134	198	20	0	66	158	73	171	18	9	R	R	6-0	200	11-12-68	1986	San Pedro de Macoris, D.R.
Valdes, Pedro	.217	14	23	1	5	1	1	0	2	1	3	0	1	L	L	6-1	190	6-29-73	1991	Loiza, P.R.
White, Derrick	.100	11	10	1	1	0	0	1	2	0	5	0	0	R	R	6-1	225	10-12-69	1991	Chandler, Ariz.

PITCHING	W	L	ERA	G	GS	CG	SV	IP	H	R	ER	BB	SO	B	T	HT	WT	DOB	1st Yr	Resides
Adams, Terry	7	7	4.33	63	0	0	1	73	72	39	35	41	73	R	R	6-3	205	3-6-73	1991	Semmes, Ala.
Beck, Rod	3	4	3.02	81	0	0	51	80	86	33	27	20	81	R	R	6-1	236	8-3-68	1986	Scottsdale, Ariz.
Clark, Mark	9	14	4.84	33	33	2	0	214	236	116	115	48	161	R	R	6-5	235	5-12-68	1988	Bath, Ill.
Fossas, Tony	0	0	9.00	8	0	0	0	4	8	4	4	6	6	L	L	6-0	198	9-23-57	1979	Fort Lauderdale, Fla.
Foster, Kevin	0	0	16.20	3	0	0	0	3	8	6	6	2	3	R	R	6-1	175	1-13-69	1988	Evanston, Ill.
Gonzalez, Jeremi	7	7	5.32	20	20	1	0	110	124	72	65	41	70	R	R	6-1	180	1-8-75	1992	Maracaibo, Ven.
Haney, Chris	0	0	7.20	5	0	0	0	5	3	4	4	1	4	L	L	6-3	210	11-16-68	1990	Barboursville, Va.
Heredia, Felix	3	0	4.08	30	0	0	0	18	19	9	8	6	16	L	L	6-0	175	6-18-76	1993	Santo Domingo, D.R.
2-team (41 Florida)	3	3	5.06	71	2	0	2	59	57	39	33	38	54							
Karchner, Matt	3	1	5.14	29	0	0	0	28	30	18	16	14	22	R	R	6-4	210	6-28-67	1989	Manassas, Va.
Miller, Kurt	0	0	0.00	3	0	0	0	4	3	0	0	0	6	R	R	6-5	220	8-24-72	1990	Bakersfield, Calif.
Morgan, Mike	0	1	7.15	5	5	0	0	23	30	21	18	15	10	R	R	6-2	220	10-8-59	1978	Park City, Utah
Mulholland, Terry	6	5	2.89	70	6	0	3	112	100	49	36	39	72	R	L	6-3	200	3-9-63	1984	Paradise Valley, Ariz.
Myers, Rodney	0	0	7.00	12	0	0	0	18	26	14	14	6	15	R	R	6-1	205	6-26-69	1990	Chandler, Ariz.
Patterson, Bob	1	1	7.52	33	0	0	1	20	36	20	17	12	17	R	L	6-1	185	5-16-59	1982	Hickory, N.C.
Pisciotta, Marc	1	2	4.09	43	0	0	0	44	44	21	20	32	31	R	R	6-5	225	8-7-70	1991	Marietta, Ga.
Speier, Justin	0	0	13.50	1	0	0	0	1	2	2	2	1	2	R	R	6-4	205	11-6-73	1995	Scottsdale, Ariz.
Steenstra, Kennie	0	0	10.80	4	0	0	0	3	7	4	4	1	4	R	R	6-5	215	10-13-70	1992	Liberty, Mo.
Stevens, Dave	1	2	4.74	31	0	0	0	38	42	20	20	17	31	R	R	6-3	210	3-4-70	1990	La Habra, Calif.
Tapani, Kevin	19	9	4.85	35	34	2	0	219	244	120	118	62	136	R	R	6-1	190	2-18-64	1986	Eden Prairie, Minn.
Telemaco, Amaury	1	1	3.90	14	0	0	0	28	23	12	12	13	18	R	R	6-3	210	1-19-74	1991	La Romana, D.R.
Trachsel, Steve	15	8	4.46	33	33	1	0	208	204	107	103	84	149	R	R	6-4	205	10-31-70	1991	Mesa, Ariz.
VanRyn, Ben	0	0	3.38	9	0	0	0	8	9	3	3	6	6	L	L	6-5	195	8-19-71	1990	San Antonio, Texas
Wengert, Don	1	5	5.07	21	6	0	0	50	55	29	28	23	41	R	R	6-2	212	11-6-69	1992	Sioux City, Iowa
2-team (10 St. Louis)	1	5	5.26	31	6	0	1	63	76	38	37	28	46							
Wood, Kerry	13	6	3.40	26	26	1	0	167	117	69	63	85	233	R	R	6-5	225	6-16-77	1995	Irving, Texas

FIELDING

Catcher	PCT	G	PO	A	E	DP	PB
Houston	.993	63	418	21	3	4	3
Martinez	.985	33	185	7	3	1	1
Servais	.994	110	652	47	4	6	3

First Base	PCT	G	PO	A	E	DP
Brown	1.000	7	32	2	0	2
Grace	.994	156	1281	118	8	82
Hernandez	1.000	3	19	1	0	2
Houston	1.000	7	32	2	0	1
Servais	1.000	1	2	1	0	0

Second Base	PCT	G	PO	A	E	DP
Alexander	.979	27	43	51	2	11
Hernandez	1.000	2	2	4	0	1
Maxwell	1.000	1	0	1	0	0
Morandini	.993	152	265	404	5	70

Third Base	PCT	G	PO	A	E	DP
Alexander	.963	19	8	18	1	1
Gaetti	.979	36	24	68	2	2
Hardtke	1.000	7	0	3	0	0
Hernandez	.958	72	45	115	7	4
Houston	.875	12	1	13	2	1
Orie	.966	57	39	101	5	7

Shortstop	PCT	G	PO	A	E	DP
Alexander	.964	50	37	71	4	15
Blauser	.965	106	129	255	14	36
Hernandez	.963	45	53	103	6	19
Nieves	.000	1	0	0	0	0

Outfield	PCT	G	PO	A	E	DP
Alexander	1.000	1	1	0	0	0
Brown	.963	102	180	1	7	0
Hardtke	.000	1	0	0	0	0
Hernandez	1.000	54	74	3	0	0
Hill	.984	34	57	3	1	0
Johnson	.975	78	154	5	4	2
Lowery	.929	22	13	0	1	0
Merced	1.000	4	3	0	0	0
Mieske	.974	62	36	1	1	0
Rodriguez	.996	114	215	7	1	1
Sosa	.975	159	334	14	9	2
Valdes	1.000	7	10	0	0	0
White	.000	1	0	0	0	0

Chicago's Jose Hernandez
Versatile Cub played everywhere in '98

First baseman Julio Zuleta
Drove in 106 runs at two minor league stops

FARM SYSTEM

Director, Minor Leagues: David Wilder

Class	Farm Team	League	W	L	Pct.	Finish*	Manager	First Yr
AAA	Iowa Cubs	Pacific Coast	85	59	.590	1st (16)	Terry Kennedy	1981
AA	West Tenn Diamond Jaxx	Southern	66	74	.471	t-7th (10)	Dave Trembley	1998
A#	Daytona (Fla.) Cubs	Florida State	67	73	.479	9th (14)	Steve Roadcap	1993
A	Rockford (Ill.) Cubbies	Midwest	71	68	.511	7th (14)	Ruben Amaro	1995
A	Williamsport (Pa.) Cubs	New York-Penn	39	36	.520	6th (14)	Bob Ralston	1994
Rookie	Mesa (Ariz.) Cubs	Arizona	29	26	.527	3rd (8)	Nate Oliver	1997

*Finish in overall standings (No. of teams in league) #Advanced level

IOWA — Class AAA

PACIFIC COAST LEAGUE

BATTING	AVG	G	AB	R	H	2B	3B	HR	RBI	BB	SO	SB	CS	B	T	HT	WT	DOB	1st Yr	Resides
Bridges, Kary	.215	64	181	25	39	10	1	0	14	11	12	0	2	L	R	5-10	165	10-27-71	1993	Hattiesburg, Miss.
Briggs, Stoney	.250	2	4	1	1	0	0	0	1	0	0	0	0	R	R	6-3	215	12-26-71	1991	Seaford, Del.
Brown, Brant	.364	3	11	1	4	0	0	0	0	0	6	0	0	L	L	6-3	205	6-22-71	1992	Porterville, Calif.
Brown, Roosevelt	.333	1	3	0	1	1	0	0	2	0	0	0	0	L	R	5-10	195	8-3-75	1993	Vicksburg, Miss.
Castleberry, Kevin	.327	23	55	11	18	2	1	1	6	5	10	1	1	L	R	5-10	170	4-22-68	1989	Midwest City, Okla.
Cline, Pat	.281	122	424	52	119	22	2	13	60	36	59	2	3	R	R	6-3	220	10-9-74	1993	Bradenton, Fla.
Ellis, Kevin	.205	27	44	5	9	0	0	0	2	1	13	1	0	R	R	6-0	220	11-21-71	1993	Waco, Texas
Franklin, Micah	.329	118	359	74	118	26	2	29	95	59	72	5	3	B	R	6-0	205	4-25-72	1990	San Francisco, Calif.
Gazarek, Marty	.256	88	238	33	61	16	0	4	16	16	38	4	3	R	R	6-2	205	6-1-73	1994	North Baltimore, Ohio
Hardtke, Jason	.288	91	333	67	96	20	1	11	53	35	46	7	7	B	R	5-10	175	9-15-71	1990	Port Washington, N.Y.
Jennings, Robin	.248	81	298	57	74	23	2	16	62	33	49	4	4	L	L	6-2	210	4-11-72	1992	Scottsdale, Ariz.
Lowery, Terrell	.297	65	246	41	73	14	1	12	49	27	63	5	2	R	R	6-3	195	10-25-70	1991	Vallejo, Calif.
Maxwell, Jason	.298	124	483	86	144	40	3	15	60	52	93	8	1	R	R	6-0	185	3-26-72	1993	Lewisburg, Tenn.
McCall, Rod	.252	114	361	78	91	19	0	30	70	64	151	0	2	L	R	6-7	235	11-4-71	1990	Stanton, Calif.
Mieske, Matt	.255	35	106	17	27	5	0	7	19	10	27	0	0	R	R	6-0	195	2-13-68	1990	Mesa, Ariz.
Nieves, Jose	.253	19	75	7	19	4	0	0	4	2	11	1	1	R	R	6-1	180	6-16-75	1992	Guacara, Ven.
Orie, Kevin	.370	24	92	27	34	8	0	9	24	12	15	1	0	R	R	6-4	215	9-1-72	1993	West Chester, Pa.
Petersen, Chris	.234	118	389	54	91	16	2	8	41	21	100	2	4	R	R	5-11	180	11-6-70	1992	Orlando, Fla.
Porter, Bo	.364	4	11	2	4	1	0	0	3	4	4	1	2	R	R	6-2	195	7-5-72	1994	Newark, N.J.
Unroe, Tim	.173	39	104	9	18	5	0	1	9	10	30	1	0	R	R	6-3	200	10-7-70	1992	Round Lake Beach, Ill.
Valdes, Pedro	.314	65	229	49	72	12	0	17	40	27	38	2	1	L	L	6-1	190	6-29-73	1991	Loiza, P.R.
White, Derrick	.363	66	251	57	91	17	2	18	76	38	48	4	5	R	R	6-1	225	10-12-69	1991	Chandler, Ariz.
Zinter, Alan	.310	129	419	82	130	23	1	23	81	75	116	3	5	B	R	6-2	200	5-19-68	1989	Tucson, Ariz.

PITCHING	W	L	ERA	G	GS	CG	SV	IP	H	R	ER	BB	SO	B	T	HT	WT	DOB	1st Yr	Resides
Adams, Terry	0	0	0.00	3	0	0	0	4	1	1	0	3	5	R	R	6-3	205	3-6-73	1991	Semmes, Ala.
Barker, Richie	3	1	4.84	16	0	0	0	22	31	14	12	5	21	R	R	6-2	210	10-29-72	1994	Malden, Mass.
Byrne, Earl	3	3	6.34	10	9	0	0	50	54	37	35	29	34	L	L	6-1	180	7-2-72	1994	Melbourne, Australia
Cole, Victor	2	2	3.74	38	2	0	0	67	77	35	28	25	69	L	R	5-10	175	1-23-68	1988	Cordova, Calif.
Farnsworth, Kyle	5	0	6.03	18	18	0	0	103	129	88	79	36	79	B	R	6-4	205	4-14-76	1995	Roswell, Ga.
Fossas, Tony	0	0	3.60	10	0	0	0	5	10	4	2	2	2	L	L	6-0	198	9-23-57	1979	Fort Lauderdale, Fla.
Foster, Kevin	5	6	6.85	17	11	1	0	67	74	52	51	38	75	R	R	6-1	175	1-13-69	1988	Evanston, Ill.
Gray, Dennis	0	0	6.23	9	0	0	0	13	9	9	9	10	8	L	L	6-6	225	12-24-69	1991	Banning, Calif.
Jimenez, Miguel	0	1	10.13	7	1	0	0	11	15	12	12	7	7	R	R	6-2	220	8-19-69	1991	Mesa, Ariz.
King, Ray	1	3	5.01	37	0	0	2	32	36	20	18	15	26	L	L	6-1	221	1-15-74	1995	Ripley, Tenn.
McNichol, Brian	0	0	7.71	1	1	0	0	7	12	6	6	1	5	L	L	6-6	215	5-20-74	1995	Woodbridge, Va.
Miller, Kurt	14	3	3.81	28	27	2	0	168	153	77	71	77	145	R	R	6-5	220	8-24-72	1990	Bakersfield, Calif.
Myers, Rodney	7	5	3.91	33	13	2	11	101	84	47	44	45	86	R	R	6-1	205	6-26-69	1990	Chandler, Ariz.
Pisciotta, Marc	3	5	6.46	28	0	0	8	31	34	24	22	16	29	R	R	6-5	225	8-7-70	1991	Marietta, Ga.
Rain, Steve	4	6	6.68	29	14	1	0	104	118	82	77	64	83	R	R	6-6	230	6-2-75	1993	Walnut, Calif.
Speier, Justin	3	3	5.05	45	0	0	12	52	52	31	29	19	49	R	R	6-4	205	11-6-73	1995	Scottsdale, Ariz.
Steenstra, Kennie	11	5	4.38	25	24	1	0	148	171	84	72	36	104	R	R	6-5	215	10-13-70	1992	Liberty, Mo.
Stevens, Dave	4	1	3.08	26	0	0	2	50	41	19	17	16	39	R	R	6-3	210	3-4-70	1990	La Habra, Calif.
Swartzbaugh, Dave	14	5	3.73	42	14	0	1	138	114	61	57	50	109	R	R	6-2	195	2-11-68	1989	Middletown, Ohio
Twiggs, Greg	2	0	4.15	7	0	0	0	9	12	6	4	6	4	R	L	5-11	165	10-15-71	1993	Winter Springs, Fla.
Wengert, Don	3	1	4.58	9	9	1	0	53	58	30	27	14	48	R	R	6-2	212	11-6-69	1992	Sioux City, Iowa
Wood, Kerry	1	0	0.00	1	1	0	0	5	1	0	0	2	11	R	R	6-5	225	6-16-77	1995	Irving, Texas
Worrell, Steve	0	0	4.20	18	0	0	0	15	25	9	7	4	14	L	L	6-2	200	11-25-69	1992	Ocala, Fla.
Young, Danny	0	0	0.00	2	0	0	0	2	1	0	0	1	1	R	L	6-4	210	11-3-71	1991	Columbus, Ohio

FIELDING

Catcher	PCT	G	PO	A	E	DP	PB
Cline	.987	112	806	50	11	3	18
Ellis	1.000	4	7	1	0	0	0
Zinter	.989	39	262	19	3	4	8

First Base	PCT	G	PO	A	E	DP
Brown	1.000	1	2	0	0	0
Ellis	1.000	1	7	1	0	1
Jennings	1.000	3	6	0	0	1
McCall	.987	84	681	57	10	74
Unroe	1.000	5	18	0	0	1
White	1.000	6	46	3	0	7
Zinter	.992	66	451	25	4	44

Second Base	PCT	G	PO	A	E	DP
Bridges	.971	23	24	42	2	6
Castleberry	.956	11	13	30	2	7
Hardtke	.951	17	28	50	4	12
Maxwell	.975	104	208	265	12	68
Petersen	.778	2	0	7	2	0
Unroe	1.000	2	1	4	0	1

Third Base	PCT	G	PO	A	E	DP
Bridges	.967	26	11	48	2	6
Castleberry	1.000	3	3	4	0	0
Franklin	.800	5	1	7	2	0
Hardtke	.944	66	40	94	8	7
Orie	.960	24	7	41	2	2
Unroe	.984	29	14	49	1	8
Zinter	.857	9	3	9	2	0

Shortstop	PCT	G	PO	A	E	DP
Maxwell	.946	22	29	41	4	11
Nieves	.960	19	35	61	4	16
Petersen	.985	113	167	347	8	78

Outfield	PCT	G	PO	A	E	DP
Bridges	.000	1	0	0	0	0
Briggs	.000	1	0	0	0	0
Brown	1.000	2	3	0	0	0
Ellis	1.000	2	3	2	0	1
Franklin	.980	94	141	4	3	0
Gazarek	.974	76	142	10	4	2
Jennings	.962	79	123	5	5	2
Lowery	.994	62	155	5	1	0
Mieske	.950	28	35	3	2	0
Porter	1.000	3	6	0	0	0
Unroe	1.000	3	4	0	0	0
Valdes	.965	60	106	3	4	0
White	.975	59	111	5	3	0
Zinter	.909	5	9	1	1	0

WEST TENN — Class AA

SOUTHERN LEAGUE

BATTING	AVG	G	AB	R	H	2B	3B	HR	RBI	BB	SO	SB	CS	B	T	HT	WT	DOB	1st Yr	Resides
Bridges, Kary	.306	48	196	30	60	7	1	0	21	18	9	6	4	L	R	5-10	165	10-27-71	1993	Hattiesburg, Miss.
Brown, Roosevelt	.263	42	160	20	42	11	0	6	24	13	30	3	1	L	R	5-10	195	8-3-75	1993	Vicksburg, Miss.
Castleberry, Kevin	.285	44	151	26	43	9	1	1	15	21	19	7	4	L	R	5-10	170	4-22-68	1989	Midwest City, Okla.
Cotton, John	.292	90	319	46	93	14	3	13	53	19	68	10	3	L	R	6-0	170	10-30-70	1989	Huntsville, Texas
Curtis, Kevin	.161	22	62	6	10	1	1	1	10	6	17	0	0	R	R	6-2	210	8-19-72	1993	Upland, Calif.
Ellis, Kevin	.172	12	29	3	5	0	0	1	2	1	3	0	0	R	R	6-0	220	11-21-71	1993	Waco, Texas
Forkerway, Trey	.197	57	152	13	30	2	0	1	6	21	28	4	2	R	R	5-10	180	5-17-71	1993	Abilene, Texas
Freeman, Ricky	.270	106	370	67	100	18	4	15	76	45	50	7	5	R	R	6-4	210	2-3-72	1994	Houston, Texas
Gazarek, Marty	.328	21	64	14	21	4	2	1	11	13	10	6	2	R	R	6-2	205	6-1-73	1994	North Baltimore, Ohio
Hall, Ronnie	.207	46	135	15	28	7	0	0	12	16	38	1	2	R	R	6-4	215	10-14-75	1993	Tustin, Calif.
Jennings, Robin	.000	2	6	0	0	0	0	0	0	0	2	0	0	L	L	6-2	210	4-11-72	1992	Scottsdale, Ariz.
Joseph, Terry	.220	37	118	24	26	2	1	2	11	11	28	3	3	R	R	5-10	190	11-20-73	1995	Harvey, La.
Manning, Nate	.193	16	57	5	11	1	0	0	6	2	14	0	2	R	R	6-2	215	12-20-73	1996	Keosauqua, Iowa
McNabb, Buck	.294	124	385	62	113	21	5	6	48	51	61	22	13	L	R	6-0	180	1-17-73	1991	Fort Walton Beach, Fla.
Meyers, Chad	.270	77	293	63	79	14	0	0	26	58	43	37	9	R	R	6-0	185	8-8-75	1996	Papillion, Neb.
Micucci, Mike	.290	53	138	20	40	11	1	0	21	17	18	0	0	L	R	5-11	190	12-15-72	1994	Emerson, N.J.
Millette, Joe	.000	1	3	0	0	0	0	0	0	0	0	0	0	R	R	6-1	185	8-12-66	1989	Lafayette, Calif.
Molina, Jose	.222	109	320	33	71	10	1	2	28	32	74	1	5	R	R	6-1	195	6-3-75	1993	Vega Alta, P.R.
Nelson, Bry	.284	32	102	10	29	6	2	2	18	12	12	4	2	B	R	5-10	205	1-27-74	1994	Crossett, Ark.
Nieves, Jose	.290	82	314	42	91	27	5	8	39	18	55	17	10	R	R	6-1	180	6-16-75	1992	Guacara, Ven.
Nunez, Raymond	.307	78	225	27	69	15	2	7	45	16	62	3	4	R	R	6-0	150	9-22-72	1990	Manzanillo, D.R.
Patel, Manny	.200	7	15	1	3	1	0	0	1	2	5	1	1	L	R	5-10	165	4-22-72	1993	Tampa, Fla.
Porter, Bo	.289	125	464	91	134	26	11	10	68	82	117	50	17	R	R	6-2	195	7-5-72	1994	Newark, N.J.
Unroe, Tim	.241	16	54	6	13	6	0	0	9	8	20	0	0	R	R	6-3	200	10-7-70	1992	Round Lake Beach, Ill.
Valette, Ramon	.218	36	101	11	22	5	2	1	9	9	25	0	0	R	R	6-1	175	1-20-72	1990	Sabana Grande, D.R.
Williams, Juan	.223	70	188	31	42	9	6	3	36	39	63	1	6	L	R	6-0	180	10-9-72	1990	Riverside, Calif.
Zuleta, Julio	.295	40	139	18	41	9	0	2	20	10	30	0	1	R	R	6-6	230	3-28-75	1993	El Dorado, Panama

PITCHING	W	L	ERA	G	GS	CG	SV	IP	H	R	ER	BB	SO	B	T	HT	WT	DOB	1st Yr	Resides
Barker, Richie	2	5	2.68	51	0	0	16	54	51	22	16	17	23	R	R	6-2	210	10-29-72	1994	Malden, Mass.
Brown, Darold	0	0	4.50	6	0	0	0	8	8	4	4	5	5	L	L	6-0	195	8-16-73	1993	San Jose, Calif.
Byrne, Earl	5	5	4.83	15	15	0	0	86	80	50	46	36	94	L	L	6-1	180	7-2-72	1994	Melbourne, Australia
Cole, Victor	2	2	2.40	19	0	0	0	30	26	12	8	11	31	L	R	5-10	175	1-23-68	1988	Cordova, Calif.
Duncan, Courtney	7	9	4.26	29	29	0	0	163	141	89	77	108	157	L	R	6-0	180	10-9-74	1996	Daphne, Ala.
Farnsworth, Kyle	8	2	2.77	13	13	0	0	81	70	32	25	21	73	B	R	6-4	205	4-14-76	1995	Roswell, Ga.
Foster, Kevin	1	0	2.25	2	0	0	0	4	5	1	1	1	5	R	R	6-1	175	1-13-69	1988	Evanston, Ill.

PITCHING	W	L	ERA	G	GS	CG	SV	IP	H	R	ER	BB	SO	B	T	HT	WT	DOB	1st Yr	Resides
Garcia, Al	4	5	4.96	25	10	0	0	78	89	47	43	16	39	B	R	6-4	175	6-11-74	1993	Buena Park, Calif.
Gissell, Chris	0	1	13.50	1	1	0	0	4	5	7	6	4	4	R	R	6-4	180	1-4-78	1996	Vancouver, Wash.
Grigsby, Benji	2	3	4.31	32	1	0	0	48	58	35	23	17	29	R	R	6-1	190	12-2-70	1992	Huntsville, Ala.
Hammack, Brandon	3	0	2.45	21	0	0	3	26	14	7	7	16	22	R	R	6-5	240	3-5-73	1995	Amarillo, Texas
Jimenez, Miguel	1	3	4.75	26	0	0	0	30	30	18	16	18	32	R	R	6-2	220	8-19-69	1991	Mesa, Ariz.
King, Ray	1	2	2.43	25	0	0	3	30	23	9	8	10	26	L	L	6-1	221	1-15-74	1995	Ripley, Tenn.
Linebarger, Keith	3	3	5.31	50	0	0	2	59	79	38	35	24	45	R	R	6-6	220	5-11-71	1992	Ringgold, Ga.
McNichol, Brian	12	9	3.72	28	26	4	0	179	170	88	74	62	168	L	L	6-6	215	5-20-74	1995	Woodbridge, Va.
Norton, Phillip	6	6	3.52	19	19	1	0	120	118	60	47	50	119	B	L	6-1	180	2-1-76	1996	Texarkana, Texas
Ricketts, Chad	0	2	3.52	13	0	0	6	15	19	7	6	4	13	R	R	6-5	225	2-12-75	1995	Thorold, Ontario
Ryan, Jason	3	13	4.88	30	25	2	0	148	172	97	80	57	121	B	R	6-3	185	1-23-76	1994	Charlotte, N.C.
Schutz, Carl	1	1	1.20	13	0	0	0	15	6	7	2	18	10	L	L	5-11	200	8-22-71	1993	Paulina, La.
2-team (33 Greenville)	2	4	4.33	46	0	0	4	52	47	36	25	50	43							
Worrell, Steve	5	1	3.66	32	0	0	1	32	40	17	13	15	37	L	L	6-2	200	11-25-69	1992	Ocala, Fla.
Young, Danny	0	2	3.67	23	1	0	0	27	22	13	11	15	20	R	L	6-4	210	11-3-71	1991	Columbus, Ohio

FIELDING

Catcher	PCT	G	PO	A	E	DP	PB
Ellis	.983	10	54	5	1	1	2
Micucci	.985	51	300	29	5	1	7
Molina	.991	104	739	108	8	2	21

First Base	PCT	G	PO	A	E	DP
Cotton	1.000	18	140	11	0	9
Curtis	1.000	2	3	0	0	1
Freeman	.989	85	695	42	8	52
Molina	.833	1	5	0	1	0
Nunez	.985	20	127	8	2	10
Zuleta	.991	32	203	18	2	19

Second Base	PCT	G	PO	A	E	DP
Bridges	.984	32	58	68	2	14
Castleberry	.967	18	19	40	2	7
Cotton	1.000	9	9	22	0	5
Forkerway	1.000	1	1	0	0	0
Meyers	.934	73	154	173	23	43
Nieves	1.000	1	0	1	0	0
Patel	.960	7	12	12	1	2
Unroe	1.000	1	2	2	0	0
Valette	.956	17	16	27	2	7

Third Base	PCT	G	PO	A	E	DP
Bridges	.977	22	8	34	1	1
Castleberry	1.000	8	2	14	0	2
Cotton	.877	29	17	47	9	4
Forkerway	1.000	4	0	7	0	0
Manning	.841	16	10	27	7	4
Millette	.667	1	2	0	1	0
Nelson	.899	28	25	46	8	9
Nunez	.900	34	16	47	7	2
Unroe	.865	15	15	30	7	1
Valette	.867	6	4	9	2	2

Shortstop	PCT	G	PO	A	E	DP
Castleberry	.833	11	11	14	5	3
Forkerway	.971	51	60	106	5	17
Nelson	1.000	7	1	4	0	2
Nieves	.934	81	130	210	24	31
Valette	.949	12	12	25	2	5

Outfield	PCT	G	PO	A	E	DP
Brown	.956	41	61	4	3	0
Castleberry	1.000	11	6	2	0	0
Cotton	.977	36	40	2	1	0
Curtis	.889	8	8	0	1	0
Ellis	.000	1	0	0	0	0
Freeman	1.000	19	28	0	0	0
Gazarek	1.000	20	38	5	0	1
Hall	.932	41	62	7	5	1
Jennings	1.000	2	1	0	0	0
Joseph	.977	28	42	0	1	0
McNabb	.979	107	181	9	4	0
Porter	.989	125	258	10	3	0
Williams	.969	42	58	4	2	1

DAYTONA — Class A

FLORIDA STATE LEAGUE

BATTING	AVG	G	AB	R	H	2B	3B	HR	RBI	BB	SO	SB	CS	B	T	HT	WT	DOB	1st Yr	Resides
Abreu, Dennis	.260	127	535	87	139	21	5	2	58	31	133	23	14	R	R	6-0	180	4-22-78	1995	Tumero, Ven.
Brown, Roosevelt	.344	68	244	49	84	15	5	9	43	23	46	3	2	L	R	5-10	195	8-3-75	1993	Vicksburg, Miss.
Cotton, John	.292	12	48	8	14	4	0	3	11	3	8	0	0	L	R	6-0	170	10-30-70	1989	Huntsville, Texas
Font, Franklin	.294	60	204	26	60	2	1	0	16	18	35	7	6	R	R	5-10	175	11-4-77	1995	Caracas, Ven.
Forkerway, Trey	.149	35	74	9	11	2	1	1	11	8	6	0	1	R	R	5-10	180	5-17-71	1993	Abilene, Texas
Fuller, Aaron	.295	79	292	63	86	17	7	4	36	64	50	18	4	B	R	5-10	170	9-7-71	1993	Sacramento, Calif.
Hall, Ronnie	.000	1	4	0	0	0	0	0	0	0	3	0	0	R	R	6-4	215	10-14-75	1993	Tustin, Calif.
Hubbard, Jeremy	.000	5	6	0	0	0	0	0	0	0	2	0	0	R	R	5-8	165	8-25-76	1997	Roseburg, Ore.
Jasco, Elinton	.314	45	156	37	49	5	4	0	24	16	34	25	4	R	R	5-10	165	5-11-75	1993	San Pedro de Macoris, D.R.
Johnson, Gary	.232	116	413	61	96	12	0	12	55	53	101	10	2	R	R	6-3	200	9-6-76	1997	Baldwin Park, Calif.
King, Brad	.293	84	276	49	81	17	0	1	37	30	37	5	6	R	R	6-2	205	12-3-74	1996	Boca Raton, Fla.
Lisanti, Bob	.100	12	10	1	1	0	0	0	1	1	4	0	0	R	R	5-10	180	5-28-73	1996	Chicago, Ill.
Manning, Nate	.269	108	427	61	115	23	1	16	71	26	89	2	4	R	R	6-2	215	12-20-73	1996	Keosauqua, Iowa
Meyers, Chad	.323	48	186	39	60	8	3	3	25	33	29	23	7	R	R	6-0	185	8-8-75	1996	Papillion, Neb.
Ramsey, Brad	.288	89	312	49	90	25	1	6	37	32	64	4	1	R	R	6-4	215	11-7-76	1997	West Monroe, La.
Rico, Diego	.276	108	366	70	101	22	7	7	58	51	76	18	7	L	L	6-0	175	3-24-76	1997	Tucson, Ariz.
Speed, Dorian	.268	85	250	43	67	11	5	6	34	20	56	13	5	R	R	6-3	195	3-1-74	1995	Tempe, Ariz.
Vieira, Scott	.370	15	54	11	20	6	0	1	13	9	12	3	0	R	R	5-11	195	8-17-73	1995	San Ramon, Calif.
Walker, Ron	.286	100	357	57	102	20	1	24	78	46	80	5	2	R	R	6-2	215	12-29-75	1997	Vincent Town, N.J.
Williams, Juan	.200	17	65	15	13	4	0	1	8	14	23	2	1	L	R	6-0	180	10-9-72	1990	Riverside, Calif.
Yedo, Carlos	.223	56	206	26	46	10	1	7	43	27	53	0	0	L	L	6-4	210	2-24-74	1994	Miami, Fla.
Zuleta, Julio	.344	94	366	69	126	25	1	16	86	35	59	6	3	R	R	6-6	230	3-28-75	1993	El Dorado, Panama

GAMES BY POSITION: C—Hubbard 4, King 75, Lisanti 12, Ramsey 70, Vieira 2. **1B**—Johnson 2, Manning 26, Vieira 5, Walker 1, Yedo 37, Zuleta 76. **2B**—Font 39, Forkerway 21, Fuller 7, Jasco 39, King 1, Meyers 48. **3B**—Cotton 5, Font 12, Forkerway 7, King 2, Manning 54, Rico 1, Walker 74. **SS**—Abreu 125, Font 14, Forkerway 6. **OF**—Brown 64, Cotton 7, Forkerway 2, Fuller 61, Hall 1, Jasco 4, Johnson 113, King 5, Meyers 1, Rico 101, Speed 79, Vieira 9, Walker 1, Williams 3.

PITCHING	W	L	ERA	G	GS	CG	SV	IP	H	R	ER	BB	SO	B	T	HT	WT	DOB	1st Yr	Resides
Brookens, Casey	3	3	6.61	23	1	0	0	33	40	30	24	22	19	R	R	6-0	185	11-24-73	1996	Fayetteville, Pa.
Cannon, Jon	0	3	3.73	7	7	1	0	31	37	22	13	12	28	R	L	6-3	195	1-1-75	1996	Los Altos, Calif.
DeJesus, Javier	5	5	5.23	43	1	0	0	53	63	34	31	24	55	L	L	5-10	198	8-3-71	1992	Fort Wayne, Ind.
Downs, Scott	8	9	3.90	27	27	2	0	162	179	83	70	55	117	L	L	6-2	180	3-17-76	1997	Louisville, Ky.
Espinal, Jose	10	10	4.73	28	22	0	0	145	165	95	76	50	117	R	R	6-1	185	8-31-76	1994	Pedernales, D.R.
Fennell, Barry	2	2	2.59	24	0	0	2	31	30	16	9	22	24	R	L	6-4	215	9-30-76	1994	Pennsauken, N.J.
Fisher, Louis	3	4	4.66	49	1	0	1	66	50	40	34	38	54	R	R	6-0	200	10-14-76	1995	Oakland, Calif.
Foster, Kevin	0	0	10.13	3	0	0	0	3	2	7	3	7	3	R	R	6-1	175	1-13-69	1988	Evanston, Ill.
Gissell, Chris	7	6	4.17	22	21	1	0	136	149	80	63	38	123	R	R	6-4	180	1-4-78	1996	Vancouver, Wash.
Hart, Len	3	3	3.55	37	0	0	2	51	52	28	20	20	46	L	L	5-11	190	10-8-73	1996	Oak Ridge, Tenn.
Hoff, Steve	0	3	7.24	6	6	0	0	27	38	25	22	12	26	L	L	6-4	205	7-1-77	1996	San Bruno, Calif.
2-team (15 Brevard)	5	11	4.87	21	21	2	0	113	131	75	61	39	71							
Markey, Barry	7	6	4.81	43	9	0	3	107	119	62	57	31	59	R	R	6-5	205	7-20-75	1995	St. Petersburg, Fla.
Norton, Phillip	4	3	3.27	10	10	0	0	66	57	30	24	26	54	B	L	6-1	180	2-1-76	1996	Texarkana, Texas
Ricketts, Chad	2	1	1.84	47	0	0	19	49	41	15	10	11	59	R	R	6-5	225	2-12-75	1995	Thorold, Ontario

PITCHING	W	L	ERA	G	GS	CG	SV	IP	H	R	ER	BB	SO	B	T	HT	WT	DOB	1st Yr	Resides
Sorzano, Ronnie	0	2	6.64	23	0	0	1	42	50	35	31	17	31	R	R	6-3	180	3-7-76	1994	Caracas, Ven.
Teut, Nate	5	3	5.48	11	11	1	0	66	88	48	40	19	54	R	L	6-7	205	3-11-76	1997	Monroe, Iowa
Yoder, Jeff	7	9	5.03	26	24	1	0	143	158	97	80	47	128	L	R	6-2	210	2-16-76	1996	Pottsville, Pa.
Young, Danny	1	1	5.19	7	0	0	0	9	9	5	5	8	6	R	L	6-4	210	11-3-71	1991	Columbus, Ohio

ROCKFORD — Class A

MIDWEST LEAGUE

BATTING	AVG	G	AB	R	H	2B	3B	HR	RBI	BB	SO	SB	CS	B	T	HT	WT	DOB	1st Yr	Resides
Abreu, Nelson	.264	89	269	38	71	13	6	7	41	31	59	8	6	R	R	5-9	180	8-16-76	1994	Tumero, Ven.
Amrhein, Mike	.317	121	457	61	145	34	1	9	87	30	47	7	4	R	R	6-2	200	6-14-75	1997	Oak Park, Ill.
Bly, Derrick	.292	135	490	64	143	40	7	4	65	58	147	10	5	R	R	6-0	200	9-19-74	1996	Tucson, Ariz.
Carter, Quincy	.248	27	101	9	25	6	0	2	14	11	18	9	2	R	R	6-3	215	10-13-77	1996	Ellenwood, Ga.
Connell, Gerald	.168	82	256	22	43	11	1	3	17	23	84	7	0	R	R	6-2	200	7-17-77	1995	Avenel, N.J.
Font, Franklin	.270	66	237	34	64	5	2	0	15	20	39	25	6	R	R	5-10	175	11-4-77	1995	Caracas, Ven.
Grubbs, Chris	.156	39	96	8	15	3	1	0	1	15	38	0	1	R	R	6-3	195	12-27-75	1996	Ocoee, Fla.
Hinske, Eric	.450	6	20	8	9	4	0	1	4	5	6	1	0	L	R	6-1	215	8-5-77	1998	Neenah, Wis.
Jasco, Elinton	.279	12	43	8	12	1	0	0	3	2	12	2	3	R	R	5-10	165	5-11-75	1993	San Pedro de Macoris, D.R.
Jimenez, Felipe	.221	120	367	46	81	11	4	1	36	28	126	36	11	R	R	6-3	200	12-22-76	1994	Camatagua, Ven.
Johnson, Jason	.241	76	232	35	56	6	1	5	22	21	43	13	5	R	R	6-2	190	2-1-76	1994	Vallejo, Calif.
King, Willie	.121	13	33	3	4	0	0	0	0	4	11	0	0	L	R	6-1	210	5-31-78	1996	Brooklyn, N.Y.
Lisanti, Bob	.227	26	75	7	17	7	0	1	14	14	18	2	0	R	R	5-10	180	5-28-73	1996	Chicago, Ill.
Longmire, Marcel	.161	40	124	10	20	4	1	0	11	13	36	6	2	R	R	6-2	220	4-18-78	1996	Vallejo, Calif.
Meadows, Tydus	.291	35	134	35	39	5	0	7	24	15	32	6	1	R	R	6-2	220	9-5-77	1998	Hardwick, Ga.
Medina, Luis	.194	10	36	2	7	2	0	0	1	2	6	1	0	R	R	6-2	200	5-14-79	1996	Valencia, Ven.
Melo, Ramon	.333	11	33	7	11	1	0	1	5	3	9	4	0	R	R	5-11	160	12-7-79	1996	Bani, D.R.
Randolph, Jaisen	.289	128	491	78	142	18	9	1	33	40	113	32	21	R	R	6-0	180	1-19-79	1997	Tampa, Fla.
Salazar, Juan	.255	100	322	39	82	20	1	4	53	44	85	7	3	B	R	6-3	240	10-31-77	1994	Valencia, Ven.
Santiago, Arnold	.218	34	110	12	24	2	1	0	9	2	21	1	1	R	R	6-3	220	10-29-75	1994	Carolina, P.R.
Schrager, Tony	.251	50	167	38	42	12	1	6	19	43	32	3	2	R	R	6-1	180	6-14-77	1998	Omaha, Neb.
Smith, Jason	.239	126	464	67	111	15	9	7	60	31	122	23	6	L	R	6-3	190	7-24-77	1997	Coatopa, Ala.
Yedo, Carlos	.290	9	31	6	9	5	0	2	10	5	8	0	0	L	L	6-4	210	2-24-74	1994	Miami, Fla.

GAMES BY POSITION: C—Amrhein 72, Grubbs 31, Lisanti 26, Longmire 4, Salazar 22. **1B**—Amrhein 33, Bly 27, Hinske 4, Longmire 5, Medina 6, Salazar 54, Santiago 28, Yedo 8. **2B**—Abreu 17, Font 66, Jasco 12, Melo 1, Schrager 50. **3B**—Abreu 30, Bly 117, Medina 4, Melo 2, Salazar 2. **SS**—Abreu 30, Bly 1, Melo 8, Smith 113. **OF**—Abreu 20, Carter 17, Connell 63, Hinske 4, Jimenez 115, Johnson 52, Longmire 24, Meadows 33, Randolph 121.

PITCHING	W	L	ERA	G	GS	CG	SV	IP	H	R	ER	BB	SO	B	T	HT	WT	DOB	1st Yr	Resides
Booker, Chris	1	2	3.36	44	1	0	4	64	47	32	24	53	78	R	R	6-3	215	12-9-76	1995	Monroeville, Ala.
Delano, Michael	2	1	5.40	5	5	0	0	23	23	17	14	17	20	L	L	6-7	205	11-9-77	1997	Las Vegas, Nev.
Fennell, Barry	2	0	0.64	17	0	0	6	28	14	2	2	12	25	R	L	6-4	215	9-30-76	1994	Pennsauken, N.J.
Garland, Jon	4	7	5.03	19	19	1	0	107	124	69	60	45	70	R	R	6-6	200	9-27-79	1997	Granada Hills, Calif.
Gissell, Chris	3	0	0.80	5	5	0	0	34	27	8	3	15	23	R	R	6-4	180	1-4-78	1996	Vancouver, Wash.
Kelley, Jason	0	0	3.78	9	0	0	0	17	9	8	7	13	14	R	R	6-1	230	11-14-75	1994	Live Oak, Fla.
Lohse, Kyle	13	8	3.22	28	26	3	0	171	158	76	61	45	121	R	R	6-2	190	10-4-78	1997	Glenn, Calif.
Magers, Mathew	2	6	2.60	50	0	0	5	52	57	26	15	32	31	L	L	6-1	190	3-31-76	1997	Gaylord, Minn.
Mallory, Andrew	2	7	7.23	33	1	0	0	61	63	59	49	43	44	R	R	6-2	160	9-25-76	1996	St. Petersburg, Fla.
Meyers, Mike	7	5	3.36	17	16	0	0	86	75	37	32	32	86	R	R	6-2	210	10-18-77	1997	Tillsonburg, Ontario
Noel, Todd	6	6	4.03	16	16	1	0	89	83	45	40	37	70	R	R	6-4	205	9-28-78	1996	Maurice, La.
Ohman, William	1	1	4.44	4	4	0	0	24	25	13	12	7	21	L	L	6-2	190	8-13-77	1998	Parker, Colo.
Palma, Ricardo	7	6	4.46	21	19	0	0	103	114	59	51	36	65	L	L	6-1	160	9-26-79	1996	Maracay, Ven.
Piersoll, Chris	2	0	3.92	27	4	1	2	60	52	28	26	20	55	R	R	6-4	195	9-25-77	1997	Carlsbad, Calif.
Polanco, Elvis	6	6	5.82	26	7	0	0	68	81	50	44	40	51	R	R	6-2	195	3-10-78	1994	Puerto Cabello, Ven.
Sorzano, Ronnie	1	1	5.68	9	0	0	2	13	25	11	8	8	9	R	R	6-3	180	3-7-76	1994	Caracas, Ven.
Sullivan, Shane	4	3	3.66	41	0	0	2	71	67	31	29	32	56	R	R	6-2	215	12-10-77	1997	Pinon Hills, Calif.
Teut, Nate	8	5	3.31	16	16	1	0	103	99	49	38	23	67	R	L	6-7	205	3-11-76	1997	Monroe, Iowa
Waligora, Tom	0	4	4.81	35	0	0	18	34	36	22	18	14	32	R	R	6-8	230	8-7-76	1997	Richmond, Va.

WILLIAMSPORT — Short-Season Class A

NEW YORK-PENN LEAGUE

BATTING	AVG	G	AB	R	H	2B	3B	HR	RBI	BB	SO	SB	CS	B	T	HT	WT	DOB	1st Yr	Resides
Boles, Kevin	.206	20	34	2	7	1	0	0	3	1	11	0	0	L	R	5-11	185	1-16-75	1998	Chicago, Ill.
Connally, Chris	.298	56	198	38	59	13	4	9	43	25	37	5	3	R	R	5-11	190	5-24-76	1998	Midland, Texas
De la Cruz, Henry	.272	66	224	36	61	8	4	3	26	23	90	16	9	R	R	6-0	175	8-25-76	1994	Santo Domingo, D.R.
Eaddy, Deon	.211	49	142	10	30	5	2	0	11	18	30	4	0	R	R	5-10	160	9-25-76	1997	Florence, S.C.
Frese, Nate	.218	54	174	28	38	8	0	2	18	16	38	5	2	R	R	6-4	190	7-10-77	1998	Norway, Iowa
Griffin, Matt	.256	64	207	32	53	11	0	4	29	24	33	13	5	R	R	6-1	192	12-24-75	1998	Miami, Fla.
Hargreaves, Brad	.260	47	131	15	34	4	0	0	18	7	22	3	1	R	R	6-0	175	10-30-77	1997	Cincinnati, Ohio
Hinske, Eric	.298	68	248	46	74	20	0	9	57	35	61	19	3	L	R	6-1	215	8-5-77	1998	Neenah, Wis.
Hubbard, Jeremy	.167	12	30	4	5	1	0	0	3	2	4	0	0	B	R	5-8	165	8-25-76	1997	Roseburg, Ore.
Kato, Takaaki	.253	58	154	19	39	10	1	0	19	24	30	1	1	L	R	5-10	190	5-1-74	1998	Kawasaki City, Japan
Longmire, Marcel	.202	58	173	20	35	6	2	4	19	9	50	5	4	R	R	6-2	220	4-18-78	1996	Vallejo, Calif.
Medina, Luis	.184	36	114	14	21	2	0	0	9	3	19	4	2	R	R	6-2	200	5-14-79	1996	Valencia, Ven.
Melo, Ramon	.382	10	34	6	13	6	0	1	4	1	4	2	1	R	R	5-11	160	12-7-79	1996	Bani, D.R.
Moreno, Mikel	.273	73	286	51	78	13	4	2	28	19	51	23	8	R	R	5-10	180	9-5-75	1998	Mesa, Ariz.
Payne, Ron	.231	48	169	27	39	9	5	2	23	16	42	8	5	L	L	6-0	180	1-9-76	1997	Waldorf, Md.
Schrager, Tony	.192	8	26	4	5	0	0	0	3	5	9	3	1	R	R	6-1	180	6-14-77	1998	Omaha, Neb.
Wallis, Michael	.202	38	89	7	18	1	2	0	5	7	18	0	0	L	L	5-11	180	8-13-75	1998	Carmichael, Calif.

GAMES BY POSITION: C—Boles 11, Hargreaves 47, Hubbard 11, Longmire 25. **1B**—Hinske 68, Kato 3, Longmire 7. **2B**—Eaddy 1, Griffin 38, Melo 4, Moreno 29, Schrager 8. **3B**—Eaddy 37, Griffin 14, Medina 36. **SS**—Eaddy 7, Frese 53, Griffin 14, Melo 5. **OF**—Connally 54, de la Cruz 65, Longmire 5, Melo 1, Moreno 36, Payne 48, Wallis 35.

PITCHING	W	L	ERA	G	GS	CG	SV	IP	H	R	ER	BB	SO	B	T	HT	WT	DOB	1st Yr	Resides
Brown, Chris	2	1	2.97	28	0	0	0	39	35	14	13	18	31	R	R	6-0	170	12-26-74	1998	Trinidad, Colo.
Bruback, Matt	2	7	3.93	14	14	0	0	66	62	46	29	45	43	R	R	6-7	185	1-12-79	1998	Sarasota, Fla.
Dant, Larry	4	3	4.12	26	0	0	0	39	41	23	18	16	29	R	R	6-4	225	9-2-76	1998	Atlantic, Iowa
Delano, Michael	4	1	2.44	9	9	0	0	44	32	16	12	24	60	L	L	6-7	205	11-9-77	1997	Las Vegas, Nev.
Delatori, Keola	2	2	3.97	11	9	0	0	48	33	25	21	35	41	R	R	6-0	180	12-23-78	1998	Schaumburg, Ill.
Gunderson, Matt	0	0	1.19	27	0	0	7	38	21	10	5	20	39	R	R	6-1	185	4-29-77	1998	Salem, Ore.
Hammons, Matt	1	1	4.24	3	3	0	0	17	13	8	8	7	14	R	R	6-3	205	4-9-77	1995	San Diego, Calif.
Krug, Dustin	1	1	1.48	27	0	0	4	30	26	6	5	8	26	R	R	6-4	205	3-6-77	1998	Kodiak, Alaska
Ohman, Will	4	4	6.46	10	7	0	0	39	39	32	28	13	35	L	L	6-2	190	8-13-77	1998	Parker, Colo.
Powalski, Richard	1	2	5.24	18	0	0	0	34	36	24	20	19	20	L	L	6-9	190	5-9-78	1997	Clearwater, Fla.
Sams, Aaron	6	5	3.43	15	14	2	0	79	66	40	30	47	72	L	L	6-1	195	4-30-76	1998	Bedford, Pa.
Torres, Leonardo	1	2	0.92	27	0	0	2	39	24	7	4	15	36	L	L	6-3	190	5-11-76	1998	Yuma, Ariz.
Wuertz, Michael	7	5	3.44	14	14	1	0	86	79	36	33	19	59	R	R	6-3	180	12-15-78	1997	Austin, Minn.
Zamarripa, Tony	4	2	3.97	17	5	0	0	45	46	23	20	17	34	R	R	6-4	240	12-17-76	1998	Austin, Texas

MESA — Rookie

ARIZONA LEAGUE

BATTING	AVG	G	AB	R	H	2B	3B	HR	RBI	BB	SO	SB	CS	B	T	HT	WT	DOB	1st Yr	Resides
Aldrup, Morey	.242	18	62	14	15	2	0	3	9	9	15	2	1	R	R	5-10	165	12-23-78	1997	Santa Ana, Calif.
Bass, Kevin	.147	23	75	8	11	1	1	1	8	6	22	1	3	B	R	6-0	210	6-22-79	1998	Fayette, Ala.
Clarke, Jason	.343	35	140	30	48	10	4	2	25	12	15	7	4	B	R	5-9	170	10-17-75	1998	Frederiksted, V.I.
Dorsett, Chris	.309	20	55	14	17	5	0	2	18	9	8	1	0	R	R	6-2	220	4-5-75	1998	Cranford, N.J.
Fukuhara, Pete	.286	49	182	37	52	16	0	3	36	25	23	5	7	R	R	5-10	175	10-21-75	1998	Palo Alto, Calif.
German, Franklin	.238	41	164	22	39	11	0	1	13	7	53	8	6	R	R	5-10	160	2-28-80	1997	Santo Domingo, D.R.
Goldbach, Jeff	.265	38	136	22	36	11	2	4	25	11	41	5	2	R	R	5-11	195	12-20-79	1998	Princeton, Ind.
Kelton, David	.265	50	181	39	48	7	5	6	29	23	58	16	3	R	R	6-3	190	12-17-79	1998	West Point, Ga.
Koen, Nate	.271	14	48	5	13	0	1	1	8	2	10	0	0	R	R	6-0	190	7-17-76	1998	Chatham, Ill.
Martinez, Daniel	.200	17	50	6	10	0	1	0	3	6	10	6	1	B	R	6-0	170	5-10-78	1996	San Cristobal, D.R.
Martinez, Dionnar	.192	25	78	13	15	3	0	0	6	7	22	4	2	B	R	6-5	175	1-15-81	1998	Barcelona, Ven.
Mauck, Matt	.240	37	125	22	30	6	4	1	16	19	45	3	1	L	R	6-3	215	2-12-79	1997	Jasper, Ind.
Meadows, Tydus	.367	27	98	25	36	8	4	3	26	17	17	6	5	R	R	6-2	220	9-5-77	1998	Hardwick, Ga.
Navarro, Ibrahim	.282	31	117	18	33	7	2	3	13	10	28	2	0	R	R	5-10	175	10-8-79	1997	Caracas, Ven.
Pinero, Juan	.264	51	201	38	53	13	4	1	18	26	30	15	7	B	R	5-10	170	1-25-78	1996	Valle de Pascua, Ven.
Robinson, Coby	.205	26	83	7	17	4	1	1	7	4	27	1	0	R	R	6-5	215	12-30-77	1998	Jonesboro, Ga.
Rohena, Omar	.143	20	56	2	8	0	0	0	4	1	20	2	1	R	R	6-2	175	8-14-80	1998	Rio Grande, P.R.
Shipp, Charles	.294	9	34	6	10	2	1	1	6	1	9	2	0	R	R	6-2	215	11-25-76	1998	Chicago, Ill.
Vieira, Scott	.500	4	12	2	6	1	0	1	4	2	0	0	0	R	R	5-11	195	8-17-73	1995	San Ramon, Calif.

GAMES BY POSITION: C—Dorsett 17, Goldbach 27, Koen 3, Mauck 16. **1B**—Bass 18, Koen 10, Dionnar Martinez 1, Mauck 19, Rohena 12, Vieira 3. **2B**—Aldrup 7, Clarke 18, German 24, Daniel Martinez 11. **3B**—Aldrup 4, German 6, Kelton 46. **SS**—Clarke 4, Daniel Martinez 2, Dionnar Martinez 23, Navarro 31. **OF**—Aldrup 6, Bass 1, Clarke 3, Fukuhara 47, German 2, Meadows 26, Pinero 48, Robinson 24, Rohena 8, Shipp 9.

PITCHING	W	L	ERA	G	GS	CG	SV	IP	H	R	ER	BB	SO	B	T	HT	WT	DOB	1st Yr	Resides
Acosta, Jhon	2	0	2.20	11	2	0	0	29	25	13	7	10	24	B	R	6-3	180	10-30-79	1996	Maracay, Ven.
Alvarez, Larry	1	1	5.54	10	0	0	1	26	24	17	16	8	15	R	R	6-4	210	9-24-79	1998	Walnut, Calif.
Batts, Nathan	3	2	5.40	13	7	0	0	37	40	31	22	34	28	R	L	6-4	185	3-30-78	1997	Mount Vernon, N.H.
Beltran, Francis	1	1	5.55	12	5	0	0	36	49	23	22	14	26	R	R	6-5	230	7-25-80	1997	Santo Domingo, D.R.
Brown, Darold	0	0	0.00	1	1	0	0	1	1	0	0	2	0	L	L	6-0	195	8-16-73	1993	San Jose, Calif.
Conroy, Ken	2	0	1.64	9	0	0	0	11	6	5	2	7	15	R	R	6-4	225	12-19-78	1998	Gastonia, N.C.
Cruz, Juan	2	4	6.10	12	5	0	0	41	61	48	28	14	36	R	R	6-2	155	10-15-80	1997	Bonao, D.R.
Ericks, Dave	0	2	4.29	11	2	0	0	21	23	19	10	17	15	R	R	6-4	180	12-4-79	1998	St. John, Ind.
Gomer, Jeramy	2	3	5.45	11	9	0	0	36	44	27	22	9	39	L	L	6-2	195	6-12-79	1998	Plant City, Fla.
Hammons, Matt	0	1	2.33	7	6	0	0	19	18	6	5	10	29	R	R	6-3	205	4-9-77	1995	San Diego, Calif.
Hardcastle, John	0	2	10.80	12	2	0	1	20	35	33	24	20	17	L	L	6-6	220	11-28-75	1998	Oakley, Calif.
Linares, Yonder	7	2	2.91	15	2	0	0	56	62	24	18	5	32	L	L	6-2	195	4-20-79	1997	Maracay, Ven.
Murphy, Matt	2	1	3.67	14	2	0	2	27	29	11	11	13	37	L	L	6-3	175	10-31-78	1998	Delano, Tenn.
Ohm, Joe	1	1	3.48	13	4	0	2	31	31	14	12	6	20	R	R	6-3	205	9-13-76	1998	Rochester, Minn.
Vracar, Paul	1	4	7.56	13	5	0	0	25	25	29	21	23	21	R	R	6-5	200	12-5-79	1997	Stoney Creek, Ontario
Waldrum, Kevin	4	1	4.67	16	0	0	1	27	27	19	14	12	23	L	R	6-4	200	3-22-79	1997	Mineral Wells, Texas
Williams, Randall	1	0	0.00	2	1	0	0	3	0	0	0	2	6	L	L	6-3	185	9-18-75	1997	Dickinson, Texas
Zambrano, Carlos	0	1	3.15	14	2	0	1	40	39	17	14	25	36	L	R	6-4	205	6-1-81	1997	Puerto Cabello, Ven.

CINCINNATI REDS

Rebuilding Reds surprise on field while restocking talent

BY JEFFREY SHELMAN

The mantra was continually the same. Younger and cheaper, Reds general manager Jim Bowden said countless times in the months leading up to the 1998 season.

At least no one can say that they weren't forewarned.

The season hadn't even begun when whatever hopes the Reds had for contending for the National League wild card were eliminated. Bowden traded scheduled Opening Day starter Dave Burba to the Cleveland Indians less than 18 hours before the start of the season, in exchange for first baseman Sean Casey.

The weekend before the All-Star Game, Bowden was back at it again. This time it was reliever Jeff Shaw–who took less money from the Reds to be able to stay near his childhood home–who was traded away to the Los Angeles Dodgers. In return, Bowden acquired two of the Dodgers' top prospects–infielder Paul Konerko and lefthander Dennis Reyes–to further stock the Reds with young talent. With any luck the young players acquired will blossom in time to contend when a new stadium opens in Cincinnati, possibly by the 2003 season.

While the Reds have moved in a direction where winning now isn't important, the team wasn't as bad as many would have thought. With a 77-85 record, the Reds actually finished a game better in 1998 than they did the previous season.

"We were supposed to lose 100 games and we proved that we were competitive and had a lot of heart," Reds manager Jack McKeon said. "The (players) had a lot of pride and even though inexperience, at times, hurt us, they were better than everybody had predicted. And to me, that's part of winning, to take a challenge and prove everybody wrong."

GEORGE GOJKOVICH

Barry Larkin

JOHN SPEAR

Jason LaRue

Players of the Year

Major League: Barry Larkin, SS

Larkin quietly put together another great season, leading the Reds with 93 runs and 271 total bases.

Minor League: Jason LaRue, c, Indy/Chatt.

LaRue showed good power with an organization-best 43 doubles, and his .350 average was sixth-best in the minor leagues.

Disproving the critics required McKeon to get a lot out of his young players. Casey, Konerko, Reyes, reliever Danny Graves and outfielder Dmitri Young all played well and showed improvement as the season progressed.

At the same time, two Reds–second baseman Bret Boone and righthander Pete Harnisch–rebounded from poor seasons. Harnisch, who battled depression during 1997, led the Reds with 14 victories, while Boone had a breakthrough offensive year, hitting .266 with 24 homers and 95 RBIs.

The Reds made history in a late-season game when they fielded an all-brother infield. Aaron Boone, Bret's younger brother, played third, while Stephen Larkin, younger brother of shortstop Barry, played first.

A couple more young players seemed likely to join the club in 1999. Catcher Jason LaRue hit a combined .350 at two stops in '98, while lashing 43 doubles. And righthander Scott Williamson, who pitched in the Rookie-level Pioneer League in '97, finished the '98 season at Triple-A Indianapolis.

Outfielder Mike Frank made an even faster leap than Williamson, arriving in Cincinnati in June, barely over a year after he was drafted in the seventh round out of Santa Clara University.

The Reds fielded just five farm teams in 1998. Notably absent was a high Class A club, though the organization had two low Class A teams, in Burlington, Iowa, and Charleston, W.Va. Charleston finished with 96 losses, a major reason the Reds' .454 overall minor league winning percentage was fifth worst in baseball.

ORGANIZATION LEADERS

BATTING		
*AVG	Jason LaRue, Indianapolis/Chattanooga	.350
R	Damian Jackson, Indianapolis	102
H	Jason LaRue, Indianapolis/Chattanooga	153
TB	Jason LaRue, Indianapolis/Chattanooga	254
2B	Jason LaRue, Indianapolis/Chattanooga	43
3B	Two tied at	10
HR	Roberto Petagine, Indianapolis	24
RBI	Roberto Petagine, Indianapolis	109
BB	Nick Presto, Chattanooga	74
SO	Darron Ingram, Chattanooga	169
SB	Travis Dawkins, Burlington	37
PITCHING		
W	Two tied at	12
L	Phil Merrell, Charleston	15
#ERA	Scott Wright, Chattanooga/Burlington	1.67
G	Mike Walker, Indianapolis	78
CG	Mark Corey, Indy/Chattanooga/Burlington	7
SV	Todd Williams, Indianapolis	26
IP	Josh Harris, Burlington	177
BB	Randi Mallard, Chattanooga/Burlington	90
SO	Josh Harris, Burlington	169

*Minimum 250 At-Bats #Minimum 75 Innings

Cincinnati REDS

Manager: Jack McKeon

1998 Record: 77-85, .475 (4th, NL Central)

BATTING	AVG	G	AB	R	H	2B	3B	HR	RBI	BB	SO	SB	CS	B	T	HT	WT	DOB	1st Yr	Resides
Boone, Aaron	.282	58	181	24	51	13	2	2	28	15	36	6	1	R	R	6-2	200	3-9-73	1994	Villa Park, Calif.
Boone, Bret	.266	157	583	76	155	38	1	24	95	48	104	6	4	R	R	5-10	180	4-6-69	1990	Orlando, Fla.
Casey, Sean	.272	96	302	44	82	21	1	7	52	43	45	1	1	L	R	6-4	215	7-2-74	1995	Pittsburgh, Pa.
Fordyce, Brook	.253	57	146	8	37	9	0	3	14	11	28	0	1	R	R	6-1	185	5-7-70	1989	Jensen Beach, Fla.
Frank, Mike	.225	28	89	14	20	6	0	0	7	7	12	0	0	L	L	6-2	190	1-14-75	1997	Santa Clara, Calif.
Garcia, Guillermo	.194	12	36	3	7	2	0	2	4	2	13	0	0	R	R	6-3	215	4-4-72	1990	Santo Domingo, D.R.
Greene, Willie	.270	111	356	57	96	18	1	14	49	56	80	6	3	L	R	5-11	192	9-23-71	1989	Haddock, Ga.
Hammonds, Jeffrey	.302	26	86	14	26	4	1	0	11	13	18	1	1	R	R	6-0	195	3-5-71	1992	Scotch Plains, N.J.
Harris, Lenny	.295	57	122	12	36	8	0	0	10	8	9	1	3	L	R	5-10	210	10-28-64	1983	Miami, Fla.
Jackson, Damian	.316	13	38	4	12	5	0	0	7	6	4	2	0	R	R	5-10	160	8-16-73	1992	Concord, Calif.
Konerko, Paul	.219	26	73	7	16	3	0	3	13	6	10	0	0	R	R	6-3	210	3-5-76	1994	Paradise Valley, Ariz.
2-team (49 L.A.)	.217	75	217	21	47	4	0	7	29	16	40	0	1							
Larkin, Barry	.309	145	538	93	166	34	10	17	72	79	69	26	3	R	R	6-0	185	4-28-64	1985	Cincinnati, Ohio
Larkin, Stephen	.333	1	3	0	1	0	0	0	0	0	1	0	0	L	L	6-0	190	7-24-73	1994	Cincinnati, Ohio
Nieves, Melvin	.252	83	119	8	30	4	0	2	17	26	42	0	0	B	R	6-2	220	12-28-71	1988	Pinehurst, N.C.
Nunnally, Jon	.207	74	174	29	36	9	0	7	20	34	38	3	4	L	R	5-10	190	11-9-71	1992	Keeling, Calif.
Perez, Eduardo	.238	84	172	20	41	4	0	4	30	21	45	0	1	R	R	6-4	225	9-11-69	1991	Calabasas, Ohio
Petagine, Roberto	.258	34	62	14	16	2	1	3	7	16	11	1	0	L	L	6-1	215	6-2-71	1990	Caracas, Ven.
Reese, Pokey	.256	59	133	20	34	2	2	1	16	14	28	3	2	R	R	5-11	180	6-10-73	1991	Columbia, S.C.
Sanders, Reggie	.268	135	481	83	129	18	6	14	59	51	137	20	9	R	R	6-1	185	12-1-67	1988	Tampa, Fla.
Stynes, Chris	.254	123	347	52	88	10	1	6	27	32	36	15	1	R	R	5-10	185	1-19-73	1991	Boca Raton, Fla.
Tarasco, Tony	.208	15	24	5	5	2	0	1	4	3	5	0	0	L	R	6-1	205	12-9-70	1988	Miami, Fla.
Taubensee, Eddie	.278	130	431	61	120	27	0	11	72	52	93	1	0	L	R	6-4	225	10-31-68	1986	Windermere, Fla.
Watkins, Pat	.265	83	147	11	39	8	1	2	15	8	26	1	3	R	R	6-2	195	9-2-72	1993	Garner, N.C.
Young, Dmitri	.310	144	536	81	166	48	1	14	83	47	94	2	4	B	R	6-2	235	10-11-73	1991	Huntington, Ind.

PITCHING	W	L	ERA	G	GS	CG	SV	IP	H	R	ER	BB	SO	B	T	HT	WT	DOB	1st Yr	Resides
Belinda, Stan	4	8	3.23	40	0	0	1	61	46	23	22	28	57	R	R	6-3	215	8-6-66	1985	Alexandria, Pa.
Bere, Jason	3	2	4.12	9	7	0	0	44	39	20	20	20	31	R	R	6-3	215	5-26-71	1990	Wilmington, Mass.
Cooke, Steve	1	0	1.50	1	1	0	0	6	4	1	1	0	3	R	L	6-6	240	1-14-70	1990	Aloha, Ore.
Glauber, Keith	0	0	2.35	3	0	0	0	8	6	2	2	1	4	R	R	6-2	190	1-18-72	1994	Morganville, N.J.
Graves, Danny	2	1	3.32	62	0	0	8	81	76	31	30	28	44	R	R	5-11	200	8-7-73	1995	Loveland, Ohio
Harnisch, Pete	14	7	3.14	32	32	2	0	209	176	79	73	64	157	R	R	6-0	228	9-23-66	1987	Lake Mary, Fla.
Hudek, John	4	2	2.43	30	0	0	0	37	27	14	10	28	40	B	R	6-2	210	8-8-66	1988	Sugar Land, Texas
2-team (28 N.Y.)	5	6	3.09	58	0	0	0	64	50	27	22	47	68							
Hutton, Mark	0	1	7.41	10	2	0	0	17	24	14	14	17	3	R	R	6-6	240	2-6-70	1989	Adelaide, Australia
Jordan, Ricardo	1	0	24.30	6	0	0	0	3	4	9	9	7	1	L	L	6-0	190	6-27-70	1990	Palm Harbor, Fla.
Klingenbeck, Scott	1	3	5.96	4	4	0	0	23	26	17	15	7	13	R	R	6-2	205	2-3-71	1992	Cincinnati, Ohio
Krivda, Rick	0	2	11.28	16	1	0	0	26	41	34	33	19	19	R	L	6-1	185	1-19-70	1991	Cockeysville, Md.
Kroon, Marc	0	0	13.50	4	0	0	0	5	7	8	8	8	4	R	R	6-2	195	4-2-73	1991	Phoenix, Ariz.
2-team (2 San Diego)	0	0	9.39	6	0	0	0	8	7	8	8	9	6							
Parris, Steve	6	5	3.73	18	16	1	0	99	89	44	41	32	77	R	R	6-0	195	12-17-67	1989	Plainfield, Ill.
Priest, Eddie	0	1	10.50	2	2	0	0	6	12	8	7	1	1	R	L	6-1	200	4-8-74	1994	Horton, Ala.
Remlinger, Mike	8	15	4.82	35	28	1	0	164	164	96	88	87	144	L	L	6-1	210	3-23-66	1987	Scottsdale, Ariz.
Reyes, Dennis	3	1	4.42	8	7	0	0	39	35	19	19	27	44	R	L	6-3	246	4-19-77	1994	Higuera de Zaragoza, Mex.
2-team (11 L.A.)	3	5	4.54	19	10	0	0	67	62	36	34	47	77							
Shaw, Jeff	2	4	1.81	39	0	0	23	50	40	11	10	12	29	R	R	6-2	200	7-7-66	1986	Washington Courthouse, Ohio
Sullivan, Scott	5	5	5.21	67	0	0	1	102	98	62	59	36	86	R	R	6-3	210	3-13-71	1993	Livingston, Ala.
Tomko, Brett	13	12	4.44	34	34	1	0	211	198	111	104	64	162	R	R	6-4	215	4-7-73	1995	San Diego, Calif.
Weathers, David	2	4	6.21	16	9	0	0	62	86	47	43	27	51	R	R	6-3	220	9-25-69	1988	Loretto, Tenn.
White, Gabe	5	5	4.01	69	3	0	9	99	86	46	44	27	83	L	L	6-2	200	11-20-71	1990	Sebring, Fla.
Williams, Todd	0	1	7.71	6	0	0	0	9	15	8	8	6	4	R	R	6-4	190	2-13-71	1991	Syracuse, N.Y.
Winchester, Scott	3	6	5.81	16	16	1	0	79	101	56	51	27	40	R	R	6-2	210	4-20-73	1995	Midland, Mich.

FIELDING

Catcher	PCT	G	PO	A	E	DP	PB
Fordyce	.978	54	288	20	7	3	0
Garcia	.988	11	74	5	1	1	2
Taubensee	.988	126	776	44	10	5	8

First Base	PCT	G	PO	A	E	DP
Casey	.994	86	643	36	4	65
Konerko	1.000	7	38	6	0	1
S. Larkin	1.000	1	6	0	0	0
Perez	.985	51	290	45	5	35
Petagine	1.000	15	46	4	0	4
Young	.994	44	304	22	2	25

Second Base	PCT	G	PO	A	E	DP
A. Boone	.000	1	0	0	1	0
B. Boone	.988	156	329	415	9	100
Reese	1.000	3	6	9	0	3
Stynes	1.000	11	15	22	0	4

Third Base	PCT	G	PO	A	E	DP
A. Boone	.950	52	37	98	7	7
Greene	.936	76	48	128	12	20
Konerko	1.000	9	2	18	0	0
Perez	1.000	1	0	2	0	0
Reese	.985	32	20	45	1	7
Stynes	.946	22	9	26	2	3

Shortstop	PCT	G	PO	A	E	DP
B. Boone	.000	1	0	0	0	0
Greene	.800	2	1	3	1	1
Jackson	.972	10	14	21	1	3
B. Larkin	.979	145	207	358	12	79
Reese	.873	18	24	24	7	7
Stynes	1.000	2	1	2	0	1

Outfield	PCT	G	PO	A	E	DP
Frank	1.000	28	60	1	0	0
Greene	1.000	28	43	1	0	0
Hammonds	.985	25	64	3	1	1
Harris	.929	32	37	2	3	0
Jackson	1.000	3	6	0	0	0
Konerko	1.000	7	8	0	0	0
Nieves	1.000	25	31	1	0	0
Nunnally	.956	70	126	5	6	0
Perez	1.000	1	1	0	0	0
Petagine	1.000	15	28	0	0	0
Sanders	.978	131	263	4	6	0
Stynes	1.000	80	123	4	0	2
Tarasco	1.000	7	10	0	0	0
Watkins	.971	77	98	1	3	0
Young	.940	105	154	3	10	0

FARM SYSTEM

Director of Player Development: Muzzy Jackson

Class	Farm Team	League	W	L	Pct.	Finish*	Manager	First Yr
AAA	Indianapolis (Ind.) Indians	International	76	67	.531	8th (14)	Dave Miley	1993
AA	Chattanooga (Tenn.) Lookouts	Southern	65	73	.471	T-7th (10)	Mark Berry	1988
A	Burlington (Iowa) Bees	Midwest	63	77	.450	13th (14)	Phillip Wellman	1997
A	Charleston (W.Va.) Alley Cats	South Atlantic	44	96	.314	14th (14)	Barry Lyons	1990
Rookie#	Billings (Mont.) Mustangs	Pioneer	40	34	.541	4th (8)	Russ Nixon	1974

*Finish in overall standings (No. of teams in league) #Advanced level

INDIANAPOLIS — Class AAA

INTERNATIONAL LEAGUE

BATTING	AVG	G	AB	R	H	2B	3B	HR	RBI	BB	SO	SB	CS	B	T	HT	WT	DOB	1st Yr	Resides
Baez, Kevin	.263	49	137	21	36	5	0	1	12	19	26	0	1	R	R	6-0	170	1-10-67	1988	New York, N.Y.
Boone, Aaron	.241	87	332	56	80	18	1	7	38	31	71	17	5	R	R	6-2	200	3-9-73	1994	Villa Park, Calif.
Casey, Sean	.326	27	95	14	31	8	1	1	13	14	10	0	0	L	R	6-4	215	7-2-74	1995	Pittsburgh, Pa.
Davis, James	.200	19	50	4	10	2	0	1	4	1	12	0	0	R	R	6-4	215	4-14-73	1995	Franklin, Ky.
Fordyce, Brook	.250	6	24	4	6	1	0	2	3	1	2	0	0	R	R	6-1	185	5-7-70	1989	Jensen Beach, Fla.
Frank, Mike	.341	22	88	8	30	4	0	0	13	7	9	1	0	L	L	6-2	190	1-14-75	1997	Santa Clara, Calif.
Garcia, Guillermo	.254	93	334	48	85	20	0	19	60	22	81	0	2	R	R	6-3	215	4-4-72	1990	Santo Domingo, D.R.
Garcia, Omar	.412	7	17	2	7	0	0	1	3	1	2	0	0	R	R	6-0	188	11-16-71	1989	Carolina, P.R.
Gibralter, Steve	.257	68	226	34	58	12	4	11	31	10	66	1	2	R	R	6-0	195	10-9-72	1990	Duncanville, Texas
Jackson, Damian	.261	131	517	102	135	36	10	6	49	62	125	25	10	R	R	5-10	160	8-16-73	1992	Concord, Calif.
Johnson, Mark	.300	116	357	65	107	33	1	22	75	68	82	2	2	L	L	6-4	230	10-17-67	1990	Pittsburgh, Pa.
Konerko, Paul	.327	39	150	25	49	8	0	8	39	19	18	1	0	R	R	6-3	210	3-5-76	1994	Paradise Valley, Ariz.
LaRue, Jason	.235	15	51	5	12	4	0	0	5	4	8	0	1	R	R	5-11	200	3-19-74	1995	Spring Branch, Texas
Marx, Tim	.154	20	52	5	8	0	1	0	6	7	13	0	0	R	R	6-2	205	11-27-68	1991	Evansville, Ind.
Mercedes, Henry	.125	8	16	1	2	0	0	0	1	1	5	0	0	R	R	6-1	210	7-23-69	1988	Eagle Point, Ore.
Mottola, Chad	.417	5	12	2	5	0	0	1	2	4	0	0	2	R	R	6-3	220	10-15-71	1992	Fort Lauderdale, Fla.
Murray, Glenn	.198	42	126	20	25	6	0	4	16	13	47	1	2	R	R	6-2	225	11-23-70	1989	Manning, S.C.
Nieves, Melvin	.283	15	53	10	15	4	0	2	13	9	11	0	0	B	R	6-2	220	12-28-71	1988	Pinehurst, N.C.
Nunnally, Jon	.252	79	290	53	73	18	2	11	53	47	71	7	4	L	R	5-10	190	11-9-71	1992	Keeling, Va.
Owens, Jayhawk	.297	16	37	5	11	4	0	2	8	4	17	0	0	R	R	6-1	213	2-10-69	1990	Cincinnati, Ohio
Petagine, Roberto	.331	102	363	79	120	30	1	24	109	70	71	3	1	L	L	6-1	215	6-2-71	1990	Caracas, Ven.
Rose, Pete	.278	43	133	19	37	7	1	3	13	8	10	1	0	L	R	6-1	180	11-16-69	1989	Cincinnati, Ohio
Tarasco, Tony	.313	90	319	53	100	19	1	16	45	43	46	3	2	L	R	6-1	205	12-9-70	1988	Miami, Fla.
Timmons, Ozzie	.263	117	327	46	86	21	3	12	36	29	65	2	2	R	R	6-2	220	9-18-70	1991	Tampa, Fla.
Watkins, Pat	.378	44	188	37	71	12	1	3	24	15	26	8	3	R	R	6-2	195	9-2-72	1993	Garner, N.C.
Williams, Jason	.266	119	406	60	108	25	1	2	45	70	63	5	2	R	R	5-8	180	12-18-73	1996	Gonzales, La.

PITCHING	W	L	ERA	G	GS	CG	SV	IP	H	R	ER	BB	SO	B	T	HT	WT	DOB	1st Yr	Resides
Bolton, Rod	12	11	3.81	29	29	1	0	177	166	82	75	64	117	R	R	6-2	190	9-23-68	1990	Chattanooga, Tenn.
Cooke, Steve	0	1	37.80	2	2	0	0	2	3	7	7	5	0	R	L	6-6	240	1-14-70	1990	Aloha, Ore.
Corey, Mark	0	1	4.50	1	1	1	0	6	4	3	3	3	2	R	R	6-2	220	11-16-74	1995	Austin, Pa.
Crowell, Jim	0	0	6.75	1	1	0	0	4	7	3	3	0	2	R	L	6-4	230	5-14-74	1995	Valparaiso, Ind.
Donnelly, Brendan	4	1	2.65	19	1	0	0	37	29	16	11	16	39	R	R	6-3	205	7-4-71	1992	Albuquerque, N.M.
Eischen, Joey	2	5	4.54	61	0	0	2	73	73	42	37	29	60	L	L	6-1	190	5-25-70	1989	West Covina, Calif.
Glauber, Keith	1	3	9.00	4	4	0	0	16	20	17	16	14	15	R	R	6-2	190	1-18-72	1994	Morganville, N.J.
Graves, Danny	1	0	1.93	13	0	0	0	14	15	3	3	3	11	R	R	5-11	200	8-7-73	1995	Loveland, Ohio
Hutton, Mark	4	6	4.43	16	16	0	0	83	91	50	41	37	47	R	R	6-6	240	2-6-70	1989	Adelaide, Australia
Jarvis, Kevin	1	0	9.00	2	2	0	0	7	10	7	7	1	5	B	R	6-2	200	8-1-69	1991	Lexington, Ky.
Jordan, Ricardo	2	4	3.49	37	6	0	0	70	70	39	27	33	52	L	L	6-0	190	6-27-70	1990	Palm Harbor, Fla.
Keyser, Brian	6	6	4.62	41	13	0	0	117	131	69	60	56	66	R	R	6-1	180	10-31-66	1989	Casper, Wyo.
Klingenbeck, Scott	6	2	2.86	10	10	0	0	63	57	26	20	10	50	R	R	6-2	205	2-3-71	1992	Cincinnati, Ohio
Kroon, Marc	3	2	5.63	39	0	0	1	46	39	29	29	47	36	R	R	6-2	195	4-2-73	1991	Phoenix, Ariz.
Martinez, Jesus	7	6	6.85	22	18	0	0	93	119	78	71	42	39	L	L	6-2	190	3-13-74	1991	Santo Domingo, D.R.
Norris, Joe	1	1	5.40	4	2	0	0	10	13	10	6	6	7	R	R	6-4	215	11-29-70	1989	Oswego, S.C.
Parris, Steve	6	1	3.84	13	13	1	0	84	74	38	36	26	102	R	R	6-0	195	12-17-67	1989	Plainfield, Ill.
Priest, Eddie	4	1	4.76	6	6	0	0	34	36	19	18	7	21	R	L	6-1	200	4-8-74	1994	Horton, Ala.
Reyes, Dennis	2	0	3.00	4	4	0	0	24	20	10	8	14	27	R	L	6-3	246	4-19-77	1994	Higuera de Zaragoza, Mex.
Ruffcorn, Scott	6	2	8.65	23	0	0	0	34	44	35	33	37	28	R	R	6-4	215	12-29-69	1991	Austin, Texas
Sauveur, Rich	0	0	3.00	7	0	0	1	9	9	8	3	4	6	L	L	6-4	170	11-23-63	1983	Falls Church, Va.
Steph, Rod	1	0	3.72	3	2	0	0	10	11	4	4	3	8	R	R	5-11	185	8-27-69	1991	Lubbock, Texas
2-team (14 Roch.)	4	4	3.45	17	2	0	0	31	36	15	12	5	25							
Tolar, Kevin	0	1	10.43	19	0	0	0	15	21	18	17	17	19	R	L	6-3	225	1-28-71	1989	Brandon, Fla.
Walker, Mike	4	8	3.17	78	3	0	6	102	86	49	36	48	63	R	R	6-1	205	10-6-66	1986	Brooksville, Fla.
Williams, Todd	0	3	2.31	53	0	0	26	58	54	19	15	24	35	R	R	6-4	190	2-13-71	1991	Syracuse, N.Y.
Williamson, Scott	0	0	3.48	5	5	0	0	21	20	9	8	9	17	R	R	6-0	185	2-17-76	1997	Friendswood, Texas
Winchester, Scott	3	2	6.67	6	5	0	0	30	39	23	22	8	12	R	R	6-2	210	4-20-73	1995	Midland, Mich.

FIELDING

Catcher	PCT	G	PO	A	E	DP	PB
Davis	.976	17	73	7	2	1	1
Fordyce	1.000	6	28	4	0	1	1
G. Garcia	.990	86	559	65	6	9	11
LaRue	1.000	14	83	11	0	1	1
Marx	.965	18	74	9	3	0	1
Mercedes	.944	5	13	4	1	0	0
Owens	.989	16	83	7	1	0	0

First Base	PCT	G	PO	A	E	DP
Casey	.991	25	205	10	2	23
G. Garcia	1.000	3	22	1	0	1
O. Garcia	1.000	2	18	0	0	2
Johnson	.993	52	410	36	3	50
Petagine	.994	68	633	53	4	76
Rose	.960	4	21	3	1	3

Second Base	PCT	G	PO	A	E	DP
Baez	.962	24	55	72	5	24
Boone	.941	7	18	14	2	6
Williams	.984	116	223	341	9	88

Third Base	PCT	G	PO	A	E	DP
Baez	.938	6	6	9	1	1
Boone	.942	77	45	213	16	21
G. Garcia	1.000	2	0	4	0	1

	PCT	G	PO	A	E	DP
Konerko	.957	39	21	68	4	8
Rose	.955	26	19	44	3	7
Timmons	1.000	1	1	0	0	0

Shortstop	PCT	G	PO	A	E	DP
Baez	.909	10	13	27	4	7
Boone	.962	7	9	16	1	3
Jackson	.938	130	227	434	44	101

Outfield	PCT	G	PO	A	E	DP
Frank	.979	22	44	2	1	1
Gibralter	.975	62	116	2	3	1
Jackson	1.000	1	3	1	0	0
Johnson	.944	26	33	1	2	0
Mottola	1.000	5	7	2	0	1
Murray	.981	32	50	1	1	0

	PCT	G	PO	A	E	DP
Nieves	.950	12	19	0	1	0
Nunnally	.951	77	146	8	8	0
Petagine	.944	20	32	2	2	0
Tarasco	1.000	70	101	3	0	1
Timmons	.986	95	133	5	2	1
Watkins	.981	44	98	5	2	3

CHATTANOOGA — Class AA

SOUTHERN LEAGUE

BATTING	AVG	G	AB	R	H	2B	3B	HR	RBI	BB	SO	SB	CS	B	T	HT	WT	DOB	1st Yr	Resides
Allen, Marlon	.234	87	312	36	73	14	0	6	33	29	91	1	5	R	R	6-6	228	3-28-73	1994	Columbus, Ga.
Baez, Kevin	.256	49	180	30	46	10	0	0	22	26	27	0	1	R	R	6-0	170	1-10-67	1988	New York, N.Y.
Brooks, Ramy	.263	19	57	7	15	3	0	2	5	7	17	0	1	R	R	6-2	180	4-12-70	1990	Blanchard, Okla.
Clark, Brady	.270	64	222	41	60	13	1	2	16	31	34	12	4	R	R	6-2	195	4-18-73	1996	Beaverton, Ore.
Davis, James	.294	37	126	11	37	5	0	2	12	8	21	0	0	R	R	6-4	215	4-14-73	1995	Franklin, Ky.
Eddie, Steve	.290	134	520	70	151	30	3	10	81	43	84	3	3	R	R	6-1	190	1-6-71	1993	Storm Lake, Iowa
Frank, Mike	.325	58	231	43	75	12	4	12	43	19	28	5	2	L	L	6-2	190	1-14-75	1997	Santa Clara, Calif.
Gibralter, Steve	.269	17	67	8	18	4	0	1	4	6	13	1	0	R	R	6-0	195	10-9-72	1990	Duncanville, Texas
Guthrie, David	.192	67	203	23	39	5	4	0	9	16	58	1	1	B	R	6-2	185	5-21-74	1995	Birmingham, Ala.
Ingram, Darron	.232	125	466	62	108	21	9	17	65	43	169	4	3	R	R	6-3	226	6-7-76	1994	Lexington, Ky.
Larkin, Stephen	.228	80	267	33	61	22	1	3	31	23	52	3	4	L	L	6-0	190	7-24-73	1994	Cincinnati, Ohio
LaRue, Jason	.365	105	386	71	141	39	8	14	82	40	60	4	3	R	R	5-11	200	3-19-74	1995	Spring Branch, Texas
Marn, Kevin	.361	20	36	8	13	3	0	0	4	5	8	2	0	R	R	6-4	205	3-23-74	1996	Broadview Heights, Ohio
Murray, Glenn	.249	60	217	35	54	16	1	8	31	42	67	3	3	R	R	6-2	225	11-23-70	1989	Manning, S.C.
Nevers, Tom	.217	58	221	30	48	9	4	7	31	17	53	1	0	R	R	6-1	175	9-13-71	1990	Edina, Minn.
Presto, Nick	.249	128	481	75	120	22	0	4	35	74	52	20	18	R	R	5-10	175	7-8-74	1996	Jupiter, Fla.
Sorg, Jay	.227	88	264	27	60	8	3	3	28	31	56	1	2	L	R	6-3	185	5-10-73	1994	Louisville, Ky.
Tidwell, Dave	.204	47	137	12	28	5	1	2	22	15	37	3	4	R	R	5-9	170	1-17-75	1997	Grenada, Miss.
Towle, Justin	.284	56	148	25	42	9	1	5	25	25	31	3	0	R	R	6-2	215	2-21-74	1992	Seattle, Wash.
Viera, Rob	.400	5	15	1	6	1	0	0	2	0	3	0	0	R	R	6-2	215	4-19-73	1996	Bradenton, Fla.

PITCHING	W	L	ERA	G	GS	CG	SV	IP	H	R	ER	BB	SO	B	T	HT	WT	DOB	1st Yr	Resides
Averette, Robert	5	8	5.11	14	14	0	0	81	97	51	46	36	32	R	R	6-2	185	9-30-76	1997	Sylacauga, Ala.
Callahan, Damon	0	0	0.00	2	0	0	0	3	1	0	0	3	0	R	R	6-3	190	12-10-75	1994	Cleveland, Tenn.
Carlyle, Buddy	0	1	5.40	1	1	0	0	5	6	3	3	0	3	L	R	6-3	175	12-21-77	1996	Bellevue, Neb.
Corey, Mark	0	4	8.20	6	6	0	0	26	32	25	24	16	6	R	R	6-2	220	11-16-74	1995	Austin, Pa.
Crowell, Jim	0	4	8.51	5	5	0	0	24	38	27	23	17	10	R	L	6-4	230	5-14-74	1995	Valparaiso, Ind.
Donnelly, Brendan	2	5	2.98	38	0	0	13	45	43	16	15	24	47	R	R	6-3	205	7-4-71	1992	Albuquerque, N.M.
Doyle, Tom	0	1	10.13	9	0	0	0	11	13	12	12	14	9	L	L	6-3	205	1-20-70	1988	Redondo Beach, Calif.
Etler, Todd	6	0	1.92	46	0	0	5	66	61	21	14	21	58	R	R	6-0	205	4-18-74	1992	Villa Hills, Ky.
Glauber, Keith	1	1	4.00	2	2	0	0	9	3	4	4	6	5	R	R	6-2	190	1-18-72	1994	Morganville, N.J.
Hunter, Rich	1	3	5.97	7	6	0	0	35	37	28	23	17	15	R	R	6-1	190	9-25-74	1993	Temecula, Calif.
Hurst, Doug	8	4	3.84	44	5	0	1	89	85	41	38	38	37	R	R	5-11	195	2-23-76	1997	Pensacola, Fla.
LeBlanc, Eric	4	3	3.93	23	7	0	0	66	56	33	29	38	49	L	R	6-0	195	7-6-73	1996	North Troy, Vt.
Lyons, Curt	0	1	9.00	3	3	0	0	7	6	7	7	8	10	R	R	6-5	240	10-17-74	1992	Richmond, Ky.
MacRae, Scott	9	4	4.43	49	5	0	0	114	105	70	56	56	67	R	R	6-3	205	8-13-74	1995	Marietta, Ga.
Mallard, Randi	1	4	4.33	13	12	0	0	60	65	37	29	58	34	R	R	6-1	180	8-11-75	1996	Tampa, Fla.
Paul, Andy	0	1	6.04	17	1	0	0	25	26	18	17	16	30	R	R	6-4	220	9-4-71	1992	Whitehouse Station, N.J.
Priest, Eddie	1	2	1.73	4	4	0	0	26	15	6	5	10	29	R	L	6-1	200	4-8-74	1994	Horton, Ala.
Puffer, Brandon	0	0	3.12	7	0	0	0	9	2	3	3	3	6	R	R	6-3	195	10-5-75	1994	Mission Viejo, Calif.
Reed, Chris	1	1	5.25	20	0	0	0	36	41	25	21	25	13	R	R	6-2	225	8-25-73	1991	Huntington Beach, Calif.
Riedling, John	3	10	5.00	24	20	0	0	103	112	70	57	60	86	R	R	5-11	190	8-29-75	1994	Pompano Beach, Fla.
Rose, Ted	11	10	4.60	29	29	1	0	168	191	97	86	66	108	L	R	6-2	185	8-23-73	1996	St. Clairsville, Ohio
Ruffcorn, Scott	3	0	1.38	10	0	0	0	13	8	3	2	6	9	R	R	6-4	215	12-29-69	1991	Austin, Texas
Ryan, Robert	1	0	2.20	16	0	0	4	16	13	4	4	6	21	L	L	6-6	230	12-28-75	1998	Benton, La.
Stidham, Phil	1	0	9.75	5	0	0	0	12	20	13	13	10	6	R	R	6-1	190	11-13-68	1991	Tulsa, Okla.
Thobe, Tom	1	0	7.50	17	0	0	0	24	32	20	20	14	11	L	L	6-6	195	9-3-69	1988	Huntington Beach, Calif.
Williamson, Scott	4	5	3.78	18	18	0	0	100	85	49	42	46	105	R	R	6-0	185	2-17-76	1997	Friendswood, Texas
Wright, Scott	2	1	2.68	26	0	0	0	44	42	15	13	12	30	R	R	6-2	210	10-15-72	1995	Medford, Wis.

FIELDING

Catcher	PCT	G	PO	A	E	DP	PB
Brooks	.977	15	72	13	2	2	5
Davis	.979	35	208	23	5	1	8
LaRue	.985	92	526	83	9	4	21
Sorg	1.000	1	1	0	0	0	0
Viera	1.000	4	29	2	0	0	1

First Base	PCT	G	PO	A	E	DP
Allen	.985	81	703	66	12	83
Davis	.000	1	0	0	0	0
LaRue	.947	2	18	0	1	4
Sorg	.996	62	512	44	2	58

Second Base	PCT	G	PO	A	E	DP
Baez	1.000	1	1	4	0	1
Eddie	1.000	9	16	23	0	6
Nevers	.947	5	8	10	1	4
Presto	.970	128	287	370	20	95

Third Base	PCT	G	PO	A	E	DP
Allen	.000	1	0	0	1	0
Baez	.000	1	0	0	0	0
Eddie	.956	110	86	215	14	27
Guthrie	.963	16	10	16	1	3
LaRue	1.000	4	2	7	0	1
Nevers	.750	2	2	4	2	0
Sorg	.854	18	10	25	6	1

Shortstop	PCT	G	PO	A	E	DP
Baez	.950	46	67	140	11	31
Eddie	.818	4	1	8	2	0
Guthrie	.959	50	78	130	9	26
Nevers	.927	48	57	145	16	33

Outfield	PCT	G	PO	A	E	DP
Brooks	1.000	1	1	0	0	0
Clark	.993	57	149	3	1	2
Eddie	1.000	21	40	1	0	1
Frank	.985	51	127	3	2	1
Gibralter	.968	15	29	1	1	1
Ingram	.986	115	203	5	3	2
Larkin	.947	70	123	3	7	1
Marn	.929	10	13	0	1	0
Murray	.956	53	87	0	4	0
Tidwell	.969	42	92	2	3	2

BURLINGTON — Class A

MIDWEST LEAGUE

BATTING	AVG	G	AB	R	H	2B	3B	HR	RBI	BB	SO	SB	CS	B	T	HT	WT	DOB	1st Yr	Resides
Baderdeen, Kevin	.250	59	212	31	53	8	0	10	28	9	75	5	1	R	R	6-3	175	1-12-77	1997	Goshen, Ind.
Baston, Stan	.119	19	67	[illegible]	8	0	0	0	3	0	22	1	[illegible]	R	R	[illegible]	190	[illegible]	[illegible]	Tallahassee, Fla.
Burress, Andy	.281	124	449	75	126	25	10	9	67	62	91	25	5	R	R	6-0	185	7-18-77	1995	McRae, Ga.
Caceres, Wilmy	.293	35	150	23	44	8	0	1	14	4	24	7	5	B	R	6-0	170	10-2-78	1997	Santo Domingo, D.R.
Campbell, Wylie	.269	75	234	33	63	8	0	0	20	34	35	18	3	B	R	5-11	180	3-27-75	1996	Fort Worth, Texas
Craig, Benny	.224	103	335	41	75	21	1	15	46	47	160	2	1	B	R	6-4	205	1-15-75	1997	Santee, Calif.
Dawkins, Travis	.264	102	367	52	97	7	6	1	30	37	60	37	10	R	R	6-1	180	5-12-79	1997	Chappells, S.C.
Larson, Brandon	.221	18	68	5	15	3	0	2	9	4	16	2	1	R	R	6-0	205	5-24-76	1997	San Antonio, Texas
Montgomery, Andre	.216	75	245	25	53	8	0	4	32	20	60	9	5	R	R	5-11	170	6-27-77	1995	Louisville, Ky.
Newman, Howard	.273	7	22	0	6	0	0	0	3	0	7	1	1	R	R	5-10	190	12-5-75	1997	Riverside, Calif.
Price, Corey	.236	52	157	17	37	11	0	0	15	16	41	4	2	B	R	6-0	165	9-18-76	1996	Mount Pleasant, Texas
Rios, Fernando	.253	119	407	49	103	13	1	5	38	42	65	16	10	R	R	6-2	175	12-15-78	1997	Glendale, Calif.
Rivera, Francisco	.172	31	93	4	16	5	0	0	6	14	15	2	0	L	R	6-2	195	10-4-79	1996	El Tejar, Mexico
Rojas, Christian	.284	40	141	27	40	5	2	8	20	9	33	5	2	R	R	6-1	170	6-23-75	1994	El Vivero, D.R.
Sorg, Jay	.257	20	74	6	19	5	0	2	10	4	13	2	0	L	R	6-3	185	5-10-73	1994	Louisville, Ky.
Suarez, Marc	.245	61	212	26	52	15	1	7	27	20	75	4	5	R	R	6-4	230	1-18-76	1997	Miami, Fla.
Tidwell, Dave	.291	39	134	21	39	10	0	2	10	17	41	6	2	R	R	5-9	170	1-17-75	1997	Grenada, Miss.
Viera, Rob	.278	33	115	11	32	6	1	2	13	5	26	0	0	R	R	6-2	215	4-19-73	1996	Bradenton, Fla.
Welsh, Eric	.259	135	525	49	136	33	3	7	68	27	112	7	6	L	L	6-3	210	9-17-76	1997	Lockport, Ill.
Williams, Mike	.143	27	84	8	12	2	0	0	4	2	40	1	1	R	R	6-2	189	12-8-73	1997	Belleville, Ill.
Wise, DeWayne	.224	127	496	61	111	15	9	2	44	41	111	27	17	L	L	6-1	172	2-24-78	1997	Chapin, S.C.

GAMES BY POSITION: C—Newman 7, Rivera 30, Sorg 2, Suarez 55, Viera 25, Williams 27. **1B**—Campbell 1, Craig 14, Price 2, Sorg 4, Welsh 125. **2B**—Baston 2, Campbell 68, Montgomery 56, Price 18. **3B**—Baderdeen 51, Baston 15, Campbell 3, Larson 18, Montgomery 11, Price 31, Sorg 15. **SS**—Caceres 35, Campbell 1, Dawkins 101, Montgomery 6, Price 1. **OF**—Baderdeen 7, Burress 120, Craig 20, Rios 117, Rojas 15, Tidwell 23, Wise 124.

PITCHING	W	L	ERA	G	GS	CG	SV	IP	H	R	ER	BB	SO	B	T	HT	WT	DOB	1st Yr	Resides
Altman, Gene	6	9	4.49	25	24	1	0	130	129	73	65	48	108	R	R	6-7	209	9-1-78	1996	Lynchburg, S.C.
Corey, Mark	12	6	2.44	20	20	6	0	140	125	55	38	36	109	R	R	6-2	220	11-16-74	1995	Austin, Pa.
Davis, Lance	4	2	1.99	25	4	0	0	54	35	17	12	29	38	R	L	5-11	165	9-1-76	1995	Polk City, Fla.
Getz, Rod	0	1	7.07	13	1	0	0	14	21	14	11	14	15	R	R	6-4	200	2-17-76	1995	Lawrenceburg, Ind.
Giuliano, Joe	3	5	3.87	44	1	0	0	81	78	41	35	35	65	R	R	6-2	175	1-1-76	1994	Hamilton, Ohio
Glauber, Keith	0	1	3.86	7	1	0	0	14	13	9	6	6	13	R	R	6-2	190	1-18-72	1994	Morganville, N.J.
Harrell, Scott	2	0	4.02	31	0	0	0	47	34	23	21	33	57	R	R	6-2	170	11-25-74	1997	Savannah, Ga.
Harris, Josh	10	12	3.05	27	27	6	0	177	166	82	60	45	169	R	R	6-3	220	10-23-77	1996	Canyon Lake, Texas
Hart, Damien	0	4	3.41	19	2	0	1	34	37	27	13	15	24	L	L	6-4	215	6-24-75	1998	Indianapolis, Ind.
Hurst, Doug	1	2	3.38	7	0	0	3	11	11	5	4	0	10	R	R	5-11	195	2-23-76	1997	Pensacola, Fla.
LeBlanc, Eric	3	3	3.02	19	6	0	0	57	51	25	19	20	41	L	R	6-0	195	7-6-73	1996	North Troy, Vt.
Mallard, Randi	9	3	3.38	14	13	2	0	83	79	41	31	32	71	R	R	6-1	180	8-11-75	1996	Tampa, Fla.
Needham, Kevin	2	5	5.36	9	9	0	0	42	46	30	25	20	22	L	L	5-10	185	1-30-75	1996	Burlington, Ontario
Peterson, Jay	3	8	6.18	16	15	0	0	63	60	52	43	49	62	B	R	6-4	198	11-2-75	1994	Commerce City, Colo.
Shepard, David	1	4	6.48	29	0	0	10	33	50	31	24	16	40	R	R	6-1	195	2-6-74	1996	Hornell, N.Y.
Stumbo, Wes	0	0	3.86	6	0	0	0	9	7	7	4	5	7	R	R	6-6	230	2-19-76	1997	Lexington, Ky.
Therneau, Dave	2	3	3.86	7	6	0	0	40	36	17	17	17	42	R	R	6-5	195	12-23-75	1998	Denton, Texas
Timm, Dan	3	1	5.74	34	1	0	1	58	50	43	37	47	62	B	R	6-1	170	4-2-76	1997	Glen Ellyn, Ill.
Whitesides, Johnny	1	7	5.06	18	10	0	0	59	70	46	33	29	42	R	R	6-4	195	3-2-78	1997	Sarasota, Fla.
Woodrum, Randy	1	0	5.33	13	0	0	0	27	25	17	16	20	24	R	L	6-5	200	2-1-76	1998	Georgetown, Ky.
Wright, Scott	0	1	0.28	27	0	0	15	32	12	4	1	8	38	R	R	6-2	210	10-15-72	1995	Medford, Wis.

CHARLESTON, W.Va. — Class A

SOUTH ATLANTIC LEAGUE

BATTING	AVG	G	AB	R	H	2B	3B	HR	RBI	BB	SO	SB	CS	B	T	HT	WT	DOB	1st Yr	Resides
Aalbers, Brady	.174	22	46	3	8	2	0	0	1	4	12	1	2	R	R	5-11	165	10-5-76	1998	Alton, Iowa
Baderdeen, Kevin	.180	31	89	10	16	3	0	2	7	4	36	2	4	R	R	6-3	175	1-12-77	1997	Goshen, Ind.
Caceres, Wilmy	.259	103	394	48	102	12	7	0	27	18	62	24	14	B	R	6-0	170	10-2-78	1997	Santo Domingo, D.R.
Copley, Travis	.232	59	211	26	49	8	0	4	21	21	59	6	2	L	R	6-4	215	1-8-76	1998	Hixson, Tenn.
Garcia, Sandro	.216	104	366	43	79	15	1	4	35	23	59	9	5	R	R	5-10	180	11-22-77	1996	Deerfield Beach, Fla.
Garrett, Scott	.175	52	171	10	30	3	0	0	14	10	58	1	0	R	R	6-5	225	3-8-74	1996	Denver, N.C.
Markray, Thad	.107	36	121	7	13	4	0	1	7	4	38	0	1	R	R	6-4	220	9-20-79	1997	Springhill, La.
Marn, Kevin	.259	96	344	40	89	19	1	4	39	28	63	15	6	R	R	6-4	205	3-23-74	1996	Broadview Heights, Ohio
Medrano, Ryan	.227	115	361	54	82	19	0	7	30	50	73	6	2	R	R	5-11	190	3-27-74	1998	El Paso, Texas
Newman, Howard	.182	3	11	1	2	0	0	1	2	0	5	0	0	R	R	5-10	190	12-5-75	1997	Riverside, Calif.
O'Hearn, Brandon	.233	113	390	36	91	21	2	7	49	31	144	4	5	R	R	6-3	200	6-24-75	1996	Butler, Ga.
Oliver, Johnny	.224	115	416	33	93	23	0	11	57	22	109	11	8	R	R	6-2	180	5-14-78	1996	Dallas, Pa.
Price, Corey	.323	36	130	19	42	6	0	1	12	12	22	6	3	B	R	6-0	165	9-18-76	1996	Mount Pleasant, Texas
Rivera, Francisco	.071	5	14	0	1	0	0	0	0	3	2	0	0	L	R	6-2	195	10-4-79	1996	El Tejar, Mexico
Rodriguez, Serafin	.282	85	323	53	91	18	0	4	28	18	53	24	6	R	R	6-0	174	10-12-78	1997	Veracruz, Mexico
Sanchez, Toby	.243	126	408	52	99	18	3	12	48	65	160	4	7	R	R	6-1	230	6-27-75	1997	Tustin, Calif.
Taylor, Corey	.214	54	173	28	37	8	3	3	19	24	46	15	4	R	R	6-0	185	10-2-74	1998	Monroe, La.
Tidwell, Dave	.265	8	34	10	9	1	0	0	1	3	9	6	0	R	R	5-9	170	1-17-75	1997	Grenada, Miss.
Toomey, Chris	.237	18	59	5	14	3	0	1	4	1	21	1	1	R	R	6-2	195	8-5-77	1998	Dana Point, Calif.
Whitehead, Braxton	.248	116	408	33	101	24	0	4	48	32	79	6	5	R	R	6-2	215	10-20-75	1997	Newton, Miss.
Williams, Mike	.222	12	27	4	6	1	0	0	3	2	13	2	1	R	R	6-2	189	12-8-73	1997	Belleville, Ill.

GAMES BY POSITION: C—Copley 12, Garrett 40, Newman 3, Rivera 2, Whitehead 75, Williams 11. **1B**—Copley 3, Garrett 1, Marn 19, O'Hearn 2, Sanchez 122, Taylor 1. **2B**—Garcia 31, Medrano 84, Price 33. **3B**—Baderdeen 21, Copley 37, Garcia 46, Markray 36, Medrano 6, Price 4. **SS**—Aalbers 21, Baderdeen 1, Caceres 103, Medrano 26, Price 1. **OF**—Baderdeen 1, Garcia 16, Marn 69, O'Hearn 95, Oliver 104, Rodriguez 83, Taylor 42, Tidwell 7, Toomey 18.

PITCHING	W	L	ERA	G	GS	CG	SV	IP	H	R	ER	BB	SO	B	T	HT	WT	DOB	1st Yr	Resides
Acevedo, Jose	9	9	3.91	25	25	2	0	159	169	74	69	40	132	R	R	6-0	185	12-18-77	1997	Santiago, D.R.
Averette, Robert	5	4	2.79	14	14	3	0	84	84	38	26	26	68	R	R	6-2	185	9-30-76	1997	Sylacauga, Ala.
Brewer, Clint	0	7	6.66	35	7	0	1	73	90	71	54	49	46	R	R	6-4	185	11-22-78	1997	Dibble, Okla.
Caddell, Carl	0	0	4.03	15	0	0	0	29	31	15	13	15	24	L	L	6-3	185	10-13-75	1996	Fort Worth, Texas
Crowell, Jim	0	4	13.20	5	5	0	0	15	28	23	22	9	9	R	L	6-4	230	5-14-74	1995	Valparaiso, Ind.
Danner, Andy	1	1	6.06	21	0	0	2	36	48	30	24	15	30	R	R	6-0	195	7-23-75	1997	Springfield, Ill.
Gardner, Nathan	6	4	3.97	45	0	0	6	77	89	41	34	33	64	R	R	5-11	195	9-10-74	1997	Newton, N.C.
Haring, Brett	2	9	3.32	38	13	2	4	108	123	48	40	26	91	R	L	5-11	180	2-7-75	1997	Mount Pleasant, Mich.
Levy, Tye	1	10	5.95	34	7	0	1	82	109	65	54	28	54	L	L	6-2	185	4-20-78	1997	Alexandria, Pa.
Merrell, Phil	5	15	4.64	26	25	4	0	149	169	91	77	43	117	R	R	6-3	190	3-11-78	1996	Nampa, Idaho
O'Toole, Ryan	0	0	11.81	4	0	0	0	5	9	10	7	9	2	R	R	6-3	190	10-2-75	1997	Irvine, Calif.
Puffer, Brandon	2	7	6.93	29	0	0	1	51	68	45	39	23	36	R	R	6-3	195	10-5-75	1994	Mission Viejo, Calif.
Robinson, Dustin	5	10	4.47	25	24	2	0	141	153	85	70	44	92	R	R	6-6	215	9-13-75	1997	Chandler, Okla.
Ryan, Robert	0	0	2.08	3	0	0	2	4	1	1	1	1	5	L	L	6-6	230	12-28-75	1998	Benton, La.
Sellers, Roger	0	1	7.67	12	0	0	0	27	39	27	23	15	13	R	R	6-0	190	7-3-77	1998	Metairie, La.
Sequea, Jacobo	3	5	6.02	13	11	0	0	55	68	42	37	33	33	R	R	6-0	175	8-31-81	1997	Anaco, Ven.
Shepard, David	2	8	5.06	16	8	2	2	48	58	41	27	9	33	R	R	6-1	195	2-6-74	1996	Hornell, N.Y.
Solano, Manny	3	2	3.21	18	1	0	0	34	38	17	12	13	18	R	R	6-0	175	5-17-78	1995	Villa Mella, D.R.

BILLINGS — Rookie

PIONEER LEAGUE

BATTING	AVG	G	AB	R	H	2B	3B	HR	RBI	BB	SO	SB	CS	B	T	HT	WT	DOB	1st Yr	Resides
Aalbers, Brady	.235	12	34	7	8	0	0	0	3	1	10	1	1	R	R	5-11	165	10-5-76	1998	Alton, Iowa
Baston, Stan	.379	12	29	8	11	1	1	0	5	11	7	1	0	R	R	6-2	180	2-12-77	1996	Tallahassee, Fla.
Beattie, Andrew	.250	43	128	36	32	8	2	4	25	34	33	3	0	B	R	5-10	170	2-28-78	1998	Clearwater, Fla.
Copley, Travis	.182	3	11	3	2	0	0	2	7	2	1	0	0	L	R	6-4	215	1-8-76	1998	Hixson, Tenn.
Dunn, Adam	.288	34	125	26	36	3	1	4	13	22	23	4	2	L	R	6-5	240	11-9-79	1998	Porter, Texas
Godfrey, Tim	.318	30	110	18	35	4	0	2	21	14	11	1	1	B	R	6-2	185	8-26-77	1999	Checotah, Okla.
Kearns, Austin	.315	30	108	17	34	9	0	1	14	23	22	1	1	R	R	6-4	210	5-20-80	1998	Lexington, Ky.
Layton, Blane	.294	59	221	56	65	20	4	7	39	33	45	3	3	L	L	6-2	190	8-17-76	1998	Plant City, Fla.
Markray, Thad	.235	70	251	43	59	11	0	2	31	33	64	1	2	R	R	6-4	220	9-20-79	1997	Springhill, La.
Matan, James	.273	74	293	61	80	13	1	18	65	39	66	0	2	R	R	6-3	230	4-18-76	1998	Kensington, Md.
Miller, Corky	.271	45	129	20	35	8	0	5	24	24	24	1	4	R	R	6-1	215	3-18-76	1998	Calimesa, Calif.
Peters, Samone	.292	72	274	44	80	22	1	13	46	13	100	0	1	R	R	6-7	260	7-30-78	1998	Alameda, Calif.
Price, Duane	.275	31	102	21	28	2	0	1	14	14	32	2	4	R	R	6-1	190	9-5-75	1998	College Station, Texas
Rivera, Francisco	.375	3	8	3	3	0	0	0	3	4	1	0	0	L	R	6-2	195	10-4-79	1996	El Tejar, Mexico
Senegal, Terence	.308	6	13	4	4	0	0	0	1	4	4	2	0	R	R	6-1	180	11-25-78	1998	Lafayette, La.
Stegall, Randy	.316	66	269	46	85	19	1	5	40	20	44	2	1	R	R	6-3	190	2-16-75	1998	Longwood, Fla.
Taylor, Corey	.200	3	10	2	2	2	0	0	1	1	6	0	0	R	R	6-0	185	10-2-74	1998	Monroe, La.
Toomey, Chris	.000	3	3	1	0	0	0	0	0	2	2	0	0	R	R	6-2	195	8-5-77	1998	Dana Point, Calif.
Vaughn, Clint	.266	74	289	46	77	18	2	12	61	26	70	2	1	R	R	6-4	225	12-30-76	1998	Edmond, Okla.
Wallis, Jacob	.238	32	105	14	25	7	0	2	20	13	29	1	1	R	R	6-2	200	2-1-80	1998	Joshua, Texas

GAMES BY POSITION: C—Miller 43, Rivera 3, Wallis 32. **1B**—Matan 7, Peters 2, Vaughn 66. **2B**—Aalbers 2, Baston 3, Beattie 6, Godfrey 27, Stegall 42. **3B**—Kearns 2, Markray 69, Stegall 6. **SS**—Aalbers 9, Baston 9, Beattie 37, Godfrey 2, Markray 2, Stegall 19. **OF**—Dunn 34, Kearns 29, Layton 56, Matan 6, Peters 70, Price 29, Senegal 4, Taylor 3, Toomey 2.

PITCHING	W	L	ERA	G	GS	CG	SV	IP	H	R	ER	BB	SO	B	T	HT	WT	DOB	1st Yr	Resides
Birdsong, Tim	4	1	1.18	19	1	0	3	38	39	13	5	17	38	R	R	6-5	210	5-4-77	1998	Bokchito, Okla.
Brown, Zadrian	0	3	6.94	16	1	0	0	23	37	18	18	12	25	R	R	6-1	172	1-5-79	1997	Warrenville, S.C.
Coffey, Todd	0	0	3.00	3	2	0	0	12	13	4	4	1	8	R	R	6-5	245	9-9-80	1998	Caroleen, N.C.
Cooper, Eric	7	2	4.37	22	3	0	5	47	49	30	23	20	48	R	R	6-4	210	9-5-77	1998	Fremont, Calif.
DeHart, Casey	3	1	5.79	15	0	0	3	23	26	20	15	22	18	L	L	6-2	180	11-1-77	1998	Burleson, Texas
Hall, Josh	5	4	5.00	14	14	1	0	81	89	53	45	33	50	R	R	6-2	170	12-16-80	1998	Lynchburg, Va.
Hart, Damien	1	0	3.00	1	0	0	0	3	4	1	1	0	4	L	L	6-4	215	6-24-75	1998	Indianapolis, Ind.
Hussman, Darrell	0	1	8.36	5	3	0	1	14	12	15	13	9	17	R	R	6-5	200	1-14-77	1998	Quartz Hill, Calif.
Iwasaki, Junichi	0	0	6.91	9	0	0	0	14	21	11	11	13	11	L	L	6-1	175	9-13-79	1998	Fukushima, Japan
Joseph, Glen	0	1	13.50	2	1	0	0	4	3	6	6	7	3	R	R	6-3	190	9-3-80	1998	Tampa, Fla.
Koronka, John	0	3	8.04	12	3	0	0	31	47	43	28	26	36	L	L	6-1	180	6-11-80	1998	Clermont, Fla.
Larman, Jayson	0	2	4.85	5	1	0	0	13	8	9	7	17	20	R	R	6-3	200	12-5-78	1998	Wayne, Okla.
Madritsch, Robert	7	3	2.80	14	13	0	0	80	72	30	25	35	87	L	L	6-2	190	2-28-76	1998	Burbank, Ill.
McEvoy, Casey	6	4	4.89	14	14	0	0	81	71	57	44	44	64	R	R	6-3	210	7-29-76	1998	Florence, Ky.
Runk, Dave	0	0	7.50	5	0	0	0	6	5	8	5	12	3	R	R	6-3	206	9-1-78	1997	Broad Top, Pa.
Russo, Dennis	1	4	8.26	17	8	0	0	57	83	56	52	32	20	R	R	6-2	180	1-10-80	1998	Auburndale, Fla.
Ryan, Robert	2	1	1.93	14	0	0	4	19	15	4	4	5	25	L	L	6-6	230	12-28-75	1998	Benton, La.
Sellers, Roger	0	1	17.18	3	0	0	0	4	8	7	7	4	5	R	R	6-0	190	7-3-77	1998	Metairie, La.
Stanley, Cody	1	1	3.03	20	0	0	1	30	32	14	10	23	19	R	R	6-2	185	9-21-78	1998	San Antonio, Texas
Therneau, Dave	3	1	3.88	9	9	0	0	51	52	27	22	16	59	R	R	6-5	195	12-23-75	1998	Denton, Texas
Woodrum, Randy	0	1	3.68	2	1	0	0	7	5	3	3	4	4	R	L	6-5	200	2-1-76	1998	Georgetown, Ky.

CLEVELAND INDIANS

Tribe secures division title, but falls short of big goal

BY JIM INGRAHAM

The Indians' goal going into the 1998 season was to make it back to the World Series, and get the last two outs in the ninth inning of Game Seven that eluded them the year before.

Six months later, they were not only still looking for those last two outs, they were still looking for the World Series.

After winning their fourth straight American League Central title, the Tribe beat the Red Sox in four games in the Division Series to advance to the AL Championship Series.

But their luck ran out against a Yankee club that owed the Tribe some payback for being sent home from the AL Division Series the year before. After taking a two-games-to-one lead, the Indians went down in three straight to a team that won 114 games in the regular season.

It was a disappointing conclusion for the Indians, who were convinced they had put together a better team for 1998 than the one that came within two outs of beating the Marlins in '97.

On paper, the team did look better. Kenny Lofton was signed as a free agent, and reinstalled at the top of the lineup. Dwight Gooden was another free agent pickup, signed to bolster the rotation. Third baseman Travis Fryman came over from the Diamondbacks in an expansion-draft-day deal. And veteran righthander Dave Burba was picked up from the Reds for highly-regarded prospect Sean Casey.

Mike Jackson, who pitched well as a setup man in '97, took his game to another level as closer, replacing an ineffective Jose Mesa and recording 40 saves. Mesa was traded to the Giants.

Manny Ramirez

Alex Ramirez

Players of the Year

Major League: Manny Ramirez, of
Ramirez led the Tribe in home runs, RBIs and runs scored while having his finest all-around season.

Minor League: Alex Ramirez, of, Buffalo
No relation to Manny, Alex led all Indians minor leaguers with 34 homers, 103 RBIs and 295 total bases.

The offense was led by right fielder Manny Ramirez, who had an MVP-caliber year, blasting 45 home runs and collecting 145 RBIs.

The starting rotation was steady, if unspectacular, with Burba, Charles Nagy, Bartolo Colon and Jaret Wright all winning between 12 and 15 games. However, the lack of a bona fide No.1 starter haunted the club in the postseason.

Like the major league club, Triple-A Buffalo had an outstanding season, but came up a little short of their ultimate goal. The Bisons fell to New Orleans in the first Triple-A World Series in Las Vegas.

But Buffalo at least had the consolation prize of the Governors' Cup for winning the International League. The team finished with the best record in the IL at 81-62, to surge past a slumping Syracuse team in the final days of the season. The Bisons then swept Syracuse in the first round of the playoffs and defeated Durham to take the IL title.

Outfielder Alex Ramirez keyed the Buffalo offensive attack, hitting .299 with 34 homers and 103 RBIs. Richie Sexson, who was named the IL's No. 2 prospect, hit .297 with 21 homers and 74 RBIs before moving up to Cleveland, where he hit another 11 home runs. Lefthander Jason Jacome led the pitching staff with a 14-2 record and 3.26 ERA.

Double-A Akron also had a successful season, finishing first in the Eastern League's Southern Division. The Aeros stumbled in the first round of the playoffs against eventual league champion Harrisburg.

Third baseman Russ Branyan, the organization's top prospect, finished the '98 season on a tear after missing much of the year with a wrist injury. He hit 16 home runs in just 163 at-bats for Akron.

ORGANIZATION LEADERS

BATTING		
*AVG	Torey Lovullo, Buffalo	.326
R	Scott Morgan, Akron	95
H	Darren Stumberger, Akron	164
TB	Alex Ramirez, Buffalo	295
2B	Darren Stumberger, Akron	39
3B	Jon Hamilton, Columbus	10
HR	Alex Ramirez, Buffalo	34
RBI	Alex Ramirez, Buffalo	103
BB	Jon Hamilton, Columbus	79
SO	Chad Whitaker, Kinston	148
SB	Marcos Scutaro, Buffalo/Akron	33
PITCHING		
W	Jason Jacome, Buffalo	14
L	Kaipo Spenser, Kinston/Columbus	13
#ERA	Chris Reinike, Watertown	1.91
G	Rich Batchelor, Buffalo	57
CG	Alberto Garza, Akron/Kinston	4
SV	David Riske, Akron/Kinston	34
IP	Frankie Sanders, Akron	186
BB	Marcus Moore, Buffalo/Akron	95
SO	Jamie Brown, Akron/Kinston	153

*Minimum 250 At-Bats #Minimum 75 Innings

Cleveland INDIANS

Manager: Mike Hargrove

1998 Record: 89-73, .549 (1st, AL Central)

BATTING	AVG	G	AB	R	H	2B	3B	HR	RBI	BB	SO	SB	CS	B	T	HT	WT	DOB	1st Yr	Resides
Alomar, Sandy	.235	117	409	45	96	26	2	6	44	18	45	0	3	R	R	6-5	215	6-18-66	1984	Westlake, Ohio
Bell, David	.262	107	340	37	89	21	2	10	41	22	54	0	4	R	R	5-10	170	9-14-72	1990	Cincinnati, Ohio
Berroa, Geronimo	.200	20	65	6	13	3	1	0	3	7	17	1	0	R	R	6-0	210	3-18-65	1984	New York, N.Y.
Borders, Pat	.238	54	160	12	38	6	0	0	6	10	40	0	2	R	R	6-2	195	5-14-63	1982	Lake Wales, Fla.
Branson, Jeff	.200	63	100	6	20	4	1	1	9	3	21	0	0	L	R	6-0	180	1-26-67	1989	Millry, Ala.
Branyan, Russell	.000	1	4	0	0	0	0	0	0	0	2	0	0	L	R	6-3	195	12-19-75	1994	Warner Robins, Ga.
Cabrera, Jolbert	.000	1	2	0	0	0	0	0	0	0	1	0	0	R	R	6-0	177	12-8-72	1991	Cartagena, Colombia
Cora, Joey	.229	24	83	16	19	4	0	0	6	11	9	2	1	B	R	5-8	162	5-14-65	1985	Caguas, P.R.
2-team (131 Seattle)	.276	155	602	111	166	27	6	6	32	73	59	15	6							
Cruz, Jacob	.000	1	1	0	0	0	0	0	0	0	1	0	0	L	L	6-0	175	1-28-73	1994	Tempe, Ariz.
Diaz, Einar	.229	17	48	8	11	1	0	2	9	3	2	0	0	R	R	5-10	165	12-28-72	1991	Chiriqui, Panama
Dunston, Shawon	.237	62	156	26	37	11	3	3	12	6	18	9	2	R	R	6-1	175	3-21-63	1982	Corona, N.Y.
Fielder, Cecil	.143	14	35	1	5	1	0	0	0	1	13	0	0	R	R	6-3	250	9-21-63	1982	Grosse Point Farms, Mich.
2-team (103 Ana.)	.233	117	416	49	97	17	1	17	68	53	111	0	1							
Fryman, Travis	.287	146	557	74	160	33	2	28	96	44	125	10	8	R	R	6-1	194	3-25-69	1987	Cantonment, Fla.
Giles, Brian	.269	112	350	56	94	19	0	16	66	73	75	10	5	L	L	5-11	195	1-20-71	1989	El Cajon, Calif.
Justice, Dave	.280	146	540	94	151	39	2	21	88	76	98	9	3	L	L	6-3	200	4-14-66	1985	Atlanta, Ga.
Lofton, Kenny	.282	154	600	101	169	31	6	12	64	87	80	54	10	L	L	6-0	180	5-31-67	1988	Tucson, Ariz.
Lovullo, Torey	.211	6	19	1	4	1	0	0	1	1	2	0	0	B	R	6-0	185	7-25-65	1987	Northridge, Calif.
Luke, Matt	.000	2	2	0	0	0	0	0	0	0	0	0	0	L	L	6-5	220	2-26-71	1992	Huntington Beach, Calif.
Manto, Jeff	.216	15	37	8	8	1	0	2	6	2	10	0	1	R	R	6-3	210	8-23-64	1985	Bristol, Pa.
2-team (16 Detroit)	.239	31	67	14	16	3	0	3	0	5	21	1	1							
Ramirez, Alex	.125	3	8	1	1	0	0	0	0	0	3	0	0	R	R	5-11	176	10-3-74	1991	Winter Haven, Fla.
Ramirez, Manny	.294	150	571	108	168	35	2	45	145	76	121	5	3	R	R	6-0	190	5-30-72	1991	Brooklyn, N.Y.
Sexson, Richie	.310	49	174	28	54	14	1	11	35	6	42	1	1	R	R	6-7	200	12-29-74	1993	Brush Prairie, Wash.
Thome, Jim	.293	123	440	89	129	34	2	30	85	90	141	1	0	L	R	6-4	225	8-27-70	1989	Aurora, Ohio
Vizquel, Omar	.288	151	576	86	166	30	6	2	50	62	64	37	12	B	R	5-9	170	4-24-67	1984	Bellevue, Wash.
Whiten, Mark	.283	88	226	31	64	14	0	6	29	29	60	2	1	B	R	6-3	215	11-25-66	1986	Pensacola, Fla.
Wilson, Enrique	.322	32	90	13	29	6	0	2	12	4	8	2	4	B	R	5-11	160	7-27-75	1992	Santo Domingo, D.R.

PITCHING	W	L	ERA	G	GS	CG	SV	IP	H	R	ER	BB	SO	B	T	HT	WT	DOB	1st Yr	Resides
Assenmacher, Paul	2	5	3.26	69	0	0	3	47	54	22	17	19	43	L	L	6-3	195	12-10-60	1983	Stone Mountain, Ga.
Burba, Dave	15	10	4.11	32	31	0	0	204	210	100	93	69	132	R	R	6-4	240	7-7-66	1987	Gilbert, Ariz.
Colon, Bartolo	14	9	3.71	31	31	6	0	204	205	91	84	79	158	R	R	6-0	185	5-24-75	1994	Puerto Plata, D.R.
Gooden, Dwight	8	6	3.76	23	23	0	0	134	135	59	56	51	83	R	R	6-2	210	11-16-64	1982	St. Petersburg, Fla.
Jackson, Mike	1	1	1.55	69	0	0	40	64	43	11	11	13	55	R	R	6-2	223	12-22-64	1984	Spring, Texas
Jacome, Jason	0	1	14.40	1	1	0	0	5	10	8	8	3	2	L	L	6-0	180	11-24-70	1991	Tucson, Ariz.
Jones, Doug	1	2	3.45	23	0	0	1	31	34	12	12	6	28	R	R	6-2	225	6-24-57	1978	Tucson, Ariz.
Karsay, Steve	0	2	5.92	11	1	0	0	24	31	16	16	6	13	R	R	6-3	210	3-24-72	1990	Tempe, Ariz.
Krivda, Rick	2	0	3.24	11	1	0	0	25	24	10	9	16	10	R	L	6-1	185	1-19-70	1991	Cockeysville, Md.
Martin, Tom	1	1	12.89	14	0	0	0	15	29	21	21	12	9	L	L	6-1	185	5-21-70	1989	Panama City, Fla.
Mesa, Jose	3	4	5.17	44	0	0	1	54	61	36	31	20	35	R	R	6-3	225	5-22-66	1982	Westlake, Ohio
Morman, Alvin	0	1	5.32	31	0	0	0	22	25	13	13	11	16	R	L	6-3	210	1-6-69	1991	Rockingham, N.C.
Nagy, Charles	15	10	5.22	33	33	2	0	210	250	139	122	66	120	L	R	6-3	200	5-5-67	1989	Westlake, Ohio
Ogea, Chad	5	4	5.61	19	9	0	0	69	74	44	43	25	43	R	R	6-2	200	11-9-70	1991	Lake Charles, La.
Plunk, Eric	3	1	4.83	37	0	0	0	41	44	23	22	15	38	R	R	6-6	220	9-3-63	1981	Riverside, Calif.
Poole, Jim	0	0	5.14	12	0	0	0	7	9	4	4	3	11	L	L	6-1	203	4-28-66	1988	Alpharetta, Ga.
Rakers, Jason	0	0	9.00	1	0	0	0	1	0	1	1	3	0	R	R	6-2	197	6-29-73	1995	Pittsburgh, Pa.
Reed, Steve	2	2	6.66	20	0	0	0	26	26	19	19	8	23	R	R	6-3	180	3-11-66	1988	Arvada, Colo.
Shuey, Paul	5	4	3.00	43	0	0	2	51	44	19	17	25	58	R	R	6-3	215	9-16-70	1992	Raleigh, N.C.
Villone, Ron	0	0	6.00	25	0	0	0	27	30	18	18	22	15	L	L	6-3	237	1-16-70	1992	Bergenfield, N.J.
Worrell, Tim	0	0	5.06	3	0	0	0	5	6	3	3	2	2	R	R	6-4	215	7-5-67	1990	Glendale, Ariz.
Wright, Jaret	12	10	4.72	32	32	1	0	193	207	109	101	87	140	R	R	6-2	230	12-29-75	1994	Anaheim, Calif.

FIELDING

Catcher	PCT	G	PO	A	E	DP	PB
Alomar	.992	111	713	42	6	7	4
Borders	.974	53	283	19	8	1	4
Diaz	.973	17	101	9	3	0	0

First Base	PCT	G	PO	A	E	DP
Bell	1.000	1	4	0	0	0
Branson	1.000	3	9	2	0	0
Fielder	.933	3	12	2	1	1
Manto	.981	7	49	2	1	4
Sexson	.984	45	321	38	6	36
Thome	.991	117	998	85	10	97

Second Base	PCT	G	PO	A	E	DP
Bell	.982	101	192	294	9	58
Branson	.960	31	35	37	3	14
Cora	.986	21	31	40	1	8
Dunston	.978	24	32	55	2	9
Lovullo	.947	5	4	14	1	3
Manto	1.000	1	0	1	0	1
Wilson	.989	22	35	52	1	6

Third Base	PCT	G	PO	A	E	DP
Bell	1.000	6	4	12	0	1
Borders	1.000	1	0	1	0	0
Branson	.913	20	5	16	2	1
Branyan	1.000	1	0	1	0	0
Fryman	.963	144	100	236	13	21
Lovullo	1.000	1	0	1	0	0
Manto	1.000	8	0	5	0	2
Wilson	1.000	2	1	0	0	0

Shortstop	PCT	G	PO	A	E	DP
Bell	1.000	1	1	0	0	0
Branson	.000	2	0	0	0	0
Cabrera	1.000	1	2	2	0	0
Dunston	.944	14	13	21	2	3
Fryman	1.000	3	1	5	0	2
Vizquel	.993	151	271	442	5	94
Wilson	.970	10	9	23	1	4

Outfield	PCT	G	PO	A	E	DP
Berroa	1.000	14	27	1	0	0
Dunston	1.000	12	18	0	0	0
Giles	.978	101	212	7	5	1
Justice	1.000	21	37	0	0	0
Lofton	.978	154	340	18	8	4
A. Ramirez	.833	3	5	0	1	0
M. Ramirez	.977	148	292	10	7	1
Sexson	1.000	3	4	0	0	0
Whiten	.971	72	124	8	4	1

Cleveland's Bartolo Colon
Led Tribe with 158 strikeouts

First baseman Richie Sexson
Hit 11 homers after promotion from Buffalo

FARM SYSTEM

Director, Minor League Operations: Mark Shapiro

Class	Farm Team	League	W	L	Pct.	Finish*	Manager	First Yr
AAA	Buffalo (N.Y.) Bisons	International	81	62	.566	+1st (14)	Jeff Datz	1995
AA	Akron (Ohio) Aeros	Eastern	81	60	.574	3rd (10)	Joel Skinner	1997
A#	Kinston (N.C.) Indians	Carolina	69	71	.493	5th (8)	Mako Oliveras	1987
A	Columbus (Ga.) RedStixx	South Atlantic	59	81	.421	12th (14)	Eric Wedge	1991
A	Watertown (N.Y.) Indians	New York-Penn	42	34	.553	5th (14)	Ted Kubiak	1989
Rookie#	Burlington (N.C.) Indians	Appalachian	31	36	.463	7th (10)	Joe Mikulik	1986

*Finish in overall standings (No. of teams in league) #Advanced level +Won league championship

BUFFALO — Class AAA

INTERNATIONAL LEAGUE

BATTING	AVG	G	AB	R	H	2B	3B	HR	RBI	BB	SO	SB	CS	B	T	HT	WT	DOB	1st Yr	Resides
Aven, Bruce	.200	5	15	4	3	1	0	1	1	6	5	3	0	R	R	5-9	180	3-4-72	1994	Orange, Texas
Betts, Todd	.229	14	35	5	8	3	0	2	6	8	7	0	0	L	R	6-0	190	6-24-73	1993	Scarborough, Ontario
Betzsold, James	.244	74	209	36	51	10	1	10	27	27	72	4	4	R	R	6-3	210	8-7-72	1994	Orange, Calif.
Branson, Jeff	.261	12	46	5	12	4	1	0	2	5	9	0	0	L	R	6-0	180	1-26-67	1989	Millry, Ala.
Cabrera, Jolbert	.318	129	494	94	157	24	1	10	45	68	71	25	15	R	R	6-0	177	12-8-72	1991	Cartagena, Colombia
Cruz, Jacob	.331	43	169	32	56	8	2	13	36	13	26	2	3	L	L	6-0	175	1-28-73	1994	Tempe, Ariz.
Diaz, Einar	.313	115	415	62	130	21	3	8	63	21	33	3	3	R	R	5-10	165	12-28-72	1991	Chiriqui, Panama
Giles, Brian	.239	13	46	5	11	2	0	2	7	6	8	0	0	L	L	5-11	195	1-20-71	1989	El Cajon, Calif.
Hiatt, Phil	.247	119	453	81	112	19	0	31	74	41	146	4	1	R	R	6-3	200	5-1-69	1990	Pensacola, Fla.
Hudler, Rex	.194	11	36	4	7	1	0	0	2	4	10	0	0	R	R	6-0	202	9-2-60	1978	Philadelphia, Pa.
Listach, Pat	.216	33	102	23	22	3	2	0	11	9	22	3	1	B	R	5-9	180	9-12-67	1988	Spring, Texas
Lovullo, Torey	.326	92	328	66	107	17	4	17	65	54	32	3	3	B	R	6-0	185	7-25-65	1987	Northridge, Calif.
Manto, Jeff	.311	62	209	46	65	11	0	23	63	58	48	4	2	R	R	6-3	210	8-23-64	1985	Bristol, Pa.
Miller, David	.267	115	415	56	111	19	2	9	54	61	72	6	8	L	L	6-4	200	12-9-73	1996	Wyndmoor, Pa.
Perry, Chan	.224	13	49	8	11	4	0	0	3	6	10	1	0	R	R	6-2	200	9-13-72	1994	Mayo, Fla.
Ramirez, Alex	.299	121	521	94	156	21	8	34	103	16	101	6	4	R	R	5-11	176	10-3-74	1991	Winter Haven, Fla.
Roberts, David	.133	5	15	2	2	0	0	0	2	0	3	2	0	L	L	5-10	172	5-31-72	1994	Oceanside, Calif.
Scutaro, Marcos	.231	8	26	3	6	3	0	0	4	0	2	0	0	R	R	5-10	170	10-30-75	1995	Yaracuy, Ven.
Selby, Bill	.254	97	334	45	85	23	0	14	52	38	50	3	0	L	R	5-9	170	6-11-70	1992	Walls, Mich.
Sexson, Richie	.297	89	344	58	102	20	1	21	74	50	68	1	2	R	R	6-7	206	12-29-74	1993	Brush Prairie, Wash.
Soliz, Steve	.223	39	112	14	25	6	0	0	9	11	23	1	1	R	R	5-10	180	1-27-71	1993	Oxnard, Calif.
Thomas, Greg	.091	4	11	1	1	1	0	0	2	1	5	0	0	L	L	6-3	200	7-19-72	1993	Canton, Ohio
Wilson, Brandon	.273	98	337	53	92	19	2	7	53	32	56	15	5	R	R	6-1	170	2-26-69	1990	Charlottesville, Va.
Wilson, Enrique	.281	56	221	40	62	13	0	4	23	19	21	8	3	B	R	5-11	160	7-27-75	1992	Santo Domingo, D.R.

PITCHING	W	L	ERA	G	GS	CG	SV	IP	H	R	ER	BB	SO	B	T	HT	WT	DOB	1st Yr	Resides
Batchelor, Rich	4	4	3.39	57	0	0	22	58	58	26	22	25	64	R	R	6-1	195	4-8-67	1990	Hartsville, S.C.
Blomdahl, Ben	2	3	4.76	35	2	0	1	70	83	43	37	17	42	R	R	6-2	185	12-30-70	1991	Riverside, Calif.
Cummings, John	0	1	5.79	21	0	0	0	19	25	15	12	4	15	L	L	6-3	200	5-10-69	1990	Laguna Niguel, Calif.
Dougherty, Tony	0	0	3.00	1	0	0	0	3	4	4	1	2	1	R	R	6-1	185	4-12-73	1994	Beaver Falls, Pa.
Driskill, Travis	0	0	9.00	1	1	0	0	6	9	6	6	1	5	R	R	6-0	185	8-1-71	1993	Austin, Texas
Flener, Huck	7	3	6.68	14	8	0	0	61	73	52	45	26	35	B	L	5-11	190	2-25-69	1990	Vacaville, Calif.
Gooden, Dwight	1	2	9.00	4	4	0	0	16	23	16	16	7	18	R	R	6-2	210	11-16-64	1982	St. Petersburg, Fla.
Grimsley, Jason	6	3	3.76	52	0	0	0	89	76	40	37	57	68	R	R	6-3	180	8-7-67	1985	Cleveland, Texas
Jacome, Jason	14	2	3.26	24	24	2	0	155	161	62	56	38	109	L	L	6-0	180	11-24-70	1991	Tucson, Ariz.
Karsay, Steve	6	4	3.76	16	14	0	0	79	89	39	33	15	63	R	R	6-3	210	3-24-72	1990	Tempe, Ariz.
Martin, Tom	3	1	6.00	41	0	0	0	36	46	25	24	13	35	L	L	6-1	185	5-21-70	1989	Panama City, Fla.
Matthews, Mike	9	6	4.63	24	23	0	0	130	137	79	67	68	86	L	L	6-2	175	10-24-73	1992	Woodbridge, Va.
Moore, Marcus	3	5	5.66	11	7	0	0	48	41	35	30	41	43	B	R	6-5	204	11-2-70	1989	Oakland, Calif.
Morman, Alvin	0	0	0.00	2	0	0	0	2	3	0	0	0	4	R	L	6-3	210	1-6-69	1991	Rockingham, N.C.
Nichting, Chris	8	6	4.39	43	5	0	1	96	104	54	47	37	97	R	R	6-1	205	5-13-66	1988	Cincinnati, Ohio
Ogea, Chad	2	1	3.61	9	9	1	0	42	42	19	17	5	34	R	R	6-2	200	11-9-70	1991	Lake Charles, La.
Poole, Jim	1	0	0.87	13	0	0	0	10	6	3	1	2	16	L	L	6-1	203	4-28-66	1988	Alpharetta, Ga.
Priest, Eddie	3	5	4.91	16	16	0	0	88	103	56	48	28	44	R	L	6-1	200	4-8-74	1994	Horton, Ala.
2-team (6 Indy)	7	6	4.87	22	22	0	0	122	139	75	66	35	65							
Rakers, Jason	8	6	4.57	21	21	1	0	126	134	70	64	38	89	R	R	6-2	197	6-29-73	1995	Pittsburgh, Pa.
Sexton, Jeff	0	0	4.07	21	0	0	1	24	25	16	11	15	15	R	R	6-2	190	10-4-71	1993	Crowder, Okla.
Shuey, Paul	0	0	2.51	11	0	0	2	14	11	4	4	6	22	R	R	6-3	215	9-16-70	1992	Raleigh, N.C.
Villone, Ron	2	2	2.01	23	0	0	7	22	20	11	5	11	28	L	L	6-3	237	1-16-70	1992	Bergenfield, N.J.
Williams, Jimmy	0	5	7.43	15	3	0	0	27	38	27	22	17	28	L	L	6-7	232	5-18-65	1984	Butler, Ala.
Young, Anthony	2	3	6.34	9	6	1	0	38	39	32	27	18	12	R	R	6-2	200	1-19-66	1987	Houston, Texas

FIELDING

Catcher	PCT	G	PO	A	E	DP	PB
Diaz	.986	112	791	70	12	7	11
Soliz	.984	39	215	27	4	1	5

First Base	PCT	G	PO	A	E	DP
Betzsold	.907	8	32	7	4	3
Hiatt	.988	73	593	57	8	64
Hudler	1.000	1	7	0	0	1
Lovullo	1.000	9	38	2	0	1
Manto	1.000	34	273	20	0	35
Perry	.971	7	65	3	2	1
Sexson	1.000	21	141	22	0	8

Second Base	PCT	G	PO	A	E	DP
Branson	1.000	6	16	11	0	4
Cabrera	1.000	1	1	1	0	0
Hudler	.917	3	6	5	1	2
Listach	1.000	19	37	40	0	4
Lovullo	.959	14	40	31	3	9
Scutaro	.938	7	12	18	2	4
Selby	.950	5	10	9	1	5
B. Wilson	.974	52	122	136	7	28
E. Wilson	.974	48	102	126	6	33

Third Base	PCT	G	PO	A	E	DP
Betts	.833	8	3	17	4	3
Branson	1.000	7	4	18	0	4
Hiatt	.000	1	0	0	0	0
Hudler	.750	4	1	5	2	0
Listach	.000	1	0	0	0	0
Lovullo	.895	74	36	135	20	16
Manto	.923	10	9	15	2	0
Scutaro	1.000	1	0	1	0	0
Selby	.963	26	17	62	3	4
B. Wilson	.940	25	11	36	3	1

Shortstop	PCT	G	PO	A	E	DP
Cabrera	.954	121	212	350	27	69
Listach	1.000	1	2	0	0	0
B. Wilson	.850	17	26	42	12	8
E. Wilson	1.000	6	6	15	0	3

Outfield	PCT	G	PO	A	E	DP
Betzsold	.970	52	90	6	3	1
Cabrera	1.000	7	22	1	0	1
Cruz	.949	43	70	5	4	0
Giles	.947	10	18	0	1	0
Hiatt	1.000	3	8	0	0	0
Hudler	1.000	3	2	1	0	0
Listach	.941	8	15	1	1	1
Miller	.985	115	251	5	4	1
Perry	1.000	2	6	0	0	0
Ramirez	.963	109	224	7	9	1
Roberts	1.000	5	12	1	0	0
Selby	1.000	16	18	3	0	0
Sexson	.978	69	129	7	3	2
Thomas	1.000	2	4	0	0	0

AKRON — Class AA

EASTERN LEAGUE

BATTING	AVG	G	AB	R	H	2B	3B	HR	RBI	BB	SO	SB	CS	B	T	HT	WT	DOB	1st Yr	Resides
Betances, Junior	.283	76	269	41	76	10	5	6	31	25	54	11	2	R	R	5-10	170	5-26-73	1991	La Vega, D.R.
Betts, Todd	.270	91	318	55	86	18	3	17	46	64	71	1	0	L	R	6-0	190	6-24-73	1993	Scarborough, Ontario
Branyan, Russell	.294	43	163	35	48	11	3	16	46	35	58	1	1	L	R	6-3	195	12-19-75	1994	Warner Robins, Ga.
Budzinski, Mark	.262	127	478	68	125	21	5	10	62	50	125	12	8	L	L	6-2	175	8-26-73	1995	Severna Park, Md.
Gross, Rafael	.069	25	58	6	4	0	0	0	3	6	21	4	3	R	R	5-10	155	8-8-74	1993	Nagua, D.R.
Gutierrez, Rick	.194	12	31	6	6	1	0	0	2	5	4	0	0	R	R	6-0	170	3-23-70	1994	Norman, Okla.
Harriss, Robin	.111	15	45	3	5	2	0	0	2	9	21	1	0	R	R	6-1	205	8-7-71	1994	San Angelo, Texas
Hayes, Heath	.207	91	329	36	68	14	1	11	46	24	95	2	3	R	R	6-3	195	2-29-72	1994	Citrus Heights, Calif.
Huelsmann, Mike	.100	9	20	4	2	0	0	1	1	4	9	1	0	B	R	5-11	165	11-21-74	1996	St. Louis, Mo.
McDonald, John	.230	132	514	68	118	18	2	2	43	43	61	17	6	R	R	5-11	175	9-24-74	1996	East Lyme, Conn.
Morgan, Scott	.294	119	456	95	134	31	4	25	89	56	124	4	5	R	R	6-7	230	7-19-73	1995	Lompoc, Calif.
Moyle, Mike	.301	39	133	19	40	5	0	4	23	17	27	1	0	R	R	6-2	200	9-8-71	1992	Dianella, Australia
Peoples, Danny	.279	60	222	30	62	19	0	8	32	29	61	1	1	R	R	6-1	207	1-20-75	1996	Round Rock, Texas
Perry, Chan	.281	54	203	36	57	17	2	5	27	23	43	3	2	R	R	6-2	200	9-13-72	1994	Mayo, Fla.
Ramirez, Peto	.184	15	49	4	9	1	0	2	8	10	17	0	0	R	R	6-2	215	9-10-72	1991	Ensenada, P.R.
Roberts, David	.361	56	227	49	82	10	5	7	33	35	30	28	6	L	L	5-10	172	5-31-72	1994	Oceanside, Calif.
Scutaro, Marcos	.316	124	462	68	146	27	6	11	62	47	71	33	16	R	R	5-10	170	10-30-75	1995	Yaracuy, Ven.
Selby, Bill	.390	20	77	15	30	7	1	3	10	3	11	0	0	L	R	5-9	170	6-11-70	1992	Walls, Mich.
Stumberger, Darren	.301	139	545	83	164	39	2	10	76	56	79	1	2	R	R	6-3	205	4-11-73	1994	Boca Raton, Fla.
Taveras, Frank	.500	2	4	2	2	0	0	0	0	1	1	0	0	L	R	6-1	158	9-6-75	1993	Santiago, D.R.
Taylor, Adam	.200	3	10	0	2	0	0	0	1	1	6	0	0	B	R	5-11	195	3-14-74	1996	Chelsea, Mich.
Thomas, Greg	.217	64	226	34	49	6	3	10	37	18	75	2	1	L	L	6-3	200	7-19-72	1993	Canton, Ohio
Whitlock, Brian	.077	9	26	1	2	1	0	0	2	1	11	0	0	R	R	6-1	180	9-16-74	1996	Sarasota, Fla.

PITCHING	W	L	ERA	G	GS	CG	SV	IP	H	R	ER	BB	SO	B	T	HT	WT	DOB	1st Yr	Resides
Atkins, Ross	7	8	4.19	40	5	0	10	77	73	39	36	31	38	R	R	6-2	195	8-7-73	1995	Miami, Fla.
Brammer, J.D.	1	0	5.23	11	0	0	3	21	21	12	12	10	23	R	R	6-4	235	1-30-75	1996	West Logan, W.Va.
Brower, Jim	13	5	3.01	23	23	2	0	156	142	60	52	38	91	R	R	6-2	205	12-29-72	1994	Minnetonka, Minn.
Brown, Jamie	1	0	2.57	1	1	0	0	7	5	2	2	1	5	R	R	6-2	205	3-31-77	1997	Gulf Breeze, Fla.
Calmus, Lance	2	5	5.50	23	2	0	0	52	55	34	32	28	23	R	R	6-5	225	1-19-73	1996	Jenks, Okla.
Camp, Jared	6	2	3.78	18	16	0	0	86	84	37	36	31	42	R	R	6-2	195	5-4-75	1995	Huntington, W.Va.
Cormier, Rheal	0	0	6.52	3	3	0	0	10	15	7	7	2	6	L	L	5-10	185	4-23-67	1989	Saint John, N.B.
DePaula, Sean	1	1	4.76	8	1	0	0	17	16	10	9	15	17	R	R	6-4	215	11-7-73	1996	Derry, N.H.
Deschenes, Marc	4	6	3.86	47	0	0	5	58	52	36	25	34	52	R	R	6-0	175	1-6-73	1995	Dracut, Mass.

PITCHING	W	L	ERA	G	GS	CG	SV	IP	H	R	ER	BB	SO	B	T	HT	WT	DOB	1st Yr	Resides
Dougherty, Tony	6	5	3.07	43	0	0	5	76	68	29	26	36	60	R	R	6-1	185	4-12-73	1994	Beaver Falls, Pa.
Driskill, Travis	3	0	3.42	5	4	0	0	26	27	12	10	7	16	R	R	6-0	185	8-1-71	1993	Austin, Texas
Flener, Huck	3	3	1.85	12	10	3	0	73	57	18	15	22	51	B	L	5-11	190	2-25-69	1990	Vacaville, Calif.
Garza, Alberto	3	0	3.86	4	4	1	0	21	24	12	9	9	19	R	R	6-3	195	5-25-77	1996	Wapato, Wash.
Martinez, Willie	9	7	4.38	26	26	2	0	154	169	92	75	44	117	R	R	6-2	165	1-4-78	1995	Barquisimeto, Ven.
Mays, Jarrod	1	0	3.47	15	0	0	1	[illegible]	[illegible]	10	10	[illegible]	[illegible]	R	R	[illegible]	190	10-8-74	[illegible]	El Dorado Springs, Mo.
Merrick, Brett	0	0	6.00	12	0	0	0	12	12	9	8	10	8	L	L	6-0	180	5-30-74	1995	Lynwood, Wash.
Moore, Marcus	2	5	4.50	23	12	0	6	82	78	49	41	54	90	B	R	6-5	204	11-2-70	1989	Oakland, Calif.
Rakers, Jason	3	1	2.59	5	5	0	0	31	35	10	9	7	27	R	R	6-2	197	6-29-73	1995	Pittsburgh, Pa.
Riske, David	0	0	0.00	2	0	0	1	3	1	0	0	1	5	R	R	6-2	175	10-23-76	1997	Kent, Wash.
Sanders, Frankie	11	8	3.48	29	29	2	0	186	175	82	72	71	108	R	R	5-11	165	8-27-75	1995	Sarasota, Fla.
Sexton, Jeff	4	2	1.57	27	0	0	11	57	41	12	10	19	49	R	R	6-2	190	10-4-71	1993	Crowder, Okla.
Shuey, Paul	0	0	54.00	1	0	0	0	0	3	2	2	1	0	R	R	6-3	215	9-16-70	1992	Raleigh, N.C.
Viano, Jacob	1	2	7.80	9	0	0	1	15	24	17	13	7	10	R	R	5-11	180	9-4-73	1993	Long Beach, Calif.
Whitten, Casey	0	0	0.00	1	0	0	0	1	1	0	0	0	0	L	L	6-0	180	5-23-72	1993	Streetsboro, Ohio

FIELDING

Catcher	PCT	G	PO	A	E	DP	PB
Harriss	.984	15	113	9	2	2	2
Hayes	.988	85	507	59	7	1	7
Moyle	.995	27	173	18	1	2	3
Ramirez	.963	15	93	12	4	1	4
Taylor	.905	3	17	2	2	0	1

First Base	PCT	G	PO	A	E	DP
Betts	.000	1	0	0	0	0
Perry	1.000	4	29	5	0	5
Stumberger	.992	135	1197	116	10	124
Thomas	1.000	4	19	0	0	3

Second Base	PCT	G	PO	A	E	DP
Betances	.948	18	29	44	4	10
Gutierrez	.978	10	17	28	1	9
Scutaro	.977	118	244	339	14	85
Selby	1.000	1	3	5	0	1

Third Base	PCT	G	PO	A	E	DP
Betances	.952	43	25	75	5	7
Betts	.972	58	48	93	4	11
Branyan	.932	41	24	72	7	7
Gross	1.000	1	0	1	0	0
Selby	.900	3	4	5	1	1
Whitlock	1.000	1	0	1	0	0

Shortstop	PCT	G	PO	A	E	DP
Betances	.952	6	4	16	1	2
McDonald	.966	132	242	407	23	91
Scutaro	.950	7	7	12	1	3

Outfield	PCT	G	PO	A	E	DP
Betances	1.000	1	3	0	0	0
Budzinski	.989	126	270	6	3	1
Gross	1.000	20	35	1	0	1
Huelsmann	1.000	8	11	1	0	0
Morgan	.976	110	201	4	5	2
Peoples	.973	45	71	2	2	1
Perry	.976	27	37	4	1	1
Roberts	.992	56	124	4	1	0
Selby	1.000	15	25	0	0	0
Taveras	1.000	2	5	0	0	0
Thomas	1.000	37	66	4	0	1
Whitlock	.000	1	0	0	0	0

KINSTON — Class A

CAROLINA LEAGUE

BATTING	AVG	G	AB	R	H	2B	3B	HR	RBI	BB	SO	SB	CS	B	T	HT	WT	DOB	1st Yr	Resides
Alvarez, Carlos	.212	10	33	3	7	0	0	1	4	4	11	2	0	R	R	6-0	170	4-28-76	1995	Bachayuero, Ven.
Benefield, Brian	.220	71	259	44	57	9	2	5	34	31	50	8	4	R	R	6-0	181	8-12-76	1997	Carrollton, Texas
Bruce, Robert	.188	55	149	11	28	4	0	2	15	4	45	3	2	R	R	6-5	225	11-13-74	1997	River Forest, Ill.
Cruz, Edgar	.152	9	33	1	5	2	0	0	3	0	9	0	0	R	R	6-3	195	8-12-78	1997	Juncos, P.R.
Dorman, John	.208	106	317	46	66	14	4	2	22	34	76	24	9	R	R	5-9	170	8-29-73	1997	Weston, Conn.
Glavine, Mike	.219	125	398	61	87	23	1	22	76	73	117	1	4	L	L	6-3	210	1-24-73	1995	Billerica, Mass.
Gonzalez, Ricky	.181	53	144	13	26	12	0	0	5	17	27	1	5	R	R	6-0	185	11-13-74	1995	Miami, Fla.
Gross, Rafael	.228	43	145	19	33	8	0	1	8	7	42	7	6	R	R	5-10	155	8-8-74	1993	Nagua, D.R.
Gutierrez, Rick	.294	4	17	2	5	1	0	1	2	1	3	0	1	R	R	6-0	170	3-23-70	1994	Norman, Okla.
Harriss, Robin	.227	44	132	19	30	6	0	0	11	16	36	1	3	R	R	6-1	205	8-7-71	1994	San Angelo, Texas
Huelsmann, Mike	.285	114	425	63	121	19	4	5	47	70	67	21	16	B	R	5-11	165	11-21-74	1996	St. Louis, Mo.
Jimenez, Ruben	.230	66	187	22	43	8	3	2	23	16	42	8	6	B	R	5-11	160	8-18-75	1993	Largo, Fla.
Kent, Troy	.240	101	329	33	79	20	1	5	33	23	84	2	3	R	R	6-1	200	9-11-73	1996	Palo Alto, Calif.
Konrady, Dennis	.236	127	419	70	99	17	3	11	49	69	59	6	5	L	R	5-11	185	9-21-74	1996	Eugene, Ore.
Mohr, Dustan	.242	134	491	60	119	23	9	19	65	39	146	8	4	R	R	6-2	210	6-19-76	1997	Hattiesburg, Miss.
Morris, Bobby	.262	25	65	11	17	2	1	2	14	6	12	2	1	L	R	6-0	175	11-22-72	1993	Munster, Ind.
Robinson, Adam	.165	24	91	9	15	3	0	3	8	11	22	4	1	R	R	6-0	185	6-28-75	1997	Long Valley, N.J.
Rodriquez, Gary	.239	45	109	9	26	3	0	0	11	15	30	3	0	L	R	5-11	165	7-17-76	1996	Keller, Texas
Russell, Jake	.128	15	39	1	5	2	0	1	1	0	13	0	0	R	R	5-11	190	3-2-74	1994	Salina, Okla.
Taylor, Adam	.167	7	18	2	3	0	0	1	3	2	8	0	1	R	R	5-11	195	3-14-74	1996	Chelsea, Mich.
Valera, Willy	.111	3	9	1	1	0	0	0	0	0	3	0	0	R	R	6-0	155	7-23-75	1993	San Cristobal, D.R.
Whitaker, Chad	.215	127	455	46	98	25	0	10	48	34	148	16	10	L	R	6-2	190	9-16-76	1995	Fort Lauderdale, Fla.
Whitlock, Brian	.212	73	198	24	42	9	3	5	30	24	74	4	1	R	R	6-1	180	9-16-74	1996	Sarasota, Fla.

GAMES BY POSITION: C—Cruz 6, Gonzalez 52, Harriss 44, Konrady 41, Russell 6, Taylor 5. **1B**—Bruce 8, Glavine 107, Kent 34, Konrady 3, Whitlock 5. **2B**—Benefield 70, Dorman 8, Gross 1, Gutierrez 1, Jimenez 34, Konrady 1, Morris 2, Whitlock 36. **3B**—Bruce 2, Gross 23, Gutierrez 2, Jimenez 7, Kent 26, Konrady 82, Russell 1, Valera 2, Whitaker 1, Whitlock 19. **SS**—Dorman 98, Gutierrez 1, Jimenez 24, Robinson 24, Valera 1, Whitlock 5. **OF**—Alvarez 9, Bruce 18, Gross 17, Huelsmann 113, Jimenez 2, Mohr 119, Morris 2, Rodriquez 29, Whitaker 119, Whitlock 11.

PITCHING	W	L	ERA	G	GS	CG	SV	IP	H	R	ER	BB	SO	B	T	HT	WT	DOB	1st Yr	Resides
Bacsik, Mike	10	9	2.88	27	27	1	0	166	147	64	53	37	128	L	L	6-3	190	11-11-77	1996	Duncanville, Texas
Brammer, J.D.	3	2	1.33	15	0	0	2	27	15	6	4	8	33	R	R	6-4	235	1-30-75	1996	West Logan, W.Va.
Brown, Jamie	11	9	3.81	27	27	2	0	173	162	91	73	44	148	R	R	6-2	205	3-31-77	1997	Gulf Breeze, Fla.
Calmus, Lance	0	1	6.75	7	1	0	0	12	14	12	9	7	10	R	R	6-5	225	1-19-73	1996	Jenks, Okla.
DePaula, Sean	3	2	2.36	28	1	0	1	50	50	20	13	18	59	R	R	6-4	215	11-7-73	1996	Derry, N.H.
Deschenes, Marc	0	0	0.00	1	0	0	0	1	0	0	0	1	2	R	R	6-0	175	1-6-73	1995	Dracut, Mass.
Drew, Tim	3	8	5.20	15	15	0	0	90	105	58	52	31	67	R	R	6-1	195	8-31-78	1997	Hahira, Ga.
Edwards, Jon	5	0	2.70	21	0	0	0	33	31	10	10	14	28	R	R	6-0	175	6-15-73	1995	Walla Walla, Wash.
Garza, Alberto	4	8	3.20	20	20	3	0	112	79	44	40	60	110	R	R	6-3	195	5-25-77	1996	Wapato, Wash.
Hamilton, Jimmy	4	6	2.75	44	0	0	4	75	61	25	23	21	83	L	L	6-3	190	8-1-75	1996	Weyers Cave, W.Va.
Hughes, Mike	1	3	4.95	9	4	0	0	36	45	26	20	8	27	L	L	6-1	192	12-5-75	1997	East Meadow, N.Y.
Koeman, Matt	0	0	1.35	4	0	0	0	7	9	8	1	1	4	R	R	6-3	200	10-13-73	1996	Manhattan, Kan.
Mackey, Jason	0	0	6.75	5	0	0	0	12	19	9	9	5	8	L	L	6-2	185	4-8-74	1993	Kelso, Wash.
Mays, Jarrod	1	1	1.59	4	4	0	0	17	12	6	3	7	10	R	R	6-4	190	10-8-74	1996	El Dorado Springs, Mo.
Merrick, Brett	0	0	9.00	2	0	0	0	2	3	2	2	1	0	L	L	6-0	180	5-30-74	1995	Lynwood, Wash.
Negrette, Richard	3	5	2.88	28	0	0	0	50	32	22	16	27	41	R	R	6-2	175	3-6-76	1994	Maracaibo, Ven.
Pirkl, Greg	2	0	2.73	14	0	0	0	26	23	10	8	7	26	R	R	6-5	225	8-7-70	1988	Surprise, Ariz.

PITCHING	W	L	ERA	G	GS	CG	SV	IP	H	R	ER	BB	SO	B	T	HT	WT	DOB	1st Yr	Resides
Reichow, Bob	0	0	23.63	2	0	0	0	3	5	7	7	2	1	R	R	6-5	220	10-10-73	1996	Temperance, Mich.
Rigdon, Paul	11	7	4.03	24	24	0	0	127	126	65	57	35	97	R	R	6-5	210	11-2-75	1996	Jacksonville, Fla.
Riske, David	1	1	2.33	53	0	0	33	54	48	15	14	15	67	R	R	6-2	175	10-23-76	1997	Kent, Wash.
Spenser, Kaipo	2	6	3.76	13	13	0	0	67	74	30	28	23	31	R	R	6-3	220	8-4-75	1998	Tempe, Ariz.
Viano, Jacob	3	0	1.54	14	0	0	1	23	14	4	4	10	21	R	R	5-11	180	9-4-73	1993	Long Beach, Calif.
Wagner, Ken	1	2	3.00	10	0	0	1	21	15	8	7	10	18	R	R	6-4	218	8-3-74	1995	West Palm Beach, Fla.
Watson, Mark	0	1	0.00	1	1	0	0	6	3	4	0	2	8	R	L	6-4	215	1-23-74	1996	Atlanta, Ga.
Whitten, Casey	1	0	3.18	9	3	0	0	17	11	6	6	7	17	L	L	6-0	180	5-23-72	1993	Streetsboro, Ohio

COLUMBUS — Class A

SOUTH ATLANTIC LEAGUE

BATTING	AVG	G	AB	R	H	2B	3B	HR	RBI	BB	SO	SB	CS	B	T	HT	WT	DOB	1st Yr	Resides
Allison, Cody	.238	74	244	27	58	11	1	5	29	22	44	2	3	L	R	6-1	200	8-8-74	1996	Odessa, Texas
Alvarez, Carlos	.260	72	265	33	69	18	3	3	34	17	62	6	4	R	R	6-0	170	4-28-76	1995	Bachayuero, Ven.
Cruz, Edgar	.247	107	396	59	98	27	0	16	65	34	97	1	0	R	R	6-3	195	8-12-78	1997	Juncos, P.R.
Edwards, Michael	.294	124	497	82	146	34	4	8	81	66	95	16	6	R	R	6-1	185	11-24-76	1995	Mechanicsburg, Pa.
Fitzgerald, Jason	.273	132	490	60	134	28	3	16	80	38	117	21	6	L	L	6-1	190	9-16-75	1997	Belle Chasse, La.
Fowler, Ben	.197	57	188	20	37	5	0	5	26	11	74	0	0	B	R	6-4	185	1-21-77	1995	Alpharetta, Ga.
Gonzalez, Luis	.272	101	320	48	87	14	1	3	32	28	63	10	3	R	R	5-11	170	6-26-79	1997	El Tigre, Ven.
Hamilton, Jon	.261	133	487	88	127	22	10	15	71	79	130	22	9	L	L	6-1	195	10-23-77	1997	San Ramon, Calif.
Kilburg, Joe	.251	121	446	81	112	19	4	7	44	67	93	24	10	L	R	5-11	180	12-20-75	1997	Bay Village, Ohio
Messner, Jake	.167	25	78	9	13	2	0	3	13	5	21	3	1	L	L	6-0	192	5-18-77	1995	Sacramento, Calif.
Munoz, Billy	.266	120	417	61	111	24	1	12	60	68	104	3	2	L	L	6-2	220	6-30-75	1998	Mesa, Ariz.
Perez, Edwin	.236	33	89	14	21	1	0	1	10	17	12	1	2	R	R	5-10	165	5-10-75	1993	Navarrete, D.R.
Rodriquez, Gary	.364	15	44	10	16	2	1	0	3	6	9	0	0	L	R	5-11	165	7-17-76	1996	Keller, Texas
Taveras, Frank	.260	84	281	31	73	12	2	5	33	10	71	1	5	L	R	6-1	158	9-6-75	1993	Santiago, D.R.
Tiller, Brad	.165	38	103	21	17	2	0	0	5	13	36	3	0	R	R	5-10	165	11-21-75	1994	Inez, Ky.
Valera, Willy	.200	6	20	4	4	0	0	1	3	2	2	0	1	R	R	6-0	155	7-23-75	1993	San Cristobal, D.R.
Williams, Jewell	.249	96	353	60	88	14	4	8	38	27	118	20	6	R	R	6-2	185	6-25-77	1995	Las Vegas, Nev.

GAMES BY POSITION: C—Allison 7, Cruz 98, Fowler 44. **1B**—Allison 20, Edwards 3, Munoz 117, Taveras 13. **2B**—Kilburg 118, Perez 5, Taveras 5, Tiller 19. **3B**—Edwards 114, Perez 9, Taveras 18, Tiller 5. **SS**—Allison 1, Gonzalez 101, Perez 11, Taveras 22, Tiller 9, Valera 6. **OF**—Alvarez 41, Fitzgerald 127, Hamilton 131, Messner 8, Rodriquez 13, Taveras 24, Tiller 1, Williams 94.

PITCHING	W	L	ERA	G	GS	CG	SV	IP	H	R	ER	BB	SO	B	T	HT	WT	DOB	1st Yr	Resides
Aracena, Juan	0	1	13.50	5	0	0	0	7	15	10	10	6	4	R	R	6-0	150	12-17-76	1994	La Vega, D.R.
Bautista, Martin	1	4	10.01	7	7	0	0	30	42	30	33	24	25	R	R	6-0	155	2-22-78	1996	San Pedro de Macoris, D.R.
Civit, Xavier	0	1	9.00	3	0	0	0	6	10	6	6	2	6	R	R	6-2	175	5-17-73	1993	Barcelona, Spain
Drew, Tim	4	3	3.79	13	13	0	0	71	68	43	30	26	64	R	R	6-1	195	8-31-78	1997	Hahira, Ga.
Guillory, Dan	3	5	3.48	20	0	0	3	34	26	14	13	9	23	R	R	6-3	205	5-12-76	1998	Baton Rouge, La.
Harrison, Scott	5	12	6.13	27	24	1	0	131	161	100	89	53	118	R	R	6-3	195	7-3-77	1995	Pinole, Calif.
Horgan, Joe	2	1	2.38	22	1	0	0	34	19	9	9	21	27	L	L	6-1	200	6-7-77	1996	Rancho Cordova, Calif.
Hughes, Mike	7	2	3.74	18	9	0	1	75	81	38	31	22	86	L	L	6-1	192	12-5-75	1997	East Meadow, N.Y.
Koeman, Matt	2	4	5.40	31	1	0	1	55	59	36	33	24	57	R	R	6-3	200	10-13-73	1996	Manhattan, Kan.
Layne, Roger	2	0	2.49	4	4	0	0	25	12	7	7	4	28	R	R	6-3	185	6-27-77	1997	Whitwell, Tenn.
McNally, Andrew	2	2	3.00	38	0	0	8	45	41	22	15	19	53	L	R	6-0	185	12-3-73	1997	Honolulu, Hawaii
Negrette, Richard	1	3	5.09	21	0	0	2	41	39	24	23	22	35	R	R	6-2	175	3-6-76	1994	Maracaibo, Ven.
Perez, Julio	0	1	8.27	9	0	0	1	16	18	17	15	10	18	R	R	6-1	163	5-18-74	1993	San Cristobal, D.R.
Pirkl, Greg	2	2	3.33	26	0	0	7	27	22	10	10	6	29	R	R	6-5	225	8-7-70	1988	Surprise, Ariz.
Reichow, Bob	2	6	5.83	39	4	0	0	79	108	69	51	31	46	R	R	6-5	220	10-10-73	1996	Temperance, Mich.
Sarmiento, Dan	1	1	7.71	6	0	0	0	9	9	11	8	9	10	L	L	5-11	203	3-28-74	1992	Tempe, Ariz.
Sido, Wilson	2	0	2.55	4	4	0	0	25	17	7	7	8	27	R	R	6-2	178	6-18-76	1998	Barahona, D.R.
Silva, Troy	4	3	3.33	16	12	1	0	76	66	29	28	32	84	R	R	6-2	205	10-15-75	1997	Atascadero, Calif.
Spenser, Kaipo	1	7	6.22	11	11	0	0	55	66	49	38	32	36	R	R	6-3	220	8-4-75	1998	Tempe, Ariz.
Spiegel, Mike	5	6	6.20	13	13	0	0	65	75	53	45	34	61	L	L	6-5	200	11-24-75	1996	Carmichael, Calif.
Turnbow, Mark	6	5	4.07	16	16	1	0	91	94	47	41	26	73	R	R	6-3	205	11-26-78	1997	Saltillo, Tenn.
Vael, Rob	0	6	10.29	9	9	0	0	42	65	51	48	21	35	R	R	6-3	200	1-8-76	1997	Tacoma, Wash.
Wagner, Ken	4	2	2.51	33	0	0	3	72	55	25	20	20	92	R	R	6-4	218	8-3-74	1995	West Palm Beach, Fla.
Watson, Mark	3	4	4.05	31	12	1	0	98	95	53	44	32	77	R	L	6-4	215	1-23-74	1996	Atlanta, Ga.

WATERTOWN — Short-Season Class A

NEW YORK-PENN LEAGUE

BATTING	AVG	G	AB	R	H	2B	3B	HR	RBI	BB	SO	SB	CS	B	T	HT	WT	DOB	1st Yr	Resides
Bender, Heath	.114	10	35	1	4	0	0	0	1	1	9	0	0	L	L	6-4	230	4-16-75	1997	Rock Island, Ill.
Dampeer, Kelly	.277	68	235	33	65	11	2	1	25	26	49	11	8	R	R	5-11	190	1-25-75	1997	Roanoke, Va.
Gordnier, Aaron	.250	36	108	17	27	7	0	3	16	22	32	7	1	R	R	5-11	185	9-4-74	1998	Carmichael, Calif.
Grindell, Nate	.259	27	81	13	21	7	0	1	13	15	9	1	2	R	R	6-1	180	4-9-77	1998	Carrollton, Texas
Haley, Ryan	.333	1	3	1	1	0	0	0	0	1	0	0	0	L	R	6-1	185	11-21-75	1997	Chandler, Okla.
Hernandez, Jesus	.241	70	257	42	62	13	5	5	43	39	49	15	0	L	L	6-2	170	6-6-77	1995	Laguna Salada, D.R.
MacMillan, Chris	.227	57	194	28	44	9	0	5	30	26	47	0	1	R	R	6-2	195	2-19-76	1998	El Monte, Calif.
Malave, Dennis	.250	6	20	1	5	0	0	1	6	0	4	2	1	L	L	5-9	165	1-6-80	1997	Caracas, Ven.
Moraga, Omar	.264	65	246	38	65	18	4	0	28	28	55	14	5	L	R	5-10	180	5-23-77	1998	Tucson, Ariz.
Patton, Barry	.067	11	30	1	2	1	0	0	1	4	14	1	0	R	R	6-2	220	10-13-75	1998	Kosciusko, Miss.
Perez, Edwin	.119	12	42	6	5	1	0	0	3	3	9	2	1	R	R	5-10	165	5-10-75	1993	Navarrete, D.R.
Powers, Jeff	.299	18	67	10	20	5	0	1	11	5	10	1	0	L	R	6-0	175	3-20-76	1998	Scottsdale, Ariz.
Pratt, Scott	.351	47	174	37	61	12	3	2	14	34	26	15	10	L	R	5-10	185	2-4-77	1998	Las Vegas, Nev.
Puffinbarger, Rusty	.167	12	24	6	4	2	0	0	4	7	6	0	0	R	R	6-3	195	6-25-76	1998	Camargo, Okla.
Rojas, Christian	.266	61	218	41	58	12	1	12	46	25	63	6	3	R	R	6-1	170	6-23-75	1994	El Vivero, D.R.
Santana, Osmany	.282	19	78	17	22	4	3	2	13	11	8	3	2	L	L	5-11	185	8-9-76	1998	San Jose, Costa Rica
Smith, Casey	.186	67	226	22	42	6	1	3	23	15	65	4	0	R	R	6-3	200	5-7-77	1997	Carrollton, Texas
Sorensen, Zach	.300	53	200	38	60	7	8	4	26	35	35	14	4	B	R	6-0	190	1-3-77	1998	Mesquite, Nev.
Upshaw, Ryan	.257	70	257	43	66	17	0	7	39	32	56	7	5	R	R	6-0	200	1-21-75	1997	Humble, Texas

GAMES BY POSITION: C—Dampeer 1, Patton 9, Puffinbarger 12, Smith 64. **1B**—Bender 10, Dampeer 17, MacMillan 47, Smith 4. **2B**—Dampeer 35, Moraga 4, Powers 2, Pratt 36. **3B**—Dampeer 4, Haley 1, MacMillan 9, Moraga 59, Perez 4. **SS**—Perez 7, Powers 15, Pratt 2, Sorensen 52. **OF**—Gordnier 28, Grindell 21, Hernandez 70, MacMillan 1, Malave 6, Perez 1, Rojas 59, Santana 19, Upshaw 33.

PITCHING	W	L	ERA	G	GS	CG	SV	IP	H	R	ER	BB	SO	B	T	HT	WT	DOB	1st Yr	Resides
Aracena, Juan	1	4	2.84	18	0	0	6	25	21	8	8	7	22	R	R	6-0	150	12-17-76	1994	La Vega, D.R.
Brown, Craig	1	2	7.23	16	0	0	1	19	29	20	15	17	19	L	L	5-9	170	8-10-76	1998	Tampa, Fla.
Carrasco, Danny	1	1	5.40	13	1	0	2	32	36	23	19	14	38	R	R	6-5	200	4-10-77	1997	Safford, Ariz.
Drese, Ryan	2	5	4.07	9	9	0	0	42	40	21	19	14	40	R	R	6-3	220	4-5-76	1998	Oakland, Calif.
Erwin, Dave	0	0	7.20	3	0	0	0	5	6	4	4	1	7	R	R	6-3	210	3-19-75	1997	Brighton, Tenn.
Escobar, Ruben	0	1	3.70	14	0	0	0	24	20	12	10	6	14	R	R	6-1	185	6-8-76	1998	Hesperia, Calif.
Everett, Matt	3	3	2.33	16	0	0	0	19	16	7	5	12	24	R	R	6-4	215	10-2-75	1998	Monroe, Ga.
Guillory, Dan	1	0	3.00	3	0	0	1	6	4	2	2	3	5	R	R	6-3	205	5-12-76	1998	Baton Rouge, La.
Jackson, Brian	0	0	11.25	1	1	0	0	4	7	6	5	3	2	R	R	6-4	190	8-12-77	1998	Tiburon, Calif.
Kearney, Ryan	1	2	1.57	20	1	0	3	46	39	16	8	10	45	R	R	6-1	190	1-9-76	1998	Nashua, N.H.
Maleski, Eric	0	0	6.00	2	0	0	0	3	5	2	2	0	3	R	R	6-2	195	7-25-76	1998	Des Plaines, Ill.
Marietta, Ron	1	1	5.09	11	11	0	0	53	55	35	30	26	41	L	L	6-0	190	8-12-77	1998	Brooklyn, N.Y.
Matsko, Rich	2	3	8.59	20	0	0	1	37	43	37	35	24	41	R	R	6-2	210	4-26-77	1998	Johnstown, Pa.
Novits, Carey	0	0	3.38	5	2	0	0	11	11	4	4	2	9	L	L	6-1	185	9-5-75	1998	San Dimas, Calif.
Percell, Brody	9	2	2.21	15	15	1	0	86	73	28	21	16	105	L	L	6-2	200	8-29-75	1998	Portland, Ore.
Reinike, Chris	10	2	1.91	15	15	0	0	90	64	21	19	33	92	R	R	6-0	195	11-16-76	1998	Gulfport, Miss.
Spiegel, Mike	1	0	0.00	1	1	0	0	6	2	1	0	5	7	L	L	6-5	200	11-24-75	1996	Carmichael, Calif.
Swinburnson, Tyler	0	1	5.01	17	0	0	4	32	30	21	18	23	29	R	R	6-4	200	8-5-75	1997	Blaine, Wash.
Vael, Rob	4	3	4.12	12	9	0	0	55	56	25	25	16	52	R	R	6-3	200	1-8-76	1997	Tacoma, Wash.
Vargas, Jose	2	2	1.45	5	5	1	0	31	28	14	5	7	22	R	R	6-0	175	3-25-77	1998	Barahona, D.R.
White, Matt	3	2	4.28	6	6	0	0	27	31	19	13	11	24	R	L	6-1	180	8-19-77	1998	Windsor, Mass.

BURLINGTON — Rookie

APPALACHIAN LEAGUE

BATTING	AVG	G	AB	R	H	2B	3B	HR	RBI	BB	SO	SB	CS	B	T	HT	WT	DOB	1st Yr	Resides
Bastardo, Angel	.240	51	179	29	43	12	0	7	25	15	59	1	3	R	R	6-0	170	4-2-79	1997	Miraflores, Ven.
Batista, Carlos	.234	54	205	15	48	8	0	7	35	2	66	2	0	R	R	6-3	174	7-3-79	1997	San Pedro de Macoris, D.R.
Centile, Raul	.320	53	181	27	58	6	1	3	22	18	36	3	4	B	R	6-0	160	5-31-79	1996	San Pedro de Macoris, D.R.
Day, Paul	.362	60	229	33	83	16	2	7	45	17	39	10	0	R	R	6-1	200	12-20-76	1998	Mission Viejo, Calif.
DePippo, Jeff	.209	39	115	16	24	6	0	1	9	10	33	0	2	R	R	5-7	170	4-29-76	1998	Garden Grove, Calif.
Esquerra, Marques	.304	55	207	32	63	8	2	4	28	12	35	11	3	B	R	6-1	185	5-17-76	1998	Tucson, Ariz.
Gallaher, T.T.	.236	43	106	19	25	3	1	1	7	30	22	4	4	R	R	5-10	185	11-5-77	1998	Middletown, Conn.
Grindell, Nate	.244	14	41	6	10	2	0	1	7	2	6	0	0	R	R	6-1	180	4-9-77	1998	Carrollton, Texas
Harding, Todd	.263	26	76	10	20	4	0	4	11	4	30	4	0	R	R	6-0	180	9-14-77	1997	Eugene, Ore.
Isturiz, Maicer	.290	55	217	33	63	8	2	2	33	17	32	16	6	B	R	5-8	155	9-12-80	1998	Barquisimeto, Ven.
Jackson, Chris	.250	7	20	1	5	1	0	0	0	0	5	0	0	R	R	6-2	200	3-7-79	1997	Birmingham, Ala.
Malave, Dennis	.279	60	208	40	58	3	5	4	19	34	59	27	13	L	L	5-9	165	1-6-80	1997	Caracas, Ven.
Minges, Tyler	.306	12	49	7	15	2	1	1	5	2	10	1	0	R	R	5-11	185	11-15-79	1998	Hamilton, Ohio
Pursell, Mike	.256	57	199	37	51	15	1	4	30	26	34	3	4	L	R	6-0	187	12-22-75	1998	Pensacola, Fla.
Silva, Carlos	.175	16	40	2	7	0	0	0	3	1	8	0	0	R	R	5-10	160	3-14-79	1996	Turmero, Ven.
Thompson, Eric	.211	55	175	27	37	6	1	0	18	14	54	10	2	L	L	6-0	170	5-1-79	1997	Fayetteville, N.C.
Ventura, Frankie	.167	3	6	1	1	0	0	0	0	0	1	0	0	R	R	6-1	180	6-4-77	1995	Santo Domingo, D.R.

GAMES BY POSITION: C—Bastardo 30, DePippo 36, Jackson 5. **1B**—Bastardo 2, Batista 53, Esquerra 3, Grindell 2, Pursell 11. **2B**—Centile 43, Esquerra 18, Grindell 1, Silva 14. **3B**—Day 48, Esquerra 15, Harding 6, Pursell 1. **SS**—Centile 14, Esquerra 5, Grindell 2, Harding 1, Isturiz 55. **OF**—DePippo 3, Esquerra 3, Gallaher 42, Grindell 8, Harding 7, Malave 58, Minges 12, Pursell 33, Thompson 53, Ventura 3.

PITCHING	W	L	ERA	G	GS	CG	SV	IP	H	R	ER	BB	SO	B	T	HT	WT	DOB	1st Yr	Resides
Bautista, Martin	3	7	4.76	13	13	1	0	74	78	49	39	35	64	R	R	6-0	155	2-22-78	1996	San Pedro de Macoris, D.R.
Berck, Darrel	2	1	5.92	16	0	0	1	38	37	29	25	23	40	R	R	6-0	170	9-27-76	1998	Atlanta, Ga.
Farmer, Jason	0	0	9.28	18	0	0	6	21	29	23	22	15	19	R	R	5-11	190	10-7-74	1998	Warrenton, Ore.
Hernandez, Mario	1	0	6.89	13	0	0	0	16	16	12	12	10	17	R	R	6-1	190	7-7-75	1998	San Pedro Sula, Honduras
Jackson, Brian	5	3	3.21	12	12	1	0	70	66	29	25	23	61	R	R	6-4	190	8-12-77	1998	Tiburon, Calif.
Koeth, Mark	0	2	10.73	20	0	0	1	28	45	40	33	22	14	R	R	6-3	215	4-11-78	1998	Carrollton, Texas
Maleski, Eric	4	2	2.05	19	0	0	5	44	37	17	10	10	47	R	R	6-2	195	7-25-76	1998	Des Plaines, Ill.
McDermott, Ryan	1	6	8.51	12	8	0	0	37	36	44	35	36	21	R	R	6-9	225	6-28-78	1996	Alamogordo, N.M.
McPadden, Mike	0	5	8.89	16	0	0	0	26	28	37	26	30	18	L	R	6-4	185	2-24-80	1998	Port St. Lucie, Fla.
Morelock, Chris	2	1	4.01	16	1	0	1	34	36	31	15	28	29	R	R	6-3	180	6-26-77	1998	Cottage Grove, Ore.
Reynolds, Jacob	1	4	7.76	10	5	0	0	29	27	28	25	26	30	R	R	6-2	200	1-7-80	1998	Huntsville, Ala.
Rosales, Rudy	0	0	13.50	1	0	0	0	2	6	3	3	1	0	R	R	6-3	220	7-9-76	1998	Tucson, Ariz.
Sabathia, C.C.	1	0	4.50	5	5	0	0	18	20	14	9	8	35	L	L	6-7	235	7-21-80	1998	Vallejo, Calif.
Sanchez, Willmen	2	1	4.82	8	4	0	1	28	25	16	15	13	26	L	L	5-11	170	2-19-79	1997	Charallaue, Ven.
Suttles, Donnie	5	3	2.87	12	11	0	0	63	40	23	20	49	77	R	R	6-2	185	1-8-77	1998	Marion, N.C.
White, Matt	4	1	1.94	8	8	0	0	46	34	14	10	24	47	R	L	6-1	180	8-19-77	1998	Windsor, Mass.

COLORADO ROCKIES

All-Star Game one of few bright spots for '98 Rockies

BY BARNEY HUTCHINSON

The baseball world's focus turned to Colorado in early July 1998, when the Rockies hosted the 69th All-Star Game.

But it was the game before the break, a 7-2 loss in San Diego, that caught Rockies owner Jerry McMorris' attention. His lackluster team fell in just more than two hours, to former Rockies righthander Andy Ashby and the Padres.

Later that month, the Rockies were swept on the road by the expansion Arizona Diamondbacks, the only team to finish behind Colorado in the National League West.

McMorris regarded those as two of the lowest moments of the season and faced his most difficult decision as owner. On the final night of the '98 season, the team fired Don Baylor, the only manager in Rockies history. Baylor's final team went 77-85, giving him a 440-469 mark in his six years.

Eight days later former Marlins skipper Jim Leyland agreed to a three-year, $6 million contract as the club's new manager.

The 1998 season began with enthusiasm over a pitching staff that was seen for the first time as a strength, with free-agent signee Darryl Kile and righthander Pedro Astacio anchoring the rotation.

But Kile, who signed a three-year, $24-million deal, led the league with 17 losses, and Astacio tied for most home runs allowed (39) with Arizona's Brian Anderson en route to a 6.23 ERA.

Second baseman Mike Lansing, who was acquired from the Expos for the organization's two best pitching prospects, proved to be another disappointment. Lansing got off to a slow start and never provided the spark the Rockies needed.

The club did have some good individual accomplishments, starting with right fielder Larry Walker winning the NL batting title with a .363 average. He also won his fourth Gold Glove. Third baseman Vinny Castilla reached career highs in home runs and RBIs while batting .319. And two Rockies–outfielder Dante Bichette and shortstop Neifi Perez–hit for the cycle, something that had never been done before in club history.

But the most encouraging sign in the disappointing year was the way rookie first baseman Todd Helton stepped in for Andres Galarraga, who had moved on to the Braves as a free agent. Helton hit an impressive .359 in the second half while finishing with 25 home runs and 97 RBIs.

Outfielder Derrick Gibson and lefthander Mike Kusiewicz looked to be next in line to help the big club. Gibson hit .292 with 14 homers and 81 RBIs for Colorado Springs in his first full season at Triple-A. Kusiewicz posted a 2.32 ERA–the best in the high minors–while going 14-7 for Double-A New Haven.

Another lefthander, Josh Kalinowski, impressed at Class A Asheville, ranking second in the minor leagues with 215 strikeouts. Kalinowski threw a no-hitter against Charleston, S.C., and also struck out 17 batters in a game against Hickory.

Team success in the organization was confined to the lowest rungs of the minor leagues, as the Rockies won the Rookie-level Arizona League with a 42-14 mark, setting a league record for most wins in a season.

Vinny Castilla

Mike Kusiewicz

Players of the Year

Major League: Vinny Castilla, 3b
Castilla finished fourth in the NL in homers and third—behind Sammy Sosa and Mark McGwire—in RBIs.

Minor League: Mike Kusiewicz, lhp, New Haven.
Kusiewicz' 2.32 ERA was the best in the high minors and his 14 wins led the organization.

ORGANIZATION LEADERS

BATTING		
*AVG	Juan Pierre, Portland	.352
R	Elvis Pena, Asheville	93
H	Juan Sosa, Salem	147
TB	Chris Kirgan, Colo. Springs/New Haven	257
2B	Rod Bair, Salem	42
3B	Juan Sosa, Salem	12
HR	Chris Kirgan, Colo. Springs/New Haven	25
RBI	Chris Kirgan, Colo. Springs/New Haven	94
BB	Two tied at	72
SO	Efrain Alamo, Asheville	141
SB	Juan Sosa, Salem	64
PITCHING		
W	Mike Kusiewicz, New Haven	14
L	Mike Vavrek, Colo. Springs/New Haven	18
#ERA	Bobby Bevel, Salem	2.26
G	Lariel Gonzalez, New Haven	58
CG	Two tied at	7
SV	David Lee, Salem	25
IP	Scott Randall, New Haven	202
BB	Steve Shoemaker, Colo. Springs/New Haven	126
SO	Josh Kalinowski, Asheville	215

*Minimum 250 At-Bats #Minimum 75 Innings

Colorado ROCKIES

Manager: Don Baylor

1998 Record: 77-85, .475 (4th, NL West)

BATTING	AVG	G	AB	R	H	2B	3B	HR	RBI	BB	SO	SB	CS	B	T	HT	WT	DOB	1st Yr	Resides
Abbott, Kurt	.254	42	71	9	18	6	0	3	15	2	19	0	0	R	R	6-0	190	6-2-69	1989	Davie, Fla.
Barry, Jeff	.176	15	34	4	6	1	0	0	2	2	11	0	0	B	R	6-0	200	9-22-68	1990	San Diego, Calif.
Bates, Jason	.189	53	74	10	14	3	0	0	3	8	21	0	0	B	R	5-11	170	1-5-71	1992	Norwalk, Calif.
Bichette, Dante	.331	161	662	97	219	48	2	22	122	28	76	14	4	R	R	6-3	235	11-18-63	1984	Palm Beach Gardens, Fla.
Burks, Ellis	.286	100	357	54	102	22	5	16	54	39	80	3	7	R	R	6-2	205	9-11-64	1983	Denver, Colo.
Castilla, Vinny	.319	162	645	108	206	28	4	46	144	40	89	5	9	R	R	6-1	185	7-4-67	1990	Oaxaca, Mexico
Clemente, Edgard	.353	11	17	2	6	0	1	0	2	2	8	0	0	R	R	6-0	170	12-15-75	1993	Guaynabo, P.R.
Colbrunn, Greg	.311	62	122	12	38	8	2	2	13	8	23	3	3	R	R	6-0	200	7-26-69	1988	Weston, Fla.
Echevarria, Angel	.379	19	29	7	11	3	0	1	9	2	3	0	0	R	R	6-4	215	5-25-71	1992	Bridgeport, Conn.
Gibson, Derrick	.429	7	21	4	9	1	0	0	2	1	4	0	0	R	R	6-2	238	2-5-75	1993	Winter Haven, Fla.
Goodwin, Curtis	.245	119	159	27	39	7	0	1	6	16	40	5	1	L	L	5-11	180	9-30-72	1991	San Leandro, Calif.
Hamilton, Darryl	.335	51	194	30	65	9	1	5	25	23	20	4	1	L	R	6-1	180	12-3-64	1986	Sugar Land, Texas
2-team (97 S.F.)	.308	148	561	95	173	28	3	6	51	82	73	13	9							
Helton, Todd	.315	152	530	78	167	37	1	25	97	53	54	3	3	L	L	6-2	195	8-20-73	1995	Powell, Tenn.
Lansing, Mike	.276	153	584	73	161	39	2	12	66	39	88	10	3	R	R	6-0	175	4-3-68	1990	Casper, Wyo.
Liriano, Nelson	.000	12	17	0	0	0	0	0	0	0	7	0	0	B	R	5-10	178	6-3-64	1983	Puerto Plata, D.R.
Manwaring, Kirt	.247	110	291	30	72	12	3	2	26	38	49	1	5	R	R	5-11	203	7-15-65	1986	Scottsdale, Ariz.
Perez, Neifi	.274	162	647	80	177	25	9	9	59	38	70	5	6	B	R	6-0	175	6-2-75	1993	Villa Mella, D.R.
Reed, Jeff	.290	113	259	43	75	17	1	9	39	37	57	0	0	L	R	6-2	190	11-12-62	1980	Elizabethton, Tenn.
Shumpert, Terry	.231	23	26	3	6	1	0	1	2	2	8	0	0	R	R	5-11	185	8-16-66	1987	Paducah, Ky.
Strittmatter, Mark	.000	4	4	0	0	0	0	0	0	0	3	0	0	R	R	6-1	200	4-4-69	1992	Ridgewood, N.J.
Vander Wal, John	.288	89	104	18	30	10	1	5	20	16	29	0	0	L	L	6-1	180	4-29-66	1987	Hudsonville, Mich.
Walker, Larry	.363	130	454	113	165	46	3	23	67	64	61	14	4	L	R	6-2	185	12-1-66	1985	Maple Ridge, B.C.
White, Derrick	.000	9	9	0	0	0	0	0	0	0	4	0	0	R	R	6-1	225	10-12-69	1991	Chandler, Ariz.
2-team (11 Chicago)	.053	20	19	1	1	0	0	1	2	0	9	0	0							

PITCHING	W	L	ERA	G	GS	CG	SV	IP	H	R	ER	BB	SO	B	T	HT	WT	DOB	1st Yr	Resides
Astacio, Pedro	13	14	6.23	35	34	0	0	209	245	160	145	74	170	R	R	6-2	195	11-28-69	1988	Miami, Fla.
Brownson, Mark	1	0	4.73	2	2	1	0	13	16	7	7	2	8	L	R	6-2	175	6-17-75	1994	Wellington, Fla.
DeJean, Mike	3	1	3.03	59	1	0	2	74	78	29	25	24	27	R	R	6-2	205	9-28-70	1992	Denham Springs, La.
DiPoto, Jerry	3	4	3.53	68	0	0	19	71	61	31	28	25	49	R	R	6-2	200	5-24-68	1989	North Olmstead, Ohio
Gonzalez, Lariel	0	0	0.00	1	0	0	0	1	0	0	0	0	0	R	R	6-4	180	5-25-76	1994	San Cristobal, D.R.
Jones, Bobby	7	8	5.22	35	20	1	0	141	153	87	82	66	109	R	L	6-0	175	4-11-72	1992	Rutherford, N.J.
Kile, Darryl	13	17	5.20	36	35	4	0	230	257	141	133	96	158	R	R	6-5	185	12-2-68	1988	Corona, Calif.
Leskanic, Curt	6	4	4.40	66	0	0	2	76	75	37	37	40	55	R	R	6-0	180	4-2-68	1990	Pineville, La.
McElroy, Chuck	6	4	2.90	78	0	0	2	68	68	23	22	24	61	L	L	6-0	195	10-1-67	1986	Friendswood, Texas
Munoz, Mike	2	2	5.66	40	0	0	3	41	53	32	26	16	24	L	L	6-2	190	7-12-65	1986	West Covina, Calif.
Rath, Fred	0	0	1.69	2	0	0	0	5	6	1	1	2	2	R	R	6-3	220	1-5-73	1995	Tampa, Fla.
Ritz, Kevin	0	2	11.00	2	2	0	0	9	17	11	11	2	3	R	R	6-4	220	6-8-65	1986	Cambridge, Ohio
Saipe, Mike	0	1	10.80	2	2	0	0	10	22	12	12	0	2	R	R	6-1	190	9-10-73	1994	San Diego, Calif.
Stoops, Jim	1	0	2.25	3	0	0	0	4	5	1	1	3	0	R	R	6-2	195	6-30-72	1995	Somerset, N.J.
Thompson, Mark	1	2	7.71	6	6	0	0	23	36	22	20	12	14	R	R	6-2	205	4-7-71	1992	Russellville, Ky.
Thomson, John	8	11	4.81	26	26	2	0	161	174	86	86	49	106	R	R	6-3	175	10-1-73	1993	Sulphur, La.
Veres, Dave	3	1	2.83	63	0	0	8	76	67	26	24	27	74	R	R	6-2	195	10-19-66	1986	Gresham, Ore.
Wainhouse, David	1	0	4.91	10	0	0	0	11	15	6	6	5	3	L	R	6-2	185	11-7-67	1989	Mercer Island, Wash.
Wright, Jamey	9	14	5.67	34	34	1	0	206	235	143	130	95	86	R	R	6-6	205	12-24-74	1993	Moore, Okla.

FIELDING

Catcher	PCT	G	PO	A	E	DP	PB
Colbrunn	.000	1	0	0	0	0	0
Manwaring	.988	108	527	49	7	6	8
Perez	.000	1	0	0	0	0	0
Reed	.986	99	452	26	7	4	1
Strittmatter	1.000	3	10	1	0	1	0

First Base	PCT	G	PO	A	E	DP
Colbrunn	.992	27	216	21	2	18
Echevarria	1.000	4	20	2	0	3
Helton	.995	146	1163	146	7	156
Vanderwal	1.000	2	8	1	0	0

Second Base	PCT	G	PO	A	E	DP
Abbott	1.000	7	13	17	0	3
Bates	.974	17	14	24	1	4
Lansing	.987	153	346	425	10	118
Liriano	1.000	3	5	2	0	1
Shumpert	1.000	6	2	14	0	3
Walker	.000	1	0	0	0	0

Third Base	PCT	G	PO	A	E	DP
Abbott	1.000	3	2	1	0	0
Bates	.000	3	0	0	0	0
Castilla	.970	162	110	315	13	39
Lansing	.000	1	0	0	0	0
Walker	.000	1	0	0	0	0

Shortstop	PCT	G	PO	A	E	DP
Abbott	1.000	7	4	6	0	2
Bates	.833	3	2	3	1	2
Castilla	.000	1	0	0	0	0
Liriano	1.000	1	0	2	0	0
Perez	.975	162	271	517	20	127

Outfield	PCT	G	PO	A	E	DP
Abbott	.929	9	13	0	1	0
Barry	1.000	10	20	1	0	0
Bichette	.965	156	288	14	11	6
Burks	.975	98	187	5	5	0
Clemente	.857	7	6	0	1	0
Colbrunn	1.000	5	6	0	0	0
Echevarria	1.000	4	3	0	0	0
Gibson	.929	7	11	2	1	0
Goodwin	.983	91	119	1	2	0
Hamilton	.990	48	103	1	1	0
Vanderwal	1.000	25	21	2	0	0
Walker	.984	123	236	8	4	2
White	1.000	2	1	0	0	0

LARRY GOREN

Larry Walker

FARM SYSTEM

Director of Player Development: Paul Egins

Class	Farm Team	League	W	L	Pct.	Finish*	Manager	First Yr
AAA	Colo. Springs (Colo.) Sky Sox	Pacific Coast	55	89	.382	15th (16)	Paul Zuvella	1993
AA	New Haven (Conn.) Ravens	Eastern	59	83	.415	9th (10)	Tim Blackwell	1994
A#	Salem (Va.) Avalanche	Carolina	62	78	.443	7th (8)	Jay Loviglio	1995
A	Asheville (N.C.) Tourists	South Atlantic	71	69	.507	7th (14)	Ron Gideon	1994
A	Portland (Ore.) Rockies	Northwest	34	42	.447	t-5th (8)	Jim Eppard	1995
Rookie	Tucson (Ariz.) Rockies	Arizona	42	14	.750	+1st (8)	P.J. Carey	1992

*Finish in overall standings (No. of teams in league) #Advanced level +Won league championship

COLORADO SPRINGS — Class AAA

PACIFIC COAST LEAGUE

BATTING	AVG	G	AB	R	H	2B	3B	HR	RBI	BB	SO	SB	CS	B	T	HT	WT	DOB	1st Yr	Resides
Barker, Tim	.266	78	252	31	67	10	0	1	27	25	43	5	6	R	R	6-0	175	6-30-68	1989	Salisbury, Md.
Barry, Jeff	.261	100	349	55	91	19	6	8	55	46	52	5	1	B	R	6-0	200	9-22-68	1990	San Diego, Calif.
Bates, Jason	.321	10	102	27	33	8	1	5	20	17	31	1	2	B	R	5-11	170	1-5-71	1992	Norwalk, Calif.
Boston, D.J.	.284	41	109	22	31	6	1	1	8	11	19	0	2	L	L	6-7	230	9-6-71	1991	Cincinnati, Ohio
Castro, Juan	.000	1	1	0	0	0	0	0	0	0	0	0	0	R	R	6-1	205	4-21-77	1996	Turmero, Ven.
Cholowsky, Dan	.243	104	342	44	83	15	2	8	39	28	72	4	2	R	R	6-0	195	10-30-70	1991	San Jose, Calif.
Clemente, Edgard	.252	135	493	79	124	21	7	22	82	40	117	5	5	R	R	6-0	170	12-15-75	1993	Guaynabo, P.R.
Coolbaugh, Mike	.277	108	386	62	107	35	2	16	75	32	93	0	3	R	R	6-1	190	6-5-72	1990	San Antonio, Texas
Echevarria, Angel	.326	85	301	50	98	21	2	15	60	14	47	0	1	R	R	6-4	215	5-25-71	1992	Bridgeport, Conn.
Gibson, Derrick	.292	126	497	84	145	20	3	14	81	35	110	14	6	R	R	6-2	238	2-5-75	1993	Winter Haven, Fla.
Kirgan, Chris	.322	26	87	12	28	6	0	3	15	3	16	0	0	R	R	6-4	235	6-29-73	1994	Littleton, Colo.
Lidle, Kevin	.267	5	15	2	4	1	1	0	1	1	8	0	0	R	R	5-11	170	3-22-72	1992	West Covina, Calif.
Liriano, Nelson	.315	87	286	44	90	16	3	7	44	39	42	8	10	B	R	5-10	178	6-3-64	1983	Puerto Plata, D.R.
Obando, Sherman	.293	55	140	23	41	12	0	8	28	25	26	3	0	R	R	6-4	215	1-23-70	1988	Changuinola, Panama
Pegues, Steve	.333	24	72	6	24	4	0	2	7	0	14	1	0	R	R	6-2	190	5-21-68	1987	Pontotoc, Miss.
Sexton, Chris	.284	132	462	88	131	22	6	2	43	72	67	7	3	R	R	5-11	180	8-3-71	1993	Cincinnati, Ohio
Shumpert, Terry	.306	97	376	66	115	29	8	12	50	35	59	11	11	R	R	5-11	185	8-16-66	1987	Paducah, Ky.
Strittmatter, Mark	.278	87	255	32	71	15	3	6	38	30	48	0	0	R	R	6-1	200	4-4-69	1992	Ridgewood, N.J.
Taylor, Jamie	.275	27	69	9	19	6	0	2	11	1	18	0	0	L	R	6-2	220	10-10-70	1992	Bloomingdale, Ohio
White, Derrick	.284	22	81	15	23	5	0	2	10	10	14	2	1	R	R	6-1	225	10-12-69	1991	Chandler, Ariz.
2-team (66 Iowa)	.343	88	332	72	114	22	2	20	86	48	62	6	6	R	R	6-1	225	10-12-69	1991	Chandler, Ariz.

PITCHING	W	L	ERA	G	GS	CG	SV	IP	H	R	ER	BB	SO	B	T	HT	WT	DOB	1st Yr	Resides
Alston, Garvin	2	4	6.45	44	0	0	5	67	85	53	48	32	69	R	R	6-2	188	12-8-71	1992	Mount Vernon, N.Y.
Beckett, Robbie	0	0	9.00	21	0	0	0	26	35	27	26	28	28	R	L	6-5	235	7-16-72	1990	Austin, Texas
Bourgeois, Steve	5	7	5.57	38	13	0	1	115	154	82	71	62	87	R	R	6-1	220	8-4-72	1993	Paulina, La.
Brownson, Mark	6	8	5.34	21	21	3	0	125	131	85	74	37	82	L	R	6-2	175	6-17-75	1994	Wellington, Fla.
Burke, John	1	0	9.00	6	0	0	0	7	5	7	7	5	8	R	R	6-4	220	2-9-70	1992	Highlands Ranch, Colo.
Cholowsky, Dan	0	0	2.00	7	0	0	0	9	6	2	2	3	2	R	R	6-0	195	10-30-70	1991	San Jose, Calif.
Cortes, David	1	0	7.71	6	0	0	0	7	14	6	6	2	5	R	R	5-11	195	10-15-73	1996	El Centro, Calif.
Farmer, Mike	7	7	5.61	28	23	0	0	127	173	107	79	56	74	B	L	6-1	200	7-3-68	1990	Gary, Ind.
Glinatsis, George	2	9	6.33	20	15	1	0	91	108	75	64	48	85	R	R	6-4	210	6-29-69	1991	Youngstown, Ohio
Jean, Domingo	3	2	5.48	36	0	0	0	48	64	33	29	25	38	R	R	6-2	175	1-9-69	1990	Chicago, Ill.
Kramer, Tom	3	6	4.60	48	3	0	9	78	76	44	40	34	67	R	R	6-0	205	1-9-68	1987	St. Bernard, Ohio
Moore, Joel	2	5	6.72	12	12	0	0	66	78	54	49	31	46	L	R	6-2	200	8-13-72	1993	Elgin, Ill.
Rath, Fred	5	1	5.08	23	0	0	4	28	37	17	16	15	20	R	R	6-3	220	1-5-73	1995	Tampa, Fla.
2-team (27 Salt Lake)	6	3	4.80	50	0	0	12	60	72	33	32	23	35							
Ritz, Kevin	0	2	8.31	4	4	0	0	17	25	23	16	9	7	R	R	6-4	220	6-8-65	1986	Cambridge, Ohio
Saipe, Mike	5	11	5.16	24	24	2	0	140	167	96	80	51	124	R	R	6-1	190	9-10-73	1994	San Diego, Calif.
Schroeffel, Scott	0	0	7.36	1	0	0	0	4	4	3	3	3	3	B	R	6-0	190	12-30-73	1996	Wexford, Pa.
Shoemaker, Stephen	2	7	9.05	15	12	0	0	63	80	68	63	63	56	L	R	6-1	195	2-3-73	1994	Phoenixville, Pa.
Stoops, Jim	1	0	1.23	11	0	0	1	15	6	6	2	8	17	R	R	6-2	195	6-30-72	1995	Somerset, N.J.
Thompson, Mark	0	1	18.90	1	1	0	0	3	10	7	7	1	1	R	R	6-2	205	4-7-71	1992	Russellville, Ky.
Vavrek, Mike	2	6	8.26	10	9	0	0	45	62	50	41	34	41	L	L	6-2	185	4-23-74	1995	Glendale Heights, Ill.
Wainhouse, David	2	3	3.60	38	0	0	4	50	47	25	20	23	44	L	R	6-2	185	11-7-67	1989	Mercer Island, Wash.
Woodson, Kerry	6	10	5.48	42	7	0	0	94	110	72	57	64	51	R	R	6-2	190	5-18-69	1989	Scottsdale, Ariz.

FIELDING

Catcher	PCT	G	PO	A	E	DP	PB
Cholowsky	.984	70	442	42	8	5	10
Lidle	1.000	5	35	4	0	0	2
Strittmatter	.991	81	504	53	5	4	2

First Base	PCT	G	PO	A	E	DP
Barry	1.000	1	7	0	0	2
Boston	.992	36	224	28	2	24
Cholowsky	1.000	10	70	10	0	8
Coolbaugh	.986	24	127	16	2	16
Echevarria	.985	48	363	25	6	44
Kirgan	.979	24	174	14	4	22
Obando	.990	24	196	8	2	16
Taylor	1.000	3	17	0	0	3
White	1.000	1	9	1	0	1

Second Base	PCT	G	PO	A	E	DP
Barker	.990	59	114	181	3	46
Bates	.952	10	7	13	1	1
Cholowsky	.714	4	1	4	2	0
Coolbaugh	1.000	2	3	5	0	2
Lidle	1.000	1	0	1	0	0
Liriano	.977	40	61	110	4	23
Sexton	1.000	3	3	3	0	1
Shumpert	.990	44	95	109	2	24

Third Base	PCT	G	PO	A	E	DP
Barker	.857	7	0	6	1	0
Barry	1.000	3	2	1	0	0
Bates	.914	20	10	22	3	1
Cholowsky	.950	11	4	15	1	1
Coolbaugh	.901	86	54	165	24	19
Liriano	.897	23	6	29	4	4
Sexton	1.000	2	1	3	0	0
Shumpert	1.000	7	3	7	0	1
Taylor	1.000	14	7	20	0	3

Shortstop	PCT	G	PO	A	E	DP
Bates	.926	22	30	45	6	16
Cholowsky	.000	1	0	0	0	0
Liriano	.882	5	4	11	2	1
Sexton	.957	126	212	346	25	81
Shumpert	1.000	5	5	13	0	6

Outfield	PCT	G	PO	A	E	DP
Barker	.000	4	0	0	1	0
Barry	.955	93	181	12	9	3
Boston	1.000	1	1	0	0	0

	PCT	G	PO	A	E	DP
Cholowsky	.818	9	8	1	2	0
Clemente	.968	128	262	8	9	3
Coolbaugh	1.000	1	3	0	0	0
Echevarria	.980	34	45	3	1	0
Gibson	.945	122	211	11	13	3
Kirgan	.000	1	0	0	0	0
Obando	.000	1	0	0	0	0
Pegues	1.000	15	27	0	0	0
Sexton	1.000	1	3	0	0	0
Shumpert	.955	35	38	4	2	1
Taylor	1.000	3	2	0	0	0
White	1.000	19	31	2	0	0

NEW HAVEN — Class AA

EASTERN LEAGUE

BATTING	AVG	G	AB	R	H	2B	3B	HR	RBI	BB	SO	SB	CS	B	T	HT	WT	DOB	1st Yr	Resides
Feuerstein, Dave	.275	133	505	61	139	13	5	6	51	23	56	18	11	R	R	6-2	200	7-19-73	1995	Scarsdale, N.Y.
Fonville, Chad	.249	54	189	26	47	2	0	0	9	23	24	16	5	B	R	5-7	155	3-5-71	1992	Midway Park, N.C.
Gambill, Chad	.191	50	152	16	29	3	0	3	9	21	53	3	2	R	R	6-2	190	11-27-74	1993	Clearwater, Fla.
Garcia, Vicente	.217	128	424	59	92	24	0	11	29	67	68	7	6	R	R	6-0	170	2-14-75	1993	Maracaibo, Ven.
Giudice, John	.250	61	212	26	53	11	1	5	31	11	55	2	3	R	R	6-1	205	6-19-71	1993	New Britain, Conn.
Gonzales, Jose	.000	2	2	0	0	0	0	0	0	0	2	0	0	R	R	6-0	205	4-25-75	1997	Lubbock, Texas
Houser, Kyle	.234	101	312	29	73	5	0	0	32	20	38	5	3	R	R	6-0	150	1-21-75	1993	Dallas, Texas
Jarrett, Link	.238	107	324	18	77	8	2	0	26	23	31	4	10	B	R	5-10	165	1-26-72	1994	Tallahassee, Fla.
Kirgan, Chris	.272	114	427	63	116	32	0	22	79	44	105	2	1	R	R	6-4	235	6-29-73	1994	Littleton, Colo.
Lidle, Kevin	.143	11	35	5	5	2	0	2	5	3	13	0	0	R	R	5-11	170	3-22-72	1992	West Covina, Calif.
Light, Tal	.166	57	181	15	30	9	1	4	24	13	62	1	4	R	R	6-3	205	11-28-73	1995	Lumberton, Texas
Monds, Wonderful	.280	122	453	76	127	32	3	9	58	33	105	41	12	R	R	6-3	190	1-11-73	1993	Fort Pierce, Fla.
Newstrom, Doug	.284	102	331	38	94	21	1	5	24	41	53	7	5	L	R	6-1	195	9-18-71	1993	Goodyear, Ariz.
Pegues, Steve	.286	17	49	6	14	2	0	1	2	4	11	2	1	R	R	6-2	190	5-21-68	1987	Pontotoc, Miss.
Petrick, Ben	.238	106	349	52	83	21	3	18	50	56	89	7	7	R	R	6-0	195	4-7-77	1996	Hillsboro, Ore.
Rennhack, Mike	.308	52	182	27	56	15	1	3	32	23	31	4	3	B	R	6-2	190	8-25-74	1992	Kissimmee, Fla.
Richardson, Brian	.100	6	20	1	2	0	0	0	2	1	4	1	0	R	R	6-2	202	8-31-75	1992	Diamond Bar, Calif.
Taylor, Jamie	.336	86	304	48	102	22	0	11	53	41	43	1	2	L	R	6-2	220	10-10-70	1992	Bloomingdale, Ohio
Whitley, Matt	.211	14	38	2	8	0	0	0	7	4	9	0	1	R	R	6-0	170	3-29-72	1995	Knoxville, Tenn.

PITCHING	W	L	ERA	G	GS	CG	SV	IP	H	R	ER	BB	SO	B	T	HT	WT	DOB	1st Yr	Resides
Beckett, Robbie	2	1	5.11	22	0	0	0	25	20	14	14	23	36	R	L	6-5	235	7-16-72	1990	Austin, Texas
Bost, Heath	4	2	3.30	41	0	0	2	46	43	20	17	11	48	R	R	6-4	200	10-13-74	1995	Taylorsville, N.C.
Brester, Jason	2	0	1.59	5	4	0	0	23	22	7	4	7	15	L	L	6-3	190	12-7-76	1995	Burlington, Wash.
Doyle, Tom	0	0	0.00	6	0	0	0	5	2	0	0	2	2	L	L	6-3	205	1-20-70	1988	Redondo Beach, Calif.
Glinatsis, George	1	2	4.10	12	2	0	2	37	32	17	17	9	41	R	R	6-4	210	6-29-69	1991	Youngstown, Ohio
Gonzalez, Lariel	0	4	4.19	58	0	0	22	58	46	30	27	40	63	R	R	6-4	180	5-25-76	1994	San Cristobal, D.R.
Hackman, Luther	3	12	5.44	28	23	1	0	139	169	102	84	54	90	R	R	6-4	195	10-10-74	1994	Columbus, Miss.
Jean, Domingo	2	2	7.00	12	5	0	1	27	30	21	21	19	17	R	R	6-2	175	1-9-69	1990	Chicago, Ill.
Kusiewicz, Mike	14	7	2.32	27	26	2	0	179	161	59	46	35	151	R	L	6-2	185	11-1-76	1995	Nepean, Ontario
Moore, Joel	4	6	3.89	13	12	0	0	81	84	42	35	26	69	L	R	6-2	200	8-13-72	1993	Elgin, Ill.
Price, Tom	4	6	3.67	38	4	0	1	69	85	33	28	7	36	L	L	6-0	190	3-19-72	1994	Edwardsville, Ill.
Randall, Scott	10	14	3.83	29	29	7	0	202	210	102	86	62	135	R	R	6-3	178	10-29-75	1995	Goleta, Calif.
Ritz, Kevin	1	2	3.71	3	3	1	0	17	17	7	7	3	14	R	R	6-4	220	6-8-65	1986	Cambridge, Ohio
Salamon, John	2	3	5.63	53	0	0	1	72	65	48	45	66	72	R	R	6-1	220	3-30-72	1991	McKees Rocks, Pa.
Shoemaker, Stephen	3	5	4.89	15	15	0	0	85	69	60	46	63	85	L	R	6-1	195	2-3-73	1994	Phoenixville, Pa.
Vavrek, Mike	5	12	5.49	19	19	0	0	115	142	83	70	49	70	L	L	6-2	185	4-23-74	1995	Glendale Heights, Ill.
Woods, Brian	1	3	3.15	31	0	0	2	34	23	15	12	22	29	L	R	6-6	212	6-7-71	1993	West Caldwell, N.J.
Zolecki, Mike	1	1	9.28	8	0	0	0	11	10	11	11	8	6	R	R	6-2	195	12-6-71	1993	South Milwaukee, Wis.

FIELDING

Catcher	PCT	G	PO	A	E	DP	PB
Gonzales	1.000	2	10	0	0	0	0
Lidle	.986	10	59	10	1	1	1
Newstrom	.981	55	391	32	8	5	9
Petrick	.991	86	534	43	5	2	10

First Base	PCT	G	PO	A	E	DP
Jarrett	1.000	1	5	1	0	0
Kirgan	.985	111	988	72	16	86
Newstrom	.988	25	228	16	3	21
Taylor	1.000	5	44	4	0	4

Second Base	PCT	G	PO	A	E	DP
Fonville	.945	12	20	32	3	5
Garcia	.967	121	247	344	20	78
Jarrett	.965	12	19	36	2	7

Third Base	PCT	G	PO	A	E	DP
Jarrett	.949	28	9	65	4	7
Light	.877	37	18	89	15	6
Richardson	.800	3	1	7	2	1
Taylor	.954	69	51	156	10	16
Whitley	.905	8	4	15	2	0

Shortstop	PCT	G	PO	A	E	DP
Houser	.956	94	138	273	19	49
Jarrett	.952	56	77	122	10	25
Whitley	1.000	4	2	7	0	1

Outfield	PCT	G	PO	A	E	DP
Feuerstein	.986	128	199	10	3	2
Fonville	1.000	32	47	1	0	0
Gambill	.958	39	63	6	3	1
Giudice	.980	59	94	6	2	0
Houser	1.000	1	0	1	0	0
Jarrett	1.000	2	1	0	0	0
Light	.900	12	8	1	1	0
Monds	.956	116	251	7	12	1
Newstrom	.857	3	6	0	1	0
Pegues	1.000	10	10	1	0	0
Petrick	1.000	1	2	0	0	0
Rennhack	.972	41	66	3	2	0
Taylor	1.000	1	2	0	0	0

SALEM — Class A

CAROLINA LEAGUE

BATTING	AVG	G	AB	R	H	2B	3B	HR	RBI	BB	SO	SB	CS	B	T	HT	WT	DOB	1st Yr	Resides
Anderson, Blake	.254	68	197	22	50	10	1	1	18	23	50	2	1	B	R	6-0	195	9-22-73	1996	Dallas, Texas
Anthony, Brian	.276	123	442	53	122	19	0	15	65	29	85	7	9	L	R	6-2	218	10-22-73	1996	Walnut Creek, Calif.
Bair, Rod	.299	114	425	62	127	42	5	8	60	24	64	12	6	R	R	5-11	190	10-29-74	1996	Tempe, Ariz.
Barthol, Blake	.290	122	441	56	128	37	2	11	68	46	94	5	3	R	R	6-0	200	4-7-73	1995	Emmaus, Pa.
Bryant, Clint	.241	123	436	46	105	12	1	8	31	23	73	7	7	R	R	6-0	180	8-29-73	1996	Kingsville, Texas
Duverge, Salvador	.214	5	14	2	3	1	0	1	2	0	4	0	0	R	R	6-0	165	5-14-76	1994	San Cristobal, D.R.
Gambill, Chad	.248	41	145	12	36	9	0	2	16	9	38	0	0	R	R	6-2	190	11-27-74	1993	Clearwater, Fla.
Hamlin, Mark	.270	57	200	29	54	16	1	8	36	19	57	0	2	R	R	6-3	220	2-9-74	1996	Augusta, Ga.
Hutchison, Bernard	.201	101	293	44	59	8	2	2	23	40	88	37	13	R	R	5-10	160	5-2-74	1996	Tallassee, Ala.
Jackson, Jeremy	.177	41	124	14	22	3	0	0	11	15	46	4	3	L	R	6-2	195	5-9-76	1997	Moline, Ill.
Keck, Brian	.274	85	263	30	72	8	3	1	24	24	39	10	11	R	R	6-3	185	1-15-74	1996	Dodge City, Kan.
Lidle, Kevin	.119	31	59	6	7	4	0	2	7	3	14	0	0	R	R	5-11	170	3-22-72	1992	West Covina, Calif.
Livingston, Doug	.270	131	514	87	139	31	1	2	58	50	98	27	5	R	R	5-8	160	4-9-74	1996	Thonotosassa, Fla.
Sosa, Juan	.278	133	529	88	147	20	12	8	47	43	83	64	16	R	R	6-1	175	8-19-75	1993	San Fran. de Macoris, D.R.
Warner, Bryan	.237	116	422	47	100	17	1	10	62	37	84	5	5	L	L	5-9	185	8-7-74	1994	Monrovia, Calif.
Whitley, Matt	.258	41	120	18	31	6	0	0	11	11	16	7	2	R	R	6-0	170	3-29-72	1995	Knoxville, Tenn.

GAMES BY POSITION: C—Anderson 28, Barthol 101, Lidle 18. **1B**—Anthony 118, Bryant 1, Keck 28. **2B**—Bryant 4, Keck 1, Lidle 1, Livingston 130, Whitley 5. **3B**—Bryant 112, Keck 23, Whitley 8. **SS**—Keck 8, Sosa 122, Whitley 14. **OF**—Anderson 1, Bair 113, Duverge 3, Gambill 14, Hamlin 48, Hutchison 101, Jackson 40, Keck 12, Warner 100.

PITCHING	W	L	ERA	G	GS	CG	SV	IP	H	R	ER	BB	SO	B	T	HT	WT	DOB	1st Yr	Resides
Bailey, Roger	0	2	8.71	3	3	0	0	10	13	11	10	11	5	R	R	6-1	180	10-3-70	1992	Tallahassee, Fla.
Bevel, Bobby	6	4	2.26	51	0	0	3	92	72	26	23	24	92	L	L	5-10	180	10-10-73	1995	West Plains, Mo.
Burke, John	0	0	1.13	2	2	0	0	8	3	1	1	7	8	R	R	6-4	220	2-9-70	1992	Highlands Ranch, Colo.
Chacon, Shawn	0	4	5.30	12	12	0	0	56	53	35	33	31	54	R	R	6-3	195	12-23-77	1996	Greeley, Colo.
Colmenares, Luis	13	6	5.05	28	28	1	0	160	187	96	90	63	117	R	R	5-11	189	11-25-76	1994	Valencia, Ven.
Doyle, Tom	5	3	4.26	18	5	0	0	57	50	38	27	21	49	L	L	6-3	205	1-20-70	1988	Redondo Beach, Calif.
Emiliano, Jamie	1	1	3.52	4	0	0	0	8	9	3	3	5	6	R	R	5-10	210	8-2-74	1995	Andrews, Texas
Garrett, Neil	0	3	5.40	12	9	0	0	45	55	28	27	11	27	R	R	6-1	170	7-4-74	1992	Joliet, Ill.
Kenady, Jake	0	2	6.75	32	0	0	0	59	53	49	44	52	43	L	L	6-4	200	9-21-73	1991	Scottsdale, Ariz.
Lee, David	3	5	3.77	54	0	0	25	57	57	26	24	15	54	R	R	6-2	200	3-12-73	1995	Pittsburgh, Pa.
Lidle, Kevin	1	1	8.64	10	0	0	0	16	22	16	16	15	6	R	R	5-11	170	3-22-72	1992	West Covina, Calif.
Macca, Chris	0	1	18.00	10	0	0	0	11	17	28	22	23	6	R	R	6-2	185	11-14-74	1995	Plant City, Fla.
Martin, Chandler	12	7	2.48	24	24	7	0	160	136	54	44	43	104	R	R	6-1	180	10-23-73	1995	Salem, Ore.
Matcuk, Steve	3	11	4.71	18	15	1	0	99	107	59	52	18	69	R	R	6-2	185	4-8-76	1996	Pasadena, Md.
Porzio, Mike	2	3	2.76	7	7	0	0	42	40	20	13	12	46	L	L	6-3	190	8-20-72	1993	Norwalk, Conn.
2-team (26 Danville)	5	5	2.58	33	18	1	2	139	114	54	40	42	141							
Romine, Jason	1	2	6.75	6	0	0	0	12	15	9	9	10	8	R	R	6-5	215	4-11-75	1995	Omak, Wash.
Rosa, Cristy	1	2	3.99	17	0	0	0	29	31	17	13	16	21	R	R	6-1	165	10-5-77	1995	Guanica, P.R.
Schroeffel, Scott	7	5	4.74	38	1	0	2	82	86	53	43	31	91	B	R	6-0	190	12-30-73	1996	Wexford, Pa.
Stepka, Tom	1	3	5.97	11	5	0	0	32	32	21	21	13	26	R	R	6-2	185	11-29-75	1996	Williamsville, N.Y.
Stoops, Jim	0	0	0.00	3	0	0	0	4	2	0	0	1	8	R	R	6-2	195	6-30-72	1995	Somerset, N.J.
Thompson, Mark	0	0	3.95	3	3	0	0	14	17	7	6	3	10	R	R	6-2	205	4-7-71	1992	Russellville, Ky.
Walls, Doug	6	13	4.47	27	26	2	0	159	145	91	79	63	169	L	R	6-3	200	3-21-74	1993	Union, Ohio
Warner, Bryan	0	0	0.00	3	0	0	0	1	1	0	0	2	0	L	L	5-9	185	8-7-74	1994	Monrovia, Calif.

ASHEVILLE — Class A

SOUTH ATLANTIC LEAGUE

BATTING	AVG	G	AB	R	H	2B	3B	HR	RBI	BB	SO	SB	CS	B	T	HT	WT	DOB	1st Yr	Resides
Alamo, Efrain	.247	130	494	67	122	25	0	16	62	25	141	18	12	R	R	6-2	190	10-5-76	1994	Canovanas, P.R.
Alviso, Jerome	.276	134	486	64	134	30	1	6	41	18	60	11	11	B	R	6-1	180	9-4-75	1997	Livermore, Calif.
Arias, Rogelio	.274	84	317	36	87	16	2	5	37	15	40	0	3	R	R	6-0	165	6-9-76	1993	Santo Domingo, D.R.
Folmar, Ryan	.000	5	14	0	0	0	0	0	0	1	11	0	0	L	R	5-11	205	11-8-74	1997	Chambersburg, Pa.
Gonzales, Jose	.190	41	121	17	23	3	0	3	11	13	38	0	2	R	R	6-0	205	4-25-75	1997	Lubbock, Texas
Jackson, Jeremy	.285	92	361	57	103	16	3	10	52	24	88	13	10	L	R	6-2	195	5-9-76	1997	Moline, Ill.
Johns, Michael	.192	59	167	18	32	5	1	2	9	7	34	3	0	R	R	6-2	190	8-26-75	1997	Fernandina Beach, Fla.
Landaeta, Luis	.220	28	91	12	20	1	0	1	9	2	14	5	3	L	L	6-0	180	3-4-77	1996	Valencia, Ven.
Lindsey, John	.275	126	472	59	130	21	3	14	73	24	114	2	4	R	R	6-3	215	1-30-77	1995	Hattiesburg, Miss.
Mitchell, Andres	.249	136	446	71	111	19	4	9	58	56	139	25	12	R	R	6-1	185	5-26-76	1996	Brentwood, Tenn.
Pena, Elvis	.287	115	428	93	123	24	4	6	48	70	85	41	12	B	R	5-11	155	9-15-76	1994	Santo Domingo, D.R.
Schwartzbauer, Whitey	.269	107	346	55	93	24	1	10	57	56	80	4	1	L	R	6-1	185	5-4-77	1996	White Bear Lake, Minn.
Sears, Todd	.290	130	459	71	133	26	2	11	82	72	89	10	4	L	R	6-6	205	10-23-75	1997	Ankeny, Iowa
Vidal, Gilbert	.298	76	275	42	82	21	0	7	42	25	63	3	1	R	R	5-10	188	4-21-75	1995	Virginia Gardens, Fla.
Zweifel, Kent	.246	64	199	34	49	11	0	11	24	19	70	1	1	R	R	6-3	210	3-21-77	1996	Klamath Falls, Ore.

GAMES BY POSITION: C—Arias 74, Folmar 2, Gonzales 40, Vidal 31. **1B**—Lindsey 112, Schwartzbauer 29, Vidal 4. **2B**—Alviso 27, Johns 5, Pena 109, Schwartzbauer 3. **3B**—Johns 13, Schwartzbauer 29, Sears 106. **SS**—Alviso 110, Johns 37. **OF**—Alamo 129, Jackson 92, Landaeta 27, Mitchell 136, Zweifel 52.

PITCHING	W	L	ERA	G	GS	CG	SV	IP	H	R	ER	BB	SO	B	T	HT	WT	DOB	1st Yr	Resides
Bailey, Roger	0	0	3.86	1	1	0	0	5	5	2	2	5	1	R	R	6-1	180	10-3-70	1992	Tallahassee, Fla.
Brueggemann, Dean	7	3	2.48	41	0	0	4	69	60	28	19	28	92	L	L	6-4	195	3-11-76	1996	Smithton, Ill.
Emiliano, Jamie	3	4	3.50	41	0	0	18	44	56	22	17	21	35	R	R	5-10	210	8-2-74	1995	Andrews, Texas
Gonzalez, Armando	0	3	4.41	11	0	0	0	16	27	11	8	8	18	R	R	6-1	195	10-12-77	1997	Pico Rivera, Calif.
Johnson, David	0	1	2.70	17	0	0	0	20	15	14	6	22	26	R	R	6-3	220	10-6-74	1997	Baxter Springs, Kan.
Kalinowski, Josh	12	10	3.92	28	28	3	0	172	159	93	75	65	215	L	L	6-2	190	12-12-76	1997	Casper, Wyo.
Kringen, Jake	6	8	4.63	28	24	0	1	146	185	90	75	29	119	L	L	6-2	215	6-25-76	1997	Elma, Wash.
Matcuk, Steve	1	3	4.62	13	7	0	1	49	60	32	25	22	32	R	R	6-2	185	4-8-76	1996	Pasadena, Md.
Miller, Justin	13	8	3.69	27	27	3	0	163	177	89	67	40	142	R	R	6-2	200	8-27-77	1997	Torrance, Calif.
Pacheco, Enemencio	0	0	6.75	2	0	0	0	4	5	5	3	1	2	R	R	6-0	160	3-30-79	1997	Santo Domingo, D.R.
Petrosian, Ara	0	3	6.66	18	0	0	0	24	30	19	18	13	32	R	R	6-4	225	3-3-75	1997	Fountain Valley, Calif.
Price, Chris	1	3	5.27	18	0	0	1	27	27	26	16	11	21	R	R	6-4	225	12-5-74	1997	Roswell, N.M.
Price, Ryan	10	7	4.12	27	26	5	0	168	178	93	77	41	145	R	R	6-3	190	1-31-78	1997	Roswell, N.M.
Rosa, Cristy	3	2	5.09	18	0	0	0	35	49	25	20	12	22	R	R	6-1	165	10-5-77	1995	Guanica, P.R.
Seifert, Ryan	7	6	4.12	36	0	0	5	87	66	44	40	37	90	R	R	6-5	215	8-14-75	1997	Chaska, Minn.
Thompson, Doug	0	0	4.70	9	1	0	0	15	17	9	8	7	17	R	R	6-1	195	7-22-76	1998	Biloxi, Miss.
Thompson, Travis	6	7	3.24	26	24	0	0	147	155	71	53	36	113	R	R	6-4	190	1-10-75	1996	Greenfield, Wis.
Thomson, John	1	0	0.00	2	2	0	0	9	5	1	0	1	12	R	R	6-3	175	10-1-73	1993	Sulphur, La.
Wrigley, Jase	1	1	5.74	13	0	0	0	16	18	11	10	4	12	R	R	6-4	220	11-6-75	1998	Atlanta, Ga.

PORTLAND — Short-Season Class A

NORTHWEST LEAGUE

BATTING	AVG	G	AB	R	H	2B	3B	HR	RBI	BB	SO	SB	CS	B	T	HT	WT	DOB	1st Yr	Resides
Castro, Juan	.237	39	139	19	33	6	1	2	18	9	37	1	0	R	R	6-1	205	4-21-77	1996	Turmero, Ven.
Duck, Kevin	.304	59	214	19	65	11	1	2	34	15	52	1	1	L	L	6-3	210	7-7-77	1998	Irvine, Calif.
Duverge, Salvador	.231	16	52	13	12	4	0	1	9	10	12	1	0	R	R	6-0	165	5-14-76	1994	San Cristobal, D.R.
Etheredge, Josh	.226	38	137	13	31	5	2	0	13	19	35	2	1	R	R	6-2	210	3-14-76	1998	Auburn, Ala.
Figgins, Chone	.283	69	269	41	76	9	3	1	26	24	56	25	4	B	R	5-8	155	1-22-78	1997	Brandon, Fla.
Franklin, Jason	.242	59	211	30	51	8	1	3	23	28	49	5	0	R	R	6-1	200	12-20-76	1997	Winter Haven, Fla.
Johnson, Erik	.274	51	186	30	51	12	0	7	30	17	26	0	0	R	R	5-11	195	3-2-77	1998	Naples, Fla.

BATTING	AVG	G	AB	R	H	2B	3B	HR	RBI	BB	SO	SB	CS	B	T	HT	WT	DOB	1st Yr	Resides
Landaeta, Luis	.297	29	111	19	33	3	2	0	12	8	16	4	4	L	L	6-0	180	3-4-77	1996	Valencia, Ven.
Leon, Richy	.231	52	186	27	43	8	1	1	18	16	20	0	4	R	R	5-8	175	6-21-76	1998	Yuma, Ariz.
Mahoney, Ricardo	.255	50	188	22	48	8	1	1	23	17	41	1	1	R	R	6-2	190	10-13-78	1996	Panama City, Panama
Nunez, Jose	.231	46	156	13	36	7	0	0	13	19	24	0	1	R	R	6-1	167	10-7-78	1996	Santo Domingo, D.R.
Pierre, Juan	.352	64	264	55	93	9	2	0	30	19	11	38	9	L	L	6-0	170	8-14-77	1998	Alexandria, La.
Rosario, Melvin	.224	61	210	30	47	4	2	0	17	26	52	12	4	L	L	6-2	175	9-22-78	1998	Carolina, P.R.
Smith, Sam	.207	21	82	10	17	5	1	1	11	4	23	1	0	R	R	6-1	180	3-21-79	1997	Jasper, Texas
Whitehurst, Tom	.262	59	233	34	61	10	2	3	39	19	47	7	2	R	R	5-11	175	7-20-77	1998	Blakely, Ga.

GAMES BY POSITION: C—Castro 29, Johnson 39, Mahoney 13. **1B**—Duck 58, Etheredge 10, Franklin 1, Johnson 2, Mahoney 16, Whitehurst 1. **2B**—Franklin 17, Leon 14, Nunez 45. **3B**—Franklin 39, Leon 25, Smith 14. **SS**—Figgins 67, Leon 12, Nunez 1. **OF**—Duverge 15, Etheredge 9, Landaeta 26, Mahoney 1, Pierre 64, Rosario 61, Whitehurst 57.

PITCHING	W	L	ERA	G	GS	CG	SV	IP	H	R	ER	BB	SO	B	T	HT	WT	DOB	1st Yr	Resides
Barboza, Carlos	0	1	2.92	14	0	0	0	25	26	12	8	14	10	R	R	6-1	188	2-21-78	1996	Maracaibo, Ven.
Bradley, Brian	3	4	4.04	10	10	0	0	49	43	27	22	26	39	R	R	6-4	185	4-23-76	1998	Chesapeake, Va.
Cameron, Ryan	0	6	6.02	18	2	0	1	40	45	30	27	24	47	R	R	6-1	180	9-13-77	1998	Williamstown, Mass.
Carter, Justin	1	1	3.78	15	2	0	0	33	41	20	14	10	35	R	L	6-2	185	3-8-77	1998	Birmingham, Ala.
Cook, Aaron	5	8	4.88	15	15	1	0	79	87	50	43	39	38	R	R	6-3	175	2-8-79	1997	Loveland, Ohio
DiFelice, Mark	4	6	3.31	15	13	0	0	82	83	45	30	11	62	R	R	6-2	190	8-23-76	1998	Havertown, Pa.
Gonzalez, Armando	0	1	3.21	5	0	0	0	14	14	6	5	3	8	R	R	6-1	195	10-12-77	1997	Pico Rivera, Calif.
Gordon, Kevin	2	2	5.52	8	7	0	0	29	31	24	18	14	20	R	R	6-3	200	9-16-76	1998	Clearwater, Fla.
Hudson, Luke	3	6	4.74	15	15	0	0	80	68	46	42	51	82	R	R	6-3	195	5-2-77	1998	Fountain Valley, Calif.
Johnson, David	0	0	3.86	6	0	0	1	5	8	2	2	1	6	R	R	6-3	220	10-6-74	1997	Baxter Springs, Kan.
Kennedy, Ryan	0	0	36.00	1	0	0	0	1	3	4	4	1	2	R	R	6-4	215	10-29-75	1996	Shubuta, Miss.
Kidd, Jake	1	0	7.46	20	0	0	3	35	49	33	29	26	20	R	R	6-6	180	2-11-78	1997	Hesperia, Calif.
Kirkpatrick, Brian	1	0	11.49	12	0	0	0	16	18	20	20	10	10	R	R	6-3	195	9-7-76	1995	King City, Calif.
Labitzke, Jesse	4	3	4.97	17	2	0	1	51	53	30	28	30	44	L	L	6-5	220	11-23-77	1996	Laramie, Wyo.
LaMattina, Ryan	4	0	3.23	18	0	0	0	31	29	14	11	18	30	R	L	6-2	210	1-14-76	1998	Fredonia, N.Y.
Mundy, Mike	2	0	2.25	21	0	0	6	24	16	9	6	5	19	L	R	6-1	185	3-26-76	1998	Belleville, N.J.
Van Buren, Jermaine	0	0	3.60	2	2	0	0	10	7	4	4	7	9	R	R	6-2	200	7-2-80	1998	Hattiesburg, Miss.
Vargas, Derrick	4	4	4.43	14	8	0	2	63	67	40	31	32	44	L	L	6-4	204	5-13-77	1997	Newark, Calif.

TUCSON — Rookie

ARIZONA LEAGUE

BATTING	AVG	G	AB	R	H	2B	3B	HR	RBI	BB	SO	SB	CS	B	T	HT	WT	DOB	1st Yr	Resides
Colina, Javier	.320	44	169	28	54	6	2	6	39	18	30	9	4	R	R	6-1	180	2-15-79	1997	Cocorote, Ven.
Easter, J.J.	.262	22	61	11	16	2	0	0	5	8	20	9	2	R	R	5-11	170	1-6-78	1998	Mount Union, Pa.
Encarnacion, Bernardo	.322	34	121	20	39	5	1	4	25	11	33	2	0	R	R	6-2	205	8-2-78	1996	Santo Domingo, D.R.
Freeman, Choo	.320	40	147	35	47	3	6	1	24	15	25	14	1	R	R	6-2	200	10-20-79	1998	Dallas, Texas
Guzman, Javier	.292	17	48	4	14	2	0	0	4	3	21	4	0	B	R	6-2	175	11-9-79	1998	Rio Piedras, P.R.
Holliday, Matt	.342	32	117	20	40	4	1	5	23	15	21	2	1	R	R	6-4	215	1-15-80	1998	Stillwater, Okla.
Morency, Vernand	.213	24	61	11	13	0	0	0	3	12	17	3	1	R	R	5-11	200	2-4-80	1998	Miami, Fla.
Paulino, Henry	.253	24	79	16	20	1	0	0	8	4	17	2	6	R	R	5-10	165	8-26-80	1997	Santo Domingo, D.R.
Reyes, Rene	.429	49	177	40	76	9	4	5	39	8	15	16	7	B	R	5-11	202	2-21-78	1996	Porlamar, Ven.
Samuel, Tomas	.304	37	112	20	34	7	2	2	17	12	40	4	9	R	R	5-11	175	7-2-79	1996	San Pedro de Macoris, D.R.
Sanchez, Agustin	.318	45	170	40	54	15	4	2	27	26	28	13	8	B	R	6-0	160	2-3-79	1997	Yauco, P.R.
Smith, Sam	.303	30	122	20	37	7	2	0	21	2	21	5	2	R	R	6-1	180	3-21-79	1997	Jasper, Texas
Sosa, Jorge	.237	45	152	23	36	6	1	2	11	12	57	4	3	B	R	6-2	177	4-28-78	1995	Santo Domingo, D.R.
Uribe, Juan	.277	40	148	25	41	5	3	0	17	12	25	8	1	R	R	5-11	173	7-22-79	1997	San Cristobal, D.R.
Vilorio, Miguel	.292	32	130	29	38	2	0	0	17	9	16	27	10	R	R	5-10	152	7-22-79	1997	Santo Domingo, D.R.
Winchester, Jeff	.208	43	125	22	26	8	0	3	16	22	46	2	1	R	R	6-0	205	1-21-80	1998	Metairie, La.

GAMES BY POSITION: C—Reyes 14, Samuel 25, Winchester 32. **1B**—Colina 2, Encarnacion 17, Reyes 34, Smith 8. **2B**—Colina 10, Paulino 22, Smith 1, Vilorio 28. **3B**—Colina 13, Holliday 24, Smith 21. **SS**—Colina 18, Uribe 40. **OF**—Easter 18, Encarnacion 9, Freeman 38, Guzman 13, Morency 23, Sanchez 43, Sosa 43.

PITCHING	W	L	ERA	G	GS	CG	SV	IP	H	R	ER	BB	SO	B	T	HT	WT	DOB	1st Yr	Resides
DePaula, Julio	5	5	3.81	17	9	0	2	54	54	30	23	18	62	R	R	6-1	160	7-27-79	1997	Santo Domingo, D.R.
Garner, Brandon	3	0	4.29	13	7	0	0	36	33	18	17	15	28	R	R	6-0	190	3-28-80	1998	Jackson, Tenn.
Gomez, Diogenes	1	0	2.55	29	0	0	12	35	30	15	10	11	28	R	R	5-11	165	3-27-79	1997	Chorrera, Panama
Hessler, John	4	0	4.50	16	0	0	1	28	23	21	14	16	13	B	R	6-2	200	8-21-74	1998	Hoven, S.D.
Iannacone, Steve	2	1	6.21	15	0	0	1	29	35	25	20	18	31	R	R	6-6	220	10-5-77	1997	Sicklerville, N.J.
Little, Rodney	2	2	3.47	19	0	0	2	36	38	18	14	21	42	R	R	6-1	182	8-14-78	1997	Combs, Ky.
Little, Roger	4	1	3.80	14	8	0	0	47	50	30	20	18	46	R	R	6-2	180	8-14-78	1997	Combs, Ky.
Pacheco, Enemencio	5	0	3.99	12	11	0	0	59	51	31	26	17	59	R	R	6-0	160	3-30-79	1997	Santo Domingo, D.R.
Roney, Matt	1	1	5.80	9	9	1	0	40	50	31	26	11	49	R	R	6-4	225	1-10-80	1998	Edmond, Okla.
Sanchez, Juan	1	1	3.86	8	0	0	1	9	11	4	4	5	10	R	R	6-1	170	11-12-78	1996	Santiago, D.R.
Thompson, Mark	0	0	0.00	1	1	0	0	3	1	0	0	0	2	R	R	6-2	205	4-7-71	1992	Russellville, Ky.
Trask, Cody	6	1	2.49	20	0	0	2	47	36	16	13	18	68	R	R	6-3	205	3-19-78	1998	Chino Hills, Calif.
Van Buren, Jermaine	7	2	2.22	12	11	1	0	65	42	20	16	22	92	R	R	6-2	200	7-2-80	1998	Hattiesburg, Miss.

DETROIT TIGERS

Rebounding Tigers hit skids, take step backward in '98

BY PAT CAPUTO

The Detroit Tigers entered the 1998 season thinking they could push the Cleveland Indians for the American League Central title, but they exited the campaign reeling.

After a 1997 season in which almost everything went right for the Tigers, almost everything went wrong in 1998, at least at the major league level.

After improving 26 games and winning 79 times in 1997, Detroit dropped off to 65 victories in 1998.

The fallout from the disappointing season was painful. Buddy Bell came close to being named AL manager of the year in 1997, but he found the pressure of losing to be difficult to handle and on Sept. 1 he was fired. Dugout coach Larry Parrish took over on an interim basis to finish the season, and was given a two-year contract after the season ended.

The Tigers' problems stemmed in large degree from a series of offseason moves in which general manager Randy Smith acquired veteran players to fill gaps until Detroit's vastly improved farm system started to pay off.

Most of those players—like Frank Castillo, Pete Incaviglia, Joe Oliver, Joe Randa, Billy Ripken, Bip Roberts and Tim Worrell—performed poorly.

By late July, Detroit was closing in on the worst record in the AL and had 10 rookies on its active roster. While that may have pointed to good times in the future, it hurt the club in '98.

Still, Smith remained encouraged. Seth Greisinger and Matt Anderson, Detroit's first-round selections in the 1996 and 1997 drafts, both made their major league debuts and held their own. Righthander Jeff Weaver, the club's first-round selection in 1998 out of Fresno State University, dominated the Class A Midwest League and didn't appear far away.

"If the guys we signed to bridge the gap came through and we won 80 games this season as opposed to 65, we wouldn't be any closer to where we want to go eventually than we are now," Smith said. "Those players weren't going to be here more than a year even if they had come though.

"You have to have the courage to stick to your plan. As far as our long-range plan, we made progress. It's up to us to be smart and not panic. We're not off track, we just hit a couple major bumps in the road."

Second baseman Damion Easley got off to a fast start before fading in the second half. Still, it was the best season of his career. First baseman Tony Clark started slowly but came around and had a good season. Center fielder Brian Hunter and right fielder Bobby Higginson both saw their production fall off but Juan Encarnacion, a legitimate five-tool player, was impressive after being called up late in the season.

Outfielder Gabe Kapler led the minor leagues with 146 RBIs for Double-A Jacksonville and rose from an unknown 57th-round pick in 1995 to become a top prospect. Catcher Robert Fick, a former All-American at Cal State Northridge, also had a big year at Jacksonville and hit well in a brief September callup.

Kapler and Fick led Jacksonville to the Southern League championship series, where it fell to Mobile. Class A West Michigan, the minors' best team in 1997, also made it to its league championship series. The Whitecaps defeated Rockford to win the Midwest League title.

Tony Clark

MEL BAILEY

Gabe Kapler

Players of the Year

Major League: Tony Clark, 1b

Clark rebounded from a slow start to lead the Tigers in home runs and RBIs for the second straight season.

Minor League: Gabe Kapler, of, Jacksonville

Kapler led the minor leagues with 146 RBIs and earned MVP honors in the Double-A Southern League.

ORGANIZATION LEADERS

BATTING

*AVG	David Roberts, Jacksonville	.326
R	Gabe Kapler, Jacksonville	113
H	Gabe Kapler, Jacksonville	176
TB	Gabe Kapler, Jacksonville	319
2B	Two tied at	47
3B	Two tied at	10
HR	Gabe Kapler, Jacksonville	28
RBI	Gabe Kapler, Jacksonville	146
BB	Rob Fick, Jacksonville	71
SO	Alex Steele, West Michigan	137
SB	Pedro Santana, West Michigan	64

PITCHING

W	David Borkowski, Jacksonville	16
L	Mike Drumright, Toledo	19
#ERA	Mark Persails, West Michigan	2.83
G	Pedro Martinez, Toledo	58
CG	Denny Harriger, Toledo	4
SV	Jose Castillo, West Michigan	28
IP	David Borkowski, Jacksonville	179
BB	Mike Drumright, Toledo	94
SO	Alan Webb, West Michigan	202

*Minimum 250 At-Bats #Minimum 75 Innings

Detroit TIGERS

Managers: Buddy Bell, Larry Parrish

1998 Record: 65-97, .401 (5th, AL Central)

BATTING	AVG	G	AB	R	H	2B	3B	HR	RBI	BB	SO	SB	CS	B	T	HT	WT	DOB	1st Yr	Resides
Alvarez, Gabe	.231	58	199	16	46	11	0	5	29	18	65	1	3	R	R	6-1	185	3-6-74	1995	El Monte, Calif.
Bako, Paul	.272	96	305	23	83	12	1	3	30	23	82	1	1	L	R	6-2	205	6-20-72	1993	Lafayette, La.
Bartee, Kimera	.194	57	98	20	19	5	1	3	15	6	35	9	5	B	R	6-0	185	7-21-72	1993	Glendale, Ariz.
Beamon, Trey	.262	28	42	4	11	4	0	0	2	5	13	1	0	L	R	6-3	192	2-11-74	1992	Garland, Texas
Berroa, Geronimo	.238	52	126	17	30	4	1	1	10	17	27	0	1	R	R	6-0	210	3-18-65	1984	New York, N.Y.
2-team (20 Cleve.)	.225	72	191	23	43	7	2	1	13	24	44	1	1							
Casanova, Raul	.143	16	42	4	6	2	0	1	3	5	10	0	0	B	R	6-0	195	8-23-72	1990	Ponce, P.R.
Catalanotto, Frank	.282	89	213	23	60	13	2	6	25	12	39	3	2	L	R	6-0	190	4-27-74	1992	Smithtown, N.Y.
Clark, Tony	.291	157	602	84	175	37	0	34	103	63	128	3	3	B	R	6-7	245	6-15-72	1990	Glendale, Ariz.
Cruz, Deivi	.260	135	454	52	118	22	3	5	45	13	55	3	4	R	R	6-0	184	11-6-75	1993	Nizao, D.R.
Easley, Damion	.271	153	594	84	161	38	2	27	100	39	112	15	5	R	R	5-11	185	11-11-69	1989	Glendale, Ariz.
Encarnacion, Juan	.329	40	164	30	54	9	4	7	21	7	31	7	4	R	R	6-3	187	3-8-76	1993	Las Matas de Farfan, D.R.
Fick, Robert	.364	7	22	6	8	1	0	3	7	2	7	1	0	L	R	6-1	189	3-15-74	1996	Thousand Oaks, Calif.
Gonzalez, Luis	.267	154	547	84	146	35	5	23	71	57	62	12	7	L	R	6-2	190	9-2-67	1988	Sugar Land, Texas
Higginson, Bob	.284	157	612	92	174	37	4	25	85	63	101	3	3	L	R	5-11	195	8-18-70	1992	Madison Heights, Mich.
Hunter, Brian	.254	142	595	67	151	29	3	4	36	36	94	42	12	R	R	6-3	180	3-25-71	1989	Vancouver, Wash.
Incaviglia, Pete	.071	7	14	0	1	0	0	0	0	1	6	0	0	R	R	6-1	230	4-2-64	1986	Colleyville, Texas
Kapler, Gabe	.200	7	25	3	5	0	1	0	0	1	4	2	0	R	R	6-2	190	8-31-75	1995	Reseda, Calif.
Manto, Jeff	.267	16	30	6	8	2	0	1	3	3	11	1	0	R	R	6-3	210	8-23-64	1985	Bristol, Pa.
Oliver, Joe	.226	50	155	8	35	8	0	4	22	7	33	0	1	R	R	6-3	220	7-24-65	1983	Orlando, Fla.
Randa, Joe	.254	138	460	56	117	21	2	9	50	41	70	8	7	R	R	5-11	190	12-18-69	1991	Overland Park, Kan.
Ripken, Billy	.270	27	74	8	20	3	0	0	5	5	10	3	2	R	R	6-1	190	12-16-64	1982	Fallston, Md.
Roberts, Bip	.248	34	113	17	28	6	0	0	9	16	14	6	1	B	R	5-7	165	10-27-63	1982	Poway, Calif.
Siddall, Joe	.185	29	65	3	12	3	0	1	6	7	25	0	0	L	R	6-1	200	10-25-67	1988	Windsor, Ontario
Tomberlin, Andy	.217	32	69	8	15	2	0	2	12	3	25	1	0	L	L	5-11	185	11-7-66	1986	Monroe, N.C.
Wood, Jason	.348	10	23	5	8	2	0	1	1	3	4	0	1	R	R	6-1	170	12-16-69	1991	Fresno, Calif.
2-team (3 Oakland)	.333	13	24	6	8	2	0	1	1	3	5	0	1							

PITCHING	W	L	ERA	G	GS	CG	SV	IP	H	R	ER	BB	SO	B	T	HT	WT	DOB	1st Yr	Resides
Anderson, Matt	5	1	3.27	42	0	0	0	44	38	16	16	31	44	R	R	6-4	200	8-17-76	1998	Houston, Texas
Bochtler, Doug	0	2	6.15	51	0	0	0	67	73	48	46	42	45	R	R	6-3	200	7-5-70	1989	West Palm Beach, Fla.
Brocail, Doug	5	2	2.73	60	0	0	0	63	47	23	19	18	55	L	R	6-5	235	5-16-67	1986	Missouri City, Texas
Brunson, Will	0	0	0.00	8	0	0	0	3	2	0	0	1	1	L	L	6-6	185	3-20-70	1992	Bulverde, Texas
Castillo, Frank	3	9	6.83	27	19	0	1	116	150	91	88	44	81	R	R	6-1	200	4-1-69	1987	Cave Creek, Ariz.
Crow, Dean	2	2	3.94	32	0	0	0	46	55	22	20	16	18	L	R	6-4	215	8-21-72	1993	Houston, Texas
Duran, Roberto	0	1	5.87	18	0	0	0	15	9	10	10	17	12	L	L	6-0	205	3-6-73	1990	Moca, D.R.
Florie, Bryce	8	9	4.80	42	16	0	0	133	141	80	71	59	97	R	R	5-11	192	5-21-70	1988	Goose Creek, S.C.
Greisinger, Seth	6	9	5.12	21	21	0	0	130	142	79	74	48	66	R	R	6-3	200	7-29-75	1996	Falls Church, Va.
Harriger, Denny	0	3	6.75	4	2	0	0	12	17	12	9	8	3	R	R	5-11	185	7-21-69	1987	Ford City, Pa.
Jones, Todd	1	4	4.97	65	0	0	28	63	58	38	35	36	57	L	R	6-3	230	4-24-68	1989	Pell City, Ala.
Keagle, Greg	0	5	5.59	9	7	0	0	39	46	26	24	20	25	R	R	6-2	195	6-28-71	1993	Horseheads, N.Y.
Moehler, Brian	14	13	3.90	33	33	4	0	221	220	103	96	56	123	R	R	6-3	235	12-31-71	1993	Marietta, Ga.
Powell, Brian	3	8	6.35	18	16	0	0	84	101	67	59	36	46	R	R	6-2	205	10-10-73	1995	Bainbridge, Ga.
Runyan, Sean	1	4	3.58	88	0	0	1	50	47	23	20	28	39	L	L	6-3	200	6-21-74	1992	Urbandale, Iowa
Sager, A.J.	4	2	6.52	31	3	0	2	59	79	47	43	23	23	R	R	6-4	220	3-3-65	1988	Toledo, Ohio
Sanders, Scott	0	2	17.69	3	2	0	0	10	24	19	19	6	6	R	R	6-4	220	3-25-69	1990	San Diego, Calif.
Santana, Marino	0	0	3.68	7	0	0	0	7	9	3	3	8	10	R	R	6-1	175	5-10-72	1990	Santo Domingo, D.R.
Thompson, Justin	11	15	4.05	34	34	5	0	222	227	114	100	79	149	L	L	6-4	215	3-8-73	1991	Montgomery, Texas
Worrell, Tim	2	6	5.98	15	9	0	0	62	66	42	41	19	47	R	R	6-4	215	7-5-67	1990	Glendale, Ariz.

FIELDING

Catcher	PCT	G	PO	A	E	DP	PB
Bako	.989	94	493	45	6	5	9
Casanova	.967	14	81	6	3	0	0
Fick	.950	3	18	1	1	0	0
Oliver	.982	48	259	16	5	2	2
Siddall	.994	27	142	15	1	3	3

First Base	PCT	G	PO	A	E	DP
Catalanotto	1.000	18	124	10	0	9
Clark	.991	142	1265	96	13	134
Fick	1.000	1	9	0	0	0
Manto	.977	10	43	0	1	3
Oliver	1.000	2	2	1	0	0
Randa	1.000	1	3	1	0	1
Ripken	1.000	2	5	0	0	0
Wood	1.000	6	36	2	0	4

Second Base	PCT	G	PO	A	E	DP
Catalanotto	.974	31	38	36	2	10
Easley	.985	140	285	439	11	102
Randa	1.000	20	24	40	0	9
Ripken	1.000	2	2	2	0	1
Roberts	1.000	1	2	3	0	3

Third Base	PCT	G	PO	A	E	DP
Alvarez	.872	55	37	93	19	6
Catalanotto	.833	3	0	5	1	1
Randa	.976	118	72	212	7	18
Ripken	1.000	2	2	5	0	1

Shortstop	PCT	G	PO	A	E	DP
Cruz	.983	135	196	445	11	100
Easley	.986	30	29	41	1	10
Ripken	.925	21	23	51	6	11
Wood	1.000	1	2	0	0	0

Outfield	PCT	G	PO	A	E	DP
Bartee	.964	29	51	3	2	0
Beamon	1.000	4	7	0	0	0
Berroa	1.000	4	4	0	0	0
Encarnacion	.985	39	60	4	1	1
Gonzalez	.988	132	233	8	3	0
Higginson	.982	153	303	18	6	3
Hunter	.988	139	386	11	5	0
Incaviglia	.000	1	0	0	0	0
Kapler	1.000	6	9	0	0	0
Manto	.000	1	0	0	0	0
Roberts	1.000	2	1	0	0	0
Siddall	.000	1	0	0	0	0
Tomberlin	1.000	5	5	0	0	0

FARM SYSTEM

Assistant General Manager: Steve Lubratich

Class	Farm Team	League	W	L	Pct.	Finish*	Manager(s)	First Yr
AAA	Toledo (Ohio) Mud Hens	International	52	89	.369	14th (14)	Gene Roof	1987
AA	Jacksonville (Fla.) Suns	Southern	86	54	.614	t-1st (10)	Dave Anderson	1995
A#	Lakeland (Fla.) Tigers	Florida State	67	72	.482	8th (14)	Mark Meleski	1960
A	West Michigan Whitecaps	Midwest	83	57	.593	+1st (14)	Bruce Fields	1997
A	Jamestown (N.Y.) Jammers	New York-Penn	32	43	.427	12th (14)	Tim Torricelli	1994
Rookie	Lakeland (Fla.) Tigers	Gulf Coast	28	32	.467	t-8th (14)	Kevin Bradshaw	1995

*Finish in overall standings (No. of teams in league) #Advanced level +Won league championship

TOLEDO — Class AAA

INTERNATIONAL LEAGUE

BATTING	AVG	G	AB	R	H	2B	3B	HR	RBI	BB	SO	SB	CS	B	T	HT	WT	DOB	1st Yr	Resides
Almanzar, Richard	.209	104	306	36	64	16	1	1	16	28	30	11	7	R	R	5-10	155	4-3-76	1993	San Francisco de Macoris, D.R.
Alvarez, Gabe	.273	67	249	37	68	15	1	20	58	30	60	3	1	R	R	6-1	185	3-6-74	1995	El Monte, Calif.
Bako, Paul	.292	13	48	5	14	3	1	1	6	1	13	0	0	L	R	6-2	205	6-20-72	1993	Lafayette, La.
Bartee, Kimera	.247	51	215	24	53	10	0	2	13	16	42	6	3	B	R	6-0	185	7-21-72	1993	Glendale, Ariz.
Beamon, Trey	.237	56	207	31	49	6	0	3	18	28	38	16	2	L	R	6-3	192	2-11-74	1992	Garland, Texas
Belk, Tim	.267	84	292	40	78	19	1	9	34	18	55	5	0	R	R	6-3	200	4-6-70	1992	Houston, Texas
Cardona, Javier	.191	47	162	12	31	4	0	5	16	9	32	0	0	R	R	6-1	185	9-15-75	1994	Dorado, P.R.
Casanova, Raul	.257	50	171	17	44	8	0	7	26	22	28	0	1	B	R	6-0	195	8-23-72	1990	Ponce, P.R.
Catalanotto, Frank	.333	28	105	20	35	6	3	4	28	14	21	0	0	L	R	6-0	190	4-27-74	1992	Smithtown, N.Y.
Cruz, Deivi	.111	2	9	1	1	1	0	0	2	2	3	0	0	R	R	6-0	184	11-6-75	1993	Nizao, D.R.
Encarnacion, Juan	.287	92	356	55	102	17	3	8	41	29	85	24	4	R	R	6-3	187	3-8-76	1993	Las Matas de Farfan, D.R.
Faries, Paul	.290	122	458	65	133	21	5	1	36	46	54	33	7	R	R	5-10	170	2-20-65	1987	San Diego, Calif.
Garcia, Luis	.258	114	407	37	105	19	4	3	31	8	59	3	2	R	R	6-0	174	5-20-75	1993	San Francisco de Macoris, D.R.
Gresham, Kris	.243	12	37	5	9	2	0	1	4	0	15	0	0	R	R	6-2	206	8-30-70	1991	Mount Pleasant, N.C.
Ibarra, Jesse	.229	81	271	22	62	9	1	9	38	30	65	1	1	B	R	6-3	195	7-12-72	1994	El Monte, Calif.
Johnson, Earl	.251	105	362	44	91	10	8	1	24	19	65	20	6	B	R	5-10	165	10-3-71	1991	Detroit, Mich.
Lindstrom, David	.000	1	3	0	0	0	0	0	0	0	1	0	0	R	R	5-10	185	8-6-74	1996	Brooklyn Park, Minn.
Marine, Del	.267	5	15	2	4	0	1	1	1	0	3	0	0	R	R	6-0	205	10-18-71	1992	Santa Monica, Calif.
Ripken, Billy	.316	5	19	3	6	1	0	0	1	2	0	0	0	R	R	6-1	190	12-16-64	1982	Fallston, Md.
Roberts, Bip	.263	6	19	2	5	0	0	0	0	2	4	2	0	B	R	5-7	165	10-27-63	1982	Poway, Calif.
Siddall, Joe	.240	43	129	16	31	5	0	4	16	11	42	2	1	L	R	6-1	200	10-25-67	1988	Windsor, Ontario
Smith, Ira	.241	91	274	28	66	18	0	2	23	17	50	8	5	R	R	5-11	185	8-4-67	1990	Chestertown, Md.
Swann, Pedro	.291	120	419	56	122	28	2	15	66	41	74	6	3	L	R	6-0	195	10-27-70	1991	Townsend, Del.
Tomberlin, Andy	.340	14	47	13	16	2	1	2	4	8	15	1	1	L	L	5-11	185	11-7-66	1986	Monroe, N.C.
Wood, Jason	.278	46	169	24	47	9	0	7	29	16	30	0	0	R	R	6-1	170	12-16-69	1991	Fresno, Calif.

PITCHING	W	L	ERA	G	GS	CG	SV	IP	H	R	ER	BB	SO	B	T	HT	WT	DOB	1st Yr	Resides
Belk, Tim	0	0	18.00	3	0	0	0	3	4	6	6	5	1	R	R	6-3	200	4-6-70	1992	Houston, Texas
Crow, Dean	2	0	1.48	24	0	0	10	24	21	8	4	3	12	L	R	6-4	215	8-21-72	1993	Houston, Texas
Darwin, David	1	0	1.29	1	1	1	0	7	4	1	1	0	5	L	L	6-0	185	12-19-73	1996	Cornelius, N.C.
Drews, Matt	5	17	6.57	27	27	1	0	149	175	120	109	78	86	R	R	6-8	230	8-29-74	1994	Sarasota, Fla.
Drumright, Mike	4	19	6.95	29	27	1	0	154	188	130	119	94	91	L	R	6-4	210	4-19-74	1995	Valley Center, Kan.
Duran, Roberto	0	0	27.00	1	0	0	0	1	1	2	2	2	1	L	L	6-0	205	3-6-73	1990	Moca, D.R.
Florie, Bryce	0	0	0.00	1	1	0	0	4	0	0	0	0	3	R	R	5-11	192	5-21-70	1988	Goose Creek, S.C.
Goldsmith, Gary	0	1	5.26	46	0	0	1	79	83	47	46	29	50	R	R	6-2	205	7-4-71	1993	Alamogordo, N.M.
Greisinger, Seth	3	4	2.91	10	10	0	0	59	50	21	19	22	37	R	R	6-3	200	7-29-75	1996	Falls Church, Va.
Harriger, Denny	5	12	4.55	22	22	4	0	142	151	78	72	48	87	R	R	5-11	185	7-21-69	1987	Ford City, Pa.
Hurst, Bill	0	1	11.42	12	0	0	0	17	21	22	22	17	13	R	R	6-7	220	4-28-70	1990	Miami, Fla.
Johnson, Craig	1	0	5.40	1	1	0	0	5	6	4	3	1	1	R	R	6-3	200	11-8-75	1997	Tuftonboro, N.H.
Keagle, Greg	5	3	4.63	15	14	0	0	82	94	48	42	32	61	R	R	6-2	195	6-28-71	1993	Horseheads, N.Y.
Martinez, Pedro	2	5	3.79	58	1	0	8	71	72	38	30	31	49	R	L	6-2	185	11-29-68	1987	Santo Domingo, D.R.
Powell, Brian	0	0	0.00	1	1	0	0	7	5	0	0	0	7	R	R	6-2	205	10-10-73	1995	Bainbridge, Ga.
Reed, Brandon	5	7	5.98	39	17	0	0	117	159	84	78	46	70	R	R	6-4	185	12-18-74	1994	Lapeer, Mich.
Roberts, Willis	3	3	4.61	39	0	0	2	55	63	33	28	28	40	R	R	6-3	175	6-19-75	1992	San Cristobal, D.R.
Sager, A.J.	1	2	3.00	14	0	0	1	24	27	8	8	13	16	R	R	6-4	220	3-3-65	1988	Toledo, Ohio
Santana, Marino	6	3	2.90	44	0	0	7	68	44	30	22	34	94	R	R	6-1	175	5-10-72	1990	Santo Domingo, D.R.
Santos, Victor	1	2	11.05	5	3	0	0	15	24	22	18	10	12	R	R	6-3	175	10-2-76	1995	Garfield, N.J.
Schmitt, Todd	0	0	11.78	15	0	0	0	18	27	25	24	26	20	R	R	6-2	170	2-12-70	1992	Clinton Township, Mich.
2-team (30 Ottawa)	1	1	6.35	45	0	0	5	51	45	40	36	51	54							
Taylor, Kerry	8	10	5.77	26	17	1	0	112	140	84	72	59	93	R	R	6-3	200	1-25-71	1989	Roseau, Minn.

FIELDING

Catcher	PCT	G	PO	A	E	DP	PB
Bako	.988	13	75	5	1	0	0
Cardona	.983	46	262	31	5	4	3
Casanova	.973	45	295	35	9	5	3
Gresham	.961	8	47	2	2	0	0
Lindstrom	1.000	1	9	0	0	0	0
Marine	.964	5	27	0	1	0	0
Siddall	.988	32	150	17	2	2	2

First Base	PCT	G	PO	A	E	DP
Belk	.987	79	683	26	9	61
Catalanotto	.984	19	106	14	2	8
Faries	.988	11	82	3	1	5
Ibarra	.969	38	261	21	9	33
Siddall	1.000	6	23	2	0	1
Wood	.987	11	70	5	1	8

Second Base	PCT	G	PO	A	E	DP
Almanzar	.967	92	194	271	16	65
Catalanotto	1.000	16	25	29	0	7
Faries	.990	43	85	121	2	27
Garcia	1.000	1	3	4	0	2

Third Base	PCT	G	PO	A	E	DP
Almanzar	.933	7	3	11	1	0
Alvarez	.923	67	38	142	15	14
Faries	.981	33	32	69	2	10
Garcia	.786	6	3	8	3	0
Gresham	.000	1	0	0	0	0
Ripken	1.000	4	3	12	0	1
Siddall	.000	1	0	0	0	0
Wood	.947	28	16	38	3	5

Shortstop	PCT	G	PO	A	E	DP
Cruz	1.000	2	2	7	0	1
Faries	.992	31	44	74	1	14
Garcia	.956	108	152	280	20	58
Wood	.973	8	13	23	1	2

Outfield	PCT	G	PO	A	E	DP
Bartee	1.000	47	124	6	0	1
Beamon	.950	46	92	3	5	1
Belk	1.000	1	1	0	0	0
Encarnacion	.973	91	168	10	5	3
Johnson	.992	104	246	11	2	3
Siddall	1.000	2	2	0	0	0
Smith	.983	66	111	3	2	0
Swann	.985	77	131	2	2	0
Tomberlin	.867	11	12	1	2	0

JACKSONVILLE — Class AA

SOUTHERN LEAGUE

BATTING	AVG	G	AB	R	H	2B	3B	HR	RBI	BB	SO	SB	CS	B	T	HT	WT	DOB	1st Yr	Resides
Barker, Glen	.280	110	453	95	127	29	6	6	54	57	120	31	7	B	R	5-10	180	5-10-71	1993	Albany, N.Y.
Bream, Scott	.291	58	206	30	60	16	3	3	36	25	41	3	1	B	R	6-1	170	11-4-70	1989	Omaha, Neb.
Cardona, Javier	.331	46	163	31	54	16	1	4	40	15	29	0	0	R	R	6-1	185	9-15-75	1994	Dorado, P.R.
Dubose, Brian	.236	46	165	30	39	10	1	7	25	13	39	4	0	L	R	6-3	208	5-17-71	1990	Detroit, Mich.
Fick, Robert	.318	130	515	101	164	47	6	18	114	71	83	8	4	L	R	6-1	189	3-15-74	1996	Thousand Oaks, Calif.
Freire, Alejandro	.275	129	494	79	136	30	0	16	78	33	83	3	1	R	R	6-2	185	8-23-74	1992	Caracas, Ven.
Hernaiz, Juan	.251	99	382	60	96	21	2	11	58	16	93	8	2	R	R	5-11	185	2-15-75	1992	Hato Rey, P.R.
Ibarra, Jesse	.100	10	30	1	3	1	0	0	1	5	14	0	0	B	R	6-3	195	7-12-72	1994	El Monte, Calif.
Kapler, Gabe	.322	139	547	113	176	47	6	28	146	66	93	6	4	R	R	6-2	190	8-31-75	1995	Reseda, Calif.
Lackey, Steve	.324	12	34	6	11	1	0	0	3	5	5	0	0	R	R	5-11	159	9-25-74	1992	Riverside, Calif.
Macias, Jose	.305	128	511	82	156	28	10	12	71	52	46	6	9	B	R	5-10	173	1-25-74	1994	Panama City, Panama
Marine, Del	.316	44	155	25	49	8	2	3	25	20	20	0	0	R	R	6-0	205	10-18-71	1992	Santa Monica, Calif.
Mitchell, Derek	.221	128	421	58	93	21	2	2	54	68	94	6	3	R	R	6-2	170	3-9-75	1996	Gurnee, Ill.
Roberts, David	.326	69	279	71	91	14	5	5	42	53	59	21	9	L	L	5-10	172	5-31-72	1994	Oceanside, Calif.
Sollmann, Scott	.077	10	26	4	2	0	0	0	1	7	4	1	1	L	L	5-10	167	5-2-75	1996	Cincinnati, Ohio
Villalobos, Carlos	.320	128	497	96	159	34	2	18	80	55	85	8	0	R	R	6-0	170	4-5-74	1994	Cartagena, Colombia

PITCHING	W	L	ERA	G	GS	CG	SV	IP	H	R	ER	BB	SO	B	T	HT	WT	DOB	1st Yr	Resides
Anderson, Matt	1	0	0.60	13	0	0	10	15	7	1	1	5	11	R	R	6-4	200	8-17-76	1998	Houston, Texas
Borkowski, Dave	16	7	4.63	28	28	3	0	179	204	99	92	54	97	R	R	6-1	200	2-7-77	1995	Sterling Heights, Mich.
Bruner, Clay	10	6	3.79	28	28	1	0	171	173	90	72	66	91	R	R	6-3	180	10-16-76	1995	Weatherford, Okla.
Cordero, Francisco	1	1	4.86	17	0	0	8	17	19	12	9	9	18	R	R	6-2	200	8-11-77	1994	Santo Domingo, D.R.
Dace, Derek	5	3	4.16	40	0	0	3	67	51	32	31	29	48	L	L	6-7	200	4-11-75	1994	Rolla, Mo.
Darwin, David	12	6	5.35	24	23	2	0	140	152	94	83	52	76	L	L	6-0	185	12-19-73	1996	Cornelius, N.C.
Davis, Keith	0	0	0.00	1	0	0	0	0	1	0	0	0	0	R	R	6-2	210	11-1-72	1994	Vacherie, La.
Durkovic, Peter	2	1	5.69	37	0	0	0	68	69	47	43	35	36	L	L	6-4	215	7-9-73	1995	Flushing, N.Y.
Hiljus, Erik	2	3	3.70	42	0	0	2	66	49	31	27	35	85	R	R	6-5	230	12-25-72	1991	Santa Clarita, Calif.
Hurst, Bill	0	0	23.14	3	0	0	0	2	4	6	6	6	3	R	R	6-7	220	4-28-70	1990	Miami, Fla.
Kimsey, Keith	0	0	22.50	3	0	0	0	4	10	10	10	3	3	R	R	6-7	200	8-15-72	1991	Lakeland, Fla.
Melendez, Dave	9	6	5.06	25	25	0	0	153	166	104	86	61	83	B	R	6-0	168	6-25-76	1996	Caguas, P.R.
Miller, Matt	3	7	7.04	13	13	0	0	61	70	49	48	50	49	L	L	6-3	175	8-2-74	1996	Lubbock, Texas
Powell, Brian	10	2	3.07	14	14	2	0	94	84	37	32	24	51	R	R	6-2	205	10-10-73	1995	Bainbridge, Ga.
Roberts, Willis	3	1	2.19	12	2	0	0	25	21	10	6	10	15	R	R	6-3	175	6-19-75	1992	San Cristobal, D.R.
Santos, Victor	4	2	4.17	6	6	0	0	37	40	20	17	15	37	R	R	6-3	175	10-2-76	1995	Garfield, N.J.
Skuse, Nick	4	6	4.76	49	0	0	13	62	54	34	33	30	74	R	R	6-7	240	1-9-72	1994	Los Gatos, Calif.
Smith, Keilan	4	3	3.64	39	1	0	0	72	69	34	29	40	54	R	R	6-4	175	12-20-73	1993	Memphis, Tenn.

FIELDING

Catcher	PCT	G	PO	A	E	DP	PB
Cardona	.976	41	208	33	6	4	0
Fick	.983	79	493	39	9	4	5
Marine	.987	28	146	11	2	1	4

First Base	PCT	G	PO	A	E	DP
Bream	1.000	3	19	3	0	3
Dubose	1.000	3	23	2	0	4
Fick	1.000	7	45	6	0	5
Freire	.987	125	1050	113	15	109
Ibarra	.960	5	21	3	1	2
Kapler	1.000	1	2	0	0	0
Marine	.974	5	31	6	1	1

Second Base	PCT	G	PO	A	E	DP
Bream	1.000	9	15	21	0	5
Lackey	.964	6	12	15	1	5
Macias	.977	127	246	354	14	85

Third Base	PCT	G	PO	A	E	DP
Bream	.979	15	12	35	1	4
Villalobos	.928	126	94	267	28	22

Shortstop	PCT	G	PO	A	E	DP
Bream	.957	10	19	26	2	5
Lackey	.920	3	6	17	2	3
Mitchell	.953	128	205	383	29	87

Outfield	PCT	G	PO	A	E	DP
Barker	1.000	109	307	16	0	7
Bream	1.000	16	45	0	0	0
Dubose	.935	24	28	1	2	0
Fick	1.000	1	2	0	0	0
Hernaiz	.935	80	124	6	9	0
Kapler	.984	139	292	12	5	3
Roberts	1.000	49	105	1	0	0
Sollmann	1.000	10	24	1	0	0

LAKELAND — Class A

FLORIDA STATE LEAGUE

BATTING	AVG	G	AB	R	H	2B	3B	HR	RBI	BB	SO	SB	CS	B	T	HT	WT	DOB	1st Yr	Resides
Airoso, Kurt	.290	109	386	69	112	24	0	15	61	67	106	7	3	R	R	6-2	190	2-12-75	1996	Tulare, Calif.
Alvarez, Julio	.000	9	13	2	0	0	0	0	0	2	5	0	0	B	R	6-0	160	3-2-79	1996	Santiago, D.R.
Bautista, Rayner	.236	32	110	11	26	4	1	0	15	6	36	0	0	R	R	5-11	155	8-17-79	1996	Nizao, D.R.
Beamon, Trey	.500	2	6	2	3	0	0	0	0	3	0	0	0	L	R	6-3	192	2-11-74	1992	Garland, Texas
Capellan, Rene	.230	55	200	24	46	6	1	1	22	6	18	1	4	R	R	5-11	160	4-24-78	1995	Santo Domingo, D.R.
Cedeno, Jesus	.238	84	286	41	68	14	2	5	39	21	66	1	3	R	R	5-11	160	6-24-76	1994	Santo Domingo, D.R.
Colquitt, Jason	.148	24	61	4	9	2	0	0	5	6	19	0	0	R	R	6-0	195	11-17-76	1998	Greenville, N.C.
Cruz, Deivi	.000	2	9	0	0	0	0	0	1	0	1	0	0	R	R	6-0	184	11-6-75	1993	Nizao, D.R.
Dubose, Brian	.314	69	258	45	81	7	3	14	48	39	51	8	3	L	R	6-3	208	5-17-71	1990	Detroit, Mich.
Encarnacion, Juan	.250	4	16	4	4	0	1	0	4	2	4	4	0	R	R	6-3	187	3-8-76	1993	Las Matas de Farfan, D.R.
Lackey, Steve	.284	102	415	68	118	14	3	3	39	31	73	19	7	R	R	5-11	159	9-25-74	1992	Riverside, Calif.
Landry, Jacques	.252	105	397	51	100	17	2	11	51	26	105	8	6	R	R	6-3	205	8-15-73	1996	La Marque, Texas
Lemonis, Chris	.281	93	327	45	92	17	1	3	48	27	46	1	1	L	R	5-11	185	8-21-73	1995	New York, N.Y.
Lindstrom, David	.246	103	337	52	83	20	2	5	42	50	46	0	3	R	R	5-10	185	8-6-74	1996	Brooklyn Park, Minn.
Lopiccolo, Jamie	.291	106	440	52	128	32	3	12	77	24	85	7	3	R	R	6-3	200	5-18-73	1995	Sterling Heights, Mich.
Marine, Del	.259	15	54	6	14	4	0	1	3	2	5	0	0	R	R	6-0	205	10-18-71	1992	Santa Monica, Calif.
Meran, Jorge	.200	7	20	0	4	3	0	0	1	0	7	0	0	R	R	6-1	168	6-18-77	1994	Santo Domingo, D.R.
Moore, LaCarlo	.290	28	100	17	29	3	2	0	13	7	17	7	3	L	R	5-10	170	1-15-76	1998	Chicago, Ill.
Parker, Chris	.176	7	17	0	3	0	0	0	0	1	6	0	0	R	R	6-2	185	8-16-79	1997	Thousand Oaks, Calif.
Runnells, T.J.	.182	6	22	3	4	1	0	0	1	0	6	0	0	R	R	5-10	160	2-15-78	1997	Greeley, Colo.
Sassanella, Jeremy	.000	1	3	0	0	0	0	0	0	0	2	0	0	B	R	6-1	225	10-21-78	1997	Auburn, Ind.
Schaffer, Jacob	.248	102	395	56	98	19	3	11	48	31	90	4	4	R	R	5-10	170	3-28-75	1997	Bloomington, Minn.
Sollmann, Scott	.252	104	401	81	101	11	4	2	35	62	52	59	17	L	L	5-10	167	5-2-75	1996	Cincinnati, Ohio
Vargas, Inakel	.143	3	7	2	1	0	1	0	2	2	3	0	0	R	R	6-0	185	3-1-78	1996	Santo Domingo, D.R.
Wakeland, Chris	.302	131	487	82	147	26	5	18	89	66	111	19	13	L	L	6-0	185	6-15-74	1996	St. Helens, Ore.

GAMES BY POSITION: C—Colquitt 24, Lindstrom 95, Marine 15, Meran 7, Parker 7, Vargas 3. **1B**—Dubose 69, Lemonis 24, Lindstrom 9, Lopiccolo 39. **2B**—Bautista 3, Capellan 37, Lackey 8, Lemonis 7, Runnells 6, Schaffer 84. **3B**—Capellan 3, Landry 99, Lemonis 40. **SS**—Alvarez 4, Bautista 32, Cruz 2, Lackey 95, Schaffer 13. **OF**—Airoso 67, Beamon 2, Cedeno 82, Encarnacion 4, Lopiccolo 24, Moore 28, Schaffer 1, Sollman 96, Wakeland 123.

PITCHING	W	L	ERA	G	GS	CG	SV	IP	H	R	ER	BB	SO	B	T	HT	WT	DOB	1st Yr	Resides
Alvord, Aaron	0	0	7.20	1	1	0	0	5	7	4	4	4	1	R	R	6-1	175	6-21-77	1996	Canton, Kan.
Anderson, Matt	1	0	0.69	17	0	0	3	26	18	4	2	8	34	R	R	6-4	200	8-17-76	1998	Houston, Texas
Ashworth, Kym	6	11	3.82	28	28	1	0	160	169	96	68	60	113	L	L	6-2	175	7-31-76	1993	Para Hills West, Australia
Bettencourt, Justin	5	7	4.04	30	13	0	1	105	106	57	47	62	86	L	L	6-2	185	12-19-73	1994	Capitola, Calif.
Castillo, Frank	1	0	0.00	1	1	0	0	5	2	0	0	0	4	R	R	6-1	200	4-1-69	1987	Cave Creek, Ariz.
Cepeda, Victor	3	0	1.99	8	2	1	0	23	8	5	5	14	22	R	R	6-0	160	4-3-78	1997	Loiza, P.R.
Cordero, Francisco	0	0	0.00	1	0	0	0	0	1	0	0	0	0	R	R	6-2	200	8-11-77	1994	Santo Domingo, D.R.
Davis, Keith	3	3	4.00	43	0	0	7	74	72	40	33	32	73	R	R	6-2	210	11-1-72	1994	Vacherie, La.
Duran, Roberto	0	0	4.15	8	0	0	0	9	4	5	4	13	9	L	L	6-0	205	3-6-73	1990	Moca, D.R.
Garcia, Apostol	5	8	5.43	34	16	1	1	119	155	89	72	52	56	R	R	6-0	155	8-3-76	1994	Las Matas de Farfan, D.R.
Hurst, Bill	0	0	0.00	2	0	0	0	4	2	0	0	0	5	R	R	6-7	220	4-28-70	1990	Miami, Fla.
Kimsey, Keith	6	1	3.92	28	4	0	2	62	56	33	27	29	52	R	R	6-7	200	8-15-72	1991	Lakeland, Fla.
Martinez, Romulo	6	3	2.63	49	0	0	16	65	63	32	19	20	34	R	R	6-1	170	12-5-76	1994	Santiago, D.R.
Miles, Chad	1	8	5.55	42	1	0	2	62	67	43	38	38	65	B	L	6-3	195	2-26-73	1994	Renton, Wash.
Mobley, Kevin	4	3	4.76	34	8	1	2	79	80	44	42	36	58	R	R	6-7	245	1-26-75	1997	Vidalia, Ga.
Quintal, Craig	8	10	5.43	21	21	2	0	128	169	91	77	23	50	R	R	6-0	190	1-21-75	1996	New Orleans, La.
Romo, Greg	5	5	4.01	12	12	3	0	76	72	46	34	30	53	L	R	6-2	165	5-14-75	1995	Wasco, Calif.
Rosario, Rafael	0	3	4.50	9	0	0	1	12	13	7	6	7	5	R	R	6-1	170	12-29-76	1995	El Seibo, D.R.
Rosario, Reynaldo	0	0	9.82	4	0	0	0	4	5	4	4	4	2	R	R	6-4	175	5-5-77	1994	Santo Domingo, D.R.
Santos, Victor	5	2	2.51	16	15	0	1	100	88	38	28	24	74	R	R	6-3	175	10-2-76	1995	Garfield, N.J.
Spear, Russell	8	7	4.73	18	17	0	0	97	101	68	51	44	78	R	R	6-3	190	8-30-77	1995	Albanvale, Australia

WEST MICHIGAN — Class A

MIDWEST LEAGUE

BATTING	AVG	G	AB	R	H	2B	3B	HR	RBI	BB	SO	SB	CS	B	T	HT	WT	DOB	1st Yr	Resides
Bunkley, Antuan	.297	129	492	74	146	32	0	8	91	47	64	4	2	R	R	6-1	205	9-20-75	1994	West Palm Beach, Fla.
Bush, Ron	.167	4	12	2	2	0	0	0	1	1	3	0	0	R	R	6-1	170	10-10-76	1998	Richmond, Va.
Grimmett, Ryan	.228	113	412	68	94	11	10	1	33	55	123	48	14	R	R	5-9	165	3-4-75	1997	Cincinnati, Ohio
Jacomino, Mandy	.209	93	273	35	57	15	0	5	40	41	63	2	1	L	R	6-2	210	6-1-74	1997	Miami, Fla.
Lauterhahn, Dan	.220	94	305	34	67	21	0	0	17	24	56	8	2	R	R	6-1	175	4-23-76	1997	Wallington, N.J.
Lignitz, Jeremiah	.176	44	125	9	22	4	0	0	12	11	45	0	0	L	R	6-2	210	5-18-77	1995	Davison, Mich.
Lindsey, Rodney	.272	45	158	37	43	7	4	3	17	22	42	24	8	R	R	5-8	175	1-28-76	1994	Opelika, Ala.
2-team (40 Clinton)	.272	85	313	69	85	11	8	7	34	39	96	60	12							
McKinney, Antonio	.071	5	14	0	1	0	0	0	2	1	4	0	0	R	R	5-10	175	1-2-78	1996	Portland, Ore.
Mora, Juan	.231	88	308	33	71	15	5	3	38	14	103	7	3	L	L	5-11	170	11-26-77	1997	Bayamon, P.R.
Ozarowski, Rich	.261	92	299	47	78	22	2	2	27	32	49	5	4	B	R	5-9	175	10-19-74	1997	Boca Raton, Fla.
Rios, Brian	.265	100	343	44	91	18	1	3	46	23	60	5	4	R	R	6-3	190	7-15-74	1996	Corona, Calif.
Rivera, Mike	.275	108	403	40	111	34	3	9	67	15	68	0	2	R	R	6-0	190	9-8-76	1997	Bayamon, P.R.
Santana, Pedro	.263	110	438	79	115	21	7	4	45	28	93	64	7	R	R	5-11	160	9-21-76	1995	San Pedro de Macoris, D.R.
Schesser, Heath	.207	93	323	48	67	14	1	0	19	33	67	1	1	R	R	6-1	190	1-7-76	1997	Manhattan, Kan.
Steele, Alex	.248	123	424	53	105	18	3	6	47	62	137	0	7	R	R	6-3	225	12-9-75	1997	Harrington Park, N.J.
Zapata, Alexis	.298	103	376	57	112	18	4	11	70	36	101	20	8	R	R	6-3	190	5-20-77	1996	Santo Domingo, D.R.

GAMES BY POSITION: C—Lignitz 42, Ozarowski 1, Rivera 106. **1B**—Bunkley 125, Jacomino 7, Rios 17. **2B**—Bush 2, Ozarowski 26, Rios 3, Santana 117. **3B**—Bush 1, Ozarowski 4, Rios 67, Schesser 76. **SS**—Bush 1, Lauterhahn 94, Mora 1, Ozarowski 48, Rios 8. **OF**—Grimmett 112, Jacomino 1, Lindsey 44, McKinney 5, Mora 68, Ozarowski 2, Steele 122, Zapata 80.

PITCHING	W	L	ERA	G	GS	CG	SV	IP	H	R	ER	BB	SO	B	T	HT	WT	DOB	1st Yr	Resides
Castillo, Jose	0	1	2.44	51	0	0	28	52	42	15	14	11	47	R	R	6-2	170	6-12-77	1994	Santo Domingo, D.R.
Johnson, Craig	14	6	2.79	26	26	3	0	165	146	66	51	22	116	R	R	6-3	200	11-8-75	1997	Tuftonboro, N.H.
Loux, Shane	7	13	4.64	28	28	2	0	157	184	96	81	52	88	R	R	6-2	205	8-31-79	1997	Gilbert, Ariz.
Miller, Matt	7	4	1.52	14	14	3	0	95	59	20	16	26	102	L	L	6-3	175	8-2-74	1996	Lubbock, Texas
Persails, Mark	11	5	2.83	39	3	0	2	92	75	33	29	29	64	R	R	6-3	190	10-25-75	1995	Vassar, Mich.
Pettyjohn, Adam	4	2	1.97	8	8	1	0	50	46	15	11	9	64	R	L	6-3	190	6-11-77	1998	Exeter, Calif.
Ramirez, Jose	4	5	4.98	22	10	1	0	72	69	49	40	31	60	L	L	6-1	170	9-1-75	1994	Santo Domingo, D.R.
Romo, Greg	7	4	2.92	16	16	0	0	96	78	42	31	25	105	L	R	6-2	165	5-14-75	1995	Wasco, Calif.
Schroeder, Chad	5	3	3.25	35	0	0	2	64	67	29	23	11	51	R	R	6-1	195	9-21-73	1996	Elgin, Ill.
Sismondo, Bobby	0	3	2.11	5	5	0	0	21	21	9	5	9	24	L	L	6-1	180	11-14-76	1998	Steubenville, Ohio
Snyder, Bill	3	1	1.82	42	0	0	2	59	40	17	12	18	84	R	R	6-0	190	1-29-75	1997	Martville, N.Y.
Viegas, Randy	4	1	3.95	52	0	0	1	55	52	29	24	24	61	L	L	6-2	175	8-22-75	1994	Roseville, Calif.
Weaver, Jeff	1	0	1.38	2	2	0	0	13	8	3	2	0	21	R	R	6-5	175	8-22-76	1998	Simi Valley, Calif.
Webb, Alan	10	7	2.93	27	27	3	0	172	110	69	56	58	202	L	L	5-10	165	9-26-79	1997	Las Vegas, Nev.
Zamarripa, Mark	6	2	2.23	35	1	0	1	73	59	19	18	34	88	R	R	6-0	175	7-28-74	1996	Los Angeles, Calif.

JAMESTOWN — Short-Season Class A

NEW YORK-PENN LEAGUE

BATTING	AVG	G	AB	R	H	2B	3B	HR	RBI	BB	SO	SB	CS	B	T	HT	WT	DOB	1st Yr	Resides
Bautista, Rayner	.207	60	222	27	46	5	4	2	15	18	67	11	2	R	R	5-11	155	8-17-79	1996	Nizao, D.R.
Besco, Derek	.235	49	183	27	43	9	1	6	18	17	30	11	3	R	R	6-2	200	1-21-76	1998	Westland, Mich.
Boone, Matt	.303	9	33	8	10	2	2	1	11	2	3	0	0	R	R	6-2	175	7-18-79	1997	Orlando, Fla.
Bush, Ron	.290	53	200	23	58	9	2	4	23	11	31	4	2	R	R	6-1	170	10-10-76	1998	Richmond, Va.
Daluz, Craig	.258	47	159	27	41	6	3	4	19	5	29	6	4	R	R	6-2	200	2-4-75	1998	Fresno, Calif.
Forbush, Nate	.231	33	117	18	27	4	0	2	16	11	29	1	1	B	R	6-2	220	11-7-75	1998	West Jordan, Utah
Hazelton, Justin	.172	27	87	9	15	3	2	0	7	15	40	1	0	R	R	6-2	175	8-9-78	1996	Philipsburg, Pa.
Inge, Brandon	.230	51	191	24	44	10	1	8	29	17	53	8	8	B	R	5-11	185	5-19-77	1998	Evington, Va.
Law, Keith	.171	33	105	11	18	5	1	1	11	10	23	3	2	R	R	6-2	165	1-12-77	1998	Hiram, Ga.
McKinney, Antonio	.308	39	130	26	40	9	0	2	17	12	26	11	3	R	R	5-10	175	1-2-78	1996	Portland, Ore.
Meran, Jorge	.273	30	110	13	30	7	1	4	20	15	24	3	1	R	R	6-1	168	6-18-77	1994	Santo Domingo, D.R.

BATTING	AVG	G	AB	R	H	2B	3B	HR	RBI	BB	SO	SB	CS	B	T	HT	WT	DOB	1st Yr	Resides
Moore, LaCarlo	.317	19	60	10	19	4	0	0	5	5	10	6	1	L	R	5-10	170	1-15-76	1998	Chicago, Ill.
Peniche, Fray	.206	11	34	3	7	0	0	1	4	1	10	0	1	R	R	6-2	185	11-2-76	1995	Santo Domingo, D.R.
Reyes, Deurys	.198	33	111	11	22	3	4	0	11	15	35	5	2	L	L	5-11	155	8-8-79	1996	Santo Domingo, D.R.
Rich, Billy	.271	62	225	42	61	9	5	5	34	28	44	7	3	R	R	6-2	205	7-26-76	1998	Meriden, Conn.
Runnells, T.J.	.238	63	239	31	57	8	1	1	25	18	47	2	0	R	R	5-10	160	2-15-78	1997	Greeley, Colo.
Torres, Andres	.234	48	192	28	45	2	0	1	21	25	60	10	[illegible]	[illegible]	[illegible]	5-11	[illegible]	[illegible]	[illegible]	Aguada, P.R.
Vargas, Inakel	.214	48	159	16	34	4	2	1	13	19	44	1	1	R	R	6-0	185	3-1-78	1996	Santo Domingo, D.R.

GAMES BY POSITION: C—Forbush 8, Inge 35, Meran 15, Vargas 19. **1B**—Besco 6, Daluz 7, Forbush 19, Law 8, Peniche 11, Vargas 29. **2B**—Bush 20, Runnells 58. **3B**—Boone 4, Bush 32, Daluz 36, Law 7. **SS**—Bautista 60, Bush 1, Law 17. **OF**—Besco 23, Hazelton 25, McKinney 31, Moore 16, Reyes 31, Rich 59, Torres 46.

PITCHING	W	L	ERA	G	GS	CG	SV	IP	H	R	ER	BB	SO	B	T	HT	WT	DOB	1st Yr	Resides
Alvord, Aaron	5	6	6.45	16	16	0	0	84	104	67	60	45	71	R	R	6-1	175	6-21-77	1996	Canton, Kan.
Buller, Sean	2	2	6.03	13	5	0	0	37	42	30	25	12	26	L	L	6-5	235	11-28-75	1998	Signal Hill, Calif.
Gutierrez, Laz	2	2	3.89	27	0	0	0	42	34	27	18	19	37	L	L	6-2	195	2-7-76	1998	Hialeah, Fla.
Heams, Shane	2	2	3.99	24	0	0	6	47	43	27	21	16	73	R	R	6-1	175	9-29-75	1995	Lambertville, Mich.
Hostetler, Jim	1	0	4.76	16	1	0	2	28	27	18	15	11	39	R	R	6-7	230	7-19-76	1998	Yorba Linda, Calif.
Keller, Kris	1	3	3.27	27	0	0	8	33	29	12	12	16	41	R	R	6-2	225	3-1-78	1996	Atlantic Beach, Fla.
Koutrouba, Tom	4	8	4.76	15	14	1	0	85	109	54	45	29	64	L	L	6-0	190	10-9-77	1998	Boston, Mass.
Madson, Bill	1	2	2.26	16	7	0	0	56	47	17	14	17	46	R	R	6-0	210	4-18-76	1998	Sheboygan, Wis.
McGowan, Brian	3	2	7.45	18	0	0	0	29	35	27	24	23	24	R	R	6-4	245	12-14-76	1998	Sunnyside, N.Y.
Pettyjohn, Adam	2	2	2.86	4	4	0	0	22	21	10	7	4	24	R	L	6-3	190	6-11-77	1998	Exeter, Calif.
Ramirez, Jose	1	0	0.00	1	0	0	0	4	4	0	0	1	5	L	L	6-1	170	9-1-75	1994	Santo Domingo, D.R.
Roberts, Richard	3	7	3.15	15	15	0	0	86	96	44	30	37	60	L	L	6-1	180	5-20-79	1997	Summer Hill, Pa.
Shea, Galen	0	1	7.71	2	0	0	1	2	3	2	2	0	3	R	R	6-3	205	7-22-76	1998	Lufkin, Texas
Sismondo, Bobby	2	0	0.71	2	2	0	0	13	7	1	1	3	19	L	L	6-1	180	11-14-76	1998	Steubenville, Ohio
Smith, Clinton	2	5	5.64	12	8	0	0	45	47	36	28	27	44	R	R	6-4	185	9-4-76	1998	Claremore, Okla.
Sosa, Franklin	0	1	6.19	19	0	0	0	36	40	28	25	17	15	R	R	5-11	170	2-27-76	1994	Los Llanos, D.R.
Weaver, Jeff	1	0	1.50	3	3	0	0	12	6	4	2	1	12	R	R	6-5	175	8-22-76	1998	Simi Valley, Calif.

LAKELAND — Rookie

GULF COAST LEAGUE

BATTING	AVG	G	AB	R	H	2B	3B	HR	RBI	BB	SO	SB	CS	B	T	HT	WT	DOB	1st Yr	Resides
Altagen, Matt	.232	33	112	14	26	7	0	0	8	15	35	3	4	R	L	6-2	180	9-5-79	1998	Malibu, Calif.
Alvarez, Julio	.342	31	114	14	39	6	2	0	15	3	26	11	6	B	R	6-0	160	3-2-79	1996	Santiago, D.R.
Boone, Matt	.293	49	191	28	56	11	4	5	29	9	42	3	2	R	R	6-2	175	7-18-79	1997	Orlando, Fla.
Cleveland, Russell	.215	31	79	5	17	3	0	0	4	11	27	1	4	R	R	6-3	205	12-26-79	1998	Las Vegas, Nev.
Daigle, Leo	.308	36	133	19	41	8	2	1	24	10	19	2	1	R	R	6-4	225	9-18-79	1998	Spring Valley, Calif.
De la Rosa, Frank	.259	32	112	17	29	8	0	1	13	7	24	1	2	R	R	6-0	180	8-26-80	1997	Santo Domingo, D.R.
Gomez, Richard	.333	47	162	42	54	11	4	6	40	21	37	20	2	R	R	5-11	190	8-19-77	1997	San Francisco de Macoris, D.R.
Hazelton, Justin	.353	4	17	1	6	2	0	0	3	1	6	0	1	R	R	6-2	175	8-9-78	1996	Philipsburg, Pa.
Jimenez, Carlos	.250	47	188	29	47	9	1	0	18	15	48	7	2	R	R	5-11	165	5-26-80	1997	San Pedro de Macoris, D.R.
Lara, Balmes	.219	17	64	7	14	2	0	1	9	2	19	0	0	R	R	6-3	180	6-19-78	1996	Santo Domingo, D.R.
Lauterhahn, Dan	.273	3	11	1	3	0	0	0	0	1	2	1	0	R	R	6-1	175	4-23-76	1997	Wallington, N.J.
Nelson, Reggie	.193	43	135	22	26	1	0	0	8	26	25	22	5	R	R	5-10	165	3-30-79	1998	San Diego, Calif.
Parker, Chris	.282	33	103	13	29	5	0	4	17	10	35	0	3	R	R	6-2	185	8-16-79	1997	Thousand Oaks, Calif.
Pender, Darrell	.279	38	129	27	36	6	3	1	15	16	44	16	3	R	R	5-10	170	1-14-79	1997	Miami, Fla.
Rodriguez, Steve	.246	36	130	19	32	6	2	4	20	16	33	2	2	R	R	6-4	210	1-28-78	1998	Arcadia, Calif.
Sassanella, Jeremy	.256	34	117	13	30	5	1	3	12	4	31	0	2	B	R	6-1	225	10-21-78	1997	Auburn, Ind.
St. Pierre, Maxim	.385	31	104	18	40	3	0	2	15	15	12	6	2	R	R	6-0	175	4-17-80	1997	Montreal, Quebec
Tiburcio, Emigdio	.356	21	73	12	26	4	5	0	12	5	23	3	0	B	R	5-10	160	8-5-80	1997	Santo Domingo, D.R.
Tolli, Barry	.179	39	117	9	21	7	1	0	10	3	41	2	2	R	R	6-2	200	8-17-79	1998	Newbury Park, Calif.

GAMES BY POSITION: C—Cleveland 25, Parker 23, St. Pierre 25. **1B**—Daigle 32, Sassanella 31. **2B**—Alvarez 23, Nelson 30, Tiburcio 12. **3B**—Alvarez 7, Boone 49, Jimenez 1, Tiburcio 8. **SS**—Jimenez 46, Lauterhahn 3, Nelson 12. **OF**—Altagen 23, de la Rosa 32, Gomez 36, Hazelton 2, Lara 17, Pender 33, Rodriguez 32, Tolli 25.

PITCHING	W	L	ERA	G	GS	CG	SV	IP	H	R	ER	BB	SO	B	T	HT	WT	DOB	1st Yr	Resides
Cepeda, Victor	4	1	3.00	18	2	0	1	45	31	18	15	11	49	R	R	6-0	160	4-3-78	1997	Loiza, P.R.
Chipperfield, Calvin	3	2	3.10	12	12	0	0	52	44	23	18	24	69	R	R	6-2	175	3-7-78	1998	Royal Oak, Mich.
Cornejo, Nate	1	0	1.26	5	0	0	1	14	12	2	2	2	9	R	R	6-5	200	9-24-79	1998	Wellington, Kan.
Diaz, Luis	2	2	2.91	25	0	0	0	53	46	21	17	23	58	R	R	6-1	180	12-3-78	1998	Aguas Buenas, P.R.
Earl, Ryan	0	0	2.93	6	4	0	0	15	18	6	5	8	11	L	L	6-6	170	8-24-80	1998	Thousand Oaks, Calif.
Hostetler, Jim	0	0	3.38	2	0	0	0	3	3	1	1	0	2	R	R	6-7	230	7-19-76	1998	Yorba Linda, Calif.
Hurst, Bill	0	0	1.59	3	0	0	0	6	2	1	1	1	7	R	R	6-7	220	4-28-70	1990	Miami, Fla.
Johnston, Rikki	2	4	4.71	11	11	0	0	50	57	27	26	18	46	L	L	6-4	185	4-2-81	1998	Victoria, Australia
Lima, Frank	5	3	4.70	12	12	1	0	59	62	39	31	14	66	R	R	6-2	190	5-20-79	1997	Santiago, D.R.
Marx, Tommy	1	3	4.29	12	12	0	0	42	33	27	20	39	38	R	L	6-7	200	9-5-79	1998	West Bloomfield, Mich.
Ramirez, Jose	1	0	3.86	2	0	0	0	7	7	3	3	4	8	L	L	6-1	170	9-1-75	1994	Santo Domingo, D.R.
Rivera, Homero	3	6	5.34	16	7	1	2	57	64	40	34	17	53	R	L	5-10	160	8-13-78	1995	Nizao, D.R.
Rosario, Rafael	1	4	9.35	22	0	0	2	43	62	49	45	18	29	R	R	6-1	170	12-29-76	1995	El Seibo, D.R.
Rosario, Reynaldo	0	1	1.99	10	0	0	1	23	21	8	5	15	17	R	R	6-4	175	5-5-77	1994	Santo Domingo, D.R.
Santana, Alfredo	3	5	4.21	22	0	0	4	36	40	26	17	12	32	R	R	6-2	180	12-24-77	1995	San Cristobal, D.R.
Whiteman, Mike	2	1	5.31	12	0	0	0	20	19	13	12	13	16	L	L	6-2	185	1-19-75	1998	Wiley Ford, W.Va.

FLORIDA MARLINS

'97 World Series champions fall to basement after fire sale

BY MIKE BERARDINO

One year after making history as the fastest expansion team to win a World Series, the Florida Marlins found themselves on the wrong side of history in 1998.

In the wake of team owner Wayne Huizenga's claim that the club lost $34 million in its championship year, the Marlins initiated an unprecedented talent selloff.

The result was a precipitous drop from first to worst. The 1998 Marlins went 54-108 to easily eclipse the 1991 Cincinnati Reds (74-88) as the worst followup to a World Series winner.

Remarkably, the payroll was slashed from $53.5 million at the end of the '97 season to $13 million by the July trading deadline. Offseason deals scattered the likes of Moises Alou, Kevin Brown, Al Leiter, Robb Nen and Devon White.

It turned out team president Don Smiley was just getting warmed up. On May 15, with the Marlins off to a 14-28 start, Smiley pulled off the so-called Deal of the Century with the Fox-owned Los Angeles Dodgers, with more than $100 million in salary obligation swapping coasts.

Five Marlins, including Gary Sheffield, headed west while Mike Piazza and Todd Zeile came to South Florida. One week later, Piazza was gone as well, shipped to the Mets for three prospects.

Four days after the season ended, Jim Leyland resigned after two seasons as Marlins manager. Leyland had three years left on his $7.5 million contract but exercised a $500,000 escape clause. Farm director John Boles, who served as interim manager for the second half of the 1996 season, assumed the role of manager after Leyland's departure.

Cliff Floyd

Brian Daubach

MORRIS FOSTOFF

Players of the Year

Major League: Cliff Floyd, of

Floyd tied for fifth in the NL with 45 doubles and led the Marlins with 22 home runs and 90 RBIs.

Minor League: Brian Daubach, of, Charlotte

Daubach's 124 RBIs were fourth best in the minor leagues and his 35 home runs tied for fifth best.

Marlins general manager Dave Dombrowski decided to stick around after a brief flirtation with the Dodgers. The only GM in Marlins history signed a five-year, $5 million extension on Sept. 8, making him the highest-paid GM in baseball history.

Smiley's protracted bid to buy the Marlins finally fell through in September. South Florida hedge-fund manager John Henry, a one-percent partner in the New York Yankees, stepped forward with a $160 million cash offer to buy the club.

Henry added assurances that he would keep the Marlins in South Florida, even if it meant using his own money to build them a new baseball-only stadium with a retractable dome.

Twenty-seven rookies paraded through the Marlins' nightmarish season. That figure represented a record for the expansion era, topping the 25 rookies used by the expansion San Diego Padres in 1969.

Rookie outfielder Mark Kotsay hit .279 with 11 homers and 68 RBIs and led the majors in outfield assists. First baseman Derrek Lee hit 17 home runs and collected 74 RBIs.

The rookie parade appears likely to continue for several seasons, but the good news is Dombrowski picked up numerous highly-regarded prospects in the firesale. Lee, outfielder Preston Wilson, lefthanders Geoff Goetz and Ed Yarnall and righthanders A.J. Burnett, Mark Johnson, Rafael Medina and Todd Noel were just some of the players acquired.

Despite the influx of talent, the losing seeped from the major leagues down through the entire organization, as only the Rookie-level Gulf Coast League Marlins finished with a winning record.

ORGANIZATION LEADERS

BATTING		
*AVG	Matt Erickson, Kane County	.324
R	Brian Daubach, Charlotte	102
H	Raul Franco, Kane County	158
TB	Brian Daubach, Charlotte	315
2B	Brian Daubach, Charlotte	45
3B	Julio Ramirez, Brevard County	12
HR	Brian Daubach, Charlotte	35
RBI	Brian Daubach, Charlotte	124
BB	Brian Daubach, Charlotte	80
SO	Nate Rolison, Portland	150
SB	Quincy Foster, Kane County	73
PITCHING		
W	Michael Tejera, Portland/Kane County	15
L	Mark Johnson, Portland	14
#ERA	A.J. Burnett, Kane County	1.97
G	Mick Pageler, Portland	60
CG	Three tied at	3
SV	Hector Almonte, Kane County	21
IP	Brandon Leese, Portland/Brevard County	174
BB	Brent Billingsley, Portland	70
SO	A.J. Burnett, Kane County	186

*Minimum 250 At-Bats #Minimum 75 Innings

Florida MARLINS

Manager: Jim Leyland

1998 Record: 54-108, .333 (5th, NL East)

BATTING	AVG	G	AB	R	H	2B	3B	HR	RBI	BB	SO	SB	CS	B	T	HT	WT	DOB	1st Yr	Resides
Berg, Dave	.313	81	182	18	57	11	0	2	21	26	46	3	0	R	R	5-11	185	9-3-70	1993	Roseville, Calif.
Bonilla, Bobby	.278	28	97	11	27	5	0	4	15	12	22	0	1	B	R	6-4	240	2-23-63	1981	Greenwich, Conn.
Booty, Josh	.158	7	19	0	3	1	0	0	3	3	8	0	0	R	R	6-3	220	4-29-75	1994	Starkville, Miss.
Cangelosi, John	.251	104	171	19	43	8	0	1	10	30	23	2	3	B	L	5-8	160	3-10-63	1982	Chicago, Ill.
Castillo, Luis	.203	44	153	21	31	3	2	1	10	22	33	3	0	B	R	5-11	175	9-12-75	1993	San Pedro de Macoris, D.R.
Counsell, Craig	.251	107	335	43	84	19	5	4	40	51	47	3	0	L	R	6-0	170	8-21-70	1992	Fort Myers Beach, Fla.
Daubach, Brian	.200	10	15	0	3	1	0	0	3	1	5	0	0	L	R	6-1	201	2-11-72	1990	Belleville, Ill.
Dunwoody, Todd	.251	116	434	53	109	27	7	5	28	21	113	5	1	L	L	6-1	195	4-11-75	1993	West Lafayette, Ind.
Eisenreich, Jim	.250	30	64	9	16	1	0	1	7	4	14	2	0	L	L	5-11	195	4-18-59	1980	Blue Springs, Mo.
Floyd, Cliff	.282	153	588	85	166	45	3	22	90	47	112	27	14	L	R	6-4	235	12-5-72	1991	Markham, Ill.
Gonzalez, Alex	.151	25	86	11	13	2	0	3	7	9	30	0	0	R	R	6-0	170	2-15-77	1994	Turmero, Ven.
Jackson, Ryan	.250	111	260	26	65	15	1	5	31	20	73	1	1	L	L	6-3	185	11-11-71	1994	Sarasota, Fla.
Johnson, Charles	.221	31	113	13	25	5	0	7	23	16	30	0	1	R	R	6-2	220	7-20-71	1992	Pembroke Pines, Fla.
Knorr, Randy	.204	15	49	4	10	4	1	2	11	1	10	0	0	R	R	6-2	215	11-12-68	1986	Covina, Calif.
Kotsay, Mark	.279	154	578	72	161	25	7	11	68	34	61	10	5	L	L	6-0	180	12-2-75	1996	Pembroke Pines, Fla.
Lee, Derrek	.233	141	454	62	106	29	1	17	74	47	120	5	2	R	R	6-5	205	9-6-75	1993	Sacramento, Calif.
Millar, Kevin	.500	2	2	1	1	0	0	0	0	1	0	0	0	R	R	6-0	185	9-24-71	1993	Encino, Calif.
Orie, Kevin	.263	48	175	23	46	8	1	6	17	14	24	1	0	R	R	6-4	215	9-1-72	1993	West Chester, Pa.
2-team (64 Chicago)	.219	112	379	47	83	22	1	8	38	32	59	2	1							
Piazza, Mike	.278	5	18	1	5	0	1	0	5	0	0	0	0	R	R	6-3	223	9-4-68	1989	Valley Forge, Pa.
Redmond, Mike	.331	37	118	10	39	9	0	2	12	5	16	0	0	R	R	6-1	185	5-5-71	1993	Spokane, Wash.
Renteria, Edgar	.282	133	517	79	146	18	2	3	31	48	78	41	22	R	R	6-1	180	8-7-75	1992	Barranquilla, Colombia
Roskos, John	.100	10	10	1	1	0	0	0	0	0	5	0	0	R	R	5-11	195	11-19-74	1993	Rio Rancho, N.M.
Sheffield, Gary	.272	40	136	21	37	11	1	6	28	26	16	4	2	R	R	5-11	205	11-18-68	1986	St. Petersburg, Fla.
Wehner, John	.227	53	88	10	20	2	0	0	5	7	12	1	0	R	R	6-3	205	6-29-67	1988	Pittsburgh, Pa.
Wilson, Preston	.065	14	31	4	2	0	0	1	1	4	13	0	0	R	R	6-2	193	7-19-74	1993	Eastover, S.C.
2-team (8 New York)	.157	22	51	7	8	2	0	1	3	6	21	1	1							
Zaun, Greg	.188	106	298	19	56	12	2	5	29	35	52	5	2	B	R	5-10	180	4-14-71	1989	Glendale, Calif.
Zeile, Todd	.291	66	234	37	68	12	1	6	39	31	34	2	3	R	R	6-1	204	9-9-65	1986	Westlake Village, Calif.
2-team (40 L.A.)	.276	106	392	59	108	18	2	13	66	41	58	3	4							

PITCHING	W	L	ERA	G	GS	CG	SV	IP	H	R	ER	BB	SO	B	T	HT	WT	DOB	1st Yr	Resides
Alfonseca, Antonio	4	6	4.08	58	0	0	8	71	75	36	32	33	46	R	R	6-5	235	4-16-72	1990	La Romana, D.R.
Barrios, Manny	0	0	3.38	2	0	0	0	3	4	1	1	2	1	R	R	6-0	185	9-21-74	1993	Rock Island, Ill.
2-team (1 L.A.)	0	0	2.45	3	0	0	0	4	4	1	1	4	1							
Darensbourg, Vic	0	7	3.68	59	0	0	1	71	52	29	29	30	74	L	L	5-10	165	11-13-70	1992	Las Vegas, Nev.
Dempster, Ryan	1	5	7.08	14	11	0	0	55	72	47	43	38	35	R	R	6-2	195	5-3-77	1995	Gibsons, B.C.
Edmondson, Brian	4	3	3.79	43	0	0	0	59	62	28	25	29	32	R	R	6-2	175	1-29-73	1991	Riverside, Calif.
2-team (10 Atlanta)	4	4	3.91	53	0	0	0	76	76	38	33	37	40							
Fontenot, Joe	0	7	6.33	8	8	0	0	43	56	34	30	20	24	R	R	6-2	185	3-20-77	1995	Scott, La.
Gonzalez, Gabe	0	0	9.00	3	0	0	0	1	1	1	1	1	0	L	L	6-1	150	5-24-72	1995	Long Beach, Calif.
Hammond, Chris	0	2	6.59	3	3	0	0	14	20	11	10	8	8	L	L	6-1	195	1-21-66	1986	Hallandale, Fla.
Henriquez, Oscar	0	0	8.55	15	0	0	0	20	26	22	19	12	19	R	R	6-6	220	1-28-74	1991	La Guaira, Ven.
Heredia, Felix	0	3	5.49	41	2	0	2	41	38	30	25	32	38	L	L	6-0	175	6-18-76	1993	Santo Domingo, D.R.
Hernandez, Livan	10	12	4.72	33	33	9	0	234	265	133	123	104	162	R	R	6-2	220	2-20-75	1996	Miami, Fla.
Larkin, Andy	3	8	9.64	17	14	0	0	75	101	87	80	55	43	R	R	6-4	190	6-27-74	1992	Medford, Ore.
Ludwick, Eric	1	4	7.44	13	6	0	0	33	46	31	27	17	27	R	R	6-5	210	12-14-71	1993	Las Vegas, Nev.
Mantei, Matt	3	4	2.96	42	0	0	9	55	38	19	18	23	63	R	R	6-1	190	7-7-73	1991	Sawyer, Mich.
Meadows, Brian	11	13	5.21	31	31	1	0	174	222	106	101	46	88	R	R	6-4	200	11-21-75	1994	Troy, Ala.
Medina, Rafael	2	6	6.01	12	12	0	0	67	76	50	45	52	49	R	R	6-3	194	2-15-75	1993	Panama City, Panama
Ojala, Kirt	2	7	4.25	41	13	1	0	125	128	71	59	59	75	L	L	6-2	200	12-24-68	1990	Portage, Mich.
Pall, Donn	0	1	5.13	23	0	0	0	33	42	19	19	7	26	R	R	6-1	180	1-11-62	1985	Bloomingdale, Ill.
Powell, Jay	4	4	4.21	33	0	0	3	36	36	19	17	22	24	R	R	6-4	225	1-9-72	1993	Madison, Miss.
Sanchez, Jesus	7	9	4.47	35	29	0	0	173	178	98	86	91	137	L	L	5-10	153	10-11-74	1992	Bani, D.R.
Speier, Justin	0	3	8.38	18	0	0	0	19	25	18	18	12	15	R	R	6-4	205	11-6-73	1995	Scottsdale, Ariz.
2-team (1 Chicago)	0	3	8.71	19	0	0	0	21	27	20	20	13	17							
Stanifer, Rob	2	4	5.63	38	0	0	1	48	54	33	30	22	30	R	R	6-2	195	3-10-72	1994	Easley, S.C.

FIELDING

Catcher	PCT	G	PO	A	E	DP	PB
Johnson	.990	31	193	10	2	2	1
Knorr	.989	15	82	7	1	2	4
Piazza	.968	4	27	3	1	1	0
Redmond	.992	37	216	25	2	3	3
Zaun	.986	88	531	47	8	12	10

First Base	PCT	G	PO	A	E	DP
Daubach	1.000	4	22	1	0	4
Eisenreich	.965	10	53	2	2	7
Jackson	.973	44	300	20	9	30
Kotsay	1.000	3	3	1	0	0
Lee	.993	132	951	114	8	116
Roskos	1.000	1	1	0	0	0

Second Base	PCT	G	PO	A	E	DP
Berg	1.000	27	57	47	0	13
Castillo	.971	44	118	113	7	34
Counsell	.991	104	237	297	5	72
Zaun	1.000	1	0	1	0	0

Third Base	PCT	G	PO	A	E	DP
Berg	.952	25	19	41	3	2
Bonilla	.922	26	18	41	5	6
Booty	.824	7	4	10	3	1
Millar	.833	2	2	3	1	1
Orie	.939	48	49	106	10	5
Wehner	1.000	8	2	10	0	0
Zeile	.971	65	43	122	5	11

Shortstop	PCT	G	PO	A	E	DP
Berg	.933	17	16	40	4	8
Gonzalez	.978	25	29	58	2	17
Renteria	.966	130	194	374	20	93

Outfield	PCT	G	PO	A	E	DP
Cangelosi	.969	45	62	1	2	0
Dunwoody	.989	111	272	9	3	4
Eisenreich	1.000	8	9	0	0	0
Floyd	.974	146	252	10	7	1
Jackson	.976	32	41	0	1	0
Kotsay	.984	145	345	20	6	2
Sheffield	.986	37	68	3	1	2
Wehner	1.000	23	25	2	0	0
Wilson	1.000	11	13	0	0	0

DAVID SEELIG

Florida's Edgar Renteria
Anchored young Marlins infield

MORRIS FOSTOFF

Outfielder Julio Ramirez
Stole 71 bases at Class A Brevard County

FARM SYSTEM

Vice President, Player Development: John Boles

Class	Farm Team	League	W	L	Pct.	Finish*	Manager	First Yr
AAA	Charlotte (N.C.) Knights	International	70	73	.490	8th (14)	Fredi Gonzalez	1995
AA	Portland (Maine) Sea Dogs	Eastern	66	75	.468	7th (10)	Lynn Jones	1994
A#	Brevard County (Fla.) Manatees	Florida State	43	97	.307	14th (14)	Rick Renteria	1994
A	Kane County (Ill.) Cougars	Midwest	69	71	.493	10th (14)	Juan Bustabad	1993
A	Utica (N.Y.) Blue Sox	New York-Penn	35	41	.461	t-9th (14)	Ken Joyce	1996
Rookie	Melbourne (Fla.) Marlins	Gulf Coast	38	22	.633	1st (14)	Jon Deeble	1992

*Finish in overall standings (No. of teams in league) #Advanced level

CHARLOTTE — Class AAA

INTERNATIONAL LEAGUE

BATTING	AVG	G	AB	R	H	2B	3B	HR	RBI	BB	SO	SB	CS	B	T	HT	WT	DOB	1st Yr	Resides
Booty, Josh	.142	38	127	9	18	3	0	3	11	7	44	0	1	R	R	6-3	220	4-29-75	1994	Starkville, Miss.
Brumfield, Jacob	.167	95	227	24	38	13	0	3	25	34	41	7	1	R	R	6-0	190	5-27-65	1983	Atlanta, Ga.
Castillo, Luis	.287	100	380	74	109	11	2	0	15	75	68	41	15	B	R	5-11	175	9-12-75	1993	San Pedro de Macoris, D.R.
Clapinski, Chris	.269	100	312	53	84	18	1	9	35	39	53	11	3	B	R	6-0	175	8-20-71	1992	Rancho Mirage, Calif.
Daubach, Brian	.316	140	497	102	157	45	4	35	124	80	114	9	3	L	R	6-1	201	2-11-72	1990	Belleville, Ill.
Dunwoody, Todd	.304	28	102	20	31	6	3	6	22	12	28	4	2	L	L	6-1	195	4-11-75	1993	West Lafayette, Ind.
Estrada, Osmani	.259	8	27	3	7	1	0	0	3	1	4	0	0	R	R	5-8	180	1-23-69	1993	Woodland Hills, Calif.
Geisler, Phil	.161	14	31	2	5	1	0	0	1	3	13	0	0	L	L	6-3	200	10-23-69	1991	Springfield, Ore.
Gonzalez, Alex	.277	108	422	71	117	20	10	10	51	28	80	4	7	R	R	6-0	170	2-15-77	1994	Turmero, Ven.
Hastings, Lionel	.242	104	265	40	64	10	2	1	21	19	55	4	3	R	R	5-9	165	1-26-73	1994	Hermosa Beach, Calif.
Hyers, Tim	.280	85	300	50	84	22	2	7	52	27	41	0	3	L	L	6-1	195	10-3-71	1990	Covington, Ga.
Jackson, Ryan	.380	13	50	5	19	4	0	2	11	4	14	2	0	L	L	6-3	185	11-11-71	1994	Sarasota, Fla.
Knorr, Randy	.328	68	201	30	66	15	0	7	39	34	41	1	2	R	R	6-2	215	11-12-68	1986	Covina, Calif.
Lucca, Lou	.290	112	397	47	115	32	0	11	51	13	75	2	6	R	R	5-11	210	10-13-70	1992	South San Francisco, Calif.
Makarewicz, Scott	.163	16	49	3	8	4	0	1	5	3	11	0	1	R	R	6-0	200	3-1-67	1989	Maitland, Fla.
Millar, Kevin	.326	14	46	14	15	3	0	4	15	9	7	1	0	R	R	6-0	185	9-24-71	1993	Encino, Calif.
Natal, Bob	.273	68	216	31	59	11	1	11	39	13	33	1	1	R	R	5-11	190	11-13-65	1987	Chula Vista, Calif.
2-team (4 Durham)	.273	72	231	31	63	12	1	11	43	13	33	2	1							
Niles, Drew	.265	16	49	5	13	1	0	1	5	6	12	0	1	B	R	6-1	175	3-17-77	1998	Irmo, S.C.
Redmond, Mike	.241	18	58	4	14	2	0	2	7	0	3	0	0	R	R	6-1	185	5-5-71	1993	Spokane, Wash.
Reese, Nate	.375	3	8	1	3	0	0	1	1	1	3	0	0	R	R	5-11	215	10-17-74	1997	Shawnee Mission, Kan.
Rigsby, Randy	.214	4	14	1	3	0	0	0	0	1	4	0	0	L	L	6-0	190	8-7-76	1998	Goldsboro, N.C.
Roskos, John	.284	115	416	54	118	23	1	10	62	43	84	0	4	R	R	5-11	195	11-19-74	1993	Rio Rancho, N.M.
Wehner, John	.325	30	83	12	27	1	0	3	15	4	16	5	1	R	R	6-3	205	6-29-67	1988	Pittsburgh, Pa.
Wilson, Preston	.278	94	356	71	99	25	3	25	77	34	121	14	6	R	R	6-2	193	7-19-74	1993	Eastover, S.C.
2-team (18 Norfolk)	.273	112	429	80	117	30	4	26	86	36	143	15	7							

PITCHING	W	L	ERA	G	GS	CG	SV	IP	H	R	ER	BB	SO	B	T	HT	WT	DOB	1st Yr	Resides
Barrios, Manny	2	0	3.70	18	1	0	0	24	19	10	10	9	22	R	R	6-0	185	9-21-74	1993	Rock Island, Ill.
Borland, Toby	3	0	2.70	19	0	0	1	37	33	12	11	21	26	R	R	6-7	175	5-29-69	1989	Quitman, La.
2-team (13 Scranton)	3	2	3.47	32	0	0	6	49	47	20	19	24	41							
Corbin, Archie	2	2	2.59	34	0	0	3	49	25	15	14	46	55	R	R	6-4	230	12-30-67	1986	Beaumont, Texas
Cornelius, Reid	3	2	4.01	8	8	1	0	49	50	25	22	13	31	R	R	6-0	200	6-2-70	1989	West Palm Beach, Fla.
Dempster, Ryan	3	1	3.27	5	5	1	0	33	33	14	12	12	24	R	R	6-2	195	5-3-77	1995	Gibsons, B.C.
Fontenot, Joe	0	1	12.00	1	1	0	0	3	4	4	4	2	0	R	R	6-2	185	3-20-77	1995	Scott, La.
Gardiner, Mike	5	7	6.01	14	14	1	0	88	107	63	59	34	53	R	R	6-0	200	10-19-65	1987	Canton, Mass.
Gonzalez, Gabe	3	9	5.48	57	4	0	2	87	101	67	53	53	41	L	L	6-1	150	5-24-72	1995	Long Beach, Calif.
Grundt, Ken	2	0	5.91	16	0	0	1	21	23	15	14	15	12	L	L	6-4	195	8-26-69	1991	Chicago, Ill.
Hammond, Chris	1	3	4.82	5	5	0	0	28	35	17	15	14	22	L	L	6-1	195	1-21-66	1986	Hallandale, Fla.
Hawblitzel, Ryan	8	5	5.59	20	19	0	0	103	133	68	64	14	72	R	R	6-2	170	4-30-71	1990	Lake Worth, Fla.
Henriquez, Oscar	1	0	2.56	26	0	0	11	32	29	12	9	12	37	R	R	6-6	220	1-28-74	1991	La Guaira, Ven.
Jacobsen, Joe	1	3	5.95	9	8	0	0	42	64	29	28	7	17	R	R	6-3	225	12-26-71	1992	Clovis, Calif.
Johnson, Dane	1	0	3.38	2	0	0	0	3	3	1	1	1	0	R	R	6-5	195	2-10-63	1993	Miami, Fla.
2-team (7 Syracuse)	2	0	3.24	9	0	0	3	8	8	3	3	6	4							
Larkin, Andy	4	1	6.37	11	10	0	0	54	55	39	38	32	41	R	R	6-4	190	6-27-74	1992	Medford, Ore.
Ludwick, Eric	1	3	3.71	8	8	0	0	27	25	17	11	13	26	R	R	6-5	210	12-14-71	1993	Las Vegas, Nev.
Mantei, Matt	1	2	5.51	16	0	0	3	16	11	10	10	18	25	R	R	6-1	190	7-7-73	1991	Sawyer, Mich.
Medina, Rafael	4	2	3.90	11	9	3	0	58	53	27	25	26	41	R	R	6-3	194	2-15-75	1993	Panama City, Panama
Mendoza, Reynol	5	10	6.19	24	18	1	0	125	163	101	86	57	59	R	R	6-0	202	10-27-70	1992	San Antonio, Texas
Pall, Donn	1	2	4.15	29	0	0	14	35	33	17	16	10	33	R	R	6-1	180	1-11-62	1985	Bloomingdale, Ill.
Ramirez, Hector	3	3	6.75	55	0	0	3	87	106	68	65	30	50	R	R	6-3	218	12-15-71	1988	El Seibo, D.R.
Stanifer, Rob	4	2	4.31	21	1	0	4	40	39	20	19	13	29	R	R	6-2	195	3-10-72	1994	Easley, S.C.
Villafuerte, Brandon	1	0	6.35	10	0	0	0	11	15	8	8	8	9	R	R	5-11	165	12-17-75	1995	Morgan Hill, Calif.
Villano, Mike	3	5	7.69	13	10	0	0	60	82	55	51	18	47	R	R	6-0	200	8-10-71	1994	Bay City, Mich.
Williams, Jimmy	4	5	5.09	19	9	0	0	53	63	33	30	24	43	L	L	6-7	232	5-18-65	1984	Butler, Ala.
2-team (15 Buffalo)	4	10	5.87	34	12	0	0	80	101	60	52	41	71							
Yarnall, Ed	4	5	6.20	15	13	2	0	70	79	60	48	39	47	L	L	6-3	234	12-4-75	1997	Coral Springs, Fla.

FIELDING

Catcher	PCT	G	PO	A	E	DP	PB
Knorr	.977	58	349	25	9	4	1
Makarewicz	.967	15	82	5	3	1	2
Natal	.982	59	342	37	7	3	3
Redmond	1.000	18	101	20	0	5	2
Reese	1.000	3	20	2	0	0	2

First Base	PCT	G	PO	A	E	DP
Daubach	.996	25	236	18	1	26
Hyers	.994	47	336	25	2	31
Jackson	1.000	5	53	5	0	5
Millar	1.000	4	28	3	0	2
Rigsby	1.000	2	20	1	0	2
Roskos	.994	76	644	38	4	64

Second Base	PCT	G	PO	A	E	DP
Castillo	.970	100	232	281	16	72
Clapinski	.978	11	19	25	1	6
Hastings	.964	37	75	112	7	24
Niles	1.000	1	1	2	0	1

Third Base	PCT	G	PO	A	E	DP
Booty	.919	37	20	94	10	7
Clapinski	.956	28	20	66	4	7
Estrada	.929	6	3	10	1	0
Hastings	.818	7	10	8	4	0
Lucca	.937	67	60	148	14	17
Millar	.846	11	6	16	4	1
Natal	1.000	2	1	2	0	0

Shortstop	PCT	G	PO	A	E	DP
Clapinski	.958	23	22	70	4	11
Estrada	1.000	1	0	3	0	1
Gonzalez	.960	107	161	322	20	74
Hastings	.875	7	11	10	3	5
Lucca	1.000	1	1	3	0	0
Niles	.921	15	23	47	6	11

Outfield	PCT	G	PO	A	E	DP
Brumfield	.958	80	107	6	5	1
Clapinski	1.000	34	47	1	0	0
Daubach	.986	104	126	10	2	1
Dunwoody	.987	28	76	2	1	1
Geisler	1.000	11	21	1	0	1
Hastings	.982	27	50	4	1	0
Hyers	1.000	46	61	1	0	0
Jackson	1.000	4	4	1	0	0
Lucca	.964	37	50	4	2	0
Makarewicz	.000	1	0	0	0	0
Rigsby	1.000	1	2	0	0	0
Roskos	1.000	1	3	0	0	0
Wehner	.939	21	29	2	2	0
Wilson	.979	91	180	8	4	0

PORTLAND — Class AA

EASTERN LEAGUE

BATTING	AVG	G	AB	R	H	2B	3B	HR	RBI	BB	SO	SB	CS	B	T	HT	WT	DOB	1st Yr	Resides
Bates, Fletcher	.274	140	537	67	147	23	5	11	60	46	118	19	6	B	R	6-1	193	3-24-74	1994	Wilmington, N.C.
Booty, Josh	.202	71	247	28	50	8	3	10	39	20	74	1	1	R	R	6-3	220	4-29-75	1994	Starkville, Miss.
Castro, Ramon	.250	31	88	9	22	3	0	3	11	8	21	0	0	R	R	6-3	225	3-1-76	1994	Vega Baja, P.R.
Cook, Hayward	.178	30	73	13	13	5	1	2	5	4	30	0	0	R	R	5-10	210	6-24-72	1994	San Jose, Calif.
Cromer, Brandon	.223	122	391	51	87	13	5	15	47	43	89	3	2	L	R	6-2	175	1-25-74	1992	Lexington, S.C.
Funaro, Joe	.285	95	340	54	97	10	4	5	28	32	44	9	6	R	R	5-9	180	3-20-73	1995	Hamden, Conn.
Garcia, Amaury	.270	137	544	79	147	19	6	13	62	45	126	23	15	R	R	5-10	160	5-20-75	1993	Santo Domingo, D.R.
Goodell, Steve	.186	48	118	13	22	6	0	1	11	26	35	0	1	R	R	6-3	196	4-23-75	1995	Danville, Calif.
Gulan, Mike	.306	46	160	24	49	16	2	5	23	10	40	3	2	R	R	6-1	190	12-18-70	1992	Steubenville, Ohio
Jones, Jaime	.281	123	438	58	123	27	0	10	63	55	118	4	1	L	L	6-3	190	8-2-76	1995	Poway, Calif.
Kuilan, Hector	.252	31	107	8	27	4	0	2	14	2	9	0	0	R	R	5-11	190	4-3-76	1994	Vega Alta, P.R.
Morales, Stephen	.300	3	10	0	3	0	0	0	3	0	2	0	0	B	R	5-11	195	5-4-78	1996	Mayaguez, P.R.
Norton, Chris	.353	22	68	12	24	4	1	6	19	12	17	0	0	R	R	6-2	215	9-21-70	1992	Maitland, Fla.
Redmond, Mike	.321	8	28	7	9	4	0	1	7	2	2	0	0	R	R	6-1	185	5-5-71	1993	Spokane, Wash.
Reeves, Glenn	.253	53	190	40	48	7	2	1	18	37	42	5	3	R	R	6-0	195	1-19-74	1993	Glen Waverly, Australia
Robertson, Ryan	.260	98	308	31	80	14	0	7	47	44	62	0	1	L	R	6-4	210	9-30-72	1996	Port Neches, Texas
Rodriguez, Victor	.284	66	222	28	63	9	1	4	19	18	26	5	4	R	R	6-1	190	10-25-76	1994	Guayama, P.R.
Rolison, Nate	.277	131	484	80	134	35	2	16	83	64	150	5	0	L	R	6-5	225	3-27-77	1995	Petal, Miss.
White, Walt	.271	70	203	23	55	9	2	6	25	16	53	1	1	R	R	6-0	195	12-12-71	1994	Torrance, Calif.

PITCHING	W	L	ERA	G	GS	CG	SV	IP	H	R	ER	BB	SO	B	T	HT	WT	DOB	1st Yr	Resides
Billingsley, Brent	6	13	3.74	28	28	0	0	171	172	90	71	70	183	L	L	6-2	200	4-19-75	1996	Chino Hills, Calif.
Burgus, Travis	2	1	1.89	38	0	0	1	57	45	16	12	29	56	L	L	6-2	190	11-6-72	1995	Mission Viejo, Calif.
Dempster, Ryan	4	3	3.22	7	7	0	0	45	34	20	16	15	33	R	R	6-2	195	5-3-77	1995	Gibsons, B.C.
DeWitt, Scott	4	4	4.53	50	3	0	1	60	61	35	30	36	64	R	L	6-3	210	10-6-74	1995	Springfield, Ore.
Duncan, Geoff	9	2	2.83	42	0	0	11	57	39	21	18	31	74	R	R	6-2	185	4-1-75	1996	Roswell, Ga.
Fontenot, Joe	3	1	3.08	7	7	0	0	38	37	16	13	13	31	R	R	6-2	185	3-20-77	1995	Scott, La.
Jacobsen, Joe	1	0	1.69	3	0	0	0	5	4	1	1	0	3	R	R	6-3	225	12-26-71	1992	Clovis, Calif.
Johnson, Mark	5	14	4.62	26	26	2	0	142	147	89	73	60	120	R	R	6-3	205	5-2-75	1996	Houston, Texas
Leese, Brandon	4	7	4.13	20	20	0	0	126	137	70	58	37	94	R	R	6-4	190	10-8-75	1996	Lincolnshire, Ill.
McCurtain, Paul	0	0	5.40	1	0	0	0	2	0	1	1	2	2	R	R	6-1	190	2-5-76	1998	Mesa, Ariz.

PITCHING	W	L	ERA	G	GS	CG	SV	IP	H	R	ER	BB	SO	B	T	HT	WT	DOB	1st Yr	Resides
Mull, Blaine	0	3	6.82	9	6	0	0	32	40	35	24	17	24	R	R	6-4	210	8-14-76	1994	Morganton, N.C.
Pageler, Mick	5	5	4.62	60	0	0	13	76	73	40	39	32	67	R	R	6-2	205	4-30-76	1996	Mesa, Ariz.
Rector, Bobby	1	1	10.45	14	1	0	0	21	31	27	24	10	15	R	R	6-1	170	9-24-74	1994	Imperial Beach, Calif.
Richards, Mark	3	8	5.38	40	7	0	9	75	96	54	45	43	56	R	R	6-6	220	6-19-74	1997	Tipp City, Ohio
Rodgers, Bobby	6	5	3.73	14	14	2	0	82	68	37	34	28	72	R	R	6-3	225	7-22-74	1996	St. Charles, Mo.
Tejera, Michael	9	5	4.11	18	18	2	0	107	113	55	49	36	97	L	L	5-9	175	10-18-76	1995	Miami, Fla.
Townsend, Dave	1	0	6.26	11	2	0	0	23	35	18	16	11	9	R	R	6-2	225	8-2-74	1996	Canton, Miss.
Vardijan, Dan	1	1	7.85	19	0	0	0	29	34	26	25	22	15	R	R	6-4	205	12-1-76	1995	Glenview, Ill.
Villafuerte, Brandon	0	2	4.97	30	0	0	1	54	68	35	30	33	52	R	R	5-11	165	12-17-75	1995	Morgan Hill, Calif.
White, Walt	0	0	0.00	3	0	0	0	2	2	0	0	1	0	R	R	6-0	195	12—71	1994	Torrance, Calif.
Yarnall, Ed	2	0	2.93	2	2	0	0	15	9	5	5	4	15	L	L	6-3	234	12-4-75	1997	Coral Springs, Fla.
2-team (7 Binghamton)	9	0	1.02	9	9	0	0	62	29	10	7	21	67							

FIELDING

Catcher	PCT	G	PO	A	E	DP	PB
Castro	.946	12	82	5	5	0	1
Kuilan	.988	30	227	26	3	3	4
Morales	1.000	3	16	3	0	0	0
Norton	.980	14	90	9	2	0	4
Redmond	.983	8	53	6	1	0	1
Robertson	.989	85	630	68	8	8	8

First Base	PCT	G	PO	A	E	DP
Goodell	1.000	1	2	0	0	0
Norton	.951	6	56	2	3	5
Robertson	1.000	4	30	4	0	1
Rolison	.989	131	1081	85	13	116

Second Base	PCT	G	PO	A	E	DP
Cromer	1.000	1	1	0	0	0
Garcia	.960	136	287	355	27	93
Rodriguez	1.000	2	2	5	0	2
White	1.000	6	14	15	0	5

Third Base	PCT	G	PO	A	E	DP
Booty	.931	68	43	159	15	20
Cromer	.904	38	23	80	11	6
Funaro	1.000	2	1	3	0	1
Goodell	.818	7	2	7	2	2
Gulan	.892	27	15	43	7	4
White	1.000	4	3	8	0	2

Shortstop	PCT	G	PO	A	E	DP
Cromer	.902	15	18	37	6	8
Funaro	.952	57	109	167	14	35
Rodriguez	.954	56	74	156	11	34
White	.935	18	30	42	5	8

Outfield	PCT	G	PO	A	E	DP
Bates	.962	139	266	9	11	2
Cook	.944	17	17	0	1	0
Cromer	.982	64	106	2	2	0
Funaro	1.000	6	6	0	0	0
Goodell	1.000	14	27	2	0	1
Gulan	1.000	3	1	0	0	0
Jones	.949	106	141	7	8	0
Reeves	1.000	50	79	5	0	0
White	.944	33	48	3	3	0

BREVARD COUNTY — Class A

FLORIDA STATE LEAGUE

BATTING	AVG	G	AB	R	H	2B	3B	HR	RBI	BB	SO	SB	CS	B	T	HT	WT	DOB	1st Yr	Resides
Callahan, David	.333	5	21	3	7	1	0	0	4	0	4	0	0	L	L	5-11	200	12-7-79	1998	Palm Bay, Fla.
Camilo, Jose	.216	101	357	34	77	16	2	3	27	23	74	10	7	L	L	5-11	177	9-28-76	1994	Trujillo Alto, P.R.
Clapinski, Chris	.071	5	14	1	1	0	1	0	4	7	2	0	0	B	R	6-0	175	8-20-71	1992	Rancho Mirage, Calif.
Conway, Scott	.167	9	24	3	4	1	0	0	0	2	5	0	0	L	L	6-3	205	10-18-78	1996	Mount Laurel, N.J.
Cook, Hayward	.198	70	243	21	48	9	2	0	16	29	78	10	2	R	R	5-10	210	6-24-72	1994	San Jose, Calif.
Garrett, Jason	.216	62	222	16	48	5	1	3	25	17	66	1	3	R	R	6-2	190	6-10-73	1995	Austin, Texas
Green, Kevin	.176	22	51	5	9	1	0	1	5	4	19	3	0	R	R	6-1	190	8-9-75	1997	Rome, N.Y.
Harvey, Aaron	.286	3	7	3	2	0	0	0	1	1	1	2	0	L	R	5-9	180	6-11-73	1995	Donvale, Australia
Heinrichs, Jon	.285	128	470	63	134	17	2	12	64	50	68	21	6	R	R	6-0	185	11-18-74	1997	La Mesa, Calif.
Jones, Jay	.221	74	262	15	58	8	0	3	25	13	34	1	3	L	R	6-0	195	10-21-74	1996	Trussville, Ala.
Kleinz, Larry	.288	88	320	48	92	23	1	7	34	46	51	1	0	R	R	6-1	205	3-3-74	1996	Hamilton Square, N.J.
Kuilan, Hector	.226	61	208	13	47	11	0	6	28	12	29	2	1	R	R	5-11	190	4-3-76	1994	Vega Alta, P.R.
Maduro, Remy	.263	65	198	17	52	7	0	0	12	21	31	0	0	L	R	5-11	185	9-18-76	1996	Hoofddorp, Netherlands
Makarewicz, Scott	.284	20	74	5	21	0	0	2	10	6	15	0	2	R	R	6-0	200	3-1-67	1989	Maitland, Fla.
Mejia, Renato	.195	32	113	9	22	1	0	1	11	6	40	1	1	R	R	6-1	190	1-2-77	1994	Hato Mayor, D.R.
Paulino, David	.175	35	97	7	17	1	0	0	5	13	31	6	0	R	R	5-10	135	11-20-79	1997	San Cristobal, D.R.
Ramirez, Julio	.279	135	559	90	156	20	12	13	58	45	147	71	27	R	R	5-11	170	8-10-77	1994	Santo Domingo, D.R.
Reese, Nate	.175	11	40	3	7	2	0	2	7	3	9	0	0	R	R	5-11	215	10-17-74	1997	Shawnee Mission, Kan.
Reyes, Dadny	.000	1	1	0	0	0	0	0	0	0	0	0	0	B	R	5-10	165	8-22-78	1997	Bonao, D.R.
Reynoso, Ismael	.216	72	231	25	50	4	2	2	19	21	50	6	2	R	R	6-0	180	6-17-78	1995	La Romana, D.R.
Schifano, Tony	.234	91	304	28	71	3	4	1	14	14	46	8	1	R	R	6-1	175	11-11-74	1997	Anaheim Hills, Calif.
Treanor, Matt	.235	80	243	24	57	8	0	3	28	38	45	3	2	R	R	6-1	188	3-3-76	1994	Anaheim, Calif.
Ugueto, Luis	.182	3	11	0	2	0	0	0	0	0	5	0	0	B	R	5-11	152	2-15-79	1996	Maracay, Ven.
Venghaus, Jeff	.181	116	375	38	68	10	4	2	23	52	91	10	8	B	R	6-0	185	9-17-74	1996	Spring, Texas
Washington, Kelley	.173	27	98	7	17	2	2	0	9	6	30	0	1	R	R	6-2	180	8-21-79	1997	Stephens City, Va.
White, Walt	.154	13	39	6	6	0	0	0	4	7	9	0	2	R	R	6-0	195	12-12-71	1994	Torrance, Calif.

GAMES BY POSITION: C—Jones 8, Kuilan 55, Makarewicz 20, Reese 10, Treanor 55. **1B**—Callahan 5, Conway 9, Garrett 57, Green 1, Jones 49, Mejia 23, Treanor 1. **2B**—Clapinski 1, Maduro 1, Paulino 17, Reyes 1, Schifano 10, Venghaus 113, White 1. **3B**—Clapinski 1, Kleinz 73, Paulino 2, Schifano 63, Treanor 1, Venghaus 1, White 1. **SS**—Camilo 1, Clapinski 1, Kleinz 1, Maduro 1, Paulino 14, Reynoso 71, Schifano 17, Ugueto 3, Washington 27, White 11. **OF**—Camilo 88, Cook 60, Green 17, Harvey 3, Heinrichs 109, Maduro 17, Mejia 8, Ramirez 135.

PITCHING	W	L	ERA	G	GS	CG	SV	IP	H	R	ER	BB	SO	B	T	HT	WT	DOB	1st Yr	Resides
Cames, Aaron	5	10	3.12	27	25	1	0	153	134	73	53	59	161	R	R	6-1	192	11-21-75	1996	Woodland, Calif.
Campos, David	0	0	12.91	6	0	0	0	8	20	11	11	4	6	L	L	5-11	170	8-31-77	1998	Kerman, Calif.
Clark, Chris	2	3	4.30	40	2	0	9	61	52	38	29	46	58	R	R	6-1	180	10-29-74	1994	Aurora, Colo.
DeYoung, Dan	1	4	6.44	6	6	2	0	36	55	28	26	4	9	R	R	6-0	210	3-24-76	1997	Libson, Iowa
2-team (20 Charlotte)	14	8	4.59	26	26	2	0	155	167	88	79	43	71							
Duncan, Geoff	1	3	2.25	17	0	0	2	32	35	15	8	9	30	R	R	6-2	185	4-1-75	1996	Roswell, Ga.
Ehlers, Corey	1	6	4.37	45	0	0	1	91	91	50	44	26	54	R	R	6-3	190	8-22-73	1997	Floresville, Texas
Fowler, Blair	3	6	4.25	28	9	1	1	91	95	54	43	44	54	R	R	6-2	185	6-25-75	1997	Everett, Wash.
Gagliano, Steve	0	0	4.85	8	0	0	0	13	15	12	7	10	7	R	R	6-3	200	8-4-77	1997	Rolling Meadows, Ill.
Garvin, Robert	1	2	5.48	15	0	0	1	23	21	16	14	14	12	R	R	6-2	165	3-14-79	1997	Charleston, S.C.
Hoff, Steve	5	8	4.11	15	15	2	0	85	93	50	39	27	45	L	L	6-4	205	7-1-77	1996	San Bruno, Calif.
Hurtado, Victor	5	11	3.87	18	18	1	0	100	105	57	43	23	59	R	R	6-4	190	6-14-77	1994	Santo Domingo, D.R.
Lara, Nelson	2	5	9.42	19	4	0	0	29	27	36	30	33	32	R	R	6-4	185	7-15-78	1995	Santo Domingo, D.R.
Leese, Brandon	1	5	5.70	8	8	0	0	47	63	36	30	7	30	R	R	6-4	190	10-8-75	1996	Lincolnshire, Ill.
Marriott, Mike	0	4	7.64	5	5	0	0	18	23	20	15	19	11	R	R	6-3	205	3-12-77	1995	Spring, Texas
Minaya, Pedro	0	2	14.46	3	3	0	0	9	20	17	15	7	6	R	R	6-3	170	7-30-77	1994	Santo Domingo, D.R.

PITCHING	W	L	ERA	G	GS	CG	SV	IP	H	R	ER	BB	SO	B	T	HT	WT	DOB	1st Yr	Resides
Moore, Chris	1	6	8.03	8	8	0	0	25	32	25	22	23	9	R	R	6-1	180	8-3-78	1997	Hazel Crest, Ill.
Morris, Alex	1	1	8.33	23	0	0	1	27	35	27	25	26	13	L	R	6-4	220	12-31-76	1996	Austin, Texas
Mull, Blaine	4	6	4.32	16	16	3	0	100	114	53	48	32	65	R	R	6-4	210	8-14-76	1994	Morganton, N.C.
Rizzo, Nick	2	0	0.98	7	0	0	0	18	15	8	2	7	7	R	R	6-0	180	1-23-74	1997	Bellmawr, N.J.
Rodgers, Bobby	1	1	4.08	7	7	0	0	35	34	17	16	7	35	R	R	6-3	225	7-22-74	1996	St. Charles, Mo.
Townsend, Dave	0	[illegible]	[illegible]	12	11	1	0	60	60	40	[illegible]	[illegible]	[illegible]	R	R	6-2	[illegible]	[illegible]	[illegible]	Canton, Miss.
Vardijan, Dan	2	0	3.00	8	0	0	0	12	15	4	4	4	8	R	R	6-4	205	12-1-76	1995	Glenview, Ill.
Vargas, Claudio	0	1	4.66	2	2	0	0	10	15	5	5	4	9	R	R	6-3	160	5-19-79	1996	Santiago, D.R.
Villafuerte, Brandon	1	0	0.93	3	0	0	0	10	7	3	1	1	6	R	R	5-11	165	12-17-75	1995	Morgan Hill, Calif.
Widerski, Jon	0	3	6.43	24	1	0	0	42	51	36	30	31	25	R	R	6-4	190	5-17-77	1995	Minneapolis, Minn.
Wyckoff, Travis	4	5	3.21	41	0	0	3	73	77	33	26	27	31	B	L	6-0	180	9-30-73	1996	Wichita, Kan.

KANE COUNTY — Class A

MIDWEST LEAGUE

BATTING	AVG	G	AB	R	H	2B	3B	HR	RBI	BB	SO	SB	CS	B	T	HT	WT	DOB	1st Yr	Resides
Bautista, Jorge	.261	84	272	33	71	16	2	7	50	40	63	3	4	R	R	5-9	185	7-12-76	1995	San Cristobal, D.R.
Donaldson, Rhodney	.219	108	334	55	73	13	0	0	45	54	56	23	10	L	R	5-11	170	4-9-74	1997	Cairo, Ga.
Erickson, Matt	.324	124	441	83	143	32	2	4	64	72	62	17	7	L	R	5-11	190	7-30-75	1997	Appleton, Wis.
Foster, Quincy	.253	134	545	90	138	14	10	0	37	51	114	73	19	L	R	6-2	175	10-30-74	1996	Hendersonville, N.C.
Franco, Raul	.287	132	551	81	158	24	0	2	51	24	52	15	12	R	R	5-11	170	1-14-76	1994	San Pedro de Macoris, D.R.
Gload, Ross	.313	132	501	77	157	41	3	12	92	58	84	7	6	L	L	6-2	195	4-5-76	1997	East Hampton, N.Y.
Green, Kevin	.156	33	96	8	15	2	0	1	8	15	32	6	5	R	R	6-1	190	8-9-75	1997	Rome, N.Y.
Harper, Brandon	.231	113	412	34	95	22	2	4	50	42	64	1	3	R	R	6-4	200	4-29-76	1997	Hobbs, N.M.
Hunter, Travis	.136	10	22	0	3	0	0	0	1	1	5	0	0	R	R	6-2	230	9-3-79	1997	La Mesa, Calif.
Melconian, Alex	.227	132	453	61	103	10	1	6	53	50	135	21	3	R	R	5-10	190	3-18-75	1997	Berwyn, Pa.
Niles, Drew	.276	26	87	12	24	4	0	0	9	12	20	2	1	B	R	6-1	175	3-17-77	1998	Irmo, S.C.
Polonia, Israel	.211	15	38	6	8	0	0	1	2	2	17	1	1	R	R	6-0	160	10-10-77	1995	San Pedro de Macoris, D.R.
Reed, Brian	.500	3	6	1	3	1	0	0	2	2	2	0	0	R	R	5-9	170	3-3-78	1997	Henderson, Nev.
Reese, Nate	.250	13	40	3	10	1	0	1	7	5	12	0	0	R	R	5-11	215	10-17-74	1997	Shawnee Mission, Kan.
Reynoso, Ismael	.188	48	144	15	27	4	0	1	9	17	34	3	3	R	R	6-0	180	6-17-78	1995	La Romana, D.R.
Rivas, Julio	.000	1	1	0	0	0	0	0	0	0	0	0	0	R	R	5-11	185	8-22-79	1998	Arlington, Va.
Roneberg, Brett	.271	68	240	35	65	7	0	3	35	25	50	2	5	L	L	6-2	205	2-5-79	1996	Cairns, Australia
Santo, Jose	.188	32	117	17	22	9	2	2	12	21	49	5	1	R	R	5-11	165	3-1-78	1995	Santiago, D.R.
Schnabel, Matt	.127	24	63	5	8	1	0	1	6	7	21	0	0	L	R	6-0	195	8-29-74	1997	Englewood, Colo.
Washington, Kelley	.247	65	239	28	59	5	0	4	21	11	75	10	8	R	R	6-2	180	8-21-79	1997	Stephens City, Va.

GAMES BY POSITION: C—Harper 110, Hunter 3, Melconian 21, Reese 9. **1B**—Bautista 10, Gload 129, Hunter 3. **2B**—Erickson 9, Franco 131, Niles 1. **3B**—Bautista 11, Erickson 102, Santos 27. **SS**—Erickson 4, Niles 12, Polonia 14, Reynoso 48, Washington 64. **OF**—Bautista 1, Donaldson 84, Foster 132, Green 32, Melconian 102, Reed 2, Reese 1, Roneberg 68, Schnabel 14.

PITCHING	W	L	ERA	G	GS	CG	SV	IP	H	R	ER	BB	SO	B	T	HT	WT	DOB	1st Yr	Resides
Akin, Aaron	1	4	3.66	12	10	0	0	52	50	28	21	20	41	R	R	6-2	190	6-13-77	1997	Pembroke Pines, Fla.
Almonte, Hector	1	5	3.95	43	0	0	21	43	51	22	19	19	51	R	R	6-2	190	10-17-75	1993	Santo Domingo, D.R.
Borges, Reece	1	2	4.71	10	0	0	0	21	24	13	11	8	8	R	R	6-3	195	4-4-76	1997	Reno, Nev.
Burnett, A.J.	10	4	1.97	20	20	0	0	119	74	27	26	45	186	R	R	6-5	204	1-3-77	1995	North Little Rock, Ark.
Comer, Scott	6	4	2.87	15	14	2	0	97	91	42	31	9	85	L	L	6-5	195	6-23-77	1996	Klamath Falls, Ore.
Gagliano, Steve	1	1	7.66	8	3	0	0	22	33	21	19	10	17	R	R	6-3	200	8-4-77	1997	Rolling Meadows, Ill.
Goetz, Geoff	1	4	4.64	9	9	0	0	43	44	22	22	24	36	L	L	5-11	163	4-3-79	1997	Lutz, Fla.
Henderson, Scott	10	7	2.99	40	1	0	4	81	64	29	27	27	96	R	R	6-3	195	2-27-75	1997	Villa Park, Calif.
Henriquez, Hector	0	5	5.29	10	8	1	0	49	55	36	29	20	30	L	L	6-2	175	8-27-78	1994	Santo Domingo, D.R.
Knotts, Gary	8	8	3.87	27	27	3	0	158	144	84	68	66	148	R	R	6-4	200	2-12-77	1996	Decatur, Ala.
Lara, Nelson	2	2	6.14	10	4	0	0	29	29	23	20	23	21	R	R	6-4	185	7-15-78	1995	Santo Domingo, D.R.
Levan, Matt	1	7	6.38	30	9	0	0	92	111	72	65	36	87	L	L	6-3	200	6-24-75	1996	Coatesville, Pa.
Lima, Cory	3	3	4.61	31	7	0	0	80	106	56	41	29	48	R	R	6-4	180	3-16-75	1997	Stone Mountain, Ga.
Marriott, Mike	2	4	3.74	10	10	0	0	53	59	31	22	18	22	R	R	6-3	205	3-12-77	1995	Spring, Texas
McClaskey, Tim	5	2	4.26	34	2	0	2	74	87	45	35	16	70	R	R	5-10	170	1-11-76	1996	Wilton, Iowa
Noel, Todd	2	2	5.30	7	5	0	0	37	45	25	22	17	26	R	R	6-4	205	9-28-78	1996	Maurice, La.
2-team (16 Rockford)	8	8	4.41	23	21	1	0	127	128	70	62	54	96							
Pearson, Jason	0	0	3.38	2	0	0	0	3	3	3	1	1	1	L	L	6-0	195	12-29-75	1998	Cambridge, Mass.
Putnicki, Billy	6	3	3.23	29	0	0	4	56	48	23	20	16	34	R	R	6-3	205	12-21-73	1997	San Antonio, Texas
Rizzo, Nick	3	2	2.91	26	0	0	0	53	49	31	17	22	33	R	R	6-0	180	1-23-74	1997	Bellmawr, N.J.
Santiago, Derek	0	1	24.00	2	1	0	0	3	9	9	8	1	6	R	R	6-1	170	10-10-75	1995	Aurora, Ill.
Tejera, Michael	6	1	2.77	10	10	0	0	55	44	20	17	13	47	L	L	5-9	175	10-18-76	1995	Miami, Fla.

UTICA — Short-Season Class A

NEW YORK-PENN LEAGUE

BATTING	AVG	G	AB	R	H	2B	3B	HR	RBI	BB	SO	SB	CS	B	T	HT	WT	DOB	1st Yr	Resides
Abreu, Miguel	.176	58	125	13	22	2	0	1	9	6	44	1	1	R	R	6-3	180	8-15-78	1995	San Pedro de Macoris, D.R.
Feliz, Joselyn	.208	32	96	8	20	6	0	2	12	2	26	0	0	R	R	6-3	225	6-2-76	1994	Santo Domingo, D.R.
Frick, Matt	.265	55	185	30	49	12	1	7	34	16	45	2	1	R	R	6-2	220	1-2-76	1998	Scottsdale, Ariz.
Green, Kevin	.375	3	8	3	3	0	0	1	2	0	1	0	0	R	R	6-1	190	8-9-75	1997	Rome, N.Y.
Hill, Willy	.270	72	270	34	73	10	4	0	19	22	48	10	9	L	R	5-9	160	9-21-76	1998	Sapulpa, Okla.
Honeycutt, Heath	.241	68	245	40	59	8	2	7	33	25	67	11	2	R	R	6-4	210	7-30-76	1998	Alpharetta, Ga.
Kelly, Heath	.232	34	95	14	22	3	1	0	10	9	29	1	1	R	R	6-1	185	2-16-76	1998	Pensacola, Fla.
Leahy, Bart	.216	49	139	13	30	9	0	1	11	9	46	3	2	R	R	6-5	225	10-19-76	1998	Glenview, Ill.
Lucca, Tony	.239	42	109	12	26	7	0	2	13	15	20	1	0	L	L	6-0	245	1-26-75	1998	Walnut Creek, Calif.
Morales, Stephen	.247	26	85	14	21	2	0	3	14	5	18	2	1	B	R	5-11	195	5-4-78	1996	Mayaguez, P.R.
Neal, Blaine	.190	53	121	13	23	4	0	0	13	23	32	2	1	L	R	6-5	205	4-6-78	1996	New Port Richey, Fla.
Padgett, Matt	.219	71	247	31	54	9	1	4	39	22	73	4	3	L	R	6-2	215	7-22-77	1998	Lexington, S.C.
Pass, Patrick	.132	15	38	5	5	0	0	1	2	5	17	2	1	R	R	6-1	215	12-31-77	1996	Decatur, Ga.
Polonia, Israel	.301	45	146	23	44	6	2	4	22	17	47	3	5	R	R	6-0	160	10-10-77	1995	San Pedro de Macoris, D.R.
Reyes, Dadny	.100	4	10	0	1	0	0	0	0	0	4	0	0	B	R	5-10	165	8-22-78	1997	Bonao, D.R.

BATTING	AVG	G	AB	R	H	2B	3B	HR	RBI	BB	SO	SB	CS	B	T	HT	WT	DOB	1st Yr	Resides
Rigsby, Randy	.302	54	179	26	54	12	2	1	16	21	42	3	4	L	L	6-0	190	8-7-76	1998	Goldsboro, N.C.
Smalls, Terrance	.275	43	102	14	28	1	0	0	6	5	13	10	4	L	R	5-10	170	11-22-75	1998	Holly Hill, S.C.
Wathan, Derek	.268	60	224	32	60	8	2	0	23	21	35	10	9	B	R	6-3	190	12-13-76	1998	Blue Springs, Mo.

GAMES BY POSITION: C—Feliz 17, Frick 38, Morales 26. **1B**—Leahy 1, Lucca 19, Neal 33, Rigsby 36. **2B**—Hill 12, Kelly 25, Polonia 22, Smalls 22. **3B**—Feliz 1, Honeycutt 65, Padgett 2, Polonia 5, Reyes 1, Smalls 6. **SS**—Kelly 2, Polonia 12, Reyes 3, Smalls 2, Wathan 59. **OF**—Abreu 55, Green 2, Hill 61, Honeycutt 1, Kelly 1, Leahy 42, Lucca 1, Neal 1, Padgett 67, Pass 12, Rigsby 16.

PITCHING	W	L	ERA	G	GS	CG	SV	IP	H	R	ER	BB	SO	B	T	HT	WT	DOB	1st Yr	Resides
Avila, David	1	1	3.57	12	0	0	0	23	26	13	9	10	13	R	R	6-5	257	10-26-75	1998	Rohnert Park, Calif.
Bair, Andy	1	2	5.28	14	0	0	0	15	14	9	9	10	12	L	L	6-5	255	1-27-77	1995	Manchester, Md.
Clackum, Scott	1	1	1.50	20	0	0	10	24	16	5	4	5	28	R	R	6-3	185	1-13-75	1998	North Augusta, S.C.
Cowan, Bobby	1	0	2.76	17	1	0	0	33	29	11	10	5	26	R	R	6-1	195	1-9-75	1998	Saugus, Calif.
Farizo, Brad	5	5	4.04	14	14	1	0	82	96	43	37	21	47	R	R	6-4	190	11-3-78	1996	Marrero, La.
Gagliano, Steve	6	4	3.31	13	12	1	0	68	67	33	25	27	66	R	R	6-3	200	8-4-77	1997	Rolling Meadows, Ill.
Garvin, Robert	0	2	5.50	5	3	0	0	18	24	12	11	8	6	R	R	6-2	165	3-14-79	1997	Charleston, S.C.
Harber, Ryan	2	6	5.55	11	6	0	0	36	46	29	22	4	38	L	L	6-4	210	9-25-76	1998	Fort Wayne, Ind.
Jupe, Eric	0	3	3.78	13	0	0	1	17	17	8	7	6	17	R	R	6-2	170	5-29-77	1998	San Antonio, Texas
Lowery, Phill	2	1	2.31	7	7	0	0	35	29	12	9	14	37	L	L	6-1	205	4-7-77	1998	Petaluma, Calif.
McCurtain, Paul	0	1	4.38	17	2	0	1	39	35	25	19	19	33	R	R	6-1	190	2-5-76	1998	Mesa, Ariz.
Moore, Chris	2	5	3.66	13	13	0	0	66	55	34	27	36	48	R	R	6-1	180	8-3-78	1997	Hazel Crest, Ill.
Noyce, David	4	2	3.52	17	0	0	2	31	23	15	12	11	28	L	L	6-5	195	3-2-77	1998	Marietta, Ga.
Olsen, Kevin	4	3	2.60	21	4	0	2	45	37	21	13	10	56	R	R	6-2	200	7-26-76	1998	Norco, Calif.
Pidgeon, Matt	6	5	3.78	14	14	0	0	79	86	41	33	22	55	R	R	6-4	200	6-25-77	1997	Eureka, Calif.
Seaman, John	0	0	6.41	14	0	0	2	27	35	19	19	9	15	R	R	6-4	190	2-14-77	1998	Wilmette, Ill.

MELBOURNE — Rookie

GULF COAST LEAGUE

BATTING	AVG	G	AB	R	H	2B	3B	HR	RBI	BB	SO	SB	CS	B	T	HT	WT	DOB	1st Yr	Resides
Aguila, Chris	.269	51	171	29	46	12	3	4	29	19	49	6	2	R	R	5-11	190	2-23-79	1997	Reno, Nev.
Bailey, Jeff	.331	37	127	21	42	10	0	2	28	19	31	3	2	R	R	6-2	195	11-19-78	1997	Kelso, Wash.
Callahan, David	.379	29	103	16	39	11	0	0	7	11	15	2	1	L	L	5-11	200	12-7-79	1998	Palm Bay, Fla.
Conway, Scott	.267	39	120	13	32	10	1	2	27	10	34	1	1	L	L	6-3	205	10-18-78	1996	Mount Laurel, N.J.
Ferrand, Francisco	.263	36	114	14	30	5	4	1	11	13	26	2	2	L	L	5-10	160	5-20-80	1997	Santo Domingo, D.R.
Foerter, Justin	.273	3	11	1	3	0	0	0	2	0	5	0	0	L	R	6-2	230	8-29-78	1998	Bordentown, N.J.
Galarraga, Luis	.188	37	80	10	15	2	0	1	10	10	37	1	0	R	R	6-4	191	12-29-79	1996	Caracas, Ven.
Louwsma, Chris	.184	22	76	7	14	3	0	0	6	5	19	0	1	R	R	6-3	195	12-25-78	1998	Sanford, Fla.
Medrano, Jesus	.286	48	175	42	50	11	1	2	15	21	30	26	7	R	R	6-0	185	9-11-78	1997	La Puente, Calif.
Mejia, Renato	.250	47	136	16	34	4	1	2	21	10	37	6	3	R	R	6-1	190	1-2-77	1994	Hato Mayor, D.R.
Paulino, David	.340	21	50	9	17	0	1	0	5	5	14	5	5	R	R	5-10	135	11-20-79	1997	San Cristobal, D.R.
Reed, Brian	.246	56	211	35	52	13	5	1	14	26	70	40	8	R	R	5-9	170	3-3-78	1997	Henderson, Nev.
Reyes, Dadny	.297	30	64	7	19	4	1	1	12	10	8	0	0	B	R	5-10	165	8-22-78	1997	Bonao, D.R.
Rivas, Julio	.148	13	27	1	4	0	0	0	3	2	11	0	0	R	R	5-11	185	8-22-79	1998	Arlington, Va.
Ugueto, Luis	.229	50	166	20	38	8	2	0	15	8	37	7	1	R	R	5-11	152	2-15-79	1996	Maracay, Ven.
Venales, Luis	.154	27	65	7	10	1	1	0	4	2	26	0	0	R	R	6-3	176	5-26-80	1997	Caracas, Ven.
Walker, Javon	.222	32	90	15	20	3	0	2	9	5	38	4	3	R	R	6-4	205	10-14-78	1997	Lafayette, La.
Zapey, Winton	.202	38	104	11	21	9	0	0	5	5	27	1	1	R	R	5-11	170	3-21-80	1997	Santo Domingo, D.R.

GAMES BY POSITION: C—Reyes 2, Rivas 13, Venales 27, Zapey 36. **1B**—Callahan 27, Conway 32, Foerter 2, Mejia 4. **2B**—Medrano 44, Paulino 2, Reyes 19. **3B**—Aguila 41, Louwsma 16, Mejia 1, Reyes 2, Zapey 1. **SS**—Medrano 1, Paulino 10, Reyes 2, Ugueto 49. **OF**—Conway 1, Ferrand 35, Galarraga 34, Mejia 44, Paulino 4, Reed 56, Walker 28.

PITCHING	W	L	ERA	G	GS	CG	SV	IP	H	R	ER	BB	SO	B	T	HT	WT	DOB	1st Yr	Resides
Anderson, Antwoine	3	1	1.35	15	0	0	3	33	23	6	5	8	37	L	L	6-3	170	11-5-78	1998	Cincinnati, Ohio
Anderson, Wes	5	2	1.39	11	11	1	0	65	44	25	10	18	66	R	R	6-4	175	9-10-79	1997	Pine Bluff, Ark.
Campos, David	3	0	0.00	9	0	0	3	23	7	1	0	10	41	L	L	5-11	170	8-31-77	1998	Kerman, Calif.
Craun, Robert	0	1	5.16	12	0	0	2	23	24	17	13	11	23	R	R	6-1	190	2-15-76	1998	Zuni, Va.
LaRoche, Jeff	0	1	2.45	4	0	0	0	7	7	6	2	3	8	L	L	6-3	185	3-17-78	1998	Fort Scott, Kan.
Lopez, Gustavo	1	3	3.60	9	1	0	2	20	17	8	8	11	16	R	R	5-9	180	12-31-78	1996	Santiago, D.R.
Minaya, Pedro	4	0	1.00	11	9	0	0	45	27	8	5	9	61	R	R	6-3	170	7-30-77	1994	Santo Domingo, D.R.
Pearson, Jason	4	0	1.57	11	3	0	2	34	28	8	6	5	36	L	L	6-0	195	12-29-75	1998	Cambridge, Mass.
Rodriguez, Marino	0	1	0.91	12	2	0	3	30	20	8	3	9	30	L	L	6-3	160	12-26-78	1996	El Seibo, D.R.
Shields, Drew	7	2	2.63	13	11	1	0	65	48	24	19	19	65	R	R	6-4	190	9-9-78	1997	Tucson, Ariz.
Thomas, Gaige	3	3	2.55	15	6	0	1	42	24	20	12	21	53	B	R	6-1	185	2-28-79	1997	Brenham, Texas
Vargas, Claudio	0	4	4.08	5	4	0	0	29	24	15	13	7	27	R	R	6-3	160	5-19-79	1996	Santiago, D.R.
Villanueva, Bill	6	2	1.88	11	11	0	0	57	46	14	12	13	54	R	R	6-4	180	10-6-78	1996	Santo Domingo, D.R.
Wesolowski, David	1	2	4.55	12	1	0	0	27	30	18	14	5	23	R	R	6-3	185	1-15-78	1996	Williamsville, N.Y.

HOUSTON ASTROS

League's top offense leads to second straight division title

BY JOSEPH DUARTE

The Astros' 1998 season will be remembered as the most successful in the organization's 37-year history.

The postseason, however, was a different story. For the second year in a row the Astros failed to advance past the National League Division Series.

The club entered the playoffs as the most feared team in the NL, featuring the league's most prolific offense and newly acquired ace lefthander Randy Johnson. But four games later it was the San Diego Padres who moved on, while the Astros went home.

Johnson, who was 10-1 with a 1.28 ERA in 11 starts after being picked up in a July 31 trade with the Mariners, lost both of his postseason starts despite a 1.93 ERA. The vaunted offense managed just eight runs in the series.

Four players scored more than 100 runs during the regular season: first baseman Jeff Bagwell, second baseman Craig Biggio and outfielders Moises Alou and Derek Bell. Biggio became only the second player this century, joining Hall of Famer Tris Speaker, to collect 50 doubles and 50 stolen bases in the same season.

Even before Johnson's arrival the Astros had compiled a formidable pitching staff. Five Astros pitchers won 10 games or more, including 19-game winner Shane Reynolds and pleasant surprise Jose Lima, who won 16 games after spending most of his career in the bullpen. Adding Johnson, who tossed shutouts in his first four Astrodome starts, took the team to a higher level.

The club experienced one of the season's most frightening moments when closer Billy Wagner was drilled in the head with a line drive in Arizona on July 16. Wagner had a concussion and spent three weeks on the disabled list.

Craig Biggio

JOHN SPEAR

Lance Berkman

Players of the Year

Major League: Craig Biggio, 2b

Biggio sparked the best offense in baseball with a .325 average, 20 home runs and 50 steals.

Minor League: Lance Berkman, of, N.O./Jack.

Berkman capped a 30-home-run season by hitting three homers in the deciding game of the Triple-A World Series.

While the Astros failed to bring home a title, the organization did not end '98 empty-handed, as New Orleans won the Triple-A World Series in Las Vegas.

Outfielder Lance Berkman finished an outstanding season with three home runs in Game Four to provide most the offense in the Zephyrs' 12-6 victory over Buffalo. Berkman, who hit 30 regular-season home runs in stops at Double-A Jackson and New Orleans, was named MVP of the Series.

While New Orleans will be remembered as the first-ever champion of the Triple-A World Series, what was more impressive was how it won. The Zephyrs survived several late-season big league call-ups and the loss of two players in the Johnson deal, and marched steadily through the Pacific Coast League playoffs, eliminating Iowa and Calgary to earn the Las Vegas trip.

Down the stretch the Zephyrs lost catcher Mitch Meluskey, first baseman J.R. Phillips, third baseman Russ Johnson and outfielder Pete Incaviglia. The biggest losses might have come with the trade for Johnson, as the club gave up middle infielder Carlos Guillen and righthander Freddy Garcia. The player to be named in the trade, lefthander John Halama, remained the rest of the season and went 12-3.

New Orleans wasn't the only championship club in the system. Short-season Auburn was named co-champion in the New York-Penn League after rain washed out the title series with Oneonta. And in the Class A Midwest League, Quad City advanced to the playoffs, but fell in the first round to Clinton.

ORGANIZATION LEADERS

BATTING		
*AVG	Mitch Meluskey, New Orleans	.353
R	Lance Berkman, New Orleans/Jackson	96
H	Chris Truby, NO/Jackson/Kissimmee	162
TB	Chris Truby, NO/Jackson/Kissimmee	306
2B	Mitch Meluskey, New Orleans	41
3B	Julio Lugo, Kissimmee	14
HR	Chris Truby, NO/Jackson/Kissimmee	31
RBI	Chris Truby, NO/Jackson/Kissimmee	112
BB	Lance Berkman, New Orleans/Jackson	97
SO	Kevin Burns, Kissimmee	124
SB	Julio Lugo, Kissimmee	51
PITCHING		
W	Eric Ireland, Quad City	14
L	Tony McKnight, Kissimmee	13
#ERA	Roy Oswalt, Auburn/GCL Astros	2.19
G	Joe Messman, Quad City	63
CG	Eric Ireland, Quad City	6
SV	Reggie Harris, New Orleans	23
IP	Eric Ireland, Quad City	206
BB	Jim Lynch, Kissimmee/Quad City	86
SO	Eric Ireland, Quad City	191

*Minimum 250 At-Bats #Minimum 75 Innings

Houston ASTROS

Manager: Larry Dierker

1998 Record: 102-60, .630 (1st, NL Central)

BATTING	AVG	G	AB	R	H	2B	3B	HR	RBI	BB	SO	SB	CS	B	T	HT	WT	DOB	1st Yr	Resides
Alou, Moises	.312	159	584	104	182	34	5	38	124	84	87	11	3	R	R	6-3	195	7-3-66	1986	Santo Domingo, D.R.
Ausmus, Brad	.269	128	412	62	111	10	4	6	45	53	60	10	3	R	R	5-11	195	4-14-69	1988	San Diego, Calif.
Bagwell, Jeff	.304	147	540	124	164	33	1	34	111	109	90	19	7	R	R	6-0	195	5-27-68	1989	Houston, Texas
Bell, Derek	.314	156	630	111	198	41	2	22	108	51	126	13	3	R	R	6-2	215	12-11-68	1987	Tampa, Fla.
Berry, Sean	.314	102	299	48	94	17	1	13	52	31	50	3	1	R	R	5-11	200	3-22-66	1986	Paso Robles, Calif.
Biggio, Craig	.325	160	646	123	210	51	2	20	88	64	113	50	8	R	R	5-11	180	12-14-65	1987	Houston, Texas
Bogar, Tim	.154	79	156	12	24	4	1	1	8	9	36	2	1	R	R	6-2	198	10-28-66	1987	Normal, Ill.
Clark, Dave	.206	93	131	12	27	7	0	0	4	14	45	1	1	L	R	6-2	210	9-3-62	1983	Germantown, Tenn.
Eusebio, Tony	.253	66	182	13	46	6	1	1	36	18	31	1	0	R	R	6-2	210	4-27-67	1985	Kissimmee, Fla.
Everett, Carl	.296	133	467	72	138	34	4	15	76	44	102	14	12	B	R	6-0	190	6-3-71	1990	Tampa, Fla.
Gutierrez, Ricky	.261	141	491	55	128	24	3	2	46	54	84	13	7	R	R	6-1	175	5-23-70	1988	Miami, Fla.
Hidalgo, Richard	.303	74	211	31	64	15	0	7	35	17	37	3	3	R	R	6-3	190	7-2-75	1991	Guarenas, Ven.
Howell, Jack	.289	24	38	4	11	5	0	1	7	4	12	0	0	L	R	6-0	190	8-18-61	1983	Celina, Texas
Incaviglia, Pete	.125	13	16	0	2	1	0	0	2	1	4	0	0	R	R	6-1	230	4-2-64	1986	Colleyville, Texas
Johnson, Russ	.231	8	13	2	3	1	0	0	0	1	5	1	0	R	R	5-10	180	2-22-73	1994	Denham Springs, La.
Meluskey, Mitch	.250	8	8	1	2	1	0	0	0	1	4	0	0	B	R	6-0	185	9-18-73	1992	Yakima, Wash.
Montgomery, Ray	.400	6	5	2	2	0	0	0	0	0	0	0	0	R	R	6-3	195	8-8-69	1990	Pearland, Texas
Phillips, J.R.	.190	36	58	4	11	0	0	2	9	7	22	0	0	L	L	6-1	185	4-29-70	1988	Moreno Valley, Calif.
Spiers, Bill	.273	123	384	66	105	27	4	4	43	45	62	11	2	L	R	6-2	190	6-5-66	1987	Cameron, S.C.
Ward, Daryle	.333	4	3	1	1	0	0	0	0	1	2	0	0	L	L	6-2	230	6-27-75	1994	Riverside, Calif.

PITCHING	W	L	ERA	G	GS	CG	SV	IP	H	R	ER	BB	SO	B	T	HT	WT	DOB	1st Yr	Resides
Bergman, Sean	12	9	3.72	31	27	1	0	172	183	81	71	42	100	R	R	6-4	225	4-11-70	1991	Joliet, Ill.
Cabrera, Jose	0	0	8.31	3	0	0	0	4	7	4	4	1	1	R	R	6-0	160	3-24-72	1991	Santiago, D.R.
Elarton, Scott	2	1	3.32	28	2	0	2	57	40	21	21	20	56	R	R	6-7	240	2-23-76	1994	Lamar, Colo.
Grzanich, Mike	0	0	18.00	1	0	0	0	1	1	2	2	2	1	R	R	6-1	180	8-24-72	1992	Champaign, Ill.
Halama, John	1	1	5.85	6	6	0	0	32	37	21	21	13	21	L	L	6-5	200	2-22-72	1994	Brooklyn, N.Y.
Hampton, Mike	11	7	3.36	32	32	1	0	212	227	92	79	81	137	R	L	5-10	180	9-9-72	1990	Houston, Texas
Harris, Reggie	0	0	6.00	6	0	0	0	6	6	4	4	2	2	R	R	6-2	217	8-12-68	1987	Waynesboro, Va.
Henry, Doug	8	2	3.04	59	0	0	2	71	55	25	24	35	59	R	R	6-4	205	12-10-63	1986	Chandler, Ariz.
Johnson, Randy	10	1	1.28	11	11	4	0	84	57	12	12	26	116	R	L	6-10	230	9-10-63	1985	Glendale, Ariz.
Lima, Jose	16	8	3.70	33	33	3	0	233	229	100	96	32	169	R	R	6-2	205	9-30-72	1989	Plant City, Fla.
Magnante, Mike	4	7	4.88	48	0	0	2	52	56	28	28	26	39	L	L	6-1	185	6-17-65	1988	Burbank, Calif.
Miller, Trever	2	0	3.04	37	1	0	1	53	57	21	18	20	30	R	L	6-4	195	5-29-73	1991	Mount Washington, Ky.
Nitkowski, C.J.	3	3	3.77	43	0	0	3	60	49	27	25	23	44	L	L	6-3	205	3-9-73	1994	Suffern, N.Y.
Powell, Jay	3	3	2.38	29	0	0	4	34	22	9	9	15	38	R	R	6-4	225	1-9-72	1993	Madison, Miss.
2-team (33 Florida)	7	7	3.33	62	0	0	7	70	58	28	26	37	62							
Reynolds, Shane	19	8	3.51	35	35	3	0	233	257	99	91	53	209	R	R	6-3	210	3-26-68	1989	Houston, Texas
Scanlan, Bob	0	1	3.08	27	0	0	0	26	24	12	9	13	9	R	R	6-7	215	8-9-66	1984	Beverly Hills, Calif.
Schourek, Pete	7	6	4.50	15	15	0	0	80	82	43	40	36	59	L	L	6-5	205	5-10-69	1987	Clifton, Va.
Wagner, Billy	4	3	2.70	58	0	0	30	60	46	19	18	25	97	L	L	5-11	180	7-25-71	1993	Pearland, Texas

FIELDING

Catcher	PCT	G	PO	A	E	DP	PB
Ausmus	.992	124	850	58	7	8	4
Eusebio	.992	54	352	19	3	2	4
Meluskey	1.000	3	9	0	0	0	1

First Base	PCT	G	PO	A	E	DP
Bagwell	.995	147	1239	129	7	114
Howell	1.000	10	63	6	0	3
Phillips	.962	12	70	6	3	7
Spiers	1.000	7	34	1	0	1

Second Base	PCT	G	PO	A	E	DP
Biggio	.980	159	318	430	15	91
Bogar	1.000	11	10	14	0	4
Johnson	1.000	1	2	2	0	0
Spiers	.958	9	10	13	1	2

Third Base	PCT	G	PO	A	E	DP
Berry	.953	87	55	150	10	13
Bogar	.909	11	4	6	1	1
Howell	1.000	2	1	5	0	0
Johnson	1.000	5	1	7	0	0
Spiers	.966	99	57	169	8	9

Shortstop	PCT	G	PO	A	E	DP
Bogar	.989	55	49	126	2	16
Gutierrez	.976	141	215	403	15	81
Spiers	.000	2	0	0	0	0

Outfield	PCT	G	PO	A	E	DP
Alou	.980	154	232	11	5	2
Bell	.973	154	282	8	8	2
Clark	.885	22	22	1	3	0
Everett	.987	123	295	12	4	3
Hidalgo	.978	72	131	3	3	1
Incaviglia	1.000	3	3	0	0	0
Montgomery	1.000	2	1	0	0	0
Phillips	1.000	6	2	0	0	0

JOHN WILLIAMSON

Jeff Bagwell

THE SPORTS GROUP

Houston's Billy Wagner
Saved 30 games for Astros

LEE SCHMID

Fast riser Chris Truby
Hit 31 home runs at three stops in Astros system

FARM SYSTEM

Director of Player Development: Tim Purpura

Class	Farm Team	League	W	L	Pct.	Finish*	Manager	First Yr
AAA	New Orleans (La.) Zephyrs	Pacific Coast	76	66	.535	+6th (16)	John Tamargo	1997
AA	Jackson (Miss.) Generals	Texas	70	70	.500	4th (8)	Jim Pankovits	1991
A#	Kissimmee (Fla.) Cobras	Florida State	64	75	.460	12th (14)	Manny Acta	1985
A	Quad City (Iowa) River Bandits	Midwest	77	62	.554	4th (14)	Mike Rojas	1993
A	Auburn (N.Y.) Doubledays	New York-Penn	43	32	.573	+3rd (14)	Lyle Yates	1982
Rookie	Kissimmee (Fla.) Astros	Gulf Coast	22	38	.367	14th (14)	Julio Linares	1985

*Finish in overall standings (No. of teams in league) #Advanced level +Won league championship

NEW ORLEANS — Class AAA

PACIFIC COAST LEAGUE

BATTING	AVG	G	AB	R	H	2B	3B	HR	RBI	BB	SO	SB	CS	B	T	HT	WT	DOB	1st Yr	Resides
Alexander, Chad	.400	2	5	1	2	0	0	0	2	0	2	0	0	R	R	6-1	190	5-22-74	1995	Lufkin, Texas
Berkman, Lance	.271	17	59	14	16	4	0	6	13	12	16	0	0	B	L	6-1	205	2-10-76	1997	New Braunfels, Texas
Butler, Rob	.274	70	223	21	61	11	1	1	29	17	19	2	2	L	L	5-11	185	4-10-70	1991	Toronto, Ontario
Candaele, Casey	.290	66	221	36	64	11	2	1	25	18	34	2	0	B	R	5-9	165	1-12-61	1983	San Luis Obispo, Calif.
2-team (44 Nashville)	.283	110	368	54	104	16	4	2	40	31	53	3	1							
Geisler, Phil	.200	23	50	3	10	2	0	0	4	4	16	0	1	L	L	6-3	200	10-23-69	1991	Springfield, Ore.
2-team (5 Nashville)	.211	28	57	4	12	2	0	0	4	5	20	0	1							
Guillen, Carlos	.291	100	374	67	109	18	4	12	51	31	61	3	4	B	R	6-1	180	9-30-75	1993	Aragua, Ven.
Hernandez, Carlos	.298	134	494	64	147	23	2	1	54	21	81	29	11	R	R	5-9	175	12-12-75	1993	Caracas, Ven.
Hidalgo, Richard	.167	10	24	0	4	2	0	0	1	3	2	0	0	R	R	6-3	190	7-2-75	1991	Guarenas, Ven.
Incaviglia, Pete	.324	76	281	57	91	10	1	23	66	34	63	11	3	R	R	6-1	230	4-2-64	1986	Colleyville, Texas
Johnson, Russ	.309	122	453	95	140	28	2	7	52	90	64	11	11	R	R	5-10	180	2-22-73	1994	Denham Springs, La.
Jones, Dax	.275	31	80	17	22	2	2	1	10	12	9	1	1	R	R	6-0	180	8-4-70	1991	Waukegan, Ill.
Makarewicz, Scott	.167	4	12	1	2	0	0	0	1	0	4	0	0	R	R	6-0	200	3-1-67	1989	Maitland, Fla.
Meluskey, Mitch	.353	121	397	76	140	41	0	17	71	85	59	2	0	B	R	6-0	185	9-18-73	1992	Yakima, Wash.
Miller, Orlando	.296	29	98	15	29	6	2	0	9	10	25	1	0	R	R	6-3	205	1-13-69	1988	Estafeta del Dorado, Panama
2-team (18 Salt Lake)	.269	68	212	31	57	16	2	2	24	25	57	2	0							
Miller, Ryan	.294	8	17	4	5	1	0	0	3	1	3	1	0	R	R	6-0	175	10-22-72	1994	Tulare, Calif.
Mitchell, Donovan	.282	49	103	16	29	5	1	3	15	9	19	2	3	L	R	5-9	175	11-27-69	1992	White Plains, N.Y.
Montgomery, Ray	.290	75	272	42	79	18	1	9	45	26	48	4	2	R	R	6-3	195	8-8-69	1990	Pearland, Texas
Neal, Mike	.231	30	91	13	21	4	1	0	6	2	16	0	0	R	R	6-1	180	11-5-71	1993	Hammond, La.
Phillips, J.R.	.302	56	225	51	68	18	0	21	60	21	65	1	1	L	L	6-1	185	4-29-70	1988	Moreno Valley, Calif.
Ramos, Ken	.295	84	217	28	64	9	0	4	30	29	24	2	0	L	L	6-1	185	6-6-67	1989	Pueblo, Colo.
2-team (18 Salt Lake)	.287	102	286	34	82	13	1	5	41	35	37	3	1							
Rivera, Luis	.232	33	82	17	19	2	1	1	7	9	8	2	1	R	R	5-10	172	1-3-64	1982	Cidra, P.R.

BATTING	AVG	G	AB	R	H	2B	3B	HR	RBI	BB	SO	SB	CS	B	T	HT	WT	DOB	1st Yr	Resides
Ronan, Marc	.244	51	123	7	30	5	0	1	10	17	25	0	0	L	R	6-2	190	9-19-69	1990	Tallahassee, Fla.
Russo, Paul	.254	93	268	33	68	15	1	12	44	30	55	0	0	R	R	5-11	215	8-26-69	1990	Tampa, Fla.
Saylor, Jamie	.364	4	11	3	4	0	1	1	3	0	0	0	0	L	R	5-11	185	9-11-74	1994	Garland, Texas
Truby, Chris	.412	5	17	6	7	1	1	1	1	1	3	1	0	R	R	6-2	190	12-9-73	1993	Mukilteo, Wash.
Ward, Daryle	.305	116	463	78	141	31	1	23	96	41	78	2	0	L	L	6-2	230	6-27-75	1994	Riverside, Calif.

PITCHING	W	L	ERA	G	GS	CG	SV	IP	H	R	ER	BB	SO	B	T	HT	WT	DOB	1st Yr	Resides
Arocha, Rene	5	4	5.45	11	11	0	0	66	86	47	40	19	44	R	R	6-0	180	2-24-66	1992	Miami, Fla.
Blais, Mike	0	0	0.00	2	0	0	0	3	1	0	0	1	1	R	R	6-5	226	10-2-71	1993	East Lyme, Conn.
Cabrera, Jose	0	0	5.40	5	0	0	1	5	2	3	3	1	6	R	R	6-0	160	3-24-72	1991	Santiago, D.R.
Diorio, Mike	4	2	5.22	21	0	0	2	29	38	24	17	11	14	R	R	6-2	200	3-1-73	1993	Pueblo, Colo.
Elarton, Scott	9	4	4.01	14	14	2	0	92	71	42	41	41	100	R	R	6-7	240	2-23-76	1994	Lamar, Colo.
Garcia, Freddy	1	0	3.14	2	2	0	0	14	14	5	5	1	13	R	R	6-4	235	10-6-76	1994	Valencia, Ven.
Grzanich, Mike	1	2	2.27	34	0	0	5	40	27	13	10	21	39	R	R	6-1	180	8-24-72	1992	Champaign, Ill.
Gutierrez, Jim	1	4	6.44	27	3	0	0	43	70	36	31	13	25	R	R	6-2	170	11-28-70	1989	Burlington, Wash.
Halama, John	12	3	3.20	17	17	4	0	121	118	48	43	16	86	L	L	6-5	200	2-22-72	1994	Brooklyn, N.Y.
Harris, Reggie	2	3	4.44	51	0	0	23	53	38	27	26	28	53	R	R	6-2	217	8-12-68	1987	Waynesboro, Va.
Lopez, Johann	7	2	5.60	45	6	0	0	80	84	52	50	28	77	R	R	6-2	210	4-4-75	1992	Agua Negra, Ven.
Milacki, Bob	10	8	3.84	29	28	2	0	190	199	96	81	51	104	R	R	6-4	225	7-28-64	1984	Lake Havasu, Ariz.
Nitkowski, C.J.	0	1	6.00	5	3	0	1	15	22	12	10	7	18	L	L	6-3	205	3-9-73	1994	Suffern, N.Y.
Ramos, Edgar	2	3	5.31	12	12	0	0	58	71	44	34	19	42	R	R	6-4	170	3-6-75	1992	Cumana, Ven.
Rivera, Roberto	5	4	2.45	54	0	0	5	62	59	22	17	15	38	L	L	6-0	200	1-1-69	1988	Bayamon, P.R.
Root, Derek	1	0	2.84	1	1	0	0	6	3	2	2	3	4	L	L	6-5	215	5-26-75	1993	Lakewood, Ohio
Salkeld, Roger	3	6	5.79	37	11	0	2	82	82	57	53	64	79	R	R	6-5	215	3-6-71	1989	Gilbert, Ariz.
Scanlan, Bob	5	4	6.46	14	12	1	0	61	90	50	44	24	35	R	R	6-7	215	8-9-66	1984	Beverly Hills, Calif.
Sikorski, Brian	5	8	5.79	15	14	1	0	84	86	57	54	32	64	R	R	6-1	190	7-27-74	1995	Roseville, Mich.
Slusarski, Joe	1	4	5.11	31	0	0	2	49	53	31	28	9	32	R	R	6-4	195	12-19-66	1989	Springfield, Ill.
Smith, Lee	1	1	6.97	10	0	0	2	10	14	8	8	4	11	R	R	6-6	270	12-4-57	1975	Castor, La.
Taylor, Scott	0	2	9.10	9	6	0	0	29	40	29	29	19	20	R	R	6-3	200	10-3-66	1989	Wichita, Kan.
Wallace, Kent	0	0	10.57	7	0	0	0	8	16	10	9	1	7	L	R	6-3	192	8-22-70	1992	Paducah, Ky.
West, David	1	1	2.56	19	2	0	0	32	26	11	9	22	33	L	L	6-6	247	9-1-64	1983	Palm City, Fla.

FIELDING

Catcher	PCT	G	PO	A	E	DP	PB
Makarewicz	1.000	4	22	1	0	0	0
Meluskey	.987	108	702	49	10	8	17
Ronan	.985	46	252	18	4	4	2
Russo	1.000	1	4	0	0	0	0

First Base	PCT	G	PO	A	E	DP
Geisler	1.000	1	1	0	0	0
Neal	1.000	3	16	2	0	1
Phillips	.995	45	349	22	2	30
Russo	.992	61	447	40	4	46
Ward	.979	54	376	45	9	48

Second Base	PCT	G	PO	A	E	DP
Candaele	.950	7	7	12	1	6
Hernandez	.983	124	243	336	10	81
Johnson	.977	10	21	22	1	7
O. Miller	.000	1	0	0	0	0
Neal	.929	7	14	12	2	3
Rivera	1.000	7	7	14	0	5

Third Base	PCT	G	PO	A	E	DP
Candaele	.964	18	11	43	2	3
Johnson	.962	110	50	204	10	19
O. Miller	1.000	1	0	2	0	0
R. Miller	1.000	1	1	5	0	1
Neal	.926	9	6	19	2	2
Rivera	1.000	6	1	4	0	0
Russo	1.000	3	1	0	0	0
Truby	.917	5	4	7	1	3

Shortstop	PCT	G	PO	A	E	DP
Candaele	1.000	1	0	3	0	1
Guillen	.943	97	145	287	26	65
Hernandez	.906	8	6	23	3	6
Johnson	1.000	3	5	9	0	2
O. Miller	.938	25	32	58	6	15
Neal	1.000	5	2	13	0	3
Rivera	.854	10	14	21	6	6
Saylor	.857	2	1	5	1	0

Outfield	PCT	G	PO	A	E	DP
Alexander	1.000	2	3	0	0	0
Berkman	1.000	17	30	0	0	0
Butler	.958	67	135	3	6	1
Candaele	.984	44	63	0	1	0
Geisler	.895	15	17	0	2	0
Hidalgo	1.000	9	17	0	0	0
Incaviglia	.955	48	62	1	3	0
Jones	.960	27	46	2	2	2
Meluskey	.000	1	0	0	0	0
Mitchell	1.000	38	60	2	0	2
Montgomery	.976	73	156	4	4	2
Neal	1.000	2	10	0	0	0
Phillips	.944	18	32	2	2	0
K. Ramos	.970	67	122	6	4	1
Rivera	.000	1	0	0	0	0
Saylor	1.000	1	2	0	0	0
Ward	.965	63	106	3	4	1

JACKSON — Class AA

TEXAS LEAGUE

BATTING	AVG	G	AB	R	H	2B	3B	HR	RBI	BB	SO	SB	CS	B	T	HT	WT	DOB	1st Yr	Resides
Alexander, Chad	.286	128	416	77	119	33	2	13	45	71	80	6	7	R	R	6-1	190	5-22-74	1995	Lufkin, Texas
Amezcua, Adan	.205	23	73	6	15	2	0	2	6	3	11	1	1	R	R	6-1	195	3-9-74	1993	Mazatlan, Mexico
Berkman, Lance	.306	122	425	82	130	34	0	24	89	85	82	6	4	B	L	6-1	205	2-10-76	1997	New Braunfels, Texas
Castro, Ramon	.256	48	168	27	43	6	0	8	25	13	31	0	1	R	R	6-3	225	3-1-76	1994	Vega Baja, P.R.
Duffy, Jim	.156	12	32	1	5	1	0	0	0	1	9	0	0	R	R	6-2	195	7-18-74	1997	Andover, N.J.
Johnson, Ric	.200	23	80	5	16	2	0	0	2	3	9	0	1	R	R	6-2	185	3-18-74	1995	Chicago, Ill.
Lopez, Pedro	.287	60	178	29	51	14	0	9	28	17	27	2	0	R	R	6-1	200	3-29-69	1988	Toa Alta, P.R.
Maddox, Garry	.351	25	94	20	33	3	2	3	14	5	20	3	2	L	R	6-3	180	10-24-74	1996	Philadelphia, Pa.
Makarewicz, Scott	.239	33	113	17	27	6	0	7	22	3	16	0	0	R	R	6-0	200	3-1-67	1989	Maitland, Fla.
Miller, Ryan	.307	102	293	36	90	20	0	3	26	9	43	6	4	R	R	6-0	175	10-22-72	1994	Tulare, Calif.
Mitchell, Donovan	.275	70	265	36	73	7	2	2	27	21	34	8	7	L	R	5-9	175	11-27-69	1992	White Plains, N.Y.
Neal, Mike	.326	103	341	53	111	27	2	17	70	39	80	4	4	R	R	6-1	180	11-5-71	1993	Hammond, La.
Owens, Billy	.264	53	159	18	42	6	0	6	28	13	17	1	1	B	R	6-1	210	4-12-71	1992	Phoenix, Ariz.
Perez, Jhonny	.285	130	439	65	125	20	0	10	39	45	72	22	11	R	R	5-10	180	10-23-76	1994	Santo Domingo, D.R.
Robles, Oscar	.200	4	5	0	1	0	0	0	0	1	1	0	0	L	R	5-11	155	4-9-76	1994	San Diego, Calif.
Sanchez, Victor	.276	117	439	65	121	29	1	23	80	21	100	4	3	R	R	5-10	180	9-20-71	1994	Stockton, Calif.
Saylor, Jamie	.292	122	462	80	135	21	6	17	66	39	91	15	10	L	R	5-11	185	9-11-74	1994	Garland, Texas
Trammell, Gary	.251	110	315	42	79	9	3	4	24	22	49	4	5	L	R	6-0	180	10-16-72	1993	Texarkana, Texas
Truby, Chris	.289	80	308	46	89	20	5	16	63	20	50	8	3	R	R	6-2	190	12-9-73	1993	Mukilteo, Wash.

PITCHING	W	L	ERA	G	GS	CG	SV	IP	H	R	ER	BB	SO	B	T	HT	WT	DOB	1st Yr	Resides
Adam, Dave	0	0	2.08	3	0	0	0	4	2	1	1	3	5	R	R	6-3	202	2-14-69	1990	Shelton, Conn.
Blais, Mike	1	2	3.08	21	0	0	1	38	40	15	13	8	37	R	R	6-5	226	10-2-71	1993	East Lyme, Conn.
Blanco, Alberto	4	4	5.76	12	12	0	0	59	65	43	38	24	60	L	L	6-1	200	6-27-76	1993	Miranda, Ven.
Diorio, Mike	2	3	2.09	32	0	0	11	43	35	16	10	21	31	R	R	6-2	200	3-1-73	1993	Pueblo, Colo.
Duncan, Sean	3	1	2.75	28	0	0	1	39	27	15	12	21	37	L	L	6-2	195	6-9-73	1994	Arlington, Texas
Garcia, Freddy	6	7	3.24	19	19	2	0	119	94	48	43	58	115	R	R	6-4	235	10-6-76	1994	Valencia, Ven.
Gutierrez, Jim	2	1	4.22	8	2	0	0	21	20	11	10	5	18	R	R	6-2	170	11-28-70	1989	Burlington, Wash.

PITCHING	W	L	ERA	G	GS	CG	SV	IP	H	R	ER	BB	SO	B	T	HT	WT	DOB	1st Yr	Resides
Hodges, Kevin	4	5	3.61	29	15	0	0	107	108	55	43	38	70	R	R	6-4	200	6-24-73	1991	Spring, Texas
Hook, Chris	2	5	6.49	15	7	0	1	43	43	36	31	30	33	R	R	6-5	195	8-4-68	1989	Florence, Ky.
2-team (15 Shreveport)	4	5	5.50	30	7	0	3	69	62	47	42	52	45							
Kester, Tim	5	5	4.19	55	0	0	6	86	90	47	40	19	51	R	R	6-4	190	12-1-71	1993	Coral Springs, Fla.
Lock, Dan	0	1	11.25	16	0	0	1	12	15	17	15	19	13	R	L	6-5	210	3-27-73	1994	Adrian, Mich.
Miller, Wade	5	0	[illegible]	10	10	0	0	62	49	23	16	27	48	R	R	6-2	185	9-13-76	1996	Reading, Pa.
Mounce, Tony	6	6	5.09	32	17	1	0	110	128	73	62	48	82	L	L	6-2	175	2-8-75	1994	Kennewick, Wash.
O'Malley, Paul	11	10	5.45	29	28	1	0	152	162	112	92	70	89	R	R	6-2	190	12-20-72	1994	Skokie, Ill.
Ramos, Edgar	2	4	6.10	17	6	0	0	49	61	34	33	12	47	R	R	6-4	170	3-6-75	1992	Cumana, Ven.
Root, Derek	4	1	3.89	7	6	0	0	44	46	24	19	17	31	L	L	6-5	215	5-26-75	1993	Lakewood, Ohio
Sikorski, Brian	6	4	4.07	15	15	0	0	97	83	50	44	44	80	R	R	6-1	190	7-27-74	1995	Roseville, Mich.
Slusarski, Joe	2	2	6.33	9	2	0	0	21	22	17	15	2	13	R	R	6-4	195	12-19-66	1989	Springfield, Ill.
Smith, Eric	1	0	5.59	6	0	0	0	10	9	6	6	5	11	R	R	6-0	185	5-17-74	1995	Garden City, Kan.
Smith, Lee	0	0	0.00	2	0	0	0	2	1	0	0	0	5	R	R	6-6	270	12-4-57	1975	Castor, La.
Wagner, Billy	0	0	0.00	3	1	0	0	3	1	0	0	0	7	L	L	5-11	180	7-25-71	1993	Pearland, Texas
Wallace, Kent	3	2	2.54	29	0	0	11	50	37	17	14	11	51	L	R	6-3	192	8-22-70	1992	Paducah, Ky.
Walter, Mike	1	7	4.66	38	0	0	3	48	48	31	25	22	55	R	R	6-1	190	10-23-74	1993	San Diego, Calif.

FIELDING

Catcher	PCT	G	PO	A	E	DP	PB
Amezcua	.985	21	121	12	2	2	4
Castro	.974	48	329	40	10	2	5
Lopez	.974	50	338	35	10	5	5
Makarewicz	.992	33	221	19	2	3	1

First Base	PCT	G	PO	A	E	DP
Lopez	1.000	1	1	0	0	0
Neal	.986	6	70	2	1	2
Owens	.985	27	246	17	4	16
Sanchez	.979	103	893	83	21	76
Trammell	1.000	2	14	2	0	1
Truby	1.000	8	43	6	0	3

Second Base	PCT	G	PO	A	E	DP
Miller	.961	38	50	72	5	14
Perez	.966	67	130	181	11	37
Robles	1.000	1	1	2	0	0
Saylor	.957	52	91	174	12	32

Third Base	PCT	G	PO	A	E	DP
Miller	.877	28	17	40	8	8
Neal	.893	55	22	78	12	4
Trammell	1.000	1	3	3	0	1
Truby	.932	70	51	155	15	15

Shortstop	PCT	G	PO	A	E	DP
Miller	.920	20	18	51	6	13
Neal	.915	34	48	70	11	19
Perez	.911	55	84	141	22	28
Saylor	.955	51	52	141	9	22

Outfield	PCT	G	PO	A	E	DP
Alexander	.977	119	197	18	5	1
Berkman	.980	118	183	9	4	4
Duffy	1.000	9	13	0	0	0
Johnson	.947	21	33	3	2	0
Maddox	1.000	23	38	2	0	1
Mitchell	.959	65	115	2	5	0
Neal	1.000	4	6	0	0	0
Saylor	.971	22	30	4	1	1
Trammell	.944	65	95	6	6	0

KISSIMMEE — Class A

FLORIDA STATE LEAGUE

BATTING	AVG	G	AB	R	H	2B	3B	HR	RBI	BB	SO	SB	CS	B	T	HT	WT	DOB	1st Yr	Resides
Adams, Jason	.250	84	268	31	67	11	2	5	32	21	57	1	3	R	R	5-11	195	11-3-73	1995	Rose Hill, Kan.
Alleyne, Roberto	.194	18	67	8	13	5	1	2	11	7	22	0	0	R	R	6-4	230	5-15-77	1994	Panama City, Panama
Amezcua, Adan	.275	72	262	40	72	19	1	8	35	22	43	2	0	R	R	6-1	195	3-9-74	1993	Mazatlan, Mexico
Barr, Tucker	.253	57	182	25	46	10	0	8	31	23	39	0	2	R	R	6-1	205	5-26-75	1996	Atlanta, Ga.
Burns, Kevin	.270	128	470	69	127	24	4	19	81	69	124	11	3	L	L	6-5	220	9-9-75	1995	El Dorado, Ark.
Chavera, Arnie	.301	84	269	46	81	17	0	12	50	35	64	0	0	L	R	5-10	195	9-24-73	1996	Arlington, Texas
Dallimore, Brian	.254	62	240	34	61	11	1	0	19	19	42	7	5	R	R	6-1	185	11-15-73	1996	Las Vegas, Nev.
Duffy, Jim	.188	24	80	7	15	2	0	1	8	4	29	1	1	R	R	6-2	195	7-18-74	1997	Andover, N.J.
Escalona, Felix	.000	3	4	0	0	0	0	0	0	0	1	0	0	R	R	6-0	185	3-12-79	1996	Puerto Cabello, Ven.
Farraez, Jesus	.242	44	132	18	32	2	1	1	11	14	36	4	0	R	R	6-3	190	10-18-72	1994	La Virginia, Ven.
Hyers, Matt	.182	10	22	4	4	1	0	0	2	4	3	0	1	B	R	5-10	170	8-8-75	1996	Covington, Ga.
Johnson, Ric	.270	103	381	67	103	17	2	6	45	34	48	20	8	R	R	6-2	185	3-18-74	1995	Chicago, Ill.
Lugo, Julio	.303	128	509	81	154	20	14	7	62	49	72	51	18	R	R	6-0	165	11-16-75	1995	Brooklyn, N.Y.
Owens, Billy	.182	10	33	4	6	0	0	2	4	4	7	0	0	B	R	6-1	210	4-12-71	1992	Phoenix, Ariz.
Parsons, Jeff	.247	34	97	11	24	2	1	0	10	15	15	5	1	R	R	5-10	165	11-16-73	1995	Shawnee, Okla.
2-team (27 St. Lucie)	.248	61	165	26	41	2	1	1	18	33	27	14	2							
Pratt, Wes	.254	19	67	9	17	2	0	1	10	6	12	1	3	R	R	6-3	195	3-5-73	1994	North East, Md.
Reeder, Jim	.228	73	228	32	52	11	3	0	24	15	30	7	1	L	R	6-1	200	3-18-75	1996	Evanston, Ill.
Robles, Oscar	.271	66	207	31	56	7	1	0	24	38	14	6	2	L	R	5-11	155	4-9-76	1994	San Diego, Calif.
Rodriguez, Noel	.245	15	53	6	13	3	0	1	8	5	3	0	0	R	R	6-3	180	12-5-73	1991	Yabucoa, P.R.
Rose, Mike	.226	18	62	9	14	4	0	3	9	8	14	1	0	B	R	6-1	185	8-25-76	1995	Sacramento, Calif.
Samboy, Nelson	.285	124	527	73	150	31	4	3	45	37	71	40	15	R	R	5-10	165	9-4-76	1994	Pedernales, D.R.
Truby, Chris	.311	52	212	36	66	16	1	14	48	19	30	6	1	R	R	6-2	190	12-9-73	1993	Mukilteo, Wash.
Vasquez, Alejandro	.053	6	19	0	1	0	0	0	0	1	9	1	0	L	L	5-11	190	7-5-77	1995	San Pedro de Macoris, D.R.
Velez, Jose	.277	98	329	38	91	11	3	3	42	18	30	6	7	B	L	6-1	160	3-6-73	1990	Mayaguez, P.R.

GAMES BY POSITION: C—Amezcua 66, Barr 48, Chavera 17, Rose 17. **1B**—Adams 8, Alleyne 1, Burns 127, Chavera 2, Owens 3. **2B**—Adams 10, Dallimore 11, Parsons 23, Robles 45, Samboy 59. **3B**—Adams 37, Dallimore 52, Escalona 1, Parsons 1, Robles 1, Samboy 1, Truby 51. **SS**—Adams 13, Hyers 7, Lugo 98, Parsons 8, Robles 21. **OF**—Alleyne 17, Duffy 23, Farraez 42, Johnson 103, Parsons 1, Pratt 19, Reeder 68, Rodriguez 15, Samboy 57, Vasquez 5, Velez 95.

PITCHING	W	L	ERA	G	GS	CG	SV	IP	H	R	ER	BB	SO	B	T	HT	WT	DOB	1st Yr	Resides
Blanco, Alberto	0	0	6.35	2	2	0	0	11	12	9	8	3	13	L	L	6-1	200	6-27-76	1993	Miranda, Ven.
Braswell, Bryan	11	9	3.95	27	26	2	0	160	176	92	70	48	118	L	L	6-1	200	6-30-75	1996	Springboro, Ohio
Duncan, Sean	2	0	3.31	23	0	0	2	33	29	13	12	17	20	L	L	6-2	195	6-9-73	1994	Arlington, Texas
Fereira, Ramon	0	0	0.00	1	0	0	0	0	2	3	3	1	0	R	R	6-1	165	2-24-79	1996	Valencia, Ven.
Garcia, Gabe	7	10	5.36	30	23	1	0	141	178	98	84	62	93	R	R	6-2	215	3-15-77	1996	Union City, Calif.
Green, Jason	2	5	3.34	51	3	0	14	67	64	34	25	32	67	R	R	6-4	190	6-5-75	1994	Port Hope, Ontario
Grzanich, Mike	1	1	6.14	4	0	0	0	7	9	7	5	5	8	R	R	6-1	180	8-24-72	1992	Champaign, Ill.
Holt, Chris	0	1	9.00	1	1	0	0	4	6	4	4	4	1	R	R	6-4	205	9-18-71	1992	Dallas, Texas
Love, Farley	0	0	4.61	11	0	0	0	14	14	9	7	12	17	R	R	6-6	200	4-21-73	1993	Eight Mile, Ala.
Love, Jeff	3	2	2.89	42	0	0	3	90	88	41	29	24	61	R	R	6-1	190	11-25-73	1996	Woodbridge, Conn.
Lynch, Jim	5	2	2.95	9	9	1	0	55	36	22	18	28	40	R	R	6-1	200	12-12-75	1994	Evansville, Ind.
Maldonado, Esteban	1	4	6.98	28	0	0	1	39	51	37	30	26	24	R	R	6-3	210	8-3-75	1996	Carolina, P.R.
McKnight, Tony	11	13	4.67	28	28	0	0	154	191	101	80	50	104	L	R	6-5	205	6-29-77	1995	Texarkana, Ark.
Mounce, Tony	1	2	6.92	5	5	0	0	26	35	22	20	13	15	L	L	6-2	175	2-8-75	1994	Kennewick, Wash.
Pascarella, Josh	0	0	2.45	2	0	0	0	4	7	3	1	2	0	R	R	5-11	180	11-11-76	1996	San Diego, Calif.

PITCHING	W	L	ERA	G	GS	CG	SV	IP	H	R	ER	BB	SO	B	T	HT	WT	DOB	1st Yr	Resides
Pipes, Joey	2	1	4.10	20	0	0	0	26	35	17	12	13	17	R	R	6-4	220	11-9-73	1998	Rolla, Mo.
Rijo, Jose	1	6	3.15	48	0	0	5	74	70	34	26	30	46	R	R	6-3	185	5-4-76	1993	La Romana, D.R.
Robertson, Jeromie	10	10	3.70	28	28	2	0	175	185	83	72	53	131	L	L	6-1	190	3-30-77	1996	Exeter, Calif.
Root, Derek	5	4	2.35	29	9	2	4	80	69	28	21	20	79	L	L	6-5	215	5-26-75	1993	Lakewood, Ohio
Schourek, Pete	0	0	1.08	2	1	0	0	8	8	1	1	4	9	L	L	6-5	205	5-10-69	1987	Clifton, Va.
Smith, Eric	2	3	6.35	9	4	0	0	28	37	22	20	16	14	R	R	6-0	185	5-17-74	1995	Garden City, Kan.
Stachler, Eric	0	2	14.90	7	0	0	0	10	17	16	16	9	9	R	R	6-3	215	4-18-73	1995	Coldwater, Ohio
Wallace, Jim	0	0	4.15	4	0	0	0	4	2	2	2	10	3	R	R	6-4	195	10-13-75	1997	Wantagh, N.Y.

QUAD CITY — Class A

MIDWEST LEAGUE

BATTING	AVG	G	AB	R	H	2B	3B	HR	RBI	BB	SO	SB	CS	B	T	HT	WT	DOB	1st Yr	Resides
Alleyne, Roberto	.234	76	248	39	58	14	2	8	33	25	73	5	2	R	R	6-4	230	5-15-77	1994	Panama City, Panama
Cathey, Joseph	.233	114	399	57	93	15	2	2	28	35	84	19	14	B	R	5-11	175	3-2-76	1997	Spring, Texas
Chapman, Scott	.238	82	277	28	66	14	1	5	28	9	67	7	5	L	R	6-2	200	1-30-78	1995	Albany, Ohio
Cole, Eric	.280	132	500	73	140	30	6	11	83	24	104	32	15	R	R	6-0	185	11-15-75	1995	Lancaster, Calif.
Cutshall, Pat	.246	114	422	52	104	20	3	5	54	33	44	15	11	R	R	5-9	175	10-29-74	1997	Beaver Falls, Pa.
Duffy, Jim	.260	37	123	16	32	8	0	3	17	9	34	5	0	R	R	6-2	195	7-18-74	1997	Andover, N.J.
Hyers, Matt	.238	58	122	22	29	6	1	0	15	20	28	8	5	B	R	5-10	170	8-8-75	1996	Covington, Ga.
Logan, Kyle	.264	110	352	50	93	22	2	4	49	36	50	22	13	L	R	6-0	196	7-11-75	1997	Hattiesburg, Miss.
Mansavage, Jay	.216	85	268	31	58	16	0	1	19	19	67	13	2	B	R	6-1	185	7-11-75	1996	Riverwoods, Ill.
McNeal, Aaron	.284	112	370	54	105	15	1	14	61	31	112	3	3	R	R	6-3	230	4-28-78	1996	Castro Valley, Calif.
Miles, Aaron	.244	108	369	42	90	22	6	2	37	25	52	28	13	B	R	5-8	170	12-15-76	1995	Antioch, Calif.
Murray, Doug	.212	21	33	4	7	0	0	1	3	1	10	0	0	L	R	6-3	215	10-9-74	1996	Orland Park, Ill.
Ochoa, Javier	.000	5	7	1	0	0	0	0	0	1	2	0	0	R	R	6-1	170	1-8-79	1996	Maracay, Ven.
Rose, Mike	.303	88	267	48	81	13	2	7	40	52	56	10	8	B	R	6-1	185	8-25-76	1995	Sacramento, Calif.
Thomas, Jim	.257	103	342	67	88	14	2	21	69	58	115	8	3	R	R	6-4	215	9-18-75	1997	Atlanta, Ga.
Vasquez, Alejandro	.114	18	35	2	4	0	0	1	5	2	4	0	1	L	L	5-11	190	7-5-77	1995	San Pedro de Macoris, D.R.
Wesson, Barry	.252	138	493	71	124	21	2	7	43	32	90	22	12	R	R	6-2	195	4-6-77	1995	Brandon, Miss.

GAMES BY POSITION: C—Chapman 57, Mansavage 1, Murray 20, Ochoa 5, Rose 81. **1B**—Alleyne 16, Duffy 3, Hyers 1, McNeal 102, Thomas 31. **2B**—Hyers 2, Mansavage 44, Miles 101. **3B**—Cathey 1, Cutshall 111, Hyers 7, Mansavage 30, Miles 1. **SS**—Cathey 112, Hyers 35, Mansavage 5. **OF**—Alleyne 38, Cole 131, Duffy 22, Logan 106, Miles 1, Rose 2, Vasquez 10, Wesson 138.

PITCHING	W	L	ERA	G	GS	CG	SV	IP	H	R	ER	BB	SO	B	T	HT	WT	DOB	1st Yr	Resides
Hamulack, Tim	0	2	3.24	52	0	0	0	58	58	23	21	26	52	L	L	6-4	215	11-14-76	1996	Edgewood, Md.
Hecht, Brian	3	6	3.41	61	0	0	22	74	63	33	28	27	66	R	R	6-4	205	11-20-77	1997	Arlington Heights, Ill.
Ireland, Eric	14	9	2.88	29	28	6	0	206	172	80	66	71	191	R	R	6-1	170	3-11-77	1996	Long Beach, Calif.
Lidge, Brad	0	1	3.27	4	4	0	0	11	10	5	4	5	6	R	R	6-3	200	12-23-76	1998	Englewood, Calif.
Love, Farley	4	2	0.90	13	0	0	3	20	6	4	2	13	30	R	R	6-6	200	4-21-73	1993	Eight Mile, Ala.
Lynch, Jim	8	6	3.39	20	17	0	0	101	80	47	38	58	97	R	R	6-1	200	12-12-75	1994	Evansville, Ind.
McCarter, Jason	5	4	4.61	47	0	0	4	70	59	41	36	39	55	R	R	6-3	210	9-26-76	1996	Seaside, Calif.
McFerrin, Chris	2	0	3.76	29	0	0	2	38	25	21	16	41	35	L	R	6-5	190	6-30-76	1995	Clovis, Calif.
Mercedes, Carlos	8	12	4.49	31	24	1	0	148	146	88	74	52	99	R	R	6-0	175	3-29-76	1994	El Seibo, D.R.
Messman, Joe	6	3	3.08	63	0	0	5	88	70	36	30	33	74	R	R	6-2	175	7-29-75	1997	Parkdale, Ore.
Ridley, Brian	0	0	5.14	8	0	0	0	7	6	4	4	1	7	B	L	5-11	180	11-11-74	1998	Waterloo, N.Y.
Rodriguez, Wilfredo	11	5	3.05	28	27	1	0	165	122	70	56	62	170	L	L	6-3	180	3-20-79	1996	San Felix, Ven.
Ryan, Jeremy	1	0	3.27	3	2	0	0	11	6	4	4	3	8	R	R	6-4	185	1-18-78	1998	Kansas City, Mo.
Santana, Johan	0	1	9.45	2	1	0	0	7	14	7	7	3	6	L	L	6-0	155	3-13-79	1996	Tovar, Ven.
Shearn, Tom	7	7	2.25	21	21	2	0	120	88	38	30	52	93	R	R	6-4	200	8-28-77	1994	Columbus, Ohio
Smith, Brandon	3	1	4.21	8	5	0	0	36	27	17	17	9	29	R	R	6-1	205	4-10-76	1998	Tyler, Texas
Wallace, Jim	0	0	15.43	8	1	0	0	7	4	12	12	13	3	R	R	6-4	195	10-13-75	1997	Wantagh, N.Y.
Zyskowski, Garrett	5	3	3.67	14	9	0	0	54	45	28	22	24	45	L	L	6-1	185	9-3-75	1998	Utica, N.Y.

AUBURN — Short-Season Class A

NEW YORK-PENN LEAGUE

BATTING	AVG	G	AB	R	H	2B	3B	HR	RBI	BB	SO	SB	CS	B	T	HT	WT	DOB	1st Yr	Resides
Buckley, Brandon	.224	26	76	5	17	4	0	0	9	12	13	0	1	R	R	6-1	200	1-25-77	1998	Danville, Calif.
Byrd, Brandon	.207	32	121	12	25	2	0	3	12	5	50	0	0	R	R	6-6	240	5-22-78	1996	Montgomery, Ala.
Carter, Charley	.330	61	218	32	72	24	1	8	42	22	35	1	1	R	R	6-2	205	12-11-75	1998	Mount Pleasant, Texas
Deshazer, Jeremy	.200	9	20	2	4	1	0	0	1	0	6	0	0	B	R	5-10	175	8-18-76	1995	Kirkland, Wash.
Dimmick, Josh	.275	13	40	5	11	4	0	0	6	3	8	0	0	B	R	6-3	225	5-5-76	1998	Wharton, Texas
Dunn, Ryan	.182	34	110	18	20	5	0	3	22	16	39	1	1	L	R	6-2	195	7-4-76	1997	Arlington, Texas
Ensberg, Morgan	.230	59	196	39	45	10	1	5	31	46	51	15	3	R	R	6-2	210	8-26-75	1998	Redondo Beach, Calif.
Escalona, Felix	.208	51	149	22	31	5	0	1	17	11	33	4	2	R	R	6-0	185	3-12-79	1996	Puerto Cabello, Ven.
Fatheree, Danny	.260	52	196	26	51	10	0	2	27	19	40	1	4	R	R	5-11	232	8-25-78	1997	Grand Prairie, Texas
Ginter, Keith	.315	71	241	55	76	22	1	8	41	60	68	10	7	R	R	5-10	190	5-5-76	1998	Fullerton, Calif.
Jordan, Kevin	.232	53	181	29	42	8	4	2	28	10	41	6	3	R	R	6-1	190	9-7-76	1998	Midland, Texas
Joyce, Jesse	.306	41	144	27	44	9	4	2	19	9	26	4	1	R	R	5-11	185	5-12-76	1998	Highland, Calif.
Matranga, David	.306	40	144	34	44	13	1	4	24	25	38	16	3	R	R	5-11	170	1-8-77	1998	Orange, Calif.
Nicholson, Derek	.310	50	168	28	52	9	1	4	34	23	34	3	2	L	R	5-11	205	6-17-76	1998	Redondo Beach, Calif.
Porter, Colin	.283	67	240	40	68	18	4	4	30	19	61	14	11	L	L	6-2	205	11-23-75	1998	Tucson, Ariz.
Yates, Chris	.254	67	224	40	57	6	5	0	24	21	48	26	11	R	L	6-0	165	8-24-75	1997	Eupora, Miss.

GAMES BY POSITION: C—Buckley 26, Dimmick 9, Fatheree 44. **1B**—Byrd 19, Carter 59, Nicholson 1. **2B**—Escalona 8, Ginter 71, Joyce 1. **3B**—Ensberg 58, Escalona 3, Jordan 2, Joyce 14. **SS**—Ensberg 1, Escalona 39, Matranga 40. **OF**—Deshazer 7, Dunn 17, Jordan 36, Joyce 18, Nicholson 38, Porter 60, Yates 65.

PITCHING	W	L	ERA	G	GS	CG	SV	IP	H	R	ER	BB	SO	B	T	HT	WT	DOB	1st Yr	Resides
Barrett, Scott	2	4	5.88	10	10	0	0	49	49	33	32	27	58	L	L	5-10	175	11-18-78	1998	Houston, Texas
Blackmore, John	5	2	4.69	19	1	0	0	56	49	31	29	25	42	R	R	6-3	200	11-5-77	1996	Plainville, Conn.
Oswalt, Roy	4	5	2.18	11	11	0	0	70	49	24	17	31	67	R	R	6-0	170	8-29-77	1997	Weir, Miss.
Pascarella, Josh	1	3	8.42	15	3	0	0	31	48	32	29	16	20	R	R	5-11	180	11-11-76	1996	San Diego, Calif.
Peguero, Darwin	5	4	2.80	20	6	0	0	64	53	30	20	31	86	B	L	6-0	165	12-5-78	1996	Hato Mayor, D.R.

PITCHING	W	L	ERA	G	GS	CG	SV	IP	H	R	ER	BB	SO	B	T	HT	WT	DOB	1st Yr	Resides
Pineda, Jairo	0	0	1.50	1	1	0	0	6	5	1	1	0	5	R	R	6-3	185	9-25-76	1997	Granada, Nicaragua
Redding, Tim	7	3	4.52	16	15	0	1	74	49	44	37	50	98	R	R	6-0	182	2-12-78	1998	Rochester, N.Y.
Ridley, Brian	3	0	3.75	17	0	0	0	24	23	12	10	9	27	B	L	5-11	180	11-11-74	1998	Waterloo, N.Y.
Rosario, Rodrigo	0	0	0.00	2	0	0	0	2	0	0	0	3	2	R	R	6-2	160	12-14-79	1996	La Romana, D.R.
Santana, Johan	7	5	4.36	15	15	1	0	87	81	52	42	21	88	L	L	6-0	155	3-13-79	1996	Tovar, Ven.
[illegible], Doug	1	0	[illegible]	[illegible]	0	0	11	21	[illegible]	10	[illegible]	10	[illegible]	R	R	6-1	[illegible]	[illegible]	1998	Orange Park, Fla.
Smith, Brandon	0	1	2.20	13	0	0	4	29	26	13	7	12	30	R	R	6-1	205	4-10-76	1998	Tyler, Texas
Sullivan, Peter	1	0	4.88	17	0	0	1	24	28	17	13	14	20	R	R	6-5	225	9-10-74	1997	Coral Gables, Fla.
Terwilliger, Rich	0	0	9.00	2	0	0	0	3	6	3	3	0	2	R	R	6-3	180	9-7-78	1998	Corning, N.Y.
Whitney, Jacob	5	5	2.98	18	13	0	0	85	92	42	28	16	64	L	L	6-1	195	5-23-76	1998	Edina, Minn.
Zyskowski, Garrett	2	0	0.00	5	0	0	0	12	5	4	0	8	9	L	L	6-1	185	9-3-75	1998	Utica, N.Y.

KISSIMMEE — Rookie

GULF COAST LEAGUE

BATTING	AVG	G	AB	R	H	2B	3B	HR	RBI	BB	SO	SB	CS	B	T	HT	WT	DOB	1st Yr	Resides
Alfaro, Jason	.242	47	178	20	43	8	0	1	18	11	24	5	5	R	R	5-10	189	11-29-77	1997	Fort Worth, Texas
Buck, John	.286	36	126	24	36	9	0	3	15	13	22	2	2	R	R	6-3	200	7-7-80	1998	Salt Lake City, Utah
Bystrowski, Robert	.149	41	134	20	20	5	0	2	14	16	37	8	4	R	R	6-1	210	9-27-76	1997	Sacramento, Calif.
Carrillo, Robert	.158	36	114	8	18	4	0	0	7	8	52	0	1	R	R	6-6	260	5-9-79	1998	San Diego, Calif.
Casilla, Luis	.212	25	66	2	14	3	0	0	10	5	20	1	3	R	R	5-11	180	4-30-79	1997	Bani, D.R.
De Aza, Modesto	.238	42	151	25	36	9	1	1	12	14	51	23	5	R	R	5-11	150	2-14-79	1996	La Romana, D.R.
De los Santos, Eddy	.135	27	74	3	10	2	0	0	8	4	32	1	2	R	R	6-1	160	12-30-78	1996	San Pedro de Macoris, D.R.
Dominguez, Luis	.282	31	110	9	31	3	1	0	13	15	17	5	8	R	R	6-0	165	3-9-80	1996	Maracay, Ven.
Linares, Rodney	.079	14	38	1	3	0	0	0	0	4	17	0	1	R	R	5-11	180	8-7-77	1997	Brooklyn, N.Y.
Ochoa, Javier	.212	34	85	7	18	2	1	0	6	14	15	1	2	R	R	6-1	170	1-8-79	1996	Maracay, Ven.
Pellicciotta, Marc	.209	36	110	14	23	3	0	2	12	8	20	3	0	R	R	5-10	180	11-30-76	1998	Berwyn, Pa.
Ramirez, Anthony	.354	20	65	8	23	4	0	0	9	7	13	3	2	L	R	6-1	200	7-21-80	1998	Carson, Calif.
Turnquist, Tyler	.283	56	219	31	62	15	4	1	29	14	23	6	5	R	R	5-11	190	11-10-75	1998	Naperville, Ill.
Vasquez, Alejandro	.335	57	209	31	70	20	2	3	23	21	34	7	7	L	L	5-11	190	7-5-77	1995	San Pedro de Macoris, D.R.
Vega, Jonathan	.200	50	180	17	36	3	2	5	25	17	62	3	3	R	R	6-3	175	3-2-79	1996	Aguadulce, Panama
Zapata, Juan	.275	50	182	17	50	10	1	0	3	10	31	5	5	R	R	5-11	160	5-30-78	1996	San Pedro de Macoris, D.R.

GAMES BY POSITION: C—Buck 26, Casilla 18, Ochoa 29, Pellicciotta 1. **1B**—Carrillo 36, Casilla 2, Dominguez 1, Turnquist 27, Vega 1. **2B**—de Aza 39, Linares 3, Pellicciotta 25. **3B**—de los Santos 4, Dominguez 27, Ramirez 14, Turnquist 19, Vega 1. **SS**—Alfaro 45, de los Santos 21, Linares 1, Vasquez 1. **OF**—Alfaro 1, Bystrowski 38, Dominguez 1, Ochoa 1, Ramirez 1, Turnquist 8, Vasquez 54, Vega 37, Zapata 49.

PITCHING	W	L	ERA	G	GS	CG	SV	IP	H	R	ER	BB	SO	B	T	HT	WT	DOB	1st Yr	Resides
Aguilar, Edwin	3	7	7.86	14	9	1	1	53	69	49	46	31	60	R	R	6-2	165	3-18-80	1996	Sarare, Ven.
Calvo, Jose	0	2	3.91	13	0	0	1	23	22	12	10	7	18	R	R	6-3	180	1-14-80	1996	Chame, Panama
Centeno, Juan	4	6	3.79	21	0	0	0	40	59	35	17	5	27	R	R	6-4	190	2-24-78	1996	San Neguilto, Panama
Fereira, Ramon	1	1	5.40	16	0	0	4	22	27	15	13	6	20	R	R	6-1	165	2-24-79	1996	Valencia, Ven.
Love, Farley	0	0	4.50	1	0	0	0	2	2	1	1	1	1	R	R	6-6	200	4-21-73	1993	Eight Mile, Ala.
Nannini, Mike	1	1	1.49	8	6	1	0	36	23	6	6	13	39	R	R	5-11	175	8-9-80	1998	Henderson, Nev.
Oswalt, Roy	1	1	2.25	4	4	0	0	16	10	6	4	1	27	R	R	6-0	170	8-29-77	1997	Weir, Miss.
Pineda, Jairo	2	6	3.93	12	12	1	0	73	74	45	32	17	83	R	R	6-3	185	9-25-76	1997	Granada, Nicaragua
Pipes, Joey	0	0	1.23	4	0	0	1	7	5	1	1	2	7	R	R	6-4	220	11-9-73	1998	Rolla, Mo.
Rosario, Rodrigo	2	2	4.12	13	12	0	0	68	61	36	31	30	65	R	R	6-2	160	12-14-79	1996	La Romana, D.R.
Ryan, Jeremy	1	0	1.69	4	4	0	0	16	7	4	3	0	18	R	R	6-4	185	1-18-78	1998	Kansas City, Mo.
Stanford, Derek	2	4	4.27	12	11	0	0	53	53	32	25	25	52	R	R	6-2	190	9-6-78	1998	Temple, Texas
Terwilliger, Rich	1	2	4.45	12	0	0	1	28	34	16	14	12	31	R	R	6-3	180	9-7-78	1998	Corning, N.Y.
Wallace, Jim	1	1	4.70	13	0	0	1	31	29	18	16	9	26	R	R	6-4	195	10-13-75	1997	Wantagh, N.Y.
Walter, Mike	0	0	0.00	3	0	0	1	4	2	0	0	1	6	R	R	6-1	190	10-23-74	1993	San Diego, Calif.
Wheeler, Mike	0	1	3.60	4	0	0	0	5	8	2	2	2	5	R	R	6-1	175	10-25-77	1996	Cincinnati, Ohio
Wilkerson, Byron	3	3	4.67	18	2	0	0	52	49	35	27	24	54	R	R	6-4	205	8-15-76	1998	Temple, Texas

KANSAS CITY ROYALS

Royals escape basement with best finish since 1995

BY ALAN ESKEW

The Kansas City Royals took small steps forward in 1998, finishing third in the American League Central Division while winning five more games than in 1997. It was the first time since 1995 they did not land in the basement.

The first order of business in 1999 will be improving on the major leagues' worst home record. The Royals had a disappointing 29-51 home record—the worst in club history—and were outscored 492-353 at Kauffman Stadium.

On the road the Royals were solid, going 43-38. Only the New York Yankees won more away games in the AL than the Royals.

The club sorely missed righthander Kevin Appier's presence in the rotation. Appier made just three September starts after having shoulder surgery in March. Tim Belcher, who went 14-14 with a 4.27 ERA, was the closest thing the team had to an ace.

Offensively, third baseman Dean Palmer, an All-Star Game selection, and second baseman Jose Offerman had career years. Palmer hit .278 with 34 homers and 119 RBIs. Hal McRae, who had 133 RBIs in 1982, is the only Royal to have more RBIs in a season. Offerman set career highs in nearly every offensive category. Both, however, were free agents and may have priced themselves out of the Royals' market with their strong seasons.

Johnny Damon matured into a .277 hitter with 30 doubles, 10 triples, 18 home runs and 26 stolen bases in his third full season in the majors. He may be joined in the outfield in 1999 by rookies Carlos Beltran and Jeremy Giambi, who had breakthrough 1998 seasons in the minors.

Dean Palmer

Jeremy Giambi

Players of the Year

Major League: Dean Palmer, 3b

Palmer was the Royals' most consistent power threat and led the team with 34 homers and 119 RBIs.

Minor League: Jeremy Giambi, of, Omaha

Giambi's .372 average and .469 on-base percentage led all of the minor leagues in 1998.

Giambi led the minor leagues with a .372 batting average and was named the Pacific Coast League's rookie of the year. Beltran hit .352 with 14 homers and 44 RBIs in 47 games with Double-A Wichita after starting the 1998 season with Class A Wilmington.

Second baseman Carlos Febles also will be in the running for a job. Febles, a slick fielder, hit .326 with Wichita and led the Texas League with 51 stolen bases.

■ The farm system was highlighted by Wilmington winning the Carolina League championship. The record of the six minor league affiliates was 390-309, which tied the Blue Jays for the top organizational winning percentage at .558.

■ Triple-A Omaha outfielder Chris Hatcher led the minor leagues with 46 home runs. Omaha finished second in team homers with 215.

■ The Royals will move their low Class A affiliate from Lansing in the Midwest League to Charleston, W.Va., in the South Atlantic League in 1999.

■ The lowlight of the major league season came in a June 2 loss to the Angels, which included two bench-clearing brawls, five hit batters and a dozen ejections. AL president Gene Budig came down hard on manager Tony Muser, suspending him for eight games. Shortstop Felix Martinez, who threw a sucker-punch that prolonged the fights, drew a five-game suspension. Martinez had found controversy earlier in the season when he kicked Twins outfielder Otis Nixon in the jaw during a play at second base. He was banished to the minors after the June brawl.

■ The club has been without an owner since the 1993 death of founder Ewing Kauffman. New York lawyer Miles Prentice emerged as the front-runner to purchase the club.

ORGANIZATION LEADERS

BATTING		
*AVG	Jeremy Giambi, Omaha	.372
R	Carlos Febles, Wichita	110
H	Chris Hatcher, Omaha	150
TB	Chris Hatcher, Omaha	313
2B	Two tied at	31
3B	Two tied at	9
HR	Chris Hatcher, Omaha	46
RBI	Chris Hatcher, Omaha	106
BB	Carlos Febles, Wichita	80
SO	Juan LeBron, Lansing	129
SB	Carlos Febles, Wichita	51
PITCHING		
W	Scott Mullen, Wichita/Wilmington	16
L	Two tied at	11
#ERA	Lance Carter, Wilmington/Lansing	2.14
G	Allen McDill, Omaha	61
CG	Aaron Lineweaver, Wilmington	5
SV	Bart Evans, Omaha	27
IP	Aaron Lineweaver, Wilmington	168
BB	Phil Grundy, Omaha/Wichita	75
SO	Chad Durbin, Wilmington	162

*Minimum 250 At-Bats #Minimum 75 Innings

Kansas City ROYALS

Manager: Tony Muser

1998 Record: 72-89, .444 (3rd, AL Central)

BATTING	AVG	G	AB	R	H	2B	3B	HR	RBI	BB	SO	SB	CS	B	T	HT	WT	DOB	1st Yr	Resides
Allensworth, Jermaine	.205	30	73	15	15	5	0	0	3	9	17	7	0	R	R	6-0	190	1-11-72	1993	Anderson, Ind.
Beltran, Carlos	.276	14	58	12	16	5	3	0	7	3	12	3	0	B	R	6-0	175	4-24-77	1995	Manati, P.R.
Brown, Dermal	.000	5	3	2	0	0	0	0	0	0	1	0	0	L	R	5-11	210	3-27-78	1996	Orlando, Fla.
Conine, Jeff	.256	93	309	30	79	26	0	8	43	26	68	3	0	R	R	6-1	220	6-27-66	1988	Weston, Fla.
Damon, Johnny	.277	161	642	104	178	30	10	18	66	58	84	26	12	L	L	6-2	190	11-5-73	1992	Overland Park, Kan.
Dye, Jermaine	.234	60	214	24	50	5	1	5	23	11	46	2	2	R	R	6-4	220	1-28-74	1993	Leawood, Kan.
Fasano, Sal	.227	74	216	21	49	10	0	8	31	10	56	1	0	R	R	6-2	220	8-10-71	1993	Joliet, Ill.
Febles, Carlos	.400	11	25	5	10	1	2	0	2	4	7	2	1	R	R	5-11	170	5-24-76	1994	La Romana, D.R.
Giambi, Jeremy	.224	18	58	6	13	4	0	2	8	11	9	0	1	L	L	6-0	185	9-30-74	1996	Covina, Calif.
Halter, Shane	.221	86	204	17	45	12	0	2	13	12	38	2	5	R	R	6-0	180	11-8-69	1991	Overland Park, Kan.
Hansen, Jed	.000	4	3	0	0	0	0	0	0	0	3	0	0	R	R	6-1	195	8-19-72	1994	Olympia, Wash.
Hatcher, Chris	.067	8	15	0	1	0	0	0	1	1	7	0	0	R	R	6-3	220	1-7-69	1990	Carter Lake, Iowa
King, Jeff	.263	131	486	83	128	17	1	24	93	42	73	10	2	R	R	6-1	190	12-26-64	1986	Hamilton, Mont.
Leius, Scott	.174	17	46	2	8	0	0	0	4	1	6	0	0	R	R	6-3	208	9-24-65	1986	Minnetonka, Minn.
Lopez, Mendy	.243	74	206	18	50	10	2	1	15	12	40	5	2	R	R	6-2	190	10-15-74	1992	Santo Domingo, D.R.
Mack, Shane	.280	66	207	30	58	15	1	6	29	15	36	8	2	R	R	6-0	190	12-7-63	1985	Las Vegas, Nev.
2-team (3 Oakland)	.278	69	209	31	58	15	1	6	29	15	36	8	2							
Macfarlane, Mike	.091	3	11	1	1	0	0	0	0	0	2	0	0	R	R	6-1	210	4-12-64	1985	Overland Park, Kan.
Martinez, Felix	.129	34	85	7	11	1	1	0	5	5	21	3	1	B	R	6-0	180	5-18-74	1993	Nagua, D.R.
Morris, Hal	.309	127	472	50	146	27	2	1	40	32	52	1	0	L	L	6-2	195	4-9-65	1986	Orlando, Fla.
Offerman, Jose	.315	158	607	102	191	28	13	7	66	89	96	45	12	B	R	6-0	190	11-8-68	1988	San Pedro de Macoris, D.R.
Ortiz, Hector	.000	4	4	1	0	0	0	0	0	0	0	0	0	R	R	6-0	205	10-14-69	1988	Canovanas, P.R.
Palmer, Dean	.278	152	572	84	159	27	2	34	119	48	134	8	2	R	R	6-2	210	12-27-68	1986	Tallahassee, Fla.
Pendleton, Terry	.257	79	237	17	61	10	0	3	29	15	49	1	0	B	R	5-9	195	7-16-60	1982	Duluth, Ga.
Rivera, Luis	.247	42	89	14	22	4	0	0	7	7	17	1	1	R	R	5-10	172	1-3-64	1982	Cidra, P.R.
Rossy, Rico	.000	1	0	0	0	0	0	0	0	0	0	0	0	R	R	5-10	175	2-16-64	1985	Bayamon, P.R.
Spehr, Tim	.240	11	25	5	6	2	0	1	2	8	3	0	0	R	R	6-2	200	7-2-66	1988	Dallas, Texas
Sutton, Larry	.245	111	310	29	76	14	2	5	42	29	46	3	3	L	L	6-0	185	5-14-70	1992	Temecula, Calif.
Sweeney, Mike	.259	92	282	32	73	18	0	8	35	24	38	2	3	R	R	6-2	215	7-22-73	1991	Ontario, Calif.
Turner, Chris	.000	4	9	0	0	0	0	0	0	0	4	0	0	R	R	6-3	200	3-23-69	1991	Bowling Green, Ky.
Vitiello, Joe	.143	3	7	0	1	0	0	0	0	1	2	0	0	R	R	6-3	230	4-11-70	1991	Stoneham, Mass.
Young, Ernie	.189	25	53	2	10	3	0	1	3	2	9	2	1	R	R	6-1	234	7-8-69	1990	Mesa. Ariz.

PITCHING	W	L	ERA	G	GS	CG	SV	IP	H	R	ER	BB	SO	B	T	HT	WT	DOB	1st Yr	Resides
Appier, Kevin	1	2	7.80	3	3	0	0	15	21	13	13	5	9	R	R	6-2	200	12-6-67	1987	Paola, Kan.
Barber, Brian	2	4	6.00	8	8	0	0	42	45	28	28	13	24	R	R	6-1	190	3-4-73	1991	Orlando, Fla.
Belcher, Tim	14	14	4.27	34	34	2	0	234	247	127	111	73	130	R	R	6-3	225	10-19-61	1984	Mount Gilead, Ohio
Bevil, Brian	3	1	6.30	39	0	0	0	40	47	29	28	22	47	R	R	6-4	225	9-5-71	1991	Houston, Texas
Bones, Ricky	2	2	3.04	32	0	0	1	53	49	18	18	24	38	R	R	6-0	202	4-7-69	1986	Guayama, P.R.
Byrdak, Tim	0	0	5.40	3	0	0	0	2	5	1	1	0	1	L	L	5-11	170	10-31-73	1994	Oak Forest, Ill.
Evans, Bart	0	0	2.00	8	0	0	0	9	7	3	2	0	7	R	R	6-2	210	12-30-70	1992	Ozark, Mo.
Haney, Chris	6	6	7.03	33	12	0	0	97	125	78	76	36	51	L	L	6-3	210	11-16-68	1990	Barboursville, Va.
McDill, Allen	0	0	10.50	7	0	0	0	6	9	7	7	2	3	L	L	6-1	155	8-23-71	1992	Hot Springs, Ark.
Montgomery, Jeff	2	5	4.98	56	0	0	36	56	58	35	31	22	54	R	R	5-11	175	1-7-62	1983	Leawood, Kan.
Pichardo, Hipolito	7	8	5.13	27	18	0	1	112	126	73	64	43	55	R	R	6-1	195	8-22-69	1988	Esperanza, D.R.
Pittsley, Jim	1	1	6.59	39	2	0	0	68	88	56	50	37	44	R	R	6-7	220	4-3-74	1992	Dubois, Pa.
Rapp, Pat	12	13	5.30	32	32	1	0	188	208	117	111	107	132	R	R	6-3	215	7-13-67	1989	Sulphur, La.
Rios, Danny	0	1	6.14	5	0	0	0	7	9	9	5	6	6	R	R	6-2	192	11-11-72	1993	Hialeah, Fla.
Rosado, Jose	8	11	4.69	38	25	2	1	175	180	106	91	57	135	L	L	6-0	185	11-9-74	1994	Monte Lindo, P.R.
Rusch, Glendon	6	15	5.88	29	24	1	1	155	191	104	101	50	94	L	L	6-1	195	11-7-74	1993	Seattle, Wash.
Santiago, Jose	0	0	9.00	2	0	0	0	2	4	2	2	0	2	R	R	6-3	215	11-5-74	1994	Loiza, P.R.
Service, Scott	6	4	3.48	73	0	0	4	83	70	35	32	34	95	R	R	6-6	230	2-26-67	1986	Cincinnati, Ohio
Suppan, Jeff	0	0	0.71	4	1	0	0	13	9	1	1	1	12	R	R	6-2	210	1-2-75	1993	West Hills, Calif.
Walker, Jamie	0	1	9.87	6	2	0	0	17	30	20	19	3	15	L	L	6-2	190	7-1-71	1992	McMinnville, Tenn.
Whisenant, Matt	2	1	4.90	70	0	0	2	61	61	37	33	33	45	R	L	6-3	215	6-8-71	1990	La Canada, Calif.

FIELDING

Catcher	PCT	G	PO	A	E	DP	PB
Fasano	.996	70	421	25	2	5	2
Macfarlane	1.000	3	13	3	0	1	0
Ortiz	1.000	3	4	0	0	0	0
Spehr	1.000	11	62	2	0	0	0
Sweeney	.984	91	517	33	9	7	9
Turner	1.000	4	16	0	0	0	0

First Base	PCT	G	PO	A	E	DP
Conine	1.000	12	101	3	0	15
Fasano	1.000	5	16	0	0	2
Halter	1.000	1	2	0	0	0
King	.995	112	932	85	5	103
Morris	.990	46	349	34	4	35
Ortiz	.000	1	0	0	0	0
Sutton	1.000	6	32	3	0	5

Second Base	PCT	G	PO	A	E	DP
Febles	1.000	11	16	18	0	2
Halter	.909	6	2	8	1	0
Hansen	1.000	2	1	0	0	0
Martinez	.000	2	0	0	0	0
Offerman	.974	152	278	440	19	112
Rivera	1.000	6	5	6	0	0

Third Base	PCT	G	PO	A	E	DP
Fasano	.000	1	0	0	0	0
Halter	1.000	8	1	3	0	0
King	1.000	4	3	6	0	2
Leius	.867	15	8	18	4	2
Lopez	1.000	2	1	4	0	0
Palmer	.920	129	69	185	22	16
Pendleton	.957	23	12	32	2	1
Rivera	1.000	6	1	3	0	0

Shortstop	PCT	G	PO	A	E	DP
Halter	.964	66	73	166	9	28
Leius	1.000	2	0	1	0	0
Lopez	.955	72	101	221	15	53
Martinez	.956	32	49	80	6	23
Rivera	.961	30	41	81	5	20

Outfield	PCT	G	PO	A	E	DP
Allensworth	.982	27	54	0	1	0
Beltran	.978	14	44	0	1	0
Brown	1.000	2	1	0	0	0
Conine	.993	80	134	4	1	0
Damon	.990	158	371	10	4	1
Dye	.987	59	153	4	2	3
Giambi	1.000	9	14	1	0	0
Halter	1.000	9	13	0	0	0
Hatcher	1.000	5	7	0	0	0
Mack	.982	32	54	1	1	1
Morris	1.000	39	47	1	0	0
Sutton	.987	79	147	4	2	1
Young	1.000	24	43	2	0	0

JOHN WILLIAMSON

Kansas City's Johnny Damon
Led team with 104 runs scored

JIM McLEAN

Outfielder Carlos Beltran
Hit .352 after promotion to Double-A Wichita

FARM SYSTEM

Director, Minor League Operations: Bob Hegman

Class	Farm Team	League	W	L	Pct.	Finish*	Manager(s)	First Yr
AAA	Omaha (Neb.) Royals	Pacific Coast	79	64	.552	t-4th (16)	Ron Johnson	1969
AA	Wichita (Kan.) Wranglers	Texas	75	65	.536	3rd (8)	John Mizerock	1995
A#	Wilmington (Del.) Blue Rocks	Carolina	86	54	.614	+1st (8)	Darrell Evans/Brian Poldberg	1993
A	Lansing (Mich.) Lugnuts	Midwest	71	69	.507	t-8th (14)	Bob Herold	1996
A	Spokane (Wash.) Indians	Northwest	47	29	.618	t-1st (8)	Jeff Garber	1995
Rookie	Fort Myers (Fla.) Royals	Gulf Coast	32	28	.533	7th (14)	Andre David	1993

*Finish in overall standings (No. of teams in league) #Advanced level +Won league championship

OMAHA — Class AAA

PACIFIC COAST LEAGUE

BATTING	AVG	G	AB	R	H	2B	3B	HR	RBI	BB	SO	SB	CS	B	T	HT	WT	DOB	1st Yr	Resides
Bradshaw, Terry	.264	105	295	61	78	12	0	13	35	51	52	12	6	L	R	6-0	195	2-3-69	1990	Zuni, Va.
Carr, Jeremy	.292	49	178	40	52	14	3	5	23	19	31	19	5	R	R	5-9	180	3-30-71	1993	Boise, Idaho
Conine, Jeff	.000	2	9	0	0	0	0	0	0	0	3	0	0	R	R	6-1	220	6-27-66	1988	Weston, Fla.
Dye, Jermaine	.299	41	157	29	47	6	0	12	35	19	29	7	0	R	R	6-4	220	1-28-74	1993	Leawood, Kan.
Escamilla, Roman	.000	1	1	0	0	0	0	0	0	0	1	0	0	R	R	5-10	200	1-21-74	1996	Corpus Christi, Texas
Fasano, Sal	.214	4	14	1	3	1	0	1	2	1	4	0	1	R	R	6-2	220	8-10-71	1993	Joliet, Ill.
Giambi, Jeremy	.372	96	325	68	121	21	2	20	66	57	64	8	5	L	L	6-0	185	9-30-74	1996	Covina, Calif.
Halter, Shane	.309	22	97	15	30	6	1	1	13	6	15	4	1	R	R	6-0	180	11-8-69	1991	Overland Park, Kan.
Hansen, Jed	.278	127	417	63	116	19	7	16	56	44	125	17	9	R	R	6-1	195	8-19-72	1994	Olympia, Wash.
Hatcher, Chris	.309	126	485	84	150	21	2	46	106	25	125	8	6	R	R	6-3	220	1-7-69	1990	Carter Lake, Iowa
Hosey, Steve	.300	3	10	2	3	0	0	1	1	2	2	1	0	R	R	6-3	230	4-2-69	1989	Clovis, Calif.
Kmak, Joe	.222	24	63	6	14	3	0	2	9	7	8	0	0	R	R	6-0	205	5-3-63	1985	Foster City, Calif.
Leius, Scott	.298	71	258	40	77	10	0	15	46	17	30	7	3	R	R	6-3	208	9-24-65	1986	Minnetonka, Minn.
Long, Ryan	.203	18	59	6	12	2	0	4	8	8	13	0	0	R	R	6-2	215	2-3-73	1991	Pearland, Texas
Lopez, Mendy	.179	60	195	18	35	6	1	3	14	18	44	2	3	R	R	6-2	190	10-15-74	1992	Santo Domingo, D.R.
Martinez, Felix	.250	51	164	27	41	8	3	2	16	15	40	6	2	B	R	6-0	180	5-18-74	1993	Nagua, D.R.
Mendez, Carlos	.272	50	173	23	47	13	0	2	18	10	24	3	0	R	R	6-0	210	6-18-74	1991	Caracas, Ven.
Miller, Orlando	.246	39	114	16	28	10	0	2	15	15	32	1	0	R	R	6-3	205	1-13-69	1988	Estafeta del Dorado, Panama
Myers, Rod	.218	30	101	15	22	4	1	0	10	12	25	4	4	L	L	6-1	190	1-14-73	1991	Conroe, Texas
Ortiz, Hector	.225	63	191	17	43	7	0	0	12	9	26	0	0	R	R	6-0	205	10-14-69	1988	Canovanas, P.R.
Ortiz, Luis	.304	44	138	27	42	13	0	5	22	10	11	0	2	R	R	6-0	195	5-25-70	1991	Santo Domingo, D.R.
Pellow, Kit	.185	14	54	8	10	3	0	2	6	2	19	2	0	R	R	6-1	205	8-28-73	1996	Olathe, Kan.
Pendleton, Terry	.360	7	25	2	9	4	0	1	6	4	3	0	0	B	R	5-9	195	7-16-60	1982	Duluth, Ga.
Sisco, Steve	.280	109	371	58	104	20	0	20	58	26	58	4	6	R	R	5-10	190	12-2-69	1992	Thousand Oaks, Calif.
Stewart, Andy	.345	8	29	5	10	4	0	1	6	1	1	0	1	R	R	5-11	205	12-5-70	1990	Wilmington, Del.
Turner, Chris	.300	67	200	32	60	14	1	1	16	39	36	6	3	R	R	6-3	200	3-23-69	1991	Bowling Green, Ky.

PITCHING	W	L	ERA	G	GS	CG	SV	IP	H	R	ER	BB	SO	B	T	HT	WT	DOB	1st Yr	Resides
Thorn, Todd	9	8	3.13	26	24	4	0	149	128	60	52	28	103	L	L	6-2	175	11-4-76	1995	Stratford, Ontario
Wilson, Kris	0	3	3.75	10	2	0	1	24	19	10	10	6	20	R	R	6-4	225	8-6-76	1997	Palm Harbor, Fla.

LANSING — Class A

MIDWEST LEAGUE

BATTING	AVG	G	AB	R	H	2B	3B	HR	RBI	BB	SO	SB	CS	B	T	HT	WT	DOB	1st Yr	Resides
Brito, Juan	.245	63	212	16	52	7	0	0	22	17	41	2	2	R	R	5-11	185	11-7-79	1996	Santiago Rodriguez, D.R.
Caruso, Joe	.269	120	417	73	112	23	7	9	60	60	61	24	9	R	R	5-9	190	12-30-74	1997	Lock Haven, Pa.
Coffee, Gary	.284	83	285	52	81	21	7	8	44	55	91	5	2	R	R	6-3	250	3-13-75	1994	Atlanta, Ga.
Dillon, Joe	.261	73	268	37	70	17	2	15	43	36	57	9	2	R	R	6-2	205	8-2-75	1997	Santa Rosa, Calif.
DiPace, Danny	.265	20	49	11	13	1	0	1	7	11	14	1	0	L	R	6-2	215	4-24-75	1996	Jensen Beach, Fla.
Hill, Jeremy	.240	86	288	25	69	12	1	4	37	15	75	4	1	R	R	5-10	185	8-8-77	1996	Dallas, Texas
LeBron, Juan	.251	121	442	70	111	26	9	17	84	57	129	18	11	R	R	6-4	195	6-7-77	1995	Arroyo, P.R.
Longueira, Tony	.291	97	357	46	104	21	2	6	49	25	58	5	7	R	R	6-0	170	9-24-74	1995	Pembroke Pines, Fla.
Medrano, Steve	.259	106	340	45	88	14	5	0	29	34	39	15	3	B	R	6-0	150	10-8-77	1996	La Puente, Calif.
Metzler, Rod	.251	88	323	45	81	17	4	2	34	36	77	17	6	B	R	5-11	185	11-19-74	1997	Zionsville, Ind.
Montas, Ricardo	.229	51	140	21	32	4	1	1	14	22	28	4	2	R	R	6-1	170	3-9-77	1994	Santo Domingo, D.R.
Pitts, Rick	.229	85	249	33	57	5	4	1	21	13	62	22	6	R	R	6-1	190	3-13-76	1994	Seattle, Wash.
Radcliff, Vic	.261	66	253	42	66	15	4	5	33	26	53	12	5	R	R	5-9	180	9-23-76	1995	Beech Island, S.C.
Taveras, Jose	.281	14	57	7	16	3	0	1	7	2	14	3	1	R	R	5-11	170	12-17-76	1994	Nagua, D.R.
Tomlinson, Goefrey	.285	68	274	55	78	16	7	7	39	39	34	21	6	L	L	6-1	190	8-19-76	1997	Fort Worth, Texas
Torres, Rafael	.272	42	136	18	37	7	1	1	15	13	32	3	2	R	R	6-0	185	10-7-78	1996	Santo Domingo, D.R.
Williams, Micah	.241	77	270	43	65	8	4	2	19	18	55	33	10	R	R	6-1	185	1-30-75	1997	Phoenix, Ariz.
Willis, Dave	.281	97	374	56	105	30	5	9	50	17	69	9	2	R	R	6-5	240	7-18-74	1997	Arcadia, Calif.

GAMES BY POSITION: C—Brito 63, Hill 85. **1B**—Coffee 45, Dillon 45, DiPace 12, Longueira 11, Montas 23, Willis 17. **2B**—Caruso 47, Longueira 34, Metzler 66. **3B**—Caruso 71, Dillon 13, Longueira 6, Montas 24, Willis 38. **SS**—Caruso 2, Longueira 39, Medrano 106. **OF**—LeBron 114, Metzler 22, Pitts 78, Radcliff 60, Taveras 13, Tomlinson 60, Torres 30, Williams 61, Willis 14.

PITCHING	W	L	ERA	G	GS	CG	SV	IP	H	R	ER	BB	SO	B	T	HT	WT	DOB	1st Yr	Resides
Affeldt, Jeremy	0	3	9.53	6	3	0	0	17	27	21	18	12	8	L	L	6-4	185	6-6-79	1997	Medical Lake, Wash.
Alexander, Jordy	4	2	5.11	21	15	0	0	92	98	56	52	31	69	R	L	6-0	180	5-6-77	1996	Burnaby, B.C.
Appier, Kevin	0	0	2.25	1	1	0	0	4	4	1	1	0	5	R	R	6-2	200	12-6-67	1987	Paola, Kan.
Calero, Kiko	1	0	3.78	4	4	0	0	17	19	7	7	7	10	R	R	6-1	170	1-9-75	1996	Rio Piedras, P.R.
Carter, Aaron	5	4	3.78	43	0	0	12	79	72	40	33	36	89	R	R	6-2	190	12-19-74	1997	Adkins, Texas
Carter, Lance	3	1	0.67	15	2	0	2	40	34	6	3	9	37	R	R	6-1	190	12-18-74	1994	Bradenton, Fla.
Delaney, Donovan	0	4	3.19	25	0	0	3	37	31	19	13	26	47	R	R	5-10	200	3-24-74	1994	Bossier City, La.
Douglass, Ryan	4	8	6.17	18	18	0	0	89	122	80	61	33	45	R	R	6-3	200	12-3-78	1997	Pittsburgh, Pa.
Gonzalez, Edwin	8	3	3.40	23	22	0	0	127	120	57	48	39	106	R	R	5-10	175	8-13-77	1995	Santo Domingo, D.R.
Key, Scott	4	9	2.95	38	0	0	7	92	68	37	30	40	74	R	R	5-10	150	10-4-76	1995	Cantonment, Fla.
Maas, Steve	3	3	3.77	43	0	0	12	72	71	33	30	31	59	R	R	6-6	220	7-31-73	1996	Houston, Texas
Medina, Tomas	3	2	7.66	14	0	0	0	25	24	22	21	26	14	R	R	6-4	185	4-12-75	1994	Barquisimeto, Ven.
Montas, Ricardo	0	0	3.38	2	0	0	0	2	1	1	1	2	1	R	R	6-1	170	3—77	1994	Santo Domingo, D.R.
Moore, Griffin	0	0	18.00	1	0	0	0	1	3	2	2	0	0	R	R	6-2	195	4-29-76	1998	Columbia, Mo.
Myers, Taylor	0	0	3.60	1	1	0	0	5	5	3	2	1	1	R	R	6-0	180	11-8-77	1996	Henderson, Nev.
Pamus, Javier	0	2	13.00	7	1	0	0	9	15	14	13	6	8	R	R	6-1	195	2-11-75	1998	Santee, Calif.
Pederson, Justin	13	5	3.45	30	27	0	0	154	132	66	59	62	119	R	R	6-1	190	9-5-74	1997	Chippawa Falls, Wis.
Pichardo, Carlos	0	0	13.50	5	0	0	0	6	11	9	9	2	3	R	R	5-10	145	3-5-78	1996	Esperanza, Ven.
Ramagli, Matt	0	1	3.18	3	0	0	0	6	8	6	2	5	2	R	R	6-3	188	4-14-75	1997	Emerson, N.J.
Reichert, Dan	1	1	3.28	13	6	0	0	36	25	16	13	20	35	R	R	6-3	175	7-12-76	1997	Turlock, Calif.
Smith, Matt	0	3	3.81	9	3	0	0	26	21	12	11	14	19	L	L	6-4	220	6-2-76	1994	Grants Pass, Ore.
Solano, Francisco	2	1	2.91	4	4	0	0	22	17	8	7	14	16	R	R	5-11	179	7-14-79	1996	Santo Domingo, D.R.
Thurman, Corey	5	6	3.61	14	11	0	0	62	47	31	25	30	61	R	R	6-1	215	11-5-78	1996	Wake Village, Texas
Ward, Monty	0	0	12.00	1	0	0	0	3	8	4	4	3	4	R	R	6-1	185	10-11-76	1998	Lubbock, Texas
Williamson, Jeremy	0	0	8.31	9	0	0	0	13	18	12	12	12	7	L	L	6-3	190	8-19-74	1995	Sumrall, Miss.
Wilson, Kris	10	5	3.53	18	18	1	0	117	119	50	46	15	74	R	R	6-4	225	8-6-76	1997	Palm Harbor, Fla.
Yanz, Eric	5	6	5.42	34	4	0	2	81	91	57	49	39	78	R	R	6-3	210	11-2-74	1997	Golden, Colo.

SPOKANE — Short-Season Class A

NORTHWEST LEAGUE

BATTING	AVG	G	AB	R	H	2B	3B	HR	RBI	BB	SO	SB	CS	B	T	HT	WT	DOB	1st Yr	Resides
Calderon, Henry	.337	72	282	58	95	17	2	9	48	25	66	19	4	R	R	6-1	170	8-3-77	1996	Santo Domingo, D.R.
Curry, Mike	.251	67	227	53	57	8	2	1	25	46	41	30	7	L	R	5-10	190	2-15-77	1998	Jacksonville, Fla.
DiPace, Danny	.274	44	113	12	31	11	0	6	34	18	28	0	0	L	R	6-2	215	4-24-75	1996	Jensen Beach, Fla.
Dodson, Jeremy	.336	69	268	56	90	19	5	9	59	25	59	8	4	L	R	6-2	190	5-3-77	1998	Sherman, Texas
Freitas, Jeremy	.305	54	197	31	60	19	0	7	45	24	39	0	2	L	R	6-3	215	2-4-75	1998	Hanford, Calif.
Fry, Ryan	.233	47	146	25	34	8	1	8	26	16	40	1	2	R	R	6-0	210	1-12-76	1998	Long Beach, Calif.
Gomez, Erick	.059	4	17	1	1	0	0	0	0	0	2	0	0	L	R	6-2	240	1-21-76	1997	Wrightwood, Calif.
Hart, Corey	.242	58	157	25	38	6	0	3	21	50	38	8	4	B	R	6-0	185	9-5-75	1998	Oklahoma City, Okla.
Herrera, Pedro	.274	25	73	11	20	2	2	0	7	11	13	1	1	R	R	6-2	180	5-24-79	1996	Santo Domingo, D.R.
Ligons, Merrell	.279	51	179	34	50	7	3	0	29	28	41	15	2	B	R	5-8	165	6-22-77	1996	Compton, Calif.
Montas, Ricardo	.303	63	211	45	64	10	0	1	27	30	28	10	1	R	R	6-1	170	3-9-77	1994	Santo Domingo, D.R.
Phillips, Paul	.308	59	234	55	72	12	2	4	25	18	19	12	1	R	R	5-11	175	4-15-77	1998	York, Pa.
Rivera, Juan	.157	19	51	6	8	1	0	0	6	7	19	0	0	R	R	6-3	190	4-30-77	1995	Rio Grande, P.R.
Ruiz, Willy	.215	43	130	18	28	0	2	0	9	14	21	11	6	R	R	5-11	150	10-15-78	1996	Nagua, D.R.
Shackelford, Brian	.293	70	266	35	78	21	1	10	55	35	52	3	1	L	L	6-1	190	8-30-76	1998	McAlester, Okla.
Slemmer, Ben	.208	25	72	9	15	3	0	1	9	7	23	2	0	R	R	5-9	190	8-26-75	1998	Edwardsville, Ill.

GAMES BY POSITION: C—Herrera 22, Phillips 49, Rivera 12. **1B**—DiPace 8, Freitas 35, Gomez 4, Montas 36, Shackelford 2. **2B**—Hart 34, Ligons 8, Montas 5, Ruiz 41. **3B**—Calderon 60, Hart 13, Montas 2, Slemmer 7. **SS**—Calderon 14, DiPace 1, Hart 1, Ligons 44, Montas 24. **OF**—Curry 66, DiPace 1, Dodson 64, Fry 45, Phillips 1, Shackelford 67.

PITCHING	W	L	ERA	G	GS	CG	SV	IP	H	R	ER	BB	SO	B	T	HT	WT	DOB	1st Yr	Resides
Ammons, Cary	5	3	1.70	15	14	0	0	74	56	23	14	32	83	L	L	5-11	170	10-14-76	1998	Durant, Okla.
Bautista, Francisco	3	1	3.77	22	0	0	1	29	22	21	12	16	19	R	R	6-0	170	4-22-76	1994	El Seibo, D.R.
Burch, Matt	3	2	4.79	12	12	0	0	56	64	34	30	25	47	R	R	6-3	190	12-21-76	1998	Horseheads, N.Y.
Casper, Michael	3	2	2.87	19	0	0	1	38	42	25	12	10	23	R	R	6-0	190	8-21-74	1998	Milwaukee, Wis.
Gilfillan, Jason	0	0	4.91	6	0	0	0	7	7	5	4	6	8	R	R	6-6	215	8-31-76	1997	Blacksburg, S.C.
Hooper, Jimmy	4	2	2.78	17	0	0	1	36	39	14	11	17	36	R	R	6-0	215	6-5-75	1998	Dallas, Texas
Jackson, Jeremy	0	1	3.05	7	5	0	0	21	22	10	7	11	29	L	L	6-4	205	6-4-76	1998	Meridian, Miss.
Lee, Wayne	3	4	3.82	31	0	0	3	35	28	22	15	23	48	R	R	6-0	208	10-15-76	1998	Los Angeles, Calif.
McDaniel, Denton	1	5	4.25	29	0	0	1	36	42	25	17	19	43	L	L	5-10	200	8-12-76	1996	Austin, Texas
Morrison, Robbie	3	0	2.13	26	0	0	13	25	15	8	6	18	33	R	R	6-0	215	12-7-76	1998	Miami, Fla.
Myers, Taylor	0	0	5.79	1	1	0	0	5	4	3	3	3	1	R	R	6-0	180	11-8-77	1996	Henderson, Nev.
Pamus, Javier	2	1	5.20	12	4	0	0	36	40	30	21	16	33	R	R	6-1	195	2-11-75	1998	Santee, Calif.
Penny, Tony	2	2	2.91	28	0	0	3	53	55	25	17	20	48	R	R	6-4	165	3-23-76	1995	Newberry, S.C.
Sedlacek, Shawn	9	2	3.45	16	13	0	0	86	89	43	33	18	62	R	R	6-4	200	6-29-76	1998	Cedar Rapids, Iowa
Sonnier, Shawn	0	0	1.35	7	0	0	1	7	7	1	1	1	10	R	R	6-5	210	7-5-76	1998	Carencro, La.
Thurman, Corey	3	3	4.05	12	12	0	0	60	72	35	27	31	49	R	R	6-1	215	11-5-78	1996	Wake Village, Texas
Ward, Monty	6	1	3.79	15	15	0	0	71	66	33	30	35	76	R	R	6-1	185	10-11-76	1998	Lubbock, Texas

FORT MYERS — Rookie

GULF COAST LEAGUE

BATTING	AVG	G	AB	R	H	2B	3B	HR	RBI	BB	SO	SB	CS	B	T	HT	WT	DOB	1st Yr	Resides
Alou, Felipe	.253	44	162	20	41	7	1	2	22	8	31	6	3	R	R	5-11	165	11-29-78	1998	Santo Domingo, D.R.
Ayres, Yancy	.227	18	44	5	10	2	0	0	3	2	8	0	0	R	R	6-0	185	5-10-76	1998	Visalia, Calif.
Bryan, Sean	.202	24	84	8	17	3	0	0	6	4	20	0	0	L	R	6-1	220	5-10-78	1998	Kansas City, Mo.
Carrasco, Ricardo	.247	54	182	33	45	9	1	9	33	27	49	0	0	R	R	6-3	210	1-27-78	1996	Santo Domingo, D.R.
Felix, Hersy	.260	48	173	23	45	5	0	5	25	21	34	0	1	R	R	6-3	159	4-11-78	1996	Sosua, D.R.
Garcia, Rafael	.213	20	61	6	13	3	0	0	7	9	15	7	1	R	R	6-1	190	10-24-79	1997	Nagua, D.R.
Gettis, Byron	.216	27	88	11	19	2	0	0	4	4	20	0	0	R	R	6-2	220	3-13-80	1998	Centreville, Ill.
Goodwin, David	.367	48	177	26	65	20	0	4	33	20	33	0	0	R	R	6-1	205	3-26-76	1998	Overland Park, Kan.
Graham, Tarik	.167	33	66	13	11	1	1	0	5	11	27	5	0	R	L	5-11	185	8-11-79	1997	Orlando, Fla.
Hopper, Norris	.308	40	133	19	41	2	1	0	11	13	12	11	2	R	R	5-10	175	3-24-79	1998	Shelby, N.C.
Moore, Griffin	.231	35	117	13	27	5	0	2	12	11	11	4	1	R	R	6-2	195	4-29-76	1998	Columbia, Mo.
Nunez, Jose	.263	46	156	22	41	6	0	3	15	12	27	0	0	R	R	5-10	175	1-31-77	1995	Saicedo, D.R.
Perea, Carlos	.250	36	116	11	29	0	0	0	7	13	20	4	4	R	R	6-0	150	8-16-79	1997	Ceiba, P.R.
Player, David	.000	1	3	0	0	0	0	0	0	1	3	0	0	L	R	5-11	220	4-12-76	1998	Palatka, Fla.
Ramirez, Charlie	.305	50	200	27	61	9	2	0	23	7	35	13	5	R	R	6-1	175	6-1-79	1996	San Pedro de Macoris, D.R.
Santana, Emmanuel	.326	16	46	7	15	6	0	2	10	3	9	0	0	L	R	6-0	185	8-4-80	1998	Vega Alta, P.R.
Shanks, James	.264	42	144	21	38	9	0	0	13	18	26	10	1	R	R	6-0	185	1-26-79	1998	Appling, Ga.
Taveras, Jose	.222	7	27	4	6	1	0	1	4	2	11	0	0	R	R	5-11	170	12-17-76	1994	Nagua, D.R.
Tillis, Cameron	.154	3	13	1	2	1	0	0	1	0	4	0	0	B	R	6-2	200	2-25-77	1997	Opp, Ala.
Vann, Eric	.043	6	23	1	1	1	0	0	1	2	10	0	1	B	R	5-8	210	1-8-76	1998	Lawrence, Kan.

GAMES BY POSITION: C—Ayres 18, Felix 45, Santana 7. **1B**—Carrasco 43, Goodwin 20. **2B**—Garcia 4, Hopper 30, Nunez 1, Perea 32. **3B**—Bryan 21, Moore 1, Nunez 45. **SS**—Garcia 16, Hopper 9, Moore 34, Perea 7. **OF**—Alou 44, Gettis 24, Graham 25, Ramirez 50, Shanks 40, Taveras 6, Tillis 3, Vann 3.

PITCHING	W	L	ERA	G	GS	CG	SV	IP	H	R	ER	BB	SO	B	T	HT	WT	DOB	1st Yr	Resides
Affeldt, Jeremy	4	3	2.89	12	9	0	0	56	50	24	18	24	67	L	L	6-4	185	6-6-79	1997	Medical Lake, Wash.
Appier, Kevin	0	1	2.70	1	1	0	0	3	3	3	1	1	2	R	R	6-2	200	12-6-67	1987	Paola, Kan.
Bevil, Brian	0	0	2.25	3	3	0	0	4	4	2	1	2	7	R	R	6-4	225	9-5-71	1991	Houston, Texas
Chiasson, Scott	2	0	4.81	13	0	0	1	24	24	17	13	11	26	R	R	6-3	185	8-14-77	1998	Norwich, Conn.
Douglass, Ryan	0	3	6.65	9	2	0	0	23	30	19	17	12	11	R	R	6-3	200	12-3-78	1997	Pittsburgh, Pa.
French, Eric	0	0	7.94	3	0	0	2	6	6	5	5	5	4	R	R	6-3	200	4-14-76	1998	Austin, Texas
George, Chris	0	1	2.87	5	4	0	0	16	14	9	5	4	10	L	L	6-2	165	9-16-79	1998	Spring, Texas
Gilfillan, Jason	1	1	8.00	7	6	0	0	9	10	8	8	4	6	R	R	6-6	215	8-31-76	1997	Blacksburg, S.C.
Guerrero, Junior	4	4	3.23	13	6	0	0	61	57	24	22	19	58	R	R	6-2	175	8-21-79	1996	Santo Domingo, D.R.
Hamilton, Charles	2	1	4.38	15	0	0	0	25	25	22	12	15	19	R	R	6-4	200	12-29-78	1998	Greenville, Miss.
Haney, Chris	0	1	0.00	1	1	0	0	2	2	2	0	0	1	L	L	6-3	210	11-16-68	1990	Barboursville, Va.
Hill, Ryan	0	0	0.00	5	0	0	0	5	3	1	0	7	4	R	R	6-4	200	8-27-78	1998	Washington, Ind.
Mancha, Tony	3	1	3.34	20	0	0	3	32	33	19	12	12	25	B	R	6-2	205	10-9-78	1997	Las Cruces, N.M.
Medrano, Juan	4	3	3.52	12	8	0	1	64	57	28	25	16	27	R	R	6-3	185	12-30-78	1996	Montecristi, D.R.
Pichardo, Carlos	0	0	1.47	14	0	0	7	18	6	4	3	8	9	R	R	5-10	145	3-5-78	1996	Esperanza, Ven.
Ralston, Kris	0	1	4.50	2	0	0	0	2	5	3	1	0	2	R	R	6-2	200	8-8-71	1993	Carthage, Mo.
Russo, Mike	5	2	3.48	18	0	0	1	34	31	16	13	15	37	R	R	6-4	230	8-9-77	1998	Berwyn, Ill.
Solano, Francisco	1	3	2.64	9	6	1	0	48	44	19	14	9	29	R	R	5-11	179	7-14-79	1996	Santo Domingo, D.R.
Sopkin, Josh	0	0	6.23	6	0	0	0	9	8	6	6	9	2	R	R	6-1	190	12-14-79	1998	Blue Island, Ill.
Turner, Kyle	6	1	2.36	12	6	0	0	42	36	13	11	17	55	L	L	6-2	215	10-14-78	1998	Antioch, Calif.
Walsh, Steven	0	2	1.88	9	8	0	0	29	22	6	6	4	28	R	R	6-6	210	3-11-78	1997	Ottawa, Ontario

LOS ANGELES DODGERS

Fox era begins with blockbuster trade, disappointing finish

BY JORGE VALENCIA

One of the most remarkable seasons in Los Angeles Dodgers history saw the end of the O'Malley era of ownership, a blockbuster trade involving one of the team's most popular players, sweeping changes in the front office and on the field and a rash of injuries that decimated the roster.

Unfortunately for the Dodgers, it also included a disappointing third-place finish in the National League West in 1998.

The shakeup started March 18 when Peter O'Malley completed the $311 million sale of the club to Rupert Murdoch's Fox Group, marking the end of family ownership in the major leagues.

The tumult continued May 15 when the new ownership group brokered one of the biggest deals in baseball history. The Dodgers sent all-star catcher Mike Piazza and third baseman Todd Zeile to the Florida Marlins for outfielder Gary Sheffield, third baseman Bobby Bonilla, catcher Charles Johnson, outfielder Jim Eisenreich and minor league righthander Manuel Barrios.

On June 21, with the team mired in mediocrity and battered by injuries, came another bombshell: Team president Bob Graziano announced the firing of manager Bill Russell and longtime general manager Fred Claire.

Russell was replaced on an interim basis by Glenn Hoffman, who was managing the team's Triple-A Albuquerque affiliate, and Claire by vice president and former manager Tom Lasorda. Hoffman's promotion created a chain reaction, as Double-A San Antonio manager Ron Roenicke jumped to Albuquerque, and San Antonio hitting coach Lance Parrish took over as manager there.

A little more than a month after taking over as GM, Lasorda "guaranteed" the Dodgers would win the NL wild card and made a series of trades to try and back his bold proclamation. Among the players Lasorda acquired were closer Jeff Shaw from the Reds, and lefthander Carlos Perez and shortstop Mark Grudzielanek from the Expos.

The moves, however, were not enough to get the Dodgers back into the playoff picture. They finished third in the NL West behind the San Diego Padres and San Francisco Giants.

As the season drew to a close, the Dodgers hired Kevin Malone as GM. Days after the season ended, Malone announced Hoffman would not return as manager and began the search for a new skipper. The team announced the hiring of Davey Johnson in October.

Malone and Johnson faced a big task in revamping the Dodgers from head to toe. The only team in the organization with a winning record in 1998 was Rookie-level Great Falls, which finished fifth in the Pioneer League with a 40-35 mark. San Antonio made the Texas League playoffs by virtue of a 38-30 first half, but collapsed in the second half and fell to Wichita in the first round of postseason play.

The Missions missed third baseman Adrian Beltre, the crown jewel of the system, who was summoned by Lasorda in June after hitting .321 with 13 homers and 20 steals for San Antonio. Though he failed to distinguish himself in 195 major league at-bats, he gained some valuable experience.

Raul Mondesi

Adrian Beltre

Players of the Year

Major League: Raul Mondesi, of
For the second straight season Mondesi hit 30 homers, and his 90 RBIs in 1998 were best on the team.

Minor League: Adrian Beltre, 3b, San Antonio
Beltre earned a midseason promotion to Los Angeles after hitting .321 with 13 homers and 56 RBIs in Double-A.

ORGANIZATION LEADERS

BATTING		
*AVG	Jorge Piedra, Great Falls	.383
R	Eric Stuckenschneider, Alb./San Antonio	110
H	Angel Pena, San Antonio	162
TB	Angel Pena, San Antonio	264
2B	Two tied at	34
3B	Eric Stuckenschneider, Alb./San Antonio	17
HR	Juan Diaz, San Antonio/Vero Beach	30
RBI	Angel Pena, San Antonio	105
BB	Eric Stuckenschneider, Alb./San Antonio	88
SO	Glenn Davis, San Antonio/Vero Beach	128
SB	Ramon Moreta, Albuquerque/San Bernardino	48
PITCHING		
W	Ricky Stone, Albuquerque/San Antonio	12
L	Two tied at	15
#ERA	Ryan Moskau, San Bernardino/Yakima	2.38
G	Matt Montgomery, Albuquerque/San Bernardino	66
CG	Two tied at	3
SV	Matt Montgomery, Albuquerque/San Bernardino	28
IP	Ricky Stone, Albuquerque/San Antonio	187
BB	Two tied at	83
SO	Luke Prokopec, San Antonio/San Bernardino	173

*Minimum 250 At-Bats #Minimum 75 Innings

Los Angeles DODGERS

Managers: Bill Russell, Glenn Hoffman

1999 Record: 83-79, .512 (3rd, NL West)

BATTING	AVG	G	AB	R	H	2B	3B	HR	RBI	BB	SO	SB	CS	B	T	HT	WT	DOB	1st Yr	Resides
Beltre, Adrian	.215	77	195	18	42	9	0	7	22	14	37	3	1	R	R	5-11	165	4-7-78	1995	Santo Domingo, D.R.
Bonilla, Bobby	.237	72	236	28	56	6	1	7	30	29	37	1	1	B	R	6-4	240	2-23-63	1981	Greenwich, Conn.
2-team (28 Florida)	.249	100	333	39	83	11	1	11	45	41	59	1	2							
Castro, Juan	.195	89	220	25	43	7	0	2	14	15	37	0	0	R	R	5-10	187	6-20-72	1991	Los Mochis, Mexico
Cedeno, Roger	.242	105	240	33	58	11	1	2	17	27	57	8	2	B	R	6-1	205	8-16-74	1992	Valencia, Ven.
Cora, Alex	.121	29	33	1	4	0	1	0	0	2	8	0	0	L	R	6-0	180	10-18-75	1996	Caguas, P.R.
Cromer, Tripp	.167	6	6	1	1	0	0	1	1	0	2	0	0	R	R	6-2	160	11-21-67	1989	Lexington, S.C.
Devereaux, Mike	.308	9	13	0	4	1	0	0	1	3	2	0	1	R	R	6-0	195	4-10-63	1985	Alpharetta, Ga.
Eisenreich, Jim	.197	75	127	12	25	2	2	0	6	12	22	4	0	L	L	5-11	195	4-18-59	1980	Blue Springs, Mo.
2-team (30 Florida)	.215	105	191	21	41	3	2	1	13	16	36	6	0							
Grudzielanek, Mark	.264	51	193	11	51	6	0	2	21	5	23	7	0	R	R	6-1	170	6-30-70	1991	El Paso, Texas
2-team (105 Montreal)	.272	156	589	62	160	21	1	10	62	26	73	18	5							
Guerrero, Wilton	.283	64	180	21	51	4	3	0	7	4	33	5	2	R	R	5-11	175	10-24-74	1992	Nizao, D.R.
Hollandsworth, Todd	.269	55	175	23	47	6	4	3	20	9	42	4	3	L	L	6-2	215	4-20-73	1991	San Ramon, Calif.
Hollins, Damon	.222	5	9	1	2	0	0	0	2	0	2	0	1	R	L	5-11	180	6-12-74	1992	Vallejo, Calif.
2-team (3 Atlanta)	.200	8	15	1	3	0	0	0	2	0	3	0	1							
Howard, Tom	.184	47	76	9	14	4	0	2	4	3	15	1	0	B	R	6-2	205	12-11-64	1986	Elk Grove, Calif.
Hubbard, Trenidad	.298	94	208	29	62	9	1	7	18	18	46	9	5	R	R	5-9	185	5-11-66	1986	Houston, Texas
Johnson, Charles	.217	102	346	31	75	13	0	12	35	29	99	0	1	R	R	6-2	220	7-20-71	1992	Pembroke Pines, Fla.
2-team (31 Florida)	.218	133	459	44	100	18	0	19	58	45	129	0	2							
Karros, Eric	.296	139	507	59	150	20	1	23	87	47	93	7	2	R	R	6-4	226	11-4-67	1988	Manhattan Beach, Calif.
Konerko, Paul	.215	49	144	14	31	1	0	4	16	10	30	0	1	R	R	6-3	210	3-5-76	1994	Paradise Valley, Ariz.
LoDuca, Paul	.286	6	14	2	4	1	0	0	1	0	1	0	0	R	R	5-10	185	4-12-72	1993	Phoenix, Ariz.
Luke, Matt	.236	102	237	34	56	12	1	12	34	17	60	2	1	L	L	6-5	220	2-26-71	1992	Huntington Beach, Calif.
Metcalfe, Mike	.000	4	1	0	0	0	0	0	0	0	1	2	0	R	R	5-10	175	1-2-73	1994	Orlando, Fla.
Mondesi, Raul	.279	148	580	85	162	26	5	30	90	30	112	16	10	R	R	5-11	215	3-12-71	1988	San Cristobal, D.R.
Pena, Angel	.231	6	13	1	3	0	0	0	0	0	6	0	0	R	R	5-10	228	2-16-75	1993	San Pedro de Macoris, D.R.
Piazza, Mike	.282	37	149	20	42	5	0	9	30	11	27	0	0	R	R	6-3	223	9-4-68	1989	Valley Forge, Pa.
Prince, Tom	.185	37	81	7	15	5	1	0	5	7	24	0	0	R	R	5-11	206	8-13-64	1984	Bradenton, Fla.
Sheffield, Gary	.316	90	301	52	95	16	1	10	57	69	30	18	5	R	R	5-11	205	11-18-68	1986	St. Petersburg, Fla.
2-team (40 Florida)	.302	130	437	73	132	27	2	22	85	95	46	22	7							
Vizcaino, Jose	.262	67	237	30	62	9	0	3	29	17	35	7	3	B	R	6-1	180	3-26-68	1987	El Cajon, Calif.
Young, Eric	.285	117	452	78	129	24	1	8	43	45	32	42	13	R	R	5-9	180	5-18-67	1989	Chattanooga, Tenn.
Zeile, Todd	.253	40	158	22	40	6	1	7	27	10	24	1	1	R	R	6-1	204	9-9-65	1986	Westlake Village, Calif.

LARRY GOREN

Righthander Chan Ho Park

Led Dodgers with 191 strikeouts

MORRIS FOSTOFF

San Antonio's Angel Pena

Hit .335 in Double-A

PITCHING	W	L	ERA	G	GS	CG	SV	IP	H	R	ER	BB	SO	B	T	HT	WT	DOB	1st Yr	Resides
Barrios, Manny	0	0	0.00	1	0	0	0	1	0	0	0	2	0	R	R	6-0	185	9-21-74	1993	Rock Island, Ill.
Bohanon, Brian	5	7	2.40	14	14	2	0	97	74	35	26	36	72	L	L	6-2	219	8-1-68	1987	Houston, Texas
2-team (25 New York)	7	11	2.67	39	18	2	0	152	121	56	45	57	111							
Brunson, Will	0	1	11.57	2	0	0	0	2	3	3	3	2	1	L	L	6-6	185	3-20-70	1992	Bulverde, Texas
Bruske, Jim	3	0	3.48	35	0	0	1	44	47	18	17	19	31	R	R	6-1	185	10-7-64	1986	Tempe, Ariz.
Clontz, Brad	2	0	5.66	18	0	0	0	21	15	13	13	10	14	R	R	6-1	180	4-25-71	1992	Alpharetta, Ga.
Dreifort, Darren	8	12	4.00	32	26	1	0	180	171	84	80	57	168	R	R	6-2	211	5-3-72	1994	Wichita, Kan.
Guthrie, Mark	2	1	3.50	53	0	0	0	54	56	26	21	24	45	R	L	6-4	211	9-22-65	1987	Bradenton, Fla.
Hall, Darren	0	3	10.32	11	0	0	0	11	17	14	13	5	8	R	R	6-3	207	7-14-64	1986	Irving, Texas
Judd, Mike	0	0	15.09	7	0	0	0	11	19	19	19	9	14	R	R	6-1	217	6-30-75	1995	La Mesa, Calif.
Kubenka, Jeff	1	0	0.96	6	0	0	0	9	4	1	1	8	10	R	L	6-1	191	8-24-74	1996	Schulenburg, Texas
Lankford, Frank	0	2	5.95	12	0	0	1	20	23	13	13	7	7	R	R	6-2	190	3-26-71	1993	Atlanta, Ga.
Maloney, Sean	0	1	4.97	11	0	0	0	13	13	7	7	5	11	R	R	6-7	210	5-25-71	1993	North Kingstown, R.I.
Martinez, Ramon	7	3	2.83	15	15	1	0	102	76	41	32	41	91	B	R	6-4	184	3-22-68	1985	Santo Domingo, D.R.
McMichael, Greg	0	1	4.40	12	0	0	1	14	17	8	7	6	11	R	R	6-3	222	12-1-66	1988	Alpharetta, Ga.
Mlicki, Dave	7	3	4.05	20	20	2	0	124	120	64	56	38	78	R	R	6-4	205	6-8-68	1990	Columbus, Ohio
2-team (10 New York)	8	7	4.57	30	30	3	0	181	188	102	92	63	117							
Nomo, Hideo	2	7	5.05	12	12	2	0	68	57	39	38	38	73	R	R	6-2	210	8-31-68	1995	Kobe, Japan
Osuna, Antonio	7	1	3.06	54	0	0	6	65	50	26	22	32	72	R	R	5-11	160	4-12-73	1991	Juan Jose Rios, Mexico
Park, Chan Ho	15	9	3.71	34	34	2	0	221	199	101	91	97	191	R	R	6-2	204	6-30-73	1994	Los Angeles, Calif.
Perez, Carlos	4	4	3.24	11	11	4	0	78	67	30	28	30	46	L	L	6-3	200	4-14-71	1990	San Cristobal, D.R.
2-team (23 Montreal)	11	14	3.59	34	34	7	0	241	244	109	96	63	128							
Radinsky, Scott	6	6	2.63	62	0	0	13	62	63	21	18	20	45	L	L	6-3	221	3-3-68	1986	Simi Valley, Calif.
Rath, Gary	0	0	10.80	3	0	0	0	3	3	4	4	2	4	L	L	6-2	185	1-10-73	1994	Long Beach, Miss.
Reyes, Dennis	0	4	4.71	11	3	0	0	29	27	17	15	20	33	R	L	6-3	246	4-19-77	1994	Higuera De Zaragoza, Mex.
Shaw, Jeff	1	4	2.55	34	0	0	25	35	35	11	10	7	26	R	R	6-2	200	7-7-66	1986	Washington Courthouse, Ohio
2-team (39 Cincinnati)	3	8	2.12	73	0	0	48	85	75	22	20	19	55							
Valdes, Ismael	11	10	3.98	27	27	2	0	174	171	82	77	66	122	R	R	6-3	215	8-21-73	1991	Victoria, Mexico
Weaver, Eric	2	0	0.93	7	0	0	0	10	5	1	1	6	5	R	R	6-5	230	8-4-73	1991	Illiopolis, Ill.

FIELDING

Catcher	PCT	G	PO	A	E	DP	PB
Johnson	.992	100	715	50	6	9	5
LoDuca	1.000	4	18	2	0	1	1
Pena	1.000	4	26	2	0	0	1
Piazza	.993	37	277	25	2	1	0
Prince	1.000	32	175	14	0	2	1

First Base	PCT	G	PO	A	E	DP
Eisenreich	1.000	9	20	2	0	5
Karros	.991	136	1151	108	12	122
Konerko	.995	23	170	15	1	8
Luke	1.000	18	64	13	0	5
Zeile	1.000	1	2	0	0	0

Second Base	PCT	G	PO	A	E	DP
Castro	.984	38	47	73	2	22
Cora	1.000	4	4	8	0	3
Guerrero	.968	32	53	67	4	16
Metcalfe	.000	1	0	0	0	0
Young	.976	114	226	305	13	67

Third Base	PCT	G	PO	A	E	DP
Beltre	.925	74	31	130	13	13
Bonilla	.912	59	40	84	12	8
Castro	.929	12	6	7	1	2
Hubbard	.000	1	0	0	0	0
Konerko	.952	11	5	15	1	1
Zeile	.929	40	25	53	6	2

Shortstop	PCT	G	PO	A	E	DP
Beltre	1.000	2	1	1	0	0
Castro	.954	47	43	102	7	29
Cora	.956	21	22	21	2	6
Grudzielanek	.962	51	78	172	10	34
Guerrero	.947	14	12	24	2	6
Vizcaino	.985	66	89	169	4	32

Outfield	PCT	G	PO	A	E	DP
Bonilla	.941	12	16	0	1	0
Cedeno	.978	77	86	5	2	1
Devereaux	1.000	5	9	1	0	0
Eisenreich	.971	24	33	1	1	0
Guerrero	.857	7	6	0	1	0
Hollandsworth	.957	51	87	1	4	0
Hollins	1.000	4	7	0	0	0
Howard	1.000	29	33	2	0	0
Hubbard	.991	81	109	3	1	0
Konerko	1.000	11	12	0	0	0
Luke	.990	63	97	6	1	0
Mondesi	.980	148	284	6	6	1
Sheffield	.994	89	149	6	1	2

FARM SYSTEM

Vice President, Minor League Operations: Charlie Blaney

Class	Farm Team	League	W	L	Pct.	Finish*	Manager(s)	First Yr
AAA	Albuquerque (N.M.) Dukes	Pacific Coast	61	82	.427	13th (16)	Hoffman/ Roenicke	1963
AA	San Antonio (Texas) Missions	Texas	67	73	.479	6th (8)	Roenicke/Parrish	1977
A#	San Bernardino (Calif.) Stampede	California	55	85	.393	9th (10)	Hatcher/ Wallach	1995
A#	Vero Beach (Fla.) Dodgers	Florida State	58	81	.417	11th (14)	John Shoemaker	1980
A	Yakima (Wash.) Bears	Northwest	32	44	.421	7th (8)	Tony Harris	1988
Rookie#	Great Falls (Mont.) Dodgers	Pioneer	40	35	.533	5th (8)	Dino Ebel	1984

*Finish in overall standings (No. of teams in league) #Advanced level

ALBUQUERQUE — Class AAA

PACIFIC COAST LEAGUE

BATTING	AVG	G	AB	R	H	2B	3B	HR	RBI	BB	SO	SB	CS	B	T	HT	WT	DOB	1st Yr	Resides
Anderson, Cliff	.232	48	142	16	33	6	2	4	24	7	23	3	0	L	R	5-8	165	7-4-70	1992	Kodiak, Alaska
Anthony, Eric	.303	59	188	34	57	9	2	10	26	36	43	3	3	L	L	6-2	210	11-8-67	1986	Houston, Texas
Blanco, Henry	.269	48	134	19	36	11	0	4	23	22	27	2	0	R	R	5-11	220	8-29-71	1990	Guarenas, Ven.
Bocachica, Hiram	.238	26	101	16	24	7	1	4	16	13	24	5	3	R	R	5-11	165	3-4-76	1994	Bayamon, P.R.
Cora, Alex	.264	81	299	42	79	17	5	5	45	15	38	10	7	L	R	6-0	180	10-18-75	1996	Caguas, P.R.
Cromer, Tripp	.333	12	30	3	10	1	0	2	5	1	5	0	1	R	R	6-2	160	11-21-67	1989	Lexington, S.C.
Cuevas, Trent	.333	5	18	3	6	1	0	0	4	0	1	0	0	R	R	5-11	170	12-25-76	1995	Placentia, Calif.
Dandridge, Brad	.182	15	33	5	6	3	0	0	4	3	5	0	0	R	R	6-0	200	11-29-71	1993	Santa Maria, Calif.
Gibbs, Kevin	.125	2	8	1	1	0	0	0	1	2	1	0	0	B	R	6-2	182	4-3-74	1995	Davidsonville, Md.
Glassey, Josh	.125	6	8	1	1	1	0	0	1	1	3	1	0	L	R	6-1	190	5-6-77	1996	Del Mar, Calif.
Guerrero, Wilton	.298	30	121	15	36	3	2	1	10	9	12	11	3	R	R	5-11	175	10-24-74	1992	Nizao, D.R.
Hubbard, Trenidad	.300	11	30	6	9	0	0	3	5	5	5	2	1	R	R	5-9	185	5-11-66	1986	Houston, Texas
Ingram, Garey	.302	108	377	60	114	25	5	8	58	30	69	20	6	R	R	5-11	195	7-25-70	1990	Columbus, Ga.
Johnson, Keith	.232	82	254	32	59	5	1	6	26	10	51	6	3	R	R	5-11	200	4-17-71	1992	Stockton, Calif.
Jones, Jack	.232	15	56	7	13	1	1	1	7	2	13	1	1	R	R	5-11	165	11-7-74	1996	Modesto, Calif.
Konerko, Paul	.379	24	87	16	33	10	0	6	26	11	12	0	0	R	R	6-3	210	3-5-76	1994	Paradise Valley, Ariz.

BATTING	AVG	G	AB	R	H	2B	3B	HR	RBI	BB	SO	SB	CS	B	T	HT	WT	DOB	1st Yr	Resides
LoDuca, Paul	.319	126	451	69	144	30	3	8	58	59	40	19	7	R	R	5-10	185	4-12-72	1993	Phoenix, Ariz.
Melendez, Dan	.280	77	207	24	58	10	1	2	30	28	37	3	2	L	L	6-4	205	1-4-71	1992	Newhall, Calif.
Moreta, Ramon	.370	8	27	5	10	1	2	0	3	1	9	2	2	R	R	5-11	185	9-5-75	1994	La Romana, D.R.
Richardson, Brian	.146	11	41	5	6	0	0	1	5	3	10	0	0	R	R	6-2	202	8-31-75	1992	Diamond Bar, Calif.
Richardson, Scott	.293	108	348	59	102	21	2	10	52	25	63	19	4	R	R	6-1	175	2-19-71	1992	Rialto, Calif.
Riggs, Adam	.371	44	170	30	63	13	3	4	25	21	29	12	6	R	R	6-0	190	10-4-72	1994	Andover, N.J.
Roberge, J.P.	.303	136	475	83	144	30	1	10	67	31	64	22	6	R	R	6-0	177	9-12-72	1994	Arcadia, Calif.
Rodriguez, Steve	.227	7	22	6	5	2	0	1	3	5	4	1	0	R	R	5-9	170	11-29-70	1992	Las Vegas, Nev.
Romero, Willie	.285	114	403	50	115	21	3	10	61	25	68	23	15	R	R	5-9	192	8-5-74	1991	Maracay, Ven.
Saitta, Rich	.063	5	16	1	1	0	0	0	0	0	5	0	0	R	R	5-10	170	7-28-75	1996	Marlboro, N.J.
Sell, Chip	.316	37	136	22	43	2	2	0	10	11	23	9	6	L	R	6-2	205	6-19-71	1994	Otis, Ore.
Snow, Casey	.200	7	20	2	4	2	0	0	2	4	7	0	0	B	R	5-10	185	12-8-74	1996	Canoga Park, Calif.
Steed, Dave	.278	57	151	18	42	7	1	4	21	11	39	0	1	R	R	6-1	205	2-25-73	1993	Starkville, Miss.
Stuckenschneider, Eric	.309	71	269	50	83	13	10	7	28	44	50	18	7	R	R	6-0	200	8-24-71	1994	Freeburg, Mo.

PITCHING	W	L	ERA	G	GS	CG	SV	IP	H	R	ER	BB	SO	B	T	HT	WT	DOB	1st Yr	Resides
Babineaux, Darrin	0	0	4.50	3	0	0	0	4	4	2	2	0	4	R	R	6-4	210	7-10-74	1995	Rayne, La.
Barrios, Manny	1	3	6.00	20	2	0	0	36	47	25	24	15	33	R	R	6-0	185	9-21-74	1993	Rock Island, Ill.
Brunson, Will	5	8	4.65	34	15	1	2	120	135	69	62	40	100	L	L	6-6	185	3-20-70	1992	Bulverde, Texas
Clontz, Brad	1	2	7.71	6	0	0	0	7	11	10	6	5	12	R	R	6-1	195	4-25-71	1992	Alpharetta, Ga.
Dollar, Toby	0	1	4.70	7	0	0	0	8	14	10	4	5	3	R	R	6-3	215	12-27-74	1996	Graham, Texas
Everly, Bill	0	1	27.00	2	0	0	0	2	6	6	6	1	1	R	R	6-1	175	6-15-75	1997	Carmichaels, Pa.
Flores, Ignacio	4	10	7.11	17	17	0	0	89	113	72	70	48	63	R	R	6-2	180	5-8-75	1995	La Paz, Mexico
Herges, Matt	3	5	5.71	34	8	0	0	88	115	64	56	37	75	L	R	6-0	200	4-1-70	1992	Champaign, Ill.
Hubbs, Dan	1	2	6.86	13	0	0	0	20	23	16	15	12	25	R	R	6-2	200	1-23-71	1993	Renton, Wash.
Iglesias, Mike	7	1	3.67	39	9	0	0	96	112	43	39	29	57	R	R	6-5	223	11-9-72	1991	Castro Valley, Calif.
Judd, Mike	5	7	4.56	17	17	3	0	95	98	62	48	44	77	R	R	6-1	217	6-30-75	1995	La Mesa, Calif.
Kubenka, Jeff	2	5	2.45	28	0	0	9	40	32	11	11	12	40	R	L	6-1	191	8-24-74	1996	Schulenburg, Texas
Lagarde, Joe	1	1	3.10	14	0	0	2	20	16	7	7	7	18	R	R	5-9	180	1-17-75	1993	Winston-Salem, N.C.
Lilly, Ted	1	3	4.94	5	5	0	0	31	39	20	17	9	25	L	L	6-1	177	1-4-76	1996	Fresno, Calif.
Maloney, Sean	3	2	4.63	26	0	0	9	35	38	21	18	8	38	R	R	6-7	210	5-25-71	1993	North Kingstown, R.I.
Montgomery, Matt	0	0	0.00	3	0	0	2	3	0	0	0	2	3	R	R	6-4	210	5-13-76	1997	Anaheim, Calif.
Morse, Paul	1	1	3.00	2	2	0	0	15	8	5	5	6	11	R	R	6-2	185	2-27-73	1995	Danville, Ky.
Neal, Billy	0	0	4.66	6	0	0	1	10	11	5	5	2	6	R	R	6-0	201	9-20-71	1995	Scottsdale, Ariz.
Pearsall, J.J.	1	1	6.23	8	0	0	1	13	16	10	9	8	8	L	L	6-2	202	9-9-73	1995	Burnt Hills, N.Y.
Rath, Gary	9	7	4.52	28	24	1	1	157	184	91	79	52	119	L	L	6-2	185	1-10-73	1994	Long Beach, Miss.
Reyes, Dennis	1	4	1.11	7	7	1	0	44	31	13	7	18	56	R	L	6-3	246	4-19-77	1994	Higuera de Zaragoza, Mex.
Roach, Petie	0	0	8.22	19	0	0	0	15	20	17	14	10	12	L	L	6-2	175	9-19-70	1992	Redding, Calif.
Stone, Ricky	5	5	5.38	18	16	0	0	105	120	69	63	41	85	R	R	6-1	168	2-28-75	1994	Hamilton, Ohio
Weaver, Eric	2	5	5.55	46	0	0	3	62	65	41	38	32	63	R	R	6-5	230	8-4-73	1991	Illiopolis, Ill.
Williams, Jeff	8	8	4.98	21	21	0	0	121	160	87	67	49	93	R	L	6-0	185	6-6-72	1997	Page, Australia

FIELDING

Catcher	PCT	G	PO	A	E	DP	PB
Blanco	.985	31	243	20	4	0	4
Dandridge	.933	6	26	2	2	0	0
Glassey	.000	1	0	0	0	0	0
LoDuca	.984	91	596	69	11	2	6
Snow	1.000	2	17	0	0	0	0
Steed	.989	28	165	23	2	1	2

First Base	PCT	G	PO	A	E	DP
Anthony	.986	8	64	4	1	7
Konerko	1.000	9	32	0	0	7
LoDuca	.988	21	142	16	2	9
Melendez	1.000	67	507	37	0	50
S. Richardson	1.000	8	58	1	0	3
Roberge	.994	45	334	21	2	28
Sell	.905	3	17	2	2	4
Steed	1.000	15	116	10	0	15

Second Base	PCT	G	PO	A	E	DP
Anderson	.979	9	20	26	1	7
Cora	.667	1	2	0	1	0
Guerrero	.989	21	44	49	1	13
Ingram	.985	30	49	81	2	21
Johnson	1.000	1	1	2	0	2
Jones	1.000	2	1	2	0	0
Riggs	.954	44	82	125	10	28
Roberge	.954	34	69	77	7	19
Rodriguez	.960	5	9	15	1	4
Saitta	1.000	5	9	11	0	3

Third Base	PCT	G	PO	A	E	DP
Anderson	.934	25	15	42	4	2
Cuevas	1.000	5	4	9	0	2
Ingram	.934	23	9	48	4	1
Johnson	.926	40	15	73	7	4
Jones	.800	3	1	3	1	1
Konerko	1.000	1	0	1	0	0
LoDuca	.733	13	4	7	4	2
B. Richardson	1.000	4	4	11	0	1
S. Richardson	.571	3	2	2	3	0
Roberge	.924	53	25	96	10	6
Rodriguez	1.000	1	1	1	0	0

Shortstop	PCT	G	PO	A	E	DP
Anderson	.964	15	15	38	2	6
Cora	.959	80	124	270	17	54
Cromer	.952	8	3	17	1	2
Ingram	.667	1	1	1	1	1
Johnson	.973	42	54	127	5	26
Jones	1.000	10	11	32	0	9

Outfield	PCT	G	PO	A	E	DP
Anthony	1.000	40	55	6	0	0
Bocachica	.976	25	80	2	2	1
Dandridge	.000	2	0	0	0	0
Gibbs	1.000	2	4	0	0	0
Guerrero	1.000	8	11	0	0	0
Hubbard	1.000	10	13	1	0	0
Ingram	1.000	54	60	1	0	0
Johnson	1.000	1	1	0	0	0
Konerko	.912	21	29	2	3	0
Moreta	1.000	8	16	1	0	0
S. Richardson	.972	77	100	5	3	2
Roberge	1.000	7	6	0	0	0
Romero	.964	108	181	6	7	2
Sell	1.000	31	60	2	0	0
St'schneider	.993	71	131	2	1	0

SAN ANTONIO — Class AA

TEXAS LEAGUE

BATTING	AVG	G	AB	R	H	2B	3B	HR	RBI	BB	SO	SB	CS	B	T	HT	WT	DOB	1st Yr	Resides
Allen, Luke	.333	23	78	9	26	3	1	3	10	6	16	1	2	L	R	6-2	208	8-4-78	1997	Covington, Ga.
Anderson, Cliff	.210	29	100	13	21	3	1	2	9	1	17	0	0	L	R	5-8	165	7-4-70	1992	Kodiak, Alaska
Beltre, Adrian	.321	64	246	49	79	21	2	13	56	39	37	20	4	R	R	5-11	165	4-7-78	1995	Santo Domingo, D.R.
Bergeron, Peter	.317	109	416	81	132	17	8	8	54	61	69	33	9	L	R	6-2	185	11-9-77	1996	Greenfield, Mass.
Cooney, Kyle	.250	1	4	1	1	0	0	0	0	0	0	0	0	R	R	6-2	200	3-31-73	1994	Meriden, Conn.
Davis, Glenn	.290	20	69	14	20	2	0	6	15	10	22	2	0	B	L	6-1	200	11-25-75	1997	Aston, Pa.
Diaz, Juan	.266	56	188	26	50	13	0	13	30	15	45	0	0	R	R	6-2	228	2-19-76	1996	Santo Domingo, D.R.
Gil, Geronimo	.290	75	241	27	70	17	3	6	29	15	43	2	1	R	R	6-2	195	8-7-75	1996	Oaxaca, Mexico
Harkrider, Kip	.239	103	343	37	82	18	4	3	40	30	57	8	4	L	R	5-11	175	9-16-75	1997	Carthage, Texas
Johnson, Keith	.299	40	154	20	46	10	1	3	16	10	26	10	5	R	R	5-11	200	4-17-71	1992	Stockton, Calif.
Jones, Jack	.226	77	248	36	56	9	4	5	28	18	69	3	4	R	R	5-11	165	11-7-74	1996	Modesto, Calif.
Malave, Jaime	.255	28	55	3	14	5	0	1	4	6	10	0	0	R	R	6-0	196	3-22-75	1995	Fort Lauderdale, Fla.
Metcalfe, Mike	.282	57	213	35	60	5	5	3	19	30	24	19	15	R	R	5-10	175	1-2-73	1994	Orlando, Fla.
Mota, Tony	.243	59	222	20	54	10	6	2	22	12	36	16	8	B	R	6-1	170	10-31-77	1996	Miami, Fla.
Nelson, Charles	.233	91	236	36	55	9	0	4	19	22	34	13	5	L	L	5-10	180	8-11-71	1994	Perham, Minn.

BATTING	AVG	G	AB	R	H	2B	3B	HR	RBI	BB	SO	SB	CS	B	T	HT	WT	DOB	1st Yr	Resides
Pena, Angel	.335	126	483	81	162	32	2	22	105	48	80	9	5	R	R	5-10	228	2-16-75	1993	San Pedro de Macoris, D.R.
Pimentel, Jose	.203	90	271	34	55	4	4	4	24	17	59	16	7	R	R	6-0	160	12-3-74	1993	San Cristobal, D.R.
Rolls, Damian	.219	50	160	18	35	6	0	1	9	6	28	2	0	R	R	6-2	205	9-15-77	1996	Kansas City, Kan.
Sell, Chip	.252	64	218	36	55	12	6	3	37	22	40	6	0	L	R	6-2	205	6-19-71	1994	Otis, Ore.
Stuckenschneider, Eric	.277	72	282	60	78	16	7	3	22	44	47	16	3	R	R	6-0	200	8-24-71	1994	Freeburg, Mo.
Tucker, Jon	.297	100	360	46	107	34	2	10	64	41	74	3	5	L	L	6-4	200	12-17-76	1995	Northridge, Calif.

PITCHING	W	L	ERA	G	GS	CG	SV	IP	H	R	ER	BB	SO	B	T	HT	WT	DOB	1st Yr	Resides
Babineaux, Darrin	5	4	3.38	39	4	0	3	77	66	34	29	33	56	R	R	6-4	210	7-10-74	1995	Rayne, La.
Bland, Nate	4	2	2.78	26	0	0	0	45	56	21	14	14	34	L	L	6-5	195	12-27-74	1993	Birmingham, Ala.
Davis, Allen	2	2	3.16	6	5	0	0	31	31	13	11	9	33	L	L	6-4	195	10-1-75	1998	Ovilla, Texas
Deskins, Casey	4	8	4.87	22	16	0	0	94	118	68	51	22	64	R	L	6-3	205	4-5-72	1996	Yakima, Wash.
Dollar, Toby	6	11	5.48	23	22	2	0	143	170	97	87	39	65	R	R	6-3	215	12-27-74	1996	Graham, Texas
Garcia, Miguel	1	3	4.27	26	7	0	0	65	65	36	31	31	39	R	R	6-2	175	2-15-75	1992	Santiago, D.R.
Garrett, Hal	2	1	3.63	11	2	0	2	22	21	9	9	13	13	R	R	6-2	175	4-27-75	1993	Mount Juliet, Tenn.
Hall, Darren	0	0	10.80	2	2	0	0	2	1	2	2	1	2	R	R	6-3	207	7-14-64	1986	Irving, Texas
Herges, Matt	0	0	0.00	3	0	0	0	6	3	0	0	2	3	L	R	6-0	200	4-1-70	1992	Champaign, Ill.
Kubenka, Jeff	0	0	7.00	9	0	0	0	9	10	11	7	7	10	R	L	6-1	191	8-24-74	1996	Schulenburg, Texas
Lilly, Ted	8	4	3.30	17	17	0	0	112	114	50	41	37	96	L	L	6-1	177	1-4-76	1996	Fresno, Calif.
Masaoka, Onan	6	6	5.32	27	20	1	1	110	114	79	65	63	94	R	L	6-0	188	10-27-77	1995	Hilo, Hawaii
Mayo, Blake	2	1	1.47	13	0	0	1	18	13	3	3	6	15	R	R	6-2	210	12-18-72	1996	Gadsden, Ala.
Mitchell, Dean	2	5	3.30	46	3	0	14	79	74	31	29	22	76	R	R	5-11	175	3-19-74	1996	Waco, Texas
Neal, Billy	1	2	4.66	31	0	0	0	48	58	31	25	22	27	R	R	6-0	201	9-20-71	1995	Scottsdale, Ariz.
Pearsall, J.J.	6	5	4.38	46	4	0	0	72	71	38	35	37	63	L	L	6-2	202	9-9-73	1995	Burnt Hills, N.Y.
Prokopec, Luke	3	0	1.38	5	5	0	0	26	16	5	4	13	25	L	R	5-11	166	2-23-78	1995	Renmark, Australia
Ricabal, Dan	2	9	6.12	54	1	0	15	78	78	59	53	40	61	R	R	6-1	195	7-8-72	1994	Rosemead, Calif.
Stone, Ricky	7	2	3.84	13	13	1	0	82	76	40	35	26	69	R	R	6-1	168	2-28-75	1994	Hamilton, Ohio
Williams, Jeff	3	0	2.59	7	7	0	0	42	43	19	12	13	35	R	L	6-0	185	6-6-72	1997	Page, Australia
Zamora, Pete	3	8	4.46	12	12	0	0	67	71	52	33	27	47	L	L	6-3	185	8-13-75	1997	Mission Viejo, Calif.

FIELDING

Catcher	PCT	G	PO	A	E	DP	PB
Gil	.979	28	170	20	4	0	2
Malave	.923	5	11	1	1	0	1
Pena	.984	112	781	81	14	9	16
Sell	1.000	4	4	0	0	0	0

First Base	PCT	G	PO	A	E	DP
Davis	.993	16	133	15	1	16
Diaz	.963	44	377	18	15	27
Gil	.976	9	72	11	2	5
Sell	1.000	4	35	4	0	3
Tucker	.985	73	676	64	11	54

Second Base	PCT	G	PO	A	E	DP
Anderson	.966	12	28	29	2	4
Harkrider	.976	38	76	128	5	23
Johnson	.714	2	2	3	2	0
Jones	.952	10	17	23	2	7
Metcalfe	.950	56	117	151	14	32
Pimentel	.960	26	47	72	5	17

Third Base	PCT	G	PO	A	E	DP
Anderson	.926	12	6	19	2	1
Beltre	.910	58	41	130	17	5
Johnson	.927	14	6	32	3	4
Jones	.909	8	3	7	1	2
Malave	.750	10	5	16	7	0
Rolls	.947	48	38	124	9	7

Shortstop	PCT	G	PO	A	E	DP
Anderson	.947	5	4	14	1	3
Harkrider	.949	63	86	176	14	34
Johnson	.944	25	28	91	7	11
Jones	.936	55	65	168	16	29

Outfield	PCT	G	PO	A	E	DP
Allen	.918	23	42	3	4	0
Bergeron	.992	107	228	17	2	5
Davis	1.000	6	5	2	0	0
Gil	.923	22	36	0	3	0
Mota	.969	57	89	5	3	1
Nelson	.980	49	95	5	2	0
Pena	.000	1	0	0	0	0
Pimentel	.935	46	80	7	6	1
Sell	.984	38	60	3	1	1
St'schneider	.968	71	114	6	4	1
Tucker	.971	18	32	2	1	0

SAN BERNARDINO — Class A

CALIFORNIA LEAGUE

BATTING	AVG	G	AB	R	H	2B	3B	HR	RBI	BB	SO	SB	CS	B	T	HT	WT	DOB	1st Yr	Resides
Allen, Luke	.298	105	399	51	119	25	6	4	46	30	93	18	11	L	R	6-2	208	8-4-78	1997	Covington, Ga.
Auterson, Jeff	.188	53	149	10	28	8	2	1	19	11	45	6	5	R	R	6-2	190	2-22-78	1996	Riverside, Calif.
Bell, Ricky	.232	133	483	38	112	18	3	5	50	16	99	6	9	R	R	6-2	180	4-5-79	1997	Cincinnati, Ohio
Blanco, Henry	.316	7	19	5	6	1	0	2	3	4	6	1	0	R	R	5-11	220	8-29-71	1990	Guarenas, Ven.
Bramlett, Jeff	.196	67	148	22	29	8	2	1	15	27	62	5	2	R	R	6-1	198	4-27-76	1995	Cleveland, Tenn.
Cromer, Tripp	.400	4	15	3	6	1	0	2	6	0	2	0	0	R	R	6-2	160	11-21-67	1989	Lexington, S.C.
Crosby, Bubba	.216	56	199	25	43	9	2	0	14	17	38	3	5	L	L	5-11	185	8-11-76	1998	Bellaire, Texas
Dean, Aaron	.167	40	102	6	17	6	0	1	6	6	31	2	1	L	L	6-2	200	11-21-76	1997	Newhall, Calif.
Gallo, Ismael	.298	68	235	23	70	10	2	0	21	17	23	7	3	L	R	5-11	165	1-14-77	1997	Ontario, Calif.
Goudie, Jaime	.183	49	175	16	32	5	3	0	4	11	36	4	2	R	R	5-10	170	3-8-79	1997	Columbus, Ga.
Illig, Brett	.236	41	123	13	29	8	1	2	14	16	42	0	2	R	R	6-3	195	9-4-77	1995	Phoenixville, Pa.
Karros, Eric	.267	4	15	3	4	1	0	0	1	0	2	0	0	R	R	6-4	226	11-4-67	1988	Manhattan Beach, Calif.
Leach, Nick	.235	131	469	49	110	30	2	6	48	44	96	6	11	L	R	6-1	190	12-7-77	1996	Madera, Calif.
McCrotty, Will	.221	103	344	20	76	18	0	3	29	11	69	1	2	R	R	6-2	195	6-23-79	1997	Russellville, Ark.
Moreta, Ramon	.257	134	536	67	138	19	7	1	24	44	109	46	23	R	R	5-11	185	9-5-75	1994	La Romana, D.R.
Morimoto, Ken	.262	44	130	21	34	2	3	0	5	5	35	11	2	B	R	6-1	163	9-22-74	1995	Hilo, Hawaii
Phoenix, Wynter	.248	110	318	38	79	16	3	7	47	35	67	20	11	L	L	6-2	208	12-7-74	1996	El Cajon, Calif.
Saitta, Rich	.296	121	446	62	132	17	7	5	51	52	92	23	17	R	R	5-10	170	7-28-75	1996	Marlboro, N.J.
Snow, Casey	.281	99	335	44	94	24	2	4	42	34	75	5	6	B	R	5-10	185	12-8-74	1996	Canoga Park, Calif.
Wilson, Steve	.229	15	35	0	8	1	0	0	3	0	12	0	0	R	R	5-11	200	6-12-74	1996	Marietta, Ga.

GAMES BY POSITION: C—Blanco 4, McCrotty 102, Snow 34, Wilson 12. **1B**—Bramlett 20, Dean 11, Karros 4, Leach 117, Wilson 1. **2B**—Cromer 3, Gallo 5, Goudie 48, Morimoto 38, Saitta 57. **3B**—Bell 133, Saitta 8. **SS**—Gallo 61, Illig 41, Morimoto 1, Saitta 46. **OF**—Allen 105, Auterson 51, Bramlett 14, Crosby 54, Moreta 132, Phoenix 81, Saitta 8.

PITCHING	W	L	ERA	G	GS	CG	SV	IP	H	R	ER	BB	SO	B	T	HT	WT	DOB	1st Yr	Resides
Avery, Paul	1	1	3.05	5	4	0	0	21	21	12	7	12	16	R	L	5-11	180	1-29-77	1998	Clovis, Calif.
Bell, Scott	2	1	0.92	8	0	0	0	20	20	4	2	7	11	R	R	6-4	210	1-19-76	1998	New Orleans, La.
Burnside, Adrian	1	10	7.81	21	12	0	0	78	97	79	68	48	65	R	L	6-4	190	3-15-77	1996	Alice Springs, Australia
Cervantes, Peter	0	5	5.54	30	7	0	0	65	79	48	40	22	57	L	R	6-2	185	10-13-74	1995	Los Angeles, Calif.
Chung, Rocky	1	2	4.44	5	5	0	0	24	24	13	12	6	22	R	R	6-2	176	7-1-73	1998	Seoul, Korea
Davis, Allen	1	2	2.90	5	5	0	0	31	30	13	10	7	34	L	L	6-4	195	10-1-75	1998	Ovilla, Texas
Dotel, Melido	0	1	8.35	11	0	0	0	18	12	20	17	30	15	R	R	6-3	163	4-20-77	1994	San Cristobal, D.R.
Fischer, Mike	1	3	4.56	12	12	0	0	51	57	35	26	15	38	R	R	6-4	200	12-10-76	1998	Crestline, Ohio

PITCHING	W	L	ERA	G	GS	CG	SV	IP	H	R	ER	BB	SO	B	T	HT	WT	DOB	1st Yr	Resides
Flores, Pedro	2	4	3.10	30	10	0	3	78	75	37	27	38	56	L	L	6-0	210	3-30-77	1996	Baldwin Park, Calif.
Hall, Darren	1	0	0.00	8	2	0	0	10	4	0	0	2	8	R	R	6-3	207	7-14-64	1986	Irving, Texas
Husted, Brent	3	6	3.60	49	0	0	1	85	77	41	34	24	68	R	R	6-3	198	3-30-76	1997	San Jose, Calif.
Kramer, Matt	0	1	6.00	8	0	0	0	12	13	8	8	1	8	R	R	6-1	200	4-4-76	1996	Simi Valley, Calif.
McDonald, Matt	3	2	4.59	24	0	0	0	49	50	36	25	32	55	L	L	6-3	200	6-10-74	1994	Princeton, Ill.
Montgomery, Matt	4	6	3.19	63	0	0	26	79	69	31	28	27	81	R	R	6-4	210	5-13-76	1997	Anaheim, Calif.
Morse, Paul	7	14	5.27	30	26	0	0	154	160	110	90	77	116	R	R	6-2	185	2-27-73	1995	Danville, Ky.
Moskau, Ryan	3	3	3.46	6	6	1	0	39	37	18	15	16	31	R	L	6-3	210	8-22-77	1998	Tucson, Ariz.
Prokopec, Luke	8	5	2.69	20	20	0	0	110	98	43	33	33	148	L	R	5-11	166	2-23-78	1995	Renmark, Australia
Regalado, Maximo	3	3	4.18	14	3	0	0	47	45	30	22	24	42	R	R	6-2	165	11-18-76	1994	Montecristi, D.R.
Scott, Tim	0	1	4.50	2	2	0	0	4	4	2	2	1	2	R	R	6-2	205	11-16-66	1984	Hanford, Calif.
Stover, C.D.	3	2	4.57	13	3	0	0	41	45	23	21	11	26	R	R	6-5	225	12-8-75	1996	Citrus Heights, Calif.
Taczy, Craig	6	11	5.85	35	16	1	0	125	155	102	81	66	83	L	L	6-7	215	4-15-77	1995	Crestwood, Ill.
Valdes, Ismael	1	0	2.84	1	1	0	0	6	7	2	2	1	4	R	R	6-3	215	8-21-73	1991	Victoria, Mexico
Workman, Widd	0	1	12.60	1	1	0	0	5	10	7	7	2	1	R	R	6-1	195	5-23-74	1996	Gilbert, Ariz.
2-team (20 R. Cuca.)	8	9	5.02	21	21	0	0	113	119	91	63	54	72							
Zamora, Pete	4	1	2.09	25	5	0	6	82	43	21	19	33	77	L	L	6-3	185	8-13-75	1997	Mission Viejo, Calif.

VERO BEACH — Class A

FLORIDA STATE LEAGUE

BATTING	AVG	G	AB	R	H	2B	3B	HR	RBI	BB	SO	SB	CS	B	T	HT	WT	DOB	1st Yr	Resides
Brown, Jason	.228	85	267	23	61	13	0	4	27	26	60	0	0	R	R	6-2	205	5-22-74	1997	Rolling Hills Estates, Calif.
Cedeno, Roger	.429	6	21	5	9	0	1	1	6	5	5	1	0	B	R	6-1	205	8-16-74	1992	Valencia, Ven.
Cuevas, Trent	.259	92	324	42	84	21	2	5	41	22	52	3	0	R	R	5-11	170	12-25-76	1995	Placentia, Calif.
Davis, Glenn	.237	102	376	63	89	14	2	20	63	70	106	13	4	B	L	6-1	200	11-25-75	1997	Aston, Pa.
Diaz, Juan	.292	67	250	33	73	12	1	17	51	21	52	1	2	R	R	6-2	228	2-19-76	1996	Santo Domingo, D.R.
Glassey, Josh	.226	58	159	19	36	7	0	2	16	35	27	1	2	L	R	6-1	190	5-6-77	1996	Del Mar, Calif.
Gomera, Rafael	.232	55	168	16	39	6	1	3	13	18	56	2	6	R	R	6-1	172	9-28-77	1995	San Cristobal, D.R.
Goudie, Jaime	.322	35	115	15	37	7	1	1	8	12	24	7	4	R	R	5-10	170	3-8-79	1997	Columbus, Ga.
Jones, Jack	.167	9	30	4	5	1	1	1	3	1	7	0	0	R	R	5-11	165	11-7-74	1996	Modesto, Calif.
Kelleher, Pat	.263	58	194	20	51	7	1	1	12	17	38	8	3	L	R	6-1	185	10-27-76	1997	Paradise Valley, Ariz.
Malave, Jaime	.270	28	89	12	24	6	1	4	9	10	16	1	0	R	R	6-0	196	3-22-75	1995	Fort Lauderdale, Fla.
Mejia, Max	.260	77	288	30	75	14	2	6	26	19	58	17	8	R	R	6-0	150	7-17-77	1996	Azua, D.R.
Morimoto, Ken	.167	45	144	20	24	2	1	0	8	21	38	13	1	B	R	6-1	163	9-22-74	1995	Hilo, Hawaii
Mota, Tony	.319	61	254	45	81	18	5	7	35	18	27	13	8	B	R	6-1	170	10-01-77	[illegible]	Miami, Fla.
Newton, Kimani	.280	62	168	26	47	3	1	5	13	29	35	10	3	R	R	6-1	195	6-16-79	1996	Christiansted, V.I.
Riggs, Eric	.248	61	230	30	57	12	3	3	17	23	46	3	4	B	R	6-2	190	8-19-76	1998	Miami, Fla.
Riley, Cash	.226	124	434	47	98	16	1	9	42	31	125	12	9	R	R	6-1	180	6-4-77	1996	Dallas, Texas
Rolls, Damian	.244	73	266	28	65	9	0	0	30	23	43	13	3	R	R	6-2	205	9-15-77	1996	Kansas City, Kan.
Ruiz, Ramon	.191	18	68	10	13	4	0	0	6	5	15	2	0	R	R	5-11	190	10-24-75	1997	Montebello, Calif.
Sankey, Brian	.259	98	309	35	80	11	1	9	44	24	52	0	1	L	L	6-1	195	6-12-74	1996	Orleans, Mass.
Torres, Bernie	.253	123	415	44	105	9	3	0	29	26	62	9	7	R	R	5-9	160	9-26-79	1997	Lara, Ven.
Warren, Lance	.212	37	66	6	14	4	0	0	7	9	23	5	2	L	R	6-3	185	8-14-78	1997	Richmond Hill, Ga.

GAMES BY POSITION: C—Brown 73, Glassey 53, Malave 24, Warren 9. **1B**—Brown 4, Davis 32, Diaz 55, Glassey 3, Sankey 53. **2B**—Cuevas 42, Goudie 18, Jones 3, Morimoto 45, Torres 49. **3B**—Brown 1, Cuevas 41, Goudie 15, Jones 2, Malave 2, Rolls 73, Ruiz 17, Warren 4. **SS**—Cuevas 14, Jones 5, Riggs 59, Torres 75. **OF**—Cedeno 6, Davis 54, Glassey 1, Gomera 54, Goudie 2, Kelleher 43, Mejia 74, Mota 54, Newton 53, Riley 100, Sankey 6, Warren 5.

PITCHING	W	L	ERA	G	GS	CG	SV	IP	H	R	ER	BB	SO	B	T	HT	WT	DOB	1st Yr	Resides
Bell, Scott	0	1	5.40	1	1	0	0	5	8	4	3	0	1	R	R	6-4	210	1-19-76	1998	New Orleans, La.
Castillo, Marcos	5	15	4.99	25	25	2	0	139	141	95	77	47	77	R	R	6-2	172	2-15-79	1996	Bolivar, Ven.
Chambers, Scott	3	1	6.21	43	2	0	2	84	99	75	58	36	85	L	L	5-10	175	7-10-75	1995	Benton, Ky.
Correa, Elvis	1	5	6.57	42	2	0	1	86	118	71	63	42	54	R	R	6-1	185	11-10-78	1996	Milwaukee, Wis.
Everly, Bill	7	6	4.57	49	4	0	3	106	108	65	54	31	59	R	R	6-1	175	6-15-75	1997	Carmichaels, Pa.
Feliciano, Pedro	2	5	4.61	22	10	0	2	68	68	44	35	30	51	L	L	5-11	165	8-25-76	1995	Dorado, P.R.
Foster, Kris	3	5	6.79	24	6	0	1	53	59	45	40	27	52	R	R	6-1	200	8-30-74	1993	Lehigh Acres, Fla.
Franklin, Wayne	9	3	3.53	48	0	0	10	87	81	43	34	26	78	L	L	6-2	195	3-9-74	1996	North East, Md.
Gagne, Eric	9	7	3.74	25	25	3	0	140	118	69	58	48	144	R	R	6-2	195	1-7-76	1996	Mascouche, Quebec
Garrett, Hal	6	6	4.97	20	20	1	0	112	111	75	62	57	86	R	R	6-2	175	4-27-75	1993	Mount Juliet, Tenn.
Mayo, Blake	4	7	2.94	32	7	0	5	83	70	35	27	48	53	R	R	6-2	210	12-18-72	1996	Gadsden, Ala.
O'Shaughnessy, Jay	4	9	5.01	30	17	0	0	101	88	65	56	83	116	R	R	6-3	220	8-14-74	1995	Belmont, Mass.
Paluk, Brian	4	7	6.27	35	10	0	2	99	118	79	69	43	58	R	R	6-6	225	10-5-75	1996	Plymouth, Mich.
Regalado, Maximo	0	2	6.75	4	4	0	0	16	17	15	12	13	14	R	R	6-2	165	11-18-76	1994	Montecristi, D.R.
Simon, Ben	1	2	6.75	7	5	0	0	19	22	14	14	7	16	R	R	6-1	185	11-12-74	1996	Berlin Heights, Ohio
Valdes, Ismael	0	0	0.00	1	1	0	0	3	2	0	0	1	3	R	R	6-3	215	8-21-73	1991	Victoria, Mexico

YAKIMA — Short-Season Class A

NORTHWEST LEAGUE

BATTING	AVG	G	AB	R	H	2B	3B	HR	RBI	BB	SO	SB	CS	B	T	HT	WT	DOB	1st Yr	Resides
Auterson, Jeff	.266	74	290	43	77	26	4	6	53	26	72	9	5	R	R	6-2	190	2-22-78	1996	Riverside, Calif.
Balbuena, Mike	.167	24	48	4	8	1	0	1	7	6	13	0	0	R	R	6-0	175	12-24-78	1997	Key West, Fla.
Collins, Michael	.284	18	67	5	19	2	0	0	2	4	6	2	6	R	R	5-9	166	1-29-77	1998	Phoenix, Ariz.
Detienne, Dave	.193	32	88	10	17	3	0	0	6	7	22	6	3	R	R	6-3	190	8-16-79	1998	Dartmouth, Nova Scotia
Feliciano, Jesus	.305	73	302	47	92	7	1	0	26	32	37	34	10	L	L	5-11	150	6-6-79	1998	Bayamon, P.R.
Garcia, Ismael	.284	41	102	20	29	4	1	2	15	10	22	1	0	R	R	6-0	170	9-11-77	1998	La Puente, Calif.
Goelz, Jim	.183	69	213	20	39	6	0	0	15	28	36	9	0	R	R	5-10	170	2-13-76	1998	St. James, N.Y.
Gorr, Robb	.264	66	254	43	67	9	2	5	35	15	33	2	1	R	R	6-0	195	9-14-76	1998	Vista, Calif.
Goudie, Jaime	.275	35	138	15	38	8	2	0	16	6	16	6	1	R	R	5-10	170	3-8-79	1997	Columbus, Ga.
Greer, Matt	.286	19	49	7	14	1	1	0	8	3	16	1	0	R	R	5-11	195	5-18-76	1998	Houston, Texas
Kellner, Ryan	.273	19	55	6	15	1	1	1	5	1	22	0	0	R	R	6-2	205	12-9-77	1998	Morganton, N.C.
Newton, Kimani	.245	41	147	19	36	6	1	4	18	12	29	7	2	R	R	6-1	195	6-16-79	1996	Christiansted, V.I.
Paterson, Joe	.278	56	187	20	52	14	2	6	34	17	37	2	4	R	R	6-0	195	12-22-78	1997	Ontario, Calif.

BATTING	AVG	G	AB	R	H	2B	3B	HR	RBI	BB	SO	SB	CS	B	T	HT	WT	DOB	1st Yr	Resides
Ross, David	.309	59	191	31	59	14	1	6	25	34	49	2	2	R	R	6-2	205	3-19-77	1998	Tallahassee, Fla.
Ruiz, Ramon	.259	39	139	27	36	8	0	4	19	20	40	1	2	R	R	5-11	190	10-24-75	1997	Montebello, Calif.
Sampson, Jacob	.203	36	74	12	15	2	2	0	9	10	18	2	1	R	R	5-9	170	9-9-78	1998	University Place, Wash.
Story-Harden, Thomari	.188	47	128	19	24	5	0	0	15	19	48	1	0	R	R	6-5	204	4-6-80	1998	Richmond, Calif.
Theodorou, Nick	.278	48	133	24	37	12	0	0	11	26	26	7	5	B	R	5-11	182	6-7-75	1998	Rialto, Calif.

GAMES BY POSITION: C—Greer 18, Kellner 13, Ross 57. **1B**—Balbuena 1, Gorr 64, Story-Harden 15, Theodorou 1. **2B**—Collins 8, Garcia 21, Goelz 15, Goudie 28, Theodorou 23. **3B**—Balbuena 14, Detienne 23, Goelz 9, Goudie 6, Ruiz 39. **SS**—Collins 12, Detienne 11, Goelz 52, Sampson 20. **OF**—Auterson 73, Balbuena 2, Feliciano 73, Newton 40, Paterson 39, Story-Harden 7, Theodorou 13.

PITCHING	W	L	ERA	G	GS	CG	SV	IP	H	R	ER	BB	SO	B	T	HT	WT	DOB	1st Yr	Resides
Avery, Paul	2	1	4.24	9	3	0	0	23	23	12	11	15	16	R	L	5-11	180	1-29-77	1998	Clovis, Calif.
Balbuena, Mike	0	0	10.80	3	0	0	0	3	5	4	4	3	2	R	R	6-0	175	12-24-78	1997	Key West, Fla.
Barnsby, Scott	2	4	5.01	26	3	0	1	50	63	37	28	22	35	R	R	6-1	185	11-20-75	1998	Torrington, Conn.
Bell, Scott	0	1	2.39	11	2	0	0	38	35	19	10	16	37	R	R	6-4	210	1-19-76	1998	New Orleans, La.
Bornyk, Matt	5	3	5.56	17	5	0	2	55	63	39	34	15	34	R	R	6-2	210	1-31-79	1997	Victoria, B.C.
Bridenbaugh, Christian	4	1	5.13	17	4	0	1	47	47	29	27	24	28	L	L	6-1	185	9-26-79	1998	Martinsburg, Pa.
Burnside, Adrian	1	4	4.05	8	6	0	0	33	27	21	15	30	34	R	L	6-4	190	3-15-77	1996	Alice Springs, Australia
Caraccioli, Lance	0	5	5.18	11	7	0	0	42	43	26	24	28	44	L	L	6-4	190	12-14-77	1998	Delano, Calif.
Colyer, Steve	2	2	4.96	15	12	0	0	65	72	46	36	36	75	L	L	6-4	205	2-22-79	1998	St. Peters, Mo.
Davis, Allen	2	0	1.13	4	2	0	0	16	10	4	2	3	14	L	L	6-4	195	10-1-75	1998	Ovilla, Texas
Gomes, Tony	2	8	4.09	16	11	0	1	73	76	53	33	34	52	R	R	6-0	190	9-10-77	1998	Delano, Calif.
Harrell, Tim	5	3	3.88	13	6	0	0	53	53	30	23	24	50	R	R	6-4	215	10-31-75	1998	Weaverville, N.C.
Hebert, Cedric	1	1	3.20	4	3	0	0	20	18	9	7	9	15	R	R	6-1	175	9-19-77	1998	Kaplan, La.
Moody, Jason	1	0	3.38	9	0	0	2	13	7	5	5	13	18	R	L	5-11	175	11-6-76	1998	Charlotte, N.C.
Moskau, Ryan	3	0	1.23	9	6	0	2	37	22	11	5	13	42	R	L	6-3	210	8-22-77	1998	Tucson, Ariz.
Pourron, Joe	0	7	6.32	25	4	0	10	47	50	43	33	30	33	R	R	6-7	222	3-12-77	1997	Jonesboro, Ga.
Proctor, Scott	0	1	10.80	3	1	0	2	5	9	8	6	1	4	R	R	6-1	198	1-2-77	1998	Jensen Beach, Fla.
Simmons, Wendell	2	2	4.50	15	0	0	0	22	24	15	11	15	18	B	R	6-1	170	9-9-76	1998	Macon, Ga.
Williams, Adam	0	0	7.36	7	0	0	0	11	17	9	9	6	15	R	L	6-3	215	11-29-78	1997	Montgomery, Ala.
Williams, Joel	0	1	16.41	15	1	0	0	17	31	42	31	40	10	R	R	6-1	190	11-26-79	1998	Delano, Calif.

GREAT FALLS — Rookie

PIONEER LEAGUE

BATTING	AVG	G	AB	R	H	2B	3B	HR	RBI	BB	SO	SB	CS	B	T	HT	WT	DOB	1st Yr	Resides
Allen, Shane	.260	54	154	28	40	7	1	0	14	32	27	8	5	R	R	5-11	165	4-25-79	1997	Glenns Ferry, Idaho
Araujo, Orlany	.270	61	215	37	58	18	2	6	45	25	35	8	2	R	R	6-2	178	6-13-78	1996	Lara, Ven.
Castellano, John	.267	35	101	10	27	5	0	1	16	15	12	2	3	R	R	5-11	185	9-8-77	1998	Dix Hills, N.Y.
Collins, Michael	.308	44	143	23	44	10	3	0	18	13	19	4	2	R	R	5-9	166	1-29-77	1998	Phoenix, Ariz.
Covington, Kevin	.221	40	122	26	27	4	0	5	15	15	39	5	0	R	R	6-1	190	4-18-78	1997	Centre, Ala.
Dean, Aaron	.327	44	159	22	52	15	2	2	24	8	30	3	1	L	L	6-2	200	11-21-76	1997	Newhall, Calif.
Dempsey, Nick	.295	40	129	20	38	7	0	4	15	8	32	4	2	R	R	6-5	212	12-15-78	1997	Durban, South Africa
Detienne, Dave	.221	21	68	9	15	3	0	0	9	6	21	7	1	R	R	6-3	190	8-16-79	1998	Dartmouth, Nova Scotia
Gomera, Rafael	.333	4	12	2	4	1	0	0	1	1	2	0	0	R	R	6-1	172	9-28-77	1995	San Cristobal, D.R.
Gonzalez, Jimmy	.277	69	278	43	77	17	2	9	61	11	32	2	1	R	R	5-9	155	8-13-78	1996	Juigalpa, Nicaragua
Hernandez, John	.286	40	133	21	38	7	0	3	15	6	23	3	0	R	R	6-2	190	9-1-79	1997	La Puente, Calif.
Jaramillo, Milko	.277	63	249	30	69	10	1	4	29	14	44	7	6	B	R	5-11	165	1-21-80	1996	Caracas, Ven.
Kluver, Hayden	.250	22	64	15	16	1	0	0	10	5	10	3	1	L	L	6-1	175	3-18-80	1998	Queensland, Australia
Moreno, Omar	.218	49	119	22	26	5	0	0	10	32	31	7	2	B	R	6-0	155	3-14-80	1997	Panama City, Panama
Piedra, Jorge	.383	72	282	72	108	22	7	2	33	39	29	16	7	L	L	6-0	175	4-17-79	1997	Van Nuys, Calif.
Proctor, Jerry	.255	30	106	12	27	0	5	3	19	2	31	2	2	R	R	6-5	200	3-5-78	1996	Pasadena, Calif.
Ruiz, Ramon	.200	9	25	6	5	0	0	0	1	4	0	1	0	R	R	5-11	190	10-24-75	1997	Montebello, Calif.
Thomas, Charles	.200	39	110	16	22	5	3	1	9	19	34	3	2	R	R	6-0	200	6-10-80	1998	Fresno, Calif.
Tomaszewski, Dane	.296	43	135	23	40	13	1	5	24	12	34	3	1	R	R	6-2	217	8-14-79	1997	Sydney, Australia

GAMES BY POSITION: C—Castellano 27, Hernandez 40, Tomaszewski 15. **1B**—Araujo 47, Dean 6, Dempsey 32, Tomaszewski 1. **2B**—Allen 4, Collins 13, Gonzalez 67. **3B**—Araujo 15, Collins 29, Detienne 11, Ruiz 9, Thomas 28. **SS**—Collins 6, Detienne 10, Jaramillo 62. **OF**—Allen 49, Covington 39, Gomera 2, Kluver 19, Moreno 43, Piedra 70, Proctor 29.

PITCHING	W	L	ERA	G	GS	CG	SV	IP	H	R	ER	BB	SO	B	T	HT	WT	DOB	1st Yr	Resides
Burgos, Ricardo	4	4	3.38	14	6	1	1	59	65	25	22	7	25	R	R	6-2	195	5-15-79	1998	Cayey, P.R.
Castillo, Wilson	3	4	4.76	16	10	0	1	62	57	37	33	37	47	R	R	6-3	195	12-9-78	1996	Santo Domingo, D.R.
Dotel, Melido	4	2	3.88	23	4	0	0	51	41	34	22	40	63	R	R	6-3	163	4-20-77	1994	San Cristobal, D.R.
Hebert, Cedric	6	1	2.55	11	7	0	1	53	40	20	15	21	51	R	R	6-1	175	9-19-77	1998	Kaplan, La.
Hughes, Nial	8	1	4.05	16	8	0	0	67	64	36	30	29	44	R	L	6-2	185	11-5-77	1997	Charlottetown, P.E.I.
Isenia, Derrick	2	5	6.24	15	9	0	0	58	64	58	40	33	47	R	R	6-3	170	12-24-77	1996	Willemstad, Neth. Antilles
Moody, Jason	1	1	4.67	14	2	0	2	27	25	16	14	14	35	R	L	5-11	175	11-6-76	1998	Charlotte, N.C.
Moon, Jared	1	5	10.74	19	1	0	2	33	54	44	39	32	25	R	R	6-4	190	3-2-79	1997	Redondo Beach, Calif.
Parker, Beau	4	2	3.08	16	11	0	0	73	67	33	25	32	72	R	R	6-4	185	6-7-79	1997	Vancouver, Wash.
Piedra, Alex	0	0	27.00	3	0	0	0	2	1	5	5	4	0	R	R	6-2	195	2-1-80	1998	Miami, Fla.
Regalado, Maximo	0	0	0.00	3	0	0	0	6	2	0	0	3	7	R	R	6-2	165	11-18-76	1994	Montecristi, D.R.
Rijo, Fernando	3	1	4.32	14	6	0	0	50	44	34	24	35	42	R	R	5-11	155	11-15-77	1995	La Romana, D.R.
Suares, Orlando	1	4	6.65	21	4	0	0	46	50	35	34	26	38	R	R	6-2	175	4-6-77	1996	Ciudad Dario, Nicaragua
Taylor, J.K.	2	3	3.77	15	4	0	3	43	48	26	18	14	43	L	R	6-2	170	6-11-80	1998	Louisa, Va.
Williams, Adam	1	2	5.00	10	3	0	1	27	23	16	15	23	32	R	L	6-3	215	11-29-78	1997	Montgomery, Ala.

MILWAUKEE BREWERS

Missed opportunities mark Milwaukee's return to NL

BY TOM HAUDRICOURT

If the only Brewers game you saw in 1998 was their final one, it told you all you needed to know about their first season in the National League.

The Brewers collected 10 hits and four walks against the Los Angeles Dodgers that day and also reached base on two errors. They loaded the bases three times, once with one out and once with nobody out.

Certainly, it had to be a rout for the Brewers, right?

No, a 2-1 defeat, leaving them with a discouraging 74-88 record.

"That sums up the whole year," said manager Phil Garner, who kept his job despite speculation that he'd get a pink slip. "Missed opportunities. Failure to make adjustments. Failure to get the job done. Too many times this year, when the game was on the line we didn't get the job done."

Much of the Brewers' offensive failure was tied to the injury-riddled, unproductive seasons of left fielder David Nilsson and first baseman John Jaha. Considered vital cogs in the lineup, neither was a factor in an attack that seldom roared unless right fielder Jeromy Burnitz had a big night.

Other than the 38 homers and 125 RBIs by Burnitz–the most by any lefthanded batter in the league–and the offensive contributions at the top of the lineup by all-star second baseman Fernando Vina, third baseman Jeff Cirillo and utilityman Mark Loretta, not much went right for the Brew Crew in 1998.

But offense wasn't the Brewers' only shortcoming. Injuries ravaged the starting rotation, leaving only one original member–Scott Karl–standing at the end. Before all was said and done, three pitchers who began the season in the minors were in the rotation, including Bill Pulsipher, the onetime phenom acquired from the New York Mets on July 31.

Just as damaging was the meltdown of veteran closer Doug Jones, the team MVP the previous season when he converted 36 of 38 save opportunities. His ineffectiveness forced the Brewers to remove him from the closer's role and eventually trade him to the Indians.

And to think the Brewers were bubbling with optimism after being realigned from the American League Central to the NL Central. Never in their wildest dreams did they expect a sixth consecutive losing season.

The news wasn't much more encouraging on the farm, either. Triple-A Louisville was the only team in the organization to finish in the top half of its league. The only other club to even finish at .500 was Rookie-level Ogden.

Louisville was led by second baseman Ron Belliard, who tied for fourth best in the minors with 114 runs scored. Outfielder Geoff Jenkins also spent time at Louisville, hitting .330 with seven homers and 52 RBIs there in between stints on the big league club.

Other organization highlights included 1998 first-round pick J.M. Gold, who made five starts for Ogden and was named the No. 4 prospect in the Pioneer League; outfielder Bucky Jacobsen, who led the Midwest League with 27 homers and 100 RBIs for Class A Beloit; and righthander Jose Garcia, the No. 8 prospect in the California League.

Just one year away from moving into their new facility, Miller Park, the Brewers obviously have a lot of work to do.

Jeromy Burnitz — Ron Belliard

Players of the Year

Major League: Jeromy Burnitz, of
Burnitz finished fifth in the NL with 125 RBIs and his 38 home runs tied for sixth best in the league.

Minor League: Ron Belliard, 2b, Louisville
Belliard tied for fourth best in the minors with 114 runs while hitting .321-14-73 for Louisville.

ORGANIZATION LEADERS

BATTING		
*AVG	Jeff Pickler, Ogden	.364
R	Ron Belliard, Louisville	114
H	Anthony Iopoce, El Paso	181
TB	Kevin Barker, Louisville/El Paso	278
2B	Two tied at	36
3B	Santiago Perez, Louisville/El Paso	16
HR	Kevin Barker, Louisville/El Paso	28
RBI	Kevin Barker, Louisville/El Paso	110
BB	Bucky Jacobsen, Beloit	83
SO	Bucky Jacobsen, Beloit	133
SB	Two tied at	43
PITCHING		
W	Two tied at	13
L	Jose Garcia, Stockton	12
#ERA	Jason Childers, Beloit	1.92
G	Greg Mullins, Louisville	61
CG	Two tied at	4
SV	Brian Mallette, Beloit	23
IP	Brian Passini, El Paso/Stockton	170
BB	Jose Garcia, Stockton	91
SO	Jose Garcia, Stockton	167

*Minimum 250 At-Bats #Minimum 75 Innings

Milwaukee BREWERS

Manager: Phil Garner

1998 Record: 74-88, .457 (5th, NL Central)

BATTING	AVG	G	AB	R	H	2B	3B	HR	RBI	BB	SO	SB	CS	B	T	HT	WT	DOB	1st Yr	Resides
Banks, Brian	.292	24	24	3	7	2	0	1	5	4	7	0	0	B	R	6-3	200	9-28-70	1993	Mesa, Ariz.
Belliard, Ron	.200	8	5	0	1	0	0	0	0	0	0	0	0	R	R	5-9	176	4-7-75	1994	Miami, Fla.
Burnitz, Jeromy	.263	161	609	92	160	28	1	38	125	70	158	7	4	L	R	6-0	205	4-14-69	1990	Tavernier, Fla.
Cirillo, Jeff	.321	156	604	97	194	31	1	14	68	79	88	10	4	R	R	6-2	193	9-23-69	1991	Seattle, Wash.
Grissom, Marquis	.271	142	542	57	147	28	1	10	60	24	78	13	8	R	R	5-11	192	4-17-67	1988	Fairburn, Ga.
Hamelin, Bob	.219	109	146	15	32	6	0	7	22	16	30	0	1	L	L	6-0	235	11-29-67	1988	Leawood, Kan.
Hughes, Bobby	.230	85	217	28	50	7	2	9	29	16	53	1	2	R	R	6-4	240	3-10-71	1992	North Hollywood, Calif.
Jackson, Darrin	.240	114	204	20	49	13	1	4	20	9	37	1	1	R	R	6-0	186	8-22-63	1981	Mesa, Ariz.
Jaha, John	.208	73	216	29	45	6	1	7	38	49	66	1	3	R	R	6-1	225	5-25-66	1985	Camas, Wash.
Jenkins, Geoff	.229	84	262	33	60	12	1	9	28	20	61	1	3	L	R	6-1	205	7-21-74	1996	Stateline, Nev.
Jensen, Marcus	.000	2	2	0	0	0	0	0	0	0	2	0	0	B	R	6-4	204	12-14-72	1990	Scottsdale, Ariz.
Levis, Jesse	.351	22	37	4	13	0	0	0	4	7	6	1	0	L	R	5-9	200	4-14-68	1989	Elkins Park, Pa.
Loretta, Mark	.316	140	434	55	137	29	0	6	54	42	47	9	6	R	R	6-0	180	8-14-71	1993	Laguna Niguel, Calif.
Martinez, Greg	.000	13	3	2	0	0	0	0	0	1	2	2	0	B	R	5-10	168	1-27-72	1993	Las Vegas, Nev.
Matheny, Mike	.238	108	320	24	76	13	0	6	27	11	63	1	0	R	R	6-3	205	9-22-70	1991	Weldon Springs, Mo.
Newfield, Marc	.237	93	186	15	44	7	0	3	25	19	29	0	1	R	R	6-4	225	10-19-72	1990	Huntington Beach, Calif.
Nilsson, Dave	.269	102	309	39	83	14	1	12	56	33	48	2	2	L	R	6-3	230	12-14-69	1987	Samford, Australia
Owens, Eric	.125	34	40	5	5	2	0	1	4	2	6	0	0	R	R	6-1	184	2-3-71	1992	Rocky Mount, Va.
Valentin, Jose	.224	151	428	65	96	24	0	16	49	63	105	10	7	L	R	5-10	175	10-12-69	1987	Manati, P.R.
Vina, Fernando	.311	159	637	101	198	39	7	7	45	54	46	22	16	L	R	5-9	170	4-16-69	1991	Elk Grove, Calif.

PITCHING	W	L	ERA	G	GS	CG	SV	IP	H	R	ER	BB	SO	B	T	HT	WT	DOB	1st Yr	Resides
Chouinard, Bobby	0	0	3.00	1	0	0	0	3	5	1	1	0	1	R	R	6-1	188	5-1-72	1990	Forest Grove, Ore.
De los Santos, Valerio	0	0	2.91	13	0	0	0	22	11	7	7	2	18	L	L	6-4	185	10-6-75	1993	Santo Domingo, D.R.
Eldred, Cal	4	8	4.80	23	23	0	0	133	157	82	71	61	86	R	R	6-4	235	11-24-67	1989	Chandler, Ariz.
Fox, Chad	1	4	3.95	49	0	0	0	57	56	27	25	20	64	R	R	6-3	190	9-3-70	1992	Houston, Texas
Henderson, Ryan	0	0	9.82	2	0	0	0	4	5	4	4	0	1	R	R	6-1	190	9-30-69	1992	Dana Point, Calif.
Hudson, Joe	0	0	162.00	1	0	0	0	0	2	6	6	4	0	R	R	6-1	180	9-29-70	1992	Medford, N.J.
Jones, Doug	3	4	5.17	46	0	0	12	54	65	32	31	11	43	R	R	6-2	225	6-24-57	1978	Tucson, Ariz.
Juden, Jeff	7	11	5.53	24	24	2	0	138	149	91	85	66	109	B	R	6-8	265	1-19-71	1989	Salem, Mass.
Karl, Scott	10	11	4.40	33	33	0	0	192	219	104	94	66	102	L	L	6-2	205	8-9-71	1992	Solana Beach, Calif.
Mercedes, Jose	2	2	6.75	7	5	0	0	32	42	25	24	9	11	R	R	6-1	210	3-5-71	1992	Las Palmillas, D.R.
Mullins, Greg	0	0	0.00	2	0	0	0	1	1	0	0	0	1	L	L	5-10	160	12-13-71	1995	Palatka, Fla.
Myers, Mike	2	2	2.70	70	0	0	1	50	44	19	15	22	40	L	L	6-4	205	6-26-69	1990	Charlotte, N.C.
Patrick, Bronswell	4	1	4.69	32	3	0	0	79	83	43	41	29	49	R	R	6-1	220	9-16-70	1988	Winterville, N.C.
Plunk, Eric	1	2	3.69	26	0	0	1	32	33	14	13	15	36	R	R	6-6	220	9-3-63	1981	Riverside, Calif.
Pulsipher, Bill	3	4	4.66	11	10	0	0	58	63	30	30	26	38	L	L	6-3	200	10-9-73	1992	Port St. Lucie, Fla.
2-team (15 N.Y.)	3	4	5.10	26	11	0	0	72	86	41	41	31	51							
Reyes, Alberto	5	1	3.95	50	0	0	0	57	55	26	25	31	58	R	R	6-0	165	4-10-71	1988	Santo Domingo, D.R.
Roque, Rafael	4	2	4.88	9	9	0	0	48	42	28	26	24	34	L	L	6-4	186	1-1-72	1991	Santo Domingo, D.R.
Smith, Travis	0	0	0.00	1	0	0	0	2	1	0	0	0	1	R	R	5-10	170	11-7-72	1995	Bend, Ore.
Wagner, Paul	1	5	7.11	13	9	0	0	56	67	49	44	31	37	R	R	6-1	202	11-14-67	1989	Germantown, Wis.
Weathers, David	4	1	3.21	28	0	0	0	48	44	22	17	14	43	R	R	6-3	220	9-25-69	1988	Loretto, Tenn.
2-team (16 Cinc.)	6	5	4.91	44	9	0	0	110	130	69	60	41	94							
Wickman, Bob	6	9	3.72	72	0	0	25	82	79	38	34	39	71	R	R	6-1	220	2-6-69	1990	Abrams, Wis.
Woodall, Brad	7	9	4.96	31	20	0	0	138	145	81	76	47	85	B	L	6-0	175	6-25-69	1991	Blythewood, S.C.
Woodard, Steve	10	12	4.18	34	26	0	0	166	170	83	77	33	135	L	R	6-4	235	5-15-75	1994	Hartselle, Ala.

FIELDING

Catcher	PCT	G	PO	A	E	DP	PB
Banks	1.000	5	4	0	0	0	0
Hughes	.995	72	397	29	2	5	6
Jensen	1.000	1	1	0	0	0	0
Levis	1.000	14	83	2	0	0	1
Matheny	.987	107	570	45	8	9	6
Nilsson	.970	7	31	1	1	0	1

First Base	PCT	G	PO	A	E	DP
Banks	1.000	2	8	0	0	0
Cirillo	1.000	6	50	13	0	8
Hamelin	.992	51	230	7	2	22
Jaha	.994	57	442	24	3	57
Loretta	.992	70	353	23	3	41
Nilsson	.984	49	354	22	6	43

Second Base	PCT	G	PO	A	E	DP
Belliard	.000	1	0	0	0	0
Loretta	1.000	13	12	15	0	5
Owens	.500	4	1	0	1	0
Vina	.986	158	404	468	12	135

Third Base	PCT	G	PO	A	E	DP
Banks	.000	1	0	0	0	0
Cirillo	.976	149	99	339	11	45
Loretta	1.000	22	18	33	0	9

Shortstop	PCT	G	PO	A	E	DP
Loretta	.986	56	67	144	3	39
Valentin	.963	139	173	371	21	69

Outfield	PCT	G	PO	A	E	DP
Banks	.500	1	0	1	1	0
Burnitz	.972	161	306	10	9	3
Grissom	.991	137	317	8	3	3
Hughes	1.000	3	1	0	0	0
Jackson	.982	94	106	3	2	0
Jenkins	.968	81	115	6	4	2
Loretta	.000	1	0	0	0	0
Martinez	.000	6	0	0	0	0
Newfield	.962	55	73	3	3	0
Nilsson	.963	37	50	2	2	0
Owens	1.000	16	13	2	0	0

DAVID SEELIG

Fernando Vina

FARM SYSTEM

Director of Player Development: Cecil Cooper

Class	Farm Team	League	W	L	Pct.	Finish*	Manager	First Yr
AAA	Louisville (Ky.) Redbirds	International	77	67	.535	5th (14)	Gary Allenson	1998
AA	El Paso (Texas) Diablos	Texas	69	71	.493	5th (8)	Ed Romero	1981
A#	Stockton (Calif.) Ports	California	66	74	.471	t-7th (10)	Bernie Moncallo	1979
A	Beloit (Wis.) Snappers	Midwest	64	75	.460	12th (14)	Don Money	1982
Rookie#	Helena (Mont.) Brewers	Pioneer	21	55	.276	8th (8)	Tom Houk	1985
Rookie#	Ogden (Utah) Raptors	Pioneer	38	38	.500	6th (8)	Ed Sedar	1996

*Finish in overall standings (No. of teams in league) #Advanced level

LOUISVILLE — Class AAA

INTERNATIONAL LEAGUE

BATTING	AVG	G	AB	R	H	2B	3B	HR	RBI	BB	SO	SB	CS	B	T	HT	WT	DOB	1st Yr	Resides
Banks, Brian	.291	85	299	58	87	18	1	21	66	52	72	14	3	B	R	6-3	200	9-20-70	1993	Mesa, Ariz.
Barker, Kevin	.276	124	463	59	128	26	4	23	96	36	97	2	5	L	L	6-3	205	7-26-75	1996	Mendota, Va.
Belliard, Ron	.321	133	507	114	163	36	7	14	73	69	77	33	12	R	R	5-9	176	4-7-75	1994	Miami, Fla.
Brito, Jorge	.284	77	232	34	66	17	0	9	36	22	61	3	1	R	R	6-1	188	6-22-66	1986	Athens, Ala.
Diaz, Eddy	.238	86	277	31	66	15	1	5	40	28	27	8	5	R	R	5-10	160	9-29-71	1991	Barquisimeto, Ven.
Dunn, Todd	.382	10	34	5	13	3	0	1	1	0	10	0	2	R	R	6-5	230	7-29-70	1993	Jacksonville, Fla.
Jenkins, Geoff	.330	55	215	38	71	10	4	7	52	14	39	1	1	L	R	6-1	205	7-21-74	1996	Stateline, Nev.
Jensen, Marcus	.226	74	230	29	52	13	0	10	33	33	64	0	3	B	R	6-4	204	12-14-72	1990	Scottsdale, Ariz.
Kinkade, Mike	.309	80	291	57	90	24	6	7	46	36	52	10	2	R	R	6-1	210	5-6-73	1995	Tigard, Ore.
Krause, Scott	.292	117	390	71	114	25	2	26	82	46	104	11	4	R	R	6-1	195	8-16-73	1994	Willowick, Ohio
Lopez, Mickey	.250	3	4	1	1	0	0	0	0	2	0	0	0	B	R	5-10	165	11-17-73	1995	Miami, Fla.
Martinez, Greg	.261	115	376	65	98	4	11	4	25	51	80	43	7	B	R	5-10	168	1-27-72	1993	Las Vegas, Nev.
Martinez, Pablo	.237	63	186	22	44	4	1	2	9	18	31	6	3	B	R	5-10	155	6-29-69	1989	Sabana Grande, D.R.
Nicholas, Darrell	.294	130	497	87	146	28	8	12	64	40	113	31	13	R	R	5-11	180	5-26-72	1994	Garyville, La.
Owens, Eric	.335	77	254	48	85	11	4	5	40	34	30	21	6	R	R	6-1	184	2-3-71	1992	Rocky Mount, Va.
Perez, Santiago	.271	36	133	18	36	4	3	3	14	6	31	6	3	B	R	6-2	150	12-30-75	1993	Santo Domingo, D.R.
Williamson, Antone	.204	29	103	11	21	8	1	2	19	13	19	0	0	L	R	6-1	195	7-18-73	1994	Tempe, Ariz.
Zosky, Eddie	.245	90	257	36	63	12	1	8	35	15	47	1	3	R	R	6-0	180	2-10-68	1989	Fresno, Calif.

PITCHING	W	L	ERA	G	GS	CG	SV	IP	H	R	ER	BB	SO	B	T	HT	WT	DOB	1st Yr	Resides
Beck, Greg	4	3	5.67	10	8	1	0	46	40	31	29	16	37	R	R	6-3	215	10-21-72	1994	Fort Myers, Fla.
Chouinard, Bobby	2	1	4.93	7	7	0	0	42	52	31	23	15	33	R	R	6-1	188	5-1-72	1990	Forest Grove, Ore.
Cornett, Brad	3	3	3.65	12	8	0	0	62	64	30	25	14	34	R	R	6-3	190	2-4-69	1992	Odessa, Texas
De los Santos, Valerio	0	0	3.60	5	0	0	0	5	4	2	2	0	0	L	L	6-4	185	10-6-75	1993	Santo Domingo, D.R.
Dunbar, Matt	1	3	6.14	50	0	0	0	56	74	47	38	32	45	L	L	6-0	175	10-15-68	1990	Tallahassee, Fla.
Ellis, Robert	10	10	5.63	30	28	0	0	150	171	103	94	78	79	R	R	6-5	220	12-15-70	1991	Carthage, Texas
Estrada, Horacio	0	0	3.00	2	2	0	0	12	10	4	4	5	4	L	L	6-1	185	10-19-75	1992	San Joaquin, Ven.
Greene, Rick	6	6	3.51	58	0	0	18	67	73	31	26	33	44	R	R	6-5	200	1-2-71	1992	Miami, Fla.
Henderson, Rod	11	5	2.97	22	19	1	0	121	100	45	40	39	68	R	R	6-4	195	3-11-71	1992	Glasgow, Ky.
2-team (6 Ottawa)	11	6	3.47	28	19	1	0	132	123	62	51	51	80							
Hudson, Joe	1	0	5.11	9	0	0	0	12	13	7	7	5	4	R	R	6-1	180	9-29-70	1992	Medford, N.J.
2-team (46 Pawtucket)	3	2	4.65	55	0	0	10	60	70	39	31	28	36							
Minor, Blas	1	0	5.00	3	1	0	0	9	11	6	5	2	9	R	R	6-3	200	3-20-66	1988	Gilbert, Ariz.
Mullins, Greg	1	3	3.55	61	0	0	18	66	57	26	26	23	86	L	L	5-10	160	12-13-71	1995	Palatka, Fla.
Nix, James	2	2	7.01	27	1	0	0	35	43	28	27	24	28	R	R	5-11	175	9-6-70	1992	Burton, Texas
Pasqualicchio, Mike	0	0	3.00	1	1	0	0	6	6	2	2	4	5	R	L	6-1	205	8-17-74	1995	Astoria, N.Y.
Patrick, Bronswell	3	1	4.30	6	6	0	0	38	43	21	18	9	28	R	R	6-1	220	9-16-70	1988	Winterville, N.C.
Peterson, Kyle	1	0	7.94	1	1	0	0	6	8	5	5	2	4	L	R	6-3	215	4-9-76	1997	Henderson, Nev.
Reyes, Alberto	0	1	8.31	3	2	0	0	4	5	5	4	2	5	R	R	6-0	165	4-10-71	1988	Santo Domingo, D.R.
Rodriguez, Frankie	4	3	3.77	47	3	0	2	91	88	39	38	38	88	R	R	5-9	160	1-6-73	1992	Rowland Heights, Calif.
Roque, Rafael	5	2	3.62	9	8	0	0	50	42	21	20	19	43	L	L	6-4	186	1-1-72	1991	Santo Domingo, D.R.
Ruffin, Johnny	5	3	3.00	35	2	0	0	60	40	27	20	48	57	R	R	6-3	170	7-29-71	1988	Butler, Ala.
Sadler, Al	2	2	5.40	25	0	0	0	33	29	21	20	18	39	R	R	6-6	180	2-10-72	1992	Conyers, Ga.
Smith, Travis	4	6	5.32	12	11	0	0	68	77	44	40	25	36	R	R	5-10	170	11-7-72	1995	Bend, Ore.
VanEgmond, Tim	6	11	4.44	24	20	0	0	132	132	72	65	45	99	R	R	6-2	185	5-31-69	1992	Shreveport, La.
Wagner, Paul	1	0	8.76	3	3	0	0	12	17	12	12	5	6	R	R	6-1	202	11-14-67	1989	Germantown, Wis.
Woodall, Brad	1	1	3.90	5	5	0	0	30	32	19	13	15	27	B	L	6-0	175	6-25-69	1991	Blythewood, S.C.
Wunsch, Kelly	3	1	3.83	9	8	0	0	52	53	23	22	15	36	L	L	6-5	192	7-12-72	1993	Houston, Texas

FIELDING

Catcher	PCT	G	PO	A	E	DP	PB
Banks	.976	16	111	10	3	1	3
Brito	.991	71	405	35	4	2	8
Jensen	.994	68	441	33	3	2	3

First Base	PCT	G	PO	A	E	DP
Banks	.990	10	84	11	1	10
Barker	.992	112	949	73	8	88
Diaz	1.000	2	20	1	0	5
Jensen	1.000	2	3	1	0	1
Kinkade	.993	17	137	13	1	15
Williamson	.982	11	104	5	2	12

Second Base	PCT	G	PO	A	E	DP
Belliard	.978	130	228	401	14	98
Diaz	.920	11	18	28	4	7
Lopez	1.000	1	1	1	0	0
Perez	1.000	1	0	1	0	0
Zosky	.974	10	15	23	1	7

Third Base	PCT	G	PO	A	E	DP
Banks	.933	8	4	10	1	2
Diaz	.899	31	16	46	7	6
Kinkade	.916	53	46	107	14	12
Lopez	1.000	1	0	1	0	0
Owens	.920	33	16	53	6	4
Williamson	.833	14	18	22	8	3
Zosky	.922	28	8	39	4	4

Shortstop	PCT	G	PO	A	E	DP
Belliard	1.000	2	3	7	0	2
Diaz	.948	18	21	52	4	13
P. Martinez	.937	56	68	156	15	33
Perez	.963	34	67	90	6	18
Zosky	.961	49	74	149	9	33

Outfield	PCT	G	PO	A	E	DP
Banks	.979	30	45	2	1	0
Barker	.889	9	8	0	1	0
Diaz	.969	15	28	3	1	0
Dunn	1.000	4	6	0	0	0
Jenkins	.979	50	90	3	2	1
Krause	.963	94	151	4	6	0
G. Martinez	.991	104	219	5	2	1
Nicholas	.953	114	213	11	11	1
Owens	.973	39	69	4	2	0
Zosky	1.000	1	2	0	0	0

EL PASO — Class AA

TEXAS LEAGUE

BATTING	AVG	G	AB	R	H	2B	3B	HR	RBI	BB	SO	SB	CS	B	T	HT	WT	DOB	1st Yr	Resides
Andreopoulos, Alex	.321	113	377	72	121	35	1	10	93	54	31	2	3	L	R	5-10	190	8-19-72	1995	Toronto, Ontario
Barker, Kevin	[illegible]	[illegible]	[illegible]	[illegible]	[illegible]	[illegible]	[illegible]	[illegible]	[illegible]	[illegible]	[illegible]	[illegible]	[illegible]	[illegible]	[illegible]	[illegible]	[illegible]	[illegible]	[illegible]	[illegible]
Cancel, Robinson	.323	58	158	17	51	10	0	1	30	22	32	2	2	R	R	6-0	195	5-4-76	1994	Lajas, P.R.
Correa, Miguel	.279	136	537	75	150	26	5	13	89	27	98	11	8	B	R	6-2	165	9-10-71	1990	Arroyo, P.R.
Dunn, Todd	.313	75	294	60	92	28	3	13	57	27	63	7	2	R	R	6-5	230	7-29-70	1993	Jacksonville, Fla.
Faurot, Adam	.297	101	249	27	74	13	2	1	39	9	49	10	3	R	R	5-11	175	8-7-74	1996	Blountstown, Fla.
Green, Chad	.000	7	6	0	0	0	0	0	0	1	3	0	0	B	R	5-10	180	6-28-75	1996	Cincinnati, Ohio
Groppuso, Mike	.300	119	437	100	131	36	4	25	90	65	113	2	1	R	R	6-3	195	3-9-70	1991	Lake Katrine, N.Y.
Iapoce, Anthony	.314	133	576	97	181	23	6	2	53	33	67	35	20	B	L	5-10	178	8-23-73	1994	Ridgewood, N.Y.
Kominek, Toby	.302	135	496	114	150	33	4	17	83	73	120	21	16	R	R	6-1	200	6-13-73	1995	Erie, Mich.
Lopez, Mickey	.277	120	459	81	127	24	9	2	64	46	61	12	10	B	R	5-10	165	11-17-73	1995	Miami, Fla.
Lopez, Roberto	.271	73	199	24	54	15	1	1	26	22	24	8	5	B	R	5-9	160	11-15-71	1994	Bayamon, P.R.
Nilsson, Dave	.294	5	17	4	5	3	0	0	5	2	0	1	0	L	R	6-3	230	12-14-69	1987	Samford, Australia
O'Neal, Troy	.180	16	50	2	9	2	0	0	7	5	12	0	0	R	R	5-11	185	4-24-72	1995	Newark, Del.
Perez, Richard	.292	17	24	6	7	1	0	0	1	2	5	0	0	R	R	6-2	175	1-30-73	1991	Lara, Ven.
Perez, Santiago	.306	107	454	73	139	20	13	11	64	28	70	21	11	B	R	6-2	150	12-30-75	1993	Santo Domingo, D.R.
Phair, Kelly	.275	28	102	7	28	2	0	0	8	8	17	1	2	R	R	6-2	190	6-2-73	1995	Cincinnati, Ohio
Rennhack, Mike	.289	82	256	55	74	19	3	4	38	33	52	1	2	B	R	6-2	190	8-25-74	1992	Kissimmee, Fla.

PITCHING	W	L	ERA	G	GS	CG	SV	IP	H	R	ER	BB	SO	B	T	HT	WT	DOB	1st Yr	Resides
Beck, Greg	9	7	6.70	30	15	0	0	98	135	80	73	24	76	R	R	6-3	215	10-21-72	1994	Fort Myers, Fla.
Chavez, Carlos	3	5	5.91	54	4	0	0	88	104	74	58	45	83	R	R	6-1	210	8-25-72	1997	El Paso, Texas
Cornett, Brad	0	2	5.17	3	3	0	0	16	22	16	9	5	10	R	R	6-3	190	2-4-69	1992	Odessa, Texas
Dawsey, Jason	1	3	7.96	6	6	0	0	32	34	29	28	22	19	L	L	5-8	165	5-27-74	1995	Lexington, S.C.
De los Santos, Valerio	6	2	3.92	42	4	0	10	67	81	34	29	25	62	L	L	6-4	185	10-6-75	1993	Santo Domingo, D.R.
Estrada, Horacio	5	0	4.53	8	8	0	0	50	50	27	25	21	37	L	L	6-1	185	10-19-75	1992	San Joaquin, Ven.
Gallaher, Kevin	0	0	29.25	5	0	0	0	4	2	13	13	18	3	R	R	6-3	190	8-1-68	1991	Vienna, Va.
Hardwick, Bubba	3	3	4.93	32	1	0	1	49	66	35	27	24	26	L	L	5-10	170	1-18-72	1992	Eaton Park, Fla.
Henderson, Ryan	2	0	3.68	20	0	0	5	22	22	14	9	13	20	R	R	6-1	190	9-30-69	1992	Dana Point, Calif.
Hollins, Stacy	6	3	5.19	10	9	0	0	52	59	35	30	24	31	R	R	6-3	180	7-31-72	1992	Denver, Colo.
2-team (18 Shreveport)	7	5	5.79	28	12	0	1	98	113	75	63	53	60							
Hommel, Brian	1	3	7.41	14	0	0	0	17	23	17	14	14	16	L	L	5-10	170	10-26-72	1995	Indianapolis, Ind.
Huber, Jeff	1	1	7.79	9	2	0	0	17	31	18	15	3	12	R	L	6-4	220	12-17-70	1990	Scottsdale, Ariz.
2-team (7 Midland)	1	1	7.71	16	2	0	1	23	45	24	20	6	17							
Huntsman, Scott	4	3	8.35	52	0	0	3	74	106	71	69	31	49	R	R	6-2	235	10-28-72	1994	Zanesville, Ohio
Kirkreit, Daron	1	6	6.23	18	13	0	0	74	103	57	51	39	31	R	R	6-6	225	8-7-72	1993	Norco, Calif.
2-team (10 Wichita)	2	9	6.37	28	20	0	0	112	155	91	79	55	54							
Levrault, Allen	1	5	5.89	11	11	0	0	63	77	51	41	17	46	R	R	6-3	238	8-15-77	1996	Westport, Mass.
Mercedes, Jose	0	0	10.80	1	1	0	0	3	9	4	4	0	0	R	R	6-1	210	3-5-71	1992	Las Palmillas, D.R.
Minor, Blas	1	3	4.62	8	2	0	1	25	30	14	13	3	26	R	R	6-3	200	3-20-66	1988	Gilbert, Ariz.
Nix, James	0	0	14.09	8	0	0	0	8	20	14	12	6	11	R	R	5-11	175	9-6-70	1992	Burton, Texas
Norris, Joe	3	1	6.66	40	0	0	3	53	51	46	39	48	41	R	R	6-4	215	11-29-70	1989	Oswego, S.C.
Pasqualicchio, Mike	3	5	7.65	10	9	0	0	42	61	39	36	26	31	R	L	6-1	205	8-17-74	1995	Astoria, N.Y.
Passini, Brian	5	4	2.91	12	12	1	0	80	69	35	26	28	51	L	L	6-3	195	1-24-75	1996	Hennepin, Ill.
Peterson, Kyle	3	2	4.40	7	7	1	0	43	41	24	21	16	33	L	R	6-3	215	4-9-76	1997	Henderson, Nev.
Rodriguez, Frankie	0	0	1.50	4	0	0	0	6	7	2	1	2	5	R	R	5-9	160	1-6-73	1992	Rowland Heights, Calif.
Roque, Rafael	5	6	4.40	16	16	1	0	94	113	56	46	35	70	L	L	6-4	186	1-1-72	1991	Santo Domingo, D.R.
Sadler, Al	1	0	4.12	34	0	0	6	44	44	20	20	12	37	R	R	6-6	180	2-10-72	1992	Conyers, Ga.
Wunsch, Kelly	5	6	5.95	17	17	1	0	101	127	81	67	31	70	L	L	6-5	192	7-12-72	1993	Houston, Texas

FIELDING

Catcher	PCT	G	PO	A	E	DP	PB
Andreopoulos	.988	89	509	61	7	4	5
Cancel	.979	47	280	48	7	4	8
O'Neal	.984	16	101	20	2	2	3

First Base	PCT	G	PO	A	E	DP
Barker	.995	20	198	16	1	15
Cancel	.857	4	6	0	1	1
Groppuso	.995	52	375	37	2	55
Kominek	.980	66	602	31	13	52
Nilsson	.975	5	32	7	1	4
Rennhack	.972	5	33	2	1	3

Second Base	PCT	G	PO	A	E	DP
Faurot	.922	15	23	24	4	3
M. Lopez	.954	115	281	367	31	92
R. Lopez	.915	23	31	44	7	10
R. Perez	.938	3	5	10	1	3

Third Base	PCT	G	PO	A	E	DP
Cancel	.000	1	0	0	0	0
Faurot	.915	50	38	92	12	11
Groppuso	.929	67	40	131	13	16
R. Lopez	.894	41	16	68	10	10
R. Perez	.714	3	0	5	2	2

Shortstop	PCT	G	PO	A	E	DP
M. Lopez	.885	7	4	19	3	2
R. Perez	.800	5	3	5	2	1
S. Perez	.932	107	186	310	36	63
Phair	.927	28	56	83	11	20

Outfield	PCT	G	PO	A	E	DP
Correa	.957	131	238	7	11	1
Dunn	.939	68	114	9	8	0
Faurot	1.000	6	3	1	0	0
Iapoce	.973	133	279	8	8	1
Kominek	.975	66	110	7	3	1
Rennhack	.976	27	41	0	1	0

STOCKTON — Class A

CALIFORNIA LEAGUE

BATTING	AVG	G	AB	R	H	2B	3B	HR	RBI	BB	SO	SB	CS	B	T	HT	WT	DOB	1st Yr	Resides
Alfano, Jeff	.242	113	389	39	94	21	1	4	40	37	93	7	4	R	R	6-3	210	8-16-76	1996	Visalia, Calif.
Bearden, Doug	.231	115	359	43	83	15	0	1	26	28	80	6	6	R	R	6-2	180	9-11-75	1997	Lexington, S.C.
Cancel, Robinson	.188	11	32	3	6	1	0	0	2	4	8	2	1	R	R	6-0	195	5-4-76	1994	Lajas, P.R.
Colon, Jose	.263	50	156	20	41	8	1	4	21	16	34	2	3	R	R	6-2	190	1-25-76	1995	Melbourne, Fla.
Darula, Bobby	.289	18	45	10	13	4	1	1	8	8	6	2	0	L	R	5-10	175	10-29-74	1996	New York, N.Y.
Dunn, Todd	.154	3	13	2	2	1	0	0	0	0	4	0	0	R	R	6-5	230	7-29-70	1993	Jacksonville, Fla.
Elliott, David	.281	96	317	52	89	22	3	8	44	30	56	12	8	R	R	6-2	205	8-10-73	1995	Gladstone, Mich.
Green, Chad	.344	40	151	30	52	13	2	0	17	12	22	22	5	B	R	5-10	180	6-28-75	1996	Cincinnati, Ohio
Guerrero, Sergio	.275	40	120	10	33	4	0	1	15	12	5	1	2	R	R	5-9	180	12-22-74	1995	McAllen, Texas
Jenkins, Dee	.271	50	166	24	45	8	1	4	12	19	48	6	3	L	R	5-9	175	6-28-73	1991	Columbia, S.C.
Klimek, Josh	.284	124	440	61	125	27	6	9	56	36	60	4	2	L	R	6-1	175	2-2-74	1996	St. Louis, Mo.
Macalutas, Jon	.285	138	527	72	150	31	0	6	59	40	52	6	8	R	R	6-0	190	1-3-74	1996	Stockton, Calif.
Mathis, Jared	.289	69	204	24	59	6	0	0	17	3	17	8	0	R	R	5-10	175	8-8-75	1997	Port Orange, Fla.
Phair, Kelly	.265	70	238	42	63	18	0	3	27	25	47	4	2	R	R	6-2	190	6-2-73	1995	Cincinnati, Ohio

BATTING	AVG	G	AB	R	H	2B	3B	HR	RBI	BB	SO	SB	CS	B	T	HT	WT	DOB	1st Yr	Resides
Reeder, Cory	.224	44	116	12	26	5	0	4	10	11	41	0	0	R	R	6-2	220	3-17-71	1994	Columbus, Neb.
Rodriguez, Miguel	.255	95	290	36	74	11	1	5	40	22	61	9	5	R	R	6-2	195	5-14-75	1993	El Seibo, D.R.
Schaub, Greg	.267	134	479	45	128	24	1	4	52	3	75	9	5	R	R	6-1	185	3-30-77	1995	Kirkwood, Pa.
Walther, Chris	.279	115	419	52	117	20	4	3	50	21	41	2	2	R	R	6-2	200	8-28-76	1995	Odessa, Fla.
Washam, Jason	.213	86	235	24	50	12	3	1	28	33	38	1	2	R	R	6-0	190	8-18-74	1996	Lincoln, Ill.

GAMES BY POSITION: C—Alfano 106, Cancel 10, Darula 1, Mathis 11, Reeder 24, Rodriguez 1. **1B**—Macalutas 116, Phair 1, Reeder 7, Walther 26. **2B**—Bearden 12, Guerrero 36, Jenkins 48, Mathis 22, Phair 41. **3B**—Bearden 16, Guerrero 3, Klimek 85, Phair 8, Reeder 1, Walther 43. **SS**—Bearden 91, Klimek 20, Mathis 15, Phair 30. **OF**—Colon 45, Dunn 2, Elliott 94, Green 40, Mathis 24, Rodriguez 44, Schaub 134, Walther 55, Washam 46.

PITCHING	W	L	ERA	G	GS	CG	SV	IP	H	R	ER	BB	SO	B	T	HT	WT	DOB	1st Yr	Resides
Akin, Jay	2	3	2.96	44	0	0	2	85	95	33	28	34	75	L	L	6-2	200	7-9-74	1997	Memphis, Tenn.
Alejo, Nigel	2	3	7.96	8	7	1	0	32	44	33	28	17	22	R	R	6-0	190	1-12-75	1993	Maracay, Ven.
Crossan, Clay	1	1	9.64	17	0	0	0	19	32	21	20	11	8	R	R	6-1	175	8-30-73	1996	Granite Bay, Calif.
Dawsey, Jason	4	2	3.18	19	9	0	0	62	54	28	22	27	79	L	L	5-8	165	5-27-74	1995	Lexington, S.C.
Garcia, Jose	11	12	3.67	28	28	1	0	169	147	89	69	91	167	R	R	6-3	195	4-29-78	1996	Baldwin Park, Calif.
Gutierrez, Javier	0	2	19.29	5	0	0	0	5	4	10	10	11	5	R	R	6-2	220	8-26-74	1994	Puerto la Cruz, Ven.
Hardwick, Bubba	2	1	1.61	22	0	0	4	22	17	9	4	14	26	L	L	5-10	170	1-18-72	1992	Eaton Park, Fla.
Hawkins, Al	3	4	4.55	9	9	0	0	55	60	37	28	26	32	R	R	6-2	210	1-1-78	1996	Elizabeth, N.J.
Helmer, Chad	6	7	4.02	46	0	0	6	65	45	35	29	42	76	R	R	6-4	195	9-12-75	1997	Ruskin, Fla.
Hollins, Stacy	0	0	4.50	1	1	0	0	4	3	4	2	2	3	R	R	6-3	180	7-31-72	1992	Denver, Colo.
Johnston, Doug	5	1	2.69	9	9	1	0	60	47	20	18	26	54	R	R	6-5	180	3-16-78	1996	Omaha, Neb.
Lee, Derek	5	9	4.17	30	18	1	1	136	134	70	63	48	141	L	L	6-4	185	8-20-74	1997	Fort Worth, Texas
Levrault, Allen	9	3	2.87	16	15	4	0	97	76	33	31	27	86	R	R	6-3	238	8-15-77	1996	Westport, Mass.
Loiz, Niuman	0	0	7.84	12	1	0	0	21	24	19	18	19	15	R	R	6-5	230	12-12-73	1991	Moline, Ill.
O'Reilly, John	5	6	5.20	32	11	0	1	97	101	65	56	57	95	R	R	6-2	200	8-11-74	1996	Elmwood Park, N.J.
Paredes, Roberto	1	3	3.86	43	0	0	11	47	54	30	20	27	47	R	R	6-3	170	10-16-73	1993	Santo Domingo, D.R.
Passini, Brian	5	6	3.60	15	15	1	0	90	83	39	36	31	91	L	L	6-3	195	1-24-75	1996	Hennepin, Ill.
Peterson, Kyle	4	7	3.55	17	17	0	0	96	99	54	38	33	109	L	R	6-3	215	4-9-76	1997	Henderson, Nev.
Rosado, Juan	0	1	7.65	21	0	0	1	20	27	23	17	23	21	L	L	5-11	180	8-6-74	1994	Camuy, P.R.
Zapata, Juan	1	3	6.69	25	0	0	3	35	41	34	26	26	46	R	R	6-2	175	9-3-75	1993	Bani, D.R.

BELOIT — Class A

MIDWEST LEAGUE

BATTING	AVG	G	AB	R	H	2B	3B	HR	RBI	BB	SO	SB	CS	B	T	HT	WT	DOB	1st Yr	Resides
Beatriz, Ramy	.258	87	302	42	78	9	1	4	28	22	60	17	1	L	L	5-11	165	1-15-75	1997	San Pedro de Macoris, D.R.
Caiazzo, Nick	.287	127	505	56	145	22	1	7	71	23	77	3	1	R	R	6-4	215	5-17-75	1997	Portland, Maine
Colon, Jose	.261	44	157	25	41	7	0	5	29	10	29	0	2	R	R	6-2	190	1-25-76	1995	Melbourne, Fla.
Cridland, Mark	.260	79	296	35	77	16	2	6	37	14	63	0	1	L	R	6-3	195	5-15-75	1998	Galveston, Texas
Deardorff, Jeff	.255	88	326	41	83	17	1	11	45	27	125	3	1	R	R	6-3	205	8-14-78	1997	Clermont, Fla.
Guerrero, Sergio	.267	47	191	24	51	10	0	0	20	12	17	1	5	R	R	5-9	180	12-22-74	1995	McAllen, Texas
Guillen, Jose	.299	42	147	16	44	5	2	0	12	11	45	6	4	B	R	6-0	156	8-10-79	1996	Santo Domingo, D.R.
Jacobsen, Bucky	.293	135	490	86	146	31	1	27	100	83	133	5	2	R	R	6-4	220	8-30-75	1997	Hermiston, Ore.
Jaha, John	.000	2	4	1	0	0	0	0	0	2	2	0	0	R	R	6-1	225	5-25-66	1985	Camas, Wash.
James, Brandon	.223	81	269	34	60	13	1	8	33	31	82	2	5	L	R	6-2	215	3-26-75	1997	Carmichael, Calif.
Kirby, Scott	.203	107	359	51	73	19	2	8	40	47	109	5	4	R	R	6-2	190	7-18-77	1996	Destin, Fla.
Kraus, Jake	.314	86	271	47	85	18	1	6	42	46	33	0	0	R	R	6-4	225	10-13-73	1997	Malone, Wis.
Matheny, Mike	.250	2	8	1	2	1	0	0	2	1	3	0	0	R	R	6-3	205	9-22-70	1991	Weldon Springs, Mo.
Mathis, Jared	.267	24	90	12	24	5	0	0	3	1	8	0	1	R	R	5-10	175	8-8-75	1997	Port Orange, Fla.
Moon, Brian	.256	118	438	62	112	20	1	1	54	46	62	0	1	B	R	6-0	190	7-15-77	1997	Mansfield, Ga.
Moore, Donnie	.219	61	183	14	40	5	0	2	13	9	55	2	2	R	R	6-2	184	6-12-76	1995	Dallastown, Pa.
Nilsson, Dave	.417	4	12	3	5	3	0	1	7	2	0	0	0	L	R	6-3	230	12-14-69	1987	Samford, Australia
Osilka, Garret	.260	127	492	74	128	26	3	7	32	65	118	18	11	R	R	6-1	170	9-14-77	1996	Atlantic Beach, Fla.
Rogue, Francisco	.163	15	49	2	8	0	0	0	3	0	10	0	0	R	R	6-1	170	11-22-75	1993	Herrera, D.R.
Sanchez, Wellington	.248	39	137	23	34	5	2	0	15	19	24	3	2	R	R	6-0	162	5-27-77	1995	Nagua, D.R.

GAMES BY POSITION: C—Caiazzo 37, Matheny 1, Moon 94, Rogue 11. **1B**—Caiazzo 36, Jacobsen 1, James 30, Kraus 80, Nilsson 3. **2B**—Guerrero 45, Kirby 20, Mathis 11, Osilka 68. **3B**—Deardorff 87, Guerrero 1, Kirby 50, Mathis 2. **SS**—Guillen 42, Mathis 2, Osilka 62, Sanchez 39. **OF**—Beatriz 85, Colon 40, Cridland 79, Guerrero 1, Jacobsen 132, James 23, Kirby 21, Mathis 8, Moore 58.

PITCHING	W	L	ERA	G	GS	CG	SV	IP	H	R	ER	BB	SO	B	T	HT	WT	DOB	1st Yr	Resides
Byrd, Ben	3	7	3.79	39	2	0	1	76	83	49	32	25	62	R	R	6-0	195	10-31-75	1997	Taylorsville, Utah
Childers, Jason	8	6	1.92	34	14	1	0	117	104	48	25	22	110	R	R	6-0	165	1-13-75	1997	Augusta, Ga.
Childers, Matt	3	7	5.10	14	12	3	0	67	89	55	38	20	49	R	R	6-5	195	12-3-78	1997	Augusta, Ga.
Fox, Chad	0	1	4.50	2	1	0	0	2	1	1	1	0	3	R	R	6-3	190	9-3-70	1992	Houston, Texas
Hawkins, Al	6	3	3.58	15	14	1	0	88	94	52	35	20	64	R	R	6-2	210	1-1-78	1996	Elizabeth, N.J.
Incantalupo, Todd	3	8	5.02	29	13	0	0	100	129	69	56	47	59	L	L	6-2	185	5-18-76	1997	Norwalk, Conn.
Johnston, Doug	8	2	2.47	14	14	2	0	91	77	30	25	28	71	R	R	6-5	180	3-16-78	1996	Omaha, Neb.
Kendall, Phil	5	9	4.74	27	27	3	0	152	166	94	80	54	109	R	R	6-4	208	8-22-77	1996	Jasper, Ind.
Kirst, Mark	3	3	3.48	24	0	0	2	41	38	17	16	12	44	R	R	6-4	200	5-23-75	1997	Green Bay, Wis.
Krawczyk, Jack	3	1	4.69	19	3	0	0	40	37	23	21	11	42	R	R	6-4	195	8-12-75	1998	Scottsdale, Ariz.
Mallette, Brian	2	1	3.09	50	0	0	23	55	40	23	19	29	76	R	R	6-0	185	1-19-75	1997	Glenwood, Ga.
Myers, Aaron	4	5	4.68	11	10	0	0	58	65	36	30	19	41	R	R	6-2	215	5-14-76	1994	Santa Maria, Calif.
Priebe, Kevin	1	3	2.15	43	0	0	2	54	43	17	13	37	63	R	L	6-2	225	1-1-75	1997	North Fond du Lac, Wis.
Rosado, Juan	1	1	3.95	14	2	0	0	27	29	14	12	11	24	L	L	5-11	180	8-6-74	1994	Camuy, P.R.
Schubmehl, Brian	5	5	2.49	50	0	0	3	72	51	25	20	29	79	R	R	6-1	185	11-3-74	1997	Wayland, N.Y.
Stewart, Paul	8	10	4.90	26	25	1	0	143	164	99	78	45	114	R	R	6-5	200	10-21-78	1996	Raleigh, N.C.
Tank, Travis	0	1	4.00	4	1	0	1	9	12	6	4	4	7	R	R	6-2	220	3-27-75	1996	Sheboygan Falls, Wis.
Wagner, Paul	0	1	7.20	1	1	0	0	5	7	4	4	0	3	R	R	6-1	202	11-14-67	1989	Germantown, Wis.
Zapata, Juan	1	1	2.61	16	0	0	0	21	13	7	6	7	20	R	R	6-2	175	9-3-75	1993	Bani, D.R.

HELENA — Rookie

PIONEER LEAGUE

BATTING	AVG	G	AB	R	H	2B	3B	HR	RBI	BB	SO	SB	CS	B	T	HT	WT	DOB	1st Yr	Resides
Ayala, Elio	.237	9	38	6	9	1	0	0	2	4	6	1	1	R	R	5-8	160	11-7-78	1998	Bronx, N.Y.

BATTING	AVG	G	AB	R	H	2B	3B	HR	RBI	BB	SO	SB	CS	B	T	HT	WT	DOB	1st Yr	Resides
2-team (28 Ogden)	.277	37	112	18	31	2	0	0	7	16	15	1	2							
Baez, Juan	.195	45	128	17	25	3	0	3	10	13	41	5	1	R	R	6-0	173	12-23-77	1996	Santo Domingo, D.R.
Campusano, Nicholas	.261	35	115	11	30	7	0	1	11	7	26	1	0	R	R	6-1	162	10-31-79	1997	Santo Domingo, D.R.
Ceriani, Matt	.226	45	155	24	35	7	0	2	24	26	26	0	2	R	R	6-2	210	10-9-76	1998	Oxford, Miss.
DiPrima, Giancarlo	.284	50	176	24	50	9	0	0	13	24	12	20	6	R	R	5-8	150	11-17-76	1998	Eastchester, N.Y.
Doucet, Brandon	.275	49	178	22	49	12	0	1	21	13	57	7	1	R	R	6-1	215	8-24-76	1998	Abbeville, La.
Figueroa, Eduardo	.283	41	152	27	43	13	1	3	24	29	35	1	2	L	L	6-2	205	9-9-76	1998	San Juan, P.R.
Fox, Jason	.302	43	179	40	54	13	1	5	23	15	36	21	4	B	R	6-2	185	3-30-77	1998	York, Pa.
Guthrie, Kendall	.285	49	172	25	49	13	0	4	22	23	50	1	0	R	R	6-1	195	11-29-75	1997	Flower Mound, Texas
Hall, William	.176	29	85	11	15	3	0	0	5	9	27	5	5	R	R	6-0	175	12-28-79	1998	Nettleton, Miss.
Hammond, Derry	.216	62	232	31	50	13	1	13	45	12	98	4	3	R	R	6-2	205	10-19-79	1998	West Point, Miss.
Jaramillo, Lee	.269	50	167	28	45	16	1	2	22	23	32	2	1	R	R	5-11	185	12-14-76	1998	Franksville, Wis.
Patten, Chris	.282	66	241	42	68	7	1	1	20	39	56	4	3	R	R	6-1	180	12-8-78	1997	Tempe, Ariz.
Patterson, Marty	.182	11	33	5	6	1	0	1	4	5	15	0	0	R	R	6-2	200	12-24-74	1997	Lexington, Mich.
Rojas, Eliezer	.293	38	140	22	41	4	0	0	8	11	22	13	1	R	R	6-0	170	1-14-79	1997	Santo Domingo, D.R.
Warren, Tom	.300	4	10	1	3	0	0	0	1	3	4	0	0	B	R	6-4	170	11-1-79	1997	Pasadena, Calif.
Wayne, Tyrone	.303	54	208	29	63	13	1	6	40	6	37	7	4	R	R	5-9	180	8-30-75	1998	Flushing, N.Y.
West, George	.196	47	148	16	29	7	1	2	14	18	22	1	1	R	R	6-3	205	8-25-77	1998	Collings Lakes, N.J.

GAMES BY POSITION: C—Ceriani 44, Guthrie 19, Jaramillo 15, Patterson 1. **1B**—Figueroa 40, Guthrie 20, Jaramillo 7, Patterson 7, Wayne 1, West 3. **2B**—Ayala 5, DiPrima 2, Jaramillo 1, Patten 43, Rojas 31. **3B**—Campusano 31, Jaramillo 6, Wayne 2, West 43. **SS**—Ayala 4, DiPrima 47, Hall 27, Patten 2. **OF**—Baez 41, Campusano 1, Doucet 49, Fox 43, Hammond 19, Jaramillo 21, Patten 15, Patterson 2, Warren 4, Wayne 49.

PITCHING	W	L	ERA	G	GS	CG	SV	IP	H	R	ER	BB	SO	B	T	HT	WT	DOB	1st Yr	Resides
Arcangel, Arsenio	1	2	8.84	26	0	0	0	38	53	39	37	17	30	R	R	6-2	175	3-27-77	1996	Santo Domingo, D.R.
Baez, Juan	0	1	15.00	4	0	0	0	3	4	5	5	4	1	R	R	6-0	173	12-23-77	1996	Santo Domingo, D.R.
Barton, Chris	4	8	6.75	14	14	1	0	75	104	64	56	33	59	R	R	6-5	214	7-30-76	1998	Concord, Mass.
Cavanagh, Andy	3	1	3.63	11	10	0	0	57	64	32	23	24	39	R	R	6-3	210	5-3-77	1997	Dunwoody, Ga.
Childers, Matt	1	0	.64	2	2	1	0	14	9	1	1	4	4	R	R	6-5	195	12-3-78	1997	Augusta, Ga.
Connell, Brian	1	1	3.06	11	0	0	0	18	15	11	6	15	14	L	L	6-3	200	8-4-77	1996	Clearwater, Fla.
Greeny, Burdette	1	2	8.36	24	3	0	0	38	67	44	35	21	22	R	R	6-6	215	4-23-75	1998	Port Angeles, Wash.
Guzman, Jonathan	0	0	.00	2	0	0	0	3	2	0	0	1	1	L	L	6-2	220	8-26-77	1995	Levittown, P.R.
Jones, Fontella	0	3	4.05	23	0	0	4	40	38	20	18	17	50	R	R	6-2	210	5-25-75	1998	Pass Christian, Miss.
Krawczyk, Jack	0	1	4.32	7	0	0	0	8	10	7	4	3	11	R	R	6-4	195	8-12-75	1998	Scottsdale, Ariz.
Lewis, Rickey	3	6	6.95	12	12	0	0	57	72	54	44	42	44	R	R	6-2	220	4-3-77	1998	Biloxi, Miss.
Martinez, Luis	0	9	10.13	17	10	0	0	48	64	73	54	66	47	L	L	6-6	185	1-20-80	1997	Santo Domingo, D.R.
McConnell, Gary	1	1	10.19	17	1	0	0	33	49	49	37	35	35	R	R	6-3	190	5-6-78	1998	Donalsonville, Ga.
Myers, Rob	1	5	7.79	21	0	0	0	35	54	40	30	27	25	R	R	6-1	185	8-24-76	1997	Loganville, Pa.
Penney, Mike	1	5	7.38	10	10	0	0	46	63	47	38	20	36	R	R	6-0	185	3-29-77	1998	Laguna Niguel, Calif.
Poe, Ryan	3	3	4.66	14	5	0	1	46	52	30	24	15	43	R	R	6-2	220	9-3-77	1998	Mission Viejo, Calif.
Smith, Jesse	1	3	5.66	12	6	0	1	48	50	38	30	30	28	R	R	6-2	210	5-15-76	1997	Wayne, W.Va.
Sokol, Trad	0	4	5.62	24	3	0	4	42	47	35	26	23	41	R	L	6-1	185	5-12-77	1997	Charleston, W.Va.

OGDEN — Rookie

PIONEER LEAGUE

BATTING	AVG	G	AB	R	H	2B	3B	HR	RBI	BB	SO	SB	CS	B	T	HT	WT	DOB	1st Yr	Resides
Ayala, Elio	.297	28	74	12	22	1	0	0	5	12	9	0	1	R	R	5-8	160	11-7-78	1998	Bronx, N.Y.
Bordenick, Ryan	.281	38	128	24	36	11	0	3	24	18	29	0	2	R	R	6-1	205	12-7-75	1998	Greenville, S.C.
Brito, Obispo	.333	32	120	22	40	12	2	2	19	2	20	5	0	R	R	5-11	186	3-17-78	1996	Monte Plata, D.R.
Candela, Frank	.311	67	257	72	80	9	0	0	20	39	23	43	10	R	R	5-9	180	7-26-78	1997	Peabody, Mass.
De la Cruz, Erickson	.239	54	188	29	45	8	1	0	23	19	25	2	4	R	R	5-10	160	12-6-78	1997	Santo Domingo, D.R.
Eaton, Bill	.295	35	129	28	38	6	0	1	14	10	20	3	2	R	R	6-0	170	3-23-76	1998	Lake Worth, Fla.
Fernandez, Ramon	.264	56	197	35	52	11	1	6	35	18	60	8	2	R	R	6-0	185	9-21-77	1996	Cayey, P.R.
Mackiewitz, Mac	.295	65	251	45	74	15	1	2	45	27	37	3	2	L	L	6-2	217	6-6-76	1998	Brandon, Fla.
Martinez, Alejandro	.311	60	222	35	69	12	1	5	43	22	47	2	2	B	R	6-1	210	5-22-77	1997	Santo Domingo, D.R.
Montenegro, Jose	.184	48	147	22	27	7	0	1	14	17	36	1	2	R	R	6-0	185	4-26-76	1998	South Gate, Calif.
Morrow, Alvin	.221	52	163	35	36	8	1	5	26	50	65	7	2	R	R	6-5	240	4-28-78	1997	St. Louis, Mo.
Pickler, Jeff	.364	71	280	55	102	22	0	4	49	39	25	20	8	L	R	5-10	185	1-6-76	1998	Santa Ana, Calif.
Rowan, Chris	.221	56	195	38	43	8	5	11	45	24	75	4	1	R	R	6-1	190	3-18-79	1997	Mount Vernon, N.Y.
Stinson, Kevin	.264	26	91	12	24	4	0	1	16	11	18	0	4	R	R	6-2	210	1-31-76	1996	Kirkland, Wash.
Tucent, Francisco	.305	50	164	30	50	6	2	1	23	15	30	4	3	B	R	6-2	165	6-16-77	1997	Villa Mella, D.R.

GAMES BY POSITION: C—Bordenick 34, Brito 22, Stinson 22. **1B**—Fernandez 1, Mackiewitz 59, Martinez 18. **2B**—Ayala 1, Pickler 70, Tucent 12. **3B**—Montenegro 48, Rowan 2, Tucent 34. **SS**—Ayala 25, Rowan 54, Tucent 2. **OF**—Candela 66, de la Cruz 53, Eaton 34, Fernandez 48, Morrow 42.

PITCHING	W	L	ERA	G	GS	CG	SV	IP	H	R	ER	BB	SO	B	T	HT	WT	DOB	1st Yr	Resides
Alejo, Nigel	3	1	6.00	6	3	0	0	24	32	18	16	14	23	R	R	6-0	190	1-12-75	1993	Maracay, Ven.
Arroyo, Joel	1	2	9.38	13	0	0	0	24	31	32	25	24	9	R	R	6-0	208	7-16-76	1997	Ponce, P.R.
Eye, Jake	3	4	4.65	15	14	0	0	79	75	49	41	44	64	R	R	6-1	205	12-28-74	1997	Windham, Ohio
Geitz, Scott	1	2	2.98	20	0	0	2	45	38	19	15	21	33	R	R	6-4	190	4-6-76	1998	St. Louis, Mo.
Gold, J.M.	1	0	2.61	5	5	0	0	21	21	13	6	7	15	R	R	6-5	225	4-10-80	1998	Toms River, N.J.
Harraid, Jon	1	3	7.80	19	0	0	4	30	41	30	26	23	24	R	R	6-0	190	11-23-75	1998	Ballard, Texas
Johnson, Jim	5	6	4.87	13	13	0	0	68	75	51	37	27	77	B	L	6-1	175	8-7-76	1998	San Diego, Calif.
MacKoul, Greg	0	1	5.00	7	1	0	0	9	10	6	5	13	13	R	R	6-3	190	6-26-77	1998	East Northport, N.Y.
Mathews, Dan	2	2	2.54	24	0	0	16	28	22	8	8	11	30	R	R	6-0	175	12-22-75	1998	South Bend, Ind.
Maysonet, Roberto	3	2	5.70	14	6	0	0	43	47	35	27	30	33	R	R	6-0	175	1-16-80	1998	Vega Baja, P.R.
Miller, Jim	7	5	4.63	15	15	3	0	101	105	57	52	32	75	B	R	6-6	195	8-1-75	1997	Des Plaines, Ill.
Miniel, Roberto	3	2	4.39	16	0	0	2	41	39	24	20	24	39	R	R	6-4	160	5-12-80	1996	Santo Domingo, D.R.
Minor, Blas	0	0	4.50	2	2	0	0	4	4	2	2	1	6	R	R	6-3	200	3-20-66	1988	Gilbert, Ariz.
Montero, Oscar	4	7	8.96	14	12	0	0	67	88	81	67	49	46	R	R	6-4	195	5-9-78	1997	Bolivar, Ven.
Myers, Aaron	2	0	3.46	4	4	0	0	26	32	16	10	8	8	R	R	6-2	215	5-14-76	1994	Santa Maria, Calif.
Norris, Mac	1	0	11.00	4	0	0	0	9	15	12	11	7	8	R	R	6-8	195	3-19-76	1994	Mesa, Ariz.
Pine, Chris	0	1	11.25	3	1	0	0	8	9	10	10	4	11	R	R	6-2	205	9-25-76	1998	Tigard, Ore.
Wooten, Shane	1	0	3.80	13	0	0	0	24	19	10	10	15	27	B	L	6-0	170	3-14-75	1997	Goodlettsville, Tenn.

MINNESOTA TWINS

Future uncertain for Twins after difficult 1998 campaign

BY SCOTT MILLER

The 1998 season was a difficult one for the Twins, both on and off the field.

While extending their franchise record of consecutive losing seasons to six, the Twins finished 22 games under .500 (70-92), fourth in the American League Central.

Owner Carl Pohlad's quest for a new, outdoor baseball-only stadium was met with severe resistance. Pohlad threatened to move the team to North Carolina–the club even played an exhibition game there in late March–but citizens there voted down a proposal to build a new stadium, leaving Pohlad and the Twins in no-man's land.

The result was kind of a good-news, bad-news scenario for Minnesota baseball fans. The good news, of course, was that the team wouldn't be playing in North Carolina in 1999. Pohlad signed a new, temporary, two-year lease with the Metrodome ensuring that the Twins would be there through the 2000 season. The bad news was tied in directly with the good: The team was cutting the payroll from $27 million to about $20 million for the 1999 season, meaning a young team would get even younger.

Two young players, second baseman Todd Walker and outfielder Matt Lawton, appeared ready to take on bigger roles on the club. Walker, the club's first-round draft choice in 1994, led the league in hitting for a short stretch in July and finished with a .316 average. Lawton was the most improved Twin in 1998. He rebounded from a poor start to hit .278 with a team-leading 21 home runs and 77 RBIs.

Veteran DH and native son Paul Molitor inspired with his effort by battling through nagging injuries.

Todd Walker

Mike Restovich

Players of the Year

Major League: Todd Walker, 2b

Walker led the Twins with a .316 average, 167 hits and 41 doubles after moving back to second base.

Minor League: Mike Restovich, of, Ft. Wayne/Eliz.

Restovich hit .444 in a short stint at Class A Fort Wayne after earning MVP honors in the Rookie-level Appalachian League.

Despite a broken rib, a badly sprained ankle and a sore left shoulder, Molitor hit a solid .281 with 69 RBIs.

Center fielder Otis Nixon, another of the club's few veterans, missed time with a broken jaw after he was kicked by Royals shortstop Felix Martinez during a play at second base. Nixon recovered to hit .297 and steal 37 bases.

Rookie first baseman David Ortiz also missed time after breaking the hamate bone in his right wrist. He was out nearly eight weeks. Veteran pitchers Bob Tewksbury and Mike Morgan, signed to help anchor a young staff, each spent time on the disabled list.

After the season the club announced it would not pick up 1999 contract options for Nixon and catcher Terry Steinbach, opening the door for more young players.

Third baseman Corey Koskie, who batted .301 with 26 homers and 105 RBIs for Triple-A Salt Lake, appeared ready to step in and earn a big league job in 1999. So did first baseman Doug Mientkiewicz, who led the Eastern League with a .323 average.

Other candidates for big league playing time included catcher A.J. Pierzynski, who performed well at Double-A New Britain and Salt Lake, and outfielder Jacque Jones, a .299 hitter at New Britain.

Mientkiewicz, Jones and closer Brent Stentz led New Britain to the Eastern League finals, where it fell in four games to Harrisburg. Stentz led the minor leagues with 43 saves while compiling a 1.98 ERA.

Fort Wayne advanced to the playoffs in the Midwest League, as did the Gulf Coast League Twins. Both clubs bowed out in the semifinals.

ORGANIZATION LEADERS

BATTING		
*AVG	Mike Restovich, Fort Wayne/Elizabethton	.369
R	Cleatus Davidson, Fort Myers	97
H	Two tied at	162
TB	Corey Koskie, Salt Lake	272
2B	Doug Mientkiewicz, New Britain	45
3B	Three tied at	7
HR	Corey Koskie, Salt Lake	26
RBI	Tommy Peterman, Fort Myers	110
BB	Doug Mientkiewicz, New Britain	96
SO	Jacque Jones, New Britain	134
SB	Anthony Felston, New Britain/Fort Myers	88
PITCHING		
W	Dan Perkins, Salt Lake/New Britain	18
L	Two tied at	11
#ERA	J.C. Romero, New Britain	2.19
G	Chris Garza, Fort Myers	58
CG	Four tied at	2
SV	Brent Stentz, New Britain	43
IP	Corey Spiers, Fort Myers/Fort Wayne	178
BB	Jason Bell, New Britain	61
SO	Jason Bell, New Britain	166

*Minimum 250 At-Bats #Minimum 75 Innings

Minnesota TWINS

Manager: Tom Kelly

1998 Record: 70-92, .432 (4th, AL Central)

BATTING	AVG	G	AB	R	H	2B	3B	HR	RBI	BB	SO	SB	CS	B	T	HT	WT	DOB	1st Yr	Resides
Coomer, Ron	.276	137	529	54	146	22	1	15	72	18	72	2	2	R	R	5-11	206	11-18-66	1987	Orland Park, Ill.
Cordova, Marty	.253	119	438	52	111	20	2	10	69	50	103	3	6	R	R	6-0	206	7-10-69	1989	Las Vegas, Nev.
Gates, Brent	.249	107	333	31	83	15	0	3	42	36	46	3	3	B	R	6-1	190	3-14-70	1991	Grandville, Mich.
Hocking, Denny	.202	110	198	32	40	6	1	3	15	16	44	2	1	B	R	5-10	183	4-2-70	1990	Anaheim, Calif.
Hunter, Torii	.235	6	17	0	4	1	0	0	2	2	6	0	1	R	R	6-2	201	7-18-75	1993	Pine Bluff, Ark.
Koskie, Corey	.138	11	29	2	4	0	0	1	2	2	10	0	0	L	R	6-3	217	6-28-73	1994	White Rock, B.C.
Latham, Chris	.160	34	94	14	15	1	0	1	5	13	36	4	2	B	R	6-0	195	5-26-73	1991	Las Vegas, Nev.
Lawton, Matt	.278	152	557	91	155	36	6	21	77	86	64	16	8	L	R	5-10	186	11-3-71	1991	Saucier, Miss.
Meares, Pat	.260	149	543	56	141	26	3	9	70	24	86	7	4	R	R	6-0	187	9-6-68	1990	Wichita, Kan.
Merced, Orlando	.289	63	204	22	59	12	0	5	33	17	29	1	4	L	R	6-1	195	11-2-66	1985	Orlando, Fla.
Mientkiewicz, Doug	.200	8	25	1	5	1	0	0	2	4	3	1	1	L	R	6-2	193	6-19-74	1995	Miami, Fla.
Molitor, Paul	.281	126	502	75	141	29	5	4	69	45	41	9	2	R	R	6-0	195	8-22-56	1977	Edina, Minn.
Nixon, Otis	.297	110	448	71	133	6	6	1	20	44	56	37	7	B	R	6-2	180	1-9-59	1979	Alpharetta, Ga.
Ochoa, Alex	.257	94	249	35	64	14	2	2	25	10	35	6	3	R	R	6-0	195	3-29-72	1991	Pembroke Pines, Fla.
Ortiz, David	.277	86	278	47	77	20	0	9	46	39	72	1	0	L	L	6-4	230	11-18-75	1993	Haina, D.R.
Pierzynski, A.J.	.300	7	10	1	3	0	0	0	1	1	2	0	0	L	R	6-3	218	12-30-76	1994	Jacksonville, Fla.
Shave, Jon	.250	19	40	7	10	3	0	1	5	3	10	1	2	R	R	6-0	185	11-4-67	1990	Fernandina Beach, Fla.
Stahoviak, Scott	.105	9	19	1	2	0	0	1	1	0	7	0	0	L	R	6-5	230	3-6-70	1991	Round Lake Beach, Ill.
Steinbach, Terry	.242	124	422	45	102	25	2	14	54	38	89	0	1	R	R	6-1	212	3-2-62	1983	Corcoran, Minn.
Valentin, Javier	.198	55	162	11	32	7	1	3	18	11	30	0	0	B	R	5-10	185	9-19-75	1993	Manati, P.R.
Walker, Todd	.316	143	528	84	167	41	3	12	62	47	65	19	7	L	R	6-0	181	5-25-73	1994	Bossier City, La.

PITCHING	W	L	ERA	G	GS	CG	SV	IP	H	R	ER	BB	SO	B	T	HT	WT	DOB	1st Yr	Resides
Aguilera, Rick	4	9	4.24	68	0	0	38	74	75	35	35	15	57	R	R	6-5	208	12-31-61	1983	Rancho Santa Fe, Calif.
Baptist, Travis	0	1	5.67	13	0	0	0	27	34	18	17	11	11	L	L	6-0	195	12-30-71	1990	Aloha, Ore.
Carrasco, Hector	4	2	4.38	63	0	0	1	62	75	30	30	31	46	R	R	6-2	220	10-22-69	1988	San Pedro de Macoris, D.R.
Guardado, Eddie	3	1	4.52	79	0	0	0	66	66	34	33	28	53	R	L	6-0	194	10-2-70	1991	Stockton, Calif.
Hawkins, LaTroy	7	14	5.25	33	33	0	0	190	227	126	111	61	105	R	R	6-5	204	12-21-72	1991	Gary, Ind.
Miller, Travis	0	2	3.86	14	0	0	0	23	25	10	10	11	23	R	L	6-3	209	11-2-72	1994	West Manchester, Ohio
Milton, Eric	8	14	5.64	32	32	1	0	172	195	113	108	70	107	L	L	6-3	200	8-4-75	1996	Bellefonte, Pa.
Morgan, Mike	4	2	3.49	18	17	0	0	98	108	41	38	24	50	R	R	6-2	220	10-8-59	1978	Park City, Utah
Naulty, Dan	0	2	4.94	19	0	0	0	24	25	16	13	10	15	R	R	6-6	224	1-6-70	1992	Tustin, Calif.
Radke, Brad	12	14	4.30	32	32	5	0	214	238	109	102	43	146	R	R	6-2	190	10-27-72	1991	Tampa, Fla.
Ritchie, Todd	0	0	5.63	15	0	0	0	24	30	17	15	9	21	R	R	6-3	219	11-7-71	1990	Duncanville, Texas
Rodriguez, Frank	4	6	6.56	20	11	0	0	70	88	58	51	30	62	R	R	6-0	200	12-11-72	1991	Brooklyn, N.Y.
Sampson, Benj	1	0	1.56	5	2	0	0	17	10	3	3	7	16	R	L	6-2	210	4-27-75	1993	Ankeny, Iowa
Serafini, Dan	7	4	6.48	28	9	0	0	75	95	58	54	29	46	B	L	6-1	191	1-25-74	1992	San Bruno, Calif.
Swindell, Greg	3	3	3.66	52	0	0	2	66	67	27	27	18	45	R	L	6-3	230	1-2-65	1986	Houston, Texas
Tewksbury, Bob	7	13	4.79	26	25	1	0	148	174	82	79	20	60	R	R	6-4	206	11-30-60	1981	Concord, N.H.
Trombley, Mike	6	5	3.63	77	1	0	1	97	90	41	39	41	89	R	R	6-2	203	4-14-67	1989	Fort Myers, Fla.

FIELDING

Catcher	PCT	G	PO	A	E	DP	PB
Pierzynski	1.000	6	33	2	0	1	0
Steinbach	.990	119	665	52	7	3	4
Valentin	.983	53	281	16	5	0	7

First Base	PCT	G	PO	A	E	DP
Coomer	.998	54	371	34	1	32
Gates	1.000	1	2	0	0	1
Hocking	1.000	2	3	0	0	0
Merced	.982	38	299	21	6	32
Mientkiewicz	1.000	8	61	3	0	3
Molitor	1.000	9	79	7	0	4
Ortiz	.989	71	503	46	6	51
Shave	1.000	1	1	0	0	0
Stahoviak	.975	4	35	4	1	4

Second Base	PCT	G	PO	A	E	DP
Gates	.971	21	23	43	2	8
Hocking	1.000	47	38	46	0	9
Walker	.978	140	219	363	13	72

Third Base	PCT	G	PO	A	E	DP
Coomer	.972	76	56	116	5	9
Gates	.961	77	59	113	7	5
Hocking	1.000	11	1	11	0	1
Koskie	.941	10	6	10	1	1
Shave	1.000	15	6	20	0	2

Shortstop	PCT	G	PO	A	E	DP
Gates	1.000	1	1	1	0	0
Hocking	.960	28	29	43	3	7
Meares	.966	149	263	411	24	92
Shave	.000	1	0	0	0	0

Outfield	PCT	G	PO	A	E	DP
Coomer	1.000	3	1	0	0	0
Cordova	.978	115	257	5	6	1
Hocking	.980	24	47	2	1	1
Hunter	1.000	6	8	0	0	0
Latham	.972	32	69	1	2	0
Lawton	.990	151	398	11	4	5
Merced	1.000	13	25	2	0	1
Nixon	.989	108	278	4	3	0
Ochoa	.969	74	117	8	4	0
Stahoviak	.000	1	0	0	0	0

MEL BAILEY

Matt Lawton

FARM SYSTEM

Director, Minor Leagues: Jim Rantz

Class	Farm Team	League	W	L	Pct.	Finish*	Manager	First Yr
AAA	Salt Lake (Utah) Buzz	Pacific Coast	79	64	.552	t-4th (16)	Phil Roof	1994
AA	New Britain (Conn.) Rock Cats	Eastern	83	59	.585	1st (10)	John Russell	1995
A#	Fort Myers (Fla.) Miracle	Florida State	65	73	.471	10th (14)	Mike Boulanger	1993
A	Fort Wayne (Ind.) Wizards	Midwest	79	61	.564	t-2nd (14)	Jose Marzan	1993
Rookie#	Elizabethton (Tenn.) Twins	Appalachian	38	29	.567	2nd (10)	Jon Mathews	1974
Rookie	Fort Myers (Fla.) Twins	Gulf Coast	34	26	.567	t-3rd (14)	Steve Liddle	1989

*Finish in overall standings (No. of teams in league) #Advanced level

SALT LAKE — Class AAA

Organization Statistics

PACIFIC COAST LEAGUE

BATTING	AVG	G	AB	R	H	2B	3B	HR	RBI	BB	SO	SB	CS	B	T	HT	WT	DOB	1st Yr	Resides
Beltre, Esteban	.278	133	510	84	142	24	4	2	40	30	100	26	11	R	R	5-10	180	12-26-67	1984	San Pedro de Macoris, D.R.
Buchanan, Brian	.278	133	500	74	139	29	3	17	82	36	90	14	2	R	R	6-4	220	7-21-73	1994	Clifton, Va.
Ferguson, Jeff	.206	81	223	35	46	6	1	3	20	24	42	7	2	R	R	5-10	170	6-18-73	1994	Whittier, Calif.
Horn, Jeff	.306	24	72	14	22	5	0	1	6	12	18	1	2	R	R	6-1	213	8-23-70	1992	Las Vegas, Nev.
Hunter, Torii	.337	26	92	15	31	7	0	4	20	1	13	2	2	R	R	6-2	201	7-18-75	1993	Pine Bluff, Ark.
Koskie, Corey	.301	135	505	91	152	32	5	26	105	51	104	15	7	L	R	6-3	217	6-28-73	1994	White Rock, B.C.
Latham, Chris	.324	97	377	81	122	21	4	11	51	56	99	29	5	B	R	6-0	195	5-26-73	1991	Las Vegas, Nev.
Lewis, Marc	.293	119	444	61	130	31	1	14	68	23	64	10	11	R	R	6-2	185	5-20-75	1994	Decatur, Ala.
LeCroy, Matt	.308	3	13	2	4	1	0	2	4	0	7	0	0	R	R	6-2	225	12-13-75	1997	Belton, S.C.
Molitor, Paul	.500	2	10	0	5	1	0	0	0	0	0	0	0	R	R	6-0	195	8-22-56	1977	Edina, Minn.
Moriarty, Mike	.224	64	161	21	36	8	2	3	19	22	39	2	1	R	R	6-0	180	3-8-74	1995	Clayton, N.J.
Ogden, Jamie	.250	94	272	29	68	16	0	6	32	16	65	4	2	L	L	6-5	225	1-19-72	1990	White Bear Lake, Minn.
Ortiz, David	.243	11	37	5	9	3	0	2	6	3	9	0	0	L	L	6-4	230	11-18-75	1993	Haina, D.R.
Owens, Jayhawk	.205	52	161	19	33	9	0	3	16	13	63	1	2	R	R	6-1	213	2-10-69	1990	Cincinnati, Ohio
Pierzynski, A.J.	.255	59	208	29	53	7	2	7	30	9	24	3	1	L	R	6-3	218	12-30-76	1994	Jacksonville, Fla.
Ramos, Ken	.261	18	69	6	18	4	1	1	11	6	13	1	1	L	L	6-1	185	6-6-67	1989	Pueblo, Colo.
Rupp, Chad	.291	115	413	78	120	25	3	20	89	61	105	8	3	R	R	6-2	215	9-30-71	1993	Tampa, Fla.
Shave, Jon	.338	90	317	63	107	20	1	4	41	34	46	8	9	R	R	6-0	185	11-4-67	1990	Fernandina Beach, Fla.
Smith, Jeff	.254	23	67	9	17	3	0	0	2	4	13	0	0	L	R	6-3	216	6-17-74	1996	Naples, Fla.
Stahoviak, Scott	.316	111	399	71	126	33	6	18	82	45	94	5	2	L	R	6-5	230	3-6-70	1991	Round Lake Beach, Ill.

PITCHING	W	L	ERA	G	GS	CG	SV	IP	H	R	ER	BB	SO	B	T	HT	WT	DOB	1st Yr	Resides
Baptist, Travis	8	5	3.12	21	21	1	0	130	128	53	47	41	98	L	L	6-0	195	12-30-71	1990	Aloha, Ore.
Bones, Ricky	5	1	3.42	8	8	0	0	47	41	20	18	19	41	R	R	6-0	202	4-7-69	1986	Guayama, P.R.
Bowers, Shane	9	7	5.89	33	16	2	0	110	137	76	72	40	101	R	R	6-5	220	7-27-71	1993	Covina, Calif.
Cumberland, Chris	3	2	5.93	17	1	1	0	30	37	21	20	18	19	R	L	6-1	189	1-15-73	1993	Mandeville, La.
Gandarillas, Gus	4	5	5.27	53	1	0	4	70	88	47	41	24	42	R	R	6-1	183	7-19-71	1992	Hialeah, Fla.
Harris, Jeff	8	0	5.91	25	0	0	3	32	38	24	21	19	24	R	R	6-0	195	7-4-74	1995	San Pablo, Calif.
Linton, Doug	4	4	5.99	18	14	0	0	80	106	57	53	14	60	R	R	6-1	190	9-2-65	1987	Overland Park, Kan.
Miller, Travis	3	4	4.84	34	2	0	9	58	60	33	31	31	65	R	L	6-3	209	11-2-72	1994	West Manchester, Ohio
Naulty, Dan	1	0	6.75	5	0	0	0	5	8	4	4	2	5	R	R	6-6	224	1-6-70	1992	Tustin, Calif.
Ohme, Kevin	4	3	5.01	51	0	0	6	83	90	48	46	31	47	L	L	6-1	180	4-13-71	1993	Brandon, Fla.
Perkins, Dan	5	0	4.82	7	7	1	0	47	48	30	25	20	33	R	R	6-2	193	3-15-75	1993	South Miami, Fla.
Rath, Fred	1	2	4.55	27	0	0	8	32	35	16	16	8	15	R	R	6-3	220	1-5-73	1995	Tampa, Fla.
Redman, Mark	6	7	5.53	19	18	0	0	99	111	75	61	41	88	L	L	6-5	220	1-5-74	1995	Tulsa, Okla.
Ritchie, Todd	1	3	4.15	36	0	0	4	61	55	38	28	31	62	R	R	6-3	219	11-7-71	1990	Duncanville, Texas
Rodriguez, Frank	5	7	4.67	16	16	2	0	96	97	53	50	35	79	R	R	6-0	200	12-11-72	1991	Brooklyn, N.Y.
Sampson, Benj	10	7	5.14	28	28	0	0	161	198	99	92	52	132	R	L	6-2	210	4-27-75	1993	Ankeny, Iowa
Serafini, Dan	2	4	3.71	9	8	0	0	53	56	29	22	21	39	B	L	6-1	191	1-25-74	1992	San Bruno, Calif.
Wilson, Gary	0	1	6.17	10	2	0	0	23	24	16	16	5	13	R	R	6-3	190	1-1-70	1992	Arcata, Calif.
2-team (29 Nashville)	3	6	6.04	39	5	0	1	82	101	62	55	27	52							
Wojciechowski, Steve	0	2	6.55	9	1	0	0	11	13	10	8	7	6	L	L	6-2	185	7-29-70	1991	Calumet City, Ill.

FIELDING

Catcher	PCT	G	PO	A	E	DP	PB
Horn	.994	23	148	9	1	0	1
LeCroy	1.000	2	6	0	0	0	0
Owens	.994	47	323	16	2	4	4
Pierzynski	.983	59	366	30	7	3	5
Smith	.994	22	145	9	1	2	1

First Base	PCT	G	PO	A	E	DP
Ogden	.989	14	80	9	1	6
Ortiz	.966	9	76	10	3	8
Rupp	.991	59	517	31	5	59
Shave	1.000	2	13	2	0	2
Stahoviak	.995	67	548	55	3	50

Second Base	PCT	G	PO	A	E	DP
Ferguson	.954	67	108	164	13	39
Moriarty	.964	37	59	100	6	28
Shave	.973	63	107	149	7	28

Third Base	PCT	G	PO	A	E	DP
Koskie	.935	131	83	250	23	21
Moriarty	.833	7	3	12	3	0
Shave	.800	14	2	14	4	2

Shortstop	PCT	G	PO	A	E	DP
Beltre	.967	124	173	388	19	79
Moriarty	.948	23	33	59	5	12
Shave	.875	8	11	17	4	5

Outfield	PCT	G	PO	A	E	DP
Buchanan	.969	122	244	6	8	3
Hunter	.966	24	55	1	2	0
Latham	.959	93	201	8	9	2
Lewis	.984	113	171	8	3	1
Ogden	.990	64	92	5	1	0
Ramos	1.000	17	19	1	0	0
Shave	1.000	9	16	1	0	0
Stahoviak	1.000	8	17	1	0	1

NEW BRITAIN — Class AA

EASTERN LEAGUE

BATTING	AVG	G	AB	R	H	2B	3B	HR	RBI	BB	SO	SB	CS	B	T	HT	WT	DOB	1st Yr	Resides
Allen, Chad	.262	137	504	70	132	31	7	8	82	51	78	21	9	R	R	6-1	190	2-6-75	1996	Desoto, Texas
Barnes, John	.268	20	71	9	19	4	1	0	8	9	9	1	1	R	R	6-1	205	4-24-76	1996	El Cajon, Calif.
2-team (100 Trenton)	.273	120	451	62	123	22	1	14	44	49	56	4	9							
Cey, Dan	.251	136	569	82	143	28	2	8	50	40	95	23	7	R	R	5-11	165	11-8-75	1996	Woodland Hills, Calif.

BATTING	AVG	G	AB	R	H	2B	3B	HR	RBI	BB	SO	SB	CS	B	T	HT	WT	DOB	1st Yr	Resides
Felston, Anthony	.222	12	45	5	10	2	0	0	5	6	10	2	1	L	L	5-9	170	11-26-74	1996	Leland, Miss.
Fortin, Troy	.183	23	60	3	11	4	0	0	6	5	13	0	0	R	R	5-11	209	2-24-75	1993	Lundar, Manitoba
Fraser, Joe	.204	16	49	6	10	5	0	0	4	3	8	0	0	R	R	6-0	208	8-23-74	1995	Huntington Beach, Calif.
Gunderson, Shane	.161	23	62	8	10	0	0	3	14	12	11	0	0	R	R	6-0	212	10-16-73	1995	Faribault, Minn.
Guzman, Cristian	.277	140	566	68	157	29	5	1	40	21	111	23	14	B	R	6-0	150	3-21-78	1995	Santo Domingo, D.R.
Hunter, Torii	.282	82	308	42	87	24	3	6	32	19	64	11	9	R	R	6-2	201	7-18-75	1993	Pine Bluff, Ark.
Johnson, J.J.	.256	101	371	54	95	19	3	13	48	25	103	5	5	R	R	6-0	204	8-31-73	1991	Pine Plains, N.Y.
Jones, Jacque	.299	134	518	78	155	39	3	21	85	37	134	18	11	L	L	5-10	175	4-25-75	1996	San Diego, Calif.
Mientkiewicz, Doug	.323	139	502	96	162	45	0	16	88	96	58	11	4	L	R	6-2	193	6-19-74	1995	Miami, Fla.
Moeller, Chad	.235	58	187	21	44	10	0	6	23	24	41	2	1	R	R	6-3	205	2-18-75	1996	Upland, Calif.
Moriarty, Mike	.286	38	112	22	32	8	0	4	15	17	16	0	4	R	R	6-0	180	3-8-74	1995	Clayton, N.J.
Moss, Rick	.280	65	193	17	54	9	0	2	25	20	20	0	0	L	R	6-2	185	9-18-75	1996	Lockport, Ill.
Mucker, Kelcey	.296	71	226	22	67	14	0	5	27	23	31	1	0	L	R	6-4	238	2-17-75	1993	Lawrenceburg, Ind.
Paez, Israel	.220	62	164	26	36	4	1	0	13	11	34	5	3	B	R	5-10	188	12-23-76	1994	Valencia, Ven.
Pierzynski, A.J.	.297	59	212	30	63	11	0	3	17	10	25	0	2	L	R	6-3	218	12-30-76	1994	Jacksonville, Fla.
Smith, Jeff	.274	27	84	11	23	11	0	1	12	5	21	0	0	L	R	6-3	216	6-17-74	1996	Naples, Fla.

PITCHING	W	L	ERA	G	GS	CG	SV	IP	H	R	ER	BB	SO	B	T	HT	WT	DOB	1st Yr	Resides
Bell, Jason	8	11	4.67	29	29	2	0	170	148	90	88	61	166	R	R	6-3	198	9-30-74	1995	Orlando, Fla.
Chapman, Walker	1	3	3.86	23	2	0	0	49	47	22	21	18	38	R	R	6-3	201	2-25-76	1994	Frostburg, Md.
Cobb, Trevor	6	9	5.06	27	23	1	0	133	160	81	75	49	87	L	L	6-2	189	7-13-73	1992	Marysville, Wash.
Cumberland, Chris	3	4	2.63	37	2	0	1	55	44	24	16	17	48	R	L	6-1	189	1-15-73	1993	Mandeville, La.
Gourdin, Tom	8	4	6.21	47	0	0	0	67	81	53	46	39	62	R	R	6-3	215	5-24-73	1992	Murray, Utah
Harris, Jeff	1	0	1.66	26	0	0	5	38	21	7	7	5	40	R	R	6-0	195	7-4-74	1995	San Pablo, Calif.
Lincoln, Mike	15	7	3.22	26	26	1	0	173	180	80	62	35	109	R	R	6-2	205	4-10-75	1996	Citrus Heights, Calif.
Mahaffey, Alan	2	3	4.47	34	1	0	0	52	62	27	26	17	61	L	L	6-3	205	2-2-74	1995	Springfield, Mo.
Mays, Joe	5	3	4.99	11	10	0	0	58	63	40	32	21	45	B	R	6-1	160	12-10-75	1995	Bradenton, Fla.
Niedermaier, Brad	0	0	5.00	8	1	0	0	9	14	5	5	4	8	R	R	6-2	205	2-9-73	1995	Niles, Ill.
Perkins, Dan	13	5	3.98	20	19	1	0	118	140	64	52	31	79	R	R	6-2	193	3-15-75	1993	South Miami, Fla.
Radlosky, Rob	10	3	4.02	27	19	0	0	132	127	61	59	38	117	R	R	6-2	192	1-7-74	1994	Lantana, Fla.
Redman, Mark	4	2	1.52	8	8	0	0	47	40	11	8	17	51	L	L	6-5	220	1-5-74	1995	Tulsa, Okla.
Romero, J.C.	6	3	2.19	51	1	0	2	78	48	28	19	43	79	B	L	5-11	195	6-4-76	1997	San Juan, P.R.
Stentz, Brent	1	2	1.98	57	0	0	43	59	44	13	13	28	65	R	R	6-5	225	7-24-75	1995	Brooksville, Fla.
Yeskie, Nate	0	0	16.20	1	1	0	0	2	4	3	3	2	1	R	R	6-3	185	8-13-74	1996	Henderson, Nev.

FIELDING

Catcher	PCT	G	PO	A	E	DP	PB
Fortin	.982	14	97	10	2	2	1
Moeller	.987	55	414	25	6	6	4
Pierzynski	.996	57	409	37	2	3	2
Smith	.994	23	151	15	1	1	1

First Base	PCT	G	PO	A	E	DP
Fortin	1.000	5	26	1	0	4
Fraser	1.000	2	9	0	0	0
Gunderson	1.000	1	2	1	0	0
Mientkiewicz	.991	137	1169	92	12	116
Mucker	1.000	4	16	1	0	6

Second Base	PCT	G	PO	A	E	DP
Cey	.967	135	246	373	21	97
Moriarty	.955	5	4	17	1	3
Paez	1.000	6	6	16	0	6

Third Base	PCT	G	PO	A	E	DP
Fraser	.968	14	8	22	1	2
Moriarty	.922	32	23	71	8	5
Moss	.936	62	28	104	9	13
Paez	.861	45	26	67	15	6

Shortstop	PCT	G	PO	A	E	DP
Guzman	.952	140	211	426	32	95
Moriarty	1.000	1	1	2	0	1
Paez	1.000	4	4	9	0	1

Outfield	PCT	G	PO	A	E	DP
Allen	.980	133	185	11	4	2
Barnes	1.000	17	39	2	0	1
Felston	.913	12	21	0	2	0
Hunter	.989	82	168	8	2	2
Johnson	.973	46	68	3	2	1
Jones	.968	129	288	12	10	2
Mientkiewicz	1.000	3	2	0	0	0
Mucker	1.000	11	19	0	0	0

FORT MYERS — Class A

FLORIDA STATE LEAGUE

BATTING	AVG	G	AB	R	H	2B	3B	HR	RBI	BB	SO	SB	CS	B	T	HT	WT	DOB	1st Yr	Resides
Alvarez, Rafael	.292	110	391	54	114	20	2	4	38	45	51	19	8	B	L	5-11	182	1-22-77	1994	Valencia, Ven.
Bolivar, Papo	.264	126	489	59	129	15	2	5	45	29	104	14	11	R	R	5-9	190	10-18-78	1996	Catia la Mar, Ven.
Cranford, Joey	.224	75	254	41	57	15	3	8	39	26	58	6	1	R	R	6-0	186	2-10-75	1996	Macon, Ga.
Davidson, Cleatus	.241	130	527	97	127	12	7	2	45	45	99	44	16	B	R	5-10	170	11-1-76	1994	Haines City, Fla.
Felston, Anthony	.279	114	427	74	119	8	0	0	43	83	65	86	26	L	L	5-9	170	11-26-74	1996	Leland, Miss.
Fraser, Joe	.267	34	101	25	27	3	1	3	13	15	12	3	1	R	R	6-0	208	8-23-74	1995	Huntington Beach, Calif.
Gunderson, Shane	.268	42	149	25	40	12	2	5	20	23	42	3	2	R	R	6-0	212	10-16-73	1995	Faribault, Minn.
Hacker, Steve	.247	62	251	29	62	11	0	11	38	17	40	0	1	R	R	6-5	230	9-6-74	1995	St. Louis, Mo.
Huls, Steve	.211	74	223	30	47	3	0	1	25	20	43	3	5	B	R	6-1	175	10-11-74	1996	Cold Spring, Minn.
LeCroy, Matt	.305	51	200	32	61	9	1	12	51	21	35	2	1	R	R	6-2	225	12-13-75	1997	Belton, S.C.
Lough, Aaron	.500	1	4	2	2	0	0	1	1	1	1	0	0	R	R	6-4	210	6-4-77	1998	Seattle, Wash.
Moeller, Chad	.327	66	254	37	83	24	1	6	39	31	37	2	3	R	R	6-3	205	2-18-75	1996	Upland, Calif.
Moss, Rick	.313	41	160	18	50	7	0	1	19	24	17	0	0	L	R	6-2	185	9-18-75	1996	Lockport, Ill.
Mucker, Kelcey	.338	21	71	11	24	6	0	2	9	5	10	1	0	L	R	6-4	238	2-17-75	1993	Lawrenceburg, Ind.
Peterman, Tommy	.312	135	519	71	162	36	2	20	110	63	86	2	0	L	L	6-0	230	5-5-75	1996	Marietta, Ga.
Prada, Nelson	.241	41	133	11	32	6	0	1	11	4	21	0	0	R	R	6-0	205	2-22-76	1995	Valencia, Ven.
Rivas, Luis	.281	126	463	58	130	21	5	4	51	14	75	34	8	R	R	5-10	165	8-30-79	1996	Caracas, Ven.
Schroeder, John	.207	39	135	17	28	5	0	8	24	10	53	0	0	L	R	6-3	245	10-9-75	1994	Coeur d'Alene, Idaho
Smith, Jeff	.348	6	23	4	8	2	0	0	1	1	2	1	0	L	R	6-3	216	6-17-74	1996	Naples, Fla.
Stevens, Tony	.286	3	7	0	2	0	0	0	1	0	0	0	0	B	R	5-9	140	9-18-78	1997	Keystone Heights, Fla.
Vaughn, Lateef	.288	22	59	9	17	2	1	0	8	3	12	2	3	R	R	5-9	175	10-1-75	1997	Long Beach, Calif.

GAMES BY POSITION: C—Huls 3, LeCroy 44, Lough 1, Moeller 57, Prada 40, Smith 4. **1B**—Gunderson 1, Hacker 14, Huls 2, Peterman 123, Schroeder 3. **2B**—Cranford 18, Davidson 125, Huls 1, Stevens 2, Vaughn 2. **3B**—Cranford 35, Fraser 31, Huls 54, Moss 25, Vaughn 2. **SS**—Alvarez 1, Davidson 5, Huls 12, Rivas 124. **OF**—Alvarez 102, Bolivar 124, Cranford 15, Felston 114, Gunderson 39, Mucker 18, Peterman 6, Stevens 1, Vaughn 12.

PITCHING	W	L	ERA	G	GS	CG	SV	IP	H	R	ER	BB	SO	B	T	HT	WT	DOB	1st Yr	Resides
Bauder, Mike	5	6	4.59	36	8	0	1	98	108	61	50	46	79	L	L	5-9	167	5-13-75	1996	Las Vegas, Nev.
Bean, Seth	0	0	3.78	10	0	0	1	17	16	7	7	5	19	R	R	6-1	190	3-31-75	1997	Lompoc, Calif.
Carrasco, Troy	0	4	4.53	19	4	0	0	46	52	29	23	26	35	B	L	5-10	177	1-27-75	1993	Tampa, Fla.
Chapman, Walker	4	0	1.97	24	0	0	2	50	40	17	11	15	47	R	R	6-3	201	2-25-76	1994	Frostburg, Md.
Fieldbinder, Mick	10	8	4.73	35	21	0	1	137	171	99	72	44	64	R	R	6-4	200	10-2-73	1996	Rochester, Ill.

PITCHING	W	L	ERA	G	GS	CG	SV	IP	H	R	ER	BB	SO	B	T	HT	WT	DOB	1st Yr	Resides
Garza, Chris	5	5	2.74	58	0	0	14	82	73	33	25	46	63	L	L	5-11	185	7-23-75	1996	Los Angeles, Calif.
Hooten, David	9	11	4.49	28	28	0	0	158	185	94	79	57	136	R	R	6-0	182	5-8-75	1996	Shreveport, La.
Kinney, Matt	3	2	3.13	7	7	0	0	37	31	18	13	18	39	R	R	6-4	190	12-16-76	1995	Bangor, Maine
2-team (22 Sarasota)	12	8	3.80	29	27	2	1	159	140	88	67	93	135							
LaRosa, Tom	1	2	7.91	22	3	0	0	39	37	39	34	48	29	R	R	5-10	180	6-28-75	1996	Henderson, Nev.
Malko, Bryan	0	1	6.92	7	0	0	2	13	19	14	10	9	5	R	R	6-3	205	1-23-77	1995	Piscataway, N.J.
Mays, Joe	7	2	3.04	16	15	0	0	95	101	45	32	23	83	B	R	6-1	160	12-10-75	1995	Bradenton, Fla.
Mills, Ryan	0	0	1.80	2	2	0	0	5	2	3	1	1	3	R	L	6-5	200	7-21-77	1998	Fort Myers, Fla.
Mota, Danny	3	5	2.85	19	4	0	0	47	45	21	15	22	49	R	R	6-0	170	10-9-75	1994	Santo Domingo, D.R.
Nakamura, Mike	1	3	3.45	8	6	1	0	29	28	15	11	10	21	R	R	6-0	208	9-6-76	1998	Melbourne, Australia
Niedermaier, Brad	4	2	7.88	25	0	0	3	40	59	39	35	21	44	R	R	6-2	205	2-9-73	1995	Niles, Ill.
Opipari, Mario	0	1	3.97	17	0	0	0	34	38	19	15	13	18	B	R	6-2	185	1-24-75	1996	Henderson, Nev.
Palki, Jeromy	0	4	4.76	40	0	0	4	59	51	39	31	29	48	R	R	6-0	195	4-14-76	1995	Oakland, Ore.
Roper, Chad	0	7	8.93	17	6	0	0	40	61	46	40	21	30	R	R	6-1	223	3-29-74	1992	Belton, S.C.
Spiers, Corey	9	8	3.33	24	24	1	0	151	172	70	56	38	98	L	L	5-11	197	6-19-75	1996	Houston, Texas
Yeskie, Nate	4	2	3.30	14	11	1	0	63	74	27	23	16	39	R	R	6-3	185	8-13-74	1996	Henderson, Nev.

FORT WAYNE — Class A

MIDWEST LEAGUE

BATTING	AVG	G	AB	R	H	2B	3B	HR	RBI	BB	SO	SB	CS	B	T	HT	WT	DOB	1st Yr	Resides
Borrego, Ramon	.261	119	422	61	110	18	3	5	55	59	75	17	10	B	R	5-6	160	6-7-78	1996	Valencia, Ven.
Cuddyer, Michael	.276	129	497	82	137	37	7	12	81	61	107	16	7	R	R	6-2	190	3-27-79	1997	Chesapeake, Va.
Harrison, Jamal	.278	107	389	58	108	25	3	8	49	40	93	7	5	R	R	6-4	220	7-15-77	1995	Palo Alto, Calif.
Jaworowski, Aaron	.268	51	190	28	51	14	1	3	28	16	50	0	0	L	R	6-3	210	8-7-75	1997	Ellisville, Mo.
LeCroy, Matt	.276	64	225	33	62	17	1	9	40	34	45	0	0	R	R	6-2	225	12-13-75	1997	Belton, S.C.
Lopez, Manny	.273	115	395	62	108	17	4	7	53	38	80	6	4	R	R	5-9	190	3-20-78	1996	El Portal, D.R.
McConnell, Jason	.259	91	316	52	82	12	3	2	23	31	48	19	10	B	R	5-9	170	5-21-76	1997	Magnolia, Ark.
McHenry, Joe	.257	46	144	21	37	4	2	0	11	15	46	3	0	L	R	6-1	180	5-24-76	1995	Murfreesboro, Tenn.
Orndorff, Dave	.261	99	380	68	99	20	4	6	47	44	91	30	12	R	R	5-10	175	8-10-77	1995	Shippensburg, Pa.
Pagan, Felix	.276	69	225	36	62	21	3	7	40	34	56	2	1	R	R	5-11	180	6-12-75	1997	Bayamon, P.R.
Pena, Frankie	.189	47	132	16	25	4	0	4	17	9	34	0	0	R	R	6-0	200	8-22-76	1994	Santo Domingo, D.R.
Restovich, Mike	.444	11	45	9	20	5	2	0	6	4	12	0	0	R	R	6-4	225	1-3-79	1997	Rochester, Minn.
Ryan, Mike	.318	113	412	68	131	24	6	9	72	44	92	7	4	L	R	5-10	194	7-6-77	1996	Indiana, Pa.
Schaeffer, Jon	.283	122	414	77	117	31	5	10	64	55	117	3	5	R	R	6-1	210	1-20-76	1997	Tarzana, Calif.
Shrum, Allen	.059	6	17	0	1	0	0	0	0	0	8	0	0	R	R	6-2	220	5-13-76	1998	Hermitage, Tenn.
Smith, Nester	.258	115	414	59	107	18	7	8	53	38	103	7	8	B	R	5-11	180	1-21-78	1997	Maturin Monagas, Ven.
Sutton, Bruce	.231	42	117	12	27	13	1	0	11	11	44	0	2	R	R	6-3	180	8-2-76	1997	Ada, Okla.

GAMES BY POSITION: C—LeCroy 51, Pena 44, Schaeffer 57, Shrum 5. **1B**—Harrison 51, Jaworowski 41, Pagan 5, Ryan 2, Schaeffer 51. **2B**—Borrego 47, Cuddyer 1, McConnell 31, Orndorff 69. **3B**—Borrego 27, Harrison 1, McConnell 5, Pagan 10, Ryan 109. **SS**—Borrego 5, Cuddyer 122, McConnell 17. **OF**—Borrego 40, Lopez 110, McConnell 36, McHenry 43, Orndorff 20, Pagan 30, Restovich 10, Schaeffer 4, Smith 113, Sutton 41.

PITCHING	W	L	ERA	G	GS	CG	SV	IP	H	R	ER	BB	SO	B	T	HT	WT	DOB	1st Yr	Resides
Carnes, Matt	8	5	5.37	47	10	1	5	104	119	74	62	36	92	R	R	6-3	206	8-18-75	1997	Miami, Okla.
Cosgrove, Mike	5	0	1.34	44	0	0	7	54	46	11	8	11	42	R	R	6-1	181	2-14-76	1997	Downey, Calif.
Davies, Bob	7	8	3.69	34	23	0	3	127	121	62	52	52	114	R	R	6-1	195	4-2-76	1997	Warren, Ohio
Dose, Gary	1	2	5.50	17	0	0	1	34	42	28	21	19	28	R	R	5-10	184	8-22-73	1996	Elgin, Minn.
Gandy, Josh	4	7	4.81	44	11	0	1	101	113	59	54	33	76	R	L	6-1	200	10-12-75	1997	Ringgold, Ga.
Hill, Kendall	5	3	4.35	26	12	0	1	68	65	38	33	30	50	B	R	6-3	180	7-18-74	1994	Pensacola, Fla.
Hoard, Brent	2	1	5.23	15	2	0	0	31	32	19	18	20	37	R	L	6-4	205	11-3-76	1998	Largo, Fla.
Jacobs, Jake	2	4	6.19	48	0	0	0	76	78	64	52	39	78	R	R	6-6	240	3-28-78	1996	Pensacola, Fla.
Malko, Bryan	8	3	3.98	22	11	0	0	75	72	38	33	30	53	R	R	6-3	205	1-23-77	1995	Piscataway, N.J.
Marshall, Lee	8	5	5.19	46	12	0	1	104	133	74	60	33	71	R	R	6-5	195	9-25-76	1995	Ariton, Ala.
Miller, Aaron	1	0	3.34	22	0	0	0	30	20	13	11	21	26	R	L	6-3	235	7-31-76	1997	Middletown, Del.
Mota, Danny	4	3	2.25	25	0	0	7	32	24	14	8	8	39	R	R	6-0	170	10-9-75	1994	Santo Domingo, D.R.
Nakamura, Mike	2	5	3.26	29	9	0	1	80	82	41	29	29	70	R	R	6-0	208	9-6-76	1998	Melbourne, Australia
Rincon, Juan	6	4	3.83	37	13	0	6	96	84	51	41	54	74	R	R	5-11	175	1-23-79	1996	Maracaibo, Ven.
Spiers, Corey	2	0	0.67	5	5	0	0	27	15	7	2	13	20	L	L	5-11	197	6-19-75	1996	Houston, Texas
Thomas, Brad	11	8	2.95	27	26	1	0	152	146	68	50	45	126	L	L	6-3	202	10-22-77	1996	Seven Hills, Australia
Thomas, Joe	3	3	3.28	6	6	0	0	36	32	17	13	4	31	L	L	6-3	225	1-25-75	1997	Kenmore, N.Y.
2-team (20 Michigan)	15	8	3.25	26	26	1	0	166	158	69	60	40	131							

ELIZABETHTON — Rookie

APPALACHIAN LEAGUE

BATTING	AVG	G	AB	R	H	2B	3B	HR	RBI	BB	SO	SB	CS	B	T	HT	WT	DOB	1st Yr	Resides
Almonte, Claudio	.303	62	241	45	73	10	3	6	40	18	57	12	2	R	R	6-0	187	8-2-78	1996	Los Prados, D.R.
Alvarez, Jimmy	.219	46	155	32	34	8	4	0	14	33	37	6	2	R	R	5-11	163	10-4-79	1997	Santo Domingo, D.R.
Brosam, Eric	.254	36	114	10	29	5	0	2	14	10	35	0	1	L	R	6-0	198	12-4-77	1996	Redwood Falls, Minn.
Collura, Todd	.205	28	88	14	18	6	0	1	10	3	29	0	0	R	R	6-2	210	12-7-78	1998	Boca Raton, Fla.
Hawthorne, Kyle	.301	45	193	46	58	7	2	1	21	23	31	9	4	R	R	6-2	180	3-13-78	1998	Baton Rouge, La.
Hodge, Kevin	.289	55	194	37	56	16	1	12	54	29	55	4	4	R	R	5-11	170	10-28-76	1998	College Station, Texas
Jaworowski, Aaron	.500	7	24	6	12	2	0	2	5	3	2	0	0	L	R	6-3	210	8-7-75	1997	Ellisville, Mo.
Jordan, Yustin	.257	20	74	14	19	2	0	1	3	3	20	2	0	R	R	6-3	200	8-15-78	1996	Monticello, Ark.
Kennedy, Brian	.317	26	82	11	26	4	0	1	16	15	18	0	2	L	R	6-0	190	8-9-77	1996	Lafayette, Ind.
Lorenzo, Juan	.261	44	176	33	46	8	1	6	23	7	17	4	1	B	R	6-0	169	6-10-78	1995	San Cristobal, D.R.
Marciniak, Dave	.296	54	189	46	56	8	1	4	26	47	32	5	1	R	R	6-1	190	2-3-77	1998	Avenel, N.J.
McMillin, Brian	.352	36	122	30	43	10	0	6	39	27	22	8	3	R	R	5-10	205	5-24-77	1998	Franklin, Ind.
Restovich, Mike	.355	65	242	68	86	20	1	13	64	54	58	5	2	R	R	6-4	225	1-3-79	1997	Rochester, Minn.
Selander, Craig	.286	36	119	23	34	4	0	9	33	21	20	1	1	L	R	6-2	180	8-31-76	1998	West St. Paul, Minn.
Sutton, Bruce	.154	19	39	6	6	1	0	0	2	12	13	2	1	R	R	6-3	180	8-2-76	1997	Ada, Okla.
Torres, Gabriel	.248	46	161	19	40	7	0	4	25	19	23	1	2	R	R	5-10	192	3-20-78	1996	Acarigua, Ven.
Vilorio, Leonel	.325	35	123	22	40	9	0	2	13	5	21	2	0	R	R	6-0	180	3-10-78	1996	Santo Domingo, D.R.

GAMES BY POSITION: C—Collura 23, Hodge 1, Sutton 8, Torres 46. **1B**—Alvarez 1, Brosam 35, Hodge 1, Jaworowski 6, Jordan 19, Lorenzo 13, Vilorio 3. **2B**—Alvarez 9, Hawthorne 15, Lorenzo 8, Marciniak 37. **3B**—Hodge 45, Jordan 1, Lorenzo 9, Marciniak 3. **SS**—Alvarez 32, Hawthorne 26, Hodge 1, Lorenzo 8. **OF**—Almonte 60, Kennedy 8, Lorenzo 4, McMillin 35, Restovich 60, Selander 30, Sutton 6, Vilorio 8.

PITCHING	W	L	ERA	G	GS	CG	SV	IP	H	R	ER	BB	SO	B	T	HT	WT	DOB	1st Yr	Resides
Balfour, Grant	[illegible]	[illegible]	[illegible]	[illegible]	[illegible]	[illegible]	[illegible]	[illegible]	[illegible]	[illegible]	[illegible]	[illegible]	[illegible]	[illegible]	[illegible]	[illegible]	[illegible]	[illegible]	[illegible]	Sydney, Australia
Butler, Andrew	2	1	6.57	17	0	0	0	37	37	29	27	19	56	R	R	6-4	210	11-1-76	1998	Findlay, Ohio
Coleman, Billy	0	0	2.40	8	0	0	0	15	12	4	4	3	16	R	R	6-0	195	1-12-76	1997	Benton Harbor, Mich.
Fisher, Peter	5	3	5.16	12	12	0	0	66	82	43	38	9	57	R	R	6-3	225	7-7-77	1998	Stoneham, Mass.
Fitts, Brian	5	3	3.64	12	12	0	0	59	57	27	24	23	48	R	R	6-2	175	7-25-76	1997	Gallatin, Tenn.
Flock, Rick	1	1	7.03	19	0	0	0	32	43	27	25	11	36	R	R	6-3	195	6-19-78	1997	Fort Myers, Fla.
Frederick, Kevin	1	4	4.25	17	0	0	1	30	28	21	14	10	46	B	R	6-2	200	11-4-76	1998	Louisville, Ky.
Perez, Pablo	3	5	6.41	16	7	0	0	53	73	45	38	24	39	R	R	6-0	170	8-27-73	1991	Queens, N.Y.
Rivera, Saul	3	3	2.25	23	0	0	7	36	19	10	9	19	65	R	R	5-11	165	12-7-77	1998	San Juan, P.R.
Sheets, Matt	2	3	9.00	14	8	0	0	42	52	47	42	37	39	R	R	6-2	207	9-16-77	1996	Grand Rapids, Mich.
Sturdy, Tim	5	1	4.00	12	12	0	0	70	65	38	31	27	46	R	R	6-2	182	10-8-78	1997	Albuquerque, N.M.
Vallis, Jamie	1	2	5.68	21	0	0	1	25	28	20	16	19	24	R	L	6-6	190	5-22-77	1996	Bedford, Nova Scotia
Victoria, Lester	3	0	6.68	22	0	0	3	32	37	26	24	20	43	R	L	5-11	175	6-14-76	1998	Orlando, Fla.

FORT MYERS — Rookie

GULF COAST LEAGUE

BATTING	AVG	G	AB	R	H	2B	3B	HR	RBI	BB	SO	SB	CS	B	T	HT	WT	DOB	1st Yr	Resides
Edwards, John	.118	10	34	1	4	1	0	0	3	1	8	0	0	R	R	6-1	185	6-27-78	1998	Victoria, Australia
Hacker, Steve	.208	6	24	5	5	0	0	1	3	2	2	0	0	R	R	6-5	230	9-6-74	1995	St. Louis, Mo.
Johnson, Kareem	.240	39	121	19	29	6	1	0	10	8	26	2	1	R	R	6-1	185	8-15-80	1998	Trail, B.C.
Lane, Ryan	.292	18	65	9	19	5	1	2	10	4	13	2	1	R	R	6-1	185	7-6-74	1993	Bellefontaine, Ohio
Lough, Aaron	.250	38	100	4	25	6	0	0	10	9	22	1	2	R	R	6-4	210	6-4-77	1998	Seattle, Wash.
McCorvey, Ken	.222	44	117	11	26	9	0	1	8	10	41	5	0	R	R	6-2	185	3-16-79	1997	Pensacola, Fla.
Nanita, Emmanuel	.232	42	125	22	29	6	3	0	9	14	19	5	2	R	R	6-2	187	12-25-79	1997	Santo Domingo, D.R.
Nunez, Edward	.182	4	11	3	2	0	0	0	1	0	1	4	0	L	R	5-6	145	1-13-80	1997	Caracas, Ven.
Pridie, Jon	.217	31	106	10	23	6	0	1	15	6	24	0	1	R	R	6-4	220	12-7-79	1998	Prescott, Ariz.
Rodriguez, Luis	.278	52	180	33	50	11	1	1	15	22	17	14	3	B	R	5-9	144	6-27-80	1997	Tinaco, Ven.
Sajiun, Joel	.253	36	99	12	25	6	1	2	12	9	33	1	1	R	R	6-3	215	12-16-77	1998	Hialeah, Fla.
Salazar, Ruben	.248	50	161	16	40	5	1	3	25	9	29	10	3	R	R	5-10	194	1-16-78	1997	San Felix, Ven.
Sandberg, Eric	.316	35	114	17	36	8	0	3	18	18	17	4	2	L	L	6-0	220	8-15-79	1998	Spokane, Wash.
Shrum, Allen	.331	42	127	17	42	10	0	10	25	13	27	3	2	R	R	6-2	220	5-13-76	1998	Hermitage, Tenn.
Southward, DeShawn	.267	56	165	31	44	5	1	2	24	21	33	11	4	R	R	5-11	180	5-16-78	1997	Dade City, Fla.
Stevens, Tony	.257	52	187	30	48	7	1	3	12	11	19	3	7	B	R	5-9	140	9-18-78	1997	Keystone Heights, Fla.
Torres, Franklin	.276	50	174	32	48	6	0	0	24	20	29	15	1	R	R	5-9	178	9-10-79	1996	Santiago, D.R.
Watkins, Tommy	.219	33	73	8	16	5	0	0	8	9	11	5	0	R	R	5-10	175	6-18-80	1998	Fort Myers, Fla.

GAMES BY POSITION: C—Edwards 8, Lough 24, Shrum 38. **1B**—Hacker 6, Lane 3, Lough 10, Pridie 5, Sandberg 32, Shrum 5, Torres 12. **2B**—Lane 5, Rodriguez 35, Salazar 3, Stevens 9, Torres 19, Watkins 6. **3B**—Lane 1, Pridie 14, Rodriguez 3, Salazar 44, Torres 7. **SS**—Lane 5, Rodriguez 17, Stevens 30, Watkins 22. **OF**—Johnson 34, McCorvey 40, Nanita 29, Nunez 3, Sajiun 32, Sandberg 2, Southward 54, Stevens 17.

PITCHING	W	L	ERA	G	GS	CG	SV	IP	H	R	ER	BB	SO	B	T	HT	WT	DOB	1st Yr	Resides
Blake, Peter	1	5	4.23	8	8	0	0	38	41	24	18	20	28	R	L	6-1	210	1-15-79	1997	Indianola, Iowa
Cooke, Andrew	6	1	1.29	17	2	0	2	42	33	10	6	5	42	L	L	6-3	190	2-17-81	1997	New South Wales, Australia
Denholm, Richard	1	0	7.85	13	0	0	1	18	20	17	16	9	9	R	R	6-2	180	10-31-79	1998	Orlando, Fla.
Espinal, Jose	2	0	4.62	9	5	1	1	25	23	14	13	15	15	R	R	6-2	160	12-3-79	1998	Canovanas, P.R.
Flock, Rick	0	0	0.00	2	0	0	0	4	0	0	0	2	5	R	R	6-3	195	6-19-78	1997	Fort Myers, Fla.
Foote, Joe	6	3	3.90	13	10	0	0	58	61	35	25	15	60	R	R	6-2	170	8-30-79	1997	Sterling, Va.
Frazier, Bradley	4	3	2.61	9	9	0	0	52	51	17	15	13	40	R	R	6-6	220	12-16-76	1998	Semmes, Ala.
Haigler, Phil	0	0	1.54	3	1	0	0	12	9	2	2	0	6	R	R	6-3	217	6-13-74	1996	Pascagoula, Miss.
LaRosa, Tom	0	2	1.29	4	0	0	0	7	1	4	1	7	6	R	R	5-10	180	6-28-75	1996	Henderson, Nev.
Melson, Nate	5	1	3.66	12	10	0	0	64	63	30	26	13	43	R	R	6-6	192	10-28-78	1997	Rogers, Ark.
Miller, Aaron	0	0	0.00	4	0	0	0	5	4	0	0	4	12	R	L	6-3	235	7-31-76	1997	Middletown, Del.
Mott, Tom	0	1	4.66	5	0	0	0	10	12	5	5	5	6	R	R	6-3	217	10-9-73	1994	San Luis Obispo, Calif.
Nowakowski, Brian	0	1	4.50	13	1	0	0	20	25	13	10	5	6	R	R	6-1	175	11-27-79	1997	Chicago, Ill.
Padilla, Juan	1	1	1.40	17	0	0	10	26	19	4	4	1	27	R	R	6-0	180	2-17-77	1998	Levittown, P.R.
Rojas, Frances	1	2	3.42	13	0	0	0	24	21	13	9	9	17	L	L	6-0	190	12-8-78	1997	La Guaira, Ven.
Sents, Marcus	2	5	6.43	9	9	0	0	35	36	33	25	28	24	R	R	6-3	215	8-12-80	1998	Cookeville, Tenn.
Stenger, Pat	3	1	3.86	13	4	0	1	35	57	26	15	5	23	R	R	6-6	196	10-7-78	1997	Mentor, Ohio
Underhill, Ray	2	0	2.53	14	1	0	0	21	18	9	6	8	13	R	R	6-4	185	1-26-79	1997	DeLand, Fla.
Whitfield, Jacob	0	0	13.50	7	0	0	0	8	10	14	12	10	12	L	L	6-2	200	4-10-76	1998	Tampa, Fla.
Wojciechowski, Steve	0	0	0.00	2	0	0	0	4	2	0	0	0	7	L	L	6-2	185	7-29-70	1991	Calumet City, Ill.

MONTREAL EXPOS

Expos' future looks bright enough to convince Alou to stay

BY JEFF BLAIR

The Montreal Expos went into the 1998-99 offseason not knowing for certain where they'd be playing after the '99 season, but one thing was clear: Wherever they end up, they will have a talented young core of players and a minor league system that has never had better pitching.

"I guess it's best left up to others to judge how deals turn out, especially this early and especially when it comes to pitching," Expos general manager Jim Beattie said. "But we think we have some promising arms."

It was a year of rebuilding for the Expos, beginning in the winter when Cy Young Award winner Pedro Martinez and second baseman Mike Lansing were dealt away. The club took its lumps in '98, but there were several bright spots. Things were encouraging enough that manager Felipe Alou was able to resist an offer from the Dodgers at the end of the season. Instead he reupped with the Expos for three more years.

Right fielder Vladimir Guerrero looked to be on the verge of superstardom. He caught fire in the second half and finished with a .324 average, 38 home runs and 109 RBIs. He signed a five-year, $28 million deal late in the summer.

Center fielder Rondell White was also enjoying a fine year before a midseason injury shelved him after 97 games. He finished with a .300 average and 17 home runs. First baseman Brad Fullmer, one of the top rookies in baseball, led the club with 44 doubles while batting .273.

Expos closer Ugueth Urbina was one of the best in baseball. He posted a sparkling 1.30 ERA while picking up 34 saves and striking out 94 batters in 69 innings. Dustin Hermanson stepped up to assume the No. 1 starter's role in Martinez' absence. After Hermanson, rookies Carl Pavano and Javier Vazquez were the most promising of the many young pitchers to appear for Montreal.

Beattie did a fine job of stocking up even more pitchers in his trades. Pavano and Tony Armas came over in the Martinez deal, while John Nicholson and Jake Westbrook were acquired from the Rockies for Lansing.

And a midseason deal with the Dodgers brought lefthander Ted Lilly, first baseman Jonathan Tucker, second baseman Wilton Guerrero and outfielder Peter Bergeron in exchange for lefthander Carlos Perez and shortstop Mark Grudzielanek.

The Expos continued to show their traditional depth at the Double-A level as well as at Class A. Michael Barrett finished with a spurt to challenge for the Eastern League batting title after a midseason shift from catching full-time to playing third base the majority of the time. He should find a home in Montreal in 1999.

The Expos will also try to find a spot for switch-hitting slugger Fernando Seguignol, who hit .288 with 25 home runs and 69 RBIs at Harrisburg and who, like Barrett, did not look overmatched after his end-of-season callup.

Armas, Nicholson and Westbrook made immediate contributions at Class A Jupiter. But other pitchers in the organization took significant strides, too. Jeremy Powell made his major league debut and will have a shot at the big club again in the spring, while Matt Blank's consistency earned organizational pitcher-of-the-year honors for him.

Vladimir Guerrero

Michael Barrett

Players of the Year

Major League: Vladimir Guerrero, of.

The Expos' latest phenom finished fourth in the NL with 202 hits and 367 total bases while hitting 38 home runs.

Minor League: Michael Barrett, c-3b, Harrisburg

Barrett led Expos minor leaguers with a .320 average while hitting 19 homers and driving in 87 runs.

ORGANIZATION LEADERS

BATTING		
*AVG	Michael Barrett, Harrisburg	.320
R	Milton Bradley, Jupiter/Cape Fear	109
H	Milton Bradley, Jupiter/Cape Fear	160
TB	Two tied at	238
2B	Two tied at	35
3B	Noah Hall, Jupiter/Cape Fear	7
HR	Fernando Seguignol, Ottawa/Harrisburg	31
RBI	Noah Hall, Jupiter/Cape Fear	90
BB	Talmadge Nunnari, Jupiter/Cape Fear	72
SO	Chris Schwab, Harrisburg/Jupiter	178
SB	Kenny James, Cape Fear	41
PITCHING		
W	Matt Blank, Jupiter/Cape Fear	14
L	Three tied at	11
#ERA	T.J. Tucker, Jupiter/Vermont/GCL Expos	1.38
G	Rodney Stevenson, Harrisburg/Jupiter	56
CG	Three tied at	2
SV	Ben Fleetham, Ottawa	25
IP	Matt Blank, Jupiter/Cape Fear	177
BB	Jason Baker, Harrisburg	71
SO	Matt Blank, Jupiter/Cape Fear	140

*Minimum 250 At-Bats #Minimum 75 Innings

Montreal EXPOS

Manager: Felipe Alou

1998 Record: 65-97, .401 (4th, NL East)

BATTING	AVG	G	AB	R	H	2B	3B	HR	RBI	BB	SO	SB	CS	B	T	HT	WT	DOB	1st Yr	Resides
Andrews, Shane	.238	150	492	48	117	30	1	25	69	58	137	1	6	R	R	6-1	205	8-28-71	1990	Carlsbad, N.M.
Barrett, Michael	.304	8	23	3	7	2	0	1	2	3	6	0	0	R	R	6-3	185	10-22-76	1995	West Palm Beach, Fla.
Cabrera, Orlando	.280	79	261	44	73	16	5	3	22	18	27	6	2	R	R	5-11	165	3-2-74	1994	Cartagena, Colombia
Fullmer, Brad	.273	140	505	58	138	44	2	13	73	39	70	6	6	L	R	6-1	185	1-17-75	1994	Chatsworth, Calif.
Grudzielanek, Mark	.275	105	396	51	109	15	1	8	41	21	50	11	5	R	R	6-1	170	6-30-70	1991	El Paso, Texas
Guerrero, Vladimir	.324	159	623	107	202	37	7	38	109	42	95	11	9	R	R	6-2	195	2-9-76	1993	Nizao, D.R.
Guerrero, Wilton	.284	52	222	29	63	10	6	2	20	10	30	3	0	R	R	5-11	175	10-24-74	1992	Nizao, D.R.
2-team (64 L.A.)	.284	116	402	50	114	14	9	2	27	14	63	8	2							
Henley, Bob	.304	41	115	16	35	8	1	3	18	11	26	3	0	R	R	6-2	190	1-30-73	1993	Grand Bay, Ala.
Holbert, Ray	.000	2	5	0	0	0	0	0	0	0	1	0	0	R	R	6-0	175	9-25-70	1988	Phoenix, Ariz.
2-team (8 Atlanta)	.100	10	20	2	2	0	0	0	1	2	5	0	0							
Hubbard, Mike	.145	32	55	3	8	1	0	1	3	0	17	0	0	R	R	6-1	205	2-16-71	1992	Madison Heights, Va.
Jones, Terry	.217	60	212	30	46	7	2	1	15	21	46	16	4	R	R	5-10	160	2-15-71	1993	Pinson, Ala.
Livingstone, Scott	.209	76	110	1	23	6	0	0	12	5	15	1	1	L	R	6-0	198	7-15-65	1988	Southlake, Texas
May, Derrick	.239	85	180	13	43	8	0	5	15	11	24	0	0	L	R	6-4	200	7-14-68	1986	Newark, Del.
McGuire, Ryan	.186	130	210	17	39	9	0	1	10	32	55	0	0	L	L	6-1	195	11-23-71	1993	Woodland Hills, Calif.
Mordecai, Mike	.202	73	119	12	24	4	2	3	10	9	20	1	0	R	R	5-11	175	12-13-67	1989	Pinson, Ala.
Perez, Robert	.236	52	106	9	25	1	0	1	8	2	23	0	0	R	R	6-3	230	6-4-69	1990	Bolivar, Ven.
Santangelo, F.P.	.214	122	383	53	82	18	0	4	23	44	72	7	3	B	R	5-10	165	10-24-67	1989	El Dorado Hills, Calif.
Seguignol, Fernando	.262	16	42	6	11	4	0	2	3	3	15	0	0	B	R	6-5	179	1-19-75	1993	Panama City, Panama
Stovall, DaRond	.205	62	78	11	16	2	1	2	6	6	29	1	0	B	L	6-1	185	1-3-73	1991	East St. Louis, Ill.
Vidro, Jose	.220	83	205	24	45	12	0	0	18	27	33	2	2	B	R	5-11	175	8-27-74	1992	Sabana Grande, P.R.
White, Rondell	.300	97	357	54	107	21	2	17	58	30	57	16	7	R	R	6-1	193	2-23-72	1990	Gray, Ga.
Widger, Chris	.233	125	417	36	97	18	1	15	53	29	85	6	1	R	R	6-3	195	5-21-71	1992	Pennsville, N.J.

PITCHING	W	L	ERA	G	GS	CG	SV	IP	H	R	ER	BB	SO	B	T	HT	WT	DOB	1st Yr	Resides
Batista, Miguel	3	5	3.80	56	13	0	0	135	141	66	57	65	92	R	R	6-0	160	2-19-71	1988	San Pedro de Macoris, D.R.
Bennett, Shayne	5	5	5.50	62	0	0	1	92	97	61	56	45	59	R	R	6-5	200	4-10-72	1993	Worongary, Australia
Boskie, Shawn	1	3	9.17	5	5	0	0	18	34	21	18	4	10	R	R	6-3	205	3-28-67	1986	Reno, Nev.
Bullinger, Kirk	1	0	9.00	8	0	0	0	7	14	8	7	0	2	R	R	6-2	170	10-28-69	1992	Hammond, La.
DeHart, Rick	0	0	4.82	26	0	0	1	28	34	22	15	13	14	R	L	6-1	180	3-21-70	1992	Topeka, Kan.
Hermanson, Dustin	14	11	3.13	32	30	1	0	187	163	80	65	56	154	R	R	6-3	195	12-21-72	1994	Springfield, Ohio
Johnson, Mike	0	2	14.73	2	2	0	0	7	16	12	12	2	4	L	R	6-2	175	10-3-75	1993	Edmonton, Alberta
Kline, Steve	3	6	2.76	78	0	0	1	72	62	25	22	41	76	B	L	6-2	200	8-22-72	1993	Winfield, Pa.
Maddux, Mike	3	4	3.72	51	0	0	1	56	50	24	23	15	33	L	R	6-2	188	8-27-61	1982	Las Vegas, Nev.
Moore, Trey	2	5	5.02	13	11	0	0	61	78	37	34	17	35	L	L	6-1	200	10-2-72	1994	Southlake, Texas
Pavano, Carl	6	9	4.21	24	23	0	0	135	130	70	63	43	83	R	R	6-5	230	1-8-76	1994	Southington, Conn.
Perez, Carlos	7	10	3.75	23	23	3	0	163	177	79	68	33	82	L	L	6-3	200	4-14-71	1990	San Cristobal, D.R.
Powell, Jeremy	1	5	7.92	7	6	0	0	25	27	25	22	11	14	R	R	6-5	230	6-18-76	1994	Sacramento, Calif.
Telford, Anthony	3	6	3.86	77	0	0	1	91	85	45	39	36	59	R	R	6-0	175	3-6-66	1987	Pinellas Park, Fla.
Thurman, Mike	4	5	4.70	14	13	0	0	67	60	38	35	26	32	R	R	6-5	190	7-22-73	1994	Philomath, Ore.
Urbina, Ugueth	6	3	1.30	64	0	0	34	69	37	11	10	33	94	R	R	6-2	170	2-15-74	1991	Caracas, Ven.
Valdes, Marc	1	3	7.43	20	4	0	0	36	41	34	30	21	28	R	R	6-0	170	12-20-71	1993	Tampa, Fla.
Vazquez, Javier	5	15	6.06	33	32	0	0	172	196	121	116	68	139	R	R	6-2	175	6-25-76	1994	Ponce, P.R.
Young, Tim	0	0	6.00	10	0	0	0	6	6	4	4	4	7	L	L	5-9	170	10-15-73	1996	Bristol, Fla.

FIELDING

Catcher	PCT	G	PO	A	E	DP	PB
Barrett	.964	3	23	4	1	1	0
Henley	.995	35	189	14	1	1	3
Hubbard	1.000	23	82	5	0	1	1
Widger	.983	123	752	62	14	12	14

First Base	PCT	G	PO	A	E	DP
Fullmer	.985	137	1070	78	17	81
Livingstone	.917	3	10	1	1	4
McGuire	.980	78	275	25	6	18
Mordecai	1.000	1	2	0	0	0
Seguignol	1.000	7	44	5	0	3

Second Base	PCT	G	PO	A	E	DP
Cabrera	.970	28	59	72	4	16
Guerrero	.975	52	103	130	6	25
Holbert	1.000	1	2	3	0	0
Hubbard	.000	1	0	0	0	0
Mordecai	.980	21	18	32	1	7
Santangelo	.983	35	47	71	2	7
Vidro	.975	56	78	121	5	25

Third Base	PCT	G	PO	A	E	DP
Andrews	.954	147	95	322	20	28
Barrett	.714	3	0	5	2	0
Livingstone	.938	17	6	24	2	0
Mordecai	.889	11	3	5	1	0
Santangelo	.000	1	0	0	0	0
Vidro	.900	7	4	5	1	2

Shortstop	PCT	G	PO	A	E	DP
Cabrera	.984	52	64	123	3	20
Grudzielanek	.950	105	152	283	23	56
Mordecai	.953	30	16	45	3	6

Outfield	PCT	G	PO	A	E	DP
Guerrero	.951	157	321	10	17	3
Jones	.988	60	162	4	2	3
May	.984	48	57	3	1	1
McGuire	.981	46	51	1	1	0
Perez	.852	29	20	3	4	0
Santangelo	.983	92	164	6	3	0
Seguignol	1.000	9	21	0	0	0
Stovall	.927	47	36	2	3	0
White	.996	96	260	7	1	3

MORRIS FOSTOFF

Dustin Hermanson

LARRY GOREN

Rookie Brad Fullmer
Led Expos with 44 doubles

MORRIS FOSTOFF

Jupiter's Tony Armas
Posted a 2.88 ERA in Class A Florida State League

FARM SYSTEM

Director of Player Development: David Littlefield

Class	Farm Team	League	W	L	Pct.	Finish*	Manager	First Yr
AAA	Ottawa (Ontario) Lynx	International	69	74	.483	10th (14)	Pat Kelly	1993
AA	Harrisburg (Pa.) Senators	Eastern	73	69	.514	+4th (10)	Rick Sweet	1991
A#	Jupiter (Fla.) Hammerheads	Florida State	80	60	.571	4th (14)	Doug Sisson	1998
A	Cape Fear (N.C.) Crocs	South Atlantic	80	61	.567	4th (14)	Luis Dorante	1997
A	Vermont Expos	New York-Penn	36	40	.474	8th (14)	Tony Barbone	1994
Rookie	Jupiter (Fla.) Expos	Gulf Coast	32	27	.542	6th (14)	Frank Kremblas	1998

*Finish in overall standings (No. of teams in league) #Advanced level +Won league championship

OTTAWA — Class AAA

INTERNATIONAL LEAGUE

BATTING	AVG	G	AB	R	H	2B	3B	HR	RBI	BB	SO	SB	CS	B	T	HT	WT	DOB	1st Yr	Resides
Arntzen, Brian	.231	5	13	0	3	0	0	0	0	0	4	0	0	R	R	6-3	205	1-8-70	1992	Redding, Calif.
Bady, Ed	.154	5	13	0	2	0	0	0	0	3	5	0	0	B	R	5-11	170	2-5-73	1994	Queens, N.Y.
Battle, Allen	.304	132	454	72	138	31	2	11	68	71	81	34	5	R	R	6-0	170	11-29-68	1991	Mount Olive, N.C.
Blum, Geoff	.174	8	23	1	4	0	0	0	1	3	6	0	0	B	R	6-3	193	4-26-73	1994	Chino, Calif.
Bocachica, Hiram	.195	12	41	5	8	3	1	0	5	6	14	2	0	R	R	5-11	165	3-4-76	1994	Bayamon, P.R.
Cabrera, Orlando	.232	66	272	31	63	9	4	0	26	28	27	19	9	R	R	5-11	165	3-2-74	1994	Cartagena, Colombia
Chavez, Raul	.226	11	31	2	7	0	0	0	1	5	5	0	0	R	R	5-11	175	3-18-73	1990	Valencia, Ven.
Coquillette, Trace	.254	74	252	30	64	14	0	7	40	17	38	3	3	R	R	5-11	165	6-4-74	1993	Orangevale, Calif.
Fernandez, Jose	.267	21	60	8	16	4	1	0	4	5	14	3	1	R	R	6-2	190	11-2-74	1993	Santiago, D.R.
Henley, Bob	.246	37	126	13	31	6	1	4	20	12	34	1	1	R	R	6-2	190	1-30-73	1993	Grand Bay, Ala.
Holbert, Ray	.308	86	266	38	82	17	4	2	25	29	66	10	5	R	R	6-0	175	9-25-70	1988	Phoenix, Ariz.
2-team (1 Richmond)	.307	87	267	39	82	17	4	2	25	31	67	10	5							
Hubbard, Mike	.229	20	70	9	16	5	0	0	8	3	13	0	0	R	R	6-1	205	2-16-71	1992	Madison Heights, Va.
Jones, Terry	.237	81	278	36	66	3	4	0	21	32	48	35	6	R	R	5-10	160	2-15-71	1993	Pinson, Ala.
Lukachyk, Rob	.234	73	222	34	52	13	2	5	25	22	52	13	0	L	R	6-0	185	7-24-68	1987	Sarasota, Fla.
May, Derrick	.377	21	69	16	26	6	0	6	21	13	7	0	1	L	R	6-4	200	7-14-68	1986	Newark, Del.
Mordecai, Mike	.227	6	22	2	5	2	0	0	1	3	3	0	0	R	R	5-11	175	12-13-67	1989	Pinson, Ala.
Ortiz, Nick	.094	12	32	1	3	1	0	0	0	6	10	0	0	R	R	6-0	165	7-9-73	1991	Cidra, P.R.
Pachot, John	.227	100	344	33	78	18	1	2	39	15	45	2	2	R	R	6-2	168	11-11-74	1993	Ponce, P.R.
Post, Dave	.300	93	330	59	99	23	2	6	35	28	50	7	7	R	R	5-11	170	9-3-73	1992	Kingston, N.Y.
Rodriguez, Steve	.280	75	232	24	65	11	1	1	28	15	34	6	7	R	R	5-9	170	11-29-70	1992	Las Vegas, Nev.
Samuels, Scott	.234	43	94	15	22	4	2	2	15	19	24	4	3	L	R	5-11	190	5-19-71	1992	San Jose, Calif.
Santangelo, F.P.	.250	2	8	1	2	0	0	0	1	0	3	0	0	B	R	5-10	165	10-24-67	1989	El Dorado Hills, Calif.
Saunders, Chris	.274	131	478	58	131	26	2	9	58	46	98	1	1	R	R	6-1	203	7-19-70	1992	Clovis, Calif.
Seefried, Tate	.184	38	114	10	21	3	0	3	12	17	37	0	1	L	R	6-4	180	4-22-72	1990	Tampa, Fla.
Seguignol, Fernando	.257	32	109	16	28	8	0	6	16	12	43	0	0	B	R	6-5	179	1-19-75	1993	Panama City, Panama
Stovall, DaRond	.227	44	150	15	34	7	1	8	22	21	51	6	2	B	L	6-1	185	1-3-73	1991	East St. Louis, Ill.
Thurston, Jerrey	.033	13	30	2	1	0	0	0	0	4	15	0	0	R	R	6-4	200	4-17-72	1990	Longwood, Fla.
Tinsley, Lee	.216	51	185	25	40	9	2	2	19	16	43	13	2	B	R	5-10	180	3-4-69	1987	Shelbyville, Ky.
Valdez, Trovin	.278	5	18	3	5	1	1	0	1	0	2	1	1	R	R	5-10	163	11-18-73	1993	New York, N.Y.
Vidro, Jose	.289	63	235	35	68	14	2	2	32	24	25	5	2	B	R	5-11	175	8-27-74	1992	Sabana Grande, P.R.

PITCHING	W	L	ERA	G	GS	CG	SV	IP	H	R	ER	BB	SO	B	T	HT	WT	DOB	1st Yr	Resides
Benz, Jake	1	5	5.84	25	3	0	1	49	63	34	32	24	40	L	L	5-9	162	2-27-72	1994	Pleasant Hill, Calif.
Boskie, Shawn	5	7	4.55	13	13	0	0	87	100	48	44	21	51	R	R	6-3	205	3-28-67	1986	Reno, Nev.
Bullinger, Kirk	0	0	1.06	13	0	0	3	17	16	2	2	6	7	R	R	6-2	170	10-28-69	1992	Hammond, La.
Bunch, Mel	6	6	4.59	25	19	0	0	104	101	58	53	48	99	R	R	6-1	165	11-4-71	1992	Texarkana, Texas
Cole, Jason	2	0	3.80	13	0	0	1	21	21	9	9	13	14	R	R	6-3	198	9-8-72	1994	Coventry, R.I.
DeHart, Rick	7	1	3.23	38	0	0	4	53	46	19	19	17	48	R	L	6-1	180	3-21-70	1992	Topeka, Kan.
DeSilva, John	4	2	2.61	7	7	0	0	48	42	15	14	12	25	R	R	6-0	193	9-30-67	1989	Fort Bragg, Calif.
Dixon, Tim	0	0	5.89	9	0	0	0	18	22	15	12	7	13	L	L	6-2	215	2-26-72	1995	San Jose, Calif.
Falteisek, Steve	10	11	5.46	34	22	1	0	162	186	110	98	59	83	R	R	6-2	200	1-28-72	1992	Floral Park, N.Y.
Fleetham, Ben	4	2	3.49	55	0	0	25	57	49	26	22	42	65	R	R	6-1	205	8-3-72	1994	Minneapolis, Minn.
Henderson, Rod	0	1	9.00	6	0	0	0	11	23	17	11	12	12	R	R	6-4	195	3-11-71	1992	Glasgow, Ky.
Johnson, Mike	4	9	4.29	18	18	1	0	109	105	63	52	38	88	L	R	6-2	175	10-3-75	1993	Edmonton, Alberta
Kline, Steve	0	0	0.00	2	0	0	0	3	1	0	0	0	1	B	L	6-2	200	8-22-72	1993	Winfield, Pa.
Lilly, Ted	2	2	4.85	7	7	0	0	39	45	28	21	19	49	L	L	6-1	177	1-4-76	1996	Fresno, Calif.
Long, Joey	2	4	4.40	34	1	0	0	47	53	27	23	24	41	R	L	6-2	215	7-15-70	1991	Rosewood, Ohio
McGraw, Tom	5	6	3.73	32	10	0	2	82	79	38	34	36	43	L	L	6-2	195	12-8-67	1990	Yacolt, Wash.
Moore, Trey	1	1	5.54	3	3	0	0	13	18	8	8	4	8	L	L	6-1	200	10-2-72	1994	Southlake, Texas
Morel, Ramon	4	3	5.12	12	12	1	0	65	60	38	37	30	29	R	R	6-2	200	8-15-74	1991	Villa Gonzalez, D.R.
Niebla, Ruben	0	1	5.11	6	0	0	0	12	20	12	7	4	7	L	L	5-10	175	12-19-71	1995	Calexico, Calif.
Pavano, Carl	1	0	2.41	3	3	0	0	19	12	5	5	7	14	R	R	6-5	230	1-8-76	1994	Southington, Conn.
Schmitt, Todd	1	1	3.31	30	0	0	5	33	18	15	12	25	34	R	R	6-2	170	2-12-70	1992	Clinton Township, Mich.
Scott, Darryl	0	1	3.09	8	0	0	2	12	12	6	4	5	7	R	R	6-1	185	8-6-68	1990	Prior Lake, Minn.
Smart, J.D.	2	3	4.89	6	6	0	0	35	34	22	19	11	16	R	R	6-2	185	11-12-73	1995	Austin, Texas
Thurman, Mike	7	7	3.41	19	19	0	0	106	107	50	40	49	76	R	R	6-5	190	7-22-73	1994	Philomath, Ore.
Young, Tim	1	1	2.03	20	0	0	2	27	26	14	6	12	34	L	L	5-9	170	10-15-73	1996	Bristol, Fla.

FIELDING

Catcher	PCT	G	PO	A	E	DP	PB
Arntzen	1.000	3	13	2	0	0	0
Chavez	1.000	11	71	15	0	2	2
Henley	.990	30	176	22	2	1	5
Hubbard	.992	19	121	8	1	1	3
Pachot	.986	76	475	69	8	8	3
Thurston	.971	12	65	2	2	1	1

First Base	PCT	G	PO	A	E	DP
Arntzen	1.000	1	1	0	0	0
Fernandez	1.000	4	25	3	0	6
Lukachyk	.997	39	315	24	1	22
Pachot	.981	14	93	8	2	11
Post	1.000	40	282	35	0	26
Saunders	.989	41	317	28	4	40
Seefried	.985	17	122	7	2	14
Seguignol	1.000	2	10	2	0	1
Thurston	1.000	1	2	1	0	0

Second Base	PCT	G	PO	A	E	DP
Blum	1.000	6	18	12	0	5
Cabrera	.955	21	42	63	5	14
Coquillette	.982	46	110	103	4	25
Holbert	1.000	4	2	4	0	1
Mordecai	1.000	2	3	5	0	2
Ortiz	1.000	5	17	8	0	1
Post	.930	12	21	32	4	6
Rodriguez	.972	31	46	57	3	15
Vidro	.981	30	73	79	3	21

Third Base	PCT	G	PO	A	E	DP
Coquillette	.912	22	15	37	5	4
Fernandez	.833	11	10	15	5	3
Holbert	.952	6	6	14	1	0
Post	1.000	4	1	5	0	0
Rodriguez	.833	3	4	6	2	0
Saunders	.956	83	55	162	10	11
Vidro	.955	23	18	45	3	6

Shortstop	PCT	G	PO	A	E	DP
Blum	1.000	2	1	3	0	1
Cabrera	.967	45	80	127	7	24
Holbert	.969	75	125	189	10	45
Mordecai	.958	4	6	17	1	3
Ortiz	.955	6	6	15	1	3
Post	1.000	4	4	7	0	2
Rodriguez	.884	16	18	43	8	11

Outfield	PCT	G	PO	A	E	DP
Bady	1.000	5	10	1	0	1
Battle	.974	125	253	5	7	2
Bocachica	1.000	11	23	1	0	1
Coquillette	.000	2	0	0	0	0
Fernandez	1.000	3	1	0	0	0
Jones	.980	79	193	5	4	2
Lukachyk	.962	30	47	4	2	0
May	.960	16	23	1	1	0
Post	.974	32	36	2	1	1
Rodriguez	1.000	23	32	0	0	0
Samuels	.977	25	40	2	1	0
Santangelo	1.000	1	2	0	0	0
Seguignol	.971	27	34	0	1	0
Stovall	.962	40	74	2	3	1
Tinsley	.975	43	76	3	2	0
Valdez	1.000	3	4	0	0	0

HARRISBURG — Class AA

EASTERN LEAGUE

BATTING	AVG	G	AB	R	H	2B	3B	HR	RBI	BB	SO	SB	CS	B	T	HT	WT	DOB	1st Yr	Resides
Adolfo, Carlos	.192	40	130	10	25	5	0	2	16	9	33	3	0	R	R	5-11	160	4-20-76	1994	Santo Domingo, D.R.
Bady, Ed	.252	58	123	19	31	4	1	0	2	15	30	10	2	B	R	5-11	170	2-5-73	1994	Queens, N.Y.
Barrett, Michael	.320	120	453	78	145	32	2	19	87	27	43	7	6	R	R	6-3	185	10-22-76	1995	West Palm Beach, Fla.
Bergeron, Peter	.246	34	134	22	33	8	4	0	9	17	26	8	3	L	R	6-2	185	11-9-77	1996	Greenfield, Mass.
Blum, Geoff	.309	39	139	25	43	12	3	6	21	17	24	2	1	B	R	6-3	193	4-26-73	1994	Chino, Calif.
Bocachica, Hiram	.264	80	296	39	78	18	4	4	27	21	61	20	8	R	R	5-11	165	3-4-76	1994	Bayamon, P.R.
Camilli, Jason	.111	6	18	1	2	0	0	0	1	3	5	0	0	R	R	6-0	178	10-18-75	1994	Phoenix, Ariz.
Campos, Jesus	.259	83	263	23	68	11	0	4	30	7	18	13	3	R	R	5-9	150	10-12-73	1991	San Pedro de Macoris, D.R.
Carroll, Jamey	.253	75	261	43	66	11	3	0	20	41	29	11	5	R	R	5-11	165	2-18-75	1996	Evansville, Ind.
Carvajal, Jhonny	.260	112	338	37	88	12	4	0	21	34	69	4	6	R	R	5-10	165	7-24-74	1993	Barcelona, Ven.
Coquillette, Trace	.332	49	187	40	62	10	0	9	23	15	41	10	3	R	R	5-11	165	6-4-74	1993	Orangevale, Calif.
Fernandez, Jose	.295	104	369	59	109	27	1	17	58	36	73	16	6	R	R	6-2	190	11-2-74	1993	Santiago, D.R.
Morales, Francisco	.215	96	311	25	67	11	1	9	45	30	86	1	1	R	R	6-3	180	1-31-73	1991	San Pedro de Macoris, D.R.
Ortiz, Nick	.270	56	163	18	44	11	2	6	24	18	37	2	3	R	R	6-0	165	7-9-73	1991	Cidra, P.R.
Pond, Simon	.000	2	3	0	0	0	0	0	0	1	1	0	0	L	R	6-1	175	10-27-76	1994	North Vancouver, B.C.
Post, Dave	.345	19	58	9	20	3	1	1	9	7	3	1	1	R	R	5-11	170	9-3-73	1992	Kingston, N.Y.
Samuels, Scott	.276	20	58	9	16	3	0	4	11	7	13	4	1	L	R	5-11	190	5-19-71	1992	San Jose, Calif.
Schwab, Chris	.000	3	4	0	0	0	0	0	0	1	3	0	0	R	L	6-3	215	7-25-74	1993	Eagan, Minn.
Seguignol, Fernando	.288	80	281	54	81	13	0	25	69	29	77	6	1	B	R	6-5	179	1-19-75	1993	Panama City, Panama
Stowers, Chris	.269	134	510	86	137	31	5	17	66	42	109	24	7	L	L	6-3	195	8-18-74	1996	Marietta, Ga.
Tracy, Andrew	.227	62	211	33	48	12	3	10	33	24	62	1	2	L	R	6-3	220	12-11-73	1996	Bowling Green, Ohio
Tucker, Jon	.278	25	79	13	22	7	0	3	16	18	18	0	0	L	L	6-4	200	12-17-76	1995	Northridge, Calif.
Valdez, Trovin	.256	54	121	16	31	8	1	2	10	6	21	14	2	R	R	5-10	163	11-18-73	1993	New York, N.Y.

PITCHING	W	L	ERA	G	GS	CG	SV	IP	H	R	ER	BB	SO	B	T	HT	WT	DOB	1st Yr	Resides
Baker, Jason	4	10	5.64	25	20	0	0	104	95	69	65	71	88	R	R	6-4	195	11-21-74	1993	Midland, Texas
Benz, Jake	3	1	1.08	16	0	0	4	33	19	5	4	11	31	L	L	5-9	162	2-27-72	1994	Pleasant Hill, Calif.
Cole, Jason	2	2	3.42	22	0	0	5	24	28	9	9	14	15	R	R	6-3	198	9-8-72	1994	Coventry, R.I.
Dixon, Tim	2	5	3.88	37	0	0	2	58	58	29	25	16	52	L	L	6-2	215	2-26-72	1995	San Jose, Calif.
Durocher, Jayson	0	1	3.97	10	0	0	1	11	10	8	5	6	12	R	R	6-3	195	8-18-74	1993	Scottsdale, Ariz.

PITCHING	W	L	ERA	G	GS	CG	SV	IP	H	R	ER	BB	SO	B	T	HT	WT	DOB	1st Yr	Resides
Evans, Keith	8	9	3.56	20	20	1	0	124	133	59	49	30	76	R	R	6-5	200	11-2-75	1996	Woodland Hills, Calif.
Forster, Scott	7	3	4.87	25	11	0	0	78	90	50	42	47	54	R	L	6-1	194	10-27-71	1994	Flourtown, Pa.
Johnson, Mike	3	2	6.95	7	7	0	0	34	35	27	26	10	38	L	R	6-2	175	10-3-75	1993	Edmonton, Alberta
Marquez, Robert	0	0	3.00	4	0	0	1	6	4	2	2	2	5	R	R	6-0	180	4-21-73	1995	Houston, Texas
Martinez, Ramiro	0	2	7.40	10	3	0	0	24	40	22	20	16	10	L	L	6-2	185	1-28-72	1992	Los Angeles, Calif.
McCommon, Jason	1	0	3.72	6	0	0	1	10	8	4	4	6	7	R	R	6-0	190	8-9-71	1994	Memphis, Tenn.
Mitchell, Scott	9	3	3.80	32	17	2	2	135	136	58	57	37	81	R	R	5-11	170	3-19-73	1995	Citrus Heights, Calif.
Moraga, David	1	4	4.95	19	4	0	1	40	42	27	22	22	23	L	L	6-0	184	7-8-75	1994	Suisun, Calif.
Mota, Guillermo	2	0	1.06	12	0	0	4	17	10	2	2	2	19	R	R	6-5	185	7-25-73	1991	San Pedro de Macoris, D.R.
Niebla, Ruben	0	2	4.60	24	1	0	1	43	45	23	22	6	30	L	L	5-10	175	12-19-71	1995	Calexico, Calif.
Parker, Christian	6	6	3.48	36	16	0	5	127	124	66	49	47	73	R	R	6-1	200	7-3-75	1996	Albuquerque, N.M.
Phelps, Tommy	5	4	3.62	12	10	0	0	60	57	29	24	26	26	L	L	6-3	192	3-4-74	1993	Tampa, Fla.
Powell, Jeremy	9	7	3.01	22	22	1	0	132	115	54	44	37	77	R	R	6-5	230	6-18-76	1994	Sacramento, Calif.
Smart, J.D.	3	5	2.45	14	11	2	1	77	67	23	21	18	47	R	R	6-2	185	11-12-73	1995	Austin, Texas
Stevenson, Rodney	5	0	4.35	37	0	0	8	39	32	19	19	18	47	R	R	6-2	210	3-21-74	1996	Columbus, Ga.
Young, Tim	3	3	3.79	26	0	0	3	36	28	17	15	10	52	L	L	5-9	170	10-15-73	1996	Bristol, Fla.

FIELDING

Catcher	PCT	G	PO	A	E	DP	PB
Barrett	.989	83	499	49	6	5	6
Morales	.993	64	396	45	3	2	13

First Base	PCT	G	PO	A	E	DP
Blum	1.000	1	5	0	0	0
Fernandez	.983	7	55	2	1	4
Morales	.984	16	116	9	2	17
Pond	1.000	1	7	2	0	0
Post	1.000	7	43	1	0	4
Seguignol	.983	59	485	50	9	38
Tracy	.988	52	476	36	6	53
Tucker	.989	13	83	8	1	10

Second Base	PCT	G	PO	A	E	DP
Bady	1.000	1	2	1	0	0
Blum	.971	9	13	20	1	4
Camilli	1.000	5	5	15	0	3
Carroll	.962	54	98	152	10	42
Carvajal	.978	12	13	31	1	9
Coquillette	.973	45	61	121	5	20
Ortiz	1.000	22	37	69	0	16
Post	1.000	4	3	10	0	2

Third Base	PCT	G	PO	A	E	DP
Barrett	.932	34	18	64	6	9
Blum	1.000	15	11	35	0	4
Coquillette	.600	1	0	3	2	1
Fernandez	.916	85	64	165	21	13
Ortiz	.933	11	4	24	2	2
Post	1.000	3	5	7	0	2

Shortstop	PCT	G	PO	A	E	DP
Blum	.983	15	19	39	1	9
Camilli	1.000	1	1	1	0	1
Carroll	.932	23	40	56	7	14
Carvajal	.977	96	141	278	10	66
Ortiz	.941	15	22	42	4	7
Post	1.000	1	1	3	0	0

Outfield	PCT	G	PO	A	E	DP
Adolfo	.958	34	64	4	3	0
Bady	1.000	39	65	1	0	1
Bergeron	1.000	32	67	5	0	1
Bocachica	.946	72	171	4	10	3
Campos	.970	76	129	1	4	0
Post	1.000	3	1	1	0	0
Samuels	.933	11	13	1	1	0
Schwab	1.000	1	2	0	0	0
Seguignol	1.000	16	18	0	0	0
Stowers	.984	132	243	10	4	1
Tracy	1.000	1	5	0	0	0
Tucker	1.000	13	15	1	0	0
Valdez	.935	34	29	0	2	0

JUPITER — Class A

FLORIDA STATE LEAGUE

BATTING	AVG	G	AB	R	H	2B	3B	HR	RBI	BB	SO	SB	CS	B	T	HT	WT	DOB	1st Yr	Resides
Adolfo, Carlos	.260	88	331	51	90	16	2	13	44	37	80	10	8	R	R	5-11	160	4-20-76	1994	Santo Domingo, D.R.
Arntzen, Brian	.276	17	58	10	16	3	1	1	6	4	12	0	0	R	R	6-3	205	1-8-70	1992	Redding, Calif.
Bady, Ed	.250	1	4	1	1	1	0	0	0	0	0	1	1	B	R	5-11	170	2-5-73	1994	Queens, N.Y.
Blandford, Paul	.211	12	38	9	8	1	0	1	6	7	7	0	0	R	R	5-10	175	3-29-74	1996	Elk Grove, Calif.
Blum, Geoff	.276	17	58	13	16	6	0	0	5	13	14	1	0	B	R	6-3	193	4-26-73	1994	Chino, Calif.
Bradley, Milton	.287	67	261	55	75	14	1	5	34	30	42	17	9	B	R	6-0	170	4-15-78	1996	Long Beach, Calif.
Bravo, Danny	.155	24	71	5	11	1	0	0	3	8	14	1	1	B	R	5-11	175	5-27-77	1996	Maracaibo, Ven.
Camilli, Jason	.258	89	314	45	81	15	1	2	33	35	55	9	10	R	R	6-0	178	10-18-75	1994	Phoenix, Ariz.
Carreno, Jose	.250	10	28	2	7	1	0	2	6	2	6	0	0	R	R	5-11	180	4-23-78	1996	El Tigre, Ven.
Carroll, Jamey	.261	55	222	40	58	5	0	0	14	24	26	11	4	R	R	5-11	165	2-18-75	1996	Evansville, Ind.
Chatman, Karl	.210	69	238	25	50	11	1	4	28	23	63	13	1	R	R	6-1	190	1-17-75	1996	Nacogdoches, Texas
De la Rosa, Tomas	.251	117	390	56	98	22	1	3	43	37	61	27	7	R	R	5-10	155	1-28-78	1996	La Victoria, D.R.
Gresham, Kris	.220	24	82	8	18	6	0	2	8	2	17	1	3	R	R	6-2	206	8-30-70	1991	Mount Pleasant, N.C.
Hall, Noah	.250	4	8	2	2	0	0	0	0	3	1	1	1	R	R	5-11	200	6-9-77	1996	Aptos, Calif.
Henley, Bob	.340	13	50	10	17	3	0	2	14	5	5	1	1	R	R	6-2	190	1-30-73	1993	Grand Bay, Ala.
Machado, Albenis	.125	3	8	1	1	0	1	0	0	0	1	0	0	B	R	6-0	175	3-20-79	1996	Caracas, Ven.
Mateo, Henry	.279	12	43	11	12	3	1	0	6	2	6	3	0	B	R	5-11	170	10-14-76	1995	Santurce, P.R.
Mordecai, Mike	.000	2	8	0	0	0	0	0	0	1	3	0	0	R	R	5-11	175	12-13-67	1989	Pinson, Ala.
Nunez, Jose	.229	54	166	24	38	6	0	0	9	17	33	2	1	R	R	5-8	180	3-4-76	1996	New York, N.Y.
Nunnari, Talmadge	.294	56	201	18	59	14	0	2	34	30	39	1	2	L	L	6-1	205	4-9-75	1997	Pensacola, Fla.
Pond, Simon	.238	105	344	40	82	15	1	1	32	24	58	1	4	L	R	6-1	175	10-27-76	1994	North Vancouver, B.C.
Reding, Josh	.250	4	12	2	3	1	0	0	2	0	3	0	1	R	R	6-2	165	3-7-77	1997	Anaheim, Calif.
Rivera, Luis A.	.111	7	18	1	2	0	0	0	0	1	6	0	0	R	R	6-2	205	4-3-75	1997	Miami, Fla.
Rivera, Luis J.	.250	1	4	0	1	0	0	0	2	0	1	0	0	R	R	6-3	185	12-21-77	1996	Bayamon, P.R.
Ruan, Wilken	.167	5	18	2	3	0	0	0	0	1	3	2	0	R	R	6-0	160	11-18-79	1996	La Romana, D.R.
Schneider, Brian	.272	82	302	32	82	12	1	3	30	22	38	4	4	L	R	6-1	180	11-26-76	1995	Cherryville, Pa.
Schwab, Chris	.215	120	433	56	93	19	1	23	48	40	175	7	6	R	L	6-3	215	7-25-74	1993	Eagan, Minn.
Tracy, Andrew	.267	71	251	37	67	16	1	11	53	39	69	6	4	L	R	6-3	220	12-11-73	1996	Bowling Green, Ohio
Valdez, Trovin	.264	54	220	31	58	13	3	1	31	11	28	22	7	R	R	5-10	163	11-18-73	1993	New York, N.Y.
Ware, Jeremy	.246	127	492	51	121	35	3	10	64	23	102	21	5	R	R	6-1	190	10-23-75	1995	Guelph, Ontario

GAMES BY POSITION: C—Arntzen 16, Carreno 9, Gresham 24, Henley 10, Luis A. Rivera 7, Luis J. Rivera 1, Schneider 76. **1B**—Nunez 3, Nunnari 53, Pond 15, Schwab 2, Tracy 67, Ware 1. **2B**—Blandford 2, Blum 13, Bravo 2, Camilli 47, Carroll 46, Mateo 11, Mordecai 1, Nunez 22, Pond 4. **3B**—Blandford 5, Blum 2, Bravo 23, Camilli 26, de la Rosa 1, Nunez 22, Pond 74, Reding 3, Schwab 1, Tracy 3. **SS**—Blum 2, Bravo 2, Camilli 12, Carroll 8, de la Rosa 117, Machado 2, Mordecai 1, Nunez 1, Reding 1. **OF**—Adolfo 81, Bady 1, Bradley 61, Camilli 3, Chatman 61, Hall 3, Pond 1, Ruan 5, Schwab 48, Valdez 50, Ware 112.

PITCHING	W	L	ERA	G	GS	CG	SV	IP	H	R	ER	BB	SO	B	T	HT	WT	DOB	1st Yr	Resides
Armas, Tony	12	8	2.88	27	27	1	0	153	140	63	49	59	136	R	R	6-4	175	4-29-78	1994	Puerto Piritu, Ven.
Baker, Jason	0	1	9.00	2	0	0	0	1	0	1	1	3	0	R	L	6-0	200	12-31-73	1995	Rome, N.Y.
Bell, Mike	0	1	5.14	5	0	0	0	7	16	8	4	2	5	L	L	6-2	195	10-14-72	1995	Sarasota, Fla.
Blank, Matt	5	1	2.34	8	6	0	0	42	33	14	11	10	26	L	L	6-2	200	4-5-76	1997	Arlington, Texas
Bullinger, Kirk	0	0	5.40	8	0	0	0	10	9	7	6	2	12	R	R	6-2	170	10-28-69	1992	Hammond, La.
Chiavacci, Ron	0	1	2.35	4	0	0	1	8	5	2	2	2	5	R	R	6-3	230	9-5-77	1998	Scranton, Pa.

PITCHING	W	L	ERA	G	GS	CG	SV	IP	H	R	ER	BB	SO	B	T	HT	WT	DOB	1st Yr	Resides
Civit, Xavier	0	0	4.50	13	0	0	2	18	21	9	9	3	14	R	R	6-2	175	5-17-73	1993	Barcelona, Spain
Durocher, Jayson	2	1	4.21	23	0	0	5	36	47	21	17	8	27	R	R	6-3	195	8-18-74	1993	Scottsdale, Ariz.
Evans, Keith	5	2	2.86	8	8	1	0	50	45	18	16	5	25	R	R	6-5	200	11-2-75	1996	Woodland Hills, Calif.
Forster, Scott	0	0	9.00	6	0	0	0	8	9	10	8	5	7	R	L	6-1	194	10-27-71	1994	Flourtown, Pa.
Marquez, Robert	5	4	3.86	39	0	0	3	51	60	28	22	16	46	R	R	6-0	180	4-21-73	1995	Houston, Texas
Mattes, Troy	7	6	3.07	17	10	0	0	73	73	33	25	19	42	R	R	6-7	185	8-26-75	1994	Sarasota, Fla.
Matz, Brian	1	2	6.05	15	6	0	2	42	54	31	28	19	29	L	L	6-1	195	9-23-74	1996	Towson, Md.
Moraga, David	5	2	2.80	25	0	0	0	45	37	16	14	9	38	L	L	6-0	184	7-8-75	1994	Suisun, Calif.
Mota, Guillermo	3	2	0.66	20	0	0	2	41	18	6	3	6	27	R	R	6-5	185	7-25-73	1991	San Pedro de Macoris, D.R.
Nicholson, John	10	7	4.05	27	26	0	0	153	151	81	69	59	122	B	R	6-4	205	12-6-77	1996	Houston, Texas
Niebla, Ruben	0	1	1.19	13	0	0	0	23	15	8	3	5	22	L	L	5-10	175	12-19-71	1995	Calexico, Calif.
Pavano, Carl	0	0	6.60	4	4	0	0	15	20	11	11	3	14	R	R	6-5	230	1-8-76	1994	Southington, Conn.
Phelps, Tommy	2	2	4.39	7	7	0	0	41	42	21	20	15	21	L	L	6-3	192	3-4-74	1993	Tampa, Fla.
Saylor, Ryan	2	4	2.54	27	0	0	7	46	32	15	13	15	45	L	R	5-10	175	5-20-75	1997	Greenville, Ohio
Stevenson, Rodney	0	1	2.66	19	0	0	10	24	13	7	7	6	21	R	R	6-2	210	3-21-74	1996	Columbus, Ga.
Strickland, Scott	4	3	3.39	22	11	0	2	69	64	28	26	20	51	R	R	5-11	180	4-26-76	1997	Spring, Texas
Tucker, T.J.	1	1	1.00	2	1	0	0	9	5	1	1	0	10	R	R	6-3	245	8-20-78	1997	New Port Richey, Fla.
Turman, Jimmy	3	2	3.31	8	6	1	0	35	37	20	13	12	15	R	R	6-10	210	11-10-75	1996	Gordo, Ala.
Van Gilder, Ryan	1	1	2.70	10	0	0	0	17	16	6	5	3	9	R	R	6-0	175	12-1-75	1997	Watertown, S.D.
Wagner, Matt	0	0	0.00	1	1	0	0	5	6	0	0	0	2	R	R	6-5	215	4-4-72	1994	Cedar Falls, Iowa
Westbrook, Jake	11	6	3.26	27	27	2	0	171	169	70	62	60	79	R	R	6-3	180	9-29-77	1996	Danielsville, Ga.
Woodring, Jason	1	1	3.07	35	0	0	1	44	47	22	15	13	19	R	R	6-3	190	4-2-74	1993	Trinidad, Colo.

CAPE FEAR — Class A

SOUTH ATLANTIC LEAGUE

BATTING	AVG	G	AB	R	H	2B	3B	HR	RBI	BB	SO	SB	CS	B	T	HT	WT	DOB	1st Yr	Resides
Blakeney, Mo	.244	94	307	34	75	14	3	2	32	27	75	10	12	R	R	5-10	185	1-17-73	1995	Kannapolis, N.C.
Bradley, Milton	.302	75	281	54	85	21	4	6	50	23	57	13	8	B	R	6-0	170	4-15-78	1996	Long Beach, Calif.
Bravo, Danny	.277	101	343	48	95	12	4	4	44	32	65	7	10	B	R	5-11	175	5-27-77	1996	Maracaibo, Ven.
Burkhart, Lance	.240	17	50	10	12	3	1	1	11	16	17	1	3	R	R	5-9	190	12-16-74	1997	Florissant, Mo.
Chatman, Karl	.335	65	221	41	74	11	3	8	41	26	58	12	4	R	R	6-1	190	1-17-75	1996	Nacogdoches, Texas
Forbes, Kevin	.256	58	211	24	54	10	1	4	28	15	59	5	3	R	R	5-11	200	2-17-76	1997	Marina, Calif.
Hall, Noah	.318	127	447	84	142	21	7	11	90	52	69	33	9	R	R	5-11	200	6-9-77	1996	Aptos, Calif.
Hendricks, Jason	.193	48	145	22	28	1	0	6	20	11	49	6	1	R	R	6-1	200	5-20-76	1998	Phoenix, Ariz.
Hook, Kevin	.247	47	158	21	39	5	0	0	13	20	29	6	3	R	R	6-0	180	9-14-76	1998	Clovis, Calif.
James, Kenny	.253	114	451	73	114	10	3	2	32	21	68	41	6	B	R	6-0	198	10-9-76	1995	Sebring, Fla.
Lentz, Ryan	.333	3	9	6	3	1	0	1	3	3	2	0	0	L	R	6-2	210	5-29-77	1998	Woodinville, Wash.
Mateo, Henry	.276	114	416	72	115	20	5	4	41	40	111	22	16	B	R	5-11	170	10-14-76	1995	Santurce, P.R.
Nunnari, Talmadge	.304	79	289	51	88	18	0	2	51	42	44	4	4	L	L	6-1	205	4-9-75	1997	Pensacola, Fla.
Oropeza, Willie	.229	57	192	22	44	5	1	1	18	17	44	2	4	R	R	6-1	175	10-16-75	1994	La Guaira, Ven.
Reding, Josh	.233	73	253	32	59	6	0	1	21	22	71	13	4	R	R	6-2	165	3-7-77	1997	Anaheim, Calif.
Rivera, Luis A.	.221	60	163	28	36	4	1	4	18	10	34	3	0	R	R	6-2	205	4-3-75	1997	Miami, Fla.
Rivera, Luis J.	.213	25	80	8	17	5	0	0	6	4	28	1	2	R	R	6-3	185	12-21-77	1996	Bayamon, P.R.
Sandusky, Scott	.286	53	189	16	54	5	0	1	19	11	54	3	1	R	R	6-0	180	3-6-76	1998	Arvada, Colo.
Schneider, Brian	.299	38	134	33	40	7	2	7	30	16	9	6	3	L	R	6-1	180	11-26-76	1995	Cherryville, Pa.
Zech, Scott	.286	102	304	53	87	20	2	3	45	43	48	13	8	R	R	5-11	175	6-6-74	1997	Boca Raton, Fla.

GAMES BY POSITION: C—Blakeney 1, Bravo 1, Burkhart 7, Oropeza 11, Luis A. Rivera 31, Luis J. Rivera 24, Sandusky 49, Schneider 35. **1B**—Blakeney 35, Bravo 3, Nunnari 74, Oropeza 23, Luis A. Rivera 19. **2B**—Bravo 18, Hook 14, Mateo 109, Zech 6. **3B**—Bravo 31, Burkhart 2, Lentz 3, Oropeza 29, Zech 90. **SS**—Bravo 42, Hook 31, Mateo 2, Reding 73. **OF**—Blakeney 44, Bradley 52, Chatman 57, Forbes 51, Hall 107, Hendricks 30, James 95, Nunnari 8.

PITCHING	W	L	ERA	G	GS	CG	SV	IP	H	R	ER	BB	SO	B	T	HT	WT	DOB	1st Yr	Resides
Agamennone, Brandon	2	0	3.06	6	6	1	0	35	24	15	12	6	29	R	R	6-2	190	11-6-75	1998	Crofton, Md.
Baker, Jason	1	0	9.72	5	0	0	0	8	11	9	9	8	2	R	L	6-0	200	12-31-73	1995	Rome, N.Y.
Becks, Ryan	11	6	5.30	28	22	1	0	122	140	88	72	55	72	L	L	6-3	185	4-7-76	1997	San Jose, Calif.
Blank, Matt	9	2	2.61	21	21	2	0	135	121	45	39	24	114	L	L	6-2	200	4-5-76	1997	Arlington, Texas
Hebson, Bryan	4	5	4.71	16	16	0	0	73	71	42	38	29	57	R	R	6-6	210	3-12-76	1997	Phenix City, Ala.
Julio, Jorge	2	2	5.68	6	6	0	0	32	33	20	20	12	20	R	R	6-1	190	3-3-79	1996	Caracas, Ven.
Lanzetta, Tobin	4	4	4.38	38	0	0	1	74	77	43	36	27	66	R	R	6-2	185	7-31-75	1997	Tucson, Ariz.
Lara, Yovanny	2	5	7.08	22	9	0	0	55	61	51	43	48	31	R	R	6-4	180	9-20-75	1993	San Cristobal, D.R.
Matz, Brian	3	5	2.83	17	16	0	0	99	75	35	31	28	63	L	L	6-1	195	9-23-74	1996	Towson, Md.
Perez, Julio	1	1	3.18	9	0	0	0	17	17	7	6	6	10	R	R	6-2	170	8-6-78	1997	Miami, Fla.
Plummer, Ray	0	2	8.01	31	1	0	2	48	56	43	43	18	36	L	L	5-11	190	11-1-75	1997	San Diego, Calif.
Quezada, Edward	8	8	4.10	30	19	2	0	138	136	72	63	51	82	R	R	6-2	150	1-15-75	1993	Nizao, D.R.
Ramos, Juan	4	4	2.39	25	0	0	6	38	33	13	10	5	29	R	R	6-0	160	2-1-76	1995	Santo Domingo, D.R.
Salyers, Jeremy	4	4	3.77	42	2	0	3	72	70	41	30	23	32	R	R	6-3	205	1-31-76	1996	Pound, Va.
Saylor, Ryan	4	1	2.45	24	0	0	6	37	26	10	10	7	50	L	R	5-10	175	5-20-75	1997	Greenville, Ohio
Schreiner, Jon	2	0	1.80	3	0	0	0	10	9	2	2	6	4	R	R	6-7	240	8-4-76	1998	Glendale, Wis.
Serrano, Jim	2	0	3.65	15	0	0	3	25	22	11	10	15	29	R	R	5-8	165	5-9-76	1998	Grand Junction, Colo.
Sheldon, Kyle	2	0	2.35	4	0	0	0	8	7	2	2	4	5	R	R	6-2	180	12-8-76	1998	Winter Haven, Fla.
Smart, J.D.	3	0	2.45	3	1	0	0	11	7	3	3	0	12	R	R	6-2	185	11-12-73	1995	Austin, Texas
Strickland, Scott	0	3	4.46	15	2	0	4	36	36	19	18	12	53	R	R	5-11	180	4-26-76	1997	Spring, Texas
Turman, Jimmy	8	5	4.62	21	20	0	1	111	126	69	57	30	76	R	R	6-10	210	11-10-75	1996	Gordo, Ala.
Van Gilder, Ryan	4	4	3.02	30	0	0	3	45	43	18	15	14	35	R	R	6-0	175	12-1-75	1997	Watertown, S.D.

VERMONT — Short-Season Class A

NEW YORK-PENN LEAGUE

BATTING	AVG	G	AB	R	H	2B	3B	HR	RBI	BB	SO	SB	CS	B	T	HT	WT	DOB	1st Yr	Resides
Burkhart, Lance	.295	16	44	13	13	4	1	0	5	13	13	0	0	R	R	5-9	190	12-16-74	1997	Florissant, Mo.
Dito, Robert	.286	4	7	2	2	1	0	0	0	3	2	0	0	R	R	6-1	195	7-31-77	1998	Queens Village, N.Y.
Forbes, Kevin	.000	2	4	0	0	0	0	0	0	0	3	0	0	R	R	5-11	200	2-17-76	1997	Marina, Calif.
Groebner, Mark	.253	36	95	12	24	2	1	0	14	15	28	1	1	R	R	5-11	190	12-12-74	1998	Coon Rapids, Minn.
Hammond, Jamie	.233	30	86	7	20	2	0	0	12	5	17	3	3	R	R	6-0	175	12-17-75	1998	Salisbury, Md.

BATTING	AVG	G	AB	R	H	2B	3B	HR	RBI	BB	SO	SB	CS	B	T	HT	WT	DOB	1st Yr	Resides
Hendricks, Jason	.261	7	23	4	6	1	0	0	2	0	4	2	0	R	R	6-1	200	5-20-76	1998	Phoenix, Ariz.
Hodges, Scott	.278	67	266	35	74	13	3	3	35	11	59	8	1	L	R	6-0	185	12-26-78	1997	Lexington, Ky.
Hook, Kevin	.500	5	8	1	4	1	0	0	3	0	1	0	1	R	R	6-0	180	9-14-76	1998	Clovis, Calif.
Lentz, Ryan	.251	67	231	37	58	12	1	1	23	38	34	4	4	L	R	6-2	210	5-29-77	1998	Woodinville, Wash.
Machado, Albenis	.279	58	197	31	55	5	2	1	23	32	33	11	13	B	R	6-0	175	3-20-79	1996	Caracas, Ven.
McKinley, Josh	.136	6	22	2	3	0	0	0	4	1	9	0	0	B	R	6-2	190	9-14-79	1998	York, Pa.
Myers, Tootie	.240	73	271	33	65	15	3	0	24	29	86	14	7	R	R	5-11	165	9-8-78	1997	Petal, Miss.
Na, Jim	.210	43	119	12	25	4	2	0	12	14	40	4	7	L	R	6-0	205	1-5-75	1998	Randle, Wash.
Piercy, Brad	.235	68	264	39	62	8	1	3	31	14	71	8	7	L	R	6-4	200	12-23-76	1998	Shelby, N.C.
Pittman, Thomas	.212	58	222	27	47	13	0	4	30	16	67	2	5	R	R	6-4	270	11-2-79	1997	Garyville, La.
Quero, Pedro	.289	73	273	40	79	8	1	1	30	22	45	7	12	R	R	6-4	190	11-17-77	1995	Caracas, Ven.
Rivera, Luis J.	.211	33	109	10	23	5	1	0	7	3	26	0	3	R	R	6-3	185	12-21-77	1996	Bayamon, P.R.
Urquhart, Derick	.247	76	243	32	60	15	2	0	26	31	43	13	7	L	L	5-8	175	12-20-75	1998	Florence, S.C.

GAMES BY POSITION: C—Burkhart 12, Dito 4, Piercy 33, Rivera 32. **1B**—Na 16, Pittman 58, Quero 10. **2B**—Hammond 10, Hook 1, Myers 70. **3B**—Hammond 2, Hodges 39, Lentz 37. **SS**—Hammond 19, Hook 3, Machado 55, McKinley 3. **OF**—Forbes 2, Groebner 35, Hendricks 6, Na 23, Piercy 33, Quero 65, Urquhart 76.

PITCHING	W	L	ERA	G	GS	CG	SV	IP	H	R	ER	BB	SO	B	T	HT	WT	DOB	1st Yr	Resides
Agamennone, Brandon	3	1	1.42	9	3	0	0	32	19	6	5	11	30	R	R	6-2	190	11-6-75	1998	Crofton, Md.
Arthurs, Shane	4	4	3.77	16	13	1	0	76	81	41	32	27	43	R	R	6-5	185	8-30-79	1997	Oklahoma City, Okla.
Bridges, Donnie	5	6	4.90	13	13	0	0	68	71	42	37	37	43	R	R	6-4	195	12-10-78	1997	Purvis, Miss.
Castelli, Robert	1	2	2.70	23	2	0	1	37	35	16	11	21	44	R	R	6-1	190	3-14-77	1998	Ottawa, Ill.
Dobson, Scott	1	2	7.52	17	0	0	0	20	17	22	17	23	22	R	R	6-3	194	12-13-76	1998	Alexandria, Va.
Field, Nathan	3	1	3.09	25	0	0	2	35	32	16	12	11	39	R	R	6-2	185	12-11-75	1998	Littleton, Colo.
Frierson, Andrew	0	0	3.86	2	0	0	0	5	5	2	2	1	4	L	L	6-5	250	8-11-75	1998	Mill Valley, Calif.
Julio, Jorge	3	1	2.57	7	7	0	0	42	30	12	12	15	52	R	R	6-1	190	3-3-79	1996	Caracas, Ven.
Kanovich, Jason	2	4	3.44	20	5	0	0	50	42	24	19	17	41	L	L	6-2	200	2-18-77	1998	Harrisburg, Pa.
Mangum, Mark	3	9	4.46	14	12	0	1	71	78	39	35	15	59	R	R	6-2	165	8-24-78	1997	Kingwood, Texas
Perez, Julio	2	1	2.70	12	0	0	2	23	21	10	7	6	29	R	R	6-2	170	8-6-78	1997	Miami, Fla.
Rodriguez, Cristobal	0	0	4.91	6	2	0	0	15	6	8	8	14	14	R	R	6-2	190	1-27-79	1996	Chichiriviche, Ven.
Serrano, Jim	0	0	1.17	7	0	0	5	8	3	1	1	1	12	R	R	5-8	165	5-9-76	1998	Grand Junction, Colo.
Sheldon, Kyle	0	1	2.33	21	0	0	2	27	17	8	7	3	34	R	R	6-2	180	12-8-76	1998	Winter Haven, Fla.
Tetz, Kris	5	5	3.79	17	11	0	1	76	76	41	32	19	51	R	R	6-5	220	9-3-78	1997	Lodi, Calif.
Tucker, T.J.	3	1	2.18	6	6	0	0	33	24	9	8	15	34	R	R	6-3	245	8-20-78	1997	New Port Richey, Fla.
Waldron, Brad	1	1	4.50	16	0	0	0	26	26	14	13	6	24	R	R	6-3	200	4-17-77	1998	Ottawa, Ill.
Wamback, Trevor	0	1	6.10	3	2	0	0	10	8	8	7	4	7	R	R	6-2	183	12-22-76	1998	Halifax, Nova Scotia

JUPITER — Rookie

GULF COAST LEAGUE

BATTING	AVG	G	AB	R	H	2B	3B	HR	RBI	BB	SO	SB	CS	B	T	HT	WT	DOB	1st Yr	Resides
Ackerman, Scott	.263	18	57	9	15	1	0	1	7	9	12	0	2	R	R	6-2	195	4-23-79	1997	Oregon City, Ore.
Aude, Rich	.333	2	6	1	2	1	0	0	0	1	3	0	0	R	R	6-5	220	7-13-71	1989	Chatsworth, Calif.
Blum, Geoff	.167	5	18	0	3	1	1	0	1	1	4	0	0	B	R	6-3	193	4-26-73	1994	Chino, Calif.
Carreno, Jose	.284	40	134	14	38	4	0	1	16	5	21	5	5	R	R	5-11	180	4-23-78	1996	El Tigre, Ven.
DeJesus, Wilmer	.050	6	20	0	1	0	0	0	0	2	8	0	0	R	R	6-1	190	8-10-77	1995	Caracas, Ven.
Dito, Robert	.375	9	16	3	6	1	0	1	2	2	4	0	0	R	R	6-1	195	7-31-77	1998	Queens Village, N.Y.
Edge, Michael	.168	35	101	10	17	1	1	0	5	5	42	8	3	R	R	6-0	180	8-13-79	1997	Winnabow, N.C.
Espinoza, Andres	.235	43	132	15	31	3	1	0	7	4	13	15	8	R	R	6-2	180	11-12-78	1996	Caracas, Ven.
Gonzalez, Felix	.143	27	70	5	10	0	0	0	3	4	12	4	4	R	R	5-11	150	9-18-79	1998	San Lorenzo, P.R.
Hoshina, Koji	.167	6	18	3	3	1	0	0	0	2	5	2	3	B	R	5-10	165	10-19-79	1996	Tokyo, Japan
Jefferson, Dave	.167	8	24	3	4	0	0	0	3	7	9	1	2	R	R	6-2	190	6-18-75	1993	Palo Alto, Calif.
Lugo, Felix	.232	57	194	22	45	9	6	1	26	14	69	9	6	B	R	6-2	173	8-1-80	1996	Bani, D.R.
McKinley, Josh	.269	57	208	36	56	11	5	1	19	24	40	14	13	B	R	6-2	190	9-14-79	1998	York, Pa.
Ortiz, Juan	.229	49	170	24	39	7	3	1	15	12	31	16	11	R	R	5-10	205	2-26-79	1998	Brooklyn, N.Y.
Reding, Josh	.375	2	8	2	3	1	0	0	0	0	3	1	1	R	R	6-2	165	3-7-77	1997	Anaheim, Calif.
Rosado, Omar	.179	47	145	13	26	7	0	0	10	11	38	9	8	R	R	6-1	170	11-12-80	1998	Toa Baja, P.R.
Ruan, Wilken	.239	54	201	22	48	9	3	1	19	5	43	13	13	R	R	6-0	160	11-18-79	1996	La Romana, D.R.
Saffer, Jon	.125	2	8	3	1	0	0	0	2	1	2	1	0	L	R	6-2	200	7-6-73	1992	Tucson, Ariz.
Valdez, Darlin	.000	5	11	0	0	0	0	0	0	0	3	0	0	R	R	6-1	180	2-21-80	1997	Nizao, D.R.
Van Pareren, Tim	.250	28	76	9	19	5	0	1	6	5	19	7	0	B	R	6-0	160	1-2-80	1997	Amsterdam, Netherlands
Williams, Clyde	.238	57	206	25	49	10	5	0	16	19	63	14	5	L	L	6-2	180	7-7-79	1998	Sanford, Fla.

GAMES BY POSITION: C—Ackerman 12, Carreno 38, DeJesus 6, Dito 7, Valdez 2. **1B**—Aude 1, Van Pareren 3, Williams 56. **2B**—Blum 3, Rosado 44, Van Pareren 13. **3B**—Lugo 56, Van Pareren 8. **SS**—Hoshina 5, Lugo 1, McKinley 50, Reding 2, Van Pareren 3. **OF**—Edge 21, Espinoza 43, Gonzalez 24, Ortiz 46, Rosado 1, Ruan 52, Saffer 1.

PITCHING	W	L	ERA	G	GS	CG	SV	IP	H	R	ER	BB	SO	B	T	HT	WT	DOB	1st Yr	Resides
Andujar, Jesse	1	2	3.56	18	0	0	2	30	30	17	12	11	27	R	R	6-1	175	7-23-79	1996	San Pedro de Macoris, D.R.
Baldassano, Joe	0	1	0.92	14	0	0	4	20	11	4	2	15	24	R	R	5-11	170	11-15-79	1998	Riverside, Calif.
Bullinger, Kirk	0	0	0.00	2	2	0	0	4	2	0	0	0	7	R	R	6-2	170	10-28-69	1992	Hammond, La.
Chiavacci, Ron	6	3	2.13	13	6	0	0	55	43	17	13	13	42	R	R	6-3	230	9-5-77	1998	Scranton, Pa.
Chisnall, Wes	3	5	6.19	13	11	0	0	57	83	54	39	6	39	R	R	6-4	180	7-18-80	1998	Alta Loma, Calif.
Frierson, Andrew	3	1	1.25	15	0	0	2	22	16	5	3	5	17	L	L	6-5	250	8-11-75	1998	Mill Valley, Calif.
Good, Eric	1	2	2.08	6	3	0	0	17	11	4	4	8	20	R	L	6-3	170	4-10-80	1998	Niles, Mich.
Grantham, Ryan	0	0	0.00	1	0	0	0	1	0	0	0	0	1	R	R	6-4	190	6-1-80	1998	Hamilton, Ontario
Hebson, Bryan	2	0	0.53	4	4	0	0	17	10	1	1	7	16	R	R	6-6	210	3-12-76	1997	Phenix City, Ala.
Klepacki, Edward	1	4	3.13	9	6	1	0	37	39	20	13	3	23	R	R	6-5	180	4-26-78	1998	Midwest City, Okla.
Lopez, Carlos	3	3	2.89	14	1	0	3	37	39	16	12	5	22	R	R	6-2	190	9-26-79	1996	Maracaibo, Ven.
Marrero, Darwin	1	1	1.85	14	1	0	1	39	33	10	8	4	39	R	R	6-1	192	2-9-81	1997	Valencia, Ven.
Martinez, Obispo	1	1	6.00	3	0	0	0	9	9	6	6	0	5	R	R	6-0	176	4-2-78	1996	San Cristobal, D.R.
Perez, Carlos	1	0	0.00	1	0	0	0	5	5	2	0	1	2	L	L	6-3	200	4-14-71	1990	San Cristobal, D.R.
Rodriguez, Cristobal	1	1	2.45	8	8	0	0	40	30	16	11	11	48	R	R	6-2	190	1-27-79	1996	Chichiriviche, Ven.
Schreiner, Jon	1	1	1.80	13	3	0	2	35	24	9	7	10	28	R	R	6-7	240	8-4-76	1998	Glendale, Wis.
Tucker, T.J.	1	0	0.75	7	7	0	0	36	23	5	3	5	40	R	R	6-3	245	8-20-78	1997	New Port Richey, Fla.
Urbina, Ulmer	0	1	4.50	5	0	0	0	6	3	5	3	3	9	R	R	6-1	180	4-20-80	1998	Miranda, Ven.

NEW YORK YANKEES

World Series sweep caps record-setting 114-win season

BY GEORGE KING

All season long the Yankees heard the talk: If they didn't come home with the trophy, their 114 wins would be forgotten and they would be remembered as failures.

But in the end, after they swept the San Diego Padres in the 1998 World Series, there were no doubters. The club reassumed its perch atop the baseball world by winning its 24th championship, and sparked debate as to whether it was the greatest team ever.

After setting an American League record for wins, sweeping the Rangers in the AL Division Series and beating the Indians 4-2 in the AL Championship Series before handling the Padres, they made a strong argument they were. In all, the team won 125 games in 1998.

What was remarkable about the Yankees' season was that it was the result of a complete team effort. It was not a story of individuals, though several players had tremendous individual seasons.

Center fielder Bernie Williams won the AL batting title with a .339 mark. Scott Brosius bounced back from a nightmarish 1997 with the Athletics by hitting .300 with 19 homers and 98 RBIs. David Wells won a career-high 18 games and received Cy Young consideration. David Cone won 20 games for the second time.

Derek Jeter continued to improve in his third season, batting .324, scoring 127 runs and driving in 84. His 19 homers were nine more than his career high. And he made only nine errors while handling 625 chances at shortstop.

The Yankees didn't pull off any big midseason trades as they had in the previous two years, but they did add Orlando "El Duque" Hernandez, a Cuban refugee whom they signed during the winter, to the mix in early June. Hernandez posted a 12-4 regular season record and won two more games in the playoffs.

On the farm, Triple-A Columbus failed to reach the International League playoffs but provided valuable players to the big club throughout the season. Hernandez, who made seven Columbus starts, was followed by outfielders Ricky Ledee and Shane Spencer, who took turns in the spotlight in the postseason.

Righthander Mike Buddie rode the Columbus-Bronx shuttle and hinted he had a big league future. Third baseman Mike Lowell pushed himself into the major league picture with a monster year and received a small taste of the big leagues in September.

One of the most noteworthy callups was righthander Ryan Bradley, who began the season at Class A Tampa. A first-round pick in 1997, Bradley made stops in Double-A Norwich and Columbus before reaching New York.

Tampa first baseman Nick Johnson continued to establish himself as a legitimate prospect, hitting .317 with 17 homers and 58 RBIs. And at Class A Greensboro, Jackson Melian, an 18-year-old native of Venezuela, showed enough skills to excite scouts throughout the South Atlantic League.

Both Tampa and Greensboro reached postseason play, each falling in its league's championship series. Short-season Oneonta was declared co-champion of the New York-Penn League after bad weather forced the cancellation of the league's title series against Auburn.

Derek Jeter

Ryan Bradley

Players of the Year

Major League: Derek Jeter, ss

Jeter led the American League with 127 runs and finished third with 203 hits while committing only nine errors at shortstop.

Minor League: Ryan Bradley, rhp, Colum./Nor./Tampa

Bradley worked his way from Class A Tampa to the big leagues by going 9-5 with a 2.65 ERA and 149 strikeouts.

ORGANIZATION LEADERS

BATTING		
*AVG	Shane Spencer, Columbus	.322
R	Donzell McDonald, Norwich/Tampa	86
H	Mike Lowell, Columbus	155
TB	Mike Lowell, Columbus	273
2B	Mike Berry, Columbus/Norwich	41
3B	Two tied at	10
HR	Two tied at	26
RBI	Mike Lowell, Columbus	99
BB	D'Angelo Jimenez, Columbus/Norwich	71
SO	Two tied at	139
SB	Scott Pose, Columbus	47
PITCHING		
W	Randy Flores, Tampa/Greensboro	13
L	Two tied at	13
#ERA	Brian Reith, Greensboro	2.28
G	Jay Tessmer, Columbus/Norwich	57
CG	Jim Baron, Columbus/Norwich	5
SV	Jay Tessmer, Columbus/Norwich	34
IP	Craig Lewis, Greensboro	174
BB	Jake Robbins, Tampa	72
SO	Craig Lewis, Greensboro	178

*Minimum 250 At-Bats #Minimum 75 Innings

New York YANKEES

Manager: Joe Torre

1998 Record: 114-48, .704 (1st, AL East)

BATTING	AVG	G	AB	R	H	2B	3B	HR	RBI	BB	SO	SB	CS	B	T	HT	WT	DOB	1st Yr	Resides
Brosius, Scott	.300	152	530	86	159	34	0	19	98	52	97	11	8	R	R	6-1	202	8-15-66	1987	McMinnville, Ore.
Bush, Homer	.380	45	71	17	27	3	0	1	5	5	19	6	3	R	R	5-10	175	11-11-72	1991	East St. Louis, Ill.
Curtis, Chad	.243	151	456	79	111	21	1	10	56	75	80	21	5	R	R	5-10	175	11-6-68	1989	Middleville, Mich.
Davis, Chili	.291	35	103	11	30	7	0	3	9	14	18	0	1	B	R	6-3	217	1-17-60	1978	Scottsdale, Ariz.
Figga, Mike	.250	1	4	1	1	0	0	0	0	0	1	0	0	R	R	6-0	200	7-31-70	1990	Tampa, Fla.
Girardi, Joe	.276	78	254	31	70	11	4	3	31	14	38	2	4	R	R	5-11	195	10-14-64	1986	Lake Forest, Ill.
Jeter, Derek	.324	149	626	127	203	25	8	19	84	57	119	30	6	R	R	6-3	175	6-26-74	1992	Tampa, Fla.
Knoblauch, Chuck	.265	150	603	117	160	25	4	17	64	76	70	31	12	R	R	5-9	181	7-7-68	1989	Houston, Texas
Ledee, Ricky	.241	42	79	13	19	5	2	1	12	7	29	3	1	L	L	6-2	160	11-22-73	1990	Salinas, P.R.
Lowell, Mike	.267	8	15	1	4	0	0	0	0	0	1	0	0	R	R	6-4	195	2-24-74	1995	Coral Gables, Fla.
Martinez, Tino	.281	142	531	92	149	33	1	28	123	61	83	2	1	L	R	6-2	210	12-7-67	1989	Tampa, Fla.
O'Neill, Paul	.317	152	602	95	191	40	2	24	116	57	103	15	1	L	L	6-4	215	2-25-63	1981	Cincinnati, Ohio
Posada, Jorge	.268	111	358	56	96	23	0	17	63	47	92	0	1	B	R	6-0	205	8-17-71	1991	Rio Piedras, P.R.
Raines, Tim	.290	109	321	53	93	13	1	5	47	55	49	8	3	B	R	5-8	185	9-16-59	1977	Heathrow, Fla.
Sojo, Luis	.231	54	147	16	34	3	1	0	14	4	15	1	0	R	R	5-11	174	1-3-66	1987	Barquisimeto, Ven.
Spencer, Shane	.373	27	67	18	25	6	0	10	27	5	12	0	1	R	R	5-11	210	2-20-72	1990	El Cajon, Calif.
Strawberry, Darryl	.247	101	295	44	73	11	2	24	57	46	90	8	7	L	L	6-6	215	3-12-62	1980	Rancho Mirage, Calif.
Sveum, Dale	.155	30	58	6	9	0	0	0	3	4	16	0	0	B	R	6-2	212	11-23-63	1982	Scottsdale, Ariz.
Williams, Bernie	.339	128	499	101	169	30	5	26	97	74	81	15	9	B	R	6-2	205	9-13-68	1986	Bayamon, P.R.

PITCHING	W	L	ERA	G	GS	CG	SV	IP	H	R	ER	BB	SO	B	T	HT	WT	DOB	1st Yr	Resides
Banks, Willie	1	1	10.05	9	0	0	0	14	20	16	16	12	8	R	R	6-1	200	2-27-69	1987	Miami, Fla.
Borowski, Joe	1	0	6.52	8	0	0	0	10	11	7	7	4	7	R	R	6-2	225	5-4-71	1989	Bayonne, N.J.
Bradley, Ryan	2	1	5.68	5	1	0	0	13	12	9	8	9	13	R	R	6-4	226	10-26-75	1997	Chino Hills, Calif.
Bruske, Jim	1	0	3.00	3	1	0	0	9	9	3	3	1	3	R	R	6-1	185	10-7-64	1986	Tempe, Ariz.
Buddie, Mike	4	1	5.62	24	2	0	0	42	46	29	26	13	20	R	R	6-3	210	12-12-70	1992	Berea, Ohio
Cone, David	20	7	3.55	31	31	3	0	208	186	89	82	59	209	L	R	6-1	190	1-2-63	1981	Greenwich, Conn.
Erdos, Todd	0	0	9.00	2	0	0	0	2	5	2	2	1	0	R	R	6-1	205	11-21-73	1992	Meadville, Pa.
Hernandez, Orlando	12	4	3.13	21	21	3	0	141	113	53	49	52	131	R	R	6-2	210	10-11-69	1998	Miami, Fla.
Holmes, Darren	0	3	3.33	34	0	0	2	51	53	19	19	14	31	R	R	6-0	202	4-25-66	1984	Fletcher, N.C.
Irabu, Hideki	13	9	4.06	29	28	2	0	173	148	79	78	76	126	R	R	6-4	240	5-5-69	1997	Chiba, Japan
Jerzembeck, Mike	0	1	12.79	3	2	0	0	6	9	9	9	4	1	R	R	6-1	185	5-18-72	1993	Queens Village, N.Y.
Lloyd, Graeme	3	0	1.67	50	0	0	0	38	26	10	7	6	20	L	L	6-7	234	4-9-67	1988	Gnarwarre, Australia
Mendoza, Ramiro	10	2	3.25	41	14	1	1	130	131	50	47	30	56	R	R	6-2	154	6-15-72	1992	Los Santos, Panama
Nelson, Jeff	5	3	3.79	45	0	0	3	40	44	18	17	22	35	R	R	6-8	235	11-17-66	1984	Issaquah, Wash.
Pettitte, Andy	16	11	4.24	33	32	5	0	216	226	110	102	87	146	L	L	6-5	225	6-15-72	1991	Deer Park, Texas
Rivera, Mariano	3	0	1.91	54	0	0	36	61	48	13	13	17	36	R	R	6-4	168	11-29-69	1990	La Chorrera, Panama
Stanton, Mike	4	1	5.47	67	0	0	6	79	71	51	48	26	69	L	L	6-1	215	6-2-67	1987	Houston, Texas
Tessmer, Jay	1	0	3.12	7	0	0	0	9	4	3	3	4	6	R	R	6-3	190	12-26-71	1995	Cochranton, Pa.
Wells, David	18	4	3.49	30	30	8	0	214	195	86	83	29	163	L	L	6-4	225	5-20-63	1982	Palm Harbor, Fla.

FIELDING

Catcher	PCT	G	PO	A	E	DP	PB
Figga	1.000	1	3	0	0	0	0
Girardi	.995	78	541	38	3	5	5
Posada	.994	99	586	46	4	3	7

First Base	PCT	G	PO	A	E	DP
Brosius	1.000	3	7	2	0	1
Martinez	.992	142	1182	93	10	109
Posada	1.000	1	7	1	0	2
Sojo	.991	19	107	8	1	8
Spencer	1.000	1	3	1	0	0
Sveum	.975	21	108	9	3	9

Second Base	PCT	G	PO	A	E	DP
Bush	.970	24	36	29	2	4
Knoblauch	.981	149	274	408	13	85
Sojo	1.000	8	7	14	0	4

Third Base	PCT	G	PO	A	E	DP
Brosius	.948	150	107	292	22	29
Bush	1.000	3	1	6	0	0
Lowell	1.000	7	2	6	0	2
Sojo	1.000	6	4	8	0	1
Sveum	.909	6	4	6	1	0

Shortstop	PCT	G	PO	A	E	DP
Bush	1.000	2	0	3	0	0
Jeter	.986	148	225	391	9	81
Sojo	.973	20	29	44	2	11

Outfield	PCT	G	PO	A	E	DP
Brosius	.000	1	0	0	0	0
Curtis	.984	148	306	9	5	3
Ledee	.981	42	47	4	1	0
O'Neill	.987	150	292	11	4	5
Raines	.984	47	60	3	1	2
Spencer	1.000	22	25	1	0	0
Strawberry	.905	16	19	0	2	0
Williams	.990	123	299	4	3	0

LARRY GOREN

Bernie Williams

FARM SYSTEM

Vice President, Player Development: Mark Newman

Class	Farm Team	League	W	L	Pct.	Finish*	Manager	First Yr
AAA	Columbus (Ohio) Clippers	International	67	77	.465	12th (14)	Stump Merrill	1979
AA	Norwich (Conn.) Navigators	Eastern	66	76	.465	t-7th (10)	Trey Hillman	1995
A#	Tampa (Fla.) Yankees	Florida State	72	67	.518	6th (14)	Lee Mazzilli	1994
A	Greensboro (N.C.) Bats	South Atlantic	79	63	.556	5th (14)	Tom Nieto	1990
A	Oneonta (N.Y.) Yankees	New York-Penn	45	31	.592	+2nd (14)	Joe Arnold	1967
Rookie	Tampa (Fla.) Yankees	Gulf Coast	34	26	.567	3rd (14)	Ken Dominguez	1980

*Finish in overall standings (No. of teams in league) #Advanced level +Won league championship

COLUMBUS — Class AAA

INTERNATIONAL LEAGUE

BATTING	AVG	G	AB	R	H	2B	3B	HR	RBI	BB	SO	SB	CS	B	T	HT	WT	DOB	1st Yr	Resides
Ashby, Chris	.091	5	11	0	1	0	0	0	1	3	6	0	0	R	R	6-3	196	12-15-74	1993	Boca Raton, Fla.
Bellinger, Clay	.224	115	397	35	89	20	2	9	40	35	79	6	3	R	R	6-3	195	11-18-68	1989	Oneonta, N.Y.
Berry, Mike	.287	25	87	7	25	6	0	1	9	10	14	0	0	R	R	5-10	185	8-12-70	1993	Rolling Hills, Calif.
Bierek, Kurt	.300	14	50	8	15	5	1	1	8	5	8	0	0	L	R	6-4	205	9-13-72	1993	Hillsboro, Ore.
Carpenter, Bubba	.227	63	198	28	45	14	2	7	24	36	48	3	2	L	L	6-1	185	7-23-68	1991	Winslow, Ark.
Cruz, Ivan	.265	56	204	34	54	10	0	13	36	29	44	0	0	L	L	6-3	210	5-3-68	1989	Fajardo, P.R.
Davis, Chili	.364	6	22	4	8	1	0	0	3	4	3	0	0	B	R	6-3	217	1-17-60	1978	Scottsdale, Ariz.
Figga, Mike	.280	123	461	57	129	30	3	26	95	35	109	2	2	R	R	6-0	200	7-31-70	1990	Tampa, Fla.
Fithian, Grant	.111	5	9	1	1	0	1	0	0	2	1	0	0	R	R	6-0	185	11-20-71	1994	Rockwall, Texas
Glass, Chip	.200	8	15	2	3	1	0	0	2	0	1	0	0	L	L	5-11	180	6-24-71	1994	Golden, Colo.
Gomez, Rudy	.205	67	234	34	48	6	2	6	25	26	37	5	5	R	R	5-11	180	9-14-74	1996	Miami, Fla.
Huckaby, Ken	.208	36	101	13	21	3	1	1	10	11	14	0	2	R	R	6-1	205	1-27-71	1991	Philadelphia, Pa.
Jeter, Derek	.400	1	5	2	2	2	0	0	0	0	2	0	0	R	R	6-3	175	6-26-74	1992	Tampa, Fla.
Jimenez, D'Angelo	.256	91	344	55	88	19	4	8	51	46	67	6	6	B	R	6-0	160	12-21-77	1995	Santo Domingo, D.R.
Ledee, Ricky	.283	96	360	70	102	21	1	19	41	54	108	7	2	L	L	6-2	160	11-22-73	1990	Salinas, P.R.
Lobaton, Jose	.143	6	7	0	1	1	0	0	0	0	2	0	0	R	R	5-11	154	3-29-74	1992	Acarigua, Ven.
Lowell, Mike	.304	126	510	79	155	34	3	26	99	37	85	4	0	R	R	6-4	195	2-24-74	1995	Coral Gables, Fla.
Martinez, Gabby	.237	36	131	17	31	3	1	0	8	4	22	5	3	R	R	6-2	170	1-7-74	1992	Santurce, P.R.
Matos, Francisco	.338	76	293	42	99	18	2	2	33	20	26	3	2	R	R	6-1	160	4-8-70	1988	Azua, D.R.
2-team (32 Durham)	.310	108	407	55	126	20	5	2	47	21	41	5	3							
Pose, Scott	.297	133	489	78	145	23	10	3	46	53	72	47	14	L	R	5-11	165	2-11-67	1989	West Des Moines, Iowa
Ramirez, Angel	.315	57	197	36	62	12	2	6	26	12	41	4	2	R	R	5-10	166	1-24-73	1991	Azua, D.R.
Singleton, Chris	.254	121	413	55	105	17	10	6	45	27	78	9	3	L	L	6-2	195	8-15-72	1993	Hercules, Calif.
Sojo, Luis	.217	6	23	1	5	2	0	0	2	1	1	1	0	R	R	5-11	174	1-3-66	1987	Barquisimeto, Ven.
Spencer, Shane	.322	87	342	66	110	29	1	18	67	41	59	1	3	R	R	5-11	210	2-20-72	1990	El Cajon, Calif.
Torres, Jaime	.164	16	55	2	9	1	0	0	3	3	7	0	0	R	R	6-0	176	3-12-73	1992	Aragua, Ven.
Troilo, Jason	.143	8	14	0	2	0	0	0	1	1	7	0	0	R	R	6-1	195	9-7-72	1994	Avondale, Pa.

PITCHING	W	L	ERA	G	GS	CG	SV	IP	H	R	ER	BB	SO	B	T	HT	WT	DOB	1st Yr	Resides
Alberro, Jose	8	10	4.52	46	13	1	5	127	123	76	64	69	91	R	R	6-2	190	6-29-69	1991	Arecibo, P.R.
Baron, Jim	1	5	6.09	8	7	1	0	44	54	32	30	19	28	L	L	6-3	230	2-22-74	1992	Humble, Texas
Borowski, Joe	3	3	2.93	45	0	0	4	74	66	25	24	39	67	R	R	6-2	225	5-4-71	1989	Bayonne, N.J.
Bradley, Ryan	0	1	6.19	3	3	0	0	16	15	13	11	13	12	R	R	6-4	226	10-26-75	1997	Chino Hills, Calif.
Brow, Scott	3	2	5.46	30	3	0	0	59	74	42	36	26	35	R	R	6-3	200	3-17-69	1990	Hillsboro, Ore.
Bruske, Jim	0	0	1.17	4	0	0	1	8	7	1	1	2	9	R	R	6-1	185	10-7-64	1986	Tempe, Ariz.
Buddie, Mike	5	0	2.74	26	0	0	4	43	35	15	13	15	30	R	R	6-3	210	12-12-70	1992	Berea, Ohio
Erdos, Todd	3	2	4.62	39	0	0	16	49	52	27	25	20	50	R	R	6-1	205	11-21-73	1992	Meadville, Pa.
Grahe, Joe	4	2	4.53	12	5	1	0	44	42	23	22	11	22	R	R	6-0	200	8-14-67	1989	Palm Beach Gardens, Fla.
Heredia, Wilson	4	7	6.90	23	14	0	0	89	111	78	68	49	70	R	R	6-0	175	3-30-72	1990	La Romana, D.R.
Hernandez, Orlando	6	0	3.83	7	7	0	0	42	41	19	18	17	59	R	R	6-2	210	10-11-69	1998	Miami, Fla.
Janzen, Marty	5	6	5.77	16	12	1	0	69	78	48	44	38	54	R	R	6-3	197	5-31-73	1991	Gainesville, Fla.
Jerzembeck, Mike	4	9	4.87	24	24	0	0	140	158	82	76	55	107	R	R	6-1	185	5-18-72	1993	Queens Village, N.Y.
Jordan, Ricardo	2	0	4.85	5	5	0	0	26	28	15	14	17	22	L	L	6-0	190	6-27-70	1990	Palm Harbor, Fla.
2-team (37 Indy)	4	4	3.86	42	11	0	0	96	98	54	41	50	74							
Kaufman, Brad	1	2	7.20	3	3	0	0	15	17	15	12	12	13	R	R	6-2	210	4-26-72	1993	Traer, Iowa
Lankford, Frank	5	9	5.07	15	15	3	0	94	110	60	53	32	58	R	R	6-2	190	3-26-71	1993	Atlanta, Ga.
Looney, Brian	4	4	4.47	41	10	0	0	93	97	52	46	52	63	L	L	5-10	180	6-26-69	1991	Cheshire, Conn.
Maeda, Kats	0	1	2.51	13	0	0	0	14	13	5	4	8	16	R	R	6-2	215	6-23-71	1996	Tokyo, Japan
Mimbs, Mike	0	2	6.33	12	3	0	0	27	26	23	19	24	19	L	L	6-2	188	2-13-69	1990	Macon, Ga.
Resz, Greg	3	3	4.92	12	9	0	0	53	53	35	29	23	31	L	R	6-5	215	12-25-71	1993	Springfield, Mo.
Ricken, Ray	0	3	7.32	4	3	1	1	20	24	17	16	11	17	R	R	6-5	225	8-11-73	1994	Warren, Mich.
Rose, Scott	2	0	3.75	29	0	0	2	36	43	18	15	17	27	R	R	6-3	200	5-12-70	1990	Tampa, Fla.
Shelby, Anthony	2	2	3.19	23	5	0	0	48	47	19	17	13	39	L	L	6-3	200	12-11-73	1993	Willow Springs, Ill.
Tessmer, Jay	1	1	0.49	12	0	0	5	18	8	2	1	1	14	R	R	6-3	190	12-26-71	1995	Cochranton, Pa.
Valera, Julio	1	2	6.38	8	2	0	0	18	19	13	13	7	12	R	R	6-2	215	10-13-68	1986	San Sebastian, P.R.
Williams, Shad	0	1	12.75	5	1	0	0	12	24	19	17	8	10	R	R	6-0	198	3-10-71	1991	Fresno, Calif.

FIELDING

Catcher	PCT	G	PO	A	E	DP	PB
Bellinger	.000	1	0	0	0	0	0
Figga	.988	100	680	59	9	4	16
Fithian	.947	4	17	1	1	0	0
Huckaby	.978	34	201	21	5	2	0
Torres	.990	14	88	8	1	0	0
Troilo	.923	8	30	6	3	0	0

First Base	PCT	G	PO	A	E	DP
Ashby	1.000	2	13	1	0	2
Bellinger	.993	44	264	14	2	23
Bierek	.983	13	111	6	2	12
Carpenter	.992	30	244	19	2	22
Cruz	.991	53	502	39	5	45
Figga	.983	5	53	4	1	5
Lowell	.976	4	38	3	1	1
Matos	1.000	2	16	2	0	4
Spencer	.991	12	107	7	1	9

Second Base	PCT	G	PO	A	E	DP
Bellinger	.963	13	21	31	2	11
Berry	1.000	1	0	2	0	0
Gomez	.984	66	128	179	5	43

FIELDING

	PCT	G	PO	A	E	DP
Jimenez	1.000	3	6	5	0	2
Lobaton	1.000	6	3	7	0	1
Martinez	1.000	4	7	9	0	2
Matos	.987	66	107	191	4	30
Sojo	1.000	1	1	1	0	0

Third Base	PCT	G	PO	A	E	DP
Bellinger	.955	23	10	53	3	2
Berry	.905	8	4	15	2	0
Lowell	.946	118	76	277	20	23
Matos	1.000	1	3	3	0	0

	PCT	G	PO	A	E	DP
Torres	1.000	1	1	1	0	0

Shortstop	PCT	G	PO	A	E	DP
Bellinger	.946	27	36	87	7	14
Jeter	.875	1	4	3	1	1
Jimenez	.944	87	144	297	26	61
Lowell	1.000	2	0	3	0	0
Martinez	.906	27	39	67	11	13
Matos	1.000	2	1	3	0	1
Sojo	.958	4	8	15	1	5

Outfield	PCT	G	PO	A	E	DP
Bellinger	1.000	10	11	0	0	0
Carpenter	.983	33	56	3	1	1
Cruz	1.000	1	1	0	0	0
Glass	1.000	4	8	2	0	1
Ledee	.971	79	132	1	4	0
Pose	.983	103	158	11	3	0
Ramirez	.932	39	65	4	5	0
Singleton	.974	117	251	10	7	2
Spencer	.968	66	118	4	4	0

NORWICH — Class AA

EASTERN LEAGUE

BATTING	AVG	G	AB	R	H	2B	3B	HR	RBI	BB	SO	SB	CS	B	T	HT	WT	DOB	1st Yr	Resides
Ashby, Chris	.285	126	438	65	125	24	0	11	53	65	99	17	3	R	R	6-3	196	12-15-74	1993	Boca Raton, Fla.
Berry, Mike	.293	107	399	50	117	35	2	14	63	53	58	8	2	R	R	5-10	185	8-12-70	1993	Rolling Hills, Calif.
Bierek, Kurt	.235	95	344	44	81	13	2	13	61	50	61	0	1	L	R	6-4	205	9-13-72	1993	Hillsboro, Ore.
Brown, Vick	.298	102	352	62	105	14	3	6	34	40	75	35	10	R	R	6-1	170	11-14-72	1993	Cypress, Fla.
Davis, Chili	.243	11	37	2	9	3	0	1	5	9	7	0	0	B	R	6-3	217	1-17-60	1978	Scottsdale, Ariz.
Dennis, Les	.247	32	93	12	23	5	1	0	13	24	20	2	2	R	R	6-0	175	6-3-73	1995	West Linn, Ore.
Emmons, Scott	.172	48	145	12	25	6	0	1	5	14	43	2	1	R	R	6-4	205	12-25-73	1995	Norco, Calif.
Fithian, Grant	.230	39	126	13	29	6	0	4	14	14	39	0	0	R	R	6-0	185	11-20-71	1994	Rockwall, Texas
Glass, Chip	.283	120	424	61	120	8	3	4	56	40	78	15	6	L	L	5-11	180	6-24-71	1994	Golden, Colo.
Gomez, Rudy	.312	46	189	31	59	10	2	3	20	17	28	8	6	R	R	5-11	180	9-14-74	1996	Miami, Fla.
Hinds, Rob	.226	38	106	17	24	4	0	2	8	8	27	4	1	R	R	6-0	185	4-26-71	1992	Cerritos, Calif.
Jimenez, D'Angelo	.270	40	152	21	41	6	2	2	21	25	26	5	5	B	R	6-0	160	12-21-77	1995	Santo Domingo, D.R.
Keel, David	.178	36	118	12	21	6	0	3	19	24	31	0	3	L	R	6-3	205	7-23-72	1992	Toney, Ala.
Kofler, Eric	.240	7	25	3	6	1	0	0	4	4	3	0	0	L	L	6-1	170	2-11-76	1994	Palm Harbor, Fla.
Lobaton, Jose	.254	52	177	16	45	14	1	1	21	10	36	2	2	R	R	5-11	154	3-29-74	1992	Acarigua, Ven.
McDonald, Donzell	.253	134	495	80	125	20	7	6	36	55	127	35	22	B	R	5-11	165	2-20-75	1995	Glendale, Colo.
McLamb, Brian	.179	62	196	18	35	10	0	1	11	10	67	2	3	B	R	6-3	185	12-13-72	1993	Jacksonville, Fla.
Morenz, Shea	.252	116	409	51	103	18	3	15	52	31	109	7	5	L	R	6-2	205	1-22-74	1995	San Antonio, Texas
Ramirez, Angel	.261	24	92	7	24	5	0	2	14	0	19	0	0	R	R	5-10	166	1-24-73	1991	Azua, D.R.
Torres, Jaime	.275	81	262	30	72	9	1	8	35	24	31	4	2	R	R	6-0	176	3-12-73	1992	Aragua, Ven.
Troilo, Jason	.159	23	69	8	11	5	0	1	7	4	22	0	0	R	R	6-1	195	9-7-72	1994	Avondale, Pa.
Williams, Bernie	.545	3	11	6	6	2	0	2	5	2	1	0	0	B	R	6-2	205	9-13-68	1986	Bayamon, P.R.

PITCHING	W	L	ERA	G	GS	CG	SV	IP	H	R	ER	BB	SO	B	T	HT	WT	DOB	1st Yr	Resides
Baron, Jim	0	4	2.33	23	12	4	0	97	99	35	25	20	69	L	L	6-3	230	2-22-74	1992	Humble, Texas
Bautista, Jose	0	2	15.12	3	3	0	0	8	17	16	14	4	4	R	R	6-2	207	7-25-64	1981	Cooper City, Fla.
Beverlin, Jason	3	5	3.67	25	9	0	1	81	68	34	33	38	86	L	R	6-5	220	11-27-73	1994	Royal Oak, Mich.
Bradley, Ryan	2	0	1.44	3	3	1	0	25	8	4	4	8	25	R	R	6-4	226	10-26-75	1997	Chino Hills, Calif.
De la Cruz, Francisco	0	2	7.71	2	2	0	0	5	8	13	4	4	5	R	R	6-2	175	7-9-73	1991	La Romana, D.R.
De los Santos, Luis	2	6	4.90	13	13	2	0	79	97	49	43	23	51	R	R	6-2	187	11-1-77	1995	San Pedro de Macoris, D.R.
Einertson, Darrell	3	1	1.02	17	0	0	0	35	23	7	4	10	33	R	R	6-2	190	9-4-72	1995	Urbandale, Iowa
Heredia, Wilson	2	3	5.57	5	5	0	0	32	31	22	20	9	31	R	R	6-0	175	3-30-72	1990	La Romana, D.R.
Janzen, Marty	1	7	3.89	11	7	1	0	35	42	28	15	19	38	R	R	6-3	197	5-31-73	1991	Gainesville, Fla.
Johnson, Barry	1	0	3.75	7	0	0	0	12	13	6	5	5	12	R	R	6-4	200	8-21-69	1991	Joliet, Ill.
Lail, Denny	0	0	5.40	8	0	0	0	10	15	6	6	7	9	R	R	6-1	172	9-10-74	1995	Taylorsville, N.C.
Lisio, Joe	1	0	0.00	1	0	0	0	1	1	0	0	1	1	R	R	6-2	205	8-5-73	1994	West Hempstead, N.Y.
Maeda, Kats	1	3	7.71	28	0	0	1	37	44	36	32	31	27	R	R	6-2	215	6-23-71	1996	Tokyo, Japan
Narcisse, Tyrone	1	0	5.23	29	0	0	1	53	61	38	31	26	43	R	R	6-6	220	2-4-72	1990	Port Arthur, Texas
Phillips, Ben	1	1	4.94	16	0	0	0	24	19	13	13	16	22	R	R	6-3	195	7-28-75	1996	Sheridan, Wyo.
Resz, Greg	4	0	2.83	19	3	0	0	48	46	20	15	11	47	L	R	6-5	215	12-25-71	1993	Springfield, Mo.
Ricken, Ray	5	4	4.55	14	14	0	0	87	90	46	44	35	95	R	R	6-5	225	8-11-73	1994	Warren, Mich.
Rose, Scott	2	2	6.14	26	0	0	9	37	49	26	25	10	22	R	R	6-3	200	5-12-70	1990	Tampa, Fla.
Schlomann, Brett	9	9	5.61	30	17	0	0	122	148	92	76	52	69	R	R	6-0	180	7-31-74	1994	Collinsville, Okla.
Shelby, Anthony	0	0	0.00	1	0	0	0	2	1	0	0	1	1	L	L	6-3	200	12-11-73	1993	Willow Springs, Ill.
St. Pierre, Bob	4	2	4.03	24	0	0	0	38	46	23	17	15	26	R	R	6-1	190	4-11-74	1995	Huntington, Md.
Tessmer, Jay	3	4	1.09	45	0	0	29	50	50	8	6	13	57	R	R	6-3	190	12-26-71	1995	Cochranton, Pa.
Valera, Julio	0	4	6.91	5	5	1	0	27	30	23	21	12	17	R	R	6-2	215	10-13-68	1986	San Sebastian, P.R.
Williams, Matt	8	11	4.60	31	28	2	0	160	186	93	82	66	112	B	L	6-0	185	4-12-71	1992	Virginia Beach, Va.
Williams, Shad	4	2	4.29	9	8	0	0	42	55	22	20	11	18	R	R	6-0	198	3-10-71	1991	Fresno, Calif.
Zancanaro, Dave	3	4	4.70	16	13	0	0	69	80	42	36	23	49	B	L	6-1	185	1-8-69	1990	Carmichael, Calif.

FIELDING

Catcher	PCT	G	PO	A	E	DP	PB
Emmons	.983	34	210	22	4	2	6
Fithian	.988	23	140	18	2	2	2
Torres	.993	76	526	59	4	3	6
Troilo	.957	23	124	9	6	0	1

First Base	PCT	G	PO	A	E	DP
Ashby	.971	21	150	18	5	8
Bierek	.989	94	731	72	9	56
Emmons	.988	10	77	7	1	2
Fithian	1.000	3	31	0	0	1
Gomez	1.000	3	24	1	0	0
Kofler	1.000	6	35	3	0	2
McLamb	.968	8	56	5	2	5

Second Base	PCT	G	PO	A	E	DP
Brown	.954	98	178	254	21	37
Dennis	.904	10	20	27	5	7
Gomez	1.000	17	41	53	0	8
Hinds	.957	16	21	24	2	2
McLamb	.895	4	7	10	2	2

Third Base	PCT	G	PO	A	E	DP
Berry	.927	103	59	157	17	12
Dennis	.714	1	3	2	2	0
Gomez	.917	4	6	5	1	0
McLamb	.934	39	26	59	6	4

Shortstop	PCT	G	PO	A	E	DP
Dennis	.901	18	24	49	8	3
Gomez	.885	18	29	40	9	5
Hinds	.871	7	10	17	4	3
Jimenez	.938	40	62	119	12	24
Lobaton	.941	50	61	116	11	13
McLamb	.944	10	12	22	2	4

Outfield	PCT	G	PO	A	E	DP
Ashby	.969	93	145	11	5	1
Bierek	.000	1	0	0	0	0
Glass	.984	107	235	12	4	0
Hinds	1.000	2	3	0	0	0
Keel	1.000	5	4	0	0	0
Kofler	1.000	2	3	1	0	0
McDonald	.976	128	312	8	8	1
Morenz	.988	82	158	3	2	1
Ramirez	.900	17	26	1	3	0
Williams	1.000	3	5	0	0	0

TAMPA — Class A

FLORIDA STATE LEAGUE

BATTING	AVG	G	AB	R	H	2B	3B	HR	RBI	BB	SO	SB	CS	B	T	HT	WT	DOB	1st Yr	Resides
Amerson, Gordon	.211	6	19	2	4	1	0	0	1	1	4	0	1	L	L	6-1	200	10-10-76	1994	San Bernardino, Calif.
August, Brian	[illegible]	[illegible]	[illegible]	[illegible]	[illegible]	[illegible]	[illegible]	[illegible]	[illegible]	[illegible]	[illegible]	[illegible]	[illegible]	[illegible]	[illegible]	[illegible]	[illegible]	[illegible]	[illegible]	[illegible]
Aylor, Brian	.268	17	56	8	15	4	0	2	6	2	23	4	0	L	L	6-2	200	4-6-74	1996	Midwest City, Okla.
Brown, Richard	.298	80	282	46	84	13	3	11	38	45	54	8	6	L	L	6-1	196	4-28-77	1996	Plantation, Fla.
Carey, Orlando	.160	10	25	5	4	0	0	0	1	2	7	3	0	R	R	6-1	180	2-25-76	1996	Gallatin, Tenn.
Cossins, Tim	.223	30	94	6	21	6	0	1	6	3	14	0	0	R	R	6-1	192	8-20-78	1993	Windsor, Calif.
Dennis, Les	.183	44	104	16	19	4	0	1	8	5	20	1	0	R	R	6-0	175	6-3-73	1995	West Linn, Ore.
Elwood, Brad	.333	3	3	1	1	0	0	0	1	0	0	0	0	R	R	6-1	195	10-22-75	1998	Clear Spring, Md.
Emmons, Scott	.250	13	24	3	6	2	0	0	4	4	6	1	0	R	R	6-4	205	12-25-73	1995	Norco, Calif.
Harrell, Ken	.125	18	32	3	4	1	0	0	3	0	8	2	1	R	R	6-0	193	1-29-75	1997	Las Cruces, N.M.
Hinds, Rob	.250	27	100	15	25	4	2	1	9	21	25	6	5	R	R	6-0	185	4-26-71	1992	Cerritos, Calif.
Johnson, Nick	.317	92	303	69	96	14	1	17	58	68	76	1	4	L	L	6-3	195	9-19-78	1996	Sacramento, Calif.
Jones, Aaron	.216	11	37	2	8	2	0	0	4	4	12	0	0	L	L	6-4	205	9-7-75	1997	Newport, Mich.
Kane, Ryan	.132	16	53	4	7	2	0	1	4	7	12	1	0	R	R	6-4	210	1-25-74	1995	Acton, Mass.
Keel, David	.327	27	107	18	35	3	0	3	16	18	18	3	1	L	R	6-3	205	7-23-72	1992	Toney, Ala.
Knowles, Eric	.278	95	360	46	100	16	4	2	41	30	62	3	6	R	R	6-0	190	10-21-73	1991	Miami, Fla.
Kofler, Eric	.309	87	337	50	104	25	3	10	69	19	51	1	2	L	L	6-1	170	2-11-76	1994	Palm Harbor, Fla.
Leon, Donny	.291	100	385	54	112	24	1	10	59	23	64	0	0	B	R	6-2	185	5-7-76	1995	Ponce, P.R.
Lobaton, Jose	.254	33	130	21	33	4	1	4	15	4	32	4	1	R	R	5-11	154	3-29-74	1992	Acarigua, Ven.
Martinez, Gabby	.319	44	166	26	53	8	1	5	24	5	20	21	6	R	R	6-2	170	1-7-74	1992	Santurce, P.R.
McDonald, Donzell	.333	5	18	6	6	1	2	0	2	2	7	2	0	B	R	5-11	165	2-20-75	1995	Glendale, Colo.
Montilla, Miguel	.125	10	16	2	2	1	0	0	0	4	6	0	0	R	R	6-1	175	12-18-73	1993	Miami, Fla.
Morris, Jeremy	.301	124	445	69	134	25	1	13	72	48	96	11	3	R	R	6-3	225	10-7-74	1997	Quincy, Fla.
Ottavinia, Paul	.253	57	174	25	44	13	3	5	28	14	20	2	0	L	L	6-1	190	4-22-73	1994	Flanders, N.J.
Rodriguez, Felix	.000	1	1	0	0	0	0	0	0	1	0	0	0	R	R	6-2	200	3-19-78	1998	Ponce, P.R.
Samuel, Cody	.338	47	154	27	52	15	0	6	32	20	44	0	0	R	R	6-1	252	4-10-74	1992	Redondo Beach, Calif.
Shumpert, Derek	.197	21	66	8	13	2	0	0	3	7	25	0	2	R	R	6-2	185	9-30-75	1993	St. Louis, Mo.
Smith, Rod	.245	86	327	57	80	15	2	6	35	39	70	40	14	B	R	6-0	185	9-2-75	1994	Lexington, Ky.
Sojo, Luis	.222	3	9	1	2	0	0	0	0	2	0	0	0	R	R	5-11	174	1-3-66	1987	Barquisimeto, Ven.
Thames, Marcus	.284	122	457	62	130	18	3	11	59	24	78	13	6	R	R	6-2	205	3-6-77	1997	Louisville, Miss.
Valencia, Victor	.224	122	411	53	92	18	1	16	43	26	139	0	1	R	R	6-2	185	5-13-77	1994	Maracay, Ven.
Williams, Bernie	.500	1	2	0	1	1	0	0	0	1	0	0	0	B	R	6-2	205	9-13-68	1986	Bayamon, P.R.

GAMES BY POSITION: C—Cossins 16, Elwood 3, Emmons 13, Harrell 9, Rodriguez 1, Valencia 122. **1B**—August 2, Cossins 13, Johnson 90, Jones 11, Knowles 1, Kofler 19, Samuel 12. **2B**—August 7, Cossins 1, Dennis 18, Hinds 27, Knowles 7, Lobaton 8, Montilla 2, Smith 85. **3B**—August 8, Dennis 6, Kane 16, Knowles 13, Leon 99, Montilla 4. **SS**—Dennis 19, Knowles 74, Lobaton 23, Martinez 38, Montilla 4, Sojo 3. **OF**—Amerson 4, Aylor 11, Brown 56, Carey 10, Emmons 1, Harrell 2, Keel 2, Kofler 58, McDonald 5, Morris 113, Ottavinia 41, Shumpert 14, Thames 120, Williams 1.

PITCHING	W	L	ERA	G	GS	CG	SV	IP	H	R	ER	BB	SO	B	T	HT	WT	DOB	1st Yr	Resides
Beverlin, Jason	1	3	5.63	7	5	0	0	32	37	23	20	16	15	L	R	6-5	220	11-27-73	1994	Royal Oak, Mich.
Bradley, Ryan	7	4	2.38	32	11	1	7	95	59	29	25	30	112	R	R	6-4	226	10-26-75	1997	Chino Hills, Calif.
Buchanan, Brian	0	1	22.50	1	1	0	0	2	4	7	5	8	1	L	L	6-3	190	4-23-77	1995	Oviedo, Fla.
Castillo, Alberto	0	0	13.50	12	0	0	0	11	14	17	17	25	11	L	L	6-3	200	7-5-75	1994	Miami, Fla.
Choate, Randy	1	8	5.27	13	13	0	0	70	83	57	41	22	55	L	L	6-3	180	9-5-75	1997	Tallahassee, Fla.
Cubillan, Darwin	9	2	4.71	45	1	0	1	65	79	45	34	36	70	R	R	6-2	170	11-15-74	1994	Bobure, Ven.
Day, Zach	5	8	5.49	18	17	0	0	100	142	89	61	32	69	R	R	6-4	185	6-15-78	1996	West Harrison, Ind.
De la Cruz, Andres	0	0	0.00	3	0	0	0	4	2	0	0	2	1	R	R	6-4	190	5-12-79	1996	Santo Domingo, D.R.
De la Cruz, Francisco	5	6	4.54	19	12	0	0	75	81	55	38	36	66	R	R	6-2	175	7-9-73	1991	La Romana, D.R.
De los Santos, Luis	4	2	4.19	10	10	1	0	67	69	40	31	11	33	R	R	6-2	187	11-1-77	1995	San Pedro de Macoris, D.R.
Dingman, Craig	5	4	3.18	50	0	0	7	71	48	29	25	39	95	R	R	6-4	195	3-12-74	1994	Wichita, Kan.
Flores, Randy	1	2	6.46	5	5	0	0	24	28	23	17	16	15	L	L	6-0	180	7-31-75	1997	Pico Rivera, Calif.
Hernandez, Orlando	1	1	1.00	2	2	0	0	9	3	2	1	3	15	R	R	6-2	210	10-11-69	1998	Miami, Fla.
Holmes, Darren	0	1	4.50	2	1	0	0	2	4	2	1	0	6	R	R	6-0	202	4-25-66	1984	Fletcher, N.C.
Lail, Denny	4	0	4.07	31	0	0	1	49	44	24	22	25	46	R	R	6-1	172	9-10-74	1995	Taylorsville, N.C.
Lisio, Joe	2	3	2.48	31	0	0	15	33	19	13	9	16	43	R	R	6-2	205	8-5-73	1994	West Hempstead, N.Y.
Mairena, Oswaldo	1	5	3.17	52	0	0	0	54	53	24	19	23	50	L	L	5-11	165	7-30-75	1996	Chinandega, Nicaragua
Narcisse, Tyrone	0	0	1.80	4	0	0	0	5	4	1	1	3	7	R	R	6-6	220	2-4-72	1990	Port Arthur, Texas
Nelson, Jeff	0	0	0.00	2	1	0	0	2	1	1	0	1	4	R	R	6-8	235	11-17-66	1984	Issaquah, Wash.
Phillips, Ben	3	1	1.73	23	0	0	1	42	22	12	8	36	51	R	R	6-3	195	7-28-75	1996	Sheridan, Wyo.
Rangel, Julio	2	3	5.15	10	7	0	0	44	47	30	25	30	31	R	R	6-3	160	9-28-75	1994	Panama City, Panama
Robbins, Jake	11	6	3.84	26	25	2	0	152	167	83	65	72	87	R	R	6-5	190	5-23-76	1994	Charlotte, N.C.
Rogers, Brian	0	0	4.20	3	3	0	0	15	12	7	7	14	13	R	R	6-6	210	2-13-77	1998	Carthage, N.C.
Schaffner, Eric	0	1	5.40	7	0	0	0	12	17	8	7	4	6	R	R	6-3	190	10-19-74	1994	Keizer, Ore.
Spence, Cam	9	5	3.75	21	20	2	0	127	125	66	53	38	105	R	R	6-3	195	10-11-74	1996	Lithonia, Ga.
St. Pierre, Bob	0	0	6.90	16	0	0	0	30	46	26	23	12	21	R	R	6-1	190	4-11-74	1995	Huntington, Md.
Wiggins, Scott	1	1	1.87	11	5	0	0	34	19	12	7	17	36	L	L	6-3	205	3-24-76	1997	Newport, Ky.

GREENSBORO — Class A

SOUTH ATLANTIC LEAGUE

BATTING	AVG	G	AB	R	H	2B	3B	HR	RBI	BB	SO	SB	CS	B	T	HT	WT	DOB	1st Yr	Resides
Almonte, Erick	.209	120	450	53	94	13	0	6	33	29	121	6	2	R	R	6-2	180	2-1-78	1996	Santo Domingo, D.R.
Amerson, Gordon	.222	4	18	2	4	0	0	0	2	0	1	0	0	L	L	6-1	200	10-10-76	1994	San Bernardino, Calif.
Aylor, Brian	.238	47	130	18	31	5	2	5	13	13	67	5	1	L	L	6-2	200	4-6-74	1996	Midwest City, Okla.
Butler, Allen	.269	125	469	70	126	26	1	19	81	50	139	4	3	L	R	6-3	190	1-22-75	1996	Clinchport, Va.
Carey, Orlando	.128	34	78	11	10	1	0	0	2	8	27	1	1	R	R	6-1	180	2-25-76	1996	Gallatin, Tenn.
Darjean, John	.190	23	84	9	16	2	2	0	8	6	11	6	4	R	R	6-1	175	4-3-76	1997	Baton Rouge, La.
Kidd, Scott	.274	126	468	74	128	30	0	17	58	44	118	9	6	R	R	5-10	180	1-15-74	1997	Cupertino, Calif.
Maxwell, Vernon	.234	104	418	53	98	10	7	5	35	32	121	11	2	R	R	6-3	205	10-22-76	1996	Midwest City, Okla.
Melian, Jackson	.255	135	467	66	119	18	2	8	45	41	120	15	12	R	R	6-2	190	1-7-80	1996	Barcelona, Ven.
Mirizzi, Marc	.279	103	373	57	104	29	1	11	44	31	85	4	5	B	R	6-1	190	6-17-75	1997	Los Gatos, Calif.
Montilla, Miguel	.000	1	3	0	0	0	0	0	0	0	3	0	0	R	R	6-1	175	12-18-73	1993	Miami, Fla.

BATTING	AVG	G	AB	R	H	2B	3B	HR	RBI	BB	SO	SB	CS	B	T	HT	WT	DOB	1st Yr	Resides
Pinto, Rene	.227	109	365	31	83	25	1	0	40	32	87	2	5	R	R	6-0	185	7-17-77	1994	Palo Negro, Ven.
Purkiss, Matt	.206	55	180	20	37	6	0	9	32	21	77	0	0	L	R	6-3	220	7-15-75	1997	Visalia, Calif.
Rodriguez, John	.252	119	408	64	103	18	4	10	49	64	93	14	3	L	L	6-0	185	1-20-78	1997	New York, N.Y.
Samuel, Cody	.200	14	50	7	10	0	0	1	3	5	23	0	1	R	R	6-1	252	4-10-74	1992	Redondo Beach, Calif.
Seabol, Scott	.286	71	210	24	60	11	0	7	33	13	40	2	2	R	R	6-4	200	5-17-75	1996	McKeesport, Pa.
Soules, Ryan	.268	98	332	48	89	16	2	17	54	58	107	3	1	L	R	6-2	185	2-27-76	1997	Seattle, Wash.
Staubach, Jeff	.333	2	3	0	1	0	0	0	0	1	1	0	0	R	R	6-0	215	12-28-74	1997	Dallas, Texas
Twombley, Dennis	.188	40	133	13	25	4	0	7	21	4	45	1	1	R	R	6-2	218	6-8-75	1996	San Diego, Calif.
Washington, Dion	.120	16	50	5	6	0	0	0	5	6	23	1	0	R	R	6-4	235	12-21-76	1997	Las Vegas, Nev.

GAMES BY POSITION: C—Pinto 108, Seabol 1, Staubach 2, Twombley 38. **1B**—Mirizzi 15, Purkiss 35, Samuel 14, Seabol 7, Soules 75. **2B**—Kidd 124, Mirizzi 21. **3B**—Butler 124, Mirizzi 15, Seabol 10. **SS**—Almonte 120, Mirizzi 23. **OF**—Amerson 4, Aylor 41, Carey 28, Darjean 19, Maxwell 95, Melian 131, Mirizzi 3, Rodriguez 103, Seabol 18, Washington 6.

PITCHING	W	L	ERA	G	GS	CG	SV	IP	H	R	ER	BB	SO	B	T	HT	WT	DOB	1st Yr	Resides
Blevins, Jeremy	5	8	4.81	24	23	0	0	120	121	80	64	66	110	R	R	6-3	190	10-5-77	1995	Bristol, Tenn.
Castillo, Alberto	0	0	3.72	5	0	0	0	10	8	6	4	14	13	L	L	6-3	200	7-5-75	1994	Miami, Fla.
Choate, Randy	1	5	3.00	8	8	1	0	39	46	21	13	7	32	L	L	6-3	180	9-5-75	1997	Tallahassee, Fla.
Cremer, Rick	8	1	2.50	13	13	0	0	79	56	28	22	25	79	L	L	6-4	180	4-19-77	1996	West Frankfort, Ill.
Day, Zach	1	2	2.75	7	6	1	0	36	35	22	11	6	37	R	R	6-4	185	6-15-78	1996	West Harrison, Ind.
De la Cruz, Francisco	2	1	3.98	5	3	0	0	20	15	9	9	10	18	R	R	6-2	175	7-9-73	1991	La Romana, D.R.
Eavenson, Clay	0	0	4.50	1	0	0	0	4	5	4	2	1	2	R	R	6-3	185	3-6-78	1997	Loganville, Ga.
Ellison, Jason	4	6	3.17	54	0	0	28	65	56	30	23	27	71	R	R	6-4	180	7-24-75	1996	Buffalo, Texas
Flores, Randy	12	7	2.62	21	20	2	0	131	119	48	38	33	139	L	L	6-0	180	7-31-75	1997	Pico Rivera, Calif.
Krall, Eric	0	1	6.63	14	0	0	0	19	27	21	14	18	15	L	L	6-4	215	2-27-74	1996	Meadows, Conn.
Lewis, Craig	11	6	3.37	28	26	3	0	174	170	77	65	34	178	R	R	6-5	210	12-30-76	1997	Sydney, Australia
Mathys, Jason	1	0	6.75	4	0	0	0	9	18	8	7	3	8	R	R	6-4	215	10-18-75	1998	Argyle, Wis.
McBride, Jason	0	0	11.48	7	0	0	0	13	24	21	17	10	11	R	R	6-1	175	2-10-76	1996	Pace, Fla.
Obando, Omar	2	0	4.60	21	0	0	2	29	29	15	15	9	24	R	R	6-2	180	3-23-77	1996	Chimandega, Nicaragua
Reith, Brian	6	7	2.28	20	20	3	0	118	86	42	30	32	116	R	R	6-5	190	2-28-78	1996	Fort Wayne, Ind.
Rogers, Brian	2	1	7.88	3	3	0	0	16	18	15	14	6	19	R	R	6-6	210	2-13-77	1998	Carthage, N.C.
Schaffner, Eric	5	2	4.35	14	4	0	0	39	53	26	19	7	35	R	R	6-3	190	10-19-74	1994	Keizer, Ore.
Spence, Cam	3	2	2.06	8	7	0	0	39	34	10	9	5	41	R	R	6-3	195	10-11-74	1996	Lithonia, Ga.
Spurling, Chris	1	0	3.00	1	1	0	0	6	7	2	2	1	5	R	R	6-6	240	6-28-77	1998	Englewood, Ohio
Taylor, Brien	0	1	9.59	13	1	0	0	25	26	29	27	26	17	L	L	6-3	220	12-26-71	1991	Beaufort, N.C.
Valle, Yoiset	4	2	4.18	33	1	0	1	52	53	27	24	24	55	L	L	6-3	200	6-9-78	1996	Miami Lakes, Fla.
Wallace, Chris	4	7	3.02	54	0	0	8	89	89	43	30	26	79	R	R	6-2	210	5-5-76	1997	Marion, Ohio
Wiggins, Scott	2	2	2.98	14	4	0	1	42	37	17	14	11	56	L	L	6-3	205	3-24-76	1997	Newport, Ky.
Wood, Stanton	5	2	3.90	31	2	0	1	65	57	29	28	20	67	R	R	6-2	185	12-5-76	1997	Torrance, Calif.

ONEONTA — Short-Season Class A

NEW YORK-PENN LEAGUE

BATTING	AVG	G	AB	R	H	2B	3B	HR	RBI	BB	SO	SB	CS	B	T	HT	WT	DOB	1st Yr	Resides
August, Brian	.318	70	242	48	77	22	2	7	67	35	38	5	2	R	R	6-2	180	3-7-76	1997	Newark, Del.
Candelaria, Tito	.306	23	36	6	11	0	1	0	7	4	7	0	0	L	R	6-1	170	5-9-78	1996	Manati, P.R.
Carek, Mark	.246	76	260	32	64	8	1	1	24	30	60	2	2	R	R	6-1	182	8-1-76	1998	Bowling Green, Ohio
Castri, Andrea	.290	49	138	27	40	4	1	2	21	8	43	11	0	R	R	6-4	210	6-26-74	1998	Lecce, Italy
Chambliss, Russ	.080	29	25	4	2	0	0	0	2	1	12	1	1	L	R	6-3	190	6-12-75	1997	Briarcliff Manor, N.Y.
Darjean, John	.314	64	226	43	71	9	4	2	23	18	42	16	5	R	R	6-1	175	4-3-76	1997	Baton Rouge, La.
Greene, Alan	.252	70	254	35	64	11	4	2	39	26	62	8	4	B	R	6-1	190	4-10-77	1998	Renton, Wash.
Gregg, Neal	.217	58	161	22	35	10	4	4	23	20	49	3	2	L	R	6-5	215	2-9-76	1998	Hattiesburg, Miss.
Gross, Jeremy	.200	11	10	1	2	1	0	0	0	2	6	0	0	R	R	5-10	180	5-31-76	1998	Nesbit, Miss.
Heine, Kyle	.167	27	42	3	7	1	0	1	4	2	11	0	0	R	R	6-1	190	1-25-76	1998	Arlington, Texas
Hernandez, Michel	.254	61	205	29	52	8	2	0	24	20	19	4	4	R	R	6-0	211	8-12-78	1998	Caracas, Ven.
Jones, Aaron	.299	51	157	34	47	8	2	3	31	33	31	2	1	L	L	6-4	205	9-7-75	1997	Newport, Mich.
Kane, Kevin	.200	8	10	1	2	1	0	0	0	0	7	0	0	R	R	5-10	160	11-22-73	1996	Tampa, Fla.
Olivares, Teuris	.277	73	271	44	75	15	6	4	43	26	60	14	7	R	R	6-0	164	12-15-78	1996	San Francisco de Macoris, D.R.
Rhodes, Dusty	.275	68	236	47	65	10	4	0	18	29	51	9	3	L	R	6-1	190	2-6-76	1998	Madison, N.J.
Rivera, Juan	.278	6	18	2	5	0	0	1	3	1	4	1	1	R	R	6-2	170	7-3-78	1996	Guarenas, Ven.
Vento, Mike	.304	43	148	25	45	9	3	1	23	14	28	8	3	R	R	6-0	200	5-25-78	1998	Albuquerque, N.M.
Washington, Dion	.185	47	124	14	23	4	1	2	14	19	50	1	0	R	R	6-4	235	12-21-76	1997	Las Vegas, Nev.

GAMES BY POSITION: C—Candelaria 19, Gross 3, Heine 23, Hernandez 59. **1B**—August 10, Castri 1, Gregg 49, Jones 29. **2B**—August 5, Kane 5, Olivares 73. **3B**—August 53, Castri 38, Darjean 1. **SS**—Carek 76, Olivares 4. **OF**—August 5, Chambliss 19, Darjean 63, Greene 69, Gross 3, Heine 1, Kane 1, Rhodes 68, Rivera 6, Vento 24, Washington, 13.

PITCHING	W	L	ERA	G	GS	CG	SV	IP	H	R	ER	BB	SO	B	T	HT	WT	DOB	1st Yr	Resides
Aramboles, Ricardo	1	0	1.50	1	1	0	0	6	4	2	1	1	8	R	R	6-2	170	6-30-80	1996	Santo Domingo, D.R.
Buchanan, Brian	2	2	4.15	15	5	0	0	35	34	16	16	25	32	L	L	6-3	190	4-23-77	1995	Oviedo, Fla.
Carlson, Jeff	1	0	4.28	18	0	0	0	34	33	19	16	13	21	R	R	6-5	220	11-3-75	1998	Niantic, Conn.
Carpenter, Justin	3	1	5.19	28	0	0	4	26	22	18	15	16	11	R	R	6-4	215	1-18-77	1997	Prague, Okla.
Dunn, Keith	0	0	5.40	2	0	0	1	2	2	1	1	0	0	R	R	6-2	180	4-18-78	1998	Tunica, Miss.
Jodie, Brett	7	6	2.59	15	15	1	0	94	87	40	27	21	73	R	R	6-4	210	3-25-77	1998	Lexington, S.C.
Keisler, Randy	1	1	7.45	6	2	0	1	10	14	10	8	7	11	L	L	6-3	180	2-24-76	1998	Richards, Texas
Kloes, David	1	2	7.88	17	0	0	0	24	38	26	21	12	17	R	R	6-2	225	1-2-76	1998	Harmony, Pa.
Knowles, Michael	0	4	5.73	5	5	0	0	22	22	18	14	16	12	R	R	6-5	215	7-15-79	1997	Daytona Beach, Fla.
McBride, Jason	0	1	22.50	2	0	0	0	2	3	5	5	3	1	R	R	6-1	175	2-10-76	1996	Pace, Fla.
Padua, Geraldo	8	0	3.14	15	14	0	0	86	79	40	30	29	75	R	R	6-2	165	2-9-77	1995	Santo Domingo, D.R.
Ridenour, Ryan	0	5	9.38	13	6	0	0	32	47	34	33	12	22	L	L	6-6	215	4-6-77	1998	Southlake, Texas
Rodriguez, Jorge	2	1	3.34	20	0	0	0	32	31	18	12	18	34	R	R	6-2	170	10-11-76	1996	Penuelas, P.R.
Rogers, Brian	2	2	2.31	6	6	0	0	35	23	9	9	10	34	R	R	6-6	210	2-13-77	1998	Carthage, N.C.
Shaddix, Jeff	4	1	3.94	21	0	0	1	30	27	16	13	13	28	R	R	6-3	195	9-10-75	1998	Houston, Texas
Vogtli, Robb	1	2	3.91	25	0	0	14	25	29	16	11	13	28	R	R	6-0	190	4-11-75	1998	Collins, N.Y.
Weber, Brett	4	1	3.04	19	8	1	0	68	68	28	23	13	68	R	R	6-2	180	8-21-76	1998	Glenview, Ill.
Whiteley, Shad	8	2	2.44	14	14	1	0	81	53	30	22	39	85	R	R	6-6	220	3-19-75	1998	Fort Worth, Texas
Wood, Stanton	0	0	.00	7	0	0	1	13	7	3	0	3	14	R	R	6-2	185	12-5-76	1997	Torrance, Calif.

TAMPA — Rookie

GULF COAST LEAGUE

BATTING	AVG	G	AB	R	H	2B	3B	HR	RBI	BB	SO	SB	CS	B	T	HT	WT	DOB	1st Yr	Resides
Amerson, Gordon	.270	13	37	6	10	1	0	1	7	10	15	4	1	L	L	6-1	200	10-10-76	1994	San Bernardino, Calif.
Brown, Andy	[illegible]	30	101	10	[illegible]	[illegible]	[illegible]	[illegible]	[illegible]	[illegible]	[illegible]	[illegible]	[illegible]	[illegible]	[illegible]	[illegible]	[illegible]	[illegible]	[illegible]	[illegible]
Brown, Richard	.429	6	14	6	6	0	0	2	2	1	3	2	0	L	L	6-1	196	4-28-77	1996	Plantation, Fla.
Carpenter, Bubba	.235	5	17	3	4	0	2	1	7	2	2	0	0	L	L	6-1	185	7-23-68	1991	Winslow, Ark.
Cruz, Ivan	.600	5	10	2	6	3	0	1	5	3	3	0	0	L	L	6-3	210	5-3-68	1989	Fajardo, P.R.
Degroote, Casey	.173	36	104	10	18	4	0	0	7	9	35	0	0	L	R	6-1	180	7-31-79	1998	Bartow, Fla.
Dorrmann, Brian	.254	41	130	18	33	9	0	0	11	13	10	2	3	R	R	5-9	165	12-4-75	1998	Cincinnati, Ohio
Fowler, David	.188	39	101	11	19	3	2	1	9	9	47	3	2	R	R	6-3	190	10-17-79	1998	St. Louis, Mo.
Fuentes, Omar	.310	38	126	18	39	9	0	2	12	11	14	0	1	R	R	6-1	175	4-6-80	1996	Maracay, Ven.
Garabito, Vianney	.212	48	156	17	33	5	0	2	16	10	27	3	0	R	R	6-1	185	12-12-79	1996	Santo Domingo, D.R.
Gross, Jeremy	1.000	1	1	1	1	0	0	0	0	0	0	0	0	R	R	5-10	180	5-31-76	1998	Nesbit, Miss.
Henson, Drew	.316	10	38	5	12	3	0	1	2	3	9	0	0	R	R	6-5	220	2-13-80	1998	Brighton, Mich.
Massucco, Scott	.244	26	86	10	21	1	1	1	9	6	15	2	0	R	R	6-1	190	8-20-79	1998	Delano, Calif.
Nettles, Jeff	.125	12	24	1	3	1	0	0	1	5	4	0	1	R	R	6-0	185	8-20-78	1998	Encinitas, Calif.
Paulino, Waren	.500	4	4	0	2	0	0	0	0	0	0	0	0	L	L	6-1	150	7-11-77	1995	Santo Domingo, D.R.
Rivera, Juan	.333	57	210	43	70	9	1	12	45	26	27	8	5	R	R	6-2	170	7-3-78	1996	Guarenas, Ven.
Rodriguez, Felix	.320	11	25	3	8	1	0	0	6	1	4	0	0	R	R	6-2	200	3-19-78	1998	Ponce, P.R.
Rodriguez, Junior	.277	48	159	27	44	12	1	0	24	48	60	2	8	R	R	6-0	175	9-9-77	1998	Brea, Calif.
Samuel, Cody	.429	2	7	3	3	1	0	1	2	1	0	0	0	R	R	6-1	252	4-10-74	1992	Redondo Beach, Calif.
Santana, Pedro	.246	16	61	11	15	2	0	0	7	3	18	1	0	R	R	6-1	190	5-19-79	1996	Santo Domingo, D.R.
Sein, Javier	.260	43	123	17	32	8	1	1	21	15	33	0	1	L	R	6-4	210	10-16-78	1998	Aguadilla, P.R.
Sheffield, Jeff	.244	20	41	2	10	1	0	0	4	2	18	0	0	B	R	6-2	200	6-1-79	1998	Spokane, Wash.
Shumpert, Derek	.125	6	16	3	2	0	1	0	0	4	11	1	0	R	R	6-2	185	9-30-75	1993	St. Louis, Mo.
Sziksai, Jeff	.224	35	125	12	28	4	0	0	9	11	21	0	2	R	R	6-2	190	6-25-75	1998	Asheville, N.C.
Valdez, Angel	.232	47	168	34	39	5	2	3	19	13	61	11	5	R	R	6-2	178	5-22-78	1996	Santo Domingo, D.R.
Wright, Charles	.171	17	41	11	7	0	0	0	3	4	11	2	0	L	R	6-0	185	9-6-76	1998	Miami, Fla.

GAMES BY POSITION: C—Fuentes 33, Massucco 22, F. Rodriguez 10. **1B**—Cruz 4, Garabito 9, Samuel 2, Sein 39, Valdez 16. **2B**—Dorrmann 24, Garabito 5, Sziksai 35. **3B**—Degroote 17, Garabito 34, Henson 10, Nettles 4, Sein 1. **SS**—Dorrmann 16, Garabito 1, J. Rodriguez 48. **OF**—Amerson 6, A. Brown 30, R. Brown 1, Carpenter 2, Fowler 36, Paulino 3, Rivera 56, Santana 16, Sheffield 9, Shumpert 5, Valdez 30, Wright 9.

PITCHING	W	L	ERA	G	GS	CG	SV	IP	H	R	ER	BB	SO	B	T	HT	WT	DOB	1st Yr	Resides
Acosta, Alberto	1	1	3.38	8	6	0	0	29	20	13	11	17	27	R	R	6-4	170	8-25-77	1996	Portobelo, Panama
Aramboles, Ricardo	2	1	2.93	10	9	0	0	40	33	14	13	13	44	R	R	6-2	170	6-30-80	1996	Santo Domingo, D.R.
De la Cruz, Andres	6	2	2.68	21	0	0	4	40	37	16	12	10	28	R	R	6-4	190	5-12-79	1996	Santo Domingo, D.R.
De la Cruz, Francisco	1	1	3.29	3	3	0	0	14	11	9	5	8	18	R	R	6-2	175	7-9-73	1991	La Romana, D.R.
Dunn, Keith	0	2	1.23	21	0	0	12	37	16	6	5	9	38	R	R	6-2	180	4-18-78	1998	Tunica, Miss.
Eavenson, Clay	3	4	4.98	12	3	0	0	34	38	22	19	7	25	R	R	6-3	185	3-6-78	1997	Loganville, Ga.
Garcia, Rosman	4	3	2.55	12	12	0	0	67	70	38	19	9	47	R	R	6-2	165	1-3-79	1996	San Joaquin, Ven.
Janzen, Marty	0	0	0.00	1	1	0	0	3	1	0	0	0	5	R	R	6-3	197	5-31-73	1991	Gainesville, Fla.
Klein, Cody	4	1	5.23	17	0	0	1	21	19	13	12	11	20	L	L	6-2	205	2-4-79	1997	Andrews, Texas
Knowles, Michael	2	1	2.84	8	7	0	0	38	34	15	12	16	30	R	R	6-5	215	7-15-79	1997	Daytona Beach, Fla.
Langston, David	2	2	5.74	15	0	0	0	31	45	21	20	9	26	R	R	6-5	215	12-11-78	1997	Ringgold, Ga.
Mathys, Jason	4	3	4.22	12	0	0	2	21	19	11	10	7	21	R	R	6-4	215	10-18-75	1998	Argyle, Wis.
Munoz, Marcos	0	0	3.00	2	1	0	0	3	4	1	1	0	1	R	R	6-1	215	8-16-78	1997	Orangeburg, N.Y.
Rangel, Julio	1	0	5.27	3	3	0	0	14	18	8	8	7	19	R	R	6-3	160	9-28-75	1994	Panama City, Panama
Reisinger, Justin	0	1	6.75	9	1	0	0	17	19	16	13	9	13	R	R	6-2	170	3-22-80	1998	Clarksburg, Ohio
Ridenour, Ryan	0	2	5.28	4	4	0	0	15	7	10	9	13	17	L	L	6-6	215	4-6-77	1998	Southlake, Texas
Rodriguez, Tony	1	0	1.29	6	0	0	0	7	4	1	1	8	10	R	R	6-1	220	11-8-78	1997	New York, N.Y.
Sosa, Jorby	1	1	3.77	12	3	0	1	31	39	22	13	5	26	R	R	6-2	170	9-17-78	1996	Maracay, Ven.
Spurling, Chris	2	1	2.28	13	6	0	1	51	57	21	13	11	44	R	R	6-6	240	6-28-77	1998	Englewood, Ohio
Torres, Elvin	0	0	3.60	2	0	0	0	5	3	2	2	0	2	R	R	6-1	168	8-4-78	1997	Salinas, P.R.
Wiggins, Scott	0	0	0.00	1	1	0	0	2	2	1	0	0	2	L	L	6-3	205	3-24-76	1997	Newport, Ky.

NEW YORK METS

Mets fall short of wild-card slot after second-half surge

BY MARTY NOBLE

For so long, the New York Mets appeared to be in the process of winning the 1998 National League wild card. They had starting pitching superior to that of

either of the other wild-card contenders, Mike Piazza was sizzling and Turk Wendell was pitching like Trevor Hoffman. And when they won three of four extraordinary games in Houston in mid-September, a sense of inevitability developed.

They had withstood the glut of doubleheaders, a West Coast swing and 10 games in 15 days against eventual division champions. Eight games remained.

As it turned out, had the Mets won four of the eight, they would have participated in the postseason for the first time in 11 years. Instead, they won merely twice, lost their final five games and were home before the Chicago Cubs defeated the San Francisco Giants in a one-game wild-card playoff.

And so the legacy of the 1998 Mets is not the fine run they made but the failure and fall that followed. Evidence of progress is in the eye of the beholder. The 1997 Mets won 88 games. The '98 Mets did too. Does that constitute progress? Or status quo? And isn't it regress that they finished 18 game behind the Braves after finishing 13 games behind in 1997?

In restrospect, the total of the season was less than the sum of its parts. Too many of the positives came in one late burst, leaving too many other flat periods.

For stretches, John Olerud and Piazza, who had 52 RBIs after July 31, were the offense. Olerud, who finished second in the league with a .353 average, was the team's most consistent hitter.

Al Leiter, bum knee and all, produced as splendid a season as any Mets pitcher in 13 years. Other players had hot stretches but the team was hurt by inconsistency, though a reliable defense and fundamental execution kept the team in the race.

Within a month after the end the season, the Mets had committed $123 million to Piazza and Leiter and said they would make the moves necessary to compete with the Braves. But to that point, they had achieved only status quo. It was asking a lot of a team that still had no speed, no leadoff man, an unreliable bullpen and little power in the outfield.

There appeared to be little the minor leagues could provide to help the 1999 Mets unless Paul Wilson and Jason Isringhausen were to reemerge as the pitchers they were expected to be before injuries interrupted their careers.

The real jewels of the system were at the lower levels. Class A teams St. Lucie and Capital City both won league titles. At 90-51 (.638), Capital City posted the best record in the minors and won three levels of playoffs in the South Atlantic League.

Righthander Grant Roberts, the organization's top prospect entering the '98 season, showed signs at St. Lucie that he had recovered from elbow surgery.

At Capital City, outfielder Alex Escobar had a breakthrough season, batting .310 with 27 home runs and 49 steals. Teammates Mo Bruce and Kevin Dougherty also enjoyed strong years.

The Mets' seven minor league affiliates produced a .535 winning percentage in 1998, the fourth highest in professional baseball and the highest among NL organizations. In addition to Capital City and St. Lucie, Double-A Binghamton also reached the playoffs.

John Olerud

Alex Escobar

Players of the Year

Major League: John Olerud, 1b

Olerud put together the National League's longest hitting streak at 23 games while batting .353, second-best in the league.

Minor League: Alex Escobar, of, Capital City

Escobar emerged as a top prospect, hitting .310 with 27 home runs, 91 RBIs and 49 steals in Class A.

ORGANIZATION LEADERS

BATTING		
*AVG	Todd Haney, Norfolk/St. Lucie	.345
R	Alex Escobar, Capital City	90
H	Maurice Bruce, Capital City	176
TB	Maurice Bruce, Capital City	253
2B	Todd Haney, Norfolk/St. Lucie	33
3B	Two tied at	10
HR	Alex Escobar, Capital City	27
RBI	Alex Escobar, Capital City	91
BB	Ralph Milliard, Norfolk	79
SO	Alex Escobar, Capital City	133
SB	Alex Escobar, Capital City	49
PITCHING		
W	Kevin Dougherty, Capital City	15
L	Arnold Gooch, Binghamton	14
#ERA	Mike Lyons, Binghamton/St. Lucie	2.05
G	Luis Arroyo, Norfolk/Binghamton	65
CG	Three tied at	3
SV	Two tied at	19
IP	Octavio Dotel, Norfolk/Binghamton	168
BB	Scott Sauerbeck, Norfolk	68
SO	Octavio Dotel, Norfolk/Binghamton	200

*Minimum 250 At-Bats #Minimum 75 Innings

New York METS

Manager: Bobby Valentine

1998 Record: 88-74, .543 (2nd, NL East)

BATTING	AVG	G	AB	R	H	2B	3B	HR	RBI	BB	SO	SB	CS	B	T	HT	WT	DOB	1st Yr	Resides
Agbayani, Benny	.133	11	15	1	2	0	0	0	0	1	5	0	2	R	R	6-0	225	12-28-71	1993	Aiea, Hawaii
Alfonzo, Edgardo	.278	144	557	94	155	28	2	17	78	65	77	8	3	R	R	5-11	187	11-8-73	1991	Caracas, Ven.
Allensworth, Jermaine	.204	34	54	9	11	2	0	2	4	2	16	0	2	R	R	6-0	190	1-11-72	1993	Anderson, Ind.
2-team (69 Pitt.)	.289	103	287	39	83	15	3	5	28	19	59	8	6							
Baerga, Carlos	.266	147	511	46	136	27	1	7	53	24	55	0	1	B	R	5-11	215	11-4-68	1986	Bayamon, P.R.
Becker, Rich	.190	49	100	15	19	4	2	3	10	21	42	3	1	L	L	5-10	193	2-1-72	1990	Cape Coral, Fla.
Castillo, Alberto	.205	38	83	13	17	4	0	2	7	9	17	0	2	R	R	6-0	185	2-10-70	1987	Port St. Lucie, Fla.
Fabregas, Jorge	.188	20	32	3	6	0	0	1	5	1	6	0	0	L	R	6-3	215	3-13-70	1991	Miami, Fla.
2-team (50 Arizona)	.197	70	183	11	36	4	0	2	20	14	32	0	0							
Franco, Matt	.273	103	161	20	44	7	2	1	13	23	26	0	1	L	R	6-1	210	8-19-69	1987	Thousand Oaks, Calif.
Gilbert, Shawn	.000	3	3	1	0	0	0	0	0	0	1	0	0	R	R	5-9	185	3-12-65	1987	Glendale, Ariz.
Gilkey, Bernard	.227	82	264	33	60	15	0	4	28	32	66	5	1	R	R	6-0	200	9-24-66	1985	St. Louis, Mo.
Haney, Todd	.000	3	3	0	0	0	0	0	0	1	0	0	0	R	R	5-9	165	7-30-65	1987	San Antonio, Texas
Harris, Lenny	.232	75	168	18	39	7	0	6	17	9	12	5	2	L	R	5-10	210	10-28-64	1983	Miami, Fla.
2-team (57 Cinc.)	.259	132	290	30	75	15	0	6	27	17	21	6	5							
Hundley, Todd	.161	53	124	8	20	4	0	3	12	16	55	1	1	B	R	5-11	199	5-27-69	1987	Port St. Lucie, Fla.
Huskey, Butch	.252	113	369	43	93	18	0	13	59	26	66	7	6	R	R	6-3	244	11-10-71	1989	Lawton, Okla.
Kinkade, Mike	.000	3	2	1	0	0	0	0	0	0	0	0	0	R	R	6-1	210	5-6-73	1995	Tigard, Ore.
Kirby, Wayne	.194	26	31	5	6	0	1	0	0	1	9	1	1	L	R	5-10	185	1-22-64	1983	Yorktown, Va.
Lopez, Luis	.252	117	266	37	67	13	2	2	22	20	60	2	2	B	R	5-11	166	9-4-70	1988	Cidra, P.R.
McRae, Brian	.264	159	552	79	146	36	5	21	79	80	90	20	11	B	R	6-0	195	8-27-67	1985	Leawood, Kan.
Milliard, Ralph	.000	10	1	3	0	0	0	0	0	0	1	0	0	R	R	5-11	175	12-30-73	1993	Amsterdam, Netherlands
Olerud, John	.353	160	558	91	197	36	4	22	93	95	73	2	2	L	L	6-5	220	8-5-68	1989	Phoenix, Ariz.
Ordonez, Rey	.246	153	505	46	124	20	2	1	42	23	60	3	6	R	R	5-9	159	11-11-72	1993	Miami, Fla.
Paquette, Craig	.263	8	19	3	5	2	0	0	0	0	6	1	0	R	R	6-0	190	3-28-69	1989	Tempe, Ariz.
Payton, Jay	.318	15	22	2	7	1	0	0	0	1	4	0	0	R	R	5-10	185	11-22-72	1994	Zanesville, Ohio
Phillips, Tony	.223	52	188	25	42	11	0	3	14	38	44	1	1	B	R	5-10	175	4-25-59	1978	Scottsdale, Ariz.
Piazza, Mike	.349	109	393	67	137	33	0	23	76	47	53	1	0	R	R	6-3	223	9-4-68	1989	Valley Forge, Pa.
3-team (37 L.A./5 Fla.)	.329	151	560	88	184	38	1	32	111	58	80	1	0							
Pratt, Todd	.275	41	69	9	19	9	1	2	18	2	20	0	0	R	R	6-3	230	2-9-67	1985	Sunrise, Fla.
Spehr, Tim	.137	21	51	3	7	1	0	0	3	7	16	1	0	R	R	6-2	200	7-2-66	1988	Dallas, Texas
Tatum, Jim	.180	35	50	4	9	1	2	2	13	3	19	0	0	R	R	6-2	200	10-9-67	1985	San Diego, Calif.
Wilkins, Rick	.133	5	15	3	2	0	0	0	1	2	2	0	0	L	R	6-2	215	6-4-67	1987	Jacksonville, Fla.
Wilson, Preston	.300	8	20	3	6	2	0	0	2	2	8	1	1	R	R	6-2	193	7-19-74	1993	Eastover, S.C.

MORRIS FOSTOFF

New York's Al Leiter
Led team with 17 wins

STAN DENNY

Righthander Octavio Dotel
Struck out 200 batters at two levels

PITCHING	W	L	ERA	G	GS	CG	SV	IP	H	R	ER	BB	SO	B	T	HT	WT	DOB	1st Yr	Resides
Beltran, Rigo	0	0	3.38	7	0	0	0	8	6	3	3	4	5	L	L	5-11	185	11-13-69	1991	San Diego, Calif.
Blair, Willie	1	1	3.14	11	2	0	0	29	23	10	10	10	21	R	R	6-1	185	12-18-65	1986	Lexington, Ky.
2-team (23 Arizona)	5	16	4.98	34	25	0	0	175	188	101	97	61	92							
Bohanon, Brian	2	4	3.15	25	4	0	0	54	47	21	19	21	39	L	L	6-2	219	8-1-68	1987	Houston, Texas
Clontz, Brad	0	0	9.00	2	0	0	0	3	4	3	3	2	2	R	R	6-1	195	4-25-71	1992	Alpharetta, Ga.
2-team (18 Los Angeles)	2	0	6.08	20	0	0	0	24	19	16	16	12	16							
Cook, Dennis	8	4	2.38	73	0	0	1	68	60	21	18	27	79	L	L	6-3	190	10-4-62	1985	Austin, Texas
Franco, John	0	8	3.62	61	0	0	38	65	66	28	26	29	59	L	L	5-10	185	9-17-60	1981	Staten Island, N.Y.
Hudek, John	1	4	4.00	28	0	0	0	27	23	13	12	19	28	B	R	6-2	210	8-8-66	1988	Sugar Land, Texas
Jones, Bobby	9	9	4.05	30	30	0	0	195	192	94	88	53	115	R	R	6-4	216	2-10-70	1991	Fresno, Calif.
Leiter, Al	17	6	2.47	28	28	4	0	193	151	55	53	71	174	L	L	6-3	220	10-23-65	1984	Plantation, Fla.
McMichael, Greg	5	3	4.02	52	0	0	1	54	64	31	24	29	44	R	R	6-3	222	12-1-66	1988	Alpharetta, Ga.
2-team (12 Los Angeles)	5	4	4.10	64	0	0	2	68	81	39	31	35	55							
Mlicki, Dave	1	4	5.68	10	10	1	0	57	68	38	36	25	39	R	R	6-4	205	6-8-68	1990	Columbus, Ohio
Nomo, Hideo	4	5	4.82	17	16	1	0	90	73	49	48	56	94	R	R	6-2	210	8-31-68	1995	Kobe, Japan
2-team (12 Los Angeles)	6	12	4.92	29	28	3	0	157	130	88	86	94	167							
Pulsipher, Bill	0	0	6.91	15	1	0	0	14	23	11	11	5	13	L	L	6-3	200	10-9-73	1992	Port St. Lucie, Fla.
Reed, Rick	16	11	3.48	31	31	2	0	212	208	84	82	29	153	R	R	6-1	195	8-16-65	1986	Huntington, W.Va.
Reynoso, Armando	7	3	3.82	11	11	0	0	68	64	31	29	32	40	R	R	6-0	196	5-1-66	1989	Lagos de Moreno, Mexico
Rojas, Mel	5	2	6.05	50	0	0	2	58	68	39	39	30	41	R	R	5-11	212	12-10-66	1986	Santo Domingo, D.R.
Tam, Jeff	1	1	6.28	15	0	0	0	14	13	10	10	4	8	R	R	6-1	202	8-19-70	1993	Melbourne, Fla.
Wendell, Turk	5	1	2.93	66	0	0	4	77	62	25	25	33	58	L	R	6-2	205	5-19-67	1988	Denver, Colo.
Yoshii, Masato	6	8	3.93	29	29	1	0	172	166	79	75	53	117	R	R	6-2	210	4-20-65	1998	Tokyo, Japan

Organization Statistics

FIELDING

Catcher	PCT	G	PO	A	E	DP	PB
Castillo	.990	35	193	15	2	3	1
Fabregas	.971	12	62	6	2	2	2
Hundley	1.000	2	18	2	0	0	0
Piazza	.989	99	680	57	8	5	5
Pratt	.973	16	67	4	2	1	2
Spehr	1.000	21	118	10	0	1	1
Tatum	1.000	4	11	3	0	0	0
Wilkins	.957	4	21	1	1	0	0

First Base	PCT	G	PO	A	E	DP
Franco	1.000	11	60	0	0	0
Harris	1.000	1	1	0	0	0
Olerud	.996	157	1257	116	5	119
Paquette	1.000	2	3	0	0	0
Pratt	1.000	3	11	0	0	1
Spehr	1.000	1	2	0	0	0
Tatum	1.000	9	32	1	0	1

Second Base	PCT	G	PO	A	E	DP
Baerga	.986	144	289	341	9	97
Haney	.000	1	0	0	0	0
Harris	1.000	2	1	0	0	0
Lopez	.975	50	73	86	4	16
Milliard	.833	5	3	2	1	0

Third Base	PCT	G	PO	A	E	DP
Alfonzo	.976	144	117	245	9	20
Franco	1.000	13	5	18	0	2
Gilbert	.000	1	0	0	0	0
Harris	.929	10	2	11	1	1
Kinkade	.000	1	0	0	0	0
Lopez	1.000	11	1	12	0	2
Paquette	1.000	4	2	2	0	1
Tatum	1.000	3	2	2	0	0

Shortstop	PCT	G	PO	A	E	DP
Alfonzo	.000	1	0	0	0	0
Lopez	.933	39	36	47	6	17
Milliard	.000	1	0	0	0	0
Ordonez	.975	151	265	398	17	82

Outfield	PCT	G	PO	A	E	DP
Agbayani	1.000	9	6	0	0	0
Allensworth	1.000	31	22	0	0	0
Becker	.984	41	56	4	1	0
Franco	.923	13	11	1	1	0
Gilkey	.992	77	121	9	1	1
Haney	.000	1	0	0	0	0
Harris	.988	65	79	3	1	0
Hundley	.898	34	42	2	5	0
Huskey	.978	103	167	8	4	1
Kirby	1.000	19	15	1	0	1
Lopez	.923	9	12	0	1	0
McRae	.987	154	301	8	4	3
Paquette	.000	1	0	0	0	0
Payton	1.000	9	6	1	0	0
Phillips	.967	51	87	2	3	0
Tatum	1.000	4	6	0	0	0
Wilson	.909	7	10	0	1	0

FARM SYSTEM

Director of Player Development: Jim Duquette

Class	Farm Team	League	W	L	Pct.	Finish*	Manager	First Yr
AAA	Norfolk (Va.) Tides	International	70	72	.493	7th (14)	Rick Dempsey	1969
AA	Binghamton (N.Y.) Mets	Eastern	82	60	.577	2nd (10)	John Gibbons	1992
A#	St. Lucie (Fla.) Mets	Florida State	70	66	.515	+7th (14)	Howie Freiling	1988
A	Capital City (S.C.) Bombers	South Atlantic	90	51	.638	+1st (14)	Doug Davis	1983
A	Pittsfield (N.Y.) Mets	New York-Penn	35	41	.461	t-9th (14)	Roger LaFrancois	1989
Rookie#	Kingsport (Tenn.) Mets	Appalachian	38	30	.559	t-3rd (10)	Tim Foli	1980
Rookie	Port St. Lucie (Fla.) Mets	Gulf Coast	24	35	.407	13th (14)	John Stephenson	1988

*Finish in overall standings (No. of teams in league) #Advanced level +Won league championship

NORFOLK — Class AAA

INTERNATIONAL LEAGUE

BATTING	AVG	G	AB	R	H	2B	3B	HR	RBI	BB	SO	SB	CS	B	T	HT	WT	DOB	1st Yr	Resides
Agbayani, Benny	.283	90	322	43	91	20	5	11	53	50	58	16	6	R	R	6-0	225	12-28-71	1993	Aiea, Hawaii
Azuaje, Jesus	.212	10	33	1	7	3	0	0	1	2	6	0	0	R	R	5-10	170	1-16-73	1992	Bolivar, Ven.
Bell, Mike	.182	17	44	6	8	1	0	2	8	8	7	0	0	R	R	6-2	195	12-7-74	1993	Cincinnati, Ohio
Bowers, Brent	.244	82	275	36	67	8	3	5	31	21	59	17	6	L	R	6-4	215	5-2-71	1989	Bridgeview, Ill.
Carey, Todd	.272	81	246	24	67	18	2	5	29	30	57	3	6	L	R	6-1	180	8-14-71	1992	Cumberland, R.I.
2-team (28 Pawtucket)	.255	109	329	34	84	22	2	9	39	35	70	5	6							
Castillo, Alberto	.184	21	49	4	9	2	0	1	6	11	12	0	0	R	R	6-0	185	2-10-70	1987	Port St. Lucie, Fla.
Chancey, Bailey	.000	2	2	0	0	0	0	0	0	0	2	0	0	B	R	5-8	160	8-25-74	1996	Millbrook, Ala.
Christopherson, Eric	.186	37	97	7	18	4	1	1	13	18	20	1	1	R	R	6-1	190	4-25-69	1990	Westminster, Calif.
Colon, Dennis	.269	51	160	18	43	7	0	0	9	21	21	1	2	L	L	5-10	185	8-4-73	1991	Manati, P.R.
Darden, Tony	.000	1	0	0	0	0	0	0	0	1	0	0	0	R	R	6-0	180	5-29-74	1994	Gilmer, Texas
Decker, Steve	.314	102	354	55	111	21	0	12	60	54	49	0	2	R	R	6-3	220	10-25-65	1988	Keizer, Ore.
Eenhoorn, Robert	.233	94	330	34	77	12	3	7	38	22	44	0	5	R	R	6-3	175	2-9-68	1990	Rotterdam, Holland
Franco, Matt	.368	5	19	2	7	1	0	0	1	3	1	2	0	L	R	6-1	210	8-19-69	1987	Thousand Oaks, Calif.
Gilbert, Shawn	.271	39	133	21	36	8	0	2	12	16	28	7	2	R	R	5-9	185	3-12-65	1987	Glendale, Ariz.
Haney, Todd	.345	117	440	84	152	33	4	3	51	55	44	11	2	R	R	5-9	165	7-30-65	1987	San Antonio, Texas

BATTING	AVG	G	AB	R	H	2B	3B	HR	RBI	BB	SO	SB	CS	B	T	HT	WT	DOB	1st Yr	Resides
Hundley, Todd	.433	10	30	9	13	1	0	4	15	14	10	0	0	B	R	5-11	199	5-27-69	1987	Port St. Lucie, Fla.
Hunter, Scott	.143	7	21	2	3	0	0	0	3	3	5	1	2	R	R	6-1	210	12-17-75	1994	Philadelphia, Pa.
Huskey, Butch	.250	2	8	0	2	0	0	0	3	0	1	0	0	R	R	6-3	244	11-10-71	1989	Lawton, Okla.
Kinkade, Mike	.280	30	125	12	35	5	0	1	18	3	24	6	1	R	R	6-1	210	5-6-73	1995	Tigard, Ore.
2-team (80 Louisville)	.300	110	416	60	125	20	6	8	61	39	76	16	3							
Kirby, Wayne	.309	42	162	32	50	8	3	5	23	21	18	11	5	L	R	5-10	185	1-22-64	1983	Yorktown, Va.
Landry, Todd	.063	9	16	2	1	1	0	0	2	2	4	0	0	R	L	6-4	215	8-21-72	1993	Donaldsonville, La.
Maness, Dwight	.100	6	10	1	1	0	0	0	0	0	4	2	0	R	R	6-3	188	4-3-74	1992	New Castle, Del.
Milliard, Ralph	.259	127	417	73	108	24	4	15	52	79	59	17	6	R	R	5-11	175	12-30-73	1993	Amsterdam, Netherlands
Mora, Melvin	.179	11	28	5	5	1	0	0	2	5	7	0	0	R	R	5-10	160	2-2-72	1991	Naquanqua, Ven.
Morales, Eric	.000	1	1	0	0	0	0	0	0	0	0	0	0	R	R	5-11	178	9-26-73	1992	Orlando, Fla.
Paquette, Craig	.279	15	61	11	17	1	1	3	14	1	13	2	1	R	R	6-0	190	3-28-69	1989	Tempe, Ariz.
Parker, Rick	.244	90	246	38	60	11	2	9	31	35	43	13	6	R	R	6-0	185	3-20-63	1985	Independence, Mo.
Payton, Jay	.261	82	322	45	84	14	4	8	30	26	50	12	7	R	R	5-10	185	11-22-72	1994	Zanesville, Ohio
Plantier, Phil	.143	2	7	0	1	0	0	0	1	0	1	0	0	L	R	5-11	205	1-27-69	1987	Poway, Calif.
Pratt, Todd	.356	35	118	16	42	6	0	7	30	15	19	2	0	R	R	6-3	230	2-9-67	1985	Sunrise, Fla.
Raleigh, Matt	.000	4	4	0	0	0	0	0	0	0	3	0	0	R	R	5-11	235	7-18-70	1992	Harrisburg, Pa.
Sierra, Ruben	.259	28	108	16	28	5	0	3	19	13	18	3	0	B	R	6-1	200	10-6-65	1983	San Juan, P.R.
Spehr, Tim	1.000	1	1	0	1	0	0	0	0	0	0	0	0	R	R	6-2	200	7-2-66	1988	Dallas, Texas
Tamargo, John	.000	3	8	0	0	0	0	0	0	1	3	0	0	B	R	5-9	172	5-3-75	1996	Tampa, Fla.
Wilkins, Rick	.259	45	158	17	41	13	1	1	20	14	37	1	0	L	R	6-2	215	6-4-67	1987	Jacksonville, Fla.
Wilson, Preston	.247	18	73	9	18	5	1	1	9	2	22	1	1	R	R	6-2	193	7-19-74	1993	Eastover, S.C.
Wilson, Vance	.260	46	154	18	40	3	0	4	16	9	29	0	3	R	R	5-11	190	3-17-73	1994	Mesa, Ariz.

PITCHING	W	L	ERA	G	GS	CG	SV	IP	H	R	ER	BB	SO	B	T	HT	WT	DOB	1st Yr	Resides
Arroyo, Luis	0	1	6.75	8	0	0	0	8	11	7	6	7	7	L	L	6-0	174	9-29-73	1992	Bajadero, P.R.
Aucoin, Derek	0	0	.00	3	0	0	0	4	3	0	0	0	5	R	R	6-7	235	3-27-70	1989	Boisbriand, Quebec
Beltran, Rigo	6	5	4.29	36	11	0	1	94	104	51	45	40	98	L	L	5-11	185	11-13-69	1991	San Diego, Calif.
Clontz, Brad	2	4	3.43	28	0	0	0	42	43	26	16	16	49	R	R	6-1	195	4-25-71	1992	Alpharetta, Ga.
Dotel, Octavio	8	6	3.45	17	16	1	0	99	82	47	38	43	118	R	R	6-0	160	11-25-75	1993	Santo Domingo, D.R.
Fernandez, Osvaldo	0	1	5.40	2	0	0	0	3	6	2	2	2	2	L	L	6-0	185	4-15-70	1994	Canoga Park, Calif.
Fyhrie, Mike	3	7	6.64	24	17	0	0	100	115	83	74	45	60	R	R	6-2	190	12-9-69	1991	Westminster, Calif.
Guerra, Mark	2	1	6.46	18	0	0	0	31	40	24	22	14	19	R	R	6-2	200	11-4-71	1994	Pensacola Beach, Fla.
Harris, Gene	0	0	12.00	2	0	0	0	3	3	4	4	4	3	R	R	5-11	195	12-5-64	1986	Okeechobee, Fla.
Henderson, Ryan	0	0	11.25	3	0	0	0	4	6	5	5	6	2	R	R	6-1	190	9-30-69	1992	Dana Point, Calif.
Manzanillo, Josias	4	4	3.24	13	12	1	1	78	77	35	28	31	72	R	R	6-0	190	10-16-67	1983	Hyde Park, Mass.
2-team (19 Durham)	11	10	3.98	32	26	1	2	163	170	92	72	61	133							
Maxcy, Brian	3	0	2.74	28	0	0	0	49	49	25	15	27	39	R	R	6-1	170	5-4-71	1992	Amory, Miss.
Mimbs, Mark	9	2	2.08	15	15	1	0	104	74	30	24	26	92	L	L	6-2	190	2-13-69	1990	Macon, Ga.
Pulido, Carlos	0	0	1.69	3	0	0	0	5	6	1	1	0	6	L	L	6-0	182	8-5-71	1989	Caracas, Ven.
Pulsipher, Bill	7	5	3.96	14	14	1	0	86	91	50	38	41	58	L	L	6-3	200	10-9-73	1992	Port St. Lucie, Fla.
Reynoso, Armando	0	2	10.61	2	2	0	0	9	14	11	11	4	8	R	R	6-0	196	5-1-66	1989	Lagos de Moreno, Mexico
Ruffin, Johnny	1	0	2.77	17	3	0	0	39	31	15	12	20	40	R	R	6-3	170	7-29-71	1988	Butler, Ala.
2-team (35 Louisville)	6	3	2.91	52	5	0	0	99	71	42	32	68	97							
Sauerbeck, Scott	7	13	3.93	27	27	2	0	160	178	82	70	68	119	R	L	6-3	190	11-9-71	1994	Cincinnati, Ohio
Steed, Rick	3	7	4.36	13	9	0	0	54	56	34	26	29	35	R	R	6-2	185	9-8-70	1989	West Covina, Calif.
Stewart, Scott	0	6	6.62	9	9	0	0	52	60	43	38	22	32	R	L	6-2	224	8-14-75	1994	Stanley, N.C.
Tam, Jeff	3	3	1.83	45	0	0	11	64	42	14	13	6	54	R	R	6-1	202	8-19-70	1993	Melbourne, Fla.
Trlicek, Rick	2	2	6.08	19	0	0	3	27	30	20	18	12	21	R	R	6-2	200	4-26-69	1987	Houston, Texas
Turrentine, Rich	0	0	1.42	5	0	0	1	6	4	1	1	2	9	R	R	6-0	220	5-21-71	1989	Texarkana, Ark.
Valdez, Efrain	1	0	3.92	18	0	0	1	21	23	9	9	10	15	L	L	5-11	170	6-11-66	1983	San Carlos, D.R.
Wallace, Derek	5	2	3.88	54	0	0	16	60	58	31	26	27	50	R	R	6-3	215	9-1-71	1992	Oxnard, Calif.
Wilson, Paul	4	1	4.42	7	7	0	0	39	42	19	19	9	30	R	R	6-5	235	3-28-73	1994	Orlando, Fla.

FIELDING

Catcher	PCT	G	PO	A	E	DP	PB
Castillo	.991	17	110	6	1	1	3
Christopherson	.989	30	167	13	2	3	4
Decker	.975	24	146	12	4	2	1
Hundley	.952	3	18	2	1	0	1
Pratt	.988	10	76	6	1	2	1
Wilkins	.995	26	201	12	1	2	0
V. Wilson	.990	44	348	29	4	5	5

First Base	PCT	G	PO	A	E	DP
Agbayani	1.000	4	36	0	0	5
Bell	.000	1	0	0	0	0
Carey	1.000	14	76	15	0	14
Colon	1.000	23	205	15	0	26
Decker	.994	70	580	46	4	65
Franco	1.000	1	9	1	0	2
Kinkade	1.000	2	11	2	0	0
Parker	.913	7	20	1	2	3
Payton	.976	25	227	16	6	23
Pratt	1.000	5	28	0	0	1
Wilkins	.943	6	30	3	2	4

Second Base	PCT	G	PO	A	E	DP
Azuaje	1.000	2	5	3	0	0
Eenhoorn	1.000	1	1	4	0	1
Gilbert	1.000	2	2	1	0	1
Haney	1.000	14	26	39	0	14
Milliard	.980	125	276	373	13	93
Mora	.833	2	4	1	1	0
Parker	1.000	1	2	2	0	0
Tamargo	.846	3	5	6	2	1

Third Base	PCT	G	PO	A	E	DP
Azuaje	1.000	3	5	6	0	1
Bell	.667	14	2	16	9	2
Carey	.873	49	18	78	14	6
Decker	.667	3	0	2	1	0
Franco	1.000	2	4	3	0	1
Gilbert	1.000	3	0	2	0	0
Haney	.919	41	22	69	8	13
Kinkade	.941	28	21	59	5	5
Mora	.857	5	2	4	1	0
Paquette	.906	10	3	26	3	0
Parker	.333	2	0	1	2	1

Shortstop	PCT	G	PO	A	E	DP
Azuaje	.938	4	4	11	1	3
Carey	.947	8	12	24	2	8
Eenhoorn	.968	92	140	285	14	62
Gilbert	.967	9	8	21	1	4
Haney	.942	33	41	73	7	17
Milliard	1.000	1	1	0	0	0
Paquette	.944	4	4	13	1	3

Outfield	PCT	G	PO	A	E	DP
Agbayani	.967	78	115	4	4	0
Bowers	1.000	79	160	2	0	0
Castillo	.000	1	0	0	0	0
Colon	1.000	16	17	0	0	0
Darden	.000	1	0	0	0	0
Franco	.600	2	3	0	2	0
Gilbert	.974	25	36	2	1	0
Haney	.974	27	37	1	1	0
Hundley	1.000	6	4	0	0	0
Hunter	1.000	7	9	0	0	0
Kirby	.987	40	71	5	1	0
Landry	1.000	4	8	0	0	0
Maness	1.000	3	4	0	0	0
Mora	1.000	4	2	1	0	0
Paquette	1.000	1	2	0	0	0
Parker	.974	69	103	9	3	2
Payton	.989	50	88	4	1	2
Pratt	.929	7	11	2	1	0
Sierra	1.000	26	50	1	0	0
Pr. Wilson	.958	18	44	2	2	0

BINGHAMTON — Class AA

EASTERN LEAGUE

BATTING	AVG	G	AB	R	H	2B	3B	HR	RBI	BB	SO	SB	CS	B	T	HT	WT	DOB	1st Yr	Resides
Azuaje, Jesus	.276	110	384	66	106	22	1	7	52	52	48	15	1	R	R	5-10	170	1-16-73	1992	Bolivar, Ven.
Bell, Mike	.265	78	275	47	73	14	1	14	56	35	50	3	5	R	R	6-2	195	12-7-74	1993	Cincinnati, Ohio
Chancey, Bailey	.146	25	48	1	7	2	0	0	2	6	18	0	0	B	R	5-8	160	8-25-74	1996	Millbrook, Ala.
Colon, Dennis	.285	69	256	40	73	14	3	5	37	25	16	5	1	L	L	5-10	185	8-4-73	1991	Manati, P.R.
Darden, Tony	.288	107	320	38	92	19	4	3	36	25	57	5	6	R	R	6-0	180	5-29-74	1994	Gilmer, Texas
Grifol, Pedro	.223	116	394	34	88	18	0	3	57	28	72	2	2	R	R	6-1	197	11-28-69	1991	Miami, Fla.
Hunter, Scott	.314	130	487	80	153	25	3	14	65	47	75	39	15	R	R	6-1	210	12-17-75	1994	Philadelphia, Pa.
Landry, Todd	.274	118	430	54	118	22	3	9	62	37	77	3	1	R	L	6-4	215	8-21-72	1993	Donaldsonville, La.
Long, Terrence	.297	130	455	69	135	20	10	16	58	62	105	23	11	L	L	6-1	190	2-29-76	1994	Millbrook, Ala.
Lopez, Jose	.275	92	327	47	90	23	1	10	51	18	91	7	3	R	R	6-1	175	8-4-75	1994	Haverstraw, N.Y.
Maness, Dwight	.237	27	93	15	22	3	0	3	10	14	28	3	5	R	R	6-3	188	4-3-74	1992	New Castle, Del.
Morales, Eric	.138	39	109	9	15	3	0	0	4	9	29	0	1	R	R	5-11	178	9-26-73	1992	Orlando, Fla.
Neubart, Garrett	.275	109	363	58	100	10	3	3	37	34	65	29	8	R	R	5-10	160	11-7-73	1995	Livingston, N.J.
Polanco, Enohel	.241	26	79	10	19	4	0	0	5	7	27	1	1	R	R	5-11	163	8-11-75	1992	Puerto Plata, D.R.
Raleigh, Matt	.200	47	140	22	28	6	0	6	28	29	60	1	4	R	R	5-11	235	7-18-70	1992	Harrisburg, Pa.
Rodriguez, Sammy	.125	3	8	2	1	0	0	0	1	1	0	0	0	R	R	5-9	185	8-20-75	1995	New York, N.Y.
Sanchez, Yuri	.259	93	316	47	82	14	7	3	26	35	95	11	7	L	R	6-1	165	11-11-73	1992	Lynn, Mass.
Zorrilla, Julio	.250	27	68	7	17	1	0	0	4	7	13	1	4	B	R	5-9	166	2-20-75	1993	San Pedro de Macorio, D.R.

PITCHING	W	L	ERA	G	GS	CG	SV	IP	H	R	ER	BB	SO	B	T	HT	WT	DOB	1st Yr	Resides
Arroyo, Luis	1	5	2.58	57	0	0	3	66	59	30	19	26	78	L	L	6-0	174	9-29-73	1992	Bajadero, P.R.
Arteaga, Ivan	2	1	4.74	23	4	0	1	49	57	28	26	20	40	L	R	6-2	227	7-20-72	1989	Puerto Cabello, Ven.
Arteaga, J.D.	8	7	2.80	21	18	0	0	119	122	48	37	25	97	L	L	6-3	220	8-2-74	1997	Miami, Fla.
Aucoin, Derek	0	0	6.75	12	0	0	0	16	16	12	12	15	18	R	R	6-7	235	3-27-70	1989	Boisbriand, Quebec
Brittan, Corey	1	1	3.86	9	0	0	0	9	9	4	4	4	5	R	R	6-6	196	2-23-75	1996	Scott City, Kan.
Dotel, Octavio	4	2	1.97	10	10	2	0	69	41	19	15	24	82	R	R	6-0	160	11-25-75	1993	Santo Domingo, D.R.
Fernandez, Osvaldo	0	1	4.05	7	1	0	0	13	10	7	6	6	16	L	L	6-0	185	4-15-70	1994	Canoga Park, Calif.
Figueroa, Nelson	12	3	4.66	21	21	3	0	124	133	73	64	44	116	B	R	6-1	155	5-18-74	1995	Brooklyn, N.Y.
Gooch, Arnold	11	14	3.90	27	27	2	0	164	164	92	71	60	116	R	R	6-2	210	11-12-76	1994	Doylestown, Pa.
Guerra, Mark	3	3	2.83	30	2	0	12	41	38	17	13	11	30	R	R	6-2	200	11-4-71	1994	Pensacola Beach, Fla.
Henderson, Ryan	0	3	3.35	29	0	0	4	40	34	18	15	20	39	R	R	6-1	190	9-30-69	1992	Dana Point, Calif.
Landry, Todd	0	0	0.00	4	0	0	0	3	3	0	0	0	4	R	L	6-4	215	8-21-72	1993	Donaldsonville, La.
Lyons, Mike	4	1	3.29	29	0	0	5	38	37	16	14	15	32	R	R	6-3	195	5-20-75	1996	Altamonte Springs, Fla.
McCrary, Scott	1	0	0.00	1	1	0	0	6	1	0	0	1	8	R	R	6-4	204	1-8-74	1997	Vacaville, Calif.
Murray, Dan	11	6	3.18	27	27	1	0	164	153	64	58	54	159	R	R	6-1	193	11-21-73	1995	Garden Grove, Calif.
Pontes, Dan	3	2	2.93	49	0	0	5	55	52	20	18	24	48	R	R	6-3	200	4-27-71	1993	Geneva, N.Y.
Pumphrey, Ken	1	0	4.50	3	2	0	0	8	10	4	4	3	6	R	R	6-6	208	9-10-76	1994	Glen Burnie, Md.
Steed, Rick	2	3	2.74	9	7	0	0	46	37	14	14	18	30	R	R	6-2	185	9-8-70	1989	West Covina, Calif.
Stewart, Scott	8	5	3.70	24	13	0	2	90	91	44	37	29	65	R	L	6-2	224	8-14-75	1994	Stanley, N.C.
Turrentine, Rich	1	2	2.93	28	0	0	10	31	15	10	10	17	35	R	R	6-0	220	5-21-71	1989	Texarkana, Ark.
Vasquez, Leo	1	1	4.60	14	2	0	1	29	28	16	15	25	28	L	L	6-4	190	7-1-73	1996	La Romana, D.R.
Veniard, Jay	1	0	3.94	11	0	0	0	16	17	10	7	10	16	L	L	6-4	215	8-16-74	1995	Jacksonville, Fla.
Yarnall, Ed	7	0	0.39	7	7	0	0	47	20	5	2	17	52	L	L	6-3	234	12-4-75	1997	Coral Springs, Fla.

FIELDING

Catcher	PCT	G	PO	A	E	DP	PB
Grifol	.990	114	897	81	10	11	6
Morales	.988	38	232	25	3	2	7
Rodriguez	1.000	2	19	1	0	0	1

First Base	PCT	G	PO	A	E	DP
Azuaje	1.000	1	1	0	0	0
Colon	.987	27	212	17	3	18
Landry	.992	89	765	60	7	78
Raleigh	.990	31	279	22	3	18
Rodriguez	.000	1	0	0	0	0

Second Base	PCT	G	PO	A	E	DP
Azuaje	.990	66	104	195	3	42
Bell	.957	54	84	114	9	20
Darden	1.000	16	15	40	0	5
Polanco	.667	2	0	2	1	0
Sanchez	.750	2	1	2	1	0
Zorrilla	.915	20	25	50	7	8

Third Base	PCT	G	PO	A	E	DP
Bell	.938	18	8	22	2	0
Darden	.946	55	21	85	6	6
Lopez	.896	79	36	163	23	7
Raleigh	.929	4	1	12	1	1

Shortstop	PCT	G	PO	A	E	DP
Azuaje	.982	39	54	114	3	21
Polanco	.930	23	39	54	7	12
Sanchez	.960	89	113	222	14	62

Outfield	PCT	G	PO	A	E	DP
Azuaje	1.000	4	1	0	0	0
Bell	.889	6	8	0	1	0
Chancey	1.000	12	14	0	0	0
Colon	.984	34	56	4	1	0
Darden	1.000	19	24	2	0	1
Grifol	.000	1	0	0	0	0
Hunter	.979	120	220	9	5	3
Landry	1.000	16	9	0	0	0
Long	.958	128	218	9	10	2
Maness	.953	25	39	2	2	0
Neubart	.971	95	160	9	5	1

ST. LUCIE — Class A

FLORIDA STATE LEAGUE

BATTING	AVG	G	AB	R	H	2B	3B	HR	RBI	BB	SO	SB	CS	B	T	HT	WT	DOB	1st Yr	Resides
Bell, Mike	.349	18	63	11	22	5	2	1	14	8	10	2	1	R	R	6-2	195	12-7-74	1993	Cincinnati, Ohio
Brett, Jason	.333	2	6	1	2	0	0	0	1	0	1	0	0	R	R	6-0	167	4-28-77	1997	Perry, Ga.
Chancey, Bailey	.232	54	168	33	39	5	0	0	10	36	34	27	3	B	R	5-8	160	8-25-74	1996	Millbrook, Ala.
Erickson, Corey	.225	100	346	49	78	23	4	6	33	16	88	5	2	R	R	5-11	190	1-10-77	1995	Springfield, Ill.
Gainey, Bryon	.280	88	336	47	94	15	3	19	57	16	116	1	3	L	R	6-5	215	1-23-76	1994	Mobile, Ala.
Haltiwanger, Garrick	.186	108	344	35	64	11	1	11	42	34	69	7	6	R	L	6-2	190	3-3-75	1996	Irmo, S.C.
Haney, Todd	.250	1	4	1	1	0	0	0	0	0	0	0	0	R	R	5-9	165	7-30-65	1987	San Antonio, Texas
Huff, Brent	.259	118	451	60	117	23	3	11	60	25	108	8	10	R	R	6-1	195	8-1-75	1996	Chandler, Ind.
Hundley, Todd	.214	12	42	4	9	2	0	1	6	12	8	0	1	B	R	5-11	199	5-27-69	1987	Port St. Lucie, Fla.
Lambert, Clark	.000	3	8	0	0	0	0	0	0	0	2	0	0	R	R	6-0	195	5-9-75	1997	Lewisburg, Tenn.
Mora, Melvin	.273	17	55	5	15	0	0	0	8	5	9	1	1	R	R	5-10	160	2-2-72	1991	Naquanqua, Ven.
Parsons, Jeff	.250	27	68	15	17	0	0	1	8	18	12	9	1	R	R	5-10	165	11-16-73	1995	Shawnee, Okla.
Payton, Jay	.143	3	7	0	1	0	0	0	0	3	1	0	0	R	R	5-10	185	11-22-72	1994	Zanesville, Ohio
Phillips, Jason	.464	8	28	4	13	2	0	0	2	2	1	0	0	R	R	6-1	171	9-27-76	1997	El Cajon, Calif.
Polanco, Enohel	.264	75	239	35	63	8	1	2	19	11	38	6	2	R	R	5-11	163	8-11-75	1992	Puerto Plata, D.R.
Pratt, Todd	.450	5	20	2	9	1	0	1	3	1	5	1	0	R	R	6-3	230	2-9-67	1985	Sunrise, Fla.

BATTING	AVG	G	AB	R	H	2B	3B	HR	RBI	BB	SO	SB	CS	B	T	HT	WT	DOB	1st Yr	Resides
Ramirez, Dan	.271	123	469	65	127	17	2	5	50	32	93	27	19	R	R	6-0	180	2-22-74	1992	San Pedro de Macoris, D.R.
Rodriguez, Sammy	.257	53	152	20	39	9	1	2	24	20	36	3	1	R	R	5-9	185	8-20-75	1995	New York, N.Y.
Shuck, Jason	.200	3	5	0	1	0	0	0	0	1	1	0	0	R	R	5-11	165	1-29-79	1997	Mansfield, Ark.
Spehr, Tim	.184	14	38	7	7	2	0	1	6	9	16	0	0	R	R	6-2	200	7-2-66	1988	Dallas, Texas
Tamargo, John	.242	105	347	40	84	24	1	0	33	41	60	14	7	B	R	5-9	172	5-3-75	1996	Tampa, Fla.
Tessmar, Tim	.271	100	377	40	102	21	[illegible]	1	64	[illegible]	72	11	4	L	L	[illegible]	190	[illegible]	[illegible]	Rochester Hills, Mich.
Tyner, Jason	.303	50	201	30	61	2	3	0	16	17	20	15	11	L	L	6-1	170	4-23-77	1998	Beaumont, Texas
Valera, Yohanny	.205	91	298	37	61	21	1	14	42	21	92	1	1	R	R	6-1	196	8-17-76	1993	San Cristobal, D.R.
Wilson, Vance	.063	4	16	0	1	0	0	0	0	0	5	0	0	R	R	5-11	190	3-17-73	1994	Mesa, Ariz.
Zamora, Junior	.285	99	368	58	105	17	4	10	53	25	60	4	3	R	R	6-2	193	5-3-76	1994	San Pedro de Macoris, D.R.
Zorrilla, Julio	.257	37	136	16	35	3	1	2	16	9	20	5	8	B	R	5-9	166	2-20-75	1993	San Pedro de Macoris, D.R.

GAMES BY POSITION: C—Lambert 2, Phillips 8, Pratt 2, Rodriguez 47, Spehr 8, Valera 78, Wilson 4. **1B**—Gainey 76, Huff 3, Pratt 2, Tessmar 69. **2B**—Bell 10, Erickson 41, Haney 1, Mora 8, Shuck 3, Tamargo 52, Zorrilla 32. **3B**—Bell 2, Brett 2, Erickson 54, Parsons 6, Rodriguez 2, Zamora 80. **SS**—Mora 6, Parsons 17, Polanco 74, Tamargo 48. **OF**—Bell 6, Chancey 41, Haltiwanger 92, Huff 102, Hundley 9, Mora 1, Parsons 2, Payton 3, Pratt 1, Ramirez 118, Tyner 49.

PITCHING	W	L	ERA	G	GS	CG	SV	IP	H	R	ER	BB	SO	B	T	HT	WT	DOB	1st Yr	Resides
Arteaga, Ivan	2	1	5.17	9	0	0	0	16	13	10	9	7	8	L	R	6-2	227	7-20-72	1989	Puerto Cabello, Ven.
Arteaga, J.D.	2	0	2.89	15	2	0	0	37	37	15	12	7	28	L	L	6-3	220	8-2-74	1997	Miami, Fla.
Aucoin, Derek	1	0	8.38	8	0	0	0	10	10	9	9	4	13	R	R	6-7	235	3-27-70	1989	Boisbriand, Quebec
Berger, Craig	2	0	1.29	3	0	0	0	7	7	1	1	1	2	R	R	6-4	210	10-20-75	1997	Orefield, Pa.
Brittan, Corey	4	2	3.90	34	0	0	2	67	74	35	29	14	40	R	R	6-6	196	2-23-75	1996	Scott City, Kan.
Cammack, Eric	3	2	2.02	29	0	0	11	36	22	12	8	14	53	R	R	6-1	175	8-14-75	1997	Port Neches, Texas
Corcoran, Tim	0	0	8.22	4	0	0	0	8	10	7	7	2	8	R	R	6-2	195	4-15-78	1997	Slaughter, La.
Gaskill, Derek	0	3	2.89	7	1	0	0	19	16	6	6	3	21	R	R	6-6	191	5-6-74	1992	Chesapeake, Va.
Gonzalez, Dicky	2	1	3.09	8	8	0	0	47	46	22	16	13	23	R	R	5-11	170	10-21-78	1996	Bayamon, P.R.
Gulin, Lindsay	1	1	2.33	6	4	0	0	27	16	9	7	11	19	L	L	6-3	165	11-22-76	1995	Issaquah, Wash.
Hafer, Jeff	3	3	7.99	24	0	0	1	42	63	42	37	11	37	R	R	6-1	185	10-27-74	1996	Springfield, Va.
Herbison, Brett	7	13	5.15	26	25	0	0	147	165	93	84	52	94	R	R	6-5	180	6-13-77	1995	Elgin, Ill.
Kessel, Kyle	2	7	5.14	16	16	0	0	89	101	58	51	27	61	R	L	6-0	160	6-2-76	1994	Mundelein, Ill.
Lohrman, Dave	2	3	6.75	19	1	0	0	31	39	27	23	14	27	R	R	6-6	205	9-16-75	1997	East Amherst, N.Y.
Lyons, Mike	3	2	0.89	28	0	0	9	41	28	12	4	14	27	R	R	6-3	195	5-20-75	1996	Altamonte Springs, Fla.
McCrary, Scott	8	4	2.92	37	4	0	6	92	78	40	30	18	75	R	R	6-4	204	1-8-74	1997	Vacaville, Calif.
McEntire, Ethan	5	4	2.94	22	12	0	0	86	85	38	28	58	52	L	L	6-1	194	7-19-75	1993	Clarkesville, Ga.
Pumphrey, Ken	10	6	3.16	25	25	1	0	142	126	66	50	57	99	R	R	6-6	208	9-10-76	1994	Glen Burnie, Md.
Reynoso, Armando	0	1	3.75	4	4	0	0	12	14	6	5	1	6	R	R	6-0	196	5-1-66	1989	Lagos de Moreno, Mexico
Roberts, Grant	4	5	4.23	17	17	0	0	72	72	37	34	37	70	R	R	6-3	205	9-13-77	1995	El Cajon, Calif.
Seo, Jae	3	1	2.31	8	7	0	0	35	26	13	9	10	37	R	R	6-1	215	5-24-77	1997	La Canada, Calif.
Short, Barry	2	3	4.22	22	0	0	0	43	52	24	20	23	25	R	R	6-3	182	12-15-73	1994	Mansfield, Mo.
Vasquez, Leo	3	2	2.22	24	6	0	4	69	44	20	17	24	46	L	L	6-4	196	7-1-73	1996	La Romana, D.R.
Veniard, Jay	1	1	1.80	12	0	0	1	15	8	5	3	6	10	L	L	6-4	215	8-16-74	1995	Jacksonville, Fla.
Wilson, Paul	0	1	6.38	5	5	0	0	18	23	13	13	4	16	R	R	6-5	235	3-28-73	1994	Orlando, Fla.

CAPITAL CITY — Class A

SOUTH ATLANTIC LEAGUE

BATTING	AVG	G	AB	R	H	2B	3B	HR	RBI	BB	SO	SB	CS	B	T	HT	WT	DOB	1st Yr	Resides
Bennett, Ryan	.286	57	175	20	50	6	1	2	20	18	49	2	0	R	R	6-0	195	7-26-74	1996	Waukegan, Ill.
Bruce, Mo	.341	126	516	81	176	24	4	15	74	41	107	45	15	R	R	5-10	190	5-1-75	1996	Kansas City, Mo.
Burns, Pat	.264	128	477	77	126	25	2	10	61	49	132	16	2	B	L	6-1	195	9-16-77	1996	Denton, Texas
Copeland, Brandon	.241	105	345	58	83	23	0	13	48	52	130	17	4	R	R	6-0	205	3-31-77	1996	Topeka, Kan.
Crespo, Cesar	.252	116	428	61	108	18	4	6	48	44	114	47	14	B	R	5-11	170	5-23-79	1997	Caguas, P.R.
Dina, Allen	.375	2	8	1	3	2	0	0	3	0	1	0	0	R	R	5-10	180	9-28-73	1998	Stratford, Conn.
Escobar, Alex	.310	112	416	90	129	23	5	27	91	54	133	49	7	R	R	6-1	185	9-6-78	1996	Valencia, Ven.
Espada, Angel	.261	40	157	26	41	5	1	0	14	8	15	20	5	R	R	5-9	155	8-15-75	1994	Salinas, P.R.
Johnson, Tom	.232	89	306	54	71	16	5	5	40	27	87	22	7	R	R	6-5	193	1-25-76	1996	Elizabeth, N.J.
Lambert, Clark	.130	11	23	3	3	0	0	0	1	1	6	0	0	R	R	6-0	195	5-9-75	1997	Lewisburg, Tenn.
McGrath, Sean	.172	26	87	6	15	4	0	3	9	3	28	3	2	R	R	6-0	202	4-4-76	1997	North Adams, Mass.
Miller, Kenny	.276	35	116	16	32	4	1	0	9	15	16	4	5	R	R	5-11	170	6-25-76	1997	Joliet, Ill.
Moreno, Juan	.285	113	435	69	124	22	1	10	51	36	98	31	8	R	R	6-2	175	3-19-76	1993	Monte Plata, D.R.
Patton, Cory	.266	55	154	32	41	4	0	1	14	20	43	18	5	R	R	6-2	189	10-18-75	1996	Harrisburg, Ill.
Perez, Jersen	.279	120	488	72	136	18	10	7	64	18	128	14	4	R	R	5-8	178	1-20-76	1996	Lynn, Mass.
Phillips, Jason	.271	69	251	36	68	15	1	5	37	23	35	5	2	R	R	6-1	171	9-27-76	1997	El Cajon, Calif.
Roach, Jason	.277	98	375	55	104	27	1	18	70	30	121	2	1	R	R	6-4	188	4-20-76	1997	Kinston, N.C.
Stanton, Tom	.161	29	87	4	14	3	0	2	15	9	35	0	1	L	R	6-0	208	2-3-76	1996	Middleburg, Fla.

GAMES BY POSITION: C—Bennett 52, Lambert 10, Phillips 68, Stanton 23. **1B**—Burns 114, Roach 25, Stanton 3. **2B**—Bruce 8, Crespo 108, Espada 9, McGrath 16, Moreno 1, Perez 4. **3B**—Bennett 1, Bruce 92, McGrath 5, Perez 8, Roach 40. **SS**—Bruce 3, Crespo 1, Espada 1, McGrath 4, Miller 35, Perez 100. **OF**—Bennett 1, Copeland 102, Dina 2, Escobar 101, Johnson 84, Moreno 102, Patton 42, Roach 1.

PITCHING	W	L	ERA	G	GS	CG	SV	IP	H	R	ER	BB	SO	B	T	HT	WT	DOB	1st Yr	Resides
Barry, Shawn	1	3	2.76	53	0	0	19	62	42	27	19	38	93	L	L	6-3	205	7-15-74	1997	Colchester, Conn.
Behn, Brendan	0	0	1.50	1	1	0	0	6	4	1	1	5	4	L	L	6-1	212	10-10-75	1997	Merced, Calif.
Berger, Craig	2	0	1.23	5	0	0	1	7	8	1	1	0	7	R	R	6-4	210	10-20-75	1997	Orefield, Pa.
Brito, Juan	1	1	3.80	13	0	0	1	24	21	14	10	10	17	L	L	5-10	152	2-10-76	1994	San Pedro de Macoris, D.R.
Cammack, Eric	4	0	2.81	25	0	0	8	32	17	13	10	13	49	R	R	6-1	175	8-14-75	1997	Port Neches, Texas
Corcoran, Tim	2	3	2.61	20	1	0	4	48	43	21	14	15	38	R	R	6-2	195	4-15-78	1997	Slaughter, La.
Cutchins, Todd	9	5	2.77	23	23	0	0	123	113	48	38	47	102	R	L	6-0	190	7-14-75	1996	Westlake, La.
Dougherty, Kevin	15	2	2.74	20	20	1	0	135	112	51	41	50	107	L	L	6-5	218	3-4-78	1997	Voorhees, N.J.
Estrella, Leo	10	8	3.93	20	20	3	0	119	120	66	52	23	97	R	R	6-1	172	2-20-75	1994	Puerto Plata, D.R.
Gaskill, Derek	5	5	5.47	29	7	0	0	82	83	55	50	30	95	R	R	6-6	191	5-6-74	1992	Chesapeake, Va.
Goetz, Geoff	5	4	3.96	15	15	0	0	77	68	45	34	37	68	L	L	5-11	163	4-3-79	1997	Lutz, Fla.
Gonzalez, Dicky	10	3	3.31	18	18	1	0	111	104	57	41	14	107	R	R	5-11	170	10-21-78	1996	Bayamon, P.R.
Gorman, Pat	5	5	5.01	42	0	0	5	70	74	53	39	46	66	R	R	6-2	222	8-16-77	1997	Valley Cottage, N.Y.
Johnston, Sean	2	2	3.35	11	11	0	0	54	54	28	20	31	42	L	L	6-4	187	6-28-76	1994	Highland Park, Ill.

PITCHING	W	L	ERA	G	GS	CG	SV	IP	H	R	ER	BB	SO	B	T	HT	WT	DOB	1st Yr	Resides
Lohrman, Dave	3	1	1.06	21	0	0	4	42	27	14	5	20	53	R	R	6-6	205	9-16-75	1997	East Amherst, N.Y.
Lovingood, Ray	2	1	4.83	6	6	0	0	32	33	20	17	14	27	L	L	6-6	200	4-8-78	1996	Riceville, Tenn.
Maberry, Mark	3	1	2.05	12	0	0	0	22	19	5	5	7	26	R	R	6-3	205	7-31-74	1997	Cookeville, Tenn.
McEntire, Ethan	1	0	0.00	1	1	0	0	5	3	0	0	4	2	L	L	6-1	194	7-19-75	1993	Clarkesville, Ga.
Presley, Kirk	0	0	3.00	3	0	0	0	6	7	5	2	4	9	R	R	6-3	195	4-17-75	1994	Tupelo, Miss.
Queen, Mike	1	0	3.38	2	2	0	0	8	4	4	3	4	9	L	L	6-4	220	12-5-77	1996	Gravette, Ark.
Riggan, Jerrod	4	1	3.70	14	0	0	1	41	38	21	17	14	40	R	R	6-4	185	5-16-74	1996	Brewster, Wash.
Santana, Humberto	0	1	3.31	5	3	0	1	16	14	7	6	3	20	L	L	5-11	175	3-25-77	1995	Puerto Plata, D.R.
Walker, Tyler	5	5	4.12	34	13	0	1	116	122	63	53	38	110	R	R	6-3	250	5-15-76	1997	Ross, Calif.

PITTSFIELD — Short-Season Class A

NEW YORK-PENN LEAGUE

BATTING	AVG	G	AB	R	H	2B	3B	HR	RBI	BB	SO	SB	CS	B	T	HT	WT	DOB	1st Yr	Resides
Bowring, Jason	.228	55	180	23	41	15	0	6	30	18	43	4	1	R	R	6-1	192	5-10-77	1997	San Bernardino, Calif.
Brett, Jason	.315	53	184	40	58	4	0	0	14	11	34	18	3	R	R	6-0	167	4-28-77	1997	Perry, Ga.
Champagne, Andre	.200	5	10	1	2	0	0	1	2	1	2	0	1	R	R	5-7	180	8-30-76	1998	Denver, Colo.
Cole, Brian	.250	2	8	0	2	1	0	0	1	0	1	1	0	R	R	5-9	168	9-28-78	1998	Meridian, Miss.
Dina, Allen	.299	68	278	47	83	16	5	5	39	24	34	18	5	R	R	5-10	180	9-28-73	1990	Stratford, Conn.
Lambert, Clark	.262	18	42	6	11	0	1	0	0	8	9	0	0	R	R	6-0	195	5-9-75	1997	Lewisburg, Tenn.
Ludvigsen, Marc	.202	49	129	14	26	5	1	0	7	6	48	0	0	L	L	6-4	215	5-2-77	1998	Statesville, N.C.
McGrath, Sean	.212	10	33	4	7	2	0	1	1	5	8	1	2	R	R	6-0	202	4-4-76	1997	North Adams, Mass.
Miller, Kenny	.216	68	222	25	48	9	0	1	16	21	42	7	3	R	R	5-11	170	6-25-76	1997	Joliet, Ill.
Mulvehill, Brandon	.252	56	210	24	53	6	6	1	24	9	64	11	4	R	R	6-2	185	2-24-78	1996	Pell City, Ala.
Paciorek, Tom	.107	8	28	5	3	0	0	0	0	0	7	0	0	R	R	6-4	200	1-4-76	1998	Stone Mountain, Ga.
Ramos, Kelly	.298	63	215	31	64	10	6	3	34	13	36	0	1	B	R	6-0	168	10-15-76	1994	San Pedro de Macoris, D.R.
Ribaudo, Mike	.307	39	137	12	42	8	0	3	24	0	26	3	5	R	R	6-2	175	6-21-75	1995	Sarasota, Fla.
Rodriguez, Pedro	.205	57	156	14	32	2	0	0	19	13	34	10	4	L	L	5-11	180	10-10-76	1998	Hialeah, Fla.
Snyder, Earl	.252	71	262	39	66	8	1	11	40	23	60	0	1	R	R	6-0	195	5-6-76	1998	Plainville, Conn.
Stratton, Robert	.226	34	124	18	28	5	4	6	18	11	55	3	2	R	R	6-2	220	10-7-77	1996	Santa Barbara, Calif.
Valentine, Anthony	.201	49	139	22	28	8	0	2	19	20	25	10	1	R	R	5-10	180	1-15-75	1997	Darien, Conn.
Wigginton, Ty	.239	70	272	39	65	14	4	8	29	16	72	11	2	R	R	6-0	190	10-11-77	1998	Chula Vista, Calif.

GAMES BY POSITION: C—Lambert 18, Ramos 57, Ribaudo 14. **1B**—Ludvigsen 1, Snyder 46, Valentine 39. **2B**—Brett 25, Champagne 2, McGrath 4, Wigginton 52. **3B**—Bowring 45, Brett 16, McGrath 3, Ramos 1, Ribaudo 1, Valentine 8, Wigginton 11. **SS**—Brett 10, Champagne 2, McGrath 1, Miller 67. **OF**—Bowring 1, Cole 2, Dina 68, Ludvigsen 38, McGrath 3, Mulvehill 53, Paciorek 8, Rodriguez 54, Snyder 24, Stratton 4, Valentine 1, Wigginton 4.

PITCHING	W	L	ERA	G	GS	CG	SV	IP	H	R	ER	BB	SO	B	T	HT	WT	DOB	1st Yr	Resides
Behn, Brendan	3	5	3.53	14	14	1	0	79	80	41	31	39	59	L	L	6-1	212	10-10-75	1997	Merced, Calif.
Bellhorn, Todd	3	4	3.56	15	12	0	0	68	69	31	27	20	60	R	L	6-0	210	10-13-76	1998	Oviedo, Fla.
Berger, Craig	3	3	2.32	23	0	0	7	50	54	21	13	11	43	R	R	6-4	210	10-20-75	1997	Orefield, Pa.
Berthelot, Eric	0	3	4.85	4	3	0	0	13	21	15	7	8	5	R	L	6-4	205	6-31-72	1997	Metairie, La.
Brito, Juan	3	0	9.31	10	0	0	0	19	21	20	20	9	7	L	L	5-10	152	2-10-76	1994	San Pedro de Macoris, D.R.
Carr, Timothy	0	5	5.81	23	1	0	1	48	54	44	31	29	37	R	R	6-2	180	12-20-77	1996	Westlake Village, Calif.
Cook, Andy	5	3	3.73	15	11	0	0	70	78	36	29	20	54	R	R	6-5	195	2-26-77	1998	Danville, Va.
Gresko, Michael	0	1	9.22	9	0	0	0	14	25	17	14	12	11	L	L	6-8	200	10-27-76	1996	Trenton, N.J.
2 team (5 Erie)	0	1	13.50	14	0	0	0	19	39	33	29	21	19							
Lovingood, Ray	0	2	8.10	13	4	0	0	27	29	24	24	15	17	L	L	6-6	200	4-8-78	1996	Riceville, Tenn.
Mattson, John	6	4	5.20	18	9	0	2	71	76	47	41	20	52	R	R	6-4	205	10-1-76	1997	Port Orchard, Wash.
Princi, Peter	1	3	5.75	22	0	0	3	41	47	31	26	22	38	R	R	6-3	187	2-4-76	1998	Cambridge, Mass.
Prokop, Michael	1	2	2.74	26	0	0	7	43	42	18	13	8	36	R	R	6-1	190	1-28-78	1998	Kennesaw, Ga.
Saenz, Jason	2	3	6.75	12	7	0	0	44	56	37	33	23	34	L	L	6-2	195	2-13-77	1998	Santa Ana, Calif.
Santana, Humberto	3	2	3.30	14	13	0	0	71	69	32	26	18	60	L	L	5-11	175	3-25-77	1995	Puerto Plata, D.R.
Vega, Rene	1	0	1.69	2	0	0	0	5	2	1	1	1	6	L	L	5-10	185	8-4-76	1998	Mobile, Ala.
Weslowski, Robert	1	1	11.05	2	2	0	0	7	10	11	9	5	3	R	R	6-2	165	9-23-78	1997	Marcellus, N.Y.

KINGSPORT — Rookie

APPALACHIAN LEAGUE

BATTING	AVG	G	AB	R	H	2B	3B	HR	RBI	BB	SO	SB	CS	B	T	HT	WT	DOB	1st Yr	Resides
Alvarez, Nelson	.229	21	48	8	11	1	3	0	4	4	15	1	1	R	R	6-0	175	9-27-78	1997	Orangeburg, N.Y.
Champagne, Andre	.180	42	133	19	24	6	1	0	13	15	13	4	1	R	R	5-7	180	8-30-76	1998	Denver, Colo.
Chavez, Endy	.289	33	114	26	33	8	4	0	16	17	17	10	5	L	L	6-0	170	2-7-78	1996	Valencia, Ven.
Cole, Brian	.300	56	230	36	69	13	8	5	35	7	23	15	8	R	R	5-9	168	9-28-78	1998	Meridian, Miss.
Durick, Chad	.190	11	42	6	8	2	1	1	6	3	11	0	2	R	R	6-0	175	12-28-76	1996	Port St. Lucie, Fla.
Gobbel, Gene	.307	48	150	28	46	7	0	6	19	19	28	14	4	R	R	6-3	200	8-21-76	1998	Lexington, S.C.
Guzman, Yorkis	.318	42	132	20	42	5	5	5	26	5	23	5	1	R	R	6-0	175	8-2-78	1996	Monte Cristi, D.R.
Hill, Bobby	.271	57	181	33	49	12	4	2	28	13	25	9	4	L	R	5-9	160	6-25-79	1997	Waldo, Fla.
Jenkins, Brian	.259	55	201	31	52	10	2	5	25	18	17	8	5	R	R	5-11	195	10-11-78	1997	Port St. Joe, Fla.
Johnson, Tony	.242	58	182	35	44	7	2	8	30	28	48	7	6	B	R	5-10	189	10-11-77	1996	Oakland, Calif.
Martin, Billy	.308	61	214	43	66	19	0	7	42	22	58	1	1	R	R	6-2	205	6-10-76	1998	Abilene, Texas
Meadows, Mike	.253	51	170	33	43	10	0	6	31	19	57	4	2	R	R	6-1	185	10-19-78	1996	Sanford, Fla.
Paciorek, Tom	.265	42	151	20	40	12	3	4	22	8	31	3	1	R	R	6-4	200	1-4-76	1998	Stone Mountain, Ga.
Proctor, Mark	.263	14	38	3	10	0	0	1	4	1	9	0	3	R	R	6-3	180	9-14-79	1997	Fredericksburg, Va.
Prosper, Gerard	.233	16	43	7	10	2	0	0	3	5	7	1	0	L	L	5-11	172	2-10-78	1997	Ocean Reef, Australia
Stoffels, Alex	.292	41	137	23	40	7	1	0	18	13	29	4	5	R	R	5-10	190	6-12-77	1998	San Bernardino, Calif.
Taylor, Joshua	.264	36	91	13	24	4	1	0	4	13	21	2	1	R	R	5-9	170	5-1-77	1997	Shawnee, Okla.
Velazquez, Gil	.103	12	29	2	3	1	0	0	4	2	7	2	0	R	R	6-2	170	10-17-79	1998	South Gate, Calif.

GAMES BY POSITION: C—Alvarez 16, Guzman 25, Stoffels 40. **1B**—Durick 4, Jenkins 9, Martin 9, Meadows 47, Paciorek 2. **2B**—Champagne 25, Gobbel 11, Hill 28, Taylor 16. **3B**—Champagne 4, Durick 1, Gobbel 10, Martin 43, Proctor 14, Taylor 9, Velazquez 1. **SS**—Champagne 8, Gobbel 28, Hill 24, Taylor 11, Velazquez 12. **OF**—Alvarez 1, Champagne 9, Chavez 16, Cole 55, Durick 3, Guzman 15, Hill 3, Jenkins 38, Johnson 36, Paciorek 36, Prosper 15, Stoffels 1.

PITCHING	W	L	ERA	G	GS	CG	SV	IP	H	R	ER	BB	SO	B	T	HT	WT	DOB	1st Yr	Resides
Bell, Heath	1	0	2.54	22	0	0	8	46	40	15	13	11	61	R	R	6-2	225	9-29-77	1998	Tustin, Calif.
Bohannon, Gary	6	3	2.56	10	10	1	0	59	56	19	17	5	49	R	R	6-4	175	2-19-76	1998	Harrison, Tenn.
Brito, Juan	0	2	6.57	10	0	0	0	25	30	19	18	6	20	L	L	5-10	152	2-10-76	1994	San Pedro de Macoris, D.R.
Driscoll, Randy	4	1	3.48	23	0	0	1	41	39	24	16	18	42	R	R	6-2	170	6-26-75	1998	Pittsfield, Mass.
Encarnacion, Orlando	6	1	4.56	16	16	1	0	71	71	39	36	25	40	R	R	6-0	202	3-1-79	1997	Bronx, N.Y.
German, Yon	6	5	2.34	13	13	0	0	77	63	31	20	12	75	L	L	5-11	155	2-28-78	1995	Bani, D.R.
Krystofoski, Jay	1	1	4.76	8	0	0	0	11	11	10	6	5	11	R	R	6-3	190	2-23-76	1998	Middletown, Conn.
Kurtz, Justin	1	3	5.91	17	2	0	1	35	47	25	23	21	37	R	R	6-0	175	3-8-77	1998	Orlando, Fla.
Lowe, Matt	2	4	6.42	13	8	0	0	41	50	40	29	21	31	R	R	6-4	220	4-3-79	1997	Walhalla, S.C.
Maness, Nick	5	3	4.48	13	13	0	0	64	68	41	32	30	76	R	R	6-4	195	10-17-78	1997	Robbins, N.C.
Mikkola, Shaun	0	0	6.35	4	0	0	0	6	8	4	4	5	4	R	R	6-1	190	8-3-79	1997	Largo, Fla.
Montada, Joaquin	0	0	3.86	1	0	0	0	2	1	2	1	1	4	R	R	6-2	175	8-19-77	1997	Hialeah, Fla.
Suggs, Willie	0	5	4.72	15	7	0	0	48	46	29	25	36	44	R	R	6-3	200	8-25-78	1996	Mount Vernon, Ill.
Vega, Rene	3	2	5.63	22	2	0	5	40	46	32	25	17	42	L	L	5-10	185	8-4-76	1998	Mobile, Ala.
Wheeler, David	3	0	1.44	19	0	0	5	31	12	7	5	9	26	R	R	6-2	185	2-11-76	1998	Spokane, Wash.

PORT ST. LUCIE — Rookie

GULF COAST LEAGUE

BATTING	AVG	G	AB	R	H	2B	3B	HR	RBI	BB	SO	SB	CS	B	T	HT	WT	DOB	1st Yr	Resides
Alvarez, Nelson	.321	16	56	3	18	2	1	2	6	2	11	0	0	R	R	6-0	175	9-27-78	1997	Orangeburg, N.Y.
Brazell, Craig	.298	13	47	6	14	3	1	1	6	2	13	0	0	L	R	6-3	185	5-10-80	1998	Montgomery, Ala.
Gainey, Bryon	.107	8	28	2	3	0	0	1	1	0	11	0	0	L	R	6-5	215	1-23-76	1994	Mobile, Ala.
Garcia, Alfredo	.280	54	200	42	56	13	4	7	35	14	34	20	2	R	R	6-1	175	2-21-78	1995	La Romana, D.R.
Guzman, Yorkis	.000	1	5	0	0	0	0	0	0	0	0	0	0	R	R	6-0	175	8-2-78	1996	Montecristi, D.R.
Hendricks, Ian	.263	45	152	18	40	14	3	0	14	6	48	2	3	R	R	6-0	170	11-28-76	1998	Randallstown, Md.
Hundley, Todd	.000	1	2	0	0	0	0	0	0	2	1	0	0	B	R	5-11	199	5-27-69	1987	Port St. Lucie, Fla.
Hunter, David	.143	27	70	6	10	2	0	0	4	4	30	0	0	L	L	6-5	210	5-26-80	1998	Delano, Calif.
Lopez, Jose	.211	5	19	2	4	3	0	1	6	0	5	0	0	B	R	6-2	165	7-13-79	1998	Santo Domingo, D.R.
Lugo, Roberto	.098	35	82	6	8	2	0	0	6	10	20	0	0	L	L	6-3	200	3-7-80	1998	San Sebastian, P.R.
Malinowski, Scott	.260	35	104	10	27	5	0	0	6	5	9	0	0	L	R	6-2	170	9-23-76	1998	Joliet, Ill.
Osborn, Jason	.245	19	53	3	13	2	0	0	4	1	12	0	0	R	R	6-2	190	5-28-80	1998	Bellingham, Wash.
Perich, Josh	.233	35	116	8	27	4	2	2	13	8	32	0	1	R	R	6-4	210	11-15-79	1998	Allentown, Pa.
Pratt, Todd	.250	2	4	1	1	0	0	0	0	4	1	0	0	R	R	6-3	230	2-9-67	1985	Sunrise, Fla.
Proctor, Mark	.184	20	49	3	9	1	2	0	2	2	5	0	3	R	R	6-3	180	9-14-79	1997	Fredericksburg, Va.
Prosper, Gerard	.241	11	29	5	7	0	0	0	0	4	7	0	1	L	L	5-11	172	2-10-78	1997	Ocean Reef, Australia
Rains, Nick	.261	12	23	5	6	1	1	0	2	1	10	2	1	R	R	6-1	170	8-12-78	1997	Fort Pierce, Fla.
Seale, Marvin	.220	37	132	24	29	4	5	0	7	10	40	11	3	B	R	6-0	190	6-16-79	1998	Durango, Colo.
Seo, Jae Hwan	.296	11	27	5	8	0	1	2	4	7	9	1	0	R	R	5-10	175	11-24-75	1997	Sed Ku, Korea
Shuck, Jason	.271	46	170	21	46	10	0	0	16	11	34	7	5	R	R	5-11	165	1-29-79	1997	Mansfield, Ark.
Smith, Ryan	.172	31	93	8	16	5	1	0	9	3	15	1	0	R	R	5-10	180	6-20-79	1998	Mobile, Ala.
Stratton, Robert	.261	12	46	4	12	1	0	3	13	2	15	1	0	R	R	6-2	220	10-7-77	1996	Santa Barbara, Calif.
Velazquez, Gil	.186	33	97	7	18	3	0	0	7	8	10	2	1	R	R	6-2	170	10-17-79	1998	South Gate, Calif.
Wilson, Vance	.357	10	28	5	10	5	0	2	9	0	0	0	1	R	R	5-11	190	3-17-73	1994	Mesa, Ariz.
Yancy, Michael	.212	42	137	15	29	2	1	1	12	7	27	2	5	R	R	5-11	180	3-26-79	1997	San Diego, Calif.
Zamora, Junior	.200	2	5	1	1	0	1	0	2	1	0	0	0	R	R	6-2	193	5-3-76	1994	San Pedro de Macoris, D.R.
Zardis, Alex	.186	27	86	8	16	4	0	0	3	3	17	0	0	R	R	6-3	190	2-17-78	1998	Seattle, Wash.
Zorrilla, Julio	.211	10	38	4	8	0	0	0	2	1	4	1	0	B	R	5-9	166	2-20-75	1993	San Pedro de Macoris, D.R.

GAMES BY POSITION: C—Alvarez 11, Brazell 2, Osborn 17, Pratt 1, Smith 30, Wilson 9. **1B**—Brazell 4, Gainey 8, Hunter 24, Lugo 33, Proctor 1, Rains 1, Zardis 1. **2B**—Hendricks 10, Malinowski 12, Proctor 1, Shuck 23, Velazquez 1, Zardis 10, Zorrilla 10. **3B**—Hendricks 29, Lopez 5, Malinowski 7, Osborn 1, Proctor 11, Shuck 2, Zamora 2, Zardis 9. **SS**—Malinowski 15, Proctor 8, Seale 2, Shuck 7, Velazquez 32. **OF**—Garcia 51, Hundley 1, Lugo 2, Perich 24, Pratt 1, Prosper 11, Rains 5, Seale 35, Seo 3, Shuck 13, Stratton 5, Yancy 37, Zardis 4.

PITCHING	W	L	ERA	G	GS	CG	SV	IP	H	R	ER	BB	SO	B	T	HT	WT	DOB	1st Yr	Resides
Aucoin, Derek	0	0	5.63	5	0	0	0	8	5	6	5	3	16	R	R	6-7	235	3-27-70	1989	Boisbriand, Quebec
Chivers, Jason	3	5	3.71	12	10	0	0	53	52	34	22	20	40	L	L	6-6	235	12-19-78	1997	Lancaster, Calif.
Gomez, Rafael	3	0	3.86	13	2	0	2	28	22	16	12	6	22	R	R	6-1	180	9-18-77	1995	Barahona, D.R.
Graham, Frank	0	1	4.09	3	2	0	0	11	6	5	5	5	14	R	R	6-2	180	8-7-78	1998	Johnstown, Ohio
Hafer, Jeff	0	0	3.52	4	4	0	0	8	8	3	3	1	6	R	R	6-1	185	10-27-74	1996	Springfield, Va.
Hee, Aaron	3	1	3.19	18	1	0	0	31	34	14	11	11	30	L	L	6-0	175	3-4-79	1998	Las Vegas, Nev.
Kessel, Kyle	1	1	0.64	4	4	0	0	14	5	4	1	5	19	R	L	6-0	160	6-2-76	1994	Mundelein, Ill.
Krystofoski, Jay	0	0	10.13	1	1	0	0	3	7	3	3	2	1	R	R	6-3	190	2-23-76	1998	Middletown, Conn.
Mangieri, John	1	1	6.61	16	1	0	1	31	35	29	23	20	15	R	R	6-2	196	9-24-76	1997	Howard Beach, N.Y.
Mikkola, Shaun	1	4	4.85	10	5	0	0	39	43	23	21	23	20	R	R	6-1	190	8-3-79	1997	Largo, Fla.
Moses, Stephen	0	2	4.35	14	0	0	2	20	16	11	10	14	18	R	R	6-1	185	7-7-74	1998	Ipswich, Mass.
Nunez, Jose	3	7	2.38	13	11	1	0	68	60	26	18	12	69	L	L	6-2	165	3-14-79	1996	Montecristi, D.R.
Palacios, Refugio	1	1	7.71	5	3	1	0	14	23	17	12	7	10	R	R	6-2	195	7-4-77	1998	Nayarit, Mexico
Pidgeon, Chip	0	3	9.00	16	0	0	0	25	34	27	25	13	21	R	L	6-5	250	12-26-78	1997	Shoreham, N.Y.
Rondon, Gabriel	2	1	0.50	8	1	0	3	18	10	2	1	1	17	R	R	6-1	180	9-29-77	1995	Monagas, Ven.
Seo, Jae Weong	0	0	0.00	2	0	0	0	5	4	0	0	0	5	R	R	6-1	215	5-24-77	1997	La Canada, Calif.
Sexton, Patrick	0	1	6.23	10	0	0	5	13	16	13	9	7	10	R	R	6-6	200	9-9-75	1998	Sumter, S.C.
Strange, Pat	1	1	1.42	4	4	0	0	19	18	3	3	7	19	R	R	6-5	240	8-23-80	1998	Springfield, Mass.
Ushiromatsu, Juei	0	2	4.85	16	0	0	0	26	39	19	14	11	27	L	L	6-1	165	9-21-79	1997	Akita, Japan
Weslowski, Robert	5	3	2.54	11	10	1	0	60	59	25	17	20	37	R	R	6-2	165	9-23-78	1997	Marcellus, N.Y.

OAKLAND ATHLETICS

Young nucleus arrives, provides hope for franchise in '99

BY CASEY TEFERTILLER

Through six consecutive losing seasons, the Athletics had been waiting for the good times to return to Oakland. What happened in 1998 provided some expectation that there was at least a flicker of hope for contending in the future.

The A's have slowly been attempting to rebuild the organization around a nucleus of young stars that could make it a power in the 21st century. With the likes of Eric Chavez, Ryan Christenson, Jason Giambi, Ben Grieve, A.J. Hinch and Miguel Tejada beginning to blossom, the A's believe they have the pieces in place to start construction.

The last three seasons under manager Art Howe have been an arduous and patient attempt to develop talent at the major league level, and 1998 was no different. The A's finished fourth in the American League West, being passed by the Mariners near the end of the schedule.

Up to the all-star break there were flurries when the team showed signs of contending, but overall inexperience and defensive lapses led to the slide to the bottom of the division. An inconsistent bullpen helped create many happy endings for Oakland's opponents. The team hit an AL-worst .257, down from .268 at the all-star break.

With the A's, the whole thrust is toward the future. Chavez was named Baseball America's Minor League Player of the Year, and Grieve put together one of the top rookie seasons in all of baseball, though he slumped in the second half. Giambi finally had a breakout year, hitting .295 with 25 home runs.

Young pitchers Jimmy Haynes and Blake Stein, though inconsistent, showed flashes that they may emerge as solid starters in the future. Equally important is that the A's still have a farm system loaded with young players who could provide an impact in the future. Pitchers Eric DuBose, Chris Enochs and Tim Hudson are on the verge of moving to the majors.

The A's also have high hopes for lefthander Mark Mulder, whom they signed after a prolonged negotiation period. Mulder, the second overall pick in the 1998 draft, signed for $3.2 million in early October.

The A's will enter the future without their longtime general manager Sandy Alderson, who left to take a position as executive vice president with Major League Baseball. Alderson guided the team for 17 years, through three AL championships, and held various administrative titles.

While his talents will be missed, Alderson oversaw the placement of a number of people who will guide the organization in the future, notably general manager Billy Beane, scouting director Grady Fuson and director of player development Keith Lieppman. Assurances have been made by managing partner Steve Schott that the payroll, a paltry $17 million in '98, will be expanded during the next two years.

The A's are on the cusp of maturing into contenders, and the big decision on the field will fall to Schott and his partner Ken Hofman, who must decide whether they are willing to pull the trigger and spend the money to bring players who can complement the emerging young stars. If the A's spend wisely and a little more freely, there is good reason to believe that 1998 provided a basis of experience for a team close to contending in the AL West.

Kenny Rogers

Eric Chavez

JOHN SPEAR

Players of the Year

Major League: Kenny Rogers, lhp

Rogers resurrected his career with a 16-win season for the Athletics. His 3.17 ERA was third in the American League.

Minor League: Eric Chavez, 3b, Edmon./Hunts.

BA's Minor League Player of the Year, Chavez combined to hit .327-33-126 at two levels.

ORGANIZATION LEADERS

BATTING		
*AVG	Eric Byrnes, Visalia/Southern Oregon	.357
R	Eric Chavez, Edmonton/Huntsville	104
H	Eric Chavez, Edmonton/Huntsville	173
TB	Eric Chavez, Edmonton/Huntsville	319
2B	Eric Chavez, Edmonton/Huntsville	45
3B	Esteban German, AZL Athletics	10
HR	Eric Chavez, Edmonton/Huntsville	33
RBI	Eric Chavez, Edmonton/Huntsville	126
BB	Rob DeBoer, Visalia	97
SO	Rob DeBoer, Visalia	157
SB	Kerwin Moore, Huntsville	43
PITCHING		
W	Two tied at	14
L	Bill King, Edmonton	13
#ERA	Juan Perez, Edmonton/Huntsville	2.81
G	Tim Kubinski, Edmonton	57
CG	Gil Heredia, Edmonton	6
SV	Kevin Gunther, Huntsville/Modesto	14
IP	Brett Laxton, Edmonton/Huntsville	176
BB	Brett Laxton, Edmonton/Huntsville	103
SO	Jay Witasick, Edmonton	155

*Minimum 250 At-Bats #Minimum 75 Innings

Organization Statistics

Oakland ATHLETICS

Manager: Art Howe

1998 Record: 74-88, .457 (4th, AL West)

BATTING	AVG	G	AB	R	H	2B	3B	HR	RBI	BB	SO	SB	CS	B	T	HT	WT	DOB	1st Yr	Resides
Abbott, Kurt	.268	35	123	17	33	7	1	2	9	10	34	2	1	R	R	6-0	190	6-2-69	1989	Davie, Fla.
Bellhorn, Mark	.083	11	12	1	1	1	0	0	1	3	4	2	0	B	R	6-1	190	8-23-74	1995	Oviedo, Fla.
Blowers, Mike	.237	129	409	56	97	24	2	11	71	39	116	1	0	R	R	6-2	210	4-24-65	1986	Tacoma, Wash.
Bournigal, Rafael	.225	85	209	23	47	11	0	1	19	10	11	6	1	R	R	5-11	176	5-12-66	1987	Lakeland, Fla.
Chavez, Eric	.311	16	45	6	14	4	1	0	6	3	5	1	1	L	R	6-1	195	12-7-77	1996	San Diego, Calif.
Christenson, Ryan	.257	117	370	56	95	22	2	5	40	36	106	5	6	R	R	5-11	175	3-28-74	1995	Apple Valley, Calif.
Giambi, Jason	.295	153	562	92	166	28	0	27	110	81	102	2	2	L	R	6-3	235	1-8-71	1992	Palm Desert, Calif.
Grieve, Ben	.288	155	583	94	168	41	2	18	89	85	123	2	2	L	R	6-4	226	5-4-76	1994	Arlington, Texas
Henderson, Rickey	.236	152	542	101	128	16	1	14	57	118	114	66	13	R	L	5-10	190	12-25-58	1976	Hillsborough, Calif.
Hinch, A.J.	.231	120	337	34	78	10	0	9	35	30	89	3	0	R	R	6-1	205	5-15-74	1996	Midwest City, Okla.
Lesher, Brian	.143	7	7	0	1	1	0	0	1	0	3	0	0	R	L	6-5	216	3-5-71	1992	Scottsdale, Ariz.
Mack, Shane	.000	3	2	1	0	0	0	0	0	0	0	0	0	R	R	6-0	190	12-7-63	1985	Las Vegas, Nev.
Macfarlane, Mike	.251	78	207	28	52	12	0	7	34	12	34	1	0	R	R	6-1	210	4-12-64	1985	Overland Park, Kan.
2-team (3 K.C.)	.243	81	218	29	53	12	0	7	34	12	36	1	0							
Magadan, Dave	.321	35	109	12	35	8	0	1	13	13	12	0	1	L	R	6-4	215	9-30-62	1983	Tampa, Fla.
McDonald, Jason	.251	70	175	25	44	9	0	1	16	27	33	10	4	B	R	5-7	182	3-20-72	1993	Sacramento, Calif.
Mitchell, Kevin	.228	51	127	14	29	7	1	2	21	9	26	0	0	R	R	5-11	210	1-13-62	1981	Chula Vista, Calif.
Molina, Izzy	.500	6	2	1	1	0	0	0	0	0	0	0	0	R	R	5-11	224	6-3-71	1990	Miami, Fla.
Neill, Mike	.267	6	15	2	4	1	0	0	0	2	4	0	0	L	L	6-2	190	4-27-70	1991	Seaford, Del.
Roberts, Bip	.280	61	182	28	51	11	0	1	15	15	24	10	3	B	R	5-7	165	10-27-63	1982	Poway, Calif.
2-team (34 Detroit)	.268	95	295	45	79	17	0	1	24	31	38	16	4							
Spiezio, Scott	.259	114	406	54	105	19	1	9	50	44	56	1	3	B	R	6-2	222	9-21-72	1993	Morris, Ill.
Sprague, Ed	.149	27	87	8	13	5	0	3	7	2	17	1	0	R	R	6-2	205	7-25-67	1989	Stockton, Calif.
2-team (105 Toronto)	.222	132	469	57	104	25	0	20	58	26	90	1	2							
Stairs, Matt	.294	149	523	88	154	33	1	26	106	59	93	8	3	L	R	5-9	206	2-27-69	1989	Stanley, New Brunswick
Tejada, Miguel	.233	105	365	53	85	20	1	11	45	28	86	5	6	R	R	5-9	192	5-25-76	1994	Bani, D.R.
Velandia, Jorge	.250	8	4	0	1	0	0	0	0	0	1	0	0	R	R	5-9	160	1-12-75	1992	Caracas, Ven.
Voigt, Jack	.139	57	72	7	10	4	0	1	10	6	19	5	1	R	R	6-1	178	5-17-66	1987	Venice, Fla.
Wood, Jason	.000	3	1	1	0	0	0	0	0	0	1	0	0	R	R	6-1	170	12-16-69	1991	Fresno, Calif.

PITCHING	W	L	ERA	G	GS	CG	SV	IP	H	R	ER	BB	SO	B	T	HT	WT	DOB	1st Yr	Resides
Candiotti, Tom	11	16	4.84	33	33	3	0	201	222	124	108	63	98	R	R	6-2	221	8-31-57	1979	Clayton, Calif.
Connelly, Steve	0	0	1.93	3	0	0	0	5	10	1	1	4	1	R	R	6-4	210	4-27-74	1995	Long Beach, Calif.
Dougherty, Jim	0	2	8.25	9	0	0	0	12	17	11	11	7	3	R	R	6-0	210	3-8-68	1991	Kitty Hawk, N.C.
Fetters, Mike	1	6	3.99	48	0	0	5	47	48	26	21	21	34	R	R	6-4	226	12-19-64	1986	Gilbert, Ariz.
Groom, Buddy	3	1	4.24	75	0	0	0	57	62	30	27	20	36	L	L	6-2	208	7-10-65	1987	Waxahachie, Texas
Haynes, Jimmy	11	9	5.09	33	33	1	0	194	229	124	110	88	134	R	R	6-3	180	9-5-72	1991	La Grange, Ga.
Heredia, Gil	3	3	2.74	8	6	0	0	43	43	14	13	3	27	R	R	6-1	195	10-26-65	1987	Tucson, Ariz.
Holzemer, Mark	1	0	5.59	13	0	0	0	10	13	6	6	3	3	L	L	6-0	165	8-20-69	1988	Littleton, Colo.
Mathews, T.J.	7	4	4.58	66	0	0	1	73	71	44	37	29	53	R	R	6-2	200	1-19-70	1992	Columbia, Ill.
Mohler, Mike	3	3	5.16	57	0	0	0	61	70	38	35	26	42	R	L	6-2	208	7-26-68	1990	Gonzales, La.
Oquist, Mike	7	11	6.22	31	29	0	0	175	210	125	121	57	112	R	R	6-2	189	5-30-68	1989	La Junta, Colo.
Prieto, Ariel	0	1	11.88	2	2	0	0	8	17	11	11	5	8	R	R	6-2	245	10-22-66	1995	Miami, Fla.
Rogers, Kenny	16	8	3.17	34	34	7	0	239	215	96	84	67	138	L	L	6-1	205	11-10-64	1982	Tampa, Fla.
Small, Aaron	1	1	7.25	24	0	0	0	36	51	34	29	14	19	R	R	6-5	226	11-23-71	1989	Loudon, Tenn.
Stein, Blake	5	9	6.37	24	20	1	0	117	117	92	83	71	89	R	R	6-7	210	8-3-73	1994	Folsom, La.
Taylor, Billy	4	9	3.58	70	0	0	33	73	71	37	29	22	58	R	R	6-8	230	10-16-61	1980	Thomasville, Ga.
Telgheder, Dave	0	1	3.60	8	2	0	0	20	19	12	8	6	5	R	R	6-2	223	11-11-66	1989	Slate Hill, N.Y.
Witasick, Jay	1	3	6.33	7	3	0	0	27	36	24	19	15	29	R	R	6-4	210	8-28-72	1993	Bel Air, Md.
Worrell, Tim	0	1	4.00	25	0	0	0	36	34	17	16	8	33	R	R	6-4	215	7-5-67	1990	Glendale, Ariz.
3-team (15 Det./3 Cle.)	2	7	5.24	43	9	0	0	103	106	62	60	29	82							

FIELDING

Catcher	PCT	G	PO	A	E	DP	PB
Hinch	.986	118	602	47	9	8	8
Macfarlane	.989	70	355	20	4	6	5
Molina	1.000	5	8	1	0	0	0

First Base	PCT	G	PO	A	E	DP
Blowers	1.000	8	47	0	0	3
Giambi	.990	146	1258	71	14	120
Lesher	.000	1	0	0	1	0
Magadan	1.000	7	33	3	0	3
Mitchell	1.000	2	5	0	0	1
Sprague	1.000	1	1	0	0	0
Stairs	1.000	6	45	8	0	6
Voigt	.987	27	73	2	1	8

Second Base	PCT	G	PO	A	E	DP
Bellhorn	.000	1	0	0	0	0
Bournigal	1.000	48	55	81	0	20
Roberts	.970	30	38	58	3	18
Spiezio	.975	112	195	316	13	71
Velandia	1.000	1	1	3	0	0

Third Base	PCT	G	PO	A	E	DP
Abbott	.000	1	0	0	0	0
Bellhorn	1.000	5	3	7	0	0
Blowers	.927	120	66	174	19	14
Chavez	1.000	13	11	21	0	2
Magadan	.918	30	15	52	6	7
Roberts	1.000	3	3	3	0	0
Sprague	.909	23	23	37	6	2
Voigt	1.000	2	0	1	0	0
Wood	1.000	1	0	1	0	0

Shortstop	PCT	G	PO	A	E	DP
Abbott	.909	28	40	70	11	16
Bellhorn	.000	2	0	0	0	0
Bournigal	1.000	38	53	89	0	18
Tejada	.950	104	173	325	26	74
Velandia	.916	7	4	7	1	1
Wood	1.000	2	1	2	0	1

Outfield	PCT	G	PO	A	E	DP
Abbott	1.000	5	6	0	0	0
Christenson	.983	116	284	7	5	2
Grieve	.993	151	262	8	2	0
Henderson	.988	151	326	3	4	1
Lesher	1.000	4	4	2	0	1
McDonald	.956	60	122	7	6	1
Mitchell	1.000	10	10	0	0	0
Neill	1.000	6	14	0	0	0
Roberts	.952	22	40	0	2	0
Stairs	1.000	12	23	3	0	0
Voigt	1.000	20	29	2	0	0

FARM SYSTEM

Director of Player Development: Keith Lieppman

Class	Farm Team	League	W	L	Pct.	Finish*	Manager	First Yr
AAA	Edmonton (Alberta) Trappers	Pacific Coast	76	67	.531	8th (16)	Mike Quade	1995
AA	Huntsville (Ala.) Stars	Southern	72	68	.514	3rd (10)	Jeffrey Leonard	1985
A#	Modesto (Calif.) A's	California	77	63	.550	5th (10)	Juan Navarrete	1975
A#	Visalia (Calif.) Oaks	California	67	73	.479	6th (10)	Tony DeFrancesco	1997
A	Southern Oregon Timberjacks	Northwest	43	33	.566	3rd (8)	Greg Sparks	1979
Rookie	Scottsdale (Ariz.) Athletics	Arizona	29	27	.518	4th (8)	John Kuehl	1988

*Finish in overall standings (No. of teams in league) #Advanced level

EDMONTON — Class AAA

PACIFIC COAST LEAGUE

BATTING	AVG	G	AB	R	H	2B	3B	HR	RBI	BB	SO	SB	CS	B	T	HT	WT	DOB	1st Yr	Resides
Abbott, Kurt	.400	7	25	5	10	2	0	2	4	6	8	0	1	R	R	6-0	190	6-2-69	1989	Davie, Fla.
Bellhorn, Mark	.249	87	309	57	77	20	4	10	44	62	90	6	2	B	R	6-1	190	8-23-74	1995	Oviedo, Fla.
Berryhill, Damon	.257	21	74	8	19	9	0	0	14	10	13	0	0	B	R	6-0	205	12-3-63	1984	Laguna Niguel, Calif.
Chavez, Eric	.325	47	194	38	63	18	0	11	40	12	32	2	3	L	R	6-1	195	12-7-77	1996	San Diego, Calif.
Christenson, Ryan	.261	22	88	17	23	6	1	1	7	15	24	4	1	R	R	5-11	175	3-28-74	1995	Apple Valley, Calif.
Cromer, D.T.	.294	125	504	75	148	30	3	16	85	32	93	12	6	L	L	6-2	190	3-19-71	1992	Lexington, S.C.
Lesher, Brian	.300	99	360	62	108	31	1	11	60	46	96	3	4	R	L	6-5	216	3-5-71	1992	Scottsdale, Ariz.
Martins, Eric	.279	39	129	14	36	8	0	3	16	9	22	1	0	R	R	5-9	170	11-19-72	1994	Rowland Heights, Calif.
McDonald, Jason	.233	12	43	12	10	1	1	2	5	15	11	7	0	B	R	5-7	182	3-20-72	1993	Sacramento, Calif.
McKay, Cody	.228	19	57	6	13	3	0	0	5	7	5	1	0	L	R	6-0	190	1-11-74	1996	Scottsdale, Ariz.
Menechino, Frank	.278	106	378	72	105	11	7	10	40	70	75	9	10	R	R	5-9	175	1-7-71	1993	Staten Island, N.Y.
Mitchell, Kevin	.348	6	23	4	8	2	0	0	1	1	2	0	1	R	R	5-11	210	1-13-62	1981	Chula Vista, Calif.
Molina, Izzy	.241	86	303	29	73	15	2	8	38	17	60	3	0	R	R	5-11	224	6-3-71	1990	Miami, Fla.
Morales, Willie	.194	73	242	25	47	13	0	5	30	17	47	0	1	R	R	5-10	182	9-7-72	1993	Tucson, Ariz.
Neill, Mike	.302	99	371	72	112	18	4	10	48	65	91	6	5	L	L	6-2	190	4-27-70	1991	Seaford, Del.
Sheff, Chris	.299	120	402	74	120	24	4	10	55	67	82	17	5	R	R	6-3	215	2-4-71	1992	Laguna Hills, Calif.
Spiezio, Scott	.231	5	13	3	3	1	0	1	4	3	2	0	0	B	R	6-2	222	9-21-72	1993	Morris, Ill.
Tejada, Miguel	.000	1	3	0	0	0	0	0	0	1	1	0	0	R	R	5-9	192	5-25-76	1994	Bani, D.R.
Tyler, Brad	.267	131	430	68	115	24	4	18	75	62	107	10	1	L	R	6-2	180	3-3-69	1990	Aurora, Ind.
Velandia, Jorge	.287	128	488	64	140	35	1	6	57	37	52	8	6	R	R	5-9	160	1-12-75	1992	Caracas, Ven.
Voigt, Jack	.324	18	68	10	22	6	0	4	11	8	15	1	2	R	R	6-1	178	5-17-66	1987	Venice, Fla.
Wood, Jason	.280	80	307	52	86	20	0	18	73	37	71	1	1	R	R	6-1	170	12-16-69	1991	Fresno, Calif.

PITCHING	W	L	ERA	G	GS	CG	SV	IP	H	R	ER	BB	SO	B	T	HT	WT	DOB	1st Yr	Resides
Abbott, Todd	0	0	.00	3	0	0	0	5	3	0	0	1	4	R	R	6-4	200	9-13-73	1995	Fayetteville, Ark.
Adams, Willie	0	0	12.27	2	2	0	0	4	8	5	5	1	1	R	R	6-7	225	10-8-72	1993	Scottsdale, Ariz.
Carroll, Dave	0	1	12.54	7	0	0	0	9	22	16	13	5	11	R	L	6-3	205	7-23-72	1993	Fairfax, Va.
Connelly, Steve	6	0	3.79	55	0	0	13	76	64	34	32	24	62	R	R	6-4	210	4-27-74	1995	Long Beach, Calif.
Dale, Carl	5	3	4.08	11	11	1	0	64	64	31	29	26	41	R	R	6-2	215	12-7-72	1994	Cookeville, Tenn.
Dougherty, Jim	2	1	3.75	45	0	0	6	58	57	24	24	33	45	R	R	6-0	210	3-8-68	1991	Kitty Hawk, N.C.
Hansell, Greg	0	0	1.23	13	0	0	6	15	13	2	2	3	16	R	R	6-5	224	3-12-71	1989	La Palma, Calif.
Haught, Gary	1	0	7.55	19	0	0	0	31	43	27	26	14	20	B	R	6-1	190	9-29-70	1992	Choctaw, Okla.
Heredia, Gil	10	8	3.67	29	19	6	1	145	154	69	59	18	99	R	R	6-1	195	10-26-65	1987	Tucson, Ariz.
Holzemer, Mark	1	1	3.23	30	0	0	6	39	41	15	14	11	27	L	L	6-0	165	8-20-69	1988	Littleton, Colo.
Jones, Marcus	2	0	2.53	2	2	0	0	11	14	7	3	5	4	R	R	6-5	235	3-29-75	1997	Yorba Linda, Calif.
King, Bill	8	13	6.56	24	22	0	0	121	162	95	88	42	57	R	R	6-5	215	2-18-73	1994	Chipley, Fla.
Kubinski, Tim	6	5	4.54	57	1	0	2	75	77	40	38	22	54	L	L	6-4	205	1-20-72	1993	San Luis Obispo, Calif.
Laxton, Brett	2	4	6.60	8	8	0	0	46	45	35	34	24	21	L	R	6-2	205	10-5-73	1996	Audubon, N.J.
Leyva, Julian	0	1	.00	1	0	0	0	3	3	3	0	0	3	L	R	6-0	200	2-11-78	1996	Riverside, Calif.
Manwiller, Tim	1	0	.82	2	0	0	0	11	8	1	1	2	10	R	R	6-2	205	9-5-74	1997	Annville, Pa.
Mathews, Terry	2	2	4.57	13	8	0	1	43	47	22	22	11	33	L	R	6-2	225	10-5-64	1987	Alexandria, La.
Nelson, Chris	0	1	14.46	4	1	0	0	9	16	16	15	8	4	B	R	6-2	180	1-26-73	1995	San Diego, Calif.
Nina, Elvin	0	0	.00	1	0	0	0	0	1	0	0	2	0	R	R	6-0	185	11-25-75	1997	East Orange, N.J.
Pavlas, Dave	2	2	3.10	26	3	0	1	58	51	23	20	12	41	R	R	6-7	205	8-12-62	1985	Shiner, Texas
2-team (9 Tucson)	2	4	3.80	35	3	0	2	66	66	34	28	17	49							
Perez, Juan	3	4	3.12	24	0	0	1	40	35	17	14	18	37	L	L	6-0	155	3-28-73	1992	La Romana, D.R.
Price, Jamey	0	0	1.29	2	2	0	0	7	6	1	1	0	6	L	R	6-7	220	2-11-72	1996	Pine Bluff, Ark.
Prieto, Ariel	5	1	2.56	10	10	1	0	53	47	20	15	12	50	R	R	6-2	245	10-22-66	1995	Miami, Fla.
Rigby, Brad	5	6	5.94	13	13	0	0	70	86	52	46	17	34	R	R	6-6	213	5-14-73	1994	Altamonte Springs, Fla.
Roberts, Chris	0	4	5.86	18	8	0	0	51	55	39	33	28	44	R	L	5-10	185	6-25-71	1992	Middleburg, Fla.
Stein, Blake	3	1	3.47	5	4	0	0	23	22	13	9	11	31	R	R	6-7	210	8-3-73	1994	Folsom, La.
Telgheder, Dave	1	2	7.31	3	3	0	0	16	26	14	13	3	9	R	R	6-2	223	11-11-66	1989	Slate Hill, N.Y.
Witasick, Jay	11	7	3.87	27	26	2	0	149	126	74	64	49	155	R	R	6-4	210	8-28-72	1993	Bel Air, Md.

FIELDING

Catcher	PCT	G	PO	A	E	DP	PB
Berryhill	1.000	5	39	2	0	0	0
McKay	1.000	3	16	0	0	0	0
Molina	.981	77	525	42	11	6	6
Morales	.988	64	357	39	5	2	3

First Base	PCT	G	PO	A	E	DP
Bellhorn	1.000	1	2	0	0	1
Berryhill	1.000	1	2	0	0	0
Cromer	.988	115	1015	89	13	113
Lesher	.976	16	120	3	3	15
Molina	.964	3	24	3	1	4
Morales	1.000	4	29	1	0	4
Voigt	.984	7	59	4	1	1

Second Base	PCT	G	PO	A	E	DP
Bellhorn	.994	34	63	110	1	24
Martins	.933	4	7	7	1	2
Menechino	.979	74	133	192	7	48
Spiezio	.889	4	5	3	1	1
Tyler	.970	14	32	32	2	11
Wood	.983	21	46	69	2	20

Third Base	PCT	G	PO	A	E	DP
Bellhorn	.919	44	27	86	10	9
Chavez	.935	46	34	66	7	8
Martins	.750	2	1	2	1	0
McKay	1.000	1	2	1	0	0
Tyler	.846	10	5	17	4	3
Wood	.949	41	23	89	6	9

Shortstop	PCT	G	PO	A	E	DP
Abbott	.846	6	9	13	4	4
Bellhorn	1.000	3	3	9	0	2
Martins	.833	1	1	4	1	1
Tejada	1.000	1	0	5	0	0
Valandia	[illegible]	[illegible]	[illegible]	[illegible]	[illegible]	[illegible]
Wood	.960	7	7	17	1	3

Outfield	PCT	G	PO	A	E	DP
Christenson	1.000	22	56	2	0	1
Cromer	.600	5	3	0	2	0
Lesher	.982	72	104	3	2	0
Martins	1.000	6	5	0	0	0
McDonald	1.000	[illegible]	[illegible]	[illegible]	0	[illegible]
Molina	.000	1	0	0	0	0
Neill	.971	96	165	5	5	1
Sheff	.993	118	262	10	2	3
Tyler	1.000	101	181	10	0	1
Voigt	1.000	0	0	0	0	0
Wood	.938	11	15	0	1	0

HUNTSVILLE — Class AA

SOUTHERN LEAGUE

BATTING	AVG	G	AB	R	H	2B	3B	HR	RBI	BB	SO	SB	CS	B	T	HT	WT	DOB	1st Yr	Resides
Ardoin, Danny	.248	109	363	67	90	21	0	16	62	62	87	8	4	R	R	6-0	205	7-8-74	1995	Ville Platte, La.
Bowles, Justin	.277	74	274	50	76	21	1	10	48	37	60	2	1	L	L	6-0	185	8-20-73	1996	Lake Jackson, Texas
Castro, Jose	.163	55	147	24	24	4	2	2	16	25	48	12	1	B	R	5-10	160	10-15-74	1994	Villa Vasquez, D.R.
Chavez, Eric	.328	88	335	66	110	27	1	22	86	42	61	12	4	L	R	6-1	195	12-7-77	1996	San Diego, Calif.
Encarnacion, Mario	.272	110	357	70	97	15	2	15	61	60	123	11	8	R	R	6-2	187	9-24-77	1994	Bani, D.R.
Espada, Josue	.255	51	161	29	41	7	1	1	22	27	15	7	4	R	R	5-10	175	8-30-75	1996	Carolina, P.R.
Garrison, Webster	.271	104	295	47	80	15	0	11	51	51	56	1	3	R	R	5-11	170	8-24-65	1984	Marrero, La.
Hernandez, Ramon	.296	127	479	83	142	24	1	15	98	57	61	4	5	R	R	6-0	203	5-20-76	1994	Caracas, Ven.
Luderer, Brian	.289	17	38	4	11	1	1	0	5	3	7	0	0	R	R	5-11	180	8-19-78	1996	Tarzana, Calif.
Marcinczyk, T.R.	.269	131	501	90	135	25	2	26	88	51	127	2	6	R	R	6-2	195	10-11-73	1996	Plainville, Conn.
Martins, Eric	.303	70	234	45	71	15	1	3	24	34	32	6	4	R	R	5-9	170	11-19-72	1994	Rowland Heights, Calif.
McDonald, Jason	.300	7	20	9	6	2	0	2	4	8	6	4	0	B	R	5-7	182	3-20-72	1993	Sacramento, Calif.
McKay, Cody	.286	9	21	5	6	0	0	1	1	6	5	0	0	L	R	6-0	190	1-11-74	1996	Scottsdale, Ariz.
Moore, Kerwin	.214	116	341	63	73	12	4	1	35	88	97	43	14	B	R	6-1	190	10-29-70	1988	Detroit, Mich.
Neill, Mike	.257	12	35	1	9	5	0	0	2	4	13	0	0	L	L	6-2	190	4-27-70	1991	Seaford, Del.
Ortiz, Santos	.277	94	354	70	98	24	2	6	55	48	63	22	8	R	R	5-9	160	6-13-77	1995	Santo Domingo, D.R.
Slemmer, Dave	.250	49	176	24	44	6	0	3	20	20	30	3	1	R	R	6-0	187	3-29-73	1995	Edwardsville, Ill.
Tejada, Miguel	.327	15	52	9	17	6	0	2	7	4	8	1	0	R	R	5-9	192	5-25-76	1994	Bani, D.R.
Vaz, Roberto	.295	131	457	54	135	18	5	8	62	56	63	23	16	L	L	5-9	195	3-15-75	1997	Tuscaloosa, Ala.

PITCHING	W	L	ERA	G	GS	CG	SV	IP	H	R	ER	BB	SO	B	T	HT	WT	DOB	1st Yr	Resides
Anderson, Jason	1	1	5.29	3	3	1	0	17	16	15	10	11	14	L	L	6-2	195	4-6-76	1997	Salem, Va.
Baez, Benito	3	8	5.80	34	17	0	0	123	161	92	79	64	83	L	L	6-0	160	5-6-77	1994	Bonao, D.R.
Bennett, Tom	1	1	10.16	28	0	0	3	34	19	41	38	67	43	R	R	6-4	180	5-13-76	1995	Alameda, Calif.
Berry, Jason	2	0	4.22	13	0	0	0	21	26	11	10	5	18	R	R	6-3	210	4-2-74	1993	Brockton, Mass.
Carroll, Dave	1	0	2.38	20	0	0	3	34	26	9	9	13	34	R	L	6-3	205	7-23-72	1993	Fairfax, Va.
D'Amico, Jeff	5	5	7.67	24	8	0	0	61	77	57	52	34	46	R	R	6-3	195	11-9-74	1993	Seattle, Wash.
Dale, Carl	1	1	4.61	3	3	0	0	14	13	7	7	8	10	R	R	6-2	215	12-7-72	1994	Cookeville, Tenn.
Della Ratta, Pete	0	1	11.25	5	0	0	0	8	21	12	10	4	3	R	R	6-4	220	2-14-74	1996	Gulf Breeze, Fla.
DuBose, Eric	7	6	2.70	14	14	1	0	83	86	37	25	34	66	L	L	6-3	215	5-15-76	1997	Nashville, Tenn.
Enochs, Chris	9	10	4.74	26	26	0	0	148	159	101	78	64	100	R	R	6-3	225	10-11-75	1997	Newell, W.Va.
Gunther, Kevin	3	5	5.64	45	0	0	12	67	107	66	42	20	40	R	R	6-0	200	2-6-73	1995	Yelm, Wash.
Harville, Chad	0	0	2.45	12	0	0	8	15	6	4	4	13	24	R	R	5-9	180	9-16-76	1997	Savannah, Tenn.
Hudson, Tim	10	9	4.54	22	22	2	0	135	136	84	68	71	104	R	R	6-0	160	7-14-75	1997	Salem, Ala.
Kjos, Ryan	1	0	5.40	9	0	0	0	13	9	8	8	12	7	R	R	6-5	217	3-4-73	1995	Hopkins, Minn.
Laxton, Brett	11	4	3.40	21	21	0	0	130	109	64	49	79	82	L	R	6-2	205	10-5-73	1996	Audubon, N.J.
Nelson, Chris	3	4	6.45	28	10	0	0	84	111	70	60	39	62	B	R	6-2	180	1-26-73	1995	San Diego, Calif.
O'Dell, Jake	2	5	5.17	27	9	0	0	78	84	54	45	30	69	R	R	6-1	205	9-22-73	1996	Round Rock, Texas
Perez, Juan	3	2	2.45	27	0	0	8	37	29	13	10	16	37	L	L	6-0	155	3-28-73	1992	La Romana, D.R.
Rivette, Scott	6	4	4.61	35	0	0	2	68	75	46	35	32	53	B	R	6-2	200	2-8-74	1995	Upland, Calif.
Smith, Andy	0	0	10.13	7	0	0	0	11	15	13	12	8	10	R	R	6-5	210	1-29-75	1993	Kannapolis, N.C.
Vizcaino, Luis	3	2	4.66	7	7	0	0	39	43	27	20	22	26	R	R	6-1	170	6-10-77	1995	Bani, D.R.

FIELDING

Catcher	PCT	G	PO	A	E	DP	PB
Ardoin	.985	85	555	86	10	8	15
Hernandez	.987	51	341	32	5	0	6
Luderer	.977	8	40	3	1	0	1
McKay	1.000	1	7	3	0	0	0

First Base	PCT	G	PO	A	E	DP
Ardoin	.500	1	2	0	2	0
Garrison	1.000	4	35	4	0	5
Hernandez	.970	22	183	10	6	16
Marcinczyk	.985	110	957	71	16	103
McKay	1.000	4	29	0	0	3
Slemmer	1.000	4	24	2	0	2
Vaz	.950	3	19	0	1	2

Second Base	PCT	G	PO	A	E	DP
Castro	.900	3	2	7	1	0
Garrison	.969	34	68	89	5	22
Martins	.989	37	72	105	2	30
Ortiz	.965	60	107	172	10	40
Slemmer	.960	21	41	54	4	8

Third Base	PCT	G	PO	A	E	DP
Castro	.898	13	9	35	5	1
Chavez	.935	79	54	146	14	13
Garrison	.969	35	28	67	3	8
Luderer	1.000	1	1	0	0	0
Marcinczyk	.912	11	9	22	3	1
McKay	1.000	3	1	6	0	0
Slemmer	.853	12	10	19	5	3

Shortstop	PCT	G	PO	A	E	DP
Castro	.930	31	33	99	10	20
Espada	.951	46	57	116	9	23
Martins	.929	39	39	92	10	20
McKay	1.000	1	1	1	0	0
Ortiz	.901	35	52	102	17	21
Tejada	.922	13	18	41	5	16

Outfield	PCT	G	PO	A	E	DP
Ardoin	1.000	2	3	1	0	0
Bowles	.969	69	118	6	4	2
Castro	1.000	5	4	0	0	0
Encarnacion	.969	94	181	8	6	1
Garrison	.958	25	21	2	1	1
Luderer	.000	1	0	0	0	0
Martins	.000	1	0	0	0	0
McDonald	1.000	5	10	1	0	0
McKay	.000	1	0	0	0	0
Moore	.961	103	192	7	8	2
Neill	1.000	9	21	1	0	1
Ortiz	.000	1	0	0	0	0
Slemmer	.963	16	22	4	1	0
Vaz	.962	125	218	9	9	0

MODESTO — Class A

CALIFORNIA LEAGUE

BATTING	AVG	G	AB	R	H	2B	3B	HR	RBI	BB	SO	SB	CS	B	T	HT	WT	DOB	1st Yr	Resides
Castro, Jose	.218	57	197	23	43	11	5	1	18	28	66	10	3	B	R	5-10	160	10-15-74	1994	Villa Vasquez, D.R.
Clifton, Rodney	.270	118	433	71	117	30	6	9	67	52	106	11	5	R	R	6-2	188	11-7-76	1996	Elgin, Ill.
Cosme, Caonabo	.275	124	414	48	114	24	3	2	41	27	137	16	7	R	R	6-2	190	3-18-79	1996	La Vega, D.R.
Davis, Josh	.250	51	124	13	31	3	0	1	10	16	34	4	0	R	R	6-0	185	6-13-76	1994	Locust Grove, Okla.
Davis, Monty	.304	78	280	48	85	16	3	8	44	23	45	11	5	R	R	6-1	195	12-25-77	1996	Vernon, B.C.
DaVanon, Jeff	.336	84	301	66	101	17	4	5	60	59	69	33	10	B	R	6-0	185	12-8-73	1995	Del Mar, Calif.

BATTING	AVG	G	AB	R	H	2B	3B	HR	RBI	BB	SO	SB	CS	B	T	HT	WT	DOB	1st Yr	Resides
Haynes, Nathan	.252	125	507	89	128	13	7	1	41	54	139	42	18	L	L	5-9	170	9-7-79	1997	Hercules, Calif.
Jones, Tim	.207	66	184	35	38	9	1	5	23	48	88	11	8	L	R	6-0	208	9-13-77	1995	Buena Park, Calif.
Luderer, Brian	.133	19	45	3	6	2	2	0	3	4	6	0	0	R	R	5-11	180	8-19-78	1996	Tarzana, Calif.
Martinez, Hipolito	.226	111	340	51	77	21	3	9	52	40	112	11	10	R	R	6-1	210	1-30-77	1994	Bani, D.R.
McKay, Cody	.284	107	402	59	114	25	1	6	58	40	62	2	4	L	R	6-0	190	1-11-74	1996	Scottsdale, Ariz.
Mensik, Todd	.274	111	379	56	104	26	2	14	59	63	103	1	4	L	L	6-2	195	2-27-75	1996	Orland Park, Ill.
Miller, Kevin	.230	39	126	20	29	3	2	1	13	12	35	3	0	R	R	6-1	205	6-20-77	1998	Seattle, Wash.
Pecci, Jay	.315	21	73	9	23	2	1	1	6	4	11	2	1	B	R	5-11	185	9-26-76	1998	Novato, Calif.
Piatt, Adam	.288	133	500	91	144	40	3	20	107	80	99	20	6	R	R	6-2	195	2-8-76	1997	Fort Myers, Fla.
Romano, Scott	.220	36	127	18	28	8	2	1	16	13	24	0	1	R	R	6-1	185	8-3-71	1989	Tampa, Fla.
Wolff, Mike	.291	102	320	46	93	21	1	6	46	35	38	3	1	L	L	6-3	205	2-17-73	1994	Granger, Ind.

GAMES BY POSITION: C—J. Davis 50, Luderer 17, McKay 93. **1B**—M. Davis 2, Martinez 3, McKay 2, Mensik 71, Romano 2, Wolff 85. **2B**—Castro 31, Cosme 62, M. Davis 34, Piatt 2, Romano 22. **3B**—M. Davis 4, Luderer 1, McKay 16, Piatt 125, Romano 5. **SS**—Castro 29, Cosme 62, Miller 37, Pecci 21, Piatt 3. **OF**—Clifton 109, DaVanon 73, Haynes 123, Jones 46, Martinez 94, Wolff 1.

PITCHING	W	L	ERA	G	GS	CG	SV	IP	H	R	ER	BB	SO	B	T	HT	WT	DOB	1st Yr	Resides
Abreu, Oscar	2	2	7.78	34	0	0	1	57	56	51	49	54	68	R	R	6-1	175	2-21-76	1994	Santo Domingo, D.R.
Anderson, Jason	9	4	3.46	28	24	1	0	146	147	67	56	53	110	L	L	6-2	195	4-6-76	1997	Salem, Va.
Blumenstock, Brad	2	2	8.67	15	5	0	1	36	58	40	35	22	29	R	R	6-6	225	2-19-75	1996	Marion, Ill.
Carroll, Dave	1	4	3.03	22	0	0	4	33	34	21	11	22	29	R	L	6-3	205	7-23-72	1993	Fairfax, Va.
Dale, Carl	1	2	2.37	3	3	0	0	19	15	6	5	2	14	R	R	6-2	215	12-7-72	1994	Cookeville, Tenn.
Gregg, Kevin	8	7	3.81	30	24	0	1	144	139	72	61	76	141	R	R	6-6	200	6-20-78	1996	Corvallis, Ore.
Gunther, Kevin	0	0	1.80	4	0	0	2	5	4	2	1	0	4	R	R	6-0	200	2-6-73	1995	Yelm, Wash.
Hudson, Tim	4	0	1.67	8	5	0	0	38	19	10	7	18	48	R	R	6-0	160	7-14-75	1997	Salem, Ala.
Kimball, Andrew	5	6	4.44	42	8	0	12	97	113	62	48	29	96	R	R	6-0	190	8-23-75	1997	Oshkosh, Wis.
Leyva, Julian	11	7	3.60	28	21	1	1	138	156	70	55	25	92	L	R	6-0	200	2-11-78	1996	Riverside, Calif.
Manwiller, Tim	13	6	3.17	30	21	1	1	156	150	69	55	46	129	R	R	6-2	205	9-5-74	1997	Annville, Pa.
McCall, Travis	6	2	1.84	20	0	0	4	29	17	7	6	10	25	L	L	5-11	185	12-20-77	1996	Chino Hills, Calif.
Paulino, Jose	2	4	5.53	38	0	0	1	70	79	57	43	28	53	R	R	6-3	170	1-24-77	1994	San Cristobal, D.R.
Pena, Juan	3	2	5.18	6	6	0	0	33	50	25	19	7	32	L	L	6-3	195	6-4-79	1996	Santo Domingo, D.R.
Schultz, Jeff	0	1	4.32	19	0	0	3	33	34	26	16	19	32	R	R	6-1	200	5-22-76	1998	Long Beach, Calif.
Snow, Bert	1	1	3.12	2	2	0	0	9	12	8	3	6	12	R	R	6-1	190	3-23-77	1998	Brooksville, Fla.
Vizcaino, Luis	6	3	2.74	23	16	0	0	102	72	39	31	43	108	R	R	6-1	170	6-10-77	1995	Bani, D.R.
Waites, David	1	2	5.56	22	0	0	3	23	29	18	14	16	25	R	R	6-3	220	2-2-76	1997	Albuquerque, N.M.
Wallace, Flint	2	8	5.04	32	5	0	1	61	68	38	34	22	55	R	R	6-1	185	7-21-74	1996	Clyde, Texas

VISALIA — Class A

CALIFORNIA LEAGUE

BATTING	AVG	G	AB	R	H	2B	3B	HR	RBI	BB	SO	SB	CS	B	T	HT	WT	DOB	1st Yr	Resides
Byrnes, Eric	.426	29	108	26	46	9	2	4	21	18	15	11	1	R	R	6-2	200	2-16-76	1998	Woodside, Calif.
Camilo, Juan	.223	85	220	29	49	9	0	4	27	35	75	5	4	L	R	6-0	205	6-24-78	1996	Santo Domingo, D.R.
Cesar, Dionys	.281	130	501	87	141	34	8	7	54	56	98	31	12	B	R	5-10	155	9-27-76	1994	Santo Domingo, D.R.
DeBoer, Rob	.279	125	409	83	114	25	1	15	66	97	157	6	5	R	R	5-10	205	2-4-71	1994	Omaha, Neb.
Farris, Ed	.120	9	25	2	3	0	0	0	1	1	7	0	0	L	R	6-0	205	6-3-74	1997	Harrison, Ohio
Filchner, Duane	.298	64	218	34	65	18	2	2	31	30	29	1	1	L	L	6-1	185	2-28-73	1995	Northampton, Pa.
Flores, Javier	.252	49	163	19	41	7	1	2	17	12	32	0	0	R	R	6-0	185	12-20-75	1997	Broken Arrow, Okla.
Jenkins, Dee	.261	65	268	37	70	16	3	8	37	23	67	12	6	L	R	5-9	175	6-28-73	1991	Columbia, S.C.
2-team (50 Stockton)	.265	115	434	61	115	24	4	12	49	42	115	18	9							
Koerner, Mike	.231	113	360	50	83	20	3	13	62	30	104	6	9	L	L	6-0	190	3-28-76	1997	Turnersville, N.J.
Lara, Eddie	.289	122	447	63	129	18	6	6	62	29	65	12	12	B	R	5-9	145	10-30-75	1993	Bani, D.R.
Robinson, Adam	.233	82	296	54	69	13	3	0	26	43	89	14	4	R	R	6-0	185	6-28-75	1997	Long Valley, N.J.
Rosario, Omar	.222	82	212	33	47	8	1	1	24	33	68	18	4	L	L	6-1	170	1-14-78	1996	Santo Domingo, D.R.
Russin, Tom	.296	101	388	70	115	27	1	14	74	33	62	1	2	R	R	6-2	200	9-9-73	1995	Sarasota, Fla.
Skeels, David	.225	78	222	19	50	14	1	1	35	18	42	0	1	R	R	6-2	195	6-23-73	1996	Thousand Oaks, Calif.
Slemmer, Dave	.285	67	260	39	74	16	1	9	36	28	53	3	2	R	R	6-0	187	3-29-73	1995	Edwardsville, Ill.
Soriano, Jose	.300	86	290	55	87	13	5	5	28	35	49	26	17	R	R	6-0	165	4-20-74	1992	Bani, D.R.
Sosa, Nicolas	.277	102	357	39	99	21	0	3	44	41	122	1	0	R	R	6-2	220	7-18-77	1996	Longwood, Fla.

GAMES BY POSITION: C—DeBoer 64, Flores 28, Skeels 60. **1B**—Farris 3, Filchner 1, Rosario 5, Russin 65, Slemmer 11, Sosa 82. **2B**—Cesar 22, Jenkins 65, Lara 12, Slemmer 47. **3B**—Cesar 69, Flores 14, Lara 54, Russin 8, Slemmer 10. **SS**—Cesar 12, Lara 54, Robinson 81. **OF**—Byrnes 29, Camilo 82, Cesar 28, Filchner 45, Koerner 108, Rosario 71, Russin 37, Skeels 1, Soriano 78.

PITCHING	W	L	ERA	G	GS	CG	SV	IP	H	R	ER	BB	SO	B	T	HT	WT	DOB	1st Yr	Resides
Abbott, Todd	3	3	7.13	34	0	0	1	48	71	47	38	21	49	R	R	6-4	200	9-13-73	1995	Fayetteville, Ark.
Bennett, Tom	1	0	0.00	1	1	0	0	7	1	0	0	3	9	R	R	6-4	180	5-13-76	1995	Alameda, Calif.
Berry, Jason	0	0	27.00	1	0	0	0	1	2	2	2	1	0	R	R	6-3	210	4-2-74	1993	Brockton, Mass.
Della Ratta, Pete	5	1	2.44	36	0	0	13	59	43	24	16	25	73	R	R	6-4	220	2-14-74	1996	Gulf Breeze, Fla.
DuBose, Eric	6	1	3.38	17	10	0	1	72	56	34	27	35	85	L	L	6-3	215	5-15-76	1997	Nashville, Tenn.
Faust, Jason	1	2	4.85	14	0	0	0	30	39	27	16	14	25	L	L	6-0	175	7-14-75	1997	Belleville, Ill.
Gorrell, Chris	3	5	5.20	32	0	0	2	55	65	39	32	17	53	R	R	6-2	188	1-27-76	1996	Las Vegas, Nev.
Harville, Chad	4	3	3.00	24	7	0	4	69	59	25	23	31	76	R	R	5-9	180	9-16-76	1997	Savannah, Tenn.
Holmes, Mike	9	10	4.14	31	24	2	0	152	192	86	70	21	98	R	R	6-2	200	10-11-75	1997	Greensboro, N.C.
Jensen, Jared	5	9	4.00	31	24	0	1	149	161	87	66	40	112	R	R	6-1	190	3-6-74	1997	Provo, Utah
Jones, Marcus	7	9	4.67	29	20	0	4	131	155	79	68	45	112	R	R	6-5	235	3-29-75	1997	Yorba Linda, Calif.
Mlodik, Kevin	0	1	12.00	4	0	0	0	3	9	5	4	2	1	R	R	6-1	205	8-21-74	1995	Rosholt, Wis.
Niles, Randy	6	12	4.07	31	22	0	0	148	144	92	67	54	103	R	R	6-2	200	8-28-75	1997	Key West, Fla.
Nina, Elvin	8	8	4.49	30	21	1	0	130	135	77	65	62	131	R	R	6-0	185	11-25-75	1997	East Orange, N.J.
Noriega, Ray	3	5	6.18	36	6	0	2	71	91	55	49	24	77	R	L	5-10	170	3-28-74	1996	Tucson, Ariz.
O'Dell, Jake	3	1	2.20	9	5	0	1	41	34	13	10	9	36	R	R	6-1	205	9-22-73	1996	Round Rock, Texas
Petrosian, Ara	1	2	9.82	19	0	0	2	29	40	36	32	24	24	R	R	6-4	225	3-3-75	1997	Fountain Valley, Calif.
Robertson, Doug	2	1	4.95	17	0	0	0	20	23	11	11	7	15	R	R	6-0	205	10-17-74	1996	Bath, Ill.
Skeels, David	0	0	5.40	7	0	0	0	10	8	7	6	3	6	R	R	6-2	195	6-23-73	1996	Thousand Oaks, Calif.

SOUTHERN OREGON — Short-Season Class A

NORTHWEST LEAGUE

BATTING	AVG	G	AB	R	H	2B	3B	HR	RBI	BB	SO	SB	CS	B	T	HT	WT	DOB	1st Yr	Resides
Basabe, Jesus	.265	60	204	44	54	6	2	14	40	26	71	5	3	R	R	6-2	175	5-14-77	1995	Bobures, Ven.
Byrnes, Eric	.314	42	169	36	53	10	2	7	31	16	16	6	1	R	R	6-2	200	2-16-76	1998	Woodside, Calif.
Camilo, Juan	.343	31	108	25	37	8	3	4	29	22	32	5	2	L	R	6-0	205	6-24-78	1996	Santo Domingo, D.R.
Cosbey, Chris	.286	49	185	30	53	9	4	0	20	14	33	7	2	L	L	5-9	165	11-14-74	1998	Arcadia, Calif.
Farris, Ed	.154	15	52	5	8	2	0	1	3	8	26	1	0	L	R	6-0	205	6-3-74	1997	Harrison, Ohio
Gorrie, Brad	.242	55	198	46	48	7	3	1	20	43	42	15	5	R	R	5-9	180	1-25-75	1997	Northboro, Mass.
Hall, Justin	.287	69	265	56	76	12	8	3	33	35	39	5	3	R	R	5-10	180	9-23-76	1998	Mesa, Ariz.
Hart, Jason	.258	75	295	58	76	19	1	20	69	36	67	0	1	R	R	6-4	225	9-5-77	1998	Springfield, Mo.
Howe, Matt	.278	68	255	57	71	16	3	5	47	54	45	5	2	R	R	6-0	190	9-16-76	1998	Houston, Texas
Luderer, Brian	.297	10	37	9	11	2	1	2	7	2	7	0	0	R	R	5-11	180	8-19-78	1996	Tarzana, Calif.
Nieckula, Aaron	.206	41	126	17	26	6	0	0	21	18	31	2	0	R	R	5-11	200	9-7-76	1998	Berwyn, Ill.
Pecci, Jay	.292	39	130	21	38	2	0	0	14	22	22	3	4	B	R	5-11	185	9-26-76	1998	Novato, Calif.
Pujols, Rafael	.224	54	183	24	41	6	1	3	24	21	34	3	0	R	R	6-0	165	1-20-78	1995	Bani, D.R.
Rosario, Omar	.257	29	101	18	26	4	0	3	13	15	26	5	2	L	L	6-1	170	1-14-78	1996	Santo Domingo, D.R.
Salazar, Oscar	.317	28	101	19	32	4	1	5	28	16	22	5	2	R	R	6-0	155	6-27-78	1994	Maracay, Ven.
Thomas, Gary	.203	61	207	30	42	8	1	0	21	31	42	11	2	R	R	5-7	175	9-6-79	1997	Houma, La.

GAMES BY POSITION: C—Luderer 7, Nieckula 38, Pujols 44. **1B**—Farris 5, Hart 67, Pujols 5, Rosario 1. **2B**—Gorrie 49, Hall 21, Salazar 7. **3B**—Hall 9, Hart 1, Howe 58, Pujols 1, Salazar 10. **SS**—Hall 34, Pecci 36, Salazar 6. **OF**—Basabe 48, Byrnes 40, Camilo 26, Cosbey 45, Rosario 25, Thomas 59.

PITCHING	W	L	ERA	G	GS	CG	SV	IP	H	R	ER	BB	SO	B	T	HT	WT	DOB	1st Yr	Resides
Brink, Jim	3	0	4.31	24	1	0	11	56	63	32	27	16	43	R	R	6-0	185	9-11-76	1998	Stockton, Calif.
Calandriello, Donato	1	0	3.71	6	0	0	1	17	19	8	7	8	15	L	L	6-2	210	7-1-75	1998	Caracas, Ven.
Crawford, Jeremy	0	0	13.50	2	0	0	0	3	6	4	4	3	3	L	L	6-0	185	12-27-78	1997	Chatham, Ill.
Dobis, Jason	7	4	4.25	16	12	0	0	78	76	44	37	36	46	R	R	6-2	200	1-17-76	1998	Orange, Calif.
Faust, Jason	2	0	1.42	7	0	0	0	13	9	3	2	3	17	L	L	6-0	175	7-14-75	1997	Belleville, Ill.
Garcia, Bryan	1	2	7.25	7	3	0	0	22	36	21	18	9	6	R	R	6-3	165	6-21-78	1996	Quartz Hill, Calif.
Kenny, Seth	0	0	0.00	2	0	0	0	2	2	0	0	0	3	R	R	6-2	195	7-21-76	1998	Novato, Calif.
Klein, Matt	4	1	4.15	16	2	0	3	48	56	25	22	22	43	R	R	6-1	190	5-15-75	1998	Harvey, Ill.
Montero, Agustin	2	3	8.68	14	3	0	0	37	47	42	36	26	28	R	R	6-2	185	8-26-77	1995	San Pedro de Macoris, D.R.
Moore, Brad	1	1	3.20	17	2	0	3	39	29	24	14	34	33	R	R	6-0	185	2-25-76	1998	Waterloo, Iowa
Nix, Wayne	6	6	5.32	16	15	0	0	71	76	56	42	37	56	R	R	6-5	210	9-16-76	1995	North Hills, Calif.
Nogowski, Brandon	4	4	3.71	17	8	0	1	68	74	44	28	11	66	L	L	6-0	161	5-13-76	1995	Hood River, Ore.
Oyler, Scott	4	4	3.48	22	0	0	3	54	53	28	21	29	42	R	R	6-4	200	12-16-75	1998	Portland, Ore.
Pena, Juan	1	2	2.15	8	8	0	0	46	46	21	11	10	38	L	L	6-3	195	6-4-79	1996	Santo Domingo, D.R.
Petrosian, Ara	0	0	0.00	1	0	0	0	0	0	0	0	0	1	R	R	6-4	225	3-3-75	1997	Fountain Valley, Calif.
Schultz, Jeff	1	0	0.00	2	0	0	0	5	0	0	0	1	10	R	R	6-1	200	5-22-76	1998	Long Beach, Calif.
Snow, Bert	1	3	5.64	11	8	0	0	45	52	38	28	18	35	R	R	6-1	190	3-23-77	1998	Brooksville, Fla.
Suazo, Rigoberto	0	0	0.00	2	0	0	1	1	0	0	0	1	0	R	R	6-2	180	1-10-77	1994	Villa Sombrero, D.R.
Thompson, Eric	5	2	4.45	13	12	0	0	57	60	34	28	25	51	R	R	6-2	195	9-7-77	1998	Fairborn, Ohio
Wagner, Denny	0	1	18.00	2	2	0	0	4	11	9	8	3	5	R	R	6-0	205	11-8-76	1997	Castlewood, Va.
Yates, Tyler	0	0	0.00	2	0	0	1	2	2	0	0	0	1	R	R	6-4	225	8-7-77	1998	Koloa, Hawaii

PHOENIX — Rookie

ARIZONA LEAGUE

BATTING	AVG	G	AB	R	H	2B	3B	HR	RBI	BB	SO	SB	CS	B	T	HT	WT	DOB	1st Yr	Resides
Betts, DeWayne	.195	46	123	21	24	3	2	0	21	20	36	6	5	R	R	6-0	175	6-14-80	1998	Lakewood, Calif.
De la Cruz, Jose	.237	46	156	19	37	5	2	2	26	21	29	1	0	R	R	6-1	200	1-27-78	1995	Santo Domingo, D.R.
Declet, Miguel	.222	17	45	6	10	0	0	0	6	4	12	1	0	R	R	6-3	185	9-9-79	1997	Caguas, P.R.
Forbes, Matt	.250	47	160	24	40	10	2	0	17	28	56	11	5	R	R	5-10	165	2-17-78	1998	Davenport, Iowa
German, Esteban	.307	55	202	52	62	3	10	2	28	33	43	40	8	R	R	5-9	165	12-26-78	1996	Santo Domingo, D.R.
Keith, Rusty	.318	48	179	37	57	18	4	3	39	20	21	6	3	R	R	6-0	209	9-18-77	1998	Brookings, Ore.
Mack, Tony	.252	43	127	20	32	8	1	3	17	17	44	2	2	R	R	5-11	235	9-13-75	1998	Inglewood, Calif.
Nixon, Justin	.160	40	81	20	13	3	1	1	11	23	42	3	4	L	L	6-2	205	7-25-79	1998	Corvallis, Mont.
Olivo, Miguel	.311	46	164	30	51	11	3	2	23	8	43	2	2	R	R	6-1	180	7-15-78	1996	Villa Vasquez, D.R.
Porter, Jamie	.254	34	126	25	32	10	0	0	16	19	30	7	3	R	R	6-1	195	5-16-76	1997	Bothell, Wash.
Salazar, Oscar	.324	26	102	29	33	7	5	2	18	12	15	4	1	R	R	6-0	155	6-27-78	1994	Maracay, Ven.
Scheid, Jeremy	.283	53	191	31	54	8	1	4	35	38	32	5	1	L	L	6-0	190	3-24-76	1998	Rock Springs, Wyo.
Schmidt, J.P.	.196	36	107	18	21	2	0	0	14	11	26	6	2	L	R	6-1	180	1-4-80	1998	Palmdale, Calif.
Schneidmiller, Gary	.241	38	141	21	34	4	2	1	13	13	30	3	2	R	R	6-1	185	1-26-80	1998	Chino, Calif.
Williams, George	.500	1	2	0	1	0	0	0	0	1	0	0	0	B	R	5-10	214	4-22-69	1991	West Salem, Wis.

GAMES BY POSITION: C—de la Cruz 25, Olivo 38. **1B**—de la Cruz 4, Keith 1, Scheid 52. **2B**—Declet 4, German 53, Salazar 5, Schmidt 2. **3B**—de la Cruz 15, Declet 7, Mack 1, Salazar 18, Schmidt 14, Schneidmiller 6, **SS**—Declet 5, Salazar 6, Schmidt 20, Schneidmiller 31. **OF**—Betts 43, Forbes 39, Keith 46, Mack 32, Nixon 38, Olivo 2.

PITCHING	W	L	ERA	G	GS	CG	SV	IP	H	R	ER	BB	SO	B	T	HT	WT	DOB	1st Yr	Resides
Adams, Willie	0	1	2.45	2	2	0	0	4	3	2	1	1	3	R	R	6-7	225	10-8-72	1993	Scottsdale, Ariz.
Bazzell, Shane	4	2	3.27	12	8	0	0	41	30	19	15	15	51	L	R	6-2	180	3-22-79	1998	Columbus, Miss.
Bennett, Tom	1	2	7.11	5	2	0	0	13	9	15	10	18	20	R	R	6-4	180	5-13-76	1995	Alameda, Calif.
Colome, Jesus	2	5	3.18	12	11	0	0	57	47	27	20	16	62	R	R	6-2	170	6-2-80	1996	San Pedro de Macoris, D.R.
Corniel, Henry	3	1	3.11	17	0	0	0	38	36	16	13	9	30	R	R	6-0	180	6-18-77	1994	San Pedro de Macoris, D.R.
Crawford, Jeremy	3	0	3.90	17	0	0	3	30	36	17	13	12	25	L	L	6-0	185	12-27-78	1997	Chatham, Ill.
D'Amico, Jeff	0	0	3.86	4	1	0	0	9	6	4	4	1	8	R	R	6-3	195	11-9-74	1993	Seattle, Wash.
German, Franklyn	2	1	6.13	14	12	0	0	54	69	43	37	18	46	R	R	6-5	210	1-20-80	1996	Haina, D.R.
Kenny, Seth	1	5	3.03	13	6	0	3	36	46	25	12	8	35	R	R	6-2	195	7-21-76	1998	Novato, Calif.
Meeks, Eric	2	1	4.60	12	8	0	0	43	35	22	22	19	41	R	R	6-4	205	4-12-79	1997	Orlando, Fla.
Negron, Jose	1	0	6.00	7	1	0	0	15	19	11	10	7	15	R	R	6-6	200	5-2-78	1998	Dorado, P.R.
Pitre, Diogenes	0	3	7.78	17	4	0	2	42	61	47	36	30	43	R	R	6-2	180	11-5-77	1995	Santo Domingo, D.R.
Suazo, Rigoberto	1	1	7.97	12	0	0	1	20	21	22	18	14	22	R	R	6-2	180	1-10-77	1994	Villa Sombrero, D.R.
Tauscher, Ryan	3	2	5.13	17	0	0	2	26	26	23	15	15	27	B	L	6-2	185	10-4-76	1998	Federal Way, Wash.
Taylor, Tony	4	2	5.67	20	0	0	2	33	43	25	21	13	27	R	R	6-3	180	10-28-77	1998	Tucson, Ariz.
Wagner, Denny	2	1	3.86	3	1	0	0	7	4	4	3	3	11	R	R	6-0	205	11-8-76	1997	Castlewood, Va.
Yates, Tyler	0	0	3.91	15	0	0	2	23	28	12	10	14	20	R	R	6-4	225	8-7-77	1998	Koloa, Hawaii

PHILADELPHIA PHILLIES

Encouraging signs outweigh disappointments for young club

BY PAUL HAGEN

The Phillies took a few steps forward and a few steps backward in 1998.

At first glance, the season had to be considered a success. The team achieved its stated goal of getting younger and better by winning seven more games than they had in 1997 with largely unproven players who blossomed, like Bob Abreu, Doug Glanville and Desi Relaford.

They also signed Pat Burrell, the first overall choice in the 1998 draft—in time for the University of Miami slugger to get in 37 games at Class A Clearwater.

Getting Burrell under contract so quickly, however, was offset to a certain extent by the failure to sign 1997 first-round pick J.D. Drew before the team's right to sign him expired. Drew was selected by the St. Louis Cardinals in 1998, and made his major league debut in September.

The Phillies' improvement in the won-lost record was somewhat deceiving. A year earlier, they were 38-22 down the stretch, giving them some optimism going into the offseason. But 1998 saw them five games over .500 before finishing in a 20-37 tailspin.

Abreu (acquired from the Devil Rays on the day of the expansion draft for shortstop Kevin Stocker) and Glanville (who came from the Cubs for second baseman Mickey Morandini) both proved to be keepers. Abreu hit .312 as the everyday right fielder, and Glanville batted .279 out of the leadoff spot.

Scott Rolen, who signed a four-year, $10 million contract in spring training, proved to be no flash in the pan. He ended the season batting a solid .290 with 31 homers, 110 RBIs and 120 runs.

ORGANIZATION LEADERS

BATTING

*AVG	Jon Zuber, Scranton	.325
R	Marlon Anderson, Scranton	104
H	Marlon Anderson, Scranton	176
TB	Marlon Anderson, Scranton	284
2B	Two tied at	38
3B	Marlon Anderson, Scranton	14
HR	Two tied at	24
RBI	Andy Dominique, Piedmont	102
BB	Todd Crane, Reading/Clearwater	74
SO	Carlos Duncan, Piedmont/Batavia	148
SB	Alex Fajardo, Piedmont	38

PITCHING

W	Brandon Duckworth, Clearwater/Piedmont	15
L	Kris Stevens, Reading/Clearwater	13
#ERA	Geoff Geary, Batavia	1.60
G	Kyle Kawabata, Reading/Clearwater	60
CG	Brandon Duckworth, Clearwater/Piedmont	6
SV	Brett Black, Piedmont	34
IP	Brandon Duckworth, Clearwater/Piedmont	201
BB	Kris Stevens, Reading/Clearwater	77
SO	Brandon Duckworth, Clearwater/Piedmont	165

*Minimum 250 At-Bats #Minimum 75 Innings

Curt Schilling

JOHN SPEAR

Marlon Anderson

Players of the Year

Major League: Curt Schilling, rhp
Schilling struck out 300 batters for the second year in a row and his 15 wins were tops on the Phillies.

Minor League: Marlon Anderson, 2b, Scranton/W-B
Anderson hit .306 at Triple-A and led all Phillies minor leaguers with 104 runs and 284 total bases.

The most impressive individual accomplishment of the season came from righthander Curt Schilling, who became just the fifth pitcher in baseball history to strike out 300 batters in consecutive seasons.

The rest of the rotation largely unraveled, however, leaving starting pitching as the team's biggest question mark at the end of the year.

The Phillies finally got out from under the contracts of seven players—Alex Arias, Lenny Dykstra, Gregg Jefferies, Mark Leiter, Mark Lewis, Mark Parent and Mark Portugal—at season's end, clearing a total of $17.8 million off the books.

There were no indications, however, that they planned to plow a significant portion of that back into the payroll, which was expected to be in the $30 million range for 1999.

Instead, club chairman Bill Giles continued to work toward getting a baseball-only stadium built, which team officials insisted was essential for the Phillies to compete with the large-market clubs.

There were some encouraging signs in the system, despite an August purge that cost farm director Del Unser, field coordinator Don Blasingame and seven other minor league instructors their jobs.

Second baseman Marlon Anderson hit .306 with 62 extra-base hits at Triple-A Scranton/Wilkes-Barre and looked to be the Phillies starter for 1999.

Third baseman Carlos Duncan was rated the New York-Penn League's No. 1 prospect, the first Phillies prospect in any league so honored since Rolen in 1995.

And righthander Brad Baisley and outfielder Jorge Padilla, the team's second- and third-round draft picks in June, made immediate impacts at Rookie-level Martinsville.

Philadelphia PHILLIES

Manager: Terry Francona.

1998 Record: 75-87, .463 (3rd, NL East)

BATTING	AVG	G	AB	R	H	2B	3B	HR	RBI	BB	SO	SB	CS	B	T	HT	WT	DOB	1st Yr	Resides
Abreu, Bob	.312	151	497	68	155	29	6	17	74	84	133	19	10	L	R	6-0	185	3-11-74	1991	Turmero, Ven.
Amaro, Ruben	.187	92	107	7	20	5	0	1	10	6	15	0	0	B	R	5-10	191	2-12-65	1987	Philadelphia, Pa.
Anderson, Marlon	.326	17	43	4	14	3	0	1	4	1	6	2	0	L	R	5-11	190	1-6-74	1995	Prattville, Ala.
Arias, Alex	.293	56	133	17	39	8	0	1	16	13	18	2	0	R	R	6-3	185	11-20-67	1987	Plantation, Fla.
Bennett, Gary	.290	9	31	4	9	0	0	0	3	5	5	0	0	R	R	6-0	190	4-17-72	1990	Waukegan, Ill.
Brogna, Rico	.265	153	565	77	150	36	3	20	104	49	125	7	7	L	L	6-2	200	4-18-70	1988	Watertown, Conn.
Estalella, Bobby	.188	47	165	16	31	6	1	8	20	13	49	0	0	R	R	6-1	200	8-23-74	1993	Pembroke Pines, Fla.
Glanville, Doug	.279	158	678	106	189	28	7	8	49	42	89	23	6	R	R	6-2	175	8-25-70	1991	Teaneck, N.J.
Hudler, Rex	.122	25	41	2	5	1	0	0	2	4	12	0	0	R	R	6-0	202	9-2-60	1978	Philadelphia, Pa.
Jefferies, Gregg	.294	125	483	65	142	22	3	8	48	29	27	11	3	B	R	5-10	185	8-1-67	1985	Pleasanton, Calif.
Jordan, Kevin	.276	112	250	23	69	13	0	2	27	8	30	0	0	R	R	6-1	185	10-9-69	1990	Birkdale, Australia
Lewis, Mark	.249	142	518	52	129	21	2	9	54	48	111	3	3	R	R	6-1	185	11-30-69	1988	Hamilton, Ohio
Lieberthal, Mike	.256	86	313	39	80	15	3	8	45	17	44	2	1	R	R	6-0	186	1-18-72	1990	Westlake Village, Calif.
Magee, Wendell	.293	20	75	9	22	6	1	1	11	7	11	0	0	R	R	6-0	220	8-3-72	1994	Birmingham, Ala.
Parent, Mark	.221	34	113	7	25	4	0	1	13	10	30	1	1	R	R	6-5	245	9-16-61	1979	Las Vegas, Nev.
Relaford, Desi	.245	142	494	45	121	25	3	5	41	33	87	9	5	B	R	5-8	170	9-16-73	1991	Palm Harbor, Fla.
Rolen, Scott	.290	160	601	120	174	45	4	31	110	93	141	14	7	R	R	6-4	223	4-4-75	1993	Jasper, Ind.
Sefcik, Kevin	.314	104	169	27	53	7	2	3	20	25	32	4	2	R	R	5-10	181	2-10-71	1993	Lockport, Ill.
Zuber, Jon	.244	38	45	6	11	3	1	2	6	6	9	0	0	L	L	6-0	190	12-10-69	1992	Moraga, Calif.

PITCHING	W	L	ERA	G	GS	CG	SV	IP	H	R	ER	BB	SO	B	T	HT	WT	DOB	1st Yr	Resides
Beech, Matt	3	9	5.15	21	21	0	0	117	126	78	67	63	113	L	L	6-2	194	1-20-72	1994	Voorhees, N.J.
Borland, Toby	0	0	5.00	6	0	0	0	9	8	5	5	5	9	R	R	6-7	175	5-29-69	1989	Quitman, La.
Bottalico, Ricky	1	5	6.44	39	0	0	6	43	54	31	31	25	27	L	R	6-1	217	8-26-69	1991	Rocky Hill, Conn.
Brewer, Billy	0	1	108.00	2	0	0	0	0	3	4	4	2	0	L	L	6-1	175	4-15-68	1990	Waco, Texas
Byrd, Paul	5	2	2.29	8	8	2	0	55	41	16	14	17	38	R	R	6-1	185	12-3-70	1991	Louisville, Ky.
2-team (1 Atlanta)	5	2	2.68	9	8	2	0	57	45	19	17	18	39							
Dodd, Robert	1	0	7.20	4	0	0	0	5	7	6	4	1	4	L	L	6-3	195	3-14-73	1994	Plano, Texas
Gomes, Wayne	9	6	4.24	71	0	0	1	93	94	48	44	35	86	R	R	6-2	226	1-15-73	1993	Cherry Hill, N.J.
Grace, Mike	4	7	5.48	21	15	0	0	90	116	61	55	30	46	R	R	6-4	210	6-20-70	1991	Clearwater, Fla.
Green, Tyler	6	12	5.03	27	27	0	0	159	142	97	89	85	113	R	R	6-5	208	2-18-70	1991	Englewood, Colo.
Leiter, Mark	7	5	3.55	69	0	0	23	89	67	36	35	47	84	R	R	6-3	220	4-13-63	1983	Ormond Beach, Fla.
Loewer, Carlton	7	8	6.09	21	21	1	0	123	154	86	83	39	58	B	R	6-6	220	9-24-73	1995	Eunice, La.
Nye, Ryan	0	0	27.00	1	0	0	0	1	3	3	3	0	3	R	R	6-2	195	6-24-73	1994	Cameron, Okla.
Perez, Yorkis	0	2	3.81	57	0	0	0	52	40	23	22	25	42	B	L	6-0	180	9-30-67	1983	Haina, D.R.
Portugal, Mark	10	5	4.44	26	26	3	0	166	186	88	82	32	104	R	R	6-0	190	10-30-62	1981	Barrington, R.I.
Ryan, Ken	0	0	4.37	17	1	0	0	23	21	12	11	20	16	R	R	6-3	230	10-24-68	1986	Attleboro, Mass.
Schilling, Curt	15	14	3.25	35	35	15	0	269	236	101	97	61	300	R	R	6-4	228	11-14-66	1986	Philadelphia, Pa.
Spradlin, Jerry	4	4	3.53	69	0	0	1	82	63	34	32	20	76	B	R	6-7	246	6-14-67	1988	Anaheim, Calif.
Stephenson, Garrett	0	2	9.00	6	6	0	0	23	31	24	23	19	17	R	R	6-5	208	1-2-72	1992	Kimberly, Idaho
Welch, Mike	0	2	8.27	10	2	0	0	21	26	19	19	7	15	L	R	6-2	210	8-25-72	1993	Nashua, N.H.
Whiteside, Matt	1	1	8.50	10	0	0	0	18	27	18	17	5	14	R	R	6-0	205	8-8-67	1990	Arlington, Texas
Winston, Darrin	2	2	6.12	27	0	0	1	25	31	18	17	6	11	R	L	6-0	195	7-6-66	1988	Fords, N.J.

FIELDING

Catcher	PCT	G	PO	A	E	DP	PB
Bennett	1.000	9	50	2	0	0	0
Estalella	.988	47	321	12	4	0	5
Lieberthal	.988	83	607	41	8	5	5
Parent	.987	34	211	15	3	4	5

First Base	PCT	G	PO	A	E	DP
Brogna	.996	151	1239	140	5	103
Hudler	1.000	1	8	1	0	0
Jordan	1.000	24	158	15	0	15
Zuber	1.000	4	15	1	0	1

Second Base	PCT	G	PO	A	E	DP
Anderson	.978	9	14	30	1	6
Arias	1.000	1	0	1	0	0
Jordan	.966	22	32	54	3	12
Lewis	.978	140	276	437	16	73
Sefcik	1.000	1	1	0	0	0

Third Base	PCT	G	PO	A	E	DP
Arias	1.000	5	0	1	0	0
Jordan	.929	6	5	8	1	1
Rolen	.970	159	135	318	14	27
Sefcik	.500	2	1	0	1	0

Shortstop	PCT	G	PO	A	E	DP
Arias	.985	38	43	87	2	10
Relaford	.960	137	189	380	24	72

Outfield	PCT	G	PO	A	E	DP
Abreu	.973	146	271	17	8	0
Amaro	1.000	51	27	3	0	0
Glanville	.995	158	360	14	2	1
Hudler	1.000	9	19	0	0	0
Jefferies	.994	121	168	7	1	0
Magee	.941	19	31	1	2	0
Sefcik	.989	60	87	1	1	0
Zuber	1.000	5	7	0	0	0

DAVID SEELIG

Scott Rolen

FARM SYSTEM

Director of Player Development: Del Unser/Dallas Green

Class	Farm Team	League	W	L	Pct.	Finish*	Manager	First Yr
AAA	Scranton/W-B (Pa.) Red Barons	International	67	75	.472	11th (14)	Marc Bombard	1989
AA	Reading (Pa.) Phillies	Eastern	56	85	.397	10th (10)	Al LeBoeuf	1967
A#	Clearwater (Fla.) Phillies	Florida State	82	58	.586	t-2nd (14)	Bill Dancy	1985
A	Piedmont (N.C.) Boll Weevils	South Atlantic	76	65	.539	6th (14)	Ken Oberkfell	1995
A	Batavia (N.Y.) Muckdogs	New York-Penn	43	33	.566	4th (14)	Frank Klebe	1988
Rookie#	Martinsville (Va.) Phillies	Appalachian	32	36	.471	6th (10)	Greg Legg	1988

*Finish in overall standings (No. of teams in league) #Advanced level

SCRANTON/WILKES-BARRE — Class AAA

INTERNATIONAL LEAGUE

BATTING	AVG	G	AB	R	H	2B	3B	HR	RBI	BB	SO	SB	CS	B	T	HT	WT	DOB	1st Yr	Resides
Anderson, Marlon	.306	136	575	104	176	32	14	16	86	28	77	24	12	L	R	5-11	190	1-6-74	1995	Prattville, Ala.
Angeli, Doug	.178	42	118	12	21	4	0	1	10	8	36	1	1	R	R	5-10	180	1-7-71	1993	Moore, S.C.
Barron, Tony	.272	102	375	60	102	23	1	18	62	39	83	7	4	R	R	6-0	208	8-17-66	1987	Tacoma, Wash.
Bennett, Gary	.255	86	282	33	72	18	0	10	40	25	41	0	0	R	R	6-0	190	4-17-72	1990	Waukegan, Ill.
Burton, Darren	.266	117	394	56	105	21	3	18	64	53	83	9	0	B	R	6-1	185	9-16-72	1990	Somerset, Ky.
Carver, Steve	.304	8	23	3	7	2	0	1	4	2	10	0	1	L	R	6-3	215	9-27-72	1995	Jacksonville, Fla.
Dawkins, Walt	.269	42	108	15	29	6	0	3	14	9	23	2	1	R	R	5-10	195	8-6-72	1995	Moraga, Calif.
Doster, David	.276	141	579	79	160	38	4	16	84	51	80	23	6	R	R	5-10	185	10-8-70	1993	Fort Wayne, Ind.
Estalella, Bobby	.281	76	242	49	68	14	1	17	49	66	49	0	0	R	R	6-1	200	8-23-74	1993	Pembroke Pines, Fla.
Flores, Jose	.301	98	345	53	104	18	2	6	34	49	45	12	6	R	R	5-11	180	6-28-73	1994	New York, N.Y.
Held, Dan	.266	119	398	64	106	28	3	15	57	34	102	2	3	R	R	6-1	200	10-7-70	1993	Neosho, Wis.
Listach, Pat	.221	55	204	27	45	5	2	1	12	23	47	14	4	B	R	5-9	180	9-12-67	1988	Spring, Texas
2-team (33 Buffalo)	.219	88	306	50	67	8	4	1	23	32	69	17	5							
Magee, Wendell	.290	126	507	86	147	30	7	24	72	46	102	7	7	R	R	6-0	220	8-3-72	1994	Birmingham, Ala.
McMillon, Billy	.258	77	267	42	69	16	1	13	38	34	59	6	3	L	L	5-11	179	11-17-71	1993	Sumter, S.C.
Millan, Adan	.130	8	23	5	3	1	0	1	3	5	7	0	0	R	R	6-0	195	3-26-72	1991	Montebello, Calif.
Pierce, Kirk	.077	4	13	2	1	0	0	0	0	3	2	0	0	R	R	6-3	200	5-26-73	1995	Murrieta, Calif.
Snusz, Chris	.111	3	9	0	1	1	0	0	0	0	2	0	0	R	R	6-0	190	11-8-72	1995	Buffalo, N.Y.
Zuber, Jon	.325	80	280	47	91	23	4	4	56	45	34	0	0	L	L	6-0	190	12-10-69	1992	Moraga, Calif.

PITCHING	W	L	ERA	G	GS	CG	SV	IP	H	R	ER	BB	SO	B	T	HT	WT	DOB	1st Yr	Resides
Bennett, Joel	1	2	5.29	8	7	0	0	48	51	29	28	25	35	R	R	6-1	161	1-31-70	1991	Sydney, N.Y.
2-team (18 Roch.)	11	2	4.17	26	22	1	0	149	150	75	69	62	134							
Borland, Toby	0	2	5.68	13	0	0	5	13	14	8	8	3	15	R	R	6-7	175	5-29-69	1989	Quitman, La.
Bottalico, Ricky	0	1	2.92	10	5	0	1	12	8	4	4	9	4	L	R	6-1	217	8-26-69	1991	Rocky Hill, Conn.
Brannan, Ryan	1	1	7.56	16	0	0	2	17	21	18	14	13	12	R	R	6-3	210	4-27-75	1996	Huntington Beach, Calif.
Dodd, Robert	4	1	3.24	42	0	0	6	42	37	15	15	19	41	L	L	6-3	195	3-14-73	1994	Plano, Texas
Fesh, Sean	0	0	3.00	8	0	0	0	6	3	2	2	4	4	L	L	6-2	165	11-3-72	1991	Bethel, Conn.
Fiore, Tony	4	7	4.47	41	7	0	1	95	92	53	47	52	71	R	R	6-4	210	10-12-71	1992	Oak Park, Ill.
Grace, Mike	3	6	5.04	11	10	2	0	75	92	44	42	18	39	R	R	6-4	210	6-20-70	1991	Clearwater, Fla.
Heflin, Bronson	0	0	7.20	10	0	0	0	10	12	10	8	7	9	R	R	6-3	200	8-29-71	1994	Gallatin, Tenn.
Holman, Craig	1	3	4.75	6	6	0	0	30	36	17	16	9	20	B	R	6-2	200	3-13-69	1991	Attalla, Ala.
Loewer, Carlton	7	3	2.87	12	12	5	0	94	89	34	30	22	69	B	R	6-6	220	9-24-73	1995	Eunice, La.
Maduro, Calvin	12	9	5.98	28	27	4	0	178	211	123	118	68	120	R	R	6-0	180	9-5-74	1992	Santa Cruz, Aruba
Nye, Ryan	9	6	4.05	23	22	3	0	140	139	73	63	49	118	R	R	6-2	195	6-24-73	1994	Cameron, Okla.
Perez, Yorkis	0	0	0.00	4	1	0	0	4	2	1	0	1	3	B	L	6-0	180	9-30-67	1983	Haina, D.R.
Ryan, Ken	1	0	0.00	6	0	0	1	8	7	0	0	3	9	R	R	6-3	230	10-24-68	1986	Attleboro, Mass.
Scott, Darryl	4	5	5.03	33	0	0	10	39	37	24	22	15	37	R	R	6-1	185	8-6-68	1990	Prior Lake, Minn.
2-team (8 Ottawa)	4	6	4.59	41	0	0	12	51	49	30	26	20	44							
Stephenson, Garrett	1	8	5.25	13	11	2	0	74	81	49	43	16	48	R	R	6-5	208	1-2-72	1992	Kimberly, Idaho
Thomas, Evan	0	1	8.00	2	2	0	0	9	9	8	8	6	5	R	R	5-10	180	6-14-74	1996	Pembroke Pines, Fla.
Troutman, Keith	6	3	4.24	43	0	0	0	81	80	44	38	31	78	R	R	6-1	200	5-29-73	1992	Candler, N.C.
Welch, Mike	3	4	5.97	31	6	0	2	75	98	56	50	17	32	L	R	6-2	210	8-25-72	1993	Nashua, N.H.
Whiteside, Matt	1	4	6.48	30	1	0	5	33	47	24	24	7	21	R	R	6-0	205	8-8-67	1990	Arlington, Texas
Winston, Darrin	0	2	9.51	16	2	0	0	24	40	27	25	10	18	R	L	6-0	195	7-6-66	1988	Fords, N.J.
Wolf, Randy	9	7	4.62	24	23	1	0	148	167	88	76	48	118	L	L	6-0	190	8-22-76	1997	Canoga Park, Calif.

FIELDING

Catcher	PCT	G	PO	A	E	DP	PB
Bennett	.998	69	424	35	1	3	1
Estalella	.990	67	469	25	5	3	4
Millan	1.000	6	42	0	0	0	1
Pierce	.923	4	34	2	3	0	0
Snusz	1.000	1	0	1	0	0	0

First Base	PCT	G	PO	A	E	DP
Barron	.987	9	70	8	1	6
Bennett	1.000	2	1	0	0	0
Held	.990	108	941	60	10	82
Zuber	1.000	31	245	20	0	21

Second Base	PCT	G	PO	A	E	DP
Anderson	.959	135	262	391	28	86
Doster	1.000	9	18	26	0	3
Flores	.909	2	2	8	1	1

Third Base	PCT	G	PO	A	E	DP
Doster	.951	134	87	283	19	20
Flores	.967	10	11	18	1	1
Held	.000	1	0	0	0	0

Shortstop	PCT	G	PO	A	E	DP
Angeli	.954	35	44	100	7	26
Doster	.833	1	2	3	1	1
Flores	.965	84	105	227	12	41
Listach	.949	34	36	94	7	20

Outfield	PCT	G	PO	A	E	DP
Angeli	1.000	1	3	0	0	0
Barron	.982	57	102	7	2	1
Burton	.963	106	200	8	8	1
Carver	1.000	6	8	0	0	0
Dawkins	.952	28	37	3	2	0
Listach	1.000	6	12	2	0	1
Magee	.966	124	302	7	11	1
McMillon	.986	70	133	9	2	2
Zuber	1.000	47	83	3	0	0

READING — Class AA

EASTERN LEAGUE

BATTING	AVG	G	AB	R	H	2B	3B	HR	RBI	BB	SO	SB	CS	B	T	HT	WT	DOB	1st Yr	Resides
*Alcantara, Israel	[illegible]	[illegible]	[illegible]	[illegible]	[illegible]	[illegible]	[illegible]	15	44	17	[illegible]	0	1	R	R	6-2	[illegible]	5-6-73	1991	Santo Domingo, D.R.
Amador, Manny	.252	35	103	12	26	10	1	1	11	9	20	0	0	B	R	6-0	160	11-21-75	1993	Sabana Perdida, D.R.
Angeli, Doug	.232	65	233	27	54	14	1	3	18	17	46	3	1	R	R	5-10	180	1-7-71	1993	Moore, S.C.
Carver, Steve	.260	127	458	63	119	17	0	21	88	64	108	0	3	L	R	6-3	215	9-27-72	1995	Jacksonville, Fla.
Costello, Brian	.150	45	120	7	18	6	1	1	7	7	44	2	0	R	R	6-1	195	10-4-74	1993	Orlando, Fla.
Crane, Todd	.074	9	27	2	2	0	0	1	2	2	7	1	1	R	R	6-0	185	7-2-73	1995	Roswell, Ga.
Dawkins, Walter	.255	49	161	24	41	16	1	2	19	17	29	1	4	R	R	5-10	195	8-6-72	1995	Moraga, Calif.
Francia, David	.238	68	269	29	64	12	4	3	20	13	41	6	7	L	L	6-0	180	4-16-75	1996	Mobile, Ala.
Guiliano, Matt	.226	126	439	47	99	15	2	12	44	45	102	2	4	R	R	5-9	180	10-7-72	1994	Ronkonkoma, N.Y.
Harris, Brian	.250	11	40	5	10	0	1	0	4	5	7	0	1	B	R	5-10	180	4-28-75	1997	Carmel, Ind.
Huff, Larry	.338	40	136	26	46	7	2	7	25	19	15	10	2	R	R	6-0	175	1-24-72	1994	Palm Harbor, Fla.
Key, Jeff	.196	63	224	24	44	8	0	7	24	14	69	6	0	L	R	6-1	210	11-22-74	1993	Covington, Ga.
Knupfer, Jason	.218	63	193	27	42	7	2	0	15	27	46	2	1	R	R	6-0	180	9-21-74	1996	Redwood City, Calif.
Marsters, Brandon	.231	38	143	9	33	4	2	1	7	11	34	0	1	R	R	5-10	190	3-14-75	1996	Sarasota, Fla.
Millan, Adan	.297	61	195	18	58	18	1	9	42	28	36	1	1	R	R	6-0	195	3-26-72	1994	Montebello, Calif.
Pierce, Kirk	.253	80	265	31	67	12	0	6	29	41	63	0	0	R	R	6-3	200	5-26-73	1995	Murrieta, Calif.
Raynor, Mark	.293	100	379	43	111	9	4	0	31	38	33	7	2	R	R	6-0	180	4-1-73	1995	Williamston, N.C.
Rivero, Eddie	.273	69	205	23	56	15	2	5	31	16	57	0	0	L	L	6-0	190	7-14-73	1996	Miami, Fla.
Royster, Aaron	.256	112	430	67	110	27	4	7	55	57	117	3	1	R	R	6-1	220	11-30-72	1994	Chicago, Ill.
Snusz, Chris	.321	12	28	6	9	2	0	0	1	3	6	0	0	R	R	6-0	190	11-8-72	1995	Buffalo, N.Y.
Taylor, Reggie	.273	79	337	49	92	14	6	5	22	12	73	22	10	L	R	6-1	175	1-12-77	1995	Newberry, S.C.

PITCHING	W	L	ERA	G	GS	CG	SV	IP	H	R	ER	BB	SO	B	T	HT	WT	DOB	1st Yr	Resides
Barbao, Joe	0	1	11.85	10	0	0	0	14	20	18	18	13	8	R	R	6-1	190	4-18-72	1994	Crown Point, Ind.
Barnett, Marty	0	3	6.20	5	5	0	0	25	31	17	17	13	21	R	R	6-3	210	3-10-74	1995	Harlan, Iowa
Borland, Toby	1	3	9.64	8	0	0	3	9	18	12	10	5	13	R	R	6-7	175	5-29-69	1989	Quitman, La.
Brannan, Ryan	5	4	3.56	41	0	0	6	56	55	31	22	29	42	R	R	6-3	210	4-27-75	1996	Huntington Beach, Calif.
Burger, Rob	3	11	6.03	33	19	1	0	115	119	88	77	69	102	R	R	6-1	175	3-25-76	1994	Willow Street, Pa.
Censale, Silvio	0	0	1.93	4	0	0	1	5	4	2	1	3	2	L	L	6-2	195	11-21-71	1993	Lodi, N.J.
Coggin, David	4	8	4.14	20	20	0	0	109	106	58	50	62	65	R	R	6-4	195	10-30-76	1995	Upland, Calif.
Costa, Tony	0	0	47.25	3	0	0	0	1	6	8	7	5	1	R	R	6-4	210	12-19-70	1992	Lemoore, Calif.
Davis, Jason	6	8	4.82	45	10	0	1	105	116	68	56	55	81	L	L	6-3	195	8-15-74	1996	Winters, Calif.
Fesh, Sean	3	1	1.36	31	0	0	9	33	19	8	5	19	41	L	L	6-2	165	11-3-72	1991	Bethel, Conn.
Kawabata, Kyle	1	0	3.68	7	0	0	0	7	14	8	3	2	2	R	R	6-0	195	1-2-74	1995	Kailua, Hawaii
Mejia, Javier	0	0	12.96	8	0	0	0	8	15	12	12	13	8	R	R	6-0	190	7-28-74	1996	Indio, Calif.
Nyari, Pete	1	7	5.29	53	0	0	3	65	87	41	38	37	54	R	R	5-11	200	9-4-71	1994	Erie, Pa.
Perez, Yorkis	0	0	0.00	1	1	0	0	1	0	0	0	0	1	B	L	6-0	180	9-30-67	1983	Haina, D.R.
Scott, Darryl	0	1	3.27	8	0	0	2	11	7	4	4	2	13	R	R	6-1	185	8-6-68	1990	Prior Lake, Minn.
Shumaker, Anthony	7	10	3.35	38	21	1	2	167	152	75	62	44	129	L	L	6-5	223	5-14-73	1995	Kokomo, Ind.
Smith, Hut	2	6	5.31	22	8	0	2	63	84	43	37	20	27	R	R	6-3	195	6-8-73	1992	Kannapolis, N.C.
2-team (6 Bowie)	2	9	5.83	28	13	0	2	93	116	66	60	26	39							
Stevens, Kris	8	11	5.77	25	24	1	0	147	163	99	94	70	113	R	L	6-2	180	9-19-77	1996	Fontana, Calif.
Thomas, Evan	8	5	3.35	24	24	3	0	158	180	66	59	44	134	R	R	5-10	180	6-14-74	1996	Pembroke Pines, Fla.
Uchiyama, Tomoyuki	5	6	3.94	43	5	0	1	119	129	55	52	49	96	L	R	6-1	181	8-15-68	1998	Gifu, Japan
Wolf, Randy	2	0	1.44	4	4	0	0	25	15	4	4	4	33	L	L	6-0	190	8-22-76	1997	Canoga Park, Calif.

*Loaned from Tampa Bay Devil Rays.

FIELDING

Catcher	PCT	G	PO	A	E	DP	PB
Marsters	.986	38	254	25	4	3	9
Millan	.994	24	153	11	1	2	6
Pierce	.987	74	561	61	8	3	11
Snusz	.979	7	39	7	1	0	0

First Base	PCT	G	PO	A	E	DP
Alcantara	.980	15	139	8	3	13
Carver	.988	82	697	69	9	75
Millan	1.000	11	105	4	0	11
Rivero	.987	34	286	23	4	26

Second Base	PCT	G	PO	A	E	DP
Guiliano	.987	34	69	87	2	26
Harris	.969	11	31	31	2	7
Huff	.957	5	9	13	1	1
Knupfer	.981	54	116	146	5	39
Raynor	.957	43	82	117	9	30

Third Base	PCT	G	PO	A	E	DP
Alcantara	.875	10	6	15	3	3
Amador	.846	15	10	23	6	3
Guiliano	.940	15	13	34	3	6
Huff	.972	36	29	74	3	9
Knupfer	.889	2	2	6	1	1
Millan	.860	17	10	39	8	3
Raynor	.943	49	41	92	8	5

Shortstop	PCT	G	PO	A	E	DP
Angeli	.977	62	82	178	6	45
Guiliano	.952	80	105	213	16	41
Raynor	1.000	2	2	6	0	3

Outfield	PCT	G	PO	A	E	DP
Alcantara	.875	4	7	0	1	0
Angeli	1.000	4	4	0	0	0
Carver	.940	28	45	2	3	0
Costello	.972	32	67	3	2	1
Crane	.857	9	17	1	3	0
Dawkins	.978	45	82	6	2	2
Francia	.993	67	142	8	1	3
Key	.969	59	93	2	3	0
Rivero	1.000	7	9	0	0	0
Royster	.970	99	159	5	5	1
Taylor	.944	77	164	6	10	1

CLEARWATER — Class A

FLORIDA STATE LEAGUE

BATTING	AVG	G	AB	R	H	2B	3B	HR	RBI	BB	SO	SB	CS	B	T	HT	WT	DOB	1st Yr	Resides
Amador, Manny	.276	35	105	12	29	5	0	1	14	10	21	1	2	B	R	6-0	160	11-21-75	1993	Sabana Perdida, D.R.
Burnham, Gary	.296	139	513	93	152	33	10	8	70	63	76	10	4	L	L	5-11	200	10-13-74	1997	South Windsor, Conn.
Burrell, Pat	.303	37	132	29	40	7	1	7	30	27	22	2	0	R	R	6-4	230	10-10-76	1998	Miami, Fla.
Collier, Lamonte	.259	25	81	7	21	2	1	0	5	3	15	1	1	R	R	5-9	185	4-1-75	1997	St. Louis, Mo.
Collins, Francis	.248	32	121	20	30	1	1	0	3	15	22	5	4	R	R	5-10	185	3-8-74	1997	San Francisco, Calif.
Cooley, Shannon	.218	19	55	3	12	1	0	1	6	4	10	1	0	L	R	6-1	170	6-24-74	1996	Hickory, Miss.
Costello, Brian	.243	36	136	20	33	7	1	3	15	8	41	4	2	R	R	6-1	195	10-4-74	1993	Orlando, Fla.
Crane, Todd	.270	126	440	77	119	22	5	9	57	72	88	34	8	R	R	6-0	185	7-2-73	1995	Roswell, Ga.
Estrada, Johnny	.222	37	117	8	26	8	0	0	13	5	7	0	0	B	R	5-11	195	6-27-76	1997	Fresno, Calif.
Francia, David	.278	48	194	33	54	13	0	6	23	12	30	13	4	L	L	6-0	180	4-16-75	1996	Mobile, Ala.
Harris, Brian	.277	118	437	55	121	17	6	5	65	47	56	20	13	B	R	5-10	180	4-28-75	1997	Carmel, Ind.
Key, Jeff	.335	63	212	38	71	13	4	3	45	17	45	5	8	L	R	6-1	210	11-22-74	1993	Covington, Ga.
Kiil, Harry	.275	116	397	90	109	31	3	14	70	70	109	23	6	R	R	6-0	189	4-10-74	1996	Salinas, Calif.
Marsters, Brandon	.283	76	265	33	75	12	1	6	39	16	41	2	1	R	R	5-10	190	3-14-75	1996	Sarasota, Fla.

BATTING	AVG	G	AB	R	H	2B	3B	HR	RBI	BB	SO	SB	CS	B	T	HT	WT	DOB	1st Yr	Resides
McNamara, Rusty	.291	134	529	78	154	36	1	9	94	23	44	14	7	R	R	5-9	185	1-23-75	1997	Riverside, Calif.
Raynor, Mark	.247	23	93	19	23	1	1	1	10	7	12	1	1	R	R	6-0	180	4-1-73	1995	Williamston, N.C.
Rollins, Jimmy	.244	119	495	72	121	18	9	6	35	41	62	23	9	B	R	5-8	160	11-27-78	1996	Alameda, Calif.
Snusz, Chris	.196	19	56	6	11	1	0	0	6	1	9	0	0	R	R	6-0	190	11-8-72	1995	Buffalo, N.Y.
Taylor, Greg	.275	22	51	7	14	1	0	0	11	8	5	0	2	B	R	5-11	175	10-30-73	1996	Fort Wayne, Ind.
Thompson, Nick	.274	59	186	24	51	10	1	2	23	8	40	3	3	R	R	6-0	190	8-23-74	1996	Dunwoody, Ga.
Valent, Eric	.264	34	125	24	33	8	1	5	25	16	29	1	2	L	L	6-0	200	4-4-77	1998	Anaheim, Calif.
Wesemann, Jason	.205	32	88	10	18	3	1	0	8	8	19	0	3	R	R	6-2	185	3-29-74	1996	Watertown, Wis.

GAMES BY POSITION: C—Estrada 36, Marsters 74, Snusz 17, Thompson 24, Wesemann 1. **1B**—Burnham 114, Burrell 22, Wesemann 10. **2B**—Amador 8, Harris 116, McNamara 7, Raynor 1, Taylor 13. **3B**—Amador 11, Collier 4, McNamara 121, Raynor 3, Wesemann 4. **SS**—Collier 16, Rollins 119, Taylor 4, Wesemann 9. **OF**—Burnham 1, Collier 4, Collins 29, Cooley 12, Costello 32, Crane 120, Francia 46, Key 53, Kiil 104, McNamara 1, Thompson 10, Valent 34.

PITCHING	W	L	ERA	G	GS	CG	SV	IP	H	R	ER	BB	SO	B	T	HT	WT	DOB	1st Yr	Resides
Adair, Derek	7	3	5.12	14	13	1	0	77	81	47	44	10	55	R	R	6-4	188	8-25-75	1997	Albertson, N.Y.
Allen, Buck	5	1	4.69	47	5	0	1	79	93	43	41	23	39	L	L	5-10	180	9-1-74	1996	Littleton, Colo.
Barnett, Marty	0	1	6.26	7	6	0	0	27	34	23	19	14	13	R	R	6-3	210	3-10-74	1995	Harlan, Iowa
Costa, Tony	0	1	8.25	6	2	0	0	12	9	11	11	14	5	R	R	6-4	210	12-19-70	1992	Lemoore, Calif.
Duckworth, Brandon	6	2	3.74	9	9	1	0	53	64	25	22	22	46	B	R	6-2	185	1-23-76	1997	Kearns, Utah
Eaton, Adam	9	8	4.44	24	23	1	0	132	152	68	65	47	89	R	R	6-2	190	11-23-77	1996	Snohomish, Wash.
Jacquez, Tom	9	11	4.30	29	28	2	0	170	215	102	81	31	108	L	L	6-2	195	12-29-75	1997	Stockton, Calif.
Kawabata, Kyle	4	3	2.64	53	0	0	33	65	63	25	19	16	49	R	R	6-0	195	1-2-74	1995	Kailua, Hawaii
Kershner, Jason	3	3	4.01	41	8	0	3	94	108	57	42	25	65	L	L	6-2	165	12-19-76	1995	Scottsdale, Ariz.
Knoll, Randy	1	3	6.20	5	5	0	0	20	31	17	14	11	14	R	R	6-4	190	3-21-77	1995	Riverside, Calif.
Maness, Chris	1	1	0.63	8	0	0	1	14	11	2	1	4	9	R	R	6-2	195	4-22-76	1998	Greensboro, N.C.
Mejia, Javier	3	3	4.05	32	0	0	1	47	40	22	21	19	39	R	R	6-0	190	7-28-74	1996	Indio, Calif.
Mendes, Jaime	9	3	3.58	48	0	0	3	65	74	34	26	15	48	R	R	5-10	188	4-6-73	1995	Las Cruces, N.M.
Mitchell, Courtney	4	4	3.36	55	0	0	1	78	93	37	29	19	61	B	L	5-9	178	11-20-72	1994	Garyville, La.
Rutherford, Mark	8	5	2.65	18	18	0	0	119	94	40	35	20	71	R	R	6-2	205	11-9-74	1997	Livonia, Mich.
Ryan, Ken	0	0	3.00	4	4	0	0	9	5	3	3	3	10	R	R	6-3	230	10-24-68	1986	Attleboro, Mass.
Stevens, Kris	2	2	1.55	5	5	0	0	29	20	6	5	7	14	R	L	6-2	180	9-19-77	1996	Fontana, Calif.
Whiteman, Greg	0	1	9.00	2	2	0	0	8	15	8	8	2	8	L	L	6-2	200	6-12-73	1994	Wiley Ford, W.Va.
Wimberly, Larry	7	2	3.63	14	10	0	0	72	77	30	29	12	66	L	L	6-2	185	8-22-75	1994	Winter Garden, Fla.
Yeager, Gary	4	1	3.44	41	2	0	0	81	102	42	31	25	44	R	R	6-1	190	11-6-73	1995	Pottsville, Pa.

PIEDMONT — Class A

SOUTH ATLANTIC LEAGUE

BATTING	AVG	G	AB	R	H	2B	3B	HR	RBI	BB	SO	SB	CS	B	T	HT	WT	DOB	1st Yr	Resides
Clark, Kirby	.292	86	322	46	94	29	2	6	63	26	84	2	0	L	R	6-0	200	10-6-73	1996	Toomsuba, Miss.
Collier, Lamonte	.318	45	154	21	49	11	2	1	30	24	38	4	3	R	R	5-9	185	4-1-75	1997	St. Louis, Mo.
Collins, Francis	.314	81	306	48	96	9	1	0	18	42	49	14	4	R	R	5-10	185	3-8-74	1997	San Francisco, Calif.
Dominique, Bubba	.282	133	514	82	145	38	0	24	102	61	97	0	2	R	R	6-0	210	10-30-75	1997	Reno, Nev.
Duncan, Carlos	.198	32	111	20	22	3	2	3	12	15	47	8	1	R	R	6-1	155	6-30-77	1995	San Pedro de Macoris, D.R.
Estrada, Johnny	.310	77	303	33	94	14	2	7	44	6	19	0	1	B	R	5-11	195	6-27-76	1997	Fresno, Calif.
Fajardo, Alex	.280	115	457	83	128	24	1	5	46	44	88	38	4	R	R	6-0	175	2-6-76	1995	Moca, D.R.
Fritz, Jim	.227	50	172	21	39	9	1	3	21	14	55	0	1	R	R	6-0	215	6-2-75	1997	Aloha, Ore.
Giron, Alejandro	.228	51	180	14	41	5	2	0	19	9	34	8	4	R	R	6-2	170	4-26-79	1996	Santo Domingo, D.R.
Guzman, Carlos	.285	74	228	29	65	10	0	0	26	16	46	8	13	L	L	5-9	160	6-28-78	1995	Santiago, D.R.
Johnson, Jason	.267	106	446	63	119	14	3	1	45	36	58	32	12	R	R	6-1	170	8-21-77	1996	Collinsville, Va.
Kurilla, Kevin	.199	53	181	21	36	6	0	2	15	19	56	1	0	R	R	6-4	195	2-21-75	1997	Mount Wolf, Pa.
Mejia, Juan	.195	55	164	24	32	7	3	0	13	6	50	11	1	R	R	6-0	150	11-22-75	1994	San Pedro de Macoris, D.R.
Salazar, Jeremy	.285	41	158	20	45	10	0	2	19	23	39	1	0	R	R	5-11	185	3-18-76	1998	Springfield, Ill.
Taylor, Greg	.216	66	218	24	47	9	0	0	21	14	46	1	1	B	R	5-11	175	10-30-73	1996	Fort Wayne, Ind.
Terrell, Jeff	.291	118	392	71	114	15	6	0	47	62	55	18	7	L	R	6-1	175	10-22-74	1997	Blue Springs, Mo.
Valent, Eric	.427	22	89	24	38	12	0	8	28	14	19	0	0	L	L	6-0	200	4-4-77	1998	Anaheim, Calif.
Van Iten, Bob	.260	121	461	60	120	18	2	4	58	53	69	0	1	L	R	6-1	170	7-1-77	1996	Independence, Mo.

GAMES BY POSITION: C—Clark 18, Estrada 73, Fritz 23, Salazar 40. **1B**—Clark 2, Dominique 34, Van Iten 108. **2B**—Collier 1, Mejia 25, Terrell 118. **3B**—Clark 29, Dominique 43, Duncan 28, Fritz 5, Kurilla 40, Mejia 6. **SS**—Collier 44, Duncan 4, Kurilla 14, Mejia 18, Taylor 65. **OF**—Collins 80, Fajardo 114, Giron 47, Guzman 68, Johnson 106, Valent 21.

PITCHING	W	L	ERA	G	GS	CG	SV	IP	H	R	ER	BB	SO	B	T	HT	WT	DOB	1st Yr	Resides
Bailie, Matt	0	0	.00	2	0	0	0	2	3	0	0	3	2	R	R	5-10	195	10-1-75	1998	Aloha, Ore.
Black, Brett	5	4	2.18	58	0	0	34	66	55	19	16	8	88	R	R	6-0	210	10-3-74	1997	Apopka, Fla.
Cotton, Joe	6	8	4.42	44	0	0	5	77	73	48	38	16	79	R	R	6-2	190	3-25-75	1996	Union Town, Ohio
Duckworth, Brandon	9	8	2.80	21	21	5	0	148	116	58	46	24	119	B	R	6-2	185	1-23-76	1997	Kearns, Utah
Eason, Clay	3	1	3.72	34	2	0	0	65	53	32	27	22	67	R	R	5-11	180	11-18-75	1997	Dunn, N.C.
Fenus, Justin	10	8	5.11	30	24	0	0	136	169	90	77	45	81	R	R	6-2	195	5-19-75	1996	Mountain View, Wyo.
Hootselle, Jeff	1	0	6.34	24	0	0	0	38	40	32	27	28	40	R	L	6-4	195	10-31-75	1997	Alpharetta, Ga.
Key, Calvin	5	7	4.88	26	19	2	0	120	157	85	65	34	74	R	R	6-4	205	10-17-74	1997	Jacksonville, Ark.
Manbeck, Mark	1	4	4.70	7	7	0	0	38	51	24	20	5	30	R	R	6-2	185	9-18-74	1997	Round Rock, Texas
Martinez, Caleb	2	0	6.66	13	0	0	2	26	31	23	19	4	26	L	L	6-2	205	2-10-77	1995	Hialeah, Fla.
Montero, Francisco	5	8	4.05	20	20	1	0	120	145	68	54	15	68	R	R	6-2	170	1-6-76	1994	Barahona, D.R.
Ramos, Fernando	3	2	3.35	26	0	0	2	48	41	19	18	12	53	R	R	6-1	169	5-3-76	1994	Moca, D.R.
Shipp, Kevin	10	11	3.46	28	28	3	0	185	210	99	71	26	142	R	R	5-11	190	2-8-75	1997	Baton Rouge, La.
Tilton, Ira	4	4	4.03	28	0	0	0	60	63	30	27	31	36	R	R	6-4	195	10-27-74	1996	Indianapolis, Ind.
Walker, Adam	9	0	2.04	15	15	0	0	84	60	21	19	21	114	L	L	6-7	210	5-28-76	1997	Albuquerque, N.M.
Westmoreland, Ken	3	0	1.93	5	5	0	0	33	27	11	7	17	41	R	R	6-1	205	2-26-75	1998	Decatur, Ala.

BATAVIA — Short-Season Class A

NEW YORK-PENN LEAGUE

BATTING	AVG	G	AB	R	H	2B	3B	HR	RBI	BB	SO	SB	CS	B	T	HT	WT	DOB	1st Yr	Resides
Beverly, Demetrius	.256	29	82	8	21	8	0	1	13	11	34	0	0	R	R	6-2	245	11-3-74	1998	Alameda, Calif.

BATTING	AVG	G	AB	R	H	2B	3B	HR	RBI	BB	SO	SB	CS	B	T	HT	WT	DOB	1st Yr	Resides
Beverly, Shomari	.207	9	29	2	6	1	0	0	1	1	9	0	1	R	R	6-0	165	2-16-78	1997	Alameda, Calif.
Bonilla, Elin	.181	35	72	7	13	2	1	0	9	9	21	0	0	R	R	6-0	180	12-7-77	1996	La Vega, D.R.
Carnes, Shayne	.329	66	237	52	78	15	0	6	38	29	48	3	0	L	L	6-2	200	9-16-76	1998	Nogales, Ariz.
Casillas, Uriel	.224	60	219	37	49	9	0	4	31	32	47	3	2	R	R	5-11	175	8-22-75	1997	Downey, Calif.
Deitrick, Jeremy	.132	16	53	6	7	1	1	1	7	6	16	0	2	R	R	6-1	200	9-14-76	1998	Williamsport, Pa.
DeNure, Chip	.242	48	157	13	38	6	1	3	22	4	39	6	2	R	R	6-0	190	6-5-76	1998	Los Angeles, Calif.
Duncan, Carlos	.264	71	276	55	73	23	4	5	43	29	101	13	4	R	R	6-1	155	6-30-77	1995	San Pedro de Macoris, D.R.
Maddox, Derrick	.114	29	70	7	8	2	0	0	3	13	32	0	2	L	R	6-0	182	6-18-76	1997	Penn Valley, Pa.
McGinnis, Ronnie	.146	31	103	7	15	3	0	2	10	4	41	0	1	R	R	6-3	215	8-17-76	1998	Las Vegas, Nev.
Michaels, Jason	.268	67	235	45	63	14	3	11	49	40	69	4	2	R	R	6-0	205	5-4-76	1998	Tampa, Fla.
Punto, Nick	.247	72	279	51	69	9	4	1	20	42	48	19	7	B	R	5-10	170	11-8-77	1998	Mission Viejo, Calif.
Rachels, Wes	.301	41	133	19	40	5	0	0	16	18	15	2	1	R	R	5-10	185	1-19-76	1998	Los Angeles, Calif.
Rauls, Ian	.264	57	178	27	47	7	0	0	7	26	55	9	7	L	L	6-2	170	10-2-77	1998	Trenton, N.J.
Rodeheaver, Roger	.143	28	70	9	10	2	1	0	5	11	25	0	0	R	R	6-2	215	10-16-76	1998	Carmel, Ind.
Salazar, Jeremy	.279	20	68	6	19	5	0	2	18	4	21	0	0	R	R	5-11	185	3-18-76	1998	Springfield, Ill.
Valdez, Jerry	.271	60	214	29	58	13	1	8	40	24	41	0	1	R	R	5-11	195	6-6-74	1997	El Paso, Texas
Williams, Ricky	.283	13	53	7	15	0	0	0	3	2	16	6	3	R	R	6-0	215	5-21-77	1995	Austin, Texas

GAMES BY POSITION: C—Deitrick 10, McGinnis 31, Salazar 16, Valdez 25. **1B**—Carnes 61, Rodeheaver 23. **2B**—Casillas 51, Punto 1, Rachels 26. **3B**—Casillas 6, Duncan 71. **SS**—Casillas 2, DeNure 5, Punto 71, Rodeheaver 1. **OF**—D. Beverly 23, S. Beverly 7, Bonilla 30, Carnes 5, DeNure 43, Maddox 11, Michaels 65, Rachels 1, Rauls 51, Williams 12.

PITCHING	W	L	ERA	G	GS	CG	SV	IP	H	R	ER	BB	SO	B	T	HT	WT	DOB	1st Yr	Resides
Ciesla, Dave	0	1	4.44	26	0	0	2	24	26	15	12	6	19	L	L	6-0	190	7-28-76	1998	Russellville, Ark.
Dagley, Corey	1	5	4.86	18	5	0	0	50	53	31	27	11	37	R	R	6-2	180	4-15-77	1998	Centralia, Ill.
Donovan, T.J.	2	2	3.94	23	0	0	1	32	31	17	14	6	22	R	R	6-0	195	7-20-76	1998	Bedford, Ohio
Geary, Geoff	9	1	1.60	16	15	1	0	95	78	20	17	14	101	R	R	6-0	175	8-26-76	1998	El Cajon, Calif.
Grammer, Ed	0	0	3.00	3	0	0	0	3	5	2	1	0	1	R	R	6-4	215	10-8-75	1998	Ripley, Tenn.
Hiles, Cary	2	2	2.97	25	0	0	10	30	27	11	10	13	45	R	R	5-10	175	11-29-75	1998	Memphis, Tenn.
Kubes, Greg	7	3	3.23	15	12	0	0	75	72	33	27	23	79	L	L	6-6	210	11-10-76	1998	East Bernard, Texas
Mondello, Pete	1	0	13.50	4	0	0	0	4	7	7	6	4	2	R	R	6-4	180	12-18-74	1997	Thibodaux, La.
Pilato, John	4	4	4.12	19	12	0	3	68	57	34	31	28	63	R	R	6-3	180	9-8-77	1998	Rochester, N.Y.
Pizarro, Melvin	0	0	14.11	10	0	0	0	15	21	30	23	21	14	L	L	6-1	185	3-16-78	1995	Carolina, P.R.
Serrano, Elio	3	2	2.55	13	3	0	1	35	28	13	10	10	26	R	R	6-3	180	12-4-78	1996	Valencia, Ven.
Silva, Carlos	2	3	6.35	9	7	0	0	45	61	37	32	9	27	R	R	6-4	198	4-23-79	1996	Calle los Mangos, Ven.
Wedel, Jeremy	7	6	4.38	16	15	1	0	88	102	48	43	15	65	R	R	6-0	190	11-27-76	1998	Wasco, Calif.
Westmoreland, Ken	3	1	1.43	7	7	0	0	38	33	10	6	5	39	R	R	6-1	205	2-26-75	1998	Decatur, Ala.
Wiedl, Andy	2	2	4.60	21	0	0	0	31	33	22	16	15	26	R	L	6-3	200	3-12-76	1998	Onalaska, Wis.
Zipser, Mike	0	1	2.67	19	0	0	3	27	26	10	8	8	33	R	R	5-11	195	9-14-76	1998	Las Vegas, Nev.

MARTINSVILLE — Rookie

APPALACHIAN LEAGUE

BATTING	AVG	G	AB	R	H	2B	3B	HR	RBI	BB	SO	SB	CS	B	T	HT	WT	DOB	1st Yr	Resides
Acevedo, Carlos	.237	64	249	31	59	11	3	1	25	12	32	6	6	R	R	6-0	180	1-31-81	1997	Santo Domingo, D.R.
Beverly, Shomari	.311	44	177	37	55	13	6	1	25	13	51	12	5	R	R	6-0	165	2-16-78	1997	Alameda, Calif.
Bishop, Bennie	.219	51	169	24	37	7	1	2	19	16	45	9	2	R	R	5-11	170	1-2-79	1997	Inglewood, Calif.
Bushman, Jon	.400	4	5	1	2	2	0	0	1	2	2	0	1	R	R	5-11	165	10-13-78	1997	St. Louis, Mo.
Caines, Franklyn	.207	35	116	16	24	4	0	5	18	6	35	1	1	R	R	6-2	170	1-5-77	1994	San Pedro de Macoris, D.R.
Cody, Ryan	.218	24	87	10	19	6	1	4	18	9	19	1	0	R	R	6-1	190	6-13-78	1997	Vancouver, Wash.
Deitrick, Jeremy	.292	8	24	5	7	0	0	0	5	3	5	0	1	R	R	6-1	200	9-14-76	1998	Williamsport, Pa.
Espy, Nate	.361	66	227	50	82	20	1	13	56	51	55	2	2	R	R	6-3	215	4-24-78	1998	Pensacola, Fla.
Hannahan, Buzz	.274	55	197	38	54	6	1	0	20	42	31	14	6	R	R	6-2	180	6-29-76	1998	Torrance, Calif.
Ishida, Takehito	.182	10	22	3	4	0	1	0	1	1	6	1	0	R	R	6-2	170	7-30-78	1998	Tokyo, Japan
Jewson, Ben	.261	35	119	19	31	4	0	1	11	16	48	0	1	R	R	6-3	205	6-29-79	1998	Waukesha, Wis.
Johnson, Duane	.216	27	51	9	11	2	0	0	2	8	21	3	1	B	R	6-0	180	11-19-78	1997	Reno, Nev.
Johnson, Yoan	.242	11	33	3	8	0	0	0	2	2	10	1	0	R	R	5-11	185	5-17-79	1997	Sabana de la Mar, D.R.
Marchant, Nick	.189	24	74	8	14	3	1	0	5	9	23	2	0	R	R	6-2	200	7-2-78	1997	Boise, Idaho
Martin, Jason	.233	18	43	9	10	1	0	0	3	5	8	2	0	R	R	6-0	175	10-9-77	1998	Las Vegas, Nev.
McArthur, Kennon	.214	38	126	18	27	2	2	5	17	8	56	0	0	R	R	6-2	205	10-23-79	1998	Sylacauga, Ala.
Norrell, Troy	.240	36	121	11	29	7	0	4	14	7	47	1	0	R	R	6-0	185	10-25-76	1997	Lake Jackson, Texas
Padilla, Jorge	.356	23	90	10	32	3	0	5	25	4	24	2	0	R	R	6-2	210	8-11-79	1998	Carolina, P.R.
Reyes, Ambiorix	.223	62	215	35	48	3	2	0	21	16	24	12	3	B	R	5-11	160	2-6-79	1996	Rancho Viejo, D.R.
Rojas, Alejandro	.239	50	180	24	43	7	0	1	15	24	44	23	2	B	R	5-9	145	3-2-78	1996	La Vega, D.R.

GAMES BY POSITION: C—Bushman 1, Cody 19, Deitrick 7, D. Johnson 1, McArthur 38, Norrell 11. **1B**—Caines 15, Espy 57, D. Johnson 1, Martin 1. **2B**—Hannahan 24, Ishida 1, Jewson 1, Rojas 48. **3B**—Caines 11, Hannahan 28, Ishida 1, Jewson 27, Martin 9. **SS**—Hannahan 4, Ishida 7, Martin 1, Norrell 1, Reyes 62. **OF**—Acevedo 63, Beverly 16, Bishop 49, Caines 4, Espy 1, Jewson 1, D. Johnson 22, Y. Johnson 8, Marchant 23, Norrell 17, Padilla 22.

PITCHING	W	L	ERA	G	GS	CG	SV	IP	H	R	ER	BB	SO	B	T	HT	WT	DOB	1st Yr	Resides
Bailie, Matt	4	2	2.84	24	0	0	9	32	33	13	10	6	36	R	R	5-10	195	10-1-75	1998	Aloha, Ore.
Baisley, Brad	3	2	3.58	7	7	0	0	28	27	12	11	4	14	R	R	6-9	200	8-24-79	1998	Tampa, Fla.
Blackmon, Kurt	1	2	4.12	15	5	0	1	44	51	26	20	17	26	R	R	6-1	200	6-21-76	1998	Rock Hill, S.C.
Castro, Rafael	1	1	6.75	14	1	0	0	21	37	22	16	9	14	R	R	6-2	155	5-18-77	1994	Los Llanos, D.R.
Gallardo, Stalin	0	0	2.25	2	0	0	0	4	6	3	1	1	4	R	R	5-10	180	8-2-79	1997	Barquisimeto, Ven.
Grammer, Ed	4	1	5.08	16	0	0	1	28	40	19	16	16	22	R	R	6-4	215	10-8-75	1998	Ripley, Tenn.
Lawson, Jarrod	4	3	4.04	13	13	0	0	62	65	40	28	26	38	R	R	6-4	200	4-2-79	1998	Potosi, Mo.
Madson, Ryan	3	3	4.83	12	10	0	0	54	57	38	29	20	52	L	R	6-5	175	8-28-80	1998	Moreno Valley, Calif.
Maness, Chris	2	2	3.38	19	0	0	0	32	31	17	12	12	40	R	R	6-2	195	4-22-76	1998	Greensboro, N.C.
Marifian, John	0	2	3.99	16	1	0	0	29	25	20	13	14	31	L	L	6-3	225	1-5-78	1998	Downey, Calif.
Martinez, Alex	1	3	2.92	22	0	0	0	37	30	22	12	22	28	R	R	6-0	145	11-13-78	1996	Santo Domingo, D.R.
Nunez, Franklin	2	2	2.49	6	4	0	0	25	23	10	7	8	19	R	R	6-0	165	1-18-77	1995	Nagua, D.R.
Rose, Johnathan	3	0	3.99	22	0	0	2	38	29	22	17	11	48	L	L	6-4	225	8-18-76	1997	Haw River, N.C.
Silva, Carlcs	1	4	5.05	7	7	1	0	41	48	24	23	4	21	R	R	6-4	198	4-23-79	1996	Calle los Mangos, Ven.
Tanaka, Masahiro	0	0	7.20	4	0	0	0	5	8	8	4	2	3	R	R	6-3	180	5-27-77	1998	Japan
Turnbow, Derrick	2	6	5.01	13	13	1	0	70	66	44	39	26	45	R	R	6-3	180	1-25-78	1997	Franklin, Tenn.
Wilson, Mike	1	3	4.81	9	7	0	0	39	40	25	21	13	40	R	R	6-6	222	6-12-80	1998	El Cajon, Calif.

PITTSBURGH PIRATES

Going gets tougher after '97 squad boosted expectations

BY JOHN PERROTTO

The Pirates' promotional slogan for the 1998 season was "What Baseball's All About."

Oops.

If the '98 Pirates were what baseball's all about, then the sport is in big trouble.

A year after making an amazing run at the National League Central title with just a $9 million payroll, the Pirates spent all season in the cellar or trying to avoid it. They wound up with their first 90-loss season since 1986, going 69-93.

"I don't think anyone realistically thought we were going to duplicate 1997 again," manager Gene Lamont said. "I think there were a lot of factors at work in '97. We probably played over our heads a little bit and the rest of the division was really down. Really, it was all kind of a mirage.

"We knew it'd be a lot tougher this year, especially in light of the fact that we were still rebuilding and our lineup was even younger this season."

Especially at third base, where Aramis Ramirez debuted at age 19 after only 40 games at Triple-A Nashville. Ramirez kept his head above water, but it was clear he was not ready for the major leagues.

What was most distressing was how the Pirates seemingly tanked it down the stretch, losing 25 of their last 30 games while often appearing to be just going through the motions.

That's not to say there were no highlights. First baseman Kevin Young was the first Pirate to hit 40 doubles and 25 homers in a season since Dave Parker in 1979. Catcher Jason Kendall contended for the NL batting title with a .327 average and led all catchers with 26 stolen bases. Second baseman Tony Womack's 58 steals made him the first Pirate to lead the NL in consecutive seasons since Omar Moreno in 1978-79.

The Pirates also put together a solid starting rotation with righthanders Francisco Cordova, Jon Lieber, Jason Schmidt and Jose Silva and lefthander Chris Peters. None will be older than 29 when the 1999 season begins.

Still, the Pirates were lacking.

"Our pitching staff is awesome," Kendall said. "What the challenge is now is for the rest of the team to catch up to the pitching staff. We need to give those guys more support. We need to score them some runs and play better defense behind them."

The season was doubly rough for the Pirates. Not only were they lacking at the major league level, but their six farm clubs compiled an aggregate 314-386 record for a lowly .449 winning percentage, the fourth worst in baseball.

While prospects such as Nashville outfielder Chad Hermansen took small steps forward, others like shortstop Abraham Nunez and righthander Kris Benson regressed. Even worse, lefthander Jeff Wallace (reconstructive elbow surgery) and first baseman Ron Wright (back surgery) suffered possibly career-altering injuries.

"It takes time," general manager Cam Bonifay said. "When we decided to go into this rebuilding program (prior to the '97 season), we said it would take five years. We're only through two years. I think we're making progress, I think we're getting better. Rebuilding takes time and we all have to remind ourselves to be patient."

Jason Kendall

Emil Brown

Players of the Year

Major League: Jason Kendall, c
Kendall's .411 on-base percentage sparked the Pirates offense and he led National League catchers with 26 stolen bases.

Minor League: Emil Brown, of, Carolina
The former Rule 5 pick batted .330 with 14 homers and 24 steals for Double-A Carolina.

ORGANIZATION LEADERS

BATTING		
*AVG	Darryl Brinkley, Nashville	.355
R	Emil Brown, Carolina	89
H	Emil Brown, Carolina	154
TB	Chad Hermansen, Nashville	238
2B	Kory DeHaan, Augusta	39
3B	Julian Redman, Lynchburg	10
HR	Chad Hermansen, Nashville	28
RBI	Derrick Lankford, Augusta	89
BB	Tracy Sanders, Carolina	97
SO	Corey Pointer, Lynchburg	177
SB	Victor Gutierrez, Augusta	60
PITCHING		
W	Two tied at	12
L	Jason Phillips, Nashville/Carolina	13
#ERA	Aaron France, Lynchburg	2.72
G	Ken Giard, Nashville/Carolina	57
CG	Paul Ah Yat, Carolina/Lynchburg	5
SV	David Daniels, Carolina/Lynchburg	25
IP	Paul Ah Yat, Carolina/Lynchburg	187
BB	Brian O'Connor, Carolina/Lynchburg	75
SO	Kris Lambert, Lynchburg	145

*Minimum 250 At-Bats #Minimum 75 Innings

Pittsburgh PIRATES

Manager: Gene Lamont.

1998 Record: 69-93, .426 (6th, NL Central)

BATTING	AVG	G	AB	R	H	2B	3B	HR	RBI	BB	SO	SB	CS	B	T	HT	WT	DOB	1st Yr	Resides
Allensworth, Jermaine	.309	69	233	30	72	13	3	3	24	17	43	8	4	R	R	6-0	190	1-11-72	1993	Anderson, Ind.
Bieser, Steve	.273	13	11	2	3	1	0	0	1	2	2	0	0	L	R	5-10	170	8-4-67	1989	St. Genevieve, Mo.
Brown, Adrian	.283	41	152	20	43	4	1	0	5	9	18	4	0	B	R	6-0	185	2-7-74	1992	Summit, Miss.
Brown, Emil	.256	13	39	2	10	1	0	0	3	1	11	0	0	R	R	6-2	195	12-29-74	1994	Chicago, Ill.
Collier, Lou	.246	110	334	30	82	13	6	2	34	31	70	2	2	R	R	5-10	183	8-21-73	1993	Chicago, Ill.
Garcia, Freddy	.256	56	172	27	44	11	1	9	26	18	45	0	2	R	R	6-3	219	8-1-72	1991	La Romana, D.R.
Guillen, Jose	.267	153	573	60	153	38	2	14	84	21	100	3	5	R	R	5-11	196	5-17-76	1993	San Cristobal, D.R.
Kendall, Jason	.327	149	535	95	175	36	3	12	75	51	51	26	5	R	R	6-0	190	6-26-74	1992	Torrance, Calif.
Laker, Tim	.375	14	24	2	9	1	0	1	2	1	3	0	0	R	R	6-2	175	11-27-69	1988	Simi Valley, Calif.
Martin, Al	.239	125	440	57	105	15	2	12	47	32	91	20	3	L	L	6-2	207	11-24-67	1985	Scottsdale, Ariz.
Martinez, Manny	.250	73	180	21	45	11	2	6	24	9	44	0	3	R	R	6-2	169	10-3-70	1988	San Pedro de Macoris, D.R.
Nunez, Abraham	.192	24	52	6	10	2	0	1	2	12	14	4	2	B	R	5-11	177	3-16-76	1994	Santo Domingo, D.R.
Osik, Keith	.214	39	98	8	21	4	0	0	7	13	16	1	2	R	R	6-0	198	10-22-68	1990	Shoreham, N.Y.
Polcovich, Kevin	.189	81	212	18	40	12	0	0	14	15	33	4	3	R	R	5-9	182	6-28-70	1992	Auburn, N.Y.
Ramirez, Aramis	.235	72	251	23	59	9	1	6	24	18	72	0	1	R	R	6-1	190	6-25-78	1995	Santo Domingo, D.R.
Sanford, Chance	.143	14	28	3	4	1	1	0	3	1	6	0	0	L	R	5-10	175	6-2-72	1992	Houston, Texas
Smith, Mark	.195	59	128	18	25	6	0	2	13	10	26	7	0	R	R	6-3	235	5-7-70	1991	Arcadia, Calif.
Strange, Doug	.173	90	185	8	32	8	0	0	14	10	39	1	0	B	R	6-1	185	4-13-64	1985	Greenville, S.C.
Ward, Turner	.262	123	282	33	74	13	3	9	46	27	40	5	4	B	R	6-2	200	4-11-65	1986	Satsuma, Ala.
Womack, Tony	.282	159	655	85	185	26	7	3	45	38	94	58	8	L	R	5-9	155	9-25-69	1991	Greensboro, N.C.
Young, Kevin	.270	159	592	88	160	40	2	27	108	44	127	15	7	R	R	6-3	220	6-16-69	1990	Phoenix, Ariz.

PITCHING	W	L	ERA	G	GS	CG	SV	IP	H	R	ER	BB	SO	B	T	HT	WT	DOB	1st Yr	Resides
Christiansen, Jason	3	3	2.51	60	0	0	6	65	51	22	18	27	71	R	L	6-5	246	9-21-69	1991	Omaha, Neb.
Cordova, Francisco	13	14	3.31	33	33	3	0	220	204	91	81	69	157	R	R	6-1	183	4-26-72	1996	Cerro Azul, Mexico
Dessens, Elmer	2	6	5.67	43	5	0	0	75	90	50	47	25	43	R	R	6-0	178	1-13-72	1993	Hermosillo, Mexico
Lawrence, Sean	2	1	7.32	7	3	0	0	20	25	16	16	10	12	L	L	6-4	215	9-2-70	1992	Hillside, Ill.
Lieber, Jon	8	14	4.11	29	28	2	1	171	182	93	78	40	138	L	R	6-2	227	4-2-70	1992	Birmingham, Ala.
Loaiza, Esteban	6	5	4.52	21	14	0	0	92	96	50	46	30	53	R	R	6-3	205	12-31-71	1991	Imperial Beach, Calif.
Loiselle, Rich	2	7	3.44	54	0	0	19	55	56	26	21	36	48	R	R	6-5	240	1-12-72	1991	Upland, Calif.
Martinez, Javier	0	1	4.83	37	0	0	0	41	39	32	22	34	42	R	R	6-2	210	2-5-77	1994	Bayamon, P.R.
McCurry, Jeff	1	3	6.52	16	0	0	0	19	24	14	14	9	11	R	R	6-6	220	1-21-70	1991	Houston, Texas
Peters, Chris	8	10	3.47	39	21	1	1	148	142	63	57	55	103	L	L	6-1	170	1-28-72	1993	McMurray, Pa.
Rincon, Ricardo	0	2	2.91	60	0	0	14	65	50	31	21	29	64	L	L	5-10	187	4-13-70	1997	Cuitlahuac, Mexico
Schmidt, Jason	11	14	4.07	33	33	0	0	214	228	106	97	71	158	R	R	6-5	207	1-29-73	1991	Lewiston, Idaho
Silva, Jose	6	7	4.40	18	18	1	0	100	104	55	49	30	64	R	R	6-5	230	12-19-73	1991	San Diego, Calif.
Tabaka, Jeff	2	2	3.02	37	0	0	0	51	37	19	17	22	40	R	L	6-3	200	1-17-64	1986	Clinton, Ohio
Van Poppel, Todd	1	2	5.36	18	7	0	0	47	53	32	28	18	32	R	R	6-5	210	12-9-71	1990	Southlake, Texas
Wilkins, Marc	0	0	3.52	16	0	0	0	15	13	6	6	9	17	R	R	5-11	207	10-21-70	1992	Pittsburgh, Pa.
Williams, Mike	4	2	1.94	37	1	0	0	51	39	12	11	16	59	R	R	6-3	195	7-29-68	1990	Newport, Va.

FIELDING

Catcher	PCT	G	PO	A	E	DP	PB
Kendall	.992	144	1015	58	9	10	9
Laker	1.000	1	2	0	0	0	1
Osik	1.000	26	143	12	0	1	4

First Base	PCT	G	PO	A	E	DP
Garcia	.964	4	25	2	1	2
Laker	1.000	4	33	1	0	4
Smith	1.000	6	30	4	0	3
Strange	1.000	3	2	1	0	0
Young	.994	157	1335	80	8	138

Second Base	PCT	G	PO	A	E	DP
Polcovich	1.000	15	15	37	0	9
Sanford	.500	1	1	0	1	0
Strange	1.000	9	17	18	0	6
Womack	.978	152	304	450	17	104

Third Base	PCT	G	PO	A	E	DP
Garcia	.949	47	28	102	7	9
Osik	.964	7	9	18	1	4
Polcovich	1.000	8	2	17	0	1
Ramirez	.941	71	29	114	9	12
Sanford	.900	5	4	5	1	2
Strange	.940	42	25	54	5	3

Shortstop	PCT	G	PO	A	E	DP
Collier	.960	107	148	287	18	56
Nunez	.930	23	32	61	7	12
Polcovich	.916	54	60	159	20	32
Sanford	1.000	1	0	1	0	0
Womack	1.000	2	1	1	0	0

Outfield	PCT	G	PO	A	E	DP
Allensworth	.980	66	145	4	3	2
Bieser	.000	1	0	0	0	0
Brown	.977	38	83	3	2	2
Brown	1.000	10	21	2	0	0
Guillen	.968	151	284	16	10	4
Martin	.985	114	192	6	3	1
Martinez	.989	62	92	0	1	0
Smith	.977	24	42	0	1	0
Ward	.983	97	162	7	3	1
Womack	1.000	5	4	0	0	0

GEORGE GOJKOVICH

Kevin Young

FARM SYSTEM

Director of Player Development: Paul Tinnell

Class	Farm Team	League	W	L	Pct.	Finish*	Manager	First Yr
AAA	Nashville (Tenn.) Sounds	Pacific Coast	67	76	.469	12th (16)	Trent Jewett	1998
AA	Carolina (N.C.) Mudcats	Southern	59	80	.424	9th (10)	Jeff Banister	1991
A#	Lynchburg (Va.) Hillcats	Carolina	69	71	.493	t-4th (8)	Jeff Richardson	1995
A	Augusta (Ga.) GreenJackets	South Atlantic	68	74	.479	9th (14)	Marty Brown	1988
A	Erie (Pa.) Seawolves	New York-Penn	26	50	.342	14th (14)	Tracy Woodson	1995
Rookie	Bradenton (Fla.) Pirates	Gulf Coast	25	35	.417	t-11th (14)	Woody Huyke	1967

*Finish in overall standings (No. of teams in league) #Advanced level

NASHVILLE — Class AAA

PACIFIC COAST LEAGUE

BATTING	AVG	G	AB	R	H	2B	3B	HR	RBI	BB	SO	SB	CS	B	T	HT	WT	DOB	1st Yr	Resides
Bieser, Steve	.257	82	206	30	53	11	4	1	24	33	30	13	2	L	R	5-10	170	8-4-67	1989	St. Genevieve, Mo.
Brinkley, Darryl	.355	114	372	57	132	23	3	9	51	27	53	10	8	R	R	5-11	205	12-23-68	1994	Stamford, Conn.
Brito, Luis	.231	9	26	3	6	0	0	0	0	2	3	0	0	B	R	6-0	155	4-12-71	1989	San Pedro de Macoris, D.R.
Brown, Adrian	.289	85	311	58	90	12	5	3	27	28	38	25	7	B	R	6-0	185	2-7-74	1992	Summit, Miss.
Brown, Randy	.184	14	49	8	9	1	0	1	6	4	15	1	1	R	R	5-11	160	5-1-70	1989	Houston, Texas
Canale, George	.232	46	151	10	35	8	0	5	29	8	36	0	1	L	R	6-1	195	8-11-65	1986	Roanoke, Va.
Candaele, Casey	.272	44	147	18	40	5	2	1	15	13	19	1	1	B	R	5-9	165	1-12-61	1983	San Luis Obispo, Calif.
Decker, Steve	.129	18	62	5	8	3	0	2	4	5	14	0	0	R	R	6-3	220	10-25-65	1988	Keizer, Ore.
Edge, Tim	.250	49	144	20	36	4	2	4	16	7	34	2	2	R	R	6-0	210	10-26-68	1990	Snellville, Ga.
Garcia, Freddy	.270	88	326	52	88	24	4	22	55	25	89	0	2	R	R	6-3	219	8-1-72	1991	La Romana, D.R.
Geisler, Phil	.286	5	7	1	2	0	0	0	0	1	4	0	0	L	L	6-3	200	10-23-69	1991	Springfield, Ore.
Grijak, Kevin	.286	67	227	32	65	17	0	15	40	23	34	1	4	L	R	6-2	215	8-6-70	1991	Sterling Heights, Mich.
Hermansen, Chad	.258	126	458	81	118	26	5	28	78	50	152	21	4	R	R	6-2	185	9-10-77	1995	Henderson, Nev.
Laker, Tim	.355	44	152	30	54	16	1	11	34	21	26	1	0	R	R	6-2	175	11-27-69	1988	Simi Valley, Calif.
Martinez, Manny	.240	22	75	12	18	5	0	1	6	7	20	5	3	R	R	6-2	169	10-3-70	1988	San Pedro de Macoris, D.R.
Nunez, Abraham	.249	94	366	50	91	12	3	3	32	39	73	16	8	B	R	5-11	177	3-16-76	1994	Santo Domingo, D.R.
Patzke, Jeff	.299	104	361	48	108	16	0	7	48	48	74	6	6	B	R	6-0	190	11-19-73	1992	Klamath Falls, Ore.
Peterson, Charles	.000	8	9	0	0	0	0	0	0	0	4	0	0	R	R	6-3	203	5-8-74	1993	Laurens, S.C.
Ramirez, Aramis	.274	47	168	19	46	10	0	5	18	24	28	0	2	R	R	6-1	190	6-25-78	1995	Santo Domingo, D.R.
Reyes, Jose	.667	1	3	0	2	1	0	0	0	0	1	0	0	R	R	6-1	188	5-1-73	1993	Villa Vazquez, D.R.
Rose, Pete	.208	28	72	8	15	1	0	1	12	3	13	0	0	L	R	6-1	180	11-16-69	1989	Cincinnati, Ohio
Sanford, Chance	.259	27	81	17	21	7	1	4	21	10	12	0	1	L	R	5-10	175	6-2-72	1992	Houston, Texas
Smith, Mark	.355	24	93	18	33	10	1	8	30	11	20	3	1	R	R	6-3	235	5-7-70	1991	Arcadia, Calif.
Staton, T.J.	.242	62	186	28	45	8	0	6	21	15	55	5	4	L	L	6-3	210	2-17-75	1993	Elyrla, Ohio
Sweet, Jon	.163	17	43	4	7	1	0	1	4	2	9	0	0	L	R	6-0	183	11-10-71	1994	Cincinnati, Ohio
Thobe, Steve	.000	7	11	0	0	0	0	0	1	0	2	0	0	R	R	6-7	230	5-26-72	1994	Huntington Beach, Calif.
Whitmore, Darrell	.309	105	311	58	96	19	1	21	50	36	87	3	4	L	R	6-1	220	11-18-68	1990	Miarmar, Fla.
Wimmer, Chris	.341	47	135	18	46	6	0	1	14	5	19	5	2	R	R	5-11	175	9-25-70	1992	Oklahoma City, Okla.
Wright, Ron	.214	17	56	6	12	3	0	0	9	9	18	0	0	R	R	6-1	230	1-21-76	1994	St. George, Utah

PITCHING	W	L	ERA	G	GS	CG	SV	IP	H	R	ER	BB	SO	B	T	HT	WT	DOB	1st Yr	Resides
Alvarez, Tavo	3	5	4.83	15	15	1	0	86	101	57	46	22	58	R	R	6-3	250	11-25-71	1990	Obregon, Mexico
Anderson, Jimmy	9	10	5.02	35	17	0	0	124	144	87	69	72	63	L	L	6-1	195	1-22-76	1994	Chesapeake, Va.
Benson, Kris	8	10	5.37	28	28	1	0	156	162	102	93	50	129	R	R	6-4	190	11-7-74	1996	Marietta, Ga.
Bolton, Tom	1	1	10.38	3	1	0	0	4	8	5	5	2	3	L	L	6-3	185	5-6-62	1980	Smyrna, Tenn.
Caruso, Gene	0	0	0.00	2	0	0	0	2	2	0	0	2	2	L	L	6-0	180	7-20-69	1992	Las Vegas, Nev.
Crawford, Carlos	2	2	6.18	8	5	0	0	28	25	23	19	15	11	R	R	6-2	205	10-4-71	1990	Charlotte, N.C.
Daniels, David	0	0	0.00	2	0	0	0	1	0	0	0	2	1	R	R	6-2	185	7-25-73	1996	Nashville, Tenn.
Dessens, Elmer	3	1	3.30	6	5	0	0	30	32	12	11	6	13	R	R	6-0	178	1-13-72	1993	Hermosillo, Mexico
Doman, Roger	0	0	9.22	7	1	0	0	14	16	14	14	6	9	R	R	6-5	190	1-26-73	1991	Joplin, Mo.
Evans, Dave	0	2	8.49	7	1	0	0	12	19	12	11	8	8	R	R	6-3	205	1-1-68	1990	Houston, Texas
Giard, Ken	1	2	5.71	15	0	0	0	17	17	12	11	12	16	R	R	6-3	200	4-2-73	1991	Warwick, R.I.
Halperin, Mike	0	2	5.79	11	0	0	0	14	17	9	9	9	10	L	L	5-10	170	9-8-73	1994	Naples, Fla.
Haynie, Jason	0	2	9.19	3	3	0	0	16	24	18	16	7	6	L	L	6-0	190	3-29-74	1996	Columbia, S.C.
Heredia, Julian	0	0	5.14	4	0	0	0	7	7	4	4	2	6	R	R	6-1	170	9-22-69	1989	La Romana, D.R.
Klingenbeck, Scott	2	2	6.14	6	6	0	0	29	45	24	20	7	15	R	R	6-2	205	2-3-71	1992	Cincinnati, Ohio
Lawrence, Sean	12	9	5.02	26	26	0	0	147	153	86	82	57	126	L	L	6-4	215	9-2-70	1992	Hillside, Ill.
Loiselle, Rich	0	0	0.00	4	0	0	2	5	3	0	0	0	6	R	R	6-5	240	1-12-72	1991	Upland, Calif.
Mathews, Del	1	0	10.50	4	0	0	0	6	8	8	7	6	4	L	L	6-4	215	10-31-74	1993	Fernandina Beach, Fla.
McCurry, Jeff	2	5	4.96	40	0	0	23	45	45	26	25	15	34	R	R	6-6	220	1-21-70	1991	Houston, Texas
Meacham, Rusty	2	1	3.34	15	2	0	3	30	35	14	11	8	25	R	R	6-2	175	1-27-68	1988	Palm City, Fla.
2-team (38 Memphis)	3	3	4.50	53	2	0	5	82	103	44	41	23	81							
Mintz, Steve	4	4	5.45	56	0	0	1	73	85	48	44	32	45	L	R	5-11	190	11-24-68	1990	Vero Beach, Fla.
Phillips, Jason	2	0	2.59	5	5	0	0	31	38	10	9	12	21	R	R	6-5	220	3-22-74	1992	Muncy, Pa.
Pickford, Kevin	6	1	3.49	13	12	0	0	80	84	33	31	20	59	L	L	6-3	192	3-12-75	1993	Fresno, Calif.
Rincon, Ricardo	0	0	0.00	1	0	0	0	1	0	0	0	0	1	L	L	5-10	187	4-13-70	1997	Cuitlahuac, Mexico
Ryan, Matt	4	3	4.17	51	6	0	3	86	85	50	40	36	41	R	R	6-5	190	3-20-72	1993	Oxford, Miss.
Sauveur, Rich	1	4	1.81	46	0	0	10	45	34	15	9	17	43	L	L	6-4	170	11-23-63	1983	Falls Church, Va.
Silva, Jose	0	0	4.82	3	3	0	0	9	10	5	5	4	6	R	R	6-5	230	12-19-73	1991	San Diego, Calif.
Tabaka, Jeff	0	1	7.71	4	0	0	0	5	9	4	4	0	4	R	L	6-3	200	1-17-64	1986	Clinton, Ohio
Tolar, Kevin	0	0	6.00	1	0	0	0	3	2	2	2	4	1	R	L	6-3	225	1-28-71	1989	Brandon, Fla.
Wiegandt, Scott	0	1	6.35	11	0	0	0	11	12	10	8	9	6	L	L	5-11	180	12-9-67	1989	Louisville, Ky.
Wilkins, Marc	1	0	10.38	5	0	0	0	4	3	5	5	3	4	R	R	5-11	207	10-21-70	1992	Pittsburgh, Pa.
Williams, Mike	0	2	5.59	16	4	0	1	37	36	25	23	14	34	R	R	6-3	195	7-29-68	1990	Newport, Va.
Wilson, Gary	3	5	5.98	29	3	0	1	59	77	46	39	22	39	R	R	6-3	190	1-1-70	1992	Arcata, Calif.

FIELDING

Catcher	PCT	G	PO	A	E	DP	PB
Bieser	.993	54	284	21	2	0	3
Decker	1.000	18	119	10	0	2	1
Edge	.992	40	232	22	2	0	3
Laker	.989	30	109	13	2	4	4
Reyes	1.000	1	2	0	0	0	0
Sweet	.986	15	66	7	1	1	1

First Base	PCT	G	PO	A	E	DP
Canale	.991	28	213	15	2	18
Edge	1.000	2	1	0	0	0
Garcia	.976	21	147	16	4	15
Grijak	.990	55	458	37	5	46
Laker	.984	14	114	13	2	11
Rose	.990	15	95	5	1	11
Smith	1.000	7	62	5	0	6
Thobe	1.000	5	33	5	0	3
Wright	.986	16	125	11	2	9

Second Base	PCT	G	PO	A	E	DP
Bieser	.840	4	12	9	4	1
Brito	.000	1	0	0	0	0
R. Brown	1.000	1	2	0	0	0
Candaele	.963	20	46	57	4	10
Hermansen	.842	7	17	15	6	3
Martinez	.000	1	0	0	0	0
Patzke	.975	101	209	306	13	74
Rose	1.000	3	0	1	0	1
Sanford	.974	10	15	23	1	5
Wimmer	1.000	6	14	12	0	3

Third Base	PCT	G	PO	A	E	DP
Canale	1.000	1	0	1	0	0
Candaele	.000	1	0	0	0	0
Garcia	.921	67	38	137	15	9
Ramirez	.932	46	33	77	8	8
Rose	.875	8	3	11	2	0
Sanford	1.000	6	6	7	0	0
Smith	.889	5	4	12	2	0
Wimmer	1.000	21	7	36	0	4

Shortstop	PCT	G	PO	A	E	DP
Brito	.925	8	13	24	3	4
R. Brown	.947	13	19	35	3	7
Candaele	.919	17	21	47	6	10
Nunez	.953	94	155	274	21	63
Patzke	1.000	2	0	3	0	0
Ramirez	.000	1	0	0	0	0
Sanford	.882	4	4	11	2	0
Wimmer	.926	14	18	32	4	10

Outfield	PCT	G	PO	A	E	DP
Bieser	1.000	13	23	2	0	0
Brinkley	.987	86	154	3	2	0
A. Brown	.977	80	204	7	5	0
Canale	.000	1	0	0	0	0
Garcia	.000	1	0	0	0	0
Geisler	1.000	5	4	0	0	0
Hermansen	.961	114	191	6	8	0
Martinez	.943	20	31	2	2	1
Peterson	1.000	3	1	0	0	0
Sanford	1.000	3	4	0	0	0
Smith	1.000	11	17	0	0	0
Staton	.945	56	102	2	6	0
Whitmore	.960	70	96	1	4	0

CAROLINA — Class AA

SOUTHERN LEAGUE

BATTING	AVG	G	AB	R	H	2B	3B	HR	RBI	BB	SO	SB	CS	B	T	HT	WT	DOB	1st Yr	Resides
Asche, Mike	.259	65	212	44	55	14	4	3	26	37	45	15	6	R	R	6-2	190	2-13-72	1994	Kearney, Neb.
Beasley, Tony	.286	6	7	2	2	1	0	0	1	1	2	0	0	R	R	5-8	165	12-5-66	1989	Bowling Green, Va.
Brito, Luis	.292	7	24	4	7	1	0	0	1	0	3	1	0	B	R	6-0	155	4-12-71	1989	San Pedro de Macoris, D.R.
Brown, Emil	.330	123	466	89	154	31	2	14	67	50	71	24	7	R	R	6-2	195	12-29-74	1994	Chicago, Ill.
Brown, Randy	.292	80	257	39	75	18	6	7	35	22	77	9	5	R	R	5-11	160	5-1-70	1989	Houston, Texas
Farris, Mark	.273	111	373	49	102	18	1	6	38	38	74	3	3	L	R	6-3	190	2-9-75	1994	Angleton, Texas
Figueroa, Luis	.249	117	350	54	87	9	3	0	24	71	46	6	5	B	R	5-9	158	2-16-74	1997	Vega Alta, P.R.
Furniss, Eddy	.136	16	44	1	6	1	0	0	3	4	13	0	0	L	L	6-3	225	9-18-75	1998	Nacogdoches, Texas
Grijak, Kevin	.349	46	146	29	51	8	0	9	33	18	15	1	0	L	R	6-2	215	8-6-70	1991	Sterling Heights, Mich.
Haverbusch, Kevin	.375	46	168	28	63	10	0	3	29	13	20	1	3	R	R	6-3	200	6-16-76	1997	Massapequa, N.Y.
Hernandez, Alex	.259	115	452	62	117	22	7	8	48	41	81	11	4	L	L	6-4	190	5-28-77	1995	Levittown, P.R.
Jasco, Elinton	.240	8	25	3	6	0	2	0	2	2	4	0	1	R	R	5-10	165	5-11-75	1993	San Pedro de Macoris, D.R.
Long, Garrett	.296	28	98	14	29	3	0	0	8	11	27	1	0	R	R	6-3	205	10-5-76	1995	Houston, Texas
Morris, Warren	.331	44	151	28	50	8	3	5	30	24	34	5	2	L	R	5-11	190	1-11-74	1997	Alexandria, La.
Ojeda, Miguel	.155	18	58	4	9	2	0	1	4	3	12	0	0	R	R	6-2	190	1-29-75	1993	Guaymas, Mexico
Peterson, Charles	.267	86	296	41	79	17	1	8	40	24	53	16	9	R	R	6-3	203	5-8-74	1993	Laurens, S.C.
Reyes, Jose	.189	11	37	5	7	0	1	2	7	1	9	1	1	R	R	6-1	188	5-1-73	1993	Villa Vazquez, D.R.
Sanders, Tracy	.234	113	342	69	80	18	2	22	70	97	86	3	4	L	R	6-1	210	7-26-69	1990	Port St. Lucie, Fla.
Staton, T.J.	.300	63	223	37	67	17	1	7	48	25	52	6	4	L	L	6-3	210	2-17-75	1993	Elyria, Ohio
Strange, Doug	.357	4	14	4	5	0	0	0	0	2	1	0	0	B	R	6-1	185	4-13-64	1985	Greenville, S.C.
Sweet, Jon	.227	77	238	24	54	11	1	2	44	20	18	1	2	L	R	6-0	183	11-10-71	1994	Cincinnati, Ohio
Thobe, Steve	.156	52	154	15	24	7	0	2	15	20	45	2	1	R	R	6-7	230	5-26-72	1994	Huntington Beach, Calif.
Wilson, Craig	.331	45	148	20	49	11	0	5	21	14	32	4	1	R	R	6-2	195	11-30-76	1995	Huntington Beach, Calif.
Wimmer, Chris	.271	59	218	28	59	7	1	1	20	20	32	15	8	R	R	5-11	175	9-25-70	1992	Oklahoma City, Okla.

PITCHING	W	L	ERA	G	GS	CG	SV	IP	H	R	ER	BB	SO	B	T	HT	WT	DOB	1st Yr	Resides
Ah Yat, Paul	5	5	3.63	13	13	1	0	84	84	43	34	21	60	R	L	6-1	190	10-13-74	1996	Honolulu, Hawaii
Arroyo, Bronson	9	8	5.46	23	22	1	0	127	158	91	77	51	90	R	R	6-5	180	2-24-77	1995	Brooksville, Fla.
Brown, Chad	0	2	3.66	24	0	0	0	32	30	13	13	17	21	L	L	6-0	185	12-9-71	1992	Gastonia, N.C.
2-team (5 Knoxville)	0	4	6.95	29	4	0	0	45	59	35	35	30	31							
Bussa, Todd	0	2	11.74	6	0	0	0	8	11	12	10	7	6	R	R	5-11	190	12-13-72	1991	Camanche, Ill.
Caruso, Gene	0	1	11.12	3	0	0	0	6	10	8	7	2	8	L	L	6-0	180	7-20-69	1992	Las Vegas, Nev.
Corn, Chris	2	2	5.48	8	7	0	0	46	61	31	28	14	26	R	R	6-3	170	10-4-71	1994	Louisville, Ky.
Crawford, Carlos	0	0	6.55	6	0	0	0	11	17	8	8	3	9	R	R	6-2	205	10-4-71	1990	Charlotte, N.C.
Daniels, David	4	3	2.97	35	0	0	16	39	34	15	13	16	37	R	R	6-2	185	7-25-73	1996	Nashville, Tenn.
Davis, Kane	1	11	9.24	18	16	0	0	74	102	84	76	38	39	R	R	6-3	190	6-25-75	1993	Reedy, W.Va.
De los Santos, Mariano	1	2	5.59	10	1	0	1	19	13	12	12	12	15	R	R	5-10	200	7-13-70	1989	Santo Domingo, D.R.
Dillinger, John	0	1	14.29	4	0	0	0	6	11	9	9	4	4	R	R	6-5	240	8-28-73	1992	Connellsville, Pa.
Doman, Roger	0	1	7.40	10	1	0	0	21	29	20	17	8	12	R	R	6-5	190	1-26-73	1991	Joplin, Mo.
Evans, Dave	5	4	5.24	26	3	0	0	57	56	36	33	30	52	R	R	6-3	205	1-1-68	1990	Houston, Texas
Giard, Ken	6	5	2.62	42	0	0	6	58	33	24	17	37	56	R	R	6-3	200	4-2-73	1991	Warwick, R.I.
Halperin, Mike	0	0	0.00	1	0	0	0	1	1	0	0	1	0	L	L	5-10	170	9-8-73	1994	Naples, Fla.
Haynie, Jason	5	3	3.50	17	15	0	0	80	82	37	31	28	44	L	L	6-0	190	3-29-74	1996	Columbia, S.C.
Hernandez, Elvin	3	6	5.72	27	13	0	0	102	127	73	65	31	67	R	R	6-1	185	8-20-77	1994	Laguna Salada Monte, D.R.
Kelly, Jeff	0	0	0.00	1	0	0	0	1	1	0	0	0	0	L	L	6-6	240	1-11-75	1994	Staten Island, N.Y.
Mathews, Del	2	0	2.34	22	0	0	1	42	36	14	11	17	36	L	L	6-4	215	10-31-74	1993	Fernandina Beach, Fla.
McConnell, Sam	0	1	4.50	2	1	0	0	12	15	7	6	3	5	L	L	6-5	204	12-31-75	1997	Fairfield, Ohio
O'Connor, Brian	2	4	8.25	14	13	0	0	64	86	65	59	53	41	L	L	6-2	170	1-4-77	1995	Cincinnati, Ohio
Phillips, Jason	7	13	4.71	25	25	1	0	151	161	89	79	52	114	R	R	6-5	220	3-22-74	1992	Muncy, Pa.
Pickford, Kevin	5	1	3.90	13	8	1	0	58	48	26	25	15	43	L	L	6-3	192	3-12-75	1993	Fresno, Calif.
Rincon, Ricardo	0	0	6.00	2	0	0	0	3	5	2	2	2	1	L	L	5-10	187	4-13-70	1997	Cuitlaluac, Mexico
Runion, Tony	1	2	4.82	7	0	0	0	9	11	7	5	7	11	R	R	6-3	220	12-6-71	1993	Florence, Ky.
Shaw, Curtis	0	1	9.95	3	1	0	0	6	10	8	7	6	2	L	L	6-2	205	8-16-69	1990	Bartlesville, Okla.
Temple, Jason	0	0	10.27	20	0	0	0	24	23	29	27	36	11	R	R	6-1	185	11-8-74	1993	Woodhaven, Mich.
Tolar, Kevin	1	2	2.22	42	0	0	1	49	35	12	12	33	48	R	L	6-3	225	1-28-71	1989	Brandon, Fla.
Wilkins, Marc	0	0	4.50	2	0	0	0	2	1	1	1	0	4	R	R	5-11	207	10-21-70	1992	Pittsburgh, Pa.

FIELDING

Catcher	PCT	G	PO	A	E	DP	PB
Asche	1.000	1	1	0	0	0	0
Ojeda	.991	18	108	8	1	2	2
Reyes	.974	11	68	6	2	2	1
Sweet	.996	74	423	56	2	5	4
Thobe	1.000	17	104	11	0	1	9
Wilson	.995	32	185	13	1	0	7

First Base	PCT	G	PO	A	E	DP
Farris	1.000	26	215	9	0	22
Furniss	.990	14	93	11	1	9
Grijak	.969	17	146	9	5	12
Long	1.000	1	3	3	0	0
Sanders	.985	79	686	38	11	77
Thobe	.989	14	78	8	1	11

Second Base	PCT	G	PO	A	E	DP
Asche	1.000	2	2	2	0	0
Beasley	1.000	2	2	2	0	1
Brito	.875	1	1	6	1	1
R. Brown	1.000	10	24	26	0	6
Figueroa	.982	29	72	92	3	27
Jasco	.897	6	12	14	3	2
Morris	.964	40	87	100	7	29
Wimmer	.989	55	119	143	3	42

Third Base	PCT	G	PO	A	E	DP
R. Brown	.947	7	4	14	1	1
Farris	.905	82	57	153	22	3
Haverbusch	.871	41	26	89	17	8
Strange	1.000	4	1	5	0	2
Thobe	.949	15	15	22	2	4

Shortstop	PCT	G	PO	A	E	DP
Brito	.905	5	5	14	2	4
R. Brown	.967	53	85	147	8	38
Figueroa	.943	90	128	267	24	56
Wimmer	1.000	2	1	3	0	0

Outfield	PCT	G	PO	A	E	DP
Asche	.964	54	99	7	4	1
E. Brown	.972	108	199	10	6	0
R. Brown	1.000	2	1	0	0	0
Hernandez	.955	110	217	15	11	4
Long	.915	26	42	1	4	0
Peterson	.944	75	126	9	8	5
Sanders	.000	1	0	0	0	0
Staton	.988	55	78	4	1	0
Thobe	1.000	5	6	1	0	0

LYNCHBURG — Class A

CAROLINA LEAGUE

BATTING	AVG	G	AB	R	H	2B	3B	HR	RBI	BB	SO	SB	CS	B	T	HT	WT	DOB	1st Yr	Resides
Anderson, Franklin	.083	8	12	1	1	1	0	0	1	1	3	0	0	R	R	6-1	200	9-1-75	1995	Lake City, Ga.
Antigua, Nilson	.000	3	3	0	0	0	0	0	1	0	0	0	0	R	R	6-2	175	12-14-75	1993	Monte Plata, D.R.
Asche, Mike	.320	29	103	24	33	8	0	5	13	10	17	9	0	R	R	6-2	190	2-13-72	1994	Kearney, Neb.
Brito, Luis	.239	12	46	4	11	2	0	0	1	1	7	0	0	B	R	6-0	155	4-12-71	1989	San Pedro de Macoris, D.R.
Bryant, Matt	.277	51	177	20	49	7	1	2	13	17	38	1	1	R	R	6-0	185	4-28-75	1997	Denver, Colo.
Collier, Lou	.167	5	18	4	3	2	0	0	0	2	0	2	0	R	R	5-10	183	8-21-73	1993	Chicago, Ill.
Davis, Albert	.000	1	1	0	0	0	0	0	0	0	1	0	0	R	R	5-9	175	10-5-76	1994	Alcoa, Tenn.
Furniss, Eddy	.193	31	109	7	21	7	0	2	11	17	38	1	0	L	L	6-3	225	9-18-75	1998	Nacogdoches, Texas
Haad, Yamid	.254	88	299	32	76	8	2	5	34	13	54	1	7	R	R	6-2	165	9-2-77	1995	Cartagena, Colombia
Haverbusch, Kevin	.331	49	181	25	60	12	1	8	39	9	33	4	2	R	R	6-3	200	6-16-76	1997	Massapequa, N.Y.
Hundt, Bo	.179	11	39	2	7	0	0	0	2	2	9	2	2	B	R	6-0	202	4-21-75	1996	Bremen, Ind.
Jackson, Jeff	.278	28	97	16	27	8	0	2	15	8	31	3	2	R	R	6-2	180	1-2-72	1989	Chicago, Ill.
Jasco, Elinton	.250	14	32	8	8	1	0	0	1	2	6	1	2	R	R	5-10	165	5-11-75	1993	San Pedro de Macoris, D.R.
Long, Garrett	.282	91	309	46	87	29	1	7	43	49	83	7	2	R	R	6-3	205	10-5-76	1995	Houston, Texas
Lorenzana, Luis	.237	95	283	27	67	7	2	2	24	35	62	2	2	R	R	6-0	165	11-9-78	1996	San Diego, Calif.
Mackowiak, Rob	.274	86	292	30	80	24	6	3	31	17	65	6	3	L	R	5-10	165	6-20-76	1996	Schererville, Ind.
May, Freddy	.292	126	466	64	136	23	4	5	42	51	112	26	16	L	L	6-2	190	1-24-76	1995	Seattle, Wash.
Miyake, Chris	.253	120	411	48	104	20	3	2	38	32	79	5	3	R	R	6-2	185	5-18-74	1995	San Gabriel, Calif.
Nunez, Abraham	.222	5	18	2	4	1	0	0	2	3	1	1	0	B	R	5-11	177	3-16-76	1994	Santo Domingo, D.R.
Pena, Alex	.063	5	16	1	1	1	0	0	0	0	8	0	0	R	R	6-2	176	9-9-77	1995	Santo Domingo, D.R.
Pointer, Corey	.224	118	375	70	84	25	3	18	46	53	177	12	10	R	R	6-2	205	9-2-75	1994	Waxahachie, Texas
Redman, Julian	.257	131	525	70	135	26	10	6	46	32	73	36	16	L	L	5-11	165	3-10-77	1996	Duncanville, Ala.
Reyes, Jose	.222	18	54	11	12	4	0	3	9	4	17	2	0	R	R	6-1	188	5-1-73	1993	Villa Vazquez, D.R.
Rivera, Carlos	.230	29	113	11	26	4	0	4	16	0	19	0	1	L	L	6-1	220	6-10-78	1996	Rio Grande, P.R.
Robinson, Tony	.083	3	12	3	1	0	0	0	0	2	4	2	0	R	R	6-0	185	6-11-76	1994	Diamond Bar, Calif.
Walker, Morgan	.298	105	373	46	111	24	0	14	68	22	92	1	0	R	L	6-3	215	8-7-74	1996	Missouri City, Texas
Walker, Shon	.217	19	60	9	13	3	0	3	8	8	25	0	0	L	L	6-1	180	6-9-74	1992	Cynthiana, Ky.
Wilson, Craig	.269	61	219	26	59	12	2	12	45	22	53	2	1	R	R	6-2	195	11-30-76	1995	Huntington Beach, Calif.

GAMES BY POSITION: C—Anderson 8, Antigua 1, Haad 84, Reyes 17, Wilson 42. **1B**—Furniss 30, Long 63, Rivera 23, M. Walker 23, Wilson 7. **2B**—Haverbusch 1, Jasco 9, Lorenzana 89, Mackowiak 1, Miyake 45, Nunez 1, Robinson 3. **3B**—Asche 7, Bryant 14, Haverbusch 12, Hundt 10, Mackowiak 80, Miyake 23. **SS**—Brito 12, Bryant 38, Collier 5, Haverbusch 32, Lorenzana 4, Mackowiak 1, Miyake 54, Nunez 4. **OF**—Asche 14, Davis 1, Hundt 1, Jackson 22, Long 14, Mackowiak 1, May 122, Pena 5, Pointer 110, Redman 131, M. Walker 19.

PITCHING	W	L	ERA	G	GS	CG	SV	IP	H	R	ER	BB	SO	B	T	HT	WT	DOB	1st Yr	Resides
Ah Yat, Paul	6	3	2.73	14	14	4	0	102	95	40	31	13	77	R	L	6-1	190	10-13-74	1996	Honolulu, Hawaii
Alvarado, Carlos	3	5	5.61	13	10	0	0	59	69	48	37	24	52	R	R	6-4	195	1-24-78	1995	Arecibo, P.R.
Ayers, Mike	3	3	7.59	34	0	0	0	40	53	36	34	17	31	L	L	5-10	190	12-23-73	1996	Cincinnati, Ohio
Bauer, Chuck	3	3	4.41	12	8	0	0	49	70	33	24	8	29	R	R	6-0	185	11-10-73	1995	East Greenbush, N.Y.
Buirley, Matt	1	0	6.97	13	0	0	0	21	26	22	16	15	21	R	R	6-3	205	7-21-75	1996	Gambier, Ohio
Bussa, Todd	2	4	2.25	35	0	0	14	48	45	16	12	23	54	R	R	5-11	190	12-13-72	1991	Camanche, Ill.
Corn, Chris	1	1	1.09	7	3	0	0	25	20	6	3	7	25	R	R	6-3	170	10-4-71	1994	Louisville, Ky.
Daniels, David	0	0	1.47	14	0	0	9	18	9	3	3	3	19	R	R	6-2	185	7-25-73	1996	Nashville, Tenn.
Duff, Matt	4	5	3.30	40	0	0	10	63	52	26	23	20	61	R	R	6-1	205	10-6-74	1997	Alligator, Miss.
France, Aaron	6	5	2.72	26	20	0	0	129	99	51	39	45	110	L	R	6-3	175	4-17-74	1994	Anaheim, Calif.
Gonzalez, Mike	0	3	6.67	7	7	0	0	28	40	21	21	13	22	R	L	6-2	210	5-23-78	1997	Pasadena, Texas
Guzman, Wilson	0	1	13.50	3	0	0	0	3	4	4	4	5	2	L	L	5-11	160	7-14-77	1995	Palo Verde, D.R.
Halla, Ryan	5	4	3.70	40	0	0	4	56	51	27	23	22	51	B	R	6-4	250	10-3-73	1997	Birmingham, Ala.
Kelly, Jeff	0	4	5.46	10	4	0	0	30	33	25	18	10	18	L	L	6-6	240	1-11-75	1994	Staten Island, N.Y.
Lambert, Kris	10	11	3.59	28	28	1	0	161	161	79	64	44	145	L	L	6-0	182	11-25-75	1997	Houston, Texas
Martin, Jeff	0	0	9.00	2	2	0	0	6	6	6	6	5	5	R	R	6-1	200	1-25-74	1995	Las Vegas, Nev.
McConnell, Sam	8	5	2.90	19	19	3	0	121	118	48	39	20	80	L	L	6-5	204	12-31-75	1997	Fairfield, Ohio
McDade, Neal	5	3	3.30	25	11	0	3	90	87	35	33	20	74	R	R	6-3	160	6-16-76	1996	Orange Park, Fla.
O'Connor, Brian	6	2	2.60	14	14	1	0	87	86	34	25	22	84	L	L	6-2	170	1-4-77	1995	Cincinnati, Ohio
Paugh, Rick	0	1	2.92	14	0	0	0	12	14	4	4	4	8	L	L	6-1	190	2-6-72	1994	Bridgeport, W.Va.
Paulino, Arison	0	0	14.73	2	0	0	0	4	6	6	6	3	5	R	R	6-1	170	2-2-77	1995	Ranchadero, D.R.
Runion, Tony	5	8	3.00	36	0	0	4	57	49	21	19	20	72	R	R	6-3	220	12-6-71	1993	Florence, Ky.
Temple, Jason	1	0	7.36	6	0	0	0	11	14	11	9	5	11	R	R	6-1	185	11-8-74	1993	Woodhaven, Mich.

AUGUSTA — Class A

SOUTH ATLANTIC LEAGUE

BATTING	AVG	G	AB	R	H	2B	3B	HR	RBI	BB	SO	SB	CS	B	T	HT	WT	DOB	1st Yr	Resides
Adorno, Wilson	.188	11	32	3	6	1	0	1	5	1	11	0	0	B	R	5-11	180	12-3-77	1996	Vega Alta, P.R.
Anderson, Franklin	.209	16	43	3	9	3	1	0	7	2	19	0	0	R	R	6-1	200	9-1-75	1995	Lake City, Ga.

BATTING	AVG	G	AB	R	H	2B	3B	HR	RBI	BB	SO	SB	CS	B	T	HT	WT	DOB	1st Yr	Resides
Bryant, Matt	.299	59	177	24	53	4	1	2	18	26	29	1	5	R	R	6-0	185	4-28-75	1997	Denver, Colo.
Burns, Xavier	.242	125	414	64	100	20	5	13	49	42	107	16	8	R	R	5-11	190	5-8-75	1996	Chicago, Ill.
Cloud, Casey	.220	36	91	10	20	2	0	0	13	19	24	0	0	L	R	6-0	200	5-1-75	1998	Santa Barbara, Calif.
Cortez, Santos	.105	6	19	2	2	0	0	0	2	2	3	0	0	R	R	6-0	210	1-18-75	1998	Long Beach, Calif.
Davis, J.J.	.194	30	108	11	21	0	0	4	11	0	24	1	1	R	R	6-6	230	10-25-78	1997	Pomona, Calif.
DeHaan, Kory	.314	132	475	85	149	39	8	8	75	69	114	33	13	L	R	6-2	185	7-10-76	1997	Pella, Iowa
Diaz, Diogenes	.042	9	24	1	1	0	0	0	1	3	12	0	0	R	R	6-0	190	10-10-78	1996	Villa Mella, D.R.
Elliott, Dawan	.050	8	20	1	1	1	0	0	2	2	8	0	0	L	L	6-3	200	7-30-76	1995	Long Branch, N.J.
Evans, Lee	.223	98	337	43	75	19	1	5	43	28	90	6	3	B	R	6-1	185	7-20-77	1996	Northport, Ala.
Freeman, Terrance	.254	122	398	84	101	16	3	0	31	84	69	47	24	B	R	5-10	180	1-24-75	1995	Brandon, Fla.
Furniss, Eddy	.465	24	86	32	40	7	0	9	31	24	20	1	1	L	L	6-3	225	9-18-75	1998	Nacogdoches, Texas
Gutierrez, Victor	.246	128	460	81	113	19	4	1	50	54	67	60	18	R	R	5-11	170	12-23-77	1995	Santo Domingo, D.R.
Hundt, Bo	.241	54	174	26	42	10	1	5	26	24	41	4	3	B	R	6-0	202	4-21-75	1996	Bremen, Ind.
Johnson, Eric	.237	23	76	9	18	4	0	1	12	5	24	2	2	R	R	6-0	190	11-16-74	1997	Vidalia, Ga.
Johnston, Clint	.154	20	13	2	2	0	0	0	0	2	7	0	0	L	L	6-3	205	7-2-77	1998	Vero Beach, Fla.
Lankford, Derrick	.278	127	457	72	127	25	4	22	89	59	119	8	5	L	R	6-4	220	9-21-74	1997	Harrison, Tenn.
Lara, Felix	.171	14	35	6	6	1	0	1	6	0	18	0	0	L	L	6-0	170	10-30-77	1995	San Cristobal, D.R.
Mackowiak, Rob	.243	25	70	16	17	4	0	1	8	13	19	4	2	L	R	5-10	165	6-20-76	1996	Schererville, Ind.
Maxwell, Keith	.222	22	81	8	18	4	0	2	13	2	13	2	1	R	R	6-1	205	4-18-75	1997	Bristol, Fla.
Mejias, Oliver	.219	36	96	11	21	1	1	1	10	5	27	1	2	B	R	6-1	180	9-21-76	1995	Caracas, Ven.
Nicolas, Jose	.196	55	153	23	30	6	1	3	15	19	54	2	4	R	R	6-3	210	1-1-79	1997	Miami, Fla.
Pena, Alex	.253	90	292	47	74	15	1	5	26	24	69	7	5	R	R	6-2	175	9-9-77	1995	Santo Domingo, D.R.
Reyes, Jose	.261	25	69	10	18	2	3	3	9	6	15	0	1	R	R	6-1	188	5-1-73	1993	Villa Vazquez, D.R.
Rivera, Carlos	.285	87	316	38	90	17	1	5	53	11	46	3	5	L	L	6-1	220	6-10-78	1996	Rio Grande, P.R.
Sosa, Jovanny	.226	26	93	8	21	8	1	1	14	4	31	2	2	R	R	6-2	180	4-11-80	1997	Santo Domingo, D.R.
Washington, Rico	.300	12	50	12	15	2	1	2	12	7	9	2	0	L	R	5-10	178	5-30-78	1997	Gray, Ga.

GAMES BY POSITION: C—Adorno 8, Anderson 14, Cloud 26, Diaz 8, Evans 86, Hundt 1, Reyes 14, Washington 1. **1B**—Furniss 12, Hundt 5, Lankford 59, Maxwell 8, Reyes 3, Rivera 70. **2B**—Bryant 18, Freeman 118, Mejias 12, Washington 3. **3B**—Bryant 28, Burns 85, Hundt 18, Mackowiak 4, Mejias 10, Washington 8. **SS**—Bryant 15, Gutierrez 126, Mejias 8, Washington 1. **OF**—Burns 17, Cortez 6, Davis 21, DeHaan 126, Elliott 7, Hundt 25, Johnson 22, Lankford 18, Lara 12, Mackowiak 22, Maxwell 12, Nicolas 55, Pena 88, Reyes 3, Rivera 3, Sosa 19.

PITCHING	W	L	ERA	G	GS	CG	SV	IP	H	R	ER	BB	SO	B	T	HT	WT	DOB	1st Yr	Resides
Alvarado, Carlos	4	1	3.60	14	10	0	0	50	48	20	20	24	50	R	R	6-4	195	1-24-78	1995	Arecibo, P.R.
Ayers, Mike	0	1	17.47	4	0	0	0	6	11	13	11	6	6	L	L	5-10	190	12-23-73	1996	Cincinnati, Ohio
Bacci, Tony	4	4	3.81	27	1	0	1	50	39	33	21	34	51	L	L	6-2	180	8-16-75	1997	Cory, Ill.
Bauer, Chuck	2	1	0.75	6	0	0	0	12	3	1	1	5	12	R	R	6-0	185	11-10-73	1995	East Greenbush, N.Y.
Bausher, Andy	7	10	4.43	24	21	2	0	110	112	69	54	36	119	R	L	6-3	185	8-17-76	1997	Bechtelsville, Pa.
Bravo, Franklin	1	2	4.47	20	5	0	0	46	44	27	23	30	43	R	R	6-2	170	12-24-78	1996	Santo Domingo, D.R.
Combs, Chris	5	6	3.25	33	12	0	3	97	100	51	35	28	76	L	R	6-8	225	5-19-75	1997	Raleigh, N.C.
Cook, O.J.	0	1	3.11	47	0	0	17	46	34	17	16	29	54	R	R	6-3	195	12-13-76	1995	Bethlehem, Pa.
Crawford, Danny	4	11	4.68	20	18	1	0	110	120	67	57	15	71	R	R	6-6	228	5-25-75	1997	Houston, Texas
Davis, Kane	0	0	6.00	2	2	0	0	9	8	6	6	3	6	R	R	6-3	190	6-25-75	1993	Reedy, W.Va.
Duff, Matt	1	0	3.00	10	0	0	3	9	8	3	3	4	12	R	R	6-1	205	10-6-74	1997	Alligator, Miss.
Gonzalez, Mike	4	2	2.84	11	9	0	0	51	43	24	16	26	72	R	L	6-2	210	5-23-78	1997	Pasadena, Texas
Grabow, John	6	3	5.78	17	16	0	0	72	84	59	46	34	67	L	L	6-2	185	11-4-78	1997	San Gabriel, Calif.
Guy, Brad	6	4	3.02	56	0	0	4	86	75	39	29	26	94	R	R	6-2	180	10-25-75	1997	Eureka, Calif.
Guzman, Wilson	6	3	2.57	42	0	0	4	70	55	24	20	24	73	L	L	5-11	160	7-14-77	1995	Palo Verde, D.R.
Johnston, Clint	3	3	2.75	16	11	0	0	59	42	20	18	32	68	L	L	6-3	205	7-2-77	1998	Vero Beach, Fla.
Kelly, Jeff	1	1	7.50	18	3	0	0	42	54	41	35	16	36	L	L	6-6	240	1-11-75	1994	Staten Island, N.Y.
Luttig, Chris	0	0	18.00	4	0	0	0	3	7	6	6	3	4	L	L	6-0	210	2-19-76	1997	Roscoe, Ill.
McConnell, Sam	4	3	3.20	8	8	1	0	45	36	22	16	13	35	L	L	6-5	204	12-31-75	1997	Fairfield, Ohio
Shaw, Curtis	1	0	5.00	2	2	0	0	9	8	5	5	5	6	L	L	6-2	205	8-16-69	1990	Bartlesville, Okla.
Siciliano, Jess	0	1	7.36	5	0	0	0	4	5	4	3	5	6	R	R	6-2	190	8-31-76	1996	East White Plains, N.Y.
Sparks, Steve	0	1	6.23	2	2	0	0	9	11	9	6	4	12	R	R	6-5	215	3-28-75	1998	Mobile, Ala.
Stabile, Paul	5	7	4.30	29	20	1	1	130	111	82	62	51	132	L	L	6-0	200	1-16-76	1997	Staten Island, N.Y.
Temple, Jason	0	2	8.35	13	0	0	0	18	21	18	17	26	25	R	R	6-1	185	11-8-74	1993	Woodhaven, Mich.
Williams, Larry	4	7	5.05	35	2	0	0	68	65	45	38	38	77	R	R	6-0	200	11-15-75	1996	Royersford, Pa.

ERIE — Short-Season Class A

NEW YORK-PENN LEAGUE

BATTING	AVG	G	AB	R	H	2B	3B	HR	RBI	BB	SO	SB	CS	B	T	HT	WT	DOB	1st Yr	Resides
Adorno, Wilson	.182	5	11	1	2	1	0	0	0	0	2	0	0	B	R	5-11	180	12-3-77	1996	Vega Alta, P.R.
Anderson, Franklin	.146	19	48	3	7	3	0	0	2	2	17	1	0	R	R	6-1	200	9-1-75	1995	Lake City, Ga.
Araujo, Victor	.238	17	63	9	15	2	0	2	9	1	18	1	0	R	R	6-0	180	1-16-80	1997	San Pedro de Macoris, D.R.
Bone, Billy	.345	21	58	14	20	2	0	2	11	11	12	2	1	R	R	6-1	180	1-5-76	1998	Jacksonville, Fla.
Cleto, Ambioris	.192	49	167	26	32	4	0	0	10	17	49	4	2	R	R	6-0	160	1-5-80	1996	Santo Domingo, D.R.
Cotten, Jeremy	.153	22	72	5	11	3	0	2	5	8	30	0	0	R	R	6-2	225	9-24-80	1998	Raleigh, N.C.
Cronk, Brian	.143	3	7	1	1	0	0	0	1	1	2	1	0	B	R	6-1	195	6-15-77	1998	Grand Junction, Colo.
Daggett, Jesse	.248	48	165	18	41	10	1	2	15	20	31	4	0	R	R	6-4	220	7-3-78	1998	La Crescenta, Calif.
Davis, J.J.	.270	52	196	25	53	12	2	8	39	20	54	4	1	R	R	6-6	230	10-25-78	1997	Pomona, Calif.
Diaz, Diogenes	.267	39	131	15	35	6	0	3	14	14	35	1	0	R	R	6-0	190	10-10-78	1996	Villa Mella, D.R.
Elliott, Dawan	.253	48	178	17	45	9	2	5	26	9	48	1	2	L	L	6-3	200	7-30-76	1995	Long Branch, N.J.
Hunt, Joe	.244	58	217	30	53	6	0	0	11	22	42	12	7	B	R	6-1	180	9-3-75	1996	Archer, Fla.
Jordan, Yustin	.000	2	6	0	0	0	0	0	0	1	4	0	0	R	R	6-3	200	8-15-78	1996	Monticello, Ark.
Lara, Felix	.236	36	127	18	30	7	1	1	8	4	37	6	4	L	L	6-0	170	10-30-77	1995	San Cristobal, D.R.
Maxwell, Keith	.267	66	240	43	64	15	2	8	30	29	54	0	1	R	R	6-1	205	4-18-75	1997	Bristol, Fla.
Mejias, Oliver	.258	11	31	2	8	1	0	0	4	1	8	0	0	B	R	6-1	180	9-21-76	1995	Caracas, Ven.
Nicolas, Jose	.248	66	242	33	60	8	3	6	35	22	85	6	5	R	R	6-3	210	1-1-79	1997	Miami, Fla.
Parker, Clark	.235	8	17	4	4	1	0	0	1	3	4	1	1	B	R	5-9	170	9-26-75	1997	Beverly Hills, Calif.
Ravelo, Manuel	.204	26	93	8	19	2	1	0	5	5	26	2	4	R	R	5-10	155	8-8-81	1997	Santo Domingo, D.R.
Skrehot, Shaun	.249	63	269	33	67	10	0	2	18	7	43	10	1	R	R	5-11	170	12-5-75	1998	Spring, Texas
Tolbert, Alex	.086	12	35	3	3	1	0	1	3	3	13	0	0	L	R	6-4	245	1-20-75	1997	Hendersonville, N.C.
Walker, Shon	.337	27	101	24	34	8	2	6	28	13	35	2	0	L	L	6-1	180	6-9-74	1992	Cynthiana, Ky.
Washington, Rico	.330	51	197	31	65	14	2	6	31	17	33	1	2	L	R	5-10	178	5-30-78	1997	Gray, Ga.

GAMES BY POSITION: C—Anderson 14, Daggett 31, Diaz 39, Washington 5. **1B**—Adorno 1, Daggett 8, Elliott 15, Maxwell 56, Tolbert 5, Walker 1. **2B**—Araujo 16, Bone 16, Mejias 7, Parker 5, Ravelo 15, Skrehot 23, Washington 4. **3B**—Adorno 3, Anderson 3, Bone 5, Cotten 12, Cronk 3, Jordan 2, Maxwell 1, Mejias 3, Skrehot 13, Washington 44. **SS**—Cleto 48, Skrehot 28. **OF**—Davis 51, Elliott 28, Hunt 54, Lara 32, Maxwell 10, Nicolas 66, Walker 1.

PITCHING	W	L	ERA	G	GS	CG	SV	IP	H	R	ER	BB	SO	B	T	HT	WT	DOB	1st Yr	Resides
Alvarado, David	0	3	9.14	19	3	0	0	42	64	46	43	18	41	R	R	6-3	170	4-29-78	1995	Falcon, Ven.
Bacci, Tony	2	4	5.34	6	6	0	0	30	25	24	18	10	23	L	L	6-2	180	8-16-75	1997	Cory, Ill.
Beimel, Joe	1	4	6.32	17	6	0	0	47	56	39	33	22	37	L	L	6-3	205	4-19-77	1998	La Mesa, Calif.
Bravo, Franklin	2	4	8.36	11	9	0	0	38	57	43	35	16	37	R	R	6-2	170	12-24-78	1996	Santo Domingo, D.R.
Buirley, Matt	1	1	2.86	16	0	0	4	22	12	7	7	7	31	R	R	6-3	205	7-21-75	1996	Gambier, Ohio
Burchart, Kyle	1	0	6.75	10	0	0	0	9	16	16	7	6	7	R	R	6-5	190	8-18-76	1995	Tulsa, Okla.
Classen, Ender	0	1	2.45	2	2	0	0	11	9	3	3	4	10	B	R	6-3	185	4-1-78	1996	Arecibo, P.R.
Gray, Michael	4	0	3.20	29	0	0	0	45	40	22	16	5	39	R	R	6-2	200	9-15-76	1998	Fernandina Beach, Fla.
Gresko, Mike	0	0	23.82	5	0	0	0	6	14	16	15	9	8	L	L	6-8	200	10-27-76	1996	Trenton, N.J.
Hlodan, George	2	3	6.05	20	8	0	1	58	82	44	39	15	31	R	R	6-1	170	6-25-76	1996	Elizabeth, Pa.
Johnston, Michael	0	0	4.50	2	0	0	0	2	4	4	1	1	2	L	L	6-3	180	3-30-79	1998	Colwyn, Pa.
Luttig, Chris	1	2	3.60	27	0	0	4	30	30	16	12	10	39	L	L	6-0	210	2-19-76	1997	Roscoe, Ill.
Montilla, Felix	1	5	6.28	27	1	0	1	39	53	33	27	14	32	R	R	6-1	185	3-7-80	1997	Santo Domingo, D.R.
Paulino, Arison	0	0	12.00	2	0	0	0	3	6	6	4	1	3	R	R	6-1	170	2-2-77	1995	Ranchadero, D.R.
Pavlovich, Tony	0	2	1.64	8	0	0	1	11	6	3	2	2	17	R	R	6-0	185	8-23-74	1994	Pavo, Ga.
Prater, Andy	3	3	5.76	18	11	0	0	59	60	44	38	30	44	R	R	6-4	170	9-27-77	1996	Florissant, Mo.
Rhea, Thad	4	4	3.63	12	12	0	0	62	61	37	25	24	41	B	R	6-1	180	1-27-77	1997	College Station, Texas
Siciliano, Jess	0	0	5.68	12	0	0	0	13	16	14	8	8	8	R	R	6-2	190	8-31-76	1996	East White Plains, N.Y.
Sparks, Steve	2	7	4.43	14	10	0	0	63	55	38	31	30	61	R	R	6-5	215	3-28-75	1998	Mobile, Ala.
Vogt, Robert	0	4	9.68	15	5	0	0	31	40	42	33	32	25	L	L	6-6	195	10-19-78	1996	Brandon, Fla.
Williams, Dave	2	2	3.23	22	2	0	0	47	45	21	17	14	38	L	L	6-3	215	3-12-79	1998	Camden, Del.
Williams, Larry	0	1	13.50	2	1	0	0	3	7	5	5	3	3	R	R	6-0	200	11-15-75	1996	Royersford, Pa.

BRADENTON — Rookie

GULF COAST LEAGUE

BATTING	AVG	G	AB	R	H	2B	3B	HR	RBI	BB	SO	SB	CS	B	T	HT	WT	DOB	1st Yr	Resides
Adorno, Wilson	.222	4	9	1	2	0	0	1	1	0	0	0	0	B	R	5-11	180	12-3-77	1996	Vega Alta, P.R.
Alvarez, Antonio	.247	50	190	27	47	13	1	4	29	13	24	19	1	R	R	6-1	165	5-10-79	1996	Los Teques, Ven.
Araujo, Victor	.284	24	95	18	27	1	1	1	10	5	9	11	4	R	R	6-0	180	1-16-80	1997	San Pedro de Macoris, D.R.
Burton, Willie	.222	19	63	6	14	4	1	0	5	3	26	1	0	R	R	5-10	180	11-13-78	1998	Lake Wales, Fla.
Cardona, Raynier	.215	22	65	4	14	1	1	1	5	8	13	3	1	B	R	5-11	180	8-26-80	1998	San Sebastian, P.R.
Chourio, Jorjanis	.218	26	78	8	17	3	0	1	11	2	21	4	0	R	R	6-2	175	12-18-80	1998	Burere, Ven.
Cotten, Jeremy	.314	24	86	13	27	4	0	7	22	9	29	1	0	R	R	6-2	225	9-24-80	1998	Raleigh, N.C.
Cronk, Brian	.233	27	90	11	21	4	1	3	10	12	26	1	0	B	R	6-1	195	6-15-77	1998	Grand Junction, Colo.
Diaz, David	.227	10	22	0	5	0	0	0	4	2	10	0	0	R	R	6-3	200	7-3-80	1998	Hialeah, Fla.
Harts, Jeremy	.268	34	123	21	33	9	3	1	11	7	37	10	0	B	L	6-1	185	6-6-80	1998	Decatur, Ga.
Hernandez, Jose	.317	14	41	7	13	3	0	0	7	2	6	0	0	R	R	6-1	175	11-6-80	1998	Valencia, Ven.
Johnson, Eric	.290	7	31	7	9	4	1	2	5	2	9	1	0	R	R	6-0	190	11-16-74	1997	Vidalia, Ga.
Jones, A.J.	.186	30	97	11	18	4	1	0	7	16	23	4	0	R	R	6-3	190	10-27-78	1997	Phoenix, Ariz.
Miller, Josh	.268	36	138	20	37	10	2	2	18	6	27	4	3	L	R	6-1	215	12-1-78	1998	Aiken, S.C.
Pelfrey, Bryce	.189	41	164	20	31	3	0	0	13	12	29	5	2	R	R	6-2	160	6-16-80	1998	Cantonment, Fla.
Prieto, Jonathan	.302	34	129	22	39	7	2	0	16	18	19	7	6	B	R	5-11	170	6-24-80	1997	San Bernardino, Ven.
Ravelo, Manuel	.253	24	95	11	24	1	2	1	7	3	17	9	1	R	R	5-10	155	8-8-81	1997	Santo Domingo, D.R.
Segura, Rolando	.274	28	95	15	26	6	0	3	15	7	23	2	0	R	R	6-2	180	12-21-78	1997	San Pedro de Macoris, D.R.
Sosa, Jovanny	.311	32	119	23	37	6	1	8	25	8	32	3	1	R	R	6-2	180	4-11-80	1997	Santo Domingo, D.R.
Stanton, Eric	.191	25	89	8	17	7	0	1	6	7	19	0	0	R	R	6-3	215	8-30-77	1998	Newberry, S.C.
Torres, Rommel	.222	26	81	11	18	5	0	0	3	9	18	1	1	R	R	6-1	165	1-13-79	1996	San Jose, Panama
Walker, Shon	.389	4	18	7	7	2	1	2	7	3	5	0	0	L	L	6-1	180	6-9-74	1992	Cynthiana, Ky.
Washington, Mo	.206	39	136	19	28	4	1	5	13	12	49	4	0	R	R	6-1	203	5-22-79	1997	Las Vegas, Nev.
Wright, Ron	.600	3	10	4	6	0	0	2	5	2	0	0	0	R	R	6-1	230	1-21-76	1994	St. George, Utah

GAMES BY POSITION: C—Adorno 3, Cardona 20, Diaz 10, Hernandez 13, Torres 26. **1B**—Adorno 1, Alvarez 9, Cronk 27, Segura 1, Stanton 24, Wright 1. **2B**—Alvarez 4, Araujo 5, Prieto 34, Ravelo 22. **3B**—Alvarez 29, Araujo 1, Cotten 16, Segura 19. **SS**—Alvarez 5, Araujo 16, Pelfrey 40. **OF**—Alvarez 1, Burton 15, Chourio 26, Harts 24, Johnson 7, Jones 30, Miller 19, Sosa 31, Washington 37.

PITCHING	W	L	ERA	G	GS	CG	SV	IP	H	R	ER	BB	SO	B	T	HT	WT	DOB	1st Yr	Resides
Bazan, Juan	1	0	2.93	8	0	0	1	15	11	7	5	7	9	R	R	6-0	180	4-7-78	1996	Chitre, Panama
Bennett, Jeff	2	4	4.63	13	11	0	0	47	50	29	24	13	18	R	R	6-3	190	6-10-80	1998	Brush Creek, Tenn.
Bumatay, Mike	2	3	3.18	13	5	0	1	40	46	29	14	16	37	L	L	6-0	175	10-9-79	1998	Clovis, Calif.
Classen, Ender	1	5	3.59	12	11	0	0	53	51	34	21	18	28	B	R	6-3	185	4-1-78	1996	Arecibo, P.R.
Crawford, Carlos	1	1	3.31	12	0	0	2	16	16	6	6	6	9	R	R	6-2	205	10-4-71	1990	Charlotte, N.C.
De la Cruz, Juan	1	4	3.44	11	11	0	0	50	53	29	19	9	20	R	R	6-4	185	3-21-80	1997	El Seibo, D.R.
Go, Ho Bong	2	3	4.84	13	0	0	0	35	33	25	19	11	26	R	R	6-2	180	6-4-75	1998	Seoul, Korea
Gomez, Ricardo	0	1	5.87	9	0	0	0	15	23	12	10	9	12	R	R	6-2	165	6-14-78	1995	Puerto Plata, D.R.
Gonzalez, Giovanni	2	1	7.50	14	0	0	2	24	32	23	20	16	15	R	R	6-4	225	6-18-80	1998	Ponce, P.R.
Hardebeck, Jason	0	0	4.15	2	0	0	0	4	5	2	2	3	4	L	L	6-1	175	10-22-75	1997	Lafayette, Ind.
Harris, Veon	0	0	6.08	7	0	0	0	13	13	12	9	12	16	R	R	6-0	175	3-19-77	1998	Columbus, Miss.
Johnston, Michael	1	2	3.34	13	3	0	0	30	28	17	11	10	17	L	L	6-3	180	3-30-79	1998	Colwyn, Pa.
Levesque, Ben	2	2	7.11	6	0	0	0	13	17	15	10	9	11	R	R	6-3	185	10-9-79	1998	Cary, N.C.
Marichal, Rafael	3	1	2.08	18	0	0	8	30	26	14	7	6	30	R	R	6-0	170	8-20-79	1996	Santo Domingo, D.R.
Martin, Jeff	0	0	0.00	1	0	0	0	1	4	2	0	0	0	R	R	6-1	200	1-25-74	1995	Las Vegas, Nev.
Moon, Chang	1	0	4.78	13	0	0	0	32	38	19	17	10	32	B	R	6-3	194	7-9-75	1998	Inchon, Korea
Morrobel, Juan	0	0	1.35	3	0	0	0	7	2	1	1	5	7	L	L	6-0	180	9-14-77	1995	Santo Domingo, D.R.
Paugh, Rick	0	1	5.68	4	1	0	0	6	10	4	4	0	5	L	L	6-1	190	2-6-72	1994	Bridgeport, W.Va.
Siciliano, Jess	2	1	13.50	4	0	0	0	5	7	8	7	4	1	R	R	6-2	190	8-31-76	1996	East White Plains, N.Y.
Smith, Eric	0	1	8.59	7	0	0	0	7	14	12	7	3	5	R	R	6-1	164	9-1-79	1998	Richmond, Ind.
South, Carl	0	0	24.00	8	0	0	0	6	15	17	16	13	3	R	R	6-5	210	4-14-75	1994	Roswell, Ga.
Vallejo, Etanislao	3	1	3.71	13	6	0	0	34	31	19	14	22	26	R	R	6-3	185	6-7-80	1997	San Cristobal, D.R.
White, James	1	4	7.22	12	12	0	0	39	44	37	31	30	26	R	R	6-2	185	11-6-79	1998	Chico, Calif.

ST. LOUIS CARDINALS

Lackluster season overshadowed by McGwire's heroics

BY MIKE EISENBATH

In their Summer of Power, the Cardinals found out what it was like to have a bona fide slugger. And it turned the 1998 season into something surreal.

Mark McGwire's chase of Roger Maris' single-season record of 61 homers–and the way he flew past the mark before finishing with an astounding 70–drew an intense spotlight on the ballclub despite its overall disappointing play.

Picked by many in the preseason to win the National League Central, the team struggled during a first half filled with pitching problems. Starters Matt Morris, Donovan Osborne and Alan Benes were counted upon heavily but instead spent most of the first three months on the disabled list. Benes never did return and in August underwent his second shoulder surgery in little more than a year.

Morris and Osborne eventually resumed their roles and combined for 12 victories, with Morris frequently looking like one of the league's top righthanders.

Todd Stottlemyre was the club's top healthy starter until he was traded along with shortstop Royce Clayton to the Texas Rangers in July for lefthander Darren Oliver and young third baseman Fernando Tatis.

The offense was weakened by low production from the shortstop, third base and catcher holes. Rookie Eli Marrero had been expected to step in as the everyday catcher, but he missed time after having a cancerous thyroid removed during spring training. Marrero batted .244 with four homers after coming back.

Left fielder Ron Gant had another difficult first half, then rebounded to finish with an impressive 26 homers and 67 RBIs in only 383 at-bats.

McGwire, center fielder Ray Lankford and right fielder Brian Jordan covered for many of those deficiencies, as they combined for 126 home runs and 343 RBIs. Their work and a stronger pitching staff, led by newly-crowned closer Juan Acevedo, helped the Cardinals win 20 of their last 27 games.

The summer went much better for the Cardinals' player-development department. All four of their full-season minor league teams–Triple-A Memphis, Double-A Arkansas, and Class A Prince William and Peoria–finished above .500. Arkansas finished with the best record in the Texas League, but was swept in the first round of the playoffs by eventual champion Tulsa.

Two of the organization's top young players began the season as teenagers on the Peoria roster. Pablo Ozuna led the Midwest League with a .357 batting average and 62 stolen bases. Ozuna also finished second in the minor leagues with 122 runs scored.

Lefthander Rick Ankiel was the Cardinals' top minor league pitcher with a combined 12-6 record at Peoria and Prince William. He allowed only 106 hits and struck out 222 batters in 161 innings.

Most exciting, though, was a June draft that brought outfielder J.D. Drew and righthander Chad Hutchinson. Though they were expected to be difficult to sign, the Cardinals landed both. Drew signed for a $3.15 million bonus, Hutchinson for $2.3 million.

Hutchinson made eight pro starts, including five with a 2.79 ERA at Prince William. Drew spent July and August in the farm system, then made a big league splash with a .417 batting average, five homers and 13 RBIs in 14 games in September.

Mark McGwire

Rick Ankiel

Players of the Year

Major League: Mark McGwire, 1b
BA's first Major League Player of the Year, McGwire rewrote the record books with 70 homers in 1998.

Minor League: Rick Ankiel, lhp, Pr. William/Peoria
The hard-throwing lefty led all minor leaguers with 222 strikeouts while going 12-6, 2.63 at two stops.

ORGANIZATION LEADERS

BATTING		
*AVG	Pablo Ozuna, Peoria	.357
R	Pablo Ozuna, Peoria	122
H	Pablo Ozuna, Peoria	192
TB	Joe McEwing, Memphis/Arkansas	307
2B	Joe McEwing, Memphis/Arkansas	51
3B	Two tied at	11
HR	Tyrone Horne, Memphis/Arkansas	37
RBI	Tyrone Horne, Memphis/Arkansas	140
BB	Stubby Clapp, Arkansas	86
SO	Nate Dishington, Memphis/Arkansas	179
SB	Pablo Ozuna, Peoria	62
PITCHING		
W	Two tied at	15
L	Neal Arnold, Peoria	15
#ERA	Jason Karnuth, Prince William	1.67
G	Armando Almanza, Memphis/Arkansas	59
CG	Three tied at	2
SV	Gene Stechschulte, Peoria	33
IP	Jose Jimenez, Arkansas	180
BB	Stephen Norris, Peoria	87
SO	Rick Ankiel, Prince William/Peoria	222

*Minimum 250 At-Bats #Minimum 75 Innings

St. Louis CARDINALS

Manager: Tony La Russa.

1998 Record: 83-79, .512 (3rd, NL Central)

BATTING	AVG	G	AB	R	H	2B	3B	HR	RBI	BB	SO	SB	CS	B	T	HT	WT	DOB	1st Yr	Resides
Bell, David	.222	4	9	0	2	1	0	0	0	0	3	0	0	R	R	5-10	170	9-14-72	1990	Cincinnati, Ohio
Clayton, Royce	.234	90	355	59	83	19	1	4	29	40	51	19	6	R	R	6-0	183	1-2-70	1988	Inglewood, Calif.
DeShields, Delino	.290	117	420	74	122	21	8	7	44	56	61	26	10	L	R	6-1	175	1-15-69	1987	West Palm Beach, Fla.
Drew, J.D.	.417	14	36	9	15	3	1	5	13	4	10	0	0	L	R	6-1	195	11-20-75	1997	Hahira, Ga.
Gaetti, Gary	.265	91	306	39	81	23	1	11	43	31	39	1	1	R	R	6-0	200	8-19-58	1979	Raleigh, N.C.
Gant, Ron	.240	121	383	60	92	17	1	26	67	51	92	8	0	R	R	6-0	200	3-2-65	1983	Smyrna, Ga.
Gilbert, Shawn	.500	4	2	0	1	0	0	0	0	0	1	1	0	R	R	5-9	185	3-12-65	1987	Glendale, Ariz.
2-team (3 New York)	.200	7	5	1	1	0	0	0	0	0	2	1	0							
Howard, Dave	.245	46	102	15	25	1	1	2	12	12	22	0	0	B	R	6-0	175	2-26-67	1987	Sarasota, Fla.
Hunter, Brian	.205	62	112	11	23	9	1	4	13	7	23	1	1	R	L	6-0	195	3-4-68	1987	Anaheim, Calif.
Jordan, Brian	.316	150	564	100	178	34	7	25	91	40	66	17	5	R	R	6-1	205	3-29-67	1988	Baltimore, Md.
Kelly, Pat	.216	53	153	18	33	5	0	4	14	13	48	5	1	R	R	6-0	182	10-14-67	1988	Clearwater Beach, Fla.
Lampkin, Tom	.231	93	216	25	50	12	1	6	28	24	32	3	2	L	R	5-11	183	3-4-64	1986	Boring, Ore.
Lankford, Ray	.293	154	533	94	156	37	1	31	105	86	151	26	5	L	L	5-11	180	6-5-67	1987	Modesto, Calif.
Little, Mark	.083	7	12	0	1	0	0	0	0	2	5	1	0	R	R	6-0	195	7-11-72	1994	Edwardsville, Ill.
Mabry, John	.249	142	377	41	94	22	0	9	46	30	76	0	2	L	R	6-4	195	10-17-70	1991	Warwick, Md.
Marrero, Eli	.244	83	254	28	62	18	1	4	20	28	42	6	2	R	R	6-1	180	11-17-73	1993	Miami, Fla.
McEwing, Joe	.200	10	20	5	4	1	0	0	1	1	3	0	1	R	R	5-10	170	10-19-72	1992	Bristol, Pa.
McGee, Willie	.253	120	269	27	68	10	1	3	34	14	49	7	2	B	R	6-1	185	11-2-58	1977	Hercules, Calif.
McGwire, Mark	.299	155	509	130	152	21	0	70	147	162	155	1	0	R	R	6-5	225	10-1-63	1984	Claremont, Calif.
Ordaz, Luis	.203	57	153	9	31	5	0	0	8	12	18	2	0	R	R	5-11	170	8-12-75	1993	Maracaibo, Ven.
Pagnozzi, Tom	.219	51	160	7	35	9	0	1	10	14	37	0	0	R	R	6-1	190	7-30-62	1983	Tucson, Ariz.
Polanco, Placido	.254	45	114	10	29	3	2	1	11	5	9	2	0	R	R	5-10	168	10-10-75	1994	Miami, Fla.
Tatis, Fernando	.287	55	202	27	58	16	2	8	26	24	57	7	3	R	R	5-10	170	1-1-75	1993	San Pedro de Macoris, D.R.

PITCHING	W	L	ERA	G	GS	CG	SV	IP	H	R	ER	BB	SO	B	T	HT	WT	DOB	1st Yr	Resides
Acevedo, Juan	8	3	2.56	50	9	0	15	98	83	30	28	29	56	R	R	6-2	228	5-5-70	1992	Carpentersville, Ill.
Aybar, Manny	6	6	5.98	20	14	0	0	81	90	58	54	42	57	R	R	6-1	165	10-5-74	1991	Bani, D.R.
Bottenfield, Kent	4	6	4.44	44	17	0	4	134	128	72	66	57	98	R	R	6-2	225	11-14-68	1986	Royal Palm Beach, Fla.
Brantley, Jeff	0	5	4.44	48	0	0	14	51	40	26	25	18	48	R	R	5-10	189	9-5-63	1985	Clinton, Miss.
Busby, Mike	5	2	4.50	26	2	0	0	46	45	23	23	15	33	R	R	6-4	215	12-27-72	1991	Glendale, Ariz.
Croushore, Rick	0	3	4.97	41	0	0	8	54	44	31	30	29	47	R	R	6-4	210	8-7-70	1993	Houston, Texas
Eversgerd, Bryan	0	0	9.00	8	0	0	0	6	9	7	6	2	4	R	L	6-1	185	2-11-69	1989	Centralia, Ill.
Frascatore, John	3	4	4.14	69	0	0	0	96	95	48	44	36	49	R	R	6-1	200	2-4-70	1991	Oceanside, N.Y.
Jimenez, Jose	3	0	2.95	4	3	0	0	21	22	8	7	8	12	R	R	6-3	170	7-7-73	1992	San Pedro de Macoris, D.R.
King, Curt	2	0	3.53	36	0	0	2	51	50	20	20	20	28	R	R	6-5	205	10-25-70	1994	Conshohocken, Pa.
Looper, Braden	0	1	5.40	4	0	0	0	3	5	4	2	1	4	R	R	6-5	225	10-28-74	1996	Arlington, Texas
Lowe, Sean	0	3	15.19	4	1	0	0	5	11	9	9	5	2	R	R	6-2	205	3-29-71	1992	Mesquite, Texas
Mercker, Kent	11	11	5.07	30	29	0	0	162	199	99	91	53	72	L	L	6-2	195	2-1-68	1986	Dublin, Ohio
Morris, Matt	7	5	2.53	17	17	2	0	114	101	37	32	42	79	R	R	6-5	210	8-9-74	1995	Montgomery, N.Y.
Oliver, Darren	4	4	4.26	10	10	0	0	57	64	31	27	23	29	R	L	6-2	210	10-6-70	1988	Arlington, Texas
Osborne, Donovan	5	4	4.09	14	14	1	0	84	84	42	38	22	60	L	L	6-2	195	6-21-69	1990	Carson City, Nev.
Painter, Lance	4	0	3.99	65	0	0	1	47	42	24	21	28	39	L	L	6-1	195	7-21-67	1990	Milwaukee, Wis.
Petkovsek, Mark	7	4	4.77	48	10	0	0	106	131	63	56	36	55	R	R	6-0	185	11-18-65	1987	Beaumont, Texas
Politte, Cliff	2	3	6.32	8	8	0	0	37	45	32	26	18	22	R	R	5-11	185	2-27-74	1995	St. Louis, Mo.
Raggio, Brady	1	1	15.43	4	1	0	0	7	22	12	12	3	3	R	R	6-4	210	9-17-72	1992	Danville, Calif.
Stottlemyre, Todd	9	9	3.51	23	23	3	0	161	146	74	63	51	147	L	R	6-3	195	5-20-65	1986	Yakima, Wash.
Witt, Bobby	2	5	4.94	17	5	0	0	47	55	32	26	20	28	R	R	6-2	205	5-11-64	1985	Colleyville, Texas

FIELDING

Catcher	PCT	G	PO	A	E	DP	PB
Lampkin	.986	62	331	19	5	5	4
Marrero	.991	73	426	30	4	3	1
Pagnozzi	.982	44	259	17	5	5	1

First Base	PCT	G	PO	A	E	DP
DeShields	.000	1	0	0	0	0
Gaetti	1.000	3	15	0	0	2
Hunter	1.000	10	23	1	0	2
Lampkin	1.000	2	5	0	0	0
Mabry	1.000	16	93	11	0	8
Marrero	1.000	2	1	1	0	0
McGee	1.000	1	2	2	0	0
McGwire	.992	152	1326	96	12	128

Second Base	PCT	G	PO	A	E	DP
Bell	1.000	1	0	2	0	1
DeShields	.983	111	248	274	9	66
Gaetti	.000	1	0	0	0	0
Gilbert	1.000	2	1	0	0	0
Howard	1.000	19	37	49	0	5
Kelly	.964	41	79	108	7	18
McEwing	1.000	6	9	10	0	3
Ordaz	1.000	1	2	3	0	1
Polanco	.982	14	34	21	1	10

Third Base	PCT	G	PO	A	E	DP
Bell	1.000	4	1	2	0	0
Gaetti	.985	83	47	153	3	15
Howard	1.000	14	3	2	0	0
Jordan	1.000	1	0	1	0	0
Mabry	.914	38	18	46	6	1
Ordaz	.000	2	0	0	0	0
Tatis	.927	55	35	118	12	7

Shortstop	PCT	G	PO	A	E	DP
Clayton	.970	90	140	286	13	53
Howard	.953	16	12	29	2	4
Kelly	1.000	2	0	1	0	0
Ordaz	.945	54	68	154	13	34
Polanco	.952	28	38	82	6	18
Tatis	1.000	3	1	3	0	0

Outfield	PCT	G	PO	A	E	DP
Drew	1.000	11	19	1	0	1
Gaetti	.000	1	0	0	0	0
Gant	.971	104	162	4	5	0
Howard	1.000	2	1	1	0	1
Hunter	.938	25	43	2	3	1
Jordan	.970	141	282	11	9	6
Kelly	.000	3	0	0	0	0
Lampkin	1.000	5	1	0	0	0
Lankford	.986	145	337	7	5	2
Little	1.000	7	11	0	0	0
Mabry	.971	80	95	7	3	3
McEwing	1.000	3	1	0	0	0
McGee	.938	88	101	6	7	1

FARM SYSTEM

Director of Player Development: Mike Jorgensen

Class	Farm Team	League	W	L	Pct.	Finish*	Manager	First Yr
AAA	Memphis (Tenn.) Redbirds	Pacific Coast	74	70	.514	t-9th (16)	Gaylen Pitts	1998
AA	Arkansas Travelers	Texas	80	60	.571	1st (8)	Chris Maloney	1966
A#	Prince William (Va.) Cannons	Carolina	72	67	.518	3rd (8)	Joe Cunningham	1997
A	Peoria (Ill.) Chiefs	Midwest	72	68	.514	6th (14)	Jeff Shireman	1995
A	New Jersey Cardinals	New York-Penn	34	41	.453	11th (14)	Jose Oquendo	1994
Rookie#	Johnson City (Tenn.) Cardinals	Appalachian	25	42	.373	10th (10)	Steve Turco	1975

*Finish in overall standings (No. of teams in league) #Advanced level

MEMPHIS — Class AAA

PACIFIC COAST LEAGUE

BATTING	AVG	G	AB	R	H	2B	3B	HR	RBI	BB	SO	SB	CS	B	T	HT	WT	DOB	1st Yr	Resides
Coleman, Vince	.316	20	76	15	24	5	1	1	5	10	11	8	4	B	R	6-1	185	9-22-61	1982	St. Louis, Mo.
Dishington, Nate	.265	60	200	30	53	15	1	10	34	24	88	1	1	L	R	6-3	210	1-8-75	1993	Glendale, Calif.
Drew, J.D.	.316	26	79	15	25	8	1	2	13	22	18	1	3	L	R	6-1	195	11-20-75	1997	Hahira, Ga.
Gilbert, Shawn	.269	62	216	37	58	15	2	7	32	29	53	7	4	R	R	5-9	185	3-12-65	1987	Glendale, Ariz.
Green, Scarborough	.198	26	81	11	16	5	0	0	2	8	22	1	4	B	R	5-10	170	6-9-74	1993	Florissant, Mo.
Hale, Chip	.268	132	411	60	110	21	0	8	66	62	37	1	3	L	R	5-10	175	12-2-64	1987	Tucson, Ariz.
Horne, Tyrone	.364	3	11	1	4	1	0	0	1	1	4	0	0	L	R	5-10	185	11-2-70	1989	Troy, N.C.
Kennedy, Adam	.305	74	305	36	93	22	7	4	41	12	42	15	4	L	R	6-1	180	1-10-76	1997	Riverside, Calif.
Kirby, Wayne	.282	58	227	36	64	15	3	5	32	15	33	10	2	L	R	5-10	185	1-22-64	1983	Yorktown, Va.
Little, Mark	.270	19	63	9	17	3	3	0	6	6	10	0	3	R	R	6-0	195	7-11-72	1994	Edwardsville, Ill.
2-team (69 Oklahoma)	.291	88	337	67	98	23	7	8	52	22	70	9	9							
Marrero, Eli	.238	32	130	22	31	5	0	7	21	13	23	5	4	R	R	6-1	180	11-17-73	1993	Miami, Fla.
McDonald, Keith	.318	58	170	21	54	8	0	7	22	10	30	1	1	R	R	6-2	215	2-8-73	1994	Yorba Linda, Calif.
McEwing, Joe	.334	78	329	52	110	30	7	6	46	21	39	11	10	R	R	5-10	170	10-19-72	1992	Bristol, Pa.
Mejia, Roberto	.240	49	175	23	42	5	2	8	25	5	42	10	5	R	R	5-11	160	4-14-72	1989	Hato Mayor, D.R.
Munoz, Juan	.268	117	399	54	107	17	5	4	44	29	58	9	4	L	L	5-9	170	3-27-74	1995	Miami, Fla.
Ordaz, Luis	.290	59	214	29	62	9	2	6	35	16	20	3	3	R	R	5-11	170	8-12-75	1993	Maracaibo, Ven.
Polanco, Placido	.280	70	246	36	69	19	1	1	21	16	15	6	3	R	R	5-10	168	10-10-75	1994	Miami, Fla.
Rupp, Brian	.234	112	209	26	49	10	1	0	24	29	32	5	5	R	R	6-5	185	9-20-71	1992	Florissant, Mo.
Secrist, Reed	.215	75	214	34	46	10	0	6	29	31	57	1	2	L	R	6-1	205	5-7-70	1992	Farmington, Utah
Sheaffer, Danny	.213	25	61	10	13	2	0	3	10	9	8	0	0	R	R	6-0	190	8-21-61	1981	Winston-Salem, N.C.
Stefanski, Mike	.265	95	298	34	79	19	1	6	44	23	42	1	2	R	R	6-2	190	9-12-69	1991	Redford, Mich.
Steverson, Todd	.192	66	182	17	35	8	0	6	21	35	57	4	2	R	R	6-2	185	11-15-71	1992	Inglewood, Calif.
Warner, Ron	.270	116	370	57	100	29	1	7	38	42	68	3	5	R	R	6-3	185	12-2-68	1991	Redlands, Calif.

PITCHING	W	L	ERA	G	GS	CG	SV	IP	H	R	ER	BB	SO	B	T	HT	WT	DOB	1st Yr	Resides
Acevedo, Juan	0	0	0.00	2	2	0	0	9	5	0	0	1	6	R	R	6-2	228	5-5-70	1992	Carpentersville, Ill.
Almanza, Armando	3	1	3.03	31	0	0	1	36	35	18	12	19	45	L	L	6-3	205	10-26-72	1993	El Paso, Texas
Arrandale, Matt	5	2	6.43	23	0	0	0	28	36	22	20	9	10	R	R	6-0	165	12-14-70	1993	St. Louis, Mo.
Aybar, Manny	10	0	2.60	13	13	0	0	83	62	24	24	17	63	R	R	6-1	165	10-5-74	1991	Bani, D.R.
Barnes, Brian	7	5	3.58	35	21	0	0	141	138	66	56	39	154	L	L	5-9	170	3-25-67	1989	Smyrna, Ga.
Busby, Mike	0	0	3.38	7	2	0	0	8	5	3	3	2	5	R	R	6-4	215	12-27-72	1991	Glendale, Ariz.
Croushore, Rick	0	3	4.71	23	0	0	2	29	21	16	15	9	40	R	R	6-4	210	8-7-70	1993	Houston, Texas
Eversgerd, Bryan	2	5	3.34	49	0	0	0	57	51	25	21	20	50	R	L	6-1	185	2-11-69	1989	Centralia, Ill.
Heflin, Bronson	0	0	9.00	2	0	0	0	2	2	2	2	0	1	R	R	6-3	200	8-29-71	1994	Gallatin, Tenn.
Heiserman, Rick	2	3	4.02	40	0	0	6	40	54	21	18	14	28	R	R	6-7	220	2-22-73	1994	Omaha, Neb.
King, Curt	0	1	2.10	27	0	0	12	26	31	6	6	6	23	R	R	6-5	205	10-25-70	1994	Conshohocken, Pa.
Looper, Braden	2	3	3.10	40	0	0	20	41	43	16	14	13	43	R	R	6-5	225	10-28-74	1996	Arlington, Texas
Lovingier, Kevin	5	1	3.05	39	0	0	0	59	38	22	20	33	63	L	L	6-1	190	8-29-71	1994	Mission Viejo, Calif.
Lowe, Sean	12	8	3.18	25	21	0	0	153	147	57	54	61	114	R	R	6-2	205	3-29-71	1992	Mesquite, Texas
Luebbers, Larry	11	11	4.10	29	29	2	0	173	183	90	79	47	110	R	R	6-6	190	10-11-69	1990	Florence, Ky.
Maxcy, Brian	1	1	18.00	3	0	0	0	4	8	8	8	1	4	R	R	6-1	170	5-4-71	1992	Amory, Miss.
Meacham, Rusty	1	2	5.16	38	0	0	2	52	68	30	30	15	56	R	R	6-2	175	1-27-68	1988	Palm City, Fla.
Mlicki, Doug	1	5	5.17	24	8	0	0	54	62	36	31	24	21	R	R	6-3	175	4-12-71	1992	Galloway, Ohio
2-team (7 Omaha)	2	6	5.00	31	10	0	0	67	77	42	37	26	30							
Morris, Matt	1	0	4.50	4	4	0	0	14	16	8	7	4	21	R	R	6-5	210	8-9-74	1995	Montgomery, N.Y.
Ontiveros, Steve	0	1	8.38	3	3	0	0	10	14	11	9	2	10	R	R	6-0	180	3-5-61	1982	Stafford, Texas
Osborne, Donovan	0	0	6.23	1	1	0	0	4	5	4	3	0	6	L	L	6-2	195	6-21-69	1990	Carson City, Nev.
Politte, Cliff	1	4	7.64	10	10	0	0	51	71	46	43	24	42	R	R	5-11	185	2-27-74	1995	St. Louis, Mo.
Raggio, Brady	8	9	3.07	24	23	2	0	152	156	57	52	31	100	R	R	6-4	210	9-17-72	1992	Danville, Calif.
Urbani, Tom	2	3	3.96	7	6	0	0	36	38	17	16	12	17	L	L	6-1	190	1-21-68	1990	Santa Cruz, Calif.
Weibl, Clint	0	1	6.35	1	1	0	0	6	6	5	4	2	2	R	R	6-3	180	3-17-75	1996	Dawson, Pa.

FIELDING

Catcher	PCT	G	PO	A	E	DP	PB
Marrero	.991	27	195	17	2	2	1
McDonald	1.000	32	189	15	0	3	1
Secrist	.000	1	0	0	0	0	0
Sheaffer	1.000	6	38	3	0	0	0
Stefanski	.993	85	629	55	5	10	3

First Base	PCT	G	PO	A	E	DP
Dishington	.981	39	295	19	6	30
Hale	.997	40	314	26	1	35
McDonald	.933	3	13	1	1	2
Munoz	.975	4	38	1	1	2
Rupp	.990	74	365	41	4	38
Secrist	.974	20	143	6	4	14
Sheaffer	1.000	9	54	8	0	4
Stefanski	1.000	5	16	1	0	1
Steverson	.000	1	0	0	0	0
Warner	.984	9	56	7	1	8

Second Base	PCT	G	PO	A	E	DP
Gilbert	1.000	3	6	9	0	2
Hale	.993	70	114	164	2	47
Kennedy	.961	14	30	43	3	11
McEwing	1.000	1	2	0	0	0
Ordaz	1.000	1	1	0	0	0
Polanco	.989	58	98	174	3	41
Warner	1.000	9	10	27	0	6

Third Base	PCT	G	PO	A	E	DP
Gilbert	.916	50	38	93	12	14
Hale	.733	5	3	8	4	0

	PCT	G	PO	A	E	DP
McEwing	1.000	2	0	6	0	0
Mejia	.938	45	26	110	9	8
Rupp	.958	17	7	16	1	4
Secrist	1.000	1	0	1	0	0
Sheaffer	1.000	2	0	1	0	0
Stefanski	.000	1	0	0	0	0
Warner	.965	41	29	80	4	10

Shortstop	PCT	G	PO	A	E	DP
Gilbert	1.000	1	0	2	0	0
Kennedy	.976	61	98	182	7	43
McEwing	1.000	1	3	4	0	0
Ordaz	.952	58	103	174	14	35
Polanco	.944	9	15	19	2	5
Warner	.919	18	25	54	7	13

Outfield	PCT	G	PO	A	E	DP
Coleman	.882	20	14	1	2	0
Drew	.966	25	54	3	2	1
Gilbert	1.000	13	21	2	0	0
Green	1.000	25	48	1	0	1
Kirby	.975	58	113	4	3	2
Little	.971	19	33	0	1	0
McEwing	.981	75	138	14	3	3
Munoz	.985	109	180	15	3	3
Rupp	.000	5	0	0	0	0
Secrist	.981	42	49	3	1	1
Sheaffer	.000	2	0	0	0	0
Steverson	.951	47	53	5	3	2
Warner	.967	41	55	3	2	0

ARKANSAS — Class AA

TEXAS LEAGUE

BATTING	AVG	G	AB	R	H	2B	3B	HR	RBI	BB	SO	SB	CS	B	T	HT	WT	DOB	1st Yr	Resides
Almond, Greg	.190	10	21	3	4	1	0	1	7	3	5	0	0	R	R	6-0	195	4-14-71	1993	Panama City, Fla.
Cameron, Ken	.171	40	82	7	14	1	2	0	3	6	17	0	0	L	L	6-0	185	3-1-73	1995	Tigard, Ore.
Clapp, Stubby	.278	139	514	113	143	30	9	12	57	86	100	18	10	L	R	5-8	175	2-24-73	1996	Windsor, Ontario
DeShields, Delino	.154	4	13	1	2	0	0	0	0	2	6	0	1	L	R	6-1	175	1-15-69	1987	West Palm Beach, Fla.
Dishington, Nate	.253	75	237	40	60	6	1	17	49	40	91	6	1	L	R	6-3	210	1-8-75	1993	Glendale, Calif.
Drew, J.D.	.328	19	67	18	22	3	1	5	11	13	15	2	1	L	R	6-1	195	11-20-75	1997	Hahira, Ga.
Garcia, Ossie	.245	94	200	32	49	10	3	0	24	13	35	10	6	R	R	6-1	180	10-14-73	1993	Hialeah, Fla.
Green, Scarborough	.360	18	75	16	27	2	1	2	9	6	12	9	2	B	R	5-10	170	6-9-74	1993	Florissant, Mo.
Haas, Chris	.274	132	445	75	122	27	4	20	83	73	129	1	2	L	R	6-2	210	10-15-76	1995	Paducah, Ky.
Hardge, Mike	.293	106	355	60	104	24	2	8	66	43	78	8	8	R	R	5-11	183	1-27-72	1990	Killeen, Texas
Horne, Tyrone	.312	123	443	94	138	13	3	37	139	70	97	18	7	L	R	5-10	185	11-2-70	1989	Troy, N.C.
Kennedy, Adam	.278	52	205	35	57	11	2	6	24	8	21	6	2	L	R	6-1	180	1-10-76	1997	Riverside, Calif.
Kleiner, Stacy	.258	99	333	44	86	28	1	6	57	33	79	1	2	R	R	6-0	185	1-12-75	1996	Las Vegas, Nev.
Lariviere, Jason	.255	132	435	69	111	29	5	8	58	50	58	14	6	R	R	5-10	180	9-30-73	1995	Biddeford, Maine
McEwing, Joe	.354	60	223	45	79	21	4	9	46	21	18	4	2	R	R	5-10	170	10-19-72	1992	Bristol, Pa.
Munoz, Juan	.269	28	119	16	32	9	0	0	18	3	15	0	0	L	L	5-9	170	3-27-74	1995	Miami, Fla.
Richard, Chris	.202	28	89	7	18	5	1	2	17	9	10	0	1	L	L	6-2	185	6-7-74	1995	San Diego, Calif.
Rivera, Micky	.194	64	108	11	21	7	1	1	5	6	18	0	0	R	R	5-10	175	4-14-74	1994	Racine, Wis.
Schmidt, Dave	.268	66	183	23	49	11	1	3	15	26	47	0	0	L	R	6-1	195	10-11-73	1996	Spokane, Wash.
Woolf, Jason	.265	76	294	63	78	22	5	4	16	34	84	28	5	B	R	6-1	170	6-6-77	1995	Miami, Fla.

PITCHING	W	L	ERA	G	GS	CG	SV	IP	H	R	ER	BB	SO	B	T	HT	WT	DOB	1st Yr	Resides
Almanza, Armando	4	1	3.31	28	0	0	8	33	27	13	12	18	46	L	L	6-3	205	10-26-72	1993	El Paso, Texas
Benes, Adam	0	0	6.06	12	0	0	0	16	21	12	11	2	8	L	R	6-2	195	3-12-73	1995	Evansville, Ind.
Brantley, Jeff	0	0	0.00	2	0	0	0	2	0	0	0	1	3	R	R	5-10	189	9-5-63	1985	Clinton, Miss.
Crafton, Kevin	5	1	3.23	46	0	0	1	56	52	23	20	7	44	R	R	6-1	185	5-10-74	1996	Russellville, Ark.
Detmers, Kris	9	10	4.92	27	26	0	0	154	175	100	84	78	88	B	L	6-5	215	6-22-74	1994	Nokomis, Ill.
Hall, Yates	0	0	18.62	8	0	0	0	10	16	21	20	19	2	R	R	6-2	190	3-29-73	1994	Front Royal, Va.
Heflin, Bronson	0	1	6.75	2	0	0	0	1	1	1	1	4	0	R	R	6-3	200	8-29-71	1994	Gallatin, Tenn.
Heiserman, Rick	0	3	4.96	18	0	0	9	16	20	11	9	5	9	R	R	6-7	220	2-22-73	1994	Omaha, Neb.
Jarvis, Matt	6	1	4.10	56	0	0	15	59	55	30	27	30	46	R	L	6-4	185	2-22-72	1991	Albuquerque, N.M.
Jimenez, Jose	15	6	3.11	26	26	1	0	180	156	71	62	68	88	R	R	6-3	170	7-7-73	1992	San Pedro de Macoris, D.R.
Logan, Marcus	7	7	5.51	28	20	0	0	126	162	91	77	56	66	R	R	6-0	170	5-8-72	1994	Evanston, Ill.
Lovingier, Kevin	1	0	2.63	19	0	0	0	24	20	9	7	13	26	L	L	6-1	190	8-29-71	1994	Mission Viejo, Calif.
McDougal, Mike	2	3	4.94	24	0	0	1	31	45	21	17	5	16	L	R	6-4	210	3-22-75	1994	Las Vegas, Nev.
Morris, Matt	0	0	0.00	1	0	0	1	4	4	0	0	0	2	R	R	6-5	210	8-9-74	1995	Montgomery, N.Y.
Nussbeck, Mark	4	2	5.10	10	8	0	0	42	44	30	24	18	21	L	R	6-4	180	5-25-74	1996	Kansas City, Mo.
Osborne, Donovan	2	0	4.26	5	5	0	0	19	16	9	9	3	21	L	L	6-2	195	6-21-69	1990	Carson City, Nev.
Politte, Cliff	5	3	2.96	10	10	1	0	67	56	25	22	16	61	R	R	5-11	185	2-27-74	1995	St. Louis, Mo.
Reed, Steve	4	7	6.03	32	17	0	0	116	163	92	78	31	53	R	R	6-2	205	9-24-75	1994	Juno Beach, Fla.
Weibl, Clint	12	10	5.37	25	23	0	0	139	161	86	83	53	85	R	R	6-3	180	3-17-75	1996	Dawson, Pa.
Welch, Travis	1	1	2.79	23	0	0	0	29	27	10	9	18	15	R	R	6-0	202	1-30-74	1993	Loomis, Calif.
Windham, Mike	3	4	5.09	40	5	1	0	76	86	47	43	41	49	R	R	6-1	185	3-8-72	1993	West Palm Beach, Fla.

FIELDING

Catcher	PCT	G	PO	A	E	DP	PB
Almond	1.000	5	21	1	0	0	0
Kleiner	.986	87	487	59	8	6	6
Schmidt	.993	55	274	30	2	4	6

First Base	PCT	G	PO	A	E	DP
Dishington	.982	64	540	47	11	63
Haas	1.000	9	81	2	0	9
Hardge	.983	52	396	20	7	41
Kleiner	1.000	2	15	2	0	2
Lariviere	1.000	1	2	0	0	0
Richard	.986	24	202	8	3	28
Schmidt	1.000	2	8	0	0	3

Second Base	PCT	G	PO	A	E	DP
Clapp	.978	137	332	436	17	113
DeShields	1.000	3	6	5	0	1
Kennedy	1.000	1	1	0	0	0
Rivera	.895	3	10	7	2	2

Third Base	PCT	G	PO	A	E	DP
Clapp	1.000	1	0	2	0	0
Haas	.926	112	65	209	22	28
Hardge	.975	21	14	25	1	4
Rivera	.944	39	11	40	3	4

Shortstop	PCT	G	PO	A	E	DP
Hardge	1.000	1	0	4	0	1
Kennedy	.940	51	90	143	15	34
McEwing	1.000	6	10	16	0	6
Rivera	.949	14	21	35	3	7
Woolf	.946	75	116	235	20	50

Outfield	PCT	G	PO	A	E	DP
Cameron	1.000	19	16	0	0	0
Clapp	1.000	2	1	0	0	0
Drew	.980	18	46	2	1	0
Garcia	1.000	79	114	5	0	1
Green	1.000	18	44	1	0	0
Hardge	.971	31	62	4	2	0
Horne	.964	95	155	6	6	1
Lariviere	.977	128	239	11	6	1
McEwing	.992	50	120	9	1	1
Munoz	1.000	28	47	2	0	1

PRINCE WILLIAM — Class A

CAROLINA LEAGUE

BATTING	AVG	G	AB	R	H	2B	3B	HR	RBI	BB	SO	SB	CS	B	T	HT	WT	DOB	1st Yr	Resides
Ametller, Jesus	.313	101	358	52	112	29	0	1	38	2	29	4	6	L	R	5-8	175	7-25-74	1997	San Jose, Costa Rica
Britt, Bryan	.176	86	284	23	50	6	0	9	33	13	98	1	1	R	R	6-2	220	4-16-75	1996	Wilmington, N.C.
Butler, Brent	.286	126	475	63	136	27	2	11	76	39	74	3	4	R	R	6-0	180	2-11-78	1996	Laurinburg, N.C.
Cameron, Ken	.326	42	138	22	45	12	0	3	23	24	23	8	7	L	L	6-0	185	3-1-73	1995	Tigard, Ore.

BATTING	AVG	G	AB	R	H	2B	3B	HR	RBI	BB	SO	SB	CS	B	T	HT	WT	DOB	1st Yr	Resides
Deck, Billy	.239	118	355	34	85	13	3	4	45	40	87	5	6	L	L	6-0	180	9-16-76	1995	Summerville, S.C.
Eckelman, Alex	.292	38	89	15	26	1	1	2	9	9	14	2	2	R	R	5-11	187	7-16-74	1997	St. Louis, Mo.
Falciglia, Tony	.000	4	7	0	0	0	0	0	0	0	1	0	0	R	R	5-11	185	9-29-72	1995	Bronx, N.Y.
Farley, Cordell	.291	134	546	92	159	28	11	11	59	27	145	50	17	R	R	6-0	185	3-29-73	1996	Blackstone, Va.
Feramisco, Derek	.297	72	256	39	76	23	3	2	[illegible]	20	70	[illegible]	[illegible]	R	R	6-5	195	11-7-74	1997	Clovis, Calif.
Hogan, Todd	.278	123	485	79	135	24	3	2	45	20	116	26	19	R	R	6-2	180	9-18-75	1996	Dublin, Ga.
Kennedy, Adam	.261	17	69	9	18	6	0	0	7	5	12	5	2	L	R	6-1	180	1-10-76	1997	Riverside, Calif.
Leon, Jose	.291	124	436	77	127	31	3	21	74	53	137	5	3	R	R	6-0	160	12-8-76	1994	Cayey, P.R.
Martine, Chris	.186	96	279	29	52	13	0	2	25	38	77	2	6	R	R	6-2	190	7-10-75	1997	Cherry Hill, N.J.
McNeal, Pepe	.209	57	163	17	34	7	1	4	17	9	54	0	1	R	R	6-3	205	8-11-75	1994	Thonotosassa, Fla.
Richard, Chris	.267	8	30	5	8	2	0	0	1	1	5	1	0	L	L	6-2	185	6-7-74	1995	San Diego, Calif.
Rivera, Micky	.000	7	6	1	0	0	0	0	0	0	4	0	1	R	R	5-10	175	4-14-74	1994	Racine, Wis.
Saturria, Luis	.294	129	462	70	136	25	9	12	73	28	104	26	15	R	R	6-2	165	7-21-76	1994	Boca Chica, D.R.
Tanner, Paul	.253	95	221	24	56	17	1	3	35	15	68	9	8	R	R	6-0	175	9-11-74	1996	Albuquerque, N.M.

GAMES BY POSITION: C—Falciglia 2, Martine 96, McNeal 56. **1B**—Britt 41, Deck 114, Hogan 1, Leon 3. **2B**—Ametller 88, Butler 1, Eckelman 19, Kennedy 15, Rivera 2, Tanner 50. **3B**—Butler 12, Eckelman 14, Leon 117, Tanner 11. **SS**—Butler 116, Kennedy 2, Rivera 1, Tanner 33. **OF**—Cameron 27, Deck 4, Eckelman 2, Farley 130, Feramisco 14, Hogan 122, Saturria 127, Tanner 3.

PITCHING	W	L	ERA	G	GS	CG	SV	IP	H	R	ER	BB	SO	B	T	HT	WT	DOB	1st Yr	Resides
Ankiel, Rick	9	6	2.79	21	21	1	0	126	91	46	39	38	181	L	L	6-1	210	7-19-79	1997	Fort Pierce, Fla.
Avrard, Corey	4	5	5.06	31	11	0	0	80	67	57	45	50	52	R	R	6-3	185	12-6-76	1994	Metairie, La.
Benes, Adam	1	0	1.35	10	0	0	0	13	12	6	2	4	9	L	R	6-2	195	3-12-73	1995	Evansville, Ind.
Coogan, Patrick	4	5	5.57	14	14	0	0	74	94	55	46	25	57	R	R	6-3	185	9-12-75	1997	Baton Rouge, La.
DeLeon, Jose	3	9	4.88	57	0	0	26	55	61	37	30	19	30	R	R	6-3	152	10-2-76	1994	Azua, D.R.
DeWitt, Matt	6	9	3.64	24	24	1	0	148	132	65	60	18	118	R	R	6-4	220	9-4-77	1995	Las Vegas, Nev.
Geis, John	3	1	4.35	32	0	0	0	39	49	24	19	10	27	L	L	6-2	191	12-21-73	1996	Central Square, N.Y.
Hall, Yates	1	1	7.15	5	1	0	0	11	11	10	9	6	7	R	R	6-2	190	3-29-73	1994	Front Royal, Va.
Huffaker, Mike	3	4	5.91	53	0	0	0	67	78	50	44	23	49	R	R	6-2	215	8-10-75	1997	Florence, Ala.
Hutchinson, Chad	2	0	2.79	5	5	0	0	29	20	12	9	11	31	R	R	6-5	220	2-21-77	1998	San Diego, Calif.
Jerue, Tristan	3	3	2.11	7	7	0	0	43	31	13	10	11	34	R	R	6-1	185	12-12-75	1997	Westfield, Mass.
Karnuth, Jason	8	1	1.67	16	15	2	0	108	86	26	20	14	53	R	R	6-2	190	5-15-76	1997	Glen Ellyn, Ill.
McDougal, Mike	3	0	2.81	17	2	0	0	32	38	11	10	2	28	L	R	6-4	210	3-22-75	1994	Las Vegas, Nev.
Montgomery, Greg	6	1	6.92	35	0	0	0	40	44	37	31	25	25	R	R	6-2	200	5-19-75	1996	Greenbrier, Ark.
Navarro, Jason	6	7	4.36	30	24	0	0	136	143	79	66	66	105	L	L	6-4	225	7-5-75	1997	Lilburn, Ga.
Nussbeck, Mark	3	6	3.56	14	13	0	0	86	75	40	34	16	65	L	R	6-4	180	5-25-74	1996	Kansas City, Mo.
Opipari, Mario	5	5	2.17	32	2	0	3	54	47	17	13	9	26	B	R	6-2	185	1-24-75	1996	Henderson, Nev.
Welch, Travis	0	1	2.13	12	0	0	7	13	10	4	3	6	8	R	R	6-0	202	1-30-74	1993	Loomis, Calif.
West, Adam	2	3	5.25	43	0	0	0	48	54	36	28	27	47	L	L	6-1	185	10-10-73	1994	Thousand Oaks, Calif.

PEORIA — Class A

MIDWEST LEAGUE

BATTING	AVG	G	AB	R	H	2B	3B	HR	RBI	BB	SO	SB	CS	B	T	HT	WT	DOB	1st Yr	Resides
Bevins, Andy	.244	130	508	68	124	30	3	18	98	34	145	6	4	R	R	6-3	215	10-10-75	1997	Sacramento, Calif.
Darr, Ryan	.289	12	38	7	11	2	2	0	2	2	10	0	1	R	R	6-1	180	10-28-77	1996	Corona, Calif.
Diaz, Miguel	.209	53	139	21	29	7	0	1	16	0	19	4	6	R	R	5-11	160	9-29-77	1995	San Pedro de Macoris, D.R.
Eckelman, Alex	.327	16	52	7	17	4	1	1	11	5	9	0	2	R	R	5-11	187	7-16-74	1997	St. Louis, Mo.
Feramisco, Derek	.200	26	85	18	17	4	0	1	5	8	23	1	0	R	R	6-5	195	11-7-74	1997	Clovis, Calif.
Gentry, Aaron	.237	99	279	39	66	10	2	3	27	29	98	13	4	R	R	6-2	185	5-22-75	1997	Tulsa, Okla.
Kim, Dave	.309	127	463	75	143	38	2	13	92	53	77	3	7	R	R	6-0	200	4-2-76	1997	Cherry Hill, N.J.
Lee, Jason	.264	122	382	51	101	15	5	5	47	43	103	10	10	L	R	6-1	185	4-22-77	1995	Burlington, Iowa
Maier, Taber	.269	84	271	47	73	14	1	2	28	45	52	6	5	R	R	6-0	180	2-24-75	1997	Santa Clara, Calif.
Macrory, Rob	.289	123	488	86	141	13	3	1	62	47	70	40	15	R	R	6-1	165	2-18-75	1997	Montgomery, Ala.
Nykoluk, Kevin	.280	67	218	29	61	7	0	2	24	13	34	1	4	R	R	6-0	210	4-2-75	1997	Simi Valley, Calif.
Ortega, Bill	.276	105	398	57	110	23	2	2	60	39	69	4	8	R	R	6-4	205	7-24-75	1997	San Jose, Costa Rica
Ozuna, Pablo	.357	133	538	122	192	27	10	9	62	29	56	62	26	R	R	6-0	160	8-25-78	1996	Santo Domingo, D.R.
Pagnozzi, Tom	.125	4	8	2	1	0	0	0	1	6	1	0	0	R	R	6-1	190	7-30-62	1983	Tucson, Ariz.
Quaccia, Luke	.279	131	437	68	122	31	1	11	67	46	88	4	2	L	R	6-6	220	2-27-75	1997	Oakdale, Calif.
Rupert, Bryan	.217	81	272	29	59	12	2	9	30	26	80	4	2	R	R	5-10	200	2-18-75	1997	Green Cove Spring, Fla.
Secoda, Joe	.042	10	24	2	1	0	0	0	0	0	15	0	0	R	R	6-1	190	11-19-77	1997	Fullerton, Calif.
Williams, Jovany	.215	54	158	20	34	10	1	4	21	10	43	3	1	R	R	6-2	165	1-29-77	1994	San Pedro de Macoris, D.R.

GAMES BY POSITION: C—Nykoluk 29, Pagnozzi 3, Rupert 73, Williams 47. **1B**—Bevins 9, Nykoluk 17, Quaccia 130. **2B**—Eckelman 4, Gentry 7, Maier 10, Macrory 122. **3B**—Darr 12, Eckelman 7, Gentry 77, Maier 58, Nykoluk 1. **SS**—Eckelman 5, Gentry 11, Maier 14, Ozuna 125. **OF**—Bevins 94, Diaz 48, Eckelman 1, Feramisco 23, Kim 114, Lee 112, Ortega 50, Secoda 6.

PITCHING	W	L	ERA	G	GS	CG	SV	IP	H	R	ER	BB	SO	B	T	HT	WT	DOB	1st Yr	Resides
Abell, Antonio	0	0	5.16	16	0	0	0	23	20	13	13	21	15	R	R	5-10	175	1-13-75	1994	Ekron, Ky.
Ankiel, Rick	3	0	2.06	7	7	0	0	35	15	8	8	12	41	L	L	6-1	210	7-19-79	1997	Fort Pierce, Fla.
Arnold, Neal	7	15	4.45	27	27	1	0	156	164	101	77	54	113	R	R	6-5	230	5-21-75	1997	Kearney, Neb.
Franks, Lance	4	6	2.28	58	0	0	4	75	57	23	19	20	68	R	R	5-11	180	8-20-75	1997	Russellville, Ark.
Geis, John	0	2	2.96	23	0	0	0	27	21	15	9	10	21	L	L	6-2	191	12-21-73	1996	Central Square, N.Y.
Gonzales, Rick	5	2	3.14	28	0	0	0	43	43	16	15	14	24	R	R	6-1	205	10-25-74	1998	Albuquerque, N.M.
Guzman, Toribio	1	0	7.16	13	0	0	0	16	20	19	13	15	7	R	R	6-3	165	7-6-76	1994	Peravia, D.R.
Jerue, Tristan	12	4	2.53	20	20	1	0	132	107	48	37	48	100	R	R	6-1	185	12-12-75	1997	Westfield, Mass.
Lanfranco, Otoniel	7	1	2.60	11	11	0	0	73	67	25	21	22	51	R	R	6-0	160	7-17-76	1996	Cotui, D.R.
Miller, Matt	3	1	5.18	27	2	0	0	49	50	35	28	15	38	R	R	6-0	180	6-22-74	1997	Greensburg, Ind.
Norris, Stephen	9	8	5.35	27	26	1	0	145	149	103	86	87	94	L	L	6-1	185	2-1-76	1996	Fort Worth, Texas
Riegert, Tim	1	0	4.34	31	0	0	0	37	31	21	18	24	21	L	L	6-0	180	6-29-74	1996	Orlando, Fla.
Rodriguez, Jose	2	4	4.58	40	0	0	0	39	47	32	20	19	30	L	L	6-1	205	12-18-74	1997	Cayey, P.R.
Rosario, Ruben	3	3	6.97	12	1	0	0	21	21	19	16	24	24	R	R	6-3	150	1-26-75	1993	Boca Chica, D.R.
Sheredy, Kevin	4	4	3.97	13	13	0	0	68	75	38	30	24	39	R	R	6-4	210	1-3-75	1996	Antioch, Calif.
Shibilo, Andy	1	3	8.51	7	7	0	0	31	42	30	29	11	22	R	R	6-7	220	9-16-76	1998	Belleville, N.J.
Stechschulte, Gene	4	8	2.59	57	0	0	33	66	58	26	19	21	70	R	R	6-5	210	8-12-73	1996	Kalida, Ohio
Wingerd, Josh	0	2	7.87	29	5	0	0	50	77	50	44	7	30	R	R	6-0	185	7-3-75	1997	Hood River, Ore.
Woodward, Finley	6	5	5.30	34	21	0	0	138	156	91	81	63	88	R	R	5-11	200	8-15-75	1997	Molino, Fla.

NEW JERSEY — Short-Season Class A

NEW YORK-PENN LEAGUE

BATTING	AVG	G	AB	R	H	2B	3B	HR	RBI	BB	SO	SB	CS	B	T	HT	WT	DOB	1st Yr	Resides
Alfonso, Eliezer	.246	48	175	16	43	4	1	2	19	6	49	1	0	R	R	6-0	165	2-7-79	1996	Puerto la Cruz, Ven.
Araujo, Danilo	.212	32	85	10	18	1	1	0	9	13	24	21	4	R	R	5-10	160	1-17-77	1995	Peravia, D.R.
Clark, Greg	.176	51	170	15	30	3	0	2	14	15	46	1	0	R	R	6-2	180	1-5-77	1998	Phoenix, Ariz.
Farnsworth, Troy	.257	65	218	33	56	14	1	6	37	25	64	2	4	R	R	6-2	200	2-4-76	1998	Salt Lake City, Utah
Folkers, Brandon	.241	52	133	7	32	5	1	1	16	10	50	2	2	L	L	6-2	180	8-29-75	1997	St. Petersburg, Fla.
Freeman, Brad	.249	73	253	37	63	11	3	2	26	24	45	19	10	R	R	6-2	210	9-13-75	1998	Oxford, Miss.
Hummel, Dan	.223	48	121	17	27	7	0	2	17	16	30	2	1	R	R	6-3	225	8-10-76	1998	Montgomery, N.Y.
Kelly, Chris	.262	19	61	6	16	4	0	1	6	7	17	1	0	R	R	6-3	210	5-29-77	1998	Trumbull, Conn.
Kidwell, Tommy	.244	39	123	14	30	6	0	0	9	8	17	1	2	R	R	5-9	175	11-19-76	1998	St. Petersburg, Fla.
McNaughton, Troy	.255	53	157	27	40	7	4	1	14	20	45	6	5	L	L	6-0	195	1-27-75	1998	Tacoma, Wash.
Molina, Jim	.226	58	212	25	48	9	0	2	28	13	58	22	1	R	R	6-1	210	4-9-76	1998	Miami, Fla.
Nunez, Jose	.216	55	162	17	35	6	2	1	14	9	22	5	4	R	R	5-10	175	12-8-78	1997	Cotui, D.R.
Schmidt, Todd	.141	29	78	9	11	1	0	2	7	14	24	1	0	B	R	6-3	225	10-12-74	1997	New Haven, Mo.
Secoda, Joe	.226	53	159	13	36	4	0	0	14	10	59	7	4	R	R	6-1	190	11-19-77	1997	Fullerton, Calif.
Smith, Nate	.245	42	143	17	35	5	3	0	17	13	27	4	1	R	R	6-0	180	12-27-74	1998	Las Vegas, Nev.
Snead, Esix	.233	58	193	38	45	4	4	1	16	33	54	42	11	B	R	5-10	175	6-7-76	1998	Williston, Fla.

GAMES BY POSITION: C—Alfonzo 24, Clark 43, Hummel 7, Schmidt 10. **1B**—Farnsworth 21, Folkers 41, Hummel 28. **2B**—Araujo 24, Farnsworth 3, Kidwell 38, Nunez 18. **3B**—Farnsworth 44, Kelly 9, Nunez 29. **SS**—Freeman 73, Nunez 9. **OF**—Folkers 3, McNaughton 39, Molina 57, Secoda 48, Smith 38, Snead 55.

PITCHING	W	L	ERA	G	GS	CG	SV	IP	H	R	ER	BB	SO	B	T	HT	WT	DOB	1st Yr	Resides
Bates, Casey	1	2	3.29	27	0	0	0	41	39	15	15	13	52	R	R	6-2	205	10-1-75	1998	Athens, Ga.
Garcia, Wilson	3	0	3.76	19	0	0	0	26	34	15	11	7	22	R	R	6-1	174	7-27-79	1997	Azua, D.R.
Gonzales, Rick	0	0	2.70	6	0	0	0	7	3	2	2	2	10	R	R	6-1	205	10-25-74	1998	Albuquerque, N.M.
Gooden, Derek	1	3	1.71	29	0	0	17	32	22	11	6	9	30	R	R	6-0	175	6-26-75	1997	Adel, Ga.
Griffin, Kirk	5	1	1.63	35	0	0	4	50	32	23	9	15	51	R	R	6-1	185	6-4-75	1998	Sacramento, Calif.
Gutshall, Eric	0	1	5.23	29	0	0	0	33	31	29	19	14	22	R	R	6-5	225	11-14-75	1998	Berwyn, Ill.
Guzman, Toribio	1	4	7.27	17	2	0	0	43	62	47	35	14	27	R	R	6-3	165	7-6-76	1994	Peravia, D.R.
Held, Travis	5	5	4.05	14	14	0	0	73	71	42	33	18	65	R	R	6-3	215	3-19-77	1998	Jupiter, Fla.
Hutchinson, Chad	0	1	3.52	3	3	0	0	15	15	7	6	4	20	R	R	6-5	220	2-21-77	1998	San Diego, Calif.
Lanfranco, Otoniel	1	0	1.24	5	5	0	0	29	14	5	4	13	35	R	R	6-0	160	7-17-76	1996	Cotui, D.R.
Langen, Brian	0	0	7.64	20	0	0	0	18	30	21	15	11	12	L	L	6-7	210	2-13-78	1998	Litchfield, Ill.
Ortega, Franklin	2	0	4.21	15	0	0	0	26	16	12	12	28	23	R	R	5-11	160	12-2-73	1991	San Pedro de Macoris, D.R.
Prather, Scott	4	6	3.15	15	14	0	0	71	55	30	25	30	73	L	L	6-2	185	10-8-76	1998	Atlanta, Ga.
Rosario, Ruben	2	7	5.11	16	9	0	0	49	33	33	28	37	63	R	R	6-3	150	1-26-75	1993	Boca Chica, D.R.
Shibilo, Andy	4	4	3.45	9	9	0	0	47	51	21	18	8	54	R	R	6-7	220	9-10-76	1998	Belleville, N.J.
Stemle, Steve	3	3	1.83	9	9	0	0	44	37	17	9	14	47	R	R	6-4	200	5-20-77	1998	Louisville, Ky.
Walrond, Les	2	4	4.01	13	10	0	0	52	52	31	23	24	52	L	L	6-0	195	11-7-76	1998	Tulsa, Okla.

JOHNSON CITY — Rookie

APPALACHIAN LEAGUE

BATTING	AVG	G	AB	R	H	2B	3B	HR	RBI	BB	SO	SB	CS	B	T	HT	WT	DOB	1st Yr	Resides
Banez, Marco	.197	38	137	18	27	1	2	0	7	8	26	3	2	L	L	6-1	173	9-24-79	1997	Maracay, Ven.
Bowers, Jason	.291	60	213	31	62	10	5	3	38	13	43	10	8	R	R	5-11	170	1-27-78	1998	Uniontown, Pa.
Carvajal, Ramon	.235	54	200	32	47	6	2	5	26	19	41	11	2	B	R	5-10	155	3-4-81	1997	Bani, D.R.
Dyt, Darren	.304	59	207	31	63	9	3	6	27	22	52	4	2	L	R	6-5	195	12-15-75	1998	Tulare, Calif.
Escobar, Gustavo	.236	43	127	16	30	7	0	4	17	14	25	4	3	R	R	5-10	170	1-30-80	1997	Anzoategui, Ven.
Espino, Jose	.236	47	165	29	39	3	0	9	25	13	52	7	3	R	R	6-0	164	11-6-79	1997	Cotui, D.R.
Gooden, Carl	.211	6	19	4	4	0	0	1	3	2	3	2	0	R	R	6-1	190	11-25-78	1997	Houston, Texas
Johnson, Gabe	.251	57	187	30	47	11	3	9	32	20	71	3	1	R	R	6-1	190	9-21-79	1998	Delray Beach, Fla.
Kerry, Bill	.157	31	51	7	8	2	0	0	4	12	17	0	1	R	R	5-10	200	12-15-75	1998	Ithaca, N.Y.
Ledbetter, Blake	.262	37	122	15	32	8	1	4	21	13	37	1	0	R	R	6-2	210	3-9-77	1997	Bertrand, Mo.
Lemon, Tim	.226	50	190	25	43	6	2	4	23	15	50	11	1	R	R	6-1	180	9-23-80	1998	La Mirada, Calif.
McIntyre, Remer	.231	41	104	17	24	1	0	0	9	7	40	6	2	R	R	5-10	180	11-23-78	1997	Tampa, Fla.
Ortega, Jose	.233	46	133	16	31	11	1	1	9	4	34	3	0	R	R	6-3	180	1-7-78	1996	El Tigre, Ven.
Rodriguez, Jose	.000	2	4	0	0	0	0	0	0	0	1	0	0	L	L	6-1	205	12-18-74	1997	Cayey, P.R.
Torres, Reynaldo	.286	44	147	19	42	12	0	3	20	11	53	1	2	R	R	6-5	235	3-14-79	1997	Guanica, P.R.
Vasquez, Geraldo	.145	31	62	11	9	2	3	0	5	12	21	5	1	R	R	5-11	145	11-5-79	1997	San Pedro de Macoris, D.R.
Wilson, Jack	.373	61	241	50	90	18	4	4	29	18	30	22	6	B	R	6-0	170	12-29-77	1998	Thousand Oaks, Calif.

GAMES BY POSITION: C—Johnson 38, Kerry 27, Ledbetter 24, Vasquez 1. **1B**—Banez 4, Johnson 1, Ortega 33, Torres 43. **2B**—Carvajal 39, Escobar 28, Vasquez 7. **3B**—Bowers 60, Escobar 3, Vasquez 14. **SS**—Escobar 11, Vasquez 6, Wilson 60. **OF**—Banez 34, Dyt 38, Escobar 2, Espino 47, Gooden 6, Lemon 50, McIntyre 39, Ortega 14, Torres 1.

PITCHING	W	L	ERA	G	GS	CG	SV	IP	H	R	ER	BB	SO	B	T	HT	WT	DOB	1st Yr	Resides
Acosta, Luis	0	0	19.29	1	0	0	0	2	4	5	5	3	3	R	R	6-2	180	3-18-80	1997	Puerto Piritu, Ven.
Alcantara, Alvin	1	1	5.56	31	0	0	0	44	53	32	27	11	31	L	L	6-0	145	5-25-78	1996	Santiago, D.R.
Book, Jeremy	3	3	7.04	13	13	0	0	63	85	52	49	27	45	R	R	6-4	205	8-3-77	1998	Trenton, Ill.
Christenson, Ryan	2	3	3.59	18	5	0	0	53	50	28	21	20	38	R	R	6-5	205	8-10-76	1998	Robbinsdale, Minn.
Gargano, Mike	1	5	7.87	12	8	0	0	42	54	39	37	24	29	R	R	6-2	200	7-28-78	1998	Salt Lake City, Utah
Hand, Jon	1	3	3.52	29	0	0	3	38	42	24	15	8	35	R	R	6-2	200	12-14-75	1998	Mount Pleasant, Texas
Hopson, Craig	4	3	5.66	29	0	0	0	35	41	24	22	15	27	R	R	6-1	195	2-20-79	1997	Rockford, Ill.
Lambert, Jeremy	4	4	4.92	13	11	0	0	64	73	44	35	37	30	R	R	6-1	192	1-10-79	1997	Kearns, Utah
Marr, Jason	2	2	2.12	25	0	0	10	34	23	11	8	10	36	R	R	6-1	195	9-9-75	1998	Downey, Calif.
Matew, Francisco	3	5	9.42	18	6	1	0	43	66	49	45	15	42	R	R	5-11	165	4-12-79	1997	San Pedro de Macoris, D.R.
Rayborn, Kris	1	7	11.06	10	10	0	0	35	40	48	43	47	26	L	L	6-4	170	8-10-79	1998	Purvis, Miss.
Rizo, Miguel	0	2	11.81	16	0	0	0	27	55	37	35	20	14	R	R	6-2	165	6-23-80	1997	Maracay, Ven.
Smith, Robert	3	3	5.18	14	14	0	0	64	85	47	37	34	65	L	L	6-0	170	10-23-79	1998	Lakewood, Calif.
Viles, Jeff	0	1	6.62	27	0	0	1	34	36	28	25	24	42	R	R	6-2	220	4-1-76	1998	Kansas City, Mo.
Zachery, Nicholas	0	0	0.00	1	0	0	0	1	0	0	0	2	0	L	L	6-1	195	5-9-79	1998	Loves Park, Ill.

SAN DIEGO PADRES

Series sweep doesn't lessen feat of '98 NL champions

BY JOHN MAFFEI

The facts were hard and cold.

The Padres advanced to the World Series in 1998 for only the second time in the organization's 30-year history and for the first time since 1984, then were swept aside by the Yankees.

There were so many positives, however, that the Padres refused to dwell on that one negative.

They pointed to a team record 98 victories and the second National League West title in three years. They boasted of an NL Division Series win over the heavily favored Astros, a team that won 102 games. And San Diego nearly swept the heavily favored Braves, a team that won 104 games, in the NL Championship Series.

"We had a tremendous season," Padres general manager Kevin Towers said. "We won the National League pennant, beating teams that were supposed to be better than us.

"And despite the World Series sweep, we played the Yankees tough. Twice we had late leads. From top to bottom, this organization had its greatest year."

Of that, there is little argument.

The Padres drew a team-record 2,555,901 fans. The playoffs and World Series pushed that over 3 million. None of the team's six postseason home games drew fewer than 58,988.

Bruce Bochy was named NL manager of the year in some quarters, earning praise for getting the most out of his club. His handling of the bullpen, where Brian Boehringer, Dan Miceli and Donne Wall set up closer Trevor Hoffman, was a key to the club's success. Hoffman tied an NL record with 53 saves.

Kevin Brown

JOHN SPEAR

George Arias

Players of the Year

Major League: Kevin Brown, rhp

Brown finished second in the NL with a 2.38 ERA while going 18-7 with 257 strikeouts.

Minor League: George Arias, 3b, Las Vegas

Arias ranked fourth among all minor leaguers with 36 homers and sixth with 119 RBIs.

Left fielder Greg Vaughn was credited by teammates as being the guy that carried the club through the regular season. Vaughn, who cranked 50 home runs, was the subject of regular trade rumors before the season began, but the Padres were glad they held onto him.

Pitching coach Dave Stewart's imprint was seen on a staff that saw its ERA improve from 4.98 in 1997 to 3.63, third-best in the league. Righthander Kevin Brown, who came over from the Florida Marlins, had a big hand in that improvement as well, finishing second in the NL with a 2.38 ERA.

When the club needed a lift, Towers acquired utilityman Jim Leyritz from the Red Sox in June and outfielder John Vander Wal from the Rockies in August. Both came up big in the playoffs.

Towers was happy with the development of the team's young players, who should form the nucleus of the club when a proposed new stadium opens in 2002.

As an organization, the Padres went 466-386 (.547), third-best in baseball behind the Yankees and Toronto Blue Jays.

Four minor league teams–Double-A Mobile, Class A Rancho Cucamonga, Class A Clinton and Rookie-level Idaho Falls–went to the playoffs. Mobile and Idaho Falls claimed league titles.

Las Vegas third baseman George Arias, who hit .306 with 38 home runs and 119 RBIs, and second baseman Dave Hajek were named to the Pacific Coast League all-star team, and righthanders Matt Clement and Stan Spencer made good impressions after September callups.

Mobile was named Baseball America's Team of the Year after winning 86 games in the regular season and going 6-1 in the postseason.

ORGANIZATION LEADERS

BATTING		
*AVG	Josh Loggins, Idaho Falls	.341
R	Mike Darr, Mobile	105
H	Dave Hajek, Las Vegas	177
TB	George Arias, Las Vegas	283
2B	Dave Hajek, Las Vegas	45
3B	Brian McClure, Rancho Cucamonga	11
HR	George Arias, Las Vegas	36
RBI	George Arias, Las Vegas	119
BB	Johnny Hunter, Clinton	82
SO	Pete Paciorek, Rancho Cucamonga	135
SB	Johnny Hunter, Clinton	36
PITCHING		
W	Buddy Carlyle, Mobile	14
L	Two tied at	12
#ERA	Brendan Sullivan, Mobile/Rancho Cucamonga	1.45
G	Brendan Sullivan, Mobile/Rancho Cucamonga	70
CG	Brian Lawrence, Clinton/Idaho Falls	4
SV	Brendan Sullivan, Mobile/Rancho Cucamonga	21
IP	Buddy Carlyle, Mobile	184
BB	Ben Howard, Idaho Falls	87
SO	Matt Clement, Las Vegas	160

*Minimum 250 At-Bats #Minimum 75 Innings

San Diego PADRES

Manager: Bruce Bochy. **1998 Record:** 98-64, .605 (1st, NL West)

BATTING	AVG	G	AB	R	H	2B	3B	HR	RBI	BB	SO	SB	CS	B	T	HT	WT	DOB	1st Yr	Resides
Arias, George	.194	20	36	4	7	1	1	1	4	3	16	0	0	R	R	5-11	190	3-12-72	1993	Tucson, Ariz.
Caminiti, Ken	.252	131	452	87	114	29	0	29	82	71	108	6	2	B	R	6-0	200	4-21-63	1985	Richmond, Texas
Cianfrocco, Archi	.125	40	72	4	9	3	0	1	5	5	22	1	0	R	R	6-5	215	10-6-66	1987	San Diego, Calif.
Davis, Ben	.000	1	1	0	0	0	0	0	0	0	0	0	0	B	R	6-4	205	3-10-77	1995	Aston, Pa.
Finley, Steve	.249	159	619	92	154	40	6	14	67	45	103	12	3	L	L	6-2	180	3-12-65	1987	Del Mar, Calif.
Giovanola, Ed	.230	92	139	19	32	3	3	1	9	22	22	1	2	L	R	5-10	170	3-4-69	1990	San Jose, Calif.
Gomez, Chris	.267	145	449	55	120	32	3	4	39	51	87	1	3	R	R	6-1	195	6-16-71	1992	Carlsbad, Calif.
Gwynn, Tony	.321	127	461	65	148	35	0	16	69	35	18	3	1	L	L	5-11	220	5-9-60	1981	Poway, Calif.
Hernandez, Carlos	.262	129	390	34	102	15	0	9	52	16	54	2	2	R	R	5-11	215	5-24-67	1985	Caracas, Ven.
Joyner, Wally	.298	131	439	58	131	30	1	12	80	51	44	1	2	L	L	6-2	200	6-16-62	1983	Rancho Santa Fe, Calif.
Leyritz, Jim	.266	62	143	17	38	10	0	4	18	21	40	0	0	R	R	6-0	195	12-27-63	1986	Cooper City, Fla.
Mouton, James	.190	55	63	8	12	2	1	0	7	7	11	4	3	R	R	5-9	175	12-29-68	1991	Missouri City, Texas
Myers, Greg	.246	69	171	19	42	10	0	4	20	17	36	0	1	L	R	6-2	208	4-14-66	1984	Riverside, Calif.
Rivera, Ruben	.209	95	172	31	36	7	2	6	29	28	52	5	1	R	R	6-3	200	11-14-73	1992	La Chorrera, Panama
Romero, Mandy	.000	6	9	1	0	0	0	0	0	1	3	0	0	B	R	5-11	196	10-19-67	1988	Miami, Fla.
Sheets, Andy	.242	88	194	31	47	5	3	7	29	21	62	7	2	R	R	6-2	180	11-19-71	1992	Lafayette, La.
Sweeney, Mark	.234	122	192	17	45	8	3	2	15	26	37	1	2	L	L	6-1	195	10-26-69	1991	Scottsdale, Ariz.
Vander Wal, John	.240	20	25	3	6	3	0	0	0	6	5	0	0	L	L	6-1	180	4-29-66	1987	Hudsonville, Mich.
2-team (89 Colorado)	.279	109	129	21	36	13	1	5	20	22	34	0	0							
Vaughn, Greg	.272	158	573	112	156	28	4	50	119	79	121	11	4	R	R	6-0	202	7-3-65	1986	Elk Grove, Calif.
Veras, Quilvio	.267	138	517	79	138	24	2	6	45	84	78	24	9	B	R	5-8	168	4-3-71	1990	Santo Domingo, D.R.
Williams, Eddie	.143	17	28	1	4	0	0	0	3	2	6	0	0	R	R	6-0	210	11-1-64	1983	La Mesa, Calif.

PITCHING	W	L	ERA	G	GS	CG	SV	IP	H	R	ER	BB	SO	B	T	HT	WT	DOB	1st Yr	Resides
Ashby, Andy	17	9	3.34	33	33	5	0	227	223	90	84	58	151	R	R	6-5	190	7-11-67	1986	Pittston, Pa.
Boehringer, Brian	5	2	4.36	56	1	0	0	76	75	38	37	45	67	B	R	6-2	190	1-8-69	1991	Fenton, Mo.
Brown, Kevin	18	7	2.38	36	35	7	0	257	225	77	68	49	257	R	R	6-4	200	3-14-65	1986	Macon, Ga.
Bruske, Jim	0	0	3.86	4	0	0	0	7	10	4	3	4	4	R	R	6-1	185	10-7-64	1986	Tempe, Ariz.
2-team (35 Los Angeles)	3	0	3.53	39	0	0	1	51	57	22	20	23	35							
Clement, Matt	2	0	4.61	4	2	0	0	14	15	8	7	7	13	R	R	6-3	190	8-12-74	1994	Butler, Pa.
Cunnane, Will	0	0	6.00	3	0	0	0	3	4	2	2	1	1	R	R	6-2	175	4-24-74	1993	Congers, N.Y.
Hamilton, Joey	13	13	4.27	34	34	0	0	217	220	113	103	106	147	R	R	6-4	230	9-9-70	1991	Atlanta, Ga.
Hitchcock, Sterling	9	7	3.93	39	27	2	1	176	169	83	77	48	158	L	L	6-1	192	4-29-71	1989	Brandon, Fla.
Hoffman, Trevor	4	2	1.48	66	0	0	53	73	41	12	12	21	86	R	R	6-0	205	10-13-67	1989	Southlake, Texas
Kroon, Marc	0	0	0.00	2	0	0	0	2	0	0	0	1	2	R	R	6-2	195	4-2-73	1991	Phoenix, Ariz.
Langston, Mark	4	6	5.86	22	16	0	0	81	107	55	53	41	56	R	L	6-2	185	8-20-60	1981	Anaheim Hills, Calif.
Miceli, Danny	10	5	3.22	67	0	0	2	73	64	28	26	27	70	R	R	6-0	216	9-9-70	1990	Winter Springs, Fla.
Myers, Randy	1	3	6.28	21	0	0	0	14	15	10	10	7	9	L	L	6-1	210	9-19-62	1982	Vancouver, Wash.
Ramirez, Roberto	1	0	6.14	21	0	0	0	15	12	13	10	12	17	R	L	5-11	170	8-17-72	1990	Laurel, Mexico
Reyes, Carlos	2	2	3.58	22	0	0	1	28	23	11	11	6	24	B	R	6-1	190	4-19-69	1991	Tampa, Fla.
Sanders, Scott	3	1	4.11	23	0	0	0	31	33	20	14	5	26	R	R	6-4	220	3-25-69	1990	San Diego, Calif.
Smith, Pete	3	2	4.78	10	8	0	0	43	45	23	23	18	36	R	R	6-2	200	2-27-66	1984	Smyrna, Ga.
Spencer, Stan	1	0	4.70	6	5	0	0	31	29	16	16	4	31	R	R	6-4	205	8-2-68	1991	Battleground, Wash.
VanRyn, Ben	0	1	10.13	6	0	0	0	3	3	3	3	4	1	L	L	6-5	195	8-19-71	1990	San Antonio, Texas
2-team (9 Chicago)	0	1	5.06	15	0	0	0	11	12	6	6	10	7							
Wall, Donne	5	4	2.43	46	1	0	1	70	50	20	19	32	56	R	R	6-1	180	7-11-67	1989	Houston, Texas
Wengert, Don	0	0	5.93	10	0	0	1	14	21	9	9	5	5	R	R	6-2	212	11-6-69	1992	Sioux City, Iowa

FIELDING

Catcher	PCT	G	PO	A	E	DP	PB
Davis	1.000	1	2	0	0	0	0
Hernandez	.992	122	793	54	7	6	13
Leyritz	.987	24	139	11	2	1	1
Myers	.987	52	276	29	4	4	1
Romero	.963	6	24	2	1	0	1

First Base	PCT	G	PO	A	E	DP
Arias	1.000	1	4	0	0	1
Cianfrocco	1.000	19	91	11	0	11
Hernandez	1.000	1	1	0	0	0
Joyner	.993	127	988	78	7	99
Leyritz	.993	20	134	8	1	12
Sheets	1.000	2	9	0	0	2
Sweeney	.992	21	127	5	1	11
Vanderwal	1.000	3	14	2	0	1
Williams	1.000	7	47	3	0	3

Second Base	PCT	G	PO	A	E	DP
Cianfrocco	1.000	3	3	1	0	1
Giovanola	.992	36	46	79	1	13
Sheets	.975	22	38	39	2	7
Veras	.987	132	255	406	9	88

Third Base	PCT	G	PO	A	E	DP
Arias	.931	14	4	23	2	2
Caminiti	.931	127	77	208	21	14
Cianfrocco	.875	13	7	14	3	0
Giovanola	.964	38	11	43	2	2
Leyritz	1.000	1	3	0	0	0
Sheets	.909	22	8	12	2	2

Shortstop	PCT	G	PO	A	E	DP
Giovanola	.000	1	0	0	0	0
Gomez	.980	143	181	395	12	92
Sheets	.964	39	41	93	5	18

Outfield	PCT	G	PO	A	E	DP
Cianfrocco	1.000	3	2	0	0	0
Finley	.981	157	350	12	7	5
Gwynn	.993	116	143	5	1	0
Leyritz	.000	1	0	0	0	0
Mouton	.969	33	30	1	1	0
Rivera	.973	91	104	3	3	0
Sweeney	1.000	34	37	0	0	0
Vanderwal	1.000	5	7	0	0	0
Vaughn	.993	151	270	5	2	0

JOHN WILLIAMSON

Greg Vaughn

FARM SYSTEM

Director of Player Development: Jim Skaalen

Class	Farm Team	League	W	L	Pct.	Finish*	Manager	First Yr
AAA	Las Vegas (Nev.) Stars	Pacific Coast	70	72	.493	11th (16)	Jerry Royster	1983
AA	Mobile (Ala.) BayBears	Southern	86	54	.614	+t-1st (10)	Mike Ramsey	1997
A#	Rancho Cucamonga (Calif.) Quakes	California	77	63	.550	t-4th (10)	Mike Basso	1993
A	Clinton (Iowa) LumberKings	Midwest	65	73	.471	11th (14)	Tom LeVasseur	1995
Rookie#	Idaho Falls (Idaho) Braves	Pioneer	47	29	.618	+t-1st (8)	Don Werner	1995
Rookie	Peoria (Ariz.) Padres	Arizona	23	31	.426	6th (8)	Randy Whisler	1988

*Finish in overall standings (No. of teams in league) #Advanced level +Won league championship

LAS VEGAS — Class AAA

PACIFIC COAST LEAGUE

BATTING	AVG	G	AB	R	H	2B	3B	HR	RBI	BB	SO	SB	CS	B	T	HT	WT	DOB	1st Yr	Resides
Allen, Dusty	.267	87	292	42	78	21	1	16	45	31	80	0	2	R	R	6-4	215	8-9-72	1995	Oklahoma City, Okla.
Arias, George	.308	114	435	73	134	33	4	36	119	37	108	0	1	R	R	5-11	190	3-12-72	1993	Tucson, Ariz.
Cianfrocco, Archi	.283	38	127	15	36	8	1	6	16	11	35	3	1	R	R	6-5	215	10-6-66	1987	San Diego, Calif.
Colbert, Craig	.167	5	18	0	3	1	0	0	2	0	3	0	0	R	R	6-0	190	2-13-65	1986	Pearland, Texas
Dascenzo, Doug	.192	7	26	5	5	1	0	0	2	5	2	2	0	B	L	5-8	160	6-30-64	1985	Labelle, Pa.
Devereaux, Mike	.267	34	120	19	32	10	1	2	12	9	13	1	0	R	R	6-0	195	4-10-63	1985	Alpharetta, Ga.
Giovanola, Ed	.333	4	15	4	5	0	0	0	1	2	3	0	1	L	R	5-10	170	3-4-69	1990	San Jose, Calif.
Gonzalez, Jimmy	.238	51	160	22	38	9	0	5	21	15	44	1	0	R	R	6-3	235	3-8-73	1991	Hartford, Conn.
Gubanich, Creighton	.291	86	292	48	85	22	0	19	70	30	85	1	1	R	R	6-3	200	3-27-72	1991	Phoenixville, Pa.
Guiel, Aaron	.311	60	183	33	57	15	4	5	31	28	51	5	1	L	R	5-10	190	10-5-72	1993	Langley, B.C.
Hajek, Dave	.328	130	539	85	177	45	3	4	63	23	46	14	6	R	R	5-10	165	10-14-67	1990	Colorado Springs, Colo.
Hemmings, Scot	.125	3	8	0	1	0	0	0	0	1	3	0	0	R	R	6-4	197	5-6-77	1997	Columbus, Ga.
Horsman, Brent	.500	1	2	1	1	0	0	0	0	0	1	0	0	L	R	6-3	175	7-31-76	1997	Fairfield, Calif.
LaRocca, Greg	.309	95	304	55	94	22	5	8	39	19	48	7	4	R	R	5-11	185	11-10-72	1994	Bedford, N.H.
Melo, Juan	.272	130	467	61	127	26	1	6	47	24	91	9	8	B	R	6-1	180	11-5-76	1994	Bani, D.R.
Morenz, Shea	.297	13	37	5	11	5	0	1	6	1	9	0	0	L	R	6-2	205	1-22-74	1995	San Antonio, Texas
Mouton, James	.354	50	192	38	68	17	3	4	31	17	31	15	1	R	R	5-9	175	12-29-68	1991	Missouri City, Texas
Myers, Greg	.556	3	9	0	5	0	0	0	1	0	0	0	0	L	R	6-2	208	4-14-66	1984	Riverside, Calif.
Poe, Charles	.277	118	393	56	109	25	2	8	43	26	81	6	2	R	R	6-0	185	11-9-71	1990	West Covina, Calif.
Prieto, Chris	.304	92	352	65	107	18	6	2	35	40	48	20	11	L	L	5-11	180	8-24-72	1993	Carmel, Calif.
Prieto, Rick	.266	32	79	15	21	6	1	0	8	12	22	4	2	B	R	5-10	175	8-24-72	1993	Carmel, Calif.
Rivera, Ruben	.144	30	104	9	15	3	0	3	11	11	42	4	0	R	R	6-3	200	11-14-73	1992	La Chorrera, Panama
Romero, Mandy	.290	40	131	25	38	8	0	8	22	20	25	0	1	B	R	5-11	196	10-19-67	1988	Miami, Fla.
Thompson, Jason	.271	58	192	21	52	15	1	3	17	16	49	3	3	L	L	6-4	200	6-13-71	1993	Laguna Hills, Calif.
Williams, Eddie	.336	90	307	69	103	24	0	20	77	33	66	1	1	R	R	6-0	210	11-1-64	1983	La Mesa, Calif.

PITCHING	W	L	ERA	G	GS	CG	SV	IP	H	R	ER	BB	SO	B	T	HT	WT	DOB	1st Yr	Resides
Bruske, Jim	0	1	6.00	5	0	0	1	6	8	4	4	1	2	R	R	6-1	185	10-7-64	1986	Tempe, Ariz.
Clement, Matt	10	9	3.98	27	27	1	0	172	157	94	76	85	160	R	R	6-3	190	8-12-74	1994	Butler, Pa.
Corbin, Archie	0	0	27.00	6	0	0	0	4	7	16	13	13	3	R	R	6-4	230	12-30-67	1986	Beaumont, Texas
Cunnane, Will	1	2	5.25	33	0	0	4	36	45	26	21	19	30	R	R	6-2	175	4-24-74	1993	Congers, N.Y.
Dixon, Bubba	3	3	5.92	38	0	0	2	52	60	38	34	32	42	L	L	5-10	165	1-7-72	1994	Lucedale, Miss.
Kaufman, Brad	9	9	6.39	23	22	0	0	118	148	90	84	65	83	R	R	6-2	210	4-26-72	1993	Traer, Iowa
Lomon, Kevin	2	9	5.15	30	17	0	0	124	128	78	71	62	118	R	R	6-1	195	11-20-71	1991	Cameron, Okla.
Menhart, Paul	7	6	5.34	49	2	0	4	64	79	45	38	39	50	R	R	6-2	190	3-25-69	1990	Conyers, Ga.
Murray, Heath	9	11	4.99	27	27	3	0	162	191	103	90	62	121	L	L	6-4	205	4-19-73	1994	Troy, Ohio
Newman, Alan	3	3	3.30	63	0	0	7	76	58	29	28	50	76	L	L	6-6	240	10-2-69	1988	Pineville, Calif.
Ramirez, Roberto	1	1	2.43	26	1	0	2	30	23	14	8	10	33	R	L	5-11	170	8-17-72	1990	Laurel, Mexico
Reyes, Carlos	0	0	0.00	1	0	0	0	2	1	0	0	0	2	B	R	6-1	190	4-19-69	1991	Tampa, Fla.
Ricken, Ray	0	1	10.05	3	3	0	0	14	18	17	16	10	16	R	R	6-5	225	8-11-73	1994	Warren, Mich.
Rossiter, Mike	2	2	4.39	31	0	0	2	41	44	20	20	17	34	R	R	6-6	230	6-20-73	1991	Burbank, Calif.
Sanders, Scott	1	2	3.44	15	3	0	3	37	34	14	14	12	43	R	R	6-4	220	3-25-69	1990	San Diego, Calif.
Spencer, Stan	12	6	3.93	22	22	0	0	137	120	67	60	42	136	R	R	6-4	205	8-2-68	1991	Battleground, Wash.
Tollberg, Brian	6	6	6.38	33	15	1	3	110	138	85	78	27	109	R	R	6-3	195	9-16-72	1994	Bradenton, Fla.
Veras, Dario	2	1	3.79	31	0	0	9	36	36	15	15	11	29	R	R	6-2	155	3-13-73	1991	Villa Vasquez, D.R.
Wall, Donne	2	0	4.80	3	3	0	0	15	11	8	8	8	12	R	R	6-1	180	7-11-67	1989	Houston, Texas
Wolff, Bryan	0	0	6.75	9	0	0	1	11	14	8	8	5	8	R	R	6-1	195	3-16-72	1993	St. Louis, Mo.

FIELDING

Catcher	PCT	G	PO	A	E	DP	PB
Cianfrocco	1.000	1	1	0	0	0	0
Gonzalez	.985	48	313	24	5	7	8
Gubanich	.991	68	507	43	5	2	16
Myers	1.000	3	16	1	0	0	0
Romero	.977	32	276	27	7	4	6

First Base	PCT	G	PO	A	E	DP
Allen	.988	36	299	21	4	38
Arias	1.000	4	28	2	0	1
Cianfrocco	.980	11	91	9	2	10
Gubanich	1.000	8	59	3	0	7
Romero	1.000	4	31	2	0	3
Thompson	.995	46	356	31	2	36
Williams	.990	46	352	28	4	47

Second Base	PCT	G	PO	A	E	DP
Cianfrocco	1.000	1	3	3	0	1
Hajek	.972	126	260	368	18	99
LaRocca	.969	24	46	49	3	12
Mouton	.000	1	0	0	0	0

Third Base	PCT	G	PO	A	E	DP
Arias	.947	106	70	232	17	29
Cianfrocco	.964	12	7	20	1	1
Giovanola	.941	4	1	15	1	1
Gonzalez	1.000	1	0	1	0	0
Gubanich	.857	6	4	14	3	3
Guiel	1.000	1	0	1	0	0
LaRocca	.941	26	8	40	3	3

Shortstop	PCT	G	PO	A	E	DP
Cianfrocco	1.000	1	2	1	0	0
Hajek	.000	1	0	0	0	0
LaRocca	.963	22	31	48	3	14
Melo	.965	127	214	360	21	91

Outfield	PCT	G	PO	A	E	DP
Allen	1.000	47	45	1	0	0
Cianfrocco	.941	10	15	1	1	0
Dascenzo	1.000	7	12	0	0	0
Devereaux	.980	28	47	2	1	0
Guiel	.946	50	60	10	4	1
Hemmings	.667	3	3	1	2	0
Horsman	.000	1	0	0	0	0
LaRocca	.864	19	19	0	3	0
Morenz	1.000	11	16	1	0	1
Mouton	.983	45	57	2	1	0
Poe	.977	101	163	6	4	0
C. Prieto	.969	91	174	12	6	2
R. Prieto	1.000	24	25	2	0	0
Rivera	1.000	30	53	2	0	0
Thompson	000	3	0	0	0	0

MOBILE — Class AA

SOUTHERN LEAGUE

BATTING	AVG	G	AB	R	H	2B	3B	HR	RBI	BB	SO	SB	CS	B	T	HT	WT	DOB	1st Yr	Resides
Allen, Dusty	.253	42	154	30	39	10	4	6	42	32	26	1	0	R	R	6-4	215	8-9-72	1995	Oklahoma City, Okla.
Balfe, Ryan	.232	23	69	9	16	5	1	2	11	8	10	1	0	B	R	6-1	180	11-11-75	1994	Cornwall, N.Y.
Briones, Chris	.000	2	3	0	0	0	0	0	0	0	1	0	0	R	R	5-11	205	6-5-73	1995	Brea, Calif.
Curl, John	.275	104	363	47	100	22	2	16	66	40	108	6	1	L	R	6-3	205	11-10-72	1995	Logansport, Ind.
Darr, Mike	.310	132	523	105	162	41	4	6	90	62	79	28	8	L	R	6-3	205	3-21-76	1994	Corona, Calif.
Dascenzo, Doug	.391	12	23	5	9	0	0	0	2	3	2	2	0	B	L	5-8	160	6-30-64	1985	Labelle, Pa.
Davis, Ben	.286	116	433	65	124	29	2	14	75	42	60	4	2	B	R	6-4	205	3-10-77	1995	Aston, Pa.
Faggett, Ethan	.247	54	162	22	40	2	1	3	25	16	40	7	1	L	L	6-0	190	8-21-74	1992	Burleson, Texas
Gama, Rick	.221	49	149	21	33	7	2	1	17	23	16	3	1	R	R	5-10	180	4-27-73	1995	Mexico City, Mexico
Gonzalez, Jimmy	.294	26	85	14	25	8	0	6	17	13	22	0	0	R	R	6-3	235	3-8-73	1991	Hartford, Conn.
Gonzalez, Wiklenman	.388	22	67	20	26	9	0	4	26	14	4	0	0	R	R	5-11	175	5-17-74	1992	Palo Negro, Ven.
Hazlett, Steve	.229	34	96	16	22	7	3	1	9	15	24	0	1	R	R	5-11	200	3-30-70	1991	Longmont, Colo.
Joseph, Terry	.221	39	122	20	27	6	1	1	13	18	30	6	5	R	R	5-10	190	11-20-73	1995	Harvey, La.
2-team (37 West Tenn)	.221	76	240	44	53	8	2	3	24	29	58	9	8							
Matthews, Gary	.307	72	254	62	78	15	4	7	51	55	50	11	1	B	R	6-3	200	8-25-74	1994	Canoga Park, Calif.
Mitchell, Mike	.318	134	509	72	162	32	2	15	97	61	95	0	0	L	R	6-3	205	4-5-73	1994	Camarillo, Calif.
Newhan, David	.261	121	491	89	128	26	3	12	45	68	110	27	8	L	R	5-10	180	9-7-73	1995	Yorba Linda, Calif.
Nicholson, Kevin	.215	132	488	64	105	27	3	5	52	47	114	9	5	B	R	5-10	190	3-29-76	1997	Surrey, B.C.
Powers, John	.303	127	476	92	144	27	4	12	52	76	76	9	6	L	R	5-9	165	6-2-74	1996	Scottsdale, Ariz.
Prieto, Rick	.239	72	218	30	52	9	2	4	25	21	49	9	2	B	R	5-10	175	8-24-72	1993	Carmel, Calif.
Sanchez, Marcos	.182	7	22	4	4	1	1	1	4	2	13	1	0	B	R	6-0	190	9-25-74	1992	Santo Domingo, D.R.

PITCHING	W	L	ERA	G	GS	CG	SV	IP	H	R	ER	BB	SO	B	T	HT	WT	DOB	1st Yr	Resides
Anderson, Bill	3	0	2.30	13	6	0	0	43	32	12	11	23	39	R	R	6-0	190	9-23-71	1994	Alta Loma, Calif.
Carlyle, Buddy	14	6	3.38	27	27	2	0	184	179	77	69	46	97	L	R	6-3	175	12-21-77	1996	Bellevue, Neb.
2-team (1 Chattanooga)	14	7	3.43	28	28	2	0	189	185	80	72	46	100							
Dixon, Bubba	0	3	5.27	9	0	0	0	14	15	12	8	9	6	L	L	5-10	165	1-7-72	1994	Lucedale, Miss.
Doughty, Brian	0	0	5.45	17	0	0	0	38	62	33	23	8	19	R	R	6-5	235	9-21-74	1992	Bothell, Wash.
Drumheller, Al	5	4	3.51	50	6	0	4	97	75	43	38	49	118	R	L	6-0	185	7-31-71	1993	Shenandoah, Pa.
Estes, Eric	7	4	5.30	17	16	0	0	88	117	61	52	31	72	R	R	6-4	185	9-4-72	1997	Vancouver, Wash.
Guzman, Domingo	5	2	4.50	12	8	0	1	48	51	34	24	26	39	R	R	6-3	195	4-5-75	1994	San Cristobal, D.R.
Kaufman, Brad	1	0	1.11	5	5	0	0	24	18	3	3	8	21	R	R	6-2	210	4-26-72	1993	Traer, Iowa
Kolb, Brandon	4	3	4.50	21	6	0	1	62	46	33	31	40	50	R	R	6-1	190	11-20-73	1995	Danville, Calif.
Lopez, Rodrigo	3	0	1.40	4	4	2	0	26	21	11	4	4	20	R	R	6-1	180	12-14-75	1995	Mexico City, Mexico
Newman, Eric	9	12	5.59	27	25	1	0	140	152	100	87	71	120	R	R	6-4	220	8-27-72	1995	Fremont, Calif.
Rossiter, Mike	2	0	1.79	22	0	0	0	45	34	10	9	11	46	R	R	6-6	230	6-20-73	1991	Burbank, Calif.
Sak, James	2	5	5.14	45	0	0	16	49	33	29	28	36	56	R	R	6-1	195	8-18-73	1995	Chicago, Ill.
Skrmetta, Matt	9	2	3.35	51	0	0	0	70	66	32	29	31	77	B	R	6-3	220	11-6-72	1993	Satellite Beach, Fla.
Sullivan, Brendan	1	2	1.85	35	0	0	13	39	28	8	8	16	24	R	R	6-3	190	12-15-74	1996	Washington, D.C.
Tollberg, Brian	3	2	2.41	6	6	1	0	41	31	11	11	4	45	R	R	6-3	195	9-16-72	1994	Bradonton, Fla.
Van De Weg, Ryan	2	3	9.74	6	4	0	0	20	37	24	22	10	6	R	R	6-0	180	2-24-74	1995	West Olive, Mich.
Walters, Brett	7	3	4.91	14	13	0	0	77	86	43	42	23	51	R	R	6-0	185	9-30-74	1994	Bateman, Australia
Wolff, Bryan	9	3	2.29	33	14	3	0	134	90	40	34	43	134	R	R	6-1	195	3-16-72	1993	St. Louis, Mo.

FIELDING

Catcher	PCT	G	PO	A	E	DP	PB
Briones	1.000	2	3	0	0	0	0
Davis	.994	115	920	76	6	7	10
J. Gonzalez	.988	13	74	6	1	0	1
W. Gonzalez	1.000	13	65	7	0	0	0
Sanchez	.960	4	23	1	1	0	0

First Base	PCT	G	PO	A	E	DP
Allen	1.000	6	28	1	0	1
Curl	1.000	21	150	10	0	17
J. Gonzalez	1.000	2	5	1	0	0
Mitchell	.990	121	963	91	11	102

Second Base	PCT	G	PO	A	E	DP
Gama	.985	28	59	69	2	15
Newhan	.974	112	226	306	14	72
Powers	1.000	4	13	5	0	2

Third Base	PCT	G	PO	A	E	DP
Balfe	.903	12	7	21	3	3
Hazlett	.974	15	8	29	1	1
Newhan	1.000	3	2	5	0	0
Powers	.941	111	65	204	17	10
Prieto	.789	7	1	14	4	3

Shortstop	PCT	G	PO	A	E	DP
Newhan	1.000	1	0	3	0	0
Nicholson	.937	130	201	363	38	80
Powers	.961	11	13	36	2	7

Outfield	PCT	G	PO	A	E	DP
Allen	.951	38	56	2	3	0
Curl	.949	60	90	4	5	1
Darr	.979	129	261	13	6	2
Dascenzo	1.000	7	9	1	0	0
Faggett	.932	42	66	2	5	0
Hazlett	1.000	12	18	1	0	0
Joseph	.976	36	80	2	2	0
Matthews	.995	68	184	8	1	2
Prieto	.985	51	64	2	1	0

RANCHO CUCAMONGA — Class A

CALIFORNIA LEAGUE

BATTING	AVG	G	AB	R	H	2B	3B	HR	RBI	BB	SO	SB	CS	B	T	HT	WT	DOB	1st Yr	Resides
Briones, Chris	.198	33	91	6	18	5	0	3	12	1	26	0	1	R	R	5-11	205	6-5-73	1995	Brea, Calif.
Carmona, Cesarin	.261	105	368	48	96	12	9	2	45	17	99	21	8	R	R	5-10	180	12-20-76	1994	Bani, D.R.
Dunn, Nathan	.222	41	135	13	30	7	2	3	14	15	50	3	2	R	R	6-0	190	10-17-74	1996	Pell City, Ala.
Gonzalez, Wiklenman	.288	75	292	51	84	24	2	10	59	26	54	0	0	R	R	5-11	175	5-17-74	1992	Palo Negro, Ven.
Itzoe, Josh	.228	52	149	22	34	4	0	1	17	35	41	2	2	R	R	6-0	185	12-20-74	1997	Towson, Md.
Johnson, A.J.	.308	134	539	94	166	33	5	24	94	28	98	15	10	R	R	6-3	210	2-17-73	1995	Neptune, N.J.
Joseph, Terry	.214	13	56	6	12	1	1	0	5	1	16	1	3	R	R	5-10	190	11-20-73	1995	Harvey, La.
Kennedy, Gus	.263	124	430	89	113	25	8	18	75	79	130	15	8	R	R	5-10	205	12-26-73	1994	Seligman, Ariz.
Kent, Robbie	.269	116	457	65	123	22	3	7	59	33	81	2	1	R	R	5-10	185	1-8-74	1996	Evansville, Ind.
Loyd, Brian	.305	87	318	55	97	19	1	4	35	42	45	1	4	R	R	6-2	210	12-3-73	1996	Yorba Linda, Calif.
McClure, Brian	.264	129	492	89	130	25	11	9	57	66	98	4	3	L	R	6-0	170	1-15-74	1996	Chatham, Ill.
Myers, Greg	.000	3	9	1	0	0	0	0	0	2	1	0	0	L	R	6-2	208	4-14-66	1984	Riverside, Calif.
Paciorek, Pete	.277	137	481	82	133	28	6	17	86	63	135	8	7	L	L	6-3	195	5-19-76	1995	San Gabriel, Calif.
Pernell, Brandon	.200	44	125	18	25	8	4	2	7	11	39	1	2	R	R	6-2	180	4-11-77	1995	Torrance, Calif.
Reynoso, Ben	.213	63	150	19	32	4	2	2	14	10	37	2	0	R	R	5-9	165	9-12-74	1996	Visalia, Calif.
Sanchez, Marcos	.306	56	144	30	44	10	2	6	24	10	47	1	0	B	R	6-0	190	9-25-74	1992	Santo Domingo, D.R.
Seal, Scott	.246	121	427	52	105	23	5	4	62	48	113	8	5	L	L	6-1	205	8-16-75	1997	Irvine, Calif.

BATTING	AVG	G	AB	R	H	2B	3B	HR	RBI	BB	SO	SB	CS	B	T	HT	WT	DOB	1st Yr	Resides
Thrower, Jake	.268	37	127	24	34	7	0	1	10	19	19	4	1	B	R	5-11	180	11-19-75	1997	Yuma, Ariz.

GAMES BY POSITION: C—Briones 20, Gonzalez 43, Loyd 72, Myers 2, Sanchez 21. **1B**—Johnson 2, Kent 7, Paciorek 137. **2B**—Kent 6, McClure 125, Reynoso 11, Thrower 8. **3B**—Dunn 36, Kent 93, Reynoso 13, Thrower 11. **SS**—Carmona 102, Kent 6, Reynoso 40, Thrower 3. **OF**—Dunn 2, Itzoe 29, Johnson 130, Joseph 13, Kennedy 110, Kent 1, Pernell 40, Seal 117.

PITCHING	W	L	ERA	G	GS	CG	SV	IP	H	R	ER	BB	SO	B	T	HT	WT	DOB	1st Yr	Resides
Agosto, Stevenson	5	8	6.08	23	23	0	0	108	132	83	73	68	91	L	L	5-10	175	9-2-75	1994	Rio Grande, P.R.
Carmody, Brian	3	1	2.20	8	8	0	0	49	42	14	12	9	48	L	L	6-3	195	7-1-75	1996	San Jose, Calif.
Diaz, Antonio	1	0	4.41	17	0	0	2	35	36	17	17	6	23	R	R	5-11	170	1-28-79	1997	Juncos, P.R.
Dodd, Scott	4	6	3.68	43	0	0	3	66	65	35	27	41	59	L	L	6-2	195	8-4-69	1991	Glendale, Ariz.
Doughty, Brian	2	1	2.56	16	2	0	1	32	29	14	9	8	23	R	R	6-5	235	9-21-74	1992	Bothell, Wash.
Foran, John	3	2	3.42	12	1	0	2	26	28	16	10	8	26	R	R	6-1	185	10-22-73	1995	Alford, Fla.
Guzman, Domingo	1	1	3.74	4	4	0	0	22	22	11	9	6	16	R	R	6-3	195	4-5-75	1994	San Cristobal, D.R.
Herndon, Harry	3	2	3.40	6	6	0	0	40	37	18	15	13	29	R	R	6-1	190	9-11-78	1997	Craig, Colo.
Hite, Kevin	4	0	3.02	30	0	0	12	42	36	16	14	8	45	R	R	6-1	155	7-23-74	1996	Hermitage, Tenn.
Iddon, Brent	7	4	3.63	32	19	0	1	139	149	67	56	40	110	R	R	6-2	192	2-4-76	1994	Sydney, Australia
Kolb, Brandon	0	2	3.05	4	4	0	0	21	14	8	7	18	16	R	R	6-1	190	11-20-73	1995	Danville, Calif.
Lynch, Ryan	3	3	2.95	21	2	0	1	43	34	17	14	19	35	L	L	6-4	220	8-10-74	1996	Solano Beach, Calif.
Maurer, Dave	5	2	2.70	48	0	0	5	83	56	27	25	46	93	R	L	6-2	205	2-23-75	1997	Burnsville, Minn.
Middlebrook, Jason	10	12	4.92	28	28	0	0	150	162	99	82	63	132	R	R	6-3	215	6-26-75	1996	Grass Lake, Mich.
Sullivan, Brendan	3	2	1.08	35	0	0	8	42	23	7	5	19	37	R	R	6-3	190	12-15-74	1996	Washington, D.C.
Szymborski, Tom	0	2	5.59	15	1	0	0	29	48	24	18	14	8	R	R	6-3	210	3-7-75	1996	Chicago, Ill.
Torres, Luis	4	0	4.18	42	0	0	1	65	72	36	30	26	57	R	R	6-2	228	1-13-76	1994	Manati, P.R.
Walker, Kevin	11	7	4.15	22	22	0	0	121	122	62	56	48	94	L	L	6-4	190	9-20-76	1995	Glen Rose, Texas
Witte, Dominic	0	0	4.91	7	0	0	2	11	14	6	6	1	6	R	R	6-0	200	11-25-73	1996	Richmond, Ind.
Workman, Widd	8	8	4.67	20	20	0	0	108	109	84	56	52	71	R	R	6-1	195	5-23-74	1996	Gilbert, Ariz.

CLINTON — Class A

MIDWEST LEAGUE

BATTING	AVG	G	AB	R	H	2B	3B	HR	RBI	BB	SO	SB	CS	B	T	HT	WT	DOB	1st Yr	Resides
Arauz, Leobardo	.000	5	8	1	0	0	0	0	0	4	1	0	1	B	R	5-9	176	1-18-77	1996	Los Mochis, Mexico
Burford, Kevin	.258	123	446	68	115	26	4	6	55	62	125	15	4	L	L	6-0	190	11-7-77	1997	Westminster, Calif.
Cronin, Shane	.253	112	380	34	96	16	0	3	46	28	47	6	1	R	R	6-1	210	2-26-76	1996	Renton, Wash.
Eberwein, Kevin	.296	65	247	42	73	20	3	10	38	26	66	4	2	R	R	6-4	200	3-30-77	1998	Las Vegas, Nev.
Gonzalez, Santos	.201	89	274	31	55	9	3	2	21	27	71	16	7	B	R	5-11	170	6-25-77	1994	Bani, D.R.
Halloran, Matt	.224	123	459	48	103	21	3	1	42	33	92	19	12	R	R	6-2	185	3-3-78	1996	Niceville, Fla.
Horsman, Brent	.240	67	208	25	50	9	1	3	18	15	49	10	6	L	R	6-3	175	7-31-76	1997	Fairfield, Calif.
Hunter, Johnny	.226	116	407	65	92	17	5	10	42	82	116	36	9	R	R	6-1	190	6-14-75	1997	Mansfield, Texas
Lawrence, Tony	.233	86	296	35	69	16	3	7	40	35	93	5	4	R	R	6-1	205	3-7-75	1997	Monroe, La.
Lindsey, Rodney	.271	40	155	32	42	4	4	4	17	17	54	36	4	R	R	5-8	175	1-28-76	1994	Opelika, Ala.
McDaniel, Ryan	.183	41	93	12	17	2	0	0	5	9	34	3	0	R	R	6-0	180	3-18-75	1997	Fort Worth, Texas
Nieves, Wilbert	.255	115	380	47	97	22	0	3	55	47	69	7	9	R	R	5-10	160	9-25-77	1996	Santurce, P.R.
Rakers, Jason	.256	55	172	20	44	6	3	2	21	28	53	5	2	L	R	6-0	190	8-28-75	1997	Aviston, Ill.
Ruotsinoja, Jacob	.214	96	341	50	73	16	2	7	42	44	91	3	2	L	R	6-2	195	11-11-76	1996	Seminole, Fla.
Rutherford, Daryl	.148	23	81	11	12	1	0	0	3	8	9	7	2	R	R	6-0	175	10-30-75	1995	Columbia, S.C.
Snellgrove, Clay	.239	104	368	42	88	14	2	2	30	27	32	11	9	R	R	6-0	180	11-22-74	1997	Lafayette, Ind.
Tegland, Ron	.206	13	34	4	7	1	0	1	7	4	12	0	1	R	R	6-2	212	10-18-73	1996	Oxnard, Calif.
Thrower, Jake	.290	43	145	25	42	11	1	5	27	22	22	11	3	B	R	5-11	180	11-19-75	1997	Yuma, Ariz.

GAMES BY POSITION: C—Lawrence 32, McDaniel 34, Nieves 90, Tegland 2. **1B**—Cronin 112, Eberwein 1, Hunter 1, Lawrence 11, Rakers 8, Snellgrove 17. **2B**—Gonzalez 73, Snellgrove 74. **3B**—Eberwein 51, Rakers 37, Snellgrove 13, Thrower 41. **SS**—Gonzalez 15, Halloran 123, Snellgrove 4, Thrower 3. **OF**—Arauz 5, Burford 110, Horsman 61, Hunter 107, Lindsey 40, Ruotsinoja 82, Rutherford 23, Snellgrove 1.

PITCHING	W	L	ERA	G	GS	CG	SV	IP	H	R	ER	BB	SO	B	T	HT	WT	DOB	1st Yr	Resides
Aragon, Angel	6	8	4.43	42	7	0	1	91	100	57	45	36	77	R	R	6-1	238	12-19-73	1998	Oxnard, Calif.
Camp, Shawn	3	5	2.62	47	0	0	13	55	48	19	16	20	62	R	R	6-1	190	11-18-75	1997	Fairfax, Va.
Guttormson, Rick	10	7	2.60	30	25	0	2	159	155	66	46	41	141	R	R	6-2	185	1-11-77	1997	Anacortes, Wash.
Herndon, Harry	10	8	2.99	21	21	3	0	132	119	59	44	34	101	R	R	6-1	190	9-11-78	1997	Craig, Colo.
Kramer, Aaron	1	0	2.00	3	2	0	0	9	13	4	2	2	7	B	R	6-1	210	6-25-75	1998	Glendale, Ariz.
Lawrence, Brian	5	3	2.80	12	12	2	0	80	67	34	25	13	79	R	R	6-0	195	5-14-76	1998	Linden, Texas
Lynch, Ryan	0	2	1.80	17	0	0	2	20	14	8	4	10	28	L	L	6-4	220	8-10-74	1996	Solano Beach, Calif.
Naff, Todd	1	4	4.11	42	4	0	1	85	94	53	39	55	51	R	R	6-3	215	3-22-75	1997	Bertram, Texas
Oiseth, Jon	3	6	5.99	31	5	0	0	71	85	55	47	45	52	R	L	6-3	190	10-31-74	1997	Savage, Minn.
Ortega, Wilbert	4	2	3.95	33	0	0	1	41	37	24	18	14	40	L	L	6-0	180	8-31-77	1998	El Fuerte, Mexico
Parent, Jerry	4	7	5.51	29	8	0	0	78	77	54	48	47	67	L	R	6-2	210	12-7-73	1995	Assonet, Mass.
Perry, Tim	1	3	5.06	9	8	0	0	48	50	32	27	19	37	R	R	6-0	190	8-17-77	1996	Carlsbad, N.M.
Ryan, Pat	3	5	8.05	12	12	0	0	54	63	51	48	24	37	R	R	6-3	200	11-29-74	1997	DeLand, Fla.
Serrano, Wascar	9	7	3.22	26	26	0	0	157	150	74	56	54	143	R	R	6-2	178	7-2-78	1995	Bani, D.R.
Verdugo, Orlando	0	0	2.70	6	0	0	1	10	7	3	3	3	20	R	R	5-9	176	5-22-77	1996	Los Mochis, Mexico
Viator, Dustin	3	6	5.28	42	6	0	0	92	113	67	54	33	67	R	R	6-3	192	7-12-75	1997	New Iberia, La.
Walker, Kevin	2	0	1.23	2	2	0	0	15	11	2	2	7	10	L	L	6-4	190	9-20-76	1995	Glen Rose, Texas

IDAHO FALLS — Rookie

PIONEER LEAGUE

BATTING	AVG	G	AB	R	H	2B	3B	HR	RBI	BB	SO	SB	CS	B	T	HT	WT	DOB	1st Yr	Resides
Arauz, Leobardo	.286	40	126	30	36	7	1	6	24	32	27	3	4	B	R	5-9	176	1-18-77	1996	Los Mochis, Mexico
Campbell, Sean	.291	44	165	29	48	12	1	6	37	19	43	2	4	L	R	6-3	180	4-15-77	1998	Fresno, Calif.
Cook, Jon	.462	5	13	3	6	1	0	0	3	4	1	0	1	R	R	6-1	195	4-26-77	1998	San Jose, Calif.
Dunaway, Jason	.316	67	272	54	86	16	3	2	47	38	55	20	10	R	R	6-1	177	1-12-77	1997	Durango, Colo.
Dunham, Tray	.278	49	176	34	49	15	0	0	40	26	49	0	0	L	R	6-1	185	9-8-77	1996	Shattuck, Okla.
Dusan, Joe	.290	61	210	50	61	12	1	8	50	50	66	1	5	L	L	6-1	190	7-30-77	1998	Bend, Ore.
French, Ron	.239	19	67	14	16	4	0	2	10	12	13	1	0	R	R	5-10	200	5-24-78	1998	Concord, Calif.
Garcia, Alex	.320	50	178	49	57	16	1	4	32	38	43	0	1	R	R	5-11	165	4-14-79	1996	Haina, D.R.

BATTING	AVG	G	AB	R	H	2B	3B	HR	RBI	BB	SO	SB	CS	B	T	HT	WT	DOB	1st Yr	Resides
Hazen, Mike	.307	61	202	57	62	14	3	5	30	36	50	8	4	R	L	6-1	195	1-7-76	1998	Abington, Mass.
Hemmings, Scot	.275	49	171	28	47	13	1	3	35	23	66	19	2	R	R	6-4	197	5-6-77	1997	Columbus, Ga.
Loggins, Josh	.341	71	299	66	102	20	5	8	64	35	60	8	8	R	R	6-1	190	11-29-76	1998	West Lafayette, Ind.
Owens, Jeremy	.278	69	284	61	79	16	4	8	52	36	81	30	7	R	R	6-1	200	12-9-76	1998	Johnson City, Tenn.
Pelaez, Alex	.340	63	262	52	89	17	1	8	51	29	32	3	1	R	R	5-9	200	4-6-76	1998	Chula Vista, Calif.
Schmidt, Bryan	.357	4	14	5	5	0	0	0	2	1	1	4	0	R	R	6-2	180	6-28-75	1998	Stockton, Calif.
Soto, Luis	.273	6	22	4	6	0	0	0	2	2	6	0	0	R	R	6-0	170	9-7-78	1995	Bani, D.R.
Weeks, Paul	.289	33	114	22	33	9	1	4	20	13	30	1	1	R	R	5-10	170	2-20-76	1998	Gardena, Calif.
Wickersham, Jack	.333	19	75	19	25	6	2	0	13	7	16	7	2	R	R	5-11	175	10-19-75	1998	La Canada, Calif.

GAMES BY POSITION: C—Campbell 26, Dunham 40, French 17, Soto 1. **1B**—Dunham 1, Dusan 57, Loggins 18. **2B**—Garcia 31, Loggins 2, Schmidt 1, Weeks 28, Wickersham 18. **3B**—Garcia 15, Owens 1, Pelaez 60, Weeks 3. **SS**—Dunaway 67, Garcia 6, Schmidt 3, Weeks 3, Wickersham 1. **OF**—Arauz 29, Campbell 1, Cook 5, Dusan 1, Hazen 47, Hemmings 48, Loggins 41, Owens 65.

PITCHING	W	L	ERA	G	GS	CG	SV	IP	H	R	ER	BB	SO	B	T	HT	WT	DOB	1st Yr	Resides
Bauer, Ryan	7	2	4.54	17	12	1	0	77	91	43	39	20	62	R	R	6-3	225	7-11-76	1998	Smithboro, Ill.
Bell, Casey	2	3	5.56	7	7	0	0	34	41	38	21	22	25	R	R	6-2	175	7-14-78	1998	Elkins, Ark.
Berryman, Brian	4	3	4.61	15	14	0	0	68	78	48	35	33	38	R	R	6-4	200	7-13-77	1998	Canton, Mich.
Condrey, Clay	2	1	2.55	18	0	0	5	25	31	12	7	4	19	R	R	6-3	195	11-19-75	1998	Navasota, Texas
Darr, Jerry	0	0	21.60	2	2	0	0	5	10	12	12	9	1	R	R	6-2	190	2-26-79	1997	Benton, Ark.
Diaz, Antonio	1	1	2.70	14	0	0	4	20	20	7	6	4	16	R	R	5-11	170	1-28-79	1997	Juncos, P.R.
Dobson, Mark	5	2	2.72	21	1	0	2	56	42	25	17	31	63	R	R	6-3	212	9-23-75	1998	Littleton, Colo.
Dowell, Brian	0	2	13.81	11	0	0	0	14	25	26	22	14	12	R	R	6-3	210	12-31-77	1998	Houston, Texas
Fikac, Jeremy	2	0	2.25	12	0	0	1	20	11	6	5	8	19	R	R	6-2	185	4-8-75	1998	Shiner, Texas
Forbes, Keith	3	0	5.02	21	0	0	1	38	33	27	21	38	40	R	R	6-1	195	1-28-77	1998	Malden, Mass.
Gonzalez, Francisco	1	1	2.57	5	1	0	0	7	5	7	2	4	3	R	R	6-4	190	3-21-78	1996	Bajadero, P.R.
Hawkins, Ryan	2	0	6.39	7	6	0	0	25	35	23	18	20	16	R	R	6-2	190	12-31-78	1998	Brewton, Ala.
Herrera, Misael	0	3	8.20	11	2	0	0	26	31	28	24	23	25	R	R	6-0	165	3-15-77	1995	Bani, D.R.
Howard, Ben	4	5	6.03	15	15	0	0	69	67	61	46	87	79	R	R	6-2	190	1-15-79	1997	Jackson, Tenn.
Jones, Travis	3	3	3.99	31	0	0	2	56	52	29	25	21	67	L	L	6-3	190	12-3-77	1996	Konawa, Okla.
Kramer, Aaron	4	0	2.23	6	6	0	0	36	30	14	9	10	22	B	R	6-1	210	6-25-75	1998	Glendale, Ariz.
Lawrence, Brian	3	0	2.45	4	4	2	0	22	22	7	6	5	21	R	R	6-0	195	5-14-76	1998	Linden, Texas
Luque, Roger	1	0	5.28	6	1	0	0	15	13	9	9	12	19	L	L	6-1	155	1-8-80	1997	Charallave, Ven.
Verdugo, Orlando	3	2	3.86	19	4	0	5	42	48	23	18	20	55	R	R	5-9	176	5-22-77	1996	Los Mochis, Mexico
Watkins, Steve	0	1	40.50	2	1	0	0	2	10	12	9	4	0	R	R	6-4	190	7-19-78	1998	Lubbock, Texas

PEORIA — Rookie

ARIZONA LEAGUE

BATTING	AVG	G	AB	R	H	2B	3B	HR	RBI	BB	SO	SB	CS	B	T	HT	WT	DOB	1st Yr	Resides
Ardizzone, Matt	.385	4	13	3	5	1	0	1	4	0	0	0	1	B	R	5-8	175	6-29-76	1998	Randolph, N.J.
Berroa, Cristian	.319	53	207	33	66	22	2	1	33	4	38	8	4	B	R	5-11	150	4-27-79	1996	Haina, D.R.
Boykin, Paul	.300	43	180	37	54	6	8	0	20	22	39	24	4	L	R	5-11	190	10-3-77	1998	Littleton, Colo.
Cook, Jon	.259	46	162	34	42	6	1	1	18	20	40	18	6	R	R	6-1	195	4-26-77	1998	San Jose, Calif.
Cosentino, Tony	.264	42	140	29	39	9	1	0	24	39	31	1	2	R	R	6-0	195	12-7-78	1997	Torrance, Calif.
Curry, Jesse	.194	46	180	24	35	7	3	2	20	25	88	4	2	L	L	6-4	205	10-25-78	1997	Gresham, Ore.
French, Ron	.190	18	63	9	12	4	0	0	5	3	13	1	0	R	R	5-10	200	5-24-78	1998	Concord, Calif.
Garrett, Shawn	.333	49	186	36	62	13	2	0	29	16	36	5	3	B	R	6-3	190	11-2-78	1998	Kinmundy, Ill.
Gonzalez, Franklin	.276	19	76	12	21	2	2	1	11	7	18	7	1	R	R	6-1	160	7-4-77	1995	Bani, D.R.
Guerrero, Joel	.232	37	112	10	26	3	0	0	6	19	41	11	8	B	R	5-9	160	7-7-78	1996	Santo Domingo, D.R.
Guiel, Aaron	.500	8	16	8	8	3	1	1	6	5	5	1	1	L	R	5-10	190	10-5-72	1993	Langley, B.C.
Gutierrez, Said	.253	28	91	13	23	4	1	0	14	7	26	3	2	R	R	6-0	182	3-26-80	1998	Merida, Mexico
Motley, Brittan	.242	27	91	15	22	6	1	1	11	13	36	5	2	B	R	6-2	180	10-18-78	1997	Kansas City, Mo.
Reed, Jeremy	.212	17	52	2	11	1	0	0	5	2	20	1	0	R	R	6-4	190	9-26-80	1998	Chattanooga, Tenn.
Schmidt, Bryan	.289	47	194	29	56	12	0	0	22	19	28	6	3	R	R	6-2	180	6-28-75	1998	Stockton, Calif.
Sobet, Renato	.209	30	110	15	23	1	3	1	15	6	40	4	2	R	R	6-2	165	12-30-79	1996	Haina, D.R.
Weeks, Paul	.313	7	16	4	5	1	0	0	2	6	4	4	3	R	R	5-10	170	2-20-76	1998	Gardena, Calif.

GAMES BY POSITION: C—Cosentino 19, French 8, Gutierrez 24, Reed 11. **1B**—Cosentino 9, Curry 46. **2B**—Ardizzone 3, Berroa 3, Guerrero 12, Schmidt 36, Weeks 6. **3B**—Garrett 49, Schmidt 9. **SS**—Berroa 52, Schmidt 5. **OF**—Boykin 42, Cook 45, Gonzalez 2, Guerrero 23, Guiel 8, Motley 26, Sobet 29.

PITCHING	W	L	ERA	G	GS	CG	SV	IP	H	R	ER	BB	SO	B	T	HT	WT	DOB	1st Yr	Resides
Bartosh, Cliff	3	2	3.48	13	5	0	0	44	43	23	17	16	43	L	L	6-2	175	9-5-79	1998	Duncanville, Texas
Bell, Casey	4	1	2.63	7	7	0	0	41	34	19	12	8	36	R	R	6-2	175	7-14-78	1998	Elkins, Ark.
Condrey, Clay	0	1	3.38	5	0	0	0	5	6	4	2	5	4	R	R	6-3	195	11-19-75	1998	Navasota, Texas
Darr, Jerry	1	0	3.47	7	7	0	0	23	16	10	9	12	27	R	R	6-2	190	2-26-79	1997	Benton, Ark.
Deliza, Carlos	1	1	2.82	18	1	0	1	38	33	14	12	9	34	R	R	6-1	160	12-19-77	1995	Bani, D.R.
Devine, Travis	0	2	18.00	2	2	0	0	2	6	5	4	1	3	R	R	6-5	190	12-3-79	1998	Lawrenceville, Ga.
DeLeon, Bryan	1	3	7.52	16	0	0	1	26	39	27	22	13	18	R	R	6-2	160	8-1-78	1997	Trujillo Alto, P.R.
Dowell, Brian	3	2	6.91	14	0	0	2	27	29	22	21	14	29	R	R	6-3	210	12-31-77	1998	Houston, Texas
Hawkins, Ryan	0	0	0.00	1	0	0	0	2	0	0	0	1	2	R	R	6-2	190	12-31-78	1998	Brewton, Ala.
Luque, Roger	2	1	5.79	12	6	0	0	42	59	36	27	9	38	L	L	6-1	155	1-8-80	1997	Charallave, Ven.
Meyer, John	2	5	5.66	12	11	0	0	49	54	40	31	33	46	R	R	6-5	215	6-19-79	1998	Fort Worth, Texas
Precinal, Huilberto	0	0	6.23	5	0	0	0	4	5	3	3	5	4	R	R	6-6	190	9-8-77	1995	Bani, D.R.
Ruiz, Juan	2	7	5.98	13	12	0	0	56	58	45	37	24	38	R	R	6-3	205	11-11-78	1998	Culiacan, Mexico
Silverio, Marcelino	1	1	4.03	18	0	0	1	38	35	22	17	24	38	R	R	6-3	180	3-7-79	1996	Haina, D.R.
Thomas, Dave	0	0	4.64	18	0	0	0	21	24	19	11	17	19	R	R	6-3	187	3-23-76	1998	Early, Texas
Thomas, Drew	2	5	3.53	19	0	0	3	43	47	27	17	12	40	R	R	6-2	175	12-1-75	1998	Mason City, Ill.
Watkins, Steve	1	0	1.31	9	3	0	0	21	15	4	3	10	20	R	R	6-4	190	7-19-78	1998	Lubbock, Texas

SAN FRANCISCO GIANTS

Bittersweet season ends with playoff loss to Cubs

BY MARK GONZALES

One loss prevented the San Francisco Giants from enjoying one of the most successful seasons in recent team history.

The Giants won six of their final seven games of 1998 to force a one-game playoff for the National League wild-card berth, which they lost 5-3 in Chicago.

The loss deprived the Giants of consecutive 90-win seasons for the first time since 1964-67. Nevertheless, the Giants' 179-146 record in 1997-98 trailed only the New York Yankees (210-114), Atlanta Braves (207-117) and Houston Astros (186-138).

The '98 season also saw outfielder Barry Bonds became the first player to hit at least 400 home runs and steal 400 bases in a career. Bonds hit his 400th career homer Aug. 23 off the Marlins' Kirt Ojala at Miami's Pro Player Stadium. He finished the season in 26th place on the all-time home run list with 411. His 28 stolen bases in 1998 gave him 445 on his career.

Jeff Kent arguably had a more amazing season than Bonds. Kent drove in 127 runs to set the franchise record for most RBIs by a second baseman, previously held by Rogers Hornsby, who drove in 125 in 1927.

Kent broke the record despite missing a month because of torn right knee ligaments suffered in early June. The Giants led the NL West at the time of Kent's injury but went 11-13 during his absence and fell out of first for good. They then lost 11 of their next 13 to open the second half.

Second-year general manager Brian Sabean continued his knack of landing pennant-drive talent, acquiring veteran outfielders Joe Carter from the Orioles and Ellis Burks from the Rockies. Both contributed to the club's late surge, with Carter hitting four homers and driving in 12 runs in the final week of the season.

Barry Bonds

Armando Rios

Players of the Year

Major League: Barry Bonds, of,

Bonds scored 120 runs and drove in 122 while missing his sixth 30-30 season by just two stolen bases.

Minor League: Armando Rios, of, Fresno

Rios led all Giants minor leaguers with 26 homers and 103 RBIs and earned a major league callup.

ORGANIZATION LEADERS

BATTING		
*AVG	Jalal Leach, Fresno/Shreveport	.347
R	Two tied at	87
H	Wilson Delgado, Fresno	142
TB	Benji Simonton, Shreveport/San Jose	249
2B	Frank Charles, Fresno/Shreveport	39
3B	Two tied at	7
HR	Armando Rios, Fresno	26
RBI	Armando Rios, Fresno	103
BB	Mike Byas, San Jose	81
SO	Tim Flaherty, Bakersfield	171
SB	Dante Powell, Fresno	41
PITCHING		
W	Joe Roa, Fresno	12
L	Manny Bermudez, Shreveport/San Jose	15
#ERA	Robbie Crabtree, Fresno/Shreveport/San Jose	1.75
G	Aaron Fultz, Fresno/Shreveport	64
CG	Jason Grilli, Fresno/Shreveport	3
SV	Jim Stoops, San Jose	31
IP	Ryan Jensen, Fresno/Bakersfield	174
BB	Nathan Rice, Bakersfield	78
SO	Ryan Jensen, Fresno/Bakersfield	170

*Minimum 250 At-Bats #Minimum 75 Innings

Unlike 1997, the Giants' trades didn't deplete their farm system. Class A San Jose won its first California League title since 1979, and short-season Salem-Keizer, filled with players from the 1998 draft, won the Northwest League title.

The biggest change occurred at Fresno, where the Giants' Triple-A affiliate played its first season and responded by winning the Pacific Coast League's Southern Division title before losing to Calgary in the semifinals.

Outfielder Armando Rios, originally signed by the Giants as an undrafted free agent, vaulted ahead of highly-touted prospects Dante Powell and Jacob Cruz (who was traded to the Indians in July) by hitting a career-best .301 with a team-high 26 homers and 103 RBIs for Fresno. Rios received a September callup and hit homers in his second and third at-bats.

Giuseppe Chiaramonte, who led the Cal League with 22 home runs and drove in a team-leading 87 runs for San Jose, developed into the organization's catcher of the future.

Taking advantage of five extra picks from free-agent losses, the Giants had a strong 1998 draft, and followed it up by signing their first 21 picks. Top pick Tony Torcato, a third baseman hit .291 for Salem-Keizer.

Righthander Nate Bump could be the first player from the Giants' 1998 draft to reach the majors. He went 6-1 with a 1.75 ERA in 11 starts at San Jose after starting his professional career with eight scoreless innings at Salem-Keizer.

San Francisco GIANTS

Manager: Dusty Baker.

1998 Record: 89-74, .546 (2nd, NL West)

BATTING	AVG	G	AB	R	H	2B	3B	HR	RBI	BB	SO	SB	CS	B	T	HT	WT	DOB	1st Yr	Resides
Aurilia, Rich	.266	122	413	54	110	27	2	9	49	31	62	3	3	R	R	6-0	170	9-2-71	1992	Hazlet, N.J.
Ball, Jeff	.250	2	4	0	1	0	0	0	0	0	0	0	0	R	R	5-10	185	4-17-69	1990	Merced, Calif.
Benard, Marvin	.322	121	286	41	92	21	1	3	36	34	39	11	4	L	L	5-10	180	1-20-71	1992	Scottsdale, Ariz.
Bonds, Barry	.303	156	552	120	167	44	7	37	122	130	92	28	12	L	L	6-1	206	7-24-64	1985	Redwood Shores, Calif.
Burks, Ellis	.306	42	147	22	45	6	1	5	22	19	31	8	1	R	R	6-2	205	9-11-64	1983	Denver, Colo.
2-team (100 Colorado)	.292	142	504	76	147	28	6	21	76	58	111	11	8							
Carter, Joe	.295	41	105	15	31	7	0	7	29	6	13	1	0	R	R	6-3	215	3-7-60	1981	Leawood, Kan.
Cruz, Jacob	.000	3	3	0	0	0	0	0	0	0	2	0	0	L	L	6-0	175	1-28-73	1994	Tempe, Ariz.
Delgado, Wilson	.167	10	12	1	2	1	0	0	1	1	3	0	0	B	R	5-11	165	7-15-75	1993	San Cristobal, D.R.
Diaz, Alex	.129	34	62	5	8	2	0	0	5	0	15	1	1	B	R	5-11	180	10-5-68	1987	San Sebastian, P.R.
Dunston, Shawon	.176	36	51	10	9	2	0	3	8	0	10	0	2	R	R	6-1	175	3-21-63	1982	Corona, N.Y.
Hamilton, Darryl	.294	97	367	65	108	19	2	1	26	59	53	9	8	L	R	6-1	180	12-3-64	1986	Sugar Land, Texas
Hayes, Charlie	.286	111	329	39	94	8	0	12	62	34	61	2	1	R	R	6-0	215	5-29-65	1983	Tomball, Texas
Javier, Stan	.290	135	417	63	121	13	5	4	49	65	63	21	5	B	R	6-0	195	1-9-64	1981	Santo Domingo, D.R.
Johnson, Brian	.237	99	308	34	73	8	1	13	34	28	67	0	2	R	R	6-2	210	1-8-68	1989	Chicago, Ill.
Jones, Chris	.189	43	90	14	17	2	1	2	10	8	28	2	1	R	R	6-2	210	11-16-65	1984	Phoenix, Ariz.
2-team (20 Arizona)	.190	63	121	17	23	3	1	2	13	11	37	2	1							
Kent, Jeff	.297	137	526	94	156	37	3	31	128	48	110	9	4	R	R	6-1	185	3-7-68	1989	Spicewood, Texas
Martinez, Ramon	.316	19	19	4	6	1	0	0	0	4	2	0	0	R	R	6-1	170	10-10-72	1993	Toa Alta, P.R.
Mayne, Brent	.273	94	275	26	75	15	0	3	32	37	47	2	2	L	R	6-1	190	4-19-68	1989	Corona del Mar, Calif.
Mirabelli, Doug	.235	10	17	2	4	2	0	1	4	2	6	0	0	R	R	6-1	215	10-18-70	1992	Wichita, Kan.
Mueller, Bill	.294	145	534	93	157	27	0	9	59	79	83	3	3	B	R	5-11	173	3-17-71	1993	Maryland Heights, Mo.
Powell, Dante	.500	8	4	2	2	0	0	1	1	3	0	0	0	R	R	6-2	185	8-25-73	1994	Long Beach, Calif.
Rios, Armando	.571	12	7	3	4	0	0	2	3	3	2	0	0	L	L	5-9	178	9-13-71	1994	Supply, N.C.
Sanchez, Rey	.285	109	316	44	90	14	2	2	30	16	47	0	0	R	R	5-10	180	10-5-67	1986	Trujillo Alto, P.R.
Snow, J.T.	.248	138	435	65	108	29	1	15	79	58	84	1	2	B	L	6-2	202	2-26-68	1989	Corona del Mar, Calif.

PITCHING	W	L	ERA	G	GS	CG	SV	IP	H	R	ER	BB	SO	B	T	HT	WT	DOB	1st Yr	Resides
Bailey, Cory	0	0	2.70	5	0	0	0	3	2	1	1	1	2	R	R	6-1	202	1-24-71	1991	Marion, Ill.
Brock, Chris	0	0	3.90	13	0	0	0	28	31	13	12	7	19	R	R	6-0	175	2-5-70	1992	Altamonte Springs, Fla.
Darwin, Danny	8	10	5.51	33	25	0	0	149	176	97	91	49	81	R	R	6-3	202	10-25-55	1976	Valley View, Texas
Estes, Shawn	7	12	5.06	25	25	1	0	149	150	89	84	80	136	R	L	6-2	200	2-18-73	1991	San Francisco, Calif.
Gardner, Mark	13	6	4.33	33	33	4	0	212	203	106	102	65	151	R	R	6-1	215	3-1-62	1985	Fresno, Calif.
Hartgraves, Dean	0	0	9.53	5	0	0	0	6	10	7	6	4	4	L	L	6-0	185	8-12-66	1987	Salem, Ore.
Hershiser, Orel	11	10	4.41	34	34	0	0	202	200	105	99	85	126	R	R	6-3	193	9-16-58	1979	Winter Park, Fla.
Johnstone, John	6	5	3.07	70	0	0	0	88	72	32	30	38	86	R	R	6-3	195	11-25-68	1987	Scottsdale, Ariz.
Mesa, Jose	5	3	3.52	32	0	0	0	31	30	14	12	18	28	R	R	6-3	225	5-22-66	1982	Westlake, Ohio
Morman, Alvin	0	1	5.14	9	0	0	0	7	8	4	4	3	7	R	L	6-3	210	1-6-69	1991	Rockingham, N.C.
Nen, Robb	7	7	1.52	78	0	0	40	89	59	21	15	25	110	R	R	6-5	210	11-28-69	1987	Weston, Fla.
Ortiz, Russ	4	4	4.99	22	13	0	0	88	90	51	49	46	75	R	R	6-1	190	6-5-74	1995	Norman, Okla.
Poole, Jim	1	3	5.29	26	0	0	0	32	38	20	19	9	16	L	L	6-1	203	4-28-66	1988	Alpharetta, Ga.
Reed, Steve	2	1	1.48	50	0	0	1	55	30	10	9	19	50	R	R	6-3	180	3-11-66	1988	Arvada, Colo.
Rodriguez, Rich	4	0	3.70	68	0	0	2	66	69	28	27	20	44	L	L	6-0	200	3-1-63	1984	Duluth, Ga.
Rueter, Kirk	16	9	4.36	33	33	1	0	188	193	100	91	57	102	L	L	6-2	210	12-1-70	1991	Nashville, Ill.
Tavarez, Julian	5	3	3.80	60	0	0	1	85	96	41	36	36	52	L	R	6-2	190	5-22-73	1990	Broadway Heights, Ohio

FIELDING

Catcher	PCT	G	PO	A	E	DP	PB
Johnson	.994	95	590	33	4	4	7
Mayne	.991	88	492	39	5	5	6
Mirabelli	.974	10	34	4	1	0	0

First Base	PCT	G	PO	A	E	DP
Ball	1.000	1	10	0	0	1
Carter	.990	16	87	8	1	5
Hayes	.995	45	347	34	2	37
Kent	1.000	1	1	0	0	0
Snow	.999	136	1039	93	1	99

Second Base	PCT	G	PO	A	E	DP
Dunston	1.000	1	0	1	0	1
Kent	.971	134	277	403	20	87
Martinez	1.000	14	15	20	0	7
Mueller	.968	10	16	14	1	4
Sanchez	.991	36	36	76	1	18

Third Base	PCT	G	PO	A	E	DP
Hayes	.989	46	22	67	1	6
Mueller	.952	137	83	273	18	32

Shortstop	PCT	G	PO	A	E	DP
Aurilia	.979	120	154	311	10	71
Delgado	1.000	6	3	6	0	2
Dunston	.938	9	11	4	1	0
Sanchez	.977	76	106	185	7	33

Outfield	PCT	G	PO	A	E	DP
Benard	.982	79	109	1	2	1
Bonds	.984	155	301	2	5	0
Burks	.989	41	89	1	1	0
Carter	1.000	17	15	0	0	0
Diaz	1.000	21	28	2	0	0
Dunston	.900	6	9	0	1	0
Hamilton	1.000	96	194	4	0	1
Javier	.986	121	217	0	3	1
Johnson	1.000	1	1	0	0	0
Jones	.941	29	31	1	2	0
Powell	1.000	8	2	0	0	0
Rios	1.000	5	5	0	0	0

LARRY GOREN

Jeff Kent

FARM SYSTEM

Director of Player Personnel: Dick Tidrow

Class	Farm Team	League	W	L	Pct.	Finish*	Manager	First Yr
AAA	Fresno (Calif.) Grizzlies	Pacific Coast	81	62	.566	t-2nd (16)	Jim Davenport	1998
AA	Shreveport (La.) Captains	Texas	57	83	.407	8th (8)	Mike Hart	1979
A#	Bakersfield (Calif.) Blaze	California	49	91	.350	10th (10)	Frank Reberger	1997
A#	San Jose (Calif.) Giants	California	83	57	.593	+1st (10)	Shane Turner	1988
A	Salem-Keizer (Ore.) Volcanoes	Northwest	43	33	.566	+t-3rd (8)	Keith Comstock	1997

*Finish in overall standings (No. of teams in league) #Advanced level +Won league championship

FRESNO — Class AAA

PACIFIC COAST LEAGUE

BATTING	AVG	G	AB	R	H	2B	3B	HR	RBI	BB	SO	SB	CS	B	T	HT	WT	DOB	1st Yr	Resides
Ball, Jeff	.296	124	456	81	135	29	0	21	80	55	86	5	2	R	R	5-10	185	4-17-69	1990	Merced, Calif.
Bonds, Bobby	.160	18	25	6	4	0	0	2	4	0	9	0	0	R	R	6-4	180	3-7-70	1992	San Carlos, Calif.
Canizaro, Jay	.226	45	106	23	24	6	2	6	14	17	23	0	1	R	R	5-10	175	7-4-73	1993	Orange, Texas
Charles, Frank	.500	4	10	2	5	0	0	1	1	1	2	0	0	R	R	6-4	210	2-23-69	1991	Anaheim, Calif.
Cruz, Jacob	.298	89	342	60	102	17	3	18	62	46	57	12	5	L	L	6-0	175	1-28-73	1994	Tempe, Ariz.
Delgado, Wilson	.277	127	512	87	142	22	2	12	63	52	92	9	5	B	R	5-11	165	7-15-75	1993	San Cristobal, D.R.
Diaz, Alex	.179	11	39	2	7	0	0	0	2	2	5	1	3	B	R	5-11	180	10-5-68	1987	San Sebastian, P.R.
Feliz, Pedro	.429	3	7	1	3	1	0	1	3	1	0	0	0	R	R	6-1	180	4-27-77	1994	Azua, D.R.
Guzman, Edwards	.305	102	325	50	99	17	0	9	48	24	47	1	0	L	R	5-11	205	9-11-76	1996	Naranjito, P.R.
Howard, Matt	.278	117	406	70	113	21	0	2	36	40	34	10	6	L	R	5-10	170	9-22-67	1989	San Diego, Calif.
Johnson, Brian	.316	5	19	4	6	1	0	2	3	1	5	0	0	R	R	6-2	210	1-8-68	1989	Chicago, Ill.
Jones, Chris	.267	25	60	11	16	1	3	3	8	6	12	2	1	R	R	6-2	210	11-16-65	1984	Phoenix, Ariz.
Leach, Jalal	.354	35	130	23	46	8	2	9	26	8	26	3	2	L	L	6-2	200	3-14-69	1990	Novato, Calif.
Martinez, Ramon	.313	98	364	58	114	21	2	14	59	38	42	0	3	R	R	6-1	170	10-10-72	1993	Toa Alta, P.R.
Mayes, Craig	.277	34	101	14	28	4	0	2	16	9	14	0	1	L	R	5-10	195	5-8-70	1992	Washington, Mich.
Mercedes, Henry	.216	27	88	17	19	5	2	2	11	15	28	0	0	R	R	6-1	210	7-23-69	1988	Eagle Point, Ore.
Mirabelli, Doug	.260	85	265	45	69	12	2	13	53	52	55	2	0	R	R	6-1	215	10-18-70	1992	Wichita, Kan.
Murray, Calvin	.233	33	90	16	21	3	1	3	5	12	18	3	1	R	R	5-11	185	7-30-71	1993	Houston, Texas
Powell, Dante	.230	134	448	83	103	17	3	14	52	71	138	41	9	R	R	6-2	185	8-25-73	1994	Long Beach, Calif.
Rios, Armando	.301	125	445	85	134	23	1	26	103	55	73	17	5	L	L	5-9	178	9-13-71	1994	Supply, N.C.
Torrealba, Yorvit	.182	4	11	1	2	1	0	0	1	1	4	0	0	R	R	5-11	180	7-19-78	1995	Guarenas, Ven.
Tyler, Josh	.000	3	3	0	0	0	0	0	0	1	1	0	0	R	R	6-1	185	9-6-73	1994	Green Lane, Pa.
Williams, Keith	.292	113	353	47	103	23	2	19	68	18	74	0	1	R	R	6-0	190	4-21-72	1993	Bedford, Pa.
Woods, Ken	.364	23	44	9	16	5	0	0	5	2	8	0	0	R	R	5-10	175	8-2-70	1992	Los Angeles, Calif.

PITCHING	W	L	ERA	G	GS	CG	SV	IP	H	R	ER	BB	SO	B	T	HT	WT	DOB	1st Yr	Resides
Bailey, Cory	7	2	2.47	57	0	0	10	95	79	31	26	18	76	R	R	6-1	202	1-24-71	1991	Marion, Ill.
Blood, Darin	4	5	4.66	19	19	1	0	114	138	63	59	37	63	B	R	6-2	200	8-31-74	1995	Scottsdale, Ariz.
Brock, Chris	11	3	3.29	17	17	2	0	115	111	47	42	33	112	R	R	6-0	175	2-5-70	1992	Altamonte Springs, Fla.
Brohawn, Troy	10	8	5.25	30	19	0	0	122	144	75	71	36	87	L	L	6-1	190	1-14-73	1994	Woolford, Md.
Crabtree, Robbie	0	0	11.57	3	1	0	0	5	8	7	6	2	10	R	R	6-1	175	11-25-72	1996	Anaheim, Calif.
Darwin, Jeff	2	6	6.79	56	0	0	24	54	69	44	41	10	45	R	R	6-3	180	7-6-69	1989	Gainesville, Texas
Estes, Shawn	1	0	1.80	1	1	0	0	5	3	1	1	3	6	R	L	6-2	200	2-18-73	1991	San Francisco, Calif.
Frontera, Chad	1	2	3.66	4	4	0	0	20	15	8	8	8	13	R	R	6-2	200	11-22-72	1994	Brooklyn, N.Y.
Fultz, Aaron	0	0	5.06	10	0	0	0	16	22	10	9	2	13	L	L	6-0	196	9-4-73	1992	Northport, Ala.
Grilli, Jason	2	3	5.14	8	8	0	0	42	49	30	24	18	37	R	R	6-4	185	11-11-76	1997	Baldwinsville, N.Y.
Hartgraves, Dean	2	3	3.97	38	1	0	3	70	67	35	31	19	64	L	L	6-0	185	8-12-66	1987	Salem, Ore.
Huisman, Rick	2	6	5.38	44	0	0	0	72	65	43	43	34	80	R	R	6-3	210	5-17-69	1990	Holland, Mich.
Jensen, Ryan	0	0	4.76	2	1	0	0	6	4	5	3	4	6	R	R	6-0	205	9-17-75	1996	West Valley, Utah
McMullen, Mike	1	0	5.40	2	0	0	0	3	2	2	2	2	2	R	R	6-2	185	10-13-73	1993	St. Louis, Mo.
Morman, Alvin	2	0	4.15	4	1	0	0	4	7	2	2	0	3	R	L	6-3	210	1-6-69	1991	Rockingham, N.C.
Ortiz, Russ	3	1	1.60	10	10	0	0	51	35	10	9	22	59	R	R	6-1	190	6-5-74	1995	Norman, Okla.
Phillips, Randy	4	2	5.32	9	8	0	0	44	56	30	26	8	45	R	R	6-3	210	3-18-71	1992	Pine Bluff, Ark.
Pickett, Ricky	1	1	3.86	5	0	0	0	7	6	4	3	14	11	L	L	6-1	200	1-19-70	1992	Greenville, Fla.
Plantenberg, Erik	4	5	4.42	53	1	0	1	77	78	45	38	43	67	B	L	6-1	180	10-30-68	1990	Bellevue, Wash.
Roa, Joe	12	9	5.17	27	27	2	0	162	192	102	93	32	97	R	R	6-1	194	10-11-71	1989	Hazel Park, Mich.
Rogers, Kevin	1	1	7.36	14	1	0	0	18	23	15	15	8	15	L	L	6-1	198	8-20-68	1988	Parchman, Miss.
Soderstrom, Steve	11	4	4.05	25	23	2	1	138	133	71	62	39	96	R	R	6-3	215	4-3-72	1993	Turlock, Calif.
Taulbee, Andy	0	1	12.60	1	1	0	0	5	9	7	7	2	2	R	R	6-4	210	10-5-72	1994	Atlanta, Ga.
Tavarez, Julian	0	0	19.29	1	0	0	0	2	6	5	5	0	1	L	R	6-2	190	5-22-73	1990	Broadway Heights, Ohio

FIELDING

Catcher	PCT	G	PO	A	E	DP	PB
Charles	.963	3	24	2	1	0	0
Guzman	1.000	5	20	3	0	0	2
Howard	.000	1	0	0	0	0	0
Mayes	.989	30	173	13	2	2	2
Mercedes	.995	27	187	16	1	1	4
Mirabelli	.995	83	605	50	3	11	4
Torrealba	1.000	4	22	0	0	0	1

First Base	PCT	G	PO	A	E	DP
Ball	.994	115	917	62	6	85
Mayes	1.000	2	6	1	0	1
Rios	1.000	3	27	5	0	1
Williams	.988	34	245	12	3	23

Second Base	PCT	G	PO	A	E	DP
Canizaro	.981	25	42	60	2	17
Howard	.955	26	53	75	6	14
Martinez	.982	97	209	280	9	57
Woods	.800	3	5	3	2	1

Third Base	PCT	G	PO	A	E	DP
Ball	.842	6	2	14	3	5
Feliz	1.000	1	0	2	0	0
Guzman	.931	79	60	128	14	17
Howard	.985	67	36	99	2	7
Woods	.947	8	9	9	1	1

Shortstop	PCT	G	PO	A	E	DP
Canizaro	1.000	1	0	3	0	1
Delgado	.962	126	205	373	23	76
Howard	.957	16	21	45	3	9
Martinez	.000	1	0	0	1	0
Woods	.000	1	0	0	0	0

Outfield	PCT	G	PO	A	E	DP
Bonds	1.000	3	1	0	0	0
Canizaro	1.000	4	7	1	0	0
Cruz	.963	86	152	5	6	0
Diaz	.818	7	8	1	2	0
Johnson	1.000	5	10	0	0	0
Jones	.944	13	17	0	1	0
Leach	.932	28	52	3	4	0
Murray	1.000	18	27	1	0	0
Powell	.976	132	284	2	7	0
Rios	.966	117	187	10	7	2
Williams	.929	47	63	2	5	0
Woods	.000	2	0	0	0	0

SHREVEPORT — Class AA

TEXAS LEAGUE

BATTING	AVG	G	AB	R	H	2B	3B	HR	RBI	BB	SO	SB	CS	B	T	HT	WT	DOB	1st Yr	Resides
Alguacil, Jose	.206	43	97	13	20	3	1	1	6	9	15	3	2	B	R	6-2	200	8-9-72	1993	Caracas, Ven.
Bonds, Bobby	.282	43	156	24	44	7	1	2	18	16	21	6	0	R	R	6-4	180	3-7-70	1992	San Carlos, Calif.
Canizaro, Jay	.224	83	281	47	63	7	1	12	32	53	46	5	2	R	R	5-10	175	7-4-73	1993	Orange, Texas
Charles, Frank	.287	108	411	49	118	39	1	12	66	18	93	0	2	R	R	6-4	210	2-23-69	1991	Anaheim, Calif.
Denbow, Don	.153	44	111	14	17	7	2	3	10	21	47	2	1	R	R	6-4	215	4-30-73	1993	Corsicana, Texas
Dilone, Juan	.207	36	111	13	23	8	2	4	16	10	35	3	1	B	R	6-1	188	5-10-73	1991	Higuey, D.R.
Feliz, Pedro	.264	100	364	39	96	23	2	12	50	9	62	0	1	R	R	6-1	180	4-27-77	1994	Azua, D.R.
Garland, Tim	.263	55	194	24	51	6	2	1	16	15	24	15	5	R	R	6-0	185	7-15-68	1989	Danville, Va.
Glendenning, Mike	.244	78	254	27	62	12	2	7	33	35	57	0	0	R	R	6-0	210	8-26-76	1996	West Hills, Calif.
King, Brett	.171	85	257	29	44	9	2	3	19	27	64	4	2	R	R	6-1	190	7-20-72	1993	Apopka, Fla.
Leach, Jalal	.344	72	253	43	87	17	2	10	45	36	35	10	2	L	L	6-2	200	3-14-69	1990	Novato, Calif.
Marval, Raul	.236	96	296	14	70	6	1	1	21	13	35	2	2	R	R	6-0	170	12-13-75	1993	Cabodare, Ven.
Mayes, Craig	.239	29	88	11	21	2	0	3	16	4	9	0	0	L	R	5-10	195	5-8-70	1992	Washington, Mich.
McKinley, Dan	.179	33	112	16	20	3	3	0	11	11	30	2	3	L	R	6-0	180	5-15-76	1997	Chandler, Ariz.
Minor, Damon	.239	81	289	39	69	11	1	14	52	30	51	1	0	L	L	6-7	230	1-5-74	1996	Edmond, Okla.
Morillo, Cesar	.111	10	18	1	2	0	0	0	2	1	3	0	0	B	R	5-11	180	7-21-73	1990	Eugene, Ore.
Murray, Calvin	.309	88	337	63	104	22	5	8	39	58	45	34	15	R	R	5-11	185	7-30-71	1993	Houston, Texas
Poor, Jeff	.000	2	2	0	0	0	0	0	0	0	0	0	0	R	R	6-1	195	5-23-74	1994	El Segundo, Calif.
Priess, Matt	.000	2	1	0	0	0	0	0	0	1	0	0	0	R	R	6-2	190	11-24-74	1997	Brea, Calif.
Ramirez, Peto	.250	12	24	1	6	3	0	0	3	5	7	0	0	R	R	6-2	215	9-10-72	1991	Ensenada, P.R.
Simonton, Benji	.280	45	161	19	45	7	1	5	19	19	44	5	0	R	R	6-1	225	5-12-72	1992	Pittsburg, Calif.
Smith, Scott	.333	7	15	3	5	0	0	0	1	0	4	0	0	R	R	6-3	215	10-14-71	1994	Coppell, Texas
Torrealba, Yorvit	.235	59	196	18	46	7	0	0	13	18	30	0	5	R	R	5-11	180	7-19-78	1995	Guarenas, Ven.
Tyler, Josh	.205	14	39	5	8	0	0	0	3	1	4	0	0	R	R	6-1	185	9-6-73	1994	Green Lane, Pa.
Van Rossum, Chris	.161	23	62	5	10	2	1	0	3	9	15	2	2	L	L	6-2	180	2-15-74	1996	Turlock, Calif.
Woods, Ken	.307	94	335	44	103	20	2	4	33	28	31	8	9	R	R	5-10	175	8-2-70	1992	Los Angeles, Calif.

PITCHING	W	L	ERA	G	GS	CG	SV	IP	H	R	ER	BB	SO	B	T	HT	WT	DOB	1st Yr	Resides
Bermudez, Manny	0	4	7.56	5	4	1	0	25	33	23	21	11	16	R	R	6-1	195	12-15-76	1995	Antioch, Calif.
Brester, Jason	2	8	3.82	19	19	0	0	113	117	58	48	44	79	L	L	6-3	190	12-7-76	1995	Burlington, Wash.
Corps, Edwin	2	5	3.90	46	5	0	1	92	94	47	40	32	42	R	R	5-11	190	11-3-72	1994	Carolina, P.R.
Crabtree, Robbie	2	0	1.67	26	0	0	4	54	30	11	10	16	56	R	R	6-1	175	11-25-72	1996	Anaheim, Calif.
Frontera, Chad	0	4	4.30	8	8	0	0	38	52	24	18	27	28	R	R	6-2	200	11-22-72	1994	Brooklyn, N.Y.
Fultz, Aaron	5	7	3.77	54	0	0	15	62	58	40	26	29	61	L	L	6-0	196	9-4-73	1992	Northport, Ala.
Grilli, Jason	7	10	3.79	21	21	3	0	123	113	60	52	37	100	R	R	6-4	185	11-11-76	1997	Baldwinsville, N.Y.
Grote, Jason	2	5	6.79	10	10	0	0	53	84	44	40	15	27	R	R	6-0	180	4-13-75	1994	Gresham, Ore.
Hollins, Stacy	1	2	6.46	18	3	0	1	46	54	40	33	29	29	R	R	6-3	180	7-31-72	1992	Denver, Colo.
Hook, Chris	2	0	3.86	15	0	0	2	26	19	11	11	22	12	R	R	6-5	195	8-4-68	1989	Florence, Ky.
Hutzler, Jeff	0	2	5.91	2	2	0	0	11	13	7	7	2	10	R	R	6-6	225	12-5-72	1994	San Antonio, Texas
Keith, Jeff	1	1	8.59	10	0	0	0	22	26	23	21	20	15	L	L	6-1	217	6-1-72	1994	Clifton Park, N.Y.
Linebrink, Scott	10	8	5.02	21	21	0	0	113	101	66	63	58	128	R	R	6-3	185	8-4-76	1997	Austin, Texas
Martin, Jeff	1	2	3.03	31	1	0	0	59	53	23	20	17	43	R	R	6-3	195	3-28-73	1991	Phoenix, Ariz.
McMullen, Mike	6	4	2.13	52	0	0	9	68	47	23	16	41	76	R	R	6-2	185	10-13-73	1993	St. Louis, Mo.
Nathan, Joe	1	3	8.80	4	4	0	0	15	20	15	15	9	10	R	R	6-4	195	11-22-74	1995	Circleville, N.Y.
Oropesa, Eddie	7	11	3.78	32	20	2	0	143	143	71	60	67	104	L	L	6-3	215	11-23-71	1993	Conoga Park, Calif.
Phillips, Randy	6	4	3.97	17	17	1	0	95	95	44	42	30	68	R	R	6-3	210	3-18-71	1992	Pine Bluff, Ark.
Rogers, Kevin	1	0	5.87	14	1	0	0	23	25	17	15	9	18	L	L	6-1	198	8-20-68	1988	Parchman, Miss.
Taulbee, Andy	0	1	4.02	3	3	0	0	16	17	9	7	9	10	R	R	6-4	210	10-5-72	1994	Atlanta, Ga.
Verdugo, Jason	1	2	3.72	9	1	0	1	19	17	9	8	6	27	R	R	6-2	195	3-28-75	1997	Tempe, Ariz.

FIELDING

Catcher	PCT	G	PO	A	E	DP	PB
Charles	.976	57	402	46	11	6	5
Mayes	.991	20	100	10	1	1	2
Poor	1.000	2	9	0	0	0	0
Ramirez	.982	12	48	7	1	1	3
Torrealba	.996	58	397	70	2	4	3

First Base	PCT	G	PO	A	E	DP
Charles	.993	41	387	23	3	42
Minor	.988	72	641	39	8	57
Simonton	1.000	16	154	5	0	11
Tyler	1.000	1	1	0	0	0
Woods	1.000	15	122	8	0	12

Second Base	PCT	G	PO	A	E	DP
Alguacil	1.000	10	11	14	0	2
Canizaro	.976	80	145	255	10	51
King	.991	21	39	67	1	16
Tyler	1.000	2	6	12	0	3
Woods	.980	38	87	106	4	19

Third Base	PCT	G	PO	A	E	DP
Feliz	.926	97	71	204	22	31
King	.971	13	9	24	1	2
Tyler	.923	9	9	15	2	0
Woods	.898	33	16	63	9	6

Shortstop	PCT	G	PO	A	E	DP
Alguacil	.946	19	18	35	3	7
King	.959	45	62	125	8	23
Marval	.956	86	114	259	17	45
Woods	.829	8	11	18	6	4

Outfield	PCT	G	PO	A	E	DP
Bonds	.920	29	41	5	4	1
Denbow	.979	34	45	1	1	0
Dilone	.963	31	50	2	2	0
Garland	.987	50	73	1	1	1
Glendenning	.949	68	90	3	5	0
King	.000	1	0	0	0	0
Leach	.976	66	120	4	3	1
McKinley	.966	31	53	3	2	0
Murray	.966	88	198	3	7	1
Simonton	1.000	24	35	0	0	0
Smith	1.000	3	5	0	0	0
Van Rossum	1.000	16	18	0	0	0
Woods	.000	2	0	0	0	0

BAKERSFIELD — Class A

CALIFORNIA LEAGUE

BATTING	AVG	G	AB	R	H	2B	3B	HR	RBI	BB	SO	SB	CS	B	T	HT	WT	DOB	1st Yr	Resides
Alguacil, Jose	.250	61	228	25	57	11	2	2	23	11	45	3	0	B	R	6-2	200	8-9-72	1993	Caracas, Ven.
Baeza, Art	.243	64	251	35	61	17	2	8	38	27	44	0	2	R	R	6-2	205	3-31-74	1996	West Covina, Calif.
Brown, Eric	.214	5	14	1	3	0	0	0	1	0	7	0	1	R	R	6-1	205	2-28-77	1995	La Place, La.
Casper, Brett	.194	74	237	27	46	10	3	2	18	23	75	5	4	R	R	6-3	215	11-24-75	1997	Omaha, Neb.
Delgado, Reymundo	.296	21	71	7	21	6	0	0	5	6	8	0	1	L	L	5-11	200	12-29-75	1996	Rio Piedras, P.R.
Denbow, Don	.307	29	101	18	31	4	2	2	13	22	35	0	3	R	R	6-4	215	4-30-73	1993	Corsicana, Texas
Faircloth, Chad	.257	84	288	39	74	13	3	3	30	16	78	12	2	L	R	6-0	180	4-25-75	1997	Winston-Salem, N.C.
Flaherty, Tim	.234	124	478	72	112	27	0	24	90	41	171	0	0	R	R	6-4	220	7-11-76	1997	Williamstown, Mass.
Fuentes, Joel	.282	31	117	14	33	3	0	3	17	9	31	0	2	B	R	6-0	178	5-27-76	1997	Cayey, P.R.
2-team (9 San Jose)	.288	40	146	19	42	5	0	3	19	13	40	0	3							

BATTING	AVG	G	AB	R	H	2B	3B	HR	RBI	BB	SO	SB	CS	B	T	HT	WT	DOB	1st Yr	Resides
Greene, Clay	.217	52	175	26	38	3	0	0	9	28	51	13	8	R	R	6-0	185	11-10-74	1997	Cleveland, Tenn.
Lindsey, Shawn	.333	10	27	6	9	2	0	0	2	5	6	1	2	L	L	6-2	188	4-9-77	1999	Portland, Ore.
Magruder, Chris	.304	22	92	21	28	7	0	1	4	13	16	3	0	B	R	5-11	200	4-26-77	1998	Yakima, Wash.
McKinley, Dan	.301	94	379	58	114	16	4	6	44	30	84	19	6	L	R	6-0	180	5-15-76	1997	Chandler, Ariz.
Melendez, Angel	[illegible]	12	47	4	10	1	0	1	4	1	11	1	0	R	R	6-0	192	10-21-75	1996	Caguas, P.R.
Morillo, Cesar	.184	14	38	3	7	0	0	0	6	3	10	0	0	B	R	5-11	180	7-21-73	1990	Eugene, Ore.
Mota, Pedro	.189	15	53	8	10	1	1	0	2	4	15	2	1	L	L	6-1	195	2-28-78	1995	San Pedro de Macoris, D.R.
2-team (15 San Jose)	.204	30	108	10	22	4	1	0	6	6	31	4	2							
Otero, William	.294	69	245	33	72	14	0	3	36	35	50	8	0	R	R	5-11	175	9-30-76	1997	Bayamon, P.R.
Pernalete, Marco	.232	73	190	19	44	6	0	0	12	11	52	5	1	B	R	6-1	165	10-12-78	1996	Barquisimeto, Ven.
Poor, Jeff	.208	26	77	6	16	5	0	1	4	10	15	0	0	R	R	6-1	195	5-23-74	1994	El Segundo, Calif.
Priess, Matt	.287	52	188	23	54	11	0	4	19	19	30	0	0	R	R	6-2	190	11-24-74	1997	Brea, Calif.
Prospero, Ted	.241	65	199	27	48	7	1	5	23	11	48	7	3	R	R	5-11	160	2-12-77	1995	San Pedro de Macoris, D.R.
Ramirez, Peto	.202	28	89	5	18	6	0	4	15	6	28	1	0	R	R	6-2	215	9-10-72	1991	Ensenada, P.R.
Smith, Scott	.247	49	178	27	44	11	1	4	18	18	52	2	1	R	R	6-3	215	10-14-71	1994	Coppell, Texas
Soriano, Fred	.244	72	242	38	59	9	2	4	23	22	71	9	4	R	R	5-9	160	8-5-74	1992	Bani, D.R.
Tommasini, Kevin	.212	33	99	12	21	5	1	3	11	9	26	0	1	R	R	6-1	205	1-18-75	1998	Winston, Ore.
Tyler, Josh	.268	53	220	27	59	14	1	6	43	11	32	12	2	R	R	6-1	185	9-6-73	1994	Green Lane, Pa.
2-team (50 San Jose)	.258	103	414	51	107	24	3	7	64	21	61	19	10							
Valenti, Jon	.245	113	371	52	91	23	1	6	35	57	65	2	2	R	R	6-1	195	11-26-73	1994	Bakersfield, Calif.
Wells, Zach	.210	49	143	9	30	6	3	1	14	17	52	0	3	R	R	6-4	205	2-23-77	1997	Clayton, Calif.

GAMES BY POSITION: C—Flaherty 79, Poor 19, Priess 43, Ramirez 5, Tommasini 6, Tyler 3. **1B**—Baeza 64, Delgado 3, Flaherty 18, Tyler 1, Valenti 23, Wells 35. **2B**—Alguacil 54, Fuentes 21, Morillo 1, Otero 26, Pernalete 26, Prospero 26, Tyler 4, Valenti 1. **3B**—Alguacil 2, Morillo 6, Otero 4, Prospero 17, Ramirez 3, Tyler 48, Valenti 70. **SS**—Alguacil 4, Morillo 3, Otero 43, Pernalete 40, Soriano 72, Tyler 1. **OF**—Alguacil 2, Brown 1, Casper 72, Delgado 12, Denbow 25, Faircloth 72, Flaherty 1, Fuentes 1, Greene 46, Lindsey 6, Magruder 22, McKinley 94, Melendez 12, Mota 14, Otero 1, Priess 1, Prospero 1, Ramirez 4, Smith 39, Tommasini 22, Tyler 1, Valenti 9, Wells 2.

PITCHING	W	L	ERA	G	GS	CG	SV	IP	H	R	ER	BB	SO	B	T	HT	WT	DOB	1st Yr	Resides
Bailey, Phil	2	2	5.74	20	0	0	1	31	40	22	20	23	27	L	L	6-1	190	10-4-73	1995	Benton, Ark.
Estes, Shawn	0	0	0.00	1	1	0	0	4	3	0	0	1	5	R	L	6-2	200	2-18-73	1991	San Francisco, Calif.
Esteves, Jake	0	2	4.29	14	6	0	1	36	43	30	17	12	24	R	R	6-1	200	7-31-75	1998	Auburn, Calif.
Frontera, Chad	2	6	5.40	11	11	0	0	53	63	39	32	23	29	R	R	6-2	200	11-22-72	1994	Brooklyn, N.Y.
Hutchings, Mark	0	0	6.30	6	0	0	0	10	8	7	7	7	6	R	R	6-4	200	9-18-76	1997	Farmington, Mo.
Hutzler, Jeff	1	7	5.71	51	0	0	3	80	96	64	51	31	34	R	R	6-6	225	12-5-72	1994	San Antonio, Texas
Jensen, Ryan	11	12	3.37	29	27	0	0	168	162	89	63	61	164	R	R	6-0	205	9-17-75	1996	West Valley, Utah
Joseph, Kevin	0	4	8.14	6	6	0	0	21	35	26	19	20	17	R	R	6-4	200	8-1-76	1997	Dallas, Texas
Larreal, Guillermo	1	1	4.82	9	0	0	0	19	23	14	10	2	14	R	R	6-1	175	2-3-76	1995	Maracaibo, Ven.
Luckert, Gabriel	0	0	16.20	2	0	0	0	2	5	3	3	1	1	R	R	6-1	165	7-2-75	1992	Cabudare, Ven.
Macey, Fausto	5	8	5.28	17	15	1	0	87	114	63	51	20	72	R	R	6-4	185	10-9-75	1994	Santo Domingo, D.R.
Malerich, Will	1	1	4.71	26	0	0	1	42	36	22	22	25	35	L	L	5-11	180	10-25-75	1997	Alexandria, Va.
Nielsen, Tom	1	0	7.88	4	0	0	0	8	10	11	7	5	8	R	L	6-2	170	7-28-76	1997	Coram, N.Y.
Ramirez, Erasmo	1	1	3.38	14	0	0	3	21	10	8	8	6	17	L	L	6-0	180	4-29-76	1998	Santa Ana, Calif.
Rice, Nathan	3	8	5.40	30	21	0	0	120	133	96	72	78	87	L	L	6-5	215	4-19-74	1997	Visalia, Calif.
Riley, Michael	6	12	4.50	40	15	2	2	128	130	73	64	58	110	L	L	6-2	165	1-2-75	1996	Seaford, Del.
Rogers, Kevin	0	0	2.11	12	0	0	0	21	15	9	5	4	19	L	L	6-1	198	8-20-68	1988	Parchman, Miss.
Takahashi, Kurt	0	0	4.66	5	0	0	0	10	11	7	5	3	7	R	R	6-4	215	2-22-74	1995	Clovis, Calif.
Taulbee, Andy	3	4	5.38	18	13	0	0	75	96	55	45	33	43	R	R	6-4	210	10-5-72	1994	Atlanta, Ga.
Thurmond, Travis	0	0	0.00	2	0	0	0	6	0	0	0	5	7	R	R	6-3	220	12-8-73	1992	Cornelius, Ore.
Travis, Jesse	1	7	6.08	50	6	0	9	80	96	66	54	33	58	R	R	6-1	195	11-4-74	1997	Seattle, Wash.
Valenti, Jon	1	2	7.08	9	2	0	0	20	26	21	16	13	11	R	R	6-1	195	11-26-73	1994	Bakersfield, Calif.
Verdugo, Jason	6	6	3.25	28	11	0	3	80	79	35	29	15	59	R	R	6-2	195	3-28-75	1997	Tempe, Ariz.
Wells, Matt	3	8	4.50	40	6	0	5	104	107	63	52	46	70	R	R	6-2	210	5-25-75	1996	Rocklin, Calif.

SAN JOSE — Class A

CALIFORNIA LEAGUE

BATTING	AVG	G	AB	R	H	2B	3B	HR	RBI	BB	SO	SB	CS	B	T	HT	WT	DOB	1st Yr	Resides
Bertrand, Ben	.196	13	46	3	9	3	0	0	3	3	13	0	0	R	R	6-0	195	8-5-75	1998	Corvallis, Ore.
Byas, Michael	.251	135	521	87	131	10	2	1	36	81	98	30	22	B	R	6-0	170	4-21-76	1997	Chesterfield, Mo.
Campusano, Carlos	.184	34	98	11	18	1	2	0	7	5	29	0	0	R	R	5-11	160	9-2-75	1994	Palave, D.R.
Chiaramonte, Giuseppe	.273	129	502	87	137	33	3	22	87	47	139	5	2	R	R	6-0	200	2-19-76	1997	Santa Cruz, Calif.
Dilone, Juan	.320	85	316	63	101	24	2	18	47	31	103	19	9	B	R	6-1	188	5-10-73	1991	Higuey, D.R.
Faircloth, Chad	.206	18	63	5	13	3	1	0	2	1	12	1	1	L	R	6-0	180	4-25-75	1997	Winston-Salem, N.C.
2-team (84 Bakersfield)	.248	102	351	44	87	16	4	3	32	17	90	13	3							
Fuentes, Joel	.310	9	29	5	9	2	0	0	2	4	9	0	1	B	R	6-0	178	5-27-76	1997	Cayey, P.R.
Glendenning, Mike	.250	48	176	26	44	9	0	10	33	24	66	1	1	R	R	6-0	210	8-26-76	1996	West Hills, Calif.
Gulseth, Mark	.283	119	467	72	132	38	2	9	75	50	67	2	2	L	R	6-4	215	11-12-71	1993	Callaway, Minn.
Mayes, Craig	.364	3	11	1	4	1	0	1	4	0	1	0	0	L	R	5-10	195	5-8-70	1992	Washington, Mich.
Melendez, Angel	.281	54	167	22	47	11	0	5	28	14	34	4	1	R	R	6-0	192	10-21-75	1996	Caguas, P.R.
2-team (12 Bakersfield)	.266	66	214	26	57	12	0	6	32	15	45	5	1							
Mendoza, Carlos	.214	110	365	36	78	7	3	0	20	19	64	11	8	B	R	6-0	175	11-27-79	1996	Barquisimeto, Ven.
Minor, Damon	.284	48	176	26	50	10	1	7	36	28	40	0	1	L	L	6-7	230	1-5-74	1996	Edmond, Okla.
Mota, Pedro	.218	15	55	2	12	3	0	0	4	2	16	2	1	L	L	6-1	195	2-28-78	1995	San Pedro de Macoris, D.R.
Rodriguez, Guillermo	.000	1	1	0	0	0	0	0	0	0	0	0	0	R	R	5-11	190	5-15-78	1996	Barquisimeto, Ven.
Simonton, Benji	.320	89	300	59	96	28	4	16	69	53	100	4	2	R	R	6-1	225	5-12-72	1992	Pittsburg, Calif.
Tommasini, Kevin	.200	6	25	1	5	0	0	1	1	0	4	0	1	R	R	6-1	205	1-18-75	1998	Winston, Ore.
2-team (33 Bakersfield)	.210	39	124	13	26	5	1	4	12	9	30	0	2							
Torrealba, Yorvit	.286	21	70	10	20	2	0	0	10	1	6	2	2	R	R	5-11	180	7-19-78	1995	Guarenas, Ven.
Tyler, Josh	.247	50	194	24	48	10	2	1	21	10	29	7	8	R	R	6-1	185	9-6-73	1994	Green Lane, Pa.
Van Rossum, Chris	.248	65	214	33	53	9	3	2	15	17	55	10	2	L	L	6-2	180	2-15-74	1996	Turlock, Calif.
Young, Travis	.244	133	517	79	126	21	2	4	63	61	101	27	12	R	R	6-1	185	9-8-74	1997	Albuquerque, N.M.
Zuniga, Tony	.244	113	397	52	97	20	4	8	59	39	64	1	2	R	R	6-0	185	1-13-75	1996	Santa Ana, Calif.

GAMES BY POSITION: C—Bertrand 13, Chiaramonte 105, Mayes 3, Rodriguez 1, Tommasini 1, Torrealba 19. **1B**—Gulseth 71, Minor 44, Simonton 26. **2B**—Fuentes 6, Tyler 2, Young 133. **3B**—Gulseth 1, Tommasini 3, Tyler 35, Zuniga 104. **SS**—Campusano 33, Fuentes 1,

Mendoza 110, Zuniga 2. **OF**—Byas 134, Dilone 63, Faircloth 18, Glendenning 48, Melendez 35, Mota 15, Simonton 44, Tommasini 3, Tyler 14, Van Rossum 57.

PITCHING	W	L	ERA	G	GS	CG	SV	IP	H	R	ER	BB	SO	B	T	HT	WT	DOB	1st Yr	Resides
Andra, Jeff	8	2	3.32	15	15	2	0	87	75	36	32	28	80	L	L	6-5	210	9-9-75	1997	Lenexa, Kan.
Bermudez, Manny	7	11	4.64	24	24	1	0	140	161	82	72	44	87	R	R	6-1	195	12-15-76	1995	Antioch, Calif.
Bump, Nate	6	1	1.75	11	11	0	0	62	37	13	12	24	61	R	R	6-2	185	7-24-76	1998	Monroeton, Pa.
Crabtree, Robbie	6	1	.99	24	0	0	2	54	39	6	6	8	67	R	R	6-1	175	11-25-72	1996	Anaheim, Calif.
Estrella, Luis	5	6	4.75	36	2	0	2	72	79	41	38	27	57	R	R	6-2	220	10-7-74	1996	Santa Ana, Calif.
Grote, Jason	7	2	2.45	15	15	0	0	88	85	30	24	22	88	R	R	6-0	180	4-13-75	1994	Gresham, Ore.
Johnson, Eric	0	0	9.64	5	0	0	0	5	5	7	5	9	2	R	R	6-4	195	9-12-77	1997	Newberg, Ore.
Keith, Jeff	1	1	3.77	23	0	0	0	29	28	16	12	16	29	L	L	6-1	217	6-1-72	1994	Clifton Park, N.Y.
Kiyono, Masashi	2	5	5.94	13	8	0	0	47	56	37	31	14	20	R	R	6-2	190	3-16-75	1997	Kanagawa, Japan
Knoll, Brian	7	7	3.45	42	6	1	3	115	135	47	44	21	109	R	R	6-3	200	8-4-73	1995	Corona, Calif.
Malerich, Will	2	2	2.23	20	0	0	2	32	28	14	8	14	24	L	L	5-11	180	10-25-75	1997	Alexandria, Va.
2-team (26 Bakersfield)	3	3	3.63	46	0	0	3	74	64	36	30	39	59							
Malloy, Bill	11	7	4.88	41	15	0	4	125	132	81	68	42	103	R	R	6-2	210	5-22-75	1996	Piscataway, N.J.
Nathan, Joe	8	6	3.32	22	22	0	0	122	100	51	45	48	118	R	R	6-4	195	11-22-74	1995	Circleville, N.Y.
Stoops, Jim	2	1	0.98	45	0	0	31	55	28	7	6	25	96	R	R	6-2	195	6-30-72	1995	Somerset, N.J.
Tucker, Ben	5	5	3.75	29	14	0	1	113	97	54	47	33	69	R	R	6-4	220	11-6-73	1995	Fresno, Calif.
Urban, Jeff	4	0	3.52	4	4	0	0	23	27	13	9	5	23	R	L	6-8	215	1-25-77	1998	Alexandria, Ind.
Verdugo, Jason	0	0	0.00	1	0	0	0	1	2	0	0	0	1	R	R	6-2	195	3-28-75	1997	Tempe, Ariz.
2-team (28 Bakersfield)	6	6	3.21	29	11	0	3	81	81	35	29	15	60							
Vogelsong, Ryan	0	0	7.58	4	4	0	0	19	23	16	16	4	26	R	R	6-3	195	7-22-77	1998	Carlisle, Pa.
Zerbe, Chad	2	0	3.35	23	0	0	1	38	37	16	14	12	28	L	L	6-0	190	4-27-72	1991	Tampa, Fla.

SALEM-KEIZER — Short-Season Class A

NORTHWEST LEAGUE

BATTING	AVG	G	AB	R	H	2B	3B	HR	RBI	BB	SO	SB	CS	B	T	HT	WT	DOB	1st Yr	Resides
Allen, Jeff	.293	60	215	47	63	10	5	11	47	33	64	10	5	R	R	6-1	190	6-8-76	1998	Walnut Creek, Calif.
Bertrand, Ben	.105	8	19	0	2	1	0	0	1	3	8	0	0	R	R	6-0	195	8-5-75	1998	Corvallis, Ore.
Casper, Brett	.308	7	26	2	8	1	1	0	3	2	7	0	1	R	R	6-3	215	11-24-75	1997	Omaha, Neb.
Clark, Doug	.335	59	227	49	76	8	6	3	41	32	31	12	8	L	R	6-2	190	3-5-76	1998	Springfield, Mass.
Dean, Mike	.279	52	183	29	51	7	5	2	34	19	51	13	4	R	R	5-11	190	8-2-77	1998	Okmulgee, Okla.
Frazier, Carlos	.000	11	11	0	0	0	0	0	0	0	4	0	0	R	R	5-9	175	11-1-78	1998	Smackover, Ark.
Hill, Steven	.263	55	186	40	49	4	5	0	24	10	24	18	4	B	R	5-10	180	12-10-75	1998	Stillwater, Okla.
Kenna, David	.000	5	3	0	0	0	0	0	0	2	2	0	0	L	R	6-1	200	3-16-78	1996	North Fort Myers, Fla.
Lindsey, Shawn	.277	30	101	21	28	0	1	1	6	17	22	7	2	L	L	6-2	188	4-9-77	1999	Portland, Ore.
Luster, Jeremy	.304	51	181	32	55	13	3	6	48	23	30	6	4	B	R	6-2	212	6-10-77	1999	Kennesaw, Ga.
Magruder, Chris	.333	47	177	43	59	8	5	3	18	37	21	14	7	B	R	5-11	200	4-26-77	1998	Yakima, Wash.
Mattern, Erik	.245	48	151	18	37	2	2	2	20	30	26	9	5	R	R	5-10	175	3-23-76	1998	Tucson, Ariz.
McDowell, Arturo	.221	47	172	32	38	3	2	0	18	29	46	13	2	L	L	6-1	175	9-7-79	1998	Jackson, Miss.
Mercedes, Luis	.000	4	6	0	0	0	0	0	1	0	3	0	0	R	R	6-2	165	1-13-78	1995	Nizao, D.R.
Mota, Pedro	.118	8	17	0	2	1	0	0	0	3	4	0	1	L	L	6-1	195	2-28-78	1995	San Pedro de Macoris, D.R.
Ransom, Bryan	.233	71	236	52	55	12	7	6	27	43	56	19	6	R	R	6-2	190	2-17-76	1998	Chandler, Ariz.
Rodriguez, Guillermo	.250	1	4	0	1	0	0	0	0	0	1	0	1	R	R	5-11	190	5-15-78	1996	Barquisimeto, Ven.
Serrano, Sammy	.200	48	191	41	38	12	1	9	40	9	36	2	1	R	R	6-2	205	12-3-76	1998	Woodbridge, Va.
Summers, John	.303	56	211	33	64	13	2	1	38	24	48	5	0	B	R	6-0	195	11-16-76	1998	Salt Lake City, Utah
Tommasini, Kevin	.189	20	53	9	10	3	2	1	8	6	8	3	0	R	R	6-1	205	1-18-75	1998	Winston, Ore.
Torcato, Tony	.291	59	220	31	64	15	2	3	43	14	38	4	2	L	R	6-1	195	10-25-79	1998	Woodland, Calif.
Valderrama, Carlos	.345	7	29	5	10	1	0	0	4	1	7	4	0	R	R	5-11	175	11-30-77	1995	Maracaibo, Ven.

GAMES BY POSITION: C—Bertrand 8, Dean 35, Kenna 3, Rodriguez 1, Serrano 34, Tommasini 6. **1B**—Luster 46, Summers 35, Tommasini 1. **2B**—Hill 38, Mattern 45, Mercedes 1. **3B**—Hill 12, Summers 16, Tommasini 3, Torcato 53. **SS**—Hill 6, Mattern 2, Mercedes 3, Ransom 71. **OF**—Allen 55, Casper 7, Clark 56, Frazier 11, Lindsey 23, Magruder 44, McDowell 45, Mota 7, Valderrama 2.

PITCHING	W	L	ERA	G	GS	CG	SV	IP	H	R	ER	BB	SO	B	T	HT	WT	DOB	1st Yr	Resides
Bump, Nate	0	0	0.00	2	2	0	0	8	5	0	0	3	8	R	R	6-2	185	7-24-76	1998	Monroeton, Pa.
Connolly, Keith	2	1	4.79	21	0	0	0	36	34	22	19	14	38	R	R	6-3	205	12-9-74	1998	Washingtonville, N.Y.
Esteves, Jake	0	0	2.25	1	1	0	0	4	1	1	1	0	5	R	R	6-1	200	7-31-75	1998	Auburn, Calif.
Farley, Joe	0	2	8.74	3	3	0	0	11	12	12	11	6	16	B	L	6-8	210	4-23-79	1997	Olympia, Wash.
Fields, Brian	1	1	1.80	9	0	0	0	10	8	3	2	4	11	R	L	6-1	175	8-21-74	1998	Greenville, N.C.
Goodrich, Randy	4	5	5.20	17	10	0	0	62	74	43	36	17	38	R	R	6-4	210	11-8-76	1998	Fresno, Calif.
Hills, Mark	4	1	5.03	11	10	0	0	48	47	28	27	27	34	L	L	6-0	202	8-12-78	1999	Salem, Ore.
Huller, Mike	1	1	8.03	19	0	0	0	25	27	31	22	31	14	R	L	6-1	190	8-25-77	1998	Westminister, Md.
Hutchings, Mark	0	2	5.02	8	0	0	0	14	13	12	8	15	10	R	R	6-4	200	9-18-76	1997	Farmington, Mo.
Jackson, Chris	1	1	6.80	17	7	0	0	42	43	43	32	40	27	R	R	6-1	190	1-20-80	1998	Colorado Springs, Colo.
Johnson, Eric	0	0	6.35	5	2	0	0	11	11	8	8	13	8	R	R	6-4	195	9-12-77	1997	Newberg, Ore.
Jones, Chris	5	4	4.13	14	13	0	0	72	76	40	33	17	60	R	L	6-3	185	8-29-79	1998	Charlotte, N.C.
Joseph, Kevin	1	1	4.36	23	0	0	0	43	36	25	21	27	37	R	R	6-4	200	8-1-76	1997	Dallas, Texas
Kiyono, Masashi	1	1	4.00	2	2	0	0	9	10	7	4	3	6	R	R	6-2	190	3-16-75	1997	Kanagawa, Japan
Miller, Benji	4	3	2.25	30	0	0	17	44	33	13	11	20	51	R	R	6-2	180	5-2-76	1998	Lynchburg, Va.
Nielsen, Tom	5	1	11.14	21	0	0	0	27	38	39	33	18	28	R	L	6-2	170	7-28-76	1997	Coram, N.Y.
Ojeda, Joseph	0	0	9.00	5	0	0	0	5	10	7	5	4	0	R	R	6-4	210	9-27-76	1998	Brooklyn, N.Y.
Ozias, Todd	3	4	3.94	27	0	0	2	46	38	23	20	12	51	R	R	6-1	185	8-19-76	1998	Coral Gables, Fla.
Ramirez, Erasmo	0	1	3.72	9	2	0	0	19	19	11	8	2	23	L	L	6-0	180	4-29-76	1998	Santa Ana, Calif.
Santos, Josh	4	1	4.04	11	11	1	0	49	50	28	22	19	57	L	L	6-0	195	2-3-77	1998	Oklahoma City, Okla.
Urban, Jeff	1	2	4.98	5	3	0	0	22	21	14	12	8	22	R	L	6-8	215	1-25-77	1998	Alexandria, Ind.
Vogelsong, Ryan	6	1	1.77	10	10	0	0	56	37	15	11	16	66	R	R	6-3	195	7-22-77	1998	Carlisle, Pa.

SEATTLE MARINERS

Underachieving club finishes third despite A-Rod, Griffey

BY SUSAN WADE

On the first day of 1998 spring training in Peoria, Ariz., ace lefthander Randy Johnson, successful in 43 of his previous 49 decisions, told manager Lou Piniella he couldn't pitch for the Mariners. Not for a team that hadn't offered him a contract extension after picking up his 1998 option against his wishes.

Johnson's heel-dragging cast a 6-foot-10 shadow over the team that looked certain to win the AL West title for the third time in four years, with superstars like Ken Griffey and Alex Rodriguez.

Though Griffey was overshadowed by Mark McGwire and Sammy Sosa in the home run chase, he finished with 56 for the second season in a row. For the third straight year he drove in more than 140 runs. And at age 28, he became the youngest player to reach 350 home runs.

Rodriguez had an incredible season himself, becoming the first 40-40 shortstop in history by hitting 42 home runs and stealing 46 bases. His 213 hits led the AL.

But it wasn't enough. Injuries, poor defense and baseball's best-paid, least-productive bullpen set the early tone and were among the reasons Seattle enjoyed only one day (May 12) above .500.

When, on July 31, the Mariners traded Johnson—by then 9-10, 4.33—to the Houston Astros for three minor leaguers, fans bitterly called for general manager Woody Woodward's resignation. They wailed, and a few players joined the chorus, that management had given up on the season.

But baseball's version of the Titanic had been sinking all year.

Alex Rodriguez

Ryan Anderson

Players of the Year

Major League: Alex Rodriguez, ss,
A-Rod led the AL with 213 hits while becoming the first 40-40 shortstop in major league history.

Minor League: Ryan Anderson, lhp, Wisconsin
The Little Unit struck out 152 batters in 111 innings in his professional debut at Class A Wisconsin.

Outfielder Jay Buhner suffered a knee injury that required surgery six days into the season. He finished the schedule on the disabled list after undergoing Tommy John elbow surgery.

First baseman David Segui was hurt a couple of times, once after a clubhouse shoving match with Johnson that left Segui to conclude, "He's just weird."

Johnson's 10-1, 1.28 post-trade effort helped the Astros clinch the National League Central. "If he'd pitched like he pitched when he went to Houston," Piniella said, "it would've changed our season."

The deal definitely changed the face of the club, and the three young players acquired—second baseman Carlos Guillen, righthander Freddy Garcia and lefthander John Halama—figured to get shots at starting roles in 1999, the club's first year in new Safeco Field.

The organization's most exciting prospects—lefthander Ryan Anderson and righthander Gil Meche—spent the season at Class A Wisconsin. Anderson dazzled in his first professional season, striking out 152 batters in just 111 innings. He was sidetracked briefly by minor ailments in midseason, but finished the year strong. Meche recorded 168 strikeouts of his own, while going 8-7 with a 3.44 ERA.

Class A Lancaster first baseman Brendan Kingman led the California League with a .340 average, though he was not highly regarded as a prospect.

Despite a lack of marquee talent, the organization experienced some success at nearly every level, compiling a 359-331 overall record for its six minor league clubs. Lancaster and Wisconsin reached postseason play, but both fell in the first round.

ORGANIZATION LEADERS

BATTING		
*AVG	Brendan Kingman, Lancaster	.340
R	Jason Regan, Lancaster	105
H	Cirilo Cruz, Lancaster	170
TB	Dan Rohrmeier, Tacoma	275
2B	Dan Rohrmeier, Tacoma	51
3B	Jermaine Clark, Wisconsin	13
HR	Dan Rohrmeier, Tacoma	25
RBI	Two tied at	104
BB	Jason Regan, Lancaster	106
SO	Tarrik Brock, Tacoma/Orlando	138
SB	Ramon Valera, Wisconsin	52
PITCHING		
W	Rob Luce, Orlando	12
L	Patrick Dunham, Orlando/Lancaster	11
#ERA	Neil Longo, Everett	2.26
G	Steve Gajkowski, Tacoma	53
CG	Tim Harikkala, Tacoma/Orlando	4
SV	Steve Gajkowski, Tacoma	24
IP	Brett Hinchliffe, Tacoma/Lancaster	177
BB	Brett Hinchliffe, Tacoma/Lancaster	93
SO	Gil Meche, Wisconsin	168

*Minimum 250 At-Bats #Minimum 75 Innings

Seattle MARINERS

Manager: Lou Piniella

1998 Record: 76-85, .472 (3rd, AL West)

BATTING	AVG	G	AB	R	H	2B	3B	HR	RBI	BB	SO	SB	CS	B	T	HT	WT	DOB	1st Yr	Resides
Amaral, Rich	.276	73	134	25	37	6	0	1	4	13	24	11	1	R	R	6-0	175	4-1-62	1983	Seattle, Wash.
Bell, David	.325	21	80	11	26	8	0	0	8	5	8	0	0	R	R	5-10	170	9-14-72	1990	Cincinnati, Ohio
2-team (107 Cleve.)	.274	128	420	48	115h	29	2	10	49	27	62	0	4							
Buhner, Jay	.242	72	244	33	59	7	1	15	45	38	71	0	0	R	R	6-3	210	8-13-64	1984	Issaquah, Wash.
Chavez, Raul	.000	1	1	0	0	0	0	0	0	0	0	0	0	R	R	5-11	175	3-18-73	1990	Valencia, Ven.
Cora, Joey	.283	131	519	95	147	23	6	6	26	62	50	13	5	B	R	5-8	162	5-14-65	1985	Caguas, P.R.
Cradle, Rickey	.143	5	7	0	1	0	0	0	2	1	5	1	0	R	R	6-2	180	6-20-73	1991	Cerritos, Calif.
Davis, Russ	.259	141	502	67	130	30	1	20	82	34	134	4	3	R	R	6-0	195	9-13-69	1988	Birmingham, Ala.
Ducey, Rob	.240	97	217	30	52	18	2	5	23	23	61	4	3	L	R	6-2	180	5-24-65	1984	Palm Harbor, Fla.
Gipson, Charles	.235	44	51	11	12	1	0	0	2	5	9	2	1	R	R	6-2	180	12-16-72	1992	Orange, Calif.
Griffey, Ken	.284	161	633	120	180	33	3	56	146	76	121	20	5	L	L	6-3	205	11-21-69	1987	Issaquah, Wash.
Guevara, Giomar	.231	11	13	4	3	2	0	0	0	4	4	0	0	R	R	5-8	150	10-23-72	1991	Guarenas, Ven.
Guillen, Carlos	.333	10	39	9	13	1	1	0	5	3	9	2	0	B	R	6-1	180	9-30-75	1993	Aragua, Ven.
Hill, Glenallen	.290	74	259	37	75	20	2	12	33	14	45	1	1	R	R	6-2	225	3-22-65	1983	Santa Cruz, Calif.
Huson, Jeff	.163	31	49	8	8	1	0	1	4	5	6	1	1	L	R	6-1	180	8-15-64	1986	Parker, Colo.
Ibanez, Raul	.255	37	98	12	25	7	1	2	12	5	22	0	0	L	R	6-2	210	6-2-72	1992	Miami, Fla.
Martinez, Edgar	.322	154	556	86	179	46	1	29	102	106	96	1	1	R	R	5-11	200	1-2-63	1983	Kirkland, Wash.
Marzano, John	.233	50	133	13	31	7	1	4	12	9	24	0	0	R	R	5-11	195	2-14-63	1985	Westboro, Mass.
McCarty, Dave	.278	8	18	1	5	0	0	1	2	5	4	1	0	R	L	6-5	215	11-23-69	1991	Menlo Park, Calif.
Monahan, Shane	.242	62	211	17	51	8	1	4	28	8	53	1	2	L	R	6-0	195	8-12-74	1995	Marietta, Ga.
Oliver, Joe	.224	29	85	12	19	3	0	2	10	10	15	1	0	R	R	6-3	220	7-24-65	1983	Orlando, Fla.
2-team (50 Detroit)	.225	79	240	20	54	11	0	6	32	17	48	1	1							
Perez, Robert	.171	17	35	3	6	1	0	2	6	0	5	0	0	R	R	6-3	230	6-4-69	1990	Bolivar, Ven.
Radmanovich, Ryan	.217	25	69	5	15	4	0	2	10	4	25	1	1	L	R	6-2	200	[illegible]	[illegible]	Calgary, Alberta
Rodriguez, Alex	.310	161	686	123	213	35	5	42	124	45	121	46	13	R	R	6-3	195	7-27-75	1994	Miami, Fla.
Rossy, Rico	.198	37	81	12	16	6	0	1	4	6	13	0	0	R	R	5-10	175	2-16-64	1985	Bayamon, P.R.
Segui, David	.305	143	522	79	159	36	1	19	84	49	80	3	1	B	L	6-1	202	7-19-66	1988	Kansas City, Kan.
Wilkins, Rick	.195	19	41	5	8	1	1	1	4	4	14	0	0	L	R	6-2	215	6-4-67	1987	Jacksonville, Fla.
Wilson, Dan	.252	96	325	39	82	17	1	9	44	24	56	2	1	R	R	6-3	190	3-25-69	1990	Seattle, Wash.

PITCHING	W	L	ERA	G	GS	CG	SV	IP	H	R	ER	BB	SO	B	T	HT	WT	DOB	1st Yr	Resides
Abbott, Paul	3	1	4.01	4	4	0	0	25	24	11	11	10	22	R	R	6-3	195	9-15-67	1985	Fullerton, Calif.
Ayala, Bobby	1	10	7.29	62	0	0	8	75	100	66	61	26	68	R	R	6-3	210	7-8-69	1988	Avondale, Ariz.
Bullinger, Jim	0	1	15.88	2	1	0	0	6	13	10	10	2	4	R	R	6-2	190	8-21-65	1986	Sarasota, Fla.
Cloude, Ken	8	10	6.37	30	30	0	0	155	187	116	110	80	114	R	R	6-1	180	1-9-75	1994	Baltimore, Md.
Fassero, Jeff	13	12	3.97	32	32	7	0	225	223	115	99	66	176	L	L	6-1	195	1-5-63	1984	Auburn, Wash.
Fossas, Tony	0	3	8.74	23	0	0	0	11	19	11	11	6	10	L	L	6-0	198	9-23-57	1979	Fort Lauderdale, Fla.
Gajkowski, Steve	0	0	7.27	9	0	0	0	9	14	8	7	4	3	R	R	6-2	200	12-30-69	1990	Olympia, Wash.
Holdridge, David	0	0	4.05	7	0	0	0	7	6	3	3	4	6	R	R	6-3	190	2-5-69	1988	Huntington Beach, Calif.
Johnson, Randy	9	10	4.33	23	23	6	0	160	146	90	77	60	213	R	L	6-10	230	9-10-63	1985	Glendale, Ariz.
Lira, Felipe	1	0	4.60	7	0	0	0	16	22	10	8	5	16	R	R	6-1	205	4-26-72	1990	Miranda, Ven.
Lorraine, Andrew	0	0	2.45	4	0	0	0	4	3	1	1	4	0	L	L	6-3	195	8-11-72	1993	Valencia, Calif.
McCarthy, Greg	1	2	5.01	29	0	0	0	23	18	13	13	17	25	L	L	6-2	215	10-30-68	1987	Shelton, Conn.
Moyer, Jamie	15	9	3.53	34	34	4	0	234	234	99	92	42	158	L	L	6-0	170	11-18-62	1984	Granger, Ill.
Paniagua, Jose	2	0	2.05	18	0	0	1	22	15	5	5	5	16	R	R	6-1	160	8-20-73	1991	Santo Domingo, D.R.
Slocumb, Heathcliff	2	5	5.32	57	0	0	3	68	72	40	40	44	51	R	R	6-3	220	6-7-66	1984	Richmond Hills, N.Y.
Spoljaric, Paul	4	6	6.48	53	6	0	0	83	85	67	60	55	89	L	L	6-3	210	9-24-70	1990	Kelowna, B.C.
Suzuki, Mac	1	2	7.18	6	5	0	0	26	34	23	21	15	19	R	R	6-3	195	5-31-75	1992	Kobe, Japan
Swift, Billy	11	9	5.85	29	26	0	0	145	183	103	94	51	77	R	R	6-0	191	10-27-61	1985	Paradise Valley, Ariz.
Timlin, Mike	3	3	2.95	70	0	0	19	79	78	26	26	16	60	R	R	6-4	210	3-10-66	1987	Midland, Texas
Wells, Bob	2	2	6.10	30	0	0	0	52	54	38	35	16	29	R	R	6-0	180	11-1-66	1989	Cowiche, Wash.

FIELDING

Catcher	PCT	G	PO	A	E	DP	PB
Chavez	1.000	1	3	1	0	0	0
Marzano	.997	48	317	24	1	2	5
Oliver	.984	29	174	9	3	0	1
Wilkins	1.000	6	28	2	0	0	0
Wilson	.994	94	677	34	4	6	5

First Base	PCT	G	PO	A	E	DP
Amaral	1.000	7	16	2	0	1
Bell	1.000	5	35	2	0	3
Griffey	.000	1	0	0	0	0
Huson	1.000	7	22	1	0	1
Ibanez	.990	16	93	5	1	12
Martinez	1.000	4	22	6	0	3
McCarty	1.000	2	14	0	0	0
Radmanovich	1.000	1	1	0	0	0
Segui	.999	134	1044	115	1	106
Wilkins	1.000	6	42	2	0	2

Second Base	PCT	G	PO	A	E	DP
Amaral	1.000	11	17	10	0	1
Bell	.984	14	24	39	1	11
Cora	.962	130	212	270	19	68
Guevara	1.000	5	6	9	0	2
Guillen	1.000	10	15	29	0	5
Huson	1.000	8	7	6	0	2
Rossy	1.000	6	1	12	0	1

Third Base	PCT	G	PO	A	E	DP
Amaral	.000	1	0	0	0	0
Bell	1.000	5	2	5	0	0
Davis	.905	137	56	250	32	26
Gipson	.900	4	6	3	1	0
Huson	.800	8	1	7	2	0
Rossy	1.000	25	11	44	0	5

Shortstop	PCT	G	PO	A	E	DP
Guevara	1.000	5	2	4	0	1
Huson	.000	1	0	0	0	0
Rodriguez	.976	160	271	447	18	89
Rossy	1.000	4	3	5	0	0

Outfield	PCT	G	PO	A	E	DP
Amaral	1.000	52	58	2	0	0
Bell	.000	1	0	0	0	0
Buhner	.985	70	127	5	2	2
Cradle	1.000	4	2	0	0	0
Davis	.333	3	1	0	2	0
Ducey	.970	83	126	4	4	1
Gipson	.973	36	34	2	1	1
Griffey	.988	158	408	11	5	2
Hill	.965	71	107	2	4	1
Huson	1.000	1	1	0	0	0
Ibanez	1.000	17	12	1	0	0
McCarty	1.000	5	7	0	0	0
Monahan	.992	62	117	3	1	1
Perez	1.000	17	20	1	0	0
Radmanovich	1.000	24	33	2	0	0
Segui	.000	1	0	0	0	0

JOHN WILLIAMSON

Seattle's Ken Griffey
Tied own club mark with 56 homers

MEL BAILEY

Lancaster's Brendan Kingman
Led organization with .340 average

FARM SYSTEM

Director of Player Development: Benny Looper

Class	Farm Team	League	W	L	Pct.	Finish*	Manager	First Yr
AAA	Tacoma (Wash.) Rainiers	Pacific Coast	77	67	.535	7th (16)	Dave Myers	1995
AA	Orlando (Fla.) Rays	Southern	67	71	.486	5th (10)	Dan Rohn	1997
A#	Lancaster (Calif.) JetHawks	California	78	62	.557	3rd (10)	Rick Burleson	1996
A	Wisconsin Timber Rattlers	Midwest	72	65	.526	5th (14)	Gary Varsho	1993
A	Everett (Wash.) Aquasox	Northwest	34	42	.447	t-5th (8)	Terry Pollreisz	1995
Rookie	Peoria (Ariz.) Mariners	Arizona	31	24	.564	2nd (8)	Darrin Garner	1988

*Finish in overall standings (No. of teams in league) #Advanced level

TACOMA Class AAA

PACIFIC COAST LEAGUE

BATTING	AVG	G	AB	R	H	2B	3B	HR	RBI	BB	SO	SB	CS	B	T	HT	WT	DOB	1st Yr	Resides
Berblinger, Jeff	.238	109	390	48	93	19	2	6	38	22	59	11	7	R	R	6-0	190	11-19-70	1993	Goddard, Kan.
Brito, Tilson	.259	42	143	20	37	12	1	2	12	8	29	0	1	R	R	6-0	180	5-28-72	1990	Santo Domingo, D.R.
Brock, Tarrik	.245	24	94	14	23	2	3	1	14	9	28	5	0	L	L	6-3	170	12-25-73	1991	Hawthorne, Calif.
Brundage, David	.000	1	1	1	0	0	0	0	0	1	0	0	0	L	L	6-3	190	10-6-64	1986	Salem, Ore.
Buhner, Jay	.500	2	4	2	2	2	0	0	2	2	2	0	0	R	R	6-3	210	8-13-64	1984	Issaquah, Wash.
Chavez, Raul	.223	76	233	27	52	6	0	4	34	22	41	1	2	R	R	5-11	175	3-18-73	1990	Valencia, Ven.
Cradle, Rickey	.290	82	297	53	86	25	1	12	53	24	76	9	5	R	R	6-2	180	6-20-73	1991	Cerritos, Calif.
Gipson, Charles	.241	75	278	39	67	16	2	0	11	27	50	14	11	R	R	6-2	180	12-16-72	1992	Orange, Calif.
Guillen, Carlos	.228	24	92	8	21	1	1	1	4	9	17	1	2	B	R	6-1	180	9-30-75	1993	Aragua, Ven.
2-team (100 N.O.)	.279	124	466	75	130	19	5	13	55	40	78	4	6							
Holbert, Aaron	.314	56	229	38	72	12	0	9	31	12	40	6	6	R	R	6-0	160	1-9-73	1990	Torrance, Calif.
Huckaby, Ken	.224	16	49	4	11	2	0	0	1	5	6	0	0	R	R	6-1	205	1-27-71	1991	Philadelphia, Pa.
Ibanez, Raul	.216	52	190	24	41	8	1	6	25	24	47	1	1	L	R	6-2	210	6-2-72	1992	Miami, Fla.
Jorgensen, Randy	.233	81	253	27	59	13	1	3	26	21	42	0	0	L	L	6-2	195	4-3-72	1993	Snohomish, Wash.
Maldonado, Carlos	.000	3	9	0	0	0	0	0	0	0	1	0	0	R	R	6-2	185	1-3-79	1996	Maracaibo, Ven.
McCarty, Dave	.317	108	398	73	126	30	2	11	52	59	85	9	6	R	L	6-5	215	11-23-69	1991	Menlo Park, Calif.
Monahan, Shane	.249	69	277	32	69	8	5	4	33	19	47	6	4	L	R	6-0	195	8-12-74	1995	Marietta, Ga.
Radmanovich, Ryan	.300	110	397	73	119	33	2	15	65	46	83	2	4	L	R	6-2	200	8-9-71	1993	Calgary, Alberta
Rohrmeier, Dan	.286	135	507	93	145	51	2	25	104	59	109	0	4	R	R	6-0	195	1-27-65	1987	Memphis, Tenn.
Rossy, Rico	.286	56	210	33	60	18	0	8	36	26	36	1	1	R	R	5-10	175	2-16-64	1985	Bayamon, P.R.
Sealy, Scot	.270	62	178	18	48	10	0	5	28	17	54	0	2	R	R	6-4	225	2-10-71	1992	Saraland, Ala.
Seitzer, Brad	.300	129	474	74	142	35	1	14	68	68	65	4	3	R	R	6-2	195	2-2-70	1991	Lincoln, Ill.
Simons, Mitch	.233	47	180	27	42	6	2	2	21	15	23	10	1	R	R	5-9	172	12-13-68	1991	Midwest City, Okla.
Underwood, Jake	.000	1	1	0	0	0	0	0	0	0	1	0	0	R	R	6-1	195	8-29-78	1997	Hillsboro, Ore.
Wathan, Dusty	.294	19	51	6	15	1	1	0	8	6	10	0	0	R	R	6-4	215	8-22-73	1994	Blue Springs, Mo.

PITCHING	W	L	ERA	G	GS	CG	SV	IP	H	R	ER	BB	SO	B	T	HT	WT	DOB	1st Yr	Resides
Abbott, Paul	1	0	1.20	3	3	0	0	15	9	2	2	5	20	R	R	6-3	195	9-15-67	1985	Fullerton, Calif.
Berumen, Andres	2	2	6.93	9	8	0	0	38	39	37	29	30	31	R	R	6-2	205	4-5-71	1989	Banning, Calif.
Bonilla, Denny	0	0	11.81	2	0	0	0	5	11	7	7	0	4	L	L	6-1	204	3-15-74	1992	Santo Domingo, D.R.
Bullinger, Jim	8	7	5.05	20	16	0	0	102	106	64	57	58	73	R	R	6-2	190	8-21-65	1986	Sarasota, Fla.
Cloude, Ken	0	1	6.75	1	1	0	0	4	4	3	3	1	4	R	R	6-1	180	1-9-75	1994	Baltimore, Md.
De la Rosa, Maximo	2	1	3.38	9	0	0	0	11	6	4	4	8	4	R	R	5-11	170	7-12-71	1990	Villa Mella, D.R.
Franklin, Ryan	5	6	4.51	34	16	1	1	128	148	75	64	32	90	R	R	6-3	165	3-5-73	1993	Spiro, Okla.
Gajkowski, Steve	3	3	2.57	53	0	0	24	74	60	23	21	20	61	R	R	6-2	200	12-30-69	1990	Olympia, Wash.
Garcia, Freddy	3	1	3.86	5	5	0	0	33	30	14	14	13	30	R	R	6-4	235	10-6-76	1994	Valencia, Ven.
2-team (2 N.O.)	4	1	3.64	7	7	0	0	47	44	19	19	14	43							
Harikkala, Tim	2	3	4.89	18	4	1	1	57	74	32	31	13	44	R	R	6-2	185	7-15-71	1992	Lake Worth, Fla.
Hinchliffe, Brett	10	8	4.00	25	25	2	0	160	132	80	71	88	100	R	R	6-5	190	7-21-74	1992	Detroit, Mich.
Holdridge, David	7	5	3.31	42	0	0	7	71	55	28	26	34	73	R	R	6-3	190	2-5-69	1988	Huntington Beach, Calif.
Juelsgaard, Jarod	5	5	5.60	28	21	0	0	125	131	91	78	73	89	R	R	6-3	195	6-27-68	1991	Elk Horn, Iowa
Kennison, Kyle	0	0	0.00	1	0	0	0	0	0	0	0	0	0	R	R	6-2	220	8-10-72	1996	Glenburn, Maine
Lira, Felipe	6	8	4.26	20	20	2	0	129	142	69	61	42	88	R	R	6-1	205	4-26-72	1990	Miranda, Ven.
Lorraine, Andrew	7	4	4.82	52	4	0	2	80	93	44	43	36	70	L	L	6-3	195	8-11-72	1993	Valencia, Calif.
McCarthy, Greg	1	2	4.19	19	0	0	1	19	15	14	9	22	24	L	L	6-2	215	10-30-68	1987	Shelton, Conn.
Paniagua, Jose	3	1	2.77	44	0	0	5	68	66	25	21	22	61	R	R	6-1	160	8-20-73	1991	Santo Domingo, D.R.
Seelbach, Chris	1	0	6.17	6	0	0	0	12	13	9	8	2	10	R	R	6-4	180	12-18-72	1991	Lufkin, Texas
Spencer, Sean	2	0	4.85	9	0	0	1	13	10	7	7	7	16	L	L	5-11	185	5-29-75	1996	Port Orchard, Wash.
Suzuki, Mac	9	10	4.37	28	21	2	0	132	130	70	64	70	117	R	R	6-3	195	5-31-75	1992	Kobe, Japan

FIELDING

Catcher	PCT	G	PO	A	E	DP	PB
Chavez	.990	74	523	70	6	12	2
Huckaby	1.000	15	90	4	0	0	2
Maldonado	.933	3	14	0	1	0	0
Sealy	.994	47	290	23	2	1	3
Underwood	.000	1	0	0	0	0	0
Wathan	.993	19	134	15	1	1	1

First Base	PCT	G	PO	A	E	DP
Huckaby	1.000	1	1	0	0	0
Jorgensen	.995	69	536	48	3	65
McCarty	.997	41	305	25	1	41
Rohrmeier	.989	41	319	40	4	45
Sealy	1.000	1	3	0	0	0
Seitzer	1.000	2	11	1	0	2

Second Base	PCT	G	PO	A	E	DP
Berblinger	.953	57	103	163	13	30
Brito	.957	23	45	67	5	25
Gipson	.964	11	26	27	2	12
Guillen	.982	24	49	63	2	16
Holbert	.966	17	37	49	3	12
Rossy	1.000	3	4	10	0	3
Seitzer	1.000	2	2	7	0	1
Simons	.969	15	26	37	2	8

Third Base	PCT	G	PO	A	E	DP
Berblinger	.842	22	18	30	9	2
Gipson	.955	11	5	16	1	2
Sealy	.000	2	0	0	0	0
Seitzer	.915	115	67	214	26	24

Shortstop	PCT	G	PO	A	E	DP
Brito	.891	18	43	55	12	21
Gipson	.947	15	29	42	4	11
Holbert	.939	36	68	100	11	26
Rossy	.950	51	90	138	12	43
Simons	.934	28	42	71	8	15

Outfield	PCT	G	PO	A	E	DP
Berblinger	.000	3	0	0	0	0
Brock	1.000	24	59	1	0	0
Buhner	.000	1	0	0	0	0
Cradle	1.000	73	143	5	0	2
Gipson	.955	40	82	3	4	2
Ibanez	.988	42	78	2	1	0
McCarty	.992	62	125	7	1	1
Monahan	.993	64	141	1	1	0
Radmanovich	.982	97	164	4	3	1
Rohrmeier	.952	40	58	1	3	0
Simons	1.000	1	2	0	0	0

ORLANDO — Class AA

SOUTHERN LEAGUE

BATTING	AVG	G	AB	R	H	2B	3B	HR	RBI	BB	SO	SB	CS	B	T	HT	WT	DOB	1st Yr	Resides
*Alcantara, Israel	.236	15	55	8	13	4	0	3	18	7	15	0	1	R	R	6-2	165	5-6-73	1991	Santo Domingo, D.R.
Brock, Tarrik	.277	111	372	76	103	28	7	15	65	59	110	17	9	L	L	6-3	170	12-25-73	1991	Hawthorne, Calif.
Buhner, Shawn	.241	99	348	48	84	14	2	10	49	47	98	1	3	R	R	6-2	200	8-29-72	1994	League City, Texas
Clifford, Jim	.000	1	1	0	0	0	0	0	0	0	0	0	0	L	L	6-2	225	3-23-70	1992	Seattle, Wash.
Dean, Chris	.197	62	203	26	40	12	1	2	22	32	39	3	3	B	R	5-10	178	1-3-74	1994	Hayward, Calif.
*Donato, Dan	.333	4	12	1	4	0	0	0	1	3	1	0	0	L	R	6-1	205	11-15-72	1995	Dedham, Mass.
Guevara, Giomar	.333	14	45	13	15	5	1	0	6	8	11	0	0	R	R	5-8	150	10-23-72	1991	Guarenas, Ven.
Harrison, Adonis	.230	58	191	35	44	6	2	3	21	30	30	6	4	L	R	5-9	165	9-28-76	1995	Pasadena, Calif.
*Hawkins, Kraig	.283	51	184	37	52	3	2	0	13	39	31	12	5	R	R	6-2	170	12-4-71	1992	Lake Charles, La.
Hazlett, Steve	.173	32	110	13	19	5	2	3	19	16	42	0	1	R	R	5-11	200	3-30-70	1991	Longmont, Colo.
2-team (34 Mobile)	.199	66	206	29	41	12	5	4	28	31	66	0	2							
Hills, Rich	.236	124	440	54	104	19	0	3	51	56	66	1	2	R	R	6-0	195	7-28-73	1995	Springdale, Ark.
Holbert, Aaron	.287	68	251	46	72	13	5	3	34	22	41	10	14	R	R	6-0	160	1-9-73	1990	Torrance, Calif.
Horner, Jim	.219	73	247	29	54	9	1	9	36	33	59	2	1	R	R	6-0	210	11-11-73	1996	Twin Falls, Idaho
Jorgensen, Randy	.385	7	26	4	10	3	0	0	10	4	3	0	0	L	L	6-2	195	4-3-72	1993	Snohomish, Wash.
Mathis, Joe	.251	104	395	49	99	18	5	4	41	27	84	12	11	L	R	5-11	180	8-10-74	1993	Johnston, S.C.
*Mendoza, Carlos	.338	35	139	27	47	3	3	1	19	19	18	16	2	L	L	5-11	160	11-4-74	1994	Bolivar, Ven.
Ramirez, Joel	.258	20	62	7	16	3	0	0	8	4	8	0	0	R	R	5-10	155	8-17-73	1994	Miami, Fla.
*Robinson, Kerry	.269	72	309	45	83	7	5	2	26	27	28	28	9	L	L	6-0	175	10-3-73	1994	St. Louis, Mo.
Rodriguez, Tony	.220	13	41	5	9	0	0	0	3	3	6	0	0	R	R	5-11	165	8-15-70	1991	Cidra, P.R.
Steinmann, Scott	.173	18	52	7	9	2	0	0	2	7	12	0	1	L	R	6-2	185	7-17-73	1996	Cincinnati, Ohio
Thompson, Karl	.125	2	8	1	1	0	0	0	0	1	2	0	0	R	R	6-0	180	12-30-73	1995	Diamond Bar, Calif.
Tinoco, Luis	.267	20	75	9	20	3	0	1	12	11	8	0	0	R	R	6-2	215	7-24-74	1992	Maracaibo, Ven.
Torres, Paul	.276	123	457	57	126	19	2	12	73	67	63	3	3	R	R	6-3	210	10-19-70	1989	San Lorenzo, Calif.
Wathan, Dusty	.256	69	234	32	60	10	0	2	21	28	39	3	1	R	R	6-4	215	8-22-73	1994	Blue Springs, Mo.
*Wilcox, Luke	.287	88	331	57	95	23	3	17	69	39	54	2	3	L	R	6-4	190	11-15-73	1995	St. Johns, Mich.
Wilson, Todd	.203	18	64	5	13	4	0	0	7	6	15	0	0	R	R	6-3	210	11-20-71	1994	San Diego, Calif.

PITCHING	W	L	ERA	G	GS	CG	SV	IP	H	R	ER	BB	SO	B	T	HT	WT	DOB	1st Yr	Resides
Bonilla, Denny	2	3	5.06	37	0	0	0	69	81	44	39	34	66	L	L	6-1	204	3-15-74	1992	Santo Domingo, D.R.
*Callaway, Mickey	5	6	4.42	18	17	0	0	90	103	56	44	44	57	R	R	6-2	190	5-13-75	1996	Germantown, Tenn.
Carmona, Rafael	0	3	14.29	4	4	0	0	11	18	18	18	6	11	L	R	6-2	185	10-2-72	1993	Comerio, P.R.
Chrysler, Clint	0	0	3.86	3	0	0	0	5	4	2	2	1	6	L	L	6-0	191	11-4-75	1997	St. Petersburg, Fla.
*Daniels, John	1	2	5.30	11	0	0	0	19	14	12	11	9	19	B	R	6-3	185	2-7-74	1993	Little Chute, Wis.
Davis, Tim	1	1	2.45	14	5	0	1	22	18	9	6	4	19	L	L	5-11	165	7-14-70	1992	Bristol, Fla.
De la Rosa, Maximo	6	4	3.03	42	0	0	8	62	47	23	21	24	51	R	R	5-11	170	7-12-71	1990	Villa Mella, D.R.
Delgado, Danny	0	0	0.00	1	0	0	0	1	0	0	0	0	0	R	R	6-2	180	2-10-78	1997	Miami Lakes, Fla.
Dunham, Pat	2	6	4.95	10	9	0	0	56	52	33	31	32	34	R	R	6-5	200	3-16-76	1997	Portage, Mich.

PITCHING	W	L	ERA	G	GS	CG	SV	IP	H	R	ER	BB	SO	B	T	HT	WT	DOB	1st Yr	Resides
Fitzgerald, Brian	0	0	2.08	2	0	0	1	4	5	1	1	1	4	L	L	5-11	175	12-26-74	1996	Lake Ridge, Va.
Gryboski, Kevin	0	0	9.00	2	0	0	0	5	8	5	5	1	4	R	R	6-5	240	11-15-73	1995	Plains, Pa.
Harikkala, Tim	5	7	4.53	15	15	3	0	103	112	56	52	14	55	R	R	6-2	185	7-15-71	1992	Lake Worth, Fla.
Janicki, Pete	0	1	10.80	12	0	0	0	18	24	24	22	12	13	R	R	6-4	190	1-26-71	1992	Mesa, Ariz.
*Kaufman, John	0	6	[illegible]	7	6	0	0	31	34	25	19	9	17	L	L	5-10	170	10-20-74	1996	Tampa, Fla.
Kelly, John	1	4	5.23	9	8	0	0	41	51	29	24	18	32	R	R	6-0	180	12-13-72	1994	Melbourne, Fla.
*LeRoy, John	1	0	6.45	12	0	0	0	22	22	17	16	10	12	R	R	6-3	175	4-19-75	1993	Bellevue, Wash.
Luce, Robert	12	7	5.09	27	26	1	0	168	218	103	95	49	73	B	R	6-0	168	7-19-74	1996	Rescue, Calif.
*Manon, Julio	0	2	6.10	13	0	0	0	21	22	19	14	9	22	R	R	6-1	183	7-10-73	1992	Boca Chica, D.R.
Marte, Damaso	7	6	5.27	22	20	0	0	121	136	82	71	47	99	L	L	6-0	170	2-14-75	1993	San Carlos, D.R.
Mears, Chris	0	1	9.64	1	1	0	0	5	8	5	5	2	4	R	R	6-4	180	1-20-78	1996	Victoria, B.C.
Montane, Ivan	0	0	11.57	2	0	0	0	2	3	3	3	2	0	R	R	6-2	195	6-3-73	1992	Miami, Fla.
Newton, Geronimo	4	1	5.53	21	1	0	0	41	45	27	25	22	28	L	L	6-0	165	12-31-73	1992	Christiansted, St. Croix
*Nunez, Maximo	2	0	0.77	6	0	0	2	12	5	1	1	4	14	R	R	6-5	165	1-15-73	1991	Villa Mella, D.R.
Pineiro, Joel	1	0	5.40	1	1	0	0	5	7	4	3	2	2	R	R	6-1	180	9-25-78	1997	Orlando, Fla.
Scheffer, Aaron	1	0	2.20	19	0	0	5	33	23	8	8	13	33	L	R	6-2	165	8-15-75	1994	Westland, Mich.
Seelbach, Chris	8	3	4.03	23	21	0	0	116	103	63	52	52	106	R	R	6-4	180	12-18-72	1991	Lufkin, Texas
Smith, Cam	1	3	4.62	23	1	0	0	39	32	27	20	32	49	R	R	6-3	190	9-20-73	1993	Selkirk, N.Y.
Spencer, Sean	2	1	2.95	37	0	0	18	43	33	18	14	18	43	L	L	5-11	185	5-29-75	1996	Port Orchard, Wash.
Thompson, John	3	4	6.87	19	3	0	0	38	43	31	29	20	11	R	R	6-2	215	1-18-73	1992	Spokane, Wash.
Westfall, Allan	2	1	6.88	8	0	0	0	17	19	13	13	16	13	R	R	5-11	195	5-15-75	1996	Deltona, Fla.

*Loaned from Tampa Bay Devil Rays.

FIELDING

Catcher	PCT	G	PO	A	E	DP	PB
Horner	.989	71	515	45	6	6	14
Steinmann	1.000	16	89	9	0	1	5
Thompson	1.000	2	8	2	0	0	0
Wathan	.997	55	331	21	1	2	4

First Base	PCT	G	PO	A	E	DP
Alcantara	1.000	3	17	3	0	1
Buhner	.990	72	646	35	7	64
Donato	.000	1	0	0	0	0
Jorgensen	.956	5	42	1	2	4
Mathis	1.000	1	1	0	0	0
Steinmann	.000	1	0	0	0	0
Torres	.981	44	351	17	7	25
Wathan	1.000	14	104	12	0	12
Wilson	1.000	7	34	7	0	6

Second Base	PCT	G	PO	A	E	DP
Dean	.964	61	115	176	11	38
Guevara	1.000	2	5	8	0	6
Harrison	.960	58	95	147	10	35
Hazlett	1.000	2	0	4	0	1
Hills	.960	10	15	9	1	3
Holbert	1.000	7	19	21	0	9
Ramirez	.909	4	5	5	1	0
Rodriguez	.964	7	9	18	1	3

Third Base	PCT	G	PO	A	E	DP
Alcantara	.750	1	2	1	1	0
Donato	.818	2	3	6	2	0
Hazlett	.571	3	1	3	3	0
Hills	.956	71	41	133	8	8
Steinmann	.000	1	0	0	0	0
Torres	.920	65	50	123	15	15
Wilson	.950	8	4	15	1	0

Shortstop	PCT	G	PO	A	E	DP
Guevara	.911	13	14	37	5	6
Hills	.925	50	65	133	16	30
Holbert	.965	62	95	178	10	35
Ramirez	.928	17	19	45	5	5
Rodriguez	.917	7	9	13	2	2
Torres	1.000	1	1	3	0	0

Outfield	PCT	G	PO	A	E	DP
Alcantara	1.000	2	3	0	0	0
Brock	.989	95	173	11	2	3
Hawkins	.972	47	98	5	3	0
Hazlett	1.000	16	29	2	0	0
Hills	1.000	3	4	0	0	0
Mathis	.991	93	216	5	2	2
Mendoza	.964	25	53	1	2	0
Robinson	1.000	63	135	5	0	1
Tinoco	1.000	15	23	2	0	0
Wilcox	.987	70	141	10	2	1

LANCASTER — Class A

CALIFORNIA LEAGUE

BATTING	AVG	G	AB	R	H	2B	3B	HR	RBI	BB	SO	SB	CS	B	T	HT	WT	DOB	1st Yr	Resides
Bass, Jayson	.288	110	392	80	113	26	6	21	84	40	102	31	12	L	L	6-3	220	6-22-74	1993	Seattle, Wash.
Burrows, Mike	.162	27	74	7	12	1	0	0	5	11	22	4	4	L	L	6-4	180	1-19-76	1994	American Fork, Utah
Connors, Greg	.287	27	101	17	29	11	1	6	26	3	16	0	0	R	R	6-2	185	8-22-74	1996	Smithtown, N.Y.
Cruz, Cirilo	.311	134	546	86	170	40	1	7	104	56	122	2	2	R	R	6-0	185	5-29-75	1995	Arroyo, P.R.
Dean, Chris	.256	46	168	33	43	15	2	4	26	14	28	14	4	B	R	5-10	178	1-3-74	1994	Hayward, Calif.
Espino, Fernando	.317	17	41	5	13	3	2	0	10	5	10	1	1	R	R	6-0	200	11-26-76	1994	La Vega, D.R.
French, Anton	.268	106	380	77	102	11	8	5	42	33	72	41	8	B	R	5-11	175	7-25-75	1993	St. Louis, Mo.
Guevara, Giomar	.246	19	61	15	15	4	0	0	3	14	20	1	1	R	R	5-8	150	10-23-72	1991	Guarenas, Ven.
Harrison, Adonis	.337	69	258	63	87	21	4	2	35	49	48	24	14	L	R	5-9	165	9-28-76	1995	Pasadena, Calif.
Haynes, Larry	.111	5	9	1	1	1	0	0	2	0	1	0	0	R	R	5-11	180	8-31-77	1997	West Covina, Calif.
Kingman, Brendan	.340	112	456	91	155	30	3	16	78	40	55	6	7	R	R	6-1	195	5-22-73	1992	Georges Hall, Australia
Moore, Mike	.206	19	63	12	13	3	1	3	11	5	27	0	1	R	R	6-4	200	3-7-71	1992	Beverly Hills, Calif.
Ramirez, Joel	.255	53	184	34	47	9	0	4	31	16	23	8	2	R	R	5-10	155	8-17-73	1994	Miami, Fla.
Regan, Jason	.298	124	416	105	124	26	6	19	82	106	123	9	3	R	R	5-9	165	6-30-76	1996	Belton, Texas
Sachse, Matt	.267	86	285	51	76	16	4	8	45	41	77	4	4	L	L	6-4	205	6-29-76	1995	Spokane, Wash.
Santiesteban, Francisco	.240	46	146	22	35	5	2	4	21	21	25	4	3	R	R	6-3	215	8-9-75	1998	San Jose, Costa Rica
Sturdivant, Marcus	.262	29	107	19	28	8	3	0	9	8	13	8	3	L	L	5-10	150	10-29-73	1992	Oakboro, N.C.
Thompson, Karl	.263	90	315	53	83	17	4	6	47	25	75	3	3	R	R	6-0	180	12-30-73	1995	Diamond Bar, Calif.
Tinoco, Luis	.284	108	412	61	117	20	6	6	69	38	79	5	1	R	R	6-2	215	7-24-74	1992	Maracaibo, Ven.
Vazquez, Ramon	.276	121	468	77	129	26	4	2	72	81	66	15	11	L	R	5-11	180	8-21-76	1995	Cayey, P.R.

GAMES BY POSITION: C—Connors 10, Kingman 10, Santiesteban 42, Thompson 90. **1B**—Connors 7, Cruz 87, Dean 3, Kingman 53, Ramirez 1, Sachse 1. **2B**—Dean 43, Guevara 14, Harrison 67, Ramirez 30, Regan 2. **3B**—Connors 2, Guevara 2, Kingman 24, Ramirez 2, Regan 116. **SS**—Guevara 4, Ramirez 17, Vazquez 121. **OF**—Bass 74, Burrows 25, Connors 5, Espino 15, French 91, Haynes 4, Kingman 15, Moore 16, Sachse 78, Sturdivant 27, Tinoco 96.

PITCHING	W	L	ERA	G	GS	CG	SV	IP	H	R	ER	BB	SO	B	T	HT	WT	DOB	1st Yr	Resides
Ayala, Julio	10	7	4.45	25	25	1	0	140	166	91	69	44	129	L	L	6-3	203	4-20-75	1996	Guaynabo, P.R.
Bond, Jason	7	3	4.46	20	16	1	0	81	87	53	40	38	95	L	L	5-11	175	11-11-74	1996	Scottsdale, Ariz.
Carmona, Rafael	0	1	6.23	4	4	0	0	13	12	10	9	5	11	L	R	6-2	185	10-2-72	1993	Comerio, P.R.
Derenches, Albert	0	0	2.45	9	0	0	0	18	11	5	5	12	18	B	L	6-3	190	8-17-76	1995	Tampa, Fla.
Dunham, Pat	9	5	3.46	17	17	0	0	104	97	48	40	41	88	R	R	6-5	200	3-16-76	1997	Portage, Mich.
Fitzgerald, Brian	1	2	4.20	41	0	0	1	71	79	39	33	24	48	L	L	5-11	175	12-26-74	1996	Lake Ridge, Va.
Fuentes, Brian	7	7	4.17	24	22	0	0	119	121	73	55	81	137	L	L	6-4	220	8-9-75	1996	Merced, Calif.
Gonzalez, Jose	2	0	4.24	8	1	0	0	17	17	9	8	9	17	R	R	6-0	200	3-4-77	1994	Maracaibo, Ven.
Gryboski, Kevin	5	5	2.65	37	3	0	8	85	75	35	25	31	73	R	R	6-5	240	11-15-73	1995	Plains, Pa.
Gulin, Lindsay	2	2	5.84	9	3	0	0	25	32	17	16	15	18	L	L	6-3	165	11-22-76	1995	Issaquah, Wash.
Hinchliffe, Brett	1	1	1.59	3	3	0	0	17	8	5	3	5	26	R	R	6-5	190	7-21-74	1992	Detroit, Mich.

PITCHING	W	L	ERA	G	GS	CG	SV	IP	H	R	ER	BB	SO	B	T	HT	WT	DOB	1st Yr	Resides
Janicki, Pete	2	3	8.83	15	3	0	2	35	40	34	34	14	36	R	R	6-4	190	1-26-71	1992	Mesa, Ariz.
Kaye, Justin	1	2	6.82	16	0	0	0	30	37	24	23	13	34	R	R	6-4	185	6-9-76	1995	Las Vegas, Nev.
Kelly, John	4	4	5.45	23	6	0	1	69	73	46	42	20	60	R	R	6-0	180	12-13-72	1994	Melbourne, Fla.
Kennison, Kyle	2	1	7.11	15	0	0	2	25	34	21	20	19	14	R	R	6-2	220	8-10-72	1996	Glenburn, Maine
Koehler, Russ	1	3	7.06	10	0	0	0	22	29	17	17	11	21	R	R	6-5	215	10-5-74	1995	Medford, Ore.
Mateo, Julio	0	0	6.75	1	0	0	0	1	1	1	1	1	1	R	R	6-0	190	8-22-79	1996	Bani, D.R.
Newton, Geronimo	3	0	3.13	19	0	0	2	32	30	15	11	21	30	L	L	6-0	165	12-31-73	1992	Christiansted, St. Croix
Pineiro, Joel	2	0	7.80	9	9	1	0	45	58	40	39	22	48	R	R	6-1	180	9-25-78	1997	Orlando, Fla.
Scheffer, Aaron	2	2	3.14	25	0	0	10	43	46	19	15	12	65	L	R	6-2	165	8-15-75	1994	Westland, Mich.
Smith, Cam	1	1	2.50	8	0	0	2	18	11	7	5	13	32	R	R	6-3	190	9-20-73	1993	Selkirk, N.Y.
Stark, Denny	1	2	4.29	5	5	0	0	21	18	12	10	17	21	R	R	6-2	210	10-27-74	1996	Edgerton, Ohio
Sweeney, Brian	6	0	3.63	17	4	0	0	52	41	26	21	21	48	R	R	6-2	195	6-13-74	1996	Yonkers, N.Y.
Thompson, John	3	5	7.09	10	10	0	0	47	61	45	37	20	26	R	R	6-2	215	1-18-73	1992	Spokane, Wash.
Westfall, Allan	4	3	3.12	37	0	0	5	52	39	21	18	28	55	R	R	5-11	195	5-15-75	1996	Deltona, Fla.
Wooten, Greg	2	2	7.18	6	6	0	0	31	43	26	25	12	22	R	R	6-7	210	3-30-74	1996	Eugene, Ore.
Zimmerman, Jordan	0	1	4.86	3	3	0	0	17	21	9	9	8	8	R	L	6-0	200	4-28-75	1995	Brenham, Texas

WISCONSIN — Class A

MIDWEST LEAGUE

BATTING	AVG	G	AB	R	H	2B	3B	HR	RBI	BB	SO	SB	CS	B	T	HT	WT	DOB	1st Yr	Resides
Clark, Jermaine	.324	123	448	81	145	24	13	6	55	57	64	40	14	L	R	5-10	175	9-29-76	1997	Vacaville, Calif.
Connors, Greg	.283	94	364	45	103	31	3	12	57	22	95	8	8	R	R	6-2	185	8-22-74	1996	Smithtown, N.Y.
Eady, Gerald	.170	80	235	28	40	7	5	4	23	22	101	13	4	R	R	6-2	200	10-25-75	1996	Jacksonville, Fla.
Espino, Fernando	.201	49	159	16	32	4	0	1	12	17	35	3	3	R	R	6-0	200	11-26-76	1994	La Vega, D.R.
Figueroa, Luis	.291	96	306	41	89	18	0	1	48	42	18	7	1	R	R	6-0	175	3-2-77	1995	Carolina, P.R.
Hargrove, Harvey	.241	121	449	68	108	26	7	15	62	45	118	21	7	R	R	5-11	175	10-9-75	1997	Upper Marlboro, Md.
Haynes, Larry	.231	5	13	4	3	0	0	0	0	1	2	1	0	R	R	5-11	180	8-31-77	1997	West Covina, Calif.
Johnson, Duan	.214	32	112	15	24	3	0	2	12	14	18	3	2	R	R	6-1	190	2-23-76	1995	St. Pauls, N.C.
Liverziani, Claudio	.248	106	355	43	88	20	4	3	33	30	67	16	3	L	R	6-0	185	3-4-75	1996	Novara, Italy
Lopez, Rafael	.223	35	121	11	27	5	1	1	12	9	18	0	0	R	R	6-0	195	10-22-76	1996	Miami, Fla.
Maldonado, Carlos	.174	7	23	4	4	0	0	0	1	2	1	0	0	R	R	6-2	185	1-3-79	1996	Maracaibo, Ven.
Marchiano, Mike	.288	117	444	62	128	29	3	14	74	47	72	13	5	R	R	6-0	190	2-3-75	1997	Oak Ridge, N.J.
Martinez, Victor	.136	5	22	2	3	0	0	0	2	0	5	1	0	R	R	5-11	180	3-12-78	1996	Santo Domingo, D.R.
Maynard, Scott	.174	81	236	29	41	8	1	2	17	30	70	4	4	R	R	6-2	215	8-28-77	1995	Laguna Niguel, Calif.
Moreno, Jose	.240	84	262	36	63	10	3	2	26	19	36	5	6	R	R	5-11	158	8-9-77	1995	San Pedro de Macoris, D.R.
Silvestre, Juan	.252	106	401	44	101	20	5	15	56	22	98	7	2	R	R	5-11	180	1-10-78	1994	San Pedro de Macoris, D.R.
Valera, Ramon	.298	119	423	75	126	18	4	4	40	46	94	52	19	B	R	5-11	160	8-21-75	1994	Haina, D.R.
Williams, Patrick	.240	71	229	35	55	8	0	11	36	17	78	5	1	R	R	6-3	210	10-3-77	1996	Nacogdoches, Texas

GAMES BY POSITION: C—Connors 29, Johnson 3, Lopez 31, Maldonado 7, Maynard 77, Williams 13. **1B**—Connors 26, Johnson 16, Liverziani 94, Maynard 4, Williams 17. **2B**—Clark 116, Connors 3, Figueroa 1, Martinez 1, Moreno 1, Valera 26. **3B**—Connors 23, Figueroa 88, Hargrove 6, Johnson 1, Lopez 3, Martinez 3, Maynard 1, Moreno 4, Valera 31. **SS**—Connors 1, Figueroa 1, Martinez 2, Moreno 76, Valera 68. **OF**—Clark 2, Connors 22, Eady 76, Espino 42, Hargrove 116, Haynes 4, Liverziani 1, Marchiano 103, Silvestre 70.

PITCHING	W	L	ERA	G	GS	CG	SV	IP	H	R	ER	BB	SO	B	T	HT	WT	DOB	1st Yr	Resides
Anderson, Ryan	6	5	3.23	22	22	0	0	111	86	47	40	67	152	L	L	6-10	215	7-12-79	1997	Westland, Mich.
Bello, Emerson	6	3	3.28	43	0	0	4	82	73	39	30	35	78	R	R	6-0	180	10-4-77	1995	Maracaibo, Ven.
Bienlasz, Derek	2	1	5.25	5	4	0	0	24	32	16	14	2	21	R	R	6-4	175	4-19-74	1993	Toronto, Ontario
Brea, Lesli	3	4	2.76	49	0	0	12	59	47	26	18	40	86	R	R	5-11	170	10-12-78	1996	Santo Domingo, D.R.
Chrysler, Clint	0	2	5.33	17	0	0	1	27	33	19	16	9	30	L	L	6-0	191	11-4-75	1997	St. Petersburg, Fla.
Derenches, Albert	1	2	6.07	17	0	0	2	30	38	24	20	13	29	B	L	6-3	190	8-17-76	1995	Tampa, Fla.
Gonzalez, Jose	7	4	4.52	26	3	0	0	62	68	34	31	27	68	R	R	6-0	200	3-4-77	1994	Maracaibo, Ven.
Gulin, Lindsay	1	3	3.72	13	8	0	1	48	47	24	20	20	51	L	L	6-3	165	11-22-76	1995	Issaquah, Wash.
Kaye, Justin	6	2	1.71	28	0	0	9	47	25	11	9	30	79	R	R	6-4	185	6-9-76	1995	Las Vegas, Nev.
Koehler, Russ	1	6	4.79	17	10	0	0	73	85	45	39	23	49	R	R	6-5	215	10-5-74	1995	Medford, Ore.
Meche, Gil	8	7	3.44	26	26	0	0	149	136	77	57	63	168	R	R	6-3	180	9-8-78	1996	Scott, La.
Parker, Brandon	7	6	5.22	27	26	0	0	128	121	82	74	79	152	R	R	6-1	200	12-9-75	1997	Long Beach, Miss.
Pineiro, Joel	8	4	3.19	16	16	1	0	96	92	40	34	28	84	R	R	6-1	180	9-25-78	1997	Orlando, Fla.
Schmidt, Donnie	3	4	4.33	42	0	0	4	69	67	39	33	33	52	R	R	6-1	175	2-18-75	1996	Sherwood, Ore.
Simpson, Allan	3	5	4.44	19	19	0	0	93	89	52	46	61	86	R	R	6-4	185	8-26-77	1997	Las Vegas, Nev.
Stark, Zac	6	4	4.31	44	2	0	1	77	79	43	37	37	71	R	L	6-6	205	8-7-74	1994	Leawood, Kan.
Ulloa, Enmanuel	0	0	1.80	3	0	0	0	5	4	1	1	1	5	R	R	6-2	170	11-26-78	1997	New York, N.Y.
Wells, Bob	0	1	3.00	1	1	0	0	3	4	2	1	0	2	R	R	6-0	180	11-1-66	1989	Cowiche, Wash.
Willis, Craig	4	2	2.91	13	0	0	0	22	20	13	7	8	11	R	R	6-3	195	7-8-76	1998	Ferndale, Wash.

EVERETT — Short-Season Class A

NORTHWEST LEAGUE

BATTING	AVG	G	AB	R	H	2B	3B	HR	RBI	BB	SO	SB	CS	B	T	HT	WT	DOB	1st Yr	Resides
Alcala, Juan	.163	29	104	6	17	2	1	1	7	5	25	1	1	R	R	6-2	160	4-15-78	1995	San Pedro de Macoris, D.R.
Carroll, Mark	.000	1	3	0	0	0	0	0	0	0	0	0	0	R	R	6-0	185	10-19-78	1996	Athens, N.Y.
Haynes, Larry	.241	67	241	36	58	12	1	10	41	9	69	15	3	R	R	5-11	180	8-31-77	1997	West Covina, Calif.
Kuzmic, Craig	.280	54	186	36	52	14	2	9	47	33	55	3	1	B	R	6-0	185	5-2-77	1998	Fountain Valley, Calif.
Maldonado, Carlos	.287	42	150	19	43	10	0	5	24	10	17	1	0	R	R	6-2	185	1-3-79	1996	Maracaibo, Ven.
Martinez, Victor	.344	67	288	60	99	13	2	5	32	28	48	21	8	R	R	5-11	180	3-12-78	1996	Santo Domingo, D.R.
McCorkle, Shawn	.265	47	162	27	43	6	0	7	37	24	46	1	0	L	R	6-5	230	7-14-77	1998	Newton, N.J.
Pacheco, Domingo	.262	35	107	16	28	3	0	1	12	8	24	6	0	B	R	6-1	165	11-8-78	1996	Santo Domingo, D.R.
Parker, Hubert	.187	69	214	33	40	7	1	0	13	42	60	14	6	B	R	5-10	170	6-14-79	1997	Rialto, Calif.
Robinson, Brian	.270	60	204	33	55	14	1	4	27	24	34	1	0	R	R	6-2	195	8-21-75	1998	Charlotte, N.C.
Southall, Rick	.290	67	248	40	72	19	1	8	47	39	82	0	1	L	R	6-3	225	2-9-77	1998	Beaverton, Ore.
Underwood, Jake	.200	15	40	2	8	4	0	0	3	0	11	0	0	R	R	6-1	195	8-29-78	1997	Hillsboro, Ore.
Weber, Jake	.338	75	275	75	93	20	2	11	52	67	42	14	7	L	L	5-11	188	4-22-76	1998	Wappingers Falls, N.Y.
Williams, P.J.	.220	36	141	24	31	8	3	0	4	18	35	12	6	R	R	6-2	165	5-7-77	1997	Rockdale, Texas
Woodward, Matt	.145	36	110	6	16	1	0	0	2	8	35	0	1	R	R	6-2	192	12-1-75	1998	Kirkland, Wash.

Tampa Bay DEVIL RAYS

Manager: Larry Rothschild

1998 Record: 63-99, .389 (5th, AL East)

BATTING	AVG	G	AB	R	H	2B	3B	HR	RBI	BB	SO	SB	CS	B	T	HT	WT	DOB	1st Yr	Resides
Boggs, Wade	.280	123	435	51	122	23	4	7	52	46	54	3	2	L	R	6-2	197	6-15-58	1976	Tampa, Fla.
Butler, Rich	.226	72	217	25	49	3	3	7	20	15	37	4	2	L	R	6-1	180	5-1-73	1991	East York, Ontario
Cairo, Miguel	.268	150	515	49	138	26	5	5	46	24	44	19	8	R	R	6-1	190	5-4-74	1991	Anaco, Ven.
Difelice, Mike	.230	84	248	17	57	12	3	3	23	15	56	0	0	R	R	6-2	205	5-28-69	1991	Knoxville, Tenn.
Flaherty, John	.207	91	304	21	63	11	0	3	24	22	46	0	5	R	R	6-1	202	10-21-67	1988	West Nyack, N.Y.
Kelly, Mike	.240	106	279	39	67	11	2	10	33	22	80	13	6	R	R	6-4	195	6-2-70	1991	Los Alamitos, Calif.
Laker, Tim	.200	3	5	1	1	0	0	0	0	1	1	0	1	R	R	6-2	175	11-27-69	1988	Simi Valley, Calif.
Ledesma, Aaron	.324	95	299	30	97	16	3	0	29	9	51	9	7	R	R	6-2	200	6-3-71	1990	Union City, Calif.
Martinez, Dave	.256	90	309	31	79	11	0	3	20	35	52	8	7	L	L	5-10	175	9-26-64	1983	Safety Harbor, Fla.
McClain, Scott	.100	9	20	2	2	0	0	0	0	2	6	0	0	R	R	6-3	209	5-19-72	1990	Glendale, Ariz.
McCracken, Quinton	.292	155	614	76	179	38	7	7	59	41	107	19	10	B	R	5-8	170	3-16-70	1992	Southport, N.C.
McGriff, Fred	.284	151	564	73	160	33	0	19	81	79	118	7	2	L	L	6-3	215	10-31-63	1981	Tampa, Fla.
Robinson, Kerry	.000	2	3	0	0	0	0	0	0	0	1	0	0	L	L	6-0	175	10-3-73	1994	St. Louis, Mo.
Silvestri, Dave	.071	8	14	0	1	0	0	0	0	0	2	0	0	R	R	6-0	180	9-29-67	1989	St. Louis, Mo.
Smith, Bobby	.276	117	370	44	102	15	3	11	55	34	110	5	3	R	R	6-3	190	4-10-74	1992	Oakland, Calif.
Sorrento, Paul	.225	137	435	40	98	27	0	17	57	54	133	2	3	L	R	6-2	220	11-17-65	1986	Peabody, Mass.
Stocker, Kevin	.208	112	336	37	70	11	3	6	25	27	80	5	3	B	R	6-1	175	2-13-70	1991	Spokane, Wash.
Trammell, Bubba	.286	59	199	28	57	18	1	12	35	16	45	0	2	R	R	6-2	205	11-6-71	1994	Knoxville, Tenn.
Walton, Jerome	.324	12	34	4	11	3	0	0	3	2	6	0	0	R	R	6-1	175	7-8-65	1986	Fairburn, Ga.
Winn, Randy	.278	109	338	51	94	9	9	1	17	29	69	26	12	B	R	6-2	175	6-9-74	1995	Danville, Calif.

PITCHING	W	L	ERA	G	GS	CG	SV	IP	H	R	ER	BB	SO	B	T	HT	WT	DOB	1st Yr	Resides
Aldred, Scott	0	0	3.73	48	0	0	0	31	33	13	13	12	21	L	L	6-4	195	6-12-68	1987	Lakeland, Fla.
Alvarez, Wilson	6	14	4.73	25	25	0	0	143	130	78	75	68	107	L	L	6-1	235	3-24-70	1987	Maracaibo, Ven.
Arrojo, Rolando	14	12	3.56	32	32	2	0	202	195	84	80	65	152	R	R	6-4	210	7-18-68	1997	San Jose, Costa Rica
Carlson, Dan	0	0	7.64	10	0	0	0	18	25	15	15	8	16	R	R	6-1	185	1-26-70	1990	Portland, Ore.
Duvall, Mike	0	0	6.75	3	0	0	0	4	4	3	3	2	1	R	L	6-0	185	10-11-74	1995	Morgantown, W.Va.
Eiland, Dave	0	1	20.25	1	1	0	0	3	6	6	6	3	1	R	R	6-3	205	7-5-66	1987	Dade City, Fla.
Gaillard, Eddie	0	0	5.87	6	0	0	0	8	4	5	5	3	5	R	R	6-1	200	8-13-70	1993	Denver, Colo.
Gorecki, Rick	1	2	4.86	3	3	0	0	17	15	9	9	10	7	R	R	6-3	167	8-27-73	1991	Oak Forest, Ill.
Hernandez, Roberto	2	6	4.04	67	0	0	26	71	55	33	32	41	55	R	R	6-4	235	11-11-64	1986	Cobo Rojo, P.R.
Johnson, Jason	2	5	5.70	13	13	0	0	60	74	38	38	27	36	R	R	6-6	220	10-27-73	1992	Burlington, Ky.
Lopez, Albie	7	4	2.60	54	0	0	1	80	73	31	23	32	62	R	R	6-2	205	8-18-71	1991	Mesa, Ariz.
Mecir, Jim	7	2	3.11	68	0	0	0	84	68	30	29	33	77	R	R	6-1	195	5-16-70	1991	St. James, N.Y.
Pennington, Brad	0	0	inf.	1	0	0	0	0	1	1	1	3	0	L	L	6-6	215	4-14-69	1989	Salem, Ind.
Rekar, Brian	2	8	4.98	16	15	1	0	87	95	56	48	21	55	R	R	6-3	205	6-3-72	1993	Orland Park, Ill.
Ruebel, Matt	0	2	6.23	7	1	0	0	9	11	7	6	4	6	L	L	6-2	180	10-16-69	1991	Oklahoma City, Okla.
Santana, Julio	5	6	4.23	32	19	1	0	140	144	72	66	58	60	R	R	6-0	185	1-20-73	1992	Santo Domingo, D.R.
2-team (3 Texas)	5	6	4.39	35	19	1	0	146	151	77	71	62	61							
Saunders, Tony	6	15	4.12	31	31	2	0	192	191	95	88	111	172	L	L	6-1	189	4-29-74	1992	Ellicott City, Md.
Springer, Dennis	3	11	5.45	29	17	1	0	116	120	77	70	60	46	R	R	5-10	185	2-12-65	1987	Fresno, Calif.
Tatis, Ramon	0	0	13.89	22	0	0	0	12	23	19	18	16	5	L	L	6-2	180	1-5-73	1991	Guayubin, D.R.
Wade, Terrell	1	1	5.06	2	2	0	0	11	14	6	6	2	8	L	L	6-3	204	1-25-73	1991	Rembert, S.C.
White, Rick	2	6	3.80	38	3	0	0	69	66	32	29	23	39	R	R	6-4	215	12-23-68	1990	Springfield, Ohio
Yan, Esteban	5	4	3.86	64	0	0	1	89	78	41	38	41	77	R	R	6-4	180	6-22-74	1991	La Higuera, D.R.

FIELDING

Catcher	PCT	G	PO	A	E	DP	PB
Difelice	.993	84	483	51	4	8	13
Flaherty	.993	91	541	45	4	2	5
Laker	1.000	2	5	0	0	0	1

First Base	PCT	G	PO	A	E	DP
Ledesma	1.000	2	4	0	0	1
Martinez	1.000	1	0	0	0	0
McClain	.966	5	24	4	1	1
McGriff	.995	135	1151	78	6	140
Sorrento	1.000	27	220	23	0	22

Second Base	PCT	G	PO	A	E	DP
Cairo	.978	148	279	429	16	110
Ledesma	.979	19	39	54	2	10
Silvestri	1.000	2	4	5	0	1
Smith	.968	6	11	19	1	3

Third Base	PCT	G	PO	A	E	DP
Boggs	.973	78	52	130	5	12
Ledesma	.846	7	5	6	2	0
McClain	1.000	3	2	2	0	0
Silvestri	1.000	3	1	1	0	0
Smith	.963	97	70	165	9	11

Shortstop	PCT	G	PO	A	E	DP
Ledesma	.971	58	104	165	8	51
Silvestri	.750	1	0	3	1	0
Smith	.900	7	7	20	3	4
Stocker	.979	110	185	335	11	80

Outfield	PCT	G	PO	A	E	DP
Butler	1.000	60	113	5	0	1
Kelly	1.000	93	136	4	0	1
Martinez	.994	86	161	9	1	1
McCracken	.992	153	344	18	3	3
Sorrento	1.000	18	30	0	0	0
Trammell	1.000	37	50	3	0	0
Walton	1.000	8	13	2	0	0
Winn	.980	96	192	7	4	1

LARRY GOREN

Wade Boggs

Tampa Bay's Tony Saunders
Led team with 172 strikeouts

LARRY GOREN

Charleston's Aubrey Huff
Hit .321 in professional debut

ROBERT GURGANUS

FARM SYSTEM

Director, Player Personnel: Bill Livesey

Class	Farm Team	League	W	L	Pct.	Finish*	Manager	First Yr
AAA	Durham (N.C.) Bulls	International	80	64	.556	3rd (14)	Bill Evers	1998
A#	St. Petersburg (Fla.) Devil Rays	Florida State	64	75	.460	t-11th (14)	Roy Silver	1997
A	Charleston (S.C.) RiverDogs	South Atlantic	67	74	.475	10th (14)	Greg Mahlberg	1997
A	Hudson Valley (N.Y.) Renegades	New York-Penn	50	26	.658	1st (14)	Charlie Montoyo	1996
Rookie#	Princeton (W.Va.) Devil Rays	Appalachian	38	30	.559	t-3rd (10)	David Howard	1997
Rookie	St. Petersburg (Fla.) Devil Rays	Gulf Coast	36	24	.600	2nd (14)	Bobby Ramos	1996

*Finish in overall standings (No. of teams in league) #Advanced level

DURHAM — Class AAA

INTERNATIONAL LEAGUE

BATTING	AVG	G	AB	R	H	2B	3B	HR	RBI	BB	SO	SB	CS	B	T	HT	WT	DOB	1st Yr	Resides
Blosser, Greg	.253	115	371	78	94	23	0	25	72	73	114	10	5	L	L	6-3	205	6-26-71	1989	Sarasota, Fla.
Buccheri, Jim	.305	106	351	51	107	14	3	6	34	25	28	37	13	R	R	5-11	165	11-12-68	1988	Fountain Valley, Calif.
Butler, Rich	.297	38	145	28	43	8	0	8	35	22	24	6	2	L	R	6-1	180	5-1-73	1991	East York, Ontario
Cox, Darron	.302	84	278	45	84	16	1	9	35	23	41	2	2	R	R	6-1	205	11-21-67	1989	Norman, Okla.
Cox, Steve	.253	119	430	64	109	23	2	13	67	56	100	3	4	L	L	6-4	225	10-31-74	1992	Strathmore, Calif.
De los Santos, Eddy	.273	4	11	2	3	2	0	0	2	0	6	0	0	R	R	6-2	165	2-24-78	1996	Santo Domingo, D.R.
Devarez, Cesar	.267	38	116	11	31	5	2	4	20	8	24	4	2	R	R	5-10	175	9-22-69	1988	San Francisco de Macoris, D.R.
Donato, Dan	.229	17	35	5	8	2	0	1	2	4	5	0	0	L	R	6-1	205	11-15-72	1995	Dedham, Mass.
Flaherty, John	.130	6	23	1	3	1	0	0	2	1	5	0	0	R	R	6-1	202	10-21-67	1988	West Nyack, N.Y.
Hawkins, Kraig	.261	6	23	2	6	0	0	0	1	0	2	1	0	R	R	6-2	170	12-4-71	1992	Lake Charles, La.
Kelly, Mike	.083	4	12	2	1	0	0	0	0	4	5	0	0	R	R	6-4	195	6-2-70	1991	Los Alamitos, Calif.
Kieschnick, Brooks	.130	7	23	4	3	1	0	1	2	4	8	0	1	L	R	6-4	228	6-6-72	1993	Caldwell, Texas
Laker, Tim	.239	40	134	36	32	7	0	11	26	28	32	1	1	R	R	6-2	175	11-27-69	1988	Simi Valley, Calif.
Martin, Chris	.259	131	448	71	116	26	2	8	49	62	80	19	11	R	R	6-1	170	1-25-68	1990	Los Angeles, Calif.
Matos, Francisco	.237	32	114	13	27	2	3	0	14	1	15	2	1	R	R	6-1	160	4-8-70	1988	Azua, D.R.
McClain, Scott	.299	126	472	91	141	35	0	34	109	66	113	6	2	R	R	6-3	209	5-19-72	1990	Glendale, Ariz.
Mendoza, Carlos	.269	51	201	32	54	8	0	0	11	16	29	9	9	L	L	5-11	160	11-4-74	1994	Bolivar, Ven.
Morman, Russ	.283	98	367	48	104	26	1	10	67	32	65	0	1	R	R	6-4	215	4-28-62	1983	Blue Springs, Mo.
Natal, Bob	.267	4	15	0	4	1	0	0	4	0	0	1	0	R	R	5-11	190	11-13-65	1987	Chula Vista, Calif.
Patterson, John	.301	25	73	12	22	5	0	2	11	3	12	1	1	B	R	5-9	168	2-11-67	1988	Phoenix, Ariz.
Perry, Herbert	.294	5	17	1	5	4	0	0	1	0	2	0	0	R	R	6-2	210	9-15-69	1991	Mayo, Fla.
Robinson, Kerry	.302	58	242	28	73	7	4	1	28	23	30	18	11	L	L	6-0	175	10-3-73	1994	St. Louis, Mo.
Silvestri, Dave	.277	129	480	74	133	31	2	8	56	61	73	12	9	R	R	6-0	180	9-29-67	1989	St. Louis, Mo.
Trammell, Bubba	.290	57	217	46	63	12	0	16	48	38	42	6	1	R	R	6-2	205	11-6-71	1994	Knoxville, Tenn.
Wilcox, Luke	.225	43	151	17	34	11	0	2	17	16	27	0	0	L	R	6-4	190	11-15-73	1995	St. Johns, Mich.
Winn, Randy	.285	29	123	25	35	5	2	1	16	15	24	10	4	B	R	6-2	175	6-9-74	1995	Danville, Calif.

PITCHING	W	L	ERA	G	GS	CG	SV	IP	H	R	ER	BB	SO	B	T	HT	WT	DOB	1st Yr	Resides
Aldred, Scott	2	4	5.35	7	7	0	0	35	44	26	21	14	19	L	L	6-4	195	6-12-68	1987	Lakeland, Fla.
Alvarez, Wilson	0	0	3.86	1	1	0	0	5	4	2	2	2	6	L	L	6-1	235	3-24-70	1987	Maracaibo, Ven.
Callaway, Mickey	5	3	4.53	9	8	0	0	48	49	27	24	17	19	R	R	6-2	190	5-13-75	1996	Germantown, Tenn.
Carlson, Dan	3	5	6.35	19	11	0	0	68	87	52	48	28	59	R	R	6-1	185	1-26-70	1990	Portland, Ore.
Daniels, John	2	0	1.86	4	0	0	1	10	4	2	2	3	9	B	R	6-3	185	2-7-74	1993	Little Chute, Wis.
Duvall, Mike	5	3	3.22	32	9	1	0	73	74	31	26	32	55	R	L	6-0	185	10-11-74	1995	Morgantown, W.Va.
Eichhorn, Mark	5	3	3.88	53	0	0	18	58	59	27	25	11	44	R	R	6-3	210	11-21-60	1979	Aptos, Calif.
Eiland, Dave	13	5	2.99	28	28	2	0	172	177	70	57	27	112	R	R	6-3	205	7-5-66	1987	Dade City, Fla.
Gaillard, Eddie	2	0	7.65	18	0	0	0	20	27	18	17	11	21	R	R	6-1	200	8-13-70	1993	Denver, Colo.
Hernandez, Santos	2	0	4.84	53	0	0	2	80	88	45	43	21	60	R	R	6-1	172	11-3-72	1994	Chiriqui, Panama
Johnson, Jason	1	0	2.92	2	2	0	0	12	6	4	4	2	14	R	R	6-6	220	10-27-73	1992	Burlington, Ky.
Karp, Ryan	2	6	5.30	36	5	1	1	73	76	44	43	31	64	L	L	6-4	205	4-5-70	1992	Coral Gables, Fla.
LeRoy, John	0	1	27.00	4	0	0	0	4	11	12	12	5	1	R	R	6-3	175	4-19-75	1993	Bellevue, Wash.
Lopez, Albie	0	0	0.00	2	0	0	0	3	4	0	0	1	2	R	R	6-2	205	8-18-71	1991	Mesa, Ariz.
Manzanillo, Josias	7	6	4.64	19	14	0	1	85	93	57	44	30	61	R	R	6-0	190	10-16-67	1983	Hyde Park, Mass.
Nunez, Maximo	3	6	5.00	58	0	0	5	63	67	39	35	40	53	R	R	6-5	165	1-15-73	1991	Villa Mella, D.R.
Pacheco, Alex	0	0	4.50	1	0	0	0	2	1	1	1	0	2	R	R	6-3	170	7-19-73	1990	Caracas, Ven.
Pennington, Brad	4	4	4.86	45	6	0	1	100	77	55	54	65	125	L	L	6-6	215	4-14-69	1989	Salem, Ind.
Rekar, Bryan	0	1	3.27	3	3	0	0	11	10	4	4	2	9	R	R	6-3	205	6-3-72	1993	Orland Park, Ill.
Ruebel, Matt	9	6	4.74	24	23	1	0	129	141	73	68	45	87	L	L	6-2	180	10-16-69	1991	Oklahoma City, Okla.
Rumer, Tim	7	2	7.34	26	0	0	0	38	49	34	31	18	27	L	L	6-3	205	8-8-69	1990	Princeton, N.J.
Springer, Dennis	2	3	2.87	5	5	0	0	38	34	13	12	15	23	R	R	5-10	185	2-12-65	1987	Fresno, Calif.
Tatis, Ramon	1	3	3.67	19	9	0	2	61	66	29	25	24	44	L	L	6-2	180	1-5-73	1991	Guayubin, D.R.
Wade, Terrell	1	1	4.58	4	4	0	0	20	21	12	10	12	14	L	L	6-3	204	1-25-73	1991	Rembert, S.C.
White, Rick	4	2	4.22	9	9	1	0	53	63	29	25	11	31	R	R	6-4	215	12-23-68	1990	Springfield, Ohio

FIELDING

Catcher	PCT	G	PO	A	E	DP	PB
D. Cox	.984	80	546	57	10	3	4
Devarez	.991	36	205	27	2	1	8
Donato	1.000	7	26	1	0	0	1
Flaherty	1.000	3	23	4	0	0	0
Laker	.991	32	197	19	2	3	5

First Base	PCT	G	PO	A	E	DP
D. Cox	1.000	1	4	0	0	0
S. Cox	.994	117	1010	62	7	84
Donato	1.000	3	27	1	0	2
Kieschnick	.909	2	10	0	1	0
Morman	1.000	23	199	16	0	18
Perry	1.000	3	19	2	0	3
Silvestri	1.000	4	21	2	0	1

Second Base	PCT	G	PO	A	E	DP
Buccheri	.986	17	30	38	1	3
Martin	.667	1	3	1	2	0
Matos	.990	23	38	64	1	10
Patterson	.961	16	28	46	3	13
Silvestri	.976	97	159	256	10	59

Third Base	PCT	G	PO	A	E	DP
D. Cox	.000	1	0	0	0	0
Donato	1.000	4	2	1	0	0
Martin	1.000	2	0	1	0	0
McClain	.963	125	73	241	12	20
Natal	1.000	1	0	4	0	0
Silvestri	.980	18	14	34	1	2

Shortstop	PCT	G	PO	A	E	DP
De los Santos	1.000	4	2	11	0	0
Martin	.953	128	194	349	27	78
McClain	1.000	1	2	1	0	1
Silvestri	.969	18	29	33	2	5

Outfield	PCT	G	PO	A	E	DP
Blosser	.954	91	130	15	7	2
Buccheri	1.000	71	124	4	0	0
Butler	.953	36	60	1	3	0
S. Cox	1.000	2	1	0	0	0
Hawkins	1.000	6	17	0	0	0
Kelly	.923	4	12	0	1	0
Kieschnick	1.000	5	11	0	0	0
Mendoza	.954	49	99	5	5	0
Robinson	.987	57	146	3	2	0
Silvestri	.000	1	0	0	0	0
Trammell	.983	57	110	5	2	0
Wilcox	1.000	41	98	4	0	1
Winn	.966	29	55	1	2	0

READING — Class AA

BATTING	AVG	G	AB	R	H	2B	3B	HR	RBI	BB	SO	SB	CS	B	T	HT	WT	DOB	1st Yr	Resides
Alcantara, Israel	.310	53	203	36	63	12	2	15	44	17	37	0	1	R	R	6-2	165	5-6-73	1991	Santo Domingo, D.R.

GAMES BY POSITION: 1B—Alcantara 15. **3B**—Alcantara 10. **OF**—Alcantara 4.

Player property of Devil Rays; on loan to Reading. For complete Reading statistics, see Page 196.

ORLANDO — Class AA

BATTING	AVG	G	AB	R	H	2B	3B	HR	RBI	BB	SO	SB	CS	B	T	HT	WT	DOB	1st Yr	Resides
Alcantara, Israel	.236	15	55	8	13	4	0	3	18	7	15	0	1	R	R	6-2	165	5-6-73	1991	Santo Domingo, D.R.
Donato, Dan	.333	4	12	1	4	0	0	0	1	3	1	0	0	L	R	6-1	205	11-15-72	1995	Dedham, Mass.
Hawkins, Kraig	.283	51	184	37	52	3	2	0	13	39	31	12	5	R	R	6-2	170	12-4-71	1992	Lake Charles, La.
Mendoza, Carlos	.338	35	139	27	47	3	3	1	19	19	18	16	2	L	L	5-11	160	11-4-74	1994	Bolivar, Ven.
Robinson, Kerry	.269	72	309	45	83	7	5	2	26	27	28	28	9	L	L	6-0	175	10-3-73	1994	St. Louis, Mo.
Wilcox, Luke	.287	88	331	57	95	23	3	17	69	39	54	2	3	L	R	6-4	190	11-15-73	1995	St. Johns, Mich.

PITCHING	W	L	ERA	G	GS	CG	SV	IP	H	R	ER	BB	SO	B	T	HT	WT	DOB	1st Yr	Resides
Callaway, Mickey	5	6	4.42	18	17	0	0	90	103	56	44	44	57	R	R	6-2	190	5-13-75	1996	Germantown, Tenn.
Daniels, John	1	2	5.30	11	0	0	0	19	14	12	11	9	19	B	R	6-3	185	2-7-74	1993	Little Chute, Wis.
Kaufman, John	0	5	6.66	7	6	0	0	24	34	25	18	9	17	L	L	5-10	170	10-23-74	1996	Tampa, Fla.
LeRoy, John	1	0	6.45	12	0	0	0	22	22	17	16	10	12	R	R	6-3	175	4-19-75	1993	Bellevue, Wash.
Manon, Julio	0	2	6.10	13	0	0	0	21	22	19	14	9	22	R	R	6-1	183	7-10-73	1992	Boca Chica, D.R.
Nunez, Maximo	2	0	0.77	6	0	0	2	12	5	1	1	4	14	R	R	6-5	165	1-15-73	1991	Villa Mella, D.R.

GAMES BY POSITION: 1B—Alcantara 3, Donato 1. **3B**—Alcantara 1, Donato 2. **OF**—Alcantara 2, Hawkins 47, Mendoza 25, Robinson 63, Wilcox 70.

Players property of Devil Rays; on loan to Orlando. For complete Orlando statistics, see Page 227.

ST. PETERSBURG — Class A

FLORIDA STATE LEAGUE

BATTING	AVG	G	AB	R	H	2B	3B	HR	RBI	BB	SO	SB	CS	B	T	HT	WT	DOB	1st Yr	Resides
Alcantara, Israel	.333	38	141	21	47	5	0	10	26	21	29	1	0	R	R	6-2	165	5-6-73	1991	Santo Domingo, D.R.
Anderson, Chris	.143	10	14	2	2	0	0	0	3	0	8	0	0	R	R	6-4	220	9-29-74	1996	Guthrie, Okla.
Arredondo, Hernando	.189	25	90	14	17	4	0	1	4	2	18	0	0	R	R	6-1	195	11-23-77	1996	Guaymas, Mexico
Becker, Brian	.283	129	492	64	139	27	4	8	63	43	116	1	1	R	R	6-7	220	5-26-75	1996	Tempe, Ariz.
Carr, Dustin	.256	138	516	85	132	23	5	6	52	70	86	11	4	R	R	6-0	190	6-7-75	1997	Mount Vernon, Texas
Colina, Roberto	.300	94	360	44	108	22	2	6	46	44	50	2	3	L	L	6-0	200	1-29-71	1997	San Jose, Costa Rica
Corps, Erick	.257	101	303	41	78	10	3	2	32	41	61	4	7	B	R	6-0	180	9-6-74	1992	Carolina, P.R.

BATTING	AVG	G	AB	R	H	2B	3B	HR	RBI	BB	SO	SB	CS	B	T	HT	WT	DOB	1st Yr	Resides
De los Santos, Eddy	.239	111	393	33	94	11	1	0	32	17	64	6	4	R	R	6-2	165	2-24-78	1996	Santo Domingo, D.R.
Donato, Dan	.310	43	171	21	53	12	0	1	25	10	22	1	1	L	R	6-1	205	11-15-72	1995	Dedham, Mass.
Friedholm, Scott	.200	10	15	2	3	1	0	0	1	2	3	0	0	R	R	6-3	205	3-14-75	1998	Walpole, Mass.
Garcia, Neil	.320	92	328	45	105	20	0	6	52	40	40	3	4	B	R	6-0	185	4-6-73	1994	Tustin, Calif.
Guerrero, Rafael	.226	76	252	23	57	9	1	3	18	15	32	1	4	R	R	6-2	191	12-3-74	1991	Santo Domingo, D.R.
Hawkins, Kraig	.198	30	96	15	19	1	1	0	4	11	12	9	4	R	R	6-2	170	12-4-71	1992	Lake Charles, La.
Icenia, Charlon	.000	1	0	0	0	0	0	0	0	0	0	0	0	R	R	5-11	190	1-23-79	1996	Curacao, Neth. Antilles
Kieschnick, Brooks	.248	28	105	15	26	6	0	5	18	11	18	0	0	L	R	6-4	228	6-6-72	1993	Caldwell, Texas
LeCronier, Jason	.231	36	104	13	24	4	1	3	21	4	31	1	2	L	R	6-0	180	3-30-73	1995	Lafayette, La.
Mendoza, Carlos	.313	8	32	6	10	2	0	0	8	4	3	4	2	L	L	5-11	160	11-4-74	1994	Bolivar, Ven.
Owens-Bragg, Luke	.206	33	63	9	13	1	1	0	6	13	13	0	1	B	R	5-11	170	6-6-74	1996	Orangevale, Calif.
Patterson, John	.263	6	19	4	5	2	0	1	2	1	4	0	0	B	R	5-9	168	2-11-67	1988	Phoenix, Ariz.
Perry, Herbert	.125	2	8	1	1	0	0	0	0	2	2	0	0	R	R	6-2	210	9-15-69	1991	Mayo, Fla.
Pomierski, Joe	.236	112	390	47	92	28	1	12	67	40	90	3	1	L	R	6-2	192	4-15-74	1992	Biloxi, Miss.
Quatraro, Matt	.248	73	270	36	67	14	2	4	31	31	67	4	0	R	R	6-2	205	11-14-73	1996	East Selkirk, N.Y.
Salinas, Trey	.227	22	66	7	15	3	0	1	7	6	10	0	0	R	R	6-1	190	6-29-75	1996	Corpus Christi, Texas
Sanchez, Alex	.330	128	545	77	180	17	9	1	50	31	70	66	33	L	L	5-10	179	8-26-76	1996	Miami, Fla.
Scioneaux, Damian	.185	18	54	4	10	0	0	0	1	4	8	1	0	L	R	5-8	165	6-4-75	1997	Kenner, La.

GAMES BY POSITION: C—Anderson 8, Donato 29, Friedholm 6, Garcia 60, Quatraro 49, Salinas 3. **1B**—Becker 113, Colina 23, Corps 2, Quatraro 6. **2B**—Carr 137, Corps 1, Owens-Bragg 4, Patterson 1. **3B**—Alcantara 27, Arredondo 20, Corps 63, Donato 9, Garcia 15, Owens-Bragg 16, Perry 2, Salinas 3. **SS**—Corps 32, de los Santos 111, Owens-Bragg 2. **OF**—Alcantara 8, Colina 15, Corps 1, Guerrero 73, Hawkins 29, Kieschnick 25, LeCronier 35, Mendoza 8, Owens-Bragg 4, Pomierski 98, Quatraro 2, Salinas 7, Sanchez 128, Scioneaux 17.

PITCHING	W	L	ERA	G	GS	CG	SV	IP	H	R	ER	BB	SO	B	T	HT	WT	DOB	1st Yr	Resides
Alvarez, Wilson	0	1	27.00	1	1	0	0	2	5	5	5	2	2	L	L	6-1	235	3-24-70	1987	Maracaibo, Ven.
Aquino, Julio	1	3	3.51	34	0	0	9	41	45	18	16	8	38	R	R	6-1	173	12-12-72	1991	Estorga de Guerra, D.R.
Armenta, Alfredo	1	2	4.62	6	6	0	0	25	25	16	13	11	21	L	L	6-1	185	8-23-78	1996	Chihuahua, Mexico
Belitz, Todd	2	2	5.04	7	7	0	0	45	39	28	25	14	40	L	L	6-1	218	10-23-75	1997	Huntington Beach, Calif.
Benesh, Ed	4	5	4.79	38	4	0	1	77	86	50	41	22	65	R	R	6-2	185	12-18-74	1996	Chicago Heights, Ill.
Bowers, Cedrick	5	9	4.38	28	26	0	0	150	144	89	73	80	156	R	L	6-2	210	2-10-78	1996	Chiefland, Fla.
Daniels, John	4	2	1.77	34	0	0	19	41	31	12	8	11	46	B	R	6-3	185	2-7-74	1993	Little Chute, Wis.
Duvall, Mike	0	0	2.70	2	0	0	0	3	4	1	1	2	3	R	L	6-0	185	10-11-74	1995	Morgantown, W.Va.
Enders, Trevor	10	1	2.23	51	0	0	1	69	48	20	17	15	61	R	L	6-1	205	12-22-74	1996	Houston, Texas
Gaillard, Eddie	0	0	0.00	1	1	0	0	2	1	0	0	0	2	R	R	6-1	200	8-13-70	1993	Denver, Colo.
Gardner, Lee	0	0	0.00	3	0	0	0	4	3	0	0	1	2	R	R	6-0	200	1-16-75	1998	Hartland, Mich.
Gorecki, Rick	0	0	0.00	1	1	0	0	5	4	0	0	1	7	R	R	6-3	167	8-27-70	1991	Oak Forest, Ill.
James, Dolvin	0	0	10.80	1	0	0	0	2	2	2	2	0	0	R	R	6-3	215	1-3-78	1996	Nacogdoches, Texas
Jimenez, Jason	0	2	8.53	13	0	0	0	19	24	20	18	10	15	R	L	6-2	210	1-10-76	1997	Elk Grove, Calif.
Jones, Kiki	1	0	6.00	6	0	0	0	9	7	7	6	3	6	R	R	5-11	175	6-8-70	1989	Tampa, Fla.
Kaufman, John	7	5	3.18	18	17	0	0	102	92	40	36	33	93	L	L	5-10	170	10-23-74	1996	Tampa, Fla.
Leon, Scott	1	3	4.46	16	4	0	0	36	33	23	18	17	22	R	R	6-4	180	9-8-74	1996	Topeka, Kan.
LeRoy, John	1	1	4.58	11	0	0	0	10	10	9	9	6	17	R	R	6-3	175	4-19-75	1993	Bellevue, Wash.
Lopez, Albie	0	1	18.00	1	1	0	0	1	2	2	2	0	1	R	R	6-2	205	8-18-71	1991	Mesa, Ariz.
Madison, Scott	2	0	5.36	27	1	0	0	42	53	28	25	20	18	L	L	6-2	190	9-12-74	1996	Latham, N.Y.
Manias, James	6	10	5.58	30	21	0	0	137	167	99	85	37	79	L	L	6-4	190	10-21-74	1996	Florham Park, Conn.
Manon, Julio	5	5	3.72	38	0	0	1	56	41	25	23	19	73	R	R	6-1	183	7-10-73	1992	Boca Chica, D.R.
Ortega, Pablo	5	9	4.40	28	25	2	0	155	187	104	76	39	111	B	R	6-2	170	11-7-76	1995	Nuevo Laredo, Mexico
Pujals, Denis	5	2	2.85	42	0	0	1	73	73	30	23	22	46	R	R	6-4	215	2-5-73	1996	Miami, Fla.
Rekar, Bryan	0	0	0.69	4	4	0	0	13	6	2	1	2	15	R	R	6-3	205	6-3-72	1993	Orland Park, Ill.
Wade, Terrell	0	1	3.60	3	3	0	0	15	12	8	6	7	16	L	L	6-3	204	1-25-73	1991	Rembert, S.C.
White, Matt	4	8	5.55	17	17	1	0	90	107	70	59	41	64	R	R	6-5	215	8-13-78	1996	South Pasadena, Fla.

CHARLESTON, S.C. — Class A

SOUTH ATLANTIC LEAGUE

BATTING	AVG	G	AB	R	H	2B	3B	HR	RBI	BB	SO	SB	CS	B	T	HT	WT	DOB	1st Yr	Resides
Bain, Tyler	.133	4	15	3	2	0	0	0	2	2	4	1	0	L	R	6-1	185	10-11-74	1996	Greeley, Colo.
Berns, Robert	.268	130	474	71	127	26	0	11	62	55	98	1	3	R	L	6-1	200	10-18-74	1997	San Jose, Calif.
Butler, Garrett	.246	45	171	28	42	7	0	3	25	6	29	8	3	B	R	6-2	170	5-20-76	1994	Miami, Fla.
Cruz, Luis	.190	34	137	15	26	5	1	1	11	11	28	4	1	R	R	6-0	180	1-21-77	1997	Santo Domingo, D.R.
Foulds, Kalin	.188	15	48	4	9	1	0	0	0	4	7	4	2	B	R	5-9	160	7-28-75	1998	La Mesa, Calif.
Guerrero, Rafael	.220	25	91	11	20	9	0	0	12	8	17	1	0	R	R	6-2	191	12-3-74	1991	Santo Domingo, D.R.
Hall, Toby	.321	105	377	59	121	25	1	6	50	39	32	3	7	R	R	6-3	205	10-21-75	1997	Placerville, Calif.
Hoover, Paul	.290	40	124	24	36	10	1	3	19	22	29	2	1	R	R	6-1	200	4-14-76	1997	Steubenville, Ohio
Huff, Aubrey	.321	69	265	38	85	19	1	13	54	24	40	3	1	L	R	6-4	220	12-20-76	1998	Fort Worth, Texas
Joffrion, Jack	.190	72	263	22	50	11	0	6	33	9	69	2	7	R	R	5-11	170	9-19-75	1997	Seabrook, Texas
Kelly, Kenny	.280	54	218	46	61	7	5	3	17	19	52	19	4	R	R	6-3	180	1-26-79	1997	Plant City, Fla.
Lopez-Cao, Mike	.250	14	24	2	6	0	0	0	4	4	4	2	0	L	R	5-6	180	8-14-75	1997	Miami, Fla.
Neuberger, Scott	.242	132	475	53	115	18	1	4	58	41	134	5	7	R	R	6-3	210	8-14-77	1997	Millersville, Md.
Owens-Bragg, Luke	.118	9	34	3	4	2	0	0	2	2	8	0	0	B	R	5-11	170	6-6-74	1996	Orangevale, Calif.
Perez, Nestor	.175	62	211	20	37	4	0	0	22	13	36	3	4	R	R	5-10	160	11-24-76	1997	Tenerife, Canary Islands
Pigott, Anthony	.170	29	100	9	17	3	1	2	11	2	26	0	1	R	R	6-1	195	6-13-76	1997	Wilmington, N.C.
Salinas, Trey	.265	47	147	26	39	6	1	4	17	18	22	2	1	R	R	6-1	190	6-29-75	1996	Corpus Christi, Texas
Sandberg, Jared	.183	56	191	31	35	11	0	3	25	27	76	4	0	R	R	6-3	185	3-2-78	1996	Olympia, Wash.
Scioneaux, Damian	.248	72	270	44	67	9	4	3	26	42	44	16	9	L	R	5-8	165	6-4-75	1997	Kenner, La.
Suriel, Miguel	.083	4	12	0	1	0	0	0	0	2	2	1	0	R	R	6-0	165	11-15-76	1994	Palmirito, D.R.
Trahan, Mike	.240	80	317	45	76	17	0	9	37	35	74	6	4	R	R	6-1	190	4-28-75	1997	Lake Charles, La.
Velazquez, Jose	.308	111	413	71	127	20	2	11	64	55	70	0	2	L	L	6-3	205	8-24-75	1994	Guayama, P.R.
Ware, Ryan	.268	26	82	12	22	1	0	0	4	9	21	2	2	R	R	5-11	180	2-6-76	1997	Houston, Texas
Wilder, Paul	.197	76	264	48	52	9	0	13	39	43	118	3	3	L	R	6-4	230	1-9-78	1996	Raleigh, N.C.

GAMES BY POSITION: C—Hall 102, Hoover 31, Lopez-Cao 9, Salinas 11, Suriel 4. **1B**—Berns 127, Hoover 1, Salinas 6, Suriel 1, Velazquez 11, Ware 1. **2B**—Bain 4, Cruz 34, Foulds 7, Owens-Bragg 1, Trahan 80, Ware 17. **3B**—Hoover 7, Huff 69, Lopez-Cao 1, Owens-Bragg 5, Salinas 5, Sandberg 56, Ware 1. **SS**—Foulds 1, Hoover 2, Joffrion 72, Owens-Bragg 4, Perez 62, Ware 2. **OF**—Butler 44, Foulds 5, Guerrero 25, Kelly 54, Neuberger 131, Pigott 29, Salinas 4, Scioneaux 71, Ware 3, Wilder 68.

PITCHING	W	L	ERA	G	GS	CG	SV	IP	H	R	ER	BB	SO	B	T	HT	WT	DOB	1st Yr	Resides
Bass, Aaron	0	0	23.14	2	0	0	0	2	7	6	6	3	2	L	L	6-3	220	10-1-75	1997	Bolivar, Mo.
Belitz, Todd	6	4	2.42	21	21	0	0	130	99	44	35	48	123	L	L	6-1	218	10-23-75	1997	Huntington Beach, Calif.
Box, John	7	2	2.58	55	0	0	2	77	63	28	22	10	67	R	L	6-3	180	4-30-75	1996	Houston, Texas
Brown, Elliot	2	7	4.96	40	15	0	0	107	123	72	59	40	59	B	R	6-3	185	6-7-75	1996	Metairie, La.
Carter, Roger	0	4	4.92	13	9	0	0	53	47	34	29	31	46	R	R	6-2	200	8-17-78	1997	Fort Gibson, Okla.
Cummins, Jon	1	0	8.74	8	0	0	0	11	15	15	11	11	8	R	R	6-3	210	12-9-75	1997	Frankfort, Ky.
Deckard, Ed	0	0	7.04	3	0	0	0	8	13	7	6	0	3	R	R	6-5	190	11-23-77	1996	Springfield, Mo.
Gardner, Lee	0	3	4.04	28	0	0	3	36	38	18	16	4	55	R	R	6-0	200	1-16-75	1998	Hartland, Mich.
Gonzalez, Ignacio	0	4	6.39	30	0	0	0	49	70	40	35	22	40	R	R	6-1	170	6-2-75	1997	Robstown, Texas
Hale, Mark	0	0	10.80	4	0	0	0	5	4	6	6	6	8	R	R	6-4	210	8-31-75	1996	Carefree, Ariz.
Howard, Tom	3	3	3.16	33	0	0	0	51	55	25	18	25	39	R	L	6-4	180	7-29-75	1993	Cocoa Beach, Fla.
James, Delvin	2	0	5.40	7	0	0	0	8	12	5	5	2	8	R	R	6-3	215	1-3-78	1996	Nacogdoches, Texas
Kimbrell, Mike	1	1	7.71	13	0	0	0	19	24	18	16	15	17	L	L	6-3	215	2-20-74	1996	Greenwell Springs, La.
Leon, Scott	0	1	4.24	5	2	0	0	17	15	9	8	4	15	R	R	6-4	180	9-8-74	1996	Topeka, Kan.
Madison, Scott	4	2	3.63	9	8	0	0	45	53	25	18	13	25	L	L	6-2	190	9-12-74	1996	Latham, N.Y.
Phelps, Travis	5	8	4.85	18	18	0	0	91	100	54	49	35	96	R	R	6-2	170	7-25-77	1997	Rocky Comfort, Mo.
Reyes, Eddy	4	6	2.19	56	0	0	24	62	60	23	15	12	49	R	R	6-4	200	4-24-76	1997	Miami, Fla.
Reynolds, Chris	0	0	2.70	2	0	0	0	3	2	1	1	2	5	R	R	6-4	195	2-16-76	1997	Irving, Texas
Rupe, Ryan	6	1	2.40	10	10	0	0	56	33	18	15	9	62	R	R	6-6	240	3-31-75	1998	Houston, Texas
Seay, Bobby	1	7	4.30	15	15	0	0	69	59	40	33	29	74	L	L	6-2	190	6-20-78	1996	Sarasota, Fla.
Wheeler, Dan	12	14	4.43	29	29	3	0	181	206	96	89	29	136	R	R	6-3	215	12-10-77	1997	Warwick, R.I.
White, Matt	4	3	3.82	12	12	0	0	75	72	41	32	21	59	R	R	6-5	215	8-13-78	1996	South Pasadena, Fla.
Zambrano, Victor	6	4	3.38	48	2	0	0	77	72	32	29	20	89	R	R	6-1	170	8-6-74	1994	Los Teques, Ven.

HUDSON VALLEY — Short-Season Class A

NEW YORK-PENN LEAGUE

BATTING	AVG	G	AB	R	H	2B	3B	HR	RBI	BB	SO	SB	CS	B	T	HT	WT	DOB	1st Yr	Resides
Backe, Brandon	.231	11	26	3	6	2	0	0	1	2	7	0	0	R	R	6-0	190	4-5-78	1998	Webster, Texas
Badeaux, Brooks	.300	68	267	48	80	9	4	1	36	29	47	11	4	B	R	5-10	175	10-20-76	1998	Scott, La.
Butler, Garrett	.304	68	280	47	85	14	2	2	44	23	48	21	8	B	R	6-2	170	5-20-76	1994	Miami, Fla.
Cruz, Luis	.222	63	230	36	51	4	3	7	32	19	46	4	5	R	R	6-0	180	1-21-77	1997	Santo Domingo, D.R.
Foulds, Kalin	.197	20	71	14	14	3	1	0	3	6	7	7	0	B	R	5-9	160	7-28-75	1998	La Mesa, Calif.
Goodson, Steven	.303	62	234	45	71	15	4	3	32	26	57	3	3	L	R	6-5	220	4-11-79	1998	Oklahoma City, Okla.
Hoover, Paul	.283	73	269	51	76	20	1	4	37	39	44	26	3	R	R	6-1	200	4-14-76	1997	Steubenville, Ohio
Llanos, Alex	.277	54	188	24	52	9	1	1	24	26	36	5	2	L	R	6-1	185	9-20-76	1995	Carolina, P.R.
Mahoney, Sean	.347	65	248	44	86	16	2	5	53	31	47	11	5	R	R	6-4	220	12-23-75	1998	Miami, Fla.
Marn, Josh	.207	29	82	11	17	2	0	0	8	11	19	0	1	R	R	6-0	205	7-4-76	1998	Manhattan, Kan.
Miller, Travis	.191	47	141	29	27	4	4	2	10	19	45	5	3	R	R	6-2	195	7-26-75	1997	Arlington, Texas
Pigott, Anthony	.250	9	16	3	4	1	0	0	3	1	2	1	0	R	R	6-1	195	6-13-76	1997	Wilmington, N.C.
Rand, Ian	.227	26	75	13	17	2	1	1	13	6	16	2	2	R	R	6-4	190	1-30-77	1995	La Mesa, Calif.
Sandberg, Jared	.288	73	271	49	78	15	2	12	54	42	76	13	3	R	R	6-3	185	3-2-78	1996	Olympia, Wash.
Smetek, Peter	.091	19	33	1	3	2	0	0	2	4	18	1	0	L	L	6-0	200	9-6-76	1998	Houston, Texas
Suriel, Miguel	.258	60	225	27	58	7	3	2	35	18	35	6	4	R	R	6-0	165	11-15-76	1994	Palmirito, D.R.
Ware, Ryan	.259	9	27	7	7	2	0	1	3	3	7	0	0	R	R	5-11	180	2-6-76	1997	Houston, Texas

GAMES BY POSITION: C—Hoover 52, Marn 18, Rand 1, Suriel 13. **1B**—Goodson 58, Marn 7, Suriel 12. **2B**—Backe 2, Cruz 63, Foulds 5, Llanos 8, Pigott 1, Suriel 1, Ware 3. **3B**—Hoover 1, Llanos 6, Sandberg 70, Suriel 2, Ware 2. **SS**—Backe 3, Badeaux 67, Foulds 9, Ware 2. **OF**—Backe 5, Butler 67, Foulds 6, Mahoney 61, Miller 44, Pigott 6, Rand 24, Smetek 16, Suriel 32.

PITCHING	W	L	ERA	G	GS	CG	SV	IP	H	R	ER	BB	SO	B	T	HT	WT	DOB	1st Yr	Resides
Cornejo, Jesse	6	1	3.08	34	0	0	0	50	40	21	17	22	50	L	L	6-3	190	10-26-76	1998	Wellington, Kan.
Cummins, Jon	0	0	4.98	14	0	0	0	22	24	17	12	10	25	R	R	6-3	210	12-9-75	1997	Frankfort, Ky.
Flohr, Adam	5	1	2.61	15	14	0	0	79	69	28	23	11	70	L	L	6-2	185	3-29-77	1998	Longview, Wash.
Harper, Travis	6	2	1.92	13	10	0	0	56	38	14	12	20	81	R	R	6-4	190	5-21-76	1997	Riverton, W.Va.
Hertzel, Patrick	5	3	4.01	15	15	0	0	74	66	44	33	24	56	R	R	6-5	210	7-9-76	1998	Manhattan, Kan.
James, Delvin	7	4	2.98	15	15	0	0	82	71	39	27	32	64	R	R	6-3	215	1-3-78	1996	Nacogdoches, Texas
Jimenez, Jason	5	2	1.60	29	0	0	4	39	20	13	7	13	55	R	L	6-2	210	1-10-76	1997	Elk Grove, Calif.
Kofler, Ed	6	3	3.03	16	12	0	1	77	65	34	26	24	64	R	R	6-2	165	12-23-77	1996	Palm Harbor, Fla.
Rosario, Juan	1	4	7.53	22	2	0	1	35	39	33	29	20	27	R	R	6-4	195	11-3-75	1993	Perth Amboy, N.J.
Rupe, Ryan	1	0	0.68	3	3	0	0	13	8	1	1	2	18	R	R	6-6	240	3-31-75	1998	Houston, Texas
Schuldt, Matt	3	2	2.81	33	0	0	5	42	30	15	13	20	56	R	R	6-2	205	9-17-75	1998	Sioux Falls, S.D.
Seberino, Ronni	3	2	4.15	22	5	0	0	52	47	29	24	24	61	L	L	6-1	177	5-27-79	1996	San Pedro de Macoris, D.R.
Smetek, Peter	0	0	1.69	4	0	0	0	5	6	2	1	1	7	L	L	6-0	200	9-6-76	1998	Houston, Texas
Wright, Chris	1	1	2.30	31	0	0	14	47	44	17	12	9	41	R	R	6-2	195	6-6-77	1997	Dale, Okla.
Zwemke, Bryan	1	1	7.50	12	0	0	0	18	25	18	15	13	18	R	R	6-3	185	3-21-74	1996	Aurora, Colo.

PRINCETON — Rookie

APPALACHIAN LEAGUE

BATTING	AVG	G	AB	R	H	2B	3B	HR	RBI	BB	SO	SB	CS	B	T	HT	WT	DOB	1st Yr	Resides
Arias, Jeison	.247	54	170	29	42	8	0	5	26	15	53	6	0	R	R	6-1	195	9-27-78	1996	San Jose de Ocoa, D.R.
Backe, Brandon	.250	27	92	14	23	5	1	0	7	12	31	1	1	R	R	6-0	190	4-5-78	1998	Webster, Texas
Ballard, Ryan	.258	15	31	5	8	2	0	0	2	6	7	0	0	R	R	6-3	215	9-12-75	1998	Cordova, Tenn.
Barlow, Marlon	.216	14	37	6	8	2	0	0	3	4	6	3	2	L	R	5-10	189	1-10-79	1998	Montgomery, Ala.
Chwan, Brian	.320	36	100	14	32	7	0	2	13	9	15	1	0	L	R	6-2	195	8-30-76	1998	Anaheim, Calif.
Cota, Humberto	.310	67	245	48	76	13	4	15	61	32	59	4	4	R	R	6-0	175	2-7-79	1996	San Luis Rio Colorado, Mexico
Garcia, Sandy	.216	54	171	23	37	10	0	0	21	7	40	7	5	R	R	5-11	180	2-19-79	1997	Bani, D.R.
Grummitt, Dan	.264	44	106	25	28	3	2	4	19	15	39	2	1	R	R	6-5	230	6-16-76	1998	Twinsburg, Ohio
Gunner, Chie	.293	41	116	22	34	3	3	3	16	17	30	3	1	L	R	6-2	183	7-22-78	1996	Grandview, Mo.
LaForest, Pierre Luc	.275	25	91	18	25	7	1	2	14	12	18	4	1	L	R	6-1	190	1-27-78	1995	Gatineau, Quebec
Lebron, Hector	.237	59	207	35	49	11	1	4	34	19	53	1	1	L	R	6-3	225	7-22-77	1997	Catano, P.R.
Mann, Derek	.325	68	280	63	91	10	6	1	32	32	46	16	7	L	R	6-0	165	3-8-78	1996	Midland, Ga.
Moore, Frank	.118	8	17	3	2	0	0	0	1	2	9	0	0	L	R	6-2	200	7-2-78	1998	Douglas, Ga.
Murch, Jeremy	.274	58	197	36	54	6	7	5	40	19	58	4	0	L	L	6-1	180	9-22-78	1998	Sarasota, Fla.

BATTING	AVG	G	AB	R	H	2B	3B	HR	RBI	BB	SO	SB	CS	B	T	HT	WT	DOB	1st Yr	Resides
Perez, Nestor	.258	66	244	41	63	7	0	0	25	33	29	13	8	R	R	5-10	160	11-24-76	1997	Tenerife, Canary Islands
Ramirez, Edgar	.254	53	205	31	52	11	2	8	35	14	63	7	3	R	R	6-2	165	8-7-79	1996	San Pedro de Macoris, D.R.

GAMES BY POSITION: C—Ballard 11, Chwan 18, Cota 52. **1B**—Chwan 1, Cota 1, Grummitt 20, Lebron 59. **2B**—Backe 1, Mann 66, Ramirez 1. **3B**—Backe 6, LaForest 18, Mann 1, Ramirez 47. **SS**—Backe 2, Moore 1, Perez 66. **OF**—Arias 53, Backe 13, Barlow 14, Garcia 51, Grummitt 1, Gunner 37, Lebron 1, Murch 55, Ramirez 4.

PITCHING	W	L	ERA	G	GS	CG	SV	IP	H	R	ER	BB	SO	B	T	HT	WT	DOB	1st Yr	Resides
Brown, Michael	1	2	7.41	13	6	0	0	34	38	29	28	22	28	R	R	6-4	200	10-13-76	1996	Oliver Springs, Tenn.
Cummins, Jon	1	1	4.67	9	1	0	0	17	21	15	9	12	16	R	R	6-3	210	12-9-75	1997	Frankfort, Ky.
Deckard, Ed	0	0	4.79	11	0	0	0	21	25	16	11	11	12	R	R	6-5	190	11-23-77	1996	Springfield, Mo.
Haines, Talley	2	3	5.19	27	1	0	2	43	54	32	25	17	37	R	R	6-5	200	11-16-76	1998	Cape Girardeau, Mo.
Hill, T.J.	0	1	3.60	4	0	0	0	5	5	3	2	1	4	R	R	6-2	220	7-15-75	1996	London, Ohio
Kennedy, Joe	6	4	3.74	13	13	0	0	67	66	37	28	26	44	R	L	6-4	220	5-24-79	1998	El Cajon, Calif.
Lira, James	4	1	3.75	29	0	0	14	36	36	18	15	19	51	R	R	6-1	160	5-19-77	1998	Fountain Valley, Calif.
MacGillivray, Monte	0	1	9.42	10	0	0	0	14	18	16	15	13	8	L	L	6-0	190	8-18-76	1998	Moreno Valley, Calif.
McDonald, Jon	4	2	2.61	25	0	0	0	38	34	14	11	19	35	L	L	6-0	190	12-1-76	1998	Humble, Texas
Reynolds, Chris	1	1	4.86	22	1	0	1	37	38	25	20	15	37	R	R	6-4	195	2-16-76	1997	Irving, Texas
Roberts, Marquis	3	2	5.59	8	8	0	0	37	49	30	23	12	27	L	L	5-11	180	8-29-79	1997	Fresno, Calif.
Robinson, Jeremy	6	2	3.01	13	13	0	0	72	78	34	24	9	64	L	L	6-1	205	10-13-77	1998	Gonzales, La.
Ruhl, Nathan	1	1	4.76	14	0	0	3	17	12	10	9	11	25	R	R	6-4	200	7-16-76	1996	Lee's Summit, Mo.
Standridge, Jason	4	4	7.00	12	12	0	0	63	82	61	49	28	47	R	R	6-4	205	11-9-78	1997	Birmingham, Ala.
Wright, Barrett	5	4	4.28	13	13	0	0	74	79	41	35	23	54	R	R	6-3	200	1-5-79	1997	Charlotte, N.C.
Wright, Jason	0	0	0.68	9	0	0	0	13	3	1	1	7	12	R	R	6-6	210	9-30-76	1995	Martinsville, Ind.

ST. PETERSBURG — Rookie

GULF COAST LEAGUE

BATTING	AVG	G	AB	R	H	2B	3B	HR	RBI	BB	SO	SB	CS	B	T	HT	WT	DOB	1st Yr	Resides
Batista, Angel	.212	57	226	35	48	11	2	3	23	19	67	10	8	L	L	6-3	190	1-14-80	1996	Santo Domingo, D.R.
Colina, Roberto	.364	3	11	0	4	1	0	0	2	0	1	0	0	L	L	6-0	200	1-29-71	1997	San Jose, Costa Rica
De Caster, Yurendell	.236	56	174	25	41	4	3	2	17	19	48	10	4	R	R	6-1	175	9-26-79	1996	Curacao, Neth. Antilles
Guerrero, Jason	.077	14	13	3	1	0	0	0	1	5	3	0	1	R	R	6-2	175	1-27-79	1997	Pittsburg, Calif.
Isenia, Charion	.295	42	132	25	39	10	2	0	14	8	20	7	6	R	R	5-11	190	1-23-79	1996	Curacao, Neth. Antilles
Jacobs, John	.284	51	155	21	44	12	4	2	29	15	50	7	4	R	R	6-1	185	11-7-79	1998	Rohnert Park, Calif.
Kieschnick, Brooks	.500	4	12	4	6	1	0	2	8	1	0	0	0	L	R	6-4	228	6-6-72	1993	Caldwell, Texas
Martin, Brian	.255	46	153	24	39	11	0	4	24	18	57	0	2	R	R	6-2	220	6-14-80	1998	El Centro, Calif.
Mendoza, Carlos	.444	6	18	6	8	1	0	0	4	5	0	3	1	L	L	5-11	160	11-4-74	1994	Bolivar, Ven.
Meseberg, Michael	.059	5	17	0	1	0	0	0	1	0	6	1	0	L	R	6-5	195	3-28-79	1998	Highland, Ill.
Moore, Frank	.303	39	99	13	30	4	3	1	9	4	15	7	1	L	R	6-2	200	7-2-78	1998	Douglas, Ga.
Osorio, Isrrael	.229	34	109	18	25	5	0	6	20	8	34	1	0	R	R	6-2	185	2-4-81	1997	Maracay, Ven.
Perry, Herbert	.115	8	26	1	3	0	0	0	1	3	5	0	0	R	R	6-2	210	9-15-69	1991	Mayo, Fla.
Pressley, Josh	.304	36	125	22	38	6	0	1	16	20	29	2	1	L	R	6-6	220	4-2-80	1998	Fort Lauderdale, Fla.
Ramirez, Edgar	.382	9	34	5	13	5	1	1	3	0	4	0	1	R	R	6-2	165	8-7-79	1996	San Pedro de Macoris, D.R.
Rhodes, Nick	.234	23	64	6	15	1	0	0	6	1	12	3	0	R	R	6-4	200	8-9-78	1998	Danbury, Conn.
Ryan, Kelvin	.266	57	222	34	59	10	3	3	36	10	38	2	4	R	R	6-1	185	8-10-78	1997	La Romana, D.R.
Soler, Ramon	.252	58	226	47	57	7	7	1	19	27	48	23	11	B	R	6-0	147	7-6-81	1997	Las Caobas, D.R.
Tsujita, Osamu	.288	41	118	27	34	11	4	3	27	14	35	2	4	L	R	6-4	190	6-20-77	1998	Nara, Japan
Vazquez, Carlos	.169	24	65	6	11	3	0	2	9	4	17	1	0	R	R	6-3	190	1-10-79	1997	Ponce, P.R.

GAMES BY POSITION: C—Isenia 36, Osorio 12, Rhodes 20. **1B**—Colina 1, Isenia 1, Jacobs 1, Kieschnick 2, Moore 1, Osorio 3, Pressley 24, Tsujita 27, Vazquez 14. **2B**—De Caster 40, Moore 13. **3B**—De Caster 4, Isenia 1, Jacobs 47, Perry 4, Ramirez 8, Vazquez 1. **SS**—De Caster 1, Martin 1, Moore 2, Soler 57. **OF**—Batista 57, Isenia 4, Jacobs 2, Martin 40, Mendoza 6, Meseberg 5, Moore 24, Ramirez 2, Ryan 56, Tsijita 3, Vazquez 1.

PITCHING	W	L	ERA	G	GS	CG	SV	IP	H	R	ER	BB	SO	B	T	HT	WT	DOB	1st Yr	Resides
Adam, Dave	0	1	4.50	1	1	0	0	2	3	1	1	0	1	R	R	6-3	202	2-14-69	1990	Shelton, Conn.
Alvarez, Wilson	0	0	0.00	1	1	0	0	3	2	0	0	1	4	L	L	6-1	235	3-24-70	1987	Maracaibo, Ven.
Armstrong, Charles	1	0	6.00	14	0	0	0	15	16	11	10	14	18	L	L	6-4	210	9-28-76	1998	Oakland, Calif.
Deckard, Ed	1	0	1.13	4	0	0	1	8	7	1	1	1	1	R	R	6-5	190	11-23-77	1996	Springfield, Mo.
Dickson, Patrick	1	2	5.30	14	3	0	0	19	29	17	11	5	17	L	L	6-2	200	9-27-79	1998	Dalton, Ga.
Erickson, John	3	2	3.94	19	0	0	1	30	34	21	13	17	22	R	R	6-1	215	10-19-78	1998	Oklahoma City, Okla.
Gaillard, Eddie	0	0	0.00	2	2	0	0	4	0	0	0	1	5	R	R	6-1	200	8-13-70	1993	Denver, Colo.
Garibaldi, Cecilio	1	3	5.06	22	0	0	5	27	30	16	15	9	20	R	R	6-2	190	1-5-78	1998	Guasave, Mexico
Getz, Cody	1	2	3.86	16	0	0	2	21	20	11	9	11	19	L	L	6-8	200	9-19-78	1998	Walnut Creek, Calif.
Gorecki, Rick	0	0	.00	2	2	0	0	5	3	0	0	2	5	R	R	6-3	167	8-27-73	1991	Oak Forest, Ill.
Guerrero, Jason	1	0	3.86	6	0	0	0	9	10	6	4	4	12	R	R	6-2	175	1-27-79	1997	Pittsburg, Calif.
Guevara, Daniel	0	0	5.40	4	0	0	0	3	4	3	2	2	5	L	L	6-2	174	2-2-78	1997	Valencia, Ven.
Hernandez, Luis	3	2	2.40	10	8	0	0	41	36	19	11	18	19	L	L	6-1	165	6-5-78	1996	Santo Domingo, D.R.
Hill, T.J.	0	0	2.25	7	1	0	0	12	10	4	3	3	8	R	R	6-2	220	7-15-75	1996	London, Ohio
Ledden, Ryan	0	3	8.44	14	4	0	0	27	33	26	25	16	21	R	R	6-4	195	10-19-77	1997	Lilburn, Ga.
Marin, Willy	8	0	2.28	27	0	0	2	47	39	13	12	4	43	R	R	6-1	165	7-28-78	1998	Miami, Fla.
McCormick, Terry	2	2	3.86	11	9	0	0	47	46	24	20	21	56	L	L	6-1	170	10-14-78	1997	Tampa, Fla.
McKoin, Heath	2	1	5.95	10	3	0	0	20	21	15	13	11	16	R	L	6-2	185	8-25-79	1997	Pine Bluff, Ark.
Peguero, Radhame	6	0	3.18	11	9	1	0	57	54	22	20	22	50	R	R	6-0	160	4-15-78	1996	San Pedro de Macoris, D.R.
Price, Kevin	1	0	3.51	16	0	0	0	26	20	15	10	8	22	R	R	6-9	180	3-7-79	1997	Riverton, Utah
Roberts, Marquis	1	0	0.00	3	2	0	0	9	1	0	0	1	8	L	L	5-11	180	8-29-79	1997	Fresno, Calif.
Rodriguez, Jose	3	3	4.26	12	11	0	0	63	77	38	30	12	61	R	R	6-2	160	2-27-78	1996	Cotui, D.R.
Smetek, Peter	0	0	0.00	2	0	0	0	2	0	0	0	1	1	L	L	6-0	200	9-6-76	1998	Houston, Texas
Veras, Enger	1	1	6.75	5	4	0	0	16	19	14	12	12	19	R	R	6-5	197	6-5-81	1998	Santo Domingo, D.R.
Wright, Jason	0	2	3.48	7	0	0	0	10	8	5	4	7	8	R	R	6-6	210	9-30-76	1995	Martinsville, Ind.

TEXAS RANGERS

Gonzalez, deadline deals spur Rangers to division title

BY EVAN GRANT

If nothing else, 1998 was eventful for the Texas Rangers.

The year started with an announcement that the club would be sold to Tom Hicks, and ended with the team's second playoff berth in the last three seasons. In between, the Rangers' farm system surged back to pre-1990s strength, when it was among the most productive in baseball.

Put it all together and it's easy to understand why the Rangers feel good about their chances as baseball heads toward the 21st century.

Shortly after the $250 million sale of the club was announced, the Rangers jumped out to an 18-8 start that included an April record for RBIs by Juan Gonzalez, who ended up with another MVP-worthy season. He batted a career high .318, hit 45 home runs and drove in an American League-best 157 runs.

The pitching staff had some stars as well. Righthanders Rick Helling and Aaron Sele combined for 39 wins on the season. Helling, who went 20-7, was one of just three 20-game winners in the AL. And closer John Wetteland set a team mark with his 42 saves.

Two deadline-day trades solidified the club. Third baseman Todd Zeile came over from the Marlins and shortstop Royce Clayton and righthander Todd Stottlemyre were acquired from the Cardinals. They helped the team come from 3½ games behind in the last 20 games to catch the Angels. The Rangers put Anaheim away by sweeping five head-to-head games in mid-September.

Though the season ended with a three-game sweep by the World Series champion Yankees in the Division Series, the Rangers played the Yankees close, allowing just nine runs in three games.

Juan Gonzalez

Ruben Mateo

MORRIS FOSTOFF

Players of the Year

Major League: Juan Gonzalez, of

After threatening Hack Wilson's single-season RBI mark early in the year, Gonzalez finished with 157 RBIs to lead the AL.

Minor League: Ruben Mateo, of, Tulsa

Mateo hit .404 during a 27-game midseason hitting streak, the third longest in the minor leagues in 1998.

ORGANIZATION LEADERS

BATTING

*AVG	Mike Zywica, Tulsa/Charlotte	.335
R	Shawn Gallagher, Charlotte	111
H	Mike Lamb, Charlotte	162
TB	Shawn Gallagher, Charlotte	283
2B	Shawn Gallagher, Charlotte	37
3B	Juan Piniella, Charlotte/Savannah	9
HR	Scott Sheldon, Oklahoma	29
RBI	Shawn Gallagher, Charlotte	121
BB	Travis Hafner, Savannah	68
SO	Tom Quinlan, Oklahoma	155
SB	Two tied at	51

PITCHING

W	Three tied at	13
L	Brandon Knight, Oklahoma/Tulsa	13
#ERA	Jeff Zimmerman, Tulsa/Charlotte	1.28
G	Mike Venafro, Oklahoma/Tulsa	59
CG	Ryan Glynn, Tulsa	4
SV	R.A. Dickey, Charlotte	38
IP	Derrick Cook, Charlotte	167
BB	Corey Lee, Tulsa	102
SO	Doug Davis, Charlotte	173

*Minimum 250 At-Bats #Minimum 75 Innings

The major league team's accomplishments weren't the only good stories of the year.

Three Rangers farm teams made the playoffs, and two won league championships. The organizational winning percentage jumped 40 points to .526, the eighth best in baseball. As a whole, Rangers farm clubs hadn't done that well since 1990, when the system's top players were Juan Gonzalez, Ivan Rodriguez and Dean Palmer.

Double-A Tulsa represented the heart and soul of the rebuilding effort. Most of the organization's top prospects were grouped at Tulsa in an effort to learn how to win. After an awful first half, the Drillers went 50-22 in the second half, setting a Texas League record for most wins by a team in a half.

Top prospect Ruben Mateo, who overcame a first-half shoulder separation, led the surge. Tulsa swept Arkansas in the first round of the playoffs, then beat Wichita four games to three to capture its first Texas League title since 1988.

Class A Charlotte won the Florida State League's Western Division first-half title. Shortstop Kelly Dransfeldt and outfielder Mike Zywica were the leaders and earned midseason promotions to Tulsa. First baseman Shawn Gallagher, who stuck around, reestablished himself as a top prospect by leading the league in home runs (26) and RBIs (121).

And the Rookie-level Rangers, made up mostly of 1998 draftees, won the Gulf Coast League title for the seventh time.

Texas RANGERS

Manager: Johnny Oates

1998 Record: 88-74, .543 (1st, AL West)

BATTING	AVG	G	AB	R	H	2B	3B	HR	RBI	BB	SO	SB	CS	B	T	HT	WT	DOB	1st Yr	Resides
Alicea, Luis	.274	101	259	51	71	15	3	6	33	37	40	4	3	B	R	5-9	176	7-29-65	1988	Loxahatchie, Fla.
Cedeno, Domingo	.262	61	141	19	37	9	1	2	21	10	32	2	1	B	R	6-0	170	11-4-68	1989	La Romana, D.R.
Clark, Will	.305	149	554	98	169	41	1	23	102	72	97	1	0	L	L	6-1	200	3-13-64	1985	Southlake, Texas
Clayton, Royce	.285	52	186	30	53	12	1	5	24	13	32	5	5	R	R	6-0	183	1-2-70	1988	Inglewood, Calif.
Cuyler, Milt	.500	7	6	3	3	2	0	1	3	1	0	0	0	B	R	5-10	185	10-7-68	1986	Lakeland, Fla.
Elster, Kevin	.232	84	297	33	69	10	1	8	37	33	66	0	2	R	R	6-2	205	8-3-64	1984	Henderson, Nev.
Gonzalez, Juan	.318	154	606	110	193	50	2	45	157	46	126	2	1	R	R	6-3	220	10-16-69	1986	Levittown, P.R.
Goodwin, Tom	.290	154	520	102	151	13	3	2	33	73	90	38	20	L	R	6-1	175	7-27-68	1989	Fresno, Calif.
Greer, Rusty	.306	155	598	107	183	31	5	16	108	80	93	2	4	L	L	6-0	195	1-21-69	1990	Colleyville, Texas
Haselman, Bill	.314	40	105	11	33	6	0	6	17	3	17	0	0	R	R	6-3	223	5-25-66	1987	New Castle, Wash.
Kelly, Roberto	.323	75	257	48	83	7	3	16	46	8	46	0	2	R	R	6-2	202	10-1-64	1982	Panama City, Panama
McLemore, Mark	.247	126	461	79	114	15	1	5	53	89	64	12	4	B	R	5-11	207	10-4-64	1982	Grapevine, Texas
Newson, Warren	.190	10	21	1	4	1	0	0	2	1	5	0	0	L	L	5-7	200	7-3-64	1986	Southlake, Texas
Rodriguez, Ivan	.321	145	579	88	186	40	4	21	91	32	88	9	0	R	R	5-9	205	11-30-71	1989	Vega Baja, P.R.
Sasser, Rob	.000	1	1	0	0	0	0	0	0	0	0	0	0	R	R	6-3	205	3-9-75	1993	Oakland, Calif.
Sheldon, Scott	.125	7	16	0	2	0	0	0	1	1	6	0	0	R	R	6-3	185	11-20-68	1991	Houston, Texas
Simms, Mike	.296	86	186	36	55	11	0	16	46	24	47	0	1	R	R	6-4	230	1-12-67	1985	Arlington, Texas
Stevens, Lee	.265	120	344	52	91	17	4	20	59	31	93	0	2	L	L	6-4	235	7-10-67	1986	Grapevine, Texas
Tatis, Fernando	.270	95	330	41	89	17	2	3	32	12	66	6	2	R	R	5-10	170	1-1-75	1993	San Pedro de Macoris, D.R.
Tremie, Chris	.333	2	3	2	1	1	0	0	0	1	1	0	0	R	R	6-0	200	10-17-69	1992	Houston, Texas
Zeile, Todd	.261	52	180	26	47	14	1	6	28	28	32	1	0	R	R	6-1	204	9-9-65	1986	Westlake Village, Calif.

PITCHING	W	L	ERA	G	GS	CG	SV	IP	H	R	ER	BB	SO	B	T	HT	WT	DOB	1st Yr	Resides
Bailes, Scott	1	0	6.47	46	0	0	0	40	61	33	29	11	30	L	L	6-2	171	12-18-62	1982	Springfield, Mo.
Burkett, John	9	13	5.68	32	32	0	0	195	230	131	123	46	131	R	R	6-3	215	11-28-64	1983	Southlake, Texas
Cadaret, Greg	0	0	4.70	11	0	0	0	8	11	4	4	3	5	L	L	6-3	215	2-27-62	1983	Mesa, Ariz.
2-team (39 Anaheim)	1	2	4.23	50	0	0	1	45	49	21	21	18	42							
Crabtree, Tim	6	1	3.50	64	0	0	0	85	86	40	34	35	60	R	R	6-4	205	10-13-69	1992	Jackson, Mich.
Fossas, Tony	1	0	0.00	10	0	0	0	7	3	0	0	4	7	L	L	6-0	198	9-23-57	1979	Fort Lauderdale, Fla.
2-team (23 Seattle)	1	3	5.30	33	0	0	0	19	22	11	11	10	17							
Gunderson, Eric	0	3	5.19	68	1	0	0	68	88	43	39	19	41	R	L	6-0	190	3-29-66	1987	Portland, Ore.
Helling, Rick	20	7	4.41	33	33	4	0	216	209	109	106	78	164	R	R	6-3	220	12-15-70	1992	West Fargo, N.D.
Hernandez, Xavier	6	6	3.57	46	0	0	1	58	43	27	23	30	41	R	R	6-2	195	8-16-65	1986	Missouri City, Texas
Johnson, Jonathan	0	0	8.31	1	1	0	0	4	5	4	4	5	3	R	R	6-0	180	7-16-74	1995	West Columbia, S.C.
Levine, Alan	0	1	4.50	30	0	0	0	58	68	30	29	16	19	L	R	6-3	180	5-22-68	1991	Belleville, Ill.
Loaiza, Esteban	3	6	5.90	14	14	1	0	79	103	57	52	22	55	R	R	6-3	205	12-31-71	1991	Imperial Beach, Calif.
Oliver, Darren	6	7	6.53	19	19	2	0	103	140	84	75	43	58	R	L	6-2	210	10-6-70	1988	Arlington, Texas
Patterson, Danny	2	5	4.45	56	0	0	2	61	64	31	30	19	33	R	R	6-0	180	2-17-71	1990	Arlington, Texas
Pavlik, Roger	1	1	3.86	5	0	0	1	14	16	8	6	5	8	R	R	6-2	220	10-4-67	1986	Arlington, Texas
Perisho, Matt	0	2	27.00	2	2	0	0	5	15	17	15	8	2	L	L	6-0	190	6-8-75	1993	Phoenix, Ariz.
Santana, Julio	0	0	8.44	3	0	0	0	5	7	5	5	4	1	R	R	6-0	185	1-20-73	1992	Santo Domingo, D.R.
Sele, Aaron	19	11	4.23	33	33	3	0	213	239	116	100	84	167	R	R	6-5	215	6-25-70	1991	Kirkland, Wash.
Stottlemyre, Todd	5	4	4.33	10	10	0	0	60	68	33	29	30	57	L	R	6-3	195	5-20-65	1986	Yakima, Wash.
Van Poppel, Todd	1	2	8.84	4	4	0	0	19	26	20	19	10	10	R	R	6-5	210	12-9-71	1990	Southlake, Texas
Wetteland, John	3	1	2.03	63	0	0	42	62	47	17	14	14	72	R	R	6-2	215	8-21-66	1985	Cedar Crest, N.M.
Witt, Bobby	5	4	7.66	14	13	0	0	69	95	62	59	33	30	R	R	6-2	205	5-11-64	1985	Colleyville, Texas

FIELDING

Catcher	PCT	G	PO	A	E	DP	PB
Haselman	.995	36	177	7	1	0	0
Rodriguez	.994	139	864	71	6	6	10

First Base	PCT	G	PO	A	E	DP
Clark	.989	134	1077	75	13	112
Sheldon	.000	1	0	0	0	0
Simms	.975	16	72	7	2	8
Stevens	.996	37	207	15	1	11

Second Base	PCT	G	PO	A	E	DP
Alicea	.970	45	81	111	6	26
Cedeno	.889	7	4	12	2	1
McLemore	.975	122	249	331	15	71

Third Base	PCT	G	PO	A	E	DP
Alicea	.940	26	15	32	3	1
Sheldon	1.000	3	1	4	0	2
Tatis	.945	94	74	184	15	15
Zeile	.915	52	38	91	12	7

Shortstop	PCT	G	PO	A	E	DP
Cedeno	.963	35	37	67	4	14
Clayton	.972	52	88	152	7	26
Elster	.976	84	107	255	9	49
Sheldon	.933	2	7	7	1	3

Outfield	PCT	G	PO	A	E	DP
Alicea	1.000	2	2	0	0	0
Cuyler	1.000	3	5	0	0	0
Gonzalez	.982	116	212	8	4	2
Goodwin	.992	150	370	5	3	1
Greer	.990	154	304	6	3	0
Kelly	.976	71	155	5	4	1
Newson	1.000	6	6	0	0	0
Simms	1.000	43	45	1	0	0
Stevens	1.000	7	12	0	0	0

JOHN WILLIAMSON

Royce Clayton

JOHN WILLIAMSON

Texas' Rick Helling
Tied for league lead with 20 wins

LEE SCHMID

Kelly Dransfeldt
Hit 27 home runs at two levels

FARM SYSTEM

Director of Player Development: Reid Nichols

Class	Farm Team	League	W	L	Pct.	Finish*	Manager	First Yr
AAA	Oklahoma Redhawks	Pacific Coast	74	70	.514	t-9th (16)	Greg Biagini	1983
AA	Tulsa (Okla.) Drillers	Texas	78	62	.557	+2nd (8)	Bobby Jones	1977
A#	Charlotte (Fla.) Rangers	Florida State	82	56	.594	1st (14)	James Byrd	1987
A	Savannah (Ga.) Sand Gnats	South Atlantic	66	76	.465	11th (14)	Paul Carey	1998
Rookie#	Pulaski (Va.) Rangers	Appalachian	29	37	.439	t-8th (10)	Bruce Crabbe	1997
Rookie	Port Charlotte (Fla.) Rangers	Gulf Coast	34	26	.567	+t-3rd (14)	Darryl Kennedy	1973

*Finish in overall standings (No. of teams in league) #Advanced level +Won championship

OKLAHOMA Class AAA

PACIFIC COAST LEAGUE

BATTING	AVG	G	AB	R	H	2B	3B	HR	RBI	BB	SO	SB	CS	B	T	HT	WT	DOB	1st Yr	Resides
Barberie, Bret	.305	133	502	70	153	36	4	6	55	57	85	3	3	B	R	5-11	180	8-16-67	1989	Cerritos, Calif.
Barkett, Andy	.314	80	255	38	80	17	5	4	36	35	43	3	4	L	L	6-1	205	9-5-74	1995	Raleigh, N.C.
Chamberlain, Wes	.365	27	96	16	35	7	0	5	21	7	12	0	1	R	R	6-2	219	4-13-66	1987	Chicago, Ill.
Cuyler, Milt	.000	2	6	0	0	0	0	0	0	2	4	0	1	B	R	5-10	185	10-7-68	1986	Lakeland, Fla.
Demetral, Chris	.299	57	157	26	47	6	0	4	16	20	31	3	2	L	R	5-11	175	12-8-69	1991	Sterling Heights, Mich.
Estrada, Osmani	.354	15	48	17	17	2	0	1	3	5	2	1	0	R	R	5-8	180	1-23-69	1993	Woodland Hills, Calif.
Gonzales, Rene	.219	62	196	24	43	9	0	4	22	36	30	1	3	R	R	6-3	220	9-3-61	1982	Hollywood Hills, Calif.
2-team (15 Calgary)	.217	77	240	28	52	10	0	4	23	47	38	1	3							
Hall, Joe	.253	24	87	6	22	5	1	1	15	7	13	0	0	R	R	6-0	180	3-6-66	1988	Rowlett, Texas
Lewis, T.R.	.252	53	206	37	52	12	3	4	27	21	32	4	3	R	R	6-0	180	4-17-71	1989	Jacksonville, Fla.
Little, Mark	.296	69	274	58	81	20	4	8	46	16	60	9	6	R	R	6-0	195	7-11-72	1994	Edwardsville, Ill.
Mottola, Chad	.265	74	257	29	68	13	1	2	22	18	49	8	3	R	R	6-3	220	10-15-71	1992	Fort Lauderdale, Fla.
Murphy, Mike	.216	24	74	10	16	1	0	0	5	6	23	3	1	R	R	6-2	185	1-23-72	1990	Albuquerque, N.M.
Newson, Warren	.307	111	398	75	122	21	1	21	75	66	106	7	5	L	L	5-7	200	7-3-64	1986	Southlake, Texas
Norman, Les	.305	100	380	64	116	32	2	10	51	17	79	6	2	R	R	6-1	185	2-25-69	1991	Blue Springs, Mo.
Quinlan, Tom	.278	137	539	75	150	33	3	16	97	43	155	4	0	R	R	6-3	210	3-27-68	1987	Maplewood, Minn.
Sagmoen, Marc	.268	113	403	61	108	26	6	14	65	35	86	6	2	L	L	5-11	185	4-16-71	1993	Seattle, Wash.
Sheldon, Scott	.256	131	493	74	126	31	4	29	96	62	143	2	2	R	R	6-3	185	11-20-68	1991	Houston, Texas
Stevens, Lee	.333	3	12	2	4	0	0	1	1	0	2	0	0	L	L	6-4	235	7-10-67	1986	Grapevine, Texas
Tremie, Chris	.223	78	247	35	55	10	0	0	12	24	47	1	1	R	R	6-0	200	10-17-69	1992	Houston, Texas
Voigt, Jack	.343	20	70	10	24	6	0	2	11	14	19	0	1	R	R	6-1	178	5-17-66	1987	Venice, Fla.
2-team (18 Edmonton)	.333	38	138	20	46	12	0	6	22	22	34	1	3							
Wrona, Rick	.277	100	300	46	83	15	1	5	35	15	56	1	3	R	R	6-1	195	12-10-63	1985	Tulsa, Okla.

PITCHING	W	L	ERA	G	GS	CG	SV	IP	H	R	ER	BB	SO	B	T	HT	WT	DOB	1st Yr	Resides
Bailes, Scott	0	0	0.00	1	0	0	0	1	2	0	0	0	2	L	L	6-2	171	12-18-62	1982	Springfield, Mo.
Clark, Terry	12	5	3.38	30	24	2	1	165	156	72	62	35	95	R	R	6-2	195	10-10-60	1979	Fontana, Calif.
Converse, Jim	0	0	5.14	4	0	0	1	7	8	5	4	2	4	L	R	5-9	180	8-17-71	1990	Citrus Heights, Calif.
Fossas, Tony	0	1	5.40	4	0	0	0	7	6	4	4	4	3	L	L	6-0	198	9-23-57	1979	Fort Lauderdale, Fla.
2-team (10 Iowa)	0	1	4.63	14	0	0	0	12	16	8	6	6	5							
Granger, Jeff	4	8	4.67	32	19	0	1	129	160	80	67	38	94	R	L	6-4	200	12-16-71	1993	College Station, Texas
Hernandez, Xavier	0	0	1.35	5	0	0	0	7	5	1	1	1	9	R	R	6-2	195	8-16-65	1986	Missouri City, Texas
Hurst, Jonathan	1	2	6.98	7	2	0	0	19	29	16	15	4	10	R	R	6-3	196	10-20-66	1987	Spartanburg, S.C.
Johnson, Barry	2	8	6.63	31	7	1	1	77	96	66	57	21	54	R	R	6-4	200	8-21-69	1991	Joliet, Ill.
Johnson, Jonathan	6	6	4.90	19	18	1	1	112	109	66	61	32	94	R	R	6-0	180	7-16-74	1995	West Columbia, S.C.
Knight, Brandon	0	7	9.74	16	12	0	0	65	100	75	70	29	52	L	R	6-0	170	10-1-75	1995	Oxnard, Calif.
Kolb, Dan	0	0	0.00	1	0	0	0	1	1	0	0	1	0	R	R	6-4	185	3-29-75	1995	Sterling, Ill.
Levine, Alan	1	3	4.73	12	7	0	1	53	51	33	28	17	30	L	R	6-3	180	5-22-68	1991	Belleville, Ill.
Manning, David	0	0	1.00	6	0	0	1	9	11	1	1	0	9	R	R	6-3	205	8-14-72	1992	Lantana, Fla.
Moody, Eric	6	6	3.38	45	6	0	12	101	112	51	38	23	73	R	R	6-6	185	1-6-71	1993	Williamston, S.C.
Myers, Jimmy	7	1	2.02	41	0	0	9	62	56	20	14	20	24	R	R	6-1	185	4-28-69	1987	Crowder, Okla.
Oliver, Darren	0	0	0.00	1	1	0	0	5	2	0	0	1	1	R	L	6-2	210	10-6-70	1988	Arlington, Texas
Patterson, Danny	0	0	4.50	1	0	0	0	2	4	1	1	1	2	R	R	6-0	180	2-17-71	1990	Arlington, Texas
Perisho, Matt	8	5	3.89	15	15	1	0	90	91	41	39	42	60	L	L	6-0	190	6-8-75	1993	Phoenix, Ariz.
Pickett, Ricky	6	6	3.71	24	10	2	1	80	69	39	33	52	78	L	L	6-1	200	1-19-70	1992	Greenville, Fla.
3-team (5 Fres./5 Tuc.)	7	7	4.32	34	10	2	1	92	82	51	44	75	94							
Powell, John	0	1	8.41	11	0	0	1	20	24	21	19	5	20	R	R	5-10	180	4-7-71	1994	Snellville, Ga.
Small, Mark	4	4	4.60	15	6	0	0	47	53	30	24	13	42	R	R	6-3	205	11-12-67	1989	Seattle, Wash.
Smith, Dan	0	0	6.00	1	1	0	0	6	6	4	4	1	3	R	R	6-3	210	9-15-75	1993	Girard, Kan.
Sturtze, Tanyon	3	1	3.34	13	3	0	0	35	33	13	13	18	31	R	R	6-5	190	10-12-70	1990	Worcester, Mass.
Thomas, Larry	3	0	4.40	11	0	0	0	14	16	7	7	2	14	R	L	6-1	195	10-25-69	1991	Mobile, Ala.
Van Poppel, Todd	5	5	3.72	15	13	2	0	87	88	44	36	25	69	R	R	6-5	210	12-9-71	1990	Southlake, Texas
Venafro, Mike	0	0	6.35	13	0	0	0	17	19	12	12	10	15	L	L	5-10	170	8-2-73	1995	Chantilly, Va.
Watkins, Scott	6	1	3.26	38	0	0	2	50	44	19	18	22	50	L	L	6-3	180	5-15-70	1992	Sand Springs, Okla.

FIELDING

Catcher	PCT	G	PO	A	E	DP	PB
Tremie	.995	78	498	45	3	4	2
Wrona	.977	85	461	45	12	8	11

First Base	PCT	G	PO	A	E	DP
Barkett	.994	73	612	33	4	60
Estrada	1.000	3	20	3	0	5
Gonzales	.993	18	127	6	1	13
Hall	1.000	13	94	8	0	9
Lewis	.988	25	232	11	3	10
Norman	.000	1	0	0	0	0
Sagmoen	.973	20	135	8	4	12
Stevens	1.000	1	12	1	0	1
Voigt	1.000	2	17	1	0	1
Wrona	.990	15	86	9	1	5

Second Base	PCT	G	PO	A	E	DP
Barberie	.982	110	229	321	10	67
Demetral	.980	21	47	52	2	13
Estrada	.902	7	15	22	4	4
Gonzales	.964	12	22	32	2	9
Hall	.857	1	2	4	1	0
Quinlan	.000	1	0	0	0	0

Third Base	PCT	G	PO	A	E	DP
Barberie	.667	1	0	2	1	0
Estrada	1.000	1	0	3	0	0
Gonzales	.929	10	9	30	3	1
Hall	1.000	4	1	14	0	0
Quinlan	.940	124	96	278	24	31
Wrona	1.000	2	0	1	0	0

Shortstop	PCT	G	PO	A	E	DP
Demetral	1.000	7	10	15	0	5
Estrada	.900	2	2	7	1	2
Gonzales	.968	15	22	38	2	5
Sheldon	.959	123	162	397	24	76

Outfield	PCT	G	PO	A	E	DP
Chamberlain	1.000	16	24	2	0	1
Cuyler	1.000	2	3	0	0	0
Demetral	1.000	20	33	1	0	0
Hall	.833	5	5	0	1	0
Lewis	.909	18	20	0	2	0
Little	.994	64	161	6	1	1
Mottola	.953	72	118	5	6	0
Murphy	1.000	14	19	0	0	0
Newson	.982	74	104	4	2	0
Norman	.987	80	144	11	2	3
Sagmoen	.909	91	172	9	2	3
Sheldon	1.000	2	1	0	0	0
Voigt	.963	16	25	1	1	0
Wrona	.000	1	0	0	0	0

TULSA — Class AA

TEXAS LEAGUE

BATTING	AVG	G	AB	R	H	2B	3B	HR	RBI	BB	SO	SB	CS	B	T	HT	WT	DOB	1st Yr	Resides
Barkett, Andy	.268	43	157	23	42	11	1	2	31	27	22	0	0	L	L	6-1	205	9-5-74	1995	Raleigh, N.C.
Brumbaugh, Cliff	.259	132	483	65	125	34	1	15	76	54	77	1	3	R	R	6-2	205	4-21-74	1995	New Castle, Del.
Collins, Sean	.138	11	29	3	4	1	0	0	1	6	8	0	0	R	R	5-10	166	3-3-67	1989	Venice, Calif.
*Conti, Jason	.315	130	530	125	167	31	12	15	67	63	96	19	13	L	R	5-11	180	1-27-75	1996	Cranberry Township, Pa.
Demetral, Chris	.272	45	147	22	40	9	3	4	18	33	24	2	3	L	R	5-11	175	12-8-69	1991	Sterling Heights, Mich.
Dransfeldt, Kelly	.252	58	226	43	57	15	4	9	36	18	79	8	1	R	R	6-2	195	4-16-75	1996	Morris, Ill.
*Goligoski, Jason	.218	65	202	21	44	4	2	0	10	21	44	0	2	L	R	6-1	175	10-2-71	1993	Hamilton, Mont.
Goodwin, Joe	.097	10	31	3	3	1	0	0	3	1	7	0	0	R	R	5-10	180	4-19-74	1995	New Windsor, Md.
King, Cesar	.222	90	316	40	70	16	2	3	39	30	68	1	1	R	R	6-0	175	2-28-78	1995	La Romana, D.R.
*Koeyers, Ramsey	.250	55	164	25	41	2	0	4	18	13	45	1	0	R	R	6-1	187	8-7-74	1991	Curacao, Neth. Antilles
Mateo, Ruben	.309	107	433	79	134	32	3	18	75	30	56	18	8	R	R	6-0	170	2-10-78	1995	San Cristobal, D.R.
Morris, Warren	.331	95	390	59	129	22	5	14	73	43	63	12	7	L	R	5-11	190	1-11-74	1997	Alexandria, La.
Mottola, Chad	.500	8	26	9	13	1	0	1	7	10	1	3	0	R	R	6-3	220	10-15-71	1992	Fort Lauderdale, Fla.
Murphy, Mike	.250	58	196	26	49	8	2	4	22	27	56	6	2	R	R	6-2	185	1-23-72	1990	Albuquerque, N.M.
O'Neill, Doug	.221	18	68	10	15	5	0	2	5	10	16	4	0	R	R	5-10	200	6-29-70	1991	Campbell, Calif.
Podsednik, Scott	.240	17	75	9	18	4	1	0	4	6	11	5	2	L	L	6-0	170	3-18-76	1994	West, Texas
Richards, Rowan	.222	34	126	23	28	4	0	6	23	12	25	0	1	R	R	6-0	195	5-17-74	1996	Bloomfield, N.J.
Sasser, Rob	.281	111	417	57	117	25	2	8	62	60	98	18	12	R	R	6-3	205	3-9-75	1993	Oakland, Calif.
Sergio, Tom	.256	11	39	7	10	1	1	0	0	4	1	0	0	L	R	5-9	175	6-27-75	1997	Norristown, Pa.
Smiga, Jason	.000	2	6	0	0	0	0	0	0	0	0	0	0	R	R	5-10	170	6-19-73	1996	Mesquite, Texas
*Spivey, Junior	.311	34	119	26	37	10	1	3	16	28	25	8	4	R	R	6-0	185	1-28-75	1996	Oklahoma City, Okla.
Vessel, Andrew	.238	106	408	42	97	23	0	8	49	22	63	5	5	R	R	6-3	225	3-11-75	1993	Richmond, Calif.
Zywica, Mike	.280	58	214	40	60	15	4	5	45	19	56	7	3	R	R	6-4	190	9-14-74	1996	Richton Park, Ill.

PITCHING	W	L	ERA	G	GS	CG	SV	IP	H	R	ER	BB	SO	B	T	HT	WT	DOB	1st Yr	Resides
Bailes, Scott	0	1	10.80	2	0	0	1	2	4	2	2	0	4	L	L	6-2	171	12-18-62	1982	Springfield, Mo.
Elliott, Donnie	1	1	5.79	20	0	0	2	28	24	20	18	21	25	R	R	6-4	190	9-20-68	1988	Deer Park, Texas
Glynn, Ryan	9	6	3.44	26	24	4	0	157	140	66	60	64	111	R	R	6-3	195	11-1-74	1995	Portsmouth, Va.
Hernandez, Xavier	0	0	3.00	2	2	0	0	3	3	1	1	0	2	R	R	6-2	195	8-16-65	1986	Missouri City, Texas
Hurst, Jonathan	0	1	4.50	10	1	0	0	26	25	16	13	8	23	R	R	6-3	196	10-20-66	1987	Spartanburg, S.C.

PITCHING	W	L	ERA	G	GS	CG	SV	IP	H	R	ER	BB	SO	B	T	HT	WT	DOB	1st Yr	Resides
Juarbe, Ken	0	1	5.65	7	1	0	0	14	16	10	9	11	13	L	L	6-1	170	7-15-68	1988	Ciales, P.R.
Knight, Brandon	6	6	5.11	14	14	0	0	86	94	54	49	37	87	L	R	6-0	170	10-1-75	1995	Oxnard, Calif.
Kolb, Dan	12	11	4.82	28	28	2	0	162	187	104	87	76	83	R	R	6-4	185	3-29-75	1995	Sterling, Ill.
Lee, Corey	10	9	4.51	26	25	1	0	144	105	81	72	102	132	B	L	6-2	180	12-26-74	1996	Clayton, N.C.
Lisio, Joe	0	0	8.10	9	0	0	0	13	21	13	12	8	13	R	R	6-2	205	8-5-73	1994	West Hempstead, N.Y.
Manning, David	2	0	4.85	6	0	0	0	13	13	7	7	11	15	R	R	6-3	205	8-14-72	1992	Lantana, Fla.
Martinez, Jose	2	2	7.60	7	7	0	0	34	46	34	29	14	21	R	R	6-0	165	2-4-75	1995	Santiago, D.R.
*Michalak, Chris	1	2	1.83	10	0	0	0	20	10	4	4	2	15	L	L	6-2	195	1-4-71	1993	Lemont, Ill.
Moore, Bobby	0	0	0.00	1	0	0	0	1	0	0	0	0	2	R	R	6-5	217	3-27-73	1995	Spokane, Wash.
Patterson, Danny	0	0	4.50	2	1	0	0	4	3	2	2	0	4	R	R	6-0	180	2-17-71	1990	Arlington, Texas
Pedraza, Rod	3	2	2.48	6	5	0	0	36	30	11	10	4	31	R	R	6-2	210	12-28-69	1991	Cuero, Texas
Perisho, Matt	0	0	6.00	1	1	0	0	3	3	2	2	3	1	L	L	6-0	190	6-8-75	1993	Phoenix, Ariz.
Powell, John	2	4	2.50	28	0	0	0	54	38	18	15	21	44	R	R	5-10	180	4-7-71	1994	Snellville, Ga.
Sabel, Erik	7	0	3.20	24	2	0	2	56	46	24	20	13	33	R	R	6-3	193	10-14-74	1996	West Lafayette, Ind.
Smith, Dan	13	9	5.81	26	25	1	0	153	162	101	99	58	105	R	R	6-3	210	9-15-75	1993	Girard, Kan.
Sollecito, Gabe	1	0	1.93	5	0	0	0	9	5	3	2	4	10	B	R	6-1	190	3-3-72	1993	Monterey, Calif.
Sturtze, Tanyon	1	0	5.40	1	0	0	0	2	2	1	1	2	3	R	R	6-5	190	10-12-70	1990	Worcester, Mass.
*Tuttle, Dave	1	2	2.69	36	2	0	4	74	73	30	22	29	47	R	R	6-3	190	9-29-69	1992	Los Gatos, Calif.
Van Poppel, Todd	0	0	4.50	1	1	0	0	4	2	2	2	4	2	R	R	6-5	210	12-9-71	1990	Southlake, Texas
Venafro, Mike	3	4	3.10	46	0	0	14	52	42	21	18	26	45	L	L	5-10	170	8-2-73	1995	Chantilly, Va.
Watkins, Scott	1	0	2.14	10	1	0	1	21	14	5	5	2	25	L	L	6-3	180	5-15-70	1992	Sand Springs, Okla.
Zimmerman, Jeff	3	1	1.29	41	0	0	9	63	38	16	9	20	67	R	R	6-1	200	8-9-72	1997	Fairmont, W.Va.

*Loaned from Arizona Diamondbacks.

FIELDING

Catcher	PCT	G	PO	A	E	DP	PB
Goodwin	1.000	10	61	3	0	2	0
King	.988	89	585	73	8	12	18
Koeyers	.989	50	344	29	4	3	5

First Base	PCT	G	PO	A	E	DP
Barkett	.995	43	370	23	2	45
Brumbaugh	.990	97	850	64	9	86
Demetral	1.000	1	1	0	0	0
Goligoski	1.000	1	10	0	0	0
Koeyers	1.000	1	9	0	0	0

Second Base	PCT	G	PO	A	E	DP
Demetral	1.000	4	8	8	0	1
Goligoski	.977	8	21	21	1	7
Morris	.964	88	179	274	17	63
Sasser	1.000	1	2	4	0	0
Sergio	.912	8	11	20	3	5
Spivey	.980	34	62	84	3	18

Third Base	PCT	G	PO	A	E	DP
Brumbaugh	.933	23	13	43	4	5
Demetral	1.000	4	4	8	0	0
Goligoski	.867	3	1	12	2	1
Sasser	.919	110	66	229	26	25

Shortstop	PCT	G	PO	A	E	DP
Demetral	.972	36	48	93	4	23
Dransfeldt	.950	58	81	184	14	30
Goligoski	.963	49	101	160	10	36
Smiga	.750	1	4	2	2	1

Outfield	PCT	G	PO	A	E	DP
Brumbaugh	1.000	12	18	2	0	0
Collins	1.000	8	10	0	0	0
Conti	.976	115	183	20	5	2
Mateo	.970	106	215	11	7	3
Mottola	1.000	4	5	0	0	0
Murphy	1.000	16	28	1	0	0
O'Neill	1.000	6	10	0	0	0
Podsednik	1.000	17	33	1	0	0
Richards	1.000	4	9	0	0	0
Vessel	.990	90	185	8	2	2
Zywica	.980	51	92	5	2	2

CHARLOTTE — Class A

FLORIDA STATE LEAGUE

BATTING	AVG	G	AB	R	H	2B	3B	HR	RBI	BB	SO	SB	CS	B	T	HT	WT	DOB	1st Yr	Resides
Acevedo, Luis	.000	1	4	0	0	0	0	0	0	0	1	0	0	R	R	5-11	180	11-19-77	1996	Isabela, P.R.
Cheek, Shawn	.138	32	87	7	12	4	0	2	10	2	32	0	1	R	R	6-3	215	4-30-74	1997	Albany, Ga.
Dransfeldt, Kelly	.322	67	245	46	79	17	0	18	76	29	67	7	2	R	R	6-2	195	4-16-75	1996	Morris, Ill.
Ellis, John	.231	60	208	22	48	9	0	3	25	9	43	1	2	R	R	6-1	195	8-4-75	1996	Niantic, Conn.
Gallagher, Shawn	.308	137	520	111	160	37	4	26	121	66	116	18	6	R	R	6-0	187	11-8-76	1995	Lakeland, Fla.
Goodwin, Joe	.385	10	26	5	10	3	0	0	4	4	2	0	1	R	R	5-10	180	4-19-74	1995	New Windsor, Md.
Guerrero, Pedro	.000	1	4	0	0	0	0	0	0	0	1	0	0	R	R	5-10	165	8-21-79	1996	Santo Domingo, D.R.
Lamb, Michael	.302	135	536	83	162	35	3	9	93	45	63	18	7	B	R	6-1	185	8-9-75	1997	Valinda, Calif.
Mateo, Ruben	.000	1	4	0	0	0	0	0	1	0	1	0	0	R	R	6-0	170	2-10-78	1995	San Cristobal, D.R.
Monroe, Craig	.242	132	472	73	114	26	7	17	76	66	102	50	13	R	R	6-1	195	2-27-77	1995	Texarkana, Texas
Murphy, Mike	.286	3	7	4	2	1	0	0	1	3	1	1	0	R	R	6-2	185	1-23-72	1990	Albuquerque, N.M.
Myers, Adrian	.269	122	454	84	122	20	7	6	64	55	98	51	23	R	R	5-10	175	5-10-75	1996	Bassfield, Miss.
Pena, Carlos	.273	7	22	1	6	1	0	0	3	2	8	0	1	L	L	6-2	210	5-17-78	1998	Haverhill, Mass.
Piniella, Juan	.306	61	222	37	68	8	3	2	23	25	38	23	6	R	R	5-10	160	3-13-78	1996	Stafford, Va.
Podsednik, Scott	.285	81	302	55	86	12	4	4	39	44	32	26	8	L	L	6-0	170	3-18-76	1994	West, Texas
Richards, Rowan	.274	57	212	32	58	14	1	3	22	11	48	5	8	R	R	6-0	195	5-17-74	1996	Bloomfield, N.J.
Romano, Jason	.208	7	24	3	5	1	0	0	1	2	2	1	2	R	R	6-0	185	6-24-79	1997	Tampa, Fla.
Sasser, Rob	.308	4	13	1	4	2	0	0	3	3	5	1	0	R	R	6-3	205	3-9-75	1993	Oakland, Calif.
Sergio, Tom	.294	112	453	90	133	30	7	5	39	46	59	33	10	L	R	5-9	175	6-27-75	1997	Norristown, Pa.
Smiga, Jason	.303	26	66	7	20	1	0	0	5	6	11	2	2	R	R	5-10	170	6-19-73	1996	Mesquite, Texas
Solano, Danny	.260	84	262	46	68	15	0	1	30	42	54	9	6	R	R	5-9	155	12-3-78	1997	Santo Domingo, D.R.
Taveras, Luis	.163	76	246	21	40	4	2	3	24	14	70	4	6	R	R	5-10	165	8-1-77	1995	Santiago, D.R.
Vazquez, Alex	.190	24	42	3	8	1	0	0	0	9	16	5	0	R	R	6-0	170	3-6-77	1997	Woodbridge, Va.
Warriax, Brandon	.125	5	16	2	2	0	0	0	1	1	5	0	0	R	R	6-0	165	6-23-79	1997	Maxton, N.C.
Zywica, Mike	.381	68	252	67	96	21	3	11	49	34	40	16	5	R	R	6-4	190	9-14-74	1996	Richton Park, Ill.

GAMES BY POSITION: C—Cheek 13, Ellis 60, Goodwin 8, Taveras 76. **1B**—Cheek 9, Gallagher 128, Lamb 2, Pena 4. **2B**—Guerrero 1, Myers 1, Romano 7, Sergio 108, Smiga 13, Solano 16. **3B**—Lamb 132, Sasser 3, Smiga 6. **SS**—Acevedo 1, Dransfeldt 66, Smiga 3, Solano 68, Warriax 5. **OF**—Mateo 1, Monroe 121, Myers 97, Piniella 53, Podsednik 63, Richards 10, Sergio 1, Smiga 1, Vazquez 23, Zywica 64.

PITCHING	W	L	ERA	G	GS	CG	SV	IP	H	R	ER	BB	SO	B	T	HT	WT	DOB	1st Yr	Resides
Buckles, Bucky	4	0	0.57	18	0	0	1	31	21	4	2	15	18	R	R	6-1	190	6-19-73	1994	Victorville, Calif.
Cook, Derrick	13	7	3.66	26	26	1	0	167	170	81	68	64	111	R	R	6-3	195	8-6-75	1996	Staunton, Va.
Daniel, Michael	0	2	6.00	4	0	0	0	9	11	7	6	3	4	R	R	6-3	185	11-28-75	1998	Cherokee, Ala.
Darley, Ned	0	0	3.38	3	0	0	0	3	2	1	1	0	3	L	R	6-4	225	2-27-71	1990	Alcolu, S.C.
Davis, Doug	11	7	3.24	27	27	1	0	155	129	69	56	74	173	R	L	6-3	185	9-21-75	1996	Sparks, Nev.
DeYoung, Dan	13	4	4.02	20	20	0	0	119	112	60	53	39	62	R	R	6-0	210	3-24-76	1997	Libson, Iowa
Dickey, R.A.	1	5	3.30	57	0	0	38	60	58	31	22	22	53	R	R	6-2	205	10-29-74	1997	Nashville, Tenn.
Johnson, Jonathan	0	2	4.63	3	3	0	0	12	10	6	6	4	11	R	R	6-0	180	7-16-74	1995	West Columbia, S.C.
Manning, David	0	0	0.00	7	0	0	0	8	4	4	0	6	11	R	R	6-3	205	8-14-72	1992	Lantana, Fla.

PITCHING	W	L	ERA	G	GS	CG	SV	IP	H	R	ER	BB	SO	B	T	HT	WT	DOB	1st Yr	Resides
Martinez, Jose	7	5	2.77	19	19	2	0	124	120	55	38	28	86	R	R	6-0	165	2-4-75	1995	Santiago, D.R.
McGarity, Jeremy	1	0	0.00	3	0	0	0	9	5	0	0	0	6	R	R	6-5	197	3-22-71	1989	Lakeside, Calif.
Moore, Bobby	1	3	5.23	38	1	0	6	74	86	45	43	27	51	R	R	6-5	217	3-27-73	1995	Spokane, Wash.
Mota, Henry	5	3	3.88	34	4	0	4	95	98	55	41	40	60	R	R	5-11	170	5-13-78	1995	Santo Domingo, D.R.
Pedraza, Rod	5	5	3.16	15	8	0	0	68	54	30	24	15	55	R	R	6-2	210	12-28-69	1991	Cuero, Texas
Poland, Trey	8	5	3.87	26	25	1	0	149	150	82	64	60	138	L	L	6-1	190	4-3-75	1997	Shreveport, La.
Saneaux, Francisco	3	1	3.93	17	0	0	3	37	34	21	16	16	43	R	R	6-4	180	2-16-74	1991	Santo Domingo, D.R.
Schultz, Eric	3	3	4.38	6	5	1	0	25	24	13	12	11	13	R	R	6-5	220	2-4-74	1997	St. John, Ind.
Sollecito, Gabe	5	2	0.90	37	0	0	2	60	54	13	6	14	50	B	R	6-1	190	3-3-72	1993	Monterey, Calif.
Sturtze, Tanyon	0	1	6.00	1	0	0	0	3	2	3	2	1	3	R	R	6-5	190	10-12-70	1990	Worcester, Mass.
Zimmerman, Jeff	2	1	1.26	10	0	0	0	14	10	2	2	1	14	R	R	6-1	200	8-9-72	1997	Fairmont, W.Va.

SAVANNAH — Class A

SOUTH ATLANTIC LEAGUE

BATTING	AVG	G	AB	R	H	2B	3B	HR	RBI	BB	SO	SB	CS	B	T	HT	WT	DOB	1st Yr	Resides
Castillo, Geramel	.176	22	74	7	13	2	0	2	8	3	29	2	1	B	R	6-1	160	10-3-77	1995	La Romana, D.R.
Castro, Martiroc	.225	67	209	26	47	11	2	3	25	16	69	4	1	R	R	6-0	170	12-6-76	1995	Caracas, Ven.
Cheek, Shawn	.273	18	55	7	15	4	1	1	5	3	16	1	0	R	R	6-3	215	4-30-74	1997	Albany, Ga.
Cordero, Willy	.241	112	378	35	91	10	2	1	38	21	85	21	12	R	R	6-1	155	8-20-78	1995	San Cristobal, D.R.
Cruz, Geronimo	.000	9	23	2	0	0	0	0	2	0	6	2	0	B	L	6-0	177	11-15-77	1997	New York, N.Y.
Fisher, Anthony	.269	122	458	86	123	24	5	12	39	52	104	35	16	R	R	6-1	180	1-18-75	1996	Oakdale, Minn.
Garcia, Douglas	.213	25	80	7	17	0	0	2	11	4	15	3	0	L	L	6-1	165	4-25-79	1997	Barquisimeto, Ven.
Grabowski, Jason	.270	104	352	63	95	13	6	14	52	57	93	16	9	L	R	6-3	200	5-24-76	1997	Clinton, Conn.
Hafner, Travis	.237	123	405	62	96	15	4	16	84	68	139	7	3	L	R	6-3	215	6-3-77	1997	Sykeston, N.D.
Harris, Kevin	.163	27	86	12	14	1	1	2	9	1	39	5	0	R	R	6-2	220	3-27-78	1997	Tampa, Fla.
Jaramillo, Frank	.248	101	315	50	78	12	6	10	41	37	98	8	5	R	R	5-11	170	11-28-74	1996	Franksville, Wis.
Lina, Estivinson	.212	73	217	22	46	8	2	2	12	12	72	2	3	R	R	6-0	170	10-19-76	1995	Santo Domingo, D.R.
Pena, Carlos	.325	30	117	22	38	14	0	6	20	8	26	3	2	L	L	6-2	210	5-17-78	1998	Haverhill, Mass.
Pena, Jose	.305	125	466	68	142	22	5	6	66	17	91	40	16	R	R	6-2	175	10-13-76	1995	Santiago, D.R.
Piniella, Juan	.341	72	255	51	87	13	6	3	39	30	48	28	11	R	R	5-10	160	3-13-78	1996	Stafford, Va.
Romano, Jason	.271	134	524	72	142	19	4	7	52	46	94	40	17	R	R	6-0	185	6-24-79	1997	Tampa, Fla.
Santo, Jose	.299	107	381	78	114	17	6	21	76	51	119	26	7	R	R	5-11	165	3-1-78	1995	Santiago, D.R.
Sienko, Ryan	.174	17	46	5	8	3	0	0	4	4	20	0	0	R	R	6-4	220	9-16-75	1997	Elgin, Ill.
Torres, Jason	.196	19	46	1	9	2	0	0	5	5	17	0	0	L	R	5-10	170	12-11-78	1997	Vero Beach, Fla.
Warriax, Brandon	.209	51	187	24	39	8	0	3	14	16	41	9	2	R	R	6-0	165	6-23-79	1997	Maxton, N.C.

GAMES BY POSITION: C—Cheek 12, Grabowski 60, Lina 56, Sienko 11, Torres 19. **1B**—Cheek 6, Fisher 0, Grabowski 11, Hafner 00, Jaramillo 27, Lina 4, C. Pena 27, Sienko 1. **2B**—Cordero 7, Jaramillo 8, Romano 133, Santo 1. **3B**—Cordero 2, Hafner 24, Jaramillo 18, Santo 104. **SS**—Cordero 94, Jaramillo 6, Romano 1, Warriax 47. **OF**—Castillo 22, Castro 55, Cruz 8, Fisher 115, Garcia 6, Hafner 1, Harris 21, Jaramillo 32, C. Pena 1, J. Pena 109, Piniella 71, Sienko 1.

PITCHING	W	L	ERA	G	GS	CG	SV	IP	H	R	ER	BB	SO	B	T	HT	WT	DOB	1st Yr	Resides
Allen, Rodney	0	1	3.15	4	3	0	0	20	21	11	7	4	18	R	R	6-2	205	6-29-74	1996	Lindside, W.Va.
Beltey, Jason	0	1	9.00	1	1	0	0	4	3	7	4	2	5	R	R	6-1	170	11-18-77	1997	Vancouver, Wash.
Benoit, Joaquin	4	3	3.83	15	15	1	0	80	79	41	34	18	68	R	R	6-3	160	7-26-79	1996	Santiago, D.R.
Bond, Aaron	10	10	4.37	28	27	3	0	167	184	96	81	41	119	R	R	6-2	230	12-2-76	1997	Las Vegas, Nev.
Brazoban, Melvin	3	6	4.76	18	18	0	0	87	68	50	46	48	84	R	R	6-3	165	1-20-77	1994	Santo Domingo, D.R.
Carrion, Jorge	5	5	5.65	15	13	1	1	73	71	51	46	51	38	R	R	6-1	175	12-10-76	1996	Brooklyn, N.Y.
Fleming, Emar	7	8	4.84	37	21	1	1	139	145	88	75	61	133	R	R	6-3	210	10-14-76	1996	Baltimore, Md.
Frey, Chris	1	0	0.52	7	0	0	0	15	19	8	6	8	17	R	R	6-3	210	4-15-74	1998	Etters, Pa.
Kertis, John	2	3	4.03	38	3	0	1	76	74	45	34	46	90	B	R	6-2	200	3-19-75	1996	Miami, Fla.
Lundberg, David	6	9	5.54	50	0	0	14	88	105	69	54	27	70	B	R	6-1	185	5-4-77	1997	San Diego, Calif.
Marsonek, Sam	0	0	3.86	2	2	0	0	7	7	7	3	3	4	R	R	6-6	225	7-10-78	1997	Tampa, Fla.
Miller, Matt	3	1	2.29	17	0	0	3	35	25	9	9	10	46	R	R	6-2	215	11-23-71	1997	Greenville, Miss.
Shourds, Anthony	3	7	4.10	37	0	0	3	75	60	39	34	34	68	R	R	6-3	185	10-9-76	1996	Meriden, Conn.
Siegel, Justin	1	1	1.17	7	0	0	0	15	7	3	2	10	11	L	L	6-0	170	9-3-75	1996	Marina del Ray, Calif.
Silva, Douglas	3	4	4.57	38	0	0	7	65	72	34	33	13	60	R	R	6-3	190	7-8-79	1997	Miranda, Ven.
Smith, Ryan	8	6	7.07	35	7	0	1	84	90	77	66	66	88	L	L	6-4	215	9-4-74	1996	San Diego, Calif.
Tynan, Chris	6	8	4.40	21	21	1	0	117	113	69	57	74	95	R	R	6-2	170	11-15-78	1997	Vancouver, Wash.
White, Darell	4	3	4.22	13	11	3	1	70	68	38	33	25	53	R	R	6-2	200	4-16-72	1992	Alexandria, La.

PULASKI — Rookie

APPALACHIAN LEAGUE

BATTING	AVG	G	AB	R	H	2B	3B	HR	RBI	BB	SO	SB	CS	B	T	HT	WT	DOB	1st Yr	Resides
Castaneda, Cesar	.265	56	200	33	53	9	0	6	26	21	52	1	1	R	R	6-3	210	11-30-76	1998	Los Angeles, Calif.
Castillo, Geramel	.302	38	149	23	45	9	3	1	18	16	32	4	4	B	R	6-1	160	10-3-77	1995	La Romana, D.R.
Edgar, Jason	.291	45	151	28	44	8	2	0	16	32	20	9	2	L	R	5-11	172	5-18-76	1998	Cornwall, N.Y.
Garcia, Douglas	.358	23	95	12	34	3	0	2	21	2	19	2	1	L	L	6-1	165	4-25-79	1997	Barquisimeto, Ven.
Harris, Kevin	.224	60	232	37	52	7	3	8	35	10	97	25	4	R	R	6-2	220	3-27-78	1997	Tampa, Fla.
Infante, Danny	.243	46	169	24	41	12	1	3	19	18	52	1	2	R	R	6-0	175	4-2-78	1995	Santiago, D.R.
Jaramillo, Tony	.293	17	41	9	12	0	1	1	6	11	11	1	1	L	R	5-10	175	8-16-78	1998	Dallas, Texas
Jones, Jeremy	.277	26	101	11	28	3	1	3	14	10	18	0	0	R	R	6-3	195	8-12-77	1998	Raymore, Mo
Meliah, David	.262	48	183	21	48	8	0	5	28	13	26	5	3	L	R	6-3	185	3-11-77	1998	Walla Walla, Wash.
Nina, Amuarys	.310	50	174	34	54	9	4	0	20	25	35	9	9	R	R	5-11	155	8-10-77	1995	San Cristobal, D.R.
Ottevaere, Derek	.314	54	204	32	64	11	3	3	40	20	41	5	1	R	R	6-2	215	12-24-75	1998	Houston, Texas
Romano, Jimmie	.188	11	32	5	6	0	0	0	4	2	5	1	2	R	R	5-10	185	3-31-77	1998	Tampa, Fla.
Torres, Jason	.277	44	141	20	39	5	1	0	15	20	23	2	0	L	R	5-10	170	12-11-78	1997	Vero Beach, Fla.
Warriax, Brandon	.254	61	209	33	53	11	0	1	20	20	42	2	4	R	R	6-0	165	6-23-79	1997	Maxton, N.C.
Wright, Corey	.278	39	133	41	37	4	3	3	26	45	23	14	4	L	L	5-11	165	11-26-79	1997	La Puente, Calif.

GAMES BY POSITION: C—Jones 18, Romano 10, Torres 41. **1B**—Infante 46, Ottevaere 21. **2B**—Edgar 41, Jaramillo 6, Meliah 25. **3B**—Castaneda 56, Meliah 14. **SS**—Edgar 1, Jaramillo 1, Meliah 6, Warriax 61. **OF**—Castillo 34, Edgar 1, Garcia 18, Harris 58, Nina 37, Ottevaere 14, Wright 39.

PITCHING	W	L	ERA	G	GS	CG	SV	IP	H	R	ER	BB	SO	B	T	HT	WT	DOB	1st Yr	Resides
Boublis, Daniel	4	7	4.74	13	13	0	0	74	79	50	39	14	58	R	R	6-0	190	3-7-77	1998	Cedar Rapids, Iowa
Daniel, Michael	3	1	3.64	10	2	1	1	30	29	12	12	8	27	R	R	6-3	185	11-28-75	1998	Cherokee, Ala.
Guzman, Ambiorix	6	3	3.24	9	9	2	0	67	59	30	24	7	46	R	R	6-2	160	5-20-78	1995	Santiago, D.R.
Hughes, Travis	2	6	3.89	22	3	0	2	42	30	25	18	25	48	R	R	6-5	215	5-25-78	1998	Newton, Kan.
Kosderka, Matt	3	6	[illegible]	14	11	[illegible]	[illegible]	[illegible]	[illegible]	[illegible]	[illegible]	[illegible]	[illegible]	[illegible]	[illegible]	[illegible]	[illegible]	[illegible]	[illegible]	Roseburg, Ore.
Lamarsh, Rob	1	2	5.28	11	2	0	1	29	35	22	17	11	28	R	L	6-4	245	7-14-76	1998	Alton, Ill.
Moore, Eric	0	4	5.12	17	0	0	1	32	34	25	18	16	25	R	R	6-3	203	5-26-76	1998	Houston, Texas
Rios, Romualdo	1	2	5.49	10	10	0	0	41	47	34	25	14	30	B	R	6-0	150	2-5-80	1996	Maracaibo, Ven.
Schaeffer, Mike	3	0	2.45	18	2	0	1	48	34	16	13	19	42	L	L	6-2	210	5-17-76	1998	Ballwin, Mo.
Stewart, John	4	4	3.17	13	13	1	0	77	82	42	27	10	57	R	L	6-4	180	7-9-77	1998	Streamwood, Ill.
Vigeland, Ole	0	1	6.58	11	1	0	0	26	30	21	19	19	23	R	R	6-1	185	10-26-76	1998	Redmond, Wash.
Weaver, Joseph	2	1	1.74	17	0	0	5	41	31	20	8	17	49	L	R	6-4	220	9-6-77	1998	Centerville, Miss.

PORT CHARLOTTE — Rookie

GULF COAST LEAGUE

BATTING	AVG	G	AB	R	H	2B	3B	HR	RBI	BB	SO	SB	CS	B	T	HT	WT	DOB	1st Yr	Resides
Acevedo, Luis	.000	1	2	1	0	0	0	0	0	2	0	0	0	R	R	5-11	180	11-19-77	1996	Isabela, P.R.
Baez, Ernies	.211	37	123	14	26	3	1	0	11	12	15	5	3	B	R	6-0	180	1-2-78	1998	Dorado, P.R.
Cruz, Rafael	.233	41	129	20	30	1	0	1	7	14	26	0	1	R	R	6-2	180	5-19-79	1996	Santiago, D.R.
Cubillan, Jose	.267	46	150	30	40	10	2	3	15	21	47	8	4	B	R	6-4	180	12-27-78	1996	Zulia, Ven.
Erwin, Chris	.303	27	76	12	23	5	1	1	11	1	20	0	1	R	R	6-0	195	8-25-76	1998	Alton, Ill.
Guerrero, Pedro	.290	52	186	35	54	10	2	1	25	26	42	11	7	R	R	5-10	165	8-21-79	1996	Santo Domingo, D.R.
Jimenez, Jonathan	.270	13	37	5	10	2	0	0	8	5	11	1	0	R	R	6-0	160	1-30-79	1997	Santo Domingo, D.R.
Marciante, Frank	.310	37	129	17	40	9	0	1	16	14	17	1	2	B	R	6-3	215	8-16-78	1998	Sunrise, Fla.
Medrano, David	.195	50	154	19	30	7	0	3	17	21	61	2	0	R	R	5-11	160	9-20-78	1996	Santo Domingo, D.R.
Nowlin, Cody	.272	52	202	25	55	13	2	7	34	19	42	1	4	L	R	6-3	190	11-27-79	1998	Fresno, Calif.
Pena, Carlos	.400	2	5	1	2	0	0	0	0	3	1	1	1	L	L	6-2	210	5-17-78	1998	Haverhill, Mass.
Quinones, Marcus	.261	59	203	27	53	9	4	1	22	25	34	3	7	B	R	6-1	190	2-26-76	1998	Houston, Texas
Rollins, Antwon	.210	53	210	23	44	5	1	1	16	11	60	8	8	R	R	6-0	190	3-18-80	1998	Alameda, Calif.
Ryan, Greg	.240	53	183	27	44	9	2	2	22	19	16	8	3	L	L	6-0	170	7-3-77	1998	Garden City, Mich.
Torres, Frederick	.221	32	104	13	23	5	0	3	13	5	23	1	1	R	R	6-0	165	3-16-80	1997	Santiago, D.R.
Wright, Corey	.273	11	44	6	12	2	1	0	3	7	11	3	2	L	L	5-11	165	11-26-79	1997	La Puente, Calif.

GAMES BY POSITION: C—Cruz 34, Erwin 8, Torres 25. **1B**—Erwin 1, Marciante 15, Pena 1, Ryan 44. **2B**—Erwin 1, Guerrero 51, Medrano 9. **3B**—Erwin 13, Jimenez 10, Marciante 1, Medrano 39, Quinones 1. **SS**—Acevedo 1, Jimenez 2, Quinones 57. **OF**—Baez 31, Cubillan 44, Erwin 1, Nowlin 45, Rollins 49, Ryan 6, Wright 9.

PITCHING	W	L	ERA	G	GS	CG	SV	IP	H	R	ER	BB	SO	B	T	HT	WT	DOB	1st Yr	Resides
Backsmeyer, Justin	0	0	1.13	5	1	0	0	8	9	5	1	7	4	R	R	6-4	205	1-24-80	1998	Ballwin, Mo.
Beitey, Jason	0	0	0.00	5	0	0	1	9	5	0	0	3	7	R	R	6-1	170	11-18-77	1997	Vancouver, Wash.
Belcher, B.J.	0	0	18.90	3	0	0	0	3	9	7	7	1	3	R	R	6-2	225	7-2-77	1998	Milford, Va.
Bobbitt, Josh	2	1	4.50	19	0	0	2	36	46	24	18	12	41	R	L	6-3	200	8-6-76	1998	Wichita Falls, Texas
Buckles, Bucky	0	0	0.00	2	2	0	0	3	0	0	0	0	2	R	R	6-1	190	6-19-73	1994	Victorville, Calif.
Bullock, Jeremiah	1	6	5.00	11	9	0	0	45	54	34	25	21	30	L	L	6-1	180	12-27-79	1998	Cedar Rapids, Iowa
Diaz, Billy	3	3	4.28	13	5	0	0	48	51	26	23	5	29	R	R	6-3	180	11-25-79	1997	Vega Alta, P.R.
Dittfurth, Ryan	3	2	1.34	8	6	0	0	34	25	8	5	11	33	R	R	6-6	175	10-18-79	1998	Plano, Texas
Figueroa, Carlos	6	1	3.57	19	0	0	1	40	34	17	16	11	39	L	L	6-1	190	10-5-78	1997	Carolina, P.R.
Frey, Chris	2	2	2.79	10	7	0	1	42	34	19	13	10	45	R	R	6-3	210	4-15-74	1998	Etters, Pa.
Garff, Jeff	0	0	0.00	1	0	0	0	2	3	1	0	2	2	R	R	6-4	195	12-3-75	1995	Bountiful, Utah
Hidalgo, Edgar	2	1	4.76	10	0	0	0	17	23	9	9	1	16	R	R	6-1	195	8-13-79	1998	Maracaibo, Ven.
Manning, David	0	0	5.40	3	3	0	0	5	6	3	3	1	2	R	R	6-3	205	8-14-72	1992	Lantana, Fla.
Marsonek, Sam	0	0	0.00	2	2	0	0	5	2	1	0	0	2	R	R	6-6	225	7-10-78	1997	Tampa, Fla.
McGill, Frankie	3	1	3.51	9	7	0	0	33	35	17	13	9	24	R	R	5-11	210	9-10-79	1998	Cantonment, Fla.
Pratt, Andy	4	3	3.86	12	8	0	0	56	49	25	24	14	49	L	L	5-11	160	8-27-79	1998	Mesa, Ariz.
Quarnstrom, Robert	4	1	1.56	23	0	0	12	35	16	6	6	3	37	R	L	5-11	200	10-30-76	1998	Cabot, Ark.
Ridenour, Jeff	0	2	3.53	18	0	0	0	43	48	23	17	18	29	R	R	6-3	190	7-22-76	1997	Granite City, Ill.
Roberts, Mike	2	0	3.00	3	2	0	0	12	10	4	4	0	10	R	R	6-4	220	8-28-75	1997	Wilbraham, Mass.
Sturtze, Tanyon	0	1	7.71	3	3	0	0	7	12	7	6	4	10	R	R	6-5	190	10-12-70	1990	Worcester, Mass.
Valdez, Domingo	2	2	3.09	10	5	0	0	32	24	15	11	16	27	R	R	6-3	220	6-27-80	1998	Corpus Christi, Texas

TORONTO BLUE JAYS

Clemens repeats triple crown, young players blossom

BY LARRY MILLSON

The Toronto Blue Jays learned how to win again in 1998.

Finishing with a surge, they won 88 games under first-year manager Tim Johnson for their first winning season since 1993, when they won their second consecutive World Series.

The Blue Jays made a late push for the American League wild-card berth, led by righthander Roger Clemens, who won his second consecutive triple crown and his fifth AL Cy Young Award. Clemens' last loss of the season came on May 29.

Several young players blossomed into stars on offense. Right fielder Shawn Green became the franchise's first 30-30 player with 35 homers and 35 stolen bases. Green also drove in 100 runs to rank third on the team behind Carlos Delgado and Jose Canseco. Delgado's accomplishment was impressive because offseason shoulder surgery delayed the start of his season until late April. Another bright spot was outfielder Shannon Stewart, who stole 51 bases in his first full major league season.

Roger Clemens — Pete Tucci

Players of the Year

Major League: Roger Clemens, rhp
The Rocket won 15 consecutive decisions on his way to a second straight AL triple crown and a fifth Cy Young Award.

Minor League: Pete Tucci, of, Knoxville/Dunedin
Tucci enjoyed a breakout season, leading all Blue Jays minor leaguers with 30 home runs and 112 RBIs.

The Blue Jays were two games below .500 at the end of July, but their season turned around with a series of trades that were regarded at the time as a form of surrender, as the club dealt off veterans for prospects.

DH Mike Stanley was traded to the Red Sox for righthanders Peter Munro and Jay Yennaco on July 30. The next day three more trades were made. Righthander Juan Guzman was traded to the Orioles for righthander Nerio Rodriguez and outfielder Shannon Carter; outfielder Tony Phillips was traded to the Mets for righthander Leoncio Estrella; and third baseman Ed Sprague was traded to the Athletics for righthander Scott Rivette. Then on Aug. 6, closer Randy Myers was traded to the Padres for catcher Brian Loyd and a player to be named.

The departure of Guzman allowed young righthander Kelvim Escobar to return to starting after a fling as a reliever. The results were impressive. Earlier in the season the release of Erik Hanson opened another rotation spot for young righthander Chris Carpenter.

At the other end of the spectrum, Dave Stieb, 41, made a comeback after a five-year absence and had a win and two saves.

The winning was also going on at the minor league level. The organization had the best overall record in baseball at 448-331. Three teams–Triple-A Syracuse, Double-A Knoxville and Class A Hagerstown–made their league playoffs.

Syracuse was led by minor league veteran Shannon Withem, who went 17-5 with a 3.27 ERA, and Roy Halladay, who was 9-5 with a 3.79 ERA. Halladay, the organization's top prospect, made his major league debut in September and took a no-hitter into the ninth inning in his second start on the final day of the season against the Tigers.

Righthander John Sneed had a dominating season for Hagerstown, going 16-2 with a 2.56 ERA and 210 strikeouts in 162 innings.

Jay Gibbons, Toronto's 14th-round pick in 1998, gave Medicine Hat of the Rookie-level Pioneer League its second consecutive triple crown winner by hitting .397 with 19 homers and a league-record 98 RBIs. Greg Morrison won the league's triple crown in 1997.

ORGANIZATION LEADERS

BATTING		
*AVG	Jay Gibbons, Medicine Hat	.397
R	Casey Blake, Knoxville/Dunedin	103
H	Casey Blake, Knoxville/Dunedin	183
TB	Peter Tucci, Knoxville/Dunedin	299
2B	Casey Blake, Knoxville/Dunedin	43
3B	Jorge Nunez, Hagerstown/Medicine Hat	11
HR	Peter Tucci, Knoxville/Dunedin	30
RBI	Peter Tucci, Knoxville/Dunedin	112
BB	Joe Lawrence, Dunedin	105
SO	Peter Tucci, Knoxville/Dunedin	126
SB	Billy Brown, Hagerstown/St. Catharines	39
PITCHING		
W	Shannon Withem, Syracuse	17
L	Gary Glover, Knoxville/Dunedin	11
#ERA	Clayton Andrews, Hagerstown	2.28
G	Jim Mann, Dunedin	51
CG	Two tied at	4
SV	Jim Mann, Dunedin	25
IP	Shannon Withem, Syracuse	190
BB	Joe Young, Knox./Dunedin/Hagerstown	72
SO	John Sneed, Hagerstown	210

*Minimum 250 At-Bats #Minimum 75 Innings

Toronto BLUE JAYS

Manager: Tim Johnson

1998 Record: 88-74, .543 (3rd, AL East)

BATTING	AVG	G	AB	R	H	2B	3B	HR	RBI	BB	SO	SB	CS	B	T	HT	WT	DOB	1st Yr	Resides
Brown, Kevin	.264	52	110	17	29	7	1	2	15	9	31	0	1	R	R	6-2	210	4-21-73	1994	Mount Vernon, Ind.
Canseco, Jose	.237	151	583	98	138	26	0	46	107	65	159	29	17	R	R	6-4	240	7-2-64	1982	Fort Lauderdale, Fla.
Crespo, Felipe	.262	66	130	11	34	8	1	1	15	15	27	4	3	B	R	5-11	200	3-5-73	1991	Caguas, P.R.
Cruz, Jose	.253	105	352	18	89	14	3	11	42	57	99	11	4	B	R	6-0	200	4-19-74	1995	Houston, Texas
Dalesandro, Mark	.299	32	67	8	20	5	0	2	14	1	6	0	0	R	R	6-0	195	5-14-68	1990	Chicago, Ill.
Delgado, Carlos	.292	142	530	94	155	43	1	38	115	73	139	3	0	L	R	6-3	225	6-25-72	1989	Aguadilla, P.R.
Evans, Tom	.000	7	10	0	0	0	0	0	0	1	2	0	0	R	R	6-1	180	7-9-74	1992	Kirkland, Wash.
Fernandez, Tony	.321	138	486	71	156	36	2	9	72	45	53	13	8	B	R	6-2	175	6-30-62	1980	Boca Raton, Fla.
Fletcher, Darrin	.283	124	407	37	115	23	1	9	52	25	39	0	0	L	R	6-2	200	10-3-66	1987	Oakwood, Ill.
Gonzalez, Alex	.239	158	568	70	136	28	1	13	51	28	121	21	6	R	R	6-0	190	4-8-73	1991	Miami, Fla.
Grebeck, Craig	.256	102	301	33	77	17	2	2	27	29	42	2	2	R	R	5-7	150	12-29-64	1987	Laguna Niguel, Calif.
Green, Shawn	.278	158	630	106	175	33	4	35	100	50	142	35	12	L	L	6-4	195	11-10-72	1992	Irvine, Calif.
Lennon, Pat	.500	2	4	1	2	2	0	0	0	0	1	0	0	R	R	6-2	200	4-27-68	1986	Whiteville, N.C.
Perez, Tomas	.111	6	9	1	1	0	0	0	0	1	3	0	0	B	R	5-11	177	12-29-73	1991	Barquisimeto, Ven.
Phillips, Tony	.354	13	48	9	17	5	0	1	7	9	6	0	0	B	R	5-10	175	4-25-59	1978	Scottsdale, Ariz.
Samuel, Juan	.180	43	50	14	9	2	0	1	2	7	13	13	7	R	R	5-11	190	12-9-60	1980	Pembroke Pines, Fla.
Santiago, Benito	.310	15	29	2	9	5	0	0	4	1	6	0	0	R	R	6-1	182	3-9-65	1983	La Jolla, Calif.
Sprague, Ed	.238	105	382	49	91	20	0	17	51	24	73	0	2	R	R	6-2	205	7-25-67	1989	Stockton, Calif.
Stanley, Mike	.240	98	341	49	82	13	0	22	47	56	86	2	1	R	R	6-0	190	6-25-63	1985	Maitland, Fla.
Stewart, Shannon	.279	144	516	90	144	29	3	12	55	67	77	51	18	R	R	6-1	194	2-25-74	1992	Miami, Fla.
Witt, Kevin	.143	5	7	0	1	0	0	0	0	0	3	0	0	L	R	6-4	195	1-5-76	1994	Jacksonville, Fla.

PITCHING	W	L	ERA	G	GS	CG	SV	IP	H	R	ER	BB	SO	B	T	HT	WT	DOB	1st Yr	Resides
Almanzar, Carlos	2	2	5.34	25	0	0	0	29	34	18	17	8	20	R	R	6-2	200	11-6-73	1991	Santo Domingo, D.R.
Andujar, Luis	0	0	9.53	5	0	0	0	6	12	6	6	2	1	R	R	6-2	215	11-22-72	1991	Bani, D.R.
Carpenter, Chris	12	7	4.37	33	24	1	0	175	177	97	85	61	136	R	R	6-6	220	4-27-75	1994	Raymond, N.H.
Clemens, Roger	20	6	2.65	33	33	5	0	235	169	78	69	88	271	R	R	6-4	230	8-4-62	1983	Houston, Texas
Escobar, Kelvim	7	3	3.73	22	10	0	0	80	72	37	33	35	72	R	R	6-1	205	4-11-76	1992	Caracas, Ven.
Guzman, Juan	6	12	4.41	22	22	2	0	145	133	83	71	65	113	R	R	5-11	195	10-28-66	1985	Miami, Fla.
Halladay, Roy	1	0	1.93	2	2	1	0	14	9	4	3	2	13	R	R	6-6	205	5-14-77	1995	Arvada, Colo.
Hanson, Erik	0	3	6.24	11	8	0	0	49	73	34	34	29	21	R	R	6-6	215	5-18-65	1986	Kirkland, Wash.
Hentgen, Pat	12	11	5.17	29	29	0	0	178	208	109	102	69	94	R	R	6-2	200	11-13-68	1986	Palm Harbor, Fla.
Myers, Randy	3	4	4.46	41	0	0	28	42	44	21	21	19	32	L	L	6-1	210	9-19-62	1982	Vancouver, Wash.
Person, Robert	3	1	7.04	27	0	0	6	38	45	31	30	22	31	R	R	5-11	180	1-8-69	1989	St. Louis, Mo.
Plesac, Dan	4	3	3.78	78	0	0	4	50	41	23	21	16	55	L	L	6-5	217	2-4-62	1983	Valparaiso, Ind.
Quantrill, Paul	3	4	2.59	82	0	0	7	80	88	26	23	22	59	L	R	6-1	185	11-3-68	1989	Port Hope, Ontario
Risley, Bill	3	4	5.27	44	0	0	0	55	52	37	32	34	42	R	R	6-2	215	5-29-67	1987	Farmington, N.M.
Rodriguez, Nerio	1	0	9.72	7	0	0	0	8	10	9	9	8	3	R	R	6-1	195	3-22-73	1991	San Pedro de Macoris, D.R.
2-team (6 Baltimore)	2	3	8.56	13	4	0	0	27	35	26	26	17	11							
Sinclair, Steve	0	2	3.60	24	0	0	0	15	13	7	6	5	8	L	L	6-2	190	8-2-71	1991	Victoria, B.C.
Stieb, Dave	1	2	4.83	19	3	0	2	50	58	31	27	17	27	R	R	6-0	195	7-22-57	1978	Gilroy, Calif.
VanRyn, Ben	0	1	9.00	10	0	0	0	4	6	4	4	2	3	L	L	6-5	195	8-19-71	1990	San Antonio, Texas
Williams, Woody	10	9	4.46	32	32	1	0	210	196	112	104	81	151	R	R	6-0	190	8-19-66	1988	Alvin, Texas
Withem, Shannon	0	0	3.00	1	0	0	0	3	3	1	1	2	2	R	R	6-3	185	9-21-72	1990	Canton, Mich.

FIELDING

Catcher	PCT	G	PO	A	E	DP	PB
Brown	.993	52	261	19	2	2	5
Dalesandro	.986	18	68	4	1	0	0
Fletcher	.991	121	832	49	8	1	3
Santiago	1.000	15	45	2	0	0	1

First Base	PCT	G	PO	A	E	DP
Crespo	.800	1	4	0	1	0
Dalesandro	1.000	2	5	0	0	0
Delgado	.992	141	1165	86	10	110
Samuel	1.000	3	2	0	0	0
Stanley	.995	22	171	12	1	14
Witt	1.000	1	5	1	0	0

Second Base	PCT	G	PO	A	E	DP
Crespo	.870	8	6	14	3	2
Fernandez	.975	82	129	222	9	43
Grebeck	.975	91	144	249	10	38
Perez	1.000	1	0	1	0	0
Samuel	1.000	2	2	4	0	0

Third Base	PCT	G	PO	A	E	DP
Crespo	1.000	2	1	2	0	0
Dalesandro	.889	8	3	5	1	0
Evans	.889	7	5	3	1	0
Fernandez	.963	54	32	73	4	3
Grebeck	.857	4	2	4	1	0
Sprague	.924	105	87	157	20	8

Shortstop	PCT	G	PO	A	E	DP
Gonzalez	.976	158	260	426	17	98
Grebeck	1.000	6	4	15	0	3
Perez	1.000	4	6	5	0	1

Outfield	PCT	G	PO	A	E	DP
Canseco	.960	73	116	4	5	2
Crespo	1.000	42	56	1	0	1
Cruz	.984	105	247	7	4	1
Dalesandro	.000	1	0	0	0	0
Green	.979	157	311	14	7	4
Lennon	1.000	2	3	0	0	0
Phillips	.960	13	24	0	1	0
Samuel	.882	10	15	0	2	0
Stanley	1.000	1	1	0	0	0
Stewart	.980	144	295	3	6	1

LARRY GOREN

Shawn Green

DAVID SEELIG

Toronto's Carlos Delgado
Led team with 115 RBIs

JIM McLEAN

Hagerstown's Clayton Andrews
Struck out 193 batters in Class A

FARM SYSTEM

Director of Player Development: Jim Hoff

Class	Farm Team	League	W	L	Pct.	Finish*	Manager	First Yr
AAA	Syracuse (N.Y.) Chiefs	International	80	62	.563	2nd (14)	Terry Bevington	1978
AA	Knoxville (Tenn.) Smokies	Southern	71	69	.507	4th (10)	Omar Malave	1980
A#	Dunedin (Fla.) Blue Jays	Florida State	82	58	.586	2nd (14)	Rocket Wheeler	1987
A	Hagerstown (Md.) Suns	South Atlantic	81	60	.574	2nd (14)	Marty Pevey	1993
A	St. Catharines (Ont.) Stompers	New York-Penn	38	38	.500	7th (14)	Duane Larson	1986
Rookie#	Medicine Hat (Alta.) Blue Jays	Pioneer	46	28	.622	1st (8)	Rolando Pino	1978

*Finish in overall standings (No. of teams in league) #Advanced level

SYRACUSE — Class AAA

INTERNATIONAL LEAGUE

BATTING	AVG	G	AB	R	H	2B	3B	HR	RBI	BB	SO	SB	CS	B	T	HT	WT	DOB	1st Yr	Resides
Bell, Juan	.211	12	38	4	8	4	1	0	1	1	6	0	0	B	R	5-11	175	3-29-68	1985	San Pedro de Macoris, D.R.
Brown, Kevin	.625	2	8	2	5	2	0	0	0	0	2	0	0	R	R	6-2	210	4-21-73	1994	Mount Vernon, Ind.
Candelaria, Ben	.247	69	251	28	62	13	2	7	32	23	68	2	0	L	R	5-11	167	1-29-75	1992	Hatillo, P.R.
Costo, Tim	.296	101	365	45	108	18	2	14	55	26	72	1	2	R	R	6-5	230	2-16-69	1990	Glen Ellyn, Ill.
Cruz, Jose	.298	40	141	29	42	14	1	7	23	32	32	8	4	B	R	6-0	200	4-19-74	1995	Houston, Texas
Dalesandro, Mark	.268	45	164	25	44	9	1	10	30	12	20	1	0	R	R	6-0	195	5-14-68	1990	Chicago, Ill.
Delgado, Alex	.234	82	286	22	67	14	0	6	28	25	39	2	0	R	R	6-0	160	1-11-71	1988	Palmerejo, Ven.
Delgado, Carlos	.571	2	7	4	4	2	0	1	6	2	0	0	0	L	R	6-3	225	6-25-72	1989	Aguadilla, P.R.
Evans, Tom	.300	109	400	57	120	32	1	15	55	50	74	11	7	R	R	6-1	180	7-9-74	1992	Kirkland, Wash.
Freel, Ryan	.229	37	118	19	27	4	0	2	12	26	16	9	4	R	R	5-10	175	3-8-76	1995	Jacksonville, Fla.
Grebeck, Brian	.333	1	3	0	1	0	0	0	0	0	0	0	0	R	R	5-7	160	8-31-67	1990	Cerritos, Calif.
Henry, Santiago	.194	62	216	20	42	8	1	5	25	10	55	4	5	R	R	5-10	178	7-27-72	1991	San Pedro de Macoris, D.R.
Herrera, Jose	.273	118	473	72	129	21	6	12	40	32	60	27	12	L	L	6-0	164	8-30-72	1991	Santo Domingo, D.R.
Kelly, Pat	.282	80	291	58	82	22	3	17	39	39	60	18	6	R	R	6-0	182	10-14-67	1988	Clearwater Beach, Fla.
Lennon, Pat	.290	126	438	87	127	22	4	27	95	87	121	12	4	R	R	6-2	200	4-27-68	1986	Whiteville, N.C.
Lopez, Luis	.220	11	41	6	9	0	0	1	3	6	6	0	0	R	R	6-0	200	10-5-73	1996	Spring Hill, Fla.
Melhuse, Adam	.289	12	38	4	11	3	0	1	7	7	6	0	0	B	R	6-2	185	3-27-72	1993	Stockton, Calif.
Mosquera, Julio	.213	28	94	10	20	6	0	2	4	5	12	1	0	R	R	6-0	190	1-29-72	1991	Dunedin, Fla.
Mummau, Rob	.429	3	7	0	3	1	0	0	2	0	1	0	0	R	R	5-11	185	8-21-71	1993	Clearwater, Fla.
Perez, Tomas	.252	116	404	40	102	15	4	3	37	18	67	4	7	B	R	5-11	177	12-29-73	1991	Barquisimeto, Ven.
Phillips, Tony	.250	10	32	7	8	1	0	1	4	15	10	2	1	B	R	5-10	175	4-25-59	1978	Scottsdale, Ariz.
Powell, Alonzo	.229	15	48	8	11	1	0	3	9	7	12	0	1	R	R	6-2	190	12-12-64	1983	Indianapolis, Ind.
Probst, Alan	.333	12	33	2	11	1	0	1	4	2	6	0	0	R	R	6-4	215	10-24-70	1992	Avis, Pa.
Rodriguez, Luis	.133	5	15	1	2	0	0	0	2	0	6	0	0	R	R	5-9	160	1-3-74	1991	Tampa, Fla.
Sanders, Anthony	.191	60	209	23	40	9	2	4	19	20	65	5	2	R	R	6-2	195	3-2-74	1993	Tucson, Ariz.

BATTING	AVG	G	AB	R	H	2B	3B	HR	RBI	BB	SO	SB	CS	B	T	HT	WT	DOB	1st Yr	Resides
Santiago, Benito	.227	5	22	0	5	2	0	0	2	1	3	0	0	R	R	6-1	182	3-9-65	1983	La Jolla, Calif.
Witt, Kevin	.273	126	455	71	124	20	3	23	67	53	124	3	3	L	R	6-4	195	1-5-76	1994	Jacksonville, Fla.
Woodward, Chris	.200	25	85	9	17	6	0	2	6	7	20	1	1	R	R	6-0	160	6-27-76	1995	Duarte, Calif.

PITCHING	W	L	ERA	G	GS	CG	SV	IP	H	R	ER	BB	SO	B	T	HT	WT	DOB	1st Yr	Resides
Almanzar, Carlos	3	6	2.31	30	0	0	10	51	44	21	13	13	53	R	R	6-2	200	11-6-73	1991	Santo Domingo, D.R.
Andujar, Luis	3	2	2.12	20	0	0	8	34	23	9	8	6	24	R	R	6-2	215	11-22-72	1991	Bani, D.R.
Escobar, Kelvim	2	2	3.77	13	10	0	1	60	51	26	25	24	64	R	R	6-1	205	4-11-76	1992	Caracas, Ven.
Fletcher, Paul	3	4	2.70	48	0	0	6	73	65	29	22	28	53	R	R	6-1	185	1-14-67	1988	Ravenswood, W.Va.
Graterol, Beiker	9	2	4.59	16	16	0	0	96	103	55	49	32	62	R	R	6-2	164	11-9-74	1993	Barquisimeto, Ven.
Halladay, Roy	9	5	3.79	21	21	1	0	116	107	52	49	53	71	R	R	6-6	205	5-14-77	1995	Arvada, Colo.
Harris, D.J.	1	4	3.98	25	1	0	0	41	40	20	18	21	25	R	R	5-10	190	4-11-71	1993	Las Vegas, Nev.
Johnson, Dane	1	0	3.18	7	0	0	3	6	5	2	2	5	4	R	R	6-5	195	2-10-63	1993	Miami, Fla.
Koch, Billy	0	1	14.29	2	2	0	0	6	9	9	9	5	9	R	R	6-3	218	12-14-74	1996	Clearwater, Fla.
Lukasiewicz, Mark	2	2	3.40	22	4	0	1	48	38	18	18	24	30	L	L	6-5	230	3-8-73	1994	Secaucus, N.J.
Munro, Peter	2	5	7.46	8	8	0	0	45	58	42	37	23	42	R	R	6-2	193	6-14-75	1994	Little Neck, N.Y.
2-team (18 Pawtucket)	7	9	5.06	26	25	0	0	151	169	91	85	58	117							
Person, Robert	3	3	2.29	20	6	1	6	59	38	17	15	29	55	R	R	5-11	180	1-8-69	1989	St. Louis, Mo.
Romano, Mike	8	6	4.14	27	13	1	1	117	131	66	54	53	69	R	R	6-2	195	3-3-72	1993	Chalmette, La.
Sievert, Mark	7	6	4.13	21	18	0	1	96	92	48	44	59	37	L	R	6-4	195	2-16-73	1991	Janesville, Wis.
Sinclair, Steve	3	1	2.17	43	1	0	3	50	37	15	12	23	45	L	L	6-2	190	8-2-71	1991	Victoria, B.C.
Stieb, Dave	5	4	2.73	9	9	2	0	66	44	23	20	17	47	R	R	6-0	195	7-22-57	1978	Gilroy, Calif.
VanRyn, Ben	2	1	3.51	30	0	0	2	41	34	16	16	13	30	L	L	6-5	195	8-19-71	1990	San Antonio, Texas
Withem, Shannon	17	5	3.27	28	27	4	0	190	176	72	69	58	113	R	R	6-3	185	9-21-72	1990	Canton, Mich.
Yennaco, Jay	0	3	5.35	7	6	1	0	39	55	27	23	10	27	R	R	6-4	238	11-17-75	1996	Windham, N.H.
2-team (11 Pawtucket)	3	5	5.64	18	17	2	0	99	132	70	62	26	61							

FIELDING

Catcher	PCT	G	PO	A	E	DP	PB
Brown	1.000	2	7	1	0	0	1
Dalesandro	.980	10	45	3	1	0	0
A. Delgado	.987	79	547	53	8	7	0
Melhuse	.960	8	41	7	2	0	1
Mosquera	1.000	28	145	20	0	2	1
Probst	.984	11	62	1	1	1	2
Rodriguez	1.000	5	28	2	0	1	1
Santiago	1.000	4	19	1	0	0	0

First Base	PCT	G	PO	A	E	DP
Costo	.997	41	347	26	1	34
C. Delgado	1.000	2	22	2	0	5
Lopez	1.000	1	2	0	0	0
Witt	.996	102	941	68	4	105

Second Base	PCT	G	PO	A	E	DP
Bell	1.000	2	4	5	0	2
Freel	.969	8	14	17	1	3
Grebeck	1.000	1	2	6	0	1
Henry	.973	40	70	112	5	20
Kelly	.977	79	133	211	8	58
Perez	.978	17	38	52	2	11
Phillips	1.000	1	4	2	0	0

Third Base	PCT	G	PO	A	E	DP
Costo	1.000	3	3	5	0	0
Dalesandro	.889	12	3	13	2	1
Evans	.955	108	89	208	14	15
Henry	.926	10	2	23	2	1
Lopez	.964	9	4	23	1	0
Melhuse	1.000	2	2	5	0	0
Mummau	.000	3	0	0	0	0

Shortstop	PCT	G	PO	A	E	DP
Bell	.923	9	17	31	4	9
Henry	.950	11	15	23	2	6
Perez	.977	99	167	385	13	86
Woodward	.961	25	29	69	4	15

Outfield	PCT	G	PO	A	E	DP
Candelaria	.967	65	79	8	3	2
Cruz	.991	40	99	7	1	0
Dalesandro	1.000	8	12	0	0	0
Freel	.957	28	43	2	2	0
Herrera	.988	115	241	8	3	3
Lennon	.947	80	132	11	8	1
Phillips	.933	9	13	1	1	0
Powell	.950	13	17	2	1	1
Sanders	.993	60	145	6	1	0
Witt	1.000	18	32	0	0	0

KNOXVILLE — Class AA

SOUTHERN LEAGUE

BATTING	AVG	G	AB	R	H	2B	3B	HR	RBI	BB	SO	SB	CS	B	T	HT	WT	DOB	1st Yr	Resides
Blake, Casey	.372	45	172	41	64	15	4	7	38	22	25	10	0	R	R	6-2	195	8-23-73	1996	Indianola, Iowa
Bowers, Brent	.280	27	107	19	30	5	1	2	12	16	18	9	1	L	R	6-4	215	5-2-71	1989	Bridgeview, Ill.
Candelaria, Ben	.333	36	156	33	52	8	3	10	31	9	31	0	3	L	R	5-11	167	1-29-75	1992	Hatillo, P.R.
Freel, Ryan	.286	66	252	47	72	17	3	4	36	33	32	18	9	R	R	5-10	175	3-8-76	1995	Jacksonville, Fla.
Jones, Ryan	.250	109	408	50	102	21	0	11	51	44	79	4	4	R	R	6-3	225	11-5-74	1993	Irvine, Calif.
Lopez, Luis	.313	119	450	70	141	27	1	15	85	58	55	0	2	R	R	6-0	200	10-5-73	1996	Spring Hill, Fla.
Melhuse, Adam	.300	76	240	56	72	22	0	15	43	70	39	4	4	B	R	6-2	185	3-27-72	1993	Stockton, Calif.
Mosquera, Julio	.279	12	43	4	12	1	0	0	8	4	7	0	0	R	R	6-0	190	1-29-72	1991	Dunedin, Fla.
Mummau, Rob	.291	39	141	28	41	5	2	3	28	11	24	4	1	R	R	5-11	185	8-21-71	1993	Clearwater, Fla.
Peeples, Michael	.251	113	395	58	99	16	3	7	42	36	62	20	10	R	R	5-11	170	9-3-76	1994	Green Cove Springs, Fla.
Probst, Alan	.261	79	261	53	68	22	0	10	44	35	81	2	1	R	R	6-4	215	10-24-70	1992	Avis, Pa.
Rivers, Jonathan	.268	91	302	51	81	19	4	9	49	47	62	20	13	R	R	6-2	200	8-17-74	1992	Tallassee, Ala.
Rodriguez, Luis	.412	8	17	6	7	0	1	0	1	7	5	1	0	R	R	5-9	160	1-3-74	1991	Tampa, Fla.
Sanders, Anthony	.400	6	25	9	10	2	0	4	9	2	6	0	1	R	R	6-2	195	3-2-74	1993	Tucson, Ariz.
Secrist, Reed	.240	15	50	9	12	4	1	2	8	4	14	0	0	L	R	6-1	205	5-7-70	1992	Farmington, Utah
Skett, Will	.250	65	236	33	59	13	6	3	33	20	63	4	8	R	R	5-11	190	5-22-74	1996	Encino, Calif.
Solano, Fausto	.240	85	288	49	69	22	2	10	38	34	53	4	4	R	R	5-9	144	6-19-74	1992	Santo Domingo, D.R.
Stromsborg, Ryan	.237	81	283	44	67	9	2	7	28	27	65	7	5	R	R	6-3	185	12-19-74	1996	Encino, Calif.
Thompson, Andy	.285	125	481	74	137	33	2	14	88	54	69	8	3	R	R	6-3	210	10-8-75	1995	Sun Prairie, Wis.
Tucci, Pete	.291	38	141	25	41	7	4	7	36	13	29	3	2	R	R	6-2	205	10-8-75	1996	Norwalk, Conn.
Woodward, Chris	.245	73	253	36	62	12	0	3	27	26	47	3	5	R	R	6-0	160	6-27-76	1995	Duarte, Calif.

PITCHING	W	L	ERA	G	GS	CG	SV	IP	H	R	ER	BB	SO	B	T	HT	WT	DOB	1st Yr	Resides
Bale, John	0	0	6.75	3	0	0	0	1	1	1	1	0	0	L	L	6-4	195	5-22-74	1996	Crestview, Fla.
Brown, Chad	0	2	14.85	5	4	0	0	13	29	22	22	13	10	L	L	6-0	185	12-9-71	1992	Gastonia, N.C.
Davey, Tom	5	3	3.87	48	9	0	16	77	70	35	33	52	78	R	R	6-7	215	9-11-73	1994	Canton, Mich.
Doman, Roger	3	1	4.60	22	0	0	0	29	26	15	15	10	14	R	R	6-5	190	1-26-73	1991	Joplin, Mo.
2-team (10 Carolina)	3	2	5.76	32	1	0	0	50	55	35	32	18	26							
Giron, Isabel	1	1	3.82	6	5	0	0	35	29	15	15	13	35	R	R	6-2	160	11-17-77	1995	Villa Mella, D.R.
Glover, Gary	0	5	6.75	8	8	0	0	37	41	36	28	28	14	R	R	6-5	200	12-3-76	1994	DeLand, Fla.
Gordon, Mike	8	2	5.02	44	12	0	0	113	123	82	63	64	95	L	R	6-2	195	11-30-72	1992	Quincy, Fla.
Graterol, Beiker	5	6	5.24	12	12	0	0	67	76	46	39	22	52	R	R	6-2	164	11-9-74	1993	Barquisimeto, Ven.
Halperin, Mike	5	1	2.92	35	0	0	2	49	44	16	16	24	35	L	L	5-10	170	9-8-73	1994	Naples, Fla.
2-team (1 Carolina)	5	1	2.88	36	0	0	2	50	45	16	16	25	35							
Harris, D.J.	4	2	2.77	22	0	0	2	49	52	17	15	24	31	R	R	5-10	190	4-11-71	1993	Las Vegas, Nev.

PITCHING	W	L	ERA	G	GS	CG	SV	IP	H	R	ER	BB	SO	B	T	HT	WT	DOB	1st Yr	Resides
Hartshorn, Ty	7	6	5.18	19	19	0	0	108	133	74	62	43	55	R	R	6-5	190	8-3-74	1993	Lamar, Colo.
Lawrence, Clint	1	2	6.84	7	7	0	0	25	31	24	19	23	16	L	L	6-4	200	10-19-76	1995	Oakville, Ontario
Lee, Jeremy	0	1	3.38	10	0	0	0	16	16	6	6	3	7	R	R	6-8	235	10-20-74	1993	Galesburg, Ill.
Lukasiewicz, Mark	0	0	1.93	5	0	0	1	9	6	2	2	1	16	L	L	6-5	230	3-8-73	1994	Secaucus, N.J.
McBride, Chris	10	5	4.40	35	21	1	2	155	185	102	76	37	90	L	R	6-5	210	10-13-73	1994	Leland, N.C.
McClellan, Sean	3	5	3.62	24	3	0	4	50	31	23	20	33	44	R	R	6-2	215	4-26-73	1996	Seminole, Fla.
Meiners, Doug	7	6	4.73	43	9	1	1	110	133	68	58	45	58	R	R	6-8	190	5-16-74	1992	Staten Island, N.Y.
Rivette, Scott	0	1	3.86	7	0	0	0	9	7	4	4	7	4	B	R	6-2	200	2-8-74	1995	Upland, Calif.
2-team (35 Huntsville)	6	5	4.52	42	0	0	2	78	82	50	39	39	57							
Smith, Brian	4	2	4.06	42	0	0	7	71	72	39	32	25	50	R	R	5-11	185	7-19-72	1994	Salisbury, N.C.
Stevenson, Jason	6	10	5.43	33	22	1	0	134	159	88	81	51	98	R	R	6-3	180	8-11-74	1994	Phenix City, Ala.
Veniard, Jay	0	1	9.58	11	0	0	0	10	10	12	11	12	7	L	L	6-4	215	8-16-74	1995	Jacksonville, Fla.
Young, Joe	2	7	9.68	11	9	0	0	40	52	51	43	32	31	R	R	6-4	210	4-28-75	1993	Fort McMurray, Alberta

FIELDING

Catcher	PCT	G	PO	A	E	DP	PB
Melhuse	.977	54	297	36	8	4	4
Mosquera	.983	8	51	7	1	0	2
Mummau	1.000	1	1	0	0	0	0
Probst	.982	75	445	54	9	7	3
Rodriguez	1.000	6	34	4	0	0	0
Secrist	.947	5	35	1	2	0	0

First Base	PCT	G	PO	A	E	DP
Jones	.988	66	606	50	8	66
Lopez	.995	61	529	42	3	49
Melhuse	.979	16	123	15	3	6
Secrist	1.000	1	5	0	0	0

Second Base	PCT	G	PO	A	E	DP
Freel	1.000	7	14	22	0	2
Mummau	.979	8	20	27	1	5
Peeples	.966	109	195	323	18	62

	PCT	G	PO	A	E	DP
Solano	.959	18	28	43	3	12

Third Base	PCT	G	PO	A	E	DP
Blake	.913	45	27	89	11	8
Lopez	1.000	29	19	50	0	4
Mummau	.943	17	10	23	2	2
Solano	1.000	3	0	3	0	0
Stromsborg	.895	10	5	12	2	1
Thompson	.814	44	24	72	22	8

Shortstop	PCT	G	PO	A	E	DP
Freel	.938	2	5	10	1	2
Mummau	.904	9	15	32	5	6
Solano	.931	60	96	186	21	28
Woodward	.971	72	145	220	11	59

Outfield	PCT	G	PO	A	E	DP
Bowers	.981	27	48	3	1	0
Candelaria	.938	36	58	3	4	0
Freel	.982	55	108	3	2	2
Melhuse	1.000	2	4	0	0	0
Mosquera	.000	1	0	0	0	0
Mummau	1.000	4	4	1	0	0
Rivers	.982	87	152	10	3	2
Rodriguez	.000	1	0	0	0	0
Sanders	1.000	6	15	3	0	1
Secrist	1.000	5	7	1	0	0
Skett	.960	64	116	3	5	1
Stromsborg	.992	61	128	3	1	0
Thompson	.967	63	114	3	4	0
Tucci	.957	38	64	2	3	0

DUNEDIN — Class A

FLORIDA STATE LEAGUE

BATTING	AVG	G	AB	R	H	2B	3B	HR	RBI	BB	SO	SB	CS	B	T	HT	WT	DOB	1st Yr	Resides
Abernathy, Brent	.328	124	485	85	159	36	1	3	65	44	38	35	13	R	R	6-1	185	9-23-77	1996	Marietta, Ga.
Adriana, Sharnol	.286	73	227	45	65	24	0	8	44	30	57	18	6	R	R	6-1	185	11-13-70	1991	Willemstad, Curacao
Blake, Casey	.350	88	340	62	119	28	3	11	65	30	81	9	6	R	R	6-2	195	8-23-73	1996	Indianola, Iowa
Chiaffredo, Paul	.234	80	290	34	68	19	0	4	41	16	68	1	3	R	R	6-2	195	5-30-76	1997	San Jose, Calif.
Delgado, Carlos	.313	4	16	4	5	1	0	2	7	2	4	0	0	L	R	6-3	225	6-25-72	1989	Aguadilla, P.R.
Giles, Tim	.303	102	363	53	110	20	2	18	65	31	83	3	2	L	R	6-3	215	9-12-75	1990	Gambrills, Md.
Henry, Santiago	.389	12	54	9	21	5	0	1	7	2	8	2	2	R	R	5-10	178	7-27-72	1991	San Pedro de Macoris, D.R.
Johnson, Damon	.278	94	338	48	94	17	2	4	32	17	98	16	9	R	R	6-1	195	8-22-75	1993	Crossett, Ark.
Langaigne, Selwyn	.261	128	475	52	124	7	0	0	38	37	73	21	17	L	L	6-0	185	3-22-76	1994	Las Acaias, Ven.
Lawrence, Joe	.308	125	454	102	140	31	6	11	44	105	88	15	12	R	R	6-2	190	2-13-77	1996	Lake Charles, La.
Lopez, Felipe	.385	4	13	3	5	0	1	1	1	0	3	0	0	B	R	6-0	175	5-12-80	1998	Apopka, Fla.
Loyd, Brian	.204	16	49	8	10	0	0	1	5	5	10	1	0	R	R	6-2	210	12-3-73	1996	Yorba Linda, Calif.
Maloney, Jeff	.183	94	300	43	55	7	1	10	32	23	76	6	4	B	R	6-4	190	11-27-76	1995	Basking Ridge, N.J.
Morgan, Dave	.229	28	70	9	16	4	0	5	15	12	16	0	1	R	R	6-4	215	11-19-71	1993	Needham, Mass.
Patzke, Jeff	.290	20	62	10	18	0	0	0	4	9	18	0	1	B	R	6-0	190	11-19-73	1992	Klamath Falls, Ore.
Rivers, Jonathan	.200	5	20	0	4	2	0	0	4	1	5	2	1	R	R	6-2	200	8-17-74	1992	Tallassee, Ala.
Rodriguez, Luis	.291	67	196	34	57	15	0	4	41	10	39	11	2	R	R	5-9	160	1-3-74	1991	Tampa, Fla.
Rodriguez, Mike	.216	15	37	4	8	2	0	0	2	3	4	0	0	R	R	5-11	185	4-1-75	1996	Stephenville, Texas
Santiago, Benito	.162	11	37	4	6	1	0	1	5	3	9	3	0	R	R	6-1	182	3-9-65	1983	La Jolla, Calif.
Skett, Will	.325	37	123	25	40	8	2	4	25	15	43	6	2	R	R	5-11	190	5-22-74	1996	Encino, Calif.
Stone, Craig	.267	104	356	44	95	29	2	12	53	20	125	3	6	R	R	6-2	190	7-12-75	1993	Quakers Hill, Australia
Stromsborg, Ryan	.250	30	108	12	27	5	0	2	12	5	28	1	0	R	R	6-3	185	12-19-74	1996	Encino, Calif.
Tucci, Pete	.329	92	356	72	117	30	3	23	76	29	97	8	5	R	R	6-2	205	10-8-75	1996	Norwalk, Conn.
Willis, Symmion	.036	9	28	1	1	0	0	0	1	0	11	1	0	R	R	6-4	215	11-27-72	1996	Atlanta, Ga.

GAMES BY POSITION: C—Chiaffredo 84, Loyd 15, Morgan 3, L. Rodriguez 50, M. Rodriguez 3, Santiago 5. **1B**—Adriana 8, Chiaffredo 4, Delgado 2, Giles 77, Morgan 2, Patzke 2, L. Rodriguez 4, M. Rodriguez 2, Stone 65. **2B**—Abernathy 123, Adriana 10, Henry 7, Patzke 5, M. Rodriguez 1, Stromsborg 1. **3B**—Adriana 28, Blake 86, Lawrence 4, Patzke 4, L. Rodriguez 1, M. Rodriguez 4, Stone 14, Stromsborg 13. **SS**—Adriana 14, Henry 5, Lawrence 120, Lopez 4, Stromsborg 2. **OF**—Adriana 4, Johnson 91, Langaigne 127, Maloney 46, Rivers 5, L. Rodriguez 7, M. Rodriguez 6, Skett 33, Stromsborg 16, Tucci 91, Willis 9.

PITCHING	W	L	ERA	G	GS	CG	SV	IP	H	R	ER	BB	SO	B	T	HT	WT	DOB	1st Yr	Resides
Adkins, Tim	0	1	5.92	19	0	0	1	24	32	18	16	10	18	L	L	6-0	195	5-12-74	1992	Huntington, W.Va.
Bale, John	4	5	4.64	24	9	0	4	66	68	39	34	23	78	L	L	6-4	195	5-22-74	1996	Crestview, Fla.
Bleazard, David	1	0	4.26	14	0	0	0	19	20	14	9	11	20	R	R	6-0	175	3-7-74	1996	Tooele, Utah
Bogott, Kurt	0	0	0.00	3	0	0	0	6	2	0	0	1	8	L	L	6-4	195	9-30-72	1993	Sterling, Ill.
Bowles, Brian	1	2	3.33	9	2	1	0	27	32	13	10	16	17	R	R	6-5	205	8-18-76	1995	Manhattan Beach, Calif.
Bradford, Josh	4	4	4.97	17	12	1	1	71	75	43	39	30	46	R	R	6-5	185	4-19-74	1996	Cincinnati, Ohio
Brown, Chad	1	1	2.30	3	2	0	0	16	13	8	4	3	10	L	L	6-0	185	12-9-71	1992	Gastonia, N.C.
Delgado, Ernie	7	10	3.64	44	9	2	1	119	119	57	48	59	97	R	R	6-2	190	7-21-75	1993	Tucson, Ariz.
Folkers, Ken	0	3	8.40	9	0	0	0	15	23	16	14	9	13	R	R	6-3	205	10-11-74	1997	Naperville, Ill.
Glover, Gary	7	6	4.28	19	18	0	0	109	117	66	52	36	88	R	R	6-5	200	12-3-76	1994	DeLand, Fla.
Hanson, Erik	0	0	2.25	1	1	0	0	4	4	1	1	2	5	R	R	6-6	215	5-18-65	1986	Kirkland, Wash.
Hartshorn, Ty	8	0	1.29	9	9	1	0	63	52	16	9	17	54	R	R	6-5	190	8-3-74	1993	Lamar, Colo.
Hendrickson, Mark	4	3	2.37	16	5	0	1	49	44	16	13	26	38	L	L	6-9	230	6-23-74	1998	Syracuse, N.Y.
Hibbard, Billy	0	0	0.00	2	0	0	0	4	4	0	0	2	1	R	R	6-3	198	6-24-76	1994	Orlando, Fla.
Koch, Billy	14	7	3.75	25	25	0	0	125	120	65	52	41	108	R	R	6-3	218	12-14-74	1996	Clearwater, Fla.
Lawrence, Clint	6	3	4.91	20	12	1	1	84	107	54	46	41	55	L	L	6-4	200	10-19-76	1995	Oakville, Ontario

PITCHING	W	L	ERA	G	GS	CG	SV	IP	H	R	ER	BB	SO	B	T	HT	WT	DOB	1st Yr	Resides
LaChapelle, Yan	11	8	3.99	24	24	1	0	126	114	68	56	58	126	R	R	5-10	190	10-26-75	1996	Gatineau, Quebec
Lee, Jeremy	2	0	3.90	15	0	0	0	28	26	13	12	6	18	R	R	6-8	235	10-20-74	1993	Galesburg, Ill.
Lowe, Benny	0	0	1.93	9	0	0	0	9	8	5	2	6	13	L	L	5-10	185	6-13-74	1994	Key West, Fla.
Lukasiewicz, Mark	1	1	0.84	9	0	0	0	11	7	2	1	4	8	L	L	6-5	230	3-8-73	1994	Secaucus, N.J.
Mann, Jim	0	[illegible]	3.04	51	0	0	25	50	31	19	17	24	59	R	R	6-3	225	11-17-74	1994	Holbrook, Mass.
McClellan, Sean	4	0	2.21	24	0	0	5	57	34	14	14	20	73	R	R	6-2	215	4-26-73	1996	Seminole, Fla.
Schaffer, Trevor	0	1	4.65	47	0	0	2	70	58	48	36	48	45	R	R	6-3	210	1-13-74	1996	Menlo Park, Calif.
Seale, Dustin	0	0	0.00	2	0	0	0	3	2	1	0	3	1	L	L	6-1	170	12-2-77	1997	Safford, Ariz.
Smith, Brian	1	0	3.38	4	0	0	2	11	8	4	4	3	9	R	R	5-11	185	7-19-72	1994	Salisbury, N.C.
Smith, Taylor	0	0	2.70	1	1	0	0	3	3	1	1	4	4	R	R	6-3	195	12-15-78	1997	Henderson, Nev.
Stieb, Dave	2	0	3.00	3	3	0	0	15	17	8	5	5	19	R	R	6-0	195	7-22-57	1978	Gilroy, Calif.
White, Keith	0	0	10.80	3	0	0	0	3	7	4	4	1	0	L	R	5-11	170	7-23-77	1997	Bradenton, Fla.
Young, Joe	4	1	4.63	8	8	0	0	45	50	34	23	22	43	R	R	6-4	210	4-28-75	1993	Fort McMurray, Alberta

HAGERSTOWN — Class A

SOUTH ATLANTIC LEAGUE

BATTING	AVG	G	AB	R	H	2B	3B	HR	RBI	BB	SO	SB	CS	B	T	HT	WT	DOB	1st Yr	Resides
Albaral, Randy	.239	86	234	34	56	4	1	0	19	16	48	15	3	R	R	6-2	180	2-27-77	1996	River Ridge, La.
Bagley, Lorenzo	.259	111	359	53	93	20	2	15	75	39	97	2	1	R	R	5-9	225	12-30-75	1996	Citra, Fla.
Brown, Billy	.264	44	148	22	39	8	0	2	19	19	38	12	5	R	R	6-0	195	3-9-76	1997	Plantation, Fla.
Cripps, Bobby	.265	123	423	64	112	17	3	29	88	41	123	2	3	L	R	6-2	200	5-9-77	1996	Powell River, B.C.
Hayes, Chris	.295	63	207	41	61	17	1	8	33	23	41	6	2	R	R	6-2	190	12-23-73	1995	Jacksonville, Fla.
Izturis, Cesar	.262	130	413	56	108	13	1	1	38	20	43	20	9	B	R	5-9	155	2-10-80	1996	Barquisimeto, Ven.
Morillo, Luis	.253	38	87	13	22	3	2	0	9	10	17	1	3	L	L	5-11	155	1-13-78	1996	Santo Domingo, D.R.
Morrison, Greg	.276	123	434	59	120	19	2	15	72	28	61	4	7	L	L	6-1	205	2-23-76	1995	Medicine Hat, Alberta
Nieves, Juan	.167	3	6	0	1	0	1	0	1	1	0	0	0	R	R	6-3	170	3-29-77	1996	Carabobo, Ven.
Nunez, Jorge	.250	4	16	0	4	0	0	0	1	0	1	1	0	R	R	5-10	158	3-3-78	1995	Villa Mella, D.R.
Peters, Tony	.303	104	327	58	99	12	1	10	35	25	72	15	7	R	R	6-2	210	10-28-74	1995	Mesa, Ariz.
Phelps, Josh	.265	117	385	48	102	24	1	8	44	40	80	2	0	R	R	6-3	195	5-12-78	1996	Rathdrum, Idaho
Rodriguez, Mike	.303	50	132	20	40	10	0	1	17	8	20	1	1	R	R	5-11	185	4-1-75	1996	Stephenville, Texas
Strange, Mike	.226	76	186	33	42	11	0	1	12	45	59	9	5	R	R	6-0	172	4-21-74	1994	Melbourne, Fla.
Wells, Vernon	.285	134	509	86	145	35	2	11	65	49	84	13	8	R	R	6-1	195	12-8-78	1997	Arlington, Texas
Young, Mike	.282	140	522	86	147	33	5	16	87	55	96	16	8	R	R	6-0	175	10-19-76	1997	Covina, Calif.
Zepeda, Jesse	.231	105	290	39	67	7	0	3	29	57	56	5	2	B	R	5-10	165	5-4-74	1996	Santa Maria, Calif.

GAMES BY POSITION: C—Albaral 2, Cripps 57, Peters 1, Phelps 85, Rodriguez 11. **1B**—Albaral 1, Cripps 3, Hayes 24, Morrison 106, Peters 7, Rodriguez 10, Strange 17, Zepeda 1. **2B**—Bagley 1, Izturis 2, Strange 8, Young 128, Zepeda 22. **3B**—Albaral 1, Hayes 35, Izturis 1, Nunez 4, Phelps 1, Rodriguez 1, Strange 42, Zepeda 82. **SS**—Izturis 129, Rodriguez 2, Strange 1, Young 24, Zepeda 2. **OF**—Albaral 78, Bagley 81, Brown 44, Hayes 7, Morillo 32, Morrison 1, Nieves 2, Peters 88, Phelps 1, Rodriguez 19, Strange 4, Wells 129, Young 1, Zepeda 1.

PITCHING	W	L	ERA	G	GS	CG	SV	IP	H	R	ER	BB	SO	B	T	HT	WT	DOB	1st Yr	Resides
Andrews, Clayton	10	7	2.28	27	26	2	0	162	112	59	41	46	193	R	L	6-0	175	5-15-78	1996	Largo, Fla.
Bowles, Brian	2	4	4.52	31	4	0	0	68	80	41	34	18	48	R	R	6-5	205	8-18-76	1995	Manhattan Beach, Calif.
Brackeen, Colin	4	4	2.45	37	0	0	0	55	46	18	15	19	61	L	L	6-0	200	3-8-75	1997	Arden Hills, Minn.
Casey, Joe	2	7	4.66	22	16	0	0	77	84	53	40	41	62	R	R	6-0	185	1-25-79	1997	Honeybrook, Pa.
Estrella, Leo	1	3	4.50	5	5	0	0	30	34	19	15	13	27	R	R	6-1	172	2-20-75	1994	Puerto Plata, D.R.
2-team (20 Capital City)	11	11	4.05	25	25	3	0	149	154	85	67	36	124							
Eversgerd, Randy	3	1	8.10	11	0	0	0	23	32	22	21	13	16	R	R	6-0	180	8-28-76	1997	Centralia, Ill.
Giron, Isabel	10	9	2.49	21	21	4	0	126	110	57	35	27	129	R	R	6-2	160	11-17-77	1995	Villa Mella, D.R.
Heath, Woody	11	3	2.97	24	10	0	1	94	79	42	31	27	82	R	R	6-0	170	8-19-76	1997	Issaquah, Wash.
Huff, Tim	2	0	3.81	26	0	0	0	50	62	23	21	17	30	L	L	6-0	170	12-28-74	1997	Phoenix, Ariz.
Huggins, David	0	2	7.98	12	0	0	2	15	16	15	13	14	13	R	R	6-5	190	12-19-75	1997	Chester, Texas
Kingrey, Jarrod	0	1	3.86	1	0	0	0	2	3	2	1	0	3	R	R	6-1	205	8-23-76	1998	Fortson, Ga.
McClellan, Matt	8	7	3.09	25	25	1	0	140	109	65	48	58	126	R	R	6-7	205	8-13-76	1997	Toledo, Ohio
Salley, Anthony	0	2	4.58	20	0	0	0	39	40	24	20	22	30	L	L	6-0	185	9-23-75	1997	Swansea, S.C.
Seabury, Jaron	2	1	1.65	45	0	0	17	55	37	14	10	21	48	R	R	6-4	215	1-31-76	1995	Mount Vernon, Wash.
Sneed, John	16	2	2.56	27	27	2	0	162	123	59	46	58	210	L	R	6-6	235	6-30-76	1997	Houston, Texas
Weimer, Matt	7	6	2.85	48	0	0	8	73	62	31	23	26	59	R	R	6-2	190	11-21-74	1997	Annapolis, Md.
Young, Joe	3	1	5.31	7	7	0	0	39	38	23	23	18	42	R	R	6-4	210	4-28-75	1993	Fort McMurray, Alberta

ST. CATHARINES — Short-Season Class A

NEW YORK-PENN LEAGUE

BATTING	AVG	G	AB	R	H	2B	3B	HR	RBI	BB	SO	SB	CS	B	T	HT	WT	DOB	1st Yr	Resides
Adams, Lawrence	.000	3	8	0	0	0	0	0	0	0	6	0	0	R	R	6-5	215	2-18-77	1997	Fairburn, Ga.
Barnett, Brian	.296	48	152	22	45	8	2	2	16	15	41	4	1	R	R	5-10	175	5-15-76	1997	McMinnville, Ore.
Bernhardt, Josephang	.182	59	181	18	33	11	1	2	19	17	61	0	0	R	R	6-1	165	9-22-80	1996	San Pedro de Macoris, D.R.
Brown, Billy	.275	72	280	41	77	12	3	3	34	39	51	27	12	R	R	6-0	195	3-9-76	1997	Plantation, Fla.
Bundy, Ryan	.196	47	148	20	29	6	3	6	16	13	55	2	2	R	R	6-1	210	8-5-77	1998	Everett, Wash.
Carter, Shannon	.262	24	61	8	16	3	0	1	7	4	14	2	0	L	L	6-0	170	3-23-79	1997	El Reno, Okla.
Estevez, Domingo	.306	56	209	40	64	16	6	7	33	19	26	12	7	B	R	6-2	165	7-1-77	1995	Santiago Rodriguez, D.R.
Heying, Scott	.261	46	115	15	30	6	0	0	13	12	19	1	1	L	R	5-11	175	12-26-75	1998	San Antonio, Texas
Hubbel, Travis	.125	10	16	1	2	1	0	0	1	3	9	0	0	R	R	6-1	185	6-27-79	1997	Edmonton, Alberta
Jackson, Brandon	.263	57	171	30	45	5	0	1	11	18	26	6	0	R	R	6-1	180	10-28-75	1998	Chicago, Ill.
Lebron, Jesus	.254	43	126	25	32	6	1	4	21	13	43	7	4	R	R	5-11	185	7-25-77	1998	Orlando, Fla.
Lee, Richard	.286	23	77	14	22	6	0	4	17	11	17	1	0	R	R	6-2	205	1-9-76	1998	Jackson, Miss.
Lopez, Felipe	.373	19	83	14	31	5	2	1	11	3	14	4	2	B	R	6-0	175	5-12-80	1998	Apopka, Fla.
Morillo, Luis	.200	1	5	1	1	0	0	0	0	0	4	1	0	L	L	5-11	155	1-13-78	1996	Santo Domingo, D.R.
Nieves, Juan	.274	60	208	26	57	15	1	7	38	14	31	2	2	R	R	6-3	170	3-29-77	1996	Carabobo, Ven.
Perez, Angelo	.269	40	119	11	32	9	1	2	13	7	29	3	0	R	R	6-1	168	11-14-76	1994	La Romana, D.R.
Polk, Chad	.231	50	130	25	30	4	0	3	18	31	45	8	1	B	R	6-0	190	5-24-75	1998	Coppell, Texas
Riggins, Auntwan	.167	5	12	1	2	0	0	0	0	1	3	0	0	B	R	6-1	170	6-17-76	1998	Houston, Texas
Silletti, Pete	.000	1	1	0	0	0	0	0	0	1	0	0	0	B	R	5-10	200	4-14-74	1997	West Harrison, N.Y.

BATTING	AVG	G	AB	R	H	2B	3B	HR	RBI	BB	SO	SB	CS	B	T	HT	WT	DOB	1st Yr	Resides
Thompson, Tyler	.252	70	246	42	62	17	0	4	32	46	64	6	5	R	R	6-0	205	8-28-75	1998	Bloomington, Ind.
Umbria, Jose	.237	32	97	14	23	2	0	0	13	9	22	0	0	R	R	6-2	205	1-20-78	1996	Barquisimeto, Ven.
Whitlock, Mike	.185	45	119	21	22	2	0	8	23	19	51	0	0	L	R	6-3	200	12-14-76	1995	Oakland, Calif.

GAMES BY POSITION: C—Bundy 43, Polk 19, Silletti 1, Umbria 22. **1B**—Lee 2, Nieves 33, Polk 11, Umbria 11, Whitlock 43. **2B**—Barnett 23, Estevez 39, Heying 27, Jackson 6. **3B**—Barnett 16, Bernhardt 28, Estevez 1, Heying 7, Hubbel 7, Jackson 18, Lee 12, Polk 4, Riggins 5. **SS**—Barnett 1, Bernhardt 32, Jackson 36, Lopez 18. **OF**—Barnett 4, Brown 66, Carter 20, Lebron 42, Morillo 1, Nieves 19, Perez 38, Thompson 63.

PITCHING	W	L	ERA	G	GS	CG	SV	IP	H	R	ER	BB	SO	B	T	HT	WT	DOB	1st Yr	Resides
Casey, Joe	1	2	12.27	4	3	0	0	11	18	19	15	11	9	R	R	6-0	185	1-25-79	1997	Honeybrook, Pa.
Coco, Pasqual	3	7	3.20	15	15	1	0	82	62	52	29	32	84	R	R	6-1	160	9-24-77	1995	Santo Domingo, D.R.
Eversgerd, Randy	4	2	3.12	17	2	0	0	35	35	17	12	4	34	R	R	6-0	180	8-28-76	1997	Centralia, Ill.
Gourlay, Matt	5	1	2.48	25	0	0	3	54	34	17	15	26	62	R	R	6-5	200	6-26-79	1996	Cheltenham, Australia
Gracesqui, Franklyn	1	0	6.61	11	0	0	0	16	16	12	12	12	19	B	L	6-5	200	8-20-79	1998	New York, N.Y.
Hueda, Alejandro	2	5	6.26	11	8	0	0	42	51	38	29	18	25	R	R	6-1	180	2-28-76	1996	San Jose, Costa Rica
Huggins, David	7	5	4.15	15	15	0	0	85	85	46	39	35	67	R	R	6-5	190	12-19-75	1997	Chester, Texas
Kingrey, Jarrod	0	0	0.48	25	0	0	16	38	21	7	2	17	58	R	R	6-1	205	8-23-76	1998	Fortson, Ga.
Markwell, Diegomar	3	3	5.54	17	5	0	0	52	61	39	32	35	40	L	L	6-2	165	8-8-80	1996	Curacao, Neth. Antilles
Place, Eric	4	5	6.51	19	8	0	0	55	59	47	40	22	40	R	L	5-11	205	5-27-75	1998	Torrance, Calif.
Sandoval, Marcos	1	2	6.15	10	4	0	1	41	33	32	28	22	39	R	R	6-1	160	12-29-80	1997	Carabobo, Ven.
Satterfield, Jeremy	0	1	10.38	1	1	0	0	4	3	5	5	5	6	R	R	6-3	200	12-2-75	1996	Santa Barbara, Calif.
Seale, Dustin	2	0	4.99	21	0	0	0	40	41	28	22	19	43	L	L	6-1	170	12-2-77	1997	Safford, Ariz.
Severino, Edy	0	0	2.25	2	0	0	0	4	1	1	1	3	5	R	R	6-4	180	6-8-76	1994	Yamasa, D.R.
Smith, Taylor	4	5	5.10	15	15	0	0	78	87	61	44	26	61	R	R	6-3	195	12-15-78	1997	Henderson, Nev.
Stafford, Mike	1	0	1.38	14	0	0	1	26	22	7	4	6	14	B	L	6-3	180	6-24-75	1998	Canton, Mich.

MEDICINE HAT — Rookie

PIONEER LEAGUE

BATTING	AVG	G	AB	R	H	2B	3B	HR	RBI	BB	SO	SB	CS	B	T	HT	WT	DOB	1st Yr	Resides
Barrett, Andy	.071	8	14	1	1	0	0	0	0	4	4	0	0	L	R	6-0	175	7-12-79	1997	Tacoma, Wash.
Davies, Justin	.209	54	145	36	39	4	0	0	10	34	18	11	4	L	R	6-0	170	11-10-76	1998	West Babylon, N.Y.
Davis, Jermaine	.276	32	87	15	24	5	1	2	23	10	24	2	0	R	R	6-4	230	9-9-78	1997	Chesnee, S.C.
Fleming, Ryan	.306	70	255	64	78	20	1	2	41	37	29	17	3	L	L	5-11	180	2-11-76	1998	Grove City, Ohio
Gibbons, Jay	.397	73	290	66	115	29	1	19	98	37	25	2	1	L	L	6-0	200	9-2-77	1998	Lakewood, Calif.
Guzman, Alexis	.179	36	84	11	15	0	0	0	3	6	21	1	0	B	R	6-0	160	4-23-80	1997	Brisas del Mar, Ven.
Hubbel, Travis	.297	16	37	5	11	1	1	0	5	10	10	1	0	R	R	6-1	185	6-27-79	1997	Edmonton, Alberta
Hudson, Orlando	.293	65	242	50	71	18	1	8	42	22	36	6	5	B	R	6-0	175	12-12-77	1998	Darlington, S.C.
Juarez, Jonny	.296	39	142	17	42	7	1	1	22	5	12	6	1	L	L	6-0	165	6-22-78	1996	Caracas, Ven.
Kremblas, Mike	.293	59	184	40	54	15	0	4	36	40	30	5	4	R	R	6-0	180	10-1-75	1998	Carroll, Ohio
Logan, Matt	.266	47	173	29	46	12	1	3	30	23	41	1	1	L	R	6-3	200	7-22-79	1997	Brampton, Ontario
Martelli, Tony	.192	23	52	7	10	1	0	0	8	10	13	1	3	R	R	6-0	185	2-11-75	1998	Flushing, N.Y.
Nunez, Jorge	.319	74	317	74	101	9	11	6	52	28	45	31	2	R	R	5-10	158	3-3-78	1995	Villa Mella, D.R.
Riggins, Auntwan	.248	41	153	30	38	6	1	0	18	10	34	16	1	B	R	6-1	170	6-17-76	1998	Houston, Texas
Santos, Juan	.111	15	27	2	3	0	0	0	1	8	13	0	0	B	R	6-3	186	3-14-78	1997	Bayamon, P.R.
Silletti, Pete	.000	2	1	0	0	0	0	0	0	0	1	0	0	B	R	5-10	200	4-14-74	1997	West Harrison, N.Y.
Smith, Fred	.252	66	226	44	57	11	1	5	36	26	62	11	3	R	R	6-2	172	5-27-78	1998	Lexington, Ky.
Ventura, Henry	.214	33	103	13	22	8	0	1	18	5	30	0	1	R	R	6-1	170	12-20-80	1997	Villa Mella, D.R.
Zeber, Ryan	.205	14	39	4	8	1	0	0	9	3	8	0	2	R	R	6-2	190	5-24-78	1996	Santa Ana, Calif.

GAMES BY POSITION: C—Kremblas 59, Santos 13, Silletti 1, Zeber 11. **1B**—Davis 1, Gibbons 35, Logan 39, Zeber 2. **2B**—Davies 1, Hudson 64, Martelli 16, Nunez 8. **3B**—Guzman 23, Hubbel 15, Martelli 7, Nunez 2, Riggins 40. **SS**—Guzman 14, Nunez 65. **OF**—Barrett 4, Davies 47, Davis 16, Fleming 68, Juarez 31, Silletti 1, Smith 64, Ventura 26.

PITCHING	W	L	ERA	G	GS	CG	SV	IP	H	R	ER	BB	SO	B	T	HT	WT	DOB	1st Yr	Resides
Caceres, Antonio	6	4	3.81	21	4	0	0	59	65	37	25	19	30	R	R	6-2	165	8-7-77	1995	Santo Domingo, D.R.
Cassidy, Scott	8	1	2.43	15	14	0	0	81	71	31	22	14	82	R	R	6-3	175	10-3-75	1998	Clay, N.Y.
Curtis, Mark	6	6	5.94	15	15	0	0	73	79	59	48	47	49	R	L	6-5	200	12-1-77	1997	St. Albert, Alberta
Espinal, Orlando	1	5	8.44	7	6	0	0	27	36	28	25	9	30	R	R	6-2	180	3-28-76	1994	Cienfuegos, D.R.
File, Robert	2	1	1.41	28	0	0	16	32	24	7	5	5	28	R	R	6-4	215	1-28-77	1998	Philadelphia, Pa.
Gaud, Perfecto	0	1	4.91	17	0	0	0	18	19	16	10	19	15	L	L	6-4	210	12-4-78	1998	Yauco, P.R.
Huxhold, Adam	0	0	5.40	3	0	0	0	5	4	4	3	3	3	L	L	6-1	175	8-25-76	1998	Gig Harbor, Wash.
Lynch, Pat	7	3	2.32	14	14	3	0	89	71	33	23	16	77	R	R	6-3	195	6-27-78	1996	Milton, Ontario
Montanez, Johen	0	0	7.88	6	0	0	0	8	14	7	7	2	10	R	R	6-5	215	11-21-75	1994	Araure, Ven.
Mowday, Chris	1	0	10.13	10	0	0	0	11	12	15	12	15	8	R	R	6-4	191	8-24-81	1997	Strathpine, Australia
Murray, Steve	4	1	5.71	14	10	0	0	58	77	46	37	11	41	L	L	6-1	185	6-29-80	1998	Ennismore, Ontario
Orloski, Joe	7	1	3.92	14	10	0	0	60	71	37	26	18	42	R	R	6-3	175	5-17-79	1998	Las Vegas, Nev.
Renwick, Tyler	1	1	21.38	9	0	0	0	8	10	20	19	20	7	R	R	6-3	195	8-12-78	1998	Langley, B.C.
St. Amand, Reuben	0	0	9.82	10	0	0	0	11	11	16	12	13	2	R	R	6-4	215	8-4-79	1998	Olympia, Wash.
Stafford, Mike	1	1	2.89	6	0	0	0	9	13	7	3	1	6	B	L	6-3	180	6-24-75	1998	Canton, Mich.
Stevens, Josh	1	0	2.98	25	0	0	0	42	37	17	14	13	39	R	R	6-3	200	6-6-79	1998	Mira Loma, Calif.
Woodards, Orlando	1	3	3.58	26	1	0	3	50	48	27	20	11	58	R	R	6-3	205	1-2-78	1997	Sacramento, Calif.

Minor Leagues

Inaugural Triple-A World Series highlights another record-breaking year in minors

BY LACY LUSK

Zephyrs celebrate Triple-A World Series triumph

Fifty years from now, the 1998 minor league season might best be remembered for the way it ended.

For the first time ever, a Triple-A champion was decided with a two-team, head-to-head series. In the first year after realignment pushed aside the American Association, the Pacific Coast League champion New Orleans Zephyrs won the Triple-A World Series at Cashman Field in Las Vegas.

The Buffalo Bisons, whose late-season surge lifted them to the International League title, lost three games to one after leading Game Three 2-1 in the eighth inning. Nevertheless, it was a landmark year for Buffalo as the team broke an IL single-season attendance mark and also won a Triple-A league title for the second straight year. In 1997, the Bisons claimed the last American Association crown.

National Association officials wouldn't mind the Triple-A World Series becoming an annual event, perhaps at the same site each season as the minors' equivalent to the College World Series in Omaha. The event is scheduled to be in Las Vegas in 1999 and 2000 at a cost of $750,000 a year to the city's Convention and Visitors Authority.

In its first year, the series drew an average crowd of 3,368 fans.

"For the first year, I think we found the attendance to be very acceptable," IL president Randy Mobley said. "We will not find it acceptable in year two and beyond."

While attendance was uninspiring for the World Series, it was up to 32.3 million in the regular season—a post-1940s high. The number reflects an additional 330 dates, so per-game attendance was actually down 1.9 percent. But the fact that crowds are holding steady is good news for the minors, as the 1990s building boom continues.

Off the field, the minors went through a peaceful year in the first year of a new Professional Baseball Agreement. Aside from a New York-Penn League team that had to move because of Erie's jump to Double-A and a Carolina League team already on the move, all 1998 franchises looked like they would be in the same place in 1999. Jackson (Texas), Vancouver (Pacific Coast), Pittsfield (New York-Penn), Watertown (New York-Penn) and probably St. Petersburg (Florida State) were on the endangered list for 2000.

TRIPLE-A WORLD SERIES

Las Vegas
Sept. 21-25, 1998

STANDINGS	W	L	RF	RA
New Orleans (Pacific Coast)	3	1	24	19
Buffalo (International)	1	3	19	24

SEMIFINALS: International League—Buffalo defeated Durham 3-2 in best-of-5 series. **Pacific Coast League**—New Orleans defeated Calgary 3-2 in best-of-5 series.

INDIVIDUAL BATTING LEADERS
(Minimum 10 At-Bats)

	AVG	AB	R	H	2B	3B	HR	RBI	SB
Manto, Jeff, Buffalo	.533	15	3	8	2	0	1	5	0
Ronan, Marc, NO	.500	14	1	7	0	0	1	4	0
Berkman, Lance, NO	.467	15	6	7	1	0	3	6	0
Ramos, Ken, New Orleans	.400	10	2	4	1	0	1	1	0
Hernandez, Carlos, NO	.389	18	3	7	0	0	0	1	3
Ward, Daryle, NO	.294	17	3	5	0	0	2	6	0

INDIVIDUAL PITCHING LEADERS
(Minimum 5 Innings)

	W	L	ERA	G	SV	IP	H	BB	SO
Martinez, Willie, Buffalo	0	0	1.50	1	0	6	8	1	7
Halama, John, New Orleans	1	0	2.00	1	0	9	4	2	7
Matthews, Mike, Buffalo	1	0	2.08	2	0	9	9	1	2
Scanlan, Bob, New Orleans	1	0	2.25	1	0	8	5	4	3

Most Valuable Player: Lance Berkman, of, New Orleans.

Hail To The First Champion

In as unlikely a parlay as any during the week of the Triple-A World Series, Ken Ramos and Marc Ronan hit pivotal back-to-back home runs to bring New Orleans from the brink of defeat to the brink of a championship.

One game later, Lance Berkman made sure the Zephyrs took home the first trophy in a new era for the highest level of minor league baseball.

Berkman's three home runs in Game Four carried New Orleans past Buffalo 12-6 to wrap up the series, three games to one. But the Zephyrs would have been fighting off elimination if not for the timely blasts from their seventh- and eighth-place hitters, who had six home runs in 409 regular season Triple-A at-bats.

"This is one step below the big leagues, and not everyone has the opportunity to play five or six years in the majors," said Ramos, a 31-year-old outfielder whose only 12 major league at-bats came in 1997 with the Astros. "I've been in Triple-A for six years, but this is a great moment. Winning this will be something those who don't get into the big leagues—and even those who do—will remember for the rest of our lives."

MINOR LEAGUE ALL-STARS

Selected by Baseball America

Pos.	Player, Team	AVG	AB	R	H	2B	3B	HR	RBI	BB	SO	SB
C	Michael Barrett, Harrisburg	.320	453	78	145	32	2	19	87	27	43	7
1B	Calvin Pickering, Bowie	.309	488	93	151	28	2	31	114	98	119	4
2B	Ron Belliard, Louisville	.321	507	114	163	36	7	14	73	69	77	32
3B	Eric Chavez, Huntsville/Edmonton	.327	529	104	173	45	1	33	126	54	93	14
SS	Pablo Ozuna, Peoria	.357	538	122	192	27	10	9	62	29	56	62
OF	Lance Berkman, Jackson/New Orleans	.302	484	96	146	38	0	30	102	97	98	6
	Alex Escobar, Capital City	.310	416	90	129	23	5	27	91	54	133	49
	Gabe Kapler, Jacksonville	.322	547	113	176	47	6	28	146	66	93	6
DH	Chris Hatcher, Omaha	.309	485	84	150	21	2	46	106	25	125	8

Pos.	Player, Team	W	L	ERA	G	GS	CG	SV	IP	H	BB	SO
SP	Rick Ankiel, Peoria/Prince William	12	6	2.63	28	28	1	0	161	106	50	222
	Ryan Bradley, Tampa/Norwich/Columbus	9	5	2.65	38	17	2	7	136	82	51	149
	Bruce Chen, Greenville/Richmond	15	8	3.09	28	27	1	0	163	123	67	193
	Brad Penny, High Desert	14	5	2.96	28	28	1	0	164	138	35	207
RP	Brent Stentz, New Britain	1	2	1.98	57	0	0	43	59	44	28	65

Player of the Year: Eric Chavez, Huntsville/Edmonton. **Manager of the Year:** Terry Kennedy, Iowa.

New Orleans trailed 2-1 with two out in the eighth inning of Game Three when Ramos homered to right field off Chris Nichting. Buffalo manager Jeff Datz brought in reliever Jimmy Hamilton, but it was more of the same as Ronan drove his second pitch to almost the same spot in right field. Reggie Harris saved the 3-2 victory for Bob Scanlan.

Throughout most of the regular season, the 29-year-old Ronan backed up Pacific Coast League all-star catcher Mitch Meluskey. In 123 at-bats, Ronan hit one home run. Like Ramos, he has 12 career major league at-bats (with the Cardinals in 1993). When Meluskey was promoted to the Astros in late August, Ronan became New Orleans' regular catcher.

When Ronan got his chance, though, he contributed behind the plate and at the plate. He went 7-for-14 (.500) in the series, and only Buffalo first baseman Jeff Manto, the active minor league home run leader, hit for a higher average (.533).

Lance Berkman

Oddly, both New Orleans and Buffalo were members of the disbanded American Association in 1997. Three of the AA's former teams, including Buffalo, were absorbed by the 14-team International League, while the 16-team Pacific Coast League took in New Orleans and four other clubs.

ORGANIZATION STANDINGS

Cumulative farm club standings for the 30 major league organizations:

	—1998—			1997	1996	1995
TEAM	W	L	Pct.	Pct.	Pct.	Pct.
Toronto (6)	398	315	.5582	.445	.487	.453
Kansas City (6)	390	309	.5580	.484	.521	.535
Minnesota (6)	378	312	.548	.520	.520	.514
New York-NL (7)	409	355	.535	.516	574	.536
Tampa Bay (6)	335	293	.533	.497	.466	—
San Diego (6)	368	322	.533	.486	.530	.456
Montreal (6)	370	331	.528	.483	.539	.462
Texas (6)	363	327	.526	.486	.501	.429
Oakland (6)	364	331	.524	.534	.536	.507
Boston (6)	362	333	.521	.512	.503	.493
Seattle (6)	359	331	.520	.509	.487	.469
New York-AL (6)	363	340	.516	.556	.525	.507
Chicago-NL (6)	357	336	.515	.487	.499	.546
Cleveland (6)	363	344	.513	.507	.542	.544
Houston (6)	352	343	.506	.468	.493	.515
St. Louis (6)	357	348	.506	.459	.501	.479
Philadelphia (6)	356	352	.503	.504	.493	.533
Detroit (6)	348	347	.501	.531	.501	.521
Baltimore (6)	347	348	.499	.535	.503	.479
Chicago-AL (6)	336	346	.493	.501	.430	.473
San Francisco (5)	313	326	.490	.512	.527	.514
Milwaukee (6)	335	380	.469	.490	.524	.550
Colorado (6)	323	375	.463	.479	.478	.510
Florida (6)	321	379	.459	.512	.464	.495
Anaheim (6)	327	368	.457	.484	.483	.566
Cincinnati (5)	288	347	.454	.541	.485	.569
Pittsburgh (6)	314	386	.449	499	.486	.499
Arizona (5)	246	306	.446	.501	.547	—
Los Angeles (7)	313	400	.439	.485	.494	.512
Atlanta (7)	337	431	.439	.483	.465	.453

Number of farm teams in parentheses

Through The Turnstiles

The minor league boom showed no signs of letting up in 1998.

With a total attendance of 32.3 million, more fans saw minor league baseball than in any season since the post-World War II years when more than 400 teams played in more than 50 leagues.

Five leagues and 27 teams set attendance records as the minors drew 1.8 percent more fans than in 1997. The leagues with new highs were the International, Pacific Coast, Eastern, New York-Penn and Northwest.

The flip side of the statistics: average attendance was down almost two percent, and the Northwest League broke its overall mark only because of two extra dates. In

CLASSIFICATION ALL-STARS

Selected by Baseball America

*League leader

TRIPLE-A

Pos.	Player, Team (League)	AVG	AB	R	H	2B	3B	HR	RBI	BB	SO	SB
C	Mitch Meluskey, New Orleans (Pacific Coast)	.353	397	76	140	41	0	17	71	85	59	2
1B	Roberto Petagine, Indianapolis (International)	.331	363	79	120	30	1	24	109	70	71	3
2B	Ron Belliard, Louisville (International)	.321	507	*114	163	36	7	14	73	69	77	32
3B	George Arias, Las Vegas (Pacific Coast)	.308	435	73	134	33	4	36	*119	37	108	0
SS	Jolbert Cabrera, Buffalo (International)	.318	494	94	157	24	1	10	45	68	71	25
OF	Brian Daubach, Charlotte (International)	.316	497	102	157	*45	4	*35	*124	80	114	9
	Jeremy Giambi, Omaha (Pacific Coast)	*.372	325	68	121	21	2	20	66	57	64	8
	Alex Ramirez, Buffalo (International)	.299	521	94	156	21	8	34	103	16	101	6
DH	Chris Hatcher, Omaha (Pacific Coast)	.309	485	84	150	21	2	*46	106	25	125	8

Pos.	Player, Team (League)	W	L	ERA	G	GS	CG	SV	IP	H	BB	SO
SP	Matt Clement, Las Vegas (Pacific Coast)	10	9	3.98	27	27	1	0	172	157	85	*160
	Jason Jacome, Buffalo (International)	14	2	3.26	24	24	2	0	155	161	38	109
	Kurt Miller, Iowa (Pacific Coast)	*14	3	3.81	28	27	2	0	168	153	77	145
	Shannon Withem, Syracuse (International)	*17	5	3.27	28	27	4	0	190	176	58	113
RP	Bart Evans, Omaha (Pacific Coast)	3	1	2.53	49	0	0	*27	57	50	22	54

Player of the Year: Brian Daubach, of, Charlotte. **Manager of the Year:** Terry Kennedy, Iowa.

DOUBLE-A

Pos.	Player, Team (League)	AVG	AB	R	H	2B	3B	HR	RBI	BB	SO	SB
C	Michael Barrett, Harrisburg (Eastern)	.320	453	78	145	32	2	19	87	27	43	7
1B	Calvin Pickering, Bowie (Eastern)	.309	488	93	151	28	2	*31	*114	*98	119	4
2B	Warren Morris, Tulsa (Texas)/ Carolina (Southern)	.331	541	87	179	30	8	19	103	67	97	17
3B	Eric Chavez, Huntsville (Southern)	.328	335	66	110	27	1	22	86	42	61	12
SS	Santiago Perez, El Paso (Texas)	.306	454	73	139	20	*13	11	64	28	70	21
OF	Tyrone Horne, Arkansas (Texas)	.312	443	94	138	13	3	*37	*139	70	97	18
	Gabe Kapler, Jacksonville (Southern)	.322	547	*113	*176	*47	6	*28	*146	66	93	6
	George Lombard, Greenville (Southern)	.308	422	84	130	25	4	22	65	71	140	35
DH	Doug Mientkiewicz, New Britain (Eastern)	*.323	502	*96	162	*45	0	16	88	96	58	11

Pos.	Player, Team (League)	W	L	ERA	G	GS	CG	SV	IP	H	BB	SO
SP	Bruce Chen, Greenville (Southern)	13	7	3.29	24	23	1	0	139	106	48	164
	Jose Jimenez, Arkansas (Texas)	*15	6	*3.11	26	26	1	0	180	156	68	88
	Mike Kuslewicz, New Haven (Eastern)	14	7	*2.32	27	26	2	0	179	161	35	151
	Mike Lincoln, New Britain (Eastern)	*15	7	3.22	26	26	1	0	173	180	35	109
RP	Brent Stentz, New Britain (Eastern)	1	2	1.98	57	0	0	*43	59	44	28	65

Player of the Year: Eric Chavez, 3b, Huntsville. **Manager of the Year:** Joel Skinner, Akron.

CLASS A

Pos.	Player, Team (League)	AVG	AB	R	H	2B	3B	HR	RBI	BB	SO	SB
C	Shea Hillenbrand, Michigan (Midwest)	.349	498	80	174	33	4	19	92	19	49	13
1B	Shawn Gallagher, Charlotte (Florida State)	.308	520	*111	160	*37	4	*26	*121	66	116	18
2B	Marcus Giles, Macon (South Atlantic)	.329	505	*111	166	38	3	*37	*108	*85	103	12
3B	Joe Crede, Winston-Salem (Carolina)	*.315	492	*92	155	32	3	20	*88	53	98	9
SS	Pablo Ozuna, Peoria (Midwest)	*.357	538	*122	*192	27	10	9	62	29	56	62
OF	Milton Bradley, Cape Fear (SAL)/Jupiter (FSL)	.295	542	109	160	35	5	11	84	53	99	30
	Alex Escobar, Capital City (South Atlantic)	.310	416	90	129	23	5	27	91	54	133	49
	Bucky Jacobsen, Beloit (Midwest)	.293	499	96	146	31	1	*27	*100	83	133	5
DH	Tommy Peterman, Fort Myers (Florida State)	.312	519	71	162	36	2	20	110	63	86	2

Pos.	Player, Team (League)	W	L	ERA	G	GS	CG	SV	IP	H	BB	SO
SP	Rick Ankiel, Peoria (MWL)/Prince William (CL)	12	6	2.63	28	28	1	0	161	106	50	222
	Aaron Myette, Hickory (SAL)/Winston-Salem (CL)	13	6	2.33	23	23	1	0	147	116	44	157
	Brad Penny, High Desert (California)	14	5	2.96	28	28	1	0	164	138	35	207
	John Sneed, Hagerstown (South Atlantic)	*16	2	2.56	27	27	2	0	162	123	58	210
RP	Jim Stoops, San Jose (California)/Salem(Carolina)	2	1	0.98	45	0	0	31	55	28	25	96

Player of the Year: Brad Penny, rhp, High Desert. **Manager of the Year:** Bruce Fields, West Michigan.

SHORT-SEASON

Pos.	Player, Team (League)	AVG	AB	R	H	2B	3B	HR	RBI	BB	SO	SB
C	Paul Phillips, Spokane (Northwest)	.308	234	55	72	12	2	4	25	18	19	12
1B	Nate Espy, Martinsville (Appalachian)	.361	227	50	82	20	1	13	56	51	55	2
2B	Rafael Furcal, Danville (Appalachian)	.328	268	56	88	15	4	0	23	36	29	*60
3B	Jared Sandberg, Hudson Valley (New York-Penn)	.288	271	49	78	15	2	*12	54	42	76	13
SS	Jorge Nunez, Medicine Hat (Pioneer)	.319	317	74	101	9	*11	6	52	28	45	31
OF	Jake Weber, Everett (Northwest)	.338	275	*75	93	20	2	11	52	*67	42	14
	Mike Restovich, Elizabethton (Appalachian)	.355	242	*68	86	20	1	13	64	*54	58	5
	Elpidio Guzman, Butte (Pioneer)	.331	299	70	99	16	5	9	61	24	44	40
DH	Jay Gibbons, Medicine Hat (Pioneer)	*.397	290	66	*115	*29	1	*19	*98	37	25	2

Pos.	Player, Team (League)	W	L	ERA	G	GS	CG	SV	IP	H	BB	SO
SP	Chris Mears, Everett (Northwest)	*9	1	2.74	15	15	1	0	93	86	33	67
	Brody Percell, Watertown (New York-Penn)	9	2	2.21	15	15	1	0	86	73	16	*105
	Chris Reinike, Watertown (New York-Penn)	*10	2	1.91	15	15	0	0	90	64	33	92
	Geoff Geary, Batavia (New York-Penn)	9	1	*1.60	16	15	1	0	95	78	14	101
RP	Jarrod Kingrey, St. Catharines (New York-Penn)	0	0	0.48	25	0	0	16	38	21	17	58

Player of the Year: Mike Restovich, of, Elizabethton. **Manager of the Year:** Nick Capra, Bristol.

Player of the Year

A's hitting machine Chavez earns top honor

JOHN SPEAR

Eric Chavez

Not so very long ago, Eric Chavez was a big kid with a load of talent and a lack of focus. Then Chavez grew up in a hurry.

At instructional league in 1997, Chavez sat down with Athletics farm director Keith Lieppman for a little talk about the ways of life of a professional baseball player. A few of the remarks made a big impact.

"We sat down and talked about where he expected to be, and how he planned on getting there," Lieppman said. "We wanted him to realize that he can become something special."

Chavez took the talk to heart. He went out in instructional league and became a model of devotion, then carried his commitment into the 1998 season. As a raw 20-year-old with only one year of pro ball behind him, he dominated Double-A, batting .328 with 22 home runs and 86 RBIs with Huntsville before receiving a promotion to Triple-A Edmonton. Undaunted by competing as the youngest player in the Pacific Coast League, he batted .325 with 11 homers and 40 RBIs.

Such remarkable achievements at so young an age provided the impetus for Baseball America to name Chavez its Minor League Player of the Year for 1998. He became the first A's prospect to win the award since Jose Canseco in 1985.

It's not so much the numbers Chavez posted that has the A's organization excited. It's his explosive improvement in just about every area of his game. Give him a challenge, and a few weeks later he seems to master it.

"That's one of his greatest talents," Lieppman said. "He's extremely quick at learning things. He just has an ability to integrate things very quickly."

Perhaps the most stunning level of development has been in Chavez's defense. At one point, the A's worried that Chavez' glovework was so ragged that his future might be at first base or possibly even DH. He improved so much in 1998 that the A's considered him close to a major league average third baseman. His biggest obstacle was footwork in setting up for his throws.

"He has so much talent that it is just a matter of how good he wants to be and how hard he will work to get there," Lieppman said. "So far, he has indicated he wants it very, very much."

A natural lefthanded hitter, Chavez graduated from San Diego's Mount Carmel High in 1996, after being a first-team All-American and batting .458 with 11 home runs as a senior. He refined his hitting skills in youth leagues, where he spent several years playing for former A's first baseman Mike Epstein, a nationally-known hitting specialist. The A's selected Chavez with the 10th pick in the '96 draft, and signed him to a $1.14 million bonus.

Despite all the progress he's made in his two seasons, the A's know he's not a finished product yet.

"As excited as we are about Eric, he has a lot of work to do to get there and make an impact. I mean a lot. I cannot overemphasize that," Edmonton manager Mike Quade said.

—CASEY TEFERTILLER

PREVIOUS WINNERS

1981—Mike Marshall, 1b, Albuquerque (Dodgers)
1982—Ron Kittle, of, Edmonton (White Sox)
1983—Dwight Gooden, rhp, Lynchburg (Mets)
1984—Mike Bielecki, rhp, Hawaii (Pirates)
1985—Jose Canseco, of, Huntsville/Tacoma (Athletics)
1986—Gregg Jefferies, ss, Columbia/Lynchburg/Jackson (Mets)
1987—Gregg Jefferies, ss, Jackson/Tidewater
1988—Tom Gordon, rhp, Appleton/Memphis/Omaha (Royals)
1989—Sandy Alomar, c, Las Vegas (Padres)
1990—Frank Thomas, 1b, Birmingham (White Sox)
1991—Derek Bell, of, Syracuse (Blue Jays)
1992—Tim Salmon, of, Edmonton (Angels)
1993—Manny Ramirez, of, Canton/Charlotte (Indians)
1994—Derek Jeter, ss, Tampa/Albany/Columbus (Yankees)
1995—Andruw Jones, of, Macon (Braves)
1996—Andruw Jones, of, Durham/Greenville/Richmond
1997—Paul Konerko, 1b, Albuquerque (Dodgers)

any case, the figures were nearly identical to the previous year's, which was good news for the minors.

The expanded IL and PCL also had more teams to draw from, but franchise records were set in Durham, Fresno, Indianapolis, Memphis, New Orleans, Oklahoma and Syracuse. Of that group, Durham and Fresno were new to Triple-A and Oklahoma had a new ballpark.

Durham and Memphis were expansion teams while Fresno replaced Phoenix, which made way for the Arizona Diamondbacks.

Triple-A drew almost 12.5 million fans in 1998. The best of those 30 teams was Buffalo, which drew an IL-record 743,463 fans. The Bisons didn't approach their franchise record, but they led the NA for the 11th straight year.

All three Double-A leagues showed an increase in attendance. After an eight percent jump in 1997, the EL went up another three percent overall to 3.29 million. Five of the league's 10 members (Akron, Harrisburg, New Britain, Reading and Trenton) broke their attendance marks.

Other teams with record attendance were Greenville and West Tenn (Southern); Tulsa (Texas); Lynchburg, Prince William and Salem (Carolina); Fort Myers and Jupiter (Florida State); Kane County (Midwest); Asheville and Piedmont (South Atlantic); Jamestown and Lowell (New York-Penn); and Everett and Spokane (Northwest).

If They Can Make It There

Soon after the New York-Penn League season ended, New York City made a move to attract two short-season franchises.

The Mets and Yankees both unveiled plans to move their affiliates in the NY-P to the city, part of a push by New York mayor Rudolph Giuliani to bring baseball to Brooklyn and Staten Island.

The Mets' move was further along, and the major league club announced that Pittsfield would move to a new ballpark at Coney Island (which is in Brooklyn) for the 2000 season.

The new ballpark, which is set to have a capacity of 6,500, will be on the Coney Island boardwalk, the centerpiece of a multi-million-dollar sports complex at the 12-acre Old Steeplechase Park.

The team will remain in Pittsfield at least until the new ballpark is ready.

The city set aside $50 million for the ballparks at Coney Island and Staten Island. City officials were still negotiating with Yankees owner George Steinbrenner over the Staten Island stadium, but Giuliani said he was hopeful a deal could be made.

The Yankees had already cleared the way to move a team there. They ended their 31-year affiliation with Oneonta for a two-year agreement with Watertown, a team that has been the subject of moving rumors several times in recent years.

Meanwhile, Oneonta president Sam Nader, who has kept professional baseball alive there for more than 50 years, lost his beloved Yankees affiliation in order to keep professional baseball alive in Oneonta. Oneonta becomes a Tigers farm team in 1999.

Other moves around the National Association:

■ The Jackson Generals (Texas) were sold to Nolan Ryan, his son Reid and former Astros owner Don Sanders with the intention of moving to Round Rock, Texas, for the 2000 season. The Austin area failed multiple times in an effort to get a team, but Ryan's stake in the club apparently paved the way for a move. The team will be called the Round Rock Express.

■ While Austin was No. 1 in Baseball America's early-season ranking of cities that most need a team, Sacramento was No. 2. Like Austin, Sacramento was closing in on a team of its own. Art Savage agreed to buy the Vancouver Canadians for $7.5 million, and he announced the team would move to Sacramento. The Fresno Grizzlies, who played in a college stadium in their inaugural season, could move to Sacramento instead if they fail to get a new ballpark. In either case, Sacramento also was in search of a new ballpark.

■ The Orlando Rays (Southern) announced they would move to Tallahassee. Fla., for the 2000 season. With major league baseball in St. Petersburg, Fla., now, that city's Florida State League team probably will move to Orlando when the Tallahassee shift takes place.

MINOR ADJUSTMENTS

The Midwest League, New York-Penn League and South Atlantic League saw the most affiliation changes after the 1998 season, but a few changes were made in Triple-A and significant changes were made in Double-A as well. Double-A gets two new Eastern League teams in 1999 to accommodate the addition of affiliates for the Devil Rays and Diamondbacks. Teams that switched affiliates are listed here.

TRIPLE-A	League	'98 affiliate	'99 affiliate
Calgary	Pacific Coast	White Sox	Marlins
Charlotte	International	Marlins	White Sox
Edmonton	Pacific Coast	Athletics	Angels
Vancouver	Pacific Coast	Angels	Athletics
DOUBLE-A			
Altoona	Eastern	—	Pirates
Carolina	Southern	Pirates	Rockies
El Paso	Texas	Brewers	Diamondbacks
Erie	Eastern	—	Angels
Huntsville	Southern	Athetlics	Brewers
Midland	Texas	Angels	Athletics
New Haven	Eastern	Rockies	Mariners
Orlando	Southern	Mariners	Devil Rays
CLASS A			
Augusta	South Atlantic	Pirates	Red Sox
Burlington	Midwest	Reds	White Sox
Charleston, W.Va.	South Atlantic	Reds	Royals
Clinton	Midwest	Padres	Reds
Fort Wayne	Midwest	Twins	Padres
Hickory	South Atlantic	White Sox	Pirates
Lansing	Midwest	Royals	Cubs
Michigan	Midwest	Red Sox	Astros
Quad City	Midwest	Astros	Twins
Rockford	Midwest	Cubs	Reds
SHORT-SEASON			
*Niles, Ohio	New York-Penn	Pirates	Indians
Eugene	Northwest	Braves	Cubs
Jamestown	New York-Penn	Tigers	Braves
Oneonta	New York-Penn	Yankees	Tigers
Watertown	New York-Penn	Indians	Yankees
Williamsport	New York-Penn	Cubs	Pirates

*Franchise operated in Erie in 1998

Minor League Capital

Just two retired numbers grace the green outfield walls at Rochester's Frontier Field, but they speak volumes about the city they represent.

One is 26, in honor of Joe Altobelli. The man who led the Orioles to their last World Series championship as manager in 1983 was a first baseman, successful manager and general manager for the Triple-A Red Wings. A Rochester resident since 1965, he's now the radio color analyst for the Wings.

The other retired number is 8,022–a tribute to the stockholders who saved baseball in this upstate New York city in 1957 and put Rochester Community Baseball Inc. on the map.

Tradition. Success. Continuity. Those qualities earned Rochester Baseball America's honor as Best Minor League City.

"I have always said that if I couldn't be in the major leagues, there is no place I'd rather be than Rochester," said Marv Foley, the fourth-year manager of the Red Wings. "The fans, the front office, the ballpark . . . everything about the city is first-class."

Rochester, home of Eastman Kodak and Bausch & Lomb, wore its new title well.

"There's a lot of people who knew that already," Altobelli said. "When I managed here (1971-76), more than 100 players asked me how they could play in Rochester. It's always been a very special place."

Rochester was chosen over 174 other minor league

DEPARTMENT LEADERS
Minor Leagues

*Full-season teams only

TEAM

WINS

Capital City (South Atlantic)	90
Jacksonville (Southern)	86
Mobile (Southern)	86
Wilmington (Carolina)	86
Iowa (Pacific Coast)	85

LONGEST WINNING STREAK

Cape Fear (South Atlantic)	15
Cedar Rapids (Midwest)	12
Durham (International)	11
Fresno (Pacific Coast)	11
Rockies (Arizona)	11

LOSSES

South Bend (Midwest)	100
Brevard County (Florida State)	97
Charleston, W.Va. (South Atlantic)	96
Bakersfield (California)	91
Vancouver (Pacific Coast)	90

LONGEST LOSING STREAK

Charleston, W.Va. (South Atlantic)	15
Helena (Pioneer)	15
Butte (Pioneer)	14
Augusta (South Atlantic)	12
New Haven (Eastern)	12

BATTING AVERAGE*

El Paso (Texas)	.293
New Orleans (Pacific Coast)	.291
Wichita (Texas)	.291
Jacksonville (Southern)	.290
Midland (Texas)	.290

RUNS

Lancaster (California)	909
Jacksonville (Southern)	882
Wichita (Texas)	857
Iowa (Pacific Coast)	849
Buffalo (International)	837

HOME RUNS

Iowa (Pacific Coast)	216
Omaha (Pacific Coast)	215
Buffalo (International)	206
Pawtucket (International)	187
Fresno (Pacific Coast)	184
Wichita (Texas)	184

STOLEN BASES

Capital City (South Atlantic)	295
Charlotte (Florida State)	271
Savannah (South Atlantic)	252
Fort Myers (Florida State)	222
Delmarva (South Atlantic)	211

Jeremy Giambi
.372 batting average

EARNED RUN AVERAGE*

Wilmington (Carolina)	2.97
West Michigan (Midwest)	3.01
Hagerstown (South Atlantic)	3.25
Binghamton (Eastern)	3.34
Jupiter (Florida State)	3.34

STRIKEOUTS

Greensboro (South Atlantic)	1228
Augusta (South Atlantic)	1209
Stockton (California)	1198
Danville (Carolina)	1190
Macon (South Atlantic)	1186

FIELDING AVERAGE*

Syracuse (International)	.981
Durham (International)	.980
Akron (Eastern)	.978
Iowa (Pacific Coast)	.978
Memphis (Pacific Coast)	.978

INDIVIDUAL BATTING

BATTING AVERAGE

(Minimum 383 Plate Appearances)

Jeremy Giambi, Omaha	.372
Casey Blake, Knoxville/Dunedin	.357
Pablo Ozuna, Peoria	.357
Darryl Brinkley, Nashville	.355
Mitch Meluskey, New Orleans	.353
Jason LaRue, Indy/Chattanooga	.350
Shea Hillenbrand, Michigan	.349
Mark Quinn, Wichita	.349
Jalal Leach, Fresno/Shreveport	.347
Todd Haney, Norfolk/St. Lucie	.345

RUNS

Jason Conti, Tulsa	125
Pablo Ozuna, Peoria	122
David Roberts, Buff./Akron/Jax	122
Ron Belliard, Louisville	114
Toby Kominek, El Paso	114

HITS

Pablo Ozuna, Peoria	192
Joe McEwing, Memphis/Arkansas	189
Casey Blake, Knoxville/Dunedin	183
Anthony Iapoce, El Paso	181
Alex Sanchez, St. Petersburg	180

TOP HITTING STREAKS

Casey Blake, Knoxville/Dunedin	31
Alex Ramirez, Buffalo	28
Jose Macias, Jacksonville	27
Ruben Mateo, Tulsa	27
Rudy Gomez, Norwich	25

MOST HITS, ONE GAME

Mike Eaglin, Greenville	6
Jose Gonzalez, Bristol	6
Eric Hinske, Williamsport	6
Adam Johnson, Greenville	6
Keith Mitchell, Pawtucket	6

TOTAL BASES

Marcus Giles, Macon	321
Eric Chavez, Edmonton/Huntsville	319
Gabe Kapler, Jacksonville	319
Brian Daubach, Charlotte (IL)	315
Chris Hatcher, Omaha	313

EXTRA-BASE HITS

Brian Daubach, Charlotte (IL)	84
Gabe Kapler, Jacksonville	81
Eric Chavez, Edmonton/Huntsville	79
Marcus Giles, Macon	78
Dan Rohrmeier, Tacoma	78

DOUBLES

Joe McEwing, Memphis/Arkansas	51
Dan Rohrmeier, Tacoma	51
Robert Fick, Jacksonville	47
Gabe Kapler, Jacksonville	47
Eric Chavez, Edmonton/Huntsville	45
Brian Daubach, Charlotte (IL)	45
Dave Hajek, Las Vegas	45
Doug Mientkiewicz, New Britain	45

RODGER WOOD

Marcus Giles
321 total bases

TRIPLES

Eric Stuckenschneider, Alb./San Ant.	17
Santiago Perez, Louisville/El Paso	16
Marlon Anderson, Scranton	14
Julio Lugo, Kissimmee	14
Jermaine Clark, Wisconsin	13

HOME RUNS

Chris Hatcher, Omaha	46
Marcus Giles, Macon	37
Tyrone Horne, Memphis/Arkansas	37
George Arias, Las Vegas	36
Brian Daubach, Charlotte (IL)	35
Troy Glaus, Vancouver/Midland	35
Scott McClain, Durham	34
Alex Ramierez, Buffalo	34
Eric Chavez, Edmonton/Huntsville	33

RUNS BATTED IN

Gabe Kapler, Jacksonville	146
Tyrone Horne, Memphis/Arkansas	140
Eric Chavez, Edmonton/Huntsville	126
Brian Daubach, Charlotte (IL)	124
Shawn Gallagher, Charlotte (FSL)	121

MOST RBIs, ONE GAME

Tyrone Horne, Arkansas	10
Randall Simon, Richmond	10
Eddie Williams, Las Vegas	10
Kurt Bierek, Norwich	9
Todd Dunn, El Paso	9
Scott McClain, Durham	9

STOLEN BASES

Anthony Felston, New Brit./Fort Myers	88
Quincy Foster, Kane County	73
Julio Ramirez, Brevard County	71
Alex Sanchez, St. Petersburg	66
Pedro Santana, West Michigan	64
Juan Sosa, Salem	64

CAUGHT STEALING

Alex Sanchez, St. Petersburg	33
Anthony Felston, New Brit./Fort Myers	27
Julio Ramirez, Brevard County	27
Pablo Ozuna, Peoria	26
Juan Moreta, Alb./San Bernardino	25
Juan Tolentino, Cedar Rapids	25

HIT BY PITCHES

Alex Helconian, Kane County 28
Brian Moon, Beloit.............................. 23
Jon Schaeffer, Fort Wayne 23
Xavier Burns, Augusta 22
David Eckstein, Sarasota 22
Toby Kominek, El Paso....................... 22
Cody McKay, Edm./Hunts./Modesto 22
Olmedo Saenz, Calgary 22

BASE ON BALLS

Jason Regan, Lancaster.................... 106
Mark Johnson, Birmingham 105
Joe Lawrence, Dunedin 105
Calvin Pickering, Bowie 98
Lance Berkman, New Orleans/Jackson.. 97
Rob DeBoer, Visalia 97
Tracy Sanders, Carolina 97

STRIKEOUTS

Nate Dishington, Memphis/Arkansas 179
Chris Schwab, Harrisburg/Jupiter 178
Corey Pointer, Lynchburg 177
Mike Hessman, Danville (CL) 172
Tim Flaherty, Bakersfield 171

SACRIFICE FLIES

Keith Luuloa, Vancouver/Midland 17
Mike Bell, Norfolk/Bing./St. Lucie 12
Giuseppe Chiaramonte, San Jose 12
Eddy Garavito, Frederick/Delmarva 12
Dave Hajek, Las Vegas 12
Alex Sanchez, St. Petersburg.............. 12

SACRIFICE BUNTS

Garret Osilka, Beloit 18
Joe Cathey, Quad City 17
Cristian Guzman, New Britain.............. 17
Andres Mitchell, Asheville.................... 17
Jose Moreno, Wisconsin...................... 17
Michael Peeples, Knoxville 17
Brett Taft, Wilmington 17

SLUGGING PERCENTAGE

Micah Franklin, Iowa .... .655
George Arias, Las Vegas................... .651
Chris Hatcher, Omaha .... .645
Troy Glaus, Vancouver/Midland......... .641
Marcus Giles, Macon .... .636

ON-BASE PERCENTAGE

Jeremy Giambi, Omaha..................... .469
Nick Johnson, Tampa .... .466
Mitch Meluskey, New Orleans .... .465
Jason Regan, Lancaster .... .447
Jackie Rexrode, High Des./So. Bend .. .447

BATTING AVERAGE*
By Position
(Minimum 400 Plate Appearances)

CATCHER

Mitch Meluskey, New Orleans .... .353
Jason LaRue, Indy/Chattanooga .... .350
Shea Hillenbrand, Michigan............... .349
Angel Pena, San Antonio................... .335
Alex Andreopoulos, El Paso .... .321
Toby Hall, Charleston, S.C. .... .321

FIRST BASEMEN

Brendan Kingman, Lancaster .... .340
Roberto Petagine, Indianapolis .... .331
Julio Zuleta, West Tenn/Daytona....... .331
Mario Valdez, Calgary .... .330
Danny Buxbaum, Vanc./Midland .... .327

SECOND BASEMEN

Keith Luuloa, Vancouver/Midland ..... .334
Warren Morris, Carolina/Tulsa........... .331
Marcus Giles, Macon .... .329
Brent Abernathy, Dunedin .... .328
Dave Hajek, Las Vegas .... .328

THIRD BASEMEN

Casey Blake, Knoxville/Dunedin .... .357
Todd Haney, Norfolk/St. Lucie........... .345
Mo Bruce, Capital City .... .341
Jarrod Patterson, High Desert .... .335

Rick Ankiel
222 strikeouts

Eric Chavez, Edmonton/Huntsville..... .327

SHORTSTOPS

Pablo Ozuna, Peoria .... .357
Jolbert Cabrera, Buffalo.................... .318
Joe Lawrence, Dunedin .... .308
Julio Lugo, Kissimmee...................... .303
Jose Flores, Scranton .... .301
Julius Matos, High Desert .... .301
David Lamb, Rochester/Bowie.......... .301

OUTFIELDERS

Jeremy Giambi, Omaha..................... .372
Darryl Brinkley, Nashville.................. .355
Mark Quinn, Wichita.......................... .349
Jalal Leach, Fresno/Shreveport......... .347
Derrick White, Colo. Springs/Iowa ..... .343

INDIVIDUAL PITCHING

EARNED RUN AVERAGE
(Minimum 112 Innings)

Robbie Crabtree, Fresno/Shr./San Jose 1.75
Jason Childers, Beloit 1.92
A.J. Burnett, Kane County 1.97
Tom Shearn, Quad City 2.25
Clayton Andrews, Hagerstown.......... 2.28
Brian Reith, Greensboro 2.28
Mike Kusiewicz, New Haven 2.32
Aaron Myette, Winston-Salem/Hickory .. 2.33
Tristan Jerue, Prince William/Peoria 2.43
Luke Prokopec, San Ant./San Bernardino 2.44

WINS

Dan Perkins, Salt Lake/New Britain 18
Shannon Withem, Syracuse 17
David Borkowski, Jacksonville 16
Scott Mullen, Wichita/Wilmington 16
John Sneed, Hagerstown 16

LOSSES

Mike Drumright, Toledo....................... 19
Mike Vavrek, Colo. Springs/New Haven 18
Matt Drews, Toledo............................ 17
Neal Arnold, Peoria 15
Manny Bermudez, Shreveport/San Jose.... 15
Marcos Castillo, Vero Beach............... 15
Tommy Darrell, Lake Els./Cedar Rapids 15
Phil Merrell, Charleston, W.Va............ 15
Paul Morse, Alb./San Bernardino 15
Marc Van Wormer, South Bend 15

GAMES

Mike Walker, Indianapolis................... 78
Brendan Sullivan, Mobile/Rancho Cuca. 70
Sal Urso, Trenton 69
Richie Barker, Iowa/West Tenn 67
Matt Montgomery, Alb./San Bernardino.. 66

COMPLETE GAMES

Mark Corey, Indy/Chatt./Burlington (MWL) .. 7
Chandler Martin, Salem 7
Scott Randall, New Haven 7
Brandon Duckworth, Clear./Piedmont.... 6
Mark Harriger, Lake Els./Cedar Rapids 6
Josh Harris, Burlington (MWL) 6
Gil Heredia, Edmonton 6
Eric Ireland, Quad City 6
Lou Pote, Midland................................ 6

SAVES

Brent Stentz, New Britain 43
R.A. Dickey, Charlotte (FSL)................ 38
Brett Black, Piedmont 34
David Riske, Akron/Kinston 34
Jay Tessmer, Columbus (IL)/Norwich.. 34

INNINGS PITCHED

Eric Ireland, Quad City 206
Scott Randall, New Haven 202
Brandon Duckworth, Clear./Pied. 201
Mark Harriger, Lake Els./Cedar Rapids 198
Bob Milacki, New Orleans.................. 190
Shannon Withem, Syracuse 190

BASE ON BALLS

Steve Shoemaker, Colo. Spr./N.H. 126
Courtney Duncan, West Tenn............ 108
Brett Laxton, Edmonton/Huntsville 103
Corey Lee, Tulsa............................... 102
Marcus Moore, Buffalo/Akron 95

STRIKEOUTS

Rick Ankiel, Prince William/Peoria 222
Josh Kalinowski, Asheville 215
John Sneed, Hagerstown 210
Brad Penny, High Desert 207
Alan Webb, West Michigan................ 202
Octavio Dotel, Norfolk/Binghamton.... 200
Rob Bell, Danville (CL) 197
Clayton Andrews, Hagerstown 193
Bruce Chen, Richmond/Greenville 193
Eric Ireland, Quad City 191

STRIKEOUTS/9 INNINGS*
(Starters)

A.J. Burnett, Kane County 14.07
Rick Ankiel, Prince William/Peoria.. 12.41
Ryan Anderson, Wisconsin 12.29
John Sneed, Hagerstown............... 11.69
Luis Rivera, Macon 11.46

STRIKEOUTS/9 INNINGS*
(Relievers)

Jim Stoops, Colo. Spr./Salem/S.J... 14.65
Shawn Barry, Capital City 13.57
Eric Cammack, St. Lucie/Capital City .. 13.57
Lesli Brea, Wisconsin..................... 13.19
Justin Kaye, Lancaster/Wisconsin .. 13.09
Jeff Taglienti, Michigan 13.09

BATTING AVERAGE AGAINST*
(Starters)

A.J. Burnett, Kane County .... .179
Alan Webb, West Michigan .... .181
Rick Ankiel, Prince William/Peoria..... .191
Clayton Andrews, Hagerstown.......... .195
Brian Reith, Greensboro .... .196

BATTING AVERAGE AGAINST*
(Relievers)

Jim Stoops, Colo. Spr./Salem/San Jose .141
Orber Moreno, Wichita/Wilmington .. .153
Eric Cammack, St. Lucie/Capital City .. .163
Sean Fesh, Scranton/Reading.......... .164
Jim Mann, Dunedin .... .172

MOST STRIKEOUTS IN ONE GAME

Josh Kalinowski, Asheville 17
Chad Durbin, Wilmington 16
Steve Parris, Indianapolis 16

INDIVIDUAL FIELDING

MOST ERRORS

Troy Cameron, ss, Macon.................... 66
Michael Cuddyer, ss, Fort Wayne........ 61
Danny Sandoval, ss, Hickory 57
Dennis Abreu, ss, Daytona 56
Luis Rivas, ss, Fort Myers................... 55

clubs because of several factors: its tradition (19 former Red Wings are in the Hall of Fame); its on-field success (a record 10 Governors' Cup titles in the International League and 47 winning seasons in 70 years); and its recent resurgence (record attendance in the Red Wings' first season at Frontier Field in 1997). The passionate interest from fans and media also were keys.

Drew Finally Debuts

J.D. Drew's career in the Cardinals organization opened against a backdrop of scattered boos and carefully selected music cuts.

LARRY GOREN

J.D. Drew

It didn't seem to faze him.

One day after he signed a record contract (with a $3 million bonus, $4 million in guaranteed salary and $1.5 million in incentives), Drew batted third and played center field for the Double-A Texas League's Arkansas Travelers in a 9-7 loss to Wichita. He went 2-for-4 with a single and a double. He had an RBI, scored a run and struck out once.

"It's the same game, I guess," said Drew, who spent all of the summer of 1997 and a month of the 1998 summer playing for the St. Paul Saints of the independent Northern League. "It's a fun game."

In 67 at-bats for Arkansas, he hit .328 with five homers. He went on to hit .316 with two homers in 79 Triple-A at-bats and .417 with five homers in just 36 big league at-bats.

Around the Minors

As usual, the affiliation shuffle that matched major league teams with minor league affiliates proceeded quite smoothly until the end of the signing period, when the last few pegs wouldn't go into the last few holes.

The Reds, who abandoned low Class A Charleston, W.Va., in hopes of picking up a high A team, were left in the cold with two Midwest League teams. Neither the Athletics nor Giants, who have two high Class A California League teams, would trade for a Midwest League club. The Brewers—who have two Rookie-level Pioneer League teams—are the only team aside from the A's, Giants and Reds with two affiliates in the

Manager of the Year

Kennedy looks to follow dad's career path

Terry Kennedy would enjoy following his father's career path, but he may have a problem. He could be too good at his current job.

It might be hard for Kennedy, who managed the Iowa Cubs to the best record in Triple-A to become Baseball America's 1998 Minor League Manager of the Year, to get out of the dugout.

His father was a big league player, manager, general manager and scout. Bob Kennedy managed the big league Cubs from 1963-65 and was the club's GM from 1977-81. While Bob was GM in Chicago, Terry began a 14-year major league career that included four All-Star Game appearances. Now Terry Kennedy is closing in on the majors again.

"I wouldn't mind trying what he did eventually," Kennedy said. "I would like to be a farm director or GM someday, somewhere, but I don't know how it will all work out. If I keep screwing up and winning pennants, I don't know if I'll be able to do that."

In just his fourth season managing in the minor leagues, Kennedy impressed his peers quickly. At midseason 1998, his fellow managers voted him as the Pacific Coast League's best managerial prospect. He was only one season removed from the Rookie-level Arizona League, where he was named manager of the year as his team in Mesa won a championship with a 34-20 record.

Terry Kennedy

The Cubs moved Kennedy all the way up to Iowa, where his managing style was just as effective. Kennedy was a hitting coach at Triple-A Tacoma in the Mariners system in 1995-96 and a manager at Class A St. Petersburg (Cardinals) in 1993 and short-season Vermont (Expos) in 1994.

"The (players) are still striving, whether it's Rookie ball or Triple-A," Kennedy said. "Both are striving to be the best they can and reach the big leagues. Obviously guys are more jaded in Triple-A, but luckily I didn't get any of that."

—LACY LUSK

PREVIOUS WINNERS

1981—Ed Nottle, Tacoma (Athletics)
1982—Eddie Haas, Richmond (Braves)
1983—Bill Dancy, Reading (Phillies)
1984—Sam Perlozzo, Jackson (Mets)
1985—Jim Lefebvre, Phoenix (Giants)
1986—Brad Fischer, Huntsville (Athletics)
1987—Dave Trembley, Harrisburg (Pirates)
1988—Joe Sparks, Indianapolis (Expos)
1989—Buck Showalter, Albany (Yankees)
1990—Kevin Kennedy, Albuquerque (Dodgers)
1991—Butch Hobson, Pawtucket (Red Sox)
1992—Grady Little, Greenville (Braves)
1993—Terry Francona, Birmingham (White Sox)
1994—Tim Ireland, El Paso (Brewers)
1995—Marc Bombard, Indianapolis (Reds)
1996—Carlos Tosca, Portland (Marlins)
1997—Gary Jones, Edmonton (Athletics)

TOP 100 PROSPECTS

Through consultation with scouts and player-development people, Baseball America selects its annual list of the game's top 100 minor league prospects. The list emphasizes long-range major league potential and considered only players in professional baseball who had not exhausted their major league rookie status entering the 1998 season.

The highest level each player reached in 1998 is noted in parentheses.

1. Ben Grieve, of, Athletics (Majors)
2. Paul Konerko, 1b/3b, Reds (Majors)
3. Adrian Beltre, 3b, Dodgers (Majors)
4. Kerry Wood, rhp, Cubs (Majors)
5. Aramis Ramirez, 3b, Pirates (Majors)
6. Matt White, rhp, Devil Rays (A)
7. Kris Benson, rhp, Pirates (AAA)
8. Travis Lee, 1b, Diamondbacks (Majors)
9. Carl Pavano, rhp, Expos (Majors)
10. Miguel Tejada, ss, Athletics (Majors)
11. Todd Helton, 1b, Rockies (Majors)
12. Mark Kotsay, of, Marlins (Majors)
13. Chad Hermansen, 2b, Pirates (AAA)
14. Brad Fullmer, 1b, Expos (Majors)
15. Juan Encarnacion, of, Tigers (Majors)
16. Matt Clement, rhp, Padres (Majors)
17. Ruben Mateo, of, Rangers (AA)
18. Rick Ankiel, lhp, Cardinals (A)
19. Richard Hidalgo, of, Astros (Majors)
20. Sean Casey, 1b, Reds (Majors)
21. Darnell McDonald, of, Orioles (A)
22. Brian Rose, rhp, Red Sox (Majors)
23. Ryan Anderson, lhp, Mariners (A)
24. Matt Anderson, rhp, Tigers (Majors)
25. Eric Milton, lhp, Twins (Majors)
26. Russell Branyan, 3b, Indians (Majors)
27. Bruce Chen, lhp, Braves (Majors)
28. Scott Elarton, rhp, Astros (Majors)
29. Grant Roberts, rhp, Mets (A)
30. Eric Chavez, 3b, Athletics (Majors)
31. Cesar King, c, Rangers (AA)
32. Dermal Brown, of, Royals (A)
33. Eli Marrero, c, Cardinals (Majors)
34. Mike Caruso, ss, White Sox (Majors)
35. Ryan Minor, 3b, Orioles (Majors)
36. Troy Glaus, 3b, Angels (Majors)
37. Rolando Arrojo, rhp, Devil Rays (Majors)
38. Roy Halladay, rhp, Blue Jays (Majors)
39. Braden Looper, rhp, Cardinals (Majors)
40. Ruben Rivera, of, Padres (Majors)
41. Francisco Cordero, rhp, Tigers (AA)
42. A.J. Hinch, c, Athletics (Majors)

Ben Grieve

43. Carlos Lee, 3b, White Sox (AA)
44. Luis Rivera, rhp, Braves (A)
45. John Patterson, rhp, Diamondbacks (A)
46. Ricky Ledee, of, Yankees (Majors)
47. Derrek Lee, 1b, Marlins (Majors)
48. Alex Gonzalez, ss, Marlins (Majors)
49. Ben Davis, c, Padres (Majors)
50. Willie Martinez, rhp, Indians (AA)
51. Michael Coleman, of, Red Sox (AAA)
52. Vernon Wells, of, Blue Jays (A)
53. Ben Petrick, c, Rockies (AA)
54. Jason Grilli, rhp, Giants (AAA)
55. Luis Rivas, ss, Twins (A)
56. Magglio Ordonez, of, White Sox (Majors)
57. Julio Ramirez, of, Marlins (A)
58. Ryan Brannan, rhp, Phillies (AAA)
59. Mike Judd, rhp, Dodgers (Majors)
60. Ed Yarnall, lhp, Marlins (AAA)
61. Enrique Wilson, 2b, Indians (Majors)
62. Damian Jackson, ss, Reds (Majors)
63. Corey Lee, lhp, Rangers (AA)
64. Lance Berkman, of, Astros (AAA)
65. Abraham Nunez, ss, Pirates (Majors)
66. Joe Fontenot, rhp, Marlins (Majors)
67. Shawn Chacon, rhp, Rockies (A)
68. Robbie Bell, rhp, Braves (A)
69. Brent Butler, ss, Cardinals (A)
70. Preston Wilson, of, Marlins (Majors)
71. Mike Lowell, 3b, Yankees (Majors)
72. Rafael Medina, rhp, Marlins (Majors)
73. Jarrod Washburn, lhp, Angels (Majors)
74. Ramon Hernandez, c, Athletics (AA)
75. Ramon Ortiz, rhp, Angels (AA)
76. Wade Miller, rhp, Astros (AA)
77. Karim Garcia, of, Diamondbacks (Majors)
78. Sidney Ponson, rhp, Orioles (Majors)
79. Robinson Checo, rhp, Red Sox (Majors)
80. Lorenzo Barcelo, rhp, White Sox (AA)
81. Derrick Gibson, of, Rockies (Majors)
82. Gil Meche, rhp, Mariners (A)
83. Javier Vazquez, rhp, Expos (Majors)
84. David Ortiz, 1b, Twins (Majors)
85. Nelson Lara, rhp, Marlins (A)
86. Juan Melo, ss, Padres (AAA)
87. Todd Dunwoody, of, Marlins (Majors)
88. Chris Reitsma, rhp, Red Sox (A)
89. Valerio de los Santos, lhp, Brewers (Majors)
90. Jeff Wallace, lhp, Pirates (Injured)
91. Dennis Reyes, lhp, Reds (Majors)
92. Orlando Cabrera, 2b, Expos (Majors)
93. George Lombard, of, Braves (Majors)
94. Lariel Gonzalez, rhp, Rockies (Majors)
95. Geoff Jenkins, of, Brewers (Majors)
96. Geoff Goetz, lhp, Marlins (A)
97. Daryle Ward, 1b, Astros (Majors)
98. Jackson Melian, of, Yankees (A)
99. Kevin Witt, 1b, Blue Jays (Majors)
100. Chris Enochs, rhp, Athletics (AA)

same league.

As is the case every other year with the two-year working agreements, the merry-go-round for affiliation changes was crowded. Four teams in Triple-A, six in Double-A, 10 in Class A and six in short-season leagues will have new affiliations in 1999. Also, the two expansion Double-A teams, Altoona and Erie, will start out with the Pirates and Angels, respectively.

Sometimes in conjunction with affiliation changes and sometimes not, several teams announced nickname changes. Midland, no longer an Angels team, will be the RockHounds in 1999. Omaha, still a Royals team, will be the Golden Spikes. Other names for 1999: Louisville RiverBats, Altoona Curve, Myrtle Beach Pelicans and Potomac (not Prince William) Cannons. The Rockford Cubbies and Williamsport Cubs each have new affiliates, so new names were in order for them too.

■ Four players involved in the Mets extended spring training program in Port St. Lucie, Fla., were arrested and charged with sexual battery of a 17-year-old girl. Outfielder Vicente Rosario, shortstop Jose Tucent Brea, shortstop Ruddi de la Cruz and pitcher Natividad Tavarez were all jailed after the alleged incident.

Rosario, born in the Dominican Republic, lives in New York. He was an eighth-round pick out of George Washington High by the Mets in 1997. The others are residents of the Dominican signed as nondrafted free agents in the last two years.

All but Brea were quickly released on bond.

Brea, Tavarez and a fifth player, Milton Gonzalez, were convicted in October. Sentencing was scheduled for December. Trials for de la Cruz and Rosario were scheduled for November.

■ Pronouncing, "Enough is enough," California League president Joe Gagliardi announced the league's takeover of the Visalia Oaks franchise from Japan Sports Systems.

"The league could not wait any longer because it was too much of a distressed situation," Gagliardi said. "There were bills owed to everyone from power companies to vendors."

The move unseated Japan-based chairman Keiichi Tsukamoto, who was part of the Visalia purchase orchestrated in 1989 by the late Hall of Fame pitcher Don Drysdale. Gagliardi said Tsukamoto became an absentee owner who made just one visit to Visalia during his tenure. New Oaks operator Jim Wadley said he wanted to try to upgrade facilities in Visalia before he would consider moving the team.

MINOR LEAGUES BEST TOOLS

Full season leagues only

	International League	Pacific Coast League	Eastern League	Southern League	Texas League	California League	Carolina League	Florida State League	Midwest League	South Atlantic League
	AAA	AAA	AA	AA	AA	A	A	A	A	A
Batting Prospect	Ron Belliard Louisville	Jeremy Giambi Omaha	Dernell Stenson Trenton	Eric Chavez Huntsville	Adrian Beltre San Antonio	Jose Soriano Visalia	Joe Crede Winston-Salem	Kelly Dransfeldt Charlotte	Pablo Ozuna Peoria	Alex Escobar Capital City
Power Prospect	Gabe Alvarez Toledo	George Arias Las Vegas	Fernando Seguignol Harrisburg	Eric Chavez Huntsville	Troy Glaus Midland	Juan Dilone San Jose	Mike Glavine Kinston	Peter Tucci Dunedin	Bucky Jacobsen Beloit	Alex Escobar Capital City
Base Runner	Luis Castillo Charlotte	Lou Frazier Calgary	Scott Hunter Binghamton	Dave Roberts Jacksonville	Norm Hutchins Midland	Junior Spivey High Desert	Pat Hallmark Wilmington	Anthony Felston Fort Myers	Quincy Foster Kane County	Alex Escobar Capital City
Fastest Runner	Terry Jones Ottawa	Dante Powell Fresno	Reggie Taylor Reading	George Lombard Greenville	Norm Hutchins Midland	Chad Green Stockton	Cordell Farley Prince William	Alex Sanchez St. Petersburg	Ryan Grimmett West Michigan	Cesar Crespo Capital City
Pitching Prospect	Carlton Loewer Scranton	Scott Elarton New Orleans	Ed Yarnall Bing./Portland	Bruce Chen Greenville	Freddy Garcia Jackson	John Patterson High Desert	Rick Ankiel Prince William	Ty Hartshorn Dunedin	Rick Ankiel Peoria	Matt White Charleston
Fastball	Roy Halladay Syracuse	Scott Elarton New Orleans	Octavio Dotel Binghamton	Matt Anderson Jacksonville	Freddy Garcia Jackson	Russell Jacob High Desert	Orber Moreno Wilmington	Guillermo Mota Jupiter	Ryan Anderson Wisconsin	Matt White Charleston
Breaking Pitch	Orlando Hernandez Columbus	Kris Benson Nashville	Mike Lincoln New Britain	Kevin Beirne Birmingham	Ryan Glynn Tulsa	Eric DuBose Visalia	Rob Bell Danville	Ty Hartshorn Dunedin	Matt Miller West Michigan	Derek Brown Delmarva
Control	Dave Stieb Syracuse	John Halama New Orleans	Mike Lincoln New Britain	Bruce Chen Greenville	Rob Bonanno Midland	Mike Holmes Visalia	Paul Ah Yat Lynchburg	Mark Rutherford Clearwater	Josh Harris Burlington	Clayton Andrews Hagerstown
Reliever	Todd Erdos Columbus	Jeff McCurry Nashville	Jeff Sexton Akron	Matt Anderson Jacksonville	Mike McMullen Shreveport	Jim Stoops San Jose	David Riske Kinston	R.A. Dickey Charlotte	Gene Stechschulte Peoria	Derek Brown Delmarva
Defensive Catcher	Bobby Estalella Scranton	Robert Machado Calgary	Michael Barrett Harrisburg	Ben Davis Huntsville	Angel Pena San Antonio	Cody McKay Modesto	Fernando Lunar Danville	Yohanny Valera St. Lucie	Michael Rivera West Michigan	Jayson Werth Delmarva
Defensive First Baseman	Roberto Petagine Indianapolis	Chris Pritchett Vancouver	Doug Mientkiewicz New Britain	Mike Mitchell Mobile	Jon Tucker San Antonio	Nick Leach San Bernardino	Jason Layne Wilmington	Rafael Martinez Sarasota	Aaron McNeal Quad City	Billy Munoz Columbus
Defensive Second Baseman	Ron Belliard Louisville	Ramon Martinez Fresno	Jesse Garcia Bowie	Jose Macias Jacksonville	Carlos Febles Wichita	Adonis Harrison Lancaster	Emiliano Escandon Wilmington	David Eckstein Sarasota	Raul Franco Kane County	Elvis Pena Asheville
Defensive Third Baseman	Scott McClain Durham	Tom Quinlan Oklahoma	Ryan Minor Bowie	Carlos Villalobos Jacksonville	Adrian Beltre San Antonio	Josh Klimek Stockton	Joe Crede Winston-Salem	Damian Rolls Vero Beach	Matt Erickson Kane County	Maurice Bruce Capital City
Defensive Shortstop	Tomas Perez Syracuse	Wilson Delgado Fresno	John McDonald Akron	Jose Nieves West Tenn	Santiago Perez El Paso	Carlos Mendoza San Jose	Jason Dellaero Winston-Salem	Kelly Dransfeldt Charlotte	Pablo Ozuna Peoria	Josh Reding Cape Fear
Infield Arm	Gabe Alvarez Toledo	Wilson Delgado Fresno	Ryan Minor Bowie	Jose Nieves West Tenn	Adrian Beltre San Antonio	Cesarin Carmona Rancho Cuca.	Jose Leon Prince William	Ron Walker Daytona	Steve Medrano Lansing	Cesar Crespo Capital City
Defensive Outfielder	Earl Johnson Toledo	Mark Little Oklahoma	Torii Hunter New Britain	Glen Barker Jacksonville	Peter Bergeron San Antonio	Mike Byas San Jose	Carlos Beltran Wilmington	Julio Ramirez Brevard County	Juan Tolentino Cedar Rapids	Milton Bradley Cape Fear
Outfield Arm	Juan Encarnacion Toledo	Edgard Clemente Colorado Springs	Fletcher Bates Portland	Emil Brown Carolina	Ruben Mateo Tulsa	Greg Schaub Stockton	Carlos Beltran Wilmington	Danny Ramirez St. Lucie	Juan LeBron Lansing	Jeremy Jackson Asheville
Most Exciting Player	Richie Sexson Akron	Derrick White Iowa	Fernando Seguignol Harrisburg	George Lombard Greenville	Adrian Beltre San Antonio	Adonis Harrison Lancaster	Carlos Beltran Wilmington	Kelly Dransfeldt Charlotte	Pablo Ozuna Peoria	Alex Escobar Capital City
Managerial Prospect	Dave Miley Indianapolis	Terry Kennedy Iowa	John Russell New Britain	Mike Ramsey Mobile	Ron Roenicke San Antonio	Shane Turner San Jose	Darrell Evans Wilmington	Doug Sisson Jupiter	Gary Varsho Wisconsin	Tom Nieto Greensboro

Selected at midseason 1998 by minor league managers in consultation with Baseball America

Team of the Year

Padres load up Mobile affiliate for wire-to-wire run to SL title

When an organization places most of its top prospects on one minor league club, expectations tend to run high. The San Diego Padres loaded up their Double-A affiliate in 1998, and the Mobile BayBears did not disappoint.

With prospects such as catcher Ben Davis, first baseman Mike Mitchell, third baseman John Powers, shortstop Kevin Nicholson, outfielders Mike Darr and Gary Matthews Jr., and righthander Buddy Carlyle, winning the Southern League crown was expected.

The BayBears took the Western Division's first-half crown by winning 42 games. Even though a spot in the playoffs already was assured, they went out and won 44 games and the second half, to finish the season at 86-54 (.614).

In winning the league championship, Mobile swept Huntsville and silenced Jacksonville, a team that established a league record for best team batting average (.290). Mobile won 11 of its final 12 games of the season to nail down Baseball America's 1998 Team of the Year.

"Just because they packed us with prospects, it wasn't a given that we would win it all," Mitchell said. "We worked our butts off."

That's an opinion shared by manager Mike Ramsey, who led the BayBears to a 155-122 record in 1997-98.

"It says a lot about the makeup of this team that they stayed hungry in the second half after winning the first half, and when they got to the playoffs there was no let-up whatsoever," he said.

The championship was the first minor league crown since 1966 for Mobile–a city with a rich baseball tradition, being the hometown of Hall of Famers Hank Aaron, Willie McCovey, Satchel Paige and Billy Williams. Other titles were won by Mobile teams in 1922, '47, '55 and '59.

Freitas Awards

Salt Lake headlines strong list of eligible clubs

The Class of '94 ruled the Bob Freitas Awards in 1998, as the Salt Lake Buzz, Trenton Thunder, West Michigan Whitecaps and Hudson Valley Renegades all swept in on their first year of eligibility.

The Freitas Awards annually recognize long-term success by minor league franchises at the Triple-A, Double-A, Class A and short-season levels. They are named for Bob Freitas, a longtime minor league operator, promoter and ambassador who died in 1989. Franchises are eligible for the honor in their fifth year of operation.

Salt Lake, the Triple-A winner, has led the Pacific Coast League in attendance in every year since the franchise moved to Salt Lake City from Portland, Ore., for the 1994 season. The Buzz drew 554,719 fans in 1998, and overall more than 3.1 million fans have seen a game at Franklin Covey Field, one of the most picturesque ballparks in the nation.

The Trenton Thunder has changed affiliates once during its short history, from the Tigers to the Red Sox, but it has been just as successful as the Buzz. Mercer County Waterfront Park has been a flashpoint for revitalization efforts in Trenton, and the Thunder annually is one of the few teams in the minors with average attendance greater than the listed capacity of the ballpark.

West Michigan has faced similar overflows, and the Whitecaps had to expand their young ballpark to keep up with the demands of fans. The Whitecaps are one of the best-run operations in baseball, and they led Class A baseball into the previously unheard-of territory of 500,000 fans a season.

Short-season winner Hudson Valley had more serious problems with its stadium, which was built in 71 days and was only 75 percent done when Opening Day 1994 rolled around. It took more than two years to finish Dutchess Stadium, but the Renegades have drawn fans from the beginning. Like the Cleveland Indians, they usually sell out all their games before the season ever starts.

PREVIOUS WINNERS

Triple-A
1989—Columbus (International)
1990—Pawtucket (International)
1991—Buffalo (Amer. Association)
1992—Iowa (Amer. Association)
1993—Richmond (International)
1994—Norfolk (International)
1995—Albuquerque (Pacific Coast)
1996—Indianapolis (Amer. Assoc.)
1997—Rochester (International)

Double-A
1989—El Paso (Texas)
1990—Arkansas (Texas)
1991—Reading (Eastern)
1992—Tulsa (Texas)
1993—Harrisburg (Eastern)
1994—San Antonio (Texas)
1995—Midland (Texas)
1996—Carolina (Southern)
1997—Bowie (Eastern)

Class A
1989—Durham (Carolina)
1990—San Jose (California)
1991—Asheville (South Atlantic)
1992—Springfield (Midwest)
1993—South Bend (Midwest)
1994—Kinston (Carolina)
1995—Kane County (Midwest)
1996—Wisconsin (Midwest)
1997—Rancho Cucamonga (Cal)

Short-Season
1989—Eugene (Northwest)
1990—Salt Lake City (Pioneer)
1991—Spokane (Northwest)
1992—Boise (Northwest)
1993—Billings (Pioneer)
1994—Everett (Northwest)
1995—Great Falls (Pioneer)
1996—Bluefield (Appalachian)
1997—Oneonta (New York-Penn)

INTERNATIONAL LEAGUE

Buffalo finishes strong to capture 1998 Governors' Cup

BY MATT MICHAEL

If you had said in mid-June that the Buffalo Bisons would win the 1998 Governors' Cup title, you would have been called crazy.

If you had said the same thing in mid-August, you would have been considered even crazier.

But by mid-September, you would have looked like a genius.

The Bisons, who were 11½ games out of first place in the International League's Northern Division in mid-June, rallied to win the division title by a half game over the Syracuse SkyChiefs. Buffalo then beat the SkyChiefs and Durham Bulls in the playoffs to capture the Governors' Cup trophy and advance to the inaugural Triple-A World Series in Las Vegas.

In Las Vegas, Buffalo lost three of four games to the Pacific Coast League champion New Orleans Zephyrs. The weekend before the world series, the Bisons' best home run hitter (Alex Ramirez) and leading winner (Jason Jacome) were promoted to the major leagues to help the Indians prepare for the American League playoffs.

The league championship gave Buffalo back-to-back playoff titles for the first time in the franchise's 114-year history. The Bisons went 36 years between championships before claiming the final American Association title in 1997.

Triumphant Return

The Bisons returned to the IL this season after a 28-year absence and won their first Governors' Cup championship since 1961. Buffalo was stretched to the limit in the finals, as Jacome beat the Bulls 3-1 in Game Five in Durham.

"All year long these guys have battled," Buffalo manager Jeff Datz said. "It hasn't been easy. This was not an easy task in Durham."

DIAMOND IMAGES

Buffalo's big stick
Alex Ramirez had a 28-game hitting streak

After getting crushed by Pawtucket 17-3 on Aug. 10, the Bisons were eight games behind Syracuse. But they went 18-9 down the stretch, while the SkyChiefs went 10-18. Buffalo swept Syracuse in one semifinal series, while the Bulls swept Louisville in the other one.

Wild-card winner Syracuse was the only member of the old 10-team IL to reach the playoffs. Buffalo and IL West Division champion Louisville came from the disbanded AA, while IL South champ Durham was a Triple-A expansion team after a long run in Class A.

Led by Ramirez, who socked 34 home runs and had

STANDINGS

Page	NORTH	W	L	PCT	GB	Manager	Attendance/Dates	Last Penn.
108	Buffalo Bisons (Indians)	81	62	.566	—	Jeff Datz	743,463 (68)	1998
247	Syracuse SkyChiefs (Blue Jays)	80	62	.563	½	Terry Bevington	420,488 (68)	1976
82	Pawtucket Red Sox (Red Sox)	77	64	.546	3	Ken Macha	475,659 (68)	1984
75	Rochester Red Wings (Orioles)	70	74	.486	11½	Marv Foley	515,436 (69)	1997
167	Ottawa Lynx (Expos)	69	74	.483	12	Pat Kelly	224,371 (70)	1995
195	Scranton/W-B Red Barons (Phillies)	67	75	.472	13½	Marc Bombard	406,735 (67)	None
Page	**WEST**	**W**	**L**	**PCT**	**GB**	**Manager**	**Attendance/Dates**	**Last Penn.**
155	Louisville Redbirds (Brewers)	77	67	.535	—	Gary Allenson	409,853 (72)	None
102	Indianapolis Indians (Reds)	76	67	.531	½	Dave Miley	659,237 (67)	1963
174	Columbus Clippers (Yankees)	67	77	.465	10	Stump Merrill	488,674 (69)	1996
121	Toledo Mud Hens (Tigers)	52	89	.369	23½	Gene Roof	311,652 (66)	1967
Page	**SOUTH**	**W**	**L**	**PCT**	**GB**	**Manager**	**Attendance/Dates**	**Last Penn.**
233	Durham Bulls (Devil Rays)	80	64	.556	—	Bill Evers	477,709 (72)	None
181	Norfolk Tides (Mets)	70	72	.493	9	Rick Dempsey	479,222 (69)	1985
127	Charlotte Knights (Marlins)	70	73	.490	9½	Fredi Gonzalez	299,664 (69)	1993
68	Richmond Braves (Braves)	64	80	.444	16	Jeff Cox	528,230 (71)	1994

GOVERNORS' CUP PLAYOFFS—Semifinals: Durham defeated Louisville 3-0 and Buffalo defeated Syracuse 3-0 in best-of-5 series. **Finals:** Buffalo defeated Durham 3-2 in best-of-5 series.

NOTE: Team's individual batting and pitching statistics can be found on page indicated in lefthanded column.

an IL-best 28-game hitting streak, the Bisons powered their way to the league's best record (81-62) with a franchise-record 206 homers (fourth all-time in the IL).

Buffalo, which has led the minors in attendance for 11 consecutive seasons, set an IL record with 743,463, breaking the previous mark of 693,043 set by Ottawa in 1993.

Durham, a virtual wire-to-wire leader in the South, went 19-9 in August to clinch the title. The Bulls were paced by third baseman Scott McClain, who clubbed 34 home runs to finish in a second-place tie with Ramirez behind leader Brian Daubach of Charlotte (35). Daubach also led the league in RBIs (124).

In the Triple-A all-star game, the IL downed the Pacific Coast League 8-4 behind the bat of Columbus third baseman Mike Lowell, who went 2-for-4 with a home run to win MVP honors.

Petagine Wins Again

Indianapolis first baseman Roberto Petagine became the first IL player to receive back-to-back MVP honors since the award was started in 1932. Petagine, who won the MVP with Norfolk in 1997, hit .331 with 24 homers and 109 RBIs before being promoted to the Reds in mid-August. Before the promotion, Petagine was looking to become the IL's first triple crown winner since Pawtucket's Jim Rice in 1974.

Syracuse's Shannon Withem went 17-5 with a 3.27 ERA and was named the IL's most valuable pitcher as he became just the third 17-game winner in the IL since 1967 (the others: Pawtucket's Brian Rose in 1997 and Richmond's Craig McMurtry in 1982). Withem, who had never before won more than 10 games in a season, became Syracuse's first 17-game winner since 1954.

Norfolk's Todd Haney, who hit .345, became the third player in franchise history to win a batting title. The others, Mike Vail in 1975 and Randy Milligan in 1987, were also named IL MVP. That didn't happen to Haney, but he did make the IL's postseason all-star team.

MEL BAILEY

SkyChief supreme Shannon Withem
First Syracuse 17-game winner in 44 years

Ken Macha, who kept the Pawtucket Red Sox in the thick of the IL North race until the last few days of the season, was named IL manager of the year. The PawSox were 22-25 on May 31, but went 55-39 the rest of the way to stay in the hunt with Buffalo and Syracuse.

Pawtucket's Juan Pena, the youngest pitcher in the IL, tossed the league's only no-hitter on July 22 against Durham at McCoy Stadium. Pena, 21, walked three and struck out 14 as he fired just the third nine-inning no-hitter in PawSox history. Much of the Boston Red Sox brass, including general manager Dan Duquette, was on hand for the game.

"I knew I had good stuff, but nobody can really tell if you are going to throw a no-hitter," said Pena, a Dominican Republic native who earlier in the season was stuck in an Ottawa hotel for more than a week because of a visa problem. "This is great. I really enjoyed it."

El Duque Was Here

Of the players just passing through, Cuban defector Orlando Hernandez was the most notable. The righthander made seven starts for Columbus, going 6-0 with a 3.83 ERA. He forced the Yankees' hand, as they promoted him earlier than even they had planned. He rewarded them by going 12-4 with a 3.13 ERA for a team that won an American League-record 114 games.

MEL BAILEY

Orlando Hernandez
6-0 in seven starts

"He's legit," said Columbus manager Stump Merrill just before Hernandez made his big league debut. "It's just a matter of time. The more time he gets, the better he'll be."

The Clippers also had Shane Spencer, an overnight hero in New York who became just the second major leaguer to have 10 home runs in a season of fewer than 100 at-bats. The other one: Ted Williams. At Columbus in his ninth minor league season, he hit .322 with 18 homers.

An additional player of interest was wayward Braves reliever Mark Wohlers, a former World Series-winning closer who mysteriously lost control of his pitches and failed to make Atlanta's postseason roster. In multiple stints with Richmond and visits throughout the league, he went 0-3 with a 20.43 ERA. In 12 innings, he walked 36 and allowed 21 hits.

Off the field, the IL enjoyed a stable year. The league set an attendance record with 6.4 million fans, led by franchise marks in Durham, Indianapolis and Syracuse. Indianapolis was in its third year at Victory Field and Syracuse in its second at P&C Stadium. The Bulls, who were a Braves affiliate in the Carolina League from 1980-97, made a seamless move to Triple-A with the Devil Rays.

In 1999, 13 of the IL's 14 teams will be with the same major league clubs. Only Charlotte, which switched from the Marlins to the White Sox, made a change after the season.

1998 International League Statistics

CLUB BATTING

	AVG	G	AB	R	H	2B	3B	HR	BB	SO	SB
Buffalo	[illegible]	[illegible]	[illegible]	[illegible]	[illegible]	[illegible]	[illegible]	[illegible]	[illegible]	[illegible]	[illegible]
Louisville	.277	144	4886	792	1354	259	54	159	519	1009	190
Pawtucket	.275	142	4724	763	1297	224	21	187	593	949	132
Durham	.274	144	4872	787	1335	275	22	160	581	906	148
Indianapolis	.273	143	4836	787	1322	299	28	160	587	1018	77
Scranton/W-B	.273	142	4877	746	1332	282	42	164	525	932	110
Columbus	.273	144	4972	726	1355	278	46	152	495	941	103
Rochester	.272	144	4897	703	1331	261	39	120	443	834	104
Charlotte	.271	143	4783	739	1297	274	29	153	499	1016	106
Norfolk	.268	142	4757	661	1274	238	35	110	564	841	129
Syracuse	.263	142	4682	653	1231	250	31	164	506	963	111
Toledo	.260	142	4752	595	1237	229	32	106	397	885	141
Richmond	.256	144	4733	607	1211	244	27	111	474	977	94
Ottawa	.255	143	4686	600	1194	239	34	76	482	935	165

CLUB PITCHING

	ERA	G	CG	SHO	SV	IP	H	R	ER	BB	SO
Syracuse	3.68	142	10	9	42	1232	1150	567	503	496	860
Norfolk	4.07	142	6	9	34	1242	1248	669	561	511	1043
Ottawa	4.25	143	3	6	45	1233	1263	680	582	529	906
Rochester	4.31	144	6	9	33	1254	1173	679	600	513	984
Louisville	4.44	144	2	7	38	1264	1294	702	623	531	945
Indianapolis	4.46	143	3	9	36	1242	1262	713	616	564	886
Richmond	4.51	144	4	7	32	1247	1320	702	625	487	968
Durham	4.51	144	6	7	31	1260	1332	706	632	467	961
Buffalo	4.51	143	5	4	34	1260	1350	734	632	491	973
Pawtucket	4.62	142	5	6	35	1230	1290	701	632	459	967
Columbus	4.85	144	8	5	38	1278	1366	774	688	599	975
Scranton/W-B	4.89	142	17	8	33	1254	1373	751	681	452	926
Charlotte	5.26	143	9	6	42	1235	1384	807	722	542	863
Toledo	5.37	142	8	6	29	1214	1359	811	724	578	849

CLUB FIELDING

	PCT	PO	A	E	DP		PCT	PO	A	E	DP
Syracuse	.981	3695	1560	102	156	Pawtucket	.973	3691	1429	143	121
Durham	.980	3781	1504	110	117	Norfolk	.973	3725	1501	146	158
Rochester	.977	3761	1495	126	135	Louisville	.973	3791	1571	150	137
Scranton/W-B	.976	3762	1511	132	119	Toledo	.973	3642	1427	142	132
Ottawa	.975	3700	1467	130	137	Charlotte	.972	3705	1639	155	144
Richmond	.974	3741	1449	141	139	Columbus	.972	3834	1654	160	133
Indianapolis	.973	3726	1684	149	165	Buffalo	.969	3780	1472	170	122

INDIVIDUAL BATTING LEADERS

(Minimum 389 Plate Appearances)

	AVG	G	AB	R	H	2B	3B	HR	RBI	BB	SO	SB
Haney, Todd, Norfolk	.345	117	440	84	152	33	4	3	51	55	44	11
Petagine, Roberto, Ind.	.331	102	363	79	120	30	1	24	109	70	71	3
Lovullo, Torey, Buffalo	.326	92	328	66	107	17	4	17	65	54	32	3
Belliard, Ron, Louisville	.321	133	507	114	163	36	7	14	73	69	77	33
Cabrera, Jolbert, Buffalo	.318	129	494	94	157	24	1	10	45	68	71	25
Daubach, Brian, Charlotte	.316	140	497	102	157	45	4	35	124	80	114	9
Decker, Steve, Norfolk	.314	102	354	55	111	21	0	12	60	54	49	0
Diaz, Einar, Buffalo	.313	115	415	62	130	21	3	8	63	21	33	3
Nixon, Trot, Pawtucket	.310	135	509	97	158	26	4	23	74	76	81	26
Matos, Francisco, Dur./Col.	.310	108	407	55	126	20	5	2	47	21	41	5

INDIVIDUAL PITCHING LEADERS

(Minimum 115 Innings)

	W	L	ERA	G	GS	CG	SV	IP	H	R	ER	BB	SO
Burrows, Terry, Rochester	9	6	2.92	29	15	1	0	132	104	49	43	42	112
Eiland, Dave, Durham	13	5	2.99	28	28	2	0	172	177	70	57	27	112
Jacome, Jason, Buffalo	14	2	3.26	24	24	2	0	155	161	62	56	38	109
Withem, Shannon, Syr.	17	5	3.27	28	27	4	0	190	176	72	69	58	113
Henderson, Rod, Ott./Lou.	11	6	3.47	28	19	1	0	132	123	62	51	51	80
Halladay, Roy, Syracuse	9	5	3.79	21	21	1	0	116	107	52	49	53	71
Bolton, Rod, Indianapolis	12	11	3.81	29	29	1	0	177	166	82	75	64	117
Sauerbeck, Scott, Norfolk	7	13	3.93	27	27	2	0	160	178	82	70	68	119

ALL-STAR TEAM

C—Einar Diaz, Buffalo. **1B**—Roberto Petagine, Indianapolis. **2B**—Ron Belliard, Louisville. **3B**—Scott McClain, Durham. **SS**—Jolbert Cabrera, Buffalo. **OF**—Allen Battle, Ottawa; Brian Daubach, Charlotte; Alex Ramirez, Buffalo. **DH**—Willis Otanez, Rochester. **Util**—Todd Haney, Norfolk. **SP**—Shannon Withem, Syracuse. **RP**—Todd Williams, Indianapolis.

Most Valuable Player—Roberto Petagine, Indianapolis. **Most Valuable Pitcher**—Shannon Withem, Syracuse. **Rookie of the Year**—Marlon Anderson, Scranton/Wilkes-Barre. **Manager of the Year**—Ken Macha, Pawtucket.

TOP 10 PROSPECTS

1. Alex Gonzalez, ss, Charlotte; **2.** Richie Sexson, of-1b, Buffalo; **3.** Roy Halladay, rhp, Syracuse; **4.** Ron Belliard, 2b, Louisville; **5.** Octavio Dotel, rhp, Norfolk; **6.** Gabe Alvarez, 3b, Toledo; **7.** Marlon Anderson, 2b, Scranton/Wilkes-Barre; **8.** Juan Encarnacion, of, Toledo; **9.** Carlton Loewer, rhp, Scranton/Wilkes-Barre; **10.** Ricky Ledee, of, Columbus.

DEPT. LEADERS

BATTING

G	David Doster, Scranton/W-B	141
AB	David Doster, Scranton/W-B	579
R	Ron Belliard, Louisville	114
H	Marlon Anderson, Scranton/W-B	176
TB	Brian Daubach, Charlotte	315
XBH	Brian Daubach, Charlotte	84
2B	Brian Daubach, Charlotte	45
3B	Marlon Anderson, Scranton/W-B	14
HR	Brian Daubach, Charlotte	35
RBI	Brian Daubach, Charlotte	124
SH	Greg Martinez, Louisville	10
SF	David Doster, Scranton/W-B	10
BB	Pat Lennon, Syracuse	87
IBB	Brian Daubach, Charlotte	9
HBP	Brian Daubach, Charlotte	15
	Scott Krause, Louisville	15
SO	Phil Hiatt, Buffalo	146
SB	Scott Pose, Columbus	47
CS	Jolbert Cabrera, Buffalo	15
	Luis Castillo, Charlotte	15
GIDP	Randall Simon, Richmond	22
OB%	Roberto Petagine, Indianapolis	.436
SL%	Brian Daubach, Charlotte	.634

PITCHING

G	Mike Walker, Indianapolis	78
GS	Ken Carlyle, Richmond	30
CG	Carlton Loewer, Scranton/W-B	5
ShO	Three tied at	2
GF	Four tied at	45
SV	Todd Williams, Indianapolis	26
W	Shannon Withem, Syracuse	17
L	Mike Drumright, Toledo	19
IP	Shannon Withem, Syracuse	190
H	Calvin Maduro, Scranton/W-B	211
R	Mike Drumright, Toledo	130
ER	Mike Drumright, Toledo	119
HR	Jim Farrell, Pawtucket	31
HB	Matt Drews, Toledo	16
BB	Mike Drumright, Toledo	94
SO	Juan Pena, Pawtucket	146
WP	Mark Wohlers, Richmond	17
BK	Jesus Martinez, Indianapolis	3

FIELDING

C	**AVG**	Guillermo Garcia, Ind.	.990
	PO	Einar Diaz, Buffalo	791
	A	Einar Diaz, Buffalo	70
	E	Einar Diaz, Buffalo	12
	DP	Fausto Tejero, Richmond	10
	PB	Mike Figga, Columbus	16
1B	**AVG**	Kevin Witt, Syracuse	.996
	PO	Steve Cox, Durham	1010
	A	Kevin Barker, Louisville	73
	E	Randall Simon, Richmond	11
	DP	Kevin Witt, Syracuse	105
2B	**AVG**	Jason Williams, Ind.	.984
	PO	Ralph Milliard, Norfolk	276
	A	Ron Belliard, Louisville	401
	E	Marlon Anderson, SWB	28
	DP	Ron Belliard, Louisville	98
3B	**AVG**	Willis Otanez, Rochester	.968
	PO	Willis Otanez, Rochester	91
	A	David Doster, SWB	283
	E	Torey Lovullo, Buffalo	20
		Mike Lowell, Columbus	20
	DP	Wes Helms, Richmond	24
SS	**AVG**	Tomas Perez, Syracuse	.977
	PO	Damian Jackson, Ind.	227
	A	Damian Jackson, Ind.	434
	E	Damian Jackson, Ind.	44
	DP	Damian Jackson, Ind.	101
OF	**AVG**	Earl Johnson, Toledo	.992
	PO	Wendell Magee, SWB	302
	A	Greg Blosser, Durham	15
	E	Three tied at	11
	DP	Several tied at	3

PACIFIC COAST LEAGUE

Late additions propel New Orleans to PCL crown

BY PETER BARROUQUERE

The New Orleans Zephyrs took a roundabout route to the first Triple-A World Series between the Pacific Coast League and International League champions.

The Zephyrs' route took detours to Double-A Jackson, where outfielders Lance Berkman and Chad Alexander, third baseman Chris Truby, catcher Scott Makarewicz and pitchers Derek Root and Kent Wallace were playing until callups by the Houston Astros forced them to Triple-A ahead of schedule.

JOHN SPEAR

Lance Berkman
World Series hero

They got to the title by way of Triple-A Pawtucket, from where reliever Mike Blais, who came in a trade for David West, showed up late in the season to contribute.

Shortstop Julio Lugo came the furthest, joining the Zephyrs from Class A Kissimmee a day before the playoffs began to become their everyday shortstop.

Berkman made the biggest impact. He hit three home runs and drove in six runs in the world series championship game, which New Orleans won 12-6, and was selected the series MVP. His last was a three-run homer that went out at the 433-foot mark in center field and was believed to be the longest hit at Cashman Field in Las Vegas.

"He hits some balls that just seem to take off and keep going," said Zephyrs manager John Tamargo, who managed Berkman last season at Kissimmee, where he hit 12 homers in half a season. "The ball doesn't seem like it's going to go out, then kicks into another gear.

"That was as hard a ball as I've seen hit all year. I've never been around a team that has been this close or has had such great chemistry that wanted to win so badly."

It was the second three-homer game for Berkman, the Astros' first-round draft choice out of Rice University in 1997.

He hit three consecutive home runs out of Southwestern Bell Ballpark in Oklahoma City in his second game with the Zephyrs on Aug. 21.

"God has given me a lot of ability to play the game of baseball," Berkman said. "I just happened to have a good night."

Berkman, New Orleans' youngest player at 22, hit more homers in the final game than the Bisons, who set a team record with 206 homers during the season, did during the series. Buffalo hit two.

He also managed to overshadow the Zephyrs' oldest player, 37-year-old Casey Candaele, who played every day in center field during the playoffs. Candaele hit a run-scoring triple, a home run, scored three times and made a diving catch in center in the final game.

The Zephyrs (76-66) struggled most of the second half before winning six of their last seven games to

Minor Leagues

STANDINGS

AMERICAN CONFERENCE

Page	EAST	W	L	PCT	GB	Manager	Attendance/Dates	Last Penn.
134	New Orleans Zephyrs (Astros)	76	66	.535	—	John Tamargo	519,584 (69)	1998
208	Memphis Redbirds (Cardinals)	74	70	.514	3	Gaylen Pitts	395,592 (71)	None
240	Oklahoma RedHawks (Rangers)	74	70	.514	3	Greg Biagini	491,036 (68)	None
201	Nashville Sounds (Pirates)	67	76	.469	9½	Trent Jewett	323,068 (65)	None
Page	**CENTRAL**	**W**	**L**	**PCT**	**GB**	**Manager(s)**	**Attendance/Dates**	**Last Penn.**
95	Iowa Cubs (Cubs)	85	59	.590	—	Terry Kennedy	420,713 (67)	None
141	Omaha Royals (Royals)	79	64	.552	5½	Ron Johnson	401,264 (65)	None
148	Albuquerque Dukes (Dodgers)	61	82	.427	23½	Hoffman/Debus/Roenicke	308,993 (67)	1994
115	Colorado Springs Sky Sox (Rockies)	55	89	.382	30	Paul Zuvella	220,281 (67)	1995

PACIFIC CONFERENCE

Page	SOUTH	W	L	PCT	GB	Manager	Attendance/Dates	Last Penn.
220	Fresno Grizzlies (Giants)	81	62	.566	—	Jim Davenport	359,076 (72)	None
161	Salt Lake Buzz (Twins)	79	64	.552	2	Phil Roof	554,719 (68)	1979
214	Las Vegas Stars (Padres)	70	72	.493	10½	Jerry Royster	336,005 (70)	1988
61	Tucson Sidewinders (Diamondbacks)	57	85	.401	23½	Chris Speier	300,460 (68)	1993
Page	**WEST**	**W**	**L**	**PCT**	**GB**	**Manager**	**Attendance/Dates**	**Last Penn.**
89	Calgary Cannons (White Sox)	81	62	.566	—	Tom Spencer	296,047 (63)	None
226	Tacoma Rainiers (Mariners)	77	67	.535	4½	Dave Myers	337,623 (72)	1978
189	Edmonton Trappers (Athletics)	76	67	.531	5	Mike Quade	410,414 (67)	1997
54	Vancouver Canadians (Angels)	53	90	.371	28	Mitch Seoane	284,935 (65)	1989

PLAYOFFS—Semifinals: Calgary defeated Fresno 3-2 in best-of-5 series, and New Orleans defeated Iowa 2-1 in best-of-3 (rain-shortened) series. **Finals:** New Orleans defeated Calgary 3-2 in best-of-5 series.

NOTE: Team's individual batting and pitching statistics can be found on page indicated in lefthand column.

overtake Oklahoma in the final week and win the Eastern Division of the PCL's newly-aligned American Conference by three games.

Iowa (85-59) had the PCL's best record and won the Central Division by 5½ games over Omaha. Calgary (Northern Division) and Fresno (Southern Division) tied for the best record (81-62) in the Pacific Conference.

New Orleans won a rain-abbreviated best-of-3 series from Iowa to win the American Conference, while Calgary took the Pacific Conference by winning three games of their best-of-5 series with the Grizzlies.

The PCL championship series saw the Zephyrs come back from a 2-1 deficit to Calgary and win the final two games to advance to the World Series. Veteran righthander Bob Milacki, who gave up six first-inning runs in the second game at Calgary, rebounded from a three-run first in the final game. He shut out the Cannons on one hit over the next six innings, and Candaele doubled home the winning run in the seventh in a 4-3 victory.

Royal Seasons for Giambi, Hatcher

In the regular season, the Omaha Royals drew a lot of attention with their offensive fireworks. Outfielder Jeremy Giambi led the league with a .372 batting average and a .469 on-base percentage. Teammate Chris Hatcher topped all minor leaguers with 46 home runs. Hatcher, who finished second in RBIs to Las Vegas third baseman George Arias, earned his first major league opportunity with his outstanding season, and made his big league debut with Kansas City in September.

Memphis Redbirds righthander Brady Raggio had the PCL's best ERA at 3.07, though he finished with a disappointing 8-9 record. Iowa righthanders Kurt Miller and Dave Swartzbaugh shared the lead in victories with 14. Las Vegas righthander Matt Clement used a little intimidation to capture the strikeout crown, hitting a minor league-leading 30 batters while striking out 160.

LARRY GOREN

Minors' best hitter
Omaha's Jeremy Giambi hit .372

Las Vegas infielder Greg LaRocca and Salt Lake first baseman Scott Stahoviak were the only PCL batters to hit for the cycle in 1998. LaRocca accomplished the feat against Nashville July 1, while Stahoviak did it in a game against New Orleans Aug. 3.

MEL BAILEY

Chris Hatcher
46 homers

Several premium third-base prospects made short stops in the PCL in 1998 before jumping to the big leagues. Aramis Ramirez began the season with Nashville, but made the leap to the Pittsburgh Pirates in May.

Vancouver's Troy Glaus and Edmonton's Eric Chavez each spent a couple of months in the league after beginning the season in Double-A. Chavez, who hit .325 with 11 homers and 40 RBIs in 47 games for the Trappers, was Baseball America's Minor League Player of the Year.

Record Expansion Season

The first year of the PCL's expansion from 10 to 16 teams resulted in a league record 5,959,104 fans. The league added five new teams from the disbanded American Association and a new expansion team in Memphis. In addition, Phoenix left the PCL to make way for the expansion Arizona Diamondbacks and relocated to Fresno.

Two teams–the Salt Lake Buzz and New Orleans–finished over the 500,000 mark in attendance. The Buzz, which averaged 8,158, led the league in average and total (554,719) attendance.

The Zephyrs, playing in the second season at new Zephyr Field, overcame late-season rainy weather to break their 1997 record of 507,164, finishing with a total of 519,584.

Once the 1998 season was over, the Edmonton Trappers and Vancouver Canadians swapped major league affiliates for the 1999 season. The Oakland Athletics left Edmonton after four seasons for Vancouver, while the Anaheim Angels go to Edmonton after six years in Vancouver.

Calgary will have its third parent club in as many seasons. The Cannons, who had tieups with the Pittsburgh Pirates and Chicago White Sox the last two years, will have a working agreement with the Florida Marlins, who left Charlotte (International).

It's not only affiliations that are changing. Vancouver is planning a move to Sacramento for the 2000 season, which may leave the British Columbia city without a team.

Fresno may also be somewhere else by 2000 should a stadium plan not be forthcoming. The Grizzlies, who played their first season at 6,575-seat Beiden Field on the Fresno State University campus, may be forced to relocate.

And Omaha will have a new identity in 1999. The Royals will be renamed the Golden Spikes in honor of the city's railroad history.

1998 Pacific Coast League Statistics

CLUB BATTING

	AVG	G	AB	R	H	2B	3B	HR	BB	SO	SB
New Orleans	.291	142	4823	779	1402	275	26	145	530	847	77
Las Vegas	.288	142	4950	772	1424	336	33	156	418	1055	96
Salt Lake	.284	143	4852	787	1380	285	33	144	455	1017	136
Albuquerque	.284	143	4790	709	1361	256	47	111	440	854	195
Omaha	.283	143	4819	766	1364	254	24	215	486	966	117
Colorado Springs	.281	144	4937	779	1387	277	47	134	468	958	66
Tucson	.281	142	4891	700	1373	255	45	116	445	936	70
Oklahoma	.280	144	5000	773	1402	302	35	137	506	1077	62
Iowa	.280	144	4900	849	1370	290	18	216	545	1058	53
Edmonton	.278	143	4816	767	1338	297	32	146	599	1002	91
Fresno	.278	143	4832	815	1342	243	25	184	536	911	106
Calgary	.277	143	4829	806	1337	289	23	162	496	895	100
Nashville	.271	143	4769	699	1292	251	32	161	467	1051	117
Tacoma	.270	144	4935	734	1330	310	27	128	501	951	80
Memphis	.266	144	4836	675	1285	287	39	105	476	851	103
Vancouver	.261	143	4727	571	1236	256	39	113	401	965	102

CLUB PITCHING

	ERA	G	CG	SHO	SV	IP	H	R	ER	BB	SO
Memphis	3.89	144	4	11	43	1267	1298	611	548	406	1034
Vancouver	4.33	143	16	6	31	1233	1264	680	593	529	894
Tacoma	4.37	144	8	8	42	1275	1274	698	619	576	1009
Oklahoma	4.45	144	9	6	32	1270	1351	721	628	419	938
Fresno	4.52	143	7	7	39	1248	1322	692	626	395	1011
Edmonton	4.54	143	10	6	37	1232	1298	698	622	404	919
New Orleans	4.70	142	10	5	43	1233	1310	726	644	450	945
Iowa	4.84	144	8	7	36	1257	1313	749	676	522	1053
Salt Lake	4.89	143	7	10	34	1234	1371	750	671	459	969
Albuquerque	4.91	143	6	3	30	1236	1423	780	674	492	1030
Omaha	4.94	143	5	6	46	1235	1399	772	678	420	834
Las Vegas	4.95	142	5	3	38	1247	1320	771	686	570	1107
Calgary	4.97	143	8	6	35	1242	1410	764	686	504	919
Nashville	4.98	143	2	6	44	1221	1345	772	676	484	852
Tucson	5.35	142	4	4	20	1237	1437	850	735	502	922
Colorado Springs	5.88	144	6	1	25	1229	1488	947	803	637	958

CLUB FIELDING

	PCT	PO	A	E	DP		PCT	PO	A	E	DP
Memphis	.978	3800	1580	121	157	Las Vegas	.974	3740	1521	141	157
Iowa	.978	3771	1495	121	138	Omaha	.974	3706	1453	140	138
Fresno	.976	3743	1449	126	133	Salt Lake	.973	3703	1535	146	134
Edmonton	.976	3697	1512	127	151	New Orleans	.973	3698	1468	144	144
Oklahoma	.976	3810	1599	132	136	Tacoma	.971	3824	1523	159	166
Calgary	.976	3727	1510	131	143	Nashville	.970	3664	1532	159	130
Vancouver	.974	3699	1488	138	156	Colo. Springs	.969	3686	1511	168	152
Albuquerque	.974	3709	1575	141	132	Tucson	.968	3710	1464	171	137

INDIVIDUAL BATTING LEADERS

(Minimum 389 Plate Appearances)

	AVG	G	AB	R	H	2B	3B	HR	RBI	BB	SO	SB
Giambi, Jeremy, Omaha	.372	96	325	68	121	21	2	20	66	57	64	8
Brinkley, Darryl, Nashville	.355	114	372	57	132	23	3	9	51	27	53	10
Meluskey, Mitch, NO	.353	121	397	76	140	41	0	17	71	85	59	2
White, Derrick, Iowa-CS	.343	88	332	72	114	22	2	20	86	48	62	6
Valdez, Mario, Calgary	.330	123	448	86	148	32	0	20	81	60	102	1
Franklin, Micah, Iowa	.329	118	359	74	118	26	2	29	95	59	72	5
Hajek, Dave, Las Vegas	.328	130	539	85	177	45	3	4	63	23	46	14
Latham, Chris, Salt Lake	.324	97	377	81	122	21	4	11	51	56	99	29

INDIVIDUAL PITCHING LEADERS

(Minimum 115 Innings)

	W	L	ERA	G	GS	CG	SV	IP	H	R	ER	BB	SO
Raggio, Brady, Memphis	8	9	3.07	24	23	2	0	152	156	57	52	31	100
Baptist, Travis, Salt Lake	8	5	3.12	21	21	1	0	136	128	53	47	41	98
Lowe, Sean, Memphis	12	8	3.18	25	21	0	0	153	147	57	54	61	114
Halama, John, New Orleans	12	3	3.20	17	17	4	0	121	118	48	43	16	86
Brock, Chris, Fresno	11	3	3.29	17	17	2	0	115	111	47	42	33	112
Clark, Terry, Oklahoma	12	5	3.38	30	24	2	1	165	156	72	62	35	95

ALL-STAR TEAM

C—Mitch Meluskey, New Orleans. **1B**—Mario Valdez, Calgary. **2B**—Dave Hajek, Las Vegas. **3B**—George Arias, Las Vegas. **SS**—Scott Sheldon, Oklahoma. **OF**—Jeremy Giambi, Omaha; Armando Rios, Fresno; Derrick White, Iowa-Colorado Springs. **DH**—Chris Hatcher, Omaha. **RHP**—Kurt Miller, Iowa. **LHP**—John Halama, New Orleans. **RP**—Bart Evans, Omaha.

Most Valuable Player—Chris Hatcher, Omaha. **Rookie of the Year**—Jeremy Giambi, Omaha. **Manager of the Year**—Terry Kennedy, Iowa.

TOP 10 PROSPECTS

1. Troy Glaus, 3b, Vancouver; **2.** Eric Chavez, 3b, Edmonton; **3.** Matt Clement, rhp, Las Vegas; **4.** Jeremy Giambi, of, Omaha; **5.** Braden Looper, rhp, Memphis; **6.** Scott Elarton, rhp, New Orleans; **7.** Aramis Ramirez, 3b, Nashville; **8.** Corey Koskie, 3b, Salt Lake; **9.** Mitch Meluskey, c, New Orleans; **10.** Russ Ortiz, rhp, Fresno.

DEPT. LEADERS

BATTING

G	Tom Quinlan, Oklahoma	137
AB	Dave Hajek, Las Vegas	539
	Tom Quinlan, Oklahoma	539
R	Russ Johnson, New Orleans	95
H	Dave Hajek, Las Vegas	177
TB	Chris Hatcher, Omaha	313
XBH	Dan Rohrmeier, Tacoma	78
2B	Dan Rohrmeier, Tacoma	51
3B	Edwin Diaz, Tucson	12
HR	Chris Hatcher, Omaha	46
RBI	George Arias, Las Vegas	119
SH	Craig Wilson, Calgary	9
SF	Dave Hajek, Las Vegas	12
BB	Russ Johnson, New Orleans	90
IBB	Mitch Meluskey, New Orleans	10
HBP	Olmedo Saenz, Calgary	22
SO	Tom Quinlan, Oklahoma	155
SB	Lou Frazier, Calgary	42
CS	Willie Romero, Albuquerque	15
GIDP	Paul LoDuca, Albuquerque	20
	Dan Rohrmeier, Tacoma	20
OB%	Jeremy Giambi, Omaha	.469
SL%	Micah Franklin, Iowa	.655

PITCHING

G	Alan Newman, Las Vegas	63
GS	Larry Luebbers, Memphis	29
CG	Gil Heredia, Edmonton	6
ShO	Larry Luebbers, Memphis	2
	Ricky Pickett, Fres./Tuc./Okla.	2
GF	Anthony Chavez, Vancouver	51
SV	Bart Evans, Omaha	27
W	Kurt Miller, Iowa	14
	Dave Swartzbaugh, Iowa	14
L	Bill King, Edmonton	13
IP	Bob Milacki, New Orleans	190
H	Bob Milacki, New Orleans	199
R	Brian Harrison, Omaha	116
ER	Brian Harrison, Omaha	108
HR	Rich Pratt, Calgary	29
HB	Matt Clement, Las Vegas	30
BB	Brett Hinchliffe, Tacoma	88
SO	Matt Clement, Las Vegas	160
WP	Kevin Lomon, Las Vegas	19
BK	Earl Byrne, Iowa	5
	Rich Pratt, Calgary	5

FIELDING

C	**AVG**	Doug Mirabelli, Fresno	.995
	PO	Pat Cline, Iowa	806
	A	Raul Chavez, Tacoma	70
	E	Tom Wilson, Tucson	12
		Rick Wrona, Oklahoma	12
	DP	Raul Chavez, Tacoma	12
	PB	Pat Cline, Iowa	18
1B	**AVG**	Jeff Ball, Fresno	.994
	PO	D.T. Cromer, Edmonton	1015
	A	D.T. Cromer, Edmonton	89
	E	Mario Valdez, Calgary	14
	DP	D.T. Cromer, Edmonton	113
2B	**AVG**	Carlos Hernandez, NO	.983
	PO	Dave Hajek, Las Vegas	260
	A	Dave Hajek, Las Vegas	368
	E	Jed Hansen, Omaha	24
	DP	Dave Hajek, Las Vegas	99
3B	**AVG**	Russ Johnson, NO	.962
	PO	Tom Quinlan, Oklahoma	96
	A	Tom Quinlan, Oklahoma	278
	E	Brad Seitzer, Tacoma	26
	DP	Tom Quinlan, Oklahoma	31
SS	**AVG**	Chris Petersen, Iowa	.985
	PO	Juan Melo, Las Vegas	214
	A	Jorge Velandia, Edmonton	428
	E	Benji Gil, Calgary	29
	DP	Jorge Velandia, Edmonton	93
OF	**AVG**	Brad Tyler, Edmonton	1.000
	PO	Dante Powell, Fresno	284
	A	Juan Munoz, Memphis	15
	E	Derrick Gibson, Colo. Spr.	13
	DP	Several tied at	3

EASTERN LEAGUE

Harrisburg continues dominant ways with '98 crown

BY ANDREW LINKER

If history indeed is written by the victors, then the Harrisburg Senators continue to own the ink.

All of it. Every last barrel. Every last drop.

While they were the last of four teams to qualify for the 1998 Eastern League playoffs, the Senators again emerged as the champions as they beat Akron and New Britain each in four games to win their third straight championship.

In doing so, the Senators matched the 1984-86 Vermont Reds as the only teams in the EL's 76 seasons to three-peat.

JOHN SPEAR

Calvin Pickering
EL MVP

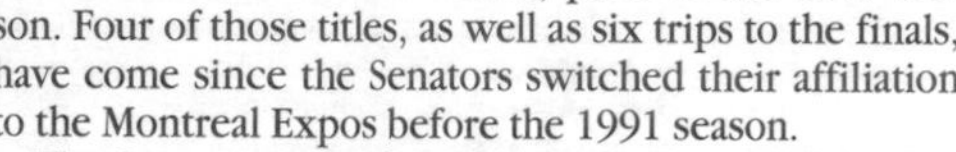

"When you work hard like this, this is what's supposed to happen," said Rick Sweet, the Senators' third manager in as many championship seasons. "When you taste this once, you want to taste it again and again."

The Senators know the taste all too well.

The title also was the fourth in six seasons for the Senators and the fifth since the franchise relocated to Harrisburg from Nashua, N.H., prior to the 1987 season. Four of those titles, as well as six trips to the finals, have come since the Senators switched their affiliation to the Montreal Expos before the 1991 season.

The Senators won their latest title the old-fashioned way as they used pitching and defense to shut down the league's two top offenses in New Britain and Akron.

In 72 postseason innings, Senators pitchers faced the minimum three batters 35 times, effectively leaving the Aeros and Rock Cats only five innings of offense in each game. Over the same span, the Senators' defense committed just three errors.

The Senators' story was one of many in the EL.

New Britain's long-suffering franchise reached the finals for the first time since 1983 when the team's prized prospect was a first-year pro named Roger Clemens.

Another New Britain pitcher, closer Brent Stentz, punctuated the franchise's return to dominance with a league-record 43 saves. Stentz, who was the league's pitcher of the year after shattering the previous record of 35 saves set by Harrisburg's Al Reyes in 1994, came within three saves of matching the all-time minor league record of 46 set in 1993 by Savannah's Jamie Cochran.

The best offensive show was turned in by Bowie first baseman Calvin Pickering (.309-31-114), who led the EL in homers and RBIs while finishing fifth in the batting race. Pickering was the only EL player to homer three times in a game; he accomplished the feat against Akron.

The top one-game performances belonged to Harrisburg third baseman Geoff Blum and Bowie outfielder Decomba Conner, who each hit for the cycle. Blum did his in order as he collected a single, double, triple and, naturally, game-winning homer in a 3-2 victory over New Haven.

Akron, the other team to lose to Harrisburg in the postseason, became the first team in Double-A history to reach the 500,000 plateau in attendance. The Aeros' total of 521,122 accounted for 16 percent of the record 3.29 million EL fans.

Akron was not the only team to set an attendance record as Reading (414,658) set its all-time high for the 11th straight season. Also reaching new single-season totals were Trenton (457,344), Harrisburg (259,381) and New Britain (181,643).

In the league's only affiliation change for 1999, New Haven ended its five-year association with the Rockies as the Ravens signed a two-year agreement with the Mariners.

STANDINGS

Page	NORTH	W	L	PCT	GB	Manager	Attendance/Dates	Last Penn.
161	New Britain Rock Cats (Twins)	83	59	.585	—	John Russell	181,643 (64)	1983
183	Binghamton Mets (Mets)	82	60	.577	1	John Gibbons	216,191 (68)	1994
128	Portland Sea Dogs (Marlins)	66	75	.468	16½	Lynn Jones	398,800 (67)	None
175	Norwich Navigators (Yankees)	66	76	.465	17	Trey Hillman	243,817 (66)	None
116	New Haven Ravens (Rockies)	59	83	.415	24	Tim Blackwell	197,342 (65)	None
Page	**SOUTH**	**W**	**L**	**PCT**	**GB**	**Manager**	**Attendance/Dates**	**Last Penn.**
109	Akron Aeros (Indians)	81	60	.574	—	Joel Skinner	521,122 (70)	None
168	Harrisburg Senators (Expos)	73	69	.514	8½	Rick Sweet	259,381 (65)	1998
83	Trenton Thunder (Red Sox)	71	70	.504	10	DeMarlo Hale	457,344 (69)	None
76	Bowie Baysox (Orioles)	71	71	.500	10½	Joe Ferguson	400,058 (67)	None
196	Reading Phillies (Phillies)	56	85	.397	25	Al LeBoeuf	414,658 (70)	1995

PLAYOFFS—Semifinals: Harrisburg defeated Akron 3-1 and New Britain defeated Binghamton 3-1 in-best-of-5 series. **Finals:** Harrisburg defeated New Britain 3-1 in best-of-5 series.

NOTE: Team's individual batting and pitching statistics can be found on page indicated in lefthand column.

1998 Eastern League Statistics

CLUB BATTING

	AVG	G	AB	R	H	2B	3B	HR	BB	SO	SB
New Britain	.273	142	4803	670	1310	297	25	97	434	882	123
Akron	.271	141	4865	758	1317	258	42	148	562	1075	123
Bowie	.269	142	4642	686	1248	201	28	126	530	951	88
Harrisburg	.266	142	4631	667	1233	251	35	142	432	920	157
Binghamton	.264	142	4691	660	1239	221	36	96	485	980	148
Portland	.260	141	4684	634	1219	217	34	119	492	1101	78
Norwich	.259	142	4659	621	1206	224	27	100	523	1007	146
Trenton	.257	141	4725	647	1214	247	20	148	471	1042	72
New Haven	.253	142	4630	578	1171	227	17	100	460	898	121
Reading	.251	141	4720	582	1184	227	36	108	470	1036	66

CLUB PITCHING

	ERA	G	CG	SHO	SV	IP	H	R	ER	BB	SO
Binghamton	3.34	142	8	13	43	1248	1151	553	463	468	1142
Akron	3.72	141	10	8	43	1251	1206	601	517	492	872
New Britain	3.87	142	5	12	51	1240	1227	611	534	425	1056
Harrisburg	3.89	142	6	8	39	1216	1180	603	526	455	865
New Haven	4.23	142	11	7	31	1226	1234	677	576	510	979
Trenton	4.23	141	5	10	41	1244	1255	670	585	470	971
Portland	4.29	141	6	6	36	1220	1245	691	582	530	1082
Norwich	4.35	142	11	4	41	1216	1327	702	588	470	969
Bowie	4.50	142	8	7	36	1197	1176	678	598	481	970
Reading	4.55	141	6	6	30	1241	1340	717	628	558	986

CLUB FIELDING

	PCT	PO	A	E	DP
Akron	.978	3753	1536	118	142
New Britain	.973	3721	1521	143	146
Harrisburg	.973	3647	1541	142	138
Trenton	.973	3733	1560	145	124
Binghamton	.973	3744	1511	145	128
Reading	.973	3723	1518	147	137
Bowie	.973	3600	1368	130	112
New Haven	.971	3678	1536	158	121
Portland	.968	3661	1491	169	137
Norwich	.967	3648	1420	174	83

INDIVIDUAL BATTING LEADERS

(Minimum 383 Plate Appearances)

	AVG	G	AB	R	H	2B	3B	HR	RBI	BB	SO	SB
Mientkiewicz, Doug, NB	.323	139	502	96	162	45	0	16	88	96	58	11
Barrett, Michael, Harrisburg	.320	120	453	78	145	32	2	19	87	27	43	7
Scutaro, Marcos, Akron	.316	124	462	68	146	27	6	11	62	47	71	33
Hunter, Scott, Binghamton	.314	130	487	80	153	25	3	14	65	47	75	39
Pickering, Calvin, Bowie	.309	139	488	93	151	28	2	31	114	98	119	4
Stumberger, Darren, Akron	.301	139	545	83	164	39	2	10	76	56	79	1
Jones, Jacque, New Britain	.299	134	518	78	155	39	3	21	85	37	134	18
Brown, Vick, Norwich	.298	102	352	62	105	14	3	6	34	40	75	35
Long, Terrence, Binghamton	.297	130	455	69	135	20	10	16	58	62	105	23
Fernandez, Jose, Harrisburg	.295	104	369	59	109	27	1	17	58	36	73	16

INDIVIDUAL PITCHING LEADERS

(Minimum 114 Innings)

	W	L	ERA	G	GS	CG	SV	IP	H	R	ER	BB	SO
Kusiewicz, Mike, New Haven	14	7	2.32	27	26	2	0	179	161	59	46	35	151
Arteaga, J.D., Binghamton	8	7	2.80	21	18	0	0	119	122	48	37	25	97
Brower, Jim, Akron	13	5	3.01	23	23	2	0	156	142	60	52	38	91
Powell, Jeremy, Harrisburg	9	7	3.01	22	22	1	0	132	115	54	44	37	77
Murray, Dan, Binghamton	11	6	3.18	27	27	1	0	164	153	64	58	54	159
Lincoln, Mike, New Britain	15	7	3.22	26	26	1	0	173	180	80	62	35	109
Shumaker, Anthony, Reading	7	10	3.35	38	21	1	2	167	152	75	62	44	129
Thomas, Evan, Reading	8	5	3.35	24	24	3	0	158	180	66	59	44	134
Sanders, Frankie, Akron	11	8	3.48	29	29	2	0	186	175	82	72	71	108
Parker, Christian, Harrisburg	6	6	3.48	36	16	0	5	127	124	66	49	47	73

ALL-STAR TEAM

C—Michael Barrett, Harrisburg. **1B**—Calvin Pickering, Bowie. **2B**—Marcos Scutaro, Akron. **3B**—Jose Fernandez, Harrisburg. **SS**—Cristian Guzman, New Britain. **OF**—Scott Hunter, Binghamton; Jacque Jones, New Britain; Dernell Stenson, Trenton. **DH**—Doug Mientkiewicz, New Britain. **RHP**—Mike Lincoln, New Britain. **LHP**—Mike Kusiewicz, New Haven. **RP**—Brent Stentz, New Britain.

Most Valuable Player—Calvin Pickering, Bowie. **Most Valuable Pitcher**—Brent Stentz, New Britain. **Rookie of the Year**—Calvin Pickering, Bowie. **Manager of the Year**—John Gibbons, Binghamton.

TOP 10 PROSPECTS

1. Michael Barrett, c-3b, Harrisburg; **2.** Dernell Stenson, of, Trenton; **3.** Jacque Jones, of, New Britain; **4.** Ed Yarnall, lhp, Binghamton/Portland; **5.** Russ Branyan, 3b, Akron; **6.** Calvin Pickering, 1b, Bowie; **7.** Fernando Seguignol, 1b-of, Harrisburg; **8.** Octavio Dotel, rhp, Binghamton; **9.** Mike Lincoln, rhp, New Britain; **10.** Cristian Guzman, ss, New Britain.

DEPT. LEADERS

BATTING

G	Fletcher Bates, Portland	140
	Cristian Guzman, New Britain	140
AB	Dan Cey, New Britain	569
R	Doug Mientkiewicz, NB	96
H	Darren Stumberger, Akron	164
TB	Calvin Pickering, Bowie	276
XBH	Jacque Jones, New Britain	63
2B	Doug Mientkiewicz, NB	45
3B	Terrence Long, Binghamton	10
HR	Calvin Pickering, Bowie	31
RBI	Calvin Pickering, Bowie	114
SH	Cristian Guzman, New Britain	17
SF	Scott Hunter, Binghamton	8
	Darren Stumberger, Akron	8
BB	Calvin Pickering, Bowie	98
IBB	Calvin Pickering, Bowie	16
HBP	Jim Chamblee, Trenton	16
SO	Ryan Minor, Bowie	152
SB	Wonderful Monds, New Haven	41
CS	Donzell McDonald, Norwich	22
GIDP	Calvin Pickering, Bowie	20
OB%	Calvin Pickering, Bowie	.434
SL%	Calvin Pickering, Bowie	.566

PITCHING

G	Sal Urso, Trenton	69
GS	Four tied at	29
CG	Scott Randall, New Haven	7
ShO	Evan Thomas, Reading	3
GF	Brent Stentz, New Britain	53
SV	Brent Stentz, New Britain	43
W	Mike Lincoln, New Britain	15
L	Three tied at	14
IP	Scott Randall, New Haven	202
H	Scott Randall, New Haven	210
R	Luther Hackman, New Haven	102
	Scott Randall, New Haven	102
ER	Kris Stevens, Reading	94
HR	Brent Billingsley, Portland	24
	Mike Vavrek, New Haven	24
HB	Mike Kusiewicz, New Haven	16
BB	Jason Baker, Harrisburg	71
	Frankie Sanders, Akron	71
SO	Brent Billingsley, Portland	183
WP	John Salamon, New Haven	22
BK	Scott Stewart, Binghamton	4

FIELDING

C	**AVG**	Jaime Torres, Norwich	.993
	PO	Pedro Grifol, Binghamton	897
	A	Pedro Grifol, Binghamton	81
	E	Pedro Grifol, Binghamton	10
	DP	Pedro Grifol, Binghamton	11
	PB	Joe DePastino, Trenton	14
1B	**AVG**	Darren Stumberger, Akron	.992
	PO	Darren Stumberger, Akron	1197
	A	Darren Stumberger, Akron	116
	E	Calvin Pickering, Bowie	20
	DP	Darren Stumberger, Akron	124
2B	**AVG**	Marcos Scutaro, Akron	.977
	PO	Amaury Garcia, Portland	287
	A	Dan Cey, New Britain	373
	E	Amaury Garcia, Portland	27
	DP	Dan Cey, New Britain	97
3B	**AVG**	Wilton Veras, Trenton	.952
	PO	Wilton Veras, Trenton	100
	A	Wilton Veras, Trenton	259
	E	Ryan Minor, Bowie	26
	DP	Ryan Minor, Bowie	27
SS	**AVG**	Jhonny Carvajal, Harr.	.977
	PO	John McDonald, Akron	242
	A	Cristian Guzman, NB	426
	E	Cristian Guzman, NB	32
	DP	Cristian Guzman, NB	95
OF	**AVG**	Mark Budzinski, Akron	.989
	PO	Donzell McDonald, Norwich	312
	A	Dernell Stenson, Trenton	15
	E	Wonderful Monds, NH	12
	DP	Johnny Isom, Bowie	5

SOUTHERN LEAGUE

Mobile grabs top honor; Kapler shines individually

BY DAVID JENKINS

When the dust settled on the 1998 Southern League season, Jacksonville's Gabe Kapler had most of the records while the Mobile BayBears wound up with most of the hardware.

The BayBears, in their second season as a league member, took both halves of the Western Division split season, then won six of seven postseason games for the championship. In the finals, the Padres' Double-A club won three of four from Kapler's Jacksonville Suns and in the process solidified Baseball America's Minor League Team of the Year award.

MEL BAILEY

Gabe Kapler
SL MVP

The BayBears placed four players on the league's postseason all-star team: catcher Ben Davis (.286-14-75), first baseman Mike Mitchell (.318-15-97), third baseman John Powers (.303-12-52) and outfielder Mike Darr (.310-6-90) Skipper Mike Ramsey was also named the league's manager of the year.

Powers was named MVP of the playoffs, going 12-for-27 with five RBIs in the BayBears' seven games against Huntsville and Jacksonville.

But the regular season–and the regular-season MVP award–belonged to Kapler.

Four league records were erased by the slugging outfielder in 1998, but the most stunning was Kapler's 146 RBIs–14 more than the old mark of 132 that had stood since 1986. Kapler's 81 extra-base hits and 319 total bases also were records. He and teammate Rob Fick both finished with 47 doubles, breaking the old mark of 44.

Jacksonville outfielder Glen Barker also put his name in the record book by playing 142 consecutive errorless games in the outfield, a mark that covered two seasons. The Suns as a team also set SL records for highest batting average (.290), most hits (1,416) and most doubles (323).

Huntsville third baseman Eric Chavez missed out on the stretch run when he was promoted to Triple-A Edmonton. But before his July callup, Chavez gave Kapler a run for the record book with 22 homers and 86 RBIs in only 88 games. He kept up his torrid hitting at Edmonton and Baseball America honored him as its Minor League Player of the Year.

Chattanooga's Jason LaRue became the first catcher to win the SL batting crown since 1980. His mark of .365 was 35 points better than runner-up Emil Brown of Carolina.

Knoxville pitcher Tom Davey was named the Southern League's MVP in the annual Double-A all-star game in New Haven, Conn. In the Southern League all-star game played earlier in the season, which had host Mobile playing the rest of the league, Kapler was named MVP in the all-stars' victory.

The West Tenn Diamond Jaxx, based in Jackson, Tenn., were a welcome addition to the league. The Jaxx replaced Memphis, which was drafted as a Triple-A expansion team, and led the Southern League in attendance at 313,775. As a whole, the league drew 2,366,234 in 1998.

STANDINGS: SPLIT SEASON

FIRST HALF					SECOND HALF				
EAST	W	L	PCT	GB	EAST	W	L	PCT	GB
Jacksonville	48	22	.686	—	Knoxville	39	31	.557	—
Knoxville	32	38	.457	16	Jacksonville	38	32	.543	1
Orlando	32	38	.457	16	Greenville	37	32	.536	1½
Carolina	31	39	.443	17	Orlando	35	33	.515	3
Greenville	30	40	.429	18	Carolina	28	41	.406	10½
WEST	W	L	PCT	GB	WEST	W	L	PCT	GB
Mobile	42	28	.600	—	Mobile	44	26	.629	—
Huntsville	40	30	.571	2	Chattanooga	40	28	.588	3
West Tenn	38	32	.543	4	Huntsville	32	38	.457	12
Birmingham	32	38	.457	10	West Tenn	28	42	.400	16
Chattanooga	25	45	.357	17	Birmingham	26	44	.371	18

PLAYOFFS—Semifinals: Jacksonville defeated Knoxville 3-0 and Mobile defeated Huntsville 3-0 in best-of-5 series. **Finals:** Mobile defeated Jacksonville 3-1 in best-of-5 series.

STANDINGS: OVERALL

Page		W	L	PCT	GB	Manager	Attendance/Dates	Last Penn.
215	Mobile BayBears (Padres)	86	54	.614	—	Mike Ramsey	271,002 (69)	1998
122	Jacksonville Suns (Tigers)	86	54	.614	—	Dave Anderson	254,882 (68)	1996
190	Huntsville Stars (Athletics)	72	68	.514	14	Jeffrey Leonard	257,915 (67)	1994
248	Knoxville Smokies (Blue Jays)	71	69	.507	15	Omar Malave	123,686 (68)	1978
227	Orlando Rays (Mariners)	67	71	.486	18	Dan Rohn	144,126 (67)	1991
69	Greenville Braves (Braves)	67	72	.482	18½	Randy Ingle	269,525 (68)	1997
96	West Tenn Diamond Jaxx (Cubs)	66	74	.471	20	Dave Trembley	313,775 (70)	None
103	Chattanooga Lookouts (Reds)	65	73	.471	20	Mark Berry	230,475 (68)	1988
202	Carolina Mudcats (Pirates)	59	80	.424	26½	Jeff Banister	230,768 (67)	1995
89	Birmingham Barons (White Sox)	58	82	.414	28	Dave Huppert	298,054 (69)	1993

NOTE: Team's individual batting and pitching statistics can be found on page indicated in lefthand column.

1998 Southern League Statistics

CLUB BATTING

	AVG	G	AB	R	H	2B	3B	HR	BB	SO	SB
Jacksonville	.290	140	4878	882	1416	323	46	133	562	908	105
Knoxville	.276	140	4701	795	1298	280	39	143	572	866	121
Huntsville	.272	140	4647	810	1266	248	23	144	685	965	161
Carolina	.271	139	4626	706	1255	239	35	106	571	911	125
Mobile	.270	140	4858	794	1312	284	39	117	630	976	124
Birmingham	.266	140	4648	670	1235	226	30	108	529	893	99
Greenville	.264	139	4668	676	1232	263	26	130	537	1036	146
West Tenn	.263	140	4698	696	1236	238	48	82	553	964	183
Chattanooga	.261	138	4687	663	1222	255	41	101	510	1007	67
Orlando	.256	138	4652	691	1192	213	41	90	595	883	116

CLUB PITCHING

	ERA	G	CG	SHO	SV	IP	H	R	ER	BB	SO
Mobile	3.85	140	9	9	35	1247	1173	616	533	489	1048
West Tenn	3.99	140	7	4	31	1237	1226	660	548	525	1073
Greenville	4.42	139	4	7	36	1235	1225	711	607	645	1097
Chattanooga	4.51	138	1	7	23	1218	1241	706	610	629	837
Jacksonville	4.57	140	8	8	36	1231	1243	710	625	524	831
Orlando	4.91	138	4	8	35	1215	1293	759	663	508	897
Knoxville	4.91	140	3	4	35	1211	1330	781	661	563	840
Huntsville	4.96	140	4	4	36	1220	1331	833	673	646	931
Carolina	5.19	139	4	6	25	1194	1298	780	688	545	863
Birmingham	5.20	140	7	5	31	1206	1304	827	696	670	992

CLUB FIELDING

	PCT	PO	A	E	DP		PCT	PO	A	E	DP
Jacksonville	.974	3694	1518	139	141	Greenville	.968	3706	1450	169	129
Mobile	.974	3742	1458	140	128	Knoxville	.968	3632	1542	170	135
Orlando	.973	3645	1437	141	127	Carolina	.967	3581	1508	171	145
Chattanooga	.972	3655	1507	150	156	Birmingham	.967	3617	1446	175	119
West Tenn	.969	3710	1455	166	98	Huntsville	.965	3661	1566	187	142

INDIVIDUAL BATTING LEADERS

(Minimum 378 Plate Appearances)

	AVG	G	AB	R	H	2B	3B	HR	RBI	BB	SO	SB
LaRue, Jason, Chattanooga	.365	105	386	71	141	39	8	14	82	40	60	4
Brown, Emil, Carolina	.330	120	466	89	154	31	2	14	67	50	71	24
Chavez, Eric, Huntsville	.328	88	335	66	110	27	1	22	86	42	61	12
Kapler, Gabe, Jacksonville	.322	139	547	113	176	47	6	28	146	66	93	6
Villalobos, Carlos, Jack	.320	128	497	96	159	34	2	18	80	55	85	8
Fick, Robert, Jacksonville	.318	130	515	101	164	47	6	18	114	71	83	8
Mitchell, Mike, Mobile	.318	134	509	72	162	32	2	15	97	61	95	0
Lopez, Luis, Knoxville	.313	119	450	70	141	27	1	15	65	50	55	0
Darr, Mike, Mobile	.310	132	523	105	162	41	4	6	90	62	79	28
Smith, Demond, Birmingham	.308	84	321	75	99	23	7	5	30	48	67	25

INDIVIDUAL PITCHING LEADERS

(Minimum 112 Innings)

	W	L	ERA	G	GS	CG	SV	IP	H	R	ER	BB	SO
Wolff, Bryan, Mobile	9	3	2.29	33	14	3	0	134	90	40	34	43	134
Chen, Bruce, Greenville	13	7	3.29	24	23	1	0	139	106	57	51	48	164
Laxton, Brett, Huntsville	11	4	3.40	21	21	0	0	130	109	64	49	79	82
Carlyle, Buddy, Chatt.-Mobile	14	7	3.43	28	28	2	0	189	185	80	72	46	100
Beirne, Kevin, Birmingham	13	9	3.44	26	26	2	0	167	142	77	64	87	153
Bowie, Micah, Greenville	11	6	3.48	30	29	1	0	163	132	73	63	64	160
Norton, Phillip, West Tenn	6	6	3.52	19	19	1	0	120	118	60	47	50	119
McNichol, Brian, West Tenn	12	9	3.72	28	26	4	0	179	170	88	74	62	168
Bruner, Clay, Jacksonville	10	6	3.79	28	28	1	0	171	173	90	72	66	91
Perez, Odalis, Greenville	6	5	4.02	23	21	0	0	132	127	67	59	53	143

ALL-STAR TEAM

C—Ben Davis, Mobile. **1B**—Mike Mitchell, Mobile. **2B**—Jose Macias, Jacksonville. **3B**—Eric Chavez, Huntsville. **SS**—Jose Nieves, West Tenn. **OF**—Emil Brown, Carolina; Mike Darr, Mobile; Gabe Kapler, Jacksonville; George Lombard, Greenville. **DH**—Robert Fick, Jacksonville. **Util**—John Powers, Mobile. **RHP**—Kevin Beirne, Birmingham. **LHP**—Bruce Chen, Greenville. **RP**—Sean Spencer, Orlando.

Most Valuable Player—Gabe Kapler, Jacksonville. **Most Outstanding Pitcher**—Bruce Chen, Greenville. **Manager of the Year**—Mike Ramsey, Mobile.

TOP 10 PROSPECTS

1. Eric Chavez, 3b, Huntsville; **2.** Bruce Chen, lhp, Greenville; **3.** Ben Davis, c, Mobile; **4.** Gary Matthews Jr., of, Mobile; **5.** George Lombard, of, Greenville; **6.** Odalis Perez, lhp, Greenville; **7.** Gabe Kapler, of, Jacksonville; **8.** Emil Brown, of, Carolina; **9.** Jose Nieves, ss, West Tenn; **10.** Jason LaRue, c, Chattanooga.

DEPT. LEADERS

BATTING

- **G** Gabe Kapler, Jacksonville 139
- Jeff Inglin, Birmingham 139
- **AB** Carlos Lee, Birmingham 549
- **R** Gabe Kapler, Jacksonville 113
- **H** Gabe Kapler, Jacksonville 176
- **TB** Gabe Kapler, Jacksonville 319
- **XBH** Gabe Kapler, Jacksonville 81
- **2B** Robert Fick, Jacksonville 47
- Gabe Kapler, Jacksonville 47
- **3B** Bo Porter, West Tenn 11
- **HR** Gabe Kapler, Jacksonville 28
- **RBI** Gabe Kapler, Jacksonville 146
- **SH** Michael Peeples, Knoxville 17
- **SF** Gabe Kapler, Jacksonville 11
- **BB** Mark Johnson, Birmingham 105
- **IBB** George Lombard, Greenville 10
- **HBP** Ramon Hernandez, Huntsville 19
- **SO** Darron Ingram, Chattanooga 169
- **SB** Bo Porter, West Tenn 50
- **CS** Mike Eaglin, Greenville 19
- **GIDP** Carlos Lee, Birmingham 32
- **OB%** Mark Johnson, Birmingham .... .443
- **SL%** Jason LaRue, Chattanooga .... .617

PITCHING

- **G** Richie Barker, West Tenn 51
- Matt Skrmetta, Mobile 51
- **GS** Three tied at 29
- **CG** Brian McNichol, West Tenn 4
- Jason Olsen, Birmingham 4
- **ShO** Tim Harikkala, Orlando 2
- Bryan Wolff, Mobile 2
- **GF** James Sak, Mobile 43
- **SV** Sean Spencer, Orlando 18
- **W** David Borkowski, Jacksonville 16
- **L** Jason Phillips, Carolina 13
- Jason Ryan, West Tenn 13
- **IP** Buddy Carlyle, Chatt.-Mobile 189
- **H** Robert Luce, Orlando 210
- **R** Dave Melendez, Jacksonville 104
- **ER** Robert Luce, Orlando 95
- **HR** David Borkowski, Jacksonville 25
- **HB** Dave Melendez, Jacksonville 15
- **BB** Courtney Duncan, West Tenn 108
- **SO** Brian McNichol, West Tenn 168
- **WP** Tom Bennett, Huntsville 18
- **BK** Jeff D'Amico, Huntsville 5

FIELDING

- **C AVG** Jon Sweet, Carolina .... .996
- **PO** Ben Davis, Mobile 920
- **A** Jose Molina, West Tenn 108
- **E** Pascual Matos, Greenville 15
- **DP** Pascual Matos, Greenville 11
- **PB** Jason LaRue, Chattanooga 21
- Jose Molina, West Tenn 21
- **1B AVG** Mike Mitchell, Mobile .... .990
- **PO** Alejandro Freire, Jack 1050
- **A** Alejandro Freire, Jack 113
- **E** T.R. Marcinczyk, Huntsville 16
- **DP** Alejandro Freire, Jack 109
- **2B AVG** Jose Macias, Jacksonville .... .977
- **PO** Nick Presto, Chattanooga 287
- **A** Nick Presto, Chattanooga 370
- **E** Mike Eaglin, Greenville 24
- **DP** Nick Presto, Chattanooga 95
- **3B AVG** Steve Eddie, Chattanooga .... .956
- **PO** Carlos Lee, Birmingham 99
- **A** Carlos Villalobos, Jack 267
- **E** Carlos Lee, Birmingham 35
- **DP** Steve Eddie, Chattanooga 27
- **SS AVG** Mark DeRosa, Greenville .... .964
- **PO** Derek Mitchell, Jack 205
- **A** Derek Mitchell, Jack 383
- **E** Kevin Nicholson, Mobile 38
- **DP** Derek Mitchell, Jack 87
- **OF AVG** Glen Barker, Jacksonville 1.000
- **PO** Glen Barker, Jacksonville 307
- **A** Manny Gonzalez, Birm 18
- **E** Alex Hernandez, Carolina 11
- **DP** Glen Barker, Jacksonville 7

TEXAS LEAGUE

Tulsa reverses fortune, storms to TL championship

BY GEORGE SCHROEDER

Bobby Jones was just getting started when he became the Tulsa Drillers' winningest manager during the 1998 season. For an encore, he presided over the team's record-setting run to the Texas League championship.

Tulsa, the Eastern Division's last-place finisher in the first half of the split-season format at 28-40, performed a complete reversal in the second half. The Drillers, with a talent upgrade from Class A Charlotte, bounced back to go 50-22.

The Drillers then beat the Wichita Wranglers—another team that made a worst-to-first reversal—in a seven-game TL championship series. It was Tulsa's first championship since 1988.

"This is an unbelievable feeling," said Jones, who had managed the Drillers since 1993.

The series was competitive, but the final game wasn't. After none of the first six games had been decided by more than two runs, Tulsa scored seven runs in the first inning of Game Seven and won 13-5. The high-scoring final illustrated well the league's offensive tendencies in 1998. Tulsa's 4.15 ERA was best in the league.

JOHN SPEAR

Adrian Beltre
Top prospect

The TL saw plenty of top prospects in 1998, perhaps more than any other minor league. Angels prospect Troy Glaus, a first-round draft pick in 1997, began his professional career in Midland and dominated the early season, hitting 19 homers before moving up to Triple-A Vancouver.

San Antonio third baseman Adrian Beltre, a preseason candidate for Minor League Player of the Year, hit .321 with 13 homers in his three months in the league. And outfield phenom J.D. Drew, the marquee talent from the 1998 draft, made his Organized Baseball debut with the Arkansas Travelers, hitting .328 in 67 at-bats.

All three finished the season in the major leagues.

The reverberations of a big June shakeup in the Los Angeles Dodgers organization were felt in San Antonio. Missions manager Ron Roenicke, who led the team to the Western Division's first-half title, was promoted to the same position at Triple-A Albuquerque and San Antonio hitting coach Lance Parrish replaced Roenicke as manager. Several prospects, including Beltre, were promoted or traded in subsequent moves by the Dodgers, leaving the Missions a shell of their first-half selves.

Arkansas, the other first-half division leader, made some news as well. Travelers outfielder Tyrone Horne, a 28-year-old minor league veteran playing in his sixth organization in four seasons, hit .312 while leading the league with 37 homers and 139 RBIs. His home run and RBI totals were franchise records and the most in the Texas League since 1964 and 1956, respectively. Horne's effort included a four-home-run game at San Antonio in which he accomplished the first "home-run cycle" ever recorded. He had 10 RBIs.

Arkansas righthander Jose Jimenez, the leader in wins (15) and ERA (3.11) threw the TL's first no-hitter since 1996 and led the Travelers to their first postseason berth since 1989.

The Travelers were swept by the Drillers in the Eastern Division playoffs, but Arkansas swept Texas League postseason honors. Horne was named the league's player of the year, Jimenez the pitcher of the year and Chris Maloney the manager of the year.

STANDINGS: SPLIT SEASON

FIRST HALF					SECOND HALF				
EAST	W	L	PCT	GB	EAST	W	L	PCT	GB
Arkansas	42	26	.618	—	Tulsa	50	22	.694	—
Jackson	35	33	.515	7	Arkansas	38	34	.528	12
Shreveport	32	36	.471	10	Jackson	35	37	.486	15
Tulsa	28	40	.412	14	Shreveport	25	47	.347	25
WEST	W	L	PCT	GB	WEST	W	L	PCT	GB
San Antonio	38	30	.559	—	Wichita	46	26	.639	—
El Paso	35	33	.515	3	El Paso	34	38	.472	12
Midland	33	35	.485	5	Midland	31	41	.431	15
Wichita	29	39	.426	9	San Antonio	29	43	.403	17

PLAYOFFS—Semifinals: Tulsa defeated Arkansas 3-0 and Wichita defeated San Antonio 3-2 in best-of-5 series. **Finals:** Tulsa defeated Wichita 4-3 in best-of-7 series.

STANDINGS: OVERALL

Page		W	L	PCT	GB	Manager(s)	Attendance/Dates	Last Penn.
209	Arkansas Travelers (Cardinals)	80	60	.571	—	Chris Maloney	190,987 (59)	1989
241	Tulsa Drillers (Rangers)	78	62	.557	2	Bobby Jones	345,097 (69)	1998
142	Wichita Wranglers (Royals)	75	65	.536	5	John Mizerock	155,353 (67)	1992
135	Jackson Generals (Astros)	70	70	.500	10	Jim Pankovits	110,595 (68)	1996
156	El Paso Diablos (Brewers)	69	71	.493	11	Ed Romero	296,609 (69)	1994
149	San Antonio Missions (Dodgers)	67	73	.479	13	Ron Roenicke/Lance Parrish	387,715 (69)	1997
55	Midland Angels (Angels)	64	76	.457	16	Don Long	190,076 (69)	1975
221	Shreveport Captains (Giants)	57	83	.407	23	Mike Hart	161,940 (68)	1995

NOTE: Team's individual batting and pitching statistics can be found on page indicated in lefthand column.

1998 Texas League Statistics

CLUB BATTING

	AVG	G	AB	R	H	2B	3B	HR	BB	SO	SB
El Paso	.293	140	4923	835	1442	298	52	105	466	894	137
Wichita	.291	140	4766	857	1389	293	37	184	533	832	111
Midland	.290	140	4857	811	1408	282	60	132	526	911	124
Jackson	.278	140	4782	724	1331	262	23	165	448	898	90
Tulsa	.271	140	4802	757	1300	274	44	121	537	941	118
San Antonio	.270	140	4726	689	1274	247	56	116	463	885	182
Arkansas	.267	140	4632	787	1237	264	46	141	559	1009	125
Shreveport	.251	140	4645	574	1165	229	32	102	457	874	102

CLUB PITCHING

	ERA	G	CG	SHO	SV	IP	H	R	ER	BB	SO
Tulsa	4.15	140	8	8	33	1236	1146	648	570	540	963
San Antonio	4.22	140	4	7	36	1229	1269	698	576	477	927
Shreveport	4.26	140	7	4	33	1217	1216	660	576	531	959
Jackson	4.28	140	4	1	35	1221	1186	691	581	504	989
Arkansas	4.64	140	3	7	35	1201	1313	707	620	489	750
Midland	5.32	140	18	5	26	1225	1431	849	724	443	961
Wichita	5.40	140	2	5	38	1213	1489	861	728	470	799
El Paso	5.73	140	4	6	29	1224	1496	912	779	535	896

CLUB FIELDING

	PCT	PO	A	E	DP
Tulsa	.974	3707	1537	138	148
Arkansas	.973	3604	1548	141	161
Shreveport	.971	3652	1597	157	132
Midland	.969	3676	1549	165	113
Wichita	.964	3640	1567	196	129
San Antonio	.963	3688	1634	205	118
Jackson	.961	3662	1582	210	120
El Paso	.960	3673	1592	218	145

INDIVIDUAL BATTING LEADERS

(Minimum 378 Plate Appearances)

	AVG	G	AB	R	H	2B	3B	HR	RBI	BB	SO	SB
Quinn, Mark, Wichita	.349	100	372	82	130	26	6	16	84	43	54	4
Pena, Angel, San Antonio	.335	126	483	81	162	32	2	22	105	48	80	9
Luuloa, Keith, Midland	.334	130	479	85	160	43	10	17	102	75	54	6
Christian, Eddie, Midland	.333	105	400	80	133	39	4	5	49	49	61	13
Morris, Warren, Tulsa	.331	95	390	59	129	22	5	14	73	43	63	12
Febles, Carlos, Wichita	.326	126	432	110	141	28	9	14	52	80	70	51
Neal, Mike, Jackson	.326	103	341	53	111	27	2	17	70	39	80	4
Gonzalez, Raul, Wichita	.325	118	455	84	148	31	1	17	80	58	53	12
Andreopoulos, Alex, El Paso	.321	113	377	72	121	35	1	10	93	54	31	2
Brown, Ray, Wichita	.318	114	402	79	128	31	1	21	96	57	57	4

INDIVIDUAL PITCHING LEADERS

(Minimum 112 Innings)

	W	L	ERA	G	GS	CG	SV	IP	H	R	ER	BB	SO
Jimenez, Jose, Arkansas	15	6	3.11	26	20	1	0	180	156	71	62	68	88
Garcia, Freddy, Jackson	6	7	3.24	19	19	2	0	119	94	48	43	58	115
Glynn, Ryan, Tulsa	9	6	3.44	26	24	4	0	157	140	66	60	64	111
Oropesa, Eddie, Shreveport	7	11	3.78	32	20	2	0	143	143	71	60	67	104
Grilli, Jason, Shreveport	7	10	3.79	21	21	3	0	123	113	60	52	37	100
Brester, Jason, Shreveport	2	8	3.82	19	19	0	0	113	117	58	48	44	79
Beaumont, Matt, Midland	9	12	4.20	34	18	1	1	129	124	81	60	67	107
Lee, Corey, Tulsa	10	9	4.51	26	25	1	0	144	105	81	72	102	132
Prihoda, Steve, Wichita	11	8	4.72	58	3	0	3	122	140	76	64	23	85
Kolb, Dan, Tulsa	12	11	4.82	28	28	2	0	162	187	104	87	76	83

ALL-STAR TEAM

C—Angel Pena, San Antonio. **1B**—Danny Buxbaum, Midland. **2B**—Carlos Febles, Wichita. **3B**—Adrian Beltre, San Antonio. **SS**—Santiago Perez, El Paso. **OF**—Peter Bergeron, San Antonio; Lance Berkman, Jackson; Jason Conti, Tulsa; Tyrone Horne, Arkansas; Mark Quinn, Wichita. **DH**—Eddie Christian, Midland. **Util**—Keith Luuloa, Midland. **RHP**—Freddy Garcia, Jackson; Jason Grilli, Shreveport; Jose Jimenez, Arkansas. **LHP**—Ted Lilly, San Antonio; Steve Prihoda, Wichita. **RP**—Jose Santiago, Wichita.

Most Valuable Player—Tyrone Horne, Arkansas. **Pitcher of the Year**—Jose Jimenez, Arkansas. **Manager of the Year**—Chris Maloney, Arkansas.

TOP 10 PROSPECTS

1. Adrian Beltre, 3b, San Antonio; **2.** Troy Glaus, 3b, Midland; **3.** J.D. Drew, of, Arkansas; **4.** Freddy Garcia, rhp, Jackson; **5.** Carlos Beltran, of, Wichita; **6.** Ruben Mateo, of, Tulsa; **7.** Angel Pena, c, San Antonio; **8.** Carlos Febles, 2b, Wichita; **9.** Peter Bergeron, of, San Antonio; **10.** Lance Berkman, of, Jackson.

DEPT. LEADERS

BATTING

G	Stubby Clapp, Arkansas	139
AB	Anthony Iapoce, El Paso	576
R	Jason Conti, Tulsa	125
H	Anthony Iapoce, El Paso	181
TB	Keith Luuloa, Midland	274
XBH	Keith Luuloa, Midland	70
2B	Keith Luuloa, Midland	43
3B	Santiago Perez, El Paso	13
HR	Tyrone Horne, Arkansas	37
RBI	Tyrone Horne, Arkansas	139
SH	Kip Harkrider, San Antonio	12
SF	Keith Luuloa, Midland	16
BB	Stubby Clapp, Arkansas	86
IBB	Lance Berkman, Jackson	10
HBP	Toby Kominek, El Paso	22
SO	Chuck Abbott, Midland	135
SB	Carlos Febles, Wichita	51
CS	Anthony Iapoce, El Paso	20
GIDP	Chuck Abbott, Midland	18
	Jason LaRiviere, Arkansas	18
OB%	Carlos, Febles, Wichita	.441
SL%	Tyrone Horne, Arkansas	.605

PITCHING

G	Steve Prihoda, Wichita	58
GS	Dan Kolb, Tulsa	28
	Paul O'Malley, Jackson	28
CG	Lou Pote, Midland	6
ShO	Several tied at	1
GF	Jose Santiago, Wichita	41
SV	Jose Santiago, Wichita	22
W	Jose Jimenez, Arkansas	15
L	Matt Beaumont, Midland	12
IP	Jose Jimenez, Arkansas	180
H	Brian Cooper, Midland	215
R	Brian Cooper, Midland	138
ER	Brian Cooper, Midland	128
HR	Brian Cooper, Midland	35
HB	Paul O'Malley, Jackson	23
BB	Corey Lee, Tulsa	102
SO	Brian Cooper, Midland	141
WP	Three tied at	15
BK	Mike Pasqualicchio, El Paso	7

FIELDING

C	AVG	Andy Stewart, Wichita	.988
	PO	Angel Pena, San Antonio	781
	A	Angel Pena, San Antonio	81
	E	Angel Pena, San Antonio	14
	DP	Cesar King, Tulsa	12
	PB	Cesar King, Tulsa	18
1B	AVG	Cliff Brumbaugh, Tulsa	.990
	PO	Ray Brown, Wichita	986
	A	Victor Sanchez, Jackson	83
	E	Ray Brown, Wichita	23
	DP	Ray Brown, Wichita	94
2B	AVG	Stubby Clapp, Arkansas	.978
	PO	Stubby Clapp, Arkansas	332
	A	Stubby Clapp, Arkansas	436
	E	Mickey Lopez, El Paso	31
	DP	Stubby Clapp, Arkansas	113
3B	AVG	Pedro Feliz, Shreveport	.926
	PO	Pedro Feliz, Shreveport	71
	A	Rob Sasser, Tulsa	229
	E	Kit Pellow, Wichita	26
		Rob Sasser, Tulsa	26
	DP	Pedro Feliz, Shreveport	31
SS	AVG	Chuck Abbott, Midland	.955
	PO	Chuck Abbott, Midland	195
	A	Chuck Abbott, Midland	337
	E	Santiago Perez, El Paso	36
	DP	Chuck Abbott, Midland	70
OF	AVG	Peter Bergeron, San Antonio	.992
	PO	Anthony Iapoce, El Paso	279
	A	Jason Conti, Tulsa	20
	E	Miguel Correa, Midland	11
	DP	Peter Bergeron, San Antonio	5

CALIFORNIA LEAGUE

San Jose rides pitching to first championship since '79

BY LANCE PUGMIRE

El Nino shriveled the attendance numbers. Brad Penny and John Patterson promised the Diamondbacks a 1-2 punch for the milennium. And the new-stadium craze of the south moved north.

Yet the most dominating topic of the 1998 California League season was the wealth of pitching in San Jose.

The Giants, who rode a league-best 3.58 team ERA to the top overall regular season record (83-57), won their first league championship series since 1979 when spot starter Luis Estrella and reliever Brian Knoll combined on an eight-hit shutout in a 1-0 road victory at Rancho Cucamonga.

JOHN SPEAR

Brad Penny
League MVP

San Jose beat the Quakes 3-1 in the best-of-5 series, allowing a series total of seven runs and an average of six hits per game. The Giants didn't even use their ace, 1998 first-round draft pick Nate Bump, because manager Shane Turner didn't want to start Bump on three days' rest.

"There was no doubt our guys stepped up when they needed to most," Turner said. "Luis was the perfect example of that. We didn't want a Game Five, but we only gave him one run. But it was good enough."

San Jose righthander Joe Nathan finished fourth in the league with a 3.32 ERA. The Giants also received sparkling seasons from lefthander Jeff Andra (8-2, 3.32) and closer Jim Stoops, who had a league-best 31 saves before being traded to the Rockies organization.

In the Valley Division playoffs, San Jose withstood losses in games started by High Desert's 20-year-old phenoms Penny and Patterson to dethrone the defending league champions.

STANDINGS: SPLIT SEASON

FIRST HALF					SECOND HALF				
VALLEY	**W**	**L**	**PCT**	**GB**	**VALLEY**	**W**	**L**	**PCT**	**GB**
San Jose	46	24	.657	—	High Desert	44	26	.629	—
Lancaster	40	30	.571	6	Modesto	42	28	.600	2
High Desert	38	32	.543	8	Lancaster	38	32	.543	6
Modesto	35	35	.500	11	San Jose	37	33	.529	7
Stockton	34	36	.486	12	Stockton	32	38	.457	12
FREEWAY	**W**	**L**	**PCT**	**GB**	**FREEWAY**	**W**	**L**	**PCT**	**GB**
R. Cucamonga	36	34	.514	—	R. Cucamonga	41	29	.586	—
Visalia	35	35	.500	1	Visalia	32	38	.457	9
Lake Elsinore	35	35	.500	1	Lake Elsinore	31	39	.443	10
San Bernardino	27	43	.386	9	San Bernardino	28	42	.400	13
Bakersfield	24	46	.343	12	Bakersfield	25	45	.357	16

PLAYOFFS—First Round: Lake Elsinore defeated Visalia 2-0 and High Desert defeated Lancaster 2-0 in best-of-3 series. **Semifinals:** Rancho Cucamonga defeated Lake Elsinore 3-0 and San Jose defeated High Desert 3-2 in best-of-5 series. **Finals:** San Jose defeated Rancho Cucamonga 3-1 in best-of-5 series.

Penny (14-5, 2.96) and Patterson (8-7, 2.83) were thrust into a first-round playoff series when the Mavericks lost their final nine regular season games, missing out on a first-round bye.

Penny, the league's MVP and pitcher of the year, led the league in wins and strikeouts (207). Patterson was the ERA champ.

Lancaster first baseman-DH Brendan Kingman, a 25-year-old Australian signed in the offseason by the Mariners after a record-setting season in the Australian League, led the league in hitting at .340.

League owners took a 15 percent attendance hit with 21 rainouts and cold weather caused by El Nino-related spring storms. San Bernardino recouped some of its losses on Aug. 8, drawing a league-record 13,762 to The Ranch.

Ownership changed hands in Stockton and Visalia, with the O'Malley family, former owners of the Los Angeles Dodgers, taking over in Stockton. San Diego-based small business owner Jim Wadley stepped up to purchase Visalia after a league takeover from debt-ridden Japan Sports Systems.

Both new owners were seeking new ballparks. Tom Seidler, a nephew of Peter O'Malley, was negotiating for a park in downtown Stockton.

STANDINGS: OVERALL

Page		W	L	PCT	GB	Manager(s)	Attendance/Dates	Last Penn.
222	San Jose Giants (Giants)	83	57	.593	—	Shane Turner	141,180 (70)	1998
82	High Desert Mavericks (Diamondbacks)	82	58	.586	1	Don Wakamatsu	151,245 (68)	1997
228	Lancaster JetHawks (Mariners)	78	62	.557	5	Rick Burleson	238,173 (69)	None
215	Rancho Cucamonga Quakes (Padres)	77	63	.550	6	Mike Basso	338,145 (66)	1994
190	Modesto A's (Athletics)	77	63	.550	6	Juan Navarrete	135,620 (67)	1984
191	Visalia Oaks (Athletics)	67	73	.479	16	Tony DeFrancesco	60,154 (65)	1978
156	Stockton Ports (Brewers)	66	74	.471	17	Bernie Moncallo	80,589 (65)	1992
56	Lake Elsinore Storm (Angels)	66	74	.471	17	Mario Mendoza	287,005 (69)	1996
150	San Bernardino Stampede (Dodgers)	55	85	.393	28	Hatcher/Vavra/Wallach	223,219 (68)	1995
221	Bakersfield Blaze (Giants)	49	91	.350	34	Frank Reberger	78,027 (69)	1989

NOTE: Team's individual batting and pitching statistics can be found on page indicated in lefthand column.

1998 California League Statistics

CLUB BATTING

	AVG	G	AB	R	H	2B	3B	HR	BB	SO	SB
Lancaster	.285	140	4882	909	1392	293	57	113	606	1004	180
High Desert	.276	140	4804	779	1327	260	64	124	491	1115	147
Visalia	.270	140	4746	739	1282	268	38	94	562	1136	147
Modesto	.268	140	4754	748	1276	271	46	90	598	1174	180
R. Cucamonga	.266	140	4790	764	1276	257	61	113	506	1129	88
Stockton	.266	140	4697	601	1250	251	24	58	360	789	103
San Jose	.261	140	4710	704	1230	245	31	105	490	1050	126
Lake Elsinore	.259	140	4760	719	1232	288	41	115	531	1128	107
Bakersfield	.250	140	4837	642	1210	238	27	93	465	1208	105
San Bernardino	.249	140	4675	516	1166	227	45	44	380	1034	164

CLUB PITCHING

	ERA	G	CG	SHO	SV	IP	H	R	ER	BB	SO
San Jose	3.58	140	4	11	40	1226	1174	567	488	396	1088
High Desert	3.84	140	3	7	34	1236	1243	676	527	430	1133
R. Cucamonga	3.94	140	0	6	38	1231	1231	661	539	513	1019
Modesto	4.03	140	3	11	35	1229	1256	692	551	499	1103
Stockton	4.16	140	9	8	29	1219	1187	686	563	593	1198
San Bernardino	4.33	140	2	9	36	1236	1233	735	594	535	1064
Visalia	4.40	140	3	7	31	1226	1328	746	599	438	1085
Lancaster	4.61	140	3	10	33	1230	1290	749	630	557	1181
Lake Elsinore	4.73	140	11	5	36	1230	1357	786	647	493	972
Bakersfield	4.75	140	3	3	28	1229	1342	823	649	526	924

CLUB FIELDING

	PCT	PO	A	E	DP
San Jose	.974	3677	1627	141	113
Lancaster	.967	3691	1513	175	108
Lake Elsinore	.966	3690	1617	186	139
R. Cuca.	.965	3693	1535	187	113
San Bern.	.964	3708	1461	192	121
Stockton	.961	3656	1382	202	110
Visalia	.959	3677	1583	225	133
High Desert	.958	3707	1558	229	118
Modesto	.958	3687	1524	227	117
Bakersfield	.955	3687	1512	247	132

INDIVIDUAL BATTING LEADERS

(Minimum 378 Plate Appearances)

	AVG	G	AB	R	H	2B	3B	HR	RBI	BB	SO	SB
Kingman, Brendan, Lancaster	.340	112	456	91	155	30	3	16	78	40	55	6
Patterson, Jarrod, High Desert	.335	131	492	89	165	34	9	18	102	66	97	9
Cruz, Cirilo, Lancaster	.311	134	546	86	170	40	1	7	104	56	122	2
Johnson, A.J., R. Cucamonga	.308	134	539	94	166	33	5	24	94	28	98	15
Barajas, Rod, High Desert	.303	113	442	67	134	26	0	23	81	25	81	1
McKinley, Dan, Bakersfield	.301	94	379	58	114	16	4	6	44	30	84	19
Matos, Julius, High Desert	.301	111	409	70	132	27	4	4	60	23	40	19
Allen, Luke, San Bernardino	.298	105	399	51	119	25	6	4	46	30	93	18
Regan, Jason, Lancaster	.298	124	416	105	124	26	6	19	82	106	123	9
Ruscin, Tom, Visalia	.296	101	388	70	115	27	1	14	74	33	62	1

INDIVIDUAL PITCHING LEADERS

(Minimum 112 Innings)

	W	L	ERA	G	GS	CG	SV	IP	H	R	ER	BB	SO
Patterson, John, High Desert	8	7	2.83	25	25	0	0	127	102	54	40	42	148
Penny, Brad, High Desert	14	5	2.96	28	28	1	0	164	138	65	54	35	207
Manwiller, Tim, Modesto	13	6	3.17	30	21	1	1	156	150	69	55	46	129
Nathan, Joe, San Jose	8	6	3.32	22	22	0	0	122	100	51	45	48	118
Jensen, Ryan, Bakersfield	11	12	3.37	29	27	0	0	168	162	89	63	61	164
Bierbrodt, Nick, High Desert	8	7	3.40	24	23	1	0	130	122	66	49	64	88
Knoll, Brian, San Jose	7	7	3.45	42	6	1	3	115	135	47	44	21	109
Anderson, Jason, Modesto	9	4	3.46	28	24	1	0	146	147	67	56	53	110
Leyva, Julian, Modesto	11	7	3.60	28	21	1	1	138	156	70	55	25	92
Iddon, Brent, R. Cucamonga	7	4	3.63	32	19	0	1	139	149	67	56	40	110

ALL-STAR TEAM

C—Giuseppe Chiaramonte, San Jose. **1B**—Cirilo Cruz, Lancaster. **2B**—Adonis Harrison, Lancaster. **3B**—Jarrod Patterson, High Desert. **SS**—Julius Matos, High Desert. **OF**—Jeff DaVanon, Modesto; Juan Dilone, San Jose; A.J. Johnson, Rancho Cucamonga. **DH**—Brendan Kingman, Lancaster. **P**—Tim Manwiller, Modesto; Brad Penny, High Desert; Luke Prokopec, San Bernardino; Jim Stoops, San Jose.

Most Valuable Player—Brad Penny, High Desert. **Pitcher of the Year**—Brad Penny, High Desert. **Rookie of the Year**—Giuseppe Chiaramonte, San Jose. **Manager of the Year**—Don Wakamatsu, High Desert.

TOP 10 PROSPECTS

1. Brad Penny, rhp, High Desert; **2.** John Patterson, rhp, High Desert; **3.** Luke Prokopec, rhp, San Bernardino; **4.** Nathan Haynes, of, Modesto; **5.** Nate Bump, rhp, San Jose; **6.** Eric DuBose, lhp, Visalia; **7.** Joe Nathan, rhp, San Jose; **8.** Jose Garcia, rhp, Stockton; **9.** Jim Stoops, rhp, San Jose; **10.** Giuseppe Chiaramonte, c, San Jose.

DEPT. LEADERS

BATTING

G	Jon Macalutas, Stockton	138
AB	Cirilo Cruz, Lancaster	546
R	Jason Regan, Lancaster	105
H	Cirilo Cruz, Lancaster	170
TB	A.J. Johnson, RC	281
XBH	Adam Piatt, Modesto	63
2B	Cirilo Cruz, Lancaster	40
	Adam Piatt, Modesto	40
3B	John Adams, High Desert	11
	Brian McClure, RC	11
HR	Tim Flaherty, Bakersfield	24
	A.J. Johnson, RC	24
RBI	Adam Piatt, Modesto	107
SH	David Davalillo, Lake Elsinore	15
SF	Giuseppe Chiaramonte, San Jose	12
BB	Jason Regan, Lancaster	106
IBB	Josh Klimek, Stockton	7
HBP	Jon Macalutas, Stockton	18
SO	Tim Flaherty, Bakersfield	171
SB	Ramon Moreta, San Bernardino	46
CS	Ramon Moreta, San Bernardino	23
GIDP	Brendan Kingman, Lancaster	20
OB%	Jason Regan, Lancaster	.447
SL%	Jarrod Patterson, High Desert	.551

PITCHING

G	Matt Montgomery, SB	63
GS	Three tied at	28
CG	Allen Levrault, Stockton	4
ShO	Several tied at	1
GF	Matt Montgomery, SB	58
SV	Jim Stoops, San Jose	31
W	Brad Penny, High Desert	14
L	Paul Morse, San Bernardino	14
IP	Jose Garcia, Stockton	169
H	Mike Holmes, Visalia	192
R	Paul Morse, San Bernardino	110
ER	Paul Morse, San Bernardino	90
HR	Jared Jensen, Visalia	16
	Eric Knott, High Desert	16
HB	Four tied at	11
BB	Jose Garcia, Stockton	91
SO	Brad Penny, High Desert	207
WP	Nathan Rice, Bakersfield	21
BK	Bill Malloy, San Jose	8

FIELDING

C	AVG	Giuseppe Chiaramonte, SJ.	.990
	PO	Jeff Alfano, Stockton	872
	A	Jeff Alfano, Stockton	107
	E	Jeff Alfano, Stockton	22
	DP	Cody McKay, Modesto	8
	PB	Jason Dewey, Lake Elsinore	30
1B	AVG	Pete Paciorek, RC	.991
	PO	Pete Paciorek, RC	1198
	A	Nick Leach, SB	83
	E	Kevin Clark, High Desert	20
	DP	Pete Paciorek, RC	97
2B	AVG	David Davalillo, LE	.976
	PO	Brian McClure, RC	249
	A	Travis Young, San Jose	404
	E	Dee Jenkins, Stock.-Vis.	20
		Junior Spivey, High Desert	20
	DP	Travis Young, San Jose	80
3B	AVG	Tony Zuniga, San Jose	.942
	PO	Ricky Bell, San Bernardino	76
	A	Ricky Bell, San Bernardino	270
	E	Adam Piatt, Modesto	32
	DP	Ricky Bell, San Bernardino	22
SS	AVG	Carlos Mendoza, San Jose.	.951
	PO	Nelson Castro, LE	185
		Julius Matos, High Desert	185
	A	Nelson Castro, LE	372
	E	Cesarin Carmona, RC	41
	DP	Nelson Castro, LE	71
OF	AVG	Gus Kennedy, RC	.991
	PO	Ramon Moreta, SB	313
	A	Kevin Ham, Lake Elsinore	19
	E	Nathan Haynes, Modesto	14
		Luis Tinoco, Lancaster	14
	DP	Kevin Ham, Lake Elsinore	4
		A.J. Johnson, RC	4

CAROLINA LEAGUE

Blue Rocks capture third Mills cup trophy in six years

BY EVAN JONES

Changing managers in the middle of a season is usually a sign of a struggling club.

But for the 1998 Wilmington Blue Rocks, the switch at the top was only a slight bump on the road to the club's third Mills Cup championship in six years. Darrell Evans, who guided the Blue Rocks to a first-half Northern Division flag and a 52-39 record, was fired by the Royals organization in July for "philosophical differences," according to farm director Bob Hegman.

RODGER WOOD

Joe Crede
CL MVP

Under new manager Brian Poldberg, the Rocks didn't miss a beat. Behind a strong pitching staff, led by righthander Aaron Lineweaver, and timely hitting, Wilmington won the division's second-half pennant and advanced directly to the finals.

There, the Blue Rocks beat Southern Division champ Winston-Salem—which also won both halves of its division—in four games. Emiliano Escandon hit a bases-loaded single in the bottom of the ninth in Game Four to give the title to Wilmington.

That finish typified the whole Wilmington season.

"During games, we might be down early, but we don't panic," Poldberg said during his team's August pennant run. "They know they will be in the game late, but nobody gets excited when they're down because they know something will happen."

Interestingly, the postseason hero for Wilmington wasn't Lineweaver, or hitters like Dermal Brown and Jose Cepeda. The series MVP was catcher Paul Phillips, who was promoted to the Blue Rocks from short-season Spokane the last weekend of the regular season. Phillips hit .357 for the series.

While the Blue Rocks were racing toward another title, most eyes in the league were focused on Winston-Salem's Joe Crede, the league's MVP.

STANDINGS: SPLIT SEASON

FIRST HALF

NORTH	W	L	PCT	GB
Wilmington	40	30	.571	—
Lynchburg	36	34	.514	4
Frederick	35	35	.500	5
Prince William	29	40	.420	10½
SOUTH	**W**	**L**	**PCT**	**GB**
Win.-Salem	41	28	.594	—
Kinston	36	34	.514	5½
Danville	31	39	.443	10½
Salem	31	39	.443	10½

SECOND HALF

NORTH	W	L	PCT	GB
Wilmington	46	24	.657	—
Prince William	43	27	.614	3
Lynchburg	33	37	.471	13
Frederick	29	41	.414	17
SOUTH	**W**	**L**	**PCT**	**GB**
Win.-Salem	38	32	.543	—
Kinston	33	37	.471	5
Salem	31	39	.443	7
Danville	27	43	.386	11

PLAYOFFS—Finals: Wilmington defeated Winston-Salem 3-1 in best-of-5 series.

For most of the second half, Crede had a serious shot at becoming the league's first triple-crown winner since Winston-Salem's Ray Jablonski in 1951. Crede ended up leading the league in both batting (.315) and RBIs (88), but he was passed in the final week in home runs by both Kinston's Mike Glavine and Prince William's Jose Leon.

On the mound, 19-year-old Prince William lefthander Rick Ankiel proved he was worth the $2.5 million signing bonus the Cardinals gave him after the 1997 draft. The league's pitcher of the year went 9-6 with a 2.79 ERA and struck out a Prince William team record 181, even after making seven starts in the Class A Midwest League. The league ERA title went to Salem's Chandler Martin, who finished at 2.48.

Pitching was supposed to be the main strength of the Danville 97s. But Danville's one-year return to the CL was underwhelming. Top prospects Rob Bell and Jason Marquis continued to slowly develop. While Bell (7-9, 3.28) led the league in strikeouts with 197, Marquis (2-12, 4.87) dropped his first 10 decisions.

The 97s, who operated in Durham, N.C., in 1997 but left to facilitate that city's move to Triple-A, were a transitional team playing while Myrtle Beach, S.C., built its new stadium for the Braves' CL affiliate. The team finished with a league-worst 58-82 record and was also a box-office bust, drawing a league-low 1,100 fans per game while sharing its ballpark with the Danville Braves of the Rookie-level Appalachian League.

STANDINGS: OVERALL

Page		W	L	PCT	GB	Manager(s)	Attendance/Dates	Last Penn.
143	Wilmington Blue Rocks (Royals)	86	54	.614	—	Evans/K. Long/Poldberg	320,540 (67)	1998
90	Winston-Salem Warthogs (White Sox)	79	60	.568	6½	Chris Cron	159,460 (68)	1993
209	Prince William Cannons (Cardinals)	72	67	.518	13½	Joe Cunningham	220,145 (64)	1989
110	Kinston Indians (Indians)	69	71	.493	17	Max Oliveras	143,309 (66)	1995
203	Lynchburg Hillcats (Pirates)	69	71	.493	17	Jeff Richardson/Jeff Livesey	113,145 (68)	1997
77	Frederick Keys (Orioles)	64	76	.457	22	Tommy Shields	301,760 (66)	1990
116	Salem Avalanche (Rockies)	62	78	.443	24	Jay Loviglio	189,069 (68)	1987
70	Danville 97s (Braves)	58	82	.414	28	Paul Runge	74,737 (66)	1967

NOTE: Team's individual batting and pitching statistics can be found on page indicated in lefthand column.

1998 Carolina League Statistics

CLUB BATTING

	AVG	G	AB	R	H	2B	3B	HR	BB	SO	SB
Prince William	.269	139	4659	651	1255	264	37	87	343	1126	153
Winston-Salem	.267	139	4645	691	1240	264	47	107	417	1061	141
Lynchburg	.262	140	4643	607	1216	259	35	103	412	1107	126
Salem	.260	140	4624	616	1202	243	29	79	396	933	187
Wilmington	.257	140	4557	618	1169	258	28	72	543	979	171
Frederick	.249	140	4574	586	1138	221	21	97	452	960	151
Kinston	.227	140	4462	570	1012	210	31	98	496	1124	121
Danville	.227	140	4595	452	1041	193	26	73	303	1095	114

CLUB PITCHING

	ERA	G	CG	SHO	SV	IP	H	R	ER	BB	SO
Wilmington	2.97	140	11	16	39	1240	1076	491	409	405	1085
Kinston	3.43	140	6	5	42	1209	1107	556	461	401	1045
Danville	3.51	140	6	10	37	1237	1165	586	482	488	1190
Lynchburg	3.64	140	9	12	44	1219	1207	602	493	368	1056
Winston-Salem	3.72	139	9	8	29	1218	1151	609	503	411	1057
Frederick	3.81	140	8	10	37	1217	1221	634	515	419	981
Prince William	3.86	139	4	8	36	1204	1143	625	517	380	952
Salem	4.45	140	11	5	30	1215	1203	688	600	490	1019

CLUB FIELDING

	PCT	PO	A	E	DP
Salem	.972	3644	1541	147	103
Kinston	.972	3628	1435	144	111
Prince William	.969	3612	1519	162	112
Winston-Salem	.969	3654	1469	164	116
Wilmington	.968	3719	1576	177	130
Frederick	.967	3652	1509	177	137
Danville	.967	3710	1376	175	106
Lynchburg	.967	3658	1478	178	117

INDIVIDUAL BATTING LEADERS

(Minimum 378 Plate Appearances)

	AVG	G	AB	R	H	2B	3B	HR	RBI	BB	SO	SB
Crede, Joe, Winston-Salem	.315	137	492	92	155	32	3	20	88	53	98	9
Bair, Rod, Salem	.299	114	425	62	127	42	5	8	60	24	64	12
Walker, Morgan, Lynchburg	.298	105	373	46	111	24	0	14	68	22	92	1
Saturria, Luis, Prince William	.294	129	462	70	136	25	9	12	73	28	104	20
May, Freddy, Lynchburg	.292	126	466	64	136	23	4	5	42	51	112	26
Leon, Jose, Prince William	.291	124	436	77	127	31	3	21	74	53	137	5
Farley, Cordell, Pr. William	.291	134	546	92	159	28	11	11	59	27	145	50
Barthol, Blake, Salem	.290	122	441	50	128	37	2	11	68	46	94	5
Heintz, Chris, Win.-Salem	.289	130	508	66	147	21	4	8	79	31	87	10
Butler, Brent, Prince William	.286	126	475	63	136	27	2	11	76	39	74	3

INDIVIDUAL PITCHING LEADERS

(Minimum 112 Innings)

	W	L	ERA	G	GS	CG	SV	IP	H	R	ER	BB	SO
Martin, Chandler, Salem	12	7	2.48	24	24	7	0	160	136	54	44	43	104
Porzio, Mike, Danville/Salem	5	5	2.58	33	18	1	2	139	114	54	40	42	141
France, Aaron, Lynchburg	6	5	2.72	26	20	0	0	129	99	51	39	45	110
Lineweaver, Aaron, Wilmington	13	5	2.79	26	26	5	0	168	136	62	52	54	116
Ankiel, Rick, Prince William	9	6	2.79	21	21	1	0	126	91	46	39	38	181
Bacsik, Mike, Kinston	10	9	2.88	27	27	1	0	166	147	64	53	37	128
McConnell, Sam, Lynchburg	8	5	2.90	19	19	3	0	121	118	48	39	20	80
McGlinchy, Kevin, Danville	9	8	2.91	22	22	1	0	142	122	55	46	29	129
Durbin, Chad, Wilmington	10	7	2.93	26	26	0	0	148	126	57	48	59	162
Thorn, Todd, Wilmington	9	8	3.13	26	24	4	0	149	128	60	52	28	103

ALL-STAR TEAM

C—Blake Barthol, Salem. **1B**—Chris Heintz, Winston-Salem. **2B**—Emiliano Escandon, Wilmington. **3B**—Joe Crede, Winston-Salem. **SS**—Brent Butler, Prince William. **OF**—Rod Bair, Salem; Cordell Farley, Prince William; Luis Saturria, Prince William. **DH**—Jose Leon, Prince William. **Util**—Dan Olson, Winston-Salem; Juan Sosa, Salem. **SP**—Rick Ankiel, Prince William. **RP**—David Riske, Kinston.

Most Valuable Player—Joe Crede, Winston-Salem. **Manager of the Year**—Chris Cron, Winston-Salem.

TOP 10 PROSPECTS

1. Rick Ankiel, lhp, Prince William; **2.** Joe Crede, 3b, Winston-Salem; **3.** Jerry Hairston, 2b, Frederick; **4.** Rob Bell, rhp, Danville; **5.** Jason Marquis, rhp, Danville; **6.** Brent Butler, ss, Prince William; **7.** Carlos Beltran, of, Wilmington; **8.** Kevin Haverbusch, 3b-ss, Lynchburg; **9.** Orber Moreno, rhp, Wilmington; **10.** Fernando Lunar, c, Danville.

DEPT. LEADERS

BATTING

G	Joe Crede, Winston-Salem	137
AB	Cordell Farley, Prince William	546
R	Joe Crede, Winston-Salem	92
	Cordell Farley, Prince William	92
H	Cordell Farley, Prince William	159
TB	Joe Crede, Winston-Salem	253
XBH	Dan Olson, Winston-Salem	56
2B	Rod Bair, Salem	42
3B	Juan Sosa, Salem	12
HR	Mike Glavine, Kinston	22
RBI	Joe Crede, Winston-Salem	88
SH	Brett Taft, Wilmington	17
SF	Joe Crede, Winston-Salem	11
BB	Emiliano Escandon, Wilm.	74
IBB	Five tied at	5
HBP	Corey Pointer, Lynchburg	17
SO	Corey Pointer, Lynchburg	177
SB	Juan Sosa, Salem	64
CS	Three tied at	19
GIDP	Chris Heintz, Winston-Salem	17
OB%	Mike Huelsmann, Kinston	.392
SL%	Jose Leon, Prince William	.521

PITCHING

G	Jose DeLeon, Prince William	57
GS	Three tied at	28
CG	Chandler Martin, Salem	7
ShO	Paul Ah Yat, Lynchburg	3
GF	David Lee, Salem	52
SV	David Riske, Kinston	33
W	Four tied at	13
L	Doug Walls, Salem	13
IP	Rob Bell, Danville	178
H	Luis Colmenares, Salem	187
R	Luis Colmenares, Salem	96
ER	Luis Colmenares, Salem	80
HR	Mike Bacsik, Kinston	17
HB	Jason Lakman, Winston-Salem	17
BB	Dwayne Jacobs, Danville	80
SO	Rob Bell, Danville	197
WP	Dwayne Jacobs, Danville	19
BK	Pat Daneker, Winston-Salem	4

FIELDING

C	AVG	Josh Paul, Win.-Salem	.997
	PO	Josh Paul, Win.-Salem	818
	A	Josh Paul, Win.-Salem	118
	E	Yamid Haad, Lynchburg	12
	DP	Fernando Lunar, Danville	9
	PB	Chip Alley, Frederick	22
1B	AVG	Mike Glavine, Kinston	.993
	PO	Brian Anthony, Salem	1010
	A	Brian Anthony, Salem	98
	E	Jim Scharrer, Danville	17
	DP	Billy Deck, Pr. William	85
2B	AVG	Liu Rodriguez, W-S	.986
	PO	Doug Livingston, Salem	266
	A	Doug Livingston, Salem	374
	E	Glenn Williams, Danville	26
	DP	Carlos Casimiro, Frederick	75
3B	AVG	Mike Hessman, Danville	.934
	PO	Joe Crede, Win.-Salem	100
	A	Joe Crede, Win.-Salem	290
	E	Joe Crede, Win.-Salem	30
	DP	Jose Leon, Prince William	24
SS	AVG	John Dorman, Kinston	.963
	PO	Juan Sosa, Salem	196
	A	Brett Taft, Wilmington	348
	E	Jason Dellaero, Win.-Salem	46
	DP	Brett Taft, Wilmington	64
OF	AVG	Todd Hogan, Pr. William	.993
	PO	Tyrone Pendergrass, Dan.	300
	A	Cordell Farley, Pr. William	13
		Jason Ross, Danville	13
	E	Luis Saturria, Pr. William	15
	DP	Five tied at	3

FLORIDA STATE LEAGUE

Korean Seo carries St. Lucie to postseason glory

BY SEAN KERNAN

The 1998 Florida State League championship series came down to one game between the Tampa Yankees and St. Lucie Mets. The Yankees had to have one thing in mind when they saw who was pitching Game Five for St. Lucie: Say it ain't Seo.

Jae Weong Seo fired 7⅔ hitless innings against the rival Yankees, striking out 12 batters, to lead the Mets to a 5-1 victory in the deciding game of the best-of-5 series. The Yankees managed just one hit, a scratch single up the middle by first baseman Nick Johnson off reliever Eric Cammack, who held on for his fourth save in St. Lucie's five postseason victories.

Nick Johnson
Top position prospect

Seo, a 21-year-old Korean righthander, didn't allow an earned run in 16 innings of postseason work. He allowed only one hit and four walks while registering 20 strikeouts in his two starts.

The Mets, who were a wild-card entry, won 2-1 in 16 innings in Game One and 4-2 in Game Two before the Yankees came back with 4-1 and 8-2 triumphs to tie the final series 2-2.

The season might best be remembered for all the home runs in the normally pitching dominated FSL. Three teams–Tampa, the Dunedin Blue Jays and Daytona Cubs–topped the previous record for home runs by a team (112 by the Lakeland Tigers in 1997).

Charlotte first baseman Shawn Gallagher, who hit for the cycle April 20 against Lakeland, made a run at the FSL triple crown, leading the league with 26 homers and 121 RBIs. But his .308 average was ninth, well behind the .350 mark of the Blue Jays' Casey Blake.

Two of Tampa's players drew rave reviews from league managers. Johnson (.317-17-58) was considered the league's top position prospect, while righthander Ryan Bradley was the top overall prospect. Bradley, a first-round pick in 1997, threw the league's only 1998 no-hitter in an 8-0 victory over Lakeland before moving on to Double-A Norwich. Bradley worked his way to the big leagues by the end of the year.

Brevard County suffered through a batting slump that saw the team get one-hit four times within the span of a month. Clearwater's Tom Jacquez was the first to shut the Manatees down. He was followed in turn by Dunedin's Ernie Delgado, St. Lucie's Ken Pumphrey and Sarasota's Andy Hazlett. The Manatees' .234 team batting average was far and away the worst in the league.

Kissimmee's Derek Root and Sarasota's Matt Kinney also threw one-hitters.

STANDINGS: SPLIT SEASON

FIRST HALF

EAST	W	L	PCT	GB
Jupiter	40	30	.571	—
St. Lucie	36	33	.522	3½
Daytona	35	35	.500	5
Kissimmee	30	40	.429	10
Vero Beach	29	41	.414	11
Brevard County	18	52	.257	22
WEST	**W**	**L**	**PCT**	**GB**
Charlotte	46	23	.667	—
Dunedin	43	27	.614	3½
Clearwater	42	28	.600	4½
Sarasota	38	31	.551	8
Lakeland	38	32	.543	8½
St. Petersburg	37	33	.529	9½
Fort Myers	30	39	.435	16
Tampa	26	44	.371	20½

SECOND HALF

EAST	W	L	PCT	GB
Jupiter	40	30	.571	—
St. Lucie	34	33	.507	4½
Kissimmee	34	35	.493	5½
Daytona	32	38	.457	8
Vero Beach	29	40	.420	10½
Brevard County	25	45	.357	15
WEST	**W**	**L**	**PCT**	**GB**
Tampa	46	23	.667	—
Clearwater	40	30	.571	6½
Sarasota	38	30	.559	7½
Dunedin	39	31	.557	7½
Charlotte	36	33	.522	10
Fort Myers	35	34	.507	11
Lakeland	29	40	.420	17
St. Petersburg	27	42	.391	19

PLAYOFFS—Semifinals: St. Lucie defeated Jupiter 2-0 and Tampa defeated Charlotte 2-0 in best-of-3 series. **Finals:** St. Lucie defeated Tampa 3-2 in best-of-5 series.

STANDINGS: OVERALL

Page		W	L	PCT	GB	Manager	Attendance/Dates	Last Penn.
242	Charlotte Rangers (Rangers)	82	56	.594	—	James Byrd	43,659 (66)	1989
196	Clearwater Phillies (Phillies)	82	58	.586	1	Bill Dancy	73,300 (67)	1993
249	Dunedin Blue Jays (Blue Jays)	82	58	.586	1	Rocket Wheeler	60,485 (69)	None
169	Jupiter Hammerheads (Expos)	80	60	.571	3	Doug Sisson	94,155 (69)	1991
84	Sarasota Red Sox (Red Sox)	76	61	.555	5½	Bob Geren	43,219 (67)	1963
176	Tampa Yankees (Yankees)	72	67	.518	10½	Lee Mazzilli	110,341 (68)	1994
183	St. Lucie Mets (Mets)	70	66	.515	11	Howie Freiling	37,189 (62)	1998
122	Lakeland Tigers (Tigers)	67	72	.482	15½	Mark Meleski	35,693 (68)	1992
97	Daytona Cubs (Cubs)	67	73	.479	16	Steve Roadcap	74,082 (63)	1995
162	Fort Myers Miracle (Twins)	65	73	.471	17	Mike Boulanger	107,110 (69)	1985
136	Kissimmee Cobras (Astros)	64	75	.460	18½	Manny Acta	41,941 (68)	None
234	St. Petersburg Devil Rays (Devil Rays)	64	75	.460	18½	Roy Silver	87,181 (69)	1997
151	Vero Beach Dodgers (Dodgers)	58	81	.417	24½	John Shoemaker	50,094 (62)	1990
129	Brevard County Manatees (Marlins)	43	97	.307	40	Rick Renteria	107,546 (67)	None

NOTE: Team's individual batting and pitching statistics can be found on page indicated in lefthand column.

1998 Florida State League Statistics

CLUB BATTING

	AVG	G	AB	R	H	2B	3B	HR	BB	SO	SB
Dunedin	.284	140	4797	763	1364	291	23	125	449	1082	162
Daytona	.281	140	4851	830	1361	240	43	119	540	1000	167
Charlotte	.277	138	4699	800	1303	262	41	110	518	915	271
Fort Myers	.273	139	4840	704	1321	217	27	94	480	863	222
Clearwater	.273	140	4829	758	1317	250	47	86	481	803	163
Tampa	.272	139	4760	712	1297	243	28	125	455	1009	128
St. Petersburg	.269	139	4827	629	1297	222	31	70	463	857	118
Kissimmee	.268	139	4720	679	1265	226	39	96	467	815	170
Lakeland	.267	139	4767	717	1271	224	34	101	481	960	145
Sarasota	.264	137	4607	711	1217	237	33	95	523	1008	164
St. Lucie	.254	137	4593	623	1168	211	30	91	394	977	147
Vero Beach	.252	139	4635	573	1167	196	28	98	465	967	134
Jupiter	.250	140	4676	638	1170	239	19	86	441	968	162
Brevard County	.234	140	4582	484	1073	150	33	61	436	969	156

CLUB PITCHING

	ERA	G	CG	SHO	SV	IP	H	R	ER	BB	SO
Jupiter	3.34	140	5	11	35	1238	1184	557	460	379	869
Charlotte	3.40	138	6	6	54	1221	1154	582	462	440	965
Dunedin	3.81	140	7	12	43	1232	1197	647	522	531	1074
St. Lucie	3.84	137	1	9	34	1207	1178	623	515	435	898
Clearwater	3.92	140	5	5	43	1254	1383	643	546	339	854
Tampa	4.10	139	6	9	32	1224	1229	725	557	567	1064
Lakeland	4.16	139	9	5	36	1215	1259	707	562	501	883
Kissimmee	4.19	139	8	7	29	1212	1321	698	564	482	889
Fort Myers	4.21	139	3	3	28	1240	1363	735	580	508	949
Sarasota	4.24	137	16	11	37	1194	1199	683	563	457	964
St. Petersburg	4.28	139	3	6	32	1236	1259	708	588	423	1019
Daytona	4.50	140	6	1	28	1219	1328	751	610	400	1004
Brevard County	4.64	140	11	8	18	1200	1309	765	618	532	814
Vero Beach	4.96	139	6	5	26	1201	1228	794	662	539	947

CLUB FIELDING

	PCT	PO	A	E	DP		PCT	PO	A	E	DP
Clearwater	.971	3762	1686	161	136	Brevard	.964	3599	1441	186	131
Jupiter	.969	3714	1645	171	127	St. Petersburg	.964	3709	1369	191	93
St. Lucie	.969	3621	1623	170	131	Kissimmee	.962	3635	1506	202	121
Charlotte	.967	3664	1521	175	116	Vero Beach	.962	3602	1443	202	100
Dunedin	.966	3697	1516	182	133	Lakeland	.961	3646	1582	213	114
Fort Myers	.965	3719	1664	193	140	Daytona	.956	3650	1480	234	114
Sarasota	.965	3583	1399	181	95	Tampa	.956	3671	1461	236	106

INDIVIDUAL BATTING LEADERS

(Minimum 378 Plate Appearances)

	AVG	G	AB	R	H	2B	3B	HR	RBI	BB	SO	SB
Blake, Casey, Dunedin	.350	88	340	62	119	28	3	11	65	30	81	9
Zuleta, Julio, Daytona	.344	94	366	69	126	25	1	16	86	35	59	6
Sanchez, Alex, St. Pete.	.330	128	545	77	180	17	9	1	50	31	70	66
Tucci, Pete, Dunedin	.329	92	356	72	117	30	3	23	76	29	97	8
Abernathy, Brent, Dunedin	.328	124	485	85	159	36	1	3	65	44	38	35
Johnson, Nick, Tampa	.317	92	303	69	96	14	1	17	58	68	76	1
Peterman, Tommy, Fort Myers	.312	135	519	71	162	36	2	20	110	63	86	2
Lawrence, Joe, Dunedin	.308	125	454	102	140	31	6	11	44	105	88	15
Gallagher, Shawn, Charlotte	.308	137	520	111	160	37	4	26	121	66	116	18
Eckstein, David, Sarasota	.306	135	503	99	154	29	4	3	58	87	51	45

INDIVIDUAL PITCHING LEADERS

(Minimum 112 Innings)

	W	L	ERA	G	GS	CG	SV	IP	H	R	ER	BB	SO
Rutherford, Mark, Clearwater	8	5	2.65	18	18	0	0	119	94	40	35	20	71
Martinez, Jose, Charlotte	7	5	2.77	19	19	2	0	124	120	55	38	28	86
Armas, Tony, Jupiter	12	8	2.88	27	27	1	0	153	140	63	49	59	136
Cames, Aaron, Brevard	5	10	3.12	27	25	1	0	153	134	73	53	59	161
Pumphrey, Ken, St. Lucie	10	6	3.16	25	25	1	0	142	126	66	50	57	99
Hazlett, Andy, Sarasota	11	7	3.19	30	22	4	1	161	154	76	57	25	135
Davis, Doug, Charlotte	11	7	3.24	27	27	1	0	155	129	69	56	74	173
Westbrook, Jake, Jupiter	11	6	3.26	27	27	2	0	171	169	70	62	60	79

ALL-STAR TEAM

C—Chad Moeller, Fort Myers; Victor Valencia, Tampa. **1B**—Shawn Gallagher, Charlotte. **2B**—Brent Abernathy, Dunedin. **3B**—Casey Blake, Dunedin. **SS**—Kelly Dransfeldt, Charlotte. **OF**—Alex Sanchez, St. Petersburg; Pete Tucci, Dunedin; Mike Zywica, Charlotte. **DH**—Tommy Peterman, Fort Myers. **Util**—David Eckstein, Sarasota; Julio Ramirez, Brevard County. **LHP**—Doug Davis, Charlotte. **RHP**—Billy Koch, Dunedin; Ken Pumphrey, St. Lucie; Mark Rutherford, Clearwater. **RP**—R.A. Dickey, Charlotte; Kyle Kawabata, Clearwater.

Most Valuable Player—Shawn Gallagher, Charlotte. **Manager of the Year**—Doug Sisson, Jupiter.

TOP 10 PROSPECTS

1. Ryan Bradley, rhp, Tampa; **2.** Matt Anderson, rhp, Lakeland; **3.** Nick Johnson, 1b, Tampa; **4.** Billy Koch, rhp, Dunedin; **5.** Julio Ramirez, of, Brevard County; **6.** Alex Sanchez, of, St. Petersburg; **7.** Pat Burrell, 1b, Clearwater; **8.** Matt White, rhp, St. Petersburg; **9.** Tony Armas, rhp, Jupiter; **10.** Pete Tucci, of, Dunedin.

DEPT. LEADERS

BATTING

G	Gary Burnham, Clearwater	139
AB	Julio Ramirez, Brevard County	559
R	Shawn Gallagher, Charlotte	111
H	Alex Sanchez, St. Petersburg	180
TB	Shawn Gallagher, Charlotte	283
XBH	Shawn Gallagher, Charlotte	67
2B	Shawn Gallagher, Charlotte	37
3B	Julio Lugo, Kissimmee	14
HR	Shawn Gallagher, Charlotte	26
RBI	Shawn Gallagher, Charlotte	121
SH	Cleatus Davidson, Fort Myers	13
SF	Alex Sanchez, St. Petersburg	12
BB	Joe Lawrence, Dunedin	105
IBB	Tommy Peterman, Fort Myers	13
HBP	David Eckstein, Sarasota	22
SO	Chris Schwab, Jupiter	175
SB	Anthony Felston, Fort Myers	86
CS	Alex Sanchez, St. Petersburg	33
GIDP	Juan Espinal, Sarasota	21
OB%	Nick Johnson, Tampa	.466
SL%	Pete Tucci, Dunedin	.624

PITCHING

G	Chris Garza, Fort Myers	58
GS	Five tied at	28
CG	Josh Garrett, Sarasota	5
	Sun Kim, Sarasota	5
ShO	Four tied at	2
GF	R.A. Dickey, Charlotte	54
SV	R.A. Dickey, Charlotte	38
W	Dan DeYoung, Char./Brevard	14
	Billy Koch, Dunedin	14
L	Marcos Castillo, Vero Beach	15
IP	Jeromie Robertson, Kissimmee	175
H	Tom Jacquez, Clearwater	215
R	Josh Garrett, Sarasota	108
ER	Josh Garrett, Sarasota	90
HR	James Manias, St. Petersburg	27
HB	John Nicholson, Jupiter	20
BB	Matt Kinney, Sarasota/FtM	93
SO	Doug Davis, Charlotte	173
WP	Matt Kinney, Sarasota/FtM	25
BK	Jeromie Robertson, Kissimmee	6
	Jae Weong Seo, St. Lucie	6

FIELDING

C	AVG	David Lindstrom, Lakeland	.993
	PO	Victor Valencia, Tampa	861
	A	David Lindstrom, Lakeland	96
	E	Victor Valencia, Tampa	19
	DP	Paul Chiaffredo, Dunedin	9
	PB	Brad Ramsey, Daytona	23
1B	AVG	Gary Burnham, Clearwater	.994
	PO	Tommy Peterman, FtM	1156
	A	Brian Becker, St. Pete.	101
	E	Shawn Gallagher, Charlotte	18
	DP	Tommy Peterman, FtM	117
2B	AVG	David Eckstein, Sarasota	.989
	PO	Cleatus Davidson, FtM	320
	A	Cleatus Davidson, FtM	403
	E	Jeff Venghaus, Brevard	28
	DP	Cleatus Davidson, FtM	98
3B	AVG	Mike Lamb, Charlotte	.931
	PO	Mike Lamb, Charlotte	98
	A	Mike Lamb, Charlotte	304
	E	Rusty McNamara, Clear.	43
	DP	Mike Lamb, Charlotte	19
SS	AVG	Jimmy Rollins, Clearwater	.952
	PO	Tomas de la Rosa, Jupiter	208
	A	Luis Rivas, Fort Myers	415
	E	Dennis Abreu, Daytona	56
	DP	Luis Rivas, Fort Myers	78
OF	AVG	Scott Sollman, Lakeland	.996
	PO	Julio Ramirez, Brevard	365
	A	Three tied at	17
	E	Corey Jenkins, Sarasota	12
		Alex Sanchez, St. Pete.	12
	DP	Jeremy Ware, Jupiter	6

MIDWEST LEAGUE

Whitecaps pick up where predecessors left off

BY BRANSON WRIGHT

The comparisons started during spring training. The pressure increased during the first few days of the regular season.

The West Michigan Whitecaps began 1998 with the task of replacing one of the best teams in recent minor league history. The 1997 Whitecaps set numerous individual and team records, including a 92-39 record–the best in the minor leagues that year.

The challenge of replacing their predecessors wasn't the only motivating factor for the Whitecaps. Most of the players were members of the '97 short-season Jamestown squad that suffered the loss of manager Dwight Lowry, who died of a heart attack during the second month of the season.

JOHN SPEAR

Alan Webb
Strikeout leader

"This entire season was dedicated to Dwight Lowry," said Whitecaps first baseman Mandy Jacomino.

The Whitecaps defeated the Rockford Cubbies three games to one in the best-of-5 Midwest League championship series, thus accomplishing what the '97 team couldn't do–bring home the title.

Pitching carried the Whitecaps all season, and the West Michigan staff got hot during the playoffs, compiling a 1.64 ERA in nine postseason games.

Lefthander Alan Webb was the club's go-to guy all year. Webb reeled off one-, two- and three-hit complete games during the regular season. He finished the season 10-7 with a 2.93 ERA and a league-leading 202 strikeouts.

But he was overshadowed by two more heralded lefties in the MWL. Peoria's Rick Ankiel, who stuck around for just seven starts, and Wisconsin's Ryan Anderson both made their professional debuts in the league. Anderson struck out 152 batters in just 111 innings and might have given Webb a run for the strikeout title had he not missed time with a sore elbow.

But the guy who stole the show in 1998 was Peoria shortstop Pablo Ozuna. The league's MVP led the Chiefs' offensive attack, scoring 122 runs and batting .357 while stealing 62 bases.

The circuit's leading power source was Beloit outfielder Bucky Jacobsen, who led the league with 27 home runs and 100 RBIs. He was a contender for the triple crown until his average dipped late in the season.

STANDINGS: SPLIT SEASON

FIRST HALF

EAST	W	L	PCT	GB
West Michigan	43	29	.597	—
Fort Wayne	41	31	.569	2
Lansing	37	35	.514	6
Michigan	36	36	.500	7
South Bend	21	51	.292	22
CENTRAL	**W**	**L**	**PCT**	**GB**
Wisconsin	39	30	.565	—
Kane County	36	36	.500	4½
Beloit	35	36	.493	5
Peoria	34	38	.472	6½
Rockford	32	39	.451	8
WEST	**W**	**L**	**PCT**	**GB**
Quad City	40	31	.563	—
Cedar Rapids	40	32	.556	½
Burlington	36	36	.500	4½
Clinton	30	40	.429	9½

SECOND HALF

EAST	W	L	PCT	GB
Michigan	43	25	.632	—
West Michigan	40	28	.588	3
Fort Wayne	38	30	.559	5
Lansing	34	34	.500	9
South Bend	19	49	.279	24
CENTRAL	**W**	**L**	**PCT**	**GB**
Rockford	39	29	.574	—
Peoria	38	30	.559	1
Wisconsin	33	35	.485	6
Kane County	33	35	.485	6
Beloit	29	39	.426	10
WEST	**W**	**L**	**PCT**	**GB**
Quad City	37	31	.544	—
Clinton	35	33	.515	2
Cedar Rapids	31	37	.456	6
Burlington	27	41	.397	10

PLAYOFFS—First Round: Clinton defeated Quad City 2-1, West Michigan defeated Michigan 2-1, Fort Wayne defeated Peoria 2-1 and Rockford defeated Wisconsin 2-1 in best-of-3 series. **Semifinals:** West Michigan defeated Clinton 2-0 and Rockford defeated Fort Wayne 2-0 in best-of-3 series. **Finals:** West Michigan defeated Rockford 3-1 in best-of-5 series.

STANDINGS: OVERALL

Page		W	L	PCT	GB	Manager	Attendance/Dates	Last Penn.
123	West Michigan Whitecaps (Tigers)	83	57	.593	—	Bruce Fields	500,083 (70)	1998
85	Michigan Battle Cats (Red Sox)	79	61	.564	4	Billy Gardner	107,137 (65)	None
163	Fort Wayne Wizards (Twins)	79	61	.564	4	Jose Marzan	214,702 (70)	None
137	Quad City River Bandits (Astros)	77	62	.554	5 ½	Mike Rojas	153,886 (64)	1990
229	Wisconsin Timber Rattlers (Mariners)	72	65	.526	9 ½	Gary Varsho	227,306 (68)	1984
210	Peoria Chiefs (Cardinals)	72	68	.514	11	Jeff Shireman	154,910 (66)	None
98	Rockford Cubbies (Cubs)	71	68	.511	11 ½	Ruben Amaro	75,600 (65)	None
144	Lansing Lugnuts (Royals)	71	69	.507	12	Bob Herold	485,815 (69)	1997
57	Cedar Rapids Kernels (Angels)	71	69	.507	12	Garry Templeton	128,742 (68)	1994
130	Kane County Cougars (Marlins)	69	71	.493	14	Juan Bustabad	481,352 (68)	None
216	Clinton LumberKings (Padres)	65	73	.471	17	Tom LeVasseur	44,401 (64)	1991
157	Beloit Snappers (Brewers)	64	75	.460	18 ½	Don Money	61,108 (65)	1995
104	Burlington Bees (Reds)	63	77	.450	20	Phillip Wellman	60,492 (67)	1977
63	South Bend Silver Hawks (Diamondbacks)	40	100	.286	43	Roly de Armas	196,793 (66)	1993

NOTE: Team's individual batting and pitching statistics can be found on page indicated in lefthand column.

1998 Midwest League Statistics

CLUB BATTING

	AVG	G	AB	R	H	2B	3B	HR	BB	SO	SB
Peoria	.274	140	4758	748	1302	247	35	82	435	992	162
Fort Wayne	.271	140	4734	742	1284	280	52	90	533	1101	117
Lansing	.261	140	4735	695	1237	247	63	89	496	989	207
Beloit	.261	139	4735	659	1236	232	18	93	482	1055	65
Michigan	.260	140	4720	685	1229	232	31	86	499	957	92
Kane County	.257	140	4602	644	1182	206	22	49	509	947	189
Wisconsin	.256	137	4602	640	1180	231	49	93	442	990	199
Rockford	.255	139	4588	637	1172	225	45	61	460	1112	203
Quad City	.253	139	4627	657	1172	230	30	92	412	992	197
West Michigan	.251	140	4705	660	1182	250	40	55	445	1078	188
Burlington	.248	140	4577	567	1137	208	34	77	423	1123	181
Clinton	.239	138	4495	592	1075	211	34	66	518	1036	194
Cedar Rapids	.238	140	4677	607	1112	216	24	87	493	1031	183
South Bend	.237	140	4599	537	1089	204	31	60	487	1148	93

CLUB PITCHING

	ERA	G	CG	SHO	SV	IP	H	R	ER	BB	SO
West Michigan	3.01	140	13	14	36	1236	1056	511	413	359	1177
Quad City	3.44	139	10	14	36	1223	1002	558	467	532	1057
Cedar Rapids	3.51	140	21	13	26	1242	1132	606	485	415	1033
Beloit	3.80	139	11	9	32	1221	1242	669	515	420	1041
Burlington	3.81	140	15	8	30	1206	1135	659	511	525	1059
Clinton	3.95	138	5	7	21	1199	1207	668	526	459	1020
Rockford	3.97	139	7	7	39	1210	1182	643	534	524	939
Kane County	3.98	140	6	11	31	1221	1220	662	540	440	1093
Michigan	3.98	140	2	7	46	1225	1243	631	542	463	1025
Wisconsin	3.98	137	1	5	34	1209	1156	642	535	578	1274
Fort Wayne	4.01	140	2	9	34	1227	1224	678	546	477	1027
Lansing	4.19	140	1	9	38	1234	1216	673	574	516	991
Peoria	4.30	140	3	3	37	1225	1222	715	585	513	896
South Bend	4.41	140	2	5	19	1195	1352	755	585	413	919

CLUB FIELDING

	PCT	PO	A	E	DP		PCT	PO	A	E	DP
Michigan	.970	3675	1415	160	109	Rockford	.965	3631	1596	192	135
Lansing	.968	3701	1544	171	132	Peoria	.963	3674	1680	203	145
Wisconsin	.968	3627	1366	163	98	Fort Wayne	.962	3680	1586	210	100
Quad City	.968	3670	1527	172	113	Clinton	.962	3596	1527	205	134
Cedar Rapids	.968	3720	1640	178	134	Burlington	.960	3618	1480	212	125
West Michigan	.967	3707	1559	177	125	Beloit	.957	3663	1531	234	106
Kane County	.966	3663	1508	183	108	South Bend	.952	3585	1619	263	104

INDIVIDUAL BATTING LEADERS

(Minimum 378 Plate Appearances)

	AVG	G	AB	R	H	2B	3B	HR	RBI	BB	SO	SB
Ozuna, Pablo, Peoria	.357	133	538	122	192	27	10	9	62	29	56	62
Hillenbrand, Shea, Michigan	.349	129	498	80	174	33	4	19	93	19	49	13
Erickson, Matt, Kane County	.324	124	441	83	143	32	2	4	64	72	62	17
Clark, Jermaine, Wisconsin	.324	123	448	81	145	24	13	6	55	57	64	40
Ryan, Mike, Fort Wayne	.318	113	412	68	131	24	6	9	72	44	92	7
Amrhein, Mike, Rockford	.317	121	457	61	145	34	1	9	87	30	47	7
Gload, Ross, Kane County	.313	132	501	77	157	41	3	12	92	58	84	7
Kim, David, Peoria	.308	127	463	75	143	38	2	13	92	53	77	3

INDIVIDUAL PITCHING LEADERS

(Minimum 112 Innings)

	W	L	ERA	G	GS	CG	SV	IP	H	R	ER	BB	SO
Childers, Jason, Beloit	8	6	1.92	34	14	1	0	117	104	48	25	22	110
Burnett, A.J., Kane County	10	4	1.97	20	20	0	0	119	74	27	26	45	186
Harriger, Mark, Cedar Rapids	8	4	2.23	16	16	3	0	117	86	37	29	38	105
Shearn, Tom, Quad City	7	7	2.25	21	21	2	0	120	88	38	30	52	93
Corey, Mark, Burlington	12	6	2.44	20	20	6	0	140	125	55	38	36	109
Fish, Steve, Cedar Rapids	10	4	2.47	30	14	3	0	128	111	52	35	28	121
Jerue, Tristan, Peoria	12	4	2.53	20	20	1	0	132	107	48	37	48	100
Guttormson, Rick, Clinton	10	7	2.60	30	25	0	2	159	155	66	46	41	141

ALL-STAR TEAM

C—Shea Hillenbrand, Michigan. **1B**—Ross Gload, Kane County. **2B**—Jermaine Clark, Wisconsin. **3B**—Matt Erickson, Kane County. **SS**—Pablo Ozuna, Peoria. **OF**—Quincy Foster, Kane County; Bucky Jacobsen, Beloit; Juan LeBron, Lansing; Rodney Lindsey, Clinton/West Michigan. **DH**—J.J. Thomas, Quad City. **RHP**—Tristan Jerue, Peoria. **LHP**—Ryan Anderson, Wisconsin. **RP**—Brian Partenheimer, Michigan; Gene Stechschulte, Peoria.

Most Valuable Player—Pablo Ozuna, Peoria. **Prospect of the Year**—Pablo Ozuna, Peoria. **Manager of the Year**—Billy Gardner, Michigan.

TOP 10 PROSPECTS

1. Pablo Ozuna, ss, Peoria; **2.** Rick Ankiel, lhp, Peoria; **3.** Ryan Anderson, lhp, Wisconsin; **4.** A.J. Burnett, rhp, Kane County; **5.** Michael Cuddyer, ss, Fort Wayne; **6.** Gil Meche, rhp, Wisconsin; **7.** Shea Hillenbrand, c, Michigan; **8.** Bucky Jacobsen, of, Beloit; **9.** Alan Webb, lhp, West Michigan; **10.** Juan LeBron, of, Lansing.

DEPT. LEADERS

BATTING

G	Barry Wesson, Quad City	138
AB	Raul Franco, Kane County	551
R	Pablo Ozuna, Peoria	122
H	Pablo Ozuna, Peoria	192
TB	Shea Hillenbrand, Michigan	272
XBH	Bucky Jacobsen, Beloit	59
2B	Ross Gload, Kane County	41
3B	Jermaine Clark, Wisconsin	13
HR	Bucky Jacobsen, Beloit	27
RBI	Bucky Jacobsen, Beloit	100
SH	Garret Osilka, Beloit	18
SF	DeWayne Wise, Burlington	9
BB	Bucky Jacobsen, Beloit	83
IBB	Ross Gload, Kane County	7
HBP	Alex Melconian, Kane County	28
SO	Benny Craig, Burlington	160
SB	Quincy Foster, Kane County	73
CS	Pablo Ozuna, Peoria	26
GIDP	Mike Amrhein, Rockford	20
OB%	Matt Erickson, Kane County	.436
SL%	Shea Hillenbrand, Michigan	.546

PITCHING

G	Joe Messman, Quad City	63
GS	Eric Ireland, Quad City	28
	Shane Loux, West Michigan	28
CG	Three tied at	6
ShO	Five tied at	2
GF	Gene Stechschulte, Peoria	51
SV	Gene Stechschulte, Peoria	33
W	Joe Thomas, Mich./Fort Wayne	15
L	Neal Arnold, Peoria	15
	Marc Van Wormer, South Bend	15
IP	Eric Ireland, Quad City	206
H	Shane Loux, West Michigan	184
R	Stephen Norris, Peoria	103
ER	Stephen Norris, Peoria	80
HR	Paul Stewart, Beloit	22
HB	Alan Webb, West Michigan	18
BB	Stephen Norris, Peoria	87
SO	Alan Webb, West Michigan	202
WP	Neal Arnold, Peoria	21
BK	Wilfredo Rodriguez, Quad City	9

FIELDING

C	**AVG**	Scott Maynard, Wisconsin	.996
	PO	Brandon Harper, Kane County	900
	A	Brian Moon, Beloit	113
	E	Brian Moon, Beloit	19
	DP	Brian Moon, Beloit	15
	PB	Shea Hillenbrand, Michigan	20
1B	**AVG**	Claudio Liverziani, Wisconsin	.996
	PO	Ariel Delgado, Cedar Rapids	1265
	A	Luke Quaccia, Peoria	97
	E	Antuan Bunkley, West Mich.	18
	DP	Luke Quaccia, Peoria	117
2B	**AVG**	Rob Macrory, Peoria	.973
	PO	Rob Macrory, Peoria	279
	A	Adam Leggett, CR	391
	E	Aaron Miles, Quad City	28
	DP	Rob Macrory, Peoria	97
3B	**AVG**	Derrick Bly, Rockford	.945
	PO	Mike Ryan, Fort Wayne	85
	A	Derrick Bly, Rockford	245
	E	Mike Ryan, Fort Wayne	32
	DP	Aaron Gentry, Peoria	20
SS	**AVG**	Steve Medrano, Lansing	.969
	PO	Jason Smith, Rockford	203
	A	Pablo Ozuna, Peoria	395
	E	Michael Cuddyer, Ft. Wayne	61
	DP	Pablo Ozuna, Peoria	80
		E.J. t'Hoen, Cedar Rapids	80
OF	**AVG**	Kyle Logan, Quad City	.993
	PO	Barry Wesson, Quad City	271
	A	Three tied at	15
	E	Abraham Nunez, South Bend	14
	DP	Brent Horsman, Clinton	4

SOUTH ATLANTIC LEAGUE

Capital City paces National Association with 90 wins

BY GENE SAPAKOFF

Talk about excitement. The Cape Fear Crocs opened 15-0, the best South Atlantic League start since the 1907 Charleston Gulls went 11-0. But by the end of the 1998 season the Crocs' torrid start was almost as distant a memory as the Gulls', because the Capital City Bombers stole the show.

Capital City finished the regular season as the only minor league team with 90 wins and went out in style by defeating Greensboro, two games to one, in the SAL championship series.

Alex Escobar
Top prospect

"To finally see it come to a culmination is really fantastic," said Capital City manager Doug Davis, who led a core group of the same players to the New York-Penn League title while at Pittsfield in 1997.

The Bombers were led by the SAL's top prospect, center fielder Alex Escobar, a native of Venezuela who blossomed in his third professional season. Escobar, 20, broke Butch Huskey's franchise record for home runs with 27, hit .310, stole 49 bases and drove in 91 runs.

With all that, he still finished 10 homers behind the league leader, Macon's Marcus Giles. The 5-foot-8, 180-pound second baseman slugged his way into the SAL all-star game, won the pregame home run contest and kept going into the second half. Giles hit 37 home runs, three short of the SAL record set by Russell Branyan of Columbus in 1996. Giles also hit .329.

Matt White, who signed a $10.2 million contract with the Devil Rays in 1996, proved his mettle with a mostly dominating first half at Charleston, S.C., including seven no-hit innings at Augusta.

Asheville righthander Josh Kalinowski (12-10, 3.92) pitched a no-hitter at Charleston, S.C., and struck out 17 batters in a game at Hickory. Delmarva righthander Matt Achilles threw the league's other no-hitter, in an April game against Hagerstown.

The SAL's Maryland teams were prospect-rich. Hagerstown had lefthander Clayton Andrews (10-7, 2.28) and righthander John Sneed (16-2, 2.56), plus outfielder Vernon Wells (.285-11-65). The Orioles' 1997 first-round picks, catcher Jayson Werth (.265-8-53) and outfielder Darnell McDonald (.261-6-44), played for Delmarva. But neither made the same impact as another '97 Orioles draft pick, lefthander Matt Riley, who fashioned a 1.19 ERA in 14 starts while striking out 136 in 83 innings.

STANDINGS: SPLIT SEASON

FIRST HALF

NORTH	W	L	PCT	GB
Hagerstown	44	26	.629	—
Cape Fear	43	27	.614	1
Delmarva	42	29	.592	2½
Charleston, W.Va.	25	44	.362	18½
CENTRAL	**W**	**L**	**PCT**	**GB**
Capital City	47	22	.681	—
Greensboro	37	33	.529	10½
Piedmont	36	34	.514	11½
Asheville	32	38	.457	15½
Charleston, S.C.	31	39	.443	16½
Hickory	25	44	.362	22
SOUTH	**W**	**L**	**PCT**	**GB**
Savannah	35	36	.493	—
Augusta	35	36	.493	—
Macon	30	40	.429	4½
Columbus	28	42	.400	6½

SECOND HALF

NORTH	W	L	PCT	GB
Delmarva	39	32	.549	—
Cape Fear	37	34	.521	2
Hagerstown	37	34	.521	2
Charleston, W.Va.	19	52	.268	20
CENTRAL	**W**	**L**	**PCT**	**GB**
Capital City	43	29	.597	—
Greensboro	42	30	.583	1
Piedmont	40	31	.563	2½
Asheville	39	31	.557	3
Charleston, S.C.	36	35	.507	6½
Hickory	31	40	.437	11½
SOUTH	**W**	**L**	**PCT**	**GB**
Macon	39	32	.549	—
Augusta	33	38	.465	6
Columbus	31	39	.443	7½
Savannah	31	40	.437	8

PLAYOFFS—First Round: Augusta defeated Macon 2-0, Hagerstown defeated Delmarva 2-0, Capital City defeated Piedmont 2-0 and Greensboro defeated Cape Fear 2-0 in best-of-3 series. **Semifinals:** Greensboro defeated Augusta 2-0 and Capital City defeated Hagerstown 2-1 in best-of-3 series. **Finals:** Capital City defeated Greensboro 2-1 in best-of-3 series.

STANDINGS: OVERALL

Page		W	L	PCT	GB	Manager	Attendance/Dates	Last Penn.
184	Capital City Bombers (Mets)	90	51	.638	—	Doug Davis	141,138 (67)	1998
250	Hagerstown Suns (Blue Jays)	81	60	.574	9	Marty Pevey	109,932 (60)	None
78	Delmarva Shorebirds (Orioles)	81	61	.570	9½	Dave Machemer	295,938 (70)	1997
170	Cape Fear Crocs (Expos)	80	61	.567	10	Luis Dorante	75,799 (68)	None
176	Greensboro Bats (Yankees)	79	63	.556	11½	Tom Nieto	160,465 (65)	1982
197	Piedmont Boll Weevils (Phillies)	76	65	.539	14	Ken Oberkfell	125,653 (69)	None
117	Asheville Tourists (Rockies)	71	69	.507	18½	Ron Gideon	148,638 (69)	1984
70	Macon Braves (Braves)	69	72	.489	21	Brian Snitker	120,009 (68)	None
203	Augusta GreenJackets (Pirates)	68	74	.479	22½	Marty Brown	162,509 (65)	1989
235	Charleston, S.C., Riverdogs (Devil Rays)	67	74	.475	23	Greg Mahlberg	234,840 (68)	None
243	Savannah Sand Gnats (Rangers)	66	76	.465	24½	Paul Carey	130,509 (66)	1996
111	Columbus Redstixx (Indians)	59	81	.421	30½	Eric Wedge	94,241 (66)	None
91	Hickory Crawdads (White Sox)	56	84	.400	33½	Mark Haley	193,258 (70)	None
104	Charleson, W.Va., Alley Cats (Reds)	44	96	.314	45½	Barry Lyons	91,219 (63)	1990

NOTE: Team's individual batting and pitching statistics can be found on page indicated in lefthand column.

1998 South Atlantic League Statistics

CLUB BATTING

	AVG	G	AB	R	H	2B	3B	HR	BB	SO	SB
Capital City	.273	141	4844	761	1324	239	36	124	448	1278	295
Piedmont	.273	141	4856	704	1324	243	27	66	484	949	146
Cape Fear	.272	141	4643	732	1261	199	37	68	451	991	201
Hagerstown	.269	141	4678	712	1258	233	22	120	476	936	124
Asheville	.266	140	4676	696	1242	242	21	111	427	1066	136
Hickory	.263	140	4817	614	1269	215	27	98	383	1080	156
Savannah	.260	142	4675	701	1215	198	50	111	451	1221	252
Delmarva	.258	142	4680	678	1207	217	45	74	432	1041	211
Macon	.258	141	4726	770	1217	245	25	173	494	1185	101
Columbus	.257	140	4718	708	1211	235	34	108	510	1148	133
Augusta	.256	142	4657	732	1190	236	37	95	540	1089	202
Charleston, S.C.	.249	141	4723	685	1177	220	18	95	492	1040	92
Greensboro	.244	142	4689	625	1144	214	22	122	458	1309	84
Charleston, W.Va.	.234	140	4497	515	1054	208	17	66	375	1124	143

CLUB PITCHING

	ERA	G	CG	SHO	SV	IP	H	R	ER	BB	SO
Hagerstown	3.25	141	9	15	28	1209	1067	567	437	438	1179
Capital City	3.47	141	5	7	45	1239	1130	619	478	468	1188
Greensboro	3.60	142	10	9	41	1243	1192	631	497	421	1228
Delmarva	3.74	142	5	9	46	1236	1160	598	513	505	1150
Piedmont	3.83	141	11	11	43	1247	1294	659	531	311	1060
Asheville	3.98	140	11	4	30	1218	1294	685	539	403	1146
Charleston, S.C.	4.04	141	3	9	29	1233	1242	657	553	391	1085
Augusta	4.15	142	5	5	33	1214	1150	707	560	520	1209
Cape Fear	4.17	141	6	10	29	1229	1202	658	569	431	911
Hickory	4.35	140	6	5	33	1247	1262	761	602	508	1065
Savannah	4.61	142	10	4	32	1219	1212	742	624	541	1068
Macon	4.62	141	3	3	32	1221	1246	814	627	558	1186
Charleston, W.Va.	4.84	140	15	3	19	1179	1378	769	634	433	868
Columbus	4.87	140	4	6	26	1208	1264	766	654	493	1114

CLUB FIELDING

	PCT	PO	A	E	DP		PCT	PO	A	E	DP
Delmarva	.970	3707	1519	159	131	Capital City	.961	3718	1587	216	136
Cape Fear	.968	3688	1587	175	87	Piedmont	.959	3740	1472	220	125
Columbus	.966	3623	1504	181	104	Savannah	.959	3656	1364	214	107
Greensboro	.965	3729	1491	189	106	Hickory	.958	3740	1637	235	118
Hagerstown	.965	3628	1486	186	124	Augusta	.958	3641	1397	223	103
Char., S.C.	.965	3699	1521	191	107	Char., W.Va.	.957	3537	1447	222	127
Asheville	.963	3653	1587	200	130	Macon	.946	3664	1282	284	89

INDIVIDUAL BATTING LEADERS

(Minimum 383 Plate Appearances)

	AVG	G	AB	R	H	2B	3B	HR	RBI	BB	SO	SB
Bruce, Maurice, Capital City	.341	126	516	81	176	24	4	15	74	41	107	45
Terrell, Jim, Hickory	.338	131	500	84	169	21	4	13	64	53	90	25
Giles, Marcus, Macon	.329	135	505	111	166	38	3	37	108	85	103	12
Hall, Toby, Charleston, S.C.	.321	105	377	59	121	25	1	6	50	39	32	3
Paz, Richard, Delmarva	.320	98	325	55	104	10	4	5	56	75	42	22
Hall, Noah, Cape Fear	.318	127	447	84	142	21	7	11	90	52	69	33
DeHaan, Kory, Augusta	.314	132	475	85	149	39	8	8	75	69	114	33
Escobar, Alex, Capital City	.310	112	416	90	129	23	5	27	91	54	133	49
Velazquez, Jose, Charleston, S.C.	.308	111	413	71	127	20	2	11	64	55	70	0
Pena, Jose, Savannah	.305	125	466	68	142	22	5	6	66	17	91	40

INDIVIDUAL PITCHING LEADERS

(Minimum 114 Innings)

	W	L	ERA	G	GS	CG	SV	IP	H	R	ER	BB	SO
Andrews, Clayton, Hagerstown	10	7	2.28	27	26	2	0	162	112	59	41	46	193
Reith, Brian, Greensboro	6	7	2.28	20	20	3	0	118	86	42	30	32	116
Belitz, Todd, Charleston, S.C.	6	4	2.42	21	21	0	0	130	99	44	35	48	123
Giron, Isabel, Hagerstown	10	9	2.49	21	21	4	0	126	110	57	35	27	129
Sneed, John, Hagerstown	16	2	2.56	27	27	2	0	162	123	59	46	58	210
Blank, Matt, Cape Fear	9	2	2.61	21	21	2	0	135	121	45	39	24	114
Flores, Randy, Greensboro	12	7	2.62	21	20	2	0	131	119	48	38	33	139
Spurgeon, Jay, Delmarva	11	3	2.64	27	20	0	0	136	112	49	40	48	103
Dougherty, Kevin, Capital City	15	2	2.74	20	20	1	0	135	112	51	41	50	107

ALL-STAR TEAM

C—Toby Hall, Charleston, S.C. **1B**—Matt Berger, Hickory. **2B**—Marcus Giles, Macon. **3B**—Maurice Bruce, Capital City. **SS**—Jersen Perez, Capital City. **OF**—Kory DeHaan, Augusta; Alex Escobar, Capital City; Noah Hall, Cape Fear. **DH**—Bobby Cripps, Hagerstown. **Util**—Jim Terrell, Hickory; Vernon Wells, Hagerstown. **RHP**—John Sneed, Hagerstown. **LHP**—Clayton Andrews, Hagerstown.

Most Valuable Player—Marcus Giles, Macon. **Most Valuable Pitcher**—Clayton Andrews, Hagerstown. **Manager of the Year**—Doug Davis, Capital City.

TOP 10 PROSPECTS

1. Alex Escobar, of, Capital City; **2.** Matt White, rhp, Charleston, S.C.; **3.** Matt Riley, lhp, Delmarva; **4.** Jayson Werth, c, Delmarva; **5.** Clayton Andrews, lhp, Hagerstown; **6.** John Sneed, rhp, Hagerstown; **7.** Milton Bradley, of, Cape Fear; **8.** Darnell McDonald, of, Delmarva; **9.** Vernon Wells, of, Hagerstown; **10.** Marcus Giles, 2b, Macon.

DEPT. LEADERS

BATTING

G	Mike Young, Hagerstown	140
AB	Darnell McDonald, Delmarva	528
R	Marcus Giles, Macon	111
H	Maurice Bruce, Capital City	176
TB	Marcus Giles, Macon	321
XBH	Marcus Giles, Macon	78
2B	Kory DeHaan, Augusta	39
3B	Jon Hamilton, Columbus	10
	Jersen Perez, Capital City	10
HR	Marcus Giles, Macon	37
RBI	Marcus Giles, Macon	108
SH	Andres Mitchell, Asheville	17
SF	Eddy Garavito, Delmarva	12
BB	Marcus Giles, Macon	85
IBB	Matt Berger, Hickory	6
	Jose Velazquez, Charleston, S.C.	6
HBP	Xavier Burns, Augusta	22
SO	Anthony Brooks, Macon	164
SB	Victor Gutierrez, Augusta	60
CS	Terrence Freeman, Augusta	24
GIDP	Erick Almonte, Greensboro	17
OB%	Richard Paz, Delmarva	.453
SL%	Marcus Giles, Macon	.636

PITCHING

G	Brett Black, Piedmont	58
GS	Dan Wheeler, Charleston, S.C.	29
CG	Brandon Duckworth, Piedmont	5
	Ryan Price, Asheville	5
ShO	Brandon Duckworth, Piedmont	3
	Isabel Giron, Hagerstown	3
GF	Three tied at	52
SV	Brett Black, Piedmont	34
W	John Sneed, Hagerstown	16
L	Phil Merrell, Charleston, W.Va.	15
IP	Kevin Shipp, Piedmont	185
H	Kevin Shipp, Piedmont	210
R	Hansel Izquierdo, Hickory	104
ER	Scott Harrison, Columbus	89
	Dan Wheeler, Charleston, S.C.	89
HR	Ryan Price, Asheville	23
HB	Hansel Izquierdo, Hickory	22
BB	Hansel Izquierdo, Hickory	76
SO	Josh Kalinowski, Asheville	215
WP	Jacob Shumate, Macon	39
BK	Pat Daneker, Hickory	6

FIELDING

C	**AVG**	Rene Pinto, Greensboro	.996
	PO	Rene Pinto, Greensboro	909
	A	Jayson Werth, Delmarva	131
	E	Josh Phelps, Hagerstown	19
	DP	Two tied at	6
	PB	Lee Evans, Augusta	32
1B	**AVG**	Bob Van Iten, Piedmont	.988
	PO	Franky Figueroa, Delmarva	1164
	A	Robert Berns, Charleston, S.C.	109
	E	Toby Sanchez, Charleston, W.Va.	23
	DP	Franky Figueroa, Delmarva	111
2B	**AVG**	Mike Young, Hagerstown	.978
	PO	Jason Romano, Savannah	305
	A	Chad Durham, Hickory	370
	E	Jason Romano, Savannah	32
		Jeff Terrell, Piedmont	32
	DP	Eddy Garavito, Delmarva	84
3B	**AVG**	Allen Butler, Greensboro	.929
	PO	Maurice Bruce, Capital City	83
	A	Allen Butler, Greensboro	230
	E	Jose Santo, Savannah	33
	DP	Maurice Bruce, Capital City	24
SS	**AVG**	Cesar Izturis, Hagerstown	.951
	PO	Cesar Izturis, Hagerstown	183
	A	Danny Sandoval, Hickory	417
	E	Danny Sandoval, Hickory	57
	DP	Danny Sandoval, Hickory	79
OF	**AVG**	Andres Mitchell, Asheville	.992
	PO	Stewart Smothers, Macon	314
	A	Jason Fitzgerald, Columbus	17
		Brandon O'Hearn, Charleston, W.Va.	17
	E	Anthony Brooks, Macon	16
	DP	Three tied at	5

NEW YORK PENN LEAGUE

Mother Nature forces NY-P to declare co-champions

BY HOWARD HERMAN

The 1998 New York-Penn League championship was decided without a pitch being thrown.

The Oneonta Yankees and Auburn Doubledays were declared co-champions after several days of heavy rain wiped out the best-of-three championship series.

Rainouts of the first two games in the series forced league officials to reduce the Oneonta-Auburn battle to a one-game, winner-take-all for the league title. Since the Yankees were the Pinckney Division champion and Auburn was the wild-card team, the game was scheduled at 58-year-old Damaschke Field in Oneonta, N.Y.

RICH ABEL

Pascual Coco
Lost no-hitter

But the real winner was Mother Nature, who would not be denied. There was no more rain, but the earlier inclement weather left the field unplayable.

"The field was mud," Oneonta manager Joe Arnold said. "It flooded most of the night, and water got underneath the tarps."

The Yankees had reached the finals by knocking off the McNamara Division champion Hudson Valley Renegades, a Devil Rays farm club that had the best record in the league at 50-26. Auburn knocked off the Stedler Division champion Batavia Muckdogs.

It was the first co-championship in the league since Jamestown and Batavia shared the crown back in 1946, and it marked the first time Auburn won a title since 1973. For Oneonta, it was the franchise's 12th championship with the Yankees and the first since 1990. It was also the last championship for the Oneonta Yankees. In mid-September, the New York Yankees ended a 32-year affiliation with the Oneonta club. The Yankees will move to Watertown in 1999.

Back in August, before the rains came, St. Catharines righthander Pasqual Coco pulled off a rare feat—he threw a no-hitter and lost. The Stompers fell 3-1 to the Jamestown Jammers on Aug. 16 in a contest that saw Coco allow no hits and just one walk. But his teammates committed five errors, three of which led to three second-inning Jamestown runs.

Oddly, the game didn't become a no-hitter until afterward. The official scorer consulted with the umpires and managers and changed an infield hit to an error—the third of the game on third baseman Josephang Bernhardt—giving Coco the league's only 1998 no-hitter.

Williamsport first baseman Eric Hinske also managed a unique accomplishment, collecting six hits in six at-bats in a June game against Auburn. Hudson Valley teammates Ian Rand and Miguel Suriel each had five hits in an August game against Lowell.

Oneonta's affiliation change was but one move in an interesting offseason. The Pirates moved their club into Williamsport, displacing the Cubs. Chicago moved its team into the short-season Northwest League, taking over in Eugene, Ore.

The Indians left Watertown for the former Erie franchise, which relocated to Niles, Ohio, for 1999. The Braves, formerly in Eugene, moved to Jamestown, formerly occupied by the Tigers. Detroit landed in Oneonta, replacing the Yankees.

Attendance went up again in 1998. A total of 1,279,493 fans went to NY-P games, an increase of more than 45,000 from the previous season.

STANDINGS

Page	McNAMARA	W	L	PCT	GB	Manager	Attendance/Dates	Last Penn.
236	Hudson Valley Renegades (Devil Rays)	50	26	.658	—	Charlie Montoyo	158,202 (38)	None
170	Vermont Expos (Expos)	36	40	.474	14	Tony Barbone	105,064 (34)	1996
185	Pittsfield Mets (Mets)	35	41	.461	15	Roger LaFrancois	84,323 (38)	1997
211	New Jersey Cardinals (Cardinals)	34	41	.453	15½	Jose Oquendo	153,445 (38)	1994
85	Lowell Spinners (Red Sox)	32	44	.421	18	Dick Berardino	174,020 (38)	None
Page	**PINCKNEY**	**W**	**L**	**PCT**	**GB**	**Manager**	**Attendance/Dates**	**Last Penn.**
177	Oneonta Yankees (Yankees)	45	31	.592	—	Joe Arnold	57,200 (35)	1998
137	Auburn Doubledays (Astros)	43	32	.573	—	Lyle Yates	52,597 (35)	1998
111	Watertown Indians (Indians)	42	34	.553	3	Ted Kubiak	28,103 (34)	1995
98	Williamsport Cubs (Cubs)	39	36	.520	5½	Bob Ralston	60,718 (37)	None
130	Utica Blue Sox (Marlins)	35	41	.461	10	Ken Joyce	58,902 (35)	1983
Page	**STEDLER**	**W**	**L**	**PCT**	**GB**	**Manager**	**Attendance/Dates**	**Last Penn.**
197	Batavia Muckdogs (Phillies)	43	33	.566	—	Frank Klebe	42,908 (37)	1963
250	St. Catharines Stompers (Blue Jays)	38	38	.500	5	Duane Larson	55,787 (37)	1986
123	Jamestown Jammers (Tigers)	32	43	.427	10½	Tom Torricelli	60,481 (38)	1991
204	Erie Seawolves (Pirates)	26	50	.342	17	Tracy Woodson	187,743 (38)	1957

PLAYOFFS—Semifinals: Oneonta defeated Hudson Valley 2-0 and Auburn defeated Batavia 2-1 in best-of-3 series. **Finals:** Series canceled due to rain; Auburn and Oneonta declared co-champions.

NOTE: Team's individual batting and pitching statistics can be found on page indicated in lefthand column.

1998 New York-Penn League Statistics

CLUB BATTING

	AVG	G	AB	R	H	2B	3B	HR	BB	SO	SB
Hudson Valley	.273	76	2683	452	732	127	28	41	305	557	117
Oneonta	.268	76	2563	417	687	121	35	30	288	580	85
Auburn	.267	75	2468	414	659	150	22	46	301	591	101
St. Catharines	.255	76	2564	389	655	134	20	55	295	631	86
Watertown	.254	76	2495	395	634	132	27	47	329	546	103
Pittsfield	.251	76	2629	364	659	113	28	48	199	600	97
Erie	.250	76	2671	363	669	125	16	54	230	682	59
Williamsport	.250	75	2433	359	609	118	24	36	235	549	111
Vermont	.250	76	2484	337	620	109	18	13	247	581	77
Batavia	.249	76	2528	387	629	125	16	44	305	678	65
Utica	.245	76	2424	325	594	99	15	34	223	607	65
Lowell	.244	76	2570	330	628	146	19	43	221	641	36
Jamestown	.241	75	2557	354	617	99	35	43	244	595	93
New Jersey	.231	75	2443	309	565	91	20	23	236	631	137

CLUB PITCHING

	ERA	G	CG	SHO	SV	IP	H	R	ER	BB	SO
Hudson Valley	3.28	76	0	7	25	691	592	325	252	245	693
Williamsport	3.43	75	3	6	13	645	553	310	246	303	539
Vermont	3.65	76	1	7	14	653	591	319	265	246	582
Watertown	3.67	76	2	6	18	652	616	326	266	250	641
New Jersey	3.70	75	0	5	21	657	597	361	270	261	659
Oneonta	3.76	76	3	5	22	656	623	349	274	264	574
Utica	3.76	76	2	4	18	637	635	330	266	217	525
Auburn	3.83	75	1	6	20	646	585	348	275	273	659
Batavia	3.85	76	2	5	20	662	660	340	283	188	599
Lowell	4.29	76	0	3	18	663	685	400	316	297	687
St. Catharines	4.46	76	1	5	21	662	629	428	328	293	606
Jamestown	4.48	75	1	2	17	661	604	404	329	278	603
Pittsfield	4.60	76	1	2	20	672	734	428	344	261	522
Erie	5.61	76	0	4	11	673	763	527	420	282	580

CLUB FIELDING

	PCT	PO	A	E	DP		PCT	PO	A	E	DP
Auburn	.966	1939	729	95	59	Batavia	.962	1985	841	112	70
Utica	.965	1910	829	98	62	Jamestown	.957	1982	840	127	54
Williamsport	.965	1934	771	98	63	Vermont	.957	1959	795	124	60
Watertown	.965	1957	769	100	59	Pittsfield	.955	2017	870	135	75
Oneonta	.963	1968	811	106	62	St. Catharines	.951	1986	793	143	55
New Jersey	.962	1970	720	105	49	Lowell	.948	1989	815	154	43
Hudson Valley	.962	2074	837	115	63	Erie	.945	2020	749	162	58

INDIVIDUAL BATTING LEADERS

(Minimum 205 Plate Appearances)

	AVG	G	AB	R	H	2B	3B	HR	RBI	BB	SO	SB
Pratt, Scott, Watertown	.351	47	174	37	61	12	3	2	14	34	26	15
Mahoney, Sean, Hudson Valley	.347	65	248	44	86	16	2	5	53	31	47	11
Carter, Charley, Auburn	.330	61	218	52	72	24	1	8	42	22	35	1
Washington, Rico, Erie	.330	51	197	31	65	14	2	6	31	17	33	1
Carnes, Shayne, Batavia	.329	66	237	52	78	15	0	6	38	29	48	3
August, Brian, Oneonta	.318	70	242	48	77	22	2	7	67	35	38	5
Ginter, Keith, Auburn	.315	71	241	55	76	22	1	8	41	60	68	10
Brett, Jason, Pittsfield	.315	53	184	40	58	4	0	0	14	11	34	18
Darjean, John, Oneonta	.314	64	226	43	71	9	4	2	23	18	42	16
Estevez, Domingo, St. Catharines	.306	56	209	40	64	16	6	7	33	19	26	12

INDIVIDUAL PITCHING LEADERS

(Minimum 61 Innings)

	W	L	ERA	G	GS	CG	SV	IP	H	R	ER	BB	SO
Geary, Geoff, Batavia	9	1	1.60	16	15	1	0	95	78	20	17	14	101
Reinike, Chris, Watertown	10	2	1.91	15	15	0	0	90	64	21	19	33	92
Hill, Terrance, Lowell	0	4	2.00	19	7	0	0	63	60	28	14	33	61
Oswalt, Roy, Auburn	4	5	2.18	11	11	0	0	70	49	24	17	31	67
Percell, Brody, Watertown	9	2	2.21	15	15	1	0	86	73	28	21	16	105
Lampley, Danny, Lowell	7	2	2.39	13	11	0	0	64	51	25	17	22	95
Whiteley, Shad, Oneonta	8	2	2.44	14	14	1	0	81	53	30	22	39	85
Jodie, Brett, Oneonta	7	6	2.59	15	15	1	0	94	87	40	27	21	73
Flohr, Adam, Hudson Valley	5	1	2.61	15	14	0	0	79	69	28	23	11	70

ALL-STAR TEAM

C—Matt Frick, Utica; Paul Hoover, Hudson Valley; Kelly Ramos, Pittsfield. **1B**—Eric Hinske, Williamsport. **2B**—Keith Ginter, Auburn. **3B**—Brooks Badeaux, Hudson Valley; Jared Sandberg, Hudson Valley. **SS**—Zach Sorensen, Watertown. **OF**—Chris Connally, Williamsport; Sean Mahoney, Hudson Valley; Angel Mendoza, Lowell; Christian Rojas, Watertown. **Util**—Rico Washington, Erie. **DH**—Shayne Carnes, Batavia. **RHP**—Geoff Geary, Batavia; Chris Reinike, Watertown. **LHP**—Adam Flohr, Hudson Valley; Darwin Peguero, Auburn; Brody Percell, Watertown.

Most Valuable Player—Brian August, Oneonta.

TOP 10 PROSPECTS

1. Carlos Duncan, 3b, Batavia; **2.** Adam Everett, ss, Lowell; **3.** Jared Sandberg, 3b, Hudson Valley; **4.** Felipe Lopez, ss, St. Catharines; **5.** Chris Reinike, rhp, Watertown; **6.** Paul Hoover, c, Hudson Valley; **7.** J.J. Davis, of, Erie; **8.** Zach Sorensen, ss, Watertown; **9.** Brody Percell, lhp, Watertown; **10.** Scott Pratt, 2b, Watertown.

DEPT. LEADERS

BATTING

G	Mark Carek, Oneonta 76
	Derek Urquhart, Vermont 76
AB	Mikel Moreno, Williamsport 286
R	Carlos Duncan, Batavia 55
	Keith Ginter, Auburn 55
H	Sean Mahoney, Hudson Valley 86
TB	Jared Sandberg, Hudson Valley 133
XBH	Charley Carter, Auburn 33
2B	Charley Carter, Auburn 24
3B	Zach Sorensen, Watertown 8
HR	Christian Rojas, Watertown 12
	Jared Sandberg, Hudson Valley 12
RBI	Brian August, Oneonta 67
SH	Brooks Badeaux, Hudson Valley 7
	Jason Brett, Pittsfield 7
SF	Nathan Frese, Williamsport 7
BB	Keith Ginter, Auburn 60
IBB	Omar Moraga, Watertown 5
HBP	Brad Freeman, New Jersey 14
SO	Carlos Duncan, Batavia 101
SB	Esix Snead, New Jersey 42
CS	Albenis Machado, Vermont 13
GIDP	Michel Hernandez, Oneonta 10
	Keith Maxwell, Erie 10
OB%	Scott Pratt, Watertown .467
SL%	Charley Carter, Auburn .560

PITCHING

G	Kirk Griffin, New Jersey 35
GS	Aaron Alvord, Jamestown 16
CG	Aaron Sams, Williamsport 2
ShO	Several tied at 1
GF	Derek Gooden, New Jersey 27
	Dustin Krug, Williamsport 27
SV	Derek Gooden, New Jersey 17
W	Chris Reinike, Watertown 10
L	Mark Mangum, Vermont 9
IP	Geoff Geary, Batavia 95
H	Tom Koutrouba, Jamestown 109
R	Aaron Alvord, Jamestown 67
ER	Aaron Alvord, Jamestown 60
HR	David Alvarado, Erie 10
HB	Johan Santana, Auburn 10
BB	Tim Hedding, Auburn 50
SO	Brody Percell, Watertown 105
WP	Brian McGowan, Jamestown 15
BK	Tom Koutrouba, Jamestown 9

FIELDING

C	**AVG**	Matt Frick, Utica .993
	PO	Casey Smith, Watertown 511
	A	Casey Smith, Watertown 69
	E	Casey Smith, Watertown 13
	DP	Michel Hernandez, Oneonta 6
	PB	Marcel Longmire, Will. 19
1B	**AVG**	Eric Hinske, Williamsport .997
	PO	Eric Hinske, Williamsport 561
	A	Eric Hinske, Williamsport 49
	E	Steven Goodson, HV 12
	DP	Eric Hinske, Williamsport 51
2B	**AVG**	Keith Ginter, Auburn .971
	PO	Tootie Myers, Vermont 144
	A	Teuris Olivares, Oneonta 199
	E	Tootie Myers, Vermont 21
	DP	Teuris Olivares, Oneonta 44
3B	**AVG**	Morgan Ensberg, Auburn .926
	PO	Jared Sandberg, HV 55
	A	Carlos Duncan, Batavia 159
		Jared Sandberg, HV 159
	E	Carlos Duncan, Batavia 24
	DP	Jared Sandberg, HV 15
SS	**AVG**	Derek Wathan, Utica .964
	PO	Kenny Miller, Pittsfield 128
	A	Mark Carek, Oneonta 246
	E	Kenny Miller, Pittsfield 29
	DP	Nick Punto, Batavia 45
OF	**AVG**	Jim Molina, New Jersey 1.000
	PO	Derek Urquhart, Vermont 164
	A	Bill Rich, Jamestown 11
	E	Joe Hunt, Erie 11
	DP	Bill Rich, Jamestown 3
		Chris Yates, Auburn 3

NORTHWEST LEAGUE

Youthful Volcanoes squad erupts for league championship

BY SUSAN WADE

Pitching coach? Piece of cake, Keith Comstock thought. Done that for six years . . . Say what? You want me to be manager, too?

Comstock arrived in Oregon in June 1998, with all the anxiety of a novice boarding-school headmaster. He was originally supposed to be the pitching coach only for the Salem-Keizer Volcanoes, but left with a gleaming championship trophy and manager-of-the-year honors in a swirl of teenage trauma and triumph.

"It threw me for a loop," Comstock said of his last-minute job change. Then his Volcanoes proceeded to do the same to the playoff-perennial Boise Hawks, sweeping the best-of-three title series.

MEL BAILEY

Jason Hart
NWL MVP

"It was amazing what Keith was able to do with so many young guys," said Spokane manager Jeff Garber, whose Indians tied for the NWL's best record (47-29) and finished tops in team ERA and batting average, yet missed the playoffs on a tiebreaker. "He stayed consistent. He benched two of his better players for not running out ground balls. He had a standard as far as effort goes, and he did not bend on that. He taught them how to be professional."

San Francisco helped by sending 17 of its top 22 draft picks, but Comstock's three first-round draft picks were high school players in a traditional college-age league. Typical personnel shifting cost Salem-Keizer nine pitchers among the 15 players promoted at one time or other to the Class A California League.

Righthander Benji Miller, who finished the season with 17 saves, was a key to Salem-Keizer's success. So was lefthander Chris Jones, 18, who showed outstanding poise and precision.

But Comstock did not have third baseman Tony Torcato, the team's top prospect, for the playoffs. The 18-year-old high-school signee from Woodland, Calif., was mending from a mouth injury. He suffered broken front teeth when he was struck by a thrown ball during a pregame warmup near the end of the season.

For the first time in the NWL's 43-year history, each division ended with two teams tied for the lead.

In the North, Boise took two games in a season-ending three-game set with Spokane to finish in a tie atop the division with the Indians. Even though the teams went 6-6 against each other, the Hawks advanced to the playoffs courtesy of a tiebreaking system. Salem-Keizer was declared Southern Division champion because it won seven of 12 games against Southern Oregon.

The Timberjacks boasted league MVP and home-run king Jason Hart (20), who also led the league in RBIs (69), extra-base hits (40) and total bases (157). Juan Pierre of defending champion Portland led the league in hitting with a .352 average and stolen bases with 38.

Everett, despite finishing 13 games out of first place, had some drawing cards at its newly remodeled stadium that drew franchise-record crowds. Righthander Chris Mears was 9-1 with a 2.74 ERA and led the league in innings pitched, and righthander Neil Longo had the second-best ERA at 2.26. Outfielder Jake Weber, the only unanimous all-star selection and a popular prospect among managers, led all hitters for most of the season. He finished first in runs (75), walks (67), on-base percentage (.471) and slugging percentage (.545).

The biggest news of the offseason was an affiliation change in Eugene. The Emeralds, an Atlanta Braves farm club for four seasons, signed a new deal with the Chicago Cubs.

The Emeralds finished last in the NWL in hitting, pitching and fielding in 1998 while compiling a league-worst 24-52 record.

STANDINGS

Page	NORTH	W	L	PCT	GB	Manager	Attendance/Dates	Last Penn.
57	*Boise Hawks (Angels)	47	29	.618	—	Tom Kotchman	152,496 (36)	1995
144	Spokane Indians (Royals)	47	29	.618	—	Jeff Garber	186,362 (38)	1990
229	Everett AquaSox (Mariners)	34	42	.447	13	Terry Pollreisz	119,396 (38)	1985
151	Yakima Bears (Dodgers)	32	44	.421	15	Tony Harris	76,049 (38)	1996
Page	**SOUTH**	**W**	**L**	**PCT**	**GB**	**Manager**	**Attendance/Dates**	**Last Penn.**
223	*Salem-Keizer Volcanoes (Giants)	43	33	.566	—	Keith Comstock	133,980 (38)	1998
192	So. Oregon Timberjacks (Athletics)	43	33	.566	—	Greg Sparks	71,822 (38)	1983
117	Portland Rockies (Rockies)	34	42	.447	9	Jim Eppard	184,172 (38)	1997
71	Eugene Emeralds (Braves)	24	52	.316	19	Jim Saul	136,310 (38)	1980

*Won playoff berth on tiebreaker

PLAYOFFS—Finals: Salem-Keizer defeated Boise 2-0 in best-of-3 series.

NOTE: Team's individual batting and pitching statistics can be found on page indicated in lefthand column.

1998 Northwest League Statistics

CLUB BATTING

	AVG	G	AB	R	H	2B	3B	HR	BB	SO	SB
Spokane	.283	76	2623	474	741	144	20	59	354	529	120
Salem-Keizer	.278	76	2619	484	727	114	49	48	337	537	139
Southern Oregon	.264	76	2617	495	692	121	30	68	379	556	78
Portland	.264	76	2638	375	697	109	19	22	250	501	98
Everett	.263	76	2643	434	695	143	16	64	329	652	98
Yakima	.259	76	2605	372	674	129	18	35	276	542	92
Boise	.258	76	2597	459	671	149	14	67	348	586	68
Eugene	.256	76	2634	367	675	122	18	52	246	610	109

CLUB PITCHING

	ERA	G	CG	SHO	SV	IP	H	R	ER	BB	SO
Spokane	3.47	76	0	2	24	675	670	357	260	301	648
Boise	3.82	76	1	5	19	665	665	371	282	237	534
Southern Oregon	4.48	76	0	3	24	669	717	433	333	292	542
Portland	4.65	76	1	5	14	666	688	416	344	322	525
Salem-Keizer	4.69	76	1	1	19	664	643	425	346	316	610
Yakima	4.75	76	0	3	21	671	695	462	354	377	576
Everett	4.87	76	1	2	15	669	727	464	362	325	517
Eugene	5.55	76	0	1	16	662	767	532	408	349	561

CLUB FIELDING

	PCT	PO	A	E	DP		PCT	PO	A	E	DP
Portland	.963	1998	823	109	59	Boise	.956	1994	934	134	60
Salem-Keizer	.960	1992	813	118	55	Yakima	.955	2013	791	133	57
Everett	.957	2007	903	130	56	So. Oregon	.952	2007	853	145	53
Spokane	.957	2025	827	128	57	Eugene	.943	1985	758	166	65

INDIVIDUAL BATTING LEADERS

(Minimum 205 Plate Appearances)

	AVG	G	AB	R	H	2B	3B	HR	RBI	BB	SO	SB
Pierre, Juan, Portland	.352	64	264	55	93	9	2	0	30	19	11	38
Martinez, Victor, Everett	.344	67	288	60	99	13	2	5	32	28	48	21
Weber, Jake, Everett	.338	75	275	75	93	20	2	11	52	67	42	14
Calderon, Henry, Spokane	.337	72	282	58	95	17	2	9	48	25	66	19
Dodson, Jeremy, Spokane	.336	69	268	56	90	19	5	9	59	25	59	8
Clark, Doug, Salem	.335	59	227	40	76	8	0	3	41	32	31	12
Magruder, Chris, Salem	.333	47	177	43	59	8	5	3	18	37	21	14
Huisman, Jason, Boise	.325	73	292	47	95	20	2	5	59	27	52	5
Ross, David, Yakima	.309	59	191	31	59	14	1	6	25	34	49	2
Phillips, Paul, Spokane	.308	59	234	55	72	12	2	4	25	18	19	12

INDIVIDUAL PITCHING LEADERS

(Minimum 61 Innings)

	W	L	ERA	G	GS	CG	SV	IP	H	R	ER	BB	SO
Ammons, Cary, Spokane	5	3	1.70	15	14	0	0	74	56	23	14	32	83
Longo, Neil, Everett	6	2	2.26	16	11	0	0	76	67	31	19	23	48
Mears, Chris, Everett	9	1	2.74	15	15	1	0	99	86	39	30	33	67
Bridges, Doug, Boise	6	2	2.98	15	15	0	0	82	73	37	27	35	63
DiFelice, Mark, Portland	4	6	3.31	15	13	0	0	82	83	45	30	11	62
Hundley, Jeff, Boise	8	3	3.40	16	16	0	0	93	77	42	35	27	89
Sedlacek, Shawn, Spokane	9	2	3.45	16	13	0	0	86	89	43	33	18	62
Nogowski, Brandon, So. Oregon	4	4	3.71	17	8	0	1	68	74	44	28	11	66
Ward, Monty, Spokane	6	1	3.79	15	15	0	0	71	66	33	30	35	76
Gomes, Tony, Yakima	2	8	4.09	16	11	0	1	73	76	53	33	34	52

ALL-STAR TEAM

C—Paul Phillips, Spokane. **1B**—Jason Hart, Southern Oregon. **2B**—Jason Huisman, Boise. **3B**—Henry Calderon, Spokane. **SS**—Chone Figgins, Portland. **OF**—Jeremy Dodson, Spokane; Juan Pierre, Portland; Jake Weber, Everett. **DH**—Bill Mott, Boise. **LHP**—Cary Ammons, Spokane; Jeff Hundley, Boise. **RHP**—Chris Mears, Everett; Shawn Sedlacek, Spokane. **RP**—Chris Demouy, Boise; Benji Miller, Salem-Keizer.

Most Valuable Player—Jason Hart, Southern Oregon. **Manager of the Year**—Keith Comstock, Salem-Keizer.

TOP 10 PROSPECTS

1. Paul Phillips, c, Spokane; **2.** Ryan Moskau, lhp, Yakima; **3.** Tony Torcato, 3b, Salem-Keizer; **4.** Chris Mears, rhp, Everett; **5.** Chris Jones, lhp, Salem-Keizer; **6.** Jake Weber, of, Everett; **7.** Steve Colyer, lhp, Yakima; **8.** Chone Figgins, ss, Portland; **9.** Jason Hart, 1b, Southern Oregon; **10.** Juan Pierre, of, Portland.

DEPT. LEADERS

BATTING

G	Jason Hart, Southern Oregon	75
	Jake Weber, Everett	75
AB	Jesus Feliciano, Yakima	302
R	Jake Weber, Everett	75
H	Victor Martinez, Everett	99
TB	Jason Hart, Southern Oregon	157
XBH	Jason Hart, Southern Oregon	40
2B	Jeff Auterson, Yakima	26
3B	Justin Hall, Southern Oregon	8
HR	Jason Hart, Southern Oregon	20
RBI	Jason Hart, Southern Oregon	69
SH	Richy Leon, Portland	8
SF	Jason Hart, Southern Oregon	8
BB	Jake Weber, Everett	67
IBB	Rick Southall, Everett	6
HBP	Darren Blakely, Boise	22
SO	Rick Southall, Everett	82
SB	Juan Pierre, Portland	38
CS	Jerry Simmons, Eugene	11
GIDP	Ricardo Montas, Spokane	10
OB%	Jake Weber, Everett	.471
SL%	Jake Weber, Everett	.545

PITCHING

G	John Wayne Lee, Spokane	31
GS	Jeff Hundley, Boise	16
	Billy Sylvester, Eugene	16
CG	Four tied at	1
ShO		0
GF	Benji Miller, Salem-Keizer	27
SV	Benji Miller, Salem-Keizer	17
W	Chris Mears, Everett	9
	Shawn Sedlacek, Spokane	9
L	Billy Sylvester, Eugene	11
IP	Chris Mears, Everett	99
H	Tommy Bond, Boise	99
R	Melqui Torres, Everett	72
ER	Melqui Torres, Everett	49
HR	Travis Brummitt, Eugene	10
HB	Travis Brummitt, Eugene	10
BB	Seferino Soto, Eugene	53
SO	Jeff Hundley, Boise	89
WP	Seferino Soto, Eugene	23
BK	Zach Frachiseur, Eugene	7

FIELDING

C	AVG	Erik Johnson, Portland	.990
	PO	David Ross, Yakima	428
	A	Paul Phillips, Spokane	62
	E	Mike Dean, Salem-Keizer	10
		David Ross, Yakima	10
	DP	Paul Phillips, Spokane	5
	PB	Juan Alcala, Everett	19
1B	AVG	Robb Gorr, Yakima	.989
	PO	Jason Hart, So. Oregon	622
	A	Robb Gorr, Yakima	46
	E	Jason Hart, So. Oregon	12
	DP	Jason Hart, So. Oregon	45
2B	AVG	Al Castro, Eugene	.944
	PO	Brad Gorrie, So. Oregon	93
	A	Jose Nunez, Portland	135
	E	Manuel Sanchez, Eugene	16
	DP	Al Castro, Eugene	28
3B	AVG	Henry Calderon, Spokane	.913
	PO	Matt Howe, So. Oregon	41
	A	Mike Christensen, Boise	180
	E	Mike Christensen, Boise	25
	DP	Asdrubal Oropeza, Eugene	13
SS	AVG	Chone Figgins, Portland	.947
	PO	Junior Brignac, Eugene	108
	A	Tre Parker, Everett	222
	E	Junior Brignac, Eugene	39
	DP	Tre Parker, Everett	37
		Cody Ransom, Salem-Keizer	37
OF	AVG	Brian Shackelford, Portland	1.000
	PO	Jesus Feliciano, Yakima	191
	A	Will Croud, Boise	14
	E	Jesus Basabe, So. Oregon	12
	DP	Jesus Feliciano, Yakima	3
		Melvin Rosario, Portland	3

APPALACHIAN LEAGUE

Experience pays off as Bristol captures Appy flag

BY JAMES BAILEY

If at first you don't succeed, try again. The Bristol Sox, who finished a distant fourth in the West Division standings in 1997, returned five starting position players from that squad and ran away with the Appalachian League's Southern Division in 1998.

DH Jason Fennell, third baseman Jose Gonzalez, first baseman Manny Lutz and outfielders Jeff Newkirk and Derek Wallace provided the leadership and much of the offense as the Sox reversed their fortune from the previous season. Lutz led the league with 17 home runs, giving him 36 in his three years in the Appy League.

The Sox finished the regular season at 42-24, then made quick work of the Princeton Devil Rays in the playoffs, scoring 25 runs in two games to sweep the best-of-3 series. Third baseman Ryan Hankins homered twice and drove in six runs as the Sox won the first game 10-6. In the final game, Bristol batted around while scoring six runs in the first inning, and the outcome was never in doubt. Lutz and Newkirk homered to carry Bristol to a 15-6 win and Bristol's first Appy League title since 1985, when it was a Tigers farm club.

With Bristol and Princeton each clinching their divisions a week before the season ended, the batting race provided more drama than the pennant race. Johnson City's Jack Wilson stormed past Burlington's Paul Day in the final days to capture the crown. The Cardinals shortstop finished at .373, Day at .362. Both were ninth-round picks in the June draft.

The stolen base title went to Danville's Rafael Furcal, who broke the Appy League record with 60. Furcal, who provided great defense at second base and explosive speed on the basepaths, was named the league's top prospect in a poll of managers. The young Dominican always seemed to find his way on base, and then his running game took over and disrupted opposing defenses.

Elizabethton outfielder Mike Restovich was widely recognized as the top hitting prospect in the league. Restovich, a second-round pick of the Minnesota Twins in 1997, was a huge success in his pro debut, leading the league in runs (68), RBIs (64), walks (54) and on-base percentage (.489).

JOHN SPEAR

Rafael Furcal
Top prospect

The sole 1998 first-round pick to play in the league was Burlington's C.C. Sabathia, rated the league's No. 3 prospect. Sabathia, a hulking prep lefthander, made just five starts for the Indians, but he garnered a lot of attention with 35 strikeouts in 18 innings of work. He was even honored as pitcher of the week after striking out 13 batters in his final start of the season.

Danville third baseman Travis Wilson, a native of New Zealand who was playing just his second season of baseball ever, was the only Appy Leaguer to hit three home runs in a game–and he did it twice, on June 22 and July 21. Oddly enough, in Danville's other 66 games he managed just three more homers to finish the year with nine.

Bristol's Newkirk hit for the cycle in a game against Martinsville on June 23. His homer that day was a grand slam, putting extra emphasis on the achievement.

That same day in Kingsport, the best pitching duel of the season unfolded as Burlington's Martin Bautista and Kingsport's Gary Bohannon traded two-hitters in the first game of a doubleheader. Kingsport managed a single run, which was enough to give Bohannon a 1-0 victory.

STANDINGS

Page	EAST	W	L	PCT	GB	Manager	Attendance/Dates	Last Penn.
236	Princeton Devil Rays (Devil Rays)	38	30	.559	—	David Howard	36,548 (32)	1994
78	Bluefield Orioles (Orioles)	33	34	.493	4½	Andy Etchebarren	39,940 (33)	1997
198	Martinsville Phillies (Phillies)	32	36	.471	6	Greg Legg	44,501 (33)	None
112	Burlington Indians (Indians)	31	36	.463	6½	Joe Mikulik	45,495 (36)	1993
71	Danville Braves (Braves)	30	38	.441	8	Franklin Stubbs	50,711 (29)	None
Page	**WEST**	**W**	**L**	**PCT**	**GB**	**Manager**	**Attendance/Dates**	**Last Penn.**
91	Bristol Sox (White Sox)	42	24	.636	—	Nick Capra	27,002 (32)	1998
163	Elizabethton Twins (Twins)	38	29	.567	4½	Jon Mathews	10,665 (30)	1990
185	Kingsport Mets (Mets)	38	30	.559	5	Tim Foli	49,579 (31)	1995
243	Pulaski Rangers (Rangers)	29	37	.439	13	Bruce Crabbe	8,812 (32)	None
211	Johnson City Cardinals (Cardinals)	25	42	.373	17½	Steve Turco	19,684 (30)	1976

PLAYOFFS—Bristol defeated Princeton 2-0 in best-of-3 series.

NOTE: Team's individual batting and pitching statistics can be found on page indicated in lefthand column.

1998 Appalachian League Statistics

CLUB BATTING

	AVG	G	AB	R	H	2B	3B	HR	BB	SO	SB
Elizabethton	.289	67	2336	462	676	127	13	70	329	490	61
Bristol	.279	66	2302	447	643	117	17	76	282	477	100
Pulaski	.276	66	2214	363	610	99	22	36	265	496	81
Burlington	.271	67	2253	335	611	100	16	46	204	529	92
Princeton	.270	68	2309	413	624	105	27	49	248	556	72
Kingsport	.268	68	2287	386	614	126	35	50	212	439	90
Johnson City	.259	67	2309	351	598	107	26	53	203	596	93
Danville	.256	68	2297	359	589	114	17	32	266	563	151
Martinsville	.256	68	2325	361	596	101	19	42	254	586	92
Bluefield	.256	67	2230	331	571	90	19	45	237	473	70

CLUB PITCHING

	ERA	G	CG	SHO	SV	IP	H	R	ER	BB	SO
Pulaski	3.99	66	6	0	11	566	552	339	251	181	485
Kingsport	4.17	68	2	5	20	602	600	346	279	228	568
Martinsville	4.25	68	2	1	13	591	618	365	279	211	481
Bluefield	4.29	67	3	6	12	579	578	342	276	211	549
Bristol	4.46	66	5	2	17	590	632	368	292	214	542
Princeton	4.64	68	0	2	20	593	640	383	306	248	505
Elizabethton	5.03	67	0	5	12	577	604	375	322	249	592
Burlington	5.05	67	2	2	15	573	560	409	322	353	545
Danville	5.30	68	3	2	12	580	638	412	342	307	475
Johnson City	6.29	67	1	1	14	580	710	469	405	298	463

CLUB FIELDING

	PCT	PO	A	E	DP		PCT	PO	A	E	DP
Princeton	.959	1780	811	111	54	Johnson City	.953	1739	732	122	48
Danville	.959	1741	778	108	69	Pulaski	.953	1698	785	123	51
Bristol	.957	1769	736	113	53	Elizabethton	.952	1700	719	123	39
Burlington	.954	1720	735	119	60	Kingsport	.952	1805	757	130	55
Bluefield	.953	1738	714	120	36	Martinsville	.949	1773	808	138	36

INDIVIDUAL BATTING LEADERS

(Minimum 184 Plate Appearances)

	AVG	G	AB	R	H	2B	3B	HR	RBI	BB	SO	SB
Wilson, Jack, Johnson City	.373	61	241	50	90	18	4	4	29	18	30	22
Day, Paul, Burlington	.362	60	229	33	83	16	2	7	45	17	39	10
Espy, Nate, Martinsville	.361	66	227	50	82	20	1	13	50	51	55	2
Restovich, Mike, Elizabeth	.355	65	242	68	86	20	1	13	64	54	58	5
Valenzuela, Mario, Bristol	.330	61	233	44	77	13	1	10	46	24	49	6
Furcal, Rafael, Danville	.328	66	268	56	88	15	4	0	23	36	29	60
Mann, Derek, Princeton	.325	68	280	63	91	10	6	1	32	32	46	16
Wilson, Travis, Danville	.323	65	269	48	87	25	5	9	48	17	54	16
Centile, Raul, Burlington	.320	53	181	27	58	6	1	3	22	18	36	0
Fennell, Jason, Bristol	.318	47	170	40	54	8	1	7	33	23	25	0

INDIVIDUAL PITCHING LEADERS

(Minimum 54 Innings)

	W	L	ERA	G	GS	CG	SV	IP	H	R	ER	BB	SO
Garcia, Sonny, Bluefield	4	2	2.04	12	8	0	0	57	39	15	13	19	77
German, Yon, Kingsport	6	5	2.34	13	13	0	0	77	63	31	20	12	75
Bohannon, Gary, Kingsport	6	3	2.56	10	10	1	0	60	56	19	17	5	49
Suttles, Donnie, Burlington	5	3	2.87	12	11	0	0	63	40	23	20	49	77
Theodile, Simeon, Bluefield	2	5	2.96	18	6	0	1	55	47	24	18	15	61
Robinson, Jeremy, Princeton	6	2	3.01	13	13	0	0	72	78	34	24	9	64
Stewart, John, Pulaski	4	4	3.17	13	13	1	0	77	82	42	27	10	57
Jackson, Brian, Burlington	5	3	3.21	12	12	1	0	70	66	29	25	23	61
Guzman, Ambiorix, Pulaski	6	3	3.24	9	9	2	0	67	59	30	24	7	46
Freeman, Kai, Bristol	6	2	3.28	11	9	1	0	58	56	28	21	21	44

ALL-STAR TEAM

C—Humberto Cota, Princeton. **1B**—Nate Espy, Martinsville. **2B**—Rafael Furcal, Danville. **3B**—Paul Day, Burlington; Travis Wilson, Danville. **SS**—Jack Wilson, Johnson City. **OF**—Brian McMillin, Elizabethton; Mike Restovich, Elizabethton; Mario Valenzuela, Bristol. **DH**—Manny Lutz, Bristol. **Util**—Brian Cole, Kingsport; Kevin Hodge, Elizabethton. **RHP**—Gary Bohannon, Kingsport. **LHP**—Jeremy Robinson, Princeton. **RP**—James Lira, Princeton.

Most Valuable Player—Mike Restovich, Elizabethton. **Pitcher of the Year**—Jeremy Robinson, Princeton. **Manager of the Year**—Nick Capra, Bristol.

TOP 10 PROSPECTS

1. Rafael Furcal, 2b, Danville; **2.** Mike Restovich, of, Elizabethton; **3.** C.C. Sabathia, lhp, Burlington; **4.** Humberto Cota, c, Princeton; **5.** Jorge Padilla, of, Martinsville; **6.** Juan Figueroa, rhp, Bristol; **7.** Brad Baisley, rhp, Martinsville; **8.** Ntema Ndungidi, of, Bluefield; **9.** Jason Standridge, rhp, Princeton; **10.** Maicer Isturiz, ss, Burlington.

DEPT. LEADERS

BATTING

G	Derek Mann, Princeton	68
AB	Derek Mann, Princeton	280
R	Mike Restovich, Elizabethton	68
H	Derek Mann, Princeton	91
TB	Manny Lutz, Bristol	157
XBH	Travis Wilson, Danville	39
2B	Travis Wilson, Danville	25
3B	Brian Cole, Kingsport	8
	Jeff Newkirk, Bristol	8
HR	Manny Lutz, Bristol	17
RBI	Mike Restovich, Elizabethton	64
SH	Nestor Perez, Princeton	17
SF	Mike Pursell, Burlington	8
BB	Mike Restovich, Elizabethton	54
IBB	Marques Esquerra, Burlington	3
HBP	Prinz Milton, Danville	9
	Mike Restovich, Elizabethton	9
SO	Kevin Harris, Pulaski	97
SB	Rafael Furcal, Danville	60
CS	Rafael Furcal, Danville	15
GIDP	Mike Restovich, Elizabethton	10
	Gabriel Torres, Elizabethton	10
OB%	Mike Restovich, Elizabethton	.489
SL%	Nate Espy, Martinsville	.630

PITCHING

G	Alvin Alcantara, Johnson City	31
GS	Robert Smith, Johnson City	14
	Aaron Taylor, Danville	14
CG	Brian Murphy, Bluefield	3
ShO	Four tied at	1
GF	Matt Bailie, Martinsville	22
	James Lira, Princeton	22
SV	James Lira, Princeton	14
W	Grant Balfour, Elizabethton	7
L	Five tied at	7
IP	Juan Figueroa, Bristol	80
	Geronimo Mendoza, Bristol	80
H	Roman Colon, Danville	92
R	Jason Standridge, Princeton	61
ER	Aaron Taylor, Danville	50
HR	Juan Figueroa, Bristol	14
HB	Donnie Suttles, Burlington	8
BB	Donnie Suttles, Burlington	49
SO	Juan Figueroa, Bristol	102
WP	Kris Rayborn, Johnson City	14
BK	Donnie Suttles, Burlington	7

FIELDING

C	AVG	Alex Stoffels, Kingsport	.991
	PO	Humberto Cota, Princeton	382
	A	Gabriel Torres, Elizabethton	69
	E	Humberto Cota, Princeton	12
		Gabriel Torres, Elizabethton	12
	DP	Gabriel Torres, Elizabethton	5
	PB	Jean Boscan, Danville	20
1B	AVG	Troy Allen, Danville	.991
	PO	Manny Lutz, Bristol	614
	A	Hector LeBron, Princeton	52
	E	Manny Lutz, Bristol	13
	DP	Troy Allen, Danville	47
2B	AVG	Derek Mann, Princeton	.966
	PO	Rafael Furcal, Danville	183
	A	Derek Mann, Princeton	210
	E	Ramon Carvajal, JC	18
	DP	Rafael Furcal, Danville	51
3B	AVG	Tim Bowers, Johnson City	.947
	PO	Travis Wilson, Danville	55
	A	Travis Wilson, Danville	150
	E	Cesar Castaneda, Pulaski	21
	DP	Travis Wilson, Danville	13
SS	AVG	Nestor Perez, Princeton	.976
	PO	Nestor Perez, Princeton	116
	A	Nestor Perez, Princeton	208
	E	Brandon Warriax, Pulaski	26
	DP	Nestor Perez, Princeton	43
OF	AVG	Jeff Newkirk, Bristol	.981
	PO	Carlos Acevedo, Martinsville	124
	A	Jose Espino, Johnson City	13
	E	Sandy Garcia, Princeton	12
	DP	Jose Espino, Johnson City	3

PIONEER LEAGUE

Gibbons shatters records in triple-crown season

BY JAMES BAILEY

It was a memorable season for the Medicine Hat Blue Jays.

First baseman Jay Gibbons became the second consecutive Blue Jay to win the Pioneer League triple crown. Two Medicine Hat players, outfielder Ryan Fleming and shortstop Jorge Nunez, collected five hits each in the same game July 21 against Butte. And the Blue Jays finished with the best overall record in the league.

Jay Gibbons
League MVP

Oh, and they didn't make the four-team playoffs.

That's right. Medicine Hat's 46-28 overall record was best in the Pioneer League in 1998, but the Jays finished second in each half, behind Great Falls and Lethbridge respectively, and they missed out on postseason play.

It might not have mattered anyhow. The Idaho Falls Braves were so hot down the stretch it probably wouldn't have made a difference who they met in the finals. Triggered by a dramatic three-run home run off the bat of third baseman Alex Palaez in the bottom of the 10th inning in an early August game against Helena, the Braves finished the season on a 19-4 tear. Palaez' blast was acknowledged as the turning point in a previously mediocre season for Idaho Falls.

The Braves stormed past Southern Division foe Ogden in the first round of the playoffs, a series that matched two bitter rivals. The clubs had engaged in a vicious brawl a month earlier, which resulted in the suspension of nearly every player on each team's roster. The suspensions were served throughout the rest of the season.

In the championship series, the Braves matched up against the Lethbridge Black Diamonds, who disposed of Great Falls in the first round. The Black Diamonds captured the first game at home, and battled tough in the second game before falling 5-4 in a 12-inning game that saw them strand 21 baserunners. The Braves stormed to a seven-run lead in Game Three, then held on for a 7-3 win that brought a PL title to Idaho Falls for the first time since 1974.

The Braves set or tied two league records in their championship season. On Aug. 25 they equaled the PL mark with seven home runs in a 24-4 win over Butte. Outfielder Josh Loggins, Pelaez and second baseman Paul Weeks each belted two home runs in the game. Three days later the Braves set a record by pounding out 12 doubles in a game against Ogden.

Gibbons had a record-setting campaign himself. His 98 RBIs broke the previous league best, set in 1997 by Medicine Hat DH Greg Morrison, who had 88 while hitting .448 with a league-record 23 home runs. Gibbons finished a whopping 33 RBIs better than Billings DH James Matan.

Gibbons' lack of a defensive position tempered league managers' excitement about his future. He ranked 10th among the league's prospects despite his awesome show with the bat.

Billings outfielder Austin Kearns, who was selected by the Cincinnati Reds in the first round of the 1998 draft, was ranked first on the list. Kearns batted .315 in 108 at-bats and surprised with his strong play in right field.

Ogden righthander J.M. Gold, the league's only other 1998 first-rounder, pitched well in five starts, and was named the No. 4 prospect.

STANDINGS: SPLIT SEASON

FIRST HALF

NORTH	W	L	PCT	GB
Great Falls	24	12	.667	—
Medicine Hat	21	16	.568	3½
Lethbridge	16	20	.444	8
Helena	12	25	.324	12½
SOUTH	**W**	**L**	**PCT**	**GB**
Ogden	22	14	.611	—
Billings	22	15	.595	½
Idaho Falls	18	18	.500	4
Butte	11	26	.297	11½

SECOND HALF

NORTH	W	L	PCT	GB
Lethbridge	27	12	.692	—
Medicine Hat	25	12	.676	1
Great Falls	16	23	.410	11
Helena	9	30	.231	18
SOUTH	**W**	**L**	**PCT**	**GB**
Idaho Falls	28	11	.718	—
Billings	18	19	.486	9
Ogden	16	23	.410	12
Butte	15	24	.385	13

PLAYOFFS—Semifinals: Lethbridge defeated Great Falls 2-1 and Idaho Falls defeated Ogden 2-0 in best-of-3 series. **Finals:** Idaho Falls defeated Lethbridge 2-1 in best-of-3 series.

STANDINGS: OVERALL

Page		W	L	PCT	GB	Manager	Attendance/Dates	Last Penn.
251	Medicine Hat Blue Jays (Blue Jays)	46	28	.622	—	Rolando Pino	34,631 (35)	1982
216	Idaho Falls Braves (Padres)	47	29	.618	—	Don Werner	62,087 (38)	1998
64	Lethbridge Black Diamonds (Diamondbacks)	43	32	.573	3½	Joe Almaraz	40,998 (37)	1980
105	Billings Mustangs (Reds)	40	34	.541	6	Russ Nixon	95,533 (34)	1997
152	Great Falls Dodgers (Dodgers)	40	35	.533	6½	Dino Ebel	74,369 (35)	1990
158	Ogden Raptors (Brewers)	38	38	.500	9	Ed Sedar	99,443 (36)	None
58	Butte Copper Kings (Angels)	26	50	.342	21	Bill Lachemann	26,061 (34)	1981
157	Helena Brewers (Brewers)	21	55	.276	26	Tom Houk	36,516 (36)	1984

NOTE: Team's individual batting and pitching statistics can be found on the page indicated in lefthand column.

1998 Pioneer League Statistics

CLUB BATTING

	AVG	G	AB	R	H	2B	3B	HR	BB	SO	SB
Idaho Falls	.304	76	2653	578	807	178	24	64	402	640	107
Medicine Hat	.286	74	2571	508	735	147	20	51	318	456	111
Ogden	.283	76	2606	494	738	140	14	42	323	519	102
Great Falls	.281	75	2604	437	733	150	27	45	267	485	88
Billings	.279	74	2512	484	701	147	13	78	333	594	25
Lethbridge	.275	75	2505	489	689	124	26	61	383	540	120
Butte	.269	76	2550	480	686	124	29	45	430	528	87
Helena	.260	76	2557	381	664	142	7	44	280	602	93

CLUB PITCHING

	ERA	G	CG	SHO	SV	IP	H	R	ER	BB	SO
Medicine Hat	4.36	74	3	2	19	642	662	407	311	236	527
Lethbridge	4.59	75	2	4	12	640	661	421	326	305	491
Great Falls	4.59	75	1	2	11	656	647	420	335	350	574
Idaho Falls	4.79	76	3	3	20	659	695	457	351	389	602
Billings	4.90	74	1	3	17	639	691	429	348	352	564
Ogden	5.36	76	3	2	24	652	703	473	388	354	541
Helena	6.51	76	2	2	10	648	819	591	469	398	531
Butte	7.55	76	5	0	10	641	875	653	538	352	534

CLUB FIELDING

	PCT	PO	A	E	DP		PCT	PO	A	E	DP
Ogden	.954	1955	837	136	93	Billings	.949	1917	818	147	82
Lethbridge	.953	1919	860	136	76	Helena	.946	1945	850	158	69
Great Falls	.953	1969	858	139	73	Medicine Hat	.946	1926	796	154	74
Idaho Falls	.951	1977	848	144	72	Butte	.942	1923	804	167	67

INDIVIDUAL BATTING LEADERS

(Minimum 205 Plate Appearances)

	AVG	G	AB	R	H	2B	3B	HR	RBI	BB	SO	SB
Gibbons, Jay, Medicine Hat	.397	73	290	66	115	29	1	19	98	37	25	2
Piedra, Jorge, Great Falls	.383	72	282	72	108	22	7	2	33	39	29	16
Pickler, Jeff, Ogden	.364	71	280	55	102	22	0	4	49	39	25	20
Cust, Jack, Lethbridge	.345	73	223	75	77	20	2	11	56	86	71	15
Loggins, Josh, Idaho Falls	.341	71	299	66	102	20	5	8	64	35	60	8
Pelaez, Alex, Idaho Falls	.340	63	262	52	89	17	1	8	51	29	32	3
Guzman, Elpidio, Butte	.331	69	299	70	99	16	5	9	61	24	44	40
Garcia, Alex, Idaho Falls	.320	60	178	49	57	16	1	4	32	38	43	0
Nunez, Jorge, Medicine Hat	.319	74	317	74	101	9	11	6	52	28	45	31
Dunaway, Jason, Idaho Falls	.316	67	272	54	86	16	3	2	47	38	55	20

INDIVIDUAL PITCHING LEADERS

(Minimum 61 Innings)

	W	L	ERA	G	GS	CG	SV	IP	H	R	ER	BB	SO
Lynch, Pat, Medicine Hat	7	3	2.32	14	14	3	0	89	71	33	23	16	77
Cassidy, Scott, Medicine Hat	8	1	2.43	15	14	0	0	81	71	31	22	14	82
Madritsch, Robert, Billings	7	3	2.80	14	13	0	0	80	72	30	25	35	87
Parker, Beau, Great Falls	4	2	3.08	16	11	0	0	73	67	33	25	32	72
Callier, Jeremy, Butte	3	9	3.54	19	11	2	0	102	102	51	40	26	78
Hughes, Nial, Great Falls	8	1	4.05	16	8	0	0	67	64	36	30	29	44
Sanchez, Simon, Lethbridge	5	3	4.11	13	13	0	0	61	72	39	28	25	37
Bido, Jose, Lethbridge	4	6	4.14	18	7	1	0	63	64	38	29	19	48
Bauer, Ryan, Idaho Falls	7	2	4.54	17	12	1	0	77	91	43	39	20	62
Berryman, Brian, Idaho Falls	4	3	4.61	15	14	0	0	68	78	48	35	33	38

ALL-STAR TEAM

C—John Hernandez, Great Falls. **1B**—Clint Vaughn, Billings. **2B**—Jimmy Gonzalez, Great Falls. **3B**—Alex Palaez, Idaho Falls. **SS**—Jorge Nunez, Medicine Hat. **OF**—Jack Cust, Lethbridge; Elpidio Guzman, Butte; Jorge Piedra, Great Falls. **DH**—Jay Gibbons, Medicine Hat. **RHP**—Scott Cassidy, Medicine Hat. **LHP**—Nial Hughes, Great Falls. **RP**—Dan Mathews, Ogden.

Most Valuable Player—Jay Gibbons, Medicine Hat. **Manager of the Year**—Rolando Pino, Medicine Hat.

TOP 10 PROSPECTS

1. Austin Kearns, of, Billings; **2.** Jorge Piedra, of, Great Falls; **3.** Jack Cust, of-1b, Lethbridge; **4.** J.M. Gold, rhp, Ogden; **5.** Elpidio Guzman, of, Butte; **6.** Adam Dunn, of, Billings; **7.** Robert Madritsch, lhp, Billings; **8.** Pat Lynch, rhp, Medicine Hat; **9.** Jorge Nunez, ss, Medicine Hat; **10.** Jay Gibbons, 1b, Medicine Hat.

DEPT. LEADERS

BATTING

G	Three tied at	74
AB	Jorge Nunez, Medicine Hat	317
R	Jack Cust, Lethbridge	75
H	Jay Gibbons, Medicine Hat	115
TB	Jay Gibbons, Medicine Hat	203
XBH	Jay Gibbons, Medicine Hat	49
2B	Jay Gibbons, Medicine Hat	29
3B	Jorge Nunez, Medicine Hat	11
HR	Jay Gibbons, Medicine Hat	19
RBI	Jay Gibbons, Medicine Hat	98
SH	Mike Collins, Great Falls	10
SF	Jay Gibbons, Medicine Hat	9
BB	Jack Cust, Lethbridge	86
IBB	Jack Cust, Lethbridge	3
	Jorge Piedra, Great Falls	3
HBP	Corky Miller, Billings	21
SO	Samone Peters, Billings	100
SB	Frank Candela, Ogden	43
CS	Three tied at	10
GIDP	Randy Stegall, Billings	15
OB%	Jack Cust, Lethbridge	.530
SL%	Jay Gibbons, Medicine Hat	.700

PITCHING

G	Travis Jones, Idaho Falls	31
GS	Adrian Ozuna, Butte	16
CG	Three tied at	3
ShO	Several tied at	1
GF	Robert File, Medicine Hat	26
SV	Robert File, Medicine Hat	16
	Dan Mathews, Ogden	16
W	Scott Cassidy, Medicine Hat	8
	Nial Hughes, Great Falls	8
L	Jeremy Callier, Butte	9
	Luis Martinez, Helena	9
IP	Jeremy Callier, Butte	102
H	Jim Miller, Ogden	105
R	Oscar Montero, Ogden	81
ER	Oscar Montero, Ogden	67
HR	Oscar Montero, Ogden	12
HB	Jim Miller, Ogden	12
BB	Ben Howard, Idaho Falls	87
SO	Robert Madritsch, Billings	87
WP	Ben Howard, Idaho Falls	17
BK	Ben Howard, Idaho Falls	6

FIELDING

C	**AVG**	Robert Hammock, Leth.	.990
	PO	Mike Kremblas, MH	394
	A	Mike Kremblas, MH	58
	E	Corky Miller, Billings	14
	DP	Corky Miller, Billings	6
	PB	Sean Campbell, Idaho Falls	14
1B	**AVG**	Mac Mackiewitz, Ogden	.984
	PO	Clint Vaughn, Billings	601
	A	Mac Mackiewitz, Ogden	40
	E	Clint Vaughn, Billings	17
	DP	Clint Vaughn, Billings	61
2B	**AVG**	Jimmy Gonzalez, Great Falls	.961
	PO	Jimmy Gonzalez, Great Falls	132
	A	Jimmy Gonzalez, Great Falls	236
	E	Chris Patten, Helena	16
	DP	Jeff Pickler, Ogden	59
3B	**AVG**	Alex Pelaez, Idaho Falls	.967
	PO	Jeff Brooks, Lethbridge	58
	A	Jeff Brooks, Lethbridge	138
		Alex Pelaez, Idaho Falls	138
	E	Jeff Brooks, Lethbridge	28
	DP	Thad Markray, Billings	14
SS	**AVG**	Milko Jaramillo, Great Falls	.927
	PO	Alex Cintron, Lethbridge	107
	A	Alex Cintron, Lethbridge	209
	E	Jorge Nunez, Medicine Hat	35
	DP	Chris Rowan, Ogden	47
OF	**AVG**	Jack Cust, Lethbridge	1.000
	PO	Elpidio Guzman, Butte	136
	A	Samone Peters, Billings	14
	E	Juan Baez, Helena	8
	DP	Samone Peters, Billings	3
		Tyrone Wayne, Helena	3

ARIZONA LEAGUE

Van Buren helps Rockies dominate expanded field

BY JAMES BAILEY

The ranks of the Rookie-level Arizona League swelled to eight teams in 1998 for the first time since 1994, with the addition of the White Sox and the Mexican All-Stars.

The Mexican team came together at the last minute when the league needed an eighth club for scheduling purposes. A co-op club made up of players from the seven participating teams in the league was considered, but when the Mexican League Academy was willing to field a team it was a better solution.

Jermaine Van Buren
ERA leader

The club was composed of promising young players under contract to Mexican League teams and played at the Diamondbacks complex in Tucson. Twelve of the Mexican League's 16 teams provided the players.

Half of the Arizona League teams played in Tucson, a departure from previous seasons when all teams played in and around Phoenix. The Diamondbacks, Mexican All-Stars, Rockies and White Sox all played at new spring training facilities in Tucson. Teams played only two games against teams in the other city.

The Mexican All-Stars didn't have much success on the field, narrowly edging out the White Sox for seventh place. But they did impress league managers with their hustling style and fundamentals.

The Rockies, however, managed to impress just about everyone with just about everything they did. They tore through the league, compiling a 42-14 record, good enough for a 10½-game bulge over the second-place team and the club's first Arizona League championship. The complex-based league, in its 11th year of operation, has no playoffs.

The Rockies dominated with a prospect-laden team, placing five players on the managers' Top 10 Prospects list. Several others, including righthander Matt Roney, Colorado's first-round pick in the 1998 draft, just missed making the list.

Rockies righthander Jermaine Van Buren captured a pitcher's version of a triple crown, leading outright in ERA (2.22) and strikeouts (92), while tying for the lead in wins (7) with Cubs lefthander Yonder Linares. Van Buren, who finished the year with short-season Portland in the Northwest League, was ranked as the league's second-best prospect. He was very polished for an 18-year-old and threw his fastball, curveball and changeup with good command.

Other Rockies to make the top prospects list were righthander Enemencio Pacheco (No. 3), shortstop Juan Uribe (No. 4), outfielder Choo Freeman (No. 7) and first baseman-catcher Rene Reyes (No. 9).

The top prospect in the league was Athletics righthander Jesus Colome, who threw a mid-90s fastball and a hard slider. Colome, a graduate of the Athletics' program in the Dominican Republic, was 2-5 with a 3.18 ERA and 62 strikeouts in 57 innings.

Three Rockies, Freeman, Roney and catcher Jeff Winchester, were the only 1998 first-round draft picks to play in the league.

STANDINGS

Page	Club	Complex Site	W	L	PCT	GB	Manager	Last Penn.
118	Rockies	Tucson	42	14	.750	—	P.J. Carey	1998
230	Mariners	Peoria	31	24	.564	10½	Darrin Garner	None
99	Cubs	Mesa	29	26	.527	12½	Nate Oliver	1997
192	Athletics	Phoenix	29	27	.518	13	John Kuehl	1995
65	Diamondbacks	Tucson	24	31	.436	17½	Mike Brumley	None
217	Padres	Peoria	23	31	.426	18	Randy Whisler	1996
—	Mexican All-Stars	Tucson	23	33	.400	19½	Abelardo Vega	None
92	White Sox	Tucson	20	34	.370	21	Tony Pena	None

PLAYOFFS—None.

NOTE: Team's individual batting and pitching statistics can be found on page indicated in lefthand column.

1998 Arizona League Statistics

CLUB BATTING

	AVG	G	AB	R	H	2B	3B	HR	BB	SO	SB
Rockies	.302	56	1939	364	585	82	26	30	189	432	124
White Sox	.280	54	1803	302	505	92	15	27	213	441	85
Diamondbacks	.274	55	1887	300	517	93	31	20	193	519	123
Padres	.269	54	1897	313	510	101	25	9	213	503	103
Athletics	.263	56	1907	353	502	92	33	20	268	459	97
Cubs	.262	55	1898	330	498	108	30	34	197	453	86
Mexican All-Stars	.258	55	1858	304	480	107	11	13	207	470	51
Mariners	.255	55	1903	289	485	85	28	14	201	486	91

CLUB PITCHING

	ERA	G	CG	SHO	SV	IP	H	R	ER	BB	SO
Mariners	3.57	55	0	3	15	497	436	270	197	213	576
Rockies	3.73	56	2	6	21	489	454	259	203	190	530
Padres	4.55	54	0	3	8	484	503	320	245	213	439
Cubs	4.60	55	0	3	8	486	539	336	248	231	419
Athletics	4.71	56	0	2	15	491	520	334	257	214	486
Diamondbacks	4.85	55	0	3	11	471	522	337	254	195	480
Mexican All-Stars	4.99	55	2	1	7	469	522	302	260	182	396
White Sox	6.19	54	0	0	7	456	586	397	314	243	437

CLUB FIELDING

	PCT	PO	A	E	DP		PCT	PO	A	E	DP
Mexico	.961	1406	615	82	37	Cubs	.947	1457	600	116	53
Athletics	.957	1474	592	93	44	Padres	.946	1453	498	111	33
Mariners	.949	1491	547	109	31	D'backs	.934	1413	549	138	47
Rockies	.947	1468	607	115	48	White Sox	.929	1369	515	145	41

INDIVIDUAL BATTING LEADERS

(Minimum 151 Plate Appearances)

	AVG	G	AB	R	H	2B	3B	HR	RBI	BB	SO	SB
Reyes, Rene, Rockies	.429	49	177	40	76	9	4	6	30	0	15	16
Battersby, Eric, White Sox	.375	43	136	34	51	15	3	5	27	29	32	4
Garza, Rolando, White Sox	.354	53	206	41	73	11	2	3	33	18	35	17
Roman, Junior, White Sox	.354	36	130	28	46	3	1	1	15	24	23	17
Clarke, Jason, Cubs	.343	35	140	30	48	10	4	2	25	12	15	7
Garrett, Shawn, Padres	.333	49	186	36	62	13	2	0	29	16	36	5
Fernandez, Alex, Mariners	.331	44	151	25	50	11	6	5	31	9	23	3
Valdez, Emanuel, Mexico	.328	50	183	31	60	18	2	1	35	20	55	5
Freeman, Choo, Rockies	.320	40	147	35	47	3	6	1	24	15	25	14
Colina, Javier, Rockies	.320	44	169	28	54	8	2	6	39	18	30	9

INDIVIDUAL PITCHING LEADERS

(Minimum 45 Innings)

	W	L	ERA	G	GS	CG	SV	IP	H	R	ER	BB	SO
Van Buren, Jermaine, Rockies	7	2	2.22	12	11	1	0	65	42	20	16	22	92
Prouty, Scott, Mariners	3	2	2.44	13	11	0	0	48	40	27	13	32	57
Trask, Cody, Rockies	6	1	2.49	20	0	0	2	47	36	16	13	18	68
Linares, Yonder, Cubs	7	2	2.91	15	2	0	0	56	62	24	18	5	32
Colome, Jesus, Athletics	2	5	3.18	12	11	0	0	57	47	27	20	16	62
Flores, Jorge, Mexico	2	2	3.40	18	3	0	2	50	52	22	19	7	53
Navarro, Joel, Mexico	4	4	3.55	13	10	0	0	66	81	34	26	13	43
Little, Roger, Rockies	4	1	3.80	14	8	0	0	47	50	30	20	18	46
DePaula, Julio, Rockies	5	5	3.81	17	9	0	2	54	54	30	23	18	62
Pacheco, Enemencio, Rockies	5	0	3.99	12	11	0	0	59	51	31	26	17	59

ALL-STAR TEAM

C—Miguel Olivo, Athletics. **1B**—Rene Reyes, Rockies. **2B**—Esteban German, Athletics. **3B**—Shawn Garrett, Padres; David Kelton, Cubs. **SS**—Cristian Berroa, Padres. **OF**—Rusty Keith, Athletics; Tydus Meadows, Cubs; Ernesto Medina, Mexican All-Stars. **DH**—Rolando Garza, White Sox. **RHP**—Jermaine Van Buren, Rockies. **LHP**—Andy Van Hekken, Mariners. **RP**—Yonder Linares, Cubs; Enmanuel Ulloa, Mariners.

Most Valuable Player—Rene Reyes, Rockies. **Manager of the Year**—P.J. Carey, Rockies.

TOP 10 PROSPECTS

1. Jesus Colome, rhp, Athletics; **2.** Jermaine Van Buren, rhp, Rockies; **3.** Enemencio Pacheco, rhp, Rockies; **4.** Juan Uribe, ss, Rockies; **5.** Cristian Berroa, ss, Padres; **6.** David Kelton, 3b, Cubs; **7.** Choo Freeman, of, Rockies; **8.** Andy Van Hekken, lhp, Mariners; **9.** Rene Reyes, 1b-c, Rockies; **10.** Casey Bell, rhp, Padres.

DEPT. LEADERS

BATTING

G	Four tied at	55
AB	Isais Rincon, Mexico	230
R	Esteban German, Athletics	52
H	Rene Reyes, Rockies	76
TB	Rene Reyes, Rockies	108
XBH	Cristian Berroa, Padres	25
	Rusty Keith, Athletics	25
2B	Cristian Berroa, Padres	22
3B	Esteban German, Athletics	10
HR	Javier Colina, Rockies	6
	David Kelton, Cubs	6
RBI	Three tied at	39
SH	Manuel Duenas, Mexico	7
SF	Rusty Keith, Athletics	8
BB	Tony Cosentino, Padres	39
IBB	Alex Fernandez, Mariners	3
HBP	Rene Reyes, Rockies	15
SO	Jesse Curry, Padres	88
SB	Esteban German, Athletics	40
CS	Miguel Vilorio, Rockies	10
GIDP	Three tied at	7
OB%	Rene Reyes, Rockies	.493
SL%	Eric Battersby, White Sox	.640

PITCHING

G	Diogenes Gomez, Rockies	29
GS	Angel Caraballo, White Sox	13
CG	Victor Angulo, Mexico	2
ShO	Matt Roney, Rockies	1
	Jermaine Van Buren, Rockies	1
GF	Diogenes Gomez, Rockies	24
SV	Diogenes Gomez, Rockies	12
W	Yonder Linares, Cubs	7
	Jermaine Van Buren, Rockies	7
L	Gerardo Garcia, Mexico	8
IP	Joel Navarro, Mexico	66
H	Angel Caraballo, White Sox	90
R	Angel Caraballo, White Sox	71
ER	Angel Caraballo, White Sox	53
HR	Andre Simpson, White Sox	8
HB	Marino Carreras, Mariners	9
	Juan Ruiz, Padres	9
BB	Samuel Walton, Mariners	45
SO	Jermaine Van Buren, Rockies	92
WP	Samuel Walton, Mariners	22
BK	Angel Caraballo, White Sox	8

FIELDING

C	AVG	Mark Carroll, Mariners	.990
	PO	J.D. Closser, Diamondbacks	311
	A	Miguel Olivo, Athletics	44
	E	J.D. Closser, Diamondbacks	12
	DP	Jose de la Cruz, Athletics	3
	PB	Miguel Olivo, Athletics	22
1B	AVG	Adan Munoz, Mexico	.988
	PO	Jeremy Scheid, Athletics	455
	A	Jeremy Scheid, Athletics	34
	E	Jesse Curry, Padres	9
		Rene Reyes, Rockies	9
	DP	Jeremy Scheid, Athletics	36
2B	AVG	Jesus Rivera, Mexico	.960
	PO	Esteban German, Athletics	87
	A	Esteban German, Athletics	116
	E	Esteban German, Athletics	13
	DP	Jesus Rivera, Mexico	23
3B	AVG	Gorky Estrella, Mariners	.903
	PO	Shawn Garrett, Padres	40
	A	Gorky Estrella, Mariners	94
		David Kelton, Cubs	94
	E	Joel Noboa, Diamondbacks	23
	DP	David Kelton, Cubs	9
SS	AVG	Francisco Arias, Mexico	.950
	PO	Francisco Arias, Mexico	90
	A	Francisco Arias, Mexico	136
	E	Ruben Castillo, Mariners	19
	DP	Gregori Valera, Diamondbacks	30
OF	AVG	Pete Fukuhara, Cubs	.989
	PO	Isais Rincon, Mexico	110
	A	Ernesto Medina, Mexico	10
	E	Rafael Perez, White Sox	11
	DP	Rusty Keith, Athletics	2

GULF COAST LEAGUE

Offensive outburst lifts Rangers to GCL championship

BY JAMES BAILEY

Catcher Fredrick Torres led the Rangers to their second Gulf Coast League title in five years in 1998, igniting a rare offensive outburst that put 24 runs on the board in three postseason games.

Torres equaled his regular season total with three home runs in the championship series. His two longballs in Game One of the finals accounted for all the Rangers runs in a 4-0 win over the Devil Rays. He belted a three-run shot in Game Two as the Rangers won 9-3 to take the title. Rangers outfielder Cody Nowlin, the team's best prospect, also homered in the final game.

Josh McKinley
Expos first-rounder

In the sudden-death semifinals the Rangers defeated the Twins 11-4 after the two clubs had tied for first in the Western Division. The Marlins, who finished with the best regular season record in the league at 38-22, fell to the Devil Rays 3-2 in 14 innings in the other semifinal contest.

The Marlins led the league with a 2.19 ERA and featured the league official ERA leader in righthander Wes Anderson (1.39). Teammate Pedro Minaya finished at 1.00, but he fell three innings short of qualifying because of a late promotion to Class A Brevard County.

Yankees outfielder Juan Rivera was named the league's top prospect. He led the league with 12 homers, 45 RBIs and 117 total bases, and was fourth in the batting race with a .333 mark. The strong-armed Venezuelan finished the season with short-season Oneonta in the New York-Penn League.

The Gulf Coast League, which is divided into three divisions, plays no interlocking games during its regular season schedule.

Other noteworthy prospects in the GCL included Braves lefthander Jung Bong and Yankees third baseman Drew Henson.

Bong, a heralded Korean pitcher signed earlier in the year by the Braves organization, showed good poise in an impressive season. He finished second in ERA with a 1.49 mark while allowing just 31 hits and 14 walks in 48 innings.

Henson, named Baseball America's 1998 High School Player of the Year after breaking the national prep record for home runs, appeared in just 10 games after signing a $2 million contract. He left early to play football at the University of Michigan, where he's a quarterback.

First-round picks from the 1998 draft to play in the GCL were Astros righthander Mike Nannini, Expos shortstop Josh McKinley, Orioles outfielders Rick Elder and Mamon Tucker, Rangers first baseman Carlos Pena, Royals lefthander Chris George, Tigers righthander Nate Cornejo and Yankees outfielder Andy Brown. They had varying degrees of success, but only Elder, who hit .340 with three homers and 26 RBIs, impressed managers enough to be ranked among the league's Top 10 Prospects.

For the second year in a row the league lost a team to the Rookie-level Arizona League. The White Sox defected, leaving the GCL with 14 clubs in 1998.

STANDINGS

Page	EAST	Complex Site	W	L	PCT	GB	Manager	Last Penn.
131	Marlins	Melbourne	38	22	.633	—	Jon Deeble	None
171	Expos	Jupiter	32	27	.542	5½	Frank Kremblas	1991
72	Braves	Orlando	25	35	.417	13	Rick Albert	1964
186	Mets	Port St. Lucie	24	35	.407	13½	John Stephenson	1997
Page	**NORTH**	**Complex Site**	**W**	**L**	**PCT**	**GB**	**Manager**	**Last Penn.**
237	Devil Rays	St. Petersburg	36	24	.600	—	Bobby Ramos	None
178	Yankees	Tampa	34	26	.567	2	Ken Dominguez	1996
124	Tigers	Lakeland	28	32	.467	8	Kevin Bradshaw	None
138	Astros	Kissimmee	22	38	.367	14	Julio Linares	1994
Page	**WEST**	**Complex Site**	**W**	**L**	**PCT**	**GB**	**Manager**	**Last Penn.**
164	Twins	Fort Myers	34	26	.567	—	Steve Liddle	None
244	Rangers	Port Charlotte	34	26	.567	—	Darryl Kennedy	1998
145	Royals	Fort Myers	32	28	.533	2	Andre David	1992
79	Orioles	Sarasota	28	32	.467	6	Butch Davis	None
86	Red Sox	Fort Myers	27	33	.450	7	Luis Aguayo	None
205	Pirates	Bradenton	25	35	.417	9	Woody Huyke	None

PLAYOFFS—Semifinals: Rangers defeated Twins and Devil Rays defeated Marlins in one-game playoffs. **Finals:** Rangers defeated Devil Rays 2-0 in best-of-3 series.

NOTE: Team's individiual batting and pitching statistics can be found on page indicated in lefthand column.

Minor Leagues

1998 Gulf Coast League Statistics

CLUB BATTING

	AVG	G	AB	R	H	2B	3B	HR	BB	SO	SB
Red Sox	.289	60	2003	347	579	107	23	39	216	367	99
Tigers	.274	60	2091	310	572	104	25	28	190	529	100
Royals	.262	60	2015	271	527	92	6	28	188	405	60
Devil Rays	.258	60	1999	322	516	103	29	31	181	492	79
Twins	.258	60	1983	280	511	102	10	29	186	371	85
Marlins	.257	59	1890	274	486	106	20	18	181	514	104
Yankees	.253	60	1955	293	495	87	13	32	226	486	41
Rangers	.251	60	1937	275	486	90	16	24	205	426	53
Pirates	.250	60	2064	294	517	101	19	45	168	471	90
Astros	.242	60	2041	237	493	100	12	18	181	470	73
Orioles	.236	60	1999	289	471	79	22	17	195	428	112
Mets	.230	59	1898	222	436	86	23	22	118	420	50
Expos	.228	59	1823	219	416	72	25	8	133	444	119
Braves	.228	59	1907	202	434	104	15	24	169	491	58

CLUB PITCHING

	ERA	G	CG	SHO	SV	IP	H	R	ER	BB	SO
Marlins	2.19	59	2	10	16	501	369	178	122	149	540
Expos	2.62	59	2	7	15	512	450	207	149	110	442
Royals	3.39	60	1	5	15	512	470	250	193	194	429
Yankees	3.42	60	0	3	21	521	496	260	198	169	463
Rangers	3.50	60	0	7	17	516	497	251	201	150	441
Braves	3.68	59	0	3	13	506	455	250	207	151	468
Red Sox	3.69	60	0	3	11	505	483	288	207	181	466
Twins	3.70	60	1	1	15	509	508	271	209	176	402
Devil Rays	3.89	60	1	4	11	522	522	282	226	203	461
Mets	3.91	59	3	3	13	498	498	282	216	191	419
Astros	4.25	60	3	3	10	531	537	316	251	187	543
Tigers	4.31	60	2	2	11	526	521	304	252	219	510
Orioles	4.57	60	0	5	13	523	564	323	266	225	373
Pirates	4.72	60	0	1	14	522	569	373	274	232	357

CLUB FIELDING

	PCT	PO	A	E	DP		PCT	PO	A	E	DP
Yankees	.962	1563	647	87	39	Astros	.956	1594	584	100	44
Marlins	.962	1504	653	86	28	Tigers	.956	1570	634	103	46
Expos	.961	1537	620	87	34	Devil Rays	.954	1567	664	107	60
Rangers	.961	1549	643	90	43	Orioles	.953	1570	654	109	54
Braves	.958	1518	629	93	40	Red Sox	.953	1514	620	106	36
Mets	.958	1493	697	95	41	Twins	.952	1527	704	113	45
Royals	.957	1535	621	97	48	Pirates	.936	1566	646	150	48

INDIVIDUAL BATTING LEADERS

(Minimum 162 Plate Appearances)

	AVG	G	AB	R	H	2B	3B	HR	RBI	BB	SO	SB
Goodwin, David, Royals	.367	48	177	26	65	20	0	4	33	20	33	0
Pena, Jose, Red Sox	.344	48	160	20	55	12	3	4	21	14	33	6
Vasquez, Alejandro, Astros	.335	57	209	31	70	20	2	3	23	21	34	7
Rivera, Juan, Yankees	.333	57	210	43	70	9	1	12	45	26	27	8
Gomez, Richard, Tigers	.333	47	162	42	54	11	4	6	40	21	37	20
Rodriguez, Carlos, Red Sox	.325	54	197	35	64	14	2	8	37	11	37	14
Brown, Tonayne, Red Sox	.316	54	225	43	71	12	4	8	38	8	32	15
Ramirez, Charlie, Royals	.305	50	200	27	61	9	2	0	23	7	35	13
Boone, Matt, Tigers	.293	49	191	28	56	11	4	5	29	9	42	3
Guerrero, Pedro, Rangers	.290	52	186	35	54	10	2	1	25	26	42	11

INDIVIDUAL PITCHING LEADERS

(Minimum 48 Innings)

	W	L	ERA	G	GS	CG	SV	IP	H	R	ER	BB	SO
Anderson, Wes, Marlins	5	2	1.39	11	11	1	0	65	44	25	10	18	66
Bong, Jung, Braves	1	1	1.49	11	10	0	0	48	31	9	8	14	56
Villanueva, Bill, Marlins	6	2	1.88	11	11	0	0	57	46	14	12	13	54
McGinnis, Johnny, Braves	2	6	1.89	13	11	0	0	62	40	23	13	17	53
Chiavacci, Ron, Expos	6	3	2.13	13	6	0	0	55	43	17	13	13	42
Spurling, Chris, Yankees	2	1	2.28	13	6	0	1	51	57	21	13	11	44
Nunez, Jose, Mets	3	7	2.38	13	11	1	0	68	60	26	18	12	69
Weslowski, Robert, Mets	5	3	2.54	11	10	1	0	60	59	25	17	20	37
Garcia, Rosman, Yankees	4	3	2.55	12	12	0	0	67	70	38	19	9	47
Frazier, Brad, Twins	4	3	2.61	9	9	0	0	52	51	17	15	13	40

ALL-STAR TEAM

C—Allen Shrum, Twins. **1B**—David Goodwin, Royals. **2B**—Pedro Guerrero, Rangers. **3B**—Matt Boone, Tigers. **SS**—Josh McKinley, Expos. **OF**—Tonayne Brown, Red Sox; Richard Gomez, Tigers; Juan Rivera, Yankees. **SP**—Wes Anderson, Marlins. **RP**—Robert Quarnstrom, Rangers.

Manager of the Year—Darryl Kennedy, Rangers.

TOP 10 PROSPECTS

1. Juan Rivera, of, Yankees; **2.** Wes Anderson, rhp, Marlins; **3.** Jung Bong, lhp, Braves; **4.** Drew Henson, 3b, Yankees; **5.** Cody Nowlin, of, Rangers; **6.** Jeremy Cotten, 3b, Pirates; **7.** Tonayne Brown, of, Red Sox; **8.** Ramon Soler, ss, Devil Rays; **9.** Rick Elder, 1b-of, Orioles; **10.** Junior Guerrero, rhp, Royals.

DEPT. LEADERS

BATTING

G	Marcus Quinones, Rangers	59
AB	Angel Batista, Devil Rays	226
	Ramon Soler, Devil Rays	226
R	Ramon Soler, Devil Rays	47
H	Tonayne Brown, Red Sox	71
TB	Juan Rivera, Yankees	117
XBH	Alejandro Vasquez, Astros	25
2B	David Goodwin, Royals	20
	Alejandro Vasquez, Astros	20
3B	Ramon Soler, Devil Rays	7
HR	Juan Rivera, Yankees	12
RBI	Juan Rivera, Yankees	45
SH	Andres Espinoza, Expos	6
	Pedro Guerrero, Rangers	6
SF	Three tied at	5
BB	Junior Rodriguez, Yankees	48
IBB	Alejandro Vasquez, Astros	4
HBP	Jose Cubillan, Rangers	16
SO	Brian Reed, Marlins	70
SB	Brian Reed, Marlins	40
CS	Josh McKinley, Expos	13
	Wilken Ruan, Expos	13
GIDP	Marcus Quinones, Rangers	10
	Juan Rivera, Yankees	10
OB%	Junior Rodriguez, Yankees	.466
SL%	Richard Gomez, Tigers	.562

PITCHING

G	Willy Marin, Devil Rays	27
GS	Several tied at	12
CG	Several tied at	1
ShO	Five tied at	1
GF	Robert Quarnstrom, Rangers	21
SV	Keith Dunn, Yankees	12
	Robert Quarnstrom, Rangers	12
W	Willy Marin, Devil Rays	8
L	Three tied at	7
IP	Jairo Pineda, Astros	73
H	Wes Chisnall, Expos	83
R	Wes Chisnall, Expos	54
ER	Edwin Aguilar, Astros	46
HR	Billy Diaz, Rangers	7
HB	Jairo Pineda, Astros	10
BB	Tommy Marx, Tigers	39
SO	Jairo Pineda, Astros	83
WP	Carl South, Pirates	17
BK	Edwin Aguilar, Astros	7

FIELDING

C	AVG	Ryan Smith, Mets	.991
	PO	Hersy Felix, Royals	304
	A	Ryan Smith, Mets	53
	E	Hersy Felix, Royals	10
		Winton Zapey, Marlins	10
	DP	Luis Venales, Marlins	4
	PB	Luis Venales, Marlins	16
1B	AVG	Derek Rix, Red Sox	.994
	PO	Clyde Williams, Expos	505
	A	Derek Rix, Red Sox	32
	E	Sam Berrien, Orioles	15
	DP	Ricardo Carrasco, Royals	39
2B	AVG	Jesus Medrano, Marlins	.984
	PO	Pedro Guerrero, Rangers	115
	A	Omar Rosado, Expos	124
	E	Three tied at	10
	DP	Yurendell de Caster, DRays	30
3B	AVG	Ruben Salazar, Twins	.940
	PO	Felix Lugo, Expos	34
	A	Ruben Salazar, Twins	126
	E	Felix Lugo, Expos	16
	DP	Brock Rumfield, Orioles	10
SS	AVG	Ramon Soler, Devil Rays	.944
	PO	Carlos Jimenez, Tigers	85
		Marcus Quinones, Rangers	85
	A	Ramon Soler, Devil Rays	209
	E	Bryce Pelfrey, Pirates	35
	DP	Ramon Soler, Devil Rays	36
OF	AVG	Wilken Ruan, Expos	.991
	PO	Tim Raines Jr., Orioles	125
	A	Angel Batista, Devil Rays	8
		Juan Rivera, Yankees	8
	E	Antwon Rollins, Rangers	7
		Jovanny Sosa, Pirates	7
	DP	Juan Rivera, Yankees	4

LATIN AMERICA

Expansion a hot topic but traditional rivals prevail in DSL

DOMINICAN SUMMER LEAGUE

For the first time in its 14-year history, the Dominican Summer League had the full participation of every major league organization in 1998. The increased support swelled the number of teams to a record 32, a 50 percent rise in just three years.

The Angels, Reds, Twins and White Sox did not participate in 1997, but the Reds fielded a full squad in 1998, the Angels and White Sox shared a team, and the Twins filled out a roster with players from several organizations. The Athletics, Dodgers and Mets each fielded two teams.

Despite spreading their young Dominican talent between two clubs, the Athletics and Dodgers again fielded the best teams. Athletics West compiled a league-best 57-12 record and ran away with the Santo Domingo West Division, while Dodgers II squeaked by in the San Pedro de Macoris Division despite a 50-14 record.

Athletics West then edged Dodgers II, the league's two-time defending champion, three games to two in a best-of-five championship series. The same two teams met in the 1996 final.

Athletics West featured both the league's player and pitcher of the year in first baseman Wilton Pena and lefthander Claudio Galvan.

Pena led the league with 19 homers and 64 RBIs, and went a team-best 7-for-19 (.389) in the final series against Dodgers II, while Galvan went 11-0 with a 1.04 ERA in the regular season and won his only start in the final.

STANDINGS

SANTO DOMINGO EAST	W	L	PCT	GB
Diamondbacks	48	23	.676	—
Dodgers I	44	23	.657	2
Brewers	43	26	.623	4
Mariners	40	28	.588	6½
Tigers	40	28	.588	6½
Marlins	30	36	.455	10½
Athletics East	26	42	.382	20½
Cardinals	25	43	.368	21½
Expos	23	45	.338	23½
Twins/Co-op*	21	46	.313	25
SANTO DOMINGO WEST	**W**	**L**	**PCT**	**GB**
Athletics West	57	12	.826	—
Yankees	42	26	.618	14½
Mets I	43	27	.614	14½
Reds	38	30	.559	18½
Rangers	37	32	.536	20
Devil Rays	34	35	.493	23
Cubs	25	44	.362	32
Pirates	23	49	.319	35½
Padres	13	57	.186	44½
SAN PEDRO de MACORIS	**W**	**L**	**PCT**	**GB**
Dodgers II	50	14	.781	—
Blue Jays	50	16	.758	1
Red Sox	37	30	.552	14½
Braves	30	36	.455	18
Angels/White Sox	28	38	.424	23
Astros	26	38	.406	24
Orioles	22	42	.344	28
Giants	17	46	.270	32½
CIBAO	**W**	**L**	**PCT**	**GB**
Indians	46	25	.648	—
Mets II	44	28	.611	2½
Royals	39	31	.557	6½
Phillies	33	37	.471	12½
Rockies	14	55	.203	31

*Players also provided by Brewers, Indians, Orioles, Red Sox

PLAYOFFS: Semifinals—Athletics West defeated Indians 2-1 and Dodgers II defeated Diamondbacks 2-1 in best-of-3 series. **Finals**—Athletics West defeated Dodgers II 3-2 in best-of-5 series.

ALL-STAR TEAM: C—Angel Matos, Rangers. **1B**—Wilton Pena, Athletics West. **2B**—Franklin Pimentel, Athletics West. **3B**—Hector Nunez, Tigers. **SS**—Isaac Garcia, Athletics West. **OF**—Yency Brazoban, Yankees; Cristian Pellerano, Athletics West; Daniel Valenzuela, Mets. **DH**—Francisco de los Santos, Mets. **RHP**—Juan Charles, Brewers. **LHP**—Claudio Galvan, Athletics West.

Player of the Year: Wilton Pena, Athletics West. **Pitcher of the Year:** Claudio Galvan, Athletics West. **Manager of the Year:** Andres Thomas, Diamondbacks.

INDIVIDUAL BATTING LEADERS

(Minimum 170 Plate Appearances)

	AVG	AB	R	H	2B	3B	HR	RBI	SB
Nunez, Hector, Tigers	**.387**	238	56	92	21	3	11	53	9
Llamas, Juan, Yankees	.383	243	55	93	16	6	7	59	4
De los Santos, F., Mets I	.371	251	65	93	20	5	9	62	16
Garcia, Isaac, A's West	.361	219	43	79	10	7	1	37	5
Pimentel, Franklin, A's West	.360	214	**78**	77	14	5	12	50	6
De la Cruz, Jovanny, Braves	.358	162	48	58	1	3	0	14	19
Valenzuela, Daniel, Mets I	.354	268	41	**95**	11	2	6	55	14
Martinez, Orlando, Reds	.349	189	38	66	12	2	8	44	14
Pichardo, Henry, Indians	.348	257	66	93	21	4	7	41	26
Morales, Victor, Blue Jays	.345	232	58	80	15	3	2	16	25
Hurtado, Omar, Reds	.340	188	37	64	12	0	8	40	4
Lantigua, Danny, Indians	.337	257	52	90	18	2	2	44	16
Rondon, Ernesto, Angels/WhSox	.337	168	38	56	6	4	0	16	35
Perez, Josue, Dodgers II	.335	167	56	56	8	7	2	17	24
Valdez, Isaac, Dodgers I	.333	228	37	76	17	2	3	42	6
Robert, Randolph, Mets I	.333	180	37	60	10	2	0	28	3
Ramirez, Frankelis, Dodgers II	.333	237	50	79	10	3	0	49	9
Pellerano, Cristian, A's West	.332	229	62	76	21	2	11	50	4
Romero, Flavio, Dodgers II	.331	148	36	49	4	3	0	13	4
Castro, Bernabel, Yankees	.330	224	**78**	74	6	4	0	17	**63**
Estevez, Jose, Mets II	.325	243	54	79	11	**10**	2	49	13
Brazoban, Yerry, Yankees	.319	251	51	80	19	2	9	46	10
Ledesma, Luis, Astros	.318	192	15	61	9	1	2	28	5
Lora, Thomas, Royals	.317	205	49	65	7	8	1	37	34
Jimenez, Manuel, Padres	.316	215	36	68	20	1	7	44	3
Astacio, Andres, Indians	.316	190	47	60	11	2	0	22	12
Villegas, Robert, Yankees	.315	165	22	52	8	1	3	22	3
Cleto, Simeon, Twins	.314	229	40	72	11	2	1	24	4
Liriano, Ruddy, Reds	.313	195	35	61	11	1	2	33	10
Belliard, Francisco, Dbacks	.312	260	41	81	**23**	0	4	55	8
Batista, Emmanuel, Red Sox	.312	215	44	67	9	2	1	30	8
Mercado, Wilkins, Royals	.311	254	43	79	16	2	2	49	8
Abreu, David, Mets I	.310	213	51	66	10	0	0	28	18
Gutierrez, Roberto, Blue Jays	.309	236	61	73	20	2	8	49	6
Richardson, Juan, Phillies	.309	152	21	47	10	0	6	33	4
Brito, Luis, Blue Jays	.308	253	50	78	12	4	3	42	20
De los Santos, N., Brewers	.306	196	32	60	11	3	3	37	6
Roque, Amauris, Tigers	.306	193	40	59	13	3	5	29	20
Ramos, Uvaldo, Blue Jays	.306	245	50	75	17	3	3	57	7
Gomez, Franklin, Yankees	.305	197	44	60	8	0	5	37	19
Matos, Angel, Rangers	.303	228	47	69	13	1	7	36	2
Moya, Wilson, Rangers	.302	215	26	65	12	0	3	30	13

	AVG	AB	R	H	2B	3B	HR	RBI	SB
Reyes, Cristian, A's West	.302	235	57	71	16	2	4	56	6
#Saba, Cesar, Red Sox	.289	197	39	57	9	**10**	2	37	2
#Pena, Wilton, A's West	.273	256	67	70	18	1	**19**	**64**	8

INDIVIDUAL PITCHING LEADERS

(Minimum 50 Innings)

	W	L	ERA	G	SV	IP	H	BB	SO
Charles, Juan, Brewers	8	1	**0.80**	21	8	80	46	14	94
Galvan, Claudio, A's West	**11**	0	1.00	13	0	90	39	14	97
Serrano, Willy, Tigers	6	1	1.04	11	0	69	34	31	59
Frias, Melvin, Dodgers II	6	2	1.14	11	0	64	42	15	42
Roche, Angel, Rangers	7	2	1.25	14	0	86	73	20	59
Ortega, Jose, Royals	4	7	1.34	25	2	54	37	16	60
Martinez, Obispo, Expos	2	4	1.46	17	3	62	45	13	74
Benitez, Fabricio, Red Sox	9	0	1.48	15	0	85	57	20	53
Reyes, Jesus, Dodgers II	3	4	1.48	11	0	51	35	45	37
Alcantara, Over, Marlins	10	3	1.56	17	1	86	60	29	78
Rosario, Melvin, Dodgers II	9	2	1.58	12	0	57	34	39	48
Coco, Martin, Dbacks	9	2	1.60	15	1	84	58	23	79
Manzueta, Roberto, Dbacks	3	1	1.62	11	0	56	31	19	64
Aguilera, Adrian, Dodgers II	6	2	1.65	11	0	60	33	33	69
Lopez, Jorge, Rods	6	1	1.75	14	5	57	46	10	45
Valverde, Jose, Dbacks	1	3	1.75	23	7	51	31	22	56
Zamora, Eric, Rangers	4	5	1.78	14	1	76	53	21	71
Sanchez, Duaner, Dbacks	2	3	1.79	14	1	50	36	24	44
Calzada, Javiel, A's West	9	0	1.80	14	0	100	74	14	77
Sanchez, S., Angels/Wh Sox	7	3	1.82	15	0	99	76	26	71
Minier, Rene, Red Sox	4	5	1.85	13	0	73	58	27	38
Mateo, Pedro, Cardinals	2	2	1.88	16	1	67	70	15	19
#Matias, A., Angels/WS	2	1	1.88	25	**15**	48	40	24	37
Colon, Jose, Indians	8	1	1.96	18	6	78	57	15	64
Mercedes, Martin, Phillies	3	5	2.00	12	0	54	46	13	50
Valdez, Fernando, Dodgers II	8	2	2.01	13	0	77	57	17	75
Lopez, Carlos, Dbacks	8	3	2.09	20	2	73	73	12	51
Franco, Jose, Yankees	3	2	2.10	10	0	64	61	13	59
Mendez, Miguel, Mets II	9	3	2.11	30	4	60	46	11	45
Diaz, Alexis, A's West	8	3	2.15	16	0	75	57	11	33
Lajara, Eudy, Marlins	2	5	2.16	12	0	71	58	28	82
Ramirez, Santiago, Astros	6	5	2.17	14	0	83	64	18	62
Zapata, Miguel, Blue Jays	8	3	2.18	16	1	91	73	23	60
Rojas, Aquilino, Mariners	5	1	2.19	28	3	70	53	19	**100**
Paredes, Robert, Mariners	8	1	2.25	13	0	64	48	25	69
Urdaneta, Lino, Dodgers I	6	1	2.20	12	0	56	43	26	44
Delgado, Joseph, Royals	8	0	2.31	15	0	82	56	34	50
Ortiz, Javier, Yankees	6	3	2.32	12	0	66	50	30	66
Linares, Ramon, Blue Jays	9	3	2.33	15	0	81	56	28	73
Perez, Franklin, Phillies	4	5	2.39	17	0	64	54	38	43
Morel, Welinton, Royals	6	2	2.40	16	0	83	66	10	41
Serrato, Alvaro, Dbacks	8	1	2.47	12	0	70	70	6	63
Chavez, Wilton, Cubs	7	5	2.48	20	1	83	58	20	84
Herrera, Carlos, Phillies	2	4	2.49	17	0	65	59	29	50
Vasquez, Luis, Astros	2	4	2.57	12	0	56	49	19	59
Arrollo, Azael, Blue Jays	3	2	2.58	27	10	60	43	16	67
Rodriguez, Enol, Reds	6	1	2.59	21	4	56	50	22	53
Marte, Neftali, Mets I	6	6	2.60	16	0	69	70	26	39
Mejia, William, Reds	5	3	2.61	14	0	62	59	27	42
Bautista, Juan, Mariners	3	1	2.65	27	1	58	51	18	69
Martinez, Martires, DRays	2	6	2.69	13	0	60	55	43	48
Zamora, Santos, Cardinals	5	2	2.69	14	0	67	55	37	40

Statistics in **boldface** indicate league leader
\# League leader but nonqualifier

VENEZUELAN SUMMER LEAGUE

Responding to a need for more development clubs in the expanding Latin America market, the Venezuelan Summer League grew from six to eight clubs in 1998, its second season of operation.

The league is open to players from all Latin American Spanish-speaking countries except Mexico, the Dominican Republic and Puerto Rico, provided players have no more than three years of professional service. The league's eight teams each had working agreements with three major league teams, with all but the Angels, Athletics, Cubs, Padres, Reds and Red Sox participating.

Though the league has no playoff, a team from Guacara, which fields two clubs, had the league's best record again. Guacara I, which finished last in the league's inaugural season, traded places with Guacara II as league champions in 1998.

Guacara I, composed of players from the Brewers, Giants and Marlins, won at a .700 clip to finish 3½ games ahead of league newcomer Montalban.

Righthander Jorge Cordova, 20, a Marlins product pitching for Guacara I, was the league's top performer. He went 6-2 and led the league with a 0.83 ERA and 119 strikeouts.

Teammate Julio Cordido, who is Brewers property, hit only .261 but led the league in runs (44), total bases (86), doubles (16) and home runs (seven).

STANDINGS

	W	L	PCT	T	GB
Guacara I	42	18	.700	0	—
Montalban	38	21	.642	1	3½
La Pradera	27	30	.475	3	13½
San Joaquin II	28	32	.467	0	14
Guacara II	28	32	.467	0	14
San Joaquin I	25	34	.425	1	16½
Miranda	25	35	.417	0	17
Universidad	24	35	.408	1	17½

PLAYOFFS: None.

AFFILIATIONS: Guacara I (Brewers, Giants, Marlins), Guacara II (Indians, Rangers, Tigers), La Pradera (Mariners, Phillies, Yankees), Miranda (Devil Rays, Diamondbacks, White Sox), Montalban (Pirates, Rockies, Twins), San Joaquin I (Astros, Dodgers, Expos), San Joaquin II (Blue Jays, Braves, Cardinals), Universidad (Mets, Orioles, Royals).

INDIVIDUAL BATTING LEADERS

(Minimum 125 At-Bats)

	AVG	AB	R	H	2B	3B	HR	RBI	SB
Hernandez, Javier, Indians	**.345**	177	35	61	13	**3**	1	23	16
Garcia, Kevin, Astros	.339	171	31	58	13	**3**	2	19	19
Blanco, Felix, Brewers	.333	153	32	51	5	2	1	18	20
Acuna, Ronald, Mets	.325	191	27	62	11	**3**	1	**38**	10
Fernandez, Medardo, Marlins	.321	162	40	52	5	1	2	19	21
Leon, Alfredo, Orioles	.313	147	23	46	11	0	2	22	5
Lopez, Victor, Mariners	.310	145	25	45	6	2	6	32	8
Timaure, Jesus, Marlins	.307	205	41	63	11	0	1	31	11
Centeno, Edwin, Orioles	.305	128	40	39	7	**3**	3	17	**31**
Canaguacan, Oscar, Yankees	.301	166	31	50	11	1	4	18	9
Lara, Rafael, Cardinals	.301	183	27	55	8	1	1	16	24
Villaneuva, Hector, Expos	.299	127	20	38	10	1	1	10	5
Cortez, Jorge, Pirates	.298	171	32	51	14	0	5	36	3
Castillo, Jose, Pirates	.291	179	31	52	9	1	1	13	23
Salinas, Yilbert, Rockies	.291	134	25	39	11	0	5	20	7
Hernandez, Argenis, Orioles	.283	145	17	41	11	1	5	25	0
Andrade, Kervin, Blue Jays	.282	177	19	50	7	1	3	21	10
Pastrano, Carlos, Blue Jays	.280	132	15	37	11	0	0	12	2
Seguera, Jorge, Tigers	.279	129	22	36	10	1	3	24	8
#Cordido, Julio, Brewers	.261	180	**44**	47	**16**	1	**7**	33	12
#Cartaya, Romy, Phillies	.184	76	12	14	2	**3**	0	9	3

INDIVIDUAL PITCHING LEADERS

(Minimum 50 Innings)

	W	L	ERA	G	SV	IP	H	BB	SO
Cordova, Jorge, Marlins	6	2	**0.83**	16	0	87	54	25	**119**
Araux, Alexis, D'backs	5	1	1.14	12	0	71	41	32	46
Tomassi, Carlos, Indians	4	3	1.19	15	0	60	49	15	49
Larrazabal, Jorge, DRays	2	2	1.31	19	1	62	45	34	48
Gomez, Deivis, Cardinals	**8**	3	1.35	16	0	80	66	25	60
Chacon, Ernesto, Yankees	3	3	1.67	15	0	65	55	22	51
Zamora, Hector, Astros	6	2	1.80	20	3	55	48	12	48
Sanchez, Aroldo, Giants	5	1	1.84	11	0	68	52	23	66
DeAbreu, Milton, Giants	6	1	2.05	11	0	66	56	25	65
Valles, Rolando, Astros	2	5	2.18	16	0	78	82	24	37
Ayala, Roberto, DRays	3	2	2.20	20	2	61	46	35	38
Anez, Omar, Orioles	3	8	2.24	18	0	76	63	38	72
Urdaneta, David, Indians	4	2	2.28	13	1	71	58	38	61
Herrera, Alex, Indians	7	4	2.30	18	3	74	70	17	68
Jauregui, Miguel, Indians	3	4	2.40	22	4	56	46	18	55
Rumbos, Jesus, Pirates	4	2	2.44	16	0	59	69	15	44
#Tovar, Angel, Yankees	0	2	2.45	31	**14**	33	24	20	35
Campos, Juan, Astros	4	5	2.50	23	2	54	43	22	38
Rojas, Ivan, Braves	3	2	2.54	25	4	60	56	18	58
Martinez, Oscar, Yankees	7	3	2.62	16	0	82	62	34	95
Moris, Carlos, Expos	5	2	2.64	22	1	75	57	32	76
Casadiego, Gerardo, Expos	1	7	2.74	15	0	69	69	28	61

Independent Leagues

Independent leagues endure rocky times; debut of Atlantic League highlights '98

BY MARK DEREWICZ

Independent baseball took another step toward respectability in the minor league landscape in 1998, especially in the crowded Northeast corridor.

Several leagues made headlines with individual success stories, while others put together solid seasons guaranteeing they'll be around for 1999.

But it wasn't all good news. Despite the almost immediate success of the newly-formed Atlantic League and stability of older circuits such as the Northern League, some franchises still couldn't attract fans.

The Heartland League was hardest hit, as it crawled to the finish line with two less teams than it had at the beginning of the season. The Tupelo Tornado and the Huntington RailKings both ceased operations in midseason, citing mounting debts and lack of community support.

Their departure left the fledgling league with four teams and directors subsequently elected to pull the plug, dissolving the league. The Cook County Cheetahs and the Dubois County Dragons were looking to join the Frontier League while the Tennessee Tomahawks were interested in the Texas-Louisiana League. With the Heartland League folding, it marked the third league in two years to bite the dust. The Big South and Prairie leagues ceased operations after the 1997 season.

Another franchise, the Grays Harbor Gulls of the Western League, also fell on hard times. The Gulls, an original team in the four-year-old league, cancelled their remaining home schedule before the start of the second half, forcing the league to send the team on the road for the remainder of the season. The club, renamed the Western Warriors, embarked on a 74-game road trip which ended with a second-half title and a playoff berth.

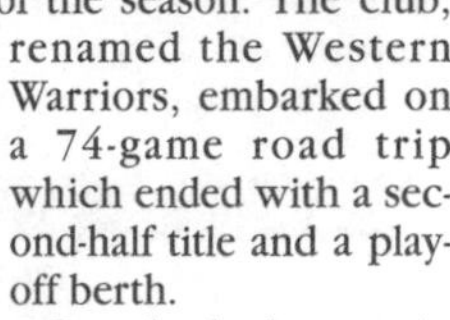

LINDA CULLEN

J.D. Drew

But the bad news in 1998 was overshadowed by the good.

The Atlantic League put up big money and offered big-name players, including several ex-major leaguers, which brought people to the park for its inaugural season.

While the jury is still out on how successful a league in the Northeast corridor can be, expectations should continue to ride high after strong years in Bridgeport, Conn., and Atlantic City, N.J.

The Bridgeport Bluefish were hailed for their part in revitalizing the city's downtown area. A new stadium was just one portion of a larger project to rebuild a once-thriving industrial town on the Eastern seaboard.

The Bluefish drew 296,145 in 67 home dates, though they shared their stadium with Newark, which did not have a home to call its own in 1998. Nonetheless, the gate count broke the record for highest attendance by a professional baseball team in Connecticut, set in 1995 by the New Haven Ravens of the Double-A Eastern League.

LEE PAYNE

Ila Borders

Somerset also did not have a home field and played all its games as the visiting team. League officials moved to rectify that situation for 1999. Lehigh Valley, Newark and Somerset will play in new ballparks when the league plans to adopt a 120-game schedule. The league was also eying expansion and a 140-game schedule for the 2000 season.

The Atlantic League may have put on a great opening act but the Northern League proved to be the show stopper for the sixth consecutive season.

Ila Borders, a lefthander for the Duluth-Superior Dukes, became the first woman to start a professional game and the first to win a decision. She beat Sioux Falls 3-1.

Mike Veeck's St. Paul Saints sold out every home date and welcomed back everybody's favorite holdout, J.D. Drew.

Drew, the Florida State University standout, played the second half of 1997 with the Saints after refusing to sign with the Phillies, who picked him second overall in that year's draft. He spent the early part of the '98 season in St. Paul before signing a four-year major league contract with the Cardinals, who selected him with the fifth overall pick in the 1998 draft. He quickly worked his way up through the minor leagues and finished the season in St. Louis.

Drew wasn't the only person to leave St. Paul. Minor league promotional guru Veeck, who co-owned the Saints since 1993, purchased the Northern League franchise in Sioux Falls. Veeck, however, may not spend much time with the Canaries in the future as he took a marketing position with the Tampa Bay Devil Rays in the offseason.

The Northern League made more headlines when officials announced plans to merge with the Northeast League, a move that could mark the beginning of an alignment between all independent leagues.

The idea was still in its infancy but both circuits felt

Player of the Year

At 26, Burkhart reaches end of line

Morgan Burkhart broke nearly every Frontier League batting record in 1998—just in time to say good-bye to the only professional team he's ever known.

Burkhart, 26, will not meet the league's age requirement in 1999, forcing the switch-hitting first baseman to look for work elsewhere. With his numbers, he had no trouble finding a new job. He was signed by the Boston Red Sox.

Burkhart hit .404 with 36 home runs and 98 RBIs for the Richmond (Ind.) Roosters to win the Frontier League triple crown and earn Baseball America's Independent Player of the Year honors.

Morgan Burkhart

His 36 homers were not only a league record but a modern independent league record as well. His 98 RBIs, 97 runs and 55 extra-base hits were all league marks as were his .404 average, .861 slugging percentage and .557 on-base percentage.

Despite that, Burkhart continued to receive little interest from scouts.

His size, 5-foot-10, 215 pounds, turned away some people, according to league commissioner Bill Lee. But his ability to play the game was undeniable.

"Guys around the league know that Morgan's a great hitter," Lee said. "But they're surprised to see how well he plays his position. He's a very smart player. He knows how to execute and knows how to win."

Burkhart spent his final year of college at Central Missouri State and helped lead the Mules to the Division II national championship in 1994.

He wasn't drafted and stayed at Central Missouri as a coach for a season before fellow assistant coach Sean McCann arranged for Burkhart to try out with the Roosters in 1995.

Four years later, he had earned four all-star team selections and three straight league MVP awards while playing in 304 consecutive games.

Baseball America's 1998 independent league all-star team:

C—Chris Coste, Fargo-Moorhead (Northern). **1B**—Morgan Burkhart, Richmond (Frontier). **2B**—Tim Howard, Amarillo (Texas-Louisiana). **3B**—John Knott, Fargo-Moorhead (Northern). **SS**—Keith Habig, Richmond (Frontier). **OF**—Jay Davis, Rio Grande Valley (Texas-Louisiana); Sean Hearn, Winnipeg (Northern); Felix Jose, Nashua (Atlantic). **DH**—Todd Pridy, Sonoma County (Western).

SP—Jeff Bittiger, Fargo-Moorhead (Northern); Daren Brown, Amarillo (Texas-Louisiana); John DeSilva, New Jersey (Northeast); Mike Smith, Mission Viejo (Western). **RP**—Chris Eddy, Atlantic City (Atlantic).

independent leagues must eventually be governed by a central administrative body in order to stabilize independent baseball across the country. It would also help teams deal with Major League Baseball in such matters as player transactions.

ATLANTIC LEAGUE

Despite two franchises playing without permanent home fields and a third club playing in a different state, the first Atlantic League season exceeded everybody's expectations.

Not only did the Bridgeport Bluefish draw 296,145 fans—an independent league record—but the entire league made plenty of noise in its inaugural season.

The Atlantic City Surf, who played in the brand new "Sand Castle," drew 189,730 in 75 home games. Up the turnpike, the Newark Bears and the Somerset Patriots played most of their games on the road while awaiting the completion of new stadiums. Still, the two teams made it through the season—a feat many other independent franchises have been unable to accomplish.

The Lehigh Valley (Pa.) Black Diamonds spent 1998 in Newburgh, N.Y., but will move into a new park in the Bethlehem-Easton area in 1999.

On the field, Bridgeport won both halves but fell to runner-up Atlantic City in the championship series, three games to one. Surf first baseman Juan Thomas, who had four home runs and seven RBIs, shared championship MVP honors with teammate Chris Eddy, who saved two games and won a third.

The league, which hired managers such as ex-big leaguers Mike Easley, Sparky Lyle and Willie Upshaw, also took an aggressive approach toward player personnel. It attracted 41 ex-major leaguers by mandating the highest salary cap in independent baseball—$190,000. That amount was due to increase to $300,000 for 1999.

Eleven Atlantic League players signed contracts with major league organizations in 1998, including Nashua outfielder Milt Cuyler, who signed with the Texas Rangers and was called up for the stretch run of the American League pennant race.

STANDINGS

FIRST HALF

	W	L	PCT	GB
Bridgeport Bluefish	31	18	.633	—
Nashua Pride	31	19	.620	½
Atlantic City Surf	30	20	.600	1½
Somerset Patriots	21	28	.429	10
Newark Bears	18	32	.360	13½
Newburgh Black Diamonds	18	32	.360	13½

SECOND HALF

	W	L	PCT	GB
Bridgeport Bluefish	33	18	.647	—
Atlantic City Surf	30	20	.600	2½
Nashua Pride	28	22	.560	4½
Newburgh Black Diamonds	24	26	.480	8½
Somerset Patriots	19	32	.373	14
Newark Bears	17	33	.340	15½

PLAYOFFS: Atlantic City defeated Bridgeport 3-1 in best-of-5 series.

MANAGERS: Atlantic City—Doc Edwards. Bridgeport—Willie Upshaw. Nashua—Mike Easler. Newark—Tom O'Malley. Newburgh—Wayne Krenchicki. Somerset—Sparky Lyle.

ATTENDANCE: Bridgeport 296,145; Atlantic City 189,730; Nashua 80,620; Newburgh 40,029. Newark and Somerset played road schedules with limited home dates.

ALL-STAR TEAM: **C**—Jorge Morales, Somerset. **1B**—Kinnis Pledger, Bridgeport. **2B**—Ryan Gorecki, Newburgh/Lehigh Valley. **3B**—Craig Worthington, Newark. **SS**—Tony Rodriguez, Nashua. **OF**—Milt Cuyler, Nashua; David Hulse, Nashua; Felix Jose, Nashua; Will Pennyfeather, Atlantic City. **DH**—Juan Thomas, Atlantic City. **Util**—Dan Fraraccio, Bridgeport. **RHP**—Mark Zappelli, Somerset. **LHP**—Dan McGee, Nashua. **RP**—Chris Eddy, Atlantic City.

Co-Most Valuable Players: Felix Jose, Nashua; Kinnis Pledger, Bridgeport. **Pitcher of the Year**: Chris Eddy, Atlantic City. **Manager of the Year**: Willie Upshaw, Bridgeport.

INDIVIDUAL BATTING LEADERS

(Minimum 270 Plate Appearances)

	AVG	AB	R	H	2B	3B	HR	RBI	SB
Jose, Felix, Nashua	.343	327	72	112	19	1	26	86	8
Pledger, Kinnis, Bridgeport	.333	348	91	116	21	1	26	91	14
Morales, Jorge, Somerset	.332	352	50	117	25	1	7	54	2
Gerecki, Ryan, Newburgh	.327	309	51	101	14	3	0	38	6
Thomas, Keith, Newark	.326	316	49	103	22	2	13	75	15
Cornelius, Brian, Bridgeport	.322	298	61	96	14	3	11	53	7
Morillo, Cesar, New.-Nash.-AC	.315	257	37	81	14	2	2	35	17
Cuyler, Milt, Nashua	.309	249	62	77	18	6	6	33	21
Viera, Jose, Newburgh	.308	247	45	76	16	3	15	52	5
Perez, Danny, Newburgh	.303	307	54	93	16	5	4	32	15

INDIVIDUAL PITCHING LEADERS

(Minimum 80 innings)

	W	L	ERA	G	SV	IP	H	BB	SO
Zappelli, Mark, Somerset	9	5	2.33	21	0	131	122	44	83
Renko, Steve, Bridgeport	6	6	2.41	16	0	97	79	25	79
Riley, Ed, Nashua	13	4	2.89	21	0	131	121	57	92
Nieves, Ernesto, Bridgeport	9	3	3.01	45	0	84	76	31	50
Magee, Dan, Nashua	11	6	3.07	20	0	123	115	71	132
Henry, Dwayne, Somerset	3	6	3.20	27	4	82	75	36	80
Murray, Matt, Newburgh	5	7	3.21	18	0	123	140	33	85
Valera, Julio, Atlantic City	6	5	3.54	11	0	81	69	13	69
Conner, Scott, Bridgeport	10	5	3.86	20	0	110	115	51	71
Telgheder, Jim, Newburgh	8	9	4.00	31	4	101	106	28	77

ATLANTIC CITY

BATTING	AVG	AB	R	H	2B	3B	HR	RBI	SB
Ahrendt, Jay, c	.270	141	26	38	6	2	2	11	1
Aude, Rich, dh	.319	163	35	52	15	1	12	37	0
Avila, Rolo, of-2b	.260	311	73	81	14	3	3	30	26
De la Vega, Javier, c	.133	15	0	2	0	0	0	2	0
Espada, Angel, ss-2b	.227	44	5	10	0	0	1	5	5
2-team (23 Newark)	.350	120	23	42	3	2	2	11	18
Fagley, Dan, c	.161	56	8	9	1	0	2	6	0
Giles, Brian, ss-2b	.296	243	56	72	12	2	8	54	4
Maysonet, Jose, ss	.250	16	1	4	1	0	1	5	0
McQuiniff, Jason, 3b-c	.250	32	2	8	2	0	0	5	0
3-team (36 Som, 7 Nash)	.180	150	11	27	8	0	0	15	1
Medina, Robert, c	.256	86	10	22	4	0	2	12	2
2-team (25 Newark)	.245	139	17	34	10	0	3	21	3
Monell, Johnny, dh-of	.320	228	34	73	12	3	4	38	1
Morillo, Cesar, ss-3b	.350	123	16	43	10	0	1	13	7
3-team (11 New, 28 Nash)	.315	257	37	81	14	2	2	35	17
Pell, Rich, 2b	.297	74	17	22	5	0	1	7	2
Pellot, Victor, 1b	.182	22	3	4	0	0	0	2	0
Pennyfeather, Will, of	.298	376	81	112	25	2	16	69	13
Quinones, Luis, 3b-2b	.202	312	32	63	13	1	6	38	4
Robinson, Darryl, 3b	.252	163	21	41	9	0	3	24	1
Rocha, Juan, of	.275	258	60	71	15	3	12	44	16
Rodriguez, Joe, c	.125	40	1	5	2	0	0	2	0
Thomas, Juan, 1b	.253	395	64	100	18	0	33	103	6
Young, Gerald, of	.293	297	69	87	24	5	4	44	12

PITCHING	W	L	ERA	G	SV	IP	H	BB	SO
Barfield, John	1	1	6.75	7	0	8	11	0	6
2-team (18 Newark)	1	6	9.43	25	1	28	48	5	24
Becker, Tom	1	0	7.20	5	0	10	12	5	9
DeJesus, Jose	1	1	6.00	2	0	9	11	5	5
Duffy, John	2	1	4.50	18	1	20	23	12	13
Eddy, Chris	6	0	0.70	38	26	39	28	6	41
Hope, John	7	8	5.33	21	0	122	138	60	73
Medero, Gadiel	5	2	4.96	25	0	85	95	35	50
Miranda, Angel	6	4	5.16	15	0	82	93	51	68
Mojica, Gonzalo	1	1	14.85	9	0	13	32	6	8
Nogowski, Brandon	0	1	5.79	4	1	14	17	5	9
2-team (2 Newark)	0	1	5.00	6	1	18	20	5	13
Ojeda, Erick	5	2	4.18	19	1	71	74	16	47
Rivera, Marco	3	3	4.96	10	0	45	44	24	29
2-team (18 Somerset)	5	6	5.66	28	0	95	117	47	46
Rodriguez, Chris	2	0	4.59	16	1	33	36	17	29
Romanoli, Paul	3	0	3.58	5	0	28	34	3	14
2-team (31 Newburgh)	5	7	2.45	36	11	73	72	24	56
Rosario, David	2	1	3.55	18	1	25	26	11	24
Santiago, Derek	1	1	1.80	5	0	15	11	5	12
Thompson, Frank	2	1	3.74	38	0	53	50	23	47
Valera, Julio	6	5	3.54	11	0	81	69	13	69
Ware, Jeff	3	4	5.71	12	0	52	47	29	39
Zimmerman, Mike	3	4	7.15	13	0	68	77	44	42

BRIDGEPORT

BATTING	AVG	AB	R	H	2B	3B	HR	RBI	SB
Bennett, Marshall, dh-of	.280	75	13	21	6	0	5	18	4
Cepeda, Malcolm, 3b	.191	152	21	29	4	0	0	19	7
Cornelius, Brian, of	.322	298	61	96	14	3	11	53	7
Davis, Gerald, of	.243	111	12	27	4	0	1	17	0
Edwards, Lamont, 3b	.284	261	39	74	7	2	4	45	7
Felder, Mike, of	.243	321	42	78	17	2	1	21	8
Fraraccio, Dan, ss	.275	305	53	84	19	2	6	42	9
Landingham, James, of-dh	.295	224	36	66	10	3	0	29	19
Marquez, Ruben, 2b-ss	.271	133	13	36	3	0	0	8	1
McGriff, Terry, c	.294	211	39	62	16	1	3	33	0
Ortiz, Asbel, 2b	.285	263	35	75	14	3	5	40	7
Pledger, Kinnis, 1b	.333	348	91	116	21	1	26	91	14
Singleton, Duane, of	.278	335	45	93	19	5	2	30	19
Trafton, Todd, dh	.256	43	8	11	3	0	0	4	1
Walker, Joe, c	.269	182	21	49	9	0	4	22	2
Wearing, Mel, dh-1b	.299	147	40	44	11	0	10	34	4

PITCHING	W	L	ERA	G	SV	IP	H	BB	SO
Ahearne, Pat	2	2	2.57	5	0	28	29	5	16
Cintron, Jose	8	3	4.31	15	0	94	86	16	51
Collazo, Rafael	1	0	4.00	5	0	9	8	3	4
Compres, Fidel	1	1	6.66	21	0	26	39	7	21
Conner, Scott	10	5	3.86	20	0	110	115	51	71
Duffy, John	0	0	6.57	9	0	12	17	6	10
2-team (18 Atlantic City)	2	1	5.29	27	1	32	40	18	23
Guilfoyle, Mike	2	2	2.28	45	30	51	39	12	56
Klemyk, Jim	2	2	4.75	33	0	55	50	39	34
Meinershagen, Adam	5	2	2.48	13	0	65	54	42	41
Nieves, Ernesto	9	3	3.01	45	0	84	76	31	50
Paige, Carey	5	3	3.66	18	1	66	59	35	65
Renko, Steve	6	6	2.41	16	0	97	79	25	79
Rosenkranz, Terry	8	2	2.15	39	1	59	31	27	61
Sontag, Alan	5	5	4.94	17	0	102	119	35	79
Yoder, Jason	0	0	4.00	10	0	18	18	5	10

NASHUA

BATTING	AVG	AB	R	H	2B	3B	HR	RBI	SB
Ahrendt, Jay, c	.233	43	9	10	4	0	1	11	1
2-team (44 Atlantic City)	.261	184	35	48	10	2	3	22	2
Beckhorn, Frank, dh	.298	121	23	36	5	2	3	17	0
Benbow, Lou, 2b-ss	.275	200	31	55	14	1	5	23	4
2-team (17 Newburgh)	.256	250	35	64	16	1	5	28	5
Bethea, Larry, 1b	.258	233	29	60	9	0	8	34	16
Boston, D.J., 1b	.294	163	32	48	13	0	9	37	4
Cuyler, Milt, of	.309	249	62	77	18	6	6	33	21
Delanuez, Rex, of	.243	37	4	9	1	0	0	6	2
2-team (23 Somerset)	.263	118	15	31	5	0	1	16	2
Diaz, Mario, 2b	.372	78	11	29	7	0	6	20	0
Fagley, Dan, c	.207	29	5	6	0	0	0	5	1
3-team (21 AC, 21 Newark)	.155	142	16	22	2	0	3	17	1
Fernandez, Emilio, 2b-3b	.125	24	2	3	0	1	0	2	0
Flores, Marcos, of	.103	29	3	3	2	0	0	3	1
Forsberg, Dana, 1b	.318	22	2	7	0	1	0	4	1
Galarza, Joel, c	.239	113	11	27	7	1	3	14	0
Gates, Leonard, 1b	.151	53	4	8	2	0	0	4	2
Green, Dario, of	.289	173	31	50	7	4	2	21	17
Gresham, Kris, c	.300	213	46	64	14	1	7	30	6
Hulse, David, of-dh	.352	230	43	81	16	2	8	42	10
Jemison, Andrew, 3b-of	.244	45	4	11	3	1	0	3	0
Jose, Felix, of	.343	327	72	112	19	1	26	86	8
Keith, Jason, 2b	.116	43	4	5	0	1	0	0	4
McQuiniff, Jason, c-3b	.188	16	4	3	0	0	0	0	0
Moore, Kevin, of-3b	.272	92	20	25	4	0	3	12	4
Moore, Michael, of	.250	132	25	33	10	0	8	19	4
Morillo, Cesar, 3b	.286	98	16	28	3	2	1	18	9
Porter, Kedric, of	.250	28	5	7	1	0	0	5	2
Robinson, Darryl, 3b	.111	18	2	2	0	0	0	3	0
2-team (45 Atlantic City)	.238	181	23	43	9	0	3	27	1
Rodriguez, Tony, ss	.284	352	60	100	18	1	6	47	36
Taylor, Matt, 3b	.207	58	9	12	2	0	0	5	1
Wilson, Todd, 3b	.281	64	9	18	0	0	1	15	1

PITCHING	W	L	ERA	G	SV	IP	H	BB	SO
Aquino, Luis	1	0	0.00	4	0	8	7	0	2
2-team (5 Newburgh)	2	2	1.87	9	0	34	30	8	23
Burgos, John	3	0	2.35	11	0	23	18	5	20
Burkindine, Larry	0	1	18.90	2	0	3	4	13	2
2-team (13 Somerset)	0	2	13.25	15	0	18	24	30	12
Calderon, Jose	3	4	3.35	14	0	54	50	22	23
Duke, Jason	2	1	5.06	9	0	27	24	18	18
Flores, Mario	2	2	7.15	6	0	23	28	10	12
Grahe, Joe	4	3	2.44	10	0	66	49	21	43
Hackett, Jason	0	1	7.00	7	0	18	23	15	12
Juarbe, Ken	3	1	3.19	28	2	48	35	31	40
MacNaught, Colin	0	1	6.55	7	0	11	19	9	4
Magee, Danny	11	6	3.07	20	0	123	115	71	132
Maldonado, Jay	2	2	5.85	17	0	40	32	38	29
Martinez, Frankie	1	1	6.83	22	1	29	29	13	15
Martinez, Sean	1	1	1.93	2	0	5	3	3	4
2-team (3 Newark)	1	2	2.25	5	0	20	13	13	11
Matulevich, Jeff	2	4	3.47	46	4	60	59	27	54
Morel, Jose	0	1	5.94	12	0	17	21	8	12
Nowell, Brian	1	0	5.89	5	0	18	22	4	5
Oliveras, Cisco	2	0	1.13	13	3	16	5	6	15
Richards, Dave	1	1	3.68	11	0	15	14	9	15
Riley, Ed	13	4	2.89	21	0	134	121	57	92
Sanchez, Geraldo	3	1	2.38	10	0	23	19	7	13
Smith, Ryan	3	5	4.17	29	2	91	99	29	58
Taylor, Tom	1	1	3.38	11	1	13	11	7	16

NEWARK

BATTING	AVG	AB	R	H	2B	3B	HR	RBI	SB
Alvarez, Luis, 1b	.295	254	38	75	12	2	2	28	4
Balint, Rob, c	.216	88	11	19	5	1	3	17	0
2-team (29 Newburgh)	.244	160	27	39	8	2	6	27	0
Bargman, Todd, of-1b	.220	100	10	22	4	0	0	5	1
Braddy, Nehemiah, of	.136	22	2	3	0	0	0	0	0
Espada, Angel, 2b-ss	.421	76	18	32	3	2	1	6	13
Estrada, Josue, of	.213	150	16	32	2	2	1	15	3
Fagley, Dan, c	.123	57	3	7	1	0	1	6	0
Giles, Brian, 2b	.238	42	6	10	2	0	0	5	1
2-team (76 Atlantic City)	.288	285	62	82	14	2	8	59	5
Green, Dario, of	.300	70	14	21	4	2	2	11	5
2-team (64 Nashua)	.292	243	45	71	11	6	4	32	22
Griffith, Tommy, of	.267	303	50	81	10	6	7	37	24
Harris, Eric, 1b	.174	69	6	12	4	0	0	6	1
McKnight, Jeff, 3b	.387	31	5	12	2	0	0	4	1
Medina, Robert, c	.226	53	7	12	6	0	1	9	1
Morillo, Cesar, ss	.278	36	5	10	1	0	0	4	1
Ramirez, Peto, c	.263	95	9	25	4	1	1	8	0
Robertson, Greg, 1b-3b	.320	125	16	40	6	1	0	18	3
Smith, Brian, of-2b	.286	248	31	71	8	2	0	20	15
Taylor, Matt, ss	.222	230	34	51	6	2	0	31	6
2-team (24 Nashua)	.219	288	43	63	8	2	0	36	7
Texidor, Jose, dh	.180	61	4	11	3	0	0	2	0
Thomas, Keith, of-dh	.326	316	49	103	22	2	13	75	15
Thurman, Gary, of	.275	109	23	30	4	2	4	17	13
Turberville, Kris, 3b-of	.056	18	5	1	0	0	0	0	1
Waggener, Jim, 2b-ss	.250	240	29	60	12	0	0	14	2
Walker, Steven, of	.234	175	34	41	5	4	9	22	9
Worthington, Craig, 3b	.265	283	42	75	14	0	12	50	0
Zabata, Charlie, c	.050	20	1	1	1	0	0	2	0

PITCHING	W	L	ERA	G	SV	IP	H	BB	SO
Apana, Matt	0	1	7.11	6	0	6	4	10	3
Barfield, John	0	5	10.53	18	1	20	37	5	18
Bennett, Jason	0	1	5.01	30	0	50	62	15	31
Cain, Tim	10	6	4.09	21	0	128	143	38	83
DeJesus, Jose	5	6	4.56	12	0	79	72	46	90
2-team (2 Atlantic City)	6	7	4.70	14	0	88	83	51	95
Givens, Brian	3	7	3.77	12	0	74	75	35	57
Hedrick, Keith	2	4	6.00	8	0	48	64	11	16
Letourneau, Jeff	1	1	4.95	4	0	20	18	9	6
Martinez, Sean	0	1	2.35	3	0	15	10	10	7
Maskivish, Joe	1	4	4.63	48	2	58	70	29	41
McHugh, Mike	0	0	11.12	7	0	6	8	9	6
Mitchell, John	3	7	5.18	14	0	83	100	23	38
Miyashita, Daisuke	1	1	5.89	9	0	18	21	6	14
Mojica, Gonzalo	0	1	12.46	5	0	9	13	6	7
3-team (11 New, 9 AC)	1	3	9.91	25	0	43	64	25	28
Nogowski, Brandon	0	0	2.25	2	0	4	3	0	4
Parotte, Frisco	1	3	10.07	11	0	22	36	13	13
Piddington, Brian	2	1	4.76	7	0	34	33	18	25
Rhodriguez, Rory	0	0	6.00	14	1	18	14	19	10
Richards, Dave	4	3	2.41	30	6	34	31	14	37
2-team (11 Nashua)	5	4	2.79	41	6	48	45	23	52
Ryan, Kevin	0	2	9.77	11	0	16	22	10	12
Sanchez, Gerardo	1	3	6.34	15	0	44	61	12	23
Vicentino, Andy	0	1	10.80	6	0	5	11	3	4
Zimmerman, Mike	1	5	7.96	6	0	32	36	24	29
2-team (13 Atlantic City)	4	9	7.40	19	0	100	113	68	71

NEWBURGH

BATTING	AVG	AB	R	H	2B	3B	HR	RBI	SB
Anderson, Milt, of	.308	104	24	32	5	1	2	15	8
Balint, Rob, c-1b	.278	72	16	20	3	1	3	10	0
Benbow, Lou, ss	.180	50	4	9	2	0	0	5	1
Blair, Brian, of	.281	335	53	94	21	8	4	51	24
Briggs, Stoney, of-1b	.333	87	21	29	6	0	8	25	9
Gorecki, Ryan, 2b-3b	.327	309	51	101	14	3	0	38	6
Hernandez, Victor, ss-3b	.237	76	12	18	2	2	2	11	5
2-team (72 Somerset)	.271	299	34	81	13	6	5	42	14
Keith, Jason, 2b	.220	41	2	9	1	0	0	2	0
2-team (18 Nashua)	.167	84	6	14	1	1	0	2	4
Martin, James, of-1b	.258	260	39	67	9	6	12	44	15
Maysonet, Jose, 2b-ss	.198	81	11	16	1	0	1	8	9
2-team (12 Atlantic City)	.206	97	12	20	2	0	2	13	9
McDonnell, John, c	.200	15	1	3	0	0	0	2	0
Merchant, Mark, dh	.254	252	33	64	14	1	8	40	1
Motley, Mel, of	.100	10	0	1	0	0	0	0	0
Pagan, Angel, ss-2b	.293	311	55	91	8	3	6	29	11
Pagano, Scott, of	.226	159	25	36	4	2	1	18	13
Pecorilli, Aldo, dh-1b	.235	85	14	20	7	0	2	18	0
Perez, Danny, of	.303	307	54	93	16	5	4	32	15
Ryder, Derek, c	.231	299	26	69	6	2	1	28	3
Viera, Jose, 3b	.308	247	45	76	16	3	15	52	5
Watkins, Sean, 1b	.235	238	22	56	12	2	5	28	0

PITCHING	W	L	ERA	G	SV	IP	H	BB	SO
Anders, Mike	0	0	8.00	7	0	9	11	8	7
Aquino, Luis	1	2	2.42	5	0	26	23	8	21
Barbao, Joe	0	1	3.00	8	2	12	17	2	3
Boze, Marshall	7	8	4.22	18	0	117	120	50	117
Campbell, Chad	1	1	5.88	6	0	26	31	16	27
Fleming, Dave	1	1	9.16	4	0	19	24	14	6
Heckman, Andy	4	4	4.65	23	0	93	106	36	63
Kammerer, James	1	5	5.00	19	0	36	42	30	21
McLaughlin, Denis	1	2	12.83	11	0	13	19	12	5
Mojica, Gonzalo	0	1	5.66	11	0	21	19	13	13
Murray, Matt	5	7	3.21	18	0	123	140	33	85
Mysel, David	1	1	2.92	9	0	12	7	5	11
Rivera, Raul	2	3	5.65	23	0	72	69	51	51
Roberts, Chris	5	2	4.56	9	0	53	58	19	37
Romanoli, Paul	2	7	1.77	31	11	46	38	21	42
Steimle, Brian	1	1	7.02	15	0	33	40	33	20
Steinmetz, Earl	0	2	4.63	4	0	23	22	9	18
Telgheder, Jim	8	9	4.00	31	4	101	106	28	77
Tyrell, Jim	1	1	4.67	9	0	17	18	9	11

SOMERSET

BATTING	AVG	AB	R	H	2B	3B	HR	RBI	SB
Arnold, Ken, ss	.249	342	43	85	12	1	3	28	17
Broach, Donald, of	.264	273	45	72	7	6	2	19	19
Delanuez, Rex, of	.272	81	11	22	4	0	1	10	0
Diorio, Andrew, 3b	.291	254	41	74	13	1	4	25	4
Forsberg, Dana, 1b	.227	110	13	25	9	0	2	13	1
2-team (8 Nashua)	.242	132	15	32	9	1	2	17	2
Goodman, Herbert, of	.159	182	20	29	5	0	5	15	7
Griggs, Rod, of	.256	262	27	67	4	2	0	19	9
Hernandez, Victor, of-2b	.283	223	22	63	11	4	3	31	9
Lukachyk, Rob, of-1b	.234	145	20	34	8	3	4	17	7
Lyle, Dane, 2b	.210	62	9	13	3	0	0	6	0
Martin, James, of	.197	71	10	14	2	2	2	11	4
2-team (69 Newburgh)	.245	331	49	81	11	8	14	55	19
McQuiniff, Jason, 3b	.157	102	5	16	6	0	0	10	1
Morales, Jorge, c	.332	352	50	117	25	1	7	54	2
Napoleon, Louie, 2b	.189	169	16	32	4	2	0	14	6
Nava, Lipso, 2b-1b	.332	202	28	67	11	2	4	31	6
Otero, Oscar, 3b	.043	23	1	1	0	0	0	0	0
Skeels, Andy, dh	.254	138	20	35	10	1	0	14	4
Szekely, Joe, dh	.107	56	2	6	0	1	1	6	1
Traxler, Brian, 1b	.256	129	12	33	9	0	5	26	0
Vazquez, Roberto, 2b	.133	15	3	2	0	0	0	0	0

PITCHING	W	L	ERA	G	SV	IP	H	BB	SO
Briscoe, John	2	4	4.12	28	9	39	42	17	41
Burkindine, Larry	0	1	12.00	13	0	15	20	17	10
Collazo, Rafael	1	2	7.56	5	0	25	29	20	11
2-team (5 Bridgeport)	2	2	6.62	10	0	34	37	23	15
Henry, Dwayne	3	6	3.20	27	4	82	75	36	80
Hoy, Wayne	6	5	4.02	13	0	63	63	22	26
Jacob, Scott	0	2	9.35	14	0	35	49	17	17

	W	L	ERA	G	SV	IP	H	BB	SO
Jolliffe, Brian	3	5	6.68	24	0	67	77	55	25
Nowell, Brian	2	4	6.32	9	0	53	66	27	38
2-team (5 Nashua)	3	4	6.21	14	0	71	88	31	43
Olsen, Mario	5	4	4.45	39	2	83	77	42	29
Pulido, Carlos	2	2	3.31	12	3	35	30	12	33
Rivera, Marco	2	3	6.30	18	0	50	73	23	17
Schmidt, Curt	2	4	4.26	40	7	68	58	30	48
Sebra, Bob	1	4	6.03	9	0	34	36	24	21
Turberville, Kris	1	3	8.89	16	1	27	37	20	26
2-team (1 Nashua)	1	3	8.89	17	1	28	39	20	27
Vanderweele, Doug	1	5	7.66	16	0	47	78	12	18
Zappelli, Mark	9	5	2.33	21	0	131	122	44	83

FRONTIER LEAGUE

The Frontier League had another solid season in 1998 and produced some of the best talent in the independent ranks, notably Richmond's Morgan Burkhart, who was named Baseball America's Independent Player of the Year.

Burkhart won the Frontier League triple crown by hitting .404 with 36 home runs and 98 RBIs, good enough to earn his third straight MVP award. The Roosters finished with the second best overall record but failed to advance to postseason play due to Evansville's domination of the Western Division in the first half and Springfield's strong second-half play.

Under the leadership of Mal Fichman, Springfield took the title for the second time in three years. It was Fichman's fourth title in six years as a Frontier League manager. He led Erie to the title in 1994 and Johnstown in 1995. His first championship with the Capitals was won in 1996.

Despite his accomplishments, the Capitals hired a new manager in the offseason. Paul Fletcher will try to make it three titles in four years when he leads the club in 1999.

The Frontier League welcomes a new franchise in 1999. O'Fallon, Mo., a suburb of St. Louis, will be the site of the league's ninth team. A 10th team was also expected be added.

STANDINGS

FIRST HALF

EAST	W	L	PCT	GB
Chillicothe Paints	23	17	.575	—
Canton Crocodiles	22	18	.550	1
Johnstown Johnnies	18	20	.474	4
Ohio Valley Redcoats	15	24	.385	7½
WEST	**W**	**L**	**PCT**	**GB**
Evansville Otters	23	16	.590	—
Richmond Roosters	23	17	.575	½
Springfield Capitals	21	16	.568	1
Kalamazoo Kodiaks	11	28	.282	12

SECOND HALF

EAST	W	L	PCT	GB
Chillicothe Paints	25	14	.641	—
Canton Crocodiles	19	20	.487	6
Johnstown Johnnies	16	23	.410	9
Ohio Valley Redcoats	11	28	.282	14
WEST	**W**	**L**	**PCT**	**GB**
Springfield Capitals	27	13	.675	—
Richmond Roosters	26	14	.650	1
Evansville Otters	20	20	.500	7
Kalamazoo Kodiaks	14	26	.350	13

PLAYOFFS: Semifinals—Chillicothe defeated Canton 2-1 and Springfield defeated Evansville 2-1 in best-of-3 series. **Finals**—Springfield defeated Chillicothe 2-1 in best-of-3 series.

MANAGERS: Canton—Theron Todd. Chillicothe—Roger Hanners. Evansville—Greg Tagert. Johnstown—Stephan Rapaglia. Kalamazoo—Alan Riffle/Andy McCauley. Ohio Valley—Greg LeMaster/Tom Waelchli. Richmond—John Cate. Springfield—Mal Fichman.

ATTENDANCE: Evansville 88,259; Chillicothe 71,782; Canton 64,519; Springfield 52,889; Johnstown 45,447; Kalamazoo 41,331; Richmond 39,978; Ohio Valley 23,933.

ALL-STAR TEAM: C—Pat Evans, Springfield. **1B**—Morgan Burkhart, Richmond. **2B**—Travis Gray, Evansville. **3B**—Mitch House, Chillicothe. **SS**—Keith Habig, Richmond. **OF**—Gator McBride, Chillicothe; Kirk Taylor, Ohio Valley; Willie Edwards, Kalamazoo. **DH**—Scott Pinoni, Chillicothe. **SP**—Jason Simontacchi, Springfield. **RP**—Sean House, Springfield.

Most Valuable Player: Morgan Burkhart, Richmond. **Most Valuable Pitcher:** Jason Simontacchi, Springfield. **Manager of the Year:** John Cate, Richmond.

INDIVIDUAL BATTING LEADERS

(Minimum 216 Plate Appearances)

	AVG	AB	R	H	2B	3B	HR	RBI	SB
Burkhart, Morgan, Rich.	.404	280	97	113	18	1	36	98	13
McBride, Gator, Chillicothe	.403	243	58	98	29	1	12	63	4
Brown, Bobby, Canton	.363	320	58	116	28	2	9	63	13
Hemme, Justin, Canton	.361	227	45	82	15	5	8	42	1
Herman, Josh, Ohio Valley	.357	210	43	75	13	0	12	48	0
Habig, Keith, Richmond	.356	289	87	103	19	4	25	89	7
Cruz, Paul, Springfield	.356	191	47	68	10	3	5	39	1
Ronca, Joe, Springfield	.344	317	56	109	21	0	16	77	1
Joseph, Eric, Evansville	.336	214	39	72	16	3	2	37	20
Evans, Pat, Springfield	.335	272	56	91	17	1	14	49	8

INDIVIDUAL PITCHING LEADERS

(Minimum 64 Innings)

	W	L	ERA	G	SV	IP	H	BB	SO
Harden, Tony, Richmond	10	1	2.36	13	0	92	83	32	66
Simontacchi, Jason, Spring.	10	2	2.95	16	0	110	103	21	92
Fidge, Darren, Kalamazoo	5	6	3.06	17	0	106	115	39	79
Arcement, Cody, Canton	7	3	3.34	15	0	102	100	30	62
Spears, Bob, Chillicothe	10	5	3.38	17	0	117	107	55	124
Irving, Jamie, Johnstown	10	4	3.41	31	2	148	176	34	88
Roberts, Mike, Chillicothe	7	1	4.22	13	0	70	81	20	50
Waller, Jerry, Kalamazoo	4	6	4.41	15	0	82	80	48	59
Schlee, Jeremy, Evansville	6	3	4.42	16	0	90	117	40	59
Prenzlin, Gregg, Canton	7	0	4.52	21	0	76	84	25	44

CANTON

BATTING	AVG	AB	R	H	2B	3B	HR	RBI	SB
Beam, Chance, c	1.000	1	1	1	0	0	0	0	0
2-team (17 Johnstown)	.250	36	4	9	1	0	1	5	2
Brown, Bobby, of-3b	.363	320	58	116	28	2	9	63	13
Copeland, Jason, 3b	.200	25	4	5	1	0	1	4	1
DeBoer, Kalen, of	.272	81	14	22	4	0	1	9	5
Doskocil, Darren, 3b	.260	169	33	44	6	1	2	24	4
Droptini, Bryan, of	.302	212	46	64	5	3	3	30	24
Girard, Charan, 2b	.292	212	24	62	9	1	0	18	12
Gracia, Tyrone, dh-3b	.263	171	29	45	6	0	4	32	8
Hemme, Justin, 1b	.361	227	45	82	15	5	8	42	1
Johnson, Danny, of	.348	66	9	23	6	1	0	8	5
Kobsik, Rick, 1b	.321	53	10	17	8	0	0	8	2
Kokinda, Steve, dh	.250	28	5	7	1	1	0	6	1
Krey, Kenny, ss	.270	178	33	48	10	1	2	17	11
Lewis, Steve, of	.205	39	4	8	0	1	0	1	2
Mitrovich, Steve, c-1b	.158	57	6	9	2	0	1	7	2
Reynolds, Chance, c	.273	256	42	70	15	1	6	43	4
Robinson, Tony, 2b-ss	.271	221	41	60	4	1	1	27	12
Rose, Carlos, of	.188	48	9	9	3	0	1	5	3
Swinton, Jermaine, of-1b	.333	297	59	99	25	2	19	83	14
Voldness, Aaron, c	.171	41	3	7	0	0	1	7	0

PITCHING	W	L	ERA	G	SV	IP	H	BB	SO
Alazaus, Shawn	4	6	5.20	16	0	106	118	34	74
Arcement, Cody	7	3	3.34	15	0	102	100	30	62
Arnold, John	5	3	5.40	13	0	78	91	40	47
Barron, Mark	0	0	4.70	6	0	15	21	14	7
Behrens, Brett	1	1	2.73	14	1	33	39	8	20
Bell, Richard	0	4	4.88	8	0	31	32	21	19
Evans, Mike	0	1	3.24	29	14	33	22	15	33
Filson, Brian	2	4	3.14	12	1	14	13	9	9
Kimoto, Kyle	0	0	7.16	11	0	16	23	5	16
Marchesano, Mike	2	1	3.46	4	0	26	22	8	23
Prenzlin, Gregg	7	3	4.52	21	0	76	84	25	44
Ramagli, Matt	1	2	5.96	4	0	26	28	8	8
Rieke, Jim	1	2	5.95	13	0	20	26	15	7
Rojas, Chris	4	4	6.65	25	0	45	43	31	33
Schulman, Jeff	0	1	18.47	6	0	6	13	8	3
Sivumaki, Cory	6	2	6.44	13	0	50	65	20	16
Snowden, Chad	1	1	14.40	4	0	5	9	1	2

CHILLICOTHE

BATTING	AVG	AB	R	H	2B	3B	HR	RBI	SB
Boggs, Ronnie, c	.266	64	7	17	1	1	3	10	0
Constantino, Tony, of	.311	212	50	66	11	6	0	21	22
Dalton, David, ss	.330	221	45	73	16	6	7	60	6
Daly, Pat, of	.250	44	10	11	0	0	2	4	0
Dockery, Tim, c	.179	28	3	5	1	0	0	4	0
Fletcher, Michael, of	.285	249	41	71	12	1	2	39	6
Flores, Freddy, ss-2b	.258	93	24	24	2	0	0	5	15
Helms, Telly, dh-3b	.278	151	27	42	6	0	6	25	1
Horning, Mike, 2b	.273	267	46	73	12	0	2	29	6
House, Mitch, 3b	.277	264	61	73	14	1	17	66	11
McBride, Gator, of	.403	243	58	98	29	1	12	63	4
Pinoni, Scott, 1b	.309	304	69	94	17	1	25	98	1
Plackemeier, Brad, c	.324	173	27	56	14	0	3	26	3
Seimetz, Dan, of-dh	.260	254	43	66	12	1	5	41	0
Walker, Corey, of	.198	121	23	24	4	1	5	18	4

PITCHING	W	L	ERA	G	SV	IP	H	BB	SO
Blanc, Rick	1	1	2.97	23	7	36	26	18	46
Byrd, Stephen	5	5	5.99	15	0	83	92	41	82
Chandler, Bobby	1	2	3.90	25	7	32	27	19	22
Collins, Donnie	2	1	2.53	30	4	32	17	20	30
Hillier, Billy	1	1	2.30	8	1	16	11	8	12
Johnson, Jeremiah	0	3	8.51	12	0	24	28	25	18
McAninch, Sam	1	2	4.33	18	1	44	48	23	34
Mycheck, Andy	0	1	16.20	3	0	2	2	4	1
Peck, John	7	4	4.75	15	0	72	94	31	35
Rask, Fred	0	2	9.31	6	0	19	28	15	12
Roberts, Mike	7	1	4.22	13	0	70	81	20	50
Scarcello, Brian	13	1	4.57	16	0	102	120	39	65
Soto, Hank	0	2	7.56	6	0	8	7	8	4
Spears, Bob	10	5	3.38	17	0	117	107	55	124
Tryon, Eric	0	0	0.00	8	0	10	3	5	10
2-team (5 Richmond)	0	2	7.36	13	0	26	34	16	22

EVANSVILLE

BATTING	AVG	AB	R	H	2B	3B	HR	RBI	SB
Bowman, L.A., ss	.235	136	16	32	4	0	0	15	9
Bowne, Jeff, of	.190	21	6	4	1	1	0	3	1
Brown, Todd, 3b	.261	134	19	35	5	0	0	10	7
Bryan, Brooks, of	.327	104	23	34	9	0	2	14	5
Cano, Matt, 3b-1b	.295	251	55	74	18	0	2	32	6
Ceriani, Matt, c	.203	59	8	12	5	0	1	11	0
Clark, Jason, of	.351	188	46	66	12	6	7	35	23
Cooper, Scott, c	.135	52	7	7	0	0	0	6	0
Cueto, Jim, of	.221	199	29	44	3	4	1	23	4
Dapprich, Scott, ss-2b	.208	120	19	25	2	0	0	15	1
Donati, John, 1b-dh	.270	89	12	24	6	0	3	13	1
Foster, Brian, 1b	.344	186	39	64	14	2	7	48	0
Giallella, Scott, c	.258	62	6	16	3	0	0	9	1
Gray, Travis, 2b-3b	.302	281	40	85	16	1	7	60	9
Holcomb, Mike, of	.277	47	6	13	2	1	1	5	2
Joseph, Eric, of	.336	214	39	72	16	3	2	37	20
Luna, Rich, 3b	.304	56	11	17	2	0	3	9	1
Mauro, Joe, c	.138	29	3	4	0	0	1	1	0
Miranda, Migdoel, of	.233	116	26	27	3	0	1	13	13
Robinson, David, of	.308	227	50	70	17	1	5	38	9
Robinson, Tony, ss-2b	.357	56	15	20	3	0	0	13	4
2-team (56 Canton)	.289	277	56	80	7	1	1	40	16
Schwieder, Nick, c	.324	34	4	11	1	0	0	8	0
Stockam, Travis, c	.167	12	1	2	0	0	0	0	0

PITCHING	W	L	ERA	G	SV	IP	H	BB	SO
Garola, Rob	2	2	3.71	26	2	63	66	20	33
Kalbrener, Jason	5	9	5.27	17	0	99	112	35	86
Kelley, Brent	1	1	5.14	2	0	7	7	4	8
Kottmeyer, Matt	6	3	3.52	36	4	46	53	7	46
May, Kyle	6	2	2.03	31	8	49	25	28	55
Miller, Mike	0	2	14.40	4	0	5	9	2	3
Murphy, Rob	2	2	5.05	31	1	46	60	15	34
Perri, Tista	7	5	5.07	17	0	110	136	18	62
Rockwell, Keith	0	0	4.58	9	0	20	23	10	8
Rodgers, Mike	4	5	5.08	17	0	96	110	44	60
Rogow, Eric	1	1	6.00	8	1	12	15	6	10
Schlee, Jeremy	6	3	4.42	16	0	90	117	40	59
Schooler, Aaron	1	0	2.11	16	0	21	17	7	17
Smith, Matt	1	0	12.00	4	0	12	14	16	11
Stadelhofer, Mike	1	0	3.86	3	0	5	6	2	3

JOHNSTOWN

BATTING	AVG	AB	R	H	2B	3B	HR	RBI	SB
Aspeslet, Preston, of	.296	226	39	67	16	0	2	21	20
Barrus, Golden, dh-c	.267	101	17	27	5	3	1	12	1
Beam, Chance, c	.229	35	3	8	1	0	1	5	2
Berliner, Seth, ss	.253	265	36	67	19	0	4	37	12
Dorsey, Jason, of	.267	150	22	40	12	2	7	30	8
Figueroa, Shaun, 2b	.296	280	50	83	6	4	2	26	21
Griffin, Justin, 3b	.222	36	6	8	0	1	0	3	3
Kalcounos, Andy, 3b-ss	.212	118	19	25	5	1	1	9	2
LaFlair, Jay, c	.235	34	2	8	1	0	0	5	1
Linder, Brian, 3b	.301	146	26	44	10	2	2	16	16
Memmert, Gabe, dh	.377	122	17	46	8	0	3	16	0
Mitchell, Rivers, of	.227	141	21	32	5	1	1	14	11
Morrill, Jim, dh	.185	27	3	5	1	0	0	4	1
Pichardo, Sandy, dh-1b	.204	54	10	11	2	0	3	9	3
Riccio, John, 1b	.305	249	44	76	21	1	10	49	3
Satcho, Rick, c	.214	173	23	37	6	0	4	22	4
Shakir, Usman, of	.118	17	3	2	0	0	0	2	0
Simmons, Leroy, of	.250	124	24	31	10	0	4	23	2
Vasquez, Danny, of	.332	313	53	104	19	10	16	65	22
Watley, Clarence, of-3b	.213	47	7	10	2	0	0	6	3

PITCHING	W	L	ERA	G	SV	IP	H	BB	SO
Allen, Rodney	0	4	6.16	4	0	19	22	7	13
Bromley, Randy	1	4	6.75	22	8	23	19	27	21
Cerbone, Marc	0	0	6.38	11	2	18	18	11	7
Collins, Heath	2	4	4.88	9	0	55	66	17	40
Cordle, Jeff	0	0	9.82	4	0	4	4	3	0
Drennen, Rich	1	0	10.97	7	0	11	17	4	9
Haro, Rosendo	1	0	5.02	12	0	14	26	6	12
Irving, Jamie	10	4	3.41	31	2	148	176	34	88
Kanemoto, Hiroshi	3	2	3.50	11	0	36	33	10	36
Kimoto, Kyle	0	1	3.38	6	0	13	14	3	10
2-team (11 Canton)	0	1	5.46	17	0	30	37	8	26
LaGrandeur, Yan	0	3	9.16	4	0	19	26	12	9
Long, Lee	6	0	3.13	11	0	55	62	18	35
Masching, Bill	2	9	4.70	17	0	105	124	49	68
Mathys, Jason	2	1	6.75	7	0	9	7	7	11
Schroeder, Chris	3	3	5.79	29	1	37	41	22	27
Sexton, Dennis	1	2	9.27	9	0	22	36	11	19
Shioya, Daisuke	0	0	5.14	4	0	7	9	3	5
Sparks, Eric	0	3	9.00	11	0	25	34	23	20
Vanderbush, Matt	0	3	9.00	5	0	21	31	17	12
Zwanch, Mike	2	0	6.00	3	0	21	21	19	16

KALAMAZOO

BATTING	AVG	AB	R	H	2B	3B	HR	RBI	SB
Bardin, Brad, c	.269	186	25	50	8	0	4	21	1
Barrow, Martin, 2b	.229	96	22	22	4	0	4	12	5
Braund, Aaron, dh	.255	102	12	26	5	0	2	13	2
Chase, Allen, 2b	.056	18	1	1	0	0	0	0	0
Clemente, Joe, c	.351	94	11	33	3	0	1	15	1
Edwards, Willie, of	.329	298	65	98	21	3	18	71	11
Hobbs, Jay, 1b-of	.330	267	44	88	19	4	8	47	3
Ikeda, Go, of	.280	246	31	69	6	3	3	18	7
Jempson, Jackie, of	.239	113	12	27	3	1	2	15	5
Kim, Young, dh	.100	10	0	1	0	0	0	0	0
Kramer, Joseph, of	.306	72	13	22	3	1	2	6	6
Mojorovich, Jelenic, 3b	.263	255	34	67	8	0	10	31	0
Poss, John, ss-2b	.251	219	30	55	10	0	3	32	1
2-team (2 Richmond)	.251	227	31	57	10	0	3	33	1
Rivera, Luis, ss	.207	140	23	29	4	2	0	12	9
Rowland, Jeff, 3b	.056	18	1	1	1	0	0	1	0
Sexton, Trent, 2b-ss	.241	166	32	40	4	0	1	13	17
Wilcox, Scot, of	.282	163	18	46	7	3	7	25	3
Zerbe, Mike, 1b-c	.255	255	47	65	18	0	13	44	2

PITCHING	W	L	ERA	G	SV	IP	H	BB	SO
Baum, Chris	1	3	6.04	8	0	51	60	37	28
Baumgardner, Chad	1	1	5.56	14	0	23	21	15	14
Estep, Rich	1	0	7.90	8	0	14	20	5	8
Fidge, Darren	5	6	3.06	17	0	106	115	39	79
Gingrich, Josh	0	2	9.62	19	2	24	32	14	21
Gray, Brett	6	7	4.55	16	0	115	118	23	91
Green, Charles	1	0	2.16	4	0	8	4	5	5
Harajiri, Yutaka	0	0	7.24	7	0	14	18	8	10
Havens, Chris	1	3	7.27	14	0	26	33	18	24
2-team (7 Richmond)	1	4	7.13	21	2	35	50	23	31
Isom, Jeff	0	3	16.71	3	0	7	21	6	2
Mycheck, Andy	0	0	3.00	2	0	3	3	2	2
2-team (3 Chillicothe)	0	1	7.71	5	0	5	5	6	3
Parra, David	0	3	10.55	7	0	21	38	16	13
2-team (3 Richmond)	0	3	9.11	10	0	27	40	20	19
Rivera, Joe	0	1	14.85	3	0	7	11	9	4
Salazar, Mike	0	0	15.43	5	0	5	12	7	3
Salvevold, Greg	1	1	5.54	2	0	13	14	6	5
Schmittle, Ray	0	4	7.56	11	0	25	34	9	14
Scott, Ron	0	2	13.81	13	2	14	19	26	15
Slattery, Alex	0	1	9.58	3	0	10	11	9	4
Spottz, Jamie	1	3	4.11	13	0	15	8	16	11

Stephens, Jon	1	2	13.30	14	0	22	44	14	13
Vitale, Anthony	1	5	7.06	10	0	51	76	17	15
Waller, Jerry	4	6	4.41	15	0	82	80	48	59
Waters, Chris	0	1	9.69	10	0	13	23	5	10
Zallie, Chris	1	0	10.38	2	0	9	12	6	3

OHIO VALLEY

BATTING	AVG	AB	R	H	2B	3B	HR	RBI	SB
Benson, Brad, dh-1b	.238	63	9	15	2	1	2	11	0
Berman, Jeff, 2b	.283	92	15	26	5	0	3	14	6
Close, Bart, of-1b	.268	82	9	22	4	1	1	8	1
Crawley, Dwayne, 1b	.154	52	5	8	2	0	0	5	2
Cunningham, Todd, of	.232	95	15	22	2	2	0	8	3
Del Gozzo, Nick, 3b-ss	.133	45	5	6	0	0	0	1	4
Dettman, Matt, 3b	.271	144	22	39	7	0	4	22	1
Dye, Anthony, of	.071	14	5	1	0	0	0	0	1
Farris, Ed, 1b	.346	104	20	36	4	1	4	23	0
Frushour, Jason, c	.267	258	26	69	10	0	4	34	3
Heise, Eric, 1b-dh	.319	116	20	37	8	2	2	14	5
Herman, Josh, dh	.357	210	43	75	13	0	12	48	0
Higgins, Bert, ss	.300	260	32	78	9	1	1	20	10
Kuempel, Tom, of	.300	90	21	27	5	0	6	19	0
Marple, Scott, of	.273	77	10	21	5	0	1	8	5
McIver, Robby, 3b	.250	44	12	11	0	2	5	9	1
McNamee, Joe, of	.245	159	19	39	9	0	7	21	4
Mumin, Gary, of	.276	127	23	35	4	0	6	17	1
Shelton, Barry, 3b	.286	98	14	28	7	0	3	17	0
Tavares, John, 2b-ss	.260	235	45	61	10	2	3	13	17
Taylor, Kirk, of	.321	290	56	93	18	3	21	62	29

PITCHING	W	L	ERA	G	SV	IP	H	BB	SO
Alleman, Derek	1	2	4.28	19	3	61	72	14	31
Anderson, Todd	2	0	4.50	25	4	28	36	14	30
Barakel, David	2	1	7.59	25	0	40	57	15	23
Boggs, Robert	4	8	7.05	18	0	83	119	44	64
Bryant, Keith	5	8	6.03	18	0	88	116	45	78
Cordle, Jeff	1	0	0.00	5	0	9	11	5	6
2-team (4 Johnstown)	1	0	5.54	9	0	13	15	8	6
English, Mike	3	7	5.78	18	0	72	83	49	63
Fischer, Kenny	3	4	6.75	16	0	72	90	17	40
Henderson, David	1	2	2.64	26	0	44	35	32	35
Pearson, Stacey	1	6	4.64	11	0	52	74	17	33
Rhodes, Brian	0	3	8.24	10	0	20	26	10	18
2-team (3 Richmond)	0	4	9.13	13	0	23	31	13	23
Scott, Ron	0	0	2.45	3	1	4	3	1	3
2-team (13 Kalamazoo)	0	2	11.50	16	3	18	22	27	18
Shanklin, Paul	2	8	6.90	11	0	59	79	32	45
Simmons, Carlos	1	3	7.43	12	3	27	31	15	32

RICHMOND

BATTING	AVG	AB	R	H	2B	3B	HR	RBI	SB
Beyna, Terry, 3b	.324	241	42	78	21	1	3	46	3
Bichelmeyer, Jason, of-1b	.280	93	24	26	3	3	5	19	0
Braughler, Matt, c	.291	230	44	67	11	2	6	43	0
Burkhart, Morgan, 1b	.404	280	97	113	18	1	36	98	13
Curry, Chris, 2b	.288	226	46	65	14	2	6	29	6
Habig, Keith, ss-of	.356	289	87	103	19	4	25	89	7
Lopez, Mark, of	.286	248	44	71	13	0	3	37	17
Love, Justin, of	.288	184	42	53	5	2	3	25	28
Pass, Joe, dh-2b	.317	290	45	92	19	0	1	34	0
Peavey, Ryan, of	.292	65	16	19	6	0	1	10	2
Poss, John, dh	.250	8	1	2	0	0	0	1	0
Riordan, Fran, of	.248	161	27	40	7	1	5	34	1
Schwade, Brian, ss-2b	.275	138	30	38	8	0	1	17	3
Spencer, Glen, of	.265	230	47	61	10	0	1	31	8
Tarleton, Tory, c	.232	82	14	19	6	0	5	20	0

PITCHING	W	L	ERA	G	SV	IP	H	BB	SO
Harden, Tony	10	1	2.36	13	0	92	83	32	66
Haro, Rosendo	0	0	18.00	3	0	4	11	1	2
2-team (12 Johnstown)	1	0	7.85	15	0	18	37	7	14
Hart, Derek	1	2	8.27	17	0	33	50	25	23
Havens, Chris	0	1	6.75	7	2	9	17	5	7
Hussar, Dan	3	5	7.24	28	8	68	77	35	61
McAdoo, Jed	10	4	5.03	19	0	106	121	40	63
Mezlak, Todd	0	2	9.82	9	0	7	9	9	8
Montfort, Jeff	6	0	5.51	12	0	64	66	42	70
Nelson, Ron	1	0	7.71	3	0	9	13	5	4
Padgett, Steven	4	4	4.90	31	6	61	71	32	50
Parra, David	0	0	3.38	3	0	5	2	4	6
Simms, Matt	1	1	6.45	6	0	22	21	21	10
Sivumaki, Cory	0	0	9.82	3	0	7	15	1	1
2-team (13 Canton)	6	2	6.87	16	0	58	80	21	17
Stephens, Jon	4	1	4.37	17	2	23	23	12	26
2-team (14 Kalamazoo)	5	3	8.80	31	2	45	67	26	39

Steppke, Terry	3	5	6.23	22	1	74	78	36	69
Thomas, Chad	1	0	7.71	19	2	28	36	21	24
Tryon, Eric	0	2	12.06	5	0	16	31	11	12
Vitale, Anthony	5	1	4.79	7	0	47	55	19	31
2-team (10 Kalamazoo)	6	6	5.97	17	0	98	131	36	46
Wright, Chris	0	0	9.00	6	0	7	0	9	6

SPRINGFIELD

BATTING	AVG	AB	R	H	2B	3B	HR	RBI	SB
Barningham, Steve, of	.285	172	28	49	6	4	3	18	6
Blackwell, John, of	.208	24	3	5	0	0	0	1	1
Bone, Billy, 3b	.304	79	14	24	1	1	5	17	7
Buckholz, A.J., 2b	.324	253	52	82	15	2	11	52	2
Bush, Darren, of	.332	304	63	101	22	5	16	66	1
Cicero, Frank, c	.185	27	4	5	0	0	1	6	0
Close, Bart, c	.364	22	8	8	3	0	0	3	0
2-team (27 Ohio Valley)	.288	104	17	30	7	1	1	11	1
Cruz, Paul, of	.356	191	47	68	10	3	5	39	1
Evans, Pat, c	.335	272	56	91	17	1	14	49	8
Farrell, Rob, of	.200	10	3	2	0	0	1	2	0
Forst, David, 3b-ss	.280	250	39	70	5	1	1	38	4
Kalcounos, Andy, 3b	.350	40	7	14	3	1	3	11	0
2-team (34 Johnstown)	.247	158	26	39	8	2	4	20	2
Lindekugel, Tyson, 1b	.245	277	41	68	14	0	8	38	3
Risinger, Ben, ss	.242	227	34	55	13	0	5	30	2
Ronca, Joe, dh-of	.344	317	56	109	21	0	16	77	1
Saalfrank, Chad, of	.237	186	42	44	6	0	2	17	9
Wiebe, Jay, of	.250	16	6	4	0	0	0	1	1

PITCHING	W	L	ERA	G	SV	IP	H	BB	SO
Austin, Swan	0	0	13.50	4	0	6	15	4	3
Beck, Matthew	6	5	5.87	16	0	84	102	36	35
Brown, Caleb	0	0	8.10	8	0	7	8	9	6
Danner, Andy	4	1	3.66	10	0	32	22	20	22
Denly, Greg	7	3	4.85	15	0	72	86	32	59
Finken, Brad	5	6	4.57	10	0	91	98	33	90
Gentner, Chris	0	0	7.04	6	0	8	9	9	5
Hoffman, J.R.	0	1	6.48	28	0	25	36	9	21
House, Sean	3	1	2.01	35	17	40	34	12	40
Kern, Brian	0	1	13.50	3	0	9	15	9	7
McGeown, John	3	0	5.20	27	0	45	53	33	46
Pavlovich, Tony	1	2	1.26	20	4	29	14	7	40
Sauget, Rich	1	1	7.20	4	0	5	6	6	5
Simontacchi, Jason	10	2	2.95	16	0	110	103	21	92
Witten, Joe	3	1	2.76	23	0	33	34	6	23
Woodman, Hank	5	5	4.91	12	0	70	71	41	64

HEARTLAND LEAGUE

The 1998 season wasn't kind to the Heartland League, which became the latest indy circuit to fold. It ceased operations Nov. 3. Eight other leagues have fallen by the wayside since the resurgence of independent leagues in 1993.

Tennessee and Dubois County were the only clubs to average more than 1,000 fans per game. It remained uncertain if any of the league's member clubs would make it to the gate in 1999. A couple of teams were looking to join the Frontier League, including the league-champion Cook County Cheetahs.

The Tupelo Tornado drew only 1,507 fans while the Huntington RailKings drew 3,515 before each franchise folded before the end of the first half.

On the field, the league had some bright spots. Lafayette's Jason Taulman pitched the only perfect game in modern independent league history until Ken Krahenbuhl pitched one later in the season in the Texas-Louisiana League.

Taulman's teammate Jason Kinchen, a former NAIA college player of the year, led the league with 24 home runs.

Cook County won the title in its first season by sweeping the Tennessee Tomahawks two games to none in the finals. The Cheetahs, who were the lowest draw in the league, were optimistic about their future with a new stadium on the way.

STANDINGS

FIRST HALF

	W	L	PCT	GB
Tennessee Tomahawks	24	11	.686	—
Cook County Cheetahs	23	11	.676	½
Lafayette Leopards	16	17	.485	7
Dubois County Dragons	15	19	.441	8½
*Tupelo Tornado	4	10	.286	9½
*Huntington RailKings	9	23	.281	13½

SECOND HALF

	W	L	PCT	GB
Tennessee Tomahawks	19	10	.655	—
Dubois County Dragons	17	17	.500	4½
Lafayette Leopards	19	22	.463	6
Cook County Cheetahs	14	18	.438	6½

*Team did not finish season.

PLAYOFFS: Cook County defeated Tennessee 2-0 in best-of-3 series.

MANAGERS: Cook County—Brian Dayett. Dubois County—Jay Welker. Huntington—Mike Richmond. Lafayette—Bob Hallas. Tennessee—Mike O'Berry. Tupelo—Steve Dillard.

ATTENDANCE: Tennessee 39,356; Dubois 31,762; Lafayette 24,418; Cook County 10,552; Huntington 3,515; Tupelo 1,507.

ALL-STAR TEAM: **C**—Erik Metzger, Lafayette. **1B**—Curtis Underwood, Tennessee. **2B**—Neil Bradshaw, Cook County. **3B**—Doyle Preston, Tennessee. **SS**—Angel Hermoso, Lafayette. **OF**—Jason Baker, Tennessee; Chris Chiprez, Dubois County; Keith Goodwin, Lafayette. **RHP**—Derek Santiago, Cook County. **LHP**—Mark Clark, Lafayette. **RP**—Michael Danley, Tennessee.

Most Valuable Player: Jason Kinchen, Lafayette.

INDIVIDUAL BATTING LEADERS

(Minimum 216 Plate Appearances)

	AVG	AB	R	H	2B	3B	HR	RBI	SB
Baker, Jason, Tennessee	.349	249	49	87	19	2	1	38	18
Overton, Chad, Dubois	.333	249	40	83	19	1	1	28	2
Goodwin, Keith, Lafayette	.331	272	58	90	11	4	11	44	21
Kinchen, Jason, Lafayette	.324	225	52	73	15	0	24	66	1
Chiprez, Chris, Dubois	.324	259	45	84	11	0	7	30	11
Metzger, Erik, Lafayette	.323	257	40	83	14	1	4	38	8
Preston, Doyle, Tennessee	.314	226	30	71	13	1	4	39	0
Michael, Jeff, Tennessee	.307	202	37	62	9	1	1	30	13
Malone, Nick, Lafayette	.306	232	33	71	14	2	0	30	13
Hermoso, Angel, Lafayette	.302	202	35	61	9	1	1	21	9
Underwood, Curtis, Tenn.	.299	224	32	67	13	0	5	39	5
Benjamin, Al, Dubois	.298	215	31	64	11	3	7	40	14
Donato, Jude, Hunt.-DC	.284	264	36	75	17	2	2	21	15
Bradshaw, Neil, Cook County	.264	235	31	62	7	1	0	18	13
Johnston, Tom, Dubois	.264	182	22	48	3	0	0	16	9

INDIVIDUAL PITCHING LEADERS

(Minimum 64 Innings)

	W	L	ERA	G	SV	IP	H	BB	SO
Santiago, Derek, Cook County	8	3	2.17	17	0	100	72	37	89
Piddington, Brian, Dubois	7	3	2.22	13	0	97	87	24	84
Hollowell, Todd, Dubois	5	3	2.40	12	0	79	64	23	59
Hedrick, Keith, Dubois	2	5	2.70	10	0	73	67	12	36
Dopson, John, Tennessee	8	1	2.85	13	0	73	71	13	61
Conner, Scott, Lafayette	4	1	2.87	12	1	78	80	19	50
Pulizzano, Tim, Cook County	4	5	2.88	15	0	100	95	25	72
Taulman, Jason, Lafayette	6	4	3.12	14	0	98	97	21	49
Calvert, Klae, Cook County	5	4	3.57	15	0	88	84	30	79
Connolly, Sean, Lafayette	3	4	3.78	16	1	79	73	40	60

NORTHEAST LEAGUE

The Albany-Colonie Diamond Dogs made it to the Northeast League finals for the fourth straight season, and for the third time the Dogs went home empty.

The New Jersey Jackals, in their first year in the league, swept the Dogs after an incredible comeback in Game One sparked their efforts.

Trailing 6-1 in the bottom of the ninth, Rogelio Nunez led off with a bunt single and eventually scored. The Jackals rallied for three more runs before Nunez came to the plate for the second time in the inning and supplied a two-run single with two outs for the game winner.

Nunez was named series MVP for his heroics. He hit only .249 during the regular season.

Perhaps the biggest news for the Northeast League was the alliance with the Northern League, announced after the season. Northern League commissioner Miles Wolff wanted to expand into the Northeast corridor for several years because he thought there were solid markets without teams.

With strong seasons 1997 and 1998, however, the Northeast League became a good fit for a merger partner. Wolff, meanwhile, purchased a Northeast franchise in Quebec City which will begin play in 1999.

The Northeast League made huge jumps in attendance in 1998 in every town but Lynn, where the Massachusetts Mad Dogs played. That franchise drew 25,000 fewer fans than in '97 and will not operate as an active franchise in 1999.

The other markets picked up the Mad Dogs' slack.

After a lackluster inaugural season in 1997, Allentown sprung to life in 1998. The city made the most of Bicentennial Park by converting the former amateur baseball and soccer field into a quirky minor league ballpark. The Ambassadors' attendance increased by 52,000 in their second season.

STANDINGS

FIRST HALF

NORTH	W	L	PCT	GB
Waterbury Spirit	22	20	.524	—
Albany-Colonie Diamond Dogs	20	22	.476	2
Massachusetts Mad Dogs	19	23	.452	3
Adirondack Lumberjacks	15	27	.357	7
SOUTH	**W**	**L**	**PCT**	**GB**
New Jersey Jackals	30	12	.714	—
Allentown Ambassadors	23	19	.548	7
Catskill Cougars	20	21	.488	9½
Elmira Pioneers	18	23	.439	11½

SECOND HALF

NORTH	W	L	PCT	GB
Albany-Colonie Diamond Dogs	27	15	.643	—
Massachusetts Mad Dogs	20	22	.476	7
Waterbury Spirit	20	22	.476	7
Adirondack Lumberjacks	19	23	.452	8
SOUTH	**W**	**L**	**PCT**	**GB**
Allentown Ambassadors	29	13	.690	—
New Jersey Jackals	23	19	.548	6
Catskill Cougars	16	26	.381	13
Elmira Pioneers	14	28	.333	15

PLAYOFFS: Semifinals—Albany-Colonie defeated Waterbury 2-0 and New Jersey defeated Allentown 2-0 in best-of-3 series. **Finals**—New Jersey defeated Albany-Colonie 2-0 in best-of-3 series.

MANAGERS: Adirondack—Kevin Graber. Albany—Charlie Sullivan. Allentown—Ed Ott. Catskill—Gates Brown/John Duffy. Elmira—Dan Shwam. Massachusetts—George Scott. New Jersey—Kash Beauchamp. Waterbury—Stan Hough.

ATTENDANCE: Allentown 122,738; New Jersey 114,796; Albany-Colonie 89,855; Adirondack 61,785; Elmira 52,436; Catskill 45,103; Massachusetts 47,123; Waterbury 46,170.

ALL-STAR TEAM: **C**—Carlos Mota, Albany-Colonie. **1B**—D.C. Olsen, New Jersey. **2B**—Billy Hall, Allentown. **3B**—Eddie Lantigua, Waterbury. **SS**—Saul Bustos, New Jersey. **OF**—Lorenzo de la Cruz, Allentown; Keith Gordon, New Jersey; Erskine Kelley, Allentown. **RHP**—Ray Davis, Allentown. **LHP**—Keith Breitenstein, Adirondack. **RP**—Juan Gonzalez, Allentown.

Player of the Year: Dan Kopriva, Albany-Colonie. **Pitcher of the Year**: John DeSilva, New Jersey. **Manager of the Year**: Ed Ott, Allentown.

INDIVIDUAL BATTING LEADERS

(Minimum 227 Plate Appearances)

	AVG	AB	R	H	2B	3B	HR	RBI	SB
Kopriva, Dan, Albany	.391	256	55	100	20	3	16	64	12
Duncan, Andres, Catskill	.345	229	35	79	15	3	0	17	30
De la Cruz, Lorenzo, Allen.	.340	291	63	99	28	5	17	85	19
Kelley, Erskine, Allentown	.340	321	80	109	24	7	12	49	20
Lantigua, Eddie, Waterbury	.339	301	43	102	20	1	5	41	3
Brown, Jarvis, Waterbury	.331	281	70	93	16	4	5	28	25
Weinheimer, Wayne, Catskill	.328	290	48	95	18	3	12	63	10
Guerrero, Juan, Catskill	.327	278	50	91	15	2	10	55	4
Naples, Brandon, Allentown	.327	321	71	105	18	4	7	48	24
Olsen, D.C., New Jersey	.327	248	47	81	21	4	13	51	0

INDIVIDUAL PITCHING LEADERS

(Minimum 67 Innings)

	W	L	ERA	G	SV	IP	H	BB	SO
DeSilva, John, New Jersey	8	1	1.56	11	0	81	53	24	90
Ponte, Ed, Waterbury	7	4	2.15	12	0	88	76	10	60
Breitenstein, Keith, Adir.	8	4	2.24	15	0	96	79	24	76
Gieras, Kevin, New Jersey	6	2	2.27	21	1	67	65	17	63
Swanson, Dave, Waterbury	7	2	2.63	17	0	110	95	33	69
Montoya, Al, Catskill	6	7	2.78	15	1	97	80	21	63
Magrini, Paul, New Jersey	9	4	2.92	17	0	102	87	38	69
Hunter, Rich, Allentown	7	4	2.94	11	0	80	79	24	52
Hueston, Steve, Mass.	6	3	3.09	38	8	82	62	46	54
Lavenia, Mark, Albany	9	4	3.33	16	0	97	109	32	54

ADIRONDACK

BATTING	AVG	AB	R	H	2B	3B	HR	RBI	SB
Carter, Keith, c	.295	44	6	13	2	0	2	8	0
Dattola, Kevin, of	.309	256	55	79	14	3	17	48	11
Davila, Vic, of-2b	.346	156	21	54	11	2	0	13	9
Doucette, Darren, 1b	.256	43	5	11	2	0	1	4	0
Flynn, Scott, 3b	.217	83	8	18	5	0	0	5	1
Gerald, Dwayne, of	.164	61	2	10	2	0	2	7	0
Gordon, Joe, 3b-of	.211	100	13	20	4	0	4	12	2
Kimbler, Doug, ss	.289	308	39	89	15	1	7	39	7
Mariano, Joe, 2b	.283	127	16	36	6	1	1	17	3
2-team (46 Albany)	.268	280	27	75	8	1	1	31	3
Mazurek, Brian, of-1b	.260	100	10	26	3	1	5	21	0
McCain, Marcus, of-2b	.286	192	30	55	7	1	0	13	19
2-team (22 Albany)	.255	259	41	66	10	1	1	19	29
Miner, Tony, 3b	.148	27	2	4	0	0	0	2	0
Mora, Mike, of	.289	291	39	84	21	2	2	35	6
Negus, Andy, of	.067	15	1	1	0	0	0	0	0
Nunez, Roman, c	.308	13	4	4	0	0	0	2	0
Porter, Kedric, of	.288	73	12	21	1	0	1	8	7
2-team (36 Mass)	.279	179	35	50	4	0	1	20	18
Reinisch, Paul, 1b-2b	.300	263	47	79	18	1	6	44	1
Santana, Ruben, 3b	.329	76	12	25	5	1	2	9	0
Sheehan, Scott, 1b	.250	16	1	4	0	0	0	1	0
Stockham, Travis, c	.257	35	7	9	3	0	0	3	0
Sutherland, Alex, c	.252	214	22	54	11	0	4	28	1
Vogel, Mike, c	.188	16	1	3	0	0	0	0	0

PITCHING	W	L	ERA	G	SV	IP	H	BB	SO
Breitenstein, Keith	8	4	2.24	15	0	96	79	24	76
Coronado, Osvaldo	2	3	3.40	33	4	50	51	10	37
Cox, Robert	1	1	8.55	20	4	20	33	8	15
Davis, Jamie	0	3	3.41	17	1	29	26	7	28
2-team (13 Albany)	1	5	5.46	30	2	56	63	16	52
Forti, Gene	1	3	4.28	17	1	34	38	25	24
Fry, Jeff	3	7	4.04	13	0	56	62	31	32
Glaze, Randy	1	0	6.23	9	0	9	7	9	9
Hogan, Dennis	6	5	3.97	19	0	91	84	33	113
Hreben, Mark	1	2	3.15	16	1	20	20	13	19
2-team (8 Waterbury)	1	3	5.34	24	1	29	38	21	29
Lancaster, Les	0	4	3.94	5	0	32	41	5	19
Larson, Toby	6	5	4.09	20	0	110	123	30	81
Maddock, Steve	0	1	3.00	10	0	18	18	11	15
2-team (6 Albany)	0	1	3.86	16	2	23	28	13	19
Mitchell, Chris	0	0	13.50	2	0	2	4	1	0
2-team (5 Elmira)	1	0	7.36	7	0	15	19	13	10
Sirianni, A.J.	2	2	5.60	21	0	18	21	5	13
Trumpour, Andy	0	2	9.90	5	0	20	29	8	15
Umbarger, Kurt	1	1	4.62	20	0	39	55	18	26
Ward, Chad	2	6	4.56	9	0	53	58	6	42

ALBANY-COLONIE

BATTING	AVG	AB	R	H	2B	3B	HR	RBI	SB
Billingsley, Kyle, of	.250	12	1	3	0	0	0	2	0
Cabrera, Francisco, of-c	.302	53	10	16	2	1	1	14	3
Castro, Jose, of	.244	123	11	30	6	1	0	13	1
Davila, Vic, 3b	.291	103	20	30	10	2	0	19	7
2-team (48 Adironack)	.324	259	41	84	21	4	0	32	16
DeLeon, Felix, 2b-ss	.301	336	62	101	21	3	2	37	22
DeLeon, Jose, of	.237	114	14	27	4	0	1	10	3
Edwards, Jerome, of	.282	277	55	78	13	1	6	29	19
Keefe, Jamie, 2b-3b	.279	111	17	31	5	1	2	15	9
Kopriva, Dan, 1b-3b	.391	256	55	100	20	3	16	64	12
Mariano, Joe, ss	.255	153	11	39	2	0	0	14	0
McCain, Marcus, of	.164	67	11	11	3	0	1	6	10
Melendez, Jorge, c	.266	109	12	29	5	0	3	12	0
Mercado, Rafael, 1b	.262	42	6	11	3	0	0	1	0
Mercedes, Luis, ss	.086	35	8	3	0	1	0	0	1
Mitchell, Tony, of	.327	49	8	16	4	0	1	6	0
Mota, Carlos, c	.283	173	20	49	10	0	3	27	3
Mueller, Jon, of	.279	280	46	78	19	0	8	52	1
Murphy, Sean, 2b-3b	.255	51	12	13	2	2	3	9	7
2-team (56 Elmira)	.289	235	45	68	14	5	6	29	22
Phillips, Gary, 3b	.289	173	23	50	14	0	1	14	1
Tegeler, Tom, c	.278	72	11	20	4	0	1	9	1
Yarbrough, Jeff, of	.125	24	3	3	1	0	0	5	1

PITCHING	W	L	ERA	G	SV	IP	H	BB	SO
Bauer, Chuck	2	0	0.36	4	0	25	12	2	28
Cerbone, Marc	0	3	7.98	7	0	15	23	8	10
Cruz, Fermin	3	1	1.80	10	0	55	43	16	54
Davis, Jamie	1	2	7.67	13	1	27	37	9	24
Hasler, Jerry	6	4	3.63	26	2	79	84	25	67
Lavenia, Mark	9	4	3.33	16	0	97	109	32	54
Legault, Kevin	6	5	5.59	18	0	97	118	33	68
Maddock, Steve	0	0	6.75	6	2	5	10	2	4
Parantala, Mark	5	1	2.17	32	2	54	53	5	42
Santana, Cesar	3	3	3.90	12	3	32	32	12	20
2-team (13 Mass)	5	6	4.26	25	4	76	74	31	49
Santiago, Sandi	1	2	4.79	20	9	21	22	10	18
Smith, Jarod	2	6	4.69	20	0	81	85	29	47
Sparks, Eric	2	1	2.52	11	1	25	18	20	27
Valdez, Rafael	3	3	4.69	19	0	40	56	13	30
Ward, Chad	2	0	3.97	18	1	23	23	4	15
2-team (9 Adirondack)	4	6	4.30	27	1	76	81	10	57
Williams, Juan	1	1	4.17	10	1	37	31	12	31

ALLENTOWN

BATTING	AVG	AB	R	H	2B	3B	HR	RBI	SB
Batiste, Kim, 3b	.307	231	44	71	21	3	10	57	1
D'Angelo, Tom, 2b	.091	22	0	2	1	0	0	1	0
De la Cruz, Lorenzo, of	.340	291	63	99	28	5	17	85	19
Hall, Billy, 2b-ss	.323	325	67	105	21	5	5	41	41
Holifield, Rick, of	.245	49	5	12	3	1	1	11	1
Keene, Andre, 1b	.316	95	23	30	6	3	8	35	7
Kelley, Erskine, of	.340	321	80	109	24	7	12	49	20
Martinez, Pablo, ss	.265	34	6	9	4	0	0	2	4
Montilla, Jose, ss	.271	218	45	59	12	1	2	20	5
Naples, Brandon, of-1b	.327	321	71	105	18	4	7	48	24
Northeimer, Jaime, c	.216	208	28	45	12	2	3	22	2
Pettiford, Torrey, 2b	.275	149	25	41	14	0	0	21	9
2-team (5 Elmira)	.268	157	26	42	14	0	0	21	10
Roberts, Robin, 1b-3b	.277	224	30	62	12	2	3	30	3
Robinson, Darryl, 1b	.267	15	1	4	1	0	0	1	0
Sadlowski, Jared, of-c	.358	151	22	54	11	4	3	26	1

PITCHING	W	L	ERA	G	SV	IP	H	BB	SO
Barbao, Joe	2	1	3.91	18	0	25	37	6	15
Beller, Steven	1	3	4.01	25	0	43	46	24	37
Davis, Ray	10	5	3.65	18	0	126	122	46	105
DaSilva, Fernando	8	3	3.58	18	0	118	123	21	82
Dillinger, John	7	3	3.57	14	0	88	96	47	66
Fry, Nolan	1	0	5.40	6	0	7	8	2	6
Gonzalez, Juan	3	2	1.91	33	17	38	32	9	35
Hunter, Rich	7	4	2.94	11	0	80	79	24	52
Kammerer, James	1	1	5.79	12	0	14	16	8	8
Kell, Rob	5	1	3.23	7	0	39	49	7	26
Losty, Kevin	0	2	8.38	5	0	10	18	5	4
Norris, Joe	2	0	1.33	8	0	27	14	7	30
Ramagli, Matt	0	2	5.71	7	0	35	57	14	12
Randall, Mark	1	2	5.40	9	1	10	12	4	8
Rohrbach, Mike	3	2	2.56	31	2	39	34	16	36
Salley, Anthony	1	0	4.70	15	0	15	13	7	13
Thobe, Tom	0	0	5.79	3	0	19	24	7	8

CATSKILL

BATTING	AVG	AB	R	H	2B	3B	HR	RBI	SB
Appel, Doug, c	.154	65	3	10	1	0	0	4	1
Burroughs, Eric, of	.277	148	26	41	9	2	1	8	15
Cunningham, Earl, of	.326	215	41	70	16	1	6	34	5
Dockery, Tim, c	.223	139	11	31	9	1	4	23	0
Duncan, Andres, ss	.345	229	35	79	15	3	0	17	30
Gates, Leonard, c	.200	25	4	5	2	0	0	1	0
2-team (3 Mass)	.200	35	4	7	2	0	0	1	0
Glenn, Brandon, of	.169	148	22	25	5	1	0	9	5

BATTING	AVG	AB	R	H	2B	3B	HR	RBI	SB
Guerrero, Juan, 3b	.327	278	50	91	15	2	10	55	4
Jimenez, Pablo, ss	.179	28	1	5	1	0	0	3	0
Johnson, Andre, of	.336	238	48	80	13	1	13	53	12
Kaber, Benji, c	.385	13	0	5	1	0	0	3	0
2-team (1 Elmira)	.333	15	0	5	1	0	0	3	0
McClendon, Tony, 2b-3b	.270	174	27	47	11	4	0	19	7
McWhite, Ray, of-1b	.223	139	16	31	5	0	4	20	3
Montero, Danny, c	.360	25	5	9	2	0	0	3	0
Pagana, Mike, 2b	.321	109	15	35	6	1	0	7	8
2-team (14 Waterbury)	.289	159	19	46	7	1	0	15	9
Peltz, Michael, c	.259	58	5	15	2	1	0	6	4
Porter, Frank, of	.300	20	1	6	1	0	0	1	1
Wallace, Tim, 2b-ss	.224	210	30	47	4	0	0	9	6
Weinheimer, Wayne, 1b	.328	290	48	95	18	3	12	63	10

PITCHING	W	L	ERA	G	SV	IP	H	BB	SO
Barron, Mark	0	1	6.39	10	0	25	40	8	15
Carter, Paul	1	4	7.90	8	0	14	25	11	10
Eannacony, Tony	0	0	3.10	27	0	49	45	16	26
Fry, Nolan	0	1	4.30	7	0	15	16	7	10
2-team (6 Allentown)	1	1	4.64	13	0	21	24	9	16
Guerrero, Jose	4	1	2.28	10	0	47	44	19	35
Jimenez, John	2	5	2.01	31	8	40	37	17	27
Lovelace, Vance	1	5	4.29	12	0	71	81	22	49
Lucey, Tim	9	6	5.00	19	0	104	125	39	63
Martinez, Johnny	5	6	3.34	14	0	94	107	25	71
Mercier, Heath	1	1	6.16	9	0	38	51	9	32
Montoya, Al	6	7	2.78	15	1	97	80	21	63
Smith, Matt	3	4	2.34	34	3	58	59	17	66
Warren, DeShawn	4	5	5.07	11	0	50	50	26	43

ELMIRA

BATTING	AVG	AB	R	H	2B	3B	HR	RBI	SB
Bennett, Mike, 1b	.280	107	14	30	7	1	0	13	3
Bethea, Scott, ss-2b	.215	130	14	28	5	0	0	12	4
De la Rosa, Juan, 3b-of	.274	223	24	61	7	1	0	23	8
Hemphill, James, of	.195	41	5	8	1	0	0	2	1
Hodge, Roy, of	.249	201	20	50	10	2	0	23	14
Lockett, Ron, 1b	.280	211	36	59	15	3	4	33	14
Mangual, Danny, ss	.271	70	14	19	1	2	1	6	3
McClendon, Travis, c	.278	180	25	50	8	1	2	21	14
Mercedes, Luis, 3b-ss	.167	18	0	3	0	0	0	3	0
2-team (11 Albany)	.113	53	8	6	0	1	0	3	1
Miller, David, c	.167	42	2	7	0	0	1	4	0
Murphy, Sean, 2b-3b	.299	184	33	55	12	3	3	20	15
Owen, Andy, of	.291	251	39	73	26	1	4	28	15
Palmer, Nate, c	.067	15	0	1	1	0	0	3	0
Pettiford, Torrey, ss	.125	8	1	1	0	0	0	0	1
Reyes, Kiko, ss	.246	61	9	15	3	0	0	4	1
2-team (51 Waterbury)	.255	220	28	56	11	1	1	20	2
Ross, Jackie, of	.200	30	2	6	1	0	0	2	1
Sawkiw, Warren, 3b-2b	.228	114	16	26	7	4	3	20	1
Taylor, Tom, of	.300	90	14	27	4	0	2	13	1
Watts, Josh, of	.190	42	4	8	4	0	0	2	2
Wingate, Ervan, ss-2b	.308	221	31	68	14	3	2	21	3
Wright, Terry, of	.305	256	39	78	11	2	1	27	19
Zachmann, Rob, 3b	.050	20	1	1	0	0	0	0	0

PITCHING	W	L	ERA	G	SV	IP	H	BB	SO
Anderson, Eric	5	8	4.93	35	0	66	70	25	45
Bourbakis, Mike	1	3	9.00	11	0	22	24	28	25
2-team (1 Massachusetts)	1	4	7.28	12	0	30	27	32	36
Brown, Duane	3	3	3.77	10	0	62	56	31	44
Crills, Brad	1	1	3.31	31	0	49	60	12	32
Forsythe, Neil	1	0	0.00	2	0	3	1	0	3
2-team (28 Waterbury)	2	1	2.63	30	6	38	34	15	27
Fuller, Duane	0	0	10.50	4	0	6	12	7	6
Garcia, Apolinar	1	1	3.66	3	0	20	19	5	19
Gonzales, Frank	2	4	4.78	30	4	75	81	25	85
Lewis, Craig	0	3	5.09	4	0	18	19	5	14
Linares, Richard	1	1	2.96	25	12	24	28	0	21
Mitchell, Chris	1	0	6.39	5	0	13	15	12	10
Morseman, Bob	1	5	6.15	7	0	34	47	17	14
Perry, Matthew	4	3	3.22	35	2	45	41	22	38
Prosser, David	5	9	4.75	20	0	91	120	24	46
Sikes, Jason	3	6	5.66	15	0	83	107	37	35
Silicato, Tom	0	1	5.25	12	1	24	26	6	6
Sullivan, Brent	0	0	12.60	6	0	5	6	8	5
Wilkerson, Steven	2	2	2.63	10	0	51	45	10	22

MASSACHUSETTS

BATTING	AVG	AB	R	H	2B	3B	HR	RBI	SB
Benes, Richie, ss	.083	12	1	1	0	0	0	1	1
Burton, Essex, 2b	.307	267	51	82	17	6	3	26	36
Cellers, Anthony, of	.238	21	2	5	1	0	0	4	1
Davis, Albert, of	.167	24	3	4	1	0	0	0	1
Davis, Eddie, of	.173	52	6	9	2	0	0	3	0
DeLeon, Sandy, c	.179	28	2	5	1	1	0	2	1
Donohue, Gregg, c	.176	17	3	3	0	0	0	2	0
Dover, Matt, c	.341	41	5	14	2	0	0	1	0
Escoto, David, 3b	.206	34	2	7	0	0	0	4	0
Gardner, Willie, 1b	.211	38	3	8	0	0	1	5	0
[illegible], 1b	.000	10	0	[illegible]	0	0	0	0	0
Gjerde, Jeff, 1b-of	.245	53	7	13	4	1	1	2	2
Jackson, Jeff, of	.191	89	7	17	3	0	2	14	6
Johnson, Andre, of	.275	51	10	14	1	0	3	9	1
2-team (67 Catskill)	.325	289	58	94	14	1	16	62	13
Keefe, Jamie, 3b	.268	41	5	11	2	1	1	5	0
King, Brion, 3b	.294	17	0	5	1	1	0	3	0
Kingsbury, Willy, c	.254	236	25	60	12	0	7	34	1
Mercado, Rafael, 1b	.270	37	1	10	0	0	0	3	0
3-team (13 Alb., 13 Adir.)	.239	109	10	26	3	0	0	7	0
Mitchell, Rivers, of	.333	39	11	13	2	0	0	3	1
Mitchell, Tony, 1b-of	.348	112	20	39	8	0	10	32	1
2-team (16 Albany)	.342	161	28	55	12	0	11	38	1
Moore, Kevin, 3b	.071	14	1	1	0	0	0	0	0
Mumin, Gary, of	.091	11	0	1	1	0	0	0	0
O'Dell, Shawn, 1b	.291	86	13	25	0	1	0	8	0
Pico, Brandon, 1b	.167	12	4	2	0	1	0	1	1
Porter, Kedric, of	.274	106	23	29	3	0	0	12	11
Rhodes, Danny, of	.279	111	20	31	9	0	2	6	5
Rosario, Victor, ss	.258	62	8	16	2	1	3	10	0
Rutherford, Daryl, of	.094	32	6	3	0	0	0	3	1
Slater, Wayne, of	.286	70	6	20	3	0	1	7	0
Soriano, Carlos, 3b-2b	.245	192	26	47	10	2	2	25	2
Stelly, Duane, 3b-ss	.261	180	24	47	8	2	0	16	5
Terry, Tony, of	.267	30	5	8	1	1	0	2	2
Valette, Ramon, ss	.266	169	27	45	9	1	5	31	11
Williams, Jerrone, of	.298	198	34	59	8	2	4	26	16

PITCHING	W	L	ERA	G	SV	IP	H	BB	SO
Bou, Edward	3	1	4.00	17	1	36	29	27	27
Bourbakis, Mike	0	1	2.35	1	0	8	3	4	11
Compres, Fidel	1	0	3.60	6	2	5	13	1	2
Forti, Gene	0	1	7.71	2	0	5	6	5	5
2-team (17 Adirondack)	1	4	4.70	19	1	38	44	30	29
Foulks, Jason	3	4	2.82	24	4	38	35	15	32
Gonsalez, Santo	3	0	7.75	19	0	34	46	30	32
Guerrero, Jose	2	3	5.77	6	0	34	39	13	23
2-team (10 Catskill)	6	4	3.75	16	0	82	83	32	58
Hackett, Jason	1	2	8.06	13	0	26	35	17	15
Hall, Brad	0	1	7.94	3	0	6	6	6	1
Hueston, Steve	6	3	3.09	38	8	82	62	46	54
Johnson, Mark	2	3	5.91	19	0	64	76	32	36
King, Matt	2	0	1.23	4	0	7	3	6	3
Macone, Mike	5	3	5.57	21	2	53	43	37	65
Manzanillo, Ravelo	2	1	2.65	5	0	34	27	8	42
Murphy, Jay	0	4	6.10	7	0	38	54	8	23
O'Flynn, Gardner	3	5	3.99	11	0	65	81	19	29
Santana, Cesar	2	3	4.53	13	1	44	42	19	29
Spivey, Chris	0	0	3.46	11	0	13	19	7	6
Thoesen, Ian	0	1	6.30	4	0	20	19	11	12
Tribe, Byron	4	6	4.22	14	0	85	61	55	112
Trumpour, Andy	0	2	15.00	2	0	9	17	5	2
2-team (5 Adirondack)	0	4	11.48	7	0	29	46	13	17
Tyus, Wayne	0	1	5.40	8	0	18	19	16	10

NEW JERSEY

BATTING	AVG	AB	R	H	2B	3B	HR	RBI	SB
Brinkley, Josh, 3b-c	.271	255	30	69	10	0	6	27	7
Bustos, Saul, ss	.293	297	56	87	21	2	15	47	11
Castleberry, Kevin, 2b	.500	10	4	5	2	0	0	1	0
Collum, Gary, of	.277	292	60	81	14	3	7	30	20
Craddox, Kenny, of	.242	157	23	38	3	2	2	10	5
Dattola, Kevin, of	.316	57	5	18	4	0	2	6	0
2-team (69 Adirondack)	.310	313	60	97	18	3	19	54	11
Gordon, Keith, of	.312	298	47	93	16	0	16	70	19
Johnson, Jace, of-2b	.183	93	13	17	8	0	0	11	1
Larkin, Garrett, 2b-1b	.238	181	29	43	7	0	2	20	7
Nunez, Rogelio, c	.249	169	17	42	1	2	3	20	7
Olsen, D.C., 1b-c	.327	248	47	81	21	4	13	51	0
Pandolfini, Ryan, 1b	.224	76	9	17	3	0	0	7	0
Paulus, Andy, of	.261	23	2	6	0	0	0	3	1
Roa, Hector, 3b	.306	108	19	33	8	0	6	24	4
Rose II, Pete, of-1b	.424	33	2	14	4	1	1	8	0
Serafin, Steven, 3b	.148	27	2	4	0	0	0	2	0
Slater, Wayne, of	.333	12	2	4	0	0	0	1	0
2-team (30 Mass.)	.293	82	8	24	3	0	1	8	0
Smith, Thomas, of	.261	23	1	6	0	0	0	4	0
Virgilio, George, 2b	.285	249	37	71	19	0	3	35	4

PITCHING	W	L	ERA	G	SV	IP	H	BB	SO
Cedeno, Blas	1	6	4.47	12	1	48	62	14	37
Collins, Ed	0	4	5.40	16	0	37	33	25	21

DeSilva, John	8	1	1.56	11	0	81	53	24	90
Dietrich, Jason	2	0	1.45	23	2	31	18	11	38
Eufemia, Frank	5	1	3.51	11	0	56	62	3	35
Gieras, Kevin	6	2	2.27	21	1	67	65	17	63
Hartmann, Pete	4	0	1.70	7	0	48	34	15	41
Hartung, Michael	4	2	2.22	40	17	45	43	13	30
High, Andy	4	2	2.77	23	1	39	29	7	47
Lovelace, Vance	0	2	4.00	2	0	9	8	5	4
2-team (12 Catskill)	1	7	4.26	14	0	80	89	27	53
Magrini, Paul	9	4	2.92	17	0	102	87	38	69
Pincavitch, Kevin	4	0	0.83	23	1	65	43	24	51
Quirk, John	0	3	7.02	14	1	17	26	8	12
Stegen, Brian	1	1	6.06	8	0	16	19	5	9
Weidert, Chris	5	3	3.49	13	0	67	82	18	45

WATERBURY

BATTING	AVG	AB	R	H	2B	3B	HR	RBI	SB
Belcher, Tim, of	.253	225	31	57	11	1	0	17	4
Brown, Jarvis, of	.331	281	70	93	16	4	5	28	25
Church, Mike, c	.260	223	23	58	13	1	1	35	0
Duross, Gabe, 1b	.287	237	24	68	12	1	1	27	1
Falciglia, Tony, c	.111	54	5	6	1	1	0	4	0
Hodge, Roy, of	.317	60	6	19	1	3	1	6	2
2-team (59 Elmira)	.264	261	26	69	11	5	1	29	16
Kingston, Kelly, of	.263	285	49	75	22	5	8	43	10
Lantigua, Eddie, 3b	.339	301	43	102	20	1	5	41	3
Lewis, Joe, ss	.261	119	14	31	1	0	0	6	2
Pagana, Mike, 2b	.220	50	4	11	1	0	0	8	1
Porzio, Nando, c	.056	18	1	1	0	0	0	1	0
Reintjes, Steve, of	.204	98	16	20	5	0	0	10	0
Reyes, Kiko, ss	.258	159	19	41	8	1	1	16	1
Ricard, Toby, 2b	.306	297	44	91	16	5	4	63	7
Shirley, Al, of	.233	43	5	10	4	0	1	4	2
Wilson, Scott, 1b-3b	.215	130	23	28	5	2	5	20	0
Wingate, Ervan, of-ss	.311	45	5	14	2	0	0	8	1
2-team (61 Elmira)	.308	266	36	82	16	3	2	29	4

PITCHING	W	L	ERA	G	SV	IP	H	BB	SO
Douglas, Bobby	0	2	5.09	11	0	18	19	13	12
Forsythe, Neil	1	1	2.86	28	6	35	33	15	24
Frazier, Ron	4	6	4.87	14	0	78	89	14	52
Hale, Mark	1	2	4.78	17	0	26	25	14	23
Hreben, Mark	0	1	10.38	8	0	9	18	8	10
Licciardi, Ron	5	4	3.78	23	0	67	77	30	40
Linares, Rich	0	1	4.26	7	3	6	5	2	4
2-team (25 Elmira)	1	2	3.23	32	15	31	33	2	25
Maddock, Steve	1	1	4.34	5	0	19	18	7	19
Mercier, Heath	2	2	2.47	28	7	47	44	13	48
2-team (9 Catskill)	3	3	4.11	37	7	85	95	22	80
Munoz, J.J.	1	1	0.90	11	1	20	12	5	21
Ponte, Ed	7	4	2.15	12	0	88	76	10	60
Santoro, Gary	6	6	3.43	15	0	100	111	22	69
Shea, John	5	5	2.67	13	0	61	60	10	30
Strahowski, Chris	1	4	3.53	26	1	43	36	27	32
Swanson, Dave	7	2	2.63	17	0	110	95	33	69
Tsamis, George	1	0	0.00	2	0	5	3	2	3

NORTHERN LEAGUE

The Northern League again attracted more fans and a wider array of talent than any other independent league.

Winnipeg slugger Sean Hearn won player of the year honors for his league-best 29 home runs. He also struck out a league-high 92 times. But the real story was Hearn and his team's struggle to catch the Fargo-Moorhead RedHawks in the highly competitive Western Division.

Led by a strong starting rotation, the Hawks compiled a 64-21 record, the best mark in Northern League history. Righthander Jeff Bittiger, a 36-year-old former major leaguer, went 12-1 with a 1.94 ERA. He combined with starters Justin Fletschock, Blaise Ilsley and Eric Schultz to post an overall 39-9 record.

Though Schultz was signed by the Yankees during the second half, the RedHawks cruised into the playoffs where they defeated Winnipeg for the Western Division title.

In the East, Thunder Bay took the first half but lost to second-half champion St. Paul in the divisional series. The RedHawks blew out the Saints in the championship series by scores of 17-6, 19-13 and 12-3.

The 1997 champion Duluth-Superior Dukes fell into their old habits, finishing with the league's worst record at 29-56. They also received bad news before the season when pitcher Allen Halley, a stellar performer during their championship run, died during his sleep in Florida.

Four franchises saw increases in attendance from 1997, including the Saints, who drew 272,210 in just 43 openings. Sioux City, Sioux Falls and Fargo-Moorhead also witnessed increases at the gate.

Thunder Bay, which will move to Schaumburg, Ill., for the 1999 season, drew 6,000 fewer fans. The decline was directly attributable to a city workers strike that began in April. The team played its early home games in Grand Forks, N.D., or at its opponent's park.

STANDINGS

FIRST HALF

EAST	W	L	PCT	GB
Thunder Bay Whiskey Jacks	22	21	.512	—
Madison Black Wolf	20	23	.465	2
St. Paul Saints	20	23	.465	2
Duluth-Superior Dukes	12	30	.286	9½
WEST	**W**	**L**	**PCT**	**GB**
Fargo-Moorhead RedHawks	31	11	.738	—
Winnipeg Goldeyes	25	18	.581	6½
Sioux City Explorers	23	20	.535	8½
Sioux Falls Canaries	18	25	.419	13½

SECOND HALF

EAST	W	L	PCT	GB
St. Paul Saints	20	23	.465	—
Thunder Bay Whiskey Jacks	18	24	.429	1½
Duluth-Superior Dukes	17	26	.395	3
Madison Black Wolf	15	28	.349	5
WEST	**W**	**L**	**PCT**	**GB**
Fargo-Moorhead RedHawks	33	10	.767	—
Winnipeg Goldeyes	33	10	.767	—
Sioux Falls Canaries	18	24	.429	14½
Sioux City Explorers	17	26	.395	16

PLAYOFFS: Semifinals—St. Paul defeated Thunder Bay 3-2 and Fargo-Moorhead defeated Winnipeg 3-1 in best-of-5 series. **Finals**—Fargo-Moorhead defeated St. Paul 3-0 in best-of-5 series.

MANAGERS: Duluth-Superior—George Mitterwald. Fargo-Moorhead—Doug Simunic. Madison—Al Gallagher. St. Paul—Marty Scott. Sioux City—Ed Nottle. Sioux Falls—Mike Burton. Thunder Bay—Jay Ward. Winnipeg—Hal Lanier.

ATTENDANCE: St. Paul 272,210; Fargo-Moorhead 182,938; Winnipeg 159,512; Sioux City 120,114; Sioux Falls 117,015; Duluth-Superior 70,105; Madison 56,462; Thunder Bay 54,566.

ALL-STAR TEAM: **C**—Chris Coste, Fargo-Moorhead. **1B**—David Kennedy, St. Paul. **2B**—Brian Duva, Winnipeg. **3B**—John Knott, Fargo-Moorhead. **SS**—Chad Akers, Fargo-Moorhead. **OF**—Tony Chance, Winnipeg; Donald Harris, Madison; Marty Neff, Sioux City. **DH**—Sean Hearn, Winnipeg. **RHP**—Jeff Bittiger, Fargo-Moorhead. **LHP**—Blaise Ilsley, Fargo-Moorhead. **RP**—Jose Prado, St. Paul.

Player of the Year: Sean Hearn, Winnipeg. **Manager of the Year**: Doug Simunic, Fargo-Moorhead.

INDIVIDUAL BATTING LEADERS

(Minimum 227 Plate Appearances)

	AVG	AB	R	H	2B	3B	HR	RBI	SB
Duva, Brian, Winnipeg	.367	357	71	131	24	1	10	46	26
Nokes, Matt, St. Paul	.351	211	30	74	15	0	8	50	0
Rogers, Lamarr, St. Paul	.338	311	61	105	19	1	1	35	29
Knott, John, Fargo	.333	267	76	89	15	1	15	61	30
Kennedy, David, St. Paul	.330	318	53	105	14	1	19	65	1
Neff, Marty, Sioux City	.329	347	55	114	33	2	15	74	12

	AVG	AB	R	H	2B	3B	HR	RBI	SB
Coste, Chris, Fargo	.328	326	59	107	17	2	10	55	6
Chance, Tony, Winnipeg	.325	314	69	102	18	0	20	81	5
Kastelic, Matt, Duluth	.325	271	37	88	20	0	6	36	20
Hine, Steve, Fargo	.323	319	59	103	22	5	3	47	17

INDIVIDUAL PITCHING LEADERS

(Minimum 67 Innings)

	W	L	ERA	G	SV	IP	H	BB	SO
Bittiger, Jeff, Fargo	12	1	1.94	16	0	97	72	16	76
Fletschock, Justin, Fargo	10	3	3.04	17	0	110	112	35	88
Schultz, Eric, Fargo	8	1	3.18	11	0	68	61	18	60
Boynewicz, Jim, Thunder Bay	7	5	3.40	19	0	132	120	37	94
Poeck, Chad, Thunder Bay	4	4	3.47	17	0	70	45	38	78
Forney, Rick, Winnipeg	11	6	3.54	19	0	130	145	20	113
Mlodik, Kevin, Fargo/Duluth	6	2	3.59	22	1	105	110	22	76
Tilmon, Pat, Thunder Bay	8	6	3.76	18	0	122	129	22	69
Badorek, Mike, Madison	8	8	3.86	21	0	154	171	37	67
DeWitt, Chris, Fargo	7	6	3.92	20	0	126	143	39	67

DULUTH-SUPERIOR

BATTING	AVG	AB	R	H	2B	3B	HR	RBI	SB
Bain, Tyler, ss	.106	47	8	5	2	0	1	4	0
Barsoom, Al, 2b-ss	.243	148	16	36	6	2	2	18	7
Briller, Chris, 3b	.290	269	43	78	12	1	3	25	8
Brito, Luis, ss	.244	217	40	53	11	3	0	24	5
Brown, Ron, of	.188	207	19	39	9	1	2	21	1
Canseco, Ozzie, 1b	.292	137	33	40	8	0	10	37	4
DeCelle, Mike, of	.109	55	2	6	2	3	0	6	1
Falciglia, Tony, c	.109	46	4	5	2	0	1	4	0
Francisco, David, of	.306	111	13	34	5	0	3	14	6
3-team (28 Mad, 24 Fargo)	.304	313	43	95	11	1	5	34	20
Gabbani, Michael, c	.000	16	0	0	0	0	0	0	0
Kastelic, Matt, of	.325	271	38	88	20	0	6	36	20
Lewis, Anthony, dh	.259	212	29	55	9	0	8	45	0
Meggers, Mike, 1b	.366	82	20	30	9	1	12	34	0
Mitrovich, Steve, c	.200	40	2	8	3	0	0	2	0
2-team (20 Winnipeg)	.220	109	11	24	5	0	3	14	0
Ralph, Brian, of	.279	247	42	69	11	1	1	17	22
Rodriguez, Javier, c	.215	242	14	52	9	1	0	29	1
Rodriguez, Ryan, 2b-ss	.242	91	8	22	5	0	0	8	2
Ross, Jackie, of	.176	34	2	6	2	0	0	5	4
Schmitz, Chris, of	.226	84	7	19	4	0	1	7	1
Switzenberg, Ty, 2b	.247	170	26	42	8	2	1	12	2
Towner, Kyle, of	.195	123	17	24	4	0	0	3	6

PITCHING	W	L	ERA	G	SV	IP	H	BB	SO
Beach, Scott	1	1	8.31	4	0	17	23	11	3
2-team (6 Winnipeg)	4	1	6.60	10	0	46	55	27	22
Borders, Ila	1	4	8.66	14	0	44	65	14	14
DeWitt, Chris	4	6	4.20	15	0	96	109	28	52
Febles, Narcisco	1	2	7.50	19	0	30	42	22	21
3-team (7 SF, 5 Mad)	1	4	8.74	31	0	45	63	36	36
Giron, Emiliano	3	2	1.27	43	18	50	31	28	54
Giron, Roberto	4	10	4.52	29	0	86	92	34	48
Glick, David	7	10	5.19	21	0	120	149	44	76
Hannah, Neal	0	2	8.31	2	0	9	12	4	4
Harvell, Pete	1	4	9.73	7	0	29	48	13	24
Heather, Scott	0	0	6.10	12	0	21	26	16	13
Hernandez, Ariel	1	5	5.20	27	0	54	63	30	38
Knollin, Chris	0	0	9.90	7	0	10	14	4	9
2-team (14 St. Paul)	0	2	9.00	21	1	33	46	21	27
Marchesano, Mike	1	3	8.10	17	0	33	45	22	30
Mlodik, Kevin	2	1	3.53	6	0	43	43	14	27
2-team (16 Fargo)	6	2	3.59	22	1	105	110	22	76
Shaver, Tony	0	0	14.81	9	0	10	29	4	8
Wagner, Rick	3	6	3.92	22	0	78	98	29	35

FARGO-MOORHEAD

BATTING	AVG	AB	R	H	2B	3B	HR	RBI	SB
Akers, Chad, ss	.310	358	79	111	30	5	8	44	12
Canseco, Ozzie, of	.333	78	17	26	8	0	5	18	3
2-team (40 Duluth)	.307	215	50	66	16	0	15	55	7
Coste, Chris, c	.328	326	59	107	17	2	10	55	6
Fink, Marc, 1b	.314	290	47	91	15	0	16	63	1
Francisco, David, of	.341	88	15	30	2	1	1	6	7
Hine, Steve, 2b	.323	319	59	103	22	5	3	47	17
Jackson, Jeff, of	.192	52	6	10	1	0	2	8	2
Knott, John, 3b	.333	267	76	89	15	1	15	61	30
Marquez, Jesus, of	.238	147	16	35	7	0	4	26	5
Motley, Darryl, dh	.290	303	56	88	18	4	12	62	1
Ottavinia, Paul, of	.409	44	11	18	4	3	1	19	1
Prodanov, Peter, of-3b	.238	235	41	56	10	1	2	30	16
Santana, Ruben, of	.222	45	3	10	3	0	0	8	0
Smith, Cory, of	.284	81	15	23	6	2	1	9	5
Wells, Forry, of	.268	291	65	78	23	1	20	57	14

PITCHING	W	L	ERA	G	SV	IP	H	BB	SO
Bittiger, Jeff	12	1	1.94	16	0	97	72	16	76
DeWitt, Chris	3	0	3.00	5	0	30	34	11	15
2-team (15 Duluth)	7	6	3.92	20	0	126	143	39	67
Fletschock, Justin	10	3	3.04	17	0	110	112	35	88
Ilsley, Blaise	9	4	5.27	17	0	94	126	12	45
Jeckell, Matt	0	2	2.40	[illegible]	[illegible]	51	47	7	11
Koch, Jack	0	0	9.53	4	0	6	7	5	3
Kunka, Tony	1	0	7.79	15	0	17	29	9	13
Lukas, Stephen	0	0	3.60	5	0	10	11	6	6
Mlodik, Kevin	4	1	3.63	16	1	62	67	8	49
Nelson, Barry	1	2	1.83	34	16	39	27	18	42
Rushing, Will	6	2	5.07	27	0	60	66	38	40
Salvevold, Greg	0	1	3.00	5	0	12	15	4	7
Schmidt, George	6	2	1.87	37	3	58	45	22	66
Schultz, Eric	8	1	3.18	11	0	68	61	18	60
Toth, Robert	0	1	7.20	1	0	5	8	3	1
Vandemark, John	4	1	5.70	6	0	30	25	10	44

MADISON

BATTING	AVG	AB	R	H	2B	3B	HR	RBI	SB
Baxter, Duke, 2b-3b	.242	306	41	74	10	2	3	22	6
Booth, Jeremy, c	.167	6	1	1	0	0	0	1	0
2-team (25 St. Paul)	.220	100	10	22	8	0	0	7	0
Campos, Jesus, of	.389	113	21	44	7	1	0	1	5
Dionne, Stephane, c	.137	51	2	7	3	0	0	3	0
Everson, Darin, 1b	.299	221	42	66	15	0	14	44	1
Francisco, David, of	.272	114	15	31	4	0	1	14	7
Grice, Dan, 3b-ss	.214	243	36	52	10	1	1	26	10
Harris, Donald, of	.276	315	58	87	18	5	18	70	4
Imrisek, Jason, dh	.256	39	6	10	2	0	0	5	0
Reyes, Gilberto, c	.203	246	19	50	6	0	7	35	1
Roper, Chad, dh-1b	.293	164	26	48	11	0	4	28	1
Sachs, Brent, 3b-of	.263	232	32	61	13	3	2	24	13
Tobiasz, Patrick, dh-1b	.071	14	1	1	0	0	0	1	0
Tokheim, David, of	.285	333	47	95	20	3	10	45	15
Vopata, Nate, ss-1b	.306	333	47	102	16	5	9	50	4
Ward, Frank, c	.000	10	1	0	0	0	0	0	0
Williams, Rodney, of	.262	130	19	34	2	1	0	12	5

PITCHING	W	L	ERA	G	SV	IP	H	BB	SO
Badorek, Mike	8	8	3.86	21	0	154	171	37	67
Bailey, Phil	0	4	8.59	18	0	15	24	16	9
Benzing, Skipp	0	0	15.43	8	0	7	11	9	5
Carl, Todd	3	9	5.01	19	0	92	97	53	83
Deremer, Brent	2	1	3.65	12	0	37	42	16	19
Deremer, Scott	4	4	3.24	39	16	42	41	16	20
Fahs, Derek	1	2	9.75	7	0	24	35	9	19
Febles, Narcisco	0	1	11.57	5	0	5	7	4	4
LaPlante, Michel	8	7	4.40	17	0	119	124	29	88
Meyer, David	2	7	5.07	18	0	94	110	55	59
Mullikin, Jamie	0	0	7.20	3	0	5	5	5	2
2-team (2 Sioux City)	0	0	6.75	5	0	8	10	6	5
Painich, Joey	0	1	9.17	19	1	36	47	23	29
Taylor, Donnie	2	0	6.21	26	0	38	45	34	42
Wagner, Matt	5	7	6.54	23	0	63	77	31	61

ST. PAUL

BATTING	AVG	AB	R	H	2B	3B	HR	RBI	SB
Booth, Jeremy, c	.223	94	9	21	8	0	0	6	0
Castillo, Benny, of	.324	71	11	23	3	0	2	12	1
2-team (25 Sioux Falls)	.253	170	23	43	7	1	6	21	2
Caston, Bernard, of	.282	156	28	44	8	1	1	15	16
2-team (23 Sioux Falls)	.253	233	42	59	10	1	3	21	22
Curtis, Brandon, dh-3b	.292	72	13	21	1	0	3	15	0
Doskocil, Darren, 2b	.222	54	8	12	2	0	2	11	2
Drew, J.D., of	.386	114	27	44	11	2	9	33	8
Evans, Chris, dh-of	.283	205	33	58	9	1	4	28	4
Johnson, Danny, of	.202	124	18	25	4	4	2	16	6
Kennedy, David, 1b	.330	318	53	105	14	1	19	65	1
Kokinda, Steve, dh	.333	15	3	5	3	0	0	2	0
Mirza, Erik, of	.176	51	4	9	2	0	0	4	4
Mulligan, Sean, dh-of	.167	12	1	2	0	0	0	2	0
Nokes, Matt, c	.351	211	30	74	15	0	8	50	0
Rodriguez, Ryan, 2b-ss	.202	89	8	18	1	1	1	6	1
2-team (26 Duluth)	.222	180	16	40	6	1	1	14	3
Rogers, Lamarr, 2b-of	.338	311	61	105	19	1	1	35	29
Senjem, Guye, c	.262	126	20	33	9	0	3	16	2
Tarpley, Andy, of	.277	321	53	89	13	0	5	40	4
Tsoukalas, John, 3b	.261	310	46	81	15	0	1	35	3
Utting, Ben, ss	.256	285	36	73	17	3	2	24	11

PITCHING	W	L	ERA	G	SV	IP	H	BB	SO
Curtis, Chris	2	1	7.59	3	0	11	13	8	7
Donnelly, Rob	3	4	4.20	31	0	94	84	50	83
Frazier, Harold	1	1	2.20	34	0	29	25	19	25

	W	L	ERA	G	SV	IP	H	BB	SO
Griffiths, Everard	6	4	4.83	18	0	101	104	50	77
Keusch, Joe	1	1	6.63	12	1	19	25	6	12
Knollin, Chris	0	2	8.61	14	1	23	32	17	18
Kosek, Kory	5	8	6.07	21	0	86	118	22	37
McRoberts, Brian	3	2	5.27	39	2	41	42	14	44
Miller, Joe	1	1	4.63	20	0	35	48	18	28
Painich, Joey	0	1	6.10	5	0	10	10	2	10
2-team (19 Madison)	0	2	8.49	24	1	47	57	25	39
Prado, Jose	0	1	2.18	36	23	33	31	13	25
Pugh, Tim	4	4	5.59	12	0	48	60	13	32
Smith, Dan	8	9	4.58	19	0	112	119	55	107
Smith, Roy	6	7	5.03	18	0	106	119	36	74

SIOUX CITY

BATTING	AVG	AB	R	H	2B	3B	HR	RBI	SB
Barwick, Neal, ss-3b	.238	21	0	5	3	0	0	2	0
Carcione, Tom, c	.245	253	24	62	8	1	4	39	0
Dalton, Dee, 3b	.266	338	54	90	21	0	6	39	2
Kopacz, Derek, of	.317	312	54	99	20	1	13	52	18
Lane, Nolan, dh	.313	300	52	94	16	3	13	43	14
Mack, Bryan, c	.300	50	9	15	2	0	1	5	0
Miranda, Jose, of	.316	38	11	12	3	0	2	5	0
Neff, Marty, 1b-of	.329	347	55	114	33	2	15	74	12
Patton, Josh, 1b-3b	.271	188	23	51	12	1	3	31	2
Powell, Chris, of	.273	143	27	39	7	2	7	27	8
Sawyer, Chris, of	.279	330	70	92	19	1	11	46	19
Tanton, Calvin, 1b	.188	48	10	9	1	0	1	4	0
Thornhill, Chad, ss	.289	270	44	78	16	1	4	42	1
Toven, John, 2b	.286	332	48	95	16	0	8	37	12

PITCHING	W	L	ERA	G	SV	IP	H	BB	SO
Allen, Chris	0	0	4.91	2	0	4	5	3	4
Ballance, Dale	1	3	7.11	6	0	32	47	16	18
2-team (12 Winnipeg)	4	6	6.11	18	0	88	113	37	51
Bedinger, Doug	9	6	4.49	20	0	116	141	44	81
Cushman, Dwayne	1	5	3.99	37	12	38	38	18	19
Fahs, Derek	2	1	5.00	15	3	18	22	4	16
2-team (7 Madison)	3	3	7.71	22	3	42	57	13	35
Gomez, Dennys	7	8	4.58	21	1	140	147	56	80
Gutierrez, Javier	2	0	3.77	6	1	14	15	9	9
Hill, Chris	4	5	4.74	33	0	63	63	26	44
Miller, Brian	4	4	5.68	36	1	71	101	38	47
Mosman, Marc	2	6	5.70	12	0	66	76	29	53
Mullikin, Jamie	0	0	6.00	2	0	3	5	1	3
Patino, Leonardo	2	2	3.96	36	2	36	40	18	38
2-team (1 Sioux Falls)	2	3	5.13	37	2	40	50	18	41
Post, Bobby	5	6	5.17	22	0	136	153	39	72
Roman, Dan	0	0	14.73	7	0	7	14	11	4

SIOUX FALLS

BATTING	AVG	AB	R	H	2B	3B	HR	RBI	SB
Batiste, Kim, 3b	.189	74	5	14	1	0	1	10	3
Berrios, Harry, of	.319	94	20	30	8	0	5	16	2
Brito, Bernardo, dh	.178	90	12	16	4	0	2	8	2
Carter, Michael, of	.339	56	15	19	6	0	4	15	3
Castillo, Benny, of	.202	99	12	20	4	1	4	9	1
Caston, Bernard, of	.195	77	14	15	2	0	2	6	6
Dour, Craig, 1b	.262	290	46	76	14	1	12	41	18
Fisher, Eric, 3b-2b	.261	134	13	35	6	0	0	10	2
Garner, Kevin, dh	.205	44	5	9	3	0	2	7	0
2-team (45 Thunder Bay)	.254	201	31	51	10	0	11	28	0
Gerald, Eddie, of	.299	321	52	96	17	4	15	50	15
Gutfeld, Marc, ss-2b	.286	255	29	73	11	0	1	24	5
Imrisek, Jason, c	.331	160	23	53	9	1	4	26	1
2-team (15 Madison)	.317	199	29	63	11	1	4	31	1
Klam, Jason, 2b-3b	.229	297	54	68	11	2	11	40	15
Marquez, Jesus, of	.220	91	8	20	4	1	2	14	3
2-team (38 Fargo)	.231	238	24	55	11	1	6	40	8
Martin, C.J., of	.308	247	37	76	15	1	7	42	5
Mendez, Sergio, c	.239	71	7	17	5	0	0	6	0
Miranda, Jose, of	.257	101	13	26	7	0	3	14	1
Rodrigues, Rich, c	.204	98	7	20	5	0	2	16	0
Tovar, Edgar, ss-3b	.295	285	41	84	9	4	6	25	7

PITCHING	W	L	ERA	G	SV	IP	H	BB	SO
Bailey, Mike	1	3	6.07	5	0	27	26	16	19
Carmon, Brad	1	4	5.65	25	2	65	72	21	35
Febles, Narcisco	0	1	10.97	7	0	11	14	10	11
Getz, Rod	0	0	13.50	5	0	8	13	9	5
Grant, Brian	4	9	6.06	19	0	107	128	44	44
Grife, Rich	2	0	5.55	27	1	36	34	29	23
Hahn, Steve	4	3	4.03	29	5	51	52	25	31
Harpe, Dan	2	3	8.71	17	0	31	44	29	19
Hartvigson, Chad	2	5	3.92	32	10	78	70	25	88
Heimes, Jay	1	0	4.15	7	0	9	10	4	4

	W	L	ERA	G	SV	IP	H	BB	SO
Hyde, Rich	4	3	4.52	14	0	94	107	34	61
Newman, Damon	5	9	5.78	21	0	104	114	47	52
Nieves, Juan	0	3	8.06	5	0	26	31	19	13
Patino, Leonardo	0	1	15.75	1	0	4	10	0	3
Ramos, Rudy	0	0	4.76	4	0	6	10	4	3
Smith, Chuck	5	3	2.62	8	0	55	44	21	70
Winkle, Ken	5	2	5.70	19	1	24	23	15	23

THUNDER BAY

BATTING	AVG	AB	R	H	2B	3B	HR	RBI	SB
Berrios, Harry, of-1b	.321	137	24	44	9	0	6	22	10
2-team (25 Sioux Falls)	.320	231	44	74	17	0	11	38	12
Buckley, Reagan, c	.254	256	31	65	13	1	12	36	3
Cardona, Ruben, 2b	.278	313	46	87	15	0	2	22	18
Colon, Frank, c	.206	34	1	7	2	0	0	3	0
Diggs, Ryan, of	.233	150	29	35	8	0	1	11	5
Dumas, Mike, 3b-of	.312	282	45	88	9	1	0	23	22
Evans, Brandon, of	.282	298	40	84	20	0	8	39	15
Garner, Kevin, dh	.268	157	26	42	7	0	9	21	0
Jesperson, Bob, p dh	.245	53	8	13	1	1	0	6	0
Jones, Ron, dh	.283	60	10	17	3	0	3	17	1
Lewis, Danny, of	.316	272	42	86	16	0	17	56	0
McDonald, Ashanti, ss	.253	292	43	74	12	1	1	26	10
Melson, Bryant, c	.125	16	3	2	0	0	0	1	0
Rios, Eduardo, 3b-1b	.274	248	34	68	16	1	8	49	2
Santiago, Angel, of	.188	48	7	9	1	0	0	1	3
See, Larry, 1b	.235	217	24	51	7	0	10	34	0
Shwartzer, Mike, c	.133	15	0	2	0	0	0	0	0
Williams, Tray, ss	.091	11	2	1	0	0	0	0	0

PITCHING	W	L	ERA	G	SV	IP	H	BB	SO
Allen, Chris	0	0	9.00	8	0	12	18	10	4
2-team (2 Sioux City)	0	0	8.04	10	0	10	23	13	8
Boynewicz, Jim	7	5	3.40	19	0	132	120	37	94
Brooks, Wes	8	9	4.69	20	0	119	129	39	74
Danielson, Bobby	2	2	4.34	39	1	37	39	17	24
Delgado, Roger	0	1	8.34	14	0	23	29	21	18
Hannah, Neal	2	3	4.82	14	0	19	23	9	12
2-team (2 Duluth)	2	5	5.93	16	0	27	35	13	16
Hart, Jason	3	1	2.62	37	15	45	27	15	56
Jesperson, Bob	0	2	6.59	24	0	29	36	21	22
Koppon, Jeff	5	9	4.56	23	1	97	117	45	94
Kragh, Ryan	1	3	6.66	16	1	26	31	17	20
Poeck, Chad	4	4	3.47	17	0	70	45	38	78
Tilmon, Pat	8	6	3.76	18	0	122	129	22	69

WINNIPEG

BATTING	AVG	AB	R	H	2B	3B	HR	RBI	SB
Baeza, Art, 3b	.316	237	32	75	9	4	6	44	3
Bargman, Todd, dh	.273	22	2	6	0	0	1	1	0
Chamberlain, Wes, of	.393	163	49	64	13	0	12	44	7
Chance, Tony, of	.325	314	69	102	18	0	20	81	5
Duva, Brian, 2b	.367	357	71	131	24	1	10	46	26
Fortin, Troy, c	.376	178	36	67	10	1	9	38	0
Hearn, Sean, of-dh	.311	318	78	99	16	1	29	80	5
Hobbie, Matt, of	.233	116	16	27	6	1	3	13	2
Kokinda, Chris, 1b-of	.321	336	74	108	24	1	14	66	8
Lydy, Scott, of	.100	10	1	1	1	0	0	2	0
MacKay, Tripp, ss	.297	354	62	105	18	3	0	29	6
Matthews, Eric, c	.220	109	15	24	8	1	3	18	0
Miranda, Jose, of	.288	80	16	23	6	0	3	18	1
3-team (33 SF, 10 SC)	.279	219	40	61	16	0	8	37	2
Mitrovich, Steve, c	.232	69	9	16	2	0	3	12	0
Reyes, Freddy, 1b	.250	32	7	8	0	0	1	5	0
Samuels, Scott, of	.300	30	7	9	1	1	2	4	3
Smith, Casey, of-2b	.294	180	28	53	6	1	5	25	14
Somrock, John, of	.119	59	4	7	1	0	0	3	0
Torti, Michael, 3b	.250	64	12	16	2	0	2	7	1
Watts, Brent, of-2b	.250	28	5	7	2	0	0	4	2

PITCHING	W	L	ERA	G	SV	IP	H	BB	SO
Aguilar, Alonzo	0	1	7.58	13	0	19	31	13	12
Anderson, Eric	8	5	6.81	18	0	106	137	36	69
Ballance, Dale	3	3	5.56	12	0	57	66	21	33
Beach, Scott	3	0	5.59	6	0	29	32	16	19
Forney, Rick	11	6	3.54	19	0	130	145	20	113
Guehne, Dan	2	0	1.03	26	3	26	18	5	15
Montgomery, Joe	7	1	3.50	32	2	54	38	26	37
Paull, Kalam	1	1	4.78	15	0	26	27	12	14
Press, Gregg	8	8	4.31	19	0	125	141	37	105
Reid, Rayon	5	1	3.92	16	0	64	63	36	74
Smith, Donnie	2	0	6.23	8	0	17	20	9	13
Sparks, Jeff	2	1	3.12	38	17	49	30	42	85
Viano, Jake	0	1	1.80	5	3	5	4	4	6
Wise, Andy	6	0	3.71	8	0	51	49	9	37

TEXAS-LOUISIANA LEAGUE

The Texas-Louisiana League championship series was a rematch of the 1997 title set . . . with the same result. The Alexandria Aces defeated the Amarillo Dillas three games to none to win their second consecutive title.

Though the Aces and Dillas were the only teams above .500 on the season, the 1998 Texas-Louisiana League mirrored the major leagues with a lot of individual drama.

Alexandria second baseman Tim Howard rewrote the record book. His .447 batting average shattered the old record by 52 points. His 148 hits in 82 games broke the previous mark of 140, set in 1995 when the league played a 100-game schedule. His 96 RBIs broke the old record of 95, also set in 1995. His 13 triples were a record. His 37 doubles tied another.

One of the strangest stories in all of baseball in 1998 involved Ken "Catfish" Krahenbuhl, who was traded from the Pacific Suns of the independent Western League to the Greenville Bluesmen for a bucket of catfish and player to be named later.

It became more than just another independent league moment when Krahenbuhl pitched a perfect game in his first start for the Bluesmen. He pitched a two-hitter in a losing effort his second time out.

News of the bizarre trade went national and everyone from CBS Late Night's David Letterman to Good Morning America to ESPN was talking about the 28-year old journeyman and his fishy tale.

Though his ERA was a respectable 3.88, Krahenbuhl went 0-6 after his perfect game and Greenville finished in the cellar.

STANDINGS

FIRST HALF

	W	L	PCT	GB
Amarillo Dillas	32	10	.762	—
Alexandria Aces	30	12	.714	2
Bayou Bullfrogs	19	23	.452	13
Abilene Prairie Dogs	18	24	.429	14
Rio Grande Valley Whitewings	17	25	.405	15
Lubbock Crickets	16	26	.381	16
Greenville Bluesmen	14	28	.333	18

SECOND HALF

	W	L	PCT	GB
Amarillo Dillas	32	10	.762	—
Alexandria Aces	28	14	.667	4
Lubbock Crickets	23	19	.548	9
Abilene Prairie Dogs	21	21	.500	11
Rio Grande Valley Whitewings	19	23	.452	13
Bayou Bullfrogs	17	25	.405	15
Greenville Bluesmen	8	34	.190	24

PLAYOFFS: Alexandria defeated Amarillo 3-0 in best-of-5 series.

MANAGERS: Abilene—Barry Jones. Alexandria—Stan Cliburn. Amarillo—Daren Brown. Bayou—Andy Skeels/Steve Dillard. Greenville—Bob Lacey. Lubbock—Glenn Sullivan. Rio Grande Valley—Eddie Dennis.

ATTENDANCE: Amarillo 142,145; Rio Grande Valley 86,656; Bayou 74,022; Alexandria 73,541; Lubbock 73,327; Abilene 53,095; Greenville 27,948.

ALL-STAR TEAM: **C**—Jack Johnson, Amarillo. **1B**—John O'Brien, Alexandria. **2B**—Tim Howard, Amarillo. **3B**—Derek Henderson, Amarillo. **SS**—Victor Rosario, Abilene. **OF**—Sean Collins, Amarillo; Jay Davis, Rio Grande Valley; Kyle Shade, Alexandria; Derek Vaughn, Lubbock. **DH**—Malvin Matos, Alexandria. **Util**—Robert Hewes, Alexandria. **P**—Greg Bicknell, Amarillo; Daren Brown, Amarillo; Jason Fawcett, Rio Grande Valley; Al Kermode, Amarillo; Tony Mack, Alexandria; Steve Ortiz, Abilene; Russell Reeder, Alexandria; Joe Stutz, Rio Grande Valley.

Most Valuable Player: Tim Howard, Amarillo. **Most Valuable Pitcher**: Daren Brown, Amarillo. **Co-Rookies of the Year**: Jason Landreth, Lubbock; Bray Woodress, Lubbock. **Manager of the Year**: Daren Brown, Amarillo.

INDIVIDUAL BATTING LEADERS

(Minimum 227 Plate Appearances)

	AVG	AB	R	H	2B	3B	HR	RBI	SB
Howard, Tim, Amarillo	.447	331	89	148	37	13	10	96	18
Davis, Jay, Rio Grande	.405	343	89	139	35	1	26	84	25
Landreth, Jason, Lubbock	.377	260	60	98	17	1	8	54	22
Wilson, Mike, Amarillo	.373	311	93	116	16	7	11	69	22
Collins, Sean, Amarillo	.371	361	96	134	19	9	12	75	41
Shade, Kyle, Alexandria	.370	349	87	129	31	3	9	84	1
DeLeon, Ray, RGV-Lubbock	.364	302	57	110	19	0	13	70	6
Hewes, Robert, Alexandria	.361	294	80	106	28	7	9	63	17
Martinez, Joey, Rio Grande	.358	215	51	77	12	3	4	26	16
Matos, Malvin, Alexandria	.356	315	76	112	23	7	26	87	9

INDIVIDUAL PITCHING LEADERS

(Minimum 67 Innings)

PITCHER, TEAM	W	L	ERA	G	SV	IP	H	BB	SO
Stutz, Joe, Rio Grande	5	5	3.04	33	3	68	61	30	58
Brown, Daren, Amarillo	15	4	3.21	20	0	137	139	21	121
Kermode, Al, Amarillo	12	3	3.93	20	0	133	145	20	118
Ortiz, Steve, Abilene	13	6	4.01	20	0	137	142	40	80
Buckman, Tom, Bayou	5	4	4.05	16	0	80	82	38	56
Reeder, Russell, Alexandria	14	2	4.24	23	0	166	179	30	93
McDermott, Toby, Lubbock	7	5	4.28	28	4	109	118	47	83
Bicknell, Greg, Amarillo	13	3	4.53	23	0	153	176	37	116
Ruiz, Rafael, Rio Grande	8	6	4.57	20	0	122	153	36	86
Arminio, Sam, Abilene	4	7	4.81	19	0	116	145	23	53

ABILENE

BATTING	AVG	AB	R	H	2B	3B	HR	RBI	SB
Abrego, Keith, of	.294	109	20	32	10	1	5	29	0
Bubela, Brent, of-1b	.313	278	46	87	18	5	1	33	4
Cairo, Sergio, of	.355	155	35	55	7	2	5	26	1
2-team (42 Rio Grande)	.323	313	58	101	22	3	9	54	4
Cedeno, Ramon, of	.325	209	30	68	15	0	11	44	2
2-team (32 Bayou)	.324	336	46	109	27	2	13	69	2
Contreras, Efrain, dh-of	.324	250	42	81	21	0	8	46	1
Hemphill, James, of	.282	117	16	33	6	0	1	13	4
Holder, Jody, 2b-of	.301	206	29	62	7	4	0	20	5
Hughes, Shawn, c	.296	294	38	87	24	3	3	45	3
Hyde, Jerod, of-1b	.191	68	13	13	5	0	2	10	2
Jones, Barry, 1b	.319	204	33	65	10	2	5	29	5
Mason, Lamont, 2b-ss	.269	208	34	56	8	0	1	13	17
3-team (9 Lubb, 15 Rio)	.283	283	51	80	16	0	2	21	18
Motes, Jeff, 3b	.285	309	55	88	12	7	3	31	11
Parra, Jose, ss	.309	178	22	55	7	1	0	19	7
Pearson, Ryan, of	.231	52	4	12	2	0	0	6	2
Perini, Mike, of	.226	146	25	33	6	0	2	15	6
Rosario, Victor, ss	.286	49	7	14	2	1	2	9	3
2-team (50 Rio Grande)	.314	255	43	80	15	2	15	61	6
Sandoval, David, 2b	.310	84	8	26	5	1	0	11	3
Takahashi, Barry, 1b	.122	49	4	6	1	0	1	5	0

PITCHING	W	L	ERA	G	SV	IP	H	BB	SO
Aiken, Greg	0	3	7.62	19	0	39	53	29	20
Arminio, Sam	4	7	4.81	19	0	116	145	23	53
Baack, John	0	2	9.47	5	0	19	31	12	5
Brown, Brandon	0	3	5.74	19	0	27	38	15	24
Glore, Jamie	1	7	7.89	15	0	59	84	17	33
Hampton, Mark	4	3	3.42	37	8	53	41	31	38
Leffingwell, Brent	0	1	4.82	3	0	9	12	7	7
Moore, Ashley	1	0	5.40	6	0	18	24	10	13
Ortiz, Steve	13	6	4.01	20	0	137	142	40	80
Phillips, Jamil	0	0	11.00	7	0	9	11	15	7
Preston, George	5	2	3.90	34	5	58	52	38	76
Rockwell, Kelth	1	1	4.34	10	1	19	19	4	9
Smith, Mike	6	7	5.56	20	0	134	169	146	88
Takahashi, Barry	4	3	6.28	16	0	39	51	13	20

ALEXANDRIA

BATTING	AVG	AB	R	H	2B	3B	HR	RBI	SB
Cole, Marvin, 2b	.319	329	68	105	19	1	8	61	12
Delafield, Wil, of	.322	329	59	106	26	4	11	68	3
Gafford, Cory, c	.266	252	48	67	10	0	9	43	2
Hewes, Robert, 3b	.361	294	80	106	28	7	9	63	17
Matos, Malvin, dh-of	.356	315	76	112	23	7	26	87	9

BATTING	AVG	AB	R	H	2B	3B	HR	RBI	SB
O'Brien, John, 1b	.351	328	89	115	21	1	32	93	1
Roland, William, ss	.304	312	60	95	19	3	9	48	3
Rothe, Ryan, of	.324	340	83	110	29	6	4	48	15
Shade, Kyle, of-3b	.370	349	87	129	31	3	9	84	1
Van Asselberg, Ricky, c	.279	136	22	38	7	0	3	16	1

PITCHING	W	L	ERA	G	SV	IP	H	BB	SO
Bawlson, Jeff	1	0	4.56	12	0	26	37	17	12
Caridad, Ron	5	6	4.86	37	18	50	47	39	48
Filson, Brian	3	1	3.68	4	0	29	32	10	21
Flores, Mario	0	2	9.35	4	0	17	30	3	7
Frisbie, James	1	1	6.00	11	0	33	41	22	3
Hartman, Kelly	6	3	6.35	23	1	74	112	30	43
Haught, Gary	2	1	2.08	3	0	26	20	8	14
2-team (3 Greenville)	3	3	3.22	6	0	45	41	13	24
Hawkins, Brandon	3	4	9.00	23	3	55	85	32	23
Mack, Tony	13	5	5.17	21	0	157	178	142	96
Moran, Eric	4	1	3.91	8	0	48	57	14	38
Reeder, Russell	14	2	4.24	23	0	166	179	30	93
White, Darell	6	0	2.85	8	0	54	48	22	48

AMARILLO

BATTING	AVG	AB	R	H	2B	3B	HR	RBI	SB
Anderson, Chris, c	.300	80	19	24	9	0	0	15	0
Collins, Sean, of-2b	.371	361	96	134	19	9	12	75	41
Cook, Jeff, of	.281	331	78	93	13	7	1	38	10
Henderson, Derek, 3b	.310	342	69	106	25	3	8	90	0
Hensley, Casey, dh-1b	.200	40	5	8	1	0	1	10	0
Hook, Kenny, ss-2b	.297	276	56	82	6	3	1	43	6
Howard, Tim, 2b-ss	.447	331	89	148	37	13	10	96	18
Johnson, Jack, c	.295	264	50	78	21	1	18	69	2
Koerner, Pat, 1b-of	.273	132	34	36	11	1	2	28	2
Maclin, Lonnie, 1b-of	.355	327	78	116	23	3	10	65	4
McAlvain, Jarrod, 1b	.284	204	35	58	21	2	4	45	0
Wilson, Mike, of	.373	311	93	116	16	7	11	69	22
Zucha, Jason, c	.125	16	6	2	0	0	0	0	0

PITCHING	W	L	ERA	G	SV	IP	H	BB	SO
Bicknoll, Greg	13	3	4.53	23	0	153	176	37	116
Boebert, Mike	10	5	4.98	21	0	128	166	42	111
Brown, Daren	15	4	3.21	20	0	137	139	21	121
Farrar, Terry	4	3	5.74	28	0	42	66	23	42
Hibbard, Billy	3	2	6.02	26	2	40	63	12	27
Kermode, Al	12	3	3.93	20	0	133	145	20	118
Neese, Josh	3	0	4.20	34	13	44	43	13	47
Patrick, Jason	3	0	4.65	29	1	50	58	19	30

BAYOU

BATTING	AVG	AB	R	H	2B	3B	HR	RBI	SB
Anderson, Jeff, 2b-3b	.281	135	26	38	9	0	2	18	2
Banks, Mike, 2b-ss	.205	39	4	8	1	0	1	2	0
Bethea, Scott, ss-2b	.328	174	34	57	6	2	2	23	6
Campaniello, Ed, of	.343	321	69	110	26	7	3	49	7
Case, Fred, c-1b	.235	85	6	20	4	1	1	16	1
Cassels, Chris, dh-of	.350	331	65	116	23	5	22	82	1
Cedeno, Ramon, of	.323	127	16	41	12	2	2	25	0
Doucet, Brandon, of	.391	23	3	9	3	0	0	4	0
Felix, Geno, 2b-3b	.267	15	1	4	0	0	0	0	0
Green, Ron, of	.196	46	6	9	0	1	0	3	3
Llanos, Bobby, 3b-of	.330	221	46	73	15	1	8	46	3
McAninch, John, 1b	.277	307	46	85	19	1	6	44	4
Oglesby, Luke, of	.158	38	6	6	2	0	0	2	3
Parnell, Dustin, p-dh	.080	25	2	2	0	0	0	0	0
Payne, Scott, ss-3b	.296	250	30	74	18	2	3	35	3
Poole, Shannon, c	.214	70	8	15	0	1	0	3	0
Poulin, Max, ss	.162	37	6	6	1	0	0	0	1
Prejean, Neil, 3b	.182	11	2	2	0	0	0	1	0
Sandoval, David, 3b	.210	157	21	33	3	1	3	17	2
2-team (24 Abilene)	.245	241	29	59	8	2	3	28	5
Skeels, Andy, c	.353	51	11	18	5	0	0	9	5
Tannehill, Jeff, c	.240	167	27	40	6	1	0	17	9
Wilson, Andy, of-2b	.345	296	58	102	16	2	0	43	30

PITCHING	W	L	ERA	G	SV	IP	H	BB	SO
Bourbakis, Mike	1	3	6.16	4	0	19	17	18	15
Buckman, Tom	5	4	4.05	16	0	80	82	38	56
Casey, Shaw	2	1	4.63	36	8	45	43	27	30
Coleman, Billy	1	1	3.79	9	0	19	19	12	11
Eave, Gary	0	2	6.29	16	0	44	56	17	25
Elliott, Donnie	4	1	2.83	6	0	35	29	12	42
Foshie, Josh	7	6	5.57	17	0	86	104	40	56
Glore, Jamie	0	1	7.50	2	0	12	14	5	9
2-team (15 Abilene)	1	8	7.82	17	0	71	98	22	42
Gray, Dave	0	2	4.43	15	0	22	18	16	14
Leiber, Zane	2	2	8.50	10	0	18	27	16	11
Masters, Dayne	2	2	6.23	15	0	35	42	15	16
Mear, Rich	1	3	12.27	8	0	22	30	38	14
Mullikin, Jamie	0	2	5.68	23	1	38	58	15	13
Mullikin, Robby	0	2	6.21	21	0	29	31	34	24
Parnell, Dustin	2	2	5.52	27	1	46	69	7	22
Periou, Todd	0	0	18.56	6	0	5	11	8	5
Perry, J.D.	1	7	5.08	13	0	62	82	28	41
Schardt, Mitch	5	6	5.56	21	2	81	104	21	45
Stadelhofer, Mike	0	1	7.20	6	3	5	3	4	3
Walker, Wade	2	0	1.93	4	0	9	9	2	6
Wilkinson, Grey	0	0	10.80	4	0	5	10	7	6

GREENVILLE

BATTING	AVG	AB	R	H	2B	3B	HR	RBI	SB
Antczak, Chuck, c	.114	35	0	4	1	0	0	3	1
Autry, Brian, 1b	.200	35	3	7	0	0	1	2	0
Aviles, Billy, 3b-2b	.240	150	14	36	6	0	2	22	1
Barnes, Nelson, of	.255	192	24	49	6	2	2	19	10
Campbell, Keiver, dh	.218	55	10	12	1	2	2	11	4
Cole, Popeye, of	.307	215	38	66	9	2	3	22	2
DiLillo, Tony, 1b	.364	11	2	4	2	0	0	2	0
Drent, Brian, of	.279	201	28	56	14	3	6	40	8
Florio, Jason, c-1b	.253	245	29	62	11	3	5	40	1
Gower, Mack, c	.182	11	2	2	0	0	0	1	0
Griffin, Bubba, c	.313	83	12	26	2	1	0	10	2
Johnson, Alphonso, ss-3b	.237	131	12	31	3	1	0	12	8
Johnson, Ryan, ss	.220	132	13	29	4	1	1	11	4
Kline, Jason, 2b	.243	37	2	9	0	1	0	3	1
Landrum, Tito, of	.342	111	18	38	7	1	5	16	8
2-team (36 Lubbock)	.323	257	49	83	16	4	9	46	15
McBride, Kip, 2b	.200	20	2	4	1	0	0	1	0
McMahan, Kenny, 1b	.273	33	5	9	3	0	1	11	1
Moore, Vince, of	.341	299	65	102	21	5	9	43	38
Robinson, Manny, 2b	.176	68	8	12	2	0	0	2	0
Sanchez, Alex, 1b	.020	178	31	58	12	3	2	37	6
Stinson, Ryan, of	.324	244	36	79	12	1	1	24	26
Stroud, Cecil, c-3b	.225	40	2	9	2	0	1	4	0
Velasquez, Arturo, 2b-ss	.260	277	40	72	6	0	0	21	5

PITCHING	W	L	ERA	G	SV	IP	H	BB	SO
Alonardo, Mike	4	4	7.88	10	0	56	70	34	21
Cantu, Alvin	2	4	5.08	12	0	67	87	25	45
Cupit, Wayne	3	2	4.23	21	2	28	31	20	16
Flores, Mario	0	2	12.91	3	0	8	20	3	6
2-team (4 Alexandria)	0	4	10.44	7	0	25	50	6	13
Hannah, Neal	4	4	8.92	14	0	37	56	18	24
Haught, Gary	1	2	4.82	3	0	19	21	5	10
Holobinko, Mike	1	8	8.15	26	1	74	117	49	45
Holter, Brian	0	0	11.25	8	0	12	20	5	6
Krahenbuhl, Ken	1	6	3.88	8	0	63	59	14	42
Lacey, Bob	0	0	5.06	4	1	5	7	0	2
Miller, Matt	1	7	2.85	8	0	54	46	19	49
Miller, Shawn	1	3	4.30	8	0	39	49	18	28
Morales, Johnny	0	3	12.09	16	1	35	57	29	21
Musset, Jose	0	2	4.38	7	2	12	21	6	9
Parks, Tommy	2	2	6.48	15	1	58	91	25	26
Robinson, Lance	0	1	4.50	5	0	8	15	2	2
2-team (20 Lubbock)	3	2	7.40	25	1	41	65	17	18
Sanchez, Alex	0	4	6.93	5	0	25	30	11	24
Schad, Jeffrey	0	0	8.41	11	0	20	32	17	4
Swearingen, Jason	2	8	6.72	13	0	83	120	21	40

LUBBOCK

BATTING	AVG	AB	R	H	2B	3B	HR	RBI	SB
Benavidez, Eric, 2b-ss	.286	308	72	88	19	1	4	44	22
Davis, Ryan, 3b	.091	11	3	1	0	0	0	0	0
2-team (13 Rio Grande)	.200	45	7	9	3	0	1	5	0
DeLeon, Roberto, ss	.237	245	35	58	9	1	5	35	8
2-team (15 Rio Grande)	.238	303	39	72	13	1	6	41	8
DeLeon, Ray, 1b	.402	219	45	88	14	0	11	55	4
2-team (21 Rio Grande)	.364	302	57	110	19	0	13	70	6
Granville, Ernie, of	.222	27	5	6	1	0	0	2	2
Hardy, Bryan, dh	.167	36	5	6	2	0	1	5	0
Hill, Jason, c-of	.345	113	21	39	11	2	5	27	1
Kagami, Clint, c	.250	16	2	4	2	0	0	1	0
Keith, Jason, 3b-ss	.281	139	28	39	10	0	3	23	3
Landreth, Jason, of-dh	.377	260	60	98	17	1	8	54	22
Landrum, Tito, of	.308	146	31	45	9	3	4	30	7
Lowery, David, 2b	.292	168	34	49	9	1	0	18	15
Martinez, Joaquin, 3b-of	.207	29	7	6	1	0	0	5	2
Marx, John, dh	.308	13	4	4	1	0	0	2	0
Mason, Lamont, of-2b	.269	26	6	7	3	0	0	3	1
Perez, Carlos, of-1b	.323	269	51	87	20	1	11	61	6
Ramirez, J.D., 3b	.327	196	51	64	16	1	10	46	4
Shuffield, Chris, of	.222	27	5	6	1	0	1	2	0
Sullivan, Drue, 1b	.235	119	14	28	8	0	0	24	4
Vaughn, Derek, of	.350	343	77	120	27	4	3	60	46
Woodress, Bray, c	.307	244	40	75	14	0	1	39	5

PITCHING	W	L	ERA	G	SV	IP	H	BB	SO
Aiken, Greg	0	1	7.90	8	1	14	22	7	6
2-team (19 Abilene)	0	4	7.69	27	1	53	75	36	26
Baine, David	4	7	6.91	21	0	113	176	38	61
Brand, Scott	0	2	9.22	8	0	14	28	8	12
Brown, Caleb	1	0	6.33	15	0	27	[illegible]	10	19
Cantu, Alvin	5	3	5.51	9	0	65	88	10	42
2-team (12 Greenville)	7	7	5.29	21	0	133	175	44	87
Felix, Ruben	1	0	10.38	13	0	13	18	13	7
Jenkins, Scott	2	1	4.00	8	1	9	10	10	8
Madigan, Brian	10	6	5.07	20	0	126	158	47	51
McDermott, Toby	7	5	4.28	28	4	109	118	47	83
McKinley, Greg	1	2	13.50	6	0	9	18	8	2
Mullikin, Robby	0	0	11.57	10	1	7	11	8	5
2-team (21 Bayou)	0	2	7.25	31	1	36	42	42	29
Nye, Richie	1	2	7.15	10	0	23	28	17	13
Peck, Jeff	2	6	9.14	17	0	65	116	26	22
Reichard, Bryan	0	0	11.57	4	0	5	10	3	2
Resendez, Oscar	2	5	6.70	10	1	47	52	38	35
2-team (4 Rio Grande)	4	6	5.87	14	1	69	72	61	53
Robinson, Lance	3	1	8.10	20	1	33	50	15	16
Wade, Travis	0	0	6.60	11	3	15	18	7	10
2-team (20 Rio Grande)	1	3	9.33	31	7	37	51	25	26
Wilder, Chris	0	2	8.44	12	1	16	23	10	11

RIO GRANDE VALLEY

BATTING	AVG	AB	R	H	2B	3B	HR	RBI	SB
Braddy, Junior, of-1b	.303	234	43	71	16	2	7	43	7
Cairo, Sergio, of	.291	158	23	46	15	1	4	28	3
Chavez, Steve, 3b	.321	137	25	44	10	0	6	31	1
Davis, Jay, of	.405	343	89	139	35	1	26	84	25
Davis, Ryan, dh	.235	34	4	8	3	0	1	5	0
DeLeon, Roberto, 2b	.241	58	4	14	4	0	1	6	0
DeLeon, Ray, 1b	.265	83	12	22	5	0	2	15	2
Ferreira, Tony, c	.091	33	3	3	1	0	0	3	0
Fitzpatrick, Eddie, c	.223	202	28	45	4	0	0	11	0
Hemphill, James, 1b	.325	40	8	13	2	0	2	9	1
2-team (31 Abilene)	.293	157	24	46	8	0	3	22	5
Hendricks, R.J., 1b	.250	80	7	20	2	0	1	13	0
Martinez, Joey, of-2b	.358	215	51	77	12	3	4	26	16
Mason, Lamont, 2b	.347	49	11	17	5	0	1	5	0
Medlin, Eddie, c	.324	37	5	12	4	0	0	4	0
Morrill, Jim, 1b	.222	18	1	4	0	0	0	0	0
Parra, Jose, ss	.243	115	26	28	4	0	1	11	11
2-team (47 Abilene)	.283	293	48	83	11	1	1	30	18
Parras, Eddie, of	.103	39	3	4	1	0	0	1	1
Polidor, Wil, 3b	.336	146	23	49	11	1	1	20	2
Ramirez, Omar, of	.338	284	66	96	18	4	12	58	26
Rice, Charles, dh-of	.232	82	10	19	2	1	3	7	1
Rosario, Victor, ss	.320	206	36	66	13	1	13	52	3
Schied, Jeremy, 1b-c	.333	12	1	4	0	0	0	3	0
Suero, Ignacio, c-1b	.393	56	16	22	6	0	5	19	0
Swindell, Mark, 2b-ss	.271	166	21	45	2	0	0	9	3
Taveras, Jose, 2b-3b	.290	131	17	38	7	1	0	19	5
Viegas, Clark, 3b	.100	10	1	1	0	0	0	1	0

PITCHING	W	L	ERA	G	SV	IP	H	BB	SO
Bargman, Cerleston	3	6	5.98	11	0	56	68	31	31
Bawlson, Jeff	1	0	0.00	2	0	2	3	0	0
2-team (12 Alexandria)	2	0	4.28	14	0	27	40	17	12
Boughton, Mike	0	1	7.14	6	0	29	38	16	16
Cuchetti, Tony	0	1	15.28	11	0	18	42	10	4
Fawcett, Jason	7	4	4.83	14	0	88	78	45	98
Fields, Kurtis	2	2	7.43	7	0	27	31	16	22
Martinez, Sergio	0	2	8.31	5	0	17	23	13	13
Mozley, Brandon	1	8	6.53	23	1	72	107	31	27
Resendez, Oscar	2	1	4.09	4	0	22	20	23	18
Rodriguez, Mario	4	2	5.79	21	1	65	78	27	39
Ruiz, Rafael	8	6	4.57	20	0	122	153	36	86
Sabino, Miguel	0	1	7.33	16	0	27	36	11	14
Schulman, Jeffrey	0	0	13.50	6	0	9	19	9	2
Stutz, Joe	5	5	3.04	33	3	68	61	30	58
Swindell, Mark	0	2	4.99	14	1	40	59	4	25
Vreonis, Joey	0	0	7.15	7	0	11	15	9	3
Wade, Travis	1	3	11.22	20	4	22	33	18	16
White, Keith	1	4	9.93	9	0	29	45	21	14

WESTERN LEAGUE

The Sonoma County Crushers won their first Western League title in 1998 with an upset over the defending champion Chico Heat.

The Heat won both halves of the Southern Division split-season schedule but couldn't handle the Crushers in the division playoffs. From there, the Crushers beat the Western Warriors in three straight games to win the league title.

The Crushers were led by first baseman Todd Pridy, whose .408 average was a league record. Pridy also broke the league mark for most hits, with 146, and his 94 RBIs tied another. He led the league with a .478 on-base percentage and a .665 slugging percentage.

In the North, the Western Warriors rallied around manager of the year Charley Kerfeld to win the second-half title despite spending the entire half on a road trip.

The Warriors began the season in Grays Harbor, Wash., but club officials could no longer pay the bills. The franchise was about to go under when the league agreed to underwrite the cost to play as a road team for the rest of the season. Tri-City president John Montero purchased new uniforms for the Warriors while Chico GM Bob Linscheid became Western's interim general manager.

The road-weary Warriors responded to their adversity by winning the second half title. They not only made the playoffs but defeated perennial power Reno to land in the finals.

STANDINGS

FIRST HALF

NORTH	W	L	PCT	GB
Reno Chukars	25	20	.556	—
Bend Bandits	24	21	.533	1
Western Warriors	20	25	.444	5
Tri-City Posse	18	27	.400	7
SOUTH	**W**	**L**	**PCT**	**GB**
Chico Heat	30	15	.667	—
Sonoma County Crushers	26	18	.591	3½
Mission Viejo Vigilantes	24	21	.533	6
Pacific Suns	12	32	.273	17½

SECOND HALF

NORTH	W	L	PCT	GB
Western Warriors	23	22	.511	—
Tri-City Posse	21	24	.467	2
Reno Chukars	20	25	.444	3
Bend Bandits	19	25	.432	3½
SOUTH	**W**	**L**	**PCT**	**GB**
Chico Heat	33	11	.750	—
Mission Viejo Vigilantes	25	20	.556	8½
Sonoma County Crushers	23	22	.511	10½
Pacific Suns	15	30	.333	18½

PLAYOFFS: Semifinals—Western Warriors defeated Reno 3-1 and Sonoma County defeated Chico 3-0 in best-of-5 series. **Finals**—Sonoma County defeated Western Warriors 3-0 in best-of-5 series.

MANAGERS: Bend—Wally Backman. Chico—Bill Plummer. Mission Viejo—Buck Rodgers. Pacific—Jim Derrington/John Wood. Reno—Butch Hughes. Sonoma County—Dick Dietz. Tri-City—Jamie Nelson/Derrel Thomas. Western—Charley Kerfeld.

ATTENDANCE: Chico 132,052; Tri-City 95,854; Sonoma County 89,598; Mission Viejo 80,208; Reno 53,930; Pacific 49,995; Bend 39,692; Western 36,046 (all but 12 home games played at opponent's stadium).

ALL-STAR TEAM: **C**—Jon Fuller, Western. **1B**—Todd Pridy, Sonoma County. **2B**—Al Harley, Chico. **3B**—Eric White, Sonoma County. **SS**—Lino Connell, Western. **OF**—Mark Charbonnet, Bend; Brett Jenkins, Reno; Vernon Spearman, Sonoma County. **DH**—Alan Burke, Mission Viejo. **P**—Tony Coscia, Sonoma County; Collin Kerley, Bend; Scott Navarro, Chico; Mike Smith, Mission Viejo; Jeff Sobkoviak, Chico.

Player of the Year: Todd Pridy, Sonoma County. **Pitcher of the Year**: Mike Smith, Mission Viejo. **Manager of the Year**: Charley Kerfeld, Western.

INDIVIDUAL BATTING LEADERS

(Minimum 243 Plate Appearances)

	AVG	AB	R	H	2B	3B	HR	RBI	SB
Pridy, Todd, Sonoma	.408	358	82	146	29	0	21	94	4
Dowler, Dee, Reno	.389	293	62	114	22	7	4	45	37
Charbonnet, Mark, Bend	.364	357	70	130	31	4	22	85	12
Spearman, Vernon, Sonoma	.363	369	89	134	21	8	2	34	40
Connell, Lino, Western	.362	370	66	134	26	9	10	56	28
Jenkins, Brett, Reno	.361	338	68	122	20	1	23	94	5
White, Eric, Sonoma	.350	309	41	108	25	0	5	51	11
Valdez, Frank, Pacific	.341	217	29	74	20	0	4	26	3
Madden, Joey, Bend	.341	358	68	122	18	3	3	38	31
Kapano, Randy, Bend	.339	307	68	104	16	0	25	76	18

INDIVIDUAL PITCHING LEADERS

(Minimum 72 Innings)

	W	L	ERA	G	SV	IP	H	BB	SO
Neier, Chris, Chico	8	2	2.94	16	0	86	73	14	49
Thurmond, Travis, Sonoma	6	5	3.05	16	0	112	99	66	134
Sobkoviak, Jeff, Chico	7	0	3.24	19	0	114	112	42	48
Navarro, Scott, Chico	10	4	3.34	19	0	121	119	40	66
Krahenbuhl, Ken, Pacific	4	5	3.51	11	0	82	92	14	51
Smith, Mike, Mission Viejo	10	6	3.52	21	0	138	144	39	121
Bergan, Tom, Chico	5	5	3.52	17	0	92	82	48	47
Campbell, Mike, Western	5	7	3.87	15	0	84	79	30	91
Coscia, Tony, Sonoma	10	4	3.88	20	0	132	136	41	131
Homan, John, Mission Viejo	3	3	3.92	24	4	78	82	33	45

BEND

BATTING	AVG	AB	R	H	2B	3B	HR	RBI	SB
Bidwell, Troy, dh	.184	49	5	9	1	0	2	8	0
Billingsley, Kyle, 1b	.304	227	37	69	15	1	7	35	7
Britt, Shane, of	.246	114	18	28	3	1	0	14	9
2-team (33 Western)	.242	223	34	54	7	1	0	25	18
Charbonnet, Mark, of	.364	357	70	130	31	4	22	85	12
Conley, Brian, ss-1b	.295	339	51	100	20	0	10	52	16
Dunn, Billy, ss	.100	20	1	2	1	0	0	4	1
Flores, Sergio, 2b	.067	15	1	1	0	0	0	1	0
Hebert, Jeff, of	.299	147	20	44	13	0	6	23	4
Kapano, Randy, 1b-3b	.339	307	68	104	16	0	25	76	18
Keefe, Jamie, ss	.221	95	17	21	3	0	1	10	7
Madden, Joey, of	.341	358	68	122	18	3	3	38	31
McGowan, Marcus, of	.233	129	21	30	6	0	0	10	14
Nadeau, Mike, 3b-2b	.325	323	67	105	17	5	4	48	27
Pergola, Jordan, c	.135	37	5	5	0	0	3	5	0
Powell, Gordon, 2b-3b	.259	294	48	76	20	3	7	37	32
Rodarte, Raul, 3b	.280	25	3	7	0	1	0	3	2
2-team (76 Reno)	.300	344	70	103	18	5	20	76	15
Val, Carter, c	.283	237	34	67	19	0	1	24	1
Vallero, Rich, c	.259	54	4	14	4	0	0	5	0

PITCHING	W	L	ERA	G	SV	IP	H	BB	SO
Bennett, Chris	0	0	12.60	1	0	5	5	6	2
Bennett, Erik	4	4	5.97	32	5	60	49	26	57
Darley, Ned	0	1	6.75	5	2	4	5	6	2
Flynt, Will	9	8	5.15	21	0	136	165	49	134
Gilich, Denny	2	0	4.41	6	0	33	34	19	33
Grennan, Steve	1	4	5.14	36	1	84	84	62	95
Kerley, Collin	12	6	4.08	21	0	148	147	45	94
Meier, Pat	8	6	4.85	18	0	106	100	74	63
Merrill, Tajah	0	2	8.27	12	0	21	29	10	19
Mitchell, Kendrick	0	3	7.15	5	0	23	26	17	23
Reiter, Morgan	1	2	11.88	5	0	17	23	16	13
Robell, Kevin	3	1	5.54	17	0	52	57	40	52
Stoecklin, Tony	1	5	3.46	38	13	55	52	22	53
Westover, Richard	2	4	5.44	38	0	43	51	26	34

CHICO

BATTING	AVG	AB	R	H	2B	3B	HR	RBI	SB
Arntzen, Brian, c	.233	73	6	17	3	0	2	11	0
Cooper, Tim, ss	.313	319	65	100	22	1	18	70	4
Durkac, Bo, 3b	.263	308	46	81	14	0	5	41	2
Funderburk, Levi, dh-of	.298	131	29	39	9	1	7	31	0
Giuffre, Guy, c	.169	89	10	15	4	0	3	11	0
Hansen, Terrel, of	.270	326	49	88	19	1	14	68	0
Harley, Al, 2b	.325	329	66	107	20	4	4	30	12
Koonce, Graham, 1b-of	.331	242	50	80	15	0	10	41	0
Lazerus, Erik, 2b-ss	.400	20	6	8	1	0	0	5	1
Mashore, Justin, of	.290	369	88	107	18	5	14	69	45
Palmer, Nate, c	.190	84	13	16	5	0	2	10	0
2-team (5 Bend)	.179	95	14	17	5	0	2	10	0
Perez, Carlos, of	.000	10	1	0	0	0	0	0	0
Rhein, Jeff, of	.264	326	58	86	18	1	11	53	18
Shamburg, Ken, dh-1b	.267	315	48	84	17	1	8	42	2
Voita, Sam, c	.296	71	9	21	3	0	1	8	1
3-team (7 Pacific, 15 MV)	.274	124	16	34	4	0	2	17	1
Wisler, Brian, of	.200	95	10	19	5	0	0	11	1

PITCHING	W	L	ERA	G	SV	IP	H	BB	SO
Beeman, Jason	1	4	6.68	19	0	31	46	21	20
Bergan, Tom	5	5	3.52	17	0	92	82	48	47
Bryant, Adam	4	3	3.19	45	3	59	45	31	55
Dawley, Joe	2	4	3.35	45	26	43	43	27	36
Montgomery, Josh	6	0	1.72	30	2	52	32	21	55
Navarro, Scott	10	4	3.34	19	0	121	119	40	66
Neier, Chris	8	2	2.94	16	0	86	73	14	49
Salcedo, Jose	11	3	5.03	19	0	111	123	38	90
Schiffhauer, Todd	1	0	3.60	4	0	5	6	2	3
Sobkoviak, Jeff	7	0	3.24	19	0	114	112	42	48
Sprinkle, Hank	5	1	1.98	43	1	55	49	30	42
Swan, Tyrone	0	0	5.40	6	0	8	9	6	2
Wisler, Brian	3	0	2.84	19	2	25	22	10	17

MISSION VIEJO

BATTING	AVG	AB	R	H	2B	3B	HR	RBI	SB
Bostic, Dwain, of	.241	54	14	13	2	0	1	8	1
Burke, Alan, 1b	.305	341	65	104	24	1	23	92	4
Curtis, Randy, of	.305	59	11	18	2	0	0	5	3
Davis, Kendrick, of	.267	165	22	44	8	0	2	15	9
2-team (37 Pacific)	.264	295	40	78	10	0	2	26	12
Edmondson, Tracy, ss-2b	.255	267	41	68	13	2	1	23	12
Gagliano, Manny, 3b	.254	284	40	72	12	0	14	46	1
Gennaro, Brad, of	.262	282	46	74	11	1	10	44	1
Grebeck, Brian, 2b-ss	.281	217	42	61	16	1	3	22	3
Kernan, Phil, of	.337	329	51	111	20	4	12	63	4
McDonnell, Tim, dh-3b	.257	175	28	45	6	0	3	20	1
Mitchell, Aaron, of	.262	61	8	16	5	0	1	10	5
2-team (9 Pacific)	.205	88	10	18	6	0	1	10	5
Moore, Michael, of	.226	133	26	30	7	1	6	16	8
Mosher, Willie, of	.222	54	2	12	0	1	2	6	1
Muro, Robert, 2b-3b	.316	266	41	84	14	1	2	34	3
Powell, Chris, of	.231	26	7	6	0	0	0	2	3
Shepherd, Bodie, c	.182	187	29	34	4	0	1	16	1
Tahan, Kevin, c	.312	141	14	44	10	0	1	21	1
Voita, Sam, c	.294	34	5	10	1	0	0	5	0

PITCHING	W	L	ERA	G	SV	IP	H	BB	SO
Belovsky, Josh	5	1	1.61	45	13	56	27	15	64
Castillo, Carlos	2	1	2.70	7	1	13	10	6	6
Ceterko, Steve	1	1	3.74	9	1	22	14	18	16
Davidson, Tim	4	0	4.13	5	0	24	27	13	10
2-team (16 Pacific)	6	6	5.28	21	0	104	120	54	73
Ehler, Dan	0	1	6.01	0	0	14	23	6	10
Ervin, Kent	4	5	7.03	13	0	65	93	25	31
Grebe, Brett	0	2	3.55	12	5	13	14	5	14
Hansen, Brent	5	8	4.55	19	0	111	120	46	79
Homan, John	3	3	3.92	24	4	78	82	33	45
Irvine, Kirk	7	6	4.46	24	0	125	127	23	85
Kishita, Kirt	1	1	3.09	12	0	12	12	3	8
Parisi, Mike	0	3	4.74	11	0	25	29	12	21
Primm, Bryce	1	1	9.00	11	0	14	19	15	13
Ritchie, Wally	4	2	6.82	13	0	34	45	13	10
Smith, Mike	10	6	3.52	21	0	138	144	39	121
Tremblay, Max	0	0	2.91	20	0	22	24	13	33
Wanders, Chad	2	0	4.44	11	0	24	27	12	8

PACIFIC

BATTING	AVG	AB	R	H	2B	3B	HR	RBI	SB
Antigua, Nilson, c	.231	268	31	62	16	1	5	22	9
Brennan, Ryan, of	.182	33	2	6	1	0	0	3	2
Combs, Marc, of	.139	36	2	5	1	0	0	0	1
Davis, Kendrick, of	.262	130	18	34	2	0	0	11	3
DiCarlo, Marc, 1b	.277	195	18	54	9	1	3	25	3
Dolias, Steve, 3b	.105	19	1	2	0	0	0	2	0
Ito, Duane, 2b-ss	.213	61	3	13	1	0	0	4	3
Konamori, Yoni, of	.088	34	2	3	0	0	0	1	0
Mitchell, Aaron, of	.074	27	2	2	1	0	0	0	0
Nunez, Bernie, dh-of	.254	244	34	62	16	0	13	40	1
Olivares, Jess, ss	.245	237	31	58	5	0	0	21	4
Ozuna, Rafael, 2b	.257	354	57	91	16	2	7	30	24
Sanchez, Alex, of	.172	93	6	16	2	1	1	8	1
Scheibe, Britton, of	.215	251	25	54	13	0	5	27	2
Seidel, Ryan, of-3b	.251	263	33	66	11	1	0	25	15
Unrat, Chris, 1b-3b	.290	276	31	80	17	0	5	32	0
Valdez, Frank, 3b	.341	217	29	74	20	0	4	26	3
Villalona, Kadir, of	.236	195	15	46	11	0	0	15	4
Voita, Sam, c	.158	19	2	3	0	0	1	4	0

PITCHING	W	L	ERA	G	SV	IP	H	BB	SO
Curran, Tighe	0	1	6.11	11	0	18	26	14	13
Davidson, Tim	2	6	5.63	16	0	80	93	41	63

PITCHING	W	L	ERA	G	SV	IP	H	BB	SO
Hollinger, Adrian	0	5	7.33	6	0	23	34	13	19
King, Eric	2	8	5.28	16	0	102	134	29	105
Krahenbuhl, Ken	4	5	3.51	11	0	82	92	14	51
Lynn, John	3	4	3.27	30	2	44	36	19	32
Moeller, Dennis	8	7	4.10	18	0	125	127	30	82
Molina, Bryan	1	2	5.01	21	0	32	33	18	10
Musset, Jose	1	3	2.21	17	2	20	15	15	19
Primm, Bryce	1	2	3.26	4	0	30	23	17	25
2-team (11 MV)	2	3	5.08	15	0	44	42	32	38
Rivera, Joe	0	0	2.45	6	0	7	8	6	4
Sanchez, Alex	3	8	5.26	14	0	89	93	52	41
Smith, Mike	0	3	4.37	13	4	23	24	8	28
Soriano, Jose	1	2	11.15	9	0	15	24	11	13
Sugar, Dylan	2	5	7.55	26	0	79	99	60	47
Verstratten, Robert	0	0	2.53	5	0	11	12	8	8

RENO

BATTING	AVG	AB	R	H	2B	3B	HR	RBI	SB
Bazzani, Matt, dh	.333	96	16	32	7	0	3	19	1
Dowler, Dee, of	.389	293	62	114	22	7	4	45	37
Glasser, Scott, 3b-ss	.169	130	22	22	5	1	0	10	5
Hagy, Gary, ss	.299	368	82	110	24	4	9	60	11
Headley, Justin, of-1b	.317	312	64	99	22	4	3	48	10
Horton, Conan, c	.220	82	11	18	1	0	3	10	2
Jenkins, Brett, of	.361	338	68	122	20	1	23	94	5
Kliner, Josh, 2b	.323	310	68	100	23	2	6	60	3
McDonnell, Tim, 3b	.262	65	11	17	3	0	1	9	0
2-team (55 MV)	.258	240	39	62	9	0	4	29	1
Olson, Cass, 1b	.229	118	19	27	5	3	2	20	2
Rodarte, Raul, 3b-of	.310	319	70	99	18	4	20	73	13
Schwenke, Matt, c	.211	266	40	56	12	0	5	36	1
Takayoshi, Todd, dh-1b	.318	311	63	99	24	1	6	61	3
Taylor, Sammy, of	.278	259	60	72	9	3	2	37	22

PITCHING	W	L	ERA	G	SV	IP	H	BB	SO
Bendik, Josh	2	6	5.18	30	3	80	106	30	64
Borges, Reece	5	4	3.71	35	10	61	60	26	46
Fernandez, Osvaldo	4	2	5.66	7	0	41	46	17	27
Frias, Miguel	2	2	8.10	24	0	50	71	31	33
Gould, Clint	4	5	5.31	13	0	61	79	22	30
Howatt, Jeff	8	3	4.51	19	0	120	147	27	51
Johnson, Carl	4	3	5.96	30	4	68	71	43	48
Mayer, Aaron	6	6	6.67	19	0	108	123	58	64
Petcka, Joe	0	1	5.40	8	0	12	13	14	10
2-team (5 Tri-City)	1	3	9.62	13	0	29	42	27	24
Pool, Matt	7	9	7.15	19	0	113	167	52	65
Robinson, Robby	0	0	9.64	7	0	9	12	4	3
Rodriguez, Mark	1	1	12.46	5	1	9	10	9	6
Tate, Seth	0	0	11.30	10	0	14	26	11	14
Urbani, Tom	2	3	4.23	8	0	55	70	9	34

SONOMA COUNTY

BATTING	AVG	AB	R	H	2B	3B	HR	RBI	SB
Ashley, Steve, c	.185	119	13	22	6	0	1	8	0
Bess, Johnny, c	.235	306	49	72	10	3	11	57	5
Bonds Jr., Bobby, of	.189	37	6	7	1	0	0	2	1
Brown, Eric, of	.286	196	24	56	8	2	2	30	6
Casey, Johnny, 2b	.265	302	55	80	13	1	4	46	0
Dietz, Steve, ss	.239	284	52	68	10	1	0	35	4
Hopgood, Scott, ss-2b	.165	91	13	15	4	0	0	7	0
Lauderdale, Jon, of	.087	23	2	2	0	0	0	0	0
McFarlin, Jason, of	.229	35	5	8	2	0	0	7	1
Mealing, Al, of	.297	300	54	89	22	5	6	50	14
Mowry, David, dh-1b	.239	289	35	69	13	0	8	42	0
Pridy, Todd, 1b-dh	.408	358	82	146	29	0	21	94	4
Simonton, Cy-Leon, of	.280	82	15	23	5	2	1	13	2
Spearman, Vernon, of	.363	369	89	134	21	8	2	34	40
White, Eric, 3b	.350	309	41	108	25	0	5	51	11

PITCHING	W	L	ERA	G	SV	IP	H	BB	SO
Basteyns, Brian	2	2	5.65	8	0	29	32	14	20
Cooper, Christian	0	1	8.04	5	0	16	20	15	15
Coscia, Tony	10	4	3.88	20	0	132	136	41	131
Crawford, Carlos	0	1	3.00	2	0	6	8	2	4
Cromwell, Nate	1	2	7.24	3	0	14	19	4	8
Frank, Kris	2	0	2.60	6	1	28	25	7	21
Goedhart, Darrell	0	1	6.86	10	0	20	28	12	12
2-team (17 Western)	4	8	7.03	27	0	97	146	51	66
Gower, Tim	5	4	3.31	34	7	54	67	12	51
Hopgood, Scott	0	0	5.40	3	0	5	6	2	6
Miller, Eric	2	2	3.81	22	9	28	27	10	29
Parisi, Mike	2	1	4.75	17	1	36	36	16	40
2-team (11 MV)	2	4	4.75	28	1	61	65	28	61
Patton, John	8	6	4.15	19	0	121	115	69	130
Shinar, Jeff	0	0	5.06	5	0	5	7	6	1
Soldate, John	1	3	7.45	21	1	39	48	20	24
Thurmond, Travis	6	5	3.05	16	0	112	99	66	134
Whitaker, Steve	4	3	5.28	12	0	61	77	36	47
Wise, Andy	0	1	9.53	3	0	6	9	6	2
Woodrow, Jim	6	5	5.42	17	0	75	92	37	40

TRI-CITY

BATTING	AVG	AB	R	H	2B	3B	HR	RBI	SB
Booth, Jeremy, 1b-c	.230	100	10	23	5	0	2	10	1
Brooks, Eric, c	.239	109	9	26	3	0	1	12	1
Gonzalez, Tony, 3b	.155	71	8	11	2	0	3	12	0
Johnson, Terry, of	.189	111	20	21	3	2	0	6	21
Lofton, James, ss	.284	394	69	112	20	3	3	34	33
Madonna, Chris, c-3b	.309	262	47	81	18	5	6	43	9
McNeely, Mike, 2b-of	.121	33	1	4	0	0	0	3	0
Newman, Mike, 3b	.087	23	1	2	1	0	0	1	0
Noles, Tremayne, 1b	.212	66	7	14	1	0	1	6	0
Paul, Corey, of	.296	304	51	90	17	1	13	58	13
Rutz, Ryan, 2b	.271	292	40	79	15	1	0	21	19
Scott, Shawn, of	.304	382	65	116	24	4	7	50	29
Simmons, Nelson, dh-1b	.289	332	35	96	17	0	12	67	1
Taylor, Sam, of-1b	.337	104	18	35	9	0	1	23	2
Vicens, Jason, 3b-1b	.313	227	23	71	8	2	0	18	4
Washington, Kyle, of	.278	291	53	81	18	2	5	43	13

PITCHING	W	L	ERA	G	SV	IP	H	BB	SO
Applegate, Bobby	1	2	7.00	7	0	27	39	10	14
Darley, Ned	5	1	0.82	38	15	44	27	10	49
2-team (5 Bend)	5	2	1.31	43	17	48	32	16	51
Elias, Joe	4	5	6.92	13	0	66	94	36	35
Gage-Cole, Kelly	0	3	10.26	8	0	17	29	13	11
Harris, Ryan	4	7	4.74	35	1	82	116	35	50
Hernandez, Jeremy	6	4	5.89	30	1	99	130	28	58
Hollinger, Adrian	0	0	5.40	2	0	5	8	3	4
2-team (6 Pacific)	0	5	6.99	8	0	28	42	16	23
Kishita, Kirt	4	4	4.47	28	0	46	57	22	36
2-team (12 MV)	5	5	4.19	40	0	58	69	25	44
Lacey, Levi	5	5	4.17	14	0	82	91	36	58
Petcka, Joe	1	2	12.46	5	0	17	29	13	14
Reardon, Kevin	0	3	11.57	6	0	14	25	8	8
Reynolds, Tim	1	0	2.39	12	1	26	22	6	15
Salazar, Mike	0	0	2.70	6	0	10	9	13	10
St. George, Nick	1	5	5.48	30	1	71	88	27	54
Thomas, Jeff	3	4	5.60	37	1	64	75	23	62
Toliver, Freddie	0	3	3.29	7	0	27	19	18	16
Torres, Mike	0	2	9.00	3	0	10	13	6	6
Walania, Al	4	1	4.47	16	0	87	97	17	35

WESTERN

BATTING	AVG	AB	R	H	2B	3B	HR	RBI	SB
Britt, Shane, of	.239	109	16	26	4	0	0	11	9
Connell, Lino, ss-2b	.362	370	66	134	26	9	10	56	28
DeMarco, Joey, 2b	.233	43	7	10	1	1	0	1	0
Fuller, Jon, c	.293	321	54	94	19	3	18	70	2
Grubb, Chris, of-ss	.276	308	43	85	10	1	3	38	11
Lewis, Tim, 3b-ss	.218	179	25	39	2	2	2	26	5
Limbrick, Byron, 2b-3b	.227	22	4	5	0	0	0	1	0
Masterson, Carter, of	.253	316	52	80	14	0	10	51	8
McDonald, Ryan, 2b-3b	.302	245	45	74	14	2	5	29	4
McDonnell, Marc, dh-c	.237	59	5	14	3	0	0	9	0
Mohler, Jacob, c	.174	23	6	4	1	0	1	3	1
Rendina, Mike, 1b-dh	.295	342	59	101	21	1	10	52	7
Sanchez, David, of	.271	332	69	90	22	7	10	59	16
Sanchez, Jimmy, of	.300	30	5	9	3	0	1	6	0
Vasquez, Chris, dh-1b	.304	359	60	109	31	0	21	70	2
Wisler, Brian, of	.000	1	0	0	0	0	0	0	0
2-team (45 Chico)	.198	96	10	19	5	0	0	11	

PITCHING	W	L	ERA	G	SV	IP	H	BB	SO
Barber, Andrew	1	0	7.84	10	0	10	15	6	6
Barnes, Keith	6	6	4.31	22	0	123	131	50	87
Campbell, Mike	5	7	3.87	15	0	84	79	30	91
Charley, Tandy	2	1	9.72	21	0	42	75	18	29
Escamilla, Jaime	2	3	5.28	49	1	44	40	29	35
Ewen, Jared	5	5	5.63	18	0	94	97	52	79
Goedhart, Darrell	4	7	7.07	17	0	78	118	39	54
Mahlberg, John	3	3	3.81	47	2	57	57	27	33
Moore, Ashley	2	3	6.60	9	0	46	59	31	15
Peterson, Mark	4	7	2.09	46	20	52	52	15	56
Schiffhauer, Todd	0	0	2.45	9	1	18	14	6	11
2-team (4 Chico)	1	0	2.70	13	1	23	20	8	14
Smith, Josh	0	0	6.26	25	0	42	54	22	22
Stewart, Mark	0	1	11.88	2	0	8	16	3	6
Wallace, Kent	3	0	1.59	3	0	23	17	2	20
Wisler, Brian	3	1	2.18	16	0	21	19	3	22
2-team (19 Chico)	6	1	2.54	35	2	46	41	13	39
Zwemke, Bryan	2	3	2.75	7	0	39	39	15	33

Foreign Leagues

MEXICAN LEAGUE

Upstart Oaxaca wins Mexican title in only third year

BY JOHN ROYSTER

For an example of how a regular season can mean nothing come playoff time, look no further than the 1998 Mexican League.

The Oaxaca Warriors, a team in their third year of existence, finished with the league's fifth-best regular season record, but took the title by sweeping the Monclova Steelers in four games in the championship series. Monclova, which had the third-best regular season record, made its first title-series appearance in 17 years.

Miguel Flores
Batting champ

And it wasn't as if the top teams, the Monterrey Sultans and Mexico City Red Devils, were just a little better than the competition during the regular season. Those teams dominated the league at 80-39 and 81-41, respectively, but both fell to Oaxaca in the first two rounds of the playoffs. The Red Devils went down 4-2 while Monterrey lost to Oaxaca in seven games.

The Warriors' run also provided an example of how much difference one player with a timely bat can make in the postseason. DH Nelson Barrera batted just .222 in 17 postseason games. But he drove in 13 runs and won two first-round games against the Red Devils with hits in the ninth and 12th innings.

Barrera, 40 and in his 22nd Mexican League season, doubled as the Warriors' manager and led the league with 110 RBIs, while hitting .321 with 15 homers. He also became the third player in league history, after Hector Espino (453) and Andres Mora (419), to hit 400 career home runs.

Oaxaca was extended to the limit in the semifinals by Monterrey, a team which had a 20-game winning streak in June and July. The Warriors won the last two games 4-1 and 7-0 in Monterrey, with Barrera hitting a two-run homer in Game Six.

The Tabasco Cattlemen, who won 17 straight to close the first half and take the South Zone title, were ousted by the Mexico City Tigers in the first round of the playoffs.

In the same year in which Cal Ripken stopped his consecutive-games streak, the Mexican League-record streak of Gerardo Sanchez ended under unusual circumstances.

Sanchez, an infielder/outfielder for the Two Laredos Owls, missed his first game since 1987 when his flight from Villahermosa to Mexico City was canceled. His streak ended at 1,415. The team made the 10-hour bus ride from Villahermosa after the previous night's game, but Sanchez and four other players decided to fly the next morning. When the Villahermosa airport was closed because of smoke from nearby forest fires, the players were stranded.

The league had co-batting champions for the first time when Monterrey second baseman Miguel Flores and Mexico City Tigers outfielder Luis Polonia finished with identical averages of .38095. Flores, who had a 32-game hitting streak at midseason, went 3-for-6 on the final day to pull even with Polonia, who sat out the Tigers' last game.

Cordoba Coffeegrowers manager Ramon Arano, the league's all-time winningest pitcher, activated himself for the last game of the season and threw 5 2/3 innings against the Tigers. Arano, 58, allowed two runs and 10 hits and left leading 3-2. The Tigers later rallied for a 5-3 win. Arano is 334-264 in 30 seasons.

Arm-twisting for a new stadium spread to Mexico at the close of the season, as both Mexico City teams threatened to move or sit out the 1999 season if the city didn't replace Social Security Stadium. The two teams share the park. The teams said if they decided not to play in 1999, they would option their players to the league's other 14 teams.

STANDINGS

NORTH ZONE	W	L	Pct.	GB
Monterrey Sultans (15.5)	80	39	.672	—
Monclova Steelers (14.5)	75	46	.620	6
Union Laguna Cotton Pickers (13)	55	67	.451	26½
Reynosa Broncos (11)	51	69	.425	29½
Saltillo Sarape Makers (11.25)	50	69	.420	30
Two Laredos Owls (11.5)	50	71	.413	31
CENTRAL ZONE	**W**	**L**	**Pct.**	**GB**
Mexico City Red Devils (16)	81	41	.664	—
Mexico City Tigers (14)	72	48	.600	8
Oaxaca Warriors (13)	68	50	.576	11
Aguascalientes Railroadmen (12)	57	63	.475	23
Cordoba Coffeegrowers (11)	37	83	.308	43
SOUTH ZONE	**W**	**L**	**Pct.**	**GB**
Tabasco Cattlemen (14.5)	66	54	.550	—
Cancun Lobstermen (15)	62	56	.525	3
Yucatan Lions (13)	57	63	.475	9
Chetumal Mayas (11.5)	51	67	.432	14
Campeche Pirates (12)	47	73	.392	19

NOTE: League played a split-season schedule. Points were awarded on the basis of finish in each half (8 for first, 7 for second, 6.5 for third, 6 for fourth, 5.5 for fifth, 5 for sixth) to determine playoff pairings.

PLAYOFFS—Quarterfinals: Oaxaca defeated Mexico City Red Devils 4-2, Mexico City Tigers defeated Tabasco 4-2, Monterrey defeated Yucatan 4-0 and Monclova defeated Cancun 4-2, in best-of-7 series. **Semifinals:** Oaxaca defeated Monterrey 4-3 and Monclova defeated Mexico City Tigers 4-3 in best-of-7 series. **Finals:** Oaxaca defeated Monclova 4-0 in best-of-7 series.

MANAGERS: Aguascalientes—Enrique Aguilar. Campeche—Carlos Paz, Roberto Mendez, Marcelo Juarez. Cancun—Francisco Estrada. Chetumal—Jesus Sommers, Raul Cano. Cordoba—Salome Barojas, Antonio Pulido, Ramon Arano. Two Laredos—Andres Mora, Porfirio Mendoza, Wilfredo Arano. Mexico City Red

Devils—Marco Vazquez. Mexico City Tigers—Dan Firova. Monclova—Aurelio Rodriguez. Monterrey—Derek Bryant. Oaxaca—Nelson Barrera. Reynosa—Leonardo Clayton. Saltillo—Marcelo Juarez, Fernando Elizondo. Tabasco—Pompeyo Davalillo. Union Laguna—Jose Guerrero. Yucatan—Gerardo Gutierrez, Jack Pierce, Carlos Paz.

REGULAR SEASON ATTENDANCE: Monterrey 541,362; Monclova 425,738; Chetumal 294,756; Cordoba 253,937; Mexico City Red Devils 231,538; Mexico City Tigers 220,218; Oaxaca 198,940; Yucatan 164,539; Tabasco 137,326; Saltillo 122,377; Union Laguna 111,170; Reynosa 106,831; Two Laredos 104,287; Aguascalientes 90,045; Cancun 82,263; Campeche 78,505.

INDIVIDUAL BATTING LEADERS

(Minimum 329 Plate Appearances)

	AVG	AB	R	H	2B	3B	HR	RBI	SB
Flores, Miguel, Monterrey	**.381**	399	87	152	32	4	4	67	32
Polonia, Luis, Tigers	**.381**	357	82	136	15	**14**	9	63	36
Espinoza, Ramon, Reds	.379	533	**114**	**202**	31	5	7	62	10
Alvarez, Hector, Oaxaca	.366	435	87	159	25	4	3	47	4
Castellano, Pedro, Reds	.354	387	71	137	31	2	13	101	5
Rojas, Homar, Oaxaca	.352	386	73	136	33	2	13	92	2
Carrillo, Matias, Tigers	.352	435	76	153	27	5	14	88	8
Carter, Michael, Laredo/UL	.351	476	72	167	21	5	4	42	35
Durazo, Erubiel, Mont.	.350	420	84	147	32	2	19	98	4
Jones, Ron, Saltillo	.349	441	59	154	26	0	11	86	0
Sherman, Darrell, Monc.	.347	320	84	111	7	3	3	29	36
Paez, Raul, Reds	.341	279	62	95	15	1	6	55	1
Magallanes, Ever, Mont.	.337	356	67	120	20	4	3	32	11
Diaz, Luis, Aguas.	.331	338	62	112	28	6	9	73	2
Azocar, Oscar, Chet.	.330	445	54	147	28	2	0	71	6
Martinez, Ray, Reds	.330	440	99	145	31	2	21	83	3
Munoz, Jooo, Reynosa	.325	431	82	140	25	12	3	60	11
Barrera, Nelson, Oaxaca	.323	387	76	125	31	1	15	**110**	2
Gregg, Tommy, Reds	.321	389	78	125	19	3	9	82	15
Ramirez, Roberto, Agu.	.320	450	77	144	23	4	8	84	7
Smith, Bubba, Mont.	.318	398	69	126	25	1	**29**	108	2
Rodriguez, Fernando, UL	.318	434	55	138	19	6	10	85	2
Fernandez, Daniel, Reds	.318	346	73	110	8	8	1	40	3
Arano, Wilfredo, Laredo	.318	321	36	102	19	2	2	43	3
Valle, Jorge, UL	.318	400	66	127	27	6	7	53	4
Cabrera, Alex, Tigers	.317	451	83	143	26	7	21	83	4
Suarez, Luis, Tigers	.316	323	46	102	8	6	5	51	4
Felix, Junior, Yucatan/UL	.316	418	73	132	27	4	19	90	12
Esquer, Ramon, Oaxaca	.315	425	94	134	17	4	7	59	13
Arredondo, Luis, Yuc.	.315	441	74	139	15	9	1	32	39
Orantes, Ramon, Agu.	.313	402	60	126	12	3	8	51	4
Castaneda, Rafael, Oax.	.313	383	61	120	16	2	6	69	1
Arano, Eloy, Chet./Reds	.313	364	39	114	8	4	0	30	13
Vega, Edgar, Aguas.	.313	297	43	93	8	6	2	38	3
Yan, Julian, Reynosa	.312	394	59	123	25	5	11	69	2
Gastelum, Sergio, Tigers	.308	429	71	132	19	4	2	46	12
Munoz, Jose, Saltillo	.305	393	84	120	9	6	2	43	**44**
DeLima Rafael, Cordoba	.304	408	61	124	21	2	2	45	10
Bruno, Julio, Tabasco	.302	467	44	141	16	1	4	60	3
Castaneda, Hector, Cor.	.302	295	35	89	18	0	7	49	1
Peguero, Julio, Can./Tab.	.301	375	52	113	14	3	3	33	21
Velazquez, Guillermo, Mont.	.301	425	85	128	23	0	12	80	2
Villanueva, Hector, Laredo	.301	372	61	112	20	0	20	56	0
Gonzalez, Denny, Tabasco	.301	359	74	108	23	1	19	61	2
Bojorquez, Victor, Reynosa	.301	409	53	123	24	7	0	33	7
Diaz, Remigio, Monterrey	.301	396	63	119	14	2	2	36	23
Fentanes, Oscar, Tabasco	.297	434	58	129	19	1	9	61	3
Vizcarra, Roberto, Aguas.	.297	445	78	132	17	5	12	67	19
Jimenez, Eduardo, Reds	.295	366	76	108	26	2	20	85	3
Zambrano, Roberto, Can.	.295	383	63	113	22	2	22	87	2
#Aganza, Ruben, Monclova	.278	439	78	122	**36**	1	15	88	4

(Other Select Players)

	AVG	AB	R	H	2B	3B	HR	RBI	SB
Stark, Matt, UL	.408	174	36	71	14	0	7	35	0
Whiten, Mark, Chet.	.382	131	38	50	15	0	5	26	5
Riley, Marquis, Aguas.	.379	66	13	25	2	0	0	7	4
Raven, Luis, Monclova	.349	149	28	52	14	1	4	34	2
Pecorilli, Aldo, Cam.	.333	117	12	39	9	0	3	18	1
Lydy, Scott, Oaxaca	.329	76	22	25	0	0	1	7	2
Hyzdu, Adam, Monterrey	.327	110	20	36	3	0	5	22	7
Chance, Tony, Monclova	.318	157	38	50	14	1	7	36	2
Bryant, Scott, Cancun	.295	217	23	64	15	1	1	32	2
Ratliff, Darryl, Cam.	.289	142	14	41	3	3	0	14	5
Rodriguez, Boi, Monc.	.280	364	61	102	22	0	8	57	14
Cole, Alex, Chet./Mont.	.279	326	48	91	8	2	2	33	29
Michel, Domingo, Cam./Yuc.	.278	385	65	107	19	1	12	62	5
Clark, Tim, Sal./Yuc.	.277	242	35	67	15	3	5	39	0
Claudio, Patricio, Tab.	.275	443	73	122	17	9	4	45	32
Meggers, Mike, Aguas./Chet.	.275	251	31	69	14	2	15	54	0
Gainer, Jay, Aguas./Oax.	.273	410	65	112	18	9	17	83	4
Tredaway, Chad, Yuc.	.269	390	44	105	20	1	5	52	3
Mulligan, Sean, Cor.	.257	113	10	29	3	1	1	12	0
Chamberlain, Wes, Cor.	.256	129	14	33	7	2	1	14	2
Pennyfeather, Will, Rey.	.253	83	12	21	4	0	2	10	2
Pagano, Scott, Can./Aguas.	.248	133	23	33	1	1	0	8	6
Mashore, Justin, Chet.	.245	49	7	12	0	0	0	1	2
Briggs, Stoney, Chet./Cor.	.239	251	39	60	5	2	8	31	21
Gordon, Keith, Cancun	.228	57	6	13	3	3	0	12	1
Pough, Clyde, Oaxaca	.227	194	47	44	7	1	7	33	6
Valrie, Kerry, Yucatan	.221	95	15	21	3	0	2	12	2
Longmire, Tony, Yuc.	.209	91	8	19	4	0	1	12	5
Hazlet, Steve, Cordoba	.170	47	2	8	1	0	1	3	0

INDIVIDUAL PITCHING LEADERS

(Minimum 98 Innings)

	W	L	ERA	G	SV	IP	H	BB	SO
Moreno, Angel, Yucatan	13	6	**1.96**	27	0	183	152	74	112
Elvira, Narciso, Mont.	**16**	4	2.00	24	0	158	130	54	114
Hernandez, Martin, Can.	10	6	2.01	18	0	134	100	41	65
Ruiz, Cecilio, Tabasco	15	7	2.22	26	0	162	149	33	54
#Metoyer, Tony, Can.	3	4	2.29	53	**32**	63	35	32	53
Young, Ray, Saltillo	9	4	2.33	15	0	108	86	58	105
Lopez, Jonas, Agu./Yuc./Tab.	9	3	2.45	26	3	121	107	39	22
Bernal, Manuel, Reds	12	5	2.52	23	0	164	154	47	75
Osuna, Ricardo, Tabasco	9	6	2.54	25	0	159	136	63	52
Rodriguez, Salvador, Yuc.	9	6	2.72	21	0	145	136	52	49
Campos, Francisco, Cam.	13	6	2.88	27	0	206	193	66	130
Manzanillo, Ravelo, Cam.	13	10	2.94	27	0	199	164	118	**144**
Soto, Fernando, Cancun	12	7	2.95	24	0	180	210	30	66
Rios, Jesus, Monclova	**16**	6	3.00	24	0	177	156	62	93
Lopez, Emigdio, Tabasco	9	7	3.01	23	0	104	109	34	41
Diaz, Rafael, Monterrey	14	4	3.02	25	0	176	146	91	117
Soto, Cruz, Cancun	9	9	3.12	37	0	121	100	79	69
Alvarez, Juan, Tabasco	10	7	3.21	24	0	146	149	62	59
Quinones, Enrique, Yuc.	7	8	3.26	22	0	132	141	28	61
Cecena, Jose, Monc.	7	1	3.29	25	0	98	86	38	45
Lopez, Rodrigo, Reds	10	6	3.35	26	0	164	165	79	95
Garibay, Daniel, Tigers	10	2	3.37	20	0	155	143	88	112
Acosta, Aaron, Laredo	12	5	3.38	23	0	149	147	73	101
Orozco, Jaime, Cordoba	9	13	3.50	23	0	157	155	29	44
Hernandez, Fernando, Mont.	12	3	3.54	31	0	114	86	90	106
Wagner, Hector, Oaxaca	8	6	3.56	22	0	137	137	50	65
#Dolarte, Jose, Monc.	6	3	3.59	60	**32**	68	61	24	38
Galvez, Randy, Reds	13	4	3.60	24	0	150	158	52	83
Hernandez, Jose, Monc.	12	7	3.60	26	0	177	200	55	70
Rodriguez, Raul, Monc.	12	7	3.73	26	0	183	201	62	90
Carranza, Javier, Can.	8	7	3.78	24	0	105	112	55	54
Cota, Marino, Oaxaca	7	3	3.79	31	0	102	123	38	66
Turgeon, Dave, Reynosa	7	8	3.88	18	0	125	139	39	87
Mora, Eleazar, Chet.	9	9	3.92	23	0	129	152	29	38
Dorame, Randey, Rey	6	13	4.03	24	0	132	143	73	71
Solis, Ricardo, Cordoba	7	9	4.04	23	0	129	158	37	36
Sanford, Mo, Aguas.	5	7	4.04	20	0	118	136	75	54
Velazquez, Israel, Cor.	4	11	4.09	22	0	123	123	56	78
Lara, Hugo, Chetumal	5	12	4.17	27	0	138	157	43	54
Huerta, Luis, Laredo	8	6	4.19	25	0	148	165	46	83
Munoz, Miguel, Rey.	3	8	4.20	24	0	139	174	32	46

(Other Select Players)

	W	L	ERA	G	SV	IP	H	BB	SO
Palacios, Vicente, Mont.	7	2	1.18	61	25	76	61	21	71
Powell, Dennis, Mont.	4	2	1.59	56	5	68	50	22	60
Lewis, Craig, Cordoba	2	2	3.14	5	0	29	25	13	12
Hurst, Jonathan, Agu./Sal.	1	1	3.71	17	5	17	15	9	12
Burgos, John, Laredo	3	10	4.35	31	2	93	120	38	50
Adam, David, Tigers	4	6	4.39	18	0	98	104	37	40
Badorek, Mike, Tigers	1	0	4.50	3	0	14	19	4	7
Barfield, John, UL	2	3	4.50	19	2	24	28	18	7
Huber, Jeff, Aguas.	4	0	4.64	15	3	21	28	10	5
Brosnan, Jason, Tigers	1	2	4.75	7	0	30	32	17	17
Williams, Jeff, Saltillo	2	2	4.78	5	0	26	30	18	10
Delgado, Tim, Saltillo	2	2	5.76	7	0	25	29	15	14
Duncan, Chip, Cordoba	1	5	7.15	13	1	39	58	22	23
Viano, Jacob, Tigers	0	1	9.00	3	0	7	8	15	3
Gray, Dennis, UL	0	2	15.32	6	0	12	19	20	11

Statistics in **boldface** indicate league leader
\# Indicates league leader but non-qualifier

FAR EAST

Yokohama ends 38 years of frustration in Japan Series

JAPAN

BY WAYNE GRACZYK

Thirty-eight years of frustration went out the window in 1998 as the Yokohama BayStars won their first pennant and Japan Series since 1960. Guided by freshman manager Hiroshi Gondo, Yokohama of the Central League defeated the Pacific League champion Seibu Lions four games to two in the Japan Series.

Nigel Wilson
33 HRs, 124 RBIs

The last time the BayStars were in postseason play, the franchise was known as the Taiyo Whales and was based in the industrial city of Kawasaki, between Tokyo and Yokohama. The club moved to its current location in 1978 and was renamed the BayStars in 1993.

The Stars got off to a mediocre start but led by superior closer Kazuhiro Sasaki, who set a Japan record with 45 saves, they took first place in the CL in May and held it the rest of the year, beating the Chunichi Dragons of Nagoya by four games.

Yokohama won with solid pitching and a super hitting lineup dubbed by the press a "machine gun" attack. It was a rare night when the BayStars failed to get at least 10 hits.

Seibu won its second straight PL title, its 13th in the last 17 years, beating the Nippon Ham Fighters by 3½ games. The Fighters blew a 9½-game midseason lead, and the race became a five-team affair by mid-September with the Kintetsu Buffaloes, Fukuoka Daiei Hawks and Orix BlueWave also joining in as contenders.

Sasaki, who had a 1-1, 0.64 record to go with his 45 saves in 51 appearances, was named Central League MVP. Seibu shortstop Kazuo Matsui was the Pacific League MVP after batting .311 and leading the league with 92 runs and 43 stolen bases.

A total of 57 foreign players saw action in 1998. Among the best were Nippon Ham DH Nigel Wilson, who led the PL with 33 home runs and 124 RBIs, and Kintetsu first baseman Phil Clark, who batted .320 with 31 homers and 114 RBIs.

The top Central League foreigners were Yokohama second baseman Bobby Rose and righthanders Nate Minchey and Ben Rivera. Rose was runner-up with 96 RBIs, and batted .325 with 19 homers. Minchey went 15-11 with a 2.75 ERA for the Hiroshima Carp. Rivera saved 27 games and won two for the Hanshin Tigers while posting a 2.38 ERA in 44 games.

Other league leaders were Yomiuri Giants slugger Hideki Matsui, who topped the CL with 34 homers and 100 RBIs, and two unrelated Suzukis who repeated as batting champions. Takanori Suzuki hit .337 for Yokohama, and Ichiro Suzuki won his fifth straight title with a .358 average for Orix. Takanori Suzuki also hit .480 in the Japan Series to win that MVP prize.

Among the lowlights during the year were an income tax-cheating scandal that resulted in 10 star players being suspended for part of the season, a record-setting 18-game losing streak by the Chiba Lotte Marines and an ugly incident involving former Los Angeles Dodgers righthander Balvino Galvez.

Throwing for Yomiuri against Hanshin on July 31, Galvez vented his anger at being removed from the game and protested several calls by firing the game ball at umpire Atsushi Kitaka as he was leaving the field. Galvez, Yomiuri's leading pitcher, was suspended by the Central League for the balance of the season.

Hard economic times in Japan were reflected in the fact that only one of 12 teams, the BayStars, enjoyed an increase in attendance over 1997. The Stars drew 1.68 million for a 10.3-percent increase, but overall Central League attendance was down 3.6 percent.

The Pacific League experienced an even worse drop of 13.5 percent.

CENTRAL LEAGUE

STANDINGS

	W	L	Pct.	GB
Yokohama BayStars	79	56	.585	—
Chunichi Dragons	75	60	.556	4
Yomiuri Giants	73	62	.541	6
Yakult Swallows	66	69	.489	13
Hiroshima Carp	60	75	.444	19
Hanshin Tigers	52	83	.385	27

INDIVIDUAL BATTING LEADERS
(Minimum 350 Plate Appearances)

	AVG	AB	R	H	2B	3B	HR	RBI	SB
Suzuki, Takanori, BayStars	**.337**	514	92	173	30	6	16	87	3
Maeda, Tomonori, Carp	.335	504	71	169	**36**	0	24	80	5
Tsuboi, Tomochika, Tigers	.327	413	63	135	26	2	2	21	7
Ogata, Koichi, Carp	.326	380	67	124	24	3	15	59	17
Rose, Bobby, BayStars	.325	468	70	152	29	4	19	96	2
Ishii, Takuro, BayStars	.314	555	**103**	**174**	34	5	7	48	**39**
Shimizu, Takayuki, Giants	.301	492	78	148	17	2	13	52	16
Takahashi, Yoshinobu, Giants	.300	466	65	140	32	1	19	75	3
Motoki, Daisuke, Giants	.297	397	49	118	18	3	9	55	3
Imaoka, Makoto, Tigers	.293	471	48	138	20	3	7	44	6
Matsui, Hideki, Giants	.292	487	**103**	142	24	3	**34**	**100**	3
Sekikawa, Koichi, Dragons	.285	382	62	109	13	2	1	36	15
Nomura, Kenjiro, Carp	.282	561	75	158	26	4	14	49	15
Komada, Norihiro, BayStars	.281	551	63	155	25	1	9	81	0
Ikeyama, Takahiro, Swallows	.275	400	63	110	20	0	18	59	3
Furuta, Atsuya, Swallows	.275	491	58	135	19	1	9	63	5
Manaka, Mitsuru, Swallows	.275	495	57	136	20	**8**	5	27	12
Shoda, Kozo, Carp	.274	376	44	103	9	0	1	17	0
Gomez, Leo, Dragons	.274	420	57	115	14	0	26	76	1
Nishi, Toshihisa, Giants	.274	424	76	116	15	1	11	33	17
Haru, Toshio, BayStars	.273	428	69	117	23	1	2	39	12
Tatsunami, Kazuyoshi, Dragons	.272	504	60	137	24	1	8	43	6

(Remaining U.S. and Latin Players)

	AVG	AB	R	H	2B	3B	HR	RBI	SB
Quezada, Alejandro, Carp	.311	61	8	19	1	0	3	9	0
Perez, Timoniel, Carp	.296	230	22	68	8	1	5	35	4
Powell, Alonzo, Tigers	.255	204	24	52	10	0	9	28	1
Hansen, Dave, Tigers	.253	400	42	101	13	1	11	55	0
Anthony, Eric, Swallows	.245	151	20	37	6	0	12	31	0
Mouton, Lyle, Swallows	.241	87	20	21	8	0	3	12	0
Hosey, Dwayne, Swallows	.233	317	35	74	12	1	13	42	4
Duncan, Mariano, Giants	.232	207	24	48	7	0	10	34	1
Malave, Jose, BayStars	.218	87	5	19	4	0	1	12	0
Wilson, Desi, Tigers	.167	24	0	4	0	0	0	3	0

INDIVIDUAL PITCHING LEADERS

(Minimum 133 Innings)

	W	L	ERA	G	SV	IP	H	BB	SO
#Sasaki, Kazuhiro, BayStars	1	1	0.64	51	**45**	56	32	13	78
Noguchi, Shigeki, Dragons	14	9	**2.34**	27	0	192	174	63	134
Kawakami, Kenshin, Dragons	14	6	2.57	26	0	161	123	51	124
Ito, Tomohito, Swallows	6	11	2.72	29	3	159	114	57	154
Mintchey, Nate, Carp	15	11	2.75	35	0	236	241	57	123
Kawaijiri, Tetsuro, Tigers	10	5	2.84	25	0	159	150	52	88
Saito, Takashi, BayStars	13	5	2.94	34	1	144	131	23	101
Kato, Shinichi, Carp	8	6	2.99	22	0	142	157	27	62
Kawasaki, Kenjiro, Swallows	**17**	10	3.04	29	0	204	195	55	94
Saito, Masaki, Giants	10	7	3.08	23	0	146	132	40	93
Miura, Daisuke, BayStars	12	7	3.18	25	0	159	138	60	119
Galvez, Balvino, Giants	9	7	3.21	18	0	137	136	39	85
Ishii, Kazuhisa, Swallows	14	6	3.30	28	0	196	149	105	**241**
Kawamura, Takeo, BayStars	8	6	3.32	26	0	146	139	46	97
Nomura, Hiroki, BayStars	13	8	3.34	28	0	178	183	29	100
Kadokura, Ken, Dragons	10	9	3.40	26	0	154	133	66	115

(Remaining U.S. and Latin Players)

	W	L	ERA	G	SV	IP	H	BB	SO
Acre, Mark, Swallows	0	2	2.34	12	0	69	47	34	58
Rivera, Ben, Tigers	2	3	2.38	44	27	53	44	19	45
May, Darrell, Tigers	4	9	3.47	21	0	130	122	55	94
Perdomo, Felix, Carp	0	0	4.15	13	0	17	15	11	6
Jarvis, Kevin, Dragons	1	2	4.41	4	0	16	18	5	7
Driskill, Travis, Swallows	0	1	4.80	7	0	15	21	6	7
Creek, Doug, Tigers	0	4	5.65	7	0	29	23	25	24
Mahomes, Pat, BayStars	0	4	5.98	10	0	44	61	29	24

PACIFIC LEAGUE

STANDINGS

	W	L	Pct.	GB
Seibu Lions	70	61	.534	—
Nippon Ham Fighters	67	65	.508	3½
Fukuoka Daiei Hawks	67	67	.500	4½
Orix BlueWave	66	66	.500	4½
Kintetsu Buffaloes	66	67	.496	5
Chiba Lotte Marines	61	71	.462	9½

INDIVIDUAL BATTING LEADERS

(Minimum 350 Plate Appearances)

	AVG	AB	R	H	2B	3B	HR	RBI	SB
Suzuki, Ichiro, BlueWave	**.358**	506	79	**181**	36	3	13	71	11
Hirai, Mitsuchika, Marines	.320	387	59	124	21	0	8	35	3
Clark, Phil, Buffaloes	.320	531	68	170	**48**	2	31	114	0
Shibahara, Hiroshi, Hawks	.314	385	54	121	14	3	2	35	18
Matsui, Kazuo, Lions	.311	575	**92**	179	38	5	9	58	43
Omura, Naoyuki, Buffaloes	.310	522	61	162	19	7	4	40	23
Kataoka, Atsushi, Fighters	.300	466	89	140	26	1	17	83	2
Hatsushiba, Kiyoshi, Marines	.296	473	68	140	38	3	25	86	0
Lopez, Luis, Hawks	.294	480	58	141	35	0	17	68	1
Franco, Julio, Marines	.290	487	78	141	27	2	18	77	7
Neel, Troy, BlueWave	.288	389	52	112	26	1	28	76	0
Fukuura, Kazuya, Marines	.284	465	61	132	32	3	3	57	1
Tani, Yoshitomo, BlueWave	.284	476	59	135	19	1	10	45	1
Martinez, Domingo, Lions	.283	491	65	139	16	1	30	95	4
Narahara, Hiroshi, Fighters	.280	364	72	102	6	4	1	25	30
Oshima, Koichi, BlueWave	.276	409	58	113	14	2	8	50	10
Takagi, Taisei, Lions	.276	504	70	139	26	2	17	84	15
Suzuki, Ken, Lions	.275	488	65	134	23	1	22	65	1
Tanaka, Yukio, Fighters	.274	420	62	115	28	0	24	63	2
Taguchi, So, BlueWave	.272	497	85	135	26	2	9	41	8
Otomo, Sasumu, Lions	.269	394	39	106	10	5	2	31	13
Kaneko, Makoto, Fighters	.263	380	53	100	10	2	4	26	11
Akiyama, Koji, Hawks	.260	423	43	110	32	4	10	49	7
Nakamura, Norihiro, Buffaloes	.260	481	74	125	14	1	32	90	1
Rhodes, Tuffy, Buffaloes	.257	494	81	127	25	0	22	70	15
Wilson, Nigel, Fighters	.255	506	65	129	13	0	**33**	**124**	1
Brooks, Jerry, Fighters	.244	459	58	112	8	1	25	73	1
#Kosaka, Makoto, Marines	.233	430	51	100	12	**8**	3	33	**43**

(Remaining U.S. and Latin Players)

	AVG	AB	R	H	2B	3B	HR	RBI	SB
Carreon, Mark, Marines	.300	227	22	68	12	0	8	37	0
Pulliam, Harvey, BlueWave	.285	326	38	93	16	0	18	62	1
Raabe, Brian, Lions	.277	83	7	23	2	0	2	12	1
Pemberton, Rudy, Lions	.275	69	10	10	0	0	5	15	2
Thompson, Ryan, Hawks	.271	107	10	29	7	0	2	16	1
Donnels, Chris, BlueWave	.264	140	17	37	9	0	5	22	1
Bonnici, James, BlueWave	.000	10	0	0	0	0	0	0	0

INDIVIDUAL PITCHING LEADERS

(Minimum 133 Innings)

	W	L	ERA	G	SV	IP	H	BB	SO
#Otsuka, Akinori, Buffaloes	3	2	2.11	49	**35**	55	43	25	74
Kanemura, Hideo, Fighters	8	8	**2.73**	31	1	135	124	37	85
Kuroki, Tomohiro, Marines	**13**	9	3.29	31	0	197	185	89	124
Ishii, Takashi, Lions	9	3	3.29	30	0	145	143	44	98
Nishimura, Motofumi, Hawks	10	10	3.36	25	0	153	163	60	69
Sekine, Hiroyuki, Fighters	9	7	3.36	25	0	161	159	44	75
Nishiguchi, Fumiya, Lions	**13**	12	3.38	33	4	181	160	73	**148**
Komiyama, Satoru, Marines	11	12	3.57	27	0	202	224	27	126
Takeda, Kazuhiro, Hawks	**13**	10	3.62	28	0	176	173	68	103
Muto, Junichiro, Marines	8	7	3.76	26	0	141	131	55	102
Shibakusa, Hiroshi, Fighters	7	11	3.90	25	0	145	144	42	44
Okamoto, Akira, Buffaloes	8	13	4.04	30	0	158	167	52	93
Iwamoto, Tsutomu, Fighters	11	8	4.11	27	0	182	186	59	110
Takamura, Hiroshi, Buffaloes	8	14	4.87	25	0	159	161	74	83

(Remaining U.S. and Latin Players)

	W	L	ERA	G	SV	IP	H	BB	SO
Warren, Brian, Marines	2	1	0.93	24	3	29	18	8	9
Davison, Scott, Marines	0	1	2.35	5	0	8	8	5	8
Schullstrom, Erik, Fighters	7	3	3.00	38	8	45	31	22	52
Mattson, Rob, Buffaloes	9	7	3.55	24	0	132	109	59	74
Mimbs, Mark, BlueWave	2	4	3.55	13	0	51	44	22	53
Hurtado, Edwin, BlueWave	8	5	3.74	49	7	113	53	54	73
Gross, Kip, Fighters	3	4	3.96	7	0	36	30	15	11
Fraser, Willie, BlueWave	5	5	4.72	24	0	109	126	41	36
Crawford, Joe, Marines	4	6	4.77	15	0	77	85	51	37
Leftwich, Phil, Buffaloes	3	4	4.81	19	0	67	64	32	38
Carrara, Giovanni, Lions	1	2	4.91	33	1	73	68	40	50
Williams, Brian, Hawks	5	6	5.60	20	1	71	57	47	64
Bross, Terry, Lions	2	3	5.74	11	0	42	35	23	28
Shouse, Brian, Buffaloes	0	2	6.49	13	0	26	40	13	20
Orellano, Rafael, Fighters	1	3	7.50	14	0	30	29	29	22

TAIWAN

BY JEFFREY WILSON

Call it the year of the import player.

The 1998 season not only saw a record number of foreign players appear in Taiwan professional baseball, but also saw them enjoy unprecedented success on the field.

Jay Kirkpatrick won the first-ever triple crown in Taiwan, batting .387 with 31 home runs and 101 RBIs for the Sinon Bulls as he was named the MVP of the Chinese Professional Baseball League. His batting average and RBIs both set league marks, while his home run total tied the league record.

A record 154 import players appeared in 1998 in the two leagues. While the Taiwan Major League was better able to hold the line, it was a revolving door all season on most CPBL teams with fans barely able to keep up with the new faces. Teams went further afield for players, recruiting the first two Cubans to play in Taiwan. But the performances of pitcher Juan Medina and catcher Alberto Hernandez failed to live up to the initial excitement.

While imports dominated the regular season, local players stepped up their play to lead their teams in the postseason.

Tim Ireland guided his third-place Taipei Gida team to a three-game playoff win over second-place Chia-nan and then upset first place Kao-ping in seven games in the Taiwan Major League championship series.

It was almost a carbon copy in the CPBL. Third-place Weichuan defeated the second-place President

Lions in a three-game playoff and then defended their league title by beating Sinon in seven games in the championship series.

The specter of a game-fixing scandal continued to haunt both leagues. In the wake of the 21 players who were convicted in 1997, rumors and accusations continued to fly that gambling was still rampant.

While police made several raids of book-making operations and several players were discretely released, prosecutors failed to indict any more players. But the scandal did claim one team. Seeing no end in sight to the questions hanging over the sport, the China Times Eagles announced in October that they were formally disbanding the team after sitting out the 1998 season. All but one of the local players on the China Times team were convicted the year before.

CPBL

STANDINGS

	W	L	Pct.	T	GB
Sinon Bulls	58	45	.563	2	—
President Lions	57	45	.559	3	½
Weichuan Dragons	56	48	.538	1	2½
China Trust Whales	54	49	.524	2	4
Mercury Tigers	50	52	.490	3	7½
Brother Elephants	33	69	.324	3	24½

INDIVIDUAL BATTING LEADERS

(Minimum 326 Plate Appearances)

	AVG	AB	R	H	2B	3B	HR	RBI	SB
Kirkpatrick, Jay, Sinon	.387	354	78	137	23	3	31	101	0
Gainey, Ty, China Trust	.376	327	66	123	25	0	21	83	2
Huang Chung-lung, Weichuan	.354	347	44	123	22	1	1	47	13
Chen Chin-mao, Weichuan	.328	332	52	109	26	0	8	60	12
Chang Tai-shan, Weichuan	.323	372	63	120	29	4	14	78	27
Tseng Chih-chen, President	.322	295	43	95	21	2	3	47	5
Wood, Ted, Brother	.321	368	72	118	33	2	19	79	11
Chen Chun-hung, CT	.314	328	65	103	16	7	16	58	26
Huang Chung-yi, Sinon	.314	430	41	135	23	4	10	46	14
Wang Kuang-hui, Brother	.305	334	70	102	12	0	9	56	5

(Remaining U.S. and Latin Players)

	AVG	AB	R	H	2B	3B	HR	RBI	SB
Heffernan, Bert, Sinon	.500	16	3	8	2	0	0	1	1
Cornelius, Brian, Mercury	.353	116	22	41	7	0	3	16	4
Mora, Melvin, Mercury	.335	164	34	55	11	2	3	11	37
Trafton, Todd, Brother	.333	192	18	64	15	1	6	30	2
Bryant, Pat, President	.324	37	5	12	2	0	1	3	0
Hall, Joe, President	.322	146	33	47	10	1	8	26	12
Hernandez, Cesar, Pres.	.316	117	21	37	5	0	3	17	6
Mulligan, Sean, Mercury	.314	35	4	11	2	0	1	2	0
Carr, Chuck, Mercury	.308	146	24	45	7	2	3	12	15
Garcia, Manny, CT	.306	36	6	11	1	0	3	8	2
Clark, Tim, Weichuan	.306	36	3	11	4	0	0	1	0
Maurer, Ron, Sinon	.305	390	70	119	31	1	9	65	6
Munoz, Jose, Brother	.305	95	14	29	5	2	0	10	3
Bullett, Scott, President	.303	300	56	91	19	3	9	64	36
Cedeno, Andujar, Pres.	.298	94	18	28	4	1	3	16	0
Martinez, Julian, President	.296	54	9	16	3	0	1	7	3
Tatis, Bernie, Weichuan	.292	390	98	114	26	4	7	29	65
Alvarez, Jorge, President	.291	86	11	19	3	0	1	7	1
Mercedes, Rafaelito, CT	.290	331	63	96	18	2	5	42	1
Raven, Luis, Mercury	.287	101	9	29	3	0	4	14	2
Traxler, Brian, CT	.287	129	17	37	6	0	2	21	0
Grebeck, Brian, Mercury	.286	14	4	3	1	0	0	1	0
Hinshaw, George, Mercury	.286	189	20	54	12	0	5	23	2
Canale, George, Weichuan	.286	56	7	16	5	0	2	6	0
Riggs, Kevin, China Trust	.278	36	5	10	0	0	0	2	1
Hernandez, Luis, Weichuan	.274	62	3	17	3	0	0	7	0
Rios, Eduardo, President	.267	30	4	8	1	1	0	2	0
Howell, Pat, Brother	.264	72	11	19	6	0	0	5	7
Francois, Manny, Weichuan	.259	212	29	55	9	1	3	25	4
Morillo, Cesar, Mercury	.241	54	5	13	2	0	2	9	0
Nunez, Raymond, CT	.231	26	2	6	2	0	0	1	0
Mendoza, Jose, Mercury	.222	27	3	6	2	0	0	3	0
Garcia, Jose, China Trust	.111	18	1	2	0	0	0	1	1
Alfonzo, Edgar, Brother	.091	11	0	1	0	0	0	0	1

INDIVIDUAL PITCHING LEADERS

(Minimum 105 Innings)

	W	L	ERA	G	SV	IP	BB	SO
Henthorne, K., China Trust	12	3	2.09	21	1	107	30	52
Kuo Yuan-chih, CT	14	3	2.50	24	0	140	46	87
Liu [illegible], Mercury	9	5	2.00	50	10	105	21	65
Rivora, Lino, Mercury	10	6	2.69	27	0	150	79	90
Rivera, Carlos, President	12	4	2.72	33	2	162	67	102
Hsieh Chang-heng, Pres.	6	12	2.98	30	0	133	43	69
Kiefer, Mark, Sinon	17	10	3.09	32	0	195	67	137
Martinez, Osvaldo, Sinon	13	10	3.17	33	0	167	58	143
Lemon, Don, President	8	9	3.18	32	3	175	58	118
Wu Chun-liang, President	14	4	3.19	37	1	132	55	70

(Remaining U.S. and Latin Players)

	W	L	ERA	G	SV	IP	BB	SO
Boze, Marshall, President	1	0	0.00	1	0	3	1	1
Smith, Willie, President	0	0	0.00	1	0	1	0	0
Henry, Dwayne, Weichuan	3	0	0.63	6	2	14	7	19
Haynes, Heath, Weichuan	0	0	1.18	19	2	38	17	24
Ettles, Mark, China Trust	2	0	1.57	7	0	23	8	10
Myers, James, Sinon	1	0	1.84	12	2	29	6	12
Mejia, Delfino, CT	0	0	1.93	5	0	9	4	7
DeLeon, Jose, China Trust	1	2	2.01	16	0	22	5	33
Drahman, Brian, President	6	3	2.22	48	18	69	26	71
Vasquez, Julian, Brother	0	1	2.48	11	3	29	9	29
Warren, Brian, CT	4	1	2.49	23	2	47	17	44
Darley, Ned, China Trust	1	1	2.50	6	1	18	9	13
Pavlas, Dave, Brother	2	2	2.56	17	1	31	10	19
Miranda, Angel, Mercury	2	2	2.78	7	0	35	34	33
Solano, Julio, Sinon	4	1	2.79	59	14	90	14	68
Jones, Al, Brother	1	5	2.95	26	10	42	18	27
Garcia, Mike, Weichuan	6	7	3.01	48	26	95	28	133
Kell, Rob, Sinon	7	3	3.03	14	0	65	32	49
Jones, Calvin, China Trust	2	2	3.08	35	17	49	15	61
Cano, Jose, Weichuan	8	8	3.16	21	1	88	42	58
Moreno, Angel, Weichuan	4	1	3.20	7	0	39	17	27
Fortugno, Tim, Sinon	3	5	3.21	61	10	98	37	96
Montalvo, Rafael, Mercury	6	4	3.25	19	0	102	39	48
Leon, Danny, Mercury	1	3	3.25	25	11	36	24	21
Garcia, Apolinar, Brother	5	5	3.27	21	4	82	40	63
Lugo, Urbano, Mercury	10	9	3.30	28	0	131	49	79
Castillo, Felipe, Weichuan	3	2	3.35	37	1	102	28	56
Ozuna, Gabriel, Weichuan	8	7	3.55	32	2	162	45	115
Caruso, Gene, Brother	7	8	3.73	20	1	135	79	108
Correa, Jose, Brother	1	4	3.73	20	0	62	22	35
Brown, Alvin, Sinon	6	8	3.75	27	0	127	78	117
Delahoya, Javier, Weichuan	1	1	3.81	11	0	28	7	26
Pena, Rafael, Weichuan	10	11	4.04	27	0	149	57	113
Treadwell, Jody, Sinon	6	8	4.17	28	1	112	46	77
Samboy, Javier, CT	0	1	4.26	7	0	6	4	5
Pulido, Carlos, Mercury	2	2	4.26	16	1	44	20	24
Hartman, Peter, Brother	1	7	4.28	20	1	80	32	66
Green, Otis, China Trust	3	6	4.33	38	1	87	52	81
Figueroa, Fernando, Mer.	0	4	4.34	11	0	47	24	19
Hurst, Jonathan, Mercury	1	4	4.45	15	3	28	12	24
Flynt, Will, Brother	0	1	4.50	1	0	4	2	0
Revenig, Todd, Weichuan	12	6	4.54	29	2	121	39	80
Tajima, Tony, Brother	8	12	4.79	29	0	126	57	91
Santiago, Sandi, CT	0	1	4.82	11	0	28	15	20
Duncan, Chip, Brother	2	3	4.91	11	0	33	25	25
Winkle, Ken, President	0	1	4.93	17	1	34	18	35
Osuna, Al, Mercury	1	2	5.02	4	0	14	7	16
Barraza, Ernesto, CT	0	5	5.03	17	1	34	24	12
Carter, Andy, President	2	5	5.26	36	2	77	48	48
Renko, Steve, China Trust	0	1	5.40	4	0	8	7	6
Reyes, Pablo, Weichuan	1	3	5.40	14	1	30	13	18
De los Santos, Mariano, CT	3	4	5.74	12	0	58	40	52
Fermin, Ramon, Brother	0	0	6.23	2	0	4	1	1
Oropesa, Eddie, President	0	2	6.28	8	1	14	11	6
Lewis, Craig, Brother	0	1	6.28	5	0	14	11	6
Acosta, Aaron, Mercury	0	1	6.38	7	0	18	7	10
Rosario, Dave, Brother	2	1	6.86	11	0	21	21	21
Auguilis, Cerade, Brother	0	0	6.97	4	0	10	9	5
Ponte, Ed, Brother	0	1	7.50	5	0	6	2	4
Delgado, Tim, Brother	0	0	7.94	2	0	5	0	3
Sorreano, Jose, Sinon	0	0	8.00	5	0	9	3	3
Brown, Clinton, Brother	0	1	8.53	5	0	19	18	6
Lovelace, Vance, CT	1	3	8.53	7	0	25	23	21
Turgeon, Dave, Brother	0	3	9.95	10	1	12	7	8
Wray, James, Weichuan	0	2	9.98	9	0	15	5	12
Ritchie, Wally, Mercury	0	1	10.80	2	0	5	4	6
Linares, Rich, Brother	0	1	13.50	3	0	5	3	2
Torres, Dilson, Mercury	0	0	21.00	4	0	3	4	3
Centeno, Jose, Mercury	0	2	27.00	4	0	1	1	0
McAndrew, Jamie, CT	0	0	36.00	3	0	1	6	1
Smith, Chuck, President	0	0	54.00	2	0	0	4	0

TAIWAN MAJOR LEAGUE

STANDINGS

	W	L	Pct.	T	GB
Kao-ping Fala	62	45	.579	1	—
Chia-nan Luka	57	48	.543	3	4
Taipei Gida	53	53	.500	2	8½
Taichung Agan	40	66	.377	2	21½

INDIVIDUAL BATTING LEADERS

(Minimum 334 Plate Appearances)

	AVG	AB	R	H	2B	3B	HR	RBI	SB
De los Santos, Luis, Kao-ping	.357	400	71	143	20	1	27	96	0
Powell, Corey, Kao-ping	.336	423	74	142	25	0	25	71	11
Guerrero, Epy, Taipei	.327	385	50	126	27	5	9	64	8
Iglesias, Luis, Chia-nan	.311	376	64	117	18	1	25	78	1
Campusano, Sil, Chia-nan	.307	417	78	128	29	0	17	64	28
Brewer, Rod, Chia-nan	.307	371	70	114	21	3	28	81	2
Strauss, Brad, Kao-ping	.306	304	66	93	23	5	8	30	25
Hung Yi-chung, Kao-ping	.302	374	38	113	21	1	4	50	3
Lu Ming-tse, Kao-ping	.301	395	50	119	25	2	5	66	2
Garcia, Leo, Taichung	.298	403	57	120	21	3	11	54	14

(Remaining U.S. and Latin Players)

	AVG	AB	R	H	2B	3B	HR	RBI	SB
Laureano, Frank, Kao-ping	.317	189	32	60	8	0	5	32	2
Horn, Sam, Taipei	.297	158	31	47	6	0	15	38	0
Vatcher, Jim, Taipei	.294	408	73	120	26	5	12	45	24
Lyden, Mitch, Taichung	.278	79	16	22	3	2	6	14	0
Gonzalez, Angel, Taichung	.258	345	41	89	15	3	11	44	10
Hernandez, Alberto, Taichung	.254	63	2	16	1	0	1	7	0
Tahan, Kevin, Taichung	.242	66	6	16	1	0	1	6	0
Goldberg, Lonnie, Taichung	.225	267	38	60	8	0	3	19	45
Pennyfeather, Will, Taipei	.315	70	11	17	4	1	3	10	2

INDIVIDUAL PITCHING LEADERS

(Minimum 108 Innings)

	W	L	ERA	G	SV	IP	BB	SO
Burlingame, Ben, Chia-nan	16	8	1.99	40	0	212	38	171
Knox, Kerry, Chia-nan	0	4	2.15	18	1	117	28	132
Hsu Ming-chieh, Taichung	7	4	2.52	17	0	118	43	81
August, Don, Kao-ping	19	5	2.56	28	0	211	50	109
Huang Ping-yang, Taipei	6	4	2.64	23	0	119	21	92
Maribel, Carlos, Chia-nan	12	12	3.12	38	1	199	65	120
Mikkelsen, Linc, Taipei	15	16	3.39	34	0	236	81	182
Wilson, Steve, Kao-ping	12	11	3.67	30	0	211	62	160
Gerstein, Ron, Kao-ping	9	6	3.71	22	0	123	59	103
Picota, Len, Taipei	11	7	3.78	32	1	147	67	147
Weber, Ben, Taipei	12	7	3.78	56	7	144	52	122

(Remaining U.S. and Latin Players)

	W	L	ERA	G	SV	IP	BB	SO
Wishnevski, R., Chia-nan/Taipei	5	3	2.08	55	18	91	29	99
Nunez, Jose, Taichung	6	5	2.71	35	7	63	10	34
Vann, Brandy, Taipei/Chia-nan	5	5	2.73	54	32	89	38	92
Osuna, Al, Taichung	1	5	2.92	12	0	77	30	86
White, Chris, Taichung	0	4	3.05	20	5	56	18	38
Cederblad, Brett, Kao-ping	3	1	3.30	10	1	60	19	32
Ettles, Mark, Chia-nan	2	2	3.55	13	1	45	10	23
Bowen, Ryan, Taichung	2	4	3.86	15	0	65	30	36
Taylor, Tommy, Taichung	2	3	4.38	13	2	37	24	20
Jersild, Aaron, Taichung	7	15	4.62	45	1	181	76	110
Medina, Juan, Taipei/Taichung	2	4	5.06	10	0	48	24	38

KOREA

The 1998 Korea Baseball Organization season will be remembered for many things, but chiefly it marked the first season foreign players were allowed to play in Korea. A total of 12 players out of a possible 16 (two per team) were signed.

Of the imports, OB Bears outfielder Tyrone Woods was by far the most successful. Woods adjusted well to Korea and thrived in his new environment. He set a new single season home run record with 42 (in a 126-game season) and was voted MVP as well. Woods-mania swept Korea and both Woods and his wife Cheryl were popular interviewees the month after the regular season had ended.

Woods, who hit 124 home runs in a 10-year minor league career in the United States from 1988-97, hit the first home run by an import player and was also the first one ejected from a game for arguing with an umpire.

Scott Baker was the standout among import pitchers with a record of 15-7.

Haitai's Lee Dae-jin struck out 10 straight batters in one game, while Hyundai pitcher Kim Su-kyung was voted rookie of the year by going 12-4 with a 2.76 ERA and 168 strikeouts in 160 innings.

—THOMAS ST. JOHN

STANDINGS

	W	L	PCT	T	GB
Hyundai Unicorns	81	45	.643	0	—
Samsung Lions	66	58	.532	2	14
LG Twins	63	62	.504	1	17½
OB Bears	61	62	.496	3	18½
Haitai Tigers	61	64	.488	1	19½
Ssangbangwool Raiders	58	66	.468	2	22
Hanwha Eagles	55	66	.455	5	23½
Lotte Giants	50	72	.410	4	29

INDIVIDUAL BATTING LEADERS

(Minimum 000 At-Bats)

	AVG	AB	R	H	2B	3B	HR	RBI	SB
Yang Jun-hyuk, Samsung	**.342**	456	80	156	30	1	27	89	15
Chun Jun-ho, Hyundai	.321	446	78	143	16	7	5	42	25
Park Jong-tae, Lotte	.318	400	58	129	24	2	13	79	1
Coolbaugh, Scott, Hyundai	.317	410	68	130	27	1	26	97	2
Chang Song-ho, Haitai	.312	485	76	145	23	1	15	49	5
Jho Won-woo, SBW	.311	479	80	149	20	4	12	62	29
Kim Ki-tae, SBW	.309	434	84	134	28	4	31	90	10
Lee Seung-yup, Samsung	.306	477	100	146	32	2	38	102	0
Woods, Tyrone, OB	.305	452	77	138	14	1	**42**	**103**	1
Lee Ho-jun, Haitai	.303	422	64	128	27	1	19	77	5
Kang Dong-woo, Samsung	.300	414	74	124	23	8	10	30	22
Kim Han-su, Samsung	.300	469	65	138	24	1	15	80	5
Kim Jae-hyun, LG	.295	482	70	142	31	3	16	76	8
Shim Jong-su, OB	.294	477	71	140	29	4	19	79	4
Kim Dae-ik, Lotte	.292	466	79	136	29	7	5	40	27
Ma Hae-young, Lotte	.292	465	77	136	33	1	15	64	4
Chong Su-kun, OB	.288	480	83	138	19	11	1	36	44
Choi Tae-won, SBW	.288	469	65	135	22	3	4	39	9

(Other Foreign Players)

	AVG	AB	R	H	2B	3B	HR	RBI	SB
Chimelis, Joel, Hanwha	.297	409	48	114	22	0	17	63	1
Felix, Junior, LG	.293	123	36	6	0	6	21	0	16
Brady, Doug, Lotte	.258	155	40	6	4	3	6	4	18
Caceres, Edgar, OB	.250	406	102	13	1	2	36	18	40
Busch, Mike, Hanwha	.213	240	51	11	1	10	28	1	20
Hare, Shawn, Haitai	.206	66	14	3	0	0	3	0	3

INDIVIDUAL PITCHING LEADERS

(Minimum 10 Victories)

	W	L	ERA	G	SV	IP	H	BB	K
Chong Myung-won, Hyundai	14	8	**1.86**	26	0	184	141	65	123
Kim Won-hyung, SBW	12	7	2.52	51	13	150	130	48	109
Kim Su-Kyung, Hyundai	12	4	2.76	31	2	160	112	73	163
Chong Min-tae, Hyundai	17	9	2.83	28	0	201	184	51	159
Choi Won-ho, Hyundai	10	5	3.04	39	1	151	118	77	112
Lee Kang-chul, Haitai	15	11	3.11	31	0	179	165	65	160
Lee Kyung-pil, OB	10	9	3.12	27	0	150	137	42	94
Moon Dong-hwan, Lotte	12	5	3.16	32	6	137	121	40	86
Chong Min-chul, Hanwha	10	7	3.16	23	0	148	133	26	97
Park Myung-won, OB	14	11	3.22	31	0	187	159	20	181
Eui Jae-young, Hyundai	13	8	3.23	26	0	164	143	69	122
Lee Dae-jin, Haitai	12	11	3.26	23	0	179	173	64	**183**
Park Chung-sik, Samsung	11	10	3.45	24	0	159	163	25	100
Kim Young-su, LG	**18**	6	3.45	32	2	175	176	52	116
Sohn Hyuk, LG	11	8	3.70	28	0	149	136	40	88

(Other Foreign Players)

	W	L	ERA	G	SV	IP	H	BB	K
Strong, Joe, Hyundai	6	5	2.95	53	27	58	64	29	54
Anderson, Mike, LG	4	7	3.56	45	21	56	53	19	30
Parra, Jose, Samsung	7	8	3.67	60	19	96	79	40	55
Baker, Scott, Samsung	15	7	4.13	26	0	172	172	81	87

Winter Baseball

Dominicans win the close ones to capture second straight Caribbean Series title

BY JOHN ROYSTER

The 1998 Caribbean World Series had plenty of close games, but it wasn't really close.

Aguilas of the Dominican Republic swept through the six-game round-robin, clinching the championship in its fifth game, a 3-0 win over Lara of Venezuela. It was the second straight title for Aguilas, who had won 10 straight Caribbean Series games after losing its first two in 1997.

Neifi Perez

But the '98 sweep didn't come easily. Each of Aguilas' first four games was in doubt in the late innings. It took 14 innings to win the opener 7-6 over Mayaguez of Puerto Rico. The next night, Aguilas scored the game-winning runs in the ninth inning when Lara closer Oscar Henriquez (Marlins) turned a game-ending double-play comebacker into a two-run throwing error and a 5-3 loss.

In its third game, Aguilas led 5-0 in the ninth and almost blew it when Mazatlan (Mexico) rallied for four runs. And on the fourth day, Mayaguez also cut a 5-0 deficit to 5-4 before the Dominicans rallied.

"You need the ball to bounce your way a couple of times to win a competition like this," said Aguilas player/manager Tony Pena, who had the decisive single in the Dominican League championship series against Licey, then deactivated himself for the Caribbean Series.

That rally, too, was set up by an enemy throwing error. Mayaguez shortstop Jose Hernandez (Cubs), the Puerto Rican League MVP, allowed what would have been the second out to reach base. After that, Aguilas got a walk, a single, a game-tying double by second baseman Neifi Perez (Rockies) and the game-winning RBI single by outfielder Patricio Claudio (Indians).

Hernandez had hit a two-run home run in the eighth to send the game into extra innings. The homer was Hernandez' 24th on the winter, leading to his selection as Baseball America's Winter League Player of the Year.

In the clinching game, Perez hit a two-run homer in the second inning and shortstop Tony Batista (Diamondbacks) added a sacrifice fly in the sixth for all the scoring Aguilas needed. Righthander Julian Tavarez (Giants) pitched six shutout innings.

Perez was named the tournament MVP after going 12-for-27 with the home run, five RBIs, six doubles and nine runs.

While the Caribbean Series will continue to rotate among the four participating nations and was set for Puerto Rico in 1999, the face of winter ball in the four competing countries changed little for the 1998-99 season. Two Dominican League clubs, Azucareros and Estrellas, were sitting out the 1998-99 season. But that was because of stadium damage caused by Hurricane Georges and not any problems with the clubs.

Talk intensified of adding Colombia, Cuba, Nicaragua and Panama to the CWS fold. But political problems and unequal competition in the region are likely to prevent expansion in the forseeble future. Cuba was an original participant when the series began in 1949 but dropped out after Fidel Castro and the Communist party came to power in 1959.

There were changes in some of the non-traditional winter leagues, though. Hawaii Winter Baseball folded after a four-year run only to be reestablished as the Maryland Fall League with teams in Bowie, Delmarva, Frederick and Wilmington, Del.

Australia, with a limited involvement from American players, also scaled back from eight to six teams, dropping Brisbane and Hunter.

1998 CARIBBEAN WORLD SERIES

Puerto la Cruz, Venezuela
Feb. 5-10, 1998

ROUND-ROBIN STANDINGS	W	L	PCT.	GB
Dominican Republic (Aguilas)	6	0	1.000	—
Puerto Rico (Mayaguez)	4	2	.667	2
Venezuela (Lara)	1	5	.167	5
Mexico (Mazatlan)	1	5	.167	5

INDIVIDUAL BATTING LEADERS

(Minimum 20 Plate Appearances)

	AVG	AB	R	H	2B	3B	HR	RBI	SB
Perez, Neifi, DR	.444	27	9	12	6	0	1	5	0
Arias, Alex, DR	.400	25	4	10	5	1	0	4	0
Munoz, Pedro, PR	.400	20	6	8	1	0	2	4	0
Robles, Javier, Mexico	.400	20	4	8	5	0	1	4	0
Cabrera, Alex, Venez	.391	23	3	9	1	0	1	2	0
Tejada, Miguel, DR	.381	21	5	8	0	0	2	5	0
Brinkley, Darryl, Mexico	.375	24	2	9	1	1	1	3	0
Hernandez, Jose, PR	.333	27	6	9	0	0	4	8	0
Franklin, Micah, DR	.333	21	3	7	4	0	0	1	0
Perez, Tomas, Venez	.318	22	4	7	0	0	0	0	0
Ordonez, Maggio, Ven	.316	19	2	6	2	0	2	3	0
Polonia, Luis, DR	.308	26	4	8	2	0	0	3	2

INDIVIDUAL PITCHING LEADERS

(Minimum 6 Innings)

	W	L	ERA	G	SV	IP	H	BB	SO
Tavarez, Julian, DR	1	0	0.00	2	0	12	7	3	1
Reyes, Dennis, Mexico	0	0	0.00	1	0	7	5	3	7
De la Rosa, Maximo, DR	1	0	0.00	1	0	6	2	3	4
Valdez, Efrain, DR	1	0	0.00	1	0	6	2	2	7
Valera, Julio, PR	1	0	1.38	2	0	13	9	5	14
Sinclair, Steve, Venez	0	0	1.50	3	0	6	3	2	6
Halladay, Roy, Venez	0	0	2.35	1	0	8	8	1	3
Gonzalez, Jeremi, Venez	0	1	3.86	1	0	7	6	3	4

ALL-TOURNAMENT TEAM: C—Guillormo Garcia, Dominican Republic. **1B**—Alex Arias, Dominican Republic. **2B**—Neifi Perez, Dominican Republic. **3B**—Miguel Tejada, Dominican Republic. **SS**—Jose Hernandez, Puerto Rico. **LF**—Luis Polonia, Dominican Republic. **CF**—Darryl Brinkley, Mexico. **RF**—Maggio Ordonez, Venezuela. **DH**—Pedro Munoz, Puerto Rico. **RHP**—Julian Tavarez, Dominican Republic. **LHP**—Dennis Reyes, Mexico. **RP**—Jose Cabrera, Dominican Republic.

Most Valuable Player—Neifi Perez, Dominican Republic.

1997-98 WINTER ALL-STAR TEAM

Selected by Baseball America

	Player, Club (League)	Organization	AVG	AB	R	H	2B	3B	HR	RBI	SB
C	Mike Sweeney, San Juan (Puerto Rico)	Royals	.302	235	34	71	14	1	12	50	3
1B	Sean Casey, Mesa (Arizona)	Indians	.396	154	23	61	9	2	3	34	1
2B	Chad Hermansen, Mesa (Arizona)	Pirates	.341	179	45	61	10	4	8	27	5
3B	Jose Oliva, Estrellas (Dom. Republic)	None*	.286	175	20	50	8	1	8	40	0
SS	Jose Hernandez, Mayaguez (Puerto Rico)	Cubs	.311	322	68	100	21	2	24	55	12
OF	Ricky Ledee, San Juan (Puerto Rico)	Yankees	.315	200	51	63	14	2	13	34	2
	Magglio Ordonez, Oriente (Venezuela)	White Sox	.305	256	36	78	17	0	16	56	14
	Ruben Sierra, Santurce (Puerto Rico)	White Sox	.297	219	37	65	17	0	16	52	3
DH	Matt Stark, Culiacan (Mexico)	None	.400	210	33	84	4	0	13	39	2
			W	**L**	**ERA**	**G**	**SV**	**IP**	**H**	**BB**	**SO**
P	Rolando Arrojo, Peoria (Arizona)	Devil Rays	5	0	1.38	9	0	39	29	8	39
	Manny Aybar, Licey (Dom. Republic)	Cardinals	6	1	1.86	11	0	58	49	14	39
	Giovanni Carrara, Lara (Venezuela)	Seibu (Japan)	10	1	1.50	17	0	108	90	22	93
	Beiker Graterol, Lara (Venezuela)	Blue Jays	12	3	2.07	21	0	113	105	35	72
RP	John Johnstone, Hermosillo (Mexico)	Athletics	1	1	1.03	29	19	35	18	22	48

PLAYER OF THE YEAR: Jose Hernandez, Mayaguez (Puerto Rico). *Deceased
Statistics include regular season, playoff and Caribbean World Series games.

PUERTO RICAN LEAGUE

Despite a power outage in the playoffs by record-setting shortstop Jose Hernandez, the Mayaguez Indians repeated as champions of the Puerto Rican League in 1997-98.

Hernandez (Cubs), 28, had one of the best seasons in Puerto Rican League history and was named Baseball America's Winter League Player of the Year. But he failed to homer in 16 playoff games as the Indians edged Caguas 4-3 in the semifinals and upset regular-season champion San Juan 5-4 in a best-of-9 championship series to reach the Caribbean World Series.

Hernandez hit 20 home runs during the regular season, breaking Orlando Cepeda's record for a native player and tying Reggie Jackson for the second highest total ever. He also led the league in runs (54), slugging (.673) and stolen bases (11), and finished among the leaders in several other categories.

Jose Hernandez

Hernandez added four more homers in the Caribbean World Series as Santurce finished second to the Dominican Republic.

Catcher Doug Mirabelli (Giants) picked up the slack for Mayaguez in its semifinal win over Caguas, hitting .480 with three homers and eight RBIs. But the Indians needed two dramatic home runs by outfielder Wil Cordero (White Sox) to overcome a 3-2 deficit. Cordero's three-run homer enabled Mayaguez to win Game Six 6-3 and he ended the series the next night with a two-run shot in the bottom of the 11th inning for a 4-2 win. Cordero stepped up in the final against San Juan, hitting .368 with six homers and 13 RBIs.

Statistics in **boldface** indicate league leader.
#Indicates league leader but non-qualifier.

STANDINGS

REGULAR SEASON	W	L	PCT	GB
San Juan Senators	40	22	.645	—
Mayaguez Indians	34	27	.557	5½
Ponce Lions	30	32	.484	10
Caguas Criollos	30	32	.484	10
Arecibo Wolves	26	35	.426	13½
Santurce Crabbers	25	37	.403	15

PLAYOFFS—Semifinals: San Juan defeated Ponce, 4-3, and Mayaguez defeated Caguas, 4-3, in best-of-7 series. **Finals:** Mayaguez defeated San Juan, 5-4, in best-of-9 series.

INDIVIDUAL BATTING LEADERS

(Minimum 167 Plate Appearances)

	AVG	AB	R	H	2B	3B	HR	RBI	SB
Garcia, Omar, Arecibo	**.375**	253	38	**95**	21	1	6	39	5
Lopez, Luis, Caguas	.330	206	25	68	10	1	3	24	3
Cruz, Ivan, Ponce	.324	222	36	72	**23**	0	15	48	1
Hernandez, Jose, Mayaguez	.323	226	**54**	73	15	2	**20**	40	**11**
Ledee, Ricky, San Juan	.315	143	37	45	9	1	9	24	2
Sweeney, Mike, San Juan	.301	176	25	53	11	1	9	40	2
Martinez, Ramon, San Juan	.297	195	35	58	14	2	0	19	1
Diaz, Alex, Mayaguez	.297	185	23	55	10	0	9	27	0
Sierra, Ruben, Santurce	.297	219	37	65	17	0	16	**52**	3
Gonzalez, Raul, San Juan	.290	183	30	53	7	0	9	26	5
Stynes, Chris, Santurce	.287	174	27	50	12	0	1	15	3
Baez, Kevin, Caguas	.286	175	21	50	8	0	3	18	1
Martinez, Carmelo, Caguas	.280	189	26	53	17	0	12	38	0
Correa, Miguel, Ponce	.278	216	32	60	14	1	6	24	9
Munoz, Pedro, Mayaguez	.274	179	20	49	11	0	5	21	0
Berg, Dave, Ponce	.272	191	28	52	10	1	0	20	10
Otero, Ricky, Arecibo	.270	204	29	55	4	**4**	3	26	6
Rossy, Rico, Arecibo	.269	167	25	45	6	0	3	13	1
Crespo, Felipe, Caguas	.269	182	28	49	11	0	8	32	4
Guzman, Edwards, Mayaguez	.267	176	22	47	8	2	0	20	4
Munoz, Jose, Mayaguez	.264	235	32	62	11	0	4	21	3
Dunwoody, Todd, Ponce	.260	200	19	52	9	2	2	22	5
Valdes, Pedro, San Juan	.257	152	21	39	9	0	10	30	0
Rodriguez, Victor, Arecibo	.251	167	19	42	4	**4**	0	8	3
Benitez, Yamil, Caguas	.251	215	34	54	10	1	10	30	7
#Valentin, Jose, Mayaguez	.218	197	27	43	9	0	6	16	**11**

INDIVIDUAL PITCHING LEADERS

(Minimum 50 Innings)

	W	L	ERA	G	SV	IP	H	BB	SO
#Evans, Bart, San Juan	**6**	1	1.78	29	7	35	29	15	45
Santiago, Jose, San Juan	5	2	**2.39**	31	**9**	53	42	23	33
Elarton, Scott, Santurce	2	4	2.53	9	0	53	38	21	40
Melendez, Dave, Ponce	5	3	2.70	16	1	60	51	17	47
Walker, Jamie, San Juan	5	1	2.77	13	0	62	60	9	40
Witasick, Jay, Caguas	**6**	5	3.03	12	0	74	60	34	**60**
#DeLeon, Luis, Mayaguez	**6**	2	3.21	20	0	34	29	7	26
Cobb, Trevor, Mayaguez	3	4	3.25	15	0	64	51	36	33
Fiore, Tony, Arecibo	4	3	3.43	10	0	60	46	22	36
Bones, Ricky, San Juan	**6**	3	3.47	13	0	80	85	14	48

Alston, Garvin, Mayaguez	3	3	3.55	15	0	63	62	23	38
Gandarillas, Gus, Arecibo	3	4	3.83	11	0	54	59	12	31
Mercado, Hector, Ponce	4	5	3.92	13	0	62	60	40	57
Mendoza, Reynol, Ponce	1	6	4.00	13	0	74	71	33	34
Valera, Julio, Mayaguez	5	2	4.14	15	0	76	84	18	45
Agosto, Stevenson, Santurce	1	2	4.33	20	1	54	54	31	31
Saler, Matt, Caguas	5	3	4.35	10	0	60	60	23	37
#Falteisek, Steve, Santurce	**6**	3	5.89	13	0	63	64	35	28

DOMINICAN LEAGUE

Despite finishing only two games over .500 in the regular season, Aguilas captured its third consecutive Dominican League title and cruised to a second straight Caribbean World Series championship.

Aguilas finished third, four games behind Licey, in the regular season and second to Licey in the league's four-team, round-robin tournament. But Aguilas turned the tables on Licey in championship series, winning 4-1, and went unbeaten at the Caribbean Series.

Julian Tavarez

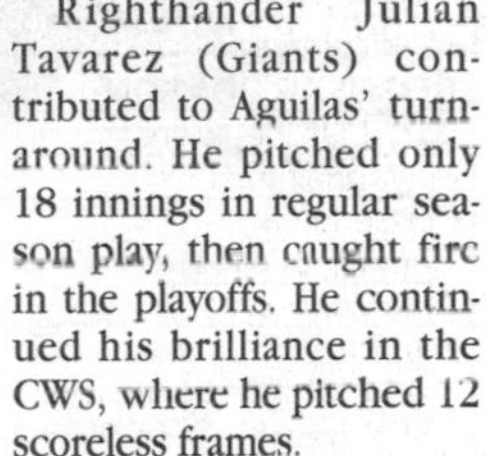

Righthander Julian Tavarez (Giants) contributed to Aguilas' turnaround. He pitched only 18 innings in regular season play, then caught fire in the playoffs. He continued his brilliance in the CWS, where he pitched 12 scoreless frames.

Estrellas first baseman Julio Franco won the batting title with a .436 mark, the highest ever by a native Dominican. Only Ralph Garr's league-record .457 in 1970-71 has topped that. Franco missed time after being hit in the helmet by a pitch, but returned for the final four games of the season to earn enough plate appearances to qualify for the title.

Estrellas third baseman Jose Oliva, a 10-year minor league veteran who played briefly in the big leagues, was posthumously named the league MVP. A car accident claimed his life on Dec. 22, 1997, but he led the league with eight home runs and 40 RBIs.

STANDINGS

REGULAR SEASON	W	L	PCT	GB
Licey Tigers	30	20	.600	—
Escogido Lions	28	22	.560	2
Aguilas	26	24	.520	4
Estrellas	24	27	.471	6½
Northeast Giants	23	28	.451	7½
Azucareros	20	30	.400	10
PLAYOFFS	**W**	**L**	**PCT**	**GB**
Licey Tigers	13	4	.765	—
Aguilas	12	6	.667	1½
Estrellas	5	12	.294	8
Escogido Lions	5	13	.278	8½

Championship Series: Aguilas defeated Licey, 4-1, in best-of-7 series.

INDIVIDUAL BATTING LEADERS

(Minimum 135 Plate Appearances)

	AVG	AB	R	H	2B	3B	HR	RBI	SB
Franco, Julio, Estrellas	**.436**	133	30	58	9	0	3	26	4
Polonia, Luis, Aguilas	.382	157	32	**60**	**15**	2	1	15	10
Cedeno, Domingo, Azucareros	.345	174	25	**60**	6	1	0	20	6
Alexander, Manny, Estrellas	.326	178	**37**	58	13	2	3	19	11
Castillo, Luis, Licey	.319	163	31	52	2	**4**	0	12	**17**
Claudio, Patricio, Aguilas	.317	123	20	39	4	**4**	1	19	9
Espinosa, Ramon, Escogido	.314	137	17	43	4	1	0	9	4
Herrera, Jose, Escogido	.305	128	19	39	6	2	1	15	6
Parra, Franklin, Northeast	.299	167	27	50	7	3	1	11	9
De la Rosa, Juan, Northeast	.299	137	28	41	8	2	2	20	3
Franco, Matt, Estrellas	.296	169	23	50	14	0	1	37	1
Sutton, Larry, Aguilas	.293	133	14	39	12	0	0	12	2
Cruz, Fausto, Northeast	.289	166	17	48	9	1	2	29	3
Oliva, Jose, Estrellas	.286	175	20	50	8	1	**8**	**40**	0
Batista, Tony, Aguilas	.268	138	23	37	9	1	3	18	3
Michel, Domingo, Northeast	.268	142	16	38	8	1	3	16	3
Latham, Chris, Estrellas	.265	162	35	43	6	0	1	13	13
Bell, Juan, Azucareros	.264	163	16	43	12	0	1	18	4
Garcia, Guillermo, Aguilas	.256	172	18	44	8	0	5	33	3
Konerko, Paul, Azucareros	.254	138	14	35	5	0	5	22	0
Cedeno, Andujar, Azucareros	.252	163	14	41	7	0	2	11	1
Tejada, Miguel, Aguilas	.245	155	20	38	9	3	3	23	5

INDIVIDUAL PITCHING LEADERS

(Minimum 40 Innings)

	W	L	ERA	G	SV	IP	H	BB	SO
#Cabrera, Jose, Aguilas	0	2	1.45	21	**11**	19	15	1	17
Hubbs, Dan, Azucareros	4	1	**1.49**	8	0	42	29	7	18
Aybar, Manny, Licey	4	1	1.96	9	0	46	37	11	33
Castillo, Carlos, Aguilas	3	3	2.16	8	0	42	33	9	35
Valdez, Efrain, Northeast	**8**	2	2.39	14	0	72	80	23	34
Mercedes, Jose, Estrellas	6	2	2.47	10	0	62	64	8	22
Manzanillo, Josias, Estrellas	5	3	2.72	11	0	56	46	14	**55**
Lima, Jose, Escogido	4	2	2.73	12	0	63	61	12	52
Yan, Esteban, Estrellas	3	2	2.85	17	4	41	43	9	29
Sanchez, Jesus, Northeast	3	3	3.21	9	0	53	45	22	43
Heredia, Julian, Estrellas	2	3	3.24	26	2	42	35	10	43
Stull, Everett, Estrellas	4	3	3.32	11	0	60	48	29	41
Roque, Rafael, Licey	5	4	3.62	12	0	60	46	24	25
Santana, Julio, Escogido	4	3	3.65	12	0	57	66	25	20
Batista, Miguel, Northeast	1	3	3.77	12	0	57	49	25	36
Parra, Jose, Aguilas	4	2	3.83	10	0	49	51	13	30
Torres, Salomon, Licey	4	1	3.95	10	0	43	49	13	21
#Reyes, Alberto, Escogido	2	1	4.01	19	**11**	25	18	13	24

VENEZUELAN LEAGUE

The Lara Cardinals rode the best pitching staff in Venezuela to the league's best regular-season record and the Venezuelan League championship in 1997-98.

Lara, with a league-best 3.01 ERA, featured three of the league's four winningest pitchers in natives Beiker Graterol (Blue Jays), Edwin Hurtado (Orix, Japan) and Giovanni Carrara (Seibu, Japan). They combined for 24 wins. Graterol, the league's pitcher of the year, led the league with nine wins and Carrara posted the best ERA at 1.30. The trio won nine more games in postseason play as the Cardinals earned a berth in the Caribbean World Series, which was played in Venezuela.

Roberto Petagine

Lara's 43-21 regular season mark was easily the league's best, but the Cardinals were challenged in the playoffs by two-time defending champion Magallanes. The strong relief pitching of Tim Crabtree (Rangers) enabled the Cardinals to hold off the Navigators and gain the second berth in the finals against the Caracas Lions, who got 16 RBIs in the round-robin tournament from Roberto Petagine (Reds).

The Cardinals held on in a tight series against Caracas, winning four games to three.

Occidente's Alex Cabrera earned MVP honors after hitting .322 with eight homers and 35 RBIs.

STANDINGS

EAST	W	L	PCT	GB
Magallanes Navigators	37	27	.578	—
Caracas Lions	35	29	.547	2
Oriente Caribbeans	30	34	.469	7
La Guaira Sharks	25	39	.391	12
WEST	**W**	**L**	**PCT**	**GB**
Lara Cardinals	43	21	.672	—
Occidente Pastora	34	30	.531	9
Aragua Tigers	26	38	.406	17
Zulia Eagles	26	38	.406	17
PLAYOFFS	**W**	**L**	**PCT**	**GB**
Caracas	12	4	.750	—
Lara	10	6	.625	2
Magallanes	8	8	.500	4
Oriente	7	9	.438	5
Pastora	3	13	.188	9

Championship Series: Lara defeated Caracas, 4-3, in best-of-7 series.

INDIVIDUAL BATTING LEADERS

(Minimum 162 Plate Appearances)

	AVG	AB	R	H	2B	3B	HR	RBI	SB
Marcano, Raul, Lara	**.329**	146	18	48	9	1	1	23	1
Owens, Eric, Caracas	.327	205	32	67	11	0	1	30	**24**
Cabrera, Alex, Occ	.322	211	31	68	**16**	1	**8**	35	4
Zambrano, Jose, Aragua	.316	133	13	42	4	1	1	25	1
Perez, Tomas, Oriente	.310	229	21	71	8	2	1	27	5
Azocar, Oscar, Aragua	.306	206	26	63	12	1	1	27	1
Garcia, Jose, Aragua	.304	191	24	58	7	1	1	23	0
Spencer, Shane, Aragua	.303	155	28	47	9	1	4	17	0
Saffer, Jon, LaGuaira	.301	229	40	69	9	7	1	14	4
Conti, Jason, Occidente	.300	140	25	42	8	0	0	11	11
Raven, Luis, Magallanes	.299	244	29	**73**	14	3	**8**	**45**	1
Delgado, Alex, Lara	.299	154	18	46	8	0	3	23	0
Ordonez, Magglio, Oriente	.298	198	27	59	15	0	8	40	12
Rodriguez, Liu, Caracas	.296	226	39	67	9	4	0	23	1
Florez, Tim, Occidente	.296	206	32	61	14	1	2	26	11
Mora, Melvin, Magallanes	.294	194	34	57	4	2	2	21	8
Ferguson, Jeff, Aragua	.289	197	35	57	9	1	1	16	3
Munoz, Orlando, Zulia	.289	194	28	56	10	1	0	26	5
Norton, Greg, LaGuaira	.288	160	24	46	14	0	6	34	3
Freire, Alejandro, Mag	.286	168	24	48	10	0	3	18	2
Mendez, Carlos, Caracas	.284	176	20	50	6	0	4	28	0
Cairo, Miguel, Lara	.282	202	34	57	8	2	1	10	15
Abreu, Bob, Caracas	.277	155	32	43	7	3	7	33	8
Belk, Tim, LaGuaira	.277	155	18	43	11	0	0	20	1
Leach, Jalal, Zulia	.276	221	26	61	9	5	1	36	2
Martinez, Carlos, LaGuaira	.269	160	13	43	5	0	1	22	1
Prieto, Alejandro, LaGuaira	.267	176	18	47	6	1	0	14	1
Garcia, Vicente, Occidente	.266	207	25	55	11	2	1	19	1
Alvarez, Rafael, LaGuaira	.265	196	32	52	7	**8**	1	26	3
Castellano, Pedro, Aragua	.265	185	20	49	10	0	2	15	0
#Little, Mark, Zulia	.234	192	**42**	45	6	5	2	19	13

INDIVIDUAL PITCHING LEADERS

(Minimum 48 Innings)

	W	L	ERA	G	SV	IP	H	BB	SO
Carrara, Giovanni, Lara	7	1	**1.30**	12	0	76	63	11	**64**
Graterol, Beiker, Lara	**9**	1	1.67	14	0	81	70	19	50
Pratt, Rich, Magallanes	6	1	1.96	11	0	69	61	24	31
Henderson, Rod, LaGuaira	6	3	2.03	12	0	80	60	33	36
Van Poppel, Todd, Zulia	3	2	2.27	11	0	67	50	32	45
Michalak, Chris, Occidente	5	0	2.47	11	0	66	47	22	31
Gonzalez, Jeremi, Zulia	5	0	2.58	9	0	59	49	23	47
Treadwell, Jody, Caracas	6	2	2.59	10	0	56	46	10	32
Rincon, Juan, Lara	5	1	2.59	20	0	49	38	34	22
#Hernandez, Santos, Occ	1	2	2.75	32	**21**	39	30	11	30
Driskill, Travis, Oriente	5	4	2.78	13	0	71	56	23	33
Pulido, Carlos, Magallanes	4	2	2.92	13	0	74	74	21	39
Hurtado, Edwin, Lara	8	4	2.99	15	0	87	90	39	60
Daal, Omar, Caracas	3	3	3.03	11	0	65	69	15	47
Lira, Felipe, LaGuaira	4	6	3.24	16	2	72	70	16	30
Gonzalez, Jose, Occidente	2	3	3.51	17	0	51	43	28	31
Gutierrez, Javier, Oriente	4	2	3.54	15	0	48	45	33	34

MEXICAN PACIFIC LEAGUE

The Mazatlan Deer staged one of the greatest comebacks in Mexican Pacific League history by erasing a 3-0 deficit in games to beat the Navojoa Mayos 4-3 in the league's best-of-seven championship series.

Mazatlan went right to the wire, scoring the winning run in Game Seven on a bases-loaded walk in extra innings. Earlier it overcame a gem by Navojoa's Juan Palafox in Game Five, breaking up his no-hitter in the ninth inning en route to a 3-1 victory.

Mazatlan finished the regular season with a losing record but won three consecutive playoff series, including beating Navojoa twice. Navojoa gained a second chance because league rules provide that the team with the best record that loses in the first round advances to the next round. The Los Mochis Sugarcane Growers, who finished the season with the best overall record, fell to Navojoa in the semifinals, setting up another showdown between Mazatlan and Navojoa.

Veteran first baseman Matt Stark of Culiacan won the league batting title with a .372 average—51 points more than his nearest competitor. Stark also had the best average in the quarterfinals (.714) as Culiacan swept Guasave 4-0, and in the semifinals (.438) as Culiacan lost 4-2 to Mazatlan.

STANDINGS

REGULAR SEASON	W	L	PCT	GB
Los Mochis Sugarcane Growers	38	23	.623	—
Culiacan Tomato Growers	34	25	.576	3
Navojoa Mayos	31	31	.500	7½
Mazatlan Deer	30	32	.484	8½
Mexicali Eagles	28	32	.467	9½
Guasave Cottoneers	28	32	.467	9½
Obregon Yaquis	27	34	.443	11
Hermosillo Orange Growers	27	34	.443	11

PLAYOFFS—Quarterfinals: Culiacan defeated Guasave, 4-0; Los Mochis defeated Mexicali, 4-0; and Mazatlan defeated Navojoa, 4-2, in best-of-7 series. **Semifinals:** Mazatlan defeated Culiacan, 4-2, and Navojoa defeated Los Mochis, 4-3, in best-of-7 series. **Finals:** Mazatlan defeated Navojoa, 4-3, in best-of 7 series.

INDIVIDUAL BATTING LEADERS

(Minimum 167 Plate Appearances)

	AVG	AB	R	H	2B	3B	HR	RBI	SB
Stark, Matt, Culiacan	**.372**	180	28	**67**	4	0	11	30	2
Durazo, Erubiel, Hermosillo	.321	184	20	59	7	0	7	28	3
Seitzer, Brad, Guasave	.316	212	26	**67**	10	0	5	34	0
Stairs, Matt, Navojoa	.303	188	34	57	9	1	11	36	7
Ball, Jeff, Hermosillo	.298	198	24	59	7	0	8	31	6
Fernandez, Daniel, Maz	.295	200	31	59	7	1	1	14	6
Martinez, Greg, Guasave	.292	192	40	56	1	1	0	15	18
Benard, Marvin, Culiacan	.292	144	17	42	11	0	1	17	5
White, Derrick, Mexicali	.289	225	39	65	14	0	9	**43**	7
Brinkley, Darryl, Mexicali	.284	236	**46**	**67**	11	0	11	27	13
Fentanes, Oscar, Guasave	.284	148	19	42	8	0	2	13	4
Sherman, Darrell, Culiacan	.282	209	37	59	13	**3**	0	15	**15**
Millar, Kevin, Navojoa	.279	204	18	57	15	0	4	33	3
Helms, Wes, Mazatlan	.279	222	32	62	10	0	7	36	1
Velasquez, Guillermo, Cul	.278	223	34	62	10	0	10	42	1
Flores, Miguel, Hermosillo	.277	191	17	53	11	0	0	16	6
Estrada, Hector, Los Mochis	.275	182	19	50	**16**	0	5	30	0
Garcia, Cornelio, Hermosillo	.273	209	26	57	6	0	1	10	9
Tellez, Alonso, Obregon	.269	238	31	64	13	0	5	23	2
Magallanes, Ever, Culiacan	.269	216	27	58	4	0	5	25	5
Vizcarra, Roberto, Obregon	.268	205	23	55	10	1	4	32	5
Robles, Javier, Mazatlan	.268	194	27	52	10	1	3	14	6
Diaz, Remigio, Navojoa	.267	217	29	58	9	0	0	13	0
Martinez, Grimaldo, Mexicali	.266	188	19	50	12	0	2	16	0
Carrillo, Matias, Guasave	.265	196	24	52	5	**3**	3	25	4
Lukachyk, Rob, Los Mochis	.265	181	28	48	12	1	5	31	5
Myers, Rod, Los Mochis	.264	148	27	39	6	1	1	17	13
Montalvo, Ivan, Los Mochis	.262	149	18	39	5	0	5	22	3
Martinez, Ray, Mexicali	.260	204	21	53	13	0	3	35	1
#Smith, Bubba, Mazatlan	.240	229	21	55	7	1	**12**	39	1

INDIVIDUAL PITCHING LEADERS

(Minimum 50 Innings)

	W	L	ERA	G	SV	IP	H	BB	SO
#Johnstone, John, Hermosillo	1	1	1.03	29	**19**	35	18	22	48
Miranda, Julio, Culiacan	1	0	**1.59**	22	0	51	44	19	29
Garcia, Jose, Mazatlan	2	2	2.13	27	0	55	51	16	27
Rodriguez, Salvador, Obr	6	5	2.15	11	0	80	72	31	46
Barraza, Ernesto, Culiacan	5	1	2.25	13	0	80	70	38	43
Osuna, Ricardo, Mexicali	**7**	1	2.34	12	0	77	69	34	43
Bernal, Manuel, Obregon	5	3	2.48	12	0	65	51	29	25
Heredia, Gil, Hermosillo	6	3	2.63	12	0	86	71	19	59
Garibay, Daniel, Mazatlan	4	4	2.64	14	0	85	69	36	52
Palacios, Vicente, Mexicali	2	5	2.64	14	0	92	80	31	**64**
Leyva, Edgar, Guasave	2	2	2.68	11	0	54	40	36	38
Lopez, Emigdio, Los Mochis	6	3	2.69	13	0	80	75	30	36
Elvira, Narciso, Hermosillo	4	5	2.77	11	0	62	59	31	27
Purata, Julio, Guasave	4	3	2.90	11	0	62	56	26	42
Heredia, Hector, Navojoa	4	6	3.05	11	0	59	51	23	21
Jones, Bobby, Obregon	2	5	3.07	10	0	59	54	37	20
Soto, Fernando, Obregon	3	3	3.09	14	0	58	50	22	34
Acosta, Aaron, Mazatlan	1	5	3.15	13	0	69	58	45	54
Hernandez, Martin, Culiacan	5	3	3.21	12	0	70	61	28	27
Higuera, Teddy, Los Mochis	3	4	3.29	11	0	63	56	35	43

ARIZONA FALL LEAGUE

The high-scoring Peoria Javelinas hit their way to their second Arizona Fall League title in four years in 1997. Peoria pounded out 18 runs in the deciding game of the league's best-of-3 championship series, defeating the Grand Canyon Rafters 18-4.

Led by batting champion Brad Fullmer (Expos), who hit .414, the Javelinas set an AFL record for team batting average (.317). The Javelinas had seven regulars over .300 in a year when a wave of offensive records were set.

Brad Fullmer

Other records set in the 1997 season: Mesa's Chad Hermansen (Pirates) scored 45 runs; Peoria outfielder Ryan Jackson (Marlins) had the highest slugging percentage (.685); Mesa third baseman Russ Branyan (Indians) struck out 83 times; and Mesa first baseman Ron Wright (Pirates) tied the mark for homers with 11.

Hermansen (Pirates), who played second base during the Fall League season before moving to left field in 1998 at Triple-A Nashville, was named the AFL's top prospect by league managers. Hermansen hit .341 with eight homers for the Saguaros.

Peoria righthander Rolando Arrojo (Devil Rays) led the league in ERA at 1.38 while going 5-0. Arrojo went on to become Tampa Bay's top pitcher during its 1998 expansion season, earning a spot on the American League all-star team.

STANDINGS

NORTH	W	L	PCT	GB
Peoria Javelinas	28	17	.622	—
Sun Cities Solar Sox	22	23	.489	6
Scottsdale Scorpions	20	25	.444	8
SOUTH	**W**	**L**	**PCT**	**GB**
Grand Canyon Rafters	29	16	.644	—
Phoenix Desert Dogs	21	24	.467	8
Mesa Saguaros	15	30	.333	14

Championship Series—Peoria defeated Grand Canyon, 2-1, in best-of-3 series.

INDIVIDUAL BATTING LEADERS

(Minimum 120 Plate Appearances)

	AVG	AB	R	H	2B	3B	HR	RBI	SB
Fullmer, Brad, Peoria	**.414**	116	27	48	**15**	0	4	29	4
Casey, Sean, Mesa	.396	154	23	**61**	9	2	3	34	1
Jackson, Ryan, Peoria	.378	127	25	48	12	3	7	33	4
Jackson, Damian, Scott	.374	139	32	52	11	4	1	15	11
LoDuca, Paul, Peoria	.363	124	35	45	14	0	0	15	2
Sexton, Chris, Scottsdale	.351	134	27	47	8	1	0	17	5
Gipson, Charles, Peoria	.346	130	26	45	4	3	0	12	10
Hermansen, Chad, Mesa	.341	179	**45**	**61**	10	4	8	27	5
Roberge, J.P., Peoria	.336	116	19	39	5	1	2	21	8
Watkins, Pat, Scottsdale	.336	131	22	44	11	2	3	19	**13**
Barker, Kevin, Sun Cities	.331	127	19	42	11	2	3	28	1
McKinley, Dan, Scottsdale	.331	124	20	41	7	3	0	10	8
Riggs, Adam, Peoria	.317	139	26	44	9	4	5	37	3
Smith, Robert, GC	.316	171	27	54	12	1	4	24	9
Kotsay, Mark, Peoria	.313	150	32	47	11	3	3	20	6
Bush, Homer, Phoenix	.308	143	27	44	9	1	5	18	4
Buchanan, Brian, Phoenix	.299	154	25	46	12	0	10	29	2
Koskie, Corey, Sun Cities	.299	107	27	32	9	1	10	21	5
Boone, Aaron, Scottsdale	.297	138	23	41	8	1	5	26	3
Jenkins, Geoff, Sun Cities	.297	138	28	41	11	0	10	**38**	1
Matthews, Gary, Sun Cities	.293	123	23	36	6	0	1	13	3
Brown, Emil, GC	.290	107	22	31	5	2	6	20	8
Ward, Daryle, Sun Cities	.289	135	18	39	11	1	5	20	1
Anderson, Marlon, GC	.289	149	22	43	2	2	3	33	10
Wilson, Preston, GC	.286	168	31	48	14	2	10	32	4
Simmons, Brian, Mesa	.284	148	23	42	7	**5**	4	19	11
Long, Ryan, Sun Cities	.276	116	17	32	10	1	2	11	0
Lee, Travis, Grand Canyon	.267	150	20	40	11	2	2	22	1
#Wright, Ron, Mesa	.217	157	25	04	7	1	**11**	35	0

INDIVIDUAL PITCHING LEADERS

(Minimum 35 Innings)

	W	L	ERA	G	SV	IP	H	BB	SO
Arrojo, Rolando, Peoria	**5**	0	**1.38**	9	0	39	29	8	39
Schoeneweis, Scott, Scottsdale	3	2	1.98	8	0	36	33	7	31
Medina, Rafael, Sun Cities	0	4	2.09	9	0	39	24	13	44
#Boyd, Jason, Grand Canyon	**5**	0	2.16	16	1	25	14	7	27
#Speier, Justin, Mesa	2	4	2.28	19	8	24	22	6	22
Sikorski, Brian, Sun Cities	4	2	2.41	9	0	41	35	12	40
Montgomery, Steve, Peoria	**5**	1	2.54	9	0	39	29	10	46
Sauerback, Scott, Grand Canyon	1	1	2.68	9	0	37	37	14	32
Munro, Peter, Phoenix	1	2	2.79	9	0	42	35	11	37
Rocker, John, Grand Canyon	2	1	2.85	9	0	41	30	9	39
Johnson, Mike, Peoria	3	1	3.07	10	0	41	37	11	41
Perisho, Matt, Phoenix	0	1	3.46	9	0	42	34	9	40
Rain, Steve, Mesa	2	1	4.07	9	0	42	39	13	40
Olsen, Jason, Mesa	0	5	4.14	11	0	37	44	11	22
Smith, Dan, Scottsdale	**5**	2	4.40	11	0	43	54	20	30
Hinchliffe, Brett, Peoria	3	1	4.50	9	0	42	45	11	43
#Shoemaker, Steve, Scottsdale	1	5	4.91	9	0	37	36	17	**49**
#Kubenka, Jeff, Peoria	4	2	4.97	10	0	38	44	10	**49**
#Ford, Ben, Phoenix	1	3	6.33	19	**8**	21	23	9	33

HAWAII WINTER BASEBALL

After two consecutive second-place finishes, the Honolulu Sharks finally took home the hardware in 1997. The Sharks pulled off a dramatic 9-8 win over the Hilo Stars to take Hawaii Winter Baseball's final championship.

Honolulu third baseman Carlos Villalobos (Mariners) was named MVP of the game after going 3-for-4 with the game-winning hit in the bottom of the ninth inning. The only drawback on the day for Villalobos came after the game when his nose was broken in the postgame pileup.

West Oahu first baseman Nobuhiko Matsunaka set a league record with his .372 average, topping the previous mark held by another Japanese player, Hiroki Kokubo, who hit .370 in 1994.

Hawaii Winter Baseball, which began in 1993 as a winter league for promising players from the lower levels of the minor leagues and Japan, ceased operations following the 1997 season. A new league based in Maryland took its place in the fall of 1998.

STANDINGS

OUTRIGGER	W	L	PCT	GB
Honolulu Sharks	27	27	.500	—
West Oahu Canefires	26	27	.491	½
VOLCANO	**W**	**L**	**PCT**	**GB**
Hilo Stars	29	24	.547	—
Maui Stingrays	25	29	.463	4½

Championship Series: Honolulu defeated Hilo in 1-game playoff.

INDIVIDUAL BATTING LEADERS
(Minimum 146 Plate Appearances)

	AVG	AB	R	H	2B	3B	HR	RBI	SB
Matsunaka, Nobuhiko, WO	**.372**	191	33	**71**	**18**	4	7	**37**	4
Johnson, Ric, Hilo	.335	158	17	53	11	1	0	17	12
Fick, Rob, Honolulu	.329	146	23	48	14	1	3	30	3
Barrett, Michael, WO	.314	175	23	55	7	0	2	24	2
Long, Terrance, WO	.302	182	**35**	55	13	**7**	4	16	7
Pickering, Calvin, Maui	.301	153	21	46	9	0	**10**	29	0
Bates, Fletcher, West Oahu	.297	175	29	52	9	3	7	31	9
Casimiro, Carlos, Maui	.293	150	18	44	9	1	1	15	5
Winn, Randy, Maui	.283	138	18	39	10	0	0	17	7
Kapler, Gabe, Honolulu	.282	188	31	53	11	2	3	23	6
Minor, Damon, Honolulu	.278	158	29	44	12	1	8	34	2
Budzinski, Mark, Hilo	.276	145	23	40	8	5	2	21	3
Funaro, Joe, Maui	.271	170	20	46	14	3	0	17	2
Villalobos, Carlos, Honolulu	.271	170	25	46	5	3	3	27	1
Kennedy, Adam, Hilo	.268	179	29	48	8	1	4	20	12
Abernathy, Brent, Honolulu	.265	181	27	48	8	1	0	11	9
Hutchins, Norm, Honolulu	.255	192	33	49	6	6	5	18	**13**
Chamblee, Jim, West Oahu	.249	177	33	44	7	3	**10**	31	11
Baker, Derek, Hilo	.247	170	15	42	8	0	2	27	2
Metcalfe, Mike, Maui	.230	135	16	31	2	1	1	9	7

INDIVIDUAL PITCHING LEADERS
(Minimum 43 Innings)

	W	L	ERA	G	SV	IP	H	BB	SO
Babineaux, Darrin, Maui	3	2	**1.35**	15	0	47	26	14	39
Evans, Keith, West Oahu	**4**	3	1.69	10	0	48	38	11	54
Grilli, Jason, Honolulu	2	5	2.41	11	0	56	45	21	41
Masaoka, Onan, Hilo	1	3	2.66	9	0	44	38	19	43
Villafuerte, Brandon, WO	2	3	2.91	12	1	46	44	18	40
#Kohlmeier, Ryan, Maui	2	1	3.18	23	**8**	23	12	7	35
Kawahara, Junichi, Honolulu	3	2	3.25	11	1	53	45	13	**68**
#Hackman, Luther, Maui	**4**	3	3.32	10	1	41	31	19	25
Cooper, Brian, Honolulu	3	4	3.27	10	0	52	47	8	61
Ah Yat, Paul, West Oahu	3	2	3.74	24	3	43	37	16	42
Manon, Julio, Maui	2	4	3.80	10	0	45	41	14	47
O'Malley, Paul, Hilo	**4**	4	3.88	11	0	53	52	22	30
#Grundy, Phil, West Oahu	**4**	3	4.37	18	2	45	43	18	39
#Kurano, Shinji, West Oahu	**4**	5	4.58	12	0	57	58	21	45

AUSTRALIAN LEAGUE

The Melbourne Reds went from worst to first in the 1997-98 Australian Baseball League, sweeping the Gold Coast Cougars in the playoff finals a year after finishing in last place.

The Reds won 4-3 and 4-0 to take the best-of-3 series. Third baseman Myles Barnden hit decisive home runs in both games. His solo shot was the go-ahead run in the first game, and a three-run homer in the eighth inning sealed the second.

Brendan Kingman

The final game was a pitching duel between Reds righthander Jason Beverlin (Yankees) and Cougars righty Paxton Crawford (Red Sox). Beverlin's six shutout innings were the decisive factor. It was just his third win in three months.

The Reds became the first team to win three ABL championships. They previously won in 1990 and '95. In 1998, they worked their way through the league's new round-robin playoff format along with the Cougars. Sydney and the Melbourne Monarchs failed to advance from the three-game tournament.

Sydney first baseman Brendan Kingman was named MVP after setting league records with his .487 average, 28 home runs and 66 RBIs. Kingman won the batting title by 99 points. Off that performance, Kingman was signed as a free agent by the Seattle Mariners and went on to win the Class A California League batting title in 1998, at .340.

Monarchs lefthander Erick Nelson (Braves) earned pitcher of the year honors after going 7-1 with a 2.83 ERA.

STANDINGS

REGULAR SEASON	W	L	PCT	GB
Melbourne Monarchs	32	20	.615	—
Sydney Storm	32	22	.592	1
Melbourne Reds	30	21	.588	1½
Gold Coast Cougars	31	22	.584	1½
Perth Heat	30	23	.566	2½
Adelaide Giants	26	27	.490	6½
Brisbane Bandits	20	33	.377	12½
Hunter Eagles	10	43	.188	22½
PLAYOFFS	**W**	**L**	**PCT**	**GB**
Melbourne Reds	2	1	.667	—
Gold Coast Cougars	2	1	.667	—
Melbourne Monarchs	1	2	.333	1
Sydney Storm	1	2	.333	1

Championship Series: Melbourne Reds defeated Gold Coast, 2-0, in best-of-3 series.

INDIVIDUAL BATTING LEADERS
(Minimum 165 Plate Appearances)

	AVG	AB	R	H	2B	3B	HR	RBI	SB
Kingman, Brendan, Sydney	**.487**	156	58	76	12	0	**28**	**66**	3
Burton, Adam, Reds	.388	165	**66**	64	15	0	21	55	18
Jelks, Greg, Perth	.379	169	51	64	13	0	21	48	3
Byrne, Clayton, Monarchs	.377	175	37	66	13	0	10	44	7
Hinton, Steve, Brisbane	.375	208	53	**78**	13	0	20	63	8
Gorman, Paul, Gold Coast	.370	173	46	64	7	0	17	49	2
McDonald, Grant, Brisbane	.369	187	44	69	16	2	18	49	8
Tunkin, Scott, Sydney	.360	189	53	68	12	0	15	36	4
Buckley, Matthew, GC	.351	208	44	73	**21**	2	12	45	7
Utting, Ben, Reds	.346	153	34	53	13	**3**	7	34	10
Jones, Sean, Perth	.342	146	33	50	6	0	13	32	5
Wells, Michael, Hunter	.324	179	28	58	13	0	16	44	1
Johnson, Ron, Gold Coast	.321	190	52	61	13	0	22	**66**	4
Stone, Craig, Sydney	.318	179	41	57	4	1	21	55	6
Barker, Glen, Brisbane	.314	185	35	58	11	2	7	20	20
Williams, Glenn, Sydney	.313	166	28	52	9	0	13	33	2
#Durrington, Trent, GC	.299	167	43	50	7	0	3	22	**28**
#Ivanoff, Jay, Adelaide	.210	100	15	21	4	**3**	2	15	2

INDIVIDUAL PITCHING LEADERS
(Minimum 40 Innings)

	W	L	ERA	G	SV	IP	H	BB	SO
Williams, Jeff, Brisbane	4	2	**2.08**	8	0	48	43	23	34
Nelson, Erick, Monarchs	7	1	2.83	15	0	70	60	29	61
Iddon, Brent, Sydney	**8**	2	3.07	15	0	94	82	21	83
Bennett, Shayne, Adelaide	6	4	3.36	14	0	78	73	10	84
Ahearne, Pat, Reds	3	4	3.51	9	0	56	53	21	43
Weaver, Eric, Adelaide	5	2	3.97	8	0	48	47	19	59
McBride, Chris, Sydney	6	4	4.02	15	0	87	82	26	70
Dale, Phil, Monarchs	**8**	3	4.03	14	0	109	107	19	**95**
Cederblad, Brett, Gold Coast	5	3	4.46	13	0	73	82	17	62
#Molina, Gabe, Perth	4	1	4.46	18	**7**	34	24	28	45
May, Warren, Reds	6	1	5.11	19	1	62	73	13	43
Crawford, Paxton, Gold Coast	4	3	5.26	15	0	79	86	32	51
Bowie, Micah, Monarchs	2	5	5.27	12	0	55	55	36	50
Eissens, Simon, Perth	5	2	5.40	18	0	55	64	13	32
Smith, Keilan, Brisbane	5	4	5.72	13	1	57	59	39	42
Moylan, Peter, Perth	5	5	5.77	12	0	53	57	22	33
LaGarde, Joe, Adelaide	5	4	5.91	14	0	75	82	42	69
Hogan, Rob, Reds	5	2	5.97	16	0	57	72	26	33

College Baseball

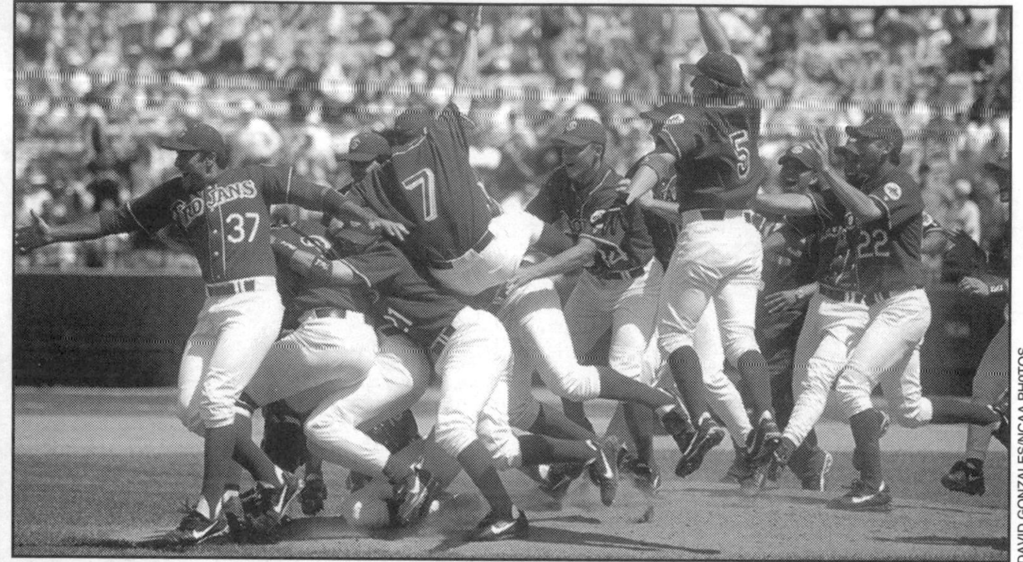

DAVID GONZALES/NCAA PHOTOS

Trojan Triumph
Southern California celebrates its 12th NCAA title

Southern California outslugs Arizona State in battle of two storied, Pac-10 opponents

BY JOHN MANUEL

It seemed that retro was cool in college baseball in 1998.

Seniors came back for their final seasons, and players such as Southern California righthander Seth Etherton and Louisiana State first baseman Eddy Furniss reaped the benefits of passing up the professional ranks for another year. Traditional powers Arizona State and USC made their way through the College World Series field to meet in the championship game, a match of two storied programs with the most CWS titles in history.

Super senior
Seth Etherton

When the Trojans outlasted the Sun Devils 21-14 in a four-hour slugfest, it seemed an old order had been restored to the sport. It was USC's 12th championship, leaving the Sun Devils further behind in second place with five.

But two months after the Trojans marched home with their championship trophy, college baseball was rocked by the biggest news to hit the sport since aluminum bats and the designated hitter were introduced for the 1974 season.

The NCAA baseball rules committee recommended major changes to those aluminum bats–bats that had helped cause offenses to explode throughout college baseball in the last 25 seasons. The recommended changes, which will force manufacturers to produce aluminum bats that perform more like wood bats, were approved swiftly by the NCAA executive committee for implementation in August 1999.

So take one long, last look around at the college baseball landscape. Because the events of 1998 ensure that radical, profound change will be coming to the sport in the very near future.

Back To The Summit

That landscape was dominated in 1998 by the Pacific-10 Conference, specifically the South Division. The Six-Pac, as the members–Arizona, Arizona State, California, Southern California, Stanford and UCLA–are known, seemed to get nudged aside in the '90s by the Southeastern Conference on the national scene.

The SEC produced five CWS champions from 1990-97, with four of the titles going to Louisiana State. SEC teams thrived in the power-hitting, smashmouth style of baseball that worked well in regional play.

Southern California played that style well, though. The Trojans were brimming with power throughout their lineup, led by senior third baseman Morgan Ensberg (21 home runs), junior outfielder Brad Ticehurst (18) and sophomore catcher Eric Munson (16). They hit a team-record 114 home runs on the season.

Moreover, USC had Etherton, an All-American who led the nation in strikeouts with 182 and helped lead the Trojans into Omaha with a 13-3, 3.23 record. For added measure, the Trojans had the nation's top closer, senior righthander Jack Krawczyk, who set an NCAA record with 23 saves.

Krawczyk's last save came in the wild title game, which featured 39 hits, nine home runs and the first Six-Pac champion since Stanford in 1988. When Krawczyk got the last out, the Trojans had their first championship since 1978.

Tournament MVP Wes Rachels, a senior second baseman, accounted for five of Southern California's 23 hits in the title game and drove in seven of its 21 runs.

Arizona State used an opportunistic offense and strong pitching—they had the field's best team ERA—to move from the CWS' sixth seed to the championship game.

BILL SETLIFF

Series MVP
USC's Wes Rachels

But its ace, junior lefthander Ryan Mills, lasted only one trip through the order against the Trojans. He gave up six runs in one-plus inning. After two innings, two homers by Robb Gorr and one by Rachels, Southern California led 8-0.

The Sun Devils closed within a run on two occasions before Krawczyk shut the door in the eighth, and before junior DH (and winning pitcher in relief) Jason Lane blasted a ninth-inning grand slam to cap the win.

The Bat Imbroglio

The 21-14 slugfest capped the most offensive season in college history. It got out of control in Omaha, where Rosenblatt Stadium doesn't help matters with 360-foot power alleys. The eight teams in the '98 series combined for a .318 average and 62 home runs, shattering the records set in 1995 of .303 and 48.

It was the third straight CWS without a shutout. Southern California hit .378 for the tournament and the average game featured 16.2 runs, a full run better than the previous record. The championship game was the highest-scoring game in tournament history and lasted 3 hours, 59 minutes.

For the season, records were set for Division I in batting average (.306), per-game scoring (7.12 a team) and home runs per game (1.06). The collective ERA for Division I teams was 6.12.

All this offense spurred the changes in aluminum bats. By 2000, bats will get slimmer, heavier and, in effect, deader. The rules changes:

■ Mandate a "maximum batted-ball exit velocity" of 93 mph. That's the speed of the ball off the bat, with 93 mph being the high-end performance for a wood bat. Current aluminum models have tested as high as 113 mph.

■ Decrease the maximum diameter of bat heads from 2¾ inches to 2⅝ inches.

■ Reduce the "length to weight unit differential"

COLLEGE WORLD SERIES

Omaha, Nebraska
May 29-June 6, 1998

STANDINGS

BRACKET ONE	W	L	RF	RA
Arizona State	3	1	48	37
Long Beach State	2	2	18	24
Miami	1	2	8	16
Florida State	0	2	14	18

Bracket One Final: Arizona State 14, Long Beach State 4

BRACKET TWO	W	L	RF	RA
Southern California	5	1	62	44
Louisiana State	2	2	29	30
Mississippi State	1	2	23	30
Florida	0	2	23	26

Bracket Two Final: USC 7, Louisiana State 3
CHAMPIONSHIP GAME: USC 21, Arizona State 14

INDIVIDUAL BATTING LEADERS

(Minimum 12 At-Bats)

	AVG	AB	R	H	2B	3B	HR	RBI	SB
Lane, Jason, USC	.517	29	9	15	4	0	4	9	0
Munson, Eric, USC	.476	21	6	10	1	0	2	5	1
Freitas, Jeremy, USC	.440	25	9	11	1	0	1	5	1
Arguelles, Rudy, ASU	.429	21	8	9	0	0	0	5	0
Bloomquist, Willie, ASU	.429	21	6	9	0	0	1	5	0
Beinbrink, Andrew, ASU	.429	14	5	6	0	0	3	8	1
Thoms, Rusty, MSU	.429	14	5	6	0	0	1	4	0
Phelps, Jeff, ASU	.421	19	4	8	2	0	1	6	0

INDIVIDUAL PITCHING LEADERS

(Minimum 7 Innings)

	W	L	ERA	G	SV	IP	H	BB	SO
Santos, Alex, Miami	1	0	0.00	1	0	8	4	1	8
Fogg, Josh, Florida	0	0	1.86	2	0	10	10	7	0
Krawczyk, Jack, USC	1	0	3.68	4	2	7	8	2	7
Kramer, Aaron, ASU	0	0	4.38	4	2	12	11	3	6
Gallo, Mike, LBSU	0	1	4.50	2	0	12	15	4	11

ALL-TOURNAMENT TEAM

C—Eric Munson, Southern California. **1B**—Robb Gorr, Southern California. **2B**—Wes Rachels, Southern California. **3B**—Andrew Beinbrink, Arizona State. **SS**—Michael Collins, Arizona State. **OF**—Rudy Arguelles, Arizona State; Cedrick Harris, Louisiana State; Brad Ticehurst, Southern California. **DH**—Jason Lane, Southern California. **P**—Jack Krawczyk, Southern California; Alex Santos, Miami.

Most Outstanding Player—Wes Rachels, USC.

CHAMPIONSHIP GAME

Trojans 21, Sun Devils 14

USC	ab	r	h	bi	ARIZONA ST.	ab	r	h	bi
Rachels 2b	7	3	5	7	Bloomquist 2b	6	0	1	0
Hanoian lf	2	1	0	0	Arguelles cf	5	2	1	2
Perry pr-cf	1	0	1	0	Moreno rf	6	2	2	1
Gorr 1b	5	3	2	5	Beinbrink 3b	2	2	1	3
Munson c	6	1	2	0	Phelps 1b	4	1	2	2
Ensberg 3b	4	3	2	1	Delucchi lf	5	1	1	1
Ticehurst rf	5	2	1	2	Myers dh	5	3	4	1
Lane dh-p	6	2	3	4	Halvorson c	5	2	3	0
Freitas cf-lf	6	3	5	1	Collins ss	3	1	1	4
DePippo pr-lf	0	0	0	0					
Davidson ss	4	3	2	0					
Totals	**46**	**21**	**23**	**20**	**Totals**	**41**	**14**	**16**	**14**

Southern California	**351 002 325—21**
Arizona State	**050 300 510—14**

E—Davidson (19). **DP**—Arizona State 2. **LOB**—Southern California 7, Arizona State 8. **2B**—Rachels (16), Ensberg (22), Lane (18), Freitas (11), Moreno (16). **HR**—Rachels (3), Gorr 2 (16), Ticehurst (18), Lane (14), Beinbrink (12), Phelps (5), Myers (8), Collins (4). **SB**—Ensberg (20), Freitas (4), Davidson (17), Moreno (27). **S**—Hanoian (14), Collins 2 (7). **SF**—Gorr (4), Beinbrink (8).

USC	ip	h	r	er	bb	so	ARIZ. ST.	ip	h	r	er	bb	so
Currier	1⅓	5	5	5	1	3	Mills L	1	6	6	6	1	1
Lane W	⅓	4	3	0	2	1	Kramer	5	6	5	5	0	1
Immel	3	4	4	4	2	1	Pennington	1⅓	5	5	5	3	1
Weibling	⅔	3	2	2	0	1	Lowery	1	4	4	4	2	0
Krawczyk S	1⅔	0	0	0	0	1	Crumpton	⅔	2	1	1	0	0

Mills faced three batters in second.

PB—Halvorson 2. **HBP**—by Kramer (Ensberg). **T**—3:59. **A**—24,456.

College Baseball

from five to three. In other words, 34-ounce bats that currently weigh 29 ounces will weigh no less than 31 ounces, without the grip.

Southwest Missouri State athletic director Bill Rowe, the rules committee chairman, said there were three reasons for the changes.

"First is the fear of litigation," he said. "We didn't want to have a player get hurt or killed and have the NCAA sued on this. Second, we just had a lot of people who watch college baseball and asked how long this kind of offense can go on. Third, we needed to do something to restore the integrity of the game. We felt in part that with all the high scores, that balance had been lost."

All the changes were originally approved by the NCAA board of directors to go into effect for the 1999 season. The NCAA executive committee instead delayed the changes until August 1999, giving bat manufacturers such as Easton Sports and Hillerich & Bradsby, maker of Louisville Slugger, extra time to develop new bats that conform to the standards and time to exhaust their inventories.

Bill Thurston, a member of the rules committee and head baseball coach at Division III Amherst (Mass.) College, said the committee wants to continue to use aluminum bats in college, though.

"We need aluminum bats that are durable but that act like wood," he said. "The manufacturers have long said that would be easy to do. If we went to wood bats or composite bats, I'm concerned about the quality of wood many schools would get."

Getting Better All The Time

At the same time it was approving bat changes, the

COLLEGE WORLD SERIES CHAMPIONS: 1947-98

Year	Champion	Coach	Record	Runner-Up	MVP
1947	California*	Clint Evans	31-10	Yale	None selected
1948	Southern California	Sam Barry	40-12	Yale	None selected
1949	Texas*	Bibb Falk	23-7	Wake Forest	Charles Teague, 2b, Wake Forest
1950	Texas	Bibb Falk	27-6	Washington State	Ray VanCleef, of, Rutgers
1951	Oklahoma*	Jack Baer	19-9	Tennessee	Sid Hatfield, 1b-p, Tennessee
1952	Holy Cross	Jack Berry	21-3	Missouri	Jim O'Neill, p, Holy Cross
1953	Michigan	Ray Fisher	21-9	Texas	J.L. Smith, p, Texas
1954	Missouri	Hi Simmons	22-4	Rollins	Tom Yewcic, c, Michigan State
1955	Wake Forest	Taylor Sanford	29-7	Western Michigan	Tom Borland, p, Oklahoma State
1956	Minnesota	Dick Siebert	33-9	Arizona	Jerry Thomas, p, Minnesota
1957	California*	George Wolfman	35-10	Penn State	Cal Emery, 1b-p, Penn State
1958	Southern California	Rod Dedeaux	35-7	Missouri	Bill Thom, p, Southern California
1959	Oklahoma State	Toby Greene	27-5	Arizona	Jim Dobson, 3b, Oklahoma State
1960	Minnesota	Dick Siebert	34-7	Southern California	John Erickson, 2b, Minnesota
1961	Southern California*	Rod Dedeaux	43-9	Oklahoma State	Littleton Fowler, p, Oklahoma State
1962	Michigan	Don Lund	31-13	Santa Clara	Bob Garibaldi, p, Santa Clara
1963	Southern California	Rod Dedeaux	37-16	Arizona	Bud Hollowell, c, Southern California
1964	Minnesota	Dick Siebert	31-12	Missouri	Joe Ferris, p, Maine
1965	Arizona State	Bobby Winkles	54-8	Ohio State	Sal Bando, 3b, Arizona State
1966	Ohio State	Marty Karow	27-6	Oklahoma State	Steve Arlin, p, Ohio State
1967	Arizona State	Bobby Winkles	53-12	Houston	Ron Davini, c, Arizona State
1968	Southern California*	Rod Dedeaux	45-14	Southern Illinois	Bill Seinsoth, 1b, Southern California
1969	Arizona State	Bobby Winkles	56-11	Tulsa	John Dolinsek, of, Arizona State
1970	Southern California	Rod Dedeaux	51-13	Florida State	Gene Ammann, p, Florida State
1971	Southern California	Rod Dedeaux	53-13	Southern Illinois	Jerry Tabb, 1b, Tulsa
1972	Southern California	Rod Dedeaux	50-13	Arizona State	Russ McQueen, p, Southern California
1973	Southern California*	Rod Dedeaux	51-11	Arizona State	Dave Winfield, of-p, Minnesota
1974	Southern California	Rod Dedeaux	50-20	Miami (Fla.)	George Milke, p, Southern California
1975	Texas	Cliff Gustafson	56-6	South Carolina	Mickey Reichenbach, 1b, Texas
1976	Arizona	Jerry Kindall	56-17	Eastern Michigan	Steve Powers, dh-p, Arizona
1977	Arizona State	Jim Brock	57-12	South Carolina	Bob Horner, 3b, Arizona State
1978	Southern California*	Rod Dedeaux	54-9	Arizona State	Rod Boxberger, p, Southern California
1979	Cal State Fullerton	Augie Garrido	60-14	Arkansas	Tony Hudson, p, Cal State Fullerton
1980	Arizona	Jerry Kindall	45-21	Hawaii	Terry Francona, of, Arizona
1981	Arizona State	Jim Brock	55-13	Oklahoma State	Stan Holmes, of, Arizona State
1982	Miami (Fla.)*	Ron Fraser	57-18	Wichita State	Dan Smith, p, Miami (Fla.)
1983	Texas*	Cliff Gustafson	66-14	Alabama	Calvin Schiraldi, p, Texas
1984	Cal State Fullerton	Augie Garrido	66-20	Texas	John Fishel, of, Cal State Fullerton
1985	Miami (Fla.)*	Ron Fraser	64-16	Texas	Greg Ellena, dh, Miami (Fla.)
1986	Arizona	Jerry Kindall	49-19	Florida State	Mike Senne, of, Arizona
1987	Stanford	Mark Marquess	53-17	Oklahoma State	Paul Carey, of, Stanford
1988	Stanford	Mark Marquess	46-23	Arizona State	Lee Plemel, p, Stanford
1989	Wichita State	Gene Stephenson	68-16	Texas	Greg Brummett, p, Wichita State
1990	Georgia	Steve Webber	52-19	Oklahoma State	Mike Rebhan, p, Georgia
1991	Louisiana State*	Skip Bertman	55-18	Wichita State	Gary Hymel, c, Louisiana State
1992	Pepperdine*	Andy Lopez	48-11	Cal State Fullerton	Phil Nevin, 3b, Cal State Fullerton
1993	Louisiana State	Skip Bertman	53-17	Wichita State	Todd Walker, 2b, Louisiana State
1994	Oklahoma*	Larry Cochell	50-17	Georgia Tech	Chip Glass, of, Oklahoma
1995	Cal State Fullerton*	Augie Garrido	57-9	Southern California	Mark Kotsay, of-lhp, Cal State Fullerton
1996	Louisiana State*	Skip Bertman	52-15	Miami (Fla.)	Pat Burrell, 3b, Miami
1997	Louisiana State*	Skip Bertman	57-13	Alabama	Brandon Larson, ss, Louisiana State
1998	Southern California	Mike Gillespie	49-17	Arizona State	Wes Rachels, 2b, Southern California

*Undefeated

NCAA executive committee approved a plan expanding the Division I baseball tournament field from 48 teams to 64.

The expansion was trumpeted by its sponsor, the American Baseball Coaches Association, as the most important baseball legislation in 20 years.

"We're really on cloud nine," said Dave Keilitz, the ABCA's executive director. "For nine years, we've worked on this issue, and to have it pass is personally and professionally gratifying. I don't think you can overstate how great this is for college baseball."

The expansion adds a week to the college season, pushing the College World Series back a week. The 1999 CWS, the 50th to be held in Omaha, will begin June 11.

Every conference champion (as designated by each conference) gets a bid to the tournament. There will be 29 automatic bids and 35 at-large bids. Play-in games become a thing of the past.

The tournament will include 16 four-team, double-elimination regionals that will retain the current $50,000 minimum bid for host schools. The 16 winners will advance to super-regionals, to be held at predetermined sites. The super-regionals will be best two-out-of-three series. The eight surviving teams advance to Omaha.

Six-Pac Era Ends

In 1998, the Six-Pac was the elite conference in college baseball. It featured national champion Southern California and Stanford, which set a record by topping Baseball America's Top 25 poll for 14 consecutive weeks.

It had BA's College Player of the Year in Stanford righthander Jeff Austin, Freshman of the Year in California second baseman Xavier Nady and Coach of the Year in Arizona State's Pat Murphy. What it did not have, however, was the conference champion. Washington, which won the Northern Division, upset Stanford in the Pac-10 tournament, gaining the conference's automatic berth in regional play.

But 1998 proved to be the last for divisional play in the Pac-10. The Six-Pac, born in 1979, effectively died in May when Portland State, a member of the conference in baseball and wrestling, dropped out. Portland State became the 40th Division I institution–the 12th

NCAA TOURNAMENT

PLAY-IN SERIES

(Best-of-3)

Oral Roberts (Mid-Continent) def. Butler (Midwestern), 2-0.
Fordham (Atlantic 10) def. Howard (Mid-Eastern Athletic), 2-0.
Southeast Missouri State (Ohio Valley) def. Southern (Southwestern Athletic), 2-0.
Monmouth (Northeast) def. Navy (Patriot), 2-1.
Harvard (Ivy) def. LeMoyne (Metro Atlantic), 2-0.

REGIONALS

(Double elimination)

ATLANTIC I

Site: Coral Gables, Fla.
Participants: No. 1 Miami (46-9, at large), No. 2 South Carolina (42-16, at large), No. 3 North Carolina (39-21, at large), No. 4 Texas Tech (43-18, Big 12), No. 5 Florida International (40-22, Trans American), No. 6 Bowling Green (34-19, Mid-American).
Champion: Miami (4-1).
Runner-Up: North Carolina (3-2).
Outstanding Player: Pat Burrell, dh, Miami.
Attendance: 18,869.

ATLANTIC II

Site: Tallahassee, Fla.
Participants: No. 1 Florida State (49-18, at large), No. 2 Auburn (43-16, Southeastern), No. 3 Delaware (43-8, America East), No. 4 Oklahoma (40-18, at large), No. 5 Rutgers (32-14, Big East), No. 6 Liberty (32-27, Big South).
Champion: Florida State (4-0).
Runner-Up: Auburn (3-2).
Outstanding Player: Matt Diaz, of, Florida State.
Attendance: 21,385.

CENTRAL

Site: College Station, Texas.
Participants: No. 1 Rice (45-15, Western Athletic), No. 2 Texas A&M (43-18, at large), No. 3 Washington (39-15, Pacific-10), No. 4 Mississippi State (37-20, at large), No. 5 UNC Charlotte (43-17, at large), No. 6 Oral Roberts (44-18, play in/Mid-Continent).
Champion: Mississippi State (4-1).
Runner-Up: Texas A&M (3-2).
Outstanding Player: Brooks Bryan, of, Mississippi State.
Attendance: 53,287.

EAST

Site: Clemson, S.C.
Participants: No. 1 Southern California (40-15, at large), No. 2 Clemson (42-14, at large), No. 3 Virginia Commonwealth (44-13, at large), No. 4 South Alabama (39-17, at large), No. 5 The Citadel (36-22, Southern), No. 6 Fordham (27-18, play in/Atlantic 10).
Champion: Southern California (4-1).
Runner-Up: South Alabama (3-2).
Outstanding Player: Eric Munson, dh, Southern California.
Attendance: 19,022.

MIDWEST

Site: Wichita, Kan.
Participants: No. 1 Wichita State (55-5, Missouri Valley), No. 2 Georgia Tech (38-20, at large), No. 3 Arizona State (34-21, at large), No. 4 Arkansas (37-19, at large), No. 5 Oklahoma State (38-19, at large), No. 6 Southeast Missouri State (32-22, play in/Ohio Valley)
Champion: Arizona State (4-1).
Runner-Up: Georgia Tech (3-2).
Outstanding Player: Mikel Moreno, of, Arizona State.
Attendance: 50,603.

SOUTH I

Site: Gainesville, Fla.
Participants: No. 1 Florida (42-15, at large), No. 2 Wake Forest (41-21, Atlantic Coast), No. 3 Baylor (40-18, at large), No. 4 Richmond (40-15, Colonial), No. 5 Illinois (39-19, at large), No. 6 Monmouth (30-19, play in/Northeast).
Champion: Florida (4-1).
Runner-Up: Illinois (3-2).
Outstanding Player: Mark Ellis, ss, Florida.
Attendance: 22,999.

SOUTH II

Site: Baton Rouge, La.
Participants: No. 1 Louisiana State (42-17, at large), No. 2 Cal State Fullerton (44-15, at large), No. 3 Tulane (47-13, Conference USA), No. 4 Southwestern Louisiana (39-20, Sun Belt), No. 5 Harvard (34-10, play in/Ivy), No. 6 Nicholls State (28-32, Southland).
Champion: Louisiana State (4-0).
Runner-Up: Cal State Fullerton (3-2).
Outstanding Player: Eddy Furniss, 1b, Louisiana State.
Attendance: 68,047.

WEST

Site: Palo Alto, Calif.
Participants: No. 1 Stanford (41-12, at large), No. 2 Alabama (43-16, at large), No. 3 Long Beach State (37-20, Big West), No. 4 North Carolina State (39-21, at large), No. 5 Minnesota (45-13, Big Ten), No. 6 Loyola Marymount (33-21, West Coast).
Champion: Long Beach State (4-1).
Runner-Up: Alabama (3-2).
Outstanding Player: Terrmel Sledge, of, Long Beach State.
Attendance: 17,683.

Player of the Year

Stanford's Austin earns nod over Pac-10 rival

Jeff Austin

Just 962 fans attended the April 3, 1998, matchup of No. 1 Stanford at No. 2 Southern California at Dedeaux Field.

As the years pass, though, thousands of college baseball fans, scouts, scouting directors and players probably will claim to have been among the crowd.

What those 962 fans witnessed was a cut above the average baseball game, whatever the level. They saw two pitchers at the top of their games, dueling pitch for pitch. One mistake was all it took to lose.

Senior righthander Seth Etherton had his best performance as a Trojan. He yielded just four hits, walked one batter and struck out 15 while throwing 130 pitches.

But he made one mistake. He hung a curveball to Cardinal center fielder Jody Gerut, who deposited the pitch over the right-field wall.

Stanford righthander Jeff Austin scattered six hits across his nine innings. In the bottom of the ninth, clinging to the one-run lead, Austin did what he does best. He made the pitches he had to make.

After a leadoff double to Eric Munson and a sacrifice bunt, Austin got a strikeout and a popout to seal the shutout and win the year's best game.

Austin didn't make a mistake that night, and he made precious few during a splendid junior season. For that, he was named Baseball America's 1998 College Player of the Year.

One game wasn't all that separates Austin from Etherton or other candidates. Austin's consistency and leading role on what was the nation's best team for most of the season put him at the forefront.

His 12-4, 3.11 record put him among the national leaders in wins and ERA. And every Friday night, Austin faced off with the Pacific-10 Conference's top starters, including first-round picks Etherton and Ryan Mills of Arizona State.

There was never a question of Austin losing his job, even with talented pitchers like Chad Hutchinson and Brent Hoard on the Stanford staff. Austin won his first nine decisions, losing the week after his showdown with Etherton.

Both pitchers admitted to a letdown after that game. It was just too good to match.

"The second my game ended the week before, I was looking forward to USC," Austin said. "If I hadn't thought that way, I probably would have lost. It takes that kind of concentration and effort to go against those guys."

Austin's bag of pitches helped Stanford win 41 games and set a record for the longest run at No. 1 in Baseball America's Top 25. But it didn't help the Cardinal win its first College World Series since 1988.

Austin won the rematch with Southern California in the last regular season series of the season, a 4-2 victory that clinched the Pac-10 South title. But Stanford won just one more game.

"I think we were a very businesslike team that approached things professionally," Austin said. "We never got too high or too low, even when we were No. 1 for (14) weeks. Maybe going into regionals, we might have gotten too excited. It came back to haunt us."

Austin was drafted by the Kansas City Royals in the first round of the 1998 draft. He had previously been drafted by the Montreal Expos in the 10th round in 1995 out of Kingwood (Texas) High. He decided not to sign at that point and went on to Stanford.

—JOHN MANUEL

PREVIOUS WINNERS

1981—Mike Sodders, 3b, Arizona State
1982—Jeff Ledbetter, of-lhp, Florida State
1983—Dave Magadan, 1b, Alabama
1984—Oddibe McDowell, of, Arizona State
1985—Pete Incaviglia, of, Oklahoma State
1986—Casey Close, of, Michigan
1987—Robin Ventura, 3b, Oklahoma State
1988—John Olerud, 1b-lhp, Washington State
1989—Ben McDonald, rhp, Louisiana State
1990—Mike Kelly, of, Arizona State
1991—David McCarty, 1b, Stanford
1992—Phil Nevin, 3b, Cal State Fullerton
1993—Brooks Kieschnick, dh-rhp, Texas
1994—Jason Varitek, c, Georgia Tech
1995—Todd Helton, 1b-lhp, Tennessee
1996—Kris Benson, rhp, Clemson
1997—J.D. Drew, of, Florida State

in the 1990s—to drop its baseball program.

That move left the league's Northern Division with just three teams—Oregon State, Washington and Washington State—so league members announced in August a shift to a nine-team conference without divisions. Oregon does not have a baseball program.

"We really didn't have a choice," Pac-10 assistant commissioner Mike Matthews said. "NCAA rules state that for a conference to have two divisions, each of them must have as many as four teams. When Portland State dropped baseball, there were no real viable alternatives that could replace it."

Under the new alignment, Pac-10 teams will play eight three-game series against league opponents. A postseason tournament was voted down by league presidents. In the Six-Pac, teams played three-game home and home series against each other, resulting in particularly fierce competition.

"I think it will help us," said California coach Bob Milano, who has been at Cal since 1978. "My friends in the Southeastern Conference, Big 12 and Atlantic Coast Conference always thought we were nuts for

1998 COLLEGE ALL-AMERICA TEAM

Selected by Baseball America

FIRST TEAM

Pos.	Player, School	YR	HT	WT	B-T	AVG	AB	R	H	2B	3B	HR	RBI	SB
C	Sammy Serrano, Stetson	Jr.	6-2	200	R-R	.457	245	71	112	23	8	13	68	8
1B	Eddy Furniss, Louisiana State	Sr.	6-4	220	L-L	.403	236	85	95	27	3	28	76	0
2B	Jeff Pickler, Tennessee	Sr.	5-10	183	L-R	.445	245	79	109	30	2	7	61	25
3B	Aubrey Huff, Miami	Jr.	6-4	220	L-R	.412	233	71	96	20	0	21	95	4
SS	Adam Everett, South Carolina	Jr.	6-1	176	R-R	.375	267	71	100	21	4	13	63	15
OF	Bubba Crosby, Rice	Jr.	5-11	185	L-L	.394	221	73	87	15	3	25	91	2
OF	Mike Curry, South Carolina	Jr.	5-11	189	L-R	.400	260	102	104	15	5	16	46	60
OF	Eric Valent, UCLA	Jr.	6-0	195	L-L	.336	220	69	74	10	1	30	73	4
DH	Damon Thames, Rice	Jr.	6-1	170	R-R	.424	283	88	120	36	7	26	115	4
UT	Brad Wilkerson, Florida	Jr.	6-0	193	L-L	.347	222	86	77	13	3	23	70	20

Pos.	Player, School	YR	HT	WT	B-T	W	L	ERA	G	SV	IP	H	BB	SO
SP	Jeff Austin, Stanford	Jr.	6-0	185	R-R	12	4	3.11	18	0	133	118	32	136
SP	Seth Etherton, Southern California	Sr.	6-1	205	R-R	13	3	3.23	18	0	137	113	29	182
SP	Mike Fischer, South Alabama	Jr.	6-4	200	R-R	11	1	2.31	20	1	125	91	23	120
SP	Alex Santos, Miami	So.	6-1	205	R-R	15	1	2.54	18	0	110	85	28	142
RP	Josh Fogg, Florida	Jr.	6-2	205	R-R	7	2	2.03	40	13	84	63	30	114
UT	Brad Wilkerson, Florida	Jr.	6-0	193	L-L	10	5	5.05	18	0	118	134	69	136

SECOND TEAM

Pos.	Player, School	YR	HT	WT	B-T	AVG	AB	R	H	2B	3B	HR	RBI	SB
C	Eric Munson, Southern California	So.	6-3	220	L-R	.392	171	45	67	15	0	16	56	6
1B	Jason Hart, SW Missouri State	Jr.	6-3	220	R-R	.416	221	71	92	15	0	28	91	6
2B	Xavier Nady, California	Fr.	6-1	185	R-R	.404	223	65	90	28	5	15	70	9
3B	Paul Day, Long Beach State	Jr.	6-1	200	R-R	.401	274	83	110	16	6	15	89	21
SS	Zach Sorensen, Wichita State	Jr.	6-1	185	B-R	.424	262	103	111	25	2	17	94	22
OF	Clinton Johnston, Vanderbilt	Jr.	6-3	200	L-L	.424	198	58	84	16	0	19	74	6
OF	Kevin Mench, Delaware	So.	6-1	205	R-R	.455	187	86	85	16	2	33	72	16
OF	Jeff Ryan, Wichita State	Jr.	5-10	180	R-R	.441	261	109	115	33	7	23	105	31
DH	Pat Magness, Wichita State	So.	6-3	225	L-R	.464	224	75	104	19	2	21	100	0
UT	Brandon Inge, Va. Commonwealth	Jr.	6-0	195	B-R	.330	212	68	70	21	5	15	61	21

Pos.	Player, School	YR	HT	WT	B-T	W	L	ERA	G	SV	IP	H	BB	SO
SP	Matt Burch, Va. Commonwealth	Jr.	6-3	185	R-R	12	4	2.59	18	0	139	113	41	122
SP	Ryan Rupe, Texas A&M	Sr.	6-6	225	R-R	11	4	2.87	15	0	113	95	23	125
SP	Jeff Weaver, Fresno State	Jr.	6-5	200	R-R	10	4	2.98	17	1	124	108	37	156
SP	Kip Wells, Baylor	Jr.	6-3	196	R-R	13	4	3.71	20	0	124	121	44	135
RP	Jack Krawczyk, Southern Cal	Sr.	6-5	195	R-R	3	2	2.01	34	23	49	46	8	51
UT	Brandon Inge, Va. Commonwealth	Jr.	6-0	195	B-R	5	2	2.09	23	11	43	27	8	59

THIRD TEAM

Pos.	Player, School	YR	HT	WT	B-T	AVG	AB	R	H	2B	3B	HR	RBI	SB
C	Josh Bard, Texas Tech	So.	6-3	205	B-R	.383	264	56	101	22	2	17	71	1
1B	Casey Bookout, Oklahoma	Jr.	6-5	235	L-R	.405	222	74	90	12	0	26	76	5
2B	Willie Bloomquist, Arizona State	So.	5-11	180	R-R	.414	263	88	109	14	9	4	61	33
3B	Brant Ust, Notre Dame	So.	6-1	190	R-R	.373	217	55	81	20	1	18	58	11
SS	Bobby Hill, Miami	So.	5-10	170	B-R	.404	240	87	97	17	0	12	59	46
OF	Chris Magruder, Washington	Jr.	6-1	200	B-R	.402	219	89	88	18	4	11	57	33
OF	Terrmel Sledge, Long Beach State	Jr.	6-0	180	L-L	.392	286	99	112	25	5	13	63	26
OF	Jason Tyner, Texas A&M	Jr.	6-1	167	L-L	.385	278	71	107	12	2	0	31	39
DH	Pat Burrell, Miami	Jr.	6-4	225	R-R	.432	118	44	51	7	0	17	47	5
UT	Jason Jennings, Baylor	So.	6-3	225	L-R	.327	211	42	69	14	0	18	58	0

Pos.	Player, School	YR	HT	WT	B-T	W	L	ERA	G	SV	IP	H	BB	SO
SP	Nate Bump, Penn State	Sr.	6-3	185	R-R	7	3	2.62	13	0	106	95	25	135
SP	Benito Flores, Cal State Fullerton	Sr.	6-1	185	L-L	12	0	3.52	18	1	123	120	34	100
SP	John Hendricks, Wake Forest	Jr.	6-1	191	L-L	13	4	3.14	27	2	143	131	34	111
SP	Shane Wright, Texas Tech	Sr.	6-2	210	R-R	14	1	2.71	21	2	153	166	20	116
RP	Robbie Morrison, Miami	Jr.	6-0	215	R-R	2	2	4.24	37	12	40	34	10	67
UT	Jason Jennings, Baylor	So.	6-3	225	L-R	11	4	5.08	20	2	117	123	53	126

Player of the Year: Jeff Austin, rhp, Stanford.
Coach of the Year: Pat Murphy, Arizona State.
Freshman of the Year: Xavier Nady, 2b, California.

Coach of the Year

ASU's Murphy travels unorthodox path to pinnacle of college game

Pat Murphy's college baseball career got off to a fitful start.

He wanted to go to Notre Dame to play football but wasn't accepted. He made pit stops at Bowling Green (where he played baseball and football) and LeMoyne (where he played basketball), but neither school worked out. So the Syracuse, N.Y., native packed up his car and headed south on Interstate 95 to pursue a boxing career.

He kept going until he got to Boca Raton, Fla., about 40 miles north of his intended target of Miami. He saw a highway sign that read, "Florida Atlantic University," and weaved his way through campus to the baseball coach's office.

It was January 1981. Steve Traylor remembers it vividly.

"He walks into my office and says, 'I was just driving down I-95 and I was wondering if you had a baseball team,' " says Traylor, now the head coach at Duke. "And I said, 'As a matter of fact, we just started one.' So he said he was going to come to school and join the team.

Pat Murphy

"We had started classes so I really didn't think anything of it. But a half-hour later he calls me from the admissions office and says, 'I'm in school. When is practice?' "

Traylor had just completed the first baseball practice in Florida Atlantic history with 12 walk-ons. Murphy became his 13th and most indispensable player on a team that went 15-16.

From those modest beginnings, Murphy has carved a unique college career, first as a player but most of all as a coach. He's risen from coaching Division III Maryville (Tenn.) College, where he went 10-21 as a 24-year-old in his first coaching job, to leading tradition-rich Arizona State, where he replaced 1,100-game winner Jim Brock.

And he's risen to the top of his profession. In his fourth season at Arizona State, Murphy led his team through the Midwest Regional as a No. 3 seed, giving him his first trip to the College World Series. His Sun Devils won their first three games in Omaha before falling to Southern California in the championship game.

For leading Arizona State back to Omaha, Pat Murphy was named Baseball America's 1998 Coach of the Year. He became the second Arizona State coach to win the award. Brock, who died shortly after leading the 1994 team to the College World Series, won it in 1988.

Murphy admitted that following a legend like Brock was a challenge that had vexed him in his career and especially in 1998, when the Sun Devils lost six straight games in March against Oklahoma, Southern California and Fresno State.

Murphy decided he needed help, so he picked up the phone and called former Nebraska football coach Tom Osborne.

"I didn't think we were going to win another game," Murphy said. "I didn't know the man, I've never met him. I called him cold and asked him if I could get a few minutes of his time. He called me back, and we ended up talking for about 35 minutes."

Osborne and Murphy spoke of the difficulty of replacing coaches of the stature of Brock and Osborne's predecessor, Bob Devaney, who won back-to-back national championships in 1970-71.

"We talked about what really helped him, his faith and what was really important to him," Murphy said. "He reminded me to keep my head down and just do my job. I haven't had a chance to thank him yet, but it really helped."

—JOHN MANUEL

PREVIOUS WINNERS

1981—Ron Fraser, Miami
1982—Gene Stephenson, Wichita State
1983—Barry Shollenberger, Alabama
1984—Augie Garrido, Cal State Fullerton
1985—Ron Polk, Mississippi State
1986—Skip Bertman, Louisiana State
Dave Snow, Loyola Marymount
1987—Mark Marquess, Stanford
1988—Jim Brock, Arizona State
1989—Dave Snow, Long Beach State
1990—Steve Webber, Georgia
1991—Jim Hendry, Creighton
1992—Andy Lopez, Pepperdine
1993—Gene Stephenson, Wichita State
1994—Jim Morris, Miami
1995—Rod Delmonico, Tennessee
1996—Skip Bertman, Louisiana State
1997—Jim Wells, Alabama

playing each other six times. We have a chance to have better records and better RPIs now because we won't be beating each other up.

"It's a necessary evil, though. I'm not happy we don't get to play Stanford, USC and UCLA six times a year."

In Other News . . .

■ Cal State Northridge's program, declared dead after the 1997 season, returned with a flourish. Coach Mike Batesole led the program to a 33-19 record despite having four players on his roster in January. The Matadors cobbled together a roster of transfers, junior-college players and freshmen after their program was restored to full-time status in September 1997.

■ The Western Athletic Conference imploded, with eight core members leaving the league. Fresno State,

Freshman of the Year

No matter what position he plays, Cal star a fixture with the bat

Opinions vary on what position California's Xavier Nady should play.

He played second base and shortstop for the Bears in 1998. Cal coach Bob Milano says he's a natural shortstop. Nady got votes for the Pacific-10's all-conference team at both positions, and the St. Louis Cardinals drafted him as a shortstop in 1997.

So what does Nady think he is?

"I think I'm probably more of a third baseman, to tell the truth," he said. "I've played the middle infield all of my life, but sooner or later I'm going to get moved, I'm sure. I don't see myself as a second baseman, although I love the position. I'd love to stick around, I just enjoyed playing it so much this year."

No matter what position he played, it was Nady's bat that carried him to the honor of Baseball America's 1998 Freshman of the Year. He hit .404 with 15 home runs and 70 RBIs, breaking Cal records for doubles and slugging percentage set by eventual big leaguers Jeff Kent and Kevin Maas.

Xavier Nady

Nady's offense was attention-getting. Stanford righthander Jeff Austin, the 1998 College Player of the Year, called Nady the toughest batter he faced all year. Not UCLA's Eric Valent, the Pac-10's all-time home run leader. Not Eric Munson, the powerful catcher of national champion Southern California.

Nady, at 6-foot-1, 185 pounds, had a knack for making contact that is rarely found in a freshman power hitter. He fanned just 40 times in 223 at-bats. Meanwhile, he had a .776 slugging percentage with 28 doubles, and his 173 total bases gave him another school record. His homer total was a school record for a freshman and seventh highest in Cal history.

"He's got great hand-eye coordination and he loves the weights," Milano said. "He is way into swinging the weights around. The reason he is so good is because he's strong without being muscle-bound. He's got athletic ability; he's strong, flexible and quick."

Milano got to coach Nady even after the Cardinals made him their fourth-round draft pick in 1997 out of Salinas (Calif.) High. "I didn't think there was any way we were going to keep him," Milano said. "I sent him a bunch of information when he got drafted, just to let him know we were still here."

"I was planning on attending college all along," Nady said. "It was going to take something dramatic to make me change my mind."

Nady chose Cal over Pepperdine, in part because of Cal's academic reputation and in part because "I had a blast on my recruiting trip." The Bears' 22-32 finish and second straight 24-loss Pac-10 South season took some of the thrill away, but Nady hopes to lead a rebound in 1999.

"This year was good for me, but next year I hope can be good for the team," he said.

BA's 1998 Freshman All-America team:

C—Scott Walter, Loyola Marymount (.383-8-67). **1B**—Todd Faulkner, Auburn (.382-20-65). **2B**—Xavier Nady, California (.404-15-70). **3B**—Garrett Atkins, UCLA (.383-9-54). **SS**—Tim Hummel, Old Dominion (.386-7-55). **OF**—Patrick Boyd, Clemson (.344-8-59); Matt Diaz, Florida State (.395-21-81); Matt Longo, Villanova (.393-12-47). **DH**—Joe Borchard, Stanford (.330-10-52). **Util**—Hayden Gliemmo, Auburn (.319-3-22; 13-3, 4.94).

P—Kip Bouknight, South Carolina (11-3, 4.07); Aaron Heilman, Notre Dame (7-3, 1.61, 9 SV); Kevin McGerry, St. John's (6-2, 2.06); Nick Stocks, Florida State (7-2, 2.35); Justin Wayne, Stanford (6-0, 3.78, 6 SV).

PREVIOUS WINNERS

1982—Cory Snyder, 3b, Brigham Young
1983—Rafael Palmeiro, of, Mississippi State
1984—Greg Swindell, lhp, Texas
1985—Jack McDowell, rhp, Stanford
Ron Wenrich, of, Georgia
1986—Robin Ventura, 3b, Oklahoma State
1987—Paul Carey, of, Stanford
1988—Kirk Dressendorfer, rhp, Texas
1989—Alex Fernandez, rhp, Miami
1990—Jeffrey Hammonds, of, Stanford
1991—Brooks Kieschnick, rhp-dh, Texas
1992—Todd Walker, 2b, Louisiana State
1993—Brett Laxton, rhp, Louisiana State
1994—R.A. Dickey, rhp, Tennessee
1995—Kyle Peterson, rhp, Stanford
1996—Pat Burrell, 3b, Miami
1997—Brian Roberts, ss, North Carolina

Hawaii, Rice, San Jose State and Texas Christian were left behind while baseball programs at Air Force, Brigham Young, Nevada-Las Vegas, New Mexico, San Diego State and Utah will leave the conference and form their own league. The WAC will play 1999 as a one-division, 11-team round-robin, then split up.

■ Furniss became the SEC's all-time leader in hits (352), home runs (80), RBIs (308) and doubles (87).

■ Four coaches reached 1,000 career victories in 1998–including two, Florida State's Mike Martin and Illinois' Itch Jones, on the same day. Also reaching the 1,000-win plateau were Arkansas' Norm DeBriyn and Hawaii's Les Murakami. They swelled the ranks of coaches to reach the mark to 20, with 12 of them active. UCLA's Gary Adams finished just short and enters 1999 with 991 wins.

■ Florida set an NCAA record when 20 consecutive batters reached base over two innings against Kentucky. Casey Smith ended the first inning with a single and a caught stealing, and the Gators' first 19 batters in the second all reached before an out was recorded. Florida, which reached the College World Series, won the game 32-10.

COLLEGE BASEBALL

NCAA DIVISION I LEADERS

TEAM BATTING

BATTING AVERAGE	G	AVG
Wichita State	63	.369
West Virginia	55	.358
Brigham Young	53	.356
Long Beach State	67	.354
New Mexico State	52	.351
Eastern Illinois	53	.349
Long Island	38	.348
Oral Roberts	65	.348
Illinois	63	.347
Jackson State	50	.346

RUNS	G	R
Wichita State	63	760
Florida State	73	638
Miami (Fla.)	63	637
Long Beach State	67	629
Florida	64	618
Oklahoma	62	606
Auburn	64	595
Tulane	63	593
Rice	63	588
Texas Tech	64	583
Louisiana State	67	583

DOUBLES	G	2B
Wichita State	63	202
New Mexico	58	181
Texas Tech	64	172
Tulane	63	168
Cal State Fullerton	64	167

TRIPLES	G	3B
Arizona	56	38
Campbell	58	35
San Diego State	57	34
Grambling State	47	33
Texas Christian	56	33

HOME RUNS	G	HR
Louisiana State	67	157
Miami (Fla.)	63	139
Florida	64	132
Wichita State	63	124
Alabama	64	122
South Carolina	62	122
Eastern Illinois	53	120
Brigham Young	53	118
Rice	63	118
Baylor	62	115
Troy State	58	115

STOLEN BASES	G	SB	ATT
Western Carolina	60	153	175
Grambling State	47	150	184
Jackson State	50	149	166
Howard	60	147	175
UNC Greensboro	58	147	185
Oral Roberts	65	147	193
Texas Tech	64	146	202
South Alabama	61	144	187
Evansville	58	143	176
Harvard	48	142	203

TEAM PITCHING

W-L PERCENTAGE	W	L	PCT
Wichita State	56	7	.889
Delaware	43	10	.811
Miami (Fla.)	51	12	.810
Tulane	48	15	.762
Virginia Commonwealth	46	15	.754
Harvard	36	12	.750
Minnesota	45	15	.750
Western Carolina	45	15	.750
Stanford	42	14	.750
Southern California	49	17	.742

EARNED RUN AVERAGE	G	ERA
St. Francis (N.Y.)	39	3.46
LeMoyne	41	3.62
Florida State	73	3.78
Butler	54	3.81
Northwestern State	60	3.82
St. John's (N.Y.)	46	3.84
Virginia Commonwealth	61	3.86
Miami (Fla.)	63	3.87
Wichita State	63	3.92
Central Florida	62	3.94

TEAM FIELDING

FIELDING AVERAGE	G	AVG
Ohio State	53	.972
Arkansas State	50	.972
Texas Christian	[illegible]	.971
Oklahoma	62	.971
South Carolina	62	.969
Northeast Louisiana	55	.969
Miami (Fla.)	63	.969
Pepperdine	54	.969
St. John's (N.Y.)	46	.969
Stanford	57	.968

INDIVIDUAL BATTING

BATTING AVERAGE
(Minimum 125 At-Bats)

	AVG	G	AB	R	H	2B	3B	HR	RBI	BB	SO	SB
Pat Magness, Wichita State	.464	60	224	75	104	19	2	21	100	65	25	0
Sammy Serrano, Stetson	.457	62	245	71	112	23	8	13	68	18	27	8
Ryan Fleming, Dayton	.455	40	156	51	71	22	4	5	43	19	10	14
Kevin Mench, Delaware	.455	52	187	86	85	16	2	33	72	36	25	16
Aaron Meyer, Dartmouth	.450	41	151	42	68	12	0	11	48	15	15	9
Jeff Pickler, Tennessee	.445	55	245	79	109	30	2	7	61	30	9	25
Muchie Dagliere, Massachusetts	.444	38	151	39	67	16	0	1	49	12	4	4
Jeff Ryan, Wichita State	.441	63	261	109	115	33	7	23	105	43	42	31
Jon Palmieri, Wake Forest	.438	64	256	73	112	30	4	12	78	31	17	12
Bob Osipower, Lafayette	.438	36	128	27	56	13	1	4	28	11	8	0
Tom Kuempel, Marshall	.435	53	184	53	80	14	1	20	60	23	27	10
Mike Conway, Dartmouth	.434	41	173	41	75	18	0	2	28	12	7	13
Sean McGowan, Boston College	.432	39	146	49	63	12	3	16	55	21	27	1
Toph Lake, Navy	.431	37	137	45	59	13	3	5	32	26	18	9
Joe McNamee, West Virginia	.429	54	191	61	82	27	2	13	66	39	42	5
Jason Trott, Ohio State	.428	52	194	53	83	10	2	8	54	22	29	5
Mike Dzurilla, St. John's (N.Y.)	.427	46	185	60	79	15	4	9	49	12	19	20
Troy McNaughton, Brig. Young	.427	53	218	76	93	25	3	22	74	42	29	10
Mike Dean, Oral Roberts	.426	60	230	57	98	15	5	11	63	18	34	26
Spencer Oborn, Brigham Young	.426	52	209	69	89	20	5	15	64	26	27	24
Clinton Johnston, Vanderbilt	.424	53	198	58	84	16	0	19	74	42	40	6
Craig Delk, Murray State	.424	52	191	47	81	18	2	6	40	23	30	2
Damon Thames, Rice	.424	63	283	88	120	36	7	26	115	13	35	4
Bo Robinson, UNC Charlotte	.424	62	250	79	106	32	2	19	100	49	18	2
Zach Sorensen, Wichita State	.424	62	262	103	111	25	2	17	94	55	33	22
Tony DeMarco, UNLV	.422	47	187	42	79	18	1	8	47	17	24	0
Chuck Lopez, Long Beach State	.422	66	268	77	113	17	4	4	52	26	29	7
Rick Hollern, Central Michigan	.421	56	178	43	75	10	2	7	41	20	24	9
Matt Peters, Texas-Pan Am	.420	49	138	33	58	8	3	1	13	10	10	11
B.J. Barns, Duquesne	.420	47	169	55	71	11	3	20	58	30	23	7
Royce Huffman, Texas Christian	.420	56	212	63	89	18	4	17	77	44	32	10
Joe McCullough, Monmouth	.420	51	212	60	89	19	5	12	79	11	18	8
Travis Copley, Tennessee	.419	45	148	38	62	16	1	5	46	16	20	3
Cristian Jung, Fairfield	.418	44	158	43	66	18	1	2	20	12	14	3
Rickie Miller, Grambling State	.417	44	127	50	53	13	5	0	30	40	18	8
Ryan Anholt, Northwestern St.	.417	60	211	64	88	14	4	16	71	39	28	13
Shayne Carnes, Alabama-Birm.	.417	53	211	64	88	18	1	23	87	40	23	7
Jamie Hammond, West Virginia	.417	55	192	45	80	8	0	0	44	19	18	19
Jason Hart, Southwest Missouri St.	.416	53	221	71	92	15	0	28	91	24	38	6
Keith Treonze, Lehigh	.415	39	135	31	56	9	3	4	37	11	22	5
Shawn Fagan, Penn State	.415	49	176	52	73	6	1	12	47	31	33	10
John Summers, Utah	.415	50	193	61	80	15	3	23	68	26	25	2
Willie Bloomquist, Arizona St.	.414	64	263	88	109	14	9	4	61	59	33	33
Kip Provines, Indiana State	.414	54	210	41	87	15	2	13	64	11	39	8
Nakia Hill, Cal St. Northridge	.414	55	232	69	96	16	3	15	41	31	36	13
Drew Corradini, Pennsylvania	.414	35	133	32	55	10	1	1	20	6	9	14
Todd Benke, Navy	.413	42	167	55	69	18	4	6	51	12	2	4
Shawn Leimbek, Iowa State	.413	39	155	37	64	14	1	5	36	17	14	3
Aubrey Huff, Miami (Fla.)	.412	63	233	71	96	20	0	21	95	39	32	4
Brian Wiese, Mississippi State	.412	64	250	71	103	24	2	14	57	26	47	11
Ryan Duncheon, Illinois State	.411	51	192	42	79	17	2	18	68	25	25	3
Dorian Cameron, Coastal Carolina	.411	58	236	57	97	17	1	3	42	15	28	12
Dave Marciniak, Rutgers	.410	46	188	58	77	24	4	6	50	20	26	5
Joe Zeccardi, Long Island	.409	37	132	41	54	6	1	15	55	29	32	3
Danny Graham, Central Conn. St.	.409	45	159	40	65	20	3	11	56	18	25	7
Brian Smith, Kent	.408	55	196	47	80	10	0	8	49	21	15	7
Ryan Browning, Tennessee Tech	.408	46	174	41	71	20	1	4	39	18	31	1
David Dalton, Liberty	.408	59	201	59	82	16	0	10	39	16	24	26
Robb Quinlan, Minnesota	.408	60	238	87	97	15	2	24	59	28	33	6
Scott Pratt, Auburn	.407	64	258	82	105	21	6	11	59	51	41	33
Nick Stefonick, Washington	.407	51	177	49	72	18	5	7	54	14	33	14
Steve Tomshack, UMBC	.407	47	182	48	74	17	3	17	59	17	20	0
David Forst, Harvard	.406	48	165	32	67	15	3	5	39	9	20	12
Louie Fernandez, Fla. Int.	.406	58	217	55	88	15	2	21	72	40	27	8
Casey Bookout, Oklahoma	.405	62	222	74	90	12	0	26	76	48	27	5
Derek Wathan, Oklahoma	.405	59	252	75	102	16	5	6	52	21	25	21

RUNS	G	R
Jeff Ryan, Wichita State	63	109
Zach Sorensen, Wichita State	62	103
Mike Curry, South Carolina	62	102
Kevin Hooper, Wichita State	57	101
Terrmel Sledge, Long Beach St.	67	99
Keith Ginter, Texas Tech	64	97
Jose Zabala, Florida State	73	92
Chris Magruder, Washington	58	89
Willie Bloomquist, Arizona St.	64	88
Brian Cox, Florida State	72	88
Damon Thames, Rice	63	88
Bobby Hill, Miami (Fla.)	63	87
Robb Quinlan, Minnesota	60	87
Tyler Thompson, Indiana State	56	87
Kevin Mench, Delaware	52	86
Brad Wilkerson, Florida	64	86

HITS	G	H
Damon Thames, Rice	63	120
Jeff Ryan, Wichita State	63	115
Chuck Lopez, Long Beach St.	66	113
Brian Cox, Florida State	72	112
Jon Palmieri, Wake Forest	64	112
Sammy Serrano, Stetson	62	112
Terrmel Sledge, Long Beach St.	67	112
Zach Sorensen, Wichita State	62	111
Paul Day, Long Beach State	67	110
Willie Bloomquist, Arizona St.	64	109
Jeff Pickler, Tennessee	55	109
Jason Tyner, Texas A&M	64	107
Bo Robinson, UNC Charlotte	62	106
Scott Pratt, Auburn	64	105
Brian Ward, North Carolina St.	64	105

SLUGGING PERCENTAGE (Minimum 125 At-Bats)	G	PCT
Kevin Mench, Delaware	52	1.091
Eddy Furniss, Louisiana State	67	.898
Jeff Ryan, Wichita State	63	.885
Sean McGowan, Boston College	39	.884
John Summers, Utah	50	.881
Damon Thames, Rice	63	.876
B.J. Barns, Duquesne	47	.876
Troy McNaughton, Brig. Young	53	.872
Jason Hart, SW Missouri State	53	.864
Jeff Tidwell, Jacksonville St.	54	.863

TOTAL BASES	G	TB
Damon Thames, Rice	63	248
Jeff Ryan, Wichita State	63	231
Eddy Furniss, Louisiana State	67	212
James Matan, UNC Charlotte	62	209
Kevin Mench, Delaware	52	204
Bo Robinson, UNC Charlotte	62	199
Brian Cox, Florida State	72	195
Matt Diaz, Florida State	72	192
Jason Hart, SW Missouri State	53	191
Zach Sorensen, Wichita State	62	191
Charley Carter, Baylor	62	190
Pat Magness, Wichita State	60	190
Troy McNaughton, Brig. Young	53	190
Sammy Serrano, Stetson	62	190

Wichita State's Pat Magness
Nation's leading hitter

Rice's Damon Thames
120 hits, 115 RBIs

DOUBLES	G	2B
Damon Thames, Rice	63	36
Robert Gonzales, New Mexico	57	35
Jeff Ryan, Wichita State	63	33
Bo Robinson, UNC Charlotte	62	32
Brian Ward, North Carolina St.	64	31
Jon Palmieri, Wake Forest	64	30
Jeff Pickler, Tennessee	55	30
Brian Hughes, Tulane	63	29
Xavier Nady, California	54	28
Brian Cox, Florida State	72	27
Eddy Furniss, Louisiana State	67	27
Eric Hinske, Arkansas	58	27
Joe McNamee, West Virginia	54	27
Aaron Rowand, CS Fullerton	60	27
Eric Riggs, Central Florida	62	26
Ty Wigginton, UNC Asheville	58	26

TRIPLES	G	3B
Jon Topolski, Baylor	61	11
David Jones, Florida A&M	41	10
Willie Bloomquist, Arizona St.	64	9
Ned French, Stetson	57	9
Sean Mignogna, Georgetown	54	9
Chris Schmitz, McNeese State	55	9

HOME RUNS	G	HR
Kevin Mench, Delaware	52	33
Jason Sparks, Tulane	62	30
Eric Valent, UCLA	57	30
Brad Cresse, Louisiana State	63	29
Eddy Furniss, Louisiana State	67	28
Jason Hart, SW Missouri State	53	28
Ryan Fry, Missouri	54	27
James Matan, UNC Charlotte	62	27
Trey McClure, Louisiana State	67	27
Casey Bookout, Oklahoma	62	26
Damon Thames, Rice	63	26
Bubba Crosby, Rice	58	25
Casey Kelley, Washington St.	49	25
Craig Kuzmic, Texas A&M	66	25
Jeff Tidwell, Jacksonville St.	54	25
Sonny Cortez, Tennessee	52	24
Mike Dwyer, Richmond	57	24
Robb Quinlan, Minnesota	60	24
Shayne Carnes, Ala.-Birm.	53	23
Andy Osbolt, Georgia	53	23
Jeff Ryan, Wichita State	63	23
Jorge Soto, Troy State	58	23
Jason Story, New Mexico State	46	23
John Summers, Utah	50	23
Brad Wilkerson, Florida	64	23
Matt Diaz, Florida State	72	22
Matt Frick, Alabama	58	22
Troy McNaughton, Brig. Young	53	22
Craig Selander, Minnesota	59	22

RUNS BATTED IN	G	RBI
Damon Thames, Rice	63	115
Jeff Ryan, Wichita State	63	105
Pat Magness, Wichita State	60	100
Bo Robinson, UNC Charlotte	62	100
Aubrey Huff, Miami (Fla.)	63	95
James Matan, UNC Charlotte	62	95
Zach Sorensen, Wichita State	62	94
Bubba Crosby, Rice	58	91
Jason Hart, SW Missouri State	53	91
Jeremy Salazar, Florida State	71	91
Brad Cresse, Louisiana State	63	90
Josh Etheredge, Auburn	63	90
Jason Sparks, Tulane	62	90
Paul Day, Long Beach State	67	89
Shayne Carnes, Ala.-Birm.	53	87
Sonny Cortez, Tennessee	52	87
Brian Cox, Florida State	72	87
Charley Carter, Baylor	62	86
Andrew Beinbrink, Arizona St.	64	85
Richard Lee, Mississippi State	65	85
Lyle Overbay, Nevada	53	85
Matt Diaz, Florida State	72	84
Kevin Jordan, Texas Tech	63	84
Trey McClure, Louisiana State	67	84

WALKS	G	BB
Brad Wilkerson, Florida	64	85
Keith Ginter, Texas Tech	64	78
Eddy Furniss, Louisiana State	67	72
Brooks Badeaux, Fla. State	73	68
Tyler Thompson, Ind. State	56	68
Jose Zabala, Florida State	73	67

STRIKEOUTS	G	SO
Jorge Soto, Troy State	58	86
Adrian Mendoza, CS Northridge	54	74
Eric Stanton, South Carolina	62	73
Grant Reed, McNeese State	55	70
Miles Durham, Texas Tech	62	67

TOUGHEST TO STRIKE OUT (Minimum 125 At-Bats)	AB	SO	Ratio
Shaun Salmon, Army	155	0	—
Kevin Kim, Northeastern	171	1	171.0
Todd Benke, Navy	167	2	83.5
Antoine Jackson, Norfolk St.	130	2	65.0
John Salter, Stanford	134	3	44.7

STOLEN BASES	G	SB	ATT
Brian Roberts, No. Carolina	65	63	76
Mike Curry, South Carolina	62	60	69
Kalin Foulds, San Diego St.	56	58	66
Juan Pierre, So. Alabama	61	54	62
Terrence Smalls, Citadel	61	49	61
Bobby Hill, Miami (Fla.)	63	46	57
Schuyler Doakes, Jack. St.	50	45	49
Herbert Wheat, Howard	46	41	43
Gerald Parr, UNC Charlotte	62	41	48
Jason Tyner, Texas A&M	64	39	46
Shawn Pearson, Old Dom.	51	38	44
John Penatello, Iona	48	38	45
Torre Tyson, Missouri	54	37	41
Jason Maule, Cent. Conn. St.	43	37	42
Ricky Rowe, Troy State	58	37	45
Billy Colome, Charleston	57	36	42
Brian Hughes, Tulane	63	35	37
Chuck Koone, West. Car.	57	35	39
John Wagler, Richmond	59	35	41
Dominic Pattie, UNC Gboro	58	35	44

HIT BY PITCH	G	HBP
David Bacani, CS Fullerton	59	30
Corky Miller, Nevada	53	29
Darren Blakely, Hawaii	56	26
Kevin Ibach, LaSalle	40	24
Bryan Kennedy, Long Beach St.	67	24

INDIVIDUAL PITCHING

EARNED RUN AVERAGE

(Minimum 60 Innings)

	W	L	ERA	G	GS	CG	SV	IP	H	R	ER	BB	SO
Aaron Heilman, Notre Dame	7	3	1.61	31	1	0	9	67	40	16	12	10	79
Jay Krystofolski, Rhode Island	5	6	1.72	11	10	7	0	68	51	27	13	14	67
Eric Gutshall, Yale	5	6	1.83	19	9	9	4	74	52	29	15	29	79
Josh Fogg, Florida	7	2	2.03	40	0	0	13	84	63	27	19	30	114
Kevin McGerry, St. John's	6	2	2.06	12	9	2	0	66	49	20	15	32	62
Brandon Emanuel, NW State	5	1	2.15	25	2	1	8	63	34	17	15	18	52
Mike Fischer, So. Alabama	11	1	2.31	20	15	7	1	125	91	33	32	23	120
Jason Parsons, UNC Greensboro	8	2	2.32	29	1	0	6	66	64	22	17	19	51
Nick Stocks, Florida State	7	2	2.35	17	11	1	0	77	65	30	20	54	81
Joe Lazewski, Valparaiso	6	3	2.43	11	11	4	0	70	64	29	19	11	60
Lee Gardner, Cent. Michigan	8	4	2.45	15	14	8	1	88	67	38	24	31	86
Chanx Martin, Beth.-Cookman	9	5	2.47	18	16	9	1	109	95	60	30	74	111
Jarrod Kingrey, Alabama	8	4	2.47	33	3	2	13	84	57	30	23	35	98
Justin Carter, South Alabama	8	3	2.52	26	2	0	5	82	77	30	23	31	83
Alex Santos, Miami (Fla.)	15	1	2.54	18	18	1	0	110	85	39	31	28	142
Matt Burch, Va. Commonwealth	12	4	2.59	18	18	11	0	139	113	50	40	41	122
Nate Bump, Penn State	7	3	2.62	13	13	6	0	106	85	42	31	25	135
Ben Birk, Minnesota	8	2	2.65	11	8	3	0	75	67	25	22	11	67
Shane Wright, Texas Tech	14	1	2.71	21	18	13	2	153	166	68	46	20	116
Ryan Spille, SE Missouri State	11	2	2.72	23	15	8	1	109	86	39	33	50	130
Santino Sarrica, St. Francis	7	2	2.73	10	10	3	0	66	58	30	20	26	61
Raul Echeverz, Tulane	7	1	2.78	19	9	0	1	74	76	36	23	27	63
Tim Kalita, Notre Dame	4	0	2.78	15	11	1	0	74	68	33	23	37	71
Jeff Urban, Ball State	8	3	2.79	15	15	5	0	81	70	37	25	22	78
David Balcer, NW State	7	3	2.84	25	7	1	1	63	59	29	20	25	49
Matt Massimi, Rider	6	4	2.84	11	11	5	0	70	63	27	22	21	62
Stephen Cowie, Duke	11	2	2.85	18	18	5	0	126	135	58	40	23	111
John Stewart, West. Michigan	9	3	2.85	18	14	11	1	107	105	41	34	11	71
Andy Warren, Sam Houston St.	6	2	2.85	14	12	5	2	88	62	32	28	29	50
Ryan Rupe, Texas A&M	11	4	2.87	15	15	7	0	113	95	43	36	23	125
Peter Bauer, South Carolina	7	0	2.93	14	11	1	0	68	59	26	22	22	68
Brian Lawrence, NW State	9	5	2.93	19	18	6	0	111	109	52	36	33	104
Steve Bechard, LeMoyne	7	4	2.95	11	11	7	0	73	63	28	24	12	46
Shane Nance, Houston	9	4	2.95	16	15	4	0	107	87	38	35	42	93
Mike Anders, Bucknell	8	3	2.96	13	11	8	0	85	93	36	28	11	73
John Bentley, Florida State	7	2	2.96	16	11	0	1	70	71	32	23	11	38
Jeff Weaver, Fresno State	10	4	2.98	17	16	9	1	124	108	50	41	37	156
Brian Moyer, Monmouth	7	1	2.98	12	11	1	0	66	75	27	22	17	59

WINS	W	L
Alex Santos, Miami (Fla.)	15	1
Shane Wright, Texas Tech	14	1
Josh Bobbitt, Tulane	13	1
Geoff Geary, Oklahoma	13	1
Darryl Roque, Miami (Fla.)	13	2
Javier Pamus, San Jose State	13	3
Seth Etherton, Southern Cal	13	3
Hayden Gliemmo, Auburn	13	3
John Hendricks, Wake Forest	13	4
Kip Wells, Baylor	13	4
Chad Berryman, Va. Commonwealth	13	4

LOSSES	W	L
Sean Richardson, Coppin State	0	13
Nick Burns, Coppin State	1	13
Mike Zirelli, Cal Poly SLO	3	12
Vannie Coles, Md.-East. Shore	1	11
Troy Young, Morehead State	1	11

APPEARANCES	G
Derrick DePriest, North Carolina	44
Josh Fogg, Florida	40
Tom Martin, Citadel	38
Robbie Morrison, Miami (Fla.)	37
Chuck Crumpton, Arizona State	36

COMPLETE GAMES	GS	CG
Shane Wright, Texas Tech	18	13
Matt Burch, Va. Commonwealth	18	11
John Hendricks, Wake Forest	15	11
John Stewart, West. Michigan	14	11
Mark Ciccarelli, Marist	11	10
Kurt Umbarger, Murray State	13	10

SAVES	G	SV
Jack Krawczyk, Southern Cal	34	23
Josh Fogg, Florida	40	13
Jarrod Kingrey, Alabama	33	13
Jason Arnold, Central Florida	28	12
Robbie Morrison, Miami (Fla.)	37	12
Marc Bluma, Wichita State	25	11
Brandon Inge, Va. Comm.	23	11
Bobby Castelli, Eastern Illinois	29	10
Van Johnson, Mississippi State	34	10

Miami's Alex Santos

Led nation with 15 wins

Kyle Kimoto, Southern Utah	24	10
Mickey Moses, Cleveland State	27	10
Joseph Ojeda, St. Francis (N.Y.)	18	10
Todd Raithel, Louisville	25	10

INNINGS	G	IP
Shane Wright, Texas Tech	21	153
John Hendricks, Wake Forest	27	143
Matt Burch, Va. Commonwealth	18	139
Seth Etherton, Southern Cal	18	137
Jeff Austin, Stanford	18	133
Philip Devey, SW Louisiana	25	132
David D'Amico, Mercer	20	131

WALKS	IP	BB
Mike MacDougal, Wake Forest	91	78
Shawn Sonnier, Louisiana Tech	123	75
Chanx Martin, Beth.-Cookman	109	74
Alan Harrison, Howard	60	73
Mike Bynum, North Carolina	99	71

Florida's Josh Fogg

7-2 record, 13 saves

STRIKEOUTS	IP	SO
Seth Etherton, Southern Cal	137	182
Brian Rogers, Citadel	119	159
Brian Wiley, Citadel	102	159
Jeff Weaver, Fresno State	124	156
Monty Ward, Texas Tech	108	151
Edwin Franco, Fla. International	113	147
Adam Pettyjohn, Fresno State	126	145
Philip Devey, SW Louisiana	132	143
Geoff Geary, Oklahoma	123	142
Alex Santos, Miami (Fla.)	110	142
Raul Garcia, Fla. International	109	140
Ryan Mills, Arizona State	115	140
John McKay, UNC Charlotte	114	138
Jim Serrano, New Mexico	116	137
Jeff Austin, Stanford	133	136
Ron Deubel, Coastal Carolina	118	136
Brad Wilkerson, Florida	118	136
Nate Bump, Penn State	106	135
Randy Keisler, Lousiana State	94	135
Kip Wells, Baylor	124	135
Josh Bobbitt, Tulane	117	133
Chuck Crowder, Georgia Tech	125	133
David D'Amico, Mercer	131	130
Ryan Spille, SE Missouri State	109	130
Casey Fossum, Texas A&M	123	129
David Walling, Arkansas	103	128
Jason Jennings, Baylor	117	126
Ryan Rupe, Texas A&M	113	125
Doug Thompson, Louisiana St.	116	124
Matt Burch, Va. Commonwealth	139	122
Jason Norton, South Alabama	105	121
Mike Fischer, South Alabama	125	120
Zack Frachiseur, Georgia	102	120
Benji Miller, Liberty	103	119
Jody Fuller, Tennessee-Martin	85	118
Jeff Nichols, Rice	120	117
James Johnson, Arizona	98	116
Shane Wright, Texas Tech	153	116

STRIKEOUTS/9 INNINGS (Minimum 50 Innings)	IP	SO	AVG
Brian Wiley, Citadel	102	159	14.1
Rik Currier, Southern Cal	71	100	12.6
Monty Ward, Texas Tech	108	151	12.5
Jody Fuller, Tenn.-Martin	85	118	12.5
Chris Pine, Oregon State	75	104	12.4
Randy Keisler, LSU	100	135	12.2
Josh Fogg, Florida	84	114	12.2
Rickey Lewis, Miss. Valley	62	83	12.1
Brian Rogers, Citadel	119	159	12.0
Mark Mulder, Michigan St.	85	113	12.0
Bryan Williamson, Jax St.	86	115	12.0
Seth Etherton, So. Cal	137	182	12.0

BASEBALL AMERICA'S COLLEGE TOP 25

BATTERS: 10 or more at-bats.
PITCHERS: 5 or more innings.
Boldface indicates selected in 1997 draft.

1. SOUTHERN CALIFORNIA

Coach: Mike Gillespie **Record:** 49-17

BATTING	AVG	AB	R	H	2B	3B	HR	RBI	SB
Munson, Eric, c	.392	171	45	67	15	0	16	56	6
Hanoian, Greg, of	.358	137	34	49	10	0	2	20	3
Casillas, Carlos, 1b	.357	14	3	5	0	0	0	2	1
Gorr, Robb, 1b	.345	278	63	96	13	3	16	79	11
Ensberg, Morgan, 3b	.344	244	74	84	22	0	21	69	20
Freitas, Jeremy, of	.340	212	57	72	11	1	14	58	4
Davidson, Seth, ss	.333	204	46	68	13	2	5	31	17
Lane, Jason, of-p	.332	232	55	77	18	1	14	50	8
Rachels, Wes, 2b	.327	251	48	82	16	1	3	36	16
Ticehurst, Brad, of	.302	202	45	61	8	1	18	54	10
Correa, Dominic, if	.270	54	13	15	3	0	0	7	2
DePippo, Jeff, c-of	.273	132	34	36	8	0	3	20	9
Townsend, Josh, c	.273	11	3	3	1	0	0	3	0
Perry, Rod, of	.247	93	12	23	1	3	1	14	3
Schultz, Kevin, if	.231	26	8	6	2	0	0	3	1

PITCHING	W	L	ERA	G	SV	IP	H	BB	SO
Krawczyk, Jack	3	2	2.01	34	23	49	46	8	51
Etherton, Seth	13	3	3.23	18	0	137	113	29	182
Flores, Ronald	0	0	3.60	11	0	15	15	3	13
Saenz, Jason	1	2	4.42	17	0	37	36	30	34
Penney, Mike	8	4	5.25	21	0	106	123	38	56
Currier, Rik	6	1	5.30	20	0	71	73	39	100
Lane, Jason	9	2	5.34	34	0	62	75	15	38
Weibling, Mike	2	0	5.47	21	1	26	34	14	22
Immel, Steve	5	1	6.17	22	0	42	49	23	37
Jones, Craig	2	2	10.09	15	0	30	40	28	29
Kramer, Shaun	0	0	11.37	8	0	6	8	5	10

2. ARIZONA STATE

Coach: Pat Murphy **Record:** 41-23

BATTING	AVG	AB	R	H	2B	3B	HR	RBI	SB
Bloomquist, Willie, of-2b	.414	263	88	109	14	9	4	61	33
Myers, Casey, dh	.386	184	35	71	17	0	8	58	1
Moreno, Mikel, of	.354	274	78	97	16	1	11	56	27
Phelps, Jeff, 1b-dh	.348	155	33	54	10	2	5	39	7
Jones, Jeremy, c	.333	123	24	41	11	1	0	23	2
Beinbrink, Andrew, 3b	.328	235	63	77	22	4	12	85	20
Gosewisch, Chip, ss	.319	69	14	22	2	1	0	13	4
Collins, Michael, ss	.285	200	44	57	12	3	4	37	7
Arguelles, Rudy, of	.278	187	55	52	4	2	0	24	9
Sitzman, Jay, of	.277	47	11	13	2	1	0	4	3
Leon, Richy, 2b-p	.272	136	30	37	8	1	4	23	1
Meier, Dan, 1b-dh	.238	172	35	41	9	1	6	26	2
Halvorson, Greg, c	.231	117	16	27	1	1	3	20	2
Delucchi, Dustin, of	.222	99	19	22	4	0	0	11	2
Ernster, Mark, if	.100	10	8	1	0	0	0	2	0

PITCHING	W	L	ERA	G	SV	IP	H	BB	SO
Crumpton, Chuck	3	7	3.00	36	5	63	65	31	61
Kramer, Aaron	8	2	3.94	29	3	75	67	21	80
Pennington, Chad	7	2	4.20	22	3	75	64	35	87
Mills, Ryan	8	4	4.68	20	0	115	110	54	140
Milner, Robby	0	0	5.27	15	0	27	25	21	25
Lowery, Phill	8	6	5.53	18	0	99	90	47	96
Leon, Richy	4	0	6.46	15	0	63	82	23	57
Call, Colin	1	0	6.52	4	0	10	9	5	7
Friedberg, Drew	0	0	6.65	19	0	22	28	14	24
Gehrke, Jay	2	1	7.36	5	0	15	13	4	8

EFF GOLDEN

Hurricane force
Miami's Pat Burrell hit .432 with 17 homers

3. MIAMI

Coach: Jim Morris **Record:** 51-12

BATTING	AVG	AB	R	H	2B	3B	HR	RBI	SB
Fleizach, Frank, 1b	.450	20	7	9	1	0	3	14	0
Burrell, Pat, 3b-dh	.432	118	44	51	7	0	17	47	5
Huff, Aubrey, 3b-1b	.412	233	71	96	20	0	21	95	4
Hill, Bobby, ss	.404	240	87	97	17	0	12	59	40
Michaels, Jason, of	.378	196	75	74	16	1	19	65	18
Crespo, Manny, 2b	.348	201	54	70	9	2	16	63	4
Alvarez, German, of	.340	188	64	64	12	2	15	51	10
Jacobson, Russ, c	.314	194	43	61	15	1	9	38	0
Seever, Brian, of	.311	167	52	52	9	2	6	20	31
Muller, Mike, c	.299	127	32	38	4	0	7	30	0
Brown, Kevin, 1b-3b	.286	112	28	32	8	0	4	32	1
Walker, Mark, of	.259	85	20	22	0	1	4	21	4
Jimerson, Charlton, of	.253	75	17	19	4	2	2	13	9
Saggese, Rick, 1b-dh	.229	131	23	30	5	2	4	29	1
Alfonso, Gus, 2b	.174	23	3	4	2	0	0	6	1
Lovelady, Greg, c	.154	26	5	4	0	0	0	1	0
Clute, Kris, 2b	.133	30	12	4	1	1	0	4	2

PITCHING	W	L	ERA	G	SV	IP	H	BB	SO
Smith, Dan	0	0	1.29	4	0	7	7	0	8
Kamalsky, Matt	1	0	2.40	15	0	30	25	20	33
Santos, Alex	15	1	2.54	18	0	110	85	28	142
Howell, Greg	4	0	3.15	32	0	40	37	12	46
Ozias, Todd	6	2	3.26	24	0	69	57	27	66
Farmer, Tom	0	0	3.60	16	1	20	16	5	13
Gil, David	3	2	3.82	10	0	38	42	20	38
Morrison, Robbie	2	2	4.24	37	12	40	34	10	67
Roque, Darryl	13	2	4.38	20	0	84	88	19	71
Gutierrez, Laz	4	1	4.75	34	1	42	42	21	45
Spassoff, Darin	2	2	5.77	13	0	53	75	24	33
Prendes, Alex	0	0	6.00	16	0	15	16	14	19
Lopez-Cao, Andrew	1	0	12.15	7	0	7	8	2	7

4. LOUISIANA STATE

Coach: Skip Bertman **Record:** 48-19

BATTING	AVG	AB	R	H	2B	3B	HR	RBI	SB
Furniss, Eddy, 1b	.403	236	85	95	27	3	28	76	0
McClure, Trey, 3b	.325	240	69	78	13	0	27	84	2
Cresse, Brad, c-dh	.323	232	55	75	12	0	29	90	0

BATTING	AVG	AB	R	H	2B	3B	HR	RBI	SB
Witten, Jeremy, of	.309	123	43	38	5	1	2	15	11
Higgins, Danny, of	.302	202	51	61	13	1	15	37	4
Harris, Cedrick, of	.298	215	45	64	5	2	10	36	5
Dalton, Josh, ss	.298	242	56	72	11	2	3	43	28
Farnhart, Clint, c-dh	.278	205	38	57	15	0	12	47	1
Bennett, Byron, of	.200	50	0	10	[illegible]	1	0	8	0
Barbler, Blair, 2b	.247	251	55	62	11	2	9	42	5
Leaumont, Jeff, of-dh	.246	122	22	30	6	0	10	26	0
Davis, Wes, of	.246	138	36	34	11	0	10	27	6
Thibodeaux, Johnnie, 3b	.207	29	9	6	0	0	1	7	1

PITCHING	W	L	ERA	G	SV	IP	H	BB	SO
Colvin, Matt	0	0	2.84	4	0	6	7	2	8
Nugent, Tim	3	0	2.87	11	1	30	18	23	36
Grace, Bryan	2	1	4.15	7	1	25	21	19	17
Thompson, Doug	12	5	4.24	24	1	116	127	42	124
Bowe, Brandon	6	3	4.34	23	1	70	84	21	77
Demouy, Chris	5	2	4.46	33	3	71	80	33	92
Ainsworth, Kurt	0	0	4.50	6	0	8	10	7	14
Keisler, Randy	9	5	4.61	27	2	94	97	33	135
Guillory, Dan	2	0	4.71	21	3	33	39	9	42
Esteves, Jake	9	3	5.03	27	2	103	129	41	100

5. FLORIDA

Coach: Andy Lopez **Record:** 46-18

BATTING	AVG	AB	R	H	2B	3B	HR	RBI	SB
Smith, Casey, of	.388	250	59	97	18	1	12	68	8
Johannes, Todd, c	.375	16	3	6	0	0	0	0	0
Nicholson, Derek, of-3b	.365	241	66	88	20	4	15	66	6
Catalanotte, Greg, of	.360	261	72	94	23	2	13	61	10
Wilkerson, Brad, 1b-p	.347	222	86	77	13	3	23	70	20
Siegel, Matt, 3b	.342	152	45	52	12	2	4	28	4
Ellis, Mark, ss	.338	225	69	76	18	0	14	51	8
Ross, David, c	.332	238	54	79	21	0	19	70	7
Martin, Ty, 2b	.309	223	58	69	11	3	7	41	5
McKinney, Pete, of	.286	35	8	10	3	1	0	4	2
Haught, Brian, dh	.282	78	18	22	2	1	5	18	6
Dill, Jason, 1b-dh	.277	213	48	59	10	0	16	51	2
Floyd, Mike, of	.273	11	2	3	1	0	1	2	0
Wood, Taylor, if	.273	11	3	3	0	0	0	1	0
Hazzard, Chuck, dh-of	.241	58	15	14	4	1	2	6	3
Seroyer, Shane, c	.182	11	2	2	1	0	0	1	0
Canales, Josh, 2b	.161	31	6	5	0	1	1	6	0

PITCHING	W	L	ERA	G	SV	IP	H	BB	SO
Fogg, Josh	7	2	2.03	40	13	75	63	30	114
Wiegandt, K.O.	1	0	2.25	4	0	7	9	2	4
Grezlovski, Ben	1	0	3.45	23	1	26	34	15	40
Bond, Tommy	5	1	4.19	15	0	60	68	27	53
Gray, Michael	8	2	4.58	24	1	51	65	17	63
Wilkerson, Brad	10	5	5.05	18	0	118	134	69	136
Rodriguez, Sergio	1	0	6.12	13	0	22	36	11	17
McClendon, Matt	9	5	6.49	21	1	110	145	43	109
Cardozo, Jeff	1	2	6.65	13	0	19	26	8	13
Rose, Tommy	2	1	8.46	10	0	26	36	14	26
McFarland, Stuart	1	0	11.30	14	0	11	29	9	16

6. STANFORD

Coach: Mark Marquess **Record:** 42-14

BATTING	AVG	AB	R	H	2B	3B	HR	RBI	SB
Gall, John, 1b	.381	239	52	91	22	2	15	63	9
Gerut, Jody, of	.335	230	64	77	18	2	18	61	13
Borchard, Joe, dh-of	.330	203	45	67	18	1	10	55	4
Day, Nick, of	.323	155	30	50	13	2	1	22	3
Hochgesang, Josh, 3b	.315	197	54	62	14	4	10	39	8
Muth, Edmund, of	.308	221	61	68	17	5	14	51	7
Salter, John, c	.299	134	23	40	0	2	4	30	2
Pecci, Jay, ss	.294	214	49	63	9	1	4	31	10
Schrager, Tony, 2b	.273	220	45	60	10	1	11	42	9
Rizzo, Jeff, 3b	.271	70	13	19	4	0	1	15	1
Alvarado, Damien, c	.260	77	14	20	2	1	1	7	0
Thompson, Craig, if	.225	40	9	9	2	1	0	4	1
Savig, Joe, if	.091	11	1	1	0	0	0	0	0

PITCHING	W	L	ERA	G	SV	IP	H	BB	SO
Coose, Austin	3	0	1.78	24	1	35	23	16	31
Austin, Jeff	12	4	3.11	18	0	133	118	32	136
Drew, Brad	1	1	3.42	11	1	24	21	11	24
Wayne, Justin	6	0	3.78	25	6	81	81	26	76
Linville, Geoff	3	0	3.86	8	0	16	15	14	17
Cogan, Tony	3	0	4.05	23	3	27	33	12	20
Hutchinson, Chad	10	5	4.89	17	0	99	92	58	115
Hoard, Brent	3	3	6.05	14	0	58	56	49	67
Young, Jason	1	1	6.35	15	1	23	23	19	29

7. FLORIDA STATE

Coach: Mike Martin **Record:** 53-20

BATTING	AVG	AB	R	H	2B	3B	HR	RBI	SB
Cox, Brian, of	.393	285	88	112	27	1	18	87	27
Diaz, Matt, of	.390	269	67	105	17	2	22	84	11
Zabala, Jose, 3b	.338	260	92	88	17	0	3	39	14
Salazar, Jeremy, c	.337	258	69	87	19	0	19	91	2
Jernigan, Karl, of	.308	211	43	65	13	1	5	42	11
Cash, Kevin, 1b-dh	.296	233	54	69	15	4	7	48	1
Klosterman, Jeremiah, c	.291	55	7	16	4	0	2	14	0
Henderson, Terry, dh-of	.286	147	40	42	7	4	4	40	1
Groves, Brett, ss	.258	252	49	65	19	2	2	42	10
Woodward, Matt, 1b	.237	114	10	27	5	0	0	13	0
Badeaux, Brooks, 2b	.236	288	72	68	12	3	0	36	11
Mayfield, Henry, dh	.234	47	9	11	2	0	0	7	2
Otero, George, dh-of	.217	83	21	18	3	2	2	12	3
McCorkel, Shawn, of	.188	16	4	3	0	0	1	1	1
Heath, Eric, of	.133	15	2	2	0	0	0	3	0

PITCHING	W	L	ERA	G	SV	IP	H	BB	SO
DiBlasi, Mike	2	1	1.14	25	4	32	20	19	38
Stocks, Nick	7	2	2.35	17	0	77	65	54	81
Bentley, John	7	2	2.96	16	1	70	71	11	38
Ginn, Chris	2	2	3.16	18	1	37	31	21	37
Crawford, Wes	9	3	3.38	18	0	123	117	48	82
Proctor, Scott	3	1	3.49	27	7	39	28	24	45
Diaz, Zach	4	0	4.13	27	0	48	51	17	37
McDonald, Jon	10	4	4.56	19	0	105	91	52	101
Chavez, Chris	8	4	4.89	18	1	85	92	47	65
Kelly, David	0	0	7.90	19	0	14	12	15	10
Smalley, Mike	1	1	9.35	16	0	17	26	22	20

8. WICHITA STATE

Coach: Gene Stephenson **Record:** 56-7

BATTING	AVG	AB	R	H	2B	3B	HR	RBI	SB
Magness, Pat, dh-1b	.464	224	75	104	19	2	21	100	0
Ryan, Jeff, of	.441	261	109	115	33	7	23	105	31
Sorensen, Zach, ss	.424	262	103	111	25	2	17	94	22
Davis, Casey, of-dh	.379	161	51	61	13	1	11	43	18
Troutman, Jeremy, dh-p	.375	32	8	12	4	1	1	13	0
Hooper, Kevin, 2b	.358	229	101	82	22	5	4	47	21
Hayes, Tim, of-p	.352	125	35	44	13	3	9	41	2
Patrick, Matt, 1b	.338	136	36	46	14	3	7	45	3
Diggs, Brian, c	.333	15	8	5	2	0	0	2	0
Preston, Brian, c	.330	227	52	75	17	0	12	46	7
Schoenhofer, Brian, of-p	.327	52	15	17	1	0	0	9	2
Hill, Koyie, 3b	.323	217	60	70	17	1	1	43	6
Blue, Joey, of	.316	247	64	78	17	2	14	77	17
Johnson, Sean, c	.300	10	3	3	1	0	0	2	0
Blasi, Blake, 2b-ss	.277	47	18	13	2	3	2	10	3
Fogarty, Ben, of	.261	46	12	12	2	0	1	7	2

PITCHING	W	L	ERA	G	SV	IP	H	BB	SO
Dobson, Matt	0	0	0.00	5	0	6	4	1	4
Neubauer, Marc	0	0	0.00	5	0	5	5	0	6
Bluma, Marc	5	0	1.74	25	11	57	45	17	56
Hayes, Tim	0	0	2.00	6	0	9	4	1	10
Lee, Tymber	2	0	2.64	15	1	31	25	8	19
Troutman, Jeremy	4	0	2.81	18	2	32	30	13	20
Schoenhofer, Brian	1	0	3.46	9	1	13	12	6	7
Humphrey, Trip	5	0	3.52	7	0	23	23	4	14
Bryan, Erich	8	3	3.68	14	1	78	87	23	53
Christensen, Ben	9	0	4.24	12	0	68	67	17	52
Bauer, Greg	4	2	4.69	15	1	48	62	19	43
Foral, Steve	10	1	5.09	15	0	87	95	25	81
Sloan, Brandon	6	1	5.15	10	0	44	50	15	29
Robertson, Nate	0	0	6.00	5	0	9	8	5	7
Drumright, Greg	2	0	6.59	13	1	27	37	3	13

9. AUBURN

Coach: Hal Baird **Record:** 46-18

BATTING	AVG	AB	R	H	2B	3B	HR	RBI	SB
Pratt, Scott, ss	.407	258	82	105	21	6	11	59	33
Faulkner, Todd, 1b-dh	.382	220	53	84	14	1	20	65	0
Kelly, Heath, 2b	.374	238	62	89	17	4	6	57	18
Wandall, Chad, 3b	.350	237	60	83	23	1	6	46	3
Etheredge, Josh, of	.340	247	71	84	19	1	21	90	4
Kersh, Jamie, 1b-dh	.333	198	46	66	14	3	5	46	3
Dunn, Casey, c	.320	275	61	88	18	0	10	67	0
Gliemmo, Hayden, of-p	.319	141	37	45	8	0	3	22	0
Rich, Dominic, of	.317	249	67	79	14	2	5	54	7
Kent, Mailon, of	.308	107	23	33	8	1	0	15	8

Alabama relief ace
Jarrod Kingrey was 8-4, 2.47 with 13 saves

BATTING	AVG	AB	R	H	2B	3B	HR	RBI	SB
Reif, Derek, of	.271	96	20	26	6	0	0	15	0
Turco, Paul, 2b-ss	.176	17	4	3	2	0	0	3	0
Bonick, Jon, c-of	.129	31	4	4	1	0	0	2	0
Zanthos, Joseph, of	.000	10	5	0	0	0	0	0	0

PITCHING	W	L	ERA	G	SV	IP	H	BB	SO
Kelly, Heath	0	0	0.00	3	0	5	4	1	0
Bean, Colter	4	3	3.56	29	7	66	63	22	57
Schoening, Brent	11	5	3.88	18	0	111	101	46	111
Merriott, Alex	0	0	4.05	6	0	7	9	3	5
Wood, Eric	4	0	4.84	24	0	58	60	9	34
Bootcheck, Chris	8	2	4.94	20	1	55	59	28	44
Gliemmo, Hayden	13	3	4.04	21	0	118	125	43	104
Jackson, J.D.	1	1	5.73	15	0	22	22	4	25
Jones, George	0	0	5.73	5	0	11	16	2	5
Knorst, Kevin	5	4	5.76	19	0	80	93	33	61
McManus, Ellis	0	0	6.52	11	0	19	26	9	10
Renfro, Jon	0	0	7.84	10	0	10	16	2	10

10. LONG BEACH STATE

Coach: Dave Snow **Record:** 43-23

BATTING	AVG	AB	R	H	2B	3B	HR	RBI	SB
Lopez, Chuck, of	.422	268	77	113	17	4	4	52	7
Day, Paul, 3b-of	.401	274	83	110	16	6	15	89	21
Sledge, Terrmel, of	.392	286	99	112	25	5	13	63	26
Luera, Michael, of	.378	37	6	14	2	1	0	9	1
Berni, Jason, dh-p	.364	217	35	79	22	0	4	48	2
Hota, Mike, of	.362	47	11	17	3	0	0	11	3
Kennedy, Bryan, c	.356	247	65	88	25	1	8	81	1
Yount, Jason, 1b	.352	233	60	82	10	1	11	57	5
Madison, Jaron, of	.333	207	43	69	8	1	2	36	8
Redfox, Scott, 3b	.330	91	21	30	6	0	2	21	1
Hall, Justin, ss	.318	261	57	83	16	3	7	56	6
Lee, Curt, 2b	.302	189	37	57	9	0	0	21	1
Grant, Daryl, p-1b	.286	28	9	8	1	0	1	8	2
Monroy, Sam, 2b	.250	60	9	15	1	0	0	4	1
Toomey, Chris, of	.231	52	14	12	4	0	1	9	0
Hill, Neville, c	.200	20	2	4	0	0	0	1	0

PITCHING	W	L	ERA	G	SV	IP	H	BB	SO
Gallo, Mike	6	2	3.41	22	0	92	94	28	66
Kordich, Dennis	5	4	3.63	29	0	52	54	25	40
Thomas, Dan	1	0	3.94	9	0	30	33	8	22
Marr, Jason	3	1	4.43	31	9	41	40	12	38
Garcia, Mike	0	0	4.50	5	0	6	4	5	6
Merrill, Darren	7	0	4.61	27	0	53	56	16	47
Berni, Jason	5	5	4.91	23	1	62	77	31	41
Balbuena, Caleb	7	3	5.17	18	0	101	112	39	81
Grant, Daryl	3	5	5.62	21	0	66	65	49	56
Leuenberger, Jeff	6	3	6.19	18	0	73	92	41	48
Veronie, Shannin	0	0	6.97	9	0	10	14	4	5
Tremblay, Max	0	0	9.00	16	0	13	20	9	15

11. TEXAS A&M

Coach: Mark Johnson **Record:** 46-20

BATTING	AVG	AB	R	H	2B	3B	HR	RBI	SB
Tyner, Jason, of	.385	278	71	107	12	2	0	31	39
Scheschuk, John, 1b	.336	217	46	73	10	4	16	68	2
Holt, Daylan, of	.316	266	51	84	22	3	7	48	5
Kuzmic, Craig, 3b	.316	244	67	77	12	5	25	72	9
Scarborough, Steve, ss	.310	229	45	71	11	3	4	42	7
Sandusky, Scott, c	.308	224	47	69	8	2	2	26	10
Truitt, Steven, of	.304	247	53	75	22	4	8	42	25
Gray, William, of	.297	37	12	11	1	0	0	6	3
Sobek, Erik, of-dh	.279	140	24	39	4	0	10	34	3
Hudson, Chad, dh	.276	98	20	27	8	1	5	17	1
Malone, Patrick, 1b	.263	19	7	5	0	0	1	4	1
Heaney, Sean, 2b	.260	242	44	63	18	0	8	51	4
Heinrichs, Darren, of	.226	31	4	7	2	0	0	5	1
Sundstrom, Ken, 3b	.190	21	3	4	0	0	0	2	0
Leonard, Steve, 1b	.179	28	6	5	2	0	0	2	1

PITCHING	W	L	ERA	G	SV	IP	H	BB	SO
French, Eric	3	1	1.46	25	6	37	27	11	38
Rupe, Ryan	11	4	2.87	15	0	113	95	23	125
Fossum, Casey	12	2	3.74	20	2	123	108	41	129
Caple, Chance	7	1	3.79	19	0	74	70	28	63
Fossum, Clancy	0	0	4.57	12	0	22	21	13	23
Scarcella, Chris	2	1	5.31	5	0	20	21	8	13
Ward, Matt	7	4	5.36	17	0	94	112	12	65
Fulbright, Chris	1	2	6.11	9	0	18	20	9	10
Russ, Chris	1	1	6.56	8	1	23	27	7	15
Holle, Kyle	1	1	6.62	10	1	18	24	7	12
Weller, Courtney	1	3	7.01	16	1	26	35	16	25
King, Shane	0	0	8.31	5	0	9	10	5	4

12. ALABAMA

Coach: Jim Wells **Record:** 46-18

BATTING	AVG	AB	R	H	2B	3B	HR	RBI	SB
Wigginton, Derek, of	.500	10	8	5	1	1	0	4	0
Keller, G.W., of-3b	.377	247	67	93	14	5	14	62	7
Phillips, Andy, 3b-ss	.351	265	65	93	11	2	21	82	5
Bounds, Drew, of	.346	182	50	63	8	1	13	43	15
Phillips, Paul, c-of	.344	273	69	94	13	3	10	38	18
Frick, Matt, c-dh	.342	222	66	76	13	4	22	60	4
Bozanich, Sam, 2b	.333	225	48	75	17	1	3	28	3
Bostic, Antonio, of	.323	65	24	21	1	2	3	13	2
Cox, Jayson, 1b	.297	212	35	63	14	0	15	46	1
Walters, Cam, if	.275	40	9	11	3	0	2	5	0
Wood, Darren, of	.272	136	25	37	6	0	3	18	5
Dragg, Jeff, 1b-of	.268	56	7	15	2	0	1	10	0
Gulledge, Kelley, c	.250	88	21	22	5	0	3	18	1
Chavers, Dan, ss	.238	172	25	41	8	0	9	34	0
Mote, David, 1b	.231	52	7	12	1	0	3	12	0
Peer, Mark, of	.226	31	6	7	0	0	0	6	1

PITCHING	W	L	ERA	G	SV	IP	H	BB	SO
Kingrey, Jarrod	8	4	2.47	33	13	84	57	35	98
Lombardi, Justin	2	0	2.70	8	0	23	19	10	22
Phillips, Paul	1	1	3.65	7	2	12	8	6	12
McWhirter, Kris	4	0	3.89	21	0	44	55	22	40
Smith, Justin	7	1	3.90	16	0	102	107	42	95
Green, B.J.	8	2	4.59	19	0	84	97	33	71
Blankenship, Jon	7	2	5.65	25	0	70	81	25	60
Fisher, Pete	7	8	5.87	18	0	104	141	32	92
Torres, Manny	1	0	6.00	6	0	9	7	6	4
Kitchens, Freddie	1	0	8.10	12	0	20	24	12	22

13. CAL STATE FULLERTON

Coach: George Horton **Record:** 47-17

BATTING	AVG	AB	R	H	2B	3B	HR	RBI	SB
Jacobs, Greg, dh-p	.389	198	56	77	20	2	8	55	11
Fukuhara, Pete, of-dh	.383	141	38	54	10	0	10	47	4
Rowand, Aaron, of	.372	242	66	90	27	4	16	72	15
Chatham, Steve, of	.362	149	45	54	12	1	7	36	9
Beck, Chris, of	.361	119	32	43	7	3	3	26	4
Moore, Ryan, 3b	.336	211	43	71	19	3	14	56	2
Fullerton, Ryan, 1b	.341	44	2	15	5	0	0	7	1
Bacani, David, 2b	.317	189	59	60	9	5	3	29	10
Duck, Kevin, 1b	.311	209	50	65	13	1	9	50	1
Patterson, Craig, c	.307	114	22	35	7	0	2	19	4
Johnson, Reed, of	.302	225	67	68	12	5	8	51	15
Baum, Chad, c	.300	20	5	6	0	0	1	1	1
Owens, Ryan, ss-2b	.288	229	50	66	17	3	10	44	13

College Baseball

Offensive cog for Huskies
Outfielder Chris Magruder hit .402 and scored 89 runs

	AVG	AB	R	H	2B	3B	HR	RBI	SB
Trentine, David, c	.277	83	17	23	5	1	2	18	2
Olszanski, Chad, ss	.265	49	15	13	3	0	0	5	7
Halcovich, Gaby, if	.200	20	9	4	0	0	0	2	1
Hernandez, Jojo, of	.083	12	0	1	0	0	0	0	0

PITCHING	W	L	ERA	G	SV	IP	H	BB	SO
Jurado, Ruben	0	0	1.88	7	0	14	16	4	9
Johnson, Adam	1	4	3.05	24	8	38	25	21	63
Smith, Jon	2	0	3.21	7	0	28	22	14	16
Flores, Benito	12	0	3.52	18	1	123	120	34	100
Ramirez, Erasmo	11	5	3.66	19	0	130	133	28	112
Hanlon, Marco	5	2	4.58	21	1	35	41	21	26
Jacobs, Greg	4	4	4.87	17	0	57	71	22	54
Saarloos, Kirk	4	2	5.15	30	3	51	62	24	57
Stewart, Jason	2	0	5.18	16	1	24	31	8	21
Carralejo, George	4	0	5.91	19	1	35	47	19	26
DeJong, Jordan	1	0	6.75	10	1	17	26	5	12
Garner, Mike	1	0	6.91	9	0	14	18	9	16

14. MISSISSIPPI STATE

Coach: Pat McMahon **Record:** 42-23

BATTING	AVG	AB	R	H	2B	3B	HR	RBI	SB
Wiese, Brian, of	.412	250	71	103	24	2	14	57	11
Lee, Richard, 1b	.357	258	71	92	20	2	19	85	4
Freeman, Brad, ss	.355	256	73	91	15	4	11	54	16
Bryan, Brooks, of	.346	237	45	82	14	2	9	50	8
Terry, Brian, dh	.333	24	5	8	2	0	1	5	0
Chapman, Travis, 3b	.327	251	55	82	17	1	10	50	1
Lotterhos, Chris, 2b	.326	129	34	42	4	3	2	18	5
Thoms, Rusty, of	.317	268	61	85	12	0	3	39	16
Willingham, Phillip, of	.314	35	8	11	1	0	2	5	1
Patton, Barry, c	.297	246	33	73	18	1	8	59	1
McGrath, Ryan, c-of	.294	17	5	5	0	0	1	3	1
Dabbs, Dustin, c-dh	.289	38	6	11	4	0	0	6	0
Thoms, Lake, 2b-ss	.260	73	13	19	4	0	1	10	3
Peeples, Matt, 2b	.258	31	9	8	0	0	0	5	0
Knott, Jon, dh	.243	169	33	41	10	1	13	42	7
West, Josh, of	.186	43	10	8	1	0	1	3	1
Hauswald, Rob, 3b	.176	17	3	3	0	1	0	2	0

PITCHING	W	L	ERA	G	SV	IP	H	BB	SO
Compton, Brian	4	0	2.24	23	1	56	41	21	72
Johnson, Van	3	0	3.27	34	10	44	38	9	32
Thoms, Hank	5	2	4.55	29	6	61	67	25	59
Jackson, Jeremy	10	3	4.61	17	0	100	126	27	91
Donovan, Kevin	2	1	4.75	17	1	30	34	11	31
Polk, Scott	0	0	4.82	22	3	37	41	18	40
Ginter, Matt	6	4	5.38	19	0	89	86	54	100
Freed, Mark	6	6	5.55	21	0	71	81	28	62
Reinike, Chris	6	6	7.17	20	0	75	102	35	74

15. RICE

Coach: Wayne Graham **Record:** 46-17

BATTING	AVG	AB	R	H	2B	3B	HR	RBI	SB
Thames, Damon, ss	.424	283	88	120	36	7	26	115	4
Crosby, Bubba, of	[illegible]	221	70	87	15	3	25	91	2
Baker, Jacob, 1b	.360	214	45	77	16	2	12	61	1
Hodge, Kevin, 3b-p	.356	239	69	85	12	4	15	64	13
Williams, Charles, of	.354	212	75	75	18	3	9	37	4
Richards, Jason, 2b	.348	230	73	80	21	2	13	51	11
Van Noy, Jerry, of	.313	32	5	10	2	0	1	6	2
Savarino, J.J., of	.311	180	40	56	8	4	1	24	5
Curry, Zane, c	.299	214	43	64	16	0	7	37	1
Berg, Justin, dh-c	.284	232	44	66	9	2	7	39	3
Kurtz-Nicholl, Jesse, 1b-p	.281	96	18	27	5	0	2	12	1
Brown, Hunter, c	.250	12	1	3	1	0	0	1	0
Fox, Matt, if	.150	20	3	3	0	0	0	1	0
Bates, Jeremy, of	.143	21	5	3	1	0	0	1	2
Michaelis, Derek, if	.083	24	2	2	1	0	0	0	0

PITCHING	W	L	ERA	G	SV	IP	H	BB	SO
Ramos, Mario	12	2	3.39	21	0	112	72	48	113
Bess, Stephen	10	2	4.37	22	1	105	98	50	73
Terrana, Peter	0	0	4.58	12	0	18	21	7	16
Nichols, Jeff	12	4	5.34	21	1	120	114	58	117
Gwyn, Marc	3	2	5.55	19	1	60	68	34	51
Baugh, Kenny	4	2	5.79	15	0	65	53	43	59
Kurtz-Nicholl, Jesse	3	2	6.02	21	5	43	47	21	39
Nemer, Spencer	0	1	9.39	8	0	8	6	11	4
Hodge, Kevin	2	2	10.80	11	2	12	15	7	11

16. SOUTH CAROLINA

Coach: Ray Tanner **Record:** 44-18

BATTING	AVG	AB	R	H	2B	3B	HR	RBI	SB
Curry, Mike, of	.400	260	102	104	15	5	16	46	60
Everett, Adam, ss	.375	267	71	100	21	4	13	63	15
Urquhart, Derick, of	.356	250	79	89	13	3	20	77	18
Bordenick, Ryan, c	.342	219	55	75	15	1	19	76	1
Poe, Adam, of	.309	243	44	75	18	3	12	54	8
Collins, Clint, 2b-p	.289	45	8	13	3	0	3	14	1
Angiolini, Tim, dh	.269	156	29	42	12	0	4	22	3
Kelly, Tripp, dh-1b	.261	115	23	30	6	0	8	23	0
Knox, Mic, 1b	.253	190	23	48	9	0	4	22	0
Stanton, Eric, 3b	.246	240	42	59	11	1	16	54	2
Lambert, Jay, 2b	.235	170	37	40	6	0	6	17	1
Jeffcoat, Bryon, 2b	.200	15	4	3	1	0	0	1	0
Whittaker, Tim, c	.200	10	2	2	0	0	1	4	0

PITCHING	W	L	ERA	G	SV	IP	H	BB	SO
Sexton, Patrick	3	2	2.65	29	2	37	38	12	19
Bauer, Peter	7	0	2.93	14	0	68	59	22	68
Pomar, Jason	4	2	3.29	28	9	38	41	24	43
Bouknight, Kip	11	3	4.07	21	0	95	87	46	86
Poston, Jamie	3	0	5.28	28	1	44	54	15	46
Kondro, Brett	6	1	5.52	16	0	77	82	39	47
Jodie, Brett	6	6	6.54	17	0	106	120	39	113
Collins, Clint	3	2	6.75	11	0	40	47	18	41
Barber, Scott	1	2	6.75	13	0	33	35	13	33

17. WASHINGTON

Coach: Ken Knutson **Record:** 41-17

BATTING	AVG	AB	R	H	2B	3B	HR	RBI	SB
Stefonick, Nick, of	.407	177	49	72	18	5	7	54	14
Magruder, Chris, of	.402	219	89	88	18	4	11	57	33
Ticen, Kevin, c-dh	.346	52	14	18	7	0	1	17	0
Lentz, Ryan, 3b	.319	226	65	72	19	1	16	65	7
Boston, Tyson, of	.318	22	8	7	4	0	2	6	0
Miller, Kevin, ss	.317	208	61	66	13	4	12	57	5
Bundy, Ryan, c	.317	164	40	52	7	3	8	25	11
Woods, Kyle, of	.314	210	48	66	12	3	14	49	20
Orgill, Pete, c-1b	.309	81	19	25	4	0	8	30	0
Na, Jim, of	.305	105	21	32	7	0	5	26	4
Williamson, Bryan, of-p	.298	94	14	28	5	0	4	21	1
Woody, Dominic, c-1b	.295	88	24	26	3	1	4	12	5
DeMar, Dwight, of	.294	17	11	5	0	2	0	7	4
Brooks, Greg, if	.286	14	4	4	2	0	0	0	0
Erickson, Ed, 1b	.283	166	35	47	9	0	14	51	2
Rittenhouse, Marc, 2b	.259	116	36	30	2	0	3	9	6
Whitemarsh, Chris, 2b	.204	54	10	11	3	1	1	6	1

PITCHING	W	L	ERA	G	SV	IP	H	BB	SO
Ferguson, Ken	3	0	3.58	14	0	28	17	15	37
Anderson, Travis	4	2	4.11	10	0	46	40	32	45

PITCHING	W	L	ERA	G	SV	IP	H	BB	SO
Massingale, Matt	6	2	4.15	25	0	35	28	12	24
Carlsen, Jeff	7	3	4.39	14	0	80	87	30	62
Gillespie, John	1	1	4.71	9	0	21	15	13	15
Lee, Wayne	1	0	4.83	23	1	32	23	11	44
Morrison, Cody	1	1	5.14	22	6	21	14	16	30
Jahn, Daniel	1	0	5.40	5	0	13	13	5	17
Heaverlo, Jeff	5	3	5.63	12	0	70	75	34	84
Hampton, Matt	4	4	5.93	13	0	68	88	29	34
Williamson, Bryan	3	0	6.89	12	0	33	35	22	20
Bomar, Mike	3	1	6.99	14	0	28	26	19	30
Linarelli, Tom	1	0	7.71	7	0	7	8	3	5
Gardner, Matt	1	0	8.10	14	0	17	18	12	13

18. SOUTH ALABAMA

Coach: Steve Kittrell **Record:** 42-19

BATTING	AVG	AB	R	H	2B	3B	HR	RBI	SB
Taylor, Seth, ss	.438	32	6	14	5	1	2	12	1
Calahan, Scott, 2b	.379	29	4	11	3	0	0	3	1
Whitehurst, Tom, of	.378	222	65	84	25	4	5	34	31
Pierre, Juan, of	.373	255	77	95	16	3	5	40	54
Wiley, Terry, 1b-2b	.311	164	27	51	9	1	6	35	2
Sutley, Andy, of-dh	.299	134	34	40	9	0	3	25	12
Wells, Eben, of	.298	171	31	51	13	3	3	36	17
Choron, Joey, 2b	.298	124	22	37	5	0	5	34	3
Hernandez, Vinnie, 3b	.277	206	48	57	14	2	6	28	2
Keats, Ben, c	.274	215	41	59	8	0	11	48	4
Jackson, Brett, dh-of	.247	182	32	45	9	0	12	42	2
Breazeale, Rob, ss	.244	176	37	43	4	0	1	16	10
Conway, Matt, 3b	.241	29	6	7	1	0	0	5	0
Bolton, Gabe, 1b	.212	104	12	22	4	1	1	17	0
Lowell, Brad, 1b	.159	44	7	7	1	0	2	10	3

PITCHING	W	L	ERA	G	SV	IP	H	BB	SO
Fischer, Mike	11	1	2.31	20	1	125	91	23	120
Cash, Wes	0	0	2.45	7	0	7	5	3	7
Carter, Justin	8	3	3.50	20	5	82	77	31	83
Norton, Jason	9	3	4.53	18	0	105	105	26	121
Cooke, Peter	2	2	4.60	12	0	43	48	16	22
McBride, Randy	3	2	5.08	23	4	51	50	20	47
Roach, Kyle	4	3	5.68	18	0	59	75	15	43
Sparks, Stephen	5	5	5.92	17	0	65	58	33	63
Moore, Quinn	0	0	14.40	4	0	5	7	3	4

19. GEORGIA TECH

Coach: Danny Hall **Record:** 41-22

BATTING	AVG	AB	R	H	2B	3B	HR	RBI	SB
Honeycutt, Heath, 3b-2b	.368	258	70	95	18	2	14	71	13
Donaghey, Stephen, 1b-p	.338	195	46	66	9	0	11	51	1
Prince, Bryan, c-dh	.337	172	41	58	11	0	5	38	3
Prather, Scott, of-p	.325	203	51	66	21	0	12	43	1
Hood, Jay, ss	.320	203	44	65	21	1	10	43	1
Basil, Jason, of-c	.313	134	28	42	11	1	3	27	3
Boggs, Matthew, 2b	.310	126	34	39	5	1	0	16	8
McQueen, Eric, c	.298	198	48	59	16	1	15	57	10
Goffena, Derik, of	.291	206	59	60	13	3	10	42	5
Brooks, Ryan, 3b	.284	141	34	40	8	1	12	38	3
Overton, Jahmal, of	.278	133	27	37	6	2	5	24	7
Atha, Jason, 2b	.256	39	10	10	1	1	1	4	1
Shoop, Lynn, of	.250	12	6	3	0	1	0	0	1
Stockton, Brad, of	.248	129	25	32	4	1	5	23	4
Rollins, Kevin, ss	.243	37	12	9	2	0	0	3	2
Vance, Cory, p-of	.148	27	2	4	1	0	0	0	0
Blue, Adam, of	.063	16	3	1	0	1	0	2	0
Mitchell, Andy, 3b-p	.000	11	0	0	0	0	0	0	0

PITCHING	W	L	ERA	G	SV	IP	H	BB	SO
Crowder, Chuck	12	4	3.03	20	0	125	105	56	133
Wrigley, Jase	5	4	3.79	30	4	74	67	37	68
Yankosky, L.J.	11	1	4.23	18	1	111	104	42	110
Young, Simon	3	2	5.07	25	1	50	53	25	68
Vance, Cory	6	4	5.96	19	0	80	95	39	102
Prather, Scott	3	4	6.03	16	1	78	87	45	98
Aaron, Robert	0	3	9.77	11	0	16	18	10	22
Bien, Jeff	0	0	11.37	6	0	6	14	5	3
Donaghey, Stephen	1	0	12.71	6	0	6	13	3	0
Mitchell, Andy	0	0	12.75	8	0	12	21	12	14

20. TULANE

Coach: Rick Jones **Record:** 48-15

BATTING	AVG	AB	R	H	2B	3B	HR	RBI	SB
Sutter, Chad, c-dh	.392	217	56	85	12	0	13	61	2
Hughes, Brian, of-c	.381	273	75	104	29	2	8	56	35
Graffagnini, Keith, 1b	.373	241	66	90	25	2	14	76	4
Sparks, Jason, of	.357	221	84	79	18	0	30	90	7
Burnham Jake, dh-c	.345	168	45	58	16	2	10	47	3
Pursell, Mike, 2b	.332	238	68	79	18	3	10	56	11
Brown, Craig, of-p	.331	148	48	49	6	0	3	22	17
McKee, Mickey, 3b	.316	98	18	31	3	0	5	26	2
Shirley, Steve, 3b	.314	159	26	50	10	1	7	31	1
Boudreaux, Paul, of	.314	156	28	49	5	0	1	22	3
Cannizaro, Andy, ss	.291	254	63	74	22	0	3	38	25
Heintz, Jay, of	.222	36	6	8	2	0	0	7	0
Llorente, Marcelo, if	.200	30	9	6	1	0	1	4	1

PITCHING	W	L	ERA	G	SV	IP	H	BB	SO
Echeverz, Raul	7	1	2.78	19	1	74	76	27	63
Bobbitt, Josh	13	1	3.09	18	0	117	105	35	133
Brown, Craig	4	3	3.49	17	1	57	55	27	58
Ardoin, Todd	5	1	3.75	32	6	36	42	6	30
Berkowitz, Jared	9	2	3.90	17	0	90	96	23	51
Melius, Barth	1	1	4.76	10	1	17	22	3	15
Bell, Scott	7	2	5.16	18	2	84	90	20	82
Whitfield, Jake	0	0	5.61	10	1	26	29	19	18
Putnam, Dylan	0	1	5.91	13	0	21	29	15	15
Lontayo, Alex	2	3	7.82	7	0	25	25	20	32

21. CLEMSON

Coach: Jack Leggett **Record:** 43-16

BATTING	AVG	AB	R	H	2B	3B	HR	RBI	SB
Padgett, Matt, of	.376	234	60	88	14	1	14	58	6
Ellis, Brian, c	.374	123	39	46	12	1	2	33	2
Singleton, Justin, 3b	.370	108	28	40	6	2	3	35	6
Harris, Jason,1b	.357	227	64	81	20	2	9	59	14
Stryhas, Paul, 3b	.355	31	6	11	5	0	0	11	0
Hyde, Justin, of	.348	46	7	16	7	1	2	12	1
Boyd, Patrick, of	.344	241	60	83	13	1	8	59	11
Nystrom, Peter, of	.309	152	47	47	11	2	6	42	2
Holstad, Brian, 3b	.301	113	27	34	3	0	1	14	15
Calitri, Mike, 3b-1b	.300	30	7	9	2	1	1	9	0
Bultmann, Kurt, 2b	.299	234	57	70	18	1	10	54	2
Roper, Doug, ss	.208	188	45	56	6	2	2	33	15
Borgert, Derek, c	.296	125	22	37	4	0	2	16	0
Stanley, Henri, dh of	.204	116	28	33	7	1	3	17	5
Stone, Casey, of	.267	86	18	23	3	1	0	14	2
LeCroy, Bradley, if	.222	27	6	6	1	0	1	6	1
Vessell, Jeff, of	.182	11	1	2	1	0	0	1	0

PITCHING	W	L	ERA	G	SV	IP	H	BB	SO
Clackum, Scott	7	1	1.11	23	9	41	21	11	42
Proto, Mike	0	0	1.45	14	0	19	14	7	17

Yellow Jacket stopper
L.J. Yankosky went 11-1 for Georgia Tech

College Baseball

Adams, Darren	0	0	3.52	7	0	8	7	1	9
Rhue, Mike	0	0	3.68	8	0	7	10	6	4
Additon, Matt	2	0	3.81	22	1	54	55	17	46
Adams, Brian	6	2	4.22	16	0	70	66	30	48
White, Matt	5	2	4.79	16	0	68	74	31	59
Mottl, Ryan	9	4	4.81	16	0	101	101	31	96
Browning, Skip	5	3	4.89	12	0	53	59	27	42
Harrison, Donovan	4	3	4.97	16	2	51	46	17	44
Paradis, Mike	5	1	5.37	11	0	55	44	39	53

22. BAYLOR

Coach: Steve Smith **Record:** 41-20

BATTING	AVG	AB	R	H	2B	3B	HR	RBI	SB
Carter, Charley, 1b	.402	246	57	99	24	2	21	86	1
Topolski, Jon, of	.344	250	74	86	7	11	19	54	22
Dodson, Jeremy, of	.342	225	69	77	19	0	13	57	19
Blair, James, of	.342	240	58	82	15	3	10	49	25
Jennings, Jason, dh-p	.327	211	42	69	14	0	18	58	0
Nelson, Eric, 2b	.317	262	63	83	16	3	13	50	15
Williams, Matt, 3b	.304	184	50	56	18	1	9	38	2
Loeb, Bryan, c	.289	128	23	37	7	3	3	26	0
Boisjoly, Eric, ss-3b	.280	50	11	14	2	0	0	3	1
Underdown, Preston, ss	.272	206	39	56	12	1	5	43	2
Polk, Chad, c	.205	127	22	26	5	1	4	17	11
Fredenburg, Denver, c	.182	11	1	2	1	0	0	1	0
Evans, Kyle, ss-p	.150	20	2	3	1	0	0	2	1

PITCHING	W	L	ERA	G	SV	IP	H	BB	SO
Scott, Josh	3	1	2.50	21	1	40	32	29	51
Bradford, Michael	3	0	2.55	20	3	35	25	12	32
Ratliff, Joe	0	0	3.38	6	0	5	6	2	5
Wells, Kip	13	4	3.71	20	0	124	121	44	135
Outlaw, Mark	3	2	3.76	25	1	38	38	19	45
Jennings, Jason	11	4	5.08	20	2	117	123	53	126
Bergman, Brett	7	7	5.31	17	0	100	110	40	84
Marcom, Matthew	1	0	5.36	18	3	47	53	12	27
Visker, Jared	0	2	5.84	12	0	25	20	20	19
Evans, Kyle	0	0	6.75	8	0	5	6	3	1

23. ILLINOIS

Coach: Itch Jones **Record:** 42-21

BATTING	AVG	AB	R	H	2B	3B	HR	RBI	SB
Peelman, Aaron, c	.444	36	12	16	3	1	4	13	1
O'Neill, Dan, of-dh	.393	206	60	81	16	3	12	48	18
Marquie, Craig, 3b	.392	209	61	82	16	3	11	58	5
Hall, Jon, 3b-1b	.389	18	5	7	1	0	0	5	1
Svihlik, D.J., 2b	.374	174	31	65	16	2	15	55	0
Rudden, Kevin, 1b	.366	205	44	75	12	3	10	47	0
Sprengard, Joe, if	.364	11	3	4	2	0	0	0	0
Rhodes, Dusty, of	.361	233	62	84	20	5	7	35	15
Ippolito, Vince, 1b	.352	54	11	19	5	0	2	15	0
Rhodes, Danny, of	.341	232	57	79	16	2	9	47	16
Whitaker, Creston, of	.333	21	13	7	1	0	0	2	5
Nieckula, Aaron, c	.332	196	38	65	12	1	5	44	17
Jackson, T.J., dh	.318	110	24	35	7	0	4	23	1
Basak, Chris, if	.304	56	15	17	3	0	0	9	2
McClure, Todd, of-dh	.285	158	27	45	11	1	5	32	9
Anderson, Jon, ss	.269	175	34	47	5	2	2	18	8
Burlage, Bob, 3b-p	.261	46	4	12	4	0	1	10	0
Targgart, Shawn, c	.235	17	2	4	0	0	2	6	0

PITCHING	W	L	ERA	G	SV	IP	H	BB	SO
Weber, Brett	10	3	3.11	21	0	107	87	28	99
Journell, Jimmy	3	1	3.82	23	5	31	23	15	41
Salter, Cody	7	6	4.03	23	2	103	130	14	49
Trayser, Tom	0	0	4.09	8	0	11	12	4	3
Anderson, Jason	6	0	4.75	18	0	66	74	22	43
Rehrer, Travis	3	1	4.82	18	1	52	38	34	70
Funk, Brian	2	0	5.55	17	1	24	32	6	16
Burlage, Bob	2	2	5.68	9	0	19	26	5	14
Zidlicky, Tom	6	5	6.15	20	0	72	91	28	56
Lavery, Tim	3	3	7.68	14	0	36	52	16	27

24. NORTH CAROLINA

Coach: Mike Roberts **Record:** 42-23

BATTING	AVG	AB	R	H	2B	3B	HR	RBI	SB
Roberts, Brian, ss	.353	258	79	91	21	2	13	49	63
Shearin, Jarrett, of	.346	254	70	88	25	3	14	68	28
Moylan, Dan, c	.340	215	50	73	14	0	10	38	8
Godwin, Tyrell, of	.337	83	19	28	8	2	4	17	1
LaMarsh, Chris, dh-2b	.336	214	53	72	10	1	6	55	2
Miano, Rob, 2b	.298	252	55	75	14	0	5	40	11
Grimsley, Richie, of	.285	256	42	73	13	3	12	62	5
Earey, Ryan, 3b-1b	.274	252	39	69	14	1	10	55	5
Madeira, Jay, 1b-p	.265	215	51	57	11	3	12	39	4
Bynum, Mike, p-1b	.215	65	5	14	3	0	1	9	0
Davidson, Kevin, of	.215	107	22	23	1	0	4	16	0
Reynolds, Wes, c	.136	44	5	6	3	0	1	6	1

Stolen base champ
UNC's Brian Roberts led the nation with 63 steals

PITCHING	W	L	ERA	G	SV	IP	H	BB	SO
Richardson, Corey	3	2	2.61	15	5	21	12	14	22
Madeira, Jay	0	0	2.95	12	0	18	15	7	14
DePriest, Derrick	7	3	3.15	44	7	114	112	35	76
Snyder, Kyle	7	6	3.53	16	0	102	104	31	88
Elmore, Chris	5	0	4.48	11	0	60	60	32	42
Earey, Ryan	4	1	4.85	12	0	13	11	13	13
Horney, Michael	3	0	5.02	15	1	38	42	21	39
Snare, Ryan	5	6	5.47	17	0	82	79	68	85
Stover, Rob	1	1	6.00	6	0	15	13	13	7
Bynum, Mike	7	4	6.11	19	0	99	105	71	95
Smith, Mark	0	0	16.03	7	0	11	31	4	9

25. TEXAS TECH

Coach: Larry Hays **Record:** 44-20

BATTING	AVG	AB	R	H	2B	3B	HR	RBI	SB
Nelson, Peter, 3b-p	.467	15	5	7	3	0	1	6	0
Martines, Scooter, 1b-of	.417	12	2	5	1	0	1	5	0
Ruiz, Ryan, of	.388	196	51	76	11	0	2	36	22
Bard, Josh, c	.383	264	56	101	22	2	17	71	1
Ginter, Keith, 2b-3b	.371	229	97	85	24	1	17	55	27
Burns, Brennan, dh	.354	192	43	68	23	1	2	38	0
Jordan, Kevin, 3b-2b	.354	263	66	93	20	5	17	84	18
Landreth, Jason, of	.343	236	63	81	16	4	11	54	28
Buckley, Brandon, c-dh	.326	92	23	30	7	1	2	13	1
Austry, Mark, 1b	.319	226	47	72	7	2	10	47	6
Tuley, David, dh-of	.316	19	6	6	1	0	0	1	0
Durham, Miles, of	.310	226	50	70	14	5	5	34	23
Huth, Jason, ss	.309	191	40	59	9	6	4	39	12
Richardson, Steve, of	.308	13	4	4	3	0	0	1	0
Rodriguez, Junior, if	.274	106	22	29	10	0	6	24	5
Smith, Joe, of-p	.227	22	4	5	0	0	0	5	1

PITCHING	W	L	ERA	G	SV	IP	H	BB	SO
Nelson, Peter	0	0	1.80	2	1	5	6	3	0
Wright, Shane	14	1	2.71	21	2	153	166	20	116
Watkins, Steve	2	0	3.26	9	0	19	21	7	17
Ward, Monty	6	4	4.65	16	0	108	109	49	151
Smith, Joe	4	3	5.13	17	0	40	60	17	32
Allison, Cade	3	3	5.22	15	0	50	63	18	51
Cornejo, Jesse	9	4	5.97	15	0	86	103	25	87
Ralston, Brad	3	4	6.28	21	5	43	56	17	54
Stewart, Zach	2	0	7.06	25	2	43	66	15	37
Cooper, Eric	1	1	10.53	7	0	20	27	11	13

CONFERENCE

Standings, Leaders

*Won conference tournament.
Boldface: NCAA regional participant/conference department leader.
#Conference department leader who is a non-qualifier

AMERICA EAST CONFERENCE

	Conference		Overall	
	W	L	W	L
***Delaware**	22	2	43	10
Northeastern	17	9	26	22
Vermont	15	12	25	21
Hofstra	14	14	20	24
Maine	12	16	24	26
Drexel	9	15	17	32
Towson	9	18	21	27
Hartford	7	19	13	32

ALL-CONFERENCE TEAM: C—Dusty Reynolds, Jr., Towson. **1B**—Darren Pulito, Sr., Delaware. **2B**—Dennis Helkowski, Sr., Drexel. **3B**—Keith Carter, Sr., Vermont. **SS**—Jason Rummel, Jr., Towson. **OF**—Tim Daley, Sr., Northeastern; Brad Eyman, Sr., Delaware; Kevin Mench, So., Delaware. **DH**—James Carolco, Sr., Hofstra. **P**—Chris Frey, Sr., Delaware; Matt Phillips, Sr., Delaware.

Player of the Year: Kevin Mench, Delaware. **Pitcher of the Year**: Matt Phillips, Delaware. **Rookie of the Year**: Bruce Boehm, Drexel. **Coach of the Year**: Bob Hannah, Delaware.

INDIVIDUAL BATTING LEADERS

(Minimum 100 At-Bats)

	AVG	AB	R	H	2B	3B	HR	RBI	SB
Mench, Kevin, Delaware	**455**	107	**88**	**85**	16	2	**33**	**72**	16
Holkowski, Dennis, Drexel	.402	189	46	76	**19**	1	2	24	**18**
Snyder, Earl, Hartford	.401	152	38	61	10	0	18	46	3
Carter, Keith, Vermont	.401	172	33	69	16	0	4	39	3
Sheedy, T.J., Maine	.401	182	59	73	14	1	2	40	9
Pulito, Darren, Delaware	.399	183	66	73	14	0	15	59	5
Rummel, Jason, Towson	.390	187	46	73	14	3	9	39	5
Forsberg, Dana, Vermont	.387	150	43	58	14	2	8	36	1
Eyman, Brad, Delaware	.385	200	58	77	16	5	15	50	9
Rikert, Wade, Vermont	.381	139	31	53	6	2	5	30	11
Reynolds, Dusty, Towson	.380	179	47	68	14	2	2	29	2
Poire, Brian, Maine	.373	185	59	69	11	2	4	39	5
Memmert, Gabe, Maine	.371	170	38	63	16	0	8	48	2
Kim, Kevin, Northeastern	.368	171	36	63	10	3	4	32	1
Caroleo, James, Hofstra	.368	117	21	43	10	0	10	37	2
Keating, Matt, Northeastern	.363	124	30	45	7	2	0	24	2
Healy, Liam, Towson	.355	166	43	59	15	1	14	52	1
Friel, Pat, Hofstra	.355	121	25	43	10	0	2	29	2
Daley. Tim, Northeastern	.352	179	38	63	9	2	13	56	0
Avila, Ryan, Towson	.350	100	16	35	3	1	2	14	6
Caputo, Tom, Hofstra	.350	140	25	49	11	0	4	26	3
Jimenez, Jose, Drexel	.347	167	33	58	10	4	6	50	4
Pena, Carlos, Northeastern	.342	146	45	50	7	1	13	52	12
#Squires, Heath, Vermont	.317	167	39	53	15	**7**	4	29	4

INDIVIDUAL PITCHING LEADERS

(Minimum 40 Innings)

	W	L	ERA	G	SV	IP	H	BB	SO
Phillips, Matt, Delaware	**11**	1	**3.25**	14	1	91	88	22	**84**
Fahs, Paul, Hofstra	4	2	3.32	12	**3**	41	38	21	20
Sage, Vic, Delaware	4	1	3.38	16	2	51	40	13	24
Spillane, Ryan, Vermont	2	4	3.53	11	0	59	57	34	40
#Fishel, Joe, Towson	4	2	3.62	17	**3**	27	28	12	30
Boehm, Bruce, Drexel	4	3	3.96	12	2	50	66	18	48
Borro, Dom, Towson	3	3	4.33	10	0	44	57	10	18
Sheehan, Michael, Drexel	2	2	4.53	12	0	52	54	37	28
Koplove, Mike, Delaware	5	1	4.60	9	0	43	44	23	42
Coppola, Scott, Hofstra	4	6	4.65	13	0	70	93	28	51
Spaulding, Jason, Vermont	5	2	4.74	17	2	44	41	24	32
Kelley, Greg, Northeastern	6	3	4.87	9	0	61	73	31	56
Dickinson, John, Maine	4	2	5.19	11	0	43	51	24	25
Zwanch, Mike, Drexel	4	6	5.29	18	1	66	80	44	76
Brazee, Chad, Northeastern	5	3	5.40	9	0	57	74	26	49
Drury, Brian, Hofstra	4	2	5.40	11	0	48	53	26	30
Frey, Chris, Delaware	8	2	5.47	13	0	72	74	25	84

BILL SETLIFF

ACC strikeout king
Georgia Tech's Chuck Crowder

ATLANTIC COAST CONFERENCE

	Conference		Overall	
	W	L	W	L
Florida State	18	4	53	20
Georgia Tech	14	9	41	22
Clemson	14	9	43	16
North Carolina State	12	9	41	23
***Wake Forest**	13	10	43	23
North Carolina	13	10	42	23
Duke	8	15	38	20
Virginia	5	18	28	26
Maryland	5	18	26	30

ALL-CONFERENCE TEAM: C—Jeremy Salazar, Sr., Florida State. **1B**—Jon Palmieri, Jr., Wake Forest. **2B**—Kurt Bultmann, Jr., Clemson. **3B**—Jeff Becker, Jr., Duke. **SS**—Brian Roberts, So., North Carolina. **OF**—Jake Weber, Sr., North Carolina State; Matt Padgett, Jr., Clemson; Brian Cox, Sr., Florida State; Jarrett Shearin, Jr., North Carolina. **DH**—Ed Conrey, So., Duke. **Util**—Vaughn Schill, So., Duke. **P**—John Hendricks, Jr., Wake Forest; Stephen Cowie, Jr., Duke; Chuck Crowder, Jr., Georgia Tech. **RP**—Scott Clackum, Sr., Clemson.

Player of the Year: Brian Roberts, North Carolina. **Rookie of the Year**: Patrick Boyd, Clemson. **Coach of the Year**: Mike Martin, Florida State.

INDIVIDUAL BATTING LEADERS

(Minimum 125 At-Bats)

	AVG	AB	R	H	2B	3B	HR	RBI	SB
Palmieri, Jon, WF	**.438**	256	73	**112**	30	4	12	78	12
Cox, Brian, Fla. State	.393	285	88	**112**	27	1	18	87	27
Ward, Brian, N.C. State	.393	267	71	105	**31**	2	11	66	5
Weber, Jake, N.C. State	.393	252	77	99	11	2	13	62	15
Diaz, Matt, Fla. State	.390	269	67	105	17	2	**22**	84	11
Piercy, Brad, N.C. State	.389	252	72	98	12	**7**	19	73	26
Padgett, Matt, Clemson	.376	234	60	88	14	1	14	58	6
Slavik, Corey, WF	.375	176	32	66	15	2	7	47	0
Honeycutt, Heath, Ga. Tech	.368	258	70	95	18	2	14	71	13
Schill, Vaughn, Duke	.367	229	74	84	20	4	14	48	5
Becker, Jeff, Duke	.366	235	61	86	20	0	7	46	4
Harris, Jason, Clemson	.357	227	64	81	20	2	9	59	14
Acevedo, Adrean, N.C. State	.356	132	30	47	8	0	4	35	4

Roberts, Brian, UNC	.353	258	79	91	21	2	13	49	**63**
Sherlock, Brian, Virginia	.351	202	46	71	19	3	10	60	4
Alleva, J.D., Duke	.346	228	39	79	19	1	8	52	0
Shearin, Jarrett, UNC	.346	254	70	88	25	3	14	68	28
Boyd, Patrick, Clemson	.344	241	66	83	13	1	8	59	11
Moylan, Dan, UNC	.340	215	50	75	11	0	10	38	8
Borrell, Danny, WF	.339	177	34	60	11	4	5	41	0
Fletcher, Michael, Duke	.339	221	50	75	18	2	11	59	10
Donaghey, Stephen, GT	.338	195	46	66	9	0	11	51	1
Zabala, Jose, Fla. State	.338	260	**92**	88	17	0	3	39	14
Prince, Brian, Ga. Tech	.337	172	41	58	11	0	5	38	3
Salazar, Jeremy, Fla. State	.337	258	69	87	19	0	19	**91**	2
LaMarsh, Chris, UNC	.336	214	53	72	10	1	6	55	2
Bronowicz, Scott, Maryland	.335	203	42	68	19	0	14	69	7
Trout, Casey, Maryland	.332	235	61	78	22	3	5	48	11
Conrey, Ed, Duke	.329	231	55	76	14	0	16	76	2
Maluchnik, Gregg, Duke	.329	210	59	69	12	2	14	53	9
Manley, Noel, N.C. State	.329	143	33	47	4	1	6	28	2
Ballard, Josh, N.C. State	.325	166	36	54	15	0	0	33	10
Prather, Scott, Ga. Tech	.325	203	51	66	21	0	12	43	1
Hood, Jay, Ga. Tech	.320	203	44	65	21	1	10	43	1
Kinsman, Ted, Virginia	.320	147	40	47	11	0	0	17	18
Lee, Craig, N.C. State	.319	163	32	52	14	3	3	38	5
Lopez, Javier, Virginia	.316	155	30	49	7	2	7	31	14
Litrownik, Jordan, Duke	.314	226	52	71	13	2	5	31	7
Basil, Jason, Ga. Tech	.313	134	28	42	11	1	3	27	3
Boggs, Matthew, Ga. Tech	.310	126	34	39	5	1	0	16	8
Nystrom, Peter, Clemson	.309	152	47	47	11	2	6	42	2
Jernigan, Karl, Fla. State	.308	211	43	65	13	1	5	42	11

INDIVIDUAL PITCHING LEADERS

(Minimum 50 Innings)

	W	L	ERA	G	SV	IP	H	BB	SO
#Clackum, Scott, Clemson	7	1	1.11	23	**9**	41	21	11	42
Stocks, Nick, Fla. State	7	2	**2.35**	17	0	77	65	54	81
Cowie, Stephen, Duke	11	2	2.85	18	0	126	135	23	111
Bentley, John, Fla. State	7	2	2.96	16	1	70	71	11	38
Crowder, Chuck, Ga. Tech	12	4	3.03	20	0	125	105	56	**133**
Hendricks, John, WF	**13**	4	3.14	27	2	143	131	34	111
DePriest, Derrick, UNC	7	3	3.15	44	7	114	112	35	76
Crawford, Wes, Fla. State	9	3	3.38	18	0	123	117	48	82
Shrout, Kevin, Virginia	6	4	3.48	18	2	72	55	39	93
Snyder, Kyle, UNC	7	6	3.53	16	0	102	104	31	88
Creswell, Brandon, Virginia	2	0	3.72	22	2	58	62	18	49
Wrigley, Jase, Ga. Tech	5	4	3.79	30	4	74	67	37	68
Additon, Matt, Clemson	2	0	3.81	22	1	54	55	17	46
Schmitt, Eric, WF	8	1	3.94	19	1	78	80	32	78
Reid, Brent, Duke	9	4	4.04	15	0	78	87	27	42
MacDougal, Mike, WF	6	5	4.15	16	0	91	79	78	86
Adams, Brian, Clemson	6	2	4.22	16	0	70	66	30	48
Yankosky, L.J., Ga. Tech	11	1	4.23	18	1	111	104	42	110
Blackmon, Kurt, N.C. State	11	5	4.27	21	1	118	127	31	103
Dupree, Brad, Duke	4	1	4.46	24	2	67	61	21	46
Elmore, Chris, UNC	5	0	4.48	11	0	60	60	32	42
McDonald, Jon, Fla. State	10	4	4.56	19	0	105	91	52	101
Ward, Jeremy, WF	10	9	4.57	25	0	104	125	38	71
Scarce, Bubba, N.C. State	8	3	4.68	23	1	83	80	48	73
White, Matt, Clemson	5	2	4.79	16	0	68	74	31	59
Mottl, Ryan, Clemson	9	4	4.81	16	0	101	101	31	96
Agamennone, Brandon, Mary.	6	7	4.87	15	0	94	113	22	96
Browning, Skip, Clemson	5	3	4.89	12	0	53	59	27	42
Chavez, Chris, Fla. State	8	4	4.89	18	1	85	92	47	65
Baker, Dustin, N.C. State	7	6	4.92	18	0	97	102	40	76

ATLANTIC-10 CONFERENCE

	Conference		Overall	
EAST	W	L	W	L
Massachusetts	15	3	27	12
***Fordham**	10	8	27	20
St. Bonaventure	8	10	21	21
Rhode Island	8	10	19	24
Temple	7	11	18	28
St. Joseph's	6	12	21	26
WEST	W	L	W	L
George Washington	13	2	33	18
Virginia Tech	10	5	28	22
Duquesne	11	7	22	25
Xavier	9	8	27	25
Dayton	5	12	21	19
LaSalle	1	15	12	28

ALL-CONFERENCE TEAM: **C**—Jason Siegfried, Jr., Dayton. **1B**—Joe Beichert, Jr., George Washington. **2B**—Muchie Dagliere, Sr., Massachusetts. **3B**—Tom Stein, Jr., Fordham. **SS**—Matt Shipley, Jr., Dayton. **OF**—B.J. Barns, So., Duquesne; Ryan Fleming, Sr., Dayton; Matt Griswold, Jr., Virginia Tech. **DH**—Jim Dallio, Sr., Xavier. **P**—Tom Baginski, Jr., George Washington; Jay Krystofolski, Jr., Rhode Island.

Player of the Year: Matt Griswold, Virginia Tech. **Pitcher of the Year**: Jay Krystofolski, Rhode Island. **Rookie of the Year**: Pat Pinkman, Virginia Tech. **Coach of the Year**: Tom Walter, George Washington.

INDIVIDUAL BATTING LEADERS

(Minimum 100 At-Bats)

	AVG	AB	R	H	2B	3B	HR	RBI	SB
Fleming, Ryan, Dayton	**.455**	156	51	**71**	**22**	4	5	43	14
Dagliere, Muchie, Mass.	.444	151	39	67	16	0	1	49	4
Barns, B.J., Duquesne	.420	169	**55**	**71**	11	3	**20**	58	7
Stahl, Josh, Duquesne	.392	125	36	49	9	4	6	42	5
Watson, Matt, Xavier	.387	142	32	55	10	1	8	41	2
Lanzilli, Kevin, RI	384	146	34	56	6	0	6	31	11
Dallio, Jim, Xavier	.382	144	31	55	8	0	12	47	0
D'Auria, Mike, Fordham	.382	131	32	50	7	0	1	28	11
Beichert, Joe, Geo. Wash.	.381	160	39	61	11	0	16	49	3
Stein, Tom, Fordham	.375	168	40	63	14	0	9	40	4
Clark, Doug, Mass.	.369	149	40	55	9	4	8	37	10
Pallotta, Jeff, Rhode Island	.369	141	29	52	11	0	0	19	9
Rouhier, Dan, Geo. Wash.	.368	114	25	42	11	0	5	28	3
Shiflett, Eric, Va. Tech	.365	189	49	69	15	0	2	23	3
Muys, Adrian, Fordham	.363	157	32	57	15	5	4	34	**24**
Griswold, Matt, Va. Tech	.361	183	47	66	18	0	9	**65**	4
Fuchs, Mike, LaSalle	.355	141	31	50	13	1	4	36	1
Siegfried, Jason, Dayton	.353	153	37	54	13	1	13	51	3
Munroe, Craig, Temple	.351	154	31	54	10	3	10	43	1
Bowman, Addison, Va. Tech	.346	205	47	**71**	18	0	7	39	4
Gautreau, Pete, Mass.	.346	133	30	46	5	4	10	47	17
Roberts, Mike, Geo. Wash.	.344	180	40	62	11	0	6	29	14
Shipley, Matt, Dayton	.344	122	34	42	12	1	10	38	4
Foutz, Chad, Va. Tech	.341	126	25	43	9	2	2	22	0
Thiebaud, Tom, St. Bona.	.341	138	26	47	9	1	3	29	12
#Bell, Pat, Dayton	.327	165	35	54	6	**7**	2	22	6

INDIVIDUAL PITCHING LEADERS

(Minimum 40 Innings)

	W	L	ERA	G	SV	IP	H	BB	SO
Krystofolski, Jay, RI	5	6	**1.72**	11	0	68	51	14	67
Young, Colin, Fordham	5	1	2.70	9	0	40	38	10	35
LaMattina, Ryan, St. Bona.	3	5	3.02	13	1	63	54	23	56
Cooke, Bill, Mass.	**8**	2	3.06	11	0	68	62	19	50
Cameron, Ryan, Mass.	5	3	3.28	13	1	71	50	35	65
Baginski, Tom, Geo. Wash.	6	4	3.30	14	0	87	72	20	**97**
Vonsossan, Ryan, Dayton	4	2	3.41	9	0	51	60	18	44
Cutter, Jared, Xavier	1	2	3.42	20	3	55	56	19	32
Reznick, Gary, Fordham	5	4	3.80	14	0	71	65	34	38
Witte, Lou, Xavier	7	5	3.89	15	0	90	92	29	77
Rosendahl, Kasey, Dayton	4	3	3.90	14	0	52	52	19	35
Davis, Jim, Duquesne	3	3	3.96	8	0	50	54	23	51
Pinkman, Pat, Va. Tech	7	2	3.97	17	2	88	78	29	82
Belicic, Adam, Geo. Wash.	7	3	4.00	13	0	74	79	42	51
McFarland, Jason, Dayton	4	3	4.17	11	0	52	58	28	25
Scullin, Jon, Rhode Island	6	1	4.26	12	1	63	71	13	35
Rain, Matt, Xavier	6	0	4.34	18	0	48	52	26	26
Zirkle, Todd, Va. Tech	5	3	4.37	14	0	56	66	24	21
Lewis, Scott, Temple	3	3	4.44	12	0	47	50	31	50
#Hand, Jon, Va. Tech	**8**	3	4.68	16	1	106	133	21	74
#Scuglikm Mike, Xavier	1	1	5.23	14	**4**	10	13	5	12

BIG EAST CONFERENCE

	Conference		Overall	
	W	L	W	L
***Rutgers**	17	3	33	16
Notre Dame	15	4	41	17
St. John's	14	7	28	17
Providence	14	8	31	22
West Virginia	13	9	37	17
Seton Hall	12	10	25	23
Connecticut	12	11	25	17
Villanova	6	15	26	21
Pittsburgh	5	16	12	27
Boston College	4	15	17	23
Georgetown	5	19	22	34

ALL-CONFERENCE TEAM: C—Scott Friedholm, Sr., Providence. **1B**—Pete Zoccolillo, Jr., Rutgers. **2B**—David Marciniak, Jr., Rutgers. **3B**—Brant Ust, So., Notre Dame. **SS**—J.J. Brock, Sr., Notre Dame. **OF**—Joe McNamee, Sr. West Virginia; Adam Neubart, Jr., Rutgers; Tyrone Wayne, Sr., St. John's. **DH**—Jeff Wagner, Jr., Notre Dame. **Util**—Dan Boublis, Jr., Villanova. **P**—Brad Lidge, Jr., Notre Dame; Kevin McGerry, Fr., St. John's; Josh Santos, Jr., Connecticut.

Player of the Year: Brant Ust, Notre Dame. **Pitcher of the Year**: Brad Lidge, Notre Dame. **Rookie of the Year**: Jake Daubert, Rutgers. **Coach of the Year**: Fred Hill, Rutgers.

INDIVIDUAL BATTING LEADERS

(Minimum 100 At-Bats)

	AVG	AB	R	H	2B	3B	HR	RBI	SB
McGowan, Sean, BC	**.432**	146	49	63	12	3	16	55	1
McNamee, Joe, West Va.	.429	191	61	82	**27**	2	13	**66**	5
Dzurilla, Mike, St. John's	.427	185	60	79	15	4	9	49	20
Hammond, Jamie, WV	.417	192	45	80	8	0	0	44	19
Marciniak, Dave, Rutgers	.410	188	58	77	24	4	6	50	5
Caudill, Clarke, Conn.	.404	166	38	67	12	2	5	44	6
Langone, Steve, BC	.401	142	41	57	13	1	9	36	3
Friedholm, Scott, Prov.	.395	200	64	79	21	2	13	**66**	16
Boublis, Dan, Villanova	.394	160	50	63	13	2	10	48	2
Longo, Matt, Villanova	.393	178	51	70	18	2	12	47	8
Zoccolillo, Pete, Rutgers	.387	199	56	77	10	1	12	59	2
Rich, Billy, Conn.	.385	174	49	67	10	2	15	58	8
Packin, Brian, Conn.	.383	141	24	54	14	0	6	34	1
Olkowski, Kevin, West Va.	.382	217	**68**	**83**	16	1	2	44	12
Williams, Lance, West Va.	.380	179	40	68	11	1	1	30	7
Carey, Pat, Prov.	.379	182	50	69	10	5	6	42	2
Hart, Matt, West Va.	.377	215	60	81	20	1	2	40	3
Ciminiello, Angelo, Prov.	.376	218	64	82	18	4	12	57	6
Bravette, John, Seton Hall	.373	166	52	62	14	1	2	25	3
Ust, Brant, ND	.373	217	55	81	20	1	**18**	58	11
Katz, Glenn, Conn.	.370	192	52	71	16	4	12	44	20
Daubert, Jake, Rutgers	.368	190	46	70	19	4	10	64	7
Mercado, Willy, Conn.	.359	131	26	47	9	0	4	30	6
Vath, Josh, Seton Hall	.359	167	33	60	9	3	7	43	7
DiPrima, Giancarlo, St.J	.350	177	49	63	11	2	2	23	**24**
Fenster, Darren, Rutgers	.355	172	35	61	11	1	1	34	6
Quirk, Mike, Boston Coll.	.352	108	20	38	15	0	1	19	1
Wayne, Tyrone, St. John's	.352	182	40	64	17	1	15	58	9
Hummel, Dan, Seton Hall	.348	161	29	56	8	0	6	40	3
#Mignogna, Sean, Georgetown	.328	177	42	58	15	**9**	3	33	17

INDIVIDUAL PITCHING LEADERS

(Minimum 40 Innings)

	W	L	ERA	G	SV	IP	H	BB	SO
Heilman, Aaron, ND	7	3	**1.61**	31	**9**	67	46	19	78
McGerry, Kevin, St.John's	6	2	2.06	12	0	66	49	33	62
Balazentis, Bob, Pittsburgh	2	4	2.35	10	1	46	43	8	53
Stamler, Keith, St. John's	4	1	2.47	13	1	51	52	16	40
Kalita, Tim, Notre Dame	4	0	2.78	15	0	74	68	37	71
Shilliday, Alex, ND	**9**	5	3.54	18	0	97	101	25	**93**
Zyskowski, Garrett, West Va.	**9**	2	3.54	15	0	89	91	39	79
Ross, Lewis, West Va.	5	2	3.62	16	4	70	78	11	73
Esslinger, Cam, Seton Hall	4	5	3.72	14	1	75	68	37	80
Benik, B.J., Seton Hall	6	3	4.05	13	0	73	77	17	47
Lidge, Brad, Notre Dame	8	2	4.15	16	0	80	72	39	**93**
Collins, Pat, St. John's	4	3	4.20	14	1	75	67	35	79
Santos, Josh, Conn.	7	4	4.42	13	0	79	97	26	91
McKeown, Chris, ND	4	2	4.47	17	0	44	51	21	37
Probst, John, Seton Hall	1	3	4.55	17	5	55	49	20	36
Connolly, Keith, Rutgers	4	3	4.60	16	1	43	52	16	42
Henry, Will, Villanova	6	2	4.68	15	0	50	48	17	48
Coughenour, Jory, Pitt.	2	2	4.70	14	1	46	53	24	30
Arizin, Matt, Georgetown	5	6	4.71	13	0	71	81	26	33
Berney, Scott, Conn.	4	2	4.71	9	0	50	65	18	28
Cummings, Jeremy, West Va.	4	2	4.72	18	2	61	67	23	53
DesRoches, Marc, Prov.	8	4	4.75	15	0	95	90	43	73

BIG SOUTH CONFERENCE

	Conference W	Conference L	Overall W	Overall L
***Liberty**	13	5	32	29
Coastal Carolina	11	7	31	29
UNC Asheville	10	8	27	32
Winthrop	10	8	35	22
Charleston Southern	9	9	24	29
Radford	7	11	17	35
Maryland-Baltimore County	3	15	10	37

ALL-CONFERENCE TEAM: **C**—Steve Tomshack, Jr., UMBC. **1B**—Rick Kobsik, Sr., Winthrop. **2B**—Mike Lombardi, Jr., Radford. **3B**—Jason Benham, Sr., Liberty. **SS**—Ty Wigginton, Sr., UNC Asheville. **OF**—Steve Wright, Sr., Liberty; Eddie Woods, Jr., UNC Asheville; Joe Colameco, Sr., Winthrop. **DH**—Jeff Collins, Sr., Radford. **P**—Mark Cisar, Sr., Charleston Southern; Dave Steffler, Jr., Winthrop.

Most Valuable Player: Jason Benham, Liberty. **Rookie of the Year**: Brooks Marzka, Coastal Carolina. **Coach of the Year**: Dave Pastors, Liberty.

INDIVIDUAL BATTING LEADERS

(Minimum 100 At-Bats)

	AVG	AB	R	H	2B	3B	HR	RBI	SB
Cameron, Dorian, Co. Car.	**.411**	236	57	**97**	17	1	3	42	12
Dalton, David, Liberty	.408	201	59	82	16	0	10	39	26
Tomshack, Steve, UMBC	.407	182	48	74	17	3	17	59	0
Benham, Jason, Liberty	.398	231	61	92	13	3	11	53	20
Crandell, Scott, UMBC	.389	180	41	70	13	3	6	38	2
Lombardi, Mike, Radford	.375	208	49	78	14	2	6	36	15
Piotraszko, Jamie, UNCA	.374	179	44	67	17	0	7	31	1
Colameco, Joe, Winthrop	.373	209	61	78	20	0	11	48	**30**
Woods, Eddie, UNCA	.368	220	46	81	11	3	13	56	2
Wright, Steve, Liberty	.366	202	46	74	14	**5**	**18**	**79**	15
Collins, Jeff, Radford	.361	191	39	69	17	1	12	51	7
Samatas, Jeremy, Co. Car.	.356	222	51	79	14	2	**18**	55	0
Siemers, Patrick, CS	.356	104	17	37	3	0	0	17	0
McClellan, Ryan, Liberty	.354	147	32	52	12	1	13	39	7
Kristowski, Jason, CS	.351	171	34	60	13	2	6	44	14
Cisar, Mark, Char. South.	.344	157	42	54	10	2	8	34	15
Miller, Trey, Liberty	.342	161	39	55	9	1	3	26	11
Carter, Chris, Co. Car.	.341	185	41	63	15	1	8	32	6
Hillier, Billy, UNC Asheville	.341	211	53	72	15	0	9	54	3
Whiting, Chris, Radford	.337	193	36	65	13	0	3	31	6
Wigginton, Ty, UNC Asheville	.336	217	**67**	73	**26**	1	16	51	10
#Kobsik, Rick, Winthrop	.322	205	50	66	15	0	**18**	66	3

INDIVIDUAL PITCHING LEADERS

(Minimum 40 Innings)

	W	L	ERA	G	SV	IP	H	BB	SO
Cisar, Mark, Char. South.	8	8	**3.08**	20	2	114	92	44	105
Steffler, Dave, Winthrop	**11**	3	3.21	17	0	104	100	18	97
Harrell, Brian, Liberty	8	4	4.20	19	0	101	113	25	73
Krooschell, Terry, Winthrop	5	2	4.31	14	0	77	75	50	76
Deubel, Ron, Co. Car.	8	8	4.44	20	0	118	118	49	**136**
Miller, Benji, Liberty	7	5	4.53	20	1	103	91	44	119
Koziara, Matt, Winthrop	6	6	4.59	16	0	82	93	38	67
Kadlec, Kit, Co. Car.	3	0	4.97	29	**9**	43	50	19	38
Hillier, Billy, UNC Asheville	5	9	4.98	16	0	87	114	39	63
MacIver, Ian, Char. South.	7	7	5.23	20	1	103	125	48	71
Harrell, Tim, Liberty	9	4	5.50	18	0	105	121	48	84
Sturkie, Scott, Co. Car.	5	2	5.71	16	0	52	56	24	56
White, Josh, UNC Asheville	7	4	5.75	16	1	83	95	45	101
Brannon, Nick, UNC Asheville	5	5	5.78	24	0	76	96	48	61
Johnson, Rett, Co. Car.	6	4	5.79	16	0	79	96	51	66

BIG TEN CONFERENCE

	Conference W	Conference L	Overall W	Overall L
Illinois	19	5	42	21
***Minnesota**	19	9	45	15
Ohio State	18	9	37	16
Penn State	15	11	28	24
Indiana	14	14	29	27
Michigan	9	15	21	27
Iowa	9	15	19	27
Northwestern	10	18	27	26
Michigan State	8	16	25	27
Purdue	9	18	23	29

ALL-CONFERENCE TEAM: C—Aaron Nieckula, Sr., Illinois. **1B**—Robb Quinlan, Jr., Minnesota. **2B**—D.J. Svihlik, So., Illinois. **3B**—Craig Marquie, So., Illinois. **SS**—Mark Carek, Sr., Ohio State. **OF**—Mike Lockwood, Jr., Ohio State; Dan O'Neill, Jr., Illinois; Craig Selander, Jr., Minnesota. **DH**—Dan Seimetz, Sr., Ohio State. **P**—Brett Weber, Sr., Illinois; Nate Bump, Sr., Penn State; Mark Mulder, Jr., Michigan State; John Seaman, Jr., Northwestern. **RP**—Jim Journell, So., Illinois.

Player of the Year: D.J. Svihlik, Illinois. **Pitcher of the Year**: Brett Weber, Illinois. **Freshman of the Year**: Jeremy Kurella, Northwestern. **Coach of the Year**: Itch Jones, Illinois.

INDIVIDUAL BATTING LEADERS

(Minimum 125 At-Bats)

	AVG	AB	R	H	2B	3B	HR	RBI	SB
Trott, Jason, Ohio State	**.428**	194	53	83	10	2	8	54	5
Fagan, Shawn, Penn State	.41[illegible]	176	62	73	6	1	12	47	10
Quinlan, Robb, Minnesota	.408	238	**87**	**97**	15	[illegible]	[illegible]	[illegible]	6
Hallada, Daryl, Purdue	.402	194	36	78	15	1	1	26	8
Lockwood, Mike, Ohio State	.401	202	72	81	14	2	18	66	8
O'Neill, Dan, Illinois	.393	206	60	81	16	3	12	48	18
Marquie, Craig, Illinois	.392	209	61	82	16	3	11	58	5
Cervenak, Mike, Michigan	.385	205	42	79	17	0	13	50	2
Childs, Brandt, Indiana	.383	175	50	67	13	1	12	52	1
Walker, Chris, Purdue	.379	169	38	64	6	4	1	23	20
Svihlik, D.J., Illinois	.374	174	31	65	16	2	15	55	0
Stritch, Mike, Northwestern	.374	179	38	67	17	1	7	49	2
Selander, Craig, Minnesota	.372	226	70	84	13	2	22	75	11
Seimetz, Dan, Ohio State	.371	175	39	65	8	0	15	46	2
Groebner, Mark, Minnesota	.370	227	70	84	17	3	17	**80**	**28**
Williamson, J.P., Nor.	.367	139	28	51	5	1	1	27	9
Rudden, Kevin, Illinois	.366	205	44	75	12	3	10	47	0
Scanlon, Matt, Minnesota	.366	243	61	89	**21**	3	7	62	3
Rhodes, Dusty, Illinois	.361	233	62	84	20	5	7	35	15
Thompson, Patrick, Nor.	.356	188	33	67	11	1	3	40	5
Scales, Bobby, Michigan	.353	173	38	61	12	2	3	26	7
Alcaraz, Jason, Michigan	.350	180	35	63	9	3	3	37	3
Baron, Brian, Northwestern	.349	152	39	53	12	4	6	33	1
Beers, Dan, Penn State	.348	181	45	63	11	1	16	60	11
Brosseau, Matt, Minnesota	.341	138	27	47	7	0	2	26	8
Rhodes, Danny, Illinois	.341	232	57	79	16	2	9	47	16
Ehrnsberger, Chad, OS	.340	141	32	48	15	1	7	40	4
Kremblas, Mike, Ohio State	.339	183	43	62	14	1	4	46	6
Campo, Michael, Penn State	.337	193	46	65	14	1	8	43	6
Boros, Steve, Iowa	.335	155	26	52	11	1	1	22	2
Mulder, Mark, Mich. State	.335	155	28	52	11	0	5	30	0
Boruta, Scott, Penn State	.333	147	43	49	9	0	6	37	9
Carek, Mark, Ohio State	.332	199	50	66	11	3	2	32	5
Kurella, Jeremy, Northwest.	.332	199	42	66	11	**6**	3	39	8
Nieckula, Aaron, Illinois	.332	196	38	65	12	1	5	44	17
Ramsey, Terry, Iowa	.331	169	35	56	8	1	8	31	7

INDIVIDUAL PITCHING LEADERS

(Minimum 50 Innings)

	W	L	ERA	G	SV	IP	H	BB	SO
Bump, Nate, Penn State	7	3	**2.62**	13	0	106	85	25	**135**
Birk, Ben, Minnesota	8	2	2.65	11	0	75	67	11	67
#Yens, Chris, Mich. State	1	2	2.77	20	**7**	26	16	12	13
Seaman, John, Northwestern	9	6	3.07	20	1	82	76	21	42
Weber, Brett, Illinois	**10**	3	3.11	21	0	107	87	28	99
Mulder, Mark, Mich. State	6	6	3.40	15	0	85	80	19	113
Smith, Chad, Indiana	7	4	3.62	13	0	82	79	30	70
Pautz, Brad, Minnesota	6	3	3.65	18	2	69	84	21	42
Murphy, Brian, Mich. State	6	4	3.73	13	0	80	79	27	60
Thompson, Eric, Ohio State	6	3	3.75	17	0	84	77	34	83
Salter, Cody, Illinois	7	6	4.03	23	2	103	130	14	49
Meccage, Jeremy, Iowa	5	4	4.55	10	0	61	61	20	45
Fry, Justin, Ohio State	7	3	4.59	16	1	96	90	31	113
McGrath, Dan, Minnesota	9	3	4.68	22	0	75	88	19	48
Anderson, Jason, Illinois	6	0	4.75	18	0	66	74	22	43
Rehrer, Travis, Illinois	3	1	4.82	18	1	52	38	34	70
Morgan, Russ, Purdue	5	2	4.97	12	0	67	73	28	68
#Fagan, Shawn, Penn State	2	4	8.49	19	**7**	41	55	17	24

BIG 12 CONFERENCE

	Conference W	Conference L	Overall W	Overall L
Texas A&M	21	9	46	20
Baylor	18	10	41	20
***Texas Tech**	18	11	44	20
Oklahoma	17	11	42	20
Missouri	17	12	36	18
Oklahoma State	15	12	40	21
Nebraska	10	13	24	20
Texas	11	18	23	32
Iowa State	10	18	20	27
Kansas State	9	19	20	32
Kansas	7	20	22	29

ALL-CONFERENCE TEAM: C—Josh Bard, So., Texas Tech; Josh Holliday, Jr., Oklahoma State. **1B**—Charley Carter, Sr., Baylor. **INF**—Keith Ginter, Sr., Texas Tech; Corey Hart, Sr., Oklahoma; Craig Kuzmic, Jr., Texas A&M; Griffin Moore, Sr., Missouri; Derek Wathan, Jr., Oklahoma. **OF**—Ryan Fry, Sr., Missouri; Willy Hill, Sr., Oklahoma; Jason Tyner, Jr., Texas A&M; Jon Topolski, Jr., Baylor. **DH**—Casey Bookout, Jr., Oklahoma. **Util**—Jason Jennings, So., Baylor. **P**—Kip Wells, Jr., Baylor; Ryan Rupe, Sr., Texas A&M; Casey Fossum, So., Texas A&M; Geoff Geary, Sr., Oklahoma; Shane Wright, Jr., Texas Tech. **RP**—Danny Prata, Jr., Oklahoma State; Chris George, Jr., Missouri.

Co-Players of the Year: Jason Jennings, Baylor; Jason Tyner, Texas A&M. **Newcomer of the Year**: Craig Kuzmic, Texas A&M. **Freshman of the Year**: Matt Smith, Oklahoma State. **Coach of the Year**: Mark Johnson, Texas A&M.

ROBERT GURGANUS

Spartan southpaw

Mark Mulder struck out 113 for Michigan State

INDIVIDUAL BATTING LEADERS

(Minimum 125 At-Bats)

	AVG	AB	R	H	2B	3B	HR	RBI	SB
Leimbek, Shawn, Iowa St.	**.413**	155	37	64	14	1	5	36	3
Bookout, Casey, Oklahoma	.405	222	74	90	12	0	26	76	5
Wathan, Derek, Oklahoma	.405	252	75	102	16	5	6	52	21
Carter, Charley, Baylor	.402	246	57	99	**24**	2	21	**86**	1
Hill, Willy, Oklahoma	.390	251	68	98	21	5	4	38	15
Ruiz, Ryan, Texas Tech	.388	196	51	76	11	0	2	36	22
Tyner, Jason, Texas A&M	.385	278	71	**107**	12	2	0	31	**39**
Bard, Josh, Texas Tech	.383	264	56	101	22	2	17	71	1
Fry, Ryan, Missouri	.377	212	77	80	18	0	**27**	78	12
Moore, Griffin, Missouri	.376	218	63	82	13	3	20	71	10
Harvey, Ken, Nebraska	.373	150	33	56	11	2	7	39	5
Ginter, Keith, Texas Tech	.371	229	**97**	85	**24**	1	17	55	27
Marn, Josh, Kansas St.	.369	206	47	76	15	0	9	52	7
Wyrick, Clint, Kansas	.369	198	53	73	17	4	5	46	27
Runk, Aaron, Iowa State	.360	175	51	63	7	5	6	24	11
Burns, Brennan, Texas Tech.	.354	192	43	68	23	1	2	38	0
Jordan, Kevin, Texas Tech	.354	263	66	93	20	5	17	84	18
Hart, Corey, Oklahoma	.347	236	69	82	23	2	10	51	7
Juday, Andy, Kansas	.347	144	30	50	11	2	1	27	8
McDonough, Matt, Iowa St.	.347	176	34	61	15	1	11	47	0
Topolski, Jon, Baylor	.344	250	74	86	7	**11**	19	54	22
Landreth, Jason, Texas Tech	.343	236	63	81	16	4	11	54	28
Dodson, Jeremy, Baylor	.342	225	69	77	19	0	13	57	19
Blair, James, Baylor	.342	240	58	82	15	3	10	49	25
Nelson, John, Kansas	.342	158	35	54	7	3	4	28	6
Kimura, Danny, Nebraska	.340	159	32	54	15	2	8	41	1
Dimmick, Josh, Kansas	.337	196	48	66	11	1	9	60	4
McCullough, Jay, Okla. St.	.337	202	43	68	13	1	9	43	4
Gasparino, Billy, Okla. St.	.336	217	72	73	17	2	13	59	23
Rallo, Mike, Missouri	.336	217	57	73	18	2	13	43	1
Scheschuk, John, Texas A&M	.336	217	46	73	10	4	16	68	2
Cox, Jason, Texas	.335	173	42	58	11	3	4	26	7
Montenegro, Jose, Oklahoma	.335	236	58	79	18	1	12	66	1
Lucas, Kevin, Oklahoma St.	.332	238	48	79	17	3	7	53	14
Jennings, Jason, Baylor	.327	211	42	69	14	0	18	58	0
Ayres, Yancy, Kansas St.	.327	202	44	66	19	3	8	43	2

INDIVIDUAL PITCHING LEADERS
(Minimum 50 Innings)

	W	L	ERA	G	SV	IP	H	BB	SO
#Silva, Andy, Kansas St.	3	1	2.66	20	**8**	24	18	11	27
Wright, Shane, Texas Tech	**14**	1	**2.71**	21	2	153	166	20	116
Rupe, Ryan, Texas A&M	11	4	2.87	15	0	113	95	23	125
Schuldt, Matt, Nebraska	4	2	3.13	10	0	55	44	25	45
Stine, Justin, Missouri	6	5	3.57	15	0	93	110	34	78
Smith, Matt, Oklahoma St.	6	3	3.61	15	0	85	79	33	90
Wells, Kip, Baylor	13	4	3.71	20	0	124	121	44	135
Fossum, Casey, Texas A&M	12	2	3.74	20	2	123	108	41	129
Caple, Chance, Texas A&M	7	1	3.79	19	0	74	70	28	63
Bludau, Frank, Oklahoma St.	4	3	4.09	21	0	62	62	11	45
Philbrick, Rusty, Kansas	4	3	4.09	17	0	73	69	31	79
Prata, Danny, Oklahoma St.	5	4	4.32	25	4	67	77	20	49
Adkins, Jon, Oklahoma St.	8	1	4.54	14	0	85	92	27	63
Pearson, Dale, Oklahoma St.	6	2	4.60	15	0	61	71	24	45
Ward, Monty, Texas Tech	6	4	4.65	16	0	108	109	49	**151**
Dunn, Scott, Texas	6	6	4.95	20	0	109	105	64	98
Geary, Geoff, Oklahoma	13	1	4.96	20	0	123	145	36	142
Hoerman, Jared, Oklahoma	7	5	4.99	14	0	60	70	26	59
Bell, Jay, Missouri	6	1	5.08	14	0	78	85	27	84
Jennings, Jason, Baylor	11	4	5.08	20	2	117	123	53	126
Allison, Cade, Texas Tech	3	3	5.22	15	0	50	63	18	51
Sirianni, Jay, Nebraska	5	4	5.24	16	0	57	61	22	44
Bergman, Brett, Baylor	7	7	5.31	17	0	100	110	40	84
Peck, Brandon, Kansas St.	4	6	5.34	17	0	93	126	30	44

BIG WEST CONFERENCE

	Conference		Overall	
NORTH	**W**	**L**	**W**	**L**
Nevada	17	10	31	22
Sacramento State	13	17	25	35
Pacific	12	17	25	22
New Mexico State	8	21	23	29
SOUTH	**W**	**L**	**W**	**L**
Cal State Fullerton	25	5	47	17
***Long Beach State**	23	7	43	23
UC Santa Barbara	11	18	18	31
Cal Poly San Luis Obispo	7	21	16	42

ALL-CONFERENCE TEAM: C—Corky Miller, Sr., Nevada. **1B**—Steve Wood, So., Cal Poly San Luis Obispo. **2B**—David Bacani, Fr., Cal State Fullerton. **3B**—Paul Day, Jr., Long Beach State. **SS**—Andre Champagne, Sr., New Mexico State. **OF**—Lyle Overbay, Jr., Nevada; Aaron Rowand, Jr., Cal State Fullerton; Terrmel Sledge, Jr., Long Beach State. **DH**—Josh Payne, Sr., Sacramento State. **Util**—Greg Jacobs, Jr., Cal State Fullerton. **P**—Jim Brink, Sr., Nevada; Benito Flores, Sr., Cal State Fullerton; Erasmo Ramirez, Sr., Cal State Fullerton. **RP**—Adam Johnson, Fr., Cal State Fullerton.

Player of the Year: Paul Day, Long Beach State. **Pitcher of the Year**: Benito Flores, Cal State Fullerton. **Coach of the Year**: George Horton, Cal State Fullerton.

INDIVIDUAL BATTING LEADERS
(Minimum 125 At-Bats)

	AVG	AB	R	H	2B	3B	HR	RBI	SB
Lopez, Chuck, Long Beach	**.422**	268	77	**113**	17	4	4	52	7
Story, Jason, New Mexico St.	.404	198	61	80	15	2	**23**	82	1
Weekly, Chris, New Mex. St.	.403	226	77	91	13	0	20	79	5
Day, Paul, Long Beach	.401	274	83	110	16	**6**	15	**89**	21
Marshall, Brandon, Sac. St.	.398	249	70	99	16	1	9	52	3
Smith, Cory, NM St.	.397	184	63	73	14	2	11	46	14
Sledge, Terrmel, Long Beach	.392	286	**99**	112	25	5	13	63	**26**
Jacobs, Greg, CS Fullerton	.389	198	56	77	20	2	8	55	11
Fukuhara, Pete, CS Fullerton	.383	141	38	54	10	0	10	47	4
Miller, Corky, Nevada	.377	191	77	72	12	1	14	63	4
Roberson, Chris, NM St.	.375	184	43	69	14	0	10	44	1
Rowand, Aaron, CS Full.	.372	242	66	90	**27**	4	16	72	15
Berni, Jason, Long Beach	.364	217	35	79	22	0	4	48	2
Inglett, Joe, Nevada	.364	162	58	59	10	3	5	40	8
Chatham, Steve, CS Full.	.362	149	45	54	12	1	7	36	9
Rizzi, Todd, New Mex. St.	.361	180	42	65	12	2	13	52	10
LaCour, Bryan, UCSB	.359	181	49	65	20	2	8	51	0
Payne, Josh, Sac. State	.357	221	68	79	18	2	18	61	2
Kennedy, Bryan, Long Beach	.356	247	65	88	25	1	8	81	1
Bollon, Jason, Sac. State	.352	236	47	83	17	1	13	68	6
Carson, Glen, Nevada	.352	216	76	76	23	0	15	67	0
Yount, Jason, Long Beach	.352	233	60	82	10	1	11	57	5
Elorduy, Dan, Sac. State	.351	225	49	79	13	2	14	64	6
Gemoll, Justin, UCSB	.351	205	44	72	20	0	9	57	4
Faltys, Jeremy, NM St.	.345	148	35	51	7	1	3	26	2
Wright, Brad, UCSB	.345	200	43	69	14	1	6	29	10
Price, Don, Nevada	.343	166	43	57	12	1	13	58	1
Champagne, Andre, NM St.	.340	191	55	65	12	2	2	32	25
Wood, Steve, Cal Poly SLO	.340	235	43	80	16	0	18	58	7
McGuire, Shawn, Sac. State	.339	127	27	43	7	2	4	19	5
Wood, Robbie, Pacific	.339	177	26	60	10	0	0	28	4
Overbay, Lyle, Nevada	.338	225	81	76	14	3	14	85	2
Martin, Justin, Nevada	.336	220	68	74	7	4	2	39	15
Moore, Ryan, CS Full.	.336	211	43	71	19	3	14	56	2

INDIVIDUAL PITCHING LEADERS
(Minimum 50 Innings)

	W	L	ERA	G	SV	IP	H	BB	SO
Gallo, Mike, Long Beach	6	2	**3.41**	22	0	92	94	28	66
Flores, Benito, CS Fullerton	**12**	0	3.52	18	1	123	120	34	100
Kordich, Dennis, Long Beach	5	4	3.63	29	0	52	54	25	40
Ramirez, Erasmo, CS Fullerton	11	5	3.66	19	0	130	133	28	**112**
#Marr, Jason, Long Beach	3	1	4.43	31	**9**	41	40	12	38
Merrill, Darren, Long Beach	7	0	4.61	27	0	53	56	16	47
Jacobs, Greg, CS Fullerton	4	4	4.87	17	0	57	71	22	54
Berni, Jason, Long Beach	5	5	4.91	23	1	62	77	31	41
Saarloos, Kirk, CS Fullerton	4	2	5.15	30	3	51	62	24	57
Balbuena, Caleb, Long Beach	7	3	5.17	18	0	101	112	39	81
Brink, Jim, Nevada	10	4	5.24	17	0	113	132	38	108
Moore, Darin, Pacific	7	5	5.36	17	2	82	105	37	77
Grant, Daryl, Long Beach	3	5	5.62	21	0	66	65	49	56
Kinto, Troy, UCSB	5	4	5.77	15	0	94	124	50	95
Zirelli, Mike, Cal Poly SLO	3	12	5.77	16	0	115	160	27	77

COLONIAL ATHLETIC ASSOCIATION

	Conference		Overall	
	W	**L**	**W**	**L**
Virginia Commonwealth	18	2	46	15
***Richmond**	15	6	41	17
James Madison	11	8	27	29
East Carolina	10	11	30	29
Old Dominion	9	12	28	29
George Mason	8	12	26	28
UNC Wilmington	6	14	21	34
William & Mary	4	16	24	28

ALL-CONFERENCE TEAM: C—Cory Whitby, Sr., Virginia Commonwealth. **1B**—Mike Dwyer, Jr., Richmond. **2B**—Nate Rewers, Jr., Richmond. **3B**—Greg Filson, So., George Mason. **SS**—Corey Hoch, Sr., James Madison. **OF**—Shawn Pearson, So., Old Dominion; Kevin Razler, Jr., James Madison; John Williamson, Fr., East Carolina. **DH**—Andy Devitt, Sr., George Mason. **P**—Matt Burch, Jr., Virginia Commonwealth; Brooks Jernigan, Jr., East Carolina. **RP**—Brandon Inge, Jr., Virginia Commonwealth.

Co-Players of the Year: Matt Burch, Virginia Commonwealth; Brandon Inge, Virginia Commonwealth. **Rookie of the Year**: Tim Hummel, Old Dominion. **Coach of the Year**: Paul Keyes, Virginia Commonwealth.

INDIVIDUAL BATTING LEADERS
(Minimum 125 At-Bats)

	AVG	AB	R	H	2B	3B	HR	RBI	SB
Razler, Kevin, JMU	**.387**	204	48	79	16	3	7	36	16
Hummel, Tim, ODU	.386	220	59	85	20	2	7	55	10
Pearson, Shawn, ODU	.380	208	65	79	17	1	4	34	**38**
Filson, Greg, George Mason	.365	200	35	73	19	1	7	54	12
Massimo, Ryan, ECU	.357	227	43	81	17	1	13	60	5
Thompson, Rich, JMU	.357	126	32	45	4	2	1	12	14
Hoch, Corey, James Madison	.356	222	67	79	14	1	8	41	15
Dwyer, Mike, Richmond	.356	247	57	**88**	19	2	**24**	**72**	1
Rewers, Nate, Richmond	.349	209	54	73	13	0	2	36	8
White, Greg, James Madison	.346	179	37	62	8	0	8	40	14
Forelli, Anthony, ODU	.341	226	45	77	14	0	10	67	5
Williamson, John, ECU	.340	194	50	66	15	0	13	38	2
Miller, Greg, James Madison	.340	153	38	52	11	1	2	23	8
Hays, Jeremy, W&M	.340	159	38	54	7	0	4	25	0
Rigsby, Randy, East Carolina	.335	242	51	81	10	1	8	42	23
Whitby, Cory, VCU	.335	200	54	67	14	0	3	47	31
Avent, John, UNCW	.333	201	46	67	9	3	8	28	16
Dubois, Jason, VCU	.333	210	40	70	16	2	9	55	0
Bush, Ron, William & Mary	.332	199	40	66	14	3	3	34	15
Bender, Eric, James Madison	.330	185	33	61	16	0	5	43	6
Inge, Brandon, VCU	.330	212	**68**	70	21	**5**	15	61	21
Jackson, Nic, Richmond	.330	230	46	76	17	0	13	55	3
Hairr, Kevin, UNCW	.328	204	46	67	**22**	3	12	46	18

INDIVIDUAL PITCHING LEADERS

(Minimum 50 Innings)

	W	L	ERA	G	SV	IP	H	BB	SO
#Inge, Brandon, VCU	5	2	2.09	23	**11**	43	27	8	59
Ashcraft, Derek, George Mason	2	4	**2.47**	11	0	58	52	14	41
Burch, Matt, VCU	12	4	[illegible]	10	0	139	113	41	**122**
Patterson, Shawn, VCU	4	0	3.08	31	5	50	49	16	[illegible]
Bailey, David, ODU	8	2	3.47	17	0	73	79	36	61
Sams, Aaron, James Madison	10	3	3.64	15	0	96	79	36	97
Cook, Andy, William & Mary	6	6	3.68	19	3	100	102	26	92
Jernigan, Brooks, East Carolina	7	3	3.74	14	1	96	100	26	105
Minton, Foye, East Carolina	4	1	3.74	16	1	67	67	10	52
Steller, Mike, George Mason	5	4	3.78	14	0	95	93	13	71
Fisher, Marc, VCU	7	3	3.88	16	0	65	80	23	46
Morris, Jason, Richmond	11	3	4.17	17	0	117	116	40	70
Herr, Nic, James Madison	5	3	4.52	19	3	88	102	27	69
Berryman, Chad, VCU	**13**	4	4.53	19	0	113	132	29	73
Brantley, Brian, ODU	4	6	4.58	15	1	79	84	34	79
Dwyer, Mike, Richmond	8	5	4.64	17	0	97	101	26	73
Outlaw, Bill, East Carolina	6	4	4.70	18	0	59	63	20	44

CONFERENCE USA

	Conference W	Conference L	Overall W	Overall L
***Tulane**	22	5	48	15
Houston	21	6	34	25
UNC Charlotte	19	8	43	19
Alabama-Birmingham	15	12	29	24
Louisville	14	13	31	24
Southern Mississippi	12	15	30	28
Memphis	12	15	24	31
South Florida	9	18	21	36
Saint Louis	4	20	10	38
Cincinnati	4	20	15	38

ALL-CONFERENCE TEAM: **C**—James McAuley, So., Louisville. **INF**—Rodney Eberly, Sr., Alabama-Birmingham; Joey Hammond, Jr., UNC Charlotte; Bo Robinson, Sr., UNC Charlotte; Jeremy Schied, Sr., Southern Miss.; Mike Terry, Sr., Alabama-Birmingham. **OF**—Shayne Carnes, Sr., Alabama-Birmingham; Brian Hughes, Sr., Tulane; James Matan, Sr., UNC Charlotte; Jason Sparks, Jr., Tulane. **DH**—Cliff Wren, Jr., Southern Miss. **P**—Josh Bobbitt, Sr., Tulane; Craig House, Jr., Memphis; Shane Nance, So., Houston; Jason Stanford, Jr., UNC Charlotte. **RP**—Todd Ardoin, Sr., Tulane.

Player of the Year: James Matan, UNC Charlotte. **Pitcher of the Year**: Josh Bobbitt, Tulane. **Freshman of the Year**: Daniel Boyd, South Florida. **Coach of the Year**: Loren Hibbs, UNC Charlotte.

INDIVIDUAL BATTING LEADERS

(Minimum 125 At-Bats)

	AVG	AB	R	H	2B	3B	HR	RBI	SB
Robinson, Bo, UNCC	**.424**	250	79	**106**	**32**	2	19	**100**	2
Carnes, Shayne, Ala.-Birm.	.417	211	64	88	18	1	23	87	7
Matan, James, UNCC	.401	257	66	103	19	3	27	95	7
Hammond, Joey, UNCC	.398	251	**84**	100	15	2	5	45	17
Sutter, Chad, Tulane	.392	217	56	85	12	0	13	61	2
Boyd, Daniel, South Florida	.391	215	49	84	13	0	13	56	8
McAuley, James, Louisville	.389	198	53	77	18	4	10	54	7
Wren, Cliff, So. Miss.	.387	217	57	84	21	4	12	58	3
Hughes, Brian, Tulane	.381	273	75	104	29	2	8	56	35
Graffagnini, Keith, Tulane	.373	241	66	90	25	2	14	76	4
Rios, Bruce, Houston	.370	192	50	71	17	1	11	55	9
Voshell, Key, Louisville	.370	230	52	65	22	5	4	41	9
Lorenz, Doug, Louisville	.367	221	41	81	24	**7**	6	55	0
Eberly, Rodney, Ala.-Birm.	.365	230	55	84	23	0	11	64	3
Schied, Jeremy, So. Miss.	.365	241	67	88	25	0	16	81	1
Cheek, Scott, So. Miss.	.363	234	50	85	17	4	13	69	4
Terry, Mike, Ala.-Birm.	.363	212	56	77	12	4	18	59	3
Sparks, Jason, Tulane	.357	221	**84**	79	18	0	**30**	90	7
Diaco, Vinnie, UNCC	.354	229	59	81	14	3	2	40	31
Bredensteiner, Brett, St. Louis	.353	170	39	60	12	1	12	44	1
Caraway, Brandon, Houston	.350	234	74	82	18	2	3	39	26
Burnham, Jake, Tulane	.345	168	45	58	16	2	10	47	3
Medrano, Mike, Houston	.344	209	50	72	14	4	12	53	12
Eaton, Bill, South Florida	.339	242	54	82	13	1	1	31	23
Albritton, Jeremy, So. Miss.	.337	187	40	63	15	3	11	47	3
Bell, Jeff, Ala.-Birm.	.333	204	47	68	12	1	7	37	11
Pursell, Mike, Tulane	.332	238	68	79	18	3	10	56	11
#Parr, Gerald, UNCC	.305	233	84	71	15	1	7	33	**41**

INDIVIDUAL PITCHING LEADERS

(Minimum 50 Innings)

	W	L	ERA	G	SV	IP	H	BB	SO
Echeverz, Raul, Tulane	7	1	**2.78**	19	1	74	76	27	63
Nance, Shane, Houston	9	4	2.95	16	0	107	87	42	93
Bobbitt, Josh, Tulane	**13**	1	3.09	18	0	117	105	35	133
Dinkinson, Tighe, Ala.-Birm.	7	2	3.14	19	0	66	57	24	41
House, Craig, Memphis	4	8	3.33	15	1	95	89	42	83
Brown, Craig, Tulane	4	3	3.49	17	1	57	55	27	58
#Raithel, Todd, Louisville	2	1	3.54	25	**10**	48	41	25	56
Adams, Eric, So. Miss.	2	1	3.55	12	0	51	59	26	39
Berkowitz, Jared, Tulane	9	2	3.90	17	0	90	96	23	51
Green, Sean, Louisville	4	3	4.31	19	1	63	62	37	40
Fortenberry, Jason, So. Miss.	7	3	4.48	18	1	70	80	15	41
Stauffer, Scott, Louisville	7	7	4.76	18	0	87	119	19	48
Baker, Ryan, UNCC	8	1	4.81	19	0	107	104	52	89
Hecker, Steve, Memphis	3	3	4.94	17	0	55	60	17	36
Bell, Scott, Tulane	7	2	5.16	18	2	84	90	20	82
Treadway, Brion, UNCC	5	4	5.19	29	5	50	48	28	56
Portell, Mick, St. Louis	1	6	5.23	13	0	62	81	24	34
Vigue, John, South Florida	5	6	5.25	15	0	84	109	25	51
McKay, John, UNCC	7	5	5.30	18	0	114	117	44	**138**
McDonald, Jon, Houston	8	4	5.33	15	0	79	94	31	55
Johnson, Drew, So. Miss.	4	5	5.34	11	0	61	64	25	52
McAdoo, Duncan, Houston	5	2	5.35	16	0	71	76	25	53
Beyer, Scott, Ala.-Birm.	4	4	5.43	21	1	63	85	25	33
Stanford, Jason, UNCC	10	3	5.50	22	1	108	112	52	97
Terry, Mike, Ala.-Birm.	5	5	5.53	14	0	85	100	25	81
Bentley, Brian, Louisville	8	4	5.74	13	0	80	103	32	60

IVY LEAGUE

GEHRIG	Conference W	Conference L	Overall W	Overall L
Princeton	13	7	25	14
Cornell	12	8	18	18
Pennsylvania	9	11	14	21
Columbia	5	15	10	31
ROLFE	**W**	**L**	**W**	**L**
***Harvard**	16	4	36	12
Yale	11	9	21	21
Dartmouth	7	13	23	18
Brown	7	13	12	34

ALL-CONFERENCE TEAM: **C**—Jason Keck, Jr., Harvard. **1B**—Aaron Meyer, So., Dartmouth. **2B**—Tommy Kidwell, Sr., Yale. **3B**—Mike Conway, Jr., Dartmouth. **SS**—Tony Coyne, So., Yale. **OF**—Brian Ralph, Sr., Harvard; Michael Hazen, Sr., Princeton; Drew Corradini, Sr., Pennsylvania. **DH**—Mark Nagata, Sr., Pennsylvania. **Util**—Peter DeYoung, Jr., Brown. **P**—Eric Gutshall, Sr., Yale; Brian Williamson, Jr., Cornell. **RP**—Mike Marcucci, Sr., Harvard.

Player of the Year: Tony Coyne, Yale. **Pitcher of the Year**: Eric Gutshall, Yale. **Rookie of the Year**: Max Krance, Princeton.

INDIVIDUAL BATTING LEADERS

(Minimum 100 At-Bats)

	AVG	AB	R	H	2B	3B	HR	RBI	SB
Meyer, Aaron, Dartmouth	**.450**	151	42	68	12	0	**11**	**48**	9
Conway, Mike, Dartmouth	.434	173	41	**75**	**18**	0	2	28	13
Corradini, Drew, Penn	.414	133	32	55	10	1	1	20	14
Forst, David, Harvard	.406	165	32	67	15	3	5	39	12
Kasper, Todd, Yale	.394	137	34	54	16	0	3	20	3
Keck, Jason, Harvard	.386	158	40	61	14	4	3	37	10
Johnstone, Ben, Yale	.381	160	41	61	6	3	2	23	**26**
Coyne, Tony, Yale	.378	156	31	59	15	2	10	43	6
Carey, Hal, Harvard	.374	174	**53**	65	16	2	2	33	25
Mauro, Craig, Cornell	.370	100	18	37	7	2	2	23	0
Hazen, Michael, Princeton	.362	138	40	50	11	**5**	6	33	24
Nagata, Mark, Penn	.361	108	24	39	8	0	9	38	0
Carlon, Joe, Penn	.359	145	36	52	14	0	9	38	6
Ralph, Brian, Harvard	.347	101	34	35	4	1	10	36	14
Griffin, Justin, Princeton	.338	130	30	44	14	3	5	36	12
Kessler, Aaron, Harvard	.337	166	41	56	11	2	3	24	22
Huling, Andrew, Harvard	.337	169	42	57	14	2	1	30	21
Evans, Matt, Princeton	.331	142	33	47	17	0	9	36	5

INDIVIDUAL PITCHING LEADERS

(Minimum 40 Innings)

	W	L	ERA	G	SV	IP	H	BB	SO
Gutshall, Eric, Yale	5	6	**1.83**	19	4	74	52	29	**79**
Vail, Garett, Harvard	5	3	2.95	12	0	58	47	18	38
Godfrey, Dan, Dartmouth	3	2	3.61	22	**5**	42	54	10	25

	W	L	ERA	G	SV	IP	H	BB	SO
Machado, Joe, Princeton	3	3	3.83	8	0	40	37	18	29
Duffell, Andrew, Harvard	3	2	4.02	10	1	40	40	14	21
Jamieson, Donny, Harvard	5	1	4.20	12	1	49	55	12	40
McDonald, Sean, Penn	4	2	4.38	9	0	49	57	26	33
Marcucci, Mike, Harvard	**7**	0	4.43	21	1	41	50	6	16
Reddy, Sudha, Yale	5	4	4.63	14	0	56	68	19	35
Williamson, Brian, Cornell	4	1	4.93	7	0	46	52	22	40
Sellers, Peter, Dartmouth	4	4	5.33	13	0	54	74	14	31
Osgood, John, Cornell	4	3	5.43	11	0	53	40	46	65
Walania, Eric, Dartmouth	4	4	5.43	12	1	58	77	13	26
Douglas, John, Cornell	2	4	5.59	10	2	47	66	19	43

METRO ATLANTIC CONFERENCE

	Conference		Overall	
NORTH	**W**	**L**	**W**	**L**
*LeMoyne	20	6	26	15
Marist	18	8	30	17
Siena	11	15	17	32
Niagara	11	15	17	23
Canisius	7	19	11	32
SOUTH	**W**	**L**	**W**	**L**
Rider	16	10	25	25
Iona	15	11	22	26
Manhattan	14	12	20	21
Fairfield	12	14	19	25
St. Peter's	6	20	7	34

MAAC North ALL-CONFERENCE TEAM: **C**—Daryl Besant, Sr., Canisius; Bill Kerry, Sr., LeMoyne. **1B**—Mike Ostrander, Jr., Siena. **2B**—Mark Drabik, Jr., Niagara. **3B**—Geoff Hoover, So., Niagara. **SS**—Vic Boccarossa, Jr., LeMoyne. **OF**—David Adair, So., Niagara; Aaron Mindel, Fr., Niagara; Todd Donovan, So., Siena. **DH**—Jim McGowan, Sr., Marist. **P**—Scott Cassidy, Sr., LeMoyne; Mark Ciccarelli, Sr., Marist.

Player of the Year: Scott Cassidy, LeMoyne. **Rookies of the Year**: Kevin Wissner, Marist; Jaime Steward, LeMoyne. **Coach of the Year**: John King, LeMoyne.

MAAC South ALL-CONFERENCE TEAM: **C**—Kyran Connelly, Sr., Iona. **1B**—Tom McDonough, Jr., Manhattan. **2B**—Cristian Jung, Jr., Farifield; Jeff Orleski, Jr., Rider. **3B**—Jeff Timperman, So., Rider. **SS**—Jeff Rowett, Sr., Manhattan; Tim Superka, Fr., Rider. **OF**—John Penatello, Jr., Iona; Michael Wenner, So., Rider; Erik Zbranak, Jr., St. Peter's. **DH**—Brian Merkle, Sr., Iona; Josh Loftin, Jr., Rider. **P**—Matt Massimi, Sr., Rider; Neil Longo, So., Manhattan.

Player of the Year: Michael Wenner, Rider. **Rookie of the Year**: Tim Superka, Rider. **Coach of the Year**: Gary Puccio, Manhattan.

INDIVIDUAL BATTING LEADERS

(Minimum 100 At-Bats)

	AVG	AB	R	H	2B	3B	HR	RBI	SB
Jung, Cristian, Fairfield	**.418**	158	43	66	**18**	1	2	20	3
O'Keefe, Liam, Iona	.402	132	25	53	6	0	7	26	5
Hoover, Geoff, Niagara	.378	127	29	48	12	0	10	41	1
Lopusznick, Tom, Fairfield	.377	151	40	57	16	1	6	44	17
Logue, Joe, Rider	.377	122	26	46	8	2	6	31	1
Besant, Daryl, Canisius	.376	141	30	53	17	0	6	28	2
Connelly, Kyran, Iona	.368	144	42	53	12	2	8	39	5
Spera, Nick, Siena	.366	123	29	45	5	3	1	16	17
Kennedy, Jack, LeMoyne	.362	141	25	51	11	1	4	24	12
Drabik, Mark, Niagara	.361	158	40	57	15	4	**11**	**53**	7
Zbranak, Erik, St. Peter's	.359	153	31	55	7	5	4	25	13
Callahan, Pat, Manhattan	.357	115	31	41	8	0	5	28	3
Wissner, Kevin, Marist	.348	155	38	54	11	1	4	28	2
McGowan, Jim, Marist	.348	164	39	57	14	1	5	33	4
Loftin, Josh, Rider	.343	166	38	57	9	4	5	30	5
Adair, David, Niagara	.340	100	27	34	9	0	2	19	3
Macchio, Paul, Fairfield	.338	145	29	49	9	0	5	27	10
Tornambe, Mike, Man.	.336	116	29	39	13	1	6	27	0
Pikolycky, Wil, Iona	.336	140	28	47	7	1	2	20	5
Wenner, Michael, Rider	.335	200	48	**67**	6	**8**	5	35	22
Cervini, Anthony, Marist	.331	166	**53**	55	6	3	5	24	10
#Penatello, John, Iona	.303	152	47	46	4	1	1	13	**38**

INDIVIDUAL PITCHING LEADERS

(Minimum 40 Innings)

	W	L	ERA	G	SV	IP	H	BB	SO
Massimi, Matt, Rider	6	4	**2.84**	11	0	70	63	21	62
Bechard, Steve, LeMoyne	7	4	2.95	11	0	73	63	12	46
Barry, Kevin, Rider	2	2	2.98	9	0	42	34	28	34
Ciccarelli, Mark, Marist	**9**	2	2.99	14	0	87	75	21	79
Cassidy, Scott, LeMoyne	7	5	3.06	13	1	82	78	15	83
Brown, Kevin, Siena	2	5	3.30	9	0	46	44	13	32
Walsh, Robin, Rider	5	2	3.60	11	0	45	57	15	22
Bruderek, Joe, Fairfield	5	2	3.64	10	0	59	64	17	38
Olore, Kevin, Marist	5	5	3.66	13	0	76	71	31	**92**
#Giard, Jeremy, Siena	0	1	3.81	22	**5**	26	21	11	20
Keilman, Ken, Niagara	6	5	3.85	11	0	63	75	21	35
Longo, Neil, Manhattan	7	4	4.11	13	1	70	75	22	52
Castrello, Steve, Iona	6	4	4.21	15	0	68	72	42	59

MID-AMERICAN CONFERENCE

	Conference		Overall	
EAST	**W**	**L**	**W**	**L**
***Bowling Green**	17	10	34	21
Kent	17	12	27	28
Miami	17	13	33	26
Ohio	13	17	31	24
Akron	10	18	20	31
Marshall	9	21	18	35
WEST	**W**	**L**	**W**	**L**
Ball State	23	8	39	18
Central Michigan	23	9	34	25
Western Michigan	16	16	26	29
Eastern Michigan	14	16	27	27
Toledo	13	17	20	32
Northern Illinois	8	23	10	39

ALL-CONFERENCE TEAM: **C**—Ben Eversole, Sr., Miami. **1B**—Tom Kuempel, Sr., Marshall. **2B**—Jess Bechard, So., Kent. **3B**—Brian Cannon, Sr., Bowling Green; Brian Smith, Sr., Kent. **SS**—Brian Dorrmann, Sr., Ball State. **OF**—Larry Bigbie, So., Ball State; John Sullivan, Sr., Miami; Bart Leahy, Sr., Ohio. **DH**—Derek Ottevaere, Jr., Western Michigan. **Util**—Justin Love, Sr., Ball State; Nick Phillips, Sr., Central Michigan. **P**—Travis Minix, So., Ball State; Jeff Hundley, Jr., Bowling Green; Lee Gardner, Sr., Central Michigan; John Stewart, Jr., Western Michigan. **RP**—Matt Speicher, Jr., Ball State.

Player of the Year: Tom Kuempel, Marshall. **Pitcher of the Year**: Jeff Hundley, Bowling Green. **Co-Freshmen of the Year**: Clark Mace, Miami; Ryan Kochen, Western Michigan. **Coach of the Year**: Rich Maloney, Ball State.

INDIVIDUAL BATTING LEADERS

(Minimum 100 At-Bats)

	AVG	AB	R	H	2B	3B	HR	RBI	SB
Kuempel, Tom, Marshall	**.435**	184	53	80	14	1	**20**	**60**	10
Hollern, Rick, Central Mich.	.421	178	43	75	10	2	7	41	9
Smith, Brian, Kent	.408	196	47	80	10	0	8	49	7
Zban, Mark, Marshall	.388	183	41	71	10	0	9	47	2
Bigbie, Larry, Ball State	.386	176	40	68	12	**5**	10	49	9
Malinowski, Scott, Ohio	.385	195	44	75	17	2	4	28	5
Pinkerton, Eric, Marshall	.385	122	28	47	8	1	6	28	2
Bechard, Jess, Kent	.379	203	58	77	**24**	2	9	54	7
Sullivan, John, Miami	.377	215	61	**81**	18	2	11	52	24
Phillips, Nick, Central Mich.	.370	192	50	71	16	1	9	49	14
Aulet, Jojo, Toledo	.368	125	28	46	5	1	0	10	19
Leahy, Bart, Ohio	.361	183	51	66	14	1	15	52	14
Sanborn, Jake, Central Mich.	.358	173	32	62	12	3	7	34	8
Arbinger, Jason, Ohio	.353	184	46	65	12	0	8	37	2
Eversole, Ben, Miami	.352	196	45	69	14	2	12	48	4
Dorrmann, Brian, Ball State	.350	214	50	75	18	1	7	46	5
Pukansky, Joe, Akron	.350	177	46	62	9	1	8	41	8
Mace, Clark, Miami	.349	209	51	73	9	1	5	39	19
Cannon, Brian, Bowl. Green	.347	190	46	66	10	1	8	45	2
Ottevaere, Derek, WM	.346	191	36	66	14	0	12	48	13
Hicks, Brian, Toledo	.345	148	27	51	9	0	5	28	0
Fetzer, Clint, East. Mich.	.344	157	32	54	8	2	2	26	8
Fitzharris, Tim, Ball State	.344	189	41	65	8	0	2	34	3
Holyszko, Anthony, W. Mich.	.344	192	35	66	9	0	0	36	3
Love, Justin, Ball State	.344	212	**62**	73	14	3	9	38	30
McClellan, Aaron, Marshall	.342	152	25	52	4	0	4	23	3
Roush, Ryan, Marshall	.342	193	46	66	18	0	12	45	13
#DeVisser, Joel, West. Mich.	.317	202	55	64	12	0	3	25	**31**

INDIVIDUAL PITCHING LEADERS

(Minimum 40 Innings)

	W	L	ERA	G	SV	IP	H	BB	SO
Stewart, Jason, East. Mich.	5	1	**2.03**	20	0	49	36	23	34
Gardner, Lee, Central Mich.	8	4	2.45	15	1	88	67	31	86
Urban, Jeff, Ball State	8	3	2.79	15	0	81	70	22	78
Stewart, John, West. Mich.	9	3	2.85	18	1	107	105	11	71
#Speicher, Matt, Ball State	1	3	2.87	24	**8**	31	26	12	31

	W	L	ERA	G	SV	IP	H	BB	SO
Minix, Travis, Ball State	9	2	3.21	19	0	81	81	17	**89**
Hundley, Jeff, Bowl. Green	**10**	4	3.23	17	0	98	79	49	81
Cabaj, Chris, Ball State	8	3	3.44	15	1	73	65	20	66
Jackson, Sage, Central Mich.	6	2	3.65	19	0	57	50	19	44
Kenny, Seth, East. Mich.	4	7	3.74	15	0	77	82	34	38
Place, Eric, West. Mich.	5	4	5.00	18	0	80	98	42	60
Wells, Chad, Ball State	4	0	4.17	18	1	41	44	15	20
Sismondo, Bobby, Ohio	8	3	4.20	12	0	79	81	22	84
Kelley, Jason, Bowl. Green	7	1	4.28	20	4	74	73	22	45
Straight, Doug, Kent	5	5	4.28	16	0	76	90	27	58
#Kommer, Phil, East. Mich.	0	1	6.97	18	**8**	21	20	23	20

MID-CONTINTENT CONFERENCE

	Conference		Overall	
EAST	**W**	**L**	**W**	**L**
C.W. Post	12	2	21	21
Youngstown State	5	6	17	31
Central Conn.	6	8	24	22
Pace	5	7	14	26
New York Tech	5	10	13	28
WEST	**W**	**L**	**W**	**L**
***Oral Roberts**	18	6	45	20
Valparaiso	13	9	31	23
Western Illinois	12	10	15	28
Chicago State	10	14	19	21
Northeastern Illinois	5	19	10	33

EASTERN DIVISION ALL-CONFERENCE TEAM: C—Chad Schultz, Sr., Youngstown State. **1B**—Mike Urtnowski, So., C.W. Post. **2B**—Tom Wigand, Jr., C.W. Post. **3B**—Ryan Nevins, So., New York Tech. **SS**—John Fodrowski, Sr., C.W. Post. **OF**—Jason Maule, Jr., Central Connecticut; Danny Graham, Sr., Central Connecticut; Blake Bendett, Sr., C.W. Post. **DH**—Tony Balcan, So., C.W. Post. **Util**—Chris Rojas, Sr., New York Tech. **P**—Adam Poturnicki, Jr., Central Connecticut; Scott Martin, Jr., Central Connecticut; Rob Bigan, Sr., New York Tech. **RP**—Hector DuPrey, Fr., C.W. Post.

WESTERN DIVISION ALL-CONFERENCE TEAM: C—Mike Dean, Jr., Oral Roberts; Craig Majdecki, Sr., Chicago State. **1B**—Todd Poepard, Jr., Valparaiso. **2B**—Scott Byrdak, Sr., Chicago State. **3B**—Billy Finn, Sr., Valparaiso. **SS**—Andrew Mosher, Jr., Oral Roberts. **OF**—John Will, Sr., Northeastern Illinois; Paul Weeks, Sr., Oral Roberts; David Keltner, Jr., Chicago State. **DH**—J.J. Swiatkowski, So., Valparaiso. **Util**—Brian Dinsmore, Sr., Oral Roberts. **P**—Joe Lazewski, Sr., Valparaiso; Matt Field, So., Western Illinois; Derek Dixon, Sr., Oral Roberts. **RP**—Bryan Reichard, Sr., Oral Roberts.

Player of the Year: Mike Dean, Oral Roberts. **Pitcher of the Year**: Derek Dixon, Oral Roberts. **Newcomer of the Year**: Tom Wigand, C.W. Post. **Co-Coaches of the Year**: Sunny Golloway, Oral Roberts; Dick Vining, C.W. Post.

INDIVIDUAL BATTING LEADERS
(Minimum 100 At-Bats)

	AVG	AB	R	H	2B	3B	HR	RBI	SB
Dean, Mike, Oral Roberts	**.426**	230	57	**98**	15	5	11	**63**	26
Graham, Danny, Cent. Conn.	.409	159	40	65	20	3	11	56	7
Stallings, Jeff, Oral Roberts	.391	233	**73**	91	12	0	5	39	27
Maule, Jason, Cent. Conn.	.386	166	54	64	10	2	3	16	**37**
Mosher, Andrew, ORU	.383	240	72	92	14	0	7	58	26
Fodrowski, John, C.W. Post	.377	151	30	57	11	0	0	23	7
Schultz, Chad, Youngstown	.376	181	46	68	**23**	0	7	31	10
Keltner, Dave, Chicago State	.372	137	41	51	16	0	5	19	12
Weeks, Paul, Oral Roberts	.366	216	64	79	16	**6**	8	46	12
Will, John, NE Illinois	.365	148	28	54	10	3	1	23	16
Gann, Bryan, Oral Roberts	.356	222	49	79	18	1	7	41	13
Mosley, Trevor, Pace	.354	113	17	40	9	0	5	37	0
Dinsmore, Brian, ORU	.353	184	42	65	12	2	8	48	19
Ciccone, Phil, Pace	.352	142	40	50	13	0	7	32	14
Byrdak, Scott, Chicago State	.350	120	21	42	9	0	0	26	7
Balcan, Tony, C.W. Post	.349	126	26	44	10	1	3	23	5
Vandeventer, Eric, ORU	.348	210	55	73	19	2	**12**	52	14
Finn, Billy, Valparaiso	.346	185	49	64	15	1	9	47	11
Kostuch, Bob, NE Illinois	.345	142	22	49	10	0	0	12	3
DeLuca, Marc, Pace	.344	131	30	45	7	3	7	27	4

INDIVIDUAL PITCHING LEADERS
(Minimum 40 Innings)

	W	L	ERA	G	SV	IP	H	BB	SO
Lazewski, Joe, Valparaiso	6	3	**2.43**	11	0	70	64	11	60
Dixon, Derek, Oral Roberts	**12**	2	3.05	18	0	115	92	51	**115**
Barrett, Dusty, Oral Roberts	6	4	3.34	13	0	70	55	33	69
Poturnicki, Adam, Cent. Conn.	7	4	3.68	15	2	88	84	37	100
Greenlee, Mark, NE Ilinois	1	7	3.86	14	2	44	39	33	37
Cohen, Jeff, C.W. Post	5	4	3.88	12	0	67	82	17	23
Duprey, Hector, C.W. Post	4	3	4.01	23	**7**	43	42	25	45
Floros, Tony, Valparaiso	2	3	4.42	12	0	55	69	15	25
Pomeroy, Jim, Valparaiso	5	4	4.43	14	1	67	65	38	62
Martin, Scott, Cent. Conn.	4	3	4.58	11	0	57	77	9	59
Rainford, Kevin, Valparaiso	6	1	4.75	11	0	61	53	36	42
#Reichard, Bryan, ORU	1	1	4.85	25	7	30	26	13	33
Nelson, Derek, Youngstown	4	3	4.93	10	0	46	43	29	35

MID-EASTERN CONFERENCE

	Conference		Overall	
NORTH	**W**	**L**	**W**	**L**
*Howard	15	0	27	33
Maryland Eastern Shore	9	7	11	41
Delaware State	6	10	8	28
Coppin State	1	14	1	44
SOUTH	**W**	**L**	**W**	**L**
Bethune-Cookman	13	5	27	29
Norfolk State	10	8	22	25
North Carolina A&T	5	10	15	36
Florida A&M	5	10	21	30

ALL-CONFERENCE TEAM: C—James Perry, So., Howard. **INF**—Chris Warren, Jr., Howard; Al Holland, Sr., North Carolina A&T; Matt Knox, So., Bethune-Cookman; Eric Crozier, So., Norfolk State. **OF**—Herbert Wheat, Sr., Howard; Chris Carmichael, Fr., Howard; David Jones, Sr., Florida A&M. **DH**—Eunique Johnson, So., Howard. **P**—David Ellyson, Sr., Norfolk State.

Player of the Year: Eunique Johnson, Howard. **Rookie of the Year**: Chris Carmichael, Howard. **Coach of the Year**: Chuck Hinton, Howard.

INDIVIDUAL BATTING LEADERS
(Minimum 100 At-Bats)

	AVG	AB	R	H	2B	3B	HR	RBI	SB
Jones, David, Fla. A&M	**.399**	158	52	63	9	**10**	4	28	24
Marsh, Mandell, UMES	.395	162	36	64	11	1	2	27	30
Johnson, Eunique, Howard	.389	162	40	63	11	1	8	41	8
Carmichael, Chris, Howard	.373	212	**60**	**79**	15	4	**11**	**60**	18
Omeir, George, Howard	.360	161	32	58	4	0	0	30	23
Perez, Felipe, UMES	.360	172	44	62	13	5	2	22	10
Dakuras, Dino, Beth.-Cook.	.355	183	36	65	15	0	3	37	6
Cobb, Floyd, Florida A&M	.350	160	53	56	11	3	0	34	18
Hinkle, Tom, Delaware St.	.346	104	20	36	7	0	3	23	1
Mosley, Rick, Delaware St.	.345	110	27	38	6	2	4	25	12
Badell, Jason, Delaware St.	.343	105	25	36	8	0	3	25	0
Defere, John, Norfolk St.	.343	140	32	48	16	2	4	27	0
Bradley, Shawn, Norfolk St.	.342	155	43	53	4	6	7	42	5
Grasso, Chris, UMES	.342	149	38	51	**18**	2	1	18	10
Wheat, Herbert, Howard	.342	149	47	51	11	6	3	42	**41**
Davis, Thornton, Fla. A&M	.337	169	40	57	15	0	10	51	3
#Hammett, Faheem, UMES	.337	172	45	58	7	5	**11**	54	12
#Ewing, Byron, Howard	.335	206	54	69	12	3	**11**	56	6

INDIVIDUAL PITCHING LEADERS
(Minimum 40 Innings)

	W	L	ERA	G	SV	IP	H	BB	SO
Martin, Chanx, Beth.-Cook.	**9**	5	**2.47**	18	1	109	95	74	**111**
Hunter, Carlton, Florida A&M	5	1	4.21	13	0	66	84	30	41
Ellyson, David, Norfolk St.	7	5	4.41	15	0	82	102	27	44
Farrow, Joshua, Florida A&M	5	3	4.52	12	0	66	63	41	62
Young, DeAntwan, Fla. A&M	4	3	4.81	16	0	43	50	22	27
King, Keith, Norfolk State	3	2	5.36	13	2	44	47	19	27
Shirtcliff, Mike, Bethune-Cook.	6	9	5.56	19	0	104	125	61	91
Coker, Jason, Bethune-Cook.	3	1	6.07	16	1	46	60	26	38
Gibson, Christopher, Norfolk St.	2	1	6.07	13	0	43	57	28	32
Ortiz, Ken, Bethune-Cook.	4	5	6.45	15	0	67	76	62	58

MIDWESTERN COLLEGIATE

	Conference		Overall	
	W	**L**	**W**	**L**
*Butler	13	5	33	21
Wisconsin-Milwaukee	14	6	33	15
Detroit	10	8	20	21
Wright State	9	11	20	34
Cleveland State	8	11	21	32
Illinois-Chicago	3	16	11	25

ALL-CONFERENCE TEAM: **C**—Justin Beasley, Sr., Butler. **1B**—Jeff Stoss, Sr., Wisconsin-Milwaukee. **2B**—Ryan O'Donovan, Sr., Butler. **3B**—Ken Poniewaz, Jr., Wisconsin-Milwaukee. **SS**—Dusty Bearn, Jr., Wright State. **OF**—Steve Johnson, Jr., Wisconsin-Milwaukee; Mike Pesci, Sr., Detroit; Josh Wilke, Sr., Butler. **DH**—Towann Jenkins, Sr., Wright State. **Util**—Dan Johnson, Fr., Butler. **P**—Ryan Harber, Jr., Butler; Mike Casper, Sr., Wisconsin-Milwaukee.

Player of the Year: Justin Beasley, Butler. **Pitcher of the Year**: Ryan Harber, Butler. **Newcomer of the Year**: Steve Johnson, Wisconsin-Milwaukee. **Coach of the Year**: Steve Farley, Butler.

INDIVIDUAL BATTING LEADERS

(Minimum 100 At-Bats)

	AVG	AB	R	H	2B	3B	HR	RBI	SB
Daguanno, Mike, Detroit	**.400**	155	42	62	5	1	13	39	3
Stoss, Jeff, Wis.-Mil.	**.400**	155	53	62	15	0	11	52	6
Beasley, Justin, Butler	.398	181	50	**72**	**19**	1	**15**	**65**	13
O'Donovan, Ryan, Butler	.369	187	45	69	17	3	4	19	7
Jarmillo, Lee, Wis.-Mil.	.366	172	40	63	16	2	6	30	15
Johnson, Steve, Wis.-Mil.	.348	178	47	62	11	3	5	33	8
Lillash, Keith, Cleveland St.	.348	187	45	65	9	4	9	39	1
Jenkins, Towann, Wright St.	.340	153	29	52	6	0	6	45	0
Beam, Dusty, Wright St.	.338	219	**54**	74	6	2	12	43	12
Wilke, Josh, Butler	.338	151	31	51	4	2	7	33	7
Bautsch, Brian, Wright St.	.336	214	29	**72**	13	1	2	40	3
Haase, Jeff, Cleveland St.	.335	158	32	53	12	3	8	37	1
Poniewaz, Ken, Wis.-Mil.	.333	168	34	56	11	0	4	37	6
Marshall, Scott, Wright St.	.329	158	19	52	9	2	0	24	2
Kein, Todd, Ill.-Chicago	.328	128	23	42	3	1	2	13	14
Gombos, Jason, Detroit	.326	172	43	56	6	2	6	35	10
Pesci, Mike, Detroit	.324	148	28	48	11	1	11	35	4
#Stosik, Bill, Wright St.	.303	178	53	54	14	1	4	20	**25**
#Olszta, Eddie, Butler	.258	132	25	34	2	**5**	1	13	6

INDIVIDUAL PITCHING LEADERS

(Minimum 40 Innings)

	W	L	ERA	G	SV	IP	H	BB	SO
Harber, Ryan, Butler	**8**	4	**2.99**	17	0	99	82	22	**88**
Justman, Josh, Wis.-Mil.	7	1	3.05	13	0	59	51	35	46
#Moses, Mickey, Cleve. St.	0	4	3.16	27	**10**	26	28	4	22
Guler, Jeremy, Butler	7	3	3.28	14	0	66	73	20	38
Casper, Mike, Wis.-Mil.	6	2	3.50	12	0	64	61	27	44
Andrzejak, Chris, Detroit	6	4	3.53	16	3	64	63	10	71
Hoane, Wes, Butler	5	4	3.72	15	0	68	67	20	44
Magill, Steve, Butler	**8**	5	3.74	26	5	89	78	40	85
Rieke, Jim, Cleveland St.	7	2	4.08	32	0	64	64	26	63
Maceri, Joe, Detroit	1	6	4.28	14	0	74	82	29	42
Carlson, Steve, Ill.-Chicago	3	4	4.43	13	1	41	44	19	40
Sanford, Casey, Wright St.	6	6	4.44	15	0	99	116	34	58

MISSOURI VALLEY CONFERENCE

	Conference W	Conference L	Overall W	Overall L
***Wichita State**	26	1	56	7
Indiana State	23	9	37	18
Southwest Missouri State	19	13	32	21
Illinois State	14	14	32	22
Evansville	13	18	28	30
Creighton	12	19	27	27
Bradley	11	21	25	30
Southern Illinois	11	21	19	35
Northern Iowa	9	22	26	30

ALL-CONFERENCE TEAM: C—Ryan Duncheon, So., Illinois State. **1B**—Jason Hart, Jr., SW Missouri State. **2B**—Kevin Hooper, Jr., Wichita State. **3B**—Pete Hennecke, Jr., Indiana State. **SS**—Zach Sorensen, Jr., Wichita State. **OF**—Jeff Ryan, Jr., Wichita State; Rick Angell, Jr., Indiana State; Jeff Allen, Jr., Illinois State. **DH**—Pat Magness, So., Wichita State. **Util**—Kevin Frederick, Sr., Creighton. **P**—Ben Christensen, So., Wichita State; Tony Harden, Sr., Indiana State; Rob Purvis, So., Bradley. **RP**—Marc Bluma, Jr., Wichita State; Scott Hoey, Jr., Northern Iowa.

Player of the Year: Jeff Ryan, Wichita State. **Pitcher of the Year**: Marc Bluma, Wichita State. **Newcomer of the Year**: Rick Angell, Indiana State. **Freshman of the Year**: Ryan Brunner, Northern Iowa. **Coach of the Year**: Gene Stephenson, Wichita State.

INDIVIDUAL BATTING LEADERS

(Minimum 125 At-Bats)

	AVG	AB	R	H	2B	3B	HR	RBI	SB
Magness, Pat, Wichita St.	**.464**	224	75	104	19	2	21	100	0
Ryan, Jeff, Wichita St.	.441	261	**109**	**115**	**33**	**7**	23	**105**	**31**
Sorensen, Zach, Wichita St.	.424	262	103	111	25	2	17	94	22
Hart, Jason, SW Missouri St.	.416	221	71	92	15	0	**28**	91	6
Provines, Kip, Indiana St.	.414	210	41	87	15	2	13	64	8
Duncheon, Ryan, Illinois St.	.411	192	42	79	17	2	18	68	3
Busse, Jeff, Bradley	.393	191	48	75	12	0	12	38	2
Cepicky, Matt, SW Mo. St.	.390	218	50	85	16	5	16	50	6
Lawler, Dan, Creighton	.388	165	35	64	10	1	4	26	1
Hennecke, Pete, Indiana St.	.386	220	56	85	19	0	8	65	3
McMillin, Brian, Evansville	.380	213	61	81	16	2	12	58	**31**
Davis, Casey, Wichita St.	.379	161	51	61	13	1	11	43	18
Jackson, Brandon, SMS	.377	236	59	89	23	2	5	41	11
Correa, Nelson, Bradley	.376	205	39	77	14	3	15	51	2
Thompson, Tyler, Indiana St.	.375	184	87	69	13	6	15	46	21
Dettman, Matt, So. Illinois	.374	198	50	74	11	2	14	54	4
Angell, Rick, Indiana St.	.363	248	71	90	12	4	11	56	23
Gripp, Ryan, Creighton	.362	196	48	71	21	2	10	56	16
Allen, Jeff, Illinois St.	.358	204	66	73	13	3	18	65	12
Hooper, Kevin, Wichita St.	.358	229	101	82	22	5	4	47	21
Woodin, Greg, Northern Iowa	.357	126	16	45	7	1	4	26	3
Carroll, Wes, Evansville	.355	248	44	88	18	2	2	39	6
Brummett, Sean, Indiana St.	.355	155	32	55	8	1	9	35	3
Schley, Joe, So. Illinois	.355	217	38	77	16	4	5	30	17
Ruggori, Steve, So. Illinois	.355	220	50	78	17	2	6	24	12
Johnson, Chad, Bradley	.354	209	44	74	9	0	19	57	0
Frederick, Kevin, Creighton	.353	204	55	72	17	5	17	67	9
Kays, Nick, SW Missouri St.	.353	207	38	73	9	2	14	50	5
Hayes, Tim, Wichita St.	.352	125	35	44	13	3	9	41	2
Broshears, Phil, Evansville	.345	197	32	68	17	1	1	33	5
Pietro, Vince, Creighton	.343	204	53	70	15	4	6	34	10
Holst, Micah, SW Missouri St.	.342	234	64	80	7	5	9	40	17
Peters, Joel, So. Illinois	.342	190	38	65	19	2	7	33	5
Patrick, Matt, Wichita St.	.338	136	36	46	14	3	7	45	3
Benson, Brad, So. Illinois	.335	194	42	65	10	1	11	42	3
Rima, Todd, Northern Iowa	.335	206	48	69	18	0	6	33	13
Brunner, Ryan, Northern Iowa	.331	130	25	43	7	0	7	29	6
Molina, Anthony, Evansville	.330	203	45	67	20	1	5	49	13

INDIVIDUAL PITCHING LEADERS

(Minimum 50 Innings)

	W	L	ERA	G	SV	IP	H	BB	SO
Bluma, Marc, Wichita St.	5	0	**1.74**	25	**11**	57	45	17	56
Bryan, Erich, Wichita St.	8	3	3.68	14	1	78	87	23	53
Vrba, Scott, Northern Iowa	6	2	3.71	10	0	68	75	9	52
Briggeman, Kevin, Nor. Iowa	4	4	3.81	14	0	87	88	31	71
Pearson, Jason, Illinois St.	5	4	3.92	18	3	62	68	12	49
Chaney, Drew, Bradley	6	2	4.14	9	0	63	84	13	47
Christensen, Ben, Wichita St.	9	0	4.24	12	0	68	67	17	52
Graman, Alex, Indiana St.	7	3	4.86	16	2	93	98	46	67
Foral, Steve, Wichita St.	**10**	1	5.09	15	0	87	95	25	81
Hoffman, David, Bradley	3	6	5.23	14	0	62	76	24	34
Harden, Tony, Indiana St.	9	2	5.23	13	0	95	106	28	75
Sterlin, Christian, Creighton	6	7	5.27	15	0	99	101	45	84
Matzenbacher, Brian, Creighton	4	4	5.36	19	1	84	110	25	66
Purvis, Rob, Bradley	7	5	5.38	14	0	95	114	44	74
Bernhardt, Mark, Indiana St.	3	2	5.40	12	0	53	68	15	41
Brummett, Sean, Indiana St.	8	2	5.42	13	1	75	97	32	51
Schullian, Chris, So. Illinois	5	5	5.51	18	0	80	107	22	55
Keating, C.J., Creighton	7	4	5.69	19	1	87	106	21	67
Walker, Ben, SW Missouri St.	6	2	5.70	12	0	73	84	29	58
Glen, Willie, Evansville	4	1	5.91	24	2	67	81	33	63
Rockness, Jon, Illinois St.	3	1	5.95	12	0	56	78	19	41
#Kremer, John, Evansville	5	9	6.36	27	6	69	91	42	**88**

NORTHEAST CONFERENCE

	Conference W	Conference L	Overall W	Overall L
***Monmouth**	10	5	30	21
St. Francis (N.Y.)	10	5	26	12
Long Island	9	6	24	14
Mount St. Mary's	6	9	9	28
Fairleigh Dickinson	6	9	15	24
Wagner	4	11	10	35

ALL-CONFERENCE TEAM: **C**—Eddie Murria, Sr., Long Island. **1B**—Joe Zeccardi, Jr., Long Island. **2B**—Joe McCullough, Sr., Monmouth. **3B**—Nick DelGozzo, Sr., Monmouth. **SS**—John Catricala, Sr., Long Island. **OF**—Andy Artale, Sr., St. Francis; Joe Francisco, Jr., Wagner; Dennis Jenks, Sr., Mount St. Mary's. **DH**—Sami Abbassi, Jr., Long Island. **P**—Brian Moyer, Jr., Monmouth; Joseph Ojeda, Jr., St. Francis.

Player of the Year: Joe McCullough, Monmouth. **Pitcher of the Year**: Santino Sarrica, St. Francis. **Newcomer of the Year**: Greg Landis, Monmouth. **Coach of the Year**: Frank Del George, St. Francis.

INDIVIDUAL BATTING LEADERS

(Minimum 100 At-Bats)

	AVG	AB	R	H	2B	3B	HR	RBI	SB
McCullough, Joe, Monmouth	**.420**	212	60	**89**	**19**	**5**	12	**79**	8
Zeccardi, Joe, Long Island	.409	132	41	54	6	1	**15**	55	3
Catricala, John, Long Island	.402	132	40	[illegible]	12	0	8	35	2
Abbassi, Sami, Long Island	.393	117	35	46	17	3	3	34	1
Francisco, Joe, Wagner	.393	140	36	55	12	1	5	17	**27**
Artale, Andy, St. Francis	.381	134	30	51	**19**	2	4	38	4
DelGozzo, Nick, Monmouth	.380	192	42	73	**19**	0	7	46	12
Barkman, Gil, Wagner	.377	122	22	46	6	4	6	28	0
Foy, Kevin, Long Island	.372	121	28	45	16	**5**	2	34	3
Jenks, Dennis, Mt. St. Mary's	.364	129	35	47	13	2	8	30	1
Bardeguez, Eric, LI	.361	144	45	52	13	1	3	24	3
Vanjonack, Will, MSM	.357	129	28	46	7	1	11	35	4
Rugg, Gordon, Wagner	.354	158	34	56	6	1	4	28	7
Ambrose, Tom, Monmouth	.349	152	51	53	11	2	7	23	9
Anderson, Jason, LI	.349	129	42	45	10	1	6	34	8
Kampf, Fred, Monmouth	.347	150	33	52	8	1	12	42	2
Landis, Greg, Monmouth	.333	195	**66**	65	9	4	3	29	19
Esposito, Paul, FDU	.331	145	38	48	9	3	6	18	6
West, George, Monmouth	.324	213	48	69	14	1	13	53	4

INDIVIDUAL PITCHING LEADERS

(Minimum 40 Innings)

	W	L	ERA	G	SV	IP	H	BB	SO
Almonte, Edwin, St. Francis	4	0	**2.66**	11	0	51	48	16	30
Sarrica, Santino, St. Francis	**7**	2	2.73	10	0	66	58	26	61
Moyer, Brian, Monmouth	**7**	1	2.98	12	0	66	75	17	59
#Ojeda, Joseph, St. Francis	0	2	3.09	18	**10**	23	13	5	26
Sapp, James, Long Island	4	4	4.39	13	0	55	49	38	32
Sevorino, Dan, Monmouth	**7**	4	4.96	14	0	74	79	33	**66**
Dorsey, Scott, Long Island	4	4	5.27	14	0	56	72	30	48
Aragona, Joe, Monmouth	5	3	5.32	13	0	71	85	50	**66**
Hinchcliff, George, FDU	4	2	5.36	8	0	42	47	14	45
Nugent, Mark, Wagner	3	7	5.82	12	0	65	83	44	44
Krajewski, Charlie, Monmouth	**7**	4	6.02	16	3	58	69	23	30

OHIO VALLEY CONFERENCE

	Conference W	Conference L	Overall W	Overall L
Eastern Illinois	17	6	37	16
***Southeast Missouri State**	15	9	32	24
Tennessee Tech	14	10	28	24
Murray State	13	11	19	33
Eastern Kentucky	12	12	24	29
Morehead State	12	12	20	34
Middle Tennessee State	9	14	17	33
Austin Peay	9	15	23	32
Tennessee-Martin	6	18	15	31

ALL-CONFERENCE TEAM: **C**—Joe Smith, Jr., Eastern Kentucky. **1B**—Mark Tomse, Jr., Eastern Illinois. **2B**—Justin Stone, Sr., Eastern Illinois. **3B**—Matt Marzec, So., Eastern Illinois. **SS**—Jason Sharp, So., Eastern Kentucky. **OF**—Ryan Browning, Sr., Tennessee Tech; Sean Lyons, Jr., Eastern Illinois; Sean Murray, Jr., Eastern Kentucky. **DH**—Matt Mason, So., Eastern Kentucky. **Util**—Craig Delk, Sr., Murray State. **P**—Ryan Spille, Jr., Southeast Missouri; Bobby Castelli, Jr., Eastern Illinois.

Player of the Year: Matt Marzec, Eastern Illinois. **Pitcher of the Year**: Ryan Spille, Southeast Missouri. **Coach of the Year**: Jim Schmitz, Eastern Illinois.

INDIVIDUAL BATTING LEADERS

(Minimum 100 At-Bats)

	AVG	AB	R	H	2B	3B	HR	RBI	SB
Delk, Craig, Murray State	**.424**	191	47	81	18	2	6	40	2
Browning, Ryan, Tenn. Tech	.408	174	41	71	20	1	4	39	1
Murray, Sean, East. Ky.	.402	209	64	**84**	16	1	16	48	11
Benhoff, Clint, East. Illinois	.396	192	51	76	20	1	18	**74**	1
Marzec, Matt, East. Illinois	.378	201	59	76	16	0	17	65	3
Hall, Scott, Tenn.-Martin	.378	180	36	68	12	1	2	24	6
Mason, Matt, East. Kentucky	.378	196	54	74	15	0	16	60	13
Attaway, Matt, Tenn. Tech.	.377	191	47	72	18	1	15	58	2
Lyons, Sean, East. Illinois	.374	211	**66**	79	**21**	3	13	47	12
Curley, Ty, Middle Tenn.	.369	157	39	58	11	1	12	47	1
Williams, Chris, Murray St.	.369	203	50	75	20	1	3	26	3
Fox, Todd, Murray State	.367	139	26	51	9	1	8	40	4
Tomse, Mark, East. Illinois	.364	176	50	64	13	1	17	52	3
Stone, Justin, East. Illinois	.364	165	38	60	9	2	5	33	20
Ralph, Taylor, Tenn. Tech	.361	183	39	66	13	3	6	31	2
Troy, Greg, Austin Peay	.358	151	33	54	11	2	5	24	9
Mikes, David, East. Illinois	.357	143	39	51	4	1	3	16	8
Wheeler, Jody, Tenn. Tech	.356	163	38	58	14	2	8	38	9
Yount, Kyle, SE Missouri St.	.351	228	30	80	12	0	5	33	5
Kennedy, Jason, More. St.	.350	103	20	36	6	1	1	23	3
Sharp, Jason, East. Ky.	.347	193	38	67	12	2	7	35	8
Moore, Mike, Tenn. Tech	.345	116	21	40	9	0	2	29	2
#Sizemore, Brad, East. Ky.	.338	216	50	73	18	**5**	6	40	22
#Marino, Charlie, SE Mo.	[illegible]	108	62	66	13	1	**21**	51	16
#Owens, Jeremy, MTS	.293	205	53	60	17	[illegible]	[illegible]	20	[illegible]

INDIVIDUAL PITCHING LEADERS

(Minimum 40 Innings)

	W	L	ERA	G	SV	IP	H	BB	SO
Castelli, Bobby, East. Illinois	7	1	**1.65**	29	**10**	55	26	29	70
Spille, Ryan, SE Missouri St.	**11**	2	2.72	23	1	109	86	50	**130**
Witten, Joe, East. Kentucky	4	4	3.95	25	4	43	50	5	34
Rauch, Jon, Morehead State	6	5	4.19	16	0	88	85	31	97
Swearingen, Jason, SE Mo. St.	7	6	4.66	23	1	110	142	17	66
Sherrill, George, Austin Peay	3	7	4.92	28	8	60	70	22	59
Peterson, Kevin, Tenn. Tech	6	3	5.05	14	0	66	84	20	44
Huesgen, Dan, SE Missouri St.	7	3	5.15	18	0	73	88	21	54
Anderson, Robert, Austin Peay	4	7	5.26	13	0	77	103	29	52
Fellers, Joe, Tenn. Tech	5	4	5.29	18	0	68	77	26	63
Patterson, John, Morehead St.	3	1	5.44	20	0	50	63	21	21
Heminover, Chad, Tenn. Tech	3	4	5.47	17	4	49	48	29	46
Massey, Seth, Austin Peay	5	5	5.49	20	0	79	81	48	78
Shelton, Chris, Austin Peay	5	2	5.67	15	0	60	64	31	64
Bedwell, Ken, Middle Tenn.	2	4	5.64	17	0	75	90	38	63

PACIFIC-10 CONFERENCE

NORTH	Conference W	Conference L	Overall W	Overall L
***Washington**	17	7	41	17
Oregon State	15	9	35	14
Washington State	12	12	25	24
Portland State	4	20	17	34

ALL-CONFERENCE TEAM: C—Ben Bertrand, Sr., Oregon State. **1B**—Casey Kelley, Jr., Washington State. **2B**—David Ferres, Jr., Portland State; Scott Randall, Jr., Washington State. **3B**—Ryan Lentz, Jr., Washington; Greg Mitchell, Sr., Washington State. **SS**—Kevin Miller, Jr., Washington. **OF**—Rob Colley, Jr., Oregon State; Rusty Keith, Jr., Portland State; Chris Magruder, Jr., Washington; Nick Stefonick, Jr., Washington. **DH**—Joe Gerber, So., Oregon State. **Util**—Rick Southall, Jr., Portland State. **P**—Andrew Checketts, Sr., Oregon State; Jeff Carlsen, Fr., Washington; Wade Parrish, So., Washington State. **RP**—Wayne Lee, Jr., Washington.

Player of the Year: Andrew Checketts, Oregon State. **Coach of the Year**: Ken Knutson, Washington.

INDIVIDUAL BATTING LEADERS

(Minimum 100 At-Bats)

	AVG	AB	R	H	2B	3B	HR	RBI	SB
Stefonick, Nick, Washington	**.407**	177	49	72	18	**5**	7	54	14
Magruder, Chris, Wash.	.402	219	**89**	**88**	18	4	11	57	**33**
Gerber, Joe, Oregon St.	.377	122	37	46	8	0	11	38	0
Keith, Rusty, Portland St.	.366	186	41	68	10	1	6	39	6
Colley, Rob, Oregon State	.362	177	43	64	6	2	6	62	2
Randall, Scott, Wash. St.	.358	187	38	67	11	3	3	28	12
Southall, Rick, Portland St.	.358	190	37	68	**22**	1	8	49	2
Bertrand, Ben, Oregon St.	.353	190	49	67	14	2	10	54	0
Hodges, Drew, Oregon St.	.350	143	43	50	10	1	6	36	3
Kelley, Casey, Wash. St.	.335	182	57	61	9	3	**25**	**68**	0
Stevenson, Shawn, WSU	.328	201	58	66	11	4	9	38	5
Lipe, Ryan, Oregon St.	.324	145	33	47	5	0	2	23	11
Ferres, David, Portland St.	.323	161	32	52	10	2	4	26	5
Grove, Jason, Wash. St.	.323	161	39	52	13	2	12	31	0
Lentz, Ryan, Washington	.319	226	65	72	19	1	16	65	7
Miller, Kevin, Washington	.317	208	61	66	13	4	12	57	5
Bundy, Ryan, Washington	.317	164	40	52	7	3	8	25	11
Bailie, Matt, Oregon St.	.315	162	47	51	8	0	9	51	1
Woods, Kyle, Washington	.314	210	48	66	12	3	14	49	20
Schader, Troy, Oregon St.	.313	166	39	52	9	0	8	38	2
Andrade, Neal, Portland St.	.308	156	32	48	10	0	7	39	2
Stranberg, Jason, Oregon St.	.306	124	36	38	9	0	2	24	16
Na, Jim, Washington	.305	105	21	32	7	0	5	26	4
Remington, Erik, Portland St.	.301	196	44	59	19	2	5	27	7
Mitchell, Greg, Wash.St.	.299	167	40	50	4	0	15	49	2

INDIVIDUAL PITCHING LEADERS

(Minimum 40 Innings)

	W	L	ERA	G	SV	IP	H	BB	SO
Checketts, Andrew, Oregon St.	**11**	1	**3.77**	13	0	86	74	19	73

	W	L	ERA	G	SV	IP	H	BB	SO
Percell, Brody, Oregon St.	5	4	3.86	13	0	70	65	20	87
Anderson, Travis, Washington	4	2	4.11	10	0	46	40	32	45
Carlsen, Jeff, Washington	7	3	4.39	14	0	80	87	30	62
Parrish, Wade, Washington St.	8	3	4.93	13	0	84	96	36	56
#Morrison, Cody, Washington	1	1	5.14	22	**6**	21	14	16	30
Pine, Chris, Oregon State	4	3	5.38	13	0	75	70	44	**104**
Heaverlo, Jeff, Washington	5	3	5.63	12	0	70	75	34	84
Gaines, Jamaal, Washington St.	4	4	5.73	13	0	75	93	19	58
Oyler, Scott, Portland St.	4	4	5.91	16	0	70	80	34	51
Hampton, Matt, Washington	4	4	5.93	13	0	68	88	29	34
Pearce, Josh, Portland St.	2	8	6.69	15	0	75	100	35	71

PACIFIC-10 CONFERENCE

	Conference		Overall	
SOUTH	**W**	**L**	**W**	**L**
Stanford	22	8	42	14
Southern California	21	9	49	17
Arizona State	18	11	41	23
Arizona	12	18	33	23
UCLA	11	19	24	33
California	5	24	22	32

ALL-CONFERENCE TEAM: C—Jason Hill, Jr., California. **1B**—John Gall, So., Stanford; Robb Gorr, Jr., Southern California. **2B**—Erik Mattern, Sr., Arizona; Xavier Nady, Fr., California. **3B**—Garrett Atkins, Fr., UCLA; Andrew Beinbrink, Jr., Arizona State; Morgan Ensberg, Sr., Southern California. **SS**—Jay Pecci, Sr., Stanford; Seth Davidson, Fr., Southern California. **OF**—Willie Bloomquist, So., Arizona State; Jody Gerut, Jr., Stanford; Colin Porter, Sr., Arizona; Eric Valent, Jr., UCLA. **P**—Jeff Austin, Jr., Stanford; Seth Etherton, Sr., Southern California; Jack Krawczyk, Sr., Southern California; Phill Lowery, Jr., Arizona State.

Player of the Year: Eric Valent, UCLA. **Co-Pitchers of the Year**: Jeff Austin, Stanford; Seth Etherton, Southern California. **Coach of the Year**: Mark Marquess, Stanford.

INDIVIDUAL BATTING LEADERS

(Minimum 125 At-Bats)

	AVG	AB	R	H	2B	3B	HR	RBI	SB
Bloomquist, Willie, Ariz. St.	**.414**	263	**88**	**109**	14	**9**	4	01	**33**
Nady, Xavier, California	.404	223	65	90	**28**	5	15	70	9
Munson, Eric, USC	.392	171	45	67	15	0	16	56	6
Oliver, Brian, California	.386	127	36	49	10	2	5	23	8
Myers, Casey, Arizona St.	.386	184	35	71	17	0	8	58	1
Atkins, Garrett, UCLA	.383	222	43	85	22	1	9	54	1
Gall, John, Stanford	.381	239	52	91	22	2	15	63	0
Hendricks, Jason, Arizona	.364	196	60	71	18	3	15	63	7
Mattern, Erik, Arizona	.363	223	78	81	12	8	7	58	5
Hanoian, Greg, USC	.358	137	34	49	10	0	2	20	3
Moreno, Mikel, Arizona St.	.354	274	78	97	16	1	11	56	27
DeRenne, Keoni, Arizona	.349	232	68	81	15	6	5	55	8
Phelps, Jeff, Arizona St.	.348	155	33	54	10	2	5	39	7
Hill, Jason, California	.347	202	41	70	15	1	12	54	10
Gorr, Robb, USC	.345	278	63	96	13	3	16	**79**	11
Gordnier, Aaron, California	.345	197	52	68	12	2	14	47	21
Ensberg, Morgan, USC	.344	244	74	84	22	0	21	69	20
Freitas, Jeremy, USC	.340	212	57	72	11	1	14	58	4
Clark, Greg, Arizona	.338	210	49	71	20	1	13	58	2
Valent, Eric, UCLA	.336	220	69	74	10	1	**30**	73	4
Gerut, Jody, Stanford	.335	230	64	77	18	2	18	61	13
Davidson, Seth, USC	.333	204	46	68	13	2	5	31	17
Green, Jason, UCLA	.333	144	23	48	11	0	3	21	2
Byrnes, Eric, UCLA	.332	244	63	81	19	2	14	52	30
Lane, Jason, USC	.332	232	55	77	18	1	14	50	8
Borchard, Joe, Stanford	.330	203	45	67	18	1	10	55	4
Beinbrink, Andrew, Ariz. St.	.328	235	63	77	22	4	12	85	20
Rachels, Wes, USC	.327	251	48	82	16	1	3	36	16
Moraga, Omar, Arizona	.326	193	44	63	19	2	4	43	8
Porter, Colin, Arizona	.326	224	68	73	14	7	14	64	23
Day, Nick, Stanford	.323	155	30	50	13	2	1	22	3
Utley, Chase, UCLA	.320	194	35	62	11	0	15	49	1
Corley, Kenny, Arizona	.316	212	50	67	12	1	12	67	7
Hochgesang, Josh, Stanford	.315	197	54	62	14	4	10	39	8
Muth, Edmund, Stanford	.308	221	61	68	17	5	14	51	7
Olson, Cassidy, UCLA	.304	191	29	58	8	0	10	47	0
Ticehurst, Brad, USC	.302	202	45	61	8	1	18	54	10

INDIVIDUAL PITCHING LEADERS

(Minimum 50 Innings)

	W	L	ERA	G	SV	IP	H	BB	SO
#Krawczyk, Jack, USC	3	2	2.01	34	**23**	49	46	8	51
Crumpton, Chuck, Arizona St.	3	7	**3.00**	36	5	63	65	31	61
Austin, Jeff, Stanford	12	4	3.11	18	0	133	118	32	136
Etherton, Seth, USC	**13**	3	3.23	18	0	137	113	29	**182**
Wayne, Justin, Stanford	6	0	3.78	25	6	01	81	25	75
Kramer, Aaron, Arizona St.	8	2	3.94	29	3	75	67	21	80
Pennington, Chad, Arizona St.	7	2	4.20	22	0	75	64	35	87
Mills, Ryan, Arizona St.	8	4	4.68	20	0	115	110	54	140
Dennis, Jason, California	6	5	4.88	21	1	98	104	36	58
Hutchinson, Chad, Stanford	10	5	4.89	17	0	99	92	58	115
Johnson, James, Arizona	7	3	5.07	16	0	98	104	45	116
Shirley, Jon, California	3	4	5.09	16	0	92	100	34	72
Penney, Mike, USC	8	4	5.25	21	0	106	123	38	56
Currier, Rik, USC	6	1	5.30	20	0	71	73	39	100
Lane, Jason, USC	9	2	5.34	34	0	62	75	15	38
Lowery, Phill, Arizona St.	8	6	5.53	18	0	99	90	47	96

Six-Pac player of year

UCLA's Eric Valent led conference with 30 home runs

PATRIOT LEAGUE

	Conference		Overall	
	W	**L**	**W**	**L**
*Navy	15	5	26	17
Bucknell	13	7	31	17
Army	12	8	16	29
Lafayette	8	12	10	26
Lehigh	7	13	13	26
Holy Cross	5	15	7	29

ALL-CONFERENCE TEAM: **C**—Mitch Hoffman, Sr., Lafayette. **1B**—Tom Stoudt, Sr., Lafayette. **2B**—Dave Apollon, Sr., Bucknell. **3B**—Bob Osipower, So., Lafayette. **SS**—Todd Benke, Sr., Navy. **OF**—Toph Lake, Sr., Navy; Shaun Salmon, So., Army; Keith Treonze, Jr., Lehigh. **DH**—Mark Zematis, So., Navy. **P**—Mike Anders, Sr., Bucknell; Shane Groover, So., Navy. **RP**—Matt Potalivo, So., Bucknell; Dave Self, Fr., Navy.

Player of the Year: Toph Lake, Navy. **Co-Pitchers of the Year**: Mike Anders, Bucknell; Shane Groover, Navy. **Coach of the Year**: Bob MacDonald, Navy.

INDIVIDUAL BATTING LEADERS

(Minimum 100 At-Bats)

	AVG	AB	R	H	2B	3B	HR	RBI	SB
Stoudt, Tom, Lafayette	**.442**	113	35	50	5	1	7	31	4
Osipower, Robert, Lafayette	.438	128	27	56	13	1	4	28	0
Lake, Toph, Navy	.431	137	45	59	13	3	5	32	9
Treonze, Keith, Lehigh	.415	135	31	56	9	3	4	37	5
Benke, Todd, Navy	.413	167	**55**	**69**	**18**	4	6	51	4
Zematis, Mark, Navy	.396	134	42	53	**18**	1	7	**58**	2
Braham, Luke, Navy	.383	128	38	49	13	3	7	40	2
Salmon, Shaun, Army	.381	155	33	59	7	3	1	23	7

McElwee, Pat, Lehigh	.377	146	42	55	11	2	7	28	2
Krone, Joe, Navy	.376	141	33	53	10	2	2	36	12
Apollon, Dave, Bucknell	.363	160	48	58	12	**8**	**8**	49	**27**
McKernan, Kevin, Lafayette	.347	118	23	41	8	1	2	24	0
MacNeely, Mike, Bucknell	.333	100	27	46	7	4	7	34	0
Damato, Micah, Lehigh	.331	124	23	41	9	2	3	25	1
Hoffman, Mitch, Lafayette	.330	112	24	37	7	0	0	10	2
Gordon, Jared, Lehigh	.319	116	27	37	8	0	2	18	1
Scioletti, Mike, Army	.305	141	19	43	7	0	7	29	3

INDIVIDUAL PITCHING LEADERS

(Minimum 40 Innings)

	W	L	ERA	G	SV	IP	H	BB	SO
McDowell, Kevin, Bucknell	6	2	**2.42**	9	0	48	30	45	49
Anders, Mike, Bucknell	**8**	3	2.96	13	0	85	93	11	**73**
Kozink, Scott, Navy	7	4	3.69	12	0	76	73	23	**73**
Groover, Shane, Navy	7	1	4.36	12	0	74	67	33	61
Heffernan, Kevin, Army	3	5	4.39	14	0	66	60	29	38
Junge, Eric, Bucknell	7	2	4.55	17	3	55	60	20	45
Kacuba, Jeremy, Lafayette	4	2	4.67	10	0	44	43	39	44
King, Jason, Army	4	4	4.76	13	0	68	73	13	33
Frey, Chris, Lehigh	3	5	5.30	10	0	53	70	21	31
Poe, Mike, Navy	2	4	5.40	10	0	47	52	10	39
Hoak, Ed, Navy	3	3	5.62	10	0	42	50	11	24
#Abell, Brian, Army	0	1	6.75	11	**4**	11	11	10	13

SOUTHEASTERN CONFERENCE

	Conference		Overall	
EAST	**W**	**L**	**W**	**L**
Florida	21	8	46	18
South Carolina	19	10	44	18
Kentucky	12	18	26	31
Tennessee	11	17	36	20
Georgia	8	21	24	30
Vanderbilt	6	24	25	28
WEST	**W**	**L**	**W**	**L**
Louisiana State	21	9	48	19
Alabama	19	10	46	18
***Auburn**	16	12	46	18
Mississippi State	14	15	42	23
Arkansas	13	14	38	21
Mississippi	13	15	30	23

ALL—CONFERENCE TEAM: C—Matt Frick, Sr., Alabama. **1B**—Eddy Furniss, Sr., Louisiana State. **2B**—Jeff Pickler, Sr., Tennesee. **3B**—Andy Phillips, Jr., Alabama. **SS**—Adam Everett, Jr., South Carolina. **OF**—Mike Curry, Jr., South Carolina; Clint Johnston, Jr., Vanderbilt; Sonny Cortez, Sr., Tennessee. **DH**—Todd Faulkner, So., Auburn. **Util**—Brad Wilkerson, Jr., Florida. **P**—David Walling, So., Arkansas; Kip Bouknight, Fr., South Carolina. **RP**—Josh Fogg, Jr., Florida.

Player of the Year: Jeff Pickler, Tennessee. **Co-Freshmen of the Year**: Hayden Gliemmo, Auburn; Todd Faulkner, Auburn. **Coach of the Year**: Ray Tanner, South Carolina.

INDIVIDUAL BATTING LEADERS

(Minimum 125 At-Bats)

	AVG	AB	R	H	2B	3B	HR	RBI	SB
Pickler, Jeff, Tennessee	**.445**	245	79	**109**	**30**	2	7	61	25
Johnston, Clint, Vanderbilt	.424	198	58	84	16	0	19	74	6
Copley, Travis, Tennessee	.419	148	38	62	16	1	5	46	3
Wiese, Brian, Miss. State	.412	250	71	103	24	2	14	57	11
Pratt, Scott, Auburn	.407	258	82	105	21	**6**	11	59	33
Furniss, Eddy, LSU	.403	236	85	95	27	3	28	76	0
Curry, Mike, South Carolina	.400	260	**102**	104	15	5	16	46	**60**
Smith, Casey, Florida	.388	250	59	97	18	1	12	68	8
Cortez, Sonny, Tennessee	.387	212	70	82	20	0	24	87	4
Loggins, Josh, Kentucky	.384	242	56	93	20	5	15	63	6
Faulkner, Todd, Auburn	.382	220	53	84	14	1	20	65	0
Henderson, Brad, Mississippi	.379	206	63	78	17	2	15	52	4
Keller, G.W., Alabama	.377	247	67	93	14	5	14	62	7
Everett, Adam, So. Carolina	.375	267	71	100	21	4	13	63	15
Kelly, Heath, Auburn	.374	238	62	89	17	4	6	57	18
Ross, Justin, Tennessee	.374	222	79	83	22	1	10	46	18
Thornhill, Mark, Georgia	.369	157	23	58	11	0	5	34	0
Huisman, Jason, Mississippi	.366	227	53	83	19	2	21	71	4
Hinske, Eric, Arkansas	.365	233	58	85	27	2	9	71	19
Nicholson, Derek, Florida	.365	241	66	88	20	4	15	66	6
Hall, Kevin, Georgia	.362	141	40	51	10	2	1	26	8
Catalanotte, Greg, Florida	.360	261	72	94	23	2	13	61	10
Lee, Richard, Miss. State	.357	258	71	92	20	2	19	85	4
Urquhart, Derick, So. Car.	.356	250	79	89	13	3	20	77	18
Freeman, Brad, Miss. State	.355	256	73	91	15	4	11	54	16
Cheatle, David, Kentucky	.352	219	54	77	18	0	2	30	3
Phillips, Andy, Alabama	.351	265	65	93	11	2	21	82	5
Wandall, Chad, Auburn	.350	237	60	83	23	1	6	46	3
Wilkerson, Brad, Florida	.347	222	86	77	13	3	23	70	20
Rounds, Drew, Alabama	.346	182	50	63	8	1	13	43	15
Bryan, Brooks, Miss. State	.346	237	45	82	14	2	9	50	8
Welsh, Jack, Arkansas	.346	217	65	75	7	2	6	47	8
Adeeb, Josh, Vanderbilt	.344	192	57	66	13	1	19	61	10
Phillips, Paul, Alabama	.344	273	69	94	13	3	10	38	18
Bordenick, Ryan, So. Car.	.342	219	55	75	15	1	19	76	1
Frick, Matt, Alabama	.342	222	66	76	13	4	22	60	4
Nye, Rodney, Arkansas	.342	228	54	78	24	0	15	69	4
Siegel, Matt, Florida	.342	152	45	52	12	2	4	28	4
Etheredge, Josh, Auburn	.340	247	71	84	19	1	21	**90**	4
Ellis, Mark, Florida	.338	225	69	76	18	0	14	51	8
Bozanich, Sam, Alabama	.333	225	48	75	17	1	3	28	3
Caldwell, Brent, Arkansas	.333	216	48	72	17	3	4	50	2
Kersh, Jamie, Auburn	.333	198	46	66	14	3	5	46	3
Ross, David, Florida	.332	238	54	79	21	0	19	70	7
Chapman, Travis, Miss. St.	.327	251	55	82	17	1	10	50	1
Osbolt, Andy, Georgia	.327	196	49	64	10	0	23	46	0
Wilson, John, Kentucky	.327	171	33	56	14	3	9	33	4
Meadows, Tydus, Vanderbilt	.326	190	46	62	6	1	12	47	13
Lotterhos, Chris, Miss. State	.326	129	34	42	4	3	2	18	5
McClure, Trey, LSU	.325	240	69	78	13	0	27	84	2
Shelton, Robert, Mississippi	.325	126	25	41	7	0	5	21	2
Cresse, Brad, LSU	.323	232	55	75	12	0	**29**	**90**	0
Hammock, Robby, Georgia	.322	205	41	66	12	3	12	46	7
Dunn, Casey, Auburn	.320	275	61	88	18	0	10	67	0
Gliemmo, Hayden, Auburn	.319	141	37	45	8	0	3	22	0
McGlone, Aaron, Kentucky	.318	220	44	70	16	0	8	45	8
Colemire, Jason, Kentucky	.317	227	44	72	23	1	15	52	3
Rich, Dominic, Auburn	.317	249	67	79	14	2	5	54	7
Thoms, Rusty, Miss. State	.317	268	61	85	12	0	3	39	16
Lundquist, Ryan, Arkansas	.315	203	68	64	18	1	13	60	4
Dill, Justin, Vanderbilt	.314	172	34	54	10	0	7	40	3
Keene, Kurt, Tennessee	.311	228	56	71	13	1	10	51	5
Figueroa, Eduardo, Tenn.	.310	184	50	57	14	1	7	40	4
Martin, Ty, Florida	.309	223	58	69	11	3	7	41	5
Poe, Adam, South Carolina	.309	243	44	75	18	3	12	54	8
Kielty, Bobby, Mississippi	.307	215	62	66	19	1	16	49	3
Dykes, Jimmy, Vanderbilt	.307	179	41	55	16	0	1	22	9
Kirby, Brian, Arkansas	.306	144	32	44	12	0	11	46	2
Higgins, Danny, LSU	.302	202	51	61	13	1	15	37	4
Jester, Joe, Arkansas	.301	186	38	56	7	1	3	25	6
Burnett, Mark, Arkansas	.301	133	40	40	6	1	1	18	10
Kata, Matt, Vanderbilt	.300	227	61	68	19	1	3	25	18

INDIVIDUAL PITCHING LEADERS

(Minimum 50 Innings)

	W	L	ERA	G	SV	IP	H	BB	SO
Fogg, Josh, Florida	7	2	**2.03**	40	**13**	84	63	30	114
Compton, Brian, Mississippi St.	4	0	2.24	23	1	56	41	21	72
Kingrey, Jarrod, Alabama	8	4	2.47	33	**13**	84	57	35	98
Vent, Kevin, Arkansas	5	0	2.77	28	3	52	47	28	50
Bauer, Peter, South Carolina	7	0	2.93	14	0	68	59	22	68
Bean, Colter, Auburn	4	3	3.56	29	7	66	63	22	57
Cramblitt, Joey, Mississippi	9	2	3.62	18	0	75	76	30	35
Smith, Justin, Alabama	7	1	3.90	16	0	102	107	42	95
Schoening, Brent, Auburn	11	5	3.88	18	0	111	101	46	111
Smith, Justin, Alabama	7	1	3.90	16	0	102	107	42	95
Bouknight, Kip, South Carolina	11	3	4.07	21	0	95	87	46	86
Bond, Tommy, Florida	5	1	4.19	15	0	60	68	27	53
Tolbert, Lance, Mississippi	5	6	4.22	16	2	85	86	35	55
Thompson, Doug, LSU	12	5	4.24	24	1	116	127	42	124
Nye, Rodney, Arkansas	3	5	4.30	22	4	59	64	20	57
Moriarity, Mike, Arkansas	6	1	4.31	18	1	77	79	32	61
Bowe, Brandon, LSU	6	3	4.34	23	1	70	84	21	77
Demouy, Chris, LSU	5	2	4.46	33	3	71	80	33	92
Yee, Damon, Vanderbilt	5	3	4.53	24	1	56	61	23	54
Thoms, Hank, Miss. State	5	2	4.55	29	6	61	67	25	59
Gray, Michael, Florida	8	2	4.58	24	1	51	65	17	63
Green, B.J., Alabama	8	2	4.59	19	0	84	97	33	71
Jackson, Jeremy, Miss. State	10	3	4.61	17	0	100	126	27	91
Keisler, Randy, LSU	9	5	4.61	27	2	94	97	33	135
Walling, David, Arkansas	10	4	4.70	18	1	103	96	25	128
Snow, Bert, Vanderbilt	5	7	4.78	16	1	90	94	43	83
Wood, Eric, Auburn	4	0	4.84	24	0	58	69	9	34
Bootcheck, Chris, Auburn	8	2	4.94	20	1	55	59	28	44
Gliemmo, Hayden, Auburn	**13**	3	4.94	21	0	118	125	43	104
Colley, Reed, Vanderbilt	3	4	5.02	23	0	66	90	20	50
Esteves, Jake, LSU	9	3	5.03	27	2	103	129	41	100
Wilkerson, Brad, Florida	10	5	5.05	18	0	118	134	69	**136**
Scott, Kurt, Tennessee	6	6	5.10	17	0	102	107	49	88
Ginter, Matt, Miss. State	6	4	5.38	19	0	89	86	54	100

	W	L	ERA	G	SV	IP	H	BB	SO
Kondro, Brett, South Carolina	6	1	5.52	16	0	77	82	39	47
Freed, Mark, Miss. State	6	6	5.55	21	0	71	81	28	62
Frachiseur, Zack, Georgia	6	7	5.63	19	0	102	118	47	120
Blankenship, Jon, Alabama	7	2	5.66	25	0	70	81	25	60
Knorst, Kevin, Auburn	5	4	5.76	19	0	80	93	33	61
Fisher, Pete, Alabama	7	8	5.87	18	0	104	141	32	92
Paxton, Josh, Kentucky	5	3	5.92	22	2	73	83	37	31
Quarnstrom, Rob, Arkansas	5	2	5.93	24	3	61	70	18	61

SOUTHERN CONFERENCE

	Conference W	Conference L	Overall W	Overall L
UNC Greensboro	22	5	40	18
***The Citadel**	21	5	37	24
Western Carolina	20	6	45	15
Furman	12	12	21	27
Wofford	10	12	15	32
Georgia Southern	9	15	22	30
Davidson	8	16	13	38
East Tennessee State	8	18	18	31
Virginia Military	7	17	14	35
Appalachian State	6	17	13	28

ALL-CONFERENCE TEAM: C—Stephen Crater, Fr., Appalachian State. **1B**—Philip Hartig, Fr., The Citadel. **2B**—Dominic Pattie, Sr., UNC Greensboro. **3B**—Mike Berrier, Jr., Appalachian State. **SS**—Chris Moore, Jr., Western Carolina. **OF**—Martin Barrow, Sr., Western Carolina; Kenny Vawter, Sr., UNC Greensboro; Linwood Davis, Sr., UNC Greensboro. **DH**—Mike DeSimone, Jr., Davidson. **P**—Mark DiFelice, Sr., Western Carolina; Lee Long, Sr., Wofford. **RP**—Tom Martin, Sr., The Citidel.

Player of the Year: Martin Barrow, Western Carolina. **Pitcher of the Year:** Mark DiFelice, Western Carolina. **Freshman of the Year:** Philip Hartig, The Citadel. **Coach of the Year:** Mike Gaski, UNC Greensboro.

INDIVIDUAL BATTING LEADERS

(Minimum 100 At-Bats)

	AVG	AB	R	H	2B	3B	HR	RBI	SB
Elerman, Brandon, ETSU	**.390**	123	32	48	9	0	7	35	0
Berrier, Mike, App. State	.381	113	32	43	11	1	6	30	2
Vawter, Kenny, UNCG	.380	205	38	78	15	2	6	47	19
Sigmon, Shane, App. State	.378	148	30	56	12	**6**	5	31	4
Smalls, Terrence, Citadel	.375	240	71	**90**	13	1	4	42	**49**
Crater, Stephen, App. State	.368	133	35	49	14	1	11	42	0
Thomas, Charles, W. Carolina	.364	209	49	76	10	2	1	29	11
Surridge, Lance, UNCG	.361	219	49	79	11	0	4	38	12
Hartig, Phillip, Citadel	.355	214	47	76	10	3	**17**	62	1
Swackhamer, Rusty, ETSU	.354	189	33	67	14	4	9	48	9
Blocker, Kevin, Wofford	.353	167	28	59	16	0	2	27	2
Moore, Chris, W. Carolina	.353	187	62	66	16	0	14	**66**	12
DeSimone, Mike, Davidson	.348	187	35	65	13	1	10	49	5
Haigler, Aaron, Citadel	.348	233	46	81	**25**	0	6	49	2
Pollock, Jody, Ga. Southern	.347	222	58	77	21	2	4	33	13
Catanzaro, Chris, VMI	.346	182	36	63	16	0	6	34	4
Wagner, Ryan, ETSU	.345	197	39	68	16	1	0	27	22
Barrow, Martin, W. Carolina	.339	254	**72**	86	16	5	4	49	30
Bright, James, Furman	.337	163	35	55	7	1	0	24	16
Cheek, Andy, App. State	.337	163	38	55	9	2	9	34	5
Anderson, John, App. State	.336	149	45	50	8	0	5	26	2
Noyce, David, Furman	.333	135	15	45	8	0	5	22	0
Koone, Chuck, W. Carolina	.332	199	60	66	15	2	6	40	35
Davis, Linwood, UNCG	.332	208	39	69	11	0	10	60	16
Nunley, Matt, ETSU	.331	139	20	46	12	1	7	30	1
Morrill, Jim, Furman	.329	167	39	55	13	0	13	44	6
Henley, Scott, Ga. Southern	.328	183	31	60	10	0	8	39	3
Easterday, Matt, Ga. Southern	.324	142	38	46	8	3	3	30	3
Wilson, Jason, ETSU	.323	189	48	61	17	3	11	33	0
Pattie, Dominic, UNCG	.322	230	61	74	9	5	4	38	35
Sloan, Stewart, Davidson	.320	172	24	55	16	2	1	37	4

INDIVIDUAL PITCHING LEADERS

(Minimum 40 Innings)

	W	L	ERA	G	SV	IP	H	BB	SO
Kirby, Aaron, W. Carolina	4	1	**1.62**	19	2	44	44	11	41
Parsons, Jason, UNCG	8	2	2.32	29	6	66	64	19	51
Martin, Tom, Citadel	5	4	2.62	38	**8**	58	65	10	61
Hancock, Rodney, Citadel	9	2	2.99	20	1	99	83	39	93
DiFelice, Mark, W. Carolina	**11**	2	3.12	15	0	98	95	21	110
Gordon, Sean, UNCG	7	0	3.36	30	2	75	71	18	69
Noyce, David, Furman	1	2	3.38	9	0	48	45	15	54
Bain, Brian, W. Carolina	8	5	3.76	15	0	89	87	48	83
Toler, Ted, UNCG	3	2	4.05	35	3	47	39	16	42
Wiley, Brian, Citadel	7	4	4.07	20	0	102	79	59	**159**
Hatchell, Kyle, Ga. Southern	2	2	4.14	18	2	46	39	35	41
Rogers, Brian, Citadel	7	6	4.16	20	0	119	112	47	**159**
McDonald, Corey, UNCG	4	3	4.19	16	0	58	46	30	62
Long, Lee, Wofford	8	4	4.22	17	1	90	108	32	78
Davidson, Chris, W. Carolina	8	1	4.69	15	0	96	109	29	87
Sauls, Clint, Ga. Southern	7	6	4.87	19	0	122	149	55	75
Surridge, Lance, UNCG	7	4	4.88	18	0	79	79	38	62
DeSimone, Mike, Davidson	4	2	4.95	27	3	44	55	18	34
David, Toby, Furman	3	3	5.13	11	0	47	49	23	34
Bates, Chip, Furman	4	5	5.14	12	1	68	77	23	70
Rowland, William, Furman	4	7	5.15	22	4	72	77	19	53
Barrow, Wes, VMI	4	6	5.33	15	0	83	98	36	68
Colvard, Ron, Citadel	6	4	5.43	25	1	68	79	26	59
Harrell, Michael, ETSU	6	6	5.49	17	0	97	127	24	69
Craun, Grayson, VMI	3	5	5.73	15	1	55	62	25	58
Washburn, Danny, Ga. Southern	3	5	5.73	13	0	66	80	26	52
Hutchinson, Brian, W. Carolina	2	2	5.80	14	0	50	57	38	35

SOUTHLAND CONFERENCE

	Conference W	Conference L	Overall W	Overall L
Northwestern State	15	8	40	20
Northeast Louisiana	13	9	33	22
McNeese State	13	10	30	26
***Nicholls State**	**13**	**11**	**28**	**34**
Southwest Texas	13	11	28	28
Sam Houston State	12	11	29	28
Texas-Arlington	9	13	20	29
Southeastern Louisiana	9	14	29	27
Texas-San Antonio	7	17	23	28

ALL-CONFERENCE TEAM: **C**—Kyle Heine, Sr., Texas-Arlington. **1B**—Ben Broussard, Jr., McNeese State. **2B**—Tyson Switzenberg, Jr., McNeese State. **3B**—Matt Mize, Jr., Texas-Arlington. **SS**—Ryan Anholt, Jr., Northwestern State. **OF**—Corey Taylor, Sr., Northeast Louisiana; Chris Schmitz, Sr., McNeese State; Jeff Juarez, Jr., Texas-San Antonio. **DH**—Billy Martin, Sr., Texas-Arlington. **P**—Brian Lawrence, Sr., Northwestern State; Cody Arcement, Sr., Nicholls State; Ben Sheets, So., Northeast Louisiana.

Player of the Year: Ryan Anholt, Northwestern State. **Hitter of the Year**: Ben Broussard, McNeese State. **Pitcher of the Year**: Brian Lawrence, Northwestern State. **Newcomer of the Year**: Ryan Anholt, Northwestern State. **Coach of the Year**: John Cohen, Northwestern State.

INDIVIDUAL BATTING LEADERS

(Minimum 100 At-Bats)

	AVG	AB	R	H	2B	3B	HR	RBI	SB
Anholt, Ryan, NW State	**.417**	211	64	88	14	4	15	71	13
Broussard, Ben, McNeese	.385	218	56	84	16	3	16	**77**	2
Schmitz, Chris, McNeese	.382	233	**69**	**89**	17	**9**	13	56	6
Mize, Matt, UT Arlington	.369	176	50	65	12	3	16	49	10
Fingleson, Gavin, SE La.	.367	237	50	87	16	1	2	19	5
Switzenberg, Tyson, McNeese	.365	241	58	88	12	3	10	53	5
Martin, Billy, UT Arlington	.363	168	33	61	13	2	13	52	0
Core, Willie, NE Louisiana	.356	149	29	53	14	2	4	42	2
Taylor, Cory, NE Louisiana	.354	189	66	67	9	2	19	53	29
Juarez, Jeff, Texas-SA	.346	182	43	63	16	3	13	54	7
Zander, Brian, NE Louisiana	.345	194	43	67	15	2	6	45	8
Landreneau, Stuart, McN.	.345	142	33	49	12	2	6	30	0
Wallis, Kent, Texas-SA	.344	180	39	62	11	3	18	62	6
Lewis, Justin, NE Louisiana	.343	161	52	62	14	1	7	48	13
Newell, Adrian, SE La.	.342	111	26	38	8	1	4	29	2
Wickersham, Jack, SW Texas	.339	233	49	79	15	1	7	36	**31**
Eddlemon, Kelly, Sam Houston	.337	175	31	59	14	0	6	32	3
Prater, Nick, Texas-SA	.335	164	42	55	16	2	3	35	10
Walters, David, SW Texas	.332	208	39	69	16	0	8	46	2
Wolfe, Jason, NE Louisiana	.331	172	44	57	15	1	7	34	8
Fikac, Jeremy, SW Texas	.327	208	44	68	15	4	8	39	7
Gremminger, Jesse, SHS	.325	157	27	51	6	0	8	31	4
Gross, Jeremy, SE La.	.324	210	51	68	18	1	**21**	58	4
Jobert, Jacques, Nicholls St.	.321	234	41	75	15	2	6	43	5
#Perret, Kevin, Nicholls St.	.285	228	49	65	**23**	5	6	40	4

INDIVIDUAL PITCHING LEADERS

(Minimum 40 Innings)

	W	L	ERA	G	SV	IP	H	BB	SO
Emanuel, Brandon, NW State	5	1	**2.15**	25	**8**	63	34	18	52
Balcer, David, NW State	7	3	2.84	25	1	63	59	25	49
Warren, Andy, Sam Houston	6	2	2.85	14	2	88	62	29	50
Lawrence, Brian, NW State	9	5	2.93	19	0	111	109	33	**104**
Orgeron, Malcolm, Nicholls St.	3	3	3.19	25	2	59	61	23	29

	W	L	ERA	G	SV	IP	H	BB	SO
Guidry, Quinn, Nicholls St.	2	2	3.27	7	0	41	44	15	31
Hastings, Aron, SE La.	2	3	3.64	17	1	42	39	24	35
Harrald, Jonathan, Sam Hous.	9	5	3.69	19	2	68	61	21	67
Williams, Blake, SW Texas	3	5	3.84	18	1	61	74	18	25
Trosclair, Shane, SE La.	4	3	3.89	16	0	42	43	18	35
Davis, Allen, NW State	8	2	4.04	10	0	85	96	17	59
Smith, Brandon, NE La.	4	4	4.13	19	2	70	74	29	61
Arcement, Cody, Nicholls St.	**10**	4	4.25	17	0	89	97	29	71
McClosky, Carl, Sam Houston	2	3	4.28	13	0	40	33	23	22
Brown, Chris, NW State	6	3	4.36	20	0	74	65	40	71
Sheets, Ben, NE La.	6	7	4.50	19	4	84	82	23	74
Thompson, Ben, Nicholls St.	0	4	4.55	14	0	65	68	32	48
Montoya, Eric, Texas-SA	5	3	4.68	22	2	75	72	59	74
Janke, Cheyenne, Nicholls St.	6	6	4.68	19	0	75	97	11	71
Klaer, Tony, SW Texas	5	7	4.74	15	0	80	92	23	48

SWAC

	Conference		Overall	
EAST	**W**	**L**	**W**	**L**
Jackson State	21	2	29	20
Alabama State	14	10	21	26
Miss. Valley State	11	13	14	23
Alcorn State	9	16	17	26
WEST	**W**	**L**	**W**	**L**
*Southern	21	3	31	16
Grambling State	16	8	32	15
Texas Southern	9	15	19	28
Prairie View A&M	2	22	8	34

ALL-CONFERENCE TEAM: C—Alva Thompson, Jr., Southern. **1B**—Lincoln Williams, Sr., Southern. **2B**—Rickie Miller, Sr., Grambling. **3B**—Antonio Banks, So., Mississippi Valley. **SS**—Schuyler Doakes, Sr., Jackson State. **OF**—Fontella Jones, Jr., Mississippi Valley; Tony Coleman, Jr., Grambling; Marlon August, Sr., Southern. **DH**—Dexter Battle, Jr., Mississippi Valley. **P**—Farrell Graham, Jr., Southern; Sonny Garcia, Sr., Texas Southern; Rickey Lewis, Jr., Mississippi Valley; David Washington, Sr., Grambling.

Player of the Year: Rickie Miller, Grambling. **Pitcher of the Year**: Farrell Graham, Southern. **Hitter of the Year**: Jason Johnson, Grambling. **Freshman of the Year**: Brandon Tellis, Jackson State. **Newcomer of the Year**: Farrell Graham, Southern. **Coach of the Year**: Wilbert Ellis, Grambling.

INDIVIDUAL BATTING LEADERS

(Minimum 100 At-Bats)

	AVG	AB	R	H	2B	3B	HR	RBI	SB
Goss, Kelvin, Jackson St.	**.440**	100	25	44	9	0	2	33	6
Banks, Antonio, Miss. Valley	.438	105	23	46	5	2	1	29	0
Hills, Chris, Jackson St.	.424	118	30	50	10	2	4	35	14
Miller, Rickie, Grambling	.417	127	50	53	13	5	0	30	8
Jones, Fontella, Miss. Valley	.390	123	37	48	10	6	2	33	7
Battle, Dexter, Miss. Valley	.385	104	27	40	5	3	10	31	1
Johnson, Jason, Grambling	.383	133	52	51	6	5	6	51	18
Mack, Ken, Texas Southern	.383	128	33	49	12	1	3	36	7
Thompson, Alva, Southern	.383	167	47	64	10	2	**16**	**58**	3
Riggins, Auntwan, Texas So.	.381	168	47	64	11	5	1	29	26
Alexander, Juan, Grambling	.379	145	47	55	7	1	2	38	32
Rosa, Dario, Alcorn St.	.378	135	41	51	11	3	2	32	16
Banks, Bryan, Southern	.375	112	51	42	7	0	4	27	21
Miller, Shalawn, Jackson St.	.375	104	39	39	7	1	4	27	16
Doakes, Schuyler, JS.	.372	180	**62**	**67**	11	3	3	44	**45**
Broom, Torry, Alabama St.	.358	134	34	48	6	0	3	37	14
Coleman, Tony, Grambling	.358	134	40	48	4	5	2	39	28
James, Louis, Jackson St.	.347	147	39	51	9	3	0	27	11
Salsman, Darryl, Texas So.	.344	125	32	43	6	0	0	16	23
Clayton, Marcus, Alcorn St.	.342	117	30	40	10	4	4	38	4
#Coleman, Alph, Texas So.	.333	156	32	52	6	**8**	1	33	11
#Ivy, Boris, Jackson St.	.327	165	45	54	**14**	2	7	50	11
#Manuel, Kenneth, Southern.	.321	156	44	50	**14**	0	10	50	2

INDIVIDUAL PITCHING LEADERS

(Minimum 35 Innings)

	W	L	ERA	G	SV	IP	H	BB	SO
Hobdy, Cedric, Grambling	3	0	**3.34**	13	0	35	24	18	24
Kidd, Marlon, Jackson State	4	0	3.63	9	0	35	26	17	31
Woods, John, Jackson State	2	2	3.72	22	3	36	34	21	34
#Lyons, Joshua, Southern	0	0	4.34	17	**4**	29	31	17	25
Hill, Terrance, Southern	6	4	4.52	15	1	90	98	32	**92**
Johnson, Jason, Grambling	4	5	4.92	10	0	68	73	16	41
Garcia, Sonny, Texas So.	7	4	4.98	14	0	78	73	29	83
Graham, Farrell, Southern	**9**	0	5.10	13	0	67	70	41	38
Washington, David, Grambling	**9**	2	5.23	12	0	64	105	25	28
White, Clinton, Jackson St.	5	2	5.29	16	0	68	74	26	60

SUN BELT CONFERENCE

	Conference		Overall	
TEAM	**W**	**L**	**W**	**L**
South Alabama	19	6	42	19
***Southwestern Louisiana**	18	7	39	22
Lamar	15	9	30	27
Arkansas State	14	11	30	20
New Orleans	13	13	29	29
Jacksonville	13	14	31	27
Western Kentucky	12	14	27	24
Texas-Pan American	11	15	18	32
Louisiana Tech	8	18	21	34
Arkansas-Little Rock	5	21	17	38

ALL-CONFERENCE TEAM: C—Ben Keats, Jr., South Alabama; Eric Matthews, Sr., Lamar. **1B**—T.J. Freeman, Jr., Western Kentucky. **2B**—Brian Myrow, Jr., Louisiana Tech; L.A. Bowman, Sr., Arkansas State. **3B**—Michael Clay, Jr., Arkansas State. **OF**—Juan Pierre, Jr., South Alabama; Tom Whitehurst, Jr., South Alabama; Matt Peters, Sr., Texas-Pan American. **DH**—Justin Hemme, Sr., Southwestern Louisiana. **P**—Justin Carter, Jr., South Alabama; Mike Fischer, Jr., South Alabama; Jason Norton, Sr., South Alabama.

Player of the Year: Juan Pierre, South Alabama. **Newcomer of the Year**: Justin Carter, South Alabama. **Freshman of the Year**: Wes Koch, Lamar. **Coach of the Year**: Steve Kittrell, South Alabama.

INDIVIDUAL BATTING LEADERS

(Minimum 125 At-Bats)

	AVG	AB	R	H	2B	3B	HR	RBI	SB
Peters, Matt, Texas-PA	**.420**	138	33	58	8	3	1	13	11
Freeman, T.J., W. Kentucky	.379	182	33	69	20	1	8	49	13
Whitehurst, Tom, So. Ala.	.378	222	65	84	**25**	4	5	34	31
Hemme, Justin, SW La.	.376	205	50	77	17	1	16	55	6
Pierre, Juan, So. Alabama	.373	255	**77**	**95**	16	3	5	40	**54**
Harer, Mac, New Orleans	.373	233	54	87	18	3	7	37	11
Bowman, L.A., Ark. State	.369	206	51	76	18	2	2	21	10
Salinas, Leo, Texas-PA	.366	172	40	63	12	1	6	40	7
Cordo, Joe, New Orleans	.365	211	41	77	12	1	13	**68**	0
Yeo, Chris, W. Kentucky	.362	196	53	71	12	1	10	53	8
Ryan, B.J., SW La.	.356	208	40	74	7	3	12	39	6
Watson, Jon, New Orleans	.356	216	59	77	16	1	11	48	4
Cantrelle, Kevin, SW La.	.349	212	49	74	14	0	8	48	7
Pierce, Jeremy, Lamar	.349	149	37	52	19	2	8	36	1
Neyland, Jeremy, SW La.	.346	191	38	66	10	0	2	20	9
Bost, Tommy, La. Tech	.346	179	51	62	13	1	12	39	12
Taylor, T.D., Texas-PA	.343	175	36	60	9	1	8	33	3
Torre, Frank, New Orleans	.343	134	26	46	8	2	4	26	2
Myrow, Brian, La. Tech	.337	208	58	70	12	1	**21**	66	4
Avans, Chris, New Orleans	.335	203	44	68	12	1	5	42	5
Benson, Larry, Ark.-LR	.333	195	26	65	9	2	0	25	9
Johnson, George, Lamar	.332	193	33	64	17	0	8	45	1
Diggs, Ryan, Jacksonville	.330	209	49	69	14	3	4	43	9
Idlett, Matt, W. Kentucky	.328	201	52	66	13	3	10	45	8
Wesley, Jabbar, Ark.-LR	.326	138	20	45	15	1	6	32	2
Clay, Michael, Ark. State	.325	206	46	67	16	0	15	54	1
Asche, Kirk, Jacksonville	.324	216	58	70	19	4	13	37	8
Matthews, Eric, Lamar	.323	186	36	60	15	2	5	28	0
Ray, Dennis, Jacksonville	.323	161	37	52	18	0	7	34	5
#Goza, Jerry, La. Tech	.255	141	26	36	3	**6**	2	19	7

INDIVIDUAL PITCHING LEADERS

(Minimum 50 Innings)

	W	L	ERA	G	SV	IP	H	BB	SO
Fischer, Mike, So. Alabama	**11**	1	**2.31**	20	1	125	91	23	120
Carter, Justin, So. Alabama	8	3	2.52	26	5	82	77	31	83
Padilla, Juan, Jacksonville	5	5	3.13	20	4	83	83	25	69
Ryan, B.J., SW La.	6	1	3.16	24	**6**	57	55	19	72
Stokley, Billy, Lamar	5	6	3.16	34	**6**	57	53	22	53
Novotney, Josh, W. Kentucky	5	5	3.70	14	0	83	76	22	64
Devey, Philip, SW La.	**11**	6	3.96	25	0	132	127	44	**143**
Cuellar, Logan, SW La.	8	4	4.14	22	1	96	97	48	96
Dobson, Mark, Ark. State	6	7	4.49	16	1	110	107	54	111
Norton, Jason, So. Alabama	9	3	4.53	18	0	105	105	26	121
Farrer, Nick, New Orleans	7	4	4.60	20	0	104	119	27	67
Cuchetti, Tony, Jacksonville	3	3	4.70	19	1	61	70	20	41
Regilio, Nick, Jacksonville	6	6	5.03	17	0	91	100	26	71
Totten, Heath, Lamar	5	2	5.07	14	0	66	70	16	55
McBride, Randy, So. Alabama	3	2	5.08	23	4	51	50	20	47
Ortiz, Omar, Texas-PA	4	4	5.12	15	1	91	97	47	89
Byrd, John, Jacksonville	6	4	5.15	14	0	65	75	34	29
Kelley, Brent, Ark. State	6	4	5.36	18	0	92	96	48	70

	W	L	ERA	G	SV	IP	H	BB	SO
Green, Scott, Texas-PA	6	4	5.50	14	0	88	81	54	87
Stemle, Steve, W. Kentucky	5	5	5.53	14	0	72	77	33	78
Hayduk, John, Ark. State	7	4	5.63	18	0	77	81	32	51
Roach, Kyle, So. Alabama	4	3	5.68	18	0	59	75	15	43
Gibson, Doug, Ark.-LR	5	9	5.77	16	0	92	112	38	59
Miller, David, New Orleans	4	6	5.90	22	2	82	95	43	68
Sparks, Stephen, So. Alabama	5	5	5.92	17	0	65	58	33	63

TRANSAMERICA CONFERENCE

	Conference		Overall	
EAST	**W**	**L**	**W**	**L**
Georgia State	11	9	23	29
Charleston	10	11	31	26
Campbell	10	11	28	30
Mercer	7	13	27	26
SOUTH	**W**	**L**	**W**	**L**
***Florida International**	15	5	41	24
Central Florida	14	7	41	21
Stetson	9	12	30	31
Florida Atlantic	6	14	29	30
WEST	**W**	**L**	**W**	**L**
Troy State	13	7	37	21
Jacksonville State	13	8	34	20
Centenary	9	12	21	36
Samford	6	14	13	43

ALL-CONFERENCE TEAM: C—Sammy Serrano, Jr., Stetson. **1B**—Jeff Tidwell, Sr., Jacksonville State. **2B**—Joey Foxhall, Jr., Charleston. **3B**—Louie Fernandez, Jr., Florida International. **SS**—Eric Riggs, Jr., Central Florida. **OF**—Jason Borghese, Sr., Troy State; Chad Campbell, Sr., Mercer; Chris Warren, Sr., Campbell. **DH**—Jorge Soto, So., Troy State. **P**—Todd Bellhorn, Sr., Central Florida; Raul Garcia, Jr., Florida International. **RP**—Jason Arnold, Fr., Central Florida.

Player of the Year: Sammy Serrano, Stetson. **Coach of the Year**: Danny Price, Florida International.

INDIVIDUAL BATTING LEADERS

(Minimum 125 At-Bats)

	AVG	AB	R	H	2B	3B	HR	RBI	SB
Serrano, Sammy, Stetson	**.457**	245	71	**112**	23	8	13	68	8
Fernandez, Louie, Fla. Int.	.406	217	55	88	15	2	21	72	8
Tidwell, Jeff, Jack. St.	.400	190	61	76	13	0	**25**	**78**	1
Riggs, Eric, Central Fla.	.394	221	64	87	**26**	4	11	67	8
Laird, Kris, Charleston	.393	173	43	68	21	0	11	69	0
Williamson, Bryan, Jack. St.	.392	171	61	67	19	0	10	54	4
Brooks, Wes, Jack. State	.386	189	76	73	17	0	21	61	5
Langston, Jay, Georgia St.	.383	201	48	77	20	3	3	48	6
Schmidt, Greg, Mercer	.381	189	45	72	22	0	11	46	3
Corbitt, Mike, Campbell	.378	185	39	70	17	0	3	34	3
Case, Fred, Troy State	.377	183	42	69	14	1	15	47	0
Colome, Billy, Charleston	.374	211	63	79	18	0	5	41	36
Croud, Will, Central Fla.	.374	211	56	79	14	4	5	38	23
Souders, Brooks, Samford	.374	203	39	76	18	1	6	49	7
Warren, Chris, Campbell	.370	211	59	78	12	7	13	57	13
French, Ned, Stetson	.368	223	55	82	10	**9**	3	29	20
Borghese, Jason, Troy St.	.365	219	73	80	11	5	15	47	14
Silfa, Hiram, Florida Int.	.361	191	35	69	12	0	6	32	9
Davis, Jeff, Campbell	.360	178	46	64	15	2	5	36	6
Morgan, Shawn, Jack. State	.359	181	45	65	14	6	7	35	8
Campbell, Chad, Mercer	.356	163	60	58	13	1	17	51	8
Blair, Jeff, Fla. Atlantic	.354	144	32	51	10	1	3	31	0
Hart, Dickie, Fla. Atlantic	.353	173	30	61	16	0	1	35	1
Molina, Jimmy, Florida Int.	.353	258	**84**	91	17	4	5	40	34
Berberich, Emmett, Stetson	.352	230	66	81	8	4	4	43	25
Worley, Kevin, Campbell	.351	231	47	81	10	8	3	39	13
Barnette, Jason, Samford	.345	206	50	71	10	2	4	26	20
McCall, Alex, Samford	.343	178	40	61	17	1	7	34	13
Branz, Tim, Stetson	.340	209	43	71	15	3	3	49	4
Hughes, Ray, Georgia St.	.339	186	41	63	12	0	2	17	2
Murphy, Tom, Fla. Atlantic	.338	154	36	52	13	0	4	32	7
May, Ryan, Samford	.337	208	45	70	18	0	4	48	13
Nunn, Jason, Jack. State	.335	161	47	54	6	3	8	30	4
Rowe, Ricky, Troy State	.330	233	52	77	13	1	9	51	**37**
Foxhall, Joey, Charleston	.327	217	52	71	10	2	3	26	19

INDIVIDUAL PITCHING LEADERS

(Minimum 50 Innings)

	W	L	ERA	G	SV	IP	H	BB	SO
#Arnold, Jason, Central Fla.	2	2	2.04	28	**12**	35	24	13	38
Morgan, Robby, Stetson	6	2	**2.60**	30	6	55	54	25	38
Gordon, Kevin, Central Fla.	3	1	2.63	19	3	51	41	24	49
Bellhorn, Todd, Central Fla.	10	2	3.09	14	0	82	74	27	64
Calandriello, Donato, Charleston	5	4	3.44	16	0	84	79	41	109
Ernsberger, Eric, Troy State	7	2	3.64	22	0	99	95	33	87
Satterfield, Troy, Central Fla.	6	3	3.65	16	1	67	70	13	38
Lubozynski, Matt, Central Fla.	7	2	3.72	16	0	85	95	14	54
Garcia, Raul, Florida Int.	10	2	3.80	18	0	109	106	48	140
Hathorn, Cypress, Jack. State	5	1	4.09	15	0	51	59	30	48
Maroth, Mike, Central Fla.	3	3	4.09	13	0	55	61	23	43
Franco, Edwin, Florida Int.	**11**	4	4.14	17	0	113	111	45	**147**
Williamson, Bryan, Jack. State	7	4	4.27	20	2	86	85	31	115
D'Amico, David, Mercer	8	7	4.33	20	0	131	131	48	130
Wright, Trey, Troy State	7	1	4.70	19	2	75	72	44	62
Parker, Matt, Mercer	8	7	4.72	21	2	114	118	33	115
Allen, J.R., Jacksonville State	8	6	4.81	17	0	97	108	46	72
Moser, Todd, Fla. Atlantic	7	9	4.89	17	0	109	127	26	102
Wentzky, Charlie, Charleston	6	5	4.96	22	1	69	81	45	62

WEST COAST CONFERENCE

	Conference		Overall	
	W	**L**	**W**	**L**
***Loyola Marymount**	21	8	34	23
Pepperdine	21	9	32	22
San Francisco	18	12	34	24
San Diego	18	12	29	30
Santa Clara	16	14	27	26
Gonzaga	10	20	16	34
St. Mary's	8	10	12	29
Portland	5	22	10	39

ALL-CONFERENCE TEAM: C—Scott Walter, Fr., Loyola Marymount. **1B**—Steve Zorn, Sr., Pepperdine. **2B**—Anthony Angel, So., Loyola Marymount. **3B**—G.J. Raymundo, Jr., Pepperdine. **SS**—David Meliah, Jr., San Francisco. **OF**—Chris Cosbey, Sr., Pepperdine; Jeff Hebert, Sr., St. Mary's; Bill Mott, Sr., Santa Clara. **DH**—David Sugden, Jr., Pepperdine; Joe Sulentor, Jr., Loyola Marymount. **Util**—Brian Mazone, Sr., San Diego; Kevin Hook, Sr., Loyola Marymount. **P**—Ryan Bulich, Sr., Santa Clara; Michael Schultz, Fr., Loyola Marymount; Brad Tucker, Jr., Pepperdine.

Player of the Year: Scott Walter, Loyola Marymount. **Pitcher of the Year**: Michael Schultz, Loyola Marymount. **Coaches of the Year**: Frank Cruz, Loyola Marymount; John Cunningham, San Diego.

INDIVIDUAL BATTING LEADERS

(Minimum 125 At-Bats)

	AVG	AB	R	H	2B	3B	HR	RBI	SB
Zorn, Steve, Pepperdine	**.397**	174	35	69	13	0	8	52	2
Omori, Gregg, San Fran.	.392	199	46	78	17	2	12	57	2
Waugh, Mike, St. Mary's	.387	142	31	55	3	1	1	20	5
Sugden, David, Pepperdine	.385	135	29	52	11	1	3	27	1
Walter, Scott, LMU	.383	209	57	80	16	1	8	**67**	8
Mott, Bill, Santa Clara	.381	202	57	77	12	**7**	13	64	**28**
Reese, Kevin, San Diego	.379	232	49	**88**	12	3	10	46	5
Hook, Kevin, LMU	.377	231	**72**	87	13	2	2	34	14
Wright, David, San Diego	.371	186	46	69	15	3	6	38	2
Fiore, Curt, LMU	.368	152	31	56	8	1	4	29	1
Hayes, Marty, San Diego	.367	169	33	62	12	0	4	37	4
Mazone, Brian, San Diego	.365	170	30	62	20	0	2	29	0
Powers, Jeff, San Diego	.364	239	45	87	17	2	5	43	4
Stokey, Adam, Gonzaga	.363	157	25	57	11	0	9	39	3
Cosbey, Chris, Pepperdine	.359	237	51	85	**22**	6	4	35	15
Riordan, Matt, LMU	.357	244	68	87	16	5	5	64	17
Hurtado, Tony, San Fran.	.354	189	49	67	15	0	7	33	7
LaPresti, Tony, San Diego	.354	195	29	69	11	1	4	42	3
Sulentor, Joe, LMU	.351	194	68	68	10	0	6	43	7
Betancourt, Tony, San Diego	.347	236	47	82	16	4	8	44	6
Raymundo, G.J., Pepperdine	.345	220	50	76	8	3	13	45	1
Queen, Matt, Santa Clara	.343	134	19	46	8	1	2	25	1
Walsh, Pat, San Fran.	.336	214	56	72	15	2	3	36	21
Hart, Bo, Gonzaga	.335	179	41	60	10	2	13	42	11
Meliah, David, San Fran.	.335	230	50	77	19	1	4	47	6
#Hebert, Jeff, St. Mary's	.327	165	33	54	14	0	**15**	48	2

INDIVIDUAL PITCHING LEADERS

(Minimum 50 Innings)

	W	L	ERA	G	SV	IP	H	BB	SO
Ohman, Will, Pepperdine	1	7	**2.80**	27	5	55	54	16	64
Crudale, Mike, Santa Clara	3	4	3.42	28	**9**	55	54	25	44
Tucker, Brad, Pepperdine	8	1	3.48	17	1	83	93	26	69
Bulich, Ryan, Santa Clara	8	3	3.83	18	0	92	101	23	55
Vallecorsa, Mark, San Diego	7	4	4.18	16	0	112	129	34	68
Buller, Sean, San Fran.	8	3	4.33	17	0	98	113	39	64
Deffner, Paul, San Fran.	2	4	4.57	23	0	67	72	28	43

	W	L	ERA	G	SV	IP	H	BB	SO
Shibilo, Andy, Pepperdine	7	4	4.65	16	0	101	105	27	**111**
Avery, Paul, Pepperdine	2	3	4.80	17	0	96	94	46	85
Gossert, Chris, San Fran.	7	3	4.88	18	0	59	65	29	42
[illegible], Brian, San Diego	**11**	3	4.88	19	1	124	141	35	68
Amundson, Mike, San Diego	[illegible]	4	4.92	17	0	53	66	23	39
Schultz, Michael, LMU	9	2	5.11	20	0	100	[illegible]	47	101
Morgan-Voyce, Jason, SM	4	5	5.30	17	1	73	101	26	56
Boyanich, Vince, Santa Clara	5	6	5.36	17	0	96	91	38	79
Bennett, Steve, Gonzaga	3	3	5.43	12	0	71	90	33	42
Jackson, Stosh, Portland	1	4	5.43	17	0	68	70	23	66

WESTERN ATHLETIC CONFERENCE

NORTH	Conference W	Conference L	Overall W	Overall L
Grand Canyon	16	14	28	27
Brigham Young	13	17	29	24
Utah	11	19	23	31
Air Force	7	23	14	39
SOUTH	**W**	**L**	**W**	**L**
***Rice**	26	4	46	17
Texas Christian	18	11	33	23
New Mexico	13	16	27	31
UNLV	13	17	31	24
WEST	**W**	**L**	**W**	**L**
Fresno State	19	11	33	28
San Diego State	18	12	32	25
San Jose State	13	17	31	23
Hawaii	12	18	34	22

ALL-CONFERENCE TEAM: **C**—Nate Forbush, Sr., Utah. **1B**—John Summers, Jr., Utah. **2B**—Sam Lunsford, Sr., Texas Christian. **3B**—Royce Huffman, Jr., Texas Christian. **SS**—Damon Thames, Jr., Rice. **OF**—Bubba Crosby, Jr., Rice; Chris Connally, Sr., Texas Christian; Damien Kolb, So., San Diego State. **DH**—Brad Winget, Sr., Brigham Young. **P**—Javier Pamus, Sr., San Jose State; Jeff Weaver, Jr., Fresno State. **RP**—Jeff Shaddix, Sr., Texas Christian.

Player of the Year: Damon Thames, Rice. **Freshman of the Year**: Robert Womack, San Diego State. **Coach of the Year**: Wayne Graham, Rice.

INDIVIDUAL BATTING LEADERS

(Minimum 125 At-Bats)

	AVG	AB	R	H	2B	3B	HR	RBI	SB
McNaughton, Troy, BYU	**.427**	218	76	93	25	3	22	74	10
Oborn, Spencer, BYU	.426	209	69	89	20	5	15	64	24
Thames, Damon, Rice	.424	283	**88**	**120**	**36**	**7**	**26**	**115**	4
DeMarco, Tony, UNLV	.422	187	42	79	18	1	8	47	0
Huffman, Royce, TCU	.420	212	63	89	18	4	17	77	10
Summers, John, Utah	.415	193	61	80	15	3	23	68	2
Forbush, Nate, Utah	.403	176	57	71	11	0	13	49	3
Pond, Ryan, BYU	.402	219	66	88	15	1	20	57	7
Pelaez, Alex, San Diego St.	.399	233	53	93	20	0	16	69	6
Crosby, Bubba, Rice	.394	221	73	87	15	3	25	91	2
Womack, Robert, SD State	.390	159	34	62	13	4	4	38	6
Yamaguchi, Lon, New Mex.	.385	221	81	85	25	1	20	56	14
Kolb, Damien, San Diego St.	.383	133	46	51	8	1	7	32	11
Connally, Chris, TCU	.378	225	72	85	19	6	17	80	12
Eberwein, Kevin, UNLV	.377	223	63	84	24	2	16	52	0
Winget, Brad, BYU	.377	191	58	72	18	0	11	43	3
Gonzales, Robert, New Mex.	.375	259	66	97	35	3	13	81	10
Foulds, Kalin, San Diego St.	.374	222	58	83	9	3	1	31	**58**
Robbins, Cory, New Mexico	.370	230	76	85	24	3	12	53	17
Aloy, Jamie, Hawaii	.367	180	51	66	12	5	0	43	2
Kerns, Rick, Grand Canyon	.362	141	41	51	11	1	9	31	4
Larsen, Jared, Utah	.362	213	60	77	15	0	7	53	0
Critchett, Buddy, GC	.361	133	34	48	10	2	2	26	6
Baker, Jacob, Rice	.360	214	45	77	16	2	12	61	4
Boomsma, Michael, Air Force	.360	161	40	58	18	1	5	43	4
Sisk, Aaron, New Mexico	.359	142	37	51	16	1	9	41	1
Armstrong, Chris, New Mex.	.357	168	39	60	16	3	7	38	3
Honma, Neal, Hawaii	.357	207	50	74	10	5	2	44	18
Farnsworth, Troy, BYU	.356	208	64	74	16	0	16	54	2
Hodge, Kevin, Rice	.356	239	69	85	12	4	15	64	13
Daluz, Craig, Fresno State	.355	242	47	86	19	1	8	42	2
Smith, Nate, UNLV	.354	147	35	52	8	5	3	34	3
Williams, Charles, Rice	.354	212	75	75	18	3	9	37	4
Wallace, Eric, Utah	.353	201	41	71	16	1	11	53	14
Ludwick, Ryan, UNLV	.352	210	57	74	21	3	14	57	5
Curtis, Bill, Grand Canyon	.351	205	42	72	18	1	6	42	3
Silva, Mark, TCU	.351	148	52	52	7	2	6	30	5
Richards, Jason, Rice	.348	230	73	80	21	2	13	51	11
Woods, Blake, Grand Canyon	.347	213	44	74	10	2	5	52	14
Gillette, Chris, UNLV	.345	194	44	67	15	2	4	34	5
Lockhart, Paul, San Diego St.	.345	145	27	50	12	3	3	27	1
[illegible]	.343	204	38	70	22	2	8	61	3
Truby, Chad, Utah	.343	210	[illegible]	72	7	0	7	41	3
Lewis, Scott, San Jose St.	.342	219	54	75	9	4	0	55	[illegible]
James, Tony, San Jose St.	.339	189	48	64	17	5	5	54	11
Lunsford, Sam, TCU	.339	213	71	74	12	5	8	46	22
Circuit, Chris, BYU	.338	201	54	68	11	1	13	57	5
Hamill, Ryan, UNLV	.338	145	38	49	8	2	16	46	2

INDIVIDUAL PITCHING LEADERS

(Minimum 50 Innings)

	W	L	ERA	G	SV	IP	H	BB	SO
Weaver, Jeff, Fresno State	10	4	**2.98**	17	1	124	108	37	**156**
Aloy, Jamie, Hawaii	4	0	3.34	12	2	59	61	15	43
Ramos, Mario, Rice	12	2	3.39	21	0	112	72	48	113
Pamus, Javier, San Jose St.	**13**	3	3.89	21	1	116	125	34	114
Pettyjohn, Adam, Fresno State	7	6	3.92	18	0	126	113	30	145
Bess, Stephen, Rice	10	2	4.37	22	1	105	98	50	73
Serrano, Jim, New Mexico	9	5	4.41	17	0	116	115	68	137
McNair, Patrick, Hawaii	5	3	4.43	14	0	69	72	50	44
Wanders, Chad, San Diego St.	9	5	4.68	17	0	90	103	38	71
Yoshimasu, Troy, Hawaii	2	2	4.75	11	0	53	70	21	22
Rowe, Casey, Fresno State	5	4	4.87	27	0	92	89	50	97
Baker, Joey, San Jose St.	6	2	5.25	16	0	62	80	21	49
Thompson, Shawn, TCU	8	7	5.26	21	1	115	116	43	108
Clinton, Ray, Utah	5	3	5.33	19	1	51	61	23	41
Nichols, Jeff, Rice	12	4	5.34	21	1	120	114	58	117
Barker, Billy, UNLV	4	4	5.38	16	0	74	87	37	58
Shaddix, Jeff, TCU	3	1	5.43	28	7	55	65	29	54
Gwyn, Marc, Rice	3	2	5.55	19	1	60	68	34	51
Ho, Randon, Hawaii	5	6	5.57	21	1	74	86	56	55
#Ladd, Todd, Air Force	1	3	5.75	25	**9**	36	40	19	31
Baugh, Kenny, Rice	4	2	5.79	15	0	65	53	43	59
Eigenhuis, Erick, San Diego St.	5	2	5.80	14	0	59	63	23	45

INDEPENDENTS

	Overall W	Overall L
Miami	51	12
CS Northridge	33	19
Southern Utah	22	21
Hawaii-Hilo	16	34

INDIVIDUAL BATTING LEADERS

(Minimum 100 At-Bats)

	AVG	AB	R	H	2B	3B	HR	RBI	SB
Burrell, Pat, Miami	.432	118	44	51	7	0	17	47	5
Hill, Nakia, CS Northridge	.414	232	69	96	16	3	15	41	13
Huff, Aubrey, Miami	.412	233	71	96	20	0	21	95	4
Hill, Bobby, Miami	.404	240	87	97	17	0	12	59	46
Downing, Phil, So. Utah	.400	170	51	68	18	1	9	38	16
Michaels, Jason, Miami	.378	196	75	74	16	1	19	65	18
Duckworth, Gavin, So. Utah	.371	167	39	62	15	1	3	32	7
Patrick, Kevin, CS North.	.359	220	41	79	20	1	5	44	9
Penick, D.J., So. Utah	.359	142	19	51	10	0	8	44	2
Crespo, Manny, Miami	.348	201	54	70	9	2	16	63	4
Ford, Brian, So. Utah	.347	101	17	35	7	1	3	16	1
Petersen, Jake, So. Utah	.346	162	40	56	11	1	14	50	6
Alvarez, German, Miami	.340	188	64	64	12	2	15	51	10
Carlson, Scott, So. Utah	.340	156	40	53	11	2	3	16	29
Cancellieri, Adam, Haw.-Hilo.	.335	164	34	55	8	5	0	15	10
McNeely, Mike, CS North.	.333	180	38	60	7	2	10	49	3

INDIVIDUAL PITCHING LEADERS

(Minimum 40 Innings)

	W	L	ERA	G	SV	IP	H	BB	SO
Santos, Alex, Miami	15	1	2.54	18	0	110	85	28	142
Howell, Greg, Miami	4	0	3.15	32	0	40	37	12	46
Ozias, Todd, Miami	6	2	3.26	24	0	69	57	27	66
Vasquez, Jose, CS Northridge	10	5	3.84	19	0	91	96	55	72
Ford, Thomas, Hawaii-Hilo	3	6	4.02	12	0	63	62	37	69
DeBiase, Jim, CS Northridge	3	2	4.14	20	2	54	49	42	54
Martin, Jeff, CS Northridge	6	2	4.20	20	2	56	66	28	49
Morrison, Robbie, Miami	2	2	4.24	37	12	40	34	10	67
Roque, Darryl, Miami	13	2	4.38	20	0	84	88	19	71
Siff, Ben, Hawaii-Hilo	2	5	4.47	12	0	56	60	31	31
Gutierrez, Laz, Miami	4	1	4.75	34	1	42	42	21	45
Novits, Carey, CS Northridge	6	2	4.76	17	1	91	108	25	73

SMALL COLLEGES

Tampa, Eastern Connecticut State capture NCAA titles

DIVISION II

Tampa lefthander Mike Valdes, the pitcher of the year in Division II, ended up winning the biggest game of 1998.

Valdes dominated top-ranked Kennesaw State's (Ga.) powerful offense as the Spartans (46-14) beat the Owls 6-1 in the national championship game in Montgomery, Ala. The 5-foot-9, 160-pound Valdes (15-1) pitched his second complete game of the tournament, retiring the first 14 batters he faced before Pat McPhee's solo home run in the fifth. He wound up with a four-hitter.

FINAL POLL

NCAA Division II

	Team	Record
1.	Tampa	46-14
2.	Kennesaw State (Ga.)	61-5
3.	West Georgia	43-17
4.	Cal State Chico	37-18
5.	Central Missouri State	39-8
6.	Alabama-Huntsville	41-17
7.	St. Joseph's (Ind.)	39-19
8.	SIU-Edwardsville	38-15
9.	Barry (Fla.)	38-20
10.	Delta State (Miss.)	39-12

The title was the third in Tampa's school history, and all have come in the 1990s. The Spartans won back-to-back titles in 1992 and 1993. This time, they finished the year with seven straight complete games.

In the final, Tampa had 14 hits. The Spartans scored two unearned runs in the fourth to take the lead for good. Shortstop Ronnie Merrill, the tournament's most outstanding player, knocked in the runs with a two-out single.

West Georgia shortstop Brian Davis, who hit .482 with 36 home runs and 102 RBIs, was named the Division II player of the year. Davis led all of Division II in runs (88), hits (107), total bases (229) and home runs.

DIVISION III

Eastern Connecticut State became just the second program in the 23-year history of the Division III tournament to win three national titles as the Warriors routed Montclair State (N.J.) 16-1 in the World Series championship game in Salem, Va.

The Warriors (40-11), who equaled the school record for wins, won four of five games in the tournament. They advanced to the title game after their 13-game winning streak was stopped by Cortland State (N.Y.).

Junior righthander Scott Czerwinski became the first Eastern Connecticut State pitcher to win three games in the NCAA tournament. He pitched the first seven innings of the championship game, and also threw a four-hitter in an opening win over Wisconsin-Oshkosh.

FINAL POLL

NCAA Division III

	Team	Record
1.	Eastern Conn. State	40-11
2.	Montclair State (N.J.)	35-11
3.	Cortland State (N.Y.)	40-5
4.	Aurora (Ill.)	33-6
5.	Wisconsin-Oshkosh	41-5
6.	North Carolina Wesleyan	42-9
7.	Anderson (Ind.)	34-15
8.	Cal Lutheran	28-15
9.	Ohio Wesleyan	36-10
10.	Methodist (N.C.)	32-13

Warriors senior second baseman Chris D'Amato was named the tournament's most outstanding player after reaching base 19 times in 22 tournament plate appearances. He went 11-for-14 (.786) overall and reached base all six times up in the championship game. Warriors closer Scott Chiasson set a national tournament record with three saves.

NAIA

Top-seeded Albertson (Idaho) College claimed its first NAIA baseball title with a 6-3 victory over Indiana Tech in the championship game of the 1998 NAIA World Series at Tulsa.

Albertson (55-8) scored all of its runs in the final with two outs in the top of the fourth inning. Second baseman Michael Diaz capped the barrage with a three-run homer. Denny Gilich (10-1), a transfer from Long Beach State, pitched 7⅓ innings for Albertson in the championship victory.

Albertson reached the World Series by defeating in-state rival and nine-time NAIA World Series champion Lewis-Clark State in regional play.

Lubbock Christian senior first baseman Keith Hart was named both NAIA and Baseball America's small college player of the year. In one of the most dominating seasons ever, Hart led NAIA players in batting (.511), runs (106), hits (138), doubles (35), triples (10), home runs (31) and RBIs (121). He was selected by the Boston Red Sox in the 32nd round of the June draft.

JUNIOR COLLEGE

Cowley County (Kan.) Community College ended the 1998 season the way it started it–as champions.

A sixth-run fifth inning helped boost the Tigers to a 15-11 win over San Jacinto (Texas) in the National Junior College Division I World Series in Grand Junction, Colo.

When the Tigers made the 10-school event for the first time in 1997, they played like they'd been there before. In 1998, they really had.

"This one was tougher," Cowley County coach Dave Burroughs said. "Last year we came in and nobody knew nothin' about us. This year people pointed at us all year long."

Cowley County outfielder Josh McMillon, who hit a two-run homer in the final game, earned tournament MVP honors.

Navarro (Texas) outfielder Brian Cole was named Division I player of the year after hitting .534 with 27 home runs and 90 RBIs. He was also selected Baseball America's junior college player of the year.

In California, perennial power Sacramento City College put the capper on a dominant 1998 season by sweeping its way through the California CC championship.

Sacramento went 3-0 in the tournament to finish 44-2 for the season.

SMALL COLLEGES

NCAA DIVISION II

WORLD SERIES

Site: Montgomery, Ala.

Participants: Chico State, Calif. (35-15); Central Missouri State (39-6); Kennesaw State, Ga. (58-4); Millersville, Pa. (37-14); New Haven, Conn. (29-9); St. Joseph's, Ind. (38-17); Tampa (42-14); West Georgia (41-15).

Champion: Tampa (4-0).

Runner-Up: Kennesaw State (3-1).

Outstanding Player: Ronnie Merrill, ss, Tampa.

ALL-AMERICA TEAM

Pos.	Player, School	Yr.	AVG	HR	RBI
C	Angel Diaz, Tampa	Sr.	.363	14	69
1B	David Goodwin, Central Missouri	Sr.	.458	18	74
2B	Sam Lee, North Alabama	Sr.	.521	6	68
3B	Nathan Cothran, Kennesaw State	Sr.	.382	11	52
SS	Brian Davis, West Georgia	Sr.	.482	36	102
OF	Allen Dina, St. Leo (Fla.)	Sr.	.484	9	56
OF	Steve Foley, Texas A&M-Kingsville	Jr.	.479	15	57
OF	Jason Jones, Kennesaw State	Jr.	.395	26	103
OF	Scott Wilcox, Mansfield (Pa.)	Sr.	.481	20	60
DH	Aaron Braund, Winona State (Minn.)	Sr.	.428	25	81
UT	Ben Slemmer, Central Missouri State	Sr.	.394	20	85

Pos.	Player, School	Yr.	W	L	ERA
SP	Chris Bowen, Kennesaw State	Jr.	12	2	2.33
SP	Rich Clover, Central Missouri State	Jr.	13	1	3.70
SP	Josh Osborn, Cal State Chico	Sr.	11	2	3.15
SP	Mike Valdes, Tampa	Jr.	15	1	3.15
RP	Nate Field, Fort Hays St. (Kan.)	Sr.	4	2	2.67

Player of the Year: Brian Davis, ss, West Georgia. **Pitcher of the Year:** Mike Valdes, lhp, Tampa.

NATIONAL LEADERS

BATTING AVERAGE

(Minimum 125 At-Bats)

Player, School	AB	H	AVG
Bob File, Philadelphia Textile	166	90	.542
Sam Lee, North Alabama	167	87	.521
Allen Dina, St. Leo (Fla.)	217	105	.484
Brian Davis, West Georgia	222	107	.482
Scott Wilcox, Mansfield (Pa.)	158	76	.481
Steve Foley, Texas A&M-Kingsville	213	102	.479
Stephen Jackson, West Florida	187	89	.476
Justin Davies, Queens (N.Y.)	160	76	.475
Trevor Timpane, North Dakota	144	68	.472
Brayden Whitney, Central Missouri	176	83	.472
Marco Crivelli, Indianapolis	191	89	.466
Bronson Bosshamer, Neb.-Kearney	142	66	.465

Department Leaders: Batting

Dept.	Player, School	G	Total
R	Brian Davis, West Georgia	58	88
H	Brian Davis, West Georgia	58	107
TB	Brian Davis, West Georgia	58	229
2B	Stephen Jackson, West Florida	49	28
3B	Willie Melendez, Savannah St. (Ga.)	49	16
HR	Brian Davis, West Georgia	58	36
RBI	Jason Jones, Kennesaw State	66	103
SB	Justin Davies, Queens (N.Y.)	38	52

EARNED RUN AVERAGE

(Minimum 60 Innings)

Player, School	IP	ER	ERA
Ryan Vogelsong, Kutztown (Pa.)	90	14	1.41
Justin Reid, UC Davis	79	16	1.82
Adam Davidson, Pfeiffer (N.C.)	76	16	1.89
B.J. Leach, Florida Southern	89	20	2.02
Fred Schwarze, Wayne St. (Mich.)	66	15	2.04
Jeremy Wedel, Armstrong (Ga.)	114	26	2.05
Brian Bradley, West Georgia	77	18	2.09
Chris Swiatkiewicz, Minn.-Duluth	82	21	2.30
Chris Bowen, Kennesaw State	120	31	2.33
Dan Mathews, Indiana-Purdue	69	18	2.35

Department Leaders: Pitching

Dept.	Player, School	G	Total
W	Mike Valdes, Tampa	17	15
SV	Eric Eckert, Millersville (Pa.)	29	13
	Nate Field, Fort Hays St. (Kan.)	24	13
SO	Danny Lampley, Wingate (N.C.)	19	179

NCAA DIVISION III

WORLD SERIES

Site: Salem, Va.

Participants: Anderson, Ind. (34-13); Aurora, Ill. (31-4); Cal Lutheran (28-13); Cortland State, N.Y. (37-3); Eastern Connecticut State (36-10); Montclair State, N.J. (31-8); North Carolina Wesleyan (41-7); Wisconsin-Oshkosh (40-3).

Champion: Eastern Connecticut State (4-1).

Runner-Up: Montclair State (4-2)

Outstanding Player: Chris D'Amato, 2b, Eastern Conn. St..

ALL-AMERICA TEAM

Pos.	Player, School	Yr.	AVG	HR	RBI
C	Josh Streit, Marietta (Ohio)	Jr.	.425	19	67
1B	Frank Beckhorn, Kean (N.J.)	Sr.	.505	10	52
	Justin Pierro, Loras (Iowa)	Sr.	.489	22	68
2B	Buzz Hannahan, St. Thomas (Minn.)	Sr.	.440	8	38
3B	Joe Fischera, McMurray (Texas)	Jr.	.429	2	39
	Lance Podlesney, East. Conn. State	Jr.	.403	7	53
SS	Mark Mason, UC San Diego	Sr.	.435	13	64
OF	John Christ, Johns Hopkins (Md.)	Jr.	.513	17	73
OF	Pat Daly, Ferrum (Va.)	Sr.	.508	24	73
OF	Pat Schultz, Mass.-Dartmouth	Sr.	.468	22	70

Pos.	Player, School	Yr.	W	L	ERA
P	David Bradley, Marietta (Ohio)	Jr.	11	1	2.29
P	Scott Chiasson, East. Conn. State	Jr.	6	2	2.51
P	Craig Glysch, Wisconsin-Oshkosh	Jr.	8	1	2.35
P	Jon Rardin, N.C. Wesleyan	Jr.	12	0	2.19

Player of the Year: Pat Schultz, of, Mass.-Dartmouth.

NATIONAL LEADERS

BATTING AVERAGE

(Minimum 100 At-Bats)

Player, School	AB	H	AVG
Aaron Kramer, St. Norbert (Wis.)	105	55	.524
Matt Hallock, Mount St. Mary (N.Y.)	112	58	.518
John Christ, Johns Hopkins (Md.)	158	81	.513
Frank Sansonetti, Staten Island (N.Y.)	108	55	.509
Pat Daly, Ferrum (Va.)	124	63	.508
Frank Beckhorn, Kean (N.J.)	111	56	.505
Greg Constantino, St. John Fisher (N.Y.)	119	59	.496
Pat Burke, King's (Pa.)	102	50	.490
Justin Pierro, Loras (Iowa)	133	65	.489
Ryan Missler, Ohio Wesleyan	171	83	.485
Brian Cutlip, Waynesburg (Pa.)	130	63	.485
Dan Morse, Tufts (Mass.)	126	61	.484

Department Leaders: Batting

Dept.	Player, School	G	Total
R	Joe Fichera, McMurry (Texas)	47	75
H	Matt McCay, N.C. Wesleyan	51	94
TB	Pat Schultz, Mass.-Dartmouth	43	164
2B	Aaron Rifkin, Chapman (Calif.)	42	26
3B	Jason Hoye, Wheaton (Mass.)	34	11
	Matt Gelotti, Southwestern (Texas)	48	11
HR	Pat Daly, Ferrum (Va.)	32	24
RBI	Pat Daly, Ferrum (Va.)	32	73
	John Christ, Johns Hopkins (Md.)	40	73
	Matt Faulken, St. Thomas (Minn.)	46	73
SB	Eric Kulbe, Cornell (Iowa)	36	41
	Jonathan Krot, East. Conn. State	49	41

EARNED RUN AVERAGE

(Minimum 50 Innings)

Player, School	IP	ER	ERA
Mike Marini, Bridgewater State (Mass.)	69	9	1.17
Brian Rudloff, Baldwin-Wallace (Ohio)	64	11	1.54
Adam Lueder, Simpson (Iowa)	57	10	1.59
Mike Dempsey, Cortland State (N.Y.)	69	13	1.70
Alex Ramsaran, Benedictine (Ill.)	55	11	1.81
Danny Woodbury, Upper Iowa	64	13	1.82
Jim LeMire, St. Norbert (Wis.)	53	11	1.87
Bob Weston, Washington & Lee (Va.)	62	13	1.88
Jason Evans, Juniata (Pa.)	52	11	1.89
Brian Toov, St. Thomas (Minn.)	56	12	1.93

Department Leaders: Pitching

Dept.	Player, School	G	Total
W	Jeff Blitstein, Chapman (Calif.)	16	12
	Jon Rardin, N.C. Wesleyan	18	12
SV	Paul Louderback, Rensselaer (N.Y.)	23	17
SO	Brian Nowell, Trinity (Texas)	17	121

SMALL COLLEGES

NAIA

WORLD SERIES

Site: Tulsa, Okla.

Participants: No. 1 Albertson, Idaho (51-7); No. 4 Bellevue, Neb. (53-12); No. 8 Culver-Stockton, Mo. (39-15); No. 3 Cumberland, Tenn. (50-12); No. 7 Indiana Tech (44-19); No. 5 Oklahoma City (42-18); No. 6 Point Park, Pa. (46-4); No. 2 St. Thomas, Fla. (53-12).

Champion: Albertson (4-1).

Runner-Up: Indiana Tech (4-2).

Outstanding Player: Chris Bradshaw, of, Oklahoma City.

ALL-AMERICA TEAM

Pos.	Player, School	Yr.	AVG	HR	RBI
C	Cameron White, Dallas Baptist	Jr.	.463	22	99
C	Brock Lowell, Birmingham-Southern	Jr.	.377	22	89
1B	Keith Hart, Lubbock Christian (Texas)	Sr.	.511	31	121
2B	Joe Bressanelli, Robert Morris (Ill.)	Jr.	.471	16	55
3B	Jeff Rowland, Union (Tenn.)	Sr.	.429	22	71
SS	Randy Stegall, Cumberland (Tenn.)	Jr.	.479	20	85
IF	Bryan Mack, Briar Cliff (Iowa)	Sr.	.459	23	75
OF	Eric Battersby, St. Mary's (Texas)	Sr.	.455	18	85
OF	John Baum, Indiana Tech	Jr.	.377	17	83
OF	Lew Ford, Dallas Baptist	Jr.	.507	14	92
OF	Dan Swift, Mayville State (N.D.)	Jr.	.468	26	87
DH	Heath Zapf, Auburn-Montgomery	Jr.	.425	21	94

Pos.	Player, School	Yr.	W	L	ERA
P	Cary Ammons, SE Oklahoma State	Sr.	14	0	2.02
P	Mark Clark, Georgia Southwestern	Sr.	13	3	1.98
P	Matt Kosderka, Willamette (Ore.)	Sr.	10	2	3.17
P	Levi Lacey, Albertson (Idaho)	Sr.	14	1	1.37

Player of the Year: Keith Hart, 1b, Lubbock Christian.

NATIONAL LEADERS

BATTING AVERAGE

(Minimum 100 At-Bats)

Player, School	AB	H	AVG
Kalin DeBoer, Sioux Falls (S.D.)	100	53	.530
Joe Pierson, Pikeville (Ky.)	137	71	.518
Keith Hart, Lubbock Christian (Texas)	270	138	.511
Joe Bressanelli, Robert Morris (Ill.)	175	89	.509
Lew Ford, Dallas Baptist	205	104	.507
Jay Wiebe, Oklahoma Baptist	178	86	.483
José Ortiz, Culver-Stockton (Mo.)	139	67	.482
Randy Stegall, Cumberland (Tenn.)	236	113	.479
Ricardo Deliz, Tiffin (Ohio)	117	55	.470
Dan Swift, Mayville State (N.D.)	156	73	.468
Joe Kellarby, Doane (Neb.)	131	61	.466
Willie DeGracia, Benedictine (Kan.)	129	60	.465

Department Leaders: Batting

Dept.	Player, School	G	Total
R	Keith Hart, Lubbock Christian	70	106
H	Keith Hart, Lubbock Christian	70	138
TB	Keith Hart, Lubbock Christian	70	286
2B	Keith Hart, Lubbock Christian	70	35
3B	Keith Hart, Lubbock Christian	70	10
HR	Keith Hart, Lubbock Christian	70	31
RBI	Keith Hart, Lubbock Christian	70	121
SB	Jeremy Burchfield, Indiana Southeast	54	50

EARNED RUN AVERAGE

(Minimum 50 Innings)

Player, School	IP	ER	ERA
Levi Lacey, Albertson (Idaho)	112	17	1.37
Ruben Escobar, The Master's (Calif.)	104	20	1.74
Luke Martin, Embry-Riddle (Fla.)	105	21	1.80
Don Smith, Valley City (N.D.)	63	13	1.85
Mark Clark, Georgia Southwestern	108	24	1.99
Cary Ammons, Southeastern Oklahoma	98	22	2.02
Brad Murray, Embry-Riddle (Fla.)	97	23	2.14
Andy Heimbach, Mt. Vernon Nazarene (Ohio)	92	22	2.16
Dave Byard, Mt. Vernon Nazarene (Ohio)	81	20	2.21

Department Leaders: Pitching

Dept.	Player, School	G	Total
W	Cary Ammons, SE Oklahoma	15	14
	Levi Lacey, Albertson (Idaho)	17	14
SO	Luke Martin, Embry-Riddle (Fla.)	23	144

JUNIOR COLLEGE

WORLD SERIES

Site: Grand Junction, Colo.

Participants: Brevard, N.C. (43-15); Central Florida (41-16); Cowley County, Kan. (50-8); DeKalb, Ga. (42-15); Dixie, Utah (40-17); Grayson County, Texas (46-17); Indian Hills, Iowa (49-9); Maple Woods, Mo. (47-11); Meridian, Miss. (50-10); San Jacinto, Texas (44-13).

Champion: Cowley County (4-1).

Runner-Up: San Jacinto (4-2).

Outstanding Player: Josh McMillen, of, Cowley County.

ALL-AMERICA TEAM

C—Curtis Sapp, Brevard (N.C.). **INF**—Mario Delgado, Yavapai (Ariz.); Randy Ruiz, Woods (Mo.); Pat Santoro, Triton (Ill.); Radames Torres, New Mexico. **OF**—Brian Cole, Navarro (Texas); Angel Rafe Boria, Allegany (Md.); Roy York, Cowley County (Kan.). **DH**—Nestor Gonzales, New Mexico. **P**—Solomon Johnson, Navarro (Texas); Craig Mosher, Southern Idaho; Michael Ziegler, Northwest Shoals (Ala.).

NATIONAL LEADERS

BATTING AVERAGE

(Minimum 100 At-Bats)

Player, School	AB	H	AVG
Pat Huntington, Monroe (N.Y.)	131	72	.550
Nick Martin, Crowder (Mo.)	131	67	.511
Raul Torres, New Mexico	107	53	.495
Angel Rafe Boria, Allegany (Md.)	148	73	.493
Marco Cunningham, Trinidad State (Colo.)	219	107	.489
Ben Emond, Seminole State (Okla.)	163	79	.485
Mario Delgado, Yavapai (Ariz.)	225	107	.476
Ronnie Branin, Utah Valley State	206	98	.476

Department Leaders: Batting

Dept.	Player, School	G	Total
HR	Radames Torres, New Mexico	50	29
RBI	Dell Lindsey, Blinn (Texas)	57	97
SB	Kyle Catrett, Central Florida	56	65

EARNED RUN AVERAGE

(Minimum 50 Innings)

Player, School	IP	ER	ERA
Nathan Kent, Motlow State (Tenn.)	92	8	0.78
Tim Redding, Monroe (N.Y.)	56	6	0.96
Matt Murphy, Wallace/Hanceville (Ala.)	70	11	1.42
Rob Cordemans, Indian River (Fla.)	98	16	1.47
Derek Devaughan, Seminole State (Okla.)	56	12	1.93

Department Leaders: Pitching

Dept.	Player, School	IP	Total
SV	David Capek, Yavapai (Ariz.)	47	9
	Zac Davis, Utah Valley State	32	9
SO	Scott Barrett, San Jacinto (Texas)	88	134
	Nathan Kent, Motlow State (Tenn.)	93	134

NJCAA DIVISION II

WORLD SERIES

Site: Millington, Tenn.

Participants: Delaware Tech (33-5); Frederick, Md. (28-10); Jefferson Davis, Ala. (44-10); Kankakee, Ill. (38-5); Kirkwood, Iowa (49-10); Lake Michigan (32-8); Redlands, Okla. (36-15); St. Louis-Forest Park (30-27).

Champion: Jefferson Davis (4-0). **Runner-Up:** Redlands (4-2).

Outstanding Player: Jeff Baumtrog, of, Jefferson Davis.

NJCAA DIVISION III

WORLD SERIES

Site: Batavia, N.Y.

Participants: Columbus State, Ohio (28-17); Eastfield, Texas (33-15); Erie, N.Y. (32-6); Gloucester County, N.J. (43-9); Norwalk, Conn. (40-4); Riverland, Minn. (21-7); Suffolk County, N.Y. (22-7); Surry, N.C. (27-13).

Champion: Norwalk (4-1). **Runner-Up**: Eastfield (5-2).

Outstanding Player: Kevin Murray, 3b, Norwalk.

CALIFORNIA JUCOS

STATE CHAMPIONSHIP

Site: Fresno.

Participants: Canada (35-7), Los Angeles Harbor (32-15), Sacramento (41-2), Saddleback (37-10)

Champion: Sacramento (3-0). **Runner-Up**: Saddleback (2-2).

Outstanding Player: Mike Neu, p, Sacramento.

High School Baseball

Fifth straight state title the charm for Vestavia Hills; Alabama school earns top national honor in prep poll

BY JOHN ROYSTER

After four straight state titles, there had to be a new horizon out there somewhere for Vestavia Hills (Ala.) High.

There was. The Rebels' 1998 Alabama 6-A championship, their fifth straight, was accompanied by their first Baseball America/National High School Baseball Coaches Association national championship.

Vestavia Hills finished 32-2, taking the state title by winning two games of a best-of-three series against arch-rival Hartselle High. The series finished on May 15, with the Rebels No. 1 in the nation. They then had to wait for four more weeks and two more polls to see if the ranking held up.

"It's really fantastic," coach Sammy Dunn said upon learning it had. "Really, you can't imagine how many people have been waiting to see if we finished No. 1."

Klein High in the Houston area came closest to eclipsing Vestavia Hills, winning the prestigious Texas 5-A championship, finishing 35-2 and rising from fourth to second in the final poll.

Vestavia Hills was on its way to its eighth straight state-finals appearance—it has won seven of them—when it ascended to No. 1 in April.

"It was an honor," Dunn said, "but we didn't know if we could keep it or not because the end of our schedule was very tough. We've been very fortunate. That's an understatement."

Both of Vestavia Hills' losses were to Hartselle, one in the regular season and one in the state finals. The Tigers, who finished 34th in the final poll and won a state-record 43 games, won the regular season game on a grand slam with two out in the seventh inning.

BONES LONG

Championship trophy
Coach Sammy Dunn, right, accepts BA/NHSBCA award from BCA executive director Jerry Miles.

They took the middle game of the best-of-three state finals behind ace pitcher Ross Dobbins, who finished 14-1.

But Vestavia Hills had 10-runned Hartselle in Game One, and it took the championship 4-2 on a three-hitter by pitchers Robert Evans and Carey Eden. All four of Vestavia Hills' runs came on two-out hits.

The Rebels had 13 come-from-behind wins, including four in their last at-bat. They had won 24 straight single-elimination games.

Vestavia Hills wasn't the only team to extend a streak of state championships in 1998.

Green Valley High of Henderson, Nev., won its sixth straight 4-A title in the school's seventh year of existence. Green Valley (32-2) featured two pitchers selected in the first six rounds of the draft: right-handers Mike Nannini (supplemental first round, Astros) and Joe Orloski (sixth round, Blue Jays).

Taylorsville (Utah) High won its fifth state championship in the 1990s. Arundel High of Gambrills, Md., won its fourth championship of the '90s, to go with two second-place finishes.

Clovis (Calif.) High, the nation's No. 2 team in 1997, finished third in 1998 by winning its second consecutive California central sectional title. California doesn't have a state championship. Clovis went 33-2 both years.

No. 16 Cretin-Derham Hall High of St. Paul, Minn., ran its winning streak to 44 over two seasons by going 29-0 in '98. Two other undefeated teams finished in the Top 50: Tottenville High of Staten Island, N.Y. (33-0, No. 7) and Edwardsville, Ill., High (40-0, No. 8).

HIGH SCHOOL TOP 25

Baseball America's final 1998 Top 25, selected in conjunction with the National High School Baseball Coaches Association.

SCHOOL, CITY	W-L	Achievement
1. Vestavia Hills (Ala.) HS	32-2	State 6-A champion*
2. Klein (Texas) HS	35-2	State 5-A champion*
3. Clovis (Calif.) HS	33-2	CIF sectional champion
4. Tate HS, Gonzalez, Fla.	32-3	State 6-A champion*
5. Owasso (Okla.) HS	45-3	State 6-A champion*
6. Green Valley HS, Henderson, Nev.	32-2	State 4-A champion*
7. Tottenville HS, Staten Island, N.Y.	33-0	State public school champion*
8. Edwardsville (Ill.) HS	40-0	State 2-A champion*
9. Hattiesburg (Miss.) HS	36-3	State 5-A champion*
10. Brighton (Mich.) HS	38-3	
11. Chatsworth (Calif.) HS	29-4	
12. La Quinta HS, Westminster, Calif.	30-2	
13. Irmo (S.C.) HS	29-3	State 4-A champion*
14. Westminster Christian HS, Miami	29-4	State 2-A champion
15. Start HS, Toledo	25-1	
16. Cretin-Derham Hall HS, St. Paul, Minn.	29-0	State 2-A champion*
17. Southridge HS, Miami	31-4	
18. Germantown (Tenn.) HS	40-4	
19. Barbe HS, Lake Charles, La.	30-5	State 5-A champion*
20. Granite Hills HS, El Cajon, Calif.	28-6	CIF sectional champion
21. Rochester HS, Rochester Hills, Mich.	31-4	
22. Wantagh (N.Y.) HS	29-1	
23. Key West (Fla.) HS	31-5	State 4-A champion
24. Midland (Mich.) HS	37-5	State Division I champion*
25. Logan HS, Union City, Calif.	25-3	

*Indicates state's highest classification

High School Baseball

Player of the Year

A man for all seasons: Michigan multi-sport star earns top honor

Drew Henson's exploits on the baseball diamond are unrivaled in recent history in Brighton, Mich.—not even by his feats on the gridiron.

Henson hit 70 home runs in his four-year Brighton High career, setting a new national record. He also drove in more runs (290) and scored more runs (259) than any prep player in history. In 1998 the shortstop hit .608 with 22 home runs and 83 RBIs while almost singlehandedly leading Brighton to the state 1-A semifinals.

Henson, Brighton's strong-armed quarterback, also took his turn on the mound, turning in a 14-1 record with a 0.86 ERA and 174 strikeouts in 82 innings. Despite those impressive numbers, there's no doubt his future lies hitting pitches, not throwing them.

"Every coach who has seen Drew play," Brighton coach Mark Carrow says, "says that he's the finest high school baseball player Michigan has ever produced."

That can be debated.

Drew Henson

But what can't be questioned is that in 1998, Drew Henson was the finest schoolboy player not just in Michigan, but in the nation. For that, he was named Baseball America's High School Player of the Year.

As Henson hit ball after ball over fences, usually in a black-pinstriped Brighton uniform that looked eerily like that of the New York Yankees, it was easy for Brighton fans, not to mention baseball scouts, to imagine him doing the same in a major league stadium in the near future. And after the Yankees—his favorite team—selected him in the third round of the 1998 draft, it became even easier to picture.

Henson signed for $2 million and spent the summer hitting .316 with one homer for the Rookie-level Gulf Coast League Yankees before reporting to the University of Michigan, where he had a scholarship to play quarterback.

The Yankees may have to share him with the Wolverines for a few years, but eventually their patience may be rewarded when one of the most prolific high school sluggers ever makes his Yankee Stadium debut.

PREVIOUS WINNERS

1992—Preston Wilson, ss-rhp, Bamberg-Ehrhardt (S.C.) High
1993—Trot Nixon, of-lhp, New Hanover High, Wilmington, N.C.
1994—Doug Million, lhp, Sarasota (Fla.) High
1995—Ben Davis, c, Malvern (Pa.) Prep
1996—Matt White, rhp, Waynesboro (Pa.) Area High
1997—Darnell McDonald, of, Cherry Creek High, Englewood, Colo.

Edwardsville kept its unbeaten team largely intact for the summer and went on to win the American Legion World Series.

Feeling The Draft

Vestavia Hills' success on the field translated to exactly zero impact on the June draft. The Rebels had no players selected.

Tate High of Gonzalez, Fla., had more players drafted than any other high school (four), including a pair of sixth-rounders, righthander Frankie McGill (Indians) and shortstop Brice Pelfrey (Pirates). Tate (32-3), a perennial national power, won the Florida 6-A title and was ranked fourth nationally.

The first high school player drafted was outfielder Corey Patterson from Harrison High in Kennesaw, Ga., who was taken third overall by the Cubs. The 5-foot-9 Patterson slugged 22 home runs in 1998, while hitting .528 with 37 stolen bases.

Patterson was outshone by Baseball America Player of the Year Drew Henson, who set national career records for runs, home runs, grand slams and RBIs, and went 14-1, 0.86 as a pitcher for Brighton (Mich.) High, which was ranked No. 10 nationally. His status as a top quarterback dropped him to the third round of the draft, but he still signed with the New York Yankees for a $2 million bonus, more than doubling the old record for a third-round pick.

Corey Patterson

In the fall, Henson began a promising college football career at the University of Michigan.

Scouts also spoke in reverent tones about a player they can't select until 1999. Josh Beckett, a junior righthander for Spring (Texas) High, went 13-2 with a 0.39 ERA, striking out 178 in 89 innings, and might have been the first selection in the '98 draft had he been eligible.

Good, Strange Performances

While Henson won notoriety for his record-break-

1998 HIGH SCHOOL ALL-AMERICA TEAM

Selected by Baseball America

FIRST TEAM

	Player, School	Yr.	AVG	AB	H	HR	RBI	SB
C	Gerald Laird, La Quinta HS, Westminster, Calif.	Sr.	.630	108	68	8	46	42
1B	Ben Diggins, Bradshaw Mountain HS, Dewey, Ariz.	Sr.	.573	89	51	11	49	5
IF	Sean Burroughs, Wilson HS, Long Beach, Calif.	Sr.	.528	89	47	7	40	12
	Felipe Lopez, Lake Brantley HS, Altamonte Springs, Fla.	Sr.	.521	73	38	7	28	35
	Mark Teixeira, Mt. St. Joseph HS, Severna Park, Md.	Sr.	.517	87	45	12	36	16
OF	Rick Elder, Sprayberry HS, Marietta, Ga.	Sr.	.509	110	56	17	44	15
	Austin Kearns, Lafayette HS, Lexington, Ky.	Sr.	.500	88	44	10	43	21
	Corey Patterson, Harrison HS, Kennesaw, Ga.	Sr.	.528	123	65	22	61	38
DH	Jeff Winchester, Archbishop Rummel HS, Metairie, La.	Sr.	.481	81	39	9	35	0
UT	Drew Henson, Brighton (Mich.) HS	Sr.	.608	112	68	22	83	16

	Player, School	Yr.	W	L	ERA	IP	H	BB	SO
P	Josh Beckett, Spring (Texas) HS	Jr.	13	2	0.39	89	31	29	178
	Chris George, Klein (Texas) HS	Sr.	15	0	1.13	110	61	33	168
	Frankie McGill, Tate HS, Gonzalez, Fla.	Sr.	15	1	0.96	94	36	41	137
	Michael Nannini, Green Valley HS, Henderson, Nev.	Sr.	10	1	0.58	73	38	8	97
	Matt Roney, Edmond North HS, Edmond, Okla.	Sr.	11	3	0.68	91	62	55	171
UT	Drew Henson, Brighton (Mich.) HS	Sr.	14	1	0.86	82	34	25	174

SECOND TEAM

	Player, School	Yr.	AVG	AB	H	HR	RBI	SB
C	Beau Craig, Grossmont HS, Santee, Calif.	Sr.	.463	108	50	12	39	14
1B	Josh Pressley, Westminster Academy, Fort Lauderdale	Sr.	.500	78	39	10	39	5
IF	Matt Holliday, Stillwater (Okla.) HS	Sr.	.473	112	53	12	43	20
	Josh McKinley, Malvern Prep, Downington, Pa.	Sr.	.500	78	39	10	39	5
	Victor Menocal, Gainesville (Ga.) HS	Sr.	.566	120	68	10	51	18
OF	Chip Ambres, West Brook HS, Beaumont, Texas	Sr.	.500	66	33	10	21	12
	Andy Brown, Richmond (Ind.) HS	Sr.	.484	91	44	7	50	6
	Choo Freeman, Dallas Christian HS, Mesquite, Texas	Sr.	.557	88	49	9	44	13
DH	Tony Torcato, Woodland (Calif.) HS	Sr.	.449	98	44	13	40	10
UT	C.C. Sabathia, Vallejo (Calif.) HS	Sr.	.563	80	45	10	39	0

	Player, School	Yr.	W	L	ERA	IP	H	BB	SO
P	J.M. Gold, Toms River North HS, Toms River, N.J.	Sr.	5	3	0.89	55	24	8	112
	Andrew Good, Rochester HS, Rochester Hills, Mich.	Sr.	12	1	1.52	69	42	15	110
	Rick Riccobono, Commack (N.Y.) HS	Sr.	7	0	0.58	48	16	21	79
	Pat Strange, Central HS, Springfield, Mass.	Sr.	4	0	0.51	55	22	17	87
	Jermaine Van Buren, Hattiesburg (Miss.) HS	Sr.	13	0	0.84	83	30	35	162
UT	C.C. Sabathia, Vallejo (Calif.) HS	Sr.	10	1	0.62	67	20	24	137

ing season, a number of other players and teams had outstanding, and often odd, achievements:

■ Righthander Josh Pressley of Westminster Academy in Fort Lauderdale picked an interesting way to nearly record a perfect game. He retired the first 20 batters sent to the plate by Santa Fe Catholic of Lakeland, Fla. He walked the 21st batter on a 3-2 pitch, then promptly picked him off first base to end the game.

Pressley, an outstanding two-way player, later became the fourth-round pick of the Tampa Bay Devil Rays as a first baseman.

■ Lefthander Mike Gosling of East High in Salt Lake City, the Minnesota Twins' 14th-round pick, struck out six batters in one inning. His regular catcher was injured for the game against Durango High of Las Vegas. Two of Gosling's curveballs went to the backstop. Another was blocked, but the reserve catcher threw the ball past the first baseman.

■ First baseman Charles Bobo of West High in Florence, S.C., hit grand slams in three straight at-bats over two games against Socastee (S.C.) and Conway (S.C.). Bobo, who wasn't drafted but drew Division I interest as a pitcher, was pinch-hit for on the third time through the order against Conway.

■ Rochester High of Rochester Hills, Mich., hit five straight home runs and six in the same inning against Troy (Mich.). In the top of the third, Domanick Squires, Andrew Good, Brett Wattles, Mike Bennion and Tom Frankhouse hit consecutive homers. After Matt Kovaleski was hit by a pitch, Jeff Buelow hit another home run. Good later became the eighth-round pick of the Arizona Diamondbacks as a pitcher.

■ Chris Martinez, a 5-foot-7, 165-pound second baseman for Chaminade of West Hills, Calif., hit a state-record 20 home runs.

"He's a freak of nature. He's an optical illusion," coach Scott Drootin said. "I can beat him in arm wrestling. I don't see a muscle on his body, but he can hit the ball far."

Notable coaching moves:

■ Ken Schreiber, the nation's fourth all-time winningest coach, abruptly retired April 27. Schreiber won 1,010 games in 37 years at LaPorte (Ind.) High and stepped down even as his team was ranked No. 1 in the Indiana 4-A poll. Schreiber's teams won seven Indiana state championships.

■ Rich Hofman, who coached Seattle Mariners shortstop Alex Rodriguez at Miami's Westminster Christian and led the school to mythical national titles in 1992 and 1995, resigned to become the new coach at Fort Lauderdale's Westminster Academy.

Amateur Baseball

Year of transition for USA Baseball results in poor showing by young American squad

BY JOHN MANUEL

A year of firsts for USA Baseball didn't include the kinds of milestones the governing body of amateur baseball in the United States hoped it would.

Yes, USA Baseball for the first time in 1998 had its own permanent home–a location where it had offices, national team trials and workouts in one place. The organization settled into its new offices in Tucson at Hi Corbett Field after a move from Trenton, N.J.

And for the first time since the mid-1980s, Mike Fiore wasn't a part of USA Baseball. Fiore, first a player and later the national team's general manager, left USA Baseball to become an agent with the Scott Boras Corporation. He was replaced by Paul Seiler.

On the field, Team USA went from first to worst. Instead of fielding a team of professionals for the 33rd World Championships in Italy–the first international tournament openly allowing professional players to represent their countries–Team USA relied again on college freshmen and sophomores.

With professionals and improved competition from the rest of the world, that decision backfired. Team USA finished a disappointing ninth in Italy, failing to reach the medal round. It was the first time the Americans had finished that low in international competition when a national team was assembled. St. John's University represented the U.S. in 1995 at the Pan American Games in Argentina and also finished ninth.

Italian Nightmare

Retired Mississippi State coach Ron Polk was entrusted with the fortunes of Team USA. A veteran of international competition and an assistant coach on the Americans' bronze-medal team at the 1996 Olympics, Polk tried to assemble a more veteran team from the national trials than the U.S. normally fields in non-Olympic years.

Of the 43 college players invited to try out, four were juniors, 13 were freshmen and the rest were sophomores. But youth won out again as only one junior, Texas A&M infielder John Scheschuk, made the trip to Italy. The average age for the Americans in Italy was 19 years, nine months–the youngest team in the 16-country field.

Still, the team was able to put together a solid exhibition season against the likes of Canada, Japan, Korea and Australia, with

Ron Polk

TEAM USA '98

BATTING	AVG	AB	R	H	2B	3B	HR	RBI	SB	College	Class
*Bryan Loeb, c	.571	7	3	4	0	0	0	3	0	Baylor	So.
*Blair Barbier, 2b	.500	8	2	4	0	0	0	2	1	Louisiana State	So.
John Scheschuk, 1b	.391	64	20	25	4	1	0	15	0	Texas A&M	Jr.
Ryan Ludwick, of	.386	127	39	49	14	3	0	27	3	UNLV	So.
Brant Ust, 3b	.378	90	16	34	10	3	0	20	1	Notre Dame	So.
John Gall, 1b-of	.371	140	30	52	15	3	5	37	5	Stanford	So.
*Matt Diaz, of	.364	11	2	4	1	1	0	4	0	Florida State	Fr.
Ryan Owens, 3b	.356	87	18	31	7	4	1	27	2	Cal State Fullerton	So.
Josh Bard, c	.350	123	22	43	11	0	2	18	0	Texas Tech	So.
*Jon Topolski, of	.339	62	15	21	2	3	1	13	5	Baylor	Jr.
Willie Bloomquist, of	.333	120	23	40	9	2	2	19	6	Arizona State	So.
*Omar Moraga, 3b	.333	9	3	3	0	0	0	1	1	Arizona	Jr.
*Kyle Woods, of	.308	13	5	4	0	0	1	3	2	Washington	So.
Eric Munson, c-1b	.300	60	16	18	5	2	2	10	0	Southern Calif.	So.
Brad Cresse, c-dh	.289	97	26	28	8	0	9	31	0	Louisiana State	So.
Seth Davidson, 2b-of	.288	73	13	21	5	0	1	11	3	Southern Calif.	Fr.
Bobby Hill, ss	.286	133	32	38	10	7	3	16	9	Miami	So.
Keoni DeRenne, 2b	.286	105	17	30	3	0	1	17	4	Arizona	Fr.
*Casey Myers, 1b	.281	32	3	9	2	1	0	7	0	Arizona State	Fr.
*Xavier Nady, 3b	.273	44	8	12	2	2	0	6	1	California	Fr.
Patrick Boyd, of	.264	91	17	24	2	0	2	15	1	Clemson	Fr.
*Brian Roberts, ss	.222	9	6	2	1	0	0	0	2	North Carolina	So.
*Kevin Mench, of	.200	5	1	1	0	0	0	1	1	Delaware	So.
Jason Jennings, p-dh	.174	23	2	4	0	0	1	5	0	Baylor	So.
*James McAuley, c	.000	5	2	0	0	0	0	1	1	Louisville	So.
TOTALS	**.326**	**1539**	**343**	**501**	**111**	**32**	**40**	**309**	**48**		

PITCHING	W	L	ERA	G	SV	IP	H	BB	SO	College	Class
*Jeff Nichols	0	0	0.00	2	0	6	6	0	7	Rice	So.
*Dan Wright	0	0	0.00	2	0	2	2	1	0	Arkansas	So.
*Aaron Heilman	0	0	0.00	1	0	1	0	1	1	Notre Dame	Fr.
Jon McDonald	2	0	1.14	8	1	24	15	3	11	Florida State	Fr.
Shane Nance	6	1	1.98	11	0	50	32	19	67	Houston	So.
Jason Jennings	4	2	2.33	9	0	39	34	13	44	Baylor	So.
Ryan Mottl	3	0	3.45	9	0	44	44	16	40	Clemson	So.
Mario Ramos	6	2	4.25	11	0	30	28	13	35	Rice	So.
Matt Ginter	1	0	4.35	12	5	21	24	4	25	Mississippi State	So.
Casey Fossum	4	1	4.41	11	2	51	61	15	58	Texas A&M	So.
*Matt Smith	0	1	4.50	1	0	2	5	0	1	Oklahoma State	Fr.
Alex Santos	2	1	4.53	9	0	46	56	9	43	Miami	So.
*Nick Stocks	0	2	5.50	9	0	18	14	12	19	Florida State	Fr.
*Ben Birk	1	1	5.56	5	0	11	11	3	15	Minnesota	So.
*Shane Wright	1	1	5.92	9	1	24	35	3	9	Texas Tech	Jr.
*Justin Wayne	0	0	8.31	2	0	9	13	2	6	Stanford	Fr.
Totals	**30**	**12**	**3.72**	**42**	**9**	**377**	**380**	**114**	**381**		

*Did not make World Championship team roster

WORLD SENIOR BASEBALL CUP

Parma, Italy
July 21-Aug. 2, 1998

ROUND-ROBIN STANDINGS

POOL A	W	L	RF	RA
Cuba	7	0	67	18
Japan	6	1	33	14
Dominican Republic	5	2	39	23
Italy	3	4	26	33
Panama	3	4	34	32
China	2	5	15	28
Spain	2	5	34	37
South Africa	0	7	12	75

POOL B	W	L	RF	RA
Australia	5	2	48	33
Nicaragua	5	2	69	37
Korea	4	3	35	34
Netherlands	4	3	45	34
United States	4	3	38	28
Canada	3	4	27	32
Chinese Taipei	3	4	36	38
Russia	0	7	12	74

GOLD MEDAL—Cuba. **SILVER MEDAL**—Korea. **BRONZE MEDAL**—Nicaragua.

FINAL STANDINGS: 1. Cuba; 2. Korea; 3. Nicaragua; 4. Italy; 5. Japan; 6. Netherlands; 7. Australia; 8. Dominican Republic; 9. United States; 10. Panama; 11. Canada; 12. China; 13. Chinese Taipei; 14. Spain; 15 (tie). South Africa, Russia.

INDIVIDUAL BATTING LEADERS

	AVG	AB	R	H	HR	RBI	SB
Orestes Kindelan, Cuba	.560	25	8	14	3	11	0
Omar Linares, Cuba	.500	22	8	11	2	5	0
Adam Burton, Australia	.500	18	9	9	0	2	3
Robelquis Bideaux, Cuba	.484	31	12	15	1	8	0
Edgard Lopez, Nicaragua	.483	29	9	14	1	3	1
Chen Chih-Yuan, Chin. Taipei	.481	27	8	13	2	6	1
Andrew Scott, Australia	.467	30	3	14	0	4	0
Manuel Rodriguez, Panama	.458	24	3	11	1	7	0
Earl Agnoly, Panama	.448	29	4	13	0	5	2
Diomedes Rodriguez, DRep	.444	27	6	12	1	4	0
Loidel Chapelli, Cuba	.444	27	7	12	3	8	0
Antonio Pacheco, Cuba	.440	25	8	11	3	14	0

INDIVIDUAL PITCHING LEADERS

	W	L	ERA	IP	H	BB	SO
Ryan Mottl, USA	1	0	0.00	8	5	2	9
Diego Ricci, Italy	1	0	0.00	8	6	1	7
Jose Contreras, Cuba	1	0	0.00	8	3	3	9
Glen Morris, South Africa	0	3	0.56	16	15	6	8
Brett Kondro, Canada	1	0	1.00	9	5	3	7
Koji Vehara, Japan	2	0	1.04	17	11	4	19
Zhanpeng Wang, China	2	0	1.04	17	13	5	12
Alex Santos, USA	0	1	1.04	9	8	1	8

AMERICAS QUALIFYING TOURNAMENT

(World Senior Baseball Cup)

Managua, Nicaragua
June 17-26, 1998

ROUND-ROBIN STANDINGS

	W	L	RF	RA
Panama	7	2	65	30
United States	7	2	57	43
Nicaragua	7	2	48	39
Canada	6	3	50	39
Dominican Republic	5	4	49	34
Venezuela	5	4	59	34
Colombia	4	5	50	43
Argentina	2	7	34	61
Mexico	1	8	37	68
Honduras	1	8	23	81

Top five teams qualify for World Senior Baseball Cup

INDIVIDUAL BATTING LEADERS

	AVG	AB	R	H	HR	RBI	SB
Earl Agnoly, Panama	.500	24	8	12	0	6	[illegible]
Henri Centeno, Venezuela	.485	33	7	16	0	3	1
Gabriel Rosario, Dom. Republic	.459	37	3	17	0	8	0
Colin Dixon, Canada	.436	39	8	17	1	7	1
Cris Colon, Venezuela	.432	37	8	16	1	13	0
Jose Solis, Panama	.432	37	8	16	3	13	0
Joe Colemeco, Canada	.417	36	8	15	0	1	4
Diomedes Rodriguez, DR	.412	34	7	14	0	4	1
Brant Ust, USA	.407	27	5	11	0	6	0
Mario Ruiz, Panama	.400	30	5	12	1	5	0
David Rivas, Panama	.400	25	6	10	0	1	0
Josh Bard, USA	.400	25	7	10	1	2	0

INDIVIDUAL PITCHING LEADERS

	W	L	ERA	IP	H	BB	SO
Cairo Murillo, Nicaragua	2	0	0.00	11	10	0	5
Franklin Rodriguez, Pan.	2	0	0.00	10	4	2	16
Matt Ginter, USA	0	0	0.00	8	4	1	11
Juan Samboy, Dom. Republic	1	0	0.00	7	3	2	6
Jose Cueto, Colombia	1	1	0.68	13	5	5	6
Mark Randall, Canada	2	0	0.90	10	5	4	7
Miguel Perez, Panama	2	0	1.13	16	10	6	12
Martin Bojorge, Nicaragua	1	0	1.13	8	3	0	10
Jason Jennings, USA	1	0	1.17	8	5	3	9

WORLD YOUTH CHAMPIONSHIPS

(16 & under)

Fairview Heights, Ill.
July 8-19, 1998

ROUND-ROBIN STANDINGS

POOL A	W	L	RF	RA
Chinese Taipei	5	0	52	10
Mexico	4	1	52	19
Brazil	2	3	30	23
Korea	2	3	26	39
South Africa	2	3	16	42
Ukraine	0	5	8	51

POOL B	W	L	RF	RA
United States	5	0	57	5
Venezuela	4	1	40	17
Australia	3	2	61	23
Japan	2	3	33	47
Italy	1	4	24	57
Czech Republic	0	5	10	76

GOLD MEDAL—United States. **SILVER MEDAL**—Chinese Taipei. **BRONZE MEDAL**—Venezuela.

TEAM USA

BATTING	AVG	AB	R	H	2B	3B	HR	RBI	SB
Carmen Pignatiello, p	1.000	4	3	4	1	1	0	3	0
Chris Patrick, 3b	.600	30	9	18	3	0	1	7	2
Ruben Salazar, of-p	.600	15	5	9	5	0	0	9	1
Jared Anderson, of	.556	9	4	5	1	0	0	2	0
Brian Horwitz, of	.481	27	10	13	5	1	0	12	1
Mark Roberts, p	.444	9	3	4	0	0	0	2	0
Kevin Melillo, 2b	.429	35	11	15	2	2	0	6	3
Landon Powell, c	.429	7	3	3	0	0	1	4	0
Tony Richie, c	.419	31	12	13	5	1	2	11	0
Matt Harrington, p	.400	5	0	2	0	0	0	0	0
Casey Kotchman, 1b	.370	27	11	10	2	0	1	8	0
Turay Alhaji, of	.353	17	6	6	1	0	1	4	0
Ron Draun, of	.333	24	7	8	0	1	0	5	2
Fritz Conrad, p	.333	3	0	1	0	0	0	1	1
Michael Hollimon, ss	.294	34	13	10	3	0	0	8	2
Dano Artman, p	.250	4	1	1	1	0	0	2	0
Sean Burnett, p	.000	3	0	0	0	0	0	0	0
Joe Torres, p	.000	1	0	0	0	0	0	0	0

PITCHING	W	L	ERA	G	SV	IP	H	BB	SO
Ruben Salazar	0	0	0.00	2	2	4	2	3	7
Fritz Conrad	1	0	1.00	1	0	9	1	4	11
Mark Roberts	2	0	1.29	2	0	14	9	3	18
Carmen Pignatiello	2	0	1.29	3	0	7	6	1	7
Dane Artman	1	0	2.00	2	0	9	8	3	13
Joe Torres	0	0	3.00	1	0	3	4	2	3
Matt Harrington	1	0	4.00	2	0	9	7	2	19
Sean Burnett	1	0	7.71	2	0	7	13	3	7

Golden Spikes Award

Burrell overcomes injury to earn award

A back injury kept Pat Burrell out of the University of Miami's lineup for 28 games in 1998. It kept Burrell from breaking Miami's all-time home run record (he finished second with 61) and kept him from joining Texas lefthander Greg Swindell and Oklahoma State third baseman Robin Ventura as a three-time first-team All-American.

But Burrell's balky back couldn't keep him from earning the Golden Spikes Award, amateur baseball's highest honor.

USA Baseball awards the Golden Spikes Award to "the player who exhibits exceptional athletic ability and exemplary sportsmanship."

This was the third time Burrell had been a Golden Spikes finalist. "I'm glad I don't have to go home and tell my friends I lost again," Burrell said in accepting the award. "I'm very excited. It's such a great feeling."

The other four finalists for the award were Stanford righthander Jeff Austin, Southern California righthander Seth Etherton, Louisiana State first baseman Eddy Furniss and Florida lefthander/outfielder Brad Wilkerson.

Burrell, a 6-foot-4, 225-pound third baseman from San Jose, Calif., baseball power Bellarmine Prep, batted .432 with 17 homers and 47 RBIs in 1998 for Miami, which finished the season ranked No. 3. For the third straight season, he helped lead Miami to the College World Series. He was MVP of Atlantic I regional, where he batted .421 with five homers.

Burrell's injury prevented Miami from breaking more NCAA records, but he left an indelible mark on college baseball since breaking in with a nation-leading .484 batting average as a freshman. Burrell hit safely in his first nine at-bats in college with four doubles and five home runs, and rarely looked back. He finished his career with a .442 average and an .886 slugging percentage.

"He really is as good a hitter in college baseball as I've seen," said Burrell's coach at Miami, Jim Morris. "He's an outstanding student, an honor student and such an outstanding person. It was really a dream to get the opportunity to coach him."

The Philadelphia Phillies drafted Burrell No. 1 overall in June and signed him to a five-year $8-million major league contract, which included a $3.15 million signing bonus.

—JOHN MANUEL

JEFF GOLDEN

Pat Burrell

PREVIOUS WINNERS

1978—Bob Horner, 3b, Arizona State
1979—Tim Wallach, 1b, Cal State Fullerton
1980—Terry Francona, of, Arizona
1981—Mike Fuentes, of, Florida State
1982—Augie Schmidt, ss, New Orleans
1983—Dave Magadan, 1b, Alabama
1984—Oddibe McDowell, of, Arizona State
1985—Will Clark, 1b, Mississippi State
1986—Mike Loynd, rhp, Florida State
1987—Jim Abbott, lhp, Michigan
1988—Robin Ventura, 3b, Oklahoma State
1989—Ben McDonald, rhp, Louisiana State
1990—Alex Fernandez, rhp, Miami-Dade CC South
1991—Mike Kelly, of, Arizona State
1992—Phil Nevin, 3b, Cal State Fullerton
1993—Darren Dreifort, rhp-dh, Wichita State
1994—Jason Varitek, c, Georgia Tech
1995—Mark Kotsay, of-lhp, Cal State Fullerton
1996—Travis Lee, 1b, San Diego State
1997—J.D. Drew, of, Florida State

all but three of the games played in Tucson.

Team USA qualified for the world tournament by tying for second with a 7-2 record at the continental qualifier in Managua, Nicaragua, in June, and headed to Italy with some confidence. The club had a 26-9 record heading to the Worlds, but Polk was cautious with the unknown professional factor looming ahead.

"We're the puppies," Polk said. "If we want to continue to send college players, we're going to have to have some cooperation from the pros so we can bring in juniors and seniors."

That lack of experience was evident in Italy, where Team USA was stunned in back-to-back, 3-1 games by the Netherlands and Korea. In both games, Team USA gave up two unearned runs on throwing errors by third baseman Brant Ust (Notre Dame).

"We played great defense all summer and we got great pitching," Polk said. "And if you look at our average for the summer (.326), it's outstanding. The problems came when we faced the other team's best guy. Our offense was shut down, and in those games our defense broke down."

The team finished with a 30-12 record for the summer, led by a pitching staff that had a 3.72 ERA and 381 strikeouts in 377 innings. Lefthander Shane Nance (Houston), just 5-foot-7, led the way all summer, pacing the club in wins and strikeouts. Lefthander Mario Ramos (Rice) tied Nance for the team lead in wins out of the bullpen, while lefthander Casey Fossum (Texas A&M) and righthanders Ryan Mottl (Clemson) and Alex Santos (Miami) helped give the Americans a formidable rotation.

The team just didn't have enough offense. Catcher-first baseman Eric Munson missed much of the summer after first leading Southern California to the

AMATEUR/YOUTH CHAMPIONS 1998

EVENT (Age Group)	Site	Champion	Runner-Up
AAABA (21 & under)	Johnstown, Pa.	Washington Senators	Philadelphia
American Legion (19 & under)	Las Vegas	Edwardsville, Ill.	State College, Pa.
National Baseball Congress (open)	Wichita	El Dorado, Kan., Broncos	Nevada, Mo., Griffons
USA Junior Olympics (16 & under)	Tucson	Dallas Tigers	Tucson Colts
Super Series (16 & under)	Marietta, Ga.	Maryland Orioles	East Cobb, Ga., Astros

AMATEUR ATHLETIC UNION (AAU)

HEADQUARTERS: Lake Buena Vista, Fla.

9 & under	Orlando	Central Florida Sun Devils	California Renegades
10 & under	Kansas City, Mo.	Florida Sharks	California Bulldogs
11 & under	Orlando	Sun Valley Park, Calif., Bums	Tidewater (Va.) Drillers
12 & under	Burnsville, Minn.	San Diego Stars	Tidewater (Va.) Drillers
13 & under (90 foot)	Lowell, Mass.	Chet Lemon's (Fla.) Juice	New England Mariners
13 & under (80 foot)	Riverside, Calif.	Tidewater (Va.) Cardinals	Placentia, Calif., Mustangs
14 & under	Concord, N.C.	Encinitas, Calif., Reds	New England Mariners
15 & under	Sarasota, Fla.	Northern California Angels	East Cobb, Ga., Astros
16 & under	Hampton Roads, Va.	East Cobb, Ga., Astros	Seminole, Fla., Predators
17 & under	Des Moines, Ia.	Indiana Bulls	Blue Springs, Mo., Sluggers
18 & under	Orlando, Fla.	West Coast Yankees	Orlando Storm

AMERICAN AMATEUR BASEBALL CONGRESS (AABC)

HEADQUARTERS: Marshall, Mich.

Roberto Clemente (8 & under)	Wheatridge, Colo.	McDonough (Ga.) Dodgers	Bayamon (P.R.) Padres
Willie Mays (10 & under)	Collierville, Tenn.	Fayette County (Ga.) Rockies	Puerto Rico Marlins
Pee Wee Reese (12 & under)	Toa Baja, P.R.	Puerto Rico Orioles	Houston
Sandy Koufax (14 & under)	Jersey City, N.J.	West Covina, Calif.	Toledo, Ohio
Mickey Mantle (16 & under)	McKinney, Texas	Memphis, Tenn.	Orange County, Calif.
Connie Mack (18 & under)	Farmington, N.M.	Cincinnati Midland Redskins	Dallas Mustangs
Stan Musial (open)	Battle Creek, Mich.	Canton, Ohio	Flint, Mich.

BABE RUTH BASEBALL

HEADQUARTERS: Trenton, N.J.

Bambino (11-12)	Vincennes, Ind.	West Palm Beach, Fla.	Kennewick, Wash.
13-Prep	Cape Coral, Fla.	Meridian, Miss.	Shoreview, Minn.
13-15	Pine Bluff, Ark.	Oakland	Pine Bluff, Ark.
16	Loudoun County, Va.	Bakersfield, Calif.	Nederland, Texas
16-18	Manteo, N.C.	Columbia Basin, Wash.	San Gabriel Valley, Calif.

CONTINENTAL AMATEUR BASEBALL ASSOCIATION (CABA)

HEADQUARTERS: Westerville, Ohio

9 & under	Charles City, Ia.	San Juan (P.R.) Indians	Wichita Rebels
10 & under	Aurelia, Ia.	Germantown (Tenn.) Giants	East Cobb, Ga.
11 & under	Tarkio, Mo.	San Diego Sting	Maryland Orioles
12 & under	Omaha	Omaha Pacesetters	Miami Dream Team
13 & under	Broken Arrow, Okla.	Germantown (Tenn.) Giants	West Covina (Calif.) Dukes
14 & under	Dublin, Ohio	East Cobb (Ga.) Astros	Palos Park (Ill.) Cougars
15 & under	Crystal Lake, Ill.	Bayamon (P.R.) Maceteros	Honolulu Rainbows
16 & under	Arlington, Texas	Dallas Tigers	Corpus Christi (Texas) Magic
High school age	Cleveland	Brooklyn Bergen Beach	Nashville, Tenn.
18 & under	Homestead, Fla.	Bayside (N.Y.) Yankees	East Cobb (Ga.) Stallions
College age	Chicago	Bloomington, Ill.	Wheaton, Ill.
Unlimited age	Eau Claire, Wis.	Illinois Badgers	Lombard (Ill.) Orioles

DIXIE BASEBALL

HEADQUARTERS: Montgomery, Ala.

Dixie Triple-A (10 & under)	Hattiesburg, Miss.	Covington, Ga.	Goodlettsville, Tenn.
Dixie Youth (12 & under)	Hattiesburg, Miss.	Lee County, Ga.	Bartow, Fla.
Dixie 13	Troy, Ala.	St. Charles Parish, La.	Goodlettsville, Tenn.
Dixie Boys (13-14)	Eufaula, Ala.	Columbia County, Ga.	Gonzales, La.
Dixie Pre-Majors (15-16)	North Charleston, S.C.	Marion County, Fla.	Valdosta, Ga.
Dixie Majors (15-18)	Florence, S.C.	Montgomery, Ala.	Monroe, La.

DIZZY DEAN BASEBALL

HEADQUARTERS: Europa, Miss.

Minor League (9-10)	East Brainerd, Tenn.	Rome, Ga.	Spring-Klein, Texas
Freshman (11-12)	Grenada, Miss.	Northport, Ala.	Spring-Klein, Texas
Sophomore (13-14)	Ellisville, Miss.	Baton Rouge, La.	North Jackson, Miss.
Junior (15-16)	Boynton, Ga.	Cincinnati	Tallahassee, Fla.
Senior (17-18)	Pelham, Ala.	Pelham, Ala.	Panama City, Fla.

HAP DUMONT BASEBALL

HEADQUARTERS: Wichita

10 & under	Harrison, Ark.	Houston Bandits	Wichita White Sox
11 & under	Russell, Kan.	Fort Worth (Texas) Stars	Houston Blue Jays
12 & under	Houston	Shaw Park (Ga.) White Sox	Texas Mustangs
13 & under	Casper, Wyom.	Toledo (Ohio) River Dogs	Houston Outlaws
14 & under	Norman, Okla.	Oklahoma Sooners	Mississippi Blazers

AMATEUR/YOUTH CHAMPIONS 1998

LITTLE LEAGUE BASEBALL

HEADQUARTERS: Williamsport, Pa.

Little League (11-12)	Williamsport, Pa.	Toms River, N.J.	Kashima, Japan
Junior League (13)	Taylor, Mich.	Mission Viejo, Calif.	Waco, Texas
Senior League (14-15)	Kissimmee, Fla.	Diamond Bar, Calif.	Orlando
Big League (16-18)	Fort Lauderdale	California	Venezuela

NATIONAL AMATEUR BASEBALL FEDERATION (NABF)

HEADQUARTERS: Bowie, Md.

Rookie (10 & under)	Cincinnati	California Bums	Cincinnati Pirates Trucking
Freshman (12 & under)	Sylvania, Ohio	East Cobb (Ga.) Mavericks	Oklahoma 89s
Sophomore (14 & under)	Miamisburg, Ohio	Surrey (B.C.) Thunder	Franklin (Tenn.) Astros
Junior (16 & under)	Northville, Mich.	Bayside (N.Y.) Yankees	Gambrills, Md.
High School (17 & under)	Clarksville, Tenn.	Twitty City (Tenn.) Hallmark	Germantown, Tenn.
Senior (18 & under)	Evansville, Ind.	East Cobb (Ga.) Astros	Olympia, Wash.
College (22 & under)	Louisville	Maryland Bombers	Miami Valley (Ohio) Bulldogs
Major (open)	Louisville	Youngstown (Ohio) Tamburro's	Chicago Clout

PONY BASEBALL

HEADQUARTERS: Washington, Pa.

Mustang (9-10)	Irving, Texas	Santa Clarita, Calif.	Pembroke Lakes, Fla.
Bronco (11-12)	Monterey, Calif.	Taiwan	Bayamon, P.R.
Pony (13-14)	Washington, Pa.	Taiwan	Washington, Pa.
Colt (15-16)	Lafayette, Ind.	East Cobb (Ga.) Mavericks	Kauai, Hawaii
Palomino (17-18)	Greensboro, N.C.	Marietta (Ga.) Tigers	Greensboro, N.C.

REVIVING BASEBALL IN INNERCITIES (RBI)

HEADQUARTERS: New York

Junior (13-15)	Lake Buena Vista, Fla.	San Juan, P.R.	Philadelphia
Senior (16-18)	Lake Buena Vista, Fla.	Atlanta	San Juan, P.R.

UNITED STATES AMATEUR BASEBALL ASSOCIATION

HEADQUARTERS: Edmonds, Wash.

11 & under	Albuquerque	Las Vegas	Fresno
12 & under	Albuquerque	Hawaii Sharks	Puyallup (Wash.) Hurricanes
14 & under	Las Vegas	Las Vegas Yard Dawgs	Desert Valley, Calif.
15 & under	Victoria, B.C.	Seattle River Dawgs	Kent (Wash.) Cubs
16 & under	West Jordan, Utah	Taylorsville, Utah	Marysville, Wash.
18 & under	Hoquiam, Wash.	Seattle Triple Play	Hawaii All-Stars

U.S. SLO-PITCH SOFTBALL ASSOCIATION (USSSA)

HEADQUARTERS: Petersburg, Va.

9 & under	Joplin, Mo.	Dallas Texans	Houston Rebels
10 & under	Slidell, La.	Houston Sharks	Columbus (Ohio) Cobras
11 & under	Kansas City, Mo.	Memphis Tigers	Houston Indians
12 & under	Hutchinson, Kan.	Wichita Warriors	Texas Titans
13 & under	Tulsa, Okla.	Houston Panthers	Antonio (Mo.) Marlins
14 & under	Sterling Heights, Mich.	Houston Sluggers	Tulsa Indians
15 & under	Winter Haven, Fla.	Clearwater (Fla.) Rough Riders	Texas Horns
16 & under	Round Rock, Texas	East Cobb (Ga.) Astros	Austin Slam Braves
18 & under	Lakeland, Fla.	East Cobb (Ga.) Chargers	Sterling Heights, Mich.

College World Series title, then recovering from a stress fracture in his right foot. Team USA never replaced his potent bat.

Instead, right fielder Ryan Ludwick (Nevada-Las Vegas) and first baseman-outfielder John Gall (Stanford) led the offense. Polk never got comfortable with his outfield, though, rotating infielders Willie Bloomquist (Arizona State) and Seth Davidson (Southern California) into left field, searching for a spark.

It never came, leaving the future of amateurs representing the national team in serious doubt.

"We can go in there with young players and expect them to compete, but we must be realistic as to how successful that approach would be," Seiler said. "What it leaves us is a method of refinement. For every tournament, our goal is to put our best team on the field that we can.

"If we can't get major leaguers, then we should try to get Triple-A or Double-A players. Then we work from there. I think that would include independent leaguers, college seniors and juniors."

The United States scored a rare victory on the international stage in 1998, though, when USA Baseball's youth national team went 8-0 to capture the gold medal at the International Baseball Association's ninth AA World Youth (16-and-under) Championships in Fairview Heights, Ill.

The United States defeated defending champion Chinese Taipei 11-10 in the championship game, scoring seven runs in the bottom of the seventh inning to overcome a 10-4 deficit. Previously unbeaten Chinese Taipei (7-1), which outhit the Americans 20-10, had scored seven runs in the top of the inning.

Catcher Tony Richie (Bishop Kenny High, Jacksonville) triggered Team USA's comeback by launching a one-out, 400-foot grand slam, closing the gap to 10-9. Landon Powell (Apex, N.C., High), who drew a leadoff walk in the seventh as a pinch-hitter, came up a second time in the inning and delivered the game-winning hit, a two-out single that scored winning pitcher Ruben Salazar (St. John Bosco High, Inglewood, Calif.) from second base.

"I couldn't think of a better way to win this game,"

said head coach Mark McKenzie, an assistant on the first USA Baseball youth team that finished fifth in the 1997 tournament. "I thrive on overcoming adversity. These players didn't quit. That's all I care about."

The United States went 5-0 in pool play before defeating Korea 17-3 and Australia 13-2 to reach the gold-medal game. Team USA outscored its opponents 98-20. Richie (.419-2-11) was named the tournament's MVP.

Team USA's junior national team (18-and-under) took a hiatus from competition in 1998 as the World Junior Championships became an every-second-year affair. The U.S. was scheduled to participate in a continental qualifier for the '99 tournament in Cartagena, Colombia, in September but that tournament was canceled and the junior team was disbanded.

Cape Crusader

The 1997 Cape Cod League season produced five 1998 first-round draft picks. While the '98 edition of the nation's most talent-laden summer collegiate league didn't have the crop of arms of previous years, it featured Baseball America's Summer Player of the Year, Bourne outfielder Bobby Kielty, who missed capturing the league's triple crown by one home run. He finished with a .384 average, six homers and 45 RBIs.

Chatham defeated defending champion Wareham in the league's best-of-5 championship series, winning three games to two. Righthander Devon Nicholson (Sacramento City College), who transferred to Tennessee in the fall, threw 130 pitches in a gutty Game Five performance, leading the A's to the title.

Wareham had taken a 2-1 lead in the series on a 1-0, 14-inning win in Game Three as righthander Ben Sheets (Northeast Louisiana) struck out a Cape League playoff record 16 in 11 innings.

The El Dorado (Kan.) Broncos won their fourth National Baseball Congress World Series at Wichita's Laurence-Dumont Stadium by going with a more veteran lineup than usual. They got key contributions from two ex-pros: 27-year-old first baseman Grier Jones and 34-year-old catcher Terry Elliot.

Jones hit .481 with three homers and 14 RBIs as the Broncos sailed through the 32-team tournament with seven straight wins. Jones homered twice in the championship game as the Broncos beat the Nevada (Mo.) Griffins 16-7 in an all-Jayhawk League final.

The Broncos had some talented collegians as well, including the tournament MVP, third baseman Jason Aspito (Texas), who hit .520 with four homers. Lefthander Nate Robertson (Wichita State) missed most of the college season recovering from Tommy John elbow surgery, but pitched 7⅔ solid innings in the final, striking out 11, for his second win of the tournament.

Americans Reign In Williamsport

Toms River, N.J., brought the Little League World Series (11-12) title back to the United States with a thrilling 12-9 victory over Kashima, Japan, in the championship game.

In a game that featured 11 home runs, one of the most unlikeliest of sluggers stole the show for Toms River. Chris Cardone entered the championship game as a pinch-hitter and homered in consecutive at-bats.

Player of the Year

Cape's Kielty a surprise choice

Outfielder Bobby Kielty was overlooked by scouts for four years. But an MVP season in the Cape Cod League, leading to his selection as Baseball America's 1998 Summer Player of the Year, changed that.

After leading the nation's premier summer college league with a .384 average and 45 RBIs, the 6-foot-1, 210-pound switch-hitter was beseiged by offers from major league clubs.

A fourth-year junior at the University of Mississippi, where he hit .307 with 16 homers in 1998, Kielty was eligible to sign as a free agent with any team because he went undrafted–for the fifth draft in a row.

Kielty signed with Southern California out of high school but he redshirted and later transfered to Mississippi, where he missed time early in the 1998 season due to a back injury from a January skiing accident.

Finally healthy, Kielty reported to Bourne on the Cape. All he did was flirt with .400 and open scouts' eyes for the first time.

"I think by the time I was healthy and playing well for Ole Miss, the scouts had already come through and made their reports," Kielty said. "I'm just glad that I was healthy this summer. I knew coming to the Cape was my big chance."

Baseball America's Summer All-America team:

C—Ryan Duncheon, Quincy/CICL (Illinois State), .398-10-53. **1B**—John Gall, Team USA (Stanford), .371-5-37. **2B**—Kevin Hooper, El Dorado/Jayhawk (Wichita State), .357-0-17. **3B**—Garrett Atkins, Cotuit/Cape Cod (UCLA), .383-3-25. **SS**—Vaughn Schill, Orleans/Cape Cod (Duke), .315-6-33. **OF**—Matt Cepicky, Chatham/Cape Cod (Southwest Missouri State), .327-5-33; Paul Lockhart, Fairbanks-Kenai/Alaska (San Diego State), .329-3-31; Ryan Ludwick, Team USA (Nevada-Las Vegas), .386-9-27. **DH**—Bobby Kielty, Brewster/Cape Cod (Mississippi), .384-6-45. **Util**—Jason Dubois, Rocky Mount/Coastal Plain (Virginia Commonwealth), .323-16-50; 4-4, 3.40.

SP—Jeff Heaverlo, Cotuit/Cape Cod (Washington) 7-1, 3.09; Shane Nance, Team USA (Houston), 6-1, 1.98; John Rauch, Harrisonburg/ShenandoahValley (Morehead State), 8-1, 1.69; Ben Sheets, Wareham/Cape Cod (Northeast Louisiana), 4-1, 2.51; Jon Shirley, Brewster/Cape Cod (California), 8-1, 2.22. **RP**—Marc Bluma, Glacier Pilots (Alaska), 0-1, 2.70, 11 SV.

PREVIOUS WINNERS

1984—Will Clark, 1b, Team USA
Rafael Palmeiro, of, Hutchinson (Jayhawk)
1985—Jeff King, 3b, Team USA
Bob Zupcic, of, Liberal (Jayhawk)
1986—Jack Armstrong, rhp, Wareham (Cape Cod)
Mike Harkey, rhp, Fairbanks (Alaska)
1987—Cris Carpenter, rhp, Team USA
1988—Ty Griffin, 2b, Team USA
Robin Ventura, 3b, Team USA
1989—John Olerud, 1b-lhp, Palouse (Alaska)
1990—Calvin Murray, of, Anchorage Bucs (Alaska)
1991—Chris Roberts, of, Team USA
1992—Jeffrey Hammonds, of, Team USA
1993—Geoff Jenkins, of, Anchorage Bucs (Alaska)
1994—Steve Carver, 1b, Anchorage Glacier Pilots (Alaska)
1995—Travis Lee, 1b, Team USA
1996—Seth Greisinger, rhp, Team USA
1997—Pat Burrell, 3b, Team USA

Cardone's second homer, a two-run shot in the top of the sixth inning, snapped an 8-8 tie and powered the United States to its first Little League triumph in five years.

Prior to his outburst, Cardone had hit only one home run in his life and was 1-for-10 entering the final game.

"Timing's a thing of beauty," said Toms River manager Mike Gaynor, whose team went 1-2 in the 1995 World Series. "He just came through for us today."

Toms River, representing the U.S. East, went undefeated in becoming the first American team since Long Beach in 1993 to win the title. Toms River went 3-0 in pool play and knocked off favored Greenville, N.C., 5-3 in the U.S. pool championship game.

Japan hit six home runs—all solo shots—in the championship game, including three by Tetsuya Furukawa. The Far East representative reached the final by defeating the Canadian entry from Langley, B.C., 3-2 in seven innings in the international pool championship, despite 17 strikeouts by Langley righthander Jeff Duda. The 17 strikeouts broke the record of 16 set by Long Beach's Sean Burroughs, a 1998 first-round pick of the San Diego Padres who led Long Beach to the '93 title.

South Mission Viejo, Calif., which squanderded a three-run lead and lost 5-4 to Guadalupe, Mexico, in the championship game of the 1997 Little League World Series, avenged that setback when the two teams met at the '98 Junior League (13) World Series.

Both teams returned 10 players and met in a losers' bracket game. The California team won 5-0 and went on to win four straight games and the title.

Edwardsville Wins Legion Title

Edwardsville, Ill., Post 199 had the perfect prescription for winning the American Legion World Series.

Twins Ben and James Hutton pitched the last 18 innings of the tournament for Edwardsville, with Ben throwing a complete game in a 9-3 win over State College, Pa., Post 245 in the semifinals, and James getting the win and Ben the save in a 9-4 victory over Cherryville, N.C., Post 100 in the finals.

"If it wasn't going to be me out there on the mound, it might as well be someone in the family," James Hutton said.

Edwardsville did most of its damage on offense, hitting a tournament record .396 in 10 regional and World Series games. Shortstop Chad Opel was named the Legion's national player of the year. He hit .632 in national play, with eight doubles and a .714 on-base percentage. He was 11-for-11 in stolen bases.

All but one Edwardsville player came from the Edwardsville High team that went 40-0 in the spring, won the Illinois 2A championship and finished eighth in the Baseball America/National High School Baseball Coaches Association final national poll. The Tigers were one of three undefeated teams in the final Top 50.

Combined, Edwardsville's teams went 81-7 in 1998.

B.J. Garbe, a projected first-round pick in the 1999 draft, almost singlehandedly lifted Columbia Basin, Wash., to the Babe Ruth League 16-18 World Series title by going 14-for-22 (.636) with two homers, eight RBIs and two pitching wins.

COLLEGE SUMMER LEAGUES

NCAA-CERTIFIED

ATLANTIC COLLEGIATE LEAGUE

	W	L	PCT	GB
Jersey City Colonels	26	10	.722	—
Quakertown Blazers	26	10	.722	—
Jersey Pilots	24	12	.667	2
Metro New York Cadets	20	16	.556	6
New York Generals	19	17	.528	7
Nassau Collegians	17	19	.472	9
West Deptford Storm	14	22	.389	12
Delaware Gulls	9	27	.250	17
Scranton/Wilkes-Barre Twins	7	29	.194	19

PLAYOFFS: Metro New York defeated Jersey City 2-0 and Quakertown defeated Jersey 2-1 in best-of-3 semifinals. Quakertown defeated Metro New York in a one-game final.

INDIVIDUAL BATTING LEADERS

(Minimum 100 Plate Appearances)

	AVG	AB	R	H	2B	3B	HR	RBI	SB
Osipower, Bob, Quakertown	.398	123	33	49	10	2	1	25	1
Macchio, Paul, New York	.364	118	12	43	3	6	0	19	2
Martinez, Casey, Metro	[illegible]	[illegible]	10	[illegible]	0	1	0	[illegible]	0
Conway, Craig, Jersey	.354	82	19	29	5	2	1	16	8
Spadt, Eric, Quakertown	.346	133	26	46	5	6	1	22	5
Zeccardi, Joe, Metro	.337	104	22	35	7	1	2	23	4
Delehanty, Brian, JC	.333	87	19	29	4	3	1	13	5
Jackson, Aurelio, JC	.333	102	22	34	4	1	0	10	12
Lynch, Mike, Metro	.333	105	18	35	2	0	0	11	5
Kano, Pat, Delaware	.330	97	21	32	6	1	1	8	12

INDIVIDUAL PITCHING LEADERS

(Minimum 35 Innings)

	W	L	ERA	G	SV	IP	H	BB	SO
Fisher, Marc, Quakertown	4	1	1.79	10	2	40	31	12	41
Clark, Kevin, Jersey	5	1	1.81	9	1	40	26	15	28
Lenko, Jared, Quakertown	2	1	1.93	9	1	37	25	15	31
Middleton, Brian, WD	2	2	2.05	9	0	40	19	19	38
Brown, Eric, Jersey	5	1	2.24	11	0	64	65	10	47

CAPE COD LEAGUE

EAST	W	L	T	PCT	PTS
Brewster Whitecaps	26	16	1	.619	53
Chatham A's	23	18	2	.561	48
Harwich Mariners	23	21	0	.523	46
Yarmouth-Dennis Red Sox	21	23	0	.477	42
Orleans Cardinals	17	27	0	.386	34
WEST	**W**	**L**	**T**	**PCT**	**PTS**
Wareham Gatemen	25	18	1	.581	51
Bourne Braves	20	21	3	.488	43
Hyannis Mets	19	22	3	.463	41
Falmouth Commodores	20	24	0	.455	40
Cotuit Kettleers	18	22	4	.450	40

PLAYOFFS: Chatham defeated Brewster 2-0 and Wareham defeated Bourne 2-1 in best-of-3 semifinals; Chatham defeated Wareham 3-2 in best-of-5 final.

ALL-STAR TEAM: C—Chris Curry, Yarmouth-Dennis (Meridian, Miss., CC). **1B**—Jon Palmieri, Chatham (Wake Forest). **2B**—Dominic Rich, Brewster (Auburn). **3B**—Garrett Atkins, Cotuit (UCLA). **SS**—Vaughn Schill, Orleans (Duke). **OF**—Larry Bigbie, Wareham (Ball State); Matt Cepicky, Chatham (Southwest Missouri State); Scott Goodman, Hyannis (Cuesta, Calif., JC). **Util**—Bobby Kielty, Brewster (Mississippi). **P**—Jeff Heaverlo, Cotuit (Washington); Jeff House, Bourne (Stetson); Ben Sheets, Wareham (Northeast Louisiana); Jon Shirley, Brewster (California); Jeremy Ward, Chatham (Long Beach State). **RP**—Jeff House, Bourne (Stetson).

Most Valuable Player: Bobby Kielty, Brewster. **Pitchers of the Year:** Phil Devey, Wareham; Jeff Heaverlo, Cotuit.

INDIVIDUAL BATTING LEADERS
(Minimum 119 Plate Appearances)

	AVG	AB	R	H	2B	3B	HR	RBI	SB
Kielty, Bobby, Brewster	.384	151	30	58	17	1	6	45	6
Atkins, Garrett, Cotuit	.383	133	21	51	11	0	3	25	0
Bigbie, Larry, Wareham	.336	122	23	41	7	1	2	24	17
Cepicky, Matt, Chatham	.327	162	24	53	8	3	5	33	2
Nelson, Eric, Hyannis	.319	163	33	52	9	1	0	20	13
Daeley, Scott, Y-D	.318	154	35	49	6	0	0	9	29
Schill, Vaughn, Orleans	.315	165	37	52	10	2	6	33	13
Rich, Dominic, Brewster	.313	131	29	41	9	0	1	18	20
Goodman, Scott, Hyannis	.312	138	23	43	10	0	6	18	9
Santora, Jack, Hyannis	.308	107	21	33	4	0	1	8	6
Palmieri, Jon, Chatham	.307	150	21	46	9	1	0	17	1
Utley, Chase, Brewster	.304	112	19	34	5	1	1	15	9
Nye, Rodney, Harwich	.303	145	22	44	11	1	4	26	2
Slavik, Cory, Y-D	.303	109	8	33	7	0	2	25	1
Johnstone, Benjamin, Brew	.297	111	17	33	5	1	0	13	10
Thompson, Craig, Harwich	.292	120	20	35	7	1	3	12	7
Rizzo, Jeff, Cotuit	.291	117	24	34	6	0	2	7	7
Kim, Kevin, Orleans	.289	114	11	33	3	0	2	19	5
Corr, Frank, Wareham	.289	135	17	39	10	0	3	21	5
Bikowski, Scott, Falmouth	.288	125	21	36	7	2	0	15	8
Kropf, Andy, Cotuit	.288	132	14	38	7	0	2	18	4
Muth, Edmund, Y-D	.273	150	25	41	5	3	7	27	11
Holt, Daylan, Y-D	.273	154	30	42	14	1	7	26	4
Stanley, Henri, Harwich	.273	132	27	36	9	4	0	11	11
Jacobson, Russ, Falmouth	.271	140	23	38	7	0	4	25	1
Johnson, Reed, Brewster	.270	159	28	43	10	1	4	23	9
Griswold, Matt, Bourne	.269	130	21	35	10	1	1	19	3
Dzurilla, Mike, Bourne	.268	168	25	45	6	1	0	13	10
O'Brien, Mike, Bourne	.266	158	17	42	13	0	3	29	1
Durham, Miles, Brewster	.265	117	28	31	7	1	0	12	15
Stevenson, Shawn, Ware.	.265	151	29	40	4	0	1	22	19
Oborn, Spencer, Wareham	.263	152	29	40	11	1	2	15	10
Curry, Chris, Y-D	.263	137	17	36	4	0	4	20	2
Chapman, Travis, Orleans	.262	141	21	37	7	0	4	18	9
Pavlich, Matt, Falmouth	.261	134	16	35	9	0	1	24	1
Groves, Brett, Falmouth	.261	119	22	31	4	0	0	6	10

INDIVIDUAL PITCHING LEADERS
(Minimum 35 Innings)

	W	L	ERA	G	SV	IP	H	BB	SO
House, Jeff, Bourne	3	0	1.22	16	3	37	23	13	23
Devey, Phil, Wareham	5	3	1.88	11	0	72	51	35	73
Ward, Jeremy, Chatham	5	0	1.94	6	0	42	33	12	31
Collins, Pat, Orleans	3	4	2.00	10	0	76	56	31	89
Shirley, Jon, Brewster	8	1	2.22	10	0	69	59	14	45
Steller, Michael, Harwich	4	2	2.24	8	0	60	52	12	36
Graham, Tom, Hyannis	2	3	2.32	10	0	66	51	18	57
Currier, Rik, Chatham	5	3	2.37	10	0	61	35	34	63
Sheets, Ben, Wareham	4	1	2.51	10	1	68	50	22	66
Carlsen, Jeff, Bourne	4	1	2.58	9	0	38	30	25	26
Berney, Scott, Falmouth	1	3	2.60	14	2	45	45	13	27
Crowder, Chuck, Falmouth	3	3	2.72	8	0	43	29	34	49
Capel, Chance, Y-D	6	2	2.73	10	0	69	55	29	58
Balcer, David, Wareham	3	3	2.80	14	1	45	41	18	28
Bynum, Mike, Hyannis	6	1	2.82	8	0	54	39	33	47
Rhodes, Shane, Bourne	3	1	2.88	10	0	50	38	19	42
McClendon, Matt, Brewster	3	3	2.91	8	0	59	46	13	35
Withelder, Greg, Fal.	4	2	2.96	9	0	52	39	24	56
Zito, Barry, Wareham	4	2	3.03	11	0	59	60	25	81
Heaverlo, Jeff, Cotuit	7	1	3.09	11	0	67	47	27	94
Warren, Andrew, Cotuit	3	4	3.23	11	0	75	83	23	56
McDougal, Mike, Chatham	4	3	3.35	9	0	48	32	33	43
Thoms, Hank, Y-D	3	5	3.36	11	0	59	40	27	61
Mittauer, David, Orleans	0	3	3.41	12	0	37	33	24	39
McGerry, Kevin, Bourne	4	4	3.46	9	0	52	41	28	39
Dennis, Jason, Hyannis	4	3	3.58	11	1	65	49	36	65

CENTRAL ILLINOIS LEAGUE

EAST	W	L	PCT	GB
Danville	33	15	.689	—
Decatur	14	28	.333	16
Twin City	13	33	.283	19
WEST	**W**	**L**	**PCT**	**GB**
Quincy	38	10	.792	—
Bluff City	22	22	.500	14
Springfield	16	28	.364	20

PLAYOFF TOURNAMENT: Quincy 2-0, Danville 2-1, Decatur 1-1, Bluff City 0-1, Springfield 0-1, Twin City 0-1.

ALL-STAR TEAM: C—Ryan Duncheon, Quincy (Illinois State); Jonathan Kessick, Quincy (Ball State). **1B**—Brian Fuess, Bluff City (Belleville Area, Ill., CC); Ryan Feyerabend, Decatur (Indiana State). **2B**—Ryan Kyes, Springfield (Ohio). **3B**—Jason Sands, Twin City (Illinois State); Phil Willingham, Danville (Mississippi State). **SS**—Jason Shelley, Danville (Northeast Louisiana). **OF**—Josh Rabe, Quincy (Quincy); Andy Reeb, Twin City (St. Francis, Ill.); Aaron Sapp, Springfield (New Orleans); Joe Schley, Danville (Southern Illinois); Shap Stiles, Quincy (Carson-Newman, Tenn.). **Util**—Corey Artieta, Danville (Northeast Louisiana); Phil Broshears, Decatur (Evansville); John Lackaff, Quincy (Miami, Ohio). **SP**—Chris Andrzejak, Springfield (Detroit); B.J. Burkhart, Twin City (Illinois State); Chris Cabaj, Quincy (Ball State); Ryan Cox, Decatur (Southern Illinois); Jason Oglesby, Twin City (Stetson); Chris Vaught, Danville (Bowling Green). **RP**—Justin Crowell, Decatur (Parkland, Ill., CC); Tony Fontana, Danville (Bowling Green); Allan Wills, Quincy (Lewis, Ill.).

Player of the Year: Ryan Duncheon, Quincy. **Pitcher of the Year:** Chris Cabaj, Quincy.

INDIVIDUAL BATTING LEADERS
(Minimum 106 Plate Appearances)

	AVG	AB	R	H	2B	3B	HR	RBI	SB
Duncheon, Ryan, Quincy	.398	171	42	68	18	1	10	53	2
Artieta, Cory, Danville	.348	92	16	32	0	3	0	15	7
Stiles, Shap, Quincy	.346	156	44	54	8	3	3	23	22
Sapp, Aaron, Springfield	.345	142	27	49	10	1	3	28	5
Sands, Jason, Twin City	.340	153	30	52	5	3	0	23	4
Kessick, Jonathan, Quincy	.338	148	28	50	14	1	3	30	1
Schley, Joe, Danville	.336	143	39	48	6	3	0	21	28
Fuess, Brian, Bluff City	.333	144	14	48	13	0	3	25	3
Kyes, Ryan, Springfield	.326	135	19	44	14	1	2	14	7
Reeb, Andy, Twin City	.322	146	16	47	12	2	0	21	5
Hale, Jon, Bluff City	.320	100	19	32	4	2	0	4	8
Willingham, Phil, Danville	.313	144	23	45	3	1	1	25	5
Feyerabend, Ryan, Decatur	.308	146	17	45	10	1	1	20	2
Rabe, Josh, Quincy	.308	146	32	45	2	5	2	31	12
Beckman, Jason, Twin City	.308	104	12	32	1	2	0	11	9
Dawson, Travis, Bluff City	.305	118	20	36	3	1	1	18	9
Scott, Adam, Springfield	.302	129	9	39	3	1	0	12	4

INDIVIDUAL PITCHING LEADERS
(Minimum 40 Innings)

	W	L	ERA	G	SV	IP	H	BB	SO
Andrzejak, Chris, Spring	5	4	1.98	9	0	68	72	17	49
Cabaj, Chris, Quincy	9	1	2.05	10	0	70	52	16	59
Cox, Ryan, Decatur	3	2	2.06	8	0	48	44	14	35
Fontana, Tony, Danville	5	2	2.12	13	5	51	41	17	36
Wills, Allan, Quincy	3	0	2.23	20	6	48	40	6	44
Warnecke, Ryan, Bluff City	3	2	2.25	10	0	48	57	9	27
Haring, Kurt, Springfield	3	3	2.52	8	0	54	43	31	22
Vaught, Chris, Danville	5	1	2.63	8	0	51	42	23	27
Burkhart, B.J., Twin City	3	4	2.68	8	0	57	59	19	47
Oglesby, Jason, Twin City	3	3	2.70	8	0	50	43	26	34
Anderson, Jason, Danville	7	2	2.71	9	0	63	41	19	60
Snoke, Eric, Quincy	7	1	2.93	12	0	68	62	25	51

GREAT LAKES LEAGUE

	W	L	PCT	GB
Central Ohio Cows	28	11	.718	--
Columbus All-Americans	23	16	.590	5
Lima Locos	22	16	.579	5 ½
Grand Lake Mariners	23	17	.575	5 ½
Sandusky Bay Stars	11	28	.282	17
Lake County Admirals	9	28	.243	18

POST-SEASON TOURNAMENT: Columbus defeated Lima 2-0 and Grand Lake defeated Central Ohio 2-0 in semifinals. Columbus defeated Grand Lake 2-0 in finals. (Regular season determines official league champion.)

ALL-STAR TEAM: C—Matt Gajewski, Columbus (Indiana State). **1B**—Bucky O'Hara, Lima (Presbyterian, S.C.). **2B**—Chad Ehrnsberger, Central Ohio (Ohio State). **3B**—Mike Conway, Columbus (Dartmouth). **SS**—Tim Olson, Columbus (Hutchinson, Kan., CC). **OF**—Robert Bobeda, Lima (Michigan); Julian Gonzalez, Sandusky (Virginia); Jason Turner, Central Ohio (Ohio State). **DH**—Matt Mason, Grand Lake (Eastern Kentucky). **P**—Jeremy Cummings, Columbus (West Virginia); Justin Fry, Central Ohio (Ohio State); Brandon Miller, Lima (Evansville); Jake Sutter, Grand Lake (Kellogg, Mich., CC).

Most Valuable Player: Jason Turner, Central Ohio. **Pitcher of the Year**: Jeremy Cummings, Central Ohio.

INDIVIDUAL BATTING LEADERS
(Minimum 100 Plate Appearances)

	AVG	AB	R	H	2B	3B	HR	RBI	SB
Thomas, Mark, LC	.398	118	16	47	9	2	0	10	4
Gonzalez, Julian, Sandusky	.361	97	20	35	7	0	5	17	5
Turner, Jason, Central Ohio	.357	126	22	45	12	2	3	33	4
Conway, Mike, Columbus	.357	98	16	35	6	0	0	20	3
Angell, Ricky, Grand Lake	.348	89	18	31	4	6	2	11	14
Ury, Josh, Sandusky	.344	122	26	42	3	0	1	10	7
Bobeda, Robert, Lima	.339	127	26	43	6	1	5	26	10
Olson, Tim, Columbus	.333	123	32	41	8	5	2	23	3
Estep, Joe, Central Ohio	.328	119	23	39	8	1	0	7	13
O'Hara, Bucky, Lima	.327	110	20	36	5	0	2	15	6
Mason, Matt, Grand Lake	.323	130	20	42	9	1	6	21	5

INDIVIDUAL PITCHING LEADERS
(Minimum 28 Innings)

	W	L	ERA	G	SV	IP	H	BB	SO
Cummings, Jeremy, Columbus	6	2	1.20	9	0	53	37	7	41
Miller, Brandon, Lima	5	0	1.37	8	0	39	27	10	25
Kelley, Jason, Grand Lake	3	2	1.46	6	0	37	22	12	20
Sanford, Casey, Grand Lake	3	1	1.59	7	0	45	37	10	27
Sutter, Jake, Grand Lake	4	1	1.64	9	1	33	25	15	29
Fry, Justin, Central Ohio	6	1	1.72	7	0	47	28	19	50
Wells, Chad, Grand Lake	2	1	2.23	9	0	40	34	9	26
Biniker, Jason, Sandusky	2	3	3.21	7	0	28	24	11	18
Magill, Steve, Columbus	1	2	3.21	6	1	28	23	8	37

NEW ENGLAND COLLEGIATE LEAGUE

	W	L	PCT	GB
Torrington Twisters	30	12	.714	—
Danbury Westerners	25	17	.595	5
Middletown Giants	24	18	.571	6
Rhode Island Reds	21	21	.500	9
Keene Swamp Bats	18	24	.429	12
Eastern Tides	15	27	.357	15
Central Mass Collegians	14	28	.333	16

PLAYOFFS: Torrington defeated Rhode Island 2-0 and Middletown defeated Danbury 2-0 in best-of-3 semifinals. Middletown defeated Torrington 3-1 in best-of-5 final.

ALL-STAR TEAM: C—Kevin Leighton, Danbury (Seton Hall). **1B**—Sean McGowan, Rhode Island (Boston College). **2B**—Shawn Larkin, Keene (Cypress, Calif., CC). **3B**—Shawn Fagan, Danbury (Penn State). **SS**—Fritz Sanches, Danbury (New Haven, Conn.). **OF**—Gil Barkman, Keene (Wagner); Aaron Fera, Rhode Island (Georgia College); Mark Malaska, Danbury (Akron). **DH**—Bud Blair, Central Mass (National Christian, Texas). **P**—Steven Bechard, Torrington (LeMoyne); Scott Martin, Middletown (Central Connecticut State); Kevin Olore, Middletown (Marist).

Most Valuable Player: Aaron Fera, Rhode Island. **Pitcher of the Year:** Kevin Olore, Middletown.

INDIVIDUAL BATTING LEADERS
(Minimum 113 Plate Appearances)

	AVG	AB	R	H	2B	3B	HR	RBI	SB
McGowan, Sean, RI	.417	139	26	58	9	0	8	28	2
Fera, Aaron, Rhode Island	.362	149	37	54	11	0	14	40	4
Malaska, Mark, Danbury	.356	163	40	58	8	7	11	40	11
Fagan, Shawn, Danbury	.346	153	35	53	10	0	6	31	7
O'Keefe, Mike, Rhode Island	.338	133	25	45	7	1	6	26	5
Johnson, Forrest, Torrington	.336	125	22	42	10	0	1	23	14
Leighton, Brian, Danbury	.336	140	30	47	9	0	7	32	2
Blair, Bud, Central Mass	.333	156	25	52	6	2	11	41	0
Sanches, Fritz, Danbury	.331	142	34	47	11	0	4	21	14
Katz, Glenn, Middletown	.326	135	25	44	7	1	7	28	16
Bitter, Jarrod, Torrington	.323	155	26	50	13	1	6	40	3
Barkman, Gil, Keene	.321	137	27	44	8	0	14	36	1
Wissner, Kevin, Middletown	.315	143	20	45	11	1	4	21	0

INDIVIDUAL PITCHING LEADERS
(Minimum 34 Innings)

	W	L	ERA	G	SV	IP	H	BB	SO
Poturnicki, Adam, Middletown	3	0	2.04	5	0	35	21	13	38
Bonehill, Tim, Eastern	2	2	2.23	8	1	44	39	22	49
Bennett, Steve, Torrington	4	2	2.61	7	1	38	29	16	34
Connolly, Douglas, CM	3	3	2.62	8	0	55	45	15	38
Olore, Kevin, Middletown	4	1	2.65	8	0	58	48	25	81
Kelly, Ryan, Danbury	3	3	2.70	19	2	50	33	14	47
Bechard, Steven, Torrington	6	3	2.81	9	0	64	57	10	47
Martin, Scott, Middletown	5	3	2.83	8	0	57	49	18	51
Burns, John, Eastern	3	1	2.88	6	0	41	26	20	30
Smith, Michael, Middletown	4	3	2.93	8	0	58	51	29	55

NORTHEASTERN LEAGUE

EAST	W	L	PCT	GB
Newark Raptors	27	15	.643	—
Geneva Knights	25	16	.610	1½
Wellsville Nitros	20	22	.476	7
Hornell Dodgers	15	27	.357	12
WEST	**W**	**L**	**PCT**	**GB**
Cortland Apples	24	18	.571	—
Ithaca Lakers	24	18	.571	—
Rome Indians	23	18	.561	½
Schenectady Mohawks	10	32	.238	14

PLAYOFFS: Cortland defeated Ithaca 2-1 and Geneva defeated Newark 2-0 in best-of-3 semifinals. Geneva defeated Cortland in one-game final.

INDIVIDUAL BATTING LEADERS
(Minimum 120 Plate Appearances)

	AVG	AB	R	H	2B	3B	HR	RBI	SB
Kerner, Craig, Rome	.388	129	23	50	5	6	2	33	21
Blair, Jeff, Geneva	.380	108	29	41	7	1	4	16	4
Hays, Chris, Ithaca	.358	148	23	53	16	1	3	32	6
Peck, Bryan, Wellsville	.352	182	38	64	12	4	5	15	19
Rayola, Mike, Schenectady	.343	134	17	46	11	0	6	26	2
Lakey, Aaron, Wellsville	.342	152	28	52	9	3	4	27	2
Vandemore, Tony, Wellsville	.336	137	21	46	10	0	7	43	11
Thomas, Kyle, Wellsville	.328	122	14	40	9	3	0	22	4
DeVore, Doug, Ithaca	.328	119	15	39	10	1	2	19	3
Tekulve, Chris, Cortland	.324	142	29	46	9	1	0	24	2

INDIVIDUAL PITCHING LEADERS
(Minimum 40 Innings)

	W	L	ERA	G	SV	IP	H	BB	SO
Sturkie, Scott, Wellsville	6	3	1.72	11	0	78	66	17	59
Cavey, Scott, Ithaca	5	1	1.76	6	0	41	34	13	33
McShea, Dan, Ithaca	4	3	1.88	7	0	48	37	24	34
McGee, Denny, Ithaca	6	0	2.13	8	0	42	25	32	44
Kamishima, Takashi, Well	3	0	2.23	17	8	28	11	11	32
Pines, Derek, Newark	4	1	2.25	8	0	56	52	15	40
Byrd, Corey, Newark	7	0	2.42	7	0	48	44	10	34

SAN DIEGO COLLEGIATE LEAGUE

FIRST HALF

AMERICAN	W	L	PCT	GB	NATIONAL	W	L	PCT	GB
Indians	10	3	.769	—	Padres	9	6	.600	—
Orioles	5	8	.385	5	Cubs	7	8	.467	2
Royals	4	9	.308	6	Mets	7	8	.467	2

SECOND HALF

AMERICAN	W	L	PCT	GB	NATIONAL	W	L	PCT	GB
Royals	8	6	.571	—	Cubs	11	2	.846	—
Indians	7	7	.500	1	Padres	8	6	.571	3½
Orioles	4	10	.286	4	Mets	4	11	.267	8

PLAYOFFS: Cubs defeated Padres and Royals defeated Indians in one-game semifinals. Cubs defeated Royals 2-0 in best-of-3 final.

INDIVIDUAL BATTING LEADERS
(Minimum 72 Plate Appearances)

	AVG	AB	R	H	2B	3B	HR	RBI	SB
Peters, James, Indians	.451	71	16	32	2	3	1	22	7
Vinh, Johnny, Royals	.450	80	24	36	4	2	0	15	15
Sleeth, Kyle, Mets	.443	79	14	35	8	1	0	8	5
Felice, Josh, Padres	.405	79	13	32	1	1	1	9	10
Richardson, Mike, Cubs	.392	74	14	29	2	1	3	27	12
Engel, Dustin, Indians	.354	65	25	23	3	3	0	12	9
Harrison, Craig, Royals	.350	80	14	28	2	2	1	16	0
Beare, Greg, Royals	.343	70	6	24	3	0	0	9	1
Ivory, Russell, Orioles	.338	68	16	23	2	1	0	4	16
Santoni, Tim, Indians	.333	72	11	24	3	1	3	21	9

INDIVIDUAL PITCHING LEADERS
(Minimum 30 Innings)

	W	L	ERA	G	SV	IP	H	BB	SO
Powers, Travis, Royals	4	2	1.09	11	0	45	30	14	48
Light, Dion, Indians	2	1	1.16	8	0	36	22	14	25
Harris, Toby, Padres	5	1	1.59	8	0	40	39	16	47
Crowther, Jackson, Cubs	4	3	1.59	7	0	44	35	16	45
Gray, Kevin, Mets	4	4	1.68	12	1	42	45	18	34
Thomas, Dan, Padres	4	2	1.79	7	0	43	25	18	55

SHENANDOAH VALLEY LEAGUE

	W	L	PCT	GB
Staunton Braves	24	16	.600	
Harrisonburg Turks	23	17	.575	1
Waynesboro Generals	23	17	.575	1
Front Royal Cardinals	18	22	.450	6
New Market Rebels	17	23	.425	7
Winchester Royals	15	25	.375	9

PLAYOFFS: Waynesboro defeated Harrisonburg 3-1 and Staunton defeated Front Royal 3-2 in best-of-5 semifinals. Waynesboro defeated Staunton 3-0 in best-of-5 finals.

INDIVIDUAL BATTING LEADERS

(Minimum 100 Plate Appearances)

	AVG	AB	R	H	2B	3B	HR	RBI	SB
Rewers, Nathan, FR	.388	170	39	66	11	0	1	18	16
Olkowski, Kevin, Wayne	.358	173	36	62	12	0	0	33	8
Core, Willie, Waynesboro	.348	155	24	54	11	0	2	35	6
Salargo, Steve, Staunton	.339	177	32	60	7	0	6	31	19
Asche, Kirk, New Market	.321	134	35	43	11	1	12	32	7
Haynes, Charles, FR	.315	124	22	39	11	0	9	33	1
Wenner, Michael, FR	.308	117	19	36	9	2	0	9	10
Foltynowicz, Roger, NM	.306	124	15	38	8	0	5	21	1
Campo, Michael, Wayne	.306	144	36	44	9	2	2	21	13
Anderson, Jon, Harr.	.306	108	19	33	2	1	0	9	16
Marquie, Craig, Harr.	.301	146	22	44	6	1	3	22	3
Fernandez, Luis, NM	.301	103	12	31	5	0	1	19	5
Haas, Trevor, Winchester	.298	104	17	31	4	0	0	9	2
Arnott, George, Winchester	.297	118	24	35	7	0	4	17	1
Koonin, Jason, FR	.289	135	24	39	5	2	3	18	11

INDIVIDUAL PITCHING LEADERS

(Minimum 30 Innings)

	W	L	ERA	G	SV	IP	H	BB	SO
Arnold, Jason, Staunton	0	2	1.10	22	9	33	22	11	51
Ross, Lewis, Waynesboro	5	2	1.37	12	0	59	45	7	72
Zaffis, Jerry, New Market	3	0	1.51	14	1	36	32	18	36
Bailey, David, Winchester	7	2	1.66	11	0	76	54	23	80
Rauch, Jon, Harrisonburg	8	1	1.69	12	0	85	51	24	126
Murphy, Tommy, Staunton	3	0	2.06	10	0	39	28	10	44
Jackson, Jeremy, Wayne.	5	3	2.59	13	1	66	58	15	64
Scott, Joshua, Harrisonburg	2	1	2.70	9	1	33	28	15	25
Regilio, Nicholas, Staunton	2	3	2.84	7	0	38	34	8	60
Prendes, Alex, Staunton	2	2	2.91	18	1	34	27	20	46
Cramblitt, Stephen, NM	2	2	2.91	5	0	34	26	15	30

NON-CERTIFIED LEAGUES

ALASKA LEAGUE

	League				Overall	
	W	L	PCT	GB	W	L
Kenai Peninsula Oilers	17	12	.586	—	33	18
Anchorage Bucs	17	12	.586	—	26	16
Anchorage Glacier Pilots	16	13	.555	1	27	18
Mat-Su Miners	15	14	.517	2	21	24
Alaska Goldpanners	14	15	.483	3	26	19
Hawaii Island Movers	8	21	.276	9	17	25

ALL-ALASKA TEAM: C—Dane Sardinha, Hawaii (Pepperdine). **1B**—Ryan Neill, Bucs (Oral Roberts). **2B**—Elliott Strankman, Bucs (Lewis-Clark, Idaho, State). **3B**—Mike Cervenak, Alaska (Michigan). **SS**—Brian Oxley, Mat-Su (Los Medanos, Calif., JC). **OF**—Phil Downing, Kenai (Southern Utah); Jeremy Johnson, Kenai (Southeast Missouri State); Paul Lockhart, Alaska (San Diego State). **Util**—Andrew Beinbrink, Bucs (Arizona State); Wes McCrotty, Glacier Pilots (Arkansas). **DH**—Ken Harvey, Kenai (Nebraska). **P**—Marc Bluma, Glacier Pilots (Wichita State); George Carralejo, Bucs (Cal State Fullerton); Kyle Crowell, Kenai (Houston); Jeremy Cunningham, Mat-Su (Cal Poly San Luis Obispo).

Most Valuable Player: Jeremy Cunningham, Mat-Su. **Manager of the Year:** Scott Marr, Kenai (Oral Roberts).

INDIVIDUAL BATTING LEADERS

(Minimum 100 Plate Appearances)

	AVG	AB	R	H	2B	3B	HR	RBI	SB
Clements, Jason, Kenai	.355	93	23	33	8	2	1	14	15
Beinbrink, Andrew, Bucs	.351	97	17	34	9	1	3	25	17
Hymes, Michael, Alaska	.350	100	24	35	2	1	0	9	11
Salter, John, Alaska	.345	139	21	48	11	0	1	25	3
Johnson, Jeremy, Kenai	.337	163	31	55	9	1	1	15	9
Sardinha, Dane, Hawaii	.333	147	19	49	9	4	1	26	8
Lockhart, Paul, Alaska	.329	161	41	53	5	4	3	31	8
Alvarado, Damien, Bucs	.323	127	10	41	1	0	1	[illegible]	[illegible]
Harvey, Ken, Kenai	.321	162	21	52	11	0	2	40	5
Chan, Steve, Mat-Su	.319	94	9	30	4	4	0	11	8
Downing, Phil, Kenai	.312	170	34	53	7	2	2	26	21
Neill, Ryan, Bucs	.311	135	24	42	7	4	0	17	14
Tillman, Kevin, Bucs	.311	135	25	42	6	0	0	14	9
Yamaguchi, Lon, Hawaii	.301	133	24	40	4	4	2	18	12
Belfanti, Matt, Pilots	.298	121	15	36	5	3	1	11	5
Strankman, Elliott, Bucs	.297	145	20	43	8	1	1	25	9
Hamill, Ryan, Pilots	.290	124	17	36	9	0	2	17	2
Kimura, Don, Hawaii	.289	135	19	39	4	0	1	22	10
Oxley, Brian, Mat-Su	.288	153	24	44	5	1	4	17	11
Hughes, Todd, Bucs	.287	150	36	43	2	1	1	14	35
Martines, Scooter, Hawaii	.286	98	17	28	2	1	1	6	5
Cervenak, Mike, Alaska	.282	174	38	49	12	4	5	30	4
Wood, Darrin, Pilots	.278	158	31	44	9	1	2	22	11
Wood, Steve, Pilots	.275	142	21	39	12	0	2	18	0
Nicholson, Tommy, Pilots	.273	150	24	41	6	1	1	12	4
Bozanich, Sam, Kenai	.270	122	14	33	5	0	1	17	5

INDIVIDUAL PITCHING LEADERS

(Minimum 32 Innings)

	W	L	ERA	G	SV	IP	H	BB	SO
Norris, Craig, Mat-Su	2	2	1.05	7	0	43	33	14	26
Cunningham, Jeremy, M-S	5	1	1.47	7	0	49	40	7	43
Garner, Mike, Kenai	6	2	1.87	10	0	53	44	6	34
Kalita, Tim, Mat-Su	4	4	1.93	9	0	56	47	28	43
Schultz, Mike, Bucs	2	1	2.08	8	0	39	30	22	35
Battagin, David, Hawaii	5	2	2.09	20	5	47	43	13	38
McKeown, Chris, Kenai	2	2	2.09	10	2	39	30	15	23
Whitekiller, Jerel, Kenai	3	2	2.35	18	5	38	32	11	14
Carralejo, George, Bucs	5	2	2.40	10	0	58	40	40	48
Boyanich, Vincent, Bucs	4	0	2.48	8	0	38	33	11	32
McCrotty, Wes, Pilots	2	4	2.54	10	0	50	46	20	30
Crowell, Kyle, Kenai	7	1	2.59	12	2	66	38	30	72
Jones, Ian, Hawaii	2	3	2.76	11	0	49	40	11	39
Baugh, Kenny, Kenai	4	3	2.78	12	0	58	48	24	41
Gosling, Mike, Pilots	1	2	2.83	10	1	35	32	19	35
Gwyn, Marc, Kenai	2	1	2.87	13	3	47	43	16	36

CLARK GRIFFITH COLLEGIATE LEAGUE

FIRST	W	L	PCT	GB
Pr. William	13	5	.722	--
Herndon	12	8	.600	2
Arlington	12	8	.600	2
Reston	6	13	.316	7½
S. Maryland	5	13	.278	8

SECOND	W	L	PCT	GB
Arlington	14	4	.778	—
Pr. William	11	8	.579	3½
Herndon	8	10	.444	6
Reston	8	11	.421	6½
S. Maryland	6	13	.316	8½

PLAYOFFS: Arlington defeated Prince William 2-1 in best-of-3 final.

INDIVIDUAL BATTING LEADERS

(Minimum 85 At-Bats)

	AVG	AB	R	H	2B	3B	HR	RBI	SB
Williams, Geoff, PW	.367	128	31	47	4	2	1	17	22
Thompson, Rich, Arlington	.351	114	20	40	5	2	0	9	26
Valdes, Chris, Arlington	.324	105	16	34	4	0	1	16	6
Merical, Tommy, Herndon	.320	100	17	32	9	1	0	12	11
Miller, Greg, Herndon	.316	136	29	43	8	4	0	13	21
Blasi, Blake, PW	.310	126	28	39	5	2	0	14	14
Mackey, Jeff, SM	.310	87	13	27	4	1	0	6	2
Rueffert, Mark, Herndon	.289	97	15	28	2	0	3	20	1
Daubert, Jake, Arlington	.286	126	27	36	10	2	2	23	6
Ferrell, Randy, Reston	.286	98	10	28	3	1	0	7	10

INDIVIDUAL PITCHING LEADERS

(Minimum 40 Innings)

	W	L	ERA	G	SV	IP	H	BB	SO
Fleming, Sean, PW	5	3	1.36	10	0	53	46	14	65
Brock, Tanner, Arlington	4	2	1.37	11	0	46	33	21	51
Beggs, Bryan, Arlington	7	2	1.54	14	3	41	30	23	50
McCullers, Brendan, Hern.	4	2	1.71	12	0	47	27	6	34
Robertson, Luke, PW	6	1	2.06	13	2	52	36	18	45
Edwards, Chad, Herndon	5	2	2.69	15	1	70	61	25	62
Miller, Anthony, Reston	3	2	3.54	9	0	53	50	37	41
Eagle, Corey, Herndon	7	5	3.61	15	0	77	70	15	92
Porter, David, Reston	5	4	3.71	10	0	68	55	41	64
Edwards, Brad, SM	5	4	3.88	10	0	60	54	41	75

COASTAL PLAIN LEAGUE

	W	L	PCT	GB
Rocky Mount Rockfish	31	19	.620	—
Wilmington Sharks	27	23	.540	4
Wilson Tobs	26	23	.531	4 ½
Durham Braves	24	23	.511	5 ½
Florence Redwolves	23	24	.489	6 ½
Edenton Steamers	14	33	.298	15 ½

PLAYOFFS: Wilmington defeated Rocky Mount 2-1 in best-of-3 final.

ALL-STAR TEAM: C—Todd Kasper, Rocky Mount (Yale). **1B**—Mike Dwyer, Florence (Richmond). **2B**—J.D. Alleva, Durham (Duke). **3B**—Curt Fiore, Wilson (Loyola Marymount). **SS**—Jason Rummel, Wilmington (Towson). **OF**—Hugh Quattlebaum, Durham (Amherst, Mass.); Casey Stone, Florence (Clemson); Jason Dubois, Rocky Mount (Virginia Commonwealth). **RHP**—Brion Treadway, Rocky Mount (UNC Charlotte). **LHP**—Brian Adams, Rocky Mount (Clemson). **RP**—Robert Jones, Wilmington (William & Mary).

Most Valuable Player: Jason Dubois, Rocky Mount. **Pitcher of the Year:** Brian Adams, Rocky Mount.

INDIVIDUAL BATTING LEADERS

(Minimum 135 Plate Appearances)

	AVG	AB	R	H	2B	3B	HR	RBI	SB
Fiore, Curt, Wilson	.362	174	36	63	9	4	3	33	6
Quattlebaum, Hugh, Dur.	.329	173	27	57	9	1	4	23	4
Dubois, Jason, Rocky Mount	.324	170	29	55	11	2	17	51	2
Kasper, Todd, Rocky Mount	.308	117	12	36	7	0	0	13	4
Stone, Casey, Florence	.307	166	29	51	4	0	0	14	12
Ross, Donnie, Rocky Mount	.303	142	29	43	11	1	7	32	3
Rummel, Jason, Wilson	.295	176	42	52	14	1	8	32	12
Dwyer, Mike, Florence	.294	170	29	50	6	2	6	31	2
Morrison, Derek, Wilson	.293	140	20	41	9	1	0	20	4
Lombardi, Mike, Florence	.292	161	31	47	10	0	1	16	7
Folz, Jason, Florence	.292	168	13	49	7	0	1	16	2
Faulkner, Todd, Wilmington	.291	134	28	39	8	0	6	17	3

INDIVIDUAL PITCHING LEADERS

(Minimum 40 Innings)

	W	L	ERA	G	SV	IP	H	BB	SO
Horney, Michael, Wilson	5	2	1.82	10	0	74	47	35	57
Adams, Brian, Rocky Mount	10	1	2.11	11	0	81	67	23	60
Baumann, Chad, Edenton	4	5	2.31	12	1	74	49	8	60
Treadway, Brion, RM	5	1	2.85	10	0	73	44	38	78
White, Eric, Durham	5	3	2.86	12	0	63	61	35	47
Cook, Brandt, Florence	4	4	2.92	11	0	62	39	33	37
Burns, Casey, Florence	3	2	2.92	8	0	49	37	29	58
Stoop, Chad, Edenton	3	5	3.06	15	0	71	52	45	33
Bouknight, Kip, Wilson	5	2	3.10	10	0	73	68	21	80
Gordon, Sean, Wilson	2	5	3.12	17	1	49	40	19	59
Briggs, Matt, Wilson	4	4	3.19	10	0	59	55	23	41

JAYHAWK LEAGUE

	W	L	PCT	GB
Nevada Griffons	27	12	.692	—
El Dorado Broncos	22	16	.579	4 ½
Liberal Bee Jays	23	17	.575	4 ½
Topeka Capitals	18	22	.450	9 ½
Hays Larks	15	24	.385	12
Elkhart Dusters	13	27	.325	14 ½

PLAYOFFS: None.

INDIVIDUAL BATTING LEADERS

(Minimum 100 At-Bats)

	AVG	AB	R	H	2B	3B	HR	RBI	SB
Hill, Mike, Liberal	.379	124	28	47	9	0	2	19	8
Trosclair, Brent, Liberal	.377	130	27	49	7	1	2	21	11
Hooper, Kevin, El Dorado	.357	115	27	41	3	1	0	17	9
Sampson, Chris, Elkhart	.356	104	16	37	8	1	2	15	7
Mize, Matt, Nevada	.348	138	30	48	5	3	6	29	11
Price, Donny, El Dorado	.330	112	16	37	12	0	2	14	0
Moore, Ryan, Topeka	.330	109	25	36	9	3	0	13	5
Berns, B.J., Hays	.326	129	20	42	8	4	2	20	6
Hill, Koyie, Liberal	.322	143	20	46	8	3	0	18	7
Thompson, Marc, Hays	.319	119	30	38	10	0	2	7	18
Cravens, Quinn, El Dorado	.303	109	25	33	8	1	4	23	8
Caraway, Brandon, Nevada	.301	133	30	40	2	1	3	19	5
Hesse, Josh, Liberal	.299	117	16	35	2	1	0	16	9

INDIVIDUAL PITCHING LEADERS

(Minimum 30 Innings)

	W	L	ERA	G	SV	IP	H	BB	SO
Bradford, Mike, Liberal	5	2	0.85	12	3	53	53	12	74
Matzenbach, Brian, ED	5	2	1.38	9	0	52	41	14	38
Williams, Chris, Nevada	5	3	2.03	10	2	49	44	12	34
Stanford, Jason, Hays	2	3	2.70	7	0	37	29	15	25
McClain, Jeremy, Nevada	5	1	2.82	9	1	54	45	14	58
Orr, Ben, El Dorado	1	2	2.97	6	0	33	26	14	22
Philbrick, Rusty, Topeka	5	2	3.06	11	1	62	60	18	46
Nemer, Spencer, Hays	3	4	3.10	9	0	49	52	16	39
Anderson, Derek, El Dorado	1	2	3.26	5	0	30	41	6	23
Carson, Chris, Elkhart	2	4	3.45	7	0	47	48	11	46

NORTHWOODS LEAGUE

FIRST HALF

SOUTH	W	L	PCT	GB	NORTH	W	L	PCT	GB
Waterloo	24	6	.800	—	St. Cloud	21	10	.677	—
Rochester	18	12	.600	6	Wausau	14	18	.438	7½
Kenosha	15	17	.469	10	Grand Forks	11	19	.367	9½
So. Minny	14	17	.451	10½	Brainerd	7	25	.219	14½

SECOND HALF

SOUTH	W	L	PCT	GB	NORTH	W	L	PCT	GB
Waterloo	22	11	.667	—	St. Cloud	18	15	.545	—
Rochester	19	13	.594	2½	Wausau	16	15	.516	1
Kenosha	17	12	.586	3	Grand Forks	15	19	.441	3½
So. Minny	7	25	.219	14½	Brainerd	14	18	.438	3½

PLAYOFFS: Rochester defeated Waterloo 2-0 and St. Cloud defeated Wausau 2-0 in best-of-3 divisional series. St. Cloud defeated Rochester 2-0 in best-of-3 final.

ALL-STAR TEAM: C—Michael Frey, Kenosha (Austin Peay); Jeff Stevens, Rochester (UC Riverside). **1B**—Ed Erickson, Grand Forks (Washington). **2B**—Jeremy Vidales, Rochester (Oklahoma). **3B**—Dan Dement, Waterloo (Alabama-Birmingham). **SS**—Curt Lee, Kenosha (Long Beach State). **OF**—Val Pascucci, Rochester (Oklahoma); Rob Quinlan, St. Cloud (Minnesota); Chris Walker, Wausau (Purdue). **DH**—Pat O'Sullivan, St. Cloud (Freed-Hardeman, Tenn.). **Util**—Todd Fox, Rochester (Murray State); Jeff Duncan, Waterloo (Arizona State). **RHP**—Scott Albin, Rochester (Nevada); Josh Novotney, Waterloo (Western Kentucky); Kevin Davis, Rochester (Middle Tennessee State); Jordan DeJong, Grand Forks (Cal State Fullerton); Justin Reid, Kenosha (UC Davis); Matt Mahoney, St. Cloud (North Dakota). **LHP**—Tim Lavery, Waterloo (Illinois); Britt Carmichael, St. Cloud (Trinidad State, Colo., JC); Andy Cheek, St. Cloud (Appalachian State); A.J. Ampi, Kenosha (Santa Clara).

Most Valuable Player: Eric Page, St. Cloud (Memphis). **Coach of the Year:** Steve Foster, Wausau (Wisconsin-Stevens Point).

INDIVIDUAL BATTING LEADERS

(Minimum 173 Plate Appearances)

	AVG	AB	R	H	2B	3B	HR	RBI	SB
Duncan, Jeff, Waterloo	.386	153	48	59	7	2	1	24	22
Dement, Dan, Waterloo	.365	233	53	85	19	8	4	58	10
Reece, Eric, Grand Forks	.361	194	32	70	8	0	4	26	8
Lotterhos, Chris, Waterloo	.356	188	46	67	11	3	0	32	23
Quinlan, Rob, St. Cloud	.353	218	46	77	15	3	11	47	4
Scanlon, Matt, St. Cloud	.344	180	36	62	15	0	4	29	0
Vidales, Jeremy, Rochester	.344	224	39	77	11	0	3	24	4
Barmes, Clint, Kenosha	.332	217	41	72	23	1	3	37	15
Frey, Michael, Kenosha	.330	215	30	71	8	1	1	15	22
Fox, Todd, Rochester	.325	234	32	76	20	0	3	40	5
O'Sullivan, Pat, St. Cloud	.319	229	38	73	14	4	8	49	5
Hollod, Matt, Grand Forks	.317	164	34	52	10	4	3	19	4
Basak, Chris, St. Cloud	.316	158	40	50	6	3	0	19	6
Walker, Chris, Wausau	.313	227	40	71	10	5	1	23	24
Hutchinson, Barney, Roch.	.309	220	43	68	17	2	5	38	10

INDIVIDUAL PITCHING LEADERS

(Minimum 51 Innings)

	W	L	ERA	G	SV	IP	H	BB	SO
Davis, Kevin, Rochester	3	2	1.56	32	9	52	30	20	44
Albin, Scott, Rochester	9	3	1.72	14	0	94	83	22	104
Ampi, A.J., Kenosha	3	1	1.75	9	0	57	41	26	52
Lavery, Tim, Waterloo	9	1	1.87	13	0	82	56	22	62
Sierra, Abel, Rochester	3	4	2.29	8	0	55	39	26	65
Stewart, Jason, Grand Forks	5	2	2.84	14	0	76	69	40	57
Novotney, Josh, Waterloo	8	3	2.97	14	0	100	108	20	89
Mahoney, Matt, St. Cloud	6	3	3.11	13	0	75	65	26	63
Seiberlich, Eric, Wausau	2	2	3.23	24	6	53	60	23	42
Magrane, Jim, Waterloo	4	0	3.27	18	2	55	57	17	47

Amateur Draft

Drew signing, other lucrative '98 contracts may set wheels in motion for changes to draft

BY DAVID RAWNSLEY

J.D. Drew was never the first pick in the country and his bonus record was short-lived, but the 1998 draft centered so much around the former Florida State/St. Paul Saints outfielder that the rest of the '98 draft class sometimes appeared to be an afterthought.

At fields across the country, the first question between scouts was often "What do you hear about Drew today?" National beat writers, whose knowledge of amateur free agents usually extends about as far as their expense money at the end of the month, were writing columns and features. Even major league players such as prospective teammate Curt Schilling and future teammate Mark McGwire chimed in with opinions.

Drew had originally been selected with the second pick in the 1997 draft by the Philadelphia Phillies, although most everyone acknowledged that he, and not righthander Matt Anderson, the Detroit Tigers' No. 1 selection, was the most talented player eligible for the draft. But Drew's signability, even at that point, was enough to worry teams.

The Phillies quickly found they had a problem. Drew and agent Scott Boras were asking for a contract between $11 million and $12 million, basing their demands on the $10 million and $10.2 million signing bonuses that "loophole" free agents Travis Lee and Matt White had received after the 1996 draft. Philadelphia took a more conventional negotiating stance and it quickly became obvious when Drew decided not to return for his senior season at Florida State that the negotiations would be long and eventually acrimonious.

ROBERT GURGANUS

Stuck to his guns
Cardinals outfielder J.D. Drew held out for top dollar

Philadelphia's dilemma was complicated. Their top pick, whom they hoped to build their franchise around, was already being vilified for his greed by the media, the Phillies fans and the Phillies own players, led by Schilling. In addition, any offer they made Drew would serve as an expensive precedent for the 1998 draft, where the Phillies had the first pick, even if the offer was soundly rejected.

As the drama played out during the spring, Boras played the next card and had a petition filed through the Players Association with Major League Baseball's arbitrator, Dana Eischen, asking that Drew be declared a free agent. Their contention was that because the commissioner's office had unilaterally changed wording in the draft rules when Drew had played with the Saints of the independent Northern League the previous summer, Drew, as a professional, should not be subject to the 'amateur' draft.

Eischen ruled that MLB had indeed violated the Basic Agreement by changing wording in the draft rules but that he could not rule on Drew's status because Drew was not a professional player and not covered by the Basic Agreement. As could only happen

TOP 10 SIGNING BONUSES

Based on the stated bonus in major league contracts and the full compensation to be paid out in standard minor league contracts, here are the 10 largest bonuses of the draft era (as reported to the commissioner's office) that were awarded to players signing with the club that drafted them:

Player, Pos.	Club, Year (Round)	Bonus
1. #Corey Patterson, of	Cubs '98 (1)	$3,700,000
2. #Mark Mulder, lhp	Athletics '98 (1)	3,200,000
3. *Pat Burrell, 3b	Phillies '98 (1)	3,150,000
4. *J.D. Drew, of	Cardinals '98 (1)	3,000,000
5. Matt Anderson, rhp	Tigers '97 (1)	2,505,000
6. Rick Ankiel, lhp	Cardinals '97 (2)	2,500,000
7. *Chad Hutchinson, rhp	Cardinals '98 (2)	2,300,000
8. Troy Glaus, 3b	Angels '97 (1)	2,250,000
9. Ryan Anderson, lhp	Mariners '97 (1)	2,175,000
10. Kris Benson, rhp	Pirates '96 (1)	2,000,000
Ryan Mills, lhp	Twins '98 (1)	2,000,000
Drew Henson, 3b	Yankees '98 (3)	2,000,000
Felipe Lopez, ss	Blue Jays '98 (1)	2,000,000

*Signed major league contract.
#Signed contract with provision for deferred interest payments

DRAFT '98 TOP 50 PICKS

Signing bonuses do not include college scholarships, incentive bonus plans or salaries from a major league contract
*Highest level attained

Team. Player, Pos.	School	Hometown	Bonus	B'date	B-T	Ht.	Wt.	AVG	AB	H	HR	RBI	SB	'98 Assignment*
1. Phillies. Pat Burrell, 3b-1b	U. of Miami	Boulder Creek, Calif.	$3,150,000	10-10-76	R-R	6-4	225	.431	109	47	16	44	5	Clearwater (A)
3. Cubs. Corey Patterson, of	Harrison HS	Kennesaw, Ga.	3,700,000	8-13-79	L-R	5-10	175	.528	123	65	22	61	38	Did Not Play
5. Cardinals. J.D. Drew, of	None	Hahira, Ga.	3,000,000	11-20-75	L-R	6-1	200	.322	146	47	7	24	3	St. Louis
7. Reds. Austin Kearns, of	Lafayette HS	Lexington, Ky.	1,950,000	5-20-80	R-R	6-3	215	.500	88	44	10	43	21	Billings (R)
8. Blue Jays. Felipe Lopez, ss	Lake Brantley HS	Altamonte Springs, Fla.	2,000,000	5-12-80	B-R	6-0	175	.521	73	38	7	28	35	St. Catharines (A)
9. Padres. Sean Burroughs, 3b	Wilson HS	Long Beach	2,100,000	9-12-80	L-R	6-1	200	.528	89	47	7	40	12	Did Not Play
10. Rangers. Carlos Pena, 1b	Northeastern U.	Haverhill, Mass.	1,850,000	5-17-78	L-L	6-2	210	.342	146	50	13	52	12	Charlotte (A)
11. Expos. Josh McKinley, ss	Malvern Prep	Downington, Pa.	1,250,000	9-14-79	B-R	6-2	192	.500	78	39	10	39	5	Vermont (A)
12. Red Sox. Adam Everett, ss	U. of South Carolina	Kennesaw, Ga.	1,725,000	2-5-77	R-R	6-1	176	.375	267	100	13	63	15	Lowell (A)
19. Giants. Tony Torcato, 3b	Woodland HS	Woodland, Calif.	975,000	10-25-79	L-R	6-1	200	.449	98	44	13	40	10	Salem-Keizer (A)
21. Mets. Jason Tyner, of	Texas A&M U.	Beaumont, Texas	1,070,000	4-23-77	L-L	6-1	167	.385	278	107	0	31	39	St. Lucie (A)
23. Dodgers. Bubba Crosby, of	Rice U.	Houston	995,000	8-11-76	L-L	5-11	185	.394	221	87	25	91	2	San Bernardino (A)
24. Yankees. Andy Brown, of	Richmond HS	Richmond, Ind.	1,050,000	4-14-80	L-L	6-7	195	.484	91	44	7	50	6	GCL Yankees (R)
26. Orioles. Rick Elder, of-1b	Sprayberry HS	Marietta, Ga.	950,000	2-24-80	L-L	6-6	230	.509	110	56	17	44	15	GCL Orioles (R)
27. Marlins. Chip Ambres, of	Westbrook HS	Beaumont, Texas	1,500,000	12-19-79	R-R	6-1	190	.500	66	33	10	21	12	Did Not Play
29. Giants. Arturo McDowell, of	Forest Hill HS	Jackson, Miss.	937,500	9-7-79	L-L	6-1	175	.447	85	38	3	25	37	Salem-Keizer (A)
32. Cardinals. Ben Diggins, 1b	Bradshaw Mountain HS	Dewey, Ariz.	Did Not Sign	6-13-79	R-R	6-6	220	.573	89	51	11	49	5	Did Not Play
33. Expos. Brad Wilkerson, of	U. of Florida	Owensboro, Ky.	$1,000,000	6-1-77	L-L	6-3	193	.347	196	68	21	63	18	Did Not Play
35. White Sox. Aaron Rowand, of	Cal State Fullerton	Glendora, Calif.	575,000	8-29-77	R-R	6-1	200	.372	242	90	16	72	15	Hickory (A)
36. Rockies. Choo Freeman, of	Dallas Christian HS	Mesquite, Texas	1,400,000	10-20-79	R-R	6-3	195	.557	88	49	9	44	13	AZL Rockies (R)
39. Orioles. Mamon Tucker, of	South Austin HS	Austin	650,000	10-18-79	R-R	6-3	195	.515	97	50	9	47	14	GCL Orioles (R)
40. Rockies. Jeff Winchester, c	Archbishop Rummel HS	Metairie, La.	537,500	1-21-80	R-R	6-0	195	.481	81	39	9	35	0	AZL Rockies (R)
42. Phillies. Eric Valent, of	UCLA	Anaheim	615,000	4-4-77	L-L	6-0	195	.336	220	74	30	73	4	Clearwater (A)
45. Athletics. Gerald Laird, c	La Quinta HS	Westminster, Calif.	Did Not Sign	11-13-79	R-R	6-2	195	.630	108	68	8	46	42	Did Not Play
46. Cubs. David Kelton, ss	Troup County HS	La Grange, Ga.	$400,000	12-17-77	R-R	6-3	185	.600	70	42	7	37	22	AZL Cubs (R)
50. Reds. Adam Dunn, of	New Caney HS	New Caney, Texas	772,000	11-9-79	L-R	6-5	238	.533	74	40	5	16	32	Billings (R)

Team. Player, Pos.	School	Hometown	Bonus	B'date	B-T	Ht.	Wt.	W	L	ERA	IP	H	BB	SO	'98 Assignment
2. Athletics. Mark Mulder, lhp	Michigan State U.	South Holland, Ill.	3,200,000	8-5-77	L-L	6-6	200	6	6	3.40	85	80	19	113	Did Not Play
4. Royals. Jeff Austin, rhp	Stanford U.	Kingwood, Texas	Unsigned	10-19-76	R-R	6-0	185	12	4	3.11	133	118	32	136	Did Not Play
6. Twins. Ryan Mills, lhp	Arizona State U.	Scottsdale, Ariz.	$2,000,000	7-21-77	L-L	6-5	200	8	4	4.68	115	110	54	140	Fort Myers (A)
13. Brewers. J.M. Gold, rhp	Toms River North HS	Toms River, N.J.	1,675,000	4-10-80	R-R	6-5	225	5	3	0.89	55	24	8	112	Ogden (R)
14. Tigers. Jeff Weaver, rhp	Fresno State U.	Simi Valley, Calif.	1,750,000	8-22-76	R-R	6-5	220	10	4	2.98	124	108	37	156	West Michigan (A)
15. Pirates. Clint Johnston, lhp	Vanderbilt U.	Vero Beach, Fla.	1,000,000	7-2-77	L-L	6-3	200	2	0	2.66	20	10	13	26	Augusta (A)
16. White Sox. Kip Wells, rhp	Baylor U.	Sugar Land, Texas	Unsigned	4-21-77	R-R	6-3	195	13	4	3.70	124	121	44	135	Did Not Play
17. Astros. Brad Lidge, rhp	U. of Notre Dame	Englewood, Colo.	$1,070,000	12-23-76	R-R	6-3	200	8	2	4.15	80	72	39	93	Quad City (A)
18. Angels. Seth Etherton, rhp	U. of Southern California	Laguna Niguel, Calif.	1,075,000	10-17-76	R-R	6-1	205	13	3	3.23	137	113	29	182	Midland (AA)
20. Indians. C.C. Sabathia, lhp	Vallejo HS	Vallejo, Calif.	1,300,000	7-21-80	L-L	6-6	240	10	1	0.62	67	20	24	137	Burlington (R)
22. Mariners. Matt Thornton, lhp	Grand Valley State U.	Centreville, Mich.	925,000	9-15-76	L-L	6-6	210	0	1	2.61	20	18	13	33	Everett (A)
25. Giants. Nate Bump, rhp	Penn State U.	Monroeton, Pa.	750,000	7-24-76	R-R	6-3	185	7	3	2.62	106	85	25	135	San Jose (A)
28. Rockies. Matt Roney, rhp	Edmond North HS	Edmond, Okla.	1,012,500	1-10-80	R-R	6-3	225	11	3	0.68	91	62	55	171	AZL Rockies (R)
30. Royals. Matt Burch, rhp	Virginia Commonwealth U.	Elmira, N.Y.	975,000	12-21-76	R-R	6-3	185	12	4	2.59	139	113	41	122	Spokane (A)
31. Royals. Chris George, lhp	Klein HS	Klein, Texas	1,162,500	9-16-79	L-L	6-2	165	15	0	1.13	110	61	33	168	GCL Royals (R)
34. Tigers. Nate Cornejo, rhp	Wellington HS	Wellington, Kan.	865,000	9-24-79	R-R	6-5	200	4	1	0.88	42	16	3	85	GCL Tigers (R)
37. Astros. Michael Nannini, rhp	Green Valley HS	Henderson, Nev.	595,000	8-9-80	R-R	5-11	175	10	1	0.58	73	38	8	97	GCL Astros (R)
38. Giants. Chris Jones, lhp	South Mecklenburg HS	Charlotte	587,500	8-29-79	R-L	6-4	195	10	2	0.71	78	28	10	150	Salem-Keizer (A)
41. Giants. Jeff Urban, lhp	Ball State U.	Alexandria, Ind.	650,000	1-25-77	L-R	6-8	211	8	2	2.60	69	55	20	72	San Jose (A)
43. Yankees. Mark Prior, rhp	University HS	San Diego	Did Not Sign	9-7-80	R-R	6-5	220	8	4	0.91	85	50	14	88	Did Not Play
44. Phillies. Brad Baisley, rhp	Land O'Lakes HS	Land O'Lakes, Fla.	$700,000	8-24-79	R-R	6-9	205	8	3	1.10	64	34	23	86	Martinsville (R)
47. Royals. Robbie Morrison, rhp	U. of Miami	Loxahatchee, Fla.	475,000	12-7-76	R-R	6-0	215	3	1	3.72	39	32	9	63	Spokane (A)
48. Cardinals. Chad Hutchinson, rhp	Stanford U.	Del Mar, Calif.	2,300,000	2-21-77	R-R	6-5	220	10	5	4.89	99	93	58	115	Prince William (A)
49. Twins. Marcus Sents, rhp	Cookeville HS	Cookeville, Tenn.	495,000	8-12-80	R-R	6-3	215	6	3	2.66	55	31	22	92	GCL Twins (R)

in baseball's convoluted legal struggles, both sides claimed victory, but the bottom line was that Drew had to re-enter the draft.

"The ruling vindicated our position that they couldn't change the rules without our permission," said Michael Weiner, the union's associate general counsel.

"Our fundamental position that the arbitrator did not have the jurisdiction to award relief to an amateur player has been vindicated," maintained MLB Player Relations Committee counsel Rob Manfred.

The far-reaching impact of the decision was the short-term survival of the draft. Most in the scouting industry conceded that if players were able to escape the restrictions of the draft by playing in an independent league or foreign league and afterward declaring themselves free agents, the amateur draft as it exists today would be a wasted exercise.

The Phillies' Choice

On the high school and college fields during the spring, most scouts agreed that the Class of 1998 was above average in overall talent depth but that no single player stood out as the top player. This created another predicament for the Phillies as the holders of the first pick. Philadelphia scouting director Mike Arbuckle was getting far more attention in a couple of short months than normally anonymous scouts get in a lifetime.

The Phillies' deliberations narrowed down to four players. University of Miami third baseman Pat Burrell was acknowledged to have the best bat in the country but he was an immobile third baseman who was in the middle of missing half of the college season with back problems.

No. 2 pick
Michigan State's Mark Mulder

Lefthanders Mark Mulder of Michigan State and Ryan Mills of Arizona State were also candidates for the top pick. Both were mature college pitchers who could help the beleaguered Phillies staff in the near future. Mills, the whose father is former major league pitcher Dick Mills, had the better raw stuff, but Mulder, who had shot onto the national scene only during the Cape Cod League season the previous summer, was thought to be the more polished and mature pitcher.

Another son of a former major leaguer, third baseman Sean Burroughs from Wilson High in Long Beach, whose father is former American League MVP Jeff Burroughs, rounded out the Phillies' short list. Burroughs was eventually selected by the Padres in the No. 9 slot and signed for $2.1 million, a mere $2.012 million more than his father received in 1969 when he was the first pick in the country.

The intrigue over who the first pick would be lost much of its momentum when Burrell returned from his back woes in time for the NCAA regionals and immediately put on an awesome power display. Burrell hit a home run in his first at-bat, four more in the Hurricanes' Atlantic regional victory and led off the College World Series with an estimated 500-foot blast. He also passed all of the Phillies' predraft "buyer beware" medical exams.

BILL SETLIFF

Record bonus
Phillies spent $3.15 million on top pick Pat Burrell

"He has a power bat, which is one of the needs we had identified for the draft," Arbuckle said after drafting Burrell. "We felt all along that he was the player we wanted.

"His health was a concern, but we've seen all the CAT scans and MRIs and been at every practice and game he's played in since May 18. We think he's fine."

The intrigue quickly shifted back to Drew, who had returned to the Northern League to keep his skills intact. The Oakland Athletics held the second pick and were strongly considering selecting Drew as a bookend to their franchise outfielder Ben Grieve. The twist was that the A's were a small-market franchise in the midst of rebuilding and no one thought for a minute that they would consider Drew's demands.

Oakland scouting director Grady Fuson eventually decided on Mulder, but not before much soul-searching. "We're confident of Mulder's intentions and desire to play pro ball," Fuson said. "I think everyone in the organization was willing to fight it out with Drew, but that wasn't in the best interests of the organization. Mulder was too good to pass up."

Picking in the third slot with a deep and talented group of college pitchers available to them, the Cubs decided to break from their recent drafts and selected Kennesaw, Ga., high school outfielder Corey Patterson. Patterson was considered the top high school athlete in the draft, a center fielder with blazing speed and developing power.

The Kansas City Royals, with ownership problems, a tight budget and three selections in the first 31 picks, chose Stanford righthander Jeff Austin, Baseball America's College Player of the Year, with signability in mind.

Austin, a polished pitcher who was close to being major league ready, was not thought by most scouts to be the best pitching prospect on his own team, with that distinction going to righthander Chad Hutchinson. The Royals plan backfired when Austin, who was represented by Boras, took an unexpectedly hard-line negotiating stance. He still had not signed by Nov. 1.

Drew, Take Two

Where was Drew as the draft unfolded? Right where most predicted he would be, available for the St. Louis Cardinals in the No. 5 slot. Most teams quietly admitted that they had hoped Oakland would select Drew, knowing that the Cardinals had paid Boras client Rick Ankiel, a second-round choice in 1997, a then-draft record $2.5 million bonus the previous summer.

"Obviously, there's a lot of pressure on the Cardinals to handle the Drew situation with due diligence," one scouting director said. "The whole industry will be paying attention."

What the industry saw was the Cardinals quickly agreeing to terms with Drew on a complicated four-year major league contract with a $3 million signing bonus and major league contract money and incentives that could bring the total value of the contract to $8.5 million.

Drew made all the contract negotiations appear almost anticlimatic after his long-awaited professional debut. He made quick three-week stops in Double-A and Triple-A before making his major league debut for the Cardinals the night Mark McGwire hit his 61st home run. In 36 at-bats for St. Louis, Drew hit .417 with five home runs and 13 RBIs, one of the best major league debuts in memory.

Bonuses Skyrocket

The chain reaction to the Drew contract started almost immediately, with the most obvious losers being the Phillies. Faced with the possibility of losing their first pick for the second straight year or topping Drew's St. Louis contract, Philadelphia quickly negotiated a five-year major league deal with Burrell that included a $3.15 million bonus and guarantees that brought the total value to $8 million. Thus they ended up paying Burrell, a lesser player by all accounts than Drew, significantly more than they had offered Drew less than two months before.

Not only had the amateur free agent bar been raised, it had shot through the roof. There was little joy in baseball at the reality that Burrell had just been guaranteed more money than the defending World Series champion Florida Marlins were spending on their entire 1998 major league roster.

One important factor that the Burrell and Drew contracts introduced into other players' negotiations was the major league contract that allowed payments to be spread over several years. Boras, anticipating this change in the market, also demanded similarly structured contracts for Stanford pitchers Austin and Hutchinson, as did Mulder.

NO. 1 DRAFT PICKS, 1965-98

Year	Club. Player, Pos.	School	Hometown	Highest Level (#G)	'98 Team	Bonus
1965	A's. Rick Monday, of	Arizona State U.	Santa Monica, Calif.	Majors (1,996)	Out of Baseball	$104,000
1966	Mets. Steve Chilcott, c	Antelope Valley HS	Lancaster, Calif.	Triple-A (2)	Out of Baseball	75,000
1967	Yankees. Ron Blomberg, 1b	Druid Hills HS	Atlanta	Majors (461)	Out of Baseball	75,000
1968	Mets. Tim Foli, ss	Notre Dame HS	Sherman Oaks, Calif.	Majors (1,696)	Out of Baseball	75,000
1969	Senators. Jeff Burroughs, of	Wilson HS	Long Beach	Majors (1,689)	Out of Baseball	88,000
1970	Padres. Mike Ivie, c	Walker HS	Decatur, Ga.	Majors (857)	Out of Baseball	80,000
1971	White Sox. Danny Goodwin, c	Central HS	Peoria, Ill.	Majors (252)	Out of Baseball	DNS
1972	Padres. Dave Roberts, 3b	U. of Oregon	Corvallis, Ore.	Majors (709)	Out of Baseball	60,000
1973	Rangers. David Clyde, lhp	Westchester HS	Houston	Majors (84)	Out of Baseball	125,000
1974	Padres. Bill Almon, ss	Brown U.	Warwick, R.I.	Majors (1,236)	Out of Baseball	90,000
1975	Angels. Danny Goodwin, c	Southern U.	Peoria, Ill.	Majors (252)	Out of Baseball	125,000
1976	Astros. Floyd Bannister, lhp	Arizona State U.	Seattle	Majors (431)	Out of Baseball	100,000
1977	White Sox. Harold Baines, of	St. Michaels HS	St. Michaels, Md.	Majors (2,567)	Orioles	40,000
1978	Braves. Bob Horner, 3b	Arizona State U.	Glendale, Ariz.	Majors (1,020)	Out of Baseball	175,000
1979	Mariners. Al Chambers, of	Harris HS	Harrisburg, Pa.	Majors (57)	Out of Baseball	60,000
1980	Mets. Darryl Strawberry, of	Crenshaw HS	Los Angeles	Majors (1,559)	Yankees	152,500
1981	Mariners. Mike Moore, rhp	Oral Roberts U.	Eakly, Okla.	Majors (450)	Out of Baseball	100,000
1982	Cubs. Shawon Dunston, ss	Jefferson HS	New York	Majors (1,388)	Giants	100,000
1983	Twins. Tim Belcher, rhp	Mt. Vernon Naz. Coll.	Sparta, Ohio	Majors (329)	Royals	DNS
1984	Mets. Shawn Abner, of	Mechanicsburg HS	Mechanicsburg, Pa.	Majors (392)	Out of Baseball	150,000
1985	Brewers. B.J. Surhoff, c	U. of North Carolina	Rye, N.Y.	Majors (1,554)	Orioles	150,000
1986	Pirates. Jeff King, 3b	U. of Arkansas	Colorado Springs	Majors (1,180)	Royals	160,000
1987	Mariners. Ken Griffey Jr., of	Moeller HS	Cincinnati	Majors (1,375)	Mariners	169,000
1988	Padres. Andy Benes, rhp	U. of Evansville	Evansville, Ind.	Majors (295)	Diamondbacks	235,000
1989	Orioles. Ben McDonald, rhp	Louisiana State U.	Denham Springs, La.	Majors (211)	Injured	*350,000
1990	Braves. Chipper Jones, ss	The Bolles School	Jacksonville	Majors (622)	Braves	275,000
1991	Yankees. Brien Taylor, lhp	East Carteret HS	Beaufort, N.C.	Double-A (27)	Yankees (A)	1,550,000
1992	Astros. Phil Nevin, 3b	Cal State Fullerton	Placentia, Calif.	Majors (253)	Angels	700,000
1993	Mariners. Alex Rodriguez, ss	West. Christian HS	Miami	Majors (513)	Mariners	*1,000,000
1994	Mets. Paul Wilson, rhp	Florida State U.	Orlando	Majors (26)	Mets (AAA)	1,550,000
1995	Angels. Darin Erstad, of	U. of Nebraska	Jamestown, N.D.	Majors (329)	Angels	1,575,000
1996	Pirates. Kris Benson, rhp	Clemson U.	Kennesaw, Ga.	Triple-A (28)	Pirates (AAA)	2,000,000
1997	Tigers. Matt Anderson, rhp	Rice U.	Louisville	Majors (42)	Tigers	2,505,000
1998	Phillies. Pat Burrell, 3b	U. of Miami	Boulder Creek, Calif.	Class A (37)	Phillies (A)	*3,150,000

*Received major league contract with guaranteed incentives #No. of games at that level DNS—Did not sign

Hutchinson was considered to have perhaps the top arm in the country, but slid to the No. 48 slot because of his often repeated desire to continue to play quarterback for the Stanford football team, and the fact that he had turned down $1.6 million from the Braves out of high school. Perhaps not coincidentally, Hutchinson was also picked by the Cardinals and agreed to a $3.4 million contract, including a $2.3 million signing bonus. He agreed to give up his football career as part of the contract.

Oakland held firm and refused to offer Mulder a major league contract, having learned the hard way from signing former phenom Todd Van Poppel to a similar contract in 1990 that all the risk under those terms rests with the club. Mulder was able to collect a $2.944 million signing bonus with ineterest at the rate of 7 percent until the final payment was due in December 1999. That made the total value of the contract $3.2 million.

Kansas City had also held firm in refusing to offer Austin a major league deal. Austin, in turn, had revoked his eligibility at Stanford and was performing a repeat of the J.D. Drew scenario by not attending classes and maintaining his signing rights.

A WHOLE NEW BALLGAME

With the major league contracts and other innovative deals that were signed after the 1998 draft, it no longer is fair to judge the highest compensation paid to draft picks strictly on the basis of cash signing bonuses. Here are the top 12 guaranteed incentive packages of the draft era:

Player, Pos.	Club, Year (Round)	Bonus	Guarantee
1. *Matt White, rhp	Devil Rays '96 (FA)	$10,200,000	$10,200,000
2. *Travis Lee, 1b	Diamondbacks '96 (FA)	10,000,000	10,000,000
3. †Pat Burrell, 1b	Phillies '98 (1)	3,150,000	8,000,000
4. †J.D. Drew, of	Cardinals '98 (1)	3,000,000	7,000,000
5. *John Patterson, rhp	Diamondbacks '96 (FA)	6,075,000	6,075,000
6. #Drew Henson, 3b	Yankees '98 (3)	2,000,000	3,900,000
7. ^Corey Patterson, of	Cubs '98 (1)	2,895,735	3,700,000
8. †Chad Hutchinson, rhp	Cardinals '98 (2)	2,300,000	3,400,000
9. ^Mark Mulder, lhp	Athletics '98 (1)	2,944,000	3,200,000
10. *Bobby Seay, lhp	Devil Rays '96 (FA)	3,000,000	3,000,000
11. Matt Anderson, rhp	Tigers '97 (1)	2,505,000	2,505,000
12. Rick Ankiel, lhp	Cardinals '97 (2)	2,500,000	2,500,000

* First-round draft pick; declared free agent because of incorrect contract tendering.
† Signed multiyear, major league contract with guaranteed incentives.
# Signed contract with a sliding incentive scale; minimum incentive of $1.9 million is paid if Henson becomes a full-time baseball player after fourth year of college.
^ Signed contract with provison for deferred interest; bonus reflects contract's present value.

RELATIVELY SPEAKING

A number of oono of former big leaguers were selected in the 1998 draft. Here's a sampling of offspring selected:

Son's name (Father)	Club, Round
Felipe Alou Jr. (Felipe)	Astros (42)
Greg Bochy (Bruce)	Rangers (45)
Sean Burroughs (Jeff)	Padres (1)
Nate Cornejo (Mardie)	Tigers (1)
Hector Cruz Jr. (Hector)	Diamondbacks (11)
Casey Davis (Willie)	Brewers (30)
Travis Devine (Adrian)	Padres (4)
Brad Downing (Brian)	Angels (36)
Justin Dunning (Steve)	Mariners (12)
Jim Essian Jr. (Jim)	Royals (32)
Eduardo Figueroa (Ed)	Brewers (29)
Justin Hairston (Jerry)	White Sox (50)
Matt Howe (Art)	Athletics (29)
Isaac Iorg (Garth)	Blue Jays (48)
Ben Knapp (Chris)	Orioles (2)
Vince LaCorte (Frank)	Reds (26)
Adam LaRoche (Dave)	Marlins (18)
Dustin Matthews (Gary)	Cubs (46)
Mario Mendoza Jr. (Mario)	Angels (46)
Ryan Mills (Dick)	Twins (1)
Ryan Moskau (Paul)	Dodgers (6)
Bill Nahorodny Jr. (Bill)	Giants (40)
Jeff Nettles (Graig)	Yankees (47)
Mack Paciorek (Jim)	Tigers (31)
Tom Paciorek Jr. (Tom)	Mets (21)
Tim Raines Jr. (Tim)	Orioles (6)
Josh Renick (Rick)	Pirates (47)
Jason Reuss (Jerry)	Diamondbacks (26)
Shaun Rudi (Joe)	Rangers (48)
Mike Stafford (Bill)	Blue Jays (41)
Derek Wathan (John)	Marlins (2)
Matt Woodward (Woody)	Mariners (24)

"This is not a J.D. Drew situation," Royals scouting director Terry Wetzel said. "Austin is a very good pitching prospect whom we'd very much like to sign, but there is no way his value goes up by sitting out. He'll never see another offer as good as the one that we've made him just by the nature of his age and the type of pitcher he is."

One other first-round choice, righthander Kip Wells of Baylor, also took Austin's route and chose not to sign while also not returning to class, thus maintaining his eligibility to sign with the White Sox, who picked him with the 16th selection.

With signing bonuses skyrocketing, a significant number of teams chose to negotiate deals before the draft contingent on the player being available. Such prearranged deals are specifically prohibited according to major league rules but are a de facto part of the negotiating process for a large number of teams.

The first pick who was believed to have come to an agreement before the draft was Mills, the sixth selection by the Minnesota Twins, who agreed to a $2 million signing bonus while pitching for Arizona State in the College World Series.

Other first-round picks who agreed to pre-negotiated deals were Expos shortstop Josh McKinley (No. 11, $1.25 million), Pirates lefthander Clint Johnston (No. 15, $1 million), Giants third baseman Tony Torcato (No. 19, $975,000) and righthander Nate Bump (No. 25, $750,000) and Yankees outfielder Andy Brown (No. 24, $1.05 million).

Two-Sport Stars

Another factor that impacted the 1998 draft more than any previous draft were two-sport contracts. Before 1995, the entire signing bonus a draft pick received had to be paid out before the end of the calendar year following the player's contract date. A rule change that year enabled clubs to spread out payments over a period of five years if the player was a legitimate dual-sport athlete.

The rule was designed to give teams protection against dual-sport athletes taking their signing bonuses and subsequently quitting baseball to pursue the other sport, usually football.

Seven high picks took advantage of the new contract language to sign lucrative contracts. Two stood out in particular.

The Cubs agreed to terms with Patterson on a $2.895 million signing bonus shortly before Patterson was to attend classes at Georgia Tech. The first unique aspect of the contract is that while the payments were spread out over five years, they carried a guaranteed interest rate of 6.5 percent on all deferred payments, making the actual cash value of the deal $3.7 million.

The second notable factor was that Patterson did not even play football his senior year in high school and had signed a baseball scholarship with Georgia Tech. He had, however, been considered one of the top wide receivers in the country by prep football experts as a junior and his letter of intent with Georgia Tech specifically mentioned that he was welcome to join the football team at any time.

The other most notable dual-sport athlete was Brighton (Mich.) High standout Drew Henson. Along with being the nation's No. 1-ranked high school quarterback, Henson threw 95 mph off the mound and broke the national prep career home run record as a third baseman/shortstop. He undoubtedly would have been one of the first picks in the draft under different circumstances but slid all the way to the third round where the Yankees selected him.

Henson's $2 million contract not only made him by far the highest paid third-round selection in history but also enabled him to continue his football career at the University of Michigan. A provision of his contract guarantees him a minimum of $1.9 million if he turns to baseball full time after four years at Michigan, a higher amount if he leaves earlier.

Other dual-sport athletes to take advantage of the rule included Marlins first-round pick Chip Ambres ($1.5 million); Rockies supplemental first-rounder Choo Freeman ($1.4 million); Reds second-round pick Adam Dunn ($772,000); St. Louis second-round pick Tim Lemon ($650,000), the nephew of former major league outfielder Chet Lemon; and Colorado's seventh-round pick Matt Holliday ($885,000). Only Dunn, who was attending the University of Texas, had an agreement allowing him to continue playing football.

Probably the most surprising first-round selection was Matt Thornton, a lefthander from Grand Valley State (Mich.), selected by the Mariners with the 22nd pick. Thornton was primarily a basketball player before 1998 and threw only 20 innings during the spring. Many teams did not even see Thornton before the draft.

UNSIGNED PICKS

Players selected in the first 10 rounds of the 1998 draft who didn't sign by Oct. 31, and the colleges they decided to attend:

Round	Club, Player, Pos.	College
1	Royals. Jeff Austin, rhp	Not in school
	White Sox. Kip Wells, rhp	Not in school
	#Cardinals. Ben Diggins, 1b-rhp	Arizona
	#Yankees. Mark Prior, rhp	Vanderbilt
2	Athletics. Gerald Laird, c	Cypress (Calif.) JC
	Mariners. Jeff Verplancke, rhp	*Cal State Los Angeles
	Orioles. Alex Hart, rhp	Florida
3	Reds. Greg Porter, ss	Texas A&M
	Padres. Beau Craig, c	Southern California
	Rangers. Barry Zito, lhp	Grossmont (Calif.) JC
	Expos. Kevin Kelly, 3b	Duke
	Angels. Paul French, rhp	Arizona State
	Astros. Brad Busbin, rhp	Georgia Tech
	Dodgers. Alex Santos, rhp	*Miami
4	Brewers. Rhett Parrott, rhp	Georgia Tech
	Astros. Jason Van Meetren, of	Stanford
	Mets. Jason Moates, rhp	Alabama
	Yankees. Ivan Reyes, ss	Miami-Dade CC North
5	Blue Jays. Lee Delfino, ss	East Carolina
	White Sox. Steve Kelly, rhp	Georgia Tech
	Rockies. Ryan Shealy, 1b	Florida
6	Phillies. Tommy Whiteman, ss	Oklahoma
	Twins. Brad Pautz, rhp	*Minnesota
	Padres. Dale Deveraux, rhp	JC of Southern Idaho
	Braves. Victor Menocal, ss	Georgia Tech
7	Twins. Sam Taulli, lhp	Louisiana State
	Red Sox. Syketo Anderson, 2b	Chipola (Fla.) JC
8	Rangers. Brad Ticehurst, of	*Southern California
	Pirates. Chuck Crowder, lhp	*Georgia Tech
	Rockies. Justin Lincoln, rhp-3b	*Manatee (Fla.) JC
	Mets. Vince Vazquez, rhp	Miami
	Braves. Josh Karp, rhp	UCLA
9	Cubs. Steve Reba, rhp	Clemson
	Red Sox. Mark Teixeira, 3b	Georgia Tech
	Tigers. Don Sevieri, of	New Mexico
	Marlins. Mike Trussell, rhp	James Madison
	Diamondbacks. Brendan Fuller, rhp	South Florida
10	Cardinals. Pedro Zazueta, rhp	Yavapai (Ariz.) JC
	Twins. Ryan Lundquist, of	Arkansas
	Red Sox. Len Dinardo, lhp	Stetson
	White Sox. Stephen Bess, rhp	*Rice
	Rockies. Andrew Beinbrink, 3b	*Arizona State
	Angels. Justin Lehr, c-rhp	Southern California
	Orioles. Dustin Emberley, rhp	Northwestern State
	Marlins. Chris Heck, lhp	Clemson
	Braves. Charlie Bilezikjian, of	St. John's
	Devil Rays. Ben Keiter, rhp	Wichita State

#Supplemental first-round pick.
*College player returning to same school.

Ones That Got Away

The highest drafted player to pass up a chance to sign to attend school was 6-foot-6 first baseman/righthander Ben Diggins, who chose the University of Arizona over the Cardinals after being selected as a supplemental first-rounder. Diggins' situation was unique, but not of his own making.

The Cardinals had picked Drew with their first pick and selected Hutchinson with their pick following Diggins and signed both to lucrative major league deals. With the market on either side of him obviously out of sync, Diggins never really came close to agreeing to terms, turning down a reported $800,000 from St. Louis.

With signability an increasingly important and discussed aspect of the draft, it wasn't surprising that a number of players saw their draft position plummet based on their contract demands before the draft.

The most notable player whose status slipped for signability reasons was Severna Park, Md., third baseman Mark Teixeira, a switch-hitter with well-above-average power. The Red Sox reportedly offered Teixeira a first-round bonus of at least $1.3 million if he would agree to terms before the draft. But they were turned down. Word spread of Teixeira's status and he slid until the Red Sox took a flier on him in the ninth round. He chose instead to attend Georgia Tech, highlighting an astounding recruiting class by the Yellow

Jackets.

Two other potential first-round picks who appeared to price themselves out of that round were righthanders Brian Sager of Branford, Conn., and Josh Karp of Bothell, Wash. Sager, who was selected in the 13th round by the Diamondbacks, enrolled at Stanford. Karp, who was picked in the eighth round by Atlanta, enrolled at UCLA. Both were reportedly demanding upwards of $2 million to sign.

Down On The Draft

The overall mood of the industry toward the draft at the end of the year was not positive. The six highest compensation packages ever given to a player signing with the team that drafted him (Burrell, Drew, Henson, Hutchinson, Mulder and Patterson) belonged to the 1998 class and it was apparent to everyone that bonuses were out of control.

In addition, there was the overwhelming feeling that nothing could be done to redefine the entire draft process, which most people felt had evolved from a method of distributing talent to the most needy clubs to a high-stakes poker game dominated by agents and major league politics.

Baseball's new vice president of baseball operations, Sandy Alderson, addressed the issue during his first day in office.

"It's definitely an issue that needs to be addressed," said Alderson, formerly the president and general manager of the Athletics. "There are a number of ways the draft is no longer serving its original purpose. We're not redistributing the talent the way that it was intended. Even major league players are beginning to wonder if the money that is going to amateur players is being distributed the right way."

Rangers scouting director Chuck McMichael summarized his feelings and perhaps those of the whole scouting industry: "We just need to overhaul the draft, plain and simple. I know better than to think that we'll be able to roll back the type of money that we're spending, but there just has to be a better way of doing things."

Other highlights of the 1998 draft:

■ The draft was limited to 50 rounds and held over a two-day period, a departure from the unlimited-round, three-day format previously used. The change was voted in in January 1998.

■ Canadians and Puerto Ricans were noticeably absent from the upper levels of the draft. Only four Canadians were picked in the top 10 rounds, headed by shortstop Lee Delfino (Pickering, Ontario), a fifth-round pick by the Blue Jays. The first Puerto Rican selected was outfielder Jose Amador (Camuy, P.R.) by Seattle in the fourth round, continuing the island's demise as a talent hotbed.

■ Three players from the 1997 draft still under control by the teams that picked them that year were signed before the 1998 draft, or they might have figured into the early rounds. Lefthanders Steve Colyer (second round in 1997, Dodgers) and Matt Riley (third round, Orioles) were both highly regarded pitchers out of high school before attending Meramec (Mo.) Junior College and Sacramento City College, respectively. Righthander Matt Bruback of Manatee (Fla.) JC was only a 47th-round choice of the Cubs in 1997 before dramatically increasing his stock during the spring.

DRAFT '98

CLUB-BY-CLUB SELECTIONS

Boldface indicates player signed; draft order in parentheses

ANAHEIM (18)

■ **SCOUTING DIRECTOR:** Bob Fontaine

1. Seth Etherton, rhp, U. of Southern California.
2. Brandon Emanuel, rhp, Northwestern State U.
3. Paul French, rhp, Northgate HS, Concord, Calif.
4. Brian Oliver, ss, U. of California.
5. Darren Blakely, of, U. of Hawaii.
6. Jay Hood, ss, Georgia Tech.
7. Jeff Hundley, lhp, Bowling Green State U.
8. Jason Hill, c, U. of California.
9. Kevin McClain, rhp, Central Florida CC.
10. Justin Lehr, rhp-c, UC Santa Barbara.
11. Bill Mott, of, Santa Clara U.
12. Edward Welch, of, Point Grey HS, Vancouver, B.C.
13. Greg Jacobs, lhp, Cal State Fullerton.
14. Jason Huisman, ss, U. of Mississippi.
15. Jaime Germain, 3b, Jose Campeche HS, San Lorenzo, P.R.
16. Justin Ross, of, U. of Tennessee.
17. Doug Bridges, lhp, Embry-Riddle Aeronautical (Fla.) U.
18. Casey Kelley, 1b, Washington State U.
19. Justin Stino, lhp, U. of Missouri.
20. Ed Hurtado, rhp, UC Riverside.
21. Oliver Harwas, rhp, Warner Southern (Fla.) College.
22. Chad Berryman, rhp, Virginia Commonwealth U.
23. Ryan Braun, rhp, c-rhp, Edison HS, Fresno.
24. Chris Demouy, lhp, Louisiana State U.
25. Tommy Bond, rhp, U. of Florida.
26. Josh Schaffer, 3b, Esperanza HS, Yorba Linda, Calif.
27. Simon Stoner, rhp, Pasco Hernando (Fla.) CC.
28. Greg Moore, rhp, Ohlone (Calif.) JC.
29. Angel Diaz, c, U. of Tampa.
30. Ronte Langs, of, Gulf Coast (Fla.) CC.
31. Mike Leach, rhp, Florida Southern College.
32. Ryan Flanagan, rhp, Gulf Coast (Fla.) CC.
33. Kenny Corley, 1b, U. of Arizona.
34. Bobby Crosby, ss, LaQuinta HS, Cypress, Calif.
35. Ben Margalski, c, Belleville Area (Ill.) CC.
36. Mike Christensen, 3b, Florida Southern College.
37. Matt Tucek, rhp, Waxahachie (Texas) HS.
38. Chris Aronson, rhp, George Mason U.
39. Brad Downing, of, Cal Poly Pomona.
40. Will Croud, of, U. of Central Florida.
41. Doug Wakefield, lhp, Cal State Dominguez Hills.
42. Matt Lubozynski, lhp, U. of Central Florida.
43. Josh Warren, rhp, Polk (Fla.) CC.
44. John Steitz, rhp, Hopkins School, New Haven, Conn.
45. Cam Esslinger, rhp, Seton Hall U.
46. Mario Mendoza, rhp, Central Arizona JC.
47. Rudy Arguelles, of, Arizona State U.
48. Brian Ferreira, of, Manatee (Fla.) JC.
49. Bryn Wade, 2b, Biola (Calif.) U.
50. Edgardo Salgado, c, Florida Air Academy, Melbourne, Fla.

ARIZONA (30)

■ **SCOUTING DIRECTOR:** Don Mitchell

1. (Choice to Royals as compensation for Type A free agent Jay Bell).
2. (Choice to Tigers as compensation for Type A free agent Willie Blair).
3. Darryl Conyer, of, Mission Bay HS, San Diego.
4. Javier Lopez, lhp, U. of Virginia.
5. J.D. Closser, c, Monroe HS, Alexandria, Ind.
6. Brock McCarty, of, Ouachita Parish HS, Monroe, La.
7. Jeff Pass, lhp, Chrysler HS, New Castle, Ind.
8. Andrew Good, rhp, Rochester HS, Rochester Hills, Mich.
9. Brendan Fuller, rhp, Clearwater (Fla.) HS.
10. Tom Kail, of, Baldwin HS, Pittsburgh.
11. Hector Cruz, ss, Florida College.
12. Victor Hall, of, Monroe HS, Arleta, Calif.
13. Brian Sager, rhp, Branford (Conn.) HS.
14. Dan Meier, of, Arizona State U.
15. Chris Cervantes, lhp, Pima (Ariz.) CC.
16. Heath Corbett, of, McMinn County HS, Athens, Tenn.
17. Lamar Sturdivant, of, Woodbury (N.J.) HS.
18. Bret Prinz, rhp, Phoenix JC.
19. Jeff Barndollar, rhp, Saddleback (Calif.) CC.
20. John Egly, 3b, Mountain View HS, Liberty, Mo.

21. Paul Giambalvo, rhp, U. of South Florida.
22. Ryan Blake, c, Glenn HS, Kernersville, N.C.
23. Robert Hammock, c, U. of Georgia.
24. Troy Niehaus, lhp, Eastern Michigan U.
25. Steven Neal, 1b, Pratt (Kan.) CC.
26. Jason Reuss, 1b, Canyon HS, Anaheim.
27. Mario Knorr, of, El Capitan HS, Lakeside, Calif.
28. Justin Santonocito, ss, Mercyhurst (Pa.) College.
29. Mike Koplove, rhp-ss, U. of Delaware.
30. Charles Manning, lhp, Polk (Fla.) CC.
31. Carl Makowsky, rhp, Conroe (Texas) HS.
32. Mario Glaser, rhp, Edmonds (Wash.) CC.
33. Horace Lawrence, lhp, El Cerrito HS, Richmond, Calif.
34. Justin Kees, rhp, Southern Illinois U.
35. Russ Bayer, lhp, Naperville (Ill.) North HS.
36. James Rinne, of, Illinois Wesleyan U.
37. Matt White, rhp, Western Oregon U.
38. Justin Crivello, lhp, Edmonds (Wash.) CC.
39. Kirk Bolling, rhp-3b, Saddleback (Calif.) CC.
40. John Gouzd, rhp, Fairmont (W.Va.) Senior HS.
41. Justin Beasley, c, Butler U.
42. Jody Fuller, rhp, U. of Tennessee-Martin.
43. Adam Neubart, of, Rutgers U.
44. Courtney Hall, rhp, Edmonds (Wash.) CC.
45. Wilton Reynolds, of, Monte Vista HS, Spring Valley, Calif.
46. Ben Mitchell, rhp, Scottsdale (Ariz.) CC.
47. Cole Saben, rhp, Portland Lutheran HS, Portland, Ore.
48. Bryon Gribbons, rhp, Cooper City (Fla.) HS.
49. Joseph Bunton, 3b, Bell HS, Cudahy, Calif.
50. Lucas Gruner, c, Mayfair HS, Long Beach.

ATLANTA (28)

■ **SCOUTING DIRECTOR:** Paul Snyder

1. (Choice to Rockies as compensation for Type A free agent Andres Galarraga).
2. Matt Belisle, rhp, McCallum HS, Austin, Texas (Choice from Padres—52nd—as compensation for Type B free agent Greg Myers).
2. (Choice to Rockies as compensation for Type A free agent Walt Weiss).
3. Ryan Langerhans, of, Round Rock (Texas) HS.
4. Johnny McGinnis, rhp, Dacula (Ga.) HS.
5. Damien Jones, of, Vigor HS, Whistler, Ala.
6. Victor Menocal, ss, Gainesville (Ga.) HS.
7. Scott Sobkowiak, rhp, U. of Northern Iowa.
8. Josh Karp, rhp, Bothell (Wash.) HS.
9. Matt Targac, lhp, Sacred Heart HS, Hallettsville, Texas.
10. Charlie Bilezikjian, of, Port Richmond HS, Staten Island, N.Y.
11. L.J. Yankosky, rhp, Georgia Tech.
12. Greg Donato, 3b, Clovis (Calif.) HS.
13. Steve Smyth, lhp, Cypress (Calif.) JC.
14. John Ennis, rhp, Monroe HS, Panorama City, Calif.
15. Tommy Clark, of, Brunswick (Ga.) HS.
16. Rob Moravek, rhp, Simsbury (Conn.) HS.
17. Daniel Curtis, rhp, Central HS, Chattanooga.
18. Colin Stewart, of, Sonoma State (Calif.) U.
19. Zach Frachiseur, rhp, U. of Georgia.
20. Gregg Maluchnik, c, Duke U.
21. Aaron Garmong, lhp, Wayne State (Neb.) College.
22. Sean Bischofberger, c, Granite Hills HS, El Cajon, Calif.
23. Jason Mikels, rhp, Rio Linda (Calif.) HS.
24. Derrick Truitt, rhp, Columbia State (Tenn.) JC.
25. Kregg Jarvais, c, U. of Maine.
26. Brian Cox, of, Florida State U.
27. Bubba Scarce, rhp, North Carolina State U.
28. Louis Angulo, lhp, Miami-Dade CC North.
29. Tim Spooneybarger, of, Pine Forest HS, Pensacola, Fla.
30. Drue James, c, Southeastern Oklahoma State U.
31. Tim Lemke, c-3b, Immaculata HS, Belle Meade, N.J.
32. Nickolas Green, 2b, DeKalb (Ga.) JC.
33. Derek Clifton, rhp, Clear Creek HS, League City, Texas.
34. Paul Burke, c, Bellarmine (Ky.) College.
35. Marcus Hambrick, of, Robert E. Lee HS, Montgomery, Ala.
36. Philip Rosengren, rhp, Northwestern U.
37. Adrian Walker, lhp, Mission Bay HS, San Diego.
38. Kevin Benson, of, Century HS, Bismarck, N.D.
39. Casey Cheshier, 3b, San Jose State U.
40. Jerry Simmons, of, The Citadel.
41. Michael Perez, c, Palm Beach Lakes HS, West Palm Beach, Fla.
42. Eric Wise, rhp, Basic HS, Henderson, Nev.
43. Greg Birch, lhp, McArthur HS, Davie, Fla.
44. Dallas McPherson, rhp, Randleman (N.C.) HS.
45. Brad Voyles, rhp, Lincoln Memorial (Tenn.) U.
46. Josh Carter, 3b, Fallbrook (Calif.) HS.
47. Mike Gleason, rhp, Santa Fe Trail HS, Carbondale, Kan.
48. Jason King, ss, Englewood HS, Jacksonville.
49. Micah Nodah, rhp, Columbia HS, Live Oak, Fla.
50. Shaun Harper, of, Frederick Douglas HS, Atlanta.

BALTIMORE (26)

■ **SCOUTING DIRECTOR:** Gary Nickels

1. Rick Elder, of, Sprayberry HS, Marietta, Ga.
1. Mamon Tucker, of, Stephen F. Austin HS, Austin (Supplemental pick—39th—for loss of Type A free agent Randy Myers).
2. Ben Knapp, rhp, Oviedo (Fla.) HS (Choice from Blue Jays—51st—as compensation for Myers).
2. Alex Hart, rhp, Chambersburg (Pa.) Area HS.
3. Steve Bechler, rhp, South Medford HS, Medford, Ore.
4. Chris Davidson, rhp, Western Carolina U.
5. Josh Yarno, rhp, Moscow (Idaho) HS.
6. Tim Raines Jr., of, Seminole HS, Sanford, Fla.
7. Tim Nelson, 3b, Allen Hancock (Calif.) JC.
8. Randy Perez, lhp, El Capitan HS, Lakeside, Calif.
9. Francisco Monzon, c, Lorenzo Vizcarrondo HS, Carolina, P.R.
10. Dustin Emberley, rhp, Composite HS, Weyburn, Sask.
11. Eliot Tomaszewski, rhp, Sandia HS, Albuquerque.
12. Derrick Gutierrez, ss, Sandalwood HS, Jacksonville.
13. John Kremer, rhp, U. of Evansville.
14. Jason Bellamy, rhp, Conway (S.C.) HS.
15. Josh Doud, rhp, Round Rock, Texas.
16. Jason Pruitt, lhp, View Marana HS, Tucson.
17. Mike MacDougal, rhp, Wake Forest U.
18. Denis Gratton, rhp, Kitchener, Ontario.
19. Ryan Smith, rhp, Lake Howell HS, Longwood, Fla.
20. Clifton Lee, lhp, Meridian (Miss.) CC.
21. Antonio Mack, of, Boone HS, Orlando.
22. Dustin Brewer, rhp, Granite City (Ill.) HS.
23. Sam Berrien, 1b, Fort Meade (Fla.) HS.
24. William Whitecotton, rhp, North County HS, Linthicum, Md.
25. Joey Hammond, ss, UNC Charlotte.
26. Jason Mandryk, rhp, Valley Heights HS, Langton, Ontario.
27. Jared Jones, of, Walla Walla (Wash.) HS.
28. Jason Botts, 1b, Paso Robles (Calif.) HS.
29. Doug Slaten, lhp, Venice (Calif.) HS.
30. Richard Green, c, Coffee County HS, Tullahoma, Tenn.
31. Sean Fisher, lhp, Grand Rapids (Mich.) CC.
32. Troy Roberson, rhp, King's Academy, Boynton Beach, Fla.
33. Fred Brassfield, of, Bryan Station HS, Lexington, Ky.
34. Phillip Cullen, rhp, Chelan (Wash.) HS.
35. Jeffrey Gatch, rhp, Aquinas (Mich.) College.
36. Scott Moore, rhp, Cowley County (Kan.) CC.
37. Jason Benham, 3b, Liberty U.
38. Mike Smith, lhp, Fletcher (Okla.) HS.
39. Marc Houle, rhp, Des Moines Area (Iowa) CC.
40. Matt Crandall, rhp, Allen Hancock (Calif.) JC.
41. Cory Acklus, of, Cascade HS, Everett, Wash.
42. Matt Blethen, lhp-of, Havre de Grace (Md.) HS.
43. Derek Eddie, c, Seward County (Kan.) CC.
44. Selection voided.
45. Brock Ralph, of, Raymond (Alberta) HS.
46. Zack Lush, c, Florida Tech.
47. Sonny Garcia, rhp, Texas Southern U.
48. Kevin Fox, lhp, Citrus (Calif.) JC.
49. Mitch Jones, 3b, Utah Valley State JC.
50. Scott Ridenour, rhp, Potomac State (W.Va.) JC.

BOSTON (12)

■ **SCOUTING DIRECTOR:** Wayne Britton

1. Adam Everett, ss, U. of South Carolina.
2. (Choice to Cardinals as compensation for Type A free agent Dennis Eckersley).
3. Mike Maroth, lhp, U. of Central Florida.
4. Jerome Gamble, rhp, Benjamin Russell HS, Alexander City, Ala.
5. Josh Hancock, rhp, Tupelo, Miss.
6. Rick Riccobono, rhp, Commack (N.Y.) HS.
7. Syketo Anderson, 2b, Prattville (Ala.) HS.
8. Frederick Silverthorn, lhp, Pearce HS, Richardson, Texas.
9. Mark Teixeira, 3b, Mt. St. Joseph HS, Severna Park, Md.
10. Lenny Dinardo, lhp, Santa Fe HS, High Spring, Fla.
11. Carlos Rodriguez, of, Louisville.
12. David Benham, c, Liberty U.
13. Michael Rabelo, c, Ridgewood HS, New Port Richey, Fla.
14. Matt Phillips, rhp, U. of Delaware.
15. Lance Surridge, rhp, UNC Greensboro.
16. Jason Norton, rhp, U. of South Alabama.
17. Benito Flores, lhp, Cal State Fullerton.
18. Terrance Hill, lhp, Southern U.
19. Shon Norris, rhp, UNC Asheville.
20. Tony James, 2b, San Jose State U.
21. Andrew Checketts, rhp, Oregon State U.

22. Tom Linarelli, rhp, U. of Washington.
23. Andrew Larned, c, Fairfield U.
24. Josh Adeeb, of, Vanderbilt U.
25. John Hattig, ss, Piti, Guam.
26. Ben Kozlowski, lhp, Seminole (Fla.) HS.
27. James Gates, of, Butler HS, Huntsville, Ala.
28. James Blanton, rhp, Brevard (Fla.) CC.
29. Ryan Siebert, rhp, Germantown (Tenn.) HS.
30. James Garcia, of, West Torrance HS, Torrance, Calif.
31. Robert Floyd, lhp, Satsuma (Ala.) HS.
32. Keith Hart, 1b, Lubbock Christian (Texas) U.
33. Heath Heiberger, lhp, Putnam County HS, Hennepin, Ill.
34. Chad Johnson, c, Bradley U.
35. Mark Younk, c, Texas HS, Wake Village, Texas.
36. Tonayne Brown, of, Lurleen B. Wallace (Ala.) JC.
37. Tony Caridi, c, Klein (Texas) HS.
38. Dennis Tankersley, rhp, Meramec (Mo.) JC.
39. Rob Shabansky, lhp, U. of Arizona.
40. Phil Ledesma, of, Rider U.
41. Jason Fingers, rhp, Central Arizona JC.
42. Bryan Barnowski, c, Southwick-Tolland HS, Granville, Mass.
43. Ron Bohinski, ss, Lakeland (Fla.) HS.
44. John Parrado, c, Miami Lakes (Fla.) HS.
45. Jon Smithers, 3b, Florida College.
46. Chris Hart, c, Central Catholic HS, Clearwater, Fla.
47. Richard Smith, 2b, Liberty County HS, Marianna, Fla.
48. Darry Burgess, rhp, Alvin (Texas) HS.

CHICAGO/AL (16)

■ **SCOUTING DIRECTOR:** Duane Shaffer
1. Kip Wells, rhp, Baylor U.
1. Aaron Rowand, of, Cal State Fullerton (Supplemental pick—35th—for loss of Type A free agent Dave Martinez).
2. Gary Majewski, rhp, St. Pius X HS, Houston.
3. Josh Fogg, rhp, U. of Florida.
3. Daniel Mozingo, lhp, Ashtabula Harbor HS, Ashtabula, Ohio (Choice from Devil Rays—102nd—as compensation for Martinez).
4. Juan Santamarina, 3b, Gulliver Prep, Miami.
5. Steve Kelly, rhp, Fairfield HS, Hamilton, Ohio.
6. Matt Borne, rhp, U. of Kentucky.
7. Eric Fischer, lhp, Moeller HS, Cincinnati.
8. Mitch Wylie, rhp, St. Amrose (Iowa) U.
9. Gus Mosley, of, Wakulla HS, Crawfordville, Fla.
10. Stephen Bess, rhp, Rice U.
11. Mike Williams, rhp, Galveston (Texas) JC.
12. Kai Freeman, rhp, U. of Minnesota.
13. Gerald McCall, c, Meridian (Miss.) HS.
14. Solomon Johnson, lhp, Navarro (Texas) JC.
15. Nate Robertson, lhp, Wichita State U.
16. Ernesto Lowe, of, American HS, Miami.
17. Brannon Whatley, rhp, Kennesaw State (Ga.) U.
18. Chris Hamblen, c, Highlands HS, Fort Thomas, Ky.
19. Jason Stovall, lhp, Battiest HS, Bethel, Okla.
20. Erik Lohse, rhp, Hamilton Union HS, Glenn, Calif.
21. Andre Simpson, rhp, Mount Miguel HS, Lemon Grove, Calif.
22. Carlos Castillo, 2b, Miami-Dade CC North.
23. Todd Johannes, c, U. of Florida.
24. Caleb Reger, 1b, Bradshaw Mountain HS, Prescott, Ariz.
25. Mark Cochrane, c, Stoneman Douglas HS, Coral Springs, Fla.
26. Edwin Almonte, rhp, St. Francis (N.Y.) College.
27. Eric Battersby, lhp-of, St. Mary's (Texas) U.
28. Travis Edwards, of, Wilson HS, Long Beach.
29. Nelson Lopez, 3b, Monsignor Pace HS, Miami.
30. Jason Abreu, ss, Hialeah Miami Lakes HS, Miami Lakes, Fla.
31. Carlos Cline, 1b, Brookdale (N.J.) CC.
32. Todd Eames, rhp, JC of Eastern Utah.
33. Paul Reuer, of, Schaumburg (Ill.) HS.
34. Terrell Merriman, of, Averett (Va.) College.
35. Scott Atwood, 1b, North Florida CC.
36. Daniel Wells, c, Columbine HS, Littleton, Colo.
37. Jason Bernard, rhp, Gulf Coast (Fla.) CC.
38. Mark Buehrle, lhp, Jefferson (Mo.) CC.
39. Curtis Young, rhp, Grand Junction (Colo.) HS.
40. Michael Baetzel, ss, Kishwaukee (Ill.) JC.
41. Michael Mallonee, lhp, Southwestern (Calif.) JC.
42. Kevin Cameron, rhp, Joliet Catholic HS, Joliet, Ill.
43. Mike Scioletti, 3b, U.S. Military Academy.
44. Julio Guerrero, of, San Angelo (Texas) HS.
45. John Gusich, 3b, Deer Valley HS, Glendale, Ariz.
46. Vince Serafini, 1b, Lockport (Ill.) HS.
47. Nathan Boyd, rhp, Allen Academy, Bryan, Texas.
48. Ryan Costello, lhp, Milford Academy, Voorhees, N.J.
49. Ricardo Suarez, of, Miami-Dade CC North.
50. Justin Hairston, 2b, JC of DuPage (Ill.).

CHICAGO/NL (3)

■ **SCOUTING DIRECTOR:** Jim Hendry
1. Corey Patterson, of, Harrison HS, Kennesaw, Ga..
2. David Kelton, ss, Troup County HS, La Grange, Ga.
2. Jeff Goldbach, c, Princeton (Ind.) Community HS (Choice from Astros—62nd—as compensation for Type B free agent Dave Clark).
3. Kevin Bass, 3b, Fayette County HS, Fayette, Ala.
4. Jeramy Gomer, lhp, Durant HS, Plant City, Fla.
5. Aaron Sams, lhp, James Madison U.
6. Tony Schrager, 2b, Stanford U.
7. Keola De la Tori, rhp, Triton (Ill.) JC.
8. Will Ohman, lhp, Pepperdine U.
9. Steven Reba, rhp, Concordia Lutheran HS, Fort Wayne, Ind.
10. Nate Frese, ss, U. of Iowa.
11. Dustin Krug, rhp, Lassen (Calif.) JC.
12. Tony Zamarripa, rhp, Texas A&M U.
13. David Ericks, rhp, Illiana Christian HS, Lansing, Ill.
14. Thomas Lipari, lhp, Indian Hills (Iowa) JC.
15. Casy Grzecka, c, Santa Margarita HS, Laguna Niguel, Calif.
16. Omar Rohena, 3b, Casiano Cepeda HS, Rio Grande, P.R.
17. Eric Hinske, 3b, U. of Arkansas.
18. Carlton Wells, lhp, King HS, Tampa.
19. Joseph Ohm, rhp, U. of Wisconsin-La Crosse.
20. Dennis Cervenka, rhp, La Vernia (Texas) HS.
21. Larry Dant, rhp, Dana (Neb.) College.
22. Mikel Moreno, of, Arizona State U.
23. Michael Carey, rhp, Westminster (Calif.) HS.
24. Charles Redmond, of, Liberty Elyau HS, Texarkana, Texas.
25. Nick Moran, rhp, Elk Grove (Calif.) HS.
26. Eric Arnold, ss, LaPorte (Ind.) HS.
27. Tydus Meadows, of, Vanderbilt U.
28. Adam Cox, of, Thomas County Central HS, Thomasville, Ga.
29. Lawrence Alvarez, rhp, Nogales HS, Walnut, Calif.
30. Justin Smith, c, Lake Brantley HS, Longwood, Fla.
31. Leonardo Torres, lhp, Metro State (Colo.) College.
32. Matthew Griffin, ss, Southern Tech (Ga.).
33. Chris Brown, rhp, Northwestern State U.
34. Dustin Brentz, rhp, Moss Point HS, Pascagoula, Miss.
35. Matt Whitehead, rhp, Northeast Texas CC.
36. Ben Johanning, 1b, Osceola HS, Kissimmee, Fla.
37. James Lunsford, c, Grayson County (Texas) CC.
38. Chris Wood, ss, Central Florida CC.
39. Jerry Whatley, lhp, Atlanta (Texas) HS.
40. Jonathan Macklin, lhp, Hallandale (Fla.) HS.
41. Nate Beucler, rhp, Huntington Beach (Calif.) HS.
42. Kevin Boles, c, U. of South Florida.
43. Jacob Pierce, rhp, Longview (Texas) HS.
44. Juston Olson, rhp, Oak Park-River Forest HS, Oak Park, Ill.
45. Chris Connally, of, Texas Christian U.
46. Dustin Matthews, ss, Whitney Young HS, Chicago.
47. John Sprowl, ss, Bay HS, Panama City Beach, Fla.
48. Chris Kellett, c, Deltona HS, Orange City, Fla.
49. Greg Eubanks, rhp, Wellington (Fla.) HS.
50. Daniel Jackson, rhp, South Suburban (Ill.) JC.

CINCINNATI (7)

■ **SCOUTING DIRECTOR:** DeJon Watson
1. Austin Kearns, of, Lafayette HS, Lexington, Ky.
2. Adam Dunn, of, New Caney (Texas) HS.
3. Greg Porter, ss, Keller (Texas) HS.
4. Darrell Hussman, rhp, U. of Arizona.
5. Jayson Larman, rhp, Wayne (Okla.) HS.
6. Robert Madritsch, lhp, Point Park (Pa.) College.
7. Josh Hall, rhp, Glass HS, Lynchburg, Va.
8. Clint Vaughn, 1b, Oklahoma Christian U.
9. David Therneau, rhp, Bellevue (Neb.) U.
10. Jacob Wallis, c, Paschal HS, Joshua, Texas.
11. James DeHart, lhp, Texarkana (Texas) CC.
12. John Koronka, lhp, South Lake HS, Clermont, Fla.
13. Damien Hart, lhp, Coastal Carolina U.
14. Dennis Russo, rhp, Santa Fe Catholic HS, Auburndale, Fla.
15. Blane Layton, of, Jacksonville U.
16. Casey McEvoy, rhp, U. of Cincinnati.
17. Robert Ryan, lhp, U. of Southwestern Louisiana.
18. Gary Loudon, rhp, Shippensburg (Pa.) U.
19. Glen Joseph, rhp, King HS, Tampa.
20. Duane Price, of, Texas Tech.
21. Alex Kellner, c, Freedom HS, Morganton, N.C.
22. Jason France, lhp, Chandler (Ariz.) HS.
23. Travis Copley, c, U. of Tennessee.
24. Eric Cooper, rhp, Texas Tech.
25. Randy Stegall, ss, Cumberland (Tenn.) U.
26. Vince La Corte, rhp, Gavilan (Calif.) JC.

27. Cory Stewart, lhp, Boerne (Texas) HS.
28. Humberto Aguilar, 1b, Odessa (Texas) HS.
29. John Nix, rhp, Kingwood (Texas) HS.
30. Tim Birdsong, rhp, Southeastern Oklahoma State U.
31. Brad Salmon, rhp, Tate HS, Gonzalez, Fla.
32. Roger Sellers, rhp, North Central Texas JC.
33. Paul Sanchez, of, Hubbard HS, Chicago.
34. James Matan, of, UNC Charlotte.
35. Andrew Beattie, ss, St. Petersburg (Fla.) JC.
36. Chris Toomey, of, Long Beach State U.
37. Donald Caldwell, of, Jefferson HS, Tampa.
38. David Jensen, 1b, Green Valley HS, Henderson, Nev.
39. Randy Woodrum, lhp, Middle Tennessee State U.
40. Lance Cormier, rhp, Lafayette (La.) HS.
41. Justin Coffey, rhp, Chase HS, Forest City, N.C.
42. Robert Jenkins, of, Valparaiso U.
43. David Carr, of, Marquette HS, Milwaukee.
44. David Martin, c, Katy (Texas) HS.
45. Terrmel Sledge, of, Long Beach State U.
46. John Whiteside, rhp, Sunset HS, Beaverton, Ore.
47. Michael Grant, lhp, Charlotte Chritian HS, Charlotte.
48. Gerald Butt, rhp, Mayville State (N.D.) U.

CLEVELAND (20)

■ **SCOUTING DIRECTOR:** Lee MacPhail IV
1. C.C. Sabathia, lhp, Vallejo (Calif.) HS.
2. Zach Sorensen, ss, Wichita State U.
3. Scott Pratt, ss, Auburn U.
4. Ron Marietta, lhp, St. John's U.
5. Ryan Drese, rhp, U. of California.
6. Tyler Minges, of, Ross HS, Hamilton, Ohio.
7. Brody Percell, lhp, Oregon State U.
8. Chris Reinike, rhp, Mississippi State U.
9. Paul Day, 3b, Long Beach State U.
10. Michael McPadden, rhp, Port St. Lucie (Fla.) HS.
11. Jacob Reynolds, rhp, Giles County HS, Pulaski, Tenn.
12. Donnie Suttles, rhp, Western Carolina U.
13. Matt Wade, rhp, Parkview HS, Lilburn, Ga.
14. Brian Jackson, rhp, U. of Southern Colorado.
15. Matt White, lhp, Clemson U.
16. Richard Matsko, rhp, Shippensburg (Pa.) U.
17. Mark Koeth, rhp, Brookhaven HS, Carrollton, Texas.
18. T.T. Gallaher, of, U. of New Haven.
19. David Raymer, of, Sacramento CC.
20. Barry Patton, c, Mississippi State U.
21. Michael Dirosa, c, Coral Gables (Fla.) HS.
22. Carey Novits, lhp, Cal State Northridge.
23. James Sherrill, of, Monterey HS, Seaside, Calif.
24. Thomas Bost, of, Louisiana Tech.
25. Eric Mileski, rhp, Benedictine (Ill.) U.
26. Chris McMillan, 3b, Cal State Northridge.
27. Jeff DiPippo, c, U. of Southern California.
28. Rodolfo Rosales, rhp, Pima (Ariz.) CC.
29. Ruben Escobar, rhp, The Master's (Calif.) College.
30. Mike Pursell, 2b, Tulane U.
31. Marques Esquerra, ss, Point Loma Nazarene College.
32. Craig Brown, lhp, Tulane U.
33. Brian Strelitz, rhp, Temple City (Calif.) HS.
34. James Jurries, 3b, Brazoswood HS, Lake Jackson, Texas.
35. Randon Ho, lhp, U. of Hawaii.
36. Matt Ramie, 1b, Castle HS, Kanoehe, Hawaii.
37. Micah Simmons, ss, Paxon HS, Jacksonville.
38. Brian Minks, lhp, Neosho County (Kan.) CC.
39. Darrel Berck, rhp, Palomar (Calif.) JC.
40. Dan Guillory, rhp, Louisiana State U.
41. Brian Sullivan, rhp, Port St. Lucie (Fla.) HS.
42. Blake Whealy, ss, Oak Park-River Forest HS, Oak Park, Ill.
43. Dana Thomas, rhp, Fork Union (Va.) Military Academy.
44. Miguel Hernandez, 3b, Nuestra Senora HS, Bayamon, P.R.
45. Eric Bush, lhp, Washington HS, Pensacola, Fla.
46. Brandon Mauer, c, Bellevue (Wash.) CC.
47. Kevin Spaulding, rhp, Anacortes (Wash.) HS.
48. Garth Blumberg, of, Hoquiam (Wash.) HS.
49. Kevin Hooper, 2b, Wichita State U.
50. Omar Moraga, 3b, U. of Arizona.

COLORADO (17)

■ **SCOUTING DIRECTOR:** Pat Daugherty
1. (Choice to Astros as compensation for Type A free agent Darryl Kile).
1. Matt Roney, rhp, Edmond North HS, Edmond, Okla. (Choice from Braves—28th—as compensation for Type A free agent Andres Galarraga).
1. Choo Freeman, of Dallas Christian HS, Mesquite, Texas (Supplemental pick—36th—for loss of Galarraga).
1. Jeff Winchester, c, Archbishop Rummel HS, Metairie, La. (Supplemental pick—40th—for loss of Type A free agent Walt Weiss).
2. Jermaine Van Buren, rhp, Hattiesburg (Miss.) HS.
2. Jody Gerut, of, Stanford U. (Choice from Braves—71st—as compensation for Weiss).
3. Kevin Gordon, rhp, U. of Central Florida.
4. Luke Hudson, rhp, U. of Tennessee.
5. Ryan Shealy, 1b, Cardinal Gibbons HS, Fort Lauderdale.
6. Javier Guzman, of, University Garden HS, Rio Piedras, P.R.
7. Matt Holliday, 3b, Stillwater (Okla.) HS.
8. Justin Lincoln, 3b-rhp, Manatee (Fla.) JC.
9. Justin Carter, lhp, U. of South Alabama.
10. Andrew Beinbrink, 3b, Arizona State U.
11. Ryan Cameron, rhp, U. of Massachusetts.
12. Brian Brantley, rhp, Old Dominion U.
13. Juan Pierre, of, U. of South Alabama.
14. Vernand Morency, of, Northwestern HS, Miami.
15. Mark DiFelice, rhp, Western Carolina U.
16. Brandon Garner, rhp, Central Merry HS, Jackson, Tenn.
17. Josh Etheredge, 1b-of, Auburn U.
18. Jase Wrigley, rhp, Georgia Tech.
19. Doug Thompson, rhp, Louisiana State U.
20. Tom Whitehurst, of, U. of South Alabama.
21. Erik Johnson, c, U. of Central Florida.
22. Ryan LaMattina, lhp, St. Bonaventure U.
23. Richy Leon, 2b, Arizona State U.
24. Michael Mundy, rhp, Rutgers U.
25. Kevin Duck, 1b, Cal State Fullerton.
26. John Dumanich, rhp, Merced (Calif.) JC.
27. Manases Pabon, of, Hato Rey, P.R.
28. Jerry Johnson, of, Westark (Ark.) CC.
29. Aaron Geralds, of, Madison-Central HS, Madison, Wis.
30. James Hymon, ss, Leo HS, Chicago.
31. Mark Woodyard, 1b, Okaloosa Walton (Fla.) JC.
32. Greg Colbrun, rhp, Skyview HS, Billings, Mont.
33. Rocky Kirk, lhp, Cochise County (Ariz.) CC.
34. Paul Miller, of, Pleasure Ridge Park HS, Louisville.
35. Ryan Truxall, rhp, Miami-Dade CC North.
36. Geoff Boutelier, rhp, Cypress (Calif.) JC.
37. Ryan Wardinsky, ss, Flathead HS, Kalispell, Mont.
38. Tobias Bird, of, Cloverdale (Calif.) HS.
39. David Bernstine, c, Vallejo (Calif.) HS.
40. Joe Simpson, rhp, Southeastern Illinois JC.
41. Bryce Coppleters, of, Raymond (Alberta) HS.
42. Nyger Morgan, of, Willits, Calif.
43. Doug Baylor, of, Reagan HS, Austin.
44. Alfredo Amezaga, ss, St. Petersburg (Fla.) JC.
45. Frank Haase, lhp, Merced (Calif.) JC.
46. John McCanne, 3b, Mammoth HS, Mammoth Lakes, Calif.

DETROIT (14)

■ **SCOUTING DIRECTOR:** Greg Smith
1. Jeff Weaver, rhp, Fresno State U.
1. Nate Cornejo, rhp, Wellington (Kan.) HS (Supplemental pick—34th—for loss of Type A free agent Willie Blair).
2. Brandon Inge, ss-rhp, Virginia Commonwealth U.
2. Adam Pettyjohn, lhp, Fresno State U. (Choice from Diamondbacks—73rd—as compensation for Blair).
3. Tommy Marx, lhp, Brother Rice HS, West Bloomfield, Mich.
4. Andres Torres, of, Miami-Dade CC North.
5. Greg Peterson, rhp-of, St. John's U.
6. Bobby Sismondo, lhp, Ohio U.
7. Clint Smith, rhp, U. of Oklahoma.
8. Barry Tolli, of, Newbury Park HS, Thousand Oaks, Calif.
9. Donny Sevieri, of, El Dorado HS, Albuquerque.
10. Billy Rich, of, U. of Connecticut.
11. Seth Taylor, ss, U. of South Alabama.
12. Russ Cleveland, c, Chaparral HS, Las Vegas.
13. Laz Gutierrez, lhp, U. of Miami.
14. Calvin Chipperfield, rhp, Mt. San Antonio (Calif.) JC.
15. Doc Brooks, c, Central HS, Phenix City, Ala.
16. Greg Sain, 3b, West Torrance HS, Torrance, Calif.
17. Reggie Nelson, ss, Santa Ana (Calif.) JC.
18. Andrew Earley, rhp, Shaker Heights (Ohio) HS.
19. Galen Shea, rhp, Houston Baptist U.
20. Jim Hostetler, rhp, Fullerton (Calif.) JC.
21. Nate Forbush, c, U. of Utah.
22. Ryan Earl, lhp, Thousand Oaks (Calif.) HS.
23. William Madson, rhp, Carthage (Wis.) College.
24. Thomas Koutrouba, lhp, U. of Maine.
25. Derek Besco, of, U. of Michigan.
26. Craig DaLuz, 3b, Fresno State U.
27. Jason Colquitt, c, East Carolina U.

28. Lacarlo Moore, of, St. Xavier (Ill.) U.
29. Scott Lawson, lhp, Logan (Ill.) JC.
30. Keith Law, ss, DeKalb (Ga.) JC.
31. Mack Paciorek, 3b, Los Angeles CC.
32. Ron Bush, ss, College of William & Mary.
33. Brian McGowan, rhp, Queens (N.Y.) College.
34. Robert Stiehl, c, West Torrance HS, Torrance, Calif.
35. Joe Yingling, c, Camarillo (Calif.) HS.
36. Scott Stuck, rhp, Climax-Scotts HS, Climax, Mich.
37. Antoine Cameron, of, Ayala HS, Chino, Calif.
38. Edgar Varela, 3b, San Gabriel (Calif.) HS.
39. Ryan Cox, rhp, Southern Illinois U.-Edwardsville.
40. David Mendez, of, Lehman HS, Bronx, N.Y.
41. Chris Tiller, rhp, Panola (Texas) JC.
42. Kevin Estrada, ss, El Segundo (Calif.) JC.
43. Keith Perez, rhp, Holly (Mich.) HS.
44. Craig Bowser, of, Lufkin (Texas) HS.
45. Miles Luuloa, ss, Malokai HS, Kaunakakai, Hawaii.
46. Patrick Gill, rhp, Grandville (Mich.) HS.
47. Warren Trott, ss, West Torrance HS, Torrance, Calif.
48. Chris Curry, c, Meridian (Miss.) CC.

FLORIDA (27)

■ **SCOUTING DIRECTOR:** Orrin Freeman
1. Chip Ambres, of, West Brook HS, Beaumont, Texas.
2. Derek Wathan, ss, U. of Oklahoma.
3. David Callahan, 1b, Palm Bay (Fla.) HS.
4. Heath Honeycutt, 3b, Georgia Tech.
5. Matt Padgett, of, Clemson U.
6. Phill Lowery, lhp, Arizona State U.
7. Ryan Harber, lhp, Butler U.
8. Marc Sauer, rhp, Bishop Eustace HS, Gloucester, N.J.
9. Mike Trussell, rhp, Menchville HS, Newport News, Va.
10. Chris Heck, lhp, St. Joseph's (Pa.) U.
11. Matt DeMarco, ss, Gloucester Catholic HS, Gloucester City, N.J.
12. David Noyce, lhp, Furman U.
13. Paul McCurtain, rhp, U. of Oklahoma.
14. Eric Jupe, rhp, Schreiner (Texas) College.
15. Heath Kelly, 2b, Auburn U.
16. John Seaman, rhp, Northwestern U.
17. Josh Hochgesang, 3b, Stanford U.
18. Adam LaRoche, lhp-1b, Fort Scott (Kan.) HS.
19. Wendell Anderson, of, East Hartford (Conn.) HS.
20. David Campos, lhp, Fresno CC.
21. Matt Frick, c, U. of Alabama.
22. Michael Wright, c, San Jose State U.
23. Matt Krabbe, rhp, Larkin HS, Elgin, Ill.
24. Terrence Smalls, 2b-ss, The Citadel.
25. Scott Murphy, rhp, Parkview HS, Lilburn, Ga.
26. Kevin Olsen, rhp, U. of Oklahoma.
27. Willy Hill, of, U. of Oklahoma.
28. Kevin Ryan, rhp, Morton (Ill.) JC.
29. Drew Niles, ss, Bowling Green State U.
30. Vincent Harrison, ss-2b, Princeton HS, Cincinnati.
31. Jon Topolski, of, Baylor U.
32. Randy Rigsby, 3b, East Carolina U.
33. John Kocur, rhp, Cooper City (Fla.) HS.
34. Adam Bragg, of, Bishop Verot HS, Cape Coral, Fla.
35. John Moylan, c, Sacred Heart HS, San Francisco.
36. Chris Halgren, c, Mt. Hood (Ore.) CC.
37. Eric Bernhardt, rhp, Cowley County (Kan.) CC.
38. Jorge Arceo, rhp, Lincoln HS, Stockton, Calif.
39. Jeff Wagner, of, San Jacinto (Texas) JC.
40. Julio Rivas, c, Washington and Lee HS, Arlington, Va.
41. Bryan Lee, of, El Camino HS, Sacramento.
42. Daniel Pettit, rhp, North Stafford HS, Stafford, Va.
43. Shawn Sabo, rhp, Oswego (Ill.) HS.
44. Shawn Norris, ss, Alta HS, Draper, Utah.
45. Peter Selden, rhp, Monroe (N.Y.) CC.
46. Greg Mickles, of, Maple Shade (N.J.) HS.
47. Aaron Alvarez, c, Chattahoochee HS, Duluth, Ga.
48. Rigo Orozco, c, Capuchino HS, San Bruno, Calif.
49. Rudy Simpson, of, Etiwanda HS, Alta Loma, Calif.

HOUSTON (19)

■ **SCOUTING DIRECTOR:** David Lakey
1. Brad Lidge, rhp, U. of Notre Dame (Choice from Rockies—17th—as compensation for Type A free agent Darryl Kile).
1. (Choice to Giants as compensation for Type B free agent Doug Henry).
1. Mike Nannini, rhp, Green Valley HS, Henderson, Nev. (Supplemental pick—37th—for loss of Kile).
2. (Choice to Cubs—62nd—as compensation for Type B free agent Dave Clark).
3. Brad Busbin, rhp, Dr. Phillips HS, Orlando.
4. Jason Van Meetren, of, Bishop Gorman HS, Las Vegas.
5. Scott Barrett, lhp, San Jacinto (Texas) JC.
6. David Matranga, ss, Pepperdine U.
7. John Buck, c, Taylorsville HS, Salt Lake City.
8. Jesse Joyce, 3b, Cal State Los Angeles.
9. Morgan Ensberg, 3b, U. of Southern California.
10. Keith Ginter, 2b, Texas Tech.
11. Kevin Jordan, 3b-of, Texas Tech.
12. Jeremy Ryan, rhp, Maple Woods (Mo.) CC.
13. Doug Sessions, rhp, Armstrong Atlantic State (Ga.) College.
14. Jacob Baker, 3b, Rice U.
15. Charley Carter, 1b, Baylor U.
16. Derek Nicholson, of, U. of Florida.
17. Colin Porter, of, U. of Arizona.
18. Rich Terwilliger, rhp, CC of the Finger Lakes (N.Y.).
19. Bryon Wilkerson, rhp, U. of Mary Hardin-Baylor (Texas).
20. Anthony Ramirez, 3b, Carson (Calif.) HS.
21. Brian Messer, rhp, U. of New Mexico.
22. Garrett Zyskowski, lhp, West Virginia U.
23. Brandon Smith, rhp, Northeast Louisiana U.
24. Josh Dimmick, c, U. of Kansas.
25. Jacob Whitney, lhp, Iowa State U.
26. Robert Cabrillo, 1b, Montgomery HS, San Diego.
27. Robert Burns, c, Bingham HS, South Jordan, Utah.
28. Chris Sheffield, rhp, Stephen F. Austin HS, Richmond, Texas.
29. Brandon Buckley, c, Texas Tech.
30. Jordan Hunt, rhp, Evergreen HS, Vancouver, Wash.
31. Alex Dvorsky, c, Marion (Iowa) HS.
32. Bernard Gonzalez, of, Brito Miami Private HS, Miami.
33. Gavin Wright, of, Blinn (Texas) JC.
34. Ryan Humphrey, lhp, Indian River (Fla.) CC.
35. Brett Kay, c, Mater Dei HS, Villa Park, Calif.
36. Benson Barrera, rhp, Skyview HS, Nampa, Idaho.
37. Jeremy Frost, c, Oviedo (Fla.) HS.
38. Bryan Edwards, rhp, Northeast Texas CC.
39. Roberto Zaldivar, rhp, Arroyo HS, San Lorenzo, Calif.
40. Ray Leyba, lhp, Choctaw (Okla.) HS.
41. Mike McHugh, rhp, Helix HS, La Mesa, Calif.

KANSAS CITY (4)

■ **SCOUTING DIRECTOR:** Terry Wetzel
1. Jeff Austin, rhp, Stanford U.
1. Matt Burch, rhp, Virginia Commonwealth U. (Choice from Diamondbacks—30th—as compensation for Type A free agent Jay Bell).
1. Chris George, lhp, Klein (Texas) HS (Supplemental pick—31st—for loss of Bell).
2. Robbie Morrison, rhp, U. of Miami.
3. Ben Cordova, of, Marian Catholic HS, Chula Vista, Calif.
4. Monty Ward, rhp, Texas Tech.
5. Scott Chiasson, rhp, Eastern Connecticut State U.
6. Mike Curry, of, U. of South Carolina.
7. Jeremy Dodson, of, Baylor U.
8. Norris Hopper, ss, Shelby (N.C.) HS.
9. Paul Phillips, of, U. of Alabama.
10. Jeremy Jackson, lhp, Mississippi State U.
11. Cary Ammons, lhp, Southeastern Oklahoma State U.
12. Emanuel Santana, c, Maestro Ladi HS, Vega Alta, P.R.
13. Brian Shackelford, of, U. of Oklahoma.
14. Shawn Sedlacek, rhp, Iowa State U.
15. Brock Griffin, c, Jesuit HS, Portland, Ore.
16. Craig Jones, rhp, U. of Southern California.
17. Charles Hamilton, rhp, Hollandale Simmons HS, Delta, Miss.
18. Ryan Hill, rhp, Wabash Valley (Ill.) JC.
19. Aaron Fausett, of, Beaverton (Ore.) HS.
20. Javier Pamus, rhp, San Jose State U.
21. James Shanks, of, Soloman HS, North Augusta, S.C.
22. John Lee, rhp, U. of Washington.
23. Corey Hart, 2b, U. of Oklahoma.
24. Ryan Fry, of, U. of Missouri.
25. Jeremy Freitas, of, U. of Southern California.
26. Jeff Trzos, lhp, North Farmington HS, Farmington Hills, Mich.
27. Yancy Ayres, c, Kansas State U.
28. Mike Russo, rhp, Queens (N.Y.) College.
29. Sean Bryan, 3b, Maple Woods (Mo.) JC.
30. Trevor Mote, ss, Yavapai (Ariz.) JC.
31. Michael Denard, ss, Oakland (Calif.) Tech HS.
32. Jim Essian Jr., c, Troy (Mich.) HS.
33. Jason Bartz, rhp, Manatee HS, Bradenton, Fla.
34. Damon Dombrowski, rhp, Truman HS, Independence, Mo.
35. Gabe Boruff, c, Ephrata (Wash.) HS.
36. Shane Scoville, c, Ridge HS, Basking Ridge, N.J.
37. Jeffrey Jobe, rhp, Seward County (Kan.) CC.
38. Lane Crews, rhp, Glades Day HS, Belle Glade, Fla.

39. Shawn Barksdale, rhp, Wallace State (Ala.) CC.
40. Nathan Price, rhp, Cleveland, Miss.
41. Adam Lingenfelter, rhp, Buchholz HS, Gainesville, Fla.
42. Felipe Alou Jr., of, Canada (Calif.) JC.

LOS ANGELES (23)

■ **SCOUTING DIRECTOR:** Terry Reynolds

1. Bubba Crosby, of, Rice U.
2. Mike Fischer, rhp, U. of South Alabama.
3. Alex Santos, rhp, U. of Miami.
4. Eric Riggs, ss, U. of Central Florida.
5. Scott Proctor, rhp, Florida State U.
6. Ryan Moskau, rhp-1b, U. of Arizona.
7. David Ross, c, U. of Florida.
8. Thomari Story-Hardin, 1b, El Cerrito HS, Richmond, Calif.
9. Joel Williams, rhp, Yoncalla (Ore.) HS.
10. Lance Caraccioli, lhp, Northeast Louisiana U.
11. Christian Bridenbaugh, lhp, Central HS, Martinsburg, Pa.
12. J.K. Taylor, rhp, Louisa (Va.) HS.
13. C.J. Thomas, of-rhp, McLane HS, Fresno.
14. Rob Gorr, 1b-of, U. of Southern California.
15. Paul Avery, lhp, Pepperdine U.
16. James Goelz, ss, New York Tech.
17. Alex Piedra, rhp, Southridge HS, Miami.
18. Tony Richards, c, North Dakota State U.
19. Jeremy Meccage, rhp, U. of Iowa.
20. Tim Harrell, rhp, Liberty U.
21. Jacob Sampson, ss, Curtis HS, Tacoma, Wash.
22. Anthony Gomes, rhp, San Joaquin Delta (Calif.) JC.
23. Jason Moody, lhp, Spartanburg Methodist (S.C.) JC.
24. Allen Davis, lhp, Northwestern State U.
25. Scott Barnsby, rhp, U. of Massachusetts.
26. Matt Greer, c, Louisiana Tech.
27. Nick Theodorou, 2b, UCLA.
28. Corry Parrott, of, Pasadena (Calif.) CC.
29. David Baum, lhp, Martin County HS, Stuart, Fla.
30. Lloyd Turner, ss, Hephzibah (Ga.) HS.
31. Paul Brown, lhp, Citrus (Calif.) JC.
32. Darren Heal, c, Indian River (Fla.) JC.
33. Herman Dean, of, Monrovia (Calif.) HS.
34. Carlos Claudio, ss, Ora Wilma Chavez HS, Guaynabo, P.R.
35. Rashad Parker, ss, Crossroads HS, Santa Monica, Calif.
36. Curt Borland, rhp, Centaurus HS, Broomfield, Colo.
37. Josh McMillen, of, West Virginia U.
38. Josh Berndt, lhp, West HS, Oshkosh, Wis.
39. Marc-Andre Lagace, lhp, Louis Riel HS, Blackburn Hamlet, Ontario.
40. Clint Hosford, rhp, Carson Graham HS, North Vancouver, B.C.
41. Doug Vandecaveye, 3b, Tilbury (Ontario) District HS.
42. Jahseam George, lhp, JC of the Sequoias (Calif.).
43. Jorge Roman, rhp, Jose de Diego HS, Aguadilla, P.R.
44. Joey Hart, c, Grayson County (Texas) CC.
45. Brandon Smith, 1b, Cypress (Calif.) JC.
46. Steve Andrade, rhp, American River (Calif.) JC.
47. Harry Arocho, of, Benito Cerezo HS, Aguadilla, P.R.
48. Chad Marchand, rhp, Lethbridge (Alberta) CC.
49. Wayne Stone, 3b, Miller HS, Rialto, Calif.
50. Blake McGinley, lhp, Bakersfield (Calif.) JC.

MILWAUKEE (13)

■ **SCOUTING DIRECTOR:** Ken Califano

1. J.M. Gold, rhp, Toms River North HS, Toms River, N.J.
2. Nick Neugebauer, rhp, Arlington HS, Riverside, Calif.
3. Derry Hammond, of, West Point (Miss.) HS.
4. Rhett Parrott, rhp, Northwest Whitfield HS, Dalton, Ga.
5. Chris Pine, rhp, Oregon State U.
6. William Hall, ss, Nettleton (Miss.) HS.
7. Jason Fox, of, Florida Southern College.
8. Mike Penney, rhp, U. of Southern California.
9. Ryan Bordenick, c, U. of South Carolina.
10. James Johnson, lhp, U. of Arizona.
11. Jeff Pickler, 2b, U. of Tennessee.
12. Chris Barton, rhp, U. of Connecticut.
13. Heath McMurray, rhp, San Jacinto (Texas) JC.
14. Charles Kegley, rhp, Middleburg (Fla.) HS.
15. Jose Montenegro, 3b, U. of Oklahoma.
16. Hector Guadalupe, ss, Arundel HS, Gambrills, Md.
17. Steve Correa, lhp, Elk Grove (Calif.) HS.
18. Ricky Lewis, rhp, Mississippi Valley State U.
19. Scott Geitz, rhp, Southwest Missouri State U.
20. Jeff Becker, 3b, Duke U.
21. Ryan Poe, rhp, Saddleback (Calif.) CC.
22. Erik Smallwood, of, Tate HS, Gonzalez, Fla.
23. Eric Ayala, 2b, Northeast Texas CC.
24. Fontella Jones, rhp, Mississippi Valley State U.
25. Jack Krawczyk, rhp, U. of Southern California.
26. Dan Mathews, rhp, Indiana U.-Purdue U.
27. Jonathan Harraid, rhp, Sam Houston State U.
28. Tyrone Wayne, rhp, St. John's U.
29. Eduardo Figueroa, 1b, U. of Tennessee.
30. Casey Davis, of, Wichita State U.
31. Lee Jaramillo, c, U. of Wisconsin-Milwaukee.
32. Roberto Maysonet, rhp, Vega Baja, P.R.
33. Mac Mackiewitz, 1b, U. of North Florida.
34. Curt Kautsch, rhp, U. of Texas.
35. Stephen York, of, Arizona Western JC.
36. Bill Eaton, of, U. of South Florida.
37. Alfred Corbeil, c, Manatee (Fla.) CC.
38. Jonathon Kuelz, rhp, West Lutheran HS, Minnetonka, Minn.
39. Dustin Wagoner, rhp, Corona (Calif.) HS.
40. Ken Harold, c, Denham Springs (La.) HS.
41. Brian Wojtkowski, of, Peoria (Ariz.) HS.
42. Chris Vallette, rhp, Angelina (Texas) JC.
43. Pedro Gavillan, 3b, Leonard HS, Lake Worth, Fla.
44. Jeff Eure, 3b, Upper Dauphin HS, Pillow, Pa.
45. Devin Butler, 1b, Key West (Fla.) HS.
46. Nicholas Murphy, rhp, Central Florida CC.
47. Landon Jacobsen, rhp, Trinidad State (Colo.) JC.
48. Chad Christianson, lhp, Seabreeze HS, Ormond Beach, Fla.
49. Nick Wash, 3b, Picayune (Miss.) HS.
50. Michael Wojtkowski, of, Peoria (Ariz.) HS.

MINNESOTA (6)

■ **SCOUTING DIRECTOR:** Mike Radcliff

1. Ryan Mills, lhp, Arizona State U.
2. Marcus Sents, rhp, Cookeville (Tenn.) HS.
3. Brent Hoard, lhp, Stanford U.
4. Pete Fisher, rhp, U. of Alabama.
5. Mickey Blount, rhp, Kansas State U.
6. Brad Pautz, rhp, U. of Minnesota.
7. Sam Taulli, lhp, Lafayette (La.) HS.
8. John Edwards, c, Triton (Ill.) JC.
9. Saul Rivera, rhp, U. of Mobile (Ala.).
10. Ryan Lundquist, of, U. of Arkansas.
11. Jonathon Pridie, rhp, Prescott (Ariz.) HS.
12. Kareem Johnson, of, Crowe HS, Trail, B.C.
13. Kyle Hawthorne, ss, Pensacola (Fla.) JC.
14. Mike Gosling, lhp, East HS, Salt Lake City.
15. Brian Haskell, lhp, Canyon Springs HS, Moreno Valley, Calif.
16. Jose Espinal, rhp, Canovanas, P.R.
17. J.J. Putz, rhp, U. of Michigan.
18. Kevin Thompson, ss, Western Hills HS, Fort Worth.
19. Kevin Hodge, ss-3b, Rice U.
20. Brad Frazier, rhp, U. of Mobile (Ala.).
21. Marc Bluma, rhp, Wichita State U.
22. Rhett Riviere, rhp, St. Michael's Academy, Austin.
23. Andrew Butler, rhp, Bowling Green State U.
24. Juan Padilla, rhp, Jacksonville U.
25. Eric Sandberg, 1b, Ferris HS, Spokane, Wash.
26. Jason Scobie, rhp, McLennan (Texas) JC.
27. Craig Selander, of, U. of Minnesota.
28. Dave Marciniak, 2b, Rutgers U.
29. Lestor Victoria, lhp, U. of Central Florida.
30. Jonathan Muller, 3b, Arapahoe HS, Littleton, Colo.
31. Brian McMillan, of, U. of Evansville.
32. Todd Collura, c, Polk (Fla.) CC.
33. Bryan Gidge, rhp, U. of Nevada-Las Vegas.
34. Kevin Frederick, rhp, Creighton U.
35. Mack Lambert, rhp, Pearl River (La.) HS.
36. Richard Denholm, rhp, Edgewater HS, Orlando.
37. Ben Smith, rhp, Brownwood (Texas) HS.
38. Tommy Watkins, ss, Riverdale HS, Fort Myers, Fla.
39. Nathan Kent, rhp, Motlow State (Tenn.) CC.
40. Joe Maruffi, rhp, St. Pius X HS, Albuquerque.
41. Kayzell Milton, of, Homestead HS, Fremont, Calif.
42. Andy Neufeld, ss, Manatee (Fla.) CC.
43. Taylor Grant, lhp, Newport HS, Bellevue, Wash.
44. Bobby Wood, rhp, Cherry Creek HS, Englewood, Colo.
45. Ernie Bascuas, rhp, Miami-Dade CC North.
46. Mike Bradley, rhp, Dr. Phillips HS, Orlando.
47. Wade Clark, rhp, Santa Ynez HS, Los Olivos, Calif.
48. Daniel Olson, rhp, Loveland (Colo.) HS.
49. Desmond Dailey, of, Eastern Arizona JC.

MONTREAL (11)

■ **SCOUTING DIRECTOR:** Jim Fleming

1. Josh McKinley, ss, Malvern Prep, Downington, Pa.
1. Brad Wilkerson, of-lhp, U. of Florida (Supplemental pick—33rd—for loss of Type A free agent Darrin Fletcher).
2. Eric Good, lhp, Mishawaka (Ind.) HS.
3. Clyde Williams, 1b, Seminole HS, Sanford, Fla. (Choice

from Blue Jays—81st—as compensation for Fletcher).
3. Kevin Kelly, 3b, Gloucester Catholic HS, Brooklawn, N.J.
4. Rob Castelli, rhp, Eastern Illinois U.
5. Ryan Lentz, 3b, U. of Washington.
6. Wes Chisnall, rhp, Etiwanda HS, Alta Loma, Calif.
7. Brad Piercy, c, North Carolina State U.
8. Scott Sandusky, c, Texas A&M U.
9. Juan Ortiz, of, Eastern District HS, Brooklyn.
10. Ryan Grantham, rhp, Aldershot HS, Burlington, Ontario.
11. Jason Walker, lhp, Ontario (Calif.) HS.
12. Scott Dobson, rhp, North Carolina State U.
13. Jason Hendricks, of, U. of Arizona.
14. Kevin Hook, ss, Loyola Marymount U.
15. Stephen Baker, of, Rome (N.Y.) Free Academy.
16. Derick Urquhart, of, U. of South Carolina.
17. Kyle Sheldon, rhp, Florida Southern College.
18. Jim Serrano, rhp, U. of New Mexico.
19. Omar Rosado, 2b, Toa Baja, P.R.
20. Brandon Agemennone, rhp, U. of Maryland.
21. Jason Kanovich, lhp, Shippensburg (Pa.) U.
22. Trevor Wamback, rhp, Dalhousie (N.S.) U.
23. Jamie Hammond, ss, West Virginia U.
24. Joseph Clark, rhp, Chugiak HS, Eagle River, Alaska.
25. Casey Fuller, lhp, Sacramento CC.
26. Brad Waldron, rhp, Iowa State U.
27. Steve Toriz, rhp, East Los Angeles JC.
28. Richard Lane, of, Tustin (Calif.) HS.
29. Michael Castleberry, rhp, Batesville (Ark.) HS.
30. Matt Romero, of, Spanish Fork (Utah) HS.
31. Jeffrey Reboin, lhp, San Juan HS, Carmichael, Calif.
32. Andrew Frierson, lhp, JC of San Mateo (Calif.).
33. Josh Merrigan, lhp, Butler County (Kan.) CC.
34. Charles Dubuc, lhp, St. Jean College HS, Iberville, Quebec.
35. Jeff Linseln, rhp, American River (Calif.) JC.
36. Nathan Kershaw, of, Hoke County HS, Raeford, N.C.
37. Clint Dunbar, rhp, Norman (Okla.) HS.
38. Chris Richards, of, Burlington (Vt.) HS.
39. Anthony Watts, lhp, Lincoln HS, San Diego.
40. Josh Laidlaw, of, Arizona Western JC.
41. Alexandre Groleau, rhp, Edouard Montpetit HS, Longueuil, Quebec.
42. Ross Bennett, of, Central HS, Cape Girardeau, Mo.
43. Jace Brewer, ss, Washington (Okla.) HS.
44. Ron Chiavacci, rhp, Kutztown (Pa.) U.
45. Tom Perez, ss, Burroughs HS, Burbank, Calif.

NEW YORK/AL (24)

■ **SCOUTING DIRECTOR:** Lin Garrett
1. Andy Brown, of, Richmond (Ind.) HS.
1. Mark Prior, rhp, University HS, San Diego (Supplemental pick—43rd—for failure to sign 1997 first-round pick Tyrell Godwin).
2. Randy Keisler, lhp, Louisiana State U.
3. Drew Henson, 3b-rhp, Brighton (Mich.) HS.
4. Ivan Reyes, ss, Liceo Hispano Americano HS, Bayamon, P.R.
5. Brian Rogers, rhp, The Citadel.
6. Brett Jodie, rhp, U. of South Carolina.
7. Ryan Ridenour, lhp, Texas Christian U.
8. David Fowler, of, McCluer North HS, Florissant, Mo.
9. Allen Greene, of, U. of Notre Dame.
10. Damon Thames, ss, Rice U.
11. Casey DeGroote, 3b, West Vigo HS, West Terre Haute, Ind.
12. Jeffrey Sheffield, of, University HS, Spokane, Wash.
13. Charlie Isaacson, rhp, Shawnee Mission (Kan.) West HS.
14. Brett Weber, rhp, U. of Illinois.
15. Justin Reisinger, rhp, Adena HS, Clarksburg, Ohio.
16. Gabe Crecion, rhp, UCLA.
17. Jeff Shaddix, rhp, Texas Christian U.
18. Danny Delmas, rhp, Odessa (Texas) JC.
19. Brad Elwood, c, West Virginia U.
20. Dusty Rhodes, of, U. of Illinois.
21. Neal Gregg, 1b, William Carey (Miss.) College.
22. Jeff Sziksai, 2b, Western Carolina U.
23. Mark Carek, ss, Ohio State U.
24. Jason Willis, rhp, East Central (Miss.) JC.
25. Mario Gandea, rhp, Odessa (Texas) HS.
26. Javier Rodriguez, ss, Gulliver Prep, Miami.
27. Scott Massucco, c, St. Thomas Aquinas HS, Fort Lauderdale.
28. Lee Gwaltney, rhp, Aledo HS, Willow Park, Texas.
29. Adam Manley, of, JC of Southern Idaho.
30. Brian Conley, lhp, Gladewater (Texas) HS.
31. Elvis Corporan, ss, Espiritu Santo HS, Baja, P.R.
32. Jay Signorelli, rhp, Manatee (Fla.) CC.
33. Jeff Hunter, rhp, Meridian (Miss.) CC.
34. Brandon Claussen, lhp, Howard (Texas) JC.
35. Michael Gosz, ss, Treasure Valley (Ore.) CC.
36. Eric Eckenstahler, lhp, Illinois State U.
37. Jarrell McIntyre, ss, Laguna Creek HS, Elk Grove, Calif.
38. Chad Christian, lhp, Northeast Jones HS, Laurel, Miss.
39. Lucas Miller, rhp, Rolla (Mo.) HS.
40. Exavier Logan, ss, Natchez (Miss.) HS.
41. David Kloes, rhp, West Virginia U.
42. Justin Nash, rhp, Calvert Hall HS, Hunt Valley, Md.
43. Kris Ehmke, rhp, Hill (Texas) JC.
44. Marc Love, of, Coldspring (Texas) HS.
45. Jeff Moye, rhp, Hardin-Jefferson HS, Kountz, Texas.
46. Jeff Carlson, rhp, Quinnipiac (Conn.) College.
47. Jeff Nettles, 3b, Palomar (Calif.) JC.
48. Kyle Geswein, 1b, Carroll HS, Dayton, Ohio.
49. Corey Lawson, rhp, Windsor (Mo.) HS.
50. Joseph List, rhp, Beechwood HS, Fort Mitchell, Ky.

NEW YORK/NL (21)

■ **SCOUTING DIRECTOR:** Gary LaRocque
1. Jason Tyner, of, Texas A&M U.
2. Pat Strange, rhp, Central HS, Springfield, Mass.
3. Jason Saenz, lhp, U. of Southern California.
4. Jason Moates, rhp, Meridian (Miss.) CC.
5. Craig Brazell, c, Jefferson Davis HS, Montgomery, Ala.
6. Marvin Seale, of, Durango (Colo.) HS.
7. Ryan Smith, c, Mifflinburg (Pa.) Area HS.
8. Vince Vazquez, rhp, Chaminade HS, Hollywood, Fla.
9. Todd Bellhorn, lhp, U. of Central Florida.
10. Larnell Hamn, of, Potomac HS, Triangle, Va.
11. Josh Perich, of, Northwestern Lehigh HS, Slatington, Pa.
12. Ryan Budde, c, Midwest City (Okla.) HS.
13. Andy Cook, rhp, College of William & Mary.
14. Gil Velazquez, ss, Paramount (Calif.) HS.
15. David Hunter, 1b, Porterville (Calif.) JC.
16. Scott Bikowski, of, Florida Southern College.
17. Ty Wigginton, ss, UNC Asheville.
18. Brian Cole, of, Navarro (Texas) JC.
19. Frank Graham, rhp, Columbus State (Ohio) JC.
20. Jason Clements, ss, Riverside (Calif.) CC.
21. Robert Lugo, 1b, Patria la Torres Ramirez HS, San Sebastian, P.R.
22. Brian Shipp, ss, Meridian (Miss.) CC.
23. Jaime Cerda, lhp, Fresno CC.
24. William Gobbel, ss, Presbyterian (S.C.) College.
25. John Wesley, rhp, Clarke HS, Westbury, N.Y.
26. Jason Osborn, c, Sehome HS, Bellingham, Wash.
27. Justin Smith, lhp, U. of Alabama.
28. Marc Ludvigsen, of, UNC Asheville.
29. Alex Zardis, 2b, Edmonds (Wash.) CC.
30. Alex Stoffels, c, Indian Hills (Iowa) CC.
31. Rene Vega, lhp, Dominican (N.Y.) College.
32. Pedro Rodriguez, of, Rollins College.
33. Greg Halvorson, c-rhp, Arizona State U.
34. Billy Martin, 3b, U. of Texas-Arlington.
35. Edwin Franco, lhp, Florida International U.
36. Earl Snyder, 1b, U. of Hartford.
37. Michael Wodnicki, rhp, Southington (Conn.) HS.
38. Gary Bohannon, rhp, Kennesaw State (Ga.) U.
39. Justin Kurtz, rhp, Brewton Parker (Ga.) College.
40. Mike Prokop, rhp, Kennesaw State (Ga.) U.
41. Joseph Yarbrough, lhp, Hazel Green (Ala.) HS.
42. Ben Leuthard, 1b, Mission Bay HS, San Diego.
43. Tom Paciorek Jr., of, Southern (Ga.) Tech.
44. Ruben Feliciano, rhp, Bushwick HS, Brooklyn.
45. Chris Nelson, of, Pasadena (Calif.) CC.
46. Ken Chenard, rhp, Fullerton (Calif.) JC.
47. Ben Vargas, rhp, El Monte HS, Azusa, Calif.
48. Chris Taylor, of, Riverside (Calif.) CC.
49. Newton Hausmann, lhp, Red Bank Catholic HS, Colts Neck, N.Y.
50. Aaron Hee, lhp, Taft (Calif.) JC.

OAKLAND (2)

■ **SCOUTING DIRECTOR:** Grady Fuson
1. Mark Mulder, lhp, Michigan State U.
2. Gerald Laird, c, La Quinta HS, Westminster, Calif.
3. Kevin Miller, ss, U. of Washington.
4. Jeff Schultz, rhp, Cypress (Calif.) JC.
5. Jason Hart, 1b, Southwest Missouri State U.
6. Gary Schneidmiller, ss, Don Lugo HS, Chino, Calif.
7. Donato Calandriello, lhp, College of Charleston.
8. Eric Byrnes, of, UCLA.
9. Jon Adkins, rhp, Oklahoma State U.
10. Bert Snow, rhp, Vanderbilt U.
11. Jay Pecci, ss, Stanford U.
12. Eric Thompson, rhp, Ohio State U.
13. Jeff Bajenaru, rhp, Riverside (Calif.) CC.
14. Mike Lockwood, of, Ohio State U.
15. Rusty Keith, of, Portland State U.

16. Shane Bazzell, rhp, New Hope HS, Columbus, Miss.
17. Elih Velazquez, lhp, Jose Campeche HS, San Lorenzo, P.R.
18. Justin Hall, ss, Long Beach State U.
19. Justin Nixon, of, Walla Walla (Wash.) CC.
20. DeWayne Betts, of, Lakewood (Calif.) HS.
21. Casey Bookout, 1b, U. of Oklahoma.
22. Aaron Nieckula, c, U. of Illinois.
23. Tyler Yates, rhp, U. of Hawaii-Hilo.
24. Bryan Williamson, of, U. of Washington.
25. Jim Brink, rhp, U. of Nevada.
26. J.P. Schmidt, ss, Highland HS, Palmdale, Calif.
27. Jason Dobis, rhp, U. of Minnesota.
28. Matt Forbes, of, Muscatine (Iowa) CC.
29. Matt Howe, 3b, Texas Christian U.
30. Anthony Taylor, rhp, U. of Southern Colorado.
31. Michael Woods, 2b, Broadmoor HS, Baton Rouge, La.
32. Kurt Nantkes, rhp, Hibkley HS, Aurora, Colo.
33. Jose Negron, rhp, Southeastern (Iowa) CC.
34. Newt Parent, c, Phoenix (Ore.) HS.
35. Brad Moore, rhp, U. of Northern Iowa.
36. Alex Torres, lhp, Cochise County (Ariz.) CC.
37. Marshall Rubens, rhp, American River (Calif.) JC.
38. Billy Green, of, Spring (Texas) HS.
39. Bryan Ball, rhp, Taylorsville HS, Salt Lake City.
40. Zack Riera, c, Florida HS, Tallahassee, Fla.
41. James Mears, rhp, Indian Hills (Iowa) CC.
42. John Dean, of, Magnolia (Texas) HS.
43. Mike Cervenak, 3b, U. of Michigan.

PHILADELPHIA (1)

■ **SCOUTING DIRECTOR:** Mike Arbuckle
1. Pat Burrell, 3b-1b, U. of Miami.
1. Eric Valent, of, UCLA (Supplemental pick—42nd—for failure to sign 1997 first-round pick J.D. Drew).
2. Brad Baisley, rhp, Land O' Lakes (Fla.) HS.
3. Jorge Padilla, of, Florida Air Academy, Melbourne, Fla.
4. Jason Michaels, of, U. of Miami.
5. Kennon McArthur, c, Sylacauga (Ala.) HS.
6. Tommy Whiteman, ss, Midwest City (Okla.) HS.
7. Jarrod Lawson, rhp, Potosi (Mo.) HS.
8. Mike Wilson, rhp, Granite Hills HS, El Cajon, Calif.
9. Ryan Madson, rhp, Valley View HS, Moreno Valley, Calif.
10. Ken Westmoreland, rhp, U. of Alabama-Huntsville.
11. Ben Jewson, 3b, Waukesha (Wis.) North HS.
12. Ian Rauls, of, Old Dominion U.
13. Adam Peterson, rhp, Oconto Falls (Wis.) HS.
14. Greg Kubes, lhp, Sam Houston State U.
15. Geoff Geary, rhp, U. of Oklahoma.
16. Chris Pilato, rhp, Villanova U.
17. Chip DeNure, ss, Ripon (Wis.) College.
18. Nate Espy, 1b, Wallace State (Ala.) JC.
19. Jeremy Salazar, c, Florida State U.
20. Jeremy Wedel, rhp, Armstrong Atlantic State (Ga.) U.
21. Nick Punto, ss, Saddleback (Calif.) JC.
22. Matt Bailie, rhp, Oregon State U.
23. Cary Hiles, rhp, U. of Memphis.
24. Shayne Carnes, of, U. of Alabama-Birmingham.
25. Aric LeClair, lhp, Crowder (Mo.) JC.
26. Mike Zipser, rhp, U. of Nevada.
27. Ron McGinnis, c, U. of Texas-San Antonio.
28. Chris Maness, rhp, Elon (N.C.) College.
29. Andrew Weidl, lhp, Winona State (Minn.) U.
30. Kurt Blackmon, rhp, North Carolina State U.
31. Len Hannahan, 2b, U. of St. Thomas (Minn.).
32. Abraham Ayala, 3b, Bayamon, P.R.
33. Wes Rachels, 2b, U. of Southern California.
34. David Ciesla, lhp, Arkansas Tech U.
35. Pete Montrenes, rhp, Ocean View HS, Fountain Valley, Calif.
36. Roger Rodeheaver, 1b, Indiana U.
37. Ed Grammer, rhp, Union (Tenn.) U.
38. Lance Cooley, ss, Killeen (Texas) HS.
39. Jeremy Deltrick, c, Penn State U.
40. Todd Henry, rhp, Bakersfield (Calif.) JC.
41. Thomas Donovan, rhp, Elon (N.C.) College.
42. Kirk Nordness, ss, Beaverton (Ore.) HS.
43. Earnest Graham, of, Mariner HS, Fort Myers, Fla.

PITTSBURGH (15)

■ **SCOUTING DIRECTOR:** Leland Maddox
1. Clint Johnston, lhp-of, Vanderbilt U.
2. Jeremy Cotten, 3b-rhp, Fuquay-Varina (N.C.) HS.
3. Jeremy Harts, of-lhp, Columbia HS, Decatur, Ga.
4. Eddy Furniss, 1b, Louisiana State U.
5. Rayner Cardona, c, Patria la Torres Ramirez HS, San Sebastian, P.R.
6. Bryce Pelfrey, ss, Tate HS, Gonzalez, Fla.
7. James White, rhp, Chico (Calif.) HS.
8. Chuck Crowder, lhp, Georgia Tech.
9. Giovanni Gonzalez, lhp, Northwest Christian Academy, Miami.
10. David Diaz, c, Hialeah-Miami Lakes HS, Hialeah, Fla.
11. Chris Smith, lhp-of, Wantagh (N.Y.) HS.
12. Willie Burton, of, Lake Wales (Fla.) HS.
13. Ben Levesque, rhp, Cary (N.C.) HS.
14. John Breck, rhp, Bridgewater-Raritan HS, Bridgewater, N.J.
15. Craig House, rhp, U. of Memphis.
16. Russ Rohlicek, lhp, College Park HS, Pleasant Hill, Calif.
17. David William, lhp, Delaware Tech and CC.
18. Joseph Beimel, lhp, Duquesne U.
19. David Bennett, rhp, Gordonsville (Tenn.) HS.
20. Michael Johnston, lhp, Garrett (Md.) CC.
21. Mike Bumatay, lhp-of, Clovis (Calif.) HS.
22. Josh Miller, c, Silver Bluff HS, Aiken, S.C.
23. Tyson Thompson, of, Inglemoor HS, Bothell, Wash.
24. David Hawk, lhp, Vista West HS, Bakersfield, Calif.
25. Thom Ott, rhp, Greenbriar Christian Academy, Chesapeake, Va.
26. Jon Switzer, lhp, Clear Lake HS, Houston.
27. Casey Cloud, c, UCLA.
28. Stephen Sparks, rhp, U. of South Alabama.
29. Scott Gardner, lhp, Cardinal Gibbons HS, Coral Springs, Fla.
30. Matt Vorwald, rhp, Freeport (Ill.) HS.
31. Eric Tatum, lhp, Forest Hill HS, West Palm Beach, Fla.
32. Wyatt Allen, rhp, Brentwood Academy, Nashville.
33. Marcus Nettles, of, Whitney Young HS, Chicago.
34. Traviss Hodge, 1b, Highland HS, Agua Dulce, Calif.
35. Trevor Hutchinson, rhp, Torrey Pines HS, San Diego.
36. Steve Wombacher, 1b, Yavapai (Ariz.) JC.
37. Justin Fry, rhp, Ohio State U.
38. Shaun Skrehot, ss, U. of Houston.
39. Veon Harris, rhp, East Mississippi JC.
40. Jeff Ellena, ss, Walnut HS, Diamond Bar, Calif.
41. Christian Ortiz, of, Arcadia (Calif.) HS.
42. Scott Glaser, lhp, U. of South Florida.
43. Eric Stanton, 3b, U. of South Carolina.
44. Brian Walker, lhp, Westminster Christian HS, Miami.
45. Brian Cronk, 3b-of, Eastern New Mexico U.
46. Jamie Shearin, c, East Wake HS, Knightdale, N.C.
47. Josh Renick, 2b, Manatee (Fla.) JC.

ST. LOUIS (5)

■ **SCOUTING DIRECTOR:** Ed Creech
1. J.D. Drew, of, St. Paul (Northern League).
1. Ben Diggins, 1b-rhp, Bradshaw Mountain HS, Dewey Ariz. (Supplemental pick—32nd—for loss of Type A free agent Dennis Eckersley).
2. Chad Hutchinson, rhp, Stanford U.
2. Tim Lemon, of, La Mirada (Calif.) HS (Choice from Red Sox—55th—as compensation for Eckersley).
3. Gabe Johnson, c, Atlantic HS, Delray Beach, Fla.
4. Bud Smith, lhp, Los Angeles Harbor JC.
5. Steve Stemle, rhp, Western Kentucky U.
6. Kristopher Rayborn, lhp, Purvis (Miss.) HS.
7. Brad Freeman, ss-of, Mississippi State U.
8. Greg Clark, c, U. of Arizona.
9. Jack Wilson, ss, Oxnard (Calif.) JC.
10. Pedro Zazueta, rhp, Amphitheater HS, Tucson.
11. Joel Vega, lhp, Ohio Dominican College.
12. Jeff Waldron, c, Boston College.
13. Les Walrond, lhp, U. of Kansas.
14. Timothy Bowers, ss, Gulf Coast (Fla.) CC.
15. John Hernandez, of, Xaverian HS, Brooklyn.
16. Scott Prather, lhp, Georgia Tech.
17. Matt Gargano, rhp, Dixie (Utah) JC.
18. Esix Snead, of, U. of Central Florida.
19. Travis Held, rhp, U. of Central Florida.
20. Chris Kelly, 3b, Catawba (N.C.) College.
21. Jim Molina, of, Florida International U.
22. Mike Rerick, lhp, U. of North Dakota.
23. Andy Shibilo, rhp, Pepperdine U.
24. Richard Gonzales, rhp, U. of New Mexico.
25. Jon Hand, rhp, Virginia Tech.
26. Stephen Parker, rhp, Key West (Fla.) HS.
27. Ryan Christianson, rhp, U. of Nebraska-Omaha.
28. Jason Marr, rhp, Long Beach State U.
29. Jeffrey Viles, rhp, Rockhurst (Mo.) College.
30. Eric Gutshall, rhp, Yale U.
31. Troy McNaughton, rhp, Brigham Young U.
32. Troy Farnsworth, 2b, Brigham Young U.
33. Tommy Kidwell, 2b, Yale U.
34. John Boyer, ss, Bonneville HS, Ogden, Utah.
35. Dustin Hawkins, of, Bonneville HS, Ogden, Utah.

36. Andrew Ecklund, c, San Luis Obispo (Calif.) HS.
37. Brent Cordell, c, Incline HS, Incline Village, Nev.
38. Seth Jerue, ss, Westfield (Mass.) HS.
39. Victor Buttler, of, Westchester HS, Hawthorne, Calif.
40. Scott Neal, of, North HS, Bakersfield, Calif.
41. Justin Knoedler, c, Springfield (Ill.) HS.
42. Brandon Tisher, 1b, Durango (Colo.) HS.
43. Scott Sorensen, rhp, Fruita Monument HS, Grand Junction, Colo.
44. Matt Harvick, c, North HS, Bakersfield, Calif.
45. Matt Van Alsburg, of, Fort Collins (Colo.) HS.

SAN DIEGO (9)

■ **SCOUTING DIRECTOR:** Brad Sloan

1. **Sean Burroughs, 3b, Wilson HS, Long Beach.**
2. (Choice to Braves as compensation for loss of Type B free agent Greg Myers).
3. Beau Craig, c, Grossmont HS, La Mesa, Calif.
4. **Travis Devine, rhp, Dacula (Ga.) HS.**
5. **Kevin Eberwein, 3b-of, U. of Nevada-Las Vegas.**
6. Dale Deveraux, rhp, American Fork (Utah) HS.
7. **Brian Berryman, rhp, U. of Michigan.**
8. **Jeremy Owens, of, Middle Tennessee State U.**
9. **Sean Campbell, c, U. of Nevada-Las Vegas.**
10. **John Meyers, rhp, Grayson County (Texas) JC.**
11. **Josh Loggins, of, U. of Kentucky.**
12. **Joe Dusan, 1b, Sacramento CC.**
13. Thom Dreier, rhp, Oklahoma State U.
14. **Ryan Hawkins, rhp, Wallace State (Ala.) JC.**
15. **Casey Bell, rhp, Crowder (Mo.) JC.**
16. **Stephen Watkins, rhp, Lubbock, Texas.**
17. **Brian Lawrence, rhp, Northwestern State U.**
18. **Aaron Kramer, rhp, Arizona State U.**
19. **Jeremy Fikac, rhp, Southwest Texas State U.**
20. Eron Morrow, 1b, Wilson HS, Tacoma.
21. **Keith Forbes, rhp, Wallace State (Ala.) JC.**
22. **Jon Cook, of, San Francisco State U.**
23. **Jack Wickersham, 2b, Southwest Texas State U.**
24. Jerymaine Beasley, of, Spokane Falls (Wash.) CC.
25. Jonathan Segarra, lhp, Frank Phillips (Texas) JC.
26. **Ryan Bauer, rhp, Fontbonne (Mo.) College.**
27. Ralph Roberts, of, Cherryville (N.C.) HS.
28. **Jeremy Reed, c, Lookout Valley HS, Chattanooga.**
29. **Cliff Bartosh, lhp, Duncanville (Texas) HS.**
30. Eric Cyr, lhp, Seminole (Okla.) JC.
31. **Michael Hazen, of, Princeton U.**
32. Geoff Jones, lhp, Montezuma-Cortez HS, Cortez, Colo.
33. **Bryan Schmidt, ss, U. of Nebraska.**
34. Simon Mitchell, of, Bellevue (Wash.) CC.
35. Josh Barbarossa, 1b, Chesterton HS, Valparaiso, Ind.
36. Nathan Sturdivant, rhp, Westmoore HS, Oklahoma City.
37. Felix Castillo, rhp, Rio Grande, P.R.
38. Trey Hodges, rhp, Blinn (Texas) JC.
39. Jonathan Stone, c, Sacramento CC.
40. Clint Kelley, rhp, Morton (Ill.) JC.
41. Charis Britt, c, Gulf Coast (Fla.) CC.
42. **Alex Palaez, 3b, San Diego State U.**
43. Jason Jones, rhp, Kennesaw State (Ga.) U.
44. Jesse Gutierrez, c, Texas Southmost JC.

SAN FRANCISCO (25)

■ **SCOUTING DIRECTOR:** Dick Tidrow

1. **Tony Torcato, 3b, Woodland (Calif.) HS** (Choice from Astros—19th—as compensation for Type B free agent Doug Henry).
1. **Nate Bump, rhp, Penn State U.**
1. **Arturo McDowell, of, Forest Hill HS, Jackson, Miss.** (Choice from Devil Rays—28th—as compensation for Type A free agent Roberto Hernandez).
1. **Chris Jones, lhp, South Mecklenburg HS, Charlotte** (Supplemental pick—38th—for loss of Hernandez).
1. **Jeff Urban, lhp, Ball State U.** (Supplemental pick—41st—for loss of Type A free agent Wilson Alvarez).
2. **Sammy Serrano, c, Stetson U.**
2. **Chris Magruder, of, U. of Washington** (Choice from Devil Rays—72nd—as compensation for Alvarez).
3. **Mike Dean, c, Oral Roberts U.**
4. **Josh Santos, lhp, U. of Connecticut.**
5. **Ryan Vogelsong, rhp, Kutztown (Pa.) U.**
6. **Jake Esteves, rhp, Louisiana State U.**
7. **Doug Clark, of, U. of Massachusetts.**
8. **Todd Ozias, rhp, U. of Miami.**
9. **Cody Ransom, ss, Grand Canyon U.**
10. **Chris Jackson, rhp, Wasson HS, Colorado Springs.**
11. **Erasmo Ramirez, lhp, Cal State Fullerton.**
12. **Randy Goodrich, rhp, Fresno State U.**
13. **John Summers, 1b, U. of Utah.**
14. **Mike Huller, lhp, George Mason U.**
15. **Jeff Allen, of, Illinois State U.**
16. **Erik Mattern, 2b-ss, U. of Arizona.**
17. **Joseph Ojeda, rhp, St. Francis (N.Y.) U.**
18. David Brous, lhp, Del Norte HS, Crescent City, Calif.
19. Ben Quick, rhp, Riverside (Calif.) CC.
20. Santiago Narciandi, 3b, Miami (Fla.) Senior HS.
21. **Benji Miller, rhp, Liberty U.**
22. Theodore Sutton, lhp, Colton (Calif.) HS.
23. Jake Mapes, c, Riverside (Calif.) CC.
24. Ken Trapp, rhp, Alvin (Texas) CC.
25. Oscar Vargas, ss, James Logan HS, Union City, Calif.
26. Jasson Barrow, of, Canby Union HS, Canby, Ore.
27. **Steve Hill, ss, Oklahoma State U.**
28. Chad Ertel, rhp, Elmira (Ontario) District HS.
29. Kyle Middleton, rhp, Escambia HS, Pensacola, Fla.
30. Grant Abrams, ss, Tarpon Springs HS, Palm Harbor, Fla.
31. Cade Sanchez, rhp, U. of Texas-Arlington.
32. Jackson Markert, rhp, Connors State (Okla.) JC.
33. Ryan Gonzales, rhp, Riverside (Calif.) CC.
34. Travis McGreal, rhp, Heritage HS, Littleton, Colo.
35. Matt Dryer, ss, McQuaid Jesuit HS, Rochester, N.Y.
36. Josh Souza, rhp, Turlock (Calif.) HS.
37. Dan Kelly, lhp, Okaloosa Walton (Fla.) JC.
38. Winston Woods, of, Coral Shores HS, Key Largo, Fla.
39. Joel Vasquez, of, Booker HS, Sarasota, Fla.
40. Bill Nahorodny Jr., of, Clearwater (Fla.) HS.
41. Marcellus Presley, of, Sacramento CC.
42. **Carlos Frazier, of, Smackover (Ark.) HS.**
43. Scott Goodman, of, Cuesta (Calif.) JC.
44. Dorian Cameron, ss, Coastal Carolina U.
45. Cody Sudbeck, rhp, Tyler (Texas) JC.

SEATTLE (22)

■ **SCOUTING DIRECTOR:** Frank Mattox

1. **Matt Thornton, lhp, Grand Valley State (Mich.) U.**
2. Jeff Verplancke, rhp, Cal State Los Angeles.
3. **Andy Van Hekken, lhp, Holland (Mich.) HS.**
4. **Juan Amador, of, Luis Felipe Crespo HS, Camuy, P.R.**
5. **Corey Freeman, ss, King HS, Tampa.**
6. **Jake Weber, of, North Carolina State U.**
7. **Shawn McCorkle, 1b, Montclair State (N.J.) U.**
8. **Craig Kuzmic, c-3b, Texas A&M U.**
9. **Neil Longo, rhp, Manhattan College.**
10. Jason Pomar, rhp, U. of South Carolina.
11. Jarrett Shearin, of, U. of North Carolina.
12. **Justin Dunning, rhp, Stanford U.**
13. **Israel Cruz, ss, Carolina, P.R.**
14. **Schuyler Doakes, ss, Jackson State U.**
15. **Wilfredo Quintana, of, Indian Hills (Iowa) CC.**
16. **Patrick Barnes, lhp, Englewood HS, Jacksonville.**
17. **Steve Wright, of, Liberty U.**
18. **Craig Willis, rhp, Pacific Lutheran (Wash.) U.**
19. **Rick Southall, 1b-of, Portland State U.**
20. Jonathan Nelson, ss, Timpanogos HS, Orem, Utah.
21. Brandon DeJaynes, rhp, Quincy (Ill.) HS.
22. Mike Myers, ss, Bishop Verot HS, Cape Coral, Fla.
23. Brian Hartung, rhp, Sinton (Texas) HS
24. **Matt Woodward, 1b, Florida State U.**
25. Craig Helmandollar, lhp, North Stafford HS, Stafford, Va.
26. **Caleb Balbuena, rhp, Long Beach State U.**
27. **Jason Crist, lhp, Southwest Missouri State U.**
28. **Bo Robinson, 3b, UNC Charlotte.**
29. Derald Deason, of, Orange HS, Santa Ana, Calif.
30. John Rheinecker, lhp, Belleville Area (Ill.) CC.
31. Roy Wells, rhp, Volunteer State (Tenn.) CC.
32. Clay Bried, of, Apache Junction HS, Mesa, Ariz.
33. Brandon Pack, c, Cypress (Calif.) JC.
34. Nick Padilla, rhp, Cerritos (Calif.) JC.
35. Guarionez Rodriguez, 2b, Trujillo Alto, P.R.
36. Tim Dierkes, c, Mehlville HS, St. Louis.
37. Michael Kashuba, rhp, Clarence Fulton HS, Vernon, B.C.
38. Clint Patton, c, Sonora HS, Brea, Calif.
39. Aaron Kirkland, rhp, Wallace State (Ala.) CC.
40. Adam Thomas, rhp, North Miami HS.
41. Nicholas Hobbs, of, Chaparral HS, Las Vegas.
42. Geoff Comfort, of, Serra HS, Burlingame, Calif.
43. James Farris, c, Hattiesburg (Miss.) HS.
44. Israel Torres, lhp, Cerritos (Calif.) JC.
45. Drew Parkin, rhp, Aliso Niguel HS, Laguna Niguel, Calif.
46. Ernesto Durazo, 3b, Pima (Ariz.) CC.
47. Clayton McCullough, c, Rose HS, Greenville, N.C.
48. Greg Pines, c, Saddleback (Calif.) CC.
49. Scott Achison, rhp, Texas Christian U.
50. David Holliday, lhp, Anderson Shiro HS, Navasota, Texas.

TAMPA BAY (29)

■ **SCOUTING DIRECTOR:** Dan Jennings

1. (Choice to Giants as compensation for Type A free agent Roberto Hernandez).
2. (Choice to Giants as compensation for Type A free agent Wilson Alvarez).
3. (Choice to White Sox as compensation for Type A free agent Dave Martinez).
4. **Josh Pressley, 1b-rhp, Westminster Academy, Fort Lauderdale.**
5. **Aubrey Huff, 3b, U. of Miami.**
6. **Ryan Rupe, rhp, Texas A&M U.**
7. **John Jacobs, 3b, Marin Catholic HS, Kentfield, Calif.**
8. **Joseph Kennedy, lhp, Grossmont (Calif.) JC.**
9. **Brian Martin, c, Central Union HS, El Centro, Calif.**
10. Ben Keiter, rhp, Arvada (Colo.) West HS.
11. **Steven Goodson, of, Cowley County (Kan.) CC.**
12. **Adam Flohr, lhp, Portland State U.**
13. **Patrick Dickson, lhp, Dalton (Ga.) HS.**
14. **Patrick Hertzel, rhp, Kansas State U.**
15. **Charles Armstrong, lhp, Contra Costa (Calif.) JC.**
16. Neal Frendling, rhp, Lake Central HS, Dyer, Ind.
17. Mike Rodriguez, of, Cooper City (Fla.) HS.
18. **Brandon Backe, ss, Galveston (Texas) JC.**
19. Art Garland, of, Santa Ana (Calif.) JC.
20. Preston Larrison, rhp, Aurora (Ill.) West HS.
21. Darin Moore, rhp, U. of the Pacific.
22. **Daniel Grummit, 1b, Shawnee State (Ohio) U.**
23. **Robert Moore, 2b, Middle Georgia JC.**
24. Ryan Jorgensen, c, San Jacinto (Texas) JC.
25. **Joseph Haines, rhp, Freed-Hardeman (Tenn.) U.**
26. George Moran, rhp, Red Bluff (Calif.) HS.
27. **James Lira, rhp, Laredo (Texas) HS.**
28. Chad Cossette, c, Edmonds (Wash.) CC.
29. Jeremy Manning, lhp, Pitt (N.C.) CC.
30. Gary Welch, rhp, Howard (Texas) JC.
31. Chris Wailand, rhp, Manatee HS, Bradenton, Fla.
32. **Sean Mahoney, of, Florida International U.**
33. Rudolph Frolish, lhp, Ansonia (Conn.) HS.
34. **Matt Schuldt, rhp, U. of Nebraska.**
35. **Monte McGillivray, lhp, San Jacinto (Texas) JC.**
36. Tim Olson, ss, Hutchinson (Kan.) JC.
37. Brandon Medders, rhp, Hillcrest HS, Duncanville, Ala.
38. Andrew Cook, rhp, Antioch (Calif.) HS.
39. Edwin Rodriguez, 1b, Ponce (P.R.) HS.
40. Michael McCuan, rhp, Butler County (Kan.) CC.
41. Jeffrey Bruksch, rhp, Beverly Hills (Calif.) HS.
42. Dane Hutchens, rhp, McLennan (Texas) JC.
43. Brandon Culp, rhp, Wallace State (Ala.) JC.
44. Mark Carter, lhp, Hewitt-Trussville HS, Trussville, Ala.
45. Harold Goodille, of, Modesto (Calif.) JC.
46. **Cody Getz, lhp, Eastern Utah State JC.**
47. Brooks Stephens, 1b, Stetson U.
48. Michael Jacobs, c, Hilltop HS, Chula Vista, Calif.
49. Justin Hancock, ss, Bloomingdale HS, Valrico, Fla.
50. Luis Candelaria, of, Hill (Texas) JC.

TEXAS (10)

■ **SCOUTING DIRECTOR:** Chuck McMichael

1. **Carlos Pena, 1b, Northeastern U.**
2. **Cody Nowlin, of, Clovis (Calif.) HS.**
3. Barry Zito, lhp, Los Angeles Pierce JC.
4. **Antwon Rollins, of, Encinal HS, Alameda, Calif.**
5. **Ryan Dittfurth, rhp, Union HS, Tulsa.**
6. **Frankie McGill, rhp, Tate HS, Gonzalez, Fla.**
7. **John Stewart, lhp, Western Michigan U.**
8. Brad Ticehurst, of, U. of Southern California.
9. **Andrew Pratt, lhp, Chino Valley (Ariz.) HS.**
10. **Justin Backsmeyer, rhp, DeSmet HS, St. Louis.**
11. **Cesar Castaneda, 3b, Dallas Baptist U.**
12. **Dan Boublis, rhp, Villanova U.**
13. **Jeremiah Bullock, lhp, Kuna (Idaho) HS.**
14. **Derek Ottevaere, 1b, Western Michigan U.**
15. **Ole Vigeland, rhp, Washington State U.**
16. **Domingo Valdez, rhp, Moody HS, Corpus Christi, Texas.**
17. **David Meliah, ss, U. of San Francisco.**
18. **Mike Schaeffer, lhp, Saint Louis U.**
19. **Michael Daniel, rhp, Lambuth (Tenn.) U.**
20. Ryan Knox, of, Illinois State U.
21. **Matt Kosderka, rhp, Willamette (Ore.) U.**
22. John Shelley, 3b, Santa Margarita HS, Rancho Santa Margarita, Calif.
23. **Frank Marciante, 1b, Palm Beach (Fla.) JC.**
24. **Jason Edgar, 2b, U. of Connecticut.**
25. Brandon Moorhead, rhp, Franklin County HS, Gainesville, Ga.
26. **Jimmie Romano, c, U. of South Florida.**
27. **Jeremy Jones, c, Arizona State U.**
28. **Rob LaMarsh, lhp, Southern Illinois U.-Edwardsville.**
29. Ron Corona, rhp, Cypress (Calif.) JC.
30. Jaime Bubela, of, Blinn (Texas) JC.
31. **Marcos Quinones, ss, Dallas Baptist U.**
32. Greg Summers, of, Port St. Joe (Fla.) HS.
33. Ryan Cullen, lhp, Satellite HS, Satellite Beach, Fla.
34. Josh Bolingbroke, c, Pleasant Grove (Utah) HS.
35. **William Villamil, lhp, Carolina, P.R.**
36. **Eric Moore, rhp, Lambuth (Tenn.) U.**
37. Jon Harris, rhp, Maple Woods (Mo.) JC.
38. Trent Pratt, c, Tooele (Utah) HS.
39. **Greg Ryan, lhp-1b, Eastern Michigan U.**
40. Craig Mosher, lhp, JC of Southern Idaho.
41. Scott Nicholson, lhp, Lower Columbia (Wash.) JC.
42. Ross Peeples, lhp, Crisp Academy, Cordele, Ga.
43. Derrick Foster, rhp, Pell City (Ala.) HS.
44. Josh Hollingsworth, ss, Dunedin (Fla.) HS.
45. Greg Bochy, rhp, Palomar (Calif.) JC.
46. Damon Sementilli, rhp, Norwalk (Conn.) CC.
47. Roy York, of, Cowley County (Kan.) CC.
48. Shaun Rudi, of, Baker HS, Baker City, Ore.
49. Marcis Hassell, of, Sam Houston HS, Arlington, Texas.
50. Albert Montes, rhp, Socorro HS, El Paso.

TORONTO (8)

■ **SCOUTING DIRECTOR:** Tim Wilken

1. **Felipe Lopez, ss, Lake Brantley HS, Altamonte Springs, Fla.**
2. (Choice to Orioles as compensation for Type A free agent Randy Myers).
3. (Choice to Expos as compensation for Type A free agent Darrin Fletcher).
4. **Ryan Bundy, c, U. of Washington.**
5. Lee Delfino, ss, Pickering (Ontario) HS.
6. **Joe Orloski, rhp, Green Valley HS, Henderson, Nev.**
7. **Tyler Thompson, of, Indiana State U.**
8. **Mike Kremblas, c, Ohio State U.**
9. **Steve Murray, lhp, St. Peter HS, Peterborough, Ontario.**
10. **Jarrod Kingrey, rhp, U. of Alabama.**
11. Ray Aguilar, lhp, South El Monte (Calif.) HS.
12. **Eric Place, lhp, Western Michigan U.**
13. **Adam Huxhold, lhp, Lewis-Clark State (Idaho) College.**
14. **Jay Gibbons, 1b, Cal State Los Angeles.**
15. **Richard Lee, 1b, Mississippi State U.**
16. **Brandon Jackson, ss, Southwest Missouri State U.**
17. **Rueben St. Amand, rhp, Capital HS, Olympia, Wash.**
18. **Ryan Fleming, of, U. of Dayton.**
19. **Robert File, 3b, Philadelphia College of Textiles.**
20. **Auntawn Riggins, ss, Texas Southern U.**
21. **Franklyn Gracesqui, lhp, George Washington HS, New York.**
22. Adam Stern, of, St. Thomas Aquinas HS, New Britain, Conn.
23. **Justin Davies, of, Queens (N.Y.) College.**
24. Maurice Murray, of, Hawkinsville (Ga.) HS.
25. Nestor Rivera, ss, Josefa Pastrana HS, Aguas Buenase, P.R.
26. Matt Sorensen, rhp, Cerritos (Calif.) JC.
27. Noel Daniel, ss, Northside HS, Jackson, Tenn.
28. Shawn Lynn, rhp, George Henry Academy, North York, Ontario.
29. Jason Shelley, ss, Northeast Louisiana U.
30. Garris Gonce, c, Clay HS, Orange Park, Fla.
31. Ryan Houston, rhp, Escambia HS, Pensacola, Fla.
32. Jason Lind, lhp, Moon Valley HS, Phoenix.
33. Ryan Smith, rhp, South Hills HS, West Covina, Calif.
34. Robert Kramer, lhp, Fullerton (Calif.) JC.
35. Cameron Reimers, rhp, JC of Southern Idaho.
36. Lee Southard, rhp, Seminole (Okla.) JC.
37. Justin Williams, of, Columbia Basin (Wash.) JC.
38. Aaron Dean, rhp, Canada (Calif.) JC.
39. Joel Alvarado, c, Miguel Melendez HS, Cayey, P.R.
40. Brian Hutchinson, lhp, Western Carolina U.
41. **Michael Stafford, lhp, Ohio State U.**
42. Justin Valente, of, Greenwich HS, Cos Cob, Conn.
43. Travis Beckham, rhp, Port Dover (Ontario) Composite HS.
44. Greg Palmer, lhp, Clackamas (Ore.) JC.
45. Brian Ackerson, rhp, Fountain Valley (Calif.) HS.
46. D.J. Loland, rhp, Northeast Louisiana U.
47. Kenny Huff, of, Horizon HS, Scottsdale, Ariz.
48. Isaac Iorg, ss, Karns HS, Knoxville.
49. Troy Wilkins, rhp, Mountain Home (Idaho) HS.
50. Jeff Wagner, c, U. of Notre Dame.

Obituaries/Index

OBITUARIES

November 1997-October 1998

Louis Adamie, the scoreboard operator at Sportsman's Park and Busch Stadium in St. Louis for four decades, died Sept. 13 in Bridgeton, Mo. He was 83. Adamie was hired as a teenager in 1940 and worked 4,350 games for the Browns and Cardinals. He's the only scoreboard operator in the communications wing of the Hall of Fame.

Harry Anderson, an outfielder with the Phillies and Reds for five seasons, died June 11 in Greenville, Del. He was 66. In 1957, Anderson hit .268-17-61 as a Phillies rookie in 118 games. For his career, he batted .264-60-242.

Gene Autry, the Singing Cowboy of the movies who owned the Angels from their inception in 1960, died Oct. 2 in Anaheim. He was 91. An enthusiastic owner, Autry was well liked by his players. His greatest disappointment was never winning a title in 39 seasons. Autry and his wife Jackie sold a 25-percent ownership share to the Walt Disney Co. in 1996, and his death allowed Disney to purchase the remaining interest.

Jim Averill, a longtime employee of Everett in the Northwest League and the grandson of Hall of Fame outfielder Earl Averill, died Aug. 26 in Snohomish, Wash. He was 45.

Red Badgro, an outfielder for two seasons with the St. Louis Browns and a pro football hall of famer, died July 13 in Kent, Wash. He was 95. Badgro played 143 games for the Browns from 1929-30, batting .257-2-45.

Red Barrett, a former major league reliever who also had a long career as a minor league player, coach and manager, died March 8 in Leesburg, Fla. He was 84. Barrett, a righthander, went 15-17, 3.51 in 104 major league games.

Frank Baumholtz, an outfielder with the Reds, Cubs and Phillies from 1947-57, died Dec. 14, 1997, in Winter Springs, Fla. He was 79. Baumholtz hit .290-25-272 over his 10-year career. His best season came in 1952, when he hit .325-4-35 in 103 games with the Cubs.

Mark Belanger, the eight-time Gold Glove-winning shortstop for the Orioles who later became an official in the players' union, died Oct. 6 in New York. He was 54. Belanger, a native of Pittsfield, Mass., played for the Orioles from 1965-81. He won six straight Gold Gloves from 1973-78 and was an all-star in 1976. All but the last 54 of his 2,016 games were as an Oriole. He finished his career with the Dodgers in 1982. He hit .228-20-389 for his career.

Doug Blosser, a 1995 third-round draft pick by the Royals, died Jan. 24 in an automobile accident in Sarasota, Fla. He was 21. Todd Sigler, a passenger in Blosser's vehicle, also died in the accident. Blosser was the younger brother of Greg Blosser, an outfielder in the Devil Rays system.

Gene Bossard, the retired White Sox groundskeeper, died of a stroke Jan. 29 in Harvey, Ill. He was 80. He was the middle of three generations of Bossard groundskeepers. He learned the trade from his father Emil, and passed it down to his son Roger. Bossard was famous for saving the day after the infamous Disco Demolition Night in 1979. He ordered 800 yards of sod at 2 a.m., and had it laid in time for that day's game.

Larry Bradford, a former Braves reliever, died of a heart attack at Turner Field in Atlanta before the Braves' Sept. 11 game against the Marlins. He was 48. Bradford went 6-4, 2.52 with seven saves in 104 major league games, all with the Braves in 1977 and 1979-81.

Jack Brickhouse, who broadcast Cubs games for 40 years, died of cardiac arrest Aug. 6 in Chicago. He was 82. Brickhouse was the Cubs' play-by-play announcer from 1941-81, when he was succeeded by Harry Caray. He also broadcast other Chicago sports teams for years, and worked more than 5,000 baseball games. He was inducted into the media wing of the Hall of Fame in 1983.

Dolph Camilli, the 1941 National League MVP for the pennant-winning Brooklyn Dodgers, died Oct. 21, 1997, in San Mateo, Calif. He was 90. Camilli, a first baseman, played eight seasons in the minors before breaking in with the Cubs in 1933 at age 26. In '41, he batted .285 and led the NL with 34 home runs and 120 RBIs.

Al Campanis, longtime general manager of the Dodgers, died of coronary artery disease June 21 in Fullerton, Calif. He was 81. Campanis served as Dodgers GM from 1968-87, presiding over teams that won four National League pennants and the 1981 World Series. His tenure came to an abrupt end when he made his infamous remarks on the "Nightline" television show, saying blacks lacked "the necessities" to become managers and executives.

Milo Candini, a former major league righthander, died March 17 in Manteca, Calif. He was 80. Candini went 26-21, 3.92 in eight major league seasons with the Senators and Phillies.

Harry Caray, legendary broadcaster for the Cardinals, White Sox and Cubs, died Feb. 18, four days after a heart attack in Rancho Mirage, Calif. He was believed to have been between 77 and 83. Harry Christopher Carabina was no ordinary baseball announcer. His catch phrases of "Hollee cow" for the inexplicable and "It might be . . . it could be . . . it is!" to describe a home run became part of baseball vernacular. Leading the crowd in singing "Take Me Out to the Ballgame" was another of Caray's trademarks.

Slick Castleman, a former New York Giants righthander, died March 2 in Nashville. He was 84. Castleman pitched for the Giants from 1934-39, going 36-26, 4.25 in 121 games. He pitched in one World Series game against the Yankees in Game Six in 1936.

Harry Caray

Zack Clayton, a former Negro Leagues first baseman who also was the referee for the Muhammad Ali-George Foreman fight in Zaire, died Nov. 20 in Philadelphia. He was 80. Clayton played in the Negro Leagues from 1932-44, but was better known for his time with the Harlem Globetrotters basketball team.

Luciean "Lou" Clinton, an outfielder who spent eight seasons with five major league teams in the 1960s, died Dec. 6 in Wichita. He was 60. Clinton hit .247-65-269. He enjoyed his best season with the Red Sox in 1962, hitting .294-18-75 in 114 games.

Brent Crossley, a senior second baseman at Alabama State University, was found dead Aug. 19 in a Montgomery, Ala., apartment, the result of a single gunshot wound to the head. He was 21. Crossley was captain of the Hornets in 1998. He hit .323-6-36 and led the club in five offensive categories.

Jim Elder, the longtime play-by-play voice of the Double-A Arkansas Travelers, died of an apparent heart attack while walking his dog on June 25 in North Little Rock, Ark. He was 73. Elder became the play-by-play man for the Travelers in 1965 and left after the '93 season.

Mike Fornieles, a pioneer as a major league relief specialist, died Feb. 11 in St. Petersburg, Fla., of injuries sustained in a fall at his home. He was 66. Fornieles' best year was 1960, when he pitched for the Red Sox and was 10-5, 2.64 while leading the AL in saves (14) and appearances (70).

Larry Freer, head coach at Division II Bowie State University, died of a heart attack March 1 in Bowie, Md. He was 48.

Denny Galehouse, a Padres area scout and a former big league righthander, died of complications from heart disease Oct. 12 in Doylestown, Ohio. He was 86. Galehouse, who went 109-118, 3.97 in 15 big league seasons, became a scout immediately after retiring from the Pacific Coast League in 1950.

Ross "Rosey" Gilhousen, an outfielder/first baseman/pitcher who played three seasons in the minor leagues and later signed George Brett as a scout with the Royals, died Dec. 20 in Rancho Mirage, Calif. He was 81.

Carol Habben, an outfielder/third baseman in the All-American Girls Baseball League, died Jan. 10 in Ringwood, N.J. She was 63. Habben batted .231 in three seasons with Rockford (1951, 1953) and Kalamazoo (1954).

RODGER WOOD

Sam Hairston

Sam Hairston, who spent half a century in professional baseball, died Oct. 31, 1997, in Birmingham, Ala. He was 77. Hairston, a catcher, won a triple crown with the Indianapolis Clowns in the Negro Leagues in 1950, hitting .434-17-71. He later played with the White Sox. His son Jerry played in the major leagues for 14 seasons.

Allen Halley, the MVP of the 1997 championship series in the independent Northern League, died of an apparent seizure March 23 in Miami. He was 26. The righthander was drafted by the White Sox in the 30th round in 1995 out of the University of South Alabama, and spent two years in the White Sox system.

Steve Hamilton, the Morehead State University athletic director and a former big league lefthander for 12 seasons, died of cancer Dec. 2 in Morehead, Ky. He was 62. Hamilton pitched in the majors for six teams, playing in two World Series with the Yankees, in 1960 and '61. Hamilton also played two seasons with the Minneapolis Lakers of the NBA, appearing in the 1959 NBA Finals.

Charles "Teenie" Harris, one of the founders of the Pittsburgh Crawfords Negro Leagues team before it was taken over by Gus Greenlee, died June 12 in Pittsburgh. He was 89.

Fred Hatfield, who had a long career as a player, manager and coach, died May 22 in Tallahassee, Fla. He was 73. "The Mad Hatter" played for 19 seasons, nine in the majors, despite losing three years to military service in World War II. An infielder, he batted .242-25-165 in 722 big league games. After retiring as a player he became head coach at Florida State University for five years, then won four titles in his first five seasons as a minor league manager in the Cardinals and Tigers organizations in the 1970s. He also was a major league coach for the Tigers and a scout for the Athletics.

Lewis Hays, founder of PONY Baseball, died of an apparent heart attack April 11 while doing yardwork at his residence in East Washington, Pa. He was 83. Hays was sports editor of a Washington, Pa., newspaper when he founded the now-international youth baseball organization in 1951.

Jim Hearn, a righthander who pitched for 13 seasons with the Cardinals, Phillies and New York Giants, died June 10 in Boca Grande, Fla. He was 77. Hearn led the National League in ERA (2.49) in 1950, and went 17-9 for the pennant winners in 1951. He finished his career with a record of 109-89, 3.81.

Chet Hoff, who was the oldest living former major league player, died Sept. 17 in a Daytona Beach, Fla., nursing home. He was 107. Hoff pitched for the Yankees when they were still the New York Highlanders, making his debut on Sept. 6, 1911. He went 2-4, 2.49 in 23 big league games with New York and the St. Louis Browns.

Ken Hunt, a major league outfielder for six seasons, died of an apparent heart attack June 8 in Gardena, Calif. He was 62. Hunt had by far his best year with the expansion Los Angeles Angels in 1961, batting .255-25-84.

Gentry Jessup, a standout righthander for the Negro Leagues' Chicago American Giants in the 1940s, died March 26 in Springfield, Mass. Jessup played for the Birmingham Black Barons in 1940 and the Giants from 1941-49. He played in four Negro Leagues all-star games.

Mel Jones, a longtime major league and minor league executive, died Dec. 10 in St. Louis. He was 87. Jones was a longtime aide to Branch Rickey with the Cardinals and Dodgers, and was general manager of several minor league teams. He was GM of the Montreal Royals (International) when Jackie Robinson broke into Organized Baseball with the team in 1946.

Forrest "Frosty" Kennedy, one of 13 players to hit 60 home runs in a season, died June 5 in Covina, Calif. He was 72. Kennedy hit 60 home runs in a 144-game season while playing for Plainview (Southwestern) in 1956.

Buck Leonard, a Hall of Fame first baseman for the Negro Leagues' Homestead Grays, died from complications of a stroke Nov. 27 in Rocky Mount, N.C. He was 90. Leonard, who was known as the "Black Lou Gehrig," combined with Hall of Famer Josh Gibson to form a feared slugging tandem for the Grays.

Rufino Linares, a former major league outfielder, was killed in an auto accident May 16 near San Pedro de Macoris, Dominican Republic. He was 47. Linares batted .270-11-63 in four major league seasons with the Braves and Angels. More recently, he served as an instructor at the Dominican academy of Japan's Hiroshima Carp.

Johnny Lipon, a former major league shortstop and the fifth-winningest minor league manager of all time, died Aug. 17 in Houston. He was 75. Lipon managed in the minors for 30 seasons, retiring after 1992. His lifetime record was 2,176-1,071, not counting 59 games as interim manager of the major league Indians in 1971. He batted .259-10-266 in 758 major league games.

Paul List, a minor league outfielder for eight seasons before being stricken with Hodgkins Disease, died Jan. 20 in Honolulu. He was 32. List was signed by the Angels in 1987 and last played in 1996, when he batted .342-24-75 for Minot of the independent Prairie League. He played part of his career under the name Lew List.

Dick Littlefield, a lefthander who was traded nine times and sold once in the 1950s, died Nov. 20 in Detroit. He was 71. Littlefield went 33-54 with a 4.71 ERA in 243 major league games.

Vic Lombardi, who pitched in two games in the 1947 World Series for the Brooklyn Dodgers, died after heart surgery Dec. 3 in Fresno. He was 75. Lombardi went 50-51, 3.68 in 223 major league games with the Dodgers (1945-47) and Pirates (1948-50).

Roy McMillan, a two-time all-star shortstop, died Nov. 2 in Bonham, Texas. He was 67. McMillan led National League shortstops in fielding for three straight seasons from 1956-58 while with the Reds.

Russ Meyer, a righthander who appeared in three World Series in the 1950s, died Nov. 16 in Oglesby, Ill. He was 74. Meyer, who coached for the Yankees in 1992, went 94-73 with a 3.99 ERA in 319 major league games.

Charles Morrow, owner of the Columbus RedStixx of the South Atlantic League, died of cancer March 11 in Houston. He was 42. Morrow also owned the Columbus Cottonmouths minor league hockey team.

Raymond Moss, a major league righthander known for his curveball, died Aug. 9 in Chattanooga. He was 96. Moss' best season came in 1929, when he was 11-6, 5.04 for the Dodgers. He finished his career 22-18, 4.95. He was the oldest surviving former Braves player.

Jim Murray, who was one of just four sportswriters to win a Pulitzer Prize, died of cardiac arrest Aug. 16 in Los Angeles. He was 78. Murray spent 37 years of his 55-year writing career with the Los Angeles Times. He was inducted into the writers' wing of the Baseball Hall of Fame, presented the Red Smith Award for lifetime achievement and in one 16-year span was voted national sportswriter of the year 14 times—including 12 years in succession.

Boyd Odom, a special-assignment scout for the Pirates, died of heart failure July 9 at his home in Cumming, Ga. He was 76. Odom had worked for the Pirates since 1977.

Jose Oliva, a Dominican third baseman who played 10 seasons of professional baseball, died Dec. 22 in a car accident near Santo Domingo, D.R. He was 26. Oliva was playing in the Dominican League at the time of his death and led the league in RBIs, batting .287-8-40.

Harry Ornest, whose varied sports career included stints as a minor league player and owner of the Pacific Coast League's Vancouver Canadians, died July 21 in Los Angeles. He was 75. Ornest was best known as owner of the NHL's St. Louis Blues and the Canadian Football League's Toronto Argonauts, but he also brought pro baseball back to Vancouver in 1978 after a nine-year absence.

Mike Paterno, the managing general partner of the Charleston, W.Va., Alley Cats, died Nov. 9 of a heart attack in Charleston. He was 46.

Gabe Paul, a longtime executive for four major league teams, died April 26 in Rochester, N.Y. He was 88. Paul began his career as a batboy for Rochester in the International League and rose to become part-owner of the Yankees in the 1970s. His longest tenure was with the Reds, whom he joined in 1936 as assistant general manager and served until he left in 1960 to help establish the Colt .45s/Astros. A year later he joined the Indians, then went to the Yankees in 1973.

Dick Phillips, a former major league first baseman, minor league manager and the 1961 Pacific Coast League MVP, died March 29 in Burnaby, British Columbia. He was 66. Phillips batted .229-12-60 in 263 major league games with the Giants and Senators. He was named Pacific Coast League MVP after hitting .264-16-98 for Tacoma in '61, and played 12 other years in the minors. After his playing career, Phillips managed in the minor leagues for 10 years.

Shirley Povich, a sports columnist for the Washington Post for 74 years, died June 4 of a heart attack. He was 92. Povich began his journalism career as a copyboy at age 17 and later rose to sports editor at the Post. He was the only writer to cover both Lou Gehrig Day at Yankee Stadium in 1939 and the game in which Cal Ripken broke Gehrig's consecutive-game record 56 years later.

Dan Quisenberry

Dan Quisenberry, a righthander who led the American League in saves five times, died of brain cancer Sept. 30 in Leawood, Kan. He was 45. He was inducted into the Royals hall of fame on May 30 and had a career record of 56-46, 2.76 with 244 saves. His best years were with the Royals from 1979-88, when he saved 238 games and had a franchise-best 2.55 ERA.

Mickey Rocco, a major league and minor league first baseman for 18 seasons, died June 1 in St. Paul, Minn. He was 81. Rocco was a regular with the Indians during the war years. He batted .258-30-186 in 440 big league games, all with the Indians, from 1943-46.

Carlos Salazar, a longtime baseball writer for the Albuquerque Tribune and official scorer for the city's minor league games, died of congestive heart failure June 14 in Albuquerque. He was 73. Salazar had covered teams in the West Texas-New Mexico, Sophomore, Texas and Pacific Coast leagues since the 1950s.

Ed Sanicki, a former major league outfielder, died July 6 in Old Bridge, N.J. He was 74. Sanicki got just two cups of coffee with the 1949 and '51 Phillies, but the first one was memorable. He homered in his first big league at-bat, and all three of his hits (in 13 at-bats) were home runs.

Frank Scott, a pioneering player agent, died June 28 in Livingston, N.J., after a fall at a nursing home. He was 80. In the days before agents negotiated player contracts with teams, Scott carved out his niche by representing players in endorsement and public appearance deals. Scott became an agent after working as the Yankees' traveling secretary, and also worked for a time for the Major League Baseball Players Association.

Russ Sehon, a longtime scout for five organizations and a former minor league second baseman and manager, died April 11 in Olathe, Kan. He was 79. Sehon played in the minors for five seasons from 1940-49, raising his batting average in every year he played. In 1950 he became a scout for the Philadelphia Athletics, and later worked for the Milwaukee Braves, the Los Angeles and California Angels, the Mets and the Yankees.

Dewey Soriano, former president of the Pacific Coast League and the short-lived Seattle Pilots major league team, died April 6 in Seattle. He was 78. Soriano served as PCL president in the mid-1960s, before becoming part-owner and president of the Pilots. Soriano also had the unusual distinction of serving simultaneously as president and player for Yakima (Western International) from 1949-50.

Bob Starr, the play-by-play voice of the Angels until retiring in 1997 for health reasons, died of pulmonary fibrosis Aug. 3 in Orange, Calif. He was 65. Starr worked for the Angels from 1980-89 and again from 1993-97, and also broadcast the Red Sox for three years and the Cardinals for eight. He broadcast major league baseball for 28 years but was at least as well known as a football announcer, doing Los Angeles Rams and St. Louis Cardinals games.

Joel Stephens, an outfielder in the Orioles organization, died of colon cancer Sept. 30 in Tioga, Pa. He was 22. Stephens discovered he had colon cancer in November 1997, beginning an ordeal that included two emergency surgeries and six months of chemotherapy. He started to work out with Class A Frederick in July, regaining about 20 of the 60 pounds he had lost, but he left the team after cancerous lymph nodes were discovered.

Elvin Tappe, one of the Cubs coaches who rotated as manager of the team in the early 1960s in one of baseball's more bizarre experiments, died of pancreatic cancer Oct. 10 in Quincy, Ill. He was 71. Tappe, a catcher, batted .207-0-17 in six major league seasons, all with the Cubs. He became a player-coach for the team in '58. In '61, he and fellow coaches Vedie Himsl, Harry Craft and Lou Klein took turns managing the Cubs to a 64-90 finish, seventh in the eight-team National League.

Bill Tuttle, the ex-major league outfielder who used his battle with oral cancer to crusade against tobacco in baseball, died July 27 in Anoka, Minn. He was 69. Tuttle batted .259-67-443 in 11 major league seasons with the Tigers, Kansas City Athletics and Twins. He was part of the famous 13-player trade between the Tigers and A's after the 1957 season.

Elmer Valo, a longtime major league outfielder and Phillies scout, died July 19 in Palmerton, Pa. He was 77. Valo batted .282-58-601 in 1,806 major league games over 20 seasons, and lost two more years to military service. He later was an Indians minor league manager and major league coach, and a scout for the Phillies for 13 years before retiring in 1982. He served as a spring training instructor for the Phillies as recently as 1998.

Ivan Walker, public-address announcer for the Northwest League's Salem-Keizer Volcanoes, died in Everett, Wash. He was 66. Walker served from 1989-1996 as radio and public-address announcer for the Bellingham Mariners and Bellingham Giants, both formerly in the Northwest League. Walker was the father of Volcanoes owner Jerry Walker.

John Wyatt, a reliever for four major league teams in the 1960s, died April 6 in Omaha. He was 62. Wyatt, a righthander, went 42-44, 3.47 in nine big league seasons. He led the American League with 81 appearances in '64, the same year he made his only All-Star Game appearance. Wyatt also won a game in relief for the Impossible Dream Red Sox in the '67 World Series against the Cardinals.

Jerry Zimmerman, a former Twins catcher, died Sept. 9 in Neskowin, Ore. He was 63. Zimmerman batted .204-3-72 in 483 major league games. He appeared in both the 1961 and 1965 World Series, going 0-for-1 in four games.

Index

GENERAL INFORMATION